AA Greater London Street Atlas

© Copyright 1977
Geographia Ltd. and
The Automobile Association

Published by Geographia Ltd.
63 Fleet Street, London, EC4
Tel. 01–353–2701/2
and
The Automobile Association
Fanum House,
Basingstoke, Hants.
Tel. Basingstoke 201 23

Based upon the Ordnance Survey Maps with the
Sanction of the Controller of H.M. Stationery Office.

The Ordnance Survey is not responsible for the
accuracy of the National Grid on this production.

We wish to acknowledge the co-operation of
the Post Office in the preparation of the postal
information used in this atlas.

The contents of this publication are believed correct
at the time of printing. Nevertheless the Publishers
can accept no responsibility for errors or omissions
or for changes in the details given.

First Published 1977

Index Computerset
Atlas printed offset litho by
Gilbert Whitehead & Co. Ltd. (Gothic Press)
Hainault Street, New Eltham, London, SE9

Preliminary pages designed by M A Preedy MSIAD

Paper supplied by Dickinson Robinson Group

Bound by William Brendon of Tiptree, Essex

ISBN 0 09 211 490 3
AA No. 55233

AA Greater London Street Atlas

Key to sectional maps	inside front cover
AA Service	4–6
Parking in London	7–8
Hospitals	9–12
Police Stations	13–14
Embassies and Legations	15
Commonwealth Offices	16
Government and Public Offices	17
Major Spectator Sporting Venues	18
Town Halls	19
British Rail – Stations	20–21
Underground Stations and Map	22–24
Livery Halls	25
Principal Clubs	26
Museums and Art Galleries	27
Street Markets	28–29
Theatres, Cinemas, Concert Halls, etc	30–31
Legend, Indexing System	32

Central London Atlas — Map 1–4
Scale – 1:11,520
5.5 inches to 1 mile – 8.7cm to 1km

Central London Street Index

Greater London Street Atlas — Map 5–123
Scale – 1:20,000
3.17 inches to 1 mile – 5cm to 1km

Approaches to Greater London — Map 124–125

Index to Greater London Streets

Administrative Areas Map — Inside back cover

THE AUTOMOBILE ASSOCIATION
Head Office:
Fanum House,
Basingstoke, Hants.
Tel. Basingstoke 20123

AA Service in the Greater London Area and surrounding counties within the area covered by this atlas follows. For further information and details of services offered by garages see AA Members Handbook.

AA BREAKDOWN SERVICE

AA members whose vehicles break down and assistance is required while in the London Area should first telephone (01) 954 7373. An automatic queueing device ensures that calls are answered in turn, so if the ringing tone is obtained DO NOT RING OFF.

Assistance can also be obtained by ringing any other available Service Centre. Those listed below are within the area covered by this atlas:

Location		Hours of Service	Telephone Number
Banstead	Surrey	0900–1800	Burgh Heath 53797
Esher	Surrey	0900–1800	01–398 5374
Gallows Corner	Gt. London	0900–1800	Ingrebourne 42310
Gravesend	Kent	0900–1800	Gravesend 52814
Guildford	Surrey	24 hour service	Guildford 72841
Hatfield	Herts	24 hour service	Hatfield 62852
Heathrow Airport	Gt. London	0900–1800	01–897 8842
Hounslow	Gt. London	0900–1800	01–759 0107
Leatherhead	Surrey	0900–1800	Leatherhead 72085
London	Gt. London	24 hour service	01–954 7373
Northolt	Gt. London	0900–1800	01–845 6281
Purfleet	Essex	0900–1800	Purfleet 6495
Sidcup	Gt. London	0900–1800	01–300 6681
South Woodford	Gt. London	0900–1800	01–989 6567

Road Reports

Road and Weather Conditions

AA reports on road conditions are transmitted by the Post Office through its recorded Motoring Information Service. The recording covering a 50 mile radius of London gives information on major roads affected by adverse weather, road works, special events, etc.

This can be obtained by telephoning any of the following numbers:

01–246 8021	Colchester 8021	Oxford 8021
Bedford 8021	Guildford 8021	Reading 8021
Bishop's Stortford 8021	High Wycombe 8021	Southend 8021
Brighton 8021	Luton 8021	Tunbridge Wells 8021
Chelmsford 8021	Medway 8021	

Weather Centre

Members of the public may telephone or call at the centre listed below for free information about local, national and continental weather. The centre is staffed by the Meteorological Office.

London 284–286, High Holborn, W.C.1 telephone 01–836 4311.

Getting in touch with the AA

For details about joining the AA or for members wanting to obtain breakdown service or motoring information, or some other aspect of Member Services proceed as follows:

Breakdown Service or Motoring Information

Telephone the nearest Breakdown Service number as in preceding paragraphs.

Member Services

Call, or telephone at any of the AA Service Centres listed below.

AA Service Centres

All the service centres listed below have reception facilities and deal with telephone enquiries on the numbers shown. Office hours are 09.00–17.00hrs from Monday to Friday and 09.00–12.30hrs on Saturday, unless otherwise stated.

Any correspondence should be sent to the address listed in next paragraph, where to 'write'.

South-East Region

London Telephone enquiries	General, home travel information, and 24hr breakdown service	01–954 7373*
	Legal, technical, insurance, overseas travel, and other specialised subjects	01–954 7355
City	Regis House, King William Street (08.30–17.30hrs from Monday to Friday, closed Saturday)	01–626 9993
Hammersmith	162 Fulham Palace Road	01–385 3677
Stanmore	Fanum House, The Broadway	01–954 7355
Teddington	Fanum House, 7 High Street (09.00–12.00hrs Saturday)	01–977 3200
West End	Fanum House, 5 New Coventry Street	01–954 7355
Guildford	Fanum House, London Road	Guildford 72841
Slough	57 High Street (closed Wednesday afternoon, open all day Saturday)	Slough 28757

*Calls are queued and answered in turn. If ringing tone is obtained **DO NOT RING OFF**

Write: to the Regional Headquarters named on your Membership Certificate. The Regional Headquarters for the London and South-east Region is Fanum House, 7 High Street, Teddington, Middlesex, TW11 8EQ telephone 01–977 3200.

Membership Subscription or Certificate

Write to AA Membership Administration PO Box 50, Basingstoke, Hants RG21 2ED to notify changes of name, address or membership class etc.

Accommodation

The AA Members Handbook, lists AA-appointed hotels; other sources of information are the AA Guide to Hotels and Restaurants in Great Britain and Ireland, and the AA Guide to Guest Houses, Farmhouses and Inns which lists relatively low-cost meals and accommodation.

Central Booking Offices

British Transport Hotels Limited,
St. Pancras Chambers,
London, NW1 2QR
Tel 01–278 4211
Telex 27863

Centre Hotels (Cranston) Limited,
101 Great Russell Street,
London, WC1B 3LH
Tel 01–637 1661
Telex 263561

De Vere Hotels and Restaurants Limited,
7 Queen Street, Mayfair,
London, W1X 8EP
Tel 01–493 2114

Grand Metropolitan Hotels Limited,
Grand Metropolitan House,
Stratford Place,
London, W1A 4YU
Tel 01–629 6618
Telex 25971

Hotel Representative Inc,
Windsor House, 83 Kingsway,
London, WC2
Tel 01–405 5438
Telex 265497.
For Berkeley, Claridges,
Connaught, Savoy, hotels.

Imperial London Hotels Limited,
Imperial Hotel,
Russell Square,
London, WC1B 5BB
Tel 01–278 7871
Telex 263951

Ind Coope Hotels, Allied Brewery Limited,
Station Street,
Burton-on-Trent, Staffs
Tel (0283) 66587

Interchange Hotels of Great Britain,
St. Pancras Chambers,
London, NW1 2QR
Tel 01–278 2411
Telex 27863

M F North Limited (North Hotels),
58 Cromwell Road,
London, SW7 5BZ
Tel 01–589 1212
Telex 262180

Norfolk Capital Hotels Limited,
2–10 Harrington Road,
London, SW7 3ER
Tel 01–589 7000
Telex 23241

Prestige Hotels,
414 Kings Road,
London, SW1 0LJ
Tel 01–352 7397
& 01–499 5564
Telex 27659

Reo Stakis Hotels,
627 Grand Buildings,
London, WC2N 5EZ
Tel 01–930 2944
Also at
Waterloo Chambers,
Waterloo Street,
Glasgow, G2 6AY
Tel 041–221 4343

Royal London Hotels and Restaurants Limited,
Victory House,
Leicester Square,
London, WC2H 7NE
Tel 01–734 0197
Telex 24616

Strand Hotels Limited,
12 Sherwood Street,
London, W1V 8AE
Tel 01–734 6755
Telex 27474

Trust Houses Forte Hotels Limited,
71–75 Uxbridge Road,
London, W5 5SL
Tel 01–567 3444
Telex 934946

Booking Agencies

Exp-o-tel
Strand House,
Great West Road,
Brentford, Middlesex
Tel 01–568 8765
Telex 8811951
Hours:
Mon–Fri 8am–9pm (Apr–Oct)
8am–6pm (Winter)
Sat 9am–12 noon.
No Charges.

Hotel Accommodation Service Ltd Hotac
80 Wigmore Street,
London, W1H 9DQ
Tel 01–935 2555
Telex 263179
Free private telephones at
Victoria Station,
General Enquiry Office, and
Waterloo Station next to
General Post Office
Hours: Mon–Fri 9.30am–6pm
Closed Sat, Sun and Bank
Holidays. No Charges.

Hotel Bookings International Limited
65 Pound Lane,
London, NW10 2LB
Tel 01–459 1212
Telex 923616
Also branches at various
London terminals.
(Heathrow 01–897 0821
7 am–11 pm)
(Gatwick (0293) 30266
8am–11pm)
Specialising in airport traffic
Hours: 9.30am–5.30pm
Mon–Fri. No Charges.

Hotel Booking Service Ltd and Stay-By Ltd
137 Regent Street,
London, W1R
Tel 01–437 5052
Telex 262892
Hours:
Mon–Thur 9.30am–5.30pm
(5pm Fri) (1pm Sat Apr–Oct)
Closed Sun. No Charges.

Hotelguide
Faraday House,
8–10 Charing Cross Road,
London, WC2
Tel 01–836 5561
Telex 22650
Hours:
Mon–Fri 9am–5.30pm
(1pm Sat) Closed Sun.
No Charges.

In listing the above mentioned organisations the Association is recording only their existence. The Association cannot accept liability for any circumstances arising from their use by members.

The Greater London Council's parking policy of meter zones for central London (covering an area of about 40 square miles) is known as the Inner London Parking Area. This Inner Area covers the whole, or part of 12 London boroughs: Brent, Camden, Hackney, Hammersmith, Islington, Kensington and Chelsea, Lambeth, Southwark, Tower Hamlets, Wandsworth, Westminster and the City of London. Additional zones are still being created, therefore it is not possible to indicate precise boundaries, but parking in the whole of central London is now controlled.

There are also parking zones in outer London, most of which include meters.

Brief details of how meters operate are given in the Street Parking section which follows.

**Street Parking
Parking zones**

Controlled zones are indicated by signs at their boundary points, giving the hours of operation. Special regulations may also apply in areas near to the wholesale markets and where Sunday street markets are held. Street parking other than at officially designated places is prohibited during the specified hours. In many zones, some parking places may be found reserved exclusively for residents, or other classes of users specified on nearby plates.

Meter Regulations

There are some differences in the charges, and variations in the length of time for which parking is allowed.

The car must be parked within the limits of the parking bay, indicated by the white lines on the road. Also it must be facing the same direction as the traffic flow, unless angle parking is indicated by road marking.

Payment must be made immediately, although unexpired meter time, paid for by a previous occupant of the space, may be used. After the initial payment has been made, additional parking time may not be bought by making any further payments. A vehicle should be removed before the permitted time has elapsed and no vehicle may be returned to any bay in the same parking place within one hour.

If a vehicle is left at a meter beyond the time paid for, a ticket may be placed on it, to show a high rate excess charge which is payable to the local authority. This allows a further short period of parking before an offence is committed.

Waiting restrictions

The usual system of yellow lines should indicate these, but their omission does not necessarily mean there is no effective restriction. In addition, any vehicle waiting on a road may be judged to be causing 'unnecessary obstruction', without proof that other vehicles or persons may have actually been obstructed, and a prosecution could ensue.

Vehicle Removal

A car left on the road causing actual obstruction, or not left in a parking place and judged to be creating an 'unnecessary obstruction' on the highway, may be removed by the Police and held in a Pound. If a vehicle has been removed a driver should contact the nearest Police Station, who will have the details of any official removal. On collection, a substantial fee is payable for the removal, in addition to any other parking or penalty charges.

Disabled people – Orange Badge Scheme

Certain disabled drivers, passengers and institutions caring for the disabled who operate specially adapted mini-buses or similar vehicles, may apply to become members of the Orange Badge Scheme run by local authorities. The badges are for identification only and do not entitle the holder to parking concessions. Concessions derive from exceptions written into traffic regulation orders by individual local authorities, and the badges are valid throughout the country except for the following areas of central London: The cities of London and Westminster, the Borough of Kensington and Chelsea, and the Borough of Camden who operate their own concessionary schemes. Extensions to the existing regulations came into effect on 1 June 1975. They extend the eligibility for an orange badge to a blind person (as a passenger) who is registered under the National Assistance Act 1948. They allow badge holders to park for up to two hours on yellow lines except where there is a ban on loading or unloading in force at the time, or in a bus lane. They must set an orange disc at the time of arrival. The badge holder is entitled to park free of charge and without time restriction, at parking meters and where parking is limited.

Special restrictions:

No stopping Regulations apply at many dangerous junctions, at a number of school entrances, in cab parking places and on bus stop clearways. In a few areas spaces are reserved for diplomatic cars, doctors, invalid carriages and pedal cycles.

Parking at night

Cars, motor cycles, invalid carriages, pedal cycles and goods vehicles under 30cwt unladen weight not being a vehicle, in any case, to which a trailer is attached, can park without lights provided that:

a   The road is subject to a speed limit of 30mph or less.

b   No part of the vehicle is within 15 yards of a road junction.

c   The vehicle is parked close to the kerb and parallel to it, and except in one way streets, with its nearside to the kerb.

d   The vehicle is parked in a recognised parking place.

Vehicles 30cwt or more unladen weight, or carrying eight or more passengers, must show two white lights to the front and two red lights with an illuminated number plate to the rear, in any night parking situation.

Similarly, if the road is not subject to a 30mph speed limit, a vehicle left standing on the highway at night must conform to the lighting regulations as above.

Hospitals

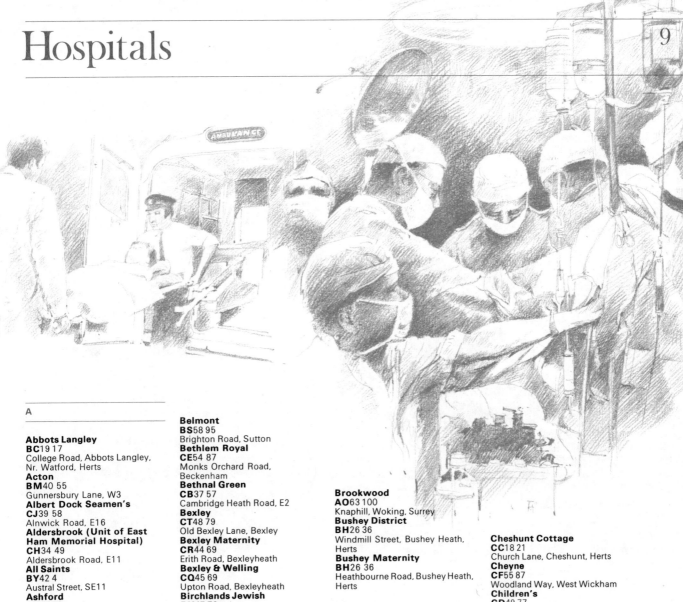

A

Abbots Langley
BC19 17
College Road, Abbots Langley,
Nr. Watford, Herts
Acton
BM40 55
Gunnersbury Lane, W3
Albert Dock Seamen's
CJ39 58
Alnwick Road, E16
**Aldersbrook (Unit of East
Ham Memorial Hospital)**
CH34 49
Aldersbrook Road, E11
All Saints
BY42 4
Austral Street, SE11
Ashford
AY48 73
London Road, Ashford
Atkinson Morley's
BP50 75
Copse Hill, Wimbledon, SW20

B

Banstead
BT59 95
Downs Road, Sutton
Barking
CN36 58
Upney Lane, Barking
Barnes
BO45 65
South Worple Way, SW14
Barnet General
BQ24 28
Wellhouse Lane, Barnet
Bearsted Memorial
BZ33 48
Lordship Road, Stoke Newington,
N16
Beckenham
CD51 87
379 Croydon Road, Beckenham
Beckenham Maternity
CE52 87
Stone Park Avenue, Beckenham
Beechcroft
AS62 100
Heathside Road, Woking, Surrey
Belgrave Children's
BY43 66
Clapham Road, SW9

Belmont
BS58 95
Brighton Road, Sutton
Bethlem Royal
CE54 87
Monks Orchard Road,
Beckenham
Bethnal Green
CB37 57
Cambridge Heath Road, E2
Bexley
CT48 79
Old Bexley Lane, Bexley
Bexley Maternity
CR44 69
Erith Road, Bexleyheath
Bexley & Welling
CQ45 69
Upton Road, Bexleyheath
Birchlands Jewish
BU47 76
Birchlands Avenue,
Wandsworth Common, SW12
Bolingbroke
BU46 76
Wandsworth Common, SW11
Botleys Park
AU56 91
Guildford Road, Chertsey, Surrey
Bow Arrow
CX46 80
Dartford, Kent
Bramley House
BZ22 30
Clayhill, Enfield
Brentford
BK43 64
Boston Manor Road, Brentford
Brentwood District
DC26 122
Crescent Drive, Brentwood, Essex
**British Home and Hospital
for Incurables**
BY49 76
Crown Lane, SW16
**British Hospital for Mothers
and Babies**
CK42 68
Samuel Street, SE18
Bromley
CH52 88
Cromwell Avenue, Bromley
Brompton
BT42 3
Fulham Road, SW3
Brook General
CK44 68
Shooters Hill Road, SE18

Brookwood
AO63 100
Knaphill, Woking, Surrey
Bushey District
BH26 36
Windmill Street, Bushey Heath,
Herts
Bushey Maternity
BH26 36
Heathbourne Road, Bushey Heath,
Herts

C

Cane Hill
BW62 104
Coulsdon
**Carshalton, Beddington &
Wallington District**
BU56 95
The Park, Carshalton
Cassel
BK49 74
Ham Common, Richmond
Caterham & District
CB64 105
Croydon Road, Caterham Valley
Cell Barnes
BK14 9
Highfield Lane, St. Albans, Herts
Central Middlesex
BN38 55
Acton Lane, NW10
Chadwell Heath
CO32 50
Grove Road, Chadwell Heath, Essex
Charing Cross
BQ42 65
Fulham Palace Road, W6
Chase Farm
BY23 29
The Ridgeway, Enfield
Cheam
BQ55 85
London Road, North Cheam
Chelsea Hospital for Women
BT42 3
Dovehouse Street, SW3

Cheshunt Cottage
CC18 21
Church Lane, Cheshunt, Herts
Cheyne
CF55 87
Woodland Way, West Wickham
Children's
CD49 77
Sydenham Road, Sydenham,
SE26
Chingford
CF27 39
Larkshall Road, Chingford, E4
Chiswick Maternity
BO42 65
Netheravon Road, Chiswick, W4
City of London Maternity
BX33 47
65 Hanley Road, N4
Clare Hall
BO20 19
South Mimms, Potters Bar, Herts
Claremont
BK53 85
St. James' Road, Surbiton
Claybury
CL29 40
Woodford Bridge, Essex
Clayponds
BL42 65
Clayponds Gardens, W5
Clerks Croft (Netherne)
BZ70 114
Bletchingley, Surrey
**Cobham & District
Cottage Hospital**
BC60 92
Portsmouth Road, Cobham,
Surrey
Colindale
BN30 37
Colindale Avenue, NW9
Connaught
CE32 48
Orford Road, Walthamstow, E17

Coppetts Wood
BU30 38
Coppetts Road, Muswell Hill, N10
Cray Valley
CP51 89
St. Pauls' Cray
Croydon General
BZ54 87
London Road, Croydon
Cuddington
BR60 94
Banstead, Surrey
Cumberland House
BU52 86
Whitford Gardens, Mitcham

D

Dagenham
CS37 59
Rainham Road South, Dagenham
Dame Gertrude Young
BJ39 54
Castlebar Hill, W5
Darenth Park
CZ48 80
Watling Street, Dartford, Kent
Dorking General
BJ72 119
Horsham Road, Dorking, Surrey
Dreadnought Seamen's
CF43 67
King William Walk, Greenwich, SE10
Dulwich
CA45 67
East Dulwich Grove, SE22

E

Eastern
CC35 48
Homerton Grove, Homerton, E9
East Ham Memorial
CJ36 58
Shrewsbury Road, Forest Gate, E7
Eastman Dental
BX49 2
Grays Inn Road, WC1
East Surrey
BU70 121
Shrewsbury Road, Redhill, Surrey
Edgware General
BM29 37
Edgware
Egham Cottage
AR49 72
98 St. Jude's Road, Englefield Green, Surrey
Elizabeth Garrett-Anderson
BW38 1
144 Euston Road, NW1
Ellesmere
BB56 92
Queens Road, Walton on Thames, Surrey
Eltham & Mottingham
CK46 78
Passey Place, Eltham, SE9
Emily Jackson
CU65 107
Eardley Road, Sevenoaks, Kent
Enfield War Memorial
BZ23 30
Chase Side, Enfield
Epsom District
BN61 103
Dorking Road, Epsom, Surrey
Epsom & Ewell Cottage
BO60 94
Alexandra Road, Epsom, Surrey
Erith & District
CS43 69
Park Crescent, Erith
Evelina Children's
BZ41 4
Southwark Bridge Road, SE1

F

Farnborough
CL56 97
Farnborough Common, Orpington

Finchley Memorial
BT29 38
Granville Road, North Finchley, N12
Fitzroy Nuffield
BU39 1
10–12, Bryanston Square, W1
Florence Nightingale
BT38 1
19 Lisson Grove, NW1
(re-opening 1978)
Forest Gate
CG35 49
Forest Lane, E7
Forest
CJ26 40
Roebuck Lane, Buckhurst Hill, Essex
French
BX39 2
172–176 Shaftesbury Avenue, WC2
Friern
BV29 38
Friern Barnet Road, New Southgate, N11

G

Garrett-Anderson Maternity Home
BM36 56
40 Belsize Grove, NW3
German
CB36 57
Ritson Road, E8
Goldie Leigh
CO43 69
Lodge Hill, Bostall Heath, Abbey Wood, SE2
Goodmayes
CO32 50
Barley Lane, Goodmayes, Ilford,
Gordon
BW42 3
126 Vauxhall Bridge Road, SW1
Gravesend & North Kent
DG46 81
Bath Street, Gravesend, Kent
Great West Hatch
High Road, Chigwell, Essex
Greentrees
BY29 38
Tottenhall Road, N13
Greenwich District
CG42 68
Vanbrugh Hill, Greenwich, SE10
Grosvenor Hospital for Women
BW42 3
Vincent Square, SW1
Grovelands
BX26 38
The Bourne, Southgate, N14
Grove Park
CJ48 78
Marvels Lane, SE12
Guy's
BZ40 2
St. Thomas' Street, SE1

H

Hackney
CD35 48
Homerton High Street, E9
Halliwick
BU28 38
Friern Barnet Road, N11
Hammersmith
BP39 55
Du Cane Road, W12
Hampstead General
BU35 47
Haverstock Hill, NW3
Harefield
AX30 35
Harefield, Uxbridge
Harlington, Harmondsworth and Cranford Cottage
AZ43 63
Sipson Lane, Harlington, Hayes
Harold Wood
CW30 42
Gubbins Lane, Romford
Harperbury
BK19 18
Harper Lane, Shenley, Radlett, Herts

Harrow
BM34 45
Roxeth Hill, Harrow
Harts
CH28 40
Woodford Green, Essex
Hayes Cottage
BB39 53
Grange Road, Hayes
Hemel Hempstead General (St. Pauls Wing)
AY13 8
Allandale, Hemel Hempstead, Herts
Hemel Hempstead General (West Herts Wing)
AX13 8
Hillfield Road, Hemel Hempstead, Herts
Henderson
BS58 95
Brighton Road, Sutton
Hendon District
BP32 46
357 Hendon Way, NW4
Highlands General
BX25 29
Worlds End Lane, N21
High Wick
BL15 10
Highfield Lane, St. Albans, Herts
High Wood
DA26 42
Ongar Road, Brentwood, Essex
Hillend
BK14 9
Hillend Lane, St. Albans, Herts
Hillingdon County
AY39 53
Uxbridge
Hither Green
CF46 77
Hither Green Lane, SE13
Holloway Sanatorium
AS52 82
Virginia Water, Surrey
Honey Lane
CH20 22
Waltham Abbey, Essex
Hornsey Central
BW32 47
Park Road, Crouch End, N8
Horton
BM59 94
Long Grove Road, Epsom, Surrey
Hospital for Sick Children
BX38 2
Gt Ormond Street, WC1
Hospital for Sick Children
BQ64 103
Tadworth Court, Tadworth, Surrey
Hospital for Tropical Diseases
BW37 1
St. Pancras Way, NW1
Hospital for Women
BW39 1
Soho Square, W1
Hospital of St. John and St. Elizabeth
BT37 1
60 Grove End Road, NW8
Hounslow
BF45 64
Staines Road, Hounslow

I

Ilford Maternity
CM32 49
Eastern Avenue, Ilford
Invalid & Crippled Children
CH38 58
Balaam Street, Plaistow, E13
Italian Hospital
BX39 2
Queen Square, WC1
Iver, Denham & Langley Cottage Hospital
AV39 52
Iver, Bucks

J

Joyce Green
CW44 70
Joyce Green Lane, Dartford, Kent

Jubilee
CH29 40
Woodford Green, Essex

K

King Edward's Memorial
BK40 54
Mattock Lane, W13
King Edward's Memorial (Clay Ponds Wing)
BL42 65
South Ealing, W5
King Edward VII Hospital for Officers
BV39 1
Beaumont Street, W1
King Edward VII (Windsor Unit)
AO45 62
Windsor, Berks
King Edward VII (Old Windsor Unit)
AP47 72
Old Windsor, Berks
King George
CM32 49
Eastern Avenue, Ilford
Kingsbury
BM31 46
Honeypot Lane, Kingsbury, NW9
Kings College
BZ45 67
Denmark Hill, SE5
Kingston
BM51 85
Galsworthy Road, Kingston upon Thames

L

Lambeth
BY42 4
Brook Drive, Kennington Road, SE1
Langthorne
CF34 48
Leytonstone, E11
Leatherhead
BK64 102
Poplar Road, Leatherhead, Surrey
Leamington Park
BN39 55
Wells Farm Road, Acton, W3
Leavesden
BC19 17
College Road, Abbots Langley, Nr. Watford, Herts
Lennard
CL54 88
Lennard Road, Bromley
Lewisham
CE46 77
High Street, Lewisham, SE13
Leytonstone House
CG33 49
High Road, Leytonstone, E11
Livingstone
CW47 80
East Hill, Dartford, Kent
London, The (Whitechapel)
CB39 57
Whitechapel Road, E1
London, (Mile End)
CC38 57
275 Bancroft Road, E1
London, (St. Clements)
CD38 57
2a Bow Road, E3
London Chest
CC37 57
Bonner Road, E2
London Foot
BW38 1
33 Fitzroy Square, W1
London Jewish
CC39 57
41/51 Stepney Green, E1
London Refraction
BZ41 4
58/62 Newington Causeway, SE1
Long Grove
BN58 94
Epsom, Surrey
Long Reach
CX43 70
Long Reach, Dartford, Kent

Lugano
CJ26 40
3 Powell Road, Buckhurst Hill,
Essex

M

Mabledon
CY48 80
Nr. Dartford, Kent
**Malden Annexe
(of Springfield Hospital,
NW7)**
BN52 85
New Malden, Surrey
**Maida Vale Hospital for
Nervous Diseases**
BT38 1
4 Maida Vale, W9
Maudsley
BZ44 67
Denmark Hill, SE5
Mayday
BY53 86
Mayday Road, Thornton Heath
Memorial
CL44 68
Shooters Hill, SE18
Metropolitan
CA36 57
Kingsland Road, E8
Middlesex
BW39 1
Mortimer Street, W1
Mildmay Mission
CA38 2
Austin Street, Hackney Road, E2
Molesey
BF53 84
High Street, West Molesey, Surrey
Moorfields Eye
BZ38 2
City Road, EC1
Moorfields Eye
BX39 2
High Holborn, WC1
Mothers (S.A.)
CB35 48
143–153 Lower Clapton Road,
E5
Mount Pleasant
BF39 54
North Road, Southall
Mount Vernon
AZ29 35
Northwood
Murray House
AU57 91
Ottershaw, Surrey

N

Napsbury
BJ17 18
Napsbury, Nr. St. Albans, Herts
National Heart
BV39 1
Westmoreland Street, W1
**National Hospital for
Nervous Diseases**
BX38 2
Queen Square, WC1
National Temperance
BW38 1
Hampstead Road, NW1
Neasden
BN36 55
Brentfield Road, NW10
Nelson
BR51 85
Kingston Road, Merton,
SW20
Netherne
BW64 104
Coulsdon
New Cross
CC43 67
Avonley Road, New Cross,
SE14
New End
BT35 47
Hampstead, NW3
New Victoria
BM51 85
184 Coombe Road, Kingston
upon Thames

Normansfield
BK50 74
Kingston Road, Teddington
North Middlesex
CA28 39
Silver Street, Edmonton, N18
Northwick Park
BD33 45
Watford Road, Harrow
Northwood, Pinner & District
BC30 35
Pinner Road, Northwood
Norwood & District
BZ50 77
Hermitage Road, SE19

O

Oldchurch
CT32 50
Oldchurch Road, Romford
Ongar War Memorial
CX16 24
Shelley, Ongar, Essex
Orme Lodge
BJ29 36
Gordon Avenue, Stanmore
Orpington
CN56 97
Orpington
Ottershaw
AU57 91
Ottershaw, Surrey
Oxted & Limpsfield
CF67 114
Eastlands Way, Oxted, Surrey

P

Paddington Green Childrens'
BT39 1
Paddington Green, W2
Perivale Maternity
BH38 54
Greenford
Plaistow
CJ37 58
Samson Street, Plaistow, E13
Plaistow Maternity
CH38 58
Howards Road, Plaistow, E13
Poplar
CF39 57
East India Dock Road, E14
Port of London Isolation
DJ46 81
Denton, Nr. Gravesend, Kent
Potters Bar & District
BS20 20
Mutton Lane, Potters Bar, Herts
Prince of Wales General
CA31 48
Tottenham Green East, N15
Princess Alexandra
CM10 6
Hamstel Road, Harlow, Essex
Princess Beatrice
BS42 66
281 Old Brompton Road, SW5
Princess Louise
BQ39 55
St. Quintin Avenue, W10
**Purley & District
War Memorial**
BY59 95
Brighton Road, Purley
Putney
BQ45 65
The Lower Common, Putney, SW15

Q

Queen Charlotte's Maternity
BP41 65
Goldhawk Road, W6
Queen Elizabeth
BT62 104
Holly Lane, Banstead Wood, Surrey
Queen Elizabeth House
BU47 76
Nightingale Lane, SW12
Queen Elizabeth II
BS10 5
Howlands, Welwyn Garden City,
Herts

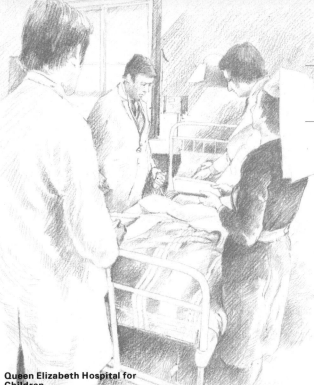

**Queen Elizabeth Hospital for
Children**
CB37 57
Hackney Road, E2
**Queen Mary's Hospital for
Children**
BV58 95
Carshalton, Surrey
Queen Mary's
CO50 79
Frognal Avenue, Sidcup
Queen Mary's
BP46 75
Roehampton Lane, SW15
Queen Mary's Maternity
BT34 47
124 Heath Street, NW3
**Queen Mary's for the
East End**
CF36 57
West Ham Lane, Stratford, E15
Queens
BZ53 87
Queens Road, Croydon
Queen Victoria
BH41 64
Green Lane, Hanwell, W7

R

Redhill General
BU71 121
Earlswood Common, Redhill,
Surrey
Rowley Bristow Orthopaedic
AW61 101
Pyrford, Nr. Woking, Surrey
Roxbourne
BF34 45
Rayners Lane, South Harrow
Royal
BL45 65
Kew Foot Road, Richmond
Royal Dental
BW40 4
32 Leicester Square, WC2
Royal Ear
BW38 1
Huntley Street, WC1
Royal Earlswood
BV72 121
Princess Road, Redhill, Surrey
Royal Eye
BY41 4
St. George's Circus, Southwark,
SE1
Royal Eye Surbiton
BL54 85
Upper Brighton Road, Surbiton,
Surrey
Royal Free
BU35 47
Pond Street, Hampstead, NW3
Royal Herbert (Military)
CK44 68
410 Shooters Hill Road, SE18

**Royal Hospital and Home for
Incurables**
BR46 75
West Hill, Putney, SW15
Royal London Homoeopathic
BX39 2
Great Ormond Street, WC1
Royal Marsden
BT42 3
Fulham Road, SW3
**Royal Marsden (Surrey
Branch)**
BT58 95
Downs Road, Sutton
Royal Masonic
BP41 65
Ravenscourt Park, W6
**Royal National Ear, Nose &
Throat**
BX38 2
Grays Inn Road, WC1
Royal National Orthopaedic
BV38 1
234 Great Portland Street, W1
Royal National Orthopaedic
BK27 36
Brockley Hill, Stanmore
Royal Northern
BX34 47
Holloway Road, N7
Royal Surrey County
AQ71 118
Farnham Road, Guildford, Surrey
Royal Waterloo
BY40 4
Waterloo Road, SE1
Rush Green
CT34 50
Dagenham Road, Romford
Russell Stoneham
CT45 69
Perry Street, Crayford

S

St. Albans City
BG12 9
Normandy Road, St. Albans, Herts
St. Andrew's
CE38 57
Devons Road, E3
St. Anne's General
BZ32 48
St. Anne's Road,
South Tottenham, N15
St. Anthony's
BQ54 85
London Road, North Cheam
St. Bartholomew's
BY39 2
West Smithfield, EC1
St. Benedict's
BV49 76
Church Lane, Tooting, SW17

St. Bernard's
BG40 54
Uxbridge Road, Southall
St. Charles'
BQ39 55
Exmoor Street, W10
St. Christopher's
CC49 77
Lawrie Park Road, SE26
St. Columba's
BT34 47
Spaniards Road, NW3
St. Ebba's
BN58 94
Hook Road, Epsom, Surrey
St. Elizabeth's
BT28 38
Mayfield Avenue, North Finchley,
N12
St. Faith's
DA27 42
London Road, Brentwood, Essex
St. Francis
CA45 67
St. Francis Road, SE22
St. George's
CV35 51
117 Suttons Lane, Hornchurch
St. George's
BV41 3
Hyde Park Corner, SW1
St. George's
BT49 76
Blackshaw Road, SW17
St. Giles'
CA44 67
St. Giles' Road, Camberwell, SE5
St. Helier
BT54 86
Wrythe Lane, Carshalton, Surrey
St. James'
BU47 76
Sarsfeld Road, SW12
St. James'
DG47 81
Trafalgar Road, Gravesend, Kent
St. John's
CF44 67
Morden Hill, SE13
St. John's
BT45 66
St. John's Hill, Battersea, SW11
**St. John's for Diseases of
the Skin**
CC35 48
Eastern Hospital,
Homerton Grove, E9
St. John's
AY38 53
Kingston Lane, Uxbridge
St. John's
BJ47 74
Amyand Park Road,
Twickenham
St. Lawrence's
BZ65 105
Caterham, Surrey
St. Leonard's
CA37 2
Nuttall Street, Kingsland Road, N1
St. Luke's
AS71 118
Warren Road, Guildford, Surrey
St. Luke's
BU42 3
Sydney Street, SW3
St. Luke's Woodside
BV31 47
Woodside Avenue, N10
St. Margaret's
CO18 23
Ongar Road, Epping, Essex
St. Mark's
BY38 2
City Road, EC1
St. Mary's
CH37 58
Upper Road, Plaistow, E13
St. Mary's Maternity
BY54 87
St. James's Road, Croydon
St. Mary's Cottage
BE51 84
Upper Sunbury Road, Hampton
St. Mary's
BT39 1
Praed Street, W2
St. Mary's
BS39 56
Harrow Road, W9

St. Mary Abbots
BS41 66
Marloes Road, W8
St. Matthew's
BZ38 2
Shepherdess Walk, N1
St. Michael's
BZ23 30
19 Chase Side Crescent, Enfield
St. Monica's
BQ36 55
Brondesbury Park, NW6
St. Nicholas
CN42 68
Tewson Road, Plumstead, SE18
St. Olave's
CC41 67
Lower Road, Rotherhithe, SE16
St. Pancras
BW37 1
4 St. Pancras Way, NW1
St. Paul's
BX39 2
Endell Street, WC2
St. Peter's
AU55 82
Guildford Road, Chertsey, Surrey
St. Peter's
BX39 2
Henrietta Street, WC2
St. Philip's
Sheffield Street, Kingsway, WC2
St. Stephen's
BQ25 28
Mays Lane, Barnet
St. Stephen's
BT43 66
Fulham Road, SW10
St. Teresa's
BQ50 75
12 The Downs, SW20
St. Thomas'
BX41 4
Lambeth Palace Road, SE1
Samaritan for Women
BU39 1
Marylebone Road, NW1
Schiff
BE61 102
Knowle Hill Park, Cobham, Surrey
**Seaman's see under
Dreadnought Sevenoaks**
Sevenoaks
CV64 108
St. John's Hill, Sevenoaks, Kent
Shabden Park
BU64 104
High Road, Chipstead, Surrey
Shaftesbury
BX39 2
172 Shaftesbury Avenue, WC2
Shenley
BL20 19
Black Lion Hill, Shenley,
St. Albans, Herts
Sidcup Cottage
CO48 79
Birkbeck Road, Sidcup
Southall-Norwood
BE41 64
The Green, Southall
**South London, for Women &
Children**
BV46 76
Clapham Common, SW4
South Middlesex
BH46 74
Mogden Lane, Isleworth
South Ockendon
DB38 60
South Road, South Ockendon,
Essex
South Western
BX45 66
Landor Road, SW9
Southwood
BV33 47
Southwood Lane, Highgate, N6
Springbok House
BJ27 36
Wood Lane, Stanmore
Springfield
BU48 76
Beechcroft Road, SW17
Staines
AW50 73
Kingston Road, Staines
Stanmore Cottage
BJ29 36
Old Church Lane, Stanmore

Stone House
CY46 80
London Road, Dartford, Kent
Sundridge
CQ67 116
Sevenoaks, Kent
Surbiton General
BL53 85
Ewell Road, Surbiton
Sutton & Cheam General
BS58 95
Cotswold Road, Sutton

T

Teddington Memorial
BH50 74
Hampton Road, Teddington
Temple Hill House
BT34 47
5 West Heath Road, NW3
Thames Ditton
BH54 84
Weston Green Road,
Thames Ditton, Surrey
The Manor
BM59 94
Christchurch Road, Epsom,
Surrey
Thomas Barlow House
BV32 47
80 Shepherds Hill, Highgate, N6
Thorpe Coombe
CF31 48
714 Forest Road,
Walthamstow, E17
Thurrock
DE40 71
Long Lane, Grays, Essex
Tolmers Park
BX16 20
Newgate Street, Nr. Hertford,
Herts
Tolworth
BM55 85
Red Lion Road, Tolworth
Tooting Bec
BV49 76
Tooting Bec Road, Tooting, SW17

U

University College
BW38 1
Gower Street, WC1
  Royal Ear
  BW38 1
  Huntley Street, WC1
  Dental
  BW38 1
  Mortimer Market, WC1
  Obstetric
  BW38 1
  Huntley Street, WC1
  Private Wing
  BW38 1
  Grafton Way, WC1
Upton
AP41 62
Slough, Berks
Uxbridge & District
AX35 44
Harefield Road, Uxbridge

V

Victoria Maternity
BR24 28
Wood Street, Barnet
Victoria
CT31 50
Pettits Lane, Romford

W

Waddon
BX54 86
Purley Way, Croydon
**Waltham Abbey
War Memorial**
CF20 21
Farm Hill Road, Waltham Abbey,
Essex

Walton General
BC55 84
Sidney Road, Walton on Thames,
Surrey
Wandle Valley
BU54 86
Mitcham Junction
Wanstead
CH31 49
Hermon Hill, Wanstead, E11
Warley
DA28 42
Warley Hill, Brentwood, Essex
Warlingham Park
CE61 105
Warlingham, Surrey
**Watford General
(Peace Memorial Wing)**
BC24 26
Rickmansworth Road, Watford,
Herts
**Watford General
(Shrodells Wing)**
BC25 26
Vicarage Road, Watford, Herts
**Watford General
(Holywell Wing)**
BB26 35
Tolpits Lane, Watford, Herts
Weir Maternity
BW47 76
Weir Road, SW12
Welfield Home & Hospital
BP12 10
Welfield Road, Hatfield, Herts
Welwyn Garden City Cottage
BQ8 5
Church Road,
Welwyn Garden City, Herts
Wembley
BK36 54
Fairview Avenue, Wembley
Western
BS43 66
Seagrave Road, W6
Western Opthalmic
BU39 1
Marylebone Road, NW1
West Hendon
BO32 46
Goldsmith Avenue, NW9
West Hill
CV46 80
Dartford, Kent
West London
BQ42 65
Hammersmith Road, W6
West Middlesex
BJ44 64
Twickenham Road, Isleworth
Westminster
BY42 4
Dean Ryle Street, SW1
Westminster Children's
BW42 3
Vincent Square, SW1
Westmoor House
BP47 75
244 Roehampton Lane, SW15
West Park
BL59 94
Epsom, Surrey
Wexham Park
AR38 52
Wexham, Slough, Berks
Weybridge
AZ56 92
Church Street, Weybridge, Surrey
Whipps Cross
CF32 48
Whipps Cross Road,
Leytonstone, E11
Whittington
BV34 47
Highgate Hill, N19
Willesden General
BP36 55
Harlesden Road, NW10
Wilson
BU52 86
Cranmer Road, Mitcham, Surrey
Wimbledon
BP50 75
Thurstan Road, Copse Hill, SW20
Woking Victoria
AS61 100
Chobham Road, Woking, Surrey
Wood Green & Southgate
BW29 38
Bounds Green Road, N11

Acton BM40 55
250 High Street, W3
Albany Street BV38 1
60 Albany Street, NW1
Arbour Square CC39 57
East Arbour Street, E1

Banstead BS61 104
High Street
Barking CM36 58
6 Ripple Road
Barkingside CM31 49
1 High Street
Barnes BO44 65
371 Lonsdale Road, SW13
Barnet BR24 28
26 High Street
Battersea BU44 66
112 Battersea Bridge Road, SW11
Beckenham CE51 87
45 High Street
Belvedere CQ42 69
2 Nuxley Road
Bethnal Green CB38 57
458 Bethnal Green Road, E2
Bexleyheath CR45 69
39 Broadway
Biggin Hill CJ61 97
195 Main Road
Blackwall CF40 57
19 Goldharbour, E14
Boreham Wood BN23 28
Elstree Way
Bow CE38 57
111 Bow Road, E3
Bow Street BX39 2
28 Bow Street, WC2
Brentford BJ43 64
The Half Acre
Brixton BY45 66
367 Brixton Road, SW9
Brockley CD45 67
4 Howson Road, SE4
Bromley CH51 88
Widmore Road
Bushey BF26 36
43 Clay Hill

Caledonian Road BX35 56
470 Caledonian Road, N7
Camberwell BZ44 67
22a Camberwell Church Street,
SE5
Cannon Row BX41 4
1 Cannon Row, SW1
Carter Street BZ42 4
292 Walworth Road, SE17
Catford CF48 77
333 Bromley Road, SE6
Chadwell Heath CP33 50
14 Wangey Road
Chelsea BU42 3
2 Lucan Place, SW3

Cheshunt BC18 21
101 Turners Hill
Chigwell CM28 40
Limes Avenue
Chingford CF26 39
Kings Head Hill, E4
Chislehurst CL50 78
47 High Street
Chiswick BO42 65
205 Chiswick High Road, W4
City Road BZ38 2
4 Shepherdess Walk, N1
Clapham BW44 66
51 Union Grove, SW8
Claybury CK29 40
Manor Road, Woodford Bridge
Cobham BC60 92
Portsmouth Road
Collier Row CS30 41
22 Collier Row Lane
Croydon BZ55 96
Fell Road

Dagenham CS35 50
561 Rainham Road South
Dalston CA36 57
39 Dalston Lane, E8
Dartford CV47 80
Instone Road
Debden CM24 31
34 Barrington Grove
Deptford CD43 67
116 Amersham Vale, SE4

Ealing BK40 54
67 Uxbridge Road, W5
Earlsfield BT48 76
522 Garratt Lane, SW17
East Dulwich CB46 77
97 Crystal Palace Road, SE22
East Ham CK37 58
4 High Street South, E6
East Molesey BG53 84
1 Walton Road
Edgware BM29 37
Whitchurch Lane
Edmonton CB28 39
320 Fore Street, N9
Eltham CK44 68
20 Well Hall Road, SE9
Enfield BZ24 30
Baker Street
Epsom BO60 94
Church Street
Esher BF56 93
113 High Street
Erith CT42 69
22 High Street

Farnborough CL55 88
Farnborough Common
Feltham BD47 74
Ashfield Avenue
Finchley BS29 38
193 Ballards Lane, N3
Forest Gate CH35 49
370 Romford Road, E7
Fulham BS43 66
Heckfield Place, SW6

Gerald Road BV42 3
5 Gerald Road, SW1
Gipsy Hill CA50 77
16 Central Hill, SE19
Golders Green BR32 46
1069 Finchley Road, NW11
Greenford BG38 54
21 Oldfield Lane
Greenwich CF43 67
31 Royal Hill, SE10

Hackney CC35 48
2 Lower Clapton Road, E5
Hainault CO28 41
Manford Way
Ham BK48 74
Ashburnham Road, Richmond
Hammersmith BQ42 65
226 Shepherds Bush Road, W6
Hampstead BT35 47
26½ Rosslyn Hill, NW3
Hampton BF51 84
68 Station Road
Harefield AX30 35
24 Rickmansworth Road
Harlesden BO36 55
75 Craven Park, NW10
Harold Hill CV28 42
Gooshays Drive
Harrow BG34 45
74 Northolt Road
Harrow Road BS38 56
325 Harrow Road, W9
Hatfield BQ11 10
St. Alban's Road East
Hayes BA39 53
755 Uxbridge Road
Hemel Hempstead AX13 8
Combe Road
Hemel Hempstead AX13 8
Combe Street
Hendon BQ31 46
133 Brent Street North, NW4

Highbury Vale BY34 47
211 Blackstock Road, N5
Highgate BV32 47
407 Archway Road, N6
Hoddesdon CE12 12
High Street
Holborn BX39 2
70 Theobalds Road, WC1
Holloway BX34 47
284 Hornsey Road, N7
Hornchurch CV34 51
74 Station Lane
Hornsey BX31 47
98 Tottenham Lane, N8
Hounslow BF45 64
5 Montague Road
Hyde Park BU40 3
North of Serpentine, W2

Ilford CL34 49
40 High Road
Isle of Dogs CF43 67
126 Manchester Road, E14
Islington BY36 56
277 Upper Street, N1

Kenley BZ60 96
94 Godstone Road
Kennington Road BY41 4
49 Kennington Road, SE1
Kensington BS41 66
72 Earl's Court Road, W8
Kentish Town BV35 47
12a Holmes Road, NW5
Kilburn BR37 55
38 Salusbury Road, NW6
Kingsbury BM32 46
3 The Mall, Kenton
**Kingston upon Thames
BK**51 84
5 High Street
Kings Cross Road BX38 2
76 Kings Cross Road, WC1

Lavender Hill BV45 66
176 Lavender Hill, SW11
Lee Road CG45 68
418 Lee High Road, SE12
Leman Street CA39 2
74 Leman Street, E1
Lewisham CE46 77
2 Ladywell Road, SE13
Leyton CF33 48
215 Francis Road, E10

Leytonstone CG34 49
470 High Road, E11
Limehouse CE40 57
29 West India Dock Road, E14
Loughton CK24 31
158 High Road

Marylebone Lane BV39 1
50 Marylebone Lane, W1
Mill Hill BN28 37
11 Deans Drive
Mitcham BU52 86
58 Cricket Green
Muswell Hill BU31 47
Fortis Green, N2

New Addington CF58 96
1 Overbury Crescent
New Malden BO52 85
184 High Street
New Southgate BV28 38
High Road, N11
Nine Elms BV43 66
147 Battersea Park Road, SW8
Norbury BX51 86
1516 London Road, SW16
Northwood BB29 35
2 Murray Road
North Woolwich CL41 68
Albert Road E16
Norwood Green BE42 64
190 Norwood Road, Southall
Notting Dale BQ40 55
58 Sirdar Road, W11
Notting Hill BR40 55
101 Ladbroke Grove, W11

Oxted CG68 115
Church Lane

Paddington BS38 56
4 Harrow Road, W2
Peckham CB44 67
117 Peckham High Street, SE15
Penge CC50 77
175 High Street, SE20
Pinner BE31 45
Bridge Street
Plaistow CH38 58
444 Barking Road, E13
Plumstead CN42 68
216 Plumstead High Street, SE18
Ponders End CC25 30
204 High Street
Potters Bar BT19 20
The Causeway
Putney BQ45 65
215 Upper Richmond Road,
SW15

Radlett BJ20 18
193 Watling Street
Rainham CV38 60
3 New Road
Richmond BK46 74
8 Red Lion Street
Rickmansworth AX26 35
High Street
Rochester Row BW42 3
63 Rochester Row, SW1
Roehampton BP47 75
117 Danebury Avenue, SW15
Romford CT31 50
19 Main Road

Rotherhithe CC41 67
99 Lower Road, SE16
Ruislip BB33 44
The Oaks

Shenley BM20 28
The Terrace, Harris Lane
Shepherds Bush BP40 55
252 Uxbridge Road, W12
Shooters Hill CK45 68
Shooters Hill, SE18
Sidcup CO49 79
87 Main Road
Southall BF40 54
67 High Street
Southgate BW26 38
25 Chase Side, N14
South Norwood CA52 87
83 High Street, SE25
Southwark BZ41 4
323 Borough High Street, SE1
Staines AW49 73
2 London Road
St. Anns Road BZ32 48
269 St. Anns Road, N15
St. John's Wood BU37 1
20½ New Court Street, NW8
St. Mary Cray CP52 89
79 High Street
Stoke Newington CA35 48
33 Stoke Newington High Street,
N16
Stoneleigh BO56 94
358 Kingston Road, Ewell
Streatham BX49 76
101 Streatham High Road, SW16
Sunbury BC50 73
67 Staines Road East
Surbiton BL54 85
1 Ditton Road, Tolworth
Sutton BC56 95
6 Carshalton Road West
Swanley CT52 89
London Road
Sydenham CC48 77
179 Dartmouth Road, SE26

Teddington BH50 74
18 Park Road
Thamesmead CP41 69
1 Tavy Bridge, SE2
Tooting BU50 76
Mitcham Road, SW17
**Tottenham Court Road
BW**39 1
56 Tottenham Court Road, W1
Tottenham CA31 48
398 High Road, N17
Tower Bridge CA41 4
209 Tooley Street, SE1
Trinity Road BU48 76
76 Trinity Road, SW17
Twickenham BJ47 74
41 London Road

Upminster CY34 51
223 St. Mary's Lane
Uxbridge AX36 53
49 Windsor Street

Vine Street BW40 3
10 Vine Street, W1

Wallington BW57 95
84 Stafford Road
Waltham Abbey CH20 21
35 Sun Street
Walthamstow CD31 48
360 Forest Road, E17
Wandsworth BS46 76
146 High Street, SW16
Wanstead CH32 49
Spratt Hall Road, E17
Wapping CB40 57
96 Wapping High Street, E1
Waterloo Pier BX40 4
Victoria Embankment, WC2
Wealdstone BH31 45
78 High Street
Welling CO45 69
60/62, High Street
Wellington Arch BV41 3
Hyde Park Corner, SW1
Welwyn Garden City BQ9 5
Stanborough Road
Wembley BK36 54
603 Harrow Road
Westcombe Park CH42 68
11 Combedale Road, SE10
West Drayton AY41 63
Station Road
West End Central BW40 3
27 Savile Row, W1
West Hampstead BS35 47
21 Fortune Green Road, E15
West Hendon BP33 46
West Hendon Broadway,
Edgware Road, NW9
West Wickham CE54 87
9 High Street
Whetstone BT27 38
1170 High Road, N20
Willesden Green BP36 55
96 High Road, NW10
Wimbledon BS50 76
15 Queens Road, SW19
Winchmore Hill BY26 38
687 Green Lanes, N21
Woodford Green CH28 40
509 High Road
Wood Green BX30 38
34 High Road, N22
Woolwich CL42 68
29 Market Street, SE18
Worcester Park BP55 85
154 Central Road

City of London Police

Snow Hill
5 Snow Hill, EC1
Bishopsgate
182 Bishopsgate, EC2
Wood Street
Wood Street, EC2

Outer London Area

Berkshire

Slough
Windsor Road, Slough
Windsor
Alma Road, Windsor

Hertfordshire

Hatfield
St. Albans Road East, Hatfield
Hemel Hempstead
Combe Street, Hemel Hempstead
Hoddesdon
High Street, Hoddesdon
Rickmansworth
Rectory Road, Rickmansworth
St. Albans
Victoria Street, St. Albans
Watford Central
Shady Lane, Clarendon Road,
Watford
Watford North
Kingsway, Garston
Welwyn Garden City
The Campus, Welwyn Garden City

Essex

Grays
Orsett Road, Grays
Harold Hill
Gooshays Drive, Harold Hill
Hornchurch
74 Station Lane, Hornchurch
Rainham
3 New Road, Rainham
Romford
Main Road, Romford
Tilbury
Dock Road, Tilbury
Upminster
223 St. Mary's Lane, Upminster
Waltham Abbey
35 Sun Street, Waltham Abbey

Kent

Dartford
Instone Road, Dartford
Farnborough
Crofton Road, Farnborough
Gravesend
Windmill Street, Gravesend
Sevenoaks
Moorewood Close, Sevenoaks
Swanley
London Road, Swanley

Surrey

Dorking
Moores Road, Dorking
Egham
High Street, Egham
Guildford
Margaret Road, Guildford
Leatherhead
44 Kingston Road, Leatherhead
Oxted
East Hill Road, Oxted
Redhill
79 Reigate Road, Redhill
Walton on Thames
New Zealand Avenue,
Walton on Thames
Woking
Heath Side Road, Woking

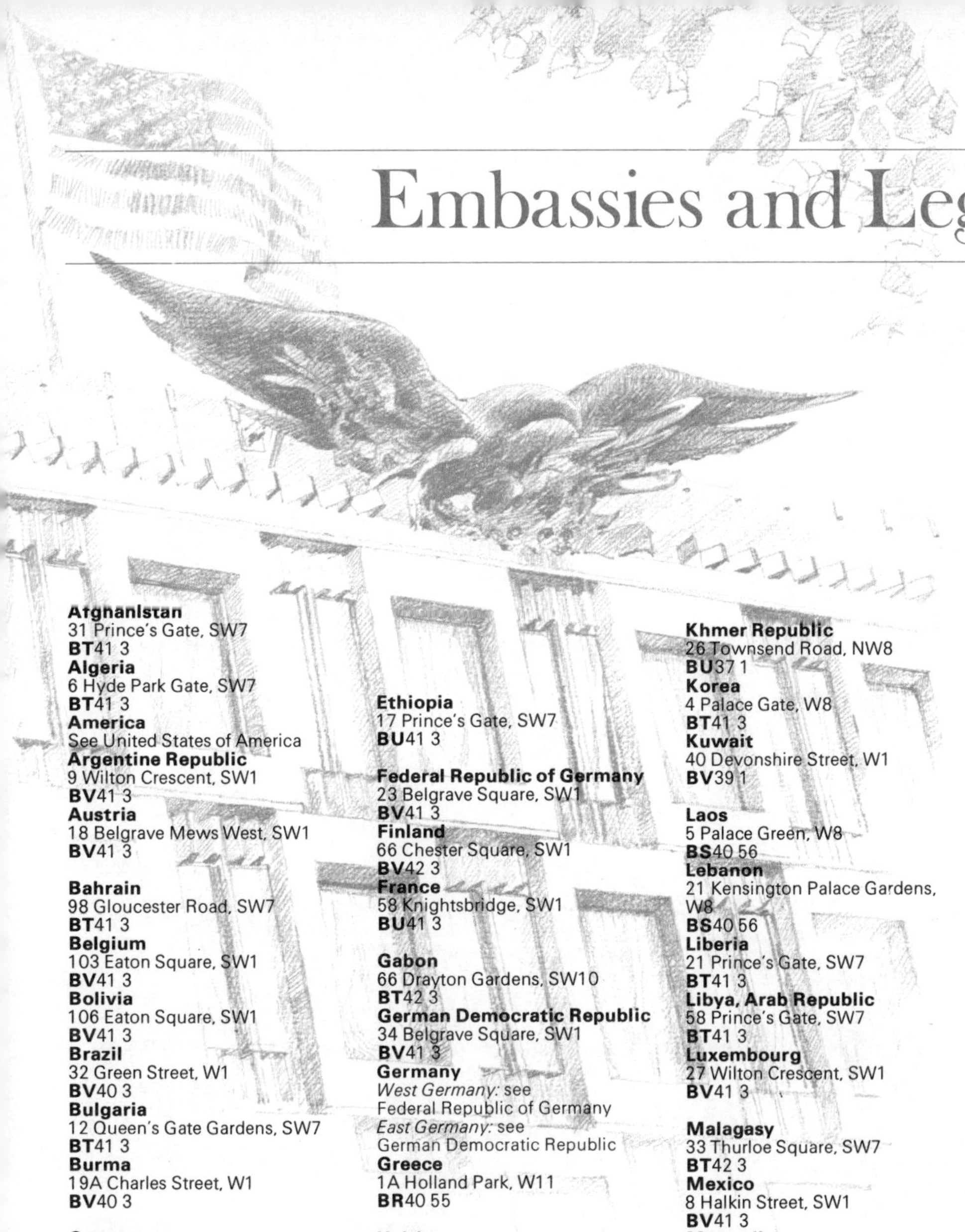

Afghanistan
31 Prince's Gate, SW7
BT41 3
Algeria
6 Hyde Park Gate, SW7
BT41 3
America
See United States of America
Argentine Republic
9 Wilton Crescent, SW1
BV41 3
Austria
18 Belgrave Mews West, SW1
BV41 3

Bahrain
98 Gloucester Road, SW7
BT41 3
Belgium
103 Eaton Square, SW1
BV41 3
Bolivia
106 Eaton Square, SW1
BV41 3
Brazil
32 Green Street, W1
BV40 3
Bulgaria
12 Queen's Gate Gardens, SW7
BT41 3
Burma
19A Charles Street, W1
BV40 3

Cameroon
84 Holland Park, W11
BR40 55
Chile
12 Devonshire Street, W1
BV39 1
China, Peoples Republic
31 Portland Place, W1
BV38 1
Colombia
3 Hans Crescent, SW1
BU41 3
Costa Rica
55 Eaton Place, SW1
BV41 3
Cuba
57 Kensington Court, W8
BS41 56
Czechoslovakia
25 Kensington Palace Gardens, W8
BS40 56

Denmark
29 Pont Street, SW1
BU41 3
Dominican Republic
4 Braemar Mansions,
Cornwall Gardens, SW7
BS41 56

Ecuador
3 Hans Crescent, SW1
BU41 3
Egypt, Arab Republic of
26 South Street, W1
BV40 3
Eire
See Ireland, Republic of
El Salvador
16 Edinburgh House,
9B Portland Place, W1
BV38 1

Ethiopia
17 Prince's Gate, SW7
BU41 3

Federal Republic of Germany
23 Belgrave Square, SW1
BV41 3
Finland
66 Chester Square, SW1
BV42 3
France
58 Knightsbridge, SW1
BU41 3

Gabon
66 Drayton Gardens, SW10
BT42 3
German Democratic Republic
34 Belgrave Square, SW1
BV41 3
Germany
West Germany: see
Federal Republic of Germany
East Germany: see
German Democratic Republic
Greece
1A Holland Park, W11
BR40 55

Haiti
17 Queen's Gate, SW7
BT41 3
Honduras
48 George Street, W1
BU39 1
Hungary
35 Eaton Place, SW1
BV41 3

Iceland
1 Eaton Terrace, SW1
BV42 3
Indonesia
38 Grosvenor Square, W1
BV40 3
Iran
16 Prince's Gate, SW7
BT41 3
Iraq
21/22 Queen's Gate, SW7
BT41 3
Ireland, Republic of
17 Grosvenor Place, SW1
BV41 3
Israel
2 Palace Green, Kensington, W8
BS40 56
Italy
14 Three King's Yard,
Davies Street, W1
BV40 3
Ivory Coast
2 Upper Belgrave Street, SW1
BV41 3

Japan
43–46 Grosvenor Street, W1
BV40 3
Jordan
6 Upper Phillimore Gardens, W8
BS41 56

Khmer Republic
26 Townsend Road, NW8
BU37 1
Korea
4 Palace Gate, W8
BT41 3
Kuwait
40 Devonshire Street, W1
BV39 1

Laos
5 Palace Green, W8
BS40 56
Lebanon
21 Kensington Palace Gardens,
W8
BS40 56
Liberia
21 Prince's Gate, SW7
BT41 3
Libya, Arab Republic
58 Prince's Gate, SW7
BT41 3
Luxembourg
27 Wilton Crescent, SW1
BV41 3

Malagasy
33 Thurloe Square, SW7
BT42 3
Mexico
8 Halkin Street, SW1
BV41 3
Mongolia
7 Kensington Court, W8
BS41 56
Morocco
49 Queen's Gate Gardens, SW7
BT41 3

Nepal
12A Kensington Palace Gardens,
W8
BS40 56
Netherlands
38 Hyde Park Gate, SW7
BT41 3
Nicaragua
8 Gloucester Road, SW7
BT41 3
Norway
25 Belgrave Square, SW1
BV41 3

Oman
64 Ennismore Gardens, SW7
BU41 3

Pakistan
35 Lowndes Square, SW1
BU41 3
Panama
29 Wellington Court,
116 Knightsbridge, SW1
BU41 3
Paraguay
Braemar Lodge,
Cornwall Gardens, SW7
BS41 56
Peru
52 Sloane Street, SW1
BU41 3
Phillipines
9A Palace Green, W8
BS40 56

Poland
47 Portland Place, W1
BV38 1
Portugal
11 Belgrave Square, SW1
BV41 3

Qatar
10 Reeves Mews, W1
BV40 3

Romania
4 Palace Green, W8
BS40 56
Russia (U.S.S.R.)
See under Soviet Union

Saudi Arabia
27 Eaton Place, SW1
BV41 3
Senegal
11 Phillimore Gardens, W8
BS41 56
Somali
60 Portland Place, W1
BV38 1
South Africa
South Africa House,
Trafalgar Square, WC2
BW40 3
Soviet Union
13 Kensington Palace Gardens,
W8
BS40 56
Spain
24 Belgrave Square, SW1
BV41 3
Sudan
3 Cleveland Row, SW1
BW40 3
Sweden
23 North Row, W1
BU40 3
Switzerland
16–18 Montagu Place, W1
BU39 1
Syria, Arab Republic
5 Eaton Terrace, SW1
BV42 3

Thailand
29/30 Queen's Gate, SW7
BT41 3
Tunisia
29 Prince's Gate, SW7
BT41 3
Turkey
43 Belgrave Square, SW1
BV41 3

United Arab Emirates
30 Prince's Gate, SW7
BT41 3
United States of America
24 Grosvenor Square, W1
BV40 3
Uruguay
48 Lennox Gardens, SW1
BU41 3

Venezuela
3 Hans Crescent, SW1
BU41 3
Viet-Nam
89 Belsize Park Gardens, NW3
BU36 56

Yemen, Arab Republic
41 South Street, W1
BV40 3
**Yemen, People's Democratic
Republic**
57 Cromwell Road, SW7
BS42 66
Yugoslavia
5 Lexham Gardens, W8
BS42 66

Zaire
26 Chesham Place, SW1
BV41 3

Australia

Australia House
Strand, WC2
BX39 2

States

New South Wales
56–57 Strand, WC2
BX40 4

Queensland
409–419 Strand, WC2
BX40 4

South Australia
50 Strand, WC2
BX40 4

Tasmania
457 Strand, WC2
BX40 4

Western Australia
115–116 Strand, WC2
BX40 4

Victoria
Victoria House, Melbourne
Place, WC2
BX39 2

Canada

Canada House
Trafalgar Square, SW1
BW40 3

Provinces

Alberta
Alberta House
37 Hill Street, W1
BV40 3

British Columbia
1 Regent Street, SW1
BW40 4

Nova Scotia
14 Pall Mall, SW1
BW40 3

Ontario
Ontario House
13 Charles II Street, SW1
BW40 3

Quebec
12 Upper Grosvenor Street, W1
BV40 3

Saskatchewan
14–16 Cockspur Street, SW1
BW40 3

New Zealand

New Zealand House
Haymarket, SW1
BW40 3

Bahamas

39 Pall Mall, SW1
BW40 3

Bangladesh

28 Queens Gate, SW7
BT41 3

Barbados

6 Upper Belgrave Street, SW1
BV41 3

Botswana

3 Buckingham Gate, SW1
BW41 3

Cyprus

93 Park Street, W1
BV40 3

Fiji

25 Upper Brook Street, W1
BV40 3

Gambia

60 Ennismore Gardens, SW7
BU41 3

Ghana

13 Belgrave Square, SW1
BV41 3

Grenada *West Indies*

Kings House
10 Haymarket, SW1
BW40 3

Guyana

3 Palace Court, Bayswater Road, W2
BS40 56

India

India House
Aldwych, WC2
BX40 4

Jamaica

48 Grosvenor Street, W1
BV40 3

Kenya

45 Portland Place, W1
BV38 1

Lesotho

16A St James's Street, SW1
BW40 3

Malawi

47 Great Cumberland Place, W1
BU39 1

Malaysia

45 Belgrave Square, SW1
BV41 3

Malta GC

24 Haymarket, SW1
BW40 3

Mauritius

153 Grand Buildings,
Northumberland Avenue,
WC2
BX40 4

Nigeria

Nigeria House
9 Northumberland Avenue, WC2
BX40 4

Sierra Leone

33 Portland Place, W1
BV38 1

Singapore

2 Wilton Crescent, SW1
BV41 3

Sri Lanka

13 Hyde Park Gardens, W2
BT40 3

Swaziland

58 Pont Street, SW1
BU41 3

Tanzania

43 Hertford Street, W1
BV40 3

Tonga

17th Floor
New Zealand House,
Haymarket, SW1
BW40 3

Trinidad & Tobago

42 Belgrave Square, SW1
BV41 3

Uganda

Uganda House
Trafalgar Square, WC2
BW40 3

Zambia

Zambia House
7–11 Cavendish Place, W1
BV39 1

Agricultural Research Council
BV38 2
160 Great Portland Street, W1
Arts Council of Great Britain
BW40 4
105 Piccadilly, W1

British Airports Authority
BV41 3
2 Buckingham Gate, SW1
British Airways Board
BV41 3
Airways Terminal, Victoria, SW1
British Broadcasting
Corporation   BV39 1
Broadcasting House, W1
British Gas Corporation
BU39 1
59 Bryanston Street, W1
British Library   BW39 1
14 Store Street, WC1
British Railways Board
BU39 1
222 Marylebone Road, NW1
British Standards Institution
BV40 3
2 Park Street, W1
British Steel Corporation
BV41 3
33 Grosvenor Place, SW1
British Tourist Authority
BW40 3
64 St James's Street, SW1
British Transport Docks
Board   BU38 1
Melbury House, Melbury Terrace,
NW1
British Waterways Board
BU38 1
Melbury House, Melbury Terrace,
NW1
Board of Customs and Excise
CA40 4
Kings Beam House, Mark Lane, EC3
Board of Inland Revenue
BX40 4
Somerset House, WC2

Central Electricity Generating
Board   BY39 2
15 Newgate Street, EC1
Central Office of Information
BY41 4
Hercules Road, SE1
Charity Commission
BW40 3
14 Ryder Street, St James's, SW1
Church Commissioners
BX41 4
1 Millbank, Westminster, SW1
Civil Aviation Authority
BX39 2
129 Kingsway, WC2
Civil Service Department
BX40 4
Whitehall, SW1
College of Arms or Heralds
College   BY40 4
Queen Victoria Street, EC4
Commission on Industrial
Relations   BW38 1
140 Gower Street, WC1
Commonwealth Development
Corporation   BV40 3
33 Hill Street, W1
Community Relations
Commission   BX40 4
15/16 Bedford Street, WC2
Corporation of London
Records Office   BZ39 2
Guildhall, EC2
Corporation of Trinity House
CA40 4
Trinity House, Tower Hill, EC3
Council on Tribunals
BW40 3
6 Spring Gardens, SW1
Criminal Injuries
Compensation Board
BX38 2
10–12 Russell Square, WC1

Crown Estate Commissioners
BW40 3
13 Carlton House Terrace, SW1

Department for National
Savings   BQ41 65
Blyth Road, W14
Department of Education and
Science   BX41 4
Elizabeth House, York Road, SE1
Department of Employment
BW40 3
8 St James's Square, SW1
Department of Health and
Social Security   BY42 4
Alexander Fleming House,
Elephant & Castle, SE1
Department of Industry
BV41 3
1 Victoria Street, SW1
Department of the
Environment   BW41 3
2 Marsham Street, SW1
Design Council   BW40 3
28 Haymarket, SW1
Development Commission
BX41 4
11 Cowley Street, SW1
Duchy of Cornwall   BV41 3
10 Buckingham Gate, SW1
Duchy of Lancaster   BX40 4
Lancaster Place, Strand, WC2

Electricity Council
BW42 3
30 Millbank, SW1
Exchequer and Audit
Department   BX41 4
Audit House, Victoria
Embankment, EC4
Export Credits Guarantee
Department   BZ39 2
PO Box 272, Aldermanbury
House, Aldermanbury, EC2

Foreign and Commonwealth
Office   BX41 4
Downing Street, SW1
Forestry Commission
BW40 3
231 Corstorphine Road,
Edinburgh EH12 7AT

Gaming Board for Great
Britain   BX39 2
Berkshire House,
168–173 High Holborn, WC1
Government Actuary
BW41 3
Steel House, Tothill Street, SW1
Government Hospitality Fund
BW40 3
2 Carlton Gardens, SW1

HM Land Registry   BX39 2
Lincoln's Inn Fields, WC2
HM Stationery Office
BY39 2
Atlantic House,
Holborn Viaduct, EC1
Historic Buildings Councils
BW40 3
25 Savile Row, W1
Home Office   BX40 4
Whitehall, SW1
Horserace Totalisator Board
BY39 2
Tote House,
8–12 New Bridge Street, EC4
Housing Corporation
BU42 3
Sloane Square House, SW1

Independant Broadcasting
Authority   BU42 3
70 Brompton Road, SW3

Institute of Geological
Sciences   BT41 3
Exhibition Road, SW7

Law Officers Department
BX39 2
Attorney-Generals Chambers,
Royal Courts of Justice, WC1
London Transport Executive
BW41 3
55 Broadway, SW1
Lord Advocates Department
BW41 3
Fielden House,
Great College Street, SW1

Medical Research Council
BV38 1
20 Park Crescent, W1
Metrication Board   BX39 2
22 Kingsway, WC2
Metropolitan Water Board
BY38 2
New River Head,
Rosebery Avenue, EC1
Ministry of Agriculture
Fish and Food
BX40 4
Whitehall Place, SW1
Ministry of Defence   BX40 4
Main Building, Whitehall, SW1
Monopolies and Mergers
Commission   BX39 2
New Court, 48 Carey Street, WC2

National Bus Company
BY39 2
55 New Street Square, EC4
National Debt Office   BZ39 2
Royex House
Aldermanbury Square, EC2
National Economic
Development Office   BW42 3
Millbank Tower, Millbank, SW1
National Freight Corporation
BV38 1
Argosy House,
215 Great Portland Street, W1
National Ports Council
BW39 1
Commonwealth House,
1 New Oxford Street, WC1
National Research
Development Council
BV41 3
Kingsgate House,
66 Victoria Street, SW1
National Theatre Office
BY40 4
Upper Ground, South Bank, SE1
National Water Council
BW41 3
1 Queen Anne's Gate, SW1
Northern Ireland Office
BW41 3
Great George Street, SW1

Office of Manpower
Economics   BX39 2
22 Kingsway, WC2
Office of Population
Censuses and Surveys
BX39 2
St Catherine's House, WC2

Patent Office   BX39 2
25 Southampton Buildings,
Chancery Lane, WC2

Political Honours Scrutiny
Committee   BX40 4
Standard House,
Northumberland Avenue, WC2
Port of London Authority
CA40 4
World Trade Centre, E1
Post Office Board   BW39 1
23 Howland Street, W1
Prices and Consumer
Protection Department
BV41 3
1 Victoria Street, SW1
Public Health Laboratory
Service   BN31 46
Colindale Avenue, NW9
Public Record Office   BX39 2
Chancery Lane, WC2
Public Trustee Office
BX39 2
Sardinia Street, Kingsway, WC2
Pilgrim Trust   BX41 4
Fielden House,
Little College Street, SW1

Registry of Friendly Societies
BV39 1
17 North Audley Street, W1
Royal Commission on
Environmental Pollution
BW41 3
Church House,
Great Smith Street, SW1
Royal Commission on
Historic Monuments
BW40 3
23 Savile Row, W1
Royal Commission
on the Press   BX40 4
Standard House,
27 Northumberland Avenue, WC2
Royal Fine Art Commission
BW40 3
2 Carlton Gardens, SW1
Royal Mint   CA40 4
Tower Hill, EC3

Social Science Research
Council   BX39 2
State House, High Holborn, WC1
Sports Council   BU42 3
70 Brompton Road, SW3
Sugar Board   CA40 4
52 Mark Lane, EC3

The British Council   BW40 3
10 Spring Gardens, SW1
The House of Lords
Record Office   BX41 4
House of Lords, SW1
The National Trust   BW41 3
42 Queen Anne's Gate, SW1
The Treasury   BW41 3
18 Parliament Street, SW1

United Kingdom Atomic
Energy Authority   BW40 3
11 Charles II Street, SW1

Value Added Tax Tribunals
BV39 1
17 North Audley Street, W1

Wine Standards Board
BZ40 4
Kennet House,
Kennet Wharf Lane, EC4

Major Spectator Sporting Venues

Association Football

Arsenal BY34 47
Avenell Road, N5
Brentford BK43 64
Griffin Park, Brentford, Middx
Charlton Athletic CJ42 68
The Valley, SE7
Chelsea BS43 66
Stamford Bridge, Fulham Road
SW6
Crystal Palace CB50 77
Selhurst Park, SE25
Fulham BQ44 65
Craven Cottage,
Stevenage Road, SW6
Millwall CC43 67
The Den, New Cross, SE14
Orient CE34 48
Leyton Stadium,
Brisbane Road, E10
**Queen's Park Rangers
BP**40 55
Loftus Road, W12
**Tottenham Hotspur
CB**29 39
White Hart Lane, N17
Watford BC25 26
Vicarage Road, Watford, Herts
West Ham United CJ37 58
Boleyn Ground, Upton Park, E13

Rugby Union

Blackheath CH43 68
Rectory Field, SE3
Harlequins BH46 74
Twickenham & Stoop Memorial
Ground, Twickenham
London Irish BC51 84
The Avenue, Sunbury on Thames
London Scottish BK45 64
Richmond Athletic Ground
London Welsh BL45 65
Old Deer Park, Kew Road,
Richmond
**Metropolitan Police
BG**54 84
Imber Court, East Molesey,
Surrey
Richmond BK45 64
Richmond Athletic Ground
Rosslyn Park BO45 65
Upper Richmond Road, SW15
St Mary's BJ50 74
Udney Park Road,
Teddington
Saracens BV25 29
Green Road, Southgate, N14
Wasps BK35 45
Repton Avenue, Sudbury

Cricket Grounds

Blackheath CH43 68
Rectory Field, SE3
Ilford CL33 49
Valentine's Park, Cranbrook
Road, Ilford
Leyton CE33 48
Youth Sports Ground,
Crawley Road, E10
Lord's BT38 1
St John's Wood, NW8
Kennington BX43 66
The Oval, SE11
Romford CU30 41
Gallows Corner Sports Ground,
Gidea Park

Athletics Centres

**Ashton Playing Fields
CJ**29 40
Woodford Green
**Crystal Palace National
Sports CA**49 77
Crystal Palace Park, SE19
**New River Sports Centre
BY**29 38
White Hart Lane, N22
**Parliament Hill Fields
BU**35 47
Gospel Oak, NW3
Victoria Park CD37 57
Victoria Park, E9
**West London Stadium
BP**39 55
Wormwood Scrubs, W12

Tennis Clubs

All England BR49 75
Church Road, SW19
**Bank of England
BO**46 75
Priory Lane, Roehampton
**Coolhurst Lawn Tennis and
Squash Club BW**32 47
Coolhurst Road, N8
Hazelwood BZ26 39
Ridge Avenue, N21
Holland Park BR41 65
1 Addison Road, W14
Hurlington BR45 75
Fulham, SW6
Paddington BS38 56
Castellain Road, W9
Queen's BR42 65
Palliser Road, W14
Roehampton BR45 65
Roehampton Lane, SW15

Greyhound Racing

Catford GE46 77
Greyhound Stadium, SE6
Crayford, Kent CT46 79
Crayford Road
Hackney Wick CE36 57
Waterden Road, E15
Harringay BZ32 48
Green Lanes, N4
Romford CS32 50
London Road
Slough, Berks AQ41 62
Uxbridge Road
Walthamstow CE29 39
Chingford Road, E17
Wembley BM35 46
Stadium Way
White City BQ40 55
Wood Lane, W12
Wimbledon BT49 76
Plough Lane, SW19

Boxing

Empire Pool BM35 46
Wembley Stadium
Empire Stadium BM35 46
Wembley Stadium
**Newington Sports Hall
BZ**42 4
Manor Place, SE17
Royal Albert Hall BT41 3
Kensington Gore, SW7
York Hall CC38 57
Old Ford Road, E2

Horse Racing

Epsom BO63 103
On B290, Epsom, Surrey
Kempton Park BD51 84
On A308, near Sunbury
Sandown Park BG55 84
On A3, near Esher
Windsor AM43 61
On A308, near Windsor

Sports Centres

Crystal Palace CA49 77
National Sports Centre,
Norwood, SE19
**Hampstead Swimming Baths
BT**36 56
Avenue Road, NW3
**Michael Sobell Sports Centre
BX**34 47
Hornsey Road, N7
**Picketts Lock Centre
CC**27 39
Picketts Lock Lane, N9
**Rainham Sports Centre
CV**38 60
Lambs Lane, Rainham, Essex
**Walnut Sports Centre
CO**54 89
Orpington, Kent

Town Halls

Greater London Council
BX41 4
The County Hall, SE1 7PB
Barking CM37 58
Civic Centre,
Dagenham, RM10 7DR
Barnet BP31 46
Town Hall, The Burroughs,
Hendon, NW4 4BG
Bexley CT42 69
Town Hall, Erith, Kent, DA8 1TL
Brent BM34 46
Town Hall, Forty Lane, Wembley
Bromley CG51 88
Town Hall, Widmore Road,
Bromley, BR1 1SB
Camden BX38 2
Town Hall,
Euston Road, NW1 2RU
City of London Corporation
BX39 2
P.O. Box 270 Guildhall, EC2P 2EJ
Croydon BZ55 87
Town Hall, Taberner House,
Park Lane, Croydon
Ealing BK40 54
Town Hall, New Broadway, W5
Enfield BZ24 30
Civic Centre, Silver Street, Enfield
Greenwich CL42 68
Town Hall, Wellington Street,
Woolwich, SE18
Hackney CB36 57
Town Hall, Mare Street, E8 1EA
Hammersmith BP42 65
Town Hall, King Street, W6 9JU
Haringey BX30 38
Civic Centre, P.O. Box
264 High Road, N22 4LE
Harrow BH31 45
Civic Centre, Harrow, Middlesex
Havering CT31 50
Town Hall, Main Road, Romford
Hillingdon BB39 53
Town Hall,
Wood End Green Road,
Hayes, UB3 2SA

Hounslow BF45 64
Civic Centre, Treaty Road,
Hounslow
Islington BY36 56
Town Hall, Upper Street, N1 20D
Kensington & Chelsea
BS41 56
Town Hall,
Kensington High Street, W8 4SQ
Kingston upon Thames
BK51 84
Guildhall, 19 High Street
Lambeth BX45 66
Town Hall, Brixton Hill, SW2 1RW
Lewisham CE47 77
Town Hall, Catford, SE6 4RU
Merton BR50 75
Town Hall, P.O. Box
364 The Broadway, SW19 7NR
Newham CK37 58
Town Hall, East Ham, E6 2RP
Redbridge CL34 49
Town Hall, High Road,
Ilford, IG1 1DD
Richmond upon Thames
BK46 74
Town Hall, York House,
Twickenham, TW1 3AA
Southwark CA44 67
Town Hall,
Peckham Road, SE5 8UB
Sutton BS56 95
Town Hall, 3 Throwley Way,
Sutton, SM1 4AB
Tower Hamlets CB37 57
Town Hall, Patriot Square, E2 9LN
Waltham Forest CE31 48
Town Hall, Forest Road,
Walthamstow, E17 4JA
Wandsworth BS46 76
Town Hall,
High Street, SW18 2PU
Westminster, City of
BW41 3
City Hall,
Victoria Street, SW1E 6QW

District Council Offices

Beaconsfield District
AP41 52
Windsor Road, Slough, SL1 2HN
Brentwood District DB27 42
Ingrave Road,
Brentwood, CM15 8AY
Broxbourne District
BC19 21
Manor House, Turners Hill,
Cheshunt, EN8 8LE
Chiltern District
(Outside area of atlas)
Elmodesham House,
42 High Street,
Amersham, HP7 0DL
Dacorum District AX13 8
Town Hall, Marlowes,
Hemel Hempstead, HP1 1HH
Dartford District CW47 80
High Street, Dartford, DA1 1DR
East Hertfordshire District
(Outside area of atlas)
Bishop's Stortford,
Hertfordshire, CM23 2EN
Elmbridge District BC54 83
Town Hall, Walton on Thames,
Surrey, KT12 1PS
Epping Forest District
CN18 22
323 High Street, Epping, Essex
Epsom and Ewell District
BN60 94
P.O. Box 5 Town Hall,
The Parade, Epsom, KT18 5BY
Gravesham District DG47 81
Civic Centre,
Gravesend, DA12 1AU
Guildford District AR71 118
Millmead House, Guildford,
Surrey, GU2 5BB
Harlow District CM11 13
Town Hall, Harlow,
Essex, CM20 1HJ

Hertsmere District BN23 28
Elstree Way, Borehamwood,
Hertfordshire
Mole Valley District
BK71 119
Pippbrook, Dorking, RH4 1SJ
Reigate and Banstead District
BS70 121
Town Hall, Reigate, RH2 0SH
Runnymede District
AX56 92
Station Road, Addlestone,
Weybridge, Surrey, KT15 2AH
St. Albans District BG13 9
16 St Peter's Street,
St Albans, AL1 3ND
Sevenoaks District
CU66 116
Argyle Road, Sevenoaks,
Kent, TN13 1HG
Slough District AO40 61
Town Hall, Bath Road, Slough
Spelthorne District
AW49 73
Knowle Green,
Staines, TW18 1XB
Surrey Heath District
(Outside area of atlas)
Bagshot Manor, Green Lane,
Bagshot, Surrey, Gl19 5NN
Tandridge District CB65 105
Caterham, Surrey, CR3 6YN
Three Rivers District
AY26 35
17–23 & 46 High Street,
Rickmansworth, WD3 1JE
Thurrock District DE42 71
Whitehall Lane, Grays,
Essex, RM17 6SL
Welwyn Hatfield District
BQ7 5
Welwyn Garden City,
Hertfordshire, AL8 6AE
Watford District BC24 26
Town Hall, Watford, WD1 3EX

British Rail - Stations

ER   Eastern Region
LMR   London Midland Region
SR   Southern Region
WR   Western Region

Abbey Wood   SR
Acton Central   LMR
Acton Main Line   WR
Addiscombe   SR
Addlestone   SR
Albany Park   SR
Anerley   SR
Angel Road   ER
Apsley   LMR
Ashford   SR
Ashtead   SR

Balham and Upper Tooting   SR
Bank   Waterloo & City
Banstead   SR
Barbican   LMR
Barking   ER
Barnehurst   SR
Barnes   SR
Barnes Bridge   SR
Bat and Ball   SR
Battersea Park   SR
Beckenham Hill   SR
Beckenham Junction   SR
Beddington Lane Halt   SR

Bush Hill Park   ER
Byfleet and New Haw   SR

Caledonian Road and Barnsbury
     LMR
Cambridge Heath   ER
Camden Road   LMR
Canning Town   ER
Cannon Street   SR
Canonbury   LMR
Carpenders Park   LMR
Carshalton   SR
Carshalton Beeches   SR
Castle Bar Park   WR
Caterham   SR
Catford   SR
Catford Bridge   SR
Chadwell Heath   ER
Charing Cross   SR
Charlton   SR
Cheam   SR
Chelsfield   SR

Bellingham   SR
Belmont   SR
Belvedere   SR
Berrylands   SR
Bethnal Green   ER
Bexley   SR
Bexleyheath   SR
Bickley   SR
Bingham Road   SR
Birkbeck   SR
Blackfriars   SR
Blackheath   SR
Black Horse Road   ER
Bookham   SR
Bowes Park   ER
Boxhill and Westhumble   SR
Brentford Central   SR
Brentwood and Warley   ER
Bricket Wood   LMR
Brimsdown   ER
Brixton   SR
Broad Street   LMR
Brockley   SR
Bromley North   SR
Bromley South   SR
Brondesbury   LMR
Brondesbury Park   LMR
Brookman's Park   ER
Bruce Grove   ER
Burnham (Bucks)   WR
Bushey   LMR

Chertsey   SR
Cheshunt   ER
Chessington North   SR
Chessington South   SR
Chingford   ER
Chipstead   SR
Chislehurst   SR
Chiswick   SR
Chorley Wood and Chenies
     LMR
Clandon   SR
Clapham   SR
Clapham Junction   SR
Clapton   ER
Claygate   SR
Clock House   SR
Cobham and Stoke D'Abernon
     SR
Coombe Road   SR
Coulsdon North   SR
Coulsdon South   SR
Crayford   SR
Crews Hill   ER
Cricklewood   LMR
Crofton Park   SR
Crouch Hill   LMR
Croxley Green   LMR
Crystal Palace   SR
Cuffley and Goff's Oak   ER
Custom House (Victoria Dock)
     ER

Dagenham Dock   ER
Dalston Junction   LMR

Dartford   SR
Datchet   SR
Deepdene   SR
Denham   WR
Denham Golf Club   WR
Denmark Hill   SR
Deptford   SR
Dorking   SR
Dorking Town   SR
Drayton Green   WR
Drayton Park   ER
Dunton Green   SR

Ealing Broadway   WR
Earlsfield   SR
Earlswood   SR
East Croydon   SR
East Dulwich   SR
East Tilbury   ER
Eden Park   SR
Effingham Junction   SR
Egham   SR
Elephant and Castle   SR
Elmers End   SR
Elmstead Woods   SR
Elstree and Borehamwood
     LMR
Eltham Park   SR
Eltham (Well Hall)   SR
Emerson Park Halt   ER
Enfield Chase   ER
Enfield Lock   ER
Enfield Town   ER
Epsom   SR
Epsom Downs   SR

Erith   SR
Esher   SR
Essex Road   ER
Euston   LMR
Ewell East   SR
Ewell West   SR
Eynsford   SR

Falconwood   SR
Farningham Road and
     Sutton-at-Hone   SR
Farringdon   LMR
Feltham   SR
Fenchurch Street   ER
Finchley Road and Frognall
     LMR
Finsbury Park   ER
Forest Gate   ER
Forest Hill   SR
Fulwell   SR

Gidea Park and Squirrels Heath
     ER
Gipsy Hill   SR
Goodmayes   ER
Gordon Hill   ER
Gospel Oak for Highgate   LMR
Grange Park   ER
Gravesend Central   SR
Grays   ER
Greenford (Central Line)   WR
Greenhithe   SR
Greenwich   SR
Grove Park   SR
Guildford   SR
Gunnersbury   LMR

Hackbridge   SR
Hackney Downs   ER
Hadley Wood   ER
Hampstead Heath   LMR
Hampton   SR
Hampton Court   SR

Hampton Wick *SR*
Hanwell *WR*
Harlesden *LMR*
Harlow Mill *ER*
Harlow Town *ER*
Harold Wood *ER*
Harringay Stadium *ER*
Harringay West *ER*
Harrow and Wealdstone *LMR*
Harrow-on-the-Hill *LMR*
Hatch End *LMR*
Hatfield *ER*
Haydons Road *SR*
Hayes *SR*
Hayes and Harlington *WR*
Headstone Lane *LMR*
Hemel Hempstead and Boxmoor
  LMR
Hendon *LMR*
Herne Hill *SR*
Hersham *SR*
Highams Park and Hale End *ER*
Highbury and Islington *LMR*
Hinchley Wood *SR*
Hither Green *SR*
Holborn Viaduct *SR*
Honor Oak Park *SR*
Hornsey *ER*
Horsley *SR*
Hounslow *SR*

Ilford *ER*
Isleworth *SR*
Iver *WR*

Kempton Park *SR*
Kemsing *SR*
Kenley *SR*
Kensal Green *LMR*
Kensal Rise *LMR*
Kent House *SR*
Kentish Town *LMR*
Kentish Town West *LMR*
Kenton *LMR*
Kew Bridge *SR*
Kew Gardens *LMR*
Kidbrooke *SR*
Kilburn High Road *LMR*
Kings Cross *ER*
King's Langley and Abbot's
  Langley *LMR*
Kingston *SR*
Kingswood and Burgh Heath
  SR
Knockholt *SR*

Ladywell *SR*
Langley (Bucks.) *WR*
Lea Bridge *ER*
Leatherhead *SR*
Lee *SR*
Lewisham *SR*
Leyton Midland Road *ER*
Leytonstone High Road *ER*
Liverpool Street *ER*
London Bridge *SR*
London Fields *ER*
London Road (Guildford) *SR*
Loughborough Junction *SR*
Lower Edmonton *ER*
Lower Sydenham *SR*

Malden Manor *SR*
Manor Park *ER*
Maryland *ER*
Marylebone *LMR*
Maze Hill *SR*
Merstham *SR*
Merton Park *SR*
Mill Hill Broadway *LMR*
Mitcham *SR*
Mitcham Junction *SR*
Moorgate *LMR*
Morden Road Halt *SR*
Morden South *SR*
Mortlake *SR*
Motspur Park *SR*
Mottingham *SR*

New Barnet *ER*
New Beckenham *SR*
New Cross *SR*
New Cross Gate *SR*
New Eltham *SR*
New Malden *SR*
New Southgate and Friern Barnet
  ER
Norbiton *SR*
Norbury *SR*
North Dulwich *SR*
Northfleet *SR*
Northolt Park *LMR*
North Sheen *SR*
Northumberland Park *ER*
North Wembley *LMR*
North Woolwich *ER*
Norwood Junction *SR*
Nunhead *SR*

Oakleigh Park *ER*
Ockendon *ER*
Orpington *SR*
Otford *SR*
Uxshott *SR*
Oxted *SR*

Paddington *WR*
Palmers Green and Southgate
  ER
Park Street and Frogmore *LMR*
Peckham Rye *SR*
Penge East *SR*
Penge West *SR*
Petts Wood *SR*
Plumstead *SR*
Ponders End *ER*
Potters Bar and South Mimms
  ER
Primrose Hill *LMR*
Purfleet *ER*
Purley *SR*
Purley Oaks *SR*
Putney *SR*

Queen's Park *LMR*
Queen's Road (Battersea) *SR*
Queen's Road Peckham *SR*

Radlett *LMR*
Rainham *ER*
Ravensbourne *SR*
Raynes Park *SR*
Rectory Road *ER*
Redhill *SR*
Reedham *SR*
Reigate *SR*
Richmond *LMR and SR*
Riddlesdown *SR*
Romford *ER*

St. Albans Abbey *LMR*
St. Albans City *LMR*
St. Helier *SR*
St. John's *SR*
St. Margaret's *SR*
St. Mary Cray *SR*
St. Pancras *LMR*
Sanderstead *SR*
Selhurst *SR*
Selsdon *SR*
Seven Kings *ER*
Sevenoaks *SR*
Seven Sisters *ER*
Shenfield and Hutton *ER*
Shepperton *SR*
Shoreham *SR*
Shortlands *SR*
Sidcup *SR*

Silver Street *ER*
Silvertown *ER*
Slade Green *SR*
Slough *WR*
Smitham *SR*
South Acton *LMR*
Southall *WR*
South Bermondsey *SR*
Southbury *ER*
South Croydon *SR*
South Greenford Halt *WR*
South Hampstead *LMR*
South Kenton *LMR*
South Merton *SR*
South Ruislip *WR*
South Tottenham *ER*
Staines Central *SR*
Stamford Hill *ER*
Stanford-le-Hope *ER*
Stepney (East) *ER*
Stoke Newington *ER*
Stonebridge Park *LMR*
Stoneleigh *SR*
Stratford *ER*
Stratford (Low Level) *ER*
Strawberry Hill *SR*
Streatham *SR*
Streatham Common *SR*
Streatham Hill *SR*
Sudbury and Harrow Road
  LMR
Sudbury Hill Harrow *LMR*
Sunbury *SR*
Sundridge Park *SR*
Sunnymeads *SR*
Surbiton *SR*
Sutton *SR*
Sutton Common *SR*
Swanley *SR*
Swanscombe Halt *SR*
Sydenham *SR*
Sydenham Hill *SR*
Syon Lane *SR*

Tadworth and Walton on the Hill
  SR
Tattenham Corner *SR*
Teddington *SR*
Thames Ditton *SR*
Theobalds Grove *ER*
Thornton Heath *SR*
Tilbury (Riverside) *ER*
Tilbury Town *ER*
Tolworth *SR*
Tooting *SR*
Tottenham Hale *ER*
Tulse Hill *SR*
Turkey Street *ER*
Twickenham *SR*

Upminster *ER*
Upper Halliford Halt *SR*
Upper Holloway *LMR*
Upper Warlingham *SR*

Vauxhall *SR*
Victoria *SR*

Waddon *SR*
Waddon Marsh Halt *SR*
Wallington *SR*
Waltham Cross and Abbey *ER*
Walthamstow *ER*
Walthamstow Queen's Road *ER*
Walthamstow St. James Street
  ER
Walthamstow Wood Street *ER*
Walton on Thames *SR*

Wandsworth Common *SR*
Wandsworth Road *SR*
Wandsworth Town *SR*
Wanstead Park *ER*
Waterloo *SR*
Watford High Street *LMR*
Watford Junction *LMR*
Watford North *LMR*
Watford West *LMR*
Welling *SR*
Wembley Central *LMR*
Wembley Hill *LMR*
Westbourne Park *WR*
West Byfleet *SR*
Westcombe Park *SR*
West Croydon *SR*
West Drayton and Yiewsley *WR*
West Dulwich *SR*
West Ealing *WR*
West End Lane *LMR*
West Hampstead Midland
  LMR
West Horndon *ER*
West Norwood *SR*
West Ruislip *WR*
West Sutton *SR*
West Wickham *SR*
Weybridge *SR*
White Hart Lane *ER*
Whitton *SR*
Whyteleafe *SR*
Whyteleafe South *SR*
Willesden Junction *LMR*
Wimbledon *SR*
Wimbledon Chase *SR*
Winchmore Hill *ER*
Windsor and Eton Central *WR*
Windsor and Eton Riverside *SR*
Woking *SR*
Woldingham *SR*
Woodgrange Park *ER*
Wood Green (Alexandra Park)
  ER
Woodmansterne *SR*
Woodside *SR*
Woolwich Arsenal *SR*
Woolwich Dockyard *SR*
Worcester Park *SR*
Worplesdon *SR*
Wraysbury *SR*

York Road *ER*

21

B'loo Bakerloo
Cent Central
Circle Circle
Dist District
Met Metropolitan
N'thn Northern
Picc Piccadilly
Vic Victoria

Acton Town *Dist and Picc*
Aldgate *Met and Circle*
Aldgate East *Dist and Met*
Aldwych *Picc*
Alperton *Picc*
Angel *N'thn*
Archway *N'thn*
Arnos Grove *Picc*
Arsenal *Picc*

Baker Street *B'loo, Met and Circle*
Balham *N'thn*
Bank *N'thn and Cent*
Barbican *Met and Circle*
Barking *Dist and Met*
Barkingside *Cent*
Barons Court *Dist and Picc*
Bayswater *Dist and Circle*
Becontree *Dist*
Belsize Park *N'thn*
Bethnal Green *Cent*
Blackfriars *Dist and Circle*
Blackhorse Lane *Vic*
Blake Hall *Cent*
Bond Street *Cent*
Borough *N'thn*
Boston Manor *Picc*
Bounds Green *Picc*

Bow Road *Met and Dist*
Brent *N'thn*
Brixton *Vic*
Bromley by Bow *Met and Dist*
Buckhurst Hill *Cent*
Burnt Oak *N'thn*
Bushey and Oxhey *B'loo*

Caledonian Road *Picc*
Camden Town *N'thn*
Cannon Street *Dist and Circle*
Canons Park *B'loo*
Carpenders Park *B'loo*
Chalk Farm *N'thn*
Chancery Lane *Cent*
Charing Cross Embankment *B'loo, N'thn, Dist and Circle*
Chigwell *Cent*
Chiswick Park *Dist*
Chorley Wood *Met*
Clapham Common *N'thn*
Clapham North *N'thn*
Clapham South *N'thn*
Cockfosters *Picc*
Colindale *N'thn*
Collier's Wood *N'thn*
Covent Garden *Picc*
Croxley *Met*

Dagenham East *Dist*
Dagenham Heathway *Dist*
Debden *Cent*
Dollis Hill *B'loo*

Ealing Broadway *Dist and Cent*
Ealing Common *Dist and Picc*
Earl's Court *Dist and Picc*
East Acton *Cent*
Eastcote *Met and Picc*
East Finchley *N'thn*
East Ham *Dist and Met*
East Putney *Dist*
Edgware *N'thn*
Edgware Road *Met, Dist, B'loo and Circle*
Elephant and Castle *N'thn and B'loo*
Elm Park *Dist*
Epping *Cent*
Euston *N'thn*
Euston Square *Circle and Met*

Fairlop *Cent*
Farringdon *Met and Circle*
Finchley Central *N'thn*
Finchley Road *B'loo and Met*
Finsbury Park *Picc and Vic*
Fulham Broadway *Dist*

Gants Hill *Cent*
Gloucester Road *Picc, Dist and Circle*
Golders Green *N'thn*
Goldhawk Road *Met*
Goodge Street *N'thn*
Grange Hill *Cent*
Great Portland Street *Met and Circle*
Greenford *Cent*

Green Park *Picc and Vic*
Gunnersbury *Dist*

Hainault *Cent*
Hammersmith *Met, Picc and Dist*
Hampstead *N'thn*
Hanger Lane *Cent*
Harlesden *B'loo*
Harrow and Wealdstone *B'loo*
Harrow-on-the-Hill *Met*
Hatch End *B'loo*
Hatton Cross *Picc*
Headstone Lane *B'loo*
Hendon Central *N'thn*
High Barnet *N'thn*
Highbury and Islington *Vic*
Highgate *N'thn*
High Street Kensington *Dist and Circle*
Hillingdon *Met and Picc*
Holborn (Kingsway) *Cent and Picc*
Holland Park *Cent*
Holloway Road *Picc*
Hornchurch *Dist*
Hounslow Central *Picc*
Hounslow East *Picc*
Hounslow West *Picc*
Hyde Park Corner *Picc*

Ickenham *Met and Picc*

Kennington *N'thn*
Kensal Green *B'loo*
Kensington (Olympia) *Dist*
Kentish Town *N'thn*
Kenton *B'loo*

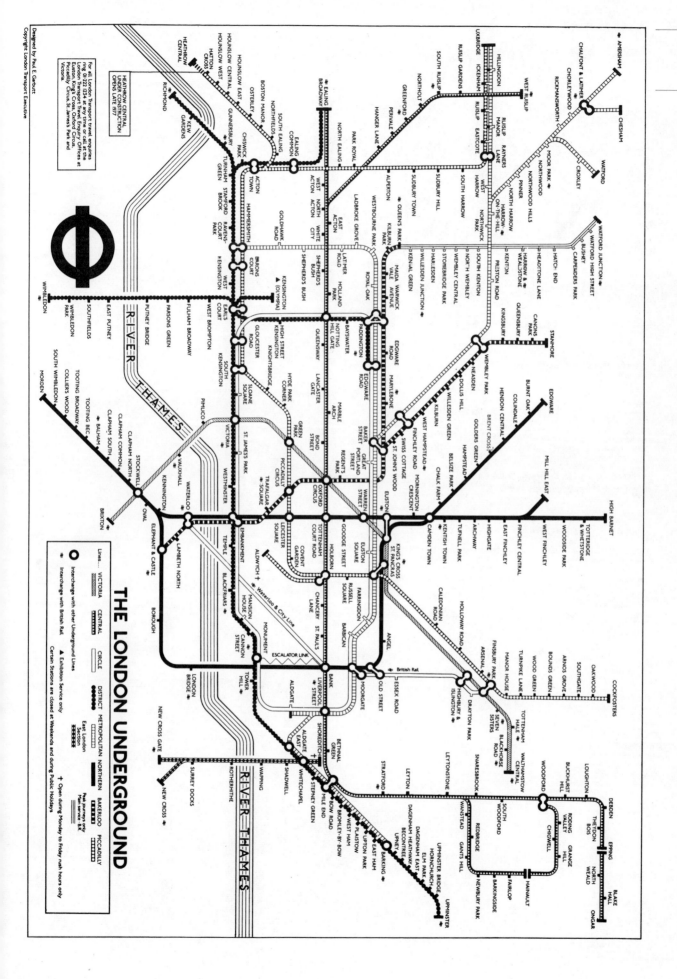

THE LONDON UNDERGROUND

Totteridge and Whetstone *N'thn*
Tower Hill *Circle and Dist*
Trafalgar Square *B'loo*
Tufnel Park *N'thn*
Turnham Green *Dist*
Turnpike Lane *Picc*

Upminster *Dist*
Upminster Bridge *Dist*
Upney *Dist*
Upton Park *Dist and Met*
Uxbridge *Met and Picc*

Vauxhall *Vic*
Victoria *Circle, Dist and Vic*

Walthamstow Central *Vic*
Wanstead *Cent*
Wapping *Met*
Warren Street *N'thn and Vic*
Warwick Avenue *B'loo*
Waterloo *N'thn and B'loo*
Watford *Met*
Watford High Street *B'loo*
Watford Junction *B'loo*
Wembley Central *B'loo*
Wembley Park *B'loo and Met*
West Acton *Cent*
Westbourne Park *Met*
West Brompton *Dist*
West Finchley *N'thn*
West Ham *Met and Dist*
West Hampstead *B'loo*
West Harrow *Met*
West Kensington *Dist*
Westminster *Circle and Dist*
West Ruislip *Cent*
Whitechapel *Met and Dist*
White City *Cent*
Willesden Green *B'loo*
Willesden Junction *B'loo*
Wimbledon *Dist*
Wimbledon Park *Dist*
Woodford *Cent*
Wood Green *Picc*
Woodside Park *N'thn*

Kew Gardens *Dist*
Kilburn *B'loo*
Kilburn Park *B'loo*
Kingsbury *B'loo*
King's Cross, St. Pancras
  N'thn, Picc, Met, Circle and Vic
Knightsbridge *Picc*

Ladbroke Grove *Met*
Lambeth North *B'loo*
Lancaster Gate *Cent*
Latimer Road *Met*
Leicester Square *N'thn and Picc*
Leyton *Cent*
Leytonstone *Cent*
Liverpool Street *Met, Circle*
  and Cent
London Bridge *N'thn*
Loughton *Cent*

Maida Vale *B'loo*
Manor House *Picc*
Mansion House *Dist and Circle*
Marble Arch *Cent*
Marylebone *B'loo*
Mile End *Cent, Met and Dist*
Mill Hill East *N'thn*
Monument *Dist and Circle*
Moorgate *N'thn, Met and Circle*
Moor Park *Met*
Morden *N'thn*
Mornington Crescent *N'thn*

Neasden *B'loo*
Newbury Park *Cent*
New Cross *Met*
New Cross Gate *Met*
North Acton *Cent*
North Ealing *Picc*
Northfields *Picc*
North Harrow *Met*
Northolt *Cent*
North Weald *Cent*
North Wembley *B'loo*
Northwick Park *Met*
Northwood *Met*
Northwood Hills *Met*
Notting Hill Gate *Cent, Dist*
  and Circle

Oakwood *Picc*
Old Street *N'thn*
Ongar *Cent*
Osterley *Picc*
Oval *N'thn*
Oxford Circus *B'loo, Cent*
  and Vic

Paddington *B'loo, Met, Dist*
  and Circle
Park Royal *Picc*
Parsons Green *Dist*
Perivale *Cent*
Piccadilly Circus *Picc and B'loo*
Pimlico *Vic*

Pinner *Met*
Plaistow *Met and Dist*
Preston Road *Met*
Putney Bridge *Dist*

Queensbury *B'loo*
Queen's Park *B'loo*
Queensway *Cent*

Ravenscourt Park *Dist*
Rayners Lane *Met and Picc*
Redbridge *Cent*
Regent's Park *B'loo*
Richmond *Dist*
Rickmansworth *Met*
Roding Valley *Cent*
Rotherhithe *Met*
Royal Oak *Met*
Ruislip *Met and Picc*
Ruislip Gardens *Cent*
Ruislip Manor *Met and Picc*
Russell Square *Picc*

St. James's Park *Dist and Circle*
St. John's Wood *B'loo*
St. Paul's *Cent*
Seven Sisters *Vic*
Shadwell *Met*
Shepherd's Bush *Cent and Met*
Shoreditch *Met*
Sloane Square *Dist and Circle*
Snaresbrook *Cent*
South Ealing *Picc*
Southfields *Dist*
Southgate *Picc*
South Harrow *Picc*
South Kensington *Picc, Dist and*
  Circle
South Kenton *B'loo*
South Ruislip *Cent*
South Wimbledon *N'thn*
South Woodford *Cent*
Stamford Brook *Dist*
Stanmore *B'loo*
Stepney Green *Dist and Met*
Stockwell *N'thn and Vic*
Stonebridge Park *B'loo*
Strand *N'thn*
Stratford *Cent*
Sudbury Hill *Picc*
Sudbury Town *Picc*
Surrey Docks *Met*
Swiss Cottage *B'loo*

Temple *Circle and Dist*
Theydon Bois *Cent*
Tooting Bec *N'thn*
Tooting Broadway *N'thn*
Tottenham Court Road *Cent*
  and N'thn
Tottenham Hale *Vic*

Apothecaries

Black Friars Lane, EC4
This charming seventeenth
century building has a most
attractive courtyard. The poet,
John Keats here became a
Licentiate. The portrait gallery
contains his picture and there are
portraits of James I and Charles I.

Armourers &
Brasiers

81 Coleman St, EC2
Historic edifice first erected about
1450 and reconstructed in 1840
by J. H. Good.

Bakers

Harp Lane, EC3
This is a modern building standing
on an historic site—the fourth
building of this Livery Company.
The first was built in 1506; the
last building fell to enemy action
in 1940. The present one dates
from 1960 and is the work of
Trehearne, Preston and Partners.

Barber-Surgeons

Monkswell Sq, EC2
Modern building adjoining the
famous Barbican site. It replaces
the ancient Hall destroyed in the
Blitz.

Brewers

Aldermanbury Sq, EC2
On its historic site, first occupied in
1420, but rebuilt in 1960 by Sir
Hubert Worthington and T. W.
Sutcliffe. It had been damaged by
enemy action in the Second
World War.

Butchers

Bartholomew Cl, EC1
The traditional Hall in
Bartholomew Close is augmented
by an additional building in
adjoining Little Britain. It is all
conveniently close to the great
traditional meat market of
Smithfield.

Carpenters

Throgmorton Ave, EC2
Although there was a Hall on this
site for at least 500 years, the
Victorian replacement was
bombed in 1941. The present Hall
dates from 1956. A commemora-
tion stone was unveiled at the
time the new foundation stone
was laid.

Clothworkers

Dunster Ct, EC3
The first Hall on this site was

built in 1456. A second was
erected in 1482, and was burned
down in the Great Fire. There
have been three others including a
Victorian one which was destroyed by bombing in 1941. The
present neo-Georgian Hall was
built in 1958. The ancient archives
survived; also among the
treasures is a loving-cup, the gift
of Samuel Pepys, Master of the
Company in 1677.

Cutlers

4 Warwick Lane, EC4
This building, is distinguished by
fine terra-cotta reliefs executed
by Benjamin Creswick in 1867.

Drapers

Throgmorton St, EC2
Part seventeenth century building
but with considerable Victorian
restoration work. It was again the
subject of careful restoration after
the Blitz, this work being carried
out in 1949. Inside there are some
fine portraits and valuables,
including the Elizabethan
Lambard Cup. The famous
mulberry tree still flourishes in the
garden.

Dyers

10 Dowgate Hill, EC4
This is a mainly Victorian building
though with some later alterations.
The Company is privileged to
keep swans on the Thames.

Fanmakers' Hall

This quaint building in the
churchyard of St. Botolph's,
Bishopsgate, was originally built
as a church school in 1861. The
entrance is still flanked by Coade
stone figures of two charity
children.

Fishmongers

London Bdge, EC4
This Victorian classical Hall was
the work of Henry Roberts and
Sir Gilbert Scott. It was the first
of the Halls to suffer fire damage
during the Second World War.
A previous Hall on that site was
destroyed in the Great Fire of
1666. This is one of the very
ancient Companies, its foundation
dating from before the reign of
Henry II.

Founders

13 St Swithin's Lne EC4
The original Hall had to be rebuilt
in 1877 but following damage in

the Second World War was again
restored in 1967.

Girdlers

Basinghall Ave, EC2
This Company met originally in
Westcheap. The medieval Hall
did not survive the Great Fire.
Its replacement was destroyed
in the Second World War, and the
present building is modern.

Goldsmiths

Foster Lne, EC2
This building has an extremely
handsome exterior which is late-
Georgian Renaissance. It stands
on the site of both the medieval
and seventeenth century fore-
runners.

Grocers

Princes St, EC2
This, the fourth Hall on the site is
mainly Victorian with some
modern restoration made neces-
sary by bomb damage. It was
unlucky enough to be damaged by
fire in 1965 and was again
restored, and re-opened in 1967.

Haberdashers

Staining Lne, EC2
A modern block called Garrard
House contains the entrance to
the new Haberdashers Hall. The
first, medieval one perished in the
Great Fire, and its replacement
was destroyed in the Second
World War.

Innholders

College St, EC4
Built in 1670 this handsome Hall
escaped the damage that afflicted
so many of the Livery Halls of the
City of London.

Ironmongers

Barbican, EC2
This building dates from 1925,
the historic original having been
destroyed in the daylight bombing
raid of 1917. This Company is
the smallest among the 'Great'
companies of the City Livery.

Leathersellers

15 St Helen's Pl, EC3
This Victorian edifice, built in
1878 was extended by the addition of a courtroom and other
offices in 1926. Damaged by air-
raids in 1941, the place was again
carefully restored and retains its
handsome and imposing entrance.
This Company is one of the oldest
in the City, dating from the four-
teenth century.

Master Mariners

The sloop *Wellington* was
purchased by the Master Mariners
from the Admiralty to be their
Company Hall in 1947. It has been
berthed permanently since
1948 in the Thames at Temple
Stairs.

Mercers

Ironmonger Lne, EC2
In Becket House after original
Hall was destroyed in 1941
bombing. Richest of the City
Livery Companies, and first in
precedence.

Merchant Taylors

30 Threadneedle St, EC2
Home of the largest of the City
Livery Companies. The medieval
Hall was replaced after the
Great Fire. The building was
burned out after a raid in 1940,
but restored in 1959 by Sir Albert
Richardson.

Painter Stainers

9 Lt Trinity Lne, EC4
The original building was rebuilt
in 1668 and a new wing added in
1880, and again in 1915.

Pewterers

Oat Lane, EC2
The present building is neo-
Georgian, rebuilt in 1960. The
original Hall dated from 1496,
and was in Lime Street, but the
new Court Room contains much
panelling and some fittings res-
cued from the old place after it
was bombed.

Plaisterers'

This modern building at No. 1,
London Wall makes a vivid
contrast with the neighbouring
portions of the Roman wall. The
decor throughout is a faithful
reproduction of the eighteenth
century Robert Adam style. The
Great Hall, with its minstrel gallery
at one end is the largest Livery
Hall in the City.

Saddlers

Gutter Lne, EC2
Home of the oldest of all City
Companies, this new Hall
built by Sylvester Sullivan was
opened in 1958. The former Hall,
destroyed in the bombing, stood in
Wood Street. This Company
claims to have been formed in
Saxon times.

Skinners

6 Dowgate Hill, EC4
The Hall has an eighteenth
century facade to a seventeenth
century building which was
rebuilt following the Great Fire of
1666. It has some large panel
paintings, the work of Sir Frank
Brangwyn in 1902.

Stationers & Newspaper
Makers

Stationers Hall, EC4
This Hall built soon after the
Great Fire was given a stone
facade in 1800 with a Victorian
wing added around 1887.
The interior suffered damage in
the Second World War but has
been carefully restored. The
ancient records, dating from 1402
also include the registration of the
First Folio of Shakespeare's
Works.

Tallowchandlers

4 Dowgate Hill, EC4
This building is mainly Victorian
reconstruction dating circa 1871.

Vintners

Upr Thames St, EC4
The medieval court room survives
from the first building which was
otherwise destroyed in the Great
Fire. The rest of the Hall dates
from 1671. Remodelling of the
exterior occurred between 1908–
1910. This is the Hall of one of the
twelve 'Great' Livery Companies
and it has rich sixteenth century
tapestries and paintings.

Wax Chandlers

Gresham St, EC2
Postwar reconstruction upon
ancient foundations. The Company itself has a history of some
500 years of prominence in the
City.

NB

Livery Halls may be visited
only by appointment. The City
Information Centre in St Paul's
Churchyard supply information in
this connection, and about special
days on which the Halls may be
open to the public.

Of the famous Livery Companies
of the City of London, only 31
have their own Livery Halls.

Principal Clubs

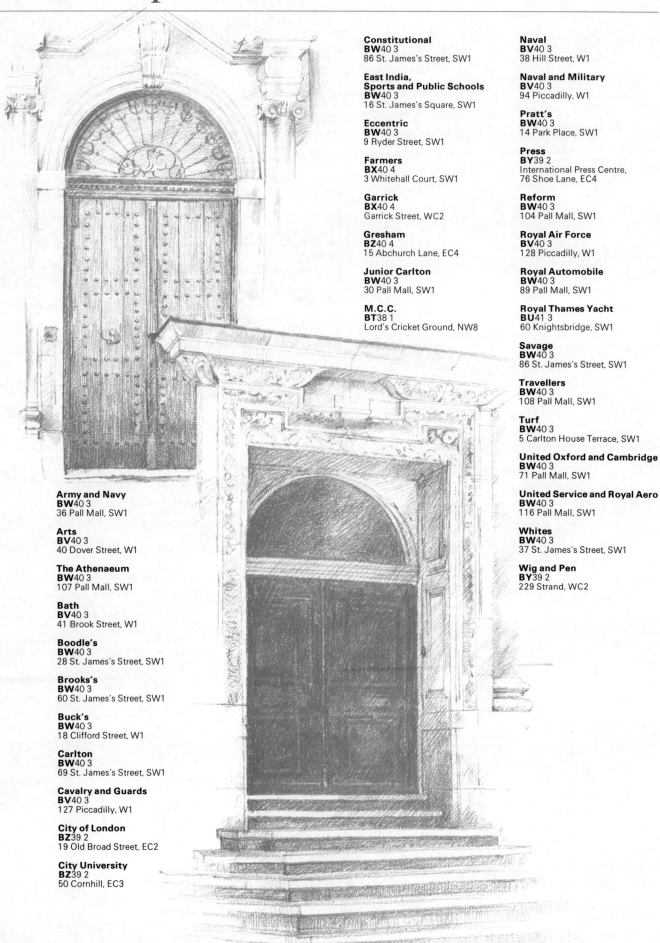

Army and Navy
BW40 3
36 Pall Mall, SW1

Arts
BV40 3
40 Dover Street, W1

The Athenaeum
BW40 3
107 Pall Mall, SW1

Bath
BV40 3
41 Brook Street, W1

Boodle's
BW40 3
28 St. James's Street, SW1

Brooks's
BW40 3
60 St. James's Street, SW1

Buck's
BW40 3
18 Clifford Street, W1

Carlton
BW40 3
69 St. James's Street, SW1

Cavalry and Guards
BV40 3
127 Piccadilly, W1

City of London
BZ39 2
19 Old Broad Street, EC2

City University
BZ39 2
50 Cornhill, EC3

Constitutional
BW40 3
86 St. James's Street, SW1

East India,
Sports and Public Schools
BW40 3
16 St. James's Square, SW1

Eccentric
BW40 3
9 Ryder Street, SW1

Farmers
BX40 4
3 Whitehall Court, SW1

Garrick
BX40 4
Garrick Street, WC2

Gresham
BZ40 4
15 Abchurch Lane, EC4

Junior Carlton
BW40 3
30 Pall Mall, SW1

M.C.C.
BT38 1
Lord's Cricket Ground, NW8

Naval
BV40 3
38 Hill Street, W1

Naval and Military
BV40 3
94 Piccadilly, W1

Pratt's
BW40 3
14 Park Place, SW1

Press
BY39 2
International Press Centre,
76 Shoe Lane, EC4

Reform
BW40 3
104 Pall Mall, SW1

Royal Air Force
BV40 3
128 Piccadilly, W1

Royal Automobile
BW40 3
89 Pall Mall, SW1

Royal Thames Yacht
BU41 3
60 Knightsbridge, SW1

Savage
BW40 3
86 St. James's Street, SW1

Travellers
BW40 3
108 Pall Mall, SW1

Turf
BW40 3
5 Carlton House Terrace, SW1

United Oxford and Cambridge
BW40 3
71 Pall Mall, SW1

United Service and Royal Aero
BW40 3
116 Pall Mall, SW1

Whites
BW40 3
37 St. James's Street, SW1

Wig and Pen
BY39 2
229 Strand, WC2

Barnet Museum
BR24 28
Wood Street, Barnet

Bear Gardens Museum
BY40 4
Bankside, Southwark SE1

Bethnal Green Museum
CB39 57
Cambridge Heath Road, E2

Borough Museum
CW47 80
Market Street, Dartford

British Museum
BW39 1
Great Russell Str. WC1

Church Farmhouse Museum
BP31 46
Church End, Hendon, NW4

City Museum
BH13 9
Hatfield Road, St, Albans

Clock Museum
Guildhall Library
BZ39 2
Aldermanbury EC2

Commonwealth Institute
BS41 66
Kensington High Street, W8

Courtauld Institute Galleries
BW38 1
Woburn Square, W1

Cuming Museum
BZ42 4
155, Walworth Road, SE17

Dulwich College Picture Gallery
CA47 77
College Road, SE21

Fenton House
BT34 47
Hampstead Grove, NW3

Forty Hall Museum
CA22 30
Forty Hill, Enfield

Foundling Hospital/Art Gallery & Museum
BX38 2
40, Brunswick Square, WC1

Geffrye Museum
CA37 2
Kingsland Road, E2

Geological Museum
BT41 3
Exhibition Road, SW7

Guards Museum
Wellington Barracks
BW41 3
Birdcage Walk, SW1

Guildford Museum & Muniment Room
AR71 118
Castle Arch, Guildford

Guildhall Art Gallery
BZ39 2
King Street, EC2

Gunnersbury Park Museum
BM41 65
Gunnersbury Park, W3

Ham House
BK47 74
Richmond

Haringey Borough Museum
CA30 39
Bruce Castle, Lordship Lane, N17

Hayward Gallery
BX40 4
South Bank, SE1

Horniman Museum
CB47 77
London Road, Forest Hill, SE23

Imperial War Museum
BY41 4
Lambeth Road, SE1

Institute of Contemporary Arts
BW41 3
Nash House, The Mall, SW1

Iveagh Bequest
BU33 47
Kenwood, Hampstead, NW3

Jewish Museum
BW38 1
Upper Woburn Place, WC1

Keats House & Museum
BU35 47
Keats Grove, Hampstead, NW3

Leighton House Art Gallery & Museum
BR41 65
Holland Park, W14

London Transport Collection
BJ44 64
Syon Park, Brentford

Marble Hill House
BK47 74
Richmond Road, Twickenham

Museum & Art Gallery
BL51 85
Fairfield West,
Kingston-upon-Thames

Museum of Mankind
BW40 3
6, Burlington Gardens, W1

Musical Museum
BK43 64
368, High Street, Brentford

National Army Museum
BU42 3
Royal Hospital Road, SW3

National Gallery
BW40 3
Trafalgar Square, WC2

National Maritime Museum
CF43 67
Romney Road, Greenwich, SE10

National Portrait Gallery
BX40 4
St. Martin's Place, WC2

National Postal Museum
BZ39 2
King Edward Street, EC1

Natural History Museum
BT41 3
Cromwell Road, SW7

Passmore Edwards Museum
CG36 58
Romford Road, E15

Percival David Foundation of Chinese Art
BW38 1
53, Gordon Square, WC1

Public Record Office Museum
BY39 2
Chancery Lane, WC2

Rotunda Museum
CK43 68
Woolwich Common, SE18

Royal Academy of Arts
BW40 3
Burlington House, Piccadilly, W1

Royal Air Force Museum
BP31 46
Hendon, NW9

Royal Society of Painters in Watercolours
BV40 3
26, Conduit Street, W1

Science Museum
BT41 3
Exhibition Road, SW7

Serpentine Gallery
BU40 3
Kensington Gardens, W2

Sevenoaks Local Museum
CU65 107
Public Library, The Drive,
Sevenoaks

Sir John Soane's Museum
BX39 2
Lincoln's Inn Fields, WC2

South London Art Gallery
CA44 67
Peckham Road, SE5

Tate Gallery
BX41 4
Millbank, SW1

The Mall Art Galleries
BW41 3
The Mall, SW1

The Museum of London
BZ39 2
London Wall, EC2

The Queen's Gallery
BV42 3
Buckingham Palace Road, SW1

Thurrock Local History Museum
DG44 71
Civic Square, Tilbury

Verulamium Museum
BF13 9
St. Michael's, St. Albans

Victoria & Albert Museum
BT41 3
Cromwell Road, SW7

Wallace Collection
BV39 1
Manchester Square, W1

Watford Art Collection
BC24 26
Central Public Library
Hemel Hempstead Road, Watford

Wellcome Medical Museum
BW38 1
Euston Road, NW1

Wellington Museum
BV41 3
Apsley House, Hyde Park
Corner W1

Whitechapel Art Gallery
CA39 2
Whitechapel High Street, E1

William Morris Gallery & Brangwyn Gift
CE31 48
Lloyd Park, Walthamstow, E17

G   General market
Ⓥ   Fruit & Vegetables
Ⓢ   Antiques
Ⓑ   Books
⚓   Flowers
Ⓐ   Animals & Birds
〰   Fish

B

Bacon Street   CA38 2
London E1
Sun am onlyⓋ
Battersea High Street
BT44 66
London SW11
Mon–Sat (Wed am only)G
Bell Lane   CA39 2
London E1
Sun am only G
Bell Street   BU39 1
London NW1
Mon–Sat G
Beresford Square   CL42 68
London SE18
Mon–Sat (Thu am only) G
Bermondsey Street   CA41 4
London SE1
Fri onlyG
Bermondsey Square   CA41 4
London SE1
Fri only Ⓢ
Berwick Street   BW39 1
London W1
Mon–Sat G
Bethnal Green Road   CA38 2
London E2
Mon–Sat G
Brick Lane   CA38 2
London E1
Sun am onlyG
Brixton Station Road
BY45 66
London SW9
Mon–Sat (Wed am only) G
Broadway   CB37 57
London E8
Mon–Sat G
Burdett Road   CD38 57
London E3
Mon–Sat G

C

Camden Passage   BY37 2
London N1
Mon–Sat (Wed until 8pm)Ⓢ

Chalton Street   BW37 1
London NW1
Mon–Sat G
Chapel Market   BY37 2
London N1
Mon–Sun am (Thu am only)G
Chatsworth Road   CC34 48
London E5
Mon–Sat G
Cheshire Street   CA38 2
London E2
Sun am only G
Choumert Road   CA45 67
London SE15
Mon–Sat (Thu am only)G
Church Street   BT39 1
London NW8
Mon–Sat G
Cobb Street   CA39 2
London E1
Sun am only G
Colomb Street   CG42 68
London SE10
Mon–Sat G
Columbia Road   CA38 2
London E2
Sun am only ⚓
Crown Street   BM40 55
Acton, London N3
Thu onlyG
Cygnet Street   CA38 2
London E1
Sun am only G

D

Dawes Street   BZ42 4
London SE17
Sun onlyG
Deptford High Street
CE43 67
London SE8
Sat only G
Devons Road   CE39 57
London E3
Mon–Sat G
Douglas Way   GD43 67
Deptford, London SE8
Fri and Sat G

E

Earlham Street   BW39 1
Holborn, London WC2
Mon–Sat G Ⓢ
Earlswood Street   CG42 68
London SE10
Mon–Sat G
East Street   BZ42 4
London SE17
Tues–Sun am (Thu am only)G
Exmouth Street   BY38 2
London EC1
Mon–Sat (Thu am only) G

F

Fairfield West   BL51 85
Kingston, Surrey
Mon am only G
Farringdon Street   BY39 2
London EC4
Mon–Sat (Thu am only) Ⓑ

G

Golborne Road   BR39 55
London W10
Mon–Sat (Thu am only) G
Goodge Place   BW39 2
London W1
Mon–SatⓋ
Goulston Street   CA39 2
London E1
Mon–Fri and Sun amG
Greenman Street   BZ36 57
Essex Road, London N1
Mon–Sat (Thu am only)Ⓥ

H

High Street   BN60 94
Epsom
Sat onlyG

High Street   CD32 48
Walthamstow, London E17
Mon–Sat G
Hildreth Street   BV47 76
Balham, London SW12
Mon–Sat (Wed am only)G
Holloway Road   BX34 47
London N7
Mon–Sat (Thu am only)G
Hoxton Street   CA37 2
London N1
Mon–Sat G

I

Inverness Street   BV37 1
London NW1
Mon–Sat G

J

Jubilee Market   BX40 4
Covent Garden, London WC2
Mon–FriG

K

Kingsland Road   CA38 2
London E8
Sat onlyG

L

Leather Lane   BY39 2
London EC1
Mon–Sat lunchtimesG
Leeds Street   CB28 39
London N18
Mon–Sat G
Leyden Street   CA39 2
London E1
Sun am only G
Lower Marsh   BY41 4
London SE1
Mon–Sat (Thu am only)G

M

Maple Road   CB51 87
Penge, London SE20
Tue–Sat (Wed am only)Ⓥ
Market Place   BK51 84
Kingston, Surrey
Mon–SatⒼ
Market Place   CT32 50
Romford, Essex
Wed, Fri & SatⒼ
Market Square   AS62 100
Woking, Surrey
Tue, Fri & SatⒼ
Middlesex Street   CA39 2
(Petticoat Lane)
London E1
Sun am onlyⒼ
Mile End Road   CC39 57
London E1
Mon–SatⒼ

N

New Goulston Street
CA39 2
London E1
Sun am onlyⒼ
Northcote Road   BU46 76
Battersea, London SW11
Mon–Sat (Wed am only)Ⓖ
North End Road   BR42 65
London W14
Mon–SatⒼ
North Street   AR71 118
Guildford, Surrey
Fri & SatⒼ

O

Old Castle Street   CA39 2
London E1
Sun am onlyⒼ

P

Petticoat Lane   CA39 2
see under Middlesex Street
Plender Street   BW37 2
London NW1
Mon–SatⓋ〰
Portobello Road   BR39 55
London W10
Mon–Sun (Thu & Sun am only)Ⓖ

Q

Queen's Crescent   BV36 56
London NW5
Mon–SatⒼ

R

Ridley Road   CA35 40
London E8
Mon–SatⒼ
Roman Road   CC38 57
London E3
Mon–SatⒼ
Rupert Street   BW40 3
London W1
Mon–SatⓋ

S

Salmon Lane   CD39 57
London E14
Mon–SatⒼ
Sclater Street   CA38 2
London E1
Sun am onlyⒼ Ⓐ
Slyfield Green   AS68 109
Guildford, Surrey
Wed & Bank HolsⒼ
Stamford Road   CO37 59
Dagenham, Essex
Mon–SatⒼ

Strutton Ground   BW41 3
London SW1
Mon–Fri & Sat amⒼ
Strype Street   CA39 2
London E1
Sun am onlyⒼ
Surrey Street   BZ55 87
Croydon, Surrey
Mon–SatⒼ

T

Tachbrook Street   BW42 3
London W1
Mon–SatⒼ
Tower Bridge Road   CA41 4
London SE1
Mon–Sat (Thu am only)Ⓖ
Toynbee Street   CA39 2
London E1
Mon–Fri & Sun am onlyⒼ
Tyler Street   CG42 68
London SE10
Mon–SatⒼ

W

Watney Street   CB39 57
London E1
Mon–SatⒼ
Well Street   CC36 57
London E9
Mon–SatⒼ
Wentworth Street   CA39 2
London E1
Mon–Fri & Sun am onlyⒼ
Westmoreland Road
CA   43 67
London SE17
Daily (Thu and Sun am only)Ⓖ
Whitechapel Road   CB39 57
London E1
Mon–SatⒼ
Whitecross Street   BZ38 2
London EC1
Mon–Sat (Thu am only)Ⓖ
Wilcox Road   BX43 66
London SW8
Mon–Sat (Thu am only)Ⓖ

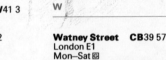

Theatres in Central London

Adelphi
BX40 4
The Strand
Albery
BX40 4
St. Martin's Lane
Aldwych
BX39 2
Aldwych
Ambassadors
BW39 1
West Street
Apollo
BW40 3
Shaftesbury Avenue

Cambridge
BX39 2
Earlham Street
Cockpit
BU38 1
Gateforth Street
Coliseum
BX40 4
St. Martin's Lane
Comedy
BW40 3
Panton Street
Cottesloe
BX40 4
National Theatre, South Bank
Criterion
BW40 3
Piccadilly

Drury Lane
BX39 2
Theatre Royal, Catherine Street
Duchess
BX40 4
Catherine Street
Duke of York's
BX40 4
St. Martin's Lane

Fortune
BX39 2
Russell Street

Garrick
BX40 4
Charing Cross Road
Globe
BW40 3
Shaftesbury Avenue

Greenwood
BZ41 4
Weston Street

Haymarket
BW40 3
Theatre Royal, Haymarket
Her Majesty's
BW40 3
Haymarket

Jeannetta Cochrane
BX39 2
Theobalds Road

Kings Road Theatre
BT42 3
Kings Road

Lyric
BW40 3
Shaftesbury Avenue
Lyttleton
BX40 4
National Theatre, South Bank

Mayfair
BV40 3
Stratton Street
Mermaid
BY40 4
Puddle Dock, Blackfriars

National Theatre
BX40 4
(Cottesloe, Lyttleton & Olivier
Theatres), South Bank
New Arts
BX40 4
(Theatre Club),
Gt. Newport Street
New London
BX39 2
Parker Street
New Victoria
BW41 3
Wilton Road

Old Vic
BY41 4
Waterloo Road
Olivier
BX40 4
National Theatre, South Bank
Open Air Theatre
BV38 1
Inner Circle, Regents Park
Open Space Theatre
BW38 1
303/307 Euston Road

Palace
BW39 1
Shaftesbury Avenue
Palladium
BW39 1
Argyll Street
Phoenix
BW39 1
Charing Cross Road
Piccadilly
BW40 3
Denman Street
Prince of Wales
BW40 3
Coventry Street

Queen's
BW40 3
Shaftesbury Avenue

Regent
BV39 1
Regent Street
Royal Court
BV42 3
Sloane Square
Royal Opera House
BX39 2
Covent Garden

Royalty
BX39 2
Portugal Street

Sadler's Wells
BY38 2
Rosebery Avenue
St. Martin's
BX40 4
West Street
Savoy
BX40 4
Strand
Shaftesbury
BX39 2
Shaftesbury Avenue
Shaw
BW38 1
Euston Road
Strand
BX40 4
Strand

Vanbrugh
BW38 1
Malet Street
Vaudeville
BX40 4
Strand

Victoria Palace
BW41 3
Victoria Street

Westminster
BW41 3
Palace Street
Whitehall
BX40 4
Whitehall
Windmill
BW40 3
Gt. Windmill Street
Wyndham's
BW40 3
Charing Cross Road

Young Vic
BY41 4
The Cut

Cinemas in Central London

ABC Bloomsbury
BX38 2
Brunswick Square
ABC
BT42 3
Fulham Road
ABC 1 & 2
BW39 1
Shaftesbury Avenue
Academy 1, 2 & 3
BW39 1
Oxford Street
Astoria
BW39 1
Charing Cross Road

Biograph
BW42 3
Wilton Road

Carlton
BW40 3
Haymarket
Casino
BW39 1
Old Compton Street
Centa
BW40 3
Piccadilly
Cinecenta
BW40 3
Panton Street
Classic
BW40 3
Charing Cross Road
Classic
BW40 3
Moulin, Great Windmill Street
Classic
BT39 1
Praed Street
Classic
BW41 3
Victoria Street
Columbia
BW40 3
Shaftesbury Avenue
Curzon
BV40 3
Curzon Street

Dominion
BW39 1
Tottenham Court Road

Empire
BW40 3
Leicester Square
Eros
BW40 3
Piccadilly Circus

Gala Royal
BU39 1
Marble Arch

Institute of Contemporary Arts
BW40 3
The Mall

Jacey
BW40 3
Leicester Square
Jacey
BX40 4
Trafalgar Square

Leicester Square Theatre
BW40 3
Leicester Square
London Pavilion
BW40 3
Piccadilly Circus

Metropole
BV41 3
Victoria Street
Minema
BU41 3
Knightsbridge

National Film Theatre 1 & 2
BX40 4
South Bank
New Victoria
BW41 3
Wilton Road

Odeon
BT39 1
Edgware Road
Odeon
BW40 3
Haymarket
Odeon
BU42 3
Kings Road
Odeon
BW40 3
Leicester Square
Odeon
BU40 3
Marble Arch
Odeon
BX40 4
St. Martin's Lane

Paris Pullman
BT42 3
Drayton Gardens
Plaza 1 & 2
BW40 3
Regent Street
Prince Charles
BW40 3
Leicester Place

Regent Theatre
BV39 1
Regent Street
Rialto
BW40 3
Coventry Street
Ritz
BW40 3
Leicester Square

Scene 1, 2, 3 & 4
BW40 3
Swiss Centre, Leicester Square
Starlight Cinema
BV40 3
Mayfair Hotel, Stratton Street
Studio 1 & 2
BW39 1
Oxford Street

The Other Cinema
BW39 1
Tottenham Street
Times Centa 1 & 2
BU38 1
Chiltern Court, Baker Street

Warner West End 1, 2, 3 & 4
BW40 3
Cranbourn Street

Concert and
Exhibition Halls in
Central London

Bishopsgate Institute
CA39 2
Bishopsgate

Caxton Hall
BW41 3
Caxton Street
Central Hall
BW41 3
Storeys Gate
Conway Hall
BX39 2
Red Lion Square

Earl's Court Ltd
BS42 66
Warwick Road

Holland Park
BR41 65
Kensington

Kingsway Hall
BX39 2
Kingsway

Olympia Ltd
BR41 65
Hammersmith Road

Purcell Rooms
BX40 4
South Bank

Queen Elizabeth Hall
BX40 4
South Bank

Royal Albert Hall
BT41 3
Kensington Gore
Royal College of Music
BT41 3
Prince Consort Road

Royal Festival Hall
BX40 4
South Bank
Royal Horticultural Society
New Hall
BW41 3
Greycoat Street
Rudolf Steiner Hall
BU38 1
Park Road

Seymour Hall
BU39 1
Seymour Place
St. Pancras Town Hall
BX38 2
Euston Road

Wigmore Hall
BV39 1
Wigmore Street

Legend, Indexing System

Index

The street name and postal district or locality of an entry is followed by a grid reference and number of the map on which the name will be found e.g. Abbey Rd, SW19 will be found in square **BT50** on map **76** and Norfolk Crescent, Sidcup in square **CN47** on map **78** (you will see from the map the latter location is in postcode boundary DA15).

The index contains some names for which there is insufficient space on the map. The adjoining thoroughfare to such roads is shown in italics e.g. *Agar Place, NW1* is off Agar Grove the latter being found in square **BW36** on map **56**.

A strict alphabetical order is followed in which Avenue, Close, Gardens etc, although abbreviated, are read as part of the preceeding name.
For example Andrews Rd comes before Andrew St, and Abbey Orchard St before Abbey Rd.

Legend

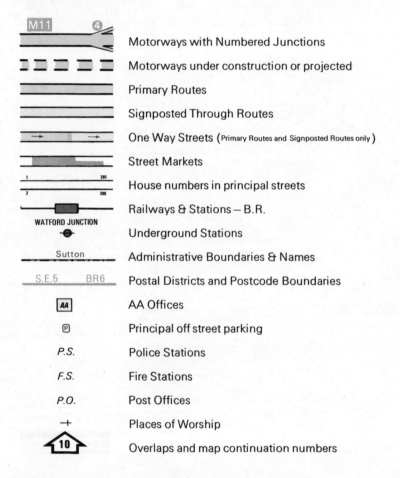

Motorways with Numbered Junctions

Motorways under construction or projected

Primary Routes

Signposted Through Routes

One Way Streets (Primary Routes and Signposted Routes only)

Street Markets

House numbers in principal streets

Railways & Stations – B.R.

WATFORD JUNCTION

Underground Stations

Sutton — Administrative Boundaries & Names

S.E.5   BR6 — Postal Districts and Postcode Boundaries

AA — AA Offices

Ⓟ — Principal off street parking

P.S. — Police Stations

F.S. — Fire Stations

P.O. — Post Offices

+ — Places of Worship

10 — Overlaps and map continuation numbers

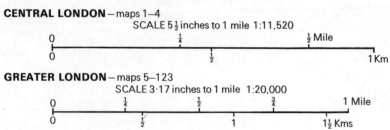

CENTRAL LONDON – maps 1–4
SCALE 5½ inches to 1 mile 1:11,520

0 .... ¼ .... ½ Mile
0 .... ½ .... 1 Km

GREATER LONDON – maps 5–123
SCALE 3·17 inches to 1 mile 1:20,000

0 ...... ¼ ...... ½ ...... ¾ ...... 1 Mile
0 ...... ½ ...... 1 ...... 1½ Kms

Central London Atlas

OXFORD STREET
Oxford Street, where specially marked, is closed
to through traffic (except buses and taxis) between
7 a.m. and 7 p.m. Monday to Saturday.

Central London Street Index

Street	Ref	Street	Ref
Abbey Gdns. NW8	BT37 1	Arne St. WC2	BX39 2
Abbey Gdns. Ms. NW8	BT37 1	Arneway St. SW1	BW41 3
Abbey Orchard St. SW1	BW41 3	Arnold Cir. E2	CA38 2
Abbey Rd. NW6	BS37 1	Arnold Est. SE1	CA41 4
Abbey Rd. Est. NW8	BS37 1	Arnside St. SE17	BZ43 4
Abbey St. SE1	CA41 4	Arthur Ct. W2	BS39 1
Abbots La. SE1	CA40 4	Arthur St. EC4	BZ40 4
Abbots Manor Est. SW1	BV42 3	Artillery La. E1	CA39 2
Abchurch La. EC4	BZ40 4	Artillery Pass. E1	CA39 2
Abercorn Clo. NW8	BT38 1	Artillery Row, SW1	BW41 3
Abercorn Ms. NW8	BT37 1	Artizan St. E1	CA39 2
Abercorn Pl. NW8	BT38 1	Arundel St. WC2	BX40 4
Aberdare Gdns. NW6	BS36 1	Ashburn Gdns. SW7	BT42 3
Aberdeen Pl. NW8	BT38 1	Ashburn Ms. SW7	BT42 3
Aberdour St. SE1	CA42 4	Ashburn Pl. SW7	BT42 3
Abingdon St. SW1	BX41 4	Ashby St. EC1	BY38 2
Acacia Gdns. NW8	BT37 1	Ashland St. SW1	BV39 1
Acacia Pl. NW8	BT37 1	Ashmill St. NW1	BU39 1
Acacia Rd. NW8	BT37 1	Ash St. E1	BW41 3
Achilles Way. W1	BV40 3	Ashworth Rd. W9	BS38 1
Acton St. WC1	BX38 2	Assam St. E1	CB39 2
Adam & Eve Ct. W1	BW39 1	Astell St. SW3	BU42 3
Adam's Row. W1	BV40 3	Aster Pl. SE1	BZ41 4
Adam St. W1	BV39 1	Astley St. SE1	CA42 4
Adam St. WC2	BX40 4	Astwood Ms. SW7	BS42 3
Addington St. SE1	BX41 4	Atherstone Ms. SW7	BT42 3
Addle Hill. EC4	BY39 2	Atterbury St. SW1	BW42 3
Addle Hill. EC4	BY40 4	Attneave St. WC1	BY38 2
Adelaide St. WC2	BX40 4	Auckland St. SE11	BX42 4
Adeline Pl. WC1	BW39 1	Auden Pl. NW1	BV37 1
Adelphi Ter. WC2	BX40 4	Audley Sq. W1	BV40 3
Adler St. E1	CB39 2	Augustus St. NW1	BV37 1
Adpar St. W2	BT39 1	Aulay St. SE1	CB43 4
Agar Gro. NW1	BW36 1	Aulton Pl. SE11	BY42 4
Agar St. WC2	BX40 4	Austin Friars, EC2	BZ39 2
Agdon St. EC1	BY38 2	Austin St. E2	CA38 2
Ainger Rd. NW3	BU37 1	Australia St. SE11	BY42 4
Ainsworth Est. NW8	BT37 1	Avebury St. N1	BZ37 2
Air St. W1	BW40 3	Aveline St. SE11	BX42 4
Albany Rd. SE5	CA43 4	Ave Maria La. EC4	BY39 2
Albany St. NW1	BV37 1	Avenue Clo. NW8	BU37 1
Albany Ter. NW1	BV38 1	Avenue Rd. NW3	BT36 1
Albany, The W1	BW40 3	Avenue, The EC3	CA40 4
Albemarle St. W1	BV40 3	Avery Row, W1	BV40 3
Albemarle Way. EC1	BY38 2	Avondale Sq. SE1	CB42 4
Alberta St. SE17	BY42 4	Avonmouth St. SE1	BZ41 4
Albert Ct. SW7	BT41 3	Avon Pl. SE1	BZ41 4
Albert Embankment, SE1	BX42 4	Aybrook St. W1	BV39 1
Albert Hall Ms. SW7	BT41 3	Aylesbury Rd. SE17	BZ42 4
Albert Ms. W8	BT41 3	Aylesbury St. EC1	BY39 2
Albert Pl. W8	BS41 3	Aylesford St. SW1	BW42 3
Albert St. NW1	BV37 1	Aylwin Est. SE1	CA41 4
Albert Ter. NW1	BV37 1	Ayres St. SE1	BZ41 4
Albert Ter. Ms. NW1	BV37 1	Babmaes St. SW1	BW40 3
Albion Cl. W2	BU40 3	Bacchus Wk. N1	CA37 2
Albion Dr. E8	CA36 2	Baches St. N1	BZ38 2
Albion Ms. W2	BU40 3	Back Church La. E1	CB39 2
Albion Pl. EC1	BY39 2	Back Hill, EC1	BY38 2
Albion St. E8	CA36 2	Bacon Gro. SE1	CA41 4
Albion St. W2	BU39 1	Bacon St. E1	CA38 2
Aldbridge St. SE17	CA42 4	Bacon St. E2	CA38 2
Aldenham St. NW1	BW37 1	Baden Pl. SE1	BZ41 4
Aldermanbury, EC2	BZ39 2	Bagford St. N1	BZ37 2
Aldermanbury Sq. EC2	BZ39 2	Bagshot St. SE17	CA42 4
Alderminster Rd. SE1	CB42 4	Bainbridge St. WC1	BW39 1
Alderney St. SW1	BV42 3	Bakers Ms. W1	BV39 1
Aldersgate St. EC1	BZ39 2	Baker's Row, E1	BY38 2
Aldford St. W1	BV40 3	Baker St. NW1	BU38 1
Aldgate, EC3	CA39 2	Balaclava Rd. SE1	CA42 4
Aldgate High St. EC3	CA39 2	Balcombe St. NW1	BU38 1
Aldwych, WC2	BX39 2	Balderton St. W1	BV39 1
Aldwych, WC2	BX40 4	Baldwin's Gdns. EC1	BY39 2
Alexander Pl. SW7	BU42 3	Baldwin St. EC1	BZ38 2
Alexander Sq. SW3	BU42 3	Baldwin Ter. N1	BZ37 2
Alexandra Ct. W9	BT38 1	Balfe St. N1	BX37 2
Alexis St. SE16	CB42 4	Balfour Ms. Pl. W1	BV40 3
Alfred Ms. W1	BW39 1	Balfour St. SE17	BZ42 4
Alfred Pl. N1	BZ37 2	Balmes Rd. N1	BZ37 2
Alfred Pl. WC1	BW39 1	Baltic St. EC1	BZ38 2
Alfreton St. SE17	CA42 4	Bankend, SE1	BZ40 4
Alice St. SE1	CA41 4	Bankside, SE1	BZ40 4
Alie St. E1	CA39 2	Banner St. EC1	BZ38 2
All Saints St. N1	BX37 2	Barford St. N1	BY37 2
All Souls Pl. W1	BV39 1	Barge House Rd. SE1	BY40 4
Allhallows La. EC4	BZ40 4	Baring St. N1	BZ37 2
Allingham St. N1	BZ37 2	Bark Pl. W2	BS40 3
Allington St. SW1	BV41 3	Barlow Pl. W1	BV40 3
Allitsen Rd. NW8	BU37 1	Barlow St. SE17	BZ42 4
Allsop Pl. NW1	BU38 1	Barnby St. NW1	BW38 1
Alma Gro. SE1	CA42 4	Barnesbury Est. N1	BX37 2
Alma Sq. NW8	BT38 1	Barnet Gro. E2	CB38 2
Almeida St. N1	BY36 2	Barnham St. SE1	CA41 4
Almorah St. N1	BZ36 2	Barnsbury Rd. N1	BY37 2
Alpha Clo. NW1	BU38 1	Barnsbury St. N1	BY36 2
Alpha Pl. SW3	BU43 3	Baroness Rd. E2	CA38 2
Alscot Rd. SE1	CA42 4	Baron's Pl. SE1	BY41 4
Alvey Est. SE17	CA42 4	Baron St. N1	BY37 2
Alvey St. SE17	CA42 4	Barrett St. W1	BV39 1
Ambergate St. SE17	BY42 4	Barrie Est. W2	BT40 3
Ambrosden Av. SW1	BW41 3	Barron Clo. WC1	BX39 2
Amelia St. SE17	BY42 4	Barrow Hill Est. NW8	BU37 1
Amen Ct. EC4	BY39 2	Barrow Hill Rd. NW8	BU37 1
America Sq. EC3	CA40 4	Barter St. WC1	BX39 2
America St. SE1	BZ40 4	Bartholomew Clo. EC1	BZ39 2
Ampthil Sq. Est. NW1	BW37 1	Bartholomew La. EC2	BZ39 2
Ampton Pl. WC1	BX38 2	Bartholomew St. EC1	BZ38 2
Ampton St. WC1	BX38 2	Bartholomew St. SE1	BZ41 4
Amwell St. EC1	BY38 2	Bartlett Ct. EC4	BY39 2
Anderson St. SW3	BU42 3	Barton St. SW1	BX41 4
Angel Ct. EC2	BZ39 2	Barton Way, NW8	BT37 1
Angel Ms. N1	BY37 2	Basil St. SW3	BU41 3
Angel Pl. SE1	BZ40 4	Basinghall Av. EC2	BZ39 2
Angel Pl. EC4	BZ40 4	Basinghall St. EC2	BZ39 2
Angel St. SE1	BZ41 4	Basire St. N1	BZ37 2
Angel St. EC1	BZ39 2	Bastwick St. EC1	BZ38 2
Anns Cl. SW1	BU41 3	Batchelor St. N1	BY37 2
Ansdell St. W8	BS41 3	Batemans Row, EC2	CA38 2
Ansdell Ter. W8	BS41 3	Bateman St. W1	BW39 1
Appleby St. E2	CA37 2	Bath Pl. EC2	CA38 2
Apple Tree Yd. SW1	BW40 3	Bath St. EC1	BZ38 2
Appold St. EC2	CA39 2	Bath Ter. SE1	BZ41 4
Aquila St. NW8	BT37 1	Bathurst Ms. W2	BT40 3
Aquinas St. SE1	BY40 4	Bathurst St. W2	BT40 3
Arcade, The EC2	CA39 2	Battle Bridge La. SE1	CA40 4
Archer St. W1	BW40 3	Battle Bridge Rd. NW1	BX37 2
Archery Clo. W2	BU39 1	Baxendale St. E2	CB38 2
Arch St. SE1	BZ41 4	Bayham Pl. NW1	BW37 1
Argent St. SE1	BY41 4	Bayham St. NW1	BV37 1
Argyle Sq. WC1	BX38 2	Bayley St. WC1	BW39 1
Argyle St. WC1	BW39 1	Baylis Rd. SE1	BY41 4
Argyle St. WC1	BX38 2	Baynes St. Nw1	BW36 1
Argyle Wk. WC1	BX38 2	Bayswater Rd. W2	BS40 3
Arlington Ave. N1	BZ37 2	Beak St. W1	BW40 3
Arlington Rd. NW1	BV37 1	Bear All. EC4	BY39 2
Arlington Sq. N1	BZ37 2	Bear Gdns. SE1	BZ40 4
Arlington St. SW1	BW40 3	Bear La. SE1	BY40 4
Arlington Way. EC1	BY38 2		

Street	Ref	Street	Ref
Bear St. WC2	BW40 3	Borers St. E1	CA39 2
Beatty St. NW1	BW37 1	Borough High St. SE1	BZ41 4
Beauchamp Pl. SW3	BU41 3	Borough Rd. SE1	BY41 4
Beauchamp St. EC1	BY39 2	Borrett Rd. SE17	BZ42 4
Beaufort Gdns. SW3	BU41 3	Boscobel Pl. SW1	BV42 3
Beaufort St. SW3	BT42 3	Boscobel St. NW8	BT38 1
Beaumont Ms. W1	BV39 1	Boss St. SE1	CA41 4
Beaumont Pl. W1	BW38 1	Boston Pl. NW1	BU38 1
Beaumont St. W1	BV39 1	Boston St. E2	CB37 2
Becket St. SE1	BZ41 4	Boswell Ct. WC1	BX39 2
Beckway St. SE17	BZ42 4	Boswell St. WC1	BX39 2
Bedale St. SE1	BZ40 4	Botolph La. EC3	CA40 4
Bedford Av. WC1	BW39 1	Boundary Rd. NW8	BS37 1
Bedfordbury, WC2	BX40 4	Boundary Row, SE1	BY41 4
Bedford Ct. WC2	BX40 4	Boundary St. E2	CA38 2
Bedford Pl. WC1	BX39 2	Bourchier St. W1	BW40 3
Bedford Row, W1	BX39 2	Bourdon Pl. W1	BV40 3
Bedford Sq. WC1	BW39 1	Bourdon St. W1	BV40 3
Bedford St. WC2	BX40 4	Bourlet Clo. W1	BW39 1
Beech St. EC2	BZ39 2	Bourne Est. EC1	BY39 2
Beeston Pl. SW1	BV41 3	Bourne St. SW1	BV42 3
Belgrave Gdns. NW8	BS37 1	Bourne Ter. W2	BS39 1
Belgrave Ms. SW1	BV41 3	Bouverie Pl. W2	BT39 1
Belgrave Ms. N. SW1	BV41 3	Bouverie St. EC4	BY39 2
Belgrave Ms. S. SW1	BV41 3	Bowden St. SE11	BY42 4
Belgrave Pl. SW1	BV41 3	Bow La. EC4	BZ39 2
Belgrave Rd. SW1	BV41 3	Bowles Rd. SE1	CB43 4
Belgrave Sq. SW1	BV41 3	Bowling Green La. EC1	BY38 2
Belgrove St. WC1	BX38 2	Bowling Green Pl. SE1	BZ41 4
Bell La. E1	CA39 2	Bowling Green Wk. N1	CA38 2
Bell St. NW1	BU39 1	Bow St. WC2	BX39 2
Bell Yard, WC2	BY39 2	Boxworth Gro. N1	BX37 2
Belsize Rd. NW6	BS37 1	Boyd St. E1	CB39 2
Belvedere Blds. SE1	BY41 4	Boyfield St. SE1	BY41 4
Belvedere Pl. SE1	BY41 4	Brackley St. EC1	BZ39 2
Belvedere Rd. SE1	BX41 4	Bracklyn Ct. N1	BZ37 2
Bemerton St. N1	BX37 2	Bracklyn St. N1	BZ37 2
Bendall Ms. NW1	BU39 1	Bradlaugh St. N1	BZ37 2
Benjamin St. EC1	BY39 2	Brad St. SE1	BY40 4
Bennet St. SW1	BW40 3	Braganza St. SE17	BY42 4
Bentinck Ms. W1	BV39 1	Braham St. E1	CA39 2
Bentinck St. W1	BV39 1	Braidwood St. SE1	CA40 4
Benyon Rd. N1	BZ37 2	Bramerton St. SW3	BU43 3
Berkeley Ms. W1	BU39 1	Bramham Gdns. SW5	BS42 3
Berkeley Sq. W1	BV40 3	Branch Pl. N1	BZ37 2
Berkeley St. W1	BV40 3	Brandon St. SE17	BZ42 4
Bermondsey Sq. SE1	CA41 4	Brangton Rd. SE11	BX42 4
Bermondsey St. SE1	CA40 4	Bratley St. E1	CB38 2
Bermondsey St. SE1	CA41 4	Bray Pl. SW3	BU42 3
Bermondsey Wall, W. SE16	CB41 4	Bread St. EC4	BZ39 2
Bernard St. WC1	BX38 2	Breams Bldgs. EC4	BY39 2
Berners Ms. W1	BW39 1	Brechin Pl. SW7	BT42 3
Berners Pl. W1	BW39 1	Bremner Rd. SW7	BT41 3
Berners Rd. N1	BY37 2	Brendon Row, SE17	BZ42 4
Berners St. W1	BW39 1	Brendon St. W1	BU39 1
Berryfield Rd. SE17	BY42 4	Bressenden Pl. SW1	BV41 3
Berry Pl. EC1	BZ38 2	Brettell St. SE17	BZ42 4
Berry St. EC1	BZ38 2	Brewer St. W1	BW40 3
Berwick St. W1	BW39 1	Brick La. E1	CA38 2
Bessborough Gdns. SW1	BW42 3	Brick La. E2	CA38 2
Bessborough Pl. SW1	BW42 3	Brick St. W1	BV40 3
Bessborough St. SW1	BW42 3	Bride La. EC4	BY39 2
Bethnal Green Rd. E1	CA38 2	Bridewell Pl. EC4	BY39 2
Bethnal Green Rd. E2	CA38 2	Bridford Ms. W1	BV39 1
Betterton St. WC2	BX39 2	Bridgefoot, SE1	BX42 4
Bevan St. N1	BZ37 2	Bridgeman St. NW8	BU37 1
Bevenden St. N1	BZ38 2	Bridge Pl. SW1	BV42 3
Bevin Ct. WC1	BX38 2	Bridge St. SW1	BX41 4
Bevin Way. WC1	BX38 2	Bridgewater Sq. EC2	BZ39 2
Bevis Marks, EC3	CA39 2	Bridgewater St. EC2	BZ39 2
Bickenhall St. W1	BV39 1	Bridgeway St. NW1	BW37 1
Bidborough St. WC1	BW38 1	Bridle La. W1	BW40 3
Bidborough St. WC1	BX38 2	Bridport Pl. N1	BZ37 2
Biddulph Rd. W9	BS38 1	Briset St. EC1	BY39 2
Billiter St. EC3	CA39 2	Bristol Gdns. W9	BS38 1
Bina Gdns. SW5	BT42 3	Bristol Ms. W9	BS38 1
Binefield St. N1	BX37 2	Britannia Row, N1	BZ37 2
Bingham Pl. W1	BV38 1	Britannia St. WC1	BX38 2
Binney St. W1	BV39 1	Britten St. SW3	BU42 3
Birchin St. EC3	BZ39 2	Britton St. EC1	BY39 2
Birdcage Wk. SW1	BW41 3	Broadbent St. W1	BV40 3
Bird St. W1	BV39 1	Broad Ct. WC2	BX39 2
Birkenhead St. WC1	BX38 2	Broadley St. NW8	BU39 1
Bishop's Bri. Rd. W2	BS39 1	Broadley Ter. NW1	BU38 1
Bishops Ct. EC4	BY39 2	Broad Sanctuary, SW1	BX41 4
Bishops Ct. WC2	BY39 2	Broad Street Av. EC2	CA39 2
Bishopsgate, EC2	CA39 2	Broad Wk. NW1	BV37 1
Bishopsgate Chyd. EC2	CA39 2	Broad Wk. W1	BU40 3
Bishop's Ter. SE11	BY42 4	Broad Walk, The W8	BS40 3
Bishop St. N1	BZ37 2	Broadwall, SE1	BY40 4
Bittern St. SE1	BZ41 4	Broadway, SW1	BW41 3
Blackall St. EC2	CA38 2	Broadwick St. W1	BW39 1
Blackburne's Ms. W1	BV40 3	Broad Yard, EC1	BY39 2
Blackfriars Bridge, EC4	BY40 4	Brockham St. SE1	BZ41 4
Blackfriars La. EC4	BY39 2	Brockley Ter. SE17	CA42 4
Blackfriars Pass. EC4	BY40 4	Brodie St. SE1	CA42 4
Blackfriars Rd. SE1	BY40 4	Broke Rd. E8	CA37 2
Blacklands Ter. SW3	BU42 3	Bromfield St. N1	BY37 2
Black Lion Yd. E1	CB39 2	Brompton Pl. SW3	BU41 3
Black Prince Rd. SE11	BX42 4	Brompton Rd. SW3	BU42 3
Blackwood St. SE17	BZ42 4	Brompton Sq. SW3	BU41 3
Blandford Ms. W1	BV39 1	Bronti Cl. SE17	BZ42 4
Blandford Sq. NW1	BU38 1	Brook Dr. SE11	BY41 4
Blandford St. W1	BV39 1	Brooke's Ct. EC1	BY39 2
Blenheim Pl. NW8	BT37 1	Brooke St. EC1	BY39 2
Blenheim Rd. NW8	BT37 1	Brook Ms. N. W2	BT40 3
Blenheim St. W1	BV39 1	Brook's Ms. W1	BV40 3
Blenheim Ter. NW8	BT37 1	Brook St. W1	BV40 3
Bletchley Ct. N1	BZ37 2	Brook St. W2	BT40 3
Bletchley St. N1	BZ37 2	Brougham Rd. E8	CB37 2
Blomfield Rd. W9	BS39 1	Brown Hart Gdns. W1	BV40 3
Blomfield Vils. W2	BS39 1	Browning Est. SE17	BZ42 4
Bloomfield St. EC2	BZ39 2	Browning Ms. W1	BV39 1
Bloomfield Ter. SW1	BV42 3	Browning St. SE17	BZ42 4
Bloomsbury Pl. WC1	BX39 2	Brownlow Ms. WC1	BX38 2
Bloomsbury Sq. WC1	BX39 2	Brownlow Rd. E8	CA37 2
Bloomsbury St. WC1	BW39 1	Brownlow St. WC1	BX39 2
Bloomsbury Way, WC1	BX39 2	Brown St. W1	BU39 1
Blossom St. E1	CA38 2	Broxwood Way, NW8	BU37 1
Blue Anchor Yd. E1	CB40 4	Brune St. E1	CA39 2
Boddys Bridge, SE1	BY40 4	Brunswick Clo. EC1	BY38 2
Bodicea St. N1	BX37 2	Brunswick Ct. SE1	CA41 4
Bolsover St. W1	BV38 1	Brunswick Pl. N1	BZ38 2
Bolt Ct. EC4	BY39 2	Brunswick Sq. WC1	BX38 2
Bolton Gdns. SW5	BS42 3	Brushfield St. E1	CA39 2
Bolton Gdns. Ms. SW10	BS42 3	Bruton La. W1	BV40 3
Bolton Rd. NW8	BS37 1	Bruton Pl. W1	BV40 3
Boltons, The SW10	BT42 3	Bruton St. W1	BV40 3
Bolton St. W1	BV40 3	Bryanston Ms. W. W1	BU39 1
Bonhill St. EC2	BZ38 2	Bryanston Pl. W1	BU39 1
Bonny St. NW1	BW36 1	Bryanston Sq. W1	BU39 1
Booths Pl. W1	BW39 1	Bryanston St. W1	BU39 1
Boot St. N1	CA38 2	Bryant Ct. E2	CA37 2
Boreham St. E2	CA38 2	Brymer Rd. SE5	CA45 4
		Buckenham St. NW1	BZ41 4
		Buckfast St. E2	CB38 2

Street	Ref
Buckingham Gate, SW1	BV41 3
Buckingham Palace Rd. SW1	BV42 3
Buckingham Pl. SW1	BW41 3
Buckingham St. WC2	BX40 4
Buckland St. N1	BZ37 2
Bucklersbury, EC4	BZ39 2
Buckle St. E1	CA39 2
Bucknall St. WC2	BW39 1
Buck St. E2	CB37 2
Budge Row, EC4	BZ40 4
Bulinga St. SW1	BX42 4
Bulls Gdns. SW3	BU42 3
Bullshead Pl. EC3	CA39 2
Bull Wf. La. EC4	BZ40 4
Bulstrode Pl. W1	BV39 1
Bulstrode St. W1	BV39 1
Bunhill Row, EC1	BZ38 2
Burdett St. SE1	BY41 4
Burge St. SE1	BZ41 4
Burgh St. N1	BY37 2
Burgundy St. SE1	CA42 4
Burleigh St. WC2	BX40 4
Burlington Arc. W1	BW40 3
Burlington Gdns. W1	BW40 3
Burman St. SE1	BY41 4
Burne St. NW1	BU39 1
Burnett St. SE1	BX42 4
Burnsall St. SW3	BU42 3
Burrell St. SE1	BY40 4
Burrows Ms. SE1	BY41 4
Burton Ct. SW3	BU42 3
Burton Gro. SE17	BZ42 4
Burton Pl. WC1	BW38 1
Burton St. WC1	BW38 1
Burwood Pl. W2	BU39 1
Bury Ct. EC3	CA39 2
Bury Pl. WC1	BX39 2
Bury St. EC3	CA39 2
Bury St. SW1	BW40 3
Bury Wk. SW3	BU42 3
Busby Pl. E2	CA38 2
Bush La. EC4	BZ40 4
Bute St. SW7	BT42 3
Buxton St. E1	CA38 2
Byng Pl. WC1	BW38 1
Byward St. EC3	CA40 4
Bywater St. SW3	BU42 3
Caesar St. E2	CA38 2
Cage St. WC1	BX39 2
Caleb St. SE1	BZ41 4
Caledonian Rd. N1	BX37 2
Caledonia St. N1	BX37 2
Cale St. SW3	BU42 3
Callow St. SW3	BT43 3
Calmington Rd. SE5	CA43 4
Calshot St. N1	BX37 2
Calthorpe St. WC1	BX38 2
Calvert Av. E2	CA38 2
Calvin St. E1	CA38 2
Cambridge Gate, NW1	BV38 1
Cambridge Gate Ms. NW1	BV38 1
Cambridge Pl. W8	BS41 3
Cambridge Sq. W2	BU39 1
Cambridge St. SW1	BV42 3
Cambridge Ter. NW1	BV38 1
Cambridge Ter. Ms. NW1	BV38 1
Camden High St. NW1	BV37 1
Camden Pass. N1	BY37 2
Camden Rd. NW1	BV37 1
Camden St. NW1	BW36 1
Camden Wk. N1	BY37 2
Camlet St. E2	CA38 2
Camley St. NW1	BW37 1
Camomile St. EC3	CA39 2
Campbell Blds. SE1	BY41 4
Campbell St. W9	BT38 1
Camperdown St. E1	CA39 2
Candover St. W1	BW39 1
Canning Ms. W8	BT41 3
Canning Pass. W8	BT41 3
Canning Pl. W8	BT41 3
Cannon Row, SW1	BX41 4
Cannon St. EC4	BZ39 2
Canon St. N1	BZ37 2
Capel Ct. EC2	BZ39 2
Capland St. NW8	BT38 1
Capper St. WC1	BW38 1
Carburton St. W1	BV38 1
Cardigan St. SE11	BY42 4
Cardinal Bourne St. SE1	BZ41 4
Cardington St. NW1	BW38 1
Carey La. EC2	BZ39 2
Carey St. WC2	BX39 2
Carlisle Av. EC3	CA39 2
Carlisle La. SE1	BX41 4
Carlisle Pl. SW1	BW41 3
Carlisle St. W1	BW39 1
Carlos Pl. W1	BV40 3
Carlton Gdns. SW1	BW40 3
Carlton Hill, NW8	BS37 1
Carlton House Ter. SW1	BW40 3
Carlton Ms. SW1	BW40 3
Carlton St. SW1	BW40 3
Carlyle Sq. SW3	BT42 3
Carmarthen St. N1	BZ37 2
Carmelite St. EC4	BY40 4
Carnaby St. W1	BW39 1
Carnegie St. N1	BX37 2
Caroline Pl. W2	BS40 3
Caroline Ter. SW1	BV42 3
Carol St. NW1	BW37 1
Carpenters Cl. SW1	BU41 3
Carpenter St. W1	BV40 3
Carriage Rd, The SW7	BT41 3
Carrington St. W1	BV40 3
Carteret St. SW1	BW41 3
Carter La. EC4	BY39 2
Carter Pl. SE17	BZ42 4
Carter St. SE17	BZ43 4
Carthusian St. EC1	BZ39 2
Carting La. WC2	BX40 4
Carton St. W1	BU39 1
Cartwright Gdns. WC1	BX38 2
Cartwright St. E1	CA40 4
Casson St. E1	CB39 2
Castellain Rd. W9	BS38 1
Castle La. SW1	BW41 3

Castlereagh St. W1 BU39 1
Castle St. EC1 BY39 2
Cathcart Rd. SW10 BS43 3
Cathedral Pl. EC4 BZ39 2
Cathedral St. SE1 BZ40 4
Catherine Pl. SW1 BW41 3
Catherine St. WC2 BX40 4
Cato St. W1 BU39 1
Catton St. WC1 BX39 2
Causton St. SW1 BW42 3
Cavaye Pl. SW10 BT42 3
Cavendish Av. NW8 BT37 1
Cavendish Clo. NW8 BT38 1
Cavendish Pl. W1 BV39 1
Cavendish Sq. W1 BV39 1
Cavendish St. N1 BZ37 2
Caversham St. SW3 BU43 3
Caxton St. SW1 BW41 3
Cayton St. EC1 BZ38 2
Centaur St. SE1 BX41 4
Central Markets, EC1 BY39 2
Central St. EC1 BZ38 2
Cerney Ms. W2 BT40 3
Chadwell St. EC1 BY38 2
Chadwick St. SW1 BW41 3
Chagford St. NW1 BU38 1
Chalcot Cres. NW1 BU37 1
Chalcot Rd. NW1 BV36 1
Chalk Farm Rd. NW1 BV36 1
Chalton St. NW1 BW37 1
Chambers St. SE16 CB41 4
Chamber St. E1 CA40 4
Chamboro St. E2 CA38 2
Chancel St. SE1 BY40 4
Chancery La. WC2 BX39 2
Chance St. E2 CA38 2
Chandos Pl. WC2 BX40 4
Chandos St. W1 BV39 1
Chantry St. N1 BY37 2
Chapel Market, N1 BY37 2
Chapel Pl. W1 BV39 1
Chapel St. NW1 BU39 1
Chapel St. SW1 BV41 3
Chapter Rd. SE17 BY42 4
Chapter St. SW1 BW42 3
Charing Cross, WC2 BX40 4
Charing Cross Rd. WC2 BW39 1
Charlbert St. NW8 BU37 1
Charles La. NW8 BU37 1
Charles Sq. N1 BZ38 2
Charles St. W1 BV40 3
Charleston St. SE17 BZ42 4
Charles 11 St. SW1 BW40 3
Charlotte Pl. W1 BW39 1
Charlotte Rd. EC2 CA38 2
Charlotte St. W1 BW39 1
Charlotte Ter. N1 BX37 2
Charlton Pl. N1 BY37 2
Charlwood Pl. SW1 BW42 3
Charlwood St. SW1 BW42 3
Charrington St. NW1 BW37 1
Charterhouse Ms. EC1 BY39 2
Charterhouse Sq. EC1 BY39 2
Charterhouse St. EC1 BY39 2
Chart St. N1 BZ38 2
Chatham St. SE17 BZ42 4
Cheapside, EC2 BZ39 2
Chelsea Bridge Rd. SW1 BV42 3
Chelsea Cloisters, SW3 BU42 3
Chelsea Embankment, SW3 BU43 3
Chelsea Man. Blds. SW3 BU42 3
Chelsea Manor Gdns. SW3 BU42 3
Chelsea Manor St. SW3 BU42 3
Chelsea Park Gdns. SW3 BT43 3
Chelsea Sq. SW3 BT42 3
Cheltenham Ter. SW3 BU42 3
Cheney Rd. NW1 BX37 2
Chenies Ms. WC1 BW38 1
Chenies Pl. NW1 BW37 1
Chenies St. WC1 BW39 1
Chequer St. EC1 BZ38 2
Cherbury Ct. N1 BZ37 2
Cherbury St. N1 BZ37 2
Chesham Ms. SW1 BV41 3
Chesham Pl. SW1 BV41 3
Chesham St. SW1 BV41 3
Chester Cl. SW1 BV41 3
Chester Ct. NW1 BV38 1
Chesterfield Gdns. W1 BV40 3
Chesterfield Hill, W1 BV40 3
Chesterfield St. W1 BV40 3
Chester Gate, NW1 BV38 1
Chester Ms. SW1 BV41 3
Chester Pl. NW1 BV38 1
Chester Rd. NW1 BV38 1
Chester Row, SW1 BV42 3
Chester Sq. SW1 BV42 3
Chester St. SW1 BV41 3
Chester Ter. NW1 BV38 1
Chester Ter. Ms. NW1 BV38 1
Chester Way, SE11 BY42 4
Chettle Cl. SE1 BZ41 4
Cheval Pl. SW7 BU41 3
Cheyne Pl. SW3 BU43 3
Chicheley St. SE1 BX41 4
Chichester Rents, WC2 BY39 2
Chichester St. SW1 BW42 3
Chichester St. W2 BS39 1
Chicksand Est. E1 CB39 2
Chicksand St. E1 CA39 2
Chiltern St. W1 BU39 1
Chilton St. E2 CA38 2
Chilworth Ms. W2 BT39 1
Chilworth St. W2 BT39 1
Chiswell St. EC1 BZ39 2
Chitty St. W1 BW39 1
Christchurch St. SW3 BU43 3
Christina St. EC2 CA38 2
Christmas St. SE1 BZ41 4
Christopher St. EC2 BZ38 2
Churchill Gdns. Est. SW1 BW43 3
Churchill Gdns. Rd. SW1 BW42 3
Church Pl. SW1 BW40 3
Church St. Est. NW8 BT38 1
Church St. W2 BT39 1
Churchway, NW1 BW38 1
Church Yd. Row, SE11 BY42 4
Churton Pl. SW1 BW42 3
Churton St. SW1 BW42 3
Circular Rd. SE1 BZ41 4
Circus Pl. EC2 BZ39 2
Circus Rd. NW8 BT38 1
Circus, The EC3 CA40 4
City Garden Row, N1 BY37 2
City Rd. EC1 BY37 2
Clabon Ms. SW1 BU41 3
Clare Mkt. WC2 BX39 2
Claremont Clo. N1 BY37 2
Claremont Sq. N1 BY37 2
Clarence Gdns. Nw1 BV38 1
Clarence Pass. NW1 BX37 2
Clarence Ter. NW1 BU38 1
Clarence Yd. SE17 BZ42 4
Clarendon Cl. W2 BU40 3
Clarendon Gdns. W9 BT38 1
Clarendon Gro. NW1 BW38 1
Clarendon Ms. W2 BU40 3
Clarendon Pl. W2 BU40 3
Clarendon St. SW1 BV42 3
Clarendon Ter. W9 BT38 1
Clareville Gro. SW7 BT42 3
Clareville St. SW7 BT42 3
Clarges Ms. W1 BV40 3
Clarges St. W1 BV40 3
Clarissa St. E8 CA37 2
Claverton St. SW1 BW42 3
Clay St. W1 BU39 1
Clayton St. SE11 BY43 4
Cleaver Sq. SE11 BY42 4
Cleaver St. SE11 BY42 4
Clements Inn, WC2 BX39 2
Clements Inn Pass. WC2 BX39 2
Clements La. EC4 BZ40 4
Clennam St. SE1 BZ41 4
Clenston Ms. W1 BU39 1
Clere Pl. EC2 BZ38 2
Clere St. EC2 BZ38 2
Clerkenwell Clo. EC1 BY38 2
Clerkenwell Grn. EC1 BY38 2
Clerkenwell Rd. EC1 BY38 2
Cleveland Gdns. W2 BT39 1
Cleveland Ms. W1 BW39 1
Cleveland Rd. N1 BZ36 2
Cleveland Row, SW1 BW40 3
Cleveland Sq. W2 BT39 1
Cleveland St. W1 BV38 1
Cleveland Ter. W2 BT39 1
Clifford St. W1 BW40 3
Clifton Ct. NW8 BT38 1
Clifton Gdns. W9 BT38 1
Clifton Hill, NW8 BS37 1
Clifton Rd. W9 BT38 1
Clifton St. EC2 CA39 2
Clifton Vils. W9 BS39 1
Clift St. N1 BZ37 2
Clinger Ct. N1 CA37 2
Clinger St. N1 CA37 2
Clink St. SE1 BZ40 4
Clipstone Ms. W1 BW38 1
Clive Ct. W9 BT38 1
Cliveden Pl. SW1 BV42 3
Cloak La. EC4 BZ40 4
Clock Pl. SE1 BY42 4
Cloth Fair, EC1 BY39 2
Cloudesley Pl. N1 BY37 2
Cloudesley Rd. N1 BY37 2
Cloudesley Sq. N1 BY37 2
Cloudesley St. N1 BY37 2
Clover Ms. SW3 BU43 3
Club Row, E2 CA38 2
Clunbury St. N1 BZ37 2
Cluny Pl. SE1 CA41 4
Coach & Horses Yd. W1 BW40 3
Cobb St. E1 CA39 2
Cobourg Rd. SE5 CA45 4
Cobourg St. NW1 BW38 1
Cochrane St. NW8 BT37 1
Cock La. EC1 BY39 2
Cockpit Yd. WC1 BX39 2
Cockspur St. SW1 BW40 3
Code St. E1 CA38 2
Colbeck Ms. SW7 BS42 3
Cold St. EC1 BY38 2
Colebrook Row, N1 BY37 2
Coleherne Ct. SW5 BS42 3
Coleherne Ms. SW10 BS42 3
Coleherne Rd. SW10 BS42 3
Coleman Fields, N1 BZ37 2
Coleman St. EC2 BZ39 2
Cole St. SE1 BZ41 4
Coley St. WC1 BX38 2
Colin St. SE1 BY40 4
College Gro. NW1 BW37 1
College Hill, EC4 BZ40 4
College Pl. NW1 BW37 1
College St. EC4 BZ40 4
Collier St. N1 BX37 2
Collingham Gdns. SW5 BS42 3
Collingham Pl. SW5 BS42 3
Collingham Rd. SW5 BS42 3
Collinson St. SE1 BZ41 4
Colnbrook St. SE1 BY41 4
Colombo St. SE1 BY40 4
Colonnade, Wc1 BX38 2
Columbia Rd. E2 CA38 2
Columbia Sq. E2 CA38 2
Colville Pl. W1 BW39 1
Colworth Gro. SE17 BZ42 4
Commercial Rd. E1 CB39 2
Commercial St. E1 CA38 2
Compton Clo. NW1 BV38 1
Compton Pass. EC1 BY38 2
Compton St. EC1 BY38 2
Comus Pl. SE17 BZ42 4
Concert Hall App. SE1 BX40 4
Conduit Ms. W2 BT39 1
Conduit Pl. W2 BT39 1
Conduit St. W1 BV40 3
Congreve St. SE17 CA42 4
Connaught Clo. W2 BU39 1
Connaught Ms. W2 BU39 1
Connaught Pl. W2 BU40 3
Connaught Sq. W2 BU39 1
Connaught St. W2 BU39 1
Cons St. SE1 BY41 4
Constitution Hill, SW1 BV41 3
Content St. SE17 BZ42 4
Conway St. W1 BW38 1
Coombs St. N1 BY37 2
Cooper's Rd. SE1 CA42 4
Cooper's Row, EC3 CA40 4
Copenhagen St. N1 BX37 2
Copperfield St. SE1 BY41 4
Copthall Av. EC2 BZ39 2
Copthall Cl. EC2 BZ39 2
Coptic St. WC1 BX39 2
Coral St. SE1 BY41 4
Coram St. WC1 BX38 2
Cork St. W1 BW40 3
Corlett St. NW1 BU39 1
Cornhill, EC3 BZ39 2
Cornwall Gdns. SW7 BS41 3
Cornwall Gdns. Wk. SW7 BS41 3
Cornwall Mews St. SW7 BT41 3
Cornwall Rd. SE1 BY40 4
Cornwall Ter. NW1 BU38 1
Coronet St. N1 CA38 2
Corporation Row, EC1 BY38 2
Corsham St. N1 BZ38 2
Cosmo Pl. WC1 BX39 2
Cosser St. SE1 BY41 4
Cosway St. NW1 BU39 1
Cotham St. SE17 BZ42 4
Cottage Pl. SW3 BU41 3
Cottage Wk. SW1 BU41 3
Cottesmore Gdns. W8 BS41 3
Cottington St. SE11 BY42 4
Cotton's Gdns. E2 CA38 2
Coulson St. SW3 BU42 3
County St. SE1 BZ41 4
Courtenay St. SE11 BX42 4
Courtfield Gdns. SW5 BS42 3
Courtfield Ms. SW7 BT42 3
Courtfield Rd. SW7 BS42 3
Cousin La. EC4 BZ40 4
Covent Gdn. WC2 BX40 4
Coventry St. W1 BW40 3
Cowan St. SE5 CA43 4
Cowcross St. EC1 BY39 2
Cowley St. SW1 BX41 4
Cowper Pl. EC2 BZ38 2
Cowper St. EC2 BZ38 2
Cox's Ct. EC1 BZ39 2
Coxson Pl. SE1 CA41 4
Craig's Ct. SW1 BX40 4
Crail Row, SE17 BZ42 4
Cramer St. W1 BV39 1
Crampton St. SE17 BY42 4
Cranbourn St. WC2 BW40 3
Cranfield Row, SE1 BY41 4
Cranleigh St. NW1 BW37 1
Cranley Gdns. SW7 BT42 3
Cranley Ms. SW7 BT42 3
Cranley Pl. SW7 BT42 3
Cranmer Ct. SW3 BU42 3
Cranwood St. EC1 BZ38 2
Craven Hill, W2 BT40 3
Craven Hill Gdns. W2 BT40 3
Craven Hill Ms. W2 BT40 3
Craven Pl. WC2 BX40 4
Craven St. WC2 BX40 4
Craven Ter. W2 BT40 3
Crawford Pl. W1 BU39 1
Crawford St. W1 BU39 1
Creasy Est. SE1 CA41 4
Creasy St. SE1 CA41 4
Creechurch La. EC3 CA39 2
Creed La. EC4 BY39 2
Cremer St. E2 CA37 2
Crescent Pl. SW3 BU42 3
Crescent Row, EC1 BZ38 2
Crescent, The EC3 CA40 4
Cresswell Gdns. SW5 BT42 3
Cresswell Pl. SW10 BT42 3
Crestfield St. WC1 BX38 2
Crimscott St. SE1 CA41 4
Crinan St. N1 BX37 2
Cripplegate St. EC1 BZ39 2
Crispin St. E1 CA39 2
Cromer Est. WC1 BX38 2
Cromer St. WC1 BX38 2
Crompton St. W2 BT38 1
Cromwell Ms. SW7 BT42 3
Cromwell Pl. SW7 BT42 3
Cromwell Rd. SW5 BS42 3
Crondale St. N1 BZ37 2
Cropley Ct. N1 BZ37 2
Cropley St. N1 BZ37 2
Cropthorne Ct. NW8 BT38 1
Crosby Row, SE1 BZ41 4
Crosby Sq. EC3 CA39 2
Cross Keys Clo. W1 BV39 1
Crosslet St. SE17 BZ42 4
Cross St. N1 BY37 2
Crosswall, EC3 CA40 4
Crown Ct. WC2 BX39 2
Crowndale Rd. NW1 BW37 1
Crown Office Row, EC4 BY40 4
Crown Pass. SW1 BW40 3
Crucifix La. SE1 CA41 4
Cruden St. N1 BY37 2
Cruikshank St. WC1 BY38 2
Crutched Friars, EC3 CA40 4
Cubitt St. WC1 BX38 2
Culford Gdns. SW3 BU42 3
Cullum St. EC3 CA40 4
Culpeper St. N1 BY37 2
Culross St. W1 BV40 3
Culworth St. NW8 BU37 1
Cumberland Gdns. WC1 BX38 2
Cumberland Gate, W1 BU40 3
Cumberland Market, NW1 BV38 1
Cumberland Pl. NW1 BV38 1
Cumberland St. SW1 BV42 3
Cumberland Ter. NW1 BV37 1
Cumming St. N1 BX37 2
Cundy St. Est. SW1 BV42 3
Cundy St. SW1 BV42 3
Cunningham Pl. NW8 BT38 1
Cureton St. SW1 BW42 3
Curlew St. Se1 CA41 4
Curnock Est. NW1 BW37 1
Cursitor St. EC4 BY39 2
Curtain Rd. EC2 CA38 2
Curtis St. SE1 CA42 4
Curzon Pl. W1 BV40 3
Curzon St. W1 BV40 3
Custom House Wf. EC3 CA40 4
Cuthbert St. W2 BT39 1
Cuthbert St. W9 BT38 1
Cutler St. E1 CA39 2
Cut, The SE1 BY41 4
Cygnet St. E1 CA38 2
Cynthia St. N1 BX37 2
Cypress Pl. W1 BW38 1
Cyprus St. EC1 BY38 2
Dacre St. SW1 BW41 3
Dagmar Pass. N1 BY37 2
Dagmar St. N1 BY37 2
Dallington St. EC1 BY38 2
Dame St. N1 BZ37 2
Danbury St. N1 BY37 2
Dane St. WC1 BX39 2
Daniel St. E2 CB38 2
Danson Rd. SE17 BY42 4
Danté Rd. SE11 BY42 4
Danube St. SW3 BU42 3
Daplyn St. E1 CB39 2
D'arblay St. W1 BW39 1
Darby St. E1 CB40 4
Dartford St. SE17 BZ43 4
Dartmouth St. SW1 BW41 3
Dartnell Rd. SE5 CA45 4
Darwin Pl. SE17 BZ42 4
Darwin St. SE17 BZ42 4
Date St. SE17 BZ42 4
Daventry St. NW1 BU39 1
Davidge St. SE1 BY41 4
David Ms. W1 BU39 1
Davies Ms. W1 BV40 3
Davies St. W1 BV39 1
Davies St. W1 BV40 3
Dawes Ho. SE17 BZ42 4
Dawes St. SE17 BZ42 4
Dawson Rd. E2 CA37 2
Deacon Way, SE17 BZ42 4
Deal St. E1 CB39 2
Dean Bradley St. BX41 4
Deanery St. W1 BV40 3
Dean Farrar St. SW1 BW41 3
Dean Ryle St. SW1 BX42 4
Dean's Ct. EC4 BY39 2
Deans Ms. W1 BV39 1
Dean Stanley St. SW1 BX41 4
Dean St. W1 BW39 1
Dean Trench St. SW1 BX41 4
De Beauvoir Cres. N1 BZ37 2
De Beauvoir Rd. N1 CA37 2
Decima St. SE1 CA41 4
Delamere Ter. W2 BS39 1
Delancey St. NW1 BV37 1
De Laune St. SE17 BY43 4
Delhi St. N1 BX37 2
Delta St. E2 CB38 2
Delverton Rd. SE17 BY42 4
Denbigh Pl. SW1 BW42 3
Denbigh St. SW1 BW42 3
Denman St. W1 BW40 3
Denmark Gro. N1 BY37 2
Denmark Pl. WC2 BW39 1
Denmark St. WC2 BW39 1
Denning Clo. NW8 BT38 1
Denny Cres. SE11 BY42 4
Denny St. SE11 BY42 4
Denyer St. SW3 BU42 3
Derby Gate, SW1 BX41 4
Derby St. W1 BV40 3
Dereham Pl. EC2 CA38 2
Dering St. W1 BV39 1
De-Vere Gdns. W8 BT41 3
Deverell St. SE1 BZ41 4
Devizes St. N1 BZ37 2
Devonia Rd. N1 BY37 2
Devonshire Clo. W1 BV39 1
Devonshire Mews, S. W1 BV39 1
Devonshire Ms. W. W1 BV38 1
Devonshire Pl. W1 BV38 1
Devonshire Pl. Ms. W1 BV38 1
Devonshire Row, EC2 CA39 2
Devonshire Sq. EC2 CA39 2
Devonshire St. W1 BV39 1
Devonshire Ter. W2 BT39 1
De Walden St. W1 BV39 1
Dewey Rd. N1 BY37 2
Dial Walk, The SW7 BS41 3
Diana Pl. NW1 BV38 1
Dibden St. N1 BY37 2
Dibdin Ho. W9 BS37 1
Dickens Est. SE16 CB41 4
Dickens Sq. SE1 BZ41 4
Dignum St. N1 BY37 2
Dingley Pl. EC1 BZ38 2
Dingley Rd. EC1 BZ38 2
Disney Pl. SE1 BZ41 4
Disney St. SE1 BZ41 4
Diss St. E2 CA38 2
Distaff La. EC4 BZ40 4
Distin St. SE11 BY42 4
Dockley Rd. SE16 CB41 4
Dock St. E1 CB40 4
Doddington Gro. SE17 BY43 4
Doddington Pl. SE17 BY43 4
Dodson St. SE1 BY41 4
Dolben St. SE1 BY40 4
Dolland St. SE11 BX42 4
Dolphin Sq. SW1 BW42 3
Dombey St. WC1 BX39 2
Dominion St. EC2 BZ39 2
Domvill Gro. SE5 CA42 4
Donegal St. N1 BX37 2
Donne Pl. SW3 BU42 3
Doon St. SE1 BY40 4
Doric Way, NW1 BW38 1
Dorrington St. EC1 BY39 2
Dorset Clo. NW1 BU39 1
Dorset Ms. SW1 BV41 3
Dorset Pl. SW1 BW42 3
Dorset Rise, EC4 BY39 2
Dorset Sq. NW1 BU38 1
Dorset St. W1 BU39 1
Doughty Ms. WC1 BX38 2
Doughty St. WC1 BX38 2
Douglas St. SW1 BW42 3
Douro Pl. W8 BS41 3
Dovehouse St. SW3 BT42 3
Dove Ms. SW5 BT42 3
Dove Row, E2 CB37 2
Dover St. W1 BV40 3
Dover Yd. W1 BW40 3
Dowgate Hill, EC4 BZ40 4
Downham Rd. N1 BZ36 2
Downing St. SW1 BX41 4
Down St. W1 BV40 3
Doyce St. SE1 BZ41 4
Doyley St. SW1 BV42 3
Draco St. SE17 BZ43 4
Drake St. WC1 BX39 2
Drapers Gdns. EC2 BZ39 2
Draycott Av. SW3 BU42 3
Draycott Pl. SW3 BU42 3
Draycott Ter. SW3 BU42 3
Drayton Gdns. SW10 BT42 3
Druid St. SE1 CA41 4
Drummond Cres. NW1 BW38 1
Drummond St. NW1 BW38 1
Drum St. E1 CA39 2
Drury La. WC2 BX39 2
Dryden St. WC2 BX39 2
Drysdale Pl. N1 CA38 2
Drysdale St. N1 CA38 2
Duchess Ms. W1 BV39 1
Duchess St. W1 BV39 1
Duchy St. SE1 BY40 4
Duck La. W1 BW39 1
Dudmaston Ms. SW3 BT42 3
Dufferin St. EC1 BZ38 2
Duke of Wellington Pl. Sw1 BV41 3
Duke of York St. SW1 BW40 3
Duke St. Hill, SE1 BZ40 4
Duke St. St. James's, SW1 BW40 3
Duke's Ms. W1 BV39 1
Duke's Pl. EC3 CA39 2
Duke's Rd. WC1 BW38 1
Duke St. SW1 BW40 3
Duke St. W1 BV39 1
Duncannon St. WC2 BX40 4
Duncan St. N1 BY37 2
Duncan Ter. N1 BY37 2
Dunloe Pl. E2 CA37 2
Dunloe St. E2 CA37 2
Dunlop Pl. SE16 CA41 4
Dunraven St. W1 BV40 3
Dunstable Ms. W1 BV39 1
Dunston Rd. E8 CA37 2
Dunston St. E8 CA37 2
Dunton Rd. SE1 CA42 4
Durant St. E2 CB37 2
Durham House St. WC2 BX40 4
Durham Pl. SW3 BU42 3
Durham St. SE11 BX43 4
Duval St. E1 CA39 2
Dyott St. WC1 BW39 1
Dyott St. WC1 BX39 2
Dysart St. EC2 BZ38 2
Eagle Ct. EC1 BY39 2
Eagle Pl. SW1 BW40 3
Eagle St. WC1 BX39 2
Eagle Wharf Rd. N1 BZ37 2
Eamont St. NW8 BU37 1
Earl Cott. SE1 CA42 4
Earlham St. WC2 BW39 1
Earlham St. WC2 BX39 2
Earl Rd. SE1 CA42 4
Earl St. EC2 BZ39 2
Earnshaw St. WC2 BW39 1
Easleys Ms. W1 BV39 1
Eastbourne Ms. W2 BT39 1
Eastbourne Ter. W2 BT39 1
Eastcastle St. W1 BW39 1
Eastcheap, EC3 BZ40 4
East Harding St. EC4 BY39 2
East La. SE16 CB41 4
Eastminster, E1 CA40 4
Easton St. WC1 BY38 2
East Rd. N1 BZ38 2
East Smithfield, E1 CA40 4
East St. EC2 BZ39 2
East St. SE17 BZ42 4
East Tenter St. E1 CA39 2
Eaton Cl. SW1 BV42 3
Eaton Gate, SW1 BV42 3
Eaton La. SW1 BV41 3
Eaton Ms. SW1 BV42 3
Eaton Ms. N. SW1 BV42 3
Eaton Ms. S. SW1 BV42 3
Eaton Ms. W. SW1 BV42 3
Eaton Pl. SW1 BV41 3
Eaton Row, SW1 BV41 3
Eaton Sq. SW1 BV42 3
Eaton Ter. SW1 BV42 3
Ebenezer St. N1 BZ38 2
Ebor St. E1 CA38 2
Ebury Bridge, SW1 BV42 3
Ebury Bridge Est. SW1 BV42 3
Ebury Bridge Rd. SW1 BV42 3
Ebury Ms. SW1 BV42 3
Ebury Ms. E. SW1 BV41 3
Ebury Sq. SW1 BV42 3
Ebury St. SW1 BV42 3
Ecclesbourne Rd. N1 BZ36 2
Eccleston Bridge, SW1 BV42 3
Eccleston Ms. SW1 BV41 3
Eccleston Ms. SW1 BV42 3
Eccleston Pl. SW1 BV42 3
Eccleston Sq. SW1 BV42 3
Eccleston St. SW1 BV41 3
Eckersley St. E1 CA38 2
Eckford St. N1 BY37 2
Edgware Rd. W2 BT38 1
Edinburgh Gate, SW1 BU41 3
Edis St. NW1 BV37 1
Edward Ms. W1 BV39 1
Egerton Cres. SW3 BU42 3
Egerton Gdns. SW3 BU41 3
Egerton Ms. SW3 BU41 3
Egerton Pl. SW3 BU41 3
Egerton Ter. SW3 BU41 3
Elba Pl. SE17 BZ42 4
Elder St. E1 CA39 2
Eldon Rd. W8 BS41 3
Eldon St. EC2 BZ39 2
Elephant & Castle, SE1 BY42 4
Elephant Rd. SE17 BZ42 4
Elgin Av. W9 BS38 1
Elgin Ms. N. W9 BS38 1
Elgin Ms. S. W9 BS38 1
Elia St. N1 BY37 2
Elim Est. SE1 BZ41 4
Elizabeth Ave. N1 BZ37 2
Elizabeth Bridge, SW1 BV42 3
Elizabeth Est. SE17 BZ43 4
Elizabeth St. SW1 BV42 3
Ellen St. E1 CB39 2
Elliott's Row, SE11 BY42 4
Ellis St. SW1 BU42 3
Elm Park Gdns. SW10 BT42 3
Elm Park La. SW3 BT42 3
Elm Park Mans. SW10 BT43 3
Elm Park Rd. SW3 BT43 3
Elm Pl. SW7 BT42 3
Elms Ms. W2 BT40 3
Elm St. WC1 BX38 2
Elm Tree Clo. NW8 BT38 1
Elm Tree Rd. NW8 BT38 1
Elnathan Ms. W9 BS38 1
Elsted St. SE17 BZ42 4
Elsworthy Rd. NW3 BU37 1
Eltham St. SE17 BZ42 4
Elvaston Ms. SW7 BT41 3
Elvaston Pl. SW7 BT41 3
Elverton St. SW1 BW42 3
Elwin St. E2 CB38 2
Ely Pl. EC1 BY39 2
Elystan Pl. SW3 BU42 3
Elystan St. SW3 BU42 3
Embankment Pl. WC2 BX40 4
Emerald St. WC1 BX39 2
Emerson Pl. SE1 BZ40 4
Emerson St. SE1 BZ40 4

Emery Hill St. SW1 BW41 3
Emperor's Gate, SW7 BS41 3
Empress St. SE17 BZ43 4
Endell St. WC2 BX39 2
Endsleigh Gdns. WC1 BW38 1
Endsleigh Pl. WC1 BW38 1
Endsleigh St. WC1 BW38 1
Enfield Rd. N1 CA36 2
Enford St. W1 BU39 1
English Gdns. SE1 CA40 4
Enid St. SE16 CA41 4
Ennismore Gdns. SW7 BT41 3
Ennismore Gdns. Ms. SW7 BU41 3
Ennismore Ms. SW7 BT41 3
Ennismore Ms. SW7 BU41 3
Ensign St. E1 CB40 4
Ensor Ms. SW7 BT42 3
Epworth St. EC2 BZ38 2
Erasmus St. SW1 BW42 3
Errol St. EC1 BZ38 2
Esmeralda Rd. SE1 CB42 4
Essex Ct. EC4 BY39 2
Essex Rd. N1 BY37 2
Essex St. EC4 BY39 2
Essex St. WC2 BY40 4
Essex Ter. EC4 BY40 4
Esterbrooke St. SW1 BW42 3
Ethel St. SE17 BZ42 4
Euston Gro. NW1 BW38 1
Euston Rd. NW1 BV38 1
Euston Sq. NW1 BW38 1
Euston St. NW1 BW38 1
Eveline Lowe Est. SE16 CB41 4
Evelyn Ct. N1 BZ37 2
Evelyn Gdns. SW7 BT42 3
Evelyn Wk. N1 BZ37 2
Evelyn Yd. W1 BW39 1
Everilda St. N1 BX37 2
Eversholt St. NW1 BW37 1
Everton Bdgs. NW1 BW38 1
Ewer St. SE1 BZ40 4
Exchange St. EC1 BZ38 2
Exeter St. WC2 BX40 4
Exhibition Rd. SW7 BT41 3
Exmouth Mkt. EC1 BY38 2
Exon St. SE17 CA42 4
Exton St. SE1 BY40 4
Eyre Ct. NW8 BT37 1
Eyre Street Hill, EC1 BY38 2
Ezra St. E2 CA38 2
Fairchild St. EC2 CA38 2
Fairclough St. E1 CB39 2
Fairfax Rd. NW6 BT36 1
Fairhazel Gdns. NW6 BT36 1
Fairholt St. SW7 BU41 3
Fairlop Pl. NW8 BT38 1
Fair St. SE1 CA41 4
Falconberg Ms. W1 BW39 1
Falcon Cl. SE1 BZ40 4
Falkirk St. N1 CA37 2
Falmouth Rd. SE1 BZ41 4
Fann St. EC1 BZ38 2
Fanshaw St. N1 CA38 2
Faraday St. SE17 BZ43 4
Farm St. W1 BV40 3
Farnham Pl. SE1 BY40 4
Farnham Royal, SE11 BX42 4
Farringdon Rd. EC1 BY38 2
Farringdon St. EC1 BY39 2
Farringdon St. EC4 BY39 2
Fashion St. E1 CA39 2
Faunce St. SE17 BY43 4
Featherstone St. EC1 BZ38 2
Felton St. N1 BZ37 2
Fenchurch Av. EC3 CA39 2
Fenchurch Bldgs. EC3 CA39 2
Fenchurch Ct. EC3 CA39 2
Fenchurch St. EC3 CA40 4
Fendall St. SE1 CA41 4
Fenning St. SE1 CA41 4
Fernsbury St. WC1 BY38 2
Fetter La. EC4 BY39 2
Field Ct. WC1 BX39 2
Fieldgate St. E1 CB39 2
Field Pl. EC1 BY37 2
Field St. WC1 BX38 2
Finch La. EC3 BZ39 2
Finchley Pl. NW8 BT37 1
Finchley Rd. NW3 BT36 1
Finck St. SE1 BX41 4
Finsbury Av. EC2 BZ39 2
Finsbury Cir. EC2 BZ39 2
Finsbury Mkt. EC2 CA38 2
Finsbury Pavement, EC2 BZ39 2
Finsbury Sq. EC2 BZ38 2
Finsbury St. EC2 BZ39 2
First St. SW3 BU42 3
Fisher St. Est. NW8 BT38 1
Fisher St. WC1 BX39 2
Fisherton St. NW8 BT38 1
Fish St. Hill, EC3 BZ40 4
Fitzalan St. SE11 BX42 4
Fitzhardinge St. W1 BV39 1
Fitzmaurice Pl. W1 BV40 3
Fitzroy Ms. W1 BW38 1
Fitzroy Rd. NW1 BU37 1
Fitzroy Sq. W1 BW38 1
Fitzroy St. W1 BW38 1
Flank St. E1 CB40 4
Flaxman Ter. WC1 BW38 1
Fleet La. EC4 BY39 2
Fleet St. EC4 BY39 2
Fleet Street Hill, E1 CB38 2
Fleming Rd. SE17 BY43 4
Fleur de Lis St. E1 CA38 2
Flinton St. SE17 CA42 4
Flint St. SE17 BZ42 4
Flitcroft St. WC2 BW39 1
Flood St. SW3 BU42 3
Flood Wk. SW3 BU43 3
Floral St. WC2 BX40 4
Florence Ct. NW8 BT38 1
Florence St. N1 BY36 2
Flower And Dean St. E1 CA39 2
Foley St. W1 BW39 1
Folgate St. E1 CA39 2
Fore St. EC2 BZ39 2
Fore Street Av. EC2 BZ39 2
Formosa St. W9 BS39 1
Forset St. W1 BU39 1
Forston St. N1 BZ37 2
Fort Pass. SE16 CA42 4
Fort Rd. SE1 CA42 4
Fort St. E1 CA39 2
Fortune St. EC1 BZ38 2
Fosbury Ms. W2 BS40 3
Foster La. EC2 BZ39 2
Foubert's Pl. W1 BW39 1
Foulis Ter. SW7 BT42 3
Fountain Ct. EC4 BY40 4
Fountain St. E2 CA38 2
Fournier St. E1 CA39 2
Fowler Rd. N1 BY37 2
Fox Ct. EC1 BY39 2
Frampton St. NW8 BT38 1
Francis St. SW1 BW42 3
Franklin's Row, SW3 BU42 3
Frazier St. SE1 BY41 4
Frean St. SE16 CB41 4
Frederick Cl. W2 BU40 3
Frederick Rd. SE17 BY43 4
Frederick St. WC1 BX38 2
Freemantle St. SE17 CA42 4
Friar St. EC4 BY39 2
Friday St. EC4 BZ40 4
Friend St. EC1 BY38 2
Frith St. W1 BW39 1
Frome St. N1 BZ37 2
Frostic Pl. E1 CA39 2
Frying Pan All. E1 CA39 2
Fulham Rd. SW10 BT42 3
Fuller St. E2 CB38 2
Fulton Ms. W2 BT40 3
Fulwood Pl. WC1 BX39 2
Furnival St. EC4 BY39 2
Fyfe Ter. N1 BX37 2
Fynes St. SW1 BW42 3
Gainford St. N1 BY37 2
Gainsford St. SE1 CA41 4
Galen Pl. WC1 BX39 2
Gambia St. SE1 BY40 4
Ganton St. W1 BW40 3
Garbutt Pl. W1 BV39 1
Garden Rd. NW8 BT38 1
Garden Row, SE1 BY41 4
Garden Wk. EC2 CA38 2
Garlick Hill, EC4 BZ40 4
Garnault Ms. EC1 BY38 2
Garnault Pl. EC1 BY38 2
Garrett St. EC1 BZ38 2
Garrick St. WC2 BX40 4
Gascoigne Pl. E2 CA38 2
Gasholder Pl. SE11 BX42 4
Gaskin St. N1 BY37 2
Gaspar Ms. SW5 BS42 3
Gateforth St. NW8 BU38 1
Gatesby St. SE17 BZ42 4
Gate St. WC2 BX39 2
Gateway, SE17 BZ43 4
Gateways, The SW3 BU42 3
Gatliff Rd. SW1 BV42 3
Gaunt St. SE1 BY41 4
Gavel St. SE17 BZ42 4
Gayfere St. SW1 BX41 4
Gaywood St. SE1 BY41 4
Gaza St. SE17 BY42 4
Gedling Pl. SE1 CA41 4
Gees Ct. W1 BV39 1
Gee St. EC1 BY38 2
Geffrye Ct. N1 CA37 2
Geffrye St. E2 CA37 2
George Inn Yd. SE1 BZ40 4
George Row, SE16 CB41 4
George's Sq. W1 CA38 2
George St. W1 BU39 1
George Yd. W1 BV40 3
Georgiana St. NW1 BW37 1
Geraldine St. SE11 BY41 4
Gerald Rd. SW1 BV42 3
Gerrard Rd. N1 BY37 2
Gerrard St. W1 BW40 3
Gerridge St. SE1 BY41 4
Gibraltar Gdns. E2 CA38 2
Gibraltar Wk. E2 CA38 2
Gibson Rd. SE11 BX42 4
Gibson Sq. N1 BY37 2
Gifford St. N1 BX37 2
Gilbert Pl. WC1 BX39 2
Gilbert Rd. SE11 BY42 4
Gilbert St. W1 BV39 1
Gilbert St. BV39 1
Gildea St. W1 BV39 1
Gillingham Ms. SW1 BV42 3
Gillingham Row, SW1 BW42 3
Gillingham St. SW1 BV42 3
Gilston Rd. SW10 BT42 3
Giltspur St. EC1 BY39 2
Gladstone St. SE1 BY41 4
Glasgow Ter. SW1 BW42 3
Glass Hill St. SE1 BY41 4
Glasshouse St. W1 BW40 3
Glasshouse Wk. SE11 BX42 4
Glebe Pl. SW3 BU43 3
Gledhow Gdns. SW5 BT42 3
Glendower Pl. SW7 BT42 3
Glengall Rd. SE15 CA42 4
Glengall Ter. SE15 CA43 4
Glentworth St. Nw1 BU38 1
Globe St. SE1 BZ41 4
Gloucester Av. NW1 BV36 1
Gloucester Cres. NW1 BV37 1
Gloucester Gdns. W2 BT39 1
Gloucester Gate, NW1 BV37 1
Gloucester Ms. W2 BT39 1
Gloucester Ms. W. W2 BT39 1
Gloucester Pl. NW1 BU38 1
Gloucester Pl. Ms. W1 BU39 1
Gloucester Rd. SW7 BT41 3
Gloucester Sq. W2 BT39 1
Gloucester St. SW1 BW42 3
Gloucester Ter. W2 BS39 1
Gloucester Way, EC1 BY38 2
Glynde Ms. SW3 BU41 3
Glyn St. SE11 BX42 4
Godfrey St. SW3 BU42 3
Goding St. SE11 BX42 4
Godliman St. EC4 BY39 2
Godwin Ct. NW1 BW37 1
Golden La. EC1 BZ38 2
Golden Sq. W1 BW40 3
Goldford Pl. NW1 BU38 1
Goldhurst Ter. NW6 BS36 1
Goldington Cres. NW1 BW37 1
Goldington St. NW1 BW37 1
Goldsmith's Row, E2 CB37 2
Goodge Pl. W1 BW39 1
Goodge St. W1 BW39 1
Goodman St. E1 CB39 2
Goodman's Yd. E1 CA40 4
Goodson St. N1 BY37 2
Goods Way, NW1 BW37 1
Goods Way, NW1 BX37 2
Goodwins Ct. WC2 BX40 4
Goose Yd. EC1 BY37 2
Gopsall St. N1 BZ37 2
Gordon Sq. WC1 BW38 1
Gordon St. WC1 BW38 1
Gore St. SW7 BT41 3
Goring St. EC3 CA39 2
Gorsuch Pl. E2 CA38 2
Gorsuch St. E2 CA38 2
Gosfield St. W1 BV39 1
Goslett Yd. WC2 BW39 1
Gosset St. E2 CA38 2
Goswell Rd. EC1 BY37 2
Gough Sq. EC4 BY39 2
Gough St. WC1 BX38 2
Goulston St. E1 CA39 2
Gower Ct. WC1 BW38 1
Gower Ms. WC1 BW39 1
Gower Pl. WC1 BW38 1
Gower St. WC1 BW38 1
Gowers Walk, E1 CB39 2
Gracechurch St. EC3 BZ40 4
Grafton Ms. W1 BW38 1
Grafton Pl. NW1 BW38 1
Grafton St. W1 BV40 3
Grafton Way, W1 BW38 1
Graham St. N1 BY37 2
Graham Ter. SW1 BV42 3
Granby's Bdgs. SE11 BX42 4
Granby St. E2 CA38 2
Granby Ter. NW1 BW37 1
Grand Av. EC1 BY39 2
Grange Ct. WC2 BX39 2
Grange St. N1 BZ37 2
Grange, The SE1 CA41 4
Grange Wk. SE1 CA41 4
Grange Yd. SE1 CA41 4
Grantbridge St. N1 BY37 2
Grantham Pl. W1 BV40 3
Grant St. N1 BY37 2
Granville Pl. W1 BV39 1
Granville Sq. WC1 BX38 2
Granville St. WC1 BX38 2
Gravel La. E1 CA39 2
Grays Inn Rd. WC1 BX38 2
Gray's Inn Sq. WC1 BX39 2
Gray St. SE1 BY41 4
Gt. Castle St. W1 BV39 1
Gt. Central St. NW1 BU39 1
Gt. Chapel St. W1 BW39 1
Gt. College St. SW1 BX41 4
Gt. Cumberland Ms. W1 BU39 1
Gt. Cumberland Pl. W1 BU39 1
Gt. Dover St. SE1 BZ41 4
Great Eastern St. EC2 CA38 2
Gt. George St. SW1 BW41 3
Gt. Guildford St. SE1 BZ40 4
Great James St. WC1 BX39 2
Gt. Marlborough St. W1 BW39 1
Great New St. EC4 BY39 2
Greatorex St. E1 CB39 2
Great Ormond St. WC1 BX39 2
Great Percy St. WC1 BX38 2
Gt. Peter St. SW1 BW41 3
Gt. Portland St. W1 BV38 1
Gt. Pulteney St. W1 BW40 3
Great Queen St. WC2 BX39 2
Gt. Russell St. WC1 BW39 1
Gt. Russell St. WC1 BX39 2
Great St. Helen's, EC3 CA39 2
Great St. Helen, S, Ec3 CA39 2
Gt. St. Thomas Apostle, EC4 BZ40 4
Gt. Scotland Yd. SW1 BX40 4
Gt. Smith St. SW1 BW41 3
Gt. Suffolk St. SE1 BY40 4
Gt. Sutton St. EC1 BY38 2
Great Swan All. EC2 BZ39 2
Gt. Tichfield St. W1 BV38 1
Gt. Tower St. EC3 CA40 4
Gt. Trinity La. EC4 BZ40 4
Great Turnstile, WC2 BX39 2
Great Winchester St. EC2 BZ39 2
Gt. Windmill St. W1 BW40 3
Greek St. W1 BW39 1
Greenberry St. NW8 BU37 1
Greencoat Pl. SW1 BW42 3
Greencoat Row, SW1 BW41 3
Green Dragon Yd. E1 CB39 2
Greenhills Rents, EC1 BY39 2
Greenland Rd. NW1 BV37 1
Greenland St. NW1 BV37 1
Green Man St. N1 BZ36 2
Green St. W1 BV40 3
Green Ter. EC1 BY38 2
Green Wk. SE1 CA41 4
Greenwell St. W1 BV38 1
Greet St. SE1 BY40 4
Grendon St. NW8 BU38 1
Grenville Ms. SW7 BT42 3
Grenville Pl. SW7 BT41 3
Grenville St. WC1 BX38 2
Gresham St. EC2 BZ39 2
Gresse St. W1 BW39 1
Greville Hall, NW6 BS37 1
Greville Pl. NW6 BS37 1
Greville Rd. NW6 BS37 1
Greville St. EC1 BY39 2
Greycoat Pl. SW1 BW41 3
Greycoat St. SW1 BW41 3
Grey Eagle St. E1 CA39 2
Greyfriars Pass. EC1 BY39 2
Griggs Pl. SE1 CA41 4
Grimsby St. E2 CA38 2
Grimthorpe Ho. EC1 BY38 2
Grindal St. SE1 BY41 4
Groom Pl. SW1 BV41 3
Grosvenor Cres. SW1 BV41 3
Grosvenor Cres. Ms. SW1 BV41 3
Grosvenor Est. SW1 BW42 3
Grosvenor Gdns. SW1 BV41 3
Grosvenor Gdns. Ms. N. SW1 BV41 3
Grosvenor Hill, W1 BV40 3
Grosvenor Pl. SW1 BV41 3
Grosvenor Rd. SW1 BV43 3
Grosvenor Sq. W1 BV40 3
Grosvenor St. W1 BV40 3
Grove Bldgs. SW3 BU43 3
Grove Ct. NW8 BT38 1
Grove End Gdns. NW8 BT37 1
Grove End Rd. NW8 BT38 1
Grove Gdns. NW8 BU38 1
Grove Hall Ct. NW8 BT38 1
Grove Wk. N1 CA38 2
Grreek Ct. W1 BW39 1
Guildford Rd. N1 CA36 2
Guildhall Bldgs. EC2 BZ39 2
Guildhall Yd. EC2 BZ39 2
Guildhouse St. SW1 BW42 3
Guilford Pl. WC1 BX38 2
Guilford St. WC1 BX38 2
Guinness Bdgs. SE11 BY42 4
Guinness Bgs. E2 CB37 2
Guinness Blds. SW3 BU42 3
Gunduff St. SE11 BY42 4
Gun St. E1 CA39 2
Gunthorpe St. E1 CA39 2
Guthrie St. SW3 BU42 3
Gutter La. EC2 BZ39 2
Guy St. SE1 BZ41 4
Gye St. SE11 BX42 4
Haberdasher St. N1 BZ38 2
Hackney Rd. E2 CA38 2
Haddon Hall St. SE1 BZ41 4
Haggerston Est. E8 CA37 2
Haggerston Rd. E8 CA36 2
Halcomb St. N1 CA37 2
Half Moon Cres. N1 BX37 2
Half Moon Pass. E1 CA39 2
Half Moon St. W1 BV40 3
Halkin Arc. SW1 BV41 3
Halkin Pl. SW1 BV41 3
Halkin St. SW1 BV41 3
Hallam St. W1 BV38 1
Hallfield Est. W2 BS39 1
Hall Gate, NW8 BT38 1
Halliford St. N1 BZ36 2
Hall Pl. W2 BT38 1
Hall Rd. NW8 BT38 1
Hall St. EC1 BY38 2
Halsey St. SW3 BU42 3
Halton Rd. N1 BY36 2
Hamilton Clo. NW8 BT38 1
Hamilton Ct. W9 BT38 1
Hamilton Gdns. NW8 BT38 1
Hamilton Pl. W1 BV40 3
Hamilton Sq. SE1 BZ41 4
Hamilton Ter. NW8 BS37 1
Hamish St. SE11 BX42 4
Hamond Sq. N1 CA37 2
Hampstead Rd. NW1 BW37 1
Hampton St. SE17 BY42 4
Hanbury St. E1 CA39 2
Hanbury St. E1 CB39 2
Hand Ct. WC1 BX39 2
Handel St. WC1 BX38 2
Hankey Pl. SE1 BZ41 4
Hanover Gate, NW1 BU38 1
Hanover Gate Mans. NW1 BU38 1
Hanover Sq. W1 BV39 1
Hanover St. W1 BV39 1
Hanover Ter. NW1 BU38 1
Hanover Ter. Ms. NW1 BU38 1
Hans Cres. SW1 BU41 3
Hanson St. W1 BW39 1
Hans Pl. SW1 BU41 3
Hans Rd. SW3 BU41 3
Hans St. SW1 BU41 3
Hanway Pl. W1 BW39 1
Hanway St. W1 BW39 1
Harbet Rd. W2 BT39 1
Harcourt St. W1 BU39 1
Harcourt Ter. SW10 BS42 3
Hardwick St. EC1 BY38 2
Hardwidge St. SE1 CA41 4
Hare Pl. EC4 BY39 2
Harewood Av. NW1 BU38 1
Harewood Pl. W1 BV39 1
Harewood Row, NW1 BU39 1
Harleyford Rd. SE11 BX43 4
Harley Gdns. SW10 BT42 3
Harley Pl. W1 BV39 1
Harley Rd. NW3 BT36 1
Harley St. W1 BV38 1
Harmsworth St. SE17 BY42 4
Harp All. EC4 BY39 2
Harper Rd. SE1 BZ41 4
Harp La. EC3 CA40 4
Harpur St. WC1 BX39 2
Harriet St. SW1 BU41 3
Harriet Wk. SW1 BU41 3
Harrington Gdns. SW7 BS42 3
Harrington Rd. SW7 BT42 3
Harrington Sq. NW1 BW37 1
Harrington St. NW1 BW38 1
Harrison St. WC1 BX38 2
Harrowby St. W1 BU39 1
Harrow Pl. E1 CA39 2
Harrow Rd. W2 BT39 1
Hart St. EC3 CA40 4
Hart St. WC2 BX39 2
Harvey St. N1 BZ37 2
Hasker St. SW3 BU42 3
Hassard St. E2 CA38 2
Hastings St. WC1 BX38 2
Hatfields, SE1 BY40 4
Hatherley Gro. W2 BS39 1
Hatherley St. SW1 BW42 3
Hatton Garden, EC1 BY39 2
Hatton Pl. EC1 BY39 2
Hatton Row, NW8 BT38 1
Hatton St. NW8 BT38 1
Hatton Wall, EC1 BY39 2
Haunch of Venison Yd. W1 BV39 1
Havelock St. N1 BX37 2
Haverstock St. N1 BY37 2
Hawes St. N1 BY36 2
Hawley Cres. NW1 BV36 1
Haydon Sq. E1 CA39 2
Haydon St. EC3 CA40 4
Hay Hill, W1 BV40 3
Hayles St. SE11 BY42 4
Haymarket, SW1 BW40 3
Hayne St. EC1 BY39 2
Hays La. SE1 BZ40 4
Hay's Ms. W1 BV40 3
Haywoods Pl. EC1 BY38 2
Headfort Pl. SW1 BV41 3
Hearn's Bdgs. SE17 BZ42 4
Hearn St. EC2 CA38 2
Heathcote St. WC1 BX38 2
Hebden Ct. E2 CA37 2
Heddon St. W1 BW40 3
Helmet Row, EC1 BZ38 2
Hemingford Rd. N1 BX37 2
Hemp Row, SE17 BZ42 4
Hemsworth Ct. N1 CA37 2
Hemsworth St. N1 CA37 2
Hemus Pl. SW3 BU42 3
Hendre Rd. SE1 CA42 4
Heneage La. EC3 CA39 2
Heneage St. E1 CA39 2
Henniker Ms. SW3 BT42 3
Henrietta Ms. WC1 BX38 2
Henrietta Pl. W1 BV39 1
Henrietta St. WC2 BX40 4
Henshaw St. SE17 BZ42 4
Henstridge Pl. NW8 BU37 1
Herbal Hill, EC1 BY38 2
Herbert Cres. SW1 BU41 3
Herbrand St. WC1 BX38 2
Hercules Rd. SE1 BX41 4
Hereford Sq. SW7 BT42 3
Hereford St. E2 CB38 2
Hermitage Wall, E1 CB40 4
Heron Pl. W1 BV39 1
Herrick St. SW1 BW42 3
Hertford Pl. W1 BW38 1
Hertford Rd. N1 CA37 2
Hertford St. W1 BV40 3
Hesper Ms. SW5 BS42 3
Heygate St. SE17 BZ42 4
Hide Pl. SW1 BW42 3
High Holborn, WC1 BX39 2
Highway, The E1 CB40 4
Hillery Rd. SE17 BZ42 4
Hillgrove Rd. NW6 BT36 1
Hill Rd. NW8 BT38 1
Hills Pl. W1 BW39 1
Hill St. W1 BV40 3
Hind Ct. EC4 BY39 2
Hinde St. W1 BV39 1
Hobart Pl. SW1 BV41 3
Hocker St. E2 CA38 2
Holbein Ms. SW1 BV42 3
Holbein Pl. SW1 BV42 3
Holborn, Ec1 BY39 2
Holborn Cir. EC1 BY39 2
Holborn Viaduct, EC1 BY39 2
Holford Pl. WC1 BY38 2
Hollen St. W1 BW39 1
Holles St. W1 BV39 1
Hollywood Rd. SW10 BT42 3
Holms St. E2 CB37 2
Holyoake Rd. SE11 BY41 4
Holyrood St. SE1 CA41 4
Holywell La. EC2 CA38 2
Holywell Row, EC2 CA38 2
Homefield Sq. N1 CA37 2
Homer Row, W1 BU39 1
Homer St. W1 BU39 1
Honduras St. EC1 BZ38 2
Honey La. EC2 BZ39 2
Hoopers Ct. SW3 BU41 3
Hopetown St. E1 CA39 2
Hopkins St. W1 BW39 1
Hopton St. SE1 BY40 4
Horatio St. E2 CA37 2
Horseferry Rd. SW1 BW41 3
Horse Guards Av. SW1 BX40 4
Horse Guards Rd. SW1 BW40 3
Horsleydown La. SE1 CA41 4
Horsley St. SE17 BZ43 4
Hosier La. EC1 BY39 2
Hotspur St. SE11 BY42 4
Houghton St. WC2 BX39 2
Houndsditch, EC3 CA39 2
Howell St. W2 BT39 1
Howick Pl. SW1 BW41 3
Howland Ms. E. W1 BW39 1
Howland Ms. W. W1 BW39 1
Howland St. W1 BW39 1
Howley Pl. W2 BT39 1
Hows St. E2 CA37 2
Hoxton Sq. N1 CA38 2
Hoxton St. N1 CA37 2
Hoyle St. W1 BW40 3
Hudson Pl. SW1 BV42 3
Huggin La. EC4 BZ40 4
Hugh Ms. SW1 BV42 3
Hugh St. SW1 BV42 3
Hull St. EC1 BZ38 2
Humphrey St. SE1 CA42 4
Hungerford Bridge, WC2 BX40 4
Hunter St. WC1 BX38 2
Huntley St. WC1 BW38 1
Hunton St. E1 CB39 2
Huntsman St. SE17 BZ42 4
Huntsworth Ms. NW1 BU38 1
Hyde Park Corner, W1 BV41 3
Hyde Park Cres. W2 BU39 1
Hyde Park Gdns. W2 BT40 3
Hyde Park Gdns. Ms. W2 BT40 3
Hyde Park Gate, SW7 BT41 3
Hyde Pk. Mans. NW1 BU39 1
Hyde Park Ms. SW7 BT41 3
Hyde Park Pl. W2 BU40 3
Hyde Park Sq. W2 BU39 1
Hyde Park St. W2 BU39 1
Hyde Rd. N1 BZ37 2
Idol La. EC3 CA40 4
Iliffe St. SE17 BY42 4
Iliffe Yd. SE17 BY42 4
Imber St. N1 BZ37 2
Imperial Institute Rd. SW7 BT41 3
India St. EC3 CA39 2
Ingestre Pl. W1 BW39 1
Inglebert St. EC1 BY38 2
Inner Circle, NW1 BV38 1
Insurance St. WC1 BY38 2
Inverness Ms. W2 BS40 3
Inverness Pl. W2 BS40 3
Inverness St. NW1 BV37 1
Inverness Ter. W2 BS39 1
Inville Rd. SE17 BZ42 4
Ireland Yd. EC4 BY39 2
Ironmonger La. EC2 BZ39 2
Ironmonger Row, EC1 BZ38 2
Irving St. WC2 BW40 3
Islington Green, N1 BY37 2
Islington High St. N1 BY37 2
Italian Wk. SE11 BX42 4
Ives St. SW3 BU42 3
Ivor Pl. NW1 BU38 1
Ivy St. N1 CA37 2
Ixworth Pl. SW3 BU42 3
Jacob St. SE1 CA41 4
Jamaica Rd. SE1 CA41 4
James St. W1 BV39 1
James St. W1 BW40 3
James St. WC2 BX39 2
Jamestown Rd. NW1 BV37 1
Jardin St. SE5 CA43 4
Jay Ms. SW7 BT41 3
Jermyn St. SW1 BW40 3
Jerome Cres. NW8 BU38 1
Jerome Pl. SE17 BZ43 4
Jerome St. E1 CA38 2
Jerrard St. N1 CA37 2

Jerusalem Pass. EC1 BY38 2
Jesmond St. SE17 BZ42 4
Jewry St. EC3 CA39 2
Joan St. SE1 BY40 4
Jockey's Fields WC1 BX39 2
Johanna St. SE1 BY41 4
John Adam St. WC2 BX40 4
John Carpenter St. EC4 BY40 4
John Felton Rd. SE16 CB41 4
John Fisher St. E1 CB40 4
John Islip St. SW1 BW42 3
John Prince's St. W1 BV39 1
John's Ms. WC1 BX38 2
Johnsons Pl. SW1 BW42 3
John St. WC1 BX38 2
Joiner St. SE1 BZ40 4
Jonathan St. SE11 BX42 4
Jones St. W1 BV40 3
Jubilee Pl. SW3 BU42 3
Judd St. WC1 BX38 2
Junction Ms. W2 BU39 1
Juxton St. SE11 BX42 4
Kay St. E2 CB37 2
Kean St. WC2 BX39 2
Keeley St. WC2 BX39 2
Kelso Pl. W8 BS41 3
Kemble St. WC2 BX39 2
Kempsford Rd. SE11 BY42 4
Kempshead Rd. SE5 CA42 4
Kendall Pl. W1 BV39 1
Kendal St. W2 BU39 1
Kendrick Ms. SW7 BT42 3
Kennings Way, SE11 BY42 4
Kenning Ter. N1 CA37 2
Kennington Gro. SE11 BX43 4
Kennington La. SE11 BX42 4
Kennington Pk. Pl. SE11 BY43 4
Kennington Pk. Rd. SE11 BY43 4
Kennington Rd. SE1 BY41 4
Kenrick Pl. W1 BV39 1
Kensington Ct. W8 BS41 3
Kensington Ct. Pl. W8 BS41 3
Kensington Gate, W8 BT41 3
Kensington Gore, SW7 BT41 3
Kensington Rd. W8 BS41 3
Kensington Sq. W8 BS41 3
Kentish Tn. Rd. NW1 BV37 1
Kenton St. WC1 BX38 2
Kent Pass. NW1 BU38 1
Kent Rd. SE1 CA42 4
Kent St. E2 CA37 2
Kent Ter. NW1 BU38 1
Keppel Row, SE1 BZ40 4
Keppel St. WC1 BW39 1
Kerbela St. E2 CB38 2
Keyse Rd. SE1 CA41 4
Keystone Cres. N1 BX37 2
Keyworth St. SE1 BY41 4
Kiffen St. EC2 BZ38 2
Kilburn Gate, NW6 BS37 1
Killick St. N1 BX37 2
King Charles St. SW1 BW41 3
King Edward St. EC1 BZ39 2
King Edward Wk. SE1 BY41 4
King Henry's Rd. NW3 BT36 1
King James St. SE1 BY41 4
King John Ct. EC2 CA38 2
Kinglake Est. SE17 CA42 4
Kinglake St. SE17 CA42 4
Kingly Ct. W1 BW40 3
Kingly St. W1 BW39 1
King & Queen St. SE17 BZ42 4
Kings Arms Ct. E1 CB39 2
King's Arms Yd. EC2 BZ39 2
King's Bench St. SE1 BY41 4
King's Bench Wk. EC4 BY40 4
Kingscote St. EC4 BY40 4
Kings Cross Rd. WC1 BX38 2
King's Head Yd. SE1 BZ40 4
Kingsland Est. E2 CA37 2
Kingsley Ms. W8 BS41 3
Kings Ms. WC1 BX38 2
Kingsmill Ter. NW8 BT37 1
Kings Pl. SE1 BZ41 4
King's Rd. SW1 BV42 3
King's Rd. SW3 BT43 3
King's Scholar's Pass. SW1 BW42 3
King's Ter. NW1 BW37 1
King St. EC2 BZ39 2
King St. SW1 BW40 3
King St. WC2 BX40 4
Kingsway, WC2 BX39 2
King William St. EC4 BZ39 2
Kinnerton Pl. N. SW1 BU41 3
Kinnerton Pl. S. SW1 BU41 3
Kinnerton St. SW1 BU41 3
Kintore St. SE1 CA42 4
Kintore Way, SE1 CA42 4
Kipling Est. SE1 BZ41 4
Kipling St. SE1 BZ41 4
Kirby Gro. SE1 CA41 4
Kirby St. EC1 BY39 2
Knaresboro' Pl. SW5 BS42 3
Knightrider St. EC4 BZ40 4
Knightsbridge, SW7 BU41 3
Knightsbridge Grn. SW1 BU41 3
Knox St. W1 BU39 1
Kynance Ms. SW7 BS41 3
Kynance Pl. SW7 BT41 3
Laburnam Ct. E2 CA37 2
Laburnam St. E2 CA37 2
Lackington St. EC2 BZ39 2
Lambeth Bridge, SW1 BX42 4
Lambeth High St. SE1 BX42 4
Lambeth Palace Rd. SE1 BX41 4
Lambeth Rd. SE1 BX41 4
Lambeth St. E1 CB39 2
Lambeth Wk. SE11 BX42 4
Lambs Bldgs. EC1 BZ38 2
Lambs Conduit Pass. WC1 BX39 2
Lambs Conduit St. WC1 BX38 2
Lambs Pass. EC1 BZ39 2
Lamb St. E1 CA39 2
Lamb Wk. SE1 CA41 4
Lamlash St. SE11 BY42 4
Lampeter St. N1 BZ37 2
Lanark Pl. W9 BT38 1
Lanark Rd. W9 BS37 1
Lancaster Ct. W2 BT40 3
Lancaster Gate, W2 BT40 3
Lancaster Ms. W2 BT40 3
Lancaster Pl. WC2 BX40 4
Lancaster St. SE1 BY41 4
Lancaster Ter. W2 BT40 3
Lancelot Pl. SW7 BU41 3
Lancing St. NW1 BW38 1
Landon Pl. SW1 BU41 3
Land St. N1 BZ38 2
Lane, The NW8 BT37 1
Lanfranc St. SE1 BY41 4
Langford Clo. NW8 BT37 1
Langford Pl. NW8 BT37 1
Langham Pl. W1 BV39 1
Langham St. W1 BV39 1
Langley Ct. WC2 BX40 4
Langley St. WC2 BX39 2
Langton Cl. WC1 BX38 2
Langtry Rd. NW6 BS37 1
Lansdowne Pl. SE1 BZ41 4
Lansdowne Row, W1 BV40 3
Lansdowne Ter. WC1 BX38 2
Lant St. SE1 BZ41 4
Larcom St. SE17 BZ42 4
Larissa St. SE17 BZ42 4
Lauderdale Rd. W9 BS38 1
Laud St. SE11 BX42 4
Launcelot St. SE1 BY41 4
Launceston Pl. W8 BT41 3
Laurence Pountney Hill, EC4 BZ40 4
Laurence Pountney La. EC4 BZ40 4
Laverton Pl. SW5 BS42 3
Lavington St. SE1 BY40 4
Lawrence La. EC2 BZ39 2
Lawson Est. SE1 BZ41 4
Law St. SE1 BZ41 4
Laxton Pl. NW1 BV38 1
Laystall St. EC1 BY38 2
Layton Rd. N1 BY37 2
Leadenhall Pl. EC3 CA39 2
Leadenhall St. EC3 CA39 2
Leake Ct. SE1 BX41 4
Leake St. SE1 BX41 4
Leather La. EC1 BY39 2
Leathermarket St. SE1 CA41 4
Lecky St. SW7 BT42 3
Leeke St. WC1 BX38 2
Lees Pl. W1 BV40 3
Lee St. E8 CA37 2
Leicester Ct. WC2 BW40 3
Leicester Pl. WC2 BW40 3
Leicester Sq. WC2 BW40 3
Leicester St. WC2 BW40 3
Leigh Hunt St. SE1 BZ41 4
Leigh St. WC1 BX38 2
Leinster Gdns. W2 BT39 1
Leinster Ms. W2 BT40 3
Leinster Pl. W2 BT39 1
Leinster Ter. W2 BT40 3
Leman Pl. E1 CB39 2
Leman St. E1 CA39 2
Lennox Gdns. SW1 BU41 3
Lennox Gdns. Ms. SW1 BU41 3
Leonard St. EC2 BZ38 2
Leopold Wk. SE11 BX42 4
Leroy St. SE1 CA41 4
Leroy St. SE1 CA42 4
Leverington Pl. N1 BZ38 2
Lever St. EC1 BY38 2
Lewisham St. SW1 BW41 3
Lewis Trust Blds. SW3 BU42 3
Lexham Gdns. W8 BS41 3
Lexham Gdns. Ms. W8 BS41 3
Lexham Wk. W8 BS41 3
Lexington St. W1 BW39 1
Lexington St. W1 BW40 3
Leyden St. E1 CA39 2
Ley St. E1 CB38 2
Library St. SE1 BY41 4
Lichfield St. WC2 BW40 3
Ligonier St. E2 CA38 2
Lilac Pl. SE11 BX42 4
Lilestone Est. NW8 BT38 1
Lilestone St. NW8 BU38 1
Lillington Gdns. Est. SW1 BW42 3
Lime St. EC3 CA40 4
Lincoln's Inn, WC2 BX39 2
Lincoln's Inn Fields, WC2 BX39 2
Lincoln St. SW3 BU42 3
Lindsey St. EC1 BY39 2
Linhope St. NW1 BU38 1
Linseys St. SE16 CB42 4
Linton St. N1 BZ37 2
Liplington Pl. NW1 BW37 1
Lisle St. WC2 BW40 3
Lisson Gro. NW8 BT38 1
Lisson St. NW1 BU39 1
Lit. Albany St. NW1 BV38 1
Lit. Argyle St. W1 BW39 1
Lit. Boltons, The SW10 BS42 3
Little Britain, EC1 BY39 2
Lit. Chester St. SW1 BV41 3
Lit. College St. SW1 BX41 4
Lit. Dorrit Ct. SE1 BZ41 4
Lit. Edward St. NW1 BV37 1
Lit. George St. SW1 BX41 4
Lit. Marlborough St. W1 BW39 1
Little New St. EC4 BY39 2
Lit. Portland St. W1 BV39 1
Little Russell St. WC1 BX39 2
Lit. St. James's St. SW1 BW40 3
Lit. Sanctuary, SW1 BW41 3
Lit. Smith St. SW1 BW41 3
Little Somerset St. E1 CA39 2
Lit. Titchfield St. W1 BW39 1
Little Turnstile, WC2 BX39 2
Livermere Rd. E8 CA37 2
Liverpool Gro. SE17 BZ42 4
Liverpool Rd. N1 BY36 2
Liverpool St. EC2 CA39 2
Livonia St. W1 BW39 1
Lizard St. EC1 BZ38 2
Lloyd Baker St. WC1 BX38 2
Lloyd's Av. EC3 CA39 2
Lloyd Sq. WC1 BY38 2
Lloyd's Row, EC1 BY38 2
Lloyd St. WC1 BY38 2
Lockyer St. SE1 BZ41 4
Lodge Rd. NW8 BT38 1
Lofting Rd. N1 BX36 2
Lolesworth St. E1 CA39 2
Lollard Pl. SE11 BY42 4
Lollard St. SE11 BX42 4
Loman St. SE1 BY41 4
Lombard La. EC4 BY39 2
Lombard St. EC3 BZ39 2
Loncroft Rd. SE5 CA43 4
London Bridge, SE1 BZ40 4
London Bridge St. SE1 BZ40 4
London Ms. W2 BT39 1
London Rd. SE1 BY41 4
London St. W2 BT39 1
London Ter. EC3 CA40 4
London Wall, EC2 BZ39 2
Long Acre, WC2 BX40 4
Longfield Est. SE1 CA42 4
Longford St. NW1 BV38 1
Long La. EC1 BY39 2
Long La. SE1 BZ41 4
Longley St. SE1 CB42 4
Longmore St. SW1 BW42 3
Long St. E2 CA38 2
Longville Rd. SE11 BY42 4
Long Wk. SE1 CA41 4
Long Yd. WC1 BX38 2
Lonsdale Sq. N1 BY36 2
Lorbet Pl. E1 CA39 2
Lorden Wk. E2 CB38 2
Lord Hills Rd. W2 BS39 1
Lord North St. SW1 BX41 4
Lorenzo St. WC1 BX38 2
Lorne Clo. NW8 BU38 1
Lorrimore Sq. SE17 BY43 4
Lothbury, Ec2 BZ39 2
Loudon Rd. NW8 BT36 1
Loughborough St. SE11 BX42 4
Lovat La. EC3 CA40 4
Love La. EC2 BZ39 2
Lwr. Belgrave St. SW1 BV41 3
Lwr. Grosvenor Pl. SW1 BV41 3
Lwr. John St. W1 BW40 3
Lower Marsh, SE1 BY41 4
Lwr. Merton Rise, NW3 BU36 1
Lwr. Newport St. WC2 BW40 3
Lwr. Sloane St. SW1 BU42 3
Lwr. Thames St. EC3 BZ40 4
Lwr. Trinity La. EC4 BZ40 4
Lowndes Cl. SW1 BV41 3
Lowndes Pl. SW1 BV41 3
Lowndes Sq. SW1 BU41 3
Lowndes St. SW1 BU41 3
Loxham St. WC1 BX38 2
Lucan Pl. SW3 BU42 3
Ludgate Cir. EC4 BY39 2
Ludgate Hill, EC4 BY39 2
Ludgate Sq. EC4 BY39 2
Luke St. EC2 CA38 2
Lumley St. W1 BV39 1
Luntly Pl. E1 CB39 2
Lupus St. SW1 BV43 3
Luton St. NW8 BT38 1
Luxborough St. W1 BV38 1
Lyall Ms. E. SW1 BV41 3
Lyall Ms. W. SW1 BV41 3
Lyall St. SW1 BV41 3
Lygon Pl. SW1 BV41 3
Lyme St. NW1 BW36 1
Lynton Est. SE1 CB42 4
Lynton Rd. SE1 CA42 4
Lyons Pl. NW8 BT38 1
Lytham St. SE17 BZ42 4
Mabledon Pl. WC1 BW38 1
Macclefield Rd. EC1 BZ38 2
Macclesfield St. W1 BW40 3
Macfarren St. NW1 BV38 1
Mackennal St. NW8 BU37 1
Macklin St. WC2 BX39 2
Mackworth St. NW1 BW38 1
Macleod St. SE17 BZ42 4
Maddox St. W1 BV40 3
Madron St. SE17 CA42 4
Magdalen St. SE1 CA40 4
Magpie All. EC4 BY39 2
Maida Av. W2 BT39 1
Maida Vale, W9 BS37 1
Maiden La. WC2 BX40 4
Maidstone Bldgs. SE1 BZ40 4
Maidstone St. E2 CB37 2
Makins St. SW3 BU42 3
Malet Pl. WC1 BW38 1
Malet St. WC1 BW38 1
Mallord St. SW3 BT43 3
Mallory St. NW8 BU38 1
Mallow St. EC1 BZ38 2
Mall, The SW1 BW41 3
Malpin Pl. SE17 BZ42 4
Malta St. EC1 BY38 2
Maltby St. SE1 CA41 4
Maltravers St. WC2 BX40 4
Malt St. SE1 CB43 4
Malvern Ct. SW7 BT42 3
Malvern Rd. E8 CB36 2
Malvern Ter. N1 BY37 2
Manchester Sq. W1 BV39 1
Manchester St. W1 BV39 1
Manciple St. SE1 BZ41 4
Mandeville Pl. W1 BV39 1
Manette St. W1 BW39 1
Manley St. NW1 BV37 1
Manningford Clo. EC1 BY38 2
Manningtree St. E1 CB39 2
Mann St. SE17 BZ43 4
Manor Pl. SE17 BY42 4
Manresa Rd. SW3 BT42 3
Mansefield Ms. W1 BV39 1
Mansefield St. W1 BV39 1
Mansell St. E1 CA39 2
Mansell St. E1 CA40 4
Mansion House St. EC2 BZ39 2
Manson Ms. SW7 BT42 3
Manson Pl. SW7 BT42 3
Mantell St. N1 BY37 2
Maple Pl. W1 BW38 1
Maple St. W1 BW39 1
Maquire St. SE1 CA41 4
Marble Arch, W1 BU40 3
Marchmont St. WC1 BX38 2
Marcia Rd. SE1 CA42 4
Mardyke St. SE17 BZ42 4
Margaret St. W1 BV39 1
Margaretta Ter. SW3 BU43 3
Margery St. WC1 BY38 2
Marine St. SE16 CB41 4
Market Ms. W1 BV40 3
Market Place, W1 BW39 1
Markham Sq. SW3 BU42 3
Markham St. SW3 BU42 3
Mark La. EC3 CA40 4
Mark St. EC2 CA38 2
Marlboro' St. SW3 BU42 3
Marlborough Ave. E8 CB37 2
Marlborough Blds. SW3 BU42 3
Marlborough Ct. W1 BW39 1
Marlborough Gro. SE1 CB42 4
Marlborough Hill, NW8 BT37 1
Marlborough Pl. NW8 BT37 1
Marlborough Rd. SW1 BW40 3
Marloes, The NW8 BT37 1
Marshall St. W1 BW39 1
Marshalsea Rd. SE1 BZ41 4
Marsham St. SW1 BW41 3
Marsland Rd. SE17 BY42 4
Martin La. EC4 BZ40 4
Martlett Ct. WC2 BX39 2
Mart St. WC2 BX40 4
Marylebone Circus, NW1 BU39 1
Marylebone High St. W1 BV39 1
Marylebone La. W1 BV39 1
Marylebone Ms. W1 BV39 1
Marylebone Pass. W1 BW39 1
Marylebone Rd. NW1 BU39 1
Marylebone St. W1 BV39 1
Marylee Way, SE11 BX42 4
Mary St. N1 BZ37 2
Mary Ter. NW1 BV37 1
Mason's Arms Ms. W1 BV40 3
Masons Av. EC2 BZ39 2
Masons Pl. EC1 BY38 2
Mason St. SE17 BZ42 4
Mason's Yd. SW1 BW40 3
Mass St. SE17 CA42 4
Matilda St. N1 BX37 2
Matthew Parker St. SW1 BW41 3
Maunsel St. SW1 BW42 3
Mawbey Est. SE1 CA42 4
Mawbey Pl. SE1 CA42 4
Mawbey Rd. SE1 CA42 4
Mayfair Pl. W1 BV40 3
Maygood St. N1 BX37 2
Mays Ct. WC2 BX40 4
Mcleod's Ms. SW7 BS41 3
Meadowbank, NW3 BU36 1
Meadow Row, SE1 BZ41 4
Mead Row, SE1 BY41 4
Meakin Est. SE1 CA41 4
Meard St. W1 BW39 1
Mecklenburgh Pl. WC1 BX38 2
Mecklenburgh Sq. WC1 BX38 2
Medburn St. NW1 BW37 1
Medway St. SW1 BW41 3
Melcombe Pl. NW1 BU39 1
Melcombe St. NW1 BU38 1
Melina Pl. NW8 BT38 1
Melior St. SE1 BZ41 4
Melton Ct. SW7 BT42 3
Melton St. NW1 BW38 1
Melville St. N1 BZ36 2
Mepham St. SE1 BX40 4
Mercer St. WC2 BW39 1
Mercer St. WC2 BX39 2
Meredith St. EC1 BY38 2
Merlin St. WC1 BY38 2
Mermaid Ct. SE1 BZ41 4
Merrick Sq. SE1 BZ41 4
Merritts Bldgs. EC2 CA38 2
Merrow St. SE17 BZ43 4
Methley St. SE11 BY42 4
Meymott St. SE1 BY40 4
Micawber St. N1 BZ38 2
Michael Faraday Ho. SE17 BZ42 4
Middlesex St. E1 CA39 2
Middle St. EC1 BZ39 2
Middle Temple La. EC4 BY39 2
Middleton Pl. EC1 BY38 2
Midfield Pl. W1 BW38 1
Midhope St. WC1 BX38 2
Midland Rd. NW1 BW37 1
Milborne Gro. SW10 BT42 3
Milcote St. SE1 BY41 4
Miles La. EC4 BZ40 4
Milford La. WC2 BX40 4
Milk St. EC2 BZ39 2
Millbank, SW1 BW42 3
Millbank, SW1 BX41 4
Miller St. NW1 BW37 1
Millman St. WC1 BX38 2
Mill Row, N1 CA37 2
Mills Ct. EC2 CA38 2
Mill's Pl. NW8 BT39 1
Millstream Rd. SE1 CA41 4
Mill St. SE1 CA41 4
Mill St. W1 BV40 3
Milner Pl. N1 BY37 2
Milner Square, N1 BY36 2
Milner St. SW3 BU42 3
Milne St. EC1 BY38 2
Milton Ct. EC2 BZ39 2
Milton St. EC2 BZ39 2
Milverton St. SE11 BY42 4
Mina Rd. SE17 CA42 4
Mincing La. EC3 CA40 4
Minera Ms. SW1 BV42 3
Minnow St. SE17 CA42 4
Minories, EC3 CA39 2
Mintern St. N1 BZ37 2
Mint St. SE1 BZ41 4
Mitchell St. EC1 BZ38 2
Mitre Ct. EC2 BZ39 2
Mitre Rd. SE1 BY41 4
Mitre St. EC3 CA39 2
Model Bldgs. WC1 BX38 2
Molyneux St. W1 BU39 1
Monck St. SW1 BW41 3
Monkton St. SE11 BY42 4
Monkwell Sq. EC2 BZ39 2
Monmouth St. WC2 BX39 2
Monnow Rd. SE1 CB42 4
Montague Cl. SE1 BZ40 4
Montague Pl. WC1 BW39 1
Montague St. WC1 BX39 2
Montagu Ms. N. W1 BU39 1
Montagu Ms. St. W1 BU39 1
Montagu Pl. W1 BU39 1
Montagu Row, W1 BU39 1
Montagu Sq. W1 BU39 1
Montagu St. W1 BU39 1
Montclare St. E2 CA38 2
Montford Pl. SE11 BY42 4
Monthope St. E1 CB39 2
Montpelier Ms. SW7 BU41 3
Montpelier Pl. SW7 BU41 3
Montpelier Sq. SW7 BU41 3
Montpelier St. SW7 BU41 3
Montpelier Ter. SW7 BU41 3
Montpelier Wk. SW7 BU41 3
Montreal Pl. WC2 BX40 4
Montrose Pl. SW1 BV41 3
Monument St. EC3 BZ40 4
Moon St. N1 BY37 2
Moore St. SW3 BU42 3
Moorfields, EC2 BZ37 2
Moorgate, EC2 BZ39 2
Moor La. EC2 BZ39 2
Moor St. W1 BW39 1
Mora St. EC1 BZ38 2
Morecombe St. SE17 BZ42 4
Moreland St. EC1 BY38 2
Moreton Pl. SW1 BW42 3
Moreton St. SW1 BW42 3
Morgan's La. SE1 CA40 4
Morley St. SE1 BY41 4
Mornington Cres. NW1 BW37 1
Mornington Pl. NW1 BV37 1
Mornington St. NW1 BV37 1
Mornington Ter. NW1 BV37 1
Morocco St. SE1 CA41 4
Morpeth Ter. SW1 BW41 3
Mortimer Cres. NW6 BS37 1
Mortimer Est. NW6 BS37 1
Mortimer Market, WC1 BW38 1
Mortimer Pl. NW6 BS37 1
Mortimer Rd. N1 CA36 2
Mortimer St. W1 BV39 1
Morton Pl. SE1 BY41 4
Morton Rd. N1 BZ36 2
Morwell St. WC1 BW39 1
Moscow Pl. W2 BS40 3
Mossop St. SW3 BU42 3
Motcomb St. SW1 BU41 3
Mountford St. E1 CB39 2
Mount Pleasant, Wc1 BY38 2
Mount Row, W1 BV40 3
Mount St. W1 BV40 3
Moxon St. W1 BV39 1
Moye St. E2 CB37 2
Mulberry Wk. SW3 BT43 3
Mulready St. Nw8 BU38 1
Mundy St. N1 CA38 2
Munster Sq. NW1 BV38 1
Munton Rd. SE17 BZ42 4
Muriel St. N1 BX37 2
Murphy St. SE1 BY41 4
Murray Gro. N1 BZ37 2
Muscovy St. EC3 CA40 4
Museum St. WC1 BX39 2
Myddelton Sq. EC1 BY38 2
Myddelton St. EC1 BY38 2
Myrtle St. N1 CA37 2
Nags Head Est. E2 CB37 2
Nags Head St. E2 CA37 2
Naish Ct. N1 BX37 2
Napier Gro. N1 BZ37 2
Napier St. N1 BY36 2
Nash St. NW1 BV38 1
Nassau St. W1 BW39 1
Navarre St. E2 CA38 2
Neal St. WC2 BX39 2
Neathouse Cl. SW1 BW42 3
Nebraska St. SE1 BZ41 4
Neckinger, SE16 CA41 4
Neckinger Est. SE16 CA41 4
Nelson Est. SE17 BZ42 4
Nelson Pl. N1 BY37 2
Nelson Sq. SE1 BY41 4
Nelson Ter. N1 BY37 2
Ness St. SE16 CB41 4
Netley St. NW1 BW38 1
Neville Ct. NW8 BT37 1
Neville St. SW7 BT42 3
Neville Ter. SW7 BT42 3
New Bond St. W1 BV39 1
New Bond St. W1 BV40 3
New Bridge St. EC4 BY39 2
New Broad St. EC2 BZ39 2
Newburgh St. W1 BW39 1
New Burlington Ms. W1 BW40 3
New Burlington Pl. W1 BW40 3
New Burlington St. W1 BW40 3
Newburn St. SE11 BX42 4
Newbury St. EC1 BZ39 2
Newcastle Ct. EC4 BY39 2
Newcastle Pl. W2 BT39 1
New Cavendish St. W1 BV39 1
New Change, EC4 BZ39 2
Newcomen St. SE1 BZ41 4
New Compton St. WC2 BW39 1
New Ct. WC2 BX39 2
Newcourt St. NW8 BU37 1
New Coventry St. W1 BW40 3
New Euston Col. NW1 BW38 1
New Fetter La. EC4 BY39 2
Newgate St. EC1 BY39 2
New Goulston St. E1 CA39 2
Newhall St. N1 BZ37 2
Newhams Row, SE1 CA41 4
Newington Butts, SE1 BY42 4
Newington Causeway, SE1 BY41 4
New Inn St. EC2 CA38 2
New Inn Yd. EC2 CA38 2
New Kent Rd. SE1 BZ41 4
Newman Pass. W1 BW39 1
Newmans Row, WC2 BX39 2
Newman St. W1 BW39 1
Newman Yd. W1 BW39 1
New Martan St. E1 CB40 4
Newnham St. E1 CA39 2
Newnham Ter. SE1 BY41 4
New North Pl. EC2 CA38 2
New North Rd. N1 BZ36 2
New North St. WC1 BX39 2
New Oxford St. WC1 BW39 1
New Oxford St. WC1 BX39 2
New Palace Yd. SW1 BX41 4
Newport Ct. WC2 BW40 3
Newport Pl. WC2 BW40 3
Newport St. SE11 BX42 4
Newport St. WC2 BW40 3
New Quebec St. W1 BU39 1
New Row, WC2 BX40 4
New Sq. WC2 BX39 2
New St. EC2 CA39 2
New Street Sq. EC4 BY39 2
Newton Gro. N1 BZ37 2
Newton St. WC2 BX39 2
New Turnstile, WC2 BX39 2
New Wharf. N1 BX37 2
Nicholas La. EC4 BZ40 4
Nicholson St. SE1 BY40 4
Nile St. N1 BZ38 2
Nile Ter. SE15 CA42 4
Noble St. EC2 BZ39 2
Noel Rd. N1 BY37 2
Noel St. W1 BW39 1
Norfolk Cres. W2 BU39 1
Norfolk Pl. W2 BT39 1
Norfolk Rd. NW8 BT37 1
Norfolk Row, SE11 BX42 4
Norfolk Sq. W2 BT39 1
Norman's Bldgs. EC1 BZ38 2
Norman St. EC1 BZ38 2
Norris St. SW1 BW40 3

Northampton Rd. EC1 BY38 2
Northampton Sq. EC1 BY38 2
North Bank, NW8 BU38 1
Northburgh St. EC1 BY38 2
North Ct. W1 BW39 1
North Cres. WC1 BW39 1
Northdown St. N1 BX37 2
Northern Bldgs. EC1 BY38 2
North Gower St. NW1 BW38 1
Northington St. WC1 BX38 2
North Ms. WC1 BX38 2
N. Moreton Ter. Ms. SW1 BW42 3
Northport St. N1 BZ37 2
North Ride, W2 BU40 3
North Row, W1 BU40 3
North Tenter St. E1 CA39 2
North Ter. SW3 BU41 3
Northumberland All. EC3 CA39 2
Northumberland Av. WC2 BX40 4
Northumberland St. WC2 BX40 4
Northwest Pl. N1 BY37 2
Northwick Clo. NW8 BT38 1
Northwick Ter. NW8 BT38 1
Norton Folgate, E1 CA39 2
Norwich St. EC4 BY39 2
Nottingham Ct. WC2 BX39 2
Nottingham Pl. W1 BV38 1
Nottingham St. W1 BV39 1
Nottingham Ter. NW1 BV38 1
Nth. Audley St. W1 BV40 3
Nth. Wharf Rd. W2 BT39 1
Nugent Ter. NW8 BT37 1
Nursery Row, SE17 BZ42 4
Nutford Pl. W1 BU39 1
Nuttall St. N1 CA37 2
Oak Ct. N1 CA38 2
Oakden St. SE11 BY42 4
Oakfield St. SW10 BT43 3
Oakley Gdns. SW3 BU43 3
Oakley Pl. SE1 CA42 4
Oakley Sq. NW1 BW37 1
Oakley St. SW3 BU42 3
Oak Tree Rd. NW8 BU38 1
Oat La. EC2 BZ39 2
Occupation Rd. SE17 BZ42 4
Odell St. SE5 CA42 4
Ogle St. W1 BW39 1
Old Bailey, EC4 BY39 2
Old Barrack Yd. SW1 BV41 3
Old Bond St. W1 BW40 3
Old Broad St. EC2 BZ39 2
Old Brompton Rd. SW5 BS42 3
Old Burlington St. W1 BW40 3
Oldbury Pl. W1 BV38 1
Old Castle St. E1 CA39 2
Old Cavendish St. W1 BV39 1
Old Change Ct. EC4 BZ39 2
Old Cheshire St. E2 CA38 2
Old Church St. SW3 BT42 3
Old Compton St. W1 BW40 3
Old Gloucester St. WC1 BX39 2
Old Jamaica Rd. SE16 CB41 4
Old Jewry, EC2 BZ39 2
Old Kent Rd. SE1 CA42 4
Old Marylebone Rd. NW1 BU39 1
Old Montague St. E1 CB39 2
Old Nichol St. E2 CA38 2
Old North St. WC1 BX39 2
Old Palace Yd. SW1 BX41 4
Old Paradise St. SE11 BX42 4
Old Park La. W1 BV40 3
Old Pye St. SW1 BW41 3
Old Quebec St. W1 BU39 1
Old Queen St. SW1 BW41 3
Old Seacoal La. EC4 BY39 2
Old Sq. WC2 BX39 2
Old St. EC1 BZ38 2
Olmar St. SE1 CB43 4
Olney Rd. SE17 BZ43 4
O'meara St. SE1 BZ40 4
Omega Pl. N1 BX37 2
Onslow Gdns. SW7 BT42 3
Onslow Ms. E. SW7 BT42 3
Onslow Ms. W. SW7 BT42 3
Onslow Sq. SW7 BT42 3
Onslow St. EC1 BY39 2
Ontario St. SE1 BY41 4
Opal St. SE11 BY42 4
Oppidans Rd. NW3 BU36 1
Orange St. WC2 BW40 3
Orb St. SE17 BZ42 4
Orchardson St. NW8 BT38 1
Orchard St. W1 BV39 1
Orde Hall St. WC1 BX39 2
Ordnance Hill, NW8 BT37 1
Orient St. SE11 BY42 4
Orme Ct. W2 BS40 3
Orme La. W2 BS40 3
Orme Sq. W2 BS40 3
Ormonde Gate, SW3 BU42 3
Ormonde Ter. NW8 BU37 1
Ormond Ms. WC1 BX38 2
Ormond Yd. SW1 BW40 3
Ormsby St. E2 CA37 2
Orsett Ms. W2 BS39 1
Orsett St. SE11 BX42 4
Orsett Ter. W2 BS39 1
Orsman Rd. N1 CA37 2
Osbert St. SW1 BW42 3
Osborne St. SE17 BZ42 4
Osborn St. E1 CA39 2
Oslo Ct. NW8 BU37 1
Osnaburgh St. NW1 BV38 1
Osnaburgh Ter. NW1 BV38 1
Ossory Rd. SE1 CB43 4
Ossulston Est. NW1 BW38 1
Ossulston St. NW1 BW37 1
Osten Ms. SW7 BS41 3
Oswin St. SE11 BY42 4
Outer Circle, NW1 BV38 1
Outram St. N1 BX37 2
Oval Rd. NW1 BV37 1
Oval Way, SE11 BX42 4
Ovington Gdns. SW3 BU41 3
Ovington Ms. SW3 BU41 3
Ovington Sq. SW3 BU41 3
Ovington St. SW3 BU42 3
Owen St. EC1 BY37 2
Oxendon St. SW1 BW40 3
Oxford Circus, W1 BV39 1
Oxford Sq. W2 BU39 1
Oxford St. W1 BV39 1
Packington St. N1 BY37 2
Packington St. N1 BZ37 2
Padbury Ct. E2 CA38 2
Paddington Basin, W2 BT39 1
Paddington St. W1 BV39 1
Page's Sq. SE1 CA42 4
Page St. SW1 BW42 3
Page's Wk. SE1 CA42 4
Paget St. EC1 BY38 2
Pakenham St. WC1 BX38 2
Palace Av. W8 BS41 3
Palace Gate, W8 BT41 3
Palace Pl. SW1 BV41 3
Palace St. SW1 BW41 3
Palissy St. E2 CA38 2
Pall Mall, SW1 BW40 3
Pall Mall E. SW1 BW40 3
Pall Mall Pl. SW1 BW40 3
Palmer St. SW1 BW41 3
Pancras La. EC4 BZ39 2
Pancras Rd. NW1 BW37 1
Panton St. SW1 BW40 3
Panyer Al. EC4 BZ39 2
Paradise Wk. SW3 BU43 3
Pardon St. EC1 BY38 2
Paris Gdn. SE1 BY40 4
Park Cl. SW1 BU41 3
Park Cres. W1 BV38 1
Park Cres. Ms. E. W1 BV38 1
Park Cres. Ms. W. W9 BV38 1
Parker St. WC2 BX39 2
Parkfield St. N1 BY37 2
Park La. W1 BV40 3
Park Mans. NW1 BU39 1
Park Pl. SW1 BW40 3
Park Pl. Vils. W2 BT39 1
Park Rd. NW8 BU38 1
Park Sq. E. NW1 BV38 1
Park Sq. Ms. NW1 BV38 1
Park Sq. W. NW1 BV38 1
Park St. W1 BV40 3
Park Village, E. NW1 BV37 1
Park Village, W. NW1 BV37 1
Park Wk. SW10 BT43 3
Parkway, NW1 BV37 1
Park West, W2 BU39 1
Park West Pl. W2 BU39 1
Parliament Sq. SW1 BX41 4
Parliament St. SW1 BX41 4
Parr St. N1 BZ37 2
Pasley Rd. SE17 BY42 4
Passmore St. SW1 BV42 3
Pastor St. SE11 BY42 4
Paternoster Row, EC4 BZ39 2
Paternoster Sq. EC4 BY39 2
Paton St. EC1 BZ38 2
Paul St. EC2 BZ38 2
Paveley St. NW8 BU38 1
Pavilion Rd. SW1 BU41 3
Pavilion St. SW1 BU41 3
Paxton Ter. SW1 BV43 3
Peabody Av. SW1 BV42 3
Peabody Blds. SE1 BY40 4
Peabody Blds. WC1 BX38 2
Peabody Blgs. SE17 BZ42 4
Peabody Sq. N1 BZ37 2
Peabody Sq. SE1 BY41 4
Peabody Trust, SW3 BU43 3
Peace St. E1 CB38 2
Peacock St. SE17 BY42 4
Pearman St. SE1 BY41 4
Pearson St. E2 CA37 2
Pear Tree Ct. EC1 BY38 2
Pear Tree St. EC1 BY38 2
Pedley St. E1 CA38 2
Peerless St. EC1 BZ38 2
Pelham Ct. SW3 BU42 3
Pelham Cres. SW7 BU42 3
Pelham Pl. SW7 BT42 3
Pelham St. SW7 BT42 3
Pelier St. SE17 BZ43 4
Pelter St. E2 CA38 2
Pembroke Cl. SW1 BV41 3
Pembroke St. N1 BX36 2
Penally Pl. N1 BZ37 2
Penfold Pl. NW1 BU39 1
Penfold St. NW8 BT38 1
Penn St. N1 BZ37 2
Penrose Gro. SE17 BZ42 4
Penrose Ho. SE17 BZ42 4
Penrose St. SE17 BZ42 4
Penryn St. NW1 BW37 1
Penry St. SE1 CA42 4
Penton Pl. SE17 BY42 4
Penton Rise, WC1 BX38 2
Penton St. N1 BY37 2
Pentonville Rd. N1 BX37 2
Pepler Rd. SE15 CA43 4
Pepper St. SE1 BZ41 4
Pepys St. EC3 CA40 4
Percival St. EC1 BY38 2
Percy Cir. WC1 BX38 2
Percy Ms. W1 BW39 1
Percy St. W1 BW39 1
Percy St. WC1 BX38 2
Perkins Rents, SW1 BW41 3
Perry's Pl. W1 BW39 1
Petersham La. SW7 BT41 3
Petersham Ms. SW7 BT41 3
Petersham Pl. SW7 BT41 3
Peter's La. EC1 BY39 2
Peter St. W1 BW40 3
Peto Pl. NW1 BV38 1
Petticoat La. E1 CA39 2
Petty France, SW1 BW41 3
Petyward, SW3 BU42 3
Phelp St. SE17 BZ43 4
Phene St. SW3 BU43 3
Philips Way, N1 BZ37 2
Phillip St. N1 CA37 2
Philpot La. EC3 CA40 4
Phipp St. EC2 CA38 2
Phoenix Pl. WC1 BX38 2
Phoenix Rd. NW1 BW38 1
Phoenix St. WC2 BW39 1
Piccadilly, W1 BV40 3
Piccadilly Circus, W1 BW40 3
Piccadilly Pl. W1 BW40 3
Pickard St. EC1 BY38 2
Pickering Ms. W2 BS39 1
Pickle Herring St. SE1 CA40 4
Pickwick St. SE1 BZ41 4
Picton Pl. W1 BV39 1
Pike Gdns. SE1 BZ40 4
Pilgrimage St. SE1 BZ41 4
Pilgrim St. EC4 BY39 2
Pilton Pl. SE17 BZ42 4
Pimlico Rd. SW1 BV42 3
Pimlico Wk. N1 CA38 2
Pinchin St. E1 CB40 4
Pindar St. EC2 CA39 2
Pindock Ms. W9 BS38 1
Pine St. EC1 BY38 2
Pitfield St. N1 CA37 2
Pitfield St. N1 CA38 2
Pit Head Ms. W1 BV40 3
Platt St. NW1 BW37 1
Playhouse Yd. EC4 BY39 2
Pleasant Pl. N1 BY36 2
Pleasant Row, NW1 BV37 1
Plender Pl. NW1 BW37 1
Plender St. NW1 BW37 1
Plough Pl. EC4 BY39 2
Plough Yd. EC2 CA38 2
Plumbers Row, E1 CB39 2
Plumtree Ct. EC4 BY39 2
Plympton Pl. NW8 BU38 1
Plympton St. NW8 BU38 1
Pocock St. SE1 BY41 4
Poets Corner, SW1 BX41 4
Poland St. W1 BW39 1
Pollen St. W1 BV39 1
Polygon Ms. W2 BU39 1
Polygon Rd. NW1 BW37 1
Pond House, SW3 BU42 3
Pond Pl. SW3 BU42 3
Ponsonby Pl. SW1 BW42 3
Ponsonby Ter. SW1 BW42 3
Pont St. Ms. SW1 BU41 3
Pont St. SW1 BU41 3
Poole St. N1 BZ37 2
Pope St. SE1 CA41 4
Popham St. N1 BZ37 2
Poplar Pl. W2 BS40 3
Poppins Ct. EC4 BY39 2
Porchester Gdns. W2 BS40 3
Porchester Pl. W2 BU39 1
Porchester Rd. W2 BS39 1
Porchester Sq. W2 BS39 1
Porchester Sq. Ms. W2 BS39 1
Porchester Ter. W2 BT40 3
Porchester Ter. W2 BT39 1
Porchester Ter. N. W2 BS39 1
Porlock St. SE1 BZ41 4
Porter St. W1 BU39 1
Porteus Rd. W2 BT39 1
Portland Pl. W1 BV38 1
Portland St. SE17 BZ42 4
Portman Bldgs. NW1 BU38 1
Portman Clo. W1 BU39 1
Portman Ms. S. W1 BV39 1
Portman Sq. W1 BV39 1
Portman St. W1 BV39 1
Portpool La. EC1 BY39 2
Portsea Ms. W2 BU39 1
Portsea Pl. W2 BU39 1
Portsoken St. E1 CA40 4
Portugal St. WC2 BX39 2
Potier St. SE1 BZ41 4
Potter's Flds. SE1 CA40 4
Poultry, EC2 BZ39 2
Poultry Av. EC1 BY39 2
Powis Pl. WC1 BX38 2
Pownall Rd. E8 CA37 2
Praed Ms. W2 BT39 1
Praed St. W2 BT39 1
Pratt Ms. NW1 BW37 1
Pratt St. NW1 BW37 1
Pratt Wk. SE11 BX42 4
Prebend St. N1 BZ37 2
Prescot St. E1 CA40 4
Preston Cl. SE1 CA42 4
Prestwood St. N1 BZ37 2
Prices St. SE1 BY40 4
Prideaux Pl. WC1 BX38 2
Primrose Hill, EC4 BY39 2
Primrose Hill Rd. NW3 BU36 1
Primrose St. EC2 CA39 2
Prince Albert Rd. NW8 BU38 1
Prince Consort Rd. SW7 BT41 3
Princelet St. E1 CA39 2
Princes Gdns. Sw7 BT41 3
Princes Gdns. Ms. SW7 BT41 3
Princes Gate, SW7 BT41 3
Princes Gate Ct. SW7 BT41 3
Princes Ms. SW7 BT41 3
Princess Rd. NW1 BV37 1
Princess St. SE1 BY41 4
Princes St. EC2 BZ39 2
Prince's St. W1 BV39 1
Princeton St. WC1 BX39 2
Prioress St. SE1 BZ41 4
Priory Green Est. N1 BX37 2
Priory Ter. NW6 BS37 1
Priory Wk. SW10 BT42 3
Priter Rd. SE16 CB41 4
Priter Way, SE16 CB41 4
Procter St. WC1 BX39 2
Profwales Ter. W8 BS41 3
Provence St. N1 BZ37 2
Providence Ct. W1 BV40 3
Providence Pl. N1 BY37 2
Provost St. N1 BZ37 2
Puddle Dock, EC4 BY40 4
Pulteney Ter. N1 BX37 2
Puma Ct. E1 CA39 2
Purbrook Est. SE1 CA41 4
Purbrook St. SE1 CA41 4
Purcell St. N1 CA37 2
Purchese St. NW1 BW37 1
Quaker St. E1 CA38 2
Quality Ct. WC2 BY39 2
Quebec Ms. W1 BU39 1
Queen Anne's Gate, SW1 BW41 3
Queen Anne St. W1 BV39 1
Queen Elizabeth St. SE1 CA41 4
Queenhithe, EC4 BZ40 4
Queen St. Pl. EC4 BZ40 4
Queensborough Ter. W2 BS40 3
Queensbridge Ct. E2 CA37 2
Queensbridge Rd. E2 CA37 2
Queensbridge Rd. E8 CA37 2
Queensbury Ms. W. SW7 BT42 3
Queensbury Pl. SW7 BT42 3
Queensbury Way, SW7 BT42 3
Queens Elm Sq. SW3 BT42 3
Queen's Gdns. W2 BT40 3
Queen's Gate, SW7 BT41 3
Queen's Gate Gdns. SW7 BT41 3
Queen's Gate Ms. SW7 BT41 3
Queen's Gate Pl. SW7 BT41 3
Queen's Gate Pl. Ms. SW7 BT41 3
Queen's Gate Ter. SW7 BT41 3
Queen's Gro. NW8 BT37 1
Queen's Gro. Studios, NW8 BT37 1
Queen's Ms. W2 BS40 3
Queen, S Head St. N1 BY37 2
Queen Sq. WC1 BX38 2
Queen's Row, SE17 BZ43 4
Queen's Ter. NW8 BT37 1
Queen St. EC4 BZ40 4
Queen St. Mayfair W1 BV40 3
Queen's Walk, SW1 BW40 3
Queensway, W2 BS39 1
Queen Victoria St. EC4 BY40 4
Quick St. N1 BY37 2
Quilp St. SE1 BZ41 4
Quilter St. E2 CA38 2
Radcot St. SE11 BY42 4
Radlett Pl. NW8 BU37 1
Radnor Ms. W2 BT39 1
Radnor Pl. W2 BT39 1
Radnor St. EC1 BZ38 2
Radnor Wk. SW3 BU42 3
Railway App. SE1 BZ40 4
Railway Pl. EC3 CA40 4
Railway St. N1 BX37 2
Rainsford St. W2 BU39 1
Raleigh St. N1 BY37 2
Ralph St. SE1 BZ41 4
Ralston St. SW3 BU42 3
Ramillies Pl. W1 BW39 1
Ramillies St. W1 BW39 1
Rampayne St. SW1 BW42 3
Ramsey St. E2 CB38 2
Randall Rd. SE11 BX42 4
Randall Row, SE11 BX42 4
Randell's Rd. N1 BX37 2
Randolph Av. W9 BS37 1
Randolph Cres. W9 BT38 1
Randolph Ms. W9 BT38 1
Randolph Rd. W9 BT38 1
Ranelagh Bri. W2 BS39 1
Ranelagh Gro. SW1 BV42 3
Ranelagh St. SW1 BW42 3
Rangoon St. EC3 CA39 2
Ranston St. NW1 BU39 1
Raphael St. SW7 BU41 3
Ratcliffe Gro. EC1 BZ38 2
Rathbone Pl. W1 BW39 1
Rathbone St. W1 BW39 1
Ravenscroft St. E2 CA37 2
Ravensdon St. SE11 BY42 4
Ravent Rd. SE11 BX42 4
Ravey St. EC2 CA38 2
Rawlings St. SW3 BU42 3
Rawstorne St. EC1 BY38 2
Raymond Bldgs. WC1 BX39 2
Ray St. EC1 BY38 2
Rector St. N1 BZ37 2
Redan Pl. W2 BS39 1
Redburn St. SW3 BU43 3
Redchurch St. E2 CA38 2
Redcliffe Gdns. SW10 BS42 3
Redcliffe Ms. SW10 BS42 3
Redcliffe Rd. SW10 BT42 3
Redcliffe Sq. SW10 BS42 3
Redcliffe St. SW10 BS43 3
Redcross Pl. SE1 BZ41 4
Redcross Way, SE1 BZ41 4
Redesdale St. SW3 BU42 3
Redhill St. NW1 BV37 1
Red Lion Ct. EC4 BY39 2
Red Lion Sq. WC1 BX39 2
Red Lion St. WC1 BX39 2
Redmead La. E1 CB40 4
Red Pl. W1 BV40 3
Reece Ms. SW7 BT42 3
Reedworth St. SE11 BY42 4
Rees St. N1 BZ37 2
Reeves Ms. W1 BV40 3
Regal La. NW1 BV37 1
Regan Way, N1 CA37 2
Regency St. SW1 BW42 3
Regent Pl. SW1 BW42 3
Regent Pl. W1 BW40 3
Regents Park Est. NW1 BV38 1
Regent's Pk. Rd. NW1 BU37 1
Regent's Pk. Ter. NW1 BV37 1
Regent Sq. WC1 BX38 2
Regent St. SW1 BW40 3
Regent St. W1 BV39 1
Remington St. N1 BY37 2
Remnant St. WC2 BX39 2
Renfrew Rd. SE11 BY42 4
Rennie St. SE1 BY40 4
Rephidim St. SE1 BZ41 4
Reston Pl. SW7 BT41 3
Reverdy Rd. SE1 CB42 4
Rex Pl. W1 BV40 3
Rheidol Ter. N1 BY37 2
Rhoda St. E2 CA38 2
Richard's Pl. SW3 BU42 3
Richmond Ave. N1 BX37 2
Richmond Bdgs. W1 BW39 1
Richmond Cres. N1 BX37 2
Richmond Ter. SW1 BX41 4
Richmond Ter. Ms. SW1 BX41 4
Ridgmount Gdns. WC1 BW39 1
Ridgmount Pl. WC1 BW39 1
Riding House St. W1 BV39 1
Rifle Ct. SE11 BY43 4
Riley Rd. SE1 CA41 4
Ring, The W2 BT40 3
Ripplevale Gro. N1 BX36 2
Risborough St. SE1 BY41 4
Risinghill St. N1 BX37 2
Ritchie St. N1 BY37 2
River Pl. N1 BZ36 2
Riverside Wk. SE1 BX41 4
River St. EC1 BY38 2
Rivington Pl. EC2 CA38 2
Rivington St. EC2 CA38 2
Roberta St. E2 CB38 2
Robert Clo. W9 BT38 1
Robert St. NW1 BV38 1
Robert St. WC2 BX40 4
Robin St. SW3 BU43 3
Rochelle St. E2 CA38 2
Rochester Row, SW1 BW42 3
Rochester St. SW1 BW41 3
Rockingham Est. SE1 BZ41 4
Rockingham St. SE1 BZ41 4
Rocliffe St. N1 BY37 2
Rodmarton St. W1 BU39 1
Rodney Ct. NW8 BT38 1
Rodney Pl. SE17 BZ42 4
Rodney Rd. SE17 BZ42 4
Rodney St. N1 BX37 2
Roger St. WC1 BX38 2
Roland Gdns. SW10 BT42 3
Roland Way, SW10 BT42 3
Rolls Bldgs. EC4 BY39 2
Rolls Pass. EC4 BY39 2
Rolls Rd. SE1 CA42 4
Romilly St. W1 BW40 3
Romney St. SW1 BW41 3
Rood La. EC3 CA40 4
Ropley St. E2 CB37 2
Rosary Gdns. SW7 BT42 3
Roscoe St. EC1 BZ38 2
Rose Alley, SE1 BZ40 4
Rosebery Av. EC1 BY38 2
Rosemaker St. EC2 BZ39 2
Rosemary St. N1 BZ37 2
Rosemoor St. SW3 BU42 3
Rose St. WC2 BX40 4
Rosoman St. EC1 BY38 2
Ross Ct. NW1 BU38 1
Rossmore Rd. NW1 BU38 1
Rotary St. SE1 BY41 4
Rotherfield St. N1 BZ36 2
Rothsay St. SE1 BZ41 4
Rotten Row, SW7 BT41 3
Rouel Rd. SE16 CB41 4
Roupell St. SE1 BY40 4
Rovington Clo. W2 BS39 1
Rowcross St. SE1 CA42 4
Royal Arc. SW1 BW40 3
Royal Av. SW3 BU42 3
Royal College St. NW1 BW36 1
Royal Exchange Bldgs. EC3 BZ39 2
Royal Hospital Rd. SW3 BU43 3
Royal Mint St. E1 CA40 4
Royal St. SE1 BX41 4
Rufford St. N1 BX37 2
Rufus St. N1 CA38 2
Rugby St. WC1 BX38 2
Rupert St. W1 BW40 3
Rushton St. N1 BZ37 2
Rushworth St. SE1 BY41 4
Russell Ct. SW1 BW40 3
Russell Pl. SW1 BW42 3
Russell Sq. WC1 BX38 2
Russell St. WC2 BX40 4
Russia Row, EC2 BZ39 2
Rutherford St. SW1 BW42 3
Rutland Gdns. SW7 BU41 3
Rutland Gate, SW7 BU41 3
Rutland Gate Ms. SW7 BU41 3
Rutland Ms. NW8 BT37 1
Rutland Ms. St. SW7 BU41 3
Rutland St. SW7 BU41 3
Ryders Ter. NW8 BT37 1
Ryder St. SW1 BW40 3
Rydon St. N1 BZ37 2
Rysbrook St. SW3 BU41 3
Sabella St. SE1 BY40 4
Sackville St. W1 BW40 3
Saffron Hill, EC1 BY39 2
Sail St. SE11 BX42 4
St. Alban's Gro. W8 BS41 3
St. Albans Ms. W2 BT39 1
St. Albans Pl. N1 BY37 2
St. Albans St. SW1 BW40 3
St. Alphages Gdns. EC2 BZ39 2
St. Andrews Hill, EC4 BY39 2
St. Andrews Hill, EC4 BY40 4
St. Andrew's Pl. NW1 BV38 1
St. Andrew St. EC4 BY39 2
St. Anne's Ct. W1 BW39 1
St. Ann's La. SW1 BW41 3
St. Ann's St. SW1 BW41 3
St. Ann's Ter. NW8 BT37 1
St. Anselm's Pl. W1 BV40 3
St. Barnabas St. SW1 BV42 3
St. Botolph St. EC3 CA39 2
St. Bride St. EC4 BY39 2
St. Chads Pl. WC1 BX38 2
St. Christopher's Pl. W1 BV39 1
St. Clare St. EC3 CA39 2
St. Clement's La. WC2 BX39 2
St. Cross St. EC1 BY39 2
St. Dunstans Hill, EC3 CA40 4
St. Dunstan's La. EC3 CA40 4
St. Edmund's Clo. NW8 BU37 1
St. Edmund's Ter. NW8 BU37 1
St. Gabriel St. SE11 BY42 4
St. George's Cir. SE1 BY41 4
St. George's Ct. SW7 BT41 3
St. George's Dr. SW1 BV42 3
St. Georges Fields, W2 BU39 1
St. George's Rd. SE1 BY41 4
St. George's Sq. SW1 BW42 3
St. George's Sq. Ms. SW1 BW42 3
St. George St. W1 BV40 3
St. Giles Circus, WC1 BW39 1
St. Giles Ct. WC2 BW39 1
St. Giles Pl. WC2 BX39 2
St. Giles High St. WC2 BW39 1
St. Helena St. WC1 BY38 2
St. Helen's Pl. EC3 CA39 2
St. James Rd. SE16 CB41 4
St. James's Mkt. SW1 BW40 3
St. James's Pl. SW1 BW40 3
St. James's Row, EC1 BY38 2
St. James's Sq. SW1 BW40 3
St. James's St. SW1 BW40 3
St. James's Ter. NW8 BU37 1
St. James's Ter. Ms. NW8 BU37 1
St. James's Wk. EC1 BY38 2
St. Johns Est. SE1 CA41 4
St. John's La. EC1 BY39 2
St. John's Sq. EC1 BY38 2
St. Johns St. EC1 BY37 2
St. John's Wood Ct. NW8 BT38 1
St. John's Wood High St. NW8 BT37 1
St. John's Wood Pk. NW8 BT37 1
St. John's Wood Rd. NW8 BT38 1
St. John's Wood Ter. NW8 BT37 1
St. Katherine's Way, E1 CA40 4
St. Leonard's Ter. SW3 BU42 3
St. Loo Av. SW3 BU43 3
St. Luke's St. SW3 BU42 3
St. Margarets Ms. WC2 BX40 4
St. Margarets Pl. SW1 BW41 3
St. Margaret St. SW1 BX41 4
St. Marks Cres. NW1 BV37 1
St. Mark's Sq. NW1 BV37 1
St. Mark St. E1 CA39 2
St. Martin's La. WC2 BX40 4
St. Martins Le Grand EC1 BZ39 2
St. Martin's Pl. WC2 BX40 4
St. Martins St. WC2 BW40 3
St. Mary at Hill, EC3 CA40 4
St. Mary Axe, EC3 CA39 2
St. Mary's Gdns. SE11 BY42 4

St. Mary's Gdns. W2 BT39 1
St. Mary's Mans. W2 BT39 1
St. Marys Path, N1 BY37 2
St. Mary's Sq. W2 BT39 1
St. Mary's Ter. W2 BT39 1
St. Mary's Wk. SE11 BY42 4
St. Mathew St. SW1 BW41 3
St. Matthews Row, E2 CB38 2
St. Michael's St. W2 BT39 1
St. Olaves Ct. EC2 BZ39 2
St. Olave's Est. SE1 CA41 4
St. Oswald's Pl. SE11 BX42 4
St. Oswulf St. SW1 BW42 3
St. Pancras Way, NW1 BW37 1
St. Paul's Churchyard, EC4 BY39 2
St. Paul's Ter. SE17 BY43 4
St. Paul St. N1 BZ37 2
St. Petersburgh Ms. W2 BS40 3
St. Peters St. N1 BY37 2
St. Stephens Clo. NW8 BU37 1
St. Swithin's La. EC4 BZ40 4
St. Thomas St. SE1 BZ40 4
St. Vincent St. W1 BV39 1
Salamanca Pl. SE11 BX42 4
Salamanca St. SE11 BX42 4
Salem Rd. W2 BS40 3
Sale Pl. W2 BU39 1
Salisbury Ct. EC4 BY39 2
Salisbury Pl. W1 BU39 1
Salisbury Row, SE17 BZ42 4
Salisbury Sq. EC4 BY39 2
Salisbury St. NW8 BU38 1
Samford St. NW8 BU38 1
Sancroft St. SE11 BX42 4
Sanctuary St. SE1 BZ41 4
Sanctuary, The SW1 BW41 3
Sandell St. SE1 BY41 4
Sandland St. WC1 BX39 2
Sandover Rd. SE5 CA43 4
Sandringham Ct. W9 BT38 1
Sandwich St. WC1 BX38 2
Sandys Row, E1 CA39 2
Sans Wk. EC1 BY38 2
Sarah St. N1 CA38 2
Sardinia St. WC2 BX39 2
Saunders St. SE11 BX42 4
Savage Gdns. EC3 CA40 4
Saville Row, W1 BW40 3
Saviours Est. SE1 CA41 4
Savoy Ct. WC2 BX40 4
Savoy Hill, WC2 BX40 4
Savoy Pl. WC2 BX40 4
Savoy St. WC2 BX40 4
Sawyer St. SE1 BZ41 4
Scala St. W1 BW39 1
Scarborough St. E1 CA39 2
Scarsdale Rd. SE5 CA43 4
Scawfell St. E2 CA37 2
Sclater St. E1 CA38 2
Scoresby St. SE1 BY40 4
Scott Ellis Gdns. NW8 BT38 1
Scott Lidgett Cres. SE16 CB41 4
Scovell Rd. SE1 BZ41 4
Scrive St. E8 CA37 2
Scrutton Pl. EC2 CA38 2
Scrutton St. EC2 CA38 2
Seacoal La. EC4 BY39 2
Seaford St. WC1 BX38 2
Seaforth Pl. SW1 BW41 3
Searles Rd. SE1 BZ42 4
Seaton Pl. NW1 BW38 1
Sebastian St. EC1 BY38 2
Sebbon St. N1 BY36 2
Secker St. SE1 BY40 4
Secretan Rd. SE5 CA42 4
Sedding St. SW1 BV42 3
Sedley Pl. W1 BV39 1
Seething La. EC3 CA40 4
Sekforde St. EC1 BY38 2
Sellon Ms. SE11 BX42 4
Selous St. NW1 BW37 1
Selwood Pl. SW7 BT42 3
Selwood Ter. SW7 BT42 3
Semley Pl. SW1 BV42 3
Serle St. WC2 BX39 2
Serpentine Rd. W2 BU40 3
Setchell Rd. SE1 CA42 4
Seven Dials, WC2 BX39 2
Seville St. SW1 BU41 3
Seward St. EC1 BY38 2
Seymour Ms. W1 BV39 1
Seymour Pl. W1 BU39 1
Seymour St. W1 BU39 1
Seymour Wk. SW10 BT42 3
Shacklewell St. E2 CA38 2
Shad Thames, SE1 CA40 4
Shaftesbury Av. W1 BW40 3
Shaftesbury Ct. N1 BZ37 2
Shaftesbury St. N1 BZ37 2
Shafto Ms. SW1 BU41 3
Shafts Ct. EC3 CA39 2
Shand St. SE1 CA41 4
Shap St. E2 CA37 2
Sharsted St. SE17 BY42 4
Shawfield St. SW3 BU42 3
Sheba St. E1 CA38 2
Sheen Gro. N1 BY37 2
Sheffield St. WC2 BX39 2
Shelton St. WC2 BX39 2
Shenfield St. N1 CA37 2
Shephard Pl. N1 BZ38 2
Shepherdess Wk. N1 BZ37 2
Shepherd Mkt. W1 BV40 3
Shepherd St. W1 BV40 3
Shepperton Rd. N1 BZ37 2
Sheraton St. W1 BW39 1
Sherborne La. EC4 BZ40 4
Sherbourne Ms. N1 BZ37 2
Sherbourne St. N1 BZ37 2
Sherlock Ms. W1 BU39 1
Sherwood St. W1 BW40 3
Shipton St. E2 CA38 2
Shirley St. N1 BX37 2
Shoe La. EC4 BY39 2
Shoreditch High St. E1 CA38 2
Shorncliffe Rd. SE1 CA42 4
Shorts Gdns. WC2 BX39 2
Short St. SE1 BY41 4
Shouldham St. W1 BU39 1
Shroton St. NW1 BU39 1
Shrubland Rd. E8 CA37 2
Shuttle St. E1 CB38 2
Sicilian Av. WC1 BX39 2
Siddons La. NW1 BU38 1
Sidford Pl. SE1 BX41 4
Sidmouth St. WC1 BX38 2
Silbury St. N1 BZ38 2
Silcote Rd. SE5 CA42 4
Silex St. SE1 BY41 4
Silk St. EC2 BZ39 2
Silver Pl. W1 BW40 3
Silvester St. SE1 BZ41 4
Simms Rd. SE1 CB42 4
Singer St. EC2 BZ38 2
Skin Market Pl. SE1 BZ40 4
Skinners La. EC4 BZ40 4
Skinner St. EC1 BY38 2
Skipton St. SE1 BY41 4
Slingsby Ms. Pl. WC2 BX40 4
Sloane Av. SW3 BU42 3
Sloane Ct. E. SW3 BV42 3
Sloane Ct. W. SW3 BU42 3
Sloane Gdns. SW1 BV42 3
Sloane Sq. SW1 BU42 3
Sloane St. SW1 BU41 3
Sloane Ter. SW1 BU42 3
Smallbrook Ms. W2 BT39 1
Smarts Pl. WC2 BX39 2
Smelbury Ter. NW1 BU38 1
Smithfield St. EC1 BY39 2
Smith Sq. SW1 BX41 4
Smith St. SW3 BU42 3
Smith Ter. SW3 BU42 3
Smyrks Rd. SE17 CA42 4
Snowdon St. EC2 CA38 2
Snowdon St. EC2 CA39 2
Snow Hill, EC1 BY39 2
Snows Fields, SE1 BZ41 4
Soho Sq. W1 BW39 1
Soho St. W1 BW39 1
Somers Cres. W2 BU39 1
Somers Ms. W2 BU39 1
Sondes St. SE17 BZ43 4
Southampton Bldgs. WC2 BY39 2
Southampton Pl. WC1 BX39 2
Southampton Row, WC1 BX39 2
Southampton St. WC2 BX40 4
South Audley St. W1 BV40 3
South Bolton Gdns. SW10 BS42 3
South Cres. WC1 BW39 1
South End, W8 BS41 3
South End Row, W8 BS41 3
Southern St. N1 BX37 2
Southgate Gro. N1 BZ36 2
Southgate Rd. N1 BZ37 2
South Lo. NW8 BT38 1
S. Moreton Ter. Ms. SW1 BW42 3
South Par. SW3 BT42 3
South Pl. EC2 BZ39 2
South Sq. WC1 BY39 2
South St. W1 BV40 3
South Ter. SW7 BU42 3
Southwark Bridge, SE1 BZ40 4
Southwark Bri. Rd. SE1 BY41 4
Southwark Gro. SE1 BZ40 4
Southwark Ms. W2 BT39 1
Southwark Pk. Rd. SE16 CA42 4
Southwark St. SE1 BY40 4
Southwell Gdns. SW7 BT41 3
South Wharf Rd. W2 BT39 1
Southwick Pl. W2 BU39 1
Southwick St. W2 BU39 1
Spanish Pl. W1 BV39 1
Spa Rd. SE16 CA41 4
Spelman St. E1 CB39 2
Spencer Ct. NW8 BT37 1
Spencer Pl. SW1 BW41 3
Spencer St. EC1 BY38 2
Spencer St. SW1 BW41 3
Spital Sq. E1 CA39 2
Spital St. E1 CA39 2
Sprimont Pl. SW3 BU42 3
Springfield Rd. NW8 BT37 1
Spring Gdns. SW1 BW40 3
Spring St. W2 BT39 1
Spurgeon St. SE1 BZ41 4
Spur Rd. SW1 BW41 3
Squirries St. E2 CB38 2
Stables Way, SE11 BY42 4
Stable Yd. SW1 BW41 3
Stable Yd. Rd. SW1 BW41 3
Stacey St. WC2 BW39 1
Stackhouse St. SW3 BU41 3
Stafford Pl. SW1 BW41 3
Stafford St. W1 BW40 3
Staff St. EC1 BZ38 2
Stag Pl. SW1 BW41 3
Stainer St. SE1 BZ40 4
Staining La. EC2 BZ39 2
Stalbridge St. NW1 BU39 1
Stamford St. SE1 BY40 4
Stamp Pl. E2 CA38 2
Stanford Pl. SE17 CA42 4
Stanford Rd. W8 BS41 3
Stanford St. SW1 BW42 3
Stanhope Blds. SE1 BZ41 4
Stanhope Gdns. SW7 BT42 3
Stanhope Gate, W1 BV40 3
Stanhope Ms. E. SW7 BT42 3
Stanhope Ms. St. SW7 BT42 3
Stanhope Ms. W. SW7 BT42 3
Stanhope Pl. W2 BU40 3
Stanhope Row, W1 BV40 3
Stanhope St. NW1 BW37 1
Stanhope Ter. W2 BT40 3
Stanley Pass. NW1 BX37 2
Stanmore Pl. NW1 BV37 1
Stanmore St. N1 BX37 2
Stannary St. SE11 BY43 4
Stanway St. N1 CA37 2
Stanworth St. SE1 CA41 4
Staple Inn, WC2 BY39 2
Staple Inn Bldgs. WC2 BY39 2
Staple St. SE1 BZ41 4
Starcross St. NW1 BW38 1
Star St. W2 BT39 1
Star Yard, WC2 BY39 2
Station Fore Ct. NW1 BW38 1
Stead St. SE17 BZ42 4
Stean St. E8 CA37 2
Steedman St. SE17 BZ42 4
Stephen & Matilda Hos. E1 CB40 4
Stephenson Way, NW1 BW38 1
Stephen St. W1 BW39 1
Sterling St. SW7 BU41 3
Sterry St. SE1 BZ41 4
Steward St. E1 CA39 2
Stewart's Gro. SW3 BT42 3
Sth. Audley St. W1 BV40 3
Sth. Eaton Pl. SW1 BV42 3
Sth. Molton La. W1 BV39 1
Sth. Molton St. W1 BV39 1
Sth. Tenter St. E1 CA40 4
Sth. Wharf Rd. W2 BT39 1
Stillington St. SW1 BW42 3
Stockleigh Hall, NW8 BU37 1
Stock St. WC2 BX39 2
Stonebridge Est. E8 CA37 2
Stone Bldgs. WC2 BX39 2
Stonecutter St. EC4 BY39 2
Stonefield St. N1 BY37 2
Stones End St. SE1 BZ41 4
Stoney La. EC3 CA39 2
Stoney St. SE1 BZ40 4
Stopford Rd. SE17 BY42 4
Store St. WC1 BW39 1
Storeys Gate, SW1 BW41 3
Story St. N1 BX36 2
Stourcliffe St. W1 BU39 1
Strand, WC2 BX40 4
Strand, Wc2 BY39 2
Strand La. WC2 BX40 4
Stratford Pl. W1 BV39 1
Strathairn St. SE1 CB42 4
Strathern Pl. W2 BT40 3
Stratton St. W1 BV40 3
Streatham St. WC1 BX39 2
Strutton Ground, SW1 BW41 3
Strype St. E1 CA39 2
Studd St. N1 BY37 2
Stukeley St. WC2 BX39 2
Sturgeon Rd. SE17 BY42 4
Sturge St. SE1 BZ41 4
Sturt St. N1 BZ37 2
Sudeley St. N1 BY37 2
Sudrey St. SE1 BZ41 4
Suffield Rd. SE17 BY42 4
Suffolk La. EC4 BZ40 4
Suffolk Pl. SW1 BW40 3
Suffolk St. SW1 BW40 3
Summers St. EC1 BY38 2
Sumner Blds. SE1 BZ40 4
Sumner Pl. SW7 BT42 3
Sumner Pl. Ms. SW7 BT42 3
Sumner St. SE1 BY40 4
Sun St. EC2 BZ39 2
Sun Street Pass. EC2 CA39 2
Surrey Gro. SE17 CA42 4
Surrey Row, SE1 BY41 4
Surrey Sq. SE17 CA42 4
Surrey St. WC2 BX40 4
Surrey Ter. SE17 CA42 4
Sussex Gdns. W2 BT39 1
Sussex Ms. NW1 BU38 1
Sussex Ms. E. W2 BT40 3
Sussex Ms. W. W2 BT40 3
Sussex Pl. W2 BT39 1
Sussex Sq. W2 BT40 3
Sussex St. SW1 BV42 3
Sutherland Av. W9 BS38 1
Sutherland Row, SW1 BV42 3
Sutherland Sq. SE17 BZ42 4
Sutherland St. SW1 BV42 3
Sutherland Wk. SE17 BZ42 4
Sutton Dwellings, SW3 BU42 3
Sutton Model Dws. EC1 BZ38 2
Sutton Row, W1 BW39 1
Swallow Pl. W1 BV39 1
Swallow St. W1 BW40 3
Swan Ct. SW3 BU42 3
Swanfield St. E2 CA38 2
Swan La. EC4 BZ40 4
Swan Mead, SE1 CA41 4
Swan St. SE1 BZ41 4
Sweeney Cres. SE1 CA41 4
Swinton Pl. WC1 BX38 2
Swinton St. WC1 BX38 2
Sydney Cl. SW7 BT42 3
Sydney Ms. SW7 BT42 3
Sydney Pl. SW7 BT42 3
Sydney St. SW3 BT42 3
Sylvia Ct. N1 BZ37 2
Symes Ms. NW1 BW37 1
Symons St. SW3 BU42 3
Tabard Gdn. Est. SE1 BZ41 4
Tabard St. SE1 BZ41 4
Tabernacle St. EC2 BZ38 2
Tachbrook Est. SW1 BW42 3
Tachbrook Ms. SW1 BW42 3
Tachbrook Ter. SW1 BW42 3
Tailworth St. E1 CB39 2
Talbot Sq. W2 BT39 1
Talbot Yd. SE1 BZ40 4
Tallis St. EC4 BY40 4
Tanfield Ct. EC4 BY39 2
Tankerton St. WC1 BX38 2
Tanner St. SE1 CA41 4
Tanswell Est. SE1 BY41 4
Tanswell St. SE1 BY41 4
Taplow St. N1 BZ37 2
Tarver Rd. SE17 BY42 4
Tatum St. SE17 BZ42 4
Taunton Ms. NW1 BU38 1
Taunton Pl. NW1 BU38 1
Tavistock Pl. WC1 BW38 1
Tavistock Pl. WC1 BX38 2
Tavistock Sq. WC1 BW38 1
Tavistock St. WC2 BX40 4
Taviton St. WC1 BW38 1
Tedworth Sq. SW3 BU42 3
Telegraph St. EC2 BZ39 2
Telford Ter. SW1 BW43 3
Temple Av. EC4 BY40 4
Temple La. EC4 BY39 2
Temple Pl. WC2 BX40 4
Temple, The EC4 BY40 4
Tenby Pl. N1 BX37 2
Tenison Ct. W1 BW40 3
Tennison Way, SE1 BX40 4
Tennis St. SE1 BZ41 4
Tenterden St. W1 BV39 1
Tenter Gro. E1 CA39 2
Tenter St. E2 BZ39 2
Terminus Pl. SW1 BV41 3
Thackeray St. W8 BS41 3
Thanet St. WC1 BX38 2
Thayer St. W1 BV39 1
Theberton St. N1 BY37 2
Theed St. SE1 BY40 4
Theobalds Rd. WC1 BX39 2
Theobald St. SE1 BZ41 4
Thirleby Rd. SW1 BW41 3
Thistle Gro. SW10 BT42 3
Thomas Doyle St. SE1 BY41 4
Thomas More St. E1 CB40 4
Thoresby St. N1 BZ38 2
Thorney St. SW1 BX42 4
Thornhaugh St. WC1 BW38 1
Thornhill Cres. N1 BX36 2
Thornhill Rd. N1 BY37 2
Thornhill Square, N1 BX36 2
Thornton Pl. W1 BU39 1
Thrale St. SE1 BZ40 4
Thrawl St. E1 CA39 2
Threadneedle St. EC2 BZ39 2
Three Kings Yd. W1 BV40 3
Three Oak La. SE1 CA41 4
Throgmorton Av. EC2 BZ39 2
Throgmorton St. EC2 BZ39 2
Thrush St. SE17 BY42 4
Thurland Rd. SE16 CB41 4
Thurloe Cl. SW7 BU42 3
Thurloe Pl. SW7 BT42 3
Thurloe Pl. Ms. SW7 BT42 3
Thurloe Sq. SW7 BU42 3
Thurloe St. SW7 BT42 3
Thurlow Ct. SW3 BU42 3
Thurlow St. SE17 BZ42 4
Thurtle Rd. E2 CA37 2
Tichborne Row, W2 BU39 1
Tilney St. W1 BV40 3
Timber St. EC1 BZ38 2
Tinworth Ho. SE11 BX42 4
Tinworth St. SE11 BX42 4
Tisdall Pl. SE17 BZ42 4
Titchfield Rd. NW8 BU37 1
Tite St. SW3 BU42 3
Tiverton St. SE1 BZ41 4
Tokenhouse Yd. EC2 BZ39 2
Tolmers Sq. NW1 BW38 1
Tomlinson Clo. E2 CA38 2
Tompion St. EC1 BY38 2
Tompson Ho. EC1 BY38 2
Tonbridge St. WC1 BX38 2
Tooks Ct. EC4 BY39 2
Tooley St. SE1 BZ40 4
Topaz St. SE11 BX42 4
Topham St. EC1 BY38 2
Torrens St. EC1 BY37 2
Torrington Pl. WC1 BW39 1
Tothill St. SW1 BW41 3
Tottenham Court Rd. W1 BW38 1
Tottenham St. W1 BW39 1
Toulmin St. SE1 BZ41 4
Tower Bridge, SE1 CA40 4
Tower Br. Northern App. E1 CA40 4
Tower Bridge Rd. SE1 CA41 4
Tower Hill, EC3 CA40 4
Tower Pl. EC3 CA40 4
Tower St. WC2 BW39 1
Townley St. SE17 BZ42 4
Townsend Est. NW8 BU37 1
Townsend Rd. NW8 BU37 1
Townsend St. SE17 BZ42 4
Toynbee St. E1 CA39 2
Tracey St. SE11 BY42 4
Trafalgar Av. SE15 CA42 4
Trafalgar Sq. WC2 BW40 3
Trafalgar St. SE17 BZ42 4
Transept St. NW1 BU39 1
Treaty St. N1 BX37 2
Trebeck St. W1 BV40 3
Tregunter Rd. SW10 BS43 3
Tresham Cres. NW8 BU38 1
Treveris St. SE1 BY40 4
Trevor Pl. SW7 BU41 3
Trevor Sq. SW7 BU41 3
Trevor St. SW7 BU41 3
Trinity Church Sq. SE1 BZ41 4
Trinity Ct. N1 CA37 2
Trinity Sq. EC3 CA40 4
Trinity St. SE1 BZ41 4
Trio Pl. SE1 BZ41 4
Triton Sq. NW1 BW38 1
Trothy Rd. SE1 CB42 4
Trump St. EC2 BZ39 2
Trundle St. SE1 BZ41 4
Tryon St. SW3 BU42 3
Tudor Pl. W1 BW39 1
Tudor St. EC4 BY40 4
Tufton St. SW1 BW41 3
Tuilerie St. E2 CB37 2
Turin St. E2 CB38 2
Turk's Row, SW3 BU42 3
Turner Sq. N1 CA37 2
Turnmill St. EC1 BY39 2
Turpentine La. SW1 BV42 3
Turquand St. SE17 BZ42 4
Turve St. E2 CA38 2
Twyford Pl. WC2 BX39 2
Twyford St. N1 BX37 2
Tybalds Est. WC1 BX39 2
Tyburn Way, W1 BU40 3
Tyer's Est. SE1 CA41 4
Tyer's Gate. SE1 CA41 4
Tyers St. SE11 BX42 4
Tyers Ter. SE11 BX42 4
Tysoe St. EC1 BY38 2
Udall St. SW1 BW42 3
Ufford St. SE1 BY41 4
Ufton Rd. N1 BZ36 2
Underwood Rd. E1 CB38 2
Underwood Row, N1 BZ38 2
Underwood St. E1 CB38 2
Underwood St. N1 BZ38 2
Union Sq. N1 BZ37 2
Union St. SE1 BY41 4
Union Wk. E2 CA38 2
University St. WC1 BW38 1
Upbrook Ms. W2 BT39 1
Upnor Way, SE17 CA42 4
Upr. Belgrave St. SW1 BV41 3
Upr. Berkeley St. W1 BU39 1
Upr. Brook St. W1 BV40 3
Upr. Grosvenor St. W1 BV40 3
Upper Ground, SE1 BY40 4
Upr. Harley St. NW1 BV38 1
Upr. James St. W1 BW40 3
Upper Marsh, SE1 BX41 4
Upr. Montagu St. W1 BU39 1
Upr. St. Martin's La. WC2 BX40 4
Upper St. N1 BY37 2
Upr. Thames St. EC4 BZ40 4
Upper Wimpole St. W1 BV39 1
Upr. Woburn Pl. WC1 BW38 1
Vale Clo. NW8 BT38 1
Vale Ct. NW8 BT38 1
Valentine Pl. SE1 BY41 4
Valentine Row, SE1 BY41 4
Vale, The SW3 BT43 3
Vandon Pass. SW1 BW41 3
Vandon St. SW1 BW41 3
Vandy St. EC2 CA38 2
Vane St. SW1 BW42 3
Varndell St. NW1 BV38 1
Vauban Est. SE16 CA41 4
Vauban St. SE16 CA41 4
Vauxhall Bridge, SW1 BX42 4
Vauxhall Bridge Rd. SW1 BW41 3
Vauxhall Cross, SW8 BX42 4
Vauxhall Gns. Est. SE11 BX42 4
Vauxhall Gro. SW8 BX43 4
Vauxhall St. SE11 BX42 4
Vauxhall Wk. SE11 BX42 4
Venables St. W9 BT38 1
Vere St. W1 BV39 1
Vernon Pl. WC1 BX39 2
Vernon Rise, WC1 BX38 2
Vernon Sq. WC1 BX38 2
Verulam Bldgs. WC1 BX39 2
Verulam St. WC1 BY39 2
Vestry St. N1 BZ38 2
Viceroy Ct. NW8 BU37 1
Victoria Emb. SW1 BX41 4
Victoria Gro. W8 BT41 3
Victoria Rd. W8 BS41 3
Victoria Sq. SW1 BU41 3
Victoria St. SW1 BV41 3
Victory Pl. SE17 BZ42 4
Vigo St. W1 BW40 3
Villa St. SE17 BZ42 4
Villiers St. WC2 BX40 4
Vincent Sq. SW1 BW42 3
Vincent St. SW1 BW42 3
Vincent Ter. N1 BY37 2
Vince St. EC1 BZ38 2
Vine Hill, EC1 BY38 2
Vine La. SE1 CA40 4
Vinery Vils. NW8 BU38 1
Vine St. EC3 CA39 2
Vine Yd. SE1 BZ41 4
Viney Wk. EC1 BY38 2
Vintners Pl. EC4 BZ40 4
Violet Hill, NW8 BT37 1
Virgil Pl. W1 BU39 1
Virgil St. SE1 BX41 4
Virginia Rd. E2 CA38 2
Viscount St. EC1 BZ39 2
Wadding St. SE17 BZ42 4
Wadham Gdns. NW3 BU37 1
Waite St. SE15 CA43 4
Waith St. EC4 BY39 2
Wakefield St. WC1 BX38 2
Wakley St. EC1 BY38 2
Walbrook, EC4 BZ40 4
Walcorde Av. SE17 BZ42 4
Walcot Sq. SE11 BY42 4
Walker Ho. NW1 BW37 1
Walkers Ct. W1 BW40 3
Walmer Pl. W1 BU39 1
Walmer St. W1 BU39 1
Walnut Tree Wk. SE11 BY42 4
Walpole St. SW3 BU42 3
Walton Pl. SW3 BU41 3
Walton St. SW3 BU42 3
Walworth Pl. SE17 BZ42 4
Walworth Rd. SE17 BZ42 4
Wansey St. SE17 BZ42 4
Wapping High St. E1 CB40 4
Wardens Gro. SE1 BZ40 4
Wardour Ms. W1 BW39 1
Wardour St. W1 BW39 1
Wardour St. W1 BW40 3
Ward St. SE11 BX42 4
Wareham St. N1 BZ37 2
Warner Pl. E2 CB37 2
Warner St. EC1 BY38 2
Warren Ms. W1 BV38 1
Warren St. W1 BV38 1
Warrington Cres. W9 BT38 1
Warwick Av. W9 BS38 1
Warwick Ct. WC1 BX39 2
Warwick Cres. W2 BT39 1
Warwick Est. W2 BS39 1
Warwick House St. SW1 BW40 3
Warwick La. EC4 BY39 2
Warwick Ms. W9 BT39 1
Warwick Ms. W2 BS39 1
Warwick Pl. SW1 BW42 3
Warwick Pl. W9 BT39 1
Warwick Row, SW1 BV41 3
Warwick Sq. EC4 BY39 2
Warwick Sq. SW1 BW42 3
Warwick Sq. Ms. SW1 BW42 3
Warwick St. W1 BW40 3
Warwick Way, SW1 BV42 3
Watergate, EC4 BY40 4
Watergate Wk. WC2 BX40 4
Waterloo Bridge, WC2 BX40 4
Waterloo Pl. SW1 BW40 3
Waterloo Rd. SE1 BX40 4
Waterloo St. EC1 BZ38 2
Waterson St. E2 CA38 2
Water St. WC2 BX40 4
Watling St. EC4 BZ39 2
Waverley Pl. NW8 BT37 1
Waverton St. W1 BV40 3
Waxwell Ter. SE1 BX41 4
Weavers' La. SE1 CA40 4
Weaver St. E1 CB38 2
Webber Row, SE1 BY41 4
Webber St. SE1 BY41 4
Webb St. SE1 CA41 4
Weighhouse St. W1 BV40 3
Weirs Pass. NW1 BW38 1
Welbeck St. W1 BV39 1
Welbeck Way, W1 BV39 1
Wellclose Sq. E1 CB40 4
Well. Ct. NW8 BT37 1
Wellers Ct. NW1 BX37 2
Wellesley Ct. NW8 BT38 1
Wellington Arch, W1 BV41 3
Wellington Pl. NW8 BT38 1
Wellington Rd. NW8 BT37 1
Wellington Row, E2 CA38 2
Wellington Sq. SW3 BU42 3
Wellington St. WC2 BX40 4
Wells Ms. W1 BW39 1
Wells Rise, NW8 BU37 1
Wells St. W1 BW39 1
Welsford Rd. SE1 CB42 4
Wenlock Ct. N1 BZ37 2
Wenlock Rd. N1 BZ37 2
Wenlock St. N1 BZ37 2
Wentworth St. E1 CA39 2
Werrington St. NW1 BW37 1
Westbourne Bri. W2 BT39 1
Westbourne Cres. W2 BT40 3
Westbourne Gdns. W2 BS39 1
Westbourne Gro. Ter. W2 BS39 1

Westbourne Pk. Ms. W2	BS39 1	Woodseer St. E1	CA39 2
Westbourne St. W2	BT40 3	Woods Ms. W1	BV40 3
Westbourne Ter. W2	BT39 1	Woods Pl. SE1	CA41 4
Westbourne Ter. Ms. W2	BT39 1	Woodstock Ms. W1	BV39 1
Westbourne Ter. Rd. W2	BT39 1	Woodstock St. W1	BV39 1
West Central Pl. WC1	BX39 2	Wood St. EC2	BZ39 2
Westcott Rd. SE17	BY43 4	Wooler St. SE17	BZ42 4
West Eaton Pl. SW1	BV42 3	Wootton St. SE1	BY41 4
Westgate Ter. SW10	BS42 3	Worgan St. SE11	BX42 4
W. Halkin St. SW1	BV41 3	Worgate St. N1	BZ37 2
West Harding St. EC4	BY39 2	Wormwood St. EC2	CA39 2
Westley St. W1	BV39 1	Woronzow Rd. NW8	BT37 1
Westminster Bridge. SW1	BX41 4	Worship St. EC2	BZ38 2
Westminster Bridge Rd. SE1	BX41 4	Wren St. WC1	BX38 2
Westmoreland Bldgs. EC1	BZ39 2	Wyclif St. EC1	BY38 2
Westmoreland Pl. SW1	BV42 3	Wyndham Ms. W1	BU39 1
Westmoreland Ter. SW1	BV42 3	Wyndham Pl. W1	BU39 1
Westmorland Rd. SE17	BZ43 4	Wyndham St. W1	BU39 1
Westmorland St. W1	BV39 1	Wynford Rd. N1	BX37 2
Weston Rise, WC1	BX38 2	Wynyard Ter. SE11	BX42 4
Weston St. SE1	BZ40 4	Wynyatt St. EC1	BY38 2
Weston St. SE1	BZ41 4	Wythburn Pl. W1	BU39 1
West Smithfield, EC1	BY39 2	Yalding Rd. SE16	CB41 4
West Sq. SE11	BY41 4	Yardley St. WC1	BY38 2
West St. EC2	BZ39 2	Yarmouth Pl. W1	BV40 3
West St. WC2	BW39 1	Yeate St. N1	BZ36 2
West Tenter St. E1	CA39 2	Yeomans Row, SW3	BU41 3
W. Warwick Pl. SW1	BV42 3	York Blds. WC2	BX40 4
Wetherby Gdns. SW5	BS42 3	York Gate, NW1	BV38 1
Wetherby Ms. SW5	BS42 3	York Pl. WC2	BX40 4
Wetherby Pl. SW7	BT42 3	York Rd. SE1	BX41 4
Weymouth Ms. W1	BV39 1	York St. W1	BU39 1
Weymouth Pl. E2	CA37 2	York Ter. NW1	BV38 1
Weymouth St. W1	BV39 1	Yorkton St. E2	CB37 2
Weymouth Ter. E2	CA37 2	York Way, N1	BX36 2
Wharfdale Rd. N1	BX37 2	York Way Ct. N1	BX37 2
Wharf Rd. N1	BZ37 2	Young St. W8	BS41 3
Wharfside, EC4	BZ40 4		
Wharncliffe Gdns. NW8	BT38 1		
Wharton St. WC1	BX38 2		
Wheat St. W1	BV39 1		
Wheler St. E1	CA38 2		
Whetstone Park, WC2	BX39 2		
Whidborne St. WC1	BX38 2		
Whiskin St. EC1	BY38 2		
Whiston Rd. E2	CA37 2		
Whitby St. E1	CA38 2		
Whitcomb St. WC2	BW40 3		
Whitechapel High St. E1	CA39 2		
Whitechapel Rd. E1	CB39 2		
Whitechurch La. E1	CB39 2		
White Conduit St. N1	BY37 2		
Whitecross Pl. EC2	BZ39 2		
Whitecross St. EC1	BZ38 2		
Whitefriars St. EC4	BY39 2		
Whitehall, SW1	BX40 4		
Whitehall Ct. SW1	BX40 4		
Whitehall Gdns. SW1	BX40 4		
Whitehall Pl. SW1	BX40 4		
White Hart St. SE11	BY42 4		
White Hart Yd. SE1	BZ40 4		
Whitehaven St. NW8	BU38 1		
Whiteheads Gro. SW3	BU42 3		
White Horse St. W1	BV40 3		
White Kennett St. E1	CA39 2		
White Lion St. N1	BY37 2		
Whites Grounds, SE1	CA41 4		
Whites Grounds Est. SE1	CA41 4		
White's Row. E1	CA39 2		
Whitfield Pl. W1	BW38 1		
Whitfield St. W1	BW38 1		
Whitgift St. SE11	BX42 4		
Whitmore Est. N1	CA37 2		
Whitmore Rd. N1	CA37 2		
Whittaker St. SW1	BV42 3		
Whittlesey St. SE1	BY40 4		
Wickham St. SE11	BX42 4		
Wicklow St. WC1	BX38 2		
Wide Gates, E1	CA39 2		
Wigmore Pl. W1	BV39 1		
Wigmore St. W1	BV39 1		
Wilbraham Pl. SW1	BU42 3		
Wild Ct. WC2	BX39 2		
Wild's Rents, SE1	BZ41 4		
Wild St. WC2	BX39 2		
Wilfred St. SW1	BW41 3		
William iv St. WC2	BX40 4		
William Rd. NW1	BV38 1		
William St. SW1	BU41 3		
Willow Gro. SE1	CA42 4		
Willow Pl. SW1	BW42 3		
Willow St. EC2	CA38 2		
Willow Wk. SE1	CA42 4		
Willy St. WC1	BX39 2		
Wilmer Gdns. N1	CA37 2		
Wilmington Sq. WC1	BY38 2		
Wilmington St. WC1	BY38 2		
Wilson St. EC2	BZ39 2		
Wilton Cres. SW1	BV41 3		
Wilton Ms. SW1	BV41 3		
Wilton Pl. SW1	BV41 3		
Wilton Rd. SW1	BV41 3		
Wilton Row, SW1	BV41 3		
Wilton Sq. N1	BZ37 2		
Wilton St. SW1	BV41 3		
Wilton Ter. SW1	BV41 3		
Wilton Vil. N1	BZ37 2		
Wiltshire Cl. SW3	BU42 3		
Wiltshire Rd. N1	BZ37 2		
Wimbolt St. E2	CB38 2		
Wimborne Ct. N1	BZ37 2		
Wimborne St. N1	BZ37 2		
Wimpole Ms. W1	BV39 1		
Wimpole St. W1	BV39 1		
Winchester Sq. SE1	BZ40 4		
Winchester St. SW1	BV42 3		
Winchester Wk. SE1	BZ40 4		
Wincott St. SE11	BY42 4		
Windmill Row, SE11	BY42 4		
Windmill St. W1	BW39 1		
Windmill Wk. SE1	BY40 4		
Windsor Pl. SW1	BW42 3		
Windsor St. N1	BY37 2		
Windsor Ter. N1	BZ38 2		
Wine Office Ct. EC4	BY39 2		
Winsland Ms. W2	BT39 1		
Winsland St. W2	BT39 1		
Winsley St. W1	BW39 1		
Winterton Pl. SW10	BT43 3		
Withers Pl. EC1	BZ38 2		
Woburn Pl. WC1	BX38 2		
Woburn Sq. WC1	BW38 1		
Woburn Wk. WC1	BW38 1		
Wolseley St. SE1	CA41 4		
Woodbridge St. EC1	BY38 2		
Woodfall St. SW3	BU42 3		

Greater London Street Atlas

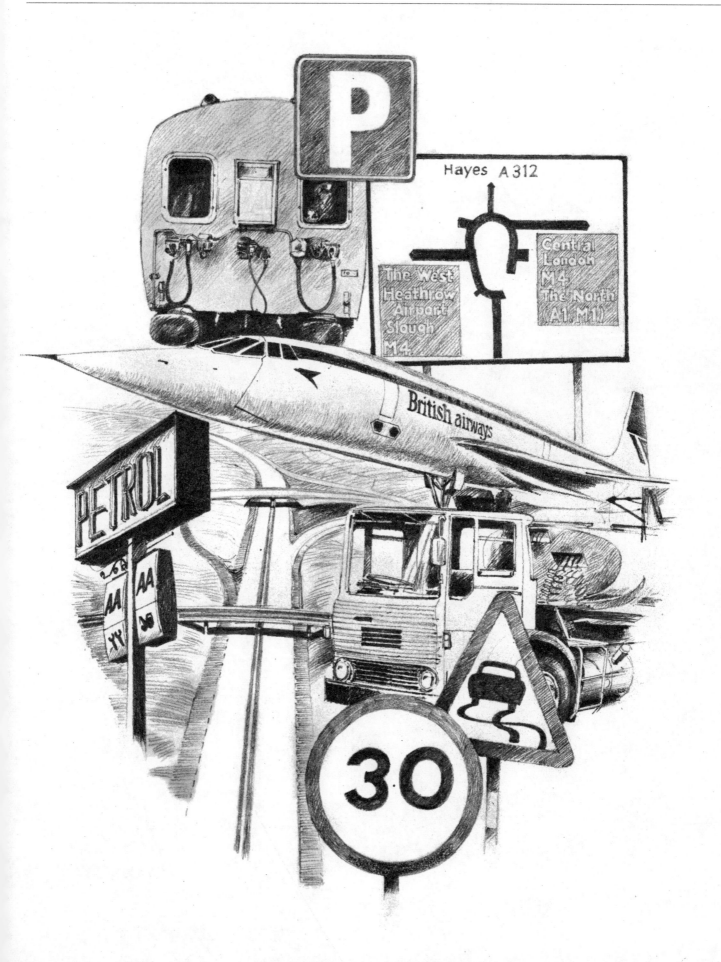

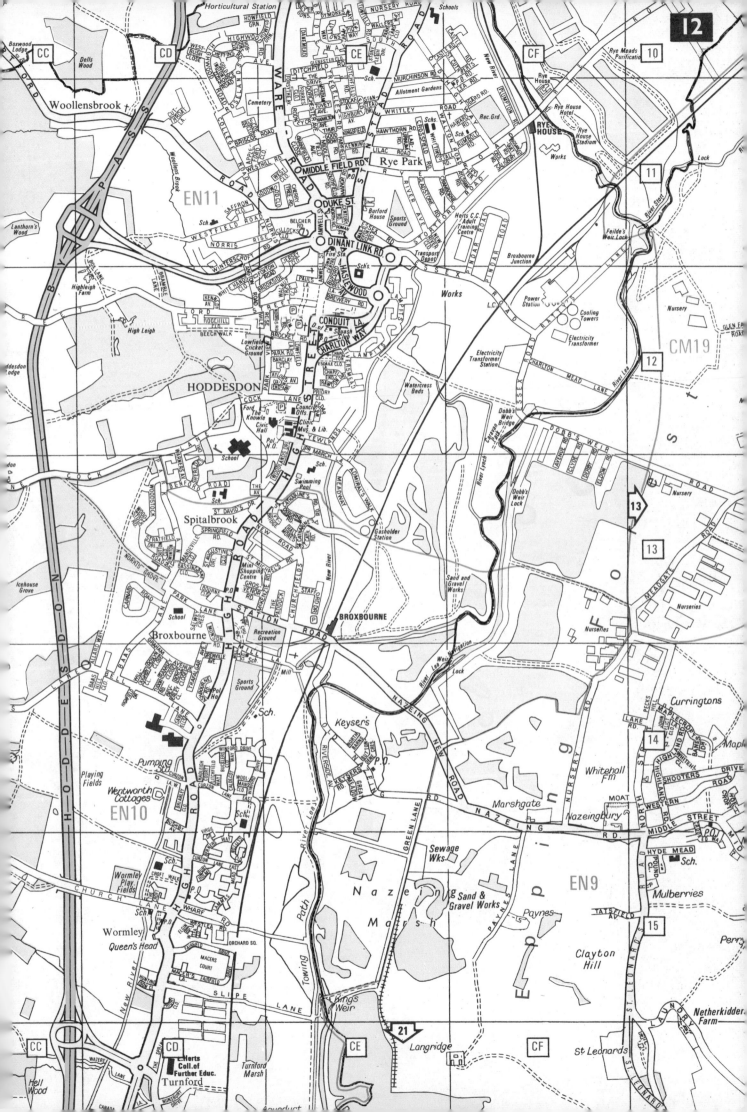

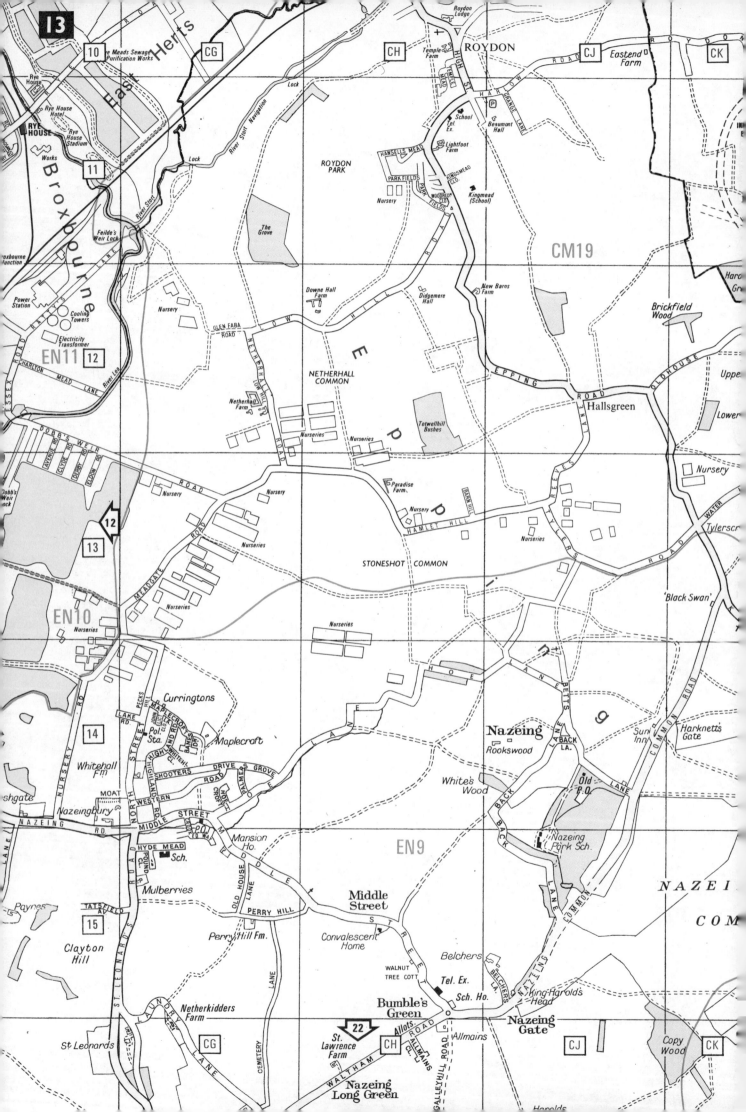

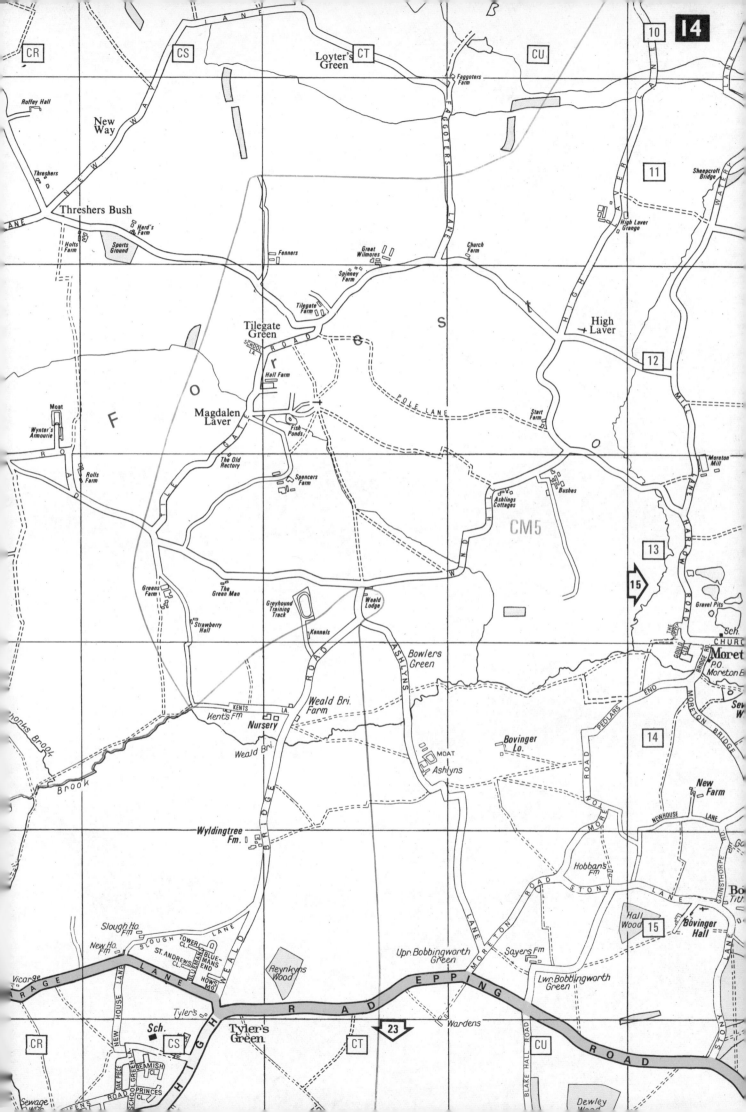

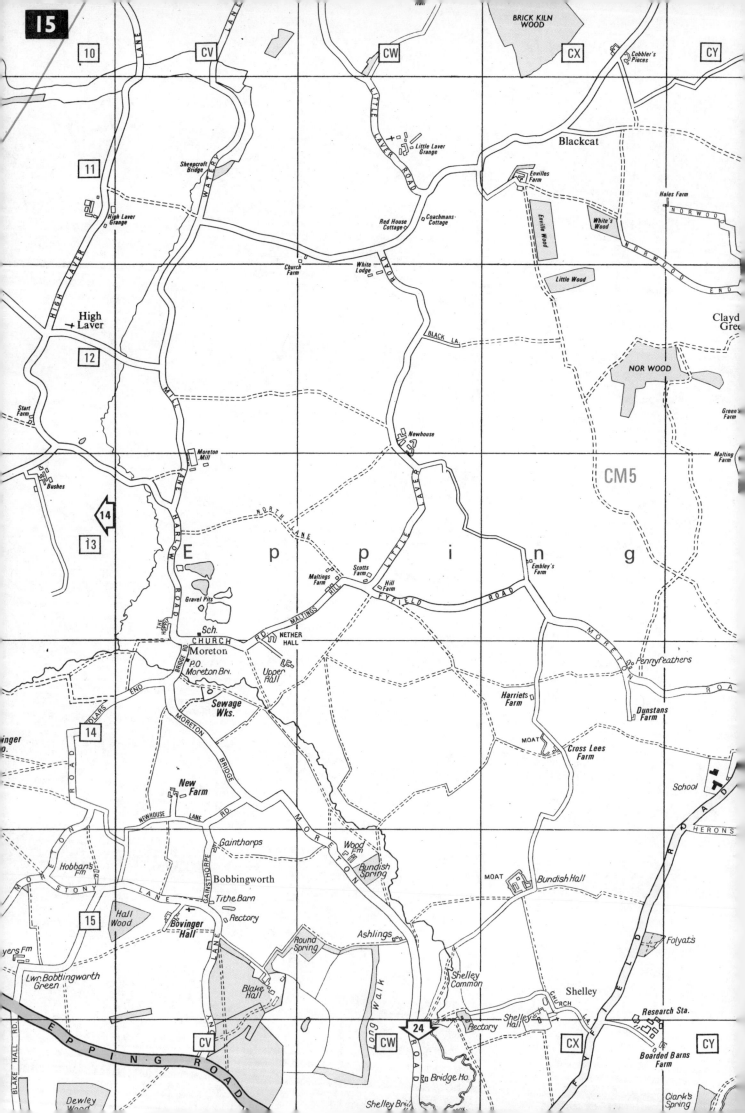

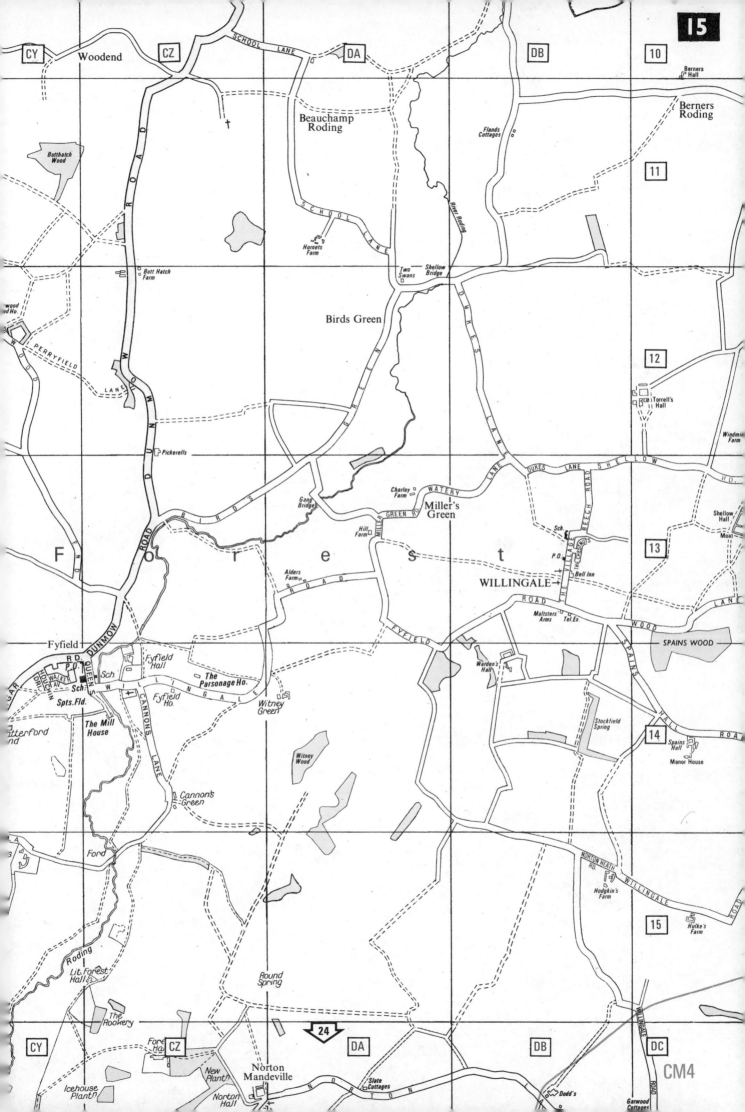

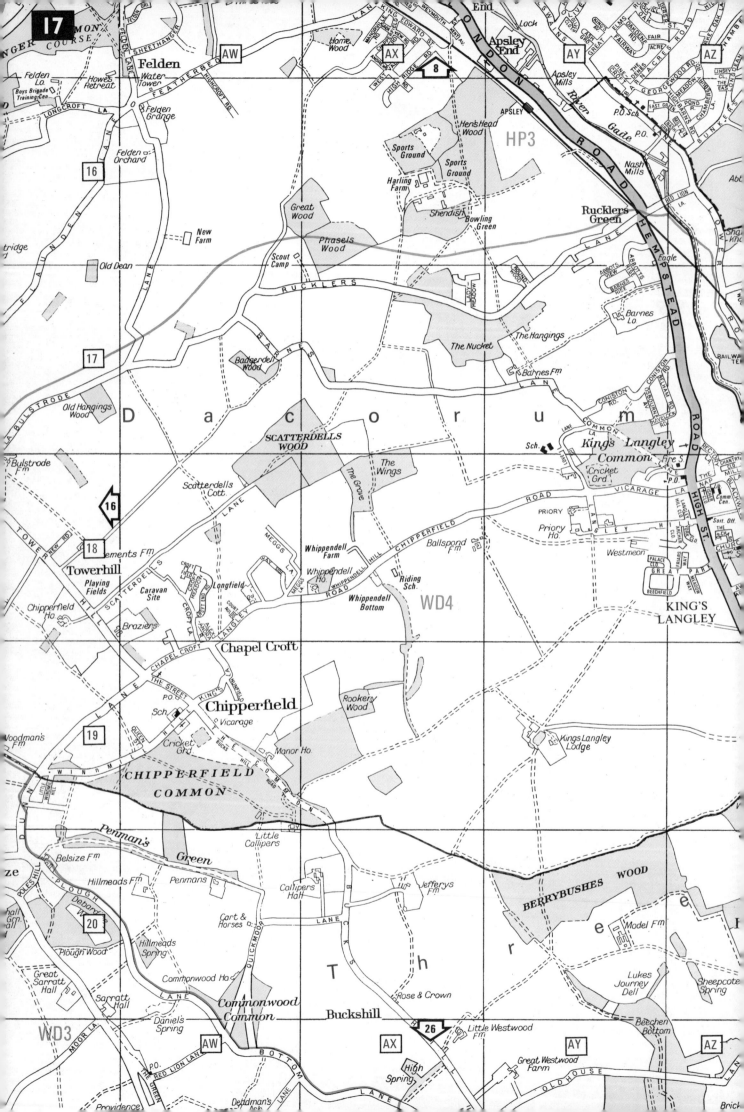

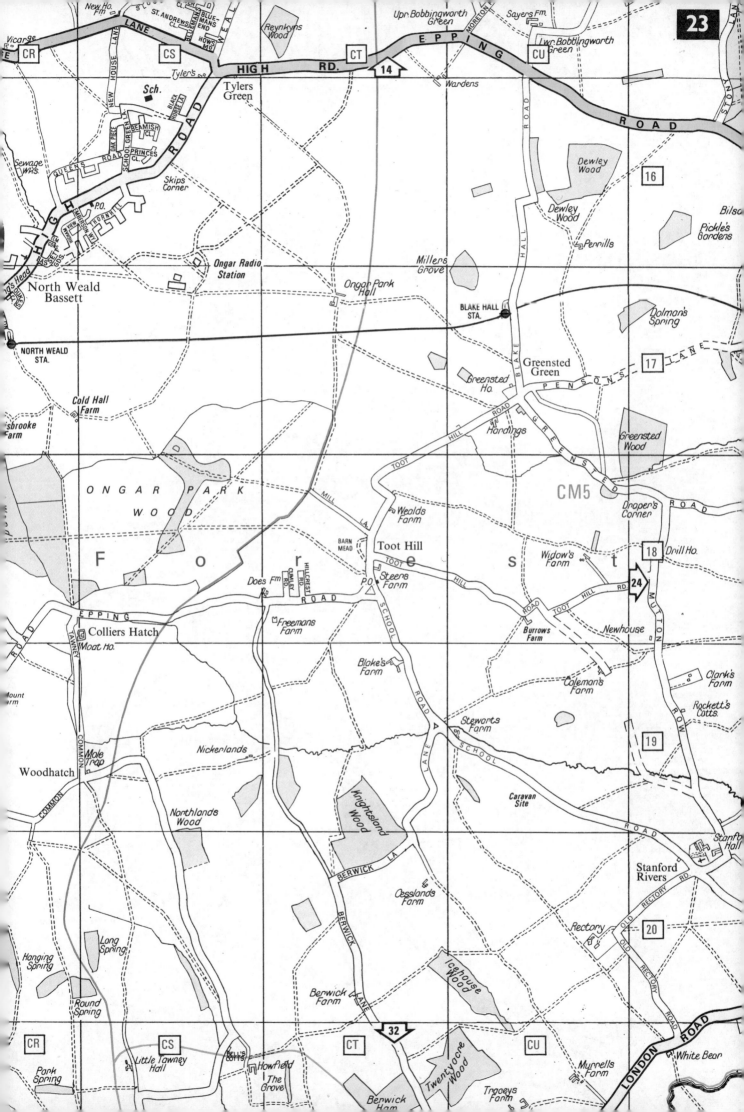

New Ho. Fm.
St. Andrews
BLUE-
MANS
END
HOWS
Upr. Bobbingworth Green
Sayers Fm.
Lwr. Bobbingworth Green
Vicarage
SLOUGH
LANE
WEALD
Reynkyns Wood
MORETON

CR
CS
CT
EPPING
CU
HIGH
RD.
14
Wardens
ROAD

Tylers
Tylers Green
Sch.
BLACK
HORSE
CL.
BEAMISH
PRINCES
CL.
CL.
16

Sewage Wks.
QUEENS
SCHOOL GREEN LA.
ROAD
OAK PIECE
ROAD
Skips Corner
HALL
Dewley Wood
BLAKE
Dewley Wood
Pennills
Bilsa
Pickle's Gardens

HORNHILL
P.O.
Ongar Radio Station
Millers Grove
Ongar Park Hall
HIGH
North Weald Bassett
NORTH WEALD STA.
BLAKE HALL STA.
Dolman's Spring

Greensted Ho.
Greensted Green
17

Cold Hall Farm
PENSONS
LANE

isbrooke Farm
ROAD
GREENSTED
Greensted Wood

Hardings
CM5
Draper's Corner
ONGAR PARK WOOD
MILL
Wealds Farm
TOOT
HILL
LA.
BARN MEAD
Toot Hill
18
Drill Ho.
F
o
r
e
s
t
24
Does Fm.
HILLCREST RD.
CUMLEY RD.
Steens Farm
P.O.
TOOT
HILL
Widow's Farm
MUTTON
Colliers Hatch
ROAD
P.O.
Freemans Farm
SCHOOL
Burrows Farm
Newhouse
ROW
EPPING
Moat Ho.
Blake's Farm
Coleman's Farm
Clark's Farm
TAWNEY
Rockett's Cotts.
Mount Farm
COMMON
Male Trap
Nickerlands
Stewarts Farm
SCHOOL
19
Woodhatch
LANE
Caravan Site
ROAD

Northlands Wood
Knightsland Wood
Stanford Hall

COMMON
BERWICK
LA.
Stanford Rivers
Hanging Spring
Long Spring
Oesslands Farm
RECTORY
OLD
Rectory
20
Round Spring
BERWICK
Icehouse Wood
OLD RECTORY
RD.

CR
CS
Little Tawney Hall
Bell's Cotts.
CT
32
CU
LONDON
White Bear
Park Spring
Howfield The Grove
Twentyacre Wood
Murrells Farm
ROAD
Benwick Ham
Benwick Farm
Tregeys Farm

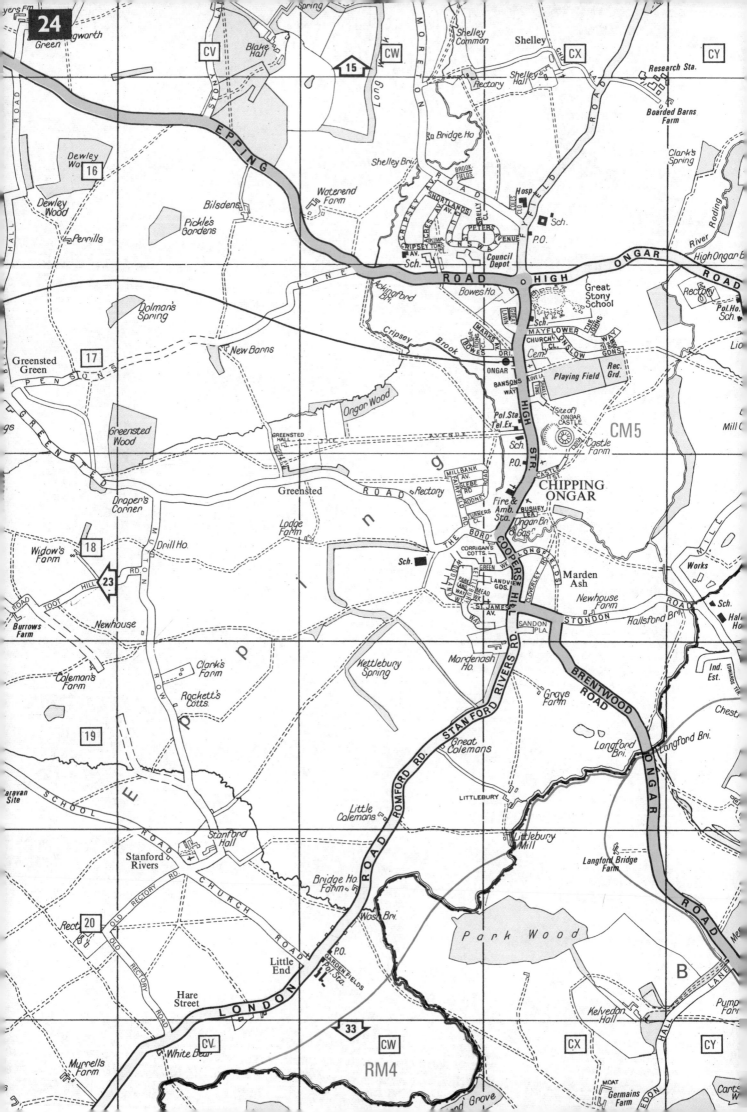

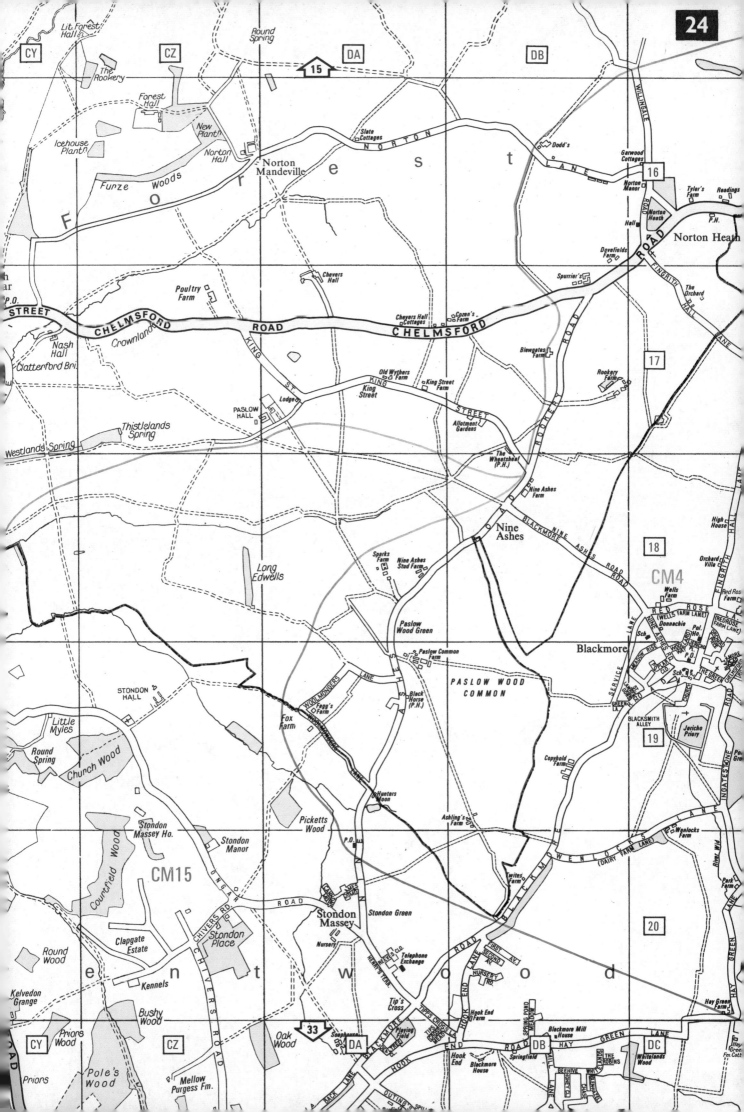

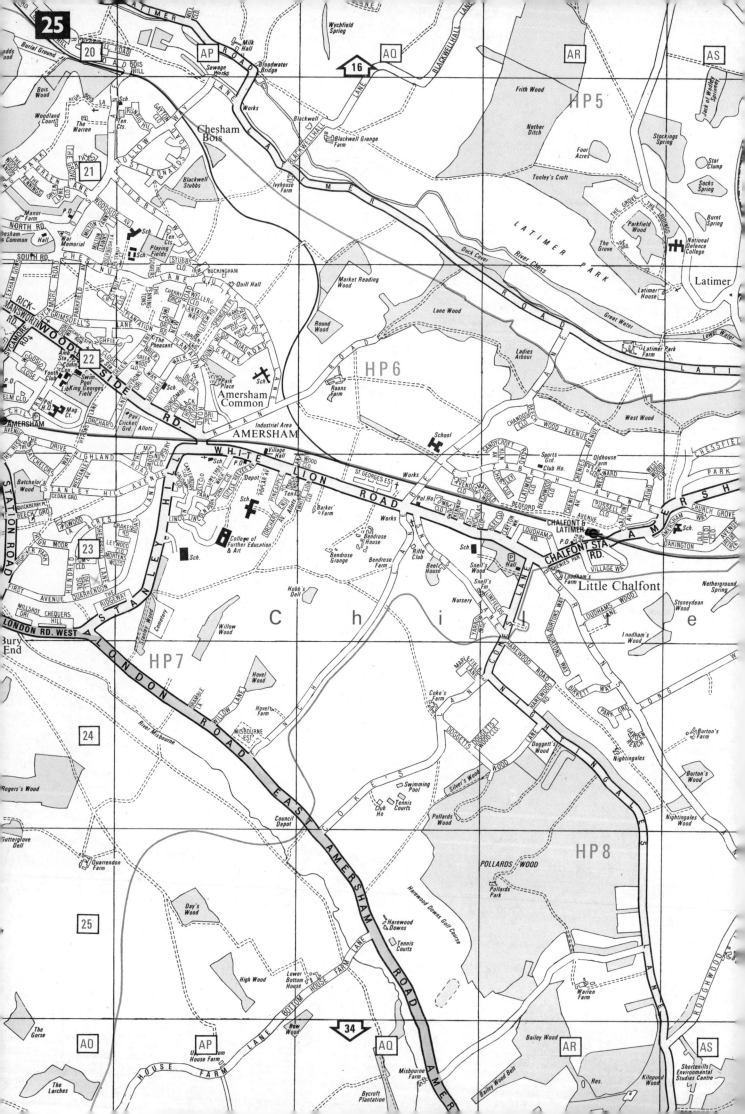

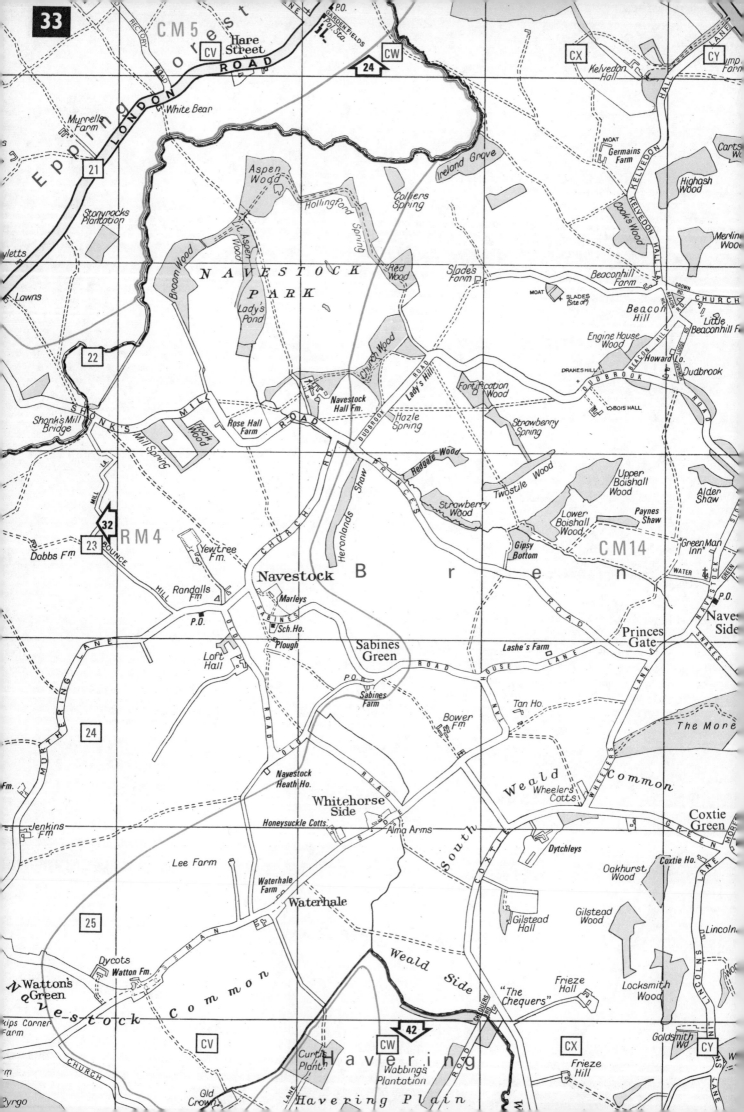

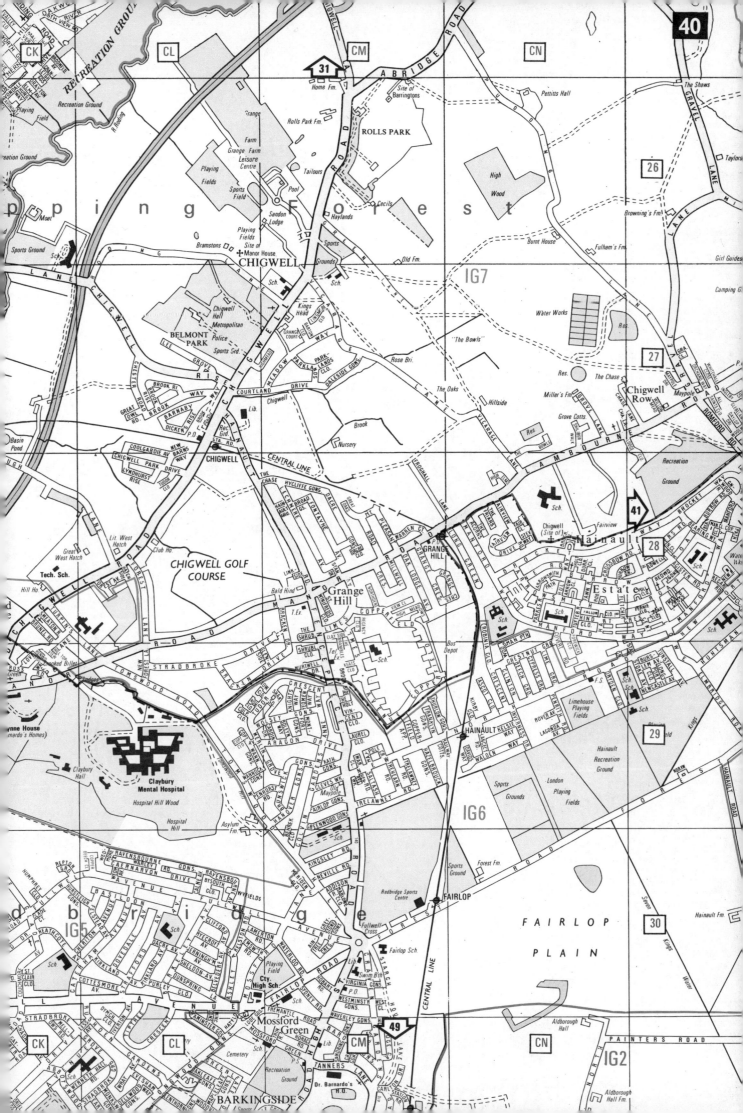

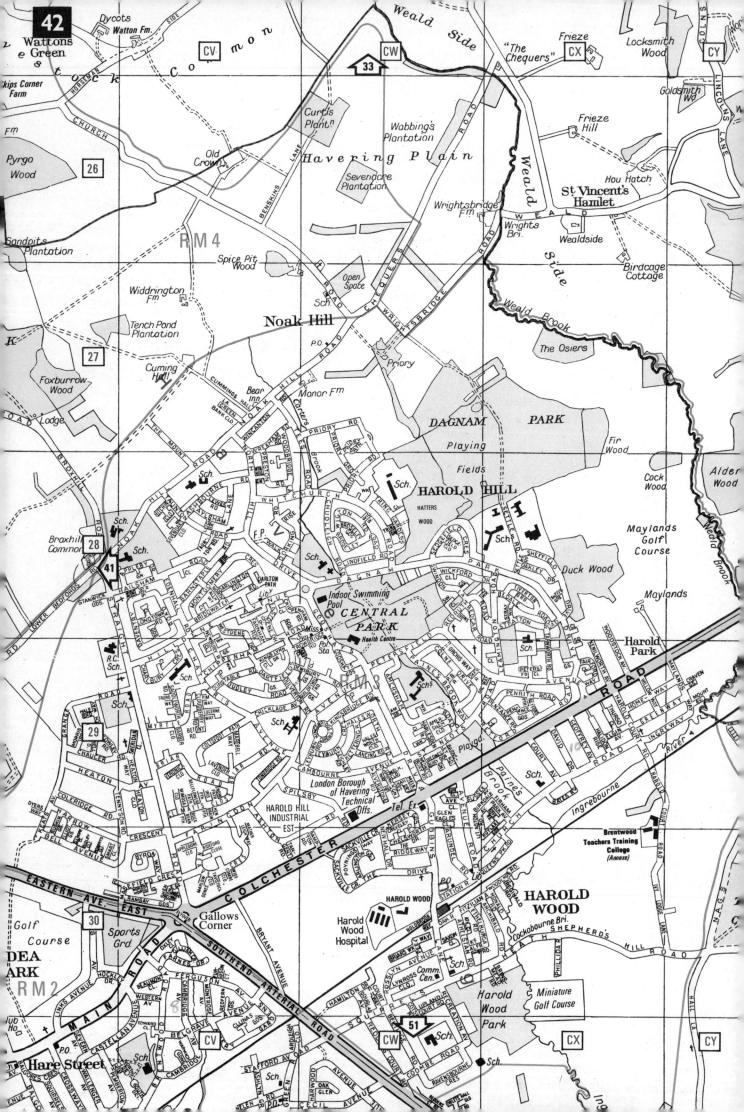

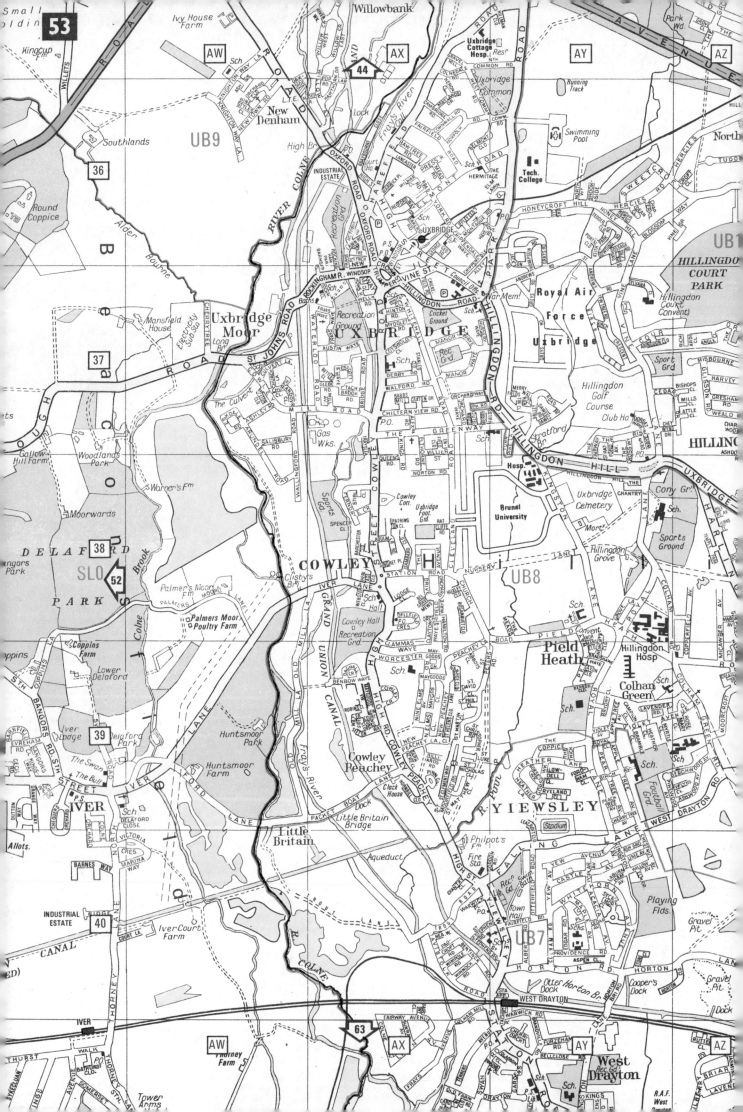

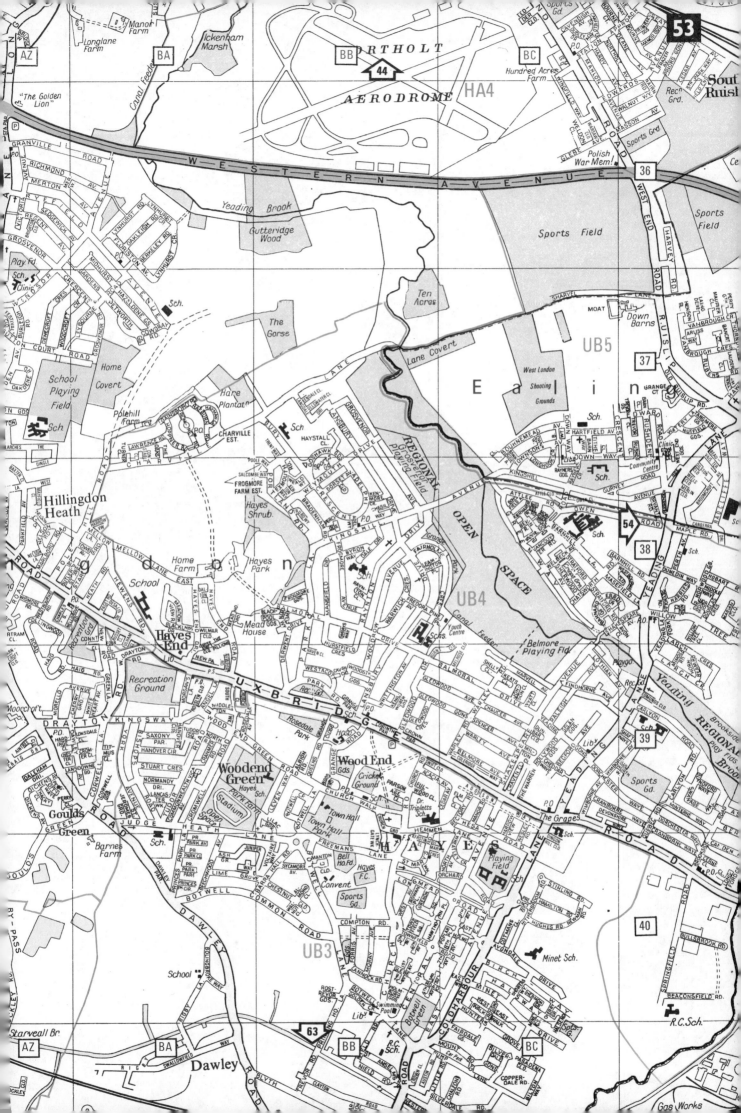

60

CV
CW
Hacton **51**
Park Corner Farm
CX
Parklands
CY
Corbets Tey
Huntsman & Hounds
Harwood Hall

RM12
36
Rainham Lo.

1 HARRIER CLO.
2 DOVE WK.
3 PEREGRINE WK.
4 EAGLE CLO.
5 FULMAR RD.
6 SWALLOW WK.
7 HERON FLIGHT AV.
8 CORMORANT WK.
9 KESTREL CLO.
10 CONDOR WK.
11 FLAMINGO WK.
12 GULL WK.
13 FALCON WAY
14 ROOK CLO.

Gerpins
Lit. Gerpins La.

Abbey Wood
Berwickpond Farm
Damyns Hall

37
Berwick Pond
Berwick Ho.

Abbey Wood La.
Berwickpond Cl.

Warwick Woods
White Post Wood

59
Cemetery
Sch.
White Post Corner
Ayletts
Warwick

38
RAINHAM
Chandlers Corner
JEWS CEMETERY
Spring Farm Pk.
Spring Cottages

1 FAGUS AV.
2 ELDER WAY
3 BETULA WK.
4 ACER AV.

RM13
1 BAILLIE CLO.
2 REDBURY CLO.
3 CRAMMERVILLE WK.
4 MAGNUM CLO.
5 NORWAY WK.

Sports Centre
Launder's Barn
Bretts
Kenningtons

39
South Hall
East Hall
Easthall
Moor Hall

U.S.

Wennington Hall
The Willows
Sch.

MARSHES
PO
The Green
Fire Sta.
Wennington
Lennard Arms

Hospital Shaw

Nethan
AVELEY
Sandy Lane

40
Hospital

St Paul's

WENNINGTON MARSHES
CV
CW **70** RM16
CX
Sports Ground
CY

Target Nº5
Target Nº4
Target Nº3
AVELEY &
Marshfoot Ho.
Sports Gnd.
London Road
Purfleet

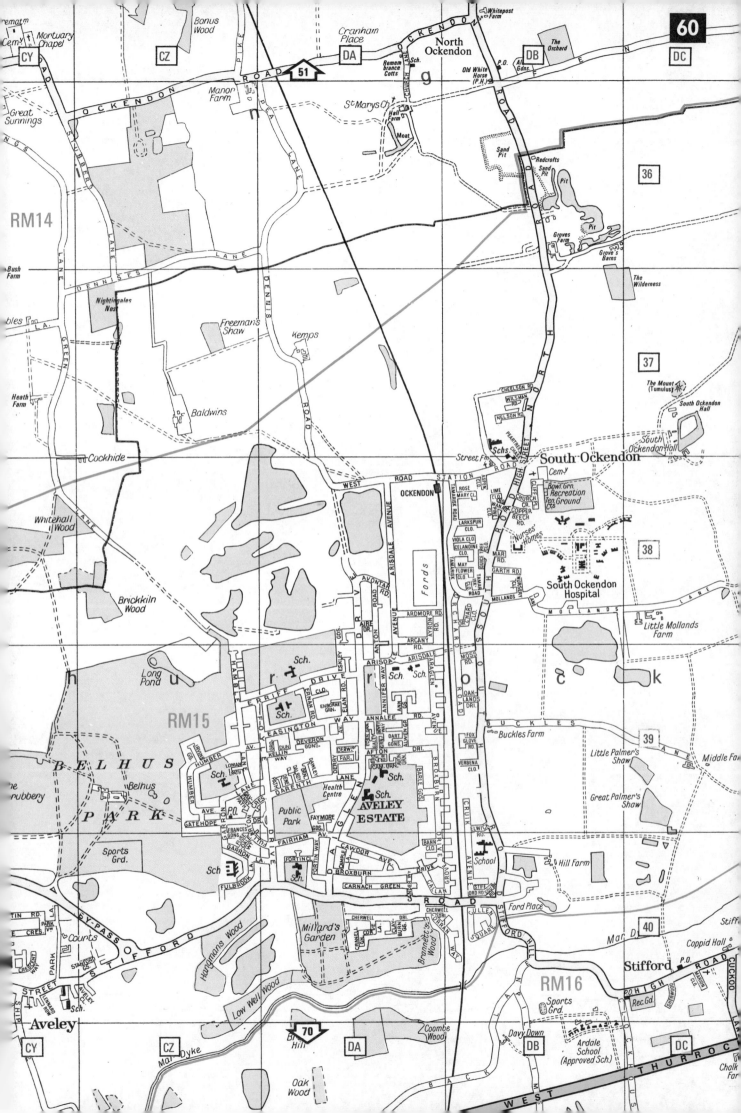

CY

CZ

DA

North Ockendon

DB

DC

RM14

Crematm
Cemy
Mortuary Chapel

Bonus Wood

Cranham Place

Whitepost Farm

The Orchard

Great Sunnings

Manor Farm

Remembrance Cotts

St Marys Ch.

Hall Farm

Moat

Old White Horse (P.H.)

P.O.

g

Sand Pit

Redcrofts

Sand Pit

Pit

36

Bush Farm

Nightingales Nest

DENNISES

Freeman's Shaw

Kemps

Groves Farm

Grove's Barns

The Wilderness

Heath Farm

Baldwins

CHEELSON RD.

WILSMAN RD.

NELSON RD.

The Mount (Tumulus)

South Ockendon Hall

37

Cockhide

Whitehall Wood

Schs.

Street Fm.

South Ockendon

Cemy

South Ockendon Hall

South Ockendon Hall

38

WEST ROAD

STATION

OCKENDON

ROSE

MARY CL.

TAMARISK ROAD

LARKSPUR CLO.

VIOLA CLO.

CELANDINE CLO.

MAY FLOWER CLO.

TAMARISK ROAD

Fords

LIME

WANT RD.

ASPEN

CHURCH

COPPER BEECH RD.

GUIDE TREE

Bowl. Grn.
Recreation Ground

Ten Cts.

Nurses' Homes

MAR. RD.

GARTH RD.

NURSERY

MOLLANDS

South Ockendon Hospital

MOLLANDS LANE

Little Mollands Farm

Brickkiln Wood

Long Pond

h

u

Sch.

ARDMORE RD.

AVRON RD.

ARCANY RD.

ARISDALE

ARRAGLEN

r

r

Sch.

Sch.

OAK-LANDS DRI.

3

k

ORCHARD ROAD

SOUTH ROAD

RM15

Sch.

Sch.

EASINGTON

DEVERON GDNS.

Health Centre

Sch.

AVELEY ESTATE

ANNALEE

DART GDNS.

AFTON

BROXBURN GDNS.

FOX GLOVE RD.

VERBENA CLO.

BUCKLES

Buckles Farm

39

Little Palmer's Shaw

Middle Fa

BELHUS

Belhus

PARK

The Shrubbery

Sports Grd.

P.O.

GATEHOPE

FRANCES GDNS.

GARRON

Public Park

FAYMORE GDNS.

FAIRHAM

Sch.

FULBROOK

FORTIN

BROXBURN

CAWDOR AVE.

CARNACH GREEN

GROVE ROAD

CRUIKS

School

Hill Farm

Great Palmer's Shaw

BY-PASS

STIFFORD

Courts

Hangmans Wood

Millard's Garden

CHERWELL

CHERWELL DRI.

Ford Place

Davy Down

Ardale School (Approved Sch.)

ROAD

Stiff

Mar D.

40

Coppid Hall

Stifford

RM16

Sports Grd.

Rec. Gd.

Aveley

CY

CZ

DA

DB

DC

Low Well Wood

Coombe Wood

Oak Wood

WEST THURROC

RM14

RM15

RM16

51

70

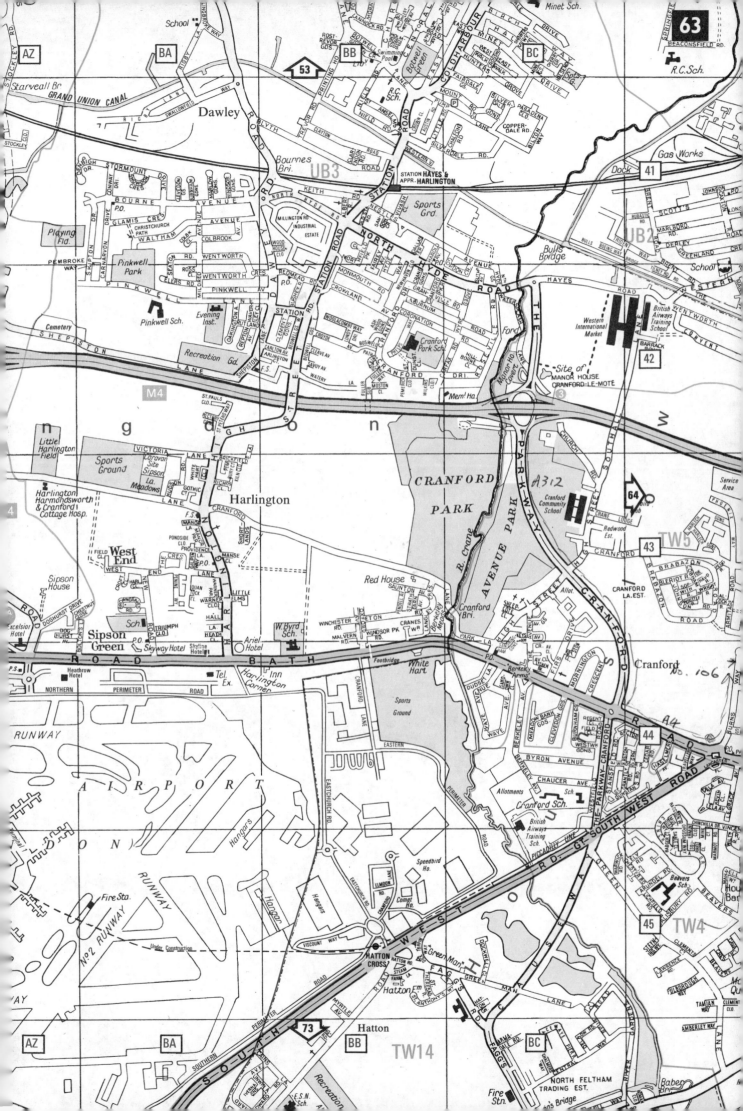

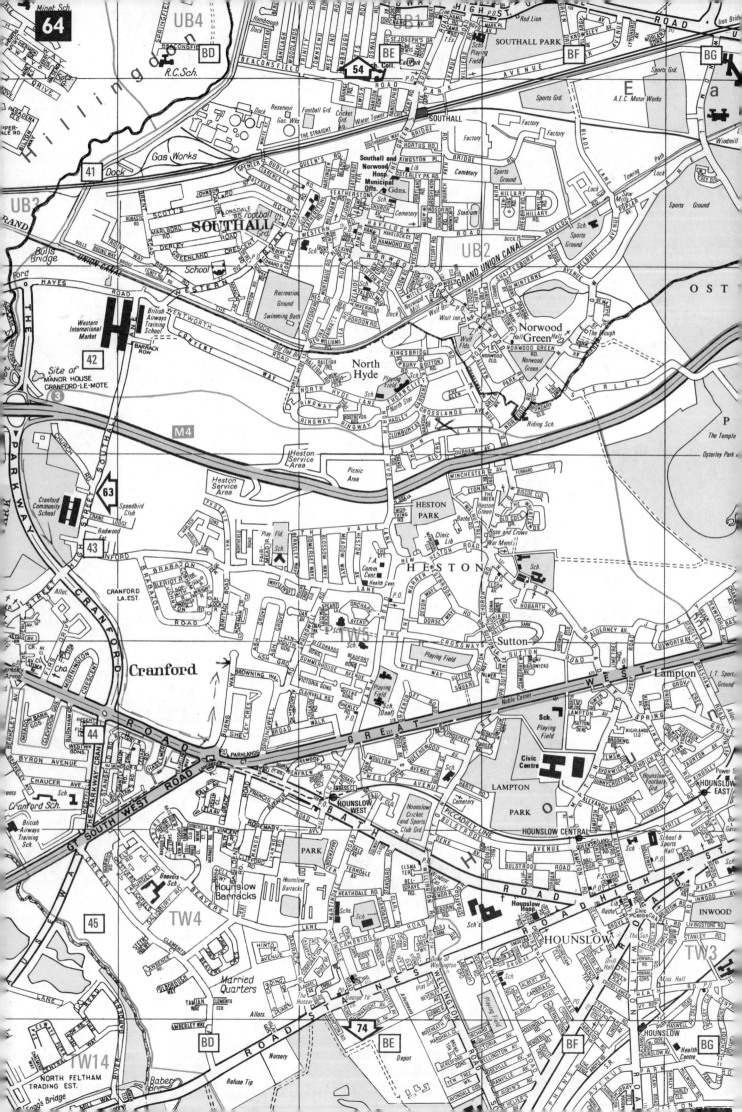

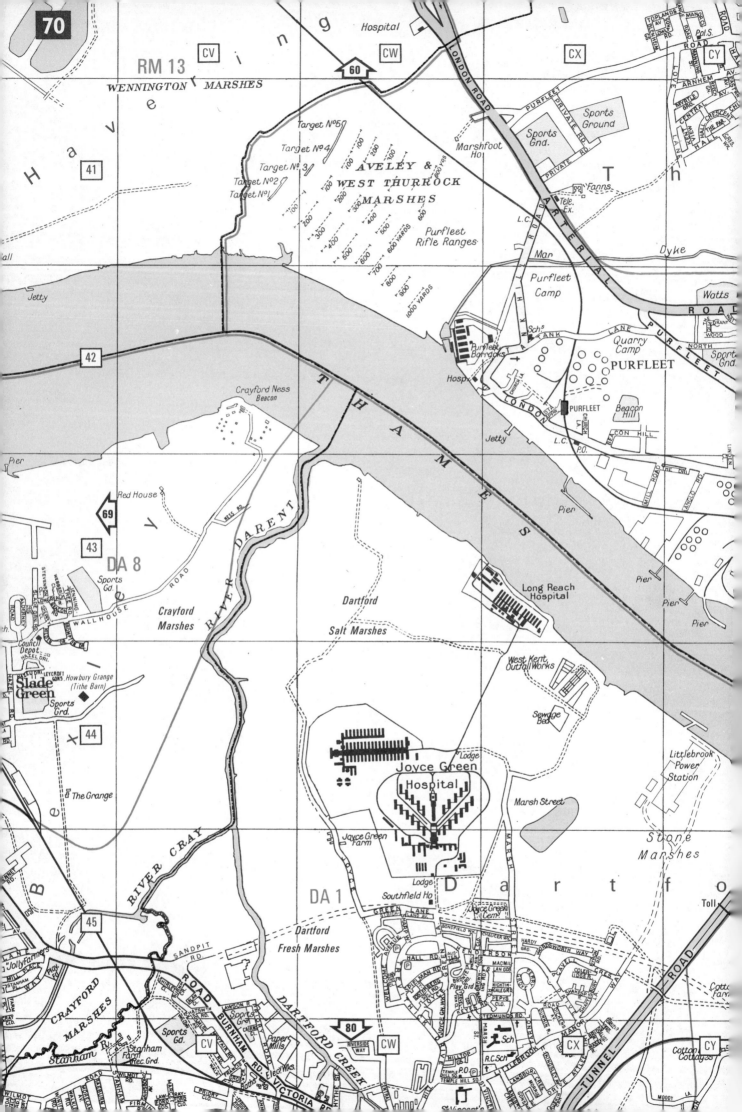

CY

CZ

DA

DB

60

41

42

43

44

45

71

80

Aveley

Low Well Wood

Broom Hill

Coombe Wood

Sports Grd.

Davy Down

Ardale School (Approved Sch.)

Rec. Gd.

Chalk Pit Farm

Oak Wood

Mar Dyke

WEST   THURROCK

r   r   o   c   k

Bramble Wood

Schools

Causeway Bri.

Sch.

BACK   LANE

ARTERIAL   ROAD

PURFLEET

Lowhouse Farm

Road

Sports Grd.

Cement Works

Stonehouse Corner

Stonehouse

BY-PASS

ROAD

LONDON

ARRAH COTTS.

JURGEN'S RD.

DARTFORD TUNNEL APPROACH

RM 16

Chalk Quarries (Disused)

WARREN

South Stifford

PALMERSTN GDS.

MOORE   AVENUE

PALMERSTON   ROAD

RM 17

Sports Grd.

West Thurrock

HILLCREST AV.

FOURTH AV.

MOTHERWELL WAY

BAY MANOR LA.

CORNWALL

FIRST AV.

Sch.

PARK A.

ROBERT

ST. CLEMENTS AV.

JUBILEE

Rec. Grd.

Cem.

SANDY

LANE

ELM

ROAD

STN. VIEW RD.

PEACOCK

MANOR RD.

STONE NESS

P.O.

FOXTON

CHARLTON

GUMLEY

EAST ST.

P.O.

BELMONT RD.

CASTLE RD.

ROSEBERY RD.

P.O.R.

P.O.

GOODYEAR T.

SCHOOLFIELD

ESSEX

WAY

FORMANOR

WAY

WILLIAM ST.

Parsonage Farm

P.O.

OVAL

Power Sta.

OLIVER   ROAD

HEDLEY

ST. CLEMENTS RD.

ST. CLEMENTS RD.

AVENUE

Piers

Pier

Wharf

Pier (Disused)

Wharf

Pier

R I V

T H A M

DA 11

St Clement's or Fiddler's Reach

Pier

Bell Wharf

Swanscombe Marshe

DARTFORD TUNNEL

d

Stoneness Lighthouse

Stone Ness

Jetty

Wharf

Greenhithe Foreshore

Paper Mills

Cricket Gd.

Sports Gd & Pav.

Cement Wks.

DA 10

Kent Portland Cement Wks.

Jetty

Johnson's Wharf

Jetties

Sports Gd. Ingress Park

Pier

Bath

HIGH   STREET

Pier

Sports Gd.

Ingress Abbey

Thames Nautic Training Coll.

Cricket

LOVERS

Old Quarry

Cement Wks.

Sewage Wks.

ST. MARYS RD.

L.C.

88

DA 9

IFIELD TER.

Greenhithe

Eagle CI.

AVENUE

LONDON

ROAD

GA

SWANS

Chalk Pit

STONE CROSSING

ELIZABETH ST.

CHURCH HILL

UPR. CHURCH HILL

CY

CZ

Stone

Old Chalk Pits

Portland Cement Wks.

CHARLES

STREET

BELL

GREENHITHE

DA

School

Play Fidlid

KNOCKHALL RD.

INGRESS GDNS.

DB

Baths

SWEYN

CRAY LANDS

Old Chalk Pit

Old Chalk Pit

Playing Fields

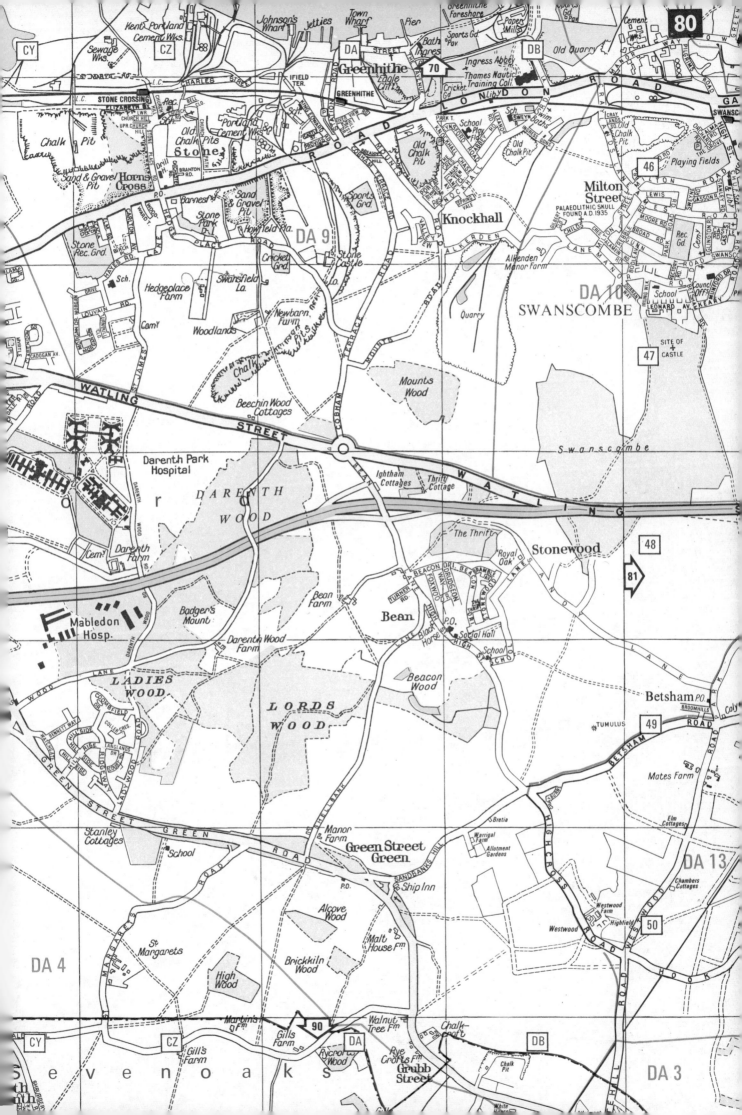

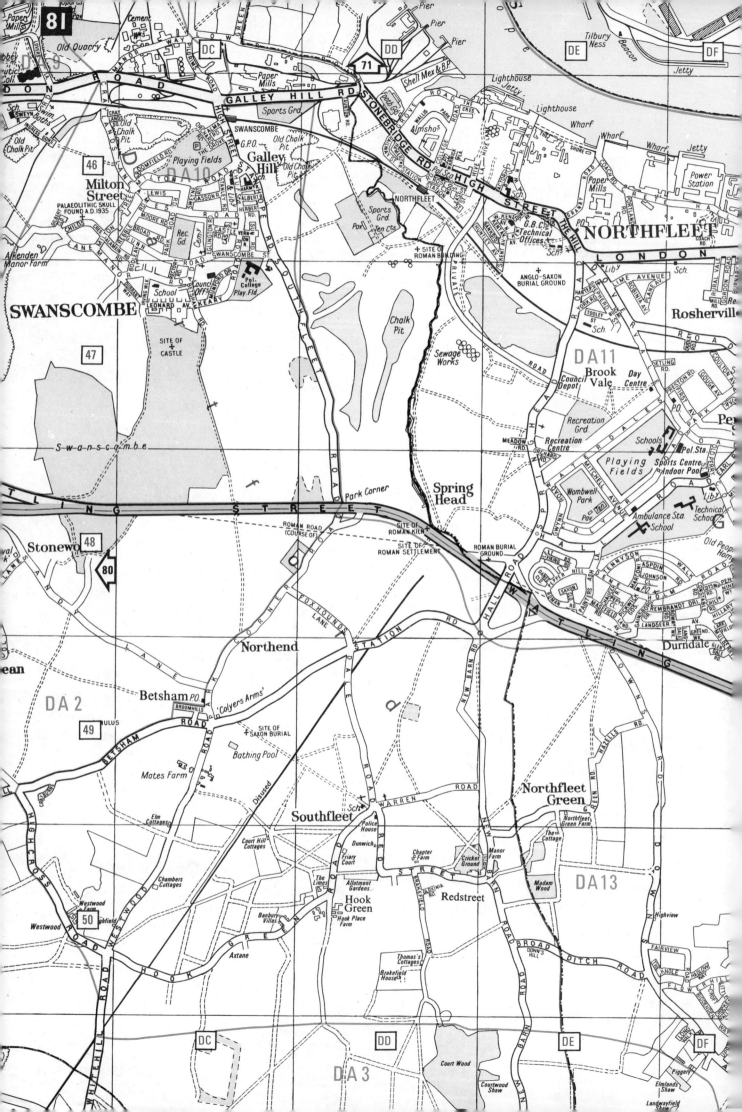

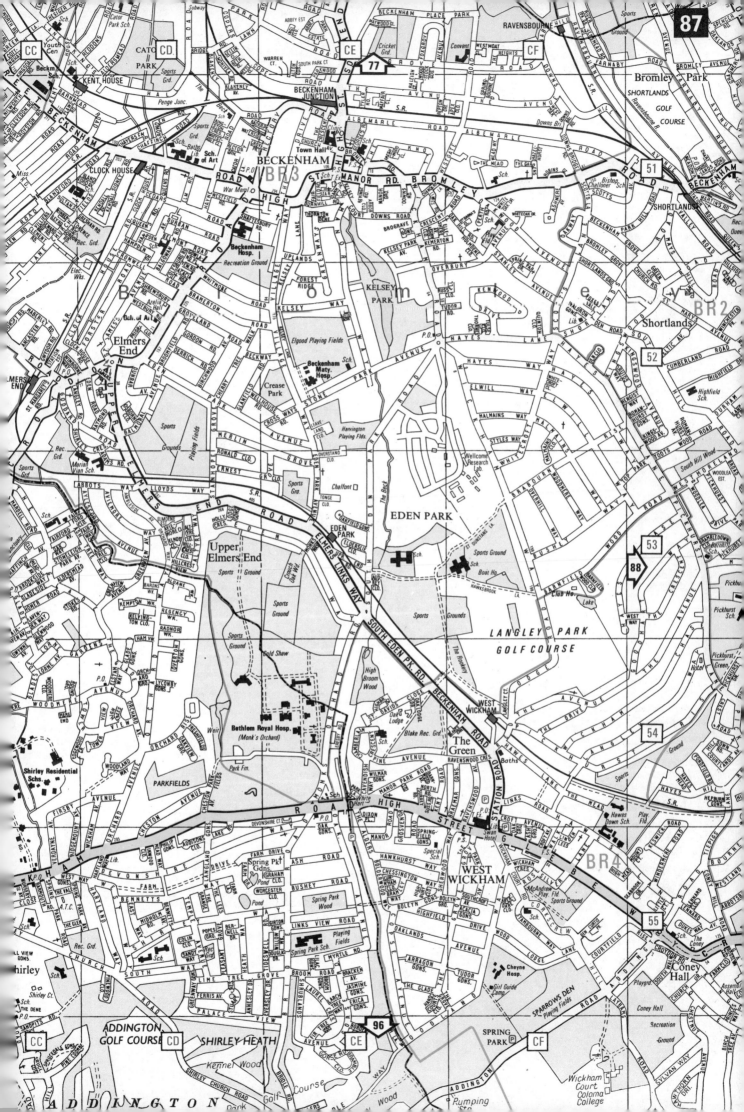

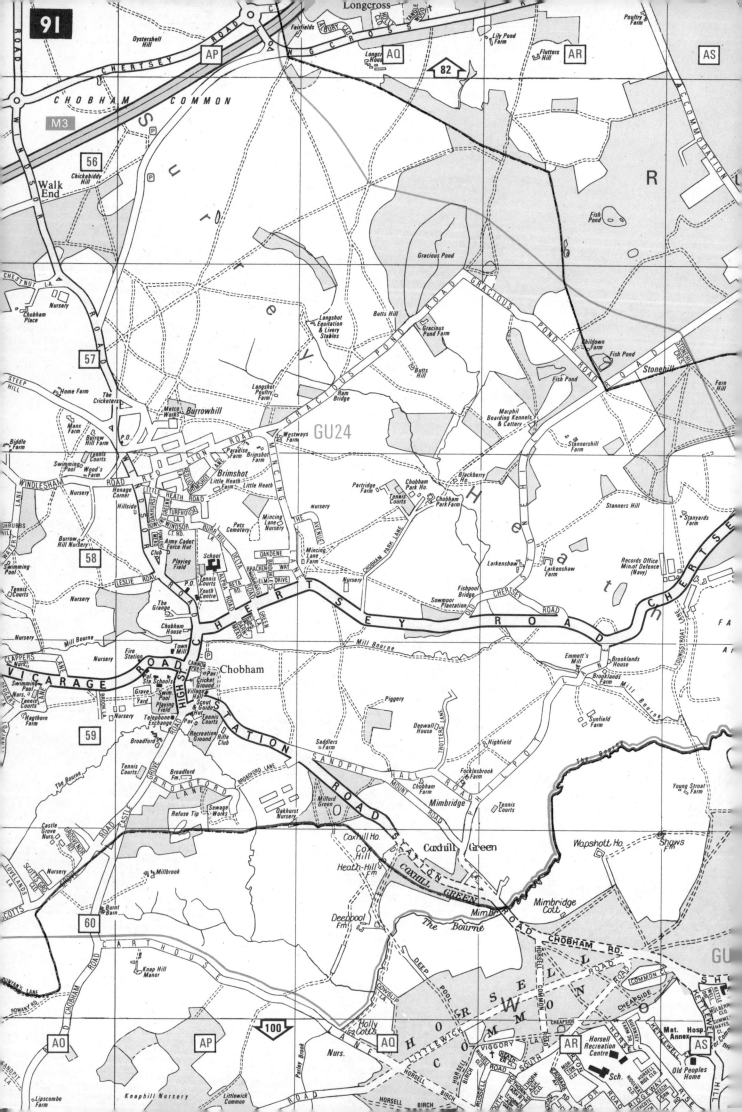

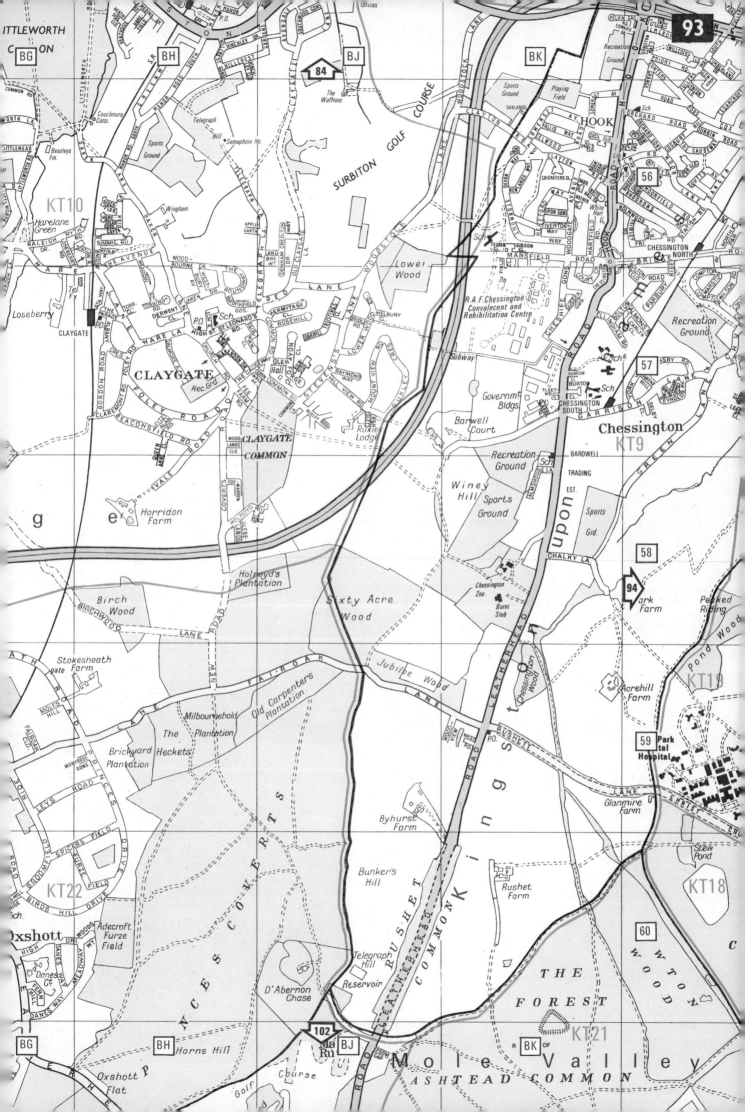

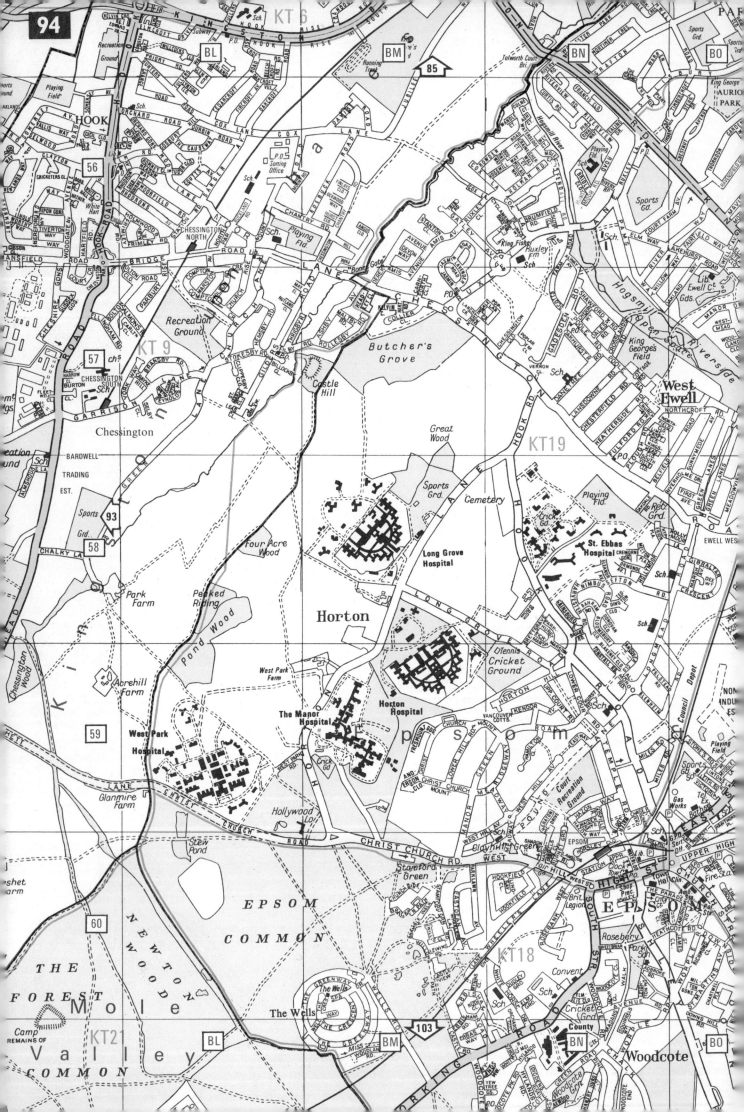

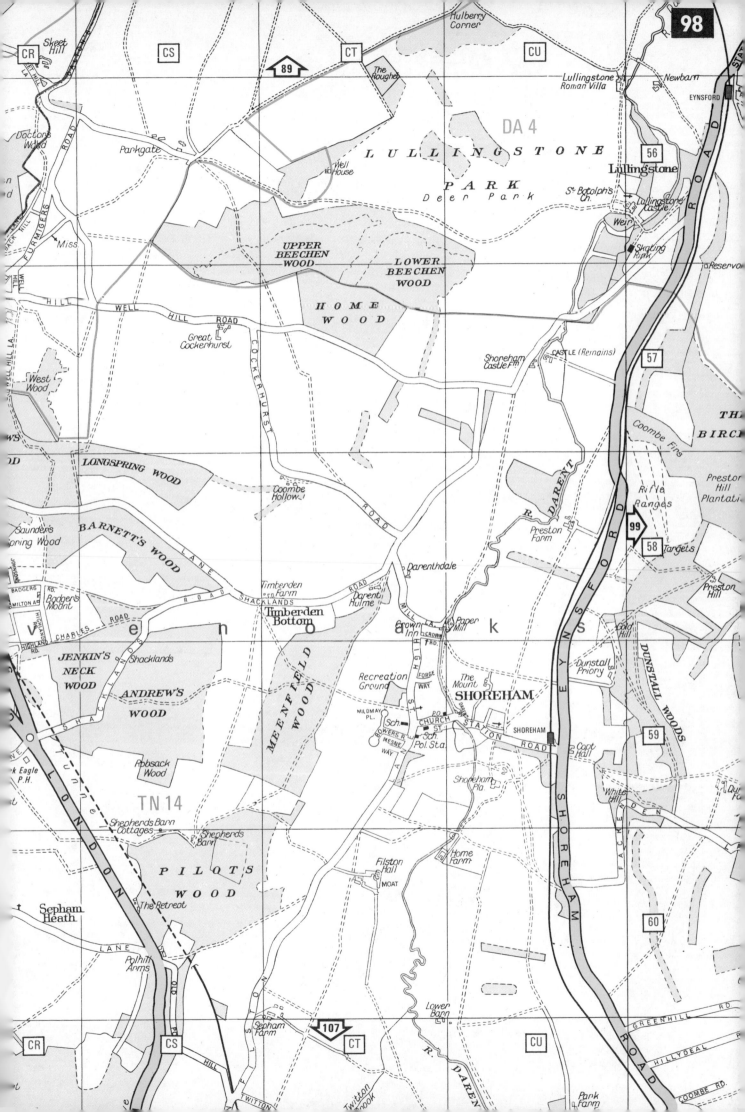

CR
CS
CT
89
CU

Hulberry Corner

Newbarn

Lullingstone Roman Villa

EYNSFORD

56

DA 4

LULLINGSTONE

The Roughet

PARK

Deer Park

St Botolph's Ch.

Lullingstone

Lullingstone Castle

Doctor's Wood

Skeet Hill

Parkgate

Well House

Weir

Skating Rink

Reservoir

FURMIGERS

ROAD

Miss.

HILL

WELL

HILL

ROAD

UPPER BEECHEN WOOD

LOWER BEECHEN WOOD

HOME WOOD

Shoreham Castle Fm

CASTLE (Remains)

57

THE BIRCH

West Wood

Great Cockerhurst

COCKERHURST

Coombe Fins

LONGSPRING WOOD

Coombe Hollow

ROAD

R. DARENT

Rifle Ranges

Preston Hill Plantation

Saunders Spring Wood

BARNETT'S WOOD

Preston Farm

99

58

Targets

Preston Hill

LANE

SHACKLANDS

Timberden Farm

ROAD

Darenthdale

BADGERS RD.

Badger's Mount

ROAD

Timberden Bottom

Darent Hulme

MILL LA.

Paper Mill

Cold Hill

V

e

n

o

Crown Inn

a

CROWN RD.

k

HIGHLAND AV.

HIGHLAND RD.

CHARLES ROAD

SHACKLANDS

Shacklands

Recreation Ground

FORGE WAY

The Mount

Dunstall Priory

DUNSTALL WOODS

JENKIN'S NECK WOOD

ANDREW'S WOOD

MEENFIELD WOOD

SHOREHAM

MILDMAY PL.

Sch.

P.O.

CHURCH ST.

STATION ROAD

Shoreham

59

Robsack Wood

BOWERS RD.

MESNE WAY

Sch.

Pol. Sta.

Capt Hall

TN 14

Black Eagle P.H.

LONDON ROAD

Shoreham Pla.

White Hill

FACKENDEN

Dur.

Shepherds Barn Cottages

Shepherds Barn

PILOTS WOOD

Home Farm

Filston Hall

MOAT

SHOREHAM ROAD

Sepham Heath

The Retreat

LANE

Polhill Arms

OLD

Sepham Farm

Lower Barn

60

R. DAREN

Park Farm

GREENHILL RD.

HILLYDEAL

CR
CS
107
CT
CU

TWITTON

Twitton Brook

R. DAREN

COOMBE RD.

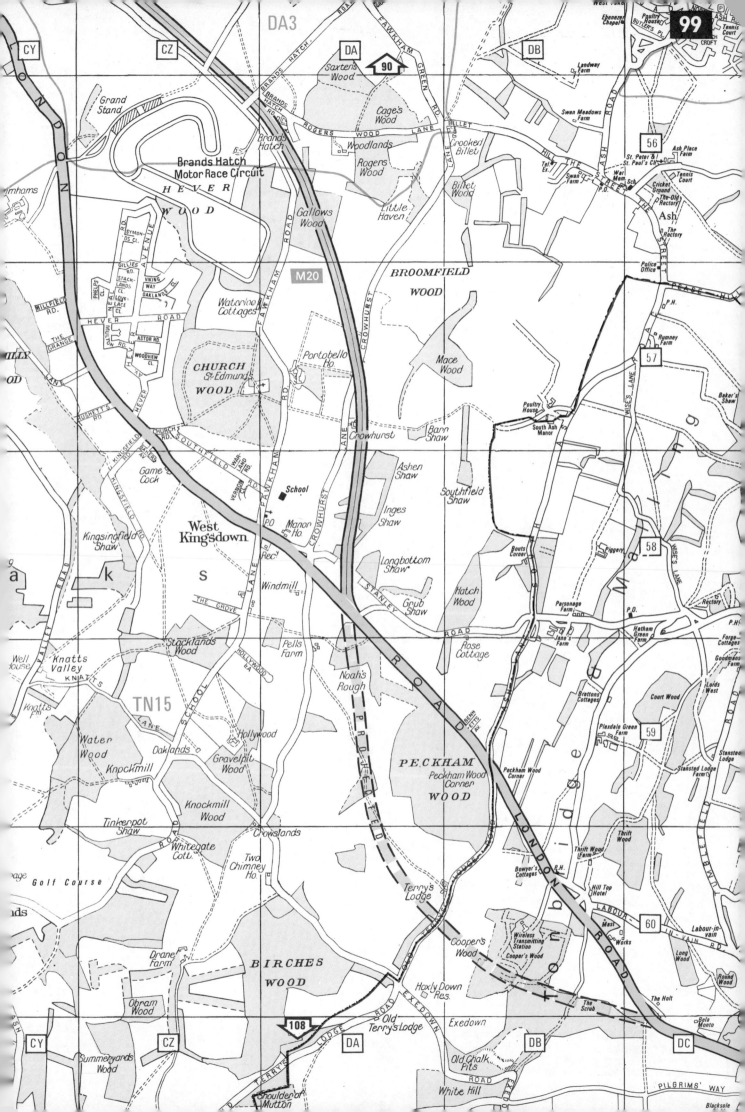

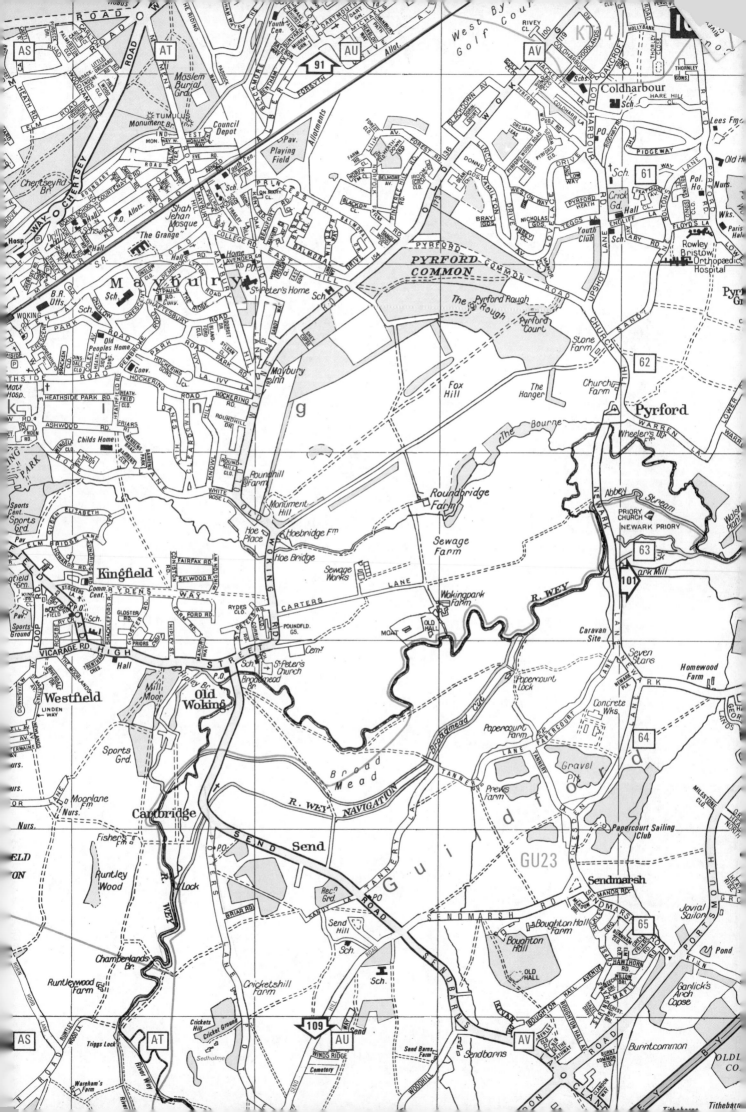

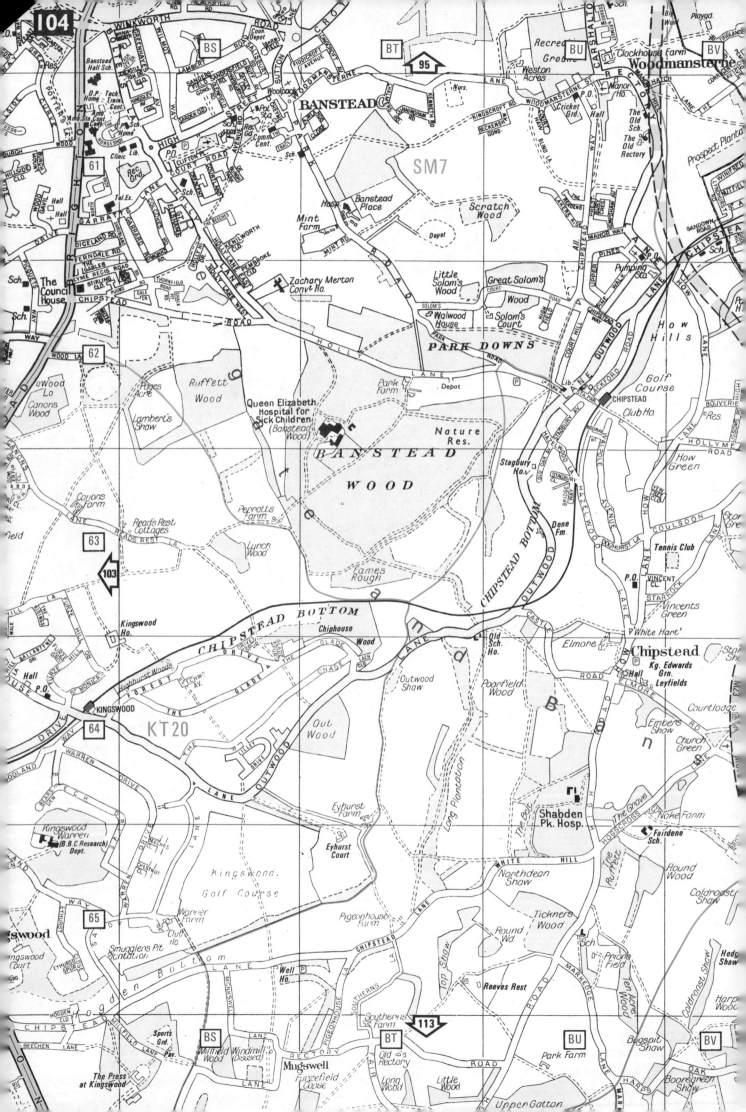

High Hill Road
Ebbuts Shaw
Greathill Shaw
Five Acre Shaw
Midgley Shaws
Honeyoak Wood
61
CG
Fickleshole Farm
Farm
Blackmans
Crookedash Shaw
Skid Hill
97
CH
CROWN
LANE
AERODROME
CJ
CK
Sr.
Cughom Lodge Wood
B
o
BIGGIN HILL
Costain Farm
Norheads
Victoria
Christy
Arthur Avenue
Sunningvale
Oaklands
Road
Cross
Victoria Gons
Magnolia Dri.
Acer Rd.
Kingsmead
Cemy.
Tel. Ex.
Recreat'n Grd.
Fire Sta.
Youth Centre
CHURCH
RD.

St Leonard's Church
Hedgers
LANE
RAILPIT RD.
Chelsham Court
62
Broom Lodge
Cony Crook
Hesiers Hill
HESIERS ROAD
BEDDLESTEAD
LANE
ROAD
Owls Wood
Mollards Wood
Jerry Reddins Shaw
Cowyard Shaw
NORHEADS
LANE
Long Coppice
Highfield Road
BEECH ROAD
KINGS ROAD
Melody
Spring
East
Alexandra
Swivelands
Bridlington
Home Wood
Sutherland
THE RICKETTS
Pimlico
Parsons Shaw
GROVE

PARK
CR3
Milberry Cottage
CHELSHAM ROAD
105
63
Beech FM.
LUMBERDINE WOOD
Ashen Shaw
Beddlested
Round Wood
Cherry Tree Shaw
Lusted Hall
Kemsley Rd.
Westmore Rd.
Goatsfield Rd.
Greenway
Crossways Rd.
Paynesfield Rd.
Johns Rd.
Georges Rd.
Cudham
Manor Ho. Manor
CROWN ROAD
Tatsfield Green

Kitchen Grove
Cheverells FM.
64
Longlands Shaw
Maesmaur
Ninehams
Westmore Green
Olde Ship
Ship Hill
Edgar Rd.
Rag Hill
Furze Corner
TATSFIELD
Middle Barns
Sch.
Tatsfield Firs
Church Lane
Church Cotts
P.

PITCHERS WOOD
TATSFIELD APPROACH
Clarkslane FM.
Clarkslane
CLARKS
WHITE LANE
LANE
Rectory
RECTORY RD.
Rectory
PILGRIMS
65
Botleyhill FM.
Botley
CLARKS
High Trees
TITSEY
ROAD
HILL
RH8
Pilgrims Lo. Farm
Clacket
g
e

Hell Shaw
Res.
TITSEY PLANTATION
Titsey Place
115
CG
CH
Titsey
CJ
Church Wood
CK
Flint Ho
TITSEY PARK
PILGRIMS WAY
BROOMLANDS LANE
Square Wood
Goldingham
FLICK

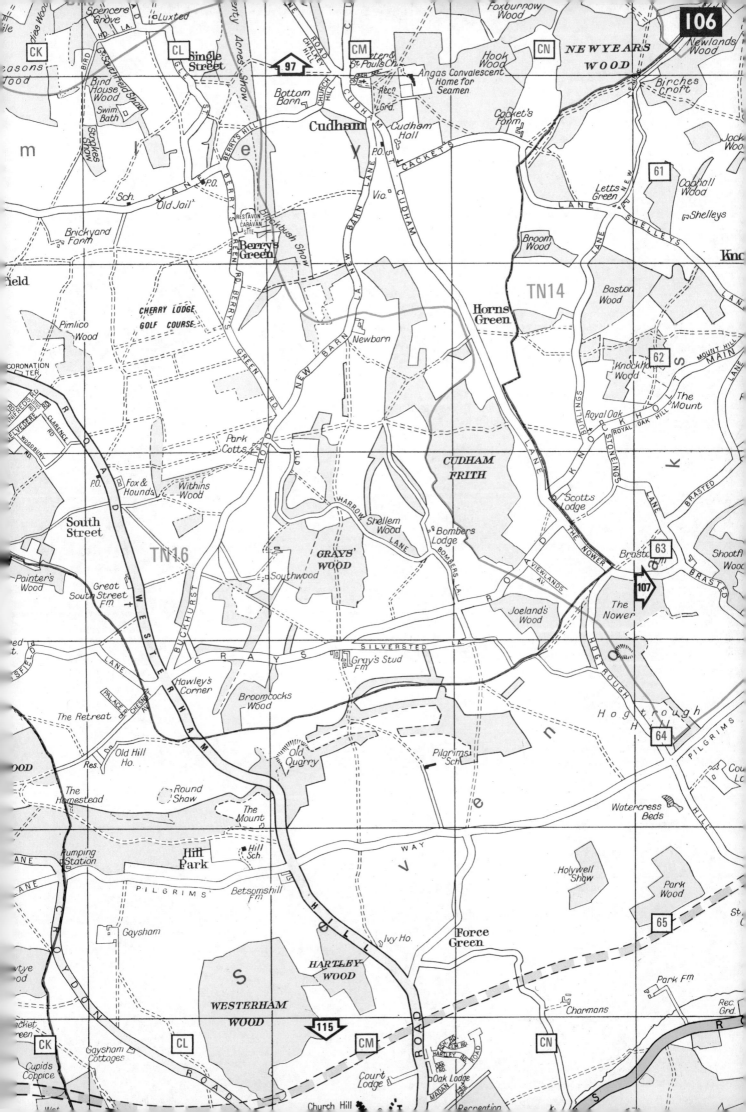

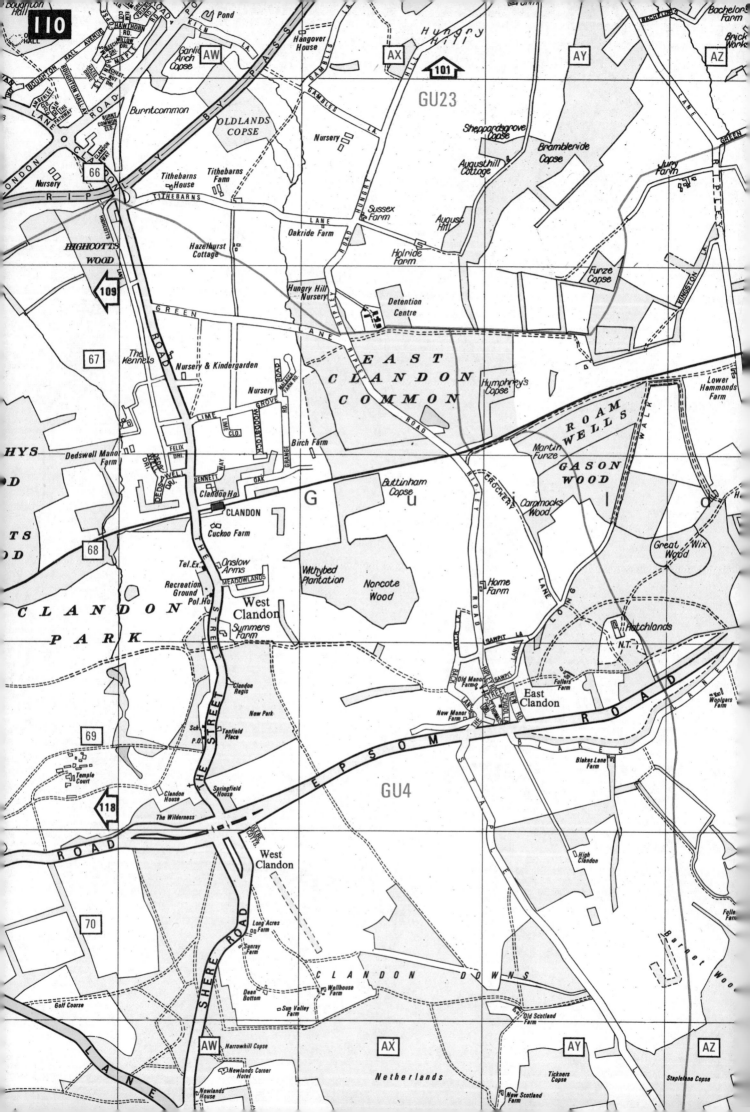

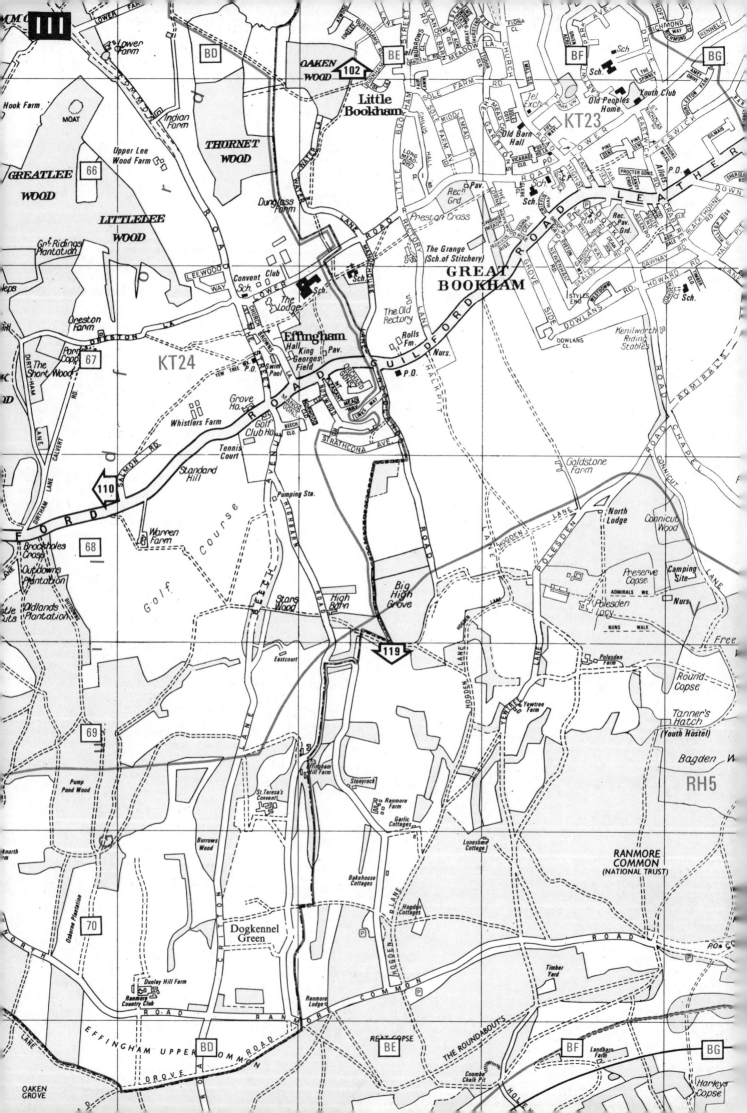

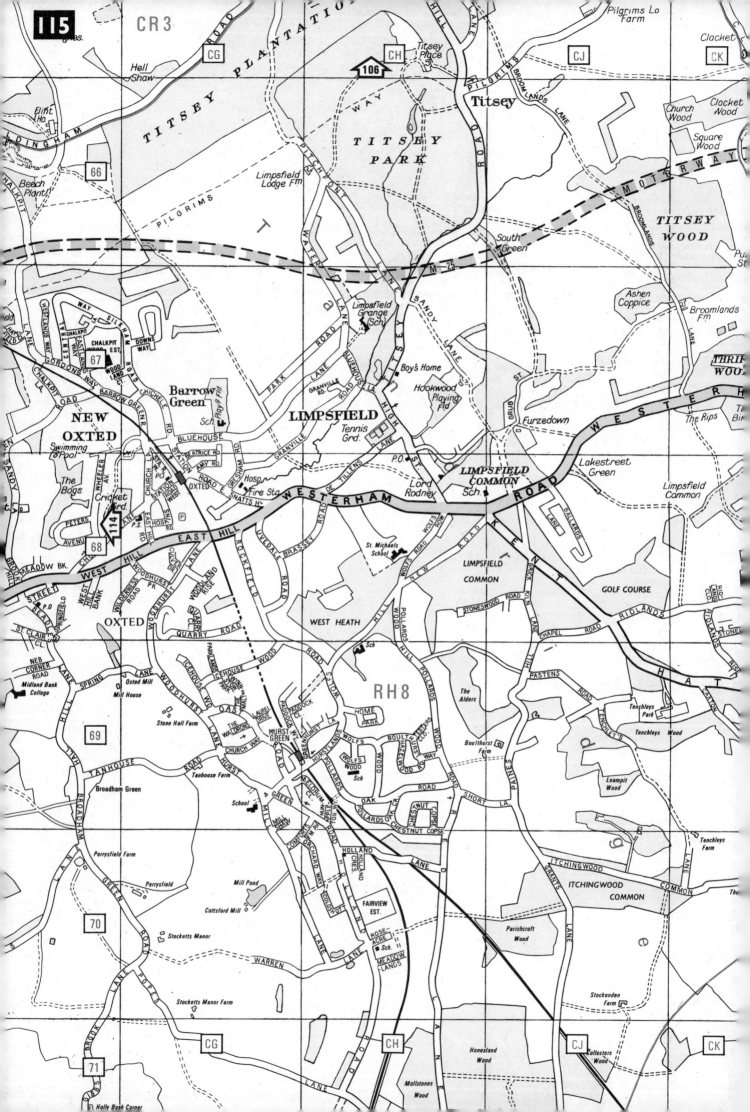

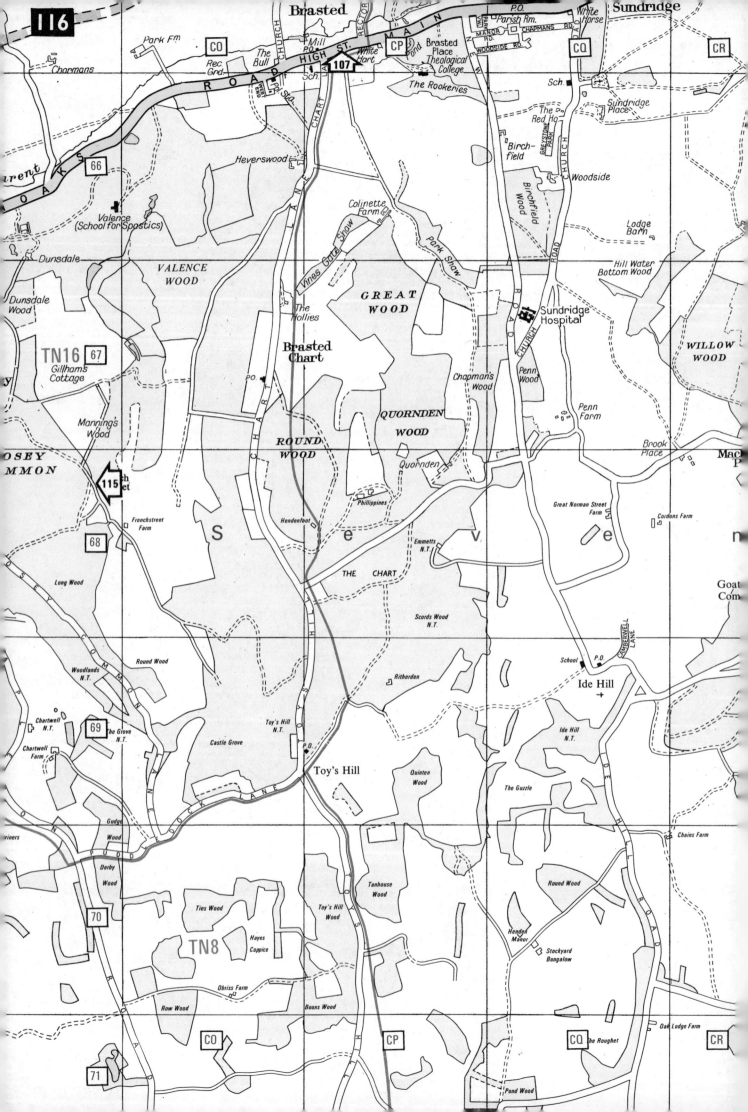

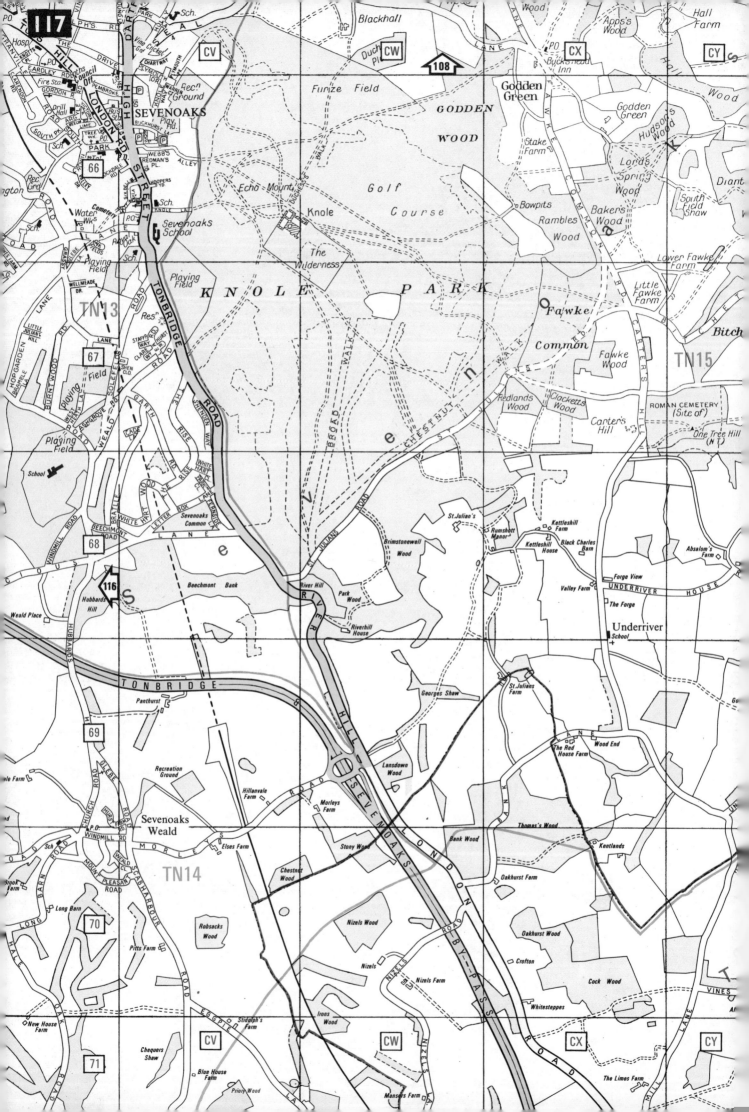

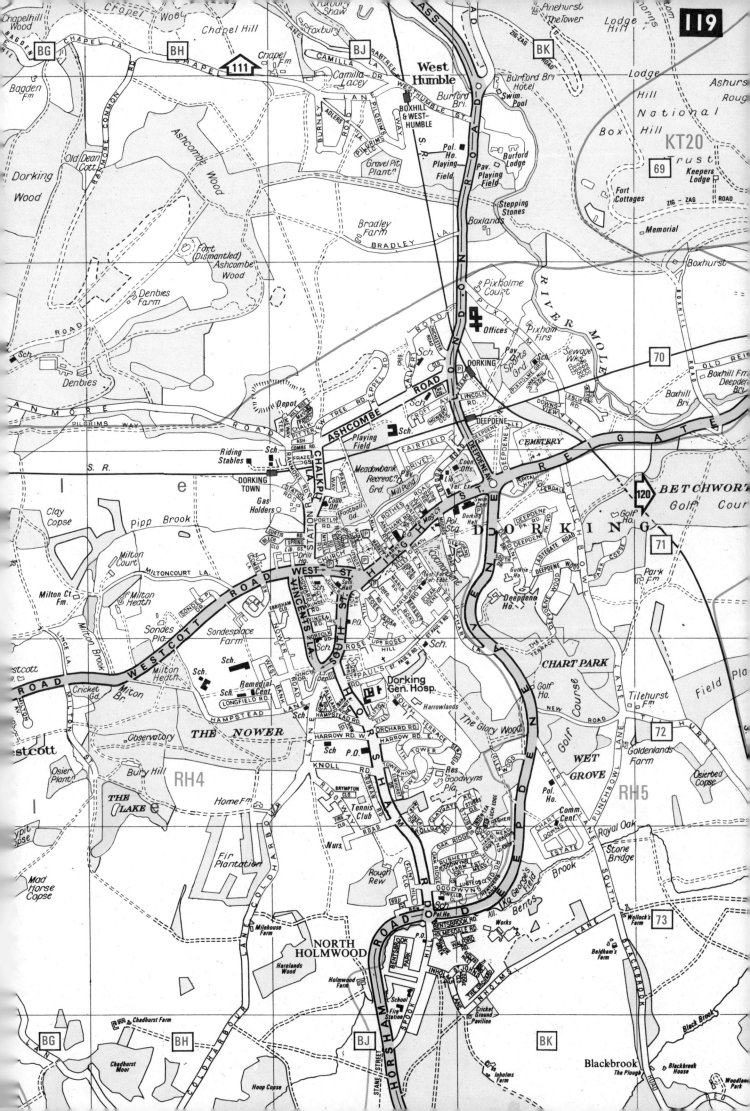

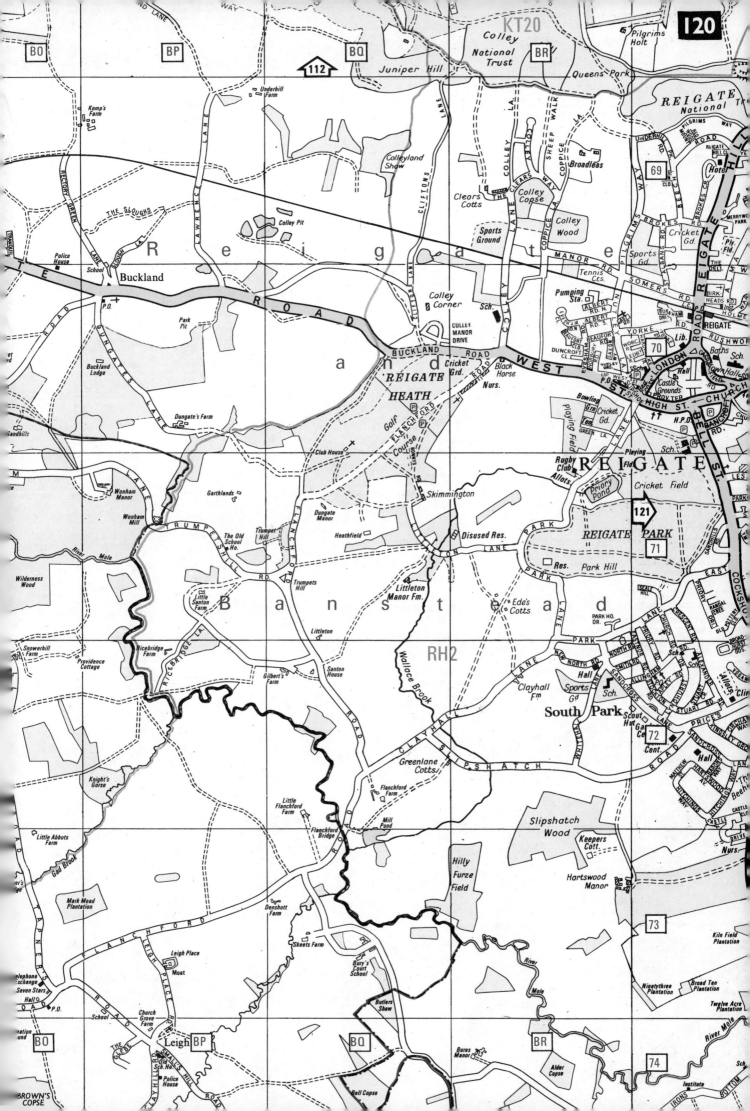

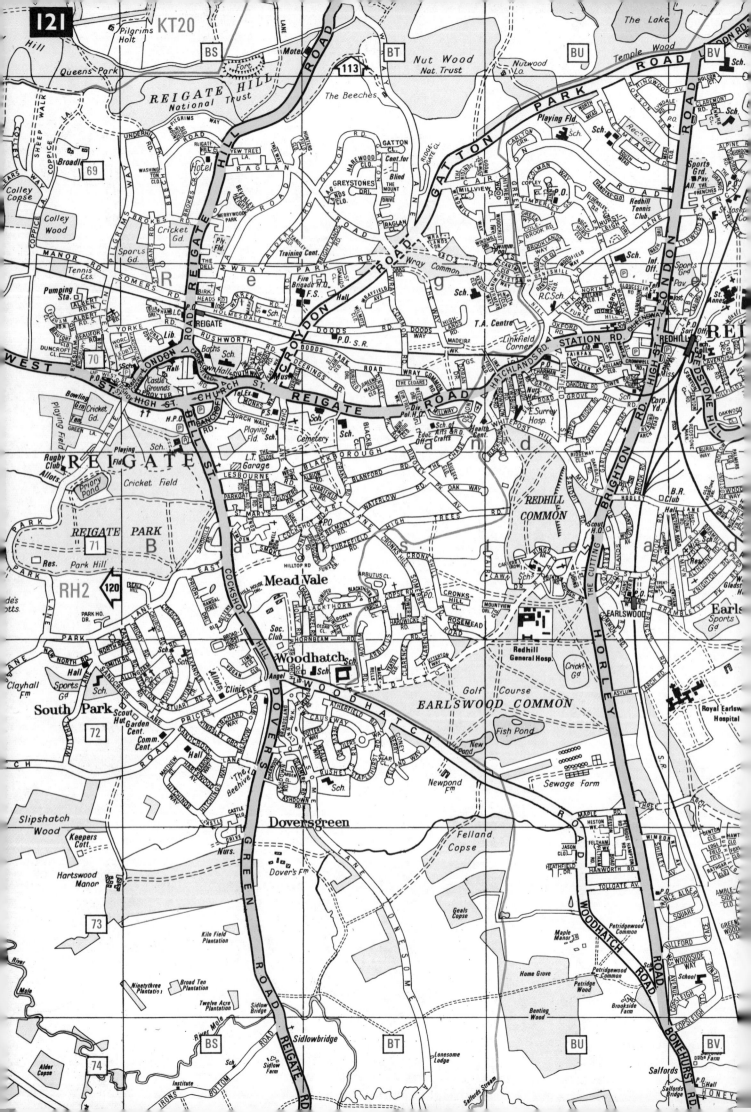

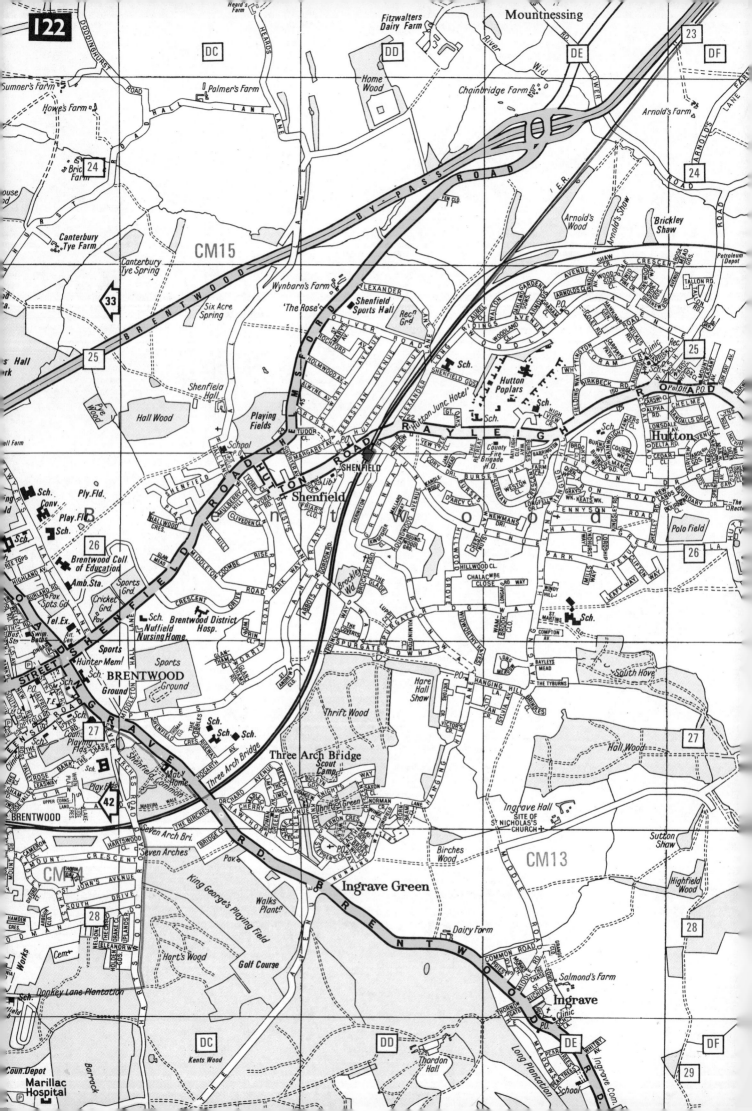

Index to Greater London Streets

Abbreviations of District Names

Amer.	Amersham	Grav.	Gravesend	Ruis.	Ruislip
Ashf.	Ashford	Grnf.	Greenford	St.Alb.	St.Albans
Ash.	Ashtead	Green.	Greenhithe	Saw.	Sawbridgeworth
Bans.	Banstead	Guil.	Guildford	Sev.	Sevenoaks
Bark.	Barking	Hmptn.	Hampton	Shep.	Shepperton
Barn.	Barnet	Harl.	Harlow	Sid.	Sidcup
Beac.	Beaconsfield	Har.	Harrow	Slou.	Slough
Beck.	Beckenham	Hart.	Hartley	Sthl.	Southall
Belv.	Belvedere	Hat.	Hatfield	Sth.Croy.	South Croydon
Berk.	Berkhamsted	Hav.	Havering-atte-Bower	S.Dnth.	South Darenth
Bet.	Betchworth	Hem.H.	Hemel Hempstead	S.Ock.	South Ockendon
Bex.	Bexley	Hert.	Hertford	Stai.	Staines
Bexh.	Bexleyheath	Hodd.	Hoddesdon	S.le H.	Stanford le Hope
Bish.	Bishops Stortford	Horn.	Hornchurch	Stan.	Stanmore
Borwd.	Boreham Wood	Hort.K.	Horton Kirby	Sun.	Sunbury-on-Thames
Brent.	Brentford	Houns.	Hounslow	Surb.	Surbiton
Brom.	Bromley	Ilf.	Ilford	Sutt.	Sutton
Brwd.	Brentwood	Ing.	Ingatestone	S.at H.	Sutton at Hone
Brox.	Broxbourne	Islw.	Isleworth	Swan.	Swanley
Buck.H.	Buckhurst Hill	Ken.	Kenley	Swans.	Swanscombe
Bush.	Bushey	Kes.	Keston	Tad.	Tadworth
Cars.	Carshalton	Kings.on T.	Kingston on Thames	Tedd.	Teddington
Cat.	Caterham	Kings.L.	Kings Langley	Th.Hth.	Thornton Heath
Ch.St.G.	Chalfont St.Giles	Leath	Leatherhead	Til.	Tilbury
Cher.	Chertsey	Long.	Longfield	Ton.	Tonbridge
Chesh.	Chesham	Loug.	Loughton	Twick.	Twickenham
Chess.	Chessington	Lthd.	Leatherhead	Upmin.	Upminster
Chig.	Chigwell	Maid.	Maidenhead	Uxb.	Uxbridge
Chis.	Chislehurst	Mitch.	Mitcham	Vir.W.	Virginia Water
Cob.	Cobham	Mord.	Morden	Wall.	Wallington
Couls.	Coulsdon	New A.G.	New Ash Green	Wal.Abb.	Waltham Abbey
Croy.	Croydon	N.Mal.	New Malden	Wal.Cr.	Waltham Cross
Dag.	Dagenham	Nthlt.	Northolt	Walt.	Walton-on-Thames
Dart.	Dartford	Nthwd.	Northwood	Warl.	Warlingham
Dor.	Dorking	Ong.	Ongar	Wat.	Watford
E.Mol.	East Molesey	Orp.	Orpington	Well.	Welling
Eden.	Edenbridge	Oxt.	Oxted	Welw.	Welwyn
Edg.	Edgware	Pnr.	Pinner	Welw.G.C.	Welwyn Garden City
Egh.	Egham	Pot.B.	Potters Bar	Wem.	Wembley
Enf.	Enfield	Pur.	Purley	West.	Westerham
Epp.	Epping	Rad.	Radlett	West Dr.	West Drayton
Eyns.	Eynsford	Rain.	Rainham	Wey.	Weybridge
Farn.	Farningham	Red.	Redhill	Whyt.	Whyteleafe
Fawk.	Fawkham	Reig.	Reigate	Wdf.Grn.	Woodford Green
Felt.	Feltham	Rich.	Richmond	W.Wick.	West Wickham
Ger.Cr.	Gerrards Cross	Rick.	Rickmansworth	Wind.	Windsor
Gdse.	Godstone	Rom.	Romford	Wok.	Woking
				Wor.Pk.	Worcester Park

General Abbreviations

All.	Alley	Fld.	Field	Pk.	Park
App.	Approach	Gdns.	Gardens	Pass.	Passage
Arc.	Arcade	Gth.	Garth	Peritr.	Perimiter
Av.	Avenue	Gte.	Gate	Pl.	Place
Bk.	Back	Gra.	Grange	Pr.	Prince,Princess
Bnk.	Bank	Gt.	Great	Prom.	Promenade
Boul.	Boulevard	Grn.	Green	Qn.	Queen
Br.	Bridge	Gro.	Grove	Ri.	Rise
Bldgs.	Buildings	Hth.	Heath	Rd.	Road
Chyd.	Churchyard	Hr.	Higher	S. Sth.	South
Circ.	Circle	Hl.	Hill	Sq.	Square
Cir.	Circus	Ho.	House	Sta.	Station
Clo.	Close	Kg.	King	St.	Street
Cor.	Corner	La.	Lane	Ter.	Terrace
Cotts.	Cottages	Lit.	Little	Trd.	Trading
Ct.	Court	Lo.	Lodge	Upr.	Upper
Cres.	Crescent	Lwr.	Lower	Vall.	Valley
Cft.	Croft	Mans.	Mansion	Vw.	View
Dr.	Drive	Mkt.	Market	Vill.	Villas
Dws.	Dwellings	Ms.	Mews	Wk.	Walk
E.	East	Mt.	Mount	W.	West
Embk.	Embankment	N. Nth.	North	Wf.	Wharf
Esp.	Esplanade	Orch.	Orchard	Wd.	Wood
Est.	Estate	Pde.	Parade	Yd.	Yard

Abberton Wk. Rain. CT37 59
Abbess Clo. SW2 BY47 76
Abbeville Rd. N8 BW31 47
Abbeville Rd. SW4 BW46 76
Abbey Av. St. Alb. BF15 9
Abbey Av. Wem. BL37 55
Abbey Cl. Wok. AV61 100
Abbey Clo. Nthlt. BE38 54
Abbey Clo. Pnr. BD31 45
Abbey Ct. Hmptn. BF51 84
Abbey Ct. St. Alb. BG14 9
Albert St.
Abbey Ct. Wal. Abb. CE20 21
Abbey Cres. Belv. CR42 69
Abbeydale Rd. Wem. BL37 55
Abbey Dr. Stai. AX52 83
Abbey Est. Beck. CE50 77
Abbeyfield Rd. SE16 CC42 67
Abbey Gdns. NW8 BT37 56
Abbey Gdns. Cher. AW53 83
Abbey Gdns. Ms. NW8 BT37 56
Abbey Gro. SE2 CO42 69
Abbey Hill Rd. Sid. CP47 79
Abbey La. E15 CF37 57
Abbey La. Beck. CE50 77
Abbey Mill End, St. Alb. BG14 9
Abbey Mill La. St. Alb. BG14 9
Abbey Orchard St. SW1 BW41 66
Abbey Park Est. Beck. CE50 77
Abbey Rd. E15 CF37 57
Abbey Rd. NW6 BS37 56
Abbey Rd. NW8 BT37 56
Abbey Rd. NW10 BM37 55
Abbey Rd. SE2 CP42 69
Abbey Rd. SW19 BT50 76
Abbey Rd. Bark. CL36 58
Abbey Rd. Belv. CP42 69
Abbey Rd. Bexh. CQ45 69
Abbey Rd. Cher. AW54 83
Abbey Rd. Croy. BY55 86
Abbey Rd. Enf. CA25 30
Abbey Rd. Est. NW8 BS37 56
Abbey Rd. Grav. DJ47 81
Abbey Rd. Green. DB46 80
Abbey Rd. Ilf. CM32 49
Abbey Rd. Shep. AZ55 83
Abbey Rd. Sth. Croy. CC58 96
Abbey Rd. Vir. W. AR53 82
Abbey Rd. Wal. Cr. CD20 21
Abbey Rd. Wok. AR62 100
Abbey St. E13 CH38 58
Abbey St. SE1 CA41 67
Abbey Ter. NW10 BL37 55
Abbey Ter. SE2 CP42 69
Abbey Vw. NW7 BO27 37
Abbey Vw. Wal. Abb. CE20 21
Abbey View Rd. St. Alb. BG13 9
Abbey Wk. E. Mol. BF52 84
Abbey Wd. La. Rain. CV37 60
Abbey Wood Rd. SE2 CO42 69
Abbot Clo. Stai. AX50 73
Bingham Dr.
Abbot Clo. Wey. AX59 92
Abbot Rd. Guil. AR71 118
Abbotsbury Clo. E15 CF37 57
Abbotsbury Clo. W14 BR41 65
Abbotsbury Gdns. Pnr. BD33 45
Abbotsbury Rd. W14 BR41 65
Abbotsbury Rd. Brom. CG55 88
Abbotsbury Rd. Mord. BS53 86
Abbots Clo. Brwd. DD26 122
Abbots Clo. Guil. AO72 118
Abbots Clo. Orp. CM54 88
Abbots Clo. Rain. CV37 60
Abbots Clo. Ruis. BD34 45
Abbots Clo. Uxb. AX39 53
Abbots Cres. Enf. BY23 29
Abbots Dr. Vir. W. AQ53 82
Abbots Dr. Wal. Abb. CH20 22
Abbotsford Av. N15 BZ31 48
Abbotsford Gdns. Wdf. Grn. CH30 40
Abbotsford Rd. Ilf. CO34 50
Abbots Gdns. N2 BT31 47
Abbots Grn. Sth. Croy. CC57 96
Abbotshall Av. N14 BW27 38
Abbotshall Rd. SE6 CF47 77
Abbots La. SE1 CA40 57
Abbots La. Ken. BZ61 105
Abbotsleigh Cl. Sutt. BS57 95
Camborne Rd.
Abbotsleigh Rd. SW16 BW49 76
Abbots Manor Est. SW1 BV42 66
Abbots Pk. SW2 BY47 76
Abbots Pk. St. Alb. BJ15 9
Abbots Pl. NW6 BS37 56
Abbot's Rd. E6 CJ37 58
Abbots Rd. Edg. BN29 37
Abbots Rd. Wat. BA19 17
Abbots Tilt Walt. BE55 84
Abbotstone Rd. SW15 BQ45 65
Abbot St. E8 CA36 57
Abbots Wk. Cat. CB64 105
Abbots Way Beck. CD53 87
Abbots Way, Guil. AU70 118
Abbots Way, Slou. AL40 61
Abbotsweld Harl. CN12 13
Abbotswell Rd. SE4 CD46 77
Abbotswood, Guil. AS69 118
Abbotswood Clo. Guil. AS69 118
Abbotswood Gdns. Ilf. CK31 49
Abbotswood Rd. SW16 BW48 76
Abbott Av. SW20 BQ51 85
Abbott Rd. E14 CF39 57
Abbotts Av. St. Alb. BH16 9
Abbotts Av. W. St. Alb. BG15 9
Abbotts Clo. Rom. CR31 50
Abbotts Clo. Swan. CU52 89
Abbotts Cres. E4 CF28 39
Abbotts Dr. Wem. BJ34 45
Abbott's Park Rd. E10 CF33 48
Abbotts Rise, Kings L. AY16 17
Abbott's Rd. Barn. BS24 29
Abbotts Rd. Mitch. BW52 86
Abbotts Rd. Sthl. BE40 54
Abbotts Rd. Sutt. BR56 94
Abbotts Vw. Kings L. AY17 17
Abbott's Wk. Bexh. CP43 69
Abbotts Wk. Wind. AM44 61
Abbscross Clo. Horn. CV33 51
Abbscross Gdns. Horn. CV33 51
Abbs Cross Rd. Horn. CV34 51
Abchurch La. EC4 BZ40 57
Abchurch Yd. EC4 BZ40 57
Abchurch La.
Abdale La. Hat. BP17 19
Abdale Rd. W12 BP40 55
Abel Clo. Hem. H. AZ13 8
Aberavon Rd. E3 CD38 57
Abercairn Rd. SW16 BW50 76
Aberconway Rd. Mord. BS52 86
Abercorn Clo. NW7 BR29 37
Abercorn Clo. NW8 BT38 56
Abercorn Cres. Har. BF33 45
Abercorn Est. Wem. BK37 54
Abercorn Gdns. Har. BK33 45
Abercorn Gdns. Rom. CO32 50
Abercorn Ms. NW8 BT37 56
Abercorn Pl. NW8 BT37 56
Abercorn Rd. NW7 BR29 37
Abercorn Rd. Stan. BK29 36
Abercrombie St. SW11 BU44 66
Abercrombie Way. Harl. CM12 13
Aberdale Gdns. Pot. B. BR19 19
Aberdale Rd. Enf. CB24 30
Aberdare Clo. W. Wick. CF55 87
Aberdare Gdns. NW6 BS36 56
Aberdare Gdns. NW7 BQ29 37
Aberdeen La. N5 BY35 47
Aberdeen Pk. N5 BY35 47
Aberdeen Pl. NW8 BT38 56
Aberdeen Rd. N5 BZ35 48
Aberdeen Rd. N18 CB28 39
Aberdeen Rd. SW19 BT51 86
Aberdeen Rd. Croy. BZ56 96
Aberdeen Rd. Har. BH30 36
Aberdeen Ter. SE3 CF44 67
Aberdeen Ter. SW19 BT51 86
Aberdour Rd. Ilf. CO34 50
Aberdour St. SE1 CA42 67
Aberfeldy St. E14 CF39 57
Aberford Gdns. SE18 CK44 68
Aberford Rd. Borwd. BM23 28
Aberfoyle Rd. SW16 BW50 76
Abergeldie Rd. SE12 CH46 78
Abernethy Rd. SE13 CG45 68
Abersham Rd. E8 CA35 48
Abery St. SE18 CN42 68
Abingdon Clo. NW1 BW36 56
Camden Sq.
Abingdon Clo. Uxb. AY37 53
Abingdon Pl. Pot. B. BS19 20
Abingdon Rd. N3 BT30 38
Abingdon Rd. SW16 BX51 86
Abingdon Rd. W8 BS41 66
Abingdon St. SW1 BX41 66
Abingdon Vill. W8 BS41 66
Abinger Av. Sutt. BQ58 94
Abinger Clo. Brom. CK52 88
Abinger Clo. Ilf. CO35 50
Abinger Clo. Wall. BX56 95
Abinger Gdns. Islw. BH45 64
Abinger Gro. SE8 CD43 67
Abinger La. Dor. BC73 119
Abinger Rd. W4 BO41 65
Ablemarle Way EC1 BY38 56
Clerkenwell Rd.
Ablett St. SE16 CC42 67
Abourne St. W9 BS38 56
Amberley Rd.
Aboyne Dr. SW20 BP51 85
Aboyne Rd. NW10 BN34 46
Aboyne Rd. SW17 BT48 76
Abridge Clo. Wal. Cr. CC21 30
Abridge Gdns. Rom. CR29 41
Abridge Rd. Chig. CM26 40
Abridge Rd. Epp. CN22 31
Abridge Way, Bark. CO37 59
Abyssinia Rd. SW11 BU45 66
Acacia Ave. Stai. AS45 62
Acacia Av. N17 BZ29 39
Acacia Av. Brent. BJ43 64
Acacia Av. Hayes BB39 53
Acacia Av. Horn. CT34 50
Acacia Av. Ruis. BC33 44
Acacia Av. Shep. AZ53 83
Acacia Av. Wem. BL35 46
Acacia Av. West Dr. AY40 53
Acacia Av. Wok. AR63 100
Acacia Clo. Orp. CM53 88
Acacia Clo. Stan. BH29 36
Acacia Dri. Wey. AV58 91
Acacia Dr. Sutt. BR54 85
Acacia Dr. Upmin. CX35 51
Acacia Gdns. Upmin. CZ33 51
Acacia Gdns. W. Wick. CF55 87
Acacia Gro. SE21 BZ48 77
Acacia Gro. N. Mal. BN52 85
Acacia Pl. NW8 BT37 56
Acacia Rd. E11 CG34 49
Acacia Rd. E17 CD32 48
Acacia Rd. N22 BY30 38
Acacia Rd. NW8 BT37 56
Acacia Rd. SW16 BX51 86
Acacia Rd. W3 BN40 55
Acacia Rd. Beck. CD52 87
Acacia Rd. Dart. CV47 80
Acacia Rd. Enf. BZ23 30
Acacia Rd. Green. CZ46 80
Acacia Rd. Guil. AR70 118
Acacia Rd. Hamptn. BF50 74
Acacia Rd. Mitch. BV51 86
Acacia Rd. Stai. AW49 73
Acacia St. Hat. BP14 10
Academy Gdns. Croy. CA54 87
Academy Gdns. Nthlt. BD37 54
Academy Rd. SE18 CK44 68
Acanthus Rd. SW11 BV45 66
Gideon Rd.
Accommodation La. West Dr. AW44 63
Accommodation Rd. Cher. AS56 91
Accomodation Rd. NW11 BR33 46
Accomodation Rd. Cher. AS55 82
Acer Av. Rain. CV38 60
Acer Rd. West. CJ61 106
Acfold Rd. SW6 BS44 66
Achilles Clo. Hem. H. AY12 8
Achilles Rd. NW6 BS35 47
Achilles St. SE14 CD43 67
Achilles Way W1 BV40 56
Acklam Rd. W10 BR39 55
Acklington Dr. NW9 BO30 37
Ackmar Rd. SW6 BS44 66
Ackroyd Dr. E3 CD39 57
Ackroydon Est. SW19 BQ47 75
Ackroyd Rd. SE23 CC47 77
Acland Cres. SE5 BZ45 67
Acland Rd. NW2 BP36 55
Linacre Rd.
Acme Rd. Wat. BC22 26
Acol Cres. Ruis. BC35 44
Acol Rd. NW6 BS36 56
Acomb Rd. Dag. CO37 59
Aconbury Rd. Dag. CO37 59
Stamford Rd.
Acorn Clo. E4 CE28 39
Lawns, The
Acorn Clo. Enf. BY23 29
Acorn Clo. Enp. CH23 31
Drapers Rd.
Acorn Gdns. SE19 CA51 87
Acorn Gdns. W3 BN39 55
Acorn Gro. Ruis. BB35 44
Acorn La. Pot. B. BX18 20
Acorn Pl. Wat. BC22 26
Acorn Pl. Est. SE15 CB44 67
Acorn Rd. Hem. H. AZ14 8
Acorns, The, Chig. CN28 40
Acorn Wk. SE16 CD40 57
Acrefield Rd. Ger. Cr. AR31 43
Acre La. SW2 BX45 66
Acre La. Cars. BV56 95
Acre Pass. Wind. AO44 61
Peascod St.
Acre Path Nthlt. BD36 54
Acre Rd. SW19 BT50 76
Acre Rd. Dag. CR36 59
Acre Rd. Kings. On T. BL51 85
Acres Av. Ong. CW16 24
Acres Gdns. Tad. BQ63 103
Acre St. SW8 BW44 66
Acre Way. Nthwd. BB30 35
Acris St. SW18 BT46 76
Acton Clo. Wal. Cr. CD19 21
Russell's Ride
Acton Est. E8 CA37 57
Acton La. NW10 BN38 55
Acton La. W3 BO41 65
Acton La. W4 BO41 65
Acton Park Ind. Est. W3 BN40 55
Acton St. WC1 BX38 56
Acuba Rd. SW18 BS47 76
Ada Gdns. E14 CF39 57
Ada Gdns. E15 CG37 58
Adair Rd. W10 BR38 55
Adam And Eve Ct. W1 BW39 56
Eastcastle St.
Adam And Eve Ms. W8 BS41 66
Adam Pl. N16 CA34 48
High St.
Adams Clo. Wem. BM34 46
Adams Gdns. Est. SE16 CC41 67
Adamson Rd. E16 CH39 58
Adamson Rd. NW3 BT36 56
Adamsrill Clo. Enf. BZ25 30
Adamsrill Rd. SE26 CC49 77
Adams Rd. N17 CA30 39
Adams Rd. Beck. CD52 87
Adam's Row W1 BV40 56
Adams Sq. Bexh. CP45 69
Adam St. W1 BV39 56
Adam St. WC2 BX40 56
Ada Pl. E2 CB37 57
Adare Wk. SW16 BX48 76
Ada Rd. SE5 CA43 67
Ada Rd. Wem BK34 45
Ada St. E8 CB37 57
Adcock Wk. Orp. CN56 97
Adderley Gdns. SE9 CL49 78
Adderley Gro. SW11 BV46 76
Culmstock Rd.
Adderley Rd. Har. BH30 36
Adderley St. E14 CF39 57
Addington Clo. Wind. AN45 61
Addington Dr. N12 BT29 38
Addington Gro. SE26 CD49 77
Addington Mans. N5 BZ35 48
Addington Rd. E3 CE38 57
Addington Rd. E16 CG38 58
Addington Rd. N4 BY32 47
Addington Rd. Croy. BY54 86
Addington Rd. Sth. Croy. CB59 96
Addington Rd. W. Wick. CF56 96
Addington Sq. SE5 BZ43 67
Addington St. SE1 BX41 66
Addington Village Rd. Croy. CD57 96
Addis Clo. Enf. CC23 30
Addiscombe Av. Croy. CB54 87
Addiscombe Clo. Har. BK32 45
Addiscombe Ct. Rd. Croy. CA54 87
Addiscombe Gro. Croy. BZ55 87
Addiscombe Rd. Croy. BZ55 87
Addiscombe Rd. Wat. BC24 26
Addison Av. N14 BV25 29
Addison Av. W11 BR40 55
Addison Av. Houns. BG44 64
Addison Av. Tedd. BJ50 74
Addison Bridge Pl. W14 BR42 65
Addison Clo. Nthwd. BB30 35
Addison Clo. Orp. CM53 88
Addison Cres. W14 BR41 65
Addison Gdns. W14 BQ41 65
Addison Gdns. Surb. BL52 85
Addison Gro. W4 BO41 65
Addison Pl. W11 BR40 55
Addison Rd. E11 CH32 49
Addison Rd. E17 CE32 48
Addison Rd. SE25 CB52 87
Addison Rd. W14 BR41 65
Addison Rd. Brom. CJ53 88
Addison Rd. Cat. BZ64 105
Addison Rd. Enf. CC23 30
Addison Rd. Guil. AS71 118
Addison Rd. Ilf. CM30 40
Addison Rd. Tedd. BJ50 74
Addison Rd. Wey. AW55 83
Addison Rd. Wok. AS62 100
Chertsey Rd.
Addisons Clo. Croy. CD55 87
Addison Way NW11 BR31 46
Addison Way Hayes BC39 53
Addison Way, Nthwd. BB30 35
Addle Hill EC4 BY39 56
Addlestone Park, Wey. AW56 92
Addlestone Rd. Wey. AY56 92
Adecroft Way E. Mol. BG52 84
Adela Av. N. Mal. BP53 85
Adelaide Av. SE4 CD45 67
Adelaide Clo. Enf. CA22 30
Adelaide Clo. Stan. BJ28 36
Adelaide Cotts. W7 BH40 54
Adelaide Gdns. Rom. CQ32 50
Adelaide Gro. W12 BP40 55
Adelaide Pl. Wey. BA56 92
Adelaide Rd. E10 CF34 48
Adelaide Rd. NW3 BT36 56
Adelaide Rd. W13 BJ40 54
Adelaide Rd. Ashf. AX49 73
Adelaide Rd. Chis. CL49 78
Adelaide Rd. Houns. BE44 64
Adelaide Rd. Ilf. CL34 49
Adelaide Rd. Rich. BL45 65
Adelaide Rd. Sthl. BE42 64
Adelaide Rd. Surb. BL53 85
Adelaide Rd. Tedd. BH50 74
Adelaide Rd. Til. DF44 71
Adelaide Rd. Walt. BC55 83
Adelaide Sq. Wind. AO44 61
Adelaide St. WC2 BX40 56
William Iv St.
Adelaide St. St. Alb. BG13 9
Adela St. W10 BR38 55
Kensal Rd.
Adele Ave. Welw. G. C. BR5 5
Adelina Gro. E1 CC39 57
Adeline Pl. WC1 BW39 56
Adelphi Cres. Hayes BB38 53
Adelphi Cres. Horn. CU34 50
Adelphi Gdns. Slou. AR41 62
Adelphi Rd. Epsom BN60 94
Adelphi Ter. WC2 BX40 56
Adam St.
Adelphi Way, Hayes BB38 53
Adeney Rd. W6 BQ43 65
Aden Gro. N16 BZ35 48
Aden Lo. N16 BZ35 48
Adenmore Rd. SE6 CE47 77
Aden Rd. Enf. CD24 30
Aden Rd. Ilf. CL33 49
Aden Ter. N5 BZ35 48
Adeyfield Gdns. Hem. H. AY13 8
Adeyfield Rd. Hem. H. AX13 8
Adhara Rd. Nthwd. BB28 35
Adie Rd. W6 BQ41 65
Adine Rd. E13 CH38 58
Adlers La. Dor. BJ69 119
Adler St. E1 CB39 57
Adley Rd. E5 CD35 48
Admaston Rd. SE18 CM43 68
Admiral Ct. Guil. AT70 118
Admiral Seymour Rd. SE9 CK45 68
Admiral, S Wk. Hodd. CE13 12
Admirals Rd. Lthd. BG66 111
Admiral's Rd. Lthd. BG67 111
Admiral St. SE8 CE44 67
Admirals Wk. NW3 BT34 47
Admirals Wk. Couls. BX63 104
Admirals Wk. St. Alb. BJ14 9
Admiralty Rd. Tedd. BH50 74
Adnams Wk. Rain. CT36 59
Adolf St. SE6 CE49 77
Adolphus Rd. N4 BY34 47
Adolphus St. SE8 CD43 67
Adomar Rd. Dag. CQ34 50
Adpar St. W2 BT39 56
Adrian Av. NW2 BP33 46
Adrian Clo. Uxb. AX30 35
Adrian Ms. SW10 BS43 66
Adrian Rd. Wat. BB19 17
Adrienne Av. Sthl. BE38 54
Adys Rd. SE15 CA45 67
Aere Clo. Orp. CN54 88
Aerodrome Rd. NW9 BO30 37
Aeroville, NW9 BO30 37
Affleck St. N1 BX37 56
Afghan Rd. SW11 BU44 66
Afton Dr. S. Ock. DA39 60
Agamemnon Rd. NW6 BR35 46
Agar Gro. NW1 BW36 56
Agar Gro. Est. NW1 BW36 56
Agar Pl. NW1 BW36 56
Agar Gro.
Agar St. WC2 BX40 56
Chandos Pl.
Agate Rd. W6 BQ41 65
Agates La. Ash. BK62 102
Agatha St. E1 CB40 57
Agaton Rd. SE9 CM48 78
Agave Rd. NW2 BQ35 46
Agdon St. EC1 BY38 56
Agincourt Rd. NW3 BU35 47
Agister Rd. Chig. CO28 41
Agnes Av. Ilf. CL34 49
Agnes Gdns. Dag. CP35 50
Agnes Rd. W3 BO40 55
Agnes St. E14 CD39 57
Agnew Rd. SE23 CC47 77
Agra Pl. E1 CB39 57
Agrarian Rd. Guil. AQ71 118
Agricola Pl. Enf. CA25 30
Main Av.
Aii. Harl. CO11 14
Aileen Wk. E15 CG36 58
Ailsa Av. Twick. BJ46 74
Ailsa Rd. Twick. BJ46 74
Ailsa St. E14 CF39 57
Ainger Rd. NW3 BU36 56
Ainsdale Clo. Orp. CM54 88
Ainsdale Cres. Pnr. BF31 45
Ainsdale Rd. W5 BK38 54
Ainsdale Rd. Wat. BD27 36
Ainsley Av. Rom. CR32 50
Ainsley St. E2 CB38 57
Ainslie Wk. SW12 BV47 76
Ainslie Wood Cres. E4 CE28 39
Ainslie Wood Gdns. E4 CE28 39
Ainslie Wood Rd. E4 CE28 39
Ainsworth Clo. NW2 BP34 46
Ainsworth Est. NW8 BT37 56
Ainsworth Rd. Croy. BY54 86
Aintree Av. E6 CK37 58
Aintree Clo. Slou. AV44 62
Aintree Clo. Uxb. AZ39 53
Aintree Cres. Ilf. CM30 40
Aintree Est. SW6 BR43 65
Aintree Gro. Upmin. CW34 51
Aintree Rd. Grnf. BJ37 54
Aintree St. SW6 BR43 65
Airdrie Clo. N1 BX36 56
Carnoustie Dr.
Airedale Hem. H. AY12 8
Wharfedale
Airedale Av. W4 BO42 65
Airedale Rd. SW12 BU47 76
Airedale Rd. W5 BK41 64
Airfield Way. Horn. CU36 59
Airfix Ct. Sun. BB51 83
Airlie Gdns. W8 BS40 56
Airlie Gdns. Ilf. CL33 49
Airmile La. Cob. BE61 102
Air St. W1 BW40 56
Glasshouse St.
Airthrie Rd. Ilf. CO34 50
Airway Clo. Wok. AQ63 100
Aisgill Av. SW5 BR42 65
Aislibie Rd. SE12 CG45 68
Aitken Rd. SE6 CE48 77
Aitken Rd. Barn. BQ25 28
Ajax Av. NW9 BO31 46
Ajax Rd. NW6 BS35 47
Akehurst St. SW15 BP46 75
Akenside Rd. NW3 BT35 47
Akerman Rd. SW9 BY44 66
Akerman Rd. Surb. BK53 84
Akers La. Rick. AU25 25
Alabama St. SE18 CM43 68
Alacross Rd. W5 BK41 64
Alamein Gdns. Dart. CY47 80
Alamein Rd. Swans. DB46 80
Alan Clo. Dart. CV45 70
Alandale Cres. Pot. B. BR19 19
Alandale Dr. Pnr. BC30 35
Alan Dri. Barn. BR25 28
Alan Gdns. Rom. CR33 50
Alan Rd. SW19 BR49 75
Alanthus Clo. SE12 CG46 78
Albacore Cres. SE13 CE46 77
Alba Gdns. NW11 BR32 46
Albain Cres. Ashf. AY48 73
Alban Av. St. Alb. BG12 9
Alban Cres. Borwd. BM23 28
Alban Cres. Farn. CX54 90
Albans La. NW11 BS33 47
West Hth. Dr.
Albans Vw. Wat. BC20 17
Albany Clo. SW14 BM45 65
Albany Clo. Bex. CP47 79
Albany Clo. Bush. BG25 27
Albany Clo. Esher BF58 93
Albany Clo. Uxb. AZ35 44
Albany Cotts. Esher. BE57 93
Albany Ct. NW9 BN30 37
Albany Cres. Edg. BM29 37
Albany Cres. Esher BH57 93
Albany Mans. SW11 BU43 66
Albany Ms. SE17 BZ43 67
Albany Rd.
Albany Pde. Brent BL43 65
Albany Rd.
Albany Pk. Av. Enf. CC23 30
Albany Pk. Rd. Kings. On T. BK50 74
Albany Pk. Rd. Lthd. BJ63 102
Albany Pass. Rich. BL46 75
Albany Pl. Brent. BK43 64
Albany Rd.
Albany Pl. Egh. AT49 72
Albany Pl. Epp. CN18 22
Albany Reach Surb. BH53 84
Albany Rd. E10 CE33 48
Albany Rd. E12 CJ35 49
Albany Rd. E17 CD32 48
Albany Rd. N4 BY32 47
Albany Rd. N18 CC28 39
Albany Rd. SE5 BZ43 67
Albany Rd. SW19 BS49 76
Albany Rd. W13 BJ39 54
Albany Rd. Belv. CQ43 69
Albany Rd. Bex. CP47 79
Albany Rd. Brent. BK43 64
Albany Rd. Brwd. DA25 33

Albany Rd. Chis.	CL49	78
Albany Rd. Enf.	CC22	30
Albany Rd. Horn.	CU33	50
Albany Rd. N. Mal.	BN52	85
Albany Rd. Rich.	BL46	75
Albert Rd.		
Albany Rd. Rom.	CQ32	50
Albany Rd. Walt.	BD56	93
Albany Rd. Wind.	AO44	61
Albany Rd. Wind.	AQ46	72
Albany St. NW1	BV37	56
Albany Ter. NW1	BV38	56
Euston Rd.		
Albany, The, W1	BW40	56
Vigo St.		
Albany, The, Wdf. Grn.	CG28	40
Albany Vw. Buck. H.	CH26	40
Alba Pl. W11	BR39	55
Portobello Rd.		
Albatross St. SE18	CM43	68
Albemarle App. Ilf.	CL32	49
Albemarle Av. Pot. B.	BS19	20
Albemarle Av. Wal. Cr.	CC17	21
Albemarle Clo. Grays.	DD41	71
Albemarle Gdns. Ilf.	CL32	49
Albemarle Gdns. N. Mal.	BN52	85
Albemarle Pk. Stan.	BK28	36
Albemarle Rd. Barn.	BU26	38
Albemarle Rd. Beck.	CE51	87
Albemarle St. W1	BV40	56
Albermarle Av. Twick.	BE47	74
Alberon Gdns. NW11	BR31	46
Alberta Av. Sutt.	BR56	94
Alberta Est. SE17	BY42	66
Alberta Rd. Enf.	CA25	30
Alberta Rd. Erith	CR44	69
Alberta St. SE17	BY42	66
Albert Av. E4	CE28	39
Albert Av. SW8	BX43	66
Albert Av. Ilf.	CM34	49
High Rd.		
Albert Br. SW3	BU43	66
Albert Br. SW11	BU43	66
Albert Br. Rd. SW11	BU43	66
Albert Carr Gdns. SW16	BX49	76
Albert Clo. N22	BW30	38
Albert Ct. SW7	BT41	66
Albert Ct. SW19	BR47	75
Albert Cres. E4	CE28	39
Albert Dri. Wok.	AU60	91
Albert Dr. SW19	BR48	75
Albert Dr. Wok.	AU61	100
Albert Embankment, SE1	BX42	66
Albert Gdns. E1	CC39	57
Albert Gdns. NW6	BR37	55
Albert Gate SW1	BU41	66
Rotten Row		
Albert Gro. SW20	BQ51	85
Albert Hall Ms. SW7	BT41	66
Prince Consort Rd.		
Albert Mans. SW11	BU44	66
Albert Pl. N3	BS30	38
Albert Pl. W8	BS41	66
Albert Rd. E10	CF34	48
Albert Rd. E17	CE32	48
Albert Rd. E18	CH31	49
Albert Rd. N4	BX33	47
Albert Rd. N15	CA32	48
Albert Rd. N22	BW30	38
Albert Rd. NW4	BQ31	46
Albert Rd. NW6	BR37	55
Albert Rd. NW7	BO28	37
Albert Rd. SE9	CK48	78
Albert Rd. SE20	CC50	77
Albert Rd. SE25	CB52	87
Albert Rd. W5	BJ38	54
Albert Rd. Ash.	BL62	103
Albert Rd. Ashf.	AY49	73
Albert Rd. Barn.	BT24	29
Albert Rd. Belv.	CQ42	69
Albert Rd. Bex.	CR47	79
Albert Rd. Brom.	CJ53	88
Albert Rd. Buck. H.	CJ27	40
Albert Rd. Dag.	CQ33	50
Albert Rd. Dart.	CV48	80
Albert Rd. Egh.	AR50	72
Albert Rd. Epsom.	BO60	94
Albert Rd. Har.	BG31	45
Albert Rd. Hayes.	BB41	63
Albert Rd. Hmptn.	BG49	74
Albert Rd. Houns.	BF45	64
Albert Rd. Ilf.	CL34	49
Albert Rd. Kings. On T.	BL51	85
Albert Rd. Mitch.	BU52	86
Albert Rd. N. Mal.	BO52	85
Albert Rd. Orp.	CO53	89
Albert Rd. Orp.	CO56	98
Albert Rd. Red.	BW68	113
Albert Rd. Rich.	BL46	75
Albert Rd. Rom.	CT32	50
Albert Rd. Sthl.	BD41	64
Albert Rd. Sutt.	BT56	95
Albert Rd. Swans.	DC46	81
Albert Rd. Tedd.	BH50	74
Albert Rd. Twick.	BH47	74
Albert Rd. Warl.	CD62	105
Albert Rd. West Dr.	AY40	53
Albert Rd. Wey.	AX55	83
Albert Rd. Wind.	AO45	61
Albert Rd. Est. Belv.	CQ42	69
Albert Rd. N. Reig.	BR70	120
Albert Rd. N. Wat.	BC24	26
Albert Rd. S. Reig.	BR70	120
Albert Rd. S. Wat.	BC24	26
Albert Sq. E15	CG35	49
Albert Sq. SW8	BX43	66
Albert St. N11	BW29	38
Albert St. N12	BT28	38
Lodge La.		
Albert St. NW1	BV37	56
Albert St. Brwd.	DB28	42
Albert St. St. Alb.	BG14	9
Albert St. Slou.	AP41	62
Albert St. Wat.	BD24	27
Queen's Rd.		
Albert St. Wind.	AN44	61
Albert Ter. NW1	BV37	56
Albert Ter. NW10	BO37	55
Albion Av. N10	BV30	38
Albion Av. SW8	BW44	66
Albion Bldgs EC1	BZ39	57
Bartholomews Clo.		
Albion Clo. W2	BU40	56
Albion St.		
Albion Clo. Rom.	CS32	50
Albion Clo. Slou.	AQ40	52
Albion Cres. Ch. St. G.	AQ27	34
Albion Dr. E8	CA36	57
Albion Est. SE16	CC41	67
Albion Gdns. W6	BP42	65
Albion Gdns. Dag.	CR35	50
Albion Gte. W2	BT40	56
Albion Gro. N16	BZ35	48
Albion Hill SE13	CE44	67
Albion Hill, Hem. H.	AX14	8
Albion Hill Loug.	CJ25	31
Albion Ms. W2	BU40	56
Albion Par. Grav.	DH46	81
Albion Pk. Loug.	CJ25	31
Albion Pl. EC1	BY39	56
Albion Pl. SE25	CB52	87
High St.		
Albion Rd. E17	CF31	48
Albion Rd. N16	BZ34	48
Albion Rd. N17	CA30	39
Reform Row		
Albion Rd. Bexh.	CR45	69
Albion Rd. Ch. St. G.	AQ27	34
Albion Rd. Grav.	DH47	81
Albion Rd. Hayes	BB39	53
Albion Rd. Houns.	BF45	64
Albion Rd. Kings. On T.	BN51	85
Albion Rd. Reig.	BT71	121
Albion Rd. St. Alb.	BH13	9
Albion Rd. Sutt.	BT57	95
Albion Rd. Twick.	BH47	74
Albion Sq. E8	CA36	57
Albion St. E15	CF37	57
Albion St. SE16	CC41	67
Albion St. W2	BU39	56
Albion St. Croy.	BY54	86
Albion Ter. E8	CA36	57
Albion Ter. Grav.	DH46	81
Albion Villas Rd. SE26	CC48	77
Albion Way, SE13	CF45	67
Albion Way, Wem.	BM34	46
Albrighton Rd. SE22	CA45	67
Albrook, Brwd.	CZ27	42
Albuhera Clo. Enf.	BY23	29
Albury Av. Islw.	BH43	64
Albury Av. Sutt.	BQ58	94
Albury Clo. Cher.	AQ55	82
Albury Clo. Hamptn.	BF50	74
Albury Dr. Pnr.	BD29	36
Albury Dr. Pnr.	BD30	36
Albury Gro. Wal. Cr.	CC18	21
Albury Ride, Wal. Cr.	CC19	21
Albury Rd. Bexh.	CQ44	69
Albury Rd. Chess.	BL56	94
Albury Rd. Guil.	AS71	118
Albury Rd. Watt.	BB57	92
Albury Wk. Wal. Cr.	CC19	21
Albyfield Brom.	CK52	88
Albyn Rd. SE8	CE44	67
Alcester Cres. E5	CB34	48
Alcester Rd. Wall.	BV56	95
Alcock Clo. Wall.	BW57	95
Alcock Rd. Houns.	BD43	64
Alcocks Clo. Tad.	BR63	103
Alcocks La. Tad.	BR64	103
Alconbury Rd. E5	CB34	48
Alcorn Clo. Sutt.	BS55	86
Aldam Pl. N16	CA34	48
High St.		
Aldborough Rd. Dag.	CS36	59
Aldborough Rd. Ilf.	CN33	49
Aldborough Rd. Upmin.	CW34	51
Aldborough Rd. N. Ilf.	CN32	49
Aldborough Rd. S. Ilf.	CN33	49
Aldborough Spur, Slou.	AP39	52
Aldbourne Rd. W12	BO40	55
Aldbridge St. SE17	CA42	67
Aldbury Av. Wem.	BM36	55
Aldbury Clo. Wat.	BD21	27
Aldbury Rd. Rick.	AV26	34
Aldbury St. SE8	CE43	67
Aldebert Ter. SW8	BX43	66
Aldeburgh Clo. E5	CB34	48
Southwold Rd.		
Aldeburgh Pl. Wdf. Grn.	CH28	40
Aldeburgh St. SE10	CH42	68
Alden Av. E15	CG38	58
Aldenham Av. Rad.	BJ21	27
Aldenham Gro. Rad.	BJ20	18
Aldenham Rd. Borwd.	BJ24	27
Aldenham Rd. Rad.	BJ21	27
Aldenham Rd. Wat.	BD25	27
Aldenham St. NW1	BW37	56
Aldenholme, Wey.	BB57	92
Aldensley Rd. W6	BP41	65
Alden Vw. Wind.	AL44	61
Alder Av. Upmin.	CW35	51
Alderbourne La. Iver	AT35	43
Alderbourne La. Slou.	AR35	43
Alderbrook Rd. SW12	BV46	76
Alderbury Rd. SW13	BP43	65
Alderbury Rd. Slou.	AS41	62
Alderbury Rd. W. Slou.	AS41	62
Alder Clo. SE15	CA43	67
Alder Clo. St. Alb.	BG17	18
Aldercoome La. Cat.	CA67	114
Alder Croft Couls.	BX57	95
Aldercroft Couls.	BX61	104
Alder Gro. NW2	BP34	46
Alderholt Way, SE15	CA43	67
Bedenham Way		
Alderley Ct. Berk.	AQ13	7
Alderman Ave. N. Slou.	AQ41	62
Alderman Av. Bark.	CO38	59
Aldermanbury, EC2	BZ39	57
Aldermanbury Sq. EC2	BZ39	57
Alderman Clo. Hat.	BQ15	10
Dixon's Hill Rd.		
Alderman's Hill N13	BX28	38
Aldermans. Wk. EC2	CA39	57
Bishopgate		
Aldermary Rd. Brom.	CH51	88
Aldermas St. W10	BQ39	55
Alderminster Rd. SE1	CB42	67
Aldermoor Rd. SE6	CD48	77
Alderney Av. Houns.	BF43	64
Alderney Gdns. Nthlt.	BE36	54
Alderney Rd. E1	CC38	57
Alderney Rd. Erith.	CU43	69
Alderney St. SW1	BV42	66
Alder Rd. SW14	BN45	65
Alder Rd. Sid.	CN48	78
Alder Rd. Uxb.	AX36	53
Alders Av. Wdf. Grn.	CG29	40
Aldersbrook Av. Enf.	CA23	30
Aldersbrook La. E12	CK34	49
Aldersbrook Rd. E11	CH34	49
Aldersbrook Rd. E12	CH34	49
Alders Clo. Edg.	BN28	37
Aldersey Gdns. Bark.	CM36	58
Aldersey Rd. Guil.	AS70	118
Aldersford Clo. SE4	CD45	67
Frendsbury Rd.		
Aldersgate St. EC1	BZ39	57
Alders Gro. E. Mol.	BG53	84
Aldersgrove Wal. Abb.	CG20	22
Roundhills		
Aldersgrove Av. SE9	CJ48	78
Aldershot Rd. NW6	BR37	55
Aldershot Rd. Guil.	AO68	109
Aldershot Rd. Guil.	AO69	118
Aldershot Ter. SE18	CK43	68
Imperial Way		
Alderside Clo. Egh.	AS49	72
Alderside Wk. Egh.	AS49	72
Aldersmead Av. Croy.	CC53	87
Aldersmead Rd. Beck.	CD50	77
Alderson St. W10	BR38	55
Kensal Rd.		
Alders Rd. Edg.	BO28	37
Alders Rd. Reig.	BS69	121
Alderstead La. Red.	BW66	113
Alders, The, N21	BY25	29
Alders, The, Felt.	BE49	74
Alders, The, Houns.	BE42	64
Alders, The, W. Wick.	CE54	87
Alderton Clo. SE5	BZ45	67
Alderton Clo. Loug.	CL24	31
Alderton Cres. NW4	BP32	46
Alderton Hall La. Loug.	CL24	31
Alderton Hill Loug.	CK25	31
Alderton Rise. Loug.	CL24	31
Alderton Rd. SE24	BZ45	67
Alderton Rd. Croy.	CA54	87
Alderton Way NW4	BP32	46
Alderton Cres.		
Alderton Way Loug.	CK25	31
Alderville Rd. SW6	BR44	65
Alder Way Swan.	CS51	89
Alderwick Dr. Houns.	BG45	64
Alderwood Clo. Cat.	CA66	114
Alderwood Rd. SE9	CM46	78
Alderwood Rom.	CO24	32
Aldford St. W1	BV40	56
Aldgate Av. E1	CA39	57
Aldgate High St. EC3	CA39	57
Aldham Hall, E11	CH32	49
Aldin Ave. Slou.	AQ41	62
Aldine Ct. W12	BQ41	65
Aldine Cres. W12	BQ41	65
Aldine St. W12	BQ41	65
Aldingham Gdns. Horn.	CU35	50
Aldington Rd. SE7	CJ41	68
Aldis Ms. SW17	BU49	76
Aldis St.		
Aldis St. SW17	BU49	76
Aldock. Welw. G. C.	BS9	5
Aldred Rd. NW6	BS35	47
Aldren Rd. SW17	BT48	76
Aldriche Cres. Croy.	CF58	96
Aldriche Way, E4	CF29	39
Aldridge Av. Edg.	BM27	37
Aldridge Av. Enf.	CE22	30
Aldridge Av. Ruis.	BD34	45
Aldridge Av. Stan.	BL30	37
Aldridge Rise N. Mal.	BO54	85
Aldridge Rd. Vill. W11	BR39	55
Aldrington Rd. SW16	BW49	76
Aldsworth Clo. W9	BS38	56
Amberley Est.		
Aldwick Clo. SE9	CM48	78
Aldwick Ct. St. Alb.	BJ14	9
Aldwick Rd. Croy.	BX55	86
Aldworth Gr. SE13	CF46	77
Aldworth Rd. E15	CG36	58
Aldwych, WC2	BX40	56
Aldwych Av. Ilf.	CM31	49
Aldwych Clo. Horn.	CU34	50
Aldykes, Hat.	BO12	10
Alers Rd. Bexh.	CP46	79
Alexander Av. NW10	BP36	55
Alexander Clo. Brom.	CH54	88
Alexander Clo. Sid.	CN46	78
Alexander Clo. Twick.	BH48	74
Alexander Ct. N14	BW25	29
Alexander Godley Clo. Ash.	BL63	103
Alexander La. Brwd.	DD25	122
Alexander Ms. W2	BS39	56
Alexander St.		
Alexander Pl. SW7	BU42	66
Alexander Rd. N19	BX34	47
Alexander Rd. Bexh.	CP44	69
Alexander Rd. Chis.	CL49	78
Alexander Rd. Couls.	BV61	104
Alexander Rd. Green.	DB46	80
Alexander Rd. Reig.	BS72	121
Alexander Sq. SW3	BU41	66
Alexander St. W2	BS39	56
Alexandra Ave. Warl.	CD62	105
Alexandra Av. N22	BW30	38
Alexandra Av. SW11	BV44	66
Alexandra Av. W4	BN43	65
Alexandra Av. Har.	BE33	45
Alexandra Av. Sthl.	BE40	54
Alexandra Av. Sutt.	BS55	86
Alexandra Clo. Ashf.	BA50	73
Alexandra Clo. Grays.	DG41	71
Alexandra Clo. Har.	BF34	45
Alexandra Clo. Stai.	AX50	73
Alexandra Cotts. SE14	CD44	67
Alexandra Ct. W9	BT38	56
Alexandra Ct. Wem.	BL35	46
Alexandra Cres. Brom.	CG50	78
Alexandra Dr. SE19	CA49	77
Alexandra Dr. Surb.	BM54	85
Alexandra Gdns. N10	BV31	47
Alexandra Gdns. W4	BO43	65
Alexandra Gdns. Cars.	BU58	95
Alexandra Gdns. Houns.	BF44	64
Alexandra Gro. N4	BY33	47
Alexandra Gro. N12	BS29	38
Alexandra Ms. NW8	BS37	56
Alexandra Pk. Rd. N10	BV30	38
Alexandra Pk. Rd. N22	BV30	38
Alexandra Pl. SE25	BZ53	87
Alexandra Pl. Croy.	CA54	87
Alexandra Rd. E6	CL38	58
Alexandra Rd. E10	CF34	48
Alexandra Rd. E17	CD32	48
Alexandra Rd. E18	CH31	49
Alexandra Rd. N8	BY31	47
Alexandra Rd. N9	CB26	39
King Edwards Rd.		
Alexandra Rd. N10	BV30	38
Alexandra Rd. N15	BZ32	48
Alexandra Rd. NW4	BQ31	46
Alexandra Rd. NW8	BS37	56
Alexandra Rd. NW8	BT37	56
Alexandra Rd. SE26	CC50	77
Alexandra Rd. SW14	BN45	65
Alexandra Rd. SW19	BR50	75
Alexandra Rd. W4	BN41	65
Alexandra Rd. Ashf.	BA50	73
Alexandra Rd. Borwd.	BN22	28
Alexandra Rd. Borwd.	BN23	28
Alexandra Rd. Brent.	BK43	64
Alexandra Rd. Brwd.	DB27	42
Alexandra Rd. Croy.	CA54	87
Alexandra Rd. Egh.	AR50	72
Alexandra Rd. Egh.	AT49	72
Alexandra Rd. Enf.	CC24	30
Alexandra Rd. Epsom.	BO60	94
Alexandra Rd. Erith	CT43	69
Alexandra Rd. Grav.	DJ47	81
Alexandra Rd. Hem. H.	AX13	8
Alexandra Rd. Houns.	BF44	64
Alexandra Rd. Kings L.	AW18	17
Alexandra Rd. Kings L.	AZ18	17
Alexandra Rd. Kings. On T.	BM50	75
Alexandra Rd. Mitch.	BU50	76
Alexandra Rd. Rain.	CT37	59
Alexandra Rd. Rich.	BL44	65
Alexandra Rd. Rick.	AW21	26
Alexandra Rd. Rom.	CP32	50
Alexandra Rd. Rom.	CQ32	50
Alexandra Rd. Rom.	CT32	50
Alexandra Rd. St. Alb.	BH13	9
Alexandra Rd. St. Alb.	BK16	18
Alexandra Rd. Slou.	AO41	61
Alexandra Rd. Surb.	BH53	84
Alexandra Rd. Til.	DF44	71
Alexandra Rd. Twick.	BK46	74
Alexandra Rd. Uxb.	AX37	53
Alexandra Rd. Warl.	CD62	105
Alexandra Rd. Wat.	BC23	26
Alexandra Rd. West.	CH63	106
Alexandra Rd. Wey.	AX56	92
Alexandra Sq. Mord.	BS53	86
Alexandra St. E16	CH39	58
Alexandra St. SE14	CD43	67
Bowerman Av.		
Alexandra Ter. Guil.	AS71	118
Alexandra Wk. SE19	CA49	77
Alexandra Way, Wal. Cr.	CD20	21
Alexandria Rd. W13	BJ40	54
Alexis St. SE16	CB42	67
Alex St. Chesh.	AO18	16
Alfan La. Dart.	CS49	79
Alford Grn. Croy.	CF57	96
Alford Pl. N1	BZ37	57
Shepherders Wk.		
Alford Rd. SW8	BW44	66
Union Gro.		
Alford Rd. Erith	CS42	69
Alfoxton Av. N15	BY31	47
Alfreda St. SW11	BV44	66
Alfred Cotts. SW17	BU49	76
Alfred Gdns. Sthl.	BE40	54
Alfred Ms. W1	BW39	56
Alfred Ms. W3	BN40	55
Alfred Pl. WC1	BW39	56
Alfred Rd. E15	CG35	49
Alfred Rd. SE25	CB53	87
Alfred Rd. W2	BS39	56
Alfred Rd. W3	BN40	55
Alfred Rd. W13	BJ40	54
Alfred Rd. Belv.	CQ42	69
Alfred Rd. Brwd.	DB27	42
Alfred Rd. Buck. H.	CJ27	40
Alfred Rd. Dart.	CW49	80
Alfred Rd. Felt.	BD48	74
Alfred Rd. Grav.	DG48	81
Alfred Rd. Kings. On T.	BL52	85
Alfred Rd. S. Ock.	CW40	60
Alfred Rd. Sutt.	BT56	95
Alfred's Gdns. Bark.	CN37	58
Alfred St. E3	CD38	57
Alfred St. E16	CG40	58
Alfred St. Grays.	DE43	71
Alfred's Way, Bark.	CM37	58
Alfreton Clo. SW19	BQ48	75
Alfreton St. SE17	CA42	67
Alfriston Surb.	BL53	85
Alfriston Av. Croy.	BX54	86
Alfriston Av. Har.	BF32	45
Alfriston Rd. SW11	BU45	66
Algar Clo. Islw.	BJ45	64
Algar Rd. Islw.	BJ45	64
Algarve Rd. SW18	BS47	76
Algernon Rd. NW4	BP32	46
Algernon Rd. NW6	BS37	56
Algernon Rd. SE13	CE45	67
Algers Clo. Loug.	CJ25	31
Algers Mead. Loug.	CJ25	31
Algers Rd. Loug.	CJ25	31
Algiers Rd. SE13	CE45	67
Alibon Gdns. Dag.	CR35	50
Alibon Rd. Dag.	CR35	50
Alice Gilliat Ct. W14	BR43	65
Alice St. SE1	CA41	67
Alicia Av. Har.	BJ31	45
Alicia Clo. Har.	BK31	45
Alicia Gdns. Har.	BJ31	45
Alie St. E1	CA39	57
Alington Cres. NW9	BN33	46
Alington Gro. Wall.	BW58	95
Aliwal Rd. SW11	BU45	66
Alkerden La. Green.	DB46	80
Alkerden Rd. W4	BO42	65
Alkham Rd. N16	CA33	48
Allan Clo. Dart.	CY47	80
Allan Clo. N. Mal.	BN53	85
Allandale Av. N3	BR31	46
Allandale Rd. Enf.	CC21	30
Allandale Rd. Horn.	CT33	50
Allanmouth Rd. E3	CD36	57
Allan Way, W3	BN39	55
Allard Clo. Orp.	CP54	89
Allard Clo. Wal. Cr.	CA17	21
Allard Cres. Bush.	BG27	36
Allard Way, Brox.	CD14	12
Allardyce St. SW9	BX45	66
Allas Rd. E2	CC38	57
Allbrook Clo. Tedd.	BH49	74
Alldicks Rd. Hem. H.	AY14	8
Allenby Av. Sth. Croy.	BZ58	96
Allenby Clo. Grnf.	BF38	54
Allenby Cres. Grays.	DD42	71
Allenby Dr. Horn.	CW33	51
Allenby Rd. SE23	CD48	77
Allenby Rd. Sthl.	BF38	54
Allenby Rd. West.	CK62	106
Allen Clo. Sun.	BC51	83
Allendale, St. Alb.	BF15	9
Allendale Av. Sthl.	BF39	54
Allendale Rd. SE5	BZ44	67
Allendale Rd. Grnf.	BJ36	54
Allendale Rd. Hem. H.	AX12	8
Allendale Rd. Hem. H.	AX13	8
Allen Edwards Dr. SW8	BX44	66
Allen Rd. E3	CD37	57
Allen Rd. N16	CA35	48
Allen Rd. Beck.	CC51	87
Allen Rd. Croy.	BX54	86
Allen Rd. Lthd.	BF66	111
Allen Rd. Rain.	CV38	60
Allen Rd. Sun.	BC51	83
Allen's Rd. Enf.	CC25	30
Allen St. W8	BS41	66
Allenswood Rd. SE9	CK45	68
Allerford Ct. Har.	BF32	45
Allerford Rd. SE6	CE48	77
Allerton Clo. Borwd.	BL22	28
Allerton Rd. N16	BZ34	48
Allerton Rd. Borwd.	BL22	28
Allerton Wk. N7	BX34	47
Andover Est.		
Allestree Rd. SW6	BR43	65
All Hallows Rd. N17	CA30	39
Roundway, The		
Alleyn Cres. SE21	BZ48	77
Alleyndale Rd. Dag.	CP34	50
Alleyn Pk. SE21	BZ47	77
Alleyn Pk. Sthl.	BE42	64
Alleyn Pk. Est. SE21	CA49	77
Alleyn Rd. SE21	BZ48	77
All Saints Clo. N9	CB27	39
All Saints Clo. Brwd.	DA21	33
All Saints Clo. Chig.	CO27	41
Romford Rd.		
All Saints Dr. SE3	CG44	68
All Saints Dr. Sth. Croy.	CA59	96
All Saints La. Rick.	AZ25	26
All Saints Pass. SW18	BS46	76
Wandsworth High St.		
All Saint's Rd. SW19	BT50	76
All Saints Rd. W3	BN41	65
All Saints Rd. W11	BR39	55
All Saints Rd. Grav.	DF47	81
All Saints Rd. Sutt.	BS55	86
All Saints St. N1	BX37	56
All Souls Pl. W1	BV39	56
Langham Pl.		
Allfarthing La. SW18	BS46	76
Allgood Clo. Mord.	BQ53	85
Allhallows La. EC4	BZ40	57
Allhusen Gdns. Slou.	AS35	43
Alliance Rd. E13	CJ38	58
Alliance Rd. SE18	CO43	69
Alliance Rd. W3	BM38	55
Allingham Ct. NW3	BU35	47
Haverstock Hill		
Allingham Rd. Reig.	BS72	121
Allingham St. N1	BZ37	57
Allington Av. N17	CA29	39
Allington Clo. SW19	BQ49	75
Allington Rd. NW4	BP32	46
Allington Rd. SW2	BX46	76
Allington Rd. W10	BR37	55
Allington Rd. Har.	BG32	45
Allington Rd. Orp.	CM55	88

Allington St. SW1 BV41 66
Allison Clo. SE3 CF44 67
Allison Clo. SE10 CF44 67
Shooters Hill Rd.
Allison Clo. Wal. Abb. CH19 22
Allison Gro. SE21 CA47 77
Allison Rd. N8 BY32 47
Allison Rd. W3 BN39 55
Allitsen Rd. NW8 BU37 56
Allmains Clo. Wal. Abb. CH16 22
Allnutts Rd Epp. CO20 23
Allnutt Way. SW4 BW46 76
Alloa Rd. SE8 CC42 67
Alloa Rd. Ilf. CO34 50
Allonby Gdns. Wem. BK33 45
Windermere Av.
Alloway Rd. E3 CD38 57
Allsop Pl. NW1 BU38 56
Allum La. Borwd. BK25 27
Allum Way N20 BT27 38
Manus Way
Allyn Clo. Stai. AV50 72
Penton Rd.
Alma Av. E4 CF29 39
Alma Av. Horn. CW35 51
Almack Rd. E5 CC35 48
Alma Cres. Har. BG34 45
Alma Cres. Sutt. BR56 94
Alma Cut, St. Alb. BH14 9
Alma Gro. SE1 CA42 67
Alma Pl. Sun. BC50 73
Alma Pl. Th. Hth. BY53 86
Alma Rd. N10 BV29 38
Alma Rd. SW18 BT45 66
Alma Rd. Berk. AP12 7
Alma Rd. Cars. BU56 95
Alma Rd. Enf. CC25 30
Alma Rd. Esher BH54 84
Alma Rd. Har. BG29 36
Alma Rd. Har. BG34 45
Alma Rd. Orp. CP55 89
Alma Rd. Reig. BS70 121
Alma Rd. St. Alb. BH14 9
Alma Rd. Sid. CO48 79
Alma Rd. Sthl. BE40 54
Alma Rd. Swans. DC46 81
Alma Rd. Wind. AM42 61
Alma Rd. Wind. AO44 61
Alma Sq. NW8 BT38 56
Alma St. E15 CF36 57
Alma St. NW5 BV36 56
Alma Ter. SW18 BT47 76
Almeida St. N1 BY36 56
Almeric Rd. SW11 BU45 66
Almer Rd. SW20 BP50 75
Almington St. N4 BX33 47
Almners Rd. Cher. AT54 82
Almond Ave. West Dr. AZ41 63
Almond Av. W5 BK41 64
Almond Av. Cars. BU55 86
Almond Av. Uxb. AZ34 44
Almond Av. Wok. AR63 100
Almond Cl. Egh. AQ50 72
Almond Cl. Grays. DG41 71
Almond Clo. SE15 CB44 67
Almond Clo. Brom. CL54 88
Almond Clo. Guil. AR68 109
Almond Clo. Guil. AR69 118
Almond Clo. Hayes BB40 53
Almond Clo. Ruis. BB34 44
Almond Clo. Ruis. BC34 44
Almond Clo. Shep. BA51 83
Almond Dr. Swan. CS51 89
Almond Gro. Brent. BJ43 64
Almond Rd. N17 CB29 39
Trulock Rd.
Almond Rd. SE16 CB42 67
Almond Rd. Epsom BN59 94
Almond Rd. Dart. CY47 80
Almonds Av. Buck. H. CH27 40
Almond Wk. Hat. BP14 10
Almond Way Borwd. BM24 28
Almond Way Brom. CL54 88
Almond Way, Har. BF30 36
Almond Way Mitch. BW53 86
Almons Way, Slou. AQ39 52
Almorah Rd. N1 BZ36 57
Almorah Rd. Houns. BD44 64
Alms Heath. Wok. AZ64 101
Almshouse La. Chess. BK58 93
Almshouse La. Enf. CB22 30
Alnwick Gro. Mord. BS52 86
Abbotsbury Rd.
Alnwick Rd. E16 CJ39 58
Alnwick Rd. SE12 CH46 78
Alperton La. Alp. BK38 54
Alpha Clo. NW1 BU38 56
Alpha Gro. E14 CE41 67
Alpha Pl. NW6 BS37 56
Alpha Pl. SW3 BU43 66
Alpha Rd. E4 CE27 39
Alpha Rd. N18 CB29 39
Alpha Rd. SE14 CD44 67
Alpha Rd. Brwd. DE25 122
Alpha Rd. Croy. CA54 87
Alpha Rd. Enf. CD24 30
Alpha Rd. Surb. BL53 85
Alpha Rd. Surb. BL54 85
Alpha Rd. Tedd. BG49 74
Alpha Rd. Uxb. AZ38 53
Alpha Rd. Wok. AP58 91
Alpha Rd. Wok. AT61 100
Alpha St. SE15 CB44 67
Alpha St. Slou. AP41 62
Alpine Av. Surb. BN55 85
Alpine Clo. Croy. CA55 87
Alpine Copse Brom. CL51 88
Alpine Rd. SE16 CC42 67
Alpine Rd. Red. BV69 121
Alpine Rd. Walt. BC54 83
Alpine St. W10 BR39 55
Alpine Wk. Bush. BH27 36
Alp St. W10 BR38 55
Alric Av. NW10 BN36 55
Alric Av. N. Mal. BO52 85
Alroy Rd. N4 BY33 47
Alscot Rd. SE1 CA42 67
Alsen Pl. N7 BX34 47
Alsen Rd. N7 BX34 47
Alsike Rd SE2 CP41 69
Alsike Rd. Belv. CP41 69
Alsike Way Belv. CQ41 69
Alsom Av. Wor. Pk. BP56 94
Alston Clo. Surb. BJ54 84
Alston Rd. N18 CB28 39
Alston Rd. SW17 BT49 76
Alston Rd. Barn. BR24 28
Alston Rd. Hem. H. AW14 8
Altair Cl. N17 CB29 39
Altair Clo. N18 CB29 39
Brantwood Rd.
Altair Way. Nthwd. BB28 35
Altash Way, SE9 CK48 78
Altenburg Av. W13 BJ41 64
Altenburg Gdns. SW11 BU45 66
Alt Gro. SW19 BR50 75
Altham Grove, Harl. CN10 6
Altham Rd. Pnr. BE29 36
Althea St. SW6 BS44 66
Althorne Gdns. E18 CG31 49
Althorne Rd. Red. BV71 121
Althorne Way Dag. CR34 50
Althorpe Gro. SW11 BT44 66
Westbridge Rd.
Althorpe Rd. Har. BG32 45
Althorpe Rd. St. Alb. BH13 9
Althorp Rd. SW17 BU47 76
Altmore Av. E6 CK36 58
Alton Av. Stan. BH29 36
Alton Clo. Bex. CQ47 79
Alton Clo. Islw. BH44 64
Alton Gdns. Beck. CE50 77
Alton Gdns. Twick. BG47 74
Alton Rd. N17 BZ31 48
Alton Rd. SW15 BP47 75
Alton Rd. Croy. BY55 86
Alton Rd. Rich. BL45 65
Alton St. E14 CE39 57
Altyre Clo. Beck. CD53 87
Altyre Rd. Croy. BZ55 87
Altyre Way Beck. CD53 87
Alvanley Gdns. NW6 BS35 47
Alva Way Wat. BD27 36
Alverstoke Rd. Rom. CW29 42
Alverstone Av. SW19 BS48 76
Alverstone Av. Barn. BU26 38
Alverstone Gdns. SE9 CM47 78
Alverstone Rd. E12 CL35 49
Alverstone Rd. NW2 BQ36 55
Alverstone Rd. N. Mal. BO52 85
Alverstone Rd. Wem. BL33 46
Alverston Gdns. SE25 CA52 87
Alverton St. SE8 CD42 67
Alveston Av. Har. BJ31 45
Alvey Est. SE17 CA42 67
Alvey St. SE17 CA42 67
Alvington Cres. E8 CA35 48
Alway Av. Epsom. BN56 94
Alwen Grn. S. Ock. DA39 60
Alwood Cres. SE12 CH46 78
Alwyn Av. W4 BN42 65
Alwyn Clo. Croy. CE57 96
Alwyne Av. Brwd. DD25 122
Alwyne La. N1 BY36 56
Alwyne Pl. N1 BZ36 57
Alwyne Rd. N1 BZ36 57
Alwyne Rd. SW19 BR50 75
Alwyne Rd. W7 BH40 54
Alwyne Sq. N1 BZ36 57
Alwyne Vill. N1 BY36 56
Alwyn Gdns. W3 BM39 55
Noel Rd.
Alwyns Clo. Cher. AW53 83
Alwyns St. Cher. AV53 82
Alyth Gdns. NW11 BS32 47
Amanda Ct. Slou. AR41 62
Amazon St. E1 CB39 57
Ambassador Clo. Houns. BE44 64
Amber Av. E17 CD30 39
Amber Croft Way Couls. BY59 95
Ambercroft Way. Couls. BY62 104
Ambercroft Way. Couls. BY63 104
Amberden Av. N3 BS31 47
Ambergate St. SE17 BY42 66
Amberley Clo. Pnr. BE31 45
Amberley Clo. Wok. AV66 109
Amberley Ct. Sid. CP49 79
Amberley Dri. Wey. AV59 91
Amberley Gdns. Enf. CA26 39
Amberley Gdns. Epsom BO56 94
Amberley Gro. SE26 CB49 77
Amberley Gro. Croy. CA54 87
Amberley Ms. W9 BS38 56
Amberley Rd. E10 CE33 48
Amberley Rd. N13 BX27 38
Amberley Rd. SE2 CP43 69
Amberley Rd. W9 BS38 56
Amberley Rd. Buck. H. CJ26 40
Amberley Rd. Enf. CA26 39
Amberley Way Houns. BD46 74
Amberley Way Mord. BR54 85
Amberley Way. Rom. CR31 50
Marlborough Rd.
Amberry Ct. Harl. CM10 6
Amber St. E15 CF36 57
Salway Rd.
Amberwood Rise N. Mal. BN53 85
Amblecote Clo. SE12 CH48 78
Amblecote Rd. SE12 CH48 78
Ambler Rd. N4 BY34 47
Ambleside Av. SW16 BW49 76
Ambleside Av. Beck. CD53 87
Ambleside Av. Horn. CU35 50
Ambleside Av. Walt. BD54 84
Ambleside Clo. E9 CC35 48
Churchill Wk.
Ambleside Clo. Red. BV73 121
Ambleside Cres. Enf. CC24 30
Ambleside Epp. CO19 23
Ambleside Gdns. Ilf. CK31 49
Ambleside Gdns. Sth. Croy. CC58 96
Ambleside Gdns. Sutt. BT57 95
Ambleside Gdns. Wem. BK33 45
Ambleside Rd. NW10 BO36 55
Ambleside Rd. Bexh. CR44 69
Ambrey Way Pur. BW58 95
Ambridge Rd. Dag. CR33 50
Ambrooke Rd. Belv. CR41 69
Sheridan Rd.
Ambrooke Rd. Belv. CR42 69
Gertrude Rd.
Ambrosden Av. SW1 BW41 66
Ambrose Av. NW11 BR33 46
Ambrose St. SE16 CB42 67
Southwark Pk. Rd.
Ambroth Clo. SE23 CB47 77
Horniman Dri.
Amelia St. SE17 BY42 66
Amen Ct. EC4 BY39 56
America St. SE1 BZ40 57
Great Guildford St.
Amerland Rd. SW18 BR46 75
Amersham Av. N18 BZ29 39
Amersham Clo. Rom. CW29 42
Amersham Dr. Rom. CW29 42
Amersham Gro. SE14 CD43 67
Amersham Rd. SE14 CD43 67
Amersham Rd. Amer. AR23 25
Amersham Rd. Ch. St. G. AQ25 25
Amersham Rd. Ch. St. G. AQ26 34
Amersham Rd. Ch. St. G. AR28 34
Amersham Rd. Croy. BZ53 87
Amersham Rd. Ger. Cr. AS31 43
Amersham Rd. Har. BH32 45
Amersham Rd. Rom. CW29 42
Amersham Val. SE14 CD43 67
Amersham Wk. Rom. CW29 42
Amersham Way. Amer. AS23 25
Amerton Ct. Wind. AO43 61
Amery Gdns. NW10 BP37 55
Amery Gdns. Rom. CV31 51
Amery Rd. Har. BJ34 45
Amesbury, Wal. Abb. CH19 22
Amesbury Av. SW2 BX48 76
Amesbury Clo. Epp. CN19 22
Amesbury Clo. Wor. Pk. BQ54 85
Amesbury Dr. E4 CE25 30
Amesbury Rd. Brom. CJ52 88
Amesbury Rd. Dag. CP36 59
Amesbury Rd. Epp. CN19 22
Amesbury Rd. Felt. BD48 74
Ames Rd. Swans. DC46 81
Amethyst Rd. E15 CF35 48
Amey Dr. Lthd. BG65 102
Amherst Av. W13 BJ39 54
Amherst Clo. Orp. CO52 89
Amherst Dr. Orp. CN52 88
Amherst Gdns. W13 BK39 54
Amherst Rd.
Amherst Hill. Sev. CT64 107
Amherst Rd. W13 BK39 54
Amherst Rd. Sev. CU64 107
Amhurst Gdns. Islw. BH44 64
Amhurst Park N16 BZ33 48
Amhurst Pass. E8 CB35 48
Amhurst Rd. E8 CA35 48
Amhurst Rd. N16 CA35 48
Amhurst Ter. E8 CB35 48
Amidas Gdns. Dag. CO35 50
Amiel St. E1 CC38 57
Colebert Av.
Amies St. SW11 BU45 66
Amis Av. Epsom BM57 94
Amis Av. Wey. AW58 92
Amis Rd. Wok. AP63 100
Amity Gro. SW20 BQ51 85
Amity Rd. E15 CG37 58
Ammiel Ter. E3 CE37 57
Amner Rd. SW11 BV46 76
Amor Pl. W6 BQ42 65
Amor Rd. W6 BQ41 65
Amos Est. SE16 CC40 57
Amott Rd. SE15 CB45 67
Amoy Pl. E14 CE40 57
Birchfield St.
Ampleforth Rd. SE2 CO41 69
Ampthill Sq. Est. BW37 56
Ampton Pl. WC1 BX38 56
Ampton St.
Ampton St. WC1 BX38 56
Amroth Clo. SE23 CB47 77
Amton Cres. Sutt. BS55 86
Amwell Clo. Enf. BZ25 30
Amwell Ct. N4 BZ33 48
Amwell Ct. Wal. Abb. CG20 22
Amwell St. EC1 BY38 56
Amwell St. Hodd. CE11 12
Amyand Cotts. Twick. BJ46 74
Amyand Park Rd
Amyand La. Twick. BJ46 74
Beaconsfield Rd.
Amyand La. Twick BJ47 74
Marble Hill Gdns
Amyand Pk. Gdns. Twick. BJ46 74
Amyand Pk. Rd.
Amyand Pk. Rd. Twick. BJ47 74
Amy Rd. Oxt. CG68 115
Amyruth Rd. SE4 CE46 77
Anatola Rd. N19 BV34 47
Ancaster Cres. N. Mal. BP53 85
Ancaster Rd. Beck. CC52 87
Ancaster St. SE18 CN43 68
Anchorage Clo. SW19 BS49 76
Anchor Cres. Wok. AO62 100
Anchor & Hope La. SE7 CH41 68
Anchor La. Hem. H. AW14 8
Anchor St. SE16 CB42 67
Anchor Yd. EC1 BZ38 57
Old St.
Ancona Rd. NW10 BP37 55
Ancona Rd. SE18 CM42 68
Andalus Rd. SW9 BX45 66
Ander Clo. Wem. BK35 45
Andermass, Wind. AL44 61
Anderson Clo. Epsom. BM59 94
Anderson Dr. Ashf. BA49 73
Anderson Rd. E9 CC36 57
Digby Rd.
Anderson Rd. Rad. BM20 19
Spencer Rd.
Anderson Rd. Wey. BA55 83
Anderson's Pl. Houns. BF45 64
Anderson St. SW3 BU42 66
Anderson St. W10 BR38 55
Kensal Rd.
Andoe Rd. SW11 BU45 66
Andover Clo. Epsom BN58 94
Andover Clo. Grnf. BF38 54
Andover Clo. Uxb. AW37 53
Andover Pl. NW6 BS37 56
Andover Rd. N7 BX34 47
Andover Rd. Orp. CN54 88
Andover Rd. Twick. BG47 74
Andover St. N7 BX34 47
Andre St. E8 CB35 48
Andrew Borde St. WC2 BW39 56
Charing Cross Rd.
Andrew Clo. Bex. CS46 79
Bourne Rd.
Andrew Pl. SW8 BW44 66
Andrews Clo. Buck. H. CJ27 40
Andrews Clo. Epsom BO60 94
Andrews Clo. Orp. CP51 89
Andrew's Crosse WC2 CM39 58
Bell Yd.
Andrew's La. Wal. Cr. CA17 21
Andrew's Rd. E8 CB37 57
Andrew St. E14 CF39 57
Andwell Clo. SE2 CO41 69
Anerley Gro. SE19 CA50 77
Anerley Hill, SE19 CA50 77
Anerley Pk. SE20 CB50 77
Anerley Pk. Rd. SE20 CB50 77
Anerley Rd. SE19 CB50 77
Anerley Rd. SE20 CB50 77
Anerley Sta. Rd. SE20 CB51 87
Anerley Val. SE19 CA50 77
Angas Ct. Wey. BA56 92
Angel Clo. N18 CA28 39
Angel Ct. EC2 BZ39 57
Throgmorton St.
Angel Ct. SW17 BU49 76
Angelfield Houns. BF45 64
Angel Hill Sutt. BS55 86
Angel Hill Dr. Sutt. BS55 86
Angel La. E15 CF36 57
Angel La. Hayes BA39 53
Angell Pk. Gdns. SW9 BY45 66
Angell Rd. SW9 BY44 66
Angel Ms. N1 BY37 56
Angel Pass. EC3 BZ40 57
Wharfside
Angel Pl. EC4 BZ40 57
Angel Pl. SE1 BZ41 67
Borough High St.
Angel Rd. N18 CB28 39
Angel Rd. Har. BH32 45
Angel Rd. Surb. BJ54 84
Angel St. EC1 BZ39 57
Angel Wk. W6 BQ42 65
Angel Way Rom. CT31 50
Angerstein La. SE3 CG43 68
Angle Clo. Uxb. AZ37 53
Anglefield Rd. Berk. AQ13 7
Angle Pl. Berk. AQ13 7
Angle Rd. Grays DB43 70
Anglers La. NW5 BV36 56
Anglesea Av. SE18 CL42 68
Anglesea Cent. Grav. DG46 81
New Rd.
Anglesea Pl. Grav. DG46 81
Clive Rd.
Anglesea Rd. SE18 CL42 68
Anglesea Rd. Kings-on-t. BK52 84
Anglesea Rd. Orp. CO53 89
Anglesea St. E1 CB38 57
Anglesey Clo. Ashf. AZ48 73
Anglesey Ct. Rd. Cars. BV57 95
Anglesey Dr. Rain. CU38 59
Anglesey Gdns. Cars. BV57 95
Anglesey Rd. Enf. CB24 30
Anglesey Rd. Wat. BD28 36
Anglesmede Cres. Pnr. BF31 45
Anglesmede Wk. Pnr. BF31 45
Angles Rd. SW16 BX49 76
Anglo Rd. E3 CD37 57
Anglo Rd. Grays. CY43 70
Angus Clo. Chess. BM56 94
Angus Dr. Ruis. BD35 45
Angus Gdns. NW9 BN30 37
Angus Rd. E13 CJ38 58
Angus St. SE14 CD43 67
Anhalt Rd. SW11 BU43 66
Ankerdine Cres. SE18 CL44 68
Anlaby Rd. Tedd. BH49 74
Anley Rd. W14 BQ41 65
Anmersh Gro. Stan. BK30 36
Annabel Clo. E14 CE39 57
Annalee Rd. S. Ock. DA39 60
Annandale Rd. SE10 CG42 68
Annandale Rd. W4 BO42 65
Annandale Rd. Croy. CB55 87
Annandale Rd. Guil. AQ71 118
Annandale Rd. Sid. CN47 78
Annan Way Rom. CS30 41
Anne Boleyn's Wk. Kings. On T. BL49 75
Anne Boleyn's Wk. Sutt. BQ57 94
Anne Of Cleves Rd. Dart. CV46 80
Annersley Walk N19 BW34 47
Girdlestone Est.
Annesley Av. NW9 BN31 46
Annesley Clo. NW10 BO34 46
Annesley Dr. Croy. CD55 87
Annesley Rd. N19 BW34 47
Annesley Rd., SE3 CH44 68
Anne St. E13 CH38 58
Anne's Wk. Cat. CA63 105
Annett Clo. Shep. BB52 83
Up. Halliford Rd.
Annette Clo. Har. BH30 36
Spencer Rd.
Annette Rd. N7 BX34 47
Annett Rd. Walt. BC54 83
Annetts Gro. N1 BZ36 57
Essex Rd.
Anne Way E. Mol. BF52 84
Anne Way, Ilf. CM29 40
Ann Gdns. S. Ock. DA39 60
Annifer Way. S. Ock. DA39 60
Anning St. EC2 CA38 57
New Inn Yd.
Annington Rd. N2 BU31 47
Annis Rd. E9 CD36 57
Ann La. SW10 BT43 66
Ann's Clo. SW1 BV41 66
Kinnerton St.
Ann St. SE18 CM42 68
Ann's Vill. W11 BQ41 65
Annsworthy Av. Th. Hth. BZ52 87
Annsworthy Cres. SE25 BZ52 87
Ansdell Rd. SE15 CC44 67
Ansdell St. W8 BS41 66
St Alban's Gro.
Ansdell Ter. W8 BS41 66
St. Alban's Gro.
Ansell Gro. Cars. BU54 86
Ansell Rd. SW17 BU48 76
Ansell Rd. Dor. BJ71 119
Anselm Rd. SW6 BS43 66
Anselm Rd. Pnr. BE29 36
Ansford Rd. Brom. CF49 77
Ansleigh Pl. W11 BQ40 55
Ansley Clo. Sth. Croy. CB60 96
Anslow Gdns. Iver AU37 52
Anson Clo. Cat. BZ63 105
Anson Clo. Rom. CR30 41
Anson Clo. St. Alb. BJ14 9
Anson Clo. St. Alb. BK10 9
Anson Rd. N7 BW35 47
Anson Rd. NW2 BF35 45
Anson Rd. Cat. BZ63 105
Anson Wk. Nthwd. BA28 35
Anstead Dr. Rain. CU37 59
Anstey Rd. E16 CH39 58
Anstey Rd. SE15 CB45 67
Anstridge Rd. SE9 CM46 78
Anthony Clo. NW7 BO28 37
Anthony Clo. Sev. CT63 107
Anthony Clo. Wat. BD26 36
Anthony Rd. SE25 CB53 87
Anthony Rd. Borwd. BL23 28
Anthony Rd. Grnf. BH37 54
Anthony Rd. Well. CO44 69
Anthony St. E1 CB39 57
Antill Rd. E3 CD38 57
Antill Rd. N15 CB31 48
Antill Ter. E1 CC39 57
Antlers Hill E4 CE24 30
Antoney's Clo. Pnr. BD30 36
Antonine Gte. St. Alb. BF14 9
Anton Rd. S. Ock. DA38 60
Anton St. E8 CB35 48
Antrim Gro. NW3 BU36 56
Antrim Mans. NW3 BU36 56
Antrim Rd. NW3 BU36 56
Antrobus Clo. Sutt. BR56 94
Antrobus Rd. W4 BN42 65
Anvil Al. Cob. BC60 92
Anworth Clo. Wdf Grn. CH29 40
Anyards Rd. Cob. BC60 92
Aperdele Rd. Lthd. BJ62 102
Aperfield Rd. Erith CT43 69
Aperfield Rd. West. CK62 106
Apers Av. Wok. AS64 100
Apex Clo. Beck. CF51 87
Apley Rd. Reig. BS72 121
Apollo Av. Brom. CH51 88
Hawes Rd.
Apollo Clo. Horn. CU34 50
Apollo Pl. SW10 BT43 66
Riley St.
Apollo Pl. SW10 BT44 66
Riley St.
Apollo Way, Hem. H. AY12 8
Apothecary St. EC4 BY39 56
New Bridge St.
Appach Rd. SW2 BY46 76
Apper St. WC1 BW38 56
Appian Way Est. Erith. CR42 69
Appleby Clo. E4 CF29 39
Appleby Clo. N15 BZ32 48
Cornwall Rd.
Appleby Clo. Twick. BG48 74
Appleby Dr. Rom. CV28 42
Appleby Grn. Rom. CV28 42
Appleby Rd. E8 CB36 57
Appleby Rd. E16 CG39 58
Appleby St. E2 CA37 57
Appleby St. Wal. Cr. BZ16 21
Applecroft, St. Alb. BF17 18
Applecroft Rd. Welw. G. C. BP8 5
Appledore Av. Bexh. CS44 69
Appledore Av. Ruis. BC34 44
Appledore Clo. SW17 BU48 76
Appledore Clo. Brom. CG53 88
Appledore Clo. Edg. BM30 37
Appledore Clo. Rom. CV30 42
Appledore Cres. Sid. CN48 78
Appleford Clo. Hodd. CD11 12
Appleford Rd. W10 BR38 55
Apple Garth, Brent. BK42 64
Applegarth Croy. CE57 96
Applegarth Av. Guil. AO70 118
Applegarth Dr. Ilf. CN31 49
Applegarth Esher BJ56 93
Applegarth Rd. W14 BQ41 65

Apple Gate Brwd.	CZ25	33
Coxtie Grn. Rd.		
Apple Gro. Enf.	CA24	30
Apple Mkt. Kings-on-t.	BK51	84
Apple Orchard, Hem. H.	AY12	8
Appleshaw Clo. Grav.	DG49	81
Chalky Bank		
Appleton Gdns. N. Mal.	BP53	85
Appleton Rd. SE9	CK45	68
Appleton Rd. Loug.	CL24	31
Appleton Way. Horn.	CV34	51
Apple Tree Av. Uxb. & West Dr.	AY39	53
Apple Tree Cres. Brwd.	DB22	33
Appletree La. Slou.	AR41	62
Appletree Wk. Chesh.	AO20	16
Cresswell Rd.		
Appletree Wk. Wat.	BC20	17
Apple Tree Yd. SW1	BW40	56
Duke Of York St.		
Appold St. EC2	CA39	57
Appold St. Erith	CT43	69
Approach Clo. N16	CA35	48
Cowper Rd.		
Approach Rd. E2	CC37	57
Approach Rd. SW20	BQ51	85
Approach Rd. Ashf.	BA49	73
Approach Rd. Barn.	BT24	29
Approach Rd. Barn.	BV24	29
Approach Rd. E. Mol.	BF53	84
Approach Rd. St. Alb.	BH14	9
Approach, The, W3	BN39	55
Approach, The, Enf.	CB23	30
Approach, The Lthd.	BE65	102
Approach, The, Orp.	CN55	88
Approach, The, Pot. B.	BR19	19
Approach, The, Upmin.	CX34	51
Apps Ct. Walt.	BD53	84
Apps Pond La. St. Alb.	BC15	8
Apps Pond La. St. Alb.	BD15	9
Aprey Gdns. NW4	BQ31	46
April Clo. Felt.	BC48	73
April Glen SE23	CC48	77
Mayow Rd.		
April Wood. Wey.	AV59	91
Apsley Clo. Har.	BG32	45
Apsley Rd. E17	CD32	48
Apsley Rd. SE25	CB52	87
Apsley Rd. N. Mal.	BN52	85
Apsley Sq. W1	BV40	56
Sth.Audley St.		
Aquila Clo. Nthwd.	BC28	35
Aquila St. NW8	BT37	56
Aquinas St. SE1	BY40	56
Arabella Dr. SW15	BO45	65
Arabia Clo. E4	CF26	39
Mornington Rd.		
Arabin Rd. SE4	CD45	67
Araglen Ave. S. Ock.	DA39	60
Aragon Av. Epsom	BP58	94
Aragon Av. Surb.	BH53	84
Aragon Clo. Hem. H.	BA11	8
Aragon Dr. Ilf.	CM29	40
Aragon Dr. Ruis.	BD33	45
Aragon Rd. E6	CJ37	58
Aragon Rd. Kings. On T.	BL49	75
Aragon Rd. Mord.	BQ53	85
Arandora Cres. Rom.	CO33	50
Arand St. W11	BQ40	55
Arbor Clo. Beck.	CE51	87
Arbor Ct. N16	BZ34	48
Arborfield Clo. Slou.	AP41	62
Arbor Rd. E4	CF27	39
Arbour Clo. Brwd.	DB28	42
Arbour Field, Wok.	AS61	100
Arbour Rd. Enf.	CC24	30
Arbour Sq. E1	CC39	57
Arbour Way. Horn.	CU35	50
Arbroath Grn. Wat.	BC27	35
Arbroath Rd. SE9	CK45	68
Arbrook La. Esher	BG57	93
Arbury Rd. E3	CD38	57
Arbury Ter. SE26	CB48	77
Arbuthnot La. Bex.	CQ47	79
Arbuthnot Rd. SE14	CC44	67
Arbutus Clo. Red.	BT71	121
Arbutus Rd. Red.	BT72	121
Arbutus St. E8	CA37	57
Arcade Pl. Rom.	CT32	50
Arcade The, E17	CE31	48
Hoe St.		
Arcade, The, EC2	CA39	57
Liverpool St.		
Arcadia Av. N3	BS30	38
Arcadian Av. Bex.	CQ46	79
Arcadian Clo. Bex.	CQ46	79
Arcadian Gdns. N22	BX29	38
Arcadian Rd. Bex.	CQ46	79
Arcadia Rd. Grav.	DF51	81
Arcadia St. E14	CE39	57
Arcany Rd. S. Ock.	DA38	60
Archbishop's Pl. SW2	BX47	76
Archdale Rd. SE22	CA46	77
Archdale Way, Egh.	AT49	72
Archel Rd. W14	BR43	65
Archer Clo. Kings L.	AZ18	17
Archer Ho. SW11	BT44	66
Archer Rd. SE25	CB52	87
Archer Rd. Orp.	CO53	89
Archers Ride. Welw. G. C.	BS9	5
Archer St. W1	BW40	56
Rupert St.		
Archers Walk SE15	CA44	67
Sumner Estate		
Archery Clo. W2	BU39	56
Archery Rd. SE9	CK46	78
Arches, The, Har.	BG34	45
Archibald Rd. E3	CE38	57
Archibald Rd. N7	BW35	47
Archibald Rd. Rom.	CW30	42
Archibald St. E3	CE38	57
Arch Rd. Walt.	BD55	84
Arch St. SE1	BZ41	67
Archway, Dor.	BJ71	119
Arch Way Rom.	CU29	41
Archway Mall N19	BW34	47
Archway Rd. N19	BU32	47
Archway St. SW13	BO45	65
Arcola St. E8	CA35	48
Arctic St. NW5	BV35	47
Arcus Rd. Brom.	CG49	78
Ardbeg Rd. SE24	BZ46	77
Arden Clo. Bush.	BH26	36
Arden Clo. Har.	BG34	45
Arden Clo. Reig.	BS72	121
Arden Cres. Dag.	CP36	59
Arden Est. N1	CA38	57
Arden Rd. N3	BR31	46
Arden Rd. W13	BJ40	54
Arden Way, St. Alb.	BK12	9
Ardern	BC31	44
Ardfern Av. SW16	BY52	86
Ardfillan Rd. SE6	CF47	77
Ardgowan Rd. SE6	CG47	78
Ardilaun Rd. N5	BZ35	48
Ardintinny St. Alb.	BH14	9
London Rd.		
Ardleigh Clo. Horn.	CV31	51
Ardleigh Gdns. Brwd.	DF26	122
Ardleigh Gdns. Sutt.	BS54	86
Ardleigh Grn. Rd. Horn.	CV32	51
Ardleigh Mews, Ilf.	CL34	49
Bengal Rd.		
Ardleigh Rd. E17	CD30	39
Ardleigh Rd. N1	CA36	57
Ardley Clo. NW10	BO34	46
Ardley Clo. SE23	CD48	77
Ardley Clo. Ruis.	BA33	44
Ardliegh Ct. Brwd.	DC26	122
Hutton Rd.		
Ardlui Rd. SE27	BZ48	77
Ardmay Gdns. Surb.	BL53	85
Ardmere Rd. SE13	CF46	77
Ardmore Av. Guil.	AQ69	118
Ardmore La. Buck. H.	CH26	40
Ardmore Rd. S. Ock.	DA38	60
Ardmore Way, Guil.	AQ69	118
Ardoch Rd. SE6	CF48	77
Ardrossan Gdns. Wor. Pk.	BP55	85
Ardross Ave. Nthwd.	BB28	35
Ardshiel Clo. SW15	BQ45	65
Bemish Rd.		
Ardshiel Dr. Red.	BU71	121
Fairlawn Dr.		
Ardsley Wood, Wey.	BB56	92
Ardwell Av. Ilf.	CM32	49
Ardwell Rd. SW2	BX48	76
Ardwick Rd. NW2	BS35	47
Argall Av. E10	CC33	48
Argent St. Grays.	DD43	71
Argon Ms. SW6	BS43	66
Argosy Gdns. Stai.	AV50	72
Argosy La. Stai.	AX47	73
Clare Rd.		
Argus Way, W3	BM41	65
Argus Way Nthlt.	BE38	54
Argyle Av. Houns.	BF46	74
Argyle Clo. W13	BJ38	54
Argyle Est. SW19	BQ48	75
Argyle Gdns. Upmin.	CY35	51
Argyle Mans. Rich.	BK48	74
Argyle Pass. N17	CB30	39
Argyle Rd.		
Argyle Pl. W6	BP42	65
Argyle Rd. E1	CC38	57
Argyle Rd. E15	CG35	49
Argyle Rd. E16	CH39	58
Argyle Rd. N12	BS28	38
Argyle Rd. N17	CB30	39
Argyle Rd. N18	CB28	39
Argyle Rd. W13	BJ38	54
Argyle Rd. W13	BJ39	54
Argyle Rd. Barn.	BQ24	28
Argyle Rd. Grays.	DD42	71
Argyle Rd. Har.	BF32	45
Argyle Rd. Houns.	BF46	74
Argyle Rd. Ilf.	CL34	49
Argyle Rd. Sev.	CU66	116
Argyle Rd. Tedd.	BH49	74
Argyle Sq. WC1	BX38	56
Argyle St. WC1	BX38	56
Argyle Wk. WC1	BX38	56
Argyll Av. Sthl.	BF40	54
Argyll Gdns. Edg.	BM30	37
Argyll Rd. W8	BS41	66
Argyll St. W1	BW39	56
Arica Rd. SE4	CD45	67
Arie Dr. S. Ock.	DA38	60
Ariel Clo. Grav.	DJ49	81
Ariel Rd. NW6	BS36	56
Arisdale Ave. S. Ock.	DA38	60
Aristotle Rd. SW4	BW45	66
Arkell Gro. SE19	BY50	76
Arkindale Rd. SE6	CF48	77
Arkley Cres. E17	CD32	48
Arkley Dr. Barn.	BP24	28
Arkley La. Barn.	BO23	28
Arkley Rd. E17	CD32	48
Arkley Rd. Barn	BP24	28
Arkley Rd. Hem. H.	AZ11	8
Arkley Vw. Barn.	BP24	28
Arklow Rd. SE14	CD43	67
Arkwright, Harl.	CN10	6
Arkwright Rd. NW3	BT35	47
Arkwright Rd. Slou.	AV44	62
Arkwright Rd. Sth. Croy.	CA58	96
Arkwright Rd. Til.	DG44	71
Arkwright St. E16	CG39	58
Arlesford Rd. SW9	BX45	66
Arlesley Clo. SW15	BR46	75
Arlingford Rd. SW2	BY46	76
Arlington N12	BS28	38
Arlington Av. N1	BZ37	57
Arlington Clo. Sid.	CN47	78
Arlington Clo. Sutt.	BS55	86
Arlington Clo. Twick.	BK46	74
Arlington Ct. Hayes.	BB42	63
Arlington Cres. Wal. Cr.	CD20	21
Arlington Dr. Cars.	BU55	86
Arlington Dr. Ruis.	BA32	44
Arlington Gdns. W4	BN42	65
Arlington Gdns. Ilf.	CL33	49
Arlington Gdns. Rom.	CW30	42
Arlington Lo. SW2	BX45	66
Arlington Pass. Tedd.	BH49	74
Arlington Rd. N14	BV27	38
Arlington Rd. NW1	BV37	56
Arlington Rd. W13	BJ39	54
Arlington Rd. Ashf.	AY49	73
Arlington Rd. Rich.	BK48	74
Arlington Rd. Surb.	BK53	84
Arlington Rd. Tedd.	BH49	74
Arlington Rd. Wdf. Grn.	CH30	40
Arlington Sq. N1	BZ37	57
Arlington St. SW1	BW40	56
Arlington Way, EC1	BY38	56
Arliss Way Nthlt.	BD37	54
Arlow Rd. N21	BY26	38
Armadale Cl. N15	CB31	48
Armadale Rd. SW6	BS43	66
Armadale Rd. Felt.	BC46	73
Armada St. SE8	CE43	67
Armfield Av. Mitch.	BU51	86
Armfield Clo. E. Mol.	BE53	84
Armfield Rd. Enf.	BZ23	30
Arminger Rd. W12	BP40	55
Armitage Clo. Rick.	AX24	26
Armitage Rd. NW11	BR33	46
Armitage Rd. SE10	CG42	68
Armitage Rd. Houns.	BD43	64
Armond Clo. Wat.	BB22	26
Armoury Way, SW18	BS46	76
Armstead Wk. Dag.	CR36	59
Armstrong Av. Wdf. Grn.	CG29	40
Armstrong Clo. Ruis.	BC32	44
Armstrong Cres. Barn.	BT24	29
Armstrong Gdns. SE7	CJ42	68
Armstrong Pl. SE18	CL42	68
Armstrong Pl. Hem. H.	AX13	8
High St.		
Armstrong Rd. W3	BO40	55
Armstrong Rd. Egh.	AR50	72
Armstrong Rd. Felt.	BE49	74
Arnal Cres. SW18	BR47	75
Arndale Est. SW18	BS46	76
Arnett Clo. Rick.	AW25	26
Arnett Way, Rick.	AW25	26
Arne Wk. SE3	CG45	68
Arneways Av. Rom.	CP31	50
Arneway St. SW1	BW41	66
Horseferry Rd.		
Arneys La. Mitch.	BV53	86
Arngask Rd. SE6	CF47	77
Arnhem Ave. S. Ock.	CW40	60
Arnhem Av. S. Ock.	CY41	70
Arnhem Dr. Croy.	CF58	96
Arnhem Dr. Croy.	CF59	96
Arnhem Way, SE22	CA46	77
Dulwich Gro.		
Arnison Rd. E. Mol.	BG52	84
Arnold Av. E. Enf.	CD22	30
Arnold Av. W. Enf.	CD22	30
Arnold Circus, E2	CA38	57
Arnold Clo. Har.	BL32	46
Arnold Cres. Islw.	BG46	74
Arnold Est. SE1	CA41	67
Arnold Gdns. N13	BY28	38
Arnold Rd. E3	CE38	57
Arnold Rd. N15	CA31	48
Arnold Rd. SW17	BU50	76
Arnold Rd. Dag.	CQ36	59
Arnold Rd. Grav.	DH48	81
Arnold Rd. Nthlt.	BE36	54
Arnold Rd. Stai.	AX50	73
Arnold Rd. Wok.	AT61	100
Arnolds Av. Brwd.	DE25	122
Arnolds Clo. Brwd.	DE25	122
Arnold's La. S. At H.	CW50	80
Arnolds La. S. At H.	CX50	80
Arnold, S Farm La. Brwd.	DF24	122
Arnos Gro. N14	BW28	38
Arnos Rd. N11	BW28	38
Arnould Av. SE5	BZ45	67
Arnside Gdns. Wem.	BK33	45
Arnside Rd. Bexh.	CR44	69
Arnside St. SE17	BZ43	67
Arnulf St. SE6	CE49	77
Arnulls Rd. SW16	BY50	76
Arodene Rd. SW2	BX46	76
Arondel Gr. N16	CA35	48
Arpley Rd. SE20	CC50	77
Arragon Gdns. SW16	BX50	76
Arragon Gdns. W. Wick.	CE55	87
Arragon Rd. Twick.	BJ47	74
Arran Clo. Erith	CS43	69
Arran Clo. Hem. H.	BA14	8
Arran Clo. Wall.	BW56	95
Arran Dr. E12	CJ33	49
Arran Dr. Stan.	BJ28	36
Arran Rd. SE6	CE48	77
Arran Wk. N1	BZ36	57
Marquess Est.		
Arran Way Esher	BF55	84
Arras Av. Mord.	BT53	86
Arrentine Clo. St. Alb.	BE14	9
Arrol Rd. Beck.	CC52	87
Arrow Rd. E3	CE38	57
Arrowscout Wk. Nthlt.	BD38	54
Arrowscout Wk. Nthlt.	BE38	54
Wayfarer Rd.		
Arrowsmith Clo. Chig.	CN28	40
Arrowsmith Path, Chig.	CN28	40
Arrowsmith Rd. Chig.	CN28	40
Arrowsmith Rd. Loug.	CK24	31
Arsenal Rd. SE9	CK44	68
Artemis Clo. Grav.	DJ47	81
Arterberry Rd. SW20	BQ50	75
Arterial Av. Rain.	CU38	59
Artesian Clo. Horn.	CT33	50
Dymoke Rd.		
Artesian Rd. W2	BS39	56
Arthingworth St. E15	CG37	58
Arthur Ct. W2	BS39	56
Queensway		
Arthurdon Rd. SE4	CE46	77
Arthur Gro. SE18	CM42	68
Arthur Henderson Ho. SW6	BR44	65
Arthur Ms. N7	BX36	56
Arthur Rd. E6	CK37	58
Arthur Rd. N7	BX34	47
Arthur Rd. N9	CA27	39
Arthur Rd. SW19	BS48	76
Arthur Rd. Kings. On T.	BM50	75
Arthur Rd. N. Mal.	BP53	85
Arthur Rd. Rom.	CP33	50
Arthur Rd. St. Alb.	BJ13	9
Arthur Rd. Slou.	AO41	61
Arthur Rd. West.	CJ61	106
Arthur Rd. Wind.	AN44	61
Arthur's Bridge Rd. Wok.	AR62	100
Arthur St. EC4	BZ40	57
Arthur St. Bush.	BD24	27
Arthur St. Erith	CT43	69
Arthur St. Grav.	DG47	81
Arthur St. Grays.	DE43	71
Arthur St. W. Grav.	DG47	81
Arthur Toft Ho. Grays	DD43	71
New Rd.		
Artichoke Hl. E1	CB40	57
Pennington St.		
Artillery Clo. Ilf.	CM32	49
Artillery La. E1	CA39	57
Artillery Pl. SE18	CK42	68
Artillery Rd. Guil.	AR70	118
Artillery Row, SW1	BW41	66
Artillery Ter. Guil.	AR70	118
Artillery Yd. EC2	CA38	57
Worship St.		
Artizan St. E1	CA39	57
Harrow Pl.		
Arty Pass. E1	CA39	57
Sandy's Row		
Arundel Av. Epsom.	BP58	94
Arundel Av. Mord.	BR52	85
Arundel Av. Sth. Croy.	CB58	96
Arundel Clo. E15	CG35	49
Arundel Clo. Bex.	CQ46	79
Arundel Clo. Croy.	BY55	86
Arundel Clo. Hamptn.	BF49	74
Arundel Clo. Hem. H.	AZ13	8
Arundel Clo. Wal. Cr.	CB17	21
Arundel Dr. Borwd.	BN24	28
Arundel Dr. Har.	BE35	45
Arundel Dr. Orp.	CO56	98
Arundel Dr. Wdf. Grn.	CH29	40
Arundel Gdns. N21	BY26	38
Arundel Gdns. W11	BR40	55
Arundel Gdns. Ilf.	CO34	50
Arundell Gdns. Edg.	BN29	37
Cressingham Rd		
Arundel Pl. N1	BY36	56
Arundel Rd. N16	CA35	48
Arundel Rd. Barn.	BU24	29
Arundel Rd. Croy.	BZ53	87
Arundel Rd. Dor.	BJ71	119
Arundel Rd. Houns.	BD45	64
Arundel Rd. Kings. On T.	BM51	85
Arundel Rd. Rom.	CW30	42
Arundel Rd. Sutt.	BR57	94
Arundel Rd. Uxb.	AW37	53
Arundel Sq. N7	BY36	56
Arundel St. WC2	BX40	56
Arundel Ter. SW13	BP43	65
Arvon Rd. N5	BY35	47
Ascalon St. SW8	BW43	66
Ascension Rd. Rom.	CS29	41
Ascham Dr. E4	CE29	39
Ascham End E17	CD30	39
Ascham St. NW5	BW35	47
Aschurch Rd. Croy.	CA54	87
Ascot Av. W5	BL41	65
Ascot Clo. Borwd.	BM25	28
Ascot Clo. Ilf.	CN29	40
Ascot Clo. Nthlt.	BF36	54
Ascot Gdns. Enf.	CC22	30
Ascot Gdns. Sthl.	BE39	54
Ascot Rd. E6	CK38	58
Ascot Rd. N15	BZ32	48
Ascot Rd. N18	CB28	39
Ascot Rd. SW17	BV50	76
Ascot Rd. Felt.	AZ48	73
Ascot Rd. Grav.	DG48	81
Ascot Rd. Orp.	CN52	88
Ascot Rd. Wat.	BB25	26
Ascots La. Hat.	BR10	5
Ashbourne Av. E18	CH31	49
Ashbourne Av. N20	BU27	38
Ashbourne Av. NW11	BR32	46
Ashbourne Av. Bexh.	CQ43	69
Ashbourne Av. Har.	BG34	45
Ashbourne Clo. N12	BS28	38
Ashbourne Clo. W5	BM39	55
Ashbourne Clo. Couls.	BW58	95
Ashbourne Clo. Couls.	BW62	104
Ashbourne Gro. NW7	BN28	37
Ashbourne Gro. SE22	CA45	67
Ashbourne Gro. W4	BO42	65
Ashbourne Rise Orp.	CM56	97
Ashbourne Rd. W5	BL38	55
Ashbourne Rd. Brox.	CD14	12
Ashbourne Rd. Mitch.	BV50	76
Ashbourne Rd. Rom.	CV28	42
Ashbourne Ter. SW19	BR50	75
Ashbridge Rd. E11	CG33	49
Ashbridge St. NW8	BU38	56
Ashbrook Rd. N19	BW33	47
Ashbrook Rd. Dag.	CR34	50
Ashbrook Rd. Wind.	AQ47	72
Ashburn Gdns. SW7	BT42	6
Ashburnham Av. Har.	BH32	4
Ashburnham Clo. N2	BT31	4
Stanley Rd.		
Ashburnham Dr. Wat.	BC27	3
Ashburnham Gdns. Har.	BH32	4
Ashburnham Gdns. Upmin.	CY33	5
Ashburnham Gro. SE10	CE43	6
Ashburnham Pl. SE10	CE43	6
Ashburnham Retreat, SE10	CE43	6
Ashburnham Rd. NW10	BQ38	5
Ashburnham Rd. SW10	BT43	6
Ashburnham Rd. Belv.	CS42	6
Ashburnham Rd. Rich.	BJ48	7
Ashburn Ms. SW7	BT42	6
Ashburn Pl. SW7	BT42	6
Ashburton Av. Croy.	CB54	8
Ashburton Av. Ilf.	CN35	4
Ashburton Clo. Croy.	CB54	8
Ashburton Ct. Pnr.	BD30	3
Ashburton Est. SW15	BQ46	7
Ashburton Gdns. Croy.	CB55	8
Ashburton Gro. N7	BY35	4
Ashburton Rd. E16	CH39	5
Ashburton Rd. Croy.	CB55	8
Ashburton Rd. Ruis.	BC34	4
Ashburton Ter. E13	CH37	5
Grasmere Rd.		
Ashbury Dr. Uxb.	AZ34	4
Ashbury Gdns. Rom.	CP32	5
Ashbury Rd. SW11	BU45	6
Ashby Av. Chess.	BM57	9
Ashby Clo. Horn.	CW33	5
Ashby Clo. Horn.	CX33	5
Ashby Gro. N1	BZ36	5
Ashby Ms. SE4	CD44	6
Ashby Rd. N15	CB32	4
Ashby Rd. SE4	CD44	6
Ashby Rd. Berk.	AO11	
Ashby Rd. Wat.	BC22	2
Ashby St. EC1	BY38	5
Ashby Way. West Dr.	AZ43	6
Ash Clo. SE20	CC51	8
Ash Clo. Brwd.	CZ25	3
Ash Clo. Cars.	BU55	8
Ash Clo. Hat.	BS16	2
Ash Clo. N. Mal.	BN51	8
Ash Clo. Orp.	CM53	8
Ash Clo. Red.	BW68	11
Ash Clo. Rom.	CR29	4
Ash Clo. Sid.	CO48	7
Ash Clo. Slou.	AT41	6
Ash Clo. Stan.	BJ29	3
Ash Clo. Swan.	CS51	8
Ash Clo. Wat.	BA19	1
Ash Clo. Welw. G. C.	BR6	
Ash Clo. Wok.	AS63	10
Ashcombe Av. Surb.	BK54	8
Ashcombe Gdns. Edg.	BM28	3
Ashcombe Pk. NW2	BO34	4
Ashcombe Rd. SW19	BS49	7
Ashcombe Rd. Cars.	BV57	9
Ashcombe Rd. Dor.	BJ70	11
Ashcombe Sq. N. Mal.	BN52	8
Ashcombe St. SW6	BS44	6
Ashcombe Ter. Tad.	BP63	10
Ash Ct. Epsom	BN56	9
Ashcroft Pnr.	BF29	3
Ashcroft Av. Sid.	CO46	7
Ashcroft Clo. Guil.	AS74	11
Ashcroft Cres. Sid.	CO46	7
Ashcroft Dr. Uxb.	AV32	4
Ashcroft Gdns. SW2	BY47	7
Trinity Rise		
Ashcroft Rise Couls.	BX57	9
Ashcroft Rise Couls	BX61	10
Ashcroft Rd. E3	CD38	5
Ashcroft Rd. Chess.	BL55	8
Ashdale. Lthd.	BF66	11
Ashdale Clo. Twick.	BF47	7
Ashdale Gro. Stan.	BH29	3
Ashdale Rd. SE12	CH47	7
Ashdale Way Twick.	BF47	7
Ashdale Clo.		
Ashdene, Pnr.	BD31	4
Ashdene Clo. Ashf.	BA50	7
Cambridge Rd.		
Ashdon Clo. Wdf. Grn.	CH29	4
Ashdon Rd. NW10	BO37	5
Ashdon Rd. Bush.	BD24	2
Ashdown Cres. Wal. Cr.	CD17	2
Ashdown Dr. Borwd.	BL23	2
Ashdowne Clo. Beck.	CE51	8
Ashdown Gdns. Sth. Croy.	CB61	10
Ashdown Rd. Enf.	CC24	3
Ashdown Rd. Epsom.	BO60	9
Ashdown Rd. Kings-on-t.	BL51	8
Ashdown Rd. Reig.	BS72	12
Ashdown Rd. Uxb.	AZ37	5
Ashdown Rd. Wat.	BD28	3
Woodhall La.		
Ashdown Wk. Rom.	CR30	4
Ash Dr. Hat.	BP14	1
Ashendene Rd. Hert.	BX13	1
Ashenden Rd. E5	CC35	4
Ashenden Rd. Guil.	AP70	11
Ashenden Wk. Slou.	AO35	4
Ashen Dr. Dart.	CU46	7
Ashen Gro. SW19	BS48	7
Ashen Gro. Farn.	CX58	9
Ashentree Ct. EC4	BY39	5
Whitefriars St.		
Ashen Vale Sth. Croy.	CC58	9
Ashes La. Ton.	DC70	11
Ashfield Av. Bush.	BF26	3
Ashfield Av. Felt.	BC47	7
Ashfield Clo. Rich.	BL47	7
Ashfield La. Chis.	CL50	7
Ashfield Pde. N14	BW26	3
Ashfield Rd. N4	BZ32	4
Ashfield Rd. N14	BW27	3

Ashfield Rd. W3 BO40 55
Ashfield Rd. Chesh. AO18 16
Ashfields Loug. CK23 31
Ashfields, Wat. BB21 26
Ashfield St. E1 CB39 57
Ashford Av. N8 BX31 47
Ashford Av. Ashf. AZ50 73
Ashford Av. Brwd. DA27 42
Ashford Av. Hayes BD39 54
Ashford Clo. E17 CD32 48
Ashford Clo. Ashf. AY49 73
Ashford Cres. Ashf. AY48 73
Ashford Cres. Enf. CC23 30
Ashford Gdns. Cob. BD61 102
Ashford Grn. Wat. BD28 36
Ashford La. Wind. AK41 61
Ashford Rd. E6 CL36 58
Ashford Rd. E18 CH30 40
Ashford Rd. N17 CD29 39
Tenterden Rd.
Ashford Rd. NW2 BQ35 46
Ashford Rd. Ashf. BA50 73
Ashford Rd. Felt. BA49 73
Ashford Rd. Iver AU37 52
Ashford Rd. Stai. AX51 83
Ashford St. N1 CA38 57
Ash Grn. Loughton CK23 31
Ash Grn. Uxb. AW36 53
Ash Gro. E8 CB37 57
Ash Gro. N13 BZ27 39
Ash Gro. NW2 BQ35 46
Ash Gro. SE20 CC51 87
Ash Gro. W5 BL41 65
Ash Gro. Enf. CA26 39
Ash Grove, Felt. DD47 73
Ash Gro. Guil. AQ70 118
Ash Gro. Hayes BA40 53
Ash Gro. Hem. H. AY15 8
Ash Gro. Houns. BD44 64
Ash Gro. Saw. CR6 6
Ash Gro. Stai. AX50 73
Ash Gro. Sthl. BF39 54
Ash Gro. Uxb. AX30 35
Ash Gro. Wem. BJ35 45
Ash Gro. West Dr. AY40 53
Ash Gro. W. Wick. CF55 87
Ashgrove Rd. Ashf. BA49 73
Ashgrove Rd. Brom. CF50 77
Ashgrove Rd. Ilf. CN33 49
Ashgrove Rd. Sev. CU67 116
Ash Hill Clo. Bush. BF26 36
Ash Hill Dr. Pnr. BD31 45
Ashington Ct. SE26 CB49 77
Ashington Rd. SW6 BR44 65
Ashlake Rd. SW16 BX49 76
Ashland Pl. W1 BV39 56
Ash La. Rom. CU29 41
Ash La. Sev. CY61 108
Ash La. Sev. DB59 99
Ash La. Wind. AL44 61
Ashlar Pl. SE18 CL42 68
Ash Latt Rd. Sev. CW63 108
Ashleigh Av. Egh. AT50 72
Ashleigh Gdns. Sutt. BS55 86
Ashleigh Gdns. Upmin. CY35 51
Ashleigh Rd. SE20 CB52 87
Ashleigh Rd. SW14 BO45 65
Ashley Av. Epsom BN60 94
Ashley Av. Ilf. CL30 40
Ashley Av. Mord. BS53 86
Ashley Clo. NW4 BQ30 37
Ashley Clo. Pnr. BC30 35
Ashley Clo. Sev. CU65 107
Ashley Clo. Walt. BB54 83
Ashley Cres. N22 BY30 38
Ashley Cres. SW11 BV45 66
Ashley Dr. Bans. BS60 95
Ashley Dr. Borwd. BN25 28
Ashley Dr. Twick. BF47 74
Ashley Dr. Walt. BC55 83
Ashley Gdns. N13 BZ28 39
Ashley Gdns. Grays. DE40 71
Ashley Gdns. Orp. CN56 97
Ashley Gdns. Rich. BK48 74
Ashley Gdns. Wem. BL34 46
Ashley Green La. Chesh. AO17 16
Ashley Green Rd. Chesh. AP15 7
Ashley La. NW4 BQ30 37
Ashley La. Croy. BY56 95
Ashley Park Av. Walt. BB55 83
Ashley Park Cres. Walt. BB54 83
Ashley Pk. Rd. Walt. BC55 83
Ashley Pl. SW1 BW41 66
Ashley Rise, Watt. BB56 92
Ashley Rd. E4 CE29 39
Ashley Rd. E7 CJ36 58
Ashley Rd. N17 CB31 48
Ashley Rd. N19 BX33 47
Ashley Rd. SW19 BS50 76
Ashley Rd. Dor. BG72 119
Ashley Rd. Enf. CC23 30
Ashley Rd. Epsom BN60 94
Ashley Rd. Hamptn. BF51 84
Ashley Rd. Rich. BL45 65
Jocelyn Rd.
Ashley Rd. St. Alb. BK13 9
Ashley Rd. Surb. BH53 84
Ashley Rd. Th. Hth. BX52 86
Ashley Rd. Uxb. AW37 53
Ashley Rd. Watt. BB56 92
Ashley Rd. Wok. AP62 100
Ashleys. Rick. AV26 34
Ashley Wk. NW7 BQ29 37
Ashling Rd. Croy. CB54 87
Ashlin Rd. E15 CF35 48
Ashlone Rd. SW15 BQ45 65
Ashlyn Clo. Bush. BE24 27
Ashlyn Gro. Horn. CV31 51
Ashlyns La. Epp. CT13 14
Ashlyns Rd. Berk. AQ13 7
Ashlyns Rd. Epp. CN18 22
Ashmead N14 BW25 29
Ashmead La. Uxb. AW34 44
Ashmead Rd. SE8 CE44 67
Ashmead Rd. Felt. BC47 73
Ashmere Av. Beck. CF51 87
Ashmere Clo. Sutt. BQ56 94
Ashmere Gdns. SW2 BX45 66
Ashmill St. NW1 BU39 56
Ashmole Pl. SW8 BX43 66
Ashmole St. SW8 BX43 66
Ashmore Gdns. Hem. H. AZ14 8
Ashmore Gro. Well. CM45 68
Ashmore La. Kes. GJ59 97
Ashmore Rd. W9 BR38 55
Ashmount Rd. N15 CA32 48
Ashmount Rd. N19 BW33 47
Ashmour Gdns. Rom. CS30 41
Ashness Gdns. Grnf. BJ36 54
Ashness Rd. SW11 BU46 76
Ash Ride Enf. BY21 29
Ashridge Clo. Har. BK32 45
Ashridge Cres. SE18 CL43 68
Ashridge Dr. St. Alb. BE18 18
Ashridge Dr. Wat. BC28 35
Ashridge Gdns. N13 BW28 38
Ashridge Gdns. Pnr. BE31 45
Ashridge La. Chesh. AR19 16
Ashridge Rise, Berk. AP12 7
Ashridge Way Mord. BR52 85
Ashridge Way Sun. BC50 73
Ash Rd. E15 CG35 49
Ash Rd. Croy. CE55 87
Ash Rd. Dart. CV47 80
Ash Rd. Dart. CW49 80
Ash Rd. Grav. DH49 81
Ash Rd. Hart. DC52 90
Ash Rd. Orp. CN57 97
Ash Rd. Sev. DB56 99
Ash Rd. Shep. AZ52 83
Ash Rd. Sutt. BR54 85
Ash Rd. West. CM66 115
Ash Rd. Wok. AS63 100
Ash Row Brom. CL54 88
Ashtead Gap, Lthd. BJ61 102
Ashtead Rd. E5 CB33 48
Ashtead Woods Rd. Ash. BK62 102
Ashton Clo. Sutt. BR56 94
Gandergreen La.
Ashton Clo. Walt. BC57 92
Ashton Gdns. Houns. BE45 64
Ashton Gdns. Rom. CQ32 50
Ashton Rd. E15 CF35 48
Ashton Rd. Enf. CD21 30
Ashton Rd. Rom. CV29 42
Ashton St. E14 CF40 57
Ashtree Av. Mitch. BT51 86
Ash Tree Clo. Croy. CD53 87
Ash Tree Dell, NW9 BN32 46
Ash Tree Field, Harl. CL10 6
Ashtree Rd. Wat. BC21 26
Ash Tree Way Croy. CD53 87
Ashtree Way, Hem. H. AW14 8
Ashurst Clo. Ken. BZ61 105
Ashurst Clo. Nthwd. BB29 35
Ashurst Dr. Ilf. CL32 49
Ashurst Dr. Shep. AY52 83
Ashurst Dr. Tad. BM68 112
Ashurst Rd. N12 BU28 38
Ashurst Rd. Barn. BU25 29
Ashurst Wk. Croy. CB55 87
Ash Vale. Rick. AU28 34
Ashvale Dr. Upmin. CZ34 51
Ashvale Gdns. Rom. CS28 41
Ashvale Gdns, Upmin. CZ34 51
Ashvale Rd. SW17 BU49 76
Ash View Gdns. Ashf. AY49 73
Ashville Rd. E11 CF34 48
Ashwater Rd. SE12 CH47 78
Ashwell Gro. N18 CA28 39
Ashwell Rd. E3 CC37 57
Ashwells Rd. Brwd. CY24 33
Ashwell St. St. Alb. BG13 9
Ashwells Way. Ch. St. G. AR27 34
Ashwin St. E8 CA36 57
Ashwood. Warl. CC63 105
Ashwood Av. Rain. CU38 59
Ashwood Av. Uxb. AZ39 53
Ashwood Gdns. Hayes. BB42 63
Ashwood Rd. E4 CF27 39
Ashwood Rd. Egh. AQ50 72
Ashwood Rd. Pot. B. BS20 20
Ashwood Rd. Wok. AS62 100
Ashworth Rd. W9 BS38 56
Askern Clo. Bexh. CP45 69
Aske St. N1 CA38 57
Pitfield St.
Askew Buildings, W12 BO41 65
Laurence Mews, W12
Askew Bldgs. W12 BP41 65
Askew Rd.
Askew Cres. W12 BO41 65
Askew Rd. W12 BO40 55
Askew Rd. Nthwd. BA27 35
Askham Ct. W12 BP40 55
Askham Rd. W12 BP40 55
Askill Dr. SW15 BR46 75
Askwith Rd. Rain. CS38 59
Aslett St. SW18 BT47 76
Asley Rd. Sev. CU65 107
Asmara Rd. NW2 BR35 46
Asmuns Hl. NW11 BS32 47
Asmuns Rd. NW11 BR32 46
Aspdin Rd. Grav. DE48 81
Aspect Row, Hem. H. AW12 8
Aspen Clo. Cob. BE61 102
Aspen Clo. Guil. AU69 118
Aspen Clo. Orp. CO56 98
Aspen Clo. S. Ock. DB38 60
Aspen Clo. West Dr. AY40 53
Aspen Copse, Brom. CK51 88
Aspen Dr. Wem. BJ34 45
Aspen Gdns. W6 BP42 65
Bridge Av.
Aspen Gdns. Mitch. BV53 86
Aspen Gro. Upmin. CW35 51
Aspenlea Rd. W6 BQ43 65
Aspen Way, Enf. CC21 30
Aspinall Rd. SE4 CC45 67
Aspinden Rd. SE16 CB42 67
Aspley Rd. SW18 BS46 76
Asplins Rd. N17 CB30 39
Assam St. E1 CB39 57
Assembly Ms. E1 CC39 57
Assembly Pass. E1 CC39 57
Assembly Wk. Cars. BU54 86
Assher Rd. Walt. BE55 84
Ass House La. Har. BF28 36
Astbury Rd. SE15 CC44 67
Astell St. SW3 BU42 66
Aster Pl. SE1 BZ41 67
Aste St. E14 CF41 67
Astey's Row, N1 BY36 56
Asthall Gdns. Ilf. CM31 49
Astle Dr. Sev. CW62 108
Astle St. SW11 BV44 66
Astley Av. NW2 BQ35 46
Astley Rd. Hem. H. AX13 8
Astley St. SE1 CA42 67
Aston Av. Har. BK33 45
Aston Clo. Sid. CO48 79
Aston Grn. Houns. BC44 63
Aston Mead. Wind. AM44 61
Aston Mews. Rom. CP33 50
Reynolds Av.
Aston Rd. SW20 BQ51 85
Approach Rd.
Aston Rd. W5 BK39 54
Aston Rd. Esher BH57 93
Astons Rd. Nthwd. BA27 35
Aston St. E14 CD39 57
Astonville St. SW18 BS47 76
Aston Way Epsom BO61 103
Aston Way, Pot. B. BT19 20
Astor Av. Rom. CS32 50
Astor Clo. Kings. On T. BM50 75
Astor Clo. Wey. AX56 92
Astoria Wk. SW9 BY45 66
Astor Rd. Sev. CZ57 99
Astra Clo. Horn. CU36 59
Astra Dr. Grav. DJ49 81
Astrop Ms. W6 BQ41 65
Astrop Ter. W6 BQ41 65
Astwick Av. Hat. BO11 10
Astwood Ms. SW7 BS42 66
Asylum Arch Rd. Red. BU72 121
Asylum Rd. SE15 CB43 67
Atalanta St. SW6 BQ44 65
Atbara Ct. Tedd. BJ50 74
Atbara Rd. Tedd. BJ50 74
Atcham Rd. Houns. BG45 64
Atheldene Rd. SW18 BS47 76
Athelney St. SE6 CE48 77
Athelstan Clo. Rom. CW30 42
Athelstane Gro. E3 CD37 57
Athelstane Rd. N4 BY34 47
Athelstan Rd. Kings-on-t. BL52 85
Villiers Rd.
Athelstan Rd. Rom. CW30 42
Athelstan Wk. Welw. G. C. BR8 5
Athelstone Rd. Har. BG30 36
Athelston Rd. Hem. H. AY15 8
Athena Clo. Har. BG34 45
Athenaeum Rd. N20 BT26 38
Athenlay Rd. SE15 CC46 77
Athens Gdns. W9 BS38 56
Atherden Rd. E5 CC35 48
Atherfield Rd. Reig. BT72 121
Atherfold Rd. SW9 BX45 66
Atherstone Ms. E7 CG36 58
Atherston Ms. SW7 BT42 66
Atherton Dr. SW19 BQ49 75
Atherton End, Saw. CQ5 6
Atherton Heights, Wem. BK36 54
Bridgewater Rd.
Atherton Pl. Har. BG31 45
Atherton Pl. Sthl. BF40 54
Atherton Rd. E7 CG35 49
Atherton Rd. SW13 BP43 65
Atherton Rd. Ilf. CK30 40
Atherton St. SW11 BU44 66
Athlone Rd. SW2 BX47 76
Athlone Sq. Wind. AO44 61
Ward Royal
Athlone St. NW5 BV36 56
Athlon Rd. Wem. BK37 54
Athol Clo. Pnr. BC30 35
Athole Gdns. Enf. CA25 30
Athol Gdns. Pnr. BC30 35
Atholl Rd. Ilf. CO33 50
Athol Rd. Erith CS42 69
Athol St. E14 CF39 57
Atkinson Clo. Orp. CN56 97
Atkinson Rd. E16 CJ39 58
Atkins Rd. E10 CE32 48
Atkins Rd. SW12 BW47 76
Atlantic Rd. SW9 BY45 66
Atlas Gdns. SE7 CJ42 68
Atlas Rd. E13 CH37 58
Atlas Rd. NW10 BO38 55
Atlas Rd. Wem. BN35 46
Atley Rd. E3 CE37 57
Atney Rd. SW15 BR45 65
Atria Rd. Nthwd. BC28 35
Atterbury St. SW1 BX42 66
Atterby Rd. N16 BY32 47
Wightman Rd.
Attewood Av. NW10 BO34 46
Attewood Rd. Nthlt. BD36 54
Attimore Clo. Welw. G. C. BP8 5
Attimore Rd. Welw. G. C. BP8 5
Attle Clo. Hayes BC38 53
Attle Clo. Uxb. AZ37 53
Attlee Dri. Dart. CW46 80
Attlee Dr. Dart. CX46 80
Attlee Rd. Hayes BC38 53
Attlee Ter. E17 CE31 48
Attneave St. WC1 BY38 56
Attwood Clo. Sth. Croy. CB60 96
Atwater Clo. SW2 BY47 76
Atwell Rd. SE15 CB44 67
Atwood, Lthd. BE65 102
Atwood Av. Rich. BM44 65
Atwood Rd. W6 BP42 65
Atwood's Alley Rich. BM44 65
Kew Gardens Rd
Atworth St. E14 CF41 67
Auberon St. E16 CK40 58
Aubert Ct. N5 BY35 47
Aubert Pk. N5 BY35 47
Aubley Ct. Twick. BG48 74
Aubrey Av. St. Alb. BK16 18
Aubrey Rd. E17 CE31 48
Aubrey Rd. N8 BX32 47
Aubrey Rd. W8 BR40 55
Aubreys Rd. Hem. H. AV14 7
Aubrey Wk. W8 BR40 55
Aubyn Hl. SE27 BZ49 77
Aubyn Sq. SW15 BP46 75
Auckland Av. Rain. CT38 59
Auckland Clo. SE19 CA51 87
Auckland Clo. Enf. CB22 30
Auckland Clo. Til. DG44 71
Auckland Gdns. SE19 CA51 87
Auckland Hl. SE27 BZ49 77
Auckland Ri. SE19 CA51 87
Auckland Rd. E10 CE34 48
Auckland Rd. SE19 CA51 87
Auckland Rd. SW11 BU45 66
Auckland Rd. Cat. CA64 105
Auckland Rd. Ilf. CL33 49
Auckland Rd. Kings. On T. BL52 85
Auckland Rd. Pot. B. BR19 19
Auckland St. SE11 BX42 66
Auden Pl. NW1 BV37 56
Audley Clo. Borwd. BM24 28
Audley Clo. Wey. AW56 92
Audley Ct. E18 CG31 49
Audley Ct. Pnr. BD30 36
Audley Dr. Warl. CC61 105
Audley Gdns. Ilf. CN34 49
Audley Gdns. Loug. CM23 31
Audley Gdns. Wal. Abb. CF20 21
Audley Pl. Sutt. BS57 95
Audley Rd. NW4 BP32 46
Audley Rd. W5 BL39 55
Audley Rd. Enf. BY23 29
Audley Rd. Rich. BL46 75
Audrey Clo. Beck. CE53 87
Audrey Gdns. Wem. BJ34 45
Audrey Rd. Ilf. CL34 49
Audrey St. E2 CB37 57
Augurs La. E13 CH38 58
Augusta Rd. Twick. BG48 74
Augustas Clo. St. Alb. BF14 9
Augusta St. E14 CE39 57
Augustine Clo. Slou. AV45 62
Augustine Rd. W14 BQ41 65
Augustine Rd. Har. BG30 36
Augustine Rd. Orp. CP52 89
Augustus Clo. Brent. BK43 64
Augustus Rd. SW19 BQ47 75
Augustus St. NW1 BV37 56
Aukingford Gdns. Ong. CW17 24
Epping Rd.
Aulay St. SE1 CB43 67
Aultone Way Cars. BU55 86
Aultone Way Sutt. BS55 86
Aulton St. SE11 BY42 66
Aurelia Gdns. Croy. BX53 86
Aurelia Rd. Croy. BX53 86
Auresford Rd. Guil. AQ71 118
Auric Clo. Grays. DG42 71
Auriel Av. Dag. CS36 59
Auriol Dr. Grnf. BG36 54
Auriol Rd. W14 BR42 65
Austell Gdns. NW7 BO27 37
Austen Clo. Green. DB46 80
Austen Clo. Til. DH44 71
Coleridge Rd.
Austen Gdns. Dart. CW45 70
Austen Pl. Guil. AS71 118
Austen Rd. Guil. AS71 118
Austen Rd. Har. BF34 45
Austenway, Ger. Cr. AR31 43
Austenwood Clo. Ger. Cr. AR30 34
Austenwood La. Ger. Cr. AR30 34
Austenwood La. Ger. Cr. AR31 43
Austin Av. Brom. CK53 88
Austin Friars EC2 BZ39 57
Austin Friars Pass. EC2 BZ39 57
Austin Friars
Austin Gdns. Surb. BM54 85
Austin Rd. SW11 BV44 66
Austin Rd. Grav. DF47 81
Austin Rd. Hayes. BB41 63
Austin Rd. Orp. CO53 89
Austins La. Uxb. BA35 44
Austins Mead, Hem. H. AT17 16
Austin, S La. Uxb. BA34 44
Austins Pl. Hem. H. AX13 8
Austin St. E2 CA38 57
Austin Waye, Uxb. AX37 53
Austral Clo. Sid. CN48 78
Longlands Rd.
Austral Dr. Horn. CV33 51
Australia Rd. W12 BP40 55
Australia Rd. Slou. AQ41 62
Austral St. SE11 BY42 66
Aust Rd. Grav. DH47 81
Autumn Clo. Enf. CB23 30
Autumn Clo. Slou. AM40 61
Autumn Gro. Welw. G. C. BS9 5
Autumn St. E3 CE37 57
Avalon Clo. W13 BJ39 54
Avalon Clo. Enf. BY23 29
Avalon Clo. Orp. CP55 89
Avalon Rd. SW6 BS44 66
Avalon Rd. W13 BJ38 54
Avalon Rd. Orp. CO55 89
Avalon Ter. Rich. BL45 65
Avarn Rd. SW17 BU50 76
Avcliffe Clo. Kings. On T. BM51 85
Avebury Est. E2 CB38 57
Avebury Pk. Surb. BK54 84
Avebury Rd. E11 CF33 48
Avebury Rd. SW19 BR51 85
Avebury Rd. Orp. CM55 88
Aveley Clo. S. Ock. CW40 60
Aveley Rd. Rom. CS31 50
Aveley Rd. Upmin. CX36 60
Aveline St. SE11 BX42 66
Aveling Park Rd. E17 CE30 39
Avelon Rd. Rain. CU37 59
Avelon Rd. Rom. CS29 41
Ave Maria La. EC4 BY39 56
Ludgate Hill
Avenell Rd. N5 BY34 47
Avening Ter. SW18 BS46 76
Avenons Rd. E13 CH38 58
Avenue App. Kings L. AZ18 17
Avenue Clo. N14 BW25 29
Avenue Clo. NW8 BU37 56
Avenue Clo. Houns. BC44 63
Avenue Clo. Rom. CW29 42
Avenue Clo. Tad. BP64 103
Avenue Clo. West Dr. AX41 63
Avenue Cres. W3 BM41 65
Avenue Cres. Houns. BC43 63
Avenue Dr. Slou. AS39 52
Avenue Elmers Surb. BL53 85
Avenue Gdns. SE25 CA51 87
Avenue Gdns. SW14 BO45 65
Avenue Gdns. W3 BM41 65
Avenue Gdns. Houns. BC43 63
Avenue Gdns. Tedd. BH50 74
Avenue Gte. SE21 CA49 77
Avenue La. Rick. AU25 25
Avenue Mews. N10 BV31 47
Queen's Av.
Avenue Ms. NW6 BS35 47
Finchley Rd.
Avenue Pk. Rd. SE27 BY48 76
Avenue Rise Bush. BF25 27
Avenue Rd. E7 CH35 49
Avenue Rd. N6 BW33 47
Avenue Rd. N12 BT28 38
Avenue Rd. N14 BV26 38
Avenue Rd. N15 BZ32 48
Avenue Rd. NW3 BT36 56
Avenue Rd. NWU0 BO37 55
Avenue Rd. SE20 CC51 87
Avenue Rd. SE25 CA51 87
Avenue Rd. SW16 BW51 86
Avenue Rd. SW20 BP51 85
Avenue Rd. W3 BM41 65
Avenue Rd. W13 BJ40 54
Avenue Rd. Bans. BS61 104
Avenue Rd. Beck. CC51 87
Avenue Rd. Belv. CR42 69
Avenue Rd. Bexh. CQ45 69
Avenue Rd. Brent. BK42 64
Avenue Rd. Brwd. DB28 42
Avenue Rd. Cat. BZ64 105
Avenue Rd. Cob. BD61 102
Avenue Rd. Epp. CM21 31
Avenue Rd. Epsom BN60 94
Avenue Rd. Erith CS43 69
Avenue Rd. Felt. BB48 73
Avenue Rd. Hmptn. BF51 84
Avenue Rd. Hodd. CF13 12
Avenue Rd. Islw. BH44 64
Avenue Rd. Kings. On T. BL52 85
Avenue Rd. Maid. AG40 61
Avenue Rd. N. Mal. BO52 85
Avenue Rd. Pnr. BE31 45
Avenue Rd. Rom. CP33 50
Avenue Rd. Rom. CW29 42
Avenue Rd. St. Alb. BH13 9
Avenue Rd. Sev. CV65 108
Avenue Rd. Stai. AU49 72
Avenue Rd. Sthl. BE40 54
Avenue Rd. Sutt. BS58 95
Avenue Rd. Tedd. BJ50 74
Avenue Rd. Wall. BW57 95
Avenue Rd. Wdf. Grn. CJ29 40
Avenue Rd. West. CK63 106
Avenue S., The, Surb. BL54 85
Avenue Ter. N. Mal. BN52 85
Avenue Ter. Wat. BE25 27
Avenue, The, E4 CF29 39
Avenue, The, E11 CH32 49
Avenue, The EC3 CA40 57
Avenue, The, N1 BV28 38
Avenue, The, N3 BS30 38
Avenue, The, N8 BY31 47
Avenue, The, N10 BW30 38
Avenue, The, N11 BV28 38
Avenue, The, N17 BZ31 48
Avenue, The, SE7 CJ43 68
Avenue, The, SE10 CF43 67
Avenue, The, SE19 CA49 77
Avenue, The, SW4 BV46 76
Avenue, The, SW17 BV48 76
Avenue, The, SW18 BU47 76
Avenue, The, W4 BO41 65
Avenue, The, W13 BJ40 54
Avenue, The Amer. AO22 25
Avenue, The, Barn. BR24 28
Avenue, The, Beck. CE51 87
Avenue, The Bet. BM70 120
Avenue, The, Bex. CP47 79
Avenue, The, Brom. CJ52 88
Avenue, The, Brwd. DC29 122
Avenue, The, Bush. BE24 27
Avenue, The, Cars. BV57 95
Avenue, The, Couls. BW61 104
Avenue, The, Croy. CA55 87
Avenue, The Egh. AT49 72
Avenue, The, Epsom BP57 94
Avenue, The, Esher BH57 93
Avenue, The Grav. DG47 81

Avenue, The, Green. DA45 70
Avenue, The Guil. AO74 118
Avenue, The, Hamptn. BE49 74
Avenue, The, Har. BH30 36
Avenue, The, Har. BH31 45
Marlborough Rd.
Avenue, The, Harl. CM9 6
Avenue, The, Hodd. CD13 12
Avenue, The, Horn. CV34 51
Avenue, The, Houns. BC44 63
Avenue, The, Houns. BF46 74
Avenue, The, Kes. CJ55 88
Avenue, The, Loug. CJ25 31
Avenue, The, Nthwd. BA29 35
Avenue, The, Orp. CN55 88
Avenue, The, Orp. CO50 79
Avenue, The, Pnr. BE29 36
Avenue, The, Pnr. BE32 45
Avenue, The, Pot. B. BS19 20
Avenue, The, Rad. BJ20 18
Avenue, The Red. BX72 121
Avenue, The, Rich. BL44 65
Avenue, The, Rom. CS31 50
Avenue, The, Stai. AR45 62
Avenue, The, Stai. AW51 83
Avenue, The, Sun. BC51 83
Avenue, The, Surb. BL53 85
Avenue, The, Sutt. BR58 94
Avenue, The, Tad. BP64 103
Avenue, The, Twick. BJ46 74
Avenue, The Uxb. AX38 53
Avenue, The, Uxb. AZ35 44
Avenue, The, Wat. BC23 26
Avenue, The, Wem. BL33 46
Avenue, The, W. Wick. CF54 87
Avenue, The, Wey. AW58 92
Avenue, The, Whyt. CB63 105
Avenue, The Wind. AQ46 72
Avenue, The Wok. AP58 91
Avenue, The, Wor. Pk. BO55 85
Avenue, The, Tad. BP65 103
Averil Gro. SW16 BY50 76
Averill St. W6 BQ43 65
Avern Rd. E. Mol. BF53 84
Avery Gdns. Ilf. CK32 49
Avery Hl. Rd. SE9 CM46 78
Avery Row, W1 BV40 56
Avey La. Wal. Abb. CG22 31
Aviary Clo. E16 CG39 58
Aviary Rd. Wok. AW61 101
Aviary St. E16 CG39 58
Lawrence St.
Aviemore Clo. Beck. CD53 87
Aviemore Way Beck. CD53 87
Avignon Rd. SE4 CC45 67
Avington Clo. Guil. AS70 118
Avington Gro. SE20 CC50 77
Avington Way SE15 CA43 67
Avior Dr. Nthwd. BB28 35
Avior Dr. Nthwd. BC28 35
Avis Sq. E1 CC39 57
Avoca Rd. SW17 BV49 76
Avon Clo. Grav. DH48 81
Avon Clo. Hayes BC38 53
Avon Clo. Sutt. BT56 95
Avon Clo. Wat. BD20 18
Avon Clo. Wey. AW57 92
Avon Clo. Wor. Pk. BP55 85
Avondale Av. N12 BS28 38
Avondale Av. NW2 BO34 46
Avondale Av. Barn. BU26 38
Avondale Av. Esher. BJ55 84
Avondale Av. Stai. AV50 72
Avondale Av. Wor. Pk. BO54 85
Avondale Clo. Loug. CK26 40
Avondale Dr.
Avondale Clo. Walt. BD56 93
Avondale Ct. E16 CG39 58
Off Avondale Rd.
Avondale Ct. E18 CH30 40
Avondale Cres. Enf. CD24 30
Avondale Cres. Ilf. CJ32 49
Avondale Dr. Loug. CK26 40
Avondale Gdns. Houns. BE46 74
Avondale Pk. W11 BR40 55
Avondale Pk. Gdns. W11 BQ40 55
Avondale Rise, SE15 CA45 67
Avondale Rd. E16 CG39 58
Avondale Rd. E17 CE33 48
Avondale Rd. N3 BT30 38
Avondale Rd. N13 BY27 38
Avondale Rd. N15 BY32 47
Avondale Rd. SE9 CK48 78
Avondale Rd. SW14 BN45 65
Avondale Rd. SW19 BS49 76
Avondale Rd. Ashf. AX48 73
Avondale Rd. Brom. CG50 78
Avondale Rd. Har. BH31 45
Avondale Rd. Hayes BC40 53
Avondale Rd. Sth. Croy. BZ57 96
Avondale Rd. Well. CP44 69
Avondale Sq. SE1 CB42 67
Avon Grn. S. Ock. DA39 60
Avonley Rd. SE14 CC43 67
Avonmead Wok. AR62 100
Silversmiths Way
Avon Ms. Pnr. BE29 36
Avonmore Pl. W14 BR42 65
Avonmore Rd.
Avonmore Rd. W14 BR42 65
Avon Path Sth. Croy. BZ57 96
Avon Pl. SE1 BZ41 67
Avon Rd. E17 CF31 48
Avon Rd. SE4 CE45 67
Avon Rd. Grnf. BF38 54
Avon Rd. Sun. BB50 73
Avon Rd. Upmin. CY32 51
Avon Sq. Hem. H. AY11 8
Avon St. SE1 BZ41 67
Avontar Rd. S. Ock. DA38 60
Avon Way E18 CH31 49
Tavistock Rd.
Avonwick Rd. Houns. BF44 64
Avril Way, E4 CF28 39
Avro Way Wall. BX57 95
Avrrit Clo. Guil. AP69 118
Awlfield Av. N17 BZ30 39
Awliscombe Rd. Well. CN44 68
Axes La. Red. BW74 121
Axe St. Bark. CM37 58
Axholme Av. Edg. BM30 37
Axminster Cres. Well. CP44 69
Axminster Rd. N7 BX34 47
Axtaine Rd. Orp. CP54 89
Axwood Epsom BN61 103
Aybrook St. W1 BV39 56
Aycliff Clo. Brom. CK52 88
Aycliffe Kings. On T. BM51 85
Cambridge Rd.
Aycliffe Rd. W12 BP40 55
Aycliffe Rd. Borwd. BL23 28
Ayebridges Av. Egh. AU50 72
Ayelands La. New. A. G. DC55 90
Aylands Rd. Enf. CC21 30
Aylesbury Cres. Slou. AO39 52
Aylesbury Rd. SE17 BZ42 67
Aylesbury Rd. Brom. CH52 88
Aylesbury St. EC1 BY38 56
Aylesbury St. NW10 BN34 46
Aylesford Av. Beck. CD53 87
Aylesford St. SW1 BW42 66
Aylesham Rd. Orp. CN54 88
Ayles Rd. Hayes BC38 53
Aylestone Av. NW6 BQ36 55
Aylett Rd. SE25 CB52 87
Aylett Rd. Islw. BH44 64
Aylett Rd. Upmin. CY34 51
Ayley Croft. Enf. CB25 30
Ayliffe Clo. Kings. On T. BM51 85
Cambridge Rd.
Aylmer Clo. Stan. BJ28 36
Aylmer Dr. Stan. BJ28 36
Aylmer Rd. E11 CG33 49
Aylmer Rd. N2 BU32 47
Aylmer Rd. W12 BO41 65
Aylmer Rd. Dag. CQ34 50
Ayloffe Rd. Dag. CQ36 59
Ayloffs Clo. Horn. CW32 51
Ayloffs Wk. Horn. CV32 51
Aylsham La. Rom. CV28 42
Aylsham Rd. Hodd. CF11 12
Aylton Est. SE16 CC41 67
Aylward Rd. SE23 CC48 77
Aylward Rd. SW20 BR51 85
Aylwards Rise Stan. BJ28 36
Aylward St. E1 CC39 57
Aylwin Est. SE1 CA41 67
Aynhoe Rd. W14 BQ42 65
Aynno St. Wat. BC25 26
Aynscombe Angle Orp. CO54 89
Aynscombe La. SW14 BN45 65
Aynscombe Path. SW14 BN44 65
Ayot Grn. Welw. BP6 5
Ayot Little Green La. Welw. BO6 5
Ayot Path Borwd. BM22 28
Ayot Rd. Welw. G. C. BP7 5
Ayot St. Peter Rd. Welw. BO5 5
Ayr Ct. W3 BM39 55
Monks Dr.
Ayres Clo. E13 CH38 58
Ayres Cres. NW10 BN36 55
Ayres St. SE1 BZ41 67
Ayr Grn. Rom. CS29 41
Ayron Rd. S. Ock. DA38 60
Ayrsome Rd. N16 CA34 48
Ayr Way Rom. CT30 41
Aysgarth Rd. SE21 BZ46 77
Aytoun Pl. SW9 BX44 66
Aytoun Rd. SW9 BX44 66
Azalea Clo. W7 BH40 54
Azalea Dr. Swan. CS52 89
Azalea Wk. Pnr. BC32 44
Azenby Rd. SE15 CA44 67
Azof St. SE10 CG42 68
Baalbec Rd. N5 BY35 47
Baas Hill Clo. Brox. CD14 12
Baas La. Brox. CD14 12
Babbacombe Clo. Chess. BK56 93
Babbacombe Gdns. Ilf. CK31 49
Babbacombe Rd. Brom. CH51 88
Babbington Ri. Wem. BM36 55
Baber Dr. Felt. BD46 74
Babington Rise, Wem. BM36 55
Babington Rd. NW4 BP31 46
Babington Rd. SW16 BW49 76
Babington Rd. Dag. CP35 50
Babington Rd. Horn. CU33 50
Babmaes St. SW1 BW40 56
Jermyn St.
Babylon La. Tad. BS67 113
Baccallay St. E3 CD39 57
Bacchus Wk. N1 CA37 57
Bachelors Acre. Wind. AO44 61
Bachelor's La. Wok. AY65 101
Baches St. N1 BZ38 57
Back Alley, Dor. BJ71 119
Back Church La. E1 CB39 57
Back Grn. Walt. BD57 93
Back Hill, EC1 BY38 56
Back La. N8 BX37 56
New Rd.
Back La. NW3 BT35 47
Flask Wk.
Back La. Bark. CM37 58
Broadway
Back La. Bex. CR47 79
Back La. Brent BK43 64
St Paul's Rd.
Back La. Brwd. DA21 33
Back La. Ch. St. G. AQ27 34
Back La. Edg. BN30 37
Back La. Grays CZ41 70
Back Lane. Guil. AW69 110
Back La. Hert. BZ12 12
Back La. Reig. BT68 113
Back La. Rich. BK48 74
Back La. Rom. CP33 50
Station Rd.
Back La. Sev. CR67 116
Back La. Sev. DB65 108
Back La. Sev. DC67 117
Back La. Ton. DB69 117
Back La. Wal. Abb. CJ14 13
Back La. Wat. BH23 27
Back River Pk. Beck. CD51 87
Back Rd. Sid. CO49 79
Back Row. SW17 BU49 76
Totterdown St.
Back St. W3 BM40 55
Back Swan Yd. SE1 CA41 67
Bermondsey St.
Back, The, Berk. AT11 7
Bacon Gro. SE1 CA41 67
Bacon La. NW9 BM31 46
Bacon La. Edg. BM30 37
Bacon Link Rom. CR29 41
Bacons Dr. Pot. B. BX18 20
Bacons La. N6 BV33 47
Bacons Mead, Uxb. AW34 44
Bacon St. E1 CA38 57
Bacon St. E2 CA38 57
Bacton St. E2 CC38 57
Digby St.
Badburgham Ct. Wal. Abb. CG20 22
Ninefields
Baddow Clo. Wdf. Grn. CJ29 40
Baden Clo. Stai. AW50 73
Baden Clo. Wey. BB57 92
Baden Pl. SE1 BZ41 67
Baden Powell Rd. Sev. CT64 107
Baden Rd. N8 BW31 47
Baden Rd. Guil. AQ69 118
Baden Rd. Ilf. CL35 49
Bader Wk. Grav. DF48 81
Hillary Av.
Bader Way. Rain. CU36 59
Badger Clo. Guil. AQ69 118
Badger Clo. Houns. BD45 64
Badgers Copse Wor. Pk. BO55 85
Badgers Croft N20 BR26 37
Badgers Cft. SE9 CL48 78
Badgers Hill, Vir. W. AR53 82
Badgers Hole Croy. CC56 96
Badgers La. Warl. CC63 105
Badgers Rd. Sev. CR58 98
Badgers Wk. N. Mal. BO51 85
Badgers Wk. Whyt. CA63 105
Badgers Wood. Slou. AO35 43
Badger Way. Hat. BP13 10
Badingham Dr. Lthd. BH65 102
Badlis Rd. E17 BW31 47
Badmaes St. SW1 BW40 56
Badminton Clo. Har. BH31 45
Badminton Clo. Nthlt. BF36 54
Badminton Pl. Brox. CD13 12
Badminton Rd. SW12 BV46 76
Badshawe Rd. Grays. DD40 71
Badsworth Rd. SE5 BZ44 67
Badwell Clo. Horn. CU36 59
Bagden Hill. Dor. BG68 111
Bagley Clo. West Dr. AY41 63
Bagley Rd. SW6 BS44 66
Bagleys Spring Clo. Rom. CQ31 50
Bagot Clo. Ash. BL61 103
Bagshot Clo. SE18 CL44 68
Bagshot Rd. Egh. AR50 72
Bagshot Rd. Enf. CA26 39
Bagshot Rd. Guil. AO66 109
Bagshot Rd. Wok. AO65 100
Bagshot St. SE17 CA42 67
Baildon St. SE8 CD43 67
Bailey Clo. Wind. AN44 61
Bailey Gdns. Rom. CO32 50
Bailey Pl. SE26 CC50 77
Bailey Rd. SW19 BT50 76
Bailey Rd. Dor. BG72 119
Bailey Rd. Ilf. CL32 49
Baillie Clo. Rain. CV39 60
Baillie Rd. Guil. AS71 118
Baillie's Wk. W5 BK41 64
Bainbridge Rd. Dag. CQ35 50
Bainbridge St. WC1 BW39 56
Baird Av. Sthl. BF40 54
Baird Clo. NW9 BN32 46
Baird Gdns. SE21 CA49 77
Baird Rd. Enf. CB24 30
Baizdon Rd. SE3 CG44 68
Bakeham La. Egh. AR50 72
Baker Hill Clo. Grav. DF49 81
Baker La. Mitch. BV51 86
Baker Rd. NW10 BN37 55
Bakers Alley, SE1 CA40 57
Abbots La.
Bakers Ave. Sev. CZ57 99
Baker's Av. E17 CE32 48
Bakers End, SW20 BR51 85
Bakers Grn. Welw. G. C. BT7 5
Baker's Hill, E5 CB33 48
Bakers Hill Barn. BS23 29
Bakers La. N6 BU32 47
North Hill
Bakers La. W5 BK40 54
Grove, The.
Bakers La. Epp. CN18 22
Bakers Md. Gdse. CC68 114
Bakers Meadow Brwd. DB22 33
Baker's Ms. W1 BV39 56
Adam St.
Bakers Rd. Uxb. AX36 53
Bakers Rd. Wal. Cr. CB18 21
Baker's Row, E15 CG37 58
Baker's Row, EC1 BY38 56
Baker St. NW1 BU38 56
Baker St. W1 BU38 56
Baker St. Enf. BZ24 30
Baker St. Pot. B. BR20 19
Baker St. Pot. B. BR21 28
Baker St. Wey. AZ56 92
Bakers Wood. Uxb. AU33 43
Bakewell Way, N. Mal. BO51 85
Balaams La. N14 BW27 38
Balaam St. E13 CH38 58
Balaclava Rd. SE1 CA42 67
Balaclava Rd. Surb. BK54 84
Balben Rd. E9 CC36 57
Balcaskie Rd. SE9 CK46 78
Balchen Rd. SE3 CJ44 68
Balchier Rd. SE22 CB46 77
Balchins La. Dor. BF72 119
Balcombe St. NW1 BU38 56
Balcorne St. E9 CC36 57
Balder Ri. SE12 CH48 78
Balderton St. W1 BV39 56
Baldocks Rd. Epp. CN21 31
Baldock St. E3 CE37 57
Baldock Way Borwd. BL23 28
Baldry Gdns. SW16 BX50 76
Baldwin Cres. SE5 BZ44 67
Baldwins. Welw. G. C. BT7 5
Baldwin's Gdns. EC1 BY39 56
Baldwin's Hill Loug. CK23 31
Baldwin's La. Rick. AZ24 26
Baldwins Pond Loug. CK23 31
Baldwins Shore. Wind. AO43 61
Baldwin St. EC1 BZ38 57
Baldwin Ter. N1 BZ37 57
Baldwyn Gdns. W3 BN40 55
Baldwyns Est. Dart. CT48 79
Baldwyn's Pk. Bex. CS48 79
Baldwyn's Rd. Bex. CS48 79
Balfern Gro. W4 BO42 65
Balfern St. SW11 BU44 66
Balfe St. N1 BX37 56
Balfont Clo. Sth. Croy. CB60 96
Balfour App. Ilf. CL34 49
Balfour Rd.
Balfour Av. W7 BH40 54
Balfour Av. Wok. AS64 100
Balfour Gro. N20 BU27 38
Balfour Ms. W1 BV40 56
Aldford St.
Balfour Of Burlington Est. W10 BQ39 55
Balfour Pl. W1 BV40 56
Alford St.
Balfour Rd. N5 BZ35 48
Balfour Rd. SE25 CB52 87
Balfour Rd. SW19 BS50 76
Balfour Rd. W3 BN39 55
Balfour Rd. W13 BJ41 64
Balfour Rd. Brom. CJ53 88
Balfour Rd. Cars. BU57 95
Balfour Rd. Grays. DE42 71
Balfour Rd. Har. BG32 45
Balfour Rd. Houns. BF45 64
Balfour Rd. Ilf. CL34 49
Balfour Rd. Sthl. BD41 64
Balfour Rd. Wey. AZ56 92
Balfour St. SE17 BZ42 67
Balgonie Rd. E4 CF26 39
Balgores Cres. Rom. CU31 50
Balgores La. Rom. CU31 50
Balgores Sq. Rom. CU31 50
Balgowan Clo. N. Mal. BO52 85
Balgowan Rd. Beck. CD52 87
Balgowan St. SE18 CN42 68
Balgrove Rd, W10 BR39 55
Balham Gro. SW12 BV47 76
Balham High Rd. SW12 BV48 76
Balham High Rd. SW17 BV48 76
Balham Hill, SW12 BV47 76
Balham New Rd. SW12 BV47 76
Balham Pk. Rd. SW12 BU47 76
Balham Rd. N9 CB27 39
Balham Station Rd. SW12 BV47 76
Ballamore Rd. Brom. CH48 78
Ballance Rd. E9 CC36 57
Ballands, S. The Lthd. BH64 102
Ballands, S. The Lthd. BH65 102
Ballantine St. SW18 BT45 66
Ballantyne Dr. Tad. BR64 103
Ballard Clo. Kings-on-t. BN50 75
Ballard Grn. Wind. AM43 61
Ballards Av. Sth. Croy. CB57 96
Ballards Clo. Dag. CR37 59
Ballards Fm. Rd. Sth. Croy. CB57 96
Ballards Grn. Tad. BR63 103
Ballard's La. N3 BS30 38
Ballard's La. N12 BS30 38
Ballards La. Oxt. CJ68 115
Ballards Rise. Sth. Croy. CB57 96
Ballards Rd. NW2 BP34 46
Ballards Rd. Dag. CR37 59
Ballards Way Sth. Croy. CB57 96
Ballast Quay SE10 CF42 67
Ballatar Clo. Wat. BD28 36
Ballater Rd. SW2 BX45 66
Ballater Rd. Sth. Croy. CA56 96
Ballina St. SE23 CC47 77
Ballingdon Rd. SW11 BV46 76
Balliol Av. E4 CG28 40
Balliol Rd. N17 BZ30 39
Balliol Rd. W10 BQ39 55
Balliol Rd. Well. CO44 69
Ball La. N14 BW27 38
Balaams La.
Balloch Rd. SE6 CF47 77
Ballogie Av. NW10 BO35 46
Ballow Close SE5 BZ43 67
Elmington Estate
Balls Pond Rd. N1 BZ36 57
Balmain Clo. W5 BK40 54
Balmer Rd. E3 CD37 57
Balmes Rd. N1 BZ37 57
Balmoral Av. Beck. CD52 87
Balmoral Clo. SW15 BQ46 75
Westleigh Ave.
Balmoral Cres. E. Mol. BF52 84
Balmoral Dr. Borwd. BN25 28
Balmoral Dr. Hayes BB38 53
Balmoral Dr. Hayes BC39 53
Balmoral Dr. Sthl. BE38 54
Balmoral Dr. Wok. AU61 100
Balmoral Gdns. W13 BJ41 64
Balmoral Gdns. Ilf. CN33 49
Balmoral Gdns. Wind. AO45 61
Balmoral Rd. E7 BZ35 48
Balmoral Rd. E10 CE34 48
Balmoral Rd. N7 BX36 56
Brewery Rd.
Balmoral Rd. Brwd. DA25 33
Balmoral Rd. Enf. CC21 30
Balmoral Rd. Har. BF35 45
Balmoral Rd. Horn. CV34 51
Balmoral Rd. Kings. On T. BL52 85
Balmoral Rd. Rom. CU32 50
Balmoral Rd. S. At H. CX50 80
Balmoral Rd. Wat. BD22 27
Balmoral Rd. Wor. Pk. BP55 85
Balmore Cres. Barn. BV25 29
Balmore St. N19 BV34 47
Balmuir Gdns. SW15 BQ45 65
Balnacraig Av. NW10 BO35 46
Balouhain Clo. Ash. BK62 102
Baltic Clo. SW19 BT50 76
Baltic St. EC1 BZ38 57
Balvernie Gro. SW18 BR47 75
Bamborough Gdns. W12 BQ41 65
Bamford Av. Wem. BL37 55
Bamford Rd. Bark. CA36 57
Bamford Rd. Brom. CF49 77
Bamford Way. Rom. CR28 41
Bampfylde Clo. Wall. BW55 86
Bampton Rd. SE23 CC48 77
Bampton Rd. Rom. CW30 42
Banbury Clo. Sutt. BS57 95
Banbury Ct. WC2 BX40 56
Long Acre
Banbury Rd. E9 CC36 57
Banbury St. SW11 BU44 66
Banbury St. Wat. BC25 26
Banbury Wk. Nthlt. BF37 54
Banchory Rd. SE3 CH43 68
Bancroft Av. N2 BU32 47
Bancroft Av. Buck. H. CH27 40
Bancroft Clo. Ashf. AZ49 73
Bancroft Clo. Reig. BS70 121
Bancroft Rd.
Bancroft Ct. Nthlt. BD37 54
Bancroft Gdns. Har. BG30 36
Bancroft Gdns. Orp. CN54 88
Bancroft Rd. E1 CC38 57
Bancroft Rd. Har. BG30 36
Bancroft Rd. Reig. BS70 121
Banders Rise, Guil. AU70 118
Band La. Egh. AS49 72
Bandon Rise Wall. BW56 95
Bangalore St. SW15 BQ45 65
Bangor Clo. Nthlt. BF35 45
Bangor Rd. Brent. BL43 65
Bangors Clo. Iver AV39 52
Bangors Rd. N. Iver AU37 52
Bangors Rd. S. Iver AV38 52
Banim St. W6 BP41 65
Banister Rd. W10 BQ38 55
Bank Av. Mitch. BT51 86
Bank Ct. Dart. CW46 80
Bank Ct. Hem. H. AX14 8
Bankfoot Rd. Brom. CG49 78
Bankhurst Rd. SE6 CD47 77
Bank La. SW15 BO46 75
Bank La. Kings-on-t. BL50 75
Bank La. Sev. CX69 117
Bank Mill La. Berk. AS13 7
Bank Pl. Brwd. DB27 42
Bankside, SE1 BY40 56
Bankside Enf. BY23 29
Bankside Sth. Croy. CA57 96
Bankside Sthl. BD40 54
Bankside Av. Nthlt. BC37 53
Bankside Clo. Bex. CS49 79
Bankside Clo. Cars. BU57 95
Bankside Clo. West. CJ62 106
Bankside Dr. Surb. BJ54 84
Banks La. Bexh. CQ45 69
Bank's La. Lthd. BC64 101
Bank St. Grav. DG46 81
Bank, The, N6 BV33 47
Bankton Rd. SW2 BY45 66
Bankwell Rd. SE13 CG45 68
Banmore Comm. Rd. Dor. BH69 119
Bann Clo. S. Ock. DA40 60
Banner St. EC1 BZ38 57
Banning St. SE10 CG42 68
Bannister Clo. SW2 BY47 76
Bannister Clo. Slou. AS41 62
Bannister Ho. E9 CC35 48
Bannisters Rd. Guil. AP71 118
Bannock Burn Rd. SE18 CN42 68
Bansons Way Ong. CX17 24
Banstead Gdns. N9 CA27 39
Banstead Rd. Cars. BT58 95
Banstead Rd. Cat. BZ64 105
Banstead Rd. Epsom BP59 94
Banstead Rd. Pur. BY59 95
Banstead Rd. S. Sutt. BT59 95
Banstead St. SE15 CB45 67
Banstead Way Wall. BX56 95
Banstock Rd. Edg. BM29 37
Banton Clo. Enf. CB23 30
Banyard Rd. SE16 CB41 67
Banyards Horn. CW32 51
Bapchild Pl. Orp. CP52 89
Okemore Gdns.
Baptist Gdns. NW5 BV36 56
Queen's Cres.
Barbara Clo. Shep. AZ53 83
Barbara St. N7 BX36 56
Barbauld Rd. N16 CA34 48

Barber Clo. N21 BY26 38
Barberry Rd. Hem. H. AW13 8
Barber's All. E13 CH38 58
Barber's Rd. E15 CE37 57
Barbican Rd. Grnf. BF39 54
Barbican Site, EC2 BZ39 57
Barb Ms. W6 BQ41 65
Shepherds Bush Rd.
Barbon Clo. WC1 BX39 56
Boswell St.
Barbot Clo. N9 CB27 39
Barchard St. SW18 BS46 76
Barchester Clo. Uxb. AX38 53
Barchester Rd. Har. BG30 36
Barchester St. E14 CE39 57
Barclay Clo. SW6 BS43 66
Barclay Clo. Lthd. BF65 102
Barclay Ct. Hodd. CE12 12
Barclay Oval. Wdf. Grn. CH28 40
Barclay Rd. E11 CG33 49
Barclay Rd. E13 CJ38 58
Barclay Rd. E17 CE32 48
Barclay Rd. N18 BZ29 39
Barclay Rd. SW6 BS43 66
Barclay Rd. Croy. BZ55 87
Barcombe Av. SW2 BX48 76
Barden Clo. Uxb. AX29 35
Barden St. SE18 CN43 68
Bardeswell Clo. Brwd. DB27 42
Bardfield Av. Rom. CP31 50
Bardinell Trd. Est. Chess BK58 93
Bardney Rd. Mord. BS52 86
Bardolph Av. Croy. CD58 96
Bardolph Rd. N7 BX35 47
Bardolph Rd. Rich. BL45 65
St. George's Rd.
Bard Rd. W10 BQ40 55
Bardsey Wk. N1 BZ36 57
Marquess Est.
Bardsley La. SE10 CF43 67
Bardwell Ct. St. Alb. BG14 9
Bardwell Rd.
Bardwell Rd. St. Alb. BG14 9
Bardwell St. N7 BX35 47
Barfett St. W10 BR38 55
Barfield Av. N20 BU27 38
Barfield Rd. E11 CG33 49
Barfield Rd. Brom. CL52 88
Barfields Loug. CL24 31
Barfields Clo. Loug. CL24 31
Barfields Cres. Red. BY70 121
Barfields Gdns. Loug. CL24 31
Barfields Path Loug. CL24 31
Barfield St. Wat. BC23 26
Barfolds Hat. BQ15 10
Barford Clo. NW4 BP30 37
Barford St. N1 BY37 56
Barforth Rd. SE15 CB45 67
Bargate Clo. SE18 CN42 68
Bargate Clo. N. Mal. BP54 85
Barge House Rd. E16 CL40 58
Barge House St. SE1 BY40 56
Barge Rd. E. Mol. BG52 84
Bargery Rd. SE6 CE47 77
Barge Wk. Kings-on-t. BK51 84
Barge Wk. Kings-on-t. BK52 84
Bargrove Av. Hem. H. AW14 8
Bargrove Cres. SE6 CD48 77
Barham Av. Borwd. BL24 28
Barham Clo. Brom. CK54 88
Barham Clo. Chis. CL49 78
Barham Clo. Grnf. BJ36 54
Barham Clo. Rom. CR30 41
Barham Clo. Wey. BA56 92
Barham Rd. SW20 BP50 75
Barham Rd. Chis. CL49 78
Barham Rd. Dart. CX47 80
Barham Rd. Epsom BN58 94
Barham Rd. Sth. Croy. BZ56 96
Baring Clo. SE12 CH48 78
Baring Rd. SE12 CH47 78
Baring Rd. Barn. BT24 29
Baring Rd. Croy. CB54 87
Baring St. N1 BZ37 57
Barker Rd. Cher. AV54 82
Barker St. SW10 BT43 66
Barker Wk. SW16 BW48 76
Barkham Rd. N17 BZ29 39
Bark Hart Rd. Orp. CO54 89
Barking By-pass Bark. CM38 58
Barking Industrial Est. Bark. CO37 59
Barking Rd. E6 CJ37 58
Barking Rd. E13 CG39 58
Barking Rd. E16 CG39 58
Barkis Way, SE16 CB42 67
Egan Way
Bark Pl. W2 BS40 56
Barkston Gdns. SW5 BS42 66
Barkston Path Borwd. BM22 28
Barkworth Rd. SE16 CB42 67
Barlborough St. SE14 CC43 67
Barlby Gdns. W10 BQ38 55
Barlby Rd. W10 BQ39 55
Barle Gdns. S. Ock. DA39 60
Barley Clo. Bush. BF25 27
Barleycorn Way. Horn. CW32 51
Barley Croft. Harl. CM13 13
Barley Croft. Harl. CN13 13
Barley Cft. Hem. H. BA13 8
Barleycroft Grn. Welw. G. C. BQ8 5
Barleycroft Rd. Welw. G. C. BQ8 5
Barley Field. Brwd. CZ22 33
Barley La. Ilf. CO33 50
Barley Mow Clo. Wok. AO62 100
Barley Mow La. Wok. AO61 100
Barley Mow Pass. W4 BN42 65
Barley Mow Rd. Egh. AR49 72
Barley Mow Way Shep. AZ52 83
Petts La.
Barlow Pl. W1 BV40 56
Bruton La.
Barlow Rd. W3 BM40 55
Barlow Rd. Hamptn. BF50 74
Barlow St. SE17 BZ42 67
Barmeston Rd. SE6 CE48 77
Barmouth Av. Grnf. BH37 54
Barmouth Rd. SW18 BT46 76
Barmouth Rd. Croy. CC55 87
Barnabas Rd. E9 CC35 48
Barnaby Way Chig. CL27 40
Barnacre Clo. Uxb. AX39 53
Barnacres Cft. Hem. H. AZ15 8
Barnacres Rd. Hem. H. AY16 17
Barnacres Rd. Hem. H. AZ15 8
Barnard Cl. SE18 CL41 68
Powis St.
Barnard Clo. Chis. CM51 88
Barnard Clo. Hem. H. AY14 8
Barnard Clo. Sun. BC50 73
Barnard Clo. Wall. BW57 95
Barnard Gdns. Hayes BC38 53
Barnard Gdns. N. Mal. BP52 85
Barnard Grn. Welw. G. C. BR8 5
Barnard Gro. E15 CG36 58
Barnard Hill, N10 BV30 38
Barnard Ms. SW11 BU45 66
Barnard Rd.
Barnardo Dr. Ilf. CM31 49
Ashurst Dr.
Barnardo St. E1 CC39 57
Barnard Rd. SW11 BU45 66
Barnard Rd. Enf. CB23 30
Barnard Rd. Saw. CQ5 6
Barnard Rd. Warl. CE63 105
Barnards Inn EC4 BY39 56
Fetter La.
Barnards Way. Beac. AO29 34
Barnby Rd. Wok. AO62 100
Barnby St. E15 CG37 58
Barnby St. NW1 BW37 56
Barn Clo. Ashf. AZ49 73
Barn Clo. Nthlt. BD37 54
Barn Clo. Welw. G. C. BQ8 5
Barn Cres. Pur. BZ60 96
Barn Cres. Stan. BK29 36
Barncroft Clo. Loug. CL25 31
Barncroft Clo. Uxb. AZ39 53
Barncroft Rd. Berk. AP13 7
Barncroft Rd. Loug. CL25 31
Barndicott. Welw. G. C. BT7 5
Barnehurst Av. Erith CS44 69
Barnehurst Clo. Erith CS44 69
Barnehurst Rd. Bexh. CR44 69
Barnend Dr. Dart. CV49 80
Barnend La. Dart. CV49 80
Barnes Alley Hmptn. BG51 84
Barnes Ave. Chesh. AO18 16
Barnes Av. SW13 BP43 65
Barnes Br. SW13 BO44 65
Barnes Br. W4 BO44 65
Barnes Clo. E12 CJ35 49
Barnes Ct. N22 BX29 38
Barnes Ct. Wdf. Grn. CJ28 40
Durham Ave.
Barnes Cray Rd. Dart. CU45 69
Barnesdale Cres. Orp. CO53 89
Barnes End N. Mal. BP53 85
Barnes High St. SW13 BO44 65
Barnes La. Kings L. AW17 17
Barnes Pikle W5 BJ40 54
Mattock La.
Barnes Pikle W5 BK40 54
Mattock La.
Barnes Rise, Kings L. AY17 17
Barnes Rd. Ilf. CM35 49
Barnes St. E14 CD39 57
Barnes Ter. SE8 CD42 67
Barnes Way, Iver AV40 52
Barnet By-pass N2 BT32 47
Barnet By-pass Barn. BO23 28
Barnet By-Pass, Hat. BO12 10
Barnet By-Pass, Hat. BP17 19
Barnet Dr. Brom. CK55 88
Barnet Gate La. Barn. BO25 28
Barnet Gro. E2 CB38 57
Barnet Hill Barn. BR24 28
Barnet La. N20 BR26 37
Barnet La. Borwd. BK25 27
Barnet Rd. Barn. BN25 28
Barnet Rd. Barn. BS21 29
Barnet Rd. Pot. B. BM18 19
Barnet Rd. Pot. B. BS20 20
Barnet Rd. St. Alb. BL17 19
Barnet Row, Guil. AR68 109
Barnets Fld. Sev. CT61 107
Barnett Clo. Lthd. BJ63 102
Barnettwood La. Lthd. & Ash. BJ63 102
Barnet Way NW7 BN27 37
Barnet Way NW7 BN28 37
Barnfield, Bans. BS60 95
Barn Field Epp. CO17 23
Barnfield, Hem. H. AY15 8
Barnfield, Iver AV39 52
Barnfield N. Mal. BN53 85
Barnfield Av. Croy. CC55 87
Barnfield Av. Kings-on-t. BK49 74
Barnfield Av. Mitch. BV52 86
Barnfield Clo. Couls. BZ63 105
Barnfield Clo. Hodd. CE11 12
Barnfield Clo. Swan. CS54 89
Barnfield Cres. Sev. CW62 108
Barnfield Gdns. Kings-on-t. BL49 75
Barnfield Gdns. Est. SE18 CL43 68
Barnfield Rd. SE18 CL43 68
Barnfield Rd. W5 BK38 54
Barnfield Rd. Belv. CQ43 69
Barnfield Rd. Edg. BN30 37
Barnfield Rd. Orp. CP52 89
Barn Field Rd. St. Alb. BK12 9
Barnfield Rd. Sev. CT65 107
Barnfield Rd. Sth. Croy. CA58 96
Barnfield Rd. Welw. G. C. BR9 5
Barnfield Way. Slou. AL40 61
Barnfield Wd. Clo. Beck. CF53 87
Barnfield Wd. Rd. Beck. CF53 87
Barnham Rd. Grnf. BG38 54
Barnham St. SE1 CA41 67
Barn Hill. Harl. CH13 13
Barnhill Pnr. BD32 45
Barn Hill, Wem. BM33 46
Barn Hill Av. Brom. CG53 88
Barnhill La. Hayes BC38 53
Barnhill Rd. Hayes BC38 53
Barnhill Rd. Wem. BN34 46
Barnhurst Path Wat. BD28 36
Barnlea Clo. Felt. BE48 74
Barn Mead Brwd. DB21 33
Barn Mead Epp. CN21 31
Coppice Row
Barn Mead. Harl. CN12 13
Barnmead Wok. AP58 91
Barnmead Gdns. Dag. CQ35 50
Barn Meadow Clo. Lthd. BE65 102
Barn Meadow La.
Barn Meadow La. Lthd. BE65 102
Barnmead Rd. Beck. CC51 87
Barnmead Rd. Dag. CQ35 50
Barn Rise, Wem. BM34 46
Barn Rd, Mitch. BV52 86
Barnsbury Clo. N. Mal. BN52 85
Barnsbury Cres. Surb. BN54 85
Barnsbury Est. N1 BX37 56
Barnsbury Gro. N7 BX36 56
Roman Way
Barnsbury La. Surb. BM55 85
Barnsbury Ms. N1 BY36 56
Brooksby St.
Barnsbury Pk. N1 BY36 56
Barnsbury Rd. N1 BY37 56
Barnsbury Sq. N1 BY36 56
Barnsbury St. N1 BY36 56
Barnsbury Ter. N1 BY36 56
Barnsdale Rd. W9 BR38 55
Barnsdale Yd. W9 BR38 55
Barnsdale Rd.
Barnsfield Pl. Uxb. AX37 53
Barns La. Wok. AV65 100
Barns Lane, Wok. AV66 109
Barnsley Rd. Rom. CW29 42
Barnsley St. E1 CB38 57
Barnstaple La. SE13 CF45 67
Lewisham High St.
Barnstaple Path Rom. CV28 42
Barnstaple Rd.
Barnstaple Rd. Rom. CV28 42
Barnstaple Rd. Ruis. BD34 45
Barn St. N16 CA34 48
Church St.
Barnway, Egh. AR49 72
Barn Way, Wem. BM33 46
Barnwell Rd. SW2 BY46 76
Barnwood Av. W. Wick. CE54 87
Barnwood Clo. W9 BS38 56
Amberley Est.
Barnwood Clo. Ruis. BA34 44
Barnwood Ct. Est. E16 CH40 58
Barnwood Rd. Guil. AP70 118
Barnyard, The, Tad. BP65 103
Baroness Rd. E2 CA38 57
Baronet Gro. N17 CB30 39
Baronet Rd. N17 CB30 39
Baron Gdns. Ilf. CM31 49
Baron Gro. Mitch. BU52 86
Baron Rd. E16 CG39 58
Baron Rd. Dag. CP33 50
Barons Ct. NW9 BN32 46
Baron's Court Rd. W14 BR42 65
Baronsfield Rd. Twick. BJ46 74
Barons Gate. Barn. BU25 29
Barons Hurst Epsom BN61 103
Barons Keep W14 BR42 65
Gliddon Rd.
Baronsmead Rd. SW13 BP44 65
Baronsmede W5 BL41 65
Baronsmere Rd. N2 BU31 47
Barons Pl. SE1 BY41 66
Barons, The. Twick. BJ46 74
Baron St. N1 BY37 56
Barons Wk. Croy. CC53 87
Barons Wk. Croy. CD53 87
Barons Way, Egh. AU50 72
Barons Way, Reig. BS72 121
Baron Wk. Mitch. BU52 86
Barque St. E14 CF42 67
Barrack La. Wind. AO44 61
Barrack Path, Wok. AP62 100
Barrack Rd. Guil. AQ69 118
Barrack Rd. Houns. BD45 64
Barrack Row, Grav. DG46 81
Barrack Row Sthl. BD42 64
Barracks, The, Wey. AW55 83
Barra Clo. Hem. H. AZ15 8
Barra Hall Rd. Hayes BB40 53
Barratt Av. N22 BX30 38
Barrenger Rd. N10 BU30 38
Barrens Brae, Wok. AT62 100
Barrens Clo. Wok. AT63 100
Barrens Pk. Wok. AT63 100
Barrets Green Rd. NW10 BN38 55
Barrett Rd. E17 CF31 48
Barrett Rd. Lthd. BG66 111
Barretts Gro. N16 CA35 48
Barretts Rd. Sev. CS63 107
Barrett St. W1 BV39 56
Barrhill Rd. SW2 BX48 76
Barricane Clo. Wok. AQ63 100
Barrie Clo. Couls. BV61 104
Barriedale, SE14 CD44 67
Barrie Est. W2 BT40 56
Barrington Clo. Loug. CM24 31
Barrington Ct. N10 BV30 38
Barrington Ct. Brwd. DE25 122
Barrington Ct. Dor. BJ72 119
Barrington
Barrington Grn. Loug. CM24 31
Barrington Rd. E12 CL36 58
Barrington Rd. N8 BW32 47
Barrington Rd. SW9 BY45 66
Barrington Rd. Bexh. CP44 69
Barrington Rd. Dor. BJ72 119
Barrington Rd. Loug. CM24 31
Barrington Rd. Pur. BW59 95
Barrington Rd. Sutt. BS54 86
Barrington Vills. SE18 CL44 68
Barrons Clo. Ong. CW17 24
Barrosa Dr. Hamptn. BE51 84
Barrosa Dr. Hamptn. BF51 84
Oldfield Rd.
Barrow Av. Cars. BU57 95
Barrow Clo. N21 BY27 38
Barrowdene Clo. Pnr. BE30 36
Paines La.
Barrowell Grn. N21 BY27 38
Barrowfield Clo. N9 CB27 39
Barrowfield La. N9 CB27 39
Barrowfield Sth. Croy. CB59 96
Barrowgate Rd. W4 BN42 65
Barrow Green Rd. Oxt. CF67 114
Barrow Grn Rd. Oxt. CU67 114
Barrow Hedges Clo. Cars. BU57 95
Barrow Hedges Way Cars. BU57 95
Barrow Hill NW8 BU37 56
Barrow Hill Wor. Pk. BO55 85
Barrow Hill Clo. Wor. Pk. BO55 85
Barrow Hill Est. NW8 BU37 56
Barrow Hill Rd. NW8 BU37 56
Barrow La. Wal. Cr. CA19 21
Barrow Point Av. Pnr. BE30 36
Barrow Point La. Pnr. BE30 36
Barrow Rd. SW16 BW50 76
Barrow Rd. Croy. BY57 95
Barrows Rd. Harl. CK11 13
Barr Rd. Grav. DJ48 81
Barr Rd. Pot. B. BT20 20
Barrs La. Wok. AO61 100
Barrs Rd. NW10 BN36 55
Barry Ave. Wind. AO43 61
Barry Av. N15 CD32 48
Craven Pk. Rd.
Barry Av. Bexh. CQ43 69
Barry Clo. Grays. DG41 71
Barry Clo. Orp. CN55 88
Barry Clo. St. Alb. BF16 18
Barry Ct. SW4 BW46 76
Barry Rd. SE22 CA46 77
Barset Rd. SE15 CC45 67
Bars, The Guil. AR71 118
Barston Rd. SE27 BZ48 77
Bartel Clo. Hem. H. BA14 8
Barter St. WC1 BX39 56
Bartholomew Clo. EC1 BY39 56
Bartholomew La. EC2 BZ39 57
Threadneedle St.
Bartholomew Rd. NW5 BW36 56
Bartholomew Sq. EC1 BZ38 57
Bartholomew St. SE1 BZ41 67
Bartholomew Vill. NW5 BW36 56
Barth Rd. SE18 CN42 68
Bartle Av. E6 CK37 58
Bartlett Ct. EC4 BY39 56
New Fetter La.
Bartlett Rd. Grav. DG47 81
Bartlett St. E14 CE39 57
Bartlett St. Sth. Croy. BZ56 96
Bartley Rd. SW2 BX46 76
Bartlow Gdns. Rom. CS30 41
Barton Av. Rom. CR33 50
Barton Clo. E9 CC35 48
Churchill Wk.
Barton Clo. Bexh. CQ46 79
Barton Clo. Chig. CM27 40
Barton Clo. Shep. AZ53 83
Barton Clo. Wey. AW57 92
Barton Grn. N. Mal. BN51 85
Barton Meadows, Ilf. CL31 49
Brandville Gdns.
Barton Rd. W14 BR42 65
Barton Rd. Horn. CU33 50
Barton Rd. Sid. CQ50 79
Barton Rd. Slou. AS41 62
Barton Rd. S. At. H. CX51 90
Bartons. The. Borwd. BK25 27
Bartons. The. Cob. BD59 93
Barton St. SW1 BX41 66
Barton Way, NW8 BT37 56
Barton Way Borwd. BM23 28
Barton Way, Rick. AZ25 26
Bartram Clo. Uxb. AZ38 53
Bartram Rd. SE4 CD46 77
Bartrams La. Barn. BT22 29
Bartrip St. E9 CD36 57
Barwick Rd. E7 CH35 49
Basden Gro. Felt. BF48 74
Basford Way. Wind. AL45 61
Bashley Rd. NW10 BN38 55
Basil Av. E6 CK38 58
Basildene Rd. Houns. BD45 64
Basildon Av. Ilf. CL30 40
Basildon Clo. Sutt. BT58 95
Basildon Rd. SE2 CO42 69
Basildon Rd. Bexh. CQ44 69
Basildon Sq. Hem. H. AY11 8
Basil St. SW3 BU41 66
Basing Clo. Surb. BH54 84
Basingdon Way, SE5 BZ45 67
Basing Dr. Bex. CQ46 79
Basing Est. N3 BS31 47
Basingfield Rd. Surb. BH54 84
Basinghall Av. EC2 BZ39 57
Basinghall Gdns. Sutt. BS58 95
Basinghall St. EC2 BZ39 57
Basing Hl. NW11 BR33 46
Basing Hl. Wem. BL34 46
Basing Rd. Rick. AV26 34
Basing St. W11 BR39 55
Basing Way N3 BS31 47
Basing Way Surb. BH54 84
Basire St. N1 BZ37 57
Baskerville Rd. SW18 BU47 76
Basket Gdns. SE9 CK46 78
Basnett Rd. SW11 BV45 66
Bassand St. SE22 CA46 77
Bassant Rd. SE18 CN43 68
Bassein Pk Rd. W12 BO41 65
Basset Clo. Wey. AW58 92
Bassett Clo. Sutt. BS58 95
Bassett Gdns. Islw. BG43 64
Bassett Rd. W10 BR39 55
Bassett Rd. Wok. AU61 100
Bassetts Clo. Orp. CL56 97
Bassett St. NW5 BV35 47
Bassetts Way Orp. CL56 97
Bassett Way Grnf. BF39 54
Bassil Rd. Hem. H. AX14 8
Bassingbourne Clo. Brox. CD13 12
Bassingburn Wk. Welw. G. C. BR8 5
Bassingham Rd. SW18 BT47 76
Bassingham Rd. Wem. BK36 54
Bastable Av. Bark. CG37 58
Bastion Rd. SE2 CO42 69
Baston Manor Rd. Brom. CH55 88
Baston Rd. Brom. CH54 88
Bastwick St. EC1 BY38 56
Basuto Rd. SW6 BS44 66
Batavia Clo. Sun. BC51 83
Batavia Rd. SE14 CD43 67
Batavia Rd. Sun. BC51 83
Batchelor St. N1 BY37 56
Batchelors Way. Amer. AO23 25
Batchwood Dr. St. Alb. BF12 9
Batchwood Gdns. St. Alb. BG12 9
Batchwood Grn. Orp. CO52 89
Batchwood Vw. St. Alb. BG12 9
Batchworth Heath Hill. Rick. AZ28 35
Batchworth La. Nthwd. AZ28 35
Bateman Rd. E4 CE29 39
Bateman Rd. Rick. AZ25 26
Bateman's Row. EC2 CA38 57
Bateman St. W1 BW39 56
Dean St.
Bates Cres. Croy. BY56 95
Bateson St. SE18 CN42 68
Gunning St.
Bateson Way. Wok. AU60 91
Bates Rd. Rom. CX29 42
Bate St. E14 CD40 57
Three Colt St.
Bates Wk. Wey. AX57 92
Bathgate Rd. SW19 BQ48 75
Bath Pass. Kings-on-t. BK51 84
Bath Pl. EC2 CA38 57
Old St.
Bath Pl. Barn. BR24 28
Bath Rd. E7 CJ36 58
Bath Rd. E15 CG36 58
Bath Rd. N9 CB27 39
Bath Rd. W4 BO42 65
Bath Rd. Dart. CU47 79
Bath Rd. Hayes BC43 63
Bath Rd. Rom. CQ32 50
Bath Rd. Slou. AN40 61
Bath Rd. Slou. AU43 62
Bath Rd. West. Dr. AX44 63
Bath St. EC1 BZ38 57
Bath St. Grav. DG46 81
Bath Ter. SE1 BZ41 67
Bathurst Av. SW19 BS51 86
Brisbane Av.
Bathurst Clo. Iver. AV41 62
Bathurst Gdns. NW10 BP37 55
Bathurst Ms. W2 BT40 56
Bathurst Rd. Hem. H. AX12 8
Bathurst Rd. Ilf. CL33 49
Bathurst St. W2 BT40 56
Bathurst Wk. Iver. AV41 62
Bathway, SE18 CL42 68
Market St.
Batley Rd. N16 CD34 48
Stoke Newington High St.
Batley Rd. Enf. BZ23 30
Batman Clo. W12 BP40 55
Batoum Gdns. W6 BQ41 65
Batson St. W12 BP41 65
Batsworth Rd. Mitch. BT52 86
Batten Av. Wok. AP63 100
Batten St. SW11 BU45 66
Batterdale Hat. BQ12 10
London Rd.
Battersby Rd. SE6 CF48 77
Battersea Br. SW3 BT43 66
Battersea Br. Rd. SW11 BU43 66
Battersea Church Rd. SW11 BT44 66
Battersea Ct. Guil. AQ70 118
Battersea High St. SW11 BT44 66
Battersea Park Est. SW11 BV44 66
Battersea Pk Rd. SW8 BU44 66
Battersea Pk. Rd. SW11 BU44 66
Battersea Ri. SW11 BT46 76
Battishill St. N1 BY36 56
Waterloo Ter.
Battle Bridge La. SE1 CA40 57
Tooley St.
Battlebridge La. Red. BY67 113
Battle Bridge Rd. NW1 BX37 56
Battledean Rd. N5 BY35 47
Battlefield Rd. St. Alb. BH12 9

Battle Rd. Erith CS42 69
Battlers Grn Dr. Rad. BH22 27
Batts Hill, Reig. & Red. BT69 121
Batts, Reig. BU69 121
Batty St. E1 CB39 57
Baudwin Rd. SE6 CG48 78
Baulk, The. SW18 BS47 76
Longfield St.
Bavant Rd. SW16 BX51 86
Bavaria Rd. N19 BX34 47
Bavent Rd. SE5 BZ44 67
Bavonne Rd. W6 BR44 65
Bawdale Rd. SE22 CA46 77
Bawdsey Av. Ilf. CN31 49
Bawtree Rd. SE14 CD43 67
Bawtree Rd. Uxb. AX36 53
Bawtry Rd. N20 BU27 38
Baxendale N20 BT27 38
Baxendale St. E2 CB38 57
Baxter Av. Red. BU70 121
Baxter Clo. Uxb. AZ38 53
Baxter Rd. E16 CJ39 58
Baxter Rd. N1 BZ36 57
Baxter Rd. N17 CB31 48
Baxter Rd. N18 CB28 39
Baxter Rd. Ilf. CL35 49
Baybrooke St. W12 BO39 55
Bay Ct. Berk. AQ13 7
Bayfield Rd. SE9 CJ45 68
Bayford Grn. Hert. BY12 11
Bayford Lane. Hert BX11 11
Bayford Rd. NW10 BQ38 55
Bayford St. E8 CB36 57
Bayham Pl. NW1 BW37 56
Bayham Rd. W4 BN41 65
Bayham Rd. W13 BJ40 54
Bayham Rd. Mord. BS52 86
Bayham Rd. Sev. CV65 108
Bayham St. NW1 BW37 56
Bayleys Hill. Sev. CT69 116
Bayleys Mead, Brwd. DE27 122
Bayley St. WC1 BW39 56
Baylin Rd. SW18 BS46 76
Baylis Rd. SE1 BY41 66
Baylis Rd. Slou. AO40 52
Bayly Rd. Dart. CX46 80
Bay Manor La. Grays. CZ43 70
Bayne Hill. Beac. AO29 34
Baynes Clo. Enf. CB23 30
Baynes St. NW1 BW36 56
Bayston Rd. N16 CA34 48
Bayswater Rd. W2 BS40 56
Baythorne St. E3 CD39 57
Baytree Rd. SW2 BX45 66
Bay Tree Wk. Wat. BC22 26
Baywood Sq. Chig. CO28 41
Bazalgette Gdns. N. Mal. BN53 85
Bazely St. E14 CF39 57
Bazile Rd. N21 BY25 29
Beachborough Rd. Brom. CF49 77
Beachcroft Rd. E11 CG34 49
Beachcroft Way N19 BX33 47
Hornsey Rise
Beach Gro. Felt. BF48 74
Beachy Rd. E3 CE36 57
Beacon Clo. Cob. BC63 101
Beacon Clo. Uxb. AX35 44
Beacon Dr. Dart. DA48 80
Beacon Gro. Cars. BV56 95
Beacon Hill. Brwd. CY22 33
Beacon Hill Grays CX42 70
Beacon Hill, Wok. AQ63 100
Beacon Hill Rd. Brwd. CX22 33
Beacon Hl. N7 BX35 47
Beacon Rd. SE13 CF46 77
Beacon Rd. Erith. CU43 69
Beaconsfield Av. Epp. CN18 22
Beaconsfield Clo. N11 BV28 38
Beaconsfield Clo. SE3 CH43 68
Beaconsfield Pl. Epsom BO59 94
Beaconsfield Rd. E10 CF34 48
Beaconsfield Rd. E16 CG38 58
Beaconsfield Rd. E17 CD32 48
Beaconsfield Rd. E18 CG30 40
Beaconsfield Rd. N9 CB27 39
Beaconsfield Rd. N11 BV27 38
Beaconsfield Rd. N15 CA31 48
Beaconsfield Rd. NW10 BO36 55
Beaconsfield Rd. SE3 CG43 68
Beaconsfield Rd. SE9 CK48 78
Beaconsfield Rd. W4 BN41 65
Beaconsfield Rd. W5 BK41 64
Beaconsfield Rd. Bex. CT48 79
Beaconsfield Rd. Brom. CJ52 88
Beaconsfield Rd. Croy. BZ53 87
Beaconsfield Rd. Enf. CC22 30
Beaconsfield Rd. Epp. CN18 22
Beaconsfield. Rd. Epsom. BN63 103
Beaconsfield Rd. Esner BH57 93
Beaconsfield Rd. Hat. BQ12 10
Beaconsfield Rd. Hayes. BD40 54
Beaconsfield Rd. N. Mal. BN51 85
Beaconsfield Rd. St. Alb. BH13 9
Beaconsfield Rd. Surb. BL54 85
Beaconsfield Rd. Twick. BJ46 74
Beaconsfield Rd. Wok. AS63 100
Beaconsfields. Sev. CT66 116
Beaconsfields Ri. Sev. CT66 116
Beaconsfield St. E6 CL39 58
Beaconsfield Ter. W4 BN42 65
Beaconsfield Ter. W14 BR41 65
Maclise Rd.
Beaconsfield Ter. Rom. CQ32 50
Beaconsfield Wk. SW6 BR44 65
Parsons Grn. La.
Beaconsfield Way. Epp. CN18 22
Beaconsfield Way Epp. CO18 23
Beacons, The Loug. CL22 31
Beacons, The, Loug. CL23 31
Beacontree Av. E17 CF30 39
Beacontree Rd. E11 CG33 49
Beacon Way Bans. BQ61 103
Beacon Way. Rick. AW26 35
Beadles La. Oxt. CF68 114
Beadman St. SE27 BY49 76
Beadnell Rd. SE23 CC47 77
Beadon Rd. W6 BQ42 65
Beadon Rd. Brom. CH52 88
Beads Hall La. Brwd. DA24 33
Beaford Gro. SW20 BR52 85
Beagle Clo. Rad. BH22 27
Beagles Clo. Orp. CP55 89
Beak St. W1 BW40 56
Bealah Rd. Sutt. BS56 95
Beal Clo. Well. CO44 69
Beale Clo. N13 BY28 38
Beale Pl. E3 CD37 57
Beale Rd. E3 CD37 57
Beales La. Wey. AZ55 83
Beales Rd. Lthd. BF67 111
Beale St. E13 CH37 58
Beale St. W. E13 CH37 58
Beale St.
Beal Rd. Ilf. CL34 49
Beam Av. Dag. CR37 59
Beaminster Gdns. Ilf. CL30 40
Beamish Clo. Epp. CS16 23
Beamish Dr. Bush. BG26 36
Beamish Rd. N9 CB26 39
Beamish Rd. Orp. CP54 89
Beam Way Dag. CS36 59
Beanacre Clo. E9 CD36 57
Beanfield Rd. Saw. CO5 6
Bean La. Dart. DA48 80
Bean Rd. Bexh. CP45 69
Beanshaw, SE9 CL49 78
Beansland Gro. Rom. CQ30 41
Bear All. EC4 BY39 56
Farringdon St.
Beardell St. SE19 CA50 77
Beardow Gro. N14 BW25 29
Beard Rd. Kings. On T. BL49 75
Beard's Hill Hamptn. BF51 84
Beard's Hill Clo. Hamptn. BF51 84
Beards Rd. Ashf. BB50 73
Bearfield Rd. Kings. On T. BL50 75
Bear Gdns. SE1 BZ40 57
Bearing Clo. Chig. CO28 41
Bearing Way. Chig. CO28 41
Bear La. SE1 BY40 56
Bear Rd. Felt. BD49 74
Bears Den, Tad. BR64 103
Bearstead Ri. SE4 CD46 77
Bear St. WC2 BW40 56
Cranbourn St.
Bearwood Clo. Pot. B. BT19
Beasley's Ait La. Sun. BC53 83
Beasley's La. Shep. BB53 83
Beatrice Av. SW16 BX52 86
Beatrice Av. Wem. BL35 46
Beatrice Clo. E13 CG38 58
Beatrice Clo. E13 CH38 58
Philip St.
Beatrice Clo. Pnr. BC31 44
Beatrice Ct. Wem. BL35 46
Beatrice Gdns. Grav. DF48 81
Beatrice Rd. E17 CE32 48
Beatrice Rd. N4 BY33 47
Beatrice Rd. N9 CC26 39
Beatrice Rd. SE1 CB42 67
Beatrice Rd. Oxt. CG68 115
Beatrice Rd. Rich. BL46 75
Albert Rd.
Beatrice Rd. Sthl. BE40 54
Beatrice St. E13 CH38 58
Beatson St. SE16 CC40 57
Beattie Clo. Lthd. BE65 102
Beatty Av. Guil. AT70 118
Beatty Rd. N16 CA35 48
Beatty Rd. Stan. BK29 36
Beatty St. NW1 BW37 56
Beattyville Gdns. Ilf. CL31 49
Beauchamp Pl. SW3 BU41 66
Beauchamp Rd. E7 CH36 58
Beauchamp Rd. SE19 BZ51 87
Beauchamp Rd. SW11 BU45 66
Beauchamp Rd. E. Mol. BF53 84
Beauchamp Rd. Sutt. BS56 95
Beauchamp Rd. Twick. BJ47 74
Beauchamp St. EC1 BY39 56
Leather La.
Beauclere Rd. W6 BP41 65
Beaufort Av. Har. BF32 45
Beaufort Av. Har. BJ31 45
Beaufort Clo. W5 BL39 55
Beaufort Clo. Reig. BR70 120
Beaufort Clo. Rom. CR31 50
Beaufort Clo. Wok. AU61 100
Beaufort Ct. Rich. BK49 74
Beaufort Dr. NW11 BS31 47
Beaufort Gdns. NW4 BQ32 46
Beaufort Gdns. SW3 BU41 66
Beaufort Gdns. SW16 BX50 76
Green La.
Beaufort Gdns. Houns. BE44 64
Beaufort Gdns. Ilf. CL33 49
Beaufort Pk. NW11 BS31 47
Beaufort Rd. W5 BL39 55
Beaufort Rd. Kings. On T. BL52 85
Beaufort Rd. Reig. BR70 120
Beaufort Rd. Rich. BK49 74
Beaufort Rd. Twick. BK47 74
Beaufort Rd. Wok. AU61 100
Beauforts, Egh. AR49 72
Beaufort St. SW3 BT43 66
Beaufort Way Epsom BP57 94
Beaufoy Rd. N17 CA29 39
Beaufoy Rd. SW11 BV44 66
Beaufoy Wk. SE11 BX42 66
Beaulieu Av. SE26 CB49 77
Beaulieu Cl. SE5 CA45 67
Beaulieu Clo. NW9 BO31 46
Beaulieu Clo. Mitch. BV51 86
Beaulieu Clo. Slou. AQ44 62
Beaulieu Clo. Twick. BK46 74
Beaulieu Dr. Pnr. BD32 45
Beaulieu Gdns. N21 BZ26 39
Beauly Way Rom. CT30 41
Beaumanor Gdns. SE9 CL49 78
Beanshaw
Beaumaris Dr. Wdf. Grn. CJ29 40
Beaumont Av. W14 BR42 65
Beaumont Av. Rich. BL45 65
Beaumont Av. St. Alb. BJ12 9
Beaumont Av. Wem. BK35 45
Beaumont Clo. Rom. CV30 42
Beaumont Cres. W14 BR42 65
Beaumont Cres. Rain. CU36 59
Beaumont Dr. Ashf. BA49 73
Beaumont Dr. Grav. DF47 81
Beaumont Gro. E1 CC38 57
Beaumont Ms. W1 BV39 56
Marylebone High St.
Beaumont Pla. Barn. BR22 28
Beaumont Pl. W1 BW38 56
Beaumont Ri. N19 BW33 47
Beaumont Rd. E10 CE33 48
Beaumont Rd. E13 CH38 58
Beaumont Rd. SE19 BZ50 77
Beaumont Rd. SW19 BR47 75
Beaumont Rd. W4 BN41 65
Beaumont Rd. Brox. CA15 12
Beaumont Rd. Orp. CM53 88
Beaumont Rd. Pur. BY60 95
Beaumont Rd. Slou. AO38 52
Beaumont Rd. Wind. AO44 61
Beaumont Sq. E1 CC39 57
Beaumont St. W1 BV39 56
Beaumont Vw. Wal. Cr. BZ16 21
Pear Tree Wk.
Beauvais Terr. Nthlt. BD38 54
Beauval Rd. SE22 CA46 77
Beaverbank Rd. SE9 CM47 78
Beaver Clo. Hamptn. BF51 84
Beaver Gro. Nthlt. BD38 54
Beaver Gro. Nthlt. BE38 54
Jetstar Way
Beaver Rd. Ilf. CP28 41
Beavers Cres. Houns. BD45 64
Beavers La. Houns. BD45 64
Beaverwood Rd. Sid. CN49 78
Beavor La. W6 BP42 65
Bebbington Rd. SE18 CN42 68
Bebletts Clo. Orp. CN56 97
Beccles Dr. Bark. CN36 58
Beccles St. E14 CD39 57
Bec Clo. Ruis. BD34 45
Beckenham Gdns. N9 CA27 39
Beckenham Gro. Brom. CF51 87
Beckenham Hill Rd. SE6 CE50 77
Beckenham Hill Rd. Beck. CE50 77
Beckenham La. Brom. CG51 88
Beckenham Pl. Pk. Beck. CE50 77
Beckenham Rd. Beck. CC51 87
Beckenham Rd. W. Wick. CE54 87
Beckenshaw Gdns. Bans. BT61 104
Beckers Est. The, N16 CB34 48
Becket Av. E6 CL38 58
Becket Clo. SE25 CB53 87
Becket Clo. Brwd. DB29 42
Becket St. SE1 BZ41 67
Beckett Av. Ken. BY61 104
Becketts Av. St. Alb. BG12 9
Becketts Clo. Houns. BC46 73
Harlington Rd. West
Becketts Clo. Orp. CN55 88
Beckett Wk. Beck. CD50 77
Beckford Rd. Croy. CA53 87
Beck La. Beck. CC52 87
Becklow Gdns. W12 BP41 65
Becklow Rd.
Becklow Rd. W12 BO41 65
Beck Rd. E8 CB37 57
Becks Rd. Sid. CQ48 79
Beckton Gdns. E6 CK39 58
Beckton Pl. Erith CR44 69
Beckton Rd. E6 CG39 58
Beckton Rd. E16 CG39 58
Beckton St. E16 CG39 58
Beckway Beck. CD52 87
Beckway Rd. SW16 BW51 86
Beckway St. SE17 BZ42 67
Beckwith Rd. SE24 BZ46 77
Beclands Rd. SW17 BV50 76
Becmead Av. SW16 BW49 76
Becmead Av. Har. BJ32 45
Becondale Rd. SE19 CA49 77
Beconsfield Rd. W11 BV28 38
Becontree Av. Dag. CO35 50
Becontree Av. Dag. CQ34 50
Bective Pl. SW15 BR45 65
Bective Rd. E7 CH35 49
Bective Rd. SW15 BR45 65
Bedale Rd. Enf. BZ22 30
Bedale Rd. Enf. BZ23 30
Bedale Rd. Rom. CX28 42
Bedale St. SE1 BZ40 57
Beddingfield St. E15 CF35 48
Beddington Fm. Rd. Croy. BX54 86
Beddington Gdns. Wall. BV57 95
Beddington Gn. Orp. CN51 88
Beddington Gro. Wall. BW56 95
Beddington La. Croy. BW53 86
Beddington Path, Orp. CN51 88
Beddington Rd. Ilf. CN33 49
Beddington Rd. Orp. CN51 88
Beddlestead La. Warl. CG62 106
Bede Clo. Pnr. BD30 36
Bedenham Way SE15 CA43 67
Hordle Prom N.
Bedens Rd. Sid. CQ50 79
Bede Rd. E3 CD39 57
Bede Rd. Rom. CP32 50
Bedfont Clo. Felt. BA46 73
Bedfont Ct. Stai. AW45 63
Bedfont La. Felt. BB47 73
Bedfont La. Felt. BC47 73
Bedfont Rd. Felt. BA47 73
Bedfont Rd. Stai. AY46 73
Bedford Ave. Amer. AR23 25
Bedford Av. WC1 BW39 56
Bedford Av. Barn. BR25 28
Bedford Av. Hayes BC39 53
Bedfordbury, WC2 BX40 56
Chandos Pl.
Bedford Clo. N10 BV29 38
Bedford Clo. Rick. AT22 25
Bedford Ct. WC2 BX40 56
Bedford St.
Bedford Cres. Enf. CD21 30
Bedford Gdns. W8 BS40 56
Bedford Gdns. Horn. CV34 51
Bedford Hill, SW12 BV47 76
Bedford Hill, SW16 BV47 76
Bedford Pk. Croy. BZ54 87
Bedford Pk. Mans. W4 BN42 65
Bedford Park Rd. St. Alb. BH13 9
Bedford Pl. WC1 BX39 56
Bedford Pl. Croy. BZ54 87
Bedford Rd. E6 CL37 58
Bedford Rd. E17 CE31 48
Bedford Rd. E18 CH30 40
Bedford Rd. N2 BU31 47
Bedford Rd. N8 BW32 47
Bedford Rd. N9 CB26 39
Bedford Rd. N15 CA31 48
Bedford Rd. N22 BX30 38
Bedford Rd. NW7 BO27 37
Bedford Rd. SW4 BX45 66
Bedford Rd. W4 BN41 65
Bedford Rd. W13 BJ40 54
Bedford Rd. Brent. BL42 65
Clayponds La.
Bedford Rd. Dart. CX47 80
Bedford Rd. Grav. DF48 81
Bedford Rd. Grays. DD42 71
Bedford Rd. Har. BG32 45
Bedford Rd. Ilf. CL34 49
Bedford Rd. Nthwd. BA27 35
Bedford Rd. Orp. CO55 89
Bedford Rd. Ruis. BB35 44
Bedford Rd. St. Alb. BH14 9
Bedford Rd. Sid. CN48 78
Bedford Rd. Twick. BG48 74
Bedford Rd. Wor. Pk. BQ55 85
Bedford Row, WC1 BX39 56
Bedford Sq. WC1 BW39 56
Bedford St. WC2 BX40 56
Bedford St. Wat. BC23 26
Bedford Ter. N7 BX34 47
Bedford Way, WC1 BW38 56
Bedgebury Gdns. SW19 BR47 75
Bedgebury Rd. SE9 CJ45 68
Bedivere Rd. Brom. CH48 78
Bedlam Gdns. E. Mol. BF52 84
Bedmond Grn. Wat. BB17 17
Bedmond Hill, Hem. H. BB16 17
Bedmond La. St. Alb. BD15 9
Bedmond La. Wat. BC16 17
Bedmond Rd. Hem. H. BA14 8
Bedmond Rd. St. Alb. BE14 9
Bedonwell Rd. Belv. CQ43 69
Bedster Gdns. E. Mol. BG51 84
Bedwardine Rd. SE19 CA50 77
Bedwell Ave. Hat. BV11 11
Bedwell Clo. Welw. G. C. BR8 5
Bedwell Gdns. E. Hayes. BB42 63
Bedwell Gdns. W. Hayes. BB42 63
Bedwell Rd. N17 CA30 39
Bedwell Rd. Belv. CQ42 69
Bedwin Way, SE16 CB42 67
Catlin St.
Beeby Rd. E16 CH39 58
Beech Ave. Lthd. BD68 111
Beech Av. N20 BU26 38
Beech Av. W3 BO40 55
Beech Av. Brent. BJ43 64
Beech Av. Brwd. DC27 122
Beech Av. Buck. H. CH27 40
Beech Av. Enf. BY21 29
Beech Av. Rad. BJ20 18
Beech Av. Ruis. BC33 44
Beech Av. Sid. CO47 79
Beech Av. Sth. Croy. BZ59 96
Beech Av. Swan. CT52 89
Beech Av. Upmin. CX35 51
Beech Cl. Hat. BP13 10
Beech Clo. N9 CB25 30
Beech Clo. SW15 BP47 75
Beech Clo. SW19 BQ50 75
Beech Clo. Ashf. BA49 73
Beech Clo. Cars. BU55 86
Beech Clo. Cob. BF59 93
Beech Clo. Dor. BH71 119
Beech Clo. Horn. CU34 50
Beech Clo. Lthd. BD67 111
Beech Clo. Walt. BD56 93
Beech Clo. West Dr. AZ41 63
Beech Clo. Wey. AY59 92
Beech Copse, Brom. CK51 88
Beech Ct. SE9 CK46 78
Beech Ct. Tedd. BK50 74
Broom Water
Beechcroft, Chis. CL50 78
Beechcroft, Guil. AO72 118
Beechcroft. S. Le H. DK42 71
Beechcroft. Ash. BL63 103
Beechcroft Av. NW11 BR33 46
Beechcroft Av. Bexh. CS44 69
Beechcroft Av. Har. BF33 45
Beechcroft Av. Ken. BZ61 105
Beechcroft Av. N. Mal. BO51 85
Beechcroft Av. Rick. BA25 26
Beechcroft Av. Sthl. BE40 54
Beechcroft Clo. SW16 BX49 76
Beechcroft Clo. Houns. BE43 64
Beechcroft Clo. Orp. CM56 97
Beechcroft Gdns. Wem. BL34 46
Beechcroft Manor, Wey. BA55 83
Beechcroft Rd. E18 CH30 40
Beechcroft Rd. SW14 BN45 65
Beechcroft Rd. SW17 BU48 76
Beechcroft Rd. Bush. BE25 27
Beechcroft Rd. Chess. BL55 85
Beechcroft Rd. Orp. CM56 97
Beechdale N21 BX27 38
Beechdale Rd. SW2 BX46 76
Beech Dell Orp. CK56 97
Beechdene, Tad. BP64 103
Beech, Dri. Berk. AR13 7
Beech Dr. N2 BU30 38
Beech Dr. Borwd. BL23 28
Beech Dr. Reig. BT70 121
Beech Dr. Saw. CP7 6
Beech Dr. Tad. BR64 103
Beech Dr. Wok. AV65 100
Beechen Clo. Pnr. BE31 45
Beechen Gro. Wat. BC24 26
Beechen La. Tad. BR66 112
Beechenlea La. Swan. CU52 89
Beechen Pl. SE23 CC48 77
Beeches Av. The, Cars. BU57 95
Beeches Clo. Tad. BS65 104
Beeches Rd. SW17 BU48 76
Beeches Rd. Sutt. BR54 85
Beeches The, Bans. BS61 104
Beeches, The, St. Alb. BG17 18
Sycamore Dr.
Beeches. The. Til. DG44 71
Beeches Wk. Cars. BT58 95
Beechey Pl. E15 CF35 48
Beech Farm Rd. Warl. CF63 105
Beechfield, Kings L. AY18 17
Beechfield, Saw. CQ6 6
Beechfield Cott. Brom. CJ51 88
Beechfield Gdns. Rom. CS33 50
Beechfield Rd. N4 BZ32 48
Beechfield Rd. SE6 CD47 77
Beechfield Rd. Brom. CJ51 88
Beechfield Rd. Erith CT43 69
Beechfield Rd. Hem. H. AW14 8
Beechfield Wk. Wal. Abb. CF21 30
Beech Gdns. W5 BL41 65
Beech Gdns. Dag. CR36 59
Beech Grn. S. Ock. CY41 70
Beech Grn. Wok. AS61 100
Beech Gro. Amer. AO23 25
Beech Gro. Cat. CA66 114
Beech Gro. Epsom BP62 103
Beech Gro. Guil. AP70 118
Beech Gro. Ilf. CN29 40
Beech Gro. Mitch. BW53 86
Beech Gro. N. Mal. BN52 85
Beech Gro. Wey. AW56 92
Beech Hall Cres. E4 CF29 39
Beech Hall Rd. E4 CF29 39
Beech Hill Barn. BT22 29
Beech Hill, Wok. AR65 100
Beech Hill Av. Barn. BT23 29
Beech Hill Ct. Berk. AR13 7
Beech Hill Gdns. Wal. Abb. CH22 31
Beechhill Rd. SE9 CL46 78
Beech House Rd. Croy. BZ55 87
Beech La. Beac. AP29 34
Beech La. Buck. H. CH27 40
Beech La. Guil. AR72 118
Beech Lawn, Guil. AS71 118
Beechlawns N2 BT28 38
Beechmont Av. Vir. W. AR53 82
Beechmont Rd. Brom. CG49 78
Beechmont Rd. Sev. CU68 116
Beechmore Gdns. Sutt. BQ55 85
Beechmore Rd. SW11 BU44 66
Beechmount Av. W7 BG39 54
Beecholme Av. Mitch. BV51 86
Beecholme Est. E5 CB34 48
Beechpark Way, Wat. BB22 26
Beech Pl. St. Alb. BG12 9
Beech Rd. N11 BX29 38
Beech Rd. SW16 BX51 86
Beech Rd. Dart. CV47 80
Beech Rd. Epsom BO61 103
Beech Rd. Felt. BB47 73
Beech Road Ong. DB13 15
Beech Rd. Orp. CO57 98
Beech Rd. Red. BW66 113
Beech Rd. Reig. BS69 121
Beech Rd. St. Alb. BH12 9
Beech Rd. Sev. CU66 116
Beech Rd. Slou. AS41 62
Beech Rd. Wat. BC22 26
Beech Rd. West. CH62 106
Beech Rd. Wey. BA56 92
Beech Row, Kings. On T. BL49 75
Beech St. E1 BZ39 57
Beech St. EC1 BZ39 57
Beech St. Rom. CS31 50
Beechtree Av. Egh. AQ50 72
Beech Tree Clo. Stan. BJ28 36
Beech Tree Clo. Stan. BK28 36
Marsh La.
Beech Tree Glade E4 CG26 40
Beech Tree La. Stai. AW51 83
Beech Tree Pl. Sutt. BS56 95
West St.
Beech Wk. NW7 BN29 37
Beech Wk. Dart. CU45 69
Beech Wk. Epsom BP59 94
Beech Wk. Hodd. CD12 12
Beech Way, NW10 BN36 55
Beechway, Bex. CP46 79
Beech Way, Croy. CC60 96
Beech Way Epsom BO61 103
Beech Way. Ger. Cr. AS33 43
Beech Way, Guil. AT70 118
Beech Way Twick. BF48 74

Beechway Clo. Wal. Cr. CA16 21
Beech Wood Ave. Amer. AR22 25
Beechwood Ave. Rick. AT24 25
Beechwood Ave. Tad. BS64 104
Beechwood Av. N3 BR31 46
Beechwood Av. Couls. BV61 104
Beechwood Av. Grnf. BF38 54
Beechwood Av. Har. BF34 45
Beechwood Av. Hayes BA40 53
Beechwood Av. Orp. CN56 97
Beechwood Av. Pot. B. BS20 20
Beechwood Av. Rich. BM44 65
Beechwood Av. Ruis. BB34 44
Beechwood Av. St. Alb. BJ12 9
Beechwood Av. Stai. AW50 73
Beechwood Av. Sun. BC50 73
Beechwood Av. Th. Hth. BY52 86
Beechwood Av. Uxb. AZ39 53
Beechwood Av. Wey. BA56 92
Beechwood Clo. NW7 BO28 37
Beechwood Clo. Amer. AR23 25
Beechwood Clo. Surb. BK54 84
Beechwood Clo. Wey. BB56 92
Beechwood Clo. Wok. AP62 100
Beechwood Cres. Bexh. CP45 69
Beechwood Dr. Kes. CJ56 97
Beechwood Dr. Wdf. Grn. CG28 40
Beechwood Gdns. W5 BL37 55
St. Anne's Gdns.
Beechwood Gdns. Cat. CB64 105
Beechwood Gdns. Har. BF34 45
Beechwood Gdns. Ilf. CK32 49
Beechwood Gdns. Rain. CU39 59
Beechwood Gdns. Slou. AR41 62
Beechwood La. Warl. CC63 105
Beechwood Manor, Wey. BB56 92
Beechwood Pk. E18 CH31 49
Beechwood Rise, Wat. BC21 26
Beechwood Rd. E8 CA36 57
Beechwood Rd. N8 BW31 47
Beechwood Rd. Cat. CB64 105
Beechwood Rd. Slou. AO39 52
Beechwood Rd. Sth. Croy. BZ58 96
Beechwood Rd. Vir. W. AQ54 82
Beechwood Rd. Wok. AP62 100
Beechwood Ter. E4 CF29 39
Larks Hall Rd.
Beechworth Clo. NW3 BS34 47
Beechy Lees Rd. Sev. CW61 108
Beecot La. Walt. BD55 84
Beecroft Rd. SE4 CD46 77
Beehive Ct. Ilf. CK32 49
Beehive Grn. Welw. G. C. BS9 5
Beehive La. Ilf. CK32 49
Beehive La. Welw. G. C. BS9 5
Beehive Rd. Stai. AV49 72
Beehive Rd. Wal. Cr. BY17 20
Beehive Whitelands Brwd. DB21 33
Beel Clo. Amer. AR23 25
Beeleigh Rd. Mord. BS52 86
Beesfield La. Farn. CX54 90
Beeston Clo. Wat. BD28 36
Beeston Pl. SW1 BV41 66
Beeston Rd. Barn. BT25 29
Berkeley Cres.
Beeston Way Felt. BD46 74
Beethoven Rd. Borwd. BK26 36
Beethoven St. W10 BR38 55
Begbie Rd. SE3 CJ44 68
Beggar's Hill Epsom BO57 94
Beggars Hollow, Enf. BZ22 30
Beggars La. Wok. AO59 91
Begonia Wk. W12 BO39 55
Du Cane Rd.
Beira St. SW12 BV47 76
Belcher Rd. Hodd. CE11 12
Belchers La. Wal. Abb. CJ15 13
Belcroft Clo. Brom. CG50 78
Hope Park
Belfairs Dr. Rom. CP33 50
Belfairs Grn. Wat. BD28 36
Heysham Dr.
Belfast Av. Slou. AO39 52
Belfast Rd. N16 CA34 48
Belfast Rd. SE25 CB52 87
Belfield Rd. Epsom BN57 94
Belfont Walk N7 BX35 47
Walters Rd.
Belford Gro. SE18 CL42 68
Belford Rd. Borwd. BL22 28
Belfort Rd. SE15 CC44 67
Belfry Ave. Uxb. AW29 35
Belgrade Rd. N16 CA35 48
Belgrade Rd. Hamptn. BF51 84
Belgrave Av. Rom. CV31 51
Belgrave Av. Wat. BB25 26
Belgrave Clo. N14 BW25 29
Belgrave Clo. W3 BM41 65
Belgrave Cres. Sun. BC51 83
Belgrave Dr. Kings L. BA17 17
Belgrave Gdns. N14 BW24 29
Belgrave Gdns. NW8 BS37 56
Belgrave Gdns. Stan. BK28 36
Belgrave Grn. N. Slou. AP40 52
Belgrave Grn. S. Slou. AP40 52
Belgrave Manor Wok. AS63 100
Brooklyn Rd.
Belgrave Ms. SW1 BV41 66
Belgrave Ms. Uxb. AX38 53
Belgrave Ms. N. SW1 BV41 66
Belgrave Ms. S. SW1 BV41 66
Belgrave Pl. SW1 BV41 66
Belgrave Rd. E10 CF33 48
Belgrave Rd. E11 CH34 49
Belgrave Rd. E13 CJ38 58
Belgrave Rd. E17 CE32 48
Belgrave Rd. SE25 CA52 87
Belgrave Rd. SW1 BV42 66
Belgrave Rd. SW13 BO43 65
Belgrave Rd. Houns. BE45 64
Belgrave Rd. Ilf. CK33 49
Belgrave Rd. Mitch. BT52 86
Belgrave Rd. Slou. AP40 52
Belgrave Rd. Sun. BC51 83
Belgrave Sq. SW1 BV41 66
Belgrave St. E1 CD39 57
Belgrave St. SW1 BV41 66
Belgrave Ter. Wdf. Grn. CH27 40
Belgrave Wk. Mitch. BT52 86
Belgravia Gdns. Brom. CF50 77
Belgravia Mews, Kings. On T. BK52 84
Belgrove St. WC1 BX38 56
Belham Rd. Kings L. AY17 17
Belham St. SE5 BZ44 67
Belhaven St. E3 CD38 57
Belinda Rd. SW9 BY45 66
Belitha Vill. N1 BX36 56
Bell Alley Houns. BF45 64
Bellamy Clo. SW5 BR42 65
Aisgill Av
Bellamy Clo. Uxb. AZ34 44
Bellamy Clo. Wat. BC23 26
Bellamy Dr. Stan. BJ30 36
Bellamy Rd. E4 CE29 39
Bellamy Rd. Wal. Cr. CD18 21
Bellamy St. SW12 BV47 76
Bellasis Av. SW2 BX48 76
Bell Av. Rom. CU30 41
Bell Av. West Dr. AY42 63
Bell Clo. Green. CZ46 80
Bell Clo. Pnr. BD30 36
Bell Clo. Ruis. BB34 44
Bell Clo. Slou. AQ39 52
Bell Clo. Wat. BC17 17
Bellclose Rd. West Dr. AY41 63
Bell Ct. Surb. BM55 85
Bell Cres. Couls. BV64 104
Bell Dr. SW18 BR47 75
Bellefield Rd. Orp. CO53 89
Bellefields Rd. SW9 BX45 66
Belle Grove Clo. Well. CN44 68
Bellegrove Rd. Well. CN44 68
Bellenden Rd. SE15 CA45 67
Belleville Rd. SW11 BU46 76
Belle Vue Grnf. BG37 54
Bellevue Gdns. SW9 BX44 66
Bellevue La. Bush. BG26 36
Bellevue Pk. Th. Hth. BZ52 87
Bellevue Rd. E17 CF30 39
Bellevue Rd. N11 BV28 38
Bellevue Rd. NW4 BQ31 46
Bellevue Rd. SW13 BP44 65
Bellevue Rd. SW17 BU47 76
Bellevue Rd. W13 BJ38 54
Belle Vue Rd. Bexh. CQ46 79
Bellevue Rd. Horn. CW33 51
Bellevue Rd. Kings-on-t. BL52 85
Belle Vue Rd. Rom. CS29 41
Belle Vue Ter. NW4 BQ31 46
Bellew St. SW17 BT48 76
Bellfield Av. Har. BG29 36
Bellfields Rd. Guil. AR69 118
Bellflower Path. Rom. CV29 42
Bell Fm. Av. Dag. CS34 50
Bell Gdns. Orp. CP53 89
Bell Grn. SE26 CD49 77
Bell Grn. La. SE26 CD49 77
Bellhouse La. Brwd. CZ25 33
Bell Ho. Rd. Rom. CS33 50
Bellingham Grn. SE6 CE48 77
Bellingham Rd. SE6 CE48 77
Bell La. E1 CA39 57
Bell La. E16 CH40 58
Bell La. NW4 BQ31 46
Bell La. Amer. AQ23 25
Bell La. Berk. AO12 7
Bell La. Berk. AP12 7
Bell La. Brox. CD14 12
Bell La. Enf. CC22 30
Bell La. Hat. BS15 11
Bell La. Hodd. CE12 12
Bell La. Lthd. BG65 102
Bell La. St. Alb. BL18 19
Bell La. Twick. BJ47 74
Bell La. Wat. BB17 17
Bell La. Wind. AM42 61
Bell La. Clo. Lthd. BG65 102
Bellman Av. Grav. DJ47 81
Bell Mead, Saw. CQ6 6
Bellmount Wood Av. Wat. BB23 26
Bellot Way, SE10 CG42 68
Bellring Clo. Belv. CR43 69
Bell Rd. E3 CF38 57
Bell Rd. E. Mol. BG53 84
Bell Rd. Enf. BZ23 30
Bell Rd. Houns. BF45 64
Bells All. SW6 BS44 66
Bells Garden Rd. SE15 CB43 67
Bells Hill Barn. BQ25 28
Bells Hill, Slou. AQ37 52
Bells Hill Grn. Slou. AQ36 52
Bells La. Slou. AT45 62
Bellstaines Pleasaunce E4 CE27 39
Bell St. NW1 BU39 56
Bell St. Reig. BS70 121
Bell St. Saw. CQ6 6
Bellswood La. Iver AT39 52
Belltrees Gro. SW16 BX49 76
Bell Vw. Wind. AM45 61
Bell View Clo. Wind. AM44 61
Bellvue Clo. Orp. CL58 97
Bell Water Gate, SE18 CL41 68
Bellweir Clo. Stai. AT48 72
Bell Wharf La. EC4 BZ40 57
Upr. Thames St.
Bellwood Rd. SE15 CC45 67
Bell Yd. WC2 BY39 56
Belmarsh Rd. Wey. AW56 92
Belmont Av. N9 CB26 30
Belmont Av. N13 BX28 38
Belmont Av. N17 BZ31 48
Belmont Av. Barn. BU25 29
Belmont Av. Guil. AP69 118
Belmont Av. N. Mal. BP52 85
Belmont Av. N. Mal. BP53 85
Belmont Av. Sthl. BE41 64
Belmont Av. Upmin. CX34 51
Belmont Av. Well. CN44 68
Belmont Av. Wem. BL37 55
Belmont Circle, Har. BJ30 36
Belmont Clo. N20 BS26 38
Belmont Clo. Barn. BU24 29
Belmont Clo. Uxb. AX36 53
Belmont Clo. Wdf. Grn. CH28 40
Belmont Ct. St. Alb. BG14 9
Belmont Hill
Belmont Gro. SE13 CF45 67
Belmont Gro. W4 BN42 65
Belmont Hall Ct. SE13 CF45 67
Belmont Hill SE13 CF45 67
Belmont Hill, St. Alb. BG14 9
Belmont La. Chis. CL49 78
Belmont La. Stan. BK29 36
Belmont Pk. SE13 CF45 67
Belmont Park Rd. E10 CE32 48
Belmont Pl. W4 BN42 65
Belmont Rise Sutt. BR57 94
Belmont Rd. E15 CG38 58
Belmont Rd. N15 BZ31 48
Belmont Rd. N17 BZ31 48
Belmont Rd. NW11 BR32 46
Belmont Rd. SW4 BW45 66
Belmont Rd. Beck. CD51 87
Belmont Rd. Bexh. CR43 69
Belmont Rd. Bush. BE24 27
Belmont Rd. Chis. CL49 78
Belmont Rd. Grays. DC43 71
Belmont Rd. Har. BH31 45
Belmont Rd. Hem. H. AY15 8
Belmont Rd. Horn. CV34 51
Belmont Rd. Ilf. CM34 49
Belmont Rd. Lthd. BJ64 102
Belmont Rd. Reig. BT71 121
Belmont Rd. Se25 CB53 87
Belmont Rd. Sutt. BS58 95
Belmont Rd. Twick. BG48 74
Belmont Rd. Uxb. AX36 53
Belmont Rd. Wall. BV56 95
Belmont St. NW1 BV36 56
Belmor, Borwd. BM25 28
Belmore Av. Hayes BC39 53
Belmore Av. Wok. AU61 100
Belmore St. SW8 BW44 66
Belper St. N1 CB36 57
Lofting Rd.
Belsham St. E9 CC36 57
Belsize Av. N13 BX29 38
Belsize Av. NW3 BT36 56
Belsize Av. W13 BJ41 64
Belsize Clo. Hem. H. AZ14 8
Belsize Cres. NW3 BT35 47
Belsize Gdns. Sutt. BS56 95
Belsize Gro. NW3 BU36 56
Belsize La. NW3 BT36 56
Belsize Ms. NW3 BT35 47
Belsize La.
Belsize Pk. NW3 BT36 56
Belsize Pk. Gdns. NW3 BT36 56
Belsize Pk. Ms. NW3 BT35 47
Belsize La.
Belsize Pl. NW3 BT35 47
Belsize La.
Belsize Rd. NW6 BS37 56
Belsize Rd. NW6 BT36 56
Belsize Rd. Har. BG29 36
Belsize Rd. Hem. H. AZ14 8
Belsize Sq. NW3 BT36 56
Belsize Ter. NW3 BT36 56
Belson Rd. SE18 CK42 68
Belswains La. Hem. H. AY15 8
Beltana Dr. Grav. DJ49 81
Beltane Dr. SW19 BQ48 75
Beltinge Rd. Rom. CW31 51
Belton Rd. E7 CH36 58
Belton Rd. E11 CG35 49
Belton Rd. N17 CA31 48
Belton Rd. NW2 BP36 55
Belton Rd. Berk. AQ12 7
Belton Rd. Sid. CO49 79
Belton Way, E3 CE39 57
Beltran Rd. SW6 BS44 66
Beltwood Rd. Belv. CS42 69
Belvedere NW9 BO30 37
Belvedere Av. SW19 BR49 75
Belvedere Av. Ilf. CL30 40
Belvedere Bldgs. SE1 BY41 66
Belvedere Clo. Esher BF56 93
Belvedere Clo. Grav. DH47 81
Belvedere Clo. Tedd. BH49 74
Belvedere Ct. N2 BT32 47
Belvedere Ct. SW15 BQ45 65
Upr. Richmond Rd.
Belvedere Dr. SW19 BR49 75
Belvedere Gdns. E. Mol. BE53 84
Belvedere Gdns. Guil. AQ69 118
Belvedere Gro. SW19 BR49 75
Belvedere Pl. SE1 BY41 66
Borough Rd.
Belvedere Rd. E10 CD33 48
Belvedere Rd. SE1 BX41 66
Belvedere Rd. SE2 CP40 59
Belvedere Rd. SE19 CA50 77
Belvedere Rd. Bexh. CQ45 69
Belvedere Rd. Brwd. CZ27 42
Belvedere Rd. West. CK62 106
Belvedere Sq. SW19 BR49 75
Belvedere Way, Har. BL32 46
Belvoir Rd. SE22 CB47 77
Belvue Clo. Nthlt. BF36 54
Belvue Rd. Nthlt. BF36 54
Bembridge Clo. NW6 BQ36 55
Bembridge Gdns. Ruis. BA34 44
Bemerton St. N1 BX37 56
Bemish Rd. SW15 BQ45 65
Bempton Dr. Ruis. BC34 44
Bemsted Rd. E17 CD31 48
Benares Rd. SE18 CN42 68
Benbow Clo. St. Alb. BJ14 9
Benbow Rd. W6 BP41 65
Benbow St. SE8 CE43 67
Benbow Waye, Uxb. AX39 53
Benbrick Rd. Guil. AQ71 118
Benbury Clo. Brom. CF49 77
Bence, The, Egh. AT52 82
Bench Fld. Sth. Croy. CA57 96
Benchley Gdns. SE23 CC46 77
Bench Manor Cres. Ger. Cr. AR30 34
Bench, The Rich. BK48 74
Back La.
Bencombe Rd. Pur. BX60 95
Bencope St. SE17 CA42 67
Bencroft Rd. SW16 BW50 76
Bendall Ms. NW1 BU39 56
Bendemeer Rd. SW15 BQ45 65
Bendish Rd. E6 CK36 58
Bendmore Av. SE2 CO42 69
Bendon Vall. SW18 BS47 76
Bendysh Rd. Bush. BE24 27
Benedict Dr. Felt. BA47 73
Benedict Rd. SW9 BX45 66
Benedict Rd. Mitch. BT52 86
Benenden Grn. Brom. CH53 88
Benenstock Rd. Stai. AW46 73
Benets Rd. Horn. CX33 51
Benett Gdns. SW16 BX51 86
Benfleet Clo. Cob. BE59 93
Benfleet Clo. Sutt. BT55 86
Benford Rd. Hodd. CD13 12
Bengal Rd. Ilf. CL35 49
Bengarth Dr. Har. BG30 36
Bengarth Rd. Nthlt. BD37 54
Bengeworth Rd. SE5 BZ45 67
Bengeworth Rd. Har. BJ34 45
Benhale Clo. Stan. BJ28 36
Benham Clo. SW11 BT45 66
Wayland Rd.
Benham Clo. Couls. BY62 104
Benham Rd. W7 BH39 54
Benham St. SW11 BT45 66
Benhill Av. Sutt. BS56 95
Benhill Rd. SE5 BZ43 67
Benhill Rd. Sutt. BT55 86
Benhill Wd. Rd. Sutt. BT55 86
Benhilton Gdns. Sutt. BS55 86
Benhurst Av. Horn. CU35 50
Benhurst Clo. Sth. Croy. CC58 96
Benhurst Ct. SW16 BY49 76
Benhurst Gdns. Sth. Croy. CC58 96
Benhurst La. SW16 BY49 76
Benin St. SE13 CF47 77
Benjamin St. EC1 BY39 56
Ben Jonson Rd. E1 CC39 57
Benledi St. E14 CF39 57
Bennerley Rd. SW11 BU46 76
Bennet St. SW1 BW40 56
Arlington St.
Bennett Clo. Well. CO44 69
Bennett Gro. SE13 CE44 67
Bennett Pk. SE3 CG45 68
Bennett Rd. E13 CJ38 58
Bennett Rd. Rom. CQ32 50
Bennetts Av. Croy. CD55 87
Bennett's Av. Grnf. BG37 54
Bennetts Av. Sev. DB59 99
Bennetts Castle La. Dag. CP35 50
Bennetts Clo. N17 CB29 39
Bennetts Clo. Cob. BC60 92
Bennetts Copse Chis. CK50 78
Wood Dr.
Bennetts End Clo. Hem. H. AY14 8
Bennetts End Rd. Hem. H. AZ14 8
Bennett St. W4 BO43 65
Bennetts Way Croy. CD55 87
Bennetts Yd. SW1 BX41 66
Marsham St.
Bennett Way. Dart. CY49 80
Bennett Way. Guil. AW68 110
Benningholme Rd. Edg. BO29 37
Bennington Av. Bark. CL36 58
Bennington Rd. N17 CA30 39
Bennington Rd. Wdf. Grn. CG29 40
Forest Dr.
Benns Alley Hamptn. BF51 84
Thames St.
Benn St. E9 CD36 57
Benrek Clo Ilf. CM30 40
Bensham Clo. Th. Hth. BZ52 87
Bensham Gro. Th. Hth. BZ51 87
Bensham La. Croy. BY54 86
Bensham Manor Rd. Th. Hth. BZ52 87
Benskin Rd. Wat. BC25 26
Benskins La. Hav. CV26 42
Benson Av. E6 CJ37 58
Benson Clo. Houns. BF45 64
Benson Clo. Slou. AQ40 52
Benson Rd. SE23 CC47 77
Benson Rd. Croy. BY55 86
Benson Rd. Grays. DD43 71
Bensor Clo. Uxb. AY39 53
Bentbrook Pk. Dor. BJ73 119
Bentfield Gdns. SE9 CJ48 78
Benthal Rd. N16 CB34 48
Bentham Ave. Wok. AU60 91
Bentham Av. Wok. AU61 100
Bentham Rd. E9 CC36 57
Ben Tillet Clo. Bark. CO36 59
Bentinck Ms. W1 BV39 56
Marylebone La.
Bentinck Rd. West Dr. AX40 53
Bentinck St. W1 BV39 56
Bentley Dr. Ilf. CM32 49
Bentley Heath La. Barn. BR21 28
Bentley Rd. N1 CA36 57
Tottenham Rd.
Bentley Rd. Slou. AN40 61
Bentleys Meadow. Sev. CW63 108
Bentley St. Grav. DH46 81
Bentley Way Stan. BJ28 36
Bentley Way Wdf. Grn. CH27 40
Benton Clo. Houns. BF45 64
Staines Rd.
Benton Rd. E16 CJ40 58
Oriental Rd.
Benton Rd. Wat. BD28 36
Benton Rd. E. Ilf. CM33 49
Benton Rd. W. Ilf. CM33 49
Bentons Harl. CN12 13
Bentons La. SE27 BZ49 77
Bentons Ri. SE27 BZ49 77
Bentry Clo. Dag. CQ34 50
Bentry Rd. Dag. CQ34 50
Bentsbrook Rd. Dor. BJ73 119
Bentsley Clo. St. Alb. BK11 9
Bentwick Clo. Ger. Cr. AR32 43
Bentworth Rd. W12 BP39 55
Benwell Rd. N7 BY35 47
Benworth St. E3 CD38 57
Benyon Rd. N1 BZ37 57
Berberis Wk. West Dr. AY42 63
Berber Rd. SW11 BU46 76
Ashness Rd.
Berceau Wk. Wat. BB23 26
Berecroft Harl. CN13 13
Beredens La. Upmin. CZ32 51
Berens Rd. NW10 BQ38 55
Berens Rd. Orp. CP53 89
Berens Way Chis. CN52 88
Beresford Av. N20 BU27 38
Beresford Av. W7 BG39 54
Beresford Av. Slou. AR40 52
Beresford Av. Surb. BM54 85
Beresford Av. Twick. BK46 74
Beresford Av. Wem. BL37 55
Beresford Dr. Wdf. Grn. CJ28 40
Beresford Gdns. Enf. CA24 30
Beresford Gdns. Houns. BE46 74
Beresford Gdns. Rom. CQ32 50
Beresford Rd. E4 CG26 40
Beresford Rd. E17 CE30 39
Beresford Rd. N2 BU31 47
Beresford Rd. N5 BZ35 48
Beresford Rd. N8 BY32 47
Beresford Rd. Dor. BJ71 119
Beresford Rd. Grav. DF47 81
Beresford Rd. Har. BG32 45
Beresford Rd. Kings. On T. BL51 85
Beresford Rd. N. Mal. BN52 85
Beresford Rd. Rick. AV26 34
Beresford Rd. St. Alb. BJ14 9
Beresford Rd. Sthl. BD40 54
Beresford Rd. Sutt. BR58 94
Beresford St. SE18 CL41 68
Beresford Ter. N5 BZ35 48
Berestead Rd. W6 BO43 65
Berestede Rd. W6 BO42 65
Berger Rd. E9 CC36 57
Bergholt Av. Ilf. CK32 49
Bergholt Cres. N16 CA33 48
Berkeley Av. Grnf. BG36 54
Berkeley Av. Houns. BC44 63
Berkeley Av. Ilf. CL30 40
Berkeley Av. Rom. CS29 41
Berkeley Av. Wal. Cr. CC20 21
Berkeley Clo. Borwd. BM25 28
Berkeley Clo. Guil. AS70 118
Berkeley Clo. Pot. B. BR19 19
Berkeley Clo. Ruis. BC34 44
Berkeley Ct. EC1 BY39 56
Briset St.
Berkeley Ct. N14 BW25 29
Berkeley Ct. Ruis. BB34 44
Berkeley Ct. Stai. AU48 72
Moor La.
Berkeley Ct. Wey. BB55 83
Berkeley Cres. Barn. BT25 29
Berkeley Cres. Dart. CW47 80
Berkeley Gdns. N21 BZ26 39
Berkeley Gdns. W8 BS40 56
Brunswick Gdns
Berkeley Gdns. Walt. BB54 83
Berkeley Ms. W1 BU39 56
Berkeley Pl. SW19 BQ50 75
Berkeley Rd. E12 CK35 49
Berkeley Rd. N8 BW32 47
Berkeley Rd. N15 BZ32 48
Berkeley Rd. NW9 BM31 46
Berkeley Rd. SW13 BP44 65
Berkeley Rd. Bexh. CP44 69
Berkeley Rd. Uxb. BA36 53
Berkeley Sq. W1 BV40 56
Berkeley St. W1 BU39 56
Berkeley Wk. N7 BX34 47
Andover Est.
Berkeley Waye Houns. BD43 64
Berkhampstead Rd. Belv. CR42 69
Berkhampsted Rd. Hem. H. AV12 7
Berkhamsted Av. Wem. BL36 55
Berkhamsted Hill, Berk. AS12 7
Berkhamsted La. Hat. BU13 11
Berkhamsted Pl. Berk. AQ12 7
Berkley Clo. Horn. CX34 51
Berkley Dr. E. Mol. BE52 84
Berkley Dr. Horn. CX34 51
Berkley Gro. NW1 BU36 56
Berkley Rd.
Berkley Rd. NW1 BU36 56
Berkley Rd. SW13 BP44 65
Berks Clo. Cat. BZ64 105
Berks Hill. Rick. AU25 25
Berkshire Gdns. N13 BX29 38
Berkshire Gdns. N18 CB28 39
Berkshire Rd. E9 CD36 57

Berkshire Sq. Mitch. BX52 86
Berkshire Ter. E9 CD36 57
Berkshire Way, Horn. CX32 51
Berkshire Way Mitch. BX52 86
Bermans Clo. Brwd. DD27 122
Hanging Hill La.
Berman's Way, NW10 BO35 46
Bermondsey Sq. SE1 CA41 67
Abbey St.
Bermondsey St. SE1 CA40 57
Bermondsey Wall. E. SE16 CB41 67
Bermondsey Wall. W. SE16 CB41 67
Mill St.
Bermuda Rd. Til. DG44 71
Bernard Av. W13 BJ41 64
Bernard Gdns. SW19 BR49 75
Bernard Rd. N15 CA32 48
Bernard Rd. Rom. CS33 50
Bernard Rd. Wall. BV56 95
Bernard St. WC1 BX38 56
Bernard St. St. Alb. BG13 9
Bernays Clo. Stan. BK29 36
Bernays Gro. SW9 BX45 66
Bernell Dr. Croy. CD55 87
Berner Est. E1 CB39 57
Berne Rd. Th. Hth. BZ52 87
Berners Dr. St. Alb. BH16 9
Berners Ms. W1 BW39 56
Berners Pl. W1 BW39 56
Berners Rd. N1 BY37 56
Berners Rd. N22 BY30 38
Berners St. W1 BW39 56
Berners Way, Brox. CD15 12
Bernville Way, Harrow. BL32 46
Kenton Rd.
Bernwell Rd. E4 CG27 40
Berota Rd. SE9 CM48 78
Berridge Est. Edg. BL29 37
Berridge Grn. Edg. BM29 37
Berridge Rd. SE19 BZ49 77
Berriman Rd. N7 BX34 47
Berriton Rd. Har. BE33 45
Berrwood Clo. Wey. AW57 92
Berry Av. Wat. BC21 26
Berry Clo. N21 BY26 38
Berry Clo. NW10 BO36 55
Berry Clo. Rick. AW26 35
Berryfield, Slou. AR39 52
Berry Grn. La. Wat. BE23 27
Berry Gro. La. Wat. BE22 27
Berry Gro. La. Wat. BF23 27
Berryhill SE9 CL45 68
Berry Hill Stan. BK28 36
Berryhill Gdns. SE9 CL45 68
Berry Ho. Rd. SW11 BU44 66
Dagnall St.
Berrylands SW20 BQ52 85
Berrylands Surb. BL53 85
Berrylands Rd. Surb. BL53 85
Berry Lane, Guil. & Wok. AO65 100
Berry La. Rick. AU25 25
Berry La. Rick. AW25 26
Berry La. Rick. AW26 35
Berry La. Walt. BD56 93
Berryman Clo. Dag. CP34 50
Bennetts Castle La.
Berrymans La. SE26 CC49 77
Berrymead, Hem. H. AY12 8
Berry Meade, Ash. BL62 103
Berrymead Gdns. W3 BN41 65
Berrymede Rd. W4 BN41 65
Berry Rd. SE17 BY42 66
Berry's Croft Rd. Stai. AX50 73
Berry's Green Rd. West. CL61 106
Berry's Hill, West. CL61 106
Berrys La. Wey. AX59 92
Berrystede Clo. Kings. On T. BM50 75
Berry St. EC1 BY38 56
Dallington St.
Berry Wk. Ash. BL63 103
Berry Way W5 BL41 65
Berry Way. Rick. AW26 35
Bertal Rd. SW17 BT49 76
Berther Rd. Horn. CV33 51
Berthon St. SE8 CE43 67
Bertie Rd. NW10 BP36 55
Bertie Rd. SE26 CC50 77
Bertram Cott. SW19 BS50 76
Bertram Gdns. E6 CK39 58
Bertram Rd. NW4 BP32 46
Bertram Rd. Enf. CA24 30
Bertram Rd. Kings. On T. BM50 75
Bertram St. N19 BV34 47
Bertram Way Enf. CA24 30
Bertrand St. SE13 CE45 67
Bert Rd. Th. Hth. BZ53 87
Berwick Av. Hayes. BD39 54
Berwick Clo. Wal. Cr. CE20 21
Queens Dr.
Berwick Cres. Sid. CN47 78
Berwick La. Ong. CT20 23
Berwick Pond Clo. Rain. CV37 60
Berwick Pond Rd. Rain. CW37 60
Berwick Rd. E16 CJ39 58
Berwick Rd. E17 CD31 48
Berwick Rd. N22 BY30 38
Berwick Rd. Borwd. BL22 28
Berwick Rd. Rain. CV37 60
Berwick Rd. Well. CO44 69
Berwick St. W1 BW39 56
Berwyn Av. Houns. BF44 64
Berwyn Rd. SE24 BY47 76
Berwyn Rd. Rich. BM45 65
Beryl Rd. W6 BQ42 65
Besant Ct. N1 BZ35 48
Besant Walk N7 BX34 47
Andover Est.
Besant Way NW10 BN35 46
Besley St. SW16 BW50 76
Bessborough Gdns. SW1 BW42 66
Vauxhall Bridge Rd.
Bessborough Pl. SW1 BW42 66
Bessborough Rd. SW15 BP47 75
Bessborough Rd. Har. BG33 45
Bessborough St. SW1 BW42 66
Bessein Pk. Rd. W12 BO41 65
Bessels Green Rd. Sev. CS65 107
Bessels Way. Sev. CS65 107
Bessemer Rd. SE5 BZ44 67
Bessemer Rd. Welw. G. C. BR7 5
Bessingby Rd. Ruis. BC34 44
Bessingham Wk. SE4 CD45 67
Frendsbury Rd.
Besson St. SE14 CC44 67
Bess St. E2 CC38 57
Bestwood St. SE8 CC42 67
Beta Rd. Wok. AP58 91
Betchworth Rd. Ilf. CN34 49
Betchworth Way Croy. CF58 96
Betenson Ave. Sev. CT64 107
Betham Rd. Grnf. BG38 54
Bethany Waye, Felt. BB47 73
Bethecar Rd. Har. BH32 45
Bethell Av. E16 CG38 58
Bethell Av. Ilf. CL33 49
Bethel Rd. Sev. CV65 108
Bethel Rd. Well. CP45 69
Bethesden Clo. Beck. CD50 77
Bethlehem Ho. E14 CD40 57
Bethnal Green Est. E2 CC38 57
Bethnal Grn Rd. E1 CA38 57
Bethnal Grn Rd. E2 CA38 57
Beth Rd. Wok. AT61 100
Princess Rd.
Bethune Av. N11 BU28 38
Bethune Rd. N16 BZ33 48
Bethune Rd. NW10 BN38 55
Bethwin Rd. SE5 BY43 66
Betley Ct. Walt. BC55 83
Betony Rd. Rom. CV29 42
Betoyne Av. E4 CG28 40
Betsham Rd. Erith CT43 69
Betsham Rd. Grav. DB49 80
Betsham Rd. Grav. DC49 81
Betsham Rd. Swans. DC47 81
Betstyle Rd. N11 BV28 38
Betterton Dr. Sid. CQ48 79
Betterton Rd. Rain. CT38 59
Betterton St. WC2 BX39 56
Bette St. E1 CB40 57
Bettles Clo. Uxb. AX37 52
Betton Pl. E2 CA37 57
Bettons Pk. E15 CG37 58
Bettridge Rd. SW6 BR44 65
Betts La. Wal. Abb. CJ14 13
Betts Rd. E16 CH39 58
Betts St. E1 CB40 57
Betts Way Surb. BJ54 84
Betula Wk. Rain. CV38 60
Between Streets, Cob. BC60 92
Beulah Av. SE26 CB49 77
Beulah Clo. Edg. BM27 37
Beulah Cres. Th. Hth. BZ51 87
Beulah Gro. Croy. BZ53 87
Beulah Hill, SE19 BY50 76
Beulah Path. E17 CE32 48
Addison Rd.
Beulah Rd. E11 CG34 49
Beulah Rd. E17 CE32 48
Beulah Rd. SW19 BR50 75
Beulah Rd. Epp. CO18 23
Beulah Rd. Horn. CV34 51
Beulah Rd. Th. Hth. BZ52 87
Beulah Wk. Cat. CD63 105
Beult Rd. Dart. CU45 69
Bevan Av. Bark. CO36 59
Bevan Clo. Hem. H. AX14 8
Bevan Ct. Croy. BY56 95
Bevan Est. Barn. BT24 29
Bevan Pl. Swan. CT52 89
Bevan Rd. SE2 CO42 69
Bevan Rd. Barn. BU24 29
Bevan St. N1 BZ37 57
Bevan Way. Horn. CW35 51
Bevenden St. N1 BZ38 57
Beverley Av. SW20 BO51 85
Beverley Av. Houns. BE45 64
Beverley Av. Sid. CN47 78
Beverley Clo. N21 BZ26 39
Beverley Clo. SW13 BP44 65
Beverley Clo. Brox. CD14 12
Beverley Clo. Chess. BK56 93
Beverley Clo. Enf. CA24 30
Beverley Clo. Horn. CW33 51
Beverley Clo. Wey. AX56 92
Beverley Clo. Wey. BB55 83
Beverley Ct. N14 BW26 38
Beverley Ct. SE4 CD45 67
Beverley Ct. W4 BN42 65
Beverley Ct. Epsom BQ59 94
Beverley Cres. Wdf. Grn. CH30 40
Beverley Dr. Edg. BM31 46
Beverley Gdns. NW11 BR33 46
Beverley Gdns. SW13 BO45 65
Beverley Gdns. Grnf. BH38 54
Beverley Gdns. Horn. CW33 51
Beverley Gdns. Stan. BJ30 36
Beverley Gdns. Wal. Cr. CB19 21
Beverley Gdns. Wem. BL33 46
Beverley Gdns. Wor. Pk. BP54 85
Beverley Heights Red. BT71 121
Cronks Hill
Beverley Hghts. Reig. BS69 121
Beverley La. Kings. On T. BO50 75
Beverley Path SW13 BO44 65
Beverley Rd. E4 CF29 39
Beverley Rd. E6 CJ38 58
Beverley Rd. SE20 CB51 87
Beverley Rd. SW13 BO45 65
Beverley Rd. W4 BO42 65
Beverley Rd. Bexh. CS44 69
Beverley Rd. Brom. CK55 88
Beverley Rd. Dag. CQ35 50
Beverley Rd. Mitch. BW52 86
Beverley Rd. N. Mal. BP52 85
Beverley Rd. Ruis. BC34 44
Beverley Rd. Sthl. BE42 64
Beverley Rd. Sun. BB51 83
Beverley Rd. Whyt. CA61 105
Beverley Rd. Wor. Pk. BQ55 85
Beverley Rd. Kings On T. BK51 84
Beverley Way N. Mal. BP52 85
Beversbrook Rd. N19 BW34 47
Beverstone Rd. SW2 BX46 76
Beverstone Rd. Th. Hth. BY52 86
Bevill Allen Clo. SW17 BU49 76
Bevil St. SE8 CE43 67
Frankham St.
Bevin Ct. WC1 BX38 56
Bevington Rd. W10 BR39 55
Bevington Rd. Beck. CE51 87
Bevington St. SE16 CB41 67
Bevin Rd. Hayes BC38 53
Bevis Clo. Dart. CY47 80
Bevis Marks, EC3 CA39 57
Bewcastle Gdns. Enf. BX24 29
Bewdley St. N1 BY36 56
Bewick St. SW8 BV44 66
Bewley Clo. Wal. Cr. CC19 21
Bewley La. Sev. DB66 117
Bewley St. E1 CC40 57
Bewlys Rd. SE27 BY49 76
Bexhill Clo. Felt. BE48 74
Bexhill Rd. N11 BW28 38
Bexhill Rd. SE4 CD46 77
Bexhill Rd. SW14 BO45 65
Bexley Clo. Dart. CT46 79
Bexley Gdns. N9 BZ27 39
Bexley La. Dart. CT46 79
Bexley La. Sid. CP49 79
Bexley Rd. SE9 CL46 78
Bexley Rd. Erith CS43 69
Bexley St. Wind. AN44 61
Beyer Gdns. Hodd. CE10 12
Beynon Rd. Cars. BU56 95
Bianca Rd. SE15 CA43 67
Bibsworth Rd. N3 BR30 37
Bicester Rd. Rich. BM45 65
Bickenhall St. W1 BU39 56
Bickersteth Rd. SW17 BU50 76
Bickerton Rd. N19 BW34 47
Bickley Cres. Brom. CK52 88
Bickley Pk. Rd. Brom. CK52 88
Bickley Rd. E10 CE33 48
Bickley Rd. Brom. CJ51 88
Bickley St. SW17 BU49 76
Bicknell Rd. SE5 BZ45 67
Bicknoller Rd. Enf. CA23 30
Bicknor Rd. Orp. CN54 88
Bidborough Clo. Brom. CG53 88
Bidborough St. WC1 BW38 56
Biddenden Way, SE9 CL49 78
Biddenden Way, Grav. DF50 81
Biddenham Turn Wat. BD21 27
Bidder St. E16 CG38 58
Biddestone Rd. N7 BX35 47
Biddulph Rd. W9 BS38 56
Biddulph Rd. Sth. Croy. BZ58 96
Bideford Av. Grnf. BJ38 54
Bideford Clo. Edg. BM30 37
Bideford Clo. Felt. BE48 74
Bideford Clo. Rom. CV30 42
Bideford Gdns. Enf. CA26 39
Bideford Rd. Brom. CG48 78
Bideford Rd. Enf. CD22 30
Bideford Rd. Ruis. BC34 44
Bideford Rd. Well. CO43 69
Bidhams Cres. Tad. BQ64 103
Bidwell Gdns. N11 BW29 38
Bidwell St. SE15 CB44 67
Bifron St. Bark. CM37 58
Big Comm. La. Red. BY70 121
Biggerstaff Rd. E15 CF37 57
Biggerstaff St. N4 BY34 47
Biggin Av. Mitch. BU51 86
Biggin Hl. SE19 BY51 86
Biggin La. Grays. DG43 71
Biggin Way, SE19 BY50 76
Bigginwood Rd. SW16 BY50 76
Big Hill, E5 CB33 48
Bigland St. E1 CB39 57
Bignell Rd. SE18 CL42 68
Bignold Rd. E7 CH35 49
Bigwood Ct. NW11 BS32 47
Bigwood Rd.
Bigwood Rd. NW11 BS32 47
Billet Clo. Horn. CV33 51
Billet Clo. Rom. CP31 50
Billet Rd.
Billet Hill. Sev. DB56 99
Billet La. Berk. AQ12 7
Billet La. Horn. CV33 51
Billet La. Iver & Slou. AT39 52
Billet Rd. E17 CC30 39
Billet Rd. Rom. CO31 50
Billet Rd. Stai. AW48 73
Billing Pl. SW10 BS43 66
Billing Rd. SW10 BS43 66
Billingsgate St. SE10 CF43 67
Billing St. SW10 BS43 66
Billington Pl. W3 BM40 55
Steyne Rd.
Billington Rd. SE14 CC43 67
Billiter Sq EC3 CA39 57
Fenchurch Av.
Billiter St. EC3 CA39 57
Billockby Clo. Chess. BL57 94
Billson St. E14 CF42 67
Billy Lows La. Pot. B. BS19 20
Bilsby Gro. SE9 CJ49 78
Bilton Clo. Slou. AV44 62
Colindale Rd.
Bilton Rd. Erith. CU43 69
Bilton Rd. Grnf. BJ37 54
Bilton Way Enf. CD23 30
Bilton Way Hayes BC41 63
Bina Gdns. SW5 BT42 66
Bincote Rd. Enf. BX24 29
Binden Rd. W12 BO41 65
Bindon Grn. Mord. BS52 86
Bayham Rd.
Binfield Rd. SW4 BX44 66
Binfield Rd. Sth. Croy. CA56 96
Binfield Rd. Wey. AY59 92
Bingfield St. N1 BX37 56
Bingham Dr. Stai. AX50 73
Bingham Pl. W1 BV38 56
Bingham Rd. Croy. CB54 87
Bingham St. N1 BZ36 57
Bingley Rd. E16 CJ39 58
Bingley Rd. Grnf. BG38 54
Bingley Rd. Sun. BC50 73
Binney St. W1 BV39 56
Binns Rd. W4 BO42 65
Binsey Wk. SE2 CP41 69
Binyon Cres. Stan. BH28 36
Birbeck Rd. Sid. CO48 79
Birbetts Rd. SE9 CK48 78
Birchall La. Welw. G. C. BT9 5
Bircham Path SE4 CD45 67
Frendsbury Rd.
Birchanger Rd. SE25 CB53 87
Birch Ave. Cat. BZ65 105
Birch Av. N13 BZ27 39
Birch Av. West Dr. AY39 53
Birch Clo. Brent. BJ43 64
Birch Clo. Buck. H. CJ27 40
Birch Clo. Rom. CR31 50
Birch Clo. Tedd. BJ49 74
Birch Clo. Wey. AX58 92
Birch Clo. Wok. AR63 100
Birch Clo. Wok. AV66 109
Birch Cres. Horn. CW31 51
Birch Cres. Uxb. AY37 53
Birchdale. Ger. Cr. AR33 43
Birchdale Clo. Wey. AX59 92
Birchdale Gdns. Rom. CP33 50
Birchdale Rd. E7 CJ35 49
Birch Dr. Hat. BP13 10
Birch Dr. Rick. AU28 34
Birchen Clo. NW9 BN34 46
Birchen Gro. NW9 BN34 46
Birches Clo. Epsom. BO61 103
Birches Clo. Pnr. BE32 45
Birches, The, N21 BX25 29
Birches The SE7 CH42 68
Birches, The, Brwd. DC27 122
Birches, The, Bush. BG25 27
Birches, The, Epp. CR16 23
Higham Vw.
Birches, The, Orp. CL56 97
Birchfield Clo. Wey. AW56 92
Birchfield Gro. Epsom BQ58 94
Birchfield Rd. Wal. Cr. CB18 21
Birchfield St. E14 CE40 57
Birch Gdns. Dag. CS34 50
Birch Grn. Hem. H. AV12 7
Birch Grn. Stai. AV48 72
Birch Gro. SE12 CG47 78
Birch Gro. W3 BM40 55
Birch Gro. Cob. BD60 93
Birch Gro. Pot. B. BS19 20
Birch Gro. Shep. BB51 83
Birch Gro. Tad. BR65 103
Birch Gro. Well. CO45 69
Birch Gro. Wind. AL44 61
Birch Hill Croy. CC56 96
Birch Hill, Wok. AR63 100
Birchington Clo. Bexh. CR44 69
Birchington Rd. N8 BW32 47
Birchington Rd. NW6 BS37 56
Birchington Rd. Surb. BL54 85
Birchington Rd. Wind. AN44 61
Birchin La. EC3 BZ39 57
Birchlands Av. SW12 BU47 76
Birch La. Pur. BX59 95
Birch Mead Orp. CL55 88
Birchmead, Wat. BB22 26
Birchmead Av. Pnr. BD31 45
Birchmead Clo. St. Alb. BG12 9
Birchmore Wk. N5 BY34 47
Birch Pl. Green. CZ46 80
Birch Rd. Berk. AO11 7
Birch Rd. Felt. BE49 74
Birch Rd. Rom. CR31 50
Birch Row Brom. CL54 88
Birch Tree Av. W. Wick. CG56 97
Birch Tree Ave Clo. Chesh. AQ18 16
Birch Tree Wk. Wat. BB22 26
Birch Tree Way Croy. CB55 87
Birch Vale. Cob. BF59 93
Birchville Ct. Bush. BH26 36
Birch Wk. Erith CS43 69
Birch Wk. Mitch. BV51 86
Birch Walk, Wey. AW59 92
Birch Way. Chesh. AO18 16
Birchway Hayes BC40 53
Birch Way, St. Alb. BK17 18
Birch Way. Warl. CD62 105
Birch Wood, Rad. BM20 19
Birchwood Wal. Abb. CG20 22
Roundhills
Birchwood Av. N10 BV31 47
Birchwood Av. Beck. CD52 87
Birchwood Av. Hat. BP11 10
Birchwood Av. Sid. CO48 79
Birchwood Av. Wall. BV55 86
Birchwood Cl. Hat. BP11 10
Birchwood Cotts. Hert. BV15 11
Birchwood Ct. N13 BY28 38
North Circular Rd.
Birchwood Ct. Edg. BN30 37
Birchwood Dr. Dart. CT49 79
Birchwood Dr. Wey. AW59 92
Birchwood Gro. Hamptn. BF50 74
Birchwood La. Cat. BY66 113
Birchwood La. Esher BG58 93
Birchwood Pk. Av. Swan. CT52 89
Birchwood Rd. SW17 BV49 76
Birchwood Rd. Orp. CM52 88
Birchwood Rd. Swan. CS51 89
Birchwood Rd. Wey. AW59 92
Birchwood Way, St. Alb. BF17 18
Birdbrook Clo. Dag. CS36 59
Birdbrook Rd. SE3 CJ45 68
Birdcage Wk. Sw1 BW41 66
Bird Clo. Uxb. AX30 35
Birdcroft Rd. Welw. G. C. BQ8 5
Bird Fm. Av. Rom. CR29 41
Birdham Clo. Brom. CK53 88
Bird House. La. Orp. CL60 97
Birdhurst Av. Sth. Croy. BZ56 96
Birdhurst Gdns. Sth. Croy. BZ56 96
Birdhurst Rise Sth. Croy. CA56 96
Birdhurst Rd. SW18 BT45 66
Birdhurst Rd. SW19 BU50 76
Birdhurst Rd. Sth. Croy. CA56 96
Bird-in-bush Rd. SE15 CB43 67
Bird-in-hand La. Brom. CJ51 88
Bird-in-hand Pass. SE23 CC48 77
Dartmouth Rd.
Bird La. Brwd. DB31 51
Bird La. Upmin. CY32 51
Bird La. Upmin. CZ31 51
Birdlington Rd. Wat. BD27 36
Birds Clo. Welw. G. C. BS9 5
Bird's Green. Ong. CZ13 15
Birds Hill Dr. Lthd. BG60 93
Birds Hill Rise. Lthd. BG60 93
Birds Hill Rd. Lthd. BG59 93
Bird St. W1 BV39 56
Bird Wk. Twick. BE47 74
Birdwood Clo. Croy. CC59 96
Birdwood Clo. Tedd. BH49 74
Birdwood Clo. Sth. Croy. CC58 96
Birkbeck Av. W3 BN40 55
Birkbeck Av. Grnf. BF37 54
Birkbeck Gdns. Wdf. Grn. CH27 40
Birkbeck Gro. W3 BN41 65
Birkbeck Hl. SE21 BY47 76
Birkbeck Pl. SE21 BZ47 77
Birkbeck Rd. E8 CA35 48
Birkbeck Rd. N8 BX31 47
Birkbeck Rd. N12 BT28 38
Birkbeck Rd. N17 CA30 39
Birkbeck Rd. NW7 BO28 37
Birkbeck Rd. SW19 BS49 76
Birkbeck Rd. W3 BN40 55
Birkbeck Rd. W5 BK42 64
Birkbeck Rd. Beck. CC51 87
Birkbeck Rd. Brwd. DE25 122
Birkbeck Rd. Enf. BZ23 30
Birkbeck Rd. Ilf. CM32 49
Birkbeck Rd. Rom. CS33 50
Birkbeck St. E2 CB38 57
Birkbeck Ter. Grnf. BG37 54
Birkbeck Way Grnf. BG37 54
Birkdale Av. Pnr. BF31 45
Birkdale Av. Rom. CW29 42
Birkdale Clo. Orp. CM54 88
Birkdale Gdns. Wat. BD27 36
Birkdale Pl. Orp. CM54 88
Birkdale Rd. SE2 CO42 69
Birkenhead Av. Kings. On T. BL51 85
Birkenhead St. WC1 BX38 56
St. Chads St.
Birkett Way. Ch. St. G. AR24 25
Birkhall Rd. SE6 CF47 77
Birkheads Rd. Reig. BS70 121
Birklands La. St. Alb. BJ15 9
Birkwood Clo. SW12 BW47 76
Birley Rd. N20 BT27 38
Birley Rd. Slou. AO39 52
Birley St. SW11 BV44 66
Birling Rd. Erith CS43 69
Birnam Rd. N4 BX34 47
Birstall Grn. Wat. BD27 36
Birstall Rd. N15 CA32 48
Biscay Rd. W6 BQ42 65
Biscoe Clo. Houns. BF43 64
Biscoe Way SE13 CF45 67
Bisenden Rd. Croy. CA55 87
Bisham Clo. Cars. BU54 86
Bisham Gdns. N6 BV33 47
Bishop Craven Clo. Enf. BY23 29
Bishop Duppas Pk. Shep. BA54 83
Watton Br. Rd.
Bishop Ken Rd. Har. BH30 36
Bishop King's Rd. W14 BR42 65
Bishop Rd. N14 BV26 38
Bishops Ave. Nthwd. BB28 35
Bishop's Av. E13 CH37 58
Bishops Av. SW6 BQ44 65
Bishops Av. Borwd. BL25 28
Bishops Av. Brom. CJ52 88
Bishops Av. Rom. CP32 50
Bishop's Av., The, N2 BT33 47
Bishop's Bri. W2 BT39 56
Bishop's Bridge Rd. W2 BS39 56
Bishop's Clo. E17 CE31 48
Bishops Clo. Couls. BY62 104
Bishop's Clo. Enf. CB23 30
Bishops Clo. Hat. BO12 10
College La.
Bishops Clo. Rich. BK48 74
Bishops Clo. St. Alb. BJ11 9
Bishops Clo. Sutt. BS55 86
Bishops Clo. Uxb. AZ37 53

Bishops Ct. EC4 BY39 56
Old Bailey
Bishop's Ct. WC2 BY39 56
Chancery La.
Bishopsfield Harl. CN12 13
Bishopsford Cars. BU53 86
Bishopsford Rd. Mord. BT54 86
Bishopsgate, EC2 CA39 57
Bishopsgate Churchyard, EC2 CA39 57
Bishopsgate Rd. Egh. AQ48 72
Bishop's Gro. N2 BU32 47
Bishops Gro. Hamptn. BE49 74
Bishop's Hall, Kings. On T. BK51 84
Bishopshall Rd. Brwd. DA25 33
Bishop's Mead, Hem. H. AW14 8
Bishopsmead Parade. Leath. BB67 110
Bishops Pk. Rd. SW6 BQ44 65
Bishop's Park Rd. SW16 BX51 86
Bishop's Rise. Hat. BO12 10
Bishops Rd. N6 BV32 47
Bishops Rd. SW6 BR44 65
Bishops Rd. W7 BH41 64
Bishop's Rd. Croy. BY54 86
Bishops Rd. Hayes BA39 53
Bishops Rd. Slou. AQ41 62
Bishop's Ter. SE11 BY42 66
Bishopsthorpe Rd. SE26 CC49 77
Bishop St. N1 BZ37 57
Bishops Wk. Chis. CM51 88
Bishops Wk. Croy. CC56 96
Bishop's Way, E2 CC37 57
Bishops Way NW10 BO36 55
Bishops Way, Egh. AU50 72
Bishopswood Rd. N6 BU33 47
Bisley Clo. Wal. Cr. CC20 21
Bisley Clo. Wor. Pk. BQ54 85
Bispham Rd. NW10 BL38 55
Bisson Rd. E15 CF37 57
Bisterne Av. E17 CF31 48
Bitchet Rd. Sev. CX67 117
Bitho Rd. West. CK61 106
Bittacy Clo. NW7 BQ29 37
Bittacy Hl. NW7 BQ29 37
Bittacy Pk. Av. NW7 BQ29 37
Bittacy Ri. NW7 BQ29 37
Bittacy Rd. NW7 BQ29 37
Bittam, S La. Cher. AU56 91
Bittern St. SE1 BZ41 67
Bittoms, The, Kings-on-t. BK52 84
Bixley Clo. Sthl. BE41 64
Blackacre Rd. Epp. CN22 31
Blackall St. EC2 CA38 57
Blackberry Clo. Shep. BB52 83
Cherry Way
Blackberry Farm Clo. Houns. BE43 64
Blackbird Hill. NW9 BN34 46
Blackbirds La. Wat. BG20 18
Blackbirds La. Wat. BG21 27
Blackborne Rd. Dag. CR36 59
Blackborough Clo. Reig. BT70 121
Blackborough Rd. Reig. BT71 121
Black Boy La. N15 BZ32 48
Black Boy Wood, St. Alb. BF18 18
Blackbridge Rd. Wok. AR63 100
Blackbrook La. Brom. CK53 88
Blackbrook Rd. Dor. BK73 119
Blackburn Rd. NW6 BS36 56
Blackburn's Ms. W1 BV40 56
Blackburn, The, Lthd. BE65 102
Lit. Bookham St.
Blackbush Av. Rom. CP32 50
Black Bush Clo. Sutt. BS57 95
Vale Copse Hl.
Black Bush Spring, Harl. CO10 6
Black Cut, St. Alb. BH14 9
Black Ditch Rd. Wal. Abb. CF21 30
Blackdon Clo. Wok. AU61 100
Blackdown Av. Wok. AV61 100
Blackdown Terr. SE18 CK43 68
Blackett St. SW15 BQ45 65
Blacketts Wood Dri. Rick. AT24 25
Blackfan Cotts. Hert. BX13 11
Black Fan Rd. Welw. G. C. BS7 5
Blackfen Rd. Sid. CN46 78
Blackfield Path. SW15 BP47 75
Roehampton High St.
Blackford Rd. Wat. BD28 36
Blackfords Path, SW15 BP47 75
Roehampton High St.
Blackfriars Br. EC4 BY40 56
Blackfriars Br. SE1 BY40 56
Blackfriars La. EC4 BY40 56
Blackfriars Rd. SE1 BY41 66
Blackhall La. Sev. CW65 108
Blackheath Av. SE10 CG43 68
Blackheath Gro. SE3 CG44 68
Blackheath Hl. SE10 CE44 67
Blackheath Pk. SE3 CG45 68
Blackheath Rise, SE13 CF44 67
Blackheath Rd. SE10 CE44 67
Blackheath Val. SE3 CG44 68
Blackheath Village, SE3 CG44 68
Black Hill Rd. Esher BE58 93
Black Horse Ave. Chesh. AO20 16
Black Horse Clo. Amer. AP22 25
Black Horse Clo. Wind. AL44 61
Black Horse Cr. Amer. AP22 25
Blackhorse La. E17 CC31 48
Blackhorse La. Croy. CB54 87
Black Horse La. Epp. CS16 23
Blackhorse La. Pot. B. BO18 19
Blackhorse La. Reig. BS68 113
Blackhorse Rd. SE8 CD43 67
Blackhorse Rd. Sid. CO49 79
Blackhorse Rd. Wok. AO63 100
Black Horse Yd. E1 CA39 57
Middlesex St.
Black Jacks La. Uxb. AW30 35
Blacklands Dr. Hayes BA38 53
Blacklands Mead, Red. BX70 121
Blacklands Rd. SE6 CF49 77
Blacklands Ter. SW3 BU42 66
Black La. Bish. CR6 6
Black Lane. Ong. CW12 15
Blackley Clo. Wat. BB22 26
Blackley Way. Guil. AP69 118
Black Lion Hill, Rad. BL19 19
Black Lion La. W6 BP42 65
Black Lion Yd. E1 CB39 57
Old Montague St.
Blackmans Clo. Dart. CV47 80
Blackman's La. War. CG60 97
Blackmore Av. Sthl. BG40 54
Blackmore Cres. Wok. AU60 91
Blackmore Cres. Wok. AU61 100
Blackmore Mead Ing. DC19 24
Blackmore Rd. Brwd. CZ22 33
Blackmore Rd. Brwd. DA21 33
Blackmore Rd. Buck. H. CK26 40
Blackmore Rd. Ing. DB18 24
Blackmore's Gro. Tedd. BJ50 74
Blacknell Clo. Har. BG29 36
Blackness La. Kes. CJ57 97
Blackness La. Wok. AS63 100
Blacknest Rd. Ascot. AO52 82
Black Pk. Rd. Slou. AS37 52
Black Path. E10 CC33 48
Blackpool Gdns. Hayes BB38 53
Blackpool Rd. SE15 CD44 67
Black Prince Clo. Wey. AY60 92
Black Prince Rd. SE1 BX42 66
Black Prince Rd. SE11 BX42 66
Black Raven Alley EC4 BZ40 57
Swan Wf.
Blackshaw Pl. N1 CD36 57
Hertford Rd.
Blackshaw Rd. SW17 BT49 76
Blackshots La. Grays. DE40 71
Blacksmith La. Guil. AU73 118
Blacksmith La. Stai. AX52 83
Blacksmith Row. Slou. AT42 62
Blacksmiths Hill Epp. CQ20 23
Blacksmith's Hill Sth. Croy. CB60 96
Blacksmiths La. Cher. AW54 83
Blacksmiths La. Orp. CP53 89
Blacksmith's La. Rain. CT37 59
Blacksmiths La. St. Alb. BF13 9
Blacksmith's La. Uxb. AU34 43
Blacks Rd. W6 BQ42 65
Blackstock Rd. N4 BY34 47
Blackstock Rd. N5 BY34 47
Blackstone Clo. Red. BU70 121
Blackstone Hill, Red. BU70 121
Blackstone Rd. NW2 BQ35 46
Blackthorn Ave. West Dr. AZ42 63
Blackthorn Clo. Reig. BT71 121
Blackthorn Clo. St. Alb. BK11 9
Blackthorn Clo. Wat. BC19 17
Blackthorn Ct. Houns. BE43 64
Blackthorne Av. Croy. CC54 87
Blackthorne Dr. E4 CF28 39
Blackthorne Gro. Bexh. CQ45 69
Blackthorne Rd. Lthd. BG66 111
Blackthorne Rd. Slou. AV45 62
Blackthorn Rd. E3 CE38 57
Blackthorn Rd. Grays. DD40 71
Blackthorn Rd. Reig. BT71 121
Blackthorn Rd. Welw. G. C. BS8 5
Blackwall La. SE10 CG41 68
Blackwall Tunnel App. E14 CF39 57
Blackwall Tunnel App. SE10 CG41 68
Blackwall Way, E14 CF40 57
Blackwater La. Hem. H. BB15 8
Blackwater St. SE22 CA46 77
Blackwell Av. Guil. AO70 118
Blackwell Dr. Wat. BD25 27
Blackwell Gdns. Edg. BM27 37
Blackwell Hall La. Chesh. AQ21 25
Blackwell Rd. Kings L. AZ18 17
Blackwell St. SW9 BY43 66
Brixton Rd.
Blackwood Av. Wey. AX59 92
Blackwood Clo. Wey. AX59 92
Blackwood St. SE17 BZ42 67
Blacthorne Cl. Hat. BO14 10
Blades Clo. Lthd. BK63 102
Bladindon Dr. Bex. CP47 79
Bladon Clo. Guil. AT70 118
Blagden's Clo. N14 BW27 38
Blagden's La. N14 BW27 38
Blagdon Rd. SE13 CE46 77
Blagdon Rd. N. Mal. BO52 85
Blagdon Wk. Tedd. BK50 74
Blagrove Rd. W10 BR39 55
Blair Av. NW9 BO33 46
Blair Av. Esher BG55 84
Blair Clo. Sid. CN46 78
Boundary Rd.
Blairderry Rd. SW2 BX48 76
Blair Dr. Sev. CU65 107
Blairhead Dr. Wat. BC27 35
Blair St. E14 CF39 57
Blake Av. Bark. CO37 59
Blake Clo. Rain. CT37 59
Blake Clo. St. Alb. BJ15 9
Blake Clo. Well. CN44 68
Blake Gdns. SW6 BS44 66
Blake Gdns. Dart. CW45 70
Blake Hall Cres. E11 CH33 49
Blake Hall Rd. E11 CH33 49
Blakehall Rd. Cars. BU57 95
Blake Hall Rd. Ong. CU17 23
Blakeley Bldgs. SE10 CG41 68
Blakeley Cotts. SE10 CG41 68
Blakemere. Welw. G. C. BQ7 5
Blakemore Rd. SW16 BX48 76
Blakemore Rd. Th. Hth. BX53 86
Blakendon Dr. Esher BH57 93
Blakeney Av. Beck. CD51 87
Blakeney Clo. N20 BT26 38
Blakeney Clo. Epsom BN59 94
Blakeney Rd. Beck. CD50 77
Blakenham Rd. SW17 BU49 76
Blaker Ct. SE7 CJ43 68
Fairlawn
Blake Rd. E16 CG38 58
Blake Rd. N11 BW29 38
Blake Rd. Croy. CA55 87
Blake Rd. Mitch. BU52 86
Blake Rd. Til. DF44 71
Blakes Av. N. Mal. BO53 85
Blakes Grn. W. Wick. CF54 87
Blakes Lane. Guil. AY69 110
Blakes La. N. Mal. BO53 85
Blakesley Av. W5 BK39 54
Blake's Rd. SE15 CA43 67
Blakes Ter. N. Mal. BP53 85
Blakesware Gdns. N9 BZ26 39
Blake Wk. Til. DH44 71
Coleridge Rd.
Blakewood Clo. Felt. BD49 74
Blanchard Pl. E8 CB36 57
Blanchard Rd.
Blanchards Hill. Guil. AS67 109
Blanchard St. E8 CB36 57
Blanchard Rd.
Blanchedowne, SE5 BZ45 67
Blanche La. Pot. B. BO20 19
Blanche St. E16 CG38 58
Blanchland Rd. Mord. BS53 86
Blanchmans Rd. Warl. CD63 105
Bland Av. SE15 CC43 67
King Arthur St.
Blandfield Rd. SW12 BV46 76
Blandford Av. Beck. CD51 87
Blandford Av. Twick. BF47 74
Blandford Clo. N2 BT32 47
Blandford Clo. Croy. BX55 86
Wandle Rd.
Blandford Clo. Wok. AT62 100
Blandford Cres. E4 CF26 39
Blandford Ms. W1 BV39 56
Blandford Rd. W4 BO41 65
Blandford Rd. W5 BK41 64
Blandford Rd. Beck. CC51 87
Blandford Rd. St. Alb. BJ13 9
Blandford Rd. Slou. AR41 62
Blandford Rd. Sthl. BF42 64
Blandford Rd. Tedd. BG49 74
Blandford Sq. NW1 BU38 56
Blandford St. W1 BV39 56
Blandford Waye Hayes. BD39 54
Bland St. SE9 CJ45 68
Blaney Cres. E6 CL38 58
Blanford Rd. Reig. BT71 121
Blanmerle Rd. SE9 CL47 78
Blann Cl. SE9 CJ46 78
Middle Pk. Av.
Blantyre St. SW10 BT43 66
Cheyne Wk.
Blashford St. SE13 CF47 77
Blawith Rd. Har. BH31 45
Blaydon Clo. N17 CB29 39
Blaydon Clo. Ruis. BB33 44
Blay's La. Egh. AQ50 72
Blean Gro. SE20 CC50 77
Bleasdale Av. Grnf. BH37 54
Blechynden St. W10 BQ40 55
Bramley Rd.
Bleddyn Clo. Sid. CP46 79
Bledlow Rise Grnf. BG37 54
Blegborough Rd. SW16 BW49 76
Blendon Dr. Bex. CP46 79
Blendon Path. Brom. CG50 78
Hope Park
Blendon Rd. Bex. CP46 79
Blendon Ter. SE18 CM42 68
Blendworth Way, SE15 CA43 67
Hordle Prom. N.
Blenheim Av. Ilf. CL32 49
Blenheim Clo. N21 BZ26 39
Blenheim Clo. SW20 BQ52 85
Blenheim Clo. Dart. CV46 80
Blenheim Clo. Grnf. BG37 54
Blenheim Clo. Rom. CS31 50
Blenheim Clo. Upmin. CZ33 51
Blenheim Clo. Wall. BW57 95
Blenheim Ct. Sid. CM48 78
Blenheim Cres. W11 BR40 55
Blenheim Cres. Ruis. BA34 44
Blenheim Cres. Sth. Croy. BZ57 96
Blenheim Dr. Well. CN44 68
Blenheim Gdns. NW2 BQ35 46
Blenheim Gdns. SW2 BX46 76
Blenheim Gdns. S. Ock. CX40 60
Blenheim Gdns. Sth. Croy. CB59 96
Blenheim Gdns. Wall. BW57 95
Blenheim Gdns. Wem. BL34 46
Blenheim Gdns. Kings On T. BM50 75
Blenheim Gro. SE15 CA44 67
Blenheim Pk. Rd. Sth. Croy. BZ58 96
Blenheim Pass. NW8 BT37 56
Blenheim Rd. E6 CJ38 58
Blenheim Rd. E15 CG35 49
Blenheim Rd. N22 BY30 38
Blenheim Rd. NW8 BT37 56
Blenheim Rd. SE20 CC50 77
Blenheim Rd. SW20 BQ52 85
Blenheim Rd. W4 BO41 65
Blenheim Rd. Barn. BQ24 28
Blenheim Rd. Brom. CK52 88
Blenheim Rd. Brwd. DA25 33
Blenheim Rd. Dart. CV46 80
Blenheim Rd. Epsom BN59 94
Blenheim Rd. Har. BF32 45
Blenheim Rd. Orp. CP55 89
Blenheim Rd. St. Alb. BH13 9
Blenheim Rd. Sid. CP47 79
Blenheim Rd. Slou. AR42 62
Blenheim Rd. Sutt. BS55 86
Blenheim St. W1 BV39 56
Blenheim Ter. NW8 BT37 56
Blenkarne Rd. SW11 BU46 76
Blenkin Clo. St. Alb. BG11 9
Bleriot Rd. Houns. BD43 64
Blessbury Rd. Edg. BM30 37
Blessington Clo. SE13 CF45 67
Blessington Rd. SE13 CF45 67
Bletchingley Clo. Red. BW68 113
Bletchingley Rd. Gdse. CB69 114
Bletchingley Rd. Red. BW68 113
Bletchingley Rd. Red. BY70 121
Bletchley Ct. N1 BZ37 57
Bletchley St. N1 BZ37 57
Blewett St. SE17 BZ42 67
Sandford Row
Bligh Rd. Grav. DG46 81
Blighs Rd. Sev. CU66 116
London Rd.
Blincoe Cl. SW19 BR48 75
Queensmere Rd.
Blind La. Bans. BU61 104
Blind La. Bet. BN72 120
Blind La. Loug. CG23 31
Blind La. Maid. AG42 61
Blind La. St. Alb. BL17 19
Blind La. Wal. Abb. CJ20 22
Blindmans La. Wal. Cr. CC18 21
Bliss Cres. SE13 CE44 67
Blissett St. SE10 CF44 67
Blithbury Rd. Dag. CO36 59
Blithdale Rd. SE2 CO42 69
Blockhouse Rd. Grays. DE43 71
Blockhouse St. SE15 CC43 67
Blockley Rd. Wem. BJ34 45
Bloemfontein Av. W12 BP40 55
Bloemfontein Rd. W12 BP40 55
Blomfield Rd. W9 BS39 56
Blomfield St. EC2 BZ39 57
Blomfield Vill. W2 BS39 56
Blomville Rd. Dag. CQ34 50
Blondel St. SW11 BV44 66
Blondin Av. W5 BK42 64
Blondin St. E3 CE37 57
Bloomburg St. SW1 BW42 66
Vincent Sq.
Bloomfield Cres. Ilf. CL32 49
Bloomfield Rise, Wat. BA19 17
Bloomfield Rd. N6 BV32 47
Bloomfield Rd. SE18 CL43 68
Bloomfield Rd. Kings-on-t. BL52 85
Bloomfield Ter. SW1 BV42 66
Bloom Gro. SE27 BY48 76
Bloomhall Rd. SE19 BZ49 77
Bloom Pk. Rd. SW6 BR43 65
Bloomsbury Clo. W5 BL40 55
Bloomsbury Clo. Epsom BN58 94
Bloomsbury Ct. Pnr. BE31 45
Bloomsbury Pl. WC1 BX39 56
Southampton Row
Bloomsbury Sq. WC1 BX39 56
Bloomsbury St. WC1 BW39 56
Bloomsbury Way, WC1 BX39 56
Blossom La. Enf. BZ23 30
Blossom St. E1 CA38 57
Blossom Way, Uxb. AY36 53
Blossom Way. West Dr. AZ42 63
Blossom Waye Houns. BE43 64
Blount St. E14 CD39 57
Bloxam Gdns. SE9 CK46 78
Bloxhall Rd. E10 CD33 48
Bloxham Cres. Hamptn. BE50 74
Blucher Rd. SE5 BZ43 67
Blue Anchor All. Rich. BL45 65
Kew Rd.
Blue Anchor La. SE16 CB42 67
Blue Anchor La. Til. DH42 71
Blue Anchor Yd. E1 CA40 57
Derby St.
Blue Ball La. Egh. AS49 72
Blue Barn La. Wey. AZ59 92
Bluebell Clo. SE26 CA49 77
Bluebell Clo. Orp. CL55 88
Blueberry Gdns. Couls. BX57 95
Blueberry Gdns. Couls. BX61 104
Blueberry La. Sev. CP61 107
Bluebridge Av. Hat. BR17 19
Bluebridge Rd. Hat. BR17 19
Bluefield Clo. Hamptn. BF49 74
Bluehouse Hill, St. Alb. BF14 9
Bluehouse La. Oxt. CG67 115
Bluehouse La. Oxt. CH67 115
Bluehouse Rd. E4 CG27 40
Bluemans. Epp. CS15 14
Bluemans End. Epp. CS15 14
Bluett Rd. St. Alb. BK17 18
Blundel La. Cob. BE61 102
Blundell Clo. St. Alb. BG11 9
Blundell Rd. Edg. BN30 37
Blundell St. N7 BX36 56
Blunesfield, Pot. B. BT19 20
Blunt Rd. Sth. Croy. BZ56 96
Blunt's Ave. West Dr. AZ44 63
Blunts La. St. Alb. BD17 18
Blunts Rd. SE9 CL46 78
Blurton Rd. E5 CC35 48
Blythe Clo. SE6 CD47 77
Blythe Hl. SE6 CD47 77
Blythe Hl. Orp. CN51 88
Blythe Hl. La. SE6 CD47 77
Blythe Mt. Welw. G. C. BQ8 5
Blythe Rd. W14 BQ41 65
Blythe Rd. Brom. CG51 88
Blythe St. E2 CB38 57
Blythe Val. SE6 CD47 77
Blyth Rd. E15 CF36 57
Blyth Rd. E17 CD33 48
Blyth Rd. W14 BQ42 65
Blyth Rd. Hayes. BB41 63
Blythswood Rd. Ilf. CO33 50
Blyth Walk, Upmin. CZ32 51
Blythway. Welw. G. C. BR6 5
Blythwood Rd. N4 BX33 47
Blythwood Rd. Pnr. BD30 36
Boadicea St. N1 BX37 56
Boar Clo. Chig. CO28 41
Hart Cres.
Boardman Av. E4 CE25 30
Board School Rd. Wok. AS61 100
Boars Rd. Harl. CR11 14
Boat House Wk. SE15 CA43 67
Bobs La. Rom. CT30 41
Bocketts La. Lthd. BH65 102
Bockhampton Rd. Kings. On T. BL50 75
Bocking St. E8 CB37 57
Boddicott Cl. SW19 BR48 75
Queensmere Rd.
Boddy's Bridge, SE1 BY40 56
Bodell Clo. Grays. DD41 71
Bodiam Clo. Enf. BZ23 30
Bodiam Rd. SW16 BW50 76
Bodicea St. N1 BX37 56
Bodle Av. Swans. DC47 81
Bodley Clo. N. Mal. BO53 85
Bodley Rd. N. Mal. BN53 85
Bodley St. SE17 BZ42 67
Wansey St.
Bodmin Rd. Mord. BS53 86
Bodmin St. SW18 BS47 76
Bodnant Gdns. SW20 BP52 85
Bodney Rd. E8 CB35 48
Bodwell Cl. Hem. H. AW13 8
Boeing Way Sthl. BC41 63
Bogey La. Orp. CK57 97
Bognor Gdns. Wat. BD28 36
Bognor Rd. Well. CP44 69
Bognor St. SW8 BW44 66
Bohun Gro. Barn. BU25 29
Boileau Rd. SW13 BP43 65
Boileau Rd. W5 BL39 55
Bois Hall Rd. Wey. AX56 92
Bois Hill. Chesh. AP20 16
Bois Moor Rd. Chesh. AO20 16
Bolden St. SE8 CE44 67
Bolderwood Way W. Wick. CE55 87
Boldmere Rd. Pnr. BD33 45
Boleyn Av. Enf. CB23 30
Boleyn Av. Epsom BP58 94
Boleyn Clo. Hem. H. BA11 8
Boleyn Dr. E. Mol. BE52 84
Boleyn Dr. Ruis. BD34 45
Boleyn Dr. St. Alb. BG14 9
Boleyn Dr. Sev. CW62 108
Boleyn Gdns. Brwd. DD27 122
Boleyn Gdns. Dag. CS36 59
Boleyn Gdns. W. Wick. CE55 87
Boleyn Gro. W. Wick. CE55 87
Boleyn Rd. E6 CJ37 58
Boleyn Rd. E7 CH36 58
Boleyn Rd. N16 CA35 48
Boleyn Way, Ilf. CM29 40
Bolina Rd. SE16 CC42 67
Bolinbroke Way, Hayes BA40 53
Bolingbroke Gro. SW11 BU46 76
Bolingbroke Rd. W14 BQ41 65
Bolingbroke Wk. SW11 BU44 66
Westbridge Rd.
Bollo Bridge Rd. W3 BM41 65
Bollo La. W3 BM41 65
Bollo La. W4 BM41 65
Bolmer Wk. Rain. CV37 60
Bolney St. SW8 BX43 66
Bolsover Gro. Red. BX68 113
Bolsover St. W1 BV38 56
Bolstead La. Mitch. BV51 86
Bolstead Pl. Mitch. BV51 86
Bolster Gro. N22 BW29 38
Bolt Cellar La. Epp. CN18 22
Bolt Ct. EC4 BY39 56
Gough Sq.
Bolter's La. Bans. BR60 94
Boltimore Clo. NW4 BQ31 46
Bolton Ave. Wind. AO45 61
Bolton Clo. Chess. BL57 94
Bolton Cres. SE5 BY43 66
Bolton Cres. Wind. AO45 61
Bolton Gdns. NW10 BQ37 55
Bolton Gdns. SW5 BS42 66
Bolton Gdns. Tedd. BJ50 74
Bolton Gdns. Ms. SW10 BT42 66
Bolton Rd. E15 CG36 58
Bolton Rd. N18 CA28 39
Bolton Rd. NW8 BS37 56
Bolton Rd. NW10 BO37 55
Bolton Rd. W4 BN43 65
Bolton Rd. Chess. BK57 93
Bolton Rd. Har. BG31 45
Bolton Rd. Wind. AO45 61
Bolton's Clo. Wok. AW61 101
Bolton's La. Hayes. AZ44 63
Bolton's La. Wok. AW61 101
Boltons, The, Sw10 BT42 66
Boltons, The, Wem. BH35 45
Bolton St. W1 BV40 56
Bolton Wk. N7 BX34 47
Andover Est.
Bolwell St. SE11 BX42 66
Boman Clo. Felt. BD46 74
Bombay St. SE16 CB42 67
Bombers La. West. CM63 106
Bomer Clo. West Dr. AZ43 63
Bomore Rd. W11 BQ40 55
Bomore St. W11 BQ40 55
Bonar Pl. Chis. CK50 78

Bonar Rd. SE15 CB43 67
Bonavere Ct. Grav. DJ49 81
Bonchester Clo. Chis. CL51 88
Bonchurch Clo. Sutt. BS57 95
Ventnor Rd.
Bonchurch Rd. W10 BR39 55
Bonchurch Rd. W13 BJ40 54
Bond Clo. Sev. CP61 107
Bond Ct. EC3 BZ39 57
Wallbrook
Bondfield Wk. Dart. CW45 70
Bond Gdns. Wall. BW56 95
Bond Rd. Mitch. BU51 86
Bond Rd. Surb. BL55 85
Bond St. E15 CG35 49
Bond St. W4 BO42 65
Chiswick Common Rd.
Bond St. W5 BK40 54
Bond St. Egh. AQ50 72
Bond St. Grays. DE43 71
Bondway, SW8 BX43 66
Bonehurst Rd. Red. BV74 121
Bonfield Av. Hayes BC38 53
Bonfield Rd. SE13 CF45 67
Bonham Gdns. Dag. CP34 50
Bonham Rd. SW2 BX46 76
Bonham Rd. Dag. CP34 50
Bonheur Rd. W4 BN41 65
Bonhill St. EC2 BZ38 57
Boniface Gdns. Har. BF29 36
Boniface Rd. Uxb. AZ34 44
Boniface Wk. Har. BF29 36
Bonks Hill, Saw. CP6 6
Bonmarche Ter. Ms. SE19 CA49 77
Gipsy Rd.
Bonner Hill Rd. Kings-on-t. BL51 85
Bonner Rd. E2 CC37 57
Bonners Clo. Wok. AR65 100
Bonnersfield Clo. Har. BH32 45
Bonnersfield La. Har. BH32 45
Bonnersfield La. Har. BJ32 45
Bonner St. E2 CC37 57
Bonneville Gdns. SW4 BW46 76
Bonney Gro. Wal. Cr. CB18 21
Bonney Way Swan. CT51 89
Bonnington Rd. Horn. CV35 51
Bonnington Sq. SW8 BX43 66
Bonnys Rd. Reig. BQ71 120
Bonny St. NW1 BW36 56
Bonser Rd. Twick. BH48 74
Bonsey Clo. Wok. AS64 100
Bonsey La. Wok. AS64 100
Bonseys La. Wok. AS58 91
Bonsor Dr. Tad. BR64 103
Bonsor St. SE5 CA43 67
Bonville Rd. Brom. CG49 78
Bookham Rd. Cob. BD63 102
Boones Rd. SE13 CG45 68
Boone St. SE13 CG45 68
Boord St. SE10 CG41 68
Boothby Rd. N19 BW34 47
Booth Dr. Stai. AX50 73
Booth Rd. NW9 BN30 37
Booth Rd. Croy. BY55 86
Booth St.
Booths Pl. W1 BW39 56
Wells St.
Boot St. N1 CA38 57
Borchester Rd. Slou. AS41 62
Bordars Rd. W7 BH39 54
Bordars Wk. W7 BH39 54
Borden Av. Enf. BZ25 30
Border Cres. SE26 CB49 77
Border Gdns. Croy. CE56 96
Bordergate, Mitch. BU51 86
Bordergate Est. Mitch. BU51 86
Border Rd. SE26 CB49 77
Borderside, Slou. AQ39 52
Border's La. Loug. CL24 31
Bordesley Rd. Mord. BS53 86
Bordon Wk. SW15 BP47 75
Boreas Walk N1 BY37 56
Nelson Pl.
Boreham Av. E16 CH39 58
Boreham Clo. E11 CF33 48
Hainault Rd.
Boreham Holt. Borwd. BL24 28
Boreham Rd. N22 BZ30 39
Boreham St. E2 CA31 48
Roda St.
Borer's Pass. EC2 CA39 57
Borgard Rd. SE18 CK42 68
Borkwood Pk. Orp. CN56 97
Borkwood Way Orp. CM56 97
Borland Rd. SE15 CC46 77
Borland Rd. Tedd. BJ50 74
Borneo St. SW15 BQ45 65
Boro, The, Ong. CW18 24
Borough Green Rd. Sev. DB64 108
Borough High St. SE1 BZ41 67
Borough Hill Croy. BY55 86
Borough Rd. SE1 BY41 66
Borough Rd. Islw. BH44 64
Borough Rd. Kings. On T. BM51 85
Borough Rd. Mitch. BU51 86
Borough Rd. West. CJ64 106
Borough, The Bet. BM71 120
Borough Way. Pot. B. BR19 19
Borrett Rd. SE17 BZ42 67
Borrodaile Rd. SW18 BS46 76
Borrowdale Hem. H. AY12 8
Lonsdale
Borrowdale Av. Har. BJ30 36
Borrowdale Clo. Ilf. CK31 49
Borrowdale Clo. Sth. Croy. CA60 96
Borrowdale Dri. Sth. Croy. CA59 96
Borthwick Rd. E15 CG35 49
Borthwick Rd. NW9 BO32 46
Broadway, The.
Borthwick St. SE8 CE42 67
Borwick Av. E17 CD31 48
Bosanquet Clo. Uxb. AX38 53
Bosbury Rd. SE6 CF48 77
Boscastle Rd. NW5 BV34 47
Boscobel Pl. SW1 BV42 66
Boscobel St. NW8 BT38 56
Boscombe Ave. Grays. DE42 71
Boscombe Av. E10 CF33 48
Boscombe Av. Horn. CV33 51
Boscombe Rd. SW17 BV50 76
Boscombe Rd. SW19 BS51 86
Boscombe Rd. W12 BP40 55
Boscombe Rd. Wor. Pk. BQ54 85
Bosenquet Rd. Hodd. CF11 12
Bosgrove E4 CF26 39
Boss Rd. E3 CE36 57
Rothbury Rd.
Boss St. SE1 CA41 67
Bostall Hill, SE2 CO42 69
Bostall Hill Rd. SE2 CP42 69
Bostall La. SE2 CO42 69
Bostall Manor Way, SE2 CO42 69
Bostall Pk. Av. Bexh. CQ43 69
Bostal Rd. Orp. CO50 79
Bostal Row, Bexh. CQ45 69
Boston Gdns. Brent. BJ42 64
Boston Gro. Ruis. BA32 44
Boston Manor Rd. Brent. BJ42 64
Boston Pk. Rd. Brent. BK43 64
Boston Pl. NW1 BU38 56
Boston Rd. E6 CK38 58
Boston Rd. E17 CE32 48
Boston Rd. W7 BH40 54
Boston Rd. Croy. BX53 86
Boston Rd. Edg. BN29 37
Boston St. E2 CB37 57
Bostonthorpe Rd. W7 BH41 64
Boston Vale W7 BJ42 64
Bosville Dr. Sev. CU65 107
Bosville Rd. Sev. CU65 107
Boswell Clo. Wal. Cr. CD18 21
Boswell Ct. WC1 BX39 56
Boswell Pth. Hayes. BB42 63
Boswell Rd. Th. Hth. BZ52 87
Boswell St. WC1 BX39 56
Boswick La. Berk. AO11 7
Bosworth Clo. E17 CD30 39
Bosworth Rd. N11 BW29 38
Bosworth Rd. W10 BR38 55
Bosworth Rd. Barn. BS24 29
Bosworth Rd. Dag. CR34 50
Botany Bay La. Chis. CM51 88
Boteley Clo. E4 CF27 39
Weale Rd.
Boterys Cross, Red. BY70 121
Botha Rd. E13 CH39 58
Bothwell Clo. E16 CH39 58
Bothwell Rd. Croy. CF58 96
Bothwell St. W6 BQ43 65
Delorme St.
Botley Rd. Chesh. AQ18 16
Botley Rd. Hem. H. AZ11 8
Botolph La. EC3 BZ40 57
Botolph Pass E3 CE38 57
Botolph Rd.
Botolph Rd E3 CE38 57
Botsford Rd. SW20 BR51 85
Botsom La. Sev. CY57 99
Bottom House Farm La. Ch. St. G. AO27 34
Bottom House Farm La. Ch. St. G. AQ25 25
Bottom La. Chesh. AP19 16
Bottom La. Rick. AW21 26
Bottrells La. Ch. St. G. AO27 34
Bott Rd. Dart. CW49 80
Botts End, Hem. H. AW12 8
Botts Ms. W2 BS39 56
Chepstow Rd.
Botwell Comm. Rd. Hayes BA40 53
Botwell Cres. Hayes BB39 53
Botwell La. Hayes BB40 53
Boucher Clo. Tedd. BH49 74
Boucher Dr. Grav. DF48 81
Bouchier Wk. Rain. CU36 59
Boughton Av. Brom. CG54 88
Boughton Rd. SE18 CN41 68
Boughton Rd. SE28 CN41 68
Boulcott St. E1 CC39 57
Boulevard, The, Pnr. BE31 45
Boulmer Rd. Uxb. AX38 53
Boulogne Rd. Croy. BZ53 87
Boulter Gdns. Horn. CU36 59
Boulthurst Way. Oxt. CH69 115
Boulton Rd. Dag. CQ34 50
Bounce Hill Rom. CU23 32
Bounces La. N9 CB27 39
Bounces Rd. N9 CB26 39
Boundaries Rd. SW12 BU48 76
Boundaries Rd. Felt. BD47 74
Boundary Clo. CM35 49
Loxford La.
Boundary Clo. Ilf. CN35 49
Loxford La.
Boundary Clo. Kings-on-t. BM52 85
Boundary Clo. Sthl. BF42 64
Boundary La. E13 CJ38 58
Boundary La. SE17 BZ43 67
Boundary La. Welw. G. C. BR9 5
Boundary Rd. E13 CJ37 58
Boundary Rd. E17 CD33 48
Boundary Rd. N9 CC25 30
Boundary Rd. N22 BY31 47
Boundary Rd. NW8 BS37 56
Boundary Rd. SW19 BT50 76
Boundary Rd. Bark. CM37 58
Boundary Rd. Ger. Cr. AR29 34
Boundary Rd. Pnr. BD33 45
Boundary Rd. Rom. CU32 50
Boundary Rd. St. Alb. BH12 9
Boundary Rd. Sid. CN46 78
Boundary Rd. Upmin. CX34 51
Boundary Rd. Wall. BV57 95
Boundary Rd. Wok. AT61 100
Boundary Rd. S. Wall. BV58 95
Boundary Row, SE1 BY41 66
Boundary St. E2 CA38 57
Boundary St. Erith CT43 69
Boundary Way Croy. CE56 96
Boundfield Rd. SE6 CG48 78
Boundry Dr. Brwd. DF26 122
Bounds Green Ind. Est. N11 BW29 38
Bounds Grn La. N11 BW29 38
Bounds Grn La. N22 BW29 38
Bourchier St. W1 BW40 56
Wardour St.
Bourdon Pl. W1 BV40 56
Bourdon St.
Bourdon Rd. SE20 CC51 87
Bourdon St. W1 BV40 56
Bourke Clo. SW2 BX47 76
Bourke Hill Couls. BU62 104
Bourke Rd. NW10 BO36 55
Bourlet Clo. W1 BW39 56
Wells St.
Bourn Av. N15 BZ31 48
Bourn Av. Barn. BT25 29
Bournbrook Rd. SE3 CJ45 68
Bourne Ave. Hayes. BA41 63
Bourne Ave. Wind. AO45 61
Bourne Av. N14 BX27 38
Bourne Av. Ruis. BD35 45
Bourne Av. Uxb. AZ38 53
Bournebridge Gdns. Ilf. CO29 41
Bournebridge La. Rom. CQ26 41
Bourne Clo. SW2 BX46 76
Bourne Clo. Brox. CD13 12
Bourne Clo. Brwd. DF26 122
Bourne Ct. Ruis. BC35 44
Bourne Cres. Wey. AW60 92
Bourne End, Horn. CX33 51
Bourne End Lane, Berk. AT15 7
Bourne End Rd. Nthwd. BB28 35
Bourne Est. EC1 BY39 56
Bournefield Rd. Whyt. CA62 105
Bourne Gdns. E4 CE28 39
Bournehall Av. Bush. BF25 27
Bournehall La. Bush. BF25 27
Bournehall Rd. Bush. BF25 27
Bourne Hill N13 BX27 38
Bourne La. Cat. BZ64 105
Bourne La. Sev. DC66 117
Bourne Mead Bex. CS46 79
Bournemead Av. Nthlt. BC37 53
Bournemead Way Nthlt. BC37 53
Bournemouth Rd. SE15 CB44 67
Bournemouth Rd. SW19 BS51 86
Bourne Pk. Gdns. Ken. CA57 96
Bourne Pk. Gdns. Ken. CA61 105
Bourne Pl. W4 BN42 65
Dukes Av.
Bourne Rd. E7 CG34 49
Bourne Rd. N8 BX32 47
Bourne Rd. Berk. AP12 7
Bourne Rd. Bex. CR47 79
Bourne Rd. Brom. CJ52 88
Bourne Rd. Bush. BF25 27
Bourne Rd. Grav. DJ48 81
Bourne Rd. Red. BW68 113
Bourne Rd. Slou. AO41 61
Bourne Rd. Vir. W. AR53 82
Bourneside, Vir. W. AQ54 82
Bourne St. SW1 BV42 66
Bourne St. Croy. BY55 86
Bourne Ter. W2 BS39 56
Bourne, The, N14 BW26 38
Bourne, The Hem. H. AT17 16
Bourne Vale Brom. CG54 88
Bournevale Rd. SW16 BX49 76
Bourne Vw. Grnf. BH36 54
Bourne Vw. Ken. BZ61 105
Bourne Way Brom. CG55 88
Bourne Way Epsom BN56 94
Bourne Way Sutt. BR56 94
Bourne Way Swan. CS52 89
Bourne Way, Wey. AX56 92
Bourne Way, Wok. AR64 100
Bournewood Rd. SE18 CO43 69
Bournewood Rd. Orp. CO54 89
Bournside Rd. Wey. AX56 92
Bournville Rd. SE6 CE47 77
Bournwell Clo. Barn. BU23 29
Bousfield Rd. SE14 CC44 67
Bousley Rise. Cher. AU57 91
Boutflower Rd. SW11 BU45 66
Bouverie Gdns. Har. BK33 45
Bouverie Pl. W2 BT39 56
Bouverie Rd. N16 CA33 48
Bouverie Rd. Couls. BV62 104
Bouverie Rd. Har. BG32 45
Bouverie St. EC4 BY39 56
Bouverie Way. Slou. AS42 62
Bouvier Rd. Enf. CC22 30
Bovay Pl. N7 BX35 47
Holloway Rd.
Bovay St. N7 BX35 47
Boveney New Rd. Wind. AM42 61
Boveney Rd. SE23 CC47 77
Boveney Rd. Wind. AL42 61
Bovey Way. S. Ock. DA39 60
Bovill Rd. SE23 CC47 77
Bovingdon Av. Wem. BM36 55
Bovingdon Cres. Wat. BD20 18
Bovingdon La. NW9 BO29 37
Bovingdon Rd. SW6 BS44 66
Bovingdon Sq. Mitch. BX52 86
Bovington Green. Hem. H. AS17 16
Bow Arrow La. Dart. CX46 80
Bowater Clo. NW9 BN32 46
Bowater Clo. NW9 BO32 46
Buck La.
Bowater Pl. SE3 CH43 68
Bowater Rd. SE18 CJ41 68
Bow Bridge Est. E3 CE38 57
Bow Common La. E3 CD38 57
Bowden Dr. Horn. CW33 51
Bowden Rd. E17 CE33 48
Bowden St. SE11 BY42 66
Bowditch, SE8 CD42 67
Bowdon Rd. E17 CE33 48
Bowen Dr. SE21 CA48 77
Bowen Rd. Har. BG33 45
Bowen St. E14 CE39 57
Bower Av. SE10 CG44 68
Bower Clo. Nthlt. BD37 54
Bower Clo. Rom. CS29 41
Bowerdeans St. SW6 BS44 66
Bowerdean St SW6 BS44 66
Bower Fm. Rd. Hav. CS27 41
Bower Hill Epp. CO19 23
Bower Hill Clo. Red. BX72 121
Bowerhill La. Red. BW71 121
Bower La. Eyns. CX57 99
Bowerman Av. SE14 CD43 67
Bowerman Rd. Grays. DG42 71
Bower Rd. Swan. CU50 79
Bowers Av. Grav. DF49 81
Mulberry Rd.
Bowers Rd. Sev. CR59 98
Bower St. E1 CC39 57
Bower Ter. Epp. CO19 23
Bower Vale Epp. CO19 23
Bowes Dr. Ong. CW17 24
Bowes-lyon Clo. Wind. AO44 61
Ward Royal
Bowes Rd. N11 BV28 38
Bowes Rd. N13 BV28 38
Bowes Rd. W3 BO40 55
Bowes Rd. Dag. CP35 50
Bowes Rd. Stai. AV50 72
Bowes Rd. Walt. BC55 83
Bowfell Rd. W6 BQ43 65
Bowford Av. Bexh. CQ44 69
Bowie Clo. SW4 BW47 76
Plummer Rd.
Bow La. EC4 BZ39 57
Bow La. N12 BT29 38
Bowlers Orchard. Ch. St. G. AQ27 34
Bowles Gro. Enf. CB21 30
Bowles Rd. SE1 CB43 67
Bowley Clo. SE19 CA49 77
Bowley St. E14 CD40 57
Bowling Green Clo. SW15 BP47 75
Bowling Green La. EC1 BY38 56
Bowling Green Rd. Wok. AP58 91
Bowling Green St. SE11 BY43 66
Bowling Green Wk. N1 CA38 57
Bowl La. St. Alb. BD11 9
Bowls Clo. Stan. BJ28 36
Bowls. The Chig. CN27 40
Bowman Av. E16 CG40 58
Bowmans Clo. Pot. B. BT19 20
Bowmans Grn. Wat. BE21 27
Bowmans Meadow Wall. BV55 86
Bowman's Pl. N7 BX34 47
Bowman's Rd. Dart. CT47 79
Bowmead, SE9 CK48 78
Bowness Cres. SW15 BO49 75
Bowness Dr. Houns. BE45 64
Bowness Rd. SE6 CE47 77
Bowness Rd. Bexh. CR44 69
Bowness Way. Horn. CU35 50
Bowood Rd. SW11 BV45 66
Bowood Rd. Enf. CC23 30
Bowring Grn. Wat. BD28 36
Bow Rd. E3 CD38 57
Bowrons Av. Wem. BK36 54
Bow St. E15 CG35 49
Bow St. WC2 BX39 56
Bowstridge La. Ch. St. G. AR27 34
Bowyer Cres. Uxb. AV32 43
Bowyers, Hem. H. AX12 8
Bowzell Rd. Sev. CT70 116
Boxall Rd. SE21 CA46 77
Boxall Rd. Dag. CQ35 50
Boxfield. Welw. G. C. BS9 5
Boxgrove Av. Guil. AT69 118
Boxgrove La. Guil. AT70 118
Boxgrove Rd. SE2 CO41 69
Boxgrove Rd. Guil. AT70 118
Boxhill Rd. Dor. BL70 120
Boxhill Rd. Tad. BL69 120
Boxhill Rd. Tad. BN68 112
Boxhill Way, Bet. BM72 120
Box La. Bark. CO37 59
Box La. Hem. H. AU16 16
Box La. Hodd. CD12 12
Boxley Rd. Mord. BT52 86
Boxley St. E16 CH40 58
Boxmoor Rd. Har. BJ31 45
Boxmoor Rd. Rom. CS28 41
Box Ridge Av. Pur. BX59 95
Box Rd. Guil. AQ67 109
Boxted Clo. Buck. H. CK26 40
Boxted Rd. Hem. H. AV12 7
Boxtree La. Har. BG30 36
Boxtree Rd. Har. BG29 36
Box Tree Wk. Orp. CP54 89
Boxwell Rd. Berk. AQ13 7
Boxwood Way, Warl. CC62 105
Boyard Rd. SE18 CL42 68
Boyce Way, E13 CH38 58
Boycroft Av. NW9 BN32 46
Boyd Av. Sthl. BE40 54
Boydell Ct. NW8 BT36 56
Boyd Rd. SW19 BT50 76
Boyd St. E1 CB39 57
Boyfield St. SE1 BY41 66
Boyland Rd. Brom. CG49 78
Boyle Av. NW4 BQ31 46
Boyle Av. Stan. BJ29 36
Boyle Fm. Rd. Surb. BJ53 84
Boyle St. W1 BW40 56
Savile Row
Boyne Rd. SE13 CF45 67
Boyne Rd. Dag. CR34 50
Boyne Ter. Ms. W11 BR40 55
Boyseland Ct. Edg. BN27 37
Boyson Rd. SE17 BZ43 67
Boythorn Way SE16 CB42 67
Bonamy Estate East The
Boyton Clo. N8 BX31 47
Boyton Rd. N8 BX31 47
Brabant Ct. EC3 BZ40 57
Philpot La.
Brabant Rd. N22 BX30 38
Brabazon Av. Wall. BX57 95
Brabazon Rd. Houns. BD43 64
Brabazon Rd. Nthlt. BF37 54
Brabazon St. E14 CE39 57
Brabourne Cres. Bexh. CQ43 69
Brabourne Rise Beck. CF53 87
Brabourn Rd. SE15 CC44 67
Bracewell Av. Grnf. BH35 45
Bracewell Rd. W10 BQ39 55
Bracewood Gdns. Croy. CA55 87
Bracey St. N4 BX33 47
Bracken Av. SW12 BV46 76
Bracken Av. Croy. CE55 87
Bracken Bri. Dr. Ruis. BD34 45
Brackenbury Gdns. W6 BP41 65
Brackenbury Rd. N3 BT31 47
Brackenbury Rd. W6 BP41 65
Bracken Clo. Slou. AO35 43
Bracken Clo. Wok. AS62 100
Brackendale N21 BX26 38
Brackendale, Pot. B. BR20 19
Brackendale, Pot. B. BS20 20
Brackendale Gdns. Upmin. CY35 51
Bracken Dene Dart. CT49 79
Brackendene, St. Alb. BE18 18
Brackendene Clo. Wok. AT61 100
Bracken Dr. Chig. CL29 40
Brackenford. Slou. AR41 62
Bracken Gdns. SW13 BP44 65
Bracken Hill Ruis. BE35 45
Bracken Hill Clo. Brom. CG51 88
Bracken Hill La. Brom. CG51 88
Bracken Path. Epsom BM60 94
Brackens, The. Enf. CA26 39
Brackens, The, Orp. CO56 98
Bracken, The, E4 CF26 39
Hortus Rd.
Bracken Way. Wok. AP58 91
Brackenwood Sun. BC51 83
Brackenwood Rd. Wok. AO63 100
Brackley, Wey. BA56 92
Brackley Rd. W4 BO42 65
Brackley Rd. Beck. CD50 77
Brackley Sq. Wdf. Grn. CJ29 40
Brackley St. EC1 BZ38 57
Viscount St.
Brackley Ter. W4 BO42 65
Bracklyn Ct. N1 BZ37 57
Bracknell Gdns. NW3 BS35 47
Bracknell Gte. NW6 BS35 47
Bracknell Pl. Hem. H. AY11 8
Bracondale Av. Grav. DF51 81
Bracondale Esher BG57 93
Bracondale Rd. SE2 CO42 69
Bradbourne Park Rd. Sev. CU65 107
Bradbourne Rd. Bex. CR47 79
Bradbourne St. SW6 BS44 66
Bradbourne Vale Rd. Sev. CT64 107
Bradbourn Rd. Sev. CU64 107
Bradbury. Rick. AU28 34
Bradbury Clo. Sthl. BE42 64
Bradbury Gdns. Slou. AR35 43
Bradbury St. N16 CA35 48
Braddon Rd. Rich. BL45 65
Braddon St. SE16 CB41 67
Braddyll St. SE10 CG42 68
Bradenham Av. Well. CO45 69
Bradenham Rd. Har. BJ31 45
Bradenham Rd. Hayes BB38 53
Braden St. W9 BS38 56
Bradfield Dr. Bark. CO35 50
Bradfield Rd. E16 CH41 68
Bradfield Rd. Ruis. BE35 45
Bradfields Av. Edg. BM28 37
Bradford Clo. SE26 CB49 77
Wells Park Rd.
Bradford Clo. Brom. CK54 88
Bradford Dr. Epsom BO57 94
Bradford Rd. SE26 CB49 77
Bradford Rd. W3 BO41 65
Warple Way
Bradford Rd. Ilf. CM33 49
Bradgate, Pot. B. BW17 20
Bradgate Clo. Pot. B. BW17 20
Bradgate Rd. SE6 CE46 77
Brading Cres. E11 CH34 49
Brading Rd. SW2 BX47 76
Brading Rd. Croy. BX53 86
Bradiston Rd. W9 BR38 55
Bradlaugh St. N1 CA37 57
Bradleigh Ave. Grays. DD42 71
Bradleigh Rd. Grays. DD42 71
Bradley Clo. N7 BX36 56
Sutterton St.
Bradley Gdns. W13 BJ39 54
Bradley La. Dor. BJ69 119
Bradley Rd. N22 BX30 38
Station Rd.
Bradley Rd. SE19 BZ50 77
Bradley Rd. Enf. CD22 30
Bradley Rd. Slou. AO40 52
Bradmore La. W6 BQ42 65
Beadon Rd.
Bradmore La. Hat. BQ16 19
Bradmore Pk. Rd. W6 BP41 65
Bradmore Way Couls. BX62 104

Bradmore Way. Hat. BR16 19
Bradshaw Clo. Wind. AM44 61
Bradshawe Waye, Uxb. AY39 53
Bradshaw Rd. Wat. BD23 27
Bradshaws. Hat. BO14 10
Bradshaw St. SE15 CB43 67
Bradstock Rd. E9 CC36 57
Bradstock Rd. Epsom BP57 94
Bradstock Rd. Est. E9 CC36 57
Brad St. SE1 BY40 56
Bradwell Av. Dag. CR34 50
Bradwell Clo. E18 CG31 49
Bradwell Rd. Buck. H. CK26 40
Brady Av. Loug. CM23 31
Brady St. Dws. E1 CB39 57
Brady St. E1 CB38 57
Brae Clo. Belv. CQ42 69
Brae Ct. Kings. On T. BM51 85
Wolverton Av.
Braefoot Ct. SW15 BQ46 75
Putney Hill
Braemar Av. N22 BX30 38
Braemar Av. NW10 BN34 46
Braemar Av. SW19 BS48 76
Braemar Av. Bexh. CS45 69
Braemar Av. Sth. Croy. BZ58 96
Braemar Av. Th. Hth. BY52 86
Braemar Av. Wem. BK36 54
Braemar Gdns. NW9 BN30 37
Braemar Gdns. Horn. CW32 51
Braemar Gdns. Horn. CX32 51
Braemar Gdns. Sid. CM48 78
Braemar Gdns. W. Wick. CF54 87
Braemar Rd. E13 CG38 58
Braemar Rd. N15 CA32 48
Braemar Rd. Brent. BK43 64
Braemar Rd. Wor. Pk. BP55 85
Braeside Beck. CE49 77
Braeside, Wey. AW59 92
Braeside Ave. Sev. CT65 107
Braeside Av. SW19 BR51 85
Braeside Clo. Pnr. BF29 36
Braeside Clo. Sev. CT65 107
Braeside Cres. Bexh. CS45 69
Braeside Rd. SW16 BW50 76
Braesmead, Red. BX71 121
Braes St. N1 BY36 56
Brafton Rd. Croy. BZ56 96
Braganza St. SE17 BY42 66
Bragmans La. Rick. AU20 16
Braham St. E1 CA39 57
Braid Av. W3 BN39 55
Braid Clo. Felt. BE48 74
Braid, The Chesh. AP18 16
Braidwood Rd. SE6 CF47 77
Braidwood St. SE1 CA40 57
Brailsford Rd. SW2 BY46 76
Brainton Av. Felt. BC47 73
Braintree Av. Ilf. CK32 49
Braintree Rd. Dag. CR34 50
Braintree Rd. Ruis. BC35 44
Braintree St. E2 CC38 57
Braithwaite Gdns. Stan. BK30 36
Brakefield Rd. Grav. DD50 81
Brakey Hill. Red. CA70 114
Brallings La. Ger. Cr. AT28 34
Bramah Rd. SW9 BY44 66
Bramall Clo. E15 CG35 49
Bramber Ct. NW10 BO36 55
Bramber Rd. N12 BU28 38
Bramber Rd. W14 BR43 65
Brambldene Clo. Wok. AR62 100
Bramble Ave. Dart. DB48 80
Bramble Banks. Cars. BV58 95
Bramblebury Rd. SE18 CM42 68
Bramble Clo. Croy. CE56 96
Bramble Clo. Guil. AP69 118
Bramble Clo. Shep. BA52 83
Bramble Clo. Uxb. AY39 53
Bramble Clo. Wat. BC20 17
Bramble Cft. Erith CS42 69
Bramble Down Stai. AW51 83
Hereford Clo.
Brambledown Clo. W. Wick. CG53 88
Brambledown Rd. Cars. BV57 95
Brambledown Rd. Sth. Croy. BZ57 96
Bramble Gdns W12 BO40 55
Wallflower St.
Bramble La. SW16 BX52 86
Bramble La. Amer. AP24 25
Bramble La. Hodd. CD12 12
Bramble La. Sev. CU67 116
Bramble La. Upmin. CY37 60
Bramble Rd. Hat. BN12 10
Brambles Clo. Brent. BJ43 64
Brambles. The Chig. CM29 40
Brambles. The West Dr. AX42 63
Brambletye Pk. Rd. BU71 121
Bramble Wk. Epsom. BM60 94
Bramblewood Clo. Cars. BU54 86
Brambling Rise, Hem. H. AY12 8
Bramcote Av. Mitch. BU52 86
Bramcote Gro. SE16 CC42 67
Bramcote Rd. SW15 BP45 65
Bramdean Cres. SE12 CH47 78
Bramdean Gdns. SE12 CH47 78
Bramerton Rd. Beck. CD52 87
Bramerton St. SW3 BU43 66
Bramfield Rd. SW11 BU46 76
Bramford Ct. N14 BW27 38
Bramford Rd. SW18 BT45 66
Bramham Gdns. SW5 BS42 66
Bramham Gdns. Chess. BK56 93
Bramhope La. SE7 CH43 68
Bramlands Clo. SW11 BU45 66
Bramley Av. Couls. BW61 104
Bramley Clo. Cher. AW54 83
Bramley Clo. Grav. DF50 81
Bramley Clo. N14 BV25 29
Bramley Clo. Orp. CL54 88
Bramley Clo. Sth. Croy. BY56 95
Bramley Clo. Swan. CT52 89
Bramley Clo. Twick. BG46 74
Bramley Ct. Well. CO44 69
Bramley Cres. Ilf. CL32 49
Bramley Gdns. Wat. BD28 36
Bramley Hill Sth. Croy. BY56 95
Bramley Pl. Dart. CU45 69
Bramley Rd. N14 BV25 29
Bramley Rd. W5 BK41 64
Bramley Rd. W10 BQ40 55
Bramley Rd. W12 BQ40 55
Shalfleet Dri. W12
Bramley Rd. Sutt. BQ58 94
Bramley Rd. Sutt. BT56 95
Bramley Shaw, Wal. Abb. CG20 22
Bramley St. W10 BQ39 55
Bramley Way, Ash BL62 103
Bramley Way W. Wick. CE55 87
Brammas Clo. Slou. AO41 61
Brampton Clo. E5 CB34 48
Comberton Rd.
Brampton Gdns. N15 BZ32 48
Brampton Rd.
Brampton Gdns. Walt. BD56 93
Brampton Gro. NW4 BP31 46
Brampton Gro. Har. BJ31 45
Brampton Gro. Wem. BL33 46
Brampton La. NW4 BQ31 46
Brampton Gro.
Brampton Pk. Rd. N8 BY31 47
High Rd.
Brampton Rd. E6 CJ38 58
Brampton Rd. N15 BZ32 48
Brampton Rd. NW9 BM31 46
Brampton Rd. SE2 CP43 69
Brampton Rd. Bexh. CP43 69
Brampton Rd. Croy. CA53 87
Brampton Rd. St. Alb. BJ13 9
Brampton Rd. Uxb. AZ37 53
Brampton Rd. Wat. BC27 35
Bramsham Gdns. Wat. BD28 36
Bramshaw Rise N. Mal. BO53 85
Bramshaw Rd. E9 CC36 57
Bramshill Clo. Chig. CN28 40
Tine Rd.
Bramshill Gdns. NW5 BV34 47
Bramshill Rd. NW10 BO37 55
Bramshot Av. SE7 CH43 68
Bramshot Way Wat. BC27 35
Bramston Rd. NW10 BP37 55
Bramwell Clo. Sun. BD51 84
Brancaster La. Pur. BZ58 96
Brancaster Rd. E12 CK35 49
Brancaster Rd. SW16 BX48 76
Brancaster Rd. Ilf. CM32 49
Brancepeth Gdns. Buck. H. CH27 40
Branch Hl. NW3 BT34 47
Branch Hl. Lo. NW3 BS34 47
Branch Pl. N1 BZ37 57
Branch Rd. E14 CD40 57
Branch Rd. Ilf. CO28 41
Branch Rd. St. Alb. BF13 9
Branch Rd. St. Alb. BG17 18
Brancker Clo. Wall. BX57 95
Brancker Rd. Har. BK31 45
Brandlehow Rd. SW15 BR45 65
Brandon Clo. Wal. Cr. CA16 21
Brandon Est. SE17 BY43 66
Brandon Gro. Ilf. CL34 49
Brandon Rd. E17 CF31 48
Brandon Rd. N7 BX36 56
Brandon Rd. Sthl. BE42 64
Brandon Rd. Sutt. BS56 95
Brandon St. SE17 BZ42 67
Brandram Rd. SE13 CG45 68
Brandreth Rd. SW17 BV48 76
Brandries, The, Wall. BW55 86
Brandsland, Reig. BS72 121
Brands Rd. Slou. AT43 62
Brand St. SE10 CF43 67
Brandum Rd. Dart. CX47 80
Brandville Gdns. Ilf. CL31 49
Brandy Way Sutt. BS57 95
Branfill Rd. Upmin. CX34 51
Brangbourne Rd. Brom. CF49 77
Brangton Rd. SE11 BX42 66
Loughborough St.
Brangwyn Cres. SW19 BT51 86
Branksea St. SW6 BR43 65
Branksome Av. N18 CA29 39
Branksome Clo. Hem. H. AZ13 8
Branksome Clo. Walt. BD54 84
Branksome Rd. SW2 BX45 66
Branksome Rd. SW19 BS51 86
Branksome Way Har. BL32 46
Branksome Way N. Mal. BN51 85
Bransby Rd. Chess. BL57 94
Branscombe Gdns. N21 BY26 38
Branscombe St. SE13 CE45 67
Bransell Clo. Swan. CS53 89
Bransgrove Rd. Edg. BL30 37
Branston Cres. Orp. CM54 88
Branstone Rd. Rich. BL44 65
Branstone St. W10 BQ38 55
Branton Rd. Green. CZ46 80
Brants Wk. W7 BH38 54
Brantwood Av. Erith. CR43 69
Brantwood Clo. E17 CE31 48
Brantwood Dri. Wey. AV60 91
Brantwood Gdns. Enf. BX24 29
Brantwood Gdns. Ilf. CK31 49
Brantwood Gdns. Wey. AV60 91
Brantwood Rd. N17 CA29 39
Brantwood Rd. SE24 BZ46 77
Brantwood Rd. Bexh. CR44 69
Brantwood Rd. Islw. BJ45 64
Brantwood Rd. Sth. Croy. BZ58 96
Brassey Rd. Oxt. CG68 115
Brassey Sq. SW11 BV45 66
Ashbury Rd.
Brassie Av. W3 BO39 55
Brasted Clo. SE26 CC49 77
Brasted Clo. Bexh. CP46 79
Brasted Hill. Sev. CO63 107
Brasted Hill. West. CO64 107
Brasted La. Sev. CO63 107
Brasted Rd. Erith CT43 69
Brathway Rd. SW18 BS47 76
Bratley St. E1 CB38 57
Weaver St.
Brattle Wood. Sev. CU68 116
Braund Av. Grnf. BF38 54
Braundton Av. Sid. CN47 78
Bravington Clo. Shep. AY53 83
Bravington Rd. W9 BR38 55
Brawell Ms. N18 CB28 39
Lyndhurst Rd.
Braxfield Rd. SE4 CD45 67
Braxted Pk. SW16 BX50 76
Brayard's Rd. SE15 CB44 67
Braybourne Clo. Uxb. AX36 53
Braybrooke Gdns. SE19 CA50 77
Fox Hill
Braybrooke St. W12 BO39 55
Braybrook St. W12 BO39 55
Brayburne Av. SW4 BW44 66
Bray Clo. Maid. AH41 61
Braycourt Av. Walt. BC54 83
Braydon Rd. N16 CA33 48
Brayfield Rd. Maid. AH41 61
Brayfield Ter. N1 BY36 56
Lofting Rd.
Bray Gdns. Wok. AV61 100
Bray Pass. E16 CG40 58
Bray Dr.
Bray Pl. SW3 BU42 66
Bray Rd. E16 CG40 58
Bray Rd. NW7 BQ29 37
Bray Rd. NW7 BR29 37
Bray Rd. Cob. BD61 102
Bray Rd. Guil. AQ71 118
Bray Rd. Maid. AG40 61
Brays Mead. Harl. CN12 13
Brays Springs Wal. Abb. CG20 22
Roundhills
Brayton Gdns. Enf. BW24 29
Braywood Av. Egh. AS50 72
Braywood Rd. SE9 CM45 68
Breach La. Dag. CR38 59
Breach La. Hert. BW12 11
Bread & Cheese La. Wal. Cr. BZ16 21
Bread St. EC4 BZ39 57
Breakfield Couls. BX57 95
Breakfield Couls. BX61 104
Break Mead. Welw. G. C. BS8 5
Breakspear Av. St. Alb. BH14 9
Breakspear Clo. Wat. BC22 26
Breakspeare Rd. Wat. BB19 17
Breakspear Rd. Ruis. AZ32 44
Breakspear Rd. Uxb. AX30 35
Breakspear Rd S. Uxb. AY31 44
Breakspears Rd. SE4 CD45 67
Breakspears Rd. Orp. CO51 89
Breakspear Way, Hem. H. BA13 8
Breaks Rd. Hat. BP12 10
Bream Gdns. E6 CL38 58
Breamore Ct. Ilf. CO34 50
Breamore Rd. Ilf. CN34 49
Breams Bldgs. EC4 BY39 56
Bream St. E3 CE36 57
Breamwater Gdns. Rich. BJ48 74
Breasley Clo. SW15 BP45 65
Brechin Pl. SW7 BT42 66
Brecknock Rd. N7 BW35 47
Brecknock Rd. N19 BW35 47
Brecknock Rd. Est. N7 BW35 47
Brecon Clo. Mitch. BX52 86
Brecon Rd. W6 BR43 65
Brecon Rd. Enf. CC24 30
Brede Clo. E6 CL38 58
Bredgar Rd. N19 BW34 47
Bredon Rd. SE5 BZ45 67
Bredon Rd. Croy. CA54 87
Bredune Ken. BZ61 105
Church Rd.
Breech La. Tad. BP66 112
Breer St. SW6 BS45 66
Breezers St. E1 CB40 57
Pennington St.
Brember Rd. Har. BG34 45
Bremer Rd. Stai. AW48 73
Bremner Rd. SW7 BT41 66
Queen's Gte.
Brenchley Av. Grav. DG49 81
Brenchley Clo. Brom. CG53 88
Brenchley Clo. Chis. CL51 88
Brenchley Rd. Orp. CN51 88
Brendans Clo. Horn. CW33 51
Brenda Rd. SW17 BU48 76
Brende Gdns. E. Mol. BF52 84
Brendon Av. NW10 BO35 46
Brendon Clo. Erith CT44 69
Brendon Dr. Esher BG57 93
Brendon Gdns. Har. BF35 45
Brendon Gdns. Ilf. CN32 49
Brendon Rd. SE9 CM48 78
Brendon Rd. Dag. CQ33 50
Brendon Row SE17 BZ42 67
Brendon St. W1 BU39 56
Brendon Way Enf. CA26 39
Brenley Clo. Mitch. BV52 86
Brenley Gdns. SE9 CJ45 68
Brennan Rd. Til. DG44 71
Brent Clo. Bex. CQ47 79
Brent Clo. Dart. CX46 80
Brentcot Clo. W13 BJ38 54
Brent Ct. NW11 BQ33 46
Highfield Av.
Brent Cres. NW10 BL37 55
Brentfield NW10 BM36 55
Brentfield Clo. NW10 BN36 55
Brentfield Gdns. NW11 BQ33 46
Brentfield Rd. NW10 BN36 55
Brentfield Rd. Dart. CX47 80
Brent Gn. NW4 BQ32 46
Brentham Halt Rd. W5 BL38 55
Brentham Way W5 BK38 54
Brenthouse St. E9 CC36 57
Brenthurst Rd. NW10 BO36 55
Brentlands Dr. Dart. CW47 80
Brentlands Dr. Dart. CX47 80
Brent La. Dart. CW47 80
Brent Lea Brent. BK43 64
Brentmead Clo. W7 BH40 54
Brentmead Gdns. NW10 BL37 55
Brentmead Pl. NW11 BQ32 46
Brenton St. E14 CD39 57
Brent Pk. Rd. NW4 BP33 46
Brent Pl. Barn. BR25 28
Brent Rd. E16 CH39 58
Brent Rd. SE18 CL43 68
Brent Rd. Brent. BK43 64
Brent Rd. Sth. Croy. CB58 96
Brent Rd. Sthl. BD41 64
Brent Side Brent. BK43 64
Brentside Clo. W13 BJ38 54
Brent St. NW4 BQ31 46
Brent Ter. NW2 BQ33 46
Brent. The. Dart. CX47 80
Brentvale Av. Sthl. BG40 54
Brentvale Av. Wem. BL37 55
Brent Vw. Rd. NW4 BP32 46
Brent Way N3 BS29 38
Brent Way Brent. BK43 64
Brent Way. Dart. CX46 80
Brent Way Wem. BM36 55
Brentwick Gdns. Brent. BL42 65
Brentwood Av. Islw. BJ45 64
Brentwood By-pass Brwd. DA25 33
Brentwood By-Pass, Brwd. DA26 42
Brentwood Clo. SE9 CM47 78
Brentwood Rd. Brwd. DD28 122
Brentwood Rd. Brwd. DF30 123
Brentwood. Rd. Grays. DG42 71
Brentwood Rd. Grays. DH41 71
Brentwood Rd. Ong. CX19 24
Brentwood Rd. Rom. CT32 50
Brereton Rd. N17 CA29 39
Bressenden Pl. SW1 BV41 66
Bressey Gro. E18 CG30 40
Bretlands Clo. Cher. AV55 82
Brett Clo. Nthlt. BD38 54
Brett Cres. NW10 BN36 55
Brettell St. SE17 BZ42 67
Merrow St.
Brettenham Av. E17 CE30 39
Brettenham Rd. E17 CD30 39
Brettenham Rd. N18 CB28 39
Brett Gdns. Dag. CQ36 59
Brettgrave Epsom BN58 94
Brett Pl. Wat. BC22 26
Brett Rd. E8 CB36 57
Brett Rd. NW10 BO37 55
Brett Rd. Barn. BQ25 28
Brewer Pl. SE18 CL42 68
Charles Grindling Wk.
Brewers La. Rich. BK46 74
Brewer St. W1 BW40 56
Brewer St. Red. BZ69 114
Brewery La. Twick. BJ47 74
London Rd.
Brewery La. Wey. AY60 92
Brewery Rd. N7 BX36 56
Brewery Rd. SE18 CM42 68
Brewery Rd. Brom. CK54 88
Brewery Rd. Hodd. CE12 12
Brewery Rd. Wok. AR62 100
Brewery Sq. Twick. BH47 74
Brewhouse La. E1 CB40 57
Wapping La.
Brewhouse St. SW15 BR45 65
Brewood Rd. Dag. CO36 59
Brewster Gdns. W10 BQ39 55
Brewster Rd. E10 CE33 48
Brian Av. Sth. Croy. CA59 96
Brian Clo. Horn. CU35 50
Brian Ct. N10 BV30 38
Briane Rd. Epsom BN58 94
Brian Rd. Rom. CP32 50
Briants Clo. Pnr. BE30 36
Briant St. SE4 CC44 67
Briar Av. SW16 BX50 76
Briarbank Rd. W13 BJ39 54
Briar Banks. Cars. BV58 95
Briar Clo. N13 BZ27 39
Briar Clo. Berk. AT11 7
Briar Clo. Buck. H. CJ27 40
Briar Clo. Islw. BH46 74
Briar Clo. Wal. Cr. CC18 21
Briar Clo. Wey. AW59 92
Briar Cres. Nthlt. BF36 54
Briardale Gdns. NW3 BS34 47
Briarfield Av. N3 BS30 38
Briar Gdns. Brom. CG54 88
Briar Gro. Sth. Croy. CB60 96
Briar Hill Pur. BX59 95
Briar La. Cars. BV58 95
Briar La. Croy. CE56 96
Briarleas Gdns. Upmin. CZ33 51
Briarley Clo. Brox. CD14 12
Briar Pass. SW16 BX52 86
Briar Pl. SW16 BX52 86
Briar Rd. NW2 BQ35 46
Briar Rd. SW16 BX52 86
Briar Rd. Bex. CS48 79
Briar Rd. Har. BK32 45
Briar Rd. Rom. CV29 42
Briar Rd. St. Alb. BK12 9
Briar Rd. Shep. AY53 83
Briar Rd. Twick. BH47 74
Briar Rd. Wat. BC20 17
Briar Rd. Wok. AT65 100
Briars Cl. N17 CB29 39
Briars Clo. N17 CB29 39
Park La.
Briar's Clo. Hat. BP12 10
Briars Lane. Hat. BP12 10
Briars, The Rick. AW21 26
Briars, The, Wal. Cr. CD19 21
Russell's Ride
Briars Wk. Rom. CW30 42
Briar's Wood. Hat. BO12 10
Briar Wk. SW15 BP45 65
Briar Wk. Edg. BN29 37
Briar Way, Berk. AR13 7
Briar Way, Guil. AT68 109
Briar Way. West Dr. AZ41 63
Briarwood Clo. NW9 BN32 46
Briarwood Dr. Nthwd. BC30 35
Briarwood Rd. SW4 BW46 76
Briarwood Rd. Epsom BP57 94
Briarwood Rd. Wok. AO63 100
Briary Clo. NW3 BT36 56
Chalcotts Est.
Briary Ct. Sid. CO49 79
Briary Gdns. Brom. CH49 78
Briary La. N9 CA27 39
Brickbarn Clo. SW10 BT43 66
Edith Gro.
Brick Ct. EC4 BY39 56
Middle Temple La.
Brickenden Ct. Wal. Abb. CG20 22
Mason Way
Brickenoon La. Hert. BZ11 12
Bricket Rd. St. Alb. BG13 9
Brickett Clo. Ruis. BA32 44
Brick Farm Clo. Rich. BM44 65
Brickfield Hat. BP14 10
Far-end
Brickfield Av. Hem. H. AZ14 8
Brickfield Clo. Brent. BK43 64
Brickfield Cotts. SE18 CN43 68
Brickfield La. Barn. BO25 28
Brickfield La. Wal. Abb. CF17 21
Brickfield Rd. E3 CE38 57
Brickfield Rd. SW19 BS49 76
Brickfield Rd. Epp. CP18 23
Brickfield Rd. Th. Hth. BY51 86
Brickfields Har. BG34 45
Brickfields La. Hayes. BA43 63
Brick Kiln Hill. Epp. CR21 32
Brick Kiln La. Oxt. CJ68 115
Brick Knoll Pk. St. Alb. BK14 9
Brick La. E1 CA38 57
Brick La. E2 CA38 57
Brick La. Enf. CB23 30
Brickmakers La. Hem. H. AZ14 8
Brick St. W1 BV40 56
Brickwall La. Ruis. BB33 44
Brickwood Clo. SE26 CB48 77
Kirkdale
Brickwood Rd. Croy. CA55 87
Brick Yd. La. Dor. BD74 119
Bride La. EC4 BY39 56
Bride St. N7 BX36 56
Bridewell Pl. EC4 BY39 56
Tudor St.
Bridford Ms. W1 BV39 56
Devonshire St.
Bridge App. NW1 BV36 56
Bridge Av. W6 BQ42 65
Bridge Av. W7 BG39 54
Bridge Av. Upmin. CX34 51
Bridge Clo. Brwd. DC28 122
Bridge Clo. Enf. CB23 30
Bridge Clo. Rom. CT32 50
Bridge Clo. Wey. AY59 92
Bridge Clo. Wok. AR62 100
Bridge Cotts. Surb. BJ54 84
Portsmouth Rd.
Bridge Ct. E10 CD33 48
Bridge End E17 CF30 39
Bridge Field. Welw. G. C. BR7 5
Bridgefield Clo. Bans. BQ61 103
Bridgefield Rd. Sutt. BS57 95
Bridgefoot, SE1 BX42 66
Bridgefoot La. Pot. B. BQ20 19
Bridge Gdns. Ashf. BA50 73
Bridge Gdns. E. Mol. BG52 84
Bridge Gate N21 BZ26 39
Bridgeham, Wey. AZ56 92
Bridge Hill, Epp. CN20 22
Bridgeland Rd. E16 CH40 58
Bridge La. NW11 BR31 46
Bridge La. SW11 BU44 66
Bridge La. Vir. W. AS53 82
Bridgeman Rd. W4 BN41 65
Bridgeman St. NW8 BU37 56
Bridgend Rd. SW18 BT45 66
Bridgend Rd. Enf. CC21 30
Bridgenhall Rd. Enf. CA23 30
Bridgen Rd. Bex. CQ47 79
Bridge Path Wat. BC23 26
Bridge Pl. SW1 BV42 66
Bridge Pl. SW6 BR45 65
Bridge Pl. Croy. BZ54 87
Bridge Pl. Wat. BD25 27
Bridger Clo. Wat. BE20 18
Bridge Rd. E6 CK36 58
Bridge Rd. E15 CF36 57
Bridge Rd. E17 CD33 48
Bridge Rd. N9 CB27 39
Bridge Rd. N22 BX30 38
Bridge Rd. NW10 BO36 55
Bridge Rd. Beck. CD50 77
Bridge Rd. Bexh. CQ45 69
Bridge Rd. Cher. AW54 83
Bridge Rd. Chess. BL56 94
Bridge Rd. Croy. BZ55 87
Bridge Rd. E. Mol. BG53 84
Bridge Rd. Epsom BO59 94
Bridge Rd. Erith CT44 69
Bridge Rd. Grays. DD42 71
Bridge Rd. Houns. BG44 64
Bridge Rd. Kings L. BA20 17

Bridge Road. Ong. CV14 15
Bridge Rd. Orp. CO53 89
Bridge Rd. Rain. CU38 59
Bridge Rd. Sthl. BE41 64
Bridge Rd. Sutt. BS57 95
Bridge Rd. Twick. BJ46 74
Bridge Rd. Uxb. AX37 53
Bridge Rd. Wall. BV56 95
Bridge Rd. Wem. BM34 46
Bridge Rd. Wey. AY56 92
Bridge Rd. East. Welw. G. C. BR8 5
Bridge Row Croy. BZ54 87
Cross Rd.
Bridges Dr. Dart. CX46 80
Bridges La. Croy. BX56 95
Bridges Pl. SW6 BR44 65
Bridges Rd. SW19 BS50 76
Bridges Rd. Stan. BH28 36
Bridge St. SW1 BX41 66
Bridge St. Berk. AR13 7
Bridge St. Guil. AR71 118
Bridge St. Hem. H. AX14 8
Bridge St. Lthd. BJ64 102
Bridge St. Pnr. BE31 45
Bridge St. Rich. BK46 74
Bridge St. Stai. AV49 72
Bridge St. Walt. BB54 83
Bridge Ter. E15 CF36 57
Bridge, The, Har. BH31 45
Bridge Vw. NW11 BR32 46
Bridge Vw. W6 BQ42 65
Bridgewater Clo. Chis. CN52 88
Bridgewater Gdns. Edg. BL30 37
Bridgewater Rd. E15 CF37 57
Bridgewater Rd. Berk. AQ12 7
Bridgewater Rd. Wem. BK36 54
Bridgewater Rd. Wey. BA57 92
Bridgewater St. EC1 BZ39 57
Viscount St.
Bridge Way N11 BW27 38
Bridge Way Bark. CN36 58
Bridge Way. Couls. BU63 104
Bridge Way Twick. BG47 74
Bridge Way, Uxb. AZ35 44
Bridgeway, Wem. BL36 55
Bridgeway St. NW1 BW37 56
Bridgewood Clo. SE20 CB50 77
Castleline Rd.
Bridgewood Rd. SW16 BW50 76
Bridgewood Rd. Wor. Pk. BP55 85
Bridgford St. SW18 BT48 76
Bridgman Rd. Tedd. BJ50 74
Bridgwater Clo. Rom. CV28 42
Bridgwater Rd. Rom. CV28 42
Bridgwater Rd. Ruis. BC35 44
Bridgwater Wk. Rom. CV28 42
Bridle Clo. Enf. CD22 30
Bridle Clo. Epsom BN56 94
Bridle Clo. St. Alb. BH12 9
Bridle End Epsom BO60 94
Bridle La. W1 BW40 56
Bridle La. Rick. AX24 26
Bridle Path Croy. BX55 86
Bridle Path. Rd. Barn. BT23 29
Bridle Path, The Wdf. Grn. CG29 40
Bridlepath Way, Felt. BB47 73
Bridle Rd. Croy. CE55 87
Bridle Rd. Epsom. BO60 94
Bridle Rd. Esher. BJ57 93
Bridle Rd. Pnr. BC32 44
Bridle, The, Rd Pur. BX58 95
Bridle, The, Way Croy. CD58 96
Bridle, The, Way Wall. BW56 95
Bridle Way, Berk. AQ12 7
Bridle Way Croy. CE56 96
Bridle Way, Hodd. CE10 12
Bridle Way, S. Hodd. CE10 12
Bridlington Clo. West. CH63 106
Bridport Av. Rom. CR32 50
Bridport Pl. N1 BZ37 57
Bridport Rd. N18 CA28 39
Bridport Rd. Grnf. BF37 54
Bridport Rd. Th. Hth. BY52 86
Bridstow Pl. W2 BS39 56
Bridwell Pl. EC4 BY39 56
Tudor St.
Brief St. SE5 BY44 66
Brier Lea. Tad. BR66 112
Brierley Croy. CE57 96
Brierley Av. N9 CC26 39
Brierley Clo. SE25 CB52 87
Brierley Clo. Horn. CU32 50
Brierley Rd. E11 CF35 48
Brierley Rd. SW12 BW48 76
Brierly St. E2 CC38 57
Royston St.
Briery Ct. Hem. H. AZ13 8
Briery Rd. Hem. H. AZ12 8
Briery Way. Amer. AP22 25
Brigadier Av. Enf. BZ22 30
Brigadier Av. Enf. BZ23 30
Brigadier Hill, Enf. BZ22 30
Brigadier Hill Enf. BZ23 30
Brightfield Rd. SE12 CG46 78
Bright Hill, Guil. AS71 118
Brightlands Rd. Reig. BT69 121
Brightling Rd. SE4 CD46 77
Brightlingsea Pl. E14 CD40 57
Brightman Rd. SW18 BT47 76
Brighton Av. E17 CD32 48
Brighton Clo. Uxb. AZ36 53
Brighton Clo. Wey. AW56 92
Burleigh Rd.
Brighton Dr. Nthlt. BF36 54
Brighton Gro. SE14 CD44 67
Brighton Rd. E6 CL38 58
Brighton Rd. E15 CG37 58
Brighton Rd. N2 BT30 38
Brighton Rd. N16 CA35 48
Brighton Rd. Couls. BW62 104
Brighton Rd. Red. BU71 121
Brighton Rd. Red. BV65 104
Brighton Rd. Surb. BK53 84
Brighton Rd. Tad. BR62 103
Brighton Rd. Tad. BR64 103
Brighton Rd. Wat. BC22 26
Brighton Rd. Wey. AX56 92
Brighton Ter. SW9 BX45 66
Brights Av. Rain. CU38 59
Brightside Av. Stai. AX50 73
Brightside Rd. SE13 CF46 77
Brightside, The, Enf. CC23 30
Bright St. E14 CE39 57
Brightwell Cres. SW17 BU49 76
Brightwell Rd. Wat. BC25 26
Brigstock Rd. Belv. CR42 69
Brigstock Rd. Couls. BV61 104
Brigstock Rd. Th. Hth. BY53 86
Brig St. E14 CF42 67
Brim Hill N2 BT31 47
Brimpsfield Clo. SE2 CO41 69
Brimsdale Rd. NW4 BQ31 46
Brimsdown Av. Enf. CD23 30
Brimshot La. Wok. AP58 91
Brimstone Clo. Orp. CP57 98
Brindles Clo. Brwd. DE27 122
Brindley St. SE14 CD44 67
Brindley Way Sthl. BF40 54
Brindwood Rd. E4 CD27 39
Brinkburn Clo. SE2 CO42 69
Brinkburn Clo. Edg. BM30 37
Brinkburn Gdns. Edg. BM31 46
Brinkley Rd. Wor. Pk. BP55 85
Brinklow Cres. SE18 CL43 68
Brinkworth Rd. Ilf. CK31 49
Brinkworth Way, E9 CD36 57
Brinley Clo. Wal. Cr. CC19 21
Brinsley Rd. Har. BG30 36
Brinsmead Rd. Rom. CX30 42
Brinsworth Clo. Twick. BG47 74
Bri Pl. Amer. AP22 25
Brisbane Av. SW19 BS50 76
Brisbane Ho. Til. DG44 71
Leicester Rd.
Brisbane Rd. E10 CE34 48
Brisbane Rd. W13 BJ40 54
Brisbane Rd. Ilf. CL33 49
Brisbane St. SE5 BZ43 67
Briscoe Clo. Hodd. CD11 12
Briscoe Rd. SW19 BT50 76
Briscoe Rd. Hodd. CD11 12
Briscoe Rd. Rain. CV37 60
Briset Rd. SE9 CJ45 68
Briset St. EC1 BY38 56
Briset Way N7 BX34 47
Andover Est.
Bristol Clo. Stai. AY46 73
Whitley Clo.
Bristol Gdns. W9 BS38 56
Bristol Park Rd. E17 CD31 48
Hervey Park Rd.
Bristol Rd. E7 CJ36 58
Bristol Rd. E15 CG36 58
Bristol Rd. Grav. DH48 81
Bristol Rd. Grnf. BF37 54
Bristol Rd. Mord. BS53 86
Bristow Av. Croy. BX56 95
Bristow Rd. SE19 CA49 77
Bristow Rd. Bexh. CQ44 69
Bristow Rd. Houns. BF45 64
Britania Dr. Grav. DJ49 81
Britania W. Y. Stai. AX47 73
Britannia Rd. N12 BT27 38
Britannia Rd. SW6 BS43 66
Britannia Rd. Brwd. DB28 42
Britannia Rd. Ilf. CL34 49
Britannia Rd. Surb. BL54 85
Britannia Row, N1 BY37 56
Britannia St. WC1 BX38 56
Britannia Wk. N1 BZ37 57
Britannia Way NW10 BM38 55
Britannia Way SW6 BS43 66
Britannia Rd.
British Gro. W4 BO42 65
British Gro. Pass. W6 BO42 65
British Legion Rd. E4 CG27 40
Briton Clo. Sth. Croy. CA59 96
Briton Cres. Sth. Croy. CA59 96
Briton Hill Rd. Sth. Croy. CA58 96
Brittain Rd. Dag. CQ34 50
Brittain Rd. Walt. BD56 93
Brittania Rd. Wal. Cr. CD20 21
Brittany St. SE11 BX42 66
Brittenden Clo. Orp. CN57 97
Brittens Clo. Guil. AQ68 109
Britten St. SW3 BU42 66
Britton Av. St. Alb. BG13 9
Britton St. EC1 BY38 56
Brixham Cres. Ruis. BC33 44
Brixham Gdns. Ilf. CN35 49
Brixham Rd. E16 CH39 58
Brixham Rd. Well. CP44 69
Brixham St. E16 CK40 58
Brixton Est. Edg. BM30 37
Brixton Hill, SW2 BX47 76
Brixton Hill Ct. SW2 BX46 76
Brixton Hill Pl. SW2 BX47 76
Brixton Oval, SW2 BY45 66
Rushcroft Rd.
Brixton Rd. Wat. BC23 26
Brixton Sta. Rd. SW9 BY45 66
Brixton Water La. SW2 BX46 76
Brnadon St. Grav. DG47 81
Broad Acre, St. Alb. BE18 18
Broad Acre Stai. AW49 73
Cherry Orch.
Broadacre Clo. Uxb. AZ34 44
Broadacres, Guil. AP69 118
Broad Acres. Hat. BO11 10
Broadbent St. W1 BV40 56
Bourdon St.
Broadbridge Clo. SE3 CH43 68
Broad Clo. Walt. BE55 84
Broadcoombe Sth. Croy. CC57 96
Broad Ct. WC2 BX39 56
Broadcroft Av. Stan. BK30 36
Broadcroft Rd. Orp. CM54 88
Broad Ditch Rd. Grav. DE50 81
Broadfield, Harl. CN10 6
Broadfield Clo. NW2 BQ34 46
Broadfield Clo. Tad. BQ63 103
Broadfield Ct. Bush. BH27 36
Broadfield La. Wat. BC26 35
Broadfield Rd. SE6 CG47 78
Broadfield Rd. Hem. H. AY13 8
Broadfields E. Mol. BG53 84
Broadfields Har. BF30 36
Broadfields, Saw. CO6 6
Broadfields, Wal. Cr. BY18 20
Broadfields Av. N21 BY26 38
Broadfields Av. Edg. BM28 37
Broadfield Sq. Enf. CB23 30
Broadfield Way Buck. H. CJ28 40
Broadfiel Pl. Welw. G. C. BP8 5
Broadford La. Wok. AP59 91
Broadford Rd. Guil. AR74 118
Broadgate, Wal. Abb. CG20 22
Broadgates Av. Barn. BS23 29
Broadgates Rd. SW18 BT47 76
Ellerton Rd.
Broad Grn. Croy. BY54 86
Broad Grn. Hert. BX12 11
Broad Grn. Av. Croy. BY54 86
Broadham Green Rd. Oxt. CF69 114
Broad High Way, Cob. BD61 102
Broadhinton Rd. SW4 BV45 66
Broadhurst. Ash. BL61 103
Broadhurst Av. Edg. BM28 37
Broadhurst Av. Ilf. CN35 49
Broadhurst Gdns. NW6 BS36 56
Broadhurst Gdns. Chig. CM28 40
Broadhurst Gdns. Reig. BS72 121
Broadhurst Gdns. Ruis. BD34 45
Broadhurst Wk. Rain. CU36 59
Broadlands Ave. Chesh. AO18 16
Broadlands Av. SW16 BX48 76
Broadlands Av. Enf. CB24 30
Broadlands Av. Shep. BA53 83
Broadlands Clo. N6 BV33 47
Broadlands Clo. Enf. CB24 30
Broadlands Dr. Warl. CC63 105
Broadlands Rd. N6 BU33 47
Broadlands Rd. Brom. CH49 78
Broadlands, The, Felt. BE48 74
Broadlands Way N. Mal. BO53 85
Broad La. N15 CA31 48
Broad La. Dart. CU49 79
Broad La. Hamptn. BE50 74
Broad Lawn, SE9 CL48 78
Broadlawns Clo. Har. BH30 36
Broadley St. NW8 BT39 56
Broadley Ter. NW1 BU38 56
Broadmark Rd. Slou. AQ40 52
Broadmead, SE6 CE48 77
Broadmead Av. Wor. Pk. BP54 85
Broadmead Clo. Pnr. BE29 36
Broad Meadow. Brwd. CZ22 33
Broadmead Rd. Wdf. Grn. CH29 40
Broadmead Strand NW9 BO30 37
Broad Oak, Wdf. Grn. CH28 40
Broad Oak Av. Enf. CC21 30
Broadoak Rd. Erith CS43 69
Broad Oaks, Surb. BM54 85
Broad Oaks Surb. BM55 85
Kingston By Pass
Broadoaks Cres. Wey. AW60 92
Broad Oaks Way Brom. CG53 88
Broad Platts. Slou. AR41 62
Broad Rd. Swans. DC46 81
Broad St. Av. EC2 CA39 57
Old Broad St.
Broad Sanctuary, SW1 BX41 66
Broadstone Rd. Horn. CU34 50
Broad St. E15 CF36 57
Broad St. Dag. CR36 59
Broad St. Guil. AO69 118
Broad St. Hem. H. AX13 8
Broad St. Tedd. BH49 74
Broad Strood, Loug. CL22 31
Broad Strood Loug. CL23 31
Broad, The, Walk, W8 BS40 56
Broad Vw. NW9 BM32 46
Broadview Ave. Grays DE41 71
Broadview Rd. SW16 BW50 76
Broad Wk. E18 CG31 49
Broad Wk. N21 BX27 38
Broad Wk. SE3 CJ44 68
Broad Wk. Cat. CA64 105
Broad Wk. Couls. BV65 104
Broad Wk. Epsom BO62 103
Broad Wk. Epsom. BQ63 103
Broad Wk. Har. BF31 45
Broad Walk. Harl. CM10 6
Broad Walk. Harl. CM11 13
Broad Wk. Houns. BD44 64
Broad Wk. Orp. CP55 89
Broad Wk. Sev. CW67 117
Broad Wk. La. NW11 BR33 46
Broad Walk N. Brwd. DD27 122
Broad Walk S. The. Brwd. DD28 122
Broad Walk. The. Nthwd. BA30 35
Broadwall, SE1 BY40 56
Broadwater, Pot. B. BS18 20
Broadwater Clo. Stai. AS47 72
Broadwater Clo. Walt. BC56 92
Broadwater Clo. Watt. BB56 92
Broadwater Clo. Wok. AU59 91
Woodham La.
Broadwater Gdns. Uxb. AW31 44
Broadwater La. Uxb. AW31 44
Broadwater Rise, Guil. AT71 118
Broadwater Rd. N17 CA30 39
Broadwater Rd. SW17 BU49 76
Broadwater Rd. Watt. BB56 92
Broadway, E13 CH37 58
Broadway, E15 CF36 57
Broadway, N16 CA33 48
Broad Way N20 BT27 38
Broadway, SW1 BW41 66
Broadway, SW16 BW49 76
Broadway W6 BQ42 65
Hammersmith Rd.
Broadway W7 BH40 54
Broadway W13 BJ40 54
Broadway, Bark. CM37 58
Broadway, Bexh. CQ45 69
Broadway, Edg. BM30 37
Broadway Epsom BP56 94
Broadway Grnf. BG38 54
Broadway Rain. CU38 59
Broadway Rom. CU30 41
Broad Way, St. Alb. BG13 9
Broadway Surb. BM54 85
Broadway Swan. CS53 89
Broadway, Til. DF44 71
Broadway Anchor Hill, Wok. AO62 100
Broadway Av. Croy. BZ53 87
Broadway Av. Harl. CP9 6
Broadway Av. Twick. BJ46 74
Broadway Church La. Berk. AT14 7
Broadway Clo. Sth. Croy. CB60 96
Broadway Clo. Wdf. Grn. CH29 40
Broadway Ct. SW19 BS50 76
Broadway Gdns. Mitch. BU52 86
Broadway Grays DE43 71
Broadway. Hat. BO12 10
Broadway Ho. Brom. CF49 77
Broadway Mkt. E8 CB37 57
Broadway Mews N21 BY26 38
Compton Rd.
Broadway, Stai. AW49 73
Broadway, The, E4 CF29 39
Broadway, The, N3 BS30 38
Broadway, The, N8 BX32 47
Broadway, The, N9 CB27 39
Fore St.
Broadway, The, NW7 BO28 37
Broadway, The, NW9 BP33 46
Broadway, The SW14 BO44 65
Terrace, The
Broadway, The, SW19 BR50 75
Broadway, The, W3 BM41 65
Gunnersbury La.
Broadway, The, W5 BK40 54
Broadway, The, Croy. BX56 95
Broadway, The, Dag. CQ34 50
Broadway, The, Har. BH30 36
Broadway, The, Horn. CU35 50
Broadway, The, Loug. CM24 31
Broadway, The, N9 CB27 39
Broadway, The, Pnr. BE29 36
Broadway, The, Stai. AX52 83
Broadway, The, Stan. BK28 36
Broadway, The, Sthl. BE40 54
Broadway, The, Surb. BH54 84
Broadway, The, Sutt. BR57 94
Broadway, The, Wat. BD24 27
Broadway, The, Wdf. Grn. CH29 40
Snakes La.
Broadway, The, Wey. AW58 92
Broadwick St. W1 BW39 56
Broadwood Av. Ruis. BB32 44
Broad Yd. EC1 BY38 56
Brocas Clo. NW3 BT36 56
Chalcotts Est.
Brocas St. Wind. AO43 61
Brockdene Dr. Nthwd. BB29 35
Brockdene Dr. Nthwd. BC29 35
Brockdish Av. Bark. CN35 49
Brockell Hurst E. Mol. BE53 84
Brockenhurst Av. Wor. Pk. BO54 85
Brockenhurst Clo. Wok. AS60 91
Brockenhurst Gdns. NW7 BO28 37
Brockenhurst Gdns. Ilf. CM35 49
Brockenhurst Rd. Croy. CB54 87
Brockenhurst Way, SW16 BW51 86
Brocket Clo. Chig. CN28 40
Brocket Rd. Grays DG41 71
Cherry Wk.
Brocket Rd. Hodd. CE12 12
Brockett Clo. Welw. G. C. BP8 5
Brocket Way, Chig. CN28 40
Brock Grn. S. Ock. DA39 60
Brockham Clo. SW19 BR49 75
Brockham Cres. Croy. CF57 96
Brockham Dr. Ilf. CM32 49
Brockhamhurst Rd. Bet. BM74 120
Brockham La. Bet. BM70 120
Brockham St. SE1 BZ41 67
Brockhill Cres. SE4 CD45 67
Brockhurst Clo. Stan. BH29 36
Brockhurst Rd. Chesh. AO18 16
Brocklebank Rd. SW18 BT47 76
Brocklehurst St. SE14 CC43 67
Brocklesby Rd. SE25 CB52 87
Brockles Mead. Harl. CM13 13
Brockley Av. Stan. BL27 37
Brockley Av. N. Stan. BL27 37
Brockley Clo. Stan. BL28 37
Brockley Combe, Wey. BA56 92
Brockley Cres. Rom. CS29 41
Brockley Cross, SE4 CD45 67
Brockley Footpath, SE15 CC45 67
Brockley Gdns. SE4 CD44 67
Brockley Gro. SE4 CD46 77
Brockley Gro. Brwd. DD26 122
Brockley Hall Rd. SE4 CD46 77
Brockley Hill Stan. BK26 36
Brockley Pk. SE23 CD47 77
Brockley Ri. SE23 CD47 77
Brockley Rd. SE4 CD45 67
Brockley Side Stan. BL28 37
Brockley Ter. SE17 CA42 67
Alvey St.
Brockley Vw. SE23 CD47 77
Brockley Way, SE4 CC46 77
Brockman Ri. Brom. CF49 77
Brock Pl. E3 CE38 57
Brock Rd. E13 CH39 58
Brocks Dr. Sutt. BR55 85
Brockside, Pot. B. BP19 19
Brockswood La. Welw. G. C. BP7 5
Brock Way. Vir. W. AR53 82
Brockway Clo. Guil. AT70 118
Brockwell Clo. Orp. CN53 88
Brockwell Ct. SW2 BY46 76
Brockwell Pk. Gdns. SE24 BY47 76
Broderick Gro. Lthd. BF66 111
Broderick Rd. SE2 CO42 69
Brodewater Rd. Borwd. BM23 28
Brodia Rd. N16 CA34 48
Brodie Rd. E4 CF26 39
Brodie Rd. Enf. BZ22 30
Brodie Rd. Guil. AS71 118
Brodie St. SE1 CA42 67
Brodlove La. E1 CC40 57
Brodrick Rd. SW17 BU48 76
Brograve Gdns. Beck. CE51 87
Brograve Rd. W17 CB31 48
Broke Fm. Dr. Orp. CP58 98
Broken Furlong. Wind. AN42 61
Broken Gate La. Uxb. AU33 43
Broken Warf, EC4 BZ40 57
Broke Rd. E8 CA37 57
Brokes Cres. Reig. BS69 121
Brokesley St. E3 CD38 57
Brokes Rd. Reig. BS69 121
Bromar Rd. SE5 CA45 67
Bromboro' Grn. Wat. BD28 36
Bromefield, Stan. BK30 36
Bromehead Rd. E1 CC39 57
Bromehead St. E1 CC39 57
Bromell's Rd. SW4 BW45 66
Brome Rd. SE9 CK45 68
Bromet Clo. Wat. BB22 26
Bromfelde Rd. SW4 BW45 66
Bromfield St. N1 BY37 56
Bromhall Rd. Dag. CO36 59
Bromhedge, SE9 CK48 78
Bromholm Rd. SE2 CO41 69
Bromleigh Clo. Wal. Cr. CD17 21
Ashdown Cres.
Bromley Av. Brom. CG50 78
Bromley Common Brom. CJ52 88
Bromley Cres. Brom. CG51 88
Bromley Cres. Ruis. BB35 44
Bromley Gdns. Brom. CG51 88
Bromley Gro. Brom. CF51 87
Bromley Hall Rd. E14 CF39 57
Lochnager St.
Bromley Hall Rd. E14 CF39 57
Bromley High St. E3 CE38 57
Bromley Hill, Brom. CG49 78
Bromley La. Chis. CM50 78
Bromley Rd. E10 CE32 48
Bromley Rd. E17 CE31 48
Bromley Rd. N17 CA30 39
Bromley Rd. N18 BZ28 39
Bromley Rd. SE6 CE47 77
Bromley Rd. Beck. CE51 87
Bromley Rd. Brom. CE47 77
Bromley Rd. Chis. CL51 88
Bromley St. E1 CC39 57
Brompton Clo. Houns. BE46 74
Brompton Dr. Erith. CU43 69
Brompton Gro. N2 BU31 47
Brompton Pk. Rd. N8 BY31 47
High Rd.
Brompton Pl. SW3 BU41 66
Brompton Rd. SW1 BU42 66
Brompton Rd. SW3 BU42 66
Brompton Rd. SW7 BU42 66
Brompton Sq. SW3 BU41 66
Bromwich Av. N6 BV34 47
Bromyard Av. W3 BO40 55
Brondesbury Ct. NW2 BQ36 55
Brondesbury Pk. NW2 BP36 55
Brondesbury Pk. NW6 BP36 55
Brondesbury Rd. NW6 BR37 55
Brondesbury Vill. NW6 BR37 55
Bronhill Ter. N17 CB30 39
Lansdowne Rd.
Bronsart Rd. SW6 BR43 65
Bronson Rd. SW20 BQ51 85
Bronsoon Way Uxb. AV34 43
Bronte Clo. Til. DH44 71
Bronte Gro. Dart. CW45 70
Bronti Clo. SE17 BZ42 67
Bronze St. SE8 CE43 67
Brook Av. Dag. CR36 59
Brook Av. Edg. BM29 37
Brook Av. Wem. BL34 46
Brookbank Av. W7 BG39 54
Brookbank Rd. SE13 CE45 67
Brook Clo. SW20 BP52 85
Brook Clo. Rom. CT30 41
Brook Clo. Ruis. BB33 44
Brook Clo. Stai. AY47 73
Brook Ct. Edg. BM28 37
Brook Cres. E4 CE28 39
Brook Cres. N9 CB28 39
Brookdale N11 BW28 38
Brookdale Av. Upmin. CX34 51
Brookdale Clo. Upmin. CX34 51
Brookdale Rd. E17 CD31 48
Brookdale Rd. SE6 CE46 77
Brookdale Rd. Bex. CQ47 79
Brookdene Av. Wat. BC26 35
Brookdene Rd. SE18 CN42 68
Brook Dr. SE11 BY41 66
Brook Dr. Har. BG31 45
Brook Dr. Rad. BH20 18
Brook Dr. Ruis. BB33 44
Brook Dr. Sun. BB50 73

Brooke Av. Har. BG34 45
Brooke Clo. Bush. BG26 36
Brookehowse Rd. SE6 CE48 77
Brook End, Saw. CP6 6
Brookend Rd. Sid. CN47 78
Brooke Rd. E5 CA34 48
Brooke Rd. E17 CF31 48
Brooke Rd. N16 CA34 48
Brooke Rd. Grays. DD42 71
Brooker Rd. Wal. Abb. CF20 21
Brooker Rd. Wal. Abb. CF21 30
Brookers Clo. Ash. BK62 102
Brooke's Ct. EC1 BY39 56
Brooke St. EC1 BY39 56
Brook Farm Rd. Cob. BD61 102
Brookfield, N6 BV34 47
Brookfield, Wok. AQ61 100
Brookfield Av. E17 CF31 48
Brookfield Av. NW7 BP29 37
Brookfield Av. W5 BK38 54
Brookfield Av. Sutt. BT56 95
Brookfield Clo. NW7 BP29 37
Brookfield Clo. Brwd. DE25 122
Brookfield Ct. Grnf. BG38 54
Brookfield Ct. Har. BK32 45
Brookfield Cres. NW7 BP29 37
Brookfield Cres. Har. BK32 45
Brookfield Gdns. Esher BH57 93
Brookfield Gdns. Wal. Cr. CC17 21
Brookfield La. Wal. Cr. CB17 21
Brookfield Pk. NW5 BV34 47
Brookfield Path Wdf. Grn. CG29 40
Oak Hill
Brookfield Rd. E9 CD36 57
Brookfield Rd. N9 CB27 39
Brookfield Rd. W4 BN41 65
Brookfields Enf. CC24 30
Brookfields, Saw. CP6 6
Brookfields Av. Mitch. BU53 86
Brook Flds. Ong. CW16 24
Brook Gdns. E4 CE28 39
Brook Gdns. SW13 BO45 65
Beverley Rd.
Brook Gdns. Kings. On T. BN51 85
Brook Grn. W6 BQ41 65
Brook Hill. Oxt. CF68 114
Brookhill Close SE18 CL42 68
Brookhill Clo. Barn. BU25 29
Brookhill Rd. SE18 CL43 68
Brookhill Rd. Barn. BT25 29
Brook Ho. Gdns. E4 CG28 40
Brookhowse Rd. SE6 CE48 77
Brookhurst Rd. Wey. AW57 92
Brookland Clo. NW11 BS31 47
Brookland Rise
Brookland Garth NW11 BS31 47
Brookland Hl. NW11 BS31 47
Brookland Ri. NW11 BS31 47
Brooklands App. Rom. CS31 50
Brooklands Av. SW19 BS48 76
Brooklands Av. Sid. CM48 78
Brooklands Clo. Rom. CS31 50
Brooklands Clo. Sun. BB51 83
Brooklands Dr. Wem. BK37 54
Brooklands Gdns. Horn. CV34 51
Brooklands Gdns. Pot. B. BR19 19
Brooklands La. Rom. CS31 50
Brooklands La. Wey. AZ56 92
Brooklands Pk. SE3 CH45 68
Brooklands Rd. Rom. CS31 50
Brooklands Rd. Surb. BH54 84
Brooklands Rd. Wey. AZ59 92
Brooklands St. SW8 BW44 66
Brooklands Way, Red. BU69 121
Brook La. SE3 CH44 68
Brook La. Bex. CP46 79
Brook La. Brom. CH50 78
Brook La. Brwd. DB22 33
Brook La. Saw. CP6 6
Brook La. Wok. AO59 91
Brooklane Field. Harl. CO12 14
Brook La. N. Brent. BK42 64
Brooklea Clo. NW9 BO30 37
Brookleys Wok. AP58 91
Brooklyn Av. SE25 CB52 87
Brooklyn Av. Loug. CK24 31
Brooklyn Clo. Wok. AS63 100
Brooklyn Ct. Loug. CK24 31
Brooklyn Gro. SE25 CB52 87
Brooklyn Rd. SE25 CB52 87
Brooklyn Rd. Brom. CJ53 88
Brooklyn Rd. Wok. AS62 100
Brooklyn Way. West Dr. AX41 63
Brookmans Ave. Grays. DE40 71
Brookman's Av. Hat. BR16 19
Brookmans Clo. Upmin. CZ33 51
Brookmead Epsom BO57 94
Brookmead Clo. Orp. CO54 89
Brookmead Rd. Croy. BW53 86
Brookmeads Est. Mitch. BU53 86
Brookmead Way Orp. CO53 89
Brook Ms. NW2 BT40 56
Brook Ms. N. W2 BT40 56
Brookmill Rd. SE8 CE44 67
Brook Parade Chig. CL27 40
Brook Path Loug. CK24 31
Brook Pl. Barn. BS25 29
Brook Rise Chig. CL27 40
Brook Rd. E7 CH35 49
Brook Rd. N8 BX31 47
Brook Rd. N22 BX31 47
Brook Rd. W4 BM43 65
Brook Rd. Borwd. BM23 28
Brook Rd. Brwd. CZ27 42
Brook Rd. Buck. H. CH27 40
Brook Rd Epp. CO20 23
Brook Rd. Grav. DF47 81
Brook Rd. Guil. AU73 118
Brook Rd. Ilf. CN32 49
Brook Rd. Loug. CK24 31
Brook Rd. Red. BU71 121
Brook Rd. Red. BW68 113
Brook Rd. Rom. CT30 41
Brook Rd. Saw. CQ6 6
Brook Rd. Surb. BL55 85
Brook Rd. Swan. CS52 89
Brook Rd. Th. Hth. BZ52 87
Brook Rd. Twick. BJ46 74
Brook Rd. Wal. Cr. CD20 21
Brook Rd. S. Brent. BK43 64
Brooks Av. E6 CK38 58
Brooksbank St. E9 CC36 57
Brooksby's Ms. N1 CB36 57
Brooksby St.
Brooksby St. N1 BY36 56
Brooksby's Wk. E9 CC35 48
Brooks Clo. SE9 CL48 78
Brooks Clo. Wey. AZ58 92
Brookscroft Rd. E17 CE30 39
Brooksfield. Welw. G. C. BS7 5
Brookshill Har. BG28 36
Brookshill Av. Stan. BG28 36
Brookshill Dr. Har. BG28 36
Brookside N21 BX25 29
Brookside Barn. BU25 29
Brookside Cars. BV56 95
Brookside, Cher. AV54 82
Brookside, Guil. AR68 109
Brookside, Hodd. CE12 12
Brookside Horn. CW32 51
Brookside, Ilf. CM29 40
Brookside Orp. CN54 88
Brookside, Pot. B. BP19 19
Brookside. Slou. AU43 62
Brookside, Uxb. AY36 53
Brook Side Wal. Abb. CG19 22
Paternoster Hill
Brookside Ave. Stai. AS45 62
Brookside Av. Ashf. AX49 73
Brookside Clo. Barn. BQ25 28
Brookside Clo. Har. BE35 45
Brookside Clo. Har. BK32 45
Brookside Cres. Hat. BN12 10
Brookside Cres. Pot. B. BX17 20
Brookside Cres. Wor. Pk. BP54 85
Green La.
Brookside Gdns. Enf. CB22 30
Brookside Rd. N9 CB28 39
Brookside Rd. N19 BW34 47
Brookside Rd. Borwd. BL22 28
Brookside Rd. Borwd. BL23 28
Brookside Rd. Grav. DF50 81
Brookside Rd. Hayes BD40 54
Brookside S. Barn. BV26 38
Brookside Wk. N3 BR29 37
Brookside Way Croy. CC53 87
Brook's Ms. W1 BV40 56
Brook's Rd. E13 CH37 58
Brook St. N17 CA30 39
High Rd.
Brook St. W1 BV40 56
Brook St. W2 BT40 56
Brook St. Belv. CR42 69
Brook St. Brwd. CY28 42
Brook St. Kings. On T. BL51 85
Brook St. Wind. AO44 61
Brooksville Av. NW6 BR37 55
Brooks Way Orp. CP51 89
Brookvale Erith CR44 69
Brookvale Rd. SW6 BR43 65
Brookview Rd. SW16 BV49 76
Brook Wk. Edg. BN29 37
Brook Wk. Guil. AR69 118
Brook Way, SE3 CH45 68
Brook Way Chig. CL27 40
Brook Way, Lthd. BJ62 102
Brook Way. Rain. CU39 59
Brookwood Av. SW13 BO44 65
Brookwood Rd. SW18 BR47 75
Brookwood Rd. Houns. BF44 64
Broom Av. Orp. CO51 89
Broom Clo. Brom. CK53 88
Broom Clo. Esher BF56 93
Broom Clo. Hat. BO14 10
Broom Clo. Tedd. BK50 74
Broom Ct. Rich. BM44 65
Lichfield Rd.
Broomcroft Av. Nthlt. BD38 54
Broome Clo. Epsom BN66 112
Broome Rd. Hamptn. BE50 74
Broome Way, SE5 BZ43 67
Broomfield E17 CS33 50
Alexandra Rd.
Broomfield, Guil. AP70 118
Broomfield, Harl. CO9 6
Broomfield, St. Alb. BG17 18
Broomfield Sun. BC51 83
Broomfield Ave. Sev. CT64 107
Broomfield Av. N13 BX28 38
Broomfield Av. Loug. CK25 31
Broomfield Ct, Wey. AZ57 92
Broomfield La. N13 BX28 38
Broomfield Pk. Dor. BG72 119
Broomfield Pl. W13 BJ40 54
Mattock La.
Broomfield Ride. Lthd. BG60 93
Broomfield Rd. N13 BX28 38
Broomfield Rd. W13 BJ40 54
Broomfield Rd. Beck. CD52 87
Broomfield Rd. Bexh. CR46 79
Broomfield Rd. Brom. CJ53 88
Broomfield Rd. Guil. AP69 118
Broomfield Rd. Rich. BL44 65
Broomfield Rd. Rom. CP33 50
Broomfield Rd. Surb. BL54 85
Broomfield Rd. Swans. DC46 81
Broomfield Rd. Tedd. BK50 74
Melbourne Rd.
Broomfield Rd. Wey. AW59 92
Broomfield St. E14 CE39 57
Broom Gdns. Croy. CE55 87
Broom Gro. Wat. BC22 26
Broomgrove Gdns. Edg. BM30 37
Broomgrove Rd. SW9 BX44 66
Stockwell Rd.
Broom Hall. Lthd. BG60 93
Broom Hall Dr. Lthd. BG60 93
Broomhall End Wok. AS61 100
Broomhall La.
Broomhall La. Wok. AS61 100
Broomhall Rd. Sth. Croy. BZ58 96
Broomhall Rd. Wok. AS61 100
Broom Hill, Hem. H. AV14 7
Broom Hill, Slou. AQ36 52
Broom Hill Ct. Wdf. Grn. CH29 40
Broomhill Rise, Bexh. CR46 79
Broomhill Rd. SW18 BS46 76
Broomhill Rd. Dart. CU46 79
Broomhill Rd. Ilf. CO34 50
Broomhill Rd. Orp. CO54 89
Broomhill Rd. Wdf. Grn. CH29 40
Broomhills, Grav. DC49 81
Broomhills. Welw. G. C. BS7 5
Broomhouse Gdns. E4 CG28 40
Abbotts Cres.
Broomhouse La. SW6 BS44 66
Broomhouse Rd. SW6 BS44 66
Broomhurst Ct. Dor. BJ72 119
Ridgeway Rd.
Broomlands La. Oxt. CJ65 106
Broomlands La. Oxt. CJ66 115
Broom Leys, St. Alb. BK12 9
Broomloan La. Sutt. BS55 86
Broom Lock, Tedd. BK50 74
Broom Water
Broom Mead Bexh. CR46 79
Broom Pk, Tedd. BK50 74
Broom Rd. Croy. CE55 87
Broom Rd. Tedd. BJ49 74
Brooms Clo. Welw. G. C. BQ6 5
Broomsleigh St. NW6 BR35 46
Broomstick Hall Rd. Wal. Abb. CG20 22
Broomstick La. Chesh. AQ18 16
Broom Water, Tedd. BK50 74
Broom Water W. Tedd. BK49 74
Broom Way. Wey. BB56 92
Broomwood Gdns. Brwd. DA25 33
Broomwood Rd. SW11 BU46 76
Broomwood Rd. Orp. CO51 89
Broseley Gdns. Rom. CW28 42
Broseley Gro. SE26 CD49 77
Broseley Rd. Rom. CW28 42
Brott St. E1 CC38 57
Mantus Rd.
Brougham Rd. E8 CB37 57
Brougham Rd. W3 BN39 55
Broughinge Rd. Borwd. BM23 28
Brough St. SW8 BX43 66
Broughton Av. N3 BR31 46
Broughton Av. Rich. BK48 74
Broughton Ct. W13 BJ40 54
Broughton Rd.
Broughton Gdns. N6 BW32 47
Broughton Hall Ave. Wok. AV66 109
Broughton Rd. SW6 BS44 66
Broughton Rd. W13 BJ40 54
Broughton Rd. Orp. CM55 88
Broughton Rd. Sev. CU61 107
Broughton Rd. Th. Hth. BY53 86
Broughton St. SW8 BV44 66
Brouncker Rd. W3 BN41 65
Brow Clo. Orp. CP54 89
Brow Cres. Orp. CP54 89
Browells La. Felt. BC48 73
Brown Clo. Til. DG45 71
Brown Clo. Wall. BX57 95
Browne Clo. Rom. CR28 41
Brownfield Est. E14 CF39 57
Brown Fields. Welw. G. C. BR7 5
Brownfield St. E14 CF39 57
Browngraves Rd. Hayes. BA43 63
Brown Hart Gdns. W1 BV40 56
Brownhill Rd. SE6 CE47 77
Browning Av. W7 BH39 54
Browning Av. Sutt. BU56 95
Browning Av. Wor. Pk. BP54 85
Browning Clo. W9 BT38 56
Randolph Av.
Browning Clo. Hamptn. BE49 74
Browning Clo. Well. CN44 68
Browning Est. SE17 BZ42 67
Browning Ho. W12 BQ39 55
Browning Ms. W1 BV39 56
New Cavendish St.
Browning Rd. E11 CG33 49
Browning Rd. E12 CK36 58
Browning Rd. Dart. CX45 70
Browning Rd. Enf. BZ22 30
Browning Rd. Enf. BZ23 30
Browning Rd. Lthd. BG66 111
Browning St. SE17 BZ42 67
Browning Wk. Til. DH44 71
Coleridge Rd.
Browning Way Houns. BD44 64
Brownlea Gdns. Ilf. CO34 50
Brownlow Ms. WC1 BX38 56
Brownlow Rd. E7 CH35 49
Brownlow Rd. E8 CA37 57
Brownlow Rd. N3 BS29 38
Brownlow Rd. N11 BW29 38
Brownlow Rd. NW10 BO36 55
Brownlow Rd. W13 BJ40 54
Brownlow Rd. Berk. AR12 7
Brownlow Rd. Borwd. BM24 28
Brownlow Rd. Croy. CA56 96
Brownlow Rd. Red. BU70 121
Brownlow St. WC1 BX39 56
Brownrigg Rd. Ashf. AZ49 73
Brown Rd. Grav. DJ47 81
Browns La. Lthd. BD67 111
Brownspring Dr. SE9 CL49 78
Browns Rd. E17 CE31 48
Brown's Rd. Surb. BL54 85
Brown St. W1 BU39 56
Brownswell Rd. N2 BT30 38
Oak La.
Brownswood Rd. N4 BY34 47
Brow, The, Wat. BC19 17
Broxash Rd. SW11 BV46 76
Broxbourne Av. E18 CH31 49
Broxbourne Rd. E7 CH34 49
Broxbourne Rd. Orp. CN54 88
Broxburn Dr. S. Ock. DA39 60
Broxburn Dr. S. Ock. DA40 60
Broxhill Rd. Hav. CT27 41
Broxholm Rd. SE27 BY48 76
Brox La. Cher. AU57 91
Brox Rd. Cher. AU57 91
Broxted Rd. SE6 CD48 77
Broxwood Way, NW3 BU37 56
Bruce Ave. Horn. CV34 51
Bruce Av. Horn. CV34 51
Bruce Av. Shep. BA53 83
Bruce Castle Rd. N17 CA30 39
Bruce Clo. Well. CO44 69
Bruce Clo. Wey. AY60 92
Bruce Dr. Sth. Croy. CC58 96
Bruce Gro. N17 CA30 39
Bruce Gro. Orp. CO54 89
Bruce Gro. Wat. BD22 27
Bruce Rd. E3 CE38 57
Bruce Rd. NW10 BN36 55
Bruce Rd. SE25 BZ52 87
Bruce Rd. Barn. BR24 28
Bruce Rd. Har. BH30 36
Bruce Rd. Mitch. BV50 76
Bruce Way, Wal. Cr. CC20 21
Brucket Rd. Welw. G. C. BN7 5
Brudenell Rd. SW17 BU48 76
Bruffs Meadow Nthlt. BD36 54
Brumfield Rd. Epsom BN56 94
Brummel Clo. Bexh. CR45 69
Brumwill Rd. W5 BL37 55
Brundall Clo. Hem. H. AX14 8
Brunel Clo. Nthlt. BE38 54
Brunel Clo. Til. DG45 71
Brunel Pl. Houns. BF39 54
Brunel Rd. SE16 CC41 67
Brunel Rd. W3 BO39 55
Brunel Rd. Wdf. Grn. CK28 40
Brunel St. E16 CG39 58
Brunel Way N15 CA31 48
Brune St. E1 CA39 57
Brunner Clo. NW11 BS32 47
Brunner Rd. E17 CD32 48
Brunner Rd. W5 BK38 54
Brunswick Av. N11 BV27 38
Brunswick Av. Upmin. CZ33 51
Brunswick Cent. WC1 BX38 56
Brunswick Clo. EC1 BY38 56
Brunswick Clo. Bexh. CP45 69
Brunswick Rd.
Brunswick Clo. Pnr. BE32 45
Brunswick Clo. Surb. BH54 84
Brunswick Ct. SE1 CA41 67
Brunswick Ct. Walt. BD55 84
Brunswick Cres. N11 BV27 38
Brunswick Gdns. W5 BL38 55
Brunswick Gdns. W8 BS40 56
Brunswick Gdns. Ilf. CM29 40
Brunswick Gro. N11 BV27 38
Brunswick Ms. W1 BU39 56
Gt. Cumberland Pl.
Brunswick Pk. SE5 BZ44 67
Brunswick Pk. Gdns. N11 BV27 38
Brunswick Pk. Rd. N11 BV27 38
Brunswick Pl. N1 BZ38 57
Brunswick Pl. SE19 CB50 77
Brunswick Pl. Grav. DH47 81
Brunswick Rd. E10 CF33 48
Brunswick Rd. N15 CA31 48
Brunswick Rd. W5 BK38 54
Brunswick Rd. Bexh. CP45 69
Brunswick Rd. Kings. On T. BM51 85
Brunswick Rd. Sutt. BS56 95
Brunswick Sq. N17 CA29 39
Brunswick Sq. WC1 BX38 56
Brunswick St. E17 CF32 48
Brunswick Ter. Wind. AO44 61
Brunswick Vil. SE5 CA44 67
Brunton Pl. E14 CD39 57
Brushfield St. E1 CA39 57
Brushwood Dri. Rick. AU24 25
Brussels Rd. SW11 BT45 66
Bruton Clo. Chis. CK50 78
Bullerswood Dr.
Bruton La. W1 BV40 56
Bruton Pl. W1 BV40 56
Bruton Rd. Mord. BT52 86
Bruton St. W1 BV40 56
Bruton Way W13 BJ39 54
Bryan Av. NW10 BP36 55
Bryan Clo. Sun. BC50 73
Bryan Rd. SE16 CD41 67
Bryanston Av. Twick. BF47 74
Bryanston Clo. Sthl. BE42 64
Bryanstone Av. Guil. AQ69 118
Bryanstone Clo. Guil. AP69 118
Bryanstone Ms. W, W1 BU39 56
Bryanstone Pl. W1 BU39 56
Bryanstone Rd. N8 BW32 47
Bryan Stone Rd. Guil. AP68 109
Bryanstone Sq. W1 BU39 56
Bryanstone St. W1 BU39 56
Bryanston Rd. Til. DH44 71
Bryant Av. Rom. CV30 42
Bryant Av. Slou. AO37 52
Bryant Rd. Nthlt. BD38 54
Bryant St. E15 CF36 57
Bryantwood Rd. N7 BY35 47
Brycedale Cres. N14 BW28 38
Bryce Rd. Dag. CP35 50
Bryden Clo. SE26 CD49 77
Bryden Gro. SE26 CD49 77
Brydges Rd. E15 CF35 48
Bryer Pl. Wind. AL45 61
Bryett Rd. N7 BX34 47
Tollington Way
Brymer Rd. SE5 CA43 67
Brympton Clo. Dor. BJ72 119
Brynford Clo. Wok. AS61 100
Brynmaer Rd. SW11 BU44 66
Brynmawr Rd. Enf. CA24 30
Bryony Clo. Uxb. AY39 53
Bryony Rd. W12 BP40 55
Bryony Rd. Guil. AT69 118
Bubblestone Rd. Sev. CU61 107
Buccleuch Cotts. E5 CB33 48
Buccleuch Rd. Slou. AQ43 62
Buccleuch Ter. E5 CB33 48
Buchanan Clo. S. Ock. CW40 60
Buchanan Gdns. NW10 BP37 55
Buchan Rd. SE15 CC45 67
Bucharest Rd. SW18 BT47 76
Buckbean Path Rom. CV29 42
Buckbean Pth. Rom. CV29 42
Buck Clo. Horn. CV32 51
Buckden Clo. SE12 CG46 78
Upwood Rd.
Buckenham St. SE1 BZ41 67
Old Kent Rd.
Buckettsland Borwd. BN22 28
Buckfast Rd. Mord. BS52 86
Buckfast St. E2 CB38 57
Buckham Thorns Rd. West. CM66 115
Buckhold Rd. SW18 BS46 76
Buckhurst Av. Cars. BU54 86
Buckhurst Av. Sev. CV66 117
Buckhurst Clo. Red. BU69 121
Buckhurst La. Sev. CV66 117
Buckhurst Rd. West. CL64 106
Buckhurst St. E1 CB38 57
Buckhurst Way Buck. H. CJ28 40
Buckingham Av. N20 BT26 38
Buckingham Av. E. Mol. BF52 84
Buckingham Av. Felt. BC46 73
Buckingham Av. Grnf. BJ37 54
Buckingham Av. Th. Hth. BY51 86
Buckingham Av. Well. CN45 68
Buckingham Clo. Enf. CA23 30
Buckingham Clo. Guil. AS70 118
Buckingham Clo. Hamptn. BE49 74
Buckingham Clo. Horn. CV32 51
Woodlands Av.
Buckingham Clo. Orp. CN54 88
Buckingham Ct. NW4 BP30 37
Buckingham Ct. Amer. AP22 25
Buckingham Gdns. E. Mol. BF51 84
Buckingham Gdns. Edg. BL29 37
Buckingham Gdns. Th. Hth. BY51 86
Buckingham Gate, SW1 BW41 66
Buckingham Hill Rd. S. Le H. DK41 71
Buckingham Ms. NW6 BS35 47
West End La.
Buckingham Ms. NW10 BO37 55
Buckingham Rd.
Buckingham Palace Rd. SW1 BV42 66
Buckingham Pl. SW1 BW41 66
Palace St.
Buckingham Rd. E10 CE34 48
Buckingham Rd. E11 CJ32 49
Buckingham Rd. E15 CG35 49
Buckingham Rd. E18 CG30 40
Buckingham Rd. N1 CA36 57
Buckingham Rd. N22 BX30 38
Buckingham Rd. NW10 BO37 55
Buckingham Rd. Borwd. BN24 28
Buckingham Rd. Edg. BL29 37
Buckingham Rd. Hamptn. BE49 74
Buckingham Rd. Har. BG32 45
Buckingham Rd. Ilf. CM34 49
Buckingham Rd. Kings. On T. BL52 85
Buckingham Rd. Mitch. BX53 86
Buckingham Rd. Rich. BK48 74
Buckingham Rd. Wat. BD22 27
Buckingham St. WC2 BX40 56
Watergate Wk.
Buckingham Ter. Sthl. BF41 64
Buckingham Way Wall. BW58 95
Buckland Ave. Slou. AQ42 62
Buckland Cres. NW3 BT36 56
Buckland Cres. Wind. AM44 61
Buckland La. Bet. BP68 112
Buckland La. Tad. BO68 112
Buckland Rise Pnr. BD30 36
Buckland Rd. E10 CF34 48
Buckland Rd. Chess. BL56 94
Buckland Rd. Orp. CN56 97
Buckland Rd. Reig. BQ70 120
Buckland Rd. Sutt. BQ58 94
Buckland Rd. Tad. BR67 112
Bucklands Rd. Tedd. BK50 74
Buckland St. N1 BZ37 57
Buckland Wk. Mord. BT53 86
Buckland Way Wor. Pk. BQ54 85
Buck La. NW9 BN32 46
Buckleigh Av. SW20 BR52 85
Buckleigh Rd. SW16 BW50 76
Buckleigh Way, SE19 CA50 77
Buckler Gdns. SE9 CK49 78
Bucklers All. SW6 BR43 65
Haldane Rd.
Bucklersbury, EC4 BZ39 57
Walbrook
Bucklers Clo. Brox. CD14 12
Buckles La. S. Ock. DB39 60
Buckle St. E1 CA39 57
Buckles Way Bans. BR61 103
Buckley Rd. NW6 BR36 55
Buckmaster Rd. SW11 BU45 66

Bucknalls Dr. St. Alb. BE19 18
Bucknalls La. Wat. BD19 18
Bucknall St. WC2 BW39 56
Buckner Rd. SW2 BX45 66
Buckner St. W10 BR38 55
Bucknills Clo. BN61 103
Bucknills Clo. Epsom BN60 94
Buckrell Rd. E4 CF27 39
Buck Rd. Grav. DE47 81
Bucks Alley. Hert. BW12 11
Bucks Av. Wat. BE26 36
Bucks Clo. Wey. AW60 92
Buckscross Rd. Grav. DF48 81
Bucks Cross Rd. Orp. CQ56 98
Buckshaw Rd. N18 CB29 39
Bucks Hill, Kings L. AX20 17
Bucks Hill, Kings L. AX21 26
Bucks Hill Rd. Kings L. AW19 17
Buckstone Clo. SE23 CC46 77
Buckstone Rd. N18 CB29 39
Buck St NW1 BV36 56
Camden High St.
Buckthorne Rd. SE4 CD46 77
Buckton Rd. Borwd. BL22 28
Buck Wk. E17 CF31 48
Bud Croft. Welw. G. C. BS7 5
Buddings Circ. Wem. BN34 46
Budd's All. Twick. BK46 74
Arlington Clo
Budebury Rd. Stai. AW49 73
Budge Row EC4 BZ40 57
Cannon St.
Budgins Hill. Orp. CO59 98
Budleigh Cres. Well. CP43 69
Budoch Dr. Ilf. CO34 50
Buer Rd. SW6 BR44 65
Buff Av. Bans. BS60 95
Buford St. Hodd. CE12 12
Bug Hill, Warl. CC63 105
Bugsby's Way, SE7 CH42 68
Bukfield Clo. Hat. BP11 10
Wellfield Rd.
Bulbourne Clo. Berk. AP12 7
Bulbourne Clo. Hem. H. AW14 8
Bulganak Rd. Th. Hth. BZ52 87
Bulinga St. SW1 BX42 66
Bulingford Clo. SE4 CD45 67
Frendsbury Rd.
Bulkeley Ave. Wind. AN44 61
Bullace Clo. Hem. H. AW13 8
Bullace La. Dart. CW46 80
Bullace Row, SE5 BZ44 67
Camberwell Rd.
Bull All. Well. CO45 69
Bullard's Pl. E2 CC38 57
Bullbanks Rd. Belv. CS42 69
Bullbeggars La. Wok. AQ61 100
Bullbeggars Rd. Gdse. CC69 114
Bullcross Ride, Wal. Cr. CB20 21
Bullen's Green La. St. Alb. BO15 10
Bullen St. SW11 BU44 66
Buller Rd. N17 CB30 39
Buller Rd. NW10 BQ38 55
Buller Rd. Bark. CN36 58
Buller Rd. Th. Hth. BZ51 87
Bullers Clo. Sid. CQ49 79
Buller Sq. SE15 CB43 67
Bullers Rd. N22 BY30 38
Bullerswood Dr. Chis. CK50 78
Bullescroft Rd. Edg. BM27 37
Bullfields, Saw. CQ5 6
Bullfinch Clo. Sev. CS64 107
Bullfinch Dene Sev. CS64 107
Bullfinch Clo.
Bullfinch La. Sev. CS64 107
Bullfinch Rd. Croy. CC59 96
Bullfinch Rd. Sth. Croy. CC58 96
Bullfinch Rd. Sth. Croy. CC58 96
Bullhead Rd. Borwd. BN23 28
Bull Hill, Lthd. BJ64 102
Bull Inn Ct. WC2 BX40 56
Strand
Bullivant St. E14 CF39 57
Bull La. N18 CA28 39
Bull La. Chis. CM50 78
Bull La. Dag. CR34 50
Bull La. Ger. Cr. AR31 43
Bull Rd. E15 CG37 58
Bullrush Cl. Hat. BP13 10
Bull's Alley SW14 BN44 65
Bullsbrook Rd. Hayes BD40 54
Bull's Cross, Enf. CB22 30
Bull's Cross Ride, Wal. Cr. CB21 30
Bulls Gdns. SW3 BU42 66
Walton St.
Bulls Head Pass. EC3 CA39 57
Gracechurch St.
Bullsland Gdns. Rick. AT25 25
Bull's La. Hat. BQ15 10
Bullsmoor Clo. Wal. Cr. CC21 30
Bullsmoor Gdns. Wal. Cr. CB21 30
Bullsmoor La. Enf. CB21 30
Bullsmoor Ride, Wal. Cr. CC21 30
Bullsmoor Way. Wal. Cr. CB21 30
Bull Stag Grn. Hat. BQ11 10
Gt. Nth. Rd.
Bull Wharf La. EC4 BZ40 57
Bull Yd. N15 CA31 48
Stamford Hill High Rd.
Bulmer Gdns. Har. BK33 45
Bulmer Ms. W11 BS40 56
Kensington Pk. Rd.
Bulmer Pl. W11 BS40 56
Bulmer Wk. Rain. CV37 60
Bulow Ct. SW6 BS44 66
Bulstrode Av. Houns. BE44 64
Bulstrode Gdns. Houns. BF45 64
Bulstrode La. Kings L. AV18 16
Bulstrode Pl. W1 BV39 56
Bulstrode Rd. Houns. BF45 64
Bulstrode St. W1 BV40 56
Bulstrode Way. Ger. Cr. AR32 43
Bulwell Cres. Wal. Cr. CD18 21
Bulwer Ct. Rd. E11 CF33 48
Bulwer Gdns. Barn. BT24 29
Bulwer Rd. E11 CF33 48
Bulwer Rd. N18 CA28 39
Bulwer Rd. Barn. BS24 29
Bulwer St. W12 BQ40 55
Bunby Rd. Slou. AP36 52
Bunce Comm. Rd. Reig. BN74 120
Buncefield La. Hem. H. AZ12 8
Bunces La. Wdf. Grn. CG29 40
Bundy's Way, Stai. AV50 72
Bungalow Rd. SE25 CA52 87
Bungalow Rd. Wok. AZ65 101
Bungalows, The, SW16 BV50 76
Bungalows, The, Bush. BE24 27
Bunhill Row, EC1 BZ38 57
Bunkers Hill, NW11 BT33 47
Bunkers Hill Belv. CR42 69
Bunkers Hill, Sid. CQ48 79
Bunker, S La. Hem. H. AZ16 17
Bunns La. NW7 BQ29 37
Bunsen St. E3 CD37 57
Kenilworth Rd.
Buntingbridge Rd. Ilf. CM32 49
Bunting Clo. Mitch. BU53 86
Bunton St. SE18 CL41 68
Bunyan Rd. E17 BW31 47
Bunyan's La. Wok. AO60 91
Bunyard Dri. Wok. AU60 91
Burbage Clo. Wal. Cr. CD19 21
Burbage Rd. SE21 BZ46 77
Burbage Rd. SE24 BZ46 77
Burberry Clo. N. Mal. BO51 85
Burbridge Rd. Shep. AZ52 83
Burbridge Way N17 CA30 39
Burcham St. E14 CE39 57
Burcharbro Rd. SE2 CP43 69
Burchell Ct. Bush. BG26 36
Burchell Rd. E10 CE33 48
Burchell Rd. SE15 CB44 67
Burchetts Way, Shep. AZ53 83
Burchett Way, Rom. CQ32 50
Burch Rd. Grav. DF46 81
Burchwall Clo. Rom. CS29 41
Burcote Rd. SW18 BT47 76
Burcote, Wey. BA57 92
Burcott Gdns. Wey. AX57 92
Burcott Rd. Pur. BY60 95
Burdenshot Hill, Guil. AQ65 100
Burdenshott Av. Rich. BM45 65
Burden Way, E11 CH34 49
Burden Way, Guil. AQ68 109
Burder Rd. N1 CA36 57
Burdett Av. SW20 BP51 85
Burdett Clo. Sid. CQ49 79
Burdett Est. E14 CE39 57
Burdett Rd. E3 CD38 57
Burdett Rd. E14 CD38 57
Burdett Rd. Croy. BZ53 87
Burdett Rd. Rich. BL44 65
Burdett St. SE1 BY41 66
Pearman St.
Burdon La. Sutt. BR57 94
Burdon Pk. Sutt. BR58 94
Burfield Clo. SW17 BT49 76
Burfield Rd. Wind. AQ46 72
Burford Clo. Dag. CP34 50
Bennetts Castle La.
Burford Clo. Ilf. CM31 49
Burford Clo. Uxb. AY35 44
Burford Gdns. N13 BX27 38
Burford La. Epsom BQ59 94
Burford Rd. E6 CK38 58
Burford Rd. E15 CF36 57
Burford Rd. SE6 CD48 77
Burford Rd. Brent. BL42 65
Burford Rd. Brom. CK52 88
Burford Rd. Sutt. BS55 86
Burford Rd. Wor. Pk. BO54 85
Burford Way Croy. CF57 96
Burgandy Croft. Welw. G. C. BR9 5
Burges Clo. Horn. CW32 51
Ernest Rd.
Burges Rd. E6 CK36 58
Burgess Av. NW9 BN32 46
Burgess Cotts. Belv. CR41 69
Burgess Hl. NW2 BS35 47
Burgess Rd. E15 CG35 49
Burgess Rd. Sutt. BS56 95
Burgess St. E14 CE39 57
Burge St. SE1 BZ41 67
Burgett Rd. Slou. AN41 61
Burghfield Epsom BO61 103
Burghfield Rd. Grav. DF50 81
Burgh Heath Rd. Epsom. BO60 94
Burghill Rd. SE26 CC49 77
Burghley Av. Borwd. BN25 28
Burghley Av. N. Mal. BN51 85
Burghley Gdns. Ilf. CO29 41
Burghley Rd. E11 CG33 49
Burghley Rd. N8 BY31 47
Burghley Rd. NW5 BV35 47
Burghley Rd. SW19 BQ49 75
Burgh Mt. Bans. BR61 103
Burgh St. N1 BY37 56
Burgh Wd. Bans. BR61 103
Burgon St. EC4 BY39 56
Carter La.
Burgos Gro. SE10 CE44 67
Burgoyne Hatch, Harl. CO10 6
Burgoyne Rd. N4 BY32 47
Burgoyne Rd. SE25 CA52 87
Burgoyne Rd. SW9 BX45 66
Burgoyne Rd. Sun. BB50 73
Burgundy St. SE1 CA42 67
Burham Clo. SE20 CC50 77
Blenheim Rd.
Burhill Gro. Pnr. BE30 36
Burhill Rd. Walt. BC58 92
Burke St. E16 CG39 58
Burland Rd. SW11 BU46 76
Burland Rd. Brwd. DB26 42
Burland Rd. Rom. CS29 41
Burlea Clo. Walt. BC56 92
Burleigh Av. Sid. CN46 78
Burleigh Av. Wall. BV55 86
Burleigh Clo. Wey. AW56 92
Burleigh Gdns. N14 BW26 38
Burleigh Gdns. Ashf. BA49 73
Burleigh Pl. Mitch. BU53 86
Burleigh Rd. Enf. CA24 30
Burleigh Rd. Hem. H. BA14 8
Burleigh Rd. St. Alb. BJ13 9
Burleigh Rd. Sutt. BR54 85
Burleigh Rd. Uxb. AZ37 53
Burleigh Rd. Wey. AW56 92
Burleigh St. WC2 BX40 56
Tavistock St.
Burleigh Way Enf. BZ24 30
Burleigh Way, Pot. B. BX18 20
Burley Clo. E4 CE28 39
Burley Clo. SW16 BW51 86
Burley Rd. E16 CJ39 58
Burliegh Mead Hat. BQ11 10
Gt. Nth. Rd.
Burlings La. Sev. CN62 106
Burlington Arcade, W1 BW40 56
Burlington Gdns.
Burlington Ave. Slou. AR41 62
Burlington Av. Rich. BM44 65
Burlington Av. Rom. CS32 50
Burlington Clo. Felt. BA47 73
Burlington Gdns. W1 BW40 56
Burlington Gdns. W3 BN40 55
Burlington Gdns. W4 BN42 65
Burlington Gdns. Rom. CQ33 50
Burlington La. W4 BN43 65
Burlington Ms. W3 BO40 55
Burlington Gdns.
Burlington Ms. E. W2 BS39 56
Shrewsbury Rd.
Burlington Ms. W. W2 BS39 56
Ledbury Rd.
Burlington Pl. Wdf. Grn. CH27 40
Burlington Rise Barn. BU26 38
Burlington Rd. N10 BV31 47
Tetherdown
Burlington Rd. N17 CB30 39
Burlington Rd. SW6 BR44 65
Burlington Rd. W4 BN42 65
Burlington Rd. Enf. BZ23 30
Burlington Rd. Islw. BG44 64
Burlington Rd. N. Mal. BO52 85
Burlington Rd. Th. Hth. BZ51 87
Burma Ct. N5 BZ35 48
Green Lanes
Burman St. SE1 BY41 66
Burma Rd. N16 BZ35 48
Burma Rd. Wok. AP53 82
Burmester Rd. SW17 BT48 76
Burnaby Cres. W4 BN43 65
Burnaby Gdns. W4 BM43 65
Burnaby Rd. Grav. DF47 81
Burnaby St. E6 CL40 58
Burnaby St. SW10 BT43 66
Burnard Pl. N7 BX35 47
Burn Brae Clo. N3 BS29 38
Burnbury Rd. SW12 BW47 76
Burn Clo. Wat. BG24 27
Burn Clo. Wey. AX56 92
Burncroft Av. Enf. CC23 30
Burne Jones Ho. W14 BR42 65
Burnell Av. Twick. BK49 74
Burnell Av. Well. CO44 69
Burnell Gdns. Stan. BK30 36
Burnell Rd. Sutt. BS56 95
Burnell Wk. Brwd. DB29 42
Burnels Av. E6 CL38 58
Burnet Av. Guil. AT69 118
Burnet Gro. Epsom BN60 94
Burnett Clo. E9 CC35 48
Churchill Wk.
Burnetts Rd. Wind. AM44 61
Burnett St. SE11 BX42 66
Burney Av. Surb. BL53 85
Burney Clo. Lthd. BG66 111
Burney Dr. Loug. CL23 31
Burney Dr. Loug. CM23 31
Burney Rd. Dor. BJ69 119
Burney St. SE10 CF43 67
Burnfoot Av. SW6 BR44 65
Burnham, Wok. AO62 100
Burnham Av. Uxb. BA35 44
Burnham Clo. E11 CJ31 49
Burnham Clo. Enf. CA22 30
Burnham Clo. Wind. AL44 61
Burnham Clo. Wok. AO62 100
Burnham Ct. NW4 BQ31 46
Burnham Cres. Dart. CV45 70
Burnham Dr. Reig. BS70 121
Burnham Dr. Wor. Pk. BQ55 85
Burnham Gdns. Hayes. BA41 63
Burnham Gdns. Houns. BC44 63
Burnham La. Guil. AT68 109
Burnham Rd. E4 CD28 39
Burnham Rd. Dag. CO36 59
Burnham Rd. Dart. CV45 70
Burnham Rd. Mord. BS53 86
Burnham Rd. Rom. CS31 50
Burnham Rd. St. Alb. BJ13 9
Burnham Rd. Sid. CQ48 79
Burnhams Rd. Lthd. BE65 102
Burnhams Rd. Lthd. BE66 111
Burnham St. E2 CC38 57
Burnham St. Kings. On T. BM51 85
Burnham Way W13 BJ41 64
Burnhill Rd. Beck. CE51 87
Burnley Rd. SW9 BX44 66
Burnsall St. SW3 BU42 66
Burns Av. Felt. BC46 73
Burns Av. Sid. CO46 79
Burns Av. Sthl. BF40 54
Burns Clo. Cob. BG61 102
Burns Clo. Erith CT44 69
Burns Clo. Hayes BB39 53
Burns Clo. Well. CO44 69
Burn Side, N9 CC27 39
Burn Side. Ash. BL62 103
Burnside, Saw. CP6 6
Burnside Cl. Hat. BP11 10
Burnside Clo. Barn. BS24 29
Burnside Clo. Twick. BJ46 74
Burnside Cres. Wem. BK37 54
Burnside Rd. E3 CD38 57
Burnside Rd. Dag. CP34 50
Burnside Ter. Harl. CQ9 6
Burns Pl. Til. DG44 71
Burns Rd. NW10 BO37 55
Burns Rd. SW11 BU44 66
Burns Rd. W13 BJ41 64
Burns Rd. Har. BH31 45
Burns Rd. Wem. BL37 55
Burns Way, Brwd. DE25 122
Burns Way Houns. BD44 64
Burnt Ash Hl. SE12 CG46 78
Burnt Ash La. Brom. CH50 78
Burnt Ash Rd. SE12 CG46 78
Burnt Common Clo. Wok. AV66 109
Burnt Farm Ride, Wal. Cr. BY20 20
Burnt Farm Rd. Enf. BY20 20
Burnthouse La. Dart. CW49 80
Burnthwaite Rd. SW6 BR43 65
Burnt Mill, Harl. CM9 6
Burntmill La. Harl. CM9 6
Burnt Oak, Edg. BM29 37
Burnt Oak La. Sid. CN46 78
Burntwood Av. Horn. CV32 51
Burntwood, Cat. CA64 105
Burntwood Clo. SW18 BU47 76
Burntwood Clo. Brwd. DE32 123
Burntwood Clo. Cat. CB64 105
Burntwood Gra. Rd. SW18 BT47 76
Burntwood La. SW17 BT48 76
Burntwood Rd. Sev. CU67 116
Burnway Horn. CW33 51
Burrage Gro. SE18 CM42 68
Burrage Pl. SE18 CL42 68
Burrage Rd. SE18 CL43 68
Burrard Rd. E16 CH39 58
Burrard Rd. NW6 BS35 47
Burr Clo. Bexh. CQ45 69
Burr Clo. St. Alb. BL17 19
Burrell Clo. Edg. BM27 37
Burrell Row, Beck. CE51 87
High St.
Burrell St. SE1 BY40 56
Burrell, The Dor. BG72 119
Burrfield Dr. Orp. CP53 89
Burr Hill La. Wok. AP58 91
Burritt Rd. Kings-on-t. BM51 85
Burroughs Gdns. NW4 BP31 46
Burroughs, The, NW4 BP31 46
Burroway Rd. Slou. AT41 62
Burrow Clo. Chig. CN28 40
Burrow Fld. Welw. G. C. BQ9 5
Burrow Grn. Chig. CN28 40
Burrow Rd. Chig. CN28 40
Burrows Clo. Lthd. BE65 102
Burrows Hill Clo. Houns. AW45 63
Burrows Hill La. Houns. AW45 63
Burrows Ms. SE1 BY41 66
Burrows Rd. NW10 BQ38 55
Burr Rd. SW18 BS47 76
Bursdon Clo. Sid. CN48 78
Burses Way, Brwd. DE25 122
Bursland Rd. Enf. CC24 30
Burslem Av. Ilf. CO29 41
Burslem St. E1 CB39 57
Burstead Clo. Cob. BD59 93
Burstead Gdns. Ilf. CO29 41
Burstock Rd. SW15 BR45 65
Burston Dr. St. Alb. BG17 18
Burston Rd. SW15 BQ45 65
Burstow Rd. SW20 BR51 85
Burtenshaw Rd. Surb. BJ53 84
Burtley Clo. N4 BZ33 48
Burton Av. Wat. BC24 26
Burton Clo. NW7 BQ28 37
Burton Clo. Chess. BK57 93
Burton Ct. SW3 BU42 66
Burton Dr. Loug. CM24 31
Burton Gdns. Houns. BE44 64
Burton Gro. SE17 BZ42 67
Burtonhole La. NW7 BQ28 37
Burton La. Wal. Cr. CA18 21
Burton Pl. WC1 BW38 56
Burton St.
Burton Rd. E18 CH31 49
Burton Rd. NW6 BR36 55
Burton Rd. SW9 BY44 66
Burton Rd. Kings. On T. BL50 75
Burton Rd. Loug. CM24 31
Burtons La. Ch. St. G. AR23 25
Burton, S La. Ch. St. G. AS25 25
Burton's Rd. Hamptn. BF49 74
Burton St. WC1 BW38 56
Burtons Way. Ch. St. G. AR23 25
Burtop Rd. SW17 BT48 76
Burt Rd. E16 CJ40 58
Burwash Rd. SE18 CM42 68
Burwell Av. Grnf. BH36 54
Burwell Clo. E1 CB39 57
Burwell Rd. E10 CD33 48
Burwood Av. Brom. CH55 88
Burwood Av. Ken. BY60 95
Burwood Av. Pnr. BC32 44
Burwood Clo. Guil. AU70 118
Burwood Clo. Reig. BT70 121
Burwood Clo. Surb. BM54 85
Burwood Clo. Walt. BD57 93
Burwood Gdns. Rain. CT38 59
Burwood Pk. Rd. Walt. BC56 92
Burwood Pl. W2 BU39 56
Burwood Rd. Watt. BB57 92
Bury Av. Ruis. BA32 44
Bury Clo. Wok. AR61 100
Bury Ct. EC3 CA39 57
Burycroft. Welw. G. C. BR6 5
Burydell La. St. Alb. BG17 18
Buryfields, Guil. AR71 118
Bury Gdns. Hat. BP12 10
Burygreen Rd. Wal. Cr. CB19 21
Bury Gro. Mord. BS53 86
Bury Hall Vill. N9 CA26 39
Bury Hill, Hem. H. AW13 8
Bury Hill Clo. Hem. H. AX13 8
Bury Holme, Brox. CD15 12
Bury La. Epp. CM17 22
Bury La. Rick. AX26 35
Bury La. Wok. AR61 100
Bury Meadows. Rick. AX26 35
Bury Pl. WC1 BX39 56
Bury Rise, Hem. H. AU16 16
Bury Rd. E4 CG25 31
Bury Rd. N22 BY30 38
Bury Rd. Dag. CR35 50
Bury Rd. Epp. CN19 22
Bury Rd. Harl. CP9 6
Bury Rd. Hem. H. AX13 8
Bury St. EC3 CA39 57
Bury St. N9 CA26 39
Bury St. SW1 BW40 56
Bury St. Guil. AR71 118
Bury St. Ruis. BA32 44
Bury St. W. N9 BZ26 39
Bury Wk. SW3 BU42 66
Busby Ms. NW5 BW36 56
Torriano Av.
Busby Pl. NW5 BW36 56
Busby St. E2 CA38 57
Bushberry Rd. E9 CD36 57
Bushbury La. Bet. BM72 120
Bushby Av. Brox. CD14 12
Bush Clo. Ilf. CM32 49
Bush Clo. Wey. AX56 92
Bush Cotts. SW18 BS46 76
Putney Br. Rd.
Bush Ct. N14 BW26 38
Bushell Gro. Bush. BG27 36
Gleed Av.
Bushell St. E1 CB40 57
Hermitage Wall
Bush Elms Rd. Horn. CU33 50
Bushetts Gro. Red. BV68 113
Bushey Av. E18 CG31 49
Bushey Av. Orp. CM54 88
Bushey Clo. Uxb. AZ34 44
Bushey Clo. Welw. G. C. BS8 5
Bushey Ct. SW20 BP51 85
Bushey Ct. Kings. On T. BK50 74
Bushey Crof. Harl. CN12 13
Bushey Gro. Rd. Bush. BD24 27
Bushey Hall Rd. Bush. BD24 27
Bushey Hill Enf. BX24 29
Bushey Hill Rd. SE5 CA44 67
Bushey La. Sutt. BS56 95
Bushey Lea Ong. CX18 24
Bushey Lees Sid. CN46 78
Fen Grove
Bushey Ley. Welw. G. C. BS8 5
Busheymill Cres. Wat. BD22 27
Bushey Mill La. Wat. BD22 27
Bushey Pk. Cotts. Tedd. BH50 74
Bushey Pk. Rd. Tedd. BJ50 74
Bushey Rd. E13 CJ37 58
Bushey Rd. N15 CA32 48
Albert Rd.
Bushey Rd. SW20 BP52 85
Bushey Rd. Hayes. BB42 63
Bushey Rd. Sutt. BS56 95
Bushey Rd. Uxb. AZ34 44
Bushey Way Beck. CF53 87
Bush Fair. Harl. CN12 13
Bushfield Clo. Edg. BM27 37
Bushfield Cres. Edg. BM27 37
Bushfield Dr. Red. BV73 121
Bushfield Rd. Hem. H. AU16 16
Bushfields Loug. CL25 31
Bush Gro. NW9 BN33 46
Bush Gro. Stan. BK29 36
Bushgrove Rd. Dag. CP35 50
Bush Hill N21 BZ26 39
Bush Hill Rd. N21 BZ25 30
Bush Hill Rd. Har. BL32 46
Bush La. EC4 BZ40 57
Bushmoor Cres. SE18 CL43 68
Bushnell Rd. SW17 BV48 76
Bush Rd. E11 CG33 49
Bush Rd. SE8 CC42 67
Bush Rd. Buck. H. CJ28 40
Bush Rd., Buck. Hill, CJ28 40
Bush Rd. Rich. BL43 65
Bush Rd. Shep. AY53 83
Bushway, Dag. CP35 50
Bushwood E11 CG33 49
Bushwood Rd. Rich. BM43 65
Bushy Hill Dr. Guil. AT69 118
Bushy Pk. Gdns. Tedd. BG49 74
Bushy Rd. E13 CJ37 58
Bushy Rd. Lthd. BF65 102
Bushy Rd. Tedd. BH50 74
Busk St. E2 CB37 57
Yorkton St.
Butcher Row, E14 CC40 57
Butcher's Rd. E16 CH39 58
Bute Av. Rich. BL48 75
Bute Ct. Wall. BV56 95
Bute Gdns. W6 BQ42 65
Bute Gdns. Wall. BW56 95
Bute Gdns. W. Wall. BW56 95

Bute Rd. Croy. BY54 86
Bute Rd. Ilf. CL31 49
Bute Rd. Wall. BW56 95
Bute St. SW7 BT42 66
Bute Wk. N1 BZ36 57
Marquess Est.
Buthfield St. W8 BS41 66
Butler Av. Har. BG33 45
Butler Ho. Grays DD43 71
Hawkes Clo.
Butler Pl. Dag. CO35 50
Butler Rd. Har. BG33 45
Butlers Clo. Wind. AL44 61
Butlers Dene Rd. Cat. CD63 105
Butlers Dr. E4 CF22 30
Butler's Pl. New. A. G. DC55 90
Butler St. E2 CC38 57
Digby St.
Butler St. Uxb. AZ38 53
Butter Cross La. Epp. CO18 23
Butterfield La. St. Alb. BH15 9
Butterfields E17 CF32 48
Butterfly La. SE9 CL46 78
Butterfly La. Borwd. BJ24 27
Butterfly Wk. Warl. CC63 105
Butter Hill Wall. BV55 86
Buttermere Gdns. Pur. BZ60 96
Buttermere Rd. SW15 BR46 75
Buttersweet Rise, Saw. CQ6 6
Butterwick W6 BQ42 65
Butterwick Wat. BE21 27
Buttesland St. N1 BZ38 57
Pitfield St.
Buttfield Clo. Dag. CR30 59
Butt Field Vw. St. Alb. BG15 9
Buttlehide. Rick. AU28 34
Buttondene Cres. Brox. CE14 12
Button Meade. Slou. AN40 61
Button St. Swan. CV53 90
Buttsbury Rd. Ilf. CM35 49
Butts Cotts. Felt. BE48 74
Butts Cres. Felt. BF48 74
Butts Farm Est. Felt. BE48 74
Butts Grn. Rd. Horn. CV32 51
Butts Head. Nthwd. BA29 35
Butts Rd. Brom. CG49 78
Butts Rd. Wok. AS62 100
Butt's, The, Brent. BK43 64
Butts, The, Bush. BG26 36
Butts. The, Sev. CU62 107
Butts, The, Sun. BD52 84
Buxted Clo. E8 CA36 57
Richmond Rd.
Buxted Rd. N12 BU28 38
Buxton Ave. Cat. CA64 105
Buxton Clo. St. Alb. BK12 9
Buxton Clo. Wdf. Grn. CJ29 40
Buxton Cres. Sutt. BR56 94
Buxton Dr. E11 CG31 49
Buxton Dr. N. Mal. BN51 85
Buxton Gdns. W3 BM40 55
Buxton La. Cat. BZ63 105
Buxton Path Wat. BD27 36
Buxton Rd. E4 CF26 39
Buxton Rd. E6 CK38 58
Buxton Rd. E15 CG35 49
Buxton Rd. E17 CD31 48
Buxton Rd. NW2 BP36 55
Buxton Rd. SW14 BO45 65
Buxton Rd. Ashf. AX49 73
Buxton Rd. Epp. CN21 31
Buxton Rd. Erith CS43 69
Buxton Rd. Grays. DF41 71
Buxton Rd. Ilf. CN32 49
Buxton Rd. Th. Hth. BY53 86
Buxton Rd. Wal. Abb. CH20 22
Buxton St. E1 CA38 57
Byam St. SW6 BT44 66
Byards Cft. SW16 BW51 86
Bycliffe Ter. Grav. DF47 81
Bycroft Rd. Sthl. BF38 54
Bycroft St. SE20 CC50 77
Parish La.
Bycullah Av. Enf. BY24 29
Bycullah Rd. Enf. BY23 29
Byegrove Rd. SW19 BT50 76
Byers Clo. Pot. B. BT20 20
Bye, The, W3 BO39 55
Bye Ways Twick. BF48 74
Byeways, The, Rick. AY27 35
Byeway, The, SW14 BN45 65
Byeway, The, Epsom BO56 94
Bye Way, The, Har. BH30 36
Byfeld Gdns. SW13 BP44 65
Byfield. Welw. G. C. BR6 5
Byfield Ct. N. Mal. BP52 85
Byfield Rd. Islw. BJ45 64
Byfleet Corner, Wey. AW60 92
Byfleet Rd. Cob. AZ59 92
Byfleet Rd. Wey. AX58 92
Byford Clo. E15 CG36 58
Bygrove Croy. CE57 96
Bygrove St. E14 CE39 57
Byland Clo. N21 BX26 38
Byland Clo. SE2 CO41 69
Finchale Rd.
Bylands, Wok. AT63 100
Byne Rd. SE26 CC50 77
Byne Rd. Cars. BU55 86
Bynes Rd. Sth. Croy. BZ57 96
Byng Dr. Pot. B. BS19 20
Byng Pl. WC1 BW38 56
Byng Rd. Barn. BQ24 28
Byng St. E14 CE41 67
Bynon Av. Bexh. CQ45 69
Byon Clo. SE26 CD49 77
Byrefield Rd. Guil. AP69 118
Byrne Rd. SW12 BV47 76
Byron Av. E12 CK36 58
Byron Av. E18 CG31 49
Byron Av. NW9 BM31 46
Byron Av. Borwd. BM25 28
Byron Av. Couls. BX61 104
Byron Av. Houns. BC44 63
Byron Av. N. Mal. BP52 85
Byron Av. Sutt. BT56 95
Byron Av. Wat. BD23 27
Byron Cl. Walt. BE54 84
Byron Clo. Hamptn. BE49 74
Byron Clo. Wok. AP62 100
Byron Ct. Enf. BY23 29
Byron Ct. Rich. BK49 74
Byron Dr. N2 BT32 47
Byron Gdns. Sutt. BT56 95
Byron Gdns. Til. DH44 71
Byron Hill Rd. Har. BG33 45
Byron Pl. Lthd. BJ64 102
Byron Rd. E10 CE33 48
Byron Rd. E17 CE31 48
Byron Rd. NW2 BP34 46
Byron Rd. NW7 BP28 37
Byron Rd. W5 BL40 55
Byron Rd. Brwd. DE26 122
Byron Rd. Har. BH30 36
Byron Rd. Har. BH32 45
Byron Rd. Sth. Croy. CB58 96
Byron Rd. Wem. BK34 45
Byron Rd. Wey. AY56 92
Byron St. E14 CE39 57
Byron Way, Hayes BB38 53
Byron Way Nthlt. BE38 54
Byron Way. Rom. CV30 42
Byron Way. West Dr. AY42 63
Bysouth Clo. Ilf. CL30 40
By The Wol. Wat. BE27 36
Bythorn St. SW9 BX45 66
Byton Rd. SW17 BU50 76
Byward Av. Felt. BD48 74
Byward St. EC3 CA40 57
Bywater St. SW3 BU42 66
By-ways, The Ash. BK62 102
Byways, The, Surb. BM53 85
Byway, The, Pot. B. BS20 20
Byway, The, Sutt. BT58 95
Bywood Av. Croy. CC53 87
Bywood Clo. Ken. BY61 104
Cabbell St. NW1 BU39 56
Cabell Rd. Guil. AO70 118
Cable St. E1 CB40 57
Cabrera Av. Vir. W. AR53 82
Cabrera Clo. Vir. W. AR53 82
Cabul Rd. SW11 BU44 66
Cacket's La. Sev. CM61 106
Cactus Wk. W12 BO39 55
Du Cane Rd
Cadbury Clo. Sun. BB50 73
Cadbury Rd. SE16 CB41 67
Cadbury Rd. Sun. BB50 73
Caddington Rd. NW2 BR34 46
Cade La. Sev. CV67 117
Cade Rd. SE10 CF44 67
Cader Rd. SW18 BT46 76
Cadet Pl. SE10 CG42 68
Cadiz Rd. Dag. CS36 59
Cadiz St. SE17 BZ42 67
Cadley Ter. SE23 CC48 77
Cadmore La. Wal. Cr. CC17 21
Cadogan Ave. Dart. CY47 80
Cadogan Av. Brwd. DE32 123
Cadogan Clo. Har. BF35 45
Cadogan Clo. Tedd. BH49 74
Cadogan Ct. SW3 BU42 66
Draycott Av.
Cadogan Ct. Sutt. BS57 95
Cadogan Gdns. E18 CH31 49
Cadogan Gdns. N3 BS30 38
Cadogan Gdns. N21 BY25 29
Cadogan Gdns. SW3 BU42 66
Cadogan Gte. SW1 BU42 66
Cadogan La. SW1 BV41 66
Cadogan Pl. SW1 BU41 66
Cadogan Rd. Surb. BK53 84
Cadogan Sq. SW1 BU41 66
Cadogan St. SW3 BU42 66
Cadogan Ter. E9 CD36 57
Cadoxton Av. N15 CA32 48
Cadwallon Rd. SE9 CL48 78
Caedmon Rd. N7 BX35 47
Caenshill Rd. Wey. AZ57 92
Caenswood Hill, Wey. AZ58 92
Caenwood Clo. Wey. AZ57 92
Caen Wood Rd. Ash. BK62 102
Caerleon Clo. Sid. CP49 79
Caerleon Ter. SE2 CO42 69
Caernaravon Clo. Hem. H. AX13 8
Caernarvon Clo, Horn. CX33 51
Caernarvon Clo. Mitch. BX52 86
Caernarvon Dr. Ilf. CL30 40
Caesar St. E2 CA38 57
Caesar's Wk. Mitch. BU53 86
Caesars Way Shep. BA53 83
Green La.
Cage Pond Rd. Rad. BL20 19
Cahir St. E14 CE42 67
Caillard Rd. Wey. AY59 92
Cains La. Felt. BA46 73
Caird St. W10 BR38 55
Cairn Av. W5 BK40 54
Cairndale Clo. Brom. CG50 78
Cairnfield Av. NW2 BO34 46
Cairns Clo. Dart. CV46 80
Cairns Rd. SW11 BU46 76
Cairn Way Stan. BH29 36
Cairo New Rd. Croy. BY55 86
Cairo Rd. E17 CE31 48
Cairo Rd. Croy. BY55 86
Caishowe Rd. Borwd. BM23 28
Caister Park Rd. E15 CG37 58
Caistor Rd. SW12 BV47 76
Caithness Gdns. Sid. CN46 78
Caithness Rd. W14 BQ41 65
Caithness Rd. Mitch. BV50 76
Calabria Rd. N5 BY36 56
Calais St SE5 BY44 66
Calbourne Av. Horn. CU35 50
Calbourne Rd. SW12 BU47 76
Calcott Clo. Brwd. DA26 42
Costead Manor Rd.
Calcot Wk. SE9 CJ49 78
Calcutta Rd. Til. DF44 71
Caldbeck Wal. Abb. CF20 22
Roundhills
Caldbeck Av. Wor. Pk. BP55 85
Caldecote Gdns. Bush. BH26 36
Caldecote La. Bush. BH26 36
Caldecot Rd. SE5 BZ44 67
Caldecot Way, Brox. CD14 12
Calder Av. Grnf. BH37 54
Calder Av. Hat. BS16 20
Calder Clo. Enf. CA24 30
Calder Gdns. Edg. BM31 46
Calderon Pl. W10 BQ39 55
St. Quintin Gdns.
Calderon Rd. E11 CF35 48
Calderville Rd. SW4 BW46 76
Calderwood St. SE18 CL42 68
Caldew St. SE5 BZ43 67
Caldwell Rd. Wat. BD28 36
Caldwell St. SW9 BX43 66
Caldwell Yd. EC4 BZ40 57
Caldy Rd. Belv. CR41 69
Caldy Wk. N1 BZ36 57
Marquess Est.
Caleb St. SE1 BZ41 67
Mint St.
Caledonian Est. N7 BX36 56
Caledonian Rd. N1 BX37 56
Caledonian Rd. N7 BX37 56
Caledonian Rd. W10 BQ39 55
Quintin Gdns.
Caledonia St. N1 BX37 56
Caledon Rd. E6 CK37 58
Caledon Rd. St. Alb. BK16 18
Caledon Rd. Wall. BV56 95
Cale St. SW3 BU42 66
Caletock St. SE10 CG42 68
Lenthorp Rd.
Caletock Way SE10 CG42 68
Glenister Rd.
Calfstock La. S. Onth. CW52 90
Calidore Clo. SW2 BX46 76
California La. Bush. BG26 36
California Rd. N. Mal. BN52 85
Caliph Clo. Grav. DJ49 81
Callander Rd. SE6 CE48 77
Callan Gro. S. Ock. DA40 60
Callard Av. N13 BY28 38
Callcott Rd. NW6 BR36 55
Callcott St. W8 BS40 56
Calley Down Cres. Croy. CF59 96
Callis Rd. E17 CD32 48
Calliston Ct. Hem. H. AY12 8
Callow Hill, Egh. AR51 82
Callow Hill, Vir. W. AR52 82
Callow St. SW3 BT43 66
Calmington Rd. SE5 CA43 67
Calmont Rd. Brom. CF50 77
Calne Av. Ilf. CL30 40
Calonne Rd. SW19 BQ49 75
Calshot Clo. Enf. BY24 29
Calshot St. N1 BX37 56
Calthorpe Gdns. Stan. BL28 37
Calthorpe Gdns. Sutt. BT55 86
Calthorpe St. WC1 BX38 56
Calton Av. SE21 CA46 77
Calton Rd. Barn. BT25 29
Calverley Cres. Dag. CR34 50
Calverley Gdns. Har. BK33 45
Calverley Gro. N19 BW33 47
Calverley Rd. Epsom. BP57 94
Calvert Av. E2 CA38 57
Calvert Clo. Belv. CR42 69
Calvert Clo. Sid. CQ50 79
Calvert Cres. Dor. BJ70 119
Calverton Rd. E6 CL37 58
Calvert Rd. SE10 CG42 68
Calvert Rd. Barn. BQ23 28
Calvert Rd. Dor. BJ70 119
Calvert Road. Leath. BC68 110
Calvert St. NW1 BV37 56
Calvin Clo. Orp. CP52 89
Calvin St. E1 CA38 57
Calydon Rd. SE7 CH42 68
Camac Rd. Twick. BG47 74
Cambalt Rd. SW15 BQ46 75
Camberley Av. SW20 BP51 85
Camberley Av. Enf. CA24 30
Cambert Way SE9 CH45 68
Camberwell Church St. SE5 BZ44 67
Camberwell Glebe SE5 BZ44 67
Camberwell Grn. SE5 BZ44 67
Camberwell Gro. SE5 BZ44 67
Camberwell La. Sev. CQ69 116
Camberwell New Rd. SE5 BY43 66
Camberwell Pass. SE5 BZ44 67
Camberwell Rd.
Camberwell Rd. SE5 BZ43 67
Camberwell Sta. Rd. SE5 BZ44 67
Cambeys Rd. Dag. CR35 50
Camborne Av. W13 BJ41 64
Camborne Rd. SW18 BS47 76
Camborne Rd. Croy. CB54 87
Camborne Rd. Mord. BQ53 85
Camborne Rd. Sid. CP48 79
Camborne Rd. Sutt. BS57 95
Camborne Rd. Well. CN44 68
Camborne Wk. Rich. BK46 74
Petersham Rd
Camborne Way Houns. BF44 64
Camborne Way. Rom. CW29 42
Cambourne Av. N9 CC26 39
Cambourne Av. Rom. CV29 42
Cambray Rd. SW12 BW47 76
Cambray Rd. Orp. CN54 88
Cambria Clo. Houns. BF45 64
Cambria Clo. Sid. CM47 78
Cambria Ct. Felt. BC47 73
Cambria Cres. Grav. DJ49 81
Cambrian Av. Ilf. CN32 49
Cambrian Clo. SE27 BY48 76
Cambrian Gro. Grav. DG47 81
Cambrian Rd. E10 CE33 48
Cambrian Rd. Rich. BL46 75
Cambrian Way, Hem. H. AY12 8
Cambria Rd. SE5 BZ45 67
Cambria St. SW6 BS43 66
Cambridge Av. NW6 BS37 56
Cambridge Av. Grnf. BH35 45
Cambridge Av. N. Mal. BO52 85
Cambridge Av. Rom. CV30 42
Cambridge Av. Well. CN45 68
Cambridge Clo. SW20 BP51 85
Cambridge Clo. Houns. BE45 64
Cambridge Clo. Wal. Cr. CC18 21
Cambridge Clo. West Dr. AX43 63
Cambridge Cotts. Rich. BM43 65
Cambridge Cres. E2 CB37 57
Cambridge Cres. Tedd. BJ49 74
Cambridge Cres. Wat. BD24 27
Cambridge Dr. SE12 CH46 78
Cambridge Dr. Ilf. CN33 49
Cambridge Dr. Pot. B. BQ19 19
Cambridge Dr. Ruis. BD34 45
Cambridge Gdns. N13 BY28 38
Cambridge Gdns. N17 BZ29 39
Great Cambridge Rd.
Cambridge Gdns. N21 BZ26 39
Cambridge Gdns. NW6 BS37 56
Cambridge Gdns. W10 BQ39 55
Cambridge Gdns. Enf. CB23 30
Cambridge Gdns. Grays. DG42 71
Cambridge Gdns. Kings-on-t. BM51 85
Cambridge Gate NW1 BV38 56
Cambridge Gate SE17 BZ43 67
Walworth Rd.
Cambridge Gate Ms. NW1 BV38 56
Albany St.
Cambridge Grn. N9 CA26 39
Cambridge Grn. SE9 CL47 78
Cambridge Gro. SE20 CB51 87
Cambridge Gro. W6 BP42 65
Cambridge Gro. Rd. Kings-on-t. BM52 85
Cambridge Hth Rd. E1 CB39 57
Cambridge Hth Rd. E2 CB39 57
Cambridge Ho. Wind. AO44 61
Ward Royal
Cambridge Ms. SW11 BU44 66
Cambridge Pde. Enf. CB23 30
Cambridge Pk. E11 CH33 49
Cambridge Pk. Twick. BK46 74
Cambridge Pk. Est. Twick. BK46 74
Cambridge Pk. Rd. E11 CG33 49
Cambridge Pl. NW6 BS37 56
Cambridge Pl. W8 BS41 66
Cambridge Pl. W9 BS38 56
Cambridge Rd. E4 CF26 39
Cambridge Rd. E11 CG32 49
Cambridge Rd. NW6 BS38 56
Cambridge Rd. SE20 CB52 87
Cambridge Rd. SW11 BU44 66
Cambridge Rd. SW13 BO44 65
Cambridge Rd. SW20 BP51 85
Cambridge Rd. W7 BH41 64
Cambridge Rd. Ashf. BA50 73
Cambridge Rd. Bark. CM36 58
Cambridge Rd. Brom. CH50 78
Cambridge Rd. Cars. BU57 95
Cambridge Rd. Hamptn. BE50 74
Cambridge Rd. Houns. BE45 64
Cambridge Rd. Ilf. CN33 49
Cambridge Rd. Kings. On T. BL51 85
Cambridge Rd. Mitch. BV52 86
Cambridge Rd. N. Mal. BN52 85
Cambridge Rd. Pnr. BE31 45
Cambridge Rd. Rich. BM43 65
Cambridge Rd. St. Alb. BJ14 9
Cambridge Rd. Saw. CQ5 6
Cambridge Rd. Sid. CN49 78
Cambridge Rd. Sthl. BE40 54
Cambridge Rd. Tedd. BH49 74
Cambridge Rd. Twick. BK46 74
Cambridge Rd. Uxb. AX36 53
Cambridge Rd. Walt. BC53 83
Cambridge Rd. Wat. BD24 27
Cambridge Rd. N. W4 BM42 65
Cambridge Rd. S. W4 BM42 65
Cambridge Row SE18 CL42 68
Cambridge Sq. W2 BU39 56
Cambridge St. SW1 BV42 66
Cambridge Ter. N9 CA26 39
Bury St. W.
Cambridge Ter. N13 BY28 38
Cambridge Ter. NW1 BV38 56
Outer Circle
Cambridge Ter. Berk. AR13 7
Cambridge Ter. Ms. NW1 BV38 56
Albany St.
Cambridge Yd. W7 BH40 54
Cambus Rd. E16 CH39 58
Camdale Rd. SE18 CN43 68
Camden Av. Felt. BD48 74
Camden Av. Hayes. BD40 54
Camden Clo. Chis. CM51 88
Camden Clo. Grays. DG42 71
Camden Gdns. Sutt. BS56 95
Camden Gdns. Th. Hth. BY52 86
Camden Gro. Chis. CL50 78
Camden High St. NW1 BV36 56
Camden Hill Rd. SE19 CA50 77
Camdenhurst St. E14 CD39 57
Camden Ms. N7 BW36 56
Murray St.
Camden Pk. Rd. NW1 BW36 56
Camden Pk. Rd. Chis. CK50 78
Camden Pass. N1 BY37 56
Camden Rd. E11 CH32 49
Camden Rd. E17 CD32 48
Camden Rd. N7 BW36 56
Camden Rd. NW1 BW36 56
Camden Rd. Bex. CQ47 79
Camden Rd. Cars. BU56 95
Camden Rd. Sev. CU64 107
Camden Rd. Sutt. BS56 95
Camden Row SE3 CG44 68
Camden Sq. NW1 BW36 56
Camden Square SE15 CA44 67
Sumner Estate
Camden St. NW1 BW36 56
Camden Ter. NW1 BW36 56
N. Villas
Camden Wk. N1 BY37 56
Camden Way, Chis. CK50 78
Camden Way Th. Hth. BY52 86
Camelia Pl. Twick. BF47 74
Camellia St. SW8 CD43 67
Camelot Clo. SW19 BR49 75
Camelot St. SE15 CB43 67
Camel Rd. E16 CJ40 58
Drew Rd.
Camera Pl. SW10 BT43 66
Cameron Cl. N20 BT27 38
Cameron Clo. N18 CB28 39
Cameron Clo. Bex. CS48 79
Cameron Clo. Brwd. DB28 42
Cameron Dr. Wal. Cr. CC20 21
Cameron Rd. SE6 CD48 77
Cameron Rd. Brom. CH53 88
Cameron Rd. Chesh. AO18 16
Cameron Rd. Croy. BY53 86
Cameron Rd. Ilf. CN33 49
Cameron St. E6 CL40 58
Camfied. Welw. G. C. BR10 5
Cam Grn. S. Ock. DA39 60
Camilla Clo. Lthd. BF66 111
Pine Dene
Camilla Dr. Dor. BJ68 111
Camilla Rd. SE16 CB42 67
Camlan Rd. Brom. CG49 78
Camlet St. E2 CA38 57
Camlet Way Barn. BS23 29
Camlet Way, St. Alb. BF13 9
Camley St. NW1 BW37 56
Camm Gdns. Surb. BH54 84
Camomile Av. Mitch. BU51 86
Camomile St. EC3 CA39 57
Campana Rd. SW6 BS44 66
Campbell Av. Ilf. CL31 49
Campbell Av. Wok. AS64 100
Campbell Cl. Rom. CT29 41
Campbell Clo. Hav. CT29 41
Havering Rd.
Campbell Clo. Ruis. BC32 44
Campbell Clo. Twick. BG47 74
Campbell Ct. NW9 BN32 46
Campbell Croft Edg. BM28 37
Campbell Est. SE18 CK44 68
Campbell Rd. E3 CE38 57
Campbell Rd. E6 CK37 58
Campbell Rd. E17 CD31 48
Campbell Rd. N17 CA30 39
Campbell Rd. W7 BH40 54
Campbell Rd. Cat. BZ64 105
Campbell Rd. Croy. BY54 86
Campbell Rd. E. Mol. BH52 84
Campbell Rd. Grav. DF47 81
Campbell Rd. Twick. BG47 74
Campbell Rd. Wey. AZ57 92
Campdale Rd. N7 BW34 47
Campden Cres. Dag. CO35 50
Campden Cres. Wem. BJ34 45
Campden Gdns. W8 BS40 56
Campden Gro. W8 BS41 66
Campden Hill W8 BS41 66
Campden Hill Gdns. W8 BS40 56
Campden Hill Pl. W8 BR40 55
Campden Hill Rd. W8 BS40 56
Campden Hill Sq. W8 BR40 55
Campden Ho. Clo. W8 BS41 66
Hornton St.
Campden Pl. W8 BR40 55
Campden Rd. Sth. Croy. CA56 96
Campden Rd. Uxb. AY34 44
Campden St. W8 BS40 56
Campen Cl. SW19 BR48 75
Queensmere Rd.
Camp End Rd. Wey. BA59 92
Camperdown St. E1 CA39 57
Leman St.
Campfield Rd. SE9 CJ47 78
Campfield Rd. St. Alb. BJ13 9
Campfield Walk, SW19 BT51 86
Brangwyn Cres.
Camphill Ct. Wey. AW59 92
Camphill Rd. Wey. AW59 92
Campion Clo. Uxb. AY39 53
Campion Ho. Islw. BG43 64
Campion Rd. SW15 BQ44 65
Campion Rd. Islw. BH44 64
Campions, Loug. CL22 31
Campions Epp. CO17 23
Campion Ter. NW2 BQ34 46
Cample Ca. S. Ock. DA40 60
Camplin Rd. Har. BL32 46
Camplin St. SE14 CC43 67
Campon Bldgs. W8 BS40 56
Camp Rd. SW19 BP49 75
Camp Rd. Cat. CD64 105
Camp Rd. Ger. Cr. AR32 43
Camp Rd. St. Alb. BH13 9
Campsbourne Rd. N8 BX31 47
Campsbourne The N8 BX31 47
Rectory Gdns.
Campsey Gdns. Dag. CO36 59
Campsey Rd. Dag. CO36 59
Campsfield Rd. N8 BX31 47
Campshill Pl. SE13 CF46 77
Campshill Rd. SE13 CF46 77
Campus Rd. E17 CD32 48
Campus, The, Welw. G. C. BQ7 5

Camp Vw. SW19 BP49 75
Camp View Rd. St. Alb. BJ14 9
Cam Rd. E15 CF37 57
Camrose Av. Edg. BL30 37
Camrose Av. Erith. CR43 69
Camrose Av. Felt. BC49 73
Camrose Clo. Mord. BS52 86
Camrose St. SE2 CO42 69
Cam Ter. Chis. CL50 78
Mill Pl.
Canada Av. N18 BZ29 39
Canada Cres. W3 BN38 55
Canada Farm Rd. S. Dnth. DA52 90
Canada La. Brox. CD16 21
Canada Rd. W3 BN39 55
Canada Rd. Cob. BD60 93
Canada Rd. Slou. AQ41 62
Canada Rd. Wey. AX59 92
Canada Way W12 BP40 55
Canadian Av. SE6 CE47 77
Canal Gro. SE15 CB43 67
Canal Head. SE15 CB44 67
Peckham High St.
Canal Pl. SE5 CA43 67
Canal Rd. E3 CD38 57
Canal Rd. Grav. DH46 81
Canal St. SE5 BZ43 67
Canal Wk. N1 BZ37 57
Canal Way NW1 BW36 56
Baynes St.
Canberra Clo. Dag. CS36 59
Canberra Clo. Horn. CV35 51
Canberra Clo. St. Alb. BH11 9
Canberra Cres. Dag. CS36 59
Canberra Dr. Hayes BD38 54
Canberra Rd. SE7 CJ43 68
Canberra Rd. Bexh. CP43 69
Canberra Sq. Til. DG44 71
Canbury Av. Kings. On T. BL51 85
Canbury Ms. SE26 CB48 77
Canbury Pk. Rd. Kings. On T. BL51 85
Canbury Pass. Kings. On T. BK51 84
Canbury Path Orp. CO52 89
Canbury Pl. Kings. On T. BL51 85
Canbury Pass.
Cancell Rd. SW9 BY44 66
Candahar Rd. SW11 BU44 66
Cander Way. S. Ock. DA40 60
Candlefield Clo. Hem. H. AZ15 8
Candlefield Rd. Hem. H. AZ15 8
Candlefield Wk. Hem. H. AZ15 8
Candler St. N15 BZ32 48
Candover Clo. West Dr. AX43 63
Candover Rd. Horn. CU33 50
Candover St. W1 BW39 56
Foley St.
Candy Croft. Lthd. BF66 111
Candy St. E3 CD37 57
Caneland Ct. Wal. Abb. CG20 22
Shernbroke Rd.
Canes La. Harl. CP13 14
Canfield Clo. Rain. CT37 59
Canfield Dr. Ruis. BC35 44
Canfield Gdns. NW6 BS36 56
Canfield Pl. NW6 BT36 56
Canfield Rd. Wdf. Grn. CK29 40
Canford Av. Nthlt. BE37 54
Canford Clo. Enf. BY23 29
Canford Dr. Wey. AW55 83
Canford Gdns. N. Mal. BN53 85
Canford Rd. SW11 BV45 66
Canham Rd. SE25 CA52 87
Canham Rd. W3 BO41 65
Canmore Gdns. SW16 BW50 76
Cannhall Rd. E11 CG35 49
Cann Hatch Tad. BR62 103
Canning Cres. N22 BX30 38
Canning Cross SE5 CC44 67
Grove La
Canning Pass. W8 BT41 66
Victoria Rd.
Canning Pla. Ms. W8 BT41 66
Canning Pla.
Canning Pl. W8 BT41 66
Canning Rd. E15 CG37 58
Canning Rd. E17 CD31 48
Canning Rd. N5 BY34 47
Canning Rd. Croy. CA55 87
Canning Rd. Har. BH31 45
Cannington Rd. Dag. CP36 59
Cannizaro Rd. SW19 BQ50 75
Cannonbury Av. Pnr. BD32 45
Cannon Clo. SW20 BQ52 85
Cannon Clo. Hamptn. BF50 74
Cannon Cres. Wok. AP59 91
Cannon Gro. Lthd. BH64 102
Cannon Hill N14 BX27 38
Cannon Hill NW6 BS35 47
Cannon Hill. Maid. AG41 61
Cannon Hill Clo. Maid. AH42 61
Cannon Hill La. SW20 BQ53 85
Cannon Hill La. SW20 BR51 85
Cannon Hill La. SW20 BR52 85
Cannon La. NW3 BT34 47
Cannon La. Pnr. BE32 45
Cannon Mill Ave. Chesh. AP20 16
Cannon Pl. NW3 BT34 47
Cannon Rd. N14 BX27 38
Cannon Rd. Bexh. CQ44 69
Cannon Rd. Wat. BD25 27
Cannon Row. SW1 BX41 66
Bridge St.
Cannon St. Rd. E1 CB39 57
Cannons Corner Edg. BL28 37
Cannon Side. Lthd. BH64 102
Cannons Lane. Ong. CZ14 15
Cannons Md. Brwd. DA20 24
Cannons Meadow. Welw. BU6 5
Cannon St. EC4 BZ39 57
Cannon St. St. Alb. BG13 9
Cannon Way E. Mol. BF52 84
Cannon Way. Lthd. BH64 102
Canon Av. Rom. CP32 50
Canon Beck Rd. SE16 CC41 67
Canonbie Rd. SE23 CC47 77
Canonbury Av. N1 BY36 56
Canonbury Rd.
Canonbury Gro. N1 BZ36 57
Canonbury La. N1 BY36 56
Canonbury Pk. N. N1 BZ36 57
Canonbury Pk. S. N1 BZ36 57
Canonbury Pl. N1 BY36 56
Canonbury Rd. N1 BY36 56
Canonbury Rd. Enf. CA23 30
Canonbury Sq. N1 BY36 56
Canonbury St. N1 BZ36 57
Canonbury Vill. N1 BY36 56
Canon Ct. Edg. BL29 37
Canon Murnane Rd. SE1 CA41 67
Canon Pk. Est. Stan. BK28 36
Canon Rd. Brom. CJ52 88
Canons Brook. Harl. CL11 13
Canons Clo. N2 BT33 47
Canons Clo. Edg. BL29 37
Canons Clo. Rad. BJ21 27
Canons Dr. Edg. BL29 37
Canons Gate. Harl. CL10 6
Canons Hill Couls. BY62 104
Canons La. Tad. BR62 103
Canonsleigh Rd. Dag. CO36 59
Canons Pk. Par. Edg. BL29 37
Canon St. N1 BZ37 57
Prebend St.
Canon's Wk. Croy. CC55 87
Canopus Way Nthwd. BC28 35
Canopus Way. Stai. AY47 73
Canrobert St. E2 CB37 57
Canrobert St. E2 CB38 57
Canterbury Av. Ilf. CK33 49
Canterbury Av. Sid. CO48 79
Canterbury Av. Slou. AO38 52
Canterbury Av. Upmin. CZ34 51
Canterbury Clo. Amer. AP23 25
Canterbury Clo. Beck. CE51 87
Tyler Rd.
Canterbury Clo. Dart. CX47 80
Canterbury Clo. Grnf. BF39 54
Canterbury Cres. SW9 BY45 66
Canterbury Gro. SE27 BY49 76
Canterbury Rd. E10 CF33 48
Canterbury Rd. NW6 BR37 55
Canterbury Rd. Borwd. BM23 28
Canterbury Rd. Croy. BX54 86
Canterbury Rd. Felt. BE48 74
Canterbury Rd. Grav. DH48 81
Canterbury Rd. Guil. AP69 118
Canterbury Rd. Har. BF32 45
Canterbury Rd. Mord. BS54 86
Canterbury Rd. Wat. BC23 26
Canterbury Ter. NW6 BS37 56
Canterbury Way. Rick. BA24 26
Cantley Gdns. SE19 CA51 87
Cantley Gdns. Ilf. CM32 49
Cantley Rd. W7 BJ41 64
Canton St. E14 CE39 57
Cantrell Rd. E3 CD38 57
Cantwell Rd. SE18 CL43 68
Canute Gdns. SE16 CC42 67
Canvey St. SE1 BZ40 57
Zoar St.
Cape Clo. Bark. CL36 58
Harts La.
Capel Av. Wall. BX56 95
Capel Clo. N20 BT27 38
Capel Clo. Brom. CK54 88
Capel Ct. EC2 BZ39 57
Bartholomew La.
Capel Gdns. Ilf. CN35 49
Capel Gdns. Pnr. BE31 45
Capella Rd. Nthwd. BB28 35
Capell Ave. Rick. AU25 25
Capell Rd. Rick. AU25 25
Capell Way. Rick. AU25 25
Capel Pl. Dart. CV49 80
Capel Rd. E7 CH35 49
Capel Rd. Barn. BU26 38
Capel Rd. Wat. BD25 27
Capel Vere Wk. Wat. BB23 26
Capener's Clo. SW1 BV41 66
Kinnerton St.
Caperne Rd. SW18 BT47 76
Cargill Rd.
Cape Rd. N17 CB31 48
Cape Rd. Enf. CB21 30
Cape Rd. St. Alb BJ13 9
Capital Ho. SE6 CE46 77
Capland St. NW8 BT38 56
Caple Rd. NW10 BO37 55
Caponfield. Welw. G. C. BS9 5
Capri Rd. Croy. CA54 87
Capstan Ride Enf. BY23 29
Capstan Sq E14 CF41 67
Capstone Rd. Brom. CG49 78
Captain Cook Clo. Ch. St. G. AQ28 34
Captains Walk. Berk. AR13 7
Capthorne Av. Har. BE33 45
Capthorne Ct. Har. BE33 45
Capworth St. E10 CE33 48
Caractacus Grn. Wat. BB25 26
Caradoc St. SE10 CG42 68
Caradon Way N15 BZ31 48
Caravelle Gdns. Nthlt. BD38 54
Javelin Way
Carberry Rd. SE19 CA50 77
Carbery Av. W3 BL41 65
Carbis Rd. E14 CD39 57
Carbone Hill. Pot. B. BW17 20
Carburton St. W1 BV38 56
Carden Rd. SE15 CB45 67
Cardiff Rd. W7 BJ41 64
Cardiff Rd. Enf. CB24 30
Cardiff Rd. Wat. BC25 26
Cardiff St. SE18 CN43 68
Cardigan Gdns. Ilf. CO34 50
Cardigan Pl. NW6 BS38 56
Cardigan Rd. E3 CD37 57
Cardigan Rd. SW13 BP44 65
Cardigan Rd. SW19 BT50 76
Cardigan Rd. Rich. BL46 75
Cardigan St. SE11 BY42 66
Cardinal Av. Borwd. BM54 85
Cardinal Av. Kings. On T. BL49 75
Cardinal Av. Mord. BR53 85
Cardinal Bourne St. SE1 BZ41 67
Burge St.
Cardinal Clo. Chis. CM50 78
Cardinal Clo. Mord. BR53 85
Cardinal Cres. N. Mal. BN51 85
Cardinal Dr. Ilf. CM29 40
Cardinal Dr. Walt. BD54 84
Cardinal Pl. SW15 BQ45 65
Cardinal Rd. Felt. BC47 73
Cardinal Rd. Ruis. BD33 45
Cardinal's Wk. Hmptn. BG50 74
Cardinals Wk. Sun. BB50 73
Seymour Way
Cardinal Way. Rain. CV37 60
Cardington Sq. Houns. BD45 64
Cardington St. NW1 BW38 56
Cardozo Rd. N7 BX35 47
Cardrew Av. N12 BT28 38
Cardrew Clo. N12 BT28 38
Cardross St. W6 BP41 65
Cardwell Rd. N7 BX35 47
Cardwell Rd. SE18 CL42 68
Cardy Rd. Hem. H. AW13 8
Carew Clo. Couls. BZ63 105
Carew Rd. N17 CB30 39
Carew Rd. W13 BK41 64
Carew Rd. Ashf. BA50 73
Carew Rd. Mitch. BV51 86
Carew Rd. Nthwd. BB29 35
Carew Rd. Th. Hth. BY52 86
Carew Rd. Wall. BW57 95
Carew St. SE5 BZ44 67
Carey Clo. Wind. AN45 61
Carey Gdns. SW8 BW44 66
Thessaly Rd.
Carey La. EC2 BZ39 57
Gutter La.
Carey Pl. Wat. BD24 27
Clifford St.
Carey Rd. Dag. CQ35 50
Carey St. WC2 BX39 56
Carfax Rd. Hayes. BB42 63
Carfax Rd. Horn. CT35 50
Carfax Sq. SW4 BW45 66
Clapham Pk. Rd.
Cargill Rd. SW18 BS47 76
Cargreen Rd. SE25 CA52 87
Carholme Rd. SE23 CD47 77
Carisbrook Av. Wat. BD23 27
Carisbrook Clo. Stan. BK30 36
Carisbrooke Av. Bex. CP47 79
Carisbrooke Clo. Enf. CA23 30
Carisbrooke Clo. Horn. CX33 51
Carisbrooke Gdns. SE15 CA43 67
Rosemary Rd.
Carisbrooke Rd. E17 CD31 48
Carisbrooke Rd. Brom. CJ52 88
Carisbrooke Rd. Mitch. BW52 86
Carisbrooke Rd. St. Alb. BF16 18
Carl Clo. Upmin. CX34 51
Carleton Av. Wall. BW57 95
Carleton Clo. Esher BG54 84
Carleton Pl. Hort. K. CY52 90
Carleton Rd. N7 BW35 47
Carleton Rd. Wal. Cr. CC17 21
Carlile Clo. E3 CD37 57
Carlingford Gdns. Mitch. BV50 76
Carlingford Rd. N15 BY31 47
Carlingford Rd. NW3 BT35 47
Carlingford Rd. Mord. BQ53 85
Carlisle Av. EC3 CA39 57
Carlisle Av. W3 BO39 55
Carlisle Av. St. Alb. BG12 9
Carlisle Clo. E3 CD37 57
Carlisle Clo. Kings. On T. BM51 85
Carlisle Gdns. Har. BK33 45
Carlisle Gdns. Ilf. CK32 49
Carlisle La. SE1 BX41 66
Carlisle Pl. N11 BW28 38
Carlisle Pl. N12 BV28 38
Oakleigh Rd.
Carlisle Pl. SW1 BW41 66
Carlisle Rd. E10 CE33 48
Carlisle Rd. N4 BY33 47
Scarborough Rd.
Carlisle Rd. NW6 BR37 55
Carlisle Rd. NW9 BN31 46
Carlisle Rd. Dart. CX46 80
Carlisle Rd. Hmptn. BF50 74
Carlisle Rd. Rom. CU32 50
Carlisle Rd. Slou. AO40 52
Carlisle Rd. Sutt. BR57 94
Carlisle St. W1 BW39 56
Soho Sq.
Carlos Pl. W1 BV40 56
Carlow St. NW1 BW37 56
Carlton Ave. Green. CZ46 80
Carlton Ave. Hayes. BB42 63
Carlton Av. N14 BW25 29
Carlton Av. Felt. BD46 74
Carlton Av. Harrow. BJ32 45
Carlton Av. Sth. Croy. BZ57 96
Carlton Av. E. Wem. BK34 45
Carlton Av. W. Wem. BJ34 45
Carlton Clo. Borwd. BN24 28
Carlton Clo. Chess. BL57 94
Carlton Clo. Edg. BM28 37
Carlton Clo. Grays. DF41 71
Carlton Clo. Wok. AT60 91
Carlton Ct. NW6 BS37 56
Carlton Cres. Sutt. BR56 94
Carlton Dr. SW15 BQ46 75
Carlton Dr. Ilf. CM31 49
Carlton Gdns. SW1 BW40 56
Carlton Gdns. W5 BK39 54
Carlton Grn. Red. BU69 121
Carlton Gro. SE15 CB44 67
Carlton Hl. NW8 BS37 56
Carlton Ho. Ter. SW1 BW40 56
Carlton Pde. Orp. CO54 89
Carlton Pk. Sev. CV64 108
Carlton Pk. Av. SW20 BQ51 85
Carlton Rd. E11 CG33 49
Carlton Rd. E12 CJ35 49
Carlton Rd. E17 CD30 39
Carlton Rd. N4 BY33 47
Carlton Rd. N11 BV28 38
Carlton Rd. N15 CA31 48
Carlton Rd. SW14 BN45 65
Carlton Rd. W4 BN41 65
Carlton Rd. W5 BK40 54
Carlton Rd. Dart. CW47 80
Carlton Rd. Dart. CX47 80
Carlton Rd. Erith. CR43 69
Carlton Rd. Grays. DF41 71
Carlton Rd. N. Mal. BO51 85
Carlton Rd. Reig. & Red. BT69 121
Carlton Rd. Rom. CT32 50
Carlton Rd. Sid. CN49 78
Carlton Rd. Slou. AQ40 52
Carlton Rd. Sth. Croy. BZ57 96
Carlton Rd. Sun. BC50 73
Carlton Rd. Walt. BC54 83
Carlton Rd. Well. CO45 69
Carlton Rd. Wok. AT60 91
Carlton Sq. E1 CC38 57
Carlton St. SW1 BW40 56
Regent St.
Carlton Ter. E7 CJ36 58
Carlton Ter. E11 CH32 49
Carlton Ter. N18 BZ27 39
Carlton Ter. SE26 CC48 77
Carlton Vale NW6 BS38 56
Carlwell St. SW17 BU49 76
Carlyle Av. NW10 BN37 55
Carlyle Av. Brom. CJ52 88
Carlyle Av. Sthl. BE40 54
Carlyle Clo. N2 BT32 47
Carlyle Clo. NW10 BN37 55
Carlyle Clo. E. Mol. BG51 84
Carlyle Gdns. Sthl. BE40 54
Carlyle Rd. E12 CK35 49
Carlyle Rd. W5 BK42 64
Carlyle Rd. Croy. CB55 87
Carlyle Rd. Stai. AV50 72
Carlyle Rd. Stai. AW50 73
Carlyle Sq. SW3 BT42 66
Carlyon Av. Har. BE35 45
Carlyon Av. Wok. AS62 100
Carlyon Clo. Wem. BL37 55
Carlyon Clo. Wok. AS62 100
Carlyon Rd. Hayes. BD39 54
Carlyon Rd. Wem. BL37 55
Carmalt Gdns. SW15 BQ45 65
Carmalt Gdns. Walt. BD56 93
Carmarthen Rd. Slou. AP40 52
Carmelite Clo. Har. BG30 36
Carmelite Rd. Har. BG30 36
Carmelite St. EC4 BY40 56
Carmelite Wk. Har. BG30 36
Carmelite Way Har. BG30 36
Carmelite Way Hart. DC53 90
Carmen St. E14 CE39 57
Carmichael Rd. SE25 CA53 87
Carminia Rd. SW17 BV48 76
Carnaby Rd. Brox. CD13 12
Carnaby St. W1 BW39 56
Carnach Grn. S. Ock. DA40 60
Carnac St. SE27 BZ48 77
Carnanton Rd. E17 CF30 39
Carnarvon Av. Enf. CA24 30
Carnarvon Clo. Orp. CP56 98
Carnarvon Dr. Hayes. BA42 63
Carnarvon Rd. E10 CF32 48
Carnarvon Rd. E15 CG36 58
Carnarvon Rd. E18 CG30 40
Carnarvon Rd. Barn. BR24 28
Carnation St. SE2 CO42 69
Carnecke Gdns. SE9 CK46 78
Carnegie Pl. SW19 BQ48 75
Carnegie Rd. St. Alb. BG11 9
Carnegie St. N1 BX37 56
Carnfield Dr. NW9 BO29 37
Carnforth Clo. Epsom BM57 94
Carnforth Gdns. Horn. CU35 50
Carnforth Rd. SW16 BW50 76
Carnoustie Dr. N1 BX36 56
Carnwath Rd. SW6 BS45 66
Carolina Rd. Th. Hth. BY51 86
Caroline Clo. Croy. CA56 96
Brownlow Rd.
Caroline Clo. West Dr. AX41 63
Caroline Ct. Ashf. AZ50 73
Caroline Ct. Stan. BJ29 36
Chase, The.
Caroline Gdns. SE15 CB43 67
Caroline Pl. W2 BS40 56
Caroline Pl. Wat. BD25 27
Caroline Pl. Ms. W2 BS40 56
Orme La.
Caroline Rd. SW19 BR50 75
Caroline St. E1 CC39 57
Caroline Ter. SW1 BV42 66
Caroline Wk. W6 BR43 65
Carol St. NW1 BW37 56
Carolyn Clo. Wok. AP63 100
Carolyn Dr. Orp. CO55 89
Caroon Dr. Rick. AW21 26
Car Park, Hem. H. AX13 8
Carpenders Av. Wat. BE27 36
Carpenter Gdns. N21 BY27 38
Carpenter Path. Brwd. DE25 122
Carpenters Arms La. Epp. CO16 23
Carpenters Ct. Twick. BH48 74
Hampton Rd.
Carpenters Pl. SW4 BW45 66
Carpenters Rd. E15 CE36 57
Carpenters Rd. Enf. CC21 30
Carpenters Way. Pot. B. BT20 20
Carpenters Wood Dri. Rick. AT24 25
Carriage, The. Rd. SW7 BT41 66
Carriageway. The. Sev. CP65 107
Carrick Dr. Sev. CU65 107
Carrick Gdns. N17 BZ30 39
Flexmere Rd.
Carrington Av. Borwd. BM25 28
Carrington Av. Houns. BF46 74
Carrington Clo. Borwd. BN25 28
Carrington Ho. SE8 CE44 67
Carrington Rd. Dart. CW46 80
Carrington Rd. Rich. BM45 65
Carrington Rd. Slou. AP40 52
Carrington St. W1 BV40 56
Carroll Av. Guil. AT70 118
Carroll Cld. E15 CG35 49
Carroll Clo. E15 CG35 49
Ash Rd.
Carroll Hill Loug. CK24 31
Carrol Pl. NW5 BV35 47
Carron Clo. E14 CE39 57
Carroun Rd. SW8 BX43 66
Carrow Rd. Dag. CO36 59
Carr Rd. E17 CD30 39
Carr Rd. Nthlt. BF36 54
Carrs La. N21 BZ25 30
Carr St. E14 CD39 57
Carshalton Gro. Sutt. BT56 95
Carshalton Pk. Rd. Cars. BU56 95
Carshalton Pk. Rd. Cars. BU57 95
Carshalton Pl. Cars. BV56 95
Carshalton Rd. Bans. BU60 95
Carshalton Rd. Mitch. BV52 86
Carshalton Rd. Sutt. BT56 95
Carshalton Rd. W. Sutt. BS56 95
Carslake Rd. SW15 BQ46 75
Carson Rd. E16 CH38 58
Carson Rd. SE21 BZ47 77
Carson Rd. Barn. BU24 29
Carstairs Rd. SE6 CF48 77
Carston Clo. SE12 CG46 78
Carston Ms. SE12 CG46 78
Carswell Clo. Brwd. DE25 122
Carswell Rd. SE6 CF47 77
Carter Clo. Rom. CR29 41
Carter Clo. Wall. BW57 95
Carter Clo. Wind. AN44 61
Carter Ct. EC4 BY39 56
Carter La.
Carter Dr. Rom. CR29 41
Carteret St. SW1 BW41 66
Carterhatch La. Enf. CA22 30
Carterhatch La. Enf. CA23 30
Carterhatch Rd. Enf. CC23 30
Carter La. EC4 BY39 56
Carter Pl. SE17 BZ42 67
Carter Rd. E13 CH37 58
Carter Rd. SW19 BT50 76
Carters Clo. Loug. CL25 31
Carters Clo. Wor. Pk. BQ55 85
Cartersfield Rd. Wal. Abb. CF21 30
Carter's Hill, Sev. CX67 117
Carter's Hl. SE9 CJ47 78
Carter's Hl. Clo. SE9 CJ47 78
Carters La. Epp. CL15 13
Carters La. Wok. AU63 100
Carters Mead. Harl. CP12 14
Carters Rd. Epsom. BO61 103
Carter's Rd. Grav. DF47 81
Carters Row, Red. BU71 121
Carter St. SE17 BZ43 67
Carters Yd. SW18 BS46 76
Wandsworth High St.
Carthew Rd. W6 BP41 65
Carthew Vill. W6 BP41 65
Carthouse La. Wok. AP60 91
Carthouse La. Wok. AQ61 100
Carting La. WC2 BX40 56
Cart La. E4 CF26 39
Station Rd.
Cartmel Clo. Red. BU70 121
Cartmell Gdns. Mord. BT53 86
Cartmel Rd. Bexh. CR44 69
Carton St. W1 BU39 56
Cartwright Gdns. WC1 BX38 56
Cartwright Rd. Dag. CQ36 59
Cartwright St. E1 CA40 57
Carve Ley. Welw. G. C. BS8 5
Carver Rd. SE24 BZ46 77
Carville Cres. Brent. BL42 65
Carville St. N7 BY34 47
Durham Rd.
Cary Rd. E11 CG35 49
Carysfort Rd. N8 BW32 47
Carysfort Rd. N16 BZ34 48
Cascade Av. N10 BW31 47
Cascade Rd. Buck. H. CJ27 40
Cascades Croy. CD58 96
Caselden Clo. Wey. AW56 92
Casella Rd. SE14 CC43 67
Casewick Rd. SE27 BY49 76
Casimir Rd. E5 CC34 48
Casino Av. SE24 BZ46 77
Casket St. E2 CA38 57
Caslon Pl. E1 CB38 57
Cudworth St.
Caslte Rd. Islw. BH44 64
Caspian St. SE5 BZ43 67
Casselden Rd. NW10 BN36 55

Cassidy Rd. SW6 BS43 66
Cassilda Rd. SE2 CO42 69
Cassiobridge Rd. Wat. BB25 26
Cassiobury Av. Felt. BB46 73
Cassiobury Dr. Wat. BB22 26
Cassiobury Pk. Av. Wat. BB24 26
Cassiobury Rd. E17 CC32 48
Cassio Rd. Wat. BC24 26
Cassius Rd. Twick. BJ46 74
Cassland Rd. E9 CC36 57
Cassland Rd. Th. Hth. BZ52 87
Casslee Rd. SE6 CD47 77
Casson St. E1 CB39 57
Castalia St. E14 CF41 67
Castellain Rd. W9 BS38 56
Castellan Av. Rom. CU31 50
Castello Av. SW15 BQ46 75
Castell Rd. Loug. CM23 31
Castells Meadows. West. CM66 115
Castelnau SW13 BP44 65
Castelnau Est. SW13 BP43 65
Castelnau Pl. SW13 BP43 65
Castelnau Row SW13 BP43 65
Lonsdale Rd
Casterbridge Rd. SE3 CH45 68
Castile Rd. SE18 CL42 68
Castillon Rd. SE6 CG48 78
Castlands Rd. SE6 CD48 77
Castle Ave. Slou. AQ43 62
Castle Av. E4 CF29 39
Castle Av. Epsom. BP58 94
Castle Av. Rain. CT36 59
Castle Av. West Dr. AY40 53
Castlebar Hill W5 BJ39 54
Castlebar Ms. W5 BJ39 54
Castlebar Pk. W5 BK39 54
Castlebar Pk. Rd. W5 BJ38 54
Castlebar Rd. W5 BK39 54
Castle Clo. E9 CD35 48
Swinnerton St.
Castle Clo. SW19 BQ48 75
Castle Clo. Bush. BF25 27
Castle Clo. Red. BZ70 114
Castle Clo. Reig. BS72 121
Castlecombe Dr. SW19 BQ47 75
Castlecombe Rd. SE9 CK49 78
Castle Ct. EC3 BZ39 57
Birchin Lane
Castledine Rd. SE20 CB50 77
Castle Dr. Ilf. CK32 49
Castle Dr. Reig. BS72 121
Castlefield Rd. Reig. BS70 121
Castlefields, Grav. DF51 81
Castleford Av. SE9 CL47 78
Castle Gdns. Dag. CO37 59
Castle Gdns. Dor. BL70 120
Castlegate, Rich. BL45 65
Castle Grn. Wey. BB55 83
Castle Grove Rd. Wok. AP59 91
Castlehaven Rd. NW1 BV36 56
Castle Hill. Berk. AR12 7
Castle Hill, Guil. AR71 118
Castle Hill Hart. DB53 90
Castle Hill. Wind. AO44 61
Castle Hill Ave. Berk. AR12 7
Castle Hill Av. Croy. CE58 96
Castle Hill Clo. Berk. AR12 7
Castle Hill Rd. Egh. AQ48 72
Castle La. SW1 BW41 66
Castleleigh Ct. Enf. BZ25 30
Castlemaine Av. Epsom BP58 94
Castlemaine Av. Sth. Croy. CA56 96
Castle Mead, Hem. H. AW14 8
Castle Ms. N12 BT28 38
Castlereagh St. W1 BU39 56
Castle Rd. N12 BT28 38
Castle Rd. NW1 BV36 56
Castle Rd. Couls. BU63 104
Castle Rd. Dag. CO37 59
Castle Rd. Enf. CD23 30
Castle Rd. Epsom. BM61 103
Castle Rd. Grays. DC43 71
Castle Rd. Hodd. CE10 12
Castle Rd. Nthlt. BF36 54
Castle Rd. St. Alb. BJ13 9
Castle Rd. Swans. DC46 81
Castle Rd. Wey. BB55 83
Castle Rd. Wok. AS60 91
Castle Sq. Guil. AR71 118
Castle Sq. Red. BZ70 114
Castle St. E6 CJ37 58
Castle St. Berk. AR13 7
Castle St. Green. DA46 80
Castle St. Guil. AR71 118
Castle St. Kings. On T. BL51 85
Castle St. Ong. CX18 24
Castle St. Red. BY70 121
Castle St. Swans. DC46 81
Castleton Av. Bexh. CS44 69
Castleton Av. Erith CS44 69
Castleton Av. Wem. BL35 46
Castleton Clo. Bans. BS61 104
Castleton Dr. Bans. BS60 95
Castleton Rd. E17 CF30 39
Castleton Rd. SE9 CJ49 78
Castleton Rd. Ilf. CO33 50
Castleton Rd. Mitch. BW52 86
Castleton Rd. Ruis. BD33 45
Castletown Rd. W14 BR42 65
Castle Vw. Epsom. BM60 94
Castleview Gdns. Ilf. CK32 49
Castle View Rd. Slou. AR42 62
Castle View Rd. Wey. AZ56 92
Castle Wk. Reig. BS70 121
High St.
Castle Way SW19 BQ48 75
Castle Way Epsom BP58 94
Castle Way Felt. BD49 74
Castlewood Dr. SE9 CK44 68
Castlewood Rd. N15 CB32 48
Castlewood Rd. N16 CB32 48
Castlewood Rd. Barn. BT24 29
Castle Yd. Rich. BK46 74
Hill St.
Castor St. E14 CE40 57
Caterham Av. Ilf. CK30 40
Caterham By-pass. Cat. CB65 105
Caterham Ct. Wal. Abb. CG20 22
Shernbroke Rd.
Caterham Dr. Couls. BY62 104
Caterham Dr. Couls. BZ63 105
Caterham Rd. SE13 CF45 67
Catesby St. SE17 BZ42 67
Catfield Gro. Felt. BF48 74
Catford Hl. SE6 CD48 77
Catford Rd. SE6 CE47 77
Cathall Rd. E11 CF34 48
Catham Clo. St. Alb. BJ14 9
Cathay St. SE16 CB41 67
Cathay Wk. Nthlt. BF37 54
Cathcart Dr. Orp. CN54 88
Cathcart Hl. N19 BW34 47
Cathcart Rd. SW10 BS43 66
Cathcart St. NW5 BV35 47
Cathedral Clo. Guil. AQ71 118
Cathedral Pl. EC4 BY39 56
Newgate St.
Cathedral St. SE1 BZ40 57
Catherall Rd. N5 BZ34 48
Catherina Ter. SW8 BX44 66
Catherine Clo. Brwd. DA25 33
Catherine Clo. Hem. H. AZ11 8
Catherine Clo. Wey. AY60 92
Catherine Ct. N14 BW25 29
Catherine Dr. Sun. BB50 73
Catherine Gdns. Houns. BG45 64
Catherine Gro. SE10 CE44 67
Catherine Pl. SW1 BW41 66
Catherine Pl. S. At. H. CX51 90
Catherine Rd. Enf. CD21 30
Catherine Rd. Rom. CU32 50
Catherine Rd. Surb. BK53 84
Catherine St. WC2 BX40 56
Catherine St. St. Alb. BG13 9
Catherine Wheel Yd. Brent. BK43 64
High St.
Cat Hill Barn. BU25 29
Cathles Rd. SW12 BV46 76
Cathnor Rd. W12 BP41 65
Catisfield Rd. Enf. CD22 30
Catkin Clo. Hem. H. AW13 8
Catlin Cres. Shep. BA53 83
Catling Clo. SE23 CC48 77
Dacres Rd.
Catlins La. Pnr. BC31 44
Catlin St. SE16 CB42 67
Catlin St. Hem. H. AW15 8
Cator Clo. Croy. CF59 96
Cator Cres. Croy. CF59 96
Cator La. Beck. CD51 87
Cato Rd. SW4 BW45 66
Cator Rd. SE26 CC50 77
Cator Rd. Cars. BU56 95
Cator St. SE15 CA43 67
Cato St. W1 BU39 56
Catsey La. Bush. BG26 36
Catsey Wds. Bush. BG26 36
Catterick Way Borwd. BL23 28
Cattistock Rd. SE9 CK49 78
Cattlegate Hill, Pot. B. BW19 20
Cattlegate Rd. Enf. BX20 20
Cattlegate Rd. Pot. B. BW19 20
Catton St. WC1 BX39 56
Cattsdell, Hem. H. AY13 8
Caulfield Rd. E6 CK37 58
Caulfield Rd. SE15 CB44 67
Causeway Felt. BC45 63
Causeway Clo. Pot. B. BT19 20
Causeway, The, N2 BT31 47
Causeway, The, SW18 BS46 76
Causeway, The, Cars. BV55 86
Causeway, The, Chess. BL56 94
Causeway, The Egh & Stai. AT49 72
Causeway, The, Esher BH57 93
Causeway, The, Pot. B. BT19 20
Causeway, The, St. Alb. BF14 9
Causeway, The, Sutt. BT58 95
Causeway, The, Tedd. BH49 74
Causeyware Rd. N9 CB26 39
Causton Rd. N6 BV33 47
Causton St. SW1 BW42 66
Cautley Av. SW4 BW46 76
Cavalry Cres. Houns. BD45 64
Cavalry Cres. Wind. AN45 61
Cavan Dr. St. Alb. BG11 9
Cavaye Pl. SW10 BT42 66
Fulham Rd.
Cavell Cres. Dart. CX45 70
Cavell Dr. Enf. BY23 29
Cavell Rd. N17 BZ29 39
Cavell Rd. Wal. Cr. CA17 21
Cavell St. E1 CB39 57
Cavendish Ave. Sev. CU64 107
Cavendish Av. N3 BS30 38
Cavendish Av. NW8 BT38 56
Cavendish Av. W13 BJ39 54
Cavendish Av. Erith. CR43 69
Cavendish Av. Har. BG35 45
Cavendish Av. Horn. CU36 59
Cavendish Av. N. Mal. BP53 85
Cavendish Av. Ruis. BC35 44
Cavendish Av. Sid. CO47 79
Cavendish Av. Wdf. Grn. CH30 40
Cavendish Av. Well. CN45 68
Cavendish Clo. N18 CB28 39
Cavendish Clo. NW6 BR36 55
Cavendish Clo. NW8 BT38 56
Cavendish Clo. SW15 BR46 75
St. John's Av.
Cavendish Clo. Amer. AQ23 25
Cavendish Clo. Hayes BB39 53
Cavendish Clo. Sun. BB50 73
Cavendish Ct. EC3 CA39 57
Houndsditch
Cavendish Cres. Borwd. BM24 28
Cavendish Cres. Horn. CU36 59
Cavendish Dr. E11 CF33 48
Cavendish Dr. Edg. BL29 37
Cavendish Dr. Esher BH56 93
Cavendish Gdns. Bark. CN35 49
Cavendish Gdns. Ilf. CL33 49
Cavendish Gdns. Red. BV70 121
Cavendish Gdns. Rom. CQ32 50
Cavendish Ms. N. W1 BV39 56
Hallam St.
Cavendish Ms. S. W1 BV39 56
Hallam St.
Cavendish Pl. W1 BV39 56
Cavendish Rd. E4 CF29 39
Cavendish Rd. N4 BY32 47
Cavendish Rd. N18 CB28 39
Cavendish Rd. NW6 BR36 55
Cavendish Rd. SW12 BV46 76
Cavendish Rd. SW19 BT50 76
Cavendish Rd. W4 BN44 65
Cavendish Rd. Barn. BQ24 28
Cavendish Rd. Chesh. AO19 16
Cavendish Rd. Croy. BY54 86
Cavendish Rd. N. Mal. BO53 85
Cavendish Rd. Red. BV70 121
Cavendish Rd. St. Alb. BH13 9
Cavendish Rd. Sun. BB50 73
Cavendish Rd. Sutt. BT57 95
Cavendish Rd. Wey. AZ58 92
Cavendish Rd. Wok. AR63 100
Cavendish Sq. W1 BV39 56
Cavendish St. N1 BZ37 57
Cavendish St. W1 BV39 56
Cavendish Way. Hat. BO12 10
Cavendish Way W. Wick. CE54 87
Cavenham Ct. Wok. AS63 100
Brooklyn Rd.
Cavenham Gdns. Horn. CV32 51
Cavenham Gdns. Ilf. CM34 49
Caveny Path. S. Ock. CZ39 60
Caverleigh Way Wor. Pk. BP54 85
Cave Rd. E13 CH37 58
Cave Rd. Rich. BK49 74
Caversham Av. N13 BY27 38
Caversham Av. Sutt. BR55 85
Caversham Rd. N15 BZ31 48
Caversham Rd. NW5 BW36 56
Caversham Rd. Kings. On T. BL51 85
Fairfield North
Caversham St. SW3 BU43 66
Caverswall St. W12 BQ39 55
Eynham Rd.
Caves Clo. Chis. CL51 88
Cave St. N1 BX37 56
Cavill's Wk. Rom. CQ27 41
Cawcott Dr. Wind. AM44 61
Cawdor Ave. S. Ock. DA40 60
Cawdor Cres. W7 BJ41 64
Cawley Rd. E9 CC37 57
Cawnpore St. SE19 CA49 77
Cawsey Way. Wok. AS62 100
Cawthorne Way NW7 BR28 37
Caxton Av. Wey. AW57 92
Caxton Dr. Uxb. AX37 53
Caxton Gro. E3 CE38 57
Caxton La. Oxt. CK69 115
Caxton Rd. N22 BX30 38
Caxton Rd. SW19 BT49 76
Caxton Rd. W12 BQ40 55
Caxton Rd. Sthl. BD41 64
Caxton St. SW1 BW41 66
Caxton St. N. E16 CG39 58
Caxton St. S. E16 CG40 58
Caxton Way, Wat. BB25 26
Caygill Clo. Brom. CG52 88
Cayley Clo. Wall. BX57 95
Cayley St. E14 CD39 57
Cayman St. SE16 CB41 67
Cayton Rd. Grnf. BH37 54
Cayton St. EC1 BZ38 57
Cazenove Rd. E17 CE30 39
Cazenove Rd. N16 CA34 48
Cearn Way Couls. BX61 104
Cecil Av. Bark. CM36 58
Cecil Av. Enf. CA24 30
Cecil Av. Horn. CW31 51
Cecil Av. Wem. BL35 46
Cecil Clo. Ashf. BA50 73
Cecil Clo. Chess. BK56 93
Cecil Ct. WC2 BX40 56
St. Martin's La.
Cecil Ct. Barn. BQ24 28
Cecil Ct. Croy. CA55 87
Cecil Cr. Hat. BP11 10
Cecile Park N8 BX32 47
Cecilia Rd. E8 CA35 48
Cecil Pk. Pnr. BE31 45
Cecil Pl. Mitch. BU53 86
Cecil Rd. E11 CG34 49
Cecil Rd. E13 CH37 58
Cecil Rd. E17 CE30 39
Cecil Rd. N10 BV30 38
Cecil Rd. N14 BW26 38
Cecil Rd. NW9 BN31 46
Cecil Rd. NW10 BN37 55
Cecil Rd. SW19 BS50 76
Cecil Rd. W3 BN39 55
Cecil Rd. Ashf. BA50 73
Cecil Rd. Croy. BX53 86
Cecil Rd. Enf. BZ24 30
Cecil Rd. Grav. DF47 81
Cecil Rd. Har. BG31 45
Cecil Rd. Hodd. CF11 12
Cecil Rd. Houns. BG44 64
Cecil Rd. Ilf. CL35 49
Cecil Rd. Iver AV39 52
Cecil Rd. Pot. B. BP19 19
Cecil Rd. Red. BV70 121
Cecil Rd. Rom. CP33 50
Cecil Rd. St. Alb. BH13 9
Cecil Rd. Sutt. BR57 94
Cecil Rd. Wal. Cr. CC19 21
Cecil St. Wat. BC22 26
Cecil Way Brom. CH54 88
Cedar Av. Barn. BU26 38
Cedar Av. Cob. BD61 102
Cedar Av. Enf. CC23 30
Cedar Av. Hayes BC39 53
Cedar Av. Rom. CQ32 50
Cedar Av. Ruis. BD35 45
Cedar Av. Sid. CN47 78
Cedar Av. Twick. BF46 74
Cedar Av. Upmin. CX35 51
Cedar Av. Wal. Cr. CC20 21
Cedar Clo. Borwd. BM24 28
Cedar Clo. Brom. CK55 88
Cedar Clo. Brwd. DE25 122
Cedar Clo. Buck. H. CJ27 40
Cedar Clo. Dor. BJ71 119
Cedar Clo. E. Mol. BH52 84
Cedar Clo. Epsom. BO60 94
Cedar Clo. Pot. B. BS18 20
Cedar Clo. Reig. BT71 121
Cedar Clo. Rom. CS31 50
Cedar Clo. Saw. CQ6 6
Cedar Clo. Stai. AW52 83
Cedar Clo. Swan. CS51 89
Cedar Clo. Warl. CD62 105
Cedar Ct. N10 BV30 38
Cedar Ct. SE9 CK46 78
Cedar Ct. Egh. AT49 72
Cedar Ct. Epp. CO19 23
Station Rd.
Cedar Ct. St. Alb. BK13 9
Cedarwood Dr.
Cedar Cres. Brom. CK55 88
Cedarcroft Rd. Chess. BL56 94
Cedar Dr. N2 BU31 47
Causeway, The,
Cedar Dr. Lthd. BH65 102
Cedar Dr. Pnr. BF29 36
Cedar Dr. S. At. H. CX51 90
Cedar Dr. Uxb. AY37 53
Cedar Gdns. Sutt. BT57 95
Cedar Gdns. Upmin. CY34 51
Cedar Grn. Hodd. CE12 12
Cedar Gro. W5 BL41 65
Cedar Gro. Amer. AO23 25
Cedar Gro. Bex. CP46 79
Cedar Gro. Sthl. BF39 54
Cedar Gro. Wey. BA56 92
Cedar Heights Rich. BL47 75
Cedar Hill Epsom BN61 103
Cedarhurst Dr. SE9 CJ46 78
Cedar Lawn, NW3 BT34 47
Cedar Lawn Av. Barn. BR25 28
Cedar Mt. SE9 CJ47 78
Cedarne Rd. SW6 BS43 66
Fulham Rd.
Cedar Pk. Gdns. Rom. CP33 50
Cedar Pk. Rd. Enf. BZ22 30
Cedar Rise N14 BV26 38
Cedar Rd. N17 CA30 39
Cedar Rd. NW2 BQ35 46
Cedar Rd. Berk. AR13 7
Cedar Rd. Brom. CJ51 88
Cedar Rd. Brwd. DE25 122
Cedar Rd. Cob. BC60 92
Cedar Rd. Croy. BZ55 87
Cedar Rd. Dart. CV47 80
Cedar Rd. E. Mol. BG52 84
Cedar Rd. Enf. BY22 29
Cedar Rd. Erith. CU44 69
Cedar Rd. Felt. BA47 73
Cedar Rd. Grav. DH49 81
Cedar Rd. Grays. DG41 71
Cedar Rd. Hat. BP13 10
Cedar Rd. Horn. CV34 51
Cedar Rd. Houns. BD44 64
Cedar Rd. Rom. CS31 50
Cedar Rd. Sutt. BT57 95
Cedar Rd. Tedd. BJ49 74
Cedar Rd. Wat. BD25 27
Cedar Rd. Wey. AZ56 92
Cedar Rd. Wok. AQ63 100
Cedars Ave. Rick. AX26 35
Cedars Av. E17 CE32 48
Cedars Av. Croy. BX55 86
Cedars Av. Mitch. BV52 86
Cedars Bans. BU60 95
Cedars Clo. NW4 BQ31 46
Cedars Clo. Ger. Cr. AS28 34
Cedars Ct. N9 CA27 39
Cedars Est. Mitch. BV52 86
Cedars Pl. SE7 CJ42 68
Charlton Church La.
Cedars Rd. E15 CG36 58
Cedars Rd. N9 CB27 39
Cedars Rd. N21 BY27 38
Cedars Rd. SW1 BO44 65
Cedars Rd. SW4 BV45 66
Cedars Rd. SW13 BO45 65
Cedars Rd. W4 BN43 65
Cedars Rd. Beck. CD51 87
Cedars Rd. Kings. On T. BK51 84
Cedars Rd. Mord. BS52 86
Cedars. The Buck. H. CH26 40
Cedars, The, Har. BG29 36
Cedars, The Reig. BT70 121
Cedars, The, Tedd. BH50 74
Cedars, The, Wey. AY59 92
Cedar St. SW19 BQ48 75
Cedars Wk. Wal. Abb. CF20 21
Cedar Ter. Rich. BL45 65
Cedar Tree Gro. SE27 BY49 76
Cedarville Gdns. SW16 BX50 76
Cedar Walk, Hem. H. AX14 8
Cedar Wk. Ken. BZ61 105
Cedar Wk. Reig. BU68 113
Cedar Wk. Tad. BR63 103
Cedar Way, Berk. AR13 7
Cedar Way, Guil. AR69 118
Cedar Way. Slou. AS42 62
Cedar Way, Sun. BB50 73
Cedarwood Dr. St. Alb. BK13 9
Cedric Av. Rom. CT31 50
Cedric Rd. SE9 CM48 78
Celandine Clo. S. Ock. DB38 60
Celandine Rd. Walt. BE56 93
Celbeck Rd. Har. BG33 45
Celia Cres. Ashf. AX50 73
Celia Rd. N19 BW35 47
Cell Barnes Clo. St. Alb. BJ14 9
Cell Barnes La. St. Alb. BJ14 9
Cell Farm Av. Wind. AQ46 72
Celtic Av. Brom. CG52 88
Celtic Rd. Wey. AY60 92
Celtic St. E14 CF39 57
Cement Block Cotts. Grays. DE43 71
Cemetery Hill, Hem. H. AX14 8
Cemetery La. SE7 CK43 68
Cemetery La. Shep. AZ54 83
Cemetery La. Wal. Abb. CG15 13
Cemetery La. Wal. Abb. CG16 22
Cemetery Rd. E7 CG35 49
Cemetery Rd. N17 CA29 39
Cemetery Rd. SE2 CO43 69
Cemmaes Court Rd. Hem. H. AX13 8
Cemmaes Mead, Hem. H. AX13 8
Cenacle Clo. NW3 BS34 47
Centaur St. SE1 BX41 66
Centenary Rd. Enf. CD24 30
Central Ave. Harl. CM11 13
Central Ave. Til. DG44 71
Central Av. E11 CF34 48
Central Av. N2 BT30 38
Central Av. N9 CA27 39
Central Av. W3 BO40 55
Central Av. E. Mol. BE52 84
Central Av. Enf. CB23 30
Central Av. Grav. DG48 81
Central Av. Harl. CM10 6
Central Av. Hayes BB40 53
Central Av. Houns. BG45 64
Central Av. Pnr. BE32 45
Central Av. S. Ock. CY41 70
Central Av. Wal. Cr. CD20 21
Central Av. Well. CN45 68
Central Cir. NW4 BP32 46
Central Dr. SW11 BU43 66
Central Dr. Horn. CW34 51
Central Dr. St. Alb. BK13 9
Central Gdns. Mord. BS53 86
Central Hill, SE19 BZ49 77
Central Mkts. EC1 BY39 56
Central Par. Hat. BO12 10
Central Pde. Croy. CF58 96
Central Pk. Av. Dag. CR34 50
Central Pk. Rd. E6 CJ37 58
Central Pl. SE25 CB52 87
Central Rd. Dart. CW46 80
Central Rd. Harl. CO9 6
Central Rd. Mord. BS53 86
Central Rd. Wem. BJ35 45
Central Rd. Wor. Pk. BP54 85
Central Sq. NW11 BS32 47
Central Sq. E. Mol. BE52 84
Central St. EC1 BZ38 57
Central St. NW1 BU39 56
Melcombe Pl.
Central Way Cars. BU57 95
Central Way Felt. BC46 73
Central Way. Oxt. CF67 114
Centre Av. Epp. CN19 22
Centre Clo. Epp. CN19 22
Centre Common Rd. Chis. CL50 78
Centre Dr. Epp. CN19 22
Centre Rd. E7 CH34 49
Centre Rd. E11 CH34 49
Centre Rd. SE18 CL42 68
Centre Rd. Dag. CR37 59
Centre St. E2 CB37 57
Centre The, Felt. BC47 73
Centre Way N9 CC27 39
Centre Way, Wal. Abb. CF21 30
Centreway Ilf. CM34 49
Century Rd. E17 CD31 48
Century Rd. Egh. AV49 72
Century Rd. Hodd. CE11 12
Century Rd. Mitch. BT52 86
Cephas Av. E1 CC38 57
Cephas St. E1 CC38 57
Ceres Rd. SE18 CN42 68
Cerise Rd. SE15 CB44 67
Cerne Clo. Hayes. BD40 54
Cerne Rd. Grav. DJ49 81
Cerne Rd. Mord. BT53 86
Cerney Ms. W2 BT40 56
Gloucester Ter.
Cervantes Ct. Nthwd. BB29 35
Cestreham Cres. Chesh. AO18 16
Ceylon Rd. W14 BQ41 65
Chace Av. Pot. B. BT19 20
Chadacre Av. Ilf. CK31 49
Chadacre Rd. Epsom BP57 94
Chadbourn St. E14 CE39 57
Chadd Dri. Brom. CK52 88
Chadfields Til. DG43 71
St. Chads Rd.
Chadville Gdns. Rom. CP32 50
Chadway, Dag. CP33 50
Chadwell Av. Rom. CO33 50
Chadwell Av. Wal. Cr. CC17 21
Chadwell By Pass. Grays. DF42 71
Chadwell Heath La. Rom. CO31 50
Chadwell Hill. Grays. DG42 71
Chadwell Rd. Grays. DE42 71
Chadwell St. EC1 BY38 56
Chadwick Av. E4 CF27 39
Chadwick Clo. Tedd. BJ50 74
Chadwick Rd. E11 CG33 49

Chadwick Rd. NW10 BO36 55
Chadwick Rd. SE15 CA44 67
Chadwick St. SW1 BW41 66
Chadwin Rd. E13 CH39 58
Chaffer's Mead. Ash. BL61 103
Chaffinch Av. Croy. CC53 87
Chaffinch Clo. Croy. CC53 87
Chaffinch La. Wat. BB26 35
Chaffinch Rd. Beck. CD51 87
Chafford Gdns. Brwd. DE32 123
Chafford Wk. Rain. CV37 60
Chafford Wk. Rain. CV38 60
Chafford Way. Grays. DD40 71
Chafford Way. Rom. CP31 50
Chagford St. NW1 BU38 56
Chailey Av. Enf. CA23 30
Chailey Pl. Walt. BE56 93
Chailey St. E5 CC34 48
Chalacoombe Clo. Brwd. DD26 122
Chalcombe Rd. SE2 CO41 69
Chalcot Clo. Sutt. BS57 95
Chalcot Cres. NW1 BU37 56
Chalcot Gdns. NW3 BU36 56
Chalcot Rd. NW1 BV36 56
Chalcots Est. NW3 BT36 56
Chalcot Sq. NW1 BV36 56
Chalcott Gdns. Surb. BK54 84
Chalcroft Rd. SE13 CG46 78
Chaldon Common Rd. Cat. BZ65 105
Chaldon Rd. SW6 BR43 65
Chaldon Rd. Cat. BZ65 105
Chaldon Way Couls. BX62 104
Chale Rd. SW2 BX46 76
Chalet Clo. Berk. AP13 7
Chalet Clo. Bex. CS49 79
Chale Walk Sutt. BS58 95
Hulverston Clo.
Chalfont Ave. Amer. AR23 25
Chalfont Av. Wem. BM36 55
Chalfont Clo. Hem. H. AZ11 8
Chalfont Grn. N9 CA27 39
Chalfont La. Ger. Cr. AU29 34
Chalfont La. Rick. AT25 25
Chalfont Rd. N7 BY35 47
Chalfont Rd. N9 CA27 39
Chalfont Rd. SE25 CA52 87
Chalfont Rd. Beac. AO28 34
Chalfont Rd. Ger. Cr. AT27 34
Chalfont Rd. Ger. Cr. AU27 34
Chalfont Rd. Hayes BC41 63
Chalfont Sta. Rd. Amer. AR23 25
Chalfont Way W13 BJ41 64
Chalford Clo. E. Mol. BF52 84
Chalforde Gdns. Rom. CU31 50
Chalford Rd. SE21 BZ49 77
Chalford Wk. Wdf. Grn. CJ30 40
Chalgrove Av. Mord. BS53 86
Chalgrove Cres. Ilf. CK30 40
Chalgrove Gdns. N3 BR31 46
Chalgrove Rd. E9 CC36 57
Chalgrove Rd. N17 CB30 39
Chalgrove Rd. Sutt. BT57 95
Chalice Clo. Wall. BW57 95
Chalice Way SW2 BX47 76
Chalkdell Fields, St. Alb. BJ11 9
Chalkenden Clo. SE20 CB50 77
Castleline Rd.
Chalkey Hill. Sev. CM60 97
Chalk Farm Rd. NW1 BV36 56
Chalk Hill, St. Alb. BF15 9
Chalk Hill. Wat. BD25 27
Chalkhill Rd. Wem. BM34 46
Chalklands, The, Wem. BN34 46
Chalk La. Ash. BL63 103
Chalk La. Barn. BU24 29
Chalk La. Epsom BN61 103
Chalk La. Harl. CR9 6
Chalk Lane. Leath. BB68 110
Chalk Pit Av. Orp. CP52 89
Chalkpit La. Dor. BJ71 119
Chalkpit La. Oxt. CF66 114
Chalkpit La. Oxt. CF67 114
Chalk Pit Rd. Bans. BS62 104
Chalk Pit Rd. Epsom. BN63 103
Chalkpit Ter. Dor. BJ70 119
Chalk Rd. E13 CH39 58
Chalk Rd. Grav. DK47 81
Chalk Road. Leath. BA69 110
Chalks Av. Saw. CP5 6
Chalkwell Pk. Av. Enf. CA24 30
Chalky Bank, Grav. DG49 81
Chalky La. Chess. BK58 93
Challenge Clo. Grav. DJ49 81
Challenge Rd. Ashf. BA48 73
Challice Way. SW2 BX47 76
Challin St. SE20 CC51 87
Challis Rd. Brent. BK42 64
Challock Clo. West. CJ61 106
Challoner Clo. N2 BT30 38
Challoner Cres. W14 BR42 65
Challoner St.
Challoners Clo. E. Mol. BG52 84
Challoner St. W14 BR42 65
Chalmers La. Reig. BT67 113
Chalmers Rd. Ashf. AZ49 73
Chalmers Rd. Bans. BT61 104
Chalmers Rd. E. Ashf. BA49 73
Chalmers St. SW8 BW44 66
Chalmers Ter. N16 CD34 48
Victorian Rd.
Chalmers Way Felt. BC46 73
Chalsey Rd. SE4 CD45 67
Chalterton Rd. N4 BY34 47
Chalton Dr. N2 BT32 47
Chalvey Gro. Slou. AN41 61
Chalvey Pk. Slou. AP41 62
Chalvey Rd. E. Slou. AO41 61
Chalvey Rd. E. Slou. AP41 62
Chalvey Rd. W. Slou. AO41 61
Chamberlain Cotts. SE5 BZ44 67
Camberwell Gro.
Chamberlain Cres. W. Wick. CE54 87
Chamberlain La. Pnr. BC31 44
Chamberlain Rd. N2 BT30 38
Chamberlain Rd. N9 CB27 39
Chamberlain Rd. W13 BJ41 64
Midhurst Rd.
Chamberlain Sq. N1 BY36 56
Lofting Rd.
Chamberlain St. NW1 BU36 56
Regents Pk. Rd.
Chamberlain Way Pnr. BC31 44
Chamberlain Way Surb. BL54 85
Chamberlayne Rd. NW10 BQ37 55
Chambersbury La. Hem. H. AZ15 8
Chambers La. NW10 BP36 55
Chambers Rd. N7 BX35 47
Chambers St. SE16 CB41 67
Chamber St. E1 CA40 57
Chambord St. E2 CA38 57
Chamersbury La. Hem. H. AZ16 17
Champion Cres. SE26 CD49 77
Champion Gro. SE5 CA45 67
Champion Hill, SE5 BZ45 67
Champion Pk. SE5 BZ44 67
Champion Rd. Upmin. CX34 51
Champions Way. Hodd. CE10 12
Champneys Clo. Sutt. BR57 94
Chancellor Gro. SE21 BZ48 77
Chancellor's Rd. W6 BQ42 65
Chancellor's St. W6 BQ42 65
Chancellor Way. Sev. CU64 107
Chancelot Rd. SE2 CO42 69
Chancel St. SE1 BY40 56
Dolben St.
Chancery La. WC2 BX39 56
Chancery La. Beck. CE51 87
Chance St. E1 CA38 57
Chance St. E2 CA38 57
Chanctonbury Chase, Red. BV70 121
Chanctonbury Clo. SE9 CL48 78
Chanctonbury Gdns. Sutt. BS57 95
Chanctonbury Way N12 BR28 37
Chandler Av. E16 CH39 58
Chandler Clo. Hamptn. BF51 84
Chandler Rd. Loug. CL23 31
Chandler's La. Rick. AY21 26
Chandlers Rd. St. Alb. BK11 9
Chandler St. E1 CB40 57
Chandos Av. E17 CE30 39
Chandos Av. N14 BW27 38
Chandos Av. N20 BT26 38
Chandos Av. W5 BK42 64
Chandos Clo. Amer. AR22 25
Chandos Clo. Buck. H. CH27 40
Chandos Cres. Edg. BL29 37
Chandos Pl. WC2 BX40 56
Chandos Rd. E15 CF35 48
Chandos Rd. N2 BT30 38
Chandos Rd. N17 CA30 39
Chandos Rd. NW2 BQ35 46
Chandos Rd. NW10 BO38 55
Chandos Rd. Borwd. BL23 28
Chandos Rd. Har. BG32 45
Chandos Rd. Pnr. BD33 45
Chandos Rd. Stai. AV49 72
Chandos St. W1 BV39 56
Chandrye Clo. SE9 CK46 78
Change Alley EC3 BZ39 57
Birchin La.
Channel Clo. Houns. BF44 64
Channelsea Rd. E15 CF37 57
Chanton Dr. Sutt. BQ58 94
Chantrey Rd. SW9 BX45 66
Chantry Av. Hat. BP13 10
Chantry Clo. Ash. BK63 102
Chantry Clo. Har. BL32 46
Chantry Clo. Kings L. AZ18 17
Chantry Clo. Sid. CQ49 79
Ellenborough La.
Chantry Clo. West Dr. AX40 53
Chantry Clo. Wind. AN44 61
Chantry Hurst Epsom BN61 103
Chantry La. Brom. CJ53 88
Chantry La. Hat. BO13 10
Chantry La. St. Alb. BK16 18
Chantry Pl. Har. BF30 36
Chantry Rd. Cher. AW54 83
Chantry Rd. Chess. BL56 94
Chantry Rd. Guil. AT73 118
Chantry Rd. Har. BF30 36
Chantry St. N1 BY37 56
Chantry, The. Harl. CO9 6
Chantry, The Uxb. AY38 53
Chantry View Rd. Guil. AR72 118
Chantry Way Rain. CS37 59
Chant St. E15 CF36 57
Chant Sw. E15 CF36 57
Chapel All. Brent. BL42 65
Chapel All. Brent. BL43 65
High St.
Chapel Av. Wey. AW56 92
Chapel Clo. N2 BU31 47
Chapel Ct.
Chapel Clo. Dart. CT46 79
Chapel Ct. N2 BU31 47
Chapel Cft. Kings L. AW19 17
Chapel End, Hodd. CE12 12
Chapel Farm Rd. SE9 CK48 78
Chapel Gro. Epsom. BQ63 103
Chapel Gro. Wey. AW56 92
Chapel Hill Dart. CT46 79
Chapel Hill. Pnr. BC32 44
Chapel Hill Crossways Lthd. BD67 111
Browns La.
Chapel Ho. Pl. E14 CE42 67
Chapel Ho. St. E14 CE42 67
Chapel La. Chig. CN27 40
Chapel La. Dor. BG68 111
Chapel La. Dor. BG72 119
Chapel La. Loug. CK24 31
Chapel La. Lthd. BG67 111
Chapel La. Ong. CV20 24
Chapel La. Pnr. BD31 45
Chapel La. Slou. AQ36 52
Chapel La. Uxb. AZ39 53
Chapel Mkt. N1 BY37 56
Chapel Park Rd. Wey. AW56 92
Chapel Pl. N17 CA29 39
White Hart La.
Chapel Pl. W1 BV39 56
Chapel Rd. SE27 BY49 76
Chapel Rd. W13 BJ40 54
Chapel Rd. Bexh. CR45 69
Chapel Rd. Epp. CN18 22
Chapel Rd. Houns. BF45 64
Chapel Rd. Mitch. BT52 86
Chapel Rd. Oxt. CJ68 115
Chapel Rd. Red. BU70 121
Chapel Rd. Tad. BQ65 103
Chapel Rd. Twick. BJ47 74
Chapel Rd. Warl. CC62 105
Chapel Row, Ilf. CL34 49
Station Rd.
Chapel Row. Uxb. AX30 35
Chapel Side W2 BS40 56
Chapel Stones N17 CA30 39
Kings Rd.
Chapel St. E15 CF36 57
Chapel St. NW1 BU39 56
Chapel St. SW1 BV41 66
Chapel St. W2 BS40 56
Chapel St. Enf. BZ24 30
Chapel St. Guil. AR71 118
Chapel St. Hem. H. AX13 8
Chapel St. Slou. AP41 62
Chapel Vw. Sth. Croy. CC57 96
Chapel Wk. NW4 BP31 46
Chapel Way Brom. CH51 88
Holwood Rd.
Chapel Way. Epsom. BQ63 103
Chapel Wood Rd. Fawk. DC55 90
Chapel Yd. N18 CB29 39
Fore St.
Chape Rd. Sev. DB64 108
Chape St. Berk. AR13 7
Chaplaincy Gdns. Horn. CW33 51
Allenby Dr.
Chaplin Cres. Sun. BB50 73
Chaplin Rd. E15 CG37 58
Chaplin Rd. NW2 BP36 55
Chaplin Rd. Dag. CQ36 59
Chaplin Rd. Wem. BK36 54
Chaplin St. SE23 CC48 77
Chapman Cres. Har. BL32 46
Chapman Rd. E9 CD36 57
Chapman Rd. Belv. CR42 69
Chapman Rd. Croy. BY54 86
Chapman's La. SE2 CP42 69
Chapman's La. Belv. CP42 69
Abbey Rd.
Chapman's La. Orp. CP51 89
Chapmans Rd. Sev. CQ65 107
Chapman St. E1 CB39 57
Chapples Clo. Loug. CM25 31
Chapter Clo. Uxb. AY36 53
Chapter Rd. NW2 BP35 46
Chapter Rd. SE17 BY42 66
Chapter St. SW1 BW42 66
Charcroft Gdns. Enf. CC24 30
Chardin Rd. W4 BO42 65
Elliott Rd.
Chardins Clo. Hem. H. AV13 7
Chardmore Rd. N16 CB33 48
Charford Rd. E16 CH39 58
Chargate Clo. Watt. BB57 92
Chargeable La. E13 CG38 58
Chargeable St. E16 CG38 58
Charing Clo. Orp. CN56 97
Charing Cross Rd. WC2 BW39 56
Charlbert St. NW8 BU37 56
Charlbury Av. Stan. BK28 36
Charlbury Clo. Rom. CV29 42
Charlbury Cres. Rom. CV29 42
Charlbury Gdns. Ilf. CN34 49
Charlbury Gro. W5 BK39 54
Charlbury Rd. Uxb. AY34 44
Charldane Rd. SE9 CL48 78
Charlecote Gro. SE26 CB48 77
Charlecote Rd. Dag. CQ34 50
Charlemont Rd. E6 CK38 58
Charles Burton Ct. E10 CD35 48
Meeson St.
Charles Clo. Sid. CO49 79
Charles Cres. Har. BG33 45
Charlesfield Way, SE9 CJ48 78
Charles Gdns. Slou. AQ39 62
Borderside
Charles Grindling Wk. SE18 CL42 68
Charles Ho. W14 BR42 65
Charles Ho. Wind. AO44 61
Ward Royal
Charles Ii St. SW1 BW40 56
Charles La. NW8 BU37 56
Charles Mills Ct. SW16 BX50 76
Charles Rd. E7 CJ36 58
Charles Rd. Dag. CS36 59
Charles Rd. Rom. CP33 50
Charles Rd. Sev. CR58 98
Charles Rd. Sev. CR59 98
Charles Rd. Stai. AX50 73
Charles Sevright Dr. NW7 BQ28 37
Charles Sq. N1 BZ38 57
Charles St. E16 CJ40 58
Charles St. SW13 BO45 65
Charles St. W1 BV40 56
Charles St. W5 BK40 54
Lancaster Rd.
Charles St. Berk. AQ13 7
Charles St. Cher. AV54 82
Charles St. Croy. BZ55 87
Charles St. Enf. CA25 30
Charles St. Epp. CO19 23
Charles St. Grays. DD43 71
Charles St. Green. CZ46 80
Charles St. Hem. H. AX14 8
Charles St. Houns. BE44 64
Charles St. Uxb. AZ38 53
Charles St. Wind. AO44 61
Charleston St. SE17 BZ42 67
Charlesworth St. N7 BX36 56
Charleville Circs. SE26 CB49 77
Charleville Rd. W14 BR42 65
Charlieville Rd. Erith CS43 69
Mill Rd.
Charlmont Rd. SW17 BU50 76
Charlock Way, Guil. AT69 118
Charlock Way, Wat. BB25 26
Charlock Way Wat. BC25 26
Charlotte Despard Av. SW11 BV44 66
Charlotte Gdns. Rom. CR29 41
Charlotte Ms. W1 BW39 56
Tottenham St.
Charlotte Pl. W1 BW39 56
Goodge St.
Charlotte Rd. EC2 CA38 57
Charlotte Rd. SW13 BO44 65
Charlotte Rd. Dag. CR36 59
Charlotte Rd. Wall. BW57 95
Charlotte Row SW4 BW45 66
North St.
Charlotte St. W1 BW39 56
Charlotte Ter. N1 BX37 56
Charlton Av. Walt. BC56 92
Charlton Church La. SE7 CJ42 68
Charlton Clo. Hodd. CE12 12
Charlton Clo. Uxb. AZ34 44
Charlton Cres. Bark. CN37 58
Charlton Dene, SE7 CJ43 68
Charlton Dr. West. CJ62 106
Charlton Gdns. Couls. BW62 104
Charlton Gs. Couls. BW58 95
Charlton Kings Rd. NW5 BW35 47
Charlton La. SE7 CJ42 68
Charlton La. Shep. BA52 83
Charlton Mead La. Hodd. CF12 12
Charlton Pk. La. SE7 CJ43 68
Charlton Pk. Rd. SE7 CJ43 68
Charlton Pl. N1 BY37 56
Charlton Rings, Wey. BB55 83
Charlton Rd. N9 CC26 39
Charlton Rd. NW10 BO37 55
Charlton Rd. SE3 CH43 68
Charlton Rd. SE7 CH43 68
Charlton Rd. Har. BK31 45
Charlton Rd. Shep. BA52 83
Charlton Rd. Shep. BA53 83
Charlton Rd. Wem. BL33 46
Charlton St. Grays DB43 70
Charlton Way, SE3 CG44 68
Charlton Way, Hodd. CE12 12
Charlwood Clo. Har. BH29 36
Charlwood Dr. Cob. BG61 102
Charlwood Pl. SW1 BW42 66
Charlwood Rd. SW15 BQ45 65
Charlwood St. SW1 BW42 66
Charlwood Ter. SW15 BQ45 65
Cardinal Pl.
Charman Rd. Red. BU70 121
Charmian Av. Stan. BK30 36
Charminster Av. SW19 BS51 86
Charminster Ct. Surb. BK54 84
Charminster Rd. SE9 CJ49 78
Charminster Rd. Wor. Pk. BQ54 85
Charmouth Ct. St. Alb. BJ12 9
Charmouth Rd. St. Alb. BJ12 9
Charmouth Rd. Well. CP44 69
Charmwood La. Orp. CO58 98
Charne. The. Sev. CU62 107
Charnock Ct. Cres. Swan. CT52 89
Charnock Rd. E5 CB34 48
Charnwood Av. SW19 BS51 86
Charnwood Clo. N. Mal. BO52 85
Charnwood Dr. E18 CH31 49
Charnwood Pl. N20 BT27 38
Charnwood Rd. SE25 BZ53 87
Charnwood Rd. Enf. CB21 30
Charnwood St. E5 CB34 48
Charrington St. NW1 BW37 56
Charriots Pl. Wind. AO44 61
Peascod St.
Charsley Clo. Amer. AR23 25
Charsley Rd. SE6 CE48 77
Chart Clo. Brom. CG51 88
Chart Downs Est. Dor. BK72 119
Chartecote Gro. SE26 CB48 77
Charter Av. Ilf. CM33 49
Charter Cres. Houns. BE45 64
Charter Dr. Bex. CQ47 79
Charterhouse Av. Wem. BK35 45
Charterhouse Bldgs. EC1 BY38 56
Goswell Rd.
Charterhouse Rd. Orp. CO55 89
Charterhouse Sq. EC1 BY39 56
Charterhouse St. EC1 BY39 56
Charteris Rd. N4 BY33 47
Charteris Rd. NW6 BR37 55
Charteris Rd. Wdf. Grn. CH29 40
Charter Rd. Kings-on-t. BM52 85
Charter Rd. E. Egh. AU50 72
Charter Rd. Sth. Egh. AU50 72
Charter Rd. W. Egh. AU50 72
Charters Clo. SE19 CA49 77
Charters Cross. Harl. CM12 13
Charter Sq. Kings-on-t. BM51 85
Charter, The, Rd. Wdf. Grn. CG29 40
Charter Way N3 BR31 46
Regents Pk. Rd.
Charter Way N14 BW25 29
Chartfield Av. SW15 BP46 75
Chartfield Rd. Reig. BT71 121
Chartfield Sq. SW15 BQ46 75
Chartham Gro. SE27 BY48 76
Royal Circus
Chartham Rd. SE25 CB52 87
Chart La. Dor. BK71 119
Chart La. Reig. BS70 121
Chart La. Reig. BT71 121
Chart La. West. CO68 116
Chart La. S. Dor. BK72 119
Chartley Av. NW2 BO34 46
Chartley Av. Stan. BH29 36
Charton Clo. Belv. CQ43 69
Chartridge Way, Hem. H. BA13 8
Chart St. N1 BZ38 57
Chart Way, Reig. BS70 121
Chartway. Sev. CV65 108
Chartwell Clo. SE9 CM48 78
Chartwell Clo. Wal. Abb. CG20 22
Mason Way
Chartwell Pl. Epsom BO60 94
Chartwell Pl. Sutt. BR55 85
Chartwell Rd. Nthwd. BB29 35
Charville Est. Hayes BA37 53
Charville La. Hayes BA38 53
Charville La. W. Uxb. AZ38 53
Charwood SE27 BY49 76
Leigham Ct. Rd.
Chasden Rd. Hem. H. AV12 7
Chase Ct. Gdns. Enf. BZ24 30
Chase Cross Rd. Rom. CS29 41
Chase End Epsom BN59 94
Chasefield Rd. SW17 BU49 76
Chase Gdns. E4 CE28 39
Chase Gdns. Twick. BG46 74
Chase Grn. Enf. BZ24 30
Chase Grn. Av. Enf. BY23 29
Chase Hill Enf. BZ24 30
Chase La. Chig. CN27 40
Chase La. Ilf. CM32 49
Chaseley St. E14 CD39 57
Chase Ridings Enf. BY23 29
Chase Rd. E18 CG30 40
Chase Rd. N14 BW25 29
Chase Rd. NW10 BO39 55
Chase Rd. W3 BO39 55
Chase Rd. Brwd. DB27 42
Chase Rd. Epsom BN59 94
Chase Side N14 BV25 29
Chase Side Enf. BZ24 30
Chase Side Av. SW20 BR51 85
Chase Side Av. Enf. BZ23 30
Chase Side Clo. Rom. CT29 41
Chase Side Cres. Enf. BZ23 30
Chaseside Gdns. Cher. AW54 83
Chase, The, E12 CJ35 49
Chase, The, SW4 BV45 66
Chase, The, SW16 BX50 76
Chase, The, SW20 BR51 85
Chase, The Ash. BK62 102
Chase, The, Bexh. CR45 69
Chase, The, Brom. CH52 88
Chase, The, Brwd. DB27 42
Chase, The, Brwd. DB28 42
Chase, The, Brwd. DE28 122
Chase, The, Chig. CM28 40
Chase, The, Couls. BW60 95
Chase, The, Edge. BM30 37
Chase, The Guil. AQ71 118
Chase, The Hem. H. AY14 8
Chase, The, Leath. BB66 110
Chase, The Lthd. BG61 102
Chase, The, Pnr. BD32 45
Chase, The, Pnr. BE31 45
Chase, The, Reig. BT71 121
Chase, The, Rom. CQ32 50
Chase, The, Rom. CT31 50
Chase, The, Rom. CT34 50
Chase, The, Stan. BJ29 36
Chase, The, Tad. BS64 104
Chase, The, Upmin. CZ34 51
Chase, The, Uxb. AZ35 44
Chase, The, Wal. Cr. BY17 20
Chase, The, Wall. BX56 95
Chase, The Wat. BB24 26
Chase. The. Sev. CW61 108
Chase, The, Trading Est. NW10 BN38 55
Chaseville Pk. Rd. N21 BX25 29
Chase Way N14 BW27 38
Chaseways, Saw. CP7 6
Chasewood Av. Enf. BY23 29
Chastilian Rd. Dart. CT47 79
Chaston St. NW5 BV35 47
Herbert St.
Chatfield Pl. W5 BL39 55
Park View Rd.
Chatfield Rd. SW11 BT45 66
Chatfield Rd. Croy. BY54 86
Chatham Av. N1 BZ38 57
Nile St.
Chatham Av. Brom. CG54 88
Chatham Clo. NW11 BS32 47
Chatham Clo. Sutt. BR54 85
Chatham Hill Rd. Sev. CV64 108
Chatham Pl. E9 CC36 57
Chatham Rd. E17 CD31 48
Chatham Rd. E18 CG30 40
Chatham Rd. SW11 BU46 76
Chatham Rd. Kings. On T. BM51 85
Chatham Rd. Orp. CM56 97
Chatham St. SE17 BZ42 67
Chatsfield, Epsom BP58 94
Chatsworth Av. NW4 BQ30 37
Chatsworth Av. SW20 BR51 85
Chatsworth Av. Brom. CH49 78
Chatsworth Av. Sid. CO47 79
Chatsworth Av. Wem. BL35 46
Chatsworth Clo. NW4 BQ30 37
Chatsworth Clo. Borwd. BM24 28
Chatsworth Ct. W8 BS42 66
Chatsworth Cres. Houns. BG45 64
Chatsworth Dr. Enf. CB26 39

Chatsworth Est. E5 CC35 48
Chatsworth Gdns. W3 BM40 55
Chatsworth Gdns. Har. BF33 45
Chatsworth Gdns. N. Mal. BO53 85
Chatsworth Pde. Orp. CM53 88
Chatsworth Pl. Tedd. BJ49 74
Chatsworth Ri. W5 BL38 55
Chatsworth Rd. E5 CC34 48
Chatsworth Rd. E15 CG35 49
Chatsworth Rd. NW2 BQ36 55
Chatsworth Rd. W4 BN43 65
Chatsworth Rd. W5 BL39 55
Chatsworth Rd. Croy. BZ55 87
Chatsworth Rd. Dart. CV45 70
Chatsworth Rd. Hayes BC38 53
Chatsworth Rd. Sutt. BQ56 94
Chatsworth Way. SE27 BY48 76
Chatteris Av. Rom. CV29 42
Chattern Hill. Ashf. AZ49 73
Chattern Rd. Ashf. BA49 73
Chatterton Rd. Brom. CJ52 88
Chatto Rd. SW11 BU46 76
Chaucer Av. Hayes BC39 53
Chaucer Av. Houns. BC44 63
Chaucer Av. Rich. BM44 65
Chaucer Clo. N11 BW28 38
Chaucer Clo. Berk. AP12 7
Chaucer Gdns. Sutt. BS55 86
Chaucer Grn. Croy. CC54 87
Chaucer Rd. E7 CH36 58
Chaucer Rd. E11 CH32 49
Chaucer Rd. E17 CF30 39
Chaucer Rd. SE24 BY46 76
Chaucer Rd. W3 BN40 55
Chaucer Rd. Ashf. AY49 73
Chaucer Rd. Grav. DE48 81
Chaucer Rd. Rom. CU29 41
Chaucer Rd. Sid. CP47 79
Chaucer Rd. Sutt. BS56 95
Chaucer Rd. Well. CN44 68
Chaucer Wk. Dart. CW45 70
Chaucer Way Dart. CX45 70
Chaucer Way. Wey. AW57 92
Chaulden Ter. Hem. H. AV14 7
Chauncey Av. Pot. B. BT20 20
Chauncey Clo. N9 CB27 39
Chave Rd. Dart. CW48 80
Chaworth Rd. Cher. AU57 91
Chealsea Cloisters SW3 BU42 66
Makins St.
Cheam Clo. Tad. BP64 103
Cheam Common Rd. Wor. Pk. BP55 85
Cheam Park Way Sutt. BQ57 94
Cheam Pl. SE5 BZ43 67
Cheam Rd. Epsom BP58 94
Cheam Rd. Sutt. BR57 94
Cheapside, EC2 BZ39 57
Cheapside Wok. AR60 91
Cheapside, Wok. AR61 100
Cheapside La. Uxb. AV34 43
Cheddar Waye Hayes BC39 53
Cheddington Rd. N18 CA27 39
Chedworth Clo. E16 CG39 58
Hallsville Rd.
Cheelson Rd. S. Ock. DA37 60
Cheffins Rd. Hodd. CD10 12
Cheguers, Welw. G. C. BQ9 5
Chelford Rd. Brom. CF49 77
Chelmer Cres. Bark. CO37 59
Chelmer Dr. Brwd. DF25 122
Chelmer Rd. E9 CC35 48
Chelmer Rd. Grays DG42 71
Chelmer Rd. Upmin. CY32 51
Chelmsford Av. Rom. CS29 41
Chelmsford Dr. Upmin. CW34 51
Chelmsford Gdns. Ilf. CK33 49
Chelmsford Rd. E11 CF33 48
Chelmsford Rd. E17 CE32 48
Chelmsford Rd. E18 CG30 40
Chelmsford Rd. N14 BW26 38
Chelmsford Rd. Brwd. DC25 122
Chelmsford Rd Ing. DC19 24
Chelmsford Rd. Ong. CZ16 24
Chelmsford Rd. Ong. DA17 24
Chelmsford Sq. NW10 BQ37 55
Chelmsford St. W6 BR43 65
Chelsea Br. BV43 66
Chelsea Br. Rd. SW1 BV42 66
Chelsea Clo. NW10 BR37 55
Chelsea Clo. Edg. BM30 37
Chelsea Clo. Hmptn. BG49 74
Chelsea Ct. SW3 BU43 66
Chelsea Embankment SW3 BU43 66
Chelsea Manor Est. SW3 BU43 66
Alpha Pl.
Chelsea Manor Gdns. SW3 BU42 66
Chelsea Manor St. SW3 BU42 66
Chelsea Pk. Gdns. SW3 BT43 66
Chelsea Sq. SW3 BT42 66
Chelsea Wk. SW3 BU43 66
Chelsfield Av. N9 CC26 39
Mottingham Rd.
Chelsfield Gdns. SE26 CC48 77
Chelsfield Hill. Orp. CP58 98
Chelsfield La. Orp. CP54 89
Chelsfield La. Orp. CR57 98
Chelsfield Rd. Orp. CP53 89
Chelsham Clo. Sutt. BR58 94
Chelsham Clo. Warl. CD62 105
Chelsham Court Rd. Warl. CF63 105
Chelsham Rd. SW4 BW45 66
Chelsham Rd. Sth. Croy. BZ57 96
Chelsham Rd. Warl. CD62 105
Chelsing Rise. Hem. H. BA14 8
Chelston Rd. Ruis. BC33 44
Chelsworth Clo. Rom. CW30 42
Chelsworth Dr. SE18 CM43 68
Chelsworth Dr. Rom. CW30 42
Cheltenham Av. Twick. BJ47 74
Cheltenham Clo. Nthlt. BF36 54
Cheltenham Gdns. E6 CK37 58
Cheltenham Gdns. Loug. CK25 31
Cheltenham Pl. W3 BM40 55
Cheltenham Pl. Har. BL31 46
Cheltenham Rd. SE15 CC45 67
Cheltenham Rd. Orp. CO55 89
Cheltenham Vil. Stai. AV46 72
Chelval St. E14 CE41 67
Chelverton Rd. SW15 BQ45 65
Chelwood Av. Hat. BP11 10
Chelwood Clo. Epsom BO59 94
Chelwood Clo. Nthwd. BA29 35
Chelwood Gdns. Rich. BM44 65
Chelwood Gdns. Pass. Rich. BM44 65
Pensford Av.
Chelwood Wk. SE4 CD45 67
Chenappa Clo. E13 CG38 58
Chenells. Hat. BO13 10
Cheney Rd. NW1 BX37 56
Cheneys Rd. E11 CG34 49
Cheney St. Pnr. BD32 45
Chenies Ave. Amer. AR23 25
Chenies Ct. Hem. H. AZ11 8
Chenies Ms. WC1 BW38 56
Chenies Par. Amer. AR23 25
Chenies Pl. NW1 BW37 56
Chenies Rd. Rick. AU23 25
Chenies St. WC1 BW39 56
Chenies, The, Dart. CT49 79
Chenies, The, Orp. CN53 88
Cheniston Clo. Wey. AV60 91
Cheniston Gdns. W8 BS41 66
Cheo Rd. Dor. BJ71 119
Chepstow Av. Horn. CW34 51
Chepstow Clo. SW15 BR46 75
Chepstow Cres. W11 BS40 56
Chepstow Cres. Ilf. CN32 49
Chepstow Gdns. Sthl. BE39 54
Chepstow Pl. W2 BS40 56
Chepstow Rise Croy. CA55 87
Chepstow Rd. W2 BS39 56
Chepstow Rd. W7 BJ41 64
Chepstow Rd. Croy. CA55 87
Chepstow Vill. W11 BR40 55
Chepstow Way SE15 CA44 67
Sumner Estate
Chequers Clo. Tad. BP66 112
Chequers Gdns. N13 BY28 38
Chequers Hill. Amer. AO23 25
Chequers La. Dag. CQ38 59
Chequers La. Tad. BP66 112
Chequers La. Wat. BD18 18
Chequers Orchard, Iver AV39 52
Chequers Rd. Brwd. CW25 33
Chequers Rd. Loug. CL25 31
Chequers Rd. Rom. CW27 42
Chequer St. EC1 BZ38 57
Chequer St. St. Alb. BG13 9
Chequers Wk. Wal. Abb. CG20 22
Mason Way
Chequers Way N13 BY28 38
Cherbury Ct. N1 BZ37 57
Cherbury St. N1 BZ37 57
Cherimoya Gdns. E. Mol. BF52 84
Cherington Rd. W7 BH40 54
Cheriton Av. Brom. CG53 88
Cheriton Av. Ilf. CK30 40
Cheriton Clo. W5 BK39 54
Cheriton Dr. SE18 CM43 68
Cheriton Sq. SW17 BV48 76
Cherkley Hill. Lthd. BK66 111
Cherries, The Slou. AQ39 52
Cherry Ave. Slou. AR41 62
Cherry Av. Brwd. DC27 122
Cherry Av. Sthl. BD40 54
Cherry Av. Swan. CS52 89
Cherry Bounce, Hem. H. AX13 8
Cherry Clo. Cars. BU55 86
Cherry Clo. Mord. BR52 85
Cherry Clo. Ruis. BB34 44
Cherrycot Hill Orp. CM56 97
Cherrycot Rise Orp. CM56 97
Cherry Cres. Brent. BJ43 64
Cherry Croft, Welw. G. C. BQ6 5
Cherrydale, Wat. BB24 26
Cherrydown Av. E4 CD27 39
Cherrydown Clo. E4 CD27 39
Cherrydown Rd. Sid. CP48 79
Cherrydown Wk. Rom. CR30 41
Cherry Gdns. Dag. CQ35 50
Cherry Garden St. SE16 CB41 67
Cherry Garth, Brent. BK42 64
Cherry Gro. Hayes BC40 53
Cherry Gro. Uxb. AZ39 53
Cherry Hill Barn. BS25 29
Cherry Hill, Rick. AW24 26
Cherry Hill, St. Alb. BF16 18
Cherry Hill Gdns. Croy. BX56 95
Cherry La. West Dr. AY42 63
Cherry Orch. Amer. AP22 25
Cherry Orchard, Ash. BM62 103
Cherry Orchard, Hem. H. AW12 8
Cherry Orchard, Slou. AQ36 52
Cherry Orchard, Stai. AW49 73
Cherry Orchard. West Dr. AY41 63
Cherry Orchard Clo. Orp. CP53 89
Cherry Orchard Gdns. E. Mol. BE52 84
Cherry Orchard La. Brom. CK55 88
Cherry Orchard Rd. Croy. BZ55 87
Cherry Orchard Rd. E. Mol. BE52 84
Cherry Ri. Ch. St. G. AR27 34
Cherry Rd. Enf. CC22 30
Cherry St. Guil. AR71 118
Cherry St. Rom. CS32 50
Cherry St. Wok. AS62 100
Cherry Tree Av. Guil. AP70 118
Cherry Tree Av. St. Alb. BK16 18
Cherry Tree Av. Stai. AW50 73
Cherry Tree Av. West Dr. AY39 53
Cherry Tree Clo. Rain. CT37 59
Cherry Tree Ct. Couls. BX62 104
Coulsdon Rd.
Cherry Tree Gdns. N2 BU31 47
Cherry Tree Gdns. Croy. BZ54 87
Oval Rd.
Cherry Tree Grn. Sth. Croy. CB60 96
Cherry Tree La. Ger. Cr. AR30 34
Cherry Tree La. Hem. H. BA11 8
Cherry Tree La. Pot. B. BS20 20
Cherry Tree La. Rain. CT38 59
Cherry Tree La. Slou. AS36 52
Cherry Tree Rise Buck. H. CJ28 40
Cherry Tree Rd. Hodd. CE11 12
Cherry Tree Rd. Wat. BC21 26
Cherry Tree Wk. Beck. CD52 87
Cherry Tree Walk. Chesh. AO18 16
Cherry Tree Wk. West. CJ61 106
Cherry Tree Wk. W. Wick. CG56 97
Cherry Tree Way, Stan. BJ28 36
Cherry Wk. Brom. CH54 88
Cherry Wk. Grays. DG41 71
Cherry Wk. Rain. CT37 59
Cherry Wk. Rick. AX23 26
Cherry Way Epsom BN57 94
Cherry Way. Hat. BP14 10
Cherry Way, Shep. BB52 83
Cherrywood Av. Egh. AQ50 72
Cherrywood Clo. Beac. AO28 34
Cherrywood Clo. Kings. On T. BM50 75
Alexandra Rd.
Cherrywood Ct. Tedd. BJ49 74
Elmfield Av.
Cherrywood Dr. SW15 BQ46 75
Cherrywood La. Mord. BR52 85
Cherston Gdns. Loug. CL24 31
Cherston Rd. Loug. CL24 31
Chertsey Bridge Rd. Cher. AX54 83
Chertsey Clo. Ken. BY61 104
Chertsey Ct. SW14 BM45 65
Chertsey Cres. Croy. CF58 96
Chertsey Cres. Croy. CF59 96
Chertsey Dr. Sutt. BR55 85
Chertsey La. Cher. AV52 82
Chertsey La. Stai. AV49 72
Chertsey La. Stai. AV51 82
Chertsey Rd. E11 CF34 48
Chertsey Rd. W4 BM42 65
Chertsey Rd. Ashf. & Sun. BA50 73
Chertsey Rd. Cher. AO56 91
Chertsey Rd. Ilf. CM35 49
Chertsey Rd. Shep. AY54 83
Chertsey Rd. Sun. & Felt. BB49 73
Chertsey Rd. Twick. BH47 74
Chertsey Rd. Twick. BJ46 74
Chertsey Rd. Wey. AW55 83
Chertsey Rd. Wey. AX59 92
Chertsey Rd. Wok. AP55 82
Chertsey Rd. Wok. AP58 91
Chertsey Rd. Wok. AS61 100
Chertsey Rd. Wok. AS62 100
Chertsey Rd. Wok. AT60 91
Chertsey St. SW17 BV49 76
Chertssey Rd. Wok. AS62 100
Cherwell Ct. Epsom BN56 94
Cherwell Dr. S. Ock. DA40 60
Cheselden Rd. Guil. AS71 118
Cheseman St. SE26 CB48 77
Chesfield Rd. Kings. On T. BL50 75
Chesham Av. Orp. CL53 88
Chesham Clo. Rom. CS31 50
Chesham Cres. SE20 CC51 87
Chesham La. Ch. St. G. AS27 34
Chesham La. Ger. Cr. AS28 34
Chesham Ms. SW1 BV41 66
Chesham Pl. SW1 BV41 66
Chesham Rd. SE20 CC51 87
Chesham Rd. SW19 BT49 76
Chesham Rd. Guil. AS71 118
Chesham Rd. Hem. H. AS17 16
Chesham Rd. Kings. On T. BM51 85
Chesham St. NW10 BN34 46
Chesham St. SW1 BV41 66
Chesham Ter. W13 BJ41 64
Cheshire Clo. Horn. CX32 51
Cheshire Clo. Mitch. BX52 86
Cheshire Ct. EC4 BY39 56
Fleet St.
Cheshire Gdns. Chess. BK57 93
Cheshire Rd. N22 BX29 38
Cheshire St. E2 CA38 57
Chesholm Rd. N16 CA34 48
Chesholm Rd. Ashf. BA50 73
Cheshunt Great Ho. Wal. Cr. CB18 21
Cheshunt Rd. E7 CH36 58
Cheshunt Rd. Belv. CR42 69
Cheshunt Wash, Wal. Cr. & Brox. CD18 21
Chesilton Rd. SW6 BR44 65
Chesil Way, Hayes BB38 53
Chesley Gdns. E6 CJ37 58
Chesney Cres. Croy. CF57 96
Chesnut Clo. Cars. BU54 86
Chesnut Gro. Mitch. BW53 86
Chess Clo. Rick. AX24 26
Chess Clo. Rick. AZ24 26
Chess Ct. E1 CA39 57
Old Castle St.
Chessfield Park. Amer. AS22 25
Chessington Av. N3 BR31 46
Chessington Av. Bexh. CQ43 69
Chessington Clo. Epsom BN57 94
Chessington Ct. Pnr. BE31 45
Chessington Hill Pk. Chess. BM57 94
Chessington Pde. Chess. BK56 93
Chessington Rd. Epsom BM57 94
Chessington Way W. Wick. CE55 87
Chess La. Rick. AX24 26
Chessmount Rise. Chesh. AO20 16
Chesson Rd. W14 BR43 65
Chess Vale Ri. Rick. AY25 26
Chess Way, Rick. AW24 26
Chesswood Way, Pnr. BD30 36
Chester Av. Rich. BL46 75
Chester Av. Twick. BE47 74
Chester Av. Upmin. CZ34 51
Chester Clo. SW1 BV41 66
Chester Clo. Ashf. BA49 73
Chester Clo. Guil. AP69 118
Chester Clo. Loug. CM23 31
Chester Clo. Sutt. BS55 86
Chester Clo. Uxb. AZ39 53
Chester Cotts. SW1 BV42 66
Bourne St
Chester Ct. NW5 BV35 47
Chester Ct. W3 BM39 55
Monks Dr.
Chester Dr. Har. BE32 45
Chesterfied Dr. Sev. CS64 107
Chesterfield Clo. Orp. CQ52 89
Chesterfield Dr. Esher. BJ55 84
Chesterfield Gdns. W1 BV40 56
Chesterfield Gro. SE22 CA46 77
Chesterfield Hill W1 BV40 56
Chesterfield Rd. E10 CF32 48
Chesterfield Rd. N3 BS29 38
Chesterfield Rd. N4 BY32 47
Chesterfield Rd. W4 BN43 65
Chesterfield Rd. Ashf. AX49 73
Chesterfield Rd. Barn. BQ25 28
Chesterfield Rd. Enf. CD22 30
Chesterfield Rd. Epsom BN57 94
Chesterfield St. W1 BV40 56
Chesterfield Wk. SE10 CF44 67
Chesterford Gdns. NW3 BS35 47
Chesterford Rd. E12 CK35 49
Chester Gdns. W13 BJ39 54
Chester Gdns. Enf. CB25 30
Chester Gdns. Mord. BT53 86
Chester Gate, NW1 BV38 56
Outer Circle
Chester Grn. Loug. CM23 31
Chester Gro. SE18 CM42 68
Chester Ms. SW1 BV41 66
Chester Path Loug. CM23 31
Chester Pl. NW1 BV38 56
Chester Ter. Ms.
Chester Rd. E7 CJ36 58
Chester Rd. E11 CH32 49
Chester Rd. E16 CG38 58
Chester Rd. E17 CC32 48
Chester Rd. N9 CB26 39
Chester Rd. N17 BZ31 48
Chester Rd. N19 BV34 47
Chester Rd. NW1 BV38 56
Chester Rd. SW19 BQ50 75
Chester Rd. Borwd. BN24 28
Chester Rd. Chig. CL27 40
Chester Rd. Houns. BC45 63
Chester Rd. Ilf. CN33 49
Chester Rd. Loug. CL23 31
Chester Rd. Nthwd. BB29 35
Chester Rd. Sid. CN46 78
Chester Rd. Wat. BC25 26
Chester Row SW1 BV42 66
Chester Sq. SW1 BV42 66
Chesters, The, N. Mal. BO51 85
Chester St. E11 CG34 49
Chester St. SW1 BV41 66
Chester Ter. NW1 BV38 56
Chester Ter. Ms. NW1 BV38 56
Chesterton Clo. Grnf. BF37 54
Chesterton Dr. Red. BX67 113
Chesterton Rd. E13 CH38 58
Chesterton Rd. W10 BQ39 55
Chesterton Ter. E13 CH38 58
Chesterton Ter. Kings-on-t. BM51 85
Chesterton Way Til. DG44 71
Brennan Rd.
Chester Way, SE11 BY42 66
Chesthunte Rd. N17 BZ30 39
Chestney St. SW11 BV44 66
Battersea Pk. Rd.
Chestnut Ave. Chesh. AO18 16
Chestnut Ave. Grays. DD41 71
Chestnut Ave. Nthwd. BB30 35
Chestnut Ave. Slou. AR41 62
Chestnut Ave. West. CL64 106
Chestnut Av. E7 CH35 49
Chestnut Av. N8 BX32 47
Chestnut Av. SW14 BO45 65
Thornton Rd
Chestnut Av. Brent. BK42 64
Chestnut Av. Buck. H. CJ27 40
Chestnut Av. Edg. BL29 37
Chestnut Av. Epsom BO56 94
Chestnut Av. Esher BF57 93
Chestnut Av. Esher BG54 84
Chestnut Av. Guil. AR72 118
Chestnut Av. Hamptn. BF50 74
Chestnut Av. Horn. CT34 50
Chestnut Av. Pnr. BD32 45
Chestnut Av. Rick. AW25 26
Chestnut Av. Tedd. BH52 84
Chestnut Av. Vir. W. AP52 82
Chestnut Av. Watt. BB58 92
Chestnut Av. Wem. BJ35 45
Chestnut Av. West Dr. AY40 53
Chestnut Av. W. Wick. CG55 88
Chestnut Av. Wey. BA57 92
Chestnut Av. N. E17 CF31 48
Chestnut Av. S. E17 CF32 48
Chestnut Clo. N14 BW25 29
Chestnut Clo. Amer. AO22 25
Chestnut Clo. Ashf. AZ49 73
Chestnut Clo. Berk. AT12 7
Chestnut Clo. Buck. H. CJ27 40
Chestnut Clo. Egh. AQ50 72
Chestnut Clo. Ger. Cr. AS30 34
Chestnut Clo. Hayes BB40 53
Chestnut Clo. Horn. CV35 51
Chestnut Clo. Orp. CO56 98
Chestnut Clo. Tad. BS65 104
Chestnut Clo. West Dr. AZ43 63
Chestnut Clo. Wey. AX56 92
Chestnut Copse. Oxt. CH69 115
Chestnut Ct. Amer. AO21 25
Chestnut Ct. N. Mal. BO52 85
Chestnut Dri. Berk. AR13 7
Chestnut Dr. E11 CH32 49
Chestnut Dr. Bexh. CP45 69
Chestnut Dr. Egh. AR50 72
Chestnut Dr. Har. BH29 36
Chestnut Dr. St. Alb. BJ12 9
Chestnut Dr. Wind. AM45 61
Chestnut Dr. Wok. AV65 100
Chestnut Gdns. Sutt. BS56 95
Elm Gro.
Chestnut Glen Horn. CU34 50
Chestnut Grn. Stai. AW49 73
Chestnut Gro. SW12 BV47 76
Chestnut Gro. W5 BK41 64
Chestnut Gro. Barn. BU25 29
Chestnut Gro. Brwd. DB27 42
Chestnut Gro. Dart. CS49 79
Chestnut Gro. Ilf. CN29 40
Chestnut Gro. Islw. BJ45 64
Chestnut Gro. N. Mal. BN52 85
Chestnut Gro. Stai. AX50 73
Chestnut Gro. Sth. Croy. CB57 96
Chestnut Gro. Wem. BJ35 45
Chestnut Gro. Wok. AS63 100
Chestnut La. Amer. AO21 25
Chestnut La. Sev. CU65 107
Chestnut La. Wey. AZ56 92
Chestnut La. Wok. AO57 91
Chestnut Rise, SE18 CM43 68
Chestnut Rise Bush. BF26 36
Chestnut Rd. N17 CA31 48
Chestnut Rd. SE27 BY48 76
Chestnut Rd. SW20 BQ51 85
Chestnut Rd. Ashf. AZ49 73
Chestnut Rd. Dart. CV47 80
Chestnut Rd. Enf. CD21 30
Chestnut Rd. Guil. AR70 118
Chestnut Rd. Kings. On T. BL50 75
Chestnut Rd. Twick. BH48 74
Chestnut Rd. Pass. Twick. BH48 74
Chestnuts, Brwd. DD26 122
Chestnuts, The, Ong. DB13 15
Chestnuts, The, Walt. BC55 83
Chestnut Wk. Ger. Cr. AS29 34
Chestnut Wk. Sev. CW67 117
Chestnut Walk, Shep. BB53 83
Chestnut Wk. Wat. BC22 26
Chestnut Walk, Watt. BB58 92
Chestnut Wk. Wdf. Grn. CH28 40
Cheston Av. Croy. CD54 87
Chesworth Clo. Erith CT44 69
Chettle Clo. SE1 BZ41 67
Spurgeon St.
Chetwode Clo. Epsom. BQ63 103
Chetwode Dr. Epsom BQ62 103
Chetwode Dr. Epsom. BQ63 103
Chetwode Rd. SW17 BU48 76
Chetwode Rd. Epsom. BQ63 103
Chetwynd Av. Barn. BU26 38
Chetwynd Rd. NW5 BV35 47
Cheval Pl. SW7 BU41 66
Cheveley Clo. Rom. CW30 42
Chevening Rd. NW6 BQ37 55
Chevening Rd. SE10 CG42 68
Chevening Rd. SE19 BZ50 77
Chevening Rd. Sev. CQ63 107
Chevenings, The, Sid. CO48 79
Cheverton Rd. N19 BW33 47
Chevet St. E9 CD35 48
Chevington Way. Horn. CV35 51
Cheviot Clo. Bans. BS61 104
Cheviot Clo. Bexh. CT44 69
Cheviot Clo. Bush. BG25 27
Cheviot Clo. Enf. BZ23 30
Cheviot Clo. Sutt. BT58 95
Cheviot Gdns. NW2 BQ34 46
Cheviot Gte. NW2 BR34 46
Cheviot Rd. SE27 BY49 76
Cheviot Rd. Horn. CU33 50
Cheviot Rd. Slou. AT42 62
Cheviots. Hat. BP14 10
Cheviots Hem. H. AY12 8
Malvern Way
Cheviot Way. Ilf. CN32 49
Chewton Rd. E17 CD31 48
Cheyham Way Sutt. BR58 94
Cheyne Av. E18 CG31 49
Cheyne Av. Twick. BE47 74
Cheyne Clo. NW4 BQ32 46
Cheyne Clo. Brom. CK55 88
Cheyne Clo. Ger. Cr. AS33 43
Cheyne Court, SW3 BU43 66
Flood St.
Cheyne Ct. Bans. BS61 104
Cheyne Gdns. SW3 BU43 66
Cheyne Hill Surb. BL52 85
Cheyne Ms. SW3 BU43 66

Cheyne Path W13 BH39 54
Cheyne Pl. SW3 BT43 66
Cheyne Rd. Ashf. BA50 73
Napier Rd.
Cheyne Row SW3 BU43 66
Cheyne Wk. N21 BY25 29
Cheyne Wk. NW4 BQ32 46
Cheyne Wk. SW3 BT43 66
Cheyne Wk. SW10 BT43 66
Cheyne Wk. Chesh. AO18 16
Cheyne Wk. Croy. CB55 87
Cheyney Row E17 CD30 39
Cheyneys Av. Edg. BK29 36
Cheywind Dr. Uxb. AY37 53
Chichele Gdns. Croy. CA56 96
Chichele Rd. NW2 BQ35 46
Chichele Rd. Oxt. CG67 115
Chicheley Gdns. Har. BG29 36
Chicheley Rd. Har. BG29 36
Chicheley St. SE1 BX41 66
Chichester Av. Ruis. BA34 44
Chichester Clo. Dor. BJ70 119
Chichester Clo. S. Ock. CW40 60
Chichester Ct. Stan. BL31 46
Chichester Dr. Pur. BX59 95
Chichester Dru. Pur. BX55 86
Chichester Gdns. Ilf. CK33 49
Chichester Rents. WC2 BY39 56
Chancery La.
Chichester Rise Grav. DH49 81
Livingstone Rd.
Chichester Rd. E11 CG34 49
Chichester Rd. N9 CB26 39
Chichester Rd. NW6 BS37 56
Chichester Rd. W2 BS39 56
Chichester Rd. Croy. CA55 87
Chichester Rd. Dor. BJ70 119
Chichester Rd. Green. CZ46 80
Chichester Row. Amer. AO22 25
Chichester St. SW1 BW42 66
Chichester Way Felt. BD46 74
Chichester Way Wat. BE20 18
Mutchetts Clo.
Chickabiddy Hill. Wok. AO56 91
Chicksand Est. E1 CB39 57
Chicksand St. E1 CA39 57
Chiddingfold N12 BS27 38
Chiddingstone Av. Bexh. CQ43 69
Chiddingstone St. SW6 BS44 66
Chieveley Rd. Bexh. CR45 69
Chigwell Hill. E1 CB40 57
Pennington St.
Chigwell Hurst Ct. Pnr. BD30 36
Chigwell La. Loug. CM24 31
Chigwell Pk. Dr. Chig. CL28 40
Chigwell Rise Chig. CL27 40
Chigwell Rd. E18 CH31 49
Chigwell Rd. Wdf. Grn. CH31 49
Chigwell Rd. Wdf. Grn. & Chig. CH31 49
Chigwell Vw. Rom. CR29 41
Chilberton Dr. Red. BW68 113
Chilberton Dr. Red. BW69 121
Chilcot Clo. E14 CE39 57
Grundy St.
Chilcott Rd. Wat. BB21 26
Childebert Rd. SW17 BV48 76
Childerditch La. Brwd. DC29 42
Childerditch La. Brwd. DD30 123
Childerditch St. Brwd. DD30 123
Childeric Rd. SE14 CD43 67
Childerley St. SW6 BR44 65
Fulham Palace St.
Childers St. SE8 CD43 67
Childsbridge La. Sev. CW62 108
Childsbridge Way. Sev. CW63 108
Childs Cres. Swans. DB46 80
Childs Hall Rd. Lthd. BE66 111
Childs La. SE19 CA50 77
Childs Pl. SW5 BS42 66
Childs St. SW5 BS42 66
Childwick Clo. Hem. H. AZ15 8
Childwick Ct. Hem. H. AZ15 8
Chilham Clo. Grnf. BJ37 54
Horsenden La. S.
Chilham Rd. SE9 CK49 78
Chilham Way Brom. CG54 88
Chillbrook Rd. Cob. BC62 101
Chillerton Rd. SW17 BV49 76
Chillingworth Gdns. Twick. BH48 74
Tower Rd.
Chillingworth Rd. N7 BY35 47
Chilmans Dri. Lthd. BF66 111
Pine Dene
Chilmark Gdns. N. Mal. BP53 85
Chilmark Gdns. Red. BX68 113
Chilmark Rd. SW16 BW51 86
Chilmead La. Red. BW69 121
Chilsey Green Rd. Cher. AV53 82
Chiltern Ave. Amer. AO22 25
Chiltern Av. Bush. BG25 27
Chiltern Av. Twick. BF47 74
Chiltern Clo. Berk. AP12 7
Chiltern Clo. Bexh. CT44 69
Chiltern Clo. Bush. BF25 27
Chiltern Clo. Uxb. AZ34 44
Chiltern Clo. Wal. Cr. BY17 20
Chiltern Dene Enf. BX24 29
Chiltern Dr. Rick. AV26 34
Chiltern Dr. Surb. BM53 85
Chiltern Gdns. NW2 BQ34 46
Chiltern Gdns. Brom. CG52 88
Chiltern Gdns. Horn. CV34 51
Chiltern Hill. Ger. Cr. AS30 34
Chiltern Rd. E3 CE38 57
Chiltern Rd. Grav. DF48 81
Chiltern Rd. Ilf. CN31 49
Chiltern Rd. Pnr. BD32 45
Chiltern Rd. St. Alb. BK11 9
Chiltern Rd. Sutt. BS58 95
Chilterns, Berk. AP12 7
Chilterns Hem. H. AY12 8
Malvern Way
Chilterns, The, Sutt. BS58 95
Chiltern St. W1 BV39 56
Chiltern Vw. Rd. Uxb. AX37 53
Chiltern Way. Wdf. Grn. CH27 40
Chilthorne Clo. SE6 CD47 77
Chilton Av. W5 BK42 64
Chilton Clo. Borwd. BL23 28
Chilton Ct. Walt. BC56 92
Chilton Gro. SE8 CC42 67
Chilton Rd. Edg. BM29 37
Chilton Rd. Grays. DG41 71
Chilton Rd. Rich. BM45 65
Chiltons, The, E18 CH30 40
Grove Hill
Chilton St. E2 CA38 57
Chilvers St. SE10 CG42 68
Chilwell Gdns. Wat. BD28 36
Chilworth Ct. SW19 BQ47 75
Windlesham Gro.
Chilworth Gdns. Sutt. BT55 86
Chilworth Ms. W2 BT39 56
Chilworth New Rd. Guil. AT74 118
Chilworth Rd. Guil. AV73 118
Chilworth St. W2 BT39 56
Chimes Av. N13 BY28 38
China La. Upmin. DE35 123
Chinbrook Cres. SE12 CH48 78
Chinbrook Rd. SE12 CH48 78
Chinchilla Dr. Houns. BD44 64
Chindits La. Brwd. DB28 42
Chine, The, N10 BW31 47
Chine, The, N21 BY25 29
Chine, The, Wem. BJ35 45
Chingdale Rd. E4 CG27 40
Chingford Av. E4 CE27 39
Chingford La. Wdf. Grn. CG28 40
Chingford Mount Rd. E4 CE28 39
Chingford Rd. E4 CE29 39
Chingley Clo. Brom. CG50 78
Chinnor Cres. Grnf. BF37 54
Chinthurst La. Guil. AS74 118
Chipka St. E14 CF41 67
Chipmunk Gro. Nthlt. BD38 54
Chipmunk Gro. Nthlt. BE38 54
Argus Way
Chippendale Alley, Uxb. AX37 53
Chippendale Rd. Orp. CO51 89
Chippendale St. E5 CC34 48
Chippendale Waye, Uxb. AX36 53
Chippenham Av. Wem. BM35 46
Chippenham Clo. Pnr. BB31 44
Chippenham Clo. Rom. CV28 42
Chippenham Gdns. NW6 BS38 56
Malvern Rd.
Chippenham Gdns. Rom. CV28 42
Chippenham Ms. W9 BS38 56
Chippenham Rd. W9 BS38 56
Chippenham Rd. Rom. CV28 42
Chippenham Wk. Rom. CV29 42
Chipperfield Clo. Upmin. CZ33 51
Chipperfield Rd. Hem. H. AT17 16
Chipperfield Rd. Hem. H. AX15 8
Chipperfield Rd. Kings L. AX18 17
Chipperfield Rd. Orp. CO51 89
Chippingfield, Harl. CP9 6
Chipstead Av. Th. Hth. BY52 86
Chipstead Clo. Couls. BV61 104
Chipstead Clo. Ger. Cr. AR30 34
Chipstead Clo. Red. BU71 121
Chipstead Ct. Wok. AP61 100
Chipstead Gdns. NW2 BP34 46
Chipstead La. Couls. BT65 104
Chipstead La. Sev. CS64 107
Chipstead La. Sev. CT64 107
Chipstead La. Tad. BR66 112
Chipstead Pk. Sev. CS64 107
Chipstead Park Clo. Sev. CS64 107
Chipstead Rd. Bans. BR62 103
Chipstead Rd. Erith CT43 69
Chipstead St. SW6 BS44 66
Chipstead Valley Rd. Couls. BV61 104
Chipstead Way Bans. BU62 104
Chip St. SW4 BW45 66
Chisenhale Rd. E3 CD37 57
Chisholm Rd. Croy. CA55 87
Chisholm Rd. Rich. BL46 75
Chisledon Wk. E9 CD36 57
Trowbridge Est.
Chislehurst Av. N12 BT29 38
Chislehurst Rd. Brom. CJ51 88
Chislehurst Rd. Orp. CN52 88
Chislehurst Rd. Rich. BL46 75
Chislehurst Rd. Sid. CO49 79
Chislet Clo. Beck. CE50 77
Abbey La.
Chisley Rd. N15 CA32 48
St. Ann's Rd.
Chiswellgreen La. St. Alb. BE16 18
Chiswell Sq. SE3 CH44 68
Chiswell St. EC1 BZ39 57
Chiswick Br. SW14 BN44 65
Chiswick Br. W4 BN44 65
Chiswick Clo. Croy. BX55 86
Chiswick Common Rd. W4 BN42 65
Chiswick Ct. Pnr. BE31 45
Chiswick High Rd. W4 BM42 65
Chiswick La. W4 BO42 65
Chiswick La. S. W4 BO42 65
Chiswick Mall W4 BO43 65
Chiswick Quay W4 BN44 65
Chiswick Rd. N9 CB27 39
Chiswick Rd. W4 BN42 65
Chiswick Staithe, W4 BN44 65
Chiswick Village, W4 BM43 65
Chitty's La. Dag. CP34 50
Chitty St. W1 BW39 56
Chittys Walk, Guil. AP68 109
Chivalry Rd. SW11 BU46 76
Chivers Rd. E4 CE28 39
Chivers Rd. Brwd. CZ20 24
Choats Manor Way Bark. CP38 59
Choats Rd. Dag. CQ38 59
Chobham Gdns. SW19 BQ48 75
Chobham Lane, Wok. AP55 82
Chobham Park La. Wok. AQ58 91
Chobham Pl. Wok. AO57 91
Chobham Rd. E15 CF35 48
Chobham Rd. AO60 91
Chobham Rd. Cher. AT57 91
Chobham Rd. Wok. AR60 91
Chobham Rd. Wok. AS61 100
Choir Grn. Wok. AP62 100
Cholmeley Cres. N6 BV33 47
Cholmeley Pk. N6 BV33 47
Cholmley Gdns. NW6 BS35 47
Fortune Gr. Rd.
Cholmley Gdns. NW6 BS36 56
Mill Lane
Cholmley Rd. Surb. BJ53 84
Cholmondeley Av. NW10 BP37 55
Cholmondeley Wk. Rich. BK46 74
Chopham Rd. Wok. AO61 100
Chorleywood Bottom. Rick. AU25 25
Chorleywood Clo. Rick. AX26 35
Nightingale Rd.
Chorleywood Cres. Orp. CN51 88
Chorleywood Rd. Rick. AW24 26
Choumert Gro. SE15 CB44 67
Choumert Rd. SE15 CA45 67
Choumert Sq. SE15 CB44 67
Chrichton St. SW8 BW44 66
Westbury St.
Chrisp St. E14 CE39 57
Christ Ch. Mt. Epsom BN59 94
Christchurch Av. N12 BT29 38
Christchurch Av. Erith CT43 69
Christchurch Av. Har. BH31 45
Christchurch Av. Har. BJ31 45
Christchurch Av. Rain. CT38 59
Christchurch Av. Tedd. BJ49 74
Christchurch Av. Wem. BL36 55
Christchurch Clo. E9 CC37 57
Northiam St.
Christchurch Clo. N12 BT29 38
Christchurch Clo. SW19 BT50 76
Christ Church Cres. Rad. BJ21 27
Christchurch Gdns. Har. BJ31 45
Christchurch Grn. Wem. BL36 55
Christchurch Hill NW3 BT34 47
Christchurch La. Barn. BR23 28
Christ Church Mt. Epsom. BM59 94
Christchurch Pk. Sutt. BT57 95
Christchurch Pass. NW3 BT34 47
Christchurch Hill
Christchurch Rd. N8 BX32 47
Christchurch Rd. SW2 BX47 76
Christ Church Rd. SW14 BM46 75
Christchurch Rd. SW19 BT51 86
Christchurch Rd. Beck. CE51 87
Fairfield Rd.
Christchurch Rd. Dart. CV47 80
Christ Church Rd. Epsom. BL59 94
Christchurch Rd. Grav. DH47 81
Christchurch Rd. Hem. H. AX13 8
Christchurch Rd. Ilf. CL33 49
Christchurch Rd. Pur. BY58 95
Christchurch Rd. Sid. CN49 78
Christchurch Rd. Surb. BL54 85
Christchurch Rd. Til. DG44 71
Christchurch Rd. Vir. W. AQ52 82
Christchurch St. SW3 BU43 66
Christchurch Way, SE10 CG42 68
Christian Fields, SW16 BY50 76
Christian Fields Av. Grav. DH49 81
Christian Sq. Wind. AO44 61
Ward Royal
Christian St. E1 CB39 57
Christie Gdns. Rom. CO32 50
Christie Rd. E9 CD36 57
Christina St. EC2 CA38 57
Christmas St. SE1 CA41 67
Tower Bridge Rd.
Christopher Av. W7 BJ41 64
Christopher Clo. Sid. CN46 78
Blackfen Rd.
Christopher Ct. Tad. BQ65 103
Christopher Gdns. Dag. CP35 50
Wren Rd.
Christopher Rd. W7 BJ41 64
Christophers Ms. W11 BR40 55
Christopher St. EC2 BZ38 57
Christy La. Lthd. BF66 111
Christy Rd. West. CJ61 106
Chryssell Rd. SW9 BY43 66
Chucer Av. Wey. AZ57 92
Chucks La. Tad. BP65 103
Chudleigh Cres. Ilf. CN35 49
Chudleigh Gdns. Sutt. BT55 86
Chudleigh Rd. NW6 BQ36 55
Chudleigh Rd. SE4 CD46 77
Chudleigh Rd. Rom. CW28 42
Chudleigh Rd. Twick. BH46 74
Chudleigh St. E1 CC39 57
Chudleigh Way Ruis. BC33 44
Chulsa Est. SE26 CB49 77
Chulsa Rd. SE26 CB49 77
Chumleigh St. SE5 CA43 67
Chumleigh Wk. Surb. BL52 85
Churcfield Rd. Welw. BT6 5
Church Alley, EC2 BZ39 57
Basinghall St.
Church Alley, Brent. BK43 64
Church Alley Croy. BY54 86
Church All. Wat. BG22 27
Church App. SE21 BZ48 77
Church App. Sev. CM61 106
Church App. Stai. AX46 73
Church Av. E4 CF29 39
Church Av. SW14 BN45 65
Church Av. Beck. CE51 87
Church Av. Nthlt. BE36 54
Church Av. Pnr. BE32 45
Church Av. Ruis. BA33 44
Church Av. Sid. CO49 79
Church Av. Sthl. BE41 64
Churchbury Clo. Enf. CA23 30
Churchbury La. Enf. BZ24 30
Churchbury Rd. SE9 CJ47 78
Churchbury Rd. Enf. BZ23 30
Church Cl. Tad. BR67 112
Church Clo. N20 BU27 38
Church Clo. SE20 CC50 77
Laurel Gro.
Church Clo. W8 BS41 66
Church Clo. Brwd. CY22 33
Church Clo. Edg. BN28 37
Church Clo. Hayes BA39 53
Church Clo. Hert. BW13 11
Church Clo. Loug. CK23 31
Church Clo. Lthd. BG65 102
Church Clo. Nthwd. BC29 35
Church Clo. Pot. B. BX18 20
Church Clo. Uxb. AW37 53
Church Clo. Uxb. AZ38 53
Church Clo. West Dr. AY41 63
Church Clo. Wey. AW56 92
Church Clo. Wok. AR61 100
Church Ct. Rich. BK46 74
Church Cres. E9 CC36 57
Church Cres. N3 BR30 37
Church Cres. N10 BV31 47
Church Cres. N20 BU27 38
Church Cres. St. Alb. BG13 9
Church Cres. Saw. CQ6 6
Church Cres. S. Ock. DB38 60
Church Cft. Clo. SW12 BV47 76
Endlesham Rd.
Churchdown, Brom. CG49 78
Church Dr. NW9 BN33 46
Church Dr. Har. BE32 45
Church Dr. Maid. AH41 61
Church Dr. Sev. CT66 116
Church Dr. W. Wick. CG55 88
Church Elm La. Dag. CR36 59
Church End. E17 CE31 48
Church End NW4 BP31 46
Church Entry, EC4 BY39 56
Carter La.
Churchfield, Harl. CO10 6
Churchfield Av. N12 BT29 38
Churchfield Av. Wey. AZ56 92
Churchfield Clo. Har. BG31 45
Church Field Path, Wal. Cr. CC18 21
Churchfield Rd. W3 BN40 55
Churchfield Rd. W7 BH41 64
Churchfield Rd. W13 BJ40 54
Churchfield Rd Ger. Cr. AR30 34
Churchfield Rd. Walt. BC54 83
Churchfield Rd. Well. CO45 69
Church Field Rd. Wey. AZ56 92
Churchfields, E18 CH30 40
Churchfields, Brox. CE13 12
Church Fields, Harl. CO10 6
Church Fields, Wok AS61 100
Churchfields Av. Felt. BE48 74
Churchfields Dart. CV48 80
Church Fields Rd. Beck. CC51 87
Church Fields Rd. Beck. CD51 87
Churchfield Way N12 BT29 38
Churchfield Av.
Church Flds. Loug. CK24 31
Church Fm. Clo. Swan. CS53 89
Church Fm. La. Sutt. BR57 94
Church Gdns. W5 BK41 64
Church Gdns. Wem. BJ35 45
Churchgate, Wal. Cr. CB18 21
Churchgate Rd. Wal. Cr. CB18 21
Churchgate St. Harl. CQ9 6
Church Grn. Walt. BD57 93
Church Gro. SE13 CE45 67
Church Gro. Amer. AS23 25
Church Gro. Hayes BB39 53
Church Gro. Kings-on-t. BK51 84
Church Gro. Slou. AR39 52
Church Hill, E17 CE31 48
Church Hill N21 BX26 38
Church Hill, SE18 CK41 68
Church Hill, SW19 BR49 75
Church Hill Barn. BU25 29
Church Hill. Cat. CA65 105
Church Hill Dart. CT45 69
Church Hill. Dart. CV48 80
Church Hill Epp. CO18 23
Church Hill. Green. CZ46 80
Church Hill Har. BH33 45
Church Hill Loug. CK24 31
Church Hill Orp. CO54 89
Church Hill. Pur. BX58 95
Church Hill, Red. BV66 113
Church Hill, Red. BX70 121
Church Hill, Sev. CM61 106
Church Hill, Uxb. AX31 44
Church Hill, Welw. G. C. BO8 5
Church Hill, Wok. AR61 100
Church Hill, Wok. AV62 100
Church Hill Clo. Warl. CC62 105
Church Hill Rd. E17 CE31 48
Church Hill Rd. Barn. BU26 38
Church Hill Rd. Surb. BL53 85
Church Hill Rd. Sutt. BQ55 85
Churchill Av. Har. BJ32 45
Churchill Av. Uxb. AZ38 53
Churchill Clo. Lthd. BH65 102
Churchill Clo. Ong. CX17 24
Churchill Cr. Hat. BQ15 10
Churchill Gdns. W3 BM39 55
Churchill Gdns. Est. SW1 BW42 66
Churchill Gdns. Rd. SW1 BV42 66
Churchill Pl. Har. BH31 45
Sandridge Clo.
Churchill Rd. E16 CJ39 58
Churchill Rd. NW2 BP36 55
Churchill Rd. NW5 BV35 47
Churchill Rd. Edg. BL29 37
Churchill Rd. Guil. AS71 118
Churchill Rd. Hort. K. CY52 90
Churchill Rd. St. Alb. BJ13 9
Churchill Rd. Slou. AS42 62
Churchill Rd. Sth. Croy. BZ58 96
Churchill Ter. E4 CE27 39
Churchill Wk. E9 CC35 48
Churchill Way Sun. BC49 73
Churchill Wd. Orp. CN53 88
Church La. E11 CG33 49
Church La. E17 CE31 48
Church La. N2 BT31 47
Church La. N8 BX31 47
Church La. N9 CA27 39
Church La. N17 CA30 39
Church La. NW9 BN32 46
Church La. NW10 BO36 55
Church La. SW17 BU49 76
Church La. SW19 BR51 85
Church La. W5 BK41 64
Church La. Berk. AR13 7
Church La. Brox. CC14 12
Church La. Brwd. DA22 33
Church La. Brwd. DB32 51
Church La. Cat. BY65 104
Church La. Chess. BL57 94
Church La. Chis. CM51 88
Church La. Couls. BV64 104
Church La. Dag. CR36 59
Church La. Enf. BZ24 30
Church La. Epp. CR16 23
Church La. Epsom. BN65 103
Church La. Epsom BQ62 103
Church La. Gdse. CC69 114
Church La. Ger. Cr. AR30 34
Church La. Grays CX42 70
Church La. Guil. AP67 109
Church La. Guil. AT66 109
Church La. Har. BH30 36
Church La. Hat. BQ12 10
Church La. Hem. H. AT17 16
Church La. Hert. BX12 11
Church La. Kings L. AZ18 17
Church La. Loug. CK24 31
Church La. Maid. AH41 61
Church Lane. Ong. CX15 15
Church La. Oxt. CF68 114
Church La. Oxt. CG68 115
Church La. Pnr. BE31 45
Church La. Pot. B. BV18 20
Church La. Red. BZ70 114
Church La. Rick. AV22 25
Church La. Rick. AW22 26
Church La. Rick. AW26 35
Church La. Rom. CP24 32
Church La. Rom. CS24 32
Church La. Rom. CT31 50
Church La. St. Alb. BM14 10
Church La. Sev. CX62 108
Heaverham Rd.
Church La. Slou. AP38 52
Church La. Slou. AQ38 52
Church La. Surb. BJ53 84
Church La. Sutt. BS56 95
Church La. Tedd. BH49 74
Church La. Twick. BJ47 74
Church La. Upmin. DA35 51
Church La. Upmin. DA36 60
Church La. Uxb. AW37 53
Church La. Wal. Cr. CB18 21
Church La. Wall. BW55 86
Church La. Warl. CC62 105
Church La. Warl. CF61 105
Church La. Wennington CV39 60
Church La. West. CJ64 106
Church Lane Ave. Couls. BV64 104
Church La. Brom. Com. CK54 88
Church La. Cl. Stai. AX46 73
Church Lane Dr. Couls. BV64 104
Churchley Rd. SE26 CB49 77
Church Leys. Harl. CN11 13
Church Manor Way, SE2 CN42 68
Church Manorway Erith CS42 69
Churchmead Clo. Barn. BU25 29
Church Meadow Surb. BK55 84
Churchmead Rd. NW10 BP36 55
Churchmore Rd. SW16 BW51 86
Church Mt. N2 BT32 47
Church Pde. Ashf. AY49 73
Church Rd.
Church Pass. EC2 BZ39 57
Gresham St.
Church Pass. Rich. BK46 74
Red Lion St.
Church Pass. Surb. BL53 85
Church Path, E11 CH32 49
Church Path, E17 CE31 48
St. Mary Rd.
Church Path, N5 BY35 47
Church Path N8 BX32 47
Tottenham La.
Church Path, N12 BT28 38
Church Path, N17 CA29 39
Church Path N20 BT28 38
Church Path, NW10 BO36 55
Church Path, SW14 BN45 65
North Worple Way
Church Path, SW19 BR51 85
Church Path, W4 BN41 65
Church Path W7 BH40 54
Church Path, Cob. BC60 92
Church Path Couls. BY62 104

Church Path Croy. BZ55 87
Church Path. Green. CZ46 80
Church Path. Mitch. BU52 86
Church Path Sthl. BE41 64
Church Pl. Mitch. BU52 86
Church Rise, SE23 CC48 77
Church Rise Chess. BL57 94
Church Rd. E10 CE33 48
Church Rd. E12 CK35 49
Church Rd. E17 BX30 38
Church Rd. N6 BV32 47
Church Rd. N17 CA30 39
Church Rd. NW4 BP31 46
Church Rd. NW10 BO36 55
Church Rd. SE19 CA51 87
Church Rd. SE26 CB50 77
Church Rd. SW13 BO44 65
Church Rd. SW19 BT51 86
Church Rd. W3 BN40 55
Church Rd. W7 BG40 54
Church Rd. Ash. BK62 102
Church Rd. Ashf. AY48 73
Church Rd. Bark. CM36 58
Church Rd. Berk. AT12 7
Church Rd. Bexh. CQ45 69
Church Rd. Brom. CH51 88
Church Rd. Brwd. CY22 33
Church Rd. Buck. H. CH26 40
Church Rd. Cat. CA65 105
Church Rd. Cat. CD65 105
Church Rd. Crockenhill CS54 89
Church Rd. Croy. BY55 86
Church Rd. E. Mol. BG52 84
Church Rd. Egh. AT49 72
Church Rd. Enf. CC25 30
Church Rd. Epsom BN57 94
Church Rd. Epsom BO59 94
Church Rd. Erith CS42 69
Church Rd. Esher BH57 93
Church Rd. Farnborough CM56 97
Church Rd. Felt. BD49 74
Church Rd. Grav. DF47 81
Church Rd. Grav. DH51 81
Church Rd. Green. CZ46 80
Church Rd. Guil. AR71 118
Church Rd. Harl. CP12 14
Church Rd. Hart. DC52 90
Church Rd. Hav. CU41 41
Church Rd. Hav. CV26 42
Church Rd. Hayes. BB40 53
Church Rd. Hem. H. BA14 8
Church Rd. Hert. BW13 11
Church Rd. Heston BF43 64
Church Rd. Houns. BC42 63
Church Rd. Ilf. CN32 49
Church Rd. Islw. BF44 64
Church Rd. Iver AU38 52
Church Rd. Ken. BZ61 105
Church Rd. Kes. CJ57 97
Church Rd. Kings-on-t. BL51 85
Church Rd. Loug. CG24 31
Church Rd. Lthd. BE65 102
Church Rd. Lthd. BF65 102
Church Rd. Lthd. BJ64 102
Church Rd. Maid. AG40 61
Church Rd. Mitch. BT51 86
Church Rd. Nthlt. BD37 54
Church Rd. Nthwd. BB29 35
Church Road. Ong. CV14 15
Church Rd. Orp. CP57 98
Church Rd. Pot. B. BS18 20
Church Rd. Pur. BX58 95
Church Rd. Red. BU71 121
Church Rd. Reig. BS71 121
Church Rd. Rich. BK49 74
Church Rd. Rich. BL45 65
Church Rd. Rom. CV23 33
Church Rd. Rom. CW30 42
Church Rd. Sev. CQ59 98
Church Rd. Sev. CQ66 116
Church Rd. Sev. CU69 116
Church Rd. Sev. CW64 108
Church Rd. Sev. CZ57 99
Church Rd. Shep. AZ54 83
Church Rd. Shortlands CG52 88
Church Rd. Sid. CO49 79
Church Rd. S. At H. CW50 80
Church Rd. Stan. BJ28 36
Church Rd. Sthl. BE41 64
Church Rd. Surb. BK54 84
Church Rd. Sutt. BR57 94
Church Rd. Swan. CV51 90
Church Rd. Swans. DC46 81
Church Rd. Tedd. BH49 74
Church Rd. Til. DF44 71
Church Rd. Til. DJ43 71
Church Rd. Uxb. AX31 44
Church Rd. Uxb. AX38 53
Church Rd. Wall. BW55 86
Church Rd. Warl. CC62 105
Church Rd. Wat. BC23 26
Church Rd. Wat. BC23 26
Church Rd. Well. CO44 69
Church Rd. Welw. G. C. BQ8 5
Church Rd. West. CJ62 106
Church Rd. West. CO65 107
Church Rd. West Dr. AX41 63
Church Rd. Wey. AW56 92
Church Rd. Wey. AY60 92
Church Rd. Whyt. CA62 105
Church Rd. Wimb. BR49 75
Church Rd. Wind. AQ46 72
Church Rd. Wok. AQ63 100
Church Rd. Wok. AR61 100
Church Rd. Wor. Pk. BO55 85
Church Row, NW3 BT35 47
Church Row, Chis. CM51 88
Church Side. Epsom. BM60 94
Church Sq. Shep. AZ54 83
Church St. E15 CG37 58
Church St. E16 CL40 58
Church St. N9 BZ26 39
Church St. NW8 BT39 56
Church St. W2 BT39 56
Church St. W4 BO43 65
Church St. Bet. BO71 120
Church St. Cob. BC61 101
Church St. Croy. BY55 86
Church St. Dag. CR36 59
Church St. Dor. BJ71 119
Church St. Enf. BZ24 30
Church St. Epsom. BO60 94
Church St. Esher BF56 93
Church St. Ewell. BP58 94
Church St. Grav. DG46 81
Church St. Grays. DE43 71
Church St. Hat. BQ12 10
Church St. Hem. H. AT17 16
Church St. Hem. H. AX12 8
Church St. Hmptn. BG51 84
Church St. Ing. DC19 24
Church St. Islw. BJ45 64
Church St. Kings-on-t. BK51 84
Clarence St.
Church St. Lthd. BD67 111
Church St. Lthd. BJ64 102
Church St. Reig. BS70 121
Church St. Rick. AY26 35
Church St. St. Alb. BG13 9
Church St. Saw. CQ6 6
Church St. Sev. CT59 98
Church St. Sev. CX64 108
Church St. Slou. AO41 61
Church St. Slou. AP41 62
Church St. Stai. AV49 72
Church St. Sun. BC52 83
Church St. Sutt. BS56 95
Church St. Twick. BJ47 74
Church St. Wal. Abb. CF20 21
Church St. Walt. BC54 83
Church St. Wat. BC24 26
Church St. Wey. AZ56 92
Church St. Wok. AS62 100
Church St. Wok. AU64 100
Church St. E. Wok. AS62 100
Church St. Est. NW8 BT38 56
Church St. N. E15 CG37 58
Church St. Pl. E15 CG37 58
Church Stretton Rd. Houns. BG46 74
Church Ter. N1 CA36 57
Mortimer Rd.
Church Ter. NW4 BP31 46
Church Ter. SE13 CG45 68
Church Ter. SW8 BW44 66
Union Gro.
Church Ter. Rich. BK46 74
Wakefield Rd
Church Ter. Wind. AM44 61
Church Vale, N2 BU31 47
Church Vale, SE23 CC48 77
Churchvale Ct. W4 BM42 65
Harvard Rd.
Church Vw. Brox. CD13 12
Church Vw. S. Ock. CY41 70
Church View, Upmin. CX34 51
Churchview Rd. Twick. BG47 74
Church Wk. NW2 BR34 46
Church Wk. NW4 BQ31 46
Church Wk. NW9 BN34 46
Church Wk. SW13 BP44 65
Church Wk. SW16 BW51 86
Church Wk. SW20 BQ52 85
Church Wk. Brent. BK43 64
Church Wk. Brox. CD13 12
Church Wk. Dart. CV48 80
Church Wk. Grav. DH47 81
Church Wk. Hayes BB39 53
Church Wk. Lthd. BJ64 102
Church Wk. Reig. BS70 121
Church Wk. Rich. BK46 74
Church Walk, Saw. CQ6 6
Church Wk. Surb. BH53 84
Church Wk. Walt. BC54 83
Church Walk, Wey. AZ55 83
Churchway N20 BT27 38
Churchway, NW1 BW38 56
Church Way Cars. BU56 95
Church Way, Edg. BM29 37
Church Way Sth. Croy. CA58 96
Churchwell Path, E9 CC35 48
Churchyard Pass. SE5 BZ44 67
Camberwell Gro.
Church Yard Row, SE11 BY42 66
Churston Av. E13 CH37 58
Churston Dr. Mord. BQ53 85
Churston Gdns. N11 BW29 38
Churton Pl. SW1 BW42 66
Churton St.
Churton St. SW1 BW42 66
Chuters Gro. Epsom BO59 94
Chyngton Clo. Sid. CN48 78
Priestlands Pk. Rd.
Cicada Rd. SW18 BT46 76
Cicely Rd. SE15 CB44 67
Cillocks Clo. Hodd. CE11 12
Cimba Wood, Grav. DJ49 81
Cinderford Way, Brom. CG49 78
Cinder Path Wok. AR63 100
College La.
Cinnamon St. E1 CB40 57
Cintra Pk. SE19 CA50 77
Cinzen Rd. N7 BY35 47
Cippenham La. Slou. AN40 61
Circle Gdns. SW19 BS51 86
Circle Gdns. Wey. AY60 92
Circle Rd, Watt. BB58 92
Circle, The, NW2 BO34 46
Circle, The, NW7 BN29 37
Circuits, The, Pnr. BD31 45
Circular Rd. N17 CA31 48
Circular Rd. SE1 BZ41 67
Falmouth Rd.
Circular Way, SE18 CK43 68
Circus Pl. EC2 BZ39 57
London Wall
Circus Rd. NW8 BT38 56
Circus St. SE10 CF43 67
Circus, The EC3 CA40 57
Minories
Cirencester St. W2 BS39 56
Cirrus Cres. Grav. DJ49 81
Cissbury Ring, N. N12 BR28 37
Cissbury Ring, S. N12 BR28 37
Cissbury Rd. N15 BZ32 48
City Garden Row, N1 BY37 56
City Rd. EC1 BY37 56
Civic Way Ilf. CM31 49
Clabon Ms. SW1 BU41 66
Clack St. SE16 CC41 67
Clacton Path SE4 CD45 67
Frendsbury Rd.
Clacton Rd. E6 CJ38 58
Clacton Rd. E17 CD32 48
Claigmar Gdns. N3 BS30 38
Claire Ct. Clo. N12 BT28 38
Woodside Av.
Clairvale Rd. Houns. BE44 64
Clairview Rd. SW16 BV49 76
Clairville Ct. Reig. BT70 121
Wray Com.
Clairy Gdns. W7 BH40 54
Clammas Waye, Uxb. AX39 53
Clamp Hill Stan. BG28 36
Clancarty Rd. SW6 BS44 66
Clandon Av. N3 BS31 47
Clandon Av. Egh. AU50 72
Clandon Clo. W3 BM41 65
Clandon Clo. Epsom BO57 94
Clandon Rd. Guil. AS71 118
Clandon Rd. Ilf. CN34 49
Clandon Rd. Wok. AV66 109
Clandon St. SE8 CE44 67
Clandon Way, Wok. AV66 109
Clanfield Way, SE15 CA43 67
Hordle Prom. W.
Clanricarde Gdns. W2 BS40 56
Clapgate La. Wal. Abb. CF18 21
Clapgate Rd. Bush. BF25 27
Clapham Com. N. Side, SW4 BU45 66
Clapham Com. S. Side, SW4 BV46 76
Clapham Com. W. Side, SW4 BU45 66
Clapham Cres. SW4 BW45 66
Clapham High St. SW4 BW45 66
Clapham Manor St. SW4 BW45 66
Clapham Pk. Est. SW2 BX47 76
Clapham Pk. Est. SW4 BW46 76
Clapham Pk. Rd. SW4 BW45 66
Clapham Rd. SW9 BX45 66
Clappers La. Wok. AO59 91
Claps Gate La. Bark. CL38 58
Clapton Common, E5 CA33 48
Clapton Pass. E5 CC35 48
Lwr. Clapton Rd.
Clapton Sq. E5 CC35 48
Clapton Ter. N16 CB33 48
Clapton Way E5 CB35 48
Clara Pl. SE18 CL42 68
Monk St.
Clare Clo. Wey. AW60 92
Clare Corner, SE9 CL47 78
Clare Cotts. Red. BY70 121
Clare Ct. Cat. CE65 105
Clare Cres. Lthd. BJ62 102
Clarecroft Way W14 BQ41 65
Claredale St. E2 CB37 57
Clare Gdns. E7 CH35 49
Clare Gdns. W11 BR39 55
Clare Gdns. Bark. CN36 58
Clare Gdns. Stan. BK28 36
Clare Hall Pl. SE16 CC42 67
Litlington St.
Clarehill Clo. Esher BF56 93
Clarehill Rd. Esher BF57 93
Clare La. N1 BZ36 57
Clare Lawn Av. SW14 BN46 75
Clare Mkt. WC2 BX39 56
Portugal St.
Claremont, Wal. Cr. CA18 21
Claremont Av. Esher BE57 93
Claremont Av. Har. BL32 46
Claremont Av. N. Mal. BP53 85
Claremont Av. Sun. BC51 83
Claremont Av. Walt. BD56 93
Claremont Av. Wok. AS63 100
Claremont Clo. E16 CL40 58
Claremont Clo. N1 BY37 56
Claremont Clo. Orp. CL56 97
Claremont Clo. Sth. Croy. CB60 96
Claremont Clo. Walt. BD56 93
Claremont Ct. Dor. BJ72 119
Rose Hill
Claremont Cres. Dart. CT45 69
Claremont Cres. Rick. BA25 26
Claremont Dr. Esher BF58 93
Claremont Dr. Wok. AS63 100
Claremont End Esher BF57 93
Claremont Est. SW2 BX47 76
Claremont Gdns. Dart. CY47 80
Claremont Gdns. Esher BF57 93
Claremont Gdns. Ilf. CN34 49
Claremont Gdns. Surb. BL52 85
Claremont Gdns. Upmin. CY33 51
Claremont Gro. Wdf. Grn. CJ29 40
Claremont La. Esher BF56 93
Claremont Pk. N3 BR30 37
Claremont Rd. E7 CH35 49
Claremont Rd. E11 CF34 48
Claremont Rd. E17 CD30 39
Claremont Rd. N6 BV31 47
Claremont Rd. NW2 BQ33 46
Claremont Rd. W9 BR37 55
Claremont Rd. W13 BJ39 54
Claremont Rd. Barn. BT22 29
Claremont Rd. Brom. CK52 88
Claremont Rd. Croy. CB54 87
Claremont Rd. Esher BH57 93
Claremont Rd. Har. BH30 36
Claremont Rd. Horn. CU32 50
Claremont Rd. Red. BV69 121
Claremont Rd. Stai. AU49 72
Claremont Rd. Surb. BL53 85
Claremont Rd. Swan. CT50 79
Claremont Rd. Tedd. BH49 74
Claremont Rd. Twick. BJ46 74
Claremont Rd. Wey. AW59 92
Claremont Rd. Wind. AO44 61
Claremont Sq. N1 BY37 56
Claremont St. E16 CL40 58
Claremont St. N18 CB29 39
Claremont St. SE10 CE43 67
Claremont Way NW2 BQ33 46
Claremount, St. Alb. BF19 18
Claremount Gdns. Epsom BQ62 103
Clarence Av. SW4 BW47 76
Clarence Av. Brom. CK52 88
Clarence Av. Ilf. CL32 49
Clarence Av. N. Mal. BN51 85
Clarence Av. Upmin. CX34 51
Clarence Clo. Bush. BH26 36
Clarence Clo. Walt. BC56 92
Clarence Cres. SW4 BW46 76
Clarence Cres. Sid. CO48 79
Clarence Cres. Wind. AO44 61
Clarence Dr. Egh. AR49 72
Clarence Gdns. NW1 BV38 56
Clarence La. SW15 BO46 75
Clarence Ms. E5 CB35 48
Clarence Pl.
Clarence Pl. E5 CB35 48
Clarence Pl. Grav. DG47 81
Clarence Rd. E5 CB35 48
Clarence Rd. E12 CJ35 49
Clarence Rd. E16 CG38 58
Clarence Rd. E17 CC30 39
Clarence Rd. N15 BZ32 48
Clarence Rd. N22 BX29 38
Clarence Rd. NW6 BR36 55
Clarence Rd. SE9 CK48 78
Clarence Rd. SW19 BS50 76
Clarence Rd. W4 BM42 65
Clarence Rd. Berk. AR13 7
Clarence Rd. Bexh. CQ45 69
Clarence Rd. Brom. CJ52 88
Clarence Rd. Brwd. DA23 33
Clarence Rd. Croy. BZ54 87
Clarence Rd. Enf. CB25 30
Clarence Rd. Grav. DH46 81
Clarence Rd. Grays. DD42 71
Clarence Rd. Red. BT72 121
Clarence Rd. Rich. BL44 65
Clarence Rd. St. Alb. BH13 9
Clarence Rd. Sid. CO48 79
Clarence Rd. Sutt. BS56 95
Clarence Rd. Tedd. BH50 74
Clarence Rd. Wall. BV56 95
Clarence Rd. Walt. BC56 92
Clarence Rd. West. CK62 106
Clarence Rd. Wind. AN44 61
Clarence Row, Grav. DG47 81
Clarence St. Egh. AS50 72
Clarence St. Kings-on-t. BK51 84
Clarence St. Rich. BL45 65
Clarence St. Stai. AV49 72
Clarence St. Sthl. BD41 64
Clarence Ter. NW1 BU38 56
Cornwall Ter.
Clarence Ter. Houns. BF45 64
Clarence Wk. SW4 BX44 66
Jeffrey's Rd.
Clarence Wk. Red. BT72 121
Clarence Way, NW1 BV36 56
Clarence Way Est. NW1 BV36 56
Clarendon Av. SE5 BZ43 67
Councillor St.
Clarendon Clo. W2 BU40 56
Clarendon Pl.
Clarendon Clo. Orp. CO52 89
Clarendon Ct. NW11 BR31 46
Finchley Rd.
Clarendon Cres. Twick. BG48 74
Clarendon Cross W11 BR40 55
Portland Rd.
Clarendon Dr. SW15 BQ45 65
Clarendon Gdns. NW4 BP31 46
Clarendon Gdns. W9 BT38 56
Clarendon Gdns. Ilf. CK33 49
Clarendon Gdns. Wem. BK35 45
Clarendon Grn. Orp. CO52 89
Clarendon Gro. NW1 BW38 56
Phoenix Rd.
Clarendon Gro. Mitch. BU52 86
Clarendon Gro. Orp. CO52 89
Clarendon Ms. W2 BU40 56
Clarendon Pl.
Clarendon Path Orp. CO52 89
Clarendon Pl. W2 BU40 56
Clarendon Ri. SE13 CF45 67
Clarendon Rd. E11 CF33 48
Clarendon Rd. E17 CE32 48
Clarendon Rd. E18 CH31 49
Clarendon Rd. N8 BX31 47
Clarendon Rd. N15 BY31 47
Clarendon Rd. N18 CB29 39
Clarendon Rd. N22 BX30 38
Clarendon Rd. SW19 BU50 76
Clarendon Rd. W5 BL38 55
Clarendon Rd. W11 BR40 55
Clarendon Rd. Ashf. AY49 73
Clarendon Rd. Borwd. BM24 28
Clarendon Rd. Croy. BY55 86
Clarendon Rd. Har. BH32 45
Clarendon Rd. Hayes. BB41 63
Clarendon Rd. Red. BU70 121
Clarendon Rd. Sev. CU65 107
Clarendon Rd. Sev. CU66 116
Clarendon Rd. Wal. Cr. CC18 21
Clarendon Rd. Wall. BW57 95
Clarendon Rd. Wat. BC24 26
Clarendon St. SW1 BV42 66
Clarendon Ter. W9 BT38 56
Maida Vale
Clarendon Way N21 BZ25 30
Clarendon Way Chis. CN52 88
Clarens St. SE6 CD48 77
Clare Rd. E11 CF32 48
Clare Rd. NW10 BP36 55
Clare Rd. Grnf. BG36 54
Clare Rd. Houns. BE45 64
Clare Rd. Stai. AX47 73
Clare St. E2 CB37 57
Clarevale Horn. CW33 51
Clareville Gro. SW7 BT42 66
Clareville Rd. Cat. CB65 105
Clareville Rd. Orp. CM55 88
Clareville St. SW7 BT42 66
Gloucester Rd.
Clare Way. Bexh. CQ44 69
Clare Way, Sev. CV67 117
Clare Wood, Lthd. BJ62 102
Clarewood Mans. SW9 BY45 66
Coldharbour La.
Clarges Ms. W1 BV40 56
Clarges St. W1 BV40 56
Claribel Rd. SW9 BY44 66
Claridge Rd. Dag. CP33 50
Clarina Rd. SE20 CC50 77
Clarissa Rd. Rom. CP33 50
Clarissa St. E8 CA37 57
Clark Clo. Erith. CU44 69
Forest Rd.
Clarke's Av. Wor. Pk. BQ54 85
Clarkes Rd. Hat. BP12 10
Clarke Way, Wat. BC21 26
Clarkhill Harl. CN12 13
Clarks La. Epp. CN19 22
Hemnall St.
Clarks La. Sev. CQ59 98
Clarks La. West. CG65 106
Clarks Mead. Bush. BG26 36
Clarkson Rd. E16 CG39 58
Clarksons, The, Bark. CM37 58
Clarkson St. E2 CB38 57
Clarks Rd. Ilf. CM34 49
Clark St. E1 CB39 57
Clatre Ct. N12 BT28 38
Claude Rd. E10 CF34 48
Claude Rd. E13 CH37 58
Claude Rd. SE15 CB44 67
Claude St. E14 CE42 67
Claudian Pl. St. Alb. BF14 9
Claudian Way. Grays. DG41 71
Claudia Pl. SW19 BR47 75
Augustus Rd.
Claughton Rd. E13 CJ37 58
Claughton Way. Brwd. DE25 122
Clauson Av. Nthlt. BF35 45
Clavell St. SE10 CF43 67
Claverdale Rd. SW2 BX47 76
Claverhambury Rd. Wal. Abb. CG18 22
Clavering Av. SW13 BP43 65
Clavering Clo. Twick. BJ49 74
Clavering Gdns. Brwd. DE32 123
Clavering Rd. E12 CJ33 49
Claverley Gdns. N3 BS30 38
Claverley Vill. N3 BS30 38
Claverley Gro.
Claverton St. SW1 BW42 66
Clave St. E1 CC40 57
Claxton Gro. W6 BQ42 65
Clay Av. Mitch. BV51 86
Claybridge Rd. SE12 CJ49 78
Clayburn Gdns. S. Ock. DA40 60
Claybury Bush. BF26 36
Claybury Broadway, Ilf. CK31 49
Claybury Rd. Wdf. Grn. CK29 40
Claydon End. Ger. Cr. AS31 43
Claydon La. Ger. Cr. AS31 43
Clay Farm Rd. SE9 CM48 78
Claygate Clo. Horn. CT35 50
Carfax Rd.
Claygate Cres. Croy. CF57 96
Claygate La. Esher BJ54 84
Claygate Rd. W13 BJ41 64
Claygate Rd. Dor. BJ72 119
Clayhall Av. Ilf. CK31 49
Clayhall La. Reig. BQ72 120
Clayhall La. Wind. AP46 72
Clay Hill Bush. BF25 27
Clay Hill Enf. BY22 29
Clay Hill, Enf. BZ22 30
Clayhill Cres. SE9 CJ49 78
Clayhill Pound La. Epsom. BM60 94
Clayhill Rd. Reig. BP74 120
Claylands Pl. SW8 BY43 66
Claylands Rd. SW8 BX43 66
Clay La. Bush. BH26 36
Clay La. Edg. BM27 37
Clay La. Epsom. BM65 103
Clay La. Guil. AR67 109
Clay La. Red. BW71 121
Clay La. Stai. AY47 73
Claypit Hill, Loug. CJ22 31
Claypole Rd. E15 CF37 57
Clayponds Av. Brent. BL42 65
Clayponds Gdns. W5 BK42 64
Clayponds La. Brent. BL42 65
Clay Ride Loug. CK25 31
Clay Side Chig. CM28 40
Clays La. E15 CF35 48
Clay's La. Loug. CL23 31
Clay St. W1 BU39 56
Dorset St.
Clayton Av. Upmin. CX35 51
Clayton Av. Wem. BL36 55
Clayton Cres. Brent. BK42 64
Clayton Croft Dart. CU48 79
Clayton Dr. Guil. AP69 118
Clayton Mead NW9 BO29 37
Clayton Rd. SE15 CB44 67

Clayton Rd. Chess. BK56 93
Clayton Rd. Epsom. BO60 94
Clayton Rd. Hayes. BB41 63
Clayton Rd. Islw. BH45 64
Clayton Rd. Rom. CS33 50
Clayton St. SE11 BY43 66
Clayton Wk. Amer. AR23 25
Clayton Waye, Uxb. AX38 53
Clay Tye Rd. Upmin. DB35 51
Claywood Clo. Orp. CN54 88
Cleanthus Rd. SE18 CL44 68
Clearbrook Way. E1 CC39 57
W. Arbour St.
Cleardene, Dor. BJ71 119
Clears, The Reig. BR69 120
Clearwell Dr. W9 BS38 56
Amberley Est.
Cleave Ave. Hayes. BB42 63
Cleave Av. Orp. CN57 97
Cleaveland Rd. Surb. BK53 84
Cleaverholme Clo. SE25 CB53 87
Cleaver Sq. SE11 BY42 66
Cleeve Hill, SE23 CB47 77
Cleeve Rd. Lthd. BJ63 102
Cleeves Clo. Hem. H. AZ11 8
Cleeves Cres. Croy. CF59 96
Clegg St. E1 CB40 57
Prusom St.
Clegg St. E13 CH37 58
Cleland Path Loug. CL23 31
Cleland. Way. Ger. Cr. AR30 34
Cleland Way. Ger. Cr. AR31 43
Clematis Clo. Rom. CV29 42
Clematis St. W12 BP40 55
Clem Attlee Ct. SW6 BR43 65
Clem Av. SW4 BW45 66
Clemence St. E14 CD39 57
Clement Clo. NW6 BQ36 55
Clement Clo. Pur. BY57 95
Clement Clo. Pur. BY61 104
Clement Clo. Slou. AQ41 62
Clement Clo. Wal. Cr. CD17 21
Clement Gdns. Hayes. BB42 63
Clementhorpe Rd. Dag. CP36 59
Clementina Rd. E10 CD33 48
Clement Mead, Lthd. BJ63 102
Clement Rd. SW19 BR49 75
Clement Rd. Beck. CC51 87
Clements Av. E16 CH40 58
Clements Ct. Houns. BD45 64
Clements Inn, WC2 BX39 56
Strand
Clement's La. EC4 BZ40 57
Clements La. Ilf. CL34 49
Clement's Pl. Brent. BK42 64
Challis Rd.
Clements Rd. E6 CK36 58
Clement's Rd. SE16 CB41 67
Clements Rd. Ilf. CL34 49
Clements Rd. Rick. AU25 25
Clement St. Swan. CV50 80
Clement Way. Upmin. CW34 51
Clenches Farm La. Sev. CU66 116
Clenches Farm Rd. Sev. CU66 116
Clendon Way. SE18 CM42 68
Polthorne Gro.
Clennam St. SE1 BZ41 67
Southwark Bridge Rd.
Clensham Ct. Sutt. BS55 86
Clensham La. Sutt. BS55 86
Clenston Ms. W1 BU39 56
Seymour Pl.
Cleremont Rd. E9 CC37 57
Clere Pl. EC2 BZ38 57
Clere St.
Clere St. EC2 BZ38 57
Clerkenwell Clo. EC1 BY38 56
Clerkenwell Grn. EC1 BY38 56
Clerkenwell Rd. EC1 BY38 56
Clerks Piece Loug. CK24 31
Clevedon Clo. N16 CA34 48
Smalley Rd.
Clevedon Gdns. Hayes. BA41 63
Clevedon Gdns. Houns. BC44 63
Clevedon Pass. N16 CA34 48
High St.
Clevedon Rd. SE20 CC51 87
Clevedon Rd. Kings-on-t. BM51 85
Clevedon Rd. Twick. BK46 74
Clevedon St. N16 CA34 48
Sanford La.
Clevehurst Clo. Slou. AQ36 52
Cleveland, Hem. H. AZ12 8
Cleveland Av. SW20 BR51 85
Cleveland Av. W4 BO42 65
Cleveland Av. Hamptn. BE50 74
Cleveland Clo. Walt. BC55 83
Cleveland Ct. W13 BJ39 54
Kent Av.
Cleveland Cres. Borwd. BN25 28
Cleveland Dr. Stai. AW51 83
Cleveland Est. E1 CC38 57
Cleveland Gdns. N4 BZ32 48
Cleveland Gdns. NW2 BQ34 46
Cleveland Gdns. SW13 BO44 65
Cleveland Gdns. W2 BT39 56
Cleveland Gdns. W13 BJ39 54
Argyle Rd.
Cleveland Gdns. Wor. Pk. BO55 85
Cleveland Gro. E1 CC38 57
Cleveland Way
Cleveland Ms. WC1 BW39 56
Maple St.
Cleveland Pk. Av. E17 CD31 48
Cleveland Pk. Cres. E17 CD31 48
Cleveland Rise Mord. BQ54 85
Cleveland Rd. E18 CH31 49
Cleveland Rd. N1 BZ36 57
Cleveland Rd. N9 CB26 39
Cleveland Rd. SW13 BO44 65
Cleveland Rd. W4 BN41 65
Cleveland Rd. W13 BJ39 54
Cleveland Rd. Ilf. CL34 49
Cleveland Rd. Islw. BJ45 64
Cleveland Rd. N. Mal. BO52 85
Cleveland Rd. Uxb. AX38 53
Cleveland Rd. Well. CG44 68
Cleveland Rd. Wor. Pk. BO55 85
Cleveland Row, SW1 BW40 56
Cleveland Sq. W2 BT39 56
Cleveland St. W1 BW38 56
Cleveland Ter. W2 BT39 56
Cleveland Way, E1 CC38 57
Cleveland Way, Hem. H. AZ12 8
Cleveley Cres. W5 BL37 55
Cleveleys Rd. E5 CB34 48
Cleverley Est. W12 BP40 55
Cleve Rd. NW6 BS36 56
Cleve Rd. Sid. CP48 79
Cleves Av. Epsom BP58 94
Cleves Clo. Cob. BC60 92
Cleves Rd. E6 CJ37 58
Cleves Rd. Rich. BK48 74
Cleves Rd. Sev. CW62 108
Cleves Wk. Ilf. CM29 40
Cleves Way Hamptn. BE50 74
Cleves Way Ruis. BD33 45
Cleves Wood, Wey. BB56 92
Clew Ave. Wind. AN44 61
Clewer Court Rd. Wind. AN43 61
Clewer Cres. Har. BG30 36
Clewer Flds. Wind. AN44 61
Clewer Hill Rd. Wind. AM44 61
Clewer Rk. Wind. AN43 61
Clichy Est. E1 CC39 57
Clifden Rd. E5 CC35 48
Clifden Rd. Brent. BK43 64
Clifden Rd. Twick. BH47 74
Cliffe End Pur. BY59 95
Cliffe Rd. Sth. Croy. BZ56 96
Cliff Gro. Grav. DG47 81
Clifford Av. SW14 BM45 65
Clifford Av. Chis. CK50 78
Clifford Av. Ilf. CL30 40
Clifford Av. Wall. BW56 95
Clifford Clo. Nthlt. BE37 54
Clifford Ct. NW9 BO35 46
Clifford Gdns. NW10 BQ37 55
Clifford Gro. SE20 CC50 77
Clifford Gro. Ashf. AZ49 73
Clifford Manor Rd. Guil. AS72 118
Clifford Rd. E16 CG38 58
Clifford Rd. E17 CF30 39
Clifford Rd. N9 CC25 30
Clifford Rd. SE25 CB52 87
Clifford Rd. Barn. BS24 29
Clifford Rd. Houns. BD45 64
Clifford Rd. Rich. BK48 74
Clifford Rd. Wem. BK36 54
Clifford's Inn, EC4 BY39 56
Fleet St.
Clifford St. W1 BW40 56
Clifford St. Wat. BD24 27
Clifford Way, NW10 BO35 46
Cliff Pl. S. Ock. DB38 60
Cliff Rd. NW1 BW36 56
Cliff Ter. SE8 CE44 67
Cliffview Rd. SE13 CE45 67
Cliff Vill. NW1 BW36 56
Cliff Wk. E16 CG39 58
Clifton Av. E17 CC31 48
Clifton Av. N3 BR30 37
Clifton Av. W12 BO41 65
Clifton Av. Felt. BD48 74
Clifton Av. Stan. BJ30 36
Clifton Av. Sutt. BS58 95
Clifton Av. Wem. BL36 55
Clifton Clo. Brwd. DE32 123
Clifton Clo. Cat. BZ65 105
Clifton Clo. Orp. CL56 97
Clifton Clo. Wall. Cr. CD18 21
Clifton Clo. Wey. AW55 83
Clifton Ct. NW8 BT38 56
Clifton Cres. SE15 CB43 67
Clifton Gdns. N15 CA32 48
Clifton Gdns. NW11 BR31 46
Clifton Gdns. W4 BN42 65
Clifton Gdns. W9 BT38 56
Clifton Gdns. Enf. BX24 29
Clifton Gdns. Uxb. AZ37 53
Clifton Hill NW8 BS37 56
Clifton Marine Par. Grav. DF46 81
Clifton Pk. Av. SW20 BQ51 85
Approach Rd.
Clifton Pl. W2 BT40 56
Clifton Pl. Bans. BS61 104
Clifton Ri. Wind. AL44 61
Clifton Rise, SE14 CD43 67
Clifton Rd. E7 CJ36 58
Clifton Rd. E16 CG39 58
Clifton Rd. N3 BT30 38
Clifton Rd. N8 BW32 47
Clifton Rd. N22 BW30 38
Clifton Rd. NW10 BP37 55
Clifton Rd. SE25 BZ52 87
Clifton Rd. SW19 BQ50 75
Clifton Rd. W9 BT38 56
Clifton Rd. Couls. BV61 104
Clifton Rd. Grav. DG46 81
Clifton Rd. Grnf. BG38 54
Clifton Rd. Har. BL32 46
Clifton Rd. Horn. CU32 50
Clifton Rd. Ilf. CM32 49
Clifton Rd. Islw. BG44 64
Clifton Rd. Kings-on-t. BL50 75
Clifton Rd. Loug. CK24 31
Clifton Rd. Sid. CN49 78
Clifton Rd. Slou. AQ41 62
Clifton Rd. Sthl. BE42 64
Clifton Rd. Tedd. BH49 74
Clifton Rd. Wall. BV56 95
Clifton Rd. Wat. BC25 26
Clifton Rd. Well. CO45 69
Cliftons La. Reig. BQ70 120
Clifton St. E8 CB36 57
Graham Rd.
Clifton St. EC2 CA39 57
Clifton St. St. Alb. BH13 9
Clifton Ter. N4 BY34 47
Cliftonville, Dor. BJ72 119
Clifton Vills. W9 BS39 56
Clifton Way, SE15 CB43 67
Clifton Way, Brwd. DE26 122
Clifton Way, Wem. BL37 55
Climb, The Rick. AW25 26
Clinch Ct. E16 CH39 58
Cline Rd. N11 BW29 38
Cline Rd. Guil. AS71 118
Clink St. SE1 BZ40 57
Clinton Av. E. Mol. BG52 84
Clinton Av. Well. CN45 68
Clinton Clo. Wok. AO62 100
Clinton Cres. Ilf. CN29 40
Clinton Rd. E3 CD38 57
Clinton Rd. E7 CH35 49
Clinton Rd. N15 BZ31 48
Clinton Rd. Lthd. BK65 102
Clipper Cres. Grav. DJ49 81
Clippesby Clo. Chess. BL57 94
Clipstone Mews, BW39 56
Clipstone Rd. Houns. BF45 64
Clipstone St. W1 BV39 56
Clissold Ct. N16 BZ34 48
Clissold Cres. N16 BZ35 48
Clissold Rd. N16 BZ34 48
Clitheroe Av. Har. BF33 45
Clitheroe Gdns. Wat. BD27 36
Clitheroe Rd. SW9 BX44 66
Clitheroe Rd. Rom. CS28 41
Clitherow Av. W7 BJ41 64
Clitherow Rd. Brent. BJ42 64
Clitterhouse Cres. NW2 BQ33 46
Clitterhouse Rd. NW2 BQ33 46
Clive Av. N18 CB29 39
Claremont St.
Clive Av. Dart. CT46 79
Clive Clo. Pot. B. BR19 19
Clive Ct. W9 BT38 56
Clive Ct. Slou. AO41 61
Clive Ct. Surb. BM55 85
Cliveden Clo. N12 BT28 38
Cliveden Clo. Brwd. DC26 122
Cliveden Pl. Shep. AZ53 83
High St.
Cliveden Rd. SW19 BR51 85
Clivedon Pl. SW1 BV42 66
Clivedon Rd. E4 CG28 40
Clive Pass. SE21 BZ48 77
Clive Rd.
Clive Rd. SE21 BZ48 77
Clive Rd. SW19 BU50 76
Clive Rd. Belv. CQ42 69
Clive Rd. Brwd. DB29 42
Clive Rd. Enf. CB24 30
Clive Rd. Esher BF56 93
Clive Rd. Felt. BC46 73
Clive Rd. Grav. DG46 81
Clive Rd. Rom. CU32 50
Clive Rd. Twick. BH49 74
Clivesdale Dr. Hayes BC40 53
Avondale Dr.
Clive Way Couls. BX62 104
Clive Way Enf. CB24 30
Clive Way. Wat. BD23 27
Cloak La. EC4 BZ40 57
Clock House Clo. Wey. AY59 92
Clockhouse La. Ashf. & Felt. AZ48 73
Clockhouse La. Egh. AT50 72
Clockhouse La. Grays DB40 60
Clockhouse La. Grays. DC40 71
Clockhouse La. Rom. CR29 41
Clock House La. Sev. CU65 107
Clock House Mead. Lthd. BF60 93
Clock Ho. Rd. Beck. CC52 87
Clock Ho. Rd. Beck. CD51 87
Clock Pl. SE17 BY42 66
Hampton St.
Clock Ter. Grav. DH46 81
Clock Tower Rd. Islw. BH45 64
Clodhouse Hill, Wok. AO64 100
Cloister Gdns. SE25 CB53 87
Cloister Gdns. Edg. BO28 37
Cloister Garth, St. Alb. BH15 9
Cloister Rd. NW2 BR34 46
Cloister Rd. W3 BN39 55
Cloisters Av. Brom. CK53 88
Cloisters, The. Rick. AY26 35
Clonard Way Pnr. BF29 36
Clonbrock Rd. N16 CA35 48
Cloncurry St. SW6 BQ44 65
Clonmell Rd. N17 BZ31 48
Clonmel Rd. SW6 BR43 65
Clonmel Rd. Tedd. BG49 74
Clonmore St. SW18 BR47 75
Clonnel Clo. Har. BG34 45
Cloonmore Av. Orp. CN56 97
Clorane Gdns. NW3 BS34 47
Close, The, E4 CF29 39
Close, The, N10 BV30 38
Close, The, N14 BW27 38
Close, The, Barn. BU25 29
Close, The, Beck. CD52 87
Close, The Bet. BM72 120
Close, The, Bex. CR47 79
Close, The, Brwd. DB27 42
Close, The, Bush. BF25 27
Close, The, Cars. BU58 95
Close, The, Dart. CV48 80
Close, The. Grays. DD41 71
Close, The, Har. BG30 36
Close, The, Hat. BR16 19
Close, The Ilf. CN32 49
Close, The, Islw. BG44 64
Close, The Iver AU38 52
Close, The, Mitch. BU52 86
Close, The, N. Mal. BN51 85
Close, The, N20 BR27 37
Close, The, Orp. CN53 88
Close, The, Pnr. BD30 36
Close, The, Pnr. BD33 45
Close, The, Pnr. BE33 45
Close, The, Pur. BX58 95
Close, The, Pur. BY58 95
Close, The, Rad. BH20 18
Close, The Reig. BS71 121
Close, The, Rich. BM45 65
Close, The. Rick. AW26 35
Close, The, Rom. CQ32 50
Close, The, Sev. CT65 107
Close, The, Sid. CO49 79
Close, The, Sutt. BR54 85
Close, The Uxb. AY36 53
Close, The Uxb. AZ37 53
Close, The, Vir. W. AR53 82
Close, The, Wem. BL36 55
Close, The, Wem. BN34 46
Close, The, Wey. AW60 92
Cloth Fair, EC1 BY39 56
Clothier St. E1 CA39 57
Cutler St.
Cloudberry Rd. Rom. CV29 42
Cloudesdale Rd. SW17 BV48 76
Cloudesley Pl. N1 BY37 56
Cloudesley Rd. N1 BY37 56
Cloudesley Rd. Bexh. CQ44 69
Cloudesley Rd. Erith CT44 69
Cloudesley Sq. N1 BY37 56
Cloudesley St. N1 BY37 56
Clova Rd. E7 CG36 58
Cloveley Av. Uxb. BA35 44
Cloveley Clo. Uxb. BA35 44
Clovelly Ave. Warl. CB63 105
Clovelly Av. NW9 BO31 46
Clovelly Ct. Horn. CW34 51
Clovelly Ct. Horn. CX34 51
Clovelly Gdns. Enf. CA26 39
Clovelly Gdns. Rom. CR30 41
Clovelly Rd. N8 BW31 47
Clovelly Rd. W4 BN41 65
Clovelly Rd. W5 BK41 64
Clovelly Rd. Bexh. CQ43 69
Clovelly Way E1 CC39 57
Jamaica St.
Clovelly Way Har. BE34 45
Cloverdale Gdns. Sid. CN46 78
Cloverfield. Welw. G. C. BR6 5
Clover Hill. Couls. BV64 104
Cloverland. Hat. BO14 10
Clover Leas, Epp. CN18 22
Cloverley Rd. Ong. CX18 24
Clover Ms. SW3 BU43 66
Clover Rd. Guil. AP69 118
Clover Way, Hem. H. AW13 8
Clove St. E13 CH38 58
Clowders Rd. SE6 CD48 77
Cloyster Wood, Edg. BK29 36
Club Gdns. Rd. Brom. CH54 88
Club Row, E1 CA38 57
Club Row, E2 CA38 57
Clump Av. Tad. BN69 120
Clump, The Rick. AW25 26
Clunas Gdns. Rom. CV31 51
Clunbury Av. Sthl. BE42 64
Cluny Ms. SW5 BS42 66
Cluny Pl. SE1 CA41 67
Clutton St. E14 CE39 57
Clydach Rd. Enf. CA24 30
Clyde Av. Sth. Croy. CB61 105
Clyde Cir. N15 CA31 48
Clyde Clo. Red. BV70 121
Clyde Clo. Upmin. CZ32 51
Clyde Pl. E10 CE33 48
Clyde Pl. SE23 CC48 77
Clyde Rd. N15 BZ31 48
Clyde Rd. N22 BW30 38
Clyde Rd. Croy. CA55 87
Clyde Rd. Hodd. CF13 12
Clyde Rd. Stai. AX47 73
Clyde Rd. Sutt. BS56 95
Clyde Rd. Wall. BW56 95
Clydesdale Av. Stan. BK31 45
Clydesdale Gdns. Rich. BM45 65
Clydesdale Rd. W11 BR39 55
Clydesdale Rd. Enf. CC24 30
Clydesdale Rd. Horn. CT33 50
Clyde Sq. Hem. H. AY11 8
Clyde St. SE8 CD43 67
Clyde Ter. SE23 CC48 77
Clyde Val. SE23 CC48 77
Clyde Way Rom. CT30 41
Clydon Clo. Erith CT43 69
Clyfford Rd. Ruis. BB35 44
Clyfton Clo. Brox. CD15 12
Clymping Dene Felt. BC47 73
Clyston Rd. Wat. BB25 26
Clyston St. SW8 BW44 66
Coach & Horses Yd. W1 BW40 56
Old Burlington St.
Coach Rd. Cher. AU57 91
Coach Rd. Dor. & Bet. BL71 120
Coach Rd. Grav. DE46 81
Coach Rd. Grav. DF46 81
Coach Rd. Sev. DA65 108
Coalecroft Rd. SW15 BQ45 65
Coaley Row, Dag. CQ37 59
Coal Rd. Til. DJ42 71
Coal Wharf Rd. W12 BQ42 65
Coalwith Rd. W6 BQ44 65
Coast Hill, Dor. BE73 119
Coast Hill La. Dor. BF72 119
Coates Hill Rd. Brom. CL51 88
Coates Rd. Borwd. BK26 36
Coates St. Harl. CM11 13
Coate St. E2 CB37 57
Coates Way, Wat. BD20 18
Coat Wicks. Beac. AO29 34
Cobb Ern. Wat. BC19 17
Cobbets Clo. Wok. AQ62 100
Cobbets Hill, Wey. AZ57 92
Cobbett, Guil. AP70 118
Cobbett Rd. SE9 CK45 68
Cobbett Rd. Twick. BF47 74
Cobbetts Av. Ilf. CJ32 49
Cobbinsend Rd. Wal. Abb. CJ18 22
Cobbins, The, Wal. Abb. CG20 22
Cobbler's Wk. Tedd. BG50 74
Cobbles, The, Brwd. DC27 122
Cobbles, The, Upmin. CZ33 51
Cobbold Est. NW10 BO36 55
Cobbold Rd. E11 CG34 49
Cobbold Rd. NW10 BO36 55
Cobbold Rd. W12 BO41 65
Cobb Rd. Berk. AP13 7
Cobbs Rd. Houns. BE45 64
Cobb St. E1 CA39 57
Leyden St.
Cobden Hill Rad. BJ21 27
Cobden Rd. E11 CG34 49
Cobden Rd. SE25 CB53 87
Cobden Rd. Orp. CM56 97
Cobden Rd. Sev. CV65 108
Cobham Av. N. Mal. BP53 85
Cobham Clo. SW11 BU46 76
Cobham Clo. Brom. CK54 88
Cobham Park Rd. Cob. BC62 101
Cobham Pk. Rd. Cob. BD62 102
Cobham Rd. E17 CF30 39
Cobham Rd. N22 BY31 47
Cobham Rd. Bark. CM37 58
St. Margaret's Rd.
Cobham Rd. Cob. & Lthd. BF62 102
Cobham Rd. Houns BC43 63
Cobham Rd. Ilf. CN34 49
Cobham Rd. Kings. On T. BM51 85
Cobham Rd. Lthd. BG64 102
Cobham St. Grav. DG47 81
Cobham Terrace Rd. Green. DA46 80
Cobham Terrace Rd. Green. DA47 80
Cobham Way. Leath. BB66 110
Cobill Clo. Horn. CV31 51
Cobland Rd. SE12 CJ49 78
Coborn Rd. E3 CD37 57
Coborn St. E3 CD38 57
Cobourg Rd. SE5 CA43 67
Cobourg St. NW1 BW38 56
Cobs Way, Wey. AW58 92
Coburgh Cres. SW2 BX47 76
Coburg Rd. N22 BX31 47
Cochrane Clo. NW8 BT37 56
Cochrane Ms. NW8 BT37 56
Cochrane Rd. SW19 BR50 75
Cochrane St. NW8 BT37 56
Cockcayne Wk. SE8 CD42 67
Cockerhurst Rd. Sev. CS57 98
Cocker Rd. Enf. CB21 30
Cockett Rd. Slou. AS41 62
Cockfosters Rd. Barn. BU22 29
Cock Gro. Berk. AO13 7
Cock Hill E1 CA39 57
New St.
Cock La. EC1 BY39 56
Cock La. Hodd. CB13 12
Cock La. Lthd. BG64 102
Cockmannings La. Orp. CP54 89
Cockmannings Rd. Orp. CP54 89
Cockpit Yd. WC1 BX39 56
Northington St.
Cock Robins La. Harl. CL7 6
Cock Robins La. Ware. CL6 6
Cocks Cres. N. Mal. BO52 85
Cocksett Av. Orp. CN57 97
Cockshot Hill, Reig. BS71 121
Cockshot Rd. Reig. BS71 121
Cockspur St. SW1 BW40 56
Cocksure La. Sid. CR48 79
Cock Yd. SE5 BZ44 67
Denmark Hill
Code St. E1 CA38 57
Codham Hall La. Brwd. DB31 51
Codicote Dr. Wat. BD20 18
Codicote Rd. Welw. BN5 5
Codicote Ter. N4 BZ34 48
Codling Way Wem. BK35 45
Codmore Cres. Chesh. AP18 16
Codmore Wood Rd. Chesh. AR20 16
Codrington Ct. Grav. DH49 81
Codrington Gdns. Grav. DH49 81
Codrington Hl. SE23 CD47 77
Codrington Ms. W11 BR39 55
Blenheim Cres.
Cody Clo. Har. BK31 45
Cody Clo. Wall. BW57 95
Alcock Clo.
Cody Rd. E16 CF38 57
Cofers Circ. Wem. BM34 46
Coftards, Slou. AR39 52
Cogan Av. E17 CD30 39
Coin St. SE1 BY40 56
Coisy St. NW5 BV36 56
Cokers La SE21 BZ47 77
Perifield
Coke, S La. Ch. St. G. AQ24 25
Coke St. E1 CB39 57
Colas Ms. NW6 BS37 56
Birchington Rd.
Colbeck Ms. SW7 BS42 66
Colberg Pl. N16 CA33 48
Colborne Way Wor. Pk. BQ55 85
Colbrook Ave. Hayes. BA41 63
Colbrook Clo. Hayes. BA41 63
Colburn Ave. Cat. CA65 105
Colburn Av. Pnr. BE29 36
Colburn Way Sutt. BT55 86
Colby Rd. SE19 CA49 77
Colby Rd. Walt. BC54 83
Colchester Av. E12 CK34 49
Colchester Dr. Pnr. BD32 45
Colchester Rd. E10 CF33 48
Colchester Rd. E17 CE32 48

Colchester Rd. Edg. BN30 37
Colchester Rd. Nthwd. BC30 35
Colchester Rd. Rom. CV30 42
Colcokes Rd. Bans. BS61 104
Cold Arbor Rd. Sev. CS65 107
Coldbath Sq. EC1 BY38 56
Topham St.
Coldbath St. SE13 CE44 67
Cold Blow Cres. Bex. CS47 79
Cold Blow La. SE14 CC43 67
Cold Blows Mitch. BU52 86
Coldershaw Rd. W13 BJ40 54
Coldfall Av. N10 BV30 38
Coldhabour Rd. Wey. AV60 91
Coldhara La. Pur. BY54 86
Coldharbour La. SE5 BZ45 67
Coldharbour La. SW9 BY45 66
Coldharbour La. Bush. BF25 27
Coldharbour La. Dor. BH74 119
Coldharbour La. Egh. AU52 82
Coldharbour La. Hayes BC41 63
Coldharbour La. Pur. CH58 97
Coldharbour La. Red. CA70 114
Coldharbour La. Ton. CZ71 117
Coldharbour La. Wok. AV61 100
Coldharbour Rd. Croy. BY56 95
Coldharbour Rd. Grav. DF48 81
Coldharbour Rd. Harl. CK11 13
Coldharbour Rd. Wok. AV61 100
Coldharbour Way Croy. BY56 95
Coldshott. Oxt. CH70 115
Coldstream Gdns. SW18 BR46 75
Colebert Av. E1 CC38 57
Colebrook Cher. AU57 91
Colebrook Av. W13 BJ39 54
Colebrook Clo. SW15 BQ47 75
Colebrooke Dr. E11 CH33 49
Colebrooke Row, N1 BY37 56
Colebrook Gdns. Loug. CM23 31
Colebrook La. Loug. CL23 31
Colebrook Path. Loug. CL23 31
Colebrook Rd. E17 CD31 48
Colebrook Rd. SW16 BX51 86
Colebrook Rd. Red. BU69 121
Coleby Path SE5 BZ43 67
Elmington Estate
Cole Ct. W6 BQ43 65
Coledale Dr. Stan. BK30 36
Coleford Clo. Loug. CL23 31
Coleford Rd. SW18 BT46 76
Colegrave Rd. E15 CF35 48
Cole Grn. Welw. G. C. BR9 5
Colegrove Rd. SE15 CA43 67
Coleherne Ct. SW5 BS42 66
Coleherne Ms. SW10 BS42 66
Coleherne Rd. SW10 BS42 65
Colehill Gdns. SW6 BR44 65
Fulham Palace Rd.
Colehill La. SW6 BR44 65
Coleman Clo. E1 CC40 57
Garnet St.
Coleman Ct. E1 CC40 57
Garnet St.
Coleman Ct. SW18 BS47 76
Coleman Flds. N1 BZ37 57
Coleman Rd. SE5 CA43 67
Coleman Rd. Belv. CR42 69
Coleman Rd. Dag. CQ36 59
Colemans Hth. SE9 CL48 78
Coleman's La. Wal. Abb. CF16 21
Coleman's La. Wal. Abb. CG16 22
Coleman St. EC2 BZ39 57
Colemorton Cres. Wind. AM42 61
Colenso Rd. E5 CC35 48
Colenso Rd. Ilf. CN33 49
Cole Pk. Gdns. Twick. BJ46 74
Cole Pk. Rd. Twick. BJ46 74
Colepits Wood Rd. SE9 CM46 78
Coleraine Rd. N8 BY31 47
Coleraine Rd. SE3 CG43 68
Coleridge Av. E12 CK36 58
Coleridge Clo. SW8 BV44 66
Coleridge Clo. Brwd. DE26 122
Byron Rd.
Coleridge Cres. Slou AV44 62
Coleridge Gdns. NW6 BT36 56
Coleridge La. N8 BX32 47
Coleridge Rd.
Coleridge Rd. E17 CD31 48
Coleridge Rd. N4 BY34 47
Coleridge Rd. N8 BW32 47
Coleridge Rd. N12 BT28 38
Coleridge Rd. Ashf. AY49 73
Coleridge Rd. Croy. CC54 87
Coleridge Rd. Dart. CX45 70
Coleridge Rd. Rom. CU29 41
Coleridge Rd. Til. DH44 71
Coleridge Wk. NW11 BS31 47
Coleridge Way Hayes BC39 53
Coleridge Way Orp. CO53 89
Coleridge Way. West Dr. AY42 63
Cole Rd. Twick. BJ46 74
Cole Rd. Wat. BC23 26
Colesburg Rd. Beck. CD52 87
Coles Clo. Ong. CX16 24
Coles Cres. Har. BF34 45
Colescroft Hill Pur. BY61 104
Colesdale, Pot. B. BX18 20
Coles Gn. Ct. NW2 BP34 46
Coles Gn. Rd. NW2 BP33 46
Coles Grn. Bush. BG26 36
Coles Grn. Loug. CL23 31
Coles Hill, Hem. H. AW12 8
Coleshill Rd. Tedd. BH50 74
Coles La. West. CP65 107
Colesmead Rd. Red. BU69 121
Colestown St. SW11 BU44 66
Cole St. SE1 BZ41 67
Cole St. SW11 BU44 66
Colet Ct. W6 BQ42 65
Colet Gdns. W14 BQ42 65
Colet Rd. Brwd. DE25 122
Colets Orch. Sev. CU61 107
Coley Av. Wok. AT62 100
Coley St. WC1 BX38 56
Colfe Rd. SE23 CD47 77
Colgrove. Welw. G. C. BQ8 5
Colham Grn. Rd. Uxb. AZ39 53
Colham Rd. Uxb. AY38 53
Colham Rd. West Dr. AY40 53
Colina Ms. N8 BY31 47
Park Rd.
Colina Rd. N15 BY32 47
Colin Clo. NW9 BO31 46
Colin Clo. Croy. CD55 87
Colin Clo. W. Wick. CG55 88
Colin Cres. NW9 BO31 46
Colindale Av. NW9 BN31 46
Colindale Av. Erith. CR43 69
Colindale Av. St. Alb. BH14 9
Colindale Rd. Slou. AV44 62
Colindeep Gdns. NW4 BP31 46
Colindeep La. NW9 BN31 46
Colin Dri. NW9 BO32 46
Colinette Rd. SW15 BQ45 65
Colin Gdns. NW9 BO32 46
Colin Pk. Rd. NW9 BO31 46
Colin Rd. NW10 BP36 55
Colin Rd. Cat. CB65 105
Colinton Rd. Ilf. CO34 50
Colin Way. Slou. AN41 61
Coliston Rd. SW18 BS47 76
Collage Gate. Harl. CM11 13
Collamore Av. SW18 BU47 76
Collapit Clo. Har. BF32 45
Collard Av. Loug. CM23 31
Collard Grn. Loug. CM23 31
College App. SE10 CF43 67
College Ave. Grays. DD42 71
College Ave. Slou. AP41 62
College Av. Egh. AT50 72
College Av. Epsom. BO60 94
College Av. Har. BH30 36
College Clo. E9 CC35 48
Churchill Wk.
College Clo. N18 CA28 39
College Clo. Har. BH29 36
College Cres. NW3 BT36 56
College Cres. Wind. AN44 61
College Cross N1 BY36 56
College Dr. Ruis. BC33 44
College Gdns. E4 CE26 39
College Gdns. N18 CA28 39
College Gdns. SE21 CA47 77
College Gdns. Enf. BZ23 30
College Gdns. Ilf. CK32 49
College Gdns. N. Mal. BO53 85
College Gn. SE19 CA50 77
College Hill, EC4 BZ40 57
College Hill Rd. Har. BH29 36
College Hill Rd. Har. BH30 36
College La. NW5 BV35 47
College La. Hat. BO13 10
College La. Wok. AR63 100
College Pl E17 CG31 49
College Pl. NW1 BW37 56
College Pl. St. Alb. BG13 9
College Rd. E17 CF32 48
College Rd. N17 CA29 39
College Rd. N21 BY27 38
College Rd. NW10 BQ37 55
College Rd. SE19 CA47 77
College Rd. SE21 CA47 77
College Rd. SW19 BT50 76
College Rd. W13 BJ39 54
College Rd. Brom. CH51 88
College Rd. Croy. BZ55 87
College Rd. Enf. BZ23 30
College Rd. Epsom BO60 94
College Rd. Grav. DD46 81
College Rd. Grays. DE42 71
College Rd. Guil. AR71 118
College Rd. Har. BH30 36
College Rd. Har. BH32 45
College Rd. Hodd. CD11 12
College Rd. Islw. BH44 64
College Rd. St. Alb. BJ14 9
College Rd. Slou. AM40 61
College Rd. Swan. CT51 89
College Rd. Wal. Cr. CB18 21
College Rd. Wat. BB19 17
College Rd. Wem. BK33 45
College Rd. Wok. AT61 100
College Slip, Brom. CH51 88
College St. EC4 BZ40 57
College St. St. Alb. BG13 9
College Ter. E3 CD38 57
College Ter. N3 BR30 37
Hendon La.
College Vw. SE9 CJ47 78
College Way. Welw. G. C. BQ7 5
Collent St. E9 CC36 57
Collerston Rd. SE10 CG42 68
Colless Rd. N15 CA32 48
Collet Rd. Sev. CW62 108
Collett Clo. Wal. Cr. CC17 21
Collett Gdns. Wal. Cr. CC17 21
Collett Clo.
Collett Rd. SE16 CB41 67
Collett Rd. Hem. H. AX13 8
Colley Hill La. Slou. AP34 43
Colley La. Reig. BR70 120
Colley La. Rick. AU24 25
Colley Manor Dr. Reig. BQ70 120
Colley Way, Reig. BR69 120
Collier Clo. Epsom. BM57 94
Collier Cres. Dart. CZ49 80
Collier Dr. Edg. BM30 37
Collier Row La. Rom. CR29 41
Collier Row Rd. Rom. CQ30 41
Colliers St. Cat. CB66 114
Collier St. N1 BX37 56
Colliers Water La. Th. Hth. BY53 86
Collindale Av. Sid. CO47 79
Collingbourne Rd. W12 BP40 55
Collingham Gdns. SW5 BS42 66
Collingham Pl. SW5 BS42 66
Collingham Rd. SW5 BS42 66
Collington Clo. Grav. DF47 81
Beresford Rd.
Collingtree Rd. SE26 CC49 77
Collingwood Av. N10 BV31 47
Collingwood Av. Surb. BN54 85
Collingwood Clo. Twick. BF46 74
Collingwood Cres. Guil. AT70 118
Collingwood Est. E1 CB38 57
Collingwood Pl. SE18 CL41 68
Rodney St.
Collingwood Rd. E17 CE32 48
Collingwood Rd. N15 CA31 48
Collingwood Rd. Mitch. BU51 86
Collingwood Rd. Sutt. BR55 85
Collingwood Rd. Uxb. AZ38 53
Collingwood St. E1 CB38 57
Collins Av. Stan. BL30 37
Collins Dr. Ruis. BD34 45
Collins Meadow. Harl. CL11 13
Collinson St. SE1 BZ41 67
Collins Rd. N5 BZ35 48
Collins St. SE3 CG44 68
Collinwood Av. Enf. CC24 30
Collinwood Gdns. Ilf. CK32 49
Collis Alley Twick. BH47 74
Albion Rd.
Coll's Rd. SE15 CC44 67
Collum Grn. Slou. AO34 43
Collyer Av. Croy. BX56 95
Collyer Pl. SE15 CA44 67
Peckham High St.
Collyer Rd. St. Alb. BK17 18
Collyer Way Croy. BX56 95
Colman Clo. Epsom BP62 103
Colman Rd. E16 CJ39 58
Colman Way, Red. BU69 121
Colmer Pl. Har. BG29 36
Colmer Rd. SW16 BX51 86
Colmore Rd. Enf. CC24 30
Colnbrook St. SE1 BY41 66
Colndale Rd. Uxb. AX35 44
Colne Ave. Rick. AW27 35
Colne Ave. West Dr. AX41 63
Colne Av. Wat. BC25 26
Colne Ct. Epsom BN56 94
Colne Dr. Rom. CW29 42
Colne Gdns. St. Alb. BL17 19
Colne Mead Rick. AW27 35
Uxbridge Rd.
Colne Orchard, Iver AV39 52
Colne Rd. E5 CD35 48
Colne Rd. N21 BZ26 39
Colne Rd. Twick. BH47 74
Colne St. E13 CH38 58
Colne Valley, Upmin. CZ32 51
Colne View Ter. St. Alb. BL15 10
Colne Way, Hem. H. AY11 8
Colne Way, Stai. AT48 72
Colney Hatch La. N10 BU29 38
Colney Hatch La. N11 BU29 38
Colney Heath La. St. Alb. BK13 9
Colney Heath La. St. Alb. BL13 10
Colney Rd. Dart. CW46 80
Cologne Rd. SW11 BT45 66
Colombo Rd. Ilf. CM33 49
Colombo St. SE1 BY40 56
Colomb St. SE10 CG42 68
Colonel's La. Cher. AW53 83
Colonial Av. Twick. BG46 74
Colonial Rd. Felt. BB47 73
Colonial Rd. Slou. AQ41 62
Colonial Way Wat. BD23 27
Colonnade, WC1 BX38 56
Herbrand St.
Colridge Av. Sutt. BU56 95
Colson Gdns. Loug. CL24 31
Colson Path. Loug. CL24 31
Colson Rd. Croy. CA55 87
Colson Rd. Loug. CL24 31
Colson Way, SW16 BW49 76
Colsterworth Rd. N15 CA31 48
Colston Av. Cars. BU56 95
Colston Ct. Cars. BU56 95
Colston Cres. Wal. Cr. BY17 20
Colston Rd. E7 CJ36 58
Colston Rd. SW14 BN45 65
Colt Hatch, Harl. CL10 6
Coltness Cres. SE2 CO42 69
Colton Gdns. N17 BZ31 48
Coltsfoot Dr. Guil. AT69 118
Coltsfoot Path Rom. CV29 42
Columbia Av. Edg. BM30 37
Columbia Av. Wor. Pk. BO54 85
Columbia Ct. N. Mal. BO54 85
Columbia Rd. E2 CA38 57
Columbia Rd. E13 CG38 58
Columbia Sq. SW14 BN45 65
Upr. Richmond Rd.
Columbine Way, SE13 CF44 67
Colvestone Cres. E8 CA35 48
Colville Est. N1 BZ37 57
Colville Gdns. W11 BR39 55
Colville Ho. W11 BR39 55
Colville Ms. W11 BR39 55
Colville Pl. W1 BW39 56
Colville Rd. E11 CF34 48
Colville Rd. E17 CD30 39
Colville Rd. N9 CB26 39
Colville Rd. W11 BR39 55
Colville Sq. W11 BR39 55
Colville Sq. Ms. W11 BR39 55
Portobello Rd.
Colville Ter. W11 BR39 55
Colvin Gdns. E4 CF27 39
Colvin Gdns. E11 CH31 49
Colvin Gdns. Ilf. CM30 40
Colvin Gdns. Wal. Cr. CC21 30
Colvin Rd. E6 CK36 58
Colvin Rd. Th. Hth. BY53 86
Colvin St W6 BQ42 65
Glenthorne Rd
Colwell Rd. SE22 CA46 77
Colwith Rd. W6 BQ43 65
Colwood Gdns. SW19 BT50 76
Colworth Gro. SE17 BZ42 67
Browning St.
Colworth Rd. E11 CG32 49
Colworth Rd. Croy. CB54 87
Colwyn Av. Grnf. BH37 54
Colwyn Cres. Houns. BG44 64
Colwyn Rd. NW2 BP34 46
Colyer Clo. SE9 CL48 78
Colyer Rd. Grav. DE48 81
Colyers Clo. Erith CS44 69
Colyers Clo. Welw. G. C. BR5 5
Colyers La. Erith CS44 69
Colyers Wk. Erith CT44 69
Colyton Clo. Well. CP44 69
Colyton Clo. Wem. BK36 54
Colyton Rd. SE22 CB46 77
Colyton Way, N18 CB28 39
Combe Av. SE3 CG43 68
Combedale Rd. SE10 CH42 68
Combe Lea Brom. CK52 88
Combemartin Rd. SW18 BR47 75
Combe Ms. SE3 CG43 68
Comber Clo. NW2 BP34 46
Comber Gro. SE5 BZ43 67
Combermere Rd. SW9 BX45 66
Combermere Rd. Mord. BS53 86
Combe Rd. N16 CD35 48
Trumans Rd.
Combe Rd. Wat. BB25 26
Comberton Rd. E5 CB34 48
Combeside, SE18 CN43 68
Combe St. Hem. H. AX13 8
Combfield Dr. Dart. CZ49 80
Combwell Cres. SE2 CO41 69
Comely Bank Rd. E17 CE32 48
Comeragh Clo. Wok. AQ63 100
Comeragh Ms. W14 BR42 65
Comeragh Rd.
Comeragh Rd. W14 BR42 65
Comerford Rd. SE4 CD45 67
Comet Clo. Wat. BB20 17
Comet Ho. Pl. SE8 CE43 67
Watson's St.
Comet Rd. Hat. BO12 10
Comet Rd. Stai. AX47 73
Comet St. SE8 CE43 67
Comforts Farm Ave. Oxt. CG70 115
Commerce Rd. N22 BX30 38
Commerce Rd. Brent. BK43 64
Commerce Way Croy. BX55 86
Commercial Dock Pass. SE16 CD41 67
Commercial Rd. E1 CB39 57
Commercial Rd. N18 CA29 39
Commercial Rd. Guil. AR71 118
Commercial Rd. Stai. AW50 73
Commercial St. E1 CA38 57
Commercial Way, SE15 CA43 67
Commercial Way, Wok. AS62 100
Commerell Pl. SE10 CG42 68
Blackwall La.
Commerell St. SE10 CG42 68
Commodore St. E1 CD38 57
Common Clo. Wok. AR60 91
Commondale SW15 BQ45 65
Commonfield Rd. Bans. BS60 95
Commonfields, Harl. CN10 6
Common Grn. Berk. AT12 7
Common La. Dart. CU48 79
Common La. Esher BJ57 93
Common La. Kings L. AY17 17
Common La. Red. BZ69 114
Common La. Wat. BH23 27
Common La. Wey. AX58 92
Common La. Wind. AO42 61
Common Meadow La. Wat. BG20 18
Common Rd. SW13 BP45 65
Common Rd. Brwd. DE28 122
Common Rd. Dor. BG70 119
Common Rd. Esher BJ57 93
Common Rd. Lthd. BE64 102
Common Rd. Red. BU71 121
Common Rd. Rick. AU24 25
Common Rd. Sev. DA65 108
Common Rd. Stan. BG28 36
Common Rd. Uxb. AX35 44
Common Rd. Wal. Abb. CJ14 13
Common Rd. Wind. AL42 61
Common Rd. Wind. AM42 61
Common Rd. Wind. AN42 61
Commonsgate Rd. Rick. AU25 25
Commonside Harl. CN13 13
Commonside Kes. CJ56 97
Commonside, Lthd. BF65 102
Commonside Mitch. BW53 86
Commonside E. Mitch. BV52 86
Commonside Rd. Harl. CN13 13
Commonside W. Mitch. BU52 86
Commons La. Hem. H. AY13 8
Commons, The, Welw. G. C. BS9 5
Common, The, W5 BL40 55
Common, The, Berk. AS12 7
Common, The, Hat. BP12 10
Common, The, Kings L. AW19 17
Common, The, Rich. BK48 74
Common, The Stan. BH27 36
Common, The, Sthl. BD42 64
Common Way Esher BG58 93
Commonwealth Av. W12 BP40 55
Commonwealth Av. Hayes BA39 53
Commonwealth Rd. N17 CB29 39
Commonwealth Rd. Cat. CB65 105
Commonwealth Way, SE2 CO42 69
Community Rd. E15 CF35 48
Como Rd. SE23 CD48 77
Como St. Rom. CS31 50
Compass Hill Rich. BL46 75
Petersham Rd
Compayne Rd. NW6 BS36 56
Comport Gr. Croy. CG59 97
Compton Av. E6 CJ37 58
Compton Av. N1 BY36 56
Compton Av. N6 BU33 47
Compton Av. Brwd. DE26 122
Compton Av. Rom. CU31 50
Compton Clo. NW1 BV38 56
Robert St.
Compton Ct. SE19 CA49 77
Compton Cres. N17 BZ29 39
Compton Cres. W4 BN43 65
Compton Cres. Chess. BL57 94
Compton Cres. Nthlt. BD37 54
Compton Gdns. St. Alb. BF16 18
Faringford Clo.
Compton Pass. EC1 BY38 56
Compton St.
Compton Pl. Wat. BE28 36
Compton Rise Pnr. BE32 45
Compton Rd. N1 BY36 56
Compton Rd. N21 BY26 38
Compton Rd. NW10 BQ38 55
Compton Rd. SW19 BR50 75
Compton Rd. Croy. CB54 87
Compton Rd. Hayes BB40 53
Compton Sq. N1 BY36 56
Canonbury Rd.
Compton St. E13 CH37 58
Compton St. EC1 BY38 56
Compton Ter. N1 BY36 56
Comreddy Clo. Enf. BY22 29
Comus Pl. SE17 CA42 67
Comus Rd. N19 BW34 47
Comyne Rd. Wat. BB21 26
Comyn Rd. SW11 BU45 66
Comyns Clo. E16 CG39 58
Comyns Rd. Dag. CR36 59
Comyns, The, Bush. BG26 36
Conaways Clo. Epsom BP58 94
Concanon Rd. SW2 BX45 66
Concert Hall App. SE1 BX40 56
Concorde Dr. Hem. H. AX13 8
Concord Rd. W3 BM38 55
Concord Rd. Enf. CB25 30
Concourse, The, N9 CB27 39
Condell Rd. SW8 BW44 66
Conder St. E14 CD39 57
Conderton Rd. SE5 BZ45 67
Condor Path Nthlt. BF37 54
Condor Rd. Stai. AX52 83
Condor Wk. Rain. CU36 59
Condover Cres. SE18 CL43 68
Condray St. SW11 BT44 66
Conduct Rd. Barn. BR25 28
Conduit Ct. WC2 BX40 56
Long Acre
Conduit La. N18 BZ28 39
Hermitage La.
Conduit La. Enf. CC25 30
Conduit La. Hodd. CE12 12
Conduit La. Sth. Croy. CA56 96
Conduit Ms. W2 BT39 56
Conduit Pl. W2 BT39 56
London St.
Conduit Rd. SE18 CL42 68
Conduit St. W1 BV40 56
Conduit Way, NW10 BM36 55
Conegar Ct. Slou. AP40 52
Conewood Pl. N5 BY34 47
Conewood St.
Conewood St. N5 BY34 47
Coney Acre, SE21 BZ47 77
Coney Berry, Reig. BT72 121
Coneybury. Red. CA70 114
Coney Cl. Hat. BP13 10
Coney Dale. Welw. G. C. BQ7 7
Coney Grn. Saw. CP5 6
Coneygrove Path Nthlt. BD36 54
Coney Hill Rd. W. Wick. CG55 88
Conference Rd. SE2 CP42 69
Congo Rd. SE18 CM42 68
Congress Rd. SE2 CP42 69
Congreve Rd. SE9 CK45 68
Congreve St. SE17 CA42 67
Conical Cnr. Enf. BZ23 30
Conifer Av. Hart. DC53 90
Conifer Av. Rom. CR28 41
Conifer Clo. Reig. BS69 121
Reigate Hill
Conifer Gdns. SW16 BX48 76
Conifers, Wey. BB56 92
Conifers Clo. Tedd. BJ50 74
Coniger Rd. SW6 BS44 66
Coningham Ms. W12 BP40 55
Percy Rd.
Coningham Rd. W12 BP40 55
Coningsby Bnk. St. Alb. BG15 9
Coningsby Cl. Hat. BQ15 10
Coningsby Cott. W5 BK41 64
Coningsby Rd.
Coningsby Dr. Pot. B. BT20 20
Coningsby Dr. Wat. BB23 26
Coningsby Gdns. E4 CE29 39
Coningsby La. Maid. AH44 61
Coningsby Rd. N4 BY33 47
Coningsby Rd. W5 BK41 64
Coningsby Rd. Sth. Croy. BZ58 96
Conington Rd. SE13 CE44 67
Conisbee Ct. N14 BW25 29
Conisborough Cres. SE6 CF48 77
Coniscliffe Rd. N13 BZ27 39
Coniston Av. Bark. CN36 58
Coniston Av. Grnf. BJ38 54
Coniston Av. Upmin. CY35 51
Coniston Av. Well. CN45 68
Coniston Clo. N20 BT27 38
Coniston Clo. W4 BN43 65
Coniston Clo. Bark. CN36 58

Coniston Clo. Bexh. CS44 69
Coniston Clo. Dart. CU47 79
Coniston Clo. Erith CT43 69
Coniston Clo. Hem. H. BA14 8
Conistone Way N7 BX36 56
Sutterton St.
Coniston Gdns. N9 CC26 39
Coniston Gdns. NW9 BN32 46
Coniston Gdns. Ilf. CK31 49
Coniston Gdns. Pnr. BC31 44
Coniston Gdns. Sutt. BT57 95
Coniston Gdns. Wem. BK33 45
Coniston Rd. N10 BV30 38
Coniston Rd. N17 CB29 39
Coniston Rd. Bexh. CS44 69
Coniston Rd. Brom. CF50 77
Coniston Rd. Couls. BW61 104
Coniston Rd. Croy. CB54 87
Coniston Rd. Kings L. AY17 17
Coniston Rd. Twick. BF46 74
Coniston Rd. Wok. AT63 100
Coniston Wk. E9 CC35 48
Churchill Wk.
Coniston Way Chess. BL55 85
Coniston Way. Horn. CU35 50
Coniston Way, Red. BU70 121
Conlan St. W10 BR38 55
Conley Rd. NW10 BO36 55
Conley St. SE10 CG42 68
Connaught App. E16 CJ39 58
Baxter Rd.
Connaught Ave. Grays. DD41 71
Connaught Av. E4 CF26 39
Connaught Av. SW14 BN45 65
Connaught Av. Ashf. AX49 73
Connaught Av. Barn. BU26 38
Connaught Av. Enf. CA23 30
Connaught Av. Houns. BE45 64
Connaught Av. Loug. CJ24 31
Connaught Clo. E10 CD34 48
Connaught Clo. W2 BU39 56
Connaught St.
Connaught Clo. Enf. CA23 30
Connaught Clo. Hem. H. AZ12 8
Connaught Clo. Sutt. BT55 86
Connaught Clo. Uxb. BA38 53
Connaught Dr. NW11 BS31 47
Connaught Gdns. N10 BW32 47
Connaught Gdns. N13 BY28 38
Connaught Hill Loug. CJ24 31
Connaught La. Ilf. CM34 49
Connaught Ms. W2 BU39 56
Connaught Pl.
Connaught Pl. W2 BU39 56
Connaught Rd. E4 CG26 40
Springfield Rd.
Connaught Rd. E11 CF33 48
Connaught Rd. E16 CJ40 58
Connaught Rd. E17 CE32 48
Connaught Rd. N4 BY33 47
Connaught Rd. NW10 BO37 55
Connaught Rd. SE18 CL42 68
Connaught Rd. W13 BJ40 54
Connaught Rd. Barn. BQ25 28
Connaught Rd. Har. BH30 36
Connaught Rd. Horn. CV34 51
Connaught Rd. Ilf. CM34 49
Connaught Rd. N. Mal. BO52 85
Connaught Rd Rich. BL46 75
Albert Rd.
Connaught Rd. St. Alb. BG12 9
Connaught Rd. Sutt. BT55 86
Connaught Rd. Tedd. BG49 74
Connaught Sq. W2 BU39 56
Connaught St. W2 BU39 56
Connaught Way N13 BY28 38
Connell Cres. W5 BL38 55
Connicut La. Lthd. BF67 111
Connington Cres. E4 CF27 39
Connop Rd. Enf. CC22 30
Connor Rd. Dag. CQ35 50
Connors All. W6 BR43 65
Bayonne Rd.
Connor St. E9 CC37 57
Lauriston Rd.
Conolly Rd. W7 BH40 54
Conquest Rd. Wey. AW56 92
Conquest St. SE1 BY41 66
Conrad Dr. Wor. Pk. BQ54 85
Conrad St. E9 CC36 57
Consfield Av. N. Mal. BP52 85
Consort Mews. Islw. BG46 74
Consort Rd. SE15 CB44 67
Cons St. SE1 BY41 66
Windmill Wk.
Constable Clo. NW11 BS32 47
Constable Clo. Hayes BA37 53
Constable Clo. Islw. BG46 74
Constable Cres. W15 CB32 48
Constable Gdns. Edg. BM30 37
Constable Rd. Grav. DF48 81
Constable Wk. SE21 CA48 77
Constance Cres. Brom. CG54 88
Constance Rd. Croy. BY54 86
Constance Rd. Enf. CA25 30
Constance Rd. Sutt. BT56 95
Constance Rd. Twick. BF47 74
Constance St. E16 CK40 58
Constantine Rd. NW3 BU35 47
Constitution Hill, SW1 BV41 66
Constitution Hill, Grav. DH47 81
Constitution Hill, Wok. AS63 100
Constitution Rise, SE18 CL44 68
Content St. SE17 BZ42 67
Contessa Clo. Orp. CM56 97
Convair Wk. Nthlt. BD37 54
Convair Wk. Nthlt. BD38 54
Kittiwake Rd.
Convent Est. SE19 BZ50 77
Convent Gdns. W5 BK42 64
Convent Gdns. W11 BR39 55
Convent Hl. SE19 BZ50 77
Convent La, Cob. BB59 92
Convent Rd. Ashf. AZ49 73
Convent Rd. Wind. AM44 61
Convent Way Sthl. BD42 64
Conway Clo. Rain. CU36 59
Conway Clo. Stan. BJ29 36
Conway Cres. Grnf. BH37 54
Conway Cres. Rom. CP33 50
Conway Dr. Ashf. BA50 73
Conway Dr. Hayes. BA41 63
Conway Gdns. Enf. CA22 30
Conway Gdns. Mitch. BW52 86
Conway Gdns. Wem. BK33 45
Conway Gro. W3 BN39 55
Conway Rd. N14 BX27 38
Conway Rd. N15 BY32 47
Conway Rd. NW2 BQ34 46
Conway Rd. SE18 CM42 68
Conway Rd. SW20 BQ51 85
Conway Rd. Felt. BD49 74
Conway Rd. Houns. BE47 74
Conway St. E13 CH38 58
Philip St.
Conway St. W1 BW38 56
Conybeare NW3 BU36 56
Quickswood
Conybury Clo. Wal. Abb. CH19 22
Conyerd Rd. Sev. DC63 108
Conyers Clo. Wdf. Grn. CG29 40
Conyers Rd. E3 CD37 57
Conyers Rd. SW16 BW49 76
Conyers Way Loug. CL24 31
Cooden Clo. Brom. CH50 78
Plaistow Lane
Cookes La. Sutt. BR57 94
Church Rd.
Cookham Hill Orp. CR55 89
Cookham Rd. Sid. CR50 79
Cookhill Rd. SE2 CO41 69
Cook's Hole Rd. Enf. BY22 29
Cook's Rd. E15 CE37 57
Cooks Rd. SE17 BY43 66
Cooks Spinney, Harl. CO10 6
Cooks Vennel, Hem. H. AW12 8
Coolfin Rd. E16 CH39 58
Coolgardie Av. E4 CF28 39
Coolgardie Av. Chig. CL27 40
Coolgardie Rd. Ashf. BA49 73
Coolhurst Rd. N8 BW32 47
Cool Oak La. NW9 BO33 46
Cool Oak Rd. NW4 BP33 46
Coomassie Rd. W9 BR38 55
Bravington Rd.
Coombe Av. Croy. CA56 96
Coombe Bank, Kings. On T. BO51 85
Coombe Clo. Edg. BL30 37
Coombe Clo. Houns. BF45 64
Coombe Cnr. N21 BY26 38
Coombe Cres. Hamptn. BE50 74
Coombe Crest, Kings. On T. BN50 75
Coombe Dri. Wey. AV57 91
Coombe Dr. Ruis. BC34 44
Coombe End, Kings. On T. BN50 75
Coombefield Clo. N. Mal. BO53 85
Coombe Gdns. SW20 BP51 85
Coombe Gdns. Berk. AP12 7
Coombe Gdns. N. Mal. BO52 85
Coombe Hill Clo. Kings. On T. BO50 75
Coombe Hill Glade, Kings. On T. BO50 75
Coombe Hill Rd. Kings. On T. BO50 75
Coombe Hill Rd. Rick. AW26 35
Coombe Ho. Chase, N. Mal. BN51 85
Coombehurst Clo. Barn. BU23 29
Coombelands La. Wey. AW57 92
Coombe La. Croy. CB56 96
Coombe La. Kings-on-t. BM51 85
Coombe Moor, Kings. On T. BO50 75
Coombe Nevile, Kings. On T. BN50 75
Coombe Pk. Kings. On T. BN49 75
Coombe Ri. Kings. On T. BN51 85
Coombe Ridings, Kings. On T. BN49 75
Coombermere Clo. Wind. AN44 61
Coombe Rd. NW10 BN34 46
Coombe Rd. SE26 CB49 77
Coombe Rd. W4 BO42 65
Coombe Rd. W13 BJ41 64
Northcroft Rd.
Coombe Rd. Bush. BG26 36
Coombe Rd. Croy. BZ56 96
Coombe Rd. Grav. DH48 81
Coombe Rd. Hamptn. BE50 74
Coombe Rd. Kings. On T. BM51 85
Coombe Rd. N. Mal. BO51 85
Coombe Rd. Rom. CW31 51
Coombe Rd. Sev. CV61 108
Coombe Springs. Kings On. T. BN51 85
Coombes Rd. Dag. CQ37 59
Coombes Rd. St. Alb. BK16 18
Coombe, The Bet. BN69 120
Coombe Vale, Ger. Cr. AS33 43
Coombe Wk. Sutt. BS55 86
Coombe Wd. Hill Pur. BZ59 96
Coombewood Dr. Rom. CR32 50
Coombe Wood Rd. Kings. On T. BN49 75
Coomb Lane, Guil. AO67 109
Coomb's St. N1 BY37 56
Remington St.
Coome Rise, Brwd. DC26 122
Coomer Rd. SW6 BR43 65
Cooper Av. E17 CD30 39
Cooper Ct. Wat. BC22 26
Cooper Cres. Cars. BU55 86
Cooper Rd. NW10 BP35 46
Cooper Rd. Croy. BY56 95
Cooper Rd. Guil. AS71 118
Coopersale Clo. Wdf. Grn. CJ29 40
Coopersale Common Epp. CP17 23
Coopersale La. Epp. CO22 32
Coopersale Lane Back La. Rom. CO23 32
Coopersale Rd. E9 CC35 48
Coopersale Rd. Epp. CO18 23
Coopersale St. Epp. CP19 23
Coopers Cl. Stai. AV49 72
Coopers Clo. Chig. CO27 41
Coopers Green La. Welw. G. C. BN10 5
Coopers Hill Ong. CX18 24
Coopers Hill La. Egh. AR49 72
Cooper's Hill Rd. Red. BX70 121
Coopers Hill Rd. Red. BY73 121
Coopers La. E10 CE33 48
Coopers La. SE12 CH48 78
Coopers La. Pot. B. BT19 20
Cooper's La. Til. DH43 71
Coopers Lane Rd. Pot. B. BU19 20
Cooper's Rd. SE1 CA42 67
Cooper's Rd. Grav. DF47 81
Coopers Rd. Pot. B. BT18 20
Cooper's Row, EC3 CA40 57
Coopers Row, Iver AU38 52
Cooper St. E16 CG39 58
Coote Gdns. Dag. CQ34 50
Coote Rd. Bexh. CQ44 69
Coote Rd. Dag. CQ34 50
Copeland Rd. E17 CE32 48
Copeland Rd. SE15 CB44 67
Copelia Rd. SE3 CG45 68
Copeman Rd. Brwd. DE26 122
Copenhagen Pl. E14 CD39 57
Copenhagen St. W1 BX37 56
Copenhagen Way Walt. BC55 83
Copen Rd. Dag. CQ33 50
Cope Pl. W8 BS41 66
Copers Cope Rd. Beck. CD50 77
Cope St. SE16 CC42 67
Copeswood Rd. Wat. BC23 26
Copford Clo. Wdf. Grn. CK29 40
Green Wk.
Copland Av. Wem. BK35 45
Copland Clo. Wem. BK35 45
Copland Rd. Wem. BL36 55
Copleigh Dr. Tad. BR63 103
Copleston Rd. SE15 CA45 67
Copley Clo. W13 BH39 54
Copley Clo. Red. BU69 121
Copley Clo. Wok. AP63 100
Copley Dene Brom. CJ51 88
Copley Pk. SW16 BX50 76
Copley Rd. Stan. BK28 36
Copley St. E1 CC39 57
Copmans Wick. Rick. AU25 25
Copnor Way, SE15 CA43 67
Hordle Prom. W.
Copperas St. SE8 CE43 67
Copperbeech Clo. NW3 BT35 47
Akenside Rd.
Copper Beech Clo. Hem. H. AV15 7
Copper Beech Clo. Ilf. CL30 40
Copper Beech Gro. Wind. AL44 61
Copper Beech Rd. S. Ock. DB38 60
Copperdale Rd. Hayes BC41 63
Copperfield, Chig. CM28 40
Copperfield Approach Chig. CM29 40
Copperfield App. Ilf. CM29 40
Copperfield Av. Uxb. AZ39 53
Copperfield Clo. Grav. DK47 81
Copperfield Ct. Lthd. BJ64 102
Kingston Rd.
Copperfield Gdns. Brwd. DA26 42
Copperfield Orchard Sev. CW62 108
Copperfields
Copperfield Rise. Wey. AV56 91
Copperfield Rd. E3 CD38 57
Copperfields. Sev. CW62 108
Copperfield St. SE1 BY41 66
Copperfield Way Chis. CM50 78
Coppermill La. E17 CC32 48
Copper Mill La. SW17 BT49 76
Coppermill La. Rick. AV29 34
Coppermill La. Uxb. AW29 35
Copper Mill Rd. Stai. AT46 72
Copper Ridge. Ger. Cr. AS28 34
Coppetts Clo. N12 BU29 38
Coppetts Rd. N10 BU29 38
Coppice Cl. Hat. BO14 10
Coppice Clo. SW20 BQ52 85
Coppice Clo. Guil. AO70 118
Coppice Clo. Ruis. BA32 44
Coppice Dr. SW15 BP46 75
Coppice Dr. Stai. AR47 72
Coppice Est. Brom. CL53 88
Coppice La. Reig. BR69 120
Coppice Path, Chig. CO28 41
Coppice Row, Epp. CM21 31
Coppice, The, Ashf. AZ50 73
School Rd.
Coppice, The, Brwd. CZ21 33
Coppice, The, Enf. BY24 29
Coppice, The, Wat. BD25 27
Coppice, The West Dr. AY39 53
Coppice Wk. N20 BS27 38
Coppice Way E18 CG31 49
Coppifs Gro. N11 BV28 38
Copping Clo. Croy. CA56 96
Coppins La. Iver AV39 52
Coppins, The, Croy. CE57 96
Coppins, The, Har. BH29 36
Coppley Way, Tad. BQ63 103
Copse Av. W. Wick. CE55 87
Copse Bnk. Sev. CW63 108
Copse Clo. Guil. AU73 118
Copse Clo. Nthwd. BA30 35
Copse Clo. West Dr. AX41 63
Copse Edge Av. Epsom. BO60 94
Copse Glade Surb. BK54 84
Copse Hill Pur. BX60 95
Copse Hill. Sutt. BS57 95
Copse Hl. SW20 BP51 85
Copse La. Beac. AP29 34
Copsem Dr. Esher BG57 93
Copsem La. Esher BG57 93
Copsem La. Lthd. BG59 93
Copse Rd. Cob. BC60 92
Copse Rd. Wok. AP62 100
Copse Side Hart. DC52 90
Copse, The, E4 CG26 40
Copse, The Lthd. BF65 102
Copse Vw. Sth. Croy. CC58 96
Copse Wood, Iver AU37 52
Copse Wood Way. Nthwd. BA30 35
Copsleigh Av. Red. BV74 121
Copsleigh Clo. Red. BV73 121
Coptfold Rd. Brwd. DB27 42
Copthall Av. EC2 BZ39 57
Copthall Bldgs. EC2 BZ39 57
Telegraph St.
Copthall Clo. EC2 BZ39 57
Copthall Clo. Ger. Cr. AS29 34
Copthall Corner. Ger. Cr. AS29 34
Copthall Ct. EC2 BZ39 57
Throgmorton St.
Copthall Dr. NW7 BP29 37
Copthall Gdns. NW7 BP29 37
Copthall Gdns. Twick. BH47 74
Copt Hall Rd. Sev. DA65 108
Copthall Rd. E. Uxb. AZ34 44
Copthall Rd. W. Uxb. AZ34 44
Copthall Way. Wey. AV58 91
Copthall Way. Wey. AW58 92
Copthorn Clo. Shep. BA53 83
Copthorne Av. SW12 BW47 76
Copthorne Av. Brom. CK55 88
Copthorne Av. Ilf. CL29 40
Copthorne Clo. Ilf. CL29 40
Copthorne Clo. Rick. AY25 26
Copthorne Gdns. Horn. CX32 51
Copthorne Rise Sth. Croy. BZ60 96
Copthorne Rd. Lthd. BJ63 102
Copthorne Rd. Rick. AY25 26
Copthorpe Ct. NW8 BT38 56
Maida Vale
Coptic St. WC1 BX39 56
Coralline Wk. SE2 CP41 69
Coral Mead. Rick. AX26 35
Coral St. SE1 BY41 66
Coram Clo. Berk. AR13 7
Coram Grn. Brwd. DE25 122
Coram St. WC1 BX38 56
Coran Clo. N9 CC26 39
Corban Rd. Houns. BF45 64
Corbar Clo. Barn. BT23 29
Corbar Clo. Barn. BT23 29
Corbet Clo. Wall. BV55 86
Corbet Pl. E1 CA39 57
Jerome St.
Corbet Rd. Epsom BO58 94
Corbets Av. Upmin. CX35 51
Corbets Tey Rd. Upmin. CX35 51
Corbett Rd. E11 CJ32 49
Corbett Rd. E17 CF31 48
Corbett Rd. N22 BX29 38
Trinity Rd.
Corbetts La. SE16 CC42 67
Rotherhithe New Rd.
Corbetts Pass. SE16 CC42 67
Rotherhithe New Rd.
Corbett St. SW8 BX43 66
Corbicum, E11 CG33 49
Corbiere Ct. SW19 BQ50 75
Thornton Rd.
Corbins La. Har. BF34 45
Corby Clo. St. Alb. BF16 18
Corby Cres. Enf. BX24 29
Corby Dr. Eng. AR50 72
Corbylands Rd. Sid. CN47 78
Corbyn St. N4 BX33 47
Corby Rd. NW10 BN37 55
Corby Way E3 CE38 57
Knapp Rd
Corcorans Brwd. DA25 33
Elizabeth Rd.
Cordelia Gdns. Stai. AY47 73
Cordelia Rd. Stai. AY47 73
Cordelia St. E14 CE39 57
Cordelia St. N7 BX36 56
Cordell Clo. Wal. Cr. CD17 21
Corder Clo. St. Alb. BF15 9
Cordons Clo. Ger. Cr. AR30 34
Cordova Rd. E3 CD38 57
Cordrey Gdns. Couls. BX57 95
Cordrey Gdns. Couls BX61 104
Cord Way, E14 CE41 67
Mellish St.
Cordwell Rd. SE13 CF46 77
Corelli Rd. SE3 CK44 68
Corfe Av. Har. BF35 45
Corfield St. E2 CB38 57
Corfton Rd. W5 BL39 55
Corinium Clo. Wem. BL35 46
Corinium Gte. St. Alb. BF14 9
Corinne Rd. N19 BW35 47
Corinthian Manorway Erith CS42 69
Corinthian Rd. Erith CS42 69
Corinthian Way Stai. AX47 73
Clare Rd.
Corinth Par. Hayes BB39 53
Corinth Rd. N7 BX35 47
Corker Way N7 BX34 47
Andover Est.
Corkran Rd. Surb. BK54 84
Corkscrew Hill W. Wick. CF55 87
Cork St. W1 BW40 56
Corlett St. NW1 BU39 56
Bell St.
Cormongers La. Red. BV70 121
Cormont Rd. SE5 BY44 66
Cormorant Wk. Rain. CU36 59
Cornbury Rd. Edg. BK29 36
Cornell Clo. Sid. CQ50 79
Cornell Way Rom. CR28 41
Cornerfield Mo. Hat. BP11 10
Corner Hall, Hem. H. AX14 8
Cornerhall Av. Hem. H. AX14 8
Corner Mead NW9 BO30 37
Corner St. E16 CH39 58
Beckton Rd.
Corney Rd. W4 BO43 65
Cornfield Clo. Uxb. AX37 53
Cornfield Rd. Bush. BF24 27
Cornfield Rd. Reig. BT71 121
Cornfields, Hem. H. AW13 8
Cornflower Ter. SE22 CB46 77
Cornford Clo. Brom. CH53 88
Cornford Gro. SW12 BV48 76
Cornhill, EC3 BZ39 57
Cornish Gro. SE20 CB51 87
Corn Mead. Welw. G. C. BQ6 5
Cornmill, Wal. Abb. CE20 21
Cornmill Dr. Orp. CN54 88
Cornmill La. SE13 CF45 67
Cornshaw Rd. Dag. CP33 50
Cornsland, Brwd. DB27 42
Cornthwaite Rd. E5 CC34 48
Cornwall Av. E2 CC38 57
Cornwall Av. N3 BS29 38
Cornwall Av. N22 BX30 38
Cornwall Av. Esher BJ57 93
Cornwall Av. Sthl. BE39 54
Cornwall Av. Well. CN45 68
Cornwall Av. Wey. AY60 92
Cornwall Clo. Bark. CN36 58
Cornwall Clo. Wal. Cr. CD20 21
Cornwall Cres. W11 BR39 55
Cornwall Cres. W11 BR40 55
Cornwall Dr. Orp. CP50 79
Cornwall Gdns. NW10 BP36 55
Cornwall Gdns. SW7 BS41 66
Cornwall Gdns. Wk. SW7 BS41 66
Cornwall Gro. W4 BO42 65
Cornwallis Av. N9 CB27 39
Cornwallis Av. SE9 CM48 78
Cornwallis Gro. N9 CB27 39
Cornwallis Rd. E17 CC31 48
Cornwallis Rd. N9 CB27 39
Cornwallis Rd. N19 BX34 47
Cornwallis Rd. Dag. CP35 50
Cornwallis Wk. SE9 CK45 68
Cornwall Lo. Kings. On T. BM50 75
Cornwall Ms. St. SW7 BT41 66
Cornwall Rd. N4 BY33 47
Cornwall Rd. N15 BZ32 48
Cornwall Rd. N18 CB28 39
Fairfield Rd.
Cornwall Rd. SE1 BY40 56
Cornwall Rd. Brwd. DA25 33
Cornwall Rd. Croy. BY55 86
Cornwall Rd. Har. BG32 45
Cornwall Rd. Pnr. BE29 36
Cornwall Rd. Ruis. BB34 44
Cornwall Rd. Ruis. BC34 44
Cornwall Rd. St. Alb. BH14 9
Cornwall Rd. Sutt. BS58 95
Cornwall Rd. Twick. BJ47 74
Cornwall Rd. Uxb. AX36 53
Cornwall St. Est. E1 CB40 57
Cornwall Ter. NW1 BU38 56
Cornwall Way, Stai. AV50 72
Cornwell Av. Grav. DH48 81
Cornwood Clo. N2 BT32 47
Cornworthy Rd. Dag. CP35 50
Corona Rd. SE12 CH47 78
Coronation Ave. Wind. AQ44 62
Coronation Av. N16 CA35 48
Coronation Av. Slou. AS39 52
Coronation Clo. Bex. CP46 79
Coronation Clo. Ilf. CM31 49
Coronation Cotts. W5 BL38 55
Coronation Cres. Grays DG41 71
Loewen Rd.
Coronation Dr. Horn. CU35 50
Coronation Hill, Epp. CN18 22
Coronation Rd. E13 CJ38 58
Coronation Rd. NW10 BL38 55
Coronation Rd. Hayes. BB42 63
Coronation Wk. Twick. BF47 74
Coroner's Ct. W6 BQ42 65
Coronet St. N1 CA38 57
Corporation Av. Houns. BE45 64
Corporation Row, EC1 BY38 56
Corporation St. E15 CG37 58
Corporation St. N7 BX35 47
Corral Gdns. Hem. H. AY13 8
Corrall Rd. N7 BX36 56
Lough Rd.
Corrance Rd. SW2 BX45 66
Corran Way. S. Ock. DA40 60
Corri Av. N14 BW28 38
Corrie Gdns. Vir. W. AR54 82
Corrie Rd. Wey. AX56 92
Corrie Rd. Wok. AT63 100
Corrigan Av. Couls. BV61 104
Corringham Ct. NW11 BS33 47
Corringham Ct. St. Alb. BH13 9
Lemsford Rd.
Corringham Rd. NW11 BS33 47
Corringham Rd. Wem. BM34 46

Corrington Ms. W11 BR40 55
Blenheim Cres.
Corringway NW11 BS33 47
Corringway W5 BL39 55
Corsair Clo. Stai. AX47 73
Corsair Rd. Stai. AX47 73
Corscoombe Clo. Kings. On T. BN49 75
Corsehill St. SW16 BW50 76
Corseley Way, E9 CD36 57
Trowbridge Est.
Corsham St. N1 BZ38 57
Corsica St. N5 BY36 56
Cortayne Rd. SW6 BR44 65
Cortis Rd. SW15 BP46 75
Cortis Ter. SW15 BP46 75
Corunna Rd. SW8 BW44 66
Corunna Ter. SW8 BW44 66
Corve La. S. Ock. DA40 60
Corville Rd. W3 BM41 65
Corwall Ave. Wind. AM42 61
Corwall Ct. SW17 BU49 76
Broadwater Rd.
Corwell Gdns. Uxb. BA39 53
Corwell La. Uxb. BA39 53
Corwood Dr. E1 CC39 57
Cory Dr. Brwd. DD26 122
Cosbycote Av. SE24 BZ46 77
Cosdach Av. Wall. BW57 95
Cosedge Cres. Croy. BY56 95
Cosmo Pl. WC1 BX39 56
Southampton Row
Cossall St. SE15 CB44 67
Cosser St. SE1 BY41 66
Costa St. SE15 CB44 67
Costead Manor Rd. Brwd. DA26 42
Coston's Av. Grnf. BG38 54
Coston's La. Grnf. BG38 54
Coston Wk. SE4 CD45 67
Frendsbury Rd.
Cosway St. NW1 BU39 56
Cotall St. E14 CE39 57
Coteford Clo. Pnr. BC32 44
Coteford St. SW17 BU49 76
Cotelands Croy. CA55 87
Cotesbach Rd. E5 CC34 48
Cotesmere Gdns. Dag. CP35 50
Cotford Rd. Th. Hth. BZ52 87
Cotham St. SE17 BZ42 67
Cotherstone, Epsom BN58 94
Cotherstone Rd. SW2 BX47 76
Cotlandswick, St. Alb. BK16 18
Cotleigh Av. Bex. CP48 79
Cotleigh Rd. NW6 BS36 56
Cotleigh Rd. Rom. CS32 50
Cotman Clo. NW11 BT32 47
Cotman Clo. SW15 BQ46 75
Cotmandene Cres. Orp. CO51 89
Cotman Gdns. Edg. BM30 37
Cotmans Ash La. Sev. CX60 99
Cotmans Ash La. Sev. CY62 108
Cotmans Clo. Hayes BC40 53
Coton Rd. Well. CO45 69
Cotsford Av. N. Mal. BN53 85
Cotswold Hem. H. AY12 8
Mendip Way
Cotswold Av. Bush. BG25 27
Cotswold Clo. Bexh. CT44 69
Cotswold Clo. St. Alb. BK11 9
Chiltern Rd.
Cotswold Clo. Slou. AN41 61
Cotswold Clo. Stai. AW49 73
Cotswold Clo. Uxb. AX37 53
Cotswold Gdns. E6 CJ38 58
Cotswold Gdns. NW2 BQ34 46
Cotswold Gdns. Brwd. DF26 122
Cotswold Gdns. Ilf. CM33 49
Cotswold Rd. Grav. DF48 81
Cotswold Rd. Hamptn. BF49 74
Cotswold Rd. Rom. CW30 42
Cotswold Rd. Sutt. BS58 95
Cotswolds. Hat. BP13 10
Cotswold St. SE27 BY49 76
Cotswold Way Enf. BX24 29
Cottage Av. Brom. CK54 88
Cottage Clo. Cher. AU57 91
Cottage Clo. Ruis. BA33 44
Cottage Farm Way, Egh. AU52 82
Cottage Gro. SE5 BZ43 67
Cottage Gro. SW9 BX45 66
Cottage Gro. Surb. BK53 84
Cottage Park Rd. Slou. AO34 43
Cottage Pl. SW3 BU41 66
Cottage Rd. Epsom BN57 94
Cottage St. E14 CE40 57
Cottage, The, Surb. BK54 84
Cottage Wk. N16 CA34 48
Smalley Rd.
Cottage Walk SE15 CA44 67
Sumner Estate
Cottage Wk. SW1 BU41 66
Cottenham Dr. SW20 BP50 75
Cottenham Pde. SW20 BP51 85
Durham Rd.
Cottenham Pk. Rd. SW20 BP51 85
Cottenham Pl. SW20 BP50 75
Cottenham Rd. E17 CD31 48
Cotterells, Hem. H. AX13 8
Cotterells Hill, Hem. H. AX13 8
Cotterill Rd. Surb. BL55 85
Cottesbrook. Slou. AU44 62
Cottesbrook St. SE14 CD43 67
Cottesmore Av. Ilf. CL30 40
Cottesmore Gdns. W8 BS41 66
Cottimore Av. Walt. BC54 83
Cottimore Cres. Walt. BC54 83
Cottimore La. Walt. BC54 83
Cottimore Ter. Walt. BC54 83
Cottingham Chase Ruis. BC34 44
Cottingham Rd. SE20 CC50 77
Cottington St. SE11 BY42 66
Cotton Av. W3 BN39 55
Cotton Hl. Brom. CF49 77
Cotton La. Green. CY46 80
Cottonmill Cres. St. Alb. BG14 9
Cottonmill La. St. Alb. BG14 9
Cotton Rd. Pot. B. BT19 20
Cotton's Gdns. E2 CA38 57
Hackney Rd.
Cotton St. E14 CF40 57
Cottrill Rd. E8 CB36 57
Couchmore Av. Esher BH55 84
Couchmore Av. Ilf. CK30 40
Coulgate St. SE4 CD45 67
Coulsdon Ct. Rd. Couls. BX61 104
Coulsdon La. Couls. BU63 104
Coulsdon Rise Couls. BX62 104
Coulsdon Rd. Cat. BZ64 105
Coulsdon Rd. Couls. BX61 104
Coulsdon Rd. Couls. BY63 104
Coulser Clo. Hem. H. AW12 8
Coulshead Ave. Guil. AQ68 109
Coulson St. SW3 BU42 66
Coulter Clo. Pot. B. BW17 20
Coulter Rd. W6 BP41 65
Coulton Av. Grav. DF47 81
Council Av. Grav. DE46 81
Councillor St. SE5 BZ43 67
Counters Clo. Hem. H. AW13 8
Countess Clo. Uxb. AX30 35
Countess Rd. NW5 BW35 47
Countisbury Av. Enf. CA26 39
Country Way Felt. BC50 73
County Gdns. Bark. CN37 58
County Gate, SE9 CM48 78
County Gate Barn. BS25 29
County Gro. SE5 BZ44 67
County Rd. Th. Hth. BY51 86
County St. SE1 BZ41 67
Coupland Ter. SE18 BU42 66
Courage Clo. Horn. CV32 51
Courage Wk. Brwd. DE25 122
Courcy Rd. N8 BY31 47
Courland Gro. SW8 BW44 66
Courlands Rd. Wey. AW55 83
Courland St. SW8 BW44 66
Coursers Rd. St. Alb. BN15 10
Course, The, SE9 CL48 78
Courtaulds, Kings L. AW18 17
Court Ave. Couls. BY63 104
Court Av. Belv. CQ42 69
Court Av. Rom. CX29 42
Court Bushes Rd. Whyt. CB63 105
Court Clo. Har. BL31 46
Court Clo. Maid. AH42 61
Court Clo. Twick. BF48 74
Court Clo. Wall. BW57 95
Court Clo. Av. Twick. BF48 74
Court Cres. Chess. BK57 93
Court Cres. Slou. AO39 52
Court Downs Rd. Beck. CE51 87
Court Dr. Croy. BX56 95
Court Dr. Stan. BL28 37
Court Dr. Sutt. BU56 95
Court Dr. Uxb. AY37 53
Courtenay Av. N6 BU33 47
Courtenay Av. Har. BG29 36
Courtenay Gdns. Har. BG30 36
Courtenay Gdns. Upmin. CY33 51
Courtenay Pl. E17 CD32 48
Courtenay Rd. E11 CG34 49
Courtenay Rd. E17 CC31 48
Courtenay Rd. Wok. AT61 100
Courtenay Rd. Wor. Pk. BQ55 85
Courtenay Sq. SE11 BY42 66
Courtenay St.
Courtenay St. SE11 BY42 66
Court Farm La. Nthlt. BF36 54
Court Farm Rd. SE9 CK48 78
Court Farm Rd. Nthlt. BF36 54
Courtfield Av. Har. BH32 45
Courtfield Cres. Har. BH32 45
Courtfield Cres. Harrow. BJ32 45
Courtfield Av.
Courtfield Gdns. SW5 BS42 66
Courtfield Gdns. W13 BJ39 54
Courtfield Gdns. Ruis. BB34 44
Courtfield Gdns. Uxb. AW34 44
Courtfield Ms. SW7 BT42 66
Courtfield Rise W. Wick. CF55 87
Courtfield Rd. SW7 BT42 66
Courtfield Rd. Ashf. AZ50 73
Court Fm. Av. Epsom BN56 94
Court Fm. Rd. Warl. CB62 105
Ct. Grn. Heights Wok. AR63 100
Fern Hill La.
Court Gro. SE9 CK46 78
Court Haw Bans. BU61 104
Court Hill Couls. BU62 104
Court Hill Sth. Croy. CA59 96
Courthill Rd. SE13 CF45 67
Courthope Rd. NW3 BU35 47
Mansfield Rd.
Courthope Rd. SW19 BR49 75
Courthope Rd. Grnf. BG37 54
Courthope Vill. SW19 BR50 75
Court House Gdns. N3 BS29 38
Court House Rd. N12 BS29 38
Courtland Av. E4 CG27 40
Courtland Av. Ilf. CK34 49
Courtland Cres. Bans. BS61 104
Courtland Dr. Chig. CL27 40
Courtlands Ave. Slou. AR42 62
Courtlands Av. NW7 BN27 37
Courtlands Av. SE12 CH46 78
Courtlands Av. SW16 BX50 76
Courtlands Av. Brom. CG54 88
Courtlands Av. Esher BE57 93
Courtlands Av. Hamptn. BE50 74
Courtlands Av. Rich. BM44 65
Courtlands Av. Est. SE12 CH46 78
Courtlands Clo. Sth. Croy. CA58 96
Courtlands Dr. Epsom BO57 94
Courtlands Dr. Wat. BB22 26
Courtlands Rd. Surb. BM54 85
Court La. SE21 CA46 77
Court La. Iver AV40 52
Court La. Wind. AK41 61
Court La. Gdns. SE21 CA47 77
Court Leas. Cob. BF60 93
Courtleet Dri. Erith CS44 69
Alberta Rd.
Courtleet Dr. Erith. CR44 69
Alberta Rd.
Courtleigh Av. Barn. BT22 29
Courtleigh Gdns. NW11 BR31 46
Courtman Rd. N17 BZ29 39
Court Mead Nthlt. BE38 54
Courtmead Clo. SE24 BZ46 77
Courtnell St. W2 BS39 56
Courtney Cres. Cars. BU57 95
Courtney Pl. Croy. BY55 86
Courtney Rd. N7 BY35 47
Courtney Rd. SE20 CC50 77
Courtney Rd. SW19 BU50 76
Courtney Rd. Croy. BY55 86
Courtney Rd. Grays. DH41 71
Court Pde. Wem. BJ34 45
Courtrai Rd. SE23 CD46 77
Court Rd. SE9 CK48 78
Court Rd. SE25 CA51 87
Court Rd. Bans. BS61 104
Court Rd. Cat. BZ65 105
Court Rd. Dart. CZ49 80
Court Rd. Cdon. CC60 114
Court Rd. Orp. CO55 89
Court Rd. Sthl. BE42 64
Court Rd. Uxb. AZ35 44
Court Side SE26 CC48 77
Round Hill
Court St. E1 CB39 57
Durward St.
Court St. Brom. CH51 88
South St.
Court, The, Ruis. BE35 45
Court. The. Warl. CD62 105
Court Way, NW9 BO31 46
Court Way W3 BN39 55
Court Way. Rom. CW30 42
Court Way Twick. BH47 74
Courtway, Wdf. Grn. CJ28 40
Courtway, The, Wat. BE27 36
Courtwood La. Croy. CD59 96
Court Wood Rd. Sev. CU65 107
Court Yard, SE9 CK46 78
Cousin La. EC4 BZ40 57
Couthurst Rd. SE3 CH43 68
Coutts Av. Chess. BL56 94
Coutts Rd. E3 CD39 57
Coval Gdns. SW14 BM45 65
Coval La. SW14 BM45 65
Coval Passage SW14 BN45 65
Upper Richmond Rd
Coval Rd. SW14 BN45 65
Coveham Cres. Cob. BC60 92
Covent Gdn. WC2 BX40 56
Coventry Clo. NW6 BS37 56
Coventry Cross Est. E3 CF38 57
Coventry Rd. E1 CB38 57
Coventry Rd. SE25 CB52 87
Coventry Rd. Ilf. CL34 49
Coventry St. W1 BW40 56
Coverack Clo. N14 BV25 29
Coverdale Hem. H. AY12 8
Wharfedale
Coverdale Clo. Stan. BJ28 36
Coverdale Gdns. Croy CA55 87
Park Hill Rise
Coverdale Rd. NW2 BQ36 55
Coverdale Rd. W12 BP41 65
Coverdales, The. Bark. CM37 58
Covert Clo. Berk. AO12 7
Coverton Rd. SW17 BU49 76
Covert Rd. Berk. AO11 7
Covert Rd. Chig. CN28 40
Coverts Rd. Leath. BH58 93
Coverts, The, Brwd. DD26 122
Covert. The. Nthwd. BA30 35
Covert, The, Orp. CN53 88
Covert Way Barn. BT23 29
Covington Gdns. SW16 BY50 76
Covington Way, SW16 BX50 76
Cowan St. SE5 CA43 67
Cowbridge La. Bark. CL36 58
Cowbridge Rd. Har. BL31 46
Cowcross St. EC1 BY39 56
Cowden Rd. Orp. CN54 88
Cowden St. SE6 CE49 77
Cowdray Rd. Uxb. BA37 53
Cowdray Way. Horn. CU35 50
Cowdrey Clo. Enf. CA23 30
Cowdrey Ct. Dart. CU47 79
Cowdrey Rd. SW19 BS49 76
Cowen Av. Har. BG34 45
Cowgate Rd. Grnf. BG37 54
Cowick Rd. SW17 BU49 76
Cowings Mead Nthlt. BD36 54
Cowland Av. Enf. CC24 30
Cow La. Grnf. BG37 54
Cow La. Wat. BD21 27
Cowleaze Rd. Kings. On T. BL51 85
Cowley Av. Cher. AV54 82
Cowley Clo. Sth. Croy. CC58 96
Cowley Cres. Uxb. AX39 53
Cowley Cres. Walt. BD56 93
Cowley Hill Borwd. BM22 28
Cowley Hill Borwd. BM23 28
Cowley La. E11 CG34 49
Cathall Rd.
Cowley La. Cher. AV54 82
Cowley Mill Rd. Uxb. AW37 53
Cowley Peachey, Uxb. AX39 53
Cowley Rd. E11 CH32 49
Cowley Rd. SW9 BY44 66
Cowley Rd. SW14 BO45 65
Cowley Rd. W3 BO40 55
Cowley Rd. Ilf. CK33 49
Cowley Rd. Rom. CU29 41
Cowley Rd. Uxb. AX38 53
Cowley St. SW1 BX41 66
Little College St.
Cowper Av. E6 CK36 58
Cowper Av. Sutt. BT56 95
Cowper Av. Til. DG44 71
Cowper Clo. Cher. AV53 82
Cowper Clo. Well. CO46 79
Cowper Gdns. N14 BV25 29
Cowper Gdns. Wall. BW57 95
Cowper Rd. N14 BV26 38
Cowper Rd. N16 CA35 48
Cowper Rd. N18 CB28 39
Cowper Rd. SW19 BT50 76
Cowper Rd. W3 BN40 55
Cowper Rd. W7 BH40 54
Cowper Rd. Belv. CQ42 69
Cowper Rd. Berk. AQ13 7
Cowper Rd. Brom. CJ52 88
Cowper Rd. Hem. H. AW14 8
Cowper Rd. Kings. On T. BL49 75
Cowper Rd. Rain. CU38 59
Cowper Rd. Welw. G. C. BR9 5
Cowper St. EC2 BZ38 57
Cowslip La. Dor. BJ67 111
Cowslip La. Wok. AQ60 91
Cowslip Rd. E18 CH31 49
Cowthorpe Rd. SW8 BW44 66
Coxdean Epsom BQ62 103
Coxdean, Epsom. BQ63 103
Coxfield Clo. Hem. H. AY13 8
Cox La. Chess. BL56 94
Cox La. Epsom BM56 94
Coxley Rise Pur. BZ56 96
Coxley Rise Pur. BZ60 96
Coxmount Rd. SE7 CJ42 68
Coxon Clo. Har. BF30 36
Cox's Ct. EC1 BZ39 57
Cox's La. Wok. AS64 100
Coxson Pl. SE1 CA41 67
Cox's Wk. SE21 CB47 77
Coxtie Green Rd. Brwd. CW25 33
Coxwell Rd. SE18 CM42 68
Coxwold Path. Chess. BL57 94
Crabbe Cres. Chesh. AO18 16
Crabbs Croft Clo. Orp. CL56 97
Crab Hill, Beck. CF50 77
Crab Hill La. Red. BX72 121
Crab La. Wat. BF21 27
Crabtree Av. Rom. CP31 50
Crabtree Av. Wem. BL37 55
Crabtree Clo. Bush. BF25 27
Crabtree Clo. Hem. H. AX14 8
Crabtree La. SW6 BQ43 65
Crabtree La. Dor. BJ68 111
Crabtree La. Hem. H. AX14 8
Crabtree La. Lthd. BF66 111
Crabtree Manorway Belv. CS41 69
Crabtree Walk SE15 CA44 67
Sumner Estate
Crace St. NW1 BW38 56
Drummond Cres.
Craddock Rd. Enf. CA24 30
Craddock's Ave. Ash BL62 103
Craddock St. NW3 BV36 56
Prince Of Wales Rd.
Cradley Rd. SE9 CM47 78
Cragg Av. Rad. BH21 27
Craigavon Rd. Hem. H. AY11 8
Craigdale Rd. Horn. CT32 50
Craig Dr. Uxb. AZ39 53
Craigen Av. Croy. CB54 87
Craigholm, SE18 CL44 68
Craigmore Tower Wok. AS63 100
Guildford Rd.
Craig Mount Rad. BJ21 27
Craigmuir Pk. Wem. BL37 55
Craignair Rd. SW2 BX47 76
Craignish Av. SW16 BX51 86
Craig Park Rd. N18 CB28 39
Craig Rd. Rich. BK49 74
Craig's Ct. SW1 BX40 56
Whitehall
Craigton Rd. SE9 CK45 68
Craig Wk. Wal. Cr. CC17 21
Davison Dr.
Craigweil Av. Rad. BJ21 27
Craigwell Av. Felt. BC48 73
Craigwell Clo. Stan. BK28 36
Craigwell Dr. Stan. BK28 36
Crail Row, SE17 BZ42 67
Darwin St.
Craithie Rd. SE12 CH46 78
Crakell Rd. BT71 121
Cramer St. W1 BV39 56
Crammavill St. Grays. DD40 71
Crammerville Wk. Rain. CV39 60
Crampshaw La. Ash. BL63 103
Crampton Rd. SE20 CC50 77
Crampton's Rd. Sev. CU63 107
Crampton St. SE17 BY42 66
Cranberry Clo. Nthlt. BE37 54
Cranberry St. E1 CB38 57
Cranborne Av. Sthl. BF42 64
Cranborne Cres. Pot. B. BR19 19
Cranborne Gdns. Upmin. CX34 51
Cranborne Rd. Hat. BP12 10
Cranborne Rd. Hodd. CE11 12
Cranborne Rd. Pot. B. BR19 19
Cranborne Rd. Wal. Cr. CC19 21
Theobalds La.
Cranborne Waye Hayes BC39 53
Cranbourne Ave. Wind. AM44 61
Cranbourne Av. E11 CH31 49
Cranbourne Av. Surb. BM55 85
Cranbourne Clo. Slou. AO40 61
Cranbourne Ct. E18 CH31 49
Cranbourne Dr. Pnr. BD32 45
Cranbourne Gdns. Ilf. CM31 49
Cranbourne Gdns. Welw. G. C. BR8 5
Cranbourne Rd. E12 CK35 49
High St.N.
Cranbourne Rd. E15 CF35 48
Cranbourne Rd. N10 BV30 38
Cranbourne Rd. Nthwd. BB31 44
Cranbourne Rd. Slou. AO40 61
Cranbourn Pass. SE16 CB41 67
Wilson Gro.
Cranbourn St. WC2 BW40 56
Long Acre
Cranbrook Clo. Brom. CH53 88
Cranbrook Dr. Esher BG55 84
Cranbrook Dr. Rom. CU31 50
Cranbrook Dr. Twick. BF47 74
Cranbrook Est. E2 CC37 57
Cranbrook Pk. N22 BX30 38
Cranbrook Rise, Ilf. CK32 49
Cranbrook Rd. SE3 CJ45 68
Cranbrook Rd. SE8 CE44 67
Cranbrook Rd. SW19 BR50 75
Cranbrook Rd. W4 BO42 65
Cranbrook Rd. Barn. BT25 29
Cranbrook Rd. Bexh. CQ44 69
Cranbrook Rd. Houns. BE45 64
Cranbrook Rd. Ilf. CL32 49
Cranbrook Rd. St. Alb. BL13 10
Cranbrook Rd. Th. Hth. BZ51 87
Cranbrook St. E2 CC37 57
Gathorne St.
Cranbrook Ter. E2 CC37 57
Roman Rd.
Cranbury Rd. SW6 BS44 66
Crane Av. W3 BO40 55
Cumberland Pk.
Crane Av. Islw. BJ46 74
Crane Ct. Epsom BN56 94
Craneford Clo. Twick. BH47 74
Craneford Way Twick. BH47 74
Crane Gdns. Hayes. BB42 63
Crane Gro. N7 BY36 56
Furlong Rd.
Cranell Grn. S. Ock. DA40 60
Crane Lo. Houns. BC43 63
Crane Pk. Rd. Twick. BF48 74
Crane Rd. Twick. BH47 74
Cranes Dr. Surb. BL52 85
Cranes Pk. Surb. BL52 85
Cranes Pk. Av. Surb. BL52 85
Cranes Pk. Cres. Surb. BL52 85
Crane St. SE10 CF42 67
Cranes Water, Hayes. BB43 63
Craneswater Pk. Sthl. BE42 64
Cranes Way Borwd. BN25 28
Crane Way Twick. BG47 74
Cranewood Clo. Wok. AS63 100
Guildford Rd.
Cranfield Cres. Pot. B. BX18 20
Cranfield Dr. Wat. BE19 18
Cranfield Rd. SE4 CD45 67
Cranfield Rd. E. Cars. BV58 95
Cranfield Rd. W. Cars. BV58 95
Cranfield Vills. SE27 BZ48 77
Norwood High St.
Cranford Av. N13 BX28 38
Cranford Av. Stai. AY47 73
Cranford Clo. SW20 BP50 75
Cranford Clo. Stai. AY47 73
Cranford Cotts. E1 CC40 57
Cranford St.
Cranford Dr. Hayes. BB42 63
Cranford Dr. Hayes BC42 63
Cranford La. Hayes. BA43 63
Cranford La. Houns. BB44 63
Cranford La. Houns. BC43 63
Cranford La. Est. Houns. BC43 63
Cranford Park Rd. Hayes. BB42 63
Cranford Pk. Rd. Hayes BC42 63
Cranford Rd. Dart. CW47 80
Cranford Rd. Hayes. BB42 63
Cranford St. E1 CC40 57
Cranham Gdns. Upmin. CZ33 51
Cranham Rd. Horn. CU32 50
Cranhurst Rd. NW2 BQ35 46
Cranleigh Clo. SE20 CB51 87
Cranleigh Clo. Bex. CR46 79
Cranleigh Clo. Orp. CN55 88
Cranleigh Clo. Sth. Croy. CB59 96
Cranleigh Dr. Swan. CT53 89
Cranleigh Gdns. N21 BY24 29
Cranleigh Gdns. SE25 CA52 87
Cranleigh Gdns. Bark. CM36 58
Cranleigh Gdns. Har. BL32 46
Cranleigh Gdns. Kings. On T. BL50 75
Cranleigh Gdns. Loug. CK25 31
Cranleigh Gdns. Sth. Croy. CB59 96
Cranleigh Gdns. Sthl. BE39 54
Cranleigh Gdns. Sutt. BS55 86
Cranleigh Rd. N15 BZ32 48
Cranleigh Rd. SW19 BR52 85
Cranleigh Rd. Esher BG54 84
Cranleigh Rd. Felt. BB49 73
Cranleigh St. NW1 BW37 56
Cranley Clo. Guil. AT70 118
Cranley Dr. Ilf. CM33 49
Cranley Dr. Ruis. BC34 44
Cranley Gdns. N10 BV31 47
Cranley Gdns. N13 BX27 38
Cranley Gdns. SW7 BT42 66
Cranley Gdns. Wall. BW57 95
Cranley Gro. Watt. BB57 92
Cranley Ms. SW7 BT42 66
Cranley Mews Ilf. CM32 49
Cranley Rd.
Cranley Pl. SW7 BT42 66
Cranley Rd. E13 CH39 58
Cranley Rd. Guil. AS70 118
Cranley Rd. Ilf. CM33 49

Cranley Rd. Watt. BB56 92
Cranmer Av. W13 BJ41 64
Cranmer Clo. Mord. BQ53 85
Cranmer Clo. Pot. B. BS18 20
Cranmer Clo. Ruis. BD33 45
Cranmer Clo. Stan. BK29 36
Cranmer Clo. Warl. CD62 105
Cranmer Gdns.
Cranmer Clo. Wey. AZ57 92
Cranmer Ct. SW3 BU42 66
Cranmer Ct. Hamptn. BF49 74
Cranmer Gdns. Dag. CS35 50
Cranmer Rd. E7 CH35 49
Cranmer Rd. SW9 BY43 66
Cranmer Rd. Croy. BY55 86
Cranmer Rd. Edg. BM27 37
Cranmer Rd. Hayes BA39 53
Cranmer Rd. Hmptn. BF49 74
Cranmer Rd. Kings. On T. BL49 75
Cranmer Rd. Mitch. BU52 86
Cranmer Rd. Sev. CT65 107
Cranmer Terr. SW17 BT49 76
Cranmer Ter. SW17 BU49 76
Tooting Gro.
Cranmore Av. Chis. CK49 78
Cranmore Av. Islw. BG43 64
Cranmore Ct. St. Alb. BH13 9
Avenue Rd.
Cranmore Lane. Leath. AZ68 110
Cranmore Pk. Est. Chis. CK50 78
Cranmore Rd. Brom. CG48 78
Cranmore Way N10 BW31 47
Cranston Clo. Reig. BS71 121
Lymden Gdns.
Cranston Est. N1 BZ37 57
Cranston Gdns. E4 CE28 39
Cranston Park Av. Upmin. CY35 51
Cranston Rd. SE23 CD47 77
Cranswick Rd. SE16 CB42 67
Crantock Rd. SE6 CE48 77
Cranwell Gro. Shep. AY52 83
Cranwich Av. N21 BZ26 39
Cranwich Rd. N16 BZ33 48
Cranwood St. EC1 BZ38 57
Cranworth Cres. E4 CF26 39
Cranworth Gdns. SW9 BY44 66
Craster Rd. SW2 BX47 76
Craven Av. W5 BK40 54
Craven Av. Felt. BC48 73
Craven Av. Sthl. BE39 54
Craven Clo. Hayes BC39 53
Craven Gdns. SW19 BS49 76
Craven Gdns. Bark. CN37 58
Craven Gdns. Ilf. CM30 40
Craven Gdns. Rom. CR28 41
Craven Gdns. Rom. CY29 42
Craven Hill W2 BT40 56
Craven Hill Gdns. W2 BT40 56
Craven Hill Ms. W2 BT40 56
Craven Ms. SW11 BV46 76
Taybridge Rd.
Craven Pk. NW10 BN37 55
Craven Pk. Rd. N15 CA32 48
Craven Pk. Rd. NW10 BO37 55
Craven Pl. WC2 BX40 56
Craven St.
Craven Rd. NW10 BO37 55
Craven Rd. W2 BT40 56
Craven Rd. W5 BK40 54
Craven Rd. Croy. CB54 87
Craven Rd. Kings. On T. BL51 85
Craven Rd. Orp. CP55 89
Craven St. WC2 BX40 56
Craven Ter. W2 BT40 56
Craven Wk. N16 CB33 48
Crawford Ave. Grays. DD40 71
Crawford Av. Wem. BK35 45
Crawford Clo. N13 BY27 38
Crawford Clo. Islw. BH44 64
Crawford Est. SE5 BZ44 67
Crawford Gdns. N13 BY27 38
Crawford Gdns. Nthlt. BE38 54
Crawford Pl. W1 BU39 56
Crawford Rd. SE5 BZ44 67
Crawford Rd. Hat. BP11 10
Crawford St. W1 BU39 56
Crawley Dr. Hem. H. AY11 8
Crawley Dr. Ruis. BB34 44
Crawley Rd. E10 CE33 48
Crawley Rd. N22 BZ30 39
Crawley Rd. Enf. CA26 39
Crawshay Clo. Sev. CU65 107
Crawshay Rd. SW9 BY44 66
Crawthew Gro. SE22 CA45 67
Cray Ave. Ash. BL61 103
Cray Av. Orp. CO54 89
Craybrooke Rd. Sid. CO49 79
Craybury End. SE9 CM48 78
Cray Clo. Dart. CU45 69
Craydene Rd. Erith CT44 69
Crayford High St. Dart. CT45 69
Crayford Rd. N7 BW35 47
Crayford Rd. Dart. CT46 79
Crayford Rd. Erith CT43 69
Crayford Way Dart. CT46 79
Crayke Hill Chess. BL57 94
Craylands Orp. CP52 89
Cray Rd. Belv. CR43 69
Cray Rd. Sid. CP50 79
Cray Rd. Swan. CR53 89
Cray Valley Rd. Orp. CO53 89
Crealock Gro. Wdf. Grn. CG28 40
Crealock St. SW18 BS46 76
Creasy St. SE1 CA41 67
Webb St.
Crebor St. SE22 CB46 77
Creden Hall Dri. Brom. CK54 88
Lwr. Gravel Rd.
Credenhill St. SW16 BW50 76
Crediton Hl. NW6 BS35 47
Crediton Rd. E16 CH39 58
Crediton Rd. NW10 BQ37 55
Crediton Way Esher BJ56 93
Credon Rd. E13 CJ37 58
Credon Rd. SE16 CB42 67
Creechurch La. EC3 CA39 57
Creed La. EC4 BY39 56
Creek Br. SE10 CE43 67
Creek Rd. SE8 CE43 67
Creek Rd. SE10 CE43 67
Creek Rd. Bark. CN38 58
Creek Rd. E. Mol. BH52 84
Creekside, SE8 CE43 67
Creekside Rain. CT38 59
Creek, The, Sun. BC53 83
Creeland Gro. SE6 CD47 77
Catford Hill
Cree Way Rom. CT29 41
Crefeld Rd. W6 BR44 65
Creffield Rd. W3 BL40 55
Creffield Rd. W5 BL40 55
Creighton Av. E6 CJ37 58
Creighton Av. N2 BU31 47
Creighton Av. N10 BU31 47
Creighton Av. St. Alb. BG15 9
Creighton Rd. N17 CA29 39
Creighton Rd. NW6 BQ37 55
Creighton Rd. W5 BK41 64
Cremarne Rd. Grav. DF47 81
Cremer St. E2 CA37 57
Cremorne Est. SW10 BT43 66
Cremorne Gdn. Epsom BN58 94
Cremorne Rd. SW10 BT43 66
Crescent Ave. Grays. DE42 71
Crescent Av. Horn. CT34 50
Crescent Ct. Surb. BK53 84
Crescent Dr. Brwd. DC26 122
Crescent Dr. Enf. CC22 30
Crescent Dr. Orp. CL53 88
Crescent (East) Barn. BT22 29
Crescent Gdns. SW19 BS48 76
Crescent Gdns. Ruis. BC33 44
Crescent Gdns. Swan. CS51 89
Crescent Gro. SW4 BW45 66
Crescent Gro. Mitch. BU53 86
Crescent La. SW4 BW45 66
Crescent Pl. SW3 BU42 66
Crescent Rise N22 BW29 38
Crescent Rise Barn. BU25 29
Crescent Rd. E4 CG26 40
Crescent Rd. E6 CJ37 58
Crescent Rd. E10 CE34 48
Crescent Rd. E13 CH37 58
Crescent Rd. E18 CH30 40
Crescent Rd. N3 BR30 37
Crescent Rd. N8 BW32 47
Crescent Rd. N9 CB26 39
Crescent Rd. N15 CH31 49
Carlingford Rd.
Crescent Rd. N22 BW30 38
Crescent Rd. SE18 CL42 68
Crescent Rd. SW20 BQ50 75
Crescent Rd. Barn. BT24 29
Crescent Rd. Beck. CE51 87
Crescent Rd. Beck. CF51 87
Crescent Rd. Brom. CH50 78
Crescent Rd. Brwd. DA28 42
Crescent Rd. Cat. CB65 105
Crescent Rd. Dag. CR34 50
Crescent Rd. Enf. BY24 29
Crescent Rd. Erith CT43 69
Crescent Rd. Hem. H. AX13 8
Crescent Rd. Kings. On T. BM50 75
Crescent Rd. Red. BZ70 114
Crescent Rd. Reig. BS71 121
Crescent Rd. Sev. CT63 107
Crescent Rd. Shep. BA53 83
Crescent Rd. Sid. CN48 78
Crescent Rd. Sthl. BE41 64
Crescent Row, EC1 BZ38 57
Baltic St.
Crescent, The, E17 CD32 48
Crescent, The, N11 BU28 38
Crescent, The, N15 CA32 48
Crescent, The, NW2 BP34 46
Crescent, The, SW13 BO44 65
Crescent, The, SW19 BS48 76
Crescent, The, W3 BN39 55
Crescent, The Ashf. AY49 73
Crescent, The, Barn. BS23 29
Crescent, The, Beck. CE51 87
Crescent, The, Bex. CP47 79
Crescent, The. Cat. CE65 105
Crescent, The, Croy. BZ53 87
Cres., The, E. Mol. BE52 84
Crescent, The Egh. AS50 72
Crescent, The, Epp. CN19 22
Crescent, The, Epsom. BM60 94
Crescent, The Grav. DD46 81
Crescent, The Grav. DF48 81
Crescent, The Green. DB46 80
Crescent, The Guil. AQ70 118
Crescent, The, Har. BG33 45
Crescent, The, Harl. CP8 6
Crescent. The. Hayes. BA43 63
Crescent, The, Ilf. CL32 49
Crescent, The, Loug. CJ25 31
Crescent, The Lthd. BJ64 102
Crescent, The, N. Mal. BN52 85
Crescent, The Reig. BS70 121
Crescent, The Rick. AZ25 26
Crescent, The, St. Alb. BF18 18
Cres. The. Sev. CV64 108
Crescent, The, Shep. BB53 83
Crescent, The, Sid. CN49 78
Crescent, The. Slou. AR41 62
Crescent, The, Surb. BL53 85
Crescent, The, Sutt. BS59 95
Crescent, The, Sutt. BT56 95
Crescent, The, Upmin. CZ33 51
Crescent, The, Wat. BB18 17
Crescent, The, Wat. BD21 27
Crescent, The, Wat. BD24 27
Crescent, The, Wem. BJ34 45
Crescent, The, W. Wick. CG53 88
Crescent, The, Wey. AZ55 83
Crescent, The, Epsom. BM61 103
Crescent Vw. Loug. CJ25 31
Crescent Wk. S. Ock. CY41 70
Crescent Way N12 BU29 38
Crescent Way. Orp. CN56 97
Crescent Way. S. Ock. CW40 60
Crescent W. Barn. BS23 29
Crescent (West) Barn. BT22 29
Crescent Wood Rd. SE26 CB48 77
Cresfield Rd. SW6 BS45 66
Cresford Clo. St. Alb. BK13 9
Cresford Rd. SW6 BS44 66
Crespigny Rd. NW4 BP32 46
Cressage Av. W4 BM43 65
Cressage Clo. Sthl. BE38 54
Cressall Mead, Lthd. BJ63 102
Cresset Rd. E9 CC36 57
Cresset St. SW4 BW45 66
Clapham Manor St.
Cressida Rd. N19 BW33 47
Cressingham Gro. Sutt. BT56 95
Cressingham Rd. SE13 CF45 67
Cressingham Rd. Edg. BN29 37
Cresswell Gdns. SW5 BT42 66
Cresswell Gdns. Houns. BE45 64
Cresswell Pk. SE3 CG45 68
Cresswell Pl. SW10 BT42 66
Cresswell Rd. SE25 CB52 87
Cresswell Rd. Ches. AO20 16
Cresswell Rd. Twick. BK46 74
Cresswell Way N21 BY26 38
Cressy Ct. E1 CC39 57
Cressy Pl. E1 CC39 57
Cressy Rd. NW3 BU35 47
Cresta Clo. Wey. AV58 91
Cresta Ct. W5 BL38 55
Crestbrook Av. N13 BY27 38
Crestbrook Pl. N13 BY27 38
Crest Dr. Enf. CC23 30
Crestfield St. WC1 BX38 56
St. Chads St.
Cresthill Ave. Grays. DE42 71
Creston Av. Wok. AP61 100
Creston Way Wor. Pk. BQ55 85
Crest Rd. NW2 BO34 46
Crest Rd. Brom. CG54 88
Crest Rd. Sth. Croy. CB57 96
Crest St. N1 BX36 56
Huntingdon St.
Crest, The, N13 BY28 38
Crest, The, NW4 BQ32 46
Crest, The, Saw. CP6 6
Crest, The, Surb. BM53 85
Crest, The, Wal. Cr. BY17 20
Crest Vw. Pnr. BD31 45
Crestview Dr. Orp. CL53 88
Crestway, SW15 BP46 75
Creswick Ct. W3 BM40 55
Creswick Ct. Welw. G. C. BQ8 5
Creswick Rd. E3 CE38 57
Creswick Rd. W3 BM40 55
Creswick Wk. NW11 BR31 46
Crete Hall Rd. Grav. DE46 81
Creton St. SE18 CL41 68
Crevington Way Horn. CV35 51
Crewdson Rd. SW9 BY43 66
Crewe Pl. NW10 BO38 55
Crewes Av. Warl. CC61 105
Crewes Clo. Warl. CC62 105
Crewes Farm La. Warl. CC62 105
Crewes La. Warl. CC61 105
Crews Hill, Enf. BX20 20
Crews St. E14 CE42 67
Crewys Rd. NW2 BR34 46
Crewys Rd. SE15 CB44 67
Crichton Av. Wall. BW56 95
Crichton Rd. Cars. BU57 95
Cricketers Arms Rd. Enf. BZ23 30
Cricketers Clo. Chess. BK56 93
Cricketfield Rd. E5 CB35 48
Cricket Field Rd. Uxb. AX37 53
Cricketfield Rd. West Dr. AX42 63
Cricket Grn. Mitch. BU52 86
Cricket Ground Rd. Chis. CL51 88
Cricket Hill, Red. BX71 121
Cricket Way, Wey. BB55 83
Cricklade Av. SW2 BX48 76
Cricklade Av. Rom. CV29 42
Cricklewood Broadway NW2 BQ35 46
Cricklewood La. NW2 BQ35 46
Cridland St. E15 CG37 58
Church St.
Crieff Ct. Tedd. BK50 74
Crieff Ct. Kings. On T. BK50 74
Upr. Teddington Rd.
Crieff Rd. SW18 BT46 76
Criffel Av. SW2 BW48 76
Crighton Gdns. Rom. CR33 50
Crimp Hill Rd. Wind. & Egh. AP47 72
Crimscott St. SE1 CA41 67
Crimsworth Rd. SW8 BW44 66
Crinan St. N1 BX37 56
Cringle St. SW8 BW43 66
Cripsey Av. Ong. CW16 24
Crispen Rd. Felt. BD49 74
Crispin Clo. Croy. BX55 86
Crispin Cres. Croy. BW55 86
Crispin Rd. Edg. BN29 37
Crispin St. E1 CA39 57
Brushfield St.
Crispin Way Slou. AO35 43
Crisp Rd. W6 BQ42 65
Criss Cres. Ger. Cr. AR30 34
Criss Gro. Ger. Cr. AR30 34
Cristowe Rd. SW6 BR44 65
Criterion Ms. N19 BW34 47
St. John's Vill.
Critton La. Dor. BD70 119
Crobars Av. Wok. AR61 100
Crockenhall Way, Grav. DF50 81
Crockenhill La. Dart. CV54 90
Crockenhill Rd. Orp. CP53 89
Crockerton Rd. SW17 BU48 76
Crockery Lane. Guil. AY68 110
Crockford Clo. Wey. AX56 92
Crockford Park Rd. Wey. AX56 92
Crockham Way, SE9 CL49 78
Crocknorth Rd. Leath. BB69 110
Crocus Field Barn. BR25 28
Croft, Harl. CL10 6
Croft Av. Dor. BJ70 119
Croft Av. W. Wick. CF54 87
Croft Clo. NW7 BO27 37
Croft Clo. Belv. CQ42 69
Croft Clo. Chis. CK49 78
Croft Clo. Hayes. BA43 63
Croft Clo. Uxb. AZ36 53
Croftdown Rd. NW5 BV34 47
Croft End Rd. Kings L. AW18 17
Crofters, Saw. CQ5 6
Crofters Mead. Croy. CD58 96
Crofters Rd. Nthwd. BB28 35
Crofters, The Hem. H. AZ14 8
Croft Fld. Kings L. AW18 17
Croft Gdns. W7 BJ41 64
Croft Gdns. Ruis. BB33 44
Croft Hill La. Tad. BR63 103
Croft La. Kings L. AW18 17
Croftleigh Av. Pur. BY57 95
Croftleigh Av. Pur. BY61 104
Croft Lodge Clo. Wdf. Grn. CH29 40
Croft Meadow, Kings L. AW18 17
Crofton Av. Bex. CP47 79
Crofton Av. Orp. CM55 88
Crofton Av. Walt. BD55 84
Crofton Clo. Cher. AU57 91
Crofton Ct. Orp. CM54 88
Crofton La. Orp. CM55 88
Crofton Pk. Rd. SE4 CD46 77
Crofton Pound Hill Orp. CM55 88
Crofton Rd. E13 CH38 58
Crofton Rd. SE5 CA44 67
Crofton Rd. Grays. DF41 71
Crofton Rd. Orp. CL55 88
Crofton Ter. Rich. BL45 65
Crofton Way, Enf. BY23 29
Croft Rd. N17 CA29 39
Durban Rd.
Croft Rd. SW16 BY51 86
Croft Rd. SW19 BT50 76
Croft Rd. Brom. CH50 78
Croft Rd. Cat. CD64 105
Croft Rd. Enf. CD23 30
Croft Rd. Ger. Cr. AS30 34
Croft Rd. Sutt. BT56 95
Croft Rd. West. CL66 115
Crofts Path, Hem. H. AZ14 8
Crofts Rd. Har. BJ32 45
Crofts, The, Shep. BB52 83
Holmbank Dr.
Crofts, The, Welw. G. C. BR9 5
Croft St. SE8 CD42 67
Croft, The, W5 BL39 55
Croft, The, Barn. BQ24 28
Croft, The, Brox. CD15 12
Croft, The, Houns. BE43 64
Croft, The, Loug. CL23 31
Croft, The, Nw10 BO37 55
Croft, The, Pnr. BE33 45
Croft, The, Ruis. BD35 45
Croft, The, St. Alb. BF16 18
Croft, The, Swan. CS51 89
Croft, The, Wem. BK35 45
Croft Wk. Brox. CD15 12
Croft Way, NW3 BS35 47
Croftway, Rich. BJ48 74
Croft Way. Sev. CT66 116
Croft Way, Sid. CN48 78
Crogsland Rd. NW1 BV36 56
Croham Clo. Sth. Croy. CA57 96
Croham Manor Rd. Sth. Croy. CA57 96
Croham Mount Sth. Croy. CA57 96
Croham Pk. Av. Sth. Croy. CA56 96
Croham Rd. Sth. Croy. BZ56 96
Croham Valley Rd. Sth. Croy. CA57 96
Croindene Rd. SW16 BX51 86
Cromar Ct. Wok. AR61 100
Cromartie Rd. N19 BW33 47
Crombie Clo. Ilf. CK32 49
Crombie Rd. Sid. CM47 78
Cromer Clo. Uxb. BA39 53
Cromer Est. WC1 BX38 56
Cromer Rd. E10 CF33 48
Cromer Rd. N17 CB30 39
Sherringham Av.
Cromer Rd. SE25 CB52 87
Cromer Rd. SW17 BV50 76
Cromer Rd. Barn. BS24 29
Cromer Rd. Horn. CV33 51
Cromer Rd. Rom. CQ32 50
Cromer Rd. Rom. CS32 50
Cromer Rd. Wat. BD22 27
Cromer Rd. Wdf. Grn. CH28 40
Cromers. Welw. G. C. BS7 5
Cromers Hyde La. Welw. G. C. BN8 5
Cromer St. WC1 BX38 56
Cromer Vill. Rd. SW18 BR46 75
Crome St. SE10 CG42 68
Cromford Clo. Orp. CN55 88
Cromford Rd. SW18 BS46 76
Cromford Way, N. Mal. BN51 85
Crompton St. W2 BT38 56
Cromwall Ct. Enf. CC25 30
Cromwell Av. N6 BV33 47
Cromwell Av. W6 BP42 65
Cromwell Av. Brom. CH52 88
Cromwell Av. N. Mal. BO53 85
Cromwell Av. Wal. Cr. CB18 21
Cromwell Clo. N2 BT31 47
Cromwell Clo. Brom. CH52 88
Cromwell Clo. Ch. St. G. AR27 34
Cromwell Clo. Walt. BC54 83
Cromwell Cres. SW5 BS42 66
Cromwell Dr. Slou. AP39 52
Cromwell Gro. W6 BQ41 65
Cromwell Ms. SW7 BT42 66
Cromwell Pl. N6 BV33 47
Cromwell Av.
Cromwell Pl. SW7 BT42 66
Cromwell Pl. SW14 BN45 65
Cromwell Rd. E7 CJ36 58
Cromwell Rd. E17 CF32 48
Cromwell Rd. N3 BT30 38
Cromwell Rd. N10 BV29 38
Cromwell Rd. SW5 BS42 66
Cromwell Rd. SW7 BS42 66
Cromwell Rd. SW19 BS49 76
Cromwell Rd. Beck. CD51 87
Cromwell Rd. Borwd. BL23 28
Cromwell Rd. Brwd. DA28 42
Cromwell Rd. Cat. BZ64 105
Cromwell Rd. Croy. BZ54 87
Cromwell Rd. Felt. BC47 73
Cromwell Rd. Grays. DD42 71
Cromwell Rd. Hayes BA39 53
Cromwell Rd. Houns. BF45 64
Cromwell Rd. Kings. On T. BL51 85
Cromwell Rd. Red. BU70 121
Cromwell Rd. Tedd. BJ50 74
Cromwell Rd. Wal. Cr. CB17 21
Cromwell Rd. Walt. BC54 83
Cromwell Rd. Wem. BL37 55
Cromwell Rd. Wor. Pk. BN55 85
Cromwells Mere Rom. CS29 41
Cromwell St. Houns. BF45 64
Cromwell Ter. Enf. BZ23 30
Crondace Rd. SW6 BS44 66
Crondall St. N1 BZ37 57
Cronks Hill, Red. BT71 121
Cronkshill Clo. Red. BT71 121
Cronkshill Rd. Red. BT71 121
Crook Clo. NW7 BR29 37
Crooked Billet, SW19 BQ50 75
Crooked Mile, Wal. Abb. CF18 21
Crooked Usage N3 BR31 46
Crooked Way. Wal. Abb. CG14 13
Crooke Rd. SE8 CC42 67
Crookham. Welw. G. C. BS7 5
Crookham Rd. SW6 BR44 65
Fulham Rd.
Crook Log. Well. CP45 69
Crookston Rd. SE9 CL45 68
Croombs Rd. E16 CJ39 58
Croom's Hl. SE10 CF43 67
Croom's Hl. Gro. SE10 CF43 67
Cropath Rd. Dag. CR35 50
Cropley Ct. N1 BZ37 57
Cropley St. N1 BZ37 57
Crosby Rd. E7 CH36 58
Crosby Rd. SE1 BZ41 67
Crosby Rd. Dag. CR37 59
Crosby Sq. EC3 CA39 57
Crosier Way, Ruis. BB34 44
Cross Acres, Wok. AV61 100
Cross Av. Wor. Pk. BP55 85
Crossbow Rd. Chig. CN28 40
Crossbrook Rd. SE3 CK44 68
Crossbrook St. Wal. Cr. CC19 21
Cross Deep Twick. BH48 74
Cross Deep Gdns. Twick. BH48 74
Crossfell Rd. Hem. H. AZ14 8
Crossfield Clo. Berk. AP13 7
Crossfield Pl. Wey. AZ57 92
Crossfield Rd. N17 BZ31 48
Crossfield Rd. NW3 BT36 56
Crossfield Rd. Hodd. CE11 12
Crossfield Rd. Red. BV70 121
Crossfields, St. Alb. BF15 9
Crossfield St. SE8 CE43 67
Crossford St. SW9 BX44 66
Lingham St.
Crossgate Edg. BM27 37
Crossgate, Grnf. BJ36 54
Crossing Epp. CO19 23
Cross Keys Sq. EC1 BZ39 57
Little Britain
Cross Keys Clo. W1 BV39 56
Marylebone La.
Cross Lances Rd. Houns. BF45 64
Crossland Rd. Th. Hth. BY53 86
Crosslands Av. W5 BL40 55
Crosslands Av. Sthl. BE42 64
Crosslands Rd. Epsom BN57 94
Cross La. EC3 CA40 57
St. Dunstan's Hill
Cross La. N8 BX31 47
Cross La. Bex. CQ47 79
Cross La. Ches. AU57 91
Cross La. Guil. AS70 118
Cross La. E. Grav. DG48 81
Cross Lane Footpath. Cher. AT57 91
Cross Lanes. Ger. Cr. AS28 34
Cross Lanes Clo. Ger. Cr. AS28 34
Cross Lane W. Grav. DG48 81
Crosslet St. SE17 BZ42 67
Townsend St.
Crossley Clo. West. CJ61 106
Crossleys. Ch. St. G. AQ28 34
Crossleys Hill. Ch. St. G. AR27 34
Crossmead, SE9 CK47 78

Cross Mead Wat. BC25 26
Crossmead Av. Grnf. BF38 54
Crossness Footpath, Belv. CQ41 69
Cross Oaks. Wind. AN44 61
Crossoaks La. Borwd. BO20 19
Crossoaks La. Pot. B. BO20 19
Crosspath, The, Rad. BJ21 27
Cross Rds. Loug. CH23 31
Cross Rd. E4 CF26 39
Cross Rd. N11 BW28 38
Cross Rd. N22 BY29 38
Cross Rd. SE5 CA44 67
Cross Rd. SW19 BS50 76
Cross Rd. Brom. CK55 88
Cross Rd. Croy. BZ54 87
Cross Rd. Dart. CV46 80
Cross Rd. Dart. CW49 80
Cross Rd. Enf. CA24 30
Cross Rd. Felt. BE49 74
Cross Rd. Har. BF34 45
Cross Rd. Har. BG31 45
Cross Rd. Har. BJ30 36
Cross Rd. Kings. On T. BL50 75
Cross Rd. Orp. CO53 89
Cross Rd. Pur. BY60 95
Cross Rd. Rom. CP33 50
Cross Rd. Rom. CR31 50
Cross Rd. Sid. CO49 79
Cross Rd. Sutt. BS58 95
Cross Rd. Sutt. BT56 95
Cross Rd. Tad. BQ64 103
Cross Rd. Wal. Cr. CD20 21
Cross Rd. Wat. BE25 27
Cross Rd. Wdf. Grn. CK29 40
Cross Rd. Wey. BA55 83
Cross St. E1 CC39 57
Commercial Rd.
Cross St. E3 CE36 57
Monier Rd.
Cross St. E15 CG36 58
Cross St. N1 BY36 56
Cross St. N18 CB28 39
Wakefield St.
Cross St. SW13 BO44 65
Cross St. Erith CT43 69
Cross St. Harl. CM11 13
Cross St. Hmptn. BG49 74
Cross St. Uxb. AX37 53
Cross St. Wat. BD24 27
Cross Street N. St. Alb. BG13 9
Crosswall, EC3 CA40 57
Crossway N12 BT29 38
Crossway N16 CA35 48
Cross Way, NW9 BO31 46
Crossway SW20 BQ52 85
Crossway, Dag. CP34 50
Crossway Enf. CA26 39
Crossway Hayes BC40 53
Crossway Orp. CM52 88
Crossway Pnr. BC30 35
Crossway Ruis. BD34 45
Crossway, Walt. BC55 83
Crossway, Wdf. Grn. CJ28 40
Crossway, Welw. G. C. BQ6 5
Cross Waye, The Uxb. AY37 53
Cross Ways N21 BZ25 30
Cross Ways. Berk. AP13 7
Crossways, Brwd. DD25 122
Crossways, Egh. AU50 72
Crossways, Guil. AP71 118
Cross Ways, Hem. H. AZ13 8
Crossways Rom. CU31 50
Crossways Sth. Croy. CD57 96
Crossways Sutt. BT57 95
Crossways La. Reig. BT67 113
Cross Ways Rd. Beck. CE52 87
Crossways Rd. Mitch. BV52 86
Crossways Rd. West. CJ63 106
Crossways. The. Couls. BX63 104
Crossways, The, Houns. BE43 64
Crossways, The. Red. BW68 113
Crossways, The, Wem. BM34 46
Crossway, The, N22 BY29 38
Cross Way, The, SE9 CJ48 78
Cross Way, The, Har. BH30 36
Crossway, The, W13 BJ38 54
Crosswell Clo. Shep. BA51 83
Charlton Rd.
Crosthwaite Av. SE5 BZ45 67
Croston St. E8 CB37 57
Crouch Av. Bark. CO37 59
Crouch Clo. Beck. CE50 77
Abbey La.
Crouch Cft. SE9 CL48 78
Crouch End Hill N8 BW33 47
Crouchfield, Hem. H. AW14 8
Crouch Hall Rd. N8 BW32 47
Crouch Hill, N4 BX32 47
Crouch Hill, N8 BX32 47
Crouch La. Wal. Cr. BZ17 21
Crouchmans Clo. SE26 CB48 77
Crouchoak La. Wey. AW56 92
Crouch Rd. NW10 BN36 55
Crouch Rd. Grays. DG42 71
Crouch Valley, Upmin. CZ33 51
Crowboro Dr. Warl. CD62 105
Crowborough Path. Wat. BD27 36
Crowborough Rd. SW17 BV50 76
Crow Clo. Warl. CD62 105
Crowder St. E1 CB40 57
Crow Grn. Brwd. DA25 33
Crow Green Rd. Brwd. CZ25 33
Crowhurst La. Sev. DA58 99
Crowhurst Rd. SW9 BY44 66
Crowhurst Rd. Sev. DB65 108
Crowhurst Way Orp. CP53 89
Crowland Ave. Hayes. BB42 63
Crowland Gdns. N14 BX26 38
Crowland Rd. N15 CA32 48
Crowland Rd. Th. Hth. BZ52 87
Crowlands Av. Rom. CR32 50
Crowland Ter. N1 BZ36 57
Crowland Wk. Mord. BS53 86
Crow La. Rom. CQ33 50
Crowley Cres. Croy. BY56 95
Crowlin Wk. N1 BZ36 57
Marquess Est.
Crown Ash Hill. West. CH60 97
Crown Ash La. West. CH61 106
Crown Clo. NW7 BO27 37
Crown Clo. Hayes. BB41 63
Crown Clo. Orp. CO56 98
Crown Ct. EC2 BZ39 57
Cheapside
Crown Ct. N10 BV29 38
Crown Ct. SE12 CH46 78
Crown Ct. WC2 BX39 56
Russell St.
Crown Ct. Brom. CK53 88
Crown Ct. Til. DG44 71
Newton Rd.
Crown Dale, SE19 BY50 76
Crowndale Rd. NW1 BW37 56
Crownfield Av. Ilf. CN32 49
Crownfield Rd. E15 CF35 48
Crownfields. Sev. CU66 116
Crown Gate. Harl. CM11 13
Crown Hill Croy. BZ55 87
Crown Hill, Wal. Abb. CK20 22
Crown Hill Rd. NW10 BO37 55
Crownhill Rd. Wdf. Grn. CK29 40
Crown La. N14 BW26 38
Crown La. SW16 BY49 76
Crown La. Brom. CJ53 88
Crown La. Chis. CM51 88
Crown La. Mord. BS52 86
Crown La. Vir. W. AR53 82
Crown La. Spur. Brom. CJ53 88
Crownmead Way Rom. CR31 50
Crown Office Row, EC4 CM40 58
Crown Par. Hayes BB39 53
Crown Pass. SW1 BW40 56
King St.
Crown Pass. Wat. BD24 27
Crown Pl. NW5 BV36 56
Raglan St.
Crown Point. Sev. CZ64 108
Crown Pt. SE19 BY50 76
Crown Rise, Wat. BD20 18
Crown Rd. N10 BV29 38
Crown Rd. N17 CB29 39
Crown Rd. Borwd. BM23 28
Crown Rd. Brwd. CY22 33
Crown Rd. Brwd. CY23 33
Crown Rd. Enf. CB24 30
Crown Rd. Grays. DD43 71
Crown Rd. Ilf. CM31 49
Crown Rd. Mord. BS52 86
Crown Rd. N. Mal. BN51 85
Crown Rd. Orp. CO56 98
Crown Rd. Sev. CT58 98
Crown Rd. Sutt. BS56 95
Crown Rd. Twick. BJ46 74
Crown Rd. Vir. W. AR53 82
Crown Rd. West. CK63 106
Crownstone Rd. SW2 BY46 76
Crown St. SE5 BZ43 67
Crown St. W3 BM40 55
Crown St. Brwd. DB27 42
Crown St. Dag. CS36 59
Crown St. Egh. AT49 72
Crown St. Har. BG33 45
Crown Ter. Rich. BL45 65
Crown Woods La. SE9 CL44 68
Crown Woods Way, SE9 CM46 78
Crowood, Egh. AV51 82
Crowshott Av. Stan. BK30 36
Crows Rd. E15 CF38 57
Crows Rd. Epp. CN18 22
Crowstone Rd. Grays. DE41 71
Crowther Av. Brent. BL42 65
Crowther Rd. SE25 CB52 87
Crowthorne St. W10 BQ39 55
Croxdale Rd. Borwd. BL23 28
Croxden Clo. Edg. BL31 46
Croxden Clo. Edg. BM31 46
Reynolds Dr.
Croxden Wk. Mord. BT53 86
Croxford Gdns. N22 BZ29 38
Croxford Way Rom. CS33 50
Croxley Clo. Orp. CO51 89
Croxley Gn. Orp. CO51 89
Croxley Rd. W9 BR38 55
Croxted Clo. SE21 BZ47 77
Croxted Rd. SE21 BZ46 77
Croxted Rd. SE24 BZ46 77
Croyde Ave. Hayes. BB42 63
Croyde Av. Grnf. BG38 54
Croyde Clo. Sid. CM47 78
Croyden Rd. Cat. CB65 105
Croydon Gro. Croy. BY54 86
Croydon La. Bans. BT61 104
Croydon Rd. E13 CG38 58
Croydon Rd. SE20 CB51 87
Croydon Rd. Beck. CC53 87
Croydon Rd. Mitch. BV52 86
Croydon Rd. Reig. BS70 121
Croydon Rd. Wall. BW56 95
Croydon Rd. Warl. CE63 105
Croydon Rd. West. CK65 106
Croydon Rd. W. Wick. CG55 88
Croyland Rd. N9 CB26 39
Croylands Surb. BL54 85
Croysdale Av. Sun. BC52 83
Crozier Rd. Uxb. BA35 44
Crozier St. SE1 BX41 66
Crozier Ter. E9 CC35 48
Crucifix La. SE1 CA41 67
Cruden Rd. Grav. DJ48 81
Cruden St. N1 BY37 56
Cruik Ave. S. Ock. DB39 60
Cruikshank Rd. E15 CG35 49
Cruikshank St. WC1 BY38 56
Crummock Gdns. NW9 BO32 46
Crumpsall St. SE2 CP42 69
Crundale Av. NW9 BM32 46
Crunden Rd. Sth. Croy. BZ57 96
Crusader Gdns. Croy. CA55 87
Crushes Clo. Brwd. DF25 122
Chelmer Dr.
Crusoe Rd. Erith CS42 69
Crusoe Rd. Mitch. BU50 76
Crutched Friars, EC3 CA40 57
Crutches La. Beac. AP29 34
Crutchfield La. Walt. BC55 83
Crutchley Rd. SE6 CG48 78
Crystal Av. Horn. CW35 51
Crystal Ct. SE19 CA49 77
Crystal Palace Pde. SE19 CA50 77
Crystal Palace Pk. Rd. SE26 CB49 77
Crystal Palace Rd. SE22 CB45 67
Crystal Palace Sta. Rd. SE19 CB50 77
Crystal Ter. SE19 BZ50 77
Crystal Vw. Ct. Brom. CF49 77
Cuba Dr. Enf. CC23 30
Cuba St. E14 CE41 67
Cubitts Clo. Welw. G. C. BR5 5
Cubitt's Cotts. SW18 BS47 76
Garratt La.
Cubitt St. WC1 BX38 56
Cubitt St. Croy. BX56 95
Cuckmans Dr. St. Alb. BF16 18
Cuckoo Av. W7 BH38 54
Cuckoo Dene W7 BG39 54
Cuckoo Hall La. N9 CC26 39
Cuckoo Hill Pnr. BD31 45
Cuckoo Hill Dr. Pnr. BD31 45
Cuckoo Hill Rd. Pnr. BD31 45
Cuckoo La. W7 BH40 54
Cuckoo La. Grays. DC40 71
Cucumber La. Hat. BU13 11
Cudas Clo. Epsom BO56 94
Cuddington Av. Wor. Pk. BO55 85
Cuddington Clo. Tad. BQ63 103
Cuddington Ct. Sutt. BQ58 94
Cuddington Way Sutt. BQ59 94
Cudham La. Sev. CM60 97
Cudham La. N. Sev. CM58 97
Cudham La. S. Sev. CM61 106
Cudham Pk. Rd. Sev. CM58 97
Cudham Rd. Orp. CL59 97
Cudham Rd. West. CK63 106
Cudham St. SE6 CF47 77
Cudworth St. E1 CB38 57
Cuff Cres. SE9 CJ46 78
Cuffley Av. Wat. BD20 18
Cuffley Hill, Wal. Cr. BY18 20
Cuff Pl. E2 CA38 57
Angela St.
Culfield Rd. Grays. DE41 71
Culford Gdns. SW3 BU42 66
Culford Gro. N1 CA36 57
Culford Ms. N1 CA36 57
Southgate Rd.
Culford Rd. N1 CA36 57
Culgaith Gdns. Enf. BX24 29
Cullen Sq. S. Ock. DB40 60
Cullen Way, NW10 BN38 55
Cullesden Rd. Ken. BY61 104
Culling Rd. SE16 CC41 67
Cullings Ct. Wal. Abb. CG20 22
Cullington Clo. BJ31 45
Cullingworth Rd. NW10 BP35 46
Culloden Rd. Enf. BY23 29
Cullum St. EC3 CA40 57
Culmington Rd. W13 BK40 54
Culmington Rd. Sth. Croy. BZ57 96
Culmore Cross, SW12 BV47 76
Culmore Rd. SE15 CB43 67
Culmstock Rd. SW11 BV46 76
Culpeper Clo. Ilf. CL29 40
Culpeper St. N1 BY37 56
Culross Cl. N15 BZ31 48
Culross St. W1 BV40 56
Culsac Rd. Surb. BL55 85
Culverden Ct. Wey. BA55 83
Culverden Rd. SW12 BW48 76
Culverden Rd. Wat. BC27 35
Culver Dr. Oxt. CG68 115
Culver Gro. Stan. BK30 36
Culverhay. Ash. BL61 103
Culverhouse Gdns. SW16 BX48 76
Culverley Rd. SE6 CE47 77
Culver Pl. SW11 BV45 66
Culver Rd. St. Alb. BH12 9
Culvers Av. Cars. BU55 86
Culvers Retreat Cars. BU54 86
Culverstone Clo. Brom. CG53 88
Culver's Way Cars. BU55 86
Culvertlands Clo. Stan. BJ28 36
Culvert La. Uxb. AW37 53
Culvert Pl. SW11 BV44 66
Culvert Rd. N15 CA32 48
Culvert Rd. SW11 BU44 66
Culvey Clo. Hart. DC53 90
Culworth St. NW8 BU37 56
Cumberland Av. NW10 BM38 55
Cumberland Av. Grav. DH47 81
Cumberland Av. Guil. AQ68 109
Cumberland Av. Horn. CW34 51
Cumberland Av. Well. CO45 69
Cumberland Clo. SW20 BQ50 75
Cumberland Clo. Amer. AQ23 25
Cumberland Clo. Hem. H. BB15 8
Cumberland Clo. Horn. CW34 51
Cumberland Clo. Twick. BJ46 74
Cumberland Ct. St. Alb. BH13 9
Carlisle Av.
Cumberland Cres. W14 BR42 65
Cumberland Dr. Bexh. CQ43 69
Cumberland Dr. Chess. BL55 85
Cumberland Dr. Dart. CW47 80
Cumberland Dr. Esher. BJ55 84
Cumberland Gdns. NW4 BQ30 37
Cumberland Gdns. WC1 BX38 56
Cumberland Gte. W1 BU40 56
Cumberland Mkt. NW1 BV38 56
Cumberland Mkt. Est. NW1 BV38 56
Cumberland Pk. W3 BN40 55
Cumberland Pl. NW1 BV38 56
Outer Circle
Cumberland Pl. Sun. BC52 83
Cumberland Rd. E12 CJ35 49
Cumberland Rd. E13 CH39 58
Cumberland Rd. E17 CD30 39
Cumberland Rd. N9 CC26 39
Cumberland Rd. N22 BX30 38
Cumberland Rd. SE25 CB53 87
Cumberland Rd. SW13 BO44 65
Cumberland Rd. W3 BN40 55
Cumberland Rd. W7 BH41 64
Cumberland Rd. Ashf. AX48 73
Cumberland Rd. Brom. CG52 88
Cumberland Rd. Har. BF32 45
Cumberland Rd. Rich. BM43 65
Cumberland Rd. Stan. BL31 46
Cumberlands Ken. BZ57 96
Cumberlands Ken. BZ61 105
Cumberland St. SW1 BV42 66
Cumberland St. Stai. AU49 72
Cumberland Ter. NW1 BV37 56
Cumberland Ter. Ms. NW1 BV37 56
Albany St.
Cumberlow Av. SE25 CA52 87
Cumberlow Pl. Hem. H. BA14 8
Cumbernauld Gdns. Sun. BB49 73
Cumberton Rd. N17 BZ30 39
Cumbrae Gdns. Surb. BK54 84
Cumbrian Av. Bexh. CT44 69
Cumbrian Gdns. NW2 BQ34 46
Cum Cum Hill. Hat. BT14 11
Cumley Rd. Epp. CT18 23
Cumming Est. N1 BZ37 57
Cummings Hall La. Rom. CV27 42
Cumming St. N1 BX37 56
Cumnor Gdns. Epsom. BP57 94
Cumnor Rd. Sutt. BT57 95
Cunard Pl. EC3 CA39 57
Bury St.
Cunard Rd. NW10 BN38 55
Cunard St. SE5 CA43 67
Cundy Rd. E16 CH39 58
Cundy St. Est. SW1 BV42 66
Cundy St. SW1 BV42 66
Cunliffe Clo. Epsom. BM65 103
Cunliffe Rd. Wor. Pk. BO56 94
Cunliffe St. SW16 BW50 76
Cunningham Av. Enf. CD21 30
Cunningham Av. Guil. AT70 118
Cunningham Av. St. Alb. BH14 9
Cunningham Clo. W. Wick. CE55 87
Cunningham Hill Rd. St. Alb. BH14 9
Cunningham Pk. Har. BG32 45
Cunningham Pl. NW8 BT38 56
Cunningham Rd. N15 CB31 48
Cunningham Rd. Bans. BT61 104
Cunningham Rd. Wal. Cr. CD17 21
Cunnington St. W4 BN41 65
Cupar Rd. SW11 BV44 66
Cupid Green Rd. Hem. H. AZ11 8
Curéton St. SW1 BW42 66
Curlew Clo. Berk. AR13 7
Curlew Clo. Croy. CC59 96
Curlew Clo. Sth. Croy. CC58 96
Curlew St. SE1 CA41 67
Curling Vale, Guil. AQ71 118
Curnick's La. SE27 BZ49 77
Curnock Est. NW1 BW37 56
Curran Av. Sid. CN46 78
Curran Av. Wall. BV55 86
Currch Path. Red. BV67 113
Currey Rd. Grnf. BG36 54
Curricle St. W3 BO40 55
Currie Hill Clo. SW19 BR49 75
Curry Ri. NW7 BQ29 37
Curry Rise, NW7 BQ29 37
Cursers Rd. St. Alb. BM17 19
Cursitor St. EC4 BY39 56
Curtain Rd. EC2 CA38 57
Curthwaite Gdns. Enf. BW24 29
Curtis Clo. Rick. AW26 35
Curtis Gdns. Dor. BJ71 119
Spring Gdns.
Curtismill Clo. Orp. CO52 89
Curtis Mill La. Rom. CT24 32
Curtismill Way Orp. CO52 89
Curtis Rd. Dor. BJ71 119
Curtis Rd. Epsom BN56 94
Curtis Rd. Hem. H. BA14 8
Curtis Rd. Horn. CW33 51
Curtis Rd. Houns. BE47 74
Curtis St. SE1 CA42 67
Curtis Way, Berk. AR13 7
Curvan Clo. Epsom BO58 94
Curve, The, W12 BP40 55
Curwen Av. E7 CH35 49
Woodford Rd.
Curwen Rd. W12 BP41 65
Curzon Av. Enf. CC25 30
Curzon Av. Stan. BJ30 36
Curzon Clo. Orp. CM56 97
Curzon Clo. Wey. AZ56 92
Curzon Cres. Bark. CN37 58
Curzon Dr. Grays. DD43 71
Curzon Ho. W5 BJ38 54
Castlebar Pk. Rd.
Curzon La. E. Brox. CD14 12
Curzon La. W. Brox. CD14 12
Curzon Pl. W1 BV40 56
Curzon St.
Curzon Pl. Pnr. BD32 45
Curzon Rd. N10 BV30 38
Curzon Rd. W5 BJ38 54
Curzon Rd. Th. Hth. BX53 86
Curzon Rd. Wey. AZ56 92
Curzon St. W1 BV40 56
Cusack Clo. Twick. BH49 74
Custom Ho. Wf. EC3 CA40 57
Cutcombe Rd. SE5 BZ44 67
Cutforth Rd. Saw. CQ5 6
Cuthbert Rd. E17 CF31 48
Cuthbert Rd. N18 CB28 39
Fairfield Rd.
Cuthbert Rd. Croy. BY55 86
Cuthill Rd. SE5 BZ44 67
Cutler's Ter. N1 CA36 57
Balls Pond Rd.
Cutler St. E1 CA39 57
Cutmere St. Grav. DG47 81
Cut, The, SE1 BY41 66
Cutthroat La. Hodd. CD11 12
Cutting, The Red. BU71 121
Cuttsfield Ter. Hem. H. AV14 7
Cuxton Clo. Bexh. CQ46 79
Cyclamen Rd. Swan. CS52 89
Cyclamen Way Epsom BN56 94
Cycle Track. Harl. CO11 14
Cygnet Av. Felt. BD47 74
Cygnet Clo. Nthwd. BA29 35
Cygnet Gdns. Grav. DF48 81
Cygnets, The, Felt. BE49 74
Cygnet St. E1 CA38 57
Sclater St.
Cymbran Ct. Hem. H. AY11 8
Cynthia St. N1 BX37 56
Cyntra Pl. E8 CB36 57
Mare St.
Cypress Av. Enf. BY21 29
Cypress Av. Twick. BG47 74
Cypress Clo. Wal. Abb. CF20 21
Cypress Gro. Ilf. CN29 40
Cypress Pl. W1 BW38 56
Maple St.
Cypress Rd. SE25 CA51 87
Cypress Rd. Guil. AR69 118
Cypress Rd. Har. BG30 36
Cypress Rd. Sun. BB51 83
Harris Way
Cyprus Av. N3 BR30 37
Cyprus Gdns. N3 BR30 37
Cyprus Pl. E2 CC37 57
Cyprus St.
Cyprus Rd. N3 BR30 37
Cyprus Rd. N9 CA27 39
Cyprus St. E2 CC37 57
Cyprus St. EC1 BY38 56
Cyrena Rd. SE22 CA46 77
Cyril Mans. SW11 BU44 66
Cyril Rd. Bexh. CQ44 69
Cyril Rd. Orp. CO54 89
Czar St. SE8 CD43 67
Dabbshill La. Nthlt. BE35 45
D'abernon Clo. Esher BF56 93
D'abernon Dr. Cob. BD61 102
Dabin Cres. SE10 CF44 67
Lindsell St.
Dacca St. SE8 CD43 67
Dace Rd. E3 CE36 57
Dacorum Way, Hem. H. AX13 8
Dacre Ave. S. Ock. CW40 60
Dacre Av. Ilf. CL30 40
Dacre Clo. Chig. CM28 40
Dacre Cres. S. Ock. CW40 60
Dacre Gdns. SE13 CG45 68
Dacre Gdns. Borwd. BN25 28
Dacre Gdns. Chig. CM28 40
Dacre Pk. SE13 CG45 68
Dacre Pl. SE13 CG45 68
Dacre Rd. E11 CG33 49
Dacre Rd. E13 CH37 58
Dacre Rd. Croy. BX54 86
Dacres Clo. SE23 CC48 77
Dacres Rd. SE23 CC48 77
Dacre St. SW1 BW41 66
Daffodil Av. Brwd. DA25 33
Daffodil St. W12 BO40 55
Dafforne Rd. SW17 BU48 76
Dagden Rd. Guil. AS73 118
Dagenham Av. Dag. CQ37 59
Dagenham Rd. E10 CD33 48
Dagenham Rd. Dag. CR35 50
Dagenham Rd. Rain. CS36 59
Dagger La. Borwd. BJ25 27
Daggs Dell Rd. Hem. H. AV12 7
Dagley La. Guil. AR73 118
Dagmar Av. Wem. BL35 46
Dagmar Gdns. NW10 BQ37 55
Dagmar Rd. N4 BY33 47
Dagmar Rd. N15 BZ32 48
Cornwall Rd.
Dagmar Rd. N22 BW30 38
Dagmar Rd. SE5 CA44 67
Dagmar Rd. SE25 CA52 87
Dagmar Rd. Dag. CS36 59
Dagmar Rd. Kings. On T. BL51 85
Dagmar Rd. Sthl. BE41 64
Dagmar Rd. Wind. AO44 61
Dagmar Ter. N1 BY37 56
Dagnall Cres. Uxb. AX39 53
Dagnall Pk. SE25 BZ53 87
Dagnall Rd. SE25 CA53 87
Dagnall St. SW11 BU44 66
Dagnam Park Clo. Rom. CX28 42
Dagnam Pk. Dr. Rom. CW28 42
Dagnam Park Gdns. Rom. CX29 42
Dagnam Park Sq. Rom. CX29 42
Dagnan Rd. SW12 BV47 76
Dagonet Gdns. Brom. CH48 78
Dagonet Rd. Brom. CH48 78
Dagwood La. Brwd. DA22 33
Dahlia Gdns. Mitch. BW52 86
Dahlia Rd. SE2 CO42 69
Dahomey Rd. SW16 BW50 76
Daiglen Dr. S. Ock. DA40 60
Daimler Cotts. SE15 CA43 67
Cronin Rd.
Daimler Way Wall. BX57 95
Daines Clo. E12 CK34 49

Dainford Clo. Brom. CF49 77
Dainton Clo. Brom. CH51 88
Daintry Way E9 CD36 57
Dairsie Rd. SE9 CL45 68
Dairy La. Eden. CL70 115
Dairy Wk. SW19 BR49 75
Daisy Dormer Ct. SW9 BX45 66
Trinity Gdns.
Daisy La. SW6 BS45 66
Daisy Rd. E18 CH30 40
Dakota Gdns. Nthlt. BD38 54
Dakota Gdns. Nthlt. BE38 54
Argus Way
Dalberg Rd. SW2 BY45 66
Dalberg Way SE2 CP41 69
Dalberg Wy. Belv. CP41 69
Dalby Rd. SW18 BT45 66
Dalcross Rd. Houns. BE44 64
Dale Av. Edg. BL30 37
Dale Av. Houns. BE45 64
Dalebury Rd. SW17 BU48 76
Dale Clo. SE3 CH45 68
Dale Clo. Barn. BS25 29
Dale Clo. Dart. CT46 79
Dale Clo. Pnr. BC30 35
Dale Clo. Wey. AW56 92
Dale Dr. Hayes BB38 53
Dale End. Dart. CT46 79
Dale Gdns. Wdf. Grn. CH28 40
Dalegarth Gdns. Pur. BZ60 96
Dale Grn. Rd. N11 BV27 38
Dale Gro. N12 BT28 38
Daleham Av. Egh. AS50 72
Daleham Dr. Uxb. AZ39 53
Daleham Gdns. NW3 BT36 56
Daleham Ms. NW3 BT35 47
Dale Pk. Av. Cars. BU55 86
Dale Pk. Rd. SE19 BZ51 87
Dale Rd. E16 CG38 58
Dale Rd. NW5 BV35 47
Dale Rd. Dart. CT46 79
Dale Rd. Grav. DD49 81
Dale Rd. Grnf. BF39 54
Dale Rd. Pur. BY59 95
Dale Rd. Sun. BB50 73
Dale Rd. Sutt. BR56 94
Dale Rd. Swan. CS51 89
Dale Rd. Walt. BB54 83
Dale Rd. Walt. BC54 83
Dale Side. Ger. Cr. AS33 43
Daleside Orp. CO56 98
Daleside Clo. Orp. CO57 98
Daleside Dr. Pot. B. BR20 19
Daleside Gdns. Chig. CM27 40
Daleside Rd. SW16 BV49 76
Daleside Rd. Epsom. BN57 94
Dale St. W4 BO42 65
Dale, The, Kes. CJ56 97
Dale, The, Wal. Abb. CG20 22
Dale Vw. Epsom. BM65 103
Daleview Erith CT44 69
Dale Vw. Wok. AQ62 100
Dale Vw. Av. E4 CF27 39
Dale Vw. Cres. E4 CF27 39
Dale Vw. Gdns. E4 CF27 39
Daleview Rd. N15 CA32 48
Dale Wd. Rd. Orp. CN54 88
Dale Wlk. Dart. CX47 80
Dalewood Gdns. Wor. Pk. BP55 85
Daley St. E9 CC36 57
Dalgarno Gdns. W10 BQ39 55
Dalgarno Way W10 BQ38 55
Dalgleish St. E14 CD39 57
Daling Way, E3 CD37 57
Dalkeith Gro. Stan. BK28 36
Dalkeith Rd. SE21 BZ47 77
Dalkeith Rd. Ilf. CM34 49
Dallas Rd. NW4 BP33 46
Dallas Rd. SE26 CB49 77
Dallas Rd. W5 BL39 55
Dallas Rd. Sutt. BR57 94
Dallas Ter. Hayes BB41 63
Dallinger Rd. SE12 CG46 78
Dalling Rd. W6 BP42 65
Dallington Clo. Walt. BD57 93
Dallington St. EC1 BY38 56
Dallin Rd. SE18 CL43 68
Dallin Rd. Bexh. CP45 69
Dalmain Rd. SE23 CC47 77
Dalmally Rd. Croy. CA54 87
Dalmeny Av. N7 BW35 47
Dalmeny Av. SW16 BY51 86
Dalmeny Clo. Wem. BK36 54
Dalmeny Cres. Houns. BG45 64
Dalmeny Rd. N7 BW34 47
Dalmeny Rd. Barn. BT25 29
Dalmeny Rd. Bexh. CR44 69
Dalmeny Rd. Cars. BV57 95
Dalmeny Rd. Wor. Pk. BP55 85
Dalmore Av. Esher BH57 93
Dalmore Rd. SE21 BZ48 77
Dalroy Clo. S. Ock. DA39 60
Dalrymple Rd. SE4 CD45 67
Dalston Gdns. Stan. BL30 37
Dalston La. E8 CA36 57
Dalton Av. Mitch. BU51 86
Dalton Clo. Hayes BA38 53
Dalton Clo. Orp. CN55 88
Dalton Rd. Har. BG30 36
Dalton's Rd. Orp. CR55 89
Dalton St. SE27 BY48 76
Dalton St. St. Alb. BG13 9
Dalwood St. SE5 CA44 67
Dalyell Rd. SW9 BX45 66
Damer Ter. SW10 BT43 66
Ashburnham Rd.
Dames Rd. E7 CH34 49
Dame St. N1 BZ37 57
Damien St. E1 CB39 57
Damon Clo. Sid. CO48 79
Damphurst Hollow, Dor. BF74 119
Danbrook Rd. SW16 BX51 86
Danbury Clo. Brwd. CZ25 33
Danbury Clo. Rom. CP31 50
Danbury Mews Wall. BV56 95
Danbury Rd. Loug. CK26 40
Danbury Rd. Rain. CT37 59
Danbury St. N1 BY37 56
Danbury Way, Wdf. Grn. CJ29 40
Danby St. SE15 CA45 67
Dancer Rd. SW6 BR44 65
Fulham Rd.
Dancer Rd. Rich. BM45 65
Dancers Hill Barn. BQ21 28
Dando Cres. SE3 CH45 68
Danebury Av. SW15 BO46 75
Daneby Rd. SE6 CE48 77
Dane Clo. Bex. CR47 79
Dane Clo. Orp. CM56 97
Dane Ct. N2 BT33 47
Danecroft Rd. SE24 BZ46 77
Danehill, Sid. CO48 79
Danehill Wk. Sid. CO48 79
Hatherley Rd.
Danehurst Gdns. Ilf. CK32 49
Danehurst St. SW6 BR44 65
Daneland Barn. BU25 29
Danemead, Hodd. CE10 12
Danemead Gdns. Nthlt. BF35 45
Danemere St. SW15 BQ45 65
Dane Rd. SW19 BT51 86
Dane Rd. W13 BK40 54
Dane Rd. Ashf. BA50 73
Dane Rd. Ilf. CM35 49
Dane Rd. Sev. CT62 107
Dane Rd. Sthl. BE40 54
Dane Rd. Warl. CC62 105
Danesbury Croy. CF57 96
Danesbury Rd. Felt. BC47 73
Danes Clo. Grav. DE48 81
Danes Clo. Lthd. BG60 93
Danescourt Cres. Sutt. BT55 86
Danescourt Gdns. Croy. CA55 87
Danescroft Av. NW4 BQ32 46
Danescroft Gdns. NW4 BQ32 46
Danesdale Rd. E9 CD36 57
Dane's Gate Har. BH31 45
Daneshill, Red. BU70 121
Danes Hill, Wok. AT62 100
Daneshill Clo. Red. BU70 121
Daneshurst St. SW6 BR44 65
Danes Rd. Rom. CS33 50
Danes, The, St. Alb. BG17 18
Park St. La.
Dane St. WC1 BX39 56
Red Lion Sq.
Danes Way Brwd. DA25 33
Daneswood Av. SE6 CF48 77
Daneswood Clo. Wey. BA56 92
Danes Wy. Lthd. BG60 93
Danethorpe Rd. Wem. BK36 54
Danetree Rd. Epsom BN57 94
Danette Gdns. Dag. CR34 50
Daneville Rd. SE5 BZ44 67
Dangan Rd. E11 CH32 49
Daniel Bolt Clo. E14 CE39 57
Daniel Pl. NW4 BP32 46
Daniel Rd. W5 BL40 55
Daniels. Welw. G. C. BS7 5
Daniels La. Warl. CD61 105
Daniels Rd. SE15 CC45 67
Dansington Rd. Well. CO45 69
Danson Cres. Well. CO45 69
Danson La. Well. CO45 69
Danson Mead, Well. CP45 69
Danson Rd. Bex. CP46 79
Dante Rd. SE11 BY42 66
Danube St. SW3 BU42 66
Danvers Rd. N8 BW31 47
Danvers St. SW3 BT43 66
Danyon Clo. Rain. CV37 60
Danyon Clo. Rain. CV38 60
Da Palma Ct. SW6 BS43 66
Racton Rd.
Dapdune Rd. Guil. AR70 118
Dapdune Wharf Rd. Guil. AR70 118
Daphne Gdns. E4 CF27 39
Gunners Gro.
Daphne St. SW18 BT46 76
Daplyn St. E1 CB39 57
D'arblay St. W1 BW39 56
Darby Cres. Sun. BD51 84
Darby Gdns. Sun. BD51 84
Darcy Av. Wall. BW56 95
D'arcy Clo. Ash. BL62 103
D, arcy Clo. Brwd. DD26 122
Darcy Clo. Couls. BY63 104
Darcy Clo. Wal. Cr. CD19 21
D'arcy Dr. Har. BK31 45
D'arcy Gdns. Dag. CQ37 59
D'arcy Gdns. Har. BK31 45
Darcy Rd. SW16 BW51 86
D'arcy Rd. Ash. BL62 103
D'arcy Rd. Sutt. BQ56 94
Dare Gdns. Dag. CQ34 50
Darent Clo. Sev. CR64 107
Darenth Hill. Dart. CY49 80
Darenth La. Sev. CT64 107
Darenth La. S. Ock. DA39 60
Darenth Rd. N16 CA33 48
Darenth Rd. Dart. CW47 80
Darenth Rd. Well. CO44 69
Darenth Wood Rd. Dart. CZ48 80
Darent Mead. S. At. H. CX51 90
Darfield Rd. SE4 CD46 77
Darfield Way, W10 BQ40 55
Darfur St. SW15 BQ45 65
Darien Rd. SW11 BT45 66
Darkes La. Pot. B. BS19 20
Dark La. Brwd. CZ28 42
Dark La. Wal. Cr. CB18 21
Darlan Rd. SW6 BR43 65
Darlaston Rd. SW19 BQ50 75
Darley Clo. Wey. AX56 92
Darley Dr. N. Mal. BN51 85
Darley Gdns. Mord. BT53 86
Darley Rd. N9 CA26 39
Darley Rd. SW11 BU46 76
Darling Rd. SE4 CE45 67
Darling Row, E1 CB38 57
Darlington Gdns. Rom. CV28 42
Darlington Path. Rom. CV28 42
Darlington Rd. SE27 BY49 76
Darnicle Hill, Wal. Cr. BY16 20
Darnley Rd. E9 CB36 57
Darnley Rd. Grav. DG47 81
Darnley Rd. Grays. DD43 71
Darnley Rd. Wdf. Grn. CH30 40
Darnley St. Grav. DG47 81
Darnley Ter. W11 BQ40 55
Darrell Clo. Slou. AS42 62
Darrell Rd. SE22 CB46 77
Darrel Rd. Rich. BM45 65
Darren Cl. N4 BX33 47
Darrick Wd. Rd. Orp. CM55 88
Darrington Rd. Borwd. BL23 28
Darr's La. Berk. AO12 7
Darsley Dr. SW8 BW44 66
Dart Clo. Upmin. CY32 51
Dartfields Rd. Rom. CV29 42
Dartford Av. N9 CC25 30
Dartford By-pass Dart. CU48 79
Dartford La. Bex. CS48 79
Dartford Rd. Bex. CS47 79
Dartford Rd. Dart. CU46 79
Dartford Rd. Dart. CX47 80
Dartford Rd. Farn. CW53 90
Dartford Rd. Sev. CV64 108
Dartford St. SE17 BZ43 67
Dartford Tunnel App. CZ43 70
Gray.
Dart Gdns. S. Ock. DA39 60
Dartmouth Ave. Wok. AU60 91
Dartmouth Grn. Wok. AU60 91
Dartmouth Gro. SE10 CF44 67
Dartmouth Hl. SE10 CF44 67
Dartmouth Pk. Av. NW5 BV34 47
Dartmouth. Pk. Hill N19 BV33 47
Dartmouth. Pk Hill NW5 BV33 47
Dartmouth Pk. Rd. NW5 BV35 47
Dartmouth Path Wok. AU60 91
Dartmouth Av.
Dartmouth Pl. SE23 CC48 77
Dartmouth Rd. E16 CH39 58
Dartmouth Rd. NW2 BQ36 55
Dartmouth Rd. NW4 BP32 46
Dartmouth Rd. SE23 CB48 77
Dartmouth Rd. SE26 CB48 77
Dartmouth Rd. Brom. CH54 88
Dartmouth Rd. Ruis. BC34 44
Dartmouth Row, SE10 CF44 67
Dartmouth St. SW1 BW41 66
Dartnell Av. Wey. AW59 92
Dartnell Cres. Wey. AW59 92
Dartnell Park Rd. Wey. AW59 92
Dartnell Pl. Wey. AW59 92
Dartnell Rd. SE5 CA43 67
Dartnell Rd. Croy. CA54 87
Dart St. W10 BR38 55
Dart, The Hem. H. AZ11 8
Darville Rd. N16 CA34 48
Darvills La. Slou. AO41 61
Darwell Clo. E6 CL37 58
Darwin Clo. Orp. CM56 97
Darwin Dr. Sthl. BF39 54
Darwin Gdns. Wat. BD28 36
Darwin Pl. SE17 BZ42 67
Darwin St.
Darwin Rd. N22 BY30 38
Darwin Rd. W5 BK42 64
Darwin Rd. Slou. AS41 62
Darwin Rd. Til. DF44 71
Darwin Rd. Well. CN45 68
Darwin St. SE17 BZ42 67
Daryngton Dr. Grnf. BG37 54
Daryngton Dr. Guil. AT70 118
Dashes, The, Harl. CN10 6
Dashwood Clo. Bexh. CR46 79
Dashwood Clo. Slou. AR42 62
Dashwood La. Grav. DG48 81
Dashwood Rd. N8 BX32 47
Dashwood Rd. Grav. DG47 81
Dasset Rd. SE27 BY49 76
Datchelor Pl. SE5 BZ44 67
Datchet Clo. Hem. H. AZ11 8
Datchet Pl. Slou. AQ44 62
Datchet Rd. SE6 CD48 77
Datchet Rd. Slou. AP42 62
Datchet Rd. Slou. AS45 62
Datchet Rd. Wind. AO43 61
Datchworth Turn, Hem. BA13 8
H.
Date St. SE17 BZ42 67
Daubeney Rd. E5 CD35 48
Daubeney Rd. N17 BZ29 39
Dault Rd. SW18 BT46 76
Davenant Rd. N19 BW34 47
Davenant Rd. Croy. BY55 86
Davenant Rd. Croy. BY56 95
Davenant St. E1 CB39 57
Davenham Ave. Nthwd. BB28 35
Davenport Rd. SE6 CE46 77
Davenport Rd. Sid. CP48 79
Daventry Av. E17 CE32 48
Daventry Clo. Slou. AV44 62
Rodney Way
Daventry Gdns. Rom. CV28 42
Daventry Grn. Rom. CV28 42
Daventry St. NW1 BU39 56
Daver Ct. W5 BK39 54
Mount Av.
Davern Clo. SE10 CG42 68
Davey St. SE15 CA43 67
David Av. Grnf. BH37 54
David Dr. Rom. CX29 42
Davidge St. SE1 BY41 66
King James St.
David Rd. Dag. CQ34 50
David Rd. Slou. AV44 62
Davidson Gdns. SW8 BX43 66
Davidson Rd. Croy. CA54 87
David's Rd. SE23 CC47 77
David St. E15 CF36 57
Davids Way, Ilf. CN29 40
Davies Clo. Rain. CV38 60
Davies La. E11 CG34 49
Davies Ms. W1 BV40 56
Davies St.
Davies St. W1 BV39 56
Davington Gdns. Dag. CO35 50
Davington Rd. Dag. CO36 59
Davis Av. Grav. DF47 81
Davison Dr. Wal. Cr. CC17 21
Davis Rd. W3 BO40 55
Davis Rd. Chess. BM56 94
Davis Rd. S. Ock. CW40 60
Davis St. E13 CH37 58
Davisville Rd. W12 BP41 65
Davos Clo. Wok. AS63 100
Davy's Pl. Grav. DJ50 81
Daw Dr. West. CJ62 106
Dawes Av. Horn. CV34 51
Dawes Av. Islw. BJ45 64
Dawes Ct. Esher BF56 93
Dawes La. Rick. AV22 25
Dawes Moor Clo. Slou. AR39 52
Dawes Rd. SW6 BR43 65
Dawes Rd. Uxb. AY37 53
Dawes St. SE17 BZ42 67
Dawley. Welw. G. C. BR6 5
Dawley Av. Uxb. BA39 53
Dawley Ct. Hem. H. AZ11 8
Dawley Grn. S. Ock. DA39 60
Dawley Par. Hayes BA40 53
Dawley Rd. Hayes BA40 53
Dawley Rd. Hayes. BB42 63
Dawlish Av. N13 BX28 38
Dawlish Av. SW18 BS48 76
Dawlish Av. Grnf. BJ37 54
Dawlish Dr. Ilf. CN35 49
Dawlish Dr. Pnr. BE32 45
Dawlish Dr. Ruis. BC34 44
Dawlish Rd. E10 CF33 48
Dawlish Rd. E10 CF34 48
Dawlish Rd. N17 CB31 48
Dawlish Rd. NW2 BQ36 55
Dawly. Welw. G. C. BR6 5
Dawnay Gdns. SW18 BT48 76
Dawnay Rd. SW18 BT48 76
Dawnay Rd. Lthd. BF66 111
Dawpool Rd. NW2 BO34 46
Daws Hill E4 CF23 30
Daws La. NW7 BO28 37
Dawson Av. Bark. CN36 58
Dawson Av. Orp. CO51 89
Dawson Clo. Wind. AN44 61
Dawson Dr. Rain. CU36 59
Dawson Gdns. Bark. CN36 58
Dawson Av.
Dawson Pl. W2 BS40 56
Dawson Rd. NW2 BQ35 46
Dawson Rd. SE17 BY42 66
Dawson Rd. Kings. On T. BL52 85
Dawson Rd. Wey. AX59 92
Dawson St. E2 CA37 57
Dax Ct. Sun. BD52 84
Daybrook Rd. SW19 BS52 86
Daye Mead. Welw. G. C. BS9 5
Daylesford Av. SW15 BP45 65
Daylop Dr. Chig. CQ27 41
Daymer BC31 44
Daymerslea Ridge, Lthd. BK64 102
Days Acre Sth. Croy. CA58 96
Daysbrook Rd. SW2 BX48 76
Days Cl. Hat. BO12 10
Days La. Brwd. DA24 33
Days La. Sid. CN47 78
Days Mo. Hat. BO12 10
Day Spring, Guil. AQ68 109
Dayton Gro. SE15 CC44 67
Deacon Clo. St. Alb. BG15 9
Creighton Av.
Deacon Rd. NW2 BP35 46
Deacon Rd. Kings. On T. BL51 85
Deacons Clo. Borwd. BM24 28
Deacons Clo. Pnr. BC30 35
Deaconsfield Rd. Hem. AY15 8
H.
Deacons Hill Wat. BD25 27
Deacon's Hill Rd. BM24 28
Borwd.
Deacons Wk. Hamptn. BF49 74
Deacon Way SE17 BZ42 67
Deadhearn La. Ch. St. AS26 34
G.
Deadmans Ash La. Rick. AW21 26
Deal Rd. SW17 BV50 76
Deal St. E1 CB39 57
Deal Tree Clo. Brwd. DA21 33
Dealtry Rd. SW15 BQ45 65
Dean Bradley St. SW1 BX41 66
Dean Clo. E9 CC35 48
Churchill Wk.
Dean Clo. Uxb. AY36 53
Dean Clo. Wind. AL45 61
Dean Clo. Wok. AV61 100
Dean Ct. Wem. BJ34 45
Deancroft Rd. Ger. Cr. AS29 34
Dean Cross St. E1 CC39 57
Commercial Rd.
Dean Dr. Stan. BL30 37
Deane Av. Ruis. BD35 45
Deane Croft Rd. Pnr. BC32 44
Deanery Rd. E15 CG36 58
Deanery Rd. Eden. CM70 115
Deanery St. W1 BV40 56
Deane Way Ruis. BC32 44
Dean Farrar St. SW1 BW41 66
Tothill St.
Dean Field. Hem. H. AT17 16
Dean Gdns. E17 CF31 48
Dean Hill Ct. SW14 BM45 65
Deanhill Rd. SW14 BM45 65
Dean La. Red. BW65 104
Dean Rd. NW2 BQ36 55
Dean Rd. Croy. BZ56 96
Dean Rd. Hamptn. BF49 74
Dean Rd. Houns. BF46 74
Dean Ryle St. SW1 BX42 66
Deansbrook Clo. Edg. BN29 37
Deansbrook Rd. Edg. BM29 37
Dean's Bldgs. SE17 BZ42 67
Deans Clo. W4 BM43 65
Whitehall Gdns.
Deans Clo. Amer. AP22 25
Deans Clo. Edg. BN29 37
Deans Clo. St. Alb. BJ11 9
Deans Clo. Slou. AQ37 52
Deans Clo. Wat. BA19 17
Dean's Ct. EC4 BY39 56
St. Paul's
Churchyard.
Deanscroft Av. NW9 BN34 46
Deans Dr. Edg. BN28 37
Deans Field. Cat. CA66 114
Deans La. Edg. BN29 37
Deans La. Tad. BP66 112
Deans Ms. W1 BV39 56
Cavendish Sq.
Deans Rd. W7 BH40 54
Deans Rd. Red. BW68 113
Deans Rd. Sutt. BS55 86
Dean Stanley St. SW1 BX41 66
Dean St. E7 CH35 49
Dean St. W1 BW39 56
Deans Wk. Couls. BY62 104
Deansway N2 BT31 47
Deansway N9 BZ27 39
Deans Way, Edg. BN28 37
Deansway, Hem. H. AY15 8
Deans Yd. SW1 BW41 66
Dean Trench St. SW1 BX41 66
Tufton St.
Dean Wk. Edg. BN29 37
Dean Wk. Lthd. BF66 111
Dean Way. Cat. BZ66 114
Dean Way. Ch. St. G. AQ27 34
Dean Wood Rd. Beac. AO30 34
Dearne Clo. Stan. BJ28 36
De'arn Gdns. Mitch. BU52 86
Deason St. E15 CF37 57
Debden Clo. Wdf. Grn. CJ29 40
Debden La. Loug. CM22 31
Debden Rd. Loug. CL22 31
Debden Wk. Horn. CU36 59
De Beauvoir Cres. N1 CA37 57
De Beauvoir Rd. N1 CA37 57
De Beauvoir Sq. N1 CA36 57
Debenham Rd. Wal. Cr. CB17 21
Debnams Rd. SE16 CC42 67
Rotherhithe New Rd.
Debohun Av. N14 BV25 29
De Burgh Pk. Bans. BS61 104
De Burgh Rd. SW19 BT50 76
Decies Way, Slou. AQ37 52
Decima St. SE1 CA41 67
Decoy Av. NW11 BR32 46
De Crespigny Pk. SE5 BZ44 67
Dedswell Drive. Guil. AW68 110
Dedworth Dr. Wind. AM44 61
Dedworth Rd. Wind. AL44 61
Dee Clo. Upmin. CZ32 51
Dee Lees. Beac. AO29 34
Deeley Rd. SW8 BW44 66
Deena Clo. W3 BL39 55
Deepdale, SW19 BQ49 75
Deepdale Av. Brom. CG52 88
Deepdene, W5 BL38 55
Ridings, The.
Deepdene, Pot. B. BQ19 19
Deepdene Av. Croy. CA55 87
Deepdene Av. Dor. BK71 119
Deepdene Av. Dor. BK73 119
Deepdene Av. Rd. Dor. BK70 119
Deepdene Clo. E18 CH31 49
Deepdene Ct. N21 BY25 29
Deepdene Dri. Dor. BK71 119
Deepdene Gdns. SW2 BX47 76
Deepdene Gdns. Dor. BJ71 119
Deepdene Pk. Rd. Dor. BK71 119
Deepdene Path. Loug. CL24 31
Deepdene Rd. SE5 BZ45 67
Deepdene Rd. Loug. CL24 31
Deepdene Rd. Well. CO45 69
Deepdene Vale, Dor. BK71 119
Deepdene Wood, Dor. BK71 119
Deepfield Way Couls. BX57 95
Deepfield Way Couls. BX61 104
Deephams Clo. N9 CC27 39
Deep Pool La. Wok. AQ60 91
Deer Barn Rd. Guil. AQ70 118
Deerbrook Rd. SE24 BY47 76
Deerdale Rd. SE24 BZ45 67
Deere Av. Rain. CU36 59
Deerfield Cotts. NW9 BO32 46
Deerhurst Rd. NW2 BQ36 55
Deerhurst Rd. SW16 BX49 76
Deerings Rd. Reig. BS70 121
Deerleap Gro. E4 CE25 30
Deerleap Rd. Dor. BF72 119
Dee Rd. E13 CG38 58
Dee Rd. Rich. BL45 65
Deer Park. Harl. CL12 13
Deer Pk. Clo. Kings. On BM50 75
T.
Crescent Rd.
Deer Pk. Gdns. Mitch. BT52 86
Deerswood Av. Hat. BP13 10
Deeside Rd. SW17 BT48 76
Dee St. E14 CF39 57
Dee, The Hem. H. AY11 8
Deeves Hall La. Pot. B. BO20 19
Dee Way Epsom BO58 94
Dee Way Rom. CT29 41
Defiant Way Wall. BX57 95
Defoe Av. Rich. BM43 65
Defoe Par. Grays. DG41 71
Defoe Rd. N16 CA34 48
Defoe Way Rom. CR29 41
De Frene Rd. SE26 CC49 77

Degema Rd. Chis. CL49 78
Dehar Cres. NW4 BP33 46
De Haviland Rd. Houns. BC43 63
De Havilland Way. AX46 73
De Havilland Clo. Hat. BO12 10
De Havilland Rd. Edg. BM30 37
De Havilland Rd. Wall. BX57 95
Dekker Rd. SE21 CA46 77
Delabole Rd. Red. BX68 113
Delacourt Rd. SE3 CH43 68
Old Dover Rd.
Delafield Rd. SE7 CH42 68
Delafield Rd. Grays. DE42 71
Delaford Clo. Hayes AW39 53
Delaford Clo. Iver AV39 52
Delaford Rd. SE15 CB42 67
Delaford Rd. SE16 CB42 67
Delaford St. SW6 BR43 65
Delagarde Rd. West. CM66 115
Delahay Rse. Berk. AQ12 7
Delamere Cres. SW9 BX45 66
Brighton Ter.
Delamere Cres. Croy. CC53 87
Delamere Gdns. NW7 BN29 37
Delamere Rd. SW20 BQ51 85
Delamere Rd. W5 BL40 55
Delamere Rd. Borwd. BM23 28
Delamere Rd. Hayes. BD40 54
Delamere Rd. Reig. BS72 121
Delamere Ter. W2 BS39 56
Delancey St. NW1 BV37 56
De La Mere Rd. Wal. Cr. CD18 21
De Lapre Clo. Orp. CP54 89
Delara Way, Wok. AR62 100
De Laune St. SE17 BY42 66
Delaware Rd. W9 BS38 56
Delawyk Cres. SE24 BZ46 77
Delbow Rd. Felt. BC46 73
Delcombe Av. Wor. Pk. BQ54 85
Delft Way, SE22 CA46 77
Dulwich Gro.
Delhi Rd. Enf. CA26 39
Delhi St. N1 BX37 56
Delia St. SW18 BS47 76
Delius Clo. Borwd. BK25 27
Dell Clo. E15 CF37 57
Dell Clo. Dor. BK67 111
Dell Clo. Lthd. BH65 102
Dell Clo. Lthd. BJ66 111
Dell Clo. Wall. BW56 95
Dell Clo. Wdf. Grn. CH27 40
Dellcott Clo. Welw. G. C. BP7 5
Dellcut Rd. Hem. H. AZ12 8
Dell Farm Rd. Ruis. BA32 44
Dellfield. St. Alb. BH14 9
Dell Field Av. Berk. AQ12 7
Dell Field Clo. Berk. AQ12 7
Dellfield Clo. Rad. BH21 27
Dellfield Clo. Wat. BC23 26
Dellfield Cres. Uxb. AX38 53
Dellfield Rd. Hat. BP12 10
Dell La. Epsom BP56 94
Dellmeadow, Wat. BB19 17
Dellors Clo. Barn. BQ25 28
Dellow St. E1 CB40 57
Dell Rise, St. Alb. BF17 18
Dell Rd. Berk. AO11 7
Dell Rd. Enf. CC22 30
Dell Rd. Epsom. BP57 94
Dell Rd. Grays. DD42 71
Dell Rd. Wat. BC22 26
Dell Rd. West Dr. AY42 63
Dell Side. Amer. AO23 25
Dellside, Uxb. AX32 44
Dell Side, Wat. BC22 26
Dellsome La. St. Alb. BO15 10
Dells, The Hem. H. AZ14 8
Dell, The, SE2 CO42 69
Dell, The, SE19 CA51 87
Dell, The, Beck. CE50 77
Dell, The, Bex. CT47 79
Dell, The, Brwd. DA29 42
Dell The, Felt. BC47 73
Dell, The. Ger. Cr. AS29 34
Dell, The, Pnr. BD30 36
Dell, The Reig. BS70 121
Dell, The, St. Alb. BJ12 9
Dell, The, Wall. BW56 95
Dell, The, Wdf. Grn. CH27 40
Dell, The, Wem. BJ35 45
Dell, The Wok. AR62 100
Dell Wk. N. Mal. BO51 85
Dell Way W13 BK39 54
Dellwood, Rick. AW26 35
Dellwood Gdns. Ilf. CL31 49
Delmar Av. Hem. H. BA14 8
Delmare Clo. SW9 BX45 66
Brighton Ter.
Delme Cres. SE3 CH44 68
Delmey Clo. Croy. CA55 87
Delmos Dr. Hem. H. AZ12 8
Deloraine St. SE8 CE44 67
Delorme St. W6 BQ43 65
Delphian Ct. SW16 BY49 76
Delsa Ct. NW2 BP34 46
Delta Gain. Wat. BD27 36
Delta Gro. Nthlt. BD37 54
Delta Gro. Nthlt. BD38 54
Kittiwake Rd.
Delta Rd. Brwd. DE25 122
Delta Rd. Wok. AP58 91
Delta Rd. Wok. AT61 100
Delta Rd. Wor. Pk. BO55 85
Delta St. E2 CB38 57
Wellington Row
Deluci Rd. Erith CS42 69
Delvan St. SE18 CL43 68
Delverton Rd. SE17 BZ42 67
Delvino Rd. SW6 BS44 66
Demesne Rd. Wall. BW57 95
Demeta Clo. Wem. BN34 46
De Montfort Rd. SW16 BX48 76
De Morgan Rd. SW6 BS45 66
Dempster Rd. SW18 BT45 66
Denberry Dr. Sid. CO48 79
Denbigh Ch. W11 BR40 55
Denbigh Clo. NW10 BO36 55
Denbigh Clo. Chis. CK50 78
Denbigh Clo. Horn. CW31 51
Denbigh Clo. Ruis. BB34 44
Denbigh Clo. Sid. CQ48 79
Riverside Rd.
Denbigh Clo. Sthl. BE39 54
Denbigh Clo. Sutt. BR56 94
Denbigh Dr. Hayes. BA41 63
Denbigh Gdns. Rich. BL46 75
Denbigh Pl. SW1 BW42 66
Denbigh Rd. E6 CJ38 58
Denbigh Rd. W11 BR40 55
Denbigh Rd. W13 BJ40 54
Denbigh Rd. Sthl. BE39 54
Denbigh Rd. Sthl. BF44 64
Denbigh St. SW1 BW42 66
Denbigh Ter. W11 BR40 55
Denbridge Rd. Brom. CK51 88
Denby Rd. Cob. BD59 93
Den Clo. Beck. CF52 87
Dendy St. SW12 BV47 76
Dene Av. Houns. BE45 64
Dene Av. Sid. CO47 79
Dene Clo. SE4 CD45 67
Dene Clo. Brom. CG54 88
Dene Clo. Dart. CT49 79
Dene Clo. Wor. Pk. BO55 85
Dene Ct. Guil. AT69 118
Denecroft Cres. Uxb. AZ37 53
Denecroft Gdns. Grays. DE41 71
Dene Dr. Orp. CO55 89
Denefield Dr. Ken. BZ61 105
Dene Gdns. W3 BM40 55
Dene Gdns. Stan. BK28 36
Dene Gdns. Surb. BJ54 84
Dene Holm Rd. Grav. DE48 81
Denehurst Gdns. NW4 BQ32 46
Denehurst Gdns. W3 BM40 55
Gunnersbury La.
Denehurst Gdns. Rich. BM45 65
Denehurst Gdns. Twick. BG47 74
Denehurst Gdns. Wdf. Grn. CH28 40
Dene Path. S. Ock. DA39 60
Dene Rd. NW11 BU26 38
Dene Rd. Ash. BL63 103
Dene Rd. Buck. H. CJ26 40
Dene Rd. Dart. CW47 80
Dene Rd. Guil. AS71 118
Dene Rd. Nthwd. BA29 35
Dene Rd. Nthwd. BB29 35
Dene St. Gdns. Dor. BJ71 119
Denes, The Hem. H. AY15 8
Dene St. Dor. BJ71 119
Dene, The, W13 BJ39 54
Templewood
Dene, The, Croy. CC55 87
Dene, The Dor. BC73 119
Dene The E. Mol. BE53 84
Dene, The, Sutt. BR59 94
Dene, The, Wem. BL35 46
Dene Walk Long. DC52 90
Denewood Barn. BT25 29
Denewood Clo. Wat. BB22 26
Denewood Rd. N6 BU32 47
Denfield, Dor. BJ72 119
Denford Rd. SE10 CG42 68
Glenforth St.
Denham Av. Uxb. AV34 43
Denham Clo. Uxb. AW34 44
Denham Ct. SE26 CB48 77
Halifax St.
Denham Cres. Mitch. BU52 86
Denham Dr. Esher BJ57 93
Denham Dr. Ilf. CM32 49
Denham Green Clo. Uxb. AW33 44
Denham Green La. Uxb. AV31 43
Denham Rd. N20 BU27 38
Denham Rd. SE10 CH42 68
Denham Rd. Egh. AT49 72
Denham Rd. Epsom BO59 94
Denham Rd. Felt. BD46 74
Denham Rd. Iver & Uxb. AU37 52
Denham Way, Bark. CN37 58
Denham Way, Uxb. AW34 44
Denholme Rd. W9 BR38 55
Denison Clo. N2 BT31 47
Denison Rd. SW19 BT50 76
Denison Rd. W5 BK38 54
Denison Rd. Felt. BB49 73
Deniston Av. Bex. CQ47 79
Denleigh Gdns. N21 BY26 38
Denleigh Gdns. E. Mol. BH53 84
Denman Dr. NW11 BS32 47
Denman Dr. Ashf. AZ50 73
Denman Dr. N. NW11 BS32 47
Denman Dr. S. NW11 BS32 47
Denman Rd. SE15 CA44 67
Denman St. W1 BW40 56
Denmark Av. SW19 BR50 75
Denmark Ct. Mord. BS53 86
Denmark Gdns. Cars. BU55 86
Denmark Gro. N1 BY37 56
Denmark Hill, SE5 BZ44 67
Denmark Pl. N8 BY31 47
Denmark Rd.
Denmark Rd. N8 BY31 47
Denmark Rd. NW6 BR37 55
Denmark Rd. SE5 BZ44 67
Denmark Rd. SE25 CB53 87
Denmark Rd. SW19 BQ50 75
Denmark Rd. W13 BJ40 54
Denmark Rd. Brom. CH51 88
Denmark Rd. Cars. BU55 86
Denmark Rd. Guil. AS71 118
Denmark Rd. Kings. On T. BL52 85
Denmark Rd. Twick. BG48 74
Denmark St. E11 CG34 49
High Rd.
Denmark St. N17 CB30 39
Denmark St. WC2 BW39 56
Denmark St. Wat. BC23 26
Denmark Wk. SE27 BZ49 77
Denmead Way, SE15 CA43 67
Hordle Prom. S.
Dennan Rd. Surb. BL54 85
Denner Rd. E4 CE27 39
Dennets, Wok. AP62 100
Dennett Rd. Croy. BY54 86
Dennetts Gro. SE14 CC44 67
Dennettsland Rd. Eden. CM70 115
Dennett's Rd. SE14 CC44 67
Denning Av. Croy. BY56 95
Denning Clo. NW8 BT38 56
Denning Rd. NW3 BT35 47
Dennington Clo. E5 CB34 48
Southwold Rd.
Dennington Pk. Rd. NW6 BS36 56
Dennis Av. Wem. BL35 46
Dennis Clo. Ashf. BA50 73
Chertsey Rd.
Dennis Clo. Red. BU69 121
Dennises La. Upmin. CZ37 60
Dennis Gdns. Stan. BK28 36
Dennis La. Stan. BJ27 36
Dennis La. Est. Stan. BJ28 36
Dennis Pk. Cres. SW20 BR51 85
Dennis Rd. E. Mol. BG52 84
Dennis Rd. Grav. DG48 81
Dennis Rd. S. Ock. DA37 60
Dennisville, Guil. AP71 118
Denny Av. Wal. Abb. CT20 21
Denny Cres. SE11 BY42 66
Denny St.
Denny Gdns. Dag. CO36 59
Denny Rd. N9 CB26 39
Denny St. SE11 BY42 66
Den Rd. Brom. CF52 87
Densham Rd. E15 CG37 58
Densley Clo. Welw. G. C. BQ7 5
Densole Clo. Beck. CD51 87
King's Hall Rd.
Densor Gdns. Est. W9 BS39 56
Densworthy Gro. N9 CC27 39
Denton Clo. Barn. BQ25 28
Denton Clo. Red. BV73 121
Denton Ct. Rd. Grav. DJ47 81
Denton Gro. Walt. BE55 84
Denton Rd. N8 BX32 47
Denton Rd. N18 CA28 39
Denton Rd. NW10 BN36 55
Denton Rd. Bex. CT48 79
Denton Rd. Twick. BK46 74
Denton Rd. Well. CP43 69
Denton St. SW18 BS46 76
Denton St. Grav. DJ47 81
Denton Ter. Bex. CT48 79
Dents Rd. SW11 BU46 76
Denver Rd. N16 CA33 48
Denver Rd. Dart. CU47 79
Denyer St. SW3 BU42 66
Denzilde Av. Uxb. AZ38 53
Denzil Rd. NW10 BO35 46
Denzil Rd. Guil. AQ71 118
Deodar Rd. SW15 BR45 65
Depot Rd. Epsom. BO60 94
Depot Rd. Houns. BG45 64
Depot St. SE5 BZ43 67
Deptford Br. SE8 CE44 67
Deptford Broadway, SE8 CE44 67
Deptford Church St. SE8 CE43 67
Deptford Ferry Rd. E14 CE42 67
Deptford Grn. SE8 CE43 67
Deptford High St. SE8 CE43 67
Deptford Strand SE8 CD42 67
De Quincey Rd. N17 BZ30 39
Derby Arms Rd. Epsom BO62 103
Derby Av. N12 BT28 38
Derby Av. Har. BG30 36
Derby Av. Rom. CS32 50
Derby Av. Upmin. CW35 51
Derby Gate, SW1 BX41 66
Derby Gro. Croy. BY54 86
Derby Hl. SE23 CC48 77
Derby Hl. Cres. SE23 CC48 77
Derby Hl. Est. SE23 CC48 77
Derby Rd. E7 CJ36 58
Derby Rd. E9 CC37 57
Derby Rd. E18 CG30 40
Derby Rd. N15 BY31 47
Derby Rd. N18 CB28 39
Derby Rd. SW14 BM45 65
Derby Rd. SW19 BS50 76
Derby Rd. Croy. BY54 86
Derby Rd. Enf. CB25 30
Derby Rd. Grays. DD43 71
Derby Rd. Grnf. BF37 54
Derby Rd. Guil. AP70 118
Derby Rd. Hodd. CF13 12
Derby Rd. Houns. BF45 64
Derby Rd. Surb. BM54 85
Derby Rd. Sutt. BR57 94
Derby Rd. Uxb. AX37 53
Derby Rd. Wat. BD24 27
Derbyshire St. E2 CB38 57
Derby Stables Rd. Epsom BO62 103
Derby St. E1 CA40 57
Derby St. W1 BV40 56
Curzon St.
Dereham Pl. EC2 CA38 57
Dereham Rd. Bark. CN35 49
Derek Av. Epsom. BM57 94
Derek Av. Wall. BV56 95
Derek Av. Wem. BM36 55
Derham Gdns. Upmin. CY34 51
Deri Av. Rain. CU38 59
Dericote Rd. E8 CB37 57
Croston St.
Deridene Clo. Stai. AY46 73
Dering Pl. Croy. BZ56 96
Dering Rd. Croy. BZ56 96
Dering St. W1 BV39 56
Derinton Rd. SW17 BU49 76
Derley Rd. Sthl. BD41 64
Dermody Gdns. SE13 CF46 77
Dermody Rd. SE13 CF46 77
Derns Wk. Couls. BY58 95
Deronda Rd. SE24 BY47 76
Derrick Av. Sth. Croy. BZ58 96
Derrick Gdns. SE7 CJ41 68
Derrick Rd. Beck. CD52 87
Derry Ave. S. Ock. DA39 60
Derry Downs Orp. CP53 89
Derry Rd. Croy. BX55 86
Derry St. W8 BS41 66
Dersingham Av. E12 CK35 49
Dersingham Rd. NW2 BR34 46
Derwent Av. N18 BZ28 39
Derwent Av. NW7 BN29 37
Derwent Av. NW9 BO32 46
Derwent Av. SW15 BO49 75
Derwent Av. Barn. BU26 38
Derwent Av. Pnr. BE29 36
Derwent Av. Uxb. AZ34 44
Derwent Clo. Dart. CU47 79
Derwent Clo. Esher BH57 93
Derwent Clo. Wey. AX56 92
Derwent Cres. N20 BT27 38
Derwent Cres. Bexh. CR44 69
Derwent Cres. Stan. BK30 36
Derwent Dr. Hayes BB39 53
Derwent Dr. Orp. CM54 88
Derwent Dr. Pur. BZ60 96
Derwent Gdns. Ilf. CK31 49
Derwent Gdns. Wem. BK33 45
Derwent Par. S. Ock DA39 60
Derwent Ri. NW9 BO32 46
Derwent Rd. N13 BX28 38
Derwent Rd. SE20 CB51 87
Derwent Rd. SE22 CA45 67
Derwent Rd. W5 BK41 64
Derwent Rd. Sthl. BE39 54
Derwent Rd. Twick. BF46 74
Derwent St. SE10 CG42 68
Derwentwater Rd. W3 BN40 55
Derwentwater Rd. Hem. H. BA14 8
Derwent Way. Horn. CU35 50
Desalis Rd. Uxb. BA38 53
Desborough Clo. Shep. AZ54 83
Ferry La.
Desborough St. W2 BS39 56
Cirencester St.
Desenfans Rd. SE21 CA46 77
Desford Ct. Ashf. AY48 73
Desford Rd. E16 CG38 58
Desford Way, Ashf. AY48 73
Desmond Rd. Wat. BB21 26
Desmond St. SE14 CD43 67
Despard Av. SW11 BV44 66
Despard Rd. N19 BW33 47
De. Tillens La. Oxt. CH68 115
Detling Clo. Horn. CV35 51
Detling Rd. Brom. CH49 78
Detling Rd. Erith CS43 69
Detling Rd. Grav. DE47 81
Deva Clo. St. Alb. BF14 9
Devana End Cars. BU55 86
Devas Rd. SW20 BQ51 85
Devas St. E3 CE38 57
Devenay Rd. E15 CG36 58
Devenish Rd. SE2 CO41 69
Deventer Cres. SE22 CA46 77
Dulwich Gro.
De Vere Gdns. W8 BT41 66
De Vere Gdns. Ilf. CK34 49
Deverell St. SE1 BZ41 67
Devereux Ct. EC4 BY40 56
Fountain Ct.
Devereux Dr. Wat. BB22 26
Devereux Rd. SW11 BU46 76
Devereux Rd. Wind. AO44 61
De Vere Wk. Wat. BB23 26
Deveron Gdns. S. Ock. DA39 60
Deveron Way Rom. CT30 41
Devils La. Egh. AU50 72
Devitt Clo. Ash. BM61 103
Devoke Way Walt. BD55 84
Devon Av. Twick. BG47 74
Devon Back, Guil. AR72 118
Devon Clo. N17 CA31 48
Devon Clo. Buck. H. CH27 40
Devon Clo. Grnf. BK37 54
Devon Clo. Ken. CA61 105
Devon Ct. W3 BM39 55
Links Rd.
Devon Ct. Hamptn. BF50 74
Devon Ct. St. Alb. BH14 9
Old London Rd.
Devon Cres. Grnf. BK37 54
Devon Cres. Red. BT70 121
Devoncroft Gdns. Twick. BJ47 74
Oak La.
Devon Gdns. N4 BY32 47
Devonia Gdns. N18 BZ29 39
Devonia Rd. N1 BY37 56
Devonport Gdns. Ilf. CK32 49
Devonport Mews W12 BP41 65
Devonport Pass. E1 CC39 57
Devonport Rd. W12 BP40 55
Devonport St. E1 CC39 57
Devon Rise N2 BT31 47
Devon Rd. Bark. CN37 58
Devon Rd. Red. BW68 113
Devon Rd. S. At. H. CX51 90
Devon Rd. Sutt. BR58 94
Devon Rd. Walt. BD56 93
Devon Rd. Wat. BD23 27
Devons Est. E3 CE38 57
Devonshire Ave. Wok. AU60 91
Devonshire Av. Dart. CU46 79
Devonshire Av. Sutt. BT57 95
Devonshire Clo. E15 CG35 49
Devonshire Clo. N13 BY27 38
Devonshire Clo. W1 BV39 56
Devonshire Ct. Croy. CD54 87
Devonshire Ct. Rich. BL44 65
Holmersdale Rd.
Devonshire Cres. NW7 BQ29 37
Devonshire Dr. SE10 CE43 67
Devonshire Dr. Surb. BK54 84
Devonshire Gdns. N17 BZ29 39
Devonshire Rd.
Devonshire Gdns. N21 BZ26 39
Devonshire Gdns. W4 BN43 65
Devonshire Gdns. S. Le H. DK41 71
Somerset Rd.
Devonshire Gro. SE15 CB43 67
Devonshire Hill La. N17 BY29 38
Devonshire Ms. S. W1 BV39 56
Devonshire Ms. W. W1 BV38 56
Devonshire Pl. W1 BV38 56
Devonshire Pl. W4 BO42 65
Devonshire Pl. Ms. W1 BV38 56
Devonshire Rd. E15 CG35 49
Devonshire Rd. E16 CH39 58
Devonshire Rd. E17 CE32 48
Devonshire Rd. N9 CC26 39
Devonshire Rd. N13 BX28 38
Devonshire Rd. N17 BZ29 39
Devonshire Rd. NW7 BQ29 37
Devonshire Rd. SE9 CK48 78
Devonshire Rd. SW19 BU50 76
Devonshire Rd. W4 BO42 65
Devonshire Rd. W5 BK41 64
Devonshire Rd. AZ56 92
Devonshire Rd. Bexh. CQ45 69
Devonshire Rd. Croy. BZ54 87
Devonshire Rd. Felt. BE48 74
Devonshire Rd. Grav. DG48 81
Devonshire Rd. Har. BG32 45
Devonshire Rd. Horn. CV34 51
Devonshire Rd. Ilf. CM33 49
Devonshire Rd. Orp. CO54 89
Devonshire Rd. Pnr. BD32 45
Devonshire Rd. Pnr. BE30 36
Devonshire Rd. Sthl. BF39 54
Devonshire Rd. Sutt. BT57 95
Devonshire Rd. Wall. BV56 95
Devonshire Row, EC2 CA39 57
Devonshire Sq. EC2 CA39 57
Devonshire Sq. Brom. CH52 88
Masons Hill
Devonshire St. W1 BV40 56
Devonshire St. W4 BO42 65
Devonshire Ter. W2 BT39 56
Devonshire Way Croy. CD55 87
Devonshire Waye Hayes BC39 53
Devons Rd. E3 CE38 57
Devon St. SE15 CB44 67
Devon Way Chess. BK56 93
Devon Way Epsom. BM56 94
Devon Waye Houns. BE43 64
De Walden St. W1 BV39 56
Marylebone St.
Dewar St. SE15 CB45 67
Dewberry St. E14 CF39 57
Dewey Rd. N1 BY37 56
Dewey Rd. Dag. CS36 59
Dewey St. SW17 BU49 76
Dewhurst Rd. W14 BQ41 65
Dewhurst Rd. Wal. Cr. CB18 21
Dewlands. Dart. CX47 80
Dewlands. Gdse. CC69 114
Dewport St. W6 BR43 65
Field Rd.
Dewsbury Clo. Pnr. BE32 45
Dewsbury Clo. Rom. CV29 42
Dewsbury Gdns. Rom. CV29 42
Dewsbury Gdns. Wor. Pk. BP55 85
Dewsbury Rd. NW10 BP35 46
Dewsbury Rd. Rom. CV29 42
Dewsbury Ter. NW1 BV36 56
Camden High St.
Dexter Clo. Grays. DD41 71
Dexter Rd. SE24 BY45 66
Dexter Rd. Barn. BQ25 28
Deyncourt Gdns. Upmin. CY34 51
Deyncourt Rd. N17 BZ30 39
Deynecourt Gdns. E11 CJ31 49
D'eynsford Rd. SE5 BZ44 67
Dial, The, Wk, W8 BS41 66
Diamedes, Stai. AX47 73
Diameter Rd. Orp. CL54 88
Diamond Clo. E7 CH35 49
Diamond Rd. Ruis. BE35 45
Diamond Rd. Slou. AQ41 62
Diamond Rd. Wat. BC22 26
Diamond St. SE15 CA43 67
Diamond Ter. SE10 CF43 67
Diana Pl. NW1 BV38 56
Diana Rd. E17 CD31 48
Dianthus Clo. SE2 CO42 69
Carnation St.
Dianthus Clo. Cher. AV54 82
Diban Av. Horn. CU35 50
Dibber Rd. SE23 CC48 77
Dibden La. Sev. CT66 116
Dibden's Cotts. SE27 BY49 76
Crown La.
Dibden St. N1 BZ37 57
Dibdin Clo. Sutt. BS55 86
Dibdin Ho. NW6 BS38 56
Dibdin Rd. NW6 BS37 56
Dibdin Rd. Sutt. BS55 86
Diceland Rd. Bans. BR61 103
Dicey Av. NW2 BQ35 46
Dickens Ave. Til. DG44 71
Dickens Av. N3 BT30 38
Dickens Av. Dart. CX45 70
Dickens Av. Uxb. AZ39 53
Dickens Clo. Hart. DC53 90
Dickens Clo. Rich. BL48 75
Dickens Clo. St. Alb. BG13 9
Dickens Dr. Chis. CM50 78
Dickens Dr. Wey. AW56 92
Dickens Est. SE1 CB41 67

Dickenson Av. Rick. AZ25 26
Dickenson Rd. N8 BX33 47
Dickenson's La. SE25 CB53 87
Dickenson's Pl. SE25 CB53 87
Dickenson Sq. Rick. AZ25 26
Dickens Rise Chig. CL27 40
Dickens Rd. E6 CJ37 58
Dickens Rd. Grav. DJ47 81
Dickens Sq. SE1 BZ41 67
Dickens St. SW8 BV44 66
Dickerage La. N. Mal. BN52 85
Dickerage Rd. Kings. On T. BN51 85
Dickson Rd. SE9 CK45 68
Dickson's Fold. Pnr. BD31 45
Dick Turpin Way. Felt. BB45 63
Didcot St. SW11 BT45 66
Digby Cres. N4 BZ34 48
Digby Est. E2 CC38 57
Digby Gdns. Dag. CR37 59
Digby Pl. Croy. CA55 87
Digby Rd. E9 CC35 48
Digby Rd. Bark. CN36 58
Digby St. E2 CC38 57
Digby Way, Wey. AY59 92
Digdag Hill, Wal. Cr. CA17 21
Digdens Rise Epsom BN61 103
Diggon St. E1 CC39 57
Dighton Rd. SW18 BT46 76
Dignum St. N1 BY37 56
Digswell Hill, Welw. G. C. BP6 5
Digswell La. Welw. G. C. BR6 5
Digswell Park Rd. Welw. G. C BQ5 5
Digswell Park Rd. Welw. G. C. BR5 5
Digswell Rise. Welw. G. C. BQ7 5
Digswell Rd. Welw. G. C. BQ7 5
Digswell St. N7 BY36 56
Holloway Rd.
Dilhorne Clo. SE12 CH48 78
Dilke St. SW3 BU43 66
Dillwyn Rd. SE26 CD49 77
Dilston Clo. Nthlt. BD38 54
Dilston Gro. SE16 CC42 67
Abbeyfield Rd.
Dilston Rd. Lthd. BJ63 102
Dilton Gdns. SW15 BP47 75
Dimes Pl. W3 BP42 65
King St.
Dimmocks La. Rick. AW21 26
Dimsdale Dr. NW9 BN33 46
Dimsdale Dr. Enf. CB25 30
Dimsdale Wk. E13 CG37 58
Dinant Link Rd. Hodd. CE11 12
Dingle Gdns. E14 CE40 57
Dingle Rd. Ashf. AZ49 73
Dingle, The Uxb. AZ38 53
Dingley Pl. EC1 BZ38 57
Dingley Rd.
Dingley Rd. EC1 BZ38 57
Dingon Hill Clo. Hayes BC39 53
Dingwall Av. Croy. BZ55 87
Dingwall Gdns. NW11 BS32 47
Dingwall Pl. Croy. BZ55 87
Dingwall Rd. SW18 BT47 76
Dingwall Rd. Cars. BU58 95
Dingwall Rd. Croy. BZ54 87
Dinmont Est. E2 CB37 57
Dinmont St. E2 CB37 57
Dinsdale Clo. Wok. AT62 100
Dinsdale Gdns. SE25 CA52 87
Dinsdale Gdns. Barn. BS25 29
Dinsdale Rd. SE3 CG43 68
Dinsmore Rd. SW12 BV47 76
Dinton Rd. SW19 BT50 76
Dinton Rd. Kings. On T. BL50 75
Dione Rd. Hem. H. AY12 8
Dippers Clo. Sev. CW62 108
Dirdene Clo. Epsom BO59 94
Dirdene Gdns. Epsom BO59 94
Dirdene Gro. Epsom BO59 94
Dirleton Rd. E15 CG37 58
Dirtham La. Leath. BC67 110
Disbrowe Rd. W6 BR43 65
Dishforth La. NW9 BO30 37
Disney Pl. SE1 BZ41 67
Disney St
Disney St. SE1 BZ41 67
Dison Clo. Enf. CC23 30
Disraeli Gdns. SW15 BR45 65
Fawe Pk. Rd.
Disraeli Rd. E7 CH36 58
Disraeli Rd. NW10 BN37 55
Disraeli Rd. SW15 BQ45 65
Disraeli Rd. W5 BK40 54
Diss St. E2 CA38 57
Distaff La. EC4 BZ39 57
Cannon St.
Distillery La. W6 BQ42 65
Distillery Wk. Brent. BL43 65
Pottery Rd.
Distin St. SE11 BY42 66
District Rd. Wem. BJ35 45
Ditch Alley SE10 CE44 67
Ditchburn St. E14 CF40 57
Ditches La. Couls. BX63 104
Ditchfield Rd. Hodd. CE10 12
Dittisham Rd. SE9 CK49 78
Ditton Clo. Surb. BJ54 84
Ditton Gra. Clo. Surb. BK54 84
Ditton Grd. Dr. Surb. BK54 84
Ditton Hill Rd. Surb. BK54 84
Ditton Lawn Surb. BJ54 84
Ditton Park Rd. Slou. AS43 62
Ditton Pl. SE20 CB51 87
Ditton Rd. Bexh. CP46 79
Ditton Rd. Slou. AR44 62
Ditton Rd. Slou. AS43 62
Ditton Rd. Sthl. BE42 64
Ditton Rd. Surb. BK55 84
Divis Way SW15 BP46 75
Dover Pk. Dr.
Dixon Pl. W. Wick. CE54 87
Dixon Rd. SE14 CD44 67
Dixon Rd. SE25 CA52 87
Dixons Alley, SE16 CB41 67
West La.
Dixon's Hill Rd. Hat. BP16 19
Dobb, S Weir Rd. Harl. CG13 13
Dobb, S Weir Rd. Hodd. CF12 12
Dobell Rd. SE9 CK46 78
Dobree Rd. NW10 BP36 55
Dobson Clo. NW6 BT36 56
Belsize Rd.
Dobson Rd. Grav. DJ49 81
Dockett Eddy La. Shep. AY54 83
Dockhead SE1 CA41 67
Jamaica Rd.
Dockland St. E16 CL40 58
Dockley Rd. SE16 CB41 67
Dock Rd. E16 CG40 58
Dock Rd. Brent. BK43 64
Dock Rd. Grays. DE43 71
Dock Rd. Grays. DF43 71
Dock St. E1 CB40 57
Dockwell Clo. Felt. BC45 63
Doctors Common Rd. Berk. AQ13 7
Doctors La. Cat. BY65 104
Docwra's Bldgs. N1 CA36 57
King Henry's Wk.
Dodbrooke Rd. SE27 BY48 76
Doddinghurst Rd. Brwd. DB23 33
Doddinghurst Rd. Brwd. DB26 42
Doddington Gro. SE17 BY43 66
Doddington Pl. SE17 BY43 66
Kennington Pk. Pl.
Dodds Cres. Wey. AW60 92
Dodds La. Ch. St. G. AQ27 34
Dodds La. Hem. H. AX10 8
Dodds La. Wey. AW60 92
Dodds Pk. Bet. BM71 120
Dodson St. SE1 BY41 66
Dod St. E14 CD39 57
Dodwood. Welw. G. C. BS8 5
Doggets Clo. Barn. BU25 29
Doggets Farm Rd. Uxb. AU33 43
Doggett Rd. SE6 CE47 77
Doggetts Way, St. Alb. BG15 9
Doggetts Wood Clo. Ch. St. G. AQ24 25
Doggetts Wood La. Ch. St. G. AQ24 25
Doghurst Ave. Hayes. AZ43 63
Doghurst Dr. West Dr. AZ43 63
Doghurst La. Couls. BU63 104
Dog Kennel Hill, SE22 CA45 67
Dog Kennel La. Hat. BP12 10
Dog Kennel La. Rick. AV25 25
Dog La. NW10 BO35 46
Dognell Grn. Welw. G. C. BP7 5
Dog Wood Clo. Grav. DF49 81
Doherty Rd. E13 CH38 58
Dolben St. SE1 BY40 56
Dolby Rd. SW6 BR44 65
Ewald Rd.
Dole St. NW7 BQ29 37
Dolland St. SE11 BX42 66
Dollis Av. N3 BR30 37
Dollis Brook Wk. Barn. BR25 28
Dollis Cres. Ruis. BD33 45
Dollis Hill Av. NW2 BP34 46
Dollis Hill La. NW2 BO35 46
Dollis Ms. N3 BS30 38
Dollis Pk.
Dollis Pk. N3 BR30 37
Dollis Valley Way Barn. BR25 28
Dolman St. SW4 BX45 66
Dolphin Clo. Surb. BK53 84
Dolphin Ct. Slou. AQ41 62
Dolphin Rd.
Dolphin Ct. Stai. AW48 73
Bremer Rd.
Dolphin La. E14 CE40 57
Dolphin Rd. Slou. AQ41 62
Dolphin Sq. SW1 BW42 66
Dombey St. WC1 BX39 56
Dome Hill. Cat. CA67 114
Dome Hill Pk. SE26 CA49 77
Dome Hill Peak. Cat. CA66 114
Domett Clo. SE5 BZ45 67
Dome Way, Red. BU70 121
Dominic Dr. SE9 CL49 78
Dominion Dri. Rom. CR29 41
Dominion Rd. Croy. CA54 87
Dominion St. EC2 BZ39 57
Dominion Way. Rain. CU38 59
Domitian Pl. Enf. CA25 30
Domville Gro. SE5 CA42 67
Donald Dr. Rom. CP32 50
Donald Rd. E13 CH37 58
Donald Rd. Croy. BX54 86
Donaldson Rd. NW6 BR37 55
Donaldson Rd. SE18 CL44 68
Doncaster Dr. Nthlt. BE35 45
Doncaster Gdns. N4 BY32 47
Stanhope Gdns.
Doncaster Gdns. Nthlt. BE35 45
Doncaster Rd. N9 CB26 39
Doncaster Way. Upmin. CW34 51
Donegal St. N1 BX37 56
Doneraile St. SW6 BQ44 65
Dongola Rd. E13 CH38 58
Dongola Rd. N17 CA31 48
Donington Av. Ilf. CM32 49
Donkey La. Enf. CB23 30
Donkey La. Farn. CX55 90
Donkey La. West Dr. AX42 63
Donnefield Av. Edg. BL29 37
Donne Gdns. Wok. AV61 100
Donne Pl. SW3 BU42 66
Donne Pl. Mitch. BV52 86
Donne Rd. Dag. CP34 50
Donnington Rd. NW10 BP36 55
Donnington Rd. Har. BK32 45
Donnington Rd. Sev. CS63 107
Donnington Rd. Wor. Pk. BP55 85
Donnybrook Rd. SW16 BW50 76
Donovan Av. N10 BV30 38
Donovan Clo. Epsom BN58 94
Don Way Rom. CT29 41
Doods Pk. Rd. Reig. BT70 121
Doods Rd. Reig. BT70 121
Doods Way, Reig. BT70 121
Doone Clo. Tedd. BJ50 74
Doon St. SE1 BY40 56
Dorado Gs. Orp. CP55 89
Doral Way Cars. BU56 95
Carshalton Pk. Rd.
Doran Dr. Reig. BT70 121
Doran Gdns. Reig. BT70 121
Doran Gro. SE18 CM43 68
Doran Mans. N2 BU32 47
Doran Wk. E15 CF36 57
Dora Rd. SW19 BS49 76
Dora St. E14 CD39 57
Dorcas Ct. St. Alb. BH14 9
Old London Rd.
Dorchester Av. N13 BZ28 39
Dorchester Av. Bex. CP47 79
Dorchester Av. Har. BF32 45
Dorchester Av. Hodd. CE11 12
Dorchester Clo. Dart. CW47 80
Dorchester Clo. Nthlt. BF35 45
Dorchester Ct. N14 BV26 38
Dorchester Ct. SE24 BZ46 77
Dorchester Dr. SE24 BZ46 77
Dorchester Gdns. E4 CE28 39
Dorchester Gdns. NW11 BS31 47
Gloucester Dr.
Dorchester Gdns. Mord. BS54 86
Dorchester Gro. W4 BO43 65
Dorchester Rd. Grav. DH48 81
Dorchester Rd. Mord. BS54 86
Dorchester Rd. Nthlt. BF35 45
Dorchester Rd. Wey. AZ55 83
Dorchester Rd. Wor. Pk. BQ54 85
Dorchester Way, Har. BL32 46
Dorchester Waye Hayes BC39 53
Dorcis Av. Bexh. CQ44 69
Dordrecht Rd. W3 BO40 55
Dore Av. E12 CL35 49
Doreen Av. NW9 BN33 46
Dorell Clo. Sthl. BE39 54
Dorian Rd. Horn. CU33 50
Doria Rd. SW6 BR44 65
Doric Way NW1 BW38 56
Dorien Rd. SW20 BQ51 85
Dorincourt, SW15 BN49 75
Dorin Ct. Wok. AV61 100
Dorinda St. N7 BY36 56
Dorinium Clo. Wem. BL35 46
Lea Gdns.
Doris Av. Erith. CR44 69
Doris Rd. E7 CH36 58
Doris Rd. Ashf. BA50 73
Doris St. SE11 BY42 66
Tracey St.
Dorking Clo. SE8 CD43 67
Dorking Rise. Rom. CV28 42
Dorking Rd. Ash. BM61 103
Dorking Rd. Guil. AU73 118
Dorking Rd. Lthd. BF66 111
Dorking Rd. Lthd. BJ64 102
Dorking Rd. Rom. CV28 42
Dorking Rd. Tad. BO67 112
Dorking Wk. Rom. CV28 42
Dorkins Way, Upmin. CZ33 51
Dorlcote Rd. SW18 BT47 76
Dorling Dr. Epsom BO59 94
Dorly Clo. Shep. BB53 83
Dormans Clo. Nthwd. BA29 35
Dorman Way, NW8 BT37 56
Dormay St. SW18 BS46 76
Dormer Clo. E15 CG36 58
Dormer Clo. Barn. BQ25 28
Dormer's Av. Sthl. BE39 54
Dormer's Rise Sthl. BF40 54
Dormer's Wells La. Sthl. BF39 54
Dormie Clo. St. Alb. BG12 9
Dormy Wood, Ruis. BB32 44
Dorncliffe Rd. SW6 BR44 65
Dornels, Slou. AR39 52
Dorney Gro. Wey. AZ55 83
Dorney Reach Rd. Maid. AJ41 61
Dorney Rise Orp. CN53 88
Dornfell St. NW6 BR35 46
Dornton Rd. SW12 BV48 76
Dornton Rd. Sth. Croy. BZ57 96
Dorothy Av. Wem. BL36 55
Dorothy Evans Clo. Bexh. CR45 69
Dorothy Gdns. Dag. CO35 50
Dorothy Rd. SW11 BU45 66
Dorrington Gdns. Horn. CV33 51
Dorrington St. EC1 BY39 56
Dorrit Way Chis. CM50 78
Dorrofield Clo. Rick. BA25 26
Dors Clo. NW9 BN33 46
Dorset Av. Hayes BB38 53
Dorset Av. Rom. CS31 50
Dorset Av. Sthl. BF42 64
Dorset Av. Well. CN45 68
Dorset Bldgs. EC4 BY39 56
Dorset Rise
Dorset Clo. NW1 BU39 56
Dorset Clo. Berk. AP12 7
Dorset Clo. Hayes BB38 53
Dorset Cres. Grav. DJ49 81
Dorset Dr. Edg. BL29 37
Dorset Dr. Wok. AT62 100
Dorset Est. E2 CA38 57
Dorset Gdns. Mitch. BX52 86
Dorset Gdns. S. Le H. DK41 71
Somerset Rd.
Dorset Ms. SW1 BV41 66
Wilton St.
Dorset Pl. E15 CF36 57
Dorset Pl. SW1 BW42 66
Rampayne St.
Dorset Rise, EC4 BY39 56
Dorset Rd. E7 CJ36 58
Dorset Rd. N15 BZ31 48
Dorset Rd. N22 BX30 38
Dorset Rd. SE9 CK48 78
Dorset Rd. SW8 BX43 66
Dorset Rd. SW19 BS51 86
Dorset Rd. W5 BK41 64
Dorset Rd. Ashf. AX48 73
Dorset Rd. Beck. CC52 87
Dorset Rd. Har. BG32 45
Dorset Rd. Mitch. BU51 86
Dorset Rd. Sutt. BS58 95
Dorset Rd. Wind. AO44 61
Dorset Sq. NW1 BU38 56
Dorset St. W1 BU39 56
Dorset Way Twick. BG47 74
Dorset Way, Wey. AX59 92
Dorset Waye Houns. BE43 64
Dorset Waye, Uxb. AY37 53
Dorville Cres. W6 BP41 65
Dorville Rd. SE12 CG46 78
Dothill Rd. SE18 CM43 68
Doubleday Rd. Loug. CM24 31
Doughty Ms. WC1 BX38 56
Roger St.
Doughty St. WC1 BX38 56
Douglas Av. E17 CD30 39
Douglas Av. N. Mal. BP52 85
Douglas Av. Rom. CW30 42
Douglas Av. Wat. BD22 27
Douglas Av. Wem. BL36 55
Douglas Clo. Guil. AR67 109
Douglas Clo. Stan. BJ28 36
Douglas Cres. Hayes. BD38 54
Douglas Dr. Croy. CE55 87
Douglas Est. N1 BZ36 57
Douglas Gdns. Berk. AP12 7
Douglas La. Stai. AS46 72
Douglas Pl. E14 CF42 67
Douglas Rd. E4 CG26 40
Douglas Rd. E16 CH39 58
Douglas Rd. N1 BZ36 57
Douglas Rd. N22 BY30 38
Douglas Rd. NW6 BR37 55
Douglas Rd. Esher BF55 84
Douglas Rd. Horn. CT32 50
Douglas Rd. Houns. BF45 64
Douglas Rd. Ilf. CO33 50
Douglas Rd. Kings-on-t. BM52 85
Douglas Rd. Slou. AO39 52
Douglas Rd. Surb. BL55 85
Douglas Rd. Well. CO44 69
Douglas Rd. Wey. AW55 83
Douglas Robinson Ct. SW16 BX50 76
Douglas Sq. Mord. BS53 86
Douglas St. SW1 BW42 66
Douglas Way, SE8 CD43 67
Dounesforth Gdns. SW18 BS47 76
Dounsell Ct. Brwd. DA25 33
Douro Pl. W8 BS41 66
Douro St. E3 CE37 57
Dovai Gro. Hamptn. BG51 84
Dovecote Av. N22 BY31 47
Dovecote Clo. Wey. AZ55 83
Dove Court. Hat. BP13 10
Dovedale Av. Har. BK32 45
Dovedale Av. Ilf. CL30 40
Dovedale Clo. Uxb. AX30 35
Dovedale Clo. Well. CO44 69
Dovedale Rise Mitch. BU50 76
Dovedale Rd. SE22 CB46 77
Dovehouse Croft, Harl. CO10 6
Dove Ho. Gdns. E4 CE27 39
Dovehouse Mead, Bark. CM37 58
Dove House St. SW3 BT42 66
Dove La. Pot. B. BT20 20
Dove Ms. SW5 BT42 66
Dove Pk. Pnr. BF29 36
Dove Park. Rick. AT25 25
Dover Clo. Rom. CS30 41
Dovercourt Av. Th. Hth. BY53 86
Dovercourt Gdns. Stan. BL28 37
Dovercourt La. Sutt. BT55 86
Dovercourt Rd. SE22 CA46 77
Doverfield Rd. SW2 BX46 76
Dover Ho. Rd. SW15 BP45 65
Doveridge Gdns. N13 BY28 38
Dove Rd. N1 BZ36 57
Dove Rd. Dart. CY47 80
Dove Row, E2 CB37 57
Dover Pk. Dr. SW15 BP46 75
Dover Rd. E12 CJ34 49
Dover Rd. N9 CC27 39
Dover Rd. SE19 BZ50 77
Dover Rd. Grav. DE47 81
Dover Rd. Rom. CQ32 50
Dover Rd. E. Grav. DF47 81
Dovers Grn. Rad. BN19 19
Dovers Green Rd. Reig. BS73 121
Doversmead, Wok. AP61 100
Dover St. W1 BV40 56
Dover Way, Rick. BA24 26
Dover Yd. W1 BW40 56
Berkeley St.
Dove's Clo. Brom. CK55 88
Dove St. E1 CC38 57
Doveton Rd. Sth. Croy. BZ56 96
Dove Wk. Rain. CU36 59
Dowanhill Rd. SE6 CF47 77
Dowdell's La. Welw. BN5 5
Dowding Pl. Stan. BJ29 36
Dowding Rd. Uxb. AY36 53
Dowding Rd. West. CJ61 106
Dowding Wk. Grav. DF48 81
Durndale La.
Dower Av. Wall. BV58 95
Dower Pk. Wind. AM45 61
Dowgate Hill, EC4 BZ40 57
Dowlans Clo. Lthd. BF67 111
Dowlans Rd. Lthd. BF67 111
Dowlas St. SE5 CA43 67
Dowlerville Rd. Orp. CN57 97
Dowlings Par. Wem. BK37 54
Bridgewater Rd.
Downage NW4 BQ30 37
Downalong Bush. BG26 36
Downbank Av. Bexh. CS44 69
Downbarns Rd. Ruis. BD34 45
Down Ct. Hat. BP14 10
Downderry Rd. Brom. CF48 77
Downe Ave. Sev. CM59 97
Downe Clo. Well. CP43 69
Down Edge, St. Alb. BF13 9
Down End, SE18 CL43 68
Moordown
Downer Dri. Rick. AV21 25
Downer Dr. Rick. AW21 26
Downe Rd. Kes. CK58 97
Downe Rd. Mitch. BU51 86
Downe Rd. Sev. CM60 97
Downers La. SW4 BW45 66
Downes Ct. N21 BY26 38
Downes Rd. St. Alb. BJ11 9
Downe Ter. Rich. BL46 75
Richmond Hill
Downfield Wor. Pk. BO54 85
Downfield Clo. W9 BS38 56
Amberley Est.
Downfield Rd. Wal. Cr. CD19 21
Downfields. Welw. G. C. BP9 5
Down Hall Rd. Kings. On T. BK51 84
Downham Rd. N1 BZ36 57
Downham Way, Brom. CF49 77
Downhills Av. N17 BZ31 48
Downhills Park Rd. N17 BZ31 48
Downhills Way N17 BZ31 48
Downhills Way N22 BZ30 39
Downhurst Av. NW7 BN28 37
Downing Av. Guil. AP71 118
Downing Clo. Har. BG31 45
Downing Dr. Grnf. BG37 54
Downing Rd. Dag. CQ37 59
Downing St. SW1 BW41 66
Downings Wd. Rick. AU28 34
Downland Clo. Couls. BV60 95
Downland Clo. Epsom BP62 103
Downland Gdns. Epsom BP62 103
Downlands Rd. Pur. BX60 95
Downlands, Wal. Abb. CG20 22
Downland Way Epsom BP62 103
Down La. Guil. AO72 118
Downleys Clo. SE9 CK48 78
Downman Rd. SE9 CK45 68
Down Pl. W6 BP42 65
Bridge Av.
Down Rd. E11 CG34 49
Down Rd. Guil. AT70 118
Down Rd. Tedd. BJ50 74
Downs Ave. Dart. CX47 80
Downs Av. Chis. CK49 78
Downs Av. Epsom BO60 94
Downs Av. Pnr. BE32 45
Downs Bri. Rd. Beck. CF51 87
Downs Ct. SW20 BQ50 75
Downs Ct. Rd. Pur. BY59 95
Downsell Rd. E15 CF35 48
Downs Est. E5 CB34 48
Downsfield Rd. E17 CD32 48
Downshall Av. Ilf. CN32 49
Downs Hill Beck. CF50 77
Downs Hill Rd. Epsom BO60 94
Downshire Hill NW3 BT35 47
Downside Epsom. BO60 94
Downside, Hem. H. AY13 8
Downside Bridge Rd. Cob. BC60 92
Downside Common Rd. Cob. BC62 101
Downside Cres. NW3 BU35 47
Downside Cres. W13 BJ38 54
Downside Gdns. Twick. BH48 74
Downside Rd. Cob. BC61 101
Downside Rd. Guil. AT71 118
Downside Rd. Sutt. BT57 95
Downside Wk. Nthlt. BE38 54
Downsland Dr. Brwd. DB27 42
Downs La. Lthd. BJ65 102
Downs Park Rd. E5 CA35 48
Downs Park Rd. E8 CA35 48
Downs Rd. E5 CB35 48
Downs Rd. Beck. CE51 87
Downs Rd. Couls. BW62 104
Downs Rd. Dor. BK68 111
Downs Rd. Enf. CA24 30
Downs Rd. Epsom BO60 94
Downs Rd. Grav. DD49 81
Downs Rd. Pur. BY59 95
Downs Rd. Slou. AR41 62
Downs Rd. Sutt. BS58 95
Downs Rd. Th. Hth. BZ51 87
Downs Side Sutt. BR59 94
Downs, The, SW20 BQ50 75
Downs, The. Harl. CN11 13
Downs, The. Lthd. BK66 111
Down St. W1 BV41 66
Down St. E. Mol. BF53 84
Downsview, Dor. BK70 119
Downs Vw. Islw. BH44 64
Downs Vw. Tad. BP64 103
Downsview Av. Wok. AS64 100
Downsview Clo. Orp. CP58 98
Downsview Clo. Swan. CT52 89
Downs View Ct. Guil. AR68 109
Downsview Gdns. SE19 BY50 76
Downsview Rd. SE19 BZ50 77
Downs View Rd. Lthd. BG67 111
Downsview Rd. Sev. CT66 116
Downs Way Epsom. BO61 103

Downsway, Guil. AV70 118
Downs Way. Lthd. BG66 111
Downs Way Orp. CN56 97
Downs Way. Oxt. CG67 115
Downsway Sth. Croy. CA59 96
Downsway Sutt. BB58 95
Downs Way. Tad. BP64 103
Downsway Whyt. CA61 105
Downs Way Ct. Tad. BP64 103
Downs Wood Epsom BP62 103
Downswood, Reig. BT69 121
Downton Av. SW2 BX48 76
Downview Clo. Cob. BC63 101
Downway N12 BU29 38
Downway Nthlt. BC37 53
Down Way Clo. Nthlt. BC37 53
Dowsett Rd. N17 CA30 39
Dowson Clo. SE5 BZ45 67
Doyce St. SE1 BZ41 67
Southwark Bridge Rd.
Doyle Gdns. NW10 BP37 55
Doyle Rd. SE25 CB52 87
Doyle Wk. Til. DH44 71
Coleridge Rd.
Doyley St. SW1 BV42 66
Doynton St. N19 BV34 47
Draco St. SE17 BZ43 67
Dragmire La. Mitch. BT52 86
Dragon La, Wey. AZ58 92
Dragoon Rd. SE8 CD42 67
Dragor Rd. NW10 BN38 55
Drake Ave. Slou. AR42 62
Drake Clo. Brwd. DB28 42
Drake Ct. Har. BE34 45
Drakefell Rd. SE4 CC44 67
Drakefell Rd. SE14 CC44 67
Drakefield Rd. SW17 BV48 76
Drakely Ct. N5 BY35 47
Highbury Hill
Drake Rd. SE4 CE45 67
Drake Rd. Croy. BX54 86
Drake Rd. Har. BE34 45
Drake Rd. Mitch. BV53 86
Drakes Av. Stai. AV49 72
Drakes Clo. Esher BF56 93
Drakes Clo. Wal. Cr. CC17 21
Drakes Dr. Nthwd. AZ30 35
Drakes Dr. St. Alb. BJ15 9
Drakes Grn. Esher BF56 93
Drakes Rd. Amer. AP23 25
Drake St. WC1 BX39 56
Theobalds Rd.
Drake St. Enf. BZ23 30
Drakewood Rd. SW16 BW50 76
Draper Clo. Belv. CQ42 69
Drapers Gdns. EC2 BZ39 57
Draper's Rd. E15 CF35 48
Drapers Rd. N17 CA31 48
Drapers Rd. Enf. BY23 29
Draw Dock Rd. SE10 CF40 57
Drax Av. SW20 BP50 75
Draxmont App. SW19 BR50 75
Draycot Rd. E11 CH32 49
Draycot Rd. Surb. BM55 85
Draycott Av. SW3 BU42 66
Draycott Av. Har. BJ32 45
Draycott Clo. Har. BJ32 45
Draycott Pl. SW3 BU42 66
Draycott Ter. SW3 BU42 66
Dray Gdn. SW2 BX46 76
Drayson Ms. W8 BS41 66
Drayton Av. W13 BJ40 54
Drayton Av. Loug. CK26 40
Drayton Av. Orp. CL54 88
Drayton Av. Pot. B. BR19 19
Drayton Br. Rd. W7 BH40 54
Drayton Br Rd. W13 BH40 54
Drayton Clo. Lthd. BH65 102
Drayton Gdns. N21 BY26 38
Drayton Gdns. SW10 BT42 66
Drayton Gdns. W13 BJ40 54
Drayton Gdns. West Dr. AX41 63
Drayton Gdns. West Dr. AY41 63
Drayton Gn. Rd. W13 BJ40 54
Drayton Grn. W13 BJ40 54
Drayton Gro. W13 BJ40 54
Drayton Pk. N5 BY34 47
Drayton Rd. E11 CF33 48
Drayton Rd. N17 CA30 39
Drayton Rd. NW10 BO37 55
Drayton Rd. W13 BJ39 54
Drayton Rd. Borwd. BM24 28
Drayton Rd. Croy. BY55 86
Drayton Waye, Harrow BJ32 45
Dreadnought St. SE10 CG41 68
Drenon Sq. Hayes BB40 53
Dresden Rd. N19 BW33 47
Dresden Walk, Wey. AZ56 92
Dresden Way, Wey. AZ56 92
Drew Av. NW7 BQ29 37
Drew Av. NW7 BR29 37
Drew Gdns. Grnf. BH36 54
Drew Rd. E16 CJ40 58
Drewstead Rd. SW16 BW48 76
Driffield Rd. E3 CD37 57
Drift La. Cob. BE62 102
Drift Rd. Wind. AG45 61
Drifts Way. Slou. AU44 62
Drift, The, Kes. CJ55 88
Drift Way, Hem. H. AY13 8
Driftway, The, Mitch. BV51 86
Streatham Rd.
Driftwood Av. St. Alb. BF16 18
Driftwood Dri. Ken. BZ58 96
Driftwood Dr. Ken. BZ62 105
Drill Hall Rd. Cher. AW54 83
Drill Hall Rd. Epsom. BP57 94
£d£ Ring Rd. Wat. BH24 27
Drinkwater Est. Felt. BC46 73
Drinkwater Rd. Har. BF34 45
Dr. Johnsons Av. SW17 BV48 76
Drive Mead Couls. BX60 95
Drive Rd. Couls. BW63 104
Drive Rd. Rick. AX26 35
Drive. Spur. Tad. BS64 104
Drive, The, E4 CF26 39
Drive, The, E18 CH31 49
Drive, The, N3 BS29 38
Drive, The, N11 BW29 38
Blake Rd.
Drive, The, NW11 BR33 46
Drive, The, SW6 BR44 65
Drive, The, SW16 BX52 86
Drive, The, SW20 BQ50 75
Drive, The, W3 BN39 55
Drive, The Amer. AO22 25
Drive, The Ashf. BA50 73
Drive, The Bans. BR62 103
Drive, The, Bark. CN30 40
Drive, The, Barn. BR24 28
Drive, The, Barn. BT25 29
Drive, The, Beck. CE51 87
Drive, The, Bex. CP47 79
Drive, The, Brwd. DB29 42
Drive, The, Buck. H. CJ26 40
Drive, The, Chis. CN51 88
Drive, The, Chis. CN52 88
Drive. The. Cob. BE60 93
Drive, The, Couls. BX60 95
Drive, The, Edg. BM28 37
Drive, The, Enf. BZ23 30
Drive, The Epsom. BM65 103
Drive, The, Epsom BO57 94
Drive, The, Erith. CR43 69
Drive, The, Esher BG54 84
Drive, The, E17 CE31 48
Drive, The, Felt. BC47 73
Drive, The Grav. DH49 81
Drive, The, Grays CX43 70
Drive, The Guil. AP71 118
Drive, The, Har. BF32 45
Drive, The, Harl. CN10 6
Drive, The, Hodd. CE11 12
Drive, The, Houns. BG44 64
Drive, The, Ilf. CK32 49
Drive, The, Kings On T. BN51 85
Drive, The, Loug. CK24 31
Drive, The Lthd. BH64 102
Drive, The, Lthd. BL65 103
Drive, The, Mord. BT53 86
Drive, The, Nthwd. BB30 35
Drive, The, Orp. CN55 88
Drive, The, Pot. B. BR19 19
Drive, The, Rad. BJ20 18
Drive, The, Rick. AW25 26
Drive, The, Rom. CS29 41
Drive, The, Rom. CW30 42
Drive, The, Saw. CQ6 6
Drive, The, Sev. CU65 107
Drive, The, Sid. CO48 79
Drive, The, Slou. AQ44 62
Drive, The, Slou. AS41 62
Drive, The Stai. AR46 72
Drive The, Surb. BL54 85
Drive, The, Sutt. BR59 94
Drive, The, Th. Hth. BZ52 87
Drive, The, Uxb. AY35 44
Drive, The, Wal. Cr. BY17 20
Drive, The, Wall. BW58 95
Drive, The Wat. BB22 26
Drive, The, Wem. BN34 46
Drive, The, W. Wick. CF54 87
Drive, The Wok. AQ63 100
Drive, The, Ger. Cr. AS29 34
Driveway, The, Pot. B. BX17 20
Dr. Williams Wk. Guil. AQ68 109
Droitwich Clo. SE26 CB48 77
Dromore Rd. SW15 BR46 75
Dronfield Gdns. Dag. CP35 50
Drood Yd. E1 CB40 57
Pennington St.
Droop St. W10 BQ38 55
Drop La. St. Alb. BF18 18
Drover La. SE15 CB43 67
Drove Rd. Dor. BC71 119
Drover's Rd. Sth. Croy BZ56 96
Drovers Way Beac. AO29 34
Drovers Way, St. Alb. BG13 9
Droveway, The Grav. DF50 81
Druce Rd. SE21 CA46 77
Drudgeon Way. Dart. DB48 80
Druids Clo. Ash BL63 103
Druid St. SE1 CA41 67
Druids Way Brom. CF52 87
Drumaline Ridge, Wor. Pk. BO55 85
Drummond Av. Rom. CS31 50
Drummond Cres. NW1 BW38 56
Drummond Dr. Stan. BH29 36
Drummond Rd. E11 CH32 49
Drummond Rd. SE16 CB41 67
Drummond Rd. Croy. BZ55 87
Drummond Rd. Guil. AR70 118
Drummond Rd. Rom. CS31 50
Drummonds' The Buck. H. CH27 40
Drummonds, The, Epp. CO18 23
Hartland Rd.
Drummond St. NW1 BW38 56
Drury La. WC2 BX39 56
Drury Rd. Har. BG33 45
Dryad St. SW15 BQ45 65
Dryburgh Gdns. NW9 BM31 46
Dryburgh Rd. SW15 BP45 65
Drycroft. Welw. G. C. BR9 5
Dryden Av. W7 BH39 54
Dryden Clo. Ilf. CN29 40
Dryden Rd. SW19 BT50 76
Dryden Rd. Enf. CA25 30
Dryden Rd. Har. BH30 36
Dryden Rd. Well. CN44 68
Dryfield Clo. NW10 BN36 55
Dryfield Rd. Edg. BN29 37
Dryfield Wk. SE8 CE43 67
Czar St.
Dryhill La. Sev. CR65 107
Dryhill Rd. Belv. CQ43 69
Dryland Av. Orp. CN56 97
Drylands Rd. N8 BX32 47
Drynham Pk. Wey. BB55 83
Drysdale Av. E4 CE26 39
Drysdale Clo. Nthwd. BB29 35
Drysdale Pl. N1 CA38 57
Drysdale St.
Drysdale St. N1 CA38 57
Duboyne Rd. NW5 BU35 47
Dubrae Clo. St. Alb. BF14 9
Ducal St. E2 CA38 57
Brick La.
Du Cane Clo. W12 BQ39 55
Du Cane Rd.
Du Cane Ct. SW17 BV47 76
Du Cane Rd. W12 BP39 55
Duchess Ms. W1 BV39 56
Duchess St.
Duchess Of Bedford's Wk. W8 BS41 66
Duchess St. W1 BV39 56
Duchy Rd. Barn. BT22 29
Duchy St. SE1 BY40 56
Ducie St. SW4 BX45 66
Duckett Rd. N4 BY32 47
Ducketts Rd. Dart. CT46 79
Duckett St. E1 CC38 57
Ducking Stool Ct. Rom. CT31 50
Duck Lane Epp. CP16 23
Ducklees La. Enf. CD24 30
Ducksfoot La. EC4 BZ40 57
Upr. Thames St.
Duck's Hill. Nthwd. AZ30 35
Duck, S Hill Rd. Nthwd. AZ31 44
Duck's Wk. Twick. BK46 74
Du Cross Dr. Stan. BK29 36
Ducross Rd. W3 BO40 55
Dudbrook Rd. Rom. CW22 33
Dudden Hill La. NW10 BO35 46
Dudley Av. Har. BK31 45
Dudley Av. Wal. Cres. CC19 21
Dudley Clo. Wey. AW55 83
Dudley Ct. NW11 BR31 46
Dudley Dr. Mord. BR54 85
Dudley Dr. Ruis. BC35 44
Dudley Gdns. W13 BJ41 64
Dudley Gdns. Har. BG33 45
Dudley Gdns. Rom. CV29 42
Dudley Gro. Epsom BN60 94
Dudley Rd. E17 CE31 48
Dudley Rd. N3 BS30 38
Dudley Rd. NW6 BR37 55
Dudley Rd. SW19 BS50 76
Dudley Rd. Ashf. AY49 73
Dudley Rd. Felt. BA47 73
Dudley Rd. Grav. DF47 81
Dudley Rd. Har. BG34 45
Dudley Rd. Ilf. CL35 49
Dudley Rd. Kings-on-t. BL52 85
Dudley Rd. Rich. BL44 65
Dudley Rd. Rom. CV29 42
Dudley Rd. Sthl. BD41 64
Dudley Rd. Walt. BC53 83
Dudlington Rd. E5 CC34 48
Dudmaston Ms. SW3 BT42 66
Dudsbury Rd. Dart. CU46 79
Dudsbury Rd. Sid. CO49 79
Dudset La. Houns. BC44 63
Dudswell La. Berk. AO10 7
Dufferin St. EC1 BZ38 57
Duffield Clo. Har. BH32 45
Duffield La. Slou. AP35 43
Duffield La. Slou. AP36 52
Duffield Pk. Slou. AQ38 52
Duffield Rd. SW11 BU45 66
Batten St.
Duffield Rd. Tad. BP65 103
Duffins Orchard. Cher. AU57 91
Duff St. E14 CE39 57
Dufours Pl. W1 BW39 56
Broadwick St.
Dugdale Hill Rd. Pot. B. BR20 19
Dugdales, Rick. AZ24 26
Duke Gdns. Ilf. CM31 49
Duke Rd.
Duke Humphrey Rd. SE3 CG44 68
Duke Of Cambridge Clo. Twick. BG46 74
Duke Of Edinburgh Rd. Sutt. BT55 86
Duke Of Wellington Pl. SW1 BV41 66
Duke Of York St. SW1 BW40 56
Duke Rd. W4 BN42 65
Duke Rd. Ilf. CM31 49
Duke St. Hill, SE1 BZ40 57
Duke St. Ms. NW8 BU38 56
Lisson Gro.
Dukes Ave. Grays. DD41 71
Duke's Av. N3 BS30 38
Duke's Av. N10 BV31 47
Dukes Av. N10 BW31 47
Duke's Av. W4 BN42 65
Dukes Av. Edg. BL29 37
Dukes Av. Epp. CN21 31
Dukes Av. Har. BE32 45
Duke's Av. Har. BH31 45
Dukes Av. Houns. BE45 64
Dukes Av. N. Mal. BO52 85
Dukes Av. Nthlt. BE36 54
Dukes Av. Twick. BK49 74
Dukes Clo. Ashf. BA49 73
Dukes Clo. Epp. CR17 23
Dukes Clo. Ger. Cr. AS33 43
Dukes Clo. Hamptn. BE49 74
Duke's Clo. Kings On T. BK49 74
Dukes Ct. E6 CL37 58
Dukes Kiln Rd. Ger. Cr. AR34 43
Dukes La. W8 BS41 66
Dukes Lane. Ong. DB12 15
Dukes Meadows W4 BN44 65
Dukes Mews N10 BV31 47
Dukes Av.
Duke's Ms. W1 BV39 56
Duke St.
Dukes Pass. E17 CF31 48
Marlowe Rd.
Duke's Pl. EC3 CA39 57
Dukes Ride. Ger. Cr. AS33 43
Dukes Rd. E6 CL37 58
Dukes Rd. W3 BM38 55
Duke's Rd. WC1 BW38 56
Dukes Rd. Walt. BD56 93
Dukesthorpe Rd. SE26 CC49 77
Duke St. W1 BV39 56
Duke St. Hodd. CE11 12
Duke St. Rich. BK46 74
Duke St. Sutt. BT56 95
Duke St. Wat. BD24 27
Duke St. Wind. AO44 61
Duke St. Wok. AS62 100
Dukes Way, Berk. AQ12 7
Dukes Way W. Wick. CG55 88
Dukes Wood Ave. Ger. Cr. AS33 43
Dukes Wood Dr. Ger. Cr. AR33 43
Dulas St. N4 BX33 47
Everleigh St.
Dulford St. W11 BR40 55
Dulka Rd. SW11 BU46 76
Dulton Clo. Hem. H. AX14 8
Dulverton Rd. SE9 CM48 78
Dulverton Rd. Rom. CV29 42
Dulverton Rd. Ruis. BC33 44
Dulverton Rd. Sth. Croy. CC58 96
Dulwich Common, SE21 CA47 77
Dulwich Rd. SE24 BY46 76
Dulwich Village, SE21 CA46 77
Dulwich Way, Rick. AZ25 26
Dulwich Wood Av. SE19 CA49 77
Dulwich Wood Pk. SE19 CA49 77
Dumbarton Av. Wal. Cr. CC20 21
Raglan Av.
Dumbarton Rd. SW2 BX46 76
Dumbreck Rd. SE9 CK45 68
Dumfries Clo. Wat. BC27 35
Dumont Rd. N16 CA34 48
Dumpton Pl. NW1 BV36 56
Dunally Park, Shep. BA54 83
Dunbar Av. SW16 BY51 86
Dunbar Av. Beck. CD52 87
Dunbar Av. Dag. CR34 50
Dunbar Clo. Hayes BC39 53
Dunbar Gdns. Dag. CR35 50
Dunbar Pl. SE27 BZ48 77
Dunbar Rd. E7 CH36 58
Dunbar Rd. N22 BY30 38
Dunbar Rd. N. Mal. BN52 85
Dunbar St. SE27 BY48 76
Dunblane Rd. SE9 CK45 68
Dunboe Pl. Shep. BA54 83
Russell Rd.
Dunbridge St. E2 CB38 57
Duncan Clo. Barn. BT24 29
Duncan Dr. Guil. AT70 118
Duncan Gro. W3 BO39 55
Duncannon Cres. Wind. AL45 61
Duncannon St. WC2 BX40 56
Adelaide St.
Duncan Rd. E8 CB37 57
Duncan Rd. Rich. BL45 65
Duncan Rd. Tad. BR62 103
Duncan Rd. Tad. BR63 103
Duncan St. N1 BY37 56
Duncan Ter. N1 BY37 56
Duncan Way Bush. BE23 27
Duncombe Clo. Amer. AP22 25
Duncombe Hl. SE23 CD47 77
Duncombe Rd. N19 BW33 47
Duncombe Rd. Berk. AP12 7
Duncrievie Rd. SE13 CF46 77
Duncroft SE18 CN43 68
Duncroft. Wind. AM45 61
Duncroft Clo. Reig. BR70 120
Dundalk Rd. SE4 CD45 67
Dundas Gdns. E. Mol. BF52 84
Dundas Rd. SE15 CC44 67
Dundee Rd. E13 CH37 58
Dundee Rd. SE25 CB53 87
Dundee St. E1 CB40 57
Green Bank
Dundela Gdns. Epsom BP56 94
Dundonald Rd. NW10 BQ37 55
Dundonald Rd. SW19 BR51 85
Dundon Gdns. SE23 CC47 77
Dundrey Cres. Red. BX68 113
Dunedin Dri. Cat. CA66 114
Dunedin Rd. E10 CE34 48
Dunedin Rd. Ilf. CM33 49
Dunedin Rd. Rain. CT38 59
Dunedin Way Hayes. BD38 54
Dunelm St. E1 CC39 57
Duneved Rd. S. Th. Hth. BY53 86
Dunewood Clo. Wey. AV59 91
Dunfield Gdns. SE6 CE49 77
Dunfield Rd. SE6 CE49 77
Dunford Rd. N7 BX35 47
Dungarvan Av. SW15 BP45 65
Dungates La. Bet. BP70 120
Dunheved Clo. Th. Hth. BY53 86
Dunheved Rd. N. Th. Hth. BY53 86
Dunheved Rd. W. Th. Hth. BY53 86
Dunholme Grn. N9 CA27 39
Dunholme La. N9 CA27 39
Dunholme Rd.
Dunholme Rd. N9 CA27 39
Dunkeld Rd. SE25 BZ52 87
Dunkeld Rd. Dag. CO34 50
Dunkellin Gro. S. Ock. DA39 60
Dunkellin Way. S. Ock. DA39 60
Dunkery Rd. SE9 CJ49 78
Dunkin Rd. Dart. CX45 70
Dunkirk Clo. Grav. DH49 81
Dunkirk St. SE27 BZ49 77
Dunlace Rd. E5 CC35 48
Dunleary Clo. Houns. BE47 74
Dunley Dr. Croy. CE57 96
Dunloe Av. N17 BZ31 48
Dunloe St. E2 CA37 57
Dunlop Pl. SE16 CA41 67
Dunlop Rd. Til. DF44 71
Dunmail Dri. Pur. CA60 96
Dunmore, Guil. AO70 118
Dunmore Rd. NW6 BR37 55
Dunmore Rd. SW20 BQ51 85
Dunmow Clo. Loug. CK25 31
Dunmow Clo. Rom. CP32 50
Dunmow Dr. Rain. CT37 59
Dunmow Gdns. Brwd. DE32 123
Dunmow Rd. E15 CF35 48
Dunmow Road. Ong. CZ13 15
Dunningford Clo. Horn. CT35 50
Dunnings La. Brwd. DC33 123
Dunnings La. Upmin. DD34 123
Dunn St. E8 CA35 48
Dunny La. Kings L. AV19 16
Dunollie Pl. NW5 BW35 47
Dunollie Rd.
Dunollie Rd. NW5 BW35 47
Dunoon Rd. SE23 CC47 77
Dunraven Dr. Enf. BY23 29
Dunraven Rd. W12 BP40 55
Dunraven St. W1 BU40 56
Green St.
Dunsany Rd. W14 BQ41 65
Dunsbury Clo. Sutt. BS58 95
Nettlecombe Clo.
Dunsdon Av. Guil. AQ71 118
Dunsfold Rise. Couls. BW60 95
Dunsfold Way Croy. CE58 96
Dunsford Cres. SW18 BS47 76
Merton Rd.
Dunsford Way SW15 BP46 75
Dover Pk. Dr.
Dunsmore Way Bush. BG25 27
Dunsmure Rd. N16 CA33 48
Dunspring La. Ilf. CL30 40
Dunstable Clo. Rom. CV29 42
Dunstable Ms. W1 BV39 56
Dunstable Rd. E. Mol. BE52 84
Dunstable Rd. Rich. BL45 65
Dunstable Rd. Rom. CV29 42
Dunstall Rd. SW20 BP50 75
Dunstall Way E. Mol. BF52 84
Dunstan Rd. NW11 BR33 46
Dunstan Rd. Couls. BW62 104
Dunstan's Gro. SE22 CB46 77
Dunstans Rd. SE22 CB47 77
Dunstar Clo. Barn. BQ24 28
Dunster Av. SW15 BP46 75
Dunster Av. Mord. BQ54 85
Dunster Clo. Rom. CS30 41
Dunster Clo. Uxb. AW30 35
Dunster Ct. EC3 CA40 57
Mincing La.
Dunster Cres. Horn. CX34 51
Dunster Dr. NW9 BN33 46
Dunster Gdns. NW6 BR36 55
Dunster Way Har. BE34 45
Dunston Rd. E8 CA37 57
Dunston Rd. SW8 BV44 66
Stanley Gro.
Dunston St. E8 CA37 57
Dunton Rd. E10 CE33 48
Dunton Rd. SE1 CA42 67
Dunton Rd. Rom. CT31 50
Duntshill Rd. SW18 BS47 76
Dunvegan Clo. E. Mol. BF52 84
Dunvegan Rd. SE9 CK45 68
Dunwich Rd. Bexh. CQ44 69
Dupont Rd. SW20 BQ51 85
Dupont St. E14 CD39 57
Duppas Av. Croy. BY56 95
Violet La.
Duppas Clo. Shep. BA53 83
Green La.
Duppas Hill La. Croy. BY56 95
Duppas Hill Rd. Croy. BY56 95
Duppas Hill Ter. Croy. BY55 86
Duppash La. Croy. BY55 86
Duppas Rd. Croy. BY55 86
Dupree Rd. SE7 CH42 68
Duraden Clo. Beck. CE50 77
Durand Clo. Cars. BU54 86
Durand Gdns. SW9 BX44 66
Durand Way, NW10 BN36 55
Durant Dr. Swan. CU50 79
Durants Pk. Av. Enf. CC24 30
Durants Rd. Enf. CC24 30
Durant St. E2 CB37 57
Durban Gdns. Dag. CS36 59
Durban Ho. E7 CJ36 58
Durban Rd. E15 CG38 58
Durban Rd. E17 CD30 39
Durban Rd. N17 CA29 39
Durban Rd. SE27 BZ49 77
Durban Rd. Beck. CD51 87
Durban Rd. Felt. BC48 73
Durban Rd. Ilf. CN33 49
Durban Rd. E. Wat. BC24 26
Durban Rd. W. Wat. BC24 26
Durbin Rd. Chess. BL56 94
Durdans Rd. Sthl. BE39 54
Durell Gdns. Dag. CP35 50
Durell Rd. Dag. CP35 50
Durfold Dr. Reig. BT70 121
Durford Cres. SW15 BP47 75
Durham Av. Brom. CG52 88
Durham Av. Houns. BE42 64
Durham Av. Rom. CV31 51
Durham Av. Wdf. Grn. CJ28 40
Durham Bldgs. SW11 BT45 66
Durham Clo. SW20 BP51 85
Durham Clo. Guil. AP69 118
Durham Hl. Brom. CG49 78
Durham Pl. SW3 BU42 66

Durham Rise, SE18 CM42 68
Durham Rd. E12 CJ35 49
Durham Rd. E16 CG38 58
Durham Rd. N2 BU31 47
Durham Rd. N7 BX34 47
Durham Rd. N9 CB27 39
Durham Rd. SW20 BP51 85
Durham Rd. W5 BK41 64
Durham Rd. Borwd. BN24 28
Durham Rd. Brom. CG52 88
Durham Rd. Dag. CS35 50
Durham Rd. Felt. BD47 74
Durham Rd. Har. BF32 45
Durham Rd. Sid. CO49 79
Durham Row, E1 CC39 57
Stepney High St.
Durham St. SE11 BX42 66
Durham Ter. W2 BS39 56
Durleston Park Dr. Lthd. BG66 111
Durley Av. Pnr. BE33 45
Durley Rd. N16 CA33 48
Durlston Rd. E5 CB34 48
Durlston Rd. Kings. On T. BL50 75
Durndale La. Grav. DF49 81
Durnell Way Loug. CL24 31
Durnford St. N15 CA32 48
Durnford St. SE10 CF43 67
Greenwich Church St.
Durning Rd. SE19 BZ49 77
Durnsford Av. SW19 BS48 76
Durnsford Rd. N11 BW30 38
Durnsford Rd. SW19 BS48 76
Duro Pl. W8 BS42 66
Durrants Clo. Rain. CV37 60
Durrants Dr. Rick. BA24 26
Durrants Hill Rd. Hem. H. AX15 8
Durrants La. Berk. AP13 7
Durrant's La. Rick. AY24 26
Durrants Rd. Berk. AP12 7
Durrant Way Orp. CM56 97
Durrant Way. Swans. DB46 80
Durrant Way, Swans. DC47 81
Durrell Rd. SW6 BR44 65
Durrell Way, Shep. BA53 83
Durrington Av. SW20 BQ50 75
Durrington Pk. Rd. SW20 BQ51 85
Durrington Rd. E5 CD35 48
Dursley Clo. SE3 CJ44 68
Dursley Gdns. SE3 CJ44 68
Dursley Rd. SE3 CJ44 68
Durward St. E1 CB39 57
Dury Falls Clo. Horn. CX33 51
Dury Rd. Barn. BR23 28
Duseley Rd. Stai. AR47 72
Duthie St. E14 CF40 57
Dutton St. SE10 CF44 67
Dutton Way, Iver AV39 52
Duxford Clo. Horn. CV36 60
Duxons Turn, Hem. H. AZ13 8
Dyall Ho. Grays DD43 71
Hawkes Clo.
Dyers Bldgs. EC1 BY39 56
Holborn
Dyers Hall Rd. E11 CF34 48
Dyer's La. SW15 BP45 65
Dyers Way Rom. CU29 41
Dyke Dr. Orp. CP54 89
Dykes Path Wok. AU61 100
Bentham Av.
Dykes Way Brom. CG52 88
Dykewood Clo. Bex. CT48 79
Dylan Rd. Belv. CR41 69
Dylways, SE5 BZ45 67
Dymchurch Clo. Ilf. CL30 40
Dymchurch Clo. Orp. CN56 97
Dymes Path SW19 BR48 75
Queensmere Rd.
Dymock St. SW6 BS45 66
Dymoke Grn. St. Alb. BJ11 9
Dymoke Rd. Horn. CT33 50
Dymokes Way, Hodd. CE10 12
Dyneley Rd. SE12 CJ49 78
Dyne Rd. NW6 BR36 55
Dynes Rd. Sev. CW62 108
Dynevor Pl. Guil. AO68 109
Dynevor Rd. N16 CA34 48
Dynevor Rd. Rich. BL46 75
Dynham Rd. NW6 BS36 56
Dyott St. WC1 BW39 56
Dyrham La. Barn. BP21 28
Dysart Av. Kings. On T. BK49 74
Dysart St. EC2 BZ38 57
Dyson Clo. Wind. AN45 61
Dyson Rd. E11 CG32 49
Dyson Rd. E15 CG36 58
Dysons Clo. Wal. Cr. CC19 21
Dyson's Rd. N18 CB29 39
Eade Rd. N4 BY33 47
Eagle Av. Rom. CQ32 50
Eagle Clo. Enf. CC24 30
Eagle Clo. Rain. CU36 59
Eagle Ct. EC1 BY39 56
Albion Pl.
Eagle Hill, SE19 BZ50 77
Eagle La. E11 CH31 49
Eagle La. Brwd. CZ22 33
Eagle Pl. E1 CC38 57
Mile End Rd.
Eagle Pl. SW1 BW40 56
Jerymyn St.
Eagle Rd. Guil. AR70 118
Eagle Rd. Wem. BK36 54
Eaglesfield Rd. SE18 CL44 68
Eagles, The, W6 BV34 47
Eagle St. WC1 BX39 56
High Holborn
Eagle Ter. Wdf. Grn. CH29 40
Eaglet Pl. E1 CC38 57
Mile End Rd.
Eagle Way, Brwd. DA29 42
Eagle Way. Hat. BP13 10
Eagle Wharf Rd. N1 BZ37 57
Eakenwalk Clo. Cher. AV53 82
Ealdham Sq. SE9 CJ45 68
Ealing Gn. W5 BK40 54
Ealing Pk. Gdns. W5 BK42 64
Ealing Pk. Ms. W5 BK41 64
Ealing Rd.
Ealing Rd. Brent. BK42 64
Ealing Rd. Nthlt. BF37 54
Ealing Rd. Wem. BL36 55
Ealing Village, W5 BL39 55
Eamont St. NW8 BU37 56
Eardemont Clo. Dart. CT45 69
Eardley Cres. SW5 BS42 66
Eardley Rd. SW16 BW49 76
Eardley Rd. Belv. CR42 69
Eardley Rd. Sev. CU65 107
Earl Cotts. SE1 CA42 67
Earldom Rd. SW15 BQ45 65
Earlesmead Rd. NW10 BQ38 55
Earlham Gro. E7 CG35 49
Earlham Gro. N22 BX29 38
Earlham St. WC2 BW39 56
Earl Rise, SE18 CM42 68
Earl Rd. SE1 CA42 67
Earl Rd. SW14 BN45 65
Earl Rd. Grav. DF48 81
Earlsbrook Rd. Red. BU71 121
Earls Ct. Gdns. SW5 BS42 66
Earl's Ct. Rd. SW5 BS41 66
Earl's Ct. Rd. W8 BS41 66
Earl's Ct. Sq. SW5 BS42 66
Earl's Cres. Har. BH31 45
Earlsferry Clo. N1 BX36 56
Carnoustie Dr.
Earlsferry Way N1 BX36 56
Earlsferry Clo.
Earlsfield Rd. SW18 BT47 76
Earlshall Rd. SE9 CK45 68
Earls La. Pot. B. BO19 19
Earlsmead Har. BE35 45
Earlsmead Rd. N15 CA32 48
Earlsmead Rd. NW10 BQ39 55
Earls Path. Loug. CJ23 31
Earls Ter. W8 BR41 65
Earlsthorpe Rd. SE26 CC49 77
Earlstoke St. EC1 BY38 56
Earlstone Gro. E9 CB37 57
Victoria Pk. Rd.
Earl St. EC2 BZ39 57
Earl St. Wat. BD24 27
Earl's Wk. W8 BS41 66
Earls Wk. Dag. CO35 50
Earlswood. Cob. BD59 93
Earlswood Av. Th. Hth. BY53 86
Earlswood Gdns. Ilf. CL31 49
Earlswood Rd. Red. BU71 121
Earlswood St. SE10 CG42 68
Early Ms. NW1 BV37 56
Arlington Rd.
Earnshaw St. WC2 BW39 56
Earsby St. W14 BR42 65
Easby Cres. Mord. BS53 86
Easebourne Rd. Dag. CP35 50
Easedale Dr. Horn. CU35 50
Easleys Ms. W1 BV39 56
Wigmore St.
East Acton La. W3 BO40 55
Eastam Cres. Brwd. DD28 122
East Arbour Sq. E1 CC39 57
East Av. E12 CK36 58
East Av. E17 CE31 48
East Av. Hayes BB40 53
East Av. Hayes BC40 53
East Av. Sthl. BE40 54
East Av. Wall. BX56 95
East Av. Watt. BB58 92
East Bank N16 CA33 48
Eastbank Rd. Hamptn. BG49 74
East Barnet Rd. Barn. BT24 29
Eastbourne Av. W3 BN39 55
Eastbourne Gdns. SW14 BN45 65
Eastbourne Ms. W2 BT39 56
Eastbourne Rd. E6 CL38 58
Eastbourne Rd. E15 CG37 58
Eastbourne Rd. N15 CA32 48
Eastbourne Rd. SW17 BV50 76
Eastbourne Rd. W4 BN43 65
Eastbourne Rd. Brent. BK42 64
Eastbourne Rd. Felt. BD48 74
Eastbourne Rd. Gdse. CC69 114
Eastbourne Ter. W2 BT39 56
Eastbournia Av. N9 CB27 39
Eastbrook Av. N9 CC26 39
Eastbrook Av. Dag. CS35 50
Eastbrook Dr. Rom. CT34 50
Eastbrook Rd. SE3 CH43 68
Eastbrook Rd. Wal. Abb. CG20 22
Eastbury Ave. Nthwd. BB28 35
Eastbury Av. Bark. CN37 58
Eastbury Av. Enf. CA23 30
Eastbury Ct. St. Alb. BH13 9
Lemsford Rd.
Eastbury Gro. W4 BO43 65
Eastbury Rd.
Eastbury Rd. W4 BO42 65
Eastbury Rd. Kings. On T. BL50 75
Eastbury Rd. Nthwd. BB28 35
Eastbury Rd. Nthwd. BB29 35
Eastbury Rd. Orp. CM53 88
Eastbury Rd. Rom. CS32 50
Eastbury Rd. Wat. BC26 35
Eastbury Sq. Bark. CN37 58
Eastbury Ter. E1 CC38 57
Eastcastle St. W1 BW39 56
Eastcheap, EC3 CA40 57
East Churchfield Rd. W3 BN40 55
Eastchurch Rd. Houns. BB44 63
East Clo. W5 BM38 55
East Clo. Barn. BV24 29
East Clo. Grnf. BG37 54
East Clo. Rain. CU38 59
Eastcombe Av. SE7 CH43 68
East Common. Ger. Cr. AS32 43
Eastcote Orp. CN54 88
Eastcote Av. E. Mol. BE53 84
Eastcote Av. Grnf. BJ35 45
Eastcote Av. Har. BF34 45
Eastcote Gdns. Well. CM44 68
Eastcote High Rd. Pnr. BC32 44
Eastcote La. N. Nthlt. BE36 54
Eastcote Rd. Har. BG34 45
Eastcote Rd. Pnr. BD32 45
Eastcote Rd. Ruis. BB33 44
Eastcote Rd. Well. CM44 68
Eastcote St. SW9 BX44 66
Eastcote Vw. Pnr. BD31 45
East Ct. Wem. BK34 45
East Cres. N11 BU28 38
East Cres. Enf. CA25 30
East Cres. Wind. AM44 61
East Cres. Rd. Grav. DH46 81
Eastcroft Rd. Epsom BO57 94
Eastdean Ave. Epsom. BM60 94
Eastdene Dr. Rom. CV28 42
Eastdown Pk. SE13 CF45 67
East Dr. SW11 BV43 66
East Dr. Cars. BU58 95
East Dr. Orp. CO53 89
East Dr. Saw. CQ6 6
East Dr. Slou. AP38 52
East Dr. Vir. W. AQ53 82
East Dr. Wat. BC21 26
East Dulwich Est. SE22 CA45 67
East Dulwich Gro. SE22 CA46 77
East Dulwich Rd. SE22 CA45 67
East End Rd. N2 BS30 38
East End Rd. N3 BS30 38
East End Way Pnr. BE31 45
East Entrance Dag. CR37 59
Eastern Ave. S. Ock. CW40 60
Eastern Av. E11 CH32 49
Eastern Av. Ilf. CH32 49
Eastern Av. Pnr. BD33 45
Eastern Av. Rom. CH32 49
Eastern Av. S. Ock. CY41 70
Eastern Av. Wal. Cr. CD20 21
Eastern Av. E. Rom. CS30 41
Eastern Av. W. Ilf. CN32 49
Eastern Industrial Est. Belv. CR41 69
Eastern Perimeter Rd. Houns. BB44 63
Eastern Rd. E13 CH37 58
Eastern Rd. E17 CF32 48
Eastern Rd. N2 BU31 47
Eastern Rd. N22 BX30 38
Eastern Rd. SE4 CE45 67
Eastern Rd. Grays. DE42 71
Eastern Rd. Rom. CT32 50
Easternville Gdns. Ilf. CM32 49
Eastern Way. Grays. DD42 71
East Ferry Rd. E14 CE42 67
Eastfield Av. Wat. BD23 27
Eastfield Gdns. Dag. CR35 50
Eastfield Rd. E17 CE31 48
Eastfield Rd. N8 BX31 47
Eastfield Rd. Brwd. DB27 42
Eastfield Rd. Dag. CQ35 50
Eastfield Rd. Enf. CC22 30
Eastfield Rd. Wal. Cr. CD19 21
Eastfields Pnr. BD32 45
Eastfields Rd. W3 BN39 55
Eastfields Rd. Mitch. BV51 86
Eastfield St. E14 CD39 57
East Flint. Hem. H. AV13 7
East Gdns. SW17 BU50 76
Eastgate Bans. BR60 94
East Gate, Harl. CM10 6
East Gate. Harl. CM11 13
Eastgate Gdns. Guil. AS71 118
East Gdn. Wok. AU62 100
Eastglade. Nthwd. BB28 35
East Glade Pnr. BE31 45
East Green, Hem. H. AY16 17
Easthall La. Rain. CV39 60
East Hall Rd. Orp. CQ54 89
East Ham Manor Way E6 CK38 58
East Ham Manor Way E16 CK38 58
East Harding St. EC4 BY39 56
East Heath Rd. NW3 BT34 47
East Hill, SW18 BS46 76
East Hill Dart. CW47 80
East Hill. Oxt. CG68 115
East Hill. Sev. CX59 99
East Hill. S. Dnth. CY51 90
East Hill Sth. Croy. CA58 96
East Hill, Wem. BM34 46
East Hill. West. CH62 106
East Hill, Wok. AU61 100
East Hill Dr. Dart. CW47 80
East Hill Rd. Oxt. CG68 115
Eastholm NW11 BS31 47
East Holme Erith CS44 69
East Holme Hayes BC40 53
E. India Dock Rd. E14 CF39 57
E. India Dock Wall Rd. E14 CF40 57
Eastington Pl. Guil. AS71 118
Maori Rd.
E. Kent Av. Grav. DE46 81
Eastlake Rd. SE5 BZ44 67
Eastlands Cres. SE21 CA46 77
Eastlands Way. Oxt. CF67 114
East La. SE16 CB41 67
Chambers St.
East La. Kings-on-t. BK52 84
High St.
East Lane. Leath. BA66 110
East La. Wat. BC18 17
East La. Wem. BJ34 45
Eastlea Av. Wat. BE22 27
Eastleigh Av. Har. BF34 45
Eastleigh Clo. NW2 BO34 46
E. Leigh Clo. Sutt. BS57 95
Eastleigh Rd. Bexh. CS44 69
Eastleigh Wk. SW15 BP47 75
East Lodge La. Enf. BW21 29
Eastman St. E1 CB38 57
Eastman Way, Hem. H. AZ12 8
Eastmead Ruis. BD34 45
E. Mead. Welw. G. C. BS9 5
Eastmead Av. Grnf. BF38 54
East Meads, Guil. AQ71 118
Eastmearn Rd. SE21 BZ48 77
East Milton Rd. Grav. DH47 81
Eastminster, E1 CA40 57
Royal Mint St.
Eastmont Rd. Esher BH55 84
Eastmoor Pl. SE7 CJ41 68
Eastmoor St.
Eastmoor St. SE7 CJ41 68
East Mount St. CB39 57
Eastney St. SE10 CF42 67
Eastnor Rd. SE9 CM47 78
Eastnor Rd. Reig. BS71 121
Easton Gdns. Borwd. BN24 28
Easton St. WC1 BY38 56
East Park, Harl. CP9 6
East Park, Saw. CQ6 6
E. Park Clo. Rom. CQ32 50
East Pl. SE27 BZ49 77
Dunkirk St.
East Ridgeway, Pot. B. BX17 20
East Rd. E11 CH32 49
East Rd. E15 CH37 58
East Rd. N1 BZ38 57
East Rd. SW19 BT50 76
East Rd. Barn. BV26 38
East Rd. Belv. CQ41 69
East Rd. Edg. BM30 37
East Rd. Enf. CC22 30
East Rd. Felt. BA47 73
East Rd. Harl. CO9 6
East Rd. Kings. On T. BL51 85
East Rd. Reig. BR70 120
East Rd. Rom. CQ31 50
East Rd. Rom. CS33 50
East Rd. Well. CO44 69
East Rd. West Dr. AY42 63
East Rd. Wey. BA57 92
East Row W10 BR38 55
Eastry Av. Brom. CG53 88
Eastry Rd. Erith. CR43 69
East Shalford La. Guil. AS73 118
East Sheen Av. SW14 BN46 75
Eastside Rd. NW11 BR31 46
East Smithfield, E1 CA40 57
East Sq. SE18 CL42 68
East St. EC2 BZ39 57
Blomfield St.
East St. SE17 BZ42 67
East St. Bark. CM36 58
East St. Bexh. CR45 69
East St. Brent. BK43 64
East St. Brom. CH51 88
East St. Epsom BO59 94
East St. Grav. DD46 81
East St. Grays. DC43 71
East St. Grays. DE43 71
East St. Hem. H. AX13 8
East St. Lthd. BF66 111
East Tenter St. E1 CA39 57
East Ter. Grav. DH46 81
East Thurrock Rd. Grays. DD43 71
East Tilbury Rd. S. Le H. DJ40 71
East Towers Pnr. BD32 45
East Vw. E4 CF28 39
East Vw. NW3 BT34 47
East Vw. Barn. BR23 28
East Vw. Hat. BU12 11
Eastview Av. SE18 CN43 68
Eastville Av. NW11 BR32 46
East Wk. Barn. BV26 38
East Wk. Hayes BC40 53
East Wk. Reig. BS70 121
Eastway, E9 CD36 57
East Way, E11 CH32 49
East Way Brom. CH54 88
East Way Croy. CD55 87
Eastway Epsom BN59 94
East Way Hayes BC40 53
Eastway Mord. BQ53 85
Eastway Ruis. BC33 44
East Way, Wal. Abb. CF21 30
Eastway Wall. BW56 95
Eastwell Clo. Beck. CD51 87
King's Hall Rd.
Eastwick Cres. Rick. AV27 34
Eastwick Dr. Lthd. BF65 102
Eastwick Hall La. Harl. CL8 6
Eastwick Park Ave. Lthd. BF66 111
Eastwick Pk. Av. Lthd. BF65 102
Eastwick Rd. Harl. CM9 6
Eastwick Rd. Lthd. BF66 111
Eastwick Rd. Walt. BC57 92
Eastwick Rd. Ware. CK9 6
Eastwick Row, Hem. H. AZ14 8
Eastwood Clo. E18 CH30 40
Viaduct, The.
Eastwood Dr. Rain. CU39 59
Eastwood Est. SW15 BP46 75
Eastwood Rd. E18 CH30 40
Eastwood Rd. N10 BV30 38
Eastwood Rd. Ilf. CO33 50
East Wood Side, Bex. CQ47 79
Eastwood St. SW16 BW50 76
Eastworth Rd. Cher. AW54 83
Eatington Rd. E10 CF32 48
Eaton Clo. SW1 BV42 66
Eaton Clo. Stan. BJ28 36
Eaton Ct. Guil. AT69 118
Eaton Dr. Kings. On T. BM50 75
Eaton Dr. Rom. CR29 41
Eaton Gte. SW1 BV42 66
Eaton Gate. Nthwd. BA29 35
Eaton La. SW1 BV41 66
Eaton Ms. N. SW1 BV41 66
Eaton Ms. Sth. SW1 BV42 66
Eaton Ms. W. SW1 BV42 66
Eaton Pk. Cob. BE60 93
Eaton Pk. Rd. N13 BY27 38
Eaton Pk. Rd. Cob. BE60 93
Eaton Pl. SW1 BV41 66
Eaton Rise W5 BK39 54
Eaton Rd. E11 CJ32 49
Eaton Rd. NW4 BQ32 46
Eaton Rd. SW9 BY45 66
Eaton Rd. Enf. CA24 30
Eaton Rd. Hem. H. AZ12 8
Eaton Rd. Houns. BG45 64
Eaton Rd. St. Alb. BJ13 9
Eaton Rd. Sid. CP48 79
Eaton Rd. Sutt. BT57 95
Eaton Row SW1 BV41 66
Eatons Mead E4 CE27 39
Eaton Sq. SW1 BV42 66
Eaton Ter. SW1 BV42 66
Eaton Ter. Ms. SW1 BV42 66
Eaton Ter.
Eatonville Rd. SW17 BU48 76
Eatonville Vills. SW17 BU48 76
Eatonville Rd.
Eaton Walk SE15 CA44 67
Sumner Estate
Eator. Welw. G. C. BS6 5
Ebbas Way, Epsom. BM61 103
Ebberns Rd. Hem. H. AY15 8
Ebbisham Clo. Dor. BJ71 119
Ebbisham Dr. SW8 BX43 66
Ebbisham La. Tad. BP64 103
Ebbisham Rd. Epsom. BM60 94
Ebbisham Rd. Epsom. BM61 103
Ebbisham Rd. Epsom BN60 94
Ebbisham Rd. Wor. Pk. BQ55 85
Ebbsfleet Rd. NW2 BR35 46
Ebdon Way, SE3 CH45 68
Ebenezer Rd. NW2 BS34 47
Ebenezer St. N1 BZ38 57
Ebenezer Wk. SW16 BW51 86
Ebner St. SW18 BS46 76
Ebor St. E1 CA38 57
Ebrington Rd. Har. BK32 45
Ebsworth St. SE23 CC47 77
Eburne Rd. N7 BX34 47
Ebury App. Rick. AX26 35
Ebury Rd.
Ebury Br. SW1 BV42 66
Ebury Br. Est. SW1 BV42 66
Ebury Br. Rd. SW1 BV42 66
Ebury Clo. Kes. CK55 88
Ebury Clo. Nthwd. BA28 35
Ebury Ms. SW1 BV42 66
Ebury Rd. Rick. AX26 35
Ebury Rd. Wat. BD24 27
Ebury Sq. SW1 BV42 66
Ebury St. SW1 BV42 66
Ecclesbourne Clo. N13 BX28 38
Cranford Av.
Ecclesbourne Gdns. N13 BY28 38
Ecclesbourne Rd. N1 BZ36 57
Ecclesbourne Rd. Th. Hth. BZ53 87
Eccles Clo. N13 BY28 38
Ecclesbourne Gdns.
Eccles Hill, Dor. BK73 119
Eccles Rd. SW11 BU45 66
Eccleston Br. SW1 BV42 66
Eccleston Clo. Orp. CM54 88
Eccleston Cres. Rom. CO33 50
Ecclestone Ct. Wem. BL35 46
Ecclestone Ms. Wem. BL35 46
Eccleston Ms. SW1 BV41 66
Eccleston Pl. SW1 BV42 66
Eccleston Pl. Wem. BL35 46
Eccleston Rd. W13 BJ40 54
Eccleston Sq. SW1 BV42 66
Eccleston Sq. Ms. SW1 BW42 66
Warwick Pl. N.
Eccleston St. SW1 BV41 66
Echo Heights E4 CE26 39
Echo Pit Rd. Guil. AS72 118
Echo Sq. Grav. DH48 81
Eckersley St. E1 CA38 57
Eckford St. N1 BY37 56
Wynford Rd.
Eckington Gdns. SE14 CC43 67
Eckstein Rd. SW11 BU45 66
Eclipse Rd. E13 CH39 58
Ecton Rd. Wey. AW56 92
Ector Rd. SE6 CG48 78
Edale Rd. SE16 CC42 67
Edbrooke Rd. W9 BS38 56
Eddington St. N4 BY33 47
Everleigh St.
Eddiscombe Rd. SW6 BR44 65
Eddy Clo. Rom. CR32 50
Eddystone Rd. SE4 CD46 77
Eddystone Wk. Stai. AY47 73
Clare Rd.
Eddy St. Berk. AQ12 7
Edenbridge Clo. Orp. CP52 89
Edenbridge Rd. E9 CC36 57
Edenbridge Rd. Enf. CA25 30
Eden Clo. Bex. CS49 79
Eden Clo. Slou. AT42 62
Eden Clo. Wem. BK37 54
Eden Clo. Wey. AW58 92
Eden Court, W5 BL39 55
Station Rd.
Edencourt Rd. SW16 BV50 76
Edendale, W3 BM40 55
Julian Av.
Edendale Rd. Bexh. CS44 69
Edenfield Gdns. Wor. Pk. BO55 85
Eden Grn. E17 CE32 48
Eden Grn. S. Ock. DA39 60
Eden Gro. N7 BX35 47
Eden Grove Rd. Wey. AY60 92

Edenhall Rd. Rom. CV28 42
Edenhurst Av. SW6 BR45 65
Eden Pk. Av. Beck. CD52 87
Eden Pk. Av. Beck. CE53 87
Eden Rd. E17 CE32 48
Eden Rd. SE27 BY49 76
Eden Rd. Beck. CD52 87
Eden Rd. Bex. CS49 79
Eden Rd. Croy. BZ56 96
Edenside Rd. Lthd. BE65 102
Edensor Gdns. W4 BO43 65
Edensor Rd. W4 BO43 65
Eden St. Kings. On T. BL51 85
Edenvale Rd. Mitch. BV50 76
Edenvale St. SW6 BS44 66
Eden Way Beck. CD53 87
Eden Way. Warl. CD62 105
Ederline Av. SW16 BX52 86
Edgar Clo. Swan. CT52 89
Edgarley Ter. SW6 BR44 65
Edgar Rd. E3 CE38 57
Edgar Rd. Houns. BE47 74
Edgar Rd. Rom. CP33 50
Edgar Rd. Sev. CW62 108
Edgar Rd. Sth. Croy. BZ58 96
Edgar Rd. West. CJ64 106
Edgar Rd. West Dr. AY40 53
Edgars Ct. Welw. G. C. BR8 5
Edgbaston Rd. Wat. BC27 35
Edgebury, Chis. CL49 78
Edgebury Est. Chis. CM49 78
Edgebury Wk. Chis. CM49 78
Edge Clo. Wey. AZ57 92
Edgecombe Clo. King. On T. BN50 75
Edgecombe Rd. E11 CG33 49
Harvey Rd.
Edgecoombe Sth. Croy. CC57 96
Edgecot Gro. N15 CA32 48
Edgefield Av. Bark. CN36 58
Edgefield Clo. Dart. CX47 80
Edge Field Clo. Red. BV73 121
Edge Hill, SE18 CL43 68
Edge Hill, SW19 BQ50 75
Edge Hill Av. N3 BS31 47
Edge Hill Ct. SW19 BQ50 75
Edgehill Gdns. Dag. CR35 50
Edgehill Gdns. Grav. DF51 81
Edgehill Rd. W13 BJ39 54
Edgehill Rd. Chis. CM48 78
Edgehill Rd. Mitch. BV51 86
Edgehill Rd. Pur. BY58 95
Edgeley, Lthd. BE65 102
Edgeley Rd. SW4 BW45 66
Edgell Clo. Vir. W. AS52 82
Edgell Rd. Stai AV49 72
Edgel St. SW18 BS45 66
Ferrier St.
Edgepoint Clo. SE27 BY49 76
Knight's Hill
Edge St. W8 BS40 56
Edgewood Dr. Orp. CN56 97
Edgewood Grn. Croy. CC54 87
Edgeworth Av. NW4 BP32 46
Edgeworth Av. Barn. BU24 29
Edgeworth Clo. NW4 BP32 46
Edgeworth Cres. NW4 BP32 46
Edgeworth Rd. SE9 CJ45 68
Edgington Rd. SW16 BW50 76
Edgwarebury Gdns. Edg. BM28 37
Edgwarebury La. Borwd. BL26 37
Edgwarebury La. Edg. BM28 37
Edgware Ct. Edg. BM29 37
Edgware Rd. NW2 BP33 46
Edgware Rd. NW9 BN30 37
Edgware Rd. W2 BT38 56
Edgware Way Edg. BK26 36
Edinar Gdns. Wind. AO44 61
Edinburgh Av. Rick. AW25 26
Edinburgh Clo. Uxb. AZ35 44
Edinburgh Ct. SW20 BQ53 85
Edinburgh Cres. Wal. Cr. CD20 21
Edinburgh Dr. Stai. AX50 73
Edinburgh Dr. Uxb. AZ35 44
Edinburgh Gte. SW1 BU41 66
Edinburgh Pl. Harl. CO9 6
Edinburgh Rd. E13 CH37 58
Edinburgh Rd. E17 CD32 48
Edinburgh Rd. N18 CB28 39
Edinburgh Rd. W7 BH41 64
Edinburgh Rd. Sutt. BT55 86
Edinburgh Way, Harl. CN9 6
Edington Rd. SE2 CO41 69
Edington Rd. Enf. CC23 30
Edison Av. Horn. CT33 50
Edison Clo. Horn. CT33 50
Edison Dr. Sthl. BF39 54
Edison Gro. SE18 CN43 68
Edison Rd. N8 BW32 47
Edison Rd. Brom. CH51 88
Church Rd.
Edison Rd. Well. CN44 68
Edis St. NW1 BV37 56
Edith Dr. N11 BW29 38
Edith Gdns. Surb. BM54 85
Edith Gro. SW10 BT43 66
Edith Ms. SW6 BS44 66
Edith Row
Edithna St. SW9 BX45 66
Edith Rd. E6 CJ36 58
Edith Rd. E15 CF35 48
Edith Rd. SE25 BZ53 87
Edith Rd. SW19 BS50 76
Edith Rd. W14 BR42 65
Edith Rd. Orp. CO56 98
Edith Rd. Rom. CP33 50
Edith Row SW6 BS44 66
Edith's Rd. Sev. CX62 108
Edith Ter. SW10 BT43 66
Edith Vill. W14 BR42 65
Edlyn Clo. Berk. AP12 7
Edmondscote W13 BJ39 54
Cleveland Rd.
Edmund Rd. Mitch. BU52 86
Edmund Rd. Orp. CP53 89
Edmund Rd. Rain. CT38 59
Edmund Rd. Well. CO45 69
Edmunds Av. Orp. CP52 89
Edmunds Clo. Hayes BD39 54
Edmunds Plover Clo. Berk. AR13 7
Edmund St. SE5 BZ43 67
Edmunds Wk. N2 BU31 47
Edmund Way, Slou. AQ39 52
Edna Rd. SW20 BQ51 85
Edna St. SW11 BU44 66
Edrick Rd. Edg. BN29 37
Edrick Wk. Edg. BN29 37
Edric Rd. SE14 CC43 67
Edridge Clo. Bush. BG25 27
Edridge Clo. Horn. CV35 51
Edridge Rd. Croy. BZ55 87
Edulf Rd. Borwd. BM23 28
Edward Av. E4 CE29 39
Edward Av. Mord. BT53 86
Edward Clo. N9 CA26 39
Edward Clo. Barn. BT25 29
Edward Clo. Hamptn. BG49 74
Edward Clo. Nthlt. BD37 54
Edward Clo. Rom. CV31 51
Edward Clo. St. Alb. BH14 9
Edward Ct. E16 CH39 58
Alexandra St.
Edwardes Sq. W8 BR41 65
Edward ii Av. Wey. AY60 92
Edward Pl. SE8 CD43 67
Edward Rd. E17 CC31 48
Edward Rd. SE20 CC50 77
Edward Rd. Barn. BT24 29
Edward Rd. Belv. CR42 69
Edward Rd. Brom. CH50 78
Edward Rd. Chis. CL49 78
Edward Rd. Couls. BW61 104
Edward Rd. Croy. CA54 87
Edward Rd. Felt. BA46 73
Edward Rd. Har. BG31 45
Edward Rd. Hmptn. BG49 74
Edward Rd. Nthlt. BD37 54
Edward Rd. Rom. CQ32 50
Edward Rd. West. CK62 106
Edwards Av. Ruis. BC36 53
Edwards Clo. Brwd. DF25 122
Edwards Clo. Wor. Pk. BQ55 85
Edwards Gdns. Swan. CS52 89
Edward's La. N16 BZ34 48
Edward Sq. Wind. AO44 61
Edwards Ter. Ong. CY19 24
Edward St. E16 CH38 58
Edward St. SE8 CD43 67
Edward St. SE14 CD43 67
Edwards Way, Brwd. DF25 122
Edward Way, Ashf. AY48 73
Edwina Gdns. Ilf. CK32 49
Edwin Av. E6 CL38 58
Edwin Clo. Bexh. CQ43 69
Edwin Clo. Rain. CT38 59
Edwin Rd. Dart. CU48 79
Edwin Rd. Edg. BN29 37
Edwin Road. Leath. BA66 110
Edwin Rd. Twick. BH47 74
Edwin St. E1 CC38 57
Edwin St. E16 CG39 58
Edwin St. Grav. DG47 81
Edwyn Clo. Barn. BQ25 28
Effie Pl. SW6 BS43 66
Effie Rd. SW6 BS43 66
Effingham Clo. Sutt. BS57 95
Effingham Ct. Wok. AS62 100
Constitution Hill
Effingham Rd. N8 BY32 47
Effingham Rd. SE12 CG46 78
Effingham Rd. Croy. BX54 86
Effingham Rd. Reig. BS71 121
Effingham Rd. Surb. BJ54 84
Effort St. SW17 BU49 76
Effra Clo. SW19 BS50 76
Effra Pde. SW2 BY46 76
Effra Rd. SW2 BY45 66
Effra Rd. SW19 BS50 76
Egan Way SE16 CB42 67
Bonamy Estate East The
Egbert St. NW1 BV36 56
Egerton Av. Swan. CT50 79
Egerton Clo. Dart. CU47 79
Egerton Clo. Pnr. BC31 44
Egerton Ct. E11 CF33 48
Egerton Cres. SW3 BU42 66
Egerton Dr. SE10 CE44 67
Egerton Gdns. NW4 BP31 46
Egerton Gdns. NW10 BQ37 55
Egerton Gdns. SW3 BU41 66
Egerton Gdns. W13 BJ39 54
Egerton Gdns. Ilf. CN34 49
Egerton Gdns. Ms. SW3 BU41 66
Egerton Ms. SW3 BU41 66
Egerton Pl. SW3 BU41 66
Egerton Pl. Wey. BA57 92
Egerton Rd. N16 CA33 48
Egerton Rd. SE25 CA52 87
Egerton Rd. Berk. AQ12 7
Egerton Rd. Guil. AP70 118
Egerton Rd. N. Mal. BO52 85
Egerton Rd. Twick. BH46 74
Egerton Rd. Wem. BL36 55
Egerton Rd. Wey. BA57 92
Egerton Ter. SW3 BU41 66
Eggpie La. Sev. & Ton. CV70 117
Egham By-pass, Egh. AS49 72
Egham Clo. Sutt. BR55 85
Egham Cres. Sutt. BQ55 85
Egham Hill, Egh. AR50 72
Egham Rd. E13 CH39 58
Eglantine La. Hort. K. CX54 90
Eglantine Rd. SW18 BT46 76
Egleston Rd. Mord. BS53 86
Egley Dr. Wok. AR64 100
Egley Rd. Wok. AR64 100
Eglington Ct. SE17 BZ43 67
Carter St.
Eglington Rd. E4 CF26 39
Eglington Rd. Swans. DC46 81
Eglinton Hill, SE18 CL43 68
Eglinton Rd. SE18 CL43 68
Eglise Rd. Warl. CD62 105
Egliston Ms. SW15 BQ45 65
Egliston Rd. SW15 BQ45 65
Egmont Av. Surb. BL54 85
Egmont Park Rd. Tad. BP66 112
Egmont Rd. N. Mal. BO52 85
Egmont Rd. Surb. BL54 85
Egmont Rd. Sutt. BT57 95
Egmont St. SE14 CC43 67
Egmont Way, Tad. BR63 103
Egremont Rd. SE27 BY48 76
Eider St. SE17 BZ42 67
Rodney Rd.
Eighth Av. E12 CK35 49
Eighth Av. Hayes BC40 53
Eileen Rd. SE25 BZ53 87
Eisenhower Dr. E6 CK39 58
Elaine Gro. NW5 BV35 47
Eland Rd. SW11 BU45 66
Eland Rd. Croy. BY55 86
Elan Rd. S. Ock. DA39 60
Elba Pl. SE17 BZ42 67
Rodney Rd.
Elberon Av. Croy. BW53 86
Elbe St. SW6 BT44 66
Elborough Rd. SE25 CB53 87
Elborough St. SW18 BS47 76
Elbury Dr. E16 CH39 58
Elcho St. SW11 BU43 66
Elcom St. W10 BR39 55
Kensal Rd.
Elcot Av. SE15 CB43 67
Elder Av. N8 BX32 47
Elderberry Rd. W5 BL41 65
Elder Ct. Bush. BH27 36
Elderfield Rd. E5 CC35 48
Elderfield Rd. Slou. AP36 52
Elderfield Wk. E11 CH32 49
Elder Oak Clo. SE20 CB51 87
Elder Rd. SE27 BZ49 77
Eldersley Clo. Red. BU69 121
Elderslie Clo. Beck. CE53 87
Elderslie Rd. SE9 CL46 78
Elder St. E1 CA39 57
Elderton Rd. SE26 CD49 77
Eldertree Pl. Mitch. BV51 86
Eldertree Way, Mitch. BV51 86
Elder Way. Rain. CV38 60
Eldon Av. Borwd. BM23 28
Eldon Av. Croy. CC55 87
Eldon Av. Houns. BF43 64
Eldon Gro. NW3 BT35 47
Eldon Pk. SE25 CB52 87
Eldon Rd. E17 CD32 48
Eldon Rd. N9 CC27 39
Eldon Rd. N22 BY30 38
Eldon Rd. NW3 BT35 47
Eldon Rd. W8 BS41 66
Eldon Rd. Cat. BZ64 105
Eldon Rd. Hodd. CF13 12
Eldon Way NW10 BM37 55
Eldon Way, SW19 BS51 86
Eldred Dr. Orp. CP54 89
Eldred Gdns. Upmin. CZ33 51
Eldred Rd. Bark. CM37 58
Eldridge Clo. Horn. CV35 51
Eleanor Av. Epsom BN58 94
Eleanor Av. St. Alb. BG12 9
Eleanor Cres. NW7 BQ28 37
Eleanor Cross Rd. Wal. Cr. CD20 21
Eleanor Gdns. Dag. CQ34 50
Eleanor Gro. SW13 BO45 65
Eleanor Rd. E8 CB36 57
Eleanor Rd. E15 CG36 58
Eleanor Rd. N11 BX29 38
Eleanor Rd. Ger. Cr. AR30 34
Eleanor Rd. Wal. Cr. CD20 21
Eleanor St. E3 CE38 57
Eleanor Way, Brwd. DB28 42
Eleanor Way, Wal. Cr. CD20 21
Electric Av. SW9 BY45 66
Electric La. SW9 BY45 66
Electric Pde. Surb. BK53 84
Elephant & Castle SE1 BY42 66
Elephant La. SE16 CC41 67
Rotherhithe St.
Elephant Rd. SE17 BZ42 67
Elers Rd. Hayes. BA42 63
Eleven Acre Rise Loug. CK24 31
Eley Rd. N18 CC28 39
Eleys Est. N18 CC28 39
Elfindale Rd. SE24 BZ46 77
Elfin Gro. Tedd. BH49 74
Elfin Rd. SE5 BY43 66
Warrior Rd.
Elford Clo. SE3 CJ45 68
Elfort Rd. N5 BY34 47
Elfrida Cres. SE6 CE49 77
Elfrida Rd. Wat. BD25 27
Elf Row, E1 CC40 57
Elfwine Rd. W7 BH39 54
Elgal Clo. Orp. CL56 97
Elgar Av. SW16 BX52 86
Elgar Av. W5 BL41 65
Elgar Av. Surb. BM54 85
Elgar Clo. Borwd. BK26 36
Elgar Clo. Uxb. AZ34 44
Elgar Gdns. Til. DG44 71
Elgar St. SE16 CD41 67
Elgin Av. W9 BS38 56
Elgin Av. Ashf. BA50 73
Elgin Av. Har. BJ30 36
Elgin Av. Rom. CX29 42
Elgin Clo. Nthwd. BB29 35
Elgin Cres. W11 BR41 65
Elgin Cres. Cat. CB64 105
Elgin Ms. W11 BR39 55
Elgin Ms. N. W9 BS38 56
Elgin Ms. S. W9 BS38 56
Elgin Rd. N22 BW30 38
Elgin Rd. Brox. CD15 12
Elgin Rd. Croy. CA55 87
Elgin Rd. Ilf. CN33 49
Elgin Rd. Sutt. BT55 86
Elgin Rd. Wal. Cr. CC18 21
Elgin Rd. Wall. BW57 95
Elgin Rd. Wey. AZ56 92
Elgin Ter. W11 BR40 55
Elgood Ave. Nthwd. BB29 35
Elias Pl. SW8 BY43 66
Elia St. N1 BY37 56
Elibank Rd. SE9 CK45 68
Elim Est. SE1 CA41 67
Elim Way, E13 CG38 58
Eliot Bank, SE23 CB48 77
Eliot Cotts. SE3 CG44 68
Eliot Dr. Har. BF34 45
Eliot Hill, SE13 CF44 67
Eliot Pk. SE13 CF44 67
Eliot Pl. SE3 CG44 68
Eliot Rd. Dag. CP35 50
Eliot Rd. Dart. CX46 80
Eliot Vale, SE3 CF44 67
Elizabethan Clo. Stai. AX47 73
Elizabethan Way, Stai. AX47 73
Elizabeth Ave. Amer. AQ23 25
Elizabeth Av. N1 BZ37 57
Elizabeth Av. Enf. DY24 20
Elizabeth Av. Ilf. CM34 49
Elizabeth Av. Stai. AX50 73
Elizabeth Br. SW1 BV42 66
Elizabeth Cl. Barn. BQ24 28
Elizabeth Clo. E14 CE39 57
Grundy St.
Elizabeth Clo. W9 BT38 56
Randolph Av.
Elizabeth Clo. Rom. CR30 41
Elizabeth Clyde Cl. N15 CA31 48
Lawrence Rd.
Elizabeth Clyde Clo. N15 CA31 48
Lawrence Road
Elizabeth Cotts. Rich. BL44 65
Elizabeth Ct. Mord. BR54 85
Elizabeth Ct. Wat. BB22 26
Elizabeth Dr. Epp. CN21 31
Elizabeth Est. SE17 BZ43 67
Elizabeth Gdns. W3 BN40 55
Elizabeth Gdns. Sun. BC52 83
Elizabeth Ms. NW3 BU36 56
Elizabeth Pl. N15 CA31 48
Elizabeth Pl. Til. DG45 71
Elizabeth Ride N9 CB26 39
Elizabeth Rd. E6 CJ37 58
Elizabeth Rd. N15 CA32 48
Elizabeth Rd. Brwd. DA23 33
Elizabeth St. SW1 BV42 66
Elizabeth St. Green. CZ46 80
Elizabeth Ter. SE9 CK46 78
Elizabeth Way Felt. BD49 74
Elizabeth Way, Harl. CK11 13
Elizabeth Way, Harl. CM9 6
Elizabeth Way Orp. CP53 89
Elizabeth Way, Slou. AP37 52
Elkington Rd. E13 CH38 58
Elkins, The Rom. CT30 41
Elkstone Rd. W10 BR39 55
Ellaline Rd. W6 BQ43 65
Ellanby Cres. N18 CB28 39
Elland Rd. SE15 CC45 67
Ellanor Gro. Uxb. AZ34 44
Ella Rd. N8 BX33 47
Ellement Clo. Pnr. BD32 45
Ellenborough Rd. N22 BY30 38
Ellenborough Rd. Sid. CP50 79
Ellenbridge Way Sth. Croy. CA58 96
Ellenbrook La. Hat. BN12 10
Ellen Clo. Brom. CJ52 88
Ellen Ct. N9 CC27 39
Densworth Gro.
Ellen St. E1 CB39 57
Elleray Rd. Tedd. BH50 74
Ellerby St. SW6 BQ44 65
Ellerdale Clo. NW3 BT35 47
Ellerdale Rd. NW3 BT35 47
Ellerdale St. SE13 CE45 67
Ellerdine Rd. Houns. BG45 64
Ellerker Gdns. Rich. BL46 75
Ellerman Av. Twick. BE47 74
Ellerman Rd. Til. DF44 71
Broadway
Ellerslie Rd. W12 BP40 55
Ellerslie Sq. SW4 BX46 76
Ellers Rd. W13 BK41 64
Ellerton Gdns. Dag. CP36 59
Ellerton Rd. SW13 BP44 65
Ellerton Rd. SW18 BT47 76
Ellerton Rd. SW20 BP50 75
Ellerton Rd. Dag. CP36 59
Ellerton Rd. Surb. BL55 85
Ellery St. SE15 CB44 67
Elles Av. Guil. AU70 118
Ellesborough Clo. Way. BD28 36
Ellesmere Av. NW7 BN27 37
Ellesmere Av. Beck. CE51 87
Ellesmere Clo. E11 CG32 49
Ellesmere Clo. Ruis. BA33 44
Ellesmere Ct. W4 BN42 65
Great W. Rd.
Ellesmere Dri. Sth. Croy. CB60 96
Ellesmere Gdns. Ilf. CK32 49
Ellesmere Gro. Barn. BR25 28
Ellesmere Rd. E3 CD37 57
Ellesmere Rd. NW10 BP35 46
Ellesmere Rd. W4 BN43 65
Ellesmere Rd. Berk. AR13 7
Ellesmere Rd. Grnf. BG38 54
Ellesmere Rd. Twick. BK46 74
Ellesmere Rd. Wey. BA57 92
Ellesmere St. E14 CE39 57
Ellias St. E1 CD39 57
Elliman Av. Slou. AP40 52
Ellingfort Rd. E8 CB36 57
Ellingham Clo. Hem. H. AZ12 8
Ellingham Rd. E15 CF35 48
Ellingham Rd. W12 BP41 65
Ellingham Rd. Chess. BK57 93
Ellingham Rd. Hem. H. AY13 8
Ellington Rd. N10 BV31 47
Ellington Rd. Felt. BB49 73
Ellington Rd. Houns. BF44 64
Ellington St. N7 BY36 56
Elliot Gdns. Rom. CU30 41
Elliot Gdns. Shep. AZ52 83
Elliot Rd. NW4 BP32 46
Elliot Rd. Stan. BJ29 36
Elliott Rd. SW9 BY43 66
Elliott Rd. W4 BO42 65
Elliott Rd. Brom. CJ52 88
Elliott Rd. Th. Hth. BY52 86
Elliotts Ct. EC4 BY39 56
Old Bailey
Elliotts Pl. N1 BY37 56
St. Peters St.
Elliotts Row, SE11 BY42 66
Elliott St. Grav. DH47 81
Ellis Ave. Ger. Cr. AS30 34
Ellis Ave. Slou. AR41 62
Ellis Av. Guil. AP71 118
Ellis Av. Rain. CU39 59
Ellis Clo. SE9 CM48 78
Elliscombe Rd. SE7 CJ42 68
Ellis David Rd. Croy. BY55 86
Ellis Farm Clo. Wok. AR64 100
Ellisfield Dri. SW15 BP47 75
Ellis Ms. SE7 CJ43 68
Ellison Dr. Wind. AM45 61
Ellison Rd. SW13 BO44 65
Ellison Rd. SW16 BW50 76
Ellison Rd. Sid. CM47 78
Ellis Rd. Couls. BX63 104
Ellis Rd. Mitch. BU53 86
Ellis St. SW1 BU42 66
Ellmore Clo. Rom. CU30 41
Ellora Rd. SW16 BW49 76
Ellsworth St. E2 CB38 57
Ellwood Gdns. Wat. BC20 17
Ellwood Gdns. Wat. BD21 27
Ellwood Ri. Ch. St. G. AR27 34
Elmar Rd. N15 BZ31 48
Elm Av. W5 BL40 55
Elm Av. Ruis. BC33 44
Elm Av. Upmin. CX35 51
Elm Av. Wat. BE26 36
Elm Bank N14 BX26 38
Elmbank Av. Barn. BQ24 28
Elmbank Av. Egh. AQ50 72
Elm Bank, Av. Guil. AQ71 118
Elm Bank Gdns. SW13 BO44 65
Elmbank Way W7 BG39 54
Elmbourne Rd. SW17 BV48 76
Elmbridge Av. Surb. BM53 85
Elmbridge Clo. Ruis. BC32 44
Elmbridge Dr. Ruis. BB32 44
Elmbridge Dr. Ruis. BC32 44
Elmbridge Rd. Ilf. CO29 41
Elmbridge Wk. E8 CB36 57
Wilman Gro.
Elmbrook Gdns. SE9 CK45 68
Elmbrook Rd. Sutt. BR56 94
Elm Clo. E11 CH32 49
Elm Clo. NW4 BQ32 46
Elm Clo. SW20 BQ52 85
Elm Clo. Amer. AO22 25
Elm Clo. Buck. H. CJ27 40
Elm Clo. Cars. BU54 86
Elm Clo. Dart. CV47 80
Elm Clo. Epp. CL15 13
Elm Clo. Har. BF32 45
Elm Clo. Hayes BC39 53
Elm Clo. Lthd. BJ64 102
Elm Clo. Rom. CR30 41
Elm Clo. Sth. Croy. BZ57 96
Elm Clo. Surb. BN54 85
Elm Clo. Twick. BF48 74
Elm Clo. Wal. Abb. CF20 21
Elm Clo. Warl. CC62 105
Elm Clo. Wok. AR61 100
Elm Clo. Wok. AW65 101
Elmcote, Rick. AY25 26
Elm Ct. Mitch. BU51 86
Elmcourt Rd. SE27 BY48 76
Elm Cres. W5 BL40 55
Elm Cres. Kings. On T. BL51 85
Elm Croft. Slou. AR44 62
Elmcroft Av. E11 CH32 49
Elmcroft Av. N9 CB25 30
Elmcroft Av. NW11 BR33 46
Elmcroft Av. Sid. CN46 78
Elmcroft Clo. E11 CH31 49
Elmcroft Clo. W5 BK39 54
Elmcroft Clo. Chess. BL55 85
Elmcroft Clo. Felt. BB46 73
Elmcroft Cres. NW11 BQ33 46
Elmcroft Cres. Har. BF31 45
Elm Croft Dr. Ashf. AZ49 73
Elmcroft Dr. Chess. BL55 85
Elmcroft Gdns. NW9 BM32 46
Elmcroft Rd. Orp. CO54 89
Elmcroft St. E5 CC35 48
Elmdale Rd. N13 BX28 38
Elmdene Surb. BN54 85
Elmdene Av. Horn. CW32 51
Elmdene Clo. Beck. CD53 87
Elmdene Est. Beck. CD53 87
Elmdene Rd. SE18 CL42 68
Elmdon Rd. Houns. BB44 63
Elmdon Rd. Houns. BE44 64
Elm Dri. Wok. AP58 91
Elm Dr. Har. BF32 45

Elm Dr. Hat. BP13 10
Elm Dr. Lthd. BJ64 102
Elm Dr. St. Alb. BK13 9
Elm Dr. Sun. BD51 84
Elm Dr. Swan. CS51 89
Elm Dr. Wal. Cr. CD17 21
Elmer Av. Hav. CT27 41
Elmer Clo. Enf. BX24 29
Elmer Clo. Rain. CU36 59
Elmer Cotts. Lthd. BJ64 102
Elmer Gdns. Edg. BM29 37
Elmer Gdns. Islw. BG45 64
Elmer Gdns. Rain. CU36 59
Elmer Rd. SE6 CF47 77
Elmers Dr. Tedd. BJ50 74
Elmers End Rd. SE20 CC51 87
Elmers End Rd. Beck. CC51 87
Elmerside Rd. Beck. CD52 87
Elmers Rd. SE25 CB54 87
Elm Field, Lthd. BF65 102
Elmfield Av. N8 BX32 47
Elmfield Av. Mitch. BV51 86
Elmfield Av. Tedd. BH49 74
Elmfield Clo. Grav. DG47 81
Elmfield Clo. Pot. B. BR20 19
Elmfield Pk. Brom. CH52 88
Elmfield Rd. E4 CF27 39
Elmfield Rd. E17 CC32 48
Elmfield Rd. N2 BT31 47
Elmfield Rd. SW17 BV48 76
Elmfield Rd. Brom. CH51 88
Elmfield Rd. Pot. B. BR20 19
Elmfield Rd. Sthl. BE41 64
Elmfield Way Sth. Croy. CA58 96
Elm Gdns. N2 BT31 47
Elm Gdns. Enf. BZ22 30
Elm Gdns. Epp. CR16 23
Elm Gdns. Epsom. BQ63 103
Elm Gdns. Esher BH57 93
Elm Gdns. Mitch. BW52 86
Elm Gdns. Welw. G. C. BP8 5
Elmgate Av. Felt. BC48 73
Elmgate Gdns. Edg. BN28 37
Elm Grn. W3 BO39 55
Elm Grn. Hem. H. AV12 7
Elm Gro. N18 BX32 47
Elm Gro. NW2 BQ35 46
Elm Gro. SE15 CA44 67
Elm Gro. SW19 BR50 75
Elm Gro. Berk. AR13 7
Elm Gro. Cat. CA64 105
Elm Gro. Epsom BN60 94
Elm Gro. Erith CS43 69
Elm Gro. Har. BF33 45
Elm Gro. Horn. CW32 51
Elm Gro. Kings. On T. BL51 85
Elm Gro. Orp. CN54 88
Elm Gro. Sutt. BS56 95
Elm Gro. Wat. BC22 26
Elm Gro. Wdf. Grn. CG28 40
Elm Gro. West Dr. AY40 53
Elm Grove Clo. Wok. AO63 100
Elmgrove Cres. Har. BH32 45
Elmgrove Gdns. Har. BJ32 45
Elmgrove Pde. Wall. BV55 86
Elm Grove Rd. SW13 BP44 65
Elmgrove Rd. W5 BL41 65
Elmgrove Rd. Cob. BD61 102
Elmgrove Rd. Croy. CB54 87
Elmgrove Rd. Har. BH32 45
Elmgrove Rd. Wey. AZ55 83
Elmhall Gdns. E11 CH32 49
Elmhurst, Belv. CQ43 69
Elmhurst Av. N2 BT31 47
Elmhurst Av. Mitch. BV50 76
Elmhurst Dr. E18 CH30 40
Elmhurst Dr. Dor. BJ72 119
Elmhurst Dr. Horn. CV33 51
Elmhurst Gdns. E18 CH30 40
Elmhurst Rd. N17 CA30 39
Elmhurst Rd. SE9 CK48 78
Elmhurst Rd. Enf. CC22 30
Elmhurst Rd. Slou. AT41 62
Elmhurst St. SW4 BW45 66
Elmhurst Way Loug. CK26 40
Elmington Clo. Bex. CR46 79
Elmington Est. SE5 BZ43 67
Elmington Rd. SE5 BZ44 67
Elmira St. SE13 CE45 67
Elm La. SE6 CD48 77
Elm Lawn Clo. Uxb. AY36 53
Elmlee Clo. Chis. CK50 78
Elmley St. SE18 CM42 68
Elm Ms. W2 BT41 66
Elm Nursery Est. Mitch. BV51 86
Elmore Rd. E11 CF34 48
Elmore Rd. Couls. BU64 104
Elmore Rd. Enf. CC22 30
Elmores Loug. CL24 31
Elmore St. N1 BZ36 57
Elm Park, SW2 BX46 76
Elm Park, Stan. BJ28 36
Elm Pk. Av. N13 CA32 48
Elm Pk. Av. Horn. CU35 50
Elm Pk. Ct. Pnr. BD31 45
Elm Pk. Gdns. NW4 BQ32 46
Elm Pk. Gdns. SW10 BT42 66
Elm Pk. Gdns. W3 BN39 55
Noel Rd.
Elm Pk. Gdns. Sth. Croy. CC58 96
Elm Pk. La. SW3 BT42 66
Elm Pk. Mans. SW10 BT43 66
Elm Pk. Pde. W3 BN39 55
Noel Rd.
Elm Pk. Rd. E10 CD33 48
Elm Pk. Rd. N3 BR29 37
Elm Pk. Rd. N21 BZ26 39
Elm Pk. Rd. SE25 CA52 87
Elm Pk. Rd. SW3 BT43 66
Elm Pk. Rd. Pnr. BD30 36
Elm Pl. SW7 BT42 66
Elm Ridge La. Wok. AS63 100
Elm Rd. E7 CG36 58
Elm Rd. E11 CF34 48
Elm Rd. E17 CF32 48
Elm Rd. N22 BY30 38
Elm Rd. SW14 BO45 65
Elm Rd. Barn. BR24 28
Elm Rd. Beck. CD51 87
Elm Rd. Chess. BK56 93
Elm Rd. Dart. CV47 80
Elm Rd. Epsom BO57 94
Elm Rd. Erith. CU44 69
Elm Rd. Esher BH57 93
Elm Rd. Felt. BA47 73
Elm Rd. Grav. DH48 81
Elm Rd. Grays. DE43 71
Elm Rd. Green. CZ46 80
Elm Rd. Hodd. CE12 12
Elm Rd. Houns. BE44 64
Elm Rd. Lthd. BJ64 102
Elm Rd. N. Mal. BN52 85
Elm Rd. Orp. CO57 98
Elm Rd. Pur. BY60 95
Elm Rd. Red. BU70 121
Elm Rd. Rom. CR30 41
Elm Rd. Sid. CO49 79
Elm Rd. S. Ock. CW40 60
Elm Rd. Th. Hth. BZ52 87
Elm Rd. Wall. BV54 86
Elm Rd. Warl. CC62 105
Elm Rd. Wem. BL35 46
Elm Rd. West. CM66 115
Elm Rd. Wind. AN45 61
Elm Rd. Wok. AR62 100
Elm Rd. Wok. AS61 100
Elm Rd. W. Sutt. BR54 85
Elm Row NW3 BT34 47
Elmroyd Av. Pot. B. BR20 19
Elmroyd Clo. Pot. B. BR20 19
Elms Av. N10 BV31 47
Elms Av. NW4 BQ32 46
Elmscott Gdns. N21 BZ25 30
Elmscott Rd. Brom. CG49 78
Elms Ct. Wem. BJ35 45
Elms Cres. SW4 BW46 76
Elmscroft Gdns. Pot. B. BR19 19
Elmsdale Rd. E17 CD31 48
Elms Fm. Rd. Horn. CV35 51
Elms Gdns. Dag. CQ35 50
Elms Gdns. Wem. BJ35 45
Elmshaw Rd. SW15 BP46 75
Elmshorn Epsom BQ61 103
Elmshurst Cres. N2 BT31 47
Elmshurst Est. N2 BT31 47
Elmshurst Rd. E7 CH36 58
Elmside Croy. CE57 96
Elmside, Guil. AQ71 118
Elmside Rd. Wem. BM34 46
Elms La. Wem. BJ34 45
Elmsleigh Av. Har. BJ31 45
Elmsleigh Ct. Sutt. BS55 86
Elmsleigh Rd. Twick. BG48 74
Elmslie Clo. Epsom BN60 94
Elms Ms. W2 BT40 56
Elms Pk. Av. Wem. BJ35 45
Elms Rd. SW4 BW46 76
Elms Rd. Ger. Cr. AS29 34
Elms Rd. Har. BH29 36
Elmstead Av. Chis. CK49 78
Elmstead Av. Wem. BL33 46
Elmstead Clo. N20 BS27 38
Elmstead Clo. Epsom BO56 94
Elmstead Clo. Sev. CT64 107
Elmstead Gdns. Wor. Pk. BP55 85
Elmstead Glade, Chis. CK50 78
Elmstead La. Chis. CK50 78
Elmstead Rd. Erith CT44 69
Elmstead Rd. Ilf. CN34 49
Elmstead Rd. Wey. AW60 92
Elmsted Cres. Well. CP43 69
Elms, The, SW13 BO45 65
Elmstone Rd. SW6 BS44 66
Elm St. WC1 BX38 56
Elmsway, Ashf. AY49 73
Elms Wood, Lthd. BE65 102
Elmsworth Av. Houns. BF44 64
Elm Ter. NW3 BS34 47
Finchley Rd.
Elm Ter. SE9 CL46 78
Elm Ter. Grays DA43 70
Elm Ter. Har. BG29 36
Elm Tree. Brwd. CZ22 33
Elmtree Av. Esher. BG54 84
Elmtree Clo. Ashf. AZ49 73
Elm Tree Clo. Cher. AV55 82
Elm Tree Clo. Nthlt. BE37 54
Elm Tree Clo. Wey. AY60 92
Elm Tree Gdns. Nthlt. BE37 54
Elm Tree Rd. NW8 BT38 56
Elmtree Rd. Tedd. BH49 74
Elm Wk. NW3 BS34 47
West Heath Rd.
Elm Wk. SW20 BQ52 85
Elm Wk. Orp. CK55 88
Elm Wk. Rad. BH21 27
Elm Wk. Rom. CU31 50
Elm Way NW3 BS33 47
West Heath Rd.
Elm Way, NW10 BO35 46
Elm Way, Brwd. DA28 42
Elm Way Epsom BN56 94
Elmway. Grays. DE40 71
Elm Way. Rick. AW26 35
Elm Way Wor. Pk. BQ55 85
Elmwood, Saw. CQ6 6
Elmwood, Welw. G. C. BP8 5
Elmwood Av. N13 BX28 38
Elmwood Av. Borwd. BM24 28
Elmwood Av. Felt. BC48 73
Elmwood Av. Har. BJ32 45
Elmwood Clo. Wall. BV55 86
Elmwood Ct. Wem. BJ34 45
Elmwood Cres. NW9 BN31 46
Elmwood Dr. Bex. CQ47 79
Elmwood Dr. Epsom BP57 94
Elmwood Gdns. W7 BH39 54
Elmwood Rd. SE24 BZ46 77
Elmwood Rd. W4 BN43 65
Elmwood Rd. Croy. BY54 86
Elmwood Rd. Mitch. BU52 86
Elmwood Rd. Red. BV69 121
Elmwood Rd. Slou. AQ40 52
Elmwood Rd. Wok. AO63 100
Elmworth Gro. SE21 BZ48 77
Elnathan Ms. W9 BS38 56
Elphinstone Rd. E17 CD30 39
Elphinstone St. N5 BY34 47
Elrick Clo. Erith CT43 69
Queen St.
Elrington Rd. E8 CB36 57
Elruge Clo. West Dr. AX41 63
Elsa Rd. Well. CO44 69
Elsa St. E14 CD39 57
Elsdale St. E9 CC36 57
Elsden Ms. E2 CC37 57
Old Ford Rd.
Elsden Rd. N17 CA30 39
Elsenham Rd. E12 CK35 49
Elsenham St. SW18 BR47 75
Elsham Rd. E11 CG34 49
Elsham Rd. W14 BR41 65
Elsham Ter. W14 BR41 65
Elsiedene Rd. N21 BZ26 39
Elsiemaud Rd. SE4 CD46 77
Elsie Rd. SE22 CA45 67
Elsinge Rd. Enf. CB22 30
Elsinore Av. Stai. AY47 73
Elsinore Rd. SE23 CD47 77
Elsley Rd. SW11 BU45 66
Elsma Ter. Houns. BE45 64
Elspeth Rd. SW11 BU45 66
Elspeth Rd. Wem. BL35 46
Elsrick Av. Mord. BS53 86
Elstan Way Croy. CD54 87
Elsted St. SE17 BZ42 67
Elsthorpe Rd. Rom. CR29 41
Elstow Clo. SE9 CL46 78
Elstow Clo. Ruis. BD33 45
Elstow Gdns. Dag. CQ37 59
Elstow Rd. Dag. CQ36 59
Elstree Gdns. N9 CB26 39
Elstree Gdns. Belv. CQ42 69
Elstree Gdns. Ilf. CM35 49
Elstree Hill N. Borwd. BK25 27
Elstree Hill S. Borwd. BK26 36
Elstree Hl. Brom. CG50 78
Elstree Rd. Bush. BG26 36
Elstree Rd. Stan. BK27 36
Elstree Rd. Wat. BH23 27
Elstree Way Borwd. BM23 28
Elswick Rd. SE13 CE44 67
Elswick St. SW6 BT44 66
Elsworthy E. Mol. BH53 84
Elsworthy Ri. NW3 BU36 56
Elsynge Rd. SW18 BT46 76
Eltham Grn. SE9 CJ46 78
Eltham Grn. Rd. SE9 CJ45 68
Eltham High St. SE9 CK46 78
Eltham Hill SE9 CJ46 78
Eltham Palace Rd. SE9 CJ46 78
Eltham Park Gdns. SE9 CL45 68
Eltham Pl. Guil. AP69 118
Eltham Rd. SE9 CG46 78
Eltham Rd. SE12 CG46 78
Eltham St. SE17 BZ42 67
Elthiron Rd. SW6 BS44 66
Elthorne Av. W7 BH41 64
Elthorne Ct. Felt. BD47 74
Elthorne Pk. Rd. W7 BH41 64
Elthorne Rd. N19 BW34 47
Elthorne Rd. NW9 BN33 46
Elthorne Rd. Uxb. AX37 52
Elthorne Way NW9 BN32 46
Elthruda Rd. SE13 CF46 77
Eltisley Rd. Ilf. CL35 49
Elton Av. Barn. BR25 28
Elton Av. Grnf. BH36 54
Elton Av. Wem. BJ35 45
Elton Clo. Kings. On T. BK50 74
Normansfield Av.
Elton Clo. Tedd. BK50 74
Elton Pl. N16 CA35 48
Elton Rd. Kings. On T. BL51 85
Elton Rd. Pur. BW59 95
Elton St. N16 CA35 48
Matthias Rd.
Elton Way Wat. BF23 27
Elvaston Ms. SW7 BT41 66
Elvaston Pl. SW7 BT41 66
Elvaston Terr. SW7 BT42 66
Elveden Clo. Wok. AW62 101
Elveden Pl. NW10 BM37 55
Elveden Rd. NW10 BM37 55
Elvendon Rd. N13 BX29 38
Elver Gdns. E2 CB38 57
Avebury Est.
Elverson Rd. SE8 CE44 67
Elverton St. SW1 BW42 66
Elvet Av. Rom. CV31 51
Elvington Dr. NW9 BO30 37
Elvington Grn. Brom. CG53 88
Elvino Rd. SE26 CC49 77
Elwell Rd. SW4 BX44 66
Elwick Rd. S. Ock. DB39 60
Elwill Way Beck. CF52 87
Elwill Way, Grav. DF51 81
Elwin St. E2 CA38 57
Elwood St. N5 BY34 47
Elwyn Gdns. SE12 CH47 78
Ely Cl. Hat. BO12 10
Ely Clo. Amer. AP23 25
Ely Clo. Erith CT44 69
Ely Clo. N. Mal. BO51 85
Ely Gdns. Borwd. BN25 28
Ely Gdns. Dag. CS34 50
Elyne Rd. N4 BY32 47
Ely Pl. EC1 BY39 56
Ely Pl. Welw. G. C. BR8 5
Ely Rd. E10 CF32 48
Ely Rd. Croy. BZ53 87
Ely Rd. Houns. BD45 64
Ely Rd. St. Alb. BJ14 9
Elysian Av. Orp. CN53 88
Elysium Pl. SW6 BR44 65
Elysium St.
Elysium St. SW6 BR44 65
Fulham Park Gdns.
Elystan Clo. Wall. BV57 95
Elystan Pl. SW3 BU42 66
Elystan St. SW3 BU42 66
Emanuel Av. W3 BN39 55
Embankment Gdns. SW3 BU43 66
Embankment Pl. WC2 BX40 56
Villiers St.
Embankment, The, SW15 BQ44 65
Embankment, The Stai. AR47 72
Embankment, The, Twick. BJ47 74
Embassy Ct. Sid. CO48 79
Emba St. SE16 CB41 67
Ember Clo. Orp. CM54 88
Ember Clo. Wey. AX56 92
Embercourt Rd. Surb. BG53 84
Ember Fm. Av. E. Mol. BG53 84
Ember Fm. Way E. Mol. BG53 84
Ember Gdns. Surb. BH53 84
Ember La. Esher BG54 84
Ember Rd. Slou. AT41 62
Emberson Way Epp. CR16 23
Embleton Rd. SE13 CE45 67
Embleton Rd. Wat. BC27 35
Embry Clo. Stan. BJ28 36
Embry Dr. Stan. BJ29 36
Embry Way Stan. BJ28 36
Emden St. SW6 BS44 66
Emerald Gdns. Dag. CR33 50
Emerald St. WC1 BX39 56
Emerson Dr. Horn. CV33 51
Emerson Gdns. Har. BL33 46
Emerson Rd. Ilf. CL33 49
Emerson St. SE1 BZ40 57
Emery Hill St. SW1 BW41 66
Emery St. SE1 BY41 66
Morley St.
Emes Rd. Erith CS43 69
Emily Pl. N7 BY35 47
Queensland Rd.
Emily St. E16 CG39 58
Jude St.
Emlyn Gdns. W12 BO41 65
Emlyn La. Lthd. BJ64 102
Emlyn Rd. W12 BO41 65
Emlyn Rd. Red. BV71 121
Emmanuel Clo. Nthw BB29 35
Emmanuel Rd. SW12 BW47 76
Emmanuel Rd. Nthw BB29 35
Emma Rd. E13 CG37 58
Emma St. E2 CB37 57
Emma Ter. E11 CG34 49
Montague Rd.
Emmett St. E14 CD40 57
Emmot Clo. NW11 BT32 47
Emmott Av. Ilf. CM32 49
Emmott St. E1 CD38 57
Emnetts Clo. Wok. AR62 100
Kirby Rd.
Emperors Gte. SW7 BS41 66
Empire Av. N18 BZ28 39
Empire Ct. Wem. BM34 46
Empire Pde. N18 BZ29 39
Empire Rd. Grnf. BJ37 54
Empire Way Wem. BL35 46
Empress Av. E4 CE29 39
Empress Av. E12 CJ34 49
Empress Av. Ilf. CK34 49
Empress Av. Wdf. Grn. CG29 40
Empress Dr. Chis. CL50 78
Empress Pl. SW6 BS42 66
Empress Rd. Grav. DJ47 81
Empress St. SE17 BZ43 67
Empson St. E3 CE38 57
Emsworth Clo. N9 CC26 39
Emsworth Rd. Ilf. CL30 40
Emsworth St. SW2 BX48 76
Emu Rd. SW8 BV44 66
Ena Rd. SW16 BX52 86
Enborne Grn. S. Ock. DA39 60
Enbrook St. W10 BR38 55
Endale Clo. Cars. BU55 86
End Av. Har. BG35 45
Endeavour Rd. Wal. Cr. CD17 21
Endeavour Way Bark. CO37 59
Endell St. WC2 BX39 56
Endensor Gdns. Est. W9 BS40 56
Enderby St. SE10 CG42 68
Enderley Clo. Har. BH30 36
Enderley Rd. Har. BH30 36
Endersby Rd. Barn. BQ25 28
Endersleigh Gdns. NW4 BP31 46
Endlebury Rd. E4 CE27 39
Endlesham Rd. SW12 BV47 76
Endsleigh Clo. Sth. Croy. CC58 96
Endsleigh Gdns. WC1 BW38 56
Endsleigh Gdns. Ilf. CK34 49
Endsleigh Gdns. Surb. BK53 84
Endsleigh Gdns. Walt. BC56 92
Endsleigh Pl. WC1 BW38 56
Endsleigh Rd. Sthl. BE42 64
Endsleigh St. WC1 BW38 56
End Way Surb. BM54 85
Endwell Rd. SE4 CD44 67
Endymion Rd. N4 BY33 47
Endymion Rd. SW2 BX46 76
Endymion Rd. Hat. BQ12 10
Enfield Clo. Uxb. AX37 52
Enfield Rd. N1 CA36 57
Enfield Rd. N8 BX32 47
Enfield Rd. W3 BM41 65
Enfield Rd. Brent. BK42 64
Enfield Rd. Enf. BW24 29
Enfield Rd. E. Brent. BK42 64
Enford St. W1 BU39 56
Engadine Croy. CA55 87
Engadine Clo. Croy. CA55 87
Engadine St. SW18 BR47 75
Engayne Gdns. Upmin. CX33 51
Engel Pk. NW7 BQ29 37
Engineer Rd. SE18 CL43 68
Englands La. NW3 BU36 56
Englands La. Loug. CL23 31
Englefield Clo. Enf. BY23 29
Englefield Clo. Orp. CN53 88
Englefield Cres. Orp. CN52 88
Englefield Path Orp. CN52 88
Englefield Rd. N1 BZ36 57
Englefield Rd. Wok. AO62 100
Engleheart Dr. Felt. BB46 73
Engleheart Dr. Felt. BC46 73
Engleheart Rd. SE6 CE47 77
Englehurst, Egh. AR50 72
Englewood Rd. SW12 BV46 76
Engliff La. Wok. AV61 100
English Gdns. Stai. AR46 72
English Grounds. SE1 CA40 57
English St. E3 CD38 57
Enid St. SE16 CA41 67
Enkel St. N7 BX34 47
Enmore Av. SE25 CB53 87
Enmore Gdns. SW14 BN46 75
Enmore Rd. SE25 CB53 87
Enmore Rd. SW15 BQ45 65
Enmore Rd. Sthl. BF38 54
Ennerdale Av. Horn. CU35 50
Ennerdale Av. Stan. BK31 45
Ennerdale Clo. St. Alb. BJ14 9
Ennerdale Dr. NW9 BN32 46
Ennerdale Gdns. Wem. BK33 45
Ennerdale Rd. Bexh. CR44 69
Ennerdale Rd. Rich. BL44 65
Ennersdale Rd. SE13 CF46 77
Ennismore Av. W4 BO42 65
Ennismore Av. Grnf. BH36 54
Ennismore Av. Guil. AS70 118
Ennismore Gdns. SW7 BU41 66
Ennismore Gdns. E. Mol. BH53 84
Ennismore Gdns. Ms. SW7 BU41 66
Ennismore Ms. SW7 BU41 66
Ennismore St. SW7 BU41 66
Ennismore Gdns.
Ennis Rd. N4 BY33 47
Ennis Rd. SE18 CM43 68
Ensign Clo. Stai. AX47 73
Ensign Dr. N13 BZ27 39
Ensign St. E1 CB40 57
Ensign Way, Stai. AX47 73
Ensleigh Rd. Red. BW68 113
Enslin Rd. SE9 CL46 78
Ensor Ms. SW7 BT42 66
Cranley Gdns.
Enstone Rd. Uxb. AY34 44
Enterdent, The Cdse. CC70 114
Entick St. E2 CC38 57
Epirus Ms. SW6 BR43 65
Epirus Rd. SW6 BR43 65
Epping Clo. Rom. CR31 50
Epping Glade E4 CF25 30
Epping New Rd. Buck. H. CH27 40
Epping Pl. N7 BY36 56
Liverpool Rd.
Epping Rd. Epp. CL14 13
Epping Rd. Epp. CL21 31
Epping Rd. Epp. CM19 22
Epping Rd. Epp. CS18 23
Epping Rd. Harl. CH11 13
Epping Rd. Ong. CT15 14
Epping Rd. Ong. CV16 24
Epping Way E4 CE25 30
Epple Rd. SW6 BR44 65
Epsom Clo. Bexh. CR45 69
Epsom Clo. Nthlt. BE35 45
Epsom Gap, Lthd. BJ61 102
Epsom La. Epsom. BP63 103
Epsom La. S. Tad. BQ64 103
Epsom Rd. E10 CF32 48
Epsom Rd. Ash. BL62 103
Epsom Rd. Croy. BY56 95
Epsom Rd. Epsom BO59 94
Epsom Rd. Guil. AS71 118
Epsom Rd. Guil. AU70 118
Epsom Road. Guil. AX69 110
Epsom Rd. Ilf. CN32 49
Epsom Rd. Lthd. BJ64 102
Epsom Rd. Mord. BR54 85
Epsom. Way. Horn. CW35 51
Epworth Pl. EC2 BZ38 57
Epworth St.
Epworth Rd. Islw. BJ43 64
Epworth St. EC2 BZ38 57
Erasmus St. SW1 BW42 66
Erconwald St. W12 BO39 55
Eresby Rd. NW6 BS36 56
Eresby Rd. Beck. CE54 87
Eresey Rd. Croy. CD54 87
Erica Ct. Swan. CT52 89
Erica Gdns. Croy. CE55 87
Erica St. W12 BP40 55
Eric Clo. E7 CH35 49
Eric Rd. E7 CH35 49
Eric Rd. NW10 BO36 55
Eric Rd. Rom. CP33 50
Eric St. E3 CD38 57
Eridge Rd. W4 BN41 65
Erin Clo. Brom. CG50 78
Elstree Hill
Erindale SE18 CM43 68
Eriswell Cres. Watt. BB57 92
Eriswell Rd. Watt. BB56 92
Erith Cres. Rom. CS30 41
Erith Rd. Belv. CR42 69
Erith Rd. Bexh. CR45 69
Erlanger Rd. SE14 CC44 67
Erlesmere Gdns. W13 BJ41 64
Ermine Clo. Houns. BD45 64
Ermine Clo. St. Alb. BF14 9
Ermine Clo. Wal. Cr. CB19 21
Ermine Side, Enf. CB25 30

Ermington Rd. SE9 CM48 78
Ermyn Clo. Lthd. BK64 102
Ermyn Way. Lthd. BK64 102
Ernald Av. E6 CK37 58
Ernan Clo. S. Ock. DA39 60
Ernan Rd. S. Ock. DA39 60
Erncroft Way Twick. BH46 74
Ernest Av. SE27 BY49 76
Ernest Gdns. W4 BM43 65
Ernest Gro. Beck. CD53 87
Ernest Gro. Clo. Beck. CE53 87
Ernest Rd. E16 CG38 58
Ernest Rd. Horn. CW32 51
Ernest Rd. Kings-on-t. BM51 85
Ernest Sq. Kings. On T. BM51 85
Ernest St. E1 CC38 57
Ernle Rd. SW20 BP50 75
Ernshaw Pl. SW15 BR46 75
Carlton Dr.
Erons Way. Grays. DG42 71
Erpingham Rd. SW15 BQ45 65
Erridge Rd. SW19 BS51 86
Erriff Dr. S. Ock. DA39 60
Errington Clo. Grays DG41 71
Cedar Rd.
Errington Rd. W9 BR38 55
Errol Gdns. Hayes BC38 53
Errol Gdns. N. Mal. BP52 85
Erroll Rd. Rom. CT31 50
Errol St. EC1 BZ38 57
Erskine Clo. Sutt. BU55 86
Erskine Hl. NW11 BS32 47
Erskine Rd. E17 CD31 48
Erskine Rd. NW3 BU36 56
Erskine Rd. Sutt. BT56 95
Esam Way SW16 BY49 76
Escombe Dri. Guil. AQ68 109
Escott Gdns. SE9 CK49 78
Escot Way Barn. BQ25 28
Escreet Gro. SE18 CL42 68
Esdaile La. Hodd. CE12 12
Esdale Gdns. Upmin. CY33 51
Esher Av. Rom. CS32 50
Esher Av. Sutt. BQ55 85
Esher Av. Walt. BC54 83
Esher Clo. Bex. CQ47 79
Esher Clo. Esher BF56 93
Esher Grn. Esher BF56 93
Esher Ms. Mitch. BU52 86
Esher Pk. Av. Esher BF56 93
Esher Pl. Av. Esher BF56 93
Esher Rd. E. Mol. BG53 84
Esher Rd. Ilf. CN34 49
Esher Rd. Walt. BE56 93
Eskdale Hem. H. AY12 8
Lonsdale
Eskdale Ave. Chesh. AO18 16
Eskdale Av. Nthlt. BE37 54
Eskdale Clo. Dart. CY47 80
Eskdale Gdns. Pur. BZ60 96
Eskdale Rd. Bexh. CR44 69
Eskdale Rd. Uxb. AW37 53
Eskley Gdns. S. Ock. DA39 60
Eskmont Ridge SE19 CA50 77
Esk Rd. E13 CH38 58
Esk Way Rom. CS29 41
Esmar Cres. NW4 BP33 46
Esmeralda Rd. SE1 CB42 67
Esmond Clo. Rain. CU36 59
Esmond Gdns. W5 BK41 64
St.Marys Rd.
Esmond Rd. NW6 BR37 55
Esmond Rd. W4 BN42 65
Esmond St. SW15 BR45 65
Esparto St. SW18 BS47 76
Essen Clo. Belv. CR42 69
Essendene Rd. Cat. CA65 105
Essenden Rd. Belv. CR42 69
Essenden Rd. Sth. Croy. BZ57 96
Essendine Rd. W9 BS38 56
Essendon Clo. Hat. BU12 11
Essendon Gdns. Welw. G. C. BR8 5
Essendon Hill. Hat. BU12 11
Essendon Rd. Hert. BV11 11
Essex Av. Islw. BH45 64
Essex Clo. E17 CC31 48
Essex Clo. Mord. BQ54 85
Essex Clo. Rom. CR31 50
Essex Clo. Ruis. BD33 45
Essex Ct. EC4 BY39 56
Middle Temple La.
Essex Ct. SW13 BP44 65
Essex Gdns. N4 BY32 47
Rutland Gdns.
Essex Gdns. Horn. CX32 51
Essex Gdns. S. Le H. DK41 71
Somerset Rd.
Essex Gro. SE19 BZ50 77
Essex La. Kings L. BA20 17
Essex Mead. Hem. H. AY10 8
Essex Pk. N3 BS29 38
Essex Pk. Ms. W3 BO40 55
Essex Pl. W4 BO42 65
Chiswick High Rd.
Essex Rd. E4 CG26 40
Essex Rd. E10 CF32 48
Essex Rd. E12 CK35 49
Essex Rd. E17 CD32 48
Essex Rd. E18 CH30 40
Essex Rd. N1 BY37 56
Essex Rd. NW10 BO36 55
Essex Rd. W3 BN40 55
Essex Rd. W4 BN42 65
Belmont Gr.
Essex Rd. Bark. CM36 58
Essex Rd. Borwd. BM24 28
Essex Rd. Dag. CS35 50
Essex Rd. Dart. CV46 80
Essex Rd. Enf. BZ24 30
Essex Rd. Grav. DG47 81
Essex Rd. Grays DA43 70
Essex Rd. Hodd. CE11 12
Essex Rd. Long. DB51 90
Essex Rd. Rom. CP33 50
Essex Rd. Rom. CR31 50
Essex Rd. Wat. BC23 26
Essex St. E7 CH35 49
Essex St. WC2 BY39 56
Essex St. St. Alb. BH13 9
Essex Vill. W8 BS41 66
Essex Way, Brwd. DB29 42
Essex Wharf E10 CC34 48
Essian St. E1 CD39 57
Estate Way E10 CE33 48
Estcourt Rd. SE25 CB53 87
Estcourt Rd. SW6 BR43 65
Estcourt Rd. Wat. BD24 27
Estella Av. N. Mal. BP52 85
Estelle Rd. NW3 BU35 47
Mansfield Rd.
Esterbrooke St. SW1 BW42 66
Este Rd. SW11 BU45 66
Esther Clo. N21 CH26 40
Esther Rd. E11 CG33 49
Estreham Rd. SW16 BW50 76
Estridge Clo. Houns. BF45 64
Staines Rd.
Eswyn Rd. SW17 BU49 76
Etchingham Ct. N12 BS29 38
Etchingham Pk. Rd. N3 BS29 38
Etchingham Rd. E15 CF35 48
Etfield Gro. Sid. CO49 79
Ethelbert Clo. Brom. CH52 88
Ethelbert Gdns. Ilf. CK32 49
Ethelbert Rd. SW20 BQ51 85
Ethelbert Rd. Brom. CH52 88
Ethelbert Rd. Dart. CW49 80
Ethelbert Rd. Erith CS43 69
Hengist Rd.
Ethelbert Rd. Orp. CP52 89
Ethelburga Rd. Rom. CW30 42
Ethelburga St. SW11 BU44 66
Etheldene Av. N10 BW31 47
Ethelden Rd. W12 BP40 55
Ethelforde Dr. Ashf. AZ49 73
Ethel Rankin Ct. SW6 BR44 65
Fulham Rd.
Ethelred Clo. Welw. G. C. BR8 5
Ethel Rd. E16 CH39 58
Ethel Rd. Ashf. AY49 73
Ethel Ter. Orp. CP58 98
Etheridge Grn. Loug. CM24 31
Etheridge Rd. Loug. CL23 31
Etherley Rd. N15 BZ32 48
Etherow St. SE22 CB46 77
Etherstone Gn. SW16 BX49 76
Etherstone Rd. SW16 BY49 76
Ethnard Rd. SE15 CB43 67
Ethorpe Clo. Ger. Cr. AS32 43
Ethronvi Rd. Bexh. CQ45 69
Etloe Rd. E10 CE34 48
Etna Rd. St. Alb. BG13 9
Eton Av. N12 BT29 38
Eton Av. NW3 BT36 56
Eton Av. Barn. BU25 29
Eton Av. Houns. BE43 64
Eton Av. N. Mal. BN53 85
Eton Av. Wem. BJ35 45
Eton Clo. Slou. AQ43 62
Eton College Rd. NW3 BU36 56
Eton Ct. Wem. BK35 45
Eton Ct. Wind. AO43 61
Eton Gdns. NW3 BU36 56
Lambolle Pl.
Eton Gro. N19 BW34 47
Wedmore St.
Eton Gro. NW9 BM31 46
Eton Gro. SE13 CG45 68
Eton Ho. SW11 BT44 66
Eton Pl. NW3 BU36 56
Eton Rd. NW3 BU36 56
Eton Rd. Hayes. BB43 63
Eton Rd. Ilf. CM35 49
Eton Rd. Orp. CO56 98
Eton Rd. Slou. AP42 62
Eton Sq. Wind. AO43 61
Eton St. Rich. BL46 75
Eton Vill. NW3 BU36 56
Etta St. SE8 CD43 67
Ettrick St. E14 CF39 57
Ettringham St. SW11 BT45 66
Petergate
Etwell Pl. Surb. BL53 85
Eugene Clo. Rom. CV31 51
Eugenia Rd. SE16 CC42 67
Eunice Gro. Chesh. AO19 16
Eureka Rd. Kings-on-t. BM51 85
Europa Rd. Hem. H. AY12 8
Eustace Pl. SE18 CK42 68
Eustace Rd. E6 CK38 58
Eustace Rd. SW6 BS43 66
Eustace Rd. Rom. CP33 50
Euston Av. Wat. BB25 26
Euston Gro. NW1 BW38 56
Euston Rd. NW1 BW38 56
Euston Rd. Croy. BX54 86
Euston Sq. NW1 BW38 56
Euston Sta. Colon. NW1 BW38 56
Euston St. NW1 BW38 56
Evandale Rd. SW9 BY44 66
Evangelist Rd. NW5 BV35 47
Evans Av. Wat. BB21 26
Evans Dale Rain. CT38 59
Evans Gro. Felt. BF48 74
Evans Gro. St. Alb. BK11 9
Evans Rd. SE6 CG48 78
Evanston Av. E4 CF29 39
Evanston Gdns. Ilf. CK32 49
Eva Rd. Rom. CP33 50
Evelina Clo. SE20 CC50 77
Evelina Rd. SE15 CC45 67
Eveline Lowe Est. SE16 CB41 67
Eveline Rd. Mitch. BU51 86
Evelyn Av. NW9 BN31 46
Evelyn Av. Ruis. BB33 44
Evelyn Clo. Twick. BF47 74
Evelyn Clo. Wok. AR63 100
Evelyn Ct. N1 BZ37 57
Evelyn Cres. Sun. BB51 83
Evelyn Dr. Pnr. BD29 36
Evelyn Gdns. SW7 BT42 66
Evelyn Gdns. Gdse. CC68 114
Evelyn Gdns. Rich. BL45 65
Kew Rd.
Evelyn Gro. W5 BL40 55
Evelyn Gro. Sthl. BE39 54
Evelyn Rd. E16 CH40 58
Evelyn Rd. E17 CF31 48
Evelyn Rd. SW19 BS49 76
Evelyn Rd. W4 BN41 65
Evelyn Rd. Barn. BU24 29
Evelyn Rd. Rich. BK48 74
Evelyn Rd. Rich. BL45 65
Evelyn Rd. Sev. CV61 108
Evelyns Clo. Uxb. AZ39 53
Evelyn St. SE8 CD42 67
Evelyn Ter. Rich. BL45 65
Evelyn Wk. N1 BZ37 57
Evelyn Way, Cob. BD61 102
Evelyn Way, Sun. BB51 83
Evelyn Way Wall. BW56 95
Evenlode Way Dag. CR34 50
Evenwood Clo. SW15 BR46 75
Everard Ave. Slou. AP41 62
Everard Av. Brom. CH54 88
Everard La. Cat. CB64 105
Everatt Cl. SW18 BR46 75
Amerland Rd.
Everdon Rd. SW13 BP43 65
Everest Clo. Grav. DF48 81
Everest Pl. Swan. CS52 89
Everest Rd. SE9 CK46 78
Everest Rd. Stai. AX47 73
Everest Way, Hem. H. AZ13 8
Everglade, West. CJ62 106
Everglade Strand NW9 BO30 37
Evergreen Oak Ave. Wind. AQ45 62
Everilda St. N1 BX37 56
Evering Rd. E5 CA34 48
Evering Rd. N16 CA34 48
Everington Rd. N10 BU30 38
Everington St. W6 BQ43 65
Everitt Rd. NW10 BN38 55
Everlands Clo. Wok. AS62 100
Everlasting La. St. Alb. BG13 9
Everleigh St. N4 BX33 47
Eve Rd. E11 CG35 49
Eve Rd. E15 CG37 58
Eve Rd. N17 CA31 48
Eve Rd. Islw. BJ45 64
Eve Rd. Wok. AT61 100
Eversfield Gdns. NW7 BO29 37
Eversfield Rd. Reig. BS70 121
Eversfield Rd. Rich. BL44 65
Eversholt St. NW1 BW37 56
Eversholt St. NW3 BU36 56
Maitland Park Vw.
Evershot Rd. N4 BX33 47
Eversleigh Gdns. Upmin. CY33 51
Eversleigh Rd. E6 CJ37 58
Eversleigh Rd. N3 BR29 37
Eversleigh Rd. SW11 BU45 66
Eversleigh Rd. Barn. BT25 29
Eversley Av. Bexh. CS44 69
Eversley Av. Wem. BM34 46
Eversley Clo. N21 BX25 29
Eversley Cres. N21 BX25 29
Eversley Cres. Islw. BG44 64
Eversley Cres. Ruis. BB34 44
Eversley Cross Bexh. CT44 69
Eversley Dr. Croy. CE55 87
Eversley Mt. N21 BX25 29
Eversley Pk. Rd. N21 BX25 29
Eversley Rd. SE7 CH43 68
Eversley Rd. SE19 BZ50 77
Eversley Rd. Surb. BL52 85
Everthorpe Rd. SE15 CA45 67
Everton Bldgs. NW1 BW38 56
Stanhope St.
Everton Dr. Stan. BL31 46
Everton Rd. Croy. CB54 87
Evesham Av. E17 CE30 39
Evesham Clo. Grnf. BF37 54
Evesham Clo. Reig. BR70 120
Evesham Clo. Sutt. BS57 95
Evesham Grn. Mord. BS53 86
Evesham Rd. E15 CG37 58
Evesham Rd. N11 BW28 38
Evesham Rd. Felt. BD46 74
Evesham Rd. Grav. DH48 81
Evesham Rd. Mord. BS53 86
Evesham Rd. Reig. BR70 120
Evesham Rd. N. Reig. BR70 120
Evesham St. W11 BQ40 55
Evesham Way SW11 BV45 66
Evesham Way Ilf. CL31 49
Evreham Rd. Iver AV39 52
Ewald Rd. SW6 BR44 65
Ewanrigg Ter. Wdf. Grn. CJ28 40
Ewart Gro. N22 BX30 38
Ewart Rd. SE23 CC47 77
Ewell By-pass Epsom BP58 94
Ewell Ct. Av. Epsom BO56 94
Ewell Downs Rd. Epsom BP59 94
Ewell Ho. Gro. Epsom BO58 94
Ewellhurst Rd. Ilf. CK30 40
Ewell Pk. Way Epsom BP57 94
Ewell Rd. Surb. BJ54 84
Ewell Rd. Surb. BL53 85
Ewell Rd. Sutt. BQ57 94
Ewelme Rd. SE23 CC47 77
Ewen Cres. SW2 BY47 76
Ewer St. SE1 BZ40 57
Ewhurst Av. Sth. Croy. CA58 96
Ewhurst Clo. Sutt. BQ58 94
Ewhurst Rd. SE4 CD46 77
Ewing St. E3 CD38 57
Maidman St.
Exbury Rd. SE6 CD48 77
Excelsior Clo. Kings-on-t. BM51 85
Washington Rd.
Exchange Bldgs. EC1 CA39 57
Cutler St.
Exchange Rd. Wat. BC24 26
Exchange St. EC1 BZ38 57
Dingley Rd.
Exchange St. Rom. CT32 50
Exedown Rd. Sev. DA60 99
Exedown Rd. Sev. DB61 108
Exeter Gdns. Ilf. CK33 49
Exeter Ho. SW15 BQ46 75
Exeter Pl. Guil. AP69 118
Exeter Rd. E16 CH39 58
Exeter Rd. E17 CE32 48
Exeter Rd. N9 CC27 39
Exeter Rd. N14 BV26 38
Exeter Rd. NW2 BR35 46
Exeter Road SE15 CA44 67
Sumner Estate
Exeter Rd. Croy. CA54 87
Exeter Rd. Dag. CR36 59
Exeter Rd. Enf. CC24 30
Exeter Rd. Felt. BE48 74
Exeter Rd. Grav. DH48 81
Exeter Rd. Har. BE34 45
Exeter Rd. Well. CN44 68
Exeter St. WC2 BX40 56
Exford Av. Ashf. AZ49 73
Exford Gdns. SE12 CH47 78
Exford Rd. SE12 CH48 78
Exhibition Rd. SW7 BT41 66
Exmoor St. W10 BQ39 55
Exmouth Dr. Hayes BB38 53
Exmouth Mkt. EC1 BY38 56
Exmouth Rd. E17 CD32 48
Exmouth Rd. Brom. CH52 88
Exmouth Rd. Grays. DD43 71
Exmouth Rd. Ruis. BD34 45
Exmouth Rd. Well. CO43 69
Exmouth St. E1 CC39 57
Exning Rd. E16 CG38 58
Exon St. SE17 CA42 67
Explorer Av. Stai. AY47 73
Exton Cres. NW10 BN36 55
Exton Gdns. Dag. CP35 50
Exton St. SE1 BY40 56
Eyhurst Av. Horn. CU34 50
Eyhurst Clo. NW2 BP34 46
Eyhurst Clo. Tad. BR65 103
Eyhurst Spur, Tad. BR65 103
Eylewood Rd. SE27 BZ49 77
Eynella Rd. SE22 CA47 77
Eynham Rd. W12 BQ39 55
Eynsford Clo. Orp. CM54 88
Eynsford Cres. Bex. CP47 79
Eynsford Ri. Eyns. CV56 99
Eynsford Rd. Farn. CW54 90
Eynsford Rd. Green. DB46 80
Eynsford Rd. Ilf. CN34 49
Eynsford Rd. Sev. CU59 98
Eynsford Rd. Swan. CS53 89
Eynsham Br. SE2 CO42 69
Eynsham Dr. SE2 CO41 69
Eynswood Dr. Sid. CO49 79
Eyot Gdns. W6 BO42 65
Eyre Clo. NW8 BT37 56
Eyre Clo. Rom. CV31 51
Eyre St. Hill EC1 BY38 56
Eythorne Rd. SW9 BY44 66
Eywood Rd. St. Alb. BG14 9
Ezra St. E2 CA38 57
Faber Gdns. NW4 BP32 46
Fabian Rd. SW6 BR43 65
Fabian St. E6 CK38 58
Fackenden La. Sev. CU60 98
Factory La. N17 CA30 39
Factory La. Croy. BY54 86
Factory Path, Stai. AV49 72
Factory Rd. E16 CK40 58
Factory Rd. Grav. DE46 81
Factory Sq. SW16 BX50 76
Factory Yd. W7 BH40 54
Faesten Way Bex. CT48 79
Faggoters La. Ong. CT11 14
Faggots Clo. Rad. BJ21 27
Fagg's Rd. Felt. BB45 63
Fagg's Rd. Felt. BC45 63
Fagus Av. Rain. CV38 60
Fair Acre, Hem. H. AY15 8
Fairacre Islw. BG44 64
Fairacre N. Mal. BO52 85
Fairacres, SW15 BP45 65
Fairacres Brom. CH53 88
Fair Acres. Cob. BD59 93
Fairacres, Ruis. BB33 44
Fair Acres. Wind. AL44 61
Fairacres Clo. Pot. B. BR20 19
Fairbairn Rd. SW9 BY44 66
Fairbank Av. Orp. CL55 88
Fairbank Rd. N17 CA31 48
Fairbourne. Cob. BD60 93
Fairbourne Rd. N17 CA31 48
Fairbridge Rd. N19 BW34 47
Fairbrook Clo. N13 BY28 38
Fairbrook Rd. N13 BY29 38
Fairburn Clo. Borwd. BM23 28
Fairby La. Hart. DC53 90
Fairby Rd. SE12 CH46 78
Fairchildes. War. CG60 97
Fairchildes Ave. Croy. CF59 96
Fair Child St. EC2 CA38 57
Gt. Eastern St.
Fair Clo. Bush. BF26 36
Fairclough St. E1 CB39 57
Faircross Av. Bark. CM36 58
Faircross Av. Rom. CS29 41
Faircross Way, St. Alb. BJ12 9
Fairdale Gdns. SW15 BP45 65
Fairdale Gdns. Hayes BC40 53
Fairdene Rd. Couls. BW62 104
Fairey Ave. Hayes. BB42 63
Fairfax Av. Epsom BP58 94
Fairfax Av. Red. BU70 121
Fairfax Clo. Walt. BC54 83
Fairfax Gdns. SE3 CJ44 68
Fairfax Pl. NW6 BT36 56
Fairfax Rd. N8 BY31 47
Fairfax Rd. NW6 BT36 56
Fairfax Rd. W4 BO41 65
Fairfax Rd. Grays. DD42 71
Fairfax Rd. Tedd. BJ50 74
Fairfax Rd. Til. DF44 71
Fairfax Rd. Wok. AT63 100
Fairfax Ter. Sthl. BE42 64
Fairfield. Lthd. BF66 111
Fairfield App. Stai. AR46 72
Fairfield Ave. Grays. DE40 71
Fairfield Ave. Slou. AR43 62
Fairfield Av. NW4 BP32 46
Fairfield Av. Edg. BM29 37
Fairfield Av. Ruis. BA33 44
Fairfield Av. Stai. AV49 72
Fairfield Av. Twick. BF47 74
Fairfield Av. Upmin. CY35 51
Fairfield Av. Wat. BD27 36
Fairfield Clo. N12 BT28 38
Torrington Park
Fairfield Clo. Enf. CC24 30
Scotland Green Rd. Nth.
Fairfield Clo. Hat. BQ11 10
Hillfield
Fairfield Clo. Rom. CU33 50
Fairfield Clo. Sid. CN46 78
Fairfield Ct. NW10 BO36 55
Fairfield Ct. NW10 BP37 55
Longstone Av.
Fairfield Ct. Wdf. Grn. CH29 40
Fairfield Rd.
Fairfield Cres. Edg. BM29 37
Fairfield Dr. SW18 BS46 76
Fairfield St.
Fairfield Dr. Brox. CD15 12
Fairfield Dr. Dor. BJ70 119
Fairfield Dr. Grnf. BK37 54
Fairfield Dr. Har. BG31 45
Fairfield E. Kings-on-t. BL51 85
Fairfield Gdns. N8 BX32 47
Elder Av.
Fairfield Gro. SE7 CJ43 68
Fairfield N. Kings. On T. BL51 85
Fairfield P. Croy. CA55 87
Fairfield Path Croy. CA55 87
Fairfield Pl. Kings BL52 85
Fairfield Rise, Guil. AP70 118
Fairfield Rd. E3 CE37 57
Fairfield Rd. E17 CD30 39
Fairfield Rd. N8 BX32 47
Fairfield Rd. N18 CB28 39
Fairfield Rd. W7 BJ41 64
Fairfield Rd. Beck. CE51 87
Fairfield Rd. Bexh. CQ44 69
Fairfield Rd. Brom. CH50 78
Fairfield Rd. Brwd. DB27 42
Fairfield Rd. Croy. BZ55 87
Fairfield Rd. Epp. CO18 23
Fairfield Rd. Hodd. CE11 12
Fairfield Rd. Ilf. CL36 58
Fairfield Rd. Kings. On T. BL51 85
Fairfield Rd. Lthd. BJ64 102
Fairfield Rd. Ong. CW18 24
Fairfield Rd. Orp. CM54 88
Fairfield Rd. Stai. AR46 72
Fairfield Rd. Sthl. BE39 54
Fairfield Rd. Uxb. AX36 53
Fairfield Rd. Wdf. Grn. CH29 40
Fairfield Rd. West Dr. AY40 53
Fairfields Croy. CA56 96
Fairfields Clo. NW9 BN32 46
Fairfields Cres. NW9 BN31 46
Fairfield S. Kings-on-t. BL52 85
Fairfields Rd. Houns. BG45 64
Fairfield St. SW18 BS45 66
Fairfield, The. Dart. CW47 80
Fairfield Wk. Wal. Cr. CD17 21
Fairfield Way Barn. BS25 29
Fairfield Way Couls. BW60 95
Fairfield Way Epsom BO56 94
Fairfield W. Kings-on-t. BL51 85
Fairfolds Wat. BE21 27
Fairfoot Rd. E3 CE38 57
Fairford Av. Bexh. CS44 69
Fairford Av. Croy. CC53 87
Fairford Clo. Croy. CC53 87
Fairford Clo. Rom. CX29 42
Fairford Clo. Wey. AV60 91
Fairford Gdns. Wor. Pk. BO55 85
Fairford Way, Rom. CX29 42
Fairgreen Barn. BU24 29
Fairgreen E. Barn. BU24 29
Fairgreen Rd. Th. Hth. BY53 86
Fairham Ave. S. Ock. DA40 60
Fairhaven Av. Croy. CC53 87
Fairhaven Cres. Wat. BC27 35
Fairhaven Rd. Red. BY67 113
Fairhazel Gdns. NW6 BS36 56
Fairholme Av. Rom. CU32 50
Fairholme Clo. N3 BR31 46
Fairholme Clo. Ash. BK62 102
Fairholme Cres. Ash. BK62 102
Fairholme Cres. Hayes BB38 53
Fairholme Gdns. N3 BR31 46
Fairholme Gdns. Upmin. CZ33 51
Fairholme Rd. W14 BR42 65
Fairholme Rd. Ashf. AY49 73
Fairholme Rd. Croy. BY54 86
Fairholme Rd. Har. BH32 45
Fairholme Rd. Sutt. BR57 94
Fairholm Est. Felt. BA47 73
Fairholm Rd. Ilf. CK32 49
Fairholt Rd. N16 BZ33 48
Fairholt St. SW7 BU41 66
Montpelier Wk.

Fairkytes Av. Horn. CV33 51
Fairland Rd. E15 CG36 58
Fairlands Av. Buck. H. CH27 40
Fairlands Av. Sutt. BS55 86
Fairlands Av. Th. Hth. BX52 86
Fairlands Rd. Guil. AO68 109
Fair La. Couls. BT66 113
Fairlawn, SE7 CJ43 68
Fair Lawn, Lthd. BE65 102
Fairlawn, Lthd. BE66 111
Fairlawn, Twick. BK46 74
Fairlawn, Wdf. Grn. CK29 40
Vicarage Rd.
Fairlawn Av. N2 BU31 47
Fairlawn Av. W4 BN42 65
Fairlawn Av. Bexh. CP44 69
Fairlawn Clo. N14 BW25 29
Fairlawn Clo. Esher BH57 93
Fairlawn Clo. Kings. On T. BN50 75
Fairlawn Ct. SE7 CJ43 68
Fairlawn
Fairlawn Ct. W4 BN42 65
Cunnington St.
Fairlawn Dr. Red. BU71 121
Fairlawn Dr. Wdf. Grn. CH29 40
Fairlawn Gdns. Sthl. BE40 54
Fairlawn Gro. W4 BN42 65
Fairlawn Gro. Bans. BT60 95
Fairlawn Pk. SE26 CD49 77
Fairlawn Rd. SW19 BR50 75
Fairlawn Rd. Sutt. BT59 95
Fairlawns, SW15 BQ46 75
Putney Hill
Fairlawns, Pnr. BD30 36
Fairlawns Sun. BC52 83
Fair Lawns. Wey. AV59 91
Fairlawns Clo. Felt. BE49 74
Fairlawns Clo. Horn. CW33 51
Herbert Rd.
Fairlawns Clo. Stai. AW50 73
Kingston Rd.
Fairlea Pl. W5 BK38 54
Fairleigh Pl. N16 CA35 48
Fairleigh Rd.
Fairley Way, Wal. Cr. CB17 21
Fairlie Gdns. SE23 CC47 77
Fairlight Ave. Wind. AO44 61
Fairlight Av. E4 CF27 39
Fairlight Av. NW10 BO37 55
Fairlight Av. Wdf. Grn. CH29 40
Fairlight Clo. E4 CF27 39
Fairlight Clo. Wor. Pk. BQ56 94
Fairlight Rd. SW17 BT49 76
Fairlop Clo. Horn. CU36 59
Fairlop Gdns. Ilf. CM29 40
Fairlop Pl. NW8 BT38 56
Fairlop Rd. E11 CF33 48
Fairlop Rd. Ilf. CM30 40
Fairmark Dr. Uxb. AZ36 53
Fairmead Brom. CK52 88
Fairmead Surb. BM54 85
Fairmead Clo. Brom. CK52 88
Fairmead Clo. N. Mal. BN52 85
Fairmead Cres. Edg. BN27 37
Fairmead Gdns. Ilf. CJ32 49
Fairmead Rd. N19 BW34 47
Fairmead Rd. Croy. BX54 86
Fairmead Rd. Houns. BD43 64
Fairmead Rd. Loug. CH25 31
Fairmile Ave. Cob. BE60 93
Fairmile Av. SW16 BW49 76
Fairmile La. Cob. BD59 93
Fairmile Pk. Rd. Cob. BE59 93
Fairmount Rd. SW2 BX46 76
Fairoak Clo. Ken. BY61 104
Fairoak Clo. Lthd. BG59 93
Fairoak Clo. Orp. CL54 88
Fairoak Dr. SE9 CM46 78
Fairoak Gdns. Rom. CT30 41
Fairoak La. Lthd. BG59 93
Fairoak La. Lthd. BH59 93
Fairshot Ct. St. Alb. BK10 9
Fairs Rd. Lthd. BJ63 102
Fair St. SE1 CA41 67
Fair St. Houns. BG45 64
Fairthorn Rd. SE7 CH42 68
Fairtrough La. Orp. CO60 98
Fair Vw. Cob. BD61 102
Fairview, Pot. B. BS18 20
Fairview Av. Brwd. DF26 122
Fairview Av. Rain. CV37 60
Fairview Av. Wem. BK36 54
Fairview Clo. E17 CD30 39
Fairview Clo. Chig. CN28 40
Fairview Clo. Epsom BO59 94
Fairview Cres. Har. BF33 45
Fairview Dr. Chig. CN28 40
Fairview Dr. Orp. CM56 97
Fairview Dr. Shep. AY53 83
Fairview Dr. Wat. BB21 26
Fairview Gdns. Wdf. Grn. CH30 40
Fairview Pl. SW2 BX47 76
Holmewood Gdns.
Fairview Rd. N15 CA32 48
Fairview Rd. SW16 BX51 86
Fairview Rd. Chig. CN28 40
Fairview Rd. Enf. BX23 29
Fairview Rd. Epsom BO59 94
Fairview Rd. Erith CT43 69
Fairview Rd. Grav. DE50 81
Fairview Rd. Sutt. BT56 95
Fairview Way, Edg. BM28 37
Fairwater Av. Well. CO45 69
Fairway SW20 BQ52 85
Fairway, Bexh. CQ46 79
Fairway Cars. BT59 95
Fairway, Cher. AW54 83
Fairway. Grays. DD40 71
Fairway, Guil. AU70 118
Fairway, Hem. H. AY15 8
Fairway Orp. CM53 88
Fairway, Saw. CQ6 6
Fairway, Wdf. Grn. CJ28 40
Fairway Av. NW9 BM31 46
Fairway Av. Borwd. BM23 28
Fairway Clo. NW11 BT33 47
Fairway Clo. Croy. CD53 87
Fairway Clo. Epsom BN55 85
Fairway Clo. St. Alb. BG17 18
Fairway Dri. Dart. CX47 80
Fairway Gdns. Ilf. CM35 49
Fairways, Ashf. AZ50 73
Fairways, Stan. BL30 37
Fairways, Tedd. BK50 74
Fairways, Wal. Abb. CG20 22
Fairways, The, Harl. CO12 14
Fairway, The, N13 BZ27 39
Fairway, The, W3 BO39 55
Fairway, The, Barn. BS25 29
Fairway, The, Brom. CK53 88
Fairway, The, E. Mol. BF52 84
Fairway, The Grav. DG48 81
Fairway, The Lthd. BJ62 102
Fairway, The, N. Mal. BN51 85
Fairway, The. Nthlt. BG36 54
Fairway. The. Nthwd. BB28 35
Fairway, The, Nw7 BN27 37
Fairway, The N14 BV25 29
Fairway, The, Ruis. BD35 45
Fairway, The, Upmin. CY33 51
Fairway, The Uxb. AY37 53
Fairway, The, Wat. BA19 17
Fairway, The, Wem. BJ34 45
Fairway, The, Wey. AZ59 92
Fairweather Clo. N15 CA31 48
Lawrence Rd.
Fairweather Rd. N16 CB32 48
Fairwood Ct. E11 CF33 48
Fairwyn Rd. SE26 CD49 77
Fairy Lawns Clo. Horn. CW33 51
Falcon Av. Brom. CK52 88
Falconberg Ms. W1 BW39 56
Sutton Row
Falcon Cl. Hat. BP13 10
Falcon Clo. SE1 BZ40 57
Falcon Clo. Saw. CP6 6
Falcon Cres. Enf. CC25 30
Falcon Dr. Stai. AX46 73
Falconer Rd. Bush. BE25 27
Falconer Rd. Ilf. CO28 41
Falconers Pk. Saw. CP6 6
Falconer Wk. N7 BX34 47
Andover Est.
Falcon Pl. N16 CA34 48
Church St.
Falcon Ridge, Berk. AR13 7
Falcon Rd. SW11 BU44 66
Falcon Rd. SW11 BU45 66
Falcon Rd. Enf. CC25 30
Falcon Rd. Guil. AR71 118
Falcon Rd. Hamptn. BE50 74
Falcon St. E13 CG38 58
Falcon Ter. Est. SW11 BU45 66
Falcon Way, Har. BL32 46
Falcon Way. Rain. CU37 59
Falcon Way Sun. BB51 83
Peregrine Rd.
Falconwood Av. Well. CM44 68
Falconwood Pde. Well. CN45 68
Falconwood Rd. Croy. CD58 96
Falcourt Clo. Sutt. BS56 95
Robin Hood La.
Falkholt St. SW7 BU42 66
Rutland St.
Falkirk Clo. Horn. CX33 51
Falkirk Gdns. Wat. BD28 36
Falkirk St. N1 CA37 57
Falkland Av. N3 BS29 38
Falkland Av. N11 BV28 38
Falkland Gdns. Dor. BJ72 119
Falkland Clo.
Falkland Gro. Dor. BJ72 119
Vincents La.
Falkland Pk. Av. SE25 CA52 87
Falkland Pl. NW5 BW35 47
Falkland Rd.
Falkland Rd. N8 BY31 47
Falkland Rd. NW5 BW35 47
Falkland Rd. Barn. BR23 28
Falkland Rd. Dor. BJ72 119
Fallaise, Egh. AS49 72
Fallaize Ave. Ilf. CL35 49
Riverdene Rd.
Falling La. West Dr. AY40 53
Falloden Way NW11 BS31 47
Fallon Trading Est. NW10 BO35 46
Fallow Clo. Chig. CN28 40
Fallow Ct. Av. N12 BT29 38
Fallowfied. Welw. G. C. BR6 5
Fallowfield Stan. BJ27 36
Fallowfield Ct. Stan. BJ27 36
Fallowfield Walk, Hem. H. AW12 8
Fallow Hurst Path, N3 BT29 38
Park Cres.
Fallsbrook Rd. SW16 BV50 76
Falmer Rd. E17 CE31 48
Falmer Rd. N15 BZ32 48
Falmer Rd. Enf. CA24 30
Falmouth Av. E4 CF28 39
Falmouth Clo. SE12 CG46 78
Taunton Rd.
Falmouth Gdns. Ilf. CJ31 49
Falmouth Rd. SE1 BZ41 67
Falmouth Rd. Walt. BD56 93
Falmouth St. E15 CF35 48
Falstaff Gdns. St. Alb. BG15 9
Fambridge Rd. SE26 CD49 77
Fambridge Rd. Dag. CR33 50
Famet Av. Pur. BZ60 96
Famet Clo. Pur. BZ60 96
Famet Wk. Pur. BZ60 96
Fane St. W14 BR43 65
Fann St. EC1 BZ38 57
Fanshawe Av. Bark. CM36 58
Fanshawe Cres. Dag. CQ35 50
Fanshawe Cres. Horn. CV32 51
Fanshawe Rd. Grays. DG41 71
Fanshawe Rd. Rich. BK49 74
Fanshaws La. Hert. BZ12 12
Fanshaw St. N1 CA38 57
Fanthorpe St. SW15 BQ45 65
Fara Cl. N7 BX36 56
Faraday Av. Sid. CO48 79
Faraday Clo. Wat. BB25 26
Faraday Rd. E15 CG36 58
Faraday Rd. SE7 CJ41 68
Faraday Rd. SW19 BS50 76
Faraday Rd. W3 BN40 55
Faraday Rd. W10 BR39 55
Faraday Rd. E. Mol. BF52 84
Faraday Rd. Sthl. BF39 54
Faraday Rd. Well. CO45 69
Faraday St. SE17 BZ43 67
Faraday Way Orp. CO52 89
Fareham Rd. Felt. BD46 74
Far End. Hat. BP14 10
Farewell Pl. Mitch. BT51 86
Farifield Clo. N12 BT28 38
Faringdon Av. Brom. CL54 88
Faringdon Av. Rom. CV30 42
Faringford Clo. St. Alb. BF16 18
Farisbarn Dri. Wey. AV59 91
Fari, S La. Wey. AV59 91
Farjoon Rd. SE3 CJ44 68
Farland Rd. Hem. H. AZ13 8
Farleigh Av. Brom. CG53 88
Farleigh Court Rd. Warl. CD60 96
Farleigh Dean Cres. Croy. CE58 96
Farleigh Dean Cres. Croy. CE59 96
Farleigh Pl. N16 CA35 48
Farleigh Rd. N16 CA35 48
Farleigh Rd. Warl. CC62 105
Farleigh Rd. Warl. CD62 105
Farleigh Rd. Wey. AW59 92
Farleton Clo. Wey. BA57 92
Farley Dr. Ilf. BT33 47
Farley Pl. SE25 CB52 87
Farley Rd. SE6 CE46 77
Farley Rd. Sth. Croy. CB58 96
Farleys Clo. Leath. BA66 110
Farlington Pl. SW15 BP47 75
Farlow Clo. Grav. DF48 81
Grieves Rd.
Farlow Rd. SW15 BQ45 65
Farlton Rd. SW18 BS47 76
Farman Gro. Nthlt. BD38 54
Wayfarer Rd.
Farm Av. NW2 BR34 46
Farm Av. SW16 BX49 76
Farm Av. Har. BE33 45
Farm Av. Orp. CM54 88
Farm Av. Swan. CS52 89
Farm Av. Wem. BK36 54
Farm Clo. Amer. AR23 25
Farm Clo. Barn. BP25 28
Farm Clo. Brwd. DE26 122
Farm Clo. Buck. H. CJ27 40
Farm Clo. Cher. AT53 82
Farm Clo. Dag. CS36 59
Farm Close. Leath. BB67 110
Farm Clo. Lthd. BG65 102
Farm Clo. Maid. AG42 61
Farm Clo. Pot. B. BW17 20
Farm Clo. Shep. AZ54 83
Farm Clo. Stai. AV49 72
Farm Clo. Sthl. BF40 54
Farm Clo. Sutt. BT57 95
Farm Clo. Wall. BW58 95
Farm Clo. Welw. G. C. BQ8 5
Farm Clo. W. Wick. CG55 88
Farmcote Rd. SE12 CH47 78
Farm Ct. NW4 BP31 46
Farm Ct. Uxb. AZ34 44
Farm Cres. Slou. AR39 52
Farmcroft, Grav. DG48 81
Farmdale Rd. SE10 CH42 68
Farmdale Rd. Cars. BU57 95
Farm Dr. Croy. CD55 87
Farm Dr. Pur. BW59 95
Farm End E4 CG25 31
Farm End. Nthwd. AZ30 35
Farmer Rd. E10 CE33 48
Farmers Clo. Wat. BC20 17
Farmers Rd. Stai. AV49 72
Farmer St. W8 BS40 56
Farmers Way. Beac. AO29 34
Farm Field, Wat. BB22 26
Farmfield Clo. N12 BS28 38
Farmfield Rd. Brom. CF49 77
Farm Fields Sth. Croy. CA59 96
Farm Hill Rd. Wal. Abb. CF20 21
Farm House Clo. Wok. AU61 100
Farmhouse Rd. SW16 BW50 76
Farmilo Rd. E17 CD33 48
Farmington Av. Sutt. BT55 86
Farmlands, Enf. CH23 31
Farmlands. Pnr. BC31 44
Farmlands, The, Nthlt. BE36 54
Farmland Wk. Chis. CL49 78
Farm La. N14 BV25 29
Farm La. SW6 BS43 66
Farm La. Ash. BM61 103
Farm La. Croy. CD55 87
Farm Lane. Leath. BB67 110
Farm La. Pur. BW58 95
Farm La. Rick. AX24 26
Farm La. Slou. AO40 52
Farmleigh Gro. Watt. BB56 92
Farmleigh Rd. N14 BW26 38
Farm Pl. W8 BS40 56
Farm Pl. Berk. AP12 7
Farm Pl. Dart. CU45 69
Farm Rd. N21 BY26 38
Farm Rd. Edg. BM29 37
Farm Rd. Epsom BN59 94
Farm Rd. Esher BF54 84
Farm Rd. Mord. BS53 86
Farm Rd. Nthwd. BA28 35
Farm Rd. Rain. CV38 60
Farm Rd. Rick. AT24 25
Farm Rd. St. Alb. BJ13 9
Farm Rd. Sev. CV63 108
Farm Rd. Stai. AU46 72
Farm Rd. Stai. AW50 73
Farm Rd. Sutt. BT57 95
Farm Rd. Warl. CD63 105
Farm Rd. Wok. AT63 100
Farmstead Rd. SE6 CE49 77
Farmstead Rd. Har. BG30 36
Farm St. W1 BV40 56
Farm, The, SW19 BQ47 75
Princes Way
Farm Vale Bex. CR46 79
Farm Wk. NW11 BR32 46
Farm Wk. Guil. AP71 118
Farm Way Buck. H. CJ28 40
Farm Way Bush. BF24 27
Farmway, Dag. CP34 50
Farmway. Hat. BP11 10
Farm Way. Horn. CU35 50
Farm Way. Nthwd. BB28 35
Farm Way, Stai. AV46 72
Farm Way Wor. Pk. BQ55 85
Farmwell Lane. Leath. AZ67 110
Farnaby Dr. Sev. CU66 116
Farnaby Rd. SE9 CJ45 68
Farnaby Rd. Brom. CF50 77
Farnan Av. E17 CE30 39
Farnan Rd. SW16 BX49 76
Farnborough Av. E17 CD31 48
Farnborough Av. Sth. Croy. CC58 96
Farnborough Com. Orp. CK55 88
Farnborough Cres. Sth. Croy. CD58 96
Farnborough Hill Orp. CM56 97
Farnborough Hill Orp. CN56 97
Farnborough Way SE15 CA43 67
Farnborough Way Orp. CL56 97
Farncombe St. SE16 CB41 67
Farndale Av. N13 BY27 38
Farndale Cres. Grnf. BG38 54
Farndon Mill La. Harl. CL9 6
Farnell Ms. SW5 BS42 66
Farnell Rd. Islw. BG45 64
Farnell Rd. Stai. AW48 73
Farnes Dr. Rom. CV30 42
Farnham Clo. N20 BT26 38
Farnham Gdns. SW20 BP51 85
Farnham Pk. La. Slou. AO37 52
Farnham Pl. SE1 BY40 56
Farnham Rd. Guil. AO72 118
Farnham Rd. Ilf. CN33 49
Farnham Rd. Rom. CV28 42
Farnham Rd. Well. CP44 69
Farnham Royal, SE11 BX43 66
Farningham By-pass Farn. CW53 90
Farningham Cres. Cat. CB65 105
Farningham Hill Swan. CV53 90
Farningham Rd. N17 CB29 39
Farningham Rd. Cat. CB65 105
Farnley Rd. E4 CG26 40
Farnley Rd. SE25 BZ52 87
Farnol Rd. Dart. CX46 80
Farn Yd. Wind. AO43 61
Faroe Rd. W14 BQ41 65
Farorna Wk. Enf. BY23 29
Farquhar Rd. SE19 CA49 77
Farquhar Rd. SW19 BS48 76
Farquharson Rd. Croy. BZ54 87
Farraline Rd. Wat. BC24 26
Farrance Est. E14 CE39 57
Farrance Rd. Rom. CQ32 50
Farrance St. E14 CD39 57
Farrant Av. N22 BY30 38
Farrant Clo. Orp. CN57 97
Farrant St. W10 BR38 55
Farr Av. Bark. CO37 59
Maybury Rd.
Farren Rd. SE23 CD48 77
Farrer Rd. N8 BW31 47
Farrer Rd. Har. BL32 46
Farriers Clo. Grav. DJ47 81
Lwr. Higham Rd.
Farrier St. NW1 BW36 56
Farringdon Clo. Pot. B. BT19 20
Farringdon Rd. EC1 BY38 56
Farringdon St. EC4 BY39 56
Farringford Rd. E15 CG36 58
Farrington Av. Orp. CO52 89
Farrow Gdns. Grays. DD40 71
Farr Rd. Enf. BZ23 30
Farthing Alley, SE1 CB41 67
Wolseley St.
Farthing Barn La. Orp. CK58 97
Farthing Clo. Dart. CW45 70
Farthing Flds. E1 CB40 57
Raine St.
Farthing Green La. Slou. AQ37 52
Farthings, Wok. AP61 100
Farthings Clo. E4 CG27 40
Bernwell Rd.
Farthings Clo. Pnr. BC32 44
Farthing St. Orp. CK57 97
Farwell Rd. Sid. CO48 79
Farwig La. Brom. CG51 88
Fashion St. E1 CA39 57
Fashoda Rd. Brom. CJ52 88
Fassett Rd. E8 CB36 57
Fassett Rd. Kings-on-t. BL52 85
Fassett Sq. E8 CB36 57
Fauconberg Rd. W4 BN43 65
Faulkners Rd. Walt. BD56 93
Faulkner St. SE14 CC44 67
Fauna Clo. Rom. CP32 50
Faunce St. SE17 BY42 66
Favart Rd. SW6 BS44 66
Faversham Av. E4 CG26 40
Faversham Av. Enf. BZ25 30
Faversham Clo. Chig. CO27 41
Faversham Rd. SE6 CD47 77
Faversham Rd. Beck. CD51 87
Croydon Rd.
Faversham Rd. Mord. BS53 86
Fawcett Est. E5 CB33 48
Fawcett Rd. NW10 BO37 55
Fawcett Rd. Croy. BZ55 87
Fawcett Rd. Wind. AN44 61
Fawcett St. SW10 BT43 66
Fawe Pk. Rd. SW15 BR45 65
Fawe St. E14 CE39 57
Fawke Comm. Rd. Sev. CX66 117
Fawkham Green Rd. Fawk. DA55 90
Fawkham Rd. Sev. CZ57 99
Fawkham Rd. S. Dnth. DB52 90
Fawley Rd. N17 CB31 48
Fawley Rd. NW6 BS35 47
Fawnbrake Av. SE24 BY46 76
Fawn Ct. Hat. BQ11 10
Fawn Rd. E13 CJ37 58
Fawn Rd. Chig. CN28 40
Fawns Manor Rd. Felt. BA47 73
Fawood Av. NW10 BN36 55
Fawsley Clo. Slou. AV44 62
Coleridge Cres.
Fawters Clo. Brwd. DE25 122
Faygate Cres. Bexh. CR46 79
Faygate Rd. SW2 BX48 76
Fay Green, Wat. BA20 17
Fayland Av. SW16 BW49 76
Fayland Est. SW16 BW49 76
Faymore Gdns. S. Ock. DA39 60
Feacey Down, Hem. H. AW12 8
Fearn Clo. Leath. BB68 110
Fearnley Rd. SE5 CA44 67
Lettsom St.
Fearnley Rd. Welw. G. C. BQ8 5
Fearnley St. Wat. BC24 26
Fearon St. SE10 CH42 68
Featherbed La. Croy. CD57 96
Featherbed La. Hem. H. AW16 17
Featherbed La. Wat. BC16 17
Featherbed La. Wat. BD16 18
Feather Dell Croft. Hat. BO12 10
Feather Dell Wood. Hat. BO12 10
Feathers La. Stai. AT48 72
Feathers Pl. SE10 CF43 67
Featherstone Av. SE23 CB48 77
Featherstone Clo. Pot. B. BT19 20
Featherstone Ct. EC1 BZ38 57
Featherstone St.
Featherstone Gdns. Borwd. BN24 28
Featherstone Rd. NW7 BP29 37
Featherstone Rd. Sthl. BE41 64
Featherstone St. EC1 BZ38 57
Featherstone Ter. Sthl. BE41 64
Featley Rd. SW9 BY45 66
Angell Rd.
Federal Rd. Grnf. BK37 54
Federal Way Wat. BD22 27
Federal Way Wat. BD23 27
Federation Rd. SE2 CO42 69
Fee Farm Rd. Esher BH57 93
Feenan Highway. Til. DG43 71
Feilding Ave. Til. DG44 71
Felbridge Av. Stan. BJ30 36
Felbridge Clo. SW16 BY49 76
Felbridge Clo. Sutt. BS58 95
Felbrigge Rd. Ilf. CN34 49
Felcott Clo. Walt. BD55 84
Felcott Rd. Walt. BD55 84
Felday Rd. SE13 CE46 77
Felden Clo. Pnr. BE29 36
Felden Clo. Wat. BD20 18
Felden Dr. Hem. H. AW15 8
Felden Lane, Hem. H. AW15 8
Felden Rd. Hem. H. AX15 8
Felden St. SW6 BR44 65
Feldwick Pl. Red. BV70 121
Ladbroke Rd.
Felgate Ms. W6 BP42 65
Felhampton Rd. SE9 CL48 78
Felhurst Cres. Dag. CR35 50
Felicia Way. Grays. DG42 71
Felix Av. N8 BX32 47
Felix Drive. Guil. AW67 110
Felix La. Shep. BB53 83
Felix Rd. W13 BJ40 54
Felix Rd. Walt. BC53 83
Felixstowe Rd. N9 CB27 39
Felixstowe Rd. N17 CA31 48
Felixstowe Rd. NW10 BP38 55
Felixstowe Rd. SE2 CO41 69
Felix St. E2 CB37 57
Cambridge Cres.
Felland Way, Reig. BT72 121
Fellbrigg Rd. SE22 CA46 77
Fellbrigg St. E1 CB38 57
Headlam St.
Fellbrook, Rich. BJ48 74
Fellowes La. St. Alb. BN15 10
Fellowes Rd. Cars. BU55 86
Fellows Rd. NW3 BT36 56
Fell Rd. Croy. BZ55 87
Felltram Way SE7 CH42 68
Felmersham Clo. SW4 BW45 66
Felmingham Rd. SE20 CC51 87
Felmongers, Harl. CO10 6
Felnex Est. NW10 BN38 55
Felsberg Rd. SW2 BX46 76
Fels Clo. Dag. CR34 50
Fels Fm. Av. Dag. CS34 50
Felsham Rd. SW15 BQ45 65
Felspar Clo. SE18 CN42 68

Felstead Av. Ilf. CL30 40
Felstead Rd. E11 CH33 49
Felstead Rd. Epsom BN59 94
Felstead Rd. Loug. CK26 40
Felstead Rd. Orp. CO55 89
Felstead Rd. Rom. CS29 41
Felstead Rd. Wal. Cr. CD19 21
Felstead St. E9 CD36 57
Felsted Rd. E16 CJ39 58
Feltham Av. E. Mol. BH52 84
Feltham Hill Rd. Ashf. AZ49 73
Feltham Hill Rd. Felt. BC49 73
Feltham Rd. Ashf. AZ49 73
Feltham Rd. Mitch. BV51 86
Feltham Rd. Red. BU73 121
Feltham Wk. Red. BU73 121
Felton Clo. Borwd. BL22 28
Felton Clo. Brom. CL53 88
Felton Lea, Sid. CN49 78
Felton Rd. W13 BK41 64
Camborne Av.
Felton Rd. Bark. CN37 58
Felton St. N1 BZ37 57
Fencepiece Rd. Chig. CM28 40
Fenchurch Av. EC3 CA39 57
Fenchurch Bldgs. EC3 CA39 57
Fenchurch St. EC3 BZ40 57
Fen Clo. Brwd. DD24 122
Fen Ct. EC3 CA39 57
Fendall Rd. Epsom BN56 94
Fendall St. SE1 CA41 67
Fendt Clo. E16 CG40 58
Rowman Av.
Fendyke Rd. Belv. CP42 69
Fenelon Pl. W14 BR42 65
Fengates Rd. Red. BU70 121
Fen Gro. Sid. CN46 78
Fenham Rd. SE15 CB43 67
Fenismead Av. Sutt. BQ58 94
Fen Lane, Upmin. DB35 51
Fen La. Upmin. DC35 123
Fenman Ct. N17 CB30 39
Shelbourne Rd.
Fenn Clo. Brom. CH50 78
Fennel Cl. Guil. AT69 118
Fennels Harl. CM13 13
Fennels Mead, Epsom BO58 94
Fennel St. SE18 CL43 68
Fennings, The Amer. AO21 25
Fenning St. SE1 CA41 67
St. Thomas St.
Fenn St. E9 CC35 48
Fenns Way, Wok. AS61 100
Fenny Croft, Hem. H. AV12 7
Fen Pond Rd. Sev. DB62 108
Fensomes Alley, Hem. H. AY13 8
Fenstanton Av. N12 BT29 38
Fen St. E16 CG40 58
Huntingdon St.
Fens Way, Swan. CU50 79
Fentiman Rd. SW8 BX43 66
Fentiman Way, Horn. CW33 51
Fenton Av. Stai. AX50 73
Fenton Clo. Red. BV70 121
Fenton Ho. Est. NW3 BT34 47
Fenton Rd. N17 BZ29 39
Fenton Rd. Red. BV70 121
Fenton's Av. E13 CH37 58
Fentum Rd. Guil. AQ69 118
Fenwick Gro. SE15 CB45 67
Fenwick Pl. SW9 BX45 66
Fenwick Rd. SE15 CB45 67
Fenwick St. SE18 CL43 68
Ferdinand Est. NW1 BV36 56
Ferdinand Pl. NW5 BV36 56
Ferdinand St. NW1 BV36 56
Ferguson Av. Grav. DH49 81
Ferguson Av. Rom. CV30 42
Ferguson Av. Surb. BL53 85
Ferguson Cres. Rom. CV30 42
Fergus Rd. N5 BY35 47
Calabria Rd.
Ferme. Pk. Rd. N4 BX32 47
Ferme. Pk. Rd. N8 BX32 47
Fermor Rd. SE23 CD47 77
Fermoy Rd. W9 BR38 55
Fermoy Rd. Grnf. BF38 54
Fern Av. Mitch. BW52 86
Fernbank Av. Horn. CV35 51
Fernbank Av. Walt. BE54 84
Fernbank Av. Wem. BH35 45
Fernbank Rd. Wey. AW56 92
Fernbrook Av. Sid. CN46 78
Fernbrook Cres. SE13 CG46 78
Fernbrook Dr. Har. BF33 45
Fernbrook Rd. SE13 CG46 78
Ferncliff Rd. E8 CB35 48
Fern Clo. Brox. CD15 12
Curzon La.E.
Fern Clo. Warl. CD62 105
Fern Cft. St. Alb. BG15 9
Ferncroft Av. N12 BU29 38
Ferncroft Av. NW3 BS34 47
Ferncroft Av. Ruis. BD34 45
Ferndale Brom. CJ51 88
Fern Dale, Guil. AP69 118
Ferndale Horn. CW32 51
Ferndale Av. E17 CF32 48
Ferndale Av. Cher. AV55 82
Ferndale Av. Houns. BE45 64
Ferndale Ct. SE3 CG43 68
Ferndale Ct. SW9 BX45 66
Ferndale Cres. Uxb. AX38 53
Ferndale Rd. E7 CH36 58
Ferndale Rd. E11 CG34 49
Ferndale Rd. N15 CA32 48
Ferndale Rd. SE25 CB53 87
Ferndale Rd. SW4 BX45 66
Ferndale Rd. SW9 BX45 66
Ferndale Rd. Ashf. AX49 73
Ferndale Rd. Bans. BR61 103
Ferndale Rd. Enf. CD22 30
Ferndale Rd. Grav. DG48 81
Ferndale Rd. Rom. CS30 41
Ferndale Rd. Wok. AS61 100
Ferndale St. E6 CL40 58
Ferndale Ter. Har. BH31 45
Ferndale Way Orp. CM56 97
Ferndell Av. Bex. CS48 79
Fern Dells. Hat. BO13 10
Fern Dene W13 BJ39 54
Dene, The.
Ferndene Rd. SE24 BZ45 67
Fernden Way. Rom. CR32 50
Ferndown Av. Orp. CM54 88
Ferndown Clo. Guil. AT71 118
Ferndown Clo. Pnr. BE29 36
Ferndown Clo. Sutt. BT57 95
Ferndown Rd. SE9 CJ47 78
Ferndown Rd. Nthwd. BC30 35
Ferndown Rd. Wat. BD27 36
Fern Dr. Felt. BC47 73
Fern Dr. Hem. H. AY14 8
Ferney Rd. Barn. BV26 38
Ferney Rd. Wey. AX59 92
Fern Gro. Welw. G. C. BQ6 5
Fernhall Dr. Ilf. CJ32 49
Fernhall La. Wal. Abb. CJ19 22
Fernham Rd. Th. Hth. BZ52 87
Fernhead Rd. W9 BR38 55
Fernhead Yd. W9 BR39 55
Fernhead Rd.
Fernheath Way Dart. CS49 79
Fernhill Harl. CN13 13
Fernhill, Kings L. BA20 17
Fern Hill, Lthd. BG60 93
Fernhill Clo. Wok. AR63 100
Fernhill Ct. E17 CF30 39
Fernhill Ct. Kings. On T. BK49 74
Fernhill Gdns. Kings. On T. BK49 74
Fernhill La. Harl. CN13 13
Fern Hill La. Wok. AR63 100
Fernhill Pk. Wok. AR63 100
Fernhill St. E16 CK40 58
Fernholme Rd. SE15 CC46 77
Fernhurst Gdns. Edg. BM29 37
Fernhurst Rd. SW6 BR44 65
Fernhurst Rd. Ashf. BA49 73
Fernhurst Rd. Croy. CB54 87
Fernie Clo. Chig. CO28 41
Fernlands Clo. Cher. AV55 82
Fern La. Houns. BE42 64
Fernlea, Lthd. BF65 102
Fernlea Rd. SW12 BV47 76
Fernlea Rd. Mitch. BV51 86
Fernleigh Ct. Har. BF30 36
Fernleigh Ct. Wem. BL34 46
Fernleigh Rd. N21 BY27 38
Fern Leys, St. Alb. BK12 9
Fernsbury St. WC1 BY38 56
Margery St.
Ferns Clo. Enf. CD21 30
Fernshaw Rd. SW10 BT43 66
Fernside, NW3 BS34 47
Fernside, NW4 BQ30 37
Fernside Buck. H. CH26 40
Fernside Av. NW7 BN27 37
Fernside Av. Felt. BC49 73
Fernside La. Sev. CV68 117
Fernside Rd. SW12 BU47 76
Fernsleigh Clo. Ger. Cr. AS29 34
Ferns Rd. E15 CG36 58
Fern St. E3 CE38 57
Fernthorpe Rd. SW16 BW50 76
Ferntower Rd. N5 BZ35 48
Fernville La. Hem. H. AX13 8
Fern Way, Wat. BC21 26
Fernways Ilf. CL35 49
Fernwood Av. SW16 BW49 76
Fernwood Av. Wem. BK36 54
Fernwood Clo. Brom. CJ51 88
Fernwood Cres. N20 BU27 38
Ferrant Clo. SE7 CJ41 68
Ferrard Clo. Houns. BF43 64
Ferrers Ave. West Dr. AX41 63
Ferrers Av. Wall. BW56 95
Ferrers Rd. SW16 BW49 76
Ferrestone Rd. N8 BX31 47
Glebe Rd.
Ferrier St. SW18 BS45 66
Ferriers Way, Epsom. BQ63 103
Ferring Clo. Har. BG33 45
Ferrings, SE21 CA48 77
Ferris Av. Croy. CD55 87
Ferris Rd. SE22 CB45 67
Ferron Rd. E5 CB34 48
Ferro Rd. Rain. CU38 59
Ferry Approach SE18 CL41 68
Ferry Av. Stai. AV50 72
Ferryhills Clo. Wat. BD27 36
Ferry La. N17 CB31 48
Ferry La. SW13 BO43 65
Lonsdale Rd.
Ferry La. Brent. BL43 65
Ferry La. Guil. AR72 118
Ferry La. Rain. CT39 59
Ferry La. Rich. BL43 65
Ferry La. Shep. AZ54 83
Ferry La. Stai. AT48 72
Ferry La. Stai. AX52 83
Ferrymead Av. Grnf. BF38 54
Ferrymead Dr. Grnf. BF37 54
Ferrymead Gdns. Grnf. BF37 54
Ferrymoor Rich. BJ48 74
Ferry Path, Cher. AW53 83
Ferry Pl. E14 CF42 67
Ferry Pl. SE18 CL41 68
Ferry Rd. SW13 BP43 65
Ferry Rd. E. Mol. BF52 84
Ferry Rd. Maid. AH41 61
Ferry Rd. Surb. BJ53 84
Ferry Rd. Tedd. BJ49 74
Ferry Rd. Twick. BJ47 74
Ferry St. E14 CF42 67
Feryby Rd. Grays. DG41 71
Fesants Croft, Harl. CO9 6
Festing Rd. SW15 BQ45 65
Festival Clo. Bex. CP47 79
Festival Clo. Erith CT43 69
Festival Clo. Uxb. AZ37 53
Fetcham Comm. La. Lthd. BF64 102
Fetcham Pk. Dr. Lthd. BH65 102
Fetter La. EC4 BY39 56
Fews La. Rom. CP31 50
Ffinch St. SE8 CE43 67
Fiddicroft Av. Bans. BS60 95
Fiddle Bri. Lane. Hat. BO12 10
Field Clo. E4 CE29 39
Field Clo. Brom. CJ51 88
Field Clo. Buck. H. CJ27 40
Field Clo. Chess. BK57 93
Field Clo. E. Mol. BF53 84
Field Clo. Houns. BC44 63
Field Clo. Rom. CO24 32
Field Clo. Ruis. BA33 44
Field Clo. Sth. Croy. CB60 96
Field Clo. Uxb. AZ34 44
Fieldcommon La. Walt. BE54 84
Field Ct. WC1 BX39 56
Field End Barn. BP24 28
Field End Couls. BW56 95
Field End. Couls. BW60 95
Field End Nthlt. BD36 54
Field End Ruis. BD36 54
Field End Twick. BH49 74
Fieldend Rd. SW16 BW51 86
Field End Rd. Pnr. BC32 44
Field Gate La. Mitch. BU52 86
Fieldgate St. E1 CB39 57
Fieldhouse Rd. SW12 BW47 76
Fieldhurst Clo. Wey. AW56 92
Fielding Av. Twick. BG48 74
Fielding Rd. W4 BN41 65
Fielding Rd. W14 BQ41 65
Fieldings Rd. Wal. Cr. CD18 21
Fieldings, The, SE23 CC47 77
Fielding Ter. W5 BL40 55
Uxbridge Rd.
Fielding Way, Brwd. DE25 122
Field La. Brent. BK43 64
Field La. Tedd. BJ49 74
Field Mead NW9 BO29 37
Field Pk. Cres. Rom. CP32 50
Field Pl. EC1 BY37 56
St. John St.
Field Pl. N. Mal. BO53 85
Field Rd. E7 CG35 49
Field Rd. E17 CE31 48
Field Rd. N17 BZ31 48
Field Rd. NW10 BQ38 55
Field Rd. W6 BR42 65
Field Rd. Felt. BC46 73
Field Rd. Slou. AT41 62
Field Rd. S. Ock. CW40 60
Field Rd. Wat. BE25 27
Fields End La. Hem. H. AU12 7
Fieldsend Rd. Sutt. BR56 94
Fields Est. E8 CB36 57
Fieldside Rd. Brom. CF49 77
Field St. WC1 BX38 56
Fieldview, SW18 BT47 76
Field Vw. Felt. BA49 73
Fieldview Rise, St. Alb. BE18 18
Field View Rd. Pot. B. BS20 20
Field Way, NW10 BN36 55
Field Way, Berk. AS14 7
Field Way Croy. CE57 96
Field Way, Dag. CO35 50
Field Way, Ger. Cr. AR29 34
Fieldway. Grays. DD40 71
Field Way. Hem. H. AT17 16
Fieldway Orp. CM53 88
Field Way. Rick. AW26 35
Field Way, Ruis. BA33 44
Fieldway Cres. N5 BY35 47
Fielding Waye, Uxb. AX38 53
Fife Ct. W3 BM39 55
Links Rd.
Fifehead Clo. Ashf. AY50 73
Fife Rd. E16 CH39 58
Fife Rd. N22 BY29 38
Fife Rd. SW14 BN46 75
Fife Rd. Kings. On T. BL51 85
Fife Ter. N1 BX37 56
Wynford Rd.
Fife Way Brom. CH51 88
White Hart Slip.
Fifeway. Lthd. BF66 111
Fifield La. Wind. AH45 61
Fifield Path SE23 CC48 77
Fifield Rd. Hem. H. AZ14 8
Fifield Rd. Maid. AH43 61
Fifield Rd. Wind. AH44 61
Fifth Av. E12 CK35 49
Fifth Av. W10 BR38 55
Fifth Av. Enf. CA25 30
Fifth Av. Harl. CM10 6
Fifth Av. Harl. CM9 6
Fifth Av. Hayes BB40 53
Fifth Av. Wat. BD21 27
Fifth Cross Rd. Twick. BG48 74
Figg's Rd. Mitch. BV50 76
Fig Tree Hill, Hem. H. AX13 8
Filby Rd. Chess. BL57 94
Filey Av. N16 CD33 48
Filey Clo. Sutt. BT57 95
Filey Clo. West. CH63 106
Filey Waye Ruis. BC34 44
Fillebrook Av. Enf. CA23 30
Fillebrook Rd. E11 CF33 48
Filmer La. Sev. CW64 108
Filmer Rd. SW6 BR44 65
Filmer Rd. Wind. AL44 61
Filston La. Sev. CS61 107
Filston Rd. Belv. CR42 69
Riverdale Rd.
Filston Rd. Erith CR42 69
Riverdale Rd.
Filston Rd. Erith CS42 69
Holly Hill Rd.
Finborough Rd. SW10 BS42 66
Finborough Rd. SW17 BU50 76
Finchale Rd. SE2 CO41 69
Finch Av. SE27 BZ49 77
Finch Cl. Hat. BP13 10
Finch Clo. NW10 BN36 55
Finch Clo. Wok. AO62 100
Finchdale, Hem. H. AW14 8
Finchdean Way, SE15 CA43 67
Finch Dr. Felt. BD47 74
Finches Dr. Guil. AU69 118
Finchingfield Av. Wdf. Grn. CJ29 40
Finch La. EC3 BZ39 57
Finch La. Amer. AP24 25
Finch La. Bush. BE24 27
Finchley Clo. Dart. CX46 80
Finchley Ct. N3 BS29 38
Finchley La. NW4 BQ31 46
Finchley Pk. N12 BT28 38
Finchley Pl. NW8 BT37 56
Finchley Rd. NW2 BR31 46
Finchley Rd. NW3 BR31 46
Finchley Rd. NW8 BR31 46
Finchley Rd. NW8 BT37 56
Finchley Rd. NW11 BR31 46
Finchley Rd. Grays. DD43 71
Finchley Way N3 BS29 38
Finchmoor Harl. CM12 13
Finch Rd. Berk. AQ12 7
Finch Rd. Guil. AR70 118
Finck St. SE1 BX41 66
Finden Rd. E7 CH35 49
Findhorne Av. Hayes BC39 53
Findhorn St. E14 CF39 57
Aberfeldy St.
Findon Clo. Har. BF34 45
Findon Gdns. Rain. CU39 59
Findon Rd. N9 CB26 39
Findon Rd. W12 BP41 65
Fine Bush La. Uxb. AZ32 44
Fingal St. SE10 CG42 68
Fingrith Hall La. Ing. DC17 24
Finians Clo. Uxb. AY36 53
Finistock Rd. W10 BQ39 55
Finland Rd. SE4 CD45 67
Finlays Clo. Chess. BM56 94
Finlay St. SW6 BQ44 65
Finnis St. E2 CB38 57
Finnymore Rd. Dag. CQ36 59
Finsbury Av. EC2 BZ39 57
Finsbury Circus, EC2 BZ39 57
Finsbury Cotts. N22 BX29 38
Finsbury Mkt. EC2 CA38 57
Finsbury Pk. Av. N4 BZ33 48
Finsbury Pk. Rd. N4 BY34 47
Finsbury Pavement, EC2 BZ39 57
Finsbury Rd. N22 BX29 38
Finsbury Sq. EC2 BZ38 57
Finsbury St. EC2 BZ39 57
Finstock Rd. W10 BQ40 55
Finucane Dr. Orp. CP54 89
Finucane Gdns. Rain. CU36 59
Finucane Rise Bush. BG27 36
Fiona Clo. Lthd. BF65 102
Firbank Dr. Wat. BE26 36
Firbank Dr. Wok. AQ63 100
Firbank La. Wok. AQ63 100
Firbank La. Wok. AR62 100
Firbank Pl. Egh. AQ50 72
Firbank Rd. SE15 CB44 67
Firbank Rd. Rom. CR28 41
Firbank Rd. St. Alb. BH11 9
Fir Clo. Walt. BC54 83
Fircroft Av. Chess. BL56 94
Fircroft Clo. Slou. AQ36 52
Fircroft Clo. Wok. AS62 100
Ockenden Rd.
Fircroft Gdns. Har. BH34 45
Fircroft Rd. SW17 BU48 76
Firdene Surb. BN54 85
Fire Bell Alley Surb. BL53 85
Firefly Clo. Wall. BX57 95
Firfield Rd. Wey. AW56 92
Fir Grange Av. Wey. AZ56 92
Fir Gro. N. Mal. BO53 85
Fir Gro. Wok. AQ63 100
Firham Park Av. Rom. CX29 42
Firhill Rd. SE6 CE49 77
Firlands, Wey. BB57 92
Firmin Rd. Dart. CV46 80
Fir Park. Harl. CL12 13
Fir Rd. Felt. BD49 74
Fir Rd. Sutt. BR54 85
Firs Ave. Wind. AM45 61
Firs Av. N10 BV31 47
Firs Av. SW14 BN45 65
Firsby Av. Croy. CC54 87
Firsby Rd. N16 CA33 48
Firs Cl. Hat. BP13 10
Firs Clo. N10 BV31 47
Firs Av.
Firs Clo. Dor. BJ72 119
Firscroft N13 BZ27 39
Firs Dri. Loug. CK23 31
Firs Dr. Houns. BC44 63
Firs Dr. Loug. CK23 31
Firsgrove Cres. Brwd. DA28 42
Firsgrove Rd. Brwd. DA28 42
Firs La. N13 BZ27 39
Firs La. N21 BZ27 39
Firs La. Pot. B. BS20 20
Firs Pk. Av. N21 BZ26 39
Firs Pk. Gdns. N21 BZ26 39
Firs Rd. Ken. BY61 104
First Ave. Amer. AO23 25
First Av. E12 CK35 49
First Av. E13 CH38 58
First Av. E17 CE32 48
First Av. N18 CC28 39
First Av. NW4 BQ31 46
First Av. SW14 BO45 65
First Av. W3 BO40 55
First Av. W10 BR38 55
First Av. Brwd. DB20 24
First Av. Dag. CR37 59
First Av. E. Mol. BE52 84
First Av. Enf. CA25 30
First Av. Epsom BO58 94
First Av. Grav. DF47 81
First Av. Grays DA43 70
First Av. Harl. CM10 6
First Av. Harl. CN10 6
First Av. Hayes BB40 53
First Av. Hayes BC40 53
Glebe Rd.
First Av. Rom. CP32 50
First Av. Walt. BC53 83
First Av. Wat. BD21 27
First Av. Well. CP43 69
First Av. Wem. BK34 45
First Clo. E. Mol. BG52 84
First Cross Rd. Twick. BH48 74
Firs, The, N20 BT26 38
Athenaeum Rd.
Firs, The, SW20 BP50 75
Firs, The, W5 BK39 54
Firs, The, Bex. CS47 79
Dartford Rd.
Firs. The Bex. CS48 79
Dartford Rd.
Firs, The, St. Alb. BJ15 9
Firs, The, Welw. G. C. BQ6 5
Firs. The. Grays. DE40 71
First Slip, Lthd. BJ62 102
First St. SW3 BU42 66
First Way SW20 BQ51 85
First Way, Guil. AQ70 118
First Way, Wem. BM35 46
Firs Wk. Nthwd. BA29 35
Firs Wk. Wdf. Grn. CH28 40
Firswood Av. Epsom BO56 94
Firth Gdns. SW6 BR44 65
Firtree Ave. West Dr. AZ41 63
Firtree Av. Mitch. BV51 86
Fir Tree Av. Slou. AP38 52
Fir Tree Clo. Epsom BO56 94
Fir Tree Clo. Epsom BQ61 103
Fir Tree Clo. Esher BG56 93
Fir Tree Clo. Hem. H. AZ14 8
Firtree Clo. Orp. CN56 97
Fir Tree Clo. Rom. CS31 50
Fir Tree Clo. Rom. CT31 50
Fir Tree Ct. Borwd. BL24 28
Fir Tree Gdns. Croy. CE56 96
Firtree Gro. Cars. BU57 95
Fir Tree Hill, Rick. AY22 26
Fir Tree Pl. Ashf. AZ49 73
Fir Tree Rd. Epsom BP61 103
Fir Tree Rd. Guil. AR69 118
Fir Tree Rd. Houns. BE45 64
Fir Tree Rd. Lthd. BK65 102
Firtree Wk. Dag. CS34 50
Fir Tree Wk. Enf. BZ24 30
Fir Tree Wk. Reig. BT70 121
Fir Wk. Sutt. BQ57 94
Firwood Av. St. Alb. BL13 10
Firwood Clo. Wok. AP63 100
Firwood Rd. Vir. W. AP53 82
Fisher Clo. Grnf. BF38 54
Fisher Clo. Kings L. AZ18 17
Fishermens Hill Grav. DD46 81
Warwick Pl.
Fisher Rd. Har. BH30 36
Fishers Ct. SE14 CC44 67
Fishers Hatch, Harl. CN10 6
Fisher's La. W4 BN42 65
Fishers La. Epp. CN19 22
Fisher St. E16 CG39 58
Fisher St. WC1 BX39 56
Fishers Way Belv. CS40 59
Fisherton St. Est. NW8 BT38 56
Fisherton St. NW8 BT38 56
Fishery Pl. Hem. H. AW14 8
Fishery Rd. Hem. H. AW14 8
Fishery Rd. Maid. AH40 61
Fishmongers Hall St. EC4 BZ40 57
Swan Wf.
Fishponds Rd. SW17 BU49 76
Fishponds Rd. Kes. CJ56 97
Fishpool St. St. Alb. BF13 9
Fish St. Hill, EC3 BZ40 57
Lwr. Thames St.
Fitzalan Rd. N3 BR31 46
Fitzalan Rd. Esher BH57 93
Fitzalan St. SE11 BX42 66
Fitzegerald Rd. Surb. BJ53 84
Fitz George Av. W14 BR42 65
Fitzgeorge Av. N. Mal. BN51 85
Fitzgerald Av. SW14 BO45 65
Fitzgerald Rd. E11 CH32 49
Fitzgerald Rd. SW14 BN45 65
Fitzhardinge St. W1 BV39 56
Fitzhugh Gro. SW18 BT46 76
Fitzilian Av. Rom. CW30 42
Fitz James Av. W14 BR42 65
Fitzjames Av. Croy. CB55 87
Fitzjohn Av. Barn. BR25 28
Fitzjohn's Av. NW3 BT35 47
Fitzmaurice Pl. W1 BV40 56
Curzon St.
Fitz Neal St. W12 BO39 55
Fitzroy Clo. Har. BH30 36
Fitzroy Gdns. SE19 CA50 77
Fitzroy Ms. NW1 BW38 56
Cleveland St.
Fitzroy Pk. N6 BU33 47
Fitzroy Rd. NW1 BU37 56
Fitzroy Sq. W1 BW38 56
Fitzroy St. W1 BW38 56
Fitzstephen Rd. Dag. CO35 50
Fitzwarren Gdns. N19 BW33 47
Fitzwilliam Av. Rich. BL44 65
Fitzwilliam Rd. SW4 BW45 66
Fitz Wygram Clo. Hamptn. BG49 74

Five Acre NW9 BO30 37
Five Acres. Chesh. AO20 16
Five Acres. Harl. CN12 13
Five Acres, St. Alb. BK16 18
Five Acres Av. St. Alb. BE18 18
Fiveash Rd. Grav. DF47 81
Five Elms Rd. Dag. CQ34 50
Five Oaks Clo. Wok. AP63 100
Five Oaks La. Chig. CQ29 41
Fivewents Swan. CU51 89
Fladbury Rd. N15 BZ32 48
Fladgate Rd. E11 CG32 49
Flags, The Hem. H. AZ13 8
Flag Wk. Pnr. BC32 44
Flambard Rd. Har. BJ32 45
Flamborough Rd. Ruis. BC34 44
Flamborough St. E14 CD39 57
Flamingo Gdns. Nthlt. BD38 54
Flamingo Gdns. Nthlt. BE38 54
Jetstar Way
Flamingo Wk. Rain. CU36 59
Flamstead Est. SE10 CG42 68
Flamstead Gdns. Dag. CP36 59
Flamstead Rd. SE7 CK42 68
Flamstead Rd. Dag. CP36 59
Flamsted Av. Wem. BM36 55
Flanchford Rd. W12 BO41 65
Flanchford Rd. Reig. BP73 120
Flanders Rd. E6 CK37 58
Flanders Rd. W4 BO42 65
Flanders Way, E9 CC36 57
Flank St. E1 CB40 57
Dock St.
Flash La. Enf. BY22 29
Flask Wk. NW3 BT35 47
Flatfield Rd. Hem. H. AZ14 8
Flaunden Bottom. Chesh. AS21 25
Flaunden Bottom. Hem. H. AS20 16
Flaunden Hill. Hem. H. AS20 16
Flaunden La. Hem. H. AT19 16
Flaunden La. Rick. AU20 16
Flavian Clo. St. Alb. BE15 9
Flaxland Hat. BP11 10
Flaxley Rd. Mord. BS54 86
Flaxman Rd. SE5 BY45 66
Flaxman Ter. WC1 BW38 56
Flaxton Rd. SE18 CM44 68
Flecker Clo. Stan. BH28 36
Fleece Rd. Surb. BK54 84
Fleeming Clo. E17 CD30 39
Pennant Ter.
Fleeming Rd. E17 CD30 39
Fleet Ave. Dart. CY47 80
Fleet Av. Upmin. CY32 51
Fleet Cl. E. Mol. BF53 84
Fleet Clo. Upmin. CY32 51
Fleetdale Par. Dart. CY47 80
Fleethall Gro. Grays. DD40 71
Fleet La. EC4 BY39 56
Fleet La. E. Mol. BE53 84
Fleet Rd. NW3 BU35 47
Fleet Rd. Dart. CY47 80
Fleet Rd. Grav. DE48 81
Fleet St. Hill. E1 CB38 57
Weaver St.
Fleet Side E. Mol. BE53 84
Fleet St. EC4 BY39 56
Fleet Way, Egh. AU52 82
Fleetwood Clo. Chess. BK57 93
Fleetwood Clo. Ch. St. G. AQ28 34
Fleetwood Rd. NW10 BP35 46
Fleetwood Rd. N. Mal. BM52 85
Fleetwood Rd. Slou. AP40 52
Fleetwood Sq. N. Mal. BM52 85
Fleetwood St. N16 CA34 48
Fleetwood Way Wat. BD28 36
Fleming Ct. W2 BT39 56
St. Mary's Ter.
Fleming Ct. Croy. BY56 95
Fleming Gdns. Til. DH44 71
Fielding Av.
Fleming Mead, Mitch. BU50 76
Fleming Rd. SE17 BY43 66
Fleming Rd. Sthl. BF39 54
Flempton Rd. E10 CD33 48
Fletcher Clo. Cher. AV57 91
Fletcher La. E10 CF33 48
Fletcher Rd. W4 BN41 65
Fletcher Rd. Cher. AU57 91
Fletcher Rd. Chig. CN28 40
Fletcher Way, Hem. H. AX12 8
Fletching Rd. E5 CC34 48
Fletch St. E1 CB40 57
Cable St.
Fletton Rd. N11 BX29 38
Fleur De Lis St. E1 CA38 57
Fleur Gates, SW19 BQ47 75
Princes Way
Flexley Wd. Welw. G. C. BR6 5
Flexmere Rd. N17 BZ30 39
Flimwell Clo. Brom. CG49 78
Flinder Clo. St. Alb. BJ14 9
Flint Clo. Lthd. BF66 111
Flint Clo. Red. BU70 121
Flint Hill Clo. Dor. BJ73 119
Flintlock Clo. Sta1. AW45 63
Flintmill Cres. SE3 CK44 68
Flinton St. SE17 CA42 67
Flint St. SE17 BZ42 67
Flint Way, St. Alb. BG11 9
Flitcroft St. WC2 BW39 56
Flockton St. SE16 CB41 67
George Row
Flodden Rd. SE5 BZ44 67
Flood St. SW3 BU42 66
Flood Wk. SW3 BU43 66
Flora Cl. E14 CE39 57
Flora Gdns. Rom. CP32 50
Flora Gdns. Est. W6 BP42 65
Flora Gro. St. Alb. BH14 9
Floral Ct. Ash. BK62 102
Floral Dr. St. Alb. BK16 18
Floral St. WC2 BX40 56
Flora St. Belv. CQ42 69
Florence Av. Enf. BZ24 30
Florence Av. Mord. BT53 86
Florence Av. Wey. AW59 92
Florence Clo. Horn. CW34 51
Florence Clo. Wat. BC21 26
Florence Ct. NW4 BP32 46
Vivian Av.
Florence Ct. NW8 BT39 56
Maida Vale
Florence Ct. W9 BT38 56
Florence Dr. Enf. BZ24 30
Florence Gdns. W4 BN43 65
Florence Gdns. Stai. AW50 73
Florence Rd. E6 CJ37 58
Florence Rd. E13 CG38 58
Florence Rd. N4 BX33 47
Florence Rd. SE2 CP42 69
Florence Rd. SE14 CD44 67
Florence Rd. SW19 BS50 76
Florence Rd. W4 BN41 65
Florence Rd. W5 BL40 55
Florence Rd. Beck. CC51 87
Florence Rd. Brom. CH51 88
Florence Rd. Felt. BC47 73
Florence Rd. Kings. On T. BL50 75
Florence Rd. Sth. Croy. BZ58 96
Florence Rd. Sthl. BD42 64
Florence Rd. Walt. BC54 83
Florence St. E16 CG38 58
Florence St. N1 BY36 56
Florence St. NW4 BQ31 46
Florence Ter. SE14 CD44 67
Florian Av. Sutt. BT56 95
Florian Rd. SW15 BR45 65
Florida Clo. Bush. BG27 36
Florida Rd. Guil. AS73 118
Florida Rd. Th. Hth. BY51 86
Florida St. E2 CB38 57
Floriston Av. Uxb. BA36 53
Floriston Clo. Stan. BJ30 36
Floriston Gdns. Stan. BJ30 36
Florys Ct. SW19 BR47 75
Floss St. SW15 BQ44 65
Flower Cres. Cher. AT57 91
Flower & Dean St. E1 CA39 57
Flowerfield. Sev. CT62 107
Flowerhill Way, Grav. DF50 81
Flower Ho. Clo. SE6 CF49 77
Flower La. NW7 BO28 37
Flower La. Gdse. CC68 114
Flowers Ms. N19 BW34 47
St. Johns Way
Flower Wk. Guil. AR72 118
Floyd Rd. SE7 CJ42 68
Floyd's La. Wok. AW61 101
Fludyer St. SE13 CG45 68
Fluys La. Epp. CO20 23
Brook Rd.
Flyover, Croy. BZ56 96
Folair Way SE16 CB42 67
Catlin St.
Fold, Harl. CL10 6
Fold Rd. Red. BV71 121
Foley Rd. Esher BH57 93
Foley St. W1 BW39 56
Folgate St. E1 CA39 57
Foliot St. W12 BO39 55
Folke La. Upmin. CZ31 51
Folkestone Gdns. SE8 CD43 67
Trundley's Rd.
Folkestone Rd. E6 CL37 58
Folkestone Rd. E15 CG37 58
Folkestone Rd. E17 CE31 48
Folkestone Rd. N18 CB28 39
Folkington Cor. N12 BR28 37
Folk La. NW9 BN30 37
Follett Clo. Wind. AQ46 72
Follett Dr. Wat. BB19 17
Follett St. E14 CF39 57
Folly Av. St. Alb. BG13 9
Folly Clo. Rad. BH21 27
Follyfield Rd. Bans. BS60 95
Folly La. E17 CD30 39
Folly La. St. Alb. BG13 9
Folly Ms. W11 BR39 55
Kensington Pk.
Folly Pathway Rad. BH21 27
Folly, The, Rad. BL20 19
Folly Wall, E14 CF41 67
Fontaine Rd. SW16 BX50 76
Fontarabia Rd. SW11 BV45 66
Fontayne Av. Chig. CM28 40
Fontayne Av. Rain. CT36 59
Fontayne Av. Rom. CT30 41
Fontenoy Rd. SW12 BV48 76
Fonteyne Gdns. Wdf. Grn. CJ30 40
Fonthill Ms. N4 BX34 47
Lennox Rd.
Fonthill Rd. N4 BX33 47
Fontley Way, SW15 BP47 75
Fontmell Clo. Ashf. AZ49 73
Fontmell Clo. St. Alb. BH12 9
Fontmell Pk. Ashf. AY49 73
Fontwell Clo. Har. BG29 36
Fontwell Clo. Nthlt. BF36 54
Fontwell Dr. Brom. CK53 88
Football La. Har. BH33 45
Footbury Hill Rd. Orp. CO54 89
Foots Cray High St. Sid. CP50 79
Foots Cray La. Sid. CP47 79
Foots Cray Rd. SE9 CL46 78
Forbes Av. Pot. B. BT19 20
Forbes St. E1 CB39 57
Forburg Rd. N16 CB33 48
Ford Bridge Clo. Cher. AW54 83
Fordbridge Rd. Ashf. AY50 73
Fordbridge Rd. Shep. BB53 83
Fordbridge Rd. Sun. BB53 83
Ford Clo. Ashf. AY50 73
Ford Clo. Bush. BG24 27
Ford Clo. Har. BG33 45
Ford Clo. Rain. CT36 59
Ford Clo. Shep. AZ52 83
Fordcroft Rd. Orp. CO53 89
Forde Av. Brom. CJ52 88
Fordel Rd. SE6 CF47 77
Ford End Wdf. Grn. CH29 40
Fordham Clo. Barn. BT24 29
Fordham Clo. West Dr. AY39 53
Fordham Rd. Barn. BT24 29
Fordham St. E1 CB39 57
Fordhook Av. W5 BL40 55
Fordingley Rd. W9 BR38 55
Fordingley Rd. Ruis. BA34 44
Fordington Rd. N6 BU32 47
Ford La. Iver AW39 53
Ford La. Rain. CT36 59
Fordmill Rd. SE6 CE48 77
Ford Rd. E3 CD37 57
Ford Rd. Ashf. AY49 73
Ford Rd. Cher. AW54 83
Ford Rd. Dag. CQ36 59
Ford Rd. Grav. DD46 81
Hive La.
Ford Rd. Wok. AT63 100
Ford's Gro. N21 BZ26 39
Ford's Pk. Rd. E16 CH39 58
Ford Sq. E1 CB39 57
Cavell St.
Ford St. E3 CD37 57
Ford St. E16 CG39 58
Fordwater Rd. Cher. AW54 83
Fordwich Clo. Orp. CN54 88
Fordwich Rd. Welw. G. C. BQ8 5
Fordwych Cres. NW2 BR35 46
Fordwych Rd. NW2 BR35 46
Fordyce Rd. SE13 CF46 77
Fordyke Rd. Dag. CQ34 50
Forebury Av. Saw. CQ6 6
Forebury Cres. Saw. CQ6 6
Forebury, The, Saw. CQ6 6
Forefield, St. Alb. BF17 18
Foreland St. SE18 CM42 68
Forel Ct. NW4 BR30 37
Foreman Ct. W6 BQ42 65
Foremark Clo. Chig. CN28 40
Fore St. Av. EC2 BZ39 57
Foreshore, SE8 CD42 67
Forest App. Wdf. Grn. CG29 40
Forest Av. E4 CG26 40
Forest Av. Chig. CL28 40
Forest Av. Hem. H. AY14 8
Forest Clo. E11 CG32 49
Forest Close. Leath. BB66 110
Forest Clo. Wal. Abb. CH22 31
Forest Clo. Wdf. Grn. CH28 40
Forest Clo. Wok. AU61 100
Forest Ct. E4 CG26 40
Forest Ct. E11 CG31 49
Forest Cres. Ash. BM61 103
Forestdale N14 BW28 38
Forest Dr. E12 CJ34 49
Forest Dr. Epp. CN21 31
Forest Dr. Kes. CK56 97
Forest Dr. Tad. BS64 104
Forest Dr. Wdf. Grn. CF29 39
Forest Dr. E. E11 CF33 48
Forest Dr. W. E11 CF33 48
Forest Edge Buck. H. CJ28 40
Forester Rd. SE15 CB45 67
Foresters Clo. Wall. BW57 95
Foresters Cres. Bexh. CR45 69
Foresters Dr. E17 CF31 48
Foresters Dr. Wall. BW57 95
Forester St. E3 CD38 57
Forest Gdns. N17 CA30 39
Bruce Gro.
Forest Gate NW9 BO32 46
Forest Glade E4 CG28 40
Forest Glade E11 CG32 49
Forest Glade Epp. CQ17 23
Forest Green Rd. Maid. AG44 61
Forest Gro. E8 CA36 57
Forest Rd.
Forest Hill Rd. SE22 CB46 77
Forest Hill Rd. SE23 CB46 77
Forestholme Clo. SE23 CC48 77
Taymount Rise
Forest La. E7 CG36 58
Forest La. E15 CG36 58
Forest La. Chig. CL28 40
Forest La. Lthd. BB65 101
Forest Mount Rd. Wdf. Grn. CF29 39
Fore St. EC2 BZ39 57
Fore St. N9 CA29 39
Fore St. N18 CA29 39
Fore St. Harl. CP9 6
Fore St. Hat. BQ12 10
Fore St. Pnr. BB31 44
Forest Ridge Beck. CE52 87
Forest Ridge Kes. CK56 97
Forest Rise E17 CF31 48
Forest Rd. E7 CH35 49
Forest Rd. E8 CA36 57
Forest Rd. E11 CF33 48
Forest Rd. E17 CB31 48
Forest Rd. N9 CB26 39
Forest Rd. N17 CB31 48
Forest Rd. Enf. CD21 30
Forest Rd. Erith. CU44 69
Forest Rd. Felt. BD48 74
Forest Rd. Ilf. CM30 40
Forest Road. Leath. BB66 110
Forest Rd. Loug. CJ24 31
Forest Rd. Lthd. BB65 101
Forest Rd. Rich. BM43 65
Forest Rd. Rom. CR31 50
Forest Rd. Sutt. BS54 86
Forest Rd. Wal. Cr. CC18 21
Forest Rd. Wdf. Grn. CH27 40
Forest Rd. Wind. AL44 61
Forest Rd. Wok. AU61 100
Forest Side E4 CG26 40
Forest Side E7 CH35 49
Capel Rd.
Forest Side Buck. H. CJ26 40
Forest Side, Epp. CM20 22
Forest Side Wor. Pk. BO54 85
Forest St. E7 CH35 49
Forest, The, E11 CG31 49
Forest Vw. E4 CF25 30
Forest Vw. E11 CG33 49
Forest Vw. Av. E10 CF32 48
Forest Vw. Rd. E12 CK35 49
Forest Vw. Rd. E17 CF30 39
Forest Vw. Rd. Loug. CJ24 31
Forest Wk. Bush. BE23 27
Forest Walk, Wey. AZ56 92
Forest Way. Ash. BL62 103
Forest Way Loug. CK24 31
Forest Way Orp. CN53 88
Forest Way Sid. CM47 78
Forest Way Wdf. Grn. CH28 40
Forfar Rd. N22 BY30 38
Forfar Rd. SW11 BV44 66
Forge Ave. Couls. BY63 104
Forge Clo. Brom. CH54 88
Forge Clo. Esher BJ57 93
Forge La. Felt. BE49 74
Forge La. Grav. DJ48 81
Forge La. Hort. K. CY52 90
Forge La. Nthwd. BB29 35
Forge La. Sun. BC52 83
Forge La. Sutt. BR57 94
Forge Way, Sev. CT59 98
Forlong Path Nthlt. BD36 54
Forman Pl. N16 CA35 48
Farleigh Rd.
Formby Av. Stan. BK31 45
Formosa St. W9 BS38 56
Formunt Clo. E16 CG39 58
Forres Clo. Hodd. CE11 12
Forres Ct. SE19 CA49 77
Forres Gdns. NW11 BS32 47
Forresters Cres. Bexh. CR45 69
Forrest Gdns. SW16 BX52 86
Forris Av. Hayes BB40 53
Forset St. W1 BU39 56
Forstall Clo. Brom. CG52 88
Forster Rd. E17 CD32 48
Forster Rd. N17 CA31 48
Forster Rd. SW2 BX47 76
Forster Rd. Beck. CD52 87
Forster Rd. Croy. BZ53 87
Forsters Clo. Rom. CQ32 50
Forston St. N1 BZ37 57
Forsythe Av. Hodd. CE11 12
Forsyth Gdns. SE17 BY43 66
Forsyth Path. Wok. AU60 91
Forsyth Pl. Enf. CA25 30
Forsyth Rd. Wok. AU60 91
Forsyth Rd. Wok. AU61 100
Forterie Gdns. Ilf. CO34 50
Fortescue Av. E8 CB36 57
Mentmore Ter.
Fortescue Av. Twick. BG48 74
Fortescue Rd. SW19 BT50 76
Fortescue Rd. Edg. BN30 37
Fortesque Rd. Wey. AY56 92
Fortess Gro. NW5 BW35 47
Fortess Rd.
Fortess Rd. NW5 BV35 47
Fortess Wk. NW5 BV35 47
Fortess Rd.
Fortess Way NW5 BV35 47
Fortess Rd.
Forth Av. W10 BR39 55
Forthbridge Rd. SW11 BV45 66
Forth Rd. Upmin. CZ32 51
Forth Way Wem. BN35 46
Fortin Clo. S. Ock. DA40 60
Fortin Way. S. Ock. DA40 60
Fortis Gn. N2 BU31 47
Fortis Gn. Av. N2 BU31 47
Fortis Gn. Rd. N10 BV31 47
Fortismere Av. N10 BV31 47
Fort La. Reig. BS68 113
Fortnum Rd. N19 BW34 47
Fortnums Acre, Stan. BH29 36
Fort Pass. SE1 CA42 67
Fort Pass. SE18 CL42 68
Sandy Hill Rd.
Fort Rd. SE1 CA42 67
Fort Rd. Guil. AS72 118
Fort Rd. Nthlt. BF36 54
Fort Rd. Tad. BM69 120
Fort Rd. Til. DH44 71
Fortrose Gdns. SW2 BX47 76
New Park Rd.
Fortune Gate Rd. NW10 BO36 55
Fortune Gate Rd. NW10 BO37 55
Fortune Gn. Rd. NW6 BS35 47
Fortune La. Borwd. BL25 28
Fortunes Mead Nthlt. BD36 54
Fortunes, The Harl. CN12 13
Fortune St. EC1 BZ38 57
Forty Acre La. E16 CG39 58
Forty Av. Wem. BL34 46
Forty Clo. Wem. BL34 46
Fortyfoot Rd. Lthd. BK64 102
Forty Hall Est. Enf. CA22 30
Forty Hill, Enf. CA22 30
Forty La. Wem. BM34 46
Forum, The, Edg. BM29 37
Forval Way. Mitch. BU53 86
Fosbury Ms. W2 BS41 66
Inverness Terr.
Foscote Ms. W9 BS39 56
Amberley Rd.
Foscote Rd. NW4 BP32 46
Foskett Rd. SW6 BR44 65
Foss Av. Croy. BY56 95
Fossdene Rd. SE7 CH42 68
Fosse, The, St. Alb. BE13 9
Fosse Way W13 BJ39 54
Fossil Rd. SE13 CE45 67
Fossington Rd. Belv. CP42 69
Fossway, Dag. CP34 50
Foster Ave. Wind. AM45 61
Foster La. EC2 BZ39 57
Foster La. Wok. AO62 100
Foster Rd. E13 CH38 58
Foster Rd. W3 BO40 55
Foster Rd. W4 BN42 65
Foster Rd. Hem. H. AW14 8
Fosters Clo. Chis. CK49 78
Foster St. NW4 BQ31 46
Foster St. Harl. CQ12 14
Foster Wk. NW4 BQ31 46
Fothergill Clo. E13 CG37 58
Fotheringham Rd. Enf. CA24 30
Fotherley Rd. AV26 34
Foubert's Pl. W1 BW39 56
Foulden Rd. N16 CA35 48
Foulis Ter. SW7 BT42 66
Foulser Rd. SW17 BU48 76
Foulsham Rd. Th. Hth. BZ52 87
Founders Gdns. SE19 BZ50 77
Hermitage Rd.
Foundry La. Slou. AT45 62
Fountain Ct. EC4 BY40 56
Fountain Dr. SE19 CA49 77
Fountain La. Sev. CZ64 108
Fountain Pl. Wal. Abb. CF20 21
Fountain Rd. SW17 BT49 76
Fountain Rd. Mitch. BU51 86
Fountain Rd. Red. BU71 121
Fountain Rd. Th. Hth. BZ51 87
Fountains Av. Felt. BE48 74
Fountains Clo. Felt. BE48 74
Fountains Cres. N14 BX26 38
Fountain St. E2 CA38 57
Columbia Rd.
Fountain Wk. Grav. DF46 81
Fountayne Rd. N15 CB31 48
Fountayne Rd. N16 CB34 48
Fount St. SW8 BW43 66
Four Acres. Cob. BE60 93
Fouracres Enf. CD23 30
Four Acres, Guil. AU69 118
Fouracres, Kings. On T. BN50 75
Four Acres, Saw. CQ6 6
Four Acres. Welw. G. C. BR9 5
Four Acres Dr. Hem. H. AY14 8
Four Acres Walk, Hem. H. AY14 8
Fourfield Clo. Epsom. BN64 103
Fourland Wk. Edg. BN29 37
Fournier St. E1 CA39 57
Fourth Ave. Harl. CK11 13
Fourth Av. E12 CK35 49
Fourth Av. W10 BR38 55
Fourth Av. Enf. CA25 30
Fourth Av. Grays DA43 70
Fourth Av. Hayes BB40 53
Fourth Av. Rom. CS33 50
Fourth Av. Wat. BD21 27
Fourth Av. Wem. BM35 46
Fourth Cross Rd. Twick. BG48 74
Fourth Dri. Couls. BW57 95
Fourth Dr. Couls. BW61 104
Fourways. St. Alb. BL13 10
Fourwents. Cob. BD60 93
Fowell St. W11 BQ40 55
Fowey Av. Ilf. CJ32 49
Fowler Clo. SW11 BT45 66
Plough Rd.
Fowler Clo. Sid. CQ49 79
Fowler Rd. E7 CH35 49
Fowler Rd. Ilf. CO28 41
Fowler Rd. Mitch. BV51 86
Fowlers Mead. Wok. AP58 91
Fowler's Wk. W5 BK38 54
Fowley Clo. Wal. Cr. CE20 21
Longcroft Dr.
Fownes St. SW11 BU45 66
Foxberry Rd. SE4 CD45 67
Foxborough Clo. Slou. AT42 62
Foxborough Gdns. SE4 CE46 77
Foxbourne Rd. SW17 BV48 76
Fox Burrow Rd. Chig. CP28 41
Foxburrows Av. Guil. AP70 118
Foxbury Av. Chis. CM50 78
Foxbury Clo. Brom. CH50 78
Foxbury Clo. Orp. CO56 98
Foxbury Dr. Orp. CO57 98
Foxbury Rd. Brom. CH50 78
Fox Clo. E1 CC38 57
Colebert Av.
Fox Clo. E16 CH39 58
Fox Clo. Orp. CO56 98
Fox Clo. Rom. CR28 41
Fox Clo. Wey. BA56 92
Fox Clo. Wok. AU61 100
Foxcombe Croy. CE57 96
Foxcombe Rd. SW15 BP47 75
Fox Ct. EC1 BY39 56
Brooke St.
Foxcroft, St. Alb. BJ14 9
Foxcroft Rd. SE18 CL44 68
Fox Dell. Nthwd. BA29 35
Foxdell Way. Ger. Cr. AS28 34
Foxearth Rd. Sth. Croy. CB58 96
Foxearth Spur Sth. Croy. CC58 96
Foxenden Rd. Guil. AS71 118
Foxes Dale SE3 CG45 68
Foxes Vale Brom. CF52 87
Foxfield Clo. Nthwd. BB29 35
Foxfield Rd. Orp. CM55 88
Foxglove Clo. Hat. BP13 10
Foxglove Rd. S. Ock. DB39 60
Foxglove St. W12 BO40 55
Foxgrove N14 BX27 38
Foxgrove Av. Beck. CE50 77
Foxgrove Dr. Wok. AT61 100
Foxgrove Path. Wat. BD28 36
Foxgrove Rd. Beck. CE50 77

Foxhall Rd. Upmin. CY35 51
Foxham Rd. N19 BW34 47
Fox Hatch. Brwd. CZ22 33
Foxherne. Slou. AR41 62
Fox Hill SE19 CA50 77
Fox Hill Kes. CJ56 97
Fox Hills Clo. Cher. AU57 91
Foxhills Rd. Cher. AT56 91
Foxhills Rd. Grays DE40 71
Brookmans Av.
Fox Hl. Gdns. SE19 CA50 77
Foxhole Rd. SE9 CK46 78
Foxholes, Wey. BA56 92
Foxholt Gdns. NW10 BN36 55
Foxhounds La. Grav. DD48 81
Fox Ho. Rd. Belv. CR42 69
Foxlake Rd. Wey. AY59 92
Foxlands Cres. Dag. CS35 50
Foxlands Rd. Dag. CS35 50
Fox La. N13 BX27 38
Fox La. W5 BL38 55
Fox La. Cat. BY64 104
Fox La. Kes. CH56 97
Fox La. Lthd. BE66 111
Fox La. North, Cher. AV54 82
Fox La. South, Cher. AV54 82
Foxley Clo. Loug. CL24 31
Foxley Clo. Red. BV73 121
Foxley Gdns. Pur. BY60 95
Foxley Hill Rd. Pur. BY59 95
Foxley La. Pur. BW59 95
Foxley Rd. SW9 BY43 66
Foxley Rd. Ken. BY60 95
Foxley Rd. Th. Hth. BY52 86
Foxleys Wat. BF27 36
Foxmanor Way Grays DA43 70
Foxmore St. SW11 BU44 66
Foxoak Hill, Watt. BB58 92
Foxon Clo. Cat. CA64 105
Foxon La. Cat. BZ64 105
Foxon La. Gdns. Cat. CA64 105
Fox Rd. E16 CG39 58
Fox Rd. Slou. AR42 62
Fox's La. Hat. BQ15 10
Fox's Path Mitch. BT51 86
Foxton Rd. Grays DB43 70
Foxton Rd. Hodd. CE12 12
Foxwarren Esher BH58 93
Fox Well Clo. Slou. AM40 61
Foxwell St. SE4 CD45 67
Foxwood Dr. Dart. DA48 80
Foxwood Rd. SE3 CG45 68
Foyle Dr. S. Ock. DA39 60
Foyle Rd. N17 CB30 39
Foyle Rd. SE3 CG43 68
Frailey Clo. Wok. AT61 100
Frailey Hill, Wok. AT61 100
Framewood Rd. Slou. AR36 52
Framfield Clo. N12 BS27 38
Framfield Rd. N5 BY35 47
Framfield Rd. W7 BH39 54
Framfield Rd. Mitch. BV50 76
Framlingham Clo. E5 CB34 48
Southwold Rd.
Framlingham Cres. SE9 CK49 78
Frampton Clo. Sutt. BS57 95
Frampton Pk. Est. E9 CC36 57
Frampton Pk. Rd. E9 CC36 57
Frampton Rd. Epp. CO17 23
Frampton Rd. Houns. BE45 64
Frampton Rd. Pot. B. BT18 20
Frampton St. NW8 BT38 56
Francemary Rd. SE4 CE46 77
Frances Gdns. S. Ock. CZ39 60
Frances Rd. E4 CE29 39
Frances Rd. Wind. AO44 61
Frances St. SE18 CK42 68
Franche Ct. Rd. SW17 BT48 76
Francis Av. Bexh. CR44 69
Francis Av. Felt. BC48 73
Francis Av. Grav. DJ49 81
Francis Av. Har. BJ32 45
Francis Av. Ilf. CM34 49
Francis Av. St. Alb. BG12 9
Franciscan Rd. SW17 BU49 76
Francis Chichester Way SW11 BV44 66
Francis Clo. Epsom BN56 94
Francis Clo. Shep. AZ52 83
Francis Gro. SW19 BR50 75
Francis Rd. E10 CF33 48
Francis Rd. N2 BU31 47
Lynmouth Rd.
Francis Rd. Cat. BZ64 105
Francis Rd. Croy. BY53 86
Francis Rd. Dart. CV46 80
Francis Rd. Grnf. BJ37 54
Francis Rd. Har. BJ32 45
Francis Rd. Houns. BD44 64
Francis Rd. Ilf. CM34 49
Francis Rd. Orp. CP52 89
Francis Rd. Pnr. BD32 45
Francis Rd. Wall. BW57 95
Francis Rd. Wat. BC24 26
Francis St. E15 CG36 58
Francis St. SW1 BW42 66
Francis St. Chesh. AO18 16
Francis St. Ilf. CM34 49
Francis Ter. N19 BW34 47
Francis Way. Grays. DH41 71
Francklyn Gdns. Edg. BM27 37
Franconia Rd. SW4 BW46 76
Frank Bailey Wk. E12 CK35 49
Frank Dixon Clo. SE21 CA47 77
Frank Dixon Way SE21 CA47 77
Frankfurt Rd. SE24 BZ46 77
Frankham St. SE8 CE43 67
Frankland Clo. Rick. AZ26 35
Frankland Clo. Wdf. Grn. CJ28 40
Frankland Rd. E4 CE28 39
Frankland Rd. Rick. AZ25 26
Franklands Dr. Wey. AW57 92
Franklin Av. Wal. Cr. CB18 21
Franklin Clo. N20 BT26 38
Franklin Clo. Kings-on-t. BM52 85
Willingham Way
Franklin Clo. St. Alb. BO14 10
Franklin Cres. Mitch. BW52 86
Franklin Pass. SE9 CK45 68
Franklin Rd. NW10 BO36 55
Franklin Rd. SE20 CC50 77
Franklin Rd. Bexh. CQ44 69
Franklin Rd. Grav. DH49 81
Franklin Rd. Wat. BC23 26
Franklins' Gro. SE15 CC44 67
Franklin Sq. SW5 BR42 65
Marchbank Rd.
Franklin's Row SW3 BU42 66
Franklin St. E3 CE38 57
Bromley High St.
Franklin St. N15 CA32 48
Franklyn Clo. Dag. CS36 59
Franklyn Cres. Wind. AL45 61
Franklyn Gdns. Ilf. CM29 40
Franklyn Rd. NW10 BO36 55
Franklyn Rd. Walt. BC53 83
Franklyns Harl. CM11 13
Franks Av. N. Mal. BN52 85
Franks La. Hort. K. CX53 90
Franks Rd. Guil. AQ69 118
Frank St. E13 CH38 58
Franks Wd. Av. Orp. CL53 88
Frankton Rd. SE15 CB44 67
Franlaw Cres. N13 BZ28 39
Franmill Rd. Horn. CU33 50
Fransfield Gro. SE26 CB48 77
Frant Clo. SE20 CC50 77
Franthorne Way SE6 CE48 77
Randlesdown Rd.
Frant Rd. Th. Hth. BY53 86
Fraser Clo. Bex. CS47 79
Dartford Rd.
Fraser Clo. Bex. CS48 79
Dartford Rd.
Fraser Rd. E17 CE32 48
Fraser Rd. N9 CB27 39
Fraser Rd. Erith CS42 69
Fraser Rd. Grnf. BJ37 54
Fraser Rd. Wal. Cr. CD17 21
Fraser St. W4 BO42 65
Frating Cres. Wdf. Grn. CH29 40
Frays Ave. West Dr. AX41 63
Frays Pl. Uxb. AX37 53
Frays Waye, Uxb. AX37 53
Frazer Av. Ruis. BD35 45
Frazer Gdns. Dor. BJ71 119
Frazier St. SE1 BY41 66
Frean St. SE16 CB41 67
Frederica Rd. E4 CF26 39
Frederick Clo. W2 BU39 56
Frederick Clo. Sutt. BR56 94
Frederick Cres. SW9 BY43 66
Frederick Cres. Enf. CC23 30
Frederick Pl. SE18 CL42 68
Frederick Rd. SE17 BY43 66
Frederick Rd. Rain. CS37 59
Frederick Rd. Sutt. BR56 94
Frederick's Pl. EC2 BZ39 57
Old Jewry
Frederick's Pl. N12 BT28 38
Frederick St. E17 CD32 48
Frederick Ter. E8 CA36 57
Haggerston Rd.
Fredora Av. Hayes BB38 53
Freeborne Gdns. Rain. CU36 59
Freedom St. SW11 BU44 66
Freedown La. Sutt. BT60 95
Freegrove Rd. N7 BX35 47
Freeland Pk. NW4 BR30 37
Freeland Rd. W5 BL40 55
Freelands Av. Sth. Croy. CC58 96
Freelands Gro. Brom. CH51 88
Freelands Rd. Brom. CH51 88
Freelands Rd. Cob. BC60 92
Freeman Ct. Chesh. AO18 16
Freeman Rd. Grav. DJ48 81
Freemantle Av. Enf. CC25 30
Freemantle Rd. Belv. CR42 69
Freemason's Rd. E16 CH39 58
Freemasons Rd. Croy. CA54 87
Free Prae Rd. Cher. AW54 83
Freke Rd. SW11 BV45 66
Fremantle Ho. Til. DG44 71
Leicester Rd.
Fremantle Rd. Ilf. CM30 40
Fremantle St. SE17 CA42 67
Fremont St. E9 CC37 57
Frencham Ct. Mitch. BT52 86
Frenchaye, Wey. AX56 92
Frenches Dr. Red. BV69 121
Frenches, The,
Frenches Rd. Red. BV69 121
Frenches, The Red. BV69 121
French Gdns. Cob. BD60 93
French Horn Lane. Hat. BP12 10
Frenchlands, Leath. BB67 110
French St. Sun. BD51 84
Frenchum Gdns. Slou. AM40 61
Frendsbury Rd. SE4 CC45 67
Frensham Dr. SW15 BO48 75
Frensham Dr. Croy. CF57 96
Frensham Rd. SE9 CM48 78
Frensham Rd. Ken. BY60 95
Frensham St. SE15 CB43 67
Frensham Way Epsom BQ61 103
Frere St. SW11 BU44 66
Freshfields Croy. CD54 87
Freshfields Av. Upmin. CX35 51
Freshford St. SW18 BT48 76
Fresh Water, Harl. CN10 6
Freshwater Clo. SW17 BV50 76
Freshwater Rd. SW17 BV50 76
Freshwater Rd. Dag. CP33 50
Freshwell Av. Rom. CP31 50
Freshwell Gdns. Brwd. DE32 123
Fresh Wharf Est. Bark. CL37 58
Fresh Wharf Rd. Bark. CL37 58
Freshwood Clo. Beck. CE51 87
Freshwood Way Wall. BV57 95
Fresley Clo. N15 BZ31 48
Clinton Rd.
Fresmount Gdns. Epsom. BM59 94
Freston Gdns. Barn. BU25 29
Freta Rd. Bexh. CQ46 79
Fretherne Rd. Welw. G. C. BQ8 5
Frewin Rd. SW18 BT47 76
Friar Rd. Hayes BD38 54
Friar Rd. Orp. CO53 89
Friars Av. N20 BU27 38
Friars Clo. N2 BT31 47
Friars Clo. Nthlt. BD38 54
Friars Gdns. W3 BN40 55
St. Dunstan's Av.
Friar's Gate, Guil. AQ71 118
Friars La. Rich. BK46 74
Friars Orchard. Lthd. BG64 102
Friar, S Av. Brwd. DD26 122
Friar, S Clo. Brwd. DD26 122
Friars Place La. W3 BN40 55
Friars Rise, Wok. AT62 100
Friars Rd. E6 CJ37 58
Friars Rd. Vir. W. AR52 82
Friars Stile Pl. Rich. BL46 75
Friars Stile Rd.
Friars Stile Rd. Rich. BL46 75
Friars, The, Chig. CN28 40
Friars, The Harl. CL12 13
Friar St. EC4 BY39 56
Carter La.
Friars Wk. N14 BV26 38
Friars Wk. SE2 CP42 69
Friars Wk. Har. BH29 36
Friars Way, N14 BV26 38
Friars Way W3 BN39 55
Friars Way Bush. BE23 27
Friars Way, Kings L. AZ18 17
Friars Wd. Croy. CD58 96
Friary Clo. N12 BU28 38
Friary Est. SE15 CB43 67
Friary La. Wdf. Grn. CH28 40
Friary Rd. N12 BT28 38
Friary Rd. SE15 CB43 67
Friary Rd. W3 BN39 55
Friary Rd. Stai. AR47 72
Friary St. Guil. AR71 118
Friary, The Wind. AR46 72
Friary Way N12 BU28 38
Friday Hill E4 CG27 40
Friday Hill Belv. CR42 69
Friday Hill West E4 CG27 40
Friday Rd. Erith CS42 69
Friday Rd. Mitch. BU50 76
Friday St. EC4 BZ39 57
Cannon St.
Frideswide Pl. NW5 BW35 47
Islip St.
Friendly St. Ms. SE8 CE44 67
Friendly St. SE8 CE44 67
Friendship Wk. Nthlt. BD38 54
Wayfarer Rd.
Friendshop Wk. Nthlt. BD38 54
Javelin Way
Friends Rd. Croy. BZ55 87
Friends Rd. Pur. BY59 95
Friend St. EC1 BY38 56
Friern Barnet La. N11 BT27 38
Friern Barnet La. N20 BT27 38
Friern Barnet Rd. N11 BU28 38
Friern Ct. N20 BT27 38
Friern Mt. Dr. N20 BT26 38
Friern Pk. N12 BT28 38
Friern Rd. SE22 CB47 77
Friern Rd. Borwd. BN25 28
Friern Watch Av. N12 BT28 38
Frieze Hill, Brwd. CX26 42
Frigo Ct. Epsom BN59 94
Frimley Av. Horn. CX33 51
Frimley Clo. Croy. CF57 96
Frimley Ct. Sid. CP49 79
Frimley Cres. Croy. CF57 96
Frimley Gdns. Mitch. BU52 86
Frimley Rd. Chess. BL56 94
Frimley Rd. Hem. H. AV13 7
Frimley Rd. Ilf. CN34 49
Frimley Vw. Wind. AL44 61
Fringewood Copse. Nthwd. AZ30 35
Frinstead Rd. Erith CS43 69
Frinsted Clo. Orp. CP52 89
Frinton Clo. Wat. BC27 35
Frinton Dr. Wdf. Grn. CF29 39
Frinton Mews Ilf. CL32 49
Bramley Cres.
Frinton Rd. E6 CJ38 58
Frinton Rd. N15 CA32 48
Frinton Rd. SW17 BV50 76
Frinton Rd. Rom. CR29 41
Frinton Rd. Sid. CQ48 79
Friston Path Chig. CN28 40
Manford Way
Friston St. SW6 BS44 66
Fritham Clo. N. Mal. BO53 85
Frith Ct. NW7 BR29 37
Frithe, The Slou. AR40 52
Frith Gdns. SW6 BR45 65
Frith Knowle Walt. BC57 92
Frith La. NW7 BR29 37
Frith Rd. E11 CF35 48
Frith Rd. Croy. BZ55 87
Frith St. W1 BW39 56
Frithville Gdns. W12 BQ40 55
Frithwald Rd. Cher. AV54 82
Frithwood Ave. Nthwd. BB29 35
Frithwood Av. Nthwd. BC29 35
Frizlands La. Dag. CR34 50
Frobish Ct. SE23 CB48 77
Sydenham Rise
Frobisher, Guil. AT70 118
Frobisher Clo. Pnr. BD33 45
Frobisher Ct. W12 BP41 65
Frobisher Cres. Stai. AY47 73
Frobisher Gdns. Stai. AY47 73
Frobisher Rd. N8 BY31 47
Frobisher Rd. St. Alb. BK14 9
Frobisher St. SE10 CG43 68
Frobisher Way, Grav. DJ49 81
Froggy La. Uxb. AU34 43
Froghall La. Chig. CM28 40
Froghole La. Eden. CN70 115
Frog La. Guil. AS66 109
Frogley Rd. SE22 CA45 67
Frogmoor La. Rick. AX27 35
Frogmore, SW18 BS46 76
Frogmore Av. Hayes BB38 53
Frogmore Clo. Sutt. BQ55 85
Frogmore Dr. Wind. AP44 62
Frogmore Farm Est. Hayes BA38 53
Frogmore Gdns. Hayes BB38 53
Frogmore Gdns. Sutt. BQ56 94
Frogmore Rd. Hem. H. AX15 8
Frognal, NW3 BT35 47
Frognal Av. Sid. CO50 79
Frognal Clo. NW3 BT35 47
Frognal Gdns. NW3 BT35 47
Frognal La. NW3 BS35 47
Frognall Av. Har. BH31 45
Frognal Pl. Sid. CO50 79
Frognal Rise NW3 BT34 47
Frognal Rd. NW3 BT36 56
Frognal Way NW3 BT35 47
Frog St. Brwd. CZ23 33
Froissart Rd. SE9 CJ46 78
Frome Sq. Hem. H. AY11 8
Frome St. N1 BZ37 57
Fromondes Rd. Sutt. BR56 94
Front La. Upmin. CZ33 51
Front, The, Berk. AT11 7
Frostic Pl. E1 CA39 57
Hopetown St.
Froude St. SW8 BV44 66
Dickens St.
Froude St. BW44 66
Robertson St.
Frowick Cl. Hat. BP15 10
Frowyke Cres. Pot. B. BP19 19
Fruen Rd. Felt. BB47 73
Fryatt Rd. N17 BZ29 39
Fryatt St. E14 CG39 58
Fry Clo. Rom. CR28 41
Fryent Clo. NW9 BM32 46
Fryent Cres. NW9 BO32 46
Fryent Fields NW9 BO32 46
Fryent Gro. NW9 BO32 46
Fryent Way NW9 BM32 46
Fryer Clo. Chesh. AO20 16
Frying Pan Alley E1 CA39 57
Bell La.
Fry Rd. E6 CJ36 58
Fry Rd. NW10 BO37 55
Fry Rd. Ashf. AX49 73
Fryston Av. Couls. BV60 95
Fryston Av. Croy. CB55 87
Fryth Mead, St. Alb. BF13 9
Fuchsia St. SE2 CO42 69
Fulbeck Dr. NW9 BO30 37
Fulbeck Way Har. BG30 36
Fulbourne Est. E1 CB38 57
Fulbourne Rd. E17 CF30 39
Fulbrook La. S. Ock. CZ40 60
Fulbrook Ms. N19 BW35 47
Tufnell Pk. Rd.
Fulbrook Rd. N19 BW35 47
Fuley Rd. West. CJ62 106
Fulford Gro. Wat. BC27 35
Fulford Rd. Cat. BZ64 105
Fulford Rd. Epsom BN57 94
Fulford St. SE16 CB41 67
Fulham Broadway SW6 BS43 66
Fulham Clo. Uxb. BA38 53
Fulham Ct. SW6 BS44 66
Fulham Est. SW6 BR43 65
Fulham High St. SW6 BR44 65
Fulham Palace Rd. SW6 BQ42 65
Fulham Palace Rd. W6 BQ42 65
Fulham Pk. Gdns. SW6 BR44 65
Fulham Pk. Rd. SW6 BR44 65
Fulham Rd. SW3 BR44 65
Fulham Rd. SW6 BR44 65
Fulham Rd. SW10 BR44 65
Fullarton Cres. S. Ock. DA40 60
Fullbrook Av. Wey. AW59 92
Fullbrooks Av. Wor. Pk. BO54 85
Fuller Clo. Orp. CN56 97
Fuller Gdns. Wat. BC22 26
Fuller Rd. Dag. CO34 50
Fuller Rd. Wat. BC22 26
Fullers Av. Surb. BL55 85
Fuller's Av. Wdf. Grn. CG29 40
Fullers Clo. Rom. CS29 41
Fullers Clo. Wal. Abb. CH20 22
Fullers La. Rom. CS29 41
Fullers Mead. Harl. CP11 14
Fuller's Rd. E18 CG30 40
Fullers St. Sev. CX63 108
Fuller St. E2 CB38 57
Fuller St. NW4 BQ31 46
Fullers Way N. Surb. BL55 85
Fullers Way S. Chess. BL56 94
Fullers Wd. Croy. CE56 96
Fullers Wood La. Red. BW71 121
Fullerton Clo. Wey. AY60 92
Fullerton Dr. Wey. AY60 92
Fullerton Rd. SW18 BT46 76
Fullerton Rd. Cars. BU58 95
Fullerton Rd. Croy. CA54 87
Fullerton Rd. Wey. AY60 92
Fullerton Way, Wey. AY60 92
Fuller Way, Hayes. BB42 63
Fuller Way, Rick. AZ25 26
Fullmer Way. Wey. AV58 91
Fullwell Av. Ilf. CK30 40
Fulmar Cres. Hem. H. AW14 8
Fulmar Rd. Rain. CU36 59
Fulmead St. SW6 BS44 66
Fulmer Common Rd. Slou. & Iver AR36 52
Fulmer Dr. Ger. Cr. AR34 43
Fulmer La. Ger. Cr. AS34 43
Fulmer Rd. Ger. Cr. AS33 43
Fulmer Way W13 BJ41 64
Fulmer Way. Ger. Cr. AS32 43
Fulready Rd. E10 CF32 48
Fulstone Clo. Houns. BE45 64
Fulthorp Rd. SE3 CG44 68
Fulton Ms. W2 BT40 56
Porchester Ter.
Fulton Rd. Wem. BM34 46
Fulton St. E16 CG39 58
George St.
Fulwell Pk. Av. Twick. BF48 74
Fulwell Rd. Tedd. BG49 74
Fulwich Rd. Dart. CW46 80
Fulwood Av. Wem. BL37 55
Fulwood Clo. Hayes BB39 53
Fulwood Gdns. Twick. BH46 74
Fulwood Pl. WC1 BX39 56
Furber St. W6 BP41 65
Furham Flds. Pnr. BF29 36
Furley Pl. N1 BY36 56
Islington Pk. St.
Furley Rd. SE15 CB44 67
Furlong Rd. N7 BY36 56
Furlong Rd. Dor. BG72 119
Furlongs, Hem. H. AW13 8
Furmage St. SW18 BS47 76
Furmigers Rd. Orp. CR56 98
Furnace Clo. Hem. H. AZ14 8
Furneaux Av. SE27 BY49 76
Furness Rd. NW10 BP37 55
Furness Rd. SW6 BS44 66
Furness Rd. Har. BF33 45
Furness Rd. Mord. BS54 86
Furness Way. Horn. CU35 50
Furnival Clo. Vir. W. AR53 82
Furnival St. EC4 BY39 56
Furrow La. E9 CC35 48
Furrows Pl. Cat. CA65 105
Furrows, The, Uxb. AX32 44
Furrows, The, Walt. BD55 84
Fursby Av. N3 BS29 38
Furse Av. St. Alb. BJ11 9
Further Acre NW9 BO30 37
Further Grn. Rd. SE6 CG47 78
Furtherground, Hem. H. AY13 8
Furzebushes La. St. Alb. BE16 18
Furzedown Dr. La. SW17 BV49 76
Furzedown Rd. SW17 BV49 76
Furzedown Rd. Sutt. BT59 95
Furze Field. Lthd. BH60 93
Furzefield Wal. Cr. CB17 21
Maybury Av.
Furzefield Clo. Chis. CL50 78
Furzefield Cres. Reig. BT71 121
Furzefield Rd. SE3 CH43 68
Furzefield Rd. Reig. BT71 121
Furzefield Rd. Welw. G. C. BR8 5
Furze Gro. Tad. BR64 103
Furzeham Rd. West Dr. AY41 63
Furze Hill Pur. BX59 95
Furze Hill, Red. BU70 121
Furze Hill, Tad. BR64 103
Furzehill Rd. Borwd. BM24 28
Furze La. Pur. BX59 95
Furzen Cr. Hat. BO14 10
Furze Rd. Hem. H. AV14 7
Furze Rd. Th. Hth. BZ52 87
Furze Rd. Wey. AV57 91
Furze St. E3 CE39 57
Furze View. Rick. AU25 25
Furze Wd. Sun. BC51 83
Fusedale Way. S. Ock. CZ40 60
Fyfield Clo. Brwd. DE32 123
Fyfield Rd. E17 CF31 48
Fyfield Rd. SW9 BY45 66
Fyfield Rd. Enf. CA24 30
Fyfield Road. Ong. CW13 15
Fyfield Road. Ong. DA13 15
Fyfield Rd. Rain. CT37 59
Fyfield Rd. Wdf. Grn. CJ29 40
Fynes St. SW1 BW42 66
Regency St.
Gable Clo. Dart. CU46 79
Gable Clo. Wat. BB19 17
Gable Ct. SE26 CB49 77
Gables Av. Ashf. AY49 73
Gables Av. Borwd. BL24 28
Gables Clo. Ger. Cr. AS28 34
Gables Clo. Slou. AQ43 62
Gables Clo. Wok. AS63 100
Gables, The, Bans. BR62 103
Gabriel St. SE23 CC47 77
Gadbrook Rd. Bet. BN73 120
Gaddesden Av. Wem. BL36 55
Gaddesden Cres. Wat. BD20 18
Gade Av. Wat. BB24 26
Gade Bk. Rick. BA24 26
Gadebridge La. Hem. H. AW12 8
Gadebridge Rd. Hem. H. AW12 8
Gade Clo. Hem. H. AW12 8
Gadesden Rd. Epsom BN57 94
Gade Side, Wat. BA21 26
Gade View Gdns. Kings L. BA19 17
Gade View Rd. Hem. H. AX15 8
Gadsden Clo. Upmin. CZ32 51
Gadwell Clo. Wat. BE21 27
Gage Rd. E16 CG39 58
Gage St. WC1 BX39 56
Boswell St.
Gainford St. N1 BY37 56
Gains Ave. E11 CF34 48

Gainsboro' Av. Dart. CV46 80
Gainsboro' Ct. Walt. BC55 83
Gainsboro' Rd. Rain. CU37 59
Gainsborough Ave. Til. DG44 71
Gainsborough Av. E12 CL35 49
Gainsborough Av. St. Alb. BH13 9
Gainsborough Dr. Grav. DE48 81
Gainsborough Gdns. NW3 BT34 47
Gainsborough Gdns. NW11 BR33 46
Gainsborough Gdns. Edg. BL30 37
Gainsborough Gdns. Grnf. BH35 45
Gainsborough Gdns. Islw. BG46 74
Gainsborough Rd. E11 CG33 49
Gainsborough Rd. E15 CG38 58
Gainsborough Rd. N12 BS28 38
Gainsborough Rd. W4 BO42 65
Gainsborough Rd. Dag. CO35 50
Gainsborough Rd. Epsom BN58 94
Gainsborough Rd. Hayes BA37 53
Gainsborough Rd. N. Mal. BN53 85
Gainsborough Rd. Rich. BL44 65
Gainsborough Rd. Wdf. Grn. CK29 40
Gainsford Rd. E17 CD31 48
Gainsford St. SE1 CA41 67
Gains' Sq. Bexh. CP45 69
Gainsthorpe Road. Ong. CV15 15
Gainswood. Welw. G. C. BR8 5
Gairloch Rd. SE5 CA44 67
Gaisford St. NW5 BW36 56
Gaitskell Rd. SE9 CM47 78
Galahad Rd. Brom. CH48 78
Galata Rd. SW13 BP43 65
Galbraith St. E14 CF41 67
Galeborough Av. Wdf. Grn. CF29 39
Gale Cres. Bans. BS62 104
Gale Grn. S. Ock. DA39 60
Galena Rd. W6 BP42 65
Galen Pl. WC1 BX39 56
Bury Pl.
Galesbury Rd. SW18 BT46 76
Gale's Gdns. E2 CB38 57
Bethnal Green Rd.
Gale St. E3 CE39 57
Gale St. Dag. CP37 59
Galesway Wdf. Grn. CK29 40
Gallants Farm Rd. Barn. BU26 38
Gallery Gdns. Nthlt. BD37 54
Gallery Rd. SE21 BZ47 77
Galley Hill, Hem. H. AV12 7
Galley Hill Rd. Grav. DC46 81
Galleyhill Rd. Wal. Abb. CG19 22
Galley La. Barn. BP22 28
Galley La. Barn. BP23 28
Galleymead Rd. Slou. AV44 62
Galleywall Rd. SE16 CB42 67
Galleywood Cres. Rom. CS29 41
Galliard Ct. N9 CC25 30
Galliard Rd. N9 CB26 39
Gallia Rd. N5 BY35 47
Calabria Rd.
Gallions Clo. Bark. CO38 59
Gallions La. Slou. AR38 52
Gallions Rd. E16 CL40 58
Gallop, The, Sth. Croy. CB57 96
Gallop, The, Sutt. BT58 95
Gallop, The Wind. AO47 72
Gallosson Rd. SE18 CN42 68
Galloway Rd. W12 BP40 55
Gallows Hill, Kings L. BA19 17
Gallowshill La. Wat. BA19 17
Gallus Sq. SE3 CH45 68
Gallys Rd. Wind. AL44 61
Galpin's Rd. Th. Hth. BX53 86
Galsworthy Av. Rom. CO33 50
Galsworthy Cres. SE3 CJ44 68
Merriman Rd.
Galsworthy Rd. NW2 BR35 46
Galsworthy Rd. Cher. AW54 83
Galsworthy Rd. Kings. On T. BM50 75
Galsworthy Rd. Til. DH44 71
Galton St. W10 BR38 55
Galveston Rd. SW15 BR46 75
Gambetta St. SW8 BV44 66
Gambia St. SE1 BY40 56
Gambles La. Wok. AX65 101
Gambles La. Wok. AX66 110
Gambole Rd. SW17 BU49 76
Games Rd. Barn. BU24 29
Gamlen Rd. SW15 BQ45 65
Gammon's La. Brox. CA16 21
Gammon's La. Wat. BB21 26
Gamuel Rd. E17 CD32 48
Gandergreen La. Sutt. BR55 85
Ganders Ash, Wat. BC20 17
Gane Clo. Wall. BX57 95
Gangers Hill. Gdse. CD67 114
Ganghill, Guil. AT69 118
Ganton St. W1 BW40 56
Kingly St.
Gants Ct. Wal. Abb. CG20 22
Gantshill Cres. Ilf. CL32 49
Gantshill Cross Ilf. CL32 49
Ganymede Pl. Hem. H. AY12 8
Gap Rd. SW19 BS49 76
Garage Rd. NW4 BP32 46
Garage Rd. W3 BM39 55
Garbrand Walk Epsom BO58 94
Garbutt Pl. W1 BV39 56
Garden Av. Bexh. CR45 69
Garden Av. Hat. BP14 10
Garden Av. Mitch. BV50 76
Garden City Edg. BM29 37
Garden Clo. E4 CE28 39
Garden Clo. SW9 BX45 66
Garden Clo. SW15 BP47 75
Bristol Gdns.
Garden Clo. Ashf. BA50 73
Garden Clo. Bans. BS61 104
Garden Clo. Hamptn. BE49 74
Garden Clo. Lthd. BK66 111
Garden Clo. Nthlt. BE37 54
Garden Clo. Ruis. BB34 44
Garden Clo. Wall. BX56 95
Garden Clo. Wat. BB23 26
Garden Clo. Wey. AX56 92
Garden Cotts. Epsom BN59 94
Garden Cotts. Orp. CP51 89
Garden Court SE15 CA44 67
Sumner Estate
Garden Ct. Rich. BL44 65
Garden End. Amer. AP22 25
Gardener Gro. Felt. BE48 74
Gardeners Rd. E3 CC37 57
Garden Fields. Ong. CW20 24
Gardenia Rd. Enf. CA25 30
Garden La. SW2 BX47 76
Garden La. Brom. CH50 78
Garden Pl. Sid. CP50 79
Garden Reach. Ch. St. G. AR24 25
Garden Rd. NW8 BT38 56
Garden Rd. SE20 CC51 87
Garden Rd. Brom. CH50 78
Garden Rd. Rich. BM45 65
Garden Rd. Sev. CV64 108
Garden Rd. Walt. BC53 83
Garden Rd. Wat. BB19 17
Garden Row SE1 BY41 66
Gardens, The, N8 BX31 47
Rectory Gdns.
Gardens, The, N16 CA33 48
Gardens, The, SE22 CB45 67
Gardens, The, Beck. CF51 87
Gardens, The, Esher BF56 93
Gardens, The, Har. BG32 45
Gardens, The, Hat. BR17 19
Gardens, The, Pnr. BE32 45
Gardens, The Wat. BB23 26
Garden St. E1 CC39 57
Garden St. Grav. D 46 81
Garden Terrace Rd. Harl. CP9 6
Garden Wk. EC2 CA38 57
Rivington St.
Garden Wk. Couls. BV65 104
Garden Way NW10 BN36 55
Garden Way. Cat. BZ64 105
Garden Way, Loug. CL22 31
Gardiner Av. NW2 BQ35 46
Gardiner's Wk. Lthd. BF66 111
Gardner Clo. E11 CH32 49
Gardner Rd. E13 CH38 58
Gardner Rd. Guil. AR70 118
Gardnor Rd. NW3 BT35 47
Flask Wk.
Gardon Clo. St. Alb. BJ13 9
Garendon Gdns. Mord. BS54 86
Garendon Rd. Mord. BS54 86
Gareth Clo. Wor. Pk. BQ55 85
Burnham Dr.
Gareth Gro. Brom. CH49 78
Garfield Pl. Wind. AO44 61
Albany Rd.
Garfield Rd. E4 CF26 39
Garfield Rd. E13 CG38 58
Garfield Rd. SW11 BV45 66
Garfield Rd. SW19 BT49 76
Garfield Rd. BJ47 74
Garfield Rd. Enf. CC24 30
Garfield Rd. Wey. AX56 92
Garfield St. Wat. BC22 26
Garford St. E14 CE40 57
Garibaldi Rd. Red. BU71 121
Garibaldi St. SE18 CN42 68
Garland Rd. SE18 CM43 68
Garland Rd. Stan. BL30 37
Garlands, Ton. CY71 117
Garlands Rd. Lthd. BJ64 102
Garlands Rd. Red. BU71 121
Garlichill Rd. Epsom BP62 103
Garlick Hill EC4 BZ40 57
Queen Victoria St.
Garlies Rd. SE23 CD48 77
Garlinge Rd. NW2 BR36 55
Garman Rd. N17 CC29 39
Garnault Ms. EC1 BY38 56
Hardwick St.
Garnault Rd. Enf. CA22 30
Garnautt Pl. EC1 BY38 56
Myddelton St.
Garner Rd. E17 CF30 39
Garners Clo. Ger. Cr. AS29 34
Garners End. Ger. Cr. AS29 34
Garners Rd. Ger. Cr. AS29 34
Garner St. E3 CB37 57
Coate St.
Garnet Rd. NW10 BO36 55
Garnet Rd. Th. Hth. BZ52 87
Garnet St. E1 CC40 57
Garnett Clo. SE9 CK45 68
Garnett Clo. Wat. BD22 27
Garnett Dr. St. Alb. BF18 18
Garnett Rd. NW3 BU35 47
Garnett Way E17 CD30 39
Mcentee Ave.
Garnham Clo. N16 CA34 48
Smalley Rd.
Garnham St. N16 CA34 48
Garnies Clo. SE15 CA43 67
Garrad's Rd. SW16 BW48 76
Garrard Clo. Bexh. CR45 69
Garrard Clo. Chis. CL49 78
Garrard Rd. Bans. BS61 104
Garratt Clo. Croy. BX56 95
Croydon Rd.
Garratt Rd. Edg. BM29 37
Garratts La. Bans. BR61 103
Garratts Rd. Bush. BG26 36
Garratt Ter. SW17 BU49 76
Garrett St. EC1 BZ38 57
Garrick Av. NW11 BR32 46
Garrick Clo. Rich. BK46 74
Green, The,
Garrick Clo. Stai. AW50 73
Garrick Clo. Walt. BC56 92
Garrick Dr. NW4 BQ30 37
Garrick Gdns. N17 CA29 39
Garrick Gdns. E. Mol. BF52 84
Garrick Rd. NW9 BO32 46
Garrick Rd. Grnf. BF38 54
Garrick Rd. Rich. BM44 65
Garrick St. WC2 BX40 56
Garrick Way NW4 BQ31 46
Garrison La. Chess. BK57 93
Gar Rd. Grav. DF47 81
Garron La. S. Ock. CZ40 60
Garrutt Rd. Upmin. CY34 51
Garry Clo. Rom. CT29 41
Garry Way Rom. CT29 41
Garside Clo. Hamptn. BF50 74
Garsington Gdns. Dart. CV48 80
Garsmouth Way Wat. BD21 27
Garson La. Stai. AR47 72
Garston Cres. Wat. BD20 18
Garston Dr. Wat. BD20 18
Garston La. Ken. BZ60 96
Garston La. Wat. BD20 18
Garston La. Wat. BD21 27
Garston Park Pde. Wat. BD20 18
Garstons. The. Lthd. BF66 111
Garth Clo. Kings. On T. BL49 75
Garth Clo. Mord. BQ54 85
Garth Clo. Ruis. BD33 45
Garth Ct. W4 BO42 65
Garth Rd.
Garthland Dr. Barn. BP25 28
Garthorne Rd. SE23 CC47 77
Garth Rd. W4 BN43 65
Garth Rd. Kings. On T. BL49 75
Garth Rd. Mord. BQ53 85
Garth Rd. Sev. CV67 117
Garth Rd. S. Ock. DB38 60
Garthside, Rich. BL49 75
Garth, The, Har. BL32 46
Garth, The, Hmptn. BF50 74
Garth, The, Wat. BA20 17
Garthway N12 BU29 38
Gartlett Rd. Wat. BC24 26
Gartmoor Gdns. SW19 BR47 75
Gartmore Rd. Ilf. CN34 49
Garton Pl. SW18 BT46 76
Garvary Rd. E16 CH39 58
Garvock Dr. Sev. CU66 116
Kippington Rd.
Garway Rd. W2 BS39 56
Gascoigne Gdns. Wdf. Grn. CG29 40
Gascoigne Pl. E2 CA38 57
Gascoigne Rd. Bark. CM37 58
Gascoigne Rd. Croy. CF58 96
Gascoigne Rd. Wey. AZ55 83
Gascony Av. NW6 BS36 56
Gascoyne Clo. Pot. B. BP19 19
Gascoyne Est. E9 CD36 57
Gascoyne Rd. E9 CC36 57
Gaselee St. E14 CF40 57
Gasholder Pl. SE11 BX42 66
Gaskarth Rd. SW12 BV46 76
Gaskarth Rd. Edg. BN30 37
Gaskell Rd. N6 BU32 47
Gaskell St. SW4 BW44 66
Gaskin St. N1 BY37 56
Gaspar Ms. SW5 BS42 66
Courtfield Gdns.
Gassiot Rd. SW17 BU49 76
Gassiot Way Sutt. BT55 86
Gastein Rd. W6 BQ43 65
Gaston Bridge Rd. Shep. BA53 83
Gaston Rd. Mitch. BV52 86
Gaston Way, Shep. BA53 83
Gas Works Rd. Sthl. BE41 64
Gataker St. SE16 CB41 67
Gatcombe Rd. N19 BW34 47
Gate End. Nthwd. BC29 35
Gateford St. NW8 BU38 56
Gateforth St. NW8 BU38 56
Gatehill. Nthwd. BB29 35
Gatehope Dr. S. Ock. CZ39 60
Gatehouse Clo. Kings. On T. BN51 85
Gateley Rd. SW9 BX45 66
Gate Rd. Wey. AZ55 83
Gatesden Rd. Lthd. BG65 102
Gates Grn. Rd. W. Wick. CG55 88
Gateshead Rd. Borwd. BL23 28
Gateside Rd. SW17 BU48 76
Gatestone Rd. SE19 CA50 77
Gate St. WC2 BX39 56
Kingsway
Gateway SE17 BZ43 67
Walworth Rd.
Gateway Clo. Nthwd. BA29 35
Gateways, Guil. AT70 118
Gateways Surb. BL53 85
Surbiton Hill Rd.
Gateways, The, SW3 BU42 66
Whiteheads Gro.
Gateway, The Wok. AU60 91
Gatewick Clo. Slou. AP40 52
Gathorne Rd. N22 BY30 38
Gathorne St. E2 CC37 57
Roman Rd.
Gatley Av. Epsom. BM56 94
Gatliff Rd. SW1 BV42 66
Gatling Rd. SE2 CO42 69
Gatton Bottom. Red. BU67 113
Gatton Clo. Reig. BT69 121
Gatton Clo. Sutt. BS58 95
Gatton Pk. Rd. Reig. & Red. BT69 121
Gatton Rd. SW17 BU49 76
Gatton Rd. Reig. BT69 121
Gattons Way Sid. CQ49 79
Gatward Grn. N9 CA27 39
Gatwick Rd. SW18 BR47 75
Gatwick Rd. Grav. DG48 81
Gatwick Way. Horn. CW34 51
Gauden Clo. SW4 BW44 66
Gauden Rd. SW4 BW44 66
Gaunt Ct. Wem. BJ35 45
Harrow Rd.
Gauntlet Clo. BJ35 45
Gauntlett Rd. Sutt. BT56 95
Gaunt St. SE1 BZ41 67
Newington Causeway
Gautrey Rd. SE15 CC44 67
Gavell Rd. Cob. BC60 92
Gaverick St. E14 CE42 67
Gaveston Dr. Berk. AQ12 7
Gavestone Clo. Wey. AY60 92
Gavestone Rd. SE12 CH47 78
Gaveston Rd. Lthd. BG63 102
Gavina Clo. Mord. BT53 86
Gavin St. SE18 CN42 68
Gaviots Clo. Ger. Cr. AS33 43
Gaviots Grn. Ger. Cr. AS33 43
Gaviots Way. Ger. Cr. AS33 43
Gawber St. E2 CC38 57
Gawsworth Clo. E15 CG35 49
Gawthorne St. E3 CE37 57
Gay Clo. NW2 BP35 46
Gaydon La. NW9 BN30 37
Gayfere Rd. Epsom BP56 94
Gayfere Rd. Ilf. CK31 49
Gayfere St. SW1 BX41 66
Gt. Peter St.
Gayford Rd. W12 BO41 65
Gay Gdns. Dag. CS35 50
Gayhurst Rd. E8 CB36 57
Gaylor Rd. Nthlt. BE35 45
Gaylor Rd. Til. DF44 71
Gaynes Ct. Upmin. CX35 51
Gaynesford Rd. SE23 CC48 77
Gaynesford Rd. Cars. BU57 95
Gaynes Hill Rd. Wdf. Grn. CK29 40
Gaynes Park Rd. Upmin. CX35 51
Gaynes Parkway. Upmin. CW34 51
Gaynes Rd. Upmin. CX34 51
Gay Rd. E15 CF37 57
Gaysham Av. Ilf. CL32 49
Gays La. Maid. AG43 61
Gayton Clo. Amer. AP21 25
Gayton Cres. NW3 BT35 47
Gayton Rd. NW3 BT35 47
Gayton Rd. Har. BH32 45
Gayville Rd. SW11 BU46 76
Gaywood Av. Wal. Cr. CC18 21
Gaywood Clo. SW2 BY47 76
Gaywood Est. SE1 BY41 66
Gaywood Rd. E17 CE31 48
Gaywood Rd. Ash. BL62 103
Gaywood St. SE1 BY41 66
Gaza St. SE17 BY42 66
Gazeley Ct. SE19 CA49 77
Gipsy Hill
Gazelle Glade, Grav. DJ49 81
Gean Wk. Hat. BP14 10
Geapins La. Upmin. CX36 60
Gear Ct. Brwd. DB26 42
Gear Dr.
Gear Dr. Brwd. DB26 42
Geariesville Gdns. Ilf. CL31 49
Geary Rd. NW10 BP35 46
Geary St. N7 BX35 47
Geddes Rd. Bush. BG24 27
Gedeney Rd. N17 BZ30 39
Gedling Pl. SE1 CA41 67
Abbey St.
Geere Rd. E15 CG37 58
Gees Ct. W1 BV39 56
Barrett St.
Gee St. EC1 BY38 56
Geffrye Ct. N1 CA37 57
Geffrye St. E2 CA37 57
Geldart Rd. SE15 CB43 67
Geldeston Rd. E5 CB34 48
Gellatly Rd. SE14 CC44 67
Gemini Gro. Nthlt. BD38 54
General Gordon Pl. SE18 CL42 68
General's Wk. The Enf. CD22 30
General Wolfe Rd. SE10 CF44 67
Genesta Glade, Grav. DJ49 81
Genesta Rd. SE18 CL43 68
Geneva Ct. N16 BZ33 48
Geneva Gdns. Rom. CQ32 50
Geneva Rd. SW9 BY45 66
Geneva Rd. Kings-on-t. BL52 85
Geneva Rd. Th. Hth. BZ53 87
Geneva Ter. SW9 BY45 66
Genever Clo. E4 CE28 39
Genista Rd. N18 CB28 39
Genoa Av. SW15 BQ46 75
Genoa Rd. SE20 CC51 87
Genotin Rd. Enf. BZ24 30
Gentian Row SE13 CF44 67
Sparta St.
Gentlemans Row Enf. BZ24 30
Gentry Gdns. E13 CH38 58
Genyn Rd. Guil. AQ71 118
Geo. Crooks Ho. Grays DD43 71
New Rd.
Geoffrey Av. Rom. CX29 42
Geoffrey Gdns. E6 CK37 58
Geoffrey Rd. SE4 CD45 67
George Avey Cft. Epp. CR16 23
Church La.
George Comberton Wk. E12 CK35 49
George Cres. N10 BV29 38
George Downing Est. N16 CA34 48
George Fifth Way Grnf. BJ37 54
George Grn. Rd. Slou. AS39 52
George Inn Yd. SE1 BZ40 57
Borough High St.
George La. E18 CH30 40
George La. SE13 CE46 77
George La. Brom. CH54 88
George Rd. E4 CE29 39
George Rd. Guil. AR70 118
George Rd. Kings. On T. BM50 75
George Rd. N. Mal. BO52 85
George Row SE16 CB41 67
Georges Clo. Orp. CP52 89
Georges Dr. Brwd. CZ25 33
George Sq. Uxb. AX36 53
George's Rd. N7 BX36 56
George's Rd. West. CJ63 106
George's Sq. N1 CA38 57
Georges Sq. SW6 BR43 65
George St. E16 CG39 58
George St. W1 BU39 56
George St. W7 BH40 54
George St. Bark. CM36 58
George St. Berk. AR13 7
George St. Chesh. AO18 16
George St. Croy. BZ55 87
George St. Grays. DD43 71
George St. Hem. H. AX13 8
George St. Houns. BE44 64
George St. Rich. BK46 74
George St. Rom. CT32 50
George St. St. Alb. BG13 9
George St. Stai. AV49 72
George St. Sthl. BE42 64
George St. Sutt. BS56 95
George St. Uxb. AX36 53
George St. Wat. BD24 27
George's Wood Rd. Hat. BS16 20
Georgette Pl. SE10 CF43 67
George V Av. Pnr. BE30 36
George V Clo. Pnr. BF31 45
Georgeville Gdns. Ilf. CL31 49
George Way, Rick. AW21 26
Georgewood Rd. Hem. H. AY16 17
George Yd. EC3 BZ39 57
Lombard St.
George Yd. W1 BV40 56
Georgiana St. NW1 BW37 56
Georgian Clo. Brom. CH54 88
Georgian Clo. Stai. AW49 73
Georgian Clo. Stan. BJ29 36
Georgian Ct. NW4 BP32 46
Foscote Rd.
Georgian Ct. Wem. BM36 55
Georgian Way, Har. BG34 45
Georgia Rd. Th. Hth. BY51 86
Geraint Rd. Brom. CH48 78
Gerald Clo. Grav. DJ47 81
Geraldine Rd. SW18 BT46 76
Geraldine St. SE11 BY41 66
St. Georges Rd.
Gerald Rd. E16 CG38 58
Gerald Rd. SW1 BV42 66
Gerald Rd. W4 BM43 65
Gerald Rd. Dag. CQ34 50
Gerard Av. Houns. BF47 74
Gerard Gdns. Rain. CT37 59
Gerard Rd. SW13 BO44 65
Gerard Rd. Har. BJ32 45
Gerda Rd. SE9 CL48 78
Gerdview Dr. Dart. CV49 80
Germini Gro. Nthlt. BD38 54
Javelin Way
Gernon Clo. Rain. CV37 60
Gernon Rd. E3 CD37 57
Gerpins La. Upmin. CW37 60
Gerrard Gdns. Pnr. BC32 44
Gerrard Pl. WC2 BW40 56
Gerrard St.
Gerrard Rd. Brwd. DB27 42
Gerrards Clo. N14 BW25 29
Gerrards Cross Rd. Slou. AQ35 43
Gerrards Cross Rd. Slou. AQ36 52
Gerrard St. N1 BY37 56
Gerrard St. W1 BW40 56
Gerridge St. SE1 BY41 66
Gertrude Rd. Belv. CR42 69
Gertrude St. SW10 BT43 66
Gervase Clo. Wem. BN34 46
Chalkhill Rd.
Gervase Rd. Edg. BN30 37
Gervase St. SE15 CB43 67
Gews Clo. Wal. Cr. CC18 21
Ghent St. SE6 CE48 77
Giant Tree Hill Bush. BG26 36
Gibbins Rd. E15 CF36 57
Gibbon Rd. SE15 CC44 67
Gibbon Rd. W3 BN40 55
Gibbon Rd. Kings. On T. BL51 85
Gibbons Rd. NW10 BN36 55
Gibbon Wk. SW15 BP45 65
Swinburne Rd.
Gibbs Av. SE19 BZ49 77
Gibbs Brook La. Oxt. CF71 114
Gibbs Clo. SE19 BZ49 77
Gibbs Clo. Wal. Cr. CC18 21
Gibbs Couch Wat. BD27 36
Gibbs Gn. Edg. BN28 37
Gibbs Grn. W14 BR42 65
Gibb's Rd. N18 CC28 39
First Av.
Gibbs Sq. SE19 BZ49 77
Gibons Clo. St. Alb. BK10 9
Gibraltar Cres. Epsom BO58 94
Gibraltar Gdns. E2 CA38 57
Bethnal Green Rd.
Gibraltar Wk. E2 CA38 57
Gibson Clo. E1 CC38 57
Colebert Av.
Gibson Clo. Chess BK56 93
Gibson Ct. Slou. AS42 62
Gibson Gdns. N16 CA34 48

Gibson Pl. Stai. AX46 73
Gibson Rd. SE11 BX42 66
Gibson Rd. Uxb. AY35 44
Gibson's Hl. SW16 BY50 76
Gibson Sq. N1 BY37 56
Gibson St. SE10 CG42 68
Gidd Hill Couls. BV61 104
Gidea Av. Rom. CU31 50
Gidea Clo. Rom. CU31 50
Gideon Clo. Belv. CR42 69
Gideon Rd. SW11 BV45 66
Giesbach Rd. N19 BW34 47
Boothby Rd.
Giffard Rd. N18 CA28 39
Giffin St. SE8 CE43 67
Gifford Gdns. W7 BG39 54
Giffordside. Grays. DG42 71
Gifford St. N1 BX36 56
Gift La. E15 CG37 58
Giggs Hill Orp. CO51 89
Giggs Hill Gdns. Surb. BJ54 84
Giggs Hill Rd. Surb. BJ54 84
Gilbert Clo. Swans. DB46 80
Gilbert Gro. Edg. BN30 37
Gilbert Ho. SE8 CE43 67
Gilbert Pl. WC1 BX39 56
Gilbert Rd. SE11 BY42 66
Gilbert Rd. SW19 BT50 76
Gilbert Rd. Belv. CQ41 69
Gilbert Rd. Brom. CH50 78
Gilbert Rd. Pnr. BD31 45
Gilbert Rd. Rom. CT31 50
Gilbert Rd. Uxb. AX30 35
Gilbert St. E15 CG35 49
Gilbert St. W1 BV39 56
Gilbert St. Enf. CC22 30
Gilbert St. Houns. BG45 64
High St.
Gilbert Way. Berk. AQ13 7
Gilbey Clo. Uxb. AZ35 44
Gilbey Rd. SW17 BU49 76
Gilbourne Rd. SE18 CN43 68
Gilda Av. Enf. CD25 30
Gilda Ct. NW7 BP30 37
Gilda Cres. N16 CB33 48
Gildenhill Rd. Swan. CV50 80
Gilden Way, Harl. CP9 6
Gilders, Saw. CP6 6
Gildersome St. SE18 CL43 68
Gilders Rd. Chess. BL57 94
Giles Clo. Rain. CV37 60
Giles Coppice SE19 CA49 77
Gilham's Av. Bans. BQ59 94
Gilkes Cres. SE21 CA46 77
Gilkes Pl. SE21 CA46 77
Gillam Way. Rain. CU36 59
Gillan Grn. Bush. BG27 36
Gill Av. E16 CH39 58
Gill Cres. Grav. DF48 81
Packham Rd.
Gillender St. E3 CF38 57
Gillespie Rd. N5 BY34 47
Gillett Av. E6 CK37 58
Gillett Pl. N16 CA35 48
Gillett St.
Gillett Rd. Th. Hth. BZ52 87
Gillett St. N16 CA35 48
Gillham Ter. N17 CB29 39
Gillian Av. St. Alb. BG15 9
Gillian Cres. Rom. CV30 42
Gillian Pk. Rd. Sutt. BR54 85
Gillian St. SE13 CE46 77
Gilliat Rd. Slou. AP40 52
Gillies Rd. Sev. CZ57 99
Gillies St. NW5 BV35 47
Gilling Ct. NW3 BU36 56
Gillingham Rd. NW2 BR34 46
Gillingham Row SW1 BW42 66
Vauxhall Bridge Rd.
Gillingham St. SW1 BW42 66
Gillman Dr. E15 CG37 58
Gillmans Rd. Orp. CO54 89
Gills Hill Rad. BH21 27
Gills Hill La. Rad. BH21 27
Gills Hollow Rad. BH21 27
Gill St. E14 CD39 57
Gillum Clo. Barn. BU26 38
Gilmais. Lthd. BG66 111
Gilman Cres. Wind. AL45 61
Gilmore Clo. Slou. AR41 62
Gilmore Clo. Uxb. AZ34 44
Gilmore Cres. Ashf. AZ49 73
Gilmore Rd. SE13 CF45 67
Gilpin Av. SW14 BN45 65
Gilpin Cres. Twick. BF47 74
Gilpin Gro. N18 CA28 39
Gilpin Rd. E5 CD35 48
Gilpins Ride. Berk. AR12 7
Gilpin Way. Hayes. BA43 63
Gilroy Clo. Rain. CT36 59
Gilroy Way Orp. CO54 89
Gilsand Wal. Abb. CG21 31
Roundhills
Gilsland Rd. Th. Hth. BZ52 87
Gilstead Rd. SW6 BS44 66
Gilston Rd. SW10 BT42 66
Gilton Rd. SE6 CG48 78
Giltspur St. EC1 BY39 56
Gilwell La. E4 CF24 30
Gimcrack Hill, Lthd. BJ64 102
Gipsy Hill SE19 CA49 77
Gipsy La. SW15 BP45 65
Gipsy La. Grays. DE43 71
Gipsy La. Hat. BR10 5
Gipsy La. Kings L. BA20 17
Gipsy Rd. SE27 BZ49 77
Gipsy Rd. Well. CP45 69
Gipsy Rd. Gdns. SE27 BZ49 77
Giraud St. E14 CE39 57
Girdler Rd. W14 BQ43 65
Girdlers Rd. W14 BQ42 65
Girdlestone Walk N19 BW34 47
Girdlestone Est.
Girdwood Rd. SW18 BR47 75
Gironde Rd. SW6 BR43 65
Girtin Rd. Bush. BF24 27
Girton Av. NW9 BM31 46
Girton Clo. Nthlt. BF36 54
Girton Gdns. Croy. CE55 87
Girton Mews N1 BY36 56
Lofting Rd.
Girton Rd. SE26 CC49 77
Girton Rd. Nthlt. BG36 54
Girton Way, Rick. BA25 26
Gisborn Gdns. Rain. CT38 59
Gisburn Rd. N8 BX31 47
Gissing Wk. N1 BY36 56
Lofting Rd.
Given Wilson Wk. E13 CG37 58
Stride Rd.
Give Wilson Wk. E13 CG37 58
Givons Gro. Lthd. BJ66 111
Gladding Rd. E12 CJ35 49
Glade Clo. Surb BK55 84
Glade Ct. Ilf. CK30 40
Glade Gdns. Croy. CD54 87
Glade La. Sthl. BF41 64
Glades. Clo. Chess. BK57 93
Gladeside N21 BX25 29
Gladeside Croy. CC53 87
Gladesmore Rd. N15 CA32 48
Glade Spur. Tad. BS64 104
Gladeswood Rd. Belv. CR42 69
Glade, The, SE7 CJ43 68
Glade, The, Brom. CJ51 88
Glade, The, Brwd. DD26 122
Glade, The, Couls. BY63 104
Glade, The, Croy CC53 87
Glade, The, Epsom BP57 94
Glade, The, Ilf. CK30 40
Glade, The Lthd. BF64 102
Glade, The, N21 BX26 38
Glade, The, Sev. CU65 107
Glade, The Stai. AW50 73
Glade, The, Sutt. BR58 94
Glade. The. Tad. BS64 104
Glade, The, Upmin. CY35 51
Glade, The, Wdf. Grn. CH27 40
Glade, The, Welw. G. C. BQ7 5
Glade, The, W. Wick. CE55 87
Gladeway, The Wal. Abb. CF20 21
Gladiator St. SE23 CD47 77
Glading Ter. N16 CA34 48
Gladsdale Dr. Pnr. BC31 44
Gladsmuir Clo. Walt. BD55 84
Gladsmuir Rd. N19 BW33 47
Gladsmuir Rd. Barn. BR23 28
Gladstone Av. E12 CK36 58
Gladstone Av. N22 BY30 38
Gladstone Av. Felt. BC46 73
Gladstone Av. Twick. BG47 74
Gladstone Mews N22 BY30 38
Pelham Rd.
Gladstone Mews SE20 CC50 77
Woodbine Gro.
Gladstone Pk. Gdns. NW2 BP35 46
Gladstone Pl. Barn. BQ24 28
Gladstone Rd. E15 CG36 58
Gladstone Rd. SW19 BS50 76
Gladstone Rd. W4 BN41 65
Gladstone Rd. Ash. BK62 102
Gladstone Rd. Buck. H. CH26 40
Gladstone Rd. Croy. BZ54 87
Gladstone Rd. Dart. CW46 80
Gladstone Rd. Hodd. CE11 12
Gladstone Rd. Kings-on-t. BM52 85
Gladstone Rd. Orp. CM56 97
Gladstone Rd. Sthl. BE41 64
Gladstone Rd. Surb. BK55 84
Gladstone Rd. Wat. BD24 27
Gladstone St. N22 BY30 38
Pelham Rd.
Gladstone St. SE1 BY41 66
Gladstone Ter. SE27 BZ49 77
Gladstone Ter. SW8 BV44 66
Gladwell Rd. N8 BX32 47
Gladwell Rd. Brom. CH50 78
Gladwyn Rd. SW15 BQ45 65
Gladys Rd. NW6 BS36 56
Glaisyer Way, Iver AU37 52
Glamis Cres. Hayes. BA41 63
Glamis Dr. Horn. CW33 51
Glamis Pl. E1 CC40 57
Glamis Rd. E1 CC40 57
Glamis Way Nthlt. BG36 54
Glamorgan Clo. Mitch. BX52 86
Glamorgan Rd. Kings. On T. BK50 74
Glanfield, Hem. H. AY12 8
Glanfield Rd. Beck. CD52 87
Glanleam Rd. Stan. BK28 36
Glan Mead, Brwd. DC26 122
Glanmor Rd. Slou. AQ40 52
Glanthams Clo. Brwd. DC27 122
Glanthams Rd. Brwd. DC27 122
Glanville Dr. Horn. CW34 51
Glanville Rd. Brom. CH52 88
Glasbrook Av. Twick. BE47 74
Glasbrook Rd. SE9 CJ47 78
Glaserton Rd. N16 CA33 48
Glasford St. SW17 BU50 76
Glasgow Rd. E13 CH37 58
Glasgow Rd. N18 CB28 39
Glasgow Ter. SW1 BW42 66
Lupus St.
Glass Hill St. SE1 BY41 66
Glasshouse Fields. E1 CC40 57
Glasshouse St. W1 BW40 56
Glasshouse Wk. SE11 BX42 66
Glasslyn Rd. N8 BW32 47
Glassmill La. Brom. CG51 88
Glassmill Clo. West Dr. AY41 63
Glass St. E2 CB38 57
Coventry Rd.
Glass Yd. SE18 CL41 68
Woolwich High St.
Glastonbury Av. Wdf. Grn. CJ29 40
Glastonbury Rd. N9 CB26 39
Chichester Rd.
Glastonbury Rd. Mord. BS54 86
Glastonbury St. NW6 BR35 46
Glaucus St. E3 CE39 57
Glazbury Rd. W14 BR42 65
Glazebrook Clo. SE21 BZ48 77
Glazebrook Rd. Tedd. BH50 74
Gleave Clo. St. Alb. BJ13 9
Glebe Av. Enf. BY24 29
Glebe Av. Har. BL31 46
Glebe Av. Mitch. BU51 86
Glebe Av. Ruis. BC36 53
Glebe Av. Uxb. BA35 44
Glebe Av. Wdf. Grn. CH29 40
Glebe Clo. W4 CO42 69
Glebe St.
Glebe Clo. Ger. Cr. AR29 34
Glebe Clo. Hat. BU12 11
Glebe Clo. Hem. H. AY15 8
Glebe Clo. Lthd. BF66 111
Glebe Clo. Sth. Croy. CA59 96
Glebe Clo. Uxb. BA35 44
Glebe Cotts. Felt. BF48 74
Glebe Cotts, Guil. AW69 110
Glebe Cotts. Hat. BU12 11
Glebe Ct. W7 BG40 54
Glebe Ct. Mitch. BU52 86
Glebe Ct. Stan. BK28 36
Glebe Cres. NW4 BQ31 46
Glebe Cres. Har. BL31 46
Glebe Gdns. N. Mal. BO54 85
Glebe Ho. Dr. Brom. CH54 88
Glebe Hyrst Sth. Croy. CA59 96
Glebeland Hat. BQ12 10
French Horn La.
Glebeland Gdns. Shep. BA53 83
Glebelands Dart. CT45 69
Glebelands Esher BH58 93
Glebelands, Harl. CN10 6
Glebelands Av. E18 CH30 40
Glebelands Av. Ilf. CM33 49
Glebelands Cl. SE5 CA45 67
Glebelands Cl. SE19 CA49 77
Glebelands Rd. Felt. BC47 73
Glebe La. Barn. BP25 28
Glebe La. Sev. CU66 116
Glebe Path Mitch. BU52 86
Glebe Pl. SW3 BU43 66
Glebe Pl. Hort. K. CY52 90
Glebe Rd. E8 CD36 57
Middleton Rd.
Glebe Rd. N3 BT30 38
Glebe Rd. N8 BX31 47
Glebe Rd. NW10 BO36 55
Glebe Rd. SW13 BP44 65
Glebe Rd. Ash. BK62 102
Glebe Rd. Brom. CH51 88
Glebe Rd. Cars. BU57 95
Glebe Rd. Dag. CR36 59
Glebe Rd. Dor. BH71 119
Glebe Rd. Egh. AV49 72
Glebe Rd. Ger. Cr. AR30 34
Glebe Rd. Grav. DF47 81
Glebe Rd. Hayes BB40 53
Glebe Rd. Ong. CW18 24
Glebe Rd. Rain. CU38 59
Glebe Rd. Red. BV65 104
Glebe Rd. Sev. CU69 116
Glebe Rd. Stai. AW49 73
Glebe Rd. Stan. BK28 36
Glebe Rd. Sutt. BR58 94
Glebe Rd. Uxb. AX37 53
Glebe Rd. Warl. CC62 105
Glebe Rd. Wind. AQ46 72
Glebe Side Twick. BH46 74
Glebe St. W4 BN42 65
Glebe Ter. E3 CE38 57
Glebe, The, SE3 CG45 68
Glebe, The, Chis. CM51 88
Glebe, The Reig. BP74 120
Glebe, The, Wat. BD20 18
Glebe, The. West Dr. AY42 63
Glebe, The, Wor. Pk. BO54 85
Glebe Way Erith CT43 69
Glebe Way Felt. BF48 74
Glebeway Horn. CW33 51
Glebe Way Sth. Croy. CA59 96
Glebeway Wdf. Grn. CJ28 40
Glebe Way W. Wick. CF55 87
Gledhow Gdns. SW5 BT42 66
Gledstanes Rd. W14 BR42 65
Gledwood Av. Hayes BB39 53
Gledwood Cres. Hayes BB39 53
Gledwood Dr. Hayes BB39 53
Gledwood Dr. Hayes BC39 53
Gledwood Gdns. Hayes BB39 53
Gleed Av. Bush. BG27 36
Gleencourt Av. Edg. BM30 37
Gleeson Dri. Orp. CN56 97
Glenaffric Av. E14 CF42 67
Glen Albyn Rd. SW19 BQ48 75
Glenalla Rd. Ruis. BB33 44
Glenalmond Rd. Har. BL31 46
Glenalyon Way SE18 CK42 68
Glena Mt. Sutt. BT56 95
Glenarm Rd. E5 CC35 48
Glen Av. Ashf. AZ49 73
Glenavon Clo. Esher BJ57 93
Glenavon Gdns. Slou. AR42 62
Glenavon Rd. E15 CG36 58
Glenbarr Clo. SE9 CL45 68
Glenbow Rd. Brom. CG50 78
Glenbrook N. Enf. BX24 29
Glenbrook Rd. NW6 BS35 47
Glenbrook S. Enf. BX24 29
Glenbuck Ct. Surb. BL53 85
Glenbuck Rd. Surb. BK53 84
Glenburnie Rd. SW17 BU48 76
Glencairn Dr. W5 BJ38 54
Glencairn Rd. SW16 BX51 86
Glen Clo. Shep. AZ52 83
Glen Clo. Tad. BR64 103
Glencoe Av. Ilf. CM33 49
Glencoe Dr. Dag. CR35 50
Glencoe Rd. Bush. BF25 27
Glencoe Rd. Wey. AZ55 83
Glen Cres. Wdf. Grn. CH29 40
Glendale Swan. CT53 89
Glendale Av. N22 BY29 38
Glendale Av. Edg. BM28 37
Glendale Av. Rom. CP33 50
Glendale Clo. SE9 CL45 68
Glendale Clo. Wok. AR62 100
Glendale Dri. Guil. AU68 109
Glendale Dr. SW19 BR49 75
Glendale Gdns. Hem. H. AW13 8
Glendale Gdns. Wem. BK33 45
Glendale Mews Beck. CE51 87
Westgate Rd.
Glendale Rd. Erith CS42 69
Glen Dale Rd. Grav. DF49 81
Glendale Wk. Wal. Cr. CD18 21
Glendall St. SW9 BX45 66
Glendarvon St. SW15 BQ45 65
Glendene Av. Leath. BB66 110
Glendish Rd. N17 CB30 39
Glendor Gdns. NW7 BN28 37
Glendower Cres. Orp. CO53 89
Glendower Gdns. SW14 BN45 65
Glendower Rd.
Glendower Pl. SW7 BT42 66
Harrington Rd.
Glendower Rd. E4 CF26 39
Glendower Rd. SW14 BN45 65
Glendown Rd. SE2 CO42 69
Glendun Ct. W3 BO40 55
Glendun Rd.
Glendun Rd. W3 BO40 55
Gleneagle Ms. SW16 BW49 76
Ambleside Av.
Gleneagle Rd. SW16 BW50 76
Gleneagles Stan. BJ29 36
Gordon Av.
Gleneagles Clo. Orp. CM54 88
Gleneagles Clo. Rom. CW29 42
Gleneagles Clo. Stai. AX46 73
Park Rd.
Gleneagles Clo. Wat. BD28 36
Gleneagles Grn. Orp. CM54 88
Gleneagles Clo.
Gleneldon Ms. SW16 BX49 76
Gleneldon Rd. SW16 BX49 76
Glenelg Rd. SW2 BX46 76
Glen End Rd. Wall. BV58 95
Glenesk Rd. SE9 CL45 68
Glenester Clo. Hodd. CE10 12
Glen Faba Rd. Harl. CG12 13
Glenfarg Rd. SE6 CF47 77
Glenferrie Rd. St. Alb. BJ13 9
Glenfield Clo. Bet. BM72 120
Glenfield Cres. Ruis. BA33 44
Glenfield Rd. SW12 BW47 76
Glenfield Rd. W13 BJ41 64
Glenfield Rd. Ashf. AZ50 73
Glenfield Rd. Bans. BS61 104
Glenfield Rd. Bet. BM72 120
Glenfield Ter. W13 BJ40 54
Glenfinlas Way SE5 BY43 66
Glenforth St. SE10 CG42 68
Glengall Causeway E14 CD41 67
Glengall Gro. E14 CE41 67
Glengall Ms. SE1 CA42 67
Glengall Rd. NW6 BR37 55
Glengall Rd. SE15 CA42 67
Glengall Rd. Bexh. CQ45 69
Glengall Rd. Edg. BM27 37
Glengall Rd. Wdf. Grn. CH29 40
Glengall Ter. SE15 CA43 67
Glen Gdns. Croy. BY55 86
Glengarnock Av. E14 CF42 67
Glengarry Rd. SE22 CA46 77
Glenham Dr. Ilf. CL32 49
Glenhaven Av. Borwd. BM24 28
Glenhazel Chase Brwd. DB21 33
Glenhead Clo. SE9 CL45 68
Glenhill Clo. N3 BS30 38
Glenhouse Rd. SE9 CL46 78
Glenhurst Av. NW5 BV35 47
Glenhurst Av. Bex. CQ47 79
Glenhurst Av. Ruis. BA33 44
Glenhurst Ri. SE19 BZ50 77
Glenhurst Rd. N12 BT28 38
Glenhurst Rd. Brent. BK43 64
Glenilla Rd. NW3 BU36 56
Glenista Rd. N18 CB28 39
Glenister Pk. Rd. SW15 BW50 76
Glenister Rd. SE10 CG42 68
Glenister St. E16 CL40 58
Glenlea Rd. SE9 CK46 78
Glenloch Rd. NW3 BU36 56
Glenloch Rd. Enf. CC23 30
Glenluce Rd. SE3 CH43 68
Glenlyn Av. St. Alb. BJ14 9
Glenlyon Rd. SE9 CL46 78
Glenmere Av. NW7 BP29 37
Glenmore Clo. Wey. AW55 83
Glenmore Rd. NW3 BU36 56
Glenmore Rd. Well. CN43 68
Glenmore Way Bark. CO37 59
Glenn Av. Pur. BY59 95
Glennie Rd. SE27 BY48 76
Glenny Rd. Bark. CM36 58
Glenparke Rd. E7 CH36 58
Glen Rise Wdf. Grn. CH29 40
Glen Rd. E13 CJ38 58
Glen Rd. E17 CD32 48
Glen Rd. Chess. BL55 85
Glenrosa St. SW6 BT44 66
Glenroy St. W12 BQ39 55
Glensdale Rd. SE4 CD45 67
Glenshiel Rd. SE9 CL46 78
Glenside Chig. CM29 40
Glenside Rd. SE18 CN42 68
Glentham Gdns. SW13 BP43 65
Glentham Rd.
Glentham Rd. SW13 BP43 65
Glen, The, Croy. CC55 87
Glen, The, Enf. BY24 29
Glen, The, Hem. H. AY11 8
Glen, The, Orp. CK55 88
Glen, The, Pnr. BC32 44
Glen, The, Pnr. BE33 45
Glen, The, Rain. CV38 60
Glen, The, Slou. AR41 62
Glen, The, Sthl. BE42 64
Glen, The, Wem. BK35 45
Glen, The Wey. AV56 91
Glenthorne Av. Croy. CB54 87
Glenthorne Clo. Sutt. BS54 86
Glenthorne Gdns. Sutt. BS54 86
Glenthorne Rd. E17 CD32 48
Glenthorne Rd. N11 BU28 38
Glenthorne Rd. W6 BP42 65
Glenthorne Rd. Kings-on-t. BL52 85
Glenthorn Gdns. Ilf. CL31 49
Glenthorpe Rd. Mord. BQ53 85
Glenton Clo. Rom. CT29 41
Glenton Rd. SE13 CG45 68
Glenton Way Rom. CT29 41
Glentrammon Av. Orp. CN57 97
Glentrammon Clo. Orp. CN56 97
Glentrammon Gdns. Orp. CN57 97
Glentrammon Rd. Orp. CN57 97
Glentworth Pl. Slou. AO40 61
Glentworth St. NW1 BU38 56
Glenure Rd. SE9 CL46 78
Glenview SE2 CP43 69
Glen Vw. Grav. DH47 81
Glenview Rd. Brom. CJ51 88
Glenview Rd. Hem. H. AW13 8
Glenville Av. Enf. BZ22 30
Glenville Av. Enf. BZ23 30
Glenville Clo. Surb. BN54 85
Glenville Gro. SE8 CD43 67
Glenville Rd. SW2 BX46 76
Glenville Rd. Kings. On T. BM51 85
Glen Way, Wat. BB22 26
Glen Wood, Dor. BK72 119
Glenwood Av. NW9 BN33 46
Glenwood Av. Rain. CU38 59
Glenwood Clo. Har. BH32 45
Glenwood Dr. Rom. CU31 50
Glenwood Gdns. Ilf. CL32 49
Glenwood Gro. NW9 BN33 46
Glenwood Rd. N15 BY32 47
Glenwood Rd. NW7 BO27 37
Glenwood Rd. SE6 CD47 77
Glenwood Rd. Epsom BP57 94
Glenwood Rd. Houns. BG45 64
Glenwood Way Croy. CC53 87
Glenworth Av. E14 CF42 67
Glevium Clo. St. Alb. BE14 9
Gliddon Rd. W14 BR42 65
Glisson Rd. Uxb. AZ37 53
Gload Cres. Orp. CP55 89
Globe Cres. E15 CG35 49
Globe La. SE18 CL41 68
Globe Rd. E15 CG35 49
Globe Rd. Horn. CU32 50
Globe Rd. Wdf. Grn. CJ29 40
Globe St. SE1 BZ41 67
Globe Ter. E2 CC38 57
Globe Rd.
Glory Mead, Dor. BJ73 119
Glossop Rd. Sth. Croy. BZ58 96
Gloster Rd. N. Mal. BO52 85
Gloster Rd. Wok. AT63 100
Gloucester Ave. Grays. DE41 71
Gloucester Av. NW1 BV36 56
Gloucester Av. Horn. CW31 51
Gloucester Av. Sid. CN48 78
Gloucester Av. Wal. Cr. CD20 21
Gloucester Av. Well. CN45 68
Gloucester Cir. SE10 CF43 67
Gloucester Clo. NW10 BN36 55
Gloucester Clo. Surb. BJ54 84
Gloucester Ct. W3 BM39 55
Links Rd.
Gloucester Ct. Rich. BM43 65
Gloucester Cres. NW1 BV37 56
Gloucester Cres. Stai. AX50 73
Gloucester Dr. N4 BY34 47
Gloucester Dr. NW11 BS31 47
Gloucester Dr. Stai. AU48 72
Gloucester Gdns. NW11 BR33 46
Gloucester Gdns. W2 BT39 56
Gloucester Gdns. Barn. BV24 29
Gloucester Gdns. Ilf. CK33 49
Gloucester Gdns. Sutt. BS55 86
Gloucester Gate NW1 BV37 56
Gloucester Gro. SE15 CA43 67
Gloucester Gro. Edg. BN30 37
Gloucester Ms. NW1 BV37 56
Albany St.
Gloucester Ms. W2 BT39 56
Gloucester Ms. W. W2 BT39 56
Gloucester Parade Sid. CO46 79
Gloucester Pl. NW1 BU38 56
Gloucester Pl. W1 BU39 56
Gloucester Pl. Wind. AO44 61
Gloucester Pl. Ms. W1 BU39 56
Gloucester Rd. E10 CE33 48
Gloucester Rd. E11 CH32 49
Gloucester Rd. E12 CK35 49
Gloucester Rd. E17 CC30 39
Gloucester Rd. N17 BZ30 39
Gloucester Rd. N18 CA28 39
Gloucester Rd. SW7 BT41 66
Gloucester Rd. W3 BN41 65
Gloucester Rd. W5 BK41 64
Gloucester Rd. Barn. BS25 29
Gloucester Rd. Belv. CQ42 69
Gloucester Rd. Brwd. DA25 33
Gloucester Rd. Croy. BZ54 87
Gloucester Rd. Dart. CU47 79

Gloucester Rd. Enf. BZ22 30
Gloucester Rd. Felt. BD47 74
Gloucester Rd. Grav. DG49 81
Gloucester Rd. Guil. AP69 118
Gloucester Rd. Har. BF32 45
Gloucester Rd. Hmptn. BF50 74
Gloucester Rd. Houns. BE45 64
Gloucester Rd. Kings. On T. BM51 85
Gloucester Rd. Red. BU70 121
Gloucester Rd. Rich. BM43 65
Gloucester Rd. Rom. CT32 50
Gloucester Rd. Tedd. BH49 74
Gloucester Rd. Twick. BG47 74
Gloucester Sq. W2 BT39 56
Gloucester St. SW1 BW42 66
Gloucester St. Red. BU70 121
Gloucester Ter. NW1 BV37 56
Outer Circle
Gloucester Ter. W2 BS39 56
Gloucester Wk. W8 BS41 66
Gloucester Way EC1 BY38 56
Glover Rd. Pnr. BD32 45
Glovers Field. Brwd. CZ22 33
Glovers Rd. Reig. BS71 121
Gloxinia Rd. Grav. DD50 81
Glycena Rd. SW11 BU45 66
Glyn Av. Barn. BT24 29
Glyn Clo. SE25 CA51 87
Grange Hill
Glyn Clo. Epsom BP58 94
Glyn Ct. SE27 BY48 76
Glynde Ms. SW3 BU41 66
Yeomans Row
Glynde Rd. Bexh. CP45 69
Glynde St. SE4 CD46 77
Glyndon Rd. SE18 CM42 68
Glyn Dr. Sid. CO49 79
Glynfield Rd. NW10 BO36 55
Glynn Rd. Enf. CC24 30
Glyn Rd. E5 CC34 48
Glyn Rd. Wor. Pk. BQ55 85
Glyn St. SE11 BX42 66
Glynswood. Ger. Cr. AS29 34
Glynwood Ct. SE26 CC48 77
Glynwood Dr.
Glynwood Dr. SE26 CC48 77
Goat Ho. Br. SE25 CB52 87
Goat La. Enf. CA22 30
Goat La. Surb. BJ55 84
Goat Rd. Mitch. BU54 86
Goatsfield Rd. West. CJ63 106
Gobions Rom. CR30 41
Gobions Av. Rom. CS29 41
Gobions Way, Pot. B. BS17 20
Goblins Grn. Welw. G. C. BQ8 5
Goblins Grn. Welw. G. C. BR8 5
Godalming Av. Wall. BX56 95
Godalming By Pass, Guil. AR70 118
Godalming Rd. E14 CE39 57
Chrisp St.
Godbold Rd. E15 CG38 58
Goddard Rd. Beck. CC52 87
Goddard Rd. Grays. DD40 71
Goddards Clo. Hert. BW13 11
Goddington Chase Orp. CO56 98
Goddington La. Orp. CO55 89
Godfrey Av. Nthlt. BE37 54
Godfrey Av. Twick. BG47 74
Godfrey Hl. SE18 CK42 68
Godfrey Rd. SE18 CK42 68
Godfrey St. E15 CF37 57
Godfrey St. SW3 BU42 66
Godfrey Way. Hou. BE47 74
Godfrey Way Houns. BG45 64
Hanworth Rd.
Godfries Clo. Welw. BU5 5
Goding St. SE11 BX42 66
Godley Rd. SW18 BT47 76
Godley Rd. Wey. AY60 92
Godliman St. EC4 BY39 56
Godlophin Clo. Sutt. BR58 94
Godman Rd. SE15 CB44 67
Godman Rd. Grays. DG41 71
Godolphin Rd. W12 BP40 55
Godolphin Rd. Beac. AO29 34
Godolphin Rd. Slou. AO40 52
Godolphin Rd. Wey. BA57 92
Godric Cres. Croy. CF58 96
Godson Rd. Croy. BY55 86
Godson St. N1 BY37 56
Godstone Hill. Gdse. CB67 114
Godstone Rd. Cat. CB65 105
Godstone Rd. Cat. CB66 114
Godstone Rd. Oxt. CE69 114
Godstone Rd. Pur. BY59 95
Godstone Rd. Red. CA70 114
Godstone Rd. Sutt. BT56 95
Godstone Rd. Twick. BJ46 74
Godstow Rd. SE2 CO41 69
Godwin Ct. NW1 BW37 56
Chalton St.
Godwin Rd. E7 CH35 49
Godwin Rd. Brom. CJ52 88
Goffers Rd. SE3 CG44 68
Goff's Cres. Wal. Cr. BZ18 21
Goff's La. Wal. Cr. BZ18 21
Goffs Rd. Ashf. BA50 73
Gogmore La. Cher. AW54 83
Goidel Clo. Wall. BW56 95
Golborne Gds. W10 BR38 55
Golborne Rd. W10 BR39 55
Golda Clo. Barn. BQ25 28
Goldbeaters Gro. Edg. BQ29 37
Goldcliff Clo. Mord. BS54 86
Goldcrest Way Bush. BG26 36
Goldcrest Way Croy. CF58 96
Gold Cft. Hem. H. AZ14 8
Golden Ct. Rich. BK46 74
George St.
Golden Cres. Hayes BB40 53
Golden Dell. Welw. G. C. BR10 5
Golden La. EC1 BZ38 57
Golden La. Est. EC1 BZ38 57
Golden Manor W7 BH40 54
Golden Sq. W1 BW40 56
Golders Clo. Edg. BM28 37
Golders Gdns. NW11 BR33 46
Golders Gn. Cres. NW11 BR33 46
Golders Gn. Rd. NW11 BQ32 46
Golders Manor Dr. NW4 BQ32 46
Golders Pk. Clo. NW11 BS33 47
Golders Rise. NW4 BQ32 46
Golders Way NW11 BR33 46
Goldhawk Rd. W12 BP41 65
Titmuss St. W12
Gold Hill Edg. BN29 37
Gold Hill. E. Ger. Cr. AR30 34
Gold Hill. N. Ger. Cr. AR30 34
Gold Hill West. Ger. Cr. AR30 34
Goldhurst Ter. NW6 BS36 56
Goldingham Av. Loug. CM23 31
Golding Rd. Sev. CV64 108
Goldings Cross. Hat. BP12 10
Goldings Hill. Loug. CK22 31
Goldings Hill Loug. CK23 31
Goldings Rise Loug. CL23 31
Goldings Rd. Loug. CL23 31
Golding St. E1 CB39 57
Goldington Clo. Hodd. CD10 12
Goldington Cres. NW1 BW37 56
Goldington St. NW1 BW37 56
Gold La. Edg. BN29 37
Goldney Rd. W9 BS38 56
Goldrings Rd. Lthd. BF60 93
Goldsboro' Rd. SW8 BW44 66
Goldsborough Cres. E4 CE27 39
Goldsdown Clo. Enf. CD23 30
Goldsdown Rd. Enf. CC23 30
Goldsell Rd. Swan. CS53 89
Goldsmid St. SE18 CN42 68
Sladedale Rd.
Goldsmith Av. E12 CK36 58
Goldsmith Av. NW9 BO32 46
Goldsmith Av. Rom. CR33 50
Goldsmith Clo. W3 BN40 55
East Acton La.
Goldsmith Clo. Har. BF33 45
Goldsmith La. NW9 BM31 46
Goldsmith Rd. E10 CE33 48
Goldsmith Rd. E17 CC30 39
Goldsmith Rd. N11 BU28 38
Goldsmith Rd. SE15 CB44 67
Goldsmith Rd. W3 BN40 55
Goldsmiths Av. W3 BN40 55
Goldsmiths Clo. Wok. AR62 100
Goldsmith's Row E2 CB37 57
Goldsmiths Sq. E2 CB37 57
Goldsmith St. EC2 BZ39 57
Gutter La.
Goldsworth Orchard, Wok. AQ62 100
Goldsworth Rd. Wok. AR62 100
Goldsworthy Gdns. SE16 CC42 67
Goldwell Rd. Th. Hth. BX52 86
Golf Clo. Bush. BD23 27
Golf Clo. Stan. BK29 36
Golf Clo. Wok. AV60 91
Golf Club Rd. Wey. AZ58 92
Golf Club Rd. Wok. AQ63 100
Golf Course Dr. Kings. On T. BN50 75
Golfe Rd. Ilf. CM34 49
Golf Links Av. Grav. DG49 81
Golford Pl. NW1 BU38 56
Lisson Gro.
Golf Ride Enf. BY21 29
Golf Rd. W5 BL39 55
Boileau Rd.
Golf Rd. Brom. CL52 88
Golf Rd. Ken. BZ62 105
Golf Side, Sutt. BR59 94
Golf Side Twick. BG48 74
Golfside Clo. N. Mal. BO51 85
Goliath Clo. Wall. BX57 95
Gollogly Terr. SE7 CJ42 68
Nadine St.
Gombards All. St. Alb. BG13 9
Gomer Gdns. Tedd. BJ50 74
Gomer Pl. Tedd. BJ49 74
Gomm Rd. SE16 CC41 67
Gomshall Av. Wall. BX56 95
Gomshall Gdns. Ken. BZ61 105
Gomshall Rd. Sutt. BQ58 94
Gonson Pl. SE8 CE43 67
Gonson St. SE8 CE43 67
Gonston Cl. SW19 BR48 75
Queensmere Rd.
Gonville Av. Rick. AZ25 26
Gonville Cres. Nthlt. BF36 54
Gonville Rd. Th. Hth. BX53 86
Gonville St. SW6 BR45 65
Putney Br. App.
Goodall Rd. E11 CF35 48
Good Clo. Couls. BY63 104
Gooden Ct. Har. BH34 45
Goodenough Rd. SW19 BR50 75
Goodenough Wy. Couls. BX63 104
Goodge Pl. W1 BW39 56
Goodge St.
Goodge St. W1 BW39 56
Goodhall St. NW10 BO38 55
Goodhews Gdns. NW4 BP30 37
Goodinge Clo. N7 BX35 47
North Rd.
Goodinge Rd. N7 BX36 56
Goodley Stock Rd. Eden. CL69 115
Goodley Stock Rd. West. CL67 115
Goodman Pk. Slou. AR40 52
Goodman Pl. Stai. AV49 72
Goodman Rd. E10 CF33 48
Goodman St. E1 CA39 57
Goodman's Yd E1 CA40 57
Goodmayes Av. Ilf. CO33 50
Goodmayes La. Ilf. CO35 50
Goodmayes Rd. Ilf. CO33 50
Goodmead Rd. Orp. CO54 89
Goodrich Clo. Wat. BC21 26
Goodrich Rd. SE22 CA46 77
Goodson Rd. NW10 BO36 55
Goods Way NW1 BW37 56
Goodway Gdns. E14 CF39 57
Goodwin Dr. Sid. CP48 79
Goodwin Gdns. Croy. BY57 95
Goodwin Rd. N9 CC26 39
Goodwin Rd. W12 BP41 65
Goodwin Rd. Croy. BY57 95
Goodwin's Ct. WC2 BX40 56
St. Martins La.
Goodwin St. N4 BY34 47
Fonthill Rd.
Goodwood Av. Horn. CW35 51
Goodwood Av. Wat. BB21 26
Goodwood Clo. Hodd. CE11 12
Goodwood Clo. Mord. BS52 86
Goodwood Cres. Grav. DH49 81
Goodwood Cres. Grav. DH50 81
Goodwood Dr. Nthlt. BF36 54
Goodwood Pde. Wat. BB21 26
Goodwood Rd. SE14 CD43 67
Goodwyn Av. NW7 BO28 37
Goodwyns Farm Est. Dor. BJ73 119
Goodwyns Rd. Dor. BJ73 119
Goodwyn's Vale N10 BV30 38
Goodyear Pl. SE5 BZ43 67
Addington Sq.
Goodyear Ter. Grays DA43 70
Goodyers Av. Rad. BH20 18
Goodyers Gdns. NW4 BQ32 46
Brent Green
Goose Acre. Welw. G. C. BR9 5
Gooseacre La. Har. BK32 45
Goose Croft. Hem. H. AV13 7
Goosefield E. Mol. BF52 84
Goose Grn. Cob. BC63 101
Goose La. Wok. AQ64 100
Gooseley La. E6 CL38 58
Goose Rye Rd. Guil. AO66 109
Goose Yd. EC1 BY37 56
St. John St.
Gooshays Dr. Rom. CW28 42
Gooshays Gdns. Rom. CW29 42
Gophir La. EC4 BZ40 57
Bush La.
Gopsall St. N1 BZ37 57
Gorden Gdns. Edg. BM30 37
Gordon Av. E4 CG29 40
Gordon Av. SW14 BO45 65
Gordon Av. Horn. CT34 50
Gordon Av. Stan. BH29 36
Gordon Av. Stan. BJ29 36
Gordon Av. Sth. Croy. BZ58 96
Gordon Av. Twick. BJ46 74
Gordonbrock Rd. SE4 CE46 77
Gordon Clo. N19 BW33 47
Highgate Hill
Gordon Clo. Cher. AV55 82
Gordon Clo. Stai. AW50 73
Gordon Ct. W12 BQ39 55
Gordon Cres. Croy. CA54 87
Gordon Cres. Hayes BC41 63
Gordondale Rd. SW19 BS48 76
Gordon Dr. Cher. AV55 82
Gordon Gro. SE5 BY44 66
Gordon Hill Enf. BZ23 30
Gordon House Rd. NW5 BV35 47
Gordon Pl. W8 BS41 66
Gordon Prom. Grav. DH46 81
Gordon Rd. E4 CG26 40
Gordon Rd. E11 CH32 49
Gordon Rd. E12 CL34 49
Gordon Rd. E15 CF35 48
Gordon Rd. E17 CD32 48
Gordon Rd. E18 CH30 40
Gordon Rd. N3 BR29 37
Gordon Rd. N9 CB27 39
Gordon Rd. N11 BW29 38
Gordon Rd. NW6 BS38 56
Gordon Rd. SE15 CB44 67
Gordon Rd. W4 BM43 65
Gordon Rd. W5 BK40 54
Gordon Rd. W13 BJ40 54
Gordon Rd. Ashf. AY48 73
Gordon Rd. Bark. CN37 58
Gordon Rd. Beck. CC51 87
Gordon Rd. Beck. CD52 87
Gordon Rd. Belv. CS42 69
Gordon Rd. Brwd. DD26 122
Gordon Rd. Cars. BU57 95
Gordon Rd. Cat. BZ64 105
Gordon Rd. Chesh. AO19 16
Gordon Rd. Dart. CV47 80
Gordon Rd. Enf. BZ23 30
Gordon Rd. Esher BH57 93
Gordon Rd. Grav. DF47 81
Gordon Rd. Grays. DF41 71
Gordon Rd. Har. BH31 45
Gordon Rd. Houns. BG45 64
Gordon Rd. Ilf. CM34 49
Gordon Rd. Kings. On T. BL51 85
Gordon Rd. Red. BV69 121
Gordon Rd. Rich. BL44 65
Gordon Rd. Rom. CQ32 50
Gordon Rd. Sev. CU66 116
Gordon Rd. Shep. BA53 83
Gordon Rd. Sid. CN46 78
Gordon Rd. Stai. AU49 72
Gordon Rd. Sthl. BE42 64
Gordon Rd. Surb. BL54 85
Gordon Rd. Wal. Abb. CE20 21
Gordon Rd. West Dr. AY40 53
Gordon Rd. Wind. AM44 61
Gordon Sq. WC1 BW38 56
Gordon St. E13 CH38 58
Gordon St. WC1 BW38 56
Gordon St. Twick. BJ46 74
Gordons Way. Oxt. CF67 114
Gordon Way Barn. BR24 28
Gordon Way. Ch. St. G. AQ27 34
Gore Clo. Wat. BC21 26
Gore Ct. NW9 BM32 46
Gorefield Pl. NW6 BS37 56
Gorelands La. Ch. St. G. AR26 34
Gore Rd. E9 CC37 57
Gore Rd. SW20 BQ51 85
Gore Rd. Dart. CY47 80
Goresbrook Rd. Dag. CO37 59
Gore St. SW7 BT41 66
Gorhambury Dr. St. Alb. BE12 9
Gorham Dr. St. Alb. BH15 9
Gorham Pl. W11 BR40 55
Mary Pl.
Goring Clo. Rom. CS30 41
Goring Gdns. Dag. CP35 50
Goring Rd. N11 BX29 38
Goring Rd. Dag. CS36 59
Goring Rd. Stai. AV49 72
Goring Rd. N. Dag. CS36 59
Goring Sq. Stai. AV49 72
Goring St. EC3 CA39 57
Houndsditch
Goring Way Grnf. BG37 54
Gorle Station St. W14 BR43 65
Gorleston Rd. N15 BZ32 48
Gorleston St. W14 BR42 65
Gorringe Pk. Av. Mitch. BU50 76
Gorse Cl. Hat. BO14 10
Gorse Hill La. Vir. W. AR52 82
Gorse Hill Rd. Vir. W. AR52 82
Gorselands Clo. Wey. AX59 92
Gorse Rise SW17 BV49 76
Gorse Rd. Croy. CE56 96
Gorse Rd. Orp. CQ54 89
Gorse Wk. West Dr. AY39 53
Gorse Way Rom. CT33 50
Gorsewood Rd. Wok. AO63 100
Gorst Rd. NW10 BN38 55
Gorst Rd. SW11 BU46 76
Gorsuch St. E2 CA38 57
Gosberton Rd. SW12 BU47 76
Gosbury Hill Chess. BL56 94
Gosden Hill Rd. Guil. AU68 109
Gosfield Rd. Dag. CR33 50
Gosfield Rd. Dag. CR34 50
Gosfield Rd. Epsom BN59 94
Gosfield St. W1 BW39 56
Gosford Gdns. Ilf. CK32 49
Gosforth La. Wat. BC27 35
Goshawk Gdns. Hayes BB38 53
Goslett Yd WC2 BW39 56
Charing Cross Rd.
Gosling Clo. Grnf. BF38 54
Gosling Green Rd. Slou. AS41 62
Gosling Way SW9 BY44 66
Gospatrick Rd. N17 BZ29 39
Gospel Oak Est. NW5 BU35 47
Gosport Rd. E17 CD32 48
Gosport Way SE15 CA43 67
Gossage Rd. SE18 CM42 68
Ancona Rd.
Gossage Rd. Uxb. AY36 53
Gossamers, The, Wat. BE21 27
Gosset St. E2 CA38 57
Goss Hill Swan. CV50 80
Gosshill Rd. Brom. CL51 88
Gossoms End. Berk. AQ12 7
Gosterwood St. SE8 CD43 67
Gostling Rd. Twick. BF47 74
Goston Gdns. Th. Hth. BY52 86
Goswell Pl. Wind. AO44 61
Goswell Rd. EC1 BY37 56
Goswell Rd. Wind. AO43 61
Gothic Clo. Dart. CW48 80
Gothic Ct. Hayes. BA43 63
Gothic Rd. Twick. BG48 74
Goudhurst Rd. Brom. CG49 78
Gouge Av. Grav. DF47 81
Gough Rd. E15 CG35 49
Gough Rd. Enf. CB23 30
Gough Sq. EC4 BY39 56
Gough St. WC1 BX38 56
Gould Cl. Hat. BP15 10
Gould Ct. SE19 CA49 77
Goulden St. SW11 BU44 66
Gould Rd. Felt. BB47 73
Gould Rd. Twick. BH47 74
Gould's Grn. Uxb. AZ40 53
Goulston St. E1 CA39 57
Goulton Rd. E5 CB35 48
Gourley St. N15 CA32 48
Gourock Rd. SE9 CL46 78
Govan St. E2 CB37 57
Whiston Rd.
Government Row, Enf. CE22 30
Govett Av. Shep. BA53 83
Gowan Av. SW6 BR44 65
Gowan Rd. NW10 BP36 55
Gower Clo. E15 CG36 58
Gower Ms. WC1 BW39 56
Gower Pl. WC1 BW38 56
Gower Rd. E7 CH36 58
Gower Rd. Islw. BH43 64
Gower Rd. Wey. BA57 92
Gowers La. Grays. DF41 71
Gowers, The Amer. AP22 25
Gowers, The, Harl. CO10 6
Gower St. WC1 BW38 56
Gowers Wk. E1 CB39 57
Gower, The, Egh. AT52 82
Gowland Pl. Beck. CD51 87
Gowlett Rd. SE15 CB45 67
Gowrie Rd. SW11 BV45 66
Graburn Way E. Mol. BG52 84
Grace Av. Bexh. CQ44 69
Gracechurch St. EC3 BZ40 57
Gracedale Rd. SW16 BV49 76
Gracefield Gdns. SW16 BX48 76
Grace Rd. Croy. BZ53 87
Grace's Alley E1 CB40 57
Ensign St.
Grace's Ms. SE5 BZ44 67
Grace's Rd. SE5 CA44 67
Grace St. E3 CE38 57
Gracious La. Sev. CU68 116
Gracious Pond Rd. Wok. AQ57 91
Gradient, The, SE26 CB49 77
Graeme Rd. Enf. BZ23 30
Graemesdyke Av. SW14 BM45 65
Graemes Dyke Rd. Berk. AQ13 7
Grafton Clo. W13 BJ39 54
Grafton Clo. Slou. AS39 52
Grafton Clo. Wey. AV60 91
Grafton Clo. Wor. Pk. BO55 85
Grafton Cres. NW1 BV36 56
Grafton Gdns. N4 CB32 48
Rutland Gdns.
Grafton Gdns. Dag. CQ34 50
Grafton Ms. W1 BW38 56
Grafton Way
Grafton Pl. NW1 BW38 56
Grafton Rd. NW5 BV35 47
Grafton Rd. W3 BN40 55
Grafton Rd. Croy. BY54 86
Grafton Rd. Dag. CQ34 50
Grafton Rd. Enf. BX24 29
Grafton Rd. Har. BG32 45
Grafton Rd. N. Mal. BO52 85
Grafton Rd. Wor. Pk. BN55 85
Grafton Sq. SW4 BW45 66
Grafton St. NW3 BS34 47
Hermitage La.
Grafton St. W1 BV40 56
Grafton Ter. NW2 BS34 47
Hermitage La.
Grafton Ter. NW5 BU35 47
Grafton Yd. NW5 BV36 56
Prince Of Wales Rd.
Graham Av. W13 BJ41 64
Graham Av. Brox. CD14 12
Graham Av. Mitch. BV51 86
Graham Clo. Croy. CE55 87
Grahame Park Est. NW9 BO30 37
Grahame Park Way NW9 BO30 37
Graham Gdns. Surb. BL54 85
Graham Rd. E8 CB36 57
Graham Rd. E13 CH38 58
Graham Rd. N15 BY31 47
Graham Rd. NW4 BP32 46
Graham Rd. SW19 BR50 75
Graham Rd. W4 BN41 65
Graham Rd. Bexh. CQ45 69
Graham Rd. Hamptn. BF49 74
Graham Rd. Har. BG31 45
Graham Rd. Mitch. BV51 86
Graham Rd. Pur. BY60 95
Graham St. N1 BY37 56
Graham Ter. SW1 BV42 66
Grainger Clo. Nthlt. BG35 45
Grainger Rd. N22 BZ30 39
Grainger Rd. Islw. BH44 64
Grampian Gdns. NW2 BR33 46
Grampians, The, W14 BQ41 65
Grampian Way. Slou. AT42 62
Granard Av. SW15 BP46 75
Granard Gdns. SW15 BP46 75
Granard Rd. SW12 BU47 76
Granary Meadow Brwd. DC22 33
Granby Rd. SE9 CK44 68
Granby Rd. Grav. DE46 81
Granby's Bldgs. SE11 BX42 66
Salamanca St.
Granby St. E2 CA38 57
Granby Ter. NW1 BW37 56
Grand Av. EC1 BY39 56
Charterhouse St.
Grand Av. N10 BV31 47
Grand Av. Surb. BM53 85
Grand Av. Wem. BM35 46
Grand Av. E. Wem. BM35 46
Grand Central Wk. SE19 CB50 77
Grand Depot Rd. SE18 CL42 68
Grand Dr. SW20 BQ52 85
Granden Rd. SW16 BX51 86
Grandfield Av. Wat. BC23 26
Grandison Rd. SW11 BU45 66
Grandison Rd. Wor. Pk. BQ55 85
Grand Pde. Surb. BM54 85
Grand Pde. Wem. BM34 46
Grand Sq. SE10 CF42 67
Grand Stand Rd. Epsom BO62 103
Grand, The, Pde. NW3 BT35 47
Finchley Rd.
Grand View Ave. West. CJ62 106
Granfield St. SW11 BT44 66
Grange Av. N12 BT28 38
Grange Av. N20 BR26 37
Grange Av. SE25 CA51 87
Grange Av. Barn. BU26 38
Grange Av. Stan. BJ30 36
Grange Av. Twick. BH48 74
Grange Av. Wdf. Grn. CH29 40
Grangecliffe Gdns. SE25 CA51 87
Grange Clo. Brwd. DE28 122
Grange Clo. Edg. BN28 37
Grange Clo. Ger. Cr. AS30 34
Grange Clo. Guil. AQ68 109
Grange Clo. Hayes BB39 53
Grange Clo. Hem. H. AZ14 8
Grange Clo. Houns. BE42 64
Grange Clo. Lthd. BK63 102
Grange Clo. N. Mal. BP53 85
Grange Clo. Red. BV67 113
Grange Clo. Sid. CO48 79
Grange Clo. Stai. AS46 72
Grange Clo. Wdf. Grn. CH29 40
Grange Ct. WC2 BX39 56
Grange Ct. Chig. CM27 40
Grange Ct. Loug. CJ25 31
Grange Ct. Nthlt. BD37 54
Grange Ct. St. Alb. BG13 9
Grange St.

Grange Ct. Shep. AZ52 83
Watersplash Rd.
Grange Ct. Wal. Abb. CE20 21
Grange Ct. Walt. BC55 83
Grange Ct. Rd. N16 CA33 48
Grange Cres. Chig. CM28 40
Grange Dr. Chis. CK50 78
Grange Dr. Orp. CP58 98
Grange Dr. Wok. AS61 100
Grange Est. N2 BT30 38
Grange Farm Clo. Har. BG34 45
Grangefields Ave. Guil. AR67 109
Grange Flds. Ger. Cr. AS30 34
Grange Gdns. N14 BW26 38
Grange Gdns. SE25 CA51 87
Grange Gdns. Bans. BS60 95
Grange Gdns. Pnr. BE31 45
Grange Gdns. Slou. AO35 43
Grange Gro. N1 BY36 56
Grange Hill SE25 CA51 87
Grange Hill Edg. BN28 37
Grangehill Pl. SE9 CK45 68
Grangehill Rd. SE9 CK45 68
Grange La. SE21 CA48 77
Grange La. Harl. CJ11 13
Grange Meadow Bans. BS60 95
Grangemill Rd. SE6 CE48 77
Grangemill Way SE6 CE48 77
Grange Mt. Lthd. BK63 102
Grange Par. Hayes BB39 53
Grange Pk. W5 BL40 55
Grange Pk. Wok. AS60 91
Grange Pk. Wok. AS61 100
Grange Pk. Av. N21 BY25 29
Grange Pk. Rd. E10 CE33 48
Grange Pk. Rd. Th. Hth. BZ52 87
Grange Pl. Stai. AW51 83
Grange Rd. E10 CE33 48
Grange Rd. E13 CG38 58
Grange Rd. E17 CD32 48
Grange Rd. N6 BU32 47
Grange Rd. N17 CB29 39
Grange Rd. NW10 BP36 55
Grange Rd. SE1 CA41 67
Grange Rd. SW13 BP44 65
Grange Rd. W4 BM42 65
Grange Rd. W5 BK40 54
Grange Rd. Borwd. BL25 28
Grange Rd. Bush. BE25 27
Grange Rd. Cat. CA66 114
Grange Rd. Chess. BL55 85
Grange Rd. E. Mol. BF53 84
Grange Rd. Edg. BN29 37
Grange Rd. Egh. AS49 72
Grange Rd. Ger. Cr. AS30 34
Grange Rd. Grav. DG47 81
Grange Rd. Grays. DD43 71
Grange Rd. Guil. AQ68 109
Grange Rd. Guil. AQ69 118
Grange Rd. Har. BG34 45
Grange Rd. Har. BJ47 74
Grange Rd. Hayes BB39 53
Grange Rd. Ilf. CL35 49
Grange Rd. Kings. On T. BL52 85
Grange Rd. Lthd. BK63 102
Grange Rd. Orp. CM55 88
Grange Rd. Rom. CU29 41
Grange Rd. Sev. CU67 116
Grange Rd. S. Ock. CW40 60
Grange Rd. Sth. Croy. BZ58 96
Grange Rd. Sthl. BE41 64
Grange Rd. Sutt. BS57 95
Grange Rd. Th. Hth. BZ52 87
Grange Rd. Walt. BE56 93
Grange Rd. Wey. AW58 92
Grange Rd. Wok. AS60 91
Granger Way. Rom. CU32 50
Grange St. N1 BZ37 57
Grange St. St. Alb. BG13 9
Grange, The. N20 BT26 38
Grange, The. NW3 BS34 47
Grange, The. SE1 CA41 67
Grange, The. SW19 BQ49 75
Grange, The. Croy. CD55 87
Grange, The. N. Mal. BP53 85
Grange, The Red. BV69 121
Grange, The. Sev. CY57 99
Grange, The. Wem. BM36 55
Grange, The. Wor. Pk. BN55 85
Grange, The Dr. N21 BY25 29
Grange Vale, Sutt. BS57 95
Grange View Rd. N20 BT26 38
Grange Wk. SE1 CA41 67
Grange Way N12 BS28 38
Grangeway NW6 BS36 56
Messina Av.
Grange Way. Erith. CU43 69
Grange Way, Iver AV39 52
Grangeway Wdf. Grn. CJ28 40
Grangeway Gdns. Ilf. CK32 49
Grangeway, The. N21 BY25 29
Grangewood Bex. CQ47 79
Hurst Rd.
Grangewood, Pot. B. BS18 20
Grangewood Ave. Grays. DF41 71
Grangewood Av. Rain. CV38 60
Grangewood Clo. Brwd. DD27 122
Grangewood Clo. Nthwd. BB29 35
Grangewood Clo. Pnr. BC32 44
Grangewood La. Beck. CD50 77
Grangewood, Slou. AR39 52
Grangewood St. E6 CJ37 58
Grangewood Ter. SE25 BZ51 87
Grange Yd. SE1 CA41 67
Granham Gdns. N9 CA27 39
Granite St. SE18 CN42 68
Granleigh Rd. E11 CG34 49
Gransden Av. E8 CB36 57
London La.
Gransden Rd. W12 BO41 65
Wendell Rd.
Grant Av. Slou. AP39 52
Grantbridge St. N1 BY37 56
Grant Clo. N14 BW26 38
Grant Clo. Shep. AZ53 83
Grantham Clo. Edg. BL27 37
Grantham Gdns. Rom. CQ32 50
Grantham Grn. Borwd. BN25 28
Grantham Pl. W1 BV40 56
Old Park La.
Grantham Rd. E12 CL34 49
Grantham Rd. SW9 BX44 66
Grantham Rd. W4 BO43 65
Grantham Way. Grays. DD40 71
Grantley Clo. Guil. AS74 118
Grantley Gdns. Guil. AQ70 118
Grantley Rd. Guil. AQ70 118
Grantley Rd. Houns. BC44 63
Grantley St. E1 CC38 57
Grantock Rd. E17 CF30 39
Granton Av. Upmin. CW34 51
Granton Rd. SW16 BW51 86
Granton Rd. Ilf. CO33 50
Granton Rd. Sid. CP50 79
Grant Pl. Croy. CA54 87
Grant Rd. SW11 BT45 66
Grant Rd. Croy. CA54 87
Grant Rd. Har. BH31 45
Grants Clo. NW7 BQ29 37
Grants La. Oxt. CJ70 115
Grant St. E13 CH38 58
Grant St. N1 BY37 56
Grantully Rd. W9 BS38 56
Grantwood Clo. Red. BV73 121
Granville Av. Felt. BC48 73
Granville Av. Houns. BF46 74
Granville Av. Slou. AO39 52
Granville Clo. Wey. AY60 92
Church Rd.
Granville Clo. Wey. BA57 92
Granville Gdns. SW16 BX51 86
Granville Gdns. W5 BL40 55
Granville Gro. SE13 CF45 67
Granville Ms. NW2 BR34 46
Granville Pk. SE13 CF45 67
Granville Pl. N12 BT29 38
High Rd. Nth. Finchley
Granville Pl. W1 BV39 56
Granville Rd. E17 CE32 48
Granville Rd. E18 CH30 40
Granville Rd. N4 BX32 47
Granville Rd. N9 CC27 39
Granville Rd. N12 BS29 38
Granville Rd. N13 BX29 38
Granville Rd. N22 BY30 38
Granville Rd. NW2 BR34 46
Granville Rd. NW6 BS37 56
Granville Rd. SW18 BR47 75
Granville Rd. SW19 BS50 76
Granville Rd. Barn. BQ24 28
Granville Rd. Berk. AP12 7
Granville Rd. Epp. CO18 23
Granville Rd. Grav. DF47 81
Granville Rd. Hayes. BB42 63
Granville Rd. Ilf. CL33 49
Granville Rd. Oxt. CG68 115
Granville Rd. St. Alb., BH13 9
Granville Rd. Sev. CU65 107
Granville Rd. Sid. CO49 79
Granville Rd. Uxb. AZ36 53
Granville Rd. Wat. BD24 27
Granville Rd. Well. CP45 69
Granville Rd. West. CM66 115
Granville Rd. Wey. BA57 92
Granville Rd. Wok. AS63 100
Granville Sq. WC1 BX38 56
Granville St. WC1 BX38 56
Wharton St.
Grape St. WC2 BX39 56
High Holborn
Grasdene Rd. SE18 CO43 69
Grasmere Av. SW15 BN49 75
Grasmere Av. SW19 BS51 86
Grasmere Av. W3 BN40 55
Grasmere Av. Houns. BF46 74
Grasmere Av. Orp. CL55 88
Grasmere Av. Ruis. BA33 44
Grasmere Av. Slou. AQ40 52
Grasmere Av. Wem. BK33 45
Grasmere Clo. Guil. AT70 118
Grasmere Clo. Hem. H. AZ14 8
Grasmere Clo. Loug. CK23 31
Grasmere Ct. N22 BX29 38
Palmerston Rd.
Grasmere Gdns. Har. BJ30 36
Grasmere Gdns. Ilf. CK32 49
Grasmere Gdns. Orp. CL55 88
Grasmere Rd. E13 CH37 58
Grasmere Rd. N10 BV30 38
Grasmere Rd. N17 CB29 39
Grasmere Rd. SE25 CB53 87
Grasmere Rd. SW16 BX49 76
Grasmere Rd. Bexh. CS44 69
Grasmere Rd. Brom. CG51 88
Grasmere Rd. Horn. CW31 51
Grasmere Rd. Orp. CL55 88
Grasmere Rd. Pur. BY59 95
Grasmere Rd. St. Alb. BJ14 9
Grasmere Way, Wey. AY59 92
Grassingham End. Ger. Cr. AS29 34
Grassingham Rd. Ger. Cr. AS29 34
Grassington Clo. St. Alb. BF18 18
W. Riding
Grassington Rd. Sid. CO49 79
Grass Mt. SE23 CB48 77
Grassmount Pur. BW58 95
Grass Pk. N3 BR30 37
Grass Warren. Welw. BU6 5
Grassway Wall. BW56 95
Grassy Clo. Hem. H. AW13 8
Grassy La. Sev. CU66 116
Grasvenor Av. Barn. BS25 29
Gratley Way SE15 CA43 67
Hordle Prom. N.
Gratton Dr. Wind. AM45 61
Gratton Rd. W14 BR41 65
Gratton Ter. NW2 BQ34 46
Gravel Clo. Chig. CO27 41
Graveley Av. Borwd. BN24 28
Graveley Ct. Hem. H. BA14 8
Gravel Hill N3 BR30 37
Broadway, The.
Gravel Hill Bexh. CR46 79
Gravel Hill. Ger. Cr. AS29 34
Gravel Hill, Hem. H. AW13 8
Gravel Hill Loug. CH23 31
Gravel Hill, Lthd. BJ64 102
Gravel Hill Sth. Croy. CC57 96
Gravel Hill, Uxb. AX35 44
Gravel Hill Clo. Bexh. CR46 79
Gravel Hill Ter. Hem. H. AW14 8
Gravel La. E1 CA39 57
Gravel La. Chig. CO26 41
Gravel La. Chig. CO27 41
Gravel La. Hem. H. AW13 8
Gravel Path. Berk. AR13 7
Gravel Path, Hem. H. AW13 8
Gravel Pit La. SE9 CM46 78
Gravel Rd. Brom. CK55 88
Gravel Rd. Twick. BH47 74
Gravel St. E1 CC40 57
Gravel Wood Clo. Chis. CM48 78
Gravely Hill. Cat. CA67 114
Graveney Gro. SE20 CC50 77
Woodbine Gro.
Graveney Rd. SW17 BU49 76
Gravesend Rd. W12 BP40 55
Gravetts La. Guil. AO09 110
Gravetts La. Guil. AP68 109
Gray Av. Dag. CQ33 50
Grayburn Clo. Ch. St. G. AQ27 34
Grayburne. Grav. DB49 80
Graydon St. SE18 CL43 68
Gray Gdns. Rain. CU36 59
Grayham Cres. N. Mal BN52 85
Grayham Rd. N. Mal. BN52 85
Graylands, Epp. CM22 31
Graylands, Wok. AS61 100
Graylands La. Swans. DB46 60
Graylands Sq. Swans. DB46 60
Grayling Rd. N16 BZ34 48
Grayling Sq. E2 CB38 57
Avebury Est.
Graylings, The, Wat. BA20 17
Grayscroft Rd. SW16 BW50 76
Graysend Clo. Gray. DD41 71
Grays Farm Rd. Orp. CO51 89
Graysfield. Welw. G. C. BS9 5
Gray's Inn Rd. WC1 BX38 56
Gray's Inn Sq. WC1 BY39 56
Gray's La. Ash. BL63 103
Grays La. Ashf. AZ49 73
Grays Pk. Rd. Slou. AQ37 52
Grays Pl. Slou. AP40 52
Grays Rd. Slou. AP40 52
Grays Rd. Uxb. AY36 53
Grays Rd. West. CL64 106
Gray St. SE1 BY41 66
Grays Wk. Brwd. DE26 122
Grayswood Gdns. SW20 BP51 85
Graywood Ct. N12 BT29 38
Grazebrook Rd. N16 BZ34 48
Grazeley Clo. Bexh. CS46 79
Gt. Acre Ct. SW4 BW45 66
Clapham Pk. Rd.
Great Benty. West Dr. AY42 63
Great Braitch La. Hat. BO10 5
Great Brays. Harl. CO11 14
Great Break. Welw. G. C. BS8 5
Gt. Brownings SE21 CA49 77
Gt. Bushey Dr. N20 BS26 38
Gt. Castle St. W1 BV39 56
Gt. Central Av. Ruis. BD35 45
Gt. Central St. NW1 BU39 56
Melcombe Sq.
Gt. Chapel St. W1 BW39 56
Gt. Chertsey Rd. W4 BN44 65
Gt. Chertsey Rd. Felt. BE48 74
Gt. Church La. W6 BQ42 65
Gt. College St. SW1 BX41 66
Gt. Cross Av. SE10 CG43 68
Gt. Cullings Rom. CT34 50
Gt. Cumberland Ms. W1 BU39 56
Seymour Pl.
Gt. Cumberland Pl. W1 BU39 56
Great Dell. Welw. G. C. BQ7 7
Gt. Dover St. SE1 BZ41 67
Greatdown Rd. W7 BH38 54
Gt. Eastern Rd. E15 CF36 57
Gt. Eastern Rd. Brwd. DB28 42
Gt. Eastern St. EC2 CA38 57
Gt. Ellshams Bans. BS61 104
Gt. Elms Rd. Brom. CJ52 88
Gt. Elms Rd. Hem. H. AY15 8
Great Field NW9 BO30 37
Greatfield Av. E6 CK38 58
Greatfield Clo. SE4 CE45 67
Greatfields Dr. Uxb. AZ39 53
Greatfields Rd. Bark. CM37 58
Great Field Strand NW9 BO30 37
Greatford Dr. Guil. AU70 118
Great Ganett. Welw. G. C. BS9 5
Gt. Gardens Rd. Horn. CU32 50
Gt. George St. SW1 BW41 66
Gt. Goodwin Dr. Guil. AT69 118
Gt. Grove Bush. BF24 27
Gt. Guildford St. SE1 BZ40 57
Greatham Rd. Bush. BD24 27
Gt. Harry Dr. SE9 CL48 78
Greatheart, Hem. H. AY12 8
Gt Heath. Hat. BP11 10
Great Hobletts Rd. Hem. H. AY13 8
Gt. Hurstend, Lthd. BE65 102
Gt. James St. WC1 BX39 56
Gt. Lawn Ong. CX17 24
Great Ley. Welw. G. C. BR9 5
Great Leylands. Harl. CO11 14
Gt. Marlborough St. W1 BW39 56
Great Meadow, Brox. CE14 12
Gt. Nelmes Chase Horn. CW32 51
Greatness La. Sev. CV64 108
Greatness Rd. Sev. CV64 108
Gt. Newport St. WC2 BW40 56
Upr. St. Martin's La.
Great Norh Rd. Hat. BQ11 10
Gt. North Rd. N2 BU31 47
Great North Rd. N20 BT26 38
Gt. North Rd. Barn. BR24 28
Great North Rd. Beac. AP29 34
Great North Rd. Hat. BT17 20
Great North Rd. Pot. B. BT18 20
Gt. North Way NW4 BP30 37
Gt. Oaks, Brwd. DD25 122
Great Oaks Chig. CM28 40
Gt. Oaks Park, Guil. AT68 109
Greatorex St. E1 CB39 57
Gt. Ormond St. WC1 BX39 56
Gt. Owl Rd. Chig. CL27 40
Great Palmers, Hem. H. AY11 8
Great Park, Kings L. AY18 17
Great Parndon. Harl. CL12 13
Gt. Percy St. WC1 BX38 56
Gt. Peter St. SW1 BX41 66
Great Plumtree, Harl. CN10 6
Gt. Portland St. W1 BV38 56
Gt. Pulteney St. W1 BW40 56
Gt. Quarry, Guil. AR72 118
Gt. Queen St. WC2 BX39 56
Gt. Queen St. Dart. CW47 80
Great Rd. Hem. H. AY13 8
Great Ropers La. Brwd. DA29 42
Gt. Russell St. WC1 BW39 56
Gt. St. Helen's EC3 CA39 57
St. Mary Axe
Gt. St. Thomas Apostle EC4 BZ40 57
Queen St.
Great Saplings SE21 CA46 77
Gt. Scotland Yd. SW1 BX40 56
Great Slades, Pot. B. BR20 19
Gt. Smith St. SW1 BW41 66
Great South West Rd. Felt. BA47 73
Gt. Spilmans SE22 CA46 77
Gt. Suffolk St. SE1 BY40 56
Gt. Sutton St. EC1 BY38 56
Gt. Swan Alley EC2 BZ39 57
Gt. Tattenhams Epsom BP62 103
Gt. Thrift Orp. CM52 88
Gt. Tichfield St. W1 BV38 56
Gt. Tower St. EC3 CA40 57
Gt. Trinity La. EC4 BZ40 57
Queen Victoria St.
Gt. Turnstile WC1 BX39 56
High Holborn
Great Warley St. Brwd. DA30 42
Great Warley St. Brwd. DB31 51
Gt. West Rd. W4 BM42 65
Gt. West Rd. Houns. BE44 64
Great Whites Rd. Hem. H. AY14 8
Gt. Winchester St. EC2 BZ39 57
Gt. Windmill St. W1 BW40 56
Greatwood Chis. CL50 78
Greatwood Clo. Cher. AU58 91
Gt. Woodcote Dr. Pur. BW58 95
Gt. Woodcote Pk. Pur. BW58 95
Greaves Pl. SW17 BU49 76
Grecian Cres. SE19 BY50 76
Greek Ct. W1 BW39 56
Old Compton St.
Greek St. W1 BW39 56
Greenacre Dart. CV48 80
Green Acre. Wind. AM44 61
Green Acre, Wok. AP61 100
Green Acre Clo. Barn. BR22 28
Greenacres SE9 CL46 78
Green Acres Croy. CA55 87
Green Acres, Hem. H. BA14 8
Green Acres, Lthd. BF65 102
Green Acres. Welw. G. C. BR9 5
Greenacres Av. Uxb. AY34 44
Greenacres Clo. Rain. CW38 60
Greenacres Dr. Stan. BJ29 36
Greenall Clo. Wal. Cr. CD18 21
Roundmoor Dr.
Green Arbour Ct. EC4 BY39 56
Old Bailey
Green Av. NW7 BN28 37
Green Av. W13 BJ41 64
Greenaway Gdns. NW3 BS35 47
Green Bank E1 CB40 57
Green Bank. N12 BS28 38
Greenbank Av. Wem. BJ35 45
Green Bank Clo. Rom. CV27 42
Greenbank Cres. NW4 BR31 46
Greenbank Rd. Wat. BA21 26
Green Banks, Upmin. CZ34 51
Green Banks Walt. BE54 84
Greenbay Rd. SE7 CJ43 68
Greenberry St. NW8 BU37 56
Greenbrook Av. Barn. BT23 29
Green Clo. NW9 BN32 46
Green Clo. NW11 BT33 47
Green Clo. Brom. CG52 88
Green Clo. Cars. BU55 86
Green Clo. Epp. CL15 13
Green Clo. Felt. BE49 74
Green Clo. Hat. BR16 19
Green Clo. Wal. Cr. CD19 21
Greencoat Pl. SW1 BW42 66
Greencoat Row SW1 BW41 66
Francis St.
Green Ct. Edg. BM29 37
Green Ct. Av. Croy. CB55 87
Green Ct. Gdns. Croy. CB54 87
Greencourt Rd. Orp. CM53 88
Green Ct. Rd. Swan. CS53 89
Greencroft, Guil. AT70 118
Green Cft. Hat. BP11 10
Greencroft Av. Ruis. BD34 45
Greencroft Gdns. NW6 BS36 56
Greencroft Gdns. Enf. CA24 30
Greencroft Rd. Houns. BE44 64
Green Curve Bans. BR60 94
Green Dale NW7 BO28 37
Green Dale SE22 BZ45 67
Green Dale Clo. SE22 CA46 77
Green Dale
Greendale Wk. Grav. DF48 81
Green Dell Way, Hem. H. AZ13 8
Green Dene. Leath. BA70 110
Green Dragon La. N21 BX25 29
Green Dragon La. Brent. BL42 65
Green Dragon Yd. E1 CB39 57
Old Montague St.
Green Dr. Sthl. BF40 54
Green East Rd. Beac. AP29 34
Green End N21 BY27 38
Green End. Chess. BK56 93
Green End. Hem. H. AV13 7
Greenend Rd. W4 BO41 65
Green End Rd. Hem. H AW14 8
Greene Walk, Berk. AR13 7
Greenfarm Clo. Orp. CN57 97
Greenfield, Welw. G. C. BQ6 5
Greenfield Av. Surb. BM54 85
Greenfield Av. Wat. BE27 36
Greenfielde End, Stai AX50 73
Greenfield End. Ger. Cr. AS29 34
Greenfield Gdns. NW2 BR34 46
Greenfield Gdns. Dag. CP37 59
Greenfield Gdns. Orp. CM54 88
Greenfield. Hat. BQ11 10
Greenfield Link-couls. BX57 95
Greenfield Rd. E1 CB39 57
Greenfield Rd. N15 CA32 48
Green Field Rd. Berk. AR13 7
Greenfield Rd. Dag. CP37 59
Greenfield Rd. Dart. CS49 79
Greenfields Loug. CL24 31
Greenfields Sthl. BF40 54
Greenfields Clo. Loug. CL24 31
Greenfield St. Wal. Abb CF20 21
Greenfield Way Har. BF31 45
Greenford Av. W7 BH38 54
Greenford Av. Sthl. BE40 54
Greenford Gdns. Grnf. BF38 54
Greenford Rd. Grnf. BG37 54
Greenford Rd. Har. BH35 45
Greenford Rd. Sthl. BG40 54
Greenford Rd. Sutt. BS56 95
Green Gdns. Orp. CM56 97
Greengate Grnf. BJ36 54
Greengate St. E13 CH37 58
Green Glade, Epp. CN22 31
Greenglades Horn. CW32 51
Greenhalgh Wk. N2 BT31 47
Greenham Rd. N10 BV30 38
Greenham Wk. Wok. AR62 100
Winnington Way
Green Haven Clo. Guil. AP68 109
Greenhayes Av. Bans. BS60 95
Greenhayes Gdns. Bans. BS61 104
Greenheys Clo. Nthwd. BB30 35
Greenheys Dr. E18 CG31 49
Greenheys Pl. Wok. AS62 100
Green Hill SE18 CK42 68
Green Hill Buck. H. CJ26 40
Green Hill. Orp. CK59 97
Greenhill Sutt. BT55 86
Greenhill Wem. BM34 46
Greenhill Ave. Cat. CB64 105
Greenhill Cres. Har. BH32 45
Greenhill Cres. Wat. BB25 26
Greenhill Gdns. Nthlt. BE37 54
Greenhill Gro. E12 CK35 49
Green Hill La. Warl. CD62 105
Greenhill Pk. NW10 BO37 55
Greenhill Pk. Barn. BS25 29
Greenhill Rd. NW10 BO37 55
Greenhill Rd. Grav. DF48 81
Greenhill Rd. Har. BH32 45
Greenhill Rd. Sev. CV61 108
Greenhills Clo. Rick. AW25 26
Greenhill's Rents. EC1 BY39 56
Cowcross St.
Green Hill Terrace SE18 CK42 68
Greenhill Ter. Nthlt. BE37 54
Greenhill Way Wem. BM34 46
Greenhithe Clo. Sid. CN47 78
Greenholm Rd. SE9 CL46 78
Green Hundred Rd. SE15 CB43 67
Greenhurst La. Oxt. CH69 115
Greenhurst Rd. SE27 BY49 76
Green Hythe Rd. Guil. AR67 109
Greening St. SE2 CP42 69
Greenland Cres. Sthl. BD41 64
Greenland Rd. NW1 BT37 56
Greenland Rd. Barn. BQ25 28
Greenlands Rd. Sev. CX63 108
Greenlands Rd. Stai. AW49 73
Greenlands Rd. Wey. AZ55 83
Green La. E4 CF24 30
Green La. NW4 BQ31 46
Green La. SE9 CL47 78
Green La. SE20 CC50 77
Green La. SW19 BS48 76
Green La. W7 BH41 64
Green La. Amer. AO21 25
Green La. Amer. AP22 25
Green La. Ash. BK62 102
Green La. Berk. AR13 7
Green La. Brox. CE15 12
Green La. Brwd. CY23 33
Green La. Brwd. DA26 42
Green La. Brwd. DA29 42

Green La. Brwd. DB25 33
Green La. Cat. BZ64 105
Green La. Cher. AV55 82
Green La. Chesh. AQ20 16
Green La. Chess. BK58 93
Green La. Chig. CM26 40
Green La. Cob. BE59 93
Green La. Dag. CP34 50
Green La. E. Mol. BF53 84
Green La. Edg. BL28 37
Green La. Egh. AT49 72
Green La. Egh. AT52 82
Green La. Egh. AU51 82
Green La. Guil. AT70 118
Green Lane. Guil. AW67 110
Green La. Har. BH34 45
Green La. Harl. CR11 14
Green La. Hem. H. BA14 8
Green La. Houns. BC45 63
Green La. Ilf. CM34 49
Green La. Ing. DB19 24
Green La. Maid. AG40 61
Green La. Maid. AG44 61
Green La. Mord. BS53 86
Green La. N. Mal. BN53 85
Green La. Nthwd. BA29 35
Green La. Pur. BW59 95
Green La. Red. BU69 121
Green La. Red. CA68 114
Green La. Reig. BR70 120
Green La. St. Alb. BG12 9
Green La. Shep. BA53 83
Green La. Slou. AQ44 62
Green La. Slou. AT44 62
Green La. Stan. BJ28 36
Green La. Sun. BB50 73
Green La. Upmin. CY37 60
Green La. Uxb. BA39 53
Green La. Wal. Abb. CJ20 22
Green La. Walt. BC57 92
Green La. Warl. CD62 105
Green La. Wat. BD26 36
Green La. Welw. G. C. BO9 5
Green La. Wey. AY59 92
Green La. Wind. AN44 61
Green La. Wok. AP58 91
Green La. Wok. AQ64 100
Green La. Wok. AZ65 101
Green La. Wor. Pk. BP54 85
Green La. Av. Walt. BD56 93
Green Lane Clo. Amer. AO21 25
Green Lane Clo. Cher. AV55 82
Green Lane Clo. Wey. AY56 92
Green La. Gdns. Th. Hth. BZ51 87
Green Lanes Epsom BO58 94
Green Lane West. Wok. AZ66 110
Greenlaw Gdns. N. Mal. BO54 85
Green Lawns. Ruis. BD33 45
Greenlaw St. SE18 CK41 68
Greenleafe Dr. Ilf. CL31 49
Greenleaf Rd. E6 CJ37 58
Greenleaf Rd. E17 CD31 48
Green Leas, Sun. BB50 73
Green Leas, Wal. Abb. CG20 22
Green Man Gdns. W13 BJ40 54
Green Man La. W13 BJ40 54
Green Man La. Felt. BC45 63
Green Manor Way. Grav. DC45 71
Green Man St. N1 BZ36 57
Green Mayes Clo. Reig. BT70 121
Green Meadow, Pot. B. BS18 20
Greenmeads, Wok. AS64 100
Green Moor Link N21 BY26 38
Greenmoor Rd. Enf. CC23 30
Greenoak Ri. West. CJ62 106
Greenock Rd. SW16 BW51 86
Greenock Rd. W3 BM41 65
Corville Rd.
Greenock Way Rom. CT29 41
Greeno Cres. Shep. AZ53 83
Green Pk. Stai. AV48 72
Vicarage Rd.
Greenpark Ct. Wem. BK36 54
Green Pl. Dart. CT46 79
Green Pond Rd. E17 CD31 48
Green Ride, Epp. CM20 22
Green Ride Loug. CH25 31
Green Rd. N14 BV25 29
Green Rd. N20 BT27 38
Green Rd. Dart. DA50 80
Green Rd. Grav. DD49 81
Green's End SE18 CL42 68
Greenshaw, Brwd. DA26 42
Greenside Bex. CQ47 79
Greenside Dag. CP33 50
Greenside Rich. BK46 74
Greenside Swan. CS51 89
Greenside Rd. W12 BP41 65
Greenside Rd. Croy. BY54 86
Greenside Rd. Wey. AZ55 83
Green Slade Ave. Ash. BM63 103
Greenstead, Saw. CQ6 6
Greenstead Av. Wdf. Grn. CJ29 40
Greenstead Clo. Brwd. DF26 122
Greenstead Clo. Wdf. Grn. CJ29 40
Greenstead Gdns.
Greenstead Gdns. SW15 BP46 75
Greenstead Gdns. Wdf. Grn. CJ29 40
Greensted Rd. Loug. CK26 40
Greens, The, Clo. Loug. CL23 31
Green St. W1 BV40 56
Green St. Dart. CX47 80
Green St. Enf. CC23 30
Green St. Hat. BS13 11
Green St. Rad. BM21 28
Green St. Rick. AU23 25
Green St. Sun. BC51 83
Green Ter. EC1 BY38 56
Green, The, E4 CF26 39
Green, The, E11 CH32 49
Green, The, E15 CG36 58
Green, The, N9 CB27 39
Green, The, N14 BW27 38
Green, The, N21 BY26 38
Green, The, W3 BO39 55
Green, The, W5 BK40 54
Green, The Amer. AO22 25
Green, The, Bexh. CR44 69
Green, The, Brom. CH48 78
Green, The, Brom. CH54 88
Green, The Epp. CM21 31
Green, The, Epsom BP59 94
Green, The Hem. H. AT18 16
Green, The, Houns. BF43 64
Green, The, Ing. DC19 24
Green, The, Mord. BR52 85
Green, The, N. Mal. BN52 85
Green, The, Orp. CL56 97
Green, The, Orp. CO50 79
Green, The, Rain. CW40 60
Green, The, Rich. BK46 74
Green, The Rick. AW21 26
Green, The Rick. AY25 26
Green, The, Sev. CV64 108
Green, The, Shep. BB52 83
Holmbank Dr.
Green, The, Sid. CO49 79
Green, The, Slou. AO41 61
Green, The, Slou. AQ43 62
Green, The, Slough. AL40 61
Green, The Stai. AS46 72
Green, The, Sthl. BE41 64
Green, The, Sutt. BS55 86
Green, The, Twick. BH47 74
Green, The Wal. Cr. CC17 21
Green, The Wat. BC22 26
Green, The, Watt. BB58 92
Green, The, Wdf. Grn. CH28 40
Green, The, Well. CM45 68
Green, The, Wem. BJ34 45
Green, The, West Dr. AX41 63
Greentiles La. Uxb. AV33 43
Green Vale W5 BL39 55
Green Vale Bexh. CP46 79
Greenvale Rd. SE9 CK45 68
Green Verges Stan. BK29 36
Green Vw. Chess. BL57 94
Greenview Av. Croy. CD53 87
Green View Clo. Hem. H. AT18 16
Greenville Clo. Cob. BD60 93
Green Wk. E4 CF26 39
Green Wk. NW4 BQ31 46
Green Wk. SE1 CA41 67
Green Wk. Dart. CT46 79
Green Wk. Ong. CW18 24
Green Wk. Ruis. BB33 44
Green Wk. Ruis. BC33 44
Green Wk. Sth. Croy. CD57 96
Green Wk. Sthl. BF42 64
Green Wk. Wdf. Grn. CK29 40
Greenway N14 BX27 38
Greenway N20 BS27 38
Green Way SE9 CJ46 78
Greenway SW20 BQ52 85
Green Way, Berk. AQ13 7
Green Way Brom. CK53 88
Greenway, Brwd. DD26 122
Greenway Chis. CL49 78
Greenway Dag. CP34 50
Greenway Har. BL32 46
Green Way Hart. DC53 90
Greenway, Hayes BC38 53
Greenway, Hem. H. AZ13 8
Greenway, Lthd. BF65 102
Greenway Pnr. BC30 35
Green Way, Red. BU69 121
Greenway, Rom. CX29 42
Green Way Sun. BC52 83
Greenway Wall. BW56 95
Greenway Wdf. Grn. CJ28 40
Greenway Av. E17 CF31 48
Greenway Clo. N16 BZ34 48
Greenway Clo. N20 BS27 38
Greenway Clo. NW9 BN30 37
Greenway Clo. Wey. AW60 92
Greenway Ct. Har. BH30 36
Greenway Dr. Stai. AX51 83
Greenway Gdns. NW9 BN30 37
Greenway Gdns. Croy. CD55 87
Greenway Gdns. Grnf. BF38 54
Greenway Rd. West. CJ63 106
Greenways Beck. CE52 87
Greenways Esher BH56 93
Greenways, Wal. Cr. BY18 20
Greenways, Wat. BB19 17
Greenways Ct. Egh. AS50 72
Greenways Est. E2 CC38 57
Greenway, The, NW9 BN30 37
Greenway, The Enf. CC21 30
Greenway, The, Epsom. BM60 94
Greenway, The, Ger. Cr. AR31 43
Greenway, The, Har. BH30 36
Green Way, The, Houns. BE45 64
Greenway, The, Orp. CO53 89
Greenway, The, Pnr. BE32 45
Greenway, The, Pot. B. BS20 20
Greenway, The. Rick. AW26 35
Greenway, The Uxb. AX37 53
Greenway, The, Uxb. AZ34 44
Greenway, The, Epsom. BM61 103
Greenwell St. W1 BV38 56
Green West Rd. Beac. AP29 34
Greenwich Church St. SE10 CF43 67
Greenwich High Rd. SE10 CE44 67
Greenwich Mkt. SE10 CF43 67
Greenwich Pk. St. SE10 CF42 67
Greenwich South St. SE10 CE44 67
Greenwood Av. Dag. CR35 50
Greenwood Av. Enf. CC23 30
Greenwood Av. Wal. Cr. CB19 21
Greenwood Clo. Amer. AP22 25
Greenwood Clo. Bush. BH26 36
Langmead Dr.
Greenwood Clo. Mord. BR52 85
Greenwood Clo. Orp. CN53 88
Greenwood Clo. Red. BV73 121
Greenwood Clo. Surb. BJ54 84
Greenwood Clo. Wey. AV59 91
Greenwood Ct. Wal. Cr. CB19 21
Greenwood Dri. E4 CF28 39
Avril Way.
Greenwood Dr. Wat. BC20 17
Greenwood Gdns. N13 BY27 38
Greenwood Gdns. Cat. CB66 114
Greenwood Gdns. Ilf. CM29 40
Greenwood Ho. Grays DD43 71
Hawkes Clo.
Greenwood La. Hamptn. BF49 74
Greenwood Pk. Kings. On. T. BO50 75
Greenwood Pl. NW5 BV35 47
Highgate Rd.
Greenwood Rd. E8 CB36 57
Greenwood Rd. E13 CH37 58
Greenwood Rd. Bex. CS49 79
Greenwood Rd. Chig. CO28 41
Greenwood Rd. Croy. BY53 86
Greenwood Rd. Islw. BH45 64
Greenwood Rd. Mitch. BW52 86
Greenwood Rd. Surb. BJ54 84
Greenwood Rd. Wok. AP63 100
Green Woods, Guil. AT70 118
Greenwood Ter. NW10 BG37 54
Greenwood Way. Sev. CT66 116
Greenwrythe Cres. Cars. BU54 86
Green Wrythe La. Cars. BT53 86
Greer Rd. Har. BG30 36
Greet Rd. Brent. BL42 65
Greet St. SE1 BY40 56
Gregor Mews. SE3 CH43 68
Gregory Av. Pot. B. BT20 20
Gregory Cres. SE9 CJ47 78
Gregory Pl. W8 BS41 66
Gregory Rd. Slou. AO34 43
Gregory Rd. Sthl. BF41 64
Greig Clo. N8 BX32 47
Greig Ter. SE17 BY43 66
Lorrimore Sq.
Grenaby Av. Croy. BZ54 87
Grenaby Rd. Croy. BZ54 87
Grenada Rd. SE7 CJ43 68
Grenade St. E14 CD40 57
Grenadier St. E16 CK40 58
Grena Gdns. Rich. BL45 65
Grena Rd. Rich. BL45 65
Grendon Gdns. Wem. BM34 46
Grendon St. NW8 BU38 56
Grenfall St. SE10 CG41 68
Grenfell Av. Horn. CT33 50
Grenfell Clo. West. CJ59 97
Grenfell Gdns. Har. BL33 46
Grenfell Gdns. Ilf. CN32 49
Grenfell Rd. W11 BQ40 55
Grenfell Rd. Mitch. BU50 76
Grennell Clo. Sutt. BT55 86
Grennell Rd. Sutt. BT55 86
Grenoble Gdns. N13 BY29 38
Grenview Ct. Ashf. AY49 73
Grenville Av. Brox. CD14 12
Grenville Clo. Wal. Cr. CC19 21
Grenville Gdns. Wdf. Grn. CJ30 40
Grenville Ms. SW7 BT42 66
Grenville Ms. Hamptn. BF49 74
Grenville Pl. NW7 BN28 37
Grenville Pl. SW7 BT41 66
Grenville Rd. N19 BX33 47
Grenville Rd. Croy. CF58 96
Grenville St. WC1 BX38 56
Guilford St.
Gresham Ave. Warl. CD62 105
Gresham Av. N20 BU28 38
Gresham Clo. Bex. CQ46 79
Gresham Clo. Enf. BZ24 30
Gresham Dr. Rom. CO32 50
Gresham Gdns. NW11 BR33 46
Gresham Rd. E6 CK37 58
Gresham Rd. E16 CH39 58
Gresham Rd. NW10 BN35 46
Gresham Rd. SE25 CB52 87
Gresham Rd. SW9 BY45 66
Gresham Rd. Beck. CD51 87
Gresham Rd. Brwd. DB27 42
Gresham Rd. Edg. BL29 37
Gresham Rd. Houns. BG44 64
Gresham Rd. Oxt. CG68 115
Gresham Rd. Stai. AV49 72
Gresham Rd. Uxb. AZ37 53
Gresham St. EC2 BZ39 57
Gresley Rd. N19 BW33 47
Gressenhall Rd. SW18 BR46 75
Gresse St. W1 BW39 56
Greswell Clo. Sid. CO48 79
Greswell Rd. SW6 BQ44 65
Greta Bank. Leath. BA66 110
Greton Rd. N17 CA29 39
Beaufoy Rd.
Greville Av. Sth. Croy. CC58 96
Greville Clo. Guil. AP70 118
Greville Clo. Hat. BQ15 10
Knolles Cres.
Greville Clo. Twick. BJ47 74
Greville Hall NW6 BS37 56
Greville Park Ave. Ash. BL62 103
Greville Park Rd. Ash. BL62 103
Greville Pl. NW6 BS38 56
Greville Rd. E17 CF31 48
Greville Rd. NW6 BS37 56
Greville Rd. Rich. BL46 75
Greville St. EC1 BY39 56
Greycaine Rd. Wat. BD22 27
Grey Clo. NW11 BT32 47
Greycoat Pl. SW1 BW41 66
Greycoat St. SW1 BW41 66
Greycott Rd. Beck. CE49 77
Grey Eagle St. E1 CA39 57
Greyfell Clo. Stan. BJ28 36
Coverdale Clo.
Greyfriars Pass. EC1 BY39 56
Newgate St.
Greyfriars Rd. Wok. AW65 101
Greygoose Park. Harl. CL12 13
Greyhound Hl. NW4 BP31 46
Greyhound La. SW16 BW50 76
Greyhound La. Grays. DG41 71
Greyhound La. Pot. B. BP20 19
Greyhound Rd. N17 CA31 48
Greyhound Rd. NW10 BP38 55
Greyhound Ter. SW16 BW51 86
Greyland Clo. Brom. CJ51 88
Greyshot Rd. SW11 BU44 66
Greys Pk. Clo. Kes. CJ56 97
Greys Rd. Uxb. AY37 53
Greystead Rd. SE23 CC47 77
Greystoke Av. Pnr. BF31 45
Greystoke Gdns. W5 BL38 55
Greystoke Gdns. Enf. BW24 29
Greystoke Lo. W5 BL38 55
Hanger La.
Greystoke Pk. Ter. W5 BK38 54
Greystoke Pl. EC4 BY39 56
Cursitor St.
Greystone Clo. Croy. CC59 96
Greystone Clo. Sth. Croy. CC58 96
Greystone Gdns. Har. BK32 45
Greystone Gdns. Ilf. CM30 40
Greystones Clo. Red. BT71 121
Hardwicke Rd.
Greystones Dr. Reig. BT69 121
Grey St. E16 CJ40 58
Greyswood St. SW16 BV50 76
Grey Towers Av. Horn. CV33 51
Grey Towers Gdns. Horn. CV33 51
Grice Ave. West. CH60 97
Gridland St. E15 CG37 58
Church St.
Grierson Rd. SE23 CC47 77
Grieves Rd. Grav. DF48 81
Griffin Av. Upmin. CZ32 51
Griffin Manor Way SE28 CM42 68
Griffin Rd. N17 CA30 39
Griffin Rd. SE18 CM42 68
Griffins. The. Grays. DD41 71
Griffin Way. Lthd. BF66 111
Griffin Way Sun. BC51 83
Griffiths Clo. Wor. Pk. BP55 85
Griffiths Rd. SW19 BS50 76
Griggs Pl. SE1 CA41 67
Grange Rd.
Griggs Rd. E10 CF32 48
Grimsby St. E2 CA38 57
Grimsdell, S La. Amer. AO22 25
Grimsdyke Cres. Barn. BQ24 28
Grimsdyke Rd. Pnr. BE29 36
Grimsel Path SE17 BY43 66
Brandon Estate
Grimshaw Clo. N6 BV33 47
Grimstone Clo. Rom. CR29 41
Grimston Rd. SW6 BR44 65
Grimston Rd. St. Alb. BH13 9
Grimthorpe Clo. St. Alb. BG12 9
Grimwade Av. Croy. CB55 87
Grimwade Cres. SE15 CC45 67
Grimwood Rd. Twick. BH47 74
Grindal St. SE1 BY41 66
Lower Marsh
Grinling Pl. SE8 CE43 67
Grinstead Rd. SE8 CD42 67
Grisedale Clo. Pur. CA60 96
Grisedale Gdns. Pur. CA60 96
Grittledon Rd. W9 BS38 56
Grittleton Av. Wem. BM36 55
Grizedale Ter. SE23 CB48 77
Grocers Hall Ct. EC2 BZ39 57
Poultry
Groombridge Clo. Walt. BC56 92
Groombridge Clo. Well. CO46 79
Groombridge Rd. E9 CC36 57
Groom Cres. SW18 BT47 76
Groomfield Clo. SW17 BV49 76
Groom Pl. SW1 BV41 66
Chapel St.
Grooms Cotts. Chesh. AQ18 16
Grosmont Rd. SE18 CN43 68
Grosse Way SW15 BP46 75
Dover Pk. Dr.
Grosvenor Av. N5 BZ35 48
Grosvenor Av. SW14 BO45 65
Grosvenor Av. Cars. BU57 95
Grosvenor Av. Har. BF33 45
Grosvenor Av. Hayes. BB37 53
Grosvenor Av. Kings L. BA17 17
Grosvenor Av. Rich. BL46 75
Grosvenor Rd.
Grosvenor Clo. Loug. CL23 31
Grosvenor Ct. N14 BW26 38
Grosvenor Ct. Guil. AT69 118
Grosvenor Ct. Mord. BS52 86
Grosvenor Cres. NW9 BM31 46
Grosvenor Cres. SW1 BV41 66
Grosvenor Cres. Dart. CV46 80
Grosvenor Cres. Uxb. AZ36 53
Grosvenor Cres. Uxb. BA37 53
Grosvenor Cres. Ms. SW1 BV41 66
Grosvenor Dr. Horn. CV33 51
Grosvenor Dr. Loug. CL23 31
Grosvenor Est. N5 BZ35 48
Grosvenor Est. SW1 BW42 66
Grosvenor Gdns. E6 CJ38 58
Grosvenor Gdns. N10 BW31 47
Grosvenor Gdns. N14 BW24 29
Grosvenor Gdns. NW2 BQ36 55
Grosvenor Gdns. NW11 BR32 46
Grosvenor Gdns. SW1 BV41 66
Grosvenor Gdns. SW14 BO45 65
Grosvenor Gdns. Kings. On T. BK50 74
Grosvenor Gdns. Upmin. CY33 51
Grosvenor Gdns. Wall. BW57 95
Grosvenor Gdns. Wdf. Grn. CH29 40
Grosvenor Gdns. Ms. N. SW1 BV41 66
Ebury St.
Grosvenor Hill SW19 BR50 75
Grosvenor Hill W1 BV40 56
Grosvenor Ms. W1 BV40 56
Grosvenor Pk. SE5 BZ43 67
Grosvenor Pk. Rd. E17 CE32 48
Grosvenor Path Loug. CM23 31
Grosvenor Pl. SW1 BV41 66
Grosvenor Rise, E. E17 CE32 48
Grosvenor Rd. E6 CJ37 58
Grosvenor Rd. E7 CH36 58
Grosvenor Rd. E10 CF33 48
Grosvenor Rd. E11 CH32 49
Grosvenor Rd. N3 BR29 37
Grosvenor Rd. N9 CB26 39
Grosvenor Rd. N10 BV30 38
Grosvenor Rd. SE25 CB52 87
Grosvenor Rd. SW1 BV43 66
Grosvenor Rd. W4 BM42 65
Grosvenor Rd. W7 BJ40 54
Grosvenor Rd. Belv. CQ43 69
Grosvenor Rd. Bexh. CP46 79
Grosvenor Rd. Borwd. BM24 28
Grosvenor Rd. Brent. BK43 64
Grosvenor Rd. Brox. CD13 12
Grosvenor Rd. Dag. CQ33 50
Grosvenor Rd. Epsom. BN63 103
Grosvenor Rd. Houns. BE45 64
Grosvenor Rd. Ilf. CM34 49
Grosvenor Rd. Nthwd. BB28 35
Grosvenor Rd. Orp. CN53 88
Grosvenor Rd. Rich. BL46 75
Grosvenor Rd. Rom. CS33 50
Grosvenor Rd. St. Alb. BH14 9
Grosvenor Rd. Stai. AW50 73
Grosvenor Rd. Sthl. BE41 64
Grosvenor Rd. Twick. BJ47 74
Grosvenor Rd. Wall. BV57 95
Grosvenor Rd. Wat. BD24 27
Grosvenor Rd. W. Wick. CE55 87
Grosvenor Rd. Wok. AO60 91
Grosvenor Sq. W1 BV40 56
Grosvenor St. W1 BV40 56
Grosvenor Ter. SE17 BZ43 67
Grosvenor Ter. Hem. H. AW14 8
Grosvenor Vale, Ruis. BB34 44
Grotes Bldgs. SE3 CG44 68
Grotes Pl. SE3 CG44 68
Groton Rd. SW18 BS48 76
Grotto Rd. Twick. BH48 74
Grotto Rd. Wey. AZ55 83
Ground Lane. Hat. BP11 10
Grove Av. N3 BS29 38
Grove Av. N10 BW30 38
Grove Av. W7 BH39 54
Grove Av. Epsom. BO60 94
Grove Av. Pnr. BE32 45
Grove Av. Sutt. BS57 95
Grove Av. Twick. BH47 74
Grove Bldgs. SW3 BU43 66
Grovebury Clo. Erith CT43 69
Grovebury Rd. SE2 CO41 69
Grove Clo. Brom. CG55 88
Grove Clo. Felt. BE49 74
Grove Clo. Ger. Cr. AR30 34
Grove Clo. Kings-on-t. BL52 85
Grove Clo. Uxb. AZ35 44
Grove Clo. Wind. AQ47 72
Grove Ct. NW8 BT38 56
Grove Ct. SE3 CH44 68
Grove Ct. E. Mol. BG53 84
Grove Ct. Tedd. BJ49 74
Cambridge Rd.
Grove Ct. Wal. Abb. CE20 21
Grove Cres. E18 CG30 40
Grove Cres. NW9 BN31 46
Grove Cres. SE5 CA44 67
Grove Cres. Felt. BE49 74
Grove Cres. Kings-on-t. BL52 85
Grove Cres. Rick. AZ24 26
Grove Cres. Walt. BC54 83
Grove Cres. Rd. E15 CF36 57
Grovedale Rd. N19 BW34 47
Grove End E18 CG30 40
Grove End. Ger. Cr. AR30 34
Grove End Gdns. NW8 BT37 56
Grove End La. Esher BG54 84
Grove End Rd. NW8 BT38 56
Grove Est. SE5 CA44 67
Grove Est. Pnr. BE32 45
Grove F. P. Kings-on-t. BL52 85
Grove Gdns. E15 CG36 58
Grove Gdns. NW4 BP31 46
Grove Gdns. NW8 BU38 56
Grove Gdns. Dag. CS34 50
Grove Gdns. Enf. CC23 30
Grove Gdns. Tedd. BJ49 74
Grove Grn. Nthwd. BA28 35
Grove Green Rd. E11 CF34 48
Grove Hall Ct. NW8 BT38 56
Grovehall Rd. Bush. BE24 27
Groveheath La. Wok. AW65 101
Grove Heath North. Wok. AW64 101
Grove Hill E18 CG30 40
Grove Hill. Ger. Cr. AR29 34
Grove Hill Har. BH33 45
Grove Hill Rd. SE5 CA45 67
Grove Hill Rd. Har. BH33 45
Grove Hill Rd. Red. BU70 121
Grove House Rd. N8 BX31 47
Groveland Av. SW16 BX50 76
Groveland Rd. Beck. CD52 87
Grovelands St. Alb. BF17 18
Ringway Rd.
Grovelands Ct. N14 BW26 38

Grovelands Rd. N13 BX28 38
Grovelands Rd. N15 CB32 48
Grovelands Rd. Orp. CO50 79
Grovelands Rd. Pur. BX59 95
Grovelands Way. Grays. DC42 71
Groveland Way N. Mal. BN53 85
Grove La. SE5 BZ44 67
Grove La. Chesh. AQ17 16
Grove La. Chig. CN27 40
Grove La. Couls. BU59 95
Grove La. Ger. Cr. AO30 34
Grove La. Kings. On T. BL52 85
Grove La. Uxb. AY38 53
Grove Lea. Hat. BP14 10
Groveley Rd. Sun. BB49 73
Grove Meadow. Welw. G. C. BT7 5
Grove Ms. W6 BQ41 65
Grove Mill La. Wat. BA22 26
Grove Mo. Hat. BO12 10
Grove Pk. E11 CH32 49
Grove Pk. NW9 BN31 46
Grove Pk. SE5 CA44 67
Grove Pk. Av. E4 CE29 39
Grove Pk. Gdns. W4 BM43 65
Grove Pk. Rd. N15 CA31 48
Grove Pk. Rd. SE9 CJ48 78
Grove Pk. Rd. W4 BM43 65
Grove Pk. Rd. Rain. CU37 59
Grove Pk. Ter. W4 BM43 65
Grove Pass. E2 CB37 57
Grove Pass. Tedd. BJ49 74
Grove Path, Wal. Cr. CB19 21
Grove Pl. NW3 BT34 47
Christchurch Hill
Grove Pl. W3 BN40 55
Grove Pl. W5 BK40 54
Grove Pl. Bark. CM36 58
Grove Pl. Croy. BY54 86
Grove Pl. Wat. BF23 27
Grove Pl. Wey. BA56 92
Grover Clo. Hem. H. AX13 8
Grove Rd. E4 CE28 39
Grove Rd. E11 CG33 49
Grove Rd. E17 CE32 48
Grove Rd. E18 CG30 40
Grove Rd. N11 BV28 38
Grove Rd. N12 BT28 38
Grove Rd. N15 CA32 48
Grove Rd. NW2 BQ36 55
Grove Rd. SW13 BO44 65
Grove Rd. SW19 BT50 76
Grove Rd. W3 BN40 55
Grove Rd. W5 BK40 54
Grove Rd. Amer. AP22 25
Grove Rd. Ash. BL62 103
Grove Rd. Barn. BU24 29
Grove Rd. Belv. CQ43 69
Grove Rd. Bexh. CS45 69
Grove Rd. Borwd. BL23 28
Grove Rd. Brent. BK42 64
Grove Rd. Cher. AV53 82
Grove Rd. E. Mol. BG52 84
Grove Rd. Edg. BM29 37
Grove Rd. Epsom. BO60 94
Grove Rd. Grav. DD46 81
Grove Rd. Grays. DD43 71
Grove Rd. Guil. AU70 118
Grove Rd. Hem. H. AW14 8
Grove Rd. Houns. BF45 64
Grove Rd. Islw. BH44 64
Grove Rd. Mitch. BV51 86
Grove Rd. Nthwd. BA29 35
Grove Rd. Oxt. CF70 114
Grove Rd. Pnr. BE32 45
Grove Rd. Rich. BL46 75
Grove Rd. Rick. AW27 35
Grove Rd. Rom. CO33 50
Grove Rd. St. Alb. BG14 9
Grove Rd. Sev. CV64 108
Grove Rd. Sev. CX64 108
Grove Rd. Shep. BA53 83
Grove Rd. Surb. BK53 84
Grove Rd. Sutt. BS57 95
Grove Rd. Twick. BG48 74
Grove Rd. Uxb. AX36 53
Grove Rd. Wind. AO44 61
Grove Rd. Wok. AS61 100
Grove Rd. W. Enf. CC22 30
Grover Rd. Wat. BD26 36
Grove Side. Lthd. BF66 111
Groveside Rd. E4 CG27 40
Grove Stile Waye, Felt. BA47 73
Grove St. N18 CA28 39
Grove St. SE8 CD42 67
Grove Ter. Tedd. BJ49 74
Grove, The, E15 CG36 58
Grove, The, N3 BS30 38
Grove, The, N4 BX33 47
Grove, The, N6 BV33 47
Grove, The, N8 BW32 47
Grove, The, N13 BY28 38
Grove, The, NW5 BV35 47
Lissenden Gdns.
Grove, The, NW9 BN32 46
Grove, The, NW11 BR33 46
Grove, The, SE21 CA47 77
Grove, The, SW16 BW49 76
Grove, The, W5 BK40 54
Grove, The Amer. AO21 25
Grove, The, Bexh. CP45 69
Grove, The, Brwd. CZ28 42
Grove, The. Cat. BZ64 105
Grove, The Chesh. AR21 25
Grove, The, Couls. BW61 104
Grove, The, Edg. BM28 37
Grove, The Egh. AT49 72
Grove, The, Enf. BY23 29
Grove, The, Epsom BO58 94
Grove, The, Epsom BO60 94
Grove, The, Esher BF54 84
Grove, The Grav. DH47 81
Grove, The, Grnf. BG39 54
Grove, The, Hat. BS16 20
Grove, The, Islw. BH44 64
Grove, The, Pot. B. BT19 20
Grove, The, Rad. BJ20 18
Grove, The. Sev. CZ58 99
Grove, The, Sid. CQ49 79
Grove, The. Slou. AQ41 62
Grove, The Swans. DC46 81
Grove, The, Tedd. BJ49 74
Grove, The, Upmin. CX35 51
Grove, The, Uxb. AZ35 44
Grove, The, Walt. BC53 83
Grove, The, West. CJ62 106
Grove, The, W. Wick. CE55 87
Grove, The, Wey. AW56 92
Grove, The Wok. AS61 100
Grove Val. SE22 CA45 67
Grove Val. Chis. CL50 78
Grove Vill. E14 CE40 57
Groveway SW9 BX44 66
Groveway Dag. CP35 50
Grove Way Esher BG54 84
Grove Way. Rick. AT25 25
Grove Way, Uxb. AX36 53
Groveway Wem. BM35 46
Grove Wd. Hill Couls. BW60 95
Grove Wood Clo. Rick. AT25 25
Grovewood Rd. Rich. BM44 65
Sandycombe Rd.
Grt. Cambridge Rd. Wal. Cr. CC19 21
Grt. Julians, Rick. AZ24 26
Grubb Rd. Oxt. CJ67 115
Grubs La. Hat. BS14 11
Grummant Rd. SE15 CA44 67
Grundy St. E14 CE39 57
Gruneisen Rd. N3 BS29 38
Gto Fox Meadow. Brwd. CZ22 33
Guardsman Clo. Brwd. DB28 42
Woodman Rd.
Gubbins La. Rom. CW29 42
Gubyon Av. SE24 BY46 76
Guerin St. E3 CD38 57
Guernsey Clo. Houns. BF43 64
Guernsey Farm Dr. Wok. AR61 100
Guernsey Gro. SE24 BZ47 77
Guernsey Rd. E11 CF33 48
Guessens Ct. Welw. G. C. BQ8 5
Guibal Rd. SE12 CH47 78
Guildables La. Eden. CK70 115
Guildersfield Rd. SW16 BX50 76
Guildford Av. Felt. BB47 73
Guildford Av. Surb. BL53 85
Guildford & Godalming By Pass, Guil. AO72 118
Guildford Gro. SE10 CE44 67
Guildford La. Guil. AU71 118
Guildford Lodge Ri. Leath. BB68 110
Guildford Park Av. Guil. AQ71 118
Guildford Park Rd. Guil. AQ71 118
Guildford Pl. Wok. AS63 100
Guildford Rd. E17 CF30 39
Guildford Rd. SW8 BX44 66
Guildford Rd. Cher. AU57 91
Guildford Rd. Cher. AV54 82
Guildford Rd. Croy. BZ53 87
Guildford Rd. Dor. BC73 119
Guildford Rd. Dor. BFG2 119
Guildford Rd. Ilf. CN34 49
Guildford Rd. Leath. BB68 110
Guildford Rd. Lthd. BE67 111
Guildford Rd. Lthd. BH65 102
Guildford Rd. Rom. CV29 42
Guildford Rd. St. Alb. BJ14 9
Guildford Rd. Wok. AS63 100
Guildford St. Stai. AW50 73
Guildford Way Wall. BX56 95
Guildhall Bldgs. EC2 BZ39 57
Basinghall St.
Guildhall Yd. EC2 BZ39 57
Gresham St.
Guildhouse St. SW1 BW42 66
Guildown Av. N12 BS28 38
Holden Rd.
Guildown Av. Guil. AQ72 118
Guildown Rd. Guil. AQ72 118
Guild Rd. SE7 CJ42 68
Guild Rd. Erith CT43 69
Guilds Way E17 CD30 39
Guileshill La. Wok. AY65 101
Guilford Pl. WC1 BX38 56
Guilford Rd. Guil. AR66 109
Guilford St. WC1 BX38 56
Guilsborough Clo. NW10 BO36 55
Guinness Bldgs. SE1 CA42 67
Guinness Bldgs. SE17 BZ42 67
Guinness Bldgs. SW3 BU42 66
Guinness Bldgs. W6 BQ42 65
Fulham Palace Rd.
Guinness Sq. SE1 CA42 67
Page's Walk
Guinness Trust SE24 BY45 66
Guinness Trust Bldgs. SW10 CN44 68
Guinness Trust Dws. N16 CA33 48
Guion Rd. SW6 BR44 65
Gulland Clo. Bush. BG24 27
Gulland Wk. N1 BZ36 57
Marquess Est.
Gullbrook, Hem. H. AW13 8
Gull Clo. Wall. BX57 95
Gulliver Clo. Nthlt. BE37 54
Gulliver Rd. Sid. CN48 78
Gulliver St. SE16 CD41 67
Gull Wk. Rain. CU37 59
Gumleigh Rd. W5 BK42 64
Gumley Gdns. Islw. BJ45 64
Gumley Rd. Grays DB43 70
Gumping Rd. Orp. CM55 88
Gundulf St. SE11 BY42 66
Gundulph Rd. Brom. CJ52 88
Gunfleet Clo. Grav. DJ47 81
Roehampton Clo.
Gun Hill. Til. DH43 71
Gunmaker's La. E3 CD37 57
Gunner La. SE18 CL42 68
Gunnersbury Ct. W3 BM41 65
Bollo La.
Gunnersbury Cres. W3 BM41 65
Gunnersbury Dr. W5 BL41 65
Gunnersbury Gdns. W3 BM41 65
Gunnersbury La. W3 BM41 65
Gunnersbury Ms. Brent. BM42 65
Gunners Gro. E4 CF27 39
Gunners Rd. SW18 BT48 76
Gunning St. SE18 CN42 68
Gunn Rd. Swans. DC46 81
Gunstor Rd. N16 CA35 48
Gunter Gro. SW10 BT43 66
Gunter Gro. Edg. BN30 37
Gunterstone Rd. W14 BR42 65
Gunthorpe St. E1 CA39 57
Wentworth St.
Gunton Rd. E5 CB34 48
Gunton Rd. SW17 BV50 76
Gurdon Rd. SE7 CH42 68
Gurnell Gro. W13 BH38 54
Gurney Clo. E15 CG35 49
Gurney Rd.
Gurney Court Rd. St. Alb. BH12 9
Gurney Cres. Croy. BX54 86
Gurney Dr. N2 BT31 47
Gurney Rd. E15 CG35 49
Gurney Rd. Cars. BU56 95
Gurney Rd. Nthlt. BC38 53
Gurnsey Clo. Houns. BF44 64
Sutton Rd.
Guthrie St. SW3 BU42 66
Cale St.
Gutter La. EC2 BZ39 57
Guyatt Gdns. Mitch. BV51 86
Ormerod Gdns.
Guy Rd. Wall. BW55 86
Guyscliff Rd. SE13 CF46 77
Guysfield Clo. Rain. CU37 59
Guysfield Dr. Rain. CU37 59
Guy St. SE1 BZ41 67
Gwendolen Av. SW15 BQ45 65
Gwendolen Clo. SW15 BQ46 75
Gwendoline Av. E13 CH37 58
Gwendwr Rd. W14 BR42 65
Gwillim Clo. Sid. CO46 79
Gwydor Rd. Beck. CC52 87
Gwydyr Rd. Brom. CG52 88
Gwynne Av. Croy. CC54 87
Gwynne Clo. Wind. AM44 61
Cawcott Dr.
Gwynne Pl. WC1 BX38 56
King's Cross Rd.
Gwynne Rd. SW11 BT44 66
Gwynne Vaughan Ave. Guil. AQ68 109
Gwynn Rd. Grav. DE48 81
Gye St. SE11 BX42 66
Gyfford Wk. Wal. Cr. CB19 21
Gylcote Clo. SE5 BZ45 67
Gyles Pk. Stan. BK29 36
Gyllyngdune Gdns. Ilf. CN34 49
Gypsy La. Slou. AP35 43
Gypsy La. Wey. AZ55 83
Haarlem Rd. W14 BQ41 65
Haberdasher St. W1 BZ38 57
Habgood Rd. Loug. CK24 31
Hackbridge Pk. Gdns. Cars. BU55 86
Hackbridge Rd. Wall. BV55 86
Hacketts La. Wok. AV60 91
Hackford Rd. SW9 BX44 66
Hackforth Clo. Barn. BP25 28
Hackington Cres. Beck. CE50 77
Hackney Gro. E8 CB36 57
Hackney Rd. E2 CA38 57
Hacombe Rd. SW19 BT50 76
Hacton Dr. Horn. CV35 51
Hacton La. Horn. CW34 51
Hacton Parkway Upmin. CW35 51
Hadden Way SE28 CN41 68
Hadden Way Grnf. BG36 54
Haddington Rd. Brom. CF48 77
Haddon Clo. Borwd. BM23 28
Haddon Clo. Enf. CB25 30
Haddon Clo. Hem. H. AZ14 8
Haddon Clo. N. Mal. BO53 85
Cromwell Av.
Haddon Gro. Sid. CN47 78
Haddonhall St. SE1 BZ41 67
Old Kent Rd.
Haddon Rd. Orp. CP53 89
Haddon Rd. Rick. AU25 25
Haddon Rd. Sutt. BS56 95
Haddo St. SE10 CE43 67
Haden Ct. N4 BY34 47
Hadfield Rd. Stai. AX47 73
Hadle&gh Ct. Brox. CD14 12
Hadleigh Clo. E1 CC38 57
Martus Rd.
Hadleigh Rd. N9 CB26 39
Hadleigh St. E2 CC38 57
Hadley Clo. N21 BY25 29
Hadley Gdns. W4 BN42 65
Hadley Gdns. Sthl. BE42 64
Hadley Grn. Rd. Barn. BR23 28
Hadley Grn. W. Barn. BR23 28
Hadley Gro. Barn. BR23 28
Hadley Highstone Barn. BR23 28
Hadley Ridge Barn. BR24 28
Hadley Rd. Barn. BS24 29
Hadley Rd. Barn. BU22 29
Hadley Rd. Barn. BX23 29
Hadley Rd. Belv. CQ42 69
Hadley Rd. Mitch. BW52 86
Hadley St. NW1 BV36 56
Hadley Way N21 BY25 29
Hadley Wd. Rd. Barn. BS23 29
Hadlow Pl. SE19 CB50 77
Hadlow Rd. Sid. CO49 79
Hadlow Rd. Well. CP43 69
Hadlow Way, Grav. DF50 81
Hadrian Clo. Stai. AY47 73
Hadrian Clo. Wall. BX57 95
Hadrian Est. E2 CB37 57
Hadrians Clo. St. Alb. BE15 9
Hadrians Ride, Enf. CA25 30
Hadrian St. SE10 CG42 68
Hadrian Way, Stai. AX47 73
Hadyn Pk. Rd. W12 BP41 65
Hafer Rd. SW11 BU45 66
Hafton Rd. SE6 CG47 78
Hagden La. Wat. BB25 26
Haggard Rd. Twick. BJ47 74
Haggerston Est. E8 CA37 57
Haggerston Rd. E8 CA36 57
Haggerston Rd. Borwd. BL22 28
Hague St. E2 CB38 57
Derbyshire St.
Ha-ha Rd. SE18 CK43 68
Haig Cres. Red. BV71 121
Haig Rd. Stan. BK28 36
Haig Rd. Uxb. AZ39 53
Haig Rd. West. CK62 106
Haig Rd. E. E13 CJ38 58
Haig Rd. W. E13 CJ38 58
Haigville Gdns. Ilf. CL31 49
Haileybury Av. Enf. CA25 30
Haileybury Rd. Orp. CO56 98
Hailey Rd. Belv. CR41 69
Hailsham Av. SW2 BX48 76
Hailsham Clo. Rom. CV28 42
Hailsham Gdns. Rom. CV28 42
Hailsham Rd. SW17 BV50 76
Hailsham Rd. Rom. CV28 42
Hailsham Ter. N18 BZ28 39
Haimo Rd. SE9 CJ46 78
Hainault Ct. E17 CF31 48
Hainault Gore, Rom. CQ32 50
Hainault Gro. Chig. CM28 40
Hainault Rd. E11 CF33 48
Hainault Rd. Chig. CL27 40
Hainault Rd. Rom. CO29 41
Hainault Rd. Rom. CQ32 50
Hainault Rd. Rom. CS30 41
Hainault St. SE9 CL47 78
Hainault St. Ilf. CM34 49
Haines Ct. Wey. BA56 92
Haines St. SW8 BW43 66
Hainford Clo. SE4 CD45 67
Frendsbury Rd.
Hainthorpe Rd. SE27 BY48 76
Halberd Ms. E5 CB34 48
Knightland Rd.
Halbutt Gdns. Dag. CQ34 50
Halbutt St. Dag. CQ34 50
Halcomb St. N1 CA37 57
Orsman Rd.
Halcot Av. Bexh. CR46 79
Halcrow St. E1 CB39 57
Halcyon Way. Horn. CW33 51
Haldane Clo. N10 BV29 38
Haldane Clo. N11 BV29 38
Hampden Rd.
Haldane Pl. SW18 BS47 76
Haldane Rd. E6 CJ38 58
Haldane Rd. SW6 BR43 65
Haldane Rd. Sthl. BG40 54
Haldan Rd. E4 CF29 39
Haldens. Welw. G. C. BR6 5
Haldon Clo. Chig. CN28 40
Arrowsmith Rd.
Haldon Rd. SW18 BR46 75
Hale Clo. E4 CF27 39
Hale Clo. Edg. BN28 37
Hale Ct. Edg. BN28 37
Hale Dr. NW7 BN29 37
Hale End. Rom. CU29 41
Halefield Rd. N17 CB30 39
Hale Gdns. N17 CB31 48
High Cross Rd.
Hale Gdns. W3 BM40 55
Hale Grove Gdns. NW7 BN28 37
Hale La. Sev. CT62 107
Hale Oak Rd. Sev. CU70 116
Hale Pit Rd. Lthd. BG66 111
Hale Rd. E6 CK38 58
Hale Rd. N17 CB31 48
Halesowen Rd. Mord. BS54 86
Hales St. SE8 CE43 67
Hale St. E14 CE40 57
Haleswood, Cob. BC60 83
Haleswood Rd. Hem. H. AZ13 8
Halesworth Clo. E5 CB34 48
Southwold Rd.
Halesworth Clo. Rom. CW29 42
Halesworth Rd. SE13 CE45 67
Halesworth Rd. Rom. CW29 42
Hale, The, E4 CF29 39
Hale, The, N17 CB31 48
Hale, The, Wem. BJ35 45
Hale Wk. W7 BH39 54
Half Acre, Brent. BK43 64
Half Acre Hill. Ger. Cr. AS30 34
Half Acre Rd. W7 BH40 54
Half End Clo. Ruis. BC32 44
Half Hide La. Wal. Cr. CC16 21
Halfhides, Wal. Abb. CF20 21
Halfield Est. W2 BT40 56
Half Moon Cres. N1 BX37 56
Half Moon La. SE24 BZ46 77
Half Moon Pass, E1 CA39 57
Braham St.
Half Moon St. W1 BV40 56
Halford Rd. E10 CF32 48
Halford Rd. SW6 BS43 66
Halford Rd. Rich. BL46 75
Halford Rd. Uxb. AZ35 44
Halfpenny Clo. Guil. AU73 118
Halfpenny La. Guil. AU71 118
Halfway Grn. Walt. BC55 83
Halfway St. Sid. CM47 78
Haliburton Rd. Twick. BJ46 74
Halidon Clo. E9 CC35 48
Churchill Wk.
Halidon Rise, Rom. CX29 42
Halidon St. E9 CC35 48
Halifax Rd. Enf. BZ23 30
Halifax Rd. Grnf. BF37 54
Halifax St. SE26 CB49 77
Haling Gro. Sth. Croy. BZ57 96
Haling Pk. Gdns. Sth. Croy. BY57 95
Haling Rd. Sth. Croy. BZ57 96
Halings La. Uxb. AU31 43
Halings La. Uxb. AV31 43
Halkin Arc. SW1 BV41 66
Motcomb St.
Halkingcroft. Slou. AR41 62
Halkin Ms. SW1 BV41 66
Motcomb St.
Halkin Pl. SW1 BV41 66
Halkin St. SW1 BV41 66
Hallam Clo. Brwd. DA22 33
Hallam Clo. Chis. CK49 78
Hallam Gdns. Pnr. BE29 36
Hallam Ms. W1 BV39 56
Hallam St.
Hallam St. W1 BV38 56
Halland Way. Nthwd. BA29 35
Hall Ave. S. Ock. CW40 60
Hall Clo. Rick. AW26 35
Hall Ct. Slou. AQ43 62
Hall Cres. S. Ock. CY41 70
Hall Dene Clo. Guil. AU70 118
Hall Dr. SE26 CB49 77
Hall Dr. W7 BH39 54
Hall Dr. Uxb. AX29 35
Halley Pl. E14 CD39 57
Halley St. E14 CD39 57
Hall Farm Clo. Stan. BJ27 36
Hall Farm Dr. Twick. BG47 74
Hallfield Est. W2 BT39 56
Hallford Way. Dart. CV46 80
Hall Gdns. E4 CD28 39
Hall Gardens. St. Alb. BN15 10
Hall Gate, NW8 BT38 56
Hall Rd.
Hall Green La. Brwd. DE26 122
Hall Gro. Welw. G. C. BS9 5
Hall Heath Clo. St. Alb. BJ12 9
Hall Hill. Oxt. CF69 114
Hall Hill. Sev. CX65 108
Halliford Clo. Shep. BB52 83
Halliford Rd. Shep. BB53 83
Halliford Rd. Sun. BB52 83
Halliford St. N1 BZ36 57
Halling, Harl. CN10 6
Hallingbury Rd. Saw. CR5 6
Halling Hill, Harl. CN10 6
Halliwell Rd. SW2 BX46 76
Halliwick Rd. N10 BV30 38
Hall La. E4 CD28 39
Hall La. NW4 BP30 37
Hall La. Brwd. DC24 122
Hall La. Brwd. DC25 122
Hall La. Hayes. BA43 63
Hall La. Upmin. CY30 42
Hall La. Upmin. CY33 51
Hallmead Sutt. BS55 86
Hall Mores, Brox. CE13 12
Hallowell Av. Croy. BX56 95
Hallowell Clo. Mitch. BV52 86
Hallowell Rd. Nthwd. BB29 35
Hallowes Cres. Wat. BC27 35
Hall Pk. Berk. AS13 7
Hall Park Gate, Berk. AS14 7
Hall Park Hill, Berk AS14 7
Hall Park Rd. Upmin. CY35 51
Hall Pl. W2 BT38 56
Hall Pl. Wok. AT61 100
Hall Place Dr. Wey. BB56 92
Hall Place Gdns. St. Alb. BH13 9
Hall Pla. Cres. Bex. CS46 79
Hall Rd. E6 CK37 58
Hall Rd. E15 CF35 48
Hall Rd. NW8 BT38 56
Hall Rd. Dart. CW45 70
Hall Rd. Grav. DE48 81
Hall Rd. Islw. BG46 74
Hall Rd. Rom. CP32 50
Hall Rd. Rom. CV31 51
Hall Rd. S. Ock. CY41 70
Hall Rd. Wall. BV58 95
Hallside Rd. Enf. CA22 30
Hall St. EC1 BY38 56
Hall St. N12 BT28 38
Hallsville Rd. E16 CG39 58
Hallswelle Rd. NW11 BR32 46
Hall Ter. S. Ock. CY41 70
Hall, The, SE3 CH45 68
Hall View SE9 CJ48 78
Hall Way Pur. BY60 95
Hallwood Ct. Welw. G. C. BR8 5
Hallwood Cres. Brwd. DC26 122
Halons Rd. SE9 CL47 78
Halpin Pl. SE17 BZ42 67
Halsbrook Rd. SE3 CJ45 68
Halsbury Clo. Stan. BJ28 36
Halsbury Rd. E. Nthlt. BG35 45
Halsbury Rd. W. Nthlt. BF35 45
Halsbury St. W12 BP40 55
Halsend Hayes BC41 63
Halsey Pl. Wat. BC22 26
Halsey St. SW3 BU42 66
Halsham Cres. Bark. CN35 49
Halsmere Rd. SE5 BY44 66
Halstead Gdns. N21 BZ26 39
Halstead Hill, Wal. Cr. CA18 21
Halstead Rd. E11 CH32 49

Halstead Rd. N21 BZ26 39
Halstead Rd. Enf. CA24 30
Halstead Rd. Erith CT44 69
Halston Cl. SW11 BU46 76
Northcote Rd.
Halstow Rd. NW10 BQ38 55
Halstow Rd. SE10 CH42 68
Halsway Hayes BC40 53
Halt Dr. S. Le H. DK42 71
Halt Hill, Egh. AS49 72
Halton Rd. N1 BY36 56
Halt Robin La. Belv. CR42 69
Halt Robin Rd.
Halt Robin Rd. Belv. CR42 69
Hambalt Rd. SW4 BW46 76
Hamberlins La. Berk. AO11 7
Hamble Clo. Ruis. BB34 44
Hambledon Gdns. SE25 CA52 87
Hambledon Hill, Epsom BN61 103
Hambledon Rd. SW18 BR47 75
Hambledon Rd. Sid. CM47 78
Hambledon Vale Epsom BN61 103
Hamble La. S. Ock. CZ39 60
Hamble St. SW6 BS45 66
Hamble Wk. Nthlt. BF37 54
Hambro Av. Brom. CH54 88
Hambrook Rd. SE25 CB52 87
Hambro Rd. SW16 BW50 76
Hambro Rd. Brwd. DB27 42
Ingrave Rd.
Hambrough Rd. Sthl. BE40 54
Ham Clo. Rich. BK48 74
Hamden Cres. Brwd. DB28 42
Hamden Cres. Dag. CR34 50
Hamelin St. E14 CF39 57
Hamerton Rd. Grav. DD46 81
Hameway, E6 CL38 58
Ham Farm Rd. Rich. BK49 74
Hamfield Clo. Oxt. CF67 114
Hamfrith Rd. E15 CG36 58
Ham Gate Av. Rich. BK48 74
Hamilton Av. N9 CB26 39
Hamilton Av. Cob. BC60 92
Hamilton Av. Hodd. CE11 12
Hamilton Av. Ilf. CL31 49
Hamilton Av. Rom. CS30 41
Hamilton Av. Surb. BM55 85
Hamilton Av. Sutt. BR54 85
Hamilton Av. Wok. AV61 100
Hamilton Cl. N17 CA31 48
Hamilton Clo. NW8 BT38 56
Hamilton Clo. Barn. BU24 29
Hamilton Clo. Cher. AV54 82
Hamilton Clo. Epsom BN59 94
Hamilton Clo. Felt. BB49 73
Hamilton Clo. Pot. B. BP20 19
Hamilton Clo. St. Alb. BF19 18
Hamilton Ct. W5 BL40 55
Hamilton Rd.
Hamilton Ct. W9 BT38 56
Hamilton Cres. N13 BY28 38
Hamilton Cres. Brwd. DB28 42
Hamilton Cres. Har. BE34 45
Hamilton Cres. Houns. BF46 74
Hamilton Dr. Rom. CW30 42
Hamilton Gdns. NW8 BT38 56
Hamilton Pk. N5 BY35 47
Hamilton Pk. Way N5 BY35 47
Hamilton Pl. SE20 CB51 87
Hamilton Pl. W1 BV40 56
Hamilton Pl. Sun. BC50 73
Hamilton Rd. E15 CG38 58
Hamilton Rd. E17 CD30 39
Hamilton Rd. N2 BT31 47
Hamilton Rd. N9 CB26 39
Hamilton Rd. NW10 BP35 46
Hamilton Rd. NW11 BQ33 46
Hamilton Rd. SE27 BZ49 77
Hamilton Rd. SW19 BS50 76
Hamilton Rd. W4 BO41 65
Hamilton Rd. W5 BL40 55
Hamilton Rd. Barn. BU24 29
Hamilton Rd. Berk. AQ13 7
Hamilton Rd. Bexh. CQ44 69
Hamilton Rd. Brent. BK43 64
Hamilton Rd. Felt. BB49 73
Hamilton Rd. Har. BH32 45
Hamilton Rd. Hayes BC40 53
Hamilton Rd. Ilf. CL35 49
Hamilton Rd. Kings L. BA20 17
Hamilton Rd. Rom. CU32 50
Hamilton Rd. St. Alb. BJ13 9
Hamilton Rd. Sid. CO49 79
Hamilton Rd. Sthl. BE40 54
Hamilton Rd. Th. Hth. BZ52 87
Hamilton Rd. Twick. BH47 74
Hamilton Rd. Uxb. AX38 53
Hamilton Rd. Wat. BC27 35
Hamilton Sq. SE1 BZ41 67
Kipling St.
Hamilton St. SE8 CD43 67
Hamilton St. Wat. BD25 27
Hamilton Ter. NW8 BT38 56
Hamilton Way N3 BS29 38
Hamilton Way. Wall. BW58 95
Hamish St. SE11 BX42 66
Lambeth Wk.
Ham La. Egh. AQ49 72
Ham La. Wind. AQ46 72
Ham La. Wind. AR45 62
Hamlea Clo. SE12 CH46 78
Hamlet Clo. Rom. CR29 41
Hamlet Clo. Wdf. Grn. CH29 40
Hamlet Gdns. W6 BP42 65
Hamlet Hill. Harl. CH13 13
Hamlet Rd. SE19 CA50 77
Hamlet Rd. Rom. CQ29 41
Hamlets Way, E3 CD38 57
Hamlet, The, Berk. AT11 7
Hamlin Cres. Pnr. BD32 43
Hamlin Rd. Sev. CT64 107
Hamlyn Gdns. SE19 CA50 77
Hammarskjold Rd. Harl. CM10 6
Hammelton Rd. Brom. CG51 88
Hammer La. Hem. H. AY13 8
Hammers Gate, St. Alb. BF16 18
Hammers La. NW7 BP28 37
Hammersley Av. E16 CG39 58
Hammersmith Br. Rd. W6 BQ42 65
Hammersmith Gro. W6 BQ41 65
Hammersmith Ter. W6 BP42 65
Hammett St. EC3 CA40 57
Minories
Hamm Moor La. Wey. AY56 92
Hammond Av. Mitch. BV51 86
Hammond Clo. Barn. BR25 28
Hammond Clo. Wal. Cr. CA16 21
Hammond Clo. Wok. AR61 100
Hammond Rd. Enf. CB23 30
Hammond Rd. Sthl. BE41 64
Hammond Rd. Wok. AR61 100
Hammond St. Rd. Wal. Cr. BZ16 21
Hammonds La. Brwd. DA29 42
Hammond St. NW5 BW36 56
Hamonde Clo. Edg. BM27 37
Hamond Sq. N1 CA37 57
Hoxton St.
Hampden Av. Beck. CD51 87
Hampden Clo. Slou. AQ37 52
Hampden Ct. N10 BV29 38
Hampden Cres. Wal. Cr. CB19 21
Hampden Gurney St. W1 BU39 56
Seymour Pl.
Hampden La. N17 CA30 39
Hampden Rd. N8 BY31 47
Hampden Rd. N10 BV29 38
Hampden Rd. N17 CB30 39
Hampden Rd. Beck. CD51 87
Hampden Rd. Ger. Cr. AR30 34
Hampden Rd. Grays. DD42 71
Hampden Rd. Har. BG30 36
Hampden Rd. Kings-on-t. BM51 85
Hampden Rd. Rom. CR29 41
Hampden Rd. Slou. AS41 62
Hampden Way N14 BV26 38
Hampden Way, Wat. BB21 26
Hampdon Pl. St. Alb. BH18 18
Hamper Mill La. Wat. BC26 35
Hampshire Clo. N18 CB28 39
Berkshire Gdns.
Hampshire Gdns. S. Le H. DK41 71
Somerset Rd.
Hampshire Rd. N22 BX29 38
Hampshire Rd. Horn. CX31 51
Hampshire St. NW5 BW36 56
Torriano Av.
Hampson Way SW8 BX44 66
Hampstead Gdns. NW3 BU35 47
Rosslyn Hill
Hampstead Gdns. NW11 BS32 47
Hampstead Gro. NW3 BT34 47
Hampstead High St. NW3 BT35 47
Hampstead Hill Gdns. NW3 BT35 47
Hampstead La. Dor. BH72 119
Hampstead Rd. NW1 BW37 56
Hampstead Rd. Dor. BJ72 119
Hampstead Sq. NW3 BT34 47
Hampstead Way NW11 BS32 47
Hampton Clo. NW6 BS38 56
Hampton Clo. SW20 BQ50 75
Hampton Ct. Av. E. Mol. BG53 84
Hampton Ct. Way Surb. BH55 84
Hampton Cres. Grav. DJ48 81
Hampton Gro. NW3 BU35 47
Pond St.
Hampton Gro. Epsom BO59 94
Hampton La. Felt. BE49 74
Hampton Mead Loug. CL24 31
Hampton Pl. NW6 BS39 56
Hampton Rise, Har. BL32 46
Hampton Rd. E4 CD28 39
Hampton Rd. E7 CH35 49
Hampton Rd. E11 CF33 48
Hampton Rd. NW6 BS38 56
Hampton Rd. Croy. BZ53 87
Hampton Rd. Ilf. CL35 49
Hampton Rd. Red. BU73 121
Hampton Rd. Tedd. BG49 74
Hampton Rd. Twick. BG48 74
Hampton Rd. Wor. Pk. BP55 85
Hampton Rd. E. Felt. BE48 74
Hampton Rd. W. Felt. BE48 74
Hampton St. SE17 BY42 66
Ham Ridings, Rich. BL49 75
Hamsey Grn. Gdns. Warl. CB61 105
Hamsey Way Sth. Croy. CB61 105
Ham Shades Clo. Sid. CO48 79
Hamstel Rd. Harl. CM10 6
Ham St. Rich. BK47 74
Ham, The, Brent. BK43 64
Ham Vw. Croy. CD53 87
Hanameel St. E16 CH40 58
Hanbury Clo. Wal. Cr. CC18 21
Hanbury Dr. West. CH60 97
Hanbury Path. Wok. AU60 91
Hanbury Rd. W3 BM41 65
Hanbury Rd. W17 CB30 39
Hanbury St. E1 CB39 57
Hanbury Wk. Bex. CS48 79
Hancock Rd. E3 CF38 57
Hancock Rd. SE19 BZ50 77
Handa Clo. Hem. H. AZ15 8
Handa Wk. N1 BZ36 57
Marquess Est.
Hand Ct. WC1 BX39 56
Sandland St.
Handcroft Rd. Croy. BY54 86
Handel Clo. Edg. BL29 37
Handel Cres. Til. DG43 71
Handel St. WC1 BX38 56
Handel Way, Edg. BM29 37
Handen Rd. SE12 CG46 78
Handford Rd. S. Ock. CW40 60
Handforth Rd. SW9 BY43 66
Hand La. Saw. CP6 6
Handley Rd. E9 CC37 57
Victoria Pk. Rd.
Handover Rd. N15 CA31 48
Handpost Hill, Pot. B. BV17 20
Handside Clo. Welw. G. C. BQ8 5
Handside Clo. Wor. Pk. BQ54 85
Handside Grn. Welw. G. C. BQ7 5
Handside La. Welw. G. C. BP9 5
Handsworth Av. E4 CF29 39
Handsworth Rd. N17 BZ31 48
Handsworth Way Wat. BC27 35
Handtrough Way, Bark. CL37 58
Fresh Wharf Rd.
Hanford Clo. SW18 BS47 76
Hanford Row, SW19 BQ50 75
Hanger Ct. W5 BL38 55
Heathcroft.
Hanger Grn. W5 BM38 55
Western Av.
Hanger Hill, Wey. AZ57 92
Hanger La. W5 BL37 55
Hanger Ruding Wat. BE27 36
Hanger Vale La. W5 BL39 55
Hang Grove Hill. Orp. CL60 97
Hanging Hill La. Brwd. DD27 122
Hankey Pl. SE1 BZ41 67
Hankins La. NW7 BO27 37
Hanks Vw. Cob. BE60 93
Hanley Clo. Wind. AL44 61
Hanley Rd. N4 BX33 47
Hanmer Walk N7 BX34 47
Andover Est.
Hannell Rd. SW6 BR43 65
Hannen Rd. SE27 BY48 76
Hannibal Rd. E1 CC39 57
Hannibal Rd. Stai. AX47 73
Hannington Rd. SW4 BV45 66
Hanover Av. Felt. BC47 73
Hanover Cir. Hayes BA39 53
Hanover Clo. Rich. BM43 65
Cambridge Rd.
Hanover Clo. Sutt. BR56 94
Hanover Ct. W12 BP40 55
Hanover Gdns. SE11 BY43 66
Hanover Gdns. Ilf. CM29 40
Hanover Gate. NW1 BU38 56
Hanover Gate Mans. NW1 BU38 56
Hanover Grn. Hem. H. AW14 8
Hanover Pk. SE15 CB44 67
Hanover Pl. WC2 BX40 56
Long Acre
Hanover Rd. NW10 BQ36 55
Hanover Rd. SW19 BT50 76
Hanover Sq. W1 BV39 56
Hanover St. W1 BV39 56
Hanover St. Croy. BY55 86
Latimer Rd.
Hanover Ter. NW1 BU38 56
Hanover Ter. Ms. NW1 BU38 56
Hanover Walk, Wey. BB55 83
Hanover Way Bexh. CP45 69
Hanover Way. Wind. AM44 61
Hansard Ms. W14 BQ41 65
Hansart Way Enf. BY23 29
Hans Cres. SW1 BU41 66
Hansells Mead. Harl. CH11 13
Hanshades Clo. Sid. CO48 79
Hanshaw Dr. Edg. BN30 37
Hansler Gro. E. Mol. BG53 84
Hansler Rd. SE22 CA46 77
Hansol Rd. Bexh. CQ46 79
Hanson Clo. SW12 BV47 76
Hanson Clo. Loug. CM23 31
Hanson Dr. Loug. CM23 31
Hanson Gdns. Sthl. BE41 64
Hanson Grn. Loug. CM23 31
Hanson St. W1 BW39 56
Hans Pl. SW1 BU41 66
Hans Rd. SW3 BU41 66
Hans St. SW1 BU41 66
Pavilion Rd.
Hanway Rd. W7 BG39 54
Hanway St. W1 BW39 56
Hanworth Clo. Felt. BE49 74
Hanworth La. Cher. AV54 82
Hanworth Rd. Felt. BC47 73
Hanworth Rd. Hamptn. BE49 74
Hanworth Rd. Houns. BE47 74
Hanworth Rd. Red. BU73 121
Hanworth Rd. Sun. BC50 73
Hanworth Trd. Est. Felt. BE48 74
Hanyards End Pot. B. BW17 20
Hill Rise
Hanyards La. Pot. B. BW17 20
Harad's Pl. E1 CB40 57
Ensign St.
Harb. Clo. Slou. AL40 61
Harben Rd. NW6 BT36 56
Harberson Rd. E15 CG37 58
Harberson Rd. SW12 BV47 76
Harberton Rd. N19 BW33 47
Harberts Rd. Harl. CL11 13
Harbet Rd. E4 CC28 39
Harbet Rd. W2 BT39 56
Harbex Clo. Bex. CR47 79
Harbinger Rd. E14 CE42 67
Harbledown Pl. Orp. CP52 89
Okemore Gdns.
Harbledown Rd. SW6 BS44 66
Harbledown Rd. Sth. Croy. CB59 96
Harbord St. SW6 BQ44 65
Harborough Av. Sid. CN47 78
Harborough Rd. SW16 BX49 76
Harbourer Clo. Ilf. CO28 41
Harbourer Rd. Ilf. CO29 41
Harbourfield Rd. Bans. BS61 104
Harbour Rd. SE5 BZ45 67
Harbridge Av. SW15 BO47 75
Harbury Rd. Cars. BU58 95
Harbut Rd. SW11 BT45 66
Harcombe Rd. N16 CA34 48
Harcourt Av. E12 CK35 49
Harcourt Av. Edg. BN27 37
Harcourt Av. Sid. CP46 79
Harcourt Av. Wall. BV56 95
Harcourt Fld. Wall. BV56 95
Harcourt La. Maid. AJ41 61
Harcourt Rd. E15 CG37 58
Harcourt Rd. N22 BW30 38
Harcourt Rd. SE4 CD45 67
Harcourt Rd. SW19 BS50 76
Harcourt Rd. Bexh. CQ45 69
Harcourt Rd. Bush. BF25 27
Harcourt Rd. Th. Hth. BX53 86
Harcourt Rd. Wall. BV56 95
Harcourt Rd. Wind. AM44 61
Harcourt St. W1 BU39 56
Harcourt Ter. SW10 BS42 66
Harcroft, Dor. BK73 119
Hardcourts Clo. W. Wick. CE55 87
Hardel Rise SW2 BY47 76
Harden Rd. Grav. DF48 81
Harden's Manor Way, SE7 CJ41 68
Harden St. SE18 CK42 68
Harders Rd. SE15 CB44 67
Harder's Rd. Ms. SE15 CB44 67
Hardess St. SE24 BY45 66
Hardie Clo. NW10 BN35 46
Hardie Rd. Dag. CS34 50
Hardinge Clo. Uxb. AZ39 53
Hardinge Rd. N18 CA29 39
Hardinge Rd. NW10 BP37 55
Hardinge St. E1 CC39 57
Harding Rd. Bexh. CQ44 69
Harding Rd. Chesh. AO18 16
Harding Rd. Epsom. BO63 103
Harding Rd. Grays. DG41 71
Hardings La. SE20 CC50 77
Hardings Row, Iver AU38 52
Hardings Wk. Welw. G. C. BT7 5
Hardley Cres. Horn. CV31 51
Hardman Rd. SE7 CH42 68
Hardman Rd. Kings. On T. BL51 85
Hardwick Clo. Stan. BK28 36
Marsh La.
Hardwicke Av. Houns. BF44 64
Hardwicke Clo. Cob. BG61 102
Hardwicke Rd. N13 BX29 38
Hardwicke Rd. W4 BN42 65
Hardwicke Rd. Reig. BS70 121
Hardwicke Rd. Rich. BK49 74
Hardwicke St. Bark. CM37 58
Hardwick Gn. W13 BJ39 54
Templewood
Hardwickke Rd. Red. BT71 121
Hardwick La. Cher. AU54 82
Hardwick St. EC1 BY38 56
Hardwidge St. SE1 CA41 67
Snows Fields
Hardy Av. Grav. DF48 81
Hardy Av. Ruis. BC35 44
Hardy Clo. Pnr. BD33 45
Hardy Gro. Dart. CX45 70
Hardy Pass. N22 BY30 38
Cranbrook Pk.
Hardy Rd. SE3 CG43 68
Hardy Rd. SW19 BS50 76
Hardy Rd. Hem. H. AY13 8
Hardy Way Enf. BY23 29
Harebell Hill, Cob. BD60 93
Harebell Way. Rom. CV29 42
Hare & Billet Rd. SE3 CF44 67
Hare Bl. Welw. G. C. BR9 5
Harebreaks, The Wat. BC21 26
Harecourt Rd. N1 BZ36 57
Hare Cres. Wat. BC19 17
Harecroft, Lthd. BF65 102
Haredale Rd. SE24 BZ45 67
Haredon Clo. SE23 CC47 77
Harefield Esher BH55 84
Harefield, Harl. CO10 6
Harefield Av. Sutt. BQ58 94
Harefield Gn. NW7 BQ29 37
Harefield Ms. SE4 CD45 67
Harefield Pl. Est. Uxb. AY35 44
Harefield Rd. N8 BW32 47
Harefield Rd. SE4 CD45 67
Harefield Rd. SW16 BX50 76
Harefield Rd. Rick. AX27 35
Harefield Rd. Sid. CP48 79
Hare Hall La. Rom. CU31 50
Hare Hill. Wey. AV57 91
Hare Hill Clo. Wok. AW61 101
Harelands Clo. Wok. AR62 100
Harelands La. Wok. AQ62 100
Hare La. Esher BG57 93
Hare La. Esher BH57 93
Hare La. Hat. BP13 10
Hare Park Clo. Hem. H. AV13 7
Hares Bank Croy. CF58 96
Haresfield Rd. Dag. CR36 59
Harestone Dri. Cat. CA66 114
Harestone Dr. Cat. CA65 105
Harestone Valley Rd. Cat. CA66 114
Hare St. SE18 CL41 68
Hare Street Springs. Harl. CL11 13
Harewood, SW15 BN49 75
Harewood, Rick. AX25 26
Harewood Av. NW1 BU38 56
Harewood Av. Nthlt. BE36 54
Harewood Clo. Nthlt. BE36 54
Harewood Clo. Reig. BT69 121
Harewood Dr. Ilf. CK30 40
Harewood Gdns. Sth. Croy. CB61 105
Harewood Hill, Epp. CN21 31
Harewood Pl. Slou. AQ41 62
Harewood Rd. SW19 BU50 76
Harewood Rd. Brwd. DA25 33
Harewood Rd. Ch. St. G. AR24 25
Harewood Rd. Islw. BH43 64
Harewood Rd. Sth. Croy. CA57 96
Harewood Rd. Wat. BC27 35
Harewood Ter. Sthl. BE42 64
Harew Pl. W1 BV39 56
Hanover Sq.
Harfield Dr. Sun. BD51 84
Harfield Gdns. SE5 CA45 67
Harfield Rd. Sun. BD51 84
Harford Clo. E4 CE26 39
Harford Dr. Wat. BB22 26
Harford Rd. E4 CE26 39
Harford St. E1 CD38 57
Harford Wk. N2 BT31 47
Hargood Rd. SE3 CJ44 68
Hargrave Pk. N19 BW34 47
Hargrave Pl. N7 BW35 47
Brecknock Rd.
Hargrave Rd. N19 BW34 47
Hargreaves Av. Wal. Cr. CB18 21
Hargreaves Clo. Wal. Cr. CB19 21
Hargwyne St. SW9 BX45 66
Haringey Gro. N8 BX31 47
Haringey Pk. N8 BX32 47
Haringey Pass N4 BY31 47
Haringey Rd. N8 BX31 47
Harkness Clo. Epsom BQ61 103
Harland Av. Croy. CA55 87
Harland Av. Sid. CM48 78
Harland Rd. SE12 CH47 78
Harlech Gdns. Houns. BD43 64
Harlech Rd. N14 BX27 38
Harlequin Av. Brent. BJ43 64
Harlequin Rd. Tedd. BJ50 74
Fairfax Rd.
Harlescott Rd. SE15 CC45 67
Harlesden Clo. Rom. CW29 42
Harlesden Gdns. NW10 BO37 55
Harlesden La. NW10 BP37 55
Harlesden Rd. NW10 BP36 55
Harlesden Rd. Rom. CW29 42
Harlesden Rd. St. Alb. BJ13 9
Harlesden Wk. Rom. CW29 42
Harleston Clo. E5 CB34 48
Southwold Rd.
Harley Clo. Wem. BK36 54
Harley Ct. Har. BG31 45
Harley Cres. Har. BG31 45
Harleyford, Brom. CJ51 88
Harleyford Rd. SE11 BX43 66
Harleyford St. SE11 BY43 66
Harley Gdns. SW10 BT42 66
Harley Gdns. Orp. CN56 97
Harley Gro. E3 CD38 57
Harley Pl. W1 BV39 56
Harley Rd. NW3 BT36 56
Harley Rd. NW10 BO37 55
Harley Rd. Har. BG31 45
Harley St. W1 BV38 56
Harling St. SE5 BZ43 67
Harlington Clo. Hayes BA43 63
Harlington High St. Hayes. BA43 63
Harlington Rd. Bexh. CQ45 69
Harlington Rd. Uxb. & Hayes AZ38 53
Harlington Rd. E. Felt. BC47 73
Harlington Rd. W. Felt. BC46 73
Harlow Common Rd. Harl. CP12 14
Harlow Gdns. Rom. CS29 41
Harlow Rd. N13 BZ27 39
Harlow Rd. Bish. CR7 6
Harlow Rd. Harl. CJ11 13
Harlow Rd. Harl. CP8 6
Harlow Rd. Harl. CR8 6
Harlow Road. Ong. CV13 15
Harlow Rd. Rain. CT37 59
Harlow Rd. Saw. CP7 6
Harlow St. Hem. H. AZ11 8
Harlton Ct. Wal. Abb. CG20 22
Harlyn Dr. Pnr. BC31 44
Harman Av. Grav. DG49 81
Harman Av. Wdf. Grn. CG29 40
Harman Clo. E4 CF28 39
Harman Clo. NW2 BR35 46
Harman Dr. NW2 BR35 46
Harman Dr. Sid. CN46 78
Harman Rd. Enf. CA25 30
Harmer Green La. Welw. G. C. BR5 5
Harmer Rd. Swans. DC46 81
Harmer St. Grav. DH46 81
Harmondsworth La. West Dr. AY43 63
Harmood St. NW1 BV36 56
Harmsworth St. SE17 BY42 66
Harmsworth Way N20 BR26 37
Harmundsworth Rd. West Dr. AY42 63
Harnage Rd. Brent. BL42 65
Harness Rd. SE28 CO41 69
Harold Ave. Hayes. BB41 63
Harold Av. Belv. CQ42 69
Harold Av. Hayes BC41 63
Harold Court Rd. Rom. CX29 42
Harold Cres. Wal. Abb. CF19 21
Harold Est. Wal. Abb. CF19 21
Harold Gibbons Ct. SE7 CJ43 68
Harold Hill Ind. Est. Rom. CV29 42
Harold Rd. E4 CF27 39
Harold Rd. E11 CG33 49
Harold Rd. E13 CH37 58
Harold Rd. N8 BX32 47

Harold Rd. N15	CA32	48
Harold Rd. NW10	BN38	55
Harold Rd. SE19	BZ50	77
Harold Rd. Dart.	CW49	80
Harold Rd. Sutt.	BT56	95
Harold Rd. Wal. Cr.	CE20	21
Harold Rd. Wdf. Grn.	CH30	40
Harolds Rd. Harl.	CK11	13
Haroldstone Rd. E17	CC32	48
Harp Alley, EC4	BY39	56
St. Bride St.		
Harpenden Rd. E12	CJ34	49
Harpenden Rd. SE27	BY48	76
Harpenden Rd. St. Alb.	BH12	9
Harper La. Rad.	BJ19	18
Harper Rd. SE1	BZ41	67
Harpers La. Brwd.	DB22	33
Harper's Yd. N17	CA30	39
Ruskin Rd.		
Harpesford Av. Vir. W.	AQ53	82
Harp La. EC3	CA40	57
Lwr. Thames St.		
Harpley Sq. E1	CC38	57
Harpour Rd. Bark.	CM36	58
Harp Rd. W7	BH38	54
Harpsfield. Hat.	BO12	10
Harps Oak La. Red.	BU66	113
Harptree Way, St. Alb.	BJ12	9
Harpur St. WC1	BX39	56
Dombey St.		
Harraden Rd. SE3	CJ44	68
Harrier Clo. Rain.	CU36	59
Harriers Clo. W5	BL40	55
Harries Cres. Wal. Abb.	CH19	22
Harries Rd. Hayes.	BD38	54
Harriet St. SW1	BU41	66
Sloane St.		
Harriet Wk. SW1	BU41	66
Harringay Gdns. N15	BY31	47
Harringay Rd. N15	BY32	47
Harring Sq. NW1	BW37	56
Harrington Clo. Wind.	AM45	61
Harrington Gdns. SW7	BS42	66
Harrington Hill, E5	CB33	48
Harrington Pl. Reig.	BS69	121
Reigate Hill		
Harrington Rd. E11	CG33	49
Harrington Rd. SE25	CB52	87
Harrington Rd. SW7	BT42	66
Harrington St. NW1	BW38	56
Harrington Ter. N18	BZ27	39
Harrington Way, SE18	CJ41	68
Harriot's La. Ash.	BK63	102
Harriott Clo. SE10	CG42	68
Tunnel Av.		
Harris La. Rad.	BM20	19
Harrison Clo. Brwd.	DE25	122
Harrison Clo. Reig.	BS71	121
Lymden Gdns.		
Harrison Dr. Epp.	CR16	23
High Rd.		
Harrison Rd. Dag.	CR36	59
Harrisons Rise Croy.	BY55	86
Harrison St. WC1	BX38	56
Harrison Way. Slou.	AL40	61
Harris Rd. Bexh.	CQ44	69
Harris Rd. Dag.	CQ35	50
Harris Rd. Wat.	BC21	26
Harris St. E17	CD33	48
Harris St. SE5	BZ43	67
Harris Way, Sun.	BB51	83
Harrogate Rd. Wat.	BD27	36
Harrold Rd. Dag.	CO35	50
Harrow Av. Enf.	CA25	30
Harrow Bottom Rd. Vir. W.	AS53	82
Harrowby St. W1	BU39	56
Harrow Clo. Chess.	BK57	93
Harrow Clo. Dor.	BJ72	119
Harrow Clo. Wey.	AW55	83
Harrow Cotts. Felt.	AZ48	73
Harrow Cres. Rom.	CU29	41
Harrowdene Clo. Wem.	BK35	45
Harrowdene Gdns. Tedd.	BJ50	74
Harrowdene Rd. Wem.	BK34	45
Harrow Dr. N9	CA26	39
Harrow Dr. Horn.	CU32	50
Harrowells, Wey.	BB55	83
Harrowes Meade Edg.	BM27	37
Harrow Gdns. Warl.	CD61	105
Harrowgate Clo. Sou.	AT42	62
Harrowgate Rd. E9	CD36	57
Harrow La. E14	CF40	57
Harrow La. West.	CM63	106
Harrow Manorway, SE2	CP40	59
Harrow Pk. Har.	BH34	45
Harrow Pl. E1	CA39	57
Harrow Rd. E6	CK37	58
Harrow Rd. E11	CG34	49
Harrow Rd. Bark.	CN37	58
Harrow Rd. Cars.	BU57	95
Harrow Rd. Felt.	AZ48	73
Harrow Rd. Ilf.	CM35	49
Harrow Rd. Sev.	CQ61	107
Harrow Rd. Slou.	AS41	62
Harrow Rd. Warl.	CD61	105
Harrow Rd. Wem.	BH34	45
Harrow Rd. E. Dor.	BJ72	119
Harrow Rd. W. Dor.	BJ72	119
Harrow View Har.	BG31	45
Harrow Vw. Hayes	BC39	53
Harrow Vw. Uxb.	BA38	53
Harrow Vw. Rd. W5	BJ38	54
Harrow Way, Shep.	BA51	83
Harrow Way Wat.	BE27	36
Harrow Weald. Har.	BG29	36
Harrow Weald Pk. Har.	BG29	36
Hart Cres. Chig.	CN28	40
Hart Dyke Cres. Swan.	CS52	89
Hartdyke Rd. Orp.	CP55	89
Hart Dyke Rd. Swan.	CS52	89
Harte Rd. Houns.	BE44	64
Hartfield Av. Borwd.	BM25	28
Hartfield Av. Nthlt.	BC37	53
Hartfield Clo. Borwd.	BM25	28
Hartfield Cres. SW19	BR50	75
Hartfield Cres. Kes.	CH55	88
Hartfield Gro. SE20	CB51	87
Hartfield Rd. SW19	BR50	75
Hartfield Rd. Chess.	BK56	93
Hartfield Rd. Kes.	CH56	97
Hartfield Ter. E3	CE37	57
Hartford Av. Har.	BJ31	45
Hartforde Rd. Borwd.	BM23	28
Hartford Pl. Grav.	DE47	81
Hartford Rd. Bex.	CR46	79
Hart Gro. W5	BM40	55
Hart Gro. Sthl.	BF39	54
Hart Gro. Clo. W5	BM40	55
Hart Gro.		
Harthall La. Hem. H.	AZ17	17
Hartham Clo. N7	BX35	47
Hartham Clo. Islw.	BJ44	64
Hartham Rd. N7	BX35	47
Hartham Rd. N17	CA30	39
Hartham Rd. Islw.	BH44	64
Hartin Clo. Uxb.	AY37	53
Harting Rd. SE9	CK49	78
Hartington Ct. W4	BM43	65
Hartington Rd. E16	CH39	58
Hartington Rd. E17	CD32	48
Hartington Rd. N17	CB30	39
Hartington Rd. SW8	BX44	66
Hartington Rd. W4	BM43	65
Hartington Rd. W13	BJ40	54
Hartington Rd. Enf.	BZ23	30
Hartington Rd. Sthl.	BE41	64
Hartington Rd. Twick.	BJ46	74
Hartismere Rd. SW6	BR43	65
Hartlake Rd. E9	CC36	57
Hartland Clo. Edg.	BM27	37
Hartland Clo. Wey.	AX58	92
Hartland Dr. Edg.	BM27	37
Hartland Dr. Ruis.	BC34	44
Hartland Gro. NW1	BV36	56
Hartland Rd.		
Hartland Rd. E15	CG36	58
Hartland Rd. N11	BU28	38
Hartland Rd. NW1	BV36	56
Hartland Rd. NW6	BR37	55
Hartland Rd. Epp.	CO19	23
Hartland Rd. Hamptn.	BF49	74
Hartland Rd. Horn.	CU34	50
Hartland Rd. Mord.	BS54	86
Hartland Rd. Wal. Cr.	CC18	21
Hartland St. NW1	BV36	56
Hartland Way Croy.	CD55	87
Hartland Way Mord.	BR54	85
Hartley Av. E6	CK37	58
Hartley Av. NW7	BK28	36
Hartley Clo. NW7	BO28	37
Hartley Clo. W3	BM40	55
Uxbridge Rd.		
Hartley Clo. Brom.	CK51	88
Hartley Clo. Slou.	AR37	52
Hartley Down Rd. Pur.	BX61	104
Hartley Hill Pur.	BX61	104
Hartley Old Rd. Pur.	BX61	104
Hartley Rd. E11	CG33	49
Hartley Rd. Croy.	BY54	86
Hartley Rd. Long.	DC51	90
Hartley Rd. Well.	CP43	69
Hartley Rd. West.	CM66	115
Hartley St. E2	CC38	57
Hartley Way Pur.	BX61	104
Hartmann Rd. E16	CJ40	58
Harton Rd. N9	CB27	39
Harton St. SE8	CE44	67
Hart Rd. Dor.	BJ71	119
Hart Rd. Harl.	CP8	6
Hart Rd. St. Alb.	BG14	9
Hart Rd. Wey.	AY60	92
Hartsbourne Av. Bush.	BG27	36
Hartsbourne Rd. Bush.	BG27	36
Hartsbourne Way, Hem. H.	BA14	8
Harts Clo. Bush.	BF23	27
Harts Gdns. Guil.	AQ69	118
Hartshill, Guil.	AO70	118
Harts Hill Clo. Uxb.	AZ36	53
Hartshill Rd. Grav.	DF48	81
Hartshill Wk. Wok.	AQ61	100
Hartshorn Gdns. E6	CL38	58
Hameway		
Hartslands Rd. Sev.	CV65	108
Hart's La. SE14	CC43	67
Harts La. Bark.	CL36	58
Hartslock Dr. SE2	CP41	69
Hartsmead Rd. SE9	CK48	78
Hartspring La. Bush.	BF23	27
Hart St. EC3	CA40	57
Mark La.		
Hart St. Brwd.	DB27	42
Hartsway Enf.	CC24	30
Hartswood Av. Reig.	BS72	121
Hartswood Clo. Brwd.	DB28	42
Hartswood Clo. Brwd.	DC28	122
Hartswood Rd. W12	BO41	65
Hartswood Rd. Brwd.	DC28	122
Hartville Rd. SE18	CO42	69
Hartwell Dr. E4	CF29	39
Hartwell St. E8	CA36	57
Dalston La.		
Harty Clo. Grays.	DD40	71
Harvard Ct. NW6	BS35	47
West End La.		
Harvard Hill, W4	BM43	65
Wolseley Gdns.		
Harvard La. W4	BN42	65
Harvard Rd.		
Harvard Rd. SE13	CF46	77
Harvard Rd. W4	BM42	65
Harvard Rd. Islw.	BH44	64
Harvard Wk. Horn.	CU35	50
Harvel Cres. SE2	CP42	69
Harvest Bnk. Rd. W. Wick.	CG55	88
Harvest End Wat.	BD21	27
Harvester Rd. Epsom	BN58	94
Harvest Rd. Bush.	BF24	27
Harvest Rd. Egh.	AR49	72
Harvest Rd. Felt.	BC48	73
Harvest Way Swan.	CS54	89
Harvey Fields, Wal. Abb.	CF20	21
Harvey Gdns. SE7	CJ42	68
Harvey Gdns. Loug.	CL24	31
Harvey Rd. E11	CG33	49
Harvey Rd. N8	BX32	47
Harvey Rd. SE5	BZ44	67
Harvey Rd. Guil.	AS71	118
Harvey Rd. Houns.	BE47	74
Harvey Rd. Ilf.	CL35	49
Harvey Rd. Nthlt.	BD36	54
Harvey Rd. Rick.	AZ25	26
Harvey Rd. St. Alb.	BK16	18
Harvey Rd. Slou.	AT41	62
Harvey Rd. Uxb.	AZ37	53
Harvey Rd. Walt.	BC54	83
Harvey's La. Rom.	CS34	50
Harvey St. N1	BZ37	57
Harvill Rd. Sid.	CP49	79
Harvil Rd. Uxb.	AX31	44
Harvington Wk. E8	CB36	57
Wilman Gro.		
Harvist Rd. NW6	BQ37	55
Harwater Dr. Loug.	CK23	31
Harwell Clo. Ruis.	BA33	44
Harwell Pass. N2	BU31	47
Harwood Av. Brom.	CH51	88
Harwood Av. Horn.	CW31	51
Harwood Av. Mitch.	BU52	86
Harwood Clo. Welw.	BU6	5
Harwood Ct. SW15	BQ45	65
Upr. Richmond Rd.		
Harwood Gdns. Wind.	AQ47	72
Harwood Hall La. Upmin.	CX36	60
Harwood Hill. Welw. G. C.	BR6	5
Harwood Rd. SW6	BS43	66
Harwood Sewells. Welw. G. C.	BR6	5
Harwoods Rd. Wat.	BC24	26
Harwoods Yd. N21	BY26	38
Wades Hill		
Harwood Ter. SW6	BS44	66
Hasedines Rd. Hem. H.	AW13	8
Haseldene Rd. St. Alb.	BK16	18
Haseldine Meadows. Hat.	BO13	10
Haselmere Av. Houns.	BD44	64
Haselrigge Rd. SW4	BW45	66
Haskard Rd. Dag.	CP35	50
Hasker St. SW3	BU42	66
Haslam Av. Sutt.	BR54	85
Haslemere Av. SW18	BS48	76
Haslemere Av. W7	BJ41	64
Haslemere Av. W13	BJ41	64
Haslemere Av. Barn.	BU26	38
Haslemere Av. Mitch.	BT51	86
Haslemere Clo. Hamptn.	BE49	74
Haslemere Clo. Wall.	BX56	95
Haslemere Gdns. N3	BR31	46
Haslemere Gdns. NW4	BQ32	46
Haslemere Rd. N8	BW33	47
Haslemere Rd. N21	BY27	38
Haslemere Rd. Bexh.	CQ44	69
Haslemere Rd. Th. Hth.	BY53	86
Haslemere Rd. Wind.	AN44	61
Haslet Rd. Wat.	BC24	26
Haslett Rd. Shep.	BB51	83
Haslewood Av. Hodd.	CE12	12
Haslewood Dr. Enf.	BY24	29
Haslock Gdns. Barn.	BS25	29
Hassard St. E2	CA38	57
Hassendean Rd. SE3	CH43	68
Hassett Rd. E9	CC36	57
Hassocks Clo. SE26	CB48	77
Hassocks Rd. SW16	BW51	86
Hassop Rd. NW2	BQ35	46
Hassop Wk. SE9	CK49	78
Hasted Rd. SE7	CJ42	68
Hastings Av. Ilf.	CL31	49
Hastings Clo. Maid.	AH42	61
Hastings Rd. E15	CG37	58
Hastings Rd. N11	BW28	38
Hastings Rd. W13	BJ40	54
Hastings Rd. Brom.	CK54	88
Hastings Rd. Croy.	CA54	87
Hastings Rd. Rom.	CU32	50
Hastings St. WC1	BX38	56
Hastings Way. Bush.	BE24	27
Hastings Way. Rick.	BA24	26
Hastingwood Rd. Harl.	CP13	14
Hatcham Pk. Rd. SE14	CC44	67
Hatcham Rd. SE15	CC43	67
Hatchard Rd. N19	BW34	47
Hatch Clo. Wey.	AW55	83
Hatchcroft, NW4	BP31	46
Hatch End. Pnr.	BE29	36
Hatchett Rd. Felt.	BA47	73
Hatch Gdns. Tad.	BQ63	103
Hatch Gro. Rom.	CQ31	50
Hatchlands Rd. Red.	BU70	121
Hatch La. E4	CF28	39
Hatch La. Bans.	BU61	104
Hatch La. West Dr.	AX43	63
Hatch La. Wok.	AZ63	101
Hatch Rd. SW16	BX51	86
Hatch Rd. Brwd.	DA25	33
Hatch Side, Chig.	CL28	40
Hatch, The, Enf.	CC23	30
Hatcliffe Clo. SE3	CG45	68
Hatcliffe St. SE10	CG42	68
Hatfield Clo. SE14	CC43	67
Reaston St.		
Hatfield Clo. Brwd.	DE26	122
Hutton Dr.		
Hatfield Clo. Horn.	CV35	51
Hatfield Clo. Ilf.	CL31	49
Hatfield Clo. Mitch.	BT52	86
Hatfield Cres. Hem. H.	AY11	8
Hatfield Mead Mord.	BS53	86
Hatfield Rd. E15	CG35	49
Hatfield Rd. W4	BN41	65
Hatfield Rd. W13	BJ40	54
Hatfield Rd. Ash.	BL62	103
Hatfield Rd. Dag.	CQ36	59
Hatfield Rd. Hat.	BU10	5
Hatfield Rd. Pot. B.	BT19	20
Hatfield Rd. St. Alb.	BH13	9
Hatfield Rd. St. Alb.	BL13	10
Hatfield Rd. Wat.	BC23	26
Hatfields, SE1	BY40	56
Hatfields Rd. Loug.	CL24	31
Hathaway Clo. Stan.	BJ28	36
Uxbridge Rd.		
Hathaway Ct. St. Alb.	BL13	10
Hatfield Rd.		
Hathaway Cres. E12	CK36	58
Hathaway Gdns. W13	BJ39	54
Hathaway Gdns. Rom.	CP32	50
Hathaway Rd. Croy.	BY54	86
Hathaway Rd. Grays.	DD41	71
Hatherleigh Clo. Chess.	BK56	93
Hatherleigh Clo. Mord.	BS52	86
Hatherleigh Gdns. Pot. B.	BT19	20
Hatherleigh Rd. Ruis.	BC34	44
Hatherleigh Way Rom.	CV30	42
Hatherley Cres. Sid.	CO48	79
Hatherley Gdns. E6	CJ37	58
Hatherley Gdns. N8	BX32	47
Hatherley Gro. W2	BS39	56
Hatherley Ms. E17	CE31	48
Hatherley Rd.		
Hatherley Rd. E17	CD31	48
Hatherley Rd. Rich.	BL44	65
Hatherley Rd. Sid.	CO49	79
Hatherley St. SW1	BW42	66
Vincent Sq.		
Hathern Gdns. SE9	CL49	78
Hatherop Rd. Hamptn.	BE50	74
Hathorne Clo. SE15	CC44	67
Hathway Rd. Grays.	DD42	71
Hathway St. SE15	CC44	67
Gibbon Rd.		
Hatley Av. Ilf.	CM31	49
Hatley Clo. N11	BU28	38
Hatley Rd. N4	BX34	47
Hatrel Dri. Horn.	CV35	51
Hatton Av. Slou.	AO38	52
Hatton Gdns. Mitch.	BU53	86
Hatton Gdn. EC1	BY38	56
Hatton Grn. Felt.	BC45	63
Hatton Rd. Croy.	BY54	86
Hatton Rd. Felt.	BA47	73
Hatton Rd. Felt.	BB45	63
Hatton Rd. Wal. Cr.	CC18	21
Hatton St. NW8	BT38	56
Hatton Wall, EC1	BY39	56
Haunch Of Venison Yd. W1	BV39	56
Brook St.		
Havana Clo. Rom.	CT32	50
Havana Rd. SW19	BS48	76
Havannah St. E14	CE41	67
Havant Rd. E17	CF31	48
Havant Way, SE15	CA43	67
Landport Way		
Havelius Clo. SE10	CG42	68
Flamstead Est.		
Havelock Ct. Sthl.	BE41	64
Havelock Pl. SE18	CL42	68
Anglesea Rd.		
Havelock Pl. Har.	BH32	45
Havelock Rd. N17	CB30	39
Havelock Rd. SW19	BT49	76
Havelock Rd. Belv.	CQ42	69
Havelock Rd. Brom.	CJ52	88
Havelock Rd. Croy.	CA55	87
Havelock Rd. Dart.	CU46	79
Havelock Rd. Grav.	DF47	81
Havelock Rd. Har.	BH31	45
Havelock Rd. Kings L.	AY17	17
Havelock Rd. Sthl.	BE41	64
Havelock St. N1	BX37	56
Havelock St. Ilf.	CL34	49
Havelock Ter. SW8	BV43	66
Havelock Wk. SE23	CC47	77
Haven Cl. Hat.	BP12	10
Haven Clo. SW19	BQ48	75
Haven Clo. Grav.	DF50	81
Haven Clo. Hayes	BB39	53
Haven Clo. Swan.	CT51	89
Haven Grn. W5	BK39	54
W. Side Rd.		
Haven Grn. Ct. W5	BK39	54
Haven Grn.		
Havenhurst Rise Enf.	BY23	29
Haven La. W5	BK39	54
Haven Pl. W5	BK40	54
Broadway, The,		
Haven Pl. Grays.	DE41	71
Haven Rd. NW1	BV36	56
Castle Rd.		
Haven Ter. W5	BK40	54
Haven Pl.		
Haven. The. Grays.	DG42	71
Haven, The, Rich.	BM45	65
Havenwood, Wem.	BM34	46
Haverfield Gdns. Rich.	BM43	65
Haverfield Rd. E3	CD38	57
Haverford Way, Edg.	BL30	37
Haverhill Rd. E4	CF26	39
Pretoria Rd.		
Haverhill Rd. SW12	BW47	76
Havering Dr. Rom.	CT31	50
Havering Gdns. Rom.	CP32	50
Havering Pl. Hav.	CS27	41
Havering Rd. Rom.	CS30	41
Havering St. E1	CC39	57
Havering Way, Bark.	CO38	59
Havers Av. Walt.	BD56	93
Haversham Clo. Twick.	BK46	74
Haversham Gra. Twick.	BK46	74
Haverstock Hl. NW3	BU35	47
Haverstock Rd. NW5	BU35	47
Haverstock St. N1	BY37	56
Haverthwaite Rd. Orp.	CM55	88
Havil St. SE5	CA43	67
Havisham Rd. Grav.	DK48	81
Hawarden Av. Wal. Cr.	CC20	21
Hawarden Gro. SE24	BZ47	77
Hawarden Rd. E17	CC31	48
Hawarden Rd. Cat.	BZ64	105
Haward Rd. Hodd.	CF11	12
Hawbridge Rd. E11	CF33	48
Hawes La. E4	CF22	30
Hawes La. W. Wick.	CF54	87
Hawes Rd. N18	CB29	39
Hawes Rd. Brom.	CH51	88
Hawes Rd. Tad.	BQ63	103
Hawes St. N1	BY36	56
Hawfield Gdns. St. Alb.	BG16	18
Hawgood St. E3	CE39	57
Hawkdene E4	CE25	30
Hawkenbury Harl.	CL12	13
Hawker Clo. Wall.	BX57	95
Hawke Rd. SE19	BZ50	77
Hawkesbury Rd. SW15	BP46	75
Hawkes Clo. Grays.	DD43	71
Hawkesfield Rd. SE23	CD48	77
Hawkesley Clo. Twick.	BJ49	74
Hawkes Rd. Mitch.	BU51	86
Hawkesworth Rd. Brom.	CH52	88
Hawkewood Rd. Sun.	BC52	83
Hawkfield Ct. Islw.	BH44	64
Hawkfield Wk. Orp.	CP55	89
Hawkhirst Rd. Ken.	BZ61	105
Hawkhurst Gdns. Rom.	CS29	41
Hawkhurst Rd. SW16	BW51	86
Hawkhurst Someroile Rd. Cob.	BF60	93
Hawkhurst Way N. Mal.	BN53	85
Hawkhurst Way W. Wick.	CE55	87
Hawkinge Wk. Orp.	CO52	89
Robin Way		
Hawkinge Way. Horn.	CV36	60
Hawkins Av. Grav.	DH49	81
Hawkins Cres. Har.	BG33	45
Hawk Park Rd. N22	BY31	47
Hawkridge Clo. Rom.	CP32	50
Hawks Brook La. Beck.	CF53	87
Hawkshaw Clo. SW2	BX47	76
Hawkshead Clo. Brom.	CG50	78
Coniston Rd.		
Hawkshead Clo. Enf.	CC21	30
Hawkshead La. Hat.	BQ17	19
Hawkshead Rd. NW10	BO36	55
Hawkshead Rd. W4	BO41	65
Hawkshead Rd. Pot. B.	BS18	20
Hawks Hill, Lthd.	BH65	102
Hawkshill Clo. Esher	BF57	93
Hawks Hill Clo. Lthd.	BH64	102
Hawkshill Way Esher	BF57	93
Hawkslade Rd. SE15	CC46	77
Hawksley Rd. N16	BZ34	48
Hawks Mews SE10	CF43	67
Luton Pl.		
Hawksmoor Grn. Brwd.	DE25	122
Hawksmoor St. W6	BQ43	65
Hawksmouth E4	CF26	39
Hawks Rd. Kings-on-t.	BL51	85
Hawkstone Rd. SE16	CC42	67
Hawks Way, Stai.	AV48	72
Hawkswood Est. Chis.	CM52	88
Hawkswood Gro. Slou.	AS36	52
Hawkswood La. Ger. Cr.	AS35	43
Hawksworth Clo. Nthwd.	BA29	35
Hawkwood Cres. E4	CE25	30
Hawkwood Dell. Lthd.	BF66	111
Hawkwood La. Chis.	CM51	88
Hawkwood Mt. E5	CB33	48
Hawkwood Ri. Lthd.	BF66	111
Hawlands Dr. Pnr.	BE33	45
Hawley Cres. NW1	BV36	56
Hawley Gdns. SE27	BY48	76
Hawley Rd. NW1	BV36	56
Hawley Rd. Dart.	CW48	80
Hawley St. NW1	BV36	56
Hawley Way, Ashf.	AZ49	73
Haws La. Stai.	AW46	73
Hawstead La. Orp.	CQ56	98
Hawstead Rd. SE6	CE46	77
Hawthorn Av. N13	BX28	38
Hawthorn Av. Brwd.	DC27	122
Hawthorn Av. Cars.	BV57	95
Hawthorn Av. Rain.	CU38	59
Hawthorn Clo. Hmptn.	BF49	74
Hawthorn Clo. Orp.	CM53	88
Hawthorn Clo. Red.	BV73	121
Hawthorn Clo. Wat.	BB22	26
Hawthorn Clo. Wok.	AS63	100
Hawthorn Cres. Croy.	CC59	96
Hawthorndene Clo. Brom.	CG55	88
Hawthorndene Rd. Brom.	CG55	88
Hawthorn Dr. Har.	BE32	45
Hawthorn Dr. Uxb.	AX36	53
Hawthorn Dr. W. Wick.	CG56	97
Hawthorne Ave. West.	CJ61	106
Hawthorne Av. Har.	BJ32	45
Hawthorne Av. Mitch.	BT51	86
Hawthorne Av. Ruis.	BC32	44
Hawthorne Av. Th. Hth.	BY51	86
Hawthorne Av. Wal. Cr.	CB19	21
Hawthorne Clo. Brom.	CK52	88
Hawthorne Clo. Sutt.	BT55	86
Hawthorne Clo. Wal. Cr.	CB19	21
Hawthorne Cres. Slou.	AP39	52
Hawthorne Cres. Sth. Croy.	CC58	96
Hawthorne Gro. NW9	BN33	46
Hawthorne La. Sev.	CT64	107
Hawthorne Pl. Epsom	BO59	94
Hawthorne Rd. Brom.	CK52	88
Hawthornes. Hat.	BO13	10
Hawthorne Way, Guil.	AT68	109

Hawthorn Farm Av. Nthlt. BE37 54
Hawthorn Gdns. W5 BK41 64
Hawthorn Gro. Enf. BZ22 30
Hawthorn Hatch, Brent. BJ43 64
Hawthorn La. Hem. H. AV13 7
Hawthorn Pl. Hayes BB40 53
Hawthorn Pl. Hayes BC40 53
Hawthorn Rd. E17 CE31 48
Hawthorn Rd. N8 BW31 47
Hawthorn Rd. N18 CA29 39
Hawthorn Rd. NW10 BP36 55
Hawthorn Rd. Bexh. CQ46 79
Hawthorn Rd. Brent. BJ43 64
Hawthorn Rd. Buck. H. CJ28 40
Hawthorn Rd. Dart. CV47 80
Hawthorn Rd. Hodd. CE11 12
Hawthorn Rd. Stai. AU49 72
Hawthorn Rd. Sutt. BT56 95
Hawthorn Rd. Wall. BV57 95
Hawthorn Rd. Wok. AR63 100
Hawthorn Rd. Wok. AV65 100
Hawthorns. Rick. AU28 34
Hawthorns Wdf. Grn. CG27 40
Hawthorns, Welw. G. C. BQ7 5
Hawthorns' The Loug. CL24 31
Hawthorn, The, Berk. AQ12 7
Hawthorn Way N9 CA27 39
Hawthorn Way. Chesh. AO18 16
Hawthorn Way, St. Alb. BF15 9
Hawthorn Way, St. Alb. BF16 18
Hawthorn Way. Shep. BA52 83
Hawthorn Way, Wey. AW58 92
Hawtrees Rad. BH21 27
Hawtrey Clo. Slou. AQ41 62
Hawtrey Dr. Ruis. BC33 44
Hawtrey Rd. NW3 BU36 56
Hawtrey Rd. Wind. AO44 61
Hawtry Av. Nthlt. BD37 54
Haxtead Rd. Brom. CH51 88
Haybourn Mead, Hem. H. AW14 8
Hayburn Way Horn. CT33 50
Hay Clo. E15 CG36 58
Haycroft Gdns. NW10 BP37 55
Haycroft Rd. SW2 BX46 76
Haycroft Rd. Surb. BK55 84
Hay Currie St. E14 CE39 57
Hayday Rd. E16 CH39 58
Hayden Ct. Wey. AW59 92
Hayden Pl. Guil. AR71 118
Haydens Clo. Orp. CP54 89
Haydens Rd. Harl. CM11 13
Hayden Way Rom. CS30 41
Haydn Av. Pur. BY60 95
Haydock Av. Nthlt. BE36 54
Haydock Clo. Horn. CW35 51
Haydock Grn. Nthlt. BF36 54
Haydon Clo. NW9 BN31 46
Haydon Dr. Pnr. BC31 44
Haydon Rd. Dag. CP34 50
Haydon Rd. Wat. BE25 27
Haydons Pk. Rd. SW19 BS49 76
Haydon Sq. E1 CA39 57
Haydons Rd. SW19 BS49 76
Haydon St. EC3 CA40 57
Hayes Chase W. Wick. CF53 87
Hayes Clo. Brom. CH55 88
Hayes Ct. SW2 BX47 76
Hayes Cres. NW11 BR32 46
Hayes Cres. Sutt. BQ56 94
Hayes Dr. Rain. CU36 59
Hayes End Clo. Hayes BA38 53
Hayes End Dr. Hayes BA38 53
Hayes End Rd. Hayes BA38 53
Hayesford Pk. Dr. Brom. CG53 88
Hayesford Pk. Est. Brom. CH53 88
Hayes Gdns. Brom. CH55 88
Hayes Hill Rd. Brom. CG54 88
Hayes La. Beck. CF52 87
Hayes La. Brom. CH54 88
Hayes La. Ken. BY61 104
Hayes La. Ken. BZ63 105
Hayes Mead Brom. CG54 88
Hayes Pl. NW1 BU40 56
Hayes Rd. Brom. CH52 88
Hayes Rd. Green. CZ47 80
Hayes Rd. Sthl. BC42 63
Hayes St. Brom. CH54 88
Hayes, The, Epsom. BN63 103
Hayes Way Beck. CF52 87
Hayes Wd. Av. Brom. CH54 88
Hayfield Clo. Bush. BF24 27
Hayfield Pass. E1 CC38 57
Hayfield Rd. Orp. CO53 89
Hay Green La. Brwd. DB21 33
Hay Green La. Ing. DC20 24
Hay Hill, W1 BV40 56
Hayland Clo. NW9 BN31 46
Hay La. NW9 BN31 46
Hay La. Slou. AR35 43
Hayles St. SE11 BY42 66
Hayling Av. Felt. BC48 73
Hayling Rd. Wat. BC27 35
Hayman Cres. Hayes BA37 53
Haymarket, SW1 BW40 56
Haymeads Dr. Esher BG57 93
Haymeads Hill. Welw. G. C. BR6 5
Haymer Gdns. Wor. Pk. BP55 85
Haymerle Rd. SE15 CB43 67
Hayne Rd. Beck. CD51 87
Haynes Clo. N17 CB29 39
Haynes Clo. SE3 CG45 68
Haynes Clo. Slou. AS42 62
Haynes Clo. Welw. G. C. BS8 5
Haynes La. SE19 CA50 77
Haynes Rd. Grav. DF48 81
Haynes Rd. Horn. CV32 51
Haynes Rd. Wem. BL36 55
Hayne St. EC1 BY39 56
Haynt Wk. SW20 BR52 85
Hayse Hill. Wind. AL44 61
Hays La. SE1 CA40 57
Haysleigh Gdns. SE20 CB51 87
Hays Ms. W1 BV40 56
Haystall Clo. Hayes BB37 53
Hays Wk. Sutt. BQ58 94
Hayter Rd. SW2 BX46 76
Hay Wk. E1 CA40 57
Hayward Clo. Bex. CS46 79
Bourne Rd.
Hayward Gdns. SW15 BQ46 75
Hayward Rd. N20 BT27 38
Haywards Clo. Brwd. DF25 122
Haywards Pl. EC1 BY38 56
Sekforde St.
Haywood Ct. Wal. Abb. CG20 22
Haywood Rise. Orp. CN56 97
Haywood Rd. Brom. CJ52 88
Haywoods Clo. Pnr. BD30 36
Hazel Ave. Guil. AR68 109
Hazel Ave. West Dr. AZ41 63
Hazel Bnk. Surb. BN54 85
Hazelbank Rd. SE6 CF48 77
Hazelbourne Rd. SW12 BV46 76
Hazelbrouck Gdns. Ilf. CM29 40
Hazelbury Av. Wat. BA19 17
Hazelbury Grn. N9 CA27 39
Hazelbury La. N9 CA27 39
Hazel Clo. N13 BZ27 39
Hazel Clo. Brent. BJ43 64
Hazel Clo. Horn. CU34 50
Hazel Clo. Mitch. BW52 86
Hazel Clo. Reig. BT71 121
Hazel Clo. Twick. BG47 74
Hazel Clo. Welw. G. C. BR5 5
Hazelcote. Wok. AW64 101
Hazel Cft. Pnr. BF29 36
Hazeldean Rd. NW10 BN36 55
Hazeldean Rd. Croy. BZ55 87
Hazeldell Rd. Hem. H. AV14 7
Hazeldene Ct. Ken. BZ61 105
Hazeldene Dr. Pnr. BD31 45
Hazeldene Gdns. Uxb. BA37 53
Hazeldene Rd. Ilf. CO34 50
Hazeldene Rd. Well. CP44 69
Hazeldon Rd. SE4 CD46 77
Hazel Dr. Erith. CU44 69
Hazel Dr. Wok. AV65 100
Hazelea Rd. Cher. AX54 83
Hazeleigh Gdns. Wdf. Grn. CK28 40
Hazel End Swan. CT53 89
Hazel Gdns. Edg. BM28 37
Hazel Gdns. Grays. DF41 71
Hazel Gr. Hat. BO14 10
Hazel Grn. Welw. G. C. BS7 5
Hazel Gro. SE26 CC49 77
Hazel Gro. Enf. CB25 30
Dimsdale Dr.
Hazel Gro. Orp. CL55 88
Hazel Gro. Rom. CQ31 50
Hazel Gro. Stai. AW50 73
Hazel Gro. Wem. BL37 55
Carlyon Rd.
Hazelhurst, Beck. CF51 87
Hazelhurst Rd. SW17 BT49 76
Hazel La. Rich. BL48 75
Hazell Clo. Egh. AQ50 72
Hazell Cres. Rom. CR29 41
Hazell Gr. Hat. BO14 10
Hazells Rd. Grav. DD49 81
Hazellville Rd. N19 BW33 47
Hazel Mead Epsom BP58 94
Hazelmere Cl. Felt. BA46 73
Hazelmere Gdns. Horn. CU32 50
Hazelmere Rd. NW6 BS37 56
Hazelmere Rd. Orp. CM52 88
Hazelmere Rd. St. Alb. BK12 9
Hazelmere Way Brom. CH53 88
Hazel Rise. Horn. CV32 51
Hazel Rd. NW10 BQ38 55
Hazel Rd. Berk. AR13 7
Hazel Rd. Dart. CV47 80
Hazel Rd. Erith. CU44 69
Hazel Rd. Reig. BT71 121
Hazel Rd. St. Alb. BF17 18
Hazel Rd. Wey. AV60 91
Hazel Rd. Wey. AW60 92
Hazel Tree Rd. Wat. BC22 26
Hazel Wk. Brom. CL53 88
Hazel Way E4 CD29 39
Hazel Way, Lthd. BG64 102
Hazel Way, Slou. AP36 52
Hazelwood. S. Le H. DK42 71
Hazelwood Clo. W5 BL41 65
Hazelwood Clo. Chesh. AO18 16
Hazelwood Ct. Surb. BL53 85
Hazelwood Cres. N13 BY28 38
Hazelwood Cres. W10 BR38 55
Hazelwood Dr. Pnr. BC30 35
Hazelwood Dr. St. Alb. BK12 9
Hazelwood Gdns. Brwd. DA25 33
Hazelwood Ho. SE8 CD42 67
Hazelwood La. N13 BY28 38
Hazelwood La. Couls. BU62 104
Hazelwood La. Couls. BU63 104
Hazelwood La. Wat. BA19 17
Hazelwood Rd. Enf. CA25 30
Hazelwood Rd. Mord. BS52 86
Hazelwood Rd. Oxt. CH69 115
Hazelwood Rd. Rick. BA25 26
Hazelwood Rd. Sev. CM59 97
Hazlebury Rd. SW6 BS44 66
Hazledene Rd. W4 BN43 65
Hazlemere Clo. Lthd. BJ63 102
Hazlemere Gdns. Wor. Pk. BP54 85
Hazlemere Rd. Ilf. CN34 49
Hazlemere Rd. Slou. AQ40 52
Hazlewell Rd. SW15 BP46 75
Hazlewood Loug. CJ25 31
Hazlewood Cres. W10 BR39 55
Hazlewood Gro. Sth. Croy. CB60 96
Hazlewood Rd. E17 CD32 48
Hazlitt Rd. W14 BR41 65
Hazon Way Epsom BN59 94
Headcorn Pl. Th. Hth. BX52 86
Headcorn Rd. N17 CA29 39
Tenterden Rd.
Headcorn Rd. Brom. CG49 78
Headcorn Rd. Th. Hth. BX52 86
Headfort Pl. SW1 BV41 66
Headingley Clo. Wal. Cr. CA16 21
Holbeck La.
Heading St. NW4 BQ31 46
Headington Rd. SW18 BT47 76
Headlam Rd. SW4 BW46 76
Headlam St. E1 CB38 57
Headley App. Ilf. CL32 49
Headley Av. Wall. BX56 95
Headley Chase, Brwd. DB28 42
Headley Clo. Epsom. BM57 94
Headley Common Rd. Epsom BN67 112
Headley Dr. Croy. CE57 96
Headley Dr. Ilf. CL32 49
Headley Heath App. Tad. BM69 120
Headley Rd. Dor. BK68 111
Headley Rd. Epsom. BM62 103
Headley Rd. Epsom. BN64 103
Headley Rd. Lthd. BK64 102
Headley St. SE15 CB44 67
Gordon Rd.
Headly Dri. Epsom. BP63 103
Head Mews, W10 BS39 56
Headstone Dr. Har. BG31 45
Headstone Gdns. Har. BG31 45
Headstone La. Har. BF31 45
Headstone Rd. Har. BG32 45
Head St. E1 CC39 57
Headway, The, Epsom BO58 94
Headworth Rd. SW17 BT48 76
Heald St. SE8 CE44 67
Heston St.
Healey Dri. Orp. CN56 97
Healey Rd. Wat. BB25 26
Healey St. NW1 BV36 56
Health Dr. Epp. CN21 31
Heards La. Brwd. DC23 122
Hearne Rd. W4 BM42 65
Hearnes Clo. Beac. AO28 34
Hearn Rise Nthlt. BD37 54
Hearn Rd. Rom. CT32 50
Hearn's Bldgs. SE17 BZ42 67
Elsted St.
Hearns Clo. Orp. CP52 89
Hearn's Meadow. Beac. AO28 34
Hearns Rise Orp. CP52 89
Hearns Rd. Orp. CP52 89
Hearn St. EC2 CA38 57
Curtain Rd.
Hearnville Rd. SW12 BV47 76
Heatham Pk. Twick. BH47 74
Heath Av. Bexh. CP43 69
Heath Av. St. Alb. BG12 9
Heathbourne Rd. Bush. BH26 36
Heathbrow, NW3 BT34 47
North End Way
Heath Clo. NW11 BS33 47
Heath Clo. W5 BL38 55
Heath Clo. Bans. BS60 95
Heath Clo. Hayes. BA43 63
Heath Clo. Hem. H. AX14 8
Heath Clo. Orp. CP54 89
Heath Clo. Pot. B. BS18 20
Heath Clo. Rom. CU31 50
Heath Clo. Stai. AX46 73
Heathclose Av. Dart. CU47 79
Heathclose Rd. Dart. CU47 79
Heathcote Av. Hat. BP11 10
Heathcote Av. Ilf. CK30 40
Heathcote Gro. E4 CF27 39
Heathcote Rd. Epsom BN60 94
Heathcote Rd. Twick. BJ46 74
Heathcote St. WC1 BX38 56
Heath Ct. W5 BL38 55
Heath Croft, NW11 BS33 47
Heathcroft, W5 BL38 55
Heathcroft Av. Sun. BB50 73
Heathcroft Grn. BB50 73
Heathdale Rd. Houns. BE45 64
Heathdene Rd. SW16 BX50 76
Heathdene Rd. Wall. BV57 95
Heathdown Rd. Wok. AU61 100
Heath Dr. NW3 BS35 47
Heath Dr. SW20 BQ52 85
Heath Dr. Pot. B. BS18 20
Heath Dr. Rom. CU30 41
Heath Dr. Sutt. BT58 95
Heath Dr. Tad. BP66 112
Heath Edge SE26 CB48 77
Heathend Rd. Bex. CT47 79
Heather Av. Rom. CS30 41
Heatherbank, SE9 CK44 68
Heatherbank Chis. CL51 88
Heather Clo. Brwd. DA25 33
Mounolid Way
Heather Clo. Hamptn. BE51 84
Heather Clo. Rom. CS30 41
Heather Clo. Tad. BR64 103
Heather Clo. Uxb. AY39 53
Heather Clo. Wey. AW58 92
Heather Clo. Wok. AR61 100
Heatherdale Clo. Kings. On T. BM50 75
Heatherdean Clo. Mitch. BT52 86
Heatherdene, Leath. BA66 110
Heatherden Grn. Iver AU37 52
Heather Dri. Rom. CS30 41
Heather Dr. Dart. CU47 79
Heather Gdns. NW11 BR32 46
Heather Gdns. Rom. CS30 41
Heather Gdns. Sutt. BS57 95
Heather Glen Rom. CS30 41
Heatherlands Sun. BC50 73
Heather La. West Dr. AY39 53
Heatherley Pl. E5 CB34 48
Heatherley St.
Heatherley St. E5 CB34 48
Heatherly Dr. Ilf. CK31 49
Heather Park Dr. Wem. BM36 55
Heather Pl. Esher BF56 93
Heather Rise Bush. BE23 27
Heather Rd. NW2 BO34 46
Heather Rd. SE12 CH48 78
Heather Rd. Welw. G. C. BQ8 5
Heatherset Gdns. SW16 BX50 76
Heatherside Dr. Vir. W. AQ53 82
Heatherside Rd. Epsom BN57 94
Heatherside Rd. Sid. CP48 79
Bexley La.
Heathers Land, Dor. BK73 119
Heatherton Ter. N3 BS30 38
Squires La.
Heathervale Rd. Wey. AW58 92
Heather Wk. Edg. BM28 37
Heather Walk, Watt. BB58 92
Heather Way, Hem. H. AX13 8
Heather Way. Pot. B. BR19 19
Heather Way Rom. CS30 41
Heather Way Stan. BH29 36
Heather Way Sth. Croy. CC58 96
Heath Farm La. St. Alb. BH12 9
Heathfield E4 CF27 39
Heathfield SW17 BU47 76
Burntwood Gra. Rd.
Heathfield, Chis. CM50 78
Heathfield. Cob. BF60 93
Heathfield Av. SW18 BT47 76
Heathfield Clo. Kes. CJ56 97
Heathfield Clo. Wok. AT62 100
Heathfield Ct. W4 BN42 65
Heathfield Ter.
Heathfield Ct. St. Alb. BH13 9
Avenue Rd.
Heathfield Dr. Red. BU73 121
Heathfield Gdns. NW11 BQ32 46
Heathfield Gdns. SW18 BT46 76
Heathfield Gdns. W4 BN42 65
Heathfield Gdns. Croy. BZ56 96
Heathfield La. Chis. CL50 78
Heathfield North Twick. BH47 74
Heathfield Pk. NW2 BQ36 55
Heathfield Rise, Ruis. BA33 44
Heathfield Rd. SW18 BT46 76
Heathfield Rd. W3 BM41 65
Heathfield Rd. Bexh. CQ45 69
Heathfield Rd. Brom. CG50 78
Heathfield Rd. Bush. BE24 27
Heathfield Rd. Croy. BZ56 96
Heathfield Rd. Kes. CJ56 97
Heathfield Rd. Sev. CT64 107
Heathfield Rd. Walt. BE56 93
Heathfield Rd. Wok. AT62 100
Heathfield South Twick. BH47 74
Heathfield Sq. SW18 BT47 76
Heathfield St. W11 BR40 55
Portland Rd.
Heathfield Ter. SE18 CN43 68
Heathfield Ter. W4 BN42 65
Heathfield Vale Sth. Croy. CC58 96
Heathfield Way, Ger. Cr. AR32 43
Heath Gdns. Twick. BH47 74
Heathgate, NW11 BS32 47
Heath Gro. SE20 CC50 77
Heath Hill, Dor. BJ71 119
Heath House La. Wok. AO64 100
Heath Hurst Rd. NW3 BT35 47
Keats Gro.
Heathland Rd. N16 CA33 48
Heathlands, NW3 BT34 47
Heathlands Clo. Sun. BC51 83
Heathlands Rise. Dart. CU46 79
Heath La. SE3 CF44 67
Heath La. Dart. CU47 79
Heath La. Dart. CV47 80
Heath La. Hem. H. AX14 8
Heathlee Rd. SE3 CG45 68
Heathley End, Chis. CM50 78
Heathmans Yd. SW6 BR44 65
Heathmead, SW19 BQ48 75
Heath Pk. Ct. Rom. CU32 50
Heath Pk. Rd. Rom. CU32 50
Heath Ri. Wok. AW65 101
Heath Ridge Grn. Cob. BF60 93
Heath Rise SW15 BQ46 75
Heath Rise Brom. CG53 88
Heath Rise, Vir. W. AR52 82
Heath Rd. SW8 BV45 66
Heath Rd. Bex. CS47 79
Heath Rd. Cat. BZ65 105
Heath Rd. Dart. CT46 79
Heath Rd. Grays. DF40 71
Heath Rd. Har. BG33 45
Heath Rd. Houns. BF45 64
Heath Rd. Lthd. BG59 93
Heath Rd. Pot. B. BS18 20
Heath Rd. Red. CB70 114
Heath Rd. Rom. CP33 50
Heath Rd. St. Alb. BH12 9
Heath Rd. Th. Hth. BZ52 87
Heath Rd. Twick. BH47 74
Heath Rd. Uxb. BA38 53
Heath Rd. Wat. BD26 36
Heath Rd. Wey. AZ56 92
Heath Rd. Wok. AS61 100
Heathrow Clo. West Dr. AW44 63
Heaths Clo. Enf. CA23 30
Heath Side, NW3 BT35 47
Heathside Esher BH55 84
Heath Side Houns. BE47 74
Heath Side Orp. CM54 88
Heathside, Wey. AZ56 92
Heathside Av. Bexh. CQ44 69
Heathside Clo. Esher BH55 84
Heathside Clo. Nthwd. BA28 35
Heathside Cres. Wok. AS62 100
Heathside Gdns. Wok. AT62 100
Heathside Park Rd. Wok. AS62 100
Heathside Rd. Nthwd. BA28 35
Heathside Rd. Wok. AS62 100
Heathstan Rd. W12 BP40 55
Heath St. NW3 BT34 47
Heath St. Bark. CM37 58
Heath St. Dart. CV47 80
Heath, The, W7 BH40 54
Lwr. Boston Rd.
Heath. The. Cat. BZ65 105
Heath, The, Rad. BJ20 18
Heathurst Rd. Sth. Croy. BZ58 96
Heath Vw. N2 BT31 47
Heath View. Leath. BB66 110
Heathview Av. Dart. CT47 79
Heath Vw. Clo. N2 BT31 47
Heathview Cres. Dart. CU47 79
Heathview Gdns. SW15 BQ47 75
Heath View Gdns. Grays. DE41 71
Heath View Rd. Grays. DE41 71
Heathview Rd. Th. Hth. BY52 86
Heath Vill. SE18 CN42 68
Heathville Rd. N19 BX33 47
Heathwall St. SW11 BU45 66
Heath Way, SE3 CH43 68
Heath Way Croy. CD55 87
Heathway, Dag. CQ34 50
Heath Way Erith CS44 69
Heathway, Iver AU37 52
Heath Way. Lthd. BB65 101
Heathway. Wdf. Grn. CJ28 40
Heath Way, West Dr. AX40 53
Heathway. Cat. BZ66 114
Heathwood Gdns. SE7 CK42 68
Heathwood Gdns. Swan. CS51 89
Heaton Av. Rom. CU29 41
Heaton Clo. Rom. CV29 42
Heaton Gra. Rd. Rom. CT30 41
Heaton Pl. E15 CF35 48
Heaton Rd. SE15 CB45 67
Heaton Rd. Mitch. BV50 76
Heaton Way. Rom. CV29 42
Heaverham Rd. Sev. CX62 108
Heaver Rd. SW11 BT45 66
Heavitree Rd. SE18 CM42 68
Hebdon Rd. SW17 BU48 76
Heber Rd. NW2 BQ35 46
Heber Rd. SE22 CA46 77
Hebron Rd. W6 BP41 65
Heckfield Pl. SW6 BS43 66
Fulham Rd.
Heckford St. E1 CC40 57
Hector St. SE18 CN42 68
Heddon Ct. Av. Barn. BU25 29
Heddon Rd. Barn. BU25 29
Heddon St. W1 BW40 56
Hedge Hill Enf. BY23 29
Hedge La. N13 BY27 38
Hedgeley, Ilf. CK31 49
Hedgeman's Rd. Dag. CP36 59
Hedgemans Way, Dag. CQ36 59
Hedge Place Rd. Green. CZ46 80
Hedgerley Gdns. Grnf. BG37 54
Hedgerley Hill. Slou. AO34 43
Hedgerley La. Slou. AP32 43
Hedge Row. Ger. Cr. AS29 34
Hedgerows, Saw. CQ6 6
Hedgers Rd. E9 CD36 57
Hedgeside, Berk. AT11 7
Hedgeside Rd. Nthwd. BA28 35
Hedge Wk. SE6 CE49 77
Lushington Rd.
Hedgeway, Guil. AQ71 118
Hedgewood Gdns. Ilf. CL31 49
Hedgley St. SE12 CG46 78
Hedingham Rd. Dag. CO35 50
Hedingham Rd. Horn. CX33 51
Hedley Av. Grays DB43 70
Hedley Rd. St. Alb. BJ13 9
Hedworth Av. Wal. Cr. CC20 21
Heene Rd. Enf. BZ23 30
Heigham Rd. E6 CJ36 58
Heighton Gdns. Croy. BY56 95
Heights Clo. Bans. BR61 103
Heights, The, SE7 CJ42 68
Heights, The, Beck. CF50 77
Heights, The, Nthlt. BE35 45
Heiron St. SE17 BY43 66
Helby Rd. SW4 BW46 76
Helder Gro. SE12 CG47 78
Helder St. Sth. Croy. BZ57 96
Heldman Clo. Islw. BG45 64
Helena Clo. Barn. BT22 29
Helena Clo. Wall. BX57 95
Helena Ct. W5 BK39 54
Eaton Rise
Helena Rd. E13 CG37 58
Helena Rd. E17 CE32 48
Helena Rd. NW10 BP35 46
Helena Rd. W5 BK39 54
Helena Rd. Wind. AO44 61
Helena St. WC1 BY38 56
Fernsbury St.
Helen Av. Felt. BC47 73
Helen Clo. E. Mol. BF52 84
Helen Rd. Horn. CV31 51
Helenslea Av. NW11 BR33 46
Helen's Pl. E2 CC38 57
Roman Rd.
Helen St. SE18 CL42 68
Helford Way, Upmin. CY33 51
Helgiford Gdns. Sun. BB50 73
Helions Rd. Harl. CL11 13
Helix Gdns. SW2 BX46 76
Helix Rd. SW2 BX46 76
Helling St. E1 CB40 57
Hermitage Wall
Helmet Row, EC1 BZ38 57
Helmsdale Clo. Rom. CT29 41
Helmsdale Rd. SW16 BW51 86
Helmsdale Rd. Rom. CT29 41
Helmsley St. E8 CB36 57
Helstone Clo. Pnr. BE29 36

Helston Pl. Wat. BB19 17
Helvetia St. SE6 CD48 77
Hemans St. SW8 BX43 66
Wandsworth Rd.
Hemberton Rd. SW9 BX45 66
Hemel Hempstead Rd. Hem. H. BB14 8
Hemel Hempstead Rd. Wat. BA21 26
Hemingford Rd. N1 BX37 56
Hemingford Rd. Sutt. BQ56 94
Hemingford Rd. Wat. BB21 26
Heming Rd. Edg. BM29 37
Hemington Av. N11 BU28 38
Hemlock Rd. W12 BO40 55
Hemmen La. Hayes BB39 53
Hemming Clo. Hamptn. BF51 84
Hemming St. E1 CB38 57
Hemming Way, Wat. BC21 26
Hemnall St. Epp. CN19 22
Hemp Row, SE17 BZ42 67
Chatham St.
Hempshaw Av. Bans. BU61 104
Hempson Ave. Slou. AR41 62
Hempstead Clo. Buck. H. CH27 40
Hempstead Rd. E17 CF31 48
Hempstead Rd. Berk. AT12 7
Hempstead Rd. Hem. H. AT16 16
Hempstead Rd. Kings L. AY16 17
Hempstead Rd. Kings L. AZ19 17
Hemsby Rd. Chess. BL57 94
Hemstal Rd. NW6 BS36 56
Hemstead Rd. St. Alb. BE14 9
Hemsted Rd. Erith CT43 69
Hemswell Dr. NW9 BO30 37
Hemsworth St. N1 CA37 57
Hemus Pl. SW3 BU42 66
Chelsea Manor St.
Hemwood Rd. Wind. AL45 61
Henbane Path. Rom. CV29 42
Henbrain Pth. Rom. CV29 42
Henbury Way Wat. BD27 36
Hen & Chickens Ct. EC4 BY39 56
Fleet St.
Henchley Clo. Guil. AU69 118
Henchman St. W12 BO39 55
Hencroft St. Slou. AP41 62
Hendale Av. NW4 BP31 46
Henderson Clo. NW10 BN36 55
Henderson Clo. St. Alb. BG11 9
Henderson Dr. Dart. CW45 70
Henderson Pl. Wat. BB17 17
Henderson Rd. E7 CJ36 58
Henderson Rd. N9 CB26 39
Henderson Rd. SW18 BU47 76
Henderson Rd. Croy. BZ53 87
Henderson Rd. West. CJ59 97
Hendham Rd. SW17 BU48 76
Hendon Av. N3 BR30 37
Hendon Clo. Islw. BJ45 64
Hendon Clo. Rom. CS29 41
Hendon La. N3 BR31 46
Hendon Pk. Mans. NW4 BQ32 46
Hendon Pk. Row, NW11 BR32 46
Hendon Rd. N9 CB27 39
Hendons Way. Maid. AG42 61
Hendon Way, Stai. AX46 73
Hendon Wood La. NW7 BO26 37
Hendre Rd. SE1 CA42 67
Hendrick Av. SW12 BU47 76
Hendricks Ter. N17 CB31 48
Heneage Cres. Croy. CF58 96
Heneage La. EC3 CA39 57
Bevis Marks
Heneage St. E1 CA39 57
Henfield Clo. Bex. CR46 79
Henfield Rd. SW19 BR51 85
Hengeld Gdns. Mitch. BT52 86
Hengist Rd. SE12 CH47 78
Hengist Rd. Erith. CR43 69
Hengist Way Brom. CF52 87
Hengrave Rd. SE23 CC46 77
Hengrove Ct. Bex. CQ47 79
Hurst Rd.
Hen Grove Cres. Ashf. AX48 73
Henhurst Rd. Grav. DJ50 81
Henley Av. Sutt. BR55 85
Henley Clo. SW11 CA44 67
Henley Clo. Grnf. BG37 54
Henley Clo. Islw. BH44 64
Henley Ct. N14 BW26 38
Henley Dr. Kings. On T. BO50 75
Henley Gdns. Pnr. BC31 44
Henley Gdns. Rom. CQ32 50
Henley Gate, Guil. AQ71 118
Henley Rd. E16 CK41 68
Henley Rd. N18 CA28 39
Henley Rd. NW10 BQ37 55
Henley Rd. Ilf. CM35 49
Henley St. SW11 BV44 66
Henley Way Felt. BD49 74
Hennel Clo. SE23 CC48 77
Henniker Gdns. E6 CJ38 58
Henniker Ms. SW3 BT44 66
Callow St.
Henniker Rd. E15 CF35 48
Henningham Rd. N17 BZ30 39
Henning St. SW11 BU44 66
Shuttleworth Rd.
Henrietta Ms. WC1 BX38 56
Brunswick Sq.
Henrietta Pl. W1 BV40 56
Henrietta St. WC2 BX40 56
Henriques St. E1 CB39 57
Henry Darlot Dr. NW7 BQ28 37
Henry Dickens Ct. W11 BQ40 55
Henry Jackson Rd. SW15 BQ45 65
Henry Prince Est. SW18 BS47 76
Henry Rd. E6 CK37 58
Henry Rd. N4 BY33 47
Henry Rd. Barn. BT25 29
Henry Rd. Slou. AO41 61
Henry's Av. Wdf. Grn. CG28 40
Henryson Rd. SE4 CD46 77
Henry's Ter. Brwd. DA20 24
Henry St. Brom. CH51 88
Henry St. Hem. H. AX15 8
Henrys Wk. Ilf. CM29 40
Henry Wells Sq. Hem. H. AY11 8
Hensford Gdns. SE26 CB48 77
Wells Park Rd.
Henshall St. N1 BZ36 57
Balls Pond Rd.
Henshawe Rd. Dag. CP34 50
Henshaw St. SE17 BZ42 67
Henslowe Rd. SE22 CB46 77
Henslow Way. Wok. AU60 91
Henson Av. NW2 BQ35 46
Henson Cl. Orp. CL55 88
Henson Path, Harrow. BK31 45
Henson Pl. Nthlt. BD37 54
Henstridge Pl. NW8 BU37 56
Hensworth Rd. Ashf. AX49 73
Henty Clo. SW11 BU43 66
Henty Wk. SW15 BP46 75
Sunnymead Rd.
Henville Rd. Brom. CH51 88
Henwick Rd. SE9 CJ45 68
Henwood Rd. SE16 CC41 67
Henwood Side Chig. CK29 40
Henwood Side Wdf. Grn. CK29 40
Hepburn Gdns. W. Wick. CG54 88
Hepple Clo. Islw. BJ44 64
Hepplestone Clo. SW15 BP46 75
Dover Pk. Dr.
Hepscott Rd. E9 CE36 57
Hepwell Rd. Grav. DG46 81
Hepworth Gdns. Bark. CQ35 50
Hepworth Rd. SW16 BX50 76
Hepworth Way, Walt. BB54 83
Heracles Clo. Wall. BX57 95
Herald St. E2 CB38 57
Birkbeck St.
Herbal Hill, EC1 BY38 56
Ray St.
Herbert Cres. SW1 BU41 66
Pavilion Rd.
Herbert Cres. Wok. AP62 100
Herbert Gdns. NW10 BP37 55
Herbert Gdns. W4 BM43 65
Magnolia Rd.
Herbert Gdns. Rom. CP33 50
Herbert Rd. E12 CK35 49
Herbert Rd. E17 CD33 48
Herbert Rd. N11 BX29 38
Herbert Rd. N15 CA32 48
Herbert Rd. NW9 BP32 46
Herbert Rd. SE18 CL43 68
Herbert Rd. SW19 BR50 75
Herbert Rd. Bexh. CQ44 69
Herbert Rd. Brom. CJ53 88
Herbert Rd. Horn. CW33 51
Herbert Rd. Ilf. CN34 49
Herbert Rd. Kings. On T. BL52 85
Herbert Rd. Sthl. BE40 54
Herbert Rd. Swan. CU50 79
Herbert Rd. Swans. DC46 81
Herbert St. E13 CH37 58
Herbert St. NW5 BV35 47
Herbert St. Hem. H. AX13 8
Herbert St. Wat. BD24 27
Herbrand St. WC1 BX38 56
Hercies Rd. Uxb. AY36 53
Hercules Pl. N7 BX34 47
Hercules Rd. SE1 BX41 66
Hercules St. N7 BX34 47
Hereford Av. Barn. BU26 38
Hereford Clo. Epsom BN60 94
Hereford Clo. Guil. AP69 118
Hereford Clo. Stai. AW51 83
Hereford Gdns. Ilf. CK33 49
Hereford Gdns. Pnr. BE32 45
Hereford Gdns. Twick. BG47 74
Hereford Ms. W2 BS39 56
Hereford Rd.
Hereford Pl. SE14 CD43 67
Hereford Retreat, SE15 CB43 67
Bird-in-bush Rd.
Hereford Rd. E11 CH32 49
Hereford Rd. W2 BS39 56
Hereford Rd. W3 BM40 55
Hereford Rd. W5 BK41 64
Hereford Rd. Felt. BD47 74
Hereford Sq. SW7 BT42 66
Hereford St. E2 CB38 57
Hereford Way Chess. BK56 93
Herent Dr. Ilf. CK31 49
Hereward Av. Pur. BY59 95
Hereward Clo. Wal. Abb. CF19 21
Hereward Gdns. N13 BY28 38
Hereward Rd. SW17 BU49 76
Herga Ct. Har. BH34 45
Herga Ct. Wat. BC23 26
Herga Rd. Har. BH31 45
Herington Gro. Brwd. DD26 122
Heriot Av. E4 CD27 39
Heriot Pl. NW5 BV35 47
Mansfield Rd.
Heriot Rd. NW4 BQ32 46
Heriot Rd. Cher. AW54 83
Heriots Clo. Stan. BJ28 36
Heritage Clo. Uxb. AX38 53
Herkomer Clo. Bush. BF25 27
Herkomer Rd. Bush. BF25 27
Herlwyn Av. Ruis. BB34 44
Herlwyn Gdns. SW17 BU49 76
Hermes St. N1 BY37 56
Hermes Wk. Nthlt. BF37 54
Hermes Way Wall. BW57 95
Hermiston Av. N8 BX32 47
Hermitage Clo. E18 CG31 49
Hermitage Clo. Enf. BY23 29
Hermitage Clo. Esher BJ57 93
Hermitage Clo. Pot. B. BT20 20
Hermitage Clo. Shep. AZ52 83
Hermitage Ct. E18 CH31 49
Hermitage Gdns. NW3 BS34 47
Hermitage Gdns. SE19 BZ50 77
Hermitage La. NW3 BS34 47
Hermitage La. SE25 CB53 87
Hermitage La. SW16 BX50 76
Hermitage Rd. SE19 BZ50 77
Hermitage Rd. Ken. BZ61 105
Hermitage Rd. Wok. AO63 100
Hermitage, The, SE23 CC47 77
Hermitage, The, SW13 BO44 65
Hermitage, The, Rich. BL46 75
Hermitage, The Uxb. AX36 53
Hermitage Wk. E18 CG31 49
Hermitage Wall, E1 CB40 57
Hermitage Way Stan. BJ30 36
Hermitage Woods Cres. Wok. AO63 100
Hermit La. N18 BZ28 39
Hermit Rd. E16 CG39 58
Hermit St. EC1 BY38 56
Rawstorne St.
Hermon Gro. Hayes BC40 53
Herndon Rd. SW18 BT46 76
Herne Clo. NW10 BN35 46
Herne Hill, SE24 BZ46 77
Herne Hill Rd. SE24 BZ45 67
Herne Ms. N18 CB28 39
Lyndhurst Rd.
Herne Pl. SE24 BY46 76
Herne Rd. Bush. BF25 27
Herne Rd. Surb. BK55 84
Herne-Shaw, Hat. BO13 10
Herns La. Welw. G. C. BS7 5
Herns Way. Welw. G. C. BS7 5
Heron Clo. E17 CD30 30
Heron Clo. Buck. H. CH26 40
Heron Clo. Guil. AQ69 118
Heron Clo. Rick. AX27 35
Heron Clo. Uxb. AX36 53
Heron Ct. Brom. CJ52 88
Heron Ct. Rich. BK46 74
Bridge St.
Heron Cres. Sid. CN48 78
Herondale Sth. Croy. CC58 96
Heron Dale, Wey. AX56 92
Herondale Av. SW18 BT47 76
Heronfield, Pot. B. BT18 20
Heron Flight Av. Rain. CU36 59
Herongate Rd. E12 CJ34 49
Herongate Rd. Wal. Cr. CD17 21
Heron Hill, Belv. CQ42 69
Heron Mews Ilf. CL34 49
Heron Rd. NW10 BO36 55
Heron Rd. SE24 BZ45 67
Heron Rd. Croy. CA54 87
Heron Rd. Twick. BJ45 64
Heronry, The, Walt. BC57 92
Heronsford, W13 BK39 54
Heronsgate, Edg. BM28 37
Heronsgate Rick. AT25 25
Herons Lane. Ong. CY14 15
Heronslea Dr. Stan. BL28 37
Heronslea Wat. BD21 27
Herons Rise Barn. BU24 29
Herons, The, E11 CG32 49
Herons Way, St. Alb. BJ15 9
Herons Wood, Harl. CL10 6
Heronswood Wal. Abb. CG20 22
Roundhills
Herons Wood Rd. Welw. G. C. BS8 5
Heronway, Brwd. DD26 122
Heron Way. Hat. BP13 10
Heron Way, Upmin. CZ33 51
Heronway, Wdf. Grn. CJ28 40
Herrick Rd. N5 BZ34 48
Herrick St. SW1 BW42 66
Herringham Rd. SE7 CJ41 68
Herring St. SE5 CA43 67
Herrongate Clo. Enf. CA23 30
Hersant Clo. NW10 BP37 55
Herschell Rd. SE23 CC47 77
Hersham Clo. SW15 BP47 75
Hersham Rd. Walt. BC55 83
Hersham Trd. Est. Walt. BE55 84
Hers St. Slou. AP41 62
Hertford Av. SW14 BN46 75
Hertford Av. Ilf. CN32 49
Hertford Clo. Barn. BT24 29
Hertford Clo. Hem. H. AY13 8
Hertford Pl. W1 BW38 56
Whitfield St.
Hertford Rd. N1 CA37 57
Hertford Rd. N2 BU31 47
Hertford Rd. Bark. CL36 58
Hertford Rd. Barn. BT24 29
Hertford Rd. Enf. CC24 30
Hertford Rd. Epsom. BM57 94
Hertford Rd. Hat. BQ11 10
Hertford Rd. Hodd. CC10 12
Hertford Rd. Welw. BU6 5
Hertford Rd. Welw. G. C. BR5 5
Hertford Sq. Mitch. BX52 86
Hertford St. W1 BV40 56
Hertford Way Mitch. BX52 86
Hertslet Rd. N7 BX34 47
Hervey Clo. N3 BS30 38
Hervey Pk. Rd. E17 CD31 48
Hervey Rd. SE3 CH44 68
Hervey Way N3 BS30 38
Hervey Clo.
Hesa Rd. Hayes BC39 53
Heseltine Rd. SE26 CD49 77
Hesiers Hill. Warl. CG62 106
Hesiers Rd. Warl. CG61 106
Hesketh Ave. Dart. CX47 80
Hesketh Pl. W11 BR40 55
Hesketh Rd. E7 CH34 49
Heslop Rd. SW12 BU47 76
Hesper Ms. SW5 BS42 66
Hesperus Cres. E14 CE42 67
Hessell St. E1 CB39 57
Hessel Rd. W13 BJ41 64
Hesselyn Dr. Rain. CU36 59
Hessle Gro. Epsom BO59 94
Hestercombe Av. SW6 BR44 65
Hester Rd. N18 CB28 39
Hester Rd. SW11 BU43 66
Heston Av. Houns. BE43 64
Heston Grange La. Houns. BE43 64
Heston Ho. SE8 CD44 67
Heston Rd. Houns. BF43 64
Heston Rd. Red. BU72 121
Heston St. SE8 CD44 67
Heston Wk. Red. BU72 121
Hetchleys, Hem. H. AW12 8
Hetherington Rd. SW4 BX45 66
Hetherington Rd. Shep. BA51 83
Hetley Gdns. SE19 CA50 77
Fox Hill
Hetley Rd. W12 BP40 55
Hetton St. W6 BQ42 65
Glenthorne Rd.
Hevelius Clo. SE10 CG42 68
Hever Ave. Sev. CZ57 99
Hever Ct. Rd. Grav. DH50 81
Hever Croft, SE9 CL49 78
Hever Gdns. Brom. CL51 88
Heverham Rd. SE18 CN42 68
Hever Rd. Sev. CZ57 99
Heversham Rd. Bexh. CR44 69
Hewens Rd. Uxb. BA38 53
Hewer St. W10 BQ39 55
Hewett Clo. Stan. BJ28 36
Stanmore Hill
Hewett Pl. Swan. CS52 89
Hewett Rd. Dag. CP35 50
Hewish Rd. N18 CA28 39
Hewitt Av. N22 BY30 38
Hewitt Rd. N8 BY32 47
Hewitts Rd. Orp. CQ57 98
Hewlett Rd. E3 CD37 57
Hexagon, The, N6 BU33 47
Hexal Rd. SE6 CG48 78
Hexham Gdns. Islw. BJ43 64
Hexham Rd. SE27 BZ48 77
Hexham Rd. Barn. BS24 29
Hexham Rd. Mord. BS54 86
Hextalls La. Red. BZ67 114
Heybourne Rd. N17 CB29 39
Heybridge Av. SW16 BX50 76
Heybridge Dr. Ilf. CM31 49
Heydons Clo. St. Alb. BG12 9
Heyford Av. SW8 BX43 66
Heyford Av. SW20 BR52 85
Heyford Rd. Mitch. BU51 86
Heyford Rd. Rad. BJ21 27
Heygate St. SE17 BZ42 67
Heynes Rd. Dag. CP35 50
Heysham Dr. Wat. BD28 36
Heysham Rd. N15 BZ32 48
Heythorp St. SW18 BR47 75
Heyworth Rd. E5 CB35 48
Heyworth Rd. E15 CG35 49
Hibbert Av. Wat. BD22 27
Hibbert Rd. E17 CD33 48
Hibbert Rd. Har. BH30 36
Hibbert Rd. Maid. AG41 61
Hibberts Alley Wind. AO44 61
Peascod St.
Hibbert St. SW11 BT45 66
Hibernia Gdns. Houns. BF45 64
Hibernia Rd. Houns. BF45 64
Hichisson Rd. SE15 CC46 77
Hickling Rd. Ilf. CL35 49
Hickman Rd. Rom. CP33 50
Hickmans Clo Gdse. CC69 114
Hicks Av. Grnf. BG37 54
Hicks St. SE8 CD42 67
Hidalgo Ct. Hem. H. AY12 8
Hide Pl. SW1 BW42 66
Hide Rd. Har. BG31 45
Hides, The, Harl. CM10 6
Higgs Row SW15 BQ45 65
Felsham Rd.
High Acres, Wat. BA19 17
Higham Av. Hem. H. AX14 8
Higham Hill Rd. E17 CD30 39
Higham La. Ton. DC70 117
Higham Pl. E17 CD31 48
Higham Rd. E17 CD30 39
Higham Rd. N17 BZ31 48
Higham Rd. Wdf. Grn. CH29 40
Highams Hill. War. CH59 97
Higham Station Av. E4 CE29 39
Highams, The, Park, Wdf. Grn. CG28 40
Higham View Epp. CR16 23
Highash Clo. S. Le H. DK42 71
Highbanks Clo. Well. CO43 69
Highbanks Rd. Hem. H. AZ16 17
High Banks Rd. Pnr. BF29 36
Highbarn Rd. Lthd. BD68 111
Highbarrow Rd. Croy. CA54 87
High Beech Sth. Croy. CA57 96
High Beeches. Ger. Cr. AR33 43
High Beeches Orp. CO57 98
High Beeches, Sid. CQ49 79
High Beech Rd. Loug. CK24 31
High Bois La. Amer. AO21 25
High Bridge, SE10 CF42 67
Highbridge Rd. Bark. CL37 58
High Bri. St. Wal. Abb. CE20 21
Highbrook Rd. SE3 CJ45 68
Highbroom Cres. W. Wick. CE54 87
Highbury Av. Hodd. CE11 12
Highbury Av. Th. Hth. BY51 86
Highbury Clo. W. Wick. CE55 87
Highbury Cres. N5 BY35 47
Highbury Gdns. Ilf. CN34 49
Highbury Gra. N5 BY35 47
Highbury Gro. N5 BY36 56
Highbury Gro. N. Mal. BN52 85
Highbury Hill, N5 BY34 47
Highbury Mews N5 BY35 47
Ronalds Rd.
Highbury New Pk. N5 BZ34 48
Highbury Pk. N5 BY35 47
Highbury Pl. N5 BY36 56
Highbury Quadrant, N5 BY34 47
Highbury Quadrant Est. N5 BZ34 48
Highbury Rd. SW19 BR49 75
Highbury Station Rd. N1 BY36 56
Highbury Ter. N5 BY35 47
High Canons Borwd. BN22 28
Highclere Clo. Ken. BZ57 96
Highclere Ct. St. Alb. BH13 9
Avenue Rd.
Highclere Dr. Hem. H. AZ15 8
Highclere Gdns. Wok. AO62 100
Highclere Rd. N. Mal. BN52 85
Highclere Rd. Wok. AO62 100
Highclere St. SE26 CD49 77
Highcliffe Dr. SW15 BO46 75
Highcliffe Gdns. Ilf. CK32 49
High Clo. Rick. AX25 26
Highcombe, SE7 CH43 68
Highcombe Clo. SE9 CJ47 78
High Ct. Wdf. Grn. CH29 40
Higham Rd.
Highcroft, NW9 BO32 46
Highcroft Av. Wem. BL36 55
Highcroft Gdns. NW11 BR32 46
Highcroft Rd. N19 BX33 47
Highcroft Rd. Hem. H. AW16 17
High Cross Rd. N17 CA31 48
Highcross Rd. Grav. DB49 80
High Cross Rd. Sev. DA66 117
Highcross Way. SW15 BP47 75
Highdaun Dr. SW16 BX52 86
High Dells. Hat. BO13 10
Highdown Wor. Pk. BO55 85
Highdown Rd. SW15 BP46 75
High Dri. Lthd BG60 93
High Dr. Cat. CE64 105
High Dr. Lthd. BG60 93
High Dr. N. Mal. BN51 85
High Elms Chig. CN28 40
High Elms, Upmin. CZ33 51
High Elms, Wdf. Grn. CH28 40
High Elms Clo. Nthwd. BA29 35
Highelms La. Wat. BC18 17
Highelms La. Wat. BD19 18
High Elms Rd. Orp. CL59 97
Higher Dr. Bans. BQ59 94
Higher Dr. Pur. BY60 95
Higher Grn. Epsom BP60 94
Higher Tubs Bush. BG26 36
High Field Bans. BU62 104
Highfield. Harl. CO11 14
Highfield Rom. CS29 41
High Fld. Wind. AM45
Highfield Av. NW9 BN32 46
Highfield Av. NW11 BQ33 46
Highfield Av. Erith CR43 69
Highfield Av. Grnf. BH35 45
Highfield Av. Orp. CN56 97
Highfield Av. Pnr. BE32 45
Highfield Av. Wem. BL34 46
Highfield Clo. NW9 BN32 46
Highfield Clo. Amer. AO22 25
Highfield Clo. Nthwd. BB30 35
Highfield Clo. Rom. CS29 41
Highfield Clo. Surb. BK54 84
Highfield Clo. Wey. AW60 92
Highfield Ct. N14 BW25 29
Highfield Cres. Horn. CW34 51
Highfield Cres. Nthwd. BB30 35
Highfield Dr. Brom. CG52 88
Highfield Dr. Brox. CD14 12
Highfield Dr. Epsom BO57 94
Highfield Dr. Uxb. AY34 44
Highfield Dr. Uxb. AY35 44
Highfield Dr. W. Wick. CE55 87
Highfield Gdns. NW11 BR32 46
Highfield Gdns. Grays. DE41 71
Highfield Grn. Epp. CN19 22
Highfield Hill SE19 BZ50 77
Highfield La. Hem. H. AY12 8
Highfield La. Hem. H. AY13 8
Highfield Pl. Epp. CN19 22
Highfield Rd. N21 BY26 38
Highfield Rd. NW11 BR32 46
Highfield Rd. W3 BM39 55
Highfield Rd. Berk. AR13 7
Highfield Rd. Bexh. CQ46 79
Highfield Rd. Brom. CK52 88
Highfield Rd. Bush. BE25 27
Highfield Rd. Cat. CB64 105
Highfield Rd. Cher. AW54 83
Highfield Rd. Chis. CN52 88
Highfield Rd. Dart. CV47 80
Highfield Rd. Felt. BC47 73
Highfield Rd. Horn. CW34 51
Highfield Rd. Islw. BH44 64
Highfield Rd. Nthwd. BB30 35
Highfield Rd. Pur. BX58 95
Highfield Rd. Rom. CS29 41
Highfield Rd. St. Alb. BJ10 9
Highfield Rd. Sun. BB53 83
Highfield Rd. Surb. BN54 85
Highfield Rd. Sutt. BU56 95
Highfield Rd. Wal. Cr. CA16 21
Highfield Rd. Walt. BC54 83
Highfield Rd. Wdf. Grn. CK29 40
Highfield Rd. West. CJ62 106
Highfield Rd. Wey. AW60 92
Highfield Rd. S. Dart. CV47 80
Highfields, Ash. BK63 102
Highfields, Leath. BB67 110
Highfields, Pot. B. BX17 20
Highfield Way. Horn. CW34 51
Highfield Way, Pot. B. BS19 20
Highfield Way, Rick. AW25 26
High Firs Swan. CT52 89
High Foleys Esher BJ57 93

High Gables Loug. CJ25 31
Highgate Av. N6 BV32 47
Highgate High St. N6 BV33 47
Highgate Hill, N19 BV33 47
Highgate La. N6 BV33 47
Highgate Rd. NW5 BV34 47
Highgate West Hill, N6 BV33 47
High Grove, SE18 CM43 68
High Gro. Welw. G. C. BQ7 5
Highgrove Rd. Dag. CP35 50
Highgrove Way Ruis. BC33 44
High Hill Est. E5 CB33 48
High Hill Rd. Warl. CF60 96
High Holborn, WC1 BX39 56
High House La. Til. DH41 71
Highland Av. W7 BH39 54
Highland Av. Brwd. DB26 42
Highland Av. Dag. CS34 50
Highland Av. Loug. CK25 31
Highland Cotts. Wall. BV56 95
Highland Croft, Beck. CE50 77
Highland Dr. Bush. BG26 36
Highland Dr. Hem. H. AZ13 8
Highland Rd. SE19 CA50 77
Highland Rd. Amer. AO23 25
Highland Rd. Bexh. CR46 79
Highland Rd. Brom. CG51 88
Highland Rd. Nthwd. BB31 44
Highland Rd. Nthwd. BC31 44
Highland Rd. Pur. BY60 95
Highland Rd. Sev. CR59 98
Highland Rd. Wal. Abb. CG14 13
Highlands. Wat. BD27 36
Highlands, Wok. AS64 100
Highlands Av. W3 BN40 55
Highlands Av. Lthd. BK64 102
Highlands. Clo. Ger. Cr. AS29 34
Highlands Clo. Houns. BF44 64
Highlands Clo. Lthd. BJ64 102
Highlands End. Ger. Cr. AS29 34
Highlands Gdns. Ilf. CK33 49
Highlands Hat. BQ11 10
Highlands Heath, SW15 BQ47 75
Bristol Gdns.
Highlands Hill. Swan. CU51 89
Highlands La. Ger. Cr. AS29 34
Highlands Pk. Lthd. BK65 102
Highlands Rd. Barn. BS25 29
Highlands Rd. Beac. AO28 34
Highlands Rd. Lthd. BJ64 102
Highlands Rd. Orp. CO54 89
Highlands Rd. Reig. BT70 121
Highlands, The, Edg. BM30 37
Highlands, The, Leath. BB66 110
Highlands, The, Pot. B. BT18 20
Highlands. The. Rick. AW26 35
High La. W7 BG39 54
High La. Warl. CD62 105
High Laver La. Ong. CU12 14
Highlea Clo. NW9 BO30 37
High Level Dr. SE26 CB49 77
High Lever Rd. W10 BQ39 55
Highmead, SE18 CN43 68
Highmead Chig. CL27 40
High Mead Har. BH32 45
High Mead W. Wick. CF55 87
Highmead Cres. Wem. BL36 55
Highmeadow Clo. Pnr. BC31 44
High Meadow Cres. NW9 BN32 46
High Meadows Chig. CM28 40
High Moor. Amer. AO23 25
Highmore Rd. SE3 CG43 68
High Oaks Enf. BX22 29
High Oaks, St. Alb. BG11 9
High Oaks Rd. Welw. G. C. BP7 5
High Ongar Rd. Ong. CX17 24
Highover Park. Amer. AO23 25
High Park Av. Leath. BB66 110
High Pk. Av. Rich. BM44 65
High Pk. Rd. Rich. BM44 65
High Pastures, Bish. CS7 6
High Path, SW19 BS51 86
High Path Rd. Guil. AU70 118
High Pine Clo. Wey. BA56 92
High Point, SE9 CL48 78
High Point, Wey. AZ56 92
High Ridge, N10 BV30 38
High Ridge, Pot. B. BX17 20
High Ridge Clo. Epsom. BO60 94
Highridge La. Bet. BM73 120
Highridge Pla. Enf. BY23 29
The Ridgeway
High Ridge Rd. Hem. H. AX16 17
High Rd. N11 BV28 38
High Rd. N22 BX29 38
High Rd. NW10 BO36 55
High Rd. NW10 BP36 55
High Rd. Brox. CD15 12
High Rd. Bush. BG26 36
High Rd. Couls. BU65 104
High Rd. E. Finchley N2 BT30 38
High Rd. Epp. CO15 14
High Rd. Epp. CO17 23
High Rd Epp. CR16 23
High Rd. Epp. CS15 14
High Rd. Grays. DC40 71
High Rd. Har. Weald BH29 36
High Rd. Hat. BU12 11
High Rd. Ilf. CL34 49
High Rd. N. Finchley N12 BT28 38
High Rd. Reig. BT67 113
High Rd. Rom. CO33 50
High Rd. Uxb. AX39 53
High Rd. Uxb. AZ34 44
High Rd. Wat. BB20 17
High Rd. Wat. BB21 26
High Rd. Wem. BK35 45
High Rd. Wey. AY59 92
High Rd. Whet. BT26 38
High Road Willesden Grn. NW10 BO36 55
High Rd. Wilmington CV48 80
High St. Ms. SW19 BR49 75
Courthope Rd.
High St. Southgate N14 BW26 38
Highshore Rd. SE15 CA44 67
High Silver Loug. CJ24 31
Highstead Cres. Erith CT43 69
Highstone, E11 CG32 49
Highstone Av. E11 CH32 49
High St. E11 CH32 49
High St. E13 CH37 58
High St. E15 CF37 57
High St. E17 CD32 48
High St. N8 BX31 47
High St. NW7 BP28 37
High St. NW10 BO37 55
High St. SE20 CB50 77
High St. SW6 BR45 65
High St. SW19 BQ49 75
High St. W3 BM40 55
High St. W5 BK40 54
High St. Bans. BS61 104
High St. Barkingside, CM31 49
High St. Barn. BR24 28
High St. Beck. CE51 87
High St. Bedmond. Wat. BB17 17
High St. Berk. AP11 7
High St. Bex. CR47 79
High St. Brent. BK43 64
High St. Brom CG51 88
High St. Brwd. DB27 42
High St. Bush. BE25 27
High St. Cars. BU56 95
High St. Cheam BR57 94
High St. Chis. CL50 78
High St. Ch. St. G. AR27 34
High St. Claygate BH57 93
High St. Cob. BC60 92
High St. Cob. BC61 101
High St. Col. Heath. BN14 10
High St. Colliers Wood, SW19 BT50 76
High St. Cranford BC43 63
High St. Croy. BZ55 87
High St. Dart. CW46 80
High St. Dart. DA48 80
High St. Dor. BJ71 119
High St. Edg. BM29 37
High St. Egh. AS49 72
High St. Elstree BK25 27
High St. E. Mol. BF52 84
High St. Epp. CN19 22
High St. Epsom BN60 94
High St. Erith CT42 69
High St. Esher BF56 93
High St. Ewell BO58 94
High St. Farn. CW53 90
High St. Farnborough CL56 97
High St. Felt. BC48 73
High St. Ger. Cr. AS30 34
High St. Grav. DD46 81
High St. Grav. DG46 81
High St. Grays DD43 71
High St. Green. DA45 70
High St. Green St. Green CN57 97
High St. Guil. AR71 118
High St. Har. BH33 45
High St. Harl. CH10 13
High St. Harl. CP9 6
High St. Hem. H. AT17 16
High St. Hem. H. AX12 8
High St. Hmptn. BF51 84
High St. Hmptn. BG51 84
High St. Hodd. CE13 12
High St. Horn. CV33 51
High St. Houns. BF45 64
High St. Iver AV39 52
High St. Kings L. AZ18 17
High St. Kings. On T. BK51 84
High St. Kings-on-t. BK52 84
High St. Lthd. BF66 111
High St. Lthd. BJ64 102
High St. Maid. AH41 61
High St. Merton, SW19 BS50 76
High St. Nthwd. BB30 35
High St. Ong. CX17 24
High St. Orp. CL59 97
High St. Orp. CO55 89
High St. Oxt. CF68 114
High St. Oxt. CH67 115
High St. Pnr. BE31 45
High St. Ponders End CC25 30
High St. Pot. B. BT19 20
High St. Pur. BY59 95
High St. Red. BU70 121
High St. Red. BV67 113
High St. Red. BX70 121
High St. Red. BZ70 114
High St. Reig. BS70 121
High St. Rick. AX26 35
High St. Rom. CT32 50
High St. Ruis. BB33 44
High St. St. Alb. BG13 9
High St. St. Alb. BK16 18
High St. St Mary Cray CP53 89
High St. S. Norwood SE25 CA52 87
High St. S. Ock. CW40 60
High St. S. Ock. DB38 60
High St. Sev. CS64 107
High St. Sev. CT58 98
High St. Sev. CU61 107
High St. Sev. CV66 117
High St. Sev. CW64 108
High St. Sev. CX62 108
High St. Sev. DC67 117
High St. Shep. AZ54 83
High St. Sid. CP50 79
High St. Slou. AO41 61
High St. Slou. AP41 62
High St. Slou. AQ44 62
High St. Slou. AU43 62
High St. Stai. AS46 72
High St. Stai. AV49 72
High St. Stai. AX46 73
High St. Sthl. BE40 54
High St. Sutt. BS56 95
High St. Swan. CT52 89
High St. Swans. DC46 81
High St. Tad. BQ65 103
High St. Tedd. BJ49 74
High St. Thames Ditton BJ54 84
High St. Th. Hth. BZ52 87
High St. Uxb. AX30 35
High St. Uxb. AX36 53
High St. Uxb. AX39 53
High St. Wal. Cr. CC18 21
High St. Wal. Cr. CD20 21
High St. Walt. BC54 83
High St. Wat. BD24 27
High St. Wealdstone BH30 36
High St. Well. CO45 69
High St. Wem. BL35 46
High St. West Dr. AX40 53
High St. Wey. AW56 92
High St. Wey. AZ56 92
High St. Whitton. BG47 74
High St. Wind. AO43 61
High St. Wind. AO44 61
High St. Wok. AP59 91
High St. Wok. AR61 100
High St. Wok. AS62 100
High St. Wok. AT64 100
High St. Wok. AW64 101
High St. W. Wick. CE54 87
High Street Green, Hem. H. AZ12 8
High Timber St. EC4 BZ40 57
Broken Wharf
Hightor Clo. Brom. CH50 78
High Tree Clo. Wey. AW56 92
High Trees, SW2 BY47 76
High Trees Croy. CD54 87
High Trees Clo. Cat. CA64 105
High Trees Rd. Reig. BT71 121
High View. Hat. BO13 10
Highview Pnr. BD31 45
High Vw. Rick. AW24 26
High Vw. Sutt. BR59 94
High Vw. Wat. BB25 26
High View Ave. Grays. DE42 71
Highview Av. Edg. BN28 37
Highview Av. Wall. BX56 95
High Vw. Clo. SE19 CA51 87
High Vw. Clo. Loug. CJ25 31
Highview Cres. Brwd DE25 122
Highview Gdns. N3 BR31 46
High View Gdns. N11 BW28 38
Highview Gdns. Edg. BN28 37
High View Gdns. Pot. B. BT20 20
Highview Gdns. Upmin. CX34 51
Highview Pk. Bans. BS61 104
High View Rd. E18 CG31 49
High View Rd. SE19 BZ50 77
Highview Rd. W13 BJ39 54
High View Rd. Guil. AO72 118
High Vw. Rd. Orp. CL58 97
High View Rd. Sid. CO49 79
Highway, The, E1 CB40 57
Highway, The, Orp. CO56 98
Highway, The, Stan. BH30 36
Highway, The, Sutt. BT58 95
Highweek Rd. N15 CA32 48
Highwold Couls. BV62 104
Highwood Av. N12 BT28 38
Highwood Av. Bush. BE23 27
Highwood Clo. Brwd. DA26 42
Highwood Clo. Ken. BZ58 96
Highwood Clo. Ken. BZ62 105
Highwood Clo. Orp. CM55 88
Highwood Dr. Orp. CM55 88
Highwood Gdns. Ilf. CK32 49
Highwood Gro. NW7 BN28 37
Highwoodhall La. Hem. H. AZ16 17
Highwood Hill NW7 BO27 37
Highwood La. Loug. CL25 31
Highwood Rd. N19 BX34 47
Highwood Rd. Hodd. CD10 12
Highwoods, Lthd. BK64 102
High Worple Har. BE33 45
Highworth Rd. N11 BW29 38
High Wych Rd. Harl. CN7 6
High Wych Rd. Harl. CN8 6
Hilary Av. Mitch. BV52 86
Hilary Clo. SW6 BS43 66
Hilary Clo. Bexh. CR44 69
Hilary Clo. Horn. CV35 51
Hilary Rd. W12 BO39 55
Hilary Rd. Hem. H. AZ13 8
Hilbert Rd. Sutt. BQ55 85
Hilborough Rd. Orp. CM56 97
Hilda May Av. Swan. CT52 89
Hilda Rd. E6 CJ36 58
Hilda Rd. E16 CG38 58
Hilda St. SW9 BY44 66
Hilda Vale Clo. Orp. CL56 97
Hilda Vale Rd. Orp. CL56 97
Hildenborough Gdns. Brom. CG50 78
Hilden Dr. Erith. CU43 69
Hildenley Clo. Red. BW67 113
Malmstone Av.
Hildens, The Dor. BG72 119
Hilders. The Ash. BM62 103
Hildreth St. SW12 BV47 76
Hildyard Rd. SW6 BS43 66
Hiley Rd. NW10 BQ38 55
Hilfield La. Wat. BF23 27
Hilfield La. S. Bush. BH25 27
Hilgrove Est. NW6 BT36 56
Hiliard Rd. Nthwd. BC30 35
Hiliary Gdns. Stan. BK30 36
Hillards Rd. Uxb. AX39 53
Hillars Hth. Rd. Couls. BX61 104
Hillary Av. Grav. DF48 81
Hillary Cres. Walt. BD54 84
Hillary Rd. Slou. AS41 62
Hillary Rd. Sthl. BF41 64
Hillbeck Clo. SE15 CB43 67
Hillbeck Way Grnf. BG37 54
Hillborne Clo. Hayes BC42 63
Hillborough Ave. Sev. CV64 108
Hillborough Clo. SW19 BT50 76
Hillbrook Rd. SW17 BU48 76
Hill Brow, Brom. CJ51 88
Hill Brow Dart. CT46 79
Hillbrow N. Mal. BO52 85
Hillbrow Clo. Bex. CS49 79
Hillbrow Rd. Brom. CG50 78
Hillbrow Rd. Esher BG56 93
Hillbury. Hat. BO13 10
Hillbury Av. Har. BJ32 45
Hillbury Clo. Warl. CC62 105
Hillbury Rd. SW17 BV48 76
Hillbury Rd. Warl. CB62 105
Hill Clo. NW2 BP34 46
Hill Clo. NW11 BS32 47
Hill Clo. Barn. BQ25 28
Hill Clo. Chesh. AP20 16
Hill Clo. Chis. CL49 78
Hill Clo. Grav. DF50 81
Hill Clo. Har. BH34 45
Hill Clo. Pur. BZ60 96
Hill Clo. Stan. BJ28 36
Hill Clo. Wok. AR61 100
Hill Common, Hem. H. AZ15 8
Hillcote Av. SW16 BY50 76
Hill Ct. SW15 BQ46 75
Putney Hill
Hill Ct. W5 BL38 55
Ridings, The,
Hillcourt Av. N12 BS29 38
Hillcourt Est. N16 BZ33 48
Hillcourt Rd. SE22 CB46 77
Hill Cres. N20 BS27 38
Hill Cres. Bex. CS47 79
Hill Cres. Har. BJ32 45
Hill Cres. Horn. CV32 51
Hill Cres. Surb. BL53 85
Hill Cres. Wor. Pk. BQ55 85
Hillcrest, N6 BV33 47
Hillcrest N21 BY26 38
Hillcrest. Hat. BO12 10
Hillcrest, Pot. B. BT20 20
Hillcrest. Sev. CU64 107
Hill Crest, Sid. CO47 79
Hillcrest Av. NW11 BR32 46
Hillcrest Av. Cher. AV55
Hillcrest Av. Edg. BM28 37
Hillcrest Av. Grays DA43 70
Hillcrest Av. Pnr. BD31 45
Hillcrest Clo. Beck. CD53 87
Hillcrest Dr. Green. DA46 80
Hill Crest Gdns. N3 BR31 46
Hillcrest Gdns. NW2 BP34 46
Hillcrest Gdns. Esher BH55 84
Hillcrest Gdns. Ruis. BD34 45
Hillcrest Rd. E17 CF30 39
Hillcrest Rd. E18 CG30 40
Hillcrest Rd. SE26 CB49 77
Hillcrest Rd. W3 BM40 55
Hillcrest Rd. W5 BL39 55
Hillcrest Rd. Brom. CH49 78
Hillcrest Rd. Dart. CT47 79
Hillcrest Rd. Epp. CT18 23
Hillcrest Rd. Guil. AP70 118
Hillcrest Rd. Horn. CU33 50
Hillcrest Rd. Loug. CJ25 31
Hillcrest Rd. Orp. CO55 89
Hillcrest Rd. Pur. BX58 95
Hillcrest Rd. Rad. BM20 19
Hill Crest Rd. West. CJ61 106
Hillcrest Rd. Whyt. CA62 105
Hillcrest Vw. Beck. CD53 87
Hillcrest Way Epp. CO19 23
Bower Hill
Hillcrest Waye. Ger. Cr. AS32 43
Hillcroft Loug. CL23 31
Hill Croft Av. Pnr. BE32 45
Hillcroft Av. Pur. BW60 95
Hillcroft Cres. W5 BK39 54
Hillcroft Cres. Ruis. BD34 45
Hillcroft Cres. Wat. BC26 35
Hillcroft Cres. Wem. BL35 46
Hillcroft Rd. Chesh. AO18 16
Hillcroome Rd. Sutt. BT57 95
Hillcross Av. Mord. BQ53 85
Hilldale Rd. Sutt. BR56 94
Hilldene Av. Rom. CV29 42
Hilldown Rd. SW16 BX50 76
Hilldown Rd. Brom. CG54 88
Hilldown Rd. Hem. H. AW12 8
Hill Dr. NW9 BN33 46
Hill Dr. SW16 BX52 86
Hilldrop Cres. N7 BW35 47
Hilldrop Est. N7 BW35 47
Hilldrop La. N7 BW35 47
Hilldrop Rd. N7 BW35 47
Hilldrop Rd. Brom. CH50 78
Hillend, SE18 CL44 68
Hill End Orp. CN55 88
Hill End La. St. Alb. BK14 9
Hill End Rd. Uxb. AX29 35
Hillerdon Av. Edg. BL28 37
Hillers Av. Uxb. AZ38 53
Hillersdon Av. SW13 BP44 65
Hillersdon Moat, Slou. AQ39 52
Hillery Rd. SE17 BZ42 67
Hill Farm Av. Wat. BC20 17
Hill Farm Clo. Wat. BC20 17
Hill Farm La. Ch. St. G. AQ26 34
Hill Farm Rd. W10 BQ39 55
Hill Farm Rd. Chesh. AO20 16
Hillfarm Rd. Ger. Cr. AS29 34
Hill Farm Rd. Uxb. BA35 44
Hillfield Av. N8 BX32 47
Hillfield Av. NW9 BO32 46
Hillfield Av. Mitch. BU53 86
Hillfield Av. Wem. BL36 55
Hillfield Clo. Guil. AU69 118
Hillfield Clo. Har. BG31 45
Hillfield Clo. Red. BV70 121
Hillfield Ct. NW3 BU35 47
Belsize Av.
Hillfield Ct. Esher BF56 93
Hillfield Pk. N10 BV31 47
Hillfield Pk. N21 BY27 38
Hillfield Pk. Ms. N10 BV31 47
Hillfield Pk.
Hillfield Rd. NW6 BR35 46
Hillfield Rd. Ger. Cr. AS29 34
Hillfield Rd. Hamptn. BE50 74
Hillfield Rd. Hem. H. AX13 8
Hillfield Rd. Red. BV70 121
Hillfield Rd. Sev. CT63 107
Hillfield Rd. Sev. CW61 108
Hillfield Sq. Ger. Cr. AS29 34
Hillfoot Av. Rom. CS30 41
Hillfoot Rd. Rom. CS30 41
Hillford Pl. Red. BV73 121
Hill Gdns. Wey. AV56 91
Hillgate Pl. W8 BS40 56
Hillgate St. W8 BS40 56
Hillgay Clo. Guil. AS70 118
Hillgay Ct. Guil. AS70 118
Hill Gro. Rom. CT31 50
Hillgrove Rd. NW6 BT36 56
Hillhouse, Wal. Abb. CG20 22
Hill Ho. Av. Stan. BH29 36
Hill Ho. Clo. N21 BY26 38
Hill House Dr. Reig. BS71 121
Hillhouse La. Wey. AZ58 92
Hill House Rd. SW16 BX49 76
Hillhouse Rd. Dart. CY47 80
Hillhurst Gdns. Cat. CA63 105
Hilliards Ct. E1 CC40 57
Hilliards Rd. Nthwd. BB30 35
Hillier Clo. Barn. BS25 29
Hillier Rd. SW11 BU46 76
Hillier Rd. Guil. AT70 118
Hilliers La. Croy. BX55 86
Hillingdon Ave. Sev. CV64 108
Hillingdon Av. Stai. AY47 73
Hillingdon Cir. Uxb. AZ36 53
Hillingdon Hill, Uxb. AY37 53
Hillingdon Ri. Sev. CV64 108
Hillingdon Rd. Bexh. CS44 69
Hillingdon Rd. Grav. DG48 81
Hillingdon Rd. Uxb. AX37 53
Hillingdon Rd. Wat. BC20 17
Hillingsdale. West. CH62 106
Hillington Gdns. Wdf. Grn. CJ30 40
Hill La. Ruis. BA33 44
Hill La. Tad. BR64 103
Hill La. Wind. AO44 61
Hill Leys Pot. B. BX17 20
Homewood Av.
Hillman Clo. Uxb. AY35 44
Hillman St. E8 CB36 57
Hillmarton Rd. N7 BX35 47
Hillmay Dr. Hem. H. AW14 8
Hillmont Rd. Esher BH55 84
Hillmore Gro. SE26 CC49 77
Hill Path, SW16 BX49 76
Hill Place St. E14 CE39 57
Hillreach, SE18 CK42 68
Hill Ri. Dart. CY49 80
Hill Ri. Dor. BJ70 119
Hill Ri. Ger. Cr. AR30 34
Hill Ri. Rick. AW26 35
Hill Ri. Slou. AT43 62
Hill Rise. N9 CB25 30
Hill Rise, NW11 BS31 47
Hill Rise, SE23 CB47 77
Hill Rise Esher. BJ55 84
Hill Rise Grnf. BG36 54
Hill Rise, Pot. B. BT20 20
Hill Rise, Pot. B. BW17 20
Hill Rise, Rich. BK46 74
Hill Rise, Ruis. BA33 44
Hill Rise, Upmin. CX34 51
Hillrise Av. Wat. BD22 27
Hill Rise Cres. Ger. Cr. AS30 34
Hillrise Rd. N19 BX33 47
Hillrise Rd. Rom. CS29 41
Hill Rd. N10 BU30 38
Hill Rd. NW8 BT38 56
Hill Rd. Amer. AO22 25
Hill Rd. Brwd. DA27 42
Hill Rd. Cars. BU57 95
Hill Rd. Dart. CW48 80
Hill Rd. Epp. CN22 31
Hill Rd. Har. BJ32 45
Hill Rd. Hem. H. AV14 7
Hill Rd. Lthd. BF64 102
Hill Rd. Mitch. BV51 86
Hill Rd. Nthwd. BA29 35
Hill Rd. Pnr. BE32 45
Hill Rd. Pur. BX59 95
Hill Rd. Sutt. BS56 95
Hillsborough Grn. Wat. BC27 35
Hillsborough Rd. SE22 CA46 77
Hills Chase, Brwd. DB28 42
Hills Clo. Watt. BB58 92
Hillside, NW9 BN31 46
Hillside, SW19 BQ50 75
Hillside Bans. BR61 103
Hillside. Barn. BT25 29
Hillside. Dart. CY49 80
Hillside Erith CS42 69
Hillside Farn. CW54 90
Hillside. Grays. DE42 71
Hillside. Hat. BP11 10
Hillside. Hat. BP12 10
Hillside. Slou. AR41 62
Hill Side Surb. BK54 84
Hillside, Uxb. AX32 44
Hillside, Vir. W. AR53 82

Hillside. Welw. G. C. BS9 5
Hillside, Wok. AR63 100
Hillside Av. N11 BU29 38
Hillside Av. Borwd. BM24 28
Hillside Av. Grav. DH48 81
Hillside Av. Pur. BY60 95
Hillside Av. Wal. Cr. CC19 21
Hillside Av. Wdf. Grn. CJ28 40
Hillside Av. Wem. BL35 46
Hillside Clo. Bans. BR61 103
Hillside Clo. Bet. BM71 120
Hillside Clo. Ch. St. G. AQ27 34
Hillside Clo. Ger. Cr. AS29 34
Hillside Clo. Mord. BR52 85
Hillside Clo. Wat. BB19 17
School Mead.
Hillside Clo. Wdf. Grn. CJ28 40
Hillside Clo. Wok. AO62 100
Hillside Ct. NW4 BQ30 37
Hillside Ct. St. Alb. BH13 9
Hillside Rd.
Hillside Cres. Enf. BZ22 30
Hillside Cres. Har. BG33 45
Hill Side Cres. Nthwd. BC30 35
Hillside Cres. Wal. Cr. CC19 21
Hillside Cres. Wat. BD25 27
Hillside Dr. Edg. BM28 37
Hillside Dr. Grav. DH48 81
Hillside Est. N15 CA32 48
Hillside Gdns. E17 CF31 48
Hillside Gdns. N6 BV32 47
Hillside Gdns. N11 BW29 38
Hillside Gdns. Barn. BR25 28
Hillside Gdns. Berk AR13 7
Hillside Gdns. Bet. BM70 120
Hillside Gdns. Edg. BL28 37
Hillside Gdns. Har. BL33 46
Hillside Gdns. Nthwd. BC29 35
Hillside Gdns. Wall. BW57 95
Hillside Gdns. Wey. AV56 91
Hillside Gdns. Est. SW2 BY48 76
Hillside Gro. N14 BW26 38
Hillside Gro. NW7 BP29 37
Hillside. Harl. CP12 14
Hillside La. Brom. CG55 88
Hillside Rise Nthwd. BC29 35
Hillside Rd. N15 CA33 48
Hillside Rd. SW2 BX48 76
Hillside Rd. W5 BL39 55
Hillside Rd. Ash. BL62 103
Hillside Rd. Brom. CG52 88
Hillside Rd. Bush. BE25 27
Hillside Rd. Couls. BX62 104
Hillside Rd. Croy. BY56 95
Hillside Rd. Dart. CT46 79
Hillside Rd. Epsom BQ58 94
Hillside Rd. Nthwd. BC29 35
Hillside Rd. Rad. BJ21 27
Hillside Rd. Rick. AU25 25
Hillside Rd. St. Alb. BH13 9
Hill Side Rd. Sev. CV65 108
Hillside Rd. Sev. CW62 108
Hillside Rd. Sthl. BE38 54
Hillside Rd. Surb. BM52 85
Hillside Rd. Sutt. BR57 94
Hillside Rd. West. CK63 106
Hillside Rd. Whyt. CB62 105
Hillside, The, Orp. CO58 98
Hillside Wk. Brwd. CZ27 42
Hills La. Nthwd. BB30 35
Hillsleigh Rd. W8 BR40 55
Hillsmead Way Sth. Croy. CB60 96
Hills Pl. W1 BW39 56
Ramillies Pl.
Hillspur Clo. Guil. AP70 118
Hillspur Rd. Guil. AP70 118
Hills Rd. Buck. H. CH26 40
Hillstowe St. E5 CC34 48
Hill St. W1 BV40 56
Hill St. Rich. BK46 74
Hill St. St. Alb. BG13 9
Hill Ter. Wat. BB19 17
Hill, The Grav. DE46 81
Hill, The, Harl. CP9 6
Hill Top, NW11 BS31 47
Hill Top Loug. CL23 31
Hilltop Mord. BS53 86
Hilltop Sutt. BR54 85
Hill Top Clo. Berk. AR13 7
Hill Top Clo. Guil. AP68 109
Hill Top Clo. Loug. CL24 31
Hilltop Clo. Wal. Cr. CA16 21
Hilltop Gdns. NW4 BP30 37
Hilltop Gdns. Dart. CW46 80
Hilltop Gdns. Orp. CN55 88
Hill Top La. Cat. BY66 113
Hill Top La. Red. BY66 113
Hilltop Ri. Lthd. BG66 111
Hilltop Ri. Lthd. BK65 102
Hilltop Rd. NW6 BS36 56
Hill Top Rd. Berk. AR13 7
Hilltop Rd. Grays DA43 70
Hilltop Rd. Kings L. BA17 17
Hilltop Rd. Reig. BS71 121
Hilltop Rd. Whyt. CA62 105
Hilltop Rd. Wind. AM45 61
Hill Top View Chig. CK29 40
Hilltop Way Stan. BJ27 36
Hillview, SW20 BP50 75
Hill Vw. Wok. AS62 100
Hill Vw. Rd.
Hillview Av. Har. BL32 46
Hillview Av. Horn. CV32 51
Hill Vw. Clo. Pnr. BE29 36
Hill View Clo. Tad. BQ64 103
Hill View Cres. Guil. AP69 118
Hill View Cres. Ilf. CK32 49
Hill Vw. Cres. Orp. CN54 88
Hillview Dr. Red. BV71 121
Hill View Dr. Well. CN44 68
Hill View Gdns. NW4 BQ31 46
Hill View Gdns. NW9 BN32 46
Hillview Gdns. Har. BF31 45
Hillview Gdns. Wal. Cr. CC17 21
Hill View Rd. NW7 BQ28 37
Hillview Rd. Chis. CL49 78
Hill Vw. Rd. Esher BJ57 93
Hill Vw. Rd. Orp. CN54 88
Hill Vw. Rd. Pnr. BE29 36
Hill View Rd. Stai. AR46 72
Hillview Rd. Sutt. BT55 86
Hill View Rd. Twick. BJ46 74
Hill Vw. Rd. Wok. AS62 100
Hillway, N6 BV34 47
Hill Way, NW9 BK33 45
Hill Waye. Ger. Cr. AS32 43
Hillwood Clo. Brwd. DD26 122
Hillwood Gro. Brwd. DD26 122
Hillworth Rd. SW2 BY47 76
Hillyard Rd. W7 BH39 54
Hillyard St. SW9 BX44 66
Hillydeal Rd. Sev. CV61 108
Hilly Field. Harl. CN13 13
Hilly Field. Harl. CO13 14
Hilly Field La. Lthd. BG64 102
Hillyfields E17 CD30 39
Hillyfields Loug. CL23 31
Hilly Fields. Welw. G. C. BT7 5
Hilly Fields Cres. SE4 CE45 67
Hillyfields Est. Loug. CL23 31
Hilsea St. E5 CC35 48
Hilton Av. N12 BT28 38
Hilton Clo. Uxb. AW37 53
Hilton Cres. Ger. Cr. AS30 34
Hilton Way Sth. Croy. CB61 105
Hilversum Cres. SE22 CA46 77
Dulwich Gro.
Himley Rd. SW17 BU49 76
Hinchcliffe Clo. Wall. BX57 95
Hinchley Clo. Esher BH55 84
Hinchley Dr. Esher BH55 84
Hinchley Way Esher BJ55 84
Hinckley Rd. SE15 CB45 67
Hind Clo. Chig. CN28 40
Hind Ct. EC4 BY39 56
Gough Sq.
Hind Cres. Erith CS43 69
Hindehead Gdns. Nthlt. BE37 54
Hindes Rd. Har. BG32 45
Hinde St. W1 BV39 56
Hind Gro. E14 CE39 57
Hindhead Clo. N16 CA33 48
Hindhead Grn. Wat. BD28 36
Hindhead Way Wall. BX56 95
Hindman's Rd. SE22 CB46 77
Hindmarsh Clo. E1 CB40 57
Hindsley Pl. SE23 CC48 77
Hinkler Clo. Wall. BX57 95
Hinkler Rd. Har. BK31 45
Hinkley Clo. Uxb. AX31 44
Hinksey Clo. Slou. AT41 62
Hinksey Path, SE2 CP41 69
Hinstock Rd. SE18 CM43 68
Hinton Av. Houns. BD45 64
Hinton Rd. N18 CA28 39
Hinton Rd. SE24 BZ45 67
Hinton Rd. Uxb. AX37 53
Hinton Rd. Wall. BW57 95
Hipley St. Wok. AT63 100
Hippodrome Pl. W11 BR40 55
Hitcham Rd. E17 CD33 48
Hitchen Hatch La. Sev. CU65 107
Hitchens Clo. Hem. H. AV13 7
Hitchings Way, Reig. BS72 121
Hitchins Clo. Rom. CV28 42
Hitherbroom Rd. Hayes BC40 53
Hitherbury Ct. Guil. AR72 118
Hitherfield Rd. SW16 BX48 76
Hitherfield Rd. Dag. CQ34 50
Hither Grn. La. SE13 CF46 77
Hithermoor Rd. Stai. AV46 72
Hithermoor Rd. Stai. AW46 73
Hither Way, Welw. G. C. BQ6 5
Hitherwell Dr. Har. BG30 36
Hitherwood Clo. Reig. BU69 121
Hither Wood Dr. SE19 CA49 77
Hive Clo. Bush. BG27 36
Hive La. Grav. DD46 81
Hive Rd. Bush. BG27 36
Hoadly Rd. SW16 BW48 76
Hobart Clo. N20 BU27 38
Hobart Gdns. Th. Hth. BZ52 87
Hobart Pl. SW1 BV41 66
Belgrave St.
Hobart Rd. Dag. CP35 50
Hobart Rd. Hayes BD38 54
Hobart Rd. Ilf. CM30 40
Hobart Rd. Til. DF44 71
Hobart Rd. Wor. Pk. BP55 85
Hobart Wk. St. Alb. BH11 9
Hobbayne Rd. W7 BG39 54
Hobbes Wk. SW15 BP46 75
Sunnymead Rd.
Hobbs Clo. St. Alb. BL13 10
Hobbs Clo. Wal. Cr. CC18 21
Hobbs Clo. Wey. AW60 92
Hobbs Cross Rd. Harl. CQ9 6
Hobbs Gn. N2 BT31 47
Hobbshill Rd. Hem. H. AY15 8
Hobbs Rd. SE27 BZ49 77
Hobbs Way. Welw. G. C. BQ8 5
Hobday St. E14 CE39 57
Hobill Wk. Surb. BL53 85
Hoblands End Chis. CN50 78
Hobsons Clo. Hodd. CD10 12
Hobsons Clo. Wal. Cr. CC18 21
Hobtoe Rd. Harl. CL10 6
Hobury St. SW10 BT43 66
Hockenden La. Swan. CR52 89
Hockering Clo. Wok. AT62 100
Hockering Gdns. Wok. AT62 100
Hockering Rd. Wok. AT62 100
Hocker St. E2 CA38 57
Arnold Circus
Hockley Av. E6 CK37 58
Hockley Dr. Rom. CU30 41
Hockley La. Slou. AQ36 52
Hocroft Rd. NW2 BR35 46
Hodder Dr. Grnf. BH37 54
Hoddesdon Rd. Belv. CR42 69
Hodds Wood Rd. Chesh. AO10 16
Hodford Rd. NW11 BR33 46
Hodham Clo. Sid. CN47 78
Hodings Rd. Harl. CL10 6
Hodings Rd. Harl. CL11 13
Hodister Clo. BZ43 67
Hodnet Gro. SE16 CC42 67
Suffolk Gro.
Hodsoll Ct. Orp. CP53 89
Hodson Cres. Orp. CP53 89
Hoe Croft. Wal. Abb. CG14 13
Hoe La. Enf. CB22 30
Hoe La. Rom. CP26 41
Hoe La. Wal. Abb. CG14 13
Hoestock Rd. Saw. CP6 6
Hoe St. E17 CE31 48
Hoe, The, Wat. BD27 36
Hofland Rd. W14 BR41 65
Hogar Rd. Wind. AM42 61
Hogarth Av. Ashf. BA50 73
Hogarth Av. Brwd. DC27 122
Hogarth Cres. Croy. BZ54 87
Hogarth Est. W4 BO42 65
Hogarth Gdns. Houns. BF43 64
Hogarth Hl. NW11 BR31 46
Hogarth Rd. SW5 BS42 66
Hogarth Rd. Edg. BM30 37
Hogarths Rd. Grays. DD40 71
Hogarth Way Hamptn. BG51 84
Hogdon Clo. Tad. BQ65 103
Hogden La. Dor. BE70 119
Hogg End La. Hem. H. & St. Alb. BA12 8
Hogg End La. St. Alb. BD12 9
Hogg La. Berk. AO14 7
Hogg La. Borwd. BJ24 27
Hogg La. Grays. DD41 71
Hog's Back, Guil. AO72 118
Hogscross La. Couls. BU65 104
Hogshill La. Cob. BC60 92
Hogshill La. Cob. BD60 93
Hogsmill Way Epsom BN56 94
Hogtrough Hill, West. CN64 106
Hogtrough La. Oxt. CE67 114
Hogtrough La. Red. BW71 121
Holbeach Gdns. Sid. CN46 78
Holbeach Rd. SE6 CE47 77
Holbeck La. Wal. Cr. CA16 21
Holbeck Row SE15 CB43 67
Holbein Ms. SW1 BV42 66
Holbein Pl. SW1 BV42 66
Holberton Gdns. NW10 BP38 55
Holborn EC1 BY39 56
Holborn Circus EC1 BY39 56
Holborn Rd. E13 CH38 58
Holborn Viaduct EC1 BY39 56
Holbrook Clo. Enf. CA23 30
Holbrook La. Chis. CM50 78
Holbrook Rd. E15 CG37 58
Holbrook Way Brom. CK53 88
Holburne Clo. SE3 CJ44 68
Holburne Gdns. SE3 CJ44 68
Holburne Rd. SE3 CJ44 68
Holcombe Dale NW7 BP27 37
Holcombe Hill NW7 BP27 37
Holcombe Rd. N17 CA31 48
Holcombe Rd. Ilf. CL33 49
Holcombe St. W6 BP42 65
Holcon Ct. Red. BV69 121
Holcroft Rd. E9 CC36 57
Holdbrook Way. Rom. CW30 42
Holden Av. N12 BS28 38
Holden Av. NW9 BN33 46
Holden Gdns. Brwd. DB28 42
Holdenhurst Av. N12 BT29 38
Holden Rd. N12 BS28 38
Holden St. SW11 BV44 66
Holden Way, Upmin. CY33 51
Holdernesse Rd. SW17 BU48 76
Holderness Way SE27 BY49 76
Holder's Hl. Av. NW4 BQ30 37
Holder's Hl. Cir. NW4 BR29 37
Holder's Hl. Cres. NW4 BQ30 37
Holder's Hl. Dr. NW4 BQ31 46
Holder's Hl. Gdns. NW4 BR30 37
Holder's Hl. Rd. NW4 BQ30 37
Holdgate St. SE7 CJ41 68
Westmoor St.
Holdings, The, Hat. BQ11 10
Hole Croft Wal. Abb. CG20 22
Roundhills
Hole Farm La. Brwd. DA30 42
Holehill La. Dor. BF71 119
Hole La. NW7 BR28 37
Holford Pl. WC1 BY38 56
Holford Rd. NW3 BT34 47
Hampstead Sq.
Holford Rd. Guil. AU70 118
Holford Rd. S. Le H. DH42 71
Holgate Av. SW11 BT45 66
Holgate Ct. Edg. BL28 37
Holgate Gdns. Dag. CR35 50
Holgate Rd. Dag. CR35 50
Holiday St. Berk. AR13 7
Holland Av. SW20 BO51 85
Holland Av. Sutt. BS57 95
Holland Clo. Barn. BT25 29
Holland Clo. Barn. BT26 38
Holland Clo. Brom. CG55 88
Holland Clo. Red. BU70 121
Holland Clo. Stan. BJ28 36
Holland Cres. Oxt. CH70 115
Holland Gdns. W14 BR41 65
Holland Gdns. Egh. AV51 82
Holland Gdns. Wat. BD21 27
Holland Gro. SW9 BY43 66
Holland La. W14 BR41 65
Holland La. Oxt CH70 115
Holland Pk. W11 BR40 55
Holland Pk. Av. W11 BR40 55
Holland Pk. Av. Ilf. CN32 49
Holland Pk. Gdns. W14 BR41 65
Holland Pk. Ms. W11 BR40 55
Holland Pk. Rd. W14 BR41 65
Holland Rd. E6 CK37 58
Holland Rd. E15 CG38 58
Holland Rd. NW10 BP37 55
Holland Rd. SE25 CB53 87
Holland Rd. W14 BQ41 65
Holland Rd. Oxt. CH70 115
Holland Rd. Wem. BK36 54
Hollands, The, Wor. Pk. BO54 85
Holland St. W8 BS41 66
Holland Villas Rd. W14 BR41 65
Holland Wk. W8 BS41 66
Holland Wk. Stan. BJ28 36
Holland Way Brom. CG55 88
Hollar Rd. N16 CA34 48
Stoke Newington High St.
Hollen St. W1 BW39 56
Wardour St.
Holles St. W1 BV39 56
Cavendish Sq.
Hollickwood Av. N12 BU29 38
Hollidge Way Dag. CR36 59
Holliers Way, Hat. BP12 10
Hollies Ave. Wey. AV60 91
Hollies Av. Sid. CN48 78
Hollies Clo. Hamptn. BF49 74
Hollies Clo. Twick. BH48 74
Hollies End NW7 BP28 37
Hollies Rd. W5 BK42 64
Hollies St. W1 BV39 56
Cavendish Sq.
Hollies, The, Wey. AX56 92
Hollies Way SW12 BV47 76
Bracken Ave.
Hollies Way, Pot. B. BT19 20
Holligrave Rd. Brom. CH51 88
Hollingbourne Av. Bexh. CQ44 69
Hollingbourne Gdns. W13 BJ39 54
Hollingbourne Rd. SE24 BZ46 77
Hollingsworth Rd. Croy. CB57 96
Hollingsworth St. N7 BX35 47
Hollington Cres. N. Mal. BO53 85
Hollington Rd. E6 CK38 58
Hollington Rd. N17 CB30 39
Sherringham Av.
Hollingworth Rd. Brom. CL53 88
Hollins Av. E15 CG38 58
Hollis Pl. Grays. DD41 71
Hollit St. N7 BY35 47
Hollman Gdns. SW16 BY50 76
Holloway Clo. West Dr. AY42 63
Holloway Hill, Cher. AU55 82
Holloway La. Rick. AU22 25
Holloway La. West Dr. AY43 63
Holloway Rd. E6 CK38 58
Holloway Rd. E11 CF34 48
Holloway Rd. SW11 BT45 66
Holloways La. Hat. BQ15 10
Holloway St. Houns. BF45 64
Hollowfield Ave. Grays. DE42 71
Hollowfield Wk. Nthlt. BE36 54
Hollow Hill La. Iver AT40 52
Hollow Hill La. Iver AU41
Hollow La. Dor. BD73 119
Hollow La. Vir. W. AR52 82
Hollow Way La. Amer. AP21 25
Holly Av. Stan. BL30 37
Holly Av. Walt. BD54 84
Holly Av. Wey. AW58 92
Hollybank Clo. Hamptn. BF49 74
Hollybank Rd. Wey. AW60 92
Holly Bank Rd. Wok. AQ64 100
Hollyberry, Hem. H. AU19 16
Hollybrawe Clo. Chis. CM50 78
Hollybush Av. St. Alb. BF15 9
Hollybush Av. St. Alb. BF16 18
Hollybush Clo. E11 CH32 49
Woodford Rd.
Holly-bush Clo. Berk. AU11 7
Hollybush Gdns. E2 CB38 57
Hollybush Hill E11 CG32 49
Holly Bush Hill NW3 BT35 47
Holly Bush Hill. Berk. AU11 7
Hollybush Hill, Slou. AQ36 52
Hollybush La. Amer. AO21 25
Holly Bush La. Hamptn. BE50 74
Hollybush. La. Hem. H. AV12 7
Hollybush La. Iver AT39 52
Hollybush La. Orp. CR57 98
Holly Bush La. Sev. CV65 108
Hollybush La. Uxb. AU34 43
Hollybush La. Welw. G. C. BR9 5
Hollybush La. Wok. AX63 101
Hollybush Pl. E2 CB38 57
Bethnal Green Rd.
Hollybush Rd. Grav. DH48 81
Hollybush Rd. Kings. On T. BL49 75
Hollybush St. E13 CH37 58
Holly Bush Vale NW3 BT35 47
Heath St.
Holly Cl. Hat. BO13 10
Holly Clo. NW10 BO36 55
Holly Clo. Buck. H. CJ27 40
Holly Clo. Cher. AQ55 82
Holly Clo. Egh. AQ50 72
Holly Clo. Felt. BE49 74
Holly Clo. Wok. AQ63 100
Hollycombe, Egh. AR49 72
Holly Cres. Beck. CD53 87
Holly Cres. Wdf. Grn. CF29 39
Holly Cres. Wind. AL44 61
Hollycroft Av. Wem. BL34 46
Hollycroft Clo. West Dr. AZ43 63
Hollycroft Gdns. West Dr. AZ43 63
Hollydale Dr. Brom. CK55 88
Hollydale Rd. SE15 CC44 67
Hollydown Way E11 CF34 48
Holly, Dri. Berk. AR13 7
Holly Dr. E4 CE26 39
Holly Dr. Pot. B. BS20 20
Holly Dr. Wind. AP46 72
Hollyfied Hat. BP14 10
Holly Field. Harl. CM12 13
Hollyfield Av. N11 BU28 38
Hollyfield Rd. Surb. BL54 85
Holly Gro. NW9 BN33 46
Holly Gro. SE15 CA44 67
Hollygrove Clo. Bush. BG26 36
Hollyhedge Bungs, SE3 CF44 67
Holly Hedge Rd. Cob. BC61 101
Holly Hedges La. Hem. H. AU18 16
Hollyhedge Ter. SE13 CF46 77
Holly Hill N21 BX25 29
Holly Hill NW3 BT35 47
Holly Hill Dr. Bans. BS61 104
Holly Hill Rd. Belv. CR41 69
Holly La. Bans. BS61 104
Holly La. Guil. AO68 109
Holly La. E. Bans. BS61 104
Holly La. W. Bans. BS62 104
Hollylodge Gdns. N6 BV33 47
Hollymead Rd. Couls. BV62 104
Hollymeoak Rd. Couls. BV62 104
Holly Mews, SW10 BT42 66
Hollymoor La. Epsom BN58 94
Holly Mt. NW3 BT35 47
Holly Bush Hill
Hollymount Clo. SE10 CF44 67
Blackheath Hill
Hollymount Rd. SE10 CF44 67
Blackheath Hill
Holly Park N3 BR31 46
Holly Park N4 BX33 47
Holly Pk. Rd. N11 BV28 38
Holly Pk. Rd. W7 BH40 54
Holly Rd. E11 CG33 49
Holly Rd. W4 BN42 65
Holly Rd. Dart. CV47 80
Holly Rd. Enf. CC21 30
Holly Rd. Hamptn. BG50 74
Holly Rd. Houns. BF45 64
Holly Rd. Orp. CO57 98
Holly Rd. Reig. BS71 121
Holly Rd. Twick. BH47 74
Holly St. E1 CB39 57
Holly St. E8 CA36 57
Holly Ter. N20 BT27 38
Hollytree Av. Swan. CT51 89
Hollytree Clo. SW19 BQ47 75
Holly Tree Clo. AQ19 16
Holly Wk. NW3 BT35 47
Holly Wk. Enf. BZ24 30
Holly Wk. Welw. G. C. BQ6 5
Holly Way Mitch. BW52 86
Hollywood Gdns. Hayes BC39 53
Hollywood La. Sev. CZ59 99
Hollywood Rd. E4 CD28 39
Hollywood Rd. SW10 BT43 66
Hollywoods Croy. CD58 96
Hollywood Way Wdf. Grn. CF29 39
Holman Ct. Epsom BP58 94
Holman Hunt Ho. W14 BR42 65
Field Rd.
Holman Rd. SW11 BT44 66
Holman Rd. Epsom BN56 94
Holmbank Dr. Shep. BB52 83
Holmbridge Gdns. Enf. CC24 30
Holmbrook Dr. NW4 BQ32 46
Holmbrook St. E9 CC35 48
Holmbury Ct. SW17 BU48 76
Holmbury Gdns. Hayes BB40 53
Holmbury Gro. Croy. CD57 96
Holmbury Vw. E5 CB33 48
Holmbush Rd. SW15 BR46 75
Holm Clo. Wey. AV59 91
Holmcote Gdns. N5 BZ35 48
Highbury New Park.
Holmcroft Way Brom. CK53 88
Holmdale Clo. Borwd. BL23 28
Holmdale Gdns. NW4 BQ32 46
Holmdale Lo. Ct. W3 BM40 55
Whitehall Gdns.
Holmdale Rd. NW6 BS35 47
Holmdale Rd. Chis. CM49 78
Holmdale Ter. N15 CA32 48
Holmdene Av. NW7 BP29 37
Holmdene Av. SE24 BZ46 77
Holmdene Av. Har. BF31 45
Holmdene Clo. Beck. CF51 87
Holmdene Rd. N15 CA33 48
Holmead Rd. SW6 BS43 66
Holmebury Cl. Bush. BH27 36
Holme Chase Mord. BR53 85
Holme Chase, Wey. BA57 92
Holme Cl. Hat. BO11 10
Holme Clo. Wal. Cr. CD19 21
Holme Lacey Rd. SE12 CG46 78
Holme Lea, Wat. BD20 18
Holme Park Borwd. BL23 28
Holme Rd. E6 CK37 58
Holme Rd. Hat. BO11 10
Holme Rd. Horn. CW33 51
Holme Rd. Horn. CX33 51
Holmes Av. E17 CD31 48
Holmes Av. NW7 BR28 37
Holmes Dale, Guil. AT70 118
Holmesdale, Wal. Cr. CC21 30
Holmesdale Av. SW14 BM45 65
Holmesdale Clo. SE25 CA52 87
Holmesdale Hill. S. Dnth. CY51 90
Holmesdale Rd. N6 BV32 47
Holmesdale Rd. Bexh. CP44 69
Holmesdale Rd. Croy. BZ53 87

Holmesdale Rd. Dor. BJ73 119
Holmesdale Rd. Red. BX71 121
Holmesdale Rd. Reig. BS70 121
Holmesdale Rd. Rich. BL44 65
Holmesdale Rd. S. Dnth. CY51 90
Holmesdale Rd. Tedd. BK50 74
Holmesley Rd. SE23 CD46 77
Holmes Rd. NW5 BV36 56
Holmes Rd. SW19 BT50 76
Holmes Rd. Twick. BH48 74
Holmes Way Stan. BH29 36
Holmethorpe Av. Red. BV69 121
Holmewood Gdns. SW2 BX47 76
Holmewood Rd. SE25 CA52 87
Holmewood Rd. SW2 BX47 76
Holmfield Av. NW4 BQ32 46
Holmfield Ct. NW3 BU35 47
Holmhurst Rd. Belv. CR42 69
Holmleigh Av. Dart. CV45 70
Holmleigh Rd. N16 CA33 48
Holmsdale Gro. Bexh. CT44 69
Holmsdale Rd. N11 BV28 38
Holmsdale Rd. Sev. CV65 108
Holmshaw Rd. SE26 CD49 77
Holmshill La. Borwd. BN21 28
Holmside Rise Wat. BC27 35
Holmside Rd. SW12 BV46 76
Holmsley Clo. N. Mal. BO53 85
Holms St. E2 CA37 57
Holmstall Av. Edg. BN30 37
Holmsworth Ct. Har. BG32 45
Holmwood Croy. BW53 86
Holmwood Kings. On T. BN49 75
Holmwood Av. Brwd. DD25 122
Holmwood Av. Sth. Croy. CA60 96
Holmwood Clo. Har. BG31 45
Holmwood Clo. Leath. BB67 110
Holmwood Clo. Nthlt. BF36 54
Holmwood Clo. Sutt. BQ58 94
Holmwood Clo. Wey. AW56 92
Holmwood Gdns. N3 BS30 38
Holmwood Gdns. Wall. BV57 95
Holmwood Gro. NW7 BN28 37
Holmwood Rd. Chess. BL56 94
Holmwood Rd. Enf. CC21 30
Holmwood Rd. Ilf. CN34 49
Holmwood Rd. Sutt. BQ58 94
Holne Chase N2 BT32 47
Holness Rd. E15 CG36 58
Holroyd Clo. Esher BJ58 93
Holroyd Rd. SW15 BQ45 65
Holroyd Rd. Leath. BH58 93
Holstein Av. Wey. AZ56 92
Holstein Way Belv. CP41 69
Holsworthy Way Chess. BK56 93
Holt Cl. N10 BV31 47
Holt Clo. Chig. CN28 40
Holton St. E1 CC38 57
Holt Rd. E16 CK40 58
Holt Rd. Wem. BJ34 45
Holtsmere Clo. Wat. BD21 27
Holt, The Hem. H. AY14 8
Holt, The, Ilf. CM29 40
Holt, The, Wall. BW56 95
Holt Way Chig. CN28 40
Holtwhites Av. Enf. BZ23 30
Holtwhite's Hill Enf. BY23 29
Holtwood Rd. Lthd. BG60 93
Holwell Ct. Hat. BU10 11
Holwell Manor Rd. Hat. BU10 11
Holwell Pl. Pnr. BE31 45
Holwell Rd. Welw. G. C. BR8 5
Holwood Clo. Walt. BD55 84
Holwood Pk. Av. Orp. CK56 97
Holwood Pl. SW4 BW45 66
Holwood Rd. Brom. CH51 88
Holybourne Av. SW15 BP47 75
Holyfield Rd. Wal. Abb. CF18 21
Holy Hedge Rd. Cob. BC60 92
Holyoake Av. Wok. AR62 100
Holyoake Cres. Wok. AR62 100
Holyoake Rd. SE11 BY42 66
Holyoake Ter. Sev. CU65 107
Holyoake Wk. N2 BT31 47
Holyoake Wk. W5 BK38 54
Holyport Rd. SW6 BQ43 65
Holyrood Av. Har. BE35 45
Holyrood Cres. St. Alb. BG15 9
Holyrood Gdns. Edg. BM31 46
Holyrood Gdns. Grays. DH42 71
Holyrood Rd. Barn. BT25 29
Holywell Hill, St. Alb. BG14 9
Holywell Hyde. Welw. G. C. BT8 5
Holywell La. EC2 CA38 57
Holywell Rd. Wat. BC25 26
Holywell Row EC2 CA38 57
Scrutton St.
Holywell Way, Stai. AY47 73
Home Clo. Brox. CD15 12
Macer's La.
Home Clo. Cars. BU55 86
Home Clo. Harl. CN11 13
Home Clo. Lthd. BG64 102
Home Clo. Nthlt. BE38 54
Homecroft Gdns. Loug. CL24 31
Homecroft Rd. N22 BY30 38
Homecroft Rd. SE26 CC49 77
Homedean Rd. Sev. CS64 107
Home Farm Clo. Esher BF57 93
Homefarm Rd. W7 BH39 54
Home Farm Rd. Brwd. DC30 42
Home Farm Rd. Rick. AZ28 35
Home Farm Way, Slou. AR37 52
Home Field, Berk. AT11 7
Homefield Hem. H. AT17 16
Homefield Wal. Abb. CH19 22
Homefield Walt. BD56 93
Homefield Av. Ilf. CN32 49
Homefield Clo. NW10 BN36 55
Homefield Clo. Epp. CO18 23
Homefield Clo. Hem. H. AZ13 8
Homefield Clo. Lthd. BK64 102
Homefield Clo. Swan. CT52 89
Homefield Clo. Wey. AV59 91
Homefield Gdns. Mitch. BT51 86
Homefield Gdns. Tad. BQ63 103
Homefield Pk. Sutt. BS57 95
Sutton Pk. Rd.
Homefield Rise Orp. CO54 89
Homefield Rd. SW19 BQ50 75
Homefield Rd. W4 BO42 65
Homefield Rd. Brom. CJ51 88
Homefield Rd. Bush. BF25 27
Homefield Rd. Couls. BY63 104
Homefield Rd. Edg. BN29 37
Homefield Rd. Rad. BH22 27
Homefield Rd. Rick. AU24 25
Homefield Rd. Sev. CT64 107
Homefield Rd. Walt. BE54 84
Homefield Rd. Warl. CC63 105
Homefield Rd. Wem. BJ35 45
Homefield St. N1 CA37 57
Regan Way
Home Fm. Clo. Epsom BQ62 103
Home Fm. Clo. Surb. BH54 84
Home Fm. Gdns. Walt. BD55 84
Home Fm. Rd. Berk. AO11 7
Home Gdns. Dag. CS34 50
Home Gdns. Dart. CW46 80
Home Hill Swan. CT50 79
Homelands, Lthd. BK64 102
Homelands Dr. SE19 CA50 77
Homeleigh Rd. SE15 CC46 77
Home Mead Stan. BK30 36
Home Mead Clo. Grav. DG47 81
Homemead Rd. Brom. CK53 88
Homemead Rd. Croy. BW53 86
Home Mo. Hat. BP11 10
Home Orchard Dart. CW46 80
Home Pk. Oxt. CH69 115
Home Pk. Rd. SW19 BR49 75
Home Pk. Wk. Kings-on-t. BK52 84
Homer Ct. Bexh. CS44 69
Homerfield. Welw. G. C. BQ7 5
Home Rd. SW11 BU44 66
Homer Rd. E9 CD36 57
Homer Rd. Croy. CC53 87
Homer Row W1 BU39 56
Homersham Rd. Kings. On T. BM51 85
Homers Rd. Wind. AL44 61
Homer St. W1 BU39 56
Homerswood La. Welw. BP6 5
Homerton Gro. E9 CC35 48
Homerton High St. E9 CC35 48
Homerton Rd. E9 CD35 48
Homerton Row E9 CC35 48
Homerton Ter. E9 CC36 57
Homesdale Rd. Brom. CJ52 88
Homesdale Rd. Cat. BZ65 105
Homesdale Rd. Orp. CN54 88
Homesfield Rd. NW11 BS32 47
Homestall, Guil. AO70 118
Homestall Rd. SE22 CC46 77
Homestead Gdns. Esher BH56 93
Homestead La. Welw. G. C. BR9 5
Homestead Paddock N14 BV25 29
Homestead Pk. NW2 BO34 46
Homestead Rd. SW6 BR43 65
Homestead Rd. Cat. BZ65 105
Homestead Rd. Dag. CQ34 50
Homestead Rd. Hat. BP11 10
Homestead Rd. Orp. CO57 98
Homestead Rd. Rick. AX26 35
Homestead Rd. Stai. AW50 73
Homestead The, Dart. CV46 80
Homestead Way, Croy. CF59 96
Homewater Av. Sun. BB51 83
Home Way, Rick. AV26 34
Homeway, Rom. CX29 42
Homewood, Slou. AR39 52
Homewood Av. Pot. B. BX17 20
Homewood Cres. Chis. CN50 78
Home Wood La. Pot. B. BW17 20
Homewood Rd. Mitch. BT52 86
Homewood Rd. St. Alb. BJ12 9
Homland Dr. Sutt. BS58 95
Hulverston Clo.
Honduras St. EC1 BZ38 57
Baltic St.
Hone Par. SE11 BX42 66
Lambeth Wk.
Honeybourne Rd. NW6 BS35 47
Honeybourne Way Orp. CM54 88
Honeybrook Rd. SW12 BW47 76
Honeybrook, Wal. Abb. CG20 22
Honey Clo. Brwd. DB21 33
Honeycrock La. Red. BV74 121
Honeycroft Loug. CL24 31
Honey Croft. Welw. G. C. BQ8 5
Honeycroft Hill, Uxb. AY36 53
Honeycross Rd. Hem. H. AV14 7
Honeyden Rd. Sid. CQ50 79
Honeyhill Harl. CN13 13
Honey Hill, Uxb. AY36 53
Honey La. EC2 BZ39 57
Cheapside
Honey La. Wal. Abb. CG20 22
Honey La. Wal. Abb. CH21 31
Honey Meade, Saw. CP7 6
Honeypot Clo. Har. BL31 46
Honeypot La. Brwd. DA27 42
Honeypot La. Sev. CX63 108
Honeypots Rd. Wok. AR64 100
Honeysett Rd. N17 CA30 39
Reform Row
Honeysuckle Bottom. Leath. BB70 110
Honeysuckle Clo. Brwd. DA25 33
Honeysuckle Clo. Rom. CV29 42
Cloudberry Rd.
Honeysuckle Gdns. Hat. BP13 10
Honeysuckle La. N22 BZ30 39
Crawley Rd.
Honeywell Rd. SW11 BU46 76
Honeywood Clo. Pot. B. BT20 20
Honeywood Rd. NW10 BO37 55
Honeywood Rd. Islw. BJ45 64
Honister Clo. Stan. BJ29 36
Honister Gdns. Stan. BK30 36
Honister Gdns. Stan. BJ29 36
Honister Gdns. Stan. BJ30 36
Honister Heights Pur. BZ60 96
Honister Pl. Stan. BJ30 36
Honiton Rd. NW6 BR37 55
Honiton Rd. Rom. CS32 50
Honiton Rd. Well. CN44 68
Honley Rd. SE6 CE47 77
Honnor Rd. Stai. AX50 73
Bingham Dr.
Honor Oak Est. SE4 CD45 67
Honor Oak Ri. SE23 CC46 77
Honor Oak Rd. SE23 CC47 77
Hood Av. N14 BV25 29
Hood Av. N14 BW26 38
Hood Av. SW14 BN46 75
Hood Av. Orp. CO53 89
Hood Clo. Croy. BY54 86
Hoodcote Gdns. N21 BY26 38
Hood Rd. SW20 BO50 75
Hood Rd. Rain. CT37 59
Hood Wk. Rom. CR30 41
Hook End La. Brwd. DB20 24
Hook End La. Brwd. DB21 33
Hook End Rd. Brwd. DA21 33
Hooke Rd. Leath. BB66 110
Hookers Rd. E17 CC31 48
Hookfarm Rd. Brom. CJ53 88
Hookfield Epsom BN60 94
Hookfield Harl. CM13 13
Hook Field, Harl. CN12 13
Hook Fields, Grav. DF48 81
Hookgate, Enf. CB21 30
Hook Grn. La. Dart. CT48 79
Hook Grn. Rd. Grav. DC50 81
Hook Heath Av. Wok. AQ63 100
Hook Heath Gdns. Wok. AQ64 100
Hook Heath Rd. Wok. AP64 100
Hook Hill Sth. Croy. CA58 96
Hook Hill La. Wok. AQ64 100
Hook Hill Pk. Wok. AQ64 100
Hooking Grn. Har. BF32 45
Hook La. Pot. B. BU19 20
Hook La. Rom. CQ25 32
Hook La. Rom. CQ26 41
Hook La. Well. CN46 78
Hook Rise N. Surb. BL55 85
Hook Rise S. Surb. BL55 85
Hook Rd. Chess. BK56 93
Hook Rd. Epsom BN57 94
Hooks Hall Dr. Dag. CS34 50
Hook, The, Barn. BT25 29
Hook Wk. Edg. BN29 37
Hookwood Rd. Orp. CP59 98
Hooley La. Red. BU71 121
Hooper Rd. E16 CH39 58
Hoopers Ct. SW3 BU41 66
Basil St.
Hooper's Ms. W3 BM40 55
Churchfield Rd.
Hooper St. E1 CB39 57
Hoopers Yd. Sev. CV66 117
Hoop La. NW11 BR33 46
Hoo, The, Harl. CP8 6
Hopedale Rd. SE7 CH43 68
Hopefield Av. NW6 BR37 55
Hope Green, Wat. BC20 17
Hope Pk. Brom. CG50 78
Hope Rd. W13 BJ40 54
Hope St. SW11 BT45 66
Hopetown St. E1 CA39 57
Hopewell Dr. Grav. DJ49 81
Hopewell St. SE5 BZ43 67
Hopfield Av. Wey. AY59 92
Hop Fields, Wok. AS61 100
Hopgarden La. Sev. CU67 116
Hop Gdns. WC2 BX40 56
Bedfordbury
Hopgood St. W12 BQ40 55
Macfarlane Rd.
Hopground Clo. St. Alb. BJ14 9
Hopkins Cres. St. Alb. BJ10 9
Hopkins St. W1 BW39 56
Hopland Rd. W14 BR42 65
Hopper's Rd. N13 BY27 38
Hopper's Rd. N21 BY27 38
Hoppett Rd. E4 CG27 40
Hoppety, The, Tad. BQ64 103
Hopping La. N1 BY36 56
St. Mary's Gro.
Hoppingwood Av. N. Mal. BO52 85
Hoppit Rd. Wal. Abb. CE19 21
Hoppner Rd. Hayes BA37 53
Hopton Gdns. N. Mal. BP53 85
Hopton Rd. SW16 BX49 76
Hopton St. SE1 BY40 56
Hopwood Wk. E8 CB36 57
Wilman Gro.
Horace Av. Rom. CS33 50
Horace Rd. E7 CH35 49
Horace Rd. Ilf. CM31 49
Horace Rd. Kings-on-t. BL52 85
Horatio St. E2 CA37 57
Horbury Cres. W11 BS40 56
Horbury Ms. W11 BR40 55
Horder Rd. SW6 BR44 65
Hordle Gdns. St. Alb. BH14 9
Hordle Promenade E. SE15 CA43 67
Hordle Promenade N. SE15 CA43 67
Hordle Promenade S. SE15 CA43 67
Hordle Promenade W. SE15 CA43 67
Horley Clo. Bexh. CR46 79
Horley Rd. SE9 CK49 78
Horley Rd. Red. BU71 121
Hormead Rd. W9 BR38 55
Hornbeam Av. Upmin. CX35 51
Hornbeam Clo. Brwd. DD27 122
Hornbeam Cres. Brent. BJ43 64
Hornbeam Gro. E4 CG27 40
Hornbeam La. E4 CG25 31
Hornbeam La. Hat. BU14 11
Hornbeam Rd. Buck. H. CJ27 40
Hornbeam Rd. Epp. CM22 31
Hornbeam Rd. Guil. AR69 118
Hornbeam Rd. Hayes BD39 54
Hornbeam Rd. Reig. BS71 121
Hornbeam Rd. Reig. BS72 121
Hornbeams, St. Alb. BE18 18
Hornbeams Av. Enf. CC21 30
Hornbeams, The, Harl. CM10 6
Hornbeam Walk, Watt. BB58 92
Hornbeam Way Brom. CL53 88
Hornbill Clo. Uxb. AX39 53
Horncastle Clo. SE12 CH47 78
Horncastle Rd. SE12 CH47 78
Hornchurch Hill Whyt. CA62 105
Hornchurch Rd. Horn. CT33 50
Horndean Clo. SW15 BP47 75
Bessborough Rd.
Horndon Clo. Rom. CS30 41
Horndon Grn. Rom. CS30 41
Horndon Rd. Rom. CS30 41
Horne Rd. Shep. AZ52 83
Hornets, The, Wat. BC24 26
Horne Way SW15 BQ44 65
Hornfair Rd. SE7 CJ43 68
Hornford Way Rom. CT33 50
Hornhatch, Guil. AT73 118
Hornhatch Clo. Guil. AT73 118
Horn Hill Rd. Rick. AU28 34
Horniman Dr. SE23 CB47 77
Horning Clo. SE9 CK49 78
Horn La. SE10 CH42 68
Horn La. W3 BN40 55
Horn La. Wdf. Grn. CH29 40
Hornminster Glen, Horn. CX34 51
Horn Pk. Clo. SE12 CH46 78
Horn Pk. La. SE12 CH46 78
Hornsby La. Grays. DG41 71
Hornsey La. N6 BX33 47
Hornsey La. Est. N19 BW33 47
Hornsey La. Gdns. N6 BW33 47
Hornsey Pk. Rd. N8 BX31 47
Hornsey Rise. N19 BW33 47
Hornsey Rise Gdns. N19 BW33 47
Hornsey St. N7 BX35 47
Hornsfield. Welw. G. C. BT7 5
Hornshay Pl. SE15 CC43 67
Hornshay St. SE15 CC43 67
Horns Meadow. West. CP65 107
Horns Rd. Ilf. CM32 49
Hornton Pl. W8 BS41 66
Hornton St.
Hornton St. W8 BS41 66
Horsa Rd. SE12 CJ47 78
Horsa Rd. Erith. CR43 69
Horsbury Cres. W11 BS40 56
Horsecroft Bans. BS62 104
Horsecroft Clo. Orp. CO54 89
Horsecroft Rd. Edg. BN29 37
Horsecroft Rd. Harl. CK11 13
Horsecroft Rd. Hem. H. AW14 8
Horse Fair Kings. On T. BL51 85
Wood St.
Horseferry Pl. SE10 CF43 67
Horseferry Rd. SW1 BW41 66
Horse Guards Av. SW1 BX40 56
Horse Guards Rd. SW1 BW40 56
Horse Hill. Chesh. AR19 16
Horselers, Hem. H. AY15 8
Horsell Birch, Wok. AQ61 100
Horsell Common Rd. Wok. AR60 91
Horsell Ct. Cher. AW54 83
Horsell Moor, Wok. AR62 100
Horsell Pk. Wok. AS61 100
Horsell Pk. Clo. Wok. AR61 100
Horsell Rise, Wok. AR61 100
Horsell Rise Clo. Wok. AR61 100
Horsell Rd. N5 BY35 47
Horsell Rd. Orp. CO51 89
Horsell Vale, Wok. AS61 100
Horsell Way, Wok. AR61 100
Horselydown La. SE1 CA41 67
Horsemonden Clo. Orp. CN54 88
Horsemoor Clo. Slou. AT42 62
Parlaunt Rd.
Horsenden Av. Grnf. BH35 45
Horsenden Cres. Grnf. BH35 45
Horsenden La. N. Grnf. BH36 54
Horsenden La. S. Grnf. BJ37 54
Horseshoe Alley SE1 BZ40 57
Bankside
Horseshoe Clo. NW2 BP34 46
Horseshoe Grn. Sutt. BS55 86
Horseshoe Hill, Wal. Abb. CJ19 22
Horseshoe La. Enf. BZ24 30
Chase Side
Horseshoe La. Guil. AT70 118
Horseshoe La. Wat. BC19 17
Horseshoe La. Wat. BD20 18
Horseshoe, The, Bans. BR61 103
Horseshoe, The, Couls. BW60 95
Horseshoe, The Hem. H. BA14 8
Horsfield Gdns. SE9 CK46 78
Horsfield Rd. SE9 CJ46 78
Horsford Rd. SW2 BX46 76
Horsham Av. N12 BU28 38
Horsham Rd. Bexh. CR46 79
Horsham Rd. Dor. BJ72 119
Horsham Rd. Felt. BA46 73
Horsham Rd. Guil. AS74 118
Horsley Clo. Epsom BN60 94
Horsley Dr. Croy. CF57 96
Horsley Rd. E4 CF27 39
Horsley Rd. Brom. CH51 88
Horsley Rd. Cob. BC64 101
Horsleys Rick. AU28 34
Long Croft Rd.
Horsley St. SE17 BZ43 67
Horsman Side. Brwd. CV25 33
Horsmonden Rd. SE4 CD46 77
Hortensia Ho. SW10 BT43 66
Hortensia Rd. SW10 BT43 66
Horticultural Pl. W4 BN42 65
Heathfield Ter.
Horton Av. NW2 BR35 46
Horton Bri. Rd. West Dr. AY40 53
Horton Cres. West Dr. AY40 53
Horton Hill Epsom BN59 94
Horton La. Epsom. BM59 94
Horton La. West Dr. AY40 53
Horton Rd. E8 CB36 57
Horton Rd. Hort. K. CY52 90
Horton Rd. Slou. AQ43 62
Horton Rd. Slou. AT44 62
Horton Rd. Slou. AU45 62
Horton Rd. Stai. AW46 73
Horton Rd. West Dr. AY40 53
Horton St. SE13 CE45 67
Horton St. Hort. K. CX52 90
Horton Way. Farn. CW54 90
Hortus Rd. E4 CF26 39
Hortus Rd. Sthl. BE41 64
Hosack Rd. SW17 BU47 76
Hoser Av. SE12 CH48 78
Hosey Common La. Eden. CM70 115
Hosey Common Rd. West. CM67 115
Hosier La. EC1 BY39 56
Hoskins Clo. Hayes. BB42 63
Hoskins Rd. Oxt. CG68 115
Hoskins St. SE10 CF42 67
Hospital Bridge Rd. Twick. BF47 74
Hospital Hill. Chesh. AO19 16
Hospital Rd. Houns. BF45 64
Hospital Rd. Sev. CV64 108
Hospital Rd. Sutt. BS59 95
Hotham Clo. E. Mol. BF52 84
Hotham Rd. SW15 BQ45 65
Hotham Rd. SW19 BT50 76
Hotham St. E15 CG37 58
Hothfield Pl. SE16 CC41 67
Hotspur Rd. Nthlt. BF37 54
Hotspur St. SE11 BY42 66
Hottsfield Hart. DC52 90
Houblon Rd. Rich. BL46 75
Houblons Hill Epp. CP19 23
Houghin Dri. Ong. CY14 15
Hough St. SE18 CL41 68
Houghton Rd. N15 CA31 48
Houghton St. WC2 BX39 56
Houlder Cres. Croy. BY57 95
Houndsditch EC3 CA39 57
Houndsfield Rd. N9 CB26 39
Hounsden Rd. N21 BX26 38
Hounslow Av. Houns. BF46 74
Hounslow Gdns. Houns. BF46 74
Hounslow Rd. Felt. BC47 73
Hounslow Rd. Felt. BD49 74
Hounslow Rd. Twick. BF46 74
House La. St. Alb. BK10 9
Housewood End, Hem. H. AW12 8
Houston Rd. SE23 CD48 77
Hove Av. E17 CD32 48
Hoveden Rd. NW2 BQ35 46
Hove St. SE15 CC43 67
Culmore Rd.
Howard Av. Bex. CP47 79
Howard Av. Epsom BP58 94
Howard Av. Slou. AO39 52
Howard Clo. N11 BV27 38
Howard Clo. NW2 BR35 46
Marnham Av.
Howard Clo. W3 BM39 55
Howard Clo. Ash. BL62 103
Howard Clo. Hamptn. BG50 74
Howard Close. Leath. BA66 110
Howard Clo. Lthd. BK65 102
Howard Clo. St. Alb. BK14 9
Howard Clo. Tad. BO66 112
Howard Clo. Wat. BC22 26
Howard Cres. Beac. AO28 34
Howard Dr. Borwd. BN24 28
Howard Gdns. SE25 CB53 87
Howard Gdns. Guil. AT70 118
Howard Lodge Rd. Brwd. CY22 33
Howard Pl. SW1 BW41 66
Howard Ridge, Guil. AT68 109
Howard Rd. E6 CK37 58
Howard Rd. E11 CG34 49
Howard Rd. E17 CE31 48
Howard Rd. N15 CA32 48
Howard Rd. N16 BZ35 48
Howard Rd. NW2 BQ35 46
Howard Rd. SE20 CC51 87
Howard Rd. SE25 CB53 87
Howard Rd. Ashf. AX49 73
Howard Rd. Bark. CM37 58
Howard Rd. Beac. AO28 34
Howard Rd. Brom. CG50 78
Howard Rd. Couls. BW61 104
Howard Rd. Dart. CX46 80
Howard Rd. Dor. BJ71 119
Howard Rd. Ilf. CL35 49
Howard Rd. Islw. BH45 64
Howard Rd. Lthd. BC64 101
Howard Rd. Lthd. BF67 111
Howard Rd. N. Mal. BO52 85
Howard Rd. Reig. BS71 121
Howard Rd. Sthl. BF39 54
Howard Rd. Surb. BL53 85
Howard Rd. Upmin. CY34 51
Howards Clo. Pnr. BC30 35

Howards Dr. Hem. H. AW12 8
Howardsgate. Welw. G. C. BQ8 5
Howards La. SW15 BP45 65
Howards La. Wey. AV57 91
Howards Rd. E13 CH38 58
Howards Rd. Wok. AS63 100
Howards Thicket. Ger. Cr. AR33 43
Howard St. WC2 BX40 56
Arundel St.
Howard St. Surb. BJ54 84
Howards Wood Dr. Ger. Cr. AR34 43
Howards Yd. SE18 CL41 68
Powis St.
Howard Wk. N2 BT31 47
Howard Way, Harl. CN10 6
Howard Way, Harl. CN9 6
Howarth Rd. SE2 CO42 69
Howberry Clo. Edg. BK29 36
Howberry Rd. Edg. BK29 36
Howberry Rd. Th. Hth. BZ51 87
Howbury La. Erith CT44 69
Howbury Rd. SE15 CC45 67
Howcroft Cres. N3 BS29 38
Howden Rd. SE25 CA51 87
Howden St. SE15 CB45 67
Howe Clo. Rom. CR30 41
Howell Clo. Rom. CP32 50
Howell Hill Clo. Epsom BQ59 94
Howell Hill Gro. Epsom BQ58 94
Howe Rd. Hem. H. AZ15 8
Howfield Grn. Hodd. CD10 12
Howgate Rd. SW14 BO45 65
Howick Pl. SW1 BW41 66
Howicks Grn. Welw. G. C. BS9 5
Howie St. SW11 BU43 66
Howitt Rd. NW3 BU36 56
Howland Garth, St. Alb. BG15 9
Howland Ms. E. W1 BW39 56
Howland St.
Howland Ms. W. W1 BW39 56
Howland St.
Howlands. Welw. G. C. BQ9 5
Howland St. W1 BW39 56
How La. Couls. BU63 104
Howlett, S La. Ruis. BA32 44
Howletts Rd. SE24 BZ46 77
Howley Pl. W2 BT39 56
Howley Rd. Croy. BY55 86
Hows Clo. Uxb. AX37 53
Howsman Rd. SW13 BP43 65
Hows Mead. Epp. CS15 14
Howson Rd. SE4 CD45 67
Howson Ter. Rich. BL46 75
Hows Rd. Uxb. AX37 53
Hows St. E2 CA37 57
Howton Pl. Bush. BG26 36
How Wood, St. Alb. BF17 18
Hoxton Mkt. N1 CA38 57
Boot St.
Hoxton Sq. N1 CA38 57
Hoxton St. N1 CA37 57
Hoylake Cres. Uxb. AZ34 44
Hoylake Gdns. Mitch. BW52 86
Hoylake Gdns. Rom. CW30 42
Hoylake Gdns. Ruis. BC33 44
Hoylake Gdns. Wat. BD28 36
Hoylake Rd. W3 BO39 55
Hoyle Rd. SW17 BU49 76
Hoy St. E16 CG40 58
Hubbard Rd. SE27 BZ49 77
Hubbards Chase, Horn. CX32 51
Hubbards Clo. Horn. CX32 51
Hubbards Hill. Sev. CU68 116
Hubbards Rd. Rick. AU25 25
Hubbard St. E15 CG37 58
Hubert Gro. SW9 BX45 66
Hubert Rd. E6 CJ38 58
Hubert Rd. Brwd. DA27 42
Hubert Rd. Rain. CT38 59
Hubert Rd. Slou. AR42 62
Huddlestone Cres. Red. BW67 113
Huddlestone Rd. E7 CG35 49
Huddlestone Rd. NW2 BP36 55
Huddleston Rd. N7 BW34 47
Hudson Clo. NW3 BU36 56
Hudson Clo. Wat. BB21 26
Hudson Pl. SW1 BW42 66
Hudson Rd. E16 CG39 58
Hudson Rd. SE18 CM42 68
Hudson Rd. Bexh. CQ44 69
Hudson Rd. Hayes. BA43 63
Hudson Rd. Kings. On T. BL51 85
Huggin Hill EC4 BZ40 57
Queen Victoria St.
Huggin's La. Hat. BQ15 10
Hughan Rd. E15 CF35 48
Hughenden Av. Har. BJ32 45
Hughenden Gdns. Nthlt. BD38 54
Hughenden Rd. St. Alb. BJ12 9
Hughenden Rd. Slou. AO39 52
Hughenden Rd. Wor. Pk. BP54 85
Hughendon Ter. E15 CF35 48
Hughes Rd. Ashf. BA50 73
Hughes Rd. Grays. DG41 71
Hughes Rd. Hayes BC40 53
Hugh Ms. SW1 BV42 66
Hugh St.
Hugh St. SW1 BV42 66
Hugo Gdns. Rain. CU36 59
Hugon Rd. SW6 BS45 66
Hugo Rd. N19 BW35 47
Huguenot Pl. SW18 BT46 76
Huguenot Rd. SE15 CB45 67
Huitt Sq. SW11 BT45 66
Winstanley Rd.
Hulletts La. Brwd. CZ24 33
Hull Pl. SE18 CN42 68
Hull Rd. Rom. CQ32 50
Hull St. EC1 BZ38 57
Hulmlea Rd. Slou. AR44 62
Hulse Av. Bark. CM36 58
Hulse Av. Rom. CR30 41
Hulsewood Clo. Dart. CU48 79
Hulton Clo. Lthd. BK65 102
Hulverston Clo. Sutt. BS58 95
Humber Ave. S. Ock. CZ39 60
Humber Dr. Upmin. CY32 51
Humber Rd. NW2 BP34 46
Humber Rd. SE3 CG43 68
Humberstone Rd. E13 CJ38 58
Humberton Clo. E9 CD35 48
Swinnerton St.
Humber Way. Slou. AT42 62
Humbolt Clo. Guil. AP70 118
Humbolt Rd. W6 BR43 65
Hume Ave. Til. DG44 71
Humes Av. W7 BH41 64
Hume Way Ruis. BC32 44
Hummer Rd. Egh. AT49 72
Humphrey Clo. Ilf. CK30 40
Humphrey Clo. Lthd. BG64 102
Humphrey St. SE1 CA42 67
Hundred Acre NW9 BO30 37
Hundred Acres La. Amer. AO23 25
Hungerdown E4 CF26 39
Hungerford Av. Slou. AP39 52
Hungerford La. WC2 BX40 56
Craven St.
Hungerford Rd. N7 BW36 56
Hungerford St. E1 CB39 57
Commercial Rd.
Hungry Hill. Wok. AX66 110
Hunsdon Est. E5 CB34 48
Hunsdon Rd. SE14 CC43 67
Hunslett St. E2 CC37 57
Royston St.
Hunsoon Dr. Sev. CU65 107
Hunston Rd. Mord. BS54 86
Hunter Av. Brwd. DD25 122
Hunter Cl. SW12 BV47 76
Balham Pk. Rd.
Hunter Clo. Pot. B. BS20 20
Huntercombe Gdns. Wat. BD28 36
Huntercombe La. Maid AK40 61
Hunter Dr. Horn. CV35 51
Hunter Rd. SW20 BQ51 85
Hunter Rd. Guil. AS71 118
Hunter Rd. Ilf. CL35 49
Hunter Rd. Th. Hth. BZ52 87
Hunters Clo. Epsom BN60 94
Hunters Clo. Hem. H. AT18 16
Huntersfield Clo. Reig. BS69 121
Hunters Gro. Har. BK31 45
Hunters Gro. Hayes BC40 53
Hunter's Gro. Rom. CR28 41
Hunters Hall Rd. Dag. CR35 50
Hunter's Hill. Ruis. BD34 45
Hunter, S La. Wat. BB20 17
Hunters Ride, St. Alb. BF19 18
Hunters Rd. Chess. BL55 85
Hunters Sq. Dag. CR35 50
Hunter St. WC1 BX38 56
Hunters Way Enf. BY23 29
Hunter's Way. Welw. G. C. BR9 5
Hunter Wk. E13 CG37 58
Hunting Clo. Esher BF56 93
Huntingdon Clo. Brox. CD15 12
Huntingdon Clo. Mitch. BX52 86
Huntingdon Gdns. Wor. Pk. BQ55 85
Huntingdon Rd. N2 BU31 47
Huntingdon Rd. N9 CC26 39
Huntingdon Rd. Red. BU70 121
Cromwell Rd.
Huntingdon St. E16 CG39 58
Huntingdon St. N1 BX36 56
Huntingdon Way Croy. CA56 96
Huntingfield Croy. CD57 96
Huntingfield Rd. SW15 BP45 65
Huntingfield Way, Egh. AU50 72
Huntings Rd. Dag. CR36 59
Huntley Av. Grav. DD46 81
Huntley Dr. N3 BS29 38
Nether St.
Huntley St. WC1 BW38 56
Huntley Way SW20 BP51 85
Huntly Rd. SE25 CA52 87
Huntonbridge Hill, Kings L. BA20 17
Hunton St. E1 CB38 57
Hunt Rd. Grav. DF48 81
Hunt Rd. Sthl. BF41 64
Hunts Clo. Guil. AO70 118
Hunt's La. E15 CF37 57
Huntsman Rd. Ilf. CQ29 41
Huntsmans Dr. Upmin. CY35 51
Huntsman St. SE17 BZ42 67
Barlow St.
Huntsmead Enf. CC24 30
Huntsmead Clo. Chis. CK50 78
Bullerswood Dr.
Hunts Mill Rd. Hem. H. AV14 7
Huntsmoor Rd. Epsom BN56 94
Huntspill St. SW17 BT48 76
Hunts Slip Rd. SE21 CA48 77
Hunt St. W11 BQ40 55
Huntsworth Ms. NW1 BU38 56
Hurley Cl. Walt. BC55 83
Hurley Rd. Grnf. BF39 54
Hurlingham Ct. SW6 BR45 65
Hurlingham Gdns. SW6 BR45 65
Hurlingham Rd. SW6 BR44 65
Hurlingham Rd. Bexh. CQ43 69
Hurlock St. N5 BY34 47
Hurlstone Rd. SE25 BZ53 87
Hurnford Clo. Sth. Croy. CA58 96
Huron Rd. SW17 BV48 76
Hurry Clo. E15 CG36 58
Hurst Av. E4 CE28 39
Hurst Av. N6 BW32 47
Hurstbourne Gdns. Bark. CM36 58
Hurstbourne Rd. SE23 CD47 77
Hurst Clo. E4 CE27 39
Hurst Clo. NW11 BS32 47
Hurst Clo. Brom. CG54 88
Hurst Clo. Chess. BM56 94
Hurst Clo. Nthlt. BE35 45
Hurst Clo. Wok. AR63 100
Hurstcourt Rd. Sutt. BS55 86
Hurst Gro. Walt. BB54 83
Hurst Cft. Guil. AS72 118
Hurstdene Av. Brom. CG54 88
Hurstdene Av. Stai. AW50 73
Hurstdene Gdns. N15 CA32 48
Hurst Dr. Tad. BP66 112
Hurst Dr. Wal. Cr. CC20 21
Hurst Farm Rd. Sev. CU69 116
Hurstfield Brom. CH53 88
Hurstfield Cres. Hayes BB39 53
Hurstfield Rd. E. Mol. BF52 84
Hurst Grn. Oxt. CG69 115
Hurst Green Rd. Oxt. CG69 115
Hurst Gro. Walt. BB54 83
Hursthead Ct. Edg. BM28 37
Hurstlands. Oxt. CH69 115
Hurstlands Clo. Horn. CV32 51
Hurst La. SE2 CP42 69
Hurst La. E. Mol. BG52 84
Hurst La. Egh. AT51 82
Hurst La. Epsom. BN65 103
Hurstleigh Clo. Red. BU69 121
Hurstleigh Dr. Red. BU69 121
Hurstleigh Gdns. Ilf. CK30 40
Hurst Pk. Av. Horn. CW35 51
Hurst Place Est. SE2 CP42 69
Hurst Rise Barn BS24 29
Hurst Rd. E17 CE31 48
Hurst Rd. N21 BY26 38
Hurst Rd. Buck. H. CJ26 40
Hurst Rd. Croy. BZ56 96
Hurst Rd. Epsom BN59 94
Hurst Rd. Erith CS44 69
Hurst Rd. Sid. CO48 79
Hurst Rd. Tad. BP65 103
Hurst Rd. Walt. BD53 84
Hurst Springs Bex. CQ47 79
Hurst St. SE24 BY46 76
Hurst St. W11 BQ40 55
Hurst Vw. Rd. Sth. Croy. CA57 96
Hurst Way, Sev. CV67 117
Hurst Way Sth. Croy. CA57 96
Hurst Way. Wok. AV60 91
Hurstwood Av. E18 CH31 49
Hurstwood Av. Bex. CQ47 79
Hurstwood Av. Brwd. DA26 42
Hurstwood Av. Erith CT44 69
Hurstwood Ct. N12 BU29 38
Woodleigh Av.
Hurstwood Ct. NW11 BR31 46
Hurstwood Dr. Brom. CK52 88
Hurstwood Rd. NW11 BR31 46
Hurtwood Rd. Walt. BE54 84
Hurworth Rd. Slou. AR41 62
Husseywell Cres. Brom. CH54 88
Hutchings St. E14 CE41 67
Hutchings Wk. NW11 BS31 47
Hutchins Clo. E15 CF36 57
Hutton Clo. Wdf. Grn. CH28 40
Hutton Dr. Brwd. DE26 122
Hutton Gdns. Har. BG29 36
Hutton Gro. N12 BS28 38
Hutton La. Har. BG29 36
Hutton Rd. Brwd. DC26 122
Hutton St. EC4 BY39 56
Dorset Rise.
Hutton Village, Brwd. DF26 122
Hutton Wk. Har. BG29 36
Huxbear St. SE4 CD46 77
Huxley Clo. Uxb. AX38 53
Huxley Dr. Rom. CO33 50
Huxley Gdns. NW10 BL38 55
Huxley Pde. N18 BZ28 39
Huxley Pl. N13 BY27 38
Huxley Rd. E10 CF34 48
Huxley Rd. N18 BZ28 39
Huxley Rd. Well. CN45 68
Huxley Sayze N18 BZ28 39
Gt. Cambridge Rd.
Huxley St. W10 BR38 55
Hyacinth Ct. Pnr. BD31 45
Nursery Rd.
Hyacinth Rd. SW15 BP47 75
Hyburn Clo. St. Alb. BE18 18
Hycliffe Gdns. Chig. CM28 40
Hyde Av. Pot. B. BS20 20
Hyde Clo. Barn. BR24 28
Hyde Cres. NW9 BO32 46
Hydefield Clo. N21 BZ26 39
Hydefield Ct. N9 CA27 39
Hyde La. SW11 BU44 66
Westbridge Rd.
Hyde La. Hem. H. AT17 16
Hyde La. Hem. H. AZ17 17
Hyde La. St. Alb. BH17 18
Hyde La. Wok. AZ63 101
Hyde Mead. Wal. Abb. CG15 13
Hyde Meadows. Hem. H. AT17 16
Hyde Pk. Av. N21 BZ26 39
Hyde Pk. Corner W1 BV41 66
Hyde Pk. Cres. W2 BU39 56
Hyde Pk. Gdns. N21 BZ26 39
Hyde Park Gdns. W2 BT40 56
Hyde Park Gdns. Ms. W2 BU39 56
Hyde Pk. Gte. SW7 BT41 66
Hyde Pk. Gte. Ms. SW7 BT41 66
Hyde Pk. Mans. NW1 BU39 56
Edgware Rd.
Hyde Pk. Pl. W2 BU40 56
Bayswater Rd.
Hyde Park Sq. W2 BU39 56
Hyde Park St. W2 BU39 56
Hyde Pl. N1 BY36 56
Compton Av.
Hyde Rd. N1 BZ37 57
Hyde Rd. Bexh. CQ44 69
Hyde Rd. Rich. BL46 75
Albert Rd.
Hyde Rd. Sth. Croy. BZ60 96
Hyde Rd. Wat. BC23 26
Hyder Rd. Grays. DH41 71
Hydeside Gdns. N9 CA27 39
Hyde St. SE8 CD43 67
Hyde Ter. Ashf. BB50 73
Hyde. The. West Dr. AY41 63
Hydethorpe Av. N9 CA27 39
Hydethorpe Rd. SW12 BW47 76
Hyde Val. SE10 CF43 67
Hyde Valley. Welw. G. C. BR9 5
Hyde Wk. Mord. BS54 86
Hyde Way N9 CA27 39
Hyde Way. Hayes. BB42 63
Hyde Way. Welw. G. C. BR8 5
Hyland Clo. Horn. CU33 50
Hylands Mews, Epsom. BM61 103
Hylands Mews Epsom BN61 103
Hylands Rd. E17 CF31 48
Hylands Rd. Epsom BN61 103
Hyland Way. Horn. CU33 50
Hylle Clo. Wind. AM44 61
Cawcott Dr.
Hylton St. SE18 CN42 68
Hyndman Gro. SE15 CB43 67
Hyndman St. SE15 CB43 67
Hyperion Ct. Hem. H. AY12 8
Hyperion Pl. Epsom BN58 94
Hyrons La. Amer. AO22 25
Hyrst Dene Sth. Croy. BY56 95
Hyson Rd. SE16 CB42 67
Hythe Av. Bexh. CQ43 69
Hythe Cl. N18 CB28 39
Hythe End Rd. Stai. AT48 72
Hythe Field Av. Egh. AU50 72
Hythe Park Rd. Egh. AV49 72
Hythe Rd. NW10 BO38 55
Hythe Rd. Stai. AU49 72
Hythe Rd. Th. Hth. BZ51 87
Hythe St. Dart. CW46 80
Hythe, The Stai. AV49 72
Hyver Hill NW7 BN26 37
Ian Sq. Enf. CC23 30
Ibbetson Path. Loug. CL24 31
Ibbotson Av. E16 CG39 58
Iberian Av. Wall. BW56 95
Ibis La. W4 BN44 65
Ibscott Clo. Dag. CS36 59
Ibsley Gdns. SW15 BP47 75
Ibsley Way Barn. BU24 29
Icehouse Wood. Oxt. CG69 115
Iceland Rd. E3 CE37 57
Ickburgh Est. E5 CB34 48
Ickburgh Rd. E5 CB34 48
Ickenham Clo. Ruis. BA34 44
Ickenham Rd. Ruis. BA33 44
Ickenham Rd. Uxb. BA34 44
Ickleton Rd. SE9 CK49 78
Icklingham Rd. Cob. BD59 93
Icknield Clo. St. Alb. BE15 9
Icknield Dr. Ilf. CL32 49
Ickworth Pk. Rd. E17 CD31 48
Ida St. E14 CF39 57
Ide Hill. Sev. CS65 107
Ide Hill Rd. Sev. CQ69 116
Iden Clo. Brom. CG52 88
Idenden Cotts. SE10 CG41 68
Idlecombe Rd. SW17 BV50 76
Idmiston Rd. E15 CG35 49
Idmiston Rd. SE27 BZ48 77
Idmiston Rd. Wor. Pk. BO54 85
Idmiston Sq. Wor. Pk. BO54 85
Idol La. EC3 CA40 57
Idonia St. SE8 CD43 67
Iffley Clo. Uxb. AX36 53
Iffley Rd. W6 BP41 65
Ifield Rd. SW10 BS43 66
Ifield Ter. Green. DA46 80
Ifield Way, Grav. DH50 81
Ightham By Pass. Sev. DB64 108
Ightham Mote, Sev. DA67 117
Ightham Rd. Erith CR43 69
Ikona Ct. Wey. BA56 92
Ilbert St. W10 BQ38 55
Ilchester Gdns. W2 BS40 56
Ilchester Pl. W14 BR41 65
Ilchester Rd. Dag. CO35 50
Ildersley Gro. SE21 BZ48 77
Ilex Clo. Egh. AQ50 72
Ilex Rd. NW10 BO36 55
Ilex Way, SW16 BY49 76
Ilford Hill, Ilf. CL34 49
Ilford La. Ilf. CL34 49
Ilfracombe Gdns. Rom. CO33 50
Ilfracombe Rd. Brom. CG48 78
Iliffe St. SE17 BY42 66
Iliffe Yd. SE17 BY42 66
Amelia St.
Ilkley Rd. E16 CJ39 58
Ilkley Rd. Wat. BD28 36
Illingworth. Wind. AM45 61
Illingworth Way. Enf. CA25 30
Ilmington Rd. Har. BK32 45
Ilminster Gdns. SW11 BU45 66
Imber Clo. N14 BW26 38
Imber Ct. E. Mol. BG54 84
Imber Gro. Esher BG54 84
Imber Pk. Rd. Esher BG54 84
Imilking La. Orp. CK59 97
Imperial Av. N16 CA35 48
Imperial Clo. Har. BF32 45
Imperial Dr. Grav. DJ49 81
Imperial Dr. Har. BF33 45
Imperial Institute Rd. SW7 BT41 66
Imperial Mews, E6 CJ37 58
Imperial Rd. N22 BX30 38
Imperial Rd. SW6 BS44 66
Imperial Rd. Felt. BB47 73
Imperial Rd. Wind. AN45 61
Imperial Sq. SW6 BS44 66
Imperial St. E3 CF38 57
Imperial Way SE18 CK43 68
Imperial Way, Chis. CM48 78
Imperial Way Croy. BY57 95
Imperial Way, Har. BL32 46
Imperial Way, Wat. BD23 27
Inca Dr. SE9 CL47 78
Ince Rd. Watt. BB57 92
Inchmery Rd. SE6 CE48 77
Indells. Hat. BO13 10
Independents Rd. SE3 CG45 68
Inderwick Rd. N8 BX32 47
India Rd. Slou. AQ41 62
India St. EC3 CA39 57
Jewry St.
India Way W12 BP40 55
Indus Rd. SE7 CJ43 68
Industrial Est. Grnf. BF37 54
Industrial Est. Iver AV40 52
Industrial Est. Mitch. BU53 86
Ingal Rd. E13 CH38 58
Ingate Pl. SW8 BV44 66
Ingatestone Rd. E12 CJ33 49
Ingatestone Rd. SE25 CB52 87
Ingatestone Rd Ing. DC19 24
Ingatestone Rd. Wdf. Grn. CH29 40
Ingelow Rd. SW8 BV44 66
Ingels Mead, Epp. CN18 22
Ingersoll Rd. W12 BP40 55
Ingersoll Rd. Enf. CC22 30
Ingestre Pl. W1 BW39 56
Ingestre Rd. E7 CH35 49
Ingham Clo. Sth. Croy. CC58 96
Ingham Rd. NW6 BS35 47
Ingham Rd. Sth. Croy. CC58 96
Inglebert St. EC1 BY38 56
Ingleboro' Dr. Pur. BZ60 96
Ingleby Clo. Dag. CR36 59
Ingleby Dr. Har. BG34 45
Ingleby Gdns. Chig. CO27 41
Lambourne Rd.
Ingleby Rd. N7 BX34 47
Tollington Way
Ingleby Rd. Dag. CR36 59
Ingleby Rd. Grays. DG41 71
Ingleby Rd. Ilf. CL33 49
Ingleby Way, Chis. CL49 78
Ingleby Way Wall. BW57 95
Ingledew Rd. SE18 CM42 68
Ingleglen, Horn. CX33 51
Inglehurst, Wey. AW58 92
Inglehurst Gdns. Ilf. CK32 49
Inglemere Rd. SE23 CC48 77
Inglemere Rd. Mitch. BU50 76
Ingles, Welw. G. C. BQ6 5
Inglesham Wk. E9 CD36 57
Trowbridge Est.
Ingleside Clo. Beck. CE50 77
Ingleside Gro. SE3 CG43 68
Inglethorpe St. SW6 BQ44 65
Ingleton Av. Well. CO46 79
Ingleton Rd. N18 CB29 39
Ingleton Rd. Cars. BU58 95
Ingleway N12 BT29 38
Inglewood Clo. Ilf. CN29 40
New North Rd.
Inglewood Copse Brom. CK51 88
Inglewood Rd. NW6 BS35 47
Inglewood Rd. Bexh. CS45 69
Inglis Rd. W5 BL40 55
Inglis Rd. Croy. CA54 87
Inglis St. SE5 BY44 66
Ingoldsby Rd. Grav. DJ47 81
Ingram Av. NW11 BT33 47
Ingram Clo. Stan. BK28 36
Ingram Ho. Kings. On T. BK51 84
Ingram Rd. N2 BU31 47
Ingram Rd. Dart. CW47 80
Ingram Rd. Grays. DE42 71
Ingram Rd. Th. Hth. BZ51 87
Ingrams Clo. Walt. BD56 93
Ingram Way Grnf. BG37 54
Ingrave Rd. Brwd. DB27 42
Ingrave Rd. Brwd. DC27 122
Ingrave Rd. Rom. CS31 50
Ingrave St. SW11 BT45 66
Ingrebourne Gdns. CY33 51
Ingrebourne Rd. Rain. CU38 59
Ingress Gdns. Green. DB46 80
Ingreway, Rom. CX29 42
Inholms La. Dor. BJ73 119
Inigo Jones Rd. SE7 CJ43 68
Inkerman Rd. NW5 BV36 56
Inkerman Rd. St. Alb. BH14 9
Inkerman Rd. Wind. AM42 61
Inkerman Rd. Wok. AP62 100
Inkerman Ter. Chesh. AO20 16
Inks Green E4 CE28 39
Inman Rd. NW10 BO37 55
Inman Rd. SW18 BT47 76
Inman's Row, Wdf. Grn. CH28 40
Inner Circ. NW1 BV38 56
Inner Pk. Rd. SW19 BQ47 75
Inner Staithe W4 BN43 65
Upper Staithe
Innes Clo. SW20 BR51 85
Innes Gdns. SW15 BP46 75
Innes Lo. SE23 CC48 77
Innes Yd. Croy. BZ55 87
Whitgift St.
Inniskilling Rd. E13 CJ37 58
Inskip Dr. Horn. CW33 51
Inskip Rd. Dag. CP33 50
Institute Pl. E8 CB35 48
Amhurst Rd.
Institute Rd Epp. CP18 23
Institution Rd. Dor. BG72 119
Instone Clo. Wall. BX57 95
Instone Rd. Dart. CV47 80
Instow Pl. N7 BY35 47
Queensland Rd.
Insurance St. WC1 BY38 56
Margery St.

Inverarey Pl. SE18 CM43 68
Inver Clo. E5 CB34 48
Southwold Rd.
Inverclyde Gdns. Rom. CP31 50
Inveresk Gdns. Wor. Pk. BO55 85
Inverine Rd. SE7 CH42 68
Invermore Pl. SE18 CM42 68
Inverna Gdns. W8 BS42 66
Inverness Av. Enf. CA23 30
Inverness Ct. W3 BM39 55
Links Rd.
Inverness Dr. Ilf. CN29 40
Inverness Gdns. W8 BS40 56
Inverness Ms. W2 BS40 56
Inverness Ter.
Inverness Pl. W2 BS40 56
Inverness Ter.
Inverness Rd. N18 CB28 39
Inverness Rd. Houns. BE45 64
Inverness Rd. Sthl. BE42 64
Inverness Rd. Wor. Pk. BQ54 85
Inverness St. NW1 BV37 56
Inverness Ter. W2 BS40 56
Inverton Rd. SE15 CC45 67
Invicta Gro. Nthlt. BE38 54
Invicta Rd. SE3 CH43 68
Invicta Rd. Dart. CX46 80
Inwood Ave. Couls. BY63 104
Inwood Av. Houns. BG45 64
Inwood Clo. Croy. CD55 87
Inwood Rd. Houns. BF45 64
Inworth St. SW11 BU44 66
Iona Clo. SE6 CD47 77
Iona Clo. SE6 CE47 77
Ravensbourne Pk.
Ionian Way, Hem. H. AY12 8
Ipplepen Rd. N15 CA32 48
Ipswich Rd. SW17 BV50 76
Ireland Yd. EC4 BY39 56
St. Andrew's Hill
Irene Rd. SW6 BS44 66
Irene Rd. Cob. BF61 102
Irene Rd. Orp. CN54 88
Ireston Rd. Grays. DD42 71
Ireton Av. Walt. BB55 83
Ireton St. E3 CE38 57
Iris Av. Bex. CQ46 79
Iris Clo. Brwd. DA25 33
Iris Ct. Pnr. BD31 45
Nursery Rd.
Iris Cres. Bexh. CQ43 69
Iris Path. Rom. CV29 42
Iris Rd. Epsom. BM56 94
Iris Way E4 CD29 39
Irkdale Av. Enf. CA23 30
Iron Bri. Rd. West Dr. AZ40 53
Irongate Wf. Rd. W2 BT39 56
Iron Mill La. Dart. CT45 69
Iron Mill Pl. Dart. CT45 69
Iron Mill Rd. SW18 BS46 76
Ironmonger La. EC2 BZ39 57
Ironmonger Row, EC1 BZ38 57
Irons Bottom Rd. Reig. BS74 121
Irons Way Rom. CS29 41
Irvine Av. Har. BJ31 45
Irvine Clo. N20 BU27 38
Irvine Gdns. S. Ock. CZ39 60
Irvine Way Orp. CN54 88
Irving Av. Nthlt. BD37 54
Irving Gro. SW9 BX44 66
Irving Rd. W14 BQ41 65
Irving St. WC2 BW40 56
Leicester Sq.
Irving Wk. Swans. DC47 81
Irving Way Swan. CS51 89
Irwin Av. SE18 CN43 68
Irwin Gdns. NW10 BP37 55
Irwin Rd. Guil. AQ71 118
Isabella Rd. E9 CC35 48
Isabel St. SW9 BX44 66
Isel Way, SE22 CA46 77
Dulwich Gro.
Isham Rd. SW16 BX51 86
Isis Dr. Upmin. CZ32 51
Isis St. SW18 BT48 76
Island Fm. Av. E. Mol. BF53 84
Island Fm. Rd. E. Mol. BE53 84
Island Rd. Mitch. BU50 76
Island Row, E14 CD39 57
Island, The Stai. AT48 72
Isla Rd. SE18 CM43 68
Islay Gdns. Houns. BD46 74
Islay Wk. N1 BZ36 57
Marquess Est.
Isledon Rd. N7 BX34 47
Islehurst Clo. Chis. CL51 88
Summer Hill
Islehurst Cr. Chis. CL51 88
Islington High St. N1 BY37 56
Islington Pk. St. N1 BY36 56
Islip Gdns. Edg. BN29 37
Islip Gdns. Nthlt. BE36 54
Islip Manor Rd. Nthlt. BE36 54
Islip St. NW5 BW35 47
Ismailia Rd. E7 CH36 58
Ismays Rd. Sev. DA66 117
Istead Rise, Grav. DF50 81
Italian Wk. SE11 BX42 66
Itchingwood Common Rd. Oxt. CJ70 115
Ivanhoe Clo. Uxb. AX39 53
Ivanhoe Dr. Har. BJ31 45
Ivanhoe Rd. SE5 CA45 67
Ivanhoe Rd. Houns. BD45 64
Ivatt Way N17 BZ31 48
Iveagh Av. NW10 BM37 55
Iveagh Clo. NW10 BM37 55
Iveagh Rd. Guil. AQ71 118
Ivedon Rd. Well. CP44 69
Ive Farm Clo. E10 CE34 48
Iveley Rd. SW4 BW44 66
Iverdale Clo. Iver AU40 52
Ivere Dr. Barn. BS25 29
Iver La. Iver & Uxb. AW39 53
Iverna Gdns. W8 BS41 66
Iverna Gdns. Felt. BA46 73
Iverson Rd. NW6 BR36 55
Ivers Way Croy. CE57 96
Ives Rd. E16 CG39 58
Ives Rd. Slou. AS41 62
Ives St. SW3 BU42 66
Ivestor Ter. SE23 CC47 77
Ivimey St. E2 CB38 57
Pollard Row
Ivinghoe Clo. Enf. BZ23 30
Ivinghoe Clo. Wat. BD21 27
Ivinghoe Rd. Bush. BG26 36
Ivinghoe Rd. Dag. CO35 50
Ivinghoe Rd. Rick. AV26 34
Ivinghoe Rd. Rick. AW26 35
Ivor Clo. Guil. AT71 118
Ivor Gro. SE9 CL47 78
Ivor Pl. NW1 BU38 56
Ivor St. NW1 BW36 56
Ivorydown, Brom. CH49 78
Ivybridge, Brox. CE13 12
Ivychimneys Rd. Epp. CN20 22
Ivy Clo. Dart. CX47 80
Ivy Clo. Har. BE35 45
Ivy Clo. Pnr. BD33 45
Ivy Clo. Sun. BD51 84
Ivy Cres. W4 BN42 65
Ivydale Rd. SE15 CC46 77
Ivydale Rd. Cars. BU55 86
Ivyday Gro. SW16 BX48 76
Ivydene E. Mol. BE53 84
Ivy Dene Clo. Red. BV73 121
Ivydene Clo. Sutt. BT56 95
Ivydene Rd. E8 CB36 57
Ivy Gdns. N8 BX32 47
Ivy Gdns. Mitch. BW52 86
Ivy House La. Berk. AR13 7
Ivy House La. Sev. CS62 107
Ivyhouse Rd. Dag. CP36 59
Ivyhouse Rd. Uxb. AZ34 44
Ivy La. Houns. BE45 64
Ivy La. Wok. AT62 100
Ivy Lodge La. Rom. CX30 42
Ivy Mill Clo. Gdse. CB69 114
Ivy Mill La. Gdse. CB69 114
Ivymount Rd. SE27 BY48 76
Ivy Pl. Surb. BL53 85
Ivy Rd. E16 CH39 58
Ivy Rd. E17 CE32 48
Ivy Rd. N14 BW26 38
Ivy Rd. NW2 BQ35 46
Ivy Rd. SE4 CD45 67
Ivy Rd. Houns. BF45 64
Ivy Rd. Surb. BM54 85
Ivy St. N1 CA37 57
Ivy Ter. Hodd. CF11 12
Ivy Wk. Dag. CQ36 59
Ixworth Pl. SW3 BU42 66
Izane Rd. Bexh. CQ45 69
Jackass La. Kes. CH57 97
Jackass La. Oxt. CD69 114
Jack Cornwell St. E12 CL35 49
Jackdaws. Welw. G. C. BT7 5
Jackets La. Nthwd. AZ29 35
Jacketts Fld. Wat. BB18 17
Jackman Ms. NW10 BO34 46
North Circular Rd.
Jackman's La. Wok. AQ63 100
Jackman St. E8 CB37 57
Jackson Clo. Epsom BN60 94
Jackson Rd. N7 BX35 47
Jackson Rd. Bark. CM37 58
Jackson Rd. Barn. BT25 29
Jackson Rd. Brom. CK55 88
Jackson Rd. Uxb. AY36 53
Jackson's La. N6 BV33 47
Jackson's Ms. NW10 BO34 46
Jackson's Pl. Croy. BZ54 87
Jackson St. SE18 CL43 68
Jacobs Clo. Wind. AM44 61
Jacobs Ladder. Warl. CB63 105
Jacob St. SE1 CB41 67
Jacobs Well Ms. W1 BV39 56
George St.
Jacob's Well Rd. Guil. AR68 109
Jaffray Pl. SE27 BY49 76
Jaffray Rd. Brom. CJ52 88
Jago Clo. SE18 CM43 68
Jago Wk. SE5 BZ43 67
Lomond Gro.
Jail La. West. CJ61 106
Jamaica Rd. SE16 CA41 67
Jamaica Rd. Th. Hth. BY53 86
Jamaica St. E1 CC39 57
James Av. NW2 BQ35 46
James Av. Dag. CQ33 50
James Clo. Bush. BE25 27
James Clo. Rom. CU32 50
James Gdns. N22 BY29 38
James Gdns. Wem. BK36 54
James Newman Ct. SE9 CL49 78
Jameson Ct. St. Alb. BH13 9
Avenue Rd.
Jameson St. W8 BS40 56
James Pass. N17 CA29 39
Church Rd.
James Rd. Dart. CT47 79
James's Cotts. Rich. BM43 65
Kew Rd.
James St. W1 BV39 56
James St. WC2 BX40 56
Long Acre
James St. Bark. CM36 58
James St. Enf. CA25 30
James St. Epp. CO17 23
James St. Houns. BG45 64
James St. Wem. BK36 54
James St. Wind. AO44 61
Peascod St.
Jamestown Rd. NW1 BV37 56
Jamnagar Clo. Stai. AV50 72
Jane Clo. Hem. H. AZ11 8
Janet St. E14 CE41 67
Janeway Pl. SE16 CB41 67
Janeway St.
Janeway St. SE16 CB41 67
Janice Mews Ilf. CL34 49
Oakfield Rd.
Jan Mead, Brwd. DD26 122
Jansen Wk. SW11 BT45 66
Wayland Rd.
Janson Clo. E15 CG35 49
Janson Rd.
Janson Rd. E15 CG35 49
Jansons Rd. N15 CA31 48
Japan Cres. N4 BX33 47
Japan Rd. Rom. CP32 50
Japonica Clo. Wok. AR62 100
Silversmiths Way
Jaqueline Clo. Nthlt. BE37 54
Jardin St. SE5 CA43 67
Jarman Clo. Hem. H. AY14 8
Jarrow Rd. N15 CB31 48
Jarrow Rd. SE16 CC42 67
Jarrow Rd. Rom. CP32 50
Jarvis Rd. Sth. Croy. BZ57 96
Jasmine Clo. Orp. CL55 88
Jasmine Clo. Red. BV73 121
Jasmine Gdns. Croy. CE55 87
Jasmine Gro. SE20 CB51 87
Jasmine Ter. West Dr. AZ41 63
Jasmine Way E. Mol. BH52 84
Jasmin Rd. Epsom. BM57 94
Jason Clo. E15 CG35 49
Jason Rd.
Jason Clo. Brwd. CZ28 42
Jason Clo. Red. BU73 121
Jason Clo, Wey. BA56 92
Jasons Hill. Chesh. AQ17 16
Jason Wk. SE9 CL49 78
Jasper Clo. Enf. CC22 30
Jasper Pass. SE19 CA50 77
Jasper Rd. SE19 CA50 77
Javelin Way Nthlt. BD38 54
Jay Ms. SW7 BT41 66
Jays Bldgs. W1 BX37 56
Rodney St.
Jebb Av. SW2 BX46 76
Jebb St. E3 CE37 57
Jedburgh Rd. E13 CJ38 58
Jedburgh St. SW11 BV45 66
Jeddo Rd. W12 BO41 65
Jeffrey Clo. Slou. AT42 62
Jeffreys Pl. NW1 BW36 56
Jeffreys St.
Jeffrey's Rd. SW4 BX44 66
Jeffreys Rd. Enf. CD24 30
Jeffrey's St. NW1 BW36 56
Jeffreys Way, Enf. CD24 30
Jeffs Rd. Sutt. BR56 94
Jeken Rd. SE9 CJ45 68
Jelf Rd. SW2 BY46 76
Jellicoe Av. Grav. DH48 81
Jellicoe Gdns. Stan. BJ29 36
Jellicoe Rd. N17 BZ29 39
Jenkins Av. St. Alb. BE18 18
Jenkins La. Bark. CL38 58
Jenkins Rd. E13 CH38 58
Jenner Pl. SW13 BP43 65
Jenner Rd. N16 CA34 48
Jenner Rd. Guil. AS71 118
Jennett Rd. Croy. BY55 86
Jennifer Rd. Brom. CG48 78
Jenningham Dr. Grays. DD40 71
Jennings Rd. SE22 CA46 77
Jennings Rd. St. Alb. BH13 9
Jennings Way Barn. BQ24 28
Jenningtree Rd. Erith. CU43 69
Jenningtree Way Belv. CS41 69
Jenny Path. Rom. CV29 42
Jenson Way SE19 CA50 77
Fox Hill
Jenton Av. Bexh. CQ44 69
Jephson Rd. E7 CJ36 58
Jephson St. SE5 BZ44 67
Grove La.
Jephtha Rd. SW18 BS46 76
Jeppo's La. Mitch. BU52 86
Jerdan Pl. SW6 BS43 66
Fulham Broadway
Jeremiah St. E14 CE39 57
Jeremys Grn. N18 CB28 39
Jericho Pl. Ing. DC19 24
Jermyn St. SW1 BW40 56
Jernigham Av. Ilf. CL30 40
Jerningham Rd. SE14 CD44 67
Jerome Cres. NW8 BU38 56
Jerome Dr. St. Alb. BF15 9
Jerome Pl. SE17 BZ43 67
Hillingdon St.
Jerome St. E1 CA38 57
Calvin St.
Jerome St. E1 CA39 57
Jerounds Harl. CL12 13
Jerrard St. SE13 CE45 67
Jersey Av. Stan. BJ30 36
Jersey Clo. Hodd. CE11 12
Jersey Dr. Orp. CM53 88
Jersey La. St. Alb. BJ12 9
Jersey La. St. Alb. BK10 9
Jersey Rd. E11 CF33 48
Jersey Rd. E16 CH39 58
Jersey Rd. SW17 BV50 76
Jersey Rd. W7 BJ41 64
Jersey Rd. Houns. BF44 64
Jersey Rd. Ilf. CL35 49
Jersey Rd. Rain. CU36 59
Jersey St. E2 CB38 57
Bethnal Green Rd.
Jerusalem Pl. EC1 BY38 56
Aylesbury St.
Jervis Av. Enf. CD21 30
Jerviston Gdns. SW16 BY50 76
Jesmond Av. Wem. BL36 55
Jesmond Rd. Croy. CA54 87
Jesmond Rd. Grays. DE40 71
Jesmond Way. Stan. BL28 37
Jessam Av. E5 CB33 48
Jessamine Pl. Dart. CW48 80
Jessamine Rd. W7 BH40 54
Jessamin Pl. Dart. CY47 80
Jessamy St. Wey. AZ55 83
Jessel Dr. Loug. CM23 31
Jesse Rd. E10 CF33 48
Jessica Rd. SW18 BT46 76
Jessiman Ter. Shep. AZ53 83
Jessop Rd. SE24 BZ45 67
Jetstar Way Nthlt. BE38 54
Jevington Way, SE12 CH47 78
Jewel Rd. E17 CE31 48
Jewels Hill. War. CH59 97
Jewry St. EC3 CA39 57
Jews Row, SW18 BS45 66
Jews Wk. SE26 CB49 77
Jeymer Av. NW2 BP35 46
Jeymer Dr. Grnf. BF37 54
Jeypore Rd. SW18 BT46 76
Jillian Clo. Hamptn. BF50 74
Jinnings, The, Welw. G. C. BS9 5
Joan Cres. SE9 CJ47 78
Joan Gdns. Dag. CQ34 50
Joan Rd. Dag. CQ34 50
Joan St. SE1 BY40 56
Jocelyn Rd. Rich. BL45 65
Jocelyns, Harl. CP9 6
Jocketts Hill, Hem. H. AV14 7
Jocketts Rd. Hem. H. AV14 7
Jockey's Fields, WC1 BX39 56
Jodrell Rd. E3 CD37 57
Joel St. Nthwd. BC31 44
Johanna St. SE1 BY41 66
John Adam St. WC2 BX40 56
Villiers St.
John Aird Ct. W2 BT39 56
Howley Pl.
John Barnes Wk. E15 CG36 58
John Bradshaw Rd. N14 BW26 38
John Burns Dr. Bark. CN36 58
John Campbell Rd. N16 CA35 48
John Carpenter St. EC4 BY40 56
John Clay Gdns. Grays DD40 71
Whitmore Av.
John Clynge Ct. SW15 BP45 65
Woodborough Rd.
John Cobb Rd. Wey. AZ57 92
John Dwight Ho. SW6 BS45 66
John Elict Clo. Wal. Abb. CG14 13
John Felton Rd. SE16 CB41 67
John Fisher St. E1 CB40 57
John Foxe Pl. Wal. Abb. CF20 21
John Islip St. SW1 BW42 66
John Newton Ct. Well. CO45 69
John Parker Clo. Dag. CR36 59
John Penn St. SE13 CE44 67
John Perrin Pl. Harrow, BL33 46
Preston Hill
John Prince's St. W1 BV39 56
John Ruskin St. SE5 BY43 66
John's Av. NW4 BQ31 46
John's Clo. Ashf. BA49 73
John's Gro. Rich. BL45 65
Kew Foot Rd.
John's La. Mord. BT53 86
John's Ms. WC1 BX38 56
Johnson Clo. Grav. DE48 81
Johnson Clo. Mitch. BV52 86
Johnson Rd. Brom. CJ53 88
Johnson Rd. Croy. BZ54 87
Johnson Rd. Houns. BD43 64
Johnsons Av. Sev. CR58 98
Johnson's Clo. Cars. BU55 86
Johnsons Dr. Hamptn. BG51 84
Johnson St. E1 CC40 57
Johnson St. Sthl. BD41 64
John's Pla. E1 CB39 57
Nelson St.
Johns Rd. West. CJ63 106
John's Ter. Croy. CA54 87
Johns, The, Ong. CX17 24
Johnstone Rd. E6 CK38 58
Johnstone Ter. NW2 BQ34 46
Johnston Grn. Guil. AQ68 109
Johnston Rd. Wdf. Grn. CH29 40
Johnston Walk, Guil. AQ68 109
John St. E15 CG37 58
John St. SE25 CB52 87
John St. WC1 BX38 56
John St. Enf. CA25 30
John St. Grays. DE43 71
John St. Houns. BE44 64
Johns Wk. Whyt. CB63 105
John Taylor Ct. Slou. AO40 61
Tuns La.
John Wilson St. SE18 CL41 68
Joiners Clo. Chesh. AQ18 16
Joiners Clo. Ger. Cr. AS29 34
Joiner St. SE1 BZ40 57
Joiners Way. Ger. Cr. AS29 34
Jolleys La. Har. BG33 45
Jolliffe Rd. Red. BW66 113
Jonathan St. SE11 BX42 66
Jones Rd. E13 CH38 58
Holborn Rd.
Jones Rd. Wal. Cr. BY18 20
Jones St. W1 BV40 56
Bourdon St.
Jones Way Slou. AO34 43
Jonson Clo. Hayes BC39 53
Joram Way, SE16 CB42 67
Egan Way
Jordan Rd. Grnf. BJ37 54
Jordans Clo. Guil. AT70 118
Beatty Av.
Jordans Clo. Islw. BH44 64
Jordans Clo. Stai. AX47 73
Jordans Clo. Wat. BB21 26
Jordans Way. Beac. AP29 34
Jordans Way. Rain. CV37 60
Jordans Way, St. Alb. BE18 18
Jordon Dr. Red. BV73 121
Josephine Ave. Tad. BR66 112
Josephine Av. SW2 BX46 76
Joseph's Rd. Guil. AR70 118
Joseph St. E3 CD38 57
Joshua St. E14 CF39 57
Joslin Rd. Grays. CY42 70
Joubert St. SW11 BU44 66
Journeys End, Slou. AP38 52
Jowett St. SE15 CA43 67
Joyce Av. N18 CA28 39
Joyce Ct. Wal. Abb. CF20 21
Joyce Grn. La. Dart. CW45 70
Joyce Grn. Wk. Dart. CW46 80
Joydens Wd. Rd. Bex. CS48 79
Joydon Dr. Rom. CO32 50
Joyners Field. Harl. CM13 13
Joy Rd. Grav. DH47 81
Jubilee Av. Rom. CR32 50
Jubilee Av. Twick. BG47 74
Jubilee Clo. NW9 BN32 46
Jubilee Clo. Rom. CR32 50
Jubilee Cotts. SE9 CK46 78
Jubilee Ct. Th. Hth. BY52 86
Jubilee Cres. E14 CF41 67
Jubilee Cres. N9 CB26 39
Jubilee Cres. Grav. DJ48 81
Jubilee Cres. Sev. DB64 108
Jubilee Cres. Wey. AX56 92
Jubilee Dr. Ruis. BD35 45
Jubilee Gdns. Sthl. BF39 54
Jubilee Pl. SW3 BU42 66
Jubilee Ri. Sev. CW64 108
Jubilee Rd. Grays DA43 70
Jubilee Rd. Grnf. BJ37 54
Jubilee Rd. Orp. CQ57 98
Jubilee Rd, St. Alb. BK16 18
Jubilee Rd. Sid. CP50 79
Jubilee Rd. Sutt. BQ57 94
Jubilee Rd. Wat. BC22 26
Jubilee St. E1 CC39 57
Jubilee Ter. Bet. BN72 120
Jubilee Ter. Dor. BJ71 119
Jubilee Way Chess. BM56 94
Judd St. WC1 BX38 56
Jude St. E16 CG39 58
Judeth Gdns. Grav. DJ49 81
Judge Heath La. Hayes BA39 53
Judges Hill, Pot. B. BU18 20
Judge St. Wat. BC22 26
Judges Wk. NW3 BT34 47
Judith Ann Ct. Upmin. CZ34 51
Judith Av. Rom. CR29 41
Juer St. SW11 BU43 66
Jug Hill, West. CG61 106
Julia Gdns. Bark. CP37 59
Julian Av. W3 BM40 55
Julian Clo. Barn. BS24 29
Julian Clo. Wok. AR62 100
Silversmiths Way
Julian Hill Har. BH34 45
Julian Hill, Wey. AZ57 92
Julian Rd. Orp. CO57 98
Julians Clo. Sev. CU67 116
Julians Way. Sev. CU67 116
Julien Rd. W5 BK42 64
Julien Rd. Couls. BW61 104
Junction App. SE13 CF45 67
Junction Ms. W2 BU39 56
Sale Pl.
Junction Rd. E13 CH37 58
Junction Rd. N9 CB26 39
Junction Rd. N19 BW35 47
Junction Rd. W5 BK42 64
Junction Rd. W17 CB31 48
Junction Rd. Ashf. BA49 73
Junction Rd. Brwd. DB28 42
Junction Rd. Dart. CV46 80
Junction Rd. Dor. BJ71 119
Junction Rd. Har. BG32 45
Junction Rd. Rom. CT31 50
Junction Rd. Sth. Croy. BZ57 96
Junction Rd. E. Rom. CQ33 50
Kenneth Rd.
Junction Rd. W. Rom. CQ33 50
June Clo. Couls. BV60 95
June La. Red. BV74 121
Juniper Av. St. Alb. BF19 18
Juniper Clo. Guil. AR68 109
Juniper Clo. Reig. BT71 121
Juniper Clo. Rick. AX27 35
Juniper Grn. Hem. H. AV13 7
Juniper Gro. Wat. BC22 26
Juniper Rd. Ilf. CL35 49
Riverdene Rd.
Juniper Rd. Reig. BT71 121
Juniper St. E1 CC40 57
Juniper Wk. Bet. BN71 120
Juniper Way, Hayes BA40 53
Juno Rd. Hem. H. AY12 8
Juno Way, SE14 CC43 67
Jupiter Dr. Hem. H. AY12 8
Jupp Rd. W. E15 CF37 57
Jupps Rd. E3 CD38 57
Jurgen's Rd. Grays CY43 70
Justice Wk. SW3 BU43 66
Lawrence St.
Justin Clo. Brent. BK43 64
Jute La. Enf. CD23 30
Jutland Rd. E13 CH38 58
Jutland Rd. SE6 CF47 77
Jutsums Av. Rom. CR32 50
Jutsums La. Rom. CR32 50
Juxon St. SE11 BX42 66
Kadona Clo. Pnr. BC32 44
Kale Rd. Belv. CQ41 69
Kambala Rd. SW11 BT44 66
Kandle Wood, Brwd. DD26 122
Kangley Bri. Rd. SE26 CD49 77
Karen Clo. Rain. CT37 59
Karen Ct. Brom. CG51 88
Karen Ter. E11 CG34 49
Montague Rd.

Karoline Gdns. Grnf. BG37 54
Kashgar Rd. SE18 CN42 68
Kashmir, Wey. AX58 92
Kashmir Rd. SE7 CJ43 68
Kassala Rd. SW11 BU44 66
Kates Croft. Welw. G. C. BR10 5
Kate St. SW12 BV47 76
Katharine St. Croy. BZ55 87
Katherine Clo. Wey. AW57 92
Katherine Gdns. SE9 CJ45 68
Katherine Gdns. Ilf. CM29 40
Katherine Rd. Twick. BJ47 74
Kathleen Av. W3 BN39 55
Kathleen Av. Wem. BL36 55
Kathleen Rd. SW11 BU45 66
Kavanagh, S Rd. Brwd. DA27 42
Kavanagh, S Ter. Brwd. DA27 42
Kayemoor Rd. Sutt. BT57 95
Kay Rd. SW9 BX44 66
Kay St. E2 CB37 57
Kay St. E15 CF36 57
New Mk. St.
Kay St. Well. CO44 69
Kean St. WC2 BX39 56
Kearn Clo. Brwd. DB26 42
Kearton Clo. Ken. BZ62 105
Keary Rd. Swans. DC47 81
Keats Av. Rom. CU30 41
Keats Clo. NW3 BU35 47
Keats Gro.
Keats Clo. Chig. CM29 40
Keats Clo. Hayes BC39 53
Keats Gdns. Til. DG44 71
Keats Gro. NW3 BT35 47
Keats La. Wind. AO43 61
Keats Rd. Belv. CS41 69
Keats Rd. Well. CN44 68
Keats Wk. Brwd. DE26 122
Keats Way Croy. CC53 87
Keats Way Grnf. BF39 54
Keats Way. West Dr. AY42 63
Keble Clo. Nthlt. BG35 45
Keble Clo. Wor. Pk. BO54 85
Keble St. SW17 BT49 76
Keble Ter. Wat. BB19 17
Kechill Gdns. Brom. CH54 88
Kedeston Ct. Sutt. BS55 86
Kedleston Dr. Orp. CN53 88
Kedleston Wk. E2 CB38 57
Keedonwood Rd. Brom. CG49 78
Keel Dr. Slou. AN40 61
Keeley Rd. Croy. BZ55 87
Keeley St. WC2 BX39 56
Keeling Rd. SE9 CJ46 78
Keemor St. SE18 CL43 68
Keensacre, Iver AU37 52
Keens Park Rd. Guil. AP68 109
Keen's Rd. Croy. BZ56 96
Keen's Yd. N1 BY36 56
St. Paul's Rd.
Keepers Walk, Vir. W. AR53 82
Keep, The, SE3 CH44 68
Keeton's Rd. SE16 CB41 67
Keevil Dr. SW19 BQ47 75
Keighley Cl. N7 BX35 47
Penn Rd.
Keighley Rd. Rom. CW29 42
Keightley Dr. SE9 CK47 78
Keildon Rd. SW11 BU45 66
Keir Hardie Ho. W6 BQ43 65
Keir Hardie Way, Bark. CO36 59
Keir, The, SW19 BQ49 75
Keith Ave. S. Dnth. CX50 80
Keith Gro. W12 BP41 65
Keith Park Cres. West. CH59 97
Keith Pk. Rd. Uxb. AY36 53
Keith Rd. E17 CD30 39
Keith Rd. Bark. CM37 58
Keith Rd. Hayes. BB41 63
Keiths Rd. Hem. H. AZ14 8
Keithway Horn. CW33 51
Kelbrook Rd. SE3 CK44 68
Kelburn Way Rain. CT38 59
Kelby Path, SE9 CL48 78
Kelceda Clo. NW2 BP34 46
Kelfield Gdns. W10 BQ39 55
Kelland Clo. N8 BW32 47
Kelland Rd. E13 CH38 58
Kellaway Rd. SE3 CJ44 68
Kellerton Rd. SE13 CG46 78
Kellett Rd. SW2 BY45 66
Kelling Gdns. Croy. BY54 86
Kellino St. SW17 BU49 76
Kelliwell Ct. SE22 CB46 77
Kellner Rd. SE28 CN41 68
Kellway Pl. W14 BR42 65
Kelly Rd. NW7 BR29 37
Kelly St. NW1 BV36 56
Kelly Way, Rom. CQ32 50
Kelman Clo. SW4 BW44 66
Kelmore Gro. SE22 CB45 67
Kelmscott Clo. E17 CD30 39
Kelmscott Clo. Wat. BC25 26
Kelmscott Cres. Wat. BC25 26
Kelmscott Gdns. W12 BP41 65
Kelmscott Rd. SW11 BU46 76
Kelross Rd. N5 BY35 47
Kelsall Clo. SE3 CH44 68
Kelsey La. Beck. CE52 87
Kelsey Pk. Av. Beck. CE51 87
Kelsey Pk. Rd. Beck. CE51 87
Kelsey Rd. Orp. CO51 89
Kelsey St. E2 CB38 57
Kelsey Way Beck. CE52 87
Kelshall Wat. BE21 27
Kelsie Way, Ilf. CN29 40
Kelso Dr. Grav. DJ49 81
Kelso Pl. W8 BS41 66
Kelso Rd. Cars. BT54 86
Kelston Rd. Ilf. CL30 40
Kelvedon Av. Watt. BB57 92
Kelvedon Clo. Kings. On T. BM50 75
Kelvedon Hall Brwd. CX21 33
Kelvedon Rd. SW6 BR43 65
Kelvedon Wk. Rain. CT37 59
Kelvedon Way, Wdf. Grn. CK29 40
Kelvin Av. N13 BX29 38
Kelvin Av. Tedd. BH50 74
Kelvinbrook E. Mol. BF52 84
Kelvin Clo. Epsom. BM57 94
Kelvin Cres. Har. BH29 36
Kelvin Dr. Twick. BJ46 74
Kelvin Gdns. Sthl. BF39 54
Kelvin Gro. SE26 CB48 77
Kelvin Gro. Chess. BK55 84
Kelvington Clo. Croy. CD53 87
Kelvington Clo. Orp. CO52 89
Kelvington Rd. SE15 CC46 77
Kelvin Pde. Orp. CN54 88
Kelvin Rd. N5 BZ35 48
Kelvin Rd. Til. DG44 71
Kelvin Rd. Well. CO45 69
Kelway Pl. W14 BR43 65
Kemble Clo. Pot. B. BT20 20
Kemble Clo, Wey. BA56 92
Kemble Dr. Brom. CK55 88
Kemble Rd. N17 CB30 39
Kemble Rd. SE23 CC47 77
Kemble Rd. Croy. BY55 86
Kemble St. WC2 BX39 56
Kemerton Rd. SE5 BZ45 67
Kemerton Rd. Beck. CE51 87
Kemerton Rd. Croy. CA54 87
Kemeys St. E9 CD35 48
Kemnal Rd. Chis. CM50 78
Kempe Clo. St. Alb. BG15 9
Kempe Rd. NW6 BQ37 55
Kempe Rd. Enf. CB21 30
Kempis Way, SE22 CA46 77
Dulwich Gro.
Kemplay Rd. NW3 BT35 47
Kemple Rd. NW6 BQ37 55
Kemp Rd. Dag. CP33 50
Kempsford Gdns. SW5 BS42 66
Kempsford Rd. SE11 BY42 66
Kempshead Rd. SE5 CA42 67
Kempshott Rd. SW16 BW50 76
Kempson Rd. SW6 BS43 66
Kempton Av. Horn. CW35 51
Kempton Av. Nthlt. BF36 54
Kempton Av. Sun. BC51 83
Kempton Clo. Erith CS43 69
Kempton Rd. E6 CK37 58
Kempton Rd. Hamptn. BE51 84
Kempton Wk. Croy. CD53 87
Kempt St. SE18 CL43 68
Kemsing Clo. Bex. CQ47 79
Kemsing Clo. Brom. CG55 88
Kemsing Clo. Th. Hth. BZ52 87
Kemsing Rd. SE10 CH42 68
Kemsing Rd. Sev. DA62 108
Kemsley Clo. Grav. DF49 81
Kemsley Rd. West. CJ63 106
Kenbrick Ms. SW7 BT43 66
Reece Ms.
Kenbury Clo. Uxb. AZ34 44
Kenbury St. SE5 BZ44 67
Kenchester St. SW8 BX43 66
Kendal Av. N18 BZ28 39
Kendal Av. W3 BM39 55
Kendal Av. Bark. CN37 58
Kendal Av. Epp. CO18 23
Kendal Av. Epp. CO19 23
Kendal Clo. Reig. BT70 121
Kendal Clo. Slou. AQ40 52
Kendal Clo. Wdf. Grn. CG27 40
Kendal Croft Horn. CU35 50
Kendal Dr. Slou. AQ40 52
Kendale Grays DG41 71
Godman Rd.
Kendale, Hem. H. AZ14 8
Kendale Clo. Hayes BB37 53
Kendale Rd. Brom. CG49 78
Kendal Gdns. N18 BZ28 39
Kendall Av. Beck. CD51 87
Kendall Av. Sth. Croy. BZ58 96
Kendall Av. S. Sth. Croy. BZ58 96
Kendall Gdns. Sutt. BT55 86
Kendall Rd. Beck. CD51 87
Kendall Rd. Islw. BJ44 64
Kendal Rd. NW10 BP35 46
Kendals Clo. Rad. BH21 27
Kendal St. W2 BU39 56
Kender Est. SE14 CC44 67
Kender St. SE14 CC44 67
Kendoa Rd. SW4 BW45 66
Kendon Clo. E11 CH32 49
Avenue, The
Kendor Av. Epsom BN59 94
Kendra Hall Rd. Sth. Croy. BY57 95
Kendrey Gdns. Twick. BH46 74
Kendrick Ms. SW7 BT42 66
Brompton Rd.
Kendrick Rd. Slou. AQ41 62
Kenelm Clo. Har. BJ34 45
Kenerne Dr. Barn. BR25 28
Kenford Clo. Wat. BC19 17
Kenilford Rd. SW12 BV47 76
Kenilworth Ave. Cob. BF60 93
Kenilworth Av. E17 CE30 39
Kenilworth Av. SW19 BS49 76
Kenilworth Av. Har. BE35 45
Kenilworth Av. Rom. CX29 42
Kenilworth Clo. Bans. BS61 104
Kenilworth Clo. Borwd. BN24 28
Kenilworth Ct. SW15 BQ45 65
Kenilworth Ct. Twick. BG48 74
Kenilworth Ct. Wat. BC23 26
Kenilworth Cres. Enf. CA22 30
Kenilworth Cres. Enf. CA23 30
Kenilworth Dr. Borwd. BN24 28
Kenilworth Dr. Rick. AZ24 26
Kenilworth Gdns. SE18 CL44 68
Kenilworth Gdns. Hayes BB39 53
Kenilworth Gdns. Horn. CV34 51
Kenilworth Gdns. Ilf. CN34 49
Kenilworth Gdns. Loug. CK25 31
Kenilworth Gdns. Stai. AX49 73
Kenilworth Gdns. Sthl. BE38 54
Kenilworth Gdns. Wat. BD28 36
Kenilworth Rd. E3 CD37 57
Kenilworth Rd. NW6 BR37 55
Kenilworth Rd. SE20 CC51 87
Kenilworth Rd. W5 BL40 55
Kenilworth Rd. Ashf. AX48 73
Kenilworth Rd. Edg. BN27 37
Kenilworth Rd. Epsom. BP56 94
Kenilworth Rd. Orp. CM53 88
Kenilworth Way Slou. AP41 62
Mere Rd.
Kenley Av. NW9 BO30 37
Kenley Clo. Bex. CR47 79
Kenley Clo. Cat. BZ63 105
Kenley Clo. Chis. CN52 88
Kenley Gdns. Horn. CW34 51
Kenley Gdns. Th. Hth. BY52 86
Kenley La. Ken. BZ61 105
Kenley Rd. SW19 BR51 85
Kenley Rd. Kings. On T. BM51 85
Kenley Rd. Twick. BJ46 74
Kenley St. W11 BR40 55
Kenley Wk. W11 BR40 55
Kenley Wk. Sutt. BQ56 94
Kenlor Rd. SW17 BT49 76
Kenmare Dr. Mitch. BU50 76
Kenmare Gdns. N13 BZ28 39
Kenmare Rd. Th. Hth. BX53 86
Kenmare Rd. Well. CP44 69
Kenmont Gdns. NW10 BP38 55
Kenmore N2 BT33 47
Kenmore Av. Har. BJ32 45
Kenmore Cres. Hayes BB38 53
Kenmore Gdns. NW10 BM37 55
Kenmore Gdns. Edg. BM30 37
Kenmore Rd. Har. BK31 45
Kenmore Rd. Ken. BY60 95
Kenmure Rd. E8 CB35 48
Kennard Rd. E15 CF36 57
Kennard Rd. N11 BU28 38
Kennard St. E16 CK40 58
Kennedy Av. Enf. CC25 30
Kennedy Av. Hodd. CD12 12
Kennedy Clo. E13 CH37 58
Kennedy Clo. Orp. CM54 88
Kennedy Clo. Pnr. BE29 36
Kennedy Clo. Wal. Cr. CD17 21
High St. Cheshunt
Kennedy Rd. W7 BH39 54
Kennedy Rd. Bark. CN37 58
Kennel Clo. Lthd. BG65 102
Kennel La. Brwd. CY23 33
Kennel La. Lthd. BF64 102
Kennelwood Cres. Croy. CF59 96
Kennel Wood Lane. Hat. BP12 10
Kenners La. Wal. Abb. CK13 13
Kennet Clo. Upmin. CZ32 51
Kenneth Av. Ilf. CL35 49
Kenneth Cres. NW2 BP35 46
Kenneth Gdns. Stan. BJ29 36
Kenneth Rd. Bans. BT61 104
Kenneth Rd. Rom. CP33 50
Kennet Rd. W9 BR38 55
Kennet Rd. Dart. CU45 69
Kennet Rd. Islw. BH45 64
Kennet Rd. Slou. AT41 62
Kenning Clo. Wind. AL45 61
Kenninghall Rd. E5 CB34 48
Kenninghall Rd. N18 CC28 39
Kenning Rd. Hodd. CE11 12
Kennings Est. SE11 BY42 66
Kenning St. SE16 CC41 67
Kennings Way, SE11 BY42 66
Kenning Ter. N1 CA37 57
Branch Pl.
Kennington Gro. SE11 BX43 66
Kennington La. SE11 BX42 66
Kennington Oval, SE11 BX43 66
Kennington Park Est. SE11 BY43 66
Kennington Pk. Gdns. SE11 BY43 66
Kennington Pk. Pl. SE11 BY43 66
Kennington Park Rd. SE11 BY43 66
Kennyland Ct. NW4 BP32 46
Kenny Rd. NW7 BR29 37
Kenrick Pl. W1 BV39 56
Dorset St.
Kenrick Sq. Red. CA70 114
Kensal Rd. W10 BR38 55
Kensal Rd. W10 BR39 55
Kensington Av. E12 CK36 58
Kensington Av. Th. Hth. BY51 86
Kensington Av. Wat. BB24 26
Kensington Church St. W8 BS40 56
Kensington Church Wk. W8 BS41 66
Holland St.
Kensington Ct. W8 BS41 66
Kensington Ct. Ms. W8 BS41 66
Kensington Ct. Pl.
Kensington Ct. Pl. W8 BS41 66
Kensington Dr. Wdf. Grn. CJ30 40
Kensington Gdns. Ilf. CK33 49
Kensington Gdns. Sq. W2 BS39 56
Kensington Gte. W8 BT41 66
Kensington Gore SW7 BT41 66
Kensington Mall W8 BS40 56
Kensington Palace Gdns. W8 BS40 56
Kensington Pk. Gdns. W11 BR40 55
Kensington Pk. Ms. W11 BR39 55
Kensington Pk. Rd. W11 BR39 55
Kensington Pl. W8 BS40 56
Kensington Rd. Brwd. DA25 33
Kensington Rd. Nthlt. BF38 54
Kensington Rd. Rom. CS32 50
Kensington Sq. W8 BS41 66
Kensington Ter. Sth. Croy. BZ57 96
Kent Av. W13 BJ39 54
Kent Av. Dag. CR39 59
Kent Av. Hem. H. AX15 8
Kent Av. Well. CN46 78
Kent Clo. Mitch. BX52 86
Kent Clo. Orp. CN57 97
Kent Clo. Stai. AX50 73
Kent Dr. Barn. BV24 29
Kent Dr. Horn. CV35 51
Kent Dr. Tedd. BH49 74
Kentford Way Nthlt. BE37 54
Kent Gdns. W13 BJ39 54
Kent Gdns. Ruis. BC32 44
Kent Gate Way. Croy. CD57 96
Kent Hatch Rd. Oxt. CJ68 115
Kent House La. Beck. CD50 77
Kentish La. Hat. BT16 20
Kentish Rd. Belv. CR42 69
Kentmere Rd. SE18 CN42 68
Kenton Av. Har. BH33 45
Kenton Av. Sthl. BF40 54
Kenton Av. Sun. BD51 84
Kenton Ct. Har. BJ32 45
Kenton Gdns. Har. BK32 45
Kenton Gdns. St. Alb. BH14 9
Kenton La. Har. BH29 36
Kenton Park Av. Har. BK31 45
Kenton Park Clo. Har. BK32 45
Kenton Park Cres. Har. BK31 45
Kenton Park Rd. Har. BK31 45
Kenton Rd. E9 CC36 57
Kenton Rd. Har. BH33 45
Kenton's La. Wind. AM44 61
Kenton St. WC1 BX38 56
Kenton Way, Hayes BB38 53
Kent Pass. NW1 BU38 56
Kent Rd. N15 CA32 48
Kent Rd. N21 BZ26 39
Kent Rd. W4 BN41 65
Kent Rd. Dag. CR35 50
Kent Rd. Dart. CV46 80
Kent Rd. E. Mol. BG52 84
Kent Rd. Grav. DG47 81
Kent Rd. Grays. DE43 71
Kent Rd. Kings-on-t. BK52 84
Kent Rd. Long. DB51 90
Kent Rd. Orp. CO53 89
Kent Rd. Rich. BM43 65
Kent Rd. W. Wick. CE54 87
Kent Rd. Wok. AT61 100
Kents La. Epp. CS14 14
Kents Pass. Hamptn. BE51 84
Kent St. E2 CA37 57
Kent St. E13 CH38 58
Kent Ter. NW1 BU38 56
Kent View S. Ock. CY41 70
Kent Vw. Gdns. Ilf. CN34 49
Kent Way SE15 CA44 67
Sumner Estate
Kent Way Surb. BL55 85
Kentwode Grn. SW13 BP43 65
Kentwyns Ri. Red. BX71 121
Kenver Av. N12 BT29 38
Kenward Rd. SE9 CJ46 78
Kenway Rain. CV38 60
Kenway Rom. CS30 41
Ken Way Wem. BN34 46
Kenway Clo. Rain. CV38 60
Kenway Dri. Amer. AQ23 25
Kenway Rd. SW5 BS42 66
Kenway Wk. Rain. CV38 60
Kenwood Av. N14 BW25 29
Kenwood Clo. West Dr. AZ43 63
Kenwood Dr. Beck. CF52 87
Kenwood Dr. Rick. AV27 34
Kenwood Dr. Walt. BC57 92
Kenwood Gdns. E18 CH31 49
Kenwood Gdns. Ilf. CL31 49
Kenwood Rd. N6 BU32 47
Kenwood Rd. N9 CB26 39
Kenworth Clo. Wal. Cr. CC20 21
Kenworthy Rd. E9 CD35 48
Kenwyn Dr. NW2 BO34 46
Kenwyn Rd. SW4 BW45 66
Kenwyn Rd. SW20 BQ51 85
Kenya Rd. SE7 CJ43 68
Kenyington Dr. Sun. BC49 73
Kenyington Pl. Har. BK32 45
Kenyons. Leath. AZ67 110
Kenyon St. SW6 BQ44 65
Keogh Rd. E15 CG36 58
Kepler Rd. SW4 BX45 66
Keppell Rd. Dor. BJ70 119
Keppel Rd. E6 CK36 58
Keppel Rd. Dag. CQ35 50
Keppel Row, SE1 BZ40 57
Great Guildford St.
Keppel Spur, Wind. AQ47 72
Keppel St. WC1 BW39 56
Malet St.
Keppel St. Wind. AO44 61
Helena Rd.
Kerbela St. E2 CA38 57
Kerbey St. E14 CE39 57
Kerdistone Clo. Pot. B. BS18 20
Kerfield Cres. SE5 BZ44 67
Kerfield Pl. SE5 BZ44 67
Kernick Clo. N7 BX36 56
Sutterton St.
Kerrill Ave. Couls. BY63 104
Kerrison Rd. E15 CF37 57
Kerrison Rd. SW11 BU45 66
Kerrison Rd. W5 BK40 54
Kerry Av. Stan. BK28 36
Kerry Clo. E16 CH39 58
Kerry Clo. Barn. BQ24 28
Kerry Clo. Upmin. CZ33 51
Kerry Dr. Upmin. CZ33 51
Kerry Rd. SE14 CD43 67
Kerry Rd. Grays. DE40 71
Kerry Ter. Wok. AT61 100
Kersey Gdns. SE9 CK49 78
Kersey Gdns. Rom. CW29 42
Kersfield Rd. SW15 BQ46 75
Kershaw Rd. Dag. CR34 50
Kersley Ms. SW11 BU44 66
Kersley Rd. N16 CA34 48
Kersley St. SW11 BU44 66
Kerstin Clo. Hayes BB40 53
Keslake Rd. NW6 BQ37 55
Kessock Clo. N15 CB32 48
Kesters Rd. Chesh. AO19 16
Kesteven Clo. Ilf. CN29 40
New North Rd.
Keston Ave. Couls. BY63 104
Keston Av. Kes. CJ56 97
Keston Av. Wey. AW59 92
Keston Clo. N18 BZ27 39
Keston Clo. Well. CP43 69
Keston Gdns. Kes. CJ56 97
Keston Rd. N17 BZ31 48
Keston Rd. SE15 CB45 67
Keston Rd. Th. Hth. BX53 86
Kestrel Av. Stai. AV48 72
Kestrel Clo. Berk. AR13 7
Kestrel Clo. Ilf. CP28 41
Kestrel Clo. Rain. CU36 59
Kestrel Grn. Hat. BP13 10
Kestrel Rd. SE24 BY46 76
Kestrel Way Croy. CF58 96
Keswick Av. SW15 BO49 75
Keswick Av. SW19 BS51 86
Keswick Av. Horn. CV33 51
Keswick Clo. Sutt. BT56 95
Keswick Dr. Enf. CC22 30
Keswick Gdns. Ilf. CK31 49
Keswick Gdns. Ruis. BA32 44
Keswick Gdns. Wem. BL35 46
Keswick Rd. SW15 BR46 75
Keswick Rd. Bexh. CR44 69
Keswick Rd. Lthd. BF66 111
Keswick Rd. Orp. CN54 88
Keswick Rd. Twick. BF46 74
Keswick Rd. W. Wick. CG55 88
Kettering Rd. Enf. CC22 30
Kettering Rd. Rom. CW29 42
Kettering St. SW16 BV50 76
Kett Gdn. SW2 BX46 76
Kettlebaston Rd. E10 CD33 48
Kettlebury Way Ong. CW18 24
Kettlewell Clo. Swan. CT51 89
Kettlewell Clo. Wok. AR61 100
Kettlewell Dri. Wok. AS60 91
Kettlewell Hill. Wok. AS60 91
Ketton Grn. Red. BW67 113
Malmstone Av.
Kevan Dr. Wok. AV65 100
Kevelioc Rd. N17 BZ30 39
Kevin Clo. Houns. BD44 64
Kevington Dr. Chis. CN52 88
Kew Bridge Rd. Brent. BL43 65
Kew Ct. W4 BM42 65
Kew Cres. Sutt. BR55 85
Kewferry Dr. Nthwd. AZ28 35
Kewferry Rd. Nthwd. BA29 35
Kew Foot Rd. Rich. BL45 65
Kew Gdns. Rd. Rich. BL43 65
Kew Grn. Rich. BL43 65
Kew Meadow Path Rich. BM44 65
Kew Palace, Rich. BL43 65
Kew Rd. Rich. BL43 65
Kew Rd. Rich. BL45 65
Key Clo. E1 CC38 57
Cambridge Heath Rd.
Keyes Rd. NW2 BQ35 46
Keyes Rd. Dart. CW45 70
Keyfield Ter. St. Alb. BG14 9
Keymer Clo. West. CJ61 106
Keymer Rd. SW2 BX48 76
Keynes Clo. N2 BU31 47
Keynsham Av. Wdf. Grn. CG28 40
Keynsham Gdns. SE9 CK46 78
Keynsham Rd. SE9 CJ46 78
Keynsham Rd. Mord. BS54 86
Keynsham Wk. Mord. BS54 86
Keyse Rd. SE1 CA41 67
Keysers Rd. Brox. CE14 12
Keysham Av. Houns. BC43 63
Keystone Cres. N1 BX37 56
Caledonian Rd.
Keywood Dr. Sun. BC50 73
Keyworth St. SE1 BY41 66
Khama Rd. SW17 BU49 76
Khartoum Rd. E13 CH38 58
Khartoum Rd. SW17 BT49 76
Khartoum Rd. Ilf. CL35 49
Khyber Rd. SW11 BU44 66
Kibworth St. SW8 BX43 66
Dorset Rd.
Kidborough Down Lthd. BF67 111
Grove Side
Kidbrooke Gdns. SE3 CH44 68
Kidbrooke Gro. SE3 CH44 68
Kidbrooke La. SE9 CK45 68
Kidbrooke Pk. Clo. SE3 CH44 68
Kidbrooke Pk. Rd. SE3 CH44 68
Kidbrooke Way, SE3 CH44 68
Kidderminster Pl. Croy. BY54 86
Kidderminster Rd. Croy. BY54 86
Kidderpore Av. NW3 BS35 47
Kidrow Way. E9 CC37 57
Cleremont Rd.
Kielder Clo. Ilf. CN29 40
New North Rd.
Kier Hardie Way Hayes BC38 53
Kilbride Ct. Hem. H. AY11 8
Kilburn Bldgs. NW6 BS37 56
Kilburn High St.
Kilburn Gate NW6 BS37 56
Kilburn High Rd. NW6 BR36 55
Kilburn La. W10 BQ38 55
Kilburn Pk. Rd. NW6 BS38 56
Kilburn Pl. NW6 BS37 56

Kilburn Priory NW6 BS37 56
Kilburn Sq. NW6 BS37 56
Kilburn Vale Est. NW6 BS37 56
Kilby Clo. Wat. BD20 18
Kilcorral Clo. Epsom BP60 94
Kildare Clo. Ruis. BD33 45
Kildare Gdns. W2 BS39 56
Kildare Rd. E16 CH39 58
Kildare Ter. W2 BS39 56
Kildonan Clo. Wat. BB23 26
Kildonan Clo. Wat. BC23 26
Kildoran Rd. SW2 BX46 76
Kilgour Rd. SE23 CD46 77
Kilgowan Rd. Ilf. CO33 50
Kilkie St. SW6 BT44 66
Killarney Rd. SW18 BT46 76
Killasser Ct. Tad. BQ65 103
Killearn Rd. SE6 CF47 77
Killester Gdns. Wor. Pk. BP56 94
Killick St. N1 BX37 56
Killieser Av. SW2 BX48 76
Killip Clo. E16 CG39 58
Killowen Av. Nthlt. BG35 45
Killowen Rd. E9 CD36 57
Killyon Rd. SW8 BW44 66
Kilmaine Rd. SW6 BR43 65
Kilmarsh St. W6 BQ42 65
Kilmartin Av. SW16 BX52 86
Kilmartin Rd. Ilf. CO34 50
Kilmartin Way Horn. CU35 50
Kilmeston Way SE15 CA43 67
Kilmington Clo. Brwd. DD27 122
Kilmington Rd. SW13 BP43 65
Kilmiston Av. Shep. BA53 83
Kilmorey Gdns. Twick. BJ46 74
Kilmorey Rd. Twick. BJ45 64
Kilmorie Rd. SE23 CD47 77
Kiln Ave. Amer. AR23 25
Kiln Clo. Hayes. BA43 63
Kilncroft, Hem. H. AZ14 8
Kiln Field Brwd. DB21 33
Kiln Field. Welw. G. C. BR6 5
Kiln Ground, Hem. H. AZ14 8
Kiln La. Bet. BN70 120
Kiln La. Chesh. AQ19 16
Kiln La. Slou. AO33 43
Kiln La. Wok. AW65 101
Kiln Meadows, Guil. AO68 109
Kiln Pl. NW5 BV35 47
Kiln Rd. Epp. CR17 23
Kilnside Esher BJ57 93
Kilravock St. W10 BR38 55
Kilrue La. Watt. BB56 92
Kilrush Ter. Wok. AT61 100
Kilsby Wk. Dag. CO36 59
Rugby Rd.
Kilsha Rd. Walt. BD53 84
Kilsmore La. Wal. Cr. CC18 21
Kilvinton Dr. Enf. BZ22 30
Kilworth Av. Brwd. DD25 122
Kimbell Gdns. SW6 BR44 65
Kimber Clo. Wind. AN45 61
Kimberley Av. E6 CK37 58
Kimberley Av. SE15 CB44 67
Kimberley Av. Ilf. CM33 49
Kimberley Av. Rom. CS32 50
Kimberley Dr. Sid. CP48 79
Kimberley Gdns. Enf. CA24 30
Kimberley Pl. Pur. BY59 95
Brighton Rd.
Kimberley Rd. E4 CG26 40
Kimberley Rd. E11 CF34 48
Kimberley Rd. E16 CG38 58
Kimberley Rd. E17 CD30 39
Kimberley Rd. N4 BY32 47
Kimberley Rd. N17 CB30 39
Kimberley Rd. N18 CB29 39
Kimberley Rd. NW6 BR37 55
Kimberley Rd. SW9 BX44 66
Kimberley Rd. Beck. CC51 87
Kimberley Rd. Croy. BY53 86
Kimberley Rd. St. Alb. BG13 9
Kimberley Way E4 CG26 40
Kimber Rd. SW18 BS47 76
Kimble Cres. Bush. BG26 36
Kimble Rd. SW19 BT50 76
Kimbolton Clo. SE12 CG46 78
Kimbolton Grn. Borwd. BN24 28
Kimbolton Row SW3 BU42 66
Fulham Rd.
Kimmeridge Gdns. SE9 CK49 78
Kimmeridge Rd. SE9 CK49 78
Kimps Way, Hem. H. AZ15 8
Kimpton Av. Brwd. DA26 42
Kimpton Clo. Wat. BD20 18
Kimpton Rd. SE5 BZ44 67
Kimpton Rd. Sutt. BR55 85
Kimptons Clo. Ong. CW16 24
Kimptons Mead, Pot. B. BQ19 19
Kimptons Mead Clo. Pot. B. BQ19 19
Kinburn Dr. Egh. AS49 72
Kinburn St. SE16 CC41 67
Kincaid Rd. SE15 CB43 67
Kinch Gro. Har. BL33 46
Kinder Scout, Hem. H. AZ14 8
Kindersley Way, Wat. BA19 17
Kinder St. E1 CB39 57
Kinfauns Av. Horn. CV32 51
Kinfauns Rd. SW2 BY48 76
Kinfauns Rd. Ilf. CO33 50
Kingaby Gdns. Rain. CU36 59
King Alfred Av. SE6 CE49 77
King Alfred Rd. Rom. CW30 42
King Arthur St. SE15 CC43 67
Kg. Charles Cres. Surb. BL54 85
King Charles's Rd. Surb. BL53 85
King Charles St. SW1 BW41 66
King Charles Wk. SW13 BR47 75
Princes Way
Kingcraig Dr. Sev. CU65 107
King David La. E1 CC40 57
Kingdon Rd. NW6 BS36 56
King Edward Av. Dart. CV46 80
King Edward Av. Rain. CV37 60
King Edward Dr. Chess. BK55 84
King Edward Dr. Grays. DF42 71
King Edward Rd. E10 CF33 48
King Edward Rd. E17 CD31 48
King Edward Rd. Barn. BS24 29
King Edward Rd. Brwd. DB27 42
King Edward Rd. Green. DA46 80
King Edward Rd. Rad. BL20 19
King Edward Rd. Rom. CT32 50
King Edward Rd. Wal. Cr. CD20 21
King Edward Rd. Wat. BE25 27
King Edwards Gdns. W3 BM40 55
King Edward's Gro. Tedd. BJ50 74
King Edward, S Rd. Ruis. BA33 44
King Edward's Rd. E9 CB37 57
King Edward's Rd. N9 CB26 39
King Edward's Rd. Bark. CM37 58
King Edward's Rd. Enf. CC24 30
King Edward St. EC1 BZ39 57
King Edward St. Hem. H. AX15 8
King Edward St. Slou. AO41 61
King Edward VII, Ave, Wind. AO43 61
King Edward Wk. SE1 BY41 66
Kingfield Clo. Wok. AS63 100
Kingfield Dr. Wok. AS63 100
Kingfield Gdns. Wok. AS63 100
Kingfield Rd. W5 BK38 54
Kingfield Rd. Wok. AS63 100
Kingfield St. E14 CF42 67
Kingfisher Clo. Brwd. DD26 122
Kingfisher Clo. Walt. BE56 93
Kingfisher Dr. Rich. BK49 74
Kingfisher Dr. Stai. AV49 72
Kingfisher Lure, Rick. AW24 26
Kingfisher Rd. Upmin. CZ33 51
Kingfisher Sq. SE8 CD43 67
Staunton St.
King George Ave. West. CJ61 106
King George Av. E16 CJ39 58
King George Av. Bush. BF25 27
King George Av. Walt. BD54 84
King George Clo. Rom. CS31 50
King George Rd. Wal. Abb. CF20 21
King George's Av. Wat. BB24 26
King Georges Dr. Wey. AW58 92
King George's Rd. Brwd. CZ25 33
King George St. SE10 CF43 67
King George Vi Av. Mitch. BU52 86
Kingham Cl. SW18 BT47 76
King Harold's Way, Bexh. CP43 69
King Harry La. St. Alb. BF14 9
King Harry St. Hem. H. AX13 8
King Henry's Dr. Croy. CF58 96
King Henry's Rd. NW3 BT36 56
Kg. Henry's Rd. Kings-on-t. BM52 85
King Henry St. N16 CA35 48
King Henry's Wk. N1 CA36 57
King James Av. Pot. B. BX18 20
King James St. SE1 BY41 66
King Jame & Tinker Rd. CA21 30
King John Ct. EC2 CA38 57
New Inn Yd.
King Johns Clo. Stai. AR46 72
King John's Ct. EC2 CA38 57
New Inn Yd.
King John St. E1 CC39 57
King John's Wk. SE9 CJ47 78
Kinglake Est. SE17 CA42 67
Kinglake St. SE17 CA42 67
Kingly St. W1 BW39 56
King & Queen St. SE17 BZ42 67
Kingsand Rd. SE12 CH48 78
Kings Arms Ct. E1 CB39 57
Old Montague St.
King's Arms Yd. EC2 BZ39 57
Kings Arms Yd. SW18 BS46 76
Wandsworth High St.
Kings Av. N10 BV31 47
King's Av. N21 BY26 38
Kings Av. W5 BK39 54
King's Av. Brom. CG50 78
King's Av. Buck. H. CJ27 40
King's Av. Cars. BU57 95
King's Av. Grnf. BF39 54
King's Av. Hem. H. AY15 8
Kings Av. Houns. BF44 64
Kings Av. N. Mal. BO52 85
Kings Av. Red. BU71 121
Kings Av. Rom. CQ32 50
Kings Av. Sun. BB49 73
King's Av. Wat. BB25 26
King's Av. Wdf. Grn. CH29 40
Kings Av. Wey. AX59 92
King's Av. Gdns. SW4 BX46 76
King's Bench St. SE1 BY41 66
Kingsbridge Av. W3 BL41 65
Kingsbridge Cir. Rom. CW29 42
Kingsbridge Clo. Rom. CW29 42
Kingsbridge Cres. Sthl. BE39 54
Kingsbridge Rd. W10 BQ39 55
Kingsbridge Rd. Bark. CM37 58
Kingsbridge Rd. Mord. BQ53 85
Kingsbridge Rd. Rom. CW29 42
Kingsbridge Rd. Sthl. BE42 64
Kingsbridge Rd. Walt. BC54 83
Kings Brook Lthd. BJ62 102
Kingston Rd.
Kingsbury Av. St. Alb. BG13 9
Kingsbury Cir. NW9 BM32 46
Kingsbury Dr. Wind. AQ47 72
Kingsbury Rd. N1 CA36 57
Kingsbury Rd. NW9 BM32 46
Kingsbury Ter. N1 CA36 57
Kingsclere Clo. SW15 BP47 75
Kingscliffe Gdns. SW19 BR47 75
Kings Clo. E10 CE33 48
Kings Clo. NW4 BQ31 46
Kings Clo. Ch. St. G. AR27 34
King's Clo. Dart. CT45 69
Kings Clo. Stai. AX50 73
King's Clo. Walt. BC54 83
Kings College Rd. NW3 BT36 56
Eton Av.
Kings College Rd. Ruis. BB32 44
Kingscote Rd. W4 BN41 65
Kingscote Rd. Croy. CB54 87
Kingscote Rd. N. Mal. BN52 85
Kingscote St. EC4 BY40 56
Tudor St.
King's Ct. E13 CH37 58
Kings Ct. SW19 BS50 76
Kings Ct. W5 BK39 54
Castlebar Pk.
King's Ct. W6 BP42 65
Kings Ct. Har. BF34 45
King's Ct. Wem. BM34 46
Kingscourt Rd. SW16 BW48 76
King's Cres. N4 BZ34 48
Kingscroft Rd. NW2 BR36 55
Kingscroft Rd. Bans. BT61 104
Kingscroft Rd. Lthd. BJ63 102
Kingscross La. Red. BW71 121
King's Cross Rd. WC1 BX38 56
Kingsdale Est. SE18 CN43 68
Kingsdale Rd. SE18 CN43 68
Kingsdale Rd. SE20 CC50 77
Kingsdale Rd. Berks. AQ13 7
Kingsdene, Tad. BP64 103
Kingsdon La. Harl. CP11 14
Kingsdown Av. W3 BO40 55
Kingsdown Av. W13 BJ41 64
Kingsdown Av. Sth. Croy. BY58 95
Kingsdowne Rd. Surb. BL54 85
Kingsdown Rd. E11 CG34 49
Kingsdown Rd. N19 BX34 47
Kingsdown Rd. Epsom BP60 94
Kingsdown Rd. Sutt. BR56 94
Kingsdown Way Brom. CH53 88
Kings Dri. Edg. BL28 37
Kings Dr. Edg. BL28 37
Kings Dr. Grav. DG48 81
King's Dr. Surb. BJ53 84
King's Dr. Surb. BM54 85
Kings Dr. Tedd. BG49 74
Kings Dr. Watt. BB58 92
King's Dr. Wem. BM34 46
Kingsend, Ruis. BA33 44
King's Farm Av. Rich. BM45 65
Kingsfield. Wind. AL44 61
Kingsfield Av. Har. BF31 45
Kingsfield Dr. Enf. CC21 30
Kingsfield Rd. Har. BG33 45
Kingsfield Rd. Sev. CZ58 99
Kingsfield Rd. Wat. BD26 36
Kingsfield Ter. Dart. CV46 80
Kingsfield Ter. Har. BG33 45
Kingsfield Way, Enf. CC21 30
Kingsford Av. Wall. BX57 95
Kings Gdns. NW6 BS36 56
Kings Gdns. Croy. BY56 95
Kings Gdns. Ilf. CM33 49
Kings Gdns. Upmin. CZ33 51
Kingsgate, Wem. BM34 46
Kingsgate Av. N3 BS31 47
Kingsgate Clo. Bexh. CQ44 69
Kingsgate Pl. NW6 BS36 56
Kingsgate Rd. NW6 BS36 56
Kings Grn. Loug. CK24 31
Kingsground, SE9 CK47 78
King's Gro. SE15 CB44 67
Kings Gro. Rom. CU32 50
King's Hall Rd. Beck. CD50 77
Kings Head Ct. EC3 BZ40 57
Fish St. Hill.
King's Head Hill E4 CE26 39
Kingshead La. Wey. AX59 92
Kings Head Pass. SW4 BW45 66
Clapham Pk. Rd.
King's Head Yd. SE1 BZ40 57
Borough High St.
Kings Highway, SE18 CN43 68
Kings Hill Loug. CK23 31
Kingshill Av. Har. BJ31 45
Kingshill Av. Hayes BB38 53
Kingshill Av. Rom. CS29 41
Kingshill Av. St. Alb. BJ11 9
Kingshill Av. Wor. Pk. BP54 85
Kingshill Dr. Har. BJ30 36
Kingshill Way. Berk. AQ14 7
Kingshold Est. E9 CC37 57
Kingshold Rd. E9 CC36 57
Kingsholm Gdns. SE9 CJ45 68
Kingshurst Rd. SE12 CH47 78
Kingsland Harl. CM12 13
Kingsland Est. E2 CA37 57
Kingsland Grn. N16 CA36 57
Kingsland High St. E8 CA36 57
Kingsland Pk. Hem. H. AW14 8
Kingsland River, Hem. H. AW14 8
Kingsland Rd. E13 CJ38 58
Kingsland Rd. Hem. H. AW14 8
King's La. Egh. AQ49 72
King's La. Sutt. BT56 95
Kings Lawn SW15 BP46 75
Kingslawn Clo. SW15 BQ45 65
Howards La.
Kingslea, Lthd. BJ63 102
Kingsley Ave. Dart. CX46 80
Kingsley Av. W13 BJ39 54
Kingsley Av. Bans. BS61 104
Kingsley Av. Borwd. BL23 28
Kingsley Av. Houns. BG44 64
Kingsley Av. Sthl. BF40 54
Kingsley Av. Sutt. BT56 95
Kingsley Av. Wal. Cr. CB18 21
Kingsley Clo. N2 BT32 47
Kingsley Clo. Dag. CR35 50
Kingsley Cres. SE19 CA51 87
Kingsley Dr. Egh. AQ50 72
Kingsley Dr. Wor. Pk. BO55 85
Kingsley Gdns. E4 CE28 39
Kingsley Gdns. Horn. CV31 51
Kingsley Gro. Reig. BS72 121
Kingsley Ms. W8 BS41 66
Stanford Rd.
Kingsley Pl. N6 BV33 47
Kingsley Rd. E7 CH36 58
Kingsley Rd. E17 CF30 39
Kingsley Rd. N13 BY28 38
Kingsley Rd. NW6 BR37 55
Kingsley Rd. SW19 BS49 76
Kingsley Rd. Brwd. DE26 122
Kingsley Rd. Croy. BY54 86
Kingsley Rd. Har. BG35 45
Kingsley Rd. Houns. BF44 64
Kingsley Rd. Ilf. CM30 40
Kingsley Rd. Orp. CN57 97
Kingsley Rd. Pnr. BE31 45
Kingsley St. SW11 BU45 66
Kingsley Wk. Grays. DG42 71
Kingsley Way N2 BT32 47
Kingsley Wood Dr. SE9 CK48 78
Kings Lynn Clo. Rom. CV29 42
Kings Lynn Dr. Rom. CV29 42
Kings Lynn Path. Rom. CV29 42
Kings Lynn Dr.
Kingsman St. SE18 CK41 68
Kingsmead Barn. BS24 29
Kings Mead, Pot. B. BX17 20
Kingsmead, Saw. CQ6 6
Kingsmead. West. CJ61 106
Kingsmead Av. N9 CB26 39
Kingsmead Av. NW9 BN33 46
Kingsmead Av. Mitch. BW52 86
Kingsmead Av. Rom. CT32 50
Kingsmead Av. Sun. BD51 84
Kingsmead Av. Surb. BM55 85
Kingsmead Av. Wor. Pk. BP55 85
Kingsmead Clo. Epsom BN57 94
Kingsmead Clo. Harl. CH11 13
Kingsmead Clo. Sid. CO48 79
Kingsmead Dr. Nthlt. BE36 54
King's Mead Est. E9 CD35 48
Kingsmead Rd. SW2 BY48 76
King's Mead Way, E9 CD35 48
Kingsmere Pk. NW9 BM33 46
Kingsmere Rd. SW19 BQ48 75
King's Ms. WC1 BX38 56
Kingsmill Gdns. Dag. CQ35 50
King's Mill La. Red. BW73 121
Kingsmill Rd. Dag. CQ35 50
Kingsmill Ter. NW8 BT37 56
Kingsmoor Harl. CL13 13
Kingsmoor Rd. Harl. CL12 13
Kingsnympton Pk. Kings. On T. BM50 75
Kings Orchard, SE9 CK46 78
King, S Chase. Brwd. DB27 42
King, S Farm Rd. Rick. AU25 25
King, S La. Kings L. AW19 17
King, S Rd. Brwd. DB27 42
Kingspark Ct. E18 CH31 49
Kingspark Ct. Ilf. CK33 49
Drive, The.
Kings Pass. Kings-on-t. BK51 84
Kings Pl. SE1 BZ41 67
Kings Pl. W4 BN42 65
Kings Pl. Buck. H. CJ27 40
King Sq. Est. EC1 BY38 56
Kings Ride Gate, Rich. BM45 65
Kingsridge Gdns. Dart. CV46 80
King's Rd. E4 CF26 39
King's Rd. E6 CJ37 58
King's Rd. E11 CG33 49
Kings Rd. N17 CA30 39
King's Rd. N18 CB28 39
King's Rd. N22 BX30 38
King's Rd. NW10 BP36 55
King's Rd. SE25 CB52 87
Kings Rd. SW1 BV42 66
King's Rd. SW14 BN45 65
King's Rd. SW19 BS50 76
Kings Rd. W5 BK39 54
Kings Rd. Bark. CM36 58
North St.
Kings Rd. Barn. BQ24 28
Kings Rd. Berk. AQ13 7
Kings Rd. Ch. St. G. AR27 34
King's Rd. Egh. AT49 72
Kings Rd. Felt. BD47 74
Kings Rd. Guil. AR70 118
Kings Rd. Guil. AS74 118
Kings Rd. Har. BE34 45
King's Rd. Kings. On T. BL51 85
King's Rd. Mitch. BV52 86
King's Rd. Orp. CN56 97
Kings Rd. Rich. BL46 75
Kings Rd. Rom. CU31 50
Kings Rd. St. Alb. BF13 9
Kings Rd. St. Alb. BK16 18
Kings Rd. Slou. AP41 62
King's Rd. Surb. BK54 84
Kings Rd. Sutt. BS58 95
King's Rd. Tedd. BG49 74
Kings Rd. Twick. BJ46 74
Kings Rd. Uxb. AX37 52
Kings Rd. Wal. Cr. CD20 21
Kings Rd. Walt. BC55 83
Kings Rd. West. CH62 106
Kings Rd. West. CJ62 106
Kings Rd. West Dr. AY41 63
Kings Rd. Wey. AW58 92
Kings Rd. Wind. AO44 61
King's Rd. Wind. AO45 61
Kings Rd. Wok. AT61 100
Kings Scholars Pass. SW1 BW41 66
Carlisle Pl.
King Stable St. Wind. AO43 61
Kings Ter. NW1 BW37 56
Plender St.
King's Ter. Islw. BJ45 64
Kingsthorpe Rd. SE26 CC49 77
Kingston Av. Felt. BB46 73
Kingston Av. Leath. BB66 110
Kingston Av. Lthd. BJ64 102
Kingston Av. Sutt. BR55 85
Kingston Av. West Dr. AY40 53
Kingston Br. Kings. On T. BK51 84
Kingston By-pass Esher BH55 84
Kingston Clo. Nthlt. BE36 54
Kingston Clo. Tedd. BJ50 74
Kingston Ct. Grav. DD46 81
Warwick Pl.
Kingston Cres. Ashf. AX49 73
Kingston Cres. Beck. CD51 87
Kingston Hall Rd. Kings-on-t. BK52 84
Kingston Hill Av. Rom. CQ30 41
Kingston Hl. Kings. On T. BM51 85
Kingston Ho. Gdns. Lthd. BJ64 102
Up. Fairfield Rd.
Kingston Lane. Leath. AZ67 110
Kingston La. Tedd. BJ49 74
Kingston La. Uxb. AY38 53
Kingston La. West Dr. AY41 63
Kingston Pk. Est. Kings. On T. BM50 75
Kingston Pl. Sthl. BE41 64
Kingston Rise, Wey. AW58 92
Kingston Rd. N9 CB27 39
Kingston Rd. SW15 BP48 75
Kingston Rd. Ashf. AY50 73
Kingston Rd. Barn. BT25 29
Kingston Rd. Epsom BO57 94
Kingston Rd. Ilf. CL35 49
Kingston Rd. Lthd. BJ62 102
Kingston Rd. N. Mal. BM52 85
Kingston Rd. Rom. CT31 50
Kingston Rd. Stai. & Ashf. AW49 73
Kingston Rd. Sun. BE51 84
Kingston Rd. Surb. BM55 85
Kingston Rd. Tedd. BJ49 74
Kingston Vale, SW15 BN49 75
Kingstown St. NW1 BV37 56
King St. E13 CH38 58
King St. EC2 BZ39 57
King St. N2 BT31 47
King St. SW1 BW40 56
King St. W3 BM40 55
King St. W6 BO42 65
King St. WC2 BX40 56
King St. Cher. AV54 82
King St. Grav. DG46 81
King St. Ong. CZ17 24
King St. Rich. BK46 74
King St. Sthl. BE41 64
King St. Twick. BJ47 74
King St. Wat. BC24 26
Kings Wk. Grays DD43 71
Argent St.
King's Wk. Kings. On T. BK51 84
Kings Wk. Sth. Croy. CB60 96
Kingsway N12 BT29 38
Kingsway NW8 BU37 56
Kingsway, SW14 BM45 65
Kingsway, WC2 BX39 56
Kingsway Croy. BX56 95
Kingsway Enf. CB25 30
Kingsway. Ger. Cr. AS30 34
Kingsway. Ger. Cr. AS31 43
King's Way Har. BH31 45
Kingsway, Hayes BA39 53
Kingsway, Iver AV39 52
Kingsway N. Mal. BQ52 85
Kingsway Orp. CM53 88
Kingsway, Pot. B. BX18 20
Kingsway, Stai. AX47 73
Kingsway, Wat. BB21 26
Kingsway, Wat. BD20 18
Kingsway, Wdf. Grn. CJ28 40
Kingsway, Wem. BL35 46
Kingsway W. Wick. CG55 88
Kingsway, Wok. AR62 100
Kingsway Av. Sth. Croy. CC58 96
Kingsway Av. Wok. AR62 100
Kingsway Cres. Har. BG31 45
Kingsway Industrial Est. N18 CC29 39
Kingsway Rd. Sutt. BR57 94
Kingsway, The, Epsom BO59 94
Kingswear Rd. NW5 BV34 47
Kingswear Rd. Ruis. BC34 44
Kingswell Ride, Pot. B. BX18 20
Kingswood Av. NW6 BR37 55
Kingswood Av. Belv. CQ42 69
Kingswood Av. Houns. BE44 64
Kingswood Av. Sth. Croy. CB61 105
Kingswood Av. Swan. CT52 89
Kingswood Av. Th. Hth. BY53 86
Kingswood Cl. Egh. AR49 72
Kingswood Clo. N20 BT26 38
Kingswood Clo. Dart. CV46 80
Kingswood Clo. Guil. AU70 118
Kingswood Clo. N. Mal. BO53 85
Kingswood Clo. Orp. CM54 88
Woodcote Rd.
Kingswood Clo. Surb. BL54 85
Kingswood Clo. Wey. AZ57 92
Kingswood Ct. Rich. BL46 75
Marchmont Rd.
Kingswood Creek, Stai. AR46 72
Kingswood Dr. SE19 CA49 77
Kingswood Dr. Cars. BU54 86
Kingswood Est. SE21 CA49 77
Kingswood La. Warl. CC61 105
Kingswood Pk. N3 BR30 37
Kingswood Pl. SE13 CG45 68

Kingswood Rise, Egh. AR49 72
Kingswood Rd. SE20 CC50 77
Kingswood Rd. SW2 BX46 76
Kingswood Rd. SW19 BR50 75
Kingswood Rd. W4 BN41 65
Kingswood Rd. Brom. CF52 87
Kingswood Rd. Ilf. CO33 50
Kingswood Rd. Sev. CT64 107
Kingswood Rd. Tad. BP64 103
Kingswood Rd. Wat. BC20 17
Kingswood Way. Croy. CC60 96
Kingswood Way Wall. BX56 95
Kingthorpe Rd. NW10 BN36 55
Kingthorpe Ter. NW10 BN36 55
Kingwell Rd. Barn. BT22 29
King William St. EC4 BZ39 57
King William Wk. SE10 CF43 67
Kingwood Av. Brom. CG52 88
Kingwood Av. Hmptn. BF50 74
Kingwood Rd. SW6 BR44 65
Kinlet Clo. SE18 CM44 68
Kinlet Rd.
Kinlet Rd. SE18 CL44 68
Kinloch Dr. NW9 BN33 46
Kinloch Dr. NW9 BO33 46
Kinloch St. N7 BX34 47
Kinloss Ct. N3 BR31 46
Kinloss Gdns.
Kinloss Gdns. N3 BR31 46
Kinloss Rd. Cars. BT54 86
Kinnaird Av. W4 BN43 65
Kinnaird Av. Brom. CG50 78
Kinnaird Clo. Brom. CG50 78
Kinnear Rd. W12 BO41 65
Kinnerton Pl. N. SW1 BU41 66
Kinnerton St.
Kinnerton Pl. S. SW1 BU41 66
Kinnerton St.
Kinnerton St. SW1 BV41 66
Kinnoul Rd. W6 BR43 65
Kinross Av. Wor. Pk. BP55 85
Kinross Clo. Har. BL32 46
Kinross Clo. Sun. BB49 73
Kinross Dr. Sun. BB49 73
Kinsale Rd. SE15 CB45 67
Kinsfield, Hodd. CE11 12
Kintore St. SE1 CA42 67
Kintore Way, SE1 CA42 67
Grange Rd.
Kints Clo. Wind. AL44 61
Kinveachy Gdns. SE7 CK42 68
Kinver Rd. North SE26 CC49 77
Kinver Rd. South SE26 CC49 77
Kipling Ave. Til. DG44 71
Kipling Estate SE1 BZ41 67
Kipling Pl. Stan. BH29 36
Kipling Rd. Bexh. CQ44 69
Kipling Rd. Dart. CX46 80
Kipling St. SE1 BZ41 67
Kipling Ter. N9 BZ27 39
Kirby Clo. Epsom BO56 94
Kirby Clo. Ilf. CN29 40
Kirby Clo. Loug. CK26 40
Kirby Est. SE16 CB41 67
Kirby Gro. SE1 CA41 67
Kirby Rd. Dart. CY47 80
Kirby Rd. Wok. AR61 100
Kirby St. EC1 BY39 56
Kirby Way Walt. BD53 84
Kircaldy Grn. Wat. BD27 36
Kirchen Rd. W13 BJ40 54
Kirkdale, SE26 CB48 77
Kirkdale Rd. E11 CG33 49
Kirkham St. SE18 CN43 68
Kirkland Av. Ilf. CL30 40
Kirkland Pl. SE10 CG41 68
Kirklands, Welw. G. C. BQ6 5
Kirk La. SE18 CM43 68
Kirklees Rd. Th. Hth. BX52 86
Kirkley Rd. SW19 BS50 76
Kirkly Clo. Sth. Croy. CA58 96
Kirkside Rd. SE3 CH43 68
Kirkstall Av. N17 BZ31 48
Kirkstall Gdns. SW2 BW47 76
Kirkstall Rd. SW2 BW47 76
Kirksted Rd. Mord. BS54 86
Kirkstone Way Brom. CG50 78
Kirkton Gdns. E2 CA38 57
Chambo Rd.
Kirkwall Pl. E2 CC38 57
Kirkwood Rd. SE15 CB44 67
Kirn Rd. W13 BJ40 54
Kirchen Rd.
Kirtley Av. SE26 CD49 77
Kirtling St. SW8 BW43 66
Gringle St.
Kirton Rd. E13 CJ37 58
Kirton Wk. Edg. BN29 37
Kirwyn Way SE5 BY43 66
Kitchener Rd. E7 CH36 58
Kitchener Rd. E17 CE30 39
Kitchener Rd. N2 BU31 47
Kitchener Rd. N17 BZ31 48
Kitchener Rd. Dag. CR36 59
Kitchener Rd. Th. Hth. BZ52 87
Kitchener's La. Red. CA70 114
Kitchenor Av. Grav. DH48 81
Kitkat Ter. E3 CE38 57
Kitley Gdns. SE19 CA51 87
Kitsbury Rd. Berk. AQ13 7
Kitsbury Ter. Berk. AQ13 7
Kitsmead La. Cher. AS55 82
Kitson Rd. SE5 BZ43 67
Kitson Rd. SW13 BP44 65
Kitswell Way, Rad. BH20 18
Kittiwake Rd. Nthlt. BD38 54
Kitto Rd. SE14 CC44 67
Kitt's End Rd. Barn. BQ21 28
Kiver Rd. N19 BW34 47
Klea Ave. SW4 BW46 76
Knapdale Clo. SE23 CB48 77
Knapmill Rd. SE6 CE48 77
Knapmill Way, SE6 CE48 77
Knappe Rd. Ashf. AY49 73
Knapp Rd. E3 CE38 57
Knaresborough Pl. SW5 BS42 66
Knaresborough Rd. SW5 BS43 66
Knatchbull Rd. NW10 BN37 55
Knatchbull Rd. SE5 BY44 66
Knatts La. Sev. CY59 99
Knatts Valley Rd. Sev. CY59 99
Knebworth Av. E17 CE30 39
Knebworth Rd. N16 CA35 48
Knee Hill, SE2 CP42 69
Knee Hill Cres. SE2 CP42 69
Knella Grn. Welw. G. C. BS8 5
Knella Rd. Welw. G. C. BR8 5
Kneller Gdns. Islw. BG46 74
Kneller Rd. SE4 CD45 67
Kneller Rd. N. Mal. BN54 85
Kneller Rd. Twick. BG46 74
Knightland Rd. E5 CB34 48
Knighton Clo. Rom. CS32 50
Knighton Clo. Sth. Croy. BY57 95
Knighton Clo. Wdf. Grn. CH28 40
Knighton Dr. Wdf. Grn. CH28 40
Knighton La. Buck. H. CH27 40
Knighton Park Rd. SE26 CC49 77
Knighton Rd. E7 CH34 49
Knighton Rd. Red. BV71 121
Knighton Rd. Rom. CS32 50
Knighton Rd. Sev. CT61 107
Knighton Way La. Uxb. AW36 53
Knightrider St. EC4 BZ39 57
Godliman St.
Knightrider St. EC4 BZ40 57
Queen Victoria St.
Knights Av. W5 BL41 65
Knightsbridge Cres. AW50 73
Knightsbridge Gdns. Rom. CS32 50
Knightsbridge Grn. SW1 BU41 66
Knightsbridge
Knightsbridge Way, Hem. H. AY13 8
Knights Clo. E9 CC35 48
Churchill Wk.
Knights Clo. Egh. AU50 72
Knights Ct. Kings-on-t. BL52 85
Knightsfield, Welw. G. C. BQ5 5
Knight's Hill, SE27 BY49 76
Knight's Hill Sq. SE27 BY49 76
Knight's Hill
Knights La. N9 CB27 39
Knight, S Way, Brwd. DD27 122
Knights Pk. Kings-on-t. BL52 85
Knight's Rd. E16 CH41 68
Knights Rd. Stan. BK28 36
Knight St. Saw. CQ6 6
Knights Walk Rom. CO24 32
Knights Way, Ilf. CM29 40
Knightswood Clo. Edg. BN27 37
Knightwood Cres. N. Mal. BO53 85
Knipp Hill, Cob. BE60 93
Knipp Hl. Cob. BE60 93
Knivett Rd. SW6 BS43 66
Knob's Hill Rd. E15 CE37 57
Knockhall Chase. Green. DB46 80
Knockholt Main Rd. Sev. CN63 106
Knockholt Rd. SE9 CJ46 78
Knockholt Rd. Sev. CO61 107
Knockholt Rd. Sev. CQ60 98
Knole La. Sev. CV66 117
Knole Rd. Dart. CU47 79
Knole Rd. Sev. CV65 108
Knole, The, SE9 CL49 78
Knole, The Grav. DF50 81
Knole Way, Sev. CV66 117
Knoll Cres. Nthwd. BB30 35
Knoll Dr. N14 BV26 38
Knolles Cr. Hat. BP15 10
Knollmead Surb. BN54 85
Knoll Rise Orp. CN54 88
Knoll Rd. SW18 BT46 76
Knoll Rd. Bex. CR47 79
Knoll Rd. Dor. BJ72 119
Knoll Rd. Sid. CO49 79
Knolls Clo. Wor. Pk. BP55 85
Knolls, The, Epsom BQ61 103
Knoll, The, W13 BK39 54
Knoll, The, Beck. CE51 87
Knoll, The, Brom. CH55 88
Knoll. The. Cob. BF60 93
Knoll, The, Orp. CN54 88
Knollys Clo. SW16 BY48 76
Knollys Rd. SW16 BX48 76
Knolton Way, Slou. AQ39 52
Knottisford St. E2 CC38 57
Knott's Grn. Rd. E10 CE32 48
Knotts Pl. Sev. CU65 107
Knowle Av. Bexh. CQ43 69
Knowle Grn. Stai. AW49 73
Knowle Gro. Vir. W. AR54 82
Knowle Grove Clo. Vir. W. AR54 82
Knowle Hill, Vir. W. AR54 82
Knowle Pk. Cob. BE61 102
Knowle Park Av. Stai. AW50 73
Knowle Rd. SW9 BY45 66
Knowle Rd. Brom. CK55 88
Knowle Rd. Twick. BH47 74
Knowles Hl. Cres. SE13 CF46 77
Knowl Hill, Wok. AT63 100
Knowlton Grn. Brom. CG53 88
Knowl Way Borwd. BL24 28
Knowsley Av. Sthl. BF40 54
Knowsley Rd. SW11 BU44 66
Knox Rd. E7 CG36 58
Knox Rd. Guil. AQ68 109
Knox St. W1 BU39 56
Knoyle St. SE14 CD43 67
Chubworthy St.
Knutsford Av. Wat. BD22 27
Knutsford St. SW8 BW44 66
Kohat Rd. SW19 BS49 76
Koh-i-noor Av. Bush. BF25 27
Kossuth St. SE10 CG42 68
Kramer Ms. SW5 BS42 66
Kuala Gdns. SW16 BX51 86
Kuhn Way, E7 CH35 49
Kydbrook Clo. Orp. CM54 88
Kylemore Rd. NW6 BS36 56
Kymberley Rd. Har. BH32 45
Kyme Rd. Rom. CT32 50
Kynance Gdns. Stan. BK30 36
Kynance Ms. SW7 BS41 66
Kynance Pl. SW7 BT41 66
Kynaston Av. N16 CA34 48
Dynevor Rd.
Kynaston Av. Th. Hth. BZ53 87
Kynaston Clo. Har. BG29 36
Kynaston Cres. Th. Hth. BZ53 87
Kynaston Rd. N16 CA34 48
Kynaston Rd. Brom. CH49 78
Kynaston Rd. Enf. BZ23 30
Kynaston Rd. Orp. CO54 89
Kynaston Rd. Th. Hth. BZ53 87
Kynaston Wood. Har. BG29 36
Kynnersley Clo. Cars. BU55 86
Kynock Rd. N18 CC28 39
Kyrle Rd. SW11 BU46 76
Kytes Dr. Wat. BD20 18
Kyverdale Rd. N16 CA33 48
Labour-in-Vain Rd. Sev. DB60 99
Laburnham Av. West Dr. AY40 53
Laburnham Ct. Stan. BK28 36
Laburnham Gdns, Upmin. CZ33 51
Laburnham Rd. Epp. CP18 23
Laburnham Way Brom. CL54 88
Laburnum Av. N9 CA27 39
Laburnum Av. N17 BZ29 39
Laburnum Av. Dart. CV47 80
Laburnum Av. Horn. CT34 50
Laburnum Av. Sutt. BU55 86
Laburnum Av. Swan. CS52 89
Laburnum Clo. E4 CD29 39
Maple Av.
Laburnum Clo. Guil. AR69 118
Laburnum Clo. Upmin. DA33 51
Laburnum Clo. Wal. Cr. CC19 21
Laburnum Cres. Sun. BC51 83
Laburnum Gdns. N21 BZ27 39
Laburnum Gro. N21 BZ27 39
Laburnum Gro. NW9 BN33 46
Laburnum Gro. Houns. BE45 64
Laburnum Gro. N. Mal. BN51 85
Laburnum Gro. St. Alb. BF16 18
Laburnum Gro. Slou. AT43 62
Laburnum Gro. Sthl. BE38 54
Laburnum Pl. SE9 CL46 78
Laburnum Pl. Egh. AQ50 72
Laburnum Rd. SW19 BT50 76
Laburnum Rd. Cher. AW54 83
Laburnum Rd. Epsom. BO60 94
Laburnum Rd. Hayes. BB42 63
Laburnum Rd. Hayes BC42 63
Laburnum Rd. Hodd. CE11 12
Laburnum Rd. Mitch. BV51 86
Laburnum Rd. Wok. AR63 100
Laburnum St. E2 CA37 57
Laburnum Wk. Horn. CV35 51
Laburnum Way, Stai. AY47 73
Laburnum Way, Wal. Cr. BY17 20
Lacey Ave. Couls. BY63 104
Lacey Clo. Egh. AU50 72
Lacey Dri. Edg. BL28 37
Lacey Grn. Couls. BY63 104
Lacey St. E3 CE37 57
Lach Clo. Tad. BT64 104
Lackford Rd. Couls. BU62 104
Lackington St. EC2 BZ39 57
Lackmore Rd. Enf. CC21 30
Lacon Rd. SE22 CB45 67
Lacy Dr. Couls. BY63 104
Lacy Rd. SW15 BQ45 65
Ladas Rd. SE27 BZ49 77
Ladbroke Cres. W11 BR39 55
Ladbroke Gro.
Ladbroke Gdns. W11 BR40 55
Ladbroke Gro. Red. BV70 121
Ladbroke Rd. W11 BR40 55
Ladbroke Rd. Enf. CA25 30
Ladbroke Rd. Epsom BN60 94
Ladbroke Rd. Red. BV70 121
Ladbroke Sq. W11 BR40 55
Ladbroke Sq Gdns. W11 BR40 55
Ladbroke Ter. W11 BR40 55
Ladbroke Wk. W11 BR40 55
Ladbrook Clo. Pnr. BE32 45
Ladbrook Cres. Sid. CP48 79
Ladbrooke Dr. Pot. B. BS19 20
Ladbrook Rd. SE25 BZ52 87
Ladbrook Rd. Slou. AO41 61
Ladderstile Ride, Kings. On T. BN49 75
Ladderswood Rd. N11 BW28 38
Ladds Way Swan. CS52 89
Ladenhatch La. Swan. CS51 89
Ladies Gro. St. Alb. BF13 9
Ladworth Lo. Est. Mitch. BV52 86
Lady Amherst's Dri. Sev. CR69 116
Ladycroft Gdns. Orp. CM56 97
Ladycroft Rd. SE13 CE45 67
Ladycroft Wk. Stan. BK30 36
Ladycroft Way Orp. CM56 97
Ladyfields, Grav. DF49 81
Ladyfields Loug. CL24 31
Ladyfields Clo. Loug. CL24 31
Ladygate La. Ruis. AZ32 44
Ladygate Rd. Dor. BK71 119
Lady Gro. Welw. G. C. BR9 5
Lady Hay Wor. Pk. BO55 85
Lady Margaret Rd. Sthl. BE40 54
Ladymeadow, Kings L. AX17 17
Ladymead Parkway, Guil. AR70 118
Lady's Clo. Wat. BC24 26
Vicarage Rd.
Ladyshot, Harl. CO10 6
Ladysmith Av. E6 CK37 58
Ladysmith Av. Ilf. CM33 49
Ladysmith Rd. E16 CG38 58
Ladysmith Rd. N17 CB30 39
Ladysmith Rd. N18 CB28 39
Ladysmith Rd. SE9 CL46 78
Ladysmith Rd. Enf. CA24 30
Ladysmith Rd. Har. BH30 36
Ladysmith Rd. Kes. CG57 97
Ladysmith Rd. St. Alb. BG13 9
Lady Somerset Rd. NW5 BV35 47
Lady Spencer Gro. St. Alb. BG14 9
Ladywell Rd. SE13 CE46 77
Ladywell St. E15 CG37 58
Ladywood Av. Orp. CN53 88
Ladywood Clo. Rick. AX24 26
Ladywood Rd. Dart. CZ49 80
Ladywood Rd. Surb. BM55 85
Lafone Av. Felt. BD48 74
Lafone St. SE1 CA41 67
Lagger Clo. Ch. St. G. AQ27 34
Lagger. The. Ch. St. G. AQ27 34
Laglands Clo. Reig. BT69 121
Lagonda Av. Ilf. CN29 40
Lagoon Rd. Orp. CO53 89
Lahore Rd. Croy. BZ53 87
Sydenham Rd.
Laindon Av. E15 CG35 49
Leytonstone Rd.
Laing Dene Nthlt. BD37 54
Laings Av. Mitch. BU51 86
Lainson St. SW18 BS47 76
Laird Ave. Grays. DE41 71
Laitwood Rd. SW12 BV47 76
Lake Av. Brom. CH50 78
Lake Av. Rain. CV37 60
Lake Av. Slou. AO40 52
Lake Clo. SW19 BR49 75
Lake Rd.
Lake Clo. Wey. AX59 92
Lakedale Rd. SE18 CG43 68
Lake End Rd. Maid. AK40 61
Lakefield Rd. N22 BY30 38
Lakefields Clo. Rain. CV37 60
Lake Gdns. Dag. CR35 50
Lake Gdns. Rich. BJ48 74
Lake Gdns. Wall. BV55 86
Lakehall Gdns. Th. Hth. BY53 86
Lakehall Rd. Th. Hth. BY53 86
Lake House Rd. E11 CH34 49
Lakehurst Rd. Epsom BO56 94
Lakeland Clo. Chig. CO28 41
Lakeland Clo. Har. BG29 36
Lakenheath N14 BW25 29
Lake Rise Rom. CT30 41
Lake Rd. SW19 BR49 75
Lake Rd. Croy. CD55 87
Lake Rd. Vir. W. AQ52 82
Lake Rd. Wal. Abb. CG14 13
Laker Pl. SW15 BR46 75
Lakers Rise Bans. BU61 104
Lakeside W13 BK39 54
Edge Hill Rd.
Lakeside Enf. BW24 29
Lakeside Rain. CV37 60
Lakeside Wall. BV56 95
Lakeside, Wey. BB55 83
Lakeside, Wok. AP63 100
Lakeside Av. Ilf. CJ31 49
Lakeside Clo. SE25 CA51 87
Lakeside Clo. Sid. CP46 79
Lakeside Clo. Wok. AP63 100
Lakeside Ct. Borwd. BM25 28
Lakeside Cres. Barn. BU25 29
Lake Side Cres. Brwd. DB27 42
Lakeside Dr. Brom. CK55 88
Lakeside Dr. Esher BG57 93
Lakeside Dr. Slou. AP37 52
Lakeside Rd. N13 BX28 38
Lakeside Rd. W14 BQ41 65
Lakeside Rd. Wal. Cr. CC17 21
Lakes Rd. Kes. CJ56 97
Lakeswood Rd. Orp. CL53 88
Lake, The, Bush. BG26 36
Lake Vw. Edg. BL28 37
Lake View, Pot. B. BT20 20
Lakeview Rd. SE27 BY49 76
Lakeview Rd. Sev. CU65 107
Lake View Rd. Well. CO45 69
Lakis Clo. NW3 BT35 47
Flask Walk.
Laleham Av. NW7 BN27 37
Laleham Rd. SE6 CF47 77
Laleham Rd. Shep. AY52 83
Laleham Rd. Stai. AV49 72
Lalor St. SW6 BR44 65
Lambarde Av. SE9 CL49 78
Lambarde Rd. Sev. CU64 107
Lamb Cl. Hat. BP13 10
Lamb Clo. Til. DH44 71
Coleridge Rd.
Lamberhurst Clo. Orp. CP54 89
Lamberhurst Rd. SE27 BY49 76
Lamberhurst Rd. Dag. CQ33 50
Lambern Ave. Slou. AS41 62
Lambert Av. Rich. BM45 65
Lambert Rd. E16 CH39 58
Lambert Rd. N12 BT28 38
Lambert Rd. SW2 BX46 76
Lambert Rd. Bans. BS60 95
Lamberts Pl. Croy. BZ54 87
Lamberts Rd. Surb. BL53 85
Lambert St. N1 BY36 56
Lambert Way N12 BT28 38
Lambeth High St. SE1 BX42 66
Lambeth Hill EC4 BZ40 57
Upper Thames St.
Lambeth Palace Rd. SE1 BX41 66
Lambeth Rd. SE1 BX41 66
Lambeth Rd. Croy. BY54 86
Lambeth St. E1 CB39 57
Lambeth Wk. SE11 BX42 66
Lamb La. E8 CB36 57
Lamble St. NW5 BV35 47
Lambley Rd. Dag. CO36 59
Lambolle Pl. NW3 BU36 56
Lambolle Rd. NW3 BU36 56
Lambourn Clo. W7 BH41 64
Lambourne Av. SW19 BR49 75
Lambourne Cres. Chig. CO27 41
Lambourne Cres. Wok. AU60 91
Lambourne Dr. Brwd. DF26 122
Lambourne Gdns. E4 CE27 39
Lambourne Gdns. Bark. CN36 58
Lambourne Rd.
Lambourne Gdns. Enf. CA23 30
Lambourne Gdns. Horn. CV34 51
Lambourne Rd. E11 CF33 48
Lambourne Rd. Bark. CN36 58
Lambourne Rd. Chig. CN28 40
Lambourne Rd. Ilf. CN34 49
Lambourn Rd. SW4 BV45 66
Lambridge Dr. Sev. CU65 107
Lambrook Ter. SW6 BR44 65
Lambs Bldgs. EC1 BZ38 57
Errol St.
Lambs Clo. Pot. B. BX18 20
Lamb's Conduit Pass, WC1 BX39 56
Red Lion Sq.
Lamb's Conduit St. WC1 BX38 56
Lambscroft Av. SE9 CJ48 78
Lambs Croft Way. Ger. Cr. AS30 34
Lambs La. Rain. CU39 59
Lambs Pass. EC1 BZ39 57
Lambs Pass. Brent. BL42 65
Lambs Ter. N9 BZ27 39
Lamb St. E1 CA39 57
Lambs Wk. Enf. BZ23 30
Lambton Av. Wal. Cr. CC19 21
Lambton Pl. W11 BS40 56
Lambton Rd. N19 BX33 47
Lambton Rd. SW20 BQ51 85
Lamb Wk. SE1 CA41 67
Lamb Yd. Wat. BD24 27
Lamerock Rd. Brom. CG49 78
Lamerton Rd. Ilf. CL30 40
Lamford Clo. N17 BZ29 39
Lamington St. W6 BP42 65
Lamlash St. SE11 BY42 66
Hayles St.
Lammas Av. Mitch. BV51 86
Lammas Ct. Stai. AU48 72
Lammas Ct. Wind. AO44 61
Lammas Dr. Stai. AU49 72
Lammas Gn. SE26 CB48 77
Lammas Hill Esher BF56 93
Lammas La. Esher BF56 93
Lammas Mead, Brox. CD15 12
Lammas Pk. Gdns. W5 BK40 54
Lammas Pk. Rd. W5 BK40 54
Lammas Rd. E9 CC36 57
Lammas Rd. E10 CD33 48
Lammas Rd. Rich. BK49 74
Lammas Rd. Wat. BD25 27
Lammermoor Rd. SW12 BV47 76
Lamont Rd. SW10 BT43 66
Lamorbey Clo. Sid. CN47 78
Lamorna Av. Grav. DH48 81
Lamorna Clo. Orp. CO54 89
Lamorna Gro. Stan. BK30 36
Lampard Gro. N16 CA33 48
Lampern Sq. E2 CB38 57
Nelson Gdns.
Lampeter Clo. Wok. AS62 100
Lampeter St. N1 BZ37 57
Lampits, Hodd. CE12 12
Lampmead Rd. SE12 CG46 78
Lamport Clo. SE18 CK42 68
Lampton Av. Houns. BF44 64
Lampton Ho. Clo. SW19 BQ49 75
Lampton Pk. Rd. Houns. BF44 64
Lampton Rd. Houns. BF44 64
Lamsey Rd. Hem. H. AX14 8
Lan Acre NW9 BO30 37
Lanark Clo. W5 BK39 54
Lanark Pl. W9 BT38 56
Lanark Rd. W9 BS38 56
Lanbury Rd. SE15 CC45 67
Lancaster Av. E18 CH31 49
Lancaster Av. SE27 BY48 76
Lancaster Av. SW19 BQ49 75
Lancaster Av. Bark. CN36 58
Lancaster Av. Barn. BT22 29
Lancaster Av. Mitch. BX53 86
Lancaster Clo. Brom. CG52 88
Lancaster Clo. Brwd. DA25 33
Lancaster Clo. Kings. On T. BK49 74
Lancaster Cotts. Rich. BL46 75
Lancaster Pk.
Lancaster Ct. SW6 BR43 65
Lancaster Ct. W2 BT40 56
Lancaster Ct. Bans. BR60 94
Lancaster Dr. NW3 BU36 56
Lancaster Dr. Horn. CU35 50
Lancaster Gdns. SW19 BR49 75
Lancaster Gdns. W2 BT40 56
Lancaster Gdns. W13 BJ40 54
Lancaster Gdns. Kings. On T. BK49 74
Lancaster Gte. W2 BT40 56
Lancaster Gds. NW3 BU36 56
Lambolle Pla.
Lancaster Gro. NW3 BT36 56
Lancaster Ms. W2 BT40 56
Lancaster Ms. Rich. BL46 75
Richmond Hill
Lancaster Pk. Rich. BL46 75
Lancaster Pl. SW19 BQ49 75
Lancaster Pl. WC2 BX40 56
Lancaster Pl. Houns. BD44 64

Lancaster Rd. E7 CH36 58
Lancaster Rd. E11 CG34 49
Lancaster Rd. E17 CC30 39
Lancaster Rd. N4 BY33 47
Lancaster Rd. N11 BW29 38
Lancaster Rd. N18 CA28 39
Lancaster Rd. NW10 BP35 46
Lancaster Rd. SE25 CA51 87
Lancaster Rd. SW19 BQ49 75
Lancaster Rd. W5 BK40 54
Lancaster Rd. W10 BQ41 65
Lancaster Rd. W11 BQ40 55
Lancaster Rd. Barn. BT24 29
Lancaster Rd. Enf. BZ23 30
Lancaster Rd Epp. CR16 23
Lancaster Rd. Har. BF32 45
Lancaster Rd. St. Alb. BH12 9
Lancaster Rd. Sthl. BE40 54
Lancaster Rd. Uxb. AX36 53
Lancaster St. SE1 BY41 66
Lancaster Way, Welw. BQ5 5
Lancaste Wk. Hayes BA39 53
Lancefield St. W10 BR38 55
Lancell St. N16 CA34 48
Lancelot Av. Wem. BK35 45
Lancelot Cres. Wem. BK35 45
Lancelot Gdns. Barn. BV26 38
Lancelot Pl. SW7 BU41 66
Lancelot Rd. Ilf. CN29 40
Lancelot Rd. Well. CO45 69
Lancelot Rd. Wem. BK35 45
Lance Rd. Har. BG33 45
Lanchester Rd. N6 BU32 47
Lancing Av. Felt. BB48 73
Lancing Gdns. N9 CA26 39
Lancing Rd. W13 BJ40 54
Drayton Gn. Rd.
Lancing Rd. Croy. BX54 86
Lancing Rd. Ilf. CM32 49
Lancing Rd. Orp. CO55 89
Lancing Rd. Rom. CW29 42
Lancing St. NW1 BW38 56
Lancing Way, Rick. AZ25 26
Landcroft Rd. SE22 CA46 77
Landells Rd. SE22 CA46 77
Lander Rd. Grays. DE42 71
Landfield St. E5 CB34 48
Landfold Clo. Rick. AY27 35
Landford Rd. SW15 BQ45 65
Landgrove Rd. SW19 BS49 76
Landguard, Saw. CQ6 6
Landmead Rd. Wal. Cr. CD18 21
Landon Pl. SW1 BU41 66
Landon Way, Ashf. BA50 73
Landor Rd. SW9 BX45 66
Landor Wk. W12 BP41 65
Landport Way, SE15 CA43 67
Landra Gdns. N21 BY25 29
Landridge Rd. SW6 BR44 65
Landrock Rd. N8 BX32 47
Landsbury Dr. Hayes BC38 53
Landscape Rd. Warl. CB63 105
Landscape Rd. Wdf. Grn. CH29 40
Landseer Av. E12 CL35 49
Landseer Av. Grav. DE48 81
Landseer Clo. Edg. BM30 37
Landseer Rd. N19 BX34 47
Landseer Rd. Enf. CB25 30
Landseer Rd. N. Mal. BN54 85
Landseer Rd. Sutt. BS57 95
Landstead Rd. SE18 CM43 68
Landview Gdns. Ong. CX18 24
Landway, The, Orp. CP52 89
Landway, The. Sev. CW63 108
Landway, The. Sev. CX62 108
Lane App. NW7 BR28 37
Lane Ave. Green. DB46 80
Lanebridge Rd. Welw. G. C. BQ7 5
Lane Clo. NW2 BP34 46
Lane Clo. Wey. AW56 92
Lane Ct. SW11 BU46 76
Thurleigh Rd.
Lane End, Bexh. CR45 69
Lane End Epsom BN60 94
Lanefield Wk. Welw. G. C. BQ8 5
Lane Gdns. Bush. BH26 36
La Plata Gro. Brwd. DA27 42
Lanercost Gdns. N14 BX26 38
Lanercost Rd. SW2 BY48 76
Lanes Av. Grav. DF48 81
Laneside, Chis. CL49 78
Laneside, Edg. BN28 37
Laneside Av. Dag. CQ33 50
Lane, The, NW8 BT37 56
Lane, The, SE3 CH45 68
Casterbridge Rd.
Lane, The, Vir. W. AS52 82
La Tourne Gdns. Orp. CM55 88
Lane Way, SW15 BP46 75
Sunnymead Rd.
Lanfranc Rd. E3 CD37 57
Langafel Clo. Long. DC51 90
Langaller La. Lthd. BF64 102
Langbourne Av. N6 BV34 47
Langbourne Way Esher BJ56 93
Langbrook Rd. SE3 CJ45 68
Lang Clo. Lthd. BF65 102
Langcroft Clo. Cars. BU55 86
Langdale Av. Mitch. BU52 86
Langdale Clo. Wok. AR61 100
Langdale Ct. Hem. H. AY12 8
Wharfedale
Langdale Cr. Bexh. CR43 69
Langdale Dr. Hayes BB37 53
Langdale Gdns. Grnf. BJ38 54
Langdale Gdns. Horn. CU35 50
Langdale Gdns. Wal. Cr. CC21 30
Langdale Rd. SE10 CE43 67
Langdale Rd. Th. Hth. BY52 86
Langdale St. E1 CB39 57
Langdale Wk. Grav. DF48 81
Langdon Ct. NW10 BO37 55
Craven Park.
Langdon Cres. E6 CL37 58
Langdon Dr. NW9 BN33 46
Langdon Pk. Rd. N6 BW33 47
Langdon Pl. SW14 BN45 65
Rosemary La.
Langdon Rd. E6 CL37 58
Langdon Rd. Brom. CH52 88
Langdon Rd. Mord. BT53 86
Langdon Shaw, Sid. CN49 78
Langford Clo. NW8 BT37 56
Langford Ct. NW8 BT37 56
Langford Cres. Barn. BU24 29
Langford Green Gdns SE5 CA45 67
Langford Pl. NW8 BT37 56
Langford Pl. Sid. CO48 79
Langford Rd. SW6 BS44 66
Langford Rd. Barn. BU24 29
Langford Rd. Wdf. Grn. CJ29 40
Langfords Buck. H. CJ27 40
Langham Clo. N15 BY31 47
Langham Rd.
Langham Ct. Horn. CV33 51
Langham Dene Ken. BY57 95
Langham Dene Ken. BY61 104
Langham Dr. Rom. CO32 50
Langham Gdns. N21 BY25 29
Langham Gdns. W13 BJ40 54
Garden Rd.
Langham Gdns. Edg. BN29 37
Langham Gdns. Rich. BK49 74
Langham Gdns. Wem. BK34 45
Langham Ho. Rich. BK49 74
Langham Pl. N15 BY31 47
Langham Pl. W1 BV39 56
Langham Pl. Egh. AS49 72
Langham Rd. N15 BY31 47
Langham Rd. SW20 BQ51 85
Langham Rd. Edg. BN29 37
Langham Rd. Tedd. BJ49 74
Langham St. W1 BV39 56
Langhedge Clo. N18 CA29 39
Langhorne Rd. Dag. CR36 59
Langland Ct. Nthwd. BA29 35
Langland Cres. E. Stan. BK30 36
Langland Cres. N. Stan. BK30 36
Langland Cres. S. Stan. BL31 46
Langland Cres. W. Stan. BK30 36
Langland Dr. Pnr. BE29 36
Langland Gdns. NW3 BS35 47
Langland Gdns. Croy. CD55 87
Langlands Dr. Dart. CZ49 80
Langlands Rise Epsom BN60 94
Langler Rd. NW10 BQ37 55
Langler Rd. NW10 BQ38 55
Langley Av. Hem. H. AY15 8
Langley Av. Ruis. BC34 44
Langley Av. Surb. BK54 84
Langley Av. Wor. Pk. BQ54 85
Langley Broom Ave. Slou. AS42 62
Langleybury La. Kings L. AZ22 26
Langley Clo. Epsom. BN63 103
Langley Clo. Rom. CV29 42
Faringdon Av.
Langley Ct. SE9 CL46 78
Langley Ct. WC2 BX40 56
Long Acre
Langley Ct. W. Wick. CF54 87
Langley Cres. E11 CH33 49
Langley Cres. Dag. CP36 59
Langley Cres. Edg. BN27 37
Langley Cres. Hayes. BB43 63
Langley Cres. St. Alb. BG12 9
Langley Dr. E11 CH33 49
Langley Dr. W3 BM41 65
Langley Dr. Brwd. DA27 42
Langley Gdns. Dag. CP36 59
Langley Gdns. Orp. CL53 88
Langley Gro. N. Mal. BN51 85
Langley High St. Slou. AT42 62
Langley Hill, Kings L. AY18 17
Langley Hill Clo. Kings L. AZ18 17
Langley La. SW8 BX43 66
Langley La. Epsom BM66 112
Langley La. Wat. BB19 17
Langley Oaks Av. Sth. Croy. CB58 96
Langley Pk. NW7 BO29 37
Langley Pk. Rd. Slou. & Iver AT40 52
Langley Pk. Rd. Sutt. BT56 95
Langley Rd. SW19 BR51 85
Langley Rd. Beck. CC52 87
Langley Rd. Kings L. AW18 17
Langley Rd. Slou. AR41 62
Langley Rd. Stai. AV50 72
Langley Rd. Sth. Croy. CC58 96
Langley Rd. Surb. BL54 85
Langley Rd. Wat. BB19 17
Langley Rd. Wat. BB22 26
Langley Rd. Well. CP43 69
Langley St. WC2 BX39 56
Langley Vale Rd. Epsom BN61 103
Langley Vale Rd. Epsom. BN63 103
Langley Wk. Wok. AS63 100
Midhope Rd.
Langley Way, Wat. BB23 26
Langley Way W. Wick. CF54 87
Langly Rd. Islw. BH44 64
Lang Mead, SE27 BY49 76
Langmead Dr. Bush. BH26 36
Langroyd Rd. SW17 BU48 76
Langshot Clo. Wey. AV59 91
Langside Av. SW15 BP45 65
Langside Cres. N14 BW27 38
Langston Rd. Loug. CM25 31
Lang St. E1 CC38 57
Langthorne Cres. Grays. DE42 71
Langthorne Rd. E11 CF34 48
Langthorne St. SW6 BQ43 65
Langton Av. E6 CL38 58
Langton Av. N20 BT26 38
Langton Av. Epsom BO59 94
Langton Clo. WC1 BX38 56
Wren St.
Langton Clo. Wey. AW55 83
Langton Ri. SE23 CB47 77
Langton Rd. NW2 BQ34 46
Langton Rd. SW9 BY43 66
Langton Rd. E. Mol. BG53 84
Langton Rd. Har. BG29 36
Langton Rd. Hodd. CD12 12
Langton St. SW10 BT43 66
Langton Way, SE3 CG44 68
Langton Way Croy. CA55 87
Langton Way, Egh. AU50 72
Langton Way. Grays. DH42 71
Langtry Rd. NW8 BT37 56
Langtry Rd. Nthlt. BD37 54
Langwood Chase Tedd. BK50 74
Broom Rd.
Langwood Gdns. Wat. BC23 26
Langworthy End. Maid. AG43 61
Lanhill Rd. W9 BS38 56
Lanier Rd. SE13 CF46 77
Lankaster Gdns. N2 BT30 38
Lankers Dr. Har. BE32 45
Lankton Clo. Beck. CF51 87
Lanleybury La. Kings L. AZ20 17
Lannock Rd. Hayes BB40 53
Lannoy Rd. SE9 CM47 78
Lanrick Rd. E14 CF39 57
Lanridge Rd. SE2 CP41 69
Lanridge Rd. Belv. CP41 69
Lansbury Av. N18 BZ28 39
Lansbury Av. Bark. CO36 59
Lansbury Av. Felt. BC46 73
Lansbury Av. Rom. CQ32 50
Lansbury Clo. NW10 BN35 46
Lansbury Cres. Dart. CX46 80
Lansbury Dr. Hayes BB37 53
Lansbury Dr. Hayes BB39 53
Lansbury Est. E14 CE39 57
Lansbury Gdns. E14 CF39 57
Lansbury Gdns. Dart. CX46 80
Lansbury Rd. Enf. CC23 30
Lansbury Way N18 CA28 39
Lansdell Rd. Mitch. BV51 86
Lansdown, Guil. AT70 118
Lansdown Clo. Wok. AP63 100
Lansdowne Av. Orp. CL54 88
Lansdowne Av. Slou. AP40 52
Lansdowne Av. Well. CP43 69
Lansdowne Clo. SW20 BQ50 75
Lansdowne Clo. Twick. BH47 74
Lansdowne Clo. Wat BD21 27
Lansdowne Ct. Pur. BY58 95
Lansdowne Ct. Wor. Pk. BP55 85
Lansdowne Cres. W11 BR40 55
Lansdowne Dr. E8 CB36 57
Lansdowne Gdns. SW8 BX44 66
Lansdowne Gdns. W11 BR41 65
Lansdowne Green Est. SW8 BX44 66
Lansdowne Gro. NW10 BO35 46
Lansdowne Hill SE27 BY48 76
Lansdowne La. SE7 CJ43 68
Lansdowne Mews SE7 CJ42 68
Lansdowne Pl. SE1 BZ41 67
Lansdowne Pl. SE19 CA50 77
Lansdowne Rise, W11 BR40 55
Lansdowne Rd. E4 CE27 39
Lansdowne Rd. E11 CG34 49
Lansdowne Rd. E17 CE32 48
Lansdowne Rd. E18 CH31 49
Lansdowne Rd. N3 BR29 37
Lansdowne Rd. N10 BW30 38
Lansdowne Rd. N17 CA30 39
Lansdowne Rd. SW20 BQ50 75
Lansdowne Rd. W11 BR40 55
Lansdowne Rd. Brom. CH50 78
Lansdowne Rd. Croy. BZ55 87
Lansdowne Rd. Epsom BN57 94
Lansdowne Rd. Har. BH33 45
Lansdowne Rd. Houns. BF45 64
Lansdowne Rd. Ilf. CN33 49
Lansdowne Rd. Pur. BX59 95
Lansdowne Rd. Stai. AW50 73
Lansdowne Rd. Stan. BK29 36
Lansdowne Rd. Til. DF44 71
Lansdowne Rd. Uxb. AZ39 53
Lansdowne Row, W1 BV40 56
Berkeley St.
Lansdowne Ter. WC1 BX38 56
Lansdowne Wk. W11 BR40 55
Lansdowne Way SW8 BW44 66
Lansdown Rd. E7 CJ36 58
Lansdown Rd. Ger. Cr. AR30 34
Lansdown Rd. Sid. CO48 79
Lansfield Av. N18 CB28 39
Lans Pl. Grav. DF47 81
Lanswell Est. SE1 BY41 66
Lantern Clo. SW15 BP45 65
Lant St. SE1 BZ41 67
Lanturn Clo. Wem. BK35 45
Lanvanor Rd. SE15 CC44 67
Lapsewood Wk. SE23 CB48 77
Lapstone Gdns. Har. BK32 45
Lapwing Clo. Hem. H. AY12 8
Lapworth Clo. Orp. CP55 89
Larbert Rd. SW16 BW50 76
Larby Pl. Epsom BO58 94
Larch Av. W3 BO40 55
Larch Av. Guil. AR69 118
Larch Av. St. Alb. BE18 18
Larch Clo. SW12 BV47 76
Larch Clo. Red. BT71 121
Larch Clo. Warl. CD63 105
Larch Cres. Epsom. BM57 94
Larch Cres. Hayes BD38 54
Larchdene Orp. CL55 88
Larches Av. SW14 BN45 65
Larches Av. Enf. CC21 30
Larches, The, N13 BZ27 39
Larches, The Uxb. AZ38 53
Larches, The, Wat. BE25 27
Larch Rd. NW2 BQ35 46
Larch Rd. Dart. CV47 80
Larch Tree Way Croy. CE55 87
Larch Way Brom. CL54 88
Larchwood Av. Rom. CR29 41
Larchwood Clo. Bans. BR61 103
Larchwood Clo. Rom. CS29 41
Larchwood Dr. Egh. AQ50 72
Larchwood Gdns. Brwd. DA25 33
Larchwood Rd. SE9 CL48 78
Larchwood Rd. Hem. H. AY12 8
Larchwood Rd. Wok. AO63 100
Larcom St. SE17 BZ42 67
Larden Rd. W3 BO40 55
Lardo Av. SW6 BR45 65
Largewood Av. Surb. BL55 85
Lark Av. Stai. AV48 72
Larkbere Rd. SE26 CD49 77
Larkfield Av. Har. BJ31 45
Larkfield Clo. Brom. CG55 88
Larkfield Rd. Rich. BL45 65
Larkfield Rd. Sev. CS65 107
Larkfield Rd. Sid. CN48 78
Lark Fields, Grav. DF48 81
Larkhall Est. SW8 BW44 66
Larkhall La. SW4 BW44 66
Larkhall Rise SW4 BW44 66
Larkin Dr. Bush. BG26 36
Larking La. Slou. AR37 52
Lark Rise. Hat. BP13 10
Lark Rise. Leath. BB69 110
Lark Row E3 CC37 57
Lark's Field Hart. DC52 90
Larksfield Gro. Enf. CB23 30
Larkshall Cres. E4 CF28 39
Larks' Hall Rd. F4 CF29 39
Larkspur Cl. N17 BZ29 39
Larkspur Clo. S. Ock. DB38 60
Larkspur Way Epsom BN56 94
Larks Rise. Chesh. AO20 16
Larkswood Rise Pnr. BD31 45
Larkswood Rd. E4 CE28 39
Larkway Clo. NW9 BN31 46
Larmans Rd. Enf. CC21 30
Larnach Rd. W6 BQ43 65
Larne Rd. Ruis. BB33 44
Larner Rd. Erith CT43 69
Larpent Av. SW15 BQ45 65
Larsen Dr. Wal. Abb. CF20 21
Larson Rd. Esher BE57 93
Lascelles Av. Har. BG33 45
Lascelles Clo. Brwd. DA25 33
Lascelles Rd. Slou. AQ42
Lascott's Rd. N22 BX29 38
Lassa Rd. SE9 CK46 78
Lassell St. SE10 CF42 67
Lasswade Rd. Cher. AV54 82
Latchett Rd. E18 CH30 40
Latchford Pl. Chig. CO28 41
Latchington Gdns. Wdf. Grn. CK29 40
Latchmere Clo. Rich. BL49 75
Latchmere Ho. Kings. On T. BL49 75
Latchmere La. Kings. On T. BL50 75
Latchmere Rd. SW11 BU44 66
Latchmere Rd. Kings. On T. BL50 75
Latchmere St. SW11 BU44 66
Burns Rd.
Latchmoor Ave. Ger. Cr. AR31 43
Latchmoor Way. Ger. Cr. AR31 43
Lateward Rd. Brent. BK43 64
Latham Clo. Twick. BJ47 74
Latham Rd. Bexh. CR46 79
Latham Rd. Twick. BH47 74
Lath Clo. West. CJ61 106
Lathkill Clo. Enf. CA26 39
Lathom Rd. E6 CK36 58
Latimer Av. E6 CK37 58
Latimer Cl. N15 CA32 48
Latimer Clo. N15 CA32 48
St. Ann's Rd.
Latimer Clo. Amer. AR23 25
Latimer Clo. Hem. H. AZ11 8
Latimer Clo. Pnr. BD30 36
Latimer Clo. Wor. Pk. BP56 94
Latimer Gdns. Pnr. BD30 36
Latimer Ms. W10 BQ39 55
Latimer Pl. W10 BQ39 55
Latimer Rd. E7 CH35 49
Latimer Rd. SW19 BS50 76
Latimer Rd. W10 BQ39 55
Latimer Rd. W11 BQ40 55
Latimer Rd. Barn. BS24 29
Latimer Rd. Chesh. AP20 16
Latimer Rd. Chesh. AP21 25
Latimer Rd. Croy. BY55 86
Latimer Rd. Tedd. BH49 74
Latimer St. E1 CC39 57
Latona Dr. Grav. DJ49 81
Latona Rd. SE15 CA43 67
Lattimore Rd. St. Alb. BH14 9
Latton Cl. Walt. BE54 84
Latton Clo. Esher BF56 93
Latton Common Rd. Harl. CO12 14
Latton Green. Harl. CN13 13
Latymer Ct. W6 BQ42 65
Latymer Rd. N9 CA26 39
Latymer Way N9 BZ27 39
Lauder Clo. Nthlt. BD37 54
Lauderdale Dr. Rich. BK48 74
Lauderdale Rd. W9 BS38 56
Laudersdale Rd. Kings L. BA20 17
Laud St. SE11 BX42 66
Laud St. Croy. BZ55 87
Laughedge La. N18 CA28 39
Laughton Rd. Nthlt. BD37 54
Launcelot Rd. Brom. CH49 78
Launceston Gdns. Grnf. BK37 54
Launceston Pl. W8 BT41 66
Launceston Rd. Grnf. BK37 54
Launch St. E14 CF41 67
Launder's La. Rain. CW39 60
Laundry La. Wal. Abb. CG15 13
Laundry La. Wal. Abb. CG16 22
Laundry Rd. E4 CF26 39
Station Rd.
Laundry Rd. W6 BR43 65
Laundry Rd. Guil. AR71 118
Lauradale Rd. N2 BU31 47
Laura Dr. Swan. CU50 79
Laura Pl. E5 CC35 48
Laurel Ave. Slou. AS41 62
Laurel Av. Egh. AQ49 72
Laurel Av. Grav. DH48 81
Laurel Av. Pot. B. BR19 19
Laurel Av. Twick. BH47 74
Laurel Bank Rd. Enf. BZ23 30
Laurel Clo. Dart. CV47 80
Laurel Clo. Ilf. CM29 40
Laurel Clo. Slou. AV44 62
Laurel Cres. Brwd. DD25 122
Laurel Cres. Croy. CE55 87
Laurel Cres. Rom. CT33 50
Laurel Cres. Wok. AU60 91
Laurel Dene Tedd. BG49 74
Laurel Dr. N21 BY26 38
Laurel Dr. Oxt. CG69 115
Laurel Gdns. E4 CE26 39
Laurel Gdns. NW7 BN27 37
Laurel Gdns. W7 BH40 54
Laurel Gdns. Houns. BE45 64
Laurel Gro. SE20 CB50 77
Laurel Gro. SE26 CC49 77
Laurel La. West Dr. AY42 63
Laurel Rd. SW13 BP44 65
Laurel Rd. SW20 BP51 85
Laurel Rd. Ger. Cr. AR30 34
Laurel Rd. St. Alb. BH13 9
Laurel Rd. Tedd. BG49 74
Laurels Rd. Iver AU37 52
Laurel St. E8 CA36 57
Laurel View N12 BS27 38
Laurel Way N20 BS27 38
Laurence Pountney Hill, EC4 BZ40 57
Cannon St.
Laurence Pountney La. EC4 BZ40 57
Laurie Gdns. W7 BH39 54
Laurie Gro. SE14 CD44 67
Laurie Rd. W7 BH39 54
Laurier Rd. NW5 BV34 47
Laurier Rd. Croy. CA54 87
Lauries Clo. Berk. AT14 7
Laurie Wk. Rom. CT31 50
Lauriston Rd. E9 CC36 57
Lauriston Rd. SW19 BQ50 75
Lausanne Rd. N8 BY31 47
Lausanne Rd. SE15 CC44 67
Lauser Rd. Stai. AX47 73
Lavell St. N16 BZ35 48
Albion Rd.
Lavender Av. NW9 BN33 46
Lavender Av. DA25 33
Lavender Av. Mitch. BU51 86
Lavender Av. Wor. Pk. BQ55 85
Lavender Clo. Cars. BV56 95
Lavender Rd.
Lavender Clo. Red. BV73 121
Lavender Clo. Rom. CV29 42
Lavender Clo. Wal. Cr. CA17 21
Peakes Way
Lavender Gdns. SW11 BU45 66
Lavender Gdns. Enf. BY22 29
Lavender Gro. E8 CA36 57
Lavender Gro. Mitch. BU51 86
Lavender Hill Enf. BY23 29
Lavender Hill Swan. CS52 89
Lavender Park Rd. Wey. AW60 92
Lavender Ri. West Dr. AZ41 63
Lavender Rd. SW11 BT45 66
Lavender Rd. Cars. BV56 95
Lavender Rd. Croy. BX53 86
Lavender Rd. Enf. BZ23 30
Lavender Rd. Epsom. BM57 94
Lavender Rd. Uxb. AY39 53
Lavender St. E15 CG36 58
Lavender Sweep, SW11 BU45 66
Lavender Vale Wall. BW57 95
Lavender Wk. SW11 BU45 66
Lavender Hill
Lavender Wk. Mitch. BV52 86
Lavender Way Croy. CC53 87
Lavener Rd. Wok. AT61 100
Lavengro Rd. SE27 BZ48 77
Lavenham Rd. SW18 BR48 75
Lavernock Rd. Bexh. CR44 69
Lavers Rd. N16 CA34 48
Laverstoke Gdns. SW15 BO47 75
Lavidge Rd. SE9 CK48 78
Lavie Ms. W10 BR38 55
Portobello Rd.
Lavina Gro. N1 BX37 56
Wharfdale Rd.
Lavington Rd. W13 BJ40 54
Lavington Rd. Croy. BX55 86
Lavington St. SE1 BY40 56
Lavinia Av. Wat. BD20 18
Lavinia Rd. Dart. CW46 80
Lavrock La. Rick. AY26 35
Lawdons Gdns. Croy. BY56 95
Lawford Clo. Wall. BX58 95
Lawford Gdns. Dart. CV46 80
Lawford Rd. NW5 BW36 56
Lawford Rd. W4 BN43 65
Lawford Rd. Clo. Rick. AU25 25
Lawless St. E14 CE40 57
Lawley Rd. N14 BV26 38
Lawley St. E5 CB35 48
Lawn Ave. West Dr. AX41 63

Lawn Clo. N9 CA26 39
Lawn Clo. Brom. CH50 78
Lawn Clo. N. Mal. BO51 85
Lawn Clo. Ruis. BB34 44
Lawn Clo. Slou. AR43 62
Lawn Clo. Swan. CS51 89
Lawn Cres. Rich. BL44 65
Lawn Farm Gro. Rom. CQ31 50
Lawnfield NW6 BQ36 55
Lawn Gdns. W7 BH40 54
Lawn La. SW8 BX43 66
Lawn La. Hem. H. AX14 8
Lawn Place SE15 CA44 67
Sumner Estate
Lawn Rd. NW3 BU35 47
Lawn Rd. Beck. CD50 77
Lawn Rd. Grav. DE46 81
Lawn Rd. Guil. AR72 118
Lawn Rd. Uxb. AX36 53
Lawns Ct. Wem. BM34 46
Avenue, The,
Lawns Cres. Grays. DE43 71
Lawnside, SE3 CG45 68
Lawns, The, E4 CE28 39
Lawns, The, SE3 CG45 68
Lawns, The, SE19 BZ51 87
Lawns, The, Pnr. BF29 36
Lawns, The, St. Alb. BG13 9
Lawns, The, Sid. CO49 79
Lawns, The, Sutt. BR57 94
Lawns, The, Welw. G. C. BQ6 5
Lawns, The, Est. SE19 BZ51 87
Lawnsway Rom. CS29 41
Lawn Ter. SE3 CG45 68
Lawn, The, Harl. CO9 6
Lawn, The, Houns. BF44 64
Lawn, The, Sthl. BF42 64
Lawrance Rd. St. Alb. BG11 9
Lawrance Sq. Grav. DF48 81
Lawrence Av. E12 CL35 49
Lawrence Av. E17 CC30 39
Lawrence Av. N13 BY28 38
Lawrence Av. NW7 BO28 37
Lawrence Av. N. Mal. BN53 85
Lawrence Av. N. Mal. BO54 85
Lawrence Ct. NW7 BO28 37
Lawrence Cres. Dag. CR34 50
Lawrence Cres. Edg. BM30 37
Lawrence Dr. Uxb. BA35 44
Lawrence Fairweather Pl. N15 CA31 48
Lawrence Rd.
Lawrence Gdns. NW7 BO27 37
Lawrence Gdns. Til. DG43 71
Lawrence Gdns. Wal. Cr. CC17 21
Lawrence Hill E4 CE27 39
Lawrence Hill Gdns. Dart. CV46 80
Lawrence Hill Rd. Dart. CV46 80
Lawrence La. EC2 BZ39 57
Trump St.
Lawrence La. Bet. BP69 120
Lawrence Rd. E3 CE38 57
Lawrence Rd. E6 CK37 58
Lawrence Rd. E13 CH37 58
Lawrence Rd. N15 CA31 48
Lawrence Rd. N18 CB28 39
Lawrence Rd. SE25 CA52 87
Lawrence Rd. W5 BK42 64
Lawrence Rd. Hamptn. BE50 74
Lawrence Rd. Hayes BA37 53
Lawrence Rd. Houns. BD45 64
Lawrence Rd. Kes. CH56 97
Lawrence Rd. Pnr. BD32 45
Lawrence Rd. Rich. BK49 74
Lawrence Rd. Rom. CU32 50
Lawrence St. E14 CF40 57
Lawrence St. E16 CG39 58
Lawrence St. NW7 BO28 37
Lawrence St. SW3 BU43 66
Lawrie Pk. Av. SE26 CB49 77
Lawrie Pk. Cres. SE26 CB49 77
Lawrie Pk. Gdns. SE26 CB49 77
Lawrie Pk. Rd. SE26 CB50 77
Lawson Est. SE1 BZ41 67
Lawson Rd. Dart. CV45 70
Lawson Rd. Enf. CC23 30
Lawson Rd. Sthl. BE38 54
Law St. SE1 BZ41 67
Lawton Rd. E3 CD38 57
Lawton Rd. E10 CF33 48
Lawton Rd. N22 BX30 38
Lawton Rd. Barn. BT24 29
Lawton Rd. Loug. CL23 31
Laxey Rd. Orp. CN57 97
Laxley Clo. SE5 BY43 66
Laxton Gdns. Red. BW67 113
Layard Rd. SE16 CB42 67
Southwark Pk. Rd.
Layard Rd. Enf. CA23 30
Layard Rd. Th. Hth. BZ51 87
Layard Sq. SE16 CB41 67
Layard Sq. SE16 CB42 67
Drummond Rd.
Layburn Cres. Slou. AT43 62
Laycock St. N1 BY36 56
Layer Gdns. W3 BM40 55
Layfield Clo. NW4 BP33 46
Layfield Cres. NW4 BP33 46
Layfield Pl. E14 CF39 57
Byron St.
Layfield Rd. NW4 BP33 46
Layhams Rd. Kes. CG59 97
Layhams Rd. W. Wick. CF55 87
Laymead Clo. Nthlt. BD36 54
Laystall St. EC1 BY38 56
Layter's Ave. Ger. Cr. AR30 34
Layter's Ave. S. Ger. Cr. AR30 34
Layter's Clo. Ger. Cr. AR30 34
Layter's End. Ger. Cr. AR30 34
Layter's Green La. Ger. Cr. AQ30 34
Layters Way. Ger. Cr. AR32 43
Layton Clo. N2 BT32 47
Layton Cotts. Brent. BL43 65
Kew Br. Rd.
Layton Ct. Wey. AZ56 92
Layton Cres. Croy. BY56 95
Layton La. Sun. BB51 83
Layton Rd. N1 BY37 56
Layton Rd. Brent. BK42 64
Layton Rd. Houns. BF45 64
Lazar Walk N7 BX34 47
Andover Est.
Leabank Clo. Har. BH34 45
Leabank Vw. N15 CB32 48
Leabourne Rd. N16 CB32 48
Lea Bushes Wat. BE21 27
Leachcroft. Ger. Cr. AQ30 34
Lea Clo. Brox. CD15 12
Lea Cres. Ruis. BB35 44
Leacroft, Stai. AW49 73
Leacroft Av. SW12 BU47 76
Leacroft Clo. West Dr. AY39 53
Leacroft Rd. Iver AV39 52
Leadale Av. E4 CD27 39
Leadenhall Pl. EC3 CA39 57
Lime St.
Leadenhall St. EC3 CA39 57
Leader Av. E12 CL35 49
Leadings, The, Wem. BN34 46
Leaf Clo. Nthwd. BA29 35
Leaf Gro. SE27 BY49 76
Leafield Clo. SW16 BY50 76
Leafield Clo. Wok. AQ62 100
Leafield Rd. SW20 BR52 85
Leafield Rd. Sutt. BS55 86
Leaford Cres. Wat. BB22 26
Leafy Gro. Kes. CJ56 97
Leafy Oak Rd. SE12 CJ49 78
Leafy Way, Brwd. DE26 122
Leagrave St. E5 CC34 48
Lea Hall Rd. E10 CE33 48
Leaholme Waye, Ruis. BA32 44
Leahurst Rd. SE13 CF46 77
Leake St. SE1 BX41 66
Lealand Rd. N15 CA32 48
Leamead Av. Nthlt. BE36 54
Leamington Av. E17 CE32 48
Leamington Av. Brom. CJ49 78
Leamington Av. Mord. BR52 85
Leamington Av. Orp. CN56 97
Leamington Clo. E12 CK35 49
Leamington Clo. Brom. CJ49 78
Leamington Clo. Houns. BG46 74
Leamington Clo. Rom. CW29 42
Leamington Cres. Har. BE34 45
Leamington Gdns. Ilf. CN34 49
Leamington Pk. W3 BN39 55
Leamington Pl. Hayes BB38 53
Leamington Pl. Hayes BC38 53
Leamington Rd. Rom. CX29 42
Leamington Rd. Sthl. BD42 64
Leamington Rd. Vill. W11 BR39 55
Leamore St. W6 BQ42 65
Leamouth Rd. E14 CF39 57
Leander Dr. Grav. DJ49 81
Leander Gdns. Wat. BE22 27
Leander Rd. SW2 BX46 76
Leander Rd. Nthlt. BF37 54
Leander Rd. Th. Hth. BX52 86
Leapale La. Guil. AR71 118
Lea Pl. Sutt. BS56 95
Lea Rd. Beck. CE51 87
Lea Rd. Enf. BZ23 30
Lea. Rd. Grays. DG42 71
Lea Rd. Hodd. CF11 12
Lea Rd. Sev. CV67 117
Lea Rd. Sthl. BE42 64
Lea Rd. Wal. Abb. CE20 21
Learoyd Gdns. E6 CL40 58
Leas Clo. Chess. BL57 94
Leas Dale, SE9 CL48 78
Leas Green, Chis. CN50 78
Lea Side, Lthd. BF65 102
Leaside Av. N10 BV31 47
Leaside Rd. E5 CB33 48
Leas La. Warl. CC62 105
Leasowes Rd. E10 CE33 48
Leas Rd. Guil. AR71 118
Leas Rd. Warl. CC62 105
Leas, The, Bush. BE23 27
Leas, The, Hem. H. AZ16 17
Leas, The, Upmin. CY33 51
Leasway, Brwd. DB27 42
Leasway, Grays. DE40 71
Leasway, Upmin. CY35 51
Leat Clo. E. Mol. BH53 84
Lea, The, Egh. AV51 82
Leather Bottle La. Belv. CQ42 69
Leather Clo. Mitch. BV51 86
Leatherdale St. E1 CC38 57
Portelet Rd.
Leather Gdns. E15 CG37 58
Leatherhead By-pass, Lthd. BH65 102
Leatherhead Clo. N16 CA33 48
Leatherhead Rd. Chess. BK59 93
Leatherhead Rd. Cob. BG61 102
Leatherhead Road. Leath. AZ68 110
Leatherhead Rd. Lthd. BF66 111
Leatherhead Rd. Lthd. BG60 93
Leatherhead Rd. Lthd. & Ash. BK64 102
Leather La. EC1 BY38 56
Leathermarket St. SE1 CA41 67
Leathwaite Rd. SW11 BU45 66
Leathwell Rd. SE8 CE44 67
Lea Vale Dart. CS45 69
Lea Valley Rd. Enf. CC24 30
Lea Valley, Trading Est. E4 CC28 39
Leaveland Clo. Beck. CE52 87
Leaver Gdns. Grnf. BH37 54
Leavesden Rd. Wat. BC22 26
Leavesden Rd. Wey. AZ56 92
Leaves Green Cres. Kes. CJ59 97
Leaves Grn. Rd. Kes. CJ58 97
Lea Vw. Wal. Abb. CE20 21
Lea View Ho. E5 CB33 48
Leavsden Rd. Stan. BJ29 36
Leaway, E10 CC33 48
Leazes Ave. Cat. BY65 104
Lebanon Av. Felt. BD49 74
Lebanon Clo. Wat. BA21 26
Lebanon Ct. Twick. BJ47 74
Lebanon Dr. Cob. BF60 93
Lebanon Gdns. SW18 BS46 76
Lebanon Gdns. West. CJ62 106
Lebanon Pk. Twick. BJ47 74
Lebanon Rd. SW18 BS46 76
Lebanon Rd. Croy. CA54 87
Lebrun Sq. SE3 CH45 68
Lechmere Av. Chig. CM28 40
Lechmere Av. Wdf. Grn. CJ30 40
Lechmere Rd. NW2 BP36 55
Leckford Rd. SW18 BT47 76
Leckwith Av. Bexh. CQ43 69
Lecky St. SW7 BT42 66
Leconfield Av. SW13 BO45 65
Leconfield Rd. N5 BZ35 48
Lectern Ct. St. Alb. BH15 9
Creighton Av.
Leda Av. Enf. CC22 30
Ledbury Ms. N. W11 BS40 56
Ledbury Ms. W. W11 BS40 56
Ledbury Pl. Croy. BZ56 96
Ledbury Rd. W11 BR39 55
Ledbury Rd. Croy. BZ56 96
Ledbury Rd. Reig. BS70 121
Ledbury St. SE15 CB43 67
Ledger Clo. Guil. AT69 118
Ledger Dri. Wey. AV56 91
Ledger La. Maid. AH44 61
Ledger's Rd. Slou. AO41 61
Ledgers Rd. Warl. CE62 105
Ledrington Rd. SE19 CA50 77
Ledway Dr. Wem. BL33 46
Lee Av. Rom. CQ32 50
Lee Bri. SE13 CF45 67
Leechcroft Av. Sid. CN46 78
Leechcroft Av. Swan. CT52 89
Leech La. Lthd. BM66 112
Lee Church St. SE13 CG45 68
Lee Clo. E17 CC30 39
Lee Conservancy Rd. E9 CD35 48
Leecroft Rd. Barn. BR24 28
Leecroft Rd. Wall. BV55 86
Leeds Pl. N4 BX33 47
Leeds Rd. Ilf. CM33 49
Leeds Rd. Slou. AP40 52
Leeds St. N18 CB28 39
Lee Farm Clo. Chesh. AQ18 16
Lee Gdns. Av. Horn. CX33 51
Leegate Ho. SE12 CG46 78
Lee Grn. SE12 CG45 68
Lee Grn. Orp. CO53 89
Lee Green La. Epsom. BM65 103
Lee Gro. Chig. CL27 40
Leeke St. WC1 BX38 56
Leeland Rd. W13 BJ40 54
Broadway
Leeland Ter. W13 BJ40 54
Leeland Way, NW10 BO35 46
Lee La. St. Alb. BH15 9
Leeming Rd. Borwd. BL22 28
Lee Pk. SE3 CG45 68
Lee Park Way, N18 CC28 39
Lee Rd. NW7 BQ29 37
Lee Rd. SE3 CG45 68
Lee Rd. SW19 BS51 86
Lee Rd. Enf. CB25 30
Lee Rd. Grnf. BK37 54
Leeside Barn. BR25 28
Leeside Cres. NW11 BR32 46
Leeson Rd. SE24 BY45 66
Mayall Rd.
Leesons Hill Chis. CN52 88
Leesons Way Orp. CN51 88
Lees Pl. W1 BV40 56
Lees Rd. Uxb. AZ38 53
Lees, The, Croy. CD55 87
Lee St. E8 CA37 57
Lee St. N11 BV28 38
Lee Ter. SE3 CG45 68
Lee Vw. Enf. BY23 29
Leeward Gdns. SW19 BR49 75
Leeway, SE8 CD42 67
Leewood Pl. Swan. CS52 89
Leewood Way. Lthd. BD67 111
Lefevre Wk. E3 CD37 57
Lefroy Rd. W12 BO41 65
Legard Rd. N5 BY34 47
Legatt Rd. SE9 CJ46 78
Leggatt Rd. E15 CF37 57
Leggatts Clo. Wat. BB21 26
Leggatts Rise, Wat. BC21 26
Leggatts Way, Wat. BB21 26
Leggatts Wood Av. Wat. BC21 26
Legge St. SE13 CF46 77
Leggfield Ter. Hem. H. AV13 7
Leghorn Rd. NW10 BO37 55
Leghorn Rd. SE18 CM42 68
Legion Clo. N1 BY36 56
Legion Ct. Mord. BS53 86
Legion Av. Rom. CS33 50
Legrace Av. Houns. BD44 64
Leicester Av. Mitch. BX52 86
Leicester Clo. Wor. Pk. BQ56 94
Leicester Ct. WC2 BW40 56
Cranbourn St.
Leicester Gdns. Ilf. CN33 49
Leicester Pl. WC2 BW40 56
Lisle St.
Leicester Rd. E11 CH32 49
Leicester Rd. N2 BU31 47
Leicester Rd. Barn. BS25 29
Leicester Rd. Croy. CA54 87
Leicester Rd. Til. DF44 71
Leicester Sq. WC2 BW40 56
Leicester St. WC2 BW40 56
Lisle St.
Leigham Av. SW16 BX48 76
Leigham Ct. Rd. SW16 BX48 76
Leigham Dr. Islw. BH43 64
Leigh Av. Ilf. BZ31 48
Leigh Clo. N. Mal. BN52 85
Leigh Clo. Wey. AV57 91
Leigh Common. Welw. G. C. BR9 5
Leigh Ct. Har. BH33 45
Leigh Cres. Croy. CE57 96
Leigh Dr. Rom. CV28 42
Leigh Gdns. NW10 BQ37 55
Leigh Hill Rd. Cob. BD60 93
Leigh Hunt St. SE1 BZ41 67
Leigh Orchard Clo. SW16 BX48 76
Ivyday Gro.
Leigh Pk. Slou. AQ43 62
Leigh Pl. Cob. BD61 102
Leigh Pl. Well. CO44 69
Leigh Place La. Gdse. CC69 114
Leigh Place Rd. Reig. BP73 120
Leigh Rd. E6 CL36 58
Leigh Rd. E10 CF33 48
Leigh Rd. N5 BY35 47
Leigh Rd. Cob. BC60 92
Leigh Rd. Grav. DG48 81
Leigh Rd. Houns. BG45 64
Leigh Rodd Wat. BF27 36
Leigh St. WC1 BX38 56
Leigh Ter. Orp. CO52 89
Leighton Av. E12 CL35 49
Leighton Av. Pnr. BE31 45
Leighton Buzzard Rd. Hem. H. AW10 8
Leighton Clo. Edg. BM30 37
Leighton Cres. NW5 BW35 47
Leighton Gro.
Leighton Gdns. NW10 BP37 55
Leighton Gdns. Sth. Croy. CB60 96
Leighton Gdns. Til. DG43 71
Leighton Gro. NW5 BW35 47
Leighton Ho. W14 BR41 65
Leighton Pl. NW5 BW35 47
Leighton Rd.
Leighton Rd. NW5 BW35 47
Leighton Rd. W13 BJ41 64
Leighton Rd. Enf. CA25 30
Leighton Rd. Har. BG30 36
Leighton St. E. Croy. BY54 86
Leighton St. W. Croy. BY54 86
Leighton Way Epsom BN60 94
Leinster Av. SW14 BN45 65
Leinster Gdns. W2 BT39 56
Leinster Ms. W2 BT40 56
Leinster Pl. W2 BT39 56
Leinster Rd. N10 BV31 47
Leinster Rd. NW6 BS38 56
Leinster Sq. W2 BS40 56
Leinster Ter. W2 BT40 56
Leith Clo. NW9 BN33 46
Leithcote Gdns. SW16 BX49 76
Leithcote Path SW16 BX48 76
Ivyday Gro.
Leith Hill Orp. CN51 88
Leith Hill Gn. Orp. CO51 89
Leith Hill
Leith Park Rd. Grav. DG47 81
Leith Rd. E3 CD39 57
Leith Rd. N22 BY30 38
Leith Rd. Epsom BO59 94
Leithsail Rd. Har. BF34 45
Lela Av. Houns. BD44 64
Leman St. E1 CA39 57
Leman St. E1 CB39 57
Good St.
Lemark Clo. Stan. BK28 36
Haig Rd.
Le May Av. SE12 CH48 78
Lemna Rd. E11 CG33 49
Lemonfield Dr. Wat. BE19 18
Lemonwell Ct. SE9 CM46 78
Lemsford Clo. N15 CB32 48
Lemsford Ct. Borwd. BN24 28
Lemsford Rd. Hat. BP11 10
Lemsford Rd. St. Alb. BH13 9
Lemsfor La. Welw. G. C. BP8 5
Lena Gdns. W6 BQ41 65
Lendal Ter. SW4 BX45 66
Lenelby Rd. Surb. BM54 85
Lenham Rd. SE12 CG45 68
Lenham Rd. Bexh. CQ43 69
Lenham Rd. Sutt. BS56 95
Lenham Rd. Th. Hth. BZ51 87
Lenmore Ave. Grays. DE41 71
Lennard Av. W. Wick. CG55 88
Lennard Clo. W. Wick. CG55 88
Lennard Rd. SE20 CC50 77
Lennard Rd. Croy. BZ54 87
Lennard Rd. Sev. CT63 107
Lennard Row. S. Ock. CW40 60
Lennox Av. E17 CE32 48
Lennox Av. Grav. DF47 81
Lennox Clo. Rom. CT32 50
Lennox Gdns. NW10 BO35 46
Lennox Gdns. SW1 BU41 66
Lennox Gdns. Croy. BY56 95
Lennox Gdns. Ilf. CK33 49
Lennox Gdns. Ms. SW1 BU41 66
Lennox Rd. E17 CD32 48
Lennox Rd. N4 BX34 47
Lennox Rd. Grav. DF46 81
Lennox Rd. E. Grav. DG47 81
Lensbury Clo. Wal. Cr. CD17 21
Lensbury Way SE2 CP41 69
Lens Rd. E7 CJ36 58
Lenthall Ave. Grays. DD41 71
Lenthall Pl. SW7 BT42 66
Gloucester Rd.
Lenthall Rd. E8 CA36 57
Lenthall Rd. Loug. CM24 31
Lenthorpe Rd. SE10 CG42 68
Lentmead Rd. Brom. CG48 78
Lenton Ri. Rich. BL45 65
Lenton St. SE18 CM42 68
Leof Cres. SE6 CE49 77
Leominster Rd. Mord. BT53 86
Leominster Wk. Mord. BT53 86
Leonard Ave. Sev. CU61 107
Leonard Av. Mord. BT53 86
Leonard Av. Rom. CS33 50
Leonard Av. Swans. DC47 81
Leonard Rd. E4 CE29 39
Leonard Rd. E7 CH35 49
Leonard Rd. N9 CA27 39
Leonard Rd. SW16 BW51 86
Leonard Rd. Sthl. BD41 64
Leonard St. E16 CK40 58
Leonard St. EC2 BZ38 57
Leonard Way, Brwd. CZ28 42
Leopold Av. SW19 BR49 75
Leopold Rd. E17 CE32 48
Leopold Rd. N2 BT31 47
Leopold Rd. N18 CB28 39
Albany Rd.
Leopold Rd. NW10 BO36 55
Leopold Rd. SW19 BR49 75
Leopold Rd. W5 BL40 55
Leopold St. E3 CD39 57
Leopold Wk. SE11 BX42 66
Leo St. SE15 CB43 67
Lepale Rd. Guil. AR71 118
Lepe Clo. Brom. CG49 78
Le Personne Rd. Cat. BZ64 105
Leppoc Rd. SW4 BW46 76
Leroy St. SE1 CA42 67
Lesbourne Rd. Reig. BS71 121
Lescombe Clo. SE23 CD48 77
Lescombe Rd. SE23 CD48 77
Lesley Clo. Bex. CR47 79
Lesley Clo. Grav. DF50 81
Lesley Clo. Swan. CS52 89
Leslie Gdns. Sutt. BS57 95
Leslie Gro. Croy. BZ54 87
Leslie Pk. Rd. Croy. CA54 87
Leslie Pl. Croy. CA54 87
Leslie Rd. E11 CF35 48
Leslie Rd. E16 CH39 58
Leslie Rd. N2 BT31 47
Leslie Rd. Dor. BK70 119
Leslie Rd. Wok. AP58 91
Lesness Rd. Belv. CR43 69
Lesney Fm. Est. Erith CT43 69
Lesney Pk. Erith CS43 69
Lesney Pk. Rd. Erith CS43 69
Lessada St. E3 CC37 57
Lessar Av. SW4 BV46 76
Lessingham Av. Ilf. CL31 49
Lessingham Rd. SW17 BU49 76
Lessing St. SE23 CD47 77
Lessington Av. Rom. CS32 50
Lessness Av. Bexh. CP43 69
Lessness Pk. Belv. CQ42 69
Lessness Rd. Belv. CR43 69
Stapley Rd.
Lessness Rd. Mord. BT53 86
Lester Av. E15 CG38 58
Leston Spur, Slou. AP39 52
Leswin Pl. N16 CA34 48
Leswin Rd.
Leswin Rd. N16 CA34 48
Letchfield Chesh. AQ19 16
Letchford Cotts. Har. BF30 36
Letchford Gdns. NW10 BP38 55
Letchford Mews NW10 BP38 55
Letchford Gdns.
Letchmore Heath Rd. Wat. BG22 27
Letchmore Hth. Rd. Wat. BG23 27
Letchmore Rd. Rad. BJ21 27
Letchmore Way Clo. Rad. BJ21 27
Letchworth Av. Felt. BB47 73
Letchworth Clo. Brom. CH53 88
Letchworth Clo. Wat. BD28 36
Letchworth Dr. Brom. CH53 88
Letchworth St. SW17 BU49 76
Lethbridge Clo. SE13 CF44 67
Letter Box La. Sev. CV68 117
Letterstone Rd. SW6 BR43 65
Varna Rd.
Lettice St. SW6 BR44 65
Lettsom St. SE5 CA44 67
Levana Ct. SW19 BR47 75
Victoria Dr.
Levcha Rd. E17 BX32 47
Levehurst Way SW4 BX44 66
Leven Clo. Wal. Cr. CC20 21
Leven Clo. Wat. BD28 36
Levendale Rd. SE23 CD48 77
Leven Dr. Wal. Cr. CC20 21
Leven Rd. E14 CF39 57
Leven Way, Hayes BB39 53
Leveret Clo. Croy. CF58 96
Leveret Clo. Croy. CF59 96
Leveret Pla. SW3 BU42 66
Denyer St.
Leverett St. SW1 BU42 66
Denyer St.
Leverholme Gdns. SE9 CL49 78
Leverson St. SW16 BW50 76
Lever Sq. Grays. DF42 71
Leverst Clo. Wat. BC20 17
Leverstock Grn. Hem. H. AZ13 8
Leverstock Green Rd. Hem. H. AZ13 8
Leverstock Green Way, Hem. H. BA13 8
Lever St. EC1 BY38 56
Leverton St. NW5 BW35 47
Leveson Rd. Grays. DG41 71
Levett Gdns. Ilf. CN35 49

Levett Rd. Bark. CN36 58
Levett Rd. Lthd. BJ63 102
Levine Gdns. Bark. CP37 59
Levylsdene, Guil. AU70 118
Lewes Clo. Nthlt. BF36 54
Lewes Rd. N12 BU28 38
Lewes Rd. Brom. CJ51 88
Lewes Rd. Rom. CV28 42
Leweston Pl. N16 CA33 48
Lewes Way, Rick. BA24 26
Lewgars Av. NW9 BN32 46
Lewin Rd. SW14 BN45 65
Lewin Rd. SW16 BW50 76
Lewin Rd. Bexh. CQ46 79
Lewins Rd. Epsom. BM60 94
Lewins, Rd. Ger. Cr. AR31 43
Lewis Av. E17 CE30 39
Lewis Clo. Brwd. DC26 122
Lewis Cres. NW10 BN35 46
Lewis Field. Guil. AO68 109
Lewis Gdns. N2 BT30 38
Lewis Gro. SE13 CF45 67
Lewisham High St. SE13 CE46 77
Lewisham Hill SE13 CF44 67
Lewisham Pk. SE13 CE46 77
Lewisham Rd. SE13 CE44 67
Lewisham St. SW1 BW41 66
Lewis La. Ger. Cr. AS30 34
Lewis Rd. Grav. DF51 81
Lewis Rd. Mitch. BT51 86
Lewis Rd. Rich. BK46 74
Red Lion St.
Lewis Rd. Sid. CP48 79
Lewis Rd. Sthl. BE41 64
Lewis Rd. Sutt. BS55 86
Lewis Rd. Swans. DC46 81
Lewis Rd. Well. CP45 69
Lewis St. NW1 BV36 56
Lewis Trust Bldgs. SW3 BU42 66
Lewville Way SE16 CB42 67
Bonamy Estate West The
Lexden Dr. Rom. CO32 50
Lexden Rd. W3 BM40 55
Lexden Rd. Mitch. BW52 86
Lexham Clo. Nthlt. BE36 54
Lexham Gdns. W8 BS42 66
Lexham Gdns. Amer. AO22 25
Lexham Gdns. Ms. W8 BS41 66
Lexham Ms. W8 BS42 66
Lexham Wk. W8 BS41 66
Lexington Clo. Borwd. BM24 28
Lexington Clo. Pur. BZ58 96
Lexington St. W1 BW39 56
Lexington Way Barn. BQ24 28
Lexington Way, Upmin. CZ32 51
Lexton Gdns. SW12 BW47 76
Leyborne Av. W13 BJ41 64
Leyborne Pk. Rich. BM44 65
Leybourne Av. Wey. AY60 92
Leybourne Clo. Brom. CH53 88
Leybourne Clo. Wey. AY60 92
Leybourne Rd. E11 CG33 49
Leybourne Rd. NW1 BV36 56
Leybourne Rd. NW9 BM32 46
Leybourne Rd. Uxb. BA37 53
Leybridge Ct. SE12 CH46 78
Leyburn Clo. E17 CE31 48
Leyburn Cres. Rom. CW29 42
Leyburn Gdns. Croy. CA55 87
Leyburn Gro. N18 CB29 39
Leyburn Rd. N18 CB29 39
Leyburn Rd. Rom. CV29 42
Leycroft Clo. Loug. CL25 31
Leycroft Gdns. Erith. CU44 69
Leyden St. E1 CA39 57
Leyes Rd. E16 CJ39 58
Leyfield Wor. Pk. BO54 85
Leyhill Clo. Swan. CT53 89
Ley Hill Rd. Hem. H. AR18 16
Leyland Av. St. Alb. BG14 9
Leyland Clo. Wal. Cr. CC17 21
Leyland Gdns. Wdf. Grn. CJ28 40
Leyland Rd. SE12 CG46 78
Leyland Rd. Enf. CD23 30
Leylands La. Slou. AV45 62
Leylang Rd. SE14 CC43 67
Leys Av. Dag. CS37 59
Leys Clo. Dag. CS36 59
Leys Clo. Har. BG32 45
Leys Clo. Uxb. AX30 35
Leysdown Av. Bexh. CS45 69
Leysdown Rd. SE9 CK48 78
Leysfield Rd. W12 BP41 65
Leys Gdns. Barn. BV25 29
Leyspring Rd. E11 CG33 49
Leys Rd. Hem. H. AY14 8
Leys Rd. Lthd. BG59 93
Leys Rd. E. Enf. CD23 30
Leys Rd. W. Enf. CD23 30
Leys, The, N2 BT31 47
Leys, The, Har. BL32 46
Ley St. Ilf. CL34 49
Leyswood Dr. Ilf. CN32 49
Leythe Rd. W3 BN41 65
Leyton Cross Rd. Dart. CT48 79
Leyton Gra. E10 CE34 48
Leyton Green Rd. E10 CF32 48
Leyton Park Rd. E10 CF34 48
Leyton Rd. E15 CF35 48
Leyton Rd. SW19 BT50 76
Leyton Sq. SE15 CB43 67
Leytonstone Rd. E15 CG36 58
Leyton Way E11 CG33 49
Leywood Clo. Amer. AP23 25
Lezayre Rd. Orp. CN57 97
Liardet Gro. SE14 CD43 67
Liardet St. SE14 CD43 67
Chubworthy St.
Liberia Rd. N5 BY36 56
Liberty Hall Rd. Wey. AW56 92
Liberty La. Wey. AW57 92
Liberty Pl. E1 CB40 57
Liberty St. SW9 BX44 66
Liberty, The, Rom. CT32 50
Libra Rd. E3 CD37 57
Wright's Rd.
Library St. SE1 BY41 66
Lichfield Gdns. Rich. BL46 75
Lichfield Gro. N3 BS30 38
Lichfield Rd. E3 CD38 57
Lichfield Rd. E6 CJ38 58
Lichfield Rd. N9 CB27 39
Winchester Rd.
Lichfield Rd. NW2 BR35 46
Lichfield Rd. Dag. CO35 50
Lichfield Rd. Houns. BD45 64
Lichfield Rd. Nthwd. BC31 44
Lichfield Rd. Rich. BL44 65
Lichfield Rd. Wdf. Grn. CG28 40
Lichfield Ter. Upmin. CZ34 51
Lichfield Way. Sth. Croy. CC58 96
Lichlade Clo. Orp. CN56 97
Lidbury Rd. NW7 BR29 37
Liddell Clo. Har. BK31 45
Liddell Gdns. NW10 BQ37 55
Lidding Rd. Har. BK32 45
Liddington Hall Dr. Guil. AP69 118
Liddington Hall New Rd. Guil. AP69 118
Liddington Rd. E15 CG37 58
Liddon Rd. E13 CH38 58
Liddon Rd. Brom. CJ52 88
Lidfield Rd. N16 BZ35 48
Lidiard Rd. SW18 BT48 76
Lidlington NW1 BW37 56
Lidyard Rd. N19 BW33 47
Liegh Sq. Wind. AL44 61
Liffler Rd. SE18 CM42 68
Liffords Pl. SW13 BO44 65
Barnes High St.
Lifford St. SW15 BQ45 65
Lightcliffe Rd. N13 BY28 38
Lightfoot Rd. N8 BX31 47
Ligonier St. E2 CA38 57
Lilac Av. Wok. AR63 100
Lilac Clo. E4 CD29 39
Lilac Clo. Guil. AR68 109
Lilac Clo. Wal. Cr. CB19 21
Greenwood Av.
Lilac Gdns. W5 BK41 64
Lilac Gdns. Croy. CE55 87
Lilac Gdns. Hayes BB39 53
Lilac Gdns. Rom. CT33 50
Lilac Gdns. Swan. CS52 89
Lilac Pl. SE11 BX42 66
Lilac Rd. Hodd. CE11 12
Lilacs Av. Enf. CC21 30
Lilac St. W12 BP40 55
Lila Pl. Swan. CT52 89
Lilburne Gdns. SE9 CK46 78
Lilburne Rd. SE9 CK46 78
Lile Cres. W7 BH39 54
Lilestone Est. NW8 BT38 56
Lilestone St. W1 BU38 56
Lilian Cres. Brwd. DE27 122
Lilian Gdns. Wdf. Grn. CH30 40
Lilian Rd. SW13 BP43 65
Lillechurch Rd. Dag. CO36 59
Lilleshall Rd. Mord. BT53 86
Lilley Clo. Brwd. CZ28 42
Lilley Dr. Tad. BS64 104
Lillian Av. W3 BM41 65
Lillian Rd. SW16 BW51 86
Lilliard Clo. Hodd. CE10 12
Lillie Br. Ms. SW6 BS43 66
Lillie Rd. SW6 BQ43 65
Lillie Rd. West. CJ62 106
Lillieshall Rd. SW4 BV45 66
Lillie Yd. SW6 BS43 66
Lillington Gdns. Est. SW1 BW42 66
Lilliput Cres. Nthlt. BE37 54
Lilliput Rd. Rom. CS33 50
Lily Gdns. Wem. BK37 54
Lily Rd. E17 CE32 48
Lilyville Rd. SW6 BR44 65
Lily Wk. Grnf. BK37 54
Limburg Rd. SW11 BU45 66
Lime Av. NW7 BO29 37
Lime Av. Brwd. DC27 122
Lime Av. Grav. DE47 81
Lime Av. Upmin. CX35 51
Lime Av. West Dr. AY40 53
Lime Clo. Buck. H. CJ27 40
Lime Clo. Cars. BU55 86
Lime Clo. Reig. BS72 121
Lime Clo. Rom. CS31 50
Lime Clo. S. Ock. DB38 60
Lime Clo. Wat. BD26 36
Lime Cres. Sun. BD51 84
Limecroft Clo. Epsom BN57 94
Limedene Clo. Pnr. BD30 36
Lime Gro. N20 BR26 37
Lime Gro. W12 BQ41 65
Lime Gro. Brwd. DB22 33
Lime Gro. Guil. AR68 109
Lime Gro. Hayes BA40 53
Lime Gro. Ilf. CN29 40
Lime Gro. N. Mal. BN52 85
Lime Gro. Orp. CL55 88
Lime Gro. Ruis. BC32 44
Lime Gro. Sid. CN46 78
Lime Gro. Twick. BH46 74
Lime Gro. Warl. CD62 105
Lime Gro. Wok. AS64 100
Lime Grove Road. Guil. AW67 110
Limehouse Causeway E14 CD40 57
Limehouse Fields Est. E14 CD39 57
Lime Meadow Av. Sth. Croy. CB60 96
Lime Pass. EC3 CA39 57
Lime St.
Lime Pit La. Sev. CS62 107
Limerick Clo. SW12 BW47 76
Limerick Gdns. Upmin. CZ33 51
Lime Rd. Epp. CN19 22
Lime Rd. Rich. BL45 65
St. Mary's Gro.
Lime Rd. Swan. CS52 89
Limerston St. SW10 BT43 66
Lime St. Pass. EC3 CA39 57
Lime St.
Limes Av. E11 CH31 49
Limes Av. N12 BT28 38
Limes Av. NW11 BR33 46
Limes Av. SE20 CB50 77
Limes Av. SW13 BO44 65
Limes Av. Cars. BU54 86
Limes Av. Chig. CM28 40
Limes Av. Croy. BX55 86
Limes Clo. Ashf. AZ49 73
Limesdale Gdns. Edg. BN30 37
Limesfield Rd. SW14 BO45 65
White Hart La.
Limesford Rd. SE15 CC45 67
Limes Gdns. SW18 BS46 76
Limes Gro. SE13 CF45 67
Limes Pl. Croy. BZ53 87
Limes Rd. Beck. CE51 87
Limes Rd. Croy. BZ53 87
Limes Rd. Egh. AS49 72
Limes Rd. Wal. Cr. CC19 21
Limes Rd. Wey. AZ56 92
Limes, The, Brom. CK55 88
Limes, The, Brwd. DC27 122
Limes, The, Welw. G. C. BS9 5
Limes, The, Av. N11 BW28 38
Limestone Wk. SE2 CP41 69
Yarnton Way
Limestone Wk. Belv. CP41 69
Yarnton Way
Lime St. E17 CD31 48
Lime St. EC3 CA40 57
Limes Wk. SE15 CC45 67
Limes Wk. W5 BM41 65
Chestnut Gro.
Limetree Av. SE20 CB51 87
Limetree Av. Surb. BG54 84
Lime Tree Clo. SW2 BX47 76
Lime Tree Gro. Croy. CD55 87
Lime Tree Pl. Mitch. BV51 86
Limetree Rd. Houns. BF44 64
Lime Tree Walk. Amer. AP23 25
Lime Tree Wk. Enf. BZ22 30
Lime Tree Wk. Sev. CU66 116
Lime Tree Wk. W. Wick. CG56 97
Lime Walk, Hem. H. AY14 8
Lime Wk. Uxb. AX35 44
Lime Way Ter. Dor. BJ70 119
Lime Wks Rd. Red. BW66 113
Limewood Clo. W13 BJ39 54
St. Stephens Rd.
Limewood Clo. Wok. AO63 100
Limewood Rd. Erith CS43 69
Limpsfield Av. SW19 BQ47 75
Limpsfield Av. Th. Hth. BX53 86
Limpsfield Rd. Sth. Croy. CB59 96
Limpsfield Rd. Warl. CC62 105
Linacre Ct. W6 BQ42 65
Colet Gdns.
Linacre Rd. NW2 BP36 55
Lince La. Dor. BG71 119
Linchfield Rd. Slou. AR44 62
Linchmere Rd. SE12 CG47 78
Lincoln Av. N14 BW27 38
Lincoln Av. SW19 BQ48 75
Lincoln Av. Rom. CS34 50
Lincoln Av. Twick. BG48 74
Lincoln Clo. SE25 CB53 87
Lincoln Clo. Erith CT44 69
Lincoln Clo. Grnf. BG37 54
Lincoln Clo. Har. BE32 45
Lincoln Clo. Horn. CX32 51
Lincoln Ct. Borwd. BN25 28
Lincoln Cres. Enf. CA25 30
Lincoln Dr. Rick. AZ24 26
Lincoln Dr. Wat. BD27 36
Lincoln Dr. Wok. AV61 100
Lincoln Est. E3 CE38 57
Lincolnes, The, NW7 BO27 37
Lincoln Gdns. Ilf. CK33 49
Lincoln Grn. Rd. Orp. CN53 88
Lincoln Ms. NW6 BR37 55
Willesden La.
Lincoln Park. Amer. AP23 25
Lincoln Rd. E7 CJ36 58
Lincoln Rd. E13 CH38 58
Lincoln Rd. E18 CH30 40
Lincoln Rd. N2 BU31 47
Lincoln Rd. N17 CB31 48
Lincoln Rd. SE25 CB52 87
Lincoln Rd. Dor. BK70 119
Lincoln Rd. Enf. CA24 30
Lincoln Rd. Erith CT44 69
Lincoln Rd. Felt. BE48 74
Lincoln Rd. Ger. Cr. AS30 34
Lincoln Rd. Guil. AP69 118
Lincoln Rd. Har. BE32 45
Lincoln Rd. Mitch. BX53 86
Lincoln Rd. N. Mal. BN52 85
Lincoln Rd. Nthwd. BB31 44
Lincoln Rd. Sid. CO49 79
Lincoln Rd. Wem. BK36 54
Lincoln Rd. Wor. Pk. BP54 85
Lincolns Field, Epp. CN18 22
Lincoln's Inn Fields WC2 BX39 56
Lincolns La. Brwd. CY25 33
Lincolns La. Brwd. CY26 42
Lincoln St. E11 CF34 48
Lincoln St. SW3 BU42 66
Lincoln Way Enf. CB25 30
Lincoln Way, Rick. AZ24 26
Lincoln Way, Sun. BB51 83
Lincombe Rd. Brom. CG48 78
Lindal Cres. Enf. BX24 29
Lindale Clo. Vir. W. AP52 82
Lindal Rd. SE4 CD46 77
Lindbergh Rd. Wall. BX57 95
Linden Av. NW10 BQ37 55
Linden Av. Couls. BV61 104
Linden Av. Dart. CV47 80
Linden Av. Enf. CB23 30
Linden Av. Houns. BF46 74
Linden Av. Ruis. BC33 44
Linden Av. Th. Hth. BY52 86
Linden Av. Wem. BL35 46
Linden Chase Rd. Sev. CU64 107
Linden Clo. N14 BW25 29
Linden Clo. Grays CY42 70
Linden Clo. Maid. AG43 61
Linden Clo. Orp. CO56 98
Linden Clo. Ruis. BC33 44
Linden Clo. Stan. BJ28 36
Linden Clo. Surb. BJ54 84
Linden Clo. Wey. AW59 92
Linden Ct. W12 BQ40 55
Linden Ct. Egh. AQ50 72
Linden Ct. Lthd. BJ64 102
Linden Rd.
Linden Cres. Grnf. BH36 54
Linden Cres. Kings-on-t. BL51 85
Linden Cres. St. Alb. BK13 9
Linden Cres. Wdf. Grn. CH29 40
Lindenfield Chis. CL51 88
Linden Gdns. W2 BS40 56
Linden Gdns. W4 BO42 65
Linden Gdns. W9 BS41 66
Linden Gdns. Enf. CB23 30
Linden Gdns. Lthd. BK64 102
Linden Gro. SE15 CB45 67
Linden Gro. SE26 CC50 77
Linden Gro. N. Mal. BO52 85
Linden Gro. Tedd. BH49 74
Linden Gro. Walt. BB55 83
Linden Gro. Warl. CD62 105
Linden Grove Est. SE15 CB45 67
Linden La. Wat. BC20 17
Linden Lawns Wem. BL35 46
Linden Lea N2 BT32 47
Linden Lea, Dor. BK72 119
Linden Lees W. Wick. CF55 87
Linden Ms. W2 BS40 56
Linden Gdns.
Linden Pit Path, Lthd. BJ64 102
Linden Rd. E17 CD32 48
Linden Rd. N10 BX31 47
Linden Rd. N11 BU27 38
Linden Rd. N15 BZ31 48
Linden Rd. Guil. AR70 118
Linden Rd. Hamptn. BF50 74
Linden Rd. Lthd. BJ64 102
Linden Sq. Sev. CT64 107
London Rd.
Lindens, The, N12 BT28 38
Lindens, The, W4 BN44 65
Hartington Rd.
Lindens, The Croy. CF57 96
Lindens, The Croy. CF57 96
Linden St. Rom. CS31 50
Lindent Ct. W12 BQ40 55
Linden Way N14 BW25 29
Linden Way Pur. BW58 95
Linden Way, Shep. BA53 83
Linden Way, Wok. AS64 100
Lindfield Gdns. Guil. AS70 118
Lindfield Rd. NW3 BT35 47
Lindfield Rd. W5 BK38 54
Lindfield Rd. Croy. CA53 87
Lindfield Rd. Rom. CW28 42
Lindisfarne SW20 BP50 75
Lindisfarne Rd. SW20 BP50 75
Lindisfarne Rd. Dag. CP34 50
Lindley Est. SE15 CB43 67
Lindley Rd. E10 CE34 48
Lindley Rd. Gdse. CC68 114
Lindley Rd. Walt. BE55 84
Lindley St. E1 CC39 57
Lindlings, Hem. H. AV14 7
Lindore Rd. SW11 BU45 66
Lindores Rd. Cars. BT54 86
Lindores Rd. Maid. AG43 61
Lindo St. SE15 CC44 67
Lind Rd. Sutt. BT56 95
Lindrop St. SW6 BT44 66
Lindsay Clo. Epsom BN60 94
Lindsay Clo. Hem. H. AZ15 8
Lindsay Clo. Stai. AX46 73
Lindsay Dr. Har. BL32 46
Lindsay Dr. Shep. BA53 83
Lindsay Rd. Hamptn. BF49 74
Lindsay Rd. Wey. AW58 92
Lindsay Rd. Wor. Pk. BP55 85
Lindsell Rd. Bark. CM37 58
Lindsell St. SE10 CF44 67
Lindsey Clo. Brwd. DA28 42
Lindsey Clo. Mitch. BX52 86
Lindsey Rd. Dag. CO35 50
Lindsey St. EC1 BY39 56
Lindsey St. Epp. CN17 22
Lindsey Way. Horn. CV32 51
Lind St. SE8 CE44 67
Lindum Pl. St. Alb. BF14 9
Lindum Rd. Tedd. BK50 74
Lindway SE27 BY49 76
Linfield Clo. Walt. BC56 92
Linfields Amer. AR23 25
Linford Clo. Harl. CM12 13
Linford End. Harl. CM12 13
Linford Rd. E17 CF31 48
Linford Rd. Grays. DG42 71
Linford St. SW8 BW44 66
Lingards Rd. SE13 CF45 67
Lingfield Ave. Dart. CX47 80
Lingfield Av. Kings. On T. BL52 85
Lingfield Av. Upmin. CW34 51
Lingfield Clo. Enf. CA25 30
Lingfield Clo. Nthwd. BB29 35
Lingfield Cres. SE9 CM45 68
Lingfield Gdns. N9 CB26 39
Lingfield Gdns. Couls. BY63 104
Lingfield Rd. SW19 BQ49 75
Lingfield Rd. Grav. DG48 81
Lingfield Rd. Wor. Pk. BQ55 85
Lingham St. SW9 BX44 66
Lingholm Way Barn. BQ24 28
Lingmere Clo. Chig. CM27 40
Ling Rd. E16 CH39 58
Ling Rd. Erith CS43 69
Lingrove Gdns. Wdf. Grn. CH27 40
Beech La.
Ling's Coppice SE21 BZ48 77
Lingwell Rd. SW17 BU48 76
Lingwood Gdns. Islw. BH43 64
Lingwood Rd. E5 CB33 48
Linhope St. NW1 BU38 56
Link Av. Wok. AU61 100
Link Dr. Hat. BP12 10
Linkfield Brom. CH53 88
Linkfield E. Mol. BF52 84
Link Field. Welw. G. C. BR10 5
Linkfield Clo. Red. BU70 121
Linkfield Gdns. Red. BU70 121
Hatchlands Rd.
Linkfield La. Red. BU70 121
Linkfield Rd. Islw. BH44 64
Linkfield St. Red. BU70 121
Link La. Wall. BW57 95
Linklea Clo. NW9 BO29 37
Link Rd. N11 BV28 38
Link Rd. Slou. AR44 62
Link Rd. Wall. BV54 86
Link Rd. Wat. BD23 27
Link Rd. Wey. AY56 92
Links Av. Mord. BS52 86
Links Av. Rom. CU30 41
Links Clo. Ash. BK62 102
Linkscroft Av. Ashf. AZ50 73
Links Dr. N20 BS26 38
Links Dr. Borwd. BL24 28
Links Dr. Rad. BH20 18
Links Gdns. SW16 BY50 76
Links Green Way. Cob. BE60 93
Linkside N12 BR29 37
Linkside Chig. CM28 40
Linkside N. Mal. BO51 85
Linkside Clo. Enf. BX24 29
Linkside Gdns. Enf. BX24 29
Links Rd. NW2 BO34 46
Links Rd. SW17 BU50 76
Links Rd. W3 BM39 55
Links Rd. Ash. BK62 102
Links Rd. Ashf. AY49 73
Links Rd. Epsom BP60 94
Links Rd. Wdf. Grn. CH28 40
Links Rd. W. Wick. CF54 87
Links Side. Enf. BX24 29
Links, The, E17 CD31 48
Links, The, Walt. BC55 83
Link St. E9 CC35 48
Links View N2 BU31 47
Gt. North Rd.
Links Vw. N3 BR29 37
Links Vw. Dart. CU47 79
Links Vw. St. Alb. BF12 9
Links View Av. Bet. BM70 120
Links Vw. Clo. Stan. BJ29 36
Links Vw. Rd. Croy. CE55 87
Links View Rd. Hamptn. BG49 74
Links Way NW4 BQ30 37
Links Way Beck. CE53 87
Links Way. Lthd. BE67 111
Links Way. Nthwd. BA29 35
Links Way, Rick. BA24 26
Linksway. Sutt. BT58 95
Link, The, W3 BM40 55
Saxon Dr.
Link, The, Enf. CD23 30
Link, The, Pnr. BD33 45
Link, The, Wem. BK33 45
Nathans Rd.
Linkway N4 BZ33 48
Vale Rd.
Linkway SW20 BP52 85
Link Way Brom. CK53 88
Link Way Dag. CP34 50
Link Way, Felt. BB47 73
Link Way, Guil. AP70 118
Linkway, Harl. CM10 6
Link Way. Harl. CM11 13
Linkway Horn. CW33 51
Linkway Pnr. BD30 36
Linkway Rich. BJ48 74
Link Way, Stai. AW50 73
Link Way, Uxb. AW32 44
Link Way, Wok. AU62 100
Linkway, Rd. Brwd. CZ27 42
Linkway, The, Barn. BS25 29
Linley Cres. Rom. CS31 50
Linley Rd. N17 CA30 39
Linnell Clo. NW11 BS32 47
Linnell Dr. NW11 BS32 47
Linnell Rd. N18 CB28 39
Fairfield Rd.
Linnell Rd. Red. BV71 121
Linnel Rd. SE5 CA44 67
Linnet Clo. Bush. BG26 36
Linnet Wk. Hat. BP13 10
Lark Rise
Linnington Ave. Chesh. AQ18 16
Linom Rd. SW4 BX45 66
Linscott Rd. E5 CC35 48
Linsey St. SE16 CB42 67
Linslade Rd. Orp. CO57 98
Linstead Ct. SE9 CN46 78
Linstead Rd. NW6 BS36 56
Linstead Way SW18 BR47 75
Linster Gro. Borwd. BN25 28
Lintaine Clo. W6 BR43 65
Moylan Rd.
Linthorpe Av. Wem. BK36 54

Linthorpe Rd. N16 CA33 48
Linthorpe Rd. Barn. BU24 29
Linton Av. Borwd. BL23 28
Linton Clo. Well. CO44 69
Anthony Rd.
Linton Ct. Rom. CT30 41
Rise Pk. Par.
Linton Ct. Stai. AX46 73
High St.
Linton Gro. SE27 BZ49 77
Linton Rd. Bark. CM36 58
Lintons La. Epsom BO59 94
Linton St. N1 BZ37 57
Linver Rd. SW6 BS44 66
Linwood, Saw. CQ6 6
Linwood Way SE15 CA43 67
Linx Walk. Leath. BB67 110
Linzee Rd. N8 BX31 47
Lion Av. Twick. BH47 74
Lionel Gdns. SE9 CJ46 78
Lionel Ms. W10 BR39 55
Telford Rd.
Lionel Oxley Ho. Grays DD43 71
New Rd.
Lionel Rd. SE9 CJ46 78
Lionel Rd. Brent. BL41 65
Lion Gate Gdns. Rich. BL45 65
Lion Grn. Rd. Couls. BW61 104
Lion La. Red. BU70 121
Lion Rd. N9 CB27 39
Lion Rd. Bexh. CQ45 69
Lion Rd. Croy. BZ53 87
Lion Rd. Twick. BH47 74
Lion Way Brent. BK43 64
Lion Wf. Islw. BJ45 64
Liphook Clo. Horn. CT35 50
Petworth Way
Liphook Cres. SE23 CC47 77
Liphook Rd. Wat. BD28 36
Lippitts Hill Loug. CG23 31
Lipsham Clo. Bans. BT60 95
Lisbon Av. Twick. BG48 74
Lisburne Rd. NW3 BU35 47
Lisford St. SE15 CA44 67
Lisgar Ter. W14 BR42 65
Liskeard Clo. Chis. CM50 78
Liskeard Gdns. SE3 CH44 68
Lisle Pl. Grays. DD41 71
Lisle St. WC2 BW40 56
Lismore, Hem. H. BA14 8
Lismore Clo. Islw. BJ44 64
Lismore Rd. N17 BZ31 48
Lismore Rd. Sth. Croy. CA57 96
Lismore Wk. N1 BZ36 57
Marquess Est.
Lissenden Gdns. NW5 BV35 47
Lissoms Rd. Couls. BV62 104
Lisson Green Est. NW8 BT39 56
Lisson Gro. NW1 BT38 56
Lisson St. NW1 BU39 56
Liss Way SE15 CA43 67
Hordle Prom. S.
Lister Ct. N16 CA34 48
Lister Gdns. N18 BZ28 39
Lister Ms. N7 BX35 47
Holloway Rd.
Lister Rd. E11 CG33 49
Lister Rd. Til. DG45 71
Liston Rd. N17 CB30 39
Liston Rd. SW4 BW45 66
Liston Way Wdf. Grn. CJ29 40
Listowell St. SW9 BY43 66
Listowel Rd. Dag. CR34 50
Listria Pk. N16 CA34 48
Litcham Spur, Slou. AO39 52
Litchfield Av. E15 CG36 58
Litchfield Av. Mord. BR54 85
Litchfield Gdns. NW10 BP36 55
Litchfield Rd. Sutt. BT56 95
Litchfield St. WC2 BW40 56
Litchfield Way NW11 BS32 47
Litchfield Way, Brox. CD14 12
Litchfield Way, Guil. AP71 118
Litford Rd. SE5 BY44 66
Lithos Rd. NW3 BS36 56
Litlington St. SE16 CB42 67
Little Acre Beck. CE52 87
Lit. Albany St. NW1 BV38 56
Lit. Argyll St. W1 BW39 56
Argyll St.
Lit. Aston Rd. Rom. CW30 42
Little Benty. West Dr. AX42 63
Little Birch Clo. Wey. AX58 92
Lit. Birches Sid. CN48 78
Little Boltons, The, SW10 BS42 66
Little Bookham St. Lthd. BE66 111
Lit. Borough, Bet. BM71 120
Lit. Bournes SE21 CA49 77
Little Brays. Harl. CO11 14
Little Britain EC1 BY39 56
Littlebrook Gdns. Wal. Cr. CC18 21
Littlebrook Manor Way Dart. CX46 80
Little Brownings SE23 CB48 77
Little Buntings. Wind. AM45 61
Little Burrow. Welw. G. C. BQ9 5
Littlebury Rd. SW4 BW45 66
Little Bury St. N9 BZ26 39
Lit. Bushey La. Bush. BF23 27
Little Chester St. SW1 BV41 66
Wilton Ms.
Little College La. EC4 BZ40 57
College St.
Little College St. SW1 BX41 66
Littlecombe SE7 CH43 68
Lit. Comm. La. Red. BY69 121
Littlecote Clo. SW19 BR47 75
Beaumont Rd.
Littlecote Pl. Pnr. BE30 36
Little Ct. W. Wick. CG55 88
Little Court Rd. Sev. CU65 107
Little Cranmore Lane. Leath. AZ67 110
Little Croft SE9 CL45 68
Littlecroft, Grav. DF50 81
Littlecroft Rd. Egh. AS49 72
Littledale SE2 CO43 69
Little Dell. Welw. G. C. BQ7 7
Little Dimocks SW12 BV48 76
Little Dorrit Ct. SE1 BZ41 67
Lit. Ealing La. W5 BK42 64
Lit. Edward St. NW1 BV37 56
Little Elms. Hayes. BA43 63
Little Ferry Rd. Twick. BJ47 74
Ferry Rd.
Littlefield Ct. West Dr. AX43 63
Littlefield Rd. Edg. BN29 37
Little Friday Hill E4 CG27 40
Lit. Friday Rd. E4 CG27 40
Little Ganett. Welw. G. C. BS9 5
Little Gaynes Gdns, Upmin. CX35 51
Little Gaynes La. Upmin. CX35 51
Little Gearies Ilf. CL31 49
Little George St. SW1 BX41 66
Gt. George St.
Lit. Gerpins La. Upmin. CW37 60
Lit. Graylings, Wat. BB20 17
Little Grn. Rick. AZ24 26
Little Green La. Cher. AV55 82
Lit. Green La. Rick. AZ24 26
Lit. Green St. NW5 BV35 47
Collage La.
Lit. Gregories La. Epp. CM21 31
Little Gro. Barn. BU25 29
Lit. Grove Bush. BF24 27
Littlegrove Field. Harl. CM11 13
Little Heath SE7 CK43 68
Little Heath Rom. CO31 50
Littleheath La. Cob. BF60 93
Little Heath Rd. Berk. AT13 7
Little Heath Rd. Bexh. CQ44 69
Littleheath Rd. Sth. Croy. CB58 96
Little Heath Rd. Wok. AP58 91
Lit. Hide, Guil. AT69 118
Little Hill. Rick. AU25 25
Little Holt E11 CH32 49
Lit. How Croft Wat. BA19 17
Abbots Rd.
Little Ilford La. E12 CK35 49
Little John Rd. W7 BH39 54
Littlejohn Rd. Orp. CO53 89
Little Julian Hill. Sev. CU67 116
Lit. Lake. Welw. G. C. BS9 5
Little Laver Road. Ong. CW11 15
Little Ley. Welw. G. C. BR9 5
Little Marlborough St. W1 BW39 56
Gt. Marlborough St.
Lit. Martins Bush. BF25 27
Littlemead Esher BG56 93
Littlemede SE9 CK48 78
Littlemore Rd. SE2 CO41 69
Littlemore Rd. Ilf. CM34 49
Lit. Moss La. Pnr. BE30 36
Little Mount. Hat. BP11 10
Little Newport St. WC2 BW40 56
Charing Cross Rd.
Little New St. EC4 BY39 56
Little Orchard. Wey. AV59 91
Lit. Orchard Clo. Pnr. BE30 36
Little Orchard Rd. Wok. AT60 91
Lit. Oxhey La. Wat. BE28 36
Little Pk. Dr. Felt. BD48 74
Little Pk. Gdns. Enf. BZ24 30
Lit. Pastures Brwd. CZ28 42
River Rd.
Lit. Pipers Clo. Wal. Cr. BZ18 21
Lit. Platt, Guil. AO70 118
Lit. Plucketts Way Buck. H. CJ26 40
Roebuck La.
Lit. Portland St. W1 BW39 56
Lit. Port Spur, Slou. AP39 52
Little Potters Bush. BG26 36
Little Pynchons. Harl. CN12 13
Lit. Queen's Rd. Tedd. BH50 74
Lit. Queen St. Dart. CW47 80
Lit. Queen St. Tedd. BH50 74
Little Redlands Brom. CK51 88
Little Reeves Ave. Amer. AP23 25
Little Rivers. Welw. G. C. BS7 5
Little Rd. Hayes. BB41 63
Little Rd. Hem. H. AY13 8
Lit. Roke Av. Ken. BY60 95
Lit. Roke Rd. Ken. BZ60 96
Littler's Clo. SW19 BT51 86
Lit. Russell St. WC1 BX39 56
Little St. James's St. SW1 BW40 56
Little St. Leonard's SW14 BO45 65
Little Sanctuary SW1 BX41 66
Broad Sanctuary
Little Somerset St. E1 CA39 57
Littlestone Clo. Beck. CE50 77
Abbey La.
Little Strand NW9 BO30 37
Little St. Guil. AQ68 109
Little Thistle. Welw. G. C. BT9 5
Lit. Thrift Orp. CM52 88
Lit. Tichfield St. W1 BW39 56
Gt. Tichfield St.
Littleton Av. E4 CG26 40
Valance Av.
Littleton Cres. Har. BH34 45
Littleton Gdns. Ashf. BA50 73
Littleton La. Guil. AQ73 118
Littleton La. Reig. BQ71 120
Littleton La. Shep. AX54 83
Littleton Rd. Har. BH34 45
Littleton St. SW18 BT48 76
Lit. Trinity La. EC4 BZ40 57
Queen Victoria St.
Lit. Turnstile WC1 BX39 56
High Holborn
Little Wade. Welw. G. C. BR9 5
Little Walk. Harl. CM11 13
Little Warley Hall La. Brwd. DC30 123
Lit. Warren Clo. Guil. AT71 118
Littlewick Rd. Wok. AP61 100
Littlewick Rd. Wok. AR60 91
Little Windmill Hill. Kings L. AV19 16
Lit. Woodcote La. Cars. BV59 95
Littlewood Rd. SE13 CF46 77
Littlewood Rd. Sev. CV64 108
Littleworth Av. Esher BG56 93
Littleworth Common Rd. Esher BG55 84
Littleworth La. Esher BG56 93
Littleworth Rd. Esher BG56 93
Lit. Youngs. Welw. G. C. BQ8 5
Liverpool Gro. SE17 BZ42 67
Liverpool Rd. E10 CF32 48
Liverpool Rd. E16 CG38 58
Liverpool Rd. W5 BK41 64
Liverpool Rd. Kings. On T. BM50 75
Liverpool Rd. St. Alb. BH13 9
Liverpool Rd. Th. Hth. BZ52 87
Liverpool Rd. Wat. BC25 26
Liverpool St. EC2 CA39 57
Livesey Pl. SE15 CB43 67
Peckham Park Rd.
Livingstone Ct. E10 CF32 48
Livingstone Gdns. Grav. DH49 81
Livingstone Rd. E15 CF37 57
Livingstone Rd. E17 CE32 48
Livingstone Rd. N13 BX29 38
Livingstone Rd. SW11 BT45 66
Winstanley Rd.
Livingstone Rd. Cat. BZ64 105
Livingstone Rd. Grav. DH49 81
Livingstone Rd. Houns. BG45 64
Livingstone Rd. Sthl. BD40 54
Livingstone Rd. Th. Hth. BZ51 87
Livingstone St. E6 CL40 58
Livingstone Ter. Rain. CT37 59
Livingstone Wk. SW11 BT45 66
Plough Rd.
Livingstone Walk, Hem. H. AY11 8
Livonia St. W1 BW39 56
Berwick St.
Lizard St. EC1 BZ38 57
Lizban St. SE3 CH43 68
Llanavor Rd. NW2 BR34 46
Llanbury Clo. Ger. Cr. AS29 34
Llanelly La. NW2 BR34 46
Llanelly Rd. NW2 BR34 46
Crewys Rd.
Llanover Rd. SE18 CL43 68
Llanover Rd. Wem. BK34 45
Llanthony Rd. Mord. BT53 86
Llewellyn St. SE16 CB41 67
Chambers St.
Lloyd Av. SW16 BX51 86
Lloyd Av. Couls. BV60 95
Lloyd Baker St. WC1 BX38 56
Lloyd Ct. Pnr. BD32 45
Lloyd Pk. Av. Croy. CA56 96
Lloyd Rd. E6 CK37 58
Lloyd Rd. E17 CC31 48
Lloyd Rd. Dag. CQ36 59
Lloyd Rd. Wor. Pk. BQ55 85
Lloyd's Av. EC3 CA39 57
Lloyds Pl. SE3 CG44 68
Lloyd Sq. WC1 BY38 56
Lloyds Row EC1 BY38 56
Lloyd St. WC1 BY38 56
Lloyds Way Beck. CD53 87
Loampit Hill SE13 CE44 67
Loampit Vale SE13 CE45 67
Loates La. Wat. BD24 27
Lobbell La. St. Alb. BL17 19
Local Board Rd. Wat. BD25 27
Locarno Rd. W3 BO41 65
High St.
Locarno Rd. Grnf. BG38 54
Lochaline St. W6 BQ43 65
Lochinvar St. SW12 BV47 76
Lochmere Clo. Erith. CR43 69
Lochnager St. E14 CF39 57
Lochnell Rd. Berk. AP12 7
Lockaber Rd. SE13 CG45 68
Lock Chase SE3 CG45 68
Locke Clo. Rain. CT36 59
Locke King Clo. Wey. AZ57 92
Locke King Rd. Wey. AZ57 92
Lockers Park La. Hem. H. AW13 8
Lockesley Dr. Orp. CN53 88
Lockesley Sq. Surb. BK53 84
Locket Rd. Har. BH30 36
Lockets Clo. Wind. AL44 61
Lockfield Av. Enf. CD23 30
Lock Grn. Slou. AR41 62
Lockhart Rd. Cob. BD60 93
Lockhart St. E3 CD38 57
Lockhurst Rd. E5 CC35 48
Lock La. Wok. AW61 101
Lockley Cres. Hat. BP11 10
Lockmead Rd. N15 CB32 48
Lockmead Rd. SE13 CF45 67
Lockner Rd. N1 CA36 57
Lock Pth. Wind. AL43 61
Lock Rd. Guil. AR69 118
Lock Rd. Rich. BK49 74
Lock's La. Mitch. BU51 86
Locksley Est. E14 CD39 57
Locksley St. E14 CD39 57
Lock St. W10 BQ40 55
Lockwood Path. Wok. AV60 91
Lockwood Rd. Ilf. CM34 49
Lockwood Sq. SE16 CB41 67
Southwark Pk. Rd.
Lockwood Wk. Rom. CT32 50
Lockwood Way, Chess. BM56 94
Lockyer Rd. Grays CY43 70
Locton Est. E3 CD37 57
Loddiges Rd. E9 CC36 57
Loder Clo. Wok. AU60 91
Loder St. SE15 CC43 67
Lodge Av. SW14 BN45 65
South Worple Way
Lodge Av. Borwd. BL25 28
Lodge Av. Croy. BX55 86
Lodge Av. Dag. CO37 59
Lodge Av. Dart. CV46 80
Lodge Av. Har. BL31 46
Lodge Av. Rom. CT32 50
Lodgebottom Rd. Lthd. BL67 112
Lodge Clo. N18 BZ28 39
Lodge Clo. Chig. CO28 41
Lodge Clo. Cob. BE61 102
Lodge Clo. Dor. BK73 119
Lodge Clo. Edg. BL29 37
Lodge Clo. Egh. AR49 72
Lodge Clo. Lthd. BG64 102
Lodge Clo. Orp. CO54 89
Lodge Clo. Slou. AO41 61
Lodge Clo. Sutt. BS56 95
Lodge Clo. Uxb. AX38 53
Lodge Clo. Wall. BV54 86
Lodge Ct. Horn. CW34 51
Lodge Cres. Orp. CO54 89
Lodge Cres. Wal. Cr. CC20 21
Lodge Dr. N13 BY28 38
Lodge Dr. Hat. BQ11 10
Lodge End, Rad. BJ20 18
Lodge Field, Welw. G. C. BR6 5
Lodge Gdns. Beck. CD53 87
Lodge Hall. Harl. CN13 13
Lodge Hill Ilf. CK31 49
Lodge Hill Pur. BY61 104
Lodge Hill Well. CO43 69
Lodge La. N12 BT28 38
Lodge La. Bex. CP46 79
Lodge La. Ch. St. G. AS23 25
Lodge La. Croy. CE57 96
Lodge La. Wal. Abb. CF21 30
Lodge La. West. CM67 115
Lodge La. Est. Rom. CR29 41
Lodge Rd. NW4 BQ31 46
Lodge Rd. NW8 BT38 56
Lodge Rd. Brom. CH50 78
Lodge Rd. Croy. BY53 86
Lodge Rd. Epp. CL20 22
Lodge Rd. Lthd. BG64 102
Lodge Rd. Sutt. BS56 95
Lodge Rd. Wall. BV56 95
Lodge Vill. Wdf. Grn. CG29 40
Lodge Way, Ashf. AY48 73
Lodge Way, Shep. BA51 83
Lodge Way. Wind. AM45 61
Lodore Gdns. NW9 BN32 46
Lodore Grn. Uxb. AY34 44
Lodore St. E14 CF39 57
Loewen Rd. Grays. DG41 71
Loftie St. SE16 CB41 67
Chambers St.
Lofting Rd. N1 BX36 56
Loftus Rd. W12 BP40 55
Logan Clo. Enf. CC23 30
Logan Ms. W8 BS42 66
Logan Pl. W8 BS42 66
Logan Rd. N9 CB27 39
Logan Rd. Wem. BK34 45
Logmore La. Dor. BF72 119
Logs Hill Chis. CK51 88
Logs Hill Clo. Chis. CK51 88
Lois Dr. Shep. BA53 83
Lolesworth St. E1 CA39 57
Wentworth St.
Lollard Pl. SE11 BY42 66
Lollard St. SE11 BX42 66
Lollesworth La. Leath. BA66 110
Loman Path. S. Ock. CZ39 60
Loman St. SE1 BY41 66
Lomas St. E1 CB39 57
Vallance Rd.
Lombard Av. N11 BW28 38
Lombard Av. Enf. CC23 30
Lombard Av. Ilf. CN33 49
Lombard La. EC4 BY39 56
Lombard Rd. SW11 BT44 66
Lombard Rd. SW19 BS51 86
Lombard St. EC3 BZ39 57
Lombard Wall, SE7 CH41 68
Lombardy Dri. Berk. AR13 7
Lomond Clo. Wem. BL36 55
Lomond Gro. SE5 BZ43 67
Loncin Mead Av. Wey. AX58 92
Londale Clo. Pnr. BE29 36
Londesborough Rd. N16 CA35 48
London Av. Gro. SE26 CB49 77
London Br. St. SE1 BZ40 57
London Br. Wk. SE1 BZ40 57
Tooley St.
London Colney By-pass, St. Alb. BL16 19
London Fields, E8 CB37 57
London Fields, E. Side, E8 CB37 57
London Fields, W. Side, E8 CB36 57
London La. E8 CB36 57
London La. Brom. CG50 78
London Lane. Leath. BC68 110
London La. Uxb. AZ38 53
London Ms. W2 CJ39 58
London St.
London Rd. E13 CH37 58
London Rd. SE1 BY41 66
London Rd. SE23 CB47 77
London Rd. SW16 BX51 86
London Rd. SW17 BU53 86
London Rd. Bark. CL37 58
London Rd. Berk. AS13 7
London Rd. Brom. CG50 78
London Rd. Brwd. CZ28 42
London Rd. Bush. BE25 27
London Rd. Cat. BZ65 105
London Rd. Ch. St. G. AR27 34
London Rd. Dart. CS46 79
London Rd. Dart. CX47 80
London Rd. Dor. BJ71 119
London Rd. Enf. BZ25 30
London Rd. Epsom BP58 94
London Rd. Farn. CX54 90
London Rd. Grav. DE46 81
London Rd Grays CX42 70
London Rd. Guil. AS71 118
London Rd. Har. BH34 45
London Rd. Harl. CP11 14
London Rd. Harl. CP13 14
London Rd. Harl. CP14 14
London Rd. Harl. CP9 6
London Rd. Hat. BQ12 10
London Rd. Hem. H. AX15 8
London Rd. Hem. H. AY16 17
London Rd. Houns. BG45 64
London Rd. Kings. On T. BL51 85
London Rd. Mitch. BU53 86
London Rd. Mitch. BV53 86
London Rd. Mord. BS53 86
London Rd. Ong. CV20 24
London Rd. Purfleet. CW42 70
London Rd. Rad. BL20 19
London Rd. Red. BU70 121
London Rd. Reig. BS70 121
London Rd. Rick. AY27 35
London Rd Rom. CO24 32
London Rd. Rom. CR32 50
London Rd. Rom. CS23 32
London Rd. St. Alb. BG13 9
London Rd, Saw. CP6 6
London Rd. Sev. CQ58 98
London Rd. Sev. CR59 98
London Rd. Sev. CS62 107
London Rd. Sev. CY56 99
London Rd. Sev. & Ton. CW70 117
London Rd. Slou. AQ43 62
London Rd. Stai. Ashf. & Felt. AW49 73
London Rd. Stan. BK28 36
London Rd. Swan. CS51 89
London Rd. Th. Hth & Croy. BX51 86
London Rd. Til. DG44 71
London Rd. Twick. BJ47 74
London Rd. Vir. W. AQ51 82
London Rd. Welw. BQ5 5
London Rd. Wem. BL35 46
London Rd. Wok. AU67 109
London Rd. East. Amer. AP24 25
London Rd. N. Red. BW67 113
London Rd. S. Red. BV68 113
London Rd. West. Amer. AO23 25
Londons Clo. Upmin. CY35 51
London Stile W4 BM42 65
Wellesley Rd.
London St. EC3 CA40 57
Fenchurch St.
London St. W2 BT39 56
London St. Cher. AW54 83
London Tilbury Rd. Rain. CV38 60
London Wall, EC2 BZ39 57
Londrina Ter. Berk. AR13 7
Lonesome La. Reig. BS72 121
Long Acre, WC2 BX40 56
Long Acre Orp. CP55 89
Longacre Pl. Cars. BV57 95
Longacre Rd. E17 CF30 39
Longacres, St. Alb. BK13 9
Longaford Way, Brwd. DE26 122
Long Arrotts, Hem. H AW12 8
Long Banks. Harl. CM12 13
Long Barn Rd. Sev. CU70 116
Longbeach Rd. SW11 BU45 66
Longberrys Rd. NW2 BR34 46
Longbottom La. Beac. AO29 34
Longbourne Way, Cher. AV53 82
Longbridge Rd. Bark. CM36 58
Longbridge Way, SE13 CF46 77
Longbury Dr. Orp. CO52 89
Long Chaulden, Hem. H. AV13 7
Longcliffe Path Wat. BC27 35
Longcroft SE9 CK48 78
Long Cft. Wat. BC26 35
Longcroft Av. Bans. BT60 95
Longcroft Dr. Wal. Cr. CD20 21
Longcroft Grn. Welw. G. C. BQ8 5
Longcroft La. Hem. H. AU17 16
Longcroft La. Welw. G. C. BQ8 5
Longcroft Rise Loug. CL25 31
Longcroft Rd. SE5 CA43 67
Longcroft Rd. Edg. BK29 36
Long Croft Rd. Rick. AU28 34
Longcrofts Wal. Abb. CG20 22
Roundhills
Longcross Rd. Cher. AP55 82
Long Deacon Rd. E4 CG26 40
Longdean Pk. Hem. H. AZ16 17
Longden Wood Av. Kes. CK56 97

Longdown La. N. Epsom BP60 94
Longdown La. S. Epsom BP61 103
Longdown Rd. SE6 CE49 77
Longdown Rd. Epsom BP60 94
Longdown Rd. Guil. AT72 118
Long Dr. W3 BO39 55
Long Dr. Grnf. BF37 54
Long Dr. Ruis. BD35 45
Long Dyke, Guil. AT69 118
Long Elmes Har. BF30 36
Long Elmes. Wat. BA20 17
Long Fallow, St. Alb. BF17 18
Longfellow Dr. Brwd. DE26 122
Longfellow Rd. E3 CD38 57
Longfellow Rd. E17 CE32 48
Longfellow Rd. Wor. Pk. BP54 85
Longfield NW9 BO29 37
Longfield, Brom. CG51 88
Longfield, Hem. H. AZ14 8
Longfield Loug. CJ25 31
Long Field. Slou. AO34 43
Longfield Av. E17 CD31 48
Longfield Av. NW7 BP29 37
Longfield Av. W5 BK40 54
Longfield Av. Enf. CC22 30
Longfield Av. Horn. CT33 50
Longfield Av. Wall. BV54 86
Longfield Av. Wem. BL33 46
Longfield Cres. SE26 CC48 77
Longfield Cres. Tad. BQ63 103
Longfield Dr. SW14 BM46 75
Longfield Est. SE1 CA42 67
Longfield. Harl. CO12 14
Longfield La. Wal. Cr. CB17 21
Longfield Rd. W5 BK40 54
Longfield Rd. Dor. BH72 119
Longfields Ong. CX18 24
Longfield St. SW18 BS47 76
Longfield Wk. W5 BK39 54
Longford Av. Felt. BB46 73
Longford Av. Stai. AY47 73
Longford Av. Sthl. BF40 54
Longford Cl. N15 CA32 48
Albert Rd.
Longford Clo. Hamptn. BF49 74
Longford Ct. Epsom BN56 94
Longford Gdns. Hayes BD40 54
Longford Gdns. Sutt. BT55 86
Longford Rd. Twick. BF47 74
Longford St. NW1 BV38 56
Longford Way Stai. AY47 73
Longford Av.
Long Grn. Chig. CN28 40
Long Gro. Beac. AO29 34
Long Gro. Rd. Epsom. BM58 94
Longhayes Av. Rom. CP31 50
Longheath Gdns. Croy. CC53 87
Long Hill. Cat. CC64 105
Longhill Rd. SE6 CF48 77
Longhook Cres. Nthlt. BC37 53
Longhouse Rd. Grays. DG41 71
Longhurst Rd. SE13 CF46 77
Longhurst Rd. Croy. CB53 87
Longhurst Road. Leath. BB68 110
Long John, Hem. H. AY14 8
Longland Dr. N20 BS27 38
Longlands Av. Couls. BV60 95
Longlands Ct. W11 BR40 55
Westbourne Gro.
Longlands, Hem. H. AY13 8
Longlands Pk. Cres. Sid. CN48 78
Longlands Rd. Sid. CN48 78
Longlands Rd. Welw. G. C. BR8 5
Long La. EC1 BY39 56
Long La. SE1 BZ41 67
Long La. Bexh. CP43 69
Long La. Croy. CB53 87
Long La. Hem. H. AS19 16
Long La. Rick. AU25 25
Long La. Rick. AV27 34
Long La. Stai. AY48 73
Long La. Uxb. AZ35 44
Longleat Rd. Enf. CA25 30
Longleat Way, Felt. BA47 73
Longlees Rick. AU28 34
Long Croft Rd.
Longleigh La. SE2 CO43 69
Long Ley. Harl. CN11 13
Long Ley. Harl. CO11 14
Longley Av. Wem. BL37 55
Longley Rd. SW17 BU50 76
Longley Rd. Croy. BY54 86
Longley Rd. Har. BG32 45
Long Leys. E4 CE29 39
Longley St. SE1 CB42 67
Long Lodge Dr. Walt. BD55 84
Longmarsh View. S. At. H. CX51 90
Long Mead NW9 BO30 37
Longmead Chis. CL51 88
Longmead, Guil. AU70 118
Long Mead. Hat. BP11 10
Longmead. Wind. AM44 61
Longmead Clo. Cat. CA64 105
Longmead Dr. Sid. CP48 79
Long Meadow NW5 BW35 47
Long Meadow, Brwd. DE27 122
Long Meadow. Lthd. BE66 111
Longmeadow Rd. Sid. CN47 78
Longmead Rd. SW17 BU49 76
Longmead Rd. Epsom BN59 94
Longmead Rd. Hayes BB40 53
Longmead Rd. Surb. BH54 84
Longmere Gdns. Tad. BQ63 103
Longmoor, Wal. Cr. CD18 21
Longmore Av. Barn. BT25 29
Longmore Clo. AV28 34
Longmore Gdns. Welw. G. C. BR8 5
Longmore Rd. Walt. BE56 93
Longmore St. SW1 BW42 66
Longnor Rd. E1 CC38 57
Long Park. Amer. AO21 25
Long Pond Rd. SE3 CG44 68
Longport Clo. Ilf. CO29 41
Long Reach. Wok. AZ65 101
Long Reach Rd. Bark. CN38 58
Longreach Rd. Erith. CU43 69
Longridge La. Sthl. BF40 54
Longridge Rd. SW5 BS42 66
Long Ridings Av. Brwd. DD25 122
Longs Clo. Wok. AW61 101
Long Shaw, Lthd. BJ63 102
Longshaw Rd. E4 CF27 39
Longshore, SE8 CD42 67
Longside Clo. Egh. AU51 82
Longspring, Wat. BC22 26
Longstaff Cres. SW18 BS46 76
Longstaff Rd. SW18 BS46 76
Longstead La. Sev. DA65 108
Longstone Av. NW10 BO37 55
Longstone Rd. SW17 BV49 76
Longstone Rd. Iver AU37 52
Long St. E2 CA38 57
Long St. Wal. Abb. CK19 22
Long String, St. Alb. BH11 9
Longthornton Rd. SW16 BW51 86
Longton Gro. SE26 CB49 77
Longtown Clo. Rom. CV28 42
Longtown Rd. Rom. CV28 42
Longview Way Rom. CS30 41
Longville Rd. SE11 BY42 66
Long Wk. SW13 BO44 65
Terrace, The.
Long Walk. Ch. St. G. AR24 25
Long Wk. Epsom. BQ63 103
Long Wk. Grav. DF51 81
Long Walk. Guil. AY68 110
Long Wk. N. Mal. BN52 85
Long Wk. Wal. Abb. CE18 21
Long Walk, The Wind. AO47 72
Longways, Stai. AV51 82
Longwood Clo. Upmin. CY35 51
Longwood Dr. SW15 BP46 75
Long Wood Dr. Beac. AP29 34
Longwood Gdns. Ilf. CK31 49
Longwood La. Amer. AO23 25
Longwood Rd. Ken. BZ61 105
Long Yd. WC1 BX38 56
Loning, The, NW9 BO31 46
Loning, The Enf. CC22 30
Lonsdale, Hem. H. AY12 8
Lonsdale Av. E6 CJ38 58
Lonsdale Av. Brwd. DE25 122
Lonsdale Av. Rom. CS32 50
Lonsdale Av. Wem. BL35 46
Lonsdale Clo. E6 CK38 58
Lonsdale Clo. Edg. BL29 37
Lonsdale Clo. Uxb. BA39 53
Lonsdale Cres. Dart. CY47 80
Lonsdale Cres. Ilf. CL32 49
Lonsdale Dr. Enf. BW24 29
Lonsdale Dr. N. Enf. BX25 29
Lonsdale Gdns. Th. Hth. BX52 86
Lonsdale Mews. Rich. BL44 65
Lonsdale Ms. Rich. BM44 65
Elizabeth Cott.
Lonsdale Pl. N1 BY36 56
Lonsdale Rd. E11 CG33 49
Lonsdale Rd. NW6 BR37 55
Lonsdale Rd. SE25 CB52 87
Lonsdale Rd. SW13 BO44 65
Lonsdale Rd. W4 BO42 65
Lonsdale Rd. W11 BR39 55
Lonsdale Rd. Bexh. CQ44 69
Lonsdale Rd. Dor. BJ71 119
Lonsdale Rd. Sthl. BD41 64
Lonsdale Rd. Wey. AZ57 92
Lonsdale Sq. N1 BY36 56
Loobert Rd. N15 CA31 48
Looe Gdns. Ilf. CL31 49
Loom La. Rad. BH22 27
Loom Pl. Rad. BJ21 27
Loop Rd. Chis. CL50 78
Loop Rd. Epsom BN61 103
Loop Rd. Wal. Abb. CE19 21
Loop Rd. Wok. AS64 100
Lopen Rd. N18 CA28 39
Loraine Clo. Enf. CC25 30
Loraine Gdns. Ash. BL62 103
Loraine Rd. N7 BX35 47
Loraine Rd. W4 BM43 65
Lord Av. Ilf. CK31 49
Lord Chancellor Wk. Kings. On T. BN51 85
Lorden Wk. E2 CB38 57
Lord Gdns. Ilf. CK31 49
Lord Hills Br. W2 BS39 56
Lord Hills Rd. W2 BS39 56
Lord Knyvetts Clo. AX46 73
Lord North St. SW1 BX41 66
Lordsbury Fld. Wall. BW58 95
Lords Clo. Felt. BE48 74
Lordship Clo. Brwd. DE26 122
Lordship Gro. N16 BZ34 48
Lordship La. SE22 CA46 77
Lordship Pk. N16 BZ34 48
Lordship Pl. SW3 BU43 66
Cheyne Row
Lordship Rd. N16 BZ33 48
Lordship Rd. Wal. Cr. CB18 21
Lordship Ter. N16 BZ34 48
Lordsmead Rd. N17 CA30 39
Lord St. E16 CK40 58
Lord St. Hodd. CB11 12
Lord Warwick St. SE18 CK41 68
Lorenzo St. WC1 BX38 56
Loretto Gdns. Har. BL31 46
Lorian Av. N12 BS28 38
Holden Rd.
Lorian Clo. N12 BS28 38
Guildown Av.
Loring Rd. N20 BU27 38
Loring Rd. Berk. AR13 7
Loring Rd. Islw. BH44 64
Loring Rd. Wind. AM44 61
Loris Rd. W6 BQ41 65
Lorne Av. Croy. CC54 87
Lorne Clo. NW8 BU38 56
Lorne Clo. Slou. AN41 61
Lorne Gdns. E11 CJ31 49
Lorne Gdns. W11 BQ41 65
Lorne Gdns. W14 BQ32 46
Lorne Gdns. Croy. CC54 87
Lorne Rd. E7 CH35 49
Lorne Rd. E17 CE32 48
Lorne Rd. N4 BX33 47
Lorne Rd. Brwd. DB28 42
Lorne Rd. Har. BH30 36
Lorne Rd. Rich. BL46 75
Albert Rd.
Lorne. The. Lthd. BF66 111
Lorn Rd. SW9 BX44 66
Lorraine Pk. Har. BH29 36
Lorriemore Rd. SE17 BY43 66
Lorrimore Sq. SE17 BY43 66
Lorton Clo. Grav. DJ48 81
Losberne Way SE16 CB42 67
Bonamy Estate West The
Loseberry Rd. Esher BG56 93
Losfield Rd. Wind. AM44
Lothair Rd. W5 BK41 64
Lothair Rd. N. N4 BY32 47
Lothair Rd. S. N4 BY33 47
Lothbury, EC2 BZ39 57
Lothian Av. Hayes BC39 53
Lothian Rd. SW9 BY44 66
Lothian Wd. Tad. BP64 103
Lothrop St. W10 BR38 55
Lots Rd. SW6 BT44 66
Lots Rd. SW10 BT43 66
Lotus Rd. West. CK62 106
Loubet St. SW17 BU50 76
Loudhams Rd. Amer. AR23 25
Loudhams Wood La. Ch. St. G. AR23 25
Loudoun Av. Ilf. CL32 49
Loudoun Rd. NW8 BT36 56
Loudwater Clo. Sun. BC52 83
Loudwater Dr. Rick. AX24 26
Loudwater Heights, Rick. AW24 26
Loudwater Hill, Rick. AX25 26
Loudwater La. Rick. AX24 26
Loudwater Rd. Sun. BC52 83
Loughborough Est. SW9 BY44 66
Loughborough Rd. SW9 BY44 66
Loughborough St. SE11 BX42 66
Loughton La. Epp. CM22 31
Loughton Way Buck. H. CJ26 40
Louisa St. E1 CC38 57
Louise Gdns. Rain. CT38 59
Louise Rd. E15 CG36 58
Louisville Rd. SW17 BV48 76
Lourdon Rd. Mews NW8 BT37 56
Lourdon Rd.
Lousehall La. Wal. Abb. CF16 21
Louvaine Rd. SW11 BT45 66
Louvain Rd. Green. CZ47 80
Louvain Way, Wat. BC19 17
Lovat Clo. NW2 BO34 46
Lovat La. EC3 CA40 57
Lovatt Clo. Edg. BM29 37
Lovatt Dr. Ruis. BB32 44
Lovatt Dr. Ruis. BC32 44
Loveday Rd. W13 BJ40 54
Love Grn. La. Iver AV39 52
Lovegrove St. SE1 CB43 67
Love Hill La. Slou. AT40 52
Lovejoy La. Wind. AL44 61
Lovekyn Clo. Kings. On T. BL51 85
Lovelace Av. Brom. CL53 88
Lovelace Clo. Lthd. BC65 101
Lovelace Clo. Sev. CZ57 99
Lovelace Dr. Wok. AV61 100
Lovelace Gdns. Bark. CO35 50
Lovelace Gdns. Surb. BK54 84
Lovelace Gdns. Walt. BD56 93
Lovelace Grn. SE9 CK45 68
Lovelace Rd. SE21 BZ48 77
Lovelace Rd. Barn. BU26 38
Lovelace Rd. Surb. BK54 84
Loveland La. Tad. BS67 113
Lovelands La. Wok. AO60 91
Love La. EC2 BZ39 57
Love La. N17 CA29 39
Love La. SE18 CL42 68
Thomas St.
Love La. SE25 CB52 87
Love La. Bex. CQ46 79
Love La. Brom. CH51 88
Love La. Grav. DH47 81
Love La. Hat. BP17 19
Love La. Iver AU39 52
Love La. Kings L. AY18 17
Love La. Mitch. BU52 86
Love La. Mord. BS54 86
Love La. Ong. CX17 24
Love La. Pnr. BE31 45
Love La. S. Ock. CW40 60
Love La. Surb. BK55 84
Love La. Sutt. BR57 94
Love La. Tad. BO67 112
Love La. Wat. BB18 17
Love La. Wdf. Grn. CK29 40
Lovel Av. Well. CO44 69
Lovel Clo. Hem. H. AW13 8
Lovel End. Ger. Cr. AR29 34
Lovelinch Cl. SE14 CC43 67
Rollins St.
Lovell Rd. Enf. CB21 30
Lovell Rd. Rich. BK48 74
Lovell Rd. Sthl. BF39 54
Lovell Wk. Rain. CT36 59
Lovel Mead. Ger. Cr. AR29 34
Lovel Rd. Ger. Cr. AR29 34
Loveridge Rd. NW6 BR36 55
Lovers La. Green. DB45 70
Lovers Wk. N3 BS29 38
Lover's Wk. SE10 CF43 67
Lover's Wk. Rom. CS28 41
Lovett Clo. Uxb. AX31 44
Lovett Dr. Cars. BT54 86
Lovetts, Rick. AZ24 26
Lovetts Pl. SW18 BS45 66
York Rd.
Lovett Way NW10 BN35 46
Love Wk. SE5 BZ44 67
Lovibonds Av. Orp. CL56 97
Lowbrook Rd. Ilf. CL35 49
Low Cross Wood La. SE21 CA48 77
Lowdell Clo. West Dr. AY39 53
Lowden Rd. N9 CB26 39
Lowden Rd. SE24 BY45 66
Lowden Rd. Sthl. BE40 54
Lowe Av. E16 CH39 58
Watford Rd.
Lowe Clo. Chig. CO28 41
Lowell St. E14 CD39 57
Lwr. Addiscombe Rd. Croy. CA54 87
Lower Barn, Hem. H. AY15 8
Lwr. Barn Rd. Pur. BZ59 96
Lwr. Bedfords Rd. Rom. CT29 41
Lower Boston Rd. W7 BH41 54
Lwr. Bridge Rd. Red. BU70 121
Lwr. Broad St. Dag. CR37 59
Lower Bury La. Epp. CN19 22
Lwr. Camden, Chis. CK50 78
Lower Church Hill. Green. CZ46 80
Lower Church St. Croy. BY55 86
Wadden New Rd.
Lwr. Church St. Croy. BY55 86
Lower Cippenham La. Slou. AM40 61
Lwr. Clapton Rd. E5 CB34 48
Lwr. Common S. SW15 BP45 65
Lwr. Coombe St. Croy. BZ56 96
Lwr. Court Rd. Epsom BN59 94
Lower Cres. S. Le H. DK41 71
Lwr. Croft Swan. CT52 89
Lwr Dagnal St. St. Alb. BG13 9
Lwr. Derby Rd. Wat. BD24 27
Lwr. Downs Rd. SW20 BQ51 85
Lwr. Drayton Pl. Croy. BY55 86
Lwr. Edgeborough Rd. Guil. AS71 118
Lower Farm Rd. Lthd. BC65 101
Lowerfield. Welw. G. C. BS8 5
Lwr. Form Wor. Pk. BQ55 85
Lwr. George St. Rich. BK46 74
George St.
Lwr. Gravel Rd. Brom. CK54 88
Lwr. Green Rd. Esher BF55 84
Lwr. Green W. Mitch. BU52 86
Lwr. Grosvenor Pl. SW1 BV41 66
Lwr. Guildford Rd. Wok. AO62 100
Lower Hall La. E4 CD28 39
Lwr. Hampton Rd. Sun. BD52 84
Lwr. Ham Rd. Kings. On T. BK50 74
Lower Hatfield Rd. Hert. BW11 11
Lwr. Higham Rd. Grav. DJ47 81
Lower Hill Rd. Epsom. BM59 94
Lwr. Hythe St. Dart. CW46 80
Lwr. James St. W1 BW40 56
Brewer St.
Lwr. John St. W1 BW40 56
Brewer St.
Lwr. Kenwood Av. Enf. BW25 29
Lower Kings Rd. Berk. AR13 7
Lwr. Maidstone Rd. N11 BW29 38
Lower Mall W6 BP42 65
Lwr. Mardyke Av. Rain. CS37 59
Lower Marsh, SE1 BY41 66
Lwr. Marsh La. Kings. On T. BL52 85
Lower Mead, Iver AU38 52
Lower Meadow. Harl. CN13 13
Lower Merton Rd. NW3 BU36 56
Lwr. Morden La. Mord. BQ53 85
Lwr. Mortlake Rd. Rich. BL45 65
Lower Paddock Rd. Wat. BE25 27
Lower Pk. Rd. Bans. BU62 104
Lwr. Park. Rd. Belv. CR41 69
Lwr. Pk. Rd. Loug. CJ25 31
Lwr. Paxton Rd. St. Alb. BH14 9
Paxton Rd.
Lower Peryers, Leath. BB67 110
Lwr. Pillory Downs. Cars. BV60 95
Lower Pyrford Rd. Wok. AW61 101
Lwr. Queen's Rd. Buck. H. CJ27 40
Lwr. Range Rd. Grav. DJ47 81
Lower Richmond Rd. SW15 BP45 65
Lower Rd. E13 CH38 58
Lower Rd. Belv. CR41 69
Lower Rd. Brwd. DE23 122
Lower Rd. Ger. Cr. AS31 43
Lower Rd. Grav. DC45 71
Lower Rd. Grav. DK47 81
Lower Rd. Har. BG34 45
Lower Rd. Hem. H. AZ16 17
Lower Rd. Ken. BY60 95
Lower Rd. Loug. CL23 31
Lower Rd. Lthd. BD67 111
Lower Rd. Lthd. BG65 102
Lower Rd. Orp. CO54 89
Lower Rd. Rain. CS37 59
Lower Rd. Red. BT71 121
Lower Rd. Rick. AU24 25
Lower Rd. Sutt. BT56 95
Lower Rd. Swan. CT50 79
Lower Rd. Uxb. AU33 43
Lower Sales, Hem. H. AV14 7
Lower Shot. Lthd. BF66 111
Lower Shot Clo. Lthd. BF66 111
Lwr. Sloane St. SW1 BV42 66
Lower Sq. Islw. BJ45 64
Lower Staithe W4 BN44 65
Lwr. Station Rd. Crayford. CT46 79
Lower Strand NW9 BO30 37
Lwr. Sunbury Rd. Hamptn. BE51 84
Lower Swaines, Epp. CN18 22
Lower Tail. Wat. BE27 36
Lwr. Teddington Rd. Kings. On T. BK50 74
Lower Ter. NW3 BT34 47
Lower Thames St. EC3 BZ40 57
Lwr. Tubs Bush. BG26 36
Lwr. Vernon Rd. Sutt. BT56 95
Lower Wood. Harl. CK12 13
Lwr. Wood Rd. Esher BJ57 93
Lower Yott. Hem. H. AY13 8
Lowestoft Clo. E5 CB34 48
Southwold Rd.
Lowestoft Rd. Wat. BC23 26
Lowe, The, Chig. CO28 41
Lowfield La. Hodd. CE12 12
Lowfield Rd. NW6 BS36 56
Lowfield Rd. W3 BM39 55
Lowfield St. Dart. CW48 80
Low Hall Clo. E4 CE26 39
Lowhall La. E17 CD32 48
Low Hill. Harl. CG12 13
Low Hill Rd. Harl. CG12 13
Lowick Rd. Har. BH31 45
Lowland Av. Brom. CH51 88
Lowlands Gdns, Rom. CR32 50
Lowlands Rd. Har. BH33 45
Lowlands Rd. Pnr. BD33 45
Lowlands Rd. S. Ock. CX40 60
Lowman Rd. N7 BX35 47
Lowndes Clo. SW1 BV41 66
Lowndes Pl. SW1 BV41 66
Lowndes Sq. SW1 BU41 66
Lowndes St. SW1 BU41 66
Lowood St. E1 CB40 57
Low Rd. Hat. BU11 11
Lowshoe La. Rom. CR30 41
Lowson Gro. Wat. BE26 36
Low Street La. Til. DJ43 71
Lowswood Clo. Nthwd. BA30 35
Lowther Dr. Enf. BW24 29
Lowther Hl. SE23 CD47 77
Lowther Rd. E17 CD30 39
Lowther Rd. N7 BY35 47
Mackenzie Rd.
Lowther Rd. SW13 BO44 65
Lowther Rd. Kings. On T. BL51 85
Lowther Rd. Stan. BL31 46
Lowth Rd. SE5 BZ44 67
Loxford Av. E6 CJ37 58
Loxford La. Ilf. CM35 49
Loxford Rd. Bark. CL36 58
Loxham Rd. E4 CE29 39
Loxham St. WC1 BX38 56
Argyle Wk.
Loxley Rd. SW18 BT47 76
Loxley Rd. Berk. AP12 7
Loxley Rd. Hamptn. BE49 74
Loxton Rd. SE23 CC47 77
Loxwood Rd. N17 CA31 48
Lubbock Rd. Chis. CK50 78
Lubbock St. SE14 CC43 67
Lubeck St. SW11 BU45 66
Lucan Dr. Stai. AX50 73
Bingham Dr.
Lucan Pl. SW3 BU42 66
Lucan Rd. Barn. BR24 28
Lucas Av. E13 CH37 58
Lucas Av. Har. BF34 45
Lucas Ct. Har. BF33 45
Lucas Ct. Wal. Abb. CG20 22
Mason Way
Lucas Rd. SE20 CC50 77
Lucas Rd. Grays. DD41 71
Lucas St. SE8 CD44 67
Lucerne Clo. N13 BX27 38
Lucerne Clo. Wok. AS63 100
Claremont Av.
Lucerne Gro. E17 CF31 48
Lucerne Ms. W8 BS40 56
Kensington Mall
Lucerne Rd. N5 BY35 47
Lucerne Rd. Orp. CN54 88
Lucerne Rd. Th. Hth. BY52 86
Lucerne Way. Rom. CV29 42
Lucie Av. Ashf. AZ50 73
Lucien Rd. SW17 BV49 76
Lucien Rd. SW19 BS48 76
Lucknow St. SE18 CN43 68
Lucks Hill, Hem. H. AV13 7
Lucorn Clo. SE12 CG46 78
Luctons Av. Buck. H. CJ26 40
Lucy Cres. W3 BN39 55
Lucy Gdns. Dag. CQ34 50
Luddesdon Rd. Erith. CR43 69
Luddington Av. Vir. W. AS51 82
Ludford Clo. NW9 BO30 37
Ludgate Circus, EC4 BY39 56
Ludgate Hill, EC4 BY39 56
Ludgate Sq. EC4 BY39 56
Creed La.
Ludlow Clo. Har. BE35 45
Ludlow Mead Wat. BC27 35
Ludlow Pl. Grays. DD41 71
Ludlow Rd. W5 BK38 54
Ludlow Rd. Felt. BB48 73
Ludlow Rd. Guil. AQ71 118
Ludlow Way, Rick. BA24 26
Ludlow Wy. N2 BT31 47
Ludovick Wk. SW15 BO45 65
Ludwick Rd. SE14 CD43 67
Luffield Rd. SE2 CO41 69
Luffman Rd. SE12 CH48 78

Lugard Rd. SE15 CB44 67
Luke St. EC2 CA38 57
Lukin Cres. E4 CF27 39
Lukin St. E1 CC39 57
Lullark Clo. West. CJ61 106
Lullingstone Av. Swan. CT52 89
Lullingstone Clo. Orp. CO50 79
Lullingstone Cres. Orp. CO50 79
Lullingstone Rd. Belv. CQ43 69
Barnfield Rd.
Lullington Garth N12 BR28 37
Lullington Garth Brom. CG50 78
Lullington Gth. Borwd. BM25 28
Lullington Rd. SE20 CB50 77
Lullington Rd. Dag. CQ36 59
Lulot St. N6 BV34 47
Lulworth Av. Houns. BF44 64
Lulworth Av. Wal. Cr. BY18 20
Lulworth Av. Wem. BK33 45
Lulworth Clo. Har. BE34 45
Lulworth Dr. Pnr. BD33 45
Lulworth Dr. Rom. CR28 41
Lulworth Gdns. Har. BE34 45
Lulworth Rd. SE9 CK48 78
Lulworth Rd. SE15 CB44 67
Lulworth Rd. Well. CN44 68
Lulworth Waye Hayes BC39 53
Lumbards. Welw. G. C. BS6 5
Lumley Gdns. Sutt. BR56 94
Lumley Rd. Sutt. BR57 94
Lumley St. W1 BV39 56
Lunar Clo. West. CJ61 106
Luna Rd. Th. Hth. BZ52 87
Lundale Rd. Dart. CX47 80
Lundale Rd. Dart. CY47 80
Lundin Wk. Wat. BD28 36
Lundy Dr. Hayes. BB42 63
Lundy St. W6 BR43 65
Field Rd.
Lundy Wk. N1 BZ36 57
Marquess Est.
Lunghurst Rd. Cat. CD63 105
Lunham Rd. SE19 CA50 77
Luntly Pl. E1 CA39 57
Chicksand St.
Lupin Clo. SW2 BY48 76
Palace Rd.
Luppit Clo. Brwd. DD26 122
Lupton St. NW5 BW35 47
Lupus St. SW1 BV42 66
Lurgan Av. W6 BQ43 65
Lurline Gdns. SW11 BV44 66
Luscombe Way, SW8 BX43 66
Lushes Rd. Loug. CL25 31
Lushington Rd. NW10 BP37 55
Lushington Rd. SE6 CE49 77
Lusted Hall La. West. CH63 106
Lusted Hall La. West. CJ62 106
Lusteds Clo. Dor. BK73 119
Lutheran Pl. SW2 BX47 76
Upr. Tulse Hill
Luther Clo. Edg. BN27 37
Luther King Rd. Harl. CM11 13
Luther Rd. Tedd. BH49 74
Luthers Clo. Brwd. CZ22 33
Luton Pl. SE10 CF43 67
Luton Rd. E13 CG38 58
Luton Rd. E13 CH38 58
Luton Rd. E17 CD31 48
Luton Rd. Sid. CP48 79
Luton St. NW8 BT37 56
Lutrell Av. SW15 BP45 65
Lutwyche Rd. SE6 CD48 77
Luxborough La. Chig. CK27 40
Luxborough Pl. W1 BV38 56
Luxborough St. W1 BV39 56
Luxemburg Gdns. W6 BQ42 65
Luxfield Rd. SE9 CK47 78
Luxford St. SE16 CC42 67
Luxmore Gdns. SE4 CD44 67
Luxmore St. SE4 CC44 67
Luxor St. SE5 BZ44 67
Luxted Rd. Orp. CL59 97
Lyall Av. SE21 CA48 77
Lyall Ms. E. SW1 BV41 66
Lyall St. SW1 BV41 66
Lyal Rd. E3 CD37 57
Lycett Pl. W12 BP41 65
Vespan Rd.
Lychen Av. Houns. BC44 63
Lych Gate Rd. Orp. CO54 89
Lych Way, Wok. AR61 100
Lyconby Gdns. Croy. CD54 87
Lycrome La. Chesh. AO17 16
Lycrome Rd. Chesh. AP17 16
Lydd Clo. Sid. CN48 78
Lydden Ct. SE9 CN46 78
Lydden Rd. SW18 BS47 76
Lyddon Gro. SW18 BS47 76
Lydd Rd. Bexh. CQ43 69
Lydeard Rd. E6 CK36 58
Lydenberg St. SE7 CJ41 68
Lydford Av. Slou. AO38 52
Lydford Rd. NW2 BQ36 55
Lydford Rd. W9 BR38 55
Lydhurst Av. SW2 BX48 76
Lydia Rd. Erith CT43 69
Lydney Clo. SW15 BR48 75
Princes Way
Lydon Rd. SW4 BW45 66
Lydstep Rd. Chis. CL49 78
Lye Green Rd. Chesh. AP18 16
Lye La. St. Alb. BF17 18
Lye Rd. Wok. AO63 100
Lyfield. Cob. BF60 93
Lyford Rd. N15 BZ32 48
Lyford Rd. SW18 BT47 76
Lyford St. SE18 CK42 68
Lyham Clo. SW2 BX46 76
Lyham Rd. SW2 BX46 76
Lymbourne Clo. Sutt. BS58 95
Lymden Gdns. Reig. BS71 121
Lyme Av. Berk. AO11 7
Lyme Farm Rd. SE12 CH45 68
Lyme Gro. Wey. AW56 92
Lymer Av. SE19 CA49 77
Lyme Regis Rd. Bans. BR62 103
Lyme Rd. Well. CO44 69
Lymescote Gdns. Sutt. BS55 86
Lyme St. NW1 BW36 56
Lyme Ter. NW1 BW36 56
Royal College St.
Lyminge Clo. Sid. CN48 78
Lyminge Gdns. SW18 BU47 76
Lymington Av. N22 BY30 38
Lymington Clo. SW16 BW51 86
Lymington Dr. Ruis. BA34 44
Lymington Gdns. Epsom BO56 94
Lymington Rd. NW6 BS36 56
Lymington Rd. Dag. CP33 50
Lympstone Gdns. SE15 CB43 67
Lynbridge Gdns. N13 BY28 38
Lynceley Gra. Epp. CO18 23
Lynch Gate, Wat. BD20 18
Lynch Gate Wk. Hayes BB40 53
Lynch, The Uxb. AX36 53
Lyncroft Av. Pnr. BE32 45
Lyncroft Gdns. NW6 BS35 47
Lyncroft Gdns. W13 BK41 64
Lyncroft Gdns. Epsom BO58 94
Lyncroft Gdns. Houns. BG46 74
Lyndale NW2 BR35 46
Lyndale Av. NW2 BR34 46
Lyndale Clo. SE3 CG43 68
Lyndale Ct. Wey. AW60 92
Parvis Rd.
Lyndale Rd. Red. BU69 121
Lynden Way Swan. CS52 89
Lyndhurst Av. N12 BU29 38
Lyndhurst Av. NW7 BO29 37
Lyndhurst Av. SW16 BW51 86
Lyndhurst Av. Pnr. BC30 35
Lyndhurst Av. Sthl. BF40 54
Lyndhurst Av. Sun. BC52 83
Lyndhurst Av. Surb. BM54 85
Lyndhurst Av. Twick. BE47 74
Lyndhurst Clo. NW10 BN34 46
Lyndhurst Clo. Bexh. CR45 69
Lyndhurst Clo. Croy. CA55 87
Selborne Rd.
Lyndhurst Ct. E18 CH30 40
Lyndhurst Dr. E10 CF33 48
Lyndhurst Dr. Horn. CV33 51
Lyndhurst Dr. N. Mal. BO53 85
Lyndhurst Dr. Sev. CT65 107
Lyndhurst Gdns. N3 BR30 37
Lyndhurst Gdns. NW3 BT35 47
Lyndhurst Gdns. Bark. CN36 58
Lyndhurst Gdns. Enf. CA24 30
Lyndhurst Gdns. Ilf. CM32 49
Lyndhurst Gdns. Pnr. BC30 35
Lyndhurst Gro. SE15 CA44 67
Lyndhurst Rise Chig. CL28 40
Lyndhurst Rd. E4 CF29 39
Lyndhurst Rd. N18 CB28 39
Lyndhurst Rd. N22 BX29 38
Lyndhurst Rd. NW3 BT35 47
Lyndhurst Rd. Bexh. CR45 69
Lyndhurst Rd. Couls. BV61 104
Lyndhurst Rd. Grnf. BF38 54
Lyndhurst Rd. Reig. BS72 121
Lyndhurst Rd. Th. Hth. BY52 86
Lyndhurst Sq. SE15 CA44 67
Lyndhurst Ter. NW3 BT35 47
Lyndhurst Way SE15 CA44 67
Lyndhurst Way, Brwd. DE26 122
Lyndhurst Way, Cher. AV55 82
Lyndhurst Way, Grav. DF51 81
Lyndhurst Way Sutt. BS58 95
Lyndon Av. Pnr. BE29 36
Lyndon Av. Sid. CN46 78
Lyndon Av. Wall. BV55 86
Lyndon Rd. Belv. CR42 69
Lyndwood Dr. Wind. AQ46 72
Lyne Clo. Vir. W. AS53 82
Lyne Crossing Rd. Cher. AT53 82
Lynegrove Av. Ashf. BA49 73
Lyneham Wk. Pnr. BB31 44
Lyne La. Cher. AT54 82
Lyne La. Vir. W. AT53 82
Lyne Rd. Vir. W. AS53 82
Lynette Av. SW4 BV46 76
Lynett Rd. Dag. CP34 50
Lyne Way, Hem. H. AV12 7
Lynford Gdns. Edg. BM27 37
Lynford Gdns. Ilf. CN34 49
Lynford Ter. N9 CA26 39
Lynhurst Cres. Uxb. BA36 53
Lynhurst Rd. Uxb. BA36 53
Lynmere Rd. Well. CO44 69
Lynmouth Av. Enf. CA25 30
Lynmouth Av. Mord. BQ53 85
Lynmouth Dr. Ruis. BC34 44
Lynmouth Gdns. Grnf. BJ37 54
Lynmouth Gdns. Houns. BD43 64
Lynmouth Rise Orp. CO52 89
Lynmouth Rd. E17 CD32 48
Lynmouth Rd. N2 BU31 47
Lynmouth Rd. N16 CA33 48
Lynmouth Rd. Grnf. BJ37 54
Lynn Clo. Ashf. BA49 73
Lynn Clo. Har. BG30 36
Lynne Clo. Croy. CC59 96
Lynne Clo. Orp. CN57 97
Lynne Clo. Sth. Croy. CC58 96
Lynne Wk. Esher BG56 93
Lynne Way NW10 BO36 55
Lynne Way Nthlt. BD37 54
Lynn Rd. E11 CG34 49
Lynn Rd. SW12 BV47 76
Lynn Rd. Ilf. CM33 49
Lynn St. Enf. BZ23 30
Lynross Clo. Rom. CW30 42
Lynsted. Clo. Bexh. CR46 79
Lynsted Gdns. SE9 CJ45 68
Lynton Av. N12 BT28 38
Lynton Av. NW9 BO31 46
Lynton Av. W13 BJ39 54
Lynton Av. Orp. CO52 89
Lynton Av. Rom. CR30 41
Lynton Av. St. Alb. BK14 9
Lynton Clo. Chess. BL56 94
Lynton Clo. Islw. BH45 64
Lynton Cres. Ilf. CL32 49
Lynton Est. SE1 CB42 67
Lynton Gdns. N11 BW29 38
Lynton Gdns. Enf. CA26 39
Lynton Mead N20 BS27 38
Lynton Rd. E4 CE28 39
Lynton Rd. E11 CF35 48
Lynton Rd. N8 BW32 47
Lynton Rd. NW6 BR38 55
Lynton Rd. SE1 CA42 67
Lynton Rd. W3 BM40 55
Lynton Rd. Croy. BY53 86
Lynton Rd. Dag. CP34 50
Lynton Rd. Grav. DG47 81
Lynton Rd. Har. BE34 45
Lynton Rd. N. Mal. BN53 85
Lynton Rd. S. Grav. DG47 81
Lynwood Ave. Slou. AR41 62
Lynwood Av. Couls. BV61 104
Lynwood Av. Egh. AS50 72
Lynwood Av. Epsom BO60 94
Lynwood Clo. E18 CJ30 40
Lynwood Clo. Har. BE34 45
Lynwood Clo. Rom. CR29 41
Lynwood Clo. Wok. AU60 91
Lynwood Dr. Rom. CR29 41
Lynwood Dr. Wor. Pk. BP55 85
Lynwood Gdns. Croy. BX56 95
Lynwood Gdns. Sthl. BE39 54
Lynwood Gro. Orp. CN54 88
Lynwood, Guil. AQ71 118
Lynwood Heights, Rick. AW25 26
Lynwood Rd. SW17 BU49 76
Lynwood Rd. W5 BK38 54
Lynwood Rd. Epsom. BO60 94
Lynwood Rd. Red. BV69 121
Lynwood Rd. Surb. BH55 84
Lyon Meade, Stan. BK30 36
Lyon Park Av. Wem. BL36 55
Lyon Rd. SW19 BT51 86
Lyon Rd. Har. BH32 45
Lyon Rd. Rom. CT33 50
Lyon Rd. Walt. BE55 84
Lyons Dene. Tad. BR67 112
Lyonsdown Av. Barn. BT25 29
Lyonsdown Rd. Barn. BS25 29
Lyons Pl. NW8 BT38 56
Lyoth Rd. Orp. CM55 88
Lyric Rd. SW13 BO44 65
Lysander Gro. N19 BW33 47
Lysander Rd. Croy. BX57 95
Lysander Rd. Ruis. BA34 44
Lysias Rd. SW12 BV46 76
Lysia St. SW6 BQ44 65
Lysons Wk. SW15 BP46 75
Swinburne Rd.
Lytchett Rd. Brom. CH50 78
Lytchet Way, Enf. CC23 30
Lytcott Gro. SE22 CA46 77
Lytham Av. Wat. BD28 36
Lytham Gro. W5 BL38 55
Lytham St. SE17 BZ42 67
Lyton Gdns. Wall. BW56 95
Lyttelton Clo. NW3 BU36 56
Lyttelton Ct. N2 BT32 47
Lyttelton Rd. E10 CE34 48
Lyttelton Rd. N2 BT32 47
Lyttleton Rd. N8 BY31 47
Lytton Av. N13 BY27 38
Lytton Av. Enf. CD22 30
Lytton Clo. Nthlt. BE36 54
Lytton Gdns. Welw. G. C. BQ8 5
Lytton Gro. SW15 BQ46 75
Lytton Rd. E11 CG33 49
Lytton Rd. Barn. BT24 29
Lytton Road. Grays. DG42 71
Lytton Rd. Pnr. BE29 36
Lytton Rd. Rom. CU32 50
Lytton Rd. Wok. AT61 100
Lyttons Way, Hodd. CE10 12
Lyveden Rd. SE3 CH43 68
Lyvedon Rd. SW17 BU50 76
Lywood Clo. Tad. BQ64 103
Mabbits Clo. St. Alb. BE18 18
Jenkins Av.
Mabel Rd. Swan. CU50 79
Mabel St. Wok. AR62 100
Maberley Ct. SE19 CB50 77
Maberley Cres. SE19 CB50 77
Maberley Rd. SE19 CA51 87
Maberley Rd. Beck. CC52 87
Mabledon Pl. WC1 BW38 56
Mablethorpe Rd. SW6 BR43 65
Mabley St. E9 CD35 48
Mabyn Rd. SE18 CN42 68
Macarthur Ter. SE7 CJ43 68
Charlton La.
Macaulay Av. Esher BH55 84
Macaulay Ct. SW4 BV45 66
Macaulay Rd. E6 CJ37 58
Macaulay Rd. SW4 BV45 66
Macaulay Rd. Cat. CA64 105
Macaulay Sq. SW4 BV45 66
Macbean St. SE18 CL41 68
Macbeth St. W6 BP42 65
Macclesfield Br. NW8 BU37 56
Macclesfield Rd. EC1 BZ38 57
Macclesfield Rd. SE25 CB53 87
Macclesfield St. W1 BW40 56
Gerrard St.
Macdonald Av. Horn. CW31 51
Macdonald Clo. Horn. CW31 51
Macdonald Rd. E7 CH35 49
Macdonald Rd. E17 CF30 39
Macdonald Rd. N11 BU28 38
Macdonald Rd. N19 BW34 47
Macdonald Rd. Dag. CR34 50
Macdonald Way. Horn. CW31 51
Macdonell Gdns. Wat. BC22 26
Macduff Rd. SW11 BV44 66
Mace La. Sev. CM60 97
Macer, S Ct. Brox. CD15 12
Macer, S La. Brox. CD15 12
Macfarlane Pl. W12 BQ40 55
Macfarlane Rd. W12 BQ40 55
Macgregor Rd. E16 CJ39 58
Machell Rd. SE15 CC45 67
Macintosh La. E9 CC35 48
High St.
Mackay Rd. SW4 BV45 66
Mackennal St. NW8 BU37 56
Mackenzie Rd. N7 BX36 56
Mackenzie Rd. Beck. CC51 87
Mackenzie Way, Grav. DH50 81
Mackeson Rd. NW3 BU35 47
Mackie Rd. SW2 BY47 76
Macklin St. WC2 BX39 56
Mackrells Rd. Red. BT72 121
Mack's Rd. SE16 CB42 67
Mackworth St. NW1 BW38 56
Maclean Rd. SE23 CD46 77
Maclennan Av. Rain. CV38 60
Macleod St. SE17 BZ42 67
Maclise Rd. W14 BR41 65
Macmillan Gdns. Dart. CX45 70
Macoma Rd. SE18 CM43 68
Macoma Ter. SE18 CM43 68
Macon Way, Upmin. CZ32 51
Macquarie Way E14 CE42 67
Macready Pl. N7 BX35 47
Macroom Rd. W9 BR38 55
Madan Rd. West. CM66 115
Madans Wk. Epsom BN61 103
Mada Rd. Orp. CL55 88
Maddams St. E3 CE38 57
Maddison Clo. Tedd. BH50 74
Maddison Way. Sev. CT65 107
Maddocks Clo. Sid. CQ49 79
Maddock Way, SE17 BY43 66
Maddox La. Lthd. BE65 102
Maddox Pk. Lthd. BE65 102
Maddox Rd. Harl. CN10 6
Maddox Rd. Harl. CN11 13
Maddox Rd. Hem. H. AZ13 8
Maddox St. W1 BV40 56
Madeira Av. Brom. CG50 78
Madeira Gro. Wdf. Grn. CJ29 40
Madeira Rd. E11 CF33 48
Madeira Rd. N13 BY28 38
Madeira Rd. Mitch. BU52 86
Madeira Rd. Wey. AV60 91
Madeira Wk. Brwd. DC27 122
Madeira Wk. Reig. BT70 121
Madeira Wk. Wind. AO44 61
Madeley Rd. W5 BK39 54
Madeline Rd. SE20 CB50 77
Madison Cres. Well. CP43 69
Madison Gdns. Brom. CG52 88
Madison Gdns. Well. CP43 69
Madras Pl. N7 BY36 56
Madras Rd. Ilf. CL35 49
Madrid Rd. SW13 BP44 65
Madrid Rd. Guil. AQ71 118
Madron St. SE17 CA42 67
Maesmaur Rd. West. CJ64 106
Mafeking Av. E6 CK37 58
Mafeking Av. Brent. BK43 64
Mafeking Av. Ilf. CM33 49
Mafeking Rd. E16 CG38 58
Mafeking Rd. N17 CB30 39
Mafeking Rd. Enf. CA24 30
Mafeking Rd. Stai. AT48 72
Magazine Pl. Lthd. BJ64 102
Magazine Rd. Cat. BY64 104
Magdala Rd. N19 BV34 47
Magdala Rd. Islw. BJ45 64
Magdala Rd. Sth. Croy. BZ57 96
Magdalen Clo. Wey. AY60 92
Magdalen Cres. Wey. AY60 92
Magdalene Gdns. E6 CL38 58
Homeway
Magdalene Pass. E1 CA40 57
Chamber St.
Magdalen Gdns. Brwd. DF25 122
Magdalen Rd. SW18 BT47 76
Magdalen St. SE1 CA40 57
Magee St. SE11 BY43 66
Magna Carta La. Stai. AR47 72
Magna Rd. Egh. AQ50 72
Magnaville Rd. Bush. BH26 36
Magnolia Clo. Kings. On T. BM50 75
Magnolia Ct. Har. BL33 46
Magnolia Dr. West. CJ61 106
Magnolia Rd. W4 BM43 65
Magnolia St. West Dr. AX42 63
Magnolia Way Epsom BN56 94
Magnum Clo. Rain. CV39 60
Magpie Alley, EC4 BY39 56
Whitefriars St.
Magpie Clo. Couls. BW58 95
Magpie Clo. Couls. BW62 104
Magpie Hall Clo. Brom. CK53 88
Magpie Hall La. Brom. CK54 88
Magpie Hall Rd. Bush. BH27 36
Magpie La. Brwd. DB30 42
Magpie La. Sev. CW60 99
Magpie Wk. Hat. BP13 10
Lark Rise
Maguire Dr. Rich. BK49 74
Maguire St. SE1 CA41 67
Mahlon Av. Ruis. BC35 44
Maida Av. E4 CE26 39
Maida Av. W2 BT39 56
Maida Rd. W2 BT40 56
Maida Rd. Belv. CR41 69
Maida Vale, W9 BS37 56
Maida Vale Rd. Dart. CU46 79
Maida Way E4 CE26 39
Maiden Erlegh Av. Bex. CQ47 79
Maidenhead Rd. Wind. AL43 61
Maiden La. WC2 BX40 56
Bedford St.
Maiden La. Dart. CU45 69
Maiden Rd. E15 CG36 58
Maidenshaw Rd. Epsom BN59 94
Maidenstone Hl. SE10 CF44 67
Maidman St. E3 CD38 57
Maid Of Honour Row Rich. BK46 74
Green, The,
Maidstone Av. Rom. CS30 41
Maidstone Bldgs. SE1 BZ40 57
Maidstone Rd. N11 BW29 38
Maidstone Rd. Grays. DD43 71
Maidstone Rd. Sev. CT64 107
Maidstone Rd. Sid. CP50 79
Maidstone St. E2 CB37 57
Main Ave. Nthwd. BA27 35
Main Av. Enf. CA25 30
Main Dr. Ger. Cr. AR32 43
Main Parade. Rick. AU24 25
Mainridge Rd. Chis. CL49 78
Main Rd. Eden. CM70 115
Main Rd. Long. DB51 90
Main Rd. Orp. CP51 89
Main Rd. Rom. CT31 50
Main Rd. Sev. CO62 107
Main Rd. Sev. CP65 107
Main Rd. Sid. CM48 78
Main Rd. S. At H. CX50 80
Main Rd. Swan. CT50 79
Main Rd. West. CJ60 97
Main Rd. West. CJ62 106
Main St. Felt. BD49 74
Maisemore St. SE15 CD43 67
Maitland Clo. SE10 CE43 67
Maitland Clo. Wey. AW60 92
Maitland Gdns. E6 CK39 58
Maitland Pk. Est. NW3 BU36 56
Maitland Pk. Rd. NW3 BU36 56
Maitland Pk. Vill. NW3 BU35 47
Maitland Rd. E15 CG36 58
Maitland Rd. SE26 CC50 77
Maize Row, E14 CD40 57
Majendie Rd. SE18 CM42 68
Major Rd. E15 CF35 48
Major Rd. SE16 CB41 67
Majors Farm Rd. Slou. AR43 62
Makepeace Av. N6 BV34 47
Makins St. SW3 BU42 66
Malacca Farm Road. Guil. AW67 110
Malam Gdns. E14 CE40 57
Wade's Pl.
Malan Clo. West. CK62 106
Malan Sq. Rain. CU36 59
Malay St. E1 CC40 57
Malbrook Rd. SW15 BP45 65
Malcolm Ct. W5 BL38 55
Malcolm Ct. Stan. BK28 36
Malcolm Cres. NW4 BP32 46
Malcolm Pl. E2 CC38 57
Malcolm Rd. E1 CC38 57
Malcolm Rd. SE20 CC50 77
Malcolm Rd. SE25 CB53 87
Malcolm Rd. SW19 BR50 75
Malcolm Rd. Couls. BW61 104
Malcolm Rd. Uxb. AY35 44
Malden Av. SE25 CB52 87
Malden Av. Grnf. BH35 45
Malden Cres. NW5 BV36 56
Malden Grn. Av. Wor. Pk. BO54 85
Malden High St. N. Mal. BO52 85
Malden Hill N. Mal. BO52 85
Malden Hill Gdns. N. Mal. BO52 85
Malden Manor, The, N. Mal. BO54 85
Malden Pk. N. Mal. BO53 85
Malden Pl. NW5 BV35 47
Grafton Ter.
Malden Rd. NW5 BV35 47
Malden Rd. Borwd. BM24 28
Malden Rd. N. Mal. BO53 85
Malden Rd. Sutt. BQ56 94
Malden Rd. Wat. BC23 26
Malden Way N. Mal. BN53 85
Maldon Clo. SE5 CA45 67
Maldon Ct. N. Mal. BP52 85
Maldon Rd. N9 CA27 39
Maldon Rd. W3 BN40 55
Maldon Rd. Rom. CS33 50
Maldon Rd. Wall. BV56 95
Maldon Wk. Wdf. Grn. CJ29 40
Malet Clo. Egh. AU50 72
Malet Pl. WC1 BW38 56
Malet St. WC1 BW38 56
Maley Av. SE27 BY48 76
Malfont Rd. SE5 CA45 67
Malford Ct. E18 CH30 40
Malford Gro. E18 CG31 49
Malham Rd. SE23 CC47 77
Malington Way NW9 BN30 37
Malins Clo. Barn. BP25 28
Mallard Clo. Barn. BT25 29
Mallard Clo. Upmin. CZ33 51
Mallard Ct. NW9 BN33 46
Mallards Rd. Wdf. Grn. CH29 40
Mallards, The, Stai. AW51 83
Staines Rd.
Mallard Wk. Sid. CP50 79
Cray Rd.
Mallard Way, NW9 BN33 46
Mallard Way, Brwd. DD26 122
Mallard Way Wat. BE21 27
Mallet Av. SE13 CF46 77
Mallet Dr. Nthlt. BE35 45
Malling Gdns. Mord. BT53 86
Malling Way Brom. CG54 88
Mallinson Rd. SW11 BU46 76
Mallinson Rd. Croy. BW55 86
Mallion Ct. Wal. Abb. CG20 22
Mallord St. SW3 BT43 66

Mallory Clo. SE4 CD45 67
Mallory Gdns. E6 CK39 58
Mallory Gdns. Barn. BV26 38
Mallory St. W1 BU38 56
Mallow Cr. Hat. BP13 10
Mallow Mead NW7 BR29 37
Mallows, The, Uxb. AZ34 44
Mallow St. EC1 BZ38 57
Mall Rd. W6 BP42 65
Mall, The, N14 BX27 38
Mall, The, SW1 BW41 66
Mall, The, SW14 BN46 75
Mall, The, W5 BK40 54
Mall, The, Brom. CH52 88
Mall, The, Har. BL33 46
Mall, The, St. Alb. BG17 18
Mall, The, Surb. BK53 84
Malmains Clo. Beck. CF53 87
Malmains Way Beck. CF52 87
Malmesbury Clo. Pnr. BC31 44
Malmesbury Rd. E3 CD38 57
Malmesbury Rd. E16 CG38 58
Malmesbury Rd. E18 CG30 40
Malmesbury Rd. Mord. BT54 86
Malmesbury Ter. E16 CG39 58
Malmesby Clo. Pnr. BB31 44
Malmes Cft. Hem. H. BA14 8
Malms Dale, Welw. G. C. BQ6 5
Malmstone Ave. Red. BW67 113
Malm. The. Rick. AX27 35
Malpas Dr. Pnr. BD32 45
Malpas Rd. SE4 CD44 67
Malpas Rd. Dag. CP36 59
Malpas Rd. Slou. AQ40 52
Malpass Rd. Grays. DH41 71
Malta Rd. E10 CE33 48
Malta Rd. Til. DF44 71
Malta St. EC1 BY38 56
Maltby Rd. Chess. BM57 94
Maltby St. SE1 CA41 67
Malt House Clo. Wind. AQ47 72
Malthouse Ct. St. Alb. BG14 9
Sopwell La.
Malthouse Dr. Felt. BD49 74
Malt House Pass. SW13 BO44 65
Terrace, The,
Malting La. Epp. CO18 23
Maltings Hill. Ong. CV13 15
Maltings, The, Kings L. BA20 17
Maltings. The. Oxt. CG69 115
Malt La. Rad. BJ21 27
Maltmans La. Ger. Cr. AR31 43
Maltman's Pk. Grnf. BG38 54
Malton Ms. W10 BR39 55
Cambridge Gdns.
Malton Rd. W10 BR39 55
Malton St. SE18 CN43 68
Maltravers St. WC2 BX40 56
Arundel St.
Malt St. SE1 CB43 67
Malus Clo. Hem. H. AZ13 8
Malus Clo. Wey. AV57 91
Malus Rd. Wey. AV57 91
Malva Cl. SW18 BS46 76
St. Ann's Hill
Malvern Av. E4 CF29 39
Malvern Av. Bexh. CQ43 69
Malvern Av. Har. BE34 45
Malvern Clo. Hat. BO12 10
Malvern Clo. Mitch. BW52 86
Malvern Clo. St. Alb. BK11 9
Chiltern Rd.
Malvern Clo. Surb. BL54 85
Malvern Clo. Uxb. AZ34 44
Malvern Ct. SW7 BT42 66
Malvern Ct. Har. BF34 45
Malvern Dr. Felt. BD49 74
Malvern Dr. Ilf. CN35 49
Malvern Dr. Wdf. Grn. CJ28 40
Malvern Gdns. NW2 BR34 46
Malvern Gdns. NW6 BR37 55
Canterbury Rd.
Malvern Gdns. Har. BL31 46
Malvern Gdns. Loug. CK25 31
Malvern Gds. W9 BR39 55
Canterbury Rd.
Malvern Ms. NW6 BS38 56
Malvern Pl. W9 BS38 56
Malvern Rd. E6 CK37 58
Malvern Rd. E8 CB36 57
Malvern Rd. E11 CG34 49
Malvern Rd. N8 BX31 47
Malvern Rd. N17 CB31 48
Malvern Rd. NW6 BS38 56
Malvern Rd. Enf. CD22 30
Malvern Rd. Grays. DF42 71
Malvern Rd. Hayes. BB43 63
Malvern Rd. Hmptn. BF50 74
Malvern Rd. Horn. CU32 50
Malvern Rd. Orp. CO56 98
Malvern Rd. Surb. BL55 85
Malvern Rd. Th. Hth. BY52 86
Malvern Ter. N1 BY37 56
Malvern Ter. N9 CA26 39
Malvern Way W13 BJ39 54
Malvern Way, Hem. H. AY12 8
Malvern Way, Rick. AZ25 26
Malverton Rd. E3 CE37 57
Malvina Av. Grav. DG48 81
Malyons Rd. SE13 CE46 77
Malyons Rd. Swan. CT50 79
Malyons Ter. SE13 CE46 77
Manan Clo. Hem. H. BA14 8
Manaton Clo. West Borwd. BK25 27
Manaton Cres. Sthl. BF39 54
Manaton Rd. SE15 CB45 67
Manbey Gro. E15 CG36 58
Manbey Pk. Rd. E15 CG36 58
Manbey Rd. E15 CG36 58
Manbey St. E15 CG36 58
Manborough Av. E6 CK38 58
Manchester Dr. W10 BR38 55
Manchester Est. E14 CF42 67
Manchester Gro. E14 CF42 67
Manchester Rd. E14 CF41 67
Manchester Rd. N15 BZ32 48
Manchester Rd. Th. Hth. BZ52 87
Manchester Row Dart. CT45 69
Manchester Sq. W1 BV39 56
Manchester St. W1 BV39 56
Manchuria Rd. SW11 BV46 76
Manciple St. SE1 BZ41 67
Mancroft Rd. Hem. H. AY14 8
Mandalay Rd. SW4 BW46 76
Mandarin St. E14 CE40 57
Salter St.
Mandeville Clo. SE3 CG43 68
Vanbrugh Pk.
Mandeville Clo. Brox. CD13 12
Mandeville Clo. Guil. AQ69 118
Mandeville Clo. Wat. BB22 26
Mandeville Clo. Welw. G. C. BQ7 7
Mandeville Ct. Egh. AT49 72
Mandeville Dr. St. Alb. BG15 9
Mandeville Dr. Surb. BK54 84
Mandeville Houses, N1 BY37 56
Mandeville Pl. W1 BV40 56
Mandeville Rise. Welw. G. C. BQ7 7
Mandeville Rd. N14 BV27 38
Mandeville Rd. Enf. CC21 30
Mandeville Rd. Islw. BJ44 64
Mandeville Rd. Nthlt. BE36 54
Mandeville Rd. Pot. B. BT19 20
Mandeville Rd. Shep. AZ53 83
Mandeville St. E5 CD34 48
Mandon St. E14 CE40 57
Salter St.
Mandrake Rd. SW17 BU48 76
Mandrell Rd. SW2 BX46 76
Manette St. W1 BW39 56
Charing Cross Rd.
Manfarm Clo. Wind. AM45 61
Manford Clo. Chig. CO28 41
Manford Cross. Chig. CO28 41
Manford Way, Chig. CN28 40
Manfred Ct. SW15 BR46 75
Manfred Rd.
Manfred Rd. SW15 BR46 75
Mangles Rd. Guil. AR69 118
Mangold Way Belv. CP41 69
Mangrove La. Hert. CA10 12
Manho La. Slou. AQ43 62
Manilla St. E14 CE41 67
Manister Rd. SE2 CO41 69
Manley Ct. N16 CA34 48
Stoke Newington High St.
Manley Rd. Hem. H. AY13 8
Manley St. NW1 BV37 56
Mannicotts. Welw. G. C. BP8 5
Manning Gdns. Har. BK33 45
Manning Rd. E17 CC32 48
Manning Rd. Dag. CR36 59
Manning Rd. Orp. CP53 89
Manning St. S. Ock. CW40 60
Manningtree Rd. Ruis. BC35 44
Manningtree St. E1 CB39 57
Mannin Rd. Rom. CO33 50
Mannn St. SE17 BZ42 67
Mannock Dr. Loug. CM23 31
Mannock Rd. N22 BY31 47
Manns Clo. Islw. BH46 74
Manns Rd. Edg. BM29 37
Manoel Rd. Twick. BG48 74
Manor Alley, W4 BO42 65
Devonshire Rd.
Manor Av. SE4 CD44 67
Manor Av. Cat. CA65 105
Manor Av. Hem. H. AX15 8
Manor Av. Horn. CV32 51
Manor Av. Houns. BD45 64
Manor Av. Nthlt. BE36 54
Manor Av. Pde. Chig. CM28 40
Grange Cres.
Manorbrook SE3 CH45 68
Manor Cl. Leath. BB67 110
Manor Clo. NW7 BN28 37
Manor Dr.
Manor Clo. NW9 BM32 46
Manor Clo. Berk. AR13 7
Manor Clo. Dag. CS36 59
Manor Clo. Dart. CS45 69
Manor Clo. Dart. CU48 79
Manor Clo. Rom. CU32 50
Manor Clo. Ruis. BB33 44
Manor Clo. S. Ock. CW40 60
Manor Clo. Stai. AW49 73
Manor Clo. Warl. CD62 105
Eglise Rd.
Manor Clo. Wok. AV61 100
Manor Clo. Wor. Pk. BO54 85
Manor Cott. Nthwd. BB30 35
Manor Cotts. N2 BT30 38
Manor Ct. N2 BU32 47
Manor Ct. N14 BW27 38
Manor Ct. SW16 BX48 76
Manor Ct. W3 BM42 65
Manor Gdns.
Manor Ct. Enf. CB21 30
Manor Ct. Wey. AZ56 92
Manor Ct. Rd. W7 BH40 54
Manor Cres. Beac. AO28 34
Manor Cres. Guil. AQ69 118
Manor Cres. Horn. CV32 51
Manor Cres. Surb. BM53 85
Manor Cres. Wey. AY60 92
Manorcroft Rd. Egh. AT50 72
Manordene Clo. Surb. BJ54 84
Manor Dr. N14 BV26 38
Manor Dr. N20 BU28 38
Manor Dr. NW7 BN28 37
Manor Dr. Epsom BO57 94
Manor Dr. Esher BH55 84
Manor Dr. Felt. BD49 74
Manor Dr. St. Alb. BF17 18
Manor Dr. Sun. BC51 83
Manor Dr. Surb. BL53 85
Manor Dr. Wem. BL35 46
Manor Dr. Wey. AW58 92
Manor Dr. N. N. Mal. BN54 85
Manor Dr. The, Wor. Pk. BO54 85
Manor Farm Av. Shep. AZ53 83
Manor Farm Est. Stai. AR46 72
Manor Farm La. Egh. AT49 72
Manor Farm Rd. SW16 BY51 86
Manor Farm Rd. Wem. BK37 54
Manor Farm Way. Beac. AO29 34
Manor Flds. SW15 BQ46 75
Manor Fm. Dr. E4 CG27 40
Manor Fm. Rd. Enf. CB21 30
Manor Gdns. N7 BX34 47
Manor Gdns. SW20 BR51 85
Manor Gdns. W3 BM42 65
Manor Gdns. Guil. AQ69 118
Manor Gdns. Hmptn. BF50 74
Manor Gdns. Lthd. BD67 111
Manor Gdns. Rich. BL45 65
Manor Gdns. Ruis. BD35 45
Manor Gdns. Sth. Croy. CA57 96
Manor Gdns. Sun. BC51 83
Manorgate Rd. Kings. On T. BM51 85
Manor Grn Rd. Epsom. BM60 94
Manor Gro. SE15 CC43 67
Manor Gro. Beck. CE51 87
Manor Gro. Leath. BB67 110
Manor Gro. Maid. AH43 61
Manor Gro. Rich. BM45 65
Manor Hall Av. NW4 BQ30 37
Manor Hall Dr. NW4 BQ30 37
Manor Hall Gdns. E10 CE33 48
Manor Hatch. Harl. CO12 14
Manor Hill Bans. BU60 95
Manor Ho. Chis. CM51 88
Manor Ho. Surb. BK55 84
Manor Ho. Wor. Pk. BN54 85
Manor Ho. Ct. Shep. AZ54 83
Church Rd.
Manor Ho. Dr. NW6 BQ36 55
Manor House Gdns. Wat. BA19 17
Manorhouse La. Lthd. BE66 111
Manor Lane Fawk. DB54 90
Manor La. Felt. BC48 73
Manor La. Ger. Cr. AR33 43
Manor La. Hayes. BA43 63
Manor La. Sun. BC51 83
Manor La. Sutt. BS56 95
Manor La. Tad. BS68 113
Manor La. Ter. SE13 CG45 68
Manor Leaze, Egh. AT49 72
Manor Mead, Wey. AZ56 92
Manor Mt. SE23 CC47 77
Manor Par. Hayes. BA43 63
Manor Pk. SE13 CF45 67
Manor Pk. Chis. CM51 88
Manor Park. Hat. BO11 10
Manor Pk. Rich. BL45 65
Manor Pk. Clo. W. Wick. CE54 87
Manor Park Cres. Edg. BM29 37
Manor Pk. Dr. Har. BF31 45
Manor Park Gdns. Edg. BM28 37
Manor Pk. Rd. E12 CJ35 49
Manor Pk. Rd. N2 BT31 47
Manor Pk. Rd. Chis. CM51 88
Manor Pk. Rd. Sutt. BT56 95
Manor Pk. Rd. W. Wick. CE54 87
Manor Pl. SE17 BY42 66
Manor Pl. Chis. CM51 88
Manor Pl. Dart. CV47 80
Manor Pl. Felt. BC47 73
Manor Pl. Mitch. BW52 86
Manor Pl. Stai. AW49 73
Manor Pl. Sutt. BS56 95
Manor Pl. Walt. BB54 83
Manor Rd. E10 CE33 48
Manor Rd. E17 CD30 39
Manor Rd. N16 BZ34 48
Manor Rd. N17 CB30 39
Manor Rd. N22 BX29 38
Manor Rd. SE25 CB52 87
Manor Rd. SW20 BR51 85
Manor Rd. W13 BJ40 54
Manor Rd. Ashf. AY49 73
Manor Rd. Bark. CN36 58
Manor Rd. Barn. BR25 28
Manor Rd. Beac. AO28 34
Manor Rd. Beck. CE51 87
Manor Rd. Bex. CR47 79
Manor Rd. Dag. CS36 59
Manor Rd. Dart. CT45 69
Manor Rd. E. Mol. BG52 84
Manor Rd. Enf. BZ23 30
Manor Rd. Erith CT43 69
Manor Rd. Grays DB43 70
Manor Rd. Grays. DE43 71
Manor Rd. Guil. AQ69 118
Manor Rd. Har. BJ32 45
Manor Rd. Harl. CP8 6
Manor Rd. Hat. BM10 5
Manor Rd. Hayes. BC39 53
Manor Rd. Hodd. CE11 12
Manor Rd. Loug. CH22 31
Manor Rd. Loug. CH23 31
Manor Rd. Loug. CH25 31
Manor Rd. Mitch. BW52 86
Manor Rd. Pot. B. BR19 19
Manor Rd. Pot. B. BS19 20
Manor Rd. Red. BW68 113
Manor Rd. Reig. BR69 120
Manor Rd. Rich. BL45 65
Manor Rd. Rom. CP27 41
Manor Rd. Rom. CP32 50
Manor Rd. Rom. CQ26 41
Manor Rd. Rom. CU32 50
Manor Rd. Ruis. BA33 44
Manor Rd. St. Alb. BH13 9
Manor Rd. St. Alb. BK16 18
Manor Rd. Sev. CP65 107
Manor Rd. Sid. CN48 78
Manor Rd. Sutt. BR57 94
Manor Rd. Swans. DB46 80
Manor Rd. Tedd. BJ49 74
Manor Rd. Til. DG44 71
Manor Rd. Twick. BG48 74
Manor Rd. Wal. Abb. CF20 21
Manor Rd. Wall. BV56 95
Manor Rd. Walt. BB54 83
Manor Rd. Wat. BC23 26
Manor Rd. Wdf. Grn. CK29 40
Manor Rd. West. CK63 106
Manor Rd. W. Wick. CE55 87
Manor Rd. Wind. AM44 61
Manor Rd. Wok. AR61 100
Manor Rd. Wok. AV65 100
Manor Rd. N. Esher BH55 84
Manor Rd. N. Wall. BV56 95
Manor Rd. S. Esher BH56 93
Manorside Barn. BR24 28
Manor Sq. Dag. CP34 50
Manor St. Berk. AR13 7
Manor, The, Way Pur. BX59 95
Manor Val. Brent. BK42 64
Manor Vw. N3 BS30 38
Manor Vw. Beck. CE51 87
High St.
Manorville Rd. Hem. H. AX15 8
Manor Way E4 CF28 39
Manor Way, NW9 BO31 46
Manor Way, SE3 CG45 68
Manor Way Bans. BU61 104
Manor Way Beck. CE51 87
Manor Way, Bex. CR47 79
Manor Way Bexh. CS45 69
Manor Way Borwd. BN23 28
Manor Way Brom. CK53 88
Manor Way, Brwd. DA27 42
Manor Way. Chesh. AO18 16
Manor Way, Egh. AS50 72
Manor Way Enf. CA26 39
Manor Way, Guil. AO72 118
Manor Way Har. BF31 45
Manor Way, Lthd. BG61 102
Manor Way Mitch. BW52 86
Manor Way Orp. CM53 88
Manor Way, Pot. B. BS18 20
Manor Way Rain. CT39 59
Manor Way, Rick. AZ24 26
Manor Way, Ruis. BB33 44
Manor Way. Sth. Croy. CA57 96
Manor Way Sthl. BD42 64
Manor Way Swans. DB45 70
Manor Way, Wal. Cr. CD18 21
Manor Way Wall. BV56 95
Manorway, Wdf. Grn. CJ28 40
Manor Way, Wok. AT64 100
Manor Way Wor. Pk. BO54 85
Manor Waye, Uxb. AX37 53
Manor Wd. Rd. Pur. BX60 95
Manresa Rd. SW3 BU42 66
Mansard Beeches SW17 BV49 76
Manscroft Rd. Hem. H. AW12 8
Manse Clo. Hayes. BA43 63
Mansel Clo. Guil. AQ68 109
Mansell Clo. Slou. AQ39 52
Mansell Clo. Wind. AM44 61
Mansell Gro. E17 CE30 39
Mansell Rd. W3 BN41 65
Mansell Rd. Grnf. BF39 54
Mansell St. E1 CA39 57
Mansel Rd. SW19 BR50 75
Manse Pde. Swan. CU52 89
Mansergh Cl. SE18 CK43 68
Stadium Rd.
Manse Rd. N16 CA34 48
Manser Rd. Rain. CT38 59
Manse Way. Swan. CU52 89
Mansfield, Saw. CO6 6
Mansfield Av. N15 BZ31 48
Mansfield Av. Barn. BU25 29
Mansfield Clo. N9 CB25 30
Mansfield Clo. Orp. CP54 89
Mansfield Clo. Wey. AZ56 92
Mansfield Dr. Hayes BB38 53
Mansfield Dr. Red. BW67 113
Mansfield Gdns. Horn. CV34 51
Mansfield Hill E4 CE26 39
Mansfield Ms. W1 BV39 56
Duchess St.
Mansfield Pl. Sth. Croy. BZ57 96
Mansfield Rd. E11 CH32 49
Mansfield Rd. E17 CD31 48
Mansfield Rd. NW3 BU35 47
Mansfield Rd. W3 BM38 55
Mansfield Rd. Chess. BK56 93
Mansfield Rd. Ilf. CL33 49
Mansfield Rd. Sth. Croy. BZ57 96
Mansfield Rd. Swan. CT50 79
Mansfield St. W1 BV39 56
Mansford St. E2 CB37 57
Manship Rd. Mitch. BV50 76
Mansion House La. EC4 BZ39 57
St. Swithin's La.
Mansion House Pl. EC4 BZ39 57
Mansion Ho. St.
Mansion House St. EC2 BZ39 57
Cornhill
Mansion La. Iver AU40 52
Mans St. SW10 BT44 66
Manson Ms. SW7 BT42 66
Manson Pl. SW7 BT42 66
Manstead Clo. Rain. CU39 59
Mansted Gdns. Rom. CP33 50
Manston Av. Sthl. BF42 64
Manston Clo. Wal. Cr. CC18 21
Manstone Rd. NW2 BR35 46
Manston Rd. Harl. CN11 13
Manston Way. Horn. CU36 59
Mantell St. N1 BY37 56
Manthorp Rd. SE18 CM42 68
Mantilla Rd. SW17 BV49 76
Mantle Rd. SE4 CD45 67
Manton Av. W7 BH41 64
Manton Clo. Hayes BB40 53
Manton Rd. SE2 CO42 69
Mantua Rd. SW11 BT45 66
Mantus Clo. E1 CC38 57
Mantus Rd.
Mantus Rd. E1 CC38 57
Manus Way N20 BT27 38
Manville Gdns. SW17 BV48 76
Manville Rd. SW17 BX48 76
Manwood Rd. SE4 CD46 77
Manwood St. E16 CK40 58
Manygate La. Shep. BA54 83
Many Gates, SW12 BV48 76
Mapel Rd. Wok. AV65 100
Mapesbury Rd. NW2 BR36 55
Mape St. E2 CB38 57
Maple Av. E4 CD28 39
Maple Av. W3 BO40 55
Maple Av. Har. BF34 45
Maple Av. St. Alb. BG11 9
Maple Av. Upmin. CX35 51
Maple Av. West Dr. AY40 53
Maple Cl. Hat. BP13 10
Maple Clo. N16 CB32 48
Timberwharf Rd.
Maple Clo. SW4 BW46 76
Clarence Av.
Maple Clo. Brwd. DC27 122
Maple Clo. Buck. H. CJ27 40
Maple Clo. Bush. BE23 27
Maple Clo. Horn. CU34 50
Maple Clo. Mitch. BV51 86
Maple Clo. Orp. CM53 88
Maple Clo. Ruis. BC32 44
Maple Ct. Egh. AQ50 72
Maple Ct. N. Mal. BO52 85
Maple Cres. Sid. CO46 79
Maple Cres. Slou. AQ40 52
Maplecroft La. Wal. Abb. CG14 13
Mapledale Av. Croy. CB55 87
Mapledene, Chis. CM50 78
Mapledene Rd. E8 CA36 57
Maplefield, St. Alb. BF18 18
Maplefield Acres. St. Alb. BF18 18
Maplefield La. Ch. St. G. AQ24 25
Maple Gdns. Edg. BO29 37
Maple Grn. Hem. H. AV12 7
Maple Gro. NW9 BN33 46
Maple Gro. W5 BK41 64
Maple Gro. Brent. BJ43 64
Maple Gro. Guil. AR69 118
Maple Gro. Sthl. BE39 54
Maple Gro. Welw. G. C. BR6 5
Maple Gro. Wok. AS64 100
Maple Hill. Hem. H. AR18 16
Maple Ho. SE8 CD43 67
Idonia St.
Mapleleafe Gdns. Ilf. CL31 49
Maple Pl. W1 BW38 56
Maple St.
Maple Pl. West Dr. AY40 53
Maple Rd. E11 CG32 49
Maple Rd. SE20 CB51 87
Maple Rd. Ash. BK63 102
Maple Rd. Dart. CV47 80
Maple Rd. Grav. DH49 81
Maple Rd. Grays. DE43 71
Maple Rd. Hayes BD38 54
Maple Rd. Red. BU72 121
Maple Rd. Surb. BK53 84
Maple Rd. Whyt. CA62 105
Maplescombe La. Farn. CX55 90
Maplescombe La. Farn. CX56 99
Maples Pl. E1 CB39 57
Raven Row
Maple Springs, Wal. Abb. CH20 22
Maplestead Rd. SW2 BX47 76
Maplestead Rd. Dag. CO37 59
Maples, The, Bans. BS60 95
Maples, The Cher. AU57 91
Maples, The Harl. CL13 13
Maple St. W1 BW39 56
Maple St. Rom. CS31 50
Maple Ter. Rick. AV28 34
Maplethorpe Rd. Th. Hth. BY52 86
Mapleton Clo. Brom. CH53 88
Mapleton Cres. SW18 BS46 76
Mapleton Rd.
Mapleton Cres. Enf. CC22 30
Mapleton Rd. SW18 BS46 76
Mapleton Rd. Enf. CB23 30
Mapleton Rd. West. CN68 115
Maple Wy. Couls. BV64 104
Maplin Clo. N21 BX25 29
Maplin Rd. E16 CH39 58
Mapperley Dr. Wdf. Grn. CG29 40
Forest Drive
Maran Way Belv. CP41 69
Marbeck Clo. Wind. AL44 61
Marble Arch W1 BU40 56
Marble Clo. W3 BM40 55
Gunnersbury La.
Marble Hill River Path, Twick. BK47 74
Orleans Rd.
Marble Hl. Clo. Twick. BJ47 74
Marble Hl. Gdns. Twick. BJ47 74
Marbles Way. Tad. BQ63 103
Marbrook Ct. SE12 CJ48 78
Marcellus Rd. N7 BX34 47
Marcet Rd. Dart. CV46 80
Marchant Rd. E11 CF34 48
Marchant St. SE14 CD43 67
Marchbank Rd. SW5 BR43 65
Marchmont Rd. Rich. BL46 75

Marchmont Rd. Wall.	BW57	95
Marchmont St. WC1	BX38	56
March Rd. Twick.	BJ47	74
March Rd. Wey.	AZ56	92
Marchwood Clo. SE5	CA43	67
Southampton Way		
Marchwood Cres. W5	BK39	54
Marcia Rd. SE1	CA42	67
Marcilly Rd. SW18	BT46	76
Marconi Rd. Grav.	DE48	81
Marconi Way Sthl.	BF39	54
Marcon Pl. E8	CB35	48
Marco Rd. W6	BP41	65
Marcus Ct. E15	CG37	58
Marcus Rd. Dart.	CU47	79
Marcus St. E15	CG37	58
Marcus St. SW18	BS46	76
Marcus Ter. SW18	BS46	76
Denton St.		
Mardale Dr. NW9	BN32	46
Mardell Rd. Croy.	CC53	87
Marden Av. Brom.	CG53	88
Marden Clo. Chig.	CO27	41
Marden Cres. Bex.	CS46	79
Marden Cres. Croy.	BX53	86
Marden Rd. N17	CA30	39
Avenue, The.		
Marden Rd. Croy.	BX53	86
Marden Rd. Rom.	CT32	50
Marden Sq. SE16	CB41	67
Drummond Rd.		
Marder Rd. W13	BJ41	64
Mardyke Rd. Harl.	CO10	6
Mardyke St. SE17	BZ42	67
Townsend St.		
Marebell Way Rom.	CV29	42
Marechal Niel Av. Sid.	CM48	78
Mareschal Rd. Guil.	AR71	118
Mares Field Croy.	CA55	87
Maresfield Gdns. NW3	BT35	47
Mare St. E8	CB37	57
Marfield Ct. N. Mal.	BO54	85
Margaret Av. E4	CE25	30
Margaret Av. Brwd.	DC26	122
Margaret Av. St. Alb.	BG12	9
Margaret Bondfield Av. Bark.	CO36	59
Margaret Bldgs. N16	CA33	48
Margaret Rd.		
Margaret Clo. Pot. B.	BT20	20
Margaret Clo. Rom.	CU32	50
Margaret Clo. Stai.	AX50	73
Margaret Ct. W1	BW39	56
Margaret St.		
Margaret Dr. Horn.	CW33	51
Margaret Rd. N16	CA33	48
Margaret Rd. Barn.	BT24	29
Margaret Rd. Bex.	CP46	79
Margaret Rd Epp.	CO18	23
Margaret Rd. Guil.	AR71	118
Margaret Rd. Rom.	CU32	50
Margaret St. W1	BV39	56
Margaretta Ter. SW3	BU43	66
Margaretting Rd. E12	CJ34	49
Margaret Way Couls.	BY58	95
Margaret Way, Ilf.	CJ32	49
Margate Rd. SW2	BX46	76
Margeholes Wat.	BE27	36
Margery Gro. Tad.	BR68	112
Margery La. Tad.	BR68	112
Margery Pk. Rd. E7	CH36	58
Margery Rd. Dag.	CP34	50
Margery St. WC1	BY38	56
Margin Dr. SW19	BQ49	75
Margravine Gdns. W6	BQ42	65
Margravine Rd. W6	BQ42	65
Marham Gdns. SW18	BU47	76
Marham Gdns. Mord.	BT53	86
Marian Clo. Hayes.	BD38	54
Marian Ct. Sutt.	BS56	95
Marian Gdns. Horn.	CW34	51
Marian Pl. E2	CB37	57
Marian Rd. SW16	BW51	86
Marian Way. NW10	BO36	55
Maria Ter. E1	CC38	57
Maricas Av. Har.	BG29	36
Marie Therese Clo. N. Mal.	BN53	85
Marigold St. SE16	CB41	67
Marina Av. N. Mal.	BP53	85
Marina Clo. Brom.	CG52	88
Marina Clo. Rom.	CS32	50
Marina Dri. Dart.	CX47	80
Marina Dr. Dart.	CW47	80
Marina Dr. Grav.	DF47	81
Marina Dr. Well.	CN44	68
Marina Gdns. Wal. Cr.	CC18	21
Marina Pl. SW8	BX44	66
Priory Gro.		
Marina Way, Hayes	AW40	53
Marina Way, Iver	AV40	52
Marina Way Tedd.	BK50	74
Fairways		
Marine Av. Well.	CO45	69
Marinefield Rd. SW6	BS44	66
Mariner Gdns. Rich.	BJ48	74
Ashburnham Rd.		
Mariner Rd. E12	CL35	49
Dersingham Av.		
Mariner Way, Hem. H.	AZ14	8
Marine St. SE16	CB41	67
Enid St.		
Marion Av. Shep.	AZ53	83
Marion Clo. Bush.	BE23	27
Marion Clo. Grays.	DC40	71
Marion Clo. Ilf.	CM29	40
Marion Cres. Orp.	CO53	89
Marion Gro. Wdf. Grn.	CG28	40
Marion Rd. NW7	BP28	37
Marion Rd. Th. Hth.	BZ53	87
Mariott Rd. Dart.	CW47	80
Marischal Rd. SE13	CF45	67
Marish La. Uxb.	AU31	43
Mariso Clo. Grays.	DG42	71
Maritime St. E3	CD38	57
Marius Rd. SW17	BV48	76
Marjorams Av. Loug.	CL23	31
Marjorie Gro. SW11	BU45	66
Markab Rd. Nthwd.	BC28	35
Markad Rd. Nthwd.	BB28	35
Mark Av. E4	CE25	30
Mark Clo. Bexh.	CQ44	69
Mark Clo. Sthl.	BF40	54
Mark Dr. Ger. Cr.	AR28	34
Marke Clo. Kes.	CK56	97
Markedge La. Couls.	BU65	104
Markedge La. Red.	BU66	113
Markenfield Rd. Guil.	AR70	118
Market Ct. W1	BW39	56
Market Pl.		
Market Field Rd. Red.	BU70	121
Market Hill, SE18	CL41	68
Market Link Rom.	CT31	50
Mkt. Meadow Pl. Orp.	CP52	89
Market Ms. W1	BV40	56
Market Oak La. Hem. H.	AZ15	8
Market Pde. SE15	CB44	67
Market Pl. N2	BU31	47
Market Pl. NW11	BS31	47
Market Pl. W1	BW39	56
Market Pl. W3	BN40	55
Market Pl. Brent.	BK43	64
Market Pl. Dart.	CW47	80
Market Pl. Dor.	BJ71	119
Market Pl. Enf.	BZ24	30
Market Pl. Ger. Cr.	AR30	34
Market Pl. Grav.	DH47	81
Market Pl. Grays.	DD40	71
Market Place. Hat.	BP12	10
Market Pl. Kings-on-t.	BK51	84
Market Pl. Rom.	CO24	32
Market Pl. Rom.	CT32	50
Market Pl. St. Alb.	BG13	9
Market Pl. Wat.	BD24	27
Market Rd. N7	BX36	56
Market Rd. Rich.	BM45	65
Market Row, SW9	BY45	66
Atlantic Rd.		
Market Sq. E14	CE39	57
Market Sq. N9	CB27	39
Market Sq. Brom.	CH51	88
Market Sq. Hem. H.	AX13	8
Market Sq. West.	CM66	115
Market St. E6	CK37	58
Market St. SE18	CL42	68
Market St. Dart.	CW47	80
Market St. Guil.	AR71	118
Market St. Harl.	CP9	6
Market St. Wat.	BC24	26
Market, The, Cars.	BT54	86
Market Way. Slou.	AU42	62
Markfield Croy.	CB58	96
Markfield Gdns. E4	CE26	39
Markfield Rd. W15	CB31	48
Markfield Rd. Cat.	CB66	114
Mark Grn. Wat.	BD28	36
Mark Hall Moors, Harl.	CO9	6
Markham Sq. SW3	BU42	66
Markham St. SW3	BU42	66
Markhole Clo. Hamptn.	BE50	74
Markhouse Av. E17	CD32	48
Mark House Rd. E17	CD32	48
Mark La. EC3	CA40	57
Mark La. Grav.	DJ47	81
Markmanor Av. E17	CD33	48
Mark Oak La. Lthd.	BF64	102
Mark Pl. Sthl.	BF40	54
Mark Rd. N22	BY30	38
Mark Rd. Hem. H.	AZ12	8
Marks Av. Grav.	DF47	81
Marks Av. Ong.	CW17	24
Marksbury Av. Rich.	BM45	65
Marks Rd. Rom.	CS32	50
Marks Rd. Warl.	CD62	105
Mark St. E1	CA39	57
Mark St. E15	CG36	58
Mark St. EC2	CA38	57
Mark St. Reig.	BS70	121
Markville Gdns. Cat.	CB66	114
Markway Sun.	BD51	84
Mark Way. Swan.	CU53	89
Markwell Clo. SE26	CB49	77
Markyate Rd. Dag.	CO35	50
Marlands Rd. Ilf.	CK31	49
Marlboro' Rd. Dart.	CV46	80
Marlboro' Rd. Sth. Croy.	BZ57	96
Marlboro' Rd. Sthl.	BD41	64
Marlboro' Rd. Wat.	BC24	26
Marlborough Av. E8	CB37	57
Marlborough Av. N14	BW27	38
Marlborough Av. Edg.	BM27	37
Marlborough Av. Ruis.	BA32	44
Marlborough Bldgs. SW3	BU42	66
Marlborough Clo. N20	BU27	38
Marlborough Clo. SW19	BU50	76
Marlborough Clo. Grays.	DE41	71
Marlborough Clo. Orp.	CN54	88
Marlborough Clo. Upmin.	CZ33	51
Marlborough Clo. Walt.	BD55	84
Marlborough Ct. W8	BS42	66
Marlborough Cres. W4	BN41	65
Marlborough Cres. Sev.	CT65	107
Marlborough Dr. Ilf.	CK31	49
Marlborough Gdns. N20	BU27	38
Marlborough Gdns. Surb.	BK54	84
Marlborough Gdns. Upmin.	CY33	51
Marlborough Gte. St. Alb.	BH13	9
Marlborough Gro. SE1	CB42	67
Marlborough Hill, NW8	BT37	56
Marlborough Hill Har.	BG32	45
Marlborough Mans. NW6	BS35	47
Marlborough Park Av. Sid.	CO47	79
Marlborough Pl. NW8	BT37	56
Marlborough Rise, Hem. H.	AY12	8
Marlborough Rd. E4	CE29	39
Marlborough Rd. E7	CJ36	58
Marlborough Rd. E15	CG35	49
Borthwick Rd.		
Marlborough Rd. E18	CH31	49
Marlborough Rd. N9	CA26	39
Marlborough Rd. N19	BW34	47
Marlborough Rd. N22	BX29	38
Marlborough Rd. SE7	CJ43	68
Marlborough Rd. SW1	BW40	56
Marlborough Rd. SW19	BT50	76
Marlborough Rd. W4	BN42	65
Marlborough Rd. W5	BK41	64
Marlborough Rd. Ashf.	AX49	73
Marlborough Rd. Bexh.	CP45	69
Marlborough Rd. Brom.	CJ52	88
Marlborough Rd. Brwd.	DA25	33
Marlborough Rd. Dag.	CO35	50
Marlborough Rd. Dor.	BJ71	119
Marlborough Rd. Felt.	BD48	74
Marlborough Rd. Har.	BH31	45
Marlborough Rd. Hmptn.	BF50	74
Marlborough Rd. Islw.	BJ44	64
Marlborough Rd. Rich.	BL46	75
Marlborough Rd. Rom.	CR31	50
Marlborough Rd. St. Alb.	BH13	9
Marlborough Rd. Slou.	AR42	62
Marlborough Rd. Sutt.	BS55	86
Marlborough Rd. Uxb.	AZ38	53
Marlborough Rd. Wok.	AT61	100
Marlborough St. SW3	BU42	66
Marle Gdns. Wal. Abb.	CF19	21
Marler Rd. SE23	CD47	77
Marlescroft Loug.	CL25	31
Marley Av. Bexh.	CP43	69
Marley Clo. Grnf.	BF37	54
Marley Clo. Wey.	AV57	91
Marley Rd. Welw. G. C.	BS9	5
Marlin Clo. Berk.	AP12	7
Marlingdene Clo. Hamptn.	BF50	74
Marlings Clo. Chis.	CN52	88
Marlings Clo. Whyt.	CA62	105
Marlings Pk. Av. Chis.	CN52	88
Marling Way, Grav.	DJ49	81
Marlin Sq. Wat.	BB19	17
Marlins Turn, Hem. H.	AW12	8
Marloes Clo. Wem.	BK35	45
Marloes Rd. W8	BS41	66
Marloes, The, NW8	BT37	56
Marlo, The, Ash.	BL62	103
Marlow Clo. SE20	CB52	87
Marlow Ct. NW6	BQ36	55
Marlow Cres. Twick.	BH46	74
Marlow Dr. Sutt.	BQ55	85
Marlowe Clo. Chis.	CM50	78
Marlowe Clo. Ilf.	CM30	40
Marlowe Gdns. Rom.	CV30	42
Marlowe Rd. E17	CF31	48
Marlowes, Hem. H.	AX14	8
Marlowe Sq. Mitch.	BV52	86
Marlowes, The, Dart.	CS45	69
Marlow Gdns. Hayes.	BA41	63
Marlow Gdns. Rom.	CV30	42
Marlow Rd. E6	CK38	58
Marlow Rd. SE20	CB52	87
Marlow Rd. Sthl.	BE41	64
Marlpit Av. Couls.	BX62	104
Marlpit La. Couls.	BW61	104
Marl St. SW18	BT45	66
Marlton St. SE10	CG42	68
Marlyns Clo. Guil.	AT68	109
Marlyns Dri. Guil.	AT68	109
Marlyns Dr. Guil.	AT69	118
Marlyon Rd. Ilf.	CO28	41
Marmadon Rd. SE18	CN42	68
Marmion App. E4	CE28	39
Marmion Clo.		
Marmion Av. E4	CD28	39
Marmion Clo. E4	CE28	39
Marmion Rd. SW11	BV45	66
Marmont Rd. SE15	CB44	67
Marmora Rd. SE22	CC46	77
Marmot Rd. Houns.	BD45	64
Marne Av. N11	BV28	38
Marnell Way Houns.	BD45	64
Marne St. W10	BR38	55
Marney Rd. SW11	BV45	66
Marnham Av. NW2	BR35	46
Marnham Cres. Grnf.	BF37	54
Marnham Rise, Hem. H.	AW12	8
Marnock Rd. SE4	CD46	77
Maroon St. E14	CD39	57
Marquess Gro. N1	BZ36	57
Marquess Rd. N1	BZ36	57
Marquis Clo. Wem.	BL36	55
Marquis Rd. N4	BX33	47
Marquis Rd. N22	BX29	38
Marquis Rd. NW1	BW36	56
Marrick Clo. SW15	BP45	65
Marrilyne Av. Enf.	CD22	30
Marriot Clo. Felt.	BA46	73
Marriot Rd. Barn.	BQ24	28
Marriots Clo.	BO32	46
Marriott Rd. E15	CG37	58
Marriott Rd. N4	BX33	47
Marriott Rd. N10	BU30	38
Mar Rd. S. Ock.	DB38	60
Marrshall Clo. Har.	BG33	45
Marryat Rd. SW19	BQ49	75
Marryat Rd. Enf.	CB21	30
Marryatt Pl. SW19	BR49	75
Marsala Rd. SE13	CE45	67
Marsden Grn. Welw. G. C.	BP8	5
Marsden Rd. N9	CB27	39
Marsden Rd. SE15	CA45	67
Marsden Rd. Welw. G. C.	BP8	5
Marsden St. NW5	BV36	56
Marshall Av. St. Alb.	BH12	9
Marshall Clo. Houns.	BE46	74
Marshall Gdns. SE1	BY41	66
London Rd.		
Marshall Rd. N17	BZ30	39
Marshalls Clo. Epsom	BN60	94
Marshalls Dr. Rom.	CT31	50
Marshall's Gro. SE18	CK42	68
Marshalls Rd. Rom.	CS31	50
Marshall's Rd. Sutt.	BS56	95
Marshall St. W1	BW39	56
Marshals Dr. St. Alb.	BJ12	9
Marshalsea Rd. SE1	BZ41	67
Marshalswick La. St. Alb.	BJ12	9
Marsham Clo. Chis.	CL49	78
Marsham La. Ger. Cr.	AS32	43
Marsham St. SW1	BW41	66
Marsham Way. Ger. Cr.	AS32	43
Marsh Av. Epsom	BO58	94
Marsh Av. Loug.	CM23	31
Marsh Av. Mitch.	BU51	86
Marshbrooke Clo. SE3	CJ45	68
Marsh Clo. NW7	BO27	37
Marshcroft Dr. Wal. Cr.	CD18	21
Southmead Cr.		
Marsh Dr. NW9	BO32	46
Marshe Clo. Pot. B.	BT19	20
Marsh Farm Rd. Twick.	BH47	74
Marshfield St. E14	CF41	67
Marshfoot Rd. Grays.	DF42	71
Marshgate La. E15	CE37	57
Marsh Grn. Rd. Dag.	CR37	59
Marsh Hill, E9	CD35	48
Marsh Hill, Wal. Abb.	CG17	22
Marsh La. E10	CE34	48
Marsh La. NW7	BN28	37
Marsh La. W17	CB30	39
Marsh La. Harl.	CQ8	6
Marsh La. Maid.	AJ40	61
Marsh La. Stan.	BK28	36
Marsh La. Wey.	AW56	92
Marshmoor Hat.	BQ14	10
Marsh Rd. Pnr.	BE31	45
Marsh Rd. Wem.	BK37	54
Marsh St. E14	CE42	67
Marsh St. Dart.	CW45	70
Marsh St. Dart.	CX45	70
Marsh St. Dart.	CX46	80
Marsland Rd. SE17	BY42	66
Marston Epsom	BN58	94
Marston Av. Chess.	BL57	94
Marston Av. Dag.	CR34	50
Marston Clo. NW6	BT36	56
Marston Clo. Hem. H.	AZ14	8
Marston Gdns. Dag.	CR34	50
Marston Rd. Hodd.	CE11	12
Marston Rd. Ilf.	CK30	40
Marston Rd. Tedd.	BJ49	74
Marston Way SE19	BY50	76
Marsworth Av. Pnr.	BD30	36
Martaban Rd. N16	CA34	48
Listria Pk.		
Martello St. E8	CB36	57
Martell Rd. SE21	BZ48	77
Marten Gte. St. Alb.	BJ11	9
Marten Rd. E17	CE30	39
Martens Av. Bexh.	CR45	69
Martens Clo. Bexh.	CS45	69
Martha Rd. E15	CG36	58
Martha St. E1	CB39	57
Marthorne Cres. Har.	BG30	36
Martian Av. Hem. H.	AZ12	8
Martin Bowes Rd. SE9	CK45	68
Martin Cl. Hat.	BP13	10
Martin Clo. Croy	CC59	96
Martin Clo. Sth. Croy.	CC58	96
Martin Clo. Warl.	CB61	105
Martin Clo. Sth. Croy.	CC58	96
Martin Cres. Croy.	BY54	86
Martindale, SW14	BN46	75
Martindale Av. Orp.	CN56	97
Martindale Rd. SW12	BV47	76
Martindale Rd. Hem. H.	AV13	7
Martindale Rd. Houns.	BE45	64
Martin Dene, Bexh.	CQ46	79
Martin Dr. Nthlt.	BE35	45
Martin Dr. Rain.	CU38	59
Martineau Dr. Dor.	BJ72	119
Martineau Rd. N5	BY35	47
Martineau St. Est. E1	CC40	57
Martingale Clo. Rich.	BK48	74
Martin Gdns. Dag.	CP35	50
Martin Gro. Mord.	BS52	86
Martin La. EC4	BZ40	57
Martin Rise, Bexh.	CQ46	79
Martin Rd. Dag.	CP35	50
Martin Rd. Dart.	CV48	80
Martin Rd. Guil.	AQ69	118
Martin Rd. Slou.	AP41	62
Martin Rd. S. Ock.	CW40	60
Martins Bldgs. SW18	BS46	76
Frogmore		
Martins Clo. Guil.	AU70	118
Martins Clo. Orp.	CP52	89
Martins Dr. Wal. Cr.	CD17	21
Martins Mt. Barn.	BS24	29
Martin's Rd. Brom.	CG51	88
Martins, The, SE26	CB49	77
Lawrie Park Gdns.		
Martins Wk. N10	BV29	38
Martin Way SW20	BQ51	85
Martin Way, Wok.	AQ62	100
Martland Rd. Wey.	AW57	92
Martlesham Clo. Horn.	CV35	51
Martlet Gro. Nthlt.	BD38	54
Javelin Way		
Martlett Ct. WC2	BX39	56
Drury La.		
Martley Dr. Ilf.	CL32	49
Mart St. WC2	BX40	56
Floral St.		
Martyr Clo. St. Alb.	BG15	9
Creighton Av.		
Martyr, S La. Wok.	AT59	91
Marvell Av. Hayes	BC39	53
Marvels Clo. SE12	CH48	78
Marvels La. SE12	CH48	78
Marville Rd. SW6	BR43	65
Marwood Clo. Well.	CO45	69
Marwood Way, SE16	CB42	67
Catlin St.		
Mary Ann's Bldgs. SE8	CE43	67
Maryatt Av. Har.	BF34	45
Marybank, SE18	CK42	68
Frances St.		
Maryfield Clo. Bex.	CT48	79
Mary Hill Clo. Ken.	BZ62	105
Mary Kingsley Pl. N6	BV33	47
Maryland. Hat.	BO13	10
Maryland Pk. E15	CG35	49
Maryland Rd. E15	CF35	48
Maryland Rd. N22	BX29	38
Maryland Rd. Th. Hth.	BY51	86
Maryland Sq. E15	CG35	49
Marylands Rd. W9	BS38	56
Maryland St. E15	CF35	48
Maryland Way Sun.	BC51	83
Marylebone High St. W1	BV39	56
Marylebone La. W1	BV39	56
Marylebone Ms. W1	BV39	56
Marylebone Rd. NW1	BU39	56
Marylebone St. W1	BV39	56
Marylee Way SE11	BX42	66
Mary Macarthur Ho. W14	BR43	65
Maryon Gro. SE7	CK42	68
Maryon Ms. NW3	BU35	47
South End Rd.		
Maryon Rd. SE7	CK42	68
Mary Pl. W11	BR40	55
Mary Rd. Guil.	AR71	118
Mary's Av. Berk.	AO12	7
Maryside. Slou.	AS41	62
Mary's Ter. Twick.	BJ47	74
Mary St. N1	BZ37	57
Mary Ter. NW1	BV37	56
Masbro' Rd. W14	BQ41	65
Mascalls Ct. SE7	CJ43	68
Victoria Way		
Mascalls Gdns. Brwd.	CZ28	42
Mascalls La. Brwd.	CZ28	42
Mascalls Rd. SE7	CJ43	68
Mascotts Clo. NW2	BP34	46
Masefield Av. Borwd.	BM25	28
Masefield Av. Stan.	BH28	36
Masefield Av. Sthl.	BF40	54
Masefield Clo. Erith	CT44	69
Masefield Clo. Rom.	CU30	41
Masefield Cres. N14	BV25	29
Masefield Cres. Rom.	CV30	42
Masefield Dr. Upmin.	CY33	51
Masefield Gdns. E6	CL38	58
Masefield La. Hayes	BC38	53
Masefield Rd. Dart.	CX46	80
Masefield Rd. Grav.	DE48	81
Masefield Rd. Grays.	DF41	71
Masefield Rd. Hamptn.	BE49	74
Mashie Rd. W3	BO39	55
Mashiters Hill Rom.	CS30	41
Mashiters Wk. Rom.	CT30	41
Maskell Rd. SW17	BT48	76
Mason Clo. E16	CH40	58
Masonic Hall Rd. Cher.	AV53	82
Mason Pl. Mitch.	BU51	86
Mason Rd. Wdf. Grn.	CG28	40
Mason's Arms Yd. W1	BV40	56
Maddox St.		
Mason's Av. EC2	BZ39	57
Masons Av. Croy.	BZ55	87
Masons Av. Har.	BH31	45
Mason's Bridge Rd. Red.	BV73	121
Masons Ct. Wem.	BM34	46
Mason's Green La. W3	BM38	55
Masons Hill, SE18	CL42	68
Masons Hill Brom.	CH52	88
Masons Paddock, Dor.	BJ70	119
Masons Pl. EC1	BY38	56
Masons Rd. Enf.	CB21	30
Mason's Rd. Hem. H.	AZ13	8
Mason St. SE17	BZ42	67
Mason's Yd. SW1	BW40	56
Duke St.		
Mason Way, Wal. Abb.	CG20	22
Massey Clo. N11	BV28	38
Grove Rd.		
Massie Rd. E8	CB36	57
Graham Rd.		
Massinger St. SE17	CA42	67
Massingham St. E1	CC38	57
Masson Av. Ruis.	BD36	54
Master Gunner Pl. SE18	CK43	68
Masterman Rd. E6	CK38	58
Masters St. E1	CC39	57
Mast House Ter. E14	CE42	67
Maswell Pk. Cres. Houns.	BG46	74
Maswell Pk. Rd. Houns.	BF46	74
Matcham Rd. E11	CG34	49
Matching Rd. Harl.	CR9	6
Matfield Clo. Brom.	CH53	88
Matfield Rd. Belv.	CR43	69
Matham Gro. SE22	CA45	67
Matham Rd. E. Mol.	BG53	84
Matheson Pl. W14	BR42	65
Matheson Rd. W14	BR43	65
Mathews Av. E6	CL37	58
Mathews La. Stai.	AV49	72
Mathews Yd. WC2	BX39	56
Shorts Gdns.		
Matilda House, E1	CB40	57
Matilda St. N1	BX37	56
Matlock Ct. SE5	BZ45	67
Matlock Cres. Sutt.	BR55	85
Matlock Cres. Wat.	BD27	36
Matlock Gdns. Horn.	CW34	51
Matlock Gdns. Sutt.	BR56	94
Matlock Pl. Sutt.	BR56	94
Matlock Rd. E10	CF32	48
Matlock Rd. Cat.	CA64	105

Matlock St. E14 CD39 57
Matlock Way, N. Mal. BN51 85
Matrimony Pl. SW8 BW44 66
Wandsworth Rd.
Matt Arnold Clo. Cob. BC60 92
Matthew Parker St. SW1 BW41 66
Matthews Av. E6 CL37 58
Folkestone Rd.
Matthews Pk. Av. E15 CG36 58
Matthews St. SW11 BU44 66
Matthew St. Reig. BS72 121
Matthias Rd. N16 BZ35 48
Mattingley Way SE15 CA43 67
Mattison Rd. N4 BY32 47
Matyr Rd. Guil. AR71 118
Maude Cres. Wat. BC22 26
Maude Rd. E17 CD32 48
Maude Rd. SE5 CA44 67
Maude Rd. Swan. CU50 79
Maudesville Cotts. W7 BH40 54
Maude Ter. E17 CD31 48
Maud Gdns. E13 CG37 58
Maud Rd.
Maud Gdns. Bark. CN37 58
Maud Rd. E10 CF34 48
Maud Rd. E13 CG37 58
Maudslay Rd. SE9 CK45 68
Maud St. E16 CG39 58
Mauleverer Rd. SW2 BX46 76
Maunder Rd. W7 BH40 54
Maunolid Way Brwd. DA25 33
Maunsel St. SW1 BW42 66
Maurice Ave. Cat. BZ64 105
Maurice Av. N22 BY30 38
Maurice Brown Clo. NW7 BQ28 37
Maurice Wk. NW11 BT31 47
Maurier Clo. Nthlt. BD38 54
Mauritius Rd. SE10 CG42 68
Maurne St. W12 BP39 55
Maury Rd. N16 CB34 48
Mauve St. E14 CF39 57
St. Leonard's Av.
Mavelstone Clo. Brom. CK51 88
Mavelstone Rd. Brom. CJ51 88
Mavis Av. Epsom BO56 94
Mavis Clo. Epsom BO56 94
Mavis Gro. Horn. CW34 51
Mawbey Est. SE1 CB42 67
Mawbey Pl. SE1 CA42 67
Mawbey Rd.
Mawbey Rd. SE1 CA42 67
Mawbey St. SW8 BX43 66
Mawney Rd. Rom. CR30 41
Mawneys Clo. Rom. CR30 41
Mawson Clo. SW20 BR51 85
Mawson Ho. EC1 BY39 56
Baldwin's Gdns.
Mawson La. W4 BO43 65
Chiswick La. S.
Maxey Gdns. Dag. CQ35 50
Maxey Rd. SE18 CM42 68
Maxey Rd. Dag. CQ35 50
Maxilla Gdns. W10 BQ39 55
Maximfeldt Rd. Erith CT42 69
Maxim Rd. N21 BY25 29
Maxim Rd. Dart. CT46 79
Maxim Rd. Erith CS42 69
Maxted Clo. Hem. H. AZ12 8
Maxted Pk. Har. BH33 45
Maxted Rd. SE15 CA45 67
Maxted Rd. Hem. H. AZ12 8
Maxwell Clo. Rick. AW27 35
Maxwell Dr. Wey. AX59 92
Maxwell Gdns. Orp. CN55 88
Maxwell Rise Wat. BE26 36
Maxwell Rd. SW6 BS43 66
Maxwell Rd. Ashf. BA50 73
Maxwell Rd. Borwd. BN23 28
Maxwell Rd. Nthwd. BA29 35
Maxwell Rd. St. Alb. BJ14 9
Maxwell Rd. Well. CO45 69
Maxwell Rd. West Dr. AY42 63
Maxwelton Av. NW7 BN28 37
Maxwelton Clo. NW7 BN28 37
Mayall Rd. SE24 BY45 66
May Av. Grav. DF47 81
May Av. Orp. CO53 89
Maybank Av. E18 CH30 40
Maybank Av. Horn. CU35 50
Maybank Av. Wem. BH35 45
Maybank Gdns. Pnr. BC32 44
Maybank Rd. E18 CH30 40
Maybank Vill. Ilf. CO33 50
Mayberry Pl. Surb. BL54 85
Maybourne Clo. SE26 CB49 77
Maybourne Rise, Wok. AR65 100
Maybrick Rd. Horn. CV32 51
Maybrook Meadow Est. Bark. CO36 59
Maybury Ave. Dart. CY47 80
Maybury Av. Wal. Cr. CB17 21
Maybury Clo. Orp. CL53 88
Maybury Clo. Tad. BR63 103
Maybury Gdns. NW10 BP36 55
Maybury Hill, Wok. AT61 100
Maybury Rd. E13 CJ38 58
Maybury Rd. Bark. CN37 58
Maybury Rd. Wok. AS62 100
Maybury St. SW17 BU49 76
Maybush Rd. Horn. CW33 51
Maychurch Clo. Stan. BK29 36
May Clo. Chess. BL57 94
May Clo. St. Alb. BG12 9
May Clo. Hem. H. AX13 8
Maycroft. Pnr. BC30 35
Maycroft Ave. Grays. DE42 71
Maycroft Rd. Wal. Cr. CA16 21
Maycross Av. Mord. BR52 85
Mayday Gdns. SE3 CK44 68
Mayday Rd. Th. Hth. BY53 86
Maye Clo. Lthd. BK65 102
Mayerne Rd. SE9 CJ46 78
Mayesbrook Rd. Bark. CN37 58
Mayesbrook Rd. Ilf. CO34 50
Mayes Clo. Swan. CU52 89
Mayes Clo. Warl. CC62 105
Mayesford Rd. Rom. CP33 50
Mayes Rd. N22 BX30 38
Mayeswood Rd. SE12 CJ48 78
Mayfair Av. Bexh. CP44 69
Mayfair Av. Ilf. CK34 49
Mayfair Av. Rom. CP32 50
Mayfair Av. Twick. BG47 74
Mayfair Av. Wor. Pk. BP54 85
Mayfair Clo. Surb. BL54 85
Mayfair Ct. Beck. CE51 87
Mayfair Gdns. N17 BZ29 39
Mayfair Gdns. Wdf. Grn. CH29 40
Mayfair Pl. W1 BV40 56
Mayfair Rd. Dart. CV46 80
Mayfair Ter. N14 BW26 38
Mayfare, Rick. BA25 26
Mayfield Bexh. CQ45 69
Church Rd.
Mayfield Wal. Abb. CF20 21
Roundhills
Mayfield, Welw. G. C. BQ6 5
Mayfield Ave. Ger. Cr. AR31 43
Mayfield Av. N12 BT28 38
Mayfield Av. N14 BW27 38
Mayfield Av. W4 BO42 65
Mayfield Av. W13 BJ41 64
Mayfield Av. Har. BJ32 45
Mayfield Av. Orp. CN54 88
Mayfield Av. Wdf. Grn. CH29 40
Mayfield Av. Wey. AW58 92
Mayfield Clo. E8 CA36 57
Forest Rd.
Mayfield Clo. Ashf. AZ50 73
Mayfield Clo. Harl. CQ9 6
Mayfield Clo. Surb. BJ54 84
Mayfield Clo. Wey. AW58 92
Mayfield Cres. N9 CB25 30
Mayfield Cres. Th. Hth. BX52 86
Mayfield Dr. Pnr. BE31 45
Mayfield Gdns. NW4 BQ32 46
Mayfield Gdns. W7 BG39 54
Mayfield Gdns. Brwd. DA26 42
Mayfield Gdns. Stai. AV50 72
Mayfield Rd. E4 CF27 39
Mayfield Rd. E8 CA36 57
Mayfield Rd. E13 CG38 58
Mayfield Rd. E17 CD30 39
Mayfield Rd. N8 BX32 47
Mayfield Rd. SW19 BR51 85
Mayfield Rd. W3 BM40 55
Mayfield Rd. Belv. CS42 69
Mayfield Rd. Brom. CK53 88
Mayfield Rd. Dag. CP33 50
Mayfield Rd. Enf. CC23 30
Mayfield Rd. Grav. DF47 81
Mayfield Rd. Sth. Croy. BZ58 96
Mayfield Rd. Sutt. BT57 95
Mayfield Rd. Th. Hth. BX52 86
Mayfield Rd. Walt. BC56 92
Mayfield Rd. Wey. AZ56 92
Mayfields. Grays. DE41 71
Mayfields, Wem. BM34 46
Mayfields Clo. Wem. BM34 46
Mayflower Av. Hem. H. AX13 8
Mayflower Clo. Ruis. BA32 44
Mayflower Clo. S. Ock. DB38 60
Mayflower Path, Brwd. DB29 42
Mayflower Rd. SW9 BX44 66
Mayflower Rd. St. Alb. BF17 18
Mayflower St. SE16 CC41 67
St. Mary Ch. St.
Mayflower Way Ong. CX17 24
Mayflower Way Slou. AO35 43
Mayfly Gdns. Nthlt. BD38 54
Seasprite Clo.
Mayford, Wok. AR64 100
Mayford Clo. SW12 BU47 76
Mayford Clo. Wok. AR64 100
Mayford Rd. SW12 BU47 76
May Gdns. Wem. BK37 54
Maygold Wk. Amer. AR23 25
Maygoods Clo. Uxb. AX39 53
Maygoods Grn. Uxb. AX39 53
Maygood St. N1 BX37 56
Maygoods Vw. Uxb. AX39 53
Maygreen Cres. Horn. CU33 50
Maygrove Rd. NW6 BR36 55
Mayh Av. Wok. AU61 100
Mayh Clo. Wok. AU61 100
Mayh Cres. Wok. AU61 100
Mayhew Clo. E4 CE27 39
Mayhill Av. SE7 CH43 68
Mayhill Rd. Barn. BR25 28
Mayh St. Wok. AU61 100
Mayland Av. Hem. H. AZ12 8
Maylands Av. Horn. CU35 50
Maylands Clo. Wat. BD28 36
Maylands Dr. Sid. CP48 79
Maylands Dr. Uxb. AX36 53
Maylands Way, Rom. CY29 42
Maylins Dr. Saw. CP6 6
Maynard Clo. Erith CT43 69
Maynard Ct. Wal. Abb. CG20 22
Shernbroke Rd.
Maynard Dr. St. Alb. BG15 9
Maynard Rd. E17 CE32 48
Maynards Horn. CW33 51
Clairvale
Mayne Av. St. Alb. BE14 9
Mayne Av. St. Alb. BF15 9
Mayo Clo. Wal. Cr. CC17 21
Mayola Rd. E5 CC35 48
Mayo Rd. NW10 BO36 55
Mayo Rd. Croy. BZ53 87
Mayo Rd. Walt. BC54 83
May Pl. Av. Dart. CU45 69
Mayplace Clo. Bexh. CR45 69
May Pl. La. SE18 CL43 68
Mayplace Rd. E. Bexh. CR45 69
Mayplace Rd. W. Bexh. CR45 69
Maypole Cres. Ilf. CM29 40
Maypole Dri. Chig. CO27 41
Maypole Rd. Orp. CQ56 98
May Rd. E4 CE29 39
May Rd. E13 CH37 58
May Rd. Dart. CW49 80
May Rd. Twick. BH47 74
Mayroyd Av. Surb. BM55 85
May's Bldgs. Ms. SE10 CF43 67
Croom's Hill
Mays Ct. WC2 BX40 56
St. Martin's La.
Mays Hill Rd. Brom. CG51 88
Mays La. E4 CF27 39
May's La. Barn. BP26 37
May's Pl. SE15 CB45 67
Scylla Rd.
Mays Rd. Tedd. BG49 74
Mayswood Gdns. Dag. CS36 59
Maythorn Clo. Wat. BB24 26
Mayton Rd. N7 BX34 47
Maytree Clo. Edg. BN27 37
Maytree Clo. Guil. AR68 109
Maytree Clo. Guil. AR69 118
Maytree Cres. Wat. BB21 26
Maytree Wk. SW2 BY48 76
Mayville Est. N16 CA35 48
Mayville Rd. E11 CG34 49
Mayville Rd. Ilf. CL35 49
Mayville St. N16 CD35 48
Woodville Rd.
May Wk. E13 CH37 58
Mayward Rd. Hem. H. AX14 8
Maywin Dr. Horn. CW33 51
Maywood Clo. Beck. CE50 77
Mazenod Av. NW6 BS36 56
Maze Rd. Rich. BM43 65
McAdam Clo. Hodd. CE11 12
Mcadam Dr. Enf. BY23 29
Mccall Cres. SE7 CK42 68
Mccarthy Rd. Felt. BD49 74
Mcdermott Rd. SE15 CB45 67
Mcdowall Rd. SE5 BZ44 67
Mcdowell Clo. E16 CH39 58
Mcentee Av. E17 CD30 39
Mcewan Clo. E15 CF37 57
Mcgrath Rd. E15 CG35 49
Mcgregor Rd. W11 BR39 55
Mcintosh Clo. Rom. CT31 50
Mcintosh Rd. Rom. CT31 50
Mckay Rd. SW20 BP50 75
Mckellar Clo. Bush. BG27 36
McKenzie Rd. Brox. CD13 12
Mckerrell Rd. SE15 CB44 67
Mcleod's Ms. SW7 BS41 66
Mcmillan St. SE8 CE43 67
McNeil Rd. SE5 CA44 67
Mead Ave. Slou. AT41 62
Mead Clo. Egh. AT50 72
Mead Clo. Grays. DD41 71
Mead Clo. Har. BG30 36
Mead Clo. Red. BU69 121
Mead Clo. Rom. CU30 41
Mead Clo. Slou. AT41 62
Mead Clo. Swan. CU53 89
Mead Clo. Uxb. AW34 44
Mead Ct. NW9 BN32 46
Mead Ct. Wal. Abb. CE20 21
Mead Ct. Wok. AP61 100
Mead Cres. E4 CF28 39
Mead Cres. Dart. CV47 80
Mead Cres. Lthd. BF66 111
Mead Cres. Sutt. BU56 95
Meadcroft SE5 BY43 66
Mead End, Ash. BL62 103
Meadfield Edg. BM27 37
Meadfield Ave. Slou. AT41 62
Meadfield Grn. Edg. BM27 37
Meadfoot Rd. SW16 BW50 76
Meadgate Av. Wdf. Grn. CK28 40
Meadgate Rd. Harl. CG13 13
Mead Gro. Croy. BY54 86
Mead Gro. Rom. CP31 50
Meadhurst Rd. Cher. AW54 83
Meadlands Dr. Rich. BK48 74
Meadow Av. Croy. CC53 87
Meadow Bk. Oxt. CF68 114
Meadow Bank N21 BX25 29
Meadowbank SE3 CG45 68
Meadowbank Surb. BL53 85
Meadow Bank Wat. BD26 36
Meadowbank Gdns. Houns. BC44 63
Meadowbank Rd. NW9 BN33 46
Meadow Brook Clo. Slou. AV44 62
Meadowbrook Rd. Dor. BJ71 119
Meadow Cl. Hat. BQ15 10
Meadow Clo. SW20 BQ52 85
Meadow Clo. Barn. BR25 28
Meadow Clo. Chis. CL49 78
Meadow Clo. Enf. CC22 30
Meadow Clo. Esher BH55 84
Meadow Clo. Houns. BF46 74
Meadow Clo. Pur. BW60 95
Meadow Clo. Rich. BL47 75
Petersham Rd.
Meadow Clo. Ruis. BB32 44
Meadow Clo. St. Alb. BF18 18
Meadow Clo. St. Alb. BK11 9
Meadow Clo. St. Alb. BK17 18
Meadow Clo. Sutt. BT55 86
Meadow Clo. Walt. BE56 93
Meadow Clo. Wind. AQ46 72
Meadow Ct. Stai. AV48 72
Moor La.
Meadowcourt Rd. SE3 CG45 68
Meadowcroft Brom. CK52 88
Meadowcroft. Ger. Cr. AR30 34
Meadow Croft. Hat. BO12 10
Meadowcroft, St. Alb. BJ15 9
Meadowcroft Rd. N13 BY27 38
Meadow Cross, Wal. Abb. CG20 22
Meadow Dell, Hat. BO12 10
Meadow Dri. Amer. AP22 25
Meadow Dr. N10 BV31 47
Meadow Dr. NW4 BQ30 37
Meadow Dr. Sev. CU65 107
Lambarde Rd.
Meadow Dr. Wok. AV65 100
Meadow Gdns. Edg. BM29 37
Meadow Gdns. Stai. AV49 72
Meadow Garth NW10 BN36 55
Meadow Grn. Welw. G. C. BQ8 5
Meadow Hill N. Mal. BO53 85
Meadow Hill Pur. BW60 95
Meadowlands, Cob. BC60 92
Meadowlands. Guil. AW68 110
Meadowlands Horn. CW33 51
Meadowlands. Oxt. CH70 115
Meadowlands. Sev. CW63 108
Meadow La. Lthd. BG64 102
Meadow La. Wind. AO43 61
Meadow Mead, Rad. BH20 18
Meadow Ms. SW8 BX43 66
Meadow Park. Ger. Cr. AR33 43
Meadow Pl. SW8 BX43 66
Meadow Rise Couls. BW60 95
Meadow Rise Ing. DC19 24
Meadow Rd. SW8 BX43 66
Meadow Rd. SW19 BT50 76
Meadow Rd. Ash. BL62 103
Meadow Rd. Ashf. BA49 73
Meadow Rd. Bark. CN36 58
Meadow Road, Berk. AQ12 7
Meadow Rd. Borwd. BM23 28
Meadow Rd. Brom. CG51 88
Meadow Rd. Bush. BF24 27
Meadow Rd. Dag. CQ36 59
Meadow Rd. Epp. CN18 22
Meadow Rd. Esher BH57 93
Meadow Rd. Felt. BE48 74
Meadow Rd. Grav. DE47 81
Meadow Rd. Grav. DG48 81
Meadow Rd. Grays. DD40 71
Meadow Rd. Guil. AT68 109
Meadow Rd. Hem. H. AZ16 17
Meadow Rd. Loug. CK25 31
Meadow Rd. Pnr. BE31 45
Meadow Rd. Rom. CS33 50
Meadow Rd. Slou. AS42 62
Meadow Rd. Sthl. BE40 54
Meadow Rd. Sutt. BU56 95
Meadow Rd. Vir. W. AP53 82
Meadow Rd. Wat. BC20 17
Meadow Row SE1 BZ41 67
Meadowside SE9 CJ45 68
Meadow Side. Dart. CW47 80
Meadowside, Lthd. BF65 102
Meadowside Walt. BD55 84
Meadowside Rd. Sutt. BR58 94
Meadowside Rd. Upmin. CY35 51
Meadows, The Amer. AP23 25
Meadows, The, Brwd. DE29 122
Meadows, The Guil. AR72 118
Meadows, The, Orp. CP57 98
Meadows, The. Sev. CQ60 98
Meadow Stile Croy. BZ55 87
Meadow, The, Chis. CM50 78
Meadow Vw. Orp. CP52 89
Meadow Vw. Sid. CO47 79
Meadowview Clo. SE6 CE49 77
Meadowview Rd. SE6 CD49 77
Meadowview Rd. Bex. CQ46 79
Meadowview Rd. Epsom BO58 94
Meadow Vw. Rd. Hayes BA38 53
Meadow Vw. Rd. Th. Hth. BY53 86
Meadow Wk. E18 CH31 49
Meadow Wk. Dag. CQ36 59
Meadow Wk. Dart. CV49 80
Meadow Wk. Epsom BO57 94
Meadow Wk. Tad. BP65 103
Meadow Wk. Wall. BV55 86
Meadow Way NW9 BN32 46
Meadow Way Chess. BL56 94
Meadow Way Chig. CM27 40
Meadow Way. Dart. CY47 80
Meadow Way, Hem. H. AW15 8
Meadow Way, Kings L. AZ18 17
Meadow Way. Leath. BA66 110
Meadow Way, Lthd. BF65 102
Meadow Way. Maid. AH44 61
Meadow Way. Maid. AJ41 61
Meadow Way Orp. CL55 88
Meadow Way. Pot. B. BS20 20
Meadow Way, Reig. BS72 121
Meadow Way. Rick. AX26 35
Meadow Way. Ruis. BC32 44
Meadow Way. St. Alb. BN15 10
Meadow Way, Saw. CR6 6
Meadow Way Tad. BR62 103
Meadow Way, Upmin. CY35 51
Meadow Way, Wat. BB17 17
Meadow Way Wem. BK35 45
Meadow Way, Wey. AW56 92
Meadow Way, Wind. AQ46 72
Meadow Waye Houns. BE43 64
Meadow Way, The, Har. BH30 36
Mead Path SW19 BT49 76
Mead Pl. E9 CC36 57
Mead Pl. Croy. BY54 86
Mead Plat. NW10 BN36 55
Mead Rd. Cat. CA65 105
Mead Rd. Chis. CM50 78
Mead Rd. Dart. CV47 80
Mead Rd. Grav. DG48 81
Mead Rd. Hayes BA38 53
Mead Rd. Rich. BK48 74
Mead Rd. Uxb. AX36 53
Mead Rd. Walt. BE56 93
Mead Row SE1 BY41 66
Westminster Bridge Rd.
Mead's La. Ilf. CN33 49
Meads Rd. N22 BY30 38
Meads Rd. Edg. BM29 37
Meads Rd. Enf. CD23 30
Meads Rd. Guil. AT70 118
Meads, The, Berk. AP12 7
Meads, The, Edg. BN29 37
Meads, The, St. Alb. BF18 18
Meads, The, Sutt. BQ55 85
Meads, The, Upmin. CZ34 51
Meads, The Uxb. AY38 53
Mead, The, W13 BJ39 54
Templewood
Mead. The Ash. BL63 103
Mead, The, Beck. CF51 87
Mead, The, Rom. CO24 32
Mead, The, Uxb. AZ34 44
Mead, The Wal. Cr. CC18 21
Mead, The, Wall. BW57 95
Mead, The, Wat. BE27 36
Mead, The, W. Wick. CF54 87
Meadvale Rd. W5 BJ38 54
Meadvale Rd. Croy. CA54 87
Mead Wk. Ong. CW18 24
Mead Wk. Slou. AT41 62
Meadway N14 BW27 38
Meadway N14 BX27 38
Mead Way NW10 BN36 55
Meadway NW11 BS32 47
Meadway SW20 BQ52 85
Meadway, Ashf. AZ49 73
Meadway Barn. BR24 28
Mead Way Beck. CF51 87
Meadway, Berk. AS12 7
Mead Way Brom. CG53 88
Mead Way Bush. BE23 27
Meadway Couls. BX62 104
Mead Way Croy. CD55 87
Meadway, Enf. CC21 30
Meadway, Epsom. M59 94
Meadway Esher BF58 93
Meadway. Grays. DE42 71
Meadway, Guil. AU68 109
Meadway, Hodd. CE13 12
Meadway Ilf. CN35 49
Meadway. Lthd. BE67 111
Meadway. Lthd. BH60 93
Meadway Rom. CT30 41
Meadway. Sev. CQ60 98
Meadway, Stai. AV50 72
Meadway, Stai. AW50 73
Meadway Surb. BN54 85
Meadway Twick. BG47 74
Meadway, Warl. CC61 105
Meadway Wdf. Grn. CJ28 40
Meadway. Welw. G. C. BR9 5
Meadway Clo. NW11 BS32 47
Meadway Clo. Barn. BS24 29
Meadway Clo. Pnr. BF29 36
High Banks Rd.
Meadway Clo. Stai. AV50 72
Meadway Clo. Stai. AW50 73
Meadway Ct. NW11 BS32 47
Meadway Dr. Wey. AX57 92
Meadway Dr. Wok. AR61 100
Meadway Gdns. Ruis. BA32 44
Meadway Gte. NW11 BS32 47
Meadway, The, SE3 CF44 67
Meadway, The, Buck. H. CJ26 40
Meadway, The, Loug. CK25 31
Meadway, The, Orp. CO56 98
Meadway, The, Pot. B. BX18 20
Mead Way. The. Sev. CT64 107
Meakin Est. SE1 CA41 67
Meald St. SE14 CD44 67
Meanley Rd. E12 CK35 49
Meard St. W1 BW39 56
Meath Clo. Orp. CO53 89
Meath Rd. E15 CG37 58
Meath Rd. Ilf. CM34 49
Meath St. SW11 BV44 66
Meautys, St. Alb. BF15 9
Mechanic's Pass. SE8 CE43 67
Mecklenburgh Pl. WC1 BX38 56
Guilford St.
Mecklenburgh Sq. WC1 BX38 56
Medburn St. NW1 BW37 56
Medcalf Rd. Enf. CD22 30
Medcroft Gdns. SW14 BM45 65
Medebourne Clo. SE3 CH45 68
Mede Clo. Stai. AR47 72
Mede Ct. Stai. AV48 72
Medfield St. SW15 BP47 75
Medhurst Cres. Grav. DJ48 81
Medhurst Gdns. Grav. DJ48 81
Median Rd. E5 CC35 48
Medina Av. Esher BH55 84
Medina Gro. N7 BY34 47
Medina Rd. N7 BY34 47
Medina Rd. Grays. DE42 71
Medlake Rd. Egh. AU50 72
Medland Clo. Wall. BV54 86
Medlar Clo. Guil. AR69 118
Medlar Clo. Nthlt. BD37 54
Medlar St. SE5 BZ44 67
Medley Rd. NW6 BS36 56
Medomsley Clo. Sid. CO48 79
Medora Rd. SW2 BX47 76
Medora Rd. Rom. CS31 50
Medusa Rd. SE6 CE46 77
Medway, Wat. BD20 18
Medway Clo. Ilf. CM35 49
Loxford La.
Medway Dr. Grnf. BH37 54
Medway Gdns. Wem. BJ35 45
Medway Ms. E3 CD37 57
Medway Pde. Grnf. BH37 54
Medway Rd. E3 CD37 57
Medway Rd. Dart. CU45 69
Medway Rd. Hem. H. AY11 8
Medway St. SW1 BW41 66
Medwin St. SW4 BX45 66
Meek St. SW10 BT43 66
Meerbrook Rd. SE3 CJ45 68
Meeson Rd. E15 CG37 58
Meeson St. E5 CD35 48
Meeting Flds. Path E9 CC36 57
Homerton Ter.

Meeting Ho. All. E1 CB40 57
Watts St.
Meeting House La. SE15 CB44 67
Meggs La. Kings L. AW18 17
Meggs Pl. E1 CB39 57
Kingward St.
Mehetabel Rd. E9 CC35 48
Melanda Clo. Chis. CK49 78
Melanie Clo. Bexh. CQ44 69
Melba Gdns. Til. DG43 71
Melba Way SE13 CE44 67
Morden St.
Melbourne Av. N13 BX29 38
Melbourne Av. W13 BJ40 54
Melbourne Av. Pnr. BF31 45
Melbourne Clo. Orp. CN54 88
Melbourne Clo. St. Alb. BH11 9
Melbourne Clo. Wall. BW56 95
Melbourne Clo. Wey. AW60 92
Melbourne Ct. SE20 CB50 77
Melbourne Ct. Welw. G. C. BP8 5
Melbourne Flds. SW9 BY44 66
Melbourne Gdns. Rom. CQ31 50
Melbourne Gro. SE22 CA45 67
Melbourne Pl. WC2 BX40 56
Melbourne Rd. E6 CK37 58
Melbourne Rd. E10 CE33 48
Melbourne Rd. E17 CD31 48
Melbourne Rd. SW19 BS51 86
Melbourne Rd. Bush. BF25 27
Melbourne Rd. Ilf. CL33 49
Melbourne Rd. Tedd. BK50 74
Melbourne Rd. Til. DF44 71
Melbourne Rd. Wal. Cr. CE20 21
Melbourne Rd. Wall. BV56 95
Melbourne Sq. SW9 BY44 66
Melbourne Way Enf. CA25 30
Melbury Av. Sthl. BF41 64
Melbury Clo. Chis. CK50 78
Melbury Clo. Esher BJ57 93
Melbury Ct. W8 BR41 65
Melbury Gdns. SW20 BP51 85
Melbury Rd. W14 BR41 65
Melbury Rd. Har. BL32 46
Melbury Ter. NW1 BU38 56
Harewood Av.
Melcombe Gdns. Har. BL32 46
Melcombe Pl. NW1 BU39 56
Melcombe St. NW1 BU38 56
Meldrum Clo. Oxt. CG69 115
Meldrum Rd. Ilf. CO34 50
Melfield Clo. SE6 CF49 77
Melford Av. Bark. CN36 58
Melford Rd. E6 CK38 58
Melford Rd. E11 CG34 49
Melford Rd. E13 CH38 58
Melford Rd. E17 CD32 48
Melford Rd. SE22 CB47 77
Melford Rd. Ilf. CM34 49
Melfort Av. Th. Hth. BY52 86
Melfort Rd. Th. Hth. BY52 86
Melgund Rd. N5 BY35 47
Melina Pl. NW8 BT38 56
Melior St. SE1 CA41 67
Weston St.
Meliot Rd. SE6 CF48 77
Melksham Clo. Rom. CW29 42
Melksham Dr. Rom. CW29 42
Melksham Gdns. Rom. CW29 42
Melksham Grn. Rom. CW29 42
Meller Clo. Croy. BX55 86
Melling St. SE18 CN43 68
Mellison Rd. SW17 BU49 76
Mellitus St. W12 BO39 55
Mellow Clo. Bans. BS60 95
Mellow La. Uxb. BA38 53
Mellow La. E. Hayes BA38 53
Mellows Rd. Ilf. CK31 49
Mellows Rd. Wall. BW56 95
Mells Cres. SE9 CK49 78
Mell St. SE10 CG42 68
Melody Rd. SW18 BT46 76
Melody Rd. West. CH62 106
Melon Pl. W8 BS41 66
Kensington Church St.
Melon Rd. SE15 CA44 67
Melrose Av. N22 BY30 38
Melrose Av. NW2 BP35 46
Melrose Av. SW16 BX52 86
Melrose Av. SW19 BR48 75
Melrose Av. Borwd. BM25 28
Melrose Av. Grnf. BF37 54
Melrose Av. Mitch. BV50 76
Melrose Av. Pot. B. BS19 20
Melrose Av. Twick. BF47 74
Melrose Clo. Grnf. BF37 54
Melrose Clo. Hayes BC39 53
Melrose Cres. Orp. CM56 97
Melrose Dr. Sthl. BF40 54
Melrose Gdns. W6 BQ41 65
Melrose Gdns. Edg. BM30 37
Melrose Gdns. N. Mal. BN52 85
Melrose Gdns. Walt. BD56 93
Melrose Pl. Wat. BB22 26
Melrose Rd. SW13 BO44 65
Melrose Rd. SW18 BR46 75
Melrose Rd. SW19 BS51 86
Melrose Rd. W3 BM41 65
Melrose Rd. Couls. BV61 104
Melrose Rd. Pnr. BE31 45
Melrose Rd. West. CJ61 106
Melrose Rd. Wey. AZ56 92
Melrose Ter. W6 BQ41 65
Melsa Rd. Mord. BT53 86
Melsted Rd. Hem. H. AW13 8
Melstock Av. Upmin. CY35 51
Meltham Way SE16 CB42 67
Egan Way
Melthorne Dr. Ruis. BD34 45
Melthorpe Gdns. SE3 CJ44 68
Melton Clo. Ruis. BD33 45
Melton Ct. SW7 BT42 66
Melton Gdns. Rom. CT33 50
Melton Pl. Epsom BN58 94
Melton Rd. Red. BW68 113
Melton St. NW1 BW38 56
Melville Av. SW20 BP50 75
Melville Av. Grnf. BH35 45
Melville Av. Sth. Croy. CA56 96
Melville Ct. W12 BP41 65
Melville Gdns. N13 BY28 38
Melville Rd. E17 CD31 48
Melville Rd. NW10 BN37 55
Melville Rd. SW13 BP44 65
Melville Rd. Rain. CU38 59
Melville Rd. Rom. CR29 41
Melville Rd. Sid. CP48 79
Melville St. N1 BZ36 57
Melvin Rd. SE20 CC51 87
Melvin Shaw, Lthd. BK64 102
Melvyn Clo. Wal. Cr. BY17 20
Melyn Clo. N19 BW35 47
Anson Rd.
Memorial Av. E15 CG38 58
Memorial Clo. Houns. BF43 64
Heston Rd.
Mendip Clo. St. Alb. BK11 9
Chiltern Rd.
Mendip Clo. Slou. AT42 62
Mendip Cres. SW11 BT45 66
Mendip Dr. NW2 BQ34 46
Mendip Rd. SW11 BT45 66
Mendip Rd. Bexh. CT44 69
Mendip Rd. Bush. BG25 27
Mendip Rd. Horn. CU33 50
Mendip Rd. Ilf. CN32 49
Mendip Way, Hem. H. AY12 8
Mendora Rd. SW6 BR43 65
Mendoza Clo. Horn. CW32 51
Menelik Rd. NW2 BR35 46
Menlo Gdns. SE19 BZ50 77
Menor Cl. Walt. BE54 84
Menotti St. E2 CB38 57
Dunbridge St.
Mense Way, Sev. CT59 98
Mentmore Clo. Har. BK32 45
Mentmore Rd. St. Alb. BG14 9
Mentmore Ter. E8 CB36 57
Meon Clo. Tad. BP64 103
Meon Rd. W3 BN41 65
Meopham Rd. Mitch. BW51 86
Mepham Cres. Har. BG29 36
Mepham Gdns. Har. BG29 36
Mepham St. SE1 BX40 56
Mera Dr. Bexh. CR45 69
Mercator Rd. SE13 CF45 67
Merceron St. E1 CB38 57
Mercer Pl. Pnr. BD30 36
Mercers, Hem. H. AY12 8
Mercers Clo. SE10 CG42 68
Tunnel Av.
Mercer's Rd. N19 BW34 47
Mercer St. WC2 BX39 56
Merchiston Rd. SE6 CF48 77
Merchland Rd. SE9 CM47 78
Mercia Gro. SE13 CF45 67
Mercian Way. Slou. AL40 61
Mercia Way Wok. AS62 100
Ch. St. W.
Mercier Rd. SW15 BR46 75
Mercury Gdns. Rom. CT31 50
Mercury Rd. Brent. BK42 64
Mercury Walk, Hem. H. AY12 8
Mercy Ter. SE13 CE45 67
Merebank La. Wall. BX56 95
Mere Clo. SW19 BQ47 75
Mere Clo. Orp. CL55 88
Meredith Av. NW2 BQ35 46
Meredith Clo. Pnr. BD29 36
Meredith Rd. Grays. DG42 71
Meredith St. E13 CH38 58
Meredith St. EC1 BY38 56
Meredyth Rd. SW13 BP44 65
Mere End. Croy. CC54 87
Merefield Gdns. Tad. BQ63 103
Mere Rd. Shep. AZ53 83
Mere Rd. Slou. AP41 62
Mere Rd. Tad. BP65 103
Mere Rd. Wey. BA55 83
Mere Side Orp. CL55 88
Meretone Clo. SE4 CD45 67
Meretune Ct. Mord. BR52 85
Merevale Cres. Mord. BT53 86
Mereway Rd. Twick. BG47 74
Merewood Clo. Brom. CL51 88
Merewood Rd. Bexh. CS44 69
Mereworth Clo. Brom. CG53 88
Mereworth Dr. SE18 CL43 68
Meriden Clo. Ilf. CM30 40
Meriden Way Wat. BE21 27
Meridian Rd. SE7 CJ43 68
Meridian Wk. N18 CA29 39
Commercial Rd.
Merifield Rd. SE9 CJ45 68
Merino Pl. Sid. CO46 79
Merivale Rd. SW15 BR45 65
Merivale Rd. Har. BG33 45
Merland Grn. Tad. BQ63 103
Merland Ri. Epsom. BQ63 103
Merle Ave. Uxb. AW30 35
Merlewood. Sev. CU65 107
Merlewood Rd. Chis. CK51 88
Merley Ct. NW9 BN33 46
Merlin Clo. Croy. CA55 87
Merlin Clo. Ilf. CP28 41
Merlin Clo. Nthlt. BD38 54
Merlin Clo. Rom. CS29 41
Merlin Cres. Edg. BL29 37
Merlin Gdns. Brom. CH48 78
Merlin Gdns. Rom. CS29 41
Merlin Gro. Beck. CD52 87
Merlin Gro. Ilf. CL29 40
Merlin Rd. E12 CJ34 49
Merlin Rd. Rom. CS29 41
Merlin Rd. Well. CO45 69
Merlins Av. Har. BE34 45
Merlin St. WC1 BY38 56
Wilmington St.
Mermagen Dr. Rain. CU36 59
Mermaid Ct. SE1 BZ41 67
Merona Clo. Uxb. AX39 53
Merredene St. SW2 BX46 76
Merrick Sq. SE1 BZ41 67
Merridene N21 BY25 29
Merrielands Cres. Bark. CQ37 59
Merrilands Rd. Wor. Pk. BQ54 85
Merrilees Rd. Sid. CN47 78
Merriman Rd. SE3 CJ44 68
Merrington Rd. SW6 BS43 66
Merrion Av. Stan. BK28 36
Merritt Rd. SE4 CD46 77
Merritts Bldgs. EC2 CA38 57
Worship St.
Merrivale N14 BW25 29
Merrivale Av. Ilf. CJ31 49
Merrow Chase, Guil. AU70 118
Merrow Common Rd. Guil. AU69 118
Merrow Croft, Guil. AU70 118
Merrow Dri. Hem. H. AV13 7
Merrow Lane, Guil. AU68 109
Merrow Rd. Sutt. BQ58 94
Merrow St. SE17 BZ43 67
Merrow St. Guil. AU69 118
Merrow Way Croy. CF57 96
Merrow Woods, Guil. AT69 118
Merry Down, Wok. AR64 100
Merryfield SE3 CG44 68
Merryfield Gdns. Stan. BK28 36
Merryfields, Uxb. AX37 53
Merryfields Wall Clo. Uxb. AY37 53
Merryhill Clo. E4 CE26 39
Merry Hill Mt. Bush. BF26 36
Merry Hill Rd. Bush. BE25 27
Merryhills Dr. Enf. BW24 29
Merrylands, Cher. AV55 82
Merrylands Rd. Lthd. BE65 102
Merrymeet Bans. BU60 95
Merrywood Pk. Reig. BS69 121
Mersey Av. Upmin. CY32 51
Mersey Pl. Hem. H. AY11 8
Mersey Rd. E17 CD31 48
Mersey Wk. Nthlt. BF37 54
Mersham Dr. NW9 BM32 46
Mersham Pl. SE20 CB51 87
Mersham Rd. Th. Hth. BZ52 87
Merstham Rd. Red. BY68 113
Merten Rd. Rom. CQ33 50
Merthyr Ter. SW13 BP43 65
Merton Abbey Sta. Rd. SW19 BT51 86
Merton Av. W4 BO42 65
Merton Av. Hart. DC52 90
Merton Av. Nthlt. BG35 45
Merton Av. Uxb. AZ36 53
Merton Gdns. Orp. CL53 88
Merton Gdns. Tad. BQ63 103
Merton Hall Gdns. SW20 BR51 85
Merton Hall Rd. SW19 BR50 75
Merton La. N6 BU34 47
Merton Mansions SW20 BQ51 85
Merton Pl. SE10 CF44 67
Merton Pl. Grays. DG42 71
Merton Ri. NW3 BU36 56
Merton Rd. E17 CF32 48
Merton Rd. SE25 CB53 87
Merton Rd. SW18 BS46 76
Merton Rd. SW19 BS50 76
Merton Rd. Bark. CN36 58
Merton Rd. Enf. BZ22 30
Merton Rd. Har. BG33 45
Merton Rd. Ilf. CN33 49
Merton Rd. Slou. AQ41 62
Merton Rd. Wat. BC24 26
Merton Spur SW20 BP52 85
Bushey Rd.
Merton Wk. Lthd. BJ62 102
Merton Way
Merton Way E. Mol. BF52 84
Merton Way, Lthd. BJ63 102
Merton Way, Uxb. AZ36 53
Merttins Rd. SE15 CC46 77
Ivydale Rd.
Mervan Rd. SW2 BY45 66
Mervyn Av. SE9 CM48 78
Mervyn Rd. W13 BJ41 64
Mervyn Rd. Shep. AZ54 83
Russell Rd.
Merwin Way. Wind. AL45 61
Messaline Av. W3 BN39 55
Messent Rd. SE9 CJ46 78
Messeter Pl. SE9 CL46 78
Messina Av. NW6 BS36 56
Messon's La. Grays. DC42 71
Metcalf Rd. Ashf. AZ49 73
Meteor St. SW11 BV45 66
Meteor Way. Wall. BX57 95
Methley St. SE11 BY42 66
Methuan Clo. Edg. BM29 37
Methuan Rd. Edg. BM29 37
Methuen Pk. N10 BV30 38
Methuen Rd. Belv. CR42 69
Methuen Rd. Bexh. CQ45 69
Methwold Rd. W10 BQ39 55
Mews End, West. CJ62 106
Mews, The, Ilf. CJ32 49
Mews, The, Rom. CT31 50
Mews, The, Saw. CQ5 6
Mews, The. Slou. AP41 62
Mews, The, Twick. BJ46 74
Bridge Rd.
Mexfield Rd. SW15 BR46 75
Meyer Grn. Enf. CB22 30
Meyer Rd. Erith CS43 69
Meymott St. SE1 BY40 56
Meynell Cres. E9 CC36 57
Meynell Rd. E9 CC36 57
Meynell Rd. Rom. CU29 41
Meyrick Rd. NW10 BP36 55
Meyrick Rd. SW11 BT45 66
Miall Rd. SE26 CD49 77
Micawber Av. Uxb. AZ39 53
Micawber St. N1 BZ38 57
Michael Faraday Ho. SE17 BZ42 67
Michael Gdns. Grav. DJ49 81
Michael Gdns. Horn. CV31 51
Michael Rd. E11 CG33 49
Michael Rd. SE25 CA52 87
Michael Rd. SW6 BS44 66
Michaels Clo. SE13 CG45 68
Michael's Rd. NW2 BQ35 46
Micheham Gdns. Tad. BQ63 103
Micheldever Rd. SE12 CG46 78
Michelham Gdns. Twick. BH48 74
Michel's Row Rich. BL45 65
Kew Foot Rd.
Michigan Av. E12 CK35 49
Michleham Down N12 BR28 37
Micklefield Rd. Hem. H. BA13 8
Mickleford Way Borwd. BL22 28
Mickleham By-pass. Dor. BJ67 111
Mickleham Clo. Orp. CN51 88
Mickleham Rd.
Mickleham Dr. Lthd. BK66 111
Mickleham Gdns. Sutt. BR57 94
Mickleham Rd. Orp. CN51 88
Mickleham Way Croy. CF57 96
Micklem Dri. Hem. H. AV13 7
Micklethwaite Rd. SW6 BS43 66
Midcot Way, Berk. AP12 7
Mid Croft, Ruis. BB33 44
Mid Cross La, Ger. Cr. AS28 34
Middfield Hat. BP12 10
Lemsford Rd.
Middle Boy Rom. CP24 32
Middle Clo. Amer. AP22 25
Middle Clo. Couls. BY63 104
Middle Cres. Uxb. AU33 43
Middle Dene NW7 BN27 37
Middlefield NW8 BT37 56
Boundary Rd.
Middle Field Av. Hodd. CE11 12
Middlefield Clo. St. Alb. BK12 9
Middlefield Cres. Ilf. CL32 49
Middle Fielde W13 BJ39 54
Templewood
Middle Field Rd. Hodd. CE11 12
Middle Furlong Bush. BF24 27
Middle Green. Brwd. DB22 33
Middlegreen. Slou. AR41 62
Middle Grn. Slou. AS40 52
Middle Grn. Stai. AX50 73
Middleham Gdns. N18 CB29 39
Middleham Rd. N18 CB29 39
Middle Hill, Hem. H. AV13 7
Middle Hill Rd. Egh. AR49 72
Middleknights Hill, Hem. H. AW12 8
Middle La. N8 BX32 47
Middle La. Epsom BO59 94
Middle La. Hem. H. AT18 16
Middle La. Tedd. BH50 74
Middle La. Mews. N8 BX32 47
Middle La.
Middle Meadow. Ch. St. G. AQ27 34
Middlemead Rd. Lthd. BE66 111
Middle Ope, Wat. BC22 26
Middle Pk. Av. SE9 CJ46 78
Middle Path. Har. BG33 45
Middle Rd. SW16 BW51 86
Middle Rd. Barn. BU25 29
Middle Rd. Berk. AQ13 7
Middle Rd. Brwd. DE28 122
Middle Rd. Har. BG34 45
Middle Rd. Lthd. BJ64 102
Up. Fairfield Rd.
Middle Rd. Uxb. AU33 43
Middle Rd. Wal. Abb. CE19 21
Middle Row W10 BR38 55
Middle Row Pl. WC1 BY39 56
High Holborn
Middlesborough Rd. N18 CB29 39
Middlesex Rd. Mitch. BX53 86
Middlesex St. E1 CA39 57
Middlesex Wharf E5 CC34 48
Southwold Rd.
Middle St. EC1 BZ39 57
Bartholomew Clo.
Middle St. Bet. BM71 120
Middle St. Croy. BZ55 87
Middle St. Wal. Abb. CG14 13
Middle Temple La. EC4 BY39 56
Middleton Av. E4 CD28 39
Middleton Av. Grnf. BG37 54
Middleton Av. Sid. CO50 79
Middleton Clo. E4 CD27 39
Middleton Dr. Pnr. BC31 44
Middleton Gdns. Ilf. CL32 49
Middleton Gro. N7 BX35 47
Middleton Hall La. Brwd. DC27 122
Middleton Ind. Est. Rd. Guil. AQ70 118
Middleton Rd. E8 CA36 57
Middleton Rd. NW11 BS33 47
Middleton Rd. Brwd. DC26 122
Middleton Rd. Cob. BD63 102
Middleton Rd. Guil. AP71 118
Middleton Rd. Hayes BA39 53
Middleton Rd. Mord. BS53 86
Middleton Rd. N. Mal. BN51 85
Middleton Rd. Rick. AW26 35
Middleton St. E2 CB38 57
Canrobert St.
Middleton Way SE13 CF45 67
Middle Wk. Wok. AS62 100
Ch. St. W.
Middleway NW11 BS32 47
Middle Way SW16 BW51 86
Middle Way Hayes BD38 54
Middle Way, Wat. BC22 26
Middle Way, The, Har. BH30 36
Middlings Ri. Sev. CT66 116
Middlings. The. Sev. CT66 116
Middlings Wood. Sev. CT66 116
Midfield Av. Bexh. CS45 69
Midfield Way Orp. CO51 89
Midford Pl. W1 BW38 56
Tottenham Court Rd.
Midholm NW11 BS31 47
Midholm Wem. BM33 46
Midholm Clo. NW11 BS31 47
Midholm Rd. Croy. CD55 87
Midhope Clo. Wok. AS63 100
Midhope Rd.
Midhope Gdns. Wok. AS63 100
Midhope Rd.
Midhope Rd. Wok. AS63 100
Midhope St. WC1 BX38 56
Argyle Wk.
Midhurst Av. N10 BV31 47
Midhurst Av. Croy. BY54 86
Midhurst Clo. Horn. CU35 50
Cowdray Way
Midhurst Hill Bexh. CR46 79
Midhurst Rd. W13 BJ41 64
Midland Mead SE16 CC42 67
Midland Rd. E10 CF33 48
Midland Rd. NW1 BW37 56
Midland Rd. Hem. H. AX13 8
Midland Ter. NW2 BQ34 46
Midland Ter. NW10 BO38 55
Midlothian Rd. E3 CD38 57
Midmoor Rd. SW12 BW47 76
Midmoor Rd. SW19 BQ50 75
Mid Sto Red. BX72 121
Midstrath Rd. NW10 BO35 46
Ballogie Av.
Midsummer Av. Houns. BE45 64
Midway, St. Alb. BF15 9
Midway Sutt. BR54 85
Midway, Walt. BC55 83
Midway Av. Egh. AT52 82
Miers Clo. E6 CL37 58
Mighell Av. Ilf. CJ32 49
Milborne Gro. SW10 BT42 66
Gilston Rd.
Milborne St. E9 CC36 57
Well St.
Milborough Cres. SE12 CG46 78
Milbourne La. Esher BG57 93
Milbourne Rd. Felt. BE49 74
Milbrook Esher BG57 93
Milburn Wk. Epsom. BO61 103
Milcote St. SE1 BY41 66
Mildenhall Rd. E5 CB35 48
Mildenhall Rd. Slou. AP39 52
Mildmay Av. N1 BZ36 57
Mildmay Gro. N1 BZ35 48
Mildmay Pk. N1 BZ35 48
Mildmay Pl. Sev. CT59 98
Mildmay Rd. N1 BZ35 48
Mildmay Rd. Rom. CS32 50
Mildmay St. N1 BZ36 57
Mildred Ave. Hayes. BA42 63
Mildred Av. Borwd. BM24 28
Mildred Av. Nthlt. BF35 45
Mildred Av. Wat. BB24 26
Mildred Clo. Dart. CX46 80
Mildred Rd. Erith CS42 69
Mildreds Rd. Guil. AS70 118
Mile Clo. Wal. Abb. CF19 21
Mile End Pl. E1 CC38 57
Mile House Clo. St. Alb. BJ15 9
Mile House La. St. Alb. BJ15 9
Mile Path, Wok. AQ63 100
Mile Rd. Wall. BV54 86
Miles La. EC4 BZ40 57
Arthur St.
Milespit Hl. NW7 BP28 37
Miles Pl. NW1 BT39 56
Miles Pl. Surb. BL52 85
Miles Rd. N8 BX31 47
Miles Rd. Epsom BN59 94
Miles Rd. Mitch. BT52 86
Miles's La. Cob. BE60 93
Miles St. SW8 BX43 66
Milestone Clo. Sutt. BT57 95
Milestone Clo. Wok. AW64 101
Milestone Rd. SE19 CA50 77
Milestone Rd. Dart. CX47 80
Miles Way N20 BU27 38
Mile, The, End E17 CC30 39
Milfoil St. W12 BP40 55
Milford Clo. SE2 CQ43 69
Milford Gdns. Edg. BM29 37
Milford Gdns. Wem. BK35 45
Milford Gro. Sutt. BT56 95
Milford La. WC2 BX39 56
Milford Rd. W13 BJ40 54
Milford Rd. Grays. DE40 71
Milford Rd. Sthl. BF40 54
Milford St. SW8 BV45 66
Milford Way SE15 CA44 67
Sumner Estate
Milhill La. Bet. BM70 120
Milhoo Ct. Wal. Abb. CG20 22
Haywood Ct.
Milking La. Kes. CJ59 97
Milk St. E16 CL40 58
Milk St. EC2 BZ39 57
Milk St. Brom. CH50 78
Milkwell Gdns. Wdf. Grn. CH29 40
Milkwell Yd. SE5 BZ44 67
Denmark Hill
Milkwood Rd. SE24 BY46 76
Milk Yd. E1 CC40 57
Millais Av. E12 CL35 49
Millais Pl. Til. DG43 71
Millais Rd. E11 CF35 48
Millais Rd. Enf. CA25 30

Millais Rd. N. Mal. BO53 85
Millais Way Epsom BN56 94
Mill Av. Uxb. AX37 53
Millbank SW1 BW42 66
Millbank Av. Ong. CW18 24
Millbrook, Wey. BB56 92
Millbrook Av. Well. CM45 68
Millbrook Ct. SW15 BR46 75
Keswick Rd.
Millbrook Gdns. Rom. CQ32 50
Millbrook Gdns. Rom. CT30 41
Millbrook Gdns. Wey. AZ57 92
Millbrook Rd. N9 CB26 39
Millbrook Rd. SW9 BY45 66
Millbrooks Rd. Bush. BE23 27
Mill Brook St. Guil. AR71 118
Mill Clo. Cars. BV55 86
Mill Clo. Chesh. AP20 16
Mill Clo. Hem. H. AZ16 17
Mill Clo. Lthd. BF65 102
Mill Clo. Wal. Cr. CD17 21
Mill Clo. Welw. G. C. BP8 5
Mill Clo. West Dr. AX41 63
Mill Corner. Barn. BR23 28
Millcrest Rd. Wal. Cr. BY17 20
Millen Clo. Wey. AW58 92
Miller Clo. Pnr. BD30 36
Miller Green Road. Ong. DA13 15
Miller Rd. SW19 BT50 76
Miller Rd. Croy. BX54 86
Miller Rd. Grav. DK48 81
Millers Av. E8 CA35 48
Miller's Clo. Chig. CO27 41
Millers Copse. Epsom. BN63 103
Millers Ct. W6 BO42 65
Millersdale Harl. CL13 13
Miller's La. Chig. CO26 41
Miller's La. Chig. CO27 41
Millers La. Wind. AP46 72
Millers Ter. E8 CA35 48
Miller St. NW1 BW37 56
Millett Rd. Grnf. BF38 54
Millfarm Av. Sun. BB50 73
Mill Farm Clo. Pnr. BD30 36
Mill Farm Cres. Houns. BE47 74
Mill Field. Berk. AR12 7
Mill Field, Harl. CP9 6
Millfield, Sun. BA51 83
Millfield Av. E17 CD30 39
Millfield La. N6 BU34 47
Millfield La. New. A. G. DC55 90
Millfield La. Tad. BR66 112
Millfield Pl. N6 BV34 47
Millfield Rd. Edg. BN30 37
Millfield Rd. Houns. BE47 74
Millfield Rd. Sev. CY57 99
Mill Fields, Saw. CQ5 6
Millfields Clo. Orp. CO52 89
Millfields Ong. CY17 24
Millfields Rd. E5 CC35 48
Millfield Wk. Hem. H. AZ15 8
Mill Gdns. SE26 CB49 77
Mill Green La. Hat. BR11 10
Millgreen Rd. Mitch. BU54 86
Mill Green Rd. Welw. G. C. BR8 5
Millgrove St. SW11 BV44 66
Dagnall St.
Mill Hedge Clo. Cob. BE61 102
Mill Hill, Brwd. DC26 122
Mill Hill Gr. NW7 BO28 37
Mill Hill Gro. W3 BN40 55
Mill Hill Rd. SW13 BP44 65
Mill Hill Rd. W3 BM41 65
Mill Hill Ter. W3 BM40 55
Mill Hl. NW3 BT34 47
Millhouse La. Wat. BB17 17
Millias Gdns. Edg. BM30 37
Millicent Rd. E10 CD33 48
Milling Rd. Edg. BN29 37
Mill La. E4 CE24 30
Mill La. NW6 BR35 46
Mill La. SE18 CL42 68
Mill La. Brox. CD14 12
Mill La. Brwd. CZ22 33
Mill La. Brwd. DB21 33
Mill La. Cars. BU56 95
Mill La. Ch. St. G. AQ27 34
Mill La. Croy. BX55 86
Mill La. Dor. BJ71 119
Mill La. Egh. AU52 82
Mill La. Epsom BO58 94
Mill La. Ger. Cr. AS32 43
Mill La. Grays DK42 70
Mill La. Harl. CQ9 6
Mill La. Kings L. AZ18 17
Mill La. Kings. On T. BL52 85
Mill La. Lthd. BJ64 102
Mill La. Ong. CT18 23
Mill Lane. Ong. CV12 15
Mill La. Ong. CY18 24
Mill La. Orp. CL58 97
Mill La. Orp. CO52 89
Mill La. Oxt. CG69 115
Mill La. Oxt. CK69 115
Mill La. Red. BW69 121
Mill La. Rom. CQ32 50
Mill La. Rom. CU23 32
Mill La. Rom. CV22 33
Mill La. St. Alb. BH18 18
Mill La. Saw. CQ6 6
Mill La. Sev. CT58 98
Mill La. Sev. CT64 107
Mill La. Sev. CV64 108
Mill La. Sev. DB64 108
Mill La. Slou. AT45 62
Mill La. Ton. CX71 117
Mill La. Wal. Cr. CD17 21
Mill La. Wdf. Grn. CG28 40
Mill La. Wey. AY60 92
Mill La. Wind. AN43 61
Mill Lane Clo. Brox. CD14 12
Millman Ms. WC1 BX38 56
Millman St. WC1 BX38 56
Millmark Gro. SE14 CD44 67
Millmarsh La. Enf. CD23 30
Millmead, Guil. AR71 118
Mill Mead, Stai. AV49 72
Mill Mead, Wey. AY59 92
Mill Mead Rd. N17 CB31 48
Millmead Ter. Guil. AR71 118
Millmead Way Loug. CK23 31
Mill Pk. Av. Horn. CW34 51
Mill Pl. E14 CD39 57
Mill Pl. Chis. CL51 88
Mill Pl. Dart. CU45 69
Mill Pl. Kings-on-t. BL52 85
Mill Pl. Slou. AR44 62
Mill Plat Islw. BJ44 64
Mill Plat Av. Islw. BJ44 64
Millpond Est. SE16 CB41 67
Mill Pond Rd. Dart. CW46 80
Mill Ridge. Edg. BL28 37
Mill Rd. E16 CH40 58
Mill Rd. SW19 BT50 76
Mill Rd. Dart. CW49 80
Mill Rd. Epsom BO59 94
Mill Rd. Erith CS43 69
Mill Rd. Esher BF55 84
Mill Rd. Eyns. CW54 90
Mill Rd. Grav. DF47 81
Mill Rd. Grays CX43 70
Mill Rd. Ilf. CL34 49
Mill Rd. S. Ock. CW40 60
Mill Rd. Twick. BG48 74
Mill Rd. West Dr. AX41 63
Mill Row N1 CA37 57
Mill Row W4 BN42 65
Belmont Rd.
Mills Clo. Uxb. AZ37 53
Mills Ct. E11 CG34 49
Harrow Rd.
Mills Cres. Sev. CW62 108
Mills Gro. E14 CF39 57
Mills Gro. NW4 BQ31 46
Mill Shaw. Oxt. CG69 115
Millshot Dri. Amer. AO23 25
Millside Cars. BU55 86
Mills Rd. Walt. BD56 93
Mills Spur, Wind. AQ47 72
Millstream La. Slou. AM40 61
Millstream Rd. SE1 CA41 67
Mill St. SE1 CA41 67
Mill St. W1 BV40 56
Mill St. Berk. AR13 7
Mill St. Hem. H. AX15 8
Mill St. Kings-on-t. BL52 85
Mill St. Red. BU71 121
Mill St. Slou. AP40 52
Mill St. Slou. AU43 62
Mill St. West. CM67 115
Mills Way, Brwd. DE26 122
Millthorn Clo. Rick. AY25 26
Mill Vale Brom. CG51 88
Millview Clo. Reig. BT69 121
Mill Vw. Gdns. Croy. CC55 87
Millwall Dock Rd. E14 CE41 67
Tiller St.
Millwall Est. E14 CE41 67
Millwards Hat. BP14 10
Millward St. SE18 CL43 68
Millward St. W10 BQ40 55
Charles Sq.
Millway NW7 BO28 37
Mill Way Bush. BE23 27
Mill Way Felt. BC46 73
Mill Way. Rick. AV26 34
Millway Gdns. Nthlt. BE36 54
Millway, Reig. BT70 121
Millwell Cres. Chig. CM28 40
Millwood Rd. Houns. BG46 74
Millwood Rd. Orp. CP52 89
Millwood St. W10 BQ39 55
Chesterton Rd.
Milman Clo. Pnr. BD30 36
Milman Rd. NW6 BQ37 55
Milmans St. SW10 BT43 66
Milne Est. SE18 CK42 68
Milne Fld. Pnr. BF29 36
Milne Gdns. SE9 CK46 78
Milne Pk. E. Croy. CF59 96
Milne Pk. W. Croy. CF59 96
Milner App. Cat. CB64 105
Milner Clo. Cat. CA64 105
Milner Dr. Cob. BE59 93
Milner Dr. Twick. BG47 74
Milner Pl. N1 BY37 56
Milner Rd. E15 CG38 58
Milner Rd. SW19 BS51 86
Milner Rd. Cat. CA64 105
Milner Rd. Dag. CP34 50
Milner Rd. Kings-on-t. BK52 84
Milner Rd. Mord. BT53 86
Milner Rd. Th. Hth. BZ52 87
Milner Sq. N1 BY36 56
Milne Way. Uxb. AW30 35
Milnthorpe Rd. W4 BN43 65
Milo Rd. SE22 CA46 77
Milroy Av. Grav. DF48 81
Milson Rd. W14 BQ41 65
Milton Ave. Ger. Cr. AR31 43
Milton Av. E6 CJ36 58
Milton Av. N6 BW33 47
Milton Av. NW9 BM31 46
Milton Av. NW10 BO37 55
Milton Av. Barn. BR25 28
Milton Av. Croy. BZ54 87
Milton Av. Dor. BG72 119
Milton Av. Grav. DH47 81
Milton Av. Horn. CT34 50
Milton Av. Sev. CR58 98
Milton Av. Sutt. BT55 86
Milton Clo. N2 BT32 47
Milton Clo. Hayes BC39 53
Milton Clo. Pnr. BE29 36
Milton Clo. Slou. AT45 62
Milton Clo. Sutt. BT55 86
Milton Ct. EC2 BZ39 57
Milton St.
Milton Ct. Kings. On T. BL49 75
Milton Ct. Uxb. AZ34 44
Miltoncourt La. Dor. BH71 119
Milton Ct. Rd. SE14 CD43 67
Milton Cres. Ilf. CM33 49
Milton Dr. Borwd. BM25 28
Milton Dr. Shep. AY52 83
Milton Flds. Ch. St. G. AQ27 34
Milton Gdns. Epsom BO60 94
Milton Gdns. Til. DG44 71
Milton Gro. N11 BW28 38
Milton Gro. N16 BZ35 48
Milton Hall Rd. Grav. DH47 81
Milton Hill. Ch. St. G. AQ27 34
Milton Lawns. Amer. AO21 25
Milton Park. N6 BW33 47
Milton Park Rd. Egh. AT50 72
Milton Pl. N7 BY35 47
George's Rd.
Milton Pl. Grav. DH46 81
Milton Rd. E17 CE31 48
Milton Rd. N6 BW33 47
Milton Rd. N15 BY31 47
Milton Rd. NW7 BP28 37
Milton Rd. NW9 BO33 46
Broadway, The.
Milton Rd NW9 BP33 46
Milton Rd. SE24 BY46 76
Milton Rd. SW14 BN45 65
Milton Rd. SW19 BT50 76
Milton Rd. W3 BN40 55
Milton Rd. W7 BH40 54
Milton Rd. Belv. CR42 69
Milton Rd. Brwd. DA28 42
Milton Rd. Cat. BZ64 105
Milton Rd. Croy. BZ54 87
Milton Rd. Egh. AS49 72
Milton Rd. Grav. DG46 81
Milton Rd. Grays. DD42 71
Milton Rd. Hamptn. BF50 74
Milton Rd. Har. BH31 45
Milton Rd. Mitch. BV50 76
Milton Rd. Rom. CU32 50
Milton Rd. Sev. CT64 107
Milton Rd. Slou. AO38 52
Milton Rd. Sutt. BS55 86
Milton Rd. Swans. DC46 81
Milton Rd. Uxb. AZ35 44
Milton Rd. Wall. BW57 95
Milton Rd. Walt. BD55 84
Milton Rd. Well. CN44 68
Milton Rd. Wey. AW57 92
Milton St. E13 CH37 58
Greenwood Rd.
Milton St. EC2 BZ39 57
Milton St. Dor. BG72 119
Milton St. Swans. DB46 80
Milton St. Wal. Abb. CF20 21
Milton St. Wat. BC22 26
Milton Way. West Dr. AY42 63
Milverton Dr. Uxb. BA35 44
Milverton Gdns. Ilf. CN34 49
Milverton Rd. NW6 BQ36 55
Milverton St. SE11 BY42 66
Milverton Way SE9 CL49 78
Milwards Harl. CL13 13
Milward St. E1 CB39 57
Mimas Rd. Hem. H. AY12 8
Mimms Hall Rd. Pot. B. BQ19 19
Mimms La. Pot. B. BN20 19
Mimms La. Rad. BM20 19
Mimosa Clo. Brwd. DA25 33
Mimosa Clo. Rom. CV29 42
Mimosa Rd. Hayes. BD39 54
Mimosa Rd. Rom. CV29 42
Mimosa St. SW6 BR44 65
Mina Ave. Slou. AR41 62
Minard Rd. SE6 CG47 78
Mina Rd. SE17 CA42 67
Mina Rd. SW19 BS51 86
Minchenden Cres. N14 BW27 38
Minchen Rd. Harl. CO10 6
Minchin Clo. Lthd. BJ64 102
Mincing La. EC3 CA40 57
Mincing La. Wok. AP58 91
Minden Rd. SE20 CB51 87
Minehead Ct. Har. BF34 45
Minehead Rd. SW16 BX49 76
Minehead Rd. Har. BF34 45
Mineral St. SE18 CM42 68
Minerva Clo. Sid. CN49 78
Minerva Dr. Wat. BB21 26
Minerva Est. E2 CB37 57
Minerva Ms. SW1 BV42 66
Minerva Rd. E4 CE29 39
Minerva Rd. NW10 BN38 55
Minerva Rd. Kings-on-t. BL51 85
Minerva St. E2 CB37 57
Minet Av. NW10 BO37 55
Minet Dr. Hayes BC40 53
Minet Gdns. NW10 BO37 55
Minet Gdns. Hayes BC40 53
Minet Rd. SW9 BY44 66
Minford Gdns. W14 BQ41 65
Minford Ho. W14 BQ41 65
Mingard Walk N7 BX34 47
Andover Est.
Ming St. E14 CE40 57
Miniver Pl. Garlick Hill EC4 BZ40 57
Queen Victoria St.
Mink Ct. Houns. BD45 64
Minnersley Wk. Reig. BS73 121
Castle Dr.
Minniedale Surb. BL53 85
Minnow St. SE17 CA42 67
Minorca Rd. Wey. AZ56 92
Minories EC3 CA39 57
Minshull St. SW8 BW44 66
Minson Rd. E9 CC37 57
Minstead Gdns. SW15 BO46 75
Minstead Way N. Mal. BO53 85
Minster Av. Sutt. BS55 86
Minster Cl. Hat. BP13 10
Minster Dr. Croy. CA56 96
Minster Gdns. E. Mol. BE52 84
Minsterley Av. Shep. BB53 83
Minster Rd. NW2 BR35 46
Minster Rd. Brom. CH50 78
Minster Walk. N8 BX31 47
Minster Way. Horn. CW33 51
Minster Way. Slou. AS41 62
Mintern Clo. N13 BY27 38
Minterne Av. Sthl. BF42 64
Minterne Way Hayes BD39 54
Mintern Rd. Har. BL32 46
Mintern St. N1 BZ37 57
Mint Gdns. Dor. BJ71 119
Minto Pl. E2 CB38 57
Mint Rd. Bans. BT61 104
Mint Rd. Wall. BV56 95
Mint St. SE1 BZ41 67
Mint Wk. Croy. BZ55 87
Mint Wk. Warl. CC62 105
Mint Wk. Wok. AP62 100
Mirabel Rd. SW6 BR43 65
Mirador Cres. Slou. AQ40 52
Miranda Rd. N19 BW33 47
Mirfield St. SE7 CJ41 68
Miriam Rd. SE18 CN42 68
Mirrie La. Uxb. AU32 43
Misbourne Ave. Ger. Cr. AR28 34
Misbourne Clo. Ger. Cr. AS28 34
Misbourne Est. Amer. AP24 25
Misbourne Rd. Uxb. AZ37 53
Misefield View Orp. CM55 88
Miskin Rd. Dart. CV47 80
Missden Dr. Hem. H. BA14 8
Missenden Gdns. Mord. BT53 86
Mission Gro. E17 CD32 48
Mission Pl. SE15 CB44 67
Mission Sq. Brent. BL43 65
Pottery Rd.
Mitcham Ct. Mitch. BU52 86
Mitcham Gdn. Vill. Mitch. BV53 86
Mitcham La. SW16 BV50 76
Mitcham Pk. Mitch. BU52 86
Mitcham Rd. E6 CK38 58
Mitcham Rd. SW17 BU49 76
Mitcham Rd. Croy. BW53 86
Mitcham Rd. Ilf. CN33 49
Mitchell Av. Grav. DE48 81
Mitchell Clo. SE2 CP42 69
Mitchell Clo. Dart. CW48 80
Mitchell Clo. St. Alb. BG15 9
Mitchell Rd. N13 BY28 38
Mitchell St. EC1 BZ38 57
Mitchell Walk. Amer. AP22 25
Mitchell Way NW10 BN36 55
Mitchison Rd. N1 BZ36 57
Mitchley Av. Pur. BZ60 96
Mitchley Gro. Sth. Croy. CB60 96
Mitchley Hill Sth. Croy. CA60 96
Mitchley Rd. N17 CB31 48
Mitchley Vw. Sth. Croy. CB60 96
Mitford Rd. N19 BX34 47
Mitre Clo. Sutt. BT57 95
Mitre Ct. EC2 BZ39 57
Wood St.
Mitre Rd. SE1 BY41 66
Mitre St. EC3 CA39 57
Mitre, The, E14 CD40 57
Mixnams La. Cher. AW52 83
Mizen Clo. Cob. BD61 102
Mizen Way, Cob. BD61 102
Moari Rd. Guil. AS70 118
Moat Clo. Brwd. DB21 33
Moat Ct. Ash. BL62 103
Woodfield La.
Moat Cres. N3 BS31 47
Basing Way
Moat Dr. E13 CJ37 58
Boundary Rd.
Moat Dr. Har. BG31 45
Moat Dr. Ruis. BB33 44
Moat Farm Rd. Nthlt. BE36 54
Moatfield Clo. Bush. BF25 27
Moatfield Rd. Bush. BF25 27
Moat La. Erith CU44 69
Moat Pl. SW9 BX45 66
Moat Pl. W3 BM39 55
Moat Side Enf. CC24 30
Durantspk Av.
Moatside Felt. BD49 74
Moat, The, N. Mal. BO51 85
Moatwood Grn. Welw. G. C. BR8 5
Modbury Gdns. NW5 BV36 56
Queen's Cres.
Modder Pl. SW15 BQ45 65
Moddy La. Slou. AP39 52
Model Cotts. SW14 BN45 65
Upr. Richmond Rd.
Model Cotts. W13 BJ41 64
Glenfield Rd.
Model Farm Clo. SE9 CK48 78
Modena St. W10 BR39 55
Kensal Rd.
Modern Ct. EC4 BY39 56
Farringdon St.
Moffat Ct. SW19 BS49 76
Gap Rd.
Moffat Gdns. Mitch. BT52 86
Moffat Rd. N13 BX29 38
Moffat Rd. SW17 BU49 76
Moffat Rd. Th. Hth. BZ51 87
Moffats Clo. Hat. BS16 20
Moffats La. Hat. BR17 19
Mogador Rd. Tad. BR67 112
Mogden La. Islw. BH46 74
Moiety St. E14 CE41 67
Moira Cl. N17 CA30 39
Moirant Gdns. Rom. CR28 41
Moira Rd. SE9 CK45 68
Moiravale, Kings. On T. BK51 84
Moir Clo. Sth. Croy. CB58 96
Mokeside, St. Alb. BF17 18
Moland Mead, SE16 CC42 67
Molash Rd. Orp. CP52 89
Mole Abbey Gdns. E. Mol. BF52 84
Mole Ct. Epsom BN56 94
Molember Rd. E. Mol. BH53 84
Mole Rd. Walt. BD56 93
Molescroft, SE9 CM48 78
Molesey Av. E. Mol. BE53 84
Molesey Clo. Walt. BE56 93
Molesey Dr. Sutt. BR55 85
Molesey Pk. Av. E. Mol. BF53 84
Molesey Pk. Clo. E. Mol. BG53 84
Molesey Pk. Rd. E. Mol. BF53 84
Molesey Rd. Walt. BD56 93
Molesford Rd. SW6 BS44 66
Molesham Clo. E. Mol. BF52 84
Molesham Way E. Mol. BF52 84
Moles Hill, Lthd. BG59 93
Moles Hl. Lthd. BG59 93
Molesworth St. SE13 CF45 67
Mole Valley Pl. Ash. BK63 102
Mollands La. S. Ock. DB38 60
Mollison Av. Enf. CD25 30
Mollison Dr. Wall. BW57 95
Mollison Way, Edg. BL30 37
Molteno Rd. Wat. BC23 26
Molyneaux St. W1 BU39 56
Molyneux Rd. Wey. AZ56 92
Momples Rd. Harl. CO10 6
Momples Rd. Harl. CO11 14
Monahan Av. Pur. BX59 95
Monarch Clo. Felt. BB47 73
Monarch Ct. N2 BT32 47
Monarch Rd. Belv. CR41 69
Ambrooke Rd.
Monarch Rd. Belv. CR42 69
Gertrude Rd.
Mona Rd. SE15 CC44 67
Monastery Gdns. Enf. BZ23 30
Mona St. E16 CG39 58
Monaveen Gdns. E. Mol. BF52 84
Monck St. SW1 BW41 66
Monclar Rd. SE5 BZ45 67
Moncrieff St. SE15 CB44 67
Money Ave. Cat. BZ64 105
Money Hill Rd. Rick. AX26 35
Money La. West Dr. AX41 63
Money Rd. Cat. BZ64 105
Mongers La. Epsom BO58 94
Monier Rd. E3 CE36 57
Monivea Rd. Beck. CD50 77
Monk Dr. E16 CG39 58
Monkey Island La. Maid. AJ42 61
Monkfrith Av. N14 BV25 29
Monkfrith Clo. N14 BV26 38
Monkfrith Way N14 BV26 38
Monkham's Av. Wdf. Grn. CH28 40
Monkham's Dr. Wdf. Grn. CH28 40
Monkham's La. Wdf. Grn. CH28 40
Monkleigh Rd. Mord. BR52 85
Monks Av. Barn. BT25 29
Monks Av. E. Mol. BE53 84
Monks Chase, Brwd. DE28 122
Monks Clo. SE2 CP42 69
New Rd.
Monks Clo. Enf. BZ23 30
Monks Clo. Ruis. BD35 45
Monks Cres. Walt. BC54 83
Monksdene Gdns. Sutt. BS55 86
Monks Dr. W3 BM39 55
Monks Grn. Lthd. BG64 102
Monks Grove Loug. CL25 31
Monks Horton Way, St. Alb. BJ12 9
Monksmead Borwd. BN24 28
Monks Orchard Dart. CV48 80
Monks Orchard Rd. Croy. CE54 87
Monk, S Clo. St. Alb. BH14 9
Monks Pk. Wem. BM36 55
Monks Pk. Gdns. Wem. BM36 55
Monks Pk. Pde. Wem. BM36 55
Monks Pl. Cat. CB64 105
Monks Rise, Welw. G. C. BQ6 5
Monks Rd. Bans. BS61 104
Monks Rd. Enf. BY23 29
Monks Rd. Vir. W. AR52 82
Monks Rd. Wind. AL44 61
Monks Wk. Welw. G. C. BQ6 5
Monks Way Beck. CE53 87
Monks Way Orp. CM54 88
Monks Way, Reig. BS70 121
Monks Way Stai. AX50 73
Bingham Dr.
Monkswell Ct. N10 BV30 38
Monkswell La. Couls. BS65 104
Monkswick Rd. Harl. CN10 6
Monkswood Av. Wal. Abb. CF20 21
Monkswood Gdns. Borwd. BN24 28
Monkswood Gdns. Ilf. CL31 49
Monkswood, Welw. G. C. BQ6 5
Monkton Rd. Well. CN44 68
Monkton St. SE11 BY42 66
Monkville Av. NW11 BR31 46
Monkwell Sq. EC2 BZ39 57
Monmouth Av. E18 CH31 49
Monmouth Av. Kings. On T. BK50 74
Monmouth Clo. Mitch. BX52 86
Monmouth Clo. Well. CO45 69
Monmouth Pl. W2 BS39 56
Monmouth Rd. E6 CK38 58
Monmouth Rd. N9 CB27 39

Monmouth Rd. W2 BS39 56
Monmouth Rd. Dag. CQ35 50
Monmouth Rd. Hayes. BB42 63
Monmouth Rd. Wat. BC24 26
Monmouth St. WC2 BX39 56
Monnery Rd. N19 BW34 47
Monnow Rd. SE1 CB42 67
Monnow Rd. S. Ock. CW40 60
Monnow Ter. Wok. AQ62 100
Monoux Gro. E17 CD30 39
Monroe Cres. Enf. CB23 30
Monroe Dr. SW14 BM46 75
Monro Gdns. Har. BH29 36
Monsell Gdns. Stai. AV49 72
Monsell Rd. N4 BY34 47
Monsey St. E1 CD38 57
Monson Rd. NW10 BP37 55
Monson Rd. SE14 CC43 67
Monson Rd. Brox. CD13 12
Monson Rd. Red. BU69 121
Mons Way Brom. CK53 88
Montacute Rd. SE6 CD47 77
Montacute Rd. Bush. BH26 36
Montacute Rd. Croy. CF58 96
Montagu Cres. N18 CB28 39
Montague Av. SE4 CD45 67
Montague Av. W7 BH40 54
Montague Av. Sth. Croy. CA59 96
Montague Clo. SE1 BZ40 57
Montague Clo. Walt. BC54 83
Montague Ct. EC1 BZ39 57
Bartholomew Cl.
Montague Gdns. W3 BM40 55
Montague Indust. Est. N18 CC28 39
Montague Pl. E14 CF40 57
Montague Pl. WC1 BW39 56
Montague Rd. E8 CB35 48
Montague Rd. E11 CG34 49
Montague Rd. N8 BX32 47
Montague Rd. N15 CB31 48
Montague Rd. N18 CB28 39
Montague Rd. NW4 BP32 46
Montague Rd. SW19 BS50 76
Montague Rd. W7 BH40 54
Montague Rd. W13 BJ39 54
Montague Rd. Berk. AQ13 7
Montague Rd. Croy. BY54 86
Montague Rd. Houns. BF45 64
Montague Rd. Rich. BL46 75
Montague Rd. Slou. AP40 52
Montague Rd. Slou. AQ44 62
Montague Rd. Sthl. BE42 64
Montague Rd. Swan. CT52 89
Montague Rd. Uxb. AX36 53
Montague St. WC1 BX39 56
Montague Way Sthl. BE41 64
Montagu Gdns. N18 CB28 39
Montagu Gdns. Wall. BW56 95
Montagu Ms. N. W1 BU39 56
Montagu Ms. S. W1 BU39 56
George St.
Montagu Pl. W1 BU39 56
Montagu Row W1 BU39 56
Montagu Sq. W1 BU39 56
Montagu St. W1 BU39 56
Montalt Rd. Wdf. Grn. CG28 40
Montana Rd. SW17 BV49 76
Montana Rd. SW20 BQ51 85
Montayne Rd. Wal. Cr. CC19 21
Montbelle Rd. SE9 CL48 78
Montcalm Clo. Brom. CH53 88
Montcalm Clo. Hayes BC38 53
Ayles Rd.
Montcalm Rd. SE7 CJ43 68
Montclare St. E2 CA38 57
Monteagle Av. Bark. CM36 58
Montecute Rd. Mord. BT53 86
Montefiore St. SW8 BV44 66
Monteith Rd. E3 CD37 57
Montem La. Slou. AO40 61
Montem Rd. SE23 CD47 77
Montem Rd. N. Mal. BO52 85
Montem St. N4 BX33 47
Montenotte Rd. N8 BW32 47
Monterey Clo. Bex. CR48 79
Monterey Clo. Bex. CS48 79
Monter Rd. E3 CE36 57
Montesole Ct. Pnr. BD30 36
Montford Pl. SE11 BY43 66
Montford Pl. SW19 BQ47 75
Montford Rd. Sev. CW62 108
Montford Rd. Sun. BC52 83
Montford St. E1 CB39 57
Montfort Gdns. Ilf. CM29 40
Montgolfier Wk. Nthlt. BD38 54
Montgolfier Wk. Nthlt. BE38 54
Wayfarer Rd.
Montgomery Av. Esher BH55 84
Montgomery Av. Hem. H. AZ13 8
Montgomery Clo. Grays. DE41 71
Montgomery Clo. Mitch. BX52 86
Montgomery Clo. Sid. CN46 78
Montgomery Cres. Rom. CV28 42
Montgomery Dr. Wal. Cr. CD17 21
Montgomery Gdns. E6 CK39 58
Montgomery Rd. W4 BN42 65
Montgomery Rd. Edg. BL29 37
Montgomery Rd. S. Dnth. CY51 90
Montholme Rd. SW11 BU46 76
Montolieu Gdns. SW15 BP46 75
Montpelier Av. N3 BT30 38
Montpelier Av. W5 BK39 54
Montpelier Av. Bex. CP47 79
Montpelier Gdns. E6 CJ38 58
Montpelier Gdns. Rom. CP33 50
Montpelier Gro. NW5 BW35 47
Montpelier Pl. SW7 BU41 66
Montpelier Ri. NW11 BR33 46
Montpelier Rise, Wem. BK33 45
Montpelier Rd. W5 BK39 54
Montpelier Rd. Pur. BY58 95
Montpelier Rd. Sutt. BT56 95
Montpelier Row, SE3 CG44 68
Montpelier Row, Twick. BK47 74
Montpelier Sq. SW7 BU41 66
Montpelier Ter.
Montpelier St. SW7 BU41 66
Montpelier Ter. SW7 BU41 66
Montpelier Vale, SE3 CG44 68
Montpelier Wk. SW7 BU41 66
Montpelier Way, NW11 BR33 46
Montpellier Rd. SE15 CB44 67
Montrave Rd. SE20 CC50 77
Montreal Pl. WC2 BX40 56
Aldwych
Montreal Rd. Ilf. CM33 49
Montreal Rd. Sev. CT65 107
Montreal Rd. Til. DG45 71
Montrell Rd. SW2 BX47 76
Montrose Ave. Slou. AR43 62
Montrose Av. NW6 BR37 55
Montrose Av. Edg. BN30 37
Montrose Av. Rom. CV30 42
Montrose Av. Sid. CO47 79
Montrose Av. Twick. BF47 74
Montrose Av. Well. CM45 68
Montrose Clo. Ashf. BA50 73
Montrose Clo. Well. CN45 68
Montrose Ct. NW9 BN30 37
Montrose Ct. NW11 BR31 46
Addison Way
Montrose Cres. N12 BT29 38
Montrose Cres. Wem. BL36 55
Montrose Gdns. Mitch. BU51 86
Montrose Gdns. Sutt. BS55 86
Montrose Gns. Lthd. BH59 93
Montrose Pl. SW1 BV41 66
Montrose Rd. Felt. BA46 73
Montrose Rd. Har. BH30 36
Montrose Walk, Wey. AZ55 83
Montrose Way. Slou. AR43 62
Montrouge Cres. Epsom BQ61 103
Montserrat Av. Wdf. Grn. CF29 39
Montserrat Rd. SW15 BR45 65
Monument Grn. Wey. AZ55 83
Monument Hill, Wey. AZ56 92
Monument La. Ger. Cr. AS29 34
Monument Rd. Wey. AZ56 92
Monument Rd. Wok. AT60 91
Monument St. EC3 BZ40 57
Monument Way, E. Wok. AT61 100
Monument Way, W. Wok. AT61 100
Monza St. E1 CC40 57
Moodkee St. SE16 CC41 67
Moody La. Dart. CX46 80
Moody St. E1 CC38 57
Moon Ct. SE12 CH45 68
Lyme Farm Rd.
Moon La. Barn. BR24 28
Moon St. N1 BY37 56
Moorcroft La. Uxb. AZ39 53
Moorcroft Rd. SW16 BW48 76
Moorcroft Way Pnr. BE32 45
Moordown, SE18 CL43 68
Moore Ave. Grays. DC42 71
Moore Ave. Til. DG44 71
Moore Clo. SW14 BN45 65
Little St. Leonard's
Moore Clo. Mitch. BV51 86
Moore Clo. Wall. BX57 95
Moore Clo. Wey. AW56 92
Moorefield Rd. N17 CA30 39
Moore Gro. Cres. Egh. AS50 72
Moorehead Way, SE3 CH45 68
Mooreland Rd. Brom. CG50 78
Moore La. Wind. AM42 61
Moorend. Welw. G. C. BS9 5
Moor End Rd. Hem. H. AX14 8
Moore Pk. Rd. SW6 BS43 66
Moore Rd. SE19 BY50 76
Moore Rd. Berk. AP12 7
Moore Rd. Swans. DC46 81
Moores Pl. Brwd. DB27 42
High St.
Moores Rd. Dor. BJ71 119
Moore St. SW3 BU42 66
Moore Walk, E7 CH35 49
Moorey Clo. E15 CG37 58
Stephen's Rd.
Moorfield Av. W5 BK38 54
Moorfield Highbank EC2 BZ39 57
St. Alphages Gdns.
Moorfield Rd. Chess. BL56 94
Moorfield Rd. Enf. CC23 30
Moorfield Rd. Guil. AR68 109
Moorfield Rd. Orp. CO54 89
Moorfield Rd. Uxb. AW33 44
Moorfield Rd. Uxb. AX39 53
Moorfields, EC2 BZ39 57
Moorfields Clo. Stai. AV51 82
Moorgate, EC2 BZ39 57
Moor Hall Rd. Harl. CQ9 6
Moorhall Rd. Uxb. AW32 44
Moorhayes Dr. Stai. AX52 83
Moor Holme, Wok. AS63 100
Moorhouse Rd. W2 BS39 56
Moorhouse Rd. Har. BK31 45
Moorhouse Rd. Oxt. CK69 115
Moorhurst Av. Wal. Cr. BY18 20
Moorland Clo. Rom. CR29 41
Moorland Rd. BY45 66
Moorland Rd. Harrow. BL32 46
Moorland Rd. Hem. H. AW14 8
Moorland Rd. West Dr. AX43 63
Moorlands Nthlt. BE37 54
Moorlands St. Alb. BH17 18
Radlett Rd.
Moorlands. Welw. G. C. BS9 5
Moorlands, The Wok. AS64 100
Moor La. EC2 BZ39 57
Moor La. Chess. BL56 94
Moor La. Rick. AY27 35
Moor La. Stai. AU48 72
Moor La. Upmin. CZ33 51
Moor La. West Dr. AX43 63
Moor La. Wok. AS64 100
Moormead Dr. Epsom BO56 94
Moor Mead Rd. Twick. BJ46 74
Moor Park Rd. Nthwd. BA29 35
Moor Rd. Chesh. AO20 16
Moorside. Welw. G. C. BS9 5
Moorside Rd. Brom. CG48 78
Moorsom Way Couls. BW62 104
Moors Rd. Sev. CU63 107
Moors Rd. Sev. CV63 108
Moors, The, Welw. G. C. BS7 5
Moor St. W1 BW39 56
Old Compton St.
Moors Wk. Welw. G. C. BS7 5
Moortown Rd. Wat. BD28 36
Moor Vw. Wat. BC25 26
Moot Clo. NW9 BM32 46
Morant Path, E14 CE40 57
Pennyfields
Morant Pl. N22 BX30 38
Morant Rd. Grays. DG41 71
Morants Court Rd. Sev. CS62 107
Morant St. E14 CE40 57
Mora Rd. NW2 BQ35 46
Mora St. EC1 BZ38 57
Morat St. SW9 BX44 66
Moravian Pl. SW10 BT43 66
Milmans St.
Moray Av. Hayes BB40 53
Moray Clo. Rom. CT29 41
Moray Mews N4 BX34 47
Durham Rd
Moray Rd. N4 BX34 47
Moray St. E2 CC38 57
Cyprus St.
Moray Way Rom. CS29 41
Morcambe Gdns. Stan. BK28 36
Morcorvo Clo. SW7 BT41 66
Mordaunt Gdns. Dag. CQ36 59
Mordaunt Rd. NW10 BN37 55
Mordaunt St. SW9 BX45 66
Morden Clo. Tad. BQ63 103
Morden Ct. Mord. BS52 86
Morden Gdns. Grnf. BH35 45
Morden Gdns. Mitch. BT52 86
Morden Hall Rd. Mord. BS52 86
Morden Hl. SE13 CF44 67
Morden Hl. Clo. SE13 CF44 67
Morden La. SE13 CF44 67
Morden Lodge Mord. BT52 86
Morden Rd. SE3 CH44 68
Morden Rd. SW19 BS50 76
Morden Rd. Mitch. BT52 86
Morden Rd. Rom. CQ33 50
Morden Rd. Ms. SE3 CH44 68
Morden St. SE13 CE44 67
Morden Way Sutt. BS54 86
Morden Wharf Rd. SE10 CG41 68
Mordon Rd. Ilf. CN33 49
Mordred Rd. SE6 CG48 78
More Av. Guil. AS70 118
Morecambe Clo. Horn. CU35 50
Morecambe St. SE17 BZ42 67
Morecambe Ter. N18 BZ28 39
More Clo. E16 CG39 58
More Clo. Pur. BY55 86
More Clo. Pur. BY59 95
Morecombe Cl. Kings. On T. BM50 75
Kingston Hill
Morecoombe Clo. Kings. On T. BM50 75
Kingston Hill
Morecote Clo. Guil. AS74 118
Moree Way, N18 CB28 39
Moreland Ave. Slou. AU43 62
Moreland Av. Dart. CU46 79
Moreland Gdns. Sthl. BF40 54
Morelands Dr. Ger. Cr. AS32 43
Moreland St. EC1 BY38 56
Moreland Way E4 CE27 39
More La. Esher BF55 84
Morella Clo. Vir. W. AR52 82
Morella Rd. SW12 BU47 76
Morello Av. Uxb. AZ39 53
Moremead Rd. SE6 CD49 77
Morena St. SE6 CE47 77
Moresby Av. Surb. BM54 85
Moresby Rd. E5 CB33 48
Mores La. Brwd. CY25 33
Moretaine Rd. Ashf. AX48 73
Moreten Gdns. Uxb. AW33 44
Moreton Av. Islw. BG44 64
Moreton Bridge. Ong. CV14 15
Moreton Clo. E5 CC34 48
Moreton Clo. N15 BZ32 48
Moreton Clo. NW7 BQ29 37
Moreton Clo. Swan. CT51 89
Moreton Clo. Wal. Cr. CB17 21
Moreton Gdns. Wdf. Grn. CK28 40
Moreton Pl. SW1 BW42 66
Moreton Rd. N15 BZ32 48
Moreton Rd. Ong. CU15 14
Moreton Road. Ong. CX13 15
Moreton Rd. Sth. Croy. BZ56 96
Moreton Rd. Wor. Pk. BP55 85
Moreton St. SW1 BW42 66
Moreton Ter. SW1 BW42 66
Moreton Way. Slou. AL40 61
Morewood Clo. Sev. CT65 107
Morford Clo. Ruis. BC33 44
Morford Way Ruis. BC33 44
Morgan Av. E17 CF31 48
Morgan Cres. Epp. CM21 31
Morgan Dr. Green. CZ47 80
Morgan Rd. N7 BY35 47
Morgan Rd. Brom. CG50 78
Morgan's La. SE1 CA40 57
Morgan's La. Hayes BA39 53
Morgan St. E3 CD38 57
Morgan St. E16 CG39 58
Morgan's Wk. SW11 BU43 66
Morgan Way. Rain. CV38 60
Morice Rd. Hodd. CD11 12
Morie St. SW18 BS45 66
Ferrier St.
Morieux Rd. E10 CD33 48
Moring Rd. SW17 BV49 76
Morkyns Wk. SE21 CA48 77
Morland Av. Croy. CA54 87
Morland Clo. NW11 BS33 47
Morland Rd. E17 CC32 48
Morland Rd. SE20 CC50 77
Morland Rd. Croy. CA54 87
Morland Rd. Dag. CR36 59
Morland Rd. Ilf. CL34 49
Morland Rd. Sutt. BT56 95
Morlands La. Egh. AV51 82
Morland Way, Wal. Cr. CD17 21
Morley Av. E4 CF29 39
Morley Av. N18 CB28 39
Morley Av. N22 BY30 38
Morley Clo. Orp. CL55 88
Morley Clo. Slou. AS41 62
Morley Cres. Edg. BN27 37
Morley Cres. Ruis. BD34 45
Morley Cres. E. Stan. BK30 36
Morley Cres. W. Stan. BK30 36
Morley Grove, Harl. CM10 6
Morley Hill, Enf. BZ22 30
Morley Ho. E5 CB34 48
Morley Rd. E10 CF33 48
Morley Rd. E15 CG37 58
Morley Rd. Bark. CM37 58
Morley Rd. Chis. CM51 88
Morley Rd. Rom. CQ32 50
Morley Rd. Sth. Croy. CA58 96
Morley Rd. Sutt. BR54 85
Morley Rd. Twick. BK46 74
Morley Sq. Grays. DG42 71
Morleys Rd. Sev. CV70 117
Morley St. SE1 BY41 66
Morna Rd. SE5 BZ44 67
Morning La. E9 CB36 57
Morning Rise, Rick. AX24 26
Morningside Est. E9 CC36 57
Morningside Rd. Wor. Pk. BP55 85
Mornington Av. W14 BR42 65
Mornington Av. Brom. CJ52 88
Mornington Av. Ilf. CL33 49
Mornington Clo. Wdf. Grn. BH28 36
Mornington Ct. Bex. CR47 79
Mornington Ct. Bex. CS47 79
Mornington Cres. NW1 BW37 56
Mornington Cres. Bex. CS47 79
Mornington Cres. Houns. BC44 63
Mornington Gro. E3 CE38 57
Mornington Pl. NW1 BW37 56
Mornington Ter.
Mornington Rd. E4 CF26 39
Mornington Rd. E11 CG33 49
Mornington Rd. SE8 CD43 67
Mornington Rd. Ashf. BA49 73
Mornington Rd. Grnf. BF39 54
Mornington Rd. Loug. CM24 31
Mornington Rd. Rad. BJ20 18
Mornington Rd. Wdf. Grn. CG28 40
Morningtons Harl. CM13 13
Mornington St. NW1 BV37 56
Mornington Ter. NW1 BV37 56
Mornington Wk. Rich. BK49 74
Morocco St. SE1 CA41 67
Morpeth Av. Borwd. BL22 28
Morpeth Gro. E9 CC37 57
Morpeth St. E2 CC38 57
Morpeth Ter. SW1 BW41 66
Morrab Gdns. Ilf. CN34 49
Morres Rd. E1 CC39 57
Morrice Clo. Slou. AS42 62
Morris Av. E12 CK35 49
Morris Clo. Ger. Cr. AS30 34
Morris Clo. Orp. CN55 88
Morris Ct. Wal. Abb. CG20 22
Morris Gdns. SW18 BS47 76
Morris Gdns. Dart. CX46 80
Morrish Rd. SW2 BX47 76
Morrison Av. N17 CA31 48
Morrison Rd. Bark. CQ37 59
Morrison Rd. Hayes BC38 53
Morrison St. SW11 BV45 66
Morris Rd. E14 CE39 57
Morris Rd. E15 CG35 49
Morris Rd. Dag. CQ34 50
Morris Rd. Grays. DG42 71
Morris Rd. Islw. BH45 64
Morris Rd. Red. BX71 121
Morris Rd. Rom. CU29 41
Morris St. E1 CB39 57
Morriston Clo. Wat. BD28 36
Morris Way, St. Alb. BK16 18
Morse Clo. E13 CG38 58
Morshead Rd. W9 BS38 56
Morston Gdns. SE9 CK49 78
Morten Clo. SW4 BW46 76
Mortens Wood. Amer. AO23 25
Morteyne Rd. N17 BZ30 39
Mortgramit Sq. SE18 CL41 68
Hare St.
Mortham St. E15 CG37 58
Mortimer Clo. SW16 BW48 76
Mortimer Cres. NW6 BS37 56
Mortimer Cres. Wor. Pk. BN55 85
Mortimer Est. NW6 BS37 56
Mortimer Mkt. WC1 BW38 56
Mortimer Pl. NW6 BS37 56
Mortimer Rd. E6 CK38 58
Mortimer Rd. N1 CA36 57
Mortimer Rd. NW10 BQ38 55
Mortimer Rd. W13 BK39 54
Mortimer Rd. Erith CS43 69
Mortimer Rd. Mitch. BU51 86
Mortimer Rd. Orp. CO55 89
Mortimer Rd. West. CJ59 97
Mortimer Sq. W11 BQ40 55
St. Ann's Rd.
Mortimer St. W1 BW39 56
Mortimer Ter. NW5 BV35 47
Mortlake Clo. Croy. BX55 86
Mortlake High St. SW14 BN45 65
Mortlake Rd. E16 CH39 58
Mortlake Rd. Ilf. CM35 49
Mortlake Rd. Rich. BM43 65
Mortmer Rd. Slou. AR41 62
Morton Clo. Wok. AR61 100
Morton Cres. N14 BW28 38
Morton Gdns. Wall. BW56 95
Morton Pl. SE1 BY41 66
Morton Rd. E15 CG36 58
Morton Rd. N1 BZ36 57
Morton Rd. Mord. BT53 86
Morton Rd. Wok. AR61 100
Morton Way N14 BW27 38
Morvale Clo. Belv. CQ42 69
Morval Rd. SW2 BY46 76
Morven Clo. Pot. B. BT19 20
Morven Rd. SW17 BU48 76
Morville St. E3 CE37 57
Morwell St. WC1 BW39 56
Moscow Pl. W2 BS40 56
Moscow Rd.
Moscow Rd. W2 BS40 56
Moscow Rd. Grav. DG46 81
Mosedale St. SE5 BZ44 67
Moselle Av. N22 BY30 38
Moselle Clo. N8 BX31 47
Moselle Pl. N17 CA29 39
High Rd.
Moselle Rd. West. CK62 106
Moselle St. N17 CA29 39
Mospey Cres. Epsom BO61 103
Mossbury Rd. SW11 BU45 66
Moss Clo. Pnr. BE30 36
Moss Clo. Rick. AX27 35
Moss Clo. Sutt. BU56 95
Mossdown Clo. Belv. CR42 69
Mossendew Clo. Uxb. AX30 35
Mossford Grn. Ilf. CL31 49
Mossford La. Ilf. CL30 40
Mossford St. E3 CD38 57
Moss Grn. Welw. G. C. BR9 5
Mosshall Cres. N12 BS29 38
Mosshall Gro. N12 BS29 38
Mossington Rd. SE16 CC42 67
Moss La. Pnr. BE30 36
Moss La. Rom. CT32 50
Mosslea Rd. SE20 CC50 77
Mosslea Rd. Brom. CJ53 88
Mosslea Rd. Orp. CL55 88
Mosslea Rd. Whyt. CA61 105
Mossop St. SW3 BU42 66
Moss Rd. Dag. CR36 59
Moss Rd. S. Ock. DB39 60
Moss Rd. Wat. BC20 17
Moss Side, St. Alb. BE18 18
Mossville Gdns. Mord. BR52 85
Moston Clo. Hayes. BB42 63
Mostyn Av. Wem. BL35 46
Mostyn Gdns. NW10 BQ37 55
Mostyn Rd. E3 CD37 57
Mostyn Rd. SW9 BY44 66
Mostyn Rd. SW19 BR51 85
Mostyn Rd. Bush. BG25 27
Mostyn Rd. Edg. BN29 37
Mostyn Ter. Red. BV71 121
Mosul Way Brom. CK53 88
Mosyer Dr. Orp. CP55 89
Motcomb St. SW1 BV41 66
Mote Rd. Lthd. BG64 102
Mote Rd. Sev. CZ68 117
Motherwell Way Grays CZ42 70
Motor Race Track, SE19 CB50 77
Motorway, 23 BY69 121
Motspur Pk. N. Mal. BO53 85
Mottingham Gdns. SE9 CJ47 78
Mottingham Rd. N9 CC26 39
Mottingham Rd. SE9 CK48 78
Mottisfont Rd. SE2 CO41 69
Mottscroft Clo. Loug. CL25 31
Motts Hill La. Tad. BP65 103
Mott St. E4 CF22 30
Mott St. E4 CF23 30
Mouchotte Clo. West. CH59 97
Moulins Rd. E9 CB36 57
Lauriston Rd.
Moulins Rd. E9 CC36 57
Moultain Hill Swan. CU52 89
Moulton Av. Houns. BE44 64
Moultrie Way, Upmin. CZ33 51
Moundfield Rd. N16 CB32 48
Mound, The, SE9 CL48 78
William Barefoot Dr.
Mt. Adon Pk. SE22 CB47 77
Mt. Angelus Rd. SW15 BO47 75
Mt. Ararat, SW20 BQ50 75
Mt. Ararat Rd. Rich. BL46 75
Mount Ash Rd. SE26 CB48 77
Mount Av. E4 CE27 39
Mount Av. W5 BK39 54
Mount Av. Brwd. DD25 122
Mount Av. Rom. CY29 42
Mount Av. Sthl. BF39 54
Mountbatten Sq. Wind. AO44 61
Ward Royal
Mountbell Rd. Stan. BJ30 36
Mount Clo. W5 BM39 55
Castlebar Rd.
Mount Clo. Barn. BV24 29
Mount Clo. Brom. CK51 88
Mount Clo. Cars. BV58 95
Mount Clo. Hem. H. AV13 7
Mount Clo. Ken. BZ57 96
Mount Clo. Ken. BZ61 105
Mount Clo. Sev. CT65 107
Mount Clo. Wok. AQ64 100
Mountcombe Clo. Surb. BL54 85
Mount Ct. W. Wick. CG55 88
Mount Cres. Brwd. DB28 42

Mt. Culver Av. Sid. CP50 79
Mt. Culver Pde. Sid. CP50 79
Maidstone Rd.
Mount Dr. Bexh. CQ46 79
Mount Dr. Har. BE32 45
Mount Dr. St. Alb. BG16 18
Mount Dr. Wem. BO34 46
Mountearl Gdns. SW16 BX48 76
Mount Echo Av. E4 CE26 39
Mount Echo Dr. E4 CE26 39
Mt. Ephraim La. SW16 BW48 76
Mt. Ephraim Rd. SW16 BW48 76
Mountfield Rd. E6 CK37 58
Mountfield Rd. N3 BR31 46
Mountfield Rd. W5 BK39 54
Mountfield Rd. Hem. H. AY13 8
Mountfield Way Orp. CP52 89
Mountford St. E1 CB39 57
Adler St.
Mountfort Cres. N1 BY36 56
Barns Sq.
Mount Gdns. SE26 CB48 77
Mountgrace Rd. Pot. B. BS19 20
Mount Gro. Edg. BN27 37
Mt. Grove Rd. N5 BY34 47
Mount Harry Rd. CU65 107
Mt. Hermon Clo. Wok. AS62 100
Mt. Hermon Rd.
Mount Hermon Rd. Wok. AR63 100
Mount Hill. Sev. CO62 107
Mount Hill La. Ger. Cr. AQ33 43
Mounthurst Rd. Brom. CG54 88
Mountjoy Clo. SE2 CO41 69
Mount La. Uxb. AU34 43
Mount Lea, Egh. AS49 72
Mountmorres Est. E1 CC39 57
Mountnessing La. Brwd. DB22 33
Mt. Nod Rd. SW16 BX48 76
Mount Pk. Cars. BV57 95
Mount Pk. Av. Har. BG34 45
Mount Pk. Av. Sth. Croy. BY58 95
Mt. Park Cres. W5 BK39 54
Mt. Park Rd. W5 BK39 54
Mount Pk. Rd. Har. BG34 45
Mount Pk. Rd. Pnr. BC32 44
Mt. Pleasant NW4 BP31 46
Church End
Mount Pleasant, WC1 BY38 56
Mount Pleasant Barn. BU24 29
Mt. Pleasant Epsom BO58 94
Mt. Pleasant, Guil. AR71 118
Mount Pleasant. Leath. AZ68 110
Mount Pleasant. Lthd. BE67 111
Mount Pleasant Ruis. BD34 45
Mount Pleasant, St. Alb. BF13 9
Mount Pleasant. Uxb. AW30 35
Mount Pleasant, Wem. BL37 55
Mount Pleasant, West. CJ62 106
Mount Pleasant, Wey. AZ55 83
Mount Pleasant Av. Brwd. DF25 122
Mt. Pleasant Cres. N4 BX33 47
Mt. Pleasant Hill, E5 CB34 48
Mt. Pleasant La. E5 CB33 48
Mount Pleasant La. St. Alb. BE18 18
Mt. Pleasant Ri. Hat. BQ11 10
Mount Pleasant Rd. E17 CD30 39
Mount Pleasant Rd. N17 CA30 39
Mount Pleasant Rd. NW10 BQ36 55
Mt. Pleasant Rd. SE13 CE46 77
Mt. Pleasant Rd. W5 BK38 54
Mount Pleasant Rd. Cat. CB65 105
Mount Pleasant Rd. Chig. CM28 40
Mount Pleasant Rd. Dart. CW46 80
Mt. Pleasant Rd. N. Mal. BN52 85
Mt. Pleasant Rd. Rom. CS29 41
Mount Pleasant Rd. Sev. CU70 116
Mt. Pleasant Vill. N4 BX33 47
Mount Pleasant Wk. Bex. CS46 79
Mount Rd. NW2 BP34 46
Mount Rd. NW4 BP32 46
Mount Rd. SE19 BZ50 77
Mount Rd. SW19 BS48 76
Mount Rd. Barn. BU25 29
Mount Rd. Bexh. CP46 79
Mount Rd. Chess. BL56 94
Mount Rd. Dag. CQ33 50
Mount Rd. Dart. CT46 79
Mount Rd Epp. CP19 23
Mount Rd. Felt. BE48 74
Mount Rd. Hayes BC41 63
Mount Rd. Ilf. CL35 49
Mount Rd. Mitch. BT51 86
Mount Rd. N. Mal. BN52 85
Mount Rd. Wok. AQ59 91
Mount Rd. Wok. AQ64 100
Mount Row W1 BV40 56
Mountsfield Clo. Stai. AW46 73
Benenstock Rd.
Mountsfield Ct. SE13 CF46 77
Mountside Felt. BE48 74
Mount Side, Guil. AQ71 118
Mount Side Stan. BH30 36
Mounts Pond Rd. SE3 CF44 67
Mounts Rd. Green. DA46 80
Mounts Rd. Green. DA47 80
Mount Stewart Av. Har. BK33 45
Mount St. W1 BV40 56
Mount St. Dor. BJ71 119
Mount, The, N20 BT27 38
High Rd. Whetstone
Mount, The, NW3 BT34 47
Heath St.
Mount, The, Brwd. DB27 42
Fairfield Rd.
Mount, The, Couls. BV61 104
Mount, The, Epsom BO58 94
Mount, The, Epsom. BP56 94
Mount, The, Esher BF57 93
Mount, The Guil. AR72 118
Mount, The Lthd. BH65 102
Mount, The, N. Mal. BO52 85
Mount, The, Pot. B. BS18 20
Mount, The Rick. AX25 26
Mount, The, Rom. CV27 42
Mount. The. Tad. BR66 112
Mount, The, Vir. W. AR53 82
Mount, The, Wal. Cr. BZ16 21
Pear Tree Wk.
Mount, The, Wem. BN34 46
Mount, The, Wey. BB55 83
Mount, The, Wok. AR62 100
Elm Rd.
Mount, The, Est. E5 CB34 48
Mount, The, Sq. NW3 BT34 47
Heath St.
Mt. Vernon NW3 BT35 47
Mount View NW7 BN27 37
Mount Vw. W5 BK38 54
Mount View Enf. BX22 29
Mountview. Nthwd. BB29 35
Mount Vw. Rick. AW26 35
Mountview Ct. N8 BY31 47
Mountview Dr. Red. BU71 121
Mt. View Rd. E4 CF26 39
Mt. View Rd. N4 BX33 47
Mount View Rd. NW9 BN32 46
Mount Vw. Rd. Esher BJ57 93
Mountview Rd. Orp. CO54 89
Mount View Rd. Wal. Cr. CA16 21
Mount Vills. SE27 BY48 76
Canterbury Gro.
Mount Way Cars. BV58 95
Mountway, Pot. B. BS18 20
Mountway Clo. Welw. G. C. BR9 5
Mountwood E. Mol. BF52 84
Mountwood Clo. Sth. Croy. CB58 96
Mover's La. Bark. CM37 58
Move St. E2 CB37 57
Mowbray Av. Wey. AY60 92
Mowbray Gdns. Dor. BJ70 119
Mowbray Rd. NW6 BR36 55
Mowbray Rd. SE19 CA51 87
Mowbray Rd. Edg. BM28 37
Mowbray Rd. Harl. CN10 6
Mowbray Rd. Rich. BK48 74
Mowbrays Clo. Rom. CS30 41
Mowbrays Rd. Rom. CS30 41
Mowbrey Gdns. Loug. CM23 31
Mowlem St. E2 CB37 57
Mowll St. SW9 BY43 66
Moxon Clo. E13 CG37 58
Whitelegg Rd.
Moxon St. W1 BV39 56
Moxon St. Barn. BR24 28
Moyers Rd. E10 CF33 48
Moylan Rd. W6 BR43 65
Moyne Pl. NW10 BM37 55
Moyser Rd. SW16 BV49 76
Mozart Sq. SW1 BV42 66
Ebury Br. Rd.
Mozart St. W10 BR38 55
Muchelney Rd. Mord. BT53 86
Muckhatch La. Egh. AT52 82
Muckingford Rd. Til. DJ42 71
Mud La. W5 BK39 54
Muggeridge Rd. Dag. CR35 50
Muirdown Av. SW14 BN45 65
Muirfield, W3 BO39 55
Muirfield Clo. Wat. BD28 36
Muirfield Grn. Wat. BC28 35
Muirfield Rd. Wat. BC28 35
Muirfield Way, Upmin. CX35 51
Muirkirk Rd. SE6 CF47 77
Muir Rd. E5 CB35 48
Muir St. E16 CK40 58
Mulbanton Ct. Chis. CM49 78
Mulberry Av. Stai. AY47 73
Mulberry Clo. E4 CE27 39
Mulberry Clo. NW3 BT35 47
Hampstead High St.
Mulberry Clo. NW4 BQ31 46
Mulberry Clo. SE7 CJ43 68
Mulberry Clo. Nthlt. BD37 54
Mulberry Clo. St. Alb. BF17 18
Wychelms
Mulberry Clo. Wok. AS60 91
Mulberry Cres. Brent. BJ43 64
Mulberry Cres. West Dr. AZ41 63
Mulberry Dr. Slou. AS42 62
Mulberry Gdns. NW4 BQ31 46
Mulberry Hill, Brwd. DC26 122
Mulberry La. Croy. CA54 87
Mulberry Rd. Grav. DF48 81
Mulberry St. E1 CB39 57
Mulberry Trees, Shep. BA54 83
Mulberry Wk. SW3 BT43 66
Mulberry Way Belv. CS41 69
Mulberry Way Ilf. CM31 49
Mulfred Way. Sev. CX62 108
Mulgrave Rd. NW10 BO35 46
Mulgrave Rd. SW6 BR43 65
Mulgrave Rd. W5 BK38 54
Mulgrave Rd. Croy. BZ55 87
Mulgrave Rd. Har. BJ34 45
Mulgrave Rd. Sutt. BR57 94
Mulgrave Rd. Wok. AP62 100
Mulholland Clo. Mitch. BV51 86
Mulkern Rd. N19 BW33 47
Mullens Rd. Egh. AT49 72
Muller Rd. SW4 BW46 76
Mullet Gdns. E2 CB38 57
St. Peters Clo.
Mullins Path, SW14 BN45 65
North Worple Way
Mullion Clo. Har. BF30 36
Mullion Wk. Wat. BD28 36
Mull Wk. N1 BZ36 57
Marquess Est.
Mulready St. NW8 BU38 56
Multi-way, W3 BO41 65
Valetta Rd.
Multon Rd. SW18 BT47 76
Multon Rd. Sev. CZ57 99
Mumford Ct. EC2 BZ39 57
Milk St.
Mumfords La. Ger. Cr. AQ31 43
Muncaster Cl. Ashf. AZ49 73
Muncaster Rd. SW11 BU45 66
Muncaster Rd. Ashf. AZ49 73
Mundania Rd. SE22 CB46 77
Munday Rd. E16 CH40 58
Mundells. Welw. G. C. BR7 5
Munden Gro. Wat. BD22 27
Munden Pl. W14 BR42 65
Munden St.
Munden St. W14 BR42 65
Mundesley Spur, Slou. AP39 52
Mundford Rd. E5 CC34 48
Mundon Gdns. Ilf. CM33 49
Mund St. W14 BR42 65
Mundy St. N1 CA38 57
Hoxton Sq.
Munford Dr. Swans. DC47 81
Mungo Pk. Clo. Bush. BG27 36
Mungo Pk. Rd. Grav. DH49 81
Mungo Pk. Rd. Rain. CU35 50
Mungo Pk. Way Orp. CP54 89
Munnings Gdns. Islw. BG46 74
Munroe Rd. Bush. BF24 27
Munro Ms. W10 BR39 55
Munstead Vw. Guil. AQ72 118
Munster Av. Houns. BE45 64
Munster Gdns. N13 BY28 38
Munster Rd. SW6 BR43 65
Munster Rd. Tedd. BJ50 74
Munster Sq. NW1 BV38 56
Munton Rd. SE17 BZ42 67
Murchinson Rd. Hodd. CE10 12
Murchison Av. Bex. CP47 79
Murchison Rd. E10 CF34 48
Murdoch Clo. Stai. AW49 73
Cherry Orch.
Murdock Cotts. E3 CD38 57
Clinton Rd.
Murdock St. SE15 CB43 67
Murfett Cl. SW19 BR48 75
Queensmere Rd.
Muriel Av. Wat. BD25 27
Muriel St. N1 BX37 56
Murillo Rd. SE13 CF45 67
Murphy St. SE1 BY41 66
Murray Av. Brom. CH52 88
Murray Av. Houns. BF46 74
Murray Clo. Pnr. BD30 36
Murray Grn. Wok. AU60 91
Murray Gro. N1 BZ37 57
Murray Ms. NW1 BW36 56
Murray Rd. NW7 BQ29 37
Murray Rd. SW19 BQ50 75
Murray Rd. W5 BK42 64
Murray Rd. Berk. AR12 7
Murray Rd. Cher. AU57 91
Murray Rd. Nthwd. BB29 35
Murray Rd. Orp. CO52 89
Murray Rd. Rich. BJ48 74
Murray Sq. E16 CH39 58
Murray St. NW1 BW36 56
Murrays Yd. SE18 CL42 68
Powis St.
Murray Ter. NW3 BT35 47
New End
Murrells Wk. Lthd. BF65 102
Murthering La. Rom. CT25 32
Murton Ct. St. Alb. BH13 9
Althorp Rd.
Murton St. EC1 BZ38 57
Lever St.
Murtwell Dr. Chig. CM29 40
Musard Rd. W6 BR43 65
Musbery St. E1 CC39 57
Muscatel Pl. SE5 CA44 67
Dalwood St.
Muschamp Rd. SE15 CA45 67
Muschamp Rd. Cars. BT55 86
Muscovy St. EC3 CA40 57
Seething La.
Museum St. WC1 BX39 56
Musgrave Clo. Barn. BT23 29
Musgrave Cres. SW6 BS43 66
Musgrave Rd. Islw. BH44 64
Musgrove Rd. SE14 CC44 67
Musjid Rd. SW11 BT44 66
Muskam Rd. Harl. CO9 6
Musk Hill, Hem. H. AV14 7
Musquash Way Houns. BD44 64
Mussenden La. Hort. K. CY53 90
Mustard Mill Rd. Stai. AV49 72
Muston Rd. E5 CB34 48
Muswell Av. N10 BV30 38
Muswell Hill, N10 BV31 47
Muswell Hill Broadway, N10 BV31 47
Muswell Hill Est. N10 BU30 38
Muswell Hill Pl. N10 BV31 47
Muswell Mews N10 BV31 47
Muswell Rd.
Muswell Rd. N10 BV31 47
Mutchetts Clo. Wat. BE20 18
Mutrix Rd. NW6 BS37 56
Mutton La. Pot. B. BQ19 19
Mutton La. Pot. B. BS20 20
Mutton Row Ong. CV18 24
Muybridge Rd. N. Mal. BN51 85
Myatt Rd. SW9 BY44 66
Myburn Clo. Hem. H. AZ14 8
Mycenae Rd. SE3 CH43 68
Mychurch Lane SE17 CA42 67
Myddelton Gdns. N21 BY26 38
Myddelton Pk. N20 BT27 38
Myddelton Pass. EC1 BY38 56
Myddelton Rd. N8 BX31 47
Myddelton Sq. EC1 BY38 56
Myddelton St. EC1 BY38 56
Myddleton Av. Enf. CA22 30
Myddleton Path, Wal. Cr. CB19 21
Myddleton Rd. N22 BX29 38
Myddleton Rd. Uxb. AX37 53
Mygrove Clo. Rain. CV37 60
Mygrove Gdns. Rain. CV37 60
Mygrove Rd. Rain. CV37 60
Mylis Clo. SE26 CB49 77
Mymms Dr. Hat. BS16 20
Mymns Cl. Epsom. BM60 94
Myra St. SE2 CO42 69
Myrdle St. E1 CB39 57
Myron Pl. SE13 CF45 67
Myrtle All. SE18 CL41 68
Hare St.
Myrtle Ave. Houns. BB45 63
Myrtle Av. Ruis. BC33 44
Myrtle Clo. Barn. BU26 38
Myrtle Clo. Erith CT44 69
Myrtle Clo. Slou. AV44 62
Coleridge Cres.
Myrtle Clo. Uxb. AY39 53
Myrtle Clo. West Dr. AY42 63
Myrtle Cres. Slou. AP40 52
Myrtledene Rd. SE2 CO42 69
Myrtle Gdns. W7 BH40 54
Myrtle Grn. Hem. H. AV13 7
Myrtle Gro. Enf. BZ22 30
Myrtle Gro. N. Mal. BN51 85
Myrtle Gro. S. Ock. CY41 70
Myrtle Pass. Dor. BJ71 119
Church St.
Myrtle Pl. Dart. CY47 80
Myrtle Rd. E6 CK37 58
Myrtle Rd. E17 CD32 48
Myrtle Rd. N13 BZ27 39
Myrtle Rd. W3 BN40 55
Myrtle Rd. Brwd. DB28 42
Myrtle Rd. Croy. CE55 87
Myrtle Rd. Dart. CV47 80
Myrtle Rd. Dor. BJ71 119
Myrtle Rd. Hamptn. BG50 74
Myrtle Rd. Houns. BF44 64
Myrtle Rd. Ilf. CL34 49
Myrtle Rd. Rom. CV29 42
Myrtle Rd. Sutt. BT56 95
Myrtleside Clo. Nthwd. BA29 35
Mysore Rd. SW11 BU45 66
Myton Rd. SE21 BZ48 77
M1 Motorway NW4 BN28 37
M1 Motorway, NW7 BN28 37
M1 Motorway Edg. BL26 37
M1. Motorway Wat. BF23 27
M4 Hayes BC42 63
Nadine St. SE7 CJ42 68
Nagle Clo. E17 CF30 39
Nag's Head Est. E2 CA37 57
Nags Head La. Well. CO45 69
Nag's Head Rd. Enf. CC24 30
Nag, S Head La. Brwd. CZ28 42
Nag, S Head La. Upmin. CY30 42
Nailsworth Cres. Red. BW68 113
Nairne Gro. SE24 BZ45 67
Nairn Grn. Wat. BC27 35
Nairn Rd. Ruis. BD35 45
Naish Ct. N1 BX37 56
Nalders Rd. Chesh. AO18 16
Naleing Common. Wal. Abb. CJ15 13
Nallhead Rd. Felt. BD49 74
Namton Dr. Th. Hth. BX52 86
Nan-clark's La. NW7 BO27 37
Nancy Downs Wat. BD26 36
Nankin St. E14 CE39 57
Nansen Rd. SW11 BV45 66
Nansen Rd. Grav. DH49 81
Nantes Pass. E1 CA39 57
Lamb St.
Nant Rd. NW2 BR34 46
Nant St. E2 CB38 57
Paradise Row
Napier Av. SW6 BR45 65
Napier Clo. W14 BR41 65
Napier Clo. West Dr. AY41 63
Napier Ct. SW6 BR45 65
Napier Dr. Bush. BE24 27
Napier Gdns. Guil. AT70 118
Napier Gro. N1 BZ37 57
Napier Pl. W14 BR41 65
Napier Rd. E6 CL37 58
Napier Rd. E11 CG35 49
Napier Rd. E15 CG37 58
Napier Rd. N17 CA31 48
Napier Rd. NW10 BP38 55
Napier Rd. SE25 CB52 87
Napier Rd. W14 BR41 65
Napier Rd. Ashf. BA50 73
Napier Rd. Belv. CQ42 69
Napier Rd. Brom. CH52 88
Napier Rd. Enf. CC25 30
Napier Rd. Grav. DF47 81
Napier Rd. Islw. BJ45 64
Napier Rd. Sth. Croy. BZ57 96
Napier Rd. Wem. BK35 45
Napier St. SE8 CD43 67
Napier Ter. N1 BY36 56
Napoleon Rd. Twick. BJ47 74
Napsbury Av. St. Alb. BK16 18
Napsbury La. St. Alb. BJ15 9
Napsbury La. St. Alb. BJ16 18
Napsbury La. St. Alb. BK18 18
Nap, The, Kings L. AZ18 17
Narbonne Av. SW4 BW46 76
Narborough St. SW6 BS44 66
Narcissus Rd. NW6 BS35 47
Narcot La. Ch. St. G. AQ27 34
Narcot Rd. Ch. St. G. AQ27 34
Narcot Way. Ch. St. G. AQ28 34
Nare Rd. S. Ock. CW40 60
Narford Rd. E5 CB34 48
Narrow La. Warl. CB63 105
Narrow St. E14 CD40 57
Narrow St. W3 BM40 55
Steyne Rd.
Narrow Way Brom. CK53 88
Nasby Clo. Islw. BH44 64
Nascot Pl. Wat. BC23 26
Nascot Rd. Wat. BC23 26
Nascot St. W12 BQ39 55
Nascot St. Wat. BC23 26
Nascot Wood Rd. Wat. BB22 26
Naseby Clo. NW6 BT36 56
Naseby Rd. SE19 BZ50 77
Naseby Rd. Dag. CR34 50
Naseby Rd. Ilf. CK30 40
Nash Dr. Red. BU69 121
Nash Grn. Brom. CH50 78
Nash Grn. Hem. H. AZ16 17
Nash La. Kes. CH57 97
Nashleigh Hill. Chesh. AO17 16
Nash Rd. N9 CC27 39
Nash Rd. SE4 CD45 67
Nash Rd. Slou. AS42 62
Nash St. NW1 BV38 56
Nasmyth St. W6 BP41 65
Nassau Rd. SW13 BO44 65
Nassau St. W1 BW39 56
Nassington Rd. NW3 BU35 47
Natal Rd. N11 BW29 38
Natal Rd. SW16 BW50 76
Natal Rd. Ilf. CL35 49
Natal Rd. Th. Hth. BZ52 87
Nathans Rd. Wem. BK33 45
Nathan Way SE28 CM42 68
Naval Row E14 CF40 57
Navarino Gro. E8 CB36 57
Navarino Rd. E8 CB36 57
Navarre Gdns. Rom. CR28 41
Navarre Rd. E6 CK37 58
Navarre St. E2 CA38 57
Navestock Cres. Wdf. Grn. CJ29 40
Navy St. SW4 BW45 66
Naylor Rd. N20 BT27 38
Naylor Rd. SE15 CB43 67
Nazeing New Rd. Brox. CE14 12
Nazeing Rd. Wal. Abb. CF14 12
Nazeing Wk. Rain. CT37 59
Neal Av. Sthl. BE38 54
Neal Ct. Wal. Abb. CG20 22
Hillhouse
Nealden St. SW9 BX45 66
Neale Clo. N2 BT31 47
Neal Rd. Sev. CZ57 99
Neals Rd. Erith CS43 69
Brook St.
Neal St. WC2 BX39 56
Neal St. Wat. BD25 27
Near Acre NW9 BO30 37
Neasden Clo. NW10 BO35 46
Neasden La. NW10 BN34 46
Neasham Rd. Dag. CO35 50
Neate St. SE5 CA43 67
Neath Gdns. Mord. BT53 86
Neathouse Pl. SW1 BW42 66
Vauxhall Bridge Rd.
Neave Cres. Rom. CV30 42
Neb Corner Rd. Oxt. CF69 114
Nebraska St. SE1 BZ41 67
Neckinger Est. SE16 CA41 67
Neckinger St. SE1 CA41 67
Nectarine Way SE13 CE44 67
Needham Clo. Wind. AM44 61
Needham Rd. W11 BS39 56
Artesian Rd.
Needham Ter. NW2 BQ34 46
Neeld Cres. NW4 BP32 46
Neeld Cres. Wem. BM35 46
Neil Clo. Ashf. BA49 73
Nelgarde Rd. SE6 CE47 77
Nella Rd. W6 BQ43 65
Nellgrove Rd. Uxb. AZ38 53
Nell Gwynne Av. Shep. BA53 83
Green La.
Nelmes Clo. Horn. CW32 51
Nelmes Cres. Horn. CW32 51
Nelmes Rd. Horn. CW33 51
Nelmes Way. Horn. CV31 51
Nelson Av. St. Alb. BJ15 9
Nelson Clo. Brwd. DB28 42
Nelson Clo. Croy. BY54 86
Nelson Clo. Rom. CR30 41
Nelson Clo. Slou. AR42 62
Nelson Clo. Uxb. AZ38 53
Nelson Clo. Walt. BC54 83
Nelson Clo. West. CK62 106
Nelson Gdns. E2 CB38 57
Bethnal Green Rd.
Nelson Gdns. Guil. AT70 118
Nelson Gdns. Houns. BF46 74
Nelson Gro. Rd. SW19 BW51 86
Nelson La. Uxb. AZ38 53
Nelson Pl. N1 BY37 56
Nelson Pl. NW6 BS38 56
Percy Rd.
Nelson Pl. W3 BM40 55
Steyne Rd.
Nelson Pl. Sid. CO49 79
Nelson Rd. E4 CE29 39
Nelson Rd. E11 CH31 49
Nelson Rd. N8 BX32 47
Nelson Rd. N9 CB27 39
Nelson Rd. N15 CA31 48
Nelson Rd. SE10 CF43 67
Nelson Rd. SW19 BS50 76
Nelson Rd. Ashf. AY49 73
Nelson Rd. Belv. CQ42 69
Nelson Rd. Brom. CJ52 88
Nelson Rd. Cat. BZ65 105
Nelson Rd. Dart. CV46 80
Nelson Rd. Enf. CC25 30
Nelson Rd. Grav. DF48 81
Nelson Rd. Har. BG33 45
Nelson Rd. Houns. BF46 74
Nelson Rd. N. Mal. BN53 85
Nelson Rd. Rain. CT37 59

Nelson Rd. Sid.	CO49	79
Nelson Rd. S. Ock.	CA37	60
Nelson Rd. Stan.	BK29	36
Nelson Rd. Uxb.	AZ38	53
Nelson Rd. Wind.	AM45	61
Nelson Sq. SE1	BY41	66
Nelson's Row SW4	BW45	66
Nelson St. E1	CB39	57
Nelson St. E6	CK37	58
Nelson St. E16	CG40	58
Nelson Ter. N1	BY37	56
Nelwyn Av. Horn.	CW32	51
Nemoure Rd. W3	BN40	55
Nepaul Rd. SW11	BU44	66
Nepean St. SW15	BP46	75
Neptune Dr. Hem. H.	AY12	8
Neptune Rd. Har.	BG32	45
Neptune St. SE16	CC41	67
Nesbit Rd. SE9	CJ45	68
Ness Rd. Erith.	CV43	70
Ness St. SE16	CB41	67
Spa Rd.		
Nesta Rd. Wdf. Grn.	CG29	40
Nestles Ave. Hayes.	BB41	63
Neston Rd. Wat.	BD22	27
Neston St. SE16	CC41	67
Nestor Av. N21	BY25	29
Nethan Dr. S. Ock.	CW40	60
Netheravon Rd. W4	BO42	65
Netheravon Rd. W7	BH40	54
Netheravon Rd. S. W4	BO42	65
Netherbury Rd. W5	BK41	64
Netherby Gdns. Enf.	BX24	29
Netherby Rd. SE23	CC47	77
Nether Clo. N3	BS29	38
Nethercourt Av. N3	BS29	38
Netherfield Gdns. Bark.	CM36	58
Netherfield Rd. N12	BS28	38
Netherfield St. W11	BR40	55
Portland Rd.		
Netherford Rd. SW4	BW44	66
Netherhall Gdns. NW3	BT36	56
Netherhall Rd. Harl.	CG12	13
Netherhall Way NW3	BT35	47
Netherhall Gdns.		
Netherland Rd. SW17	BV48	76
Netherland Rd. Barn.	BT25	29
Netherlands. The. Couls.	BW63	104
Netherleigh Pk. Red.	BX72	121
Nether Mount. Guil.	AQ71	118
Nethern Court Rd. Cat.	CE65	105
Netherne La. Couls.	BW65	104
Netherpark Dr. Rom.	CT30	41
Netherton Gro. SW10	BT43	66
Netherton Rd. Twick.	BJ46	74
Netherway, St. Alb.	BF15	9
Netherwood Rd. W14	BQ41	65
Netherwood St. Est. NW6	BR36	55
Netherwood St. NW6	BR36	55
Netley Clo. Croy.	CF57	96
Netley Clo. Sutt.	BQ56	94
Netley Dr. Walt.	BE54	84
Netley Gdns. Mord.	BT54	86
Netley Rd. E17	CD32	48
Netley Rd. Brent.	BL43	65
Netley Rd. Ilf.	CM32	49
Netley Rd. Mord.	BT54	86
Nettlecombe Clo. Sutt.	BS58	95
Nettlecroft. Hem. H.	AW14	8
Nettleden Av. Wem	BM36	55
Nettleden Rd. Berk.	AT11	7
Nettlefold Pl. SE27	BY48	76
Nettlestead Clo. Beck.	CD50	77
Nettles Ter. Guil.	AR70	118
Nettleton Rd. SE14	CC44	67
Nettleton Rd. Uxb.	AY35	44
Nettlewood Rd. SW16	BW50	76
Neuchatel Rd. SE6	CD48	77
Neusden Way	AS33	43
Nevada St. SE10	CF43	67
Nevell Rd. Grays	DG41	71
Brentwood Rd.		
Nevern Pl. SW5	BS42	66
Nevern Rd. SW5	BS42	66
Nevern Sq. SW5	BS42	66
Neville Av. N. Mal.	BN51	85
Neville Clo. NW6	BR37	55
Neville Clo. Esher.	BE57	93
Neville Clo. Pot. B.	BR19	19
Neville Clo. Sid.	CN49	78
Neville Clo. Slou.	AP36	52
Neville Ct. NW8	BT37	56
Neville Dr. N2	BT32	47
Neville Gdns. Dag.	CP34	50
Neville Rd.		
Neville Gill Clo. SW18	BS46	76
Buckhold Rd.		
Neville Pl. NW6	BR37	55
Neville Rd. E7	CH36	58
Neville Rd. NW6	BR37	55
Neville Rd. W5	BK38	54
Neville Rd. Croy.	BZ54	87
Neville Rd. Dag.	CP34	50
Neville Rd. Ilf.	CM30	40
Neville Rd. Kings. On T.	BM51	85
Neville Rd. Rich.	BK48	74
Neville's Ct. NW2	BP34	46
Neville St. SW7	BT42	66
Neville Ter. SW7	BT42	66
Neville Wk. Cars.	BU54	86
Green Wrythe La.		
Nevill Gro. Wat.	BC23	26
Nevill Rd. N16	CA34	48
Nevill Way Loug.	CK26	40
Nevin Dr. E4	CE26	39
Nevis Clo. Rom.	CT29	41
Nevis Rd. SW17	BV48	76
Newark Cres. NW10	BN38	55
Newark Grn. Borwd.	BN24	28
Newark La. Wok.	AV63	100
Newark La. Wok.	AW64	101
Newark Rd. Sth. Croy.	BZ57	96
Newark St. E1	CB39	57
Newark Way NW4	BP31	46
New Barnes Av. St. Alb.	BJ15	9
Newbarn La. Beac.	AP28	34
New Barn La. Sev.	CM62	106
New Barn La. West.	CM62	106
New Barn La. Whyt.	CA61	105
New Barn Rd. Grav.	DD49	81
New Barn Rd. Swan.	CT51	89
New Barns Av. Mitch.	BW52	86
New Barn St. E13	CH39	58
New Barns Way Chig.	CL27	40
Newberries Av. Rad.	BJ21	27
Newberry Cres. Wind.	AL44	61
Newberry Est. N1	BZ36	57
Newberry Way. Slou.	AO41	61
Newbery Rd. Erith	CT44	69
Newbiggin Path. Wat.	BD28	36
Newbold Rd. SE15	CB44	67
Asylum Rd.		
Newbolt Rd. Stan.	BH28	36
New Bond St. W1	BV39	56
Newborough Grn. N. Mal.	BN52	85
New Bowyer Pla. SE5	BZ43	67
New Brent St. NW4	BQ32	46
New Bridge Erith	CS42	69
New Bridge St. EC4	BY39	56
New Broad St. EC2	BZ39	57
New Broadway W5	BK40	54
Newburgh Rd. W3	BN40	55
Newburgh St. W1	BW39	56
Foubert's Pl.		
New Burlington Pl. W1	BW40	56
Savile Row		
New Burlington St. W1	BW40	56
Newburn St. SE11	BX42	66
Newbury Av. Enf.	CD22	30
Newbury Clo. Nthlt.	BE36	54
Newbury Clo. Rom.	CV29	42
Newbury Ct. E11	CH31	49
Newbury Gdns. Epsom	BO56	94
Newbury Gdns. Rom.	CV29	42
Newbury Gdns. Upmin.	CW34	51
Newbury Rd. E4	CF29	39
Newbury Rd. Brom.	CH52	88
Newbury Rd. Ilf.	CN32	49
Newbury Rd. Rom.	CV28	42
Newbury St. EC1	BZ39	57
Newbury Wk. Rom.	CV28	42
Newbury Way Nthlt.	BE36	54
New Butts Gdns. Slou.	AT44	62
Newby Clo. Enf.	CA23	30
Newby Pl. E14	CF39	57
Newby St. SW8	BV44	66
Newcastle Av. Ilf.	CO29	41
Newcastle Ct. EC4	BY39	56
Farringdon St.		
Newcastle Pl. W2	BT39	56
Newcastle St. W8	BS41	66
New Causeway, Reig.	BS72	121
New Cavendish St. W1	BV39	56
New Change EC4	BZ39	57
New Chapel Rd. Felt.	BC47	73
New Church Rd. SE5	BZ43	67
New City Rd. E13	CJ38	58
New Clo. SW19	BT51	86
New Clo. Felt.	BE49	74
New Close Est. Mitch.	BT51	86
Newcombe Pk. NW7	BO28	37
Newcombe Pk. Wem.	BL37	55
Newcombe Rd. Rad.	BM20	19
Newcombe St. W8	BS40	56
Newcomen Rd. E11	CG34	49
Newcomen Rd. SW11	BT45	66
Newcomen St. SE1	BZ41	67
New Compton St. WC2	BW39	56
New Ct. Dart.	CW46	80
New Ct. Uxb.	AX39	53
New Ct. Wey.	AX55	83
Newcourt St. NW8	BU37	56
New Coventry St. W1	BW40	56
Coventry St.		
Newcroft Clo. Uxb.	AY39	53
New Cross Gate SE14	CC44	67
New Cross Rd. SE14	CC43	67
New Cross Rd. Guil.	AQ69	118
Newdene Av. Nthlt.	BD37	54
Newdigate Gdn. Uxb.	AX30	35
Newdigate Rd. Uxb.	AX30	35
Newdigate Rd. East. Uxb.	AX30	35
Newell Rd. Hem. H.	AY15	8
Newell St. E14	CD39	57
New End NW3	BT35	47
New End Sq. NW3	BT35	47
New England St. St. Alb.	BG13	9
Newenham Rd. Lthd.	BF66	111
Newent Clo. Cars.	BU54	86
New Farm Dr.	CP24	32
New Farm La. Nthwd.	BB30	35
New Fetter La. EC4	BY39	56
Newfield Clo. Hamptn.	BF51	84
Newfield La. Hem. H.	AY13	8
Newfields. Welw. G. C.	BP8	5
New Fm. Av. Brom.	CH52	88
Newford Clo. Hem. H.	AZ13	8
New Ford Rd. Wal. Cr.	CD20	21
New Forest La. Chig.	CL29	40
Newgale Gdns. Edg.	BL30	37
Newgate Croy.	BZ54	87
Newgate Clo. Felt.	BE48	74
Newgate St. E4	CG27	40
Newgate St. EC1	BY39	56
Newgate St. Hert.	BX15	11
Newgatestreet Rd. Wal. Cr.	BY16	20
New Goulston St. E1	CA39	57
Middlesex St.		
New Greens Av. St. Alb.	BG11	9
Newhall Ct. Wal. Abb.	CG20	22
Mason Way		
New Hall Dr. Rom.	CW30	42
Newhams Clo. Brom.	CK52	88
Newhams Row SE1	CA41	67
Newham Way E16	CJ39	58
Newham Way Har.	BL31	46
Newhaven Clo. Hayes.	BB42	63
Newhaven Cres. Ashf.	BA49	73
Newhaven Gdns. SE9	CJ45	68
Newhaven Rd. SE25	BZ53	87
Newhaw Rd. Wey.	AX56	92
New Heston Rd. Houns.	BE43	64
New Hill Rd. Orp.	CK58	97
Newhouse Av. Rom.	CP31	50
Newhouse Clo. N. Mal.	BO54	85
Newhouse Cres. Wat.	BC19	17
New House La. Epp.	CS16	23
New House La. Grav.	DF48	81
Newhouse Lane. Ong.	CV14	15
Newhouse Pk. St. Alb.	BJ15	9
Newhouse Rd. Hem. H.	AT16	16
Newhouse Way Mord.	BT54	86
Newick Clo. Bex.	CR46	79
Newick Rd. E5	CB34	48
Newington Barrow Way N7	BX34	47
Andover Est.		
Newington Butts. SE11	BY42	66
Newington Causeway SE1	BY41	66
Newington Gn. N16	BZ35	48
Newington Gn. Rd. N1	BZ35	48
New Inn Broadway EC2	CA38	57
New Inn Yd.		
New Inn La. Guil.	AT00	100
New Inn Yd. EC2	CA38	57
New James Ct. SE15	CB45	67
New James St. SE15	CB45	67
Scylla Rd.		
New Kent Rd. SE1	BZ41	67
New King's Rd. SW6	BR44	65
New King St. SE8	CE43	67
Newland Gdns. W13	BJ41	64
Newland Rd. N8	BX31	47
Newlands Av. Rad.	BH20	18
Newlands Av. Surb.	BH54	84
Newlands Av. Wok.	AS64	100
Newlands Clo. Brwd.	DE26	122
Newlands Clo. Edg.	BL27	37
Newlands Clo. Sthl.	BE42	64
Newlands Clo. Walt.	BE56	93
Newlands Clo. Wem.	BK36	54
Newlands Ct. Wem.	BM34	46
Newlands Dr. Enf.	CB23	30
Newlands Est. SW17	BV49	76
Newlands Pk. SE26	CC50	77
Newlands Pl. Barn.	BQ25	28
Newlands Rd. SW16	BX51	86
Newlands Rd. Hem. H.	AV13	7
Newlands Rd. Wdf. Grn.	CG27	40
Newlands, The, Wall.	BW57	95
Newland St. E16	CK40	58
Newlands Wk. Wat.	BD20	18
Newlands Way Chess.	BK56	93
Newlands Wd. Croy.	CD58	96
New La. Guil.	AS66	109
New La. Wok. & Guil.	AS64	100
Newling Est. E2	CA38	57
New London St. EC3	CA40	57
Hart St.		
Newlyn Clo. St. Alb.	BE18	18
Newlyn Clo. Uxb.	AZ39	53
Newlyn Gdns. Har.	BE33	45
Newlyn Rd. N17	CA30	39
Newlyn Rd. Barn.	BR24	28
Newlyn Rd. Nw2	BQ33	46
Newlyn Rd. Well.	CN44	68
Newman Pass. W1	BW39	56
Newman St.		
Newman Rd. E13	CH38	58
Newman Rd. E17	CC32	48
Newman Rd. Brom.	CH51	88
Newman Rd. Hayes	BC40	53
Newmans Clo. Loug.	CL24	31
Newmans Dr. Brwd.	DE26	122
Newmans La. Loug.	CL24	31
Newmans Rd. Grav.	DF48	81
Newman's Row WC2	BV39	56
Gt. Turnstile		
Newman St. W1	BW39	56
Newmans Way Barn.	BT23	29
Newmarket Av. Nthlt.	BF35	45
Newmarket Grn. SE9	CJ47	78
Newmarket Way. Horn.	CW35	51
New Martan St. E1	CA40	57
New Meadows Path Rich.	BM44	65
Townmead Rd.		
Newminster Rd. Mord.	BT53	86
New Mount St. E15	CF36	57
Newnham Av. Ruis.	BD33	45
Newnham Clo. Loug.	CJ25	31
Newnham Clo. Nthlt.	BG35	45
Newnham Clo. Slou.	AQ40	52
Newnham Gdns. Nthlt.	BG36	54
Newnham Pk. Wal. Cr.	CC18	21
Newnham Pl. Grays.	DG42	71
Newnham Rd. N22	BX30	38
Newnham Ter. SE1	BY41	66
New North Pl. EC2	CA38	57
Luke St.		
New North Rd. N1	BZ36	57
New North Rd. Ilf.	CM29	40
New North Rd. Reig.	BR72	120
New North St. WC1	BX39	56
Newnton Clo. N4	BZ33	48
New Oak Rd. N2	BT30	38
New Orleans Walk N19	BW33	47
New Oxford St. WC1	BW39	56
New Pa. Hayes	BA39	53
New Pde. Ashf.	AY49	73
Church Rd.		
New Pk. Av. N13	BY27	38
New Park Clo. Nthlt.	BD36	54
New Pk. Ct. SW2	BX47	76
New Park Dr. Hem. H.	AZ13	8
New Park Rd. SW2	BW47	76
New Park Rd. Ashf.	BA49	73
New Park Rd. Hert.	BV15	11
New Park Rd. Uxb.	AX30	35
New Peachey La. Uxb.	AX39	53
New Peachey La. Clo. Uxb.	AX39	53
Newpiece Loug.	CL24	31
New Place Gdns. Upmin.	CY34	51
New Pl. Sq. SE16	CB41	67
Southwark Pk. Rd.		
New Plaistow Rd. E15	CG37	58
New Pond Rd. Guil.	AO74	118
Newport Av. E13	CH38	58
Palmer Rd.		
Newport.Ct. WC2	BW40	56
Charing Cross Rd.		
Newport Est. E3	CD38	57
Newport Mead Wat.	BD28	36
Newport Pl. WC2	BW40	56
Shaftesbury Av.		
Newport Rd. E10	CF34	48
Newport Rd. E17	CD31	48
Newport Rd. SW13	BP44	65
Newport Rd. Hayes	BA39	53
Newports, Saw.	CP6	6
Newports Swan.	CS54	89
Newport St. SE11	BX42	66
Newport St. WC2	BW41	66
Charing Cross Rd.		
Newquay Cres. Har.	BE34	45
Newquay Gdns. Wat.	BC27	35
Newquay Rd. SE6	CE48	77
New Quebec St. W1	BU39	56
New River Clo. Hodd.	CE11	12
New River Ct. N5	BZ35	48
New River Cres. N13	BY28	38
New River Gdns. N22	BY29	38
New River Wk. N1	BZ36	57
New Rd. E1	CA39	57
New Rd. E4	CE28	39
New Rd. E16	CG39	58
New Rd. N8	BX32	47
New Rd. N9	CB27	39
New Rd. N17	CA30	39
New Rd. N22	BZ30	39
New Rd. NW7	BO26	37
New Rd. NW7	BR29	37
New Rd. SE2	CP42	69
New Rd. Amer.	AP22	25
New Rd. Berk.	AS11	7
New Rd. Berks.	AP12	7
New Rd. Brent.	BK43	64
New Rd. Brox.	CD13	12
New Rd. Brwd.	DB27	42
New Rd. Ch. St. G.	AS24	25
New Rd. Dag.	CR37	59
New Rd. Dor.	BK72	119
New Rd. E. Mol.	BF52	84
New Rd. Epp.	CR19	23
New Rd. Esher	BG55	84
New Rd. Felt.	BA46	73
New Rd. Felt.	BC47	73
New Rd. Felt.	BE49	74
New Rd. Grav.	DG46	81
New Road. Guil.	AY69	110
New Rd. Har.	BH35	45
New Rd. Harl.	CP9	6
New Rd. Hayes.	BA43	63
New Rd. Ilf.	CN34	49
New Rd. Kings L.	AV18	16
New Rd. Kings. On T.	BM50	75
New Rd. Leath.	BH58	93
New Rd. Lthd	BH59	93
New Rd. Maid.	AG43	61
New Rd. Mord.	BU54	86
New Rd. Orp.	CO54	89
New Rd. Oxt.	CH68	115
New Rd. Pot. B.	BP20	19
New Rd. Rad.	BH21	27
New Rd. Rad.	BM20	19
New Rd. Rich.	BK49	74
New Rd. Rick.	AV23	25
New Rd. Rick.	AZ25	26
New Rd Rom.	CP25	32
New Rd. Shep.	AZ52	83
New Rd. Slou.	AR44	62
New Rd. Slou.	AT41	62
New Rd. S. Dnth.	CY51	90
New Rd. Stai.	AU49	72
New Rd. Swan.	CT50	79
New Rd. Swan.	CT52	89
New Rd. Tad.	BQ65	103
New Rd. Uxb.	BA38	53
New Rd. Wat.	BD24	27
New Rd. Wat.	BH23	27
New Rd. Well.	CO44	69
New Rd. Welw. G. C.	BP9	5
New Rd. Welw. G. C.	BR5	5
New Rd. Wey.	BA56	92
New Row WC2	BX40	56
Newry Rd. Twick.	BJ46	74
New St. Hill EC4	BY39	56
Lit. New St.		
New St. Hill Brom.	CH49	78
New St. Sq. EC4	BY39	56
Newsam Av. N15	BZ32	48
New Scotland Yd. SW1	BX41	66
Derby Gate		
New Spring Gdns. Brent.	BK43	64
New Sq. WC2	BX39	56
Newstead. Hat.	BO14	10
Newstead Av. Orp.	CM55	88
Newstead Ri. Cat.	CB66	114
Newstead Rd. SE12	CG47	78
Newstead Rd. Cat.	CB66	114
Newstead Wk. Cars.	BT54	86
Newstead Way SW19	BQ49	75
New St. EC2	CA39	57
New St. Berk.	AR13	7
New St. Saw.	CQ5	6
New St. Stai.	AW49	73
New St. Wat.	BD24	27
Church St.		
New St. West.	CM67	115
Newton Abbot Rd. Grav.	DF48	81
Newton Av. N10	BV30	38
Newton Av. W3	BN41	65
Newton Clo. Slou.	AS41	62
Newton Dr. Saw.	CP6	6
Newton Gro. N1	BZ37	57
Northport St.		
Newton Gro. W4	BO41	65
Newton La. Wind.	AQ46	72
Newton Rd. E15	CF35	48
Newton Rd. N15	CA32	48
Newton Rd. NW2	BQ35	46
Newton Rd. SW19	BR50	75
Newton Rd. W2	BS39	56
Newton Rd. Chig.	CO28	41
Newton Rd. Har.	BH30	36
Newton Rd. Islw.	BH44	64
Newton Rd. Pur.	BW59	95
Newton Rd. Til.	DG44	71
Newton Rd. Well.	CO45	69
Newton Rd. Wem.	BL36	55
Newtons Clo. Rain.	CT36	59
Newton St. WC2	BX39	56
Newton's Yd. SW18	BS46	76
Wandsworth High St.		
Newton Way N18	BZ28	39
Newton Wood Rd. Ash.	BL61	103
Newtown Rd. Uxb.	AW36	53
Newtown St. SW11	BV44	66
New Trinity Rd. N2	BT31	47
New Turnstile WC1	BX39	56
High Holborn		
New Wanstead E11	CG32	49
New Way La. Harl.	CR11	14
New Way Rd. NW9	BO31	46
New Wharf Rd. N1	BX37	56
New Windsor St. Uxb.	AX37	53
New Wood. Welw. G. C.	BT7	5
Newyears Green La. Uxb.	AY32	44
New Years La. Sev.	CN61	106
New Zealand Av. Walt.	BB54	83
New Zealand Way W12	BP40	55
New Zealand Way Rain.	CT38	59
Niagara Av. W5	BK42	64
Nibthwaite Rd. Har.	BH32	45
Nicholas Clo. St. Alb.	BG11	9
Nicholas Clo. Wat.	BC22	26
Nicholas Dr. Sev.	CV66	117
Nicholas Gdns. W5	BK40	54
Nicholas Gdns. Wok.	AV61	100
Nicholas La. EC4	BZ40	57
Nicholas Rd. E1	CC38	57
Nicholas Rd. Borwd.	BM25	28
Nicholas Rd. Croy.	BX56	95
Nicholas Rd. Dag.	CQ34	50
Nicholas Rd. Houns.	BF45	64
Nicholas Way, Hem. H.	AY12	8
Nicholas Way. Nthwd.	BA30	35
Nicholas Way. Sev.	CV64	108
Nicholay Rd. N19	BW33	47
Nichol Clo. N14	BW26	38
Nichol La. Brom.	CH50	78
Nicholl Rd. NW10	BO37	55
Nicholl Rd. Epp.	CN19	22
Nicholls Av. Uxb.	AZ38	53
Nichollsfield. Harl.	CO11	14
Nichols Grn. W5	BK39	54
Montpelier Rd.		
Nicholson Dr. Bush.	BG26	36
Nicholson Rd. Croy.	CA54	87
Nicholson St. SE1	BY40	56
Nickleby Rd. Grav.	DK47	81
Nicola Clo. Har.	BG30	36
Nicola Clo. Sth. Croy.	BZ57	96
Nicolas Wk. Grays.	DG41	71
Nicol End. Ger. Cr.	AR30	34
Nicoll Way Borwd.	BN24	28
Nicol Pl. NW4	BP32	46
Nicol Rd. Ger. Cr.	AR30	34
Nicolson Rd. Orp.	CP54	89
Nicosia Rd. SW18	BU47	76
Niddersdale, Hem. H.	AY12	8
Niederwald Rd. SE26	CD49	77
Nield Rd. Hayes.	BB41	63
Nigel Clo. Nthlt.	BE37	54
Nigel Ms. Ilf.	CL35	49
Nigel Playfair Av. W6	BP42	65
Nigel Rd. E7	CJ35	49
Nigel Rd. SE15	CB45	67
Nigeria Rd. SE7	CJ43	68
Nighingales La. Ch. St. G.	AR26	34
Nightingale Ave. Lthd.	BA65	101
Nightingale Av. E4	CG28	40
Nightingale Av. Leath.	BA66	110
Nightingale Av. Upmin.	CZ33	51
Nightingale Clo. E4	CF28	39
Nightingale Clo. W4	BN43	65
Nightingale Clo. Cars.	BV55	86
Nightingale Clo. Grav.	DF49	81
Nightingale Cres. SW11	BU46	76
Blenkarne Rd.		
Nightingale Cres. Leath.	BA66	110
Nightingale Cres. Lthd.	BA65	101
Nightingale Dr. Epsom.	BM57	94
Nightingale Gro. SE13	CF46	77
Nightingale Gro. Dart.	CX45	70
Nightingale La. E11	CH32	49
Nightingale La. N6	BU33	47
Nightingale La. N8	BX31	47
Nightingale La. Brom.	CJ51	88
Nightingale La. Rich.	BL47	75
Nightingale La. St. Alb.	BK15	9
Nightingale La. Sev.	CR68	116
Nightingale Pl. SE18	CL43	68
Nightingale Rd. E5	CB34	48
Nightingale Rd. N9	CC26	39
Nightingale Rd. N22	BX30	38
Nightingale Rd. NW10	BO37	55
Nightingale Rd. W7	BH40	54
Nightingale Rd. Bush.	BF25	27

Nightingale Rd. Cars. BU55 86
Nightingale Rd. Croy. CC59 96
Nightingale Rd. E. Mol. BF53 84
Nightingale Rd. Esher. BE56 93
Nightingale Rd. Guil. AR70 118
Nightingale Rd. Hmptn. BF49 74
Nightingale Road. Leath. BB66 110
Nightingale Rd. Orp. CM53 88
Nightingale Rd. Rick. AX26 35
Nightingale. Rd. Sev. CW62 108
Nightingale Rd. Sth. Croy. CC58 96
Nightingale Rd. Sth. Croy. CC58 96
Nightingales Wal. Abb. CG20 22
Roundhills
Nightingales La. Ch. St. G. AR24 25
Nightingale Sq. SW12 BV47 76
Nightingale Vale SE18 CL43 68
Nightingale Wk. SW4 BV46 76
Nightingale Way Uxb. AV33 43
Nile Rd. E13 CJ37 58
Nile St. N1 BW38 56
Nile Ter. SE15 CA42 67
Nimbus Rd. Epsom BN58 94
Nimegen Way SE22 CA46 77
Dulwich Gro.
Nimmo Dr. Bush. BG26 36
Nimrod Rd. SW17 BV50 76
Nine Acres, Clo. E12 CK35 49
Nine Ashes Rd. Brwd. DA20 24
Nine Ashes Rd. Ing. DC18 24
Nine Elms Av. Uxb. AX39 53
Nine Elms Clo. Uxb. AX39 53
Nine Elms Gro. Grav. DG47 81
Nine Elms La. SW8 BW43 66
Ninefields, Wal. Abb. CG20 22
Nineham Gdns. Cat. BZ63 105
Ninehams Clo. Cat. BZ63 105
Ninehams Rd. Cat. BZ64 105
Ninehams Rd. West. CJ64 106
Nine Styles Clo. Uxb. AW36 53
Ninhams Wd. Orp. CK56 97
Ninnings Rd. Ger. Cr. AS29 34
Ninnings Way. Ger. Cr. AS29 34
Ninth Av. Hayes BC40 53
Nisbet Ho. E9 CC35 48
Nita Rd. Brwd. DB28 42
Nithdale Rd. SE18 CL43 68
Niton Clo. Barn. BQ25 28
Niton Rd. Rich. BM45 65
Niton St. SW6 BQ43 65
Nizels La. Ton. CW71 117
Nizels Rd. Ton. CW70 117
Noak Hill Rd. Rom. CV28 42
Noble Rd. N18 CC28 39
Noble St. EC2 BZ39 57
Nobles Way, Egh. AS50 72
Nockhall Rd. Green. DB46 80
Noel Park Rd. N22 BY30 38
Noel Rd. E6 CK38 58
Noel Rd. N1 BY37 56
Noel Rd. W3 BM40 55
Noel Sq. Dag. CP35 50
Noel St. W1 BW39 56
Noke Dr. Red. BV70 121
Noke La. St. Alb. BE16 18
Nokes, The Hem. H. AW12 8
Nolan Way, E5 CB35 48
Nolton Pl. Edg. BL30 37
Nonsuch Clo. Ilf. CL29 40
Nonsuch Wk. Sutt. BQ58 94
Nora Gdns. NW4 BQ31 46
Norah St. E2 CB38 57
Nora Ter. Har. BH33 45
Norbiton Av. Kings. On T. BM51 85
Norbiton Common Rd. N. Mal. BM52 85
Norbiton Hall Kings. On T. BL51 85
Norbiton Rd. E14 CD39 57
Norbreck Gdns. NW10 BL38 55
Norbreck Pde. W5 BL38 55
Norbroke St. W12 BO40 55
Norburn St. W10 BR39 55
Chesterton Rd.
Norbury Av. Houns. BG45 64
Norbury Clo. SW16 BY51 86
Norbury Ct. Rd. SW16 BX52 86
Norbury Cres. SW16 BX51 86
Norbury Cross SW16 BX52 86
Norbury Gdns. Rom. CP32 50
Norbury Gro. NW7 BO27 37
Norbury Hl. SW16 BY50 76
Norbury Ms. SW16 BX51 86
Norbury Cres.
Norbury Rise SW16 BX52 86
Norbury Rd. E4 CE28 39
Norbury Rd. Reig. BR70 120
Norbury Rd. Th. Hth. BZ51 87
Norbury Way. Lthd. BG66 111
Norcombe Gdns. Har. BK32 45
Norcott Clo. Hayes BD38 54
Norcott Rd. N16 CB34 48
Norcroft Gdns. SE22 CB47 77
Norcutt Rd. Twick. BH47 74
Nordenfeldt Rd. Erith CS42 69
Norfield Rd. Bex. CS49 79
Norfolk Av. N13 BY29 38
Norfolk Av. N15 CA32 48
Norfolk Av. Sth. Croy. CA58 96
Norfolk Av. Wat. BD22 27
Norfolk Clo. N2 BU31 47
Park Rd.
Norfolk Clo. N13 BY29 38
Norfolk Clo. Barn. BV24 29
Norfolk Clo. Twick. BJ46 74
Norfolk Cres. W2 BU39 56
Norfolk Cres. Sid. CN47 78
Norfolk Est. E1 CC38 57
Norfolk Farm Clo. Wok. AU61 100
Norfolk Farm Rd. Wok. AU61 100
Norfolk Gdns. Bexh. CQ44 69
Norfolk Gdns. Borwd. BN24 28
Norfolk Ho. Rd. SW16 BW48 76
Norfolk Pl. W2 BT39 56
Norfolk Pl. Well. CO44 69
Norfolk Rd. E6 CK37 58
Norfolk Rd. E17 CC30 39
Norfolk Rd. NW8 BT37 56
Norfolk Rd. NW10 BO36 55
Norfolk Rd. SW19 BU50 76
Norfolk Rd. Bark. CN36 58
Norfolk Rd. Barn. BS24 29
Norfolk Rd. Dag. CR35 50
Norfolk Rd. Dor. BJ71 119
Norfolk Rd. Enf. CB25 30
Norfolk Rd. Esher BH56 93
Norfolk Rd. Felt. BD47 74
Norfolk Rd. Grav. DH46 81
Norfolk Rd. Grav. DH47 81
Norfolk Rd. Har. BF32 45
Norfolk Rd. Ilf. CN33 49
Norfolk Rd. Rick. AY26 35
Norfolk Rd. Rom. CS32 50
Norfolk Rd. Th. Hth. BZ52 87
Norfolk Rd. Upmin. CX34 51
Norfolk Rd. Uxb. AX36 53
Norfolk Row SE11 BX42 66
Old Paradise St.
Norfolk Sq. W2 BT39 56
Norfolk St. E7 CH35 49
Norfolk Ter. W6 BR42 65
Norgrove St. SW12 BV47 76
Norheads. West. CH62 106
Norheads La. West. CJ61 106
Norhyrst Av. SE25 CA52 87
Nork Gdns. Bans. BR60 94
Nork Rise Bans. BQ61 103
Nork Way Bans. BQ61 103
Norland Pl. W11 BR40 55
Norland Rd. W11 BQ40 55
Norlands Cres. Chis. CL51 88
Norland Sq. W11 BR40 55
Norley Rd. SE13 CF45 67
Norley Vale SW15 BP47 75
Norman Av. N22 BY30 38
Norman Av. Epsom BO59 94
Norman Av. Felt. BE48 74
Norman Av. Sth. Croy. BZ58 96
Norman Av. Sthl. BE40 54
Norman Av. Twick. BJ47 74
Normanby Rd. NW10 BO35 46
Norman Clo. N22 BZ30 39
Norman Av.
Norman Clo. Dart. CW47 80
Norman Clo. Orp. CM55 88
Norman Clo. Rom. CR30 41
Norman Clo. Wal. Abb. CF20 21
Norman Ct. N4 BY33 47
Norman Ct. Pot. B. BT19 20
Norman Cres. Brwd. DD27 122
Norman Cres. Houns. BD43 64
Normand Ms. W14 BR43 65
Normand Rd. W14 BR43 65
Normandy Av. Barn. BR25 28
Normandy Dr. Berk. AQ12 7
Normandy Dr. Hayes BA39 53
Normandy Rd. SW9 BY44 66
Normandy Rd. St. Alb. BG12 9
Normandy Ter. E16 CH39 58
Normandy Way Erith CT44 69
Norman Gro. E3 CD37 57
Norman Ho. Felt. BE48 74
Norman Hurst, Ashf. AZ49 73
Normanhurst Brwd. DE25 122
Rayleigh Rd.
Normanhurst Dr. Twick. BJ46 74
St. Margaret's Rd.
Normanhurst Rd. SW2 BX48 76
Normanhurst Rd. Orp. CO51 89
Normanhurst Rd. Walt. BD55 84
Norman Rd. E6 CK38 58
Norman Rd. N15 CA32 48
Norman Rd. SE10 CE43 67
Norman Rd. SW19 BT50 76
Norman Rd. Ashf. BA50 73
Norman Rd. Belv. CR41 69
Norman Rd. Dart. CW47 80
Norman Rd. Horn. CU33 50
Norman Rd. Ilf. CL35 49
Norman Rd. Sutt. BS56 95
Norman Rd. Th. Hth. BY53 86
Norman Rd. Welw. BP5 5
Norman's Bldgs. EC1 BZ38 57
Norman's Clo. NW10 BN36 55
Normans Clo. Grav. DG47 81
Normans Clo. Uxb. AY39 53
Normansfield Tedd. BK50 74
Normansfield Av. Tedd. BK50 74
Normansfield Clo. Bush. BF26 36
Normanshire Av. E4 CF28 39
Normanshire Dr. E4 CE28 39
Normansmead NW10 BN36 55
Normans, The Slou. AQ39 52
Norman St. EC1 BZ38 57
Normanton Av. SW19 BS48 76
Normanton Pk. E4 CG27 40
Normanton Rd. Sth. Croy. CA57 96
Normanton St. SE23 CC48 77
Norman Way N14 BX27 38
Norman Way W3 BM39 55
Normington Clo. SW16 BY49 76
Norrell's Dri. Leath. BB66 110
Norrells Ride. Leath. BB66 110
Norrice Lea N2 BT32 47
Norris Gro. Brox. CD13 12
Norris La. Hodd. CE11 12
Norris Rise, Hodd. CD11 12
Norris Rd. Hodd. CE12 12
Norris Rd. Stai. AV49 72
Norris St. SW1 BW40 56
Haymarket
Norroy Rd. SW15 BQ45 65
Norrys Clo. Barn. BU24 29
Norrys Rd. Barn. BU24 29
Norstead Pl. SW15 BP48 75
Norsted La. Orp. CO59 98
North Access Rd. E17 CC32 48
North Acre NW9 BO30 37
North Acre Bans. BR61 103
North Acton Rd. NW10 BN37 55
Northallerton Way. Rom. CV28 42
Northall Rd. Bexh. CS44 69
Northampton Bldgs. EC1 BY38 56
Skinner St.
Northampton Gro. N1 BZ35 48
St. Pauls Pl.
Northampton Pk. N1 BZ36 57
Northampton Rd. EC1 BY38 56
Northampton Rd. Croy. CB55 87
Northampton Rd. Enf. CD25 30
Northampton Sq. EC1 BY38 56
Northampton St. N1 BZ36 57
Northanger Rd. SW16 BX50 76
North App. Nthwd. BA27 35
North App. Wat. BB21 26
North App. Wat. BC20 17
North Ash Rd. New. A. G. DC55 90
North Audley St. W1 BV39 56
North Av. N18 CB28 39
North Av. W13 BJ39 54
North Av. Cars. BU57 95
North Av. Har. BF32 45
North Av. Hayes BC40 53
North Av. Rich. BM44 65
Sandycombe Rd.
North Av. Sthl. BE40 54
North Av. Watt. BB58 92
Northaw Rd. East, Pot. B. BW19 20
Northaw Rd. West, Pot. B. BV18 20
Northbank NW8 BU38 56
Northbank Rd. E17 CF30 39
North Barns, Brox. CE14 12
Northborough Rd. SW16 BW52 86
Northbourne Brom. CH54 88
Northbourne Rd. SW4 BW45 66
North Bridge Rd. Berk. AP12 7
Northbrook Dr. Nthwd. BB30 35
Northbrook Rd. N22 BX29 38
Northbrook Rd. SE13 CF46 77
Northbrook Rd. Barn. BR25 28
Northbrook Rd. Croy. BZ53 87
Northbrook Rd. Ilf. CL34 49
Northbrooks Harl. CM11 13
Northburgh St. EC1 BY38 56
Northchurch Rd. N1 BZ36 57
North Church Rd. Wem. BM36 55
North Circular Rd. E4 CD28 39
North Circular Rd. E17 CF30 39
North Circular Rd. N13 BY28 38
Northcliffe Dr. N20 BR26 37
Northcliffe Rd. Grav. DF47 81
North Clo. Barn. BQ25 28
North Clo. Bexh. CP45 69
North Clo. Chig. CO28 41
North Clo. Dag. CR37 59
North Clo. Dor. BK73 119
North Clo. Mord. BR52 85
North Clo. St. Alb. BF16 18
North Common, Wey. BA56 92
N. Common Rd. W5 BL40 55
Northcote, Wey. AX56 92
Northcote Av. W5 BL40 55
Northcote Av. Islw. BJ46 74
Northcote Av. Sthl. BE40 54
Northcote Av. Surb. BM54 85
Northcote Close. Leath. BA66 110
Northcote Rd. E17 CD31 48
Northcote Rd. NW10 BO36 55
Northcote Rd. SW11 BU46 76
Northcote Rd. Croy. BZ53 87
Northcote Road. Leath. BA66 110
Northcote Rd. N. Mal. BN52 85
Northcote Rd. Sid. CN49 78
Northcote Rd. Twick. BJ46 74
Northcott Av. N22 BX30 38
N. Countess Rd. E17 BX30 38
North Ct. W1 BW39 56
Chitty St.
North Cres. N3 BR30 37
North Cres. WC1 BW39 56
Store St.
Northcroft Clo. Egh. AQ49 72
Northcroft Gdns. Egh. AQ49 72
Northcroft Rd. W13 BJ41 64
Northcroft Rd. Egh. AQ49 72
Northcroft Rd. Epsom BN57 94
Northcroft Vill. Egh. AQ49 72
N. Cross Rd. SE22 CA46 77
North Cross Rd. Ilf. CM31 49
North Dene NW7 BN27 37
Northdene Chig. CM28 40
North Dene Houns. BF44 64
Northdene Gdns. N15 CA32 48
North Dolphin Rd. Sun. BB51 83
Northdon Clo. Ruis. BB34 44
North Down Sth. Croy. CA59 96
Northdown Gdns. Ilt. CN32 49
North Down La. Guil. AS72 118
Northdown Rd. Cat. CE65 105
North Down Rd. Ger. Cr. AS29 34
Northdown Rd. Hat. BP14 10
Northdown Rd. Horn. CU33 50
Northdown Rd. Long. DB51 90
Northdown Rd. Sev. CW62 108
North Down Rd. Sutt. BS58 95
Northdown Rd. Well. CO44 69
Northdowns Cres. Croy. CE58 96
North Downs Rd. Croy. CE58 96
Northdown St. N1 BX37 56
North Dr. SW11 BU43 66
North Dr. SW16 BW49 76
North Dr. Houns. BG44 64
North Dr. Orp. CN56 97
North Dr. Rom. CV31 51
North Dr. Ruis. BB33 44
North Dr. Vir. W. AO53 82
North Dr. Vir. W. AP53 82
Northeast Pl. N1 BY37 56
Chapel Mkt.
North End NW3 BT34 47
North End W14 BR43 65
Northend, Brwd. DB28 42
North End Buck. H. CJ26 40
North End Croy. BZ54 87
Northend, Hem. H. AZ14 8
North End Av. NW3 BT34 47
North End Cres. W14 BR42 65
North End Ho. W14 BR42 65
North End La. Orp. CL58 97
North End Pde. W14 BR42 65
North End Rd.
North End Rd. NW11 BS33 47
Northend Rd. Erith CT44 69
North End Rd. Wem BM34 46
North End Way NW3 BT34 47
Northern Av. N9 CA27 39
Northernhay Wk. Mord. BR52 85
Northern Rd. E13 CH37 58
Northern Rd. Slou. AO38 52
Northey Av. Sutt. BQ58 94
North Eyot Gdns. W6 BO42 65
Berestead Rd.
North Eyot St. W6 BP42 65
St Peter's Sq.
Northey St. E14 CD40 57
North Feltham Trd. Est. Felt. BC46 73
Northfield Av. Orp. CP53 89
Northfield Av. Pnr. BD31 45
Northfield Cres. Sutt. BR56 94
Abbotts Rd.
Northfield Gdns. Dag. CQ35 50
Northfield Gdns. Wat. BD22 27
Northfield Industrial Est. Wem. BM37 55
Northfield Park Clo. Hayes. BB41 63
Northfield Path Dag. CQ34 50
Northfield Pl. Wey. AZ57 92
Northfield Rd. E6 CK36 58
Northfield Rd. N16 CA33 48
Northfield Rd. W13 BJ41 64
Northfield Rd. Barn. BU24 29
Northfield Rd. Borwd. BM23 28
Northfield Rd. Cob. BC60 92
Northfield Rd. Dag. CQ35 50
Northfield Rd. Enf. CB25 30
Northfield Rd. Houns. BD43 64
Northfield Rd. Stai. AW51 83
Northfield Rd. Wal. Cr. CD19 21
Northfield Rd. Wind. AM42 61
Northfields SW18 BS45 66
Northfields, Ash. BL63 103
Northfields Rd. W3 BM39 55
North Gdns. SW19 BT50 76
North Gate, Harl. CM10 6
North Gate Path. Borwd. BL22 28
Northgate Path Borwd. BL23 28
North Gower St. NW1 BW38 56
North Gro. N6 BV33 47
North Gro. N15 BZ32 48
North Gro. Cher. AV53 82
North Gro. Harl. CO11 14
N. Harrow Est. Har. BF31 45
North Hill Av. N6 BU32 47
North Hill Dr. Rom. CV27 42
North Hill Grn. Rom. CV28 42
North Hl. N6 BU32 47
North Hyde Gdns. Hayes BC42 63
North Hyde La. Sthl. BD42 64
North Hyde Rd. Hayes. BB41 63
Northiam N12 BS28 38
Northiam St. E8 CB37 57
Northington St. WC1 BX38 56
North Kent Rd. St. Alb. BG13 9
Northlands, Pot. B. BT19 20
Northlands Av. Orp. CM56 97
Northlands St. SE5 BZ44 67
North La. Rick. AV23 25
North La. Tedd. BH50 74
North Lodge W5 BK40 54
North Lodge Clo. SW15 BQ46 75
North Mall, N9 CB27 39
North Mead, Red. BU69 121
North Ms. WC1 BX38 56
Northolm Edg. BN28 37
Northolme Gdns. Edg. BM30 37
Northolme Rise Orp. CN55 88
Northolme Rd. N5 BY35 47
Northolt Av. Ruis. BC35 44
Northolt Gdns. Grnf. BH35 45
Northolt Rd. Har. BF35 45
Northolt Way. Horn. CV36 60
North Orbital. Rick. AV25 25
North Orbital Rd. St. Alb. BE18 18
North Orbital Rd. Uxb. AV33 43
North Orbital Rd. Uxb. AW32 44
North Orbital Rd. Wat. BC20 17
North Orbital Rd. Wat. BD19 18
Northover Brom. CG48 78
North Pde. Chess. BL56 94
North Parade. Hat. BO12 10
North Pk. SE9 CK46 78
North Park. Ger. Cr. AS31 43
North Pk. Iver. AU41 62
North Park La. Gdse. CB68 114
North Pass. SW18 BS46 76
North Pl. Guil. AR71 118
North Pl. Harl. CO9 6
North Pl. Mitch. BU50 76
North Pl. Tedd. BH50 74
North Pl. Wal. Abb. CE20 21
North Pole W10 BQ40 55
North Pole La. Kes. CG57 97
Northpole Rd. W10 BQ39 55
Northport St. N1 BZ37 57
North Quay E1 CB40 57
North Ride W2 BU40 56
Northridge Rd. Grav. DH48 81
Northridge Way, Hem. H. AV14 7
North Riding, St. Alb. BF18 18
North Rd. N2 BT30 38
North Rd. N6 BV33 47
North Rd. N7 BX36 56
North Rd. N9 CB26 39
North Rd. SE18 CN42 68
North Rd. SW19 BR48 75
North Rd. SW19 BT50 76
North Rd. W5 BK41 64
North Rd. Amer. AO21 25
North Rd. Belv. CR41 69
North Rd. Berk. AQ13 7
North Rd. Brent. BL43 65
North Rd. Brom. CH51 88
North Rd. Brwd. DB26 42
North Rd. Dart. CT46 79
North Rd. Edg. BM30 37
North Rd. Felt. BA46 73
North Rd. Grays CY42 70
North Rd. Guil. AQ69 118
North Rd. Hav. CT27 41
North Rd. Hayes BA39 53
North Rd. Hodd. CE11 12
North Rd. Ilf. CN34 49
North Rd. Reig. BR72 120
North Rd. Rich. BM45 65
North Rd. Rick. AU25 25
North Rd. Rom. CQ32 50
North Rd. S. Ock. DA37 60
North Rd. Sthl. BF40 54
North Rd. Surb. BK53 84
North Rd. Wal. Cr. CD20 21
North Rd. Walt. BD56 93
North Rd. West Dr. AY41 63
North Rd. W. Wick. CE54 87
North Rd. Wok. AT61 100
North Road Av. Brwd. DB26 42
North Row W1 BU40 56
North St. Pass. E13 CH37 58
North Several SE3 CF44 67
North Side SW18 BT46 76
Northspur Rd. Sutt. BS55 86
North Sq. N9 CB27 39
North Sq. N9 CB27 39
Town Rd.
North Sq. NW11 BS32 47
Northstead Rd. SW2 BY48 76
North Strand NW9 BO30 37
North St. E13 CH37 58
North St. NW4 BQ32 46
Heriot Rd.
North St. SW4 BW45 66
North St. BJ71 119
North St. Bark. CL36 58
North St. Bexh. CR45 69
North St. Brom. CH51 88
North St. Cars. BU55 86
North St. Dart. CV47 80
North St. Dor. BG72 119
North St. Egh. AS49 72
North St. Guil. AR71 118
North St. Horn. CV33 51
North St. Islw. BJ45 64
North St. Lthd. BJ64 102
North St. Red. BU70 121
North St. Rom. CS31 50
North St. Rom. CT32 50
North St. Wal. Abb. CG14 13
North Tenter St. E1 CA39 57
North Ter. SW3 BU41 66
North, The, Glade, Bex. CQ47 79
Northumberland Alley EC3 CA39 57
Northumberland Av. E12 CJ33 49
Northumberland Av. WC2 BX40 56
Northumberland Av. Enf. CB22 30
Northumberland Av. Horn. CV32 51
Northumberland Av. Islw. BH44 64
Northumberland Av. Well. CM45 68
Northumberland Clo. Erith CS43 69
Northumberland Clo. Stai. AY46 73
Northumberland Cres. Felt. BB46 73
Northumberland Gdns. N9 CA27 39
Northumberland Gdns. Mitch. BW53 86
Northumberland Gro. N17 CB29 39
Northumberland Pk. N17 CA29 39
Northumberland Pk. Erith. CR43 69
Northumberland Pk. Clo. N17 CB29 39
Northumberland Pk.
Northumberland Pl. W2 BS39 56
Northumberland Rd. E17 CE33 48
Northumberland Rd. Barn. BT26 38
Northumberland Rd. Grav. DF50 81
Northumberland Rd. Har. BE32 45
Northumberland Rd. S. Le H. DJ41 71
Northumberland Row Twick. BH47 74
Colne Rd.
Northumberland St. WC2 BX40 56
Northumberland Way Erith CS44 69
Northumbria St. E14 CE39 57

North Verbena Gdns. W6 BP42 65
St.Peter's Sq.
North Vw. SW19 BP49 75
North View W5 BK38 54
North Vw. Ilf. CO29 41
North Vw. Pnr. BD33 45
Northview Swan. CT51 89
North View Ave. Til. DG44 71
North View Cres. NW10 BO35 46
North View Cres. Epsom BP62 103
North View Dr. Wdf. Grn. CJ30 40
North View Rd. N8 BW31 47
Northview Rd. Sev. CV64 108
North Vill. NW1 BW36 56
North Wk. Croy. CF57 96
North Wk. Sutt. BQ59 94
North Way N9 CC27 39
Northway N11 BW29 38
North Way NW9 BM31 46
Northway NW11 BS32 47
Northway, Guil. AQ69 118
North Way Mord. BR52 85
North Way Pnr. BD31 45
Northway. Rick. AX26 35
North Way, Uxb. AY36 53
Northway Wall. BW56 95
Northway Cir. NW7 BN28 37
Northway Cres. NW7 BN28 37
Northway Rd. SE5 BZ45 67
Northway Rd. Croy. CA53 87
Northways NW3 BT30 56
College Cres.
North Western Av. Wat. BG24 27
Northwest Pl. N1 BY37 56
Chapel Mkt.
North Wharf Rd. W2 BT39 56
Northwick Av. Har. BJ32 45
Northwick Circle Har. BK32 45
Northwick Clo. NW8 CJ38 58
Northwick Ter.
Northwick Rd. Wat. BD28 36
Northwick Ter. NW8 BT38 56
Northwick Wk. Har. BH33 45
Northwold Dr. Pnr. BD30 36
Northwold Est. E5 CB34 48
North Wolf W13 BJ40 54
North Wood. Grays. DG41 71
Northwood Av. Horn. CU35 50
Northwood Ave. Pur. BY59 95
Northwood Av. Wok. AO62 100
Northwood Gdns. N12 BT28 38
Northwood Gdns. Grnf. BH35 45
Northwood Gdns. Ilf. CL31 49
Northwood Hills Nthwd. BC30 35
Northwood Hills Cir. Nthwd. BC30 35
Northwood Rd. N6 BV33 47
Northwood Rd. SE23 CD47 77
Northwood Rd. Cars. BV57 95
Northwood Rd. Th. Hth. BY51 86
Northwood Rd. Uxb. AX30 35
Northwood Way. Nthwd. BB29 35
Northwood Way. Uxb. AX30 35
N. Woolwich Rd. E16 CH40 58
North Worple Way SW14 BN45 65
Nortoft Rd. Ger. Cr. AS29 34
Norton Av. Surb. BM54 85
Norton Clo. E4 CE28 39
Norton Clo. Enf. CB23 30
Norton Folgate E1 CA39 57
Norton Gdns. SW16 BX51 86
Norton Heath Rd. Ong. DB15 15
Norton La. Cob. BB63 101
Norton La. Ong. DA16 24
Norton Rd. E10 BX33 47
Dagenham Rd.
Norton Rd. Dag. CS36 59
Norton Rd. Uxb. AX38 53
Norton Rd. Wem. BK36 54
Norval Rd. Wem. BJ34 45
Norway Dr. Slou. AQ39 52
Norway Pl. E14 CD39 57
Norway St. SE10 CE43 67
Norway Wk. Rain. CV39 60
Norwich Av. Dag. CR37 59
Norwich Mews Ilf. CO33 50
Ashgrove Rd.
Norwich Rd. E7 CH35 49
Norwich Rd. E8 CB37 57
Norwich Rd. Grnf. BF37 54
Norwich Rd. Nthwd. BB31 44
Norwich Rd. Th. Hth. BZ52 87
Norwich St. EC4 BY39 56
Norwich Wk. Edg. BN29 37
Norwich Way. Rick. AZ24 26
Norwood Av. Rom. CS33 50
Norwood Av. Wem. BL37 55
Norwood Clo. Lthd. BE67 111
Norwood Clo. Sthl. BF42 64
Norwood Dr. Har. BE32 45
Norwood End. Ong. CX11 15
Norwood Gdns. Hayes BD38 54
Norwood Gdns. Sthl. BE42 64
Norwood Grn. Rd. Sthl. BF42 64
Norwood High St. SE27 BY48 76
Norwood La. Iver AU38 52
Norwood Pk. Rd. SE27 BZ49 77
Norwood Rd. Lthd. BE67 111
Norwood Rd. Sthl. BE41 64
Norwood Ter. Sthl. BF42 64
Notley St. SE5 BZ43 67
Notre Dame Est. SW4 BW46 76
Notson Rd. SE25 CB52 87
Nott Ct. WC2 BX39 56
Shorts Gdns.
Nottingham Av. E16 CJ39 58
Nottingham Pl. W1 BV38 56
Nottingham Rd. E10 CF32 48
Nottingham Rd. SW17 BU47 76
Nottingham Rd. Islw. BH44 64
Nottingham Rd. Sth. Croy. BZ56 96
Nottingham St. W1 BV39 56
Nottingham Ter. NW1 BV38 56
Allsop Pl.
Notting Hill Gte. W11 BS40 56
Nova Rd. Croy. BY54 86
Novar Rd. SE9 CM47 78
Novello St. SW6 BS44 66
Nowell Rd. SW13 BP43 65
Nower Hill Pnr. BE31 45
Nower Rd. Dor. BJ71 119
Nower, The, Sev. CN63 106
Noyna Rd. SW17 BU48 76
Nth. Birkbeck Rd. E11 CF34 48
Nth. Kent Av. Grav. DE46 81
Nth. Ockham Rd. Sth. Leath. BA66 110
Nth. Orbital Rd. Hat. BP10 5
Nth. Orbital Rd. Wat. AW25 26
Nth. Station App. Red. BX71 121
Nth. Western Av. Wat. BA21 26
Nuding Clo. SE13 CE45 67
Nuding Rd. SE13 CE45 67
Nufield Rd. Swan. CU50 79
Nugent Rd. N19 BX33 47
Nugent Rd. SE25 CA52 87
Nugents Ct. Pnr. BE30 36
Nugents Pk. Pnr. BE30 36
Nugent Ter. NW8 BT38 56
Nunappleton Way. Oxt. CH69 115
Nuneaton Rd. Dag. CP36 59
Nunfield, Kings L. AW19 17
Nunhead Cres. SE15 CB45 67
Nunhead Grn. SE15 CB45 67
Nunhead Gro. SE15 CB45 67
Nunhead La. SE15 CB45 67
Nunnery Clo. St. Alb. BH14 9
Nunns Rd. Enf. BZ23 30
Nunns Way. Grays. DE42 71
Nunsbury Dr. Brox. CD16 21
Nuns La. St. Alb. BH15 9
Nuns Walk, Vir. W. AR53 82
Nupton Dr. Barn. BQ25 28
Nursery Av. N3 BT30 38
Nursery Av. Bexh. CQ45 69
Nursery Av. Croy. CC55 87
Nursery Clo. Amer. AP23 25
Nursery Clo. Croy. CC55 87
Nursery Clo. Dart. CY47 80
Nursery Clo. Enf. CC23 30
Nursery Clo. Epsom BO58 94
Nursery Clo. Felt. BC47 73
Nursery Clo. Hamptn. BE49 74
Nursery Clo. Orp. CO54 89
Nursery Clo. Rom. CP32 50
Nursery Clo. Sev. CV64 108
Nursery Clo. S. Ock. DB38 60
Nursery Clo. Swan. CS51 89
Nursery Clo. Wdf. Grn. CH28 40
Nursery Clo. Wey. AV58 91
Nursery Clo. Wok. AR61 100
Nursery Gdns. Enf. CC23 30
Nursery Gdns. Stai. AW50 73
Nursery Gdns. Sun. BB51 83
Nursery Gdns. Sun. BC51 83
Nursery La. E7 CH36 58
Nursery La. Uxb. AX38 53
Nursery La. Rd. Slou. AR40 52
Nursery Pl. Sev. CS65 107
Nursery Rd. N14 BW26 38
Nursery Rd. SW9 BX45 66
Nursery Rd. SW19 BR50 75
Nursery Rd. Brox. CD16 21
Nursery Rd. Brwd. DB20 24
Nursery Rd. Hodd. CE10 12
Nursery Rd. Loug. CH23 31
Nursery Rd. Loug. CJ25 31
Nursery Rd. Pnr. BD31 45
Nursery Rd. Sun. BB51 83
Nursery Rd. Tad. BP66 112
Nursery Rd. Th. Hth. BZ52 87
Nursery Rd. Wal. Abb. CF14 12
Nursery Rd. Wok. AO62 100
Nursery Row SE17 BZ42 67
Nurserys. The. West. CM67 115
Nursery St. N17 CA29 39
Nursery St. SW4 BV45 66
Heath Rd.
Nursery Ter. Berk. AT11 7
Nursery, The, Erith CT43 69
Nursery Wk. NW4 BP31 46
Nursery Wk. Rom. CS32 50
Nursery Way. Stai. AR46 72
Nursery Waye, Uxb. AX37 53
Nurstead Rd. Erith. CR43 69
Nutberry Ave. Grays. DD41 71
Nutbourne St. W10 BR38 55
Nutbrook St. SE15 CA45 67
Nut Browne Rd. Dag. CQ37 59
Nutcome La. Dor. BH71 119
Nutcroft Gro. Lthd. BH64 102
Nutcroft Rd. SE15 CB43 67
Nutfield Clo. N18 CB29 39
Fore St.
Nutfield Gdns. Ilf. CO34 50
Nutfield Gdns. Nthlt. BD37 54
Nutfield Marsh Rd. Red. BW69 121
Nutfield Pl. Th. Hth. BY52 86
Nutfield Rd. E15 CF35 48
Nutfield Rd. NW2 BP34 46
Nutfield Rd. SE22 CA45 67
Nutfield Rd. Couls. BV61 104
Nutfield Rd. Red. BV70 121
Nutfield Rd. Red. BW68 113
Nutfield Rd. Red. BW69 121
Nutfield Rd. Th. Hth. BY52 86
Nutfield Way Orp. CL55 88
Nutford Pl. W1 BU39 56
Nut Gro. Welw. G. C. BQ6 5
Nuthurst Av. SW2 BX48 76
Nutlands. Sev. DB64 108
Nutley Clo. Swan. CT51 89
Nutley Gro. Reig. BR70 120
Nutley La. Reig. BR70 120
Nutley Ter. NW3 BT36 56
Nutmead Clo. Bex. CS47 79
Nuttall St. N1 CA37 57
Nutter La. E11 CH32 49
Nuttfield Clo. Rick. AZ25 26
Nutt Gro. Stan. BK27 36
Nut Tree Clo. Orp. CP55 89
Nutt St. SE15 CA43 67
Sumner Rd.
Nutty La. Shep. BA52 83
Nutwell St. SW17 BU49 76
Nutwood Av. Bet. BN71 120
Nutwood Clo. Bet. BN71 120
Nuxley Rd. Belv. CQ43 69
Nyanza St. SE18 CM43 68
Nye Bevan Est. E5 CC34 48
Nye Way. Hem. H. AT17 16
Nylands Av. Rich. BM44 65
Nymans Gdns. SW20 BP51 85
Nynehead St. SE14 CD43 67
Nyon Gro. SE6 CD48 77
Nyth Clo. Upmin. CY32 51
Oak Ave. Sev. CU67 116
Oak Ave. West Dr. AZ41 63
Oak Av. N8 BX31 47
Oak Av. N10 BV29 38
Oak Av. N17 BZ29 39
Oak Av. Croy. CE54 87
Oak Av. Egh. AU50 72
Oak Av. Enf. BX22 29
Oak Av. Hamptn. BE49 74
Oak Av. Houns. BE43 64
Oak Av. St. Alb. BF18 18
Oak Av. Upmin. CX35 51
Oak Av. Uxb. AZ34 44
Oakbank, Brwd. DF25 122
Oakbank Croy. CF57 96
Oak Bank, Wok. AS63 100
Oakbank Av. Walt. BE54 84
Oakbank Gro. SE24 BZ45 67
Oakbury Rd. SW6 BS44 66
Oak Clo. N14 BV26 38
Oak Clo. Hem. H. AY15 8
Oak Clo. Sutt. BT55 86
Oak Clo. Wal. Abb. CF20 21
Oak Clo. West Dr. AZ41 63
Oak Common W3 BO39 55
Common La.
Oak Corner, Berk. AO13 7
Oak Cottage Clo. SE6 CG47 78
Oak Ct. Barn. BU25 29
Oak Cres. E16 CG39 58
Oakcroft Clo. Wey. AV60 91
Oakcroft Rd. SE13 CF44 67
Oakcroft Rd. Chess. BL56 94
Oakcroft Rd. Wey. AV60 91
Oakcroft Vill. Chess. BL56 94
Oakdale N14 BV26 38
Oakdale, Welw. G. C. BQ6 5
Oakdale Av. Har. BL32 46
Oakdale Av. Nthwd. BC30 35
Oakdale Clo. Wat. BD28 36
Oakdale Ct. E4 CF28 39
Oakdale La. Eden. CM70 115
Oakdale Rd. E7 CH36 58
Oakdale Rd. E11 CF34 48
Oakdale Rd. E18 CH30 40
Oakdale Rd. N4 BZ32 48
Oakdale Rd. SW16 BX49 76
Oakdale Rd. Epsom BN57 94
Oakdale Rd. Wat. BD27 36
Oakdale Rd. Wey. AZ55 83
Oak Dene W13 BJ39 54
Dene, The,
Oak Dene, Tad. BR63 103
Oakdene, Wal. Cr. CD18 21
Oakdene Wok. AP58 91
Oakdene Av. Chis. CL49 78
Oakdene Av. Erith CS43 69
Oakdene Av. Surb. BJ54 84
Oakdene Clo. Bet. BN71 120
Oakdene Clo. Horn. CU32 50
Oakdene Clo. Lthd. BF67 111
Oakdene Dr. Surb. BN54 85
Oakdene Pk. N3 BR29 37
Oakdene Rd. Bet. BM72 120
Oakdene Rd. Cob. BC60 92
Oakdene Rd. Hem. H. AY15 8
Oakdene Rd. Lthd. BE65 102
Oakdene Rd. Orp. CN53 88
Oakdene Rd. Red. BU70 121
Oakdene Rd. Sev. CU64 107
Oakdene Rd. Uxb. AZ37 53
Oakdene Rd. Wat. BC21 26
Oakdene Way, St. Alb. BK13 9
Oakden St. SE11 BY42 66
Oak Dri. Berk. AR13 7
Oak Dr. Saw. CP7 6
Oaken Coppice La. Ash. BM63 103
Oaken Dr. Esher BH57 93
Oakend Way. Ger. Cr. AS32 43
Oak End Way. Wey. AV59 91
Oaken Gro. Welw. G. C. BR9 5
Oaken La. Esher BH56 93
Oakenshaw Clo. Surb. BL54 85
Oakes Gro. E4 CG27 40
Oakeshott Av. N6 BV34 47
Oakfield. Rick. AV26 34
Oakfield Ave. Slou. AN40 61
Oakfield Av. Har. BJ31 45
Oakfield Ct. N8 BX33 47
Oakfield Ct. NW11 BQ33 46
Oakfield Dr. Reig. BS69 121
Reigate Hill
Oakfield Gdns. N18 CA28 39
Oakfield Gdns. SE19 CA49 77
Oakfield Gdns. Beck. CE53 87
Oakfield Gdns. Cars. BU54 86
Oakfield Gdns. Grnf. BG38 54
Oakfield Glade, Wey. BA56 92
Oakfield La. Dart. CV48 80
Oakfield La. Kes. CJ56 97
Oakfield Pk. Rd. Dart. CV48 80
Oakfield Pl. Dart. CV48 80
Oakfield Rd. E6 CK37 58
Oakfield Rd. E17 CD30 39
Oakfield Rd. N3 BS30 38
Oakfield Rd. N4 BY32 47
Oakfield Rd. N14 BX27 38
Oakfield Rd. SE20 CB51 87
Oakfield Rd. SW19 BQ48 75
Oakfield Rd. Ash. BL62 103
Oakfield Rd. Ashf. AZ49 73
Oakfield Rd. Cob. BC60 92
Oakfield Rd. Croy. BZ54 87
Oakfield Rd. Ilf. CL34 49
Oakfield Rd. Orp. CO54 89
Oakfields, Guil. AP69 118
Oakfields. Sev. CU66 116
Oakfields Walt. BC54 83
Oakfields Rd. NW11 BR32 46
Oakfield St. SW10 BT43 66
Oakford Rd. NW5 BW35 47
Oak Gdns. Croy. CE54 87
Oak Gdns. Edg. BN30 37
Oak Glade. Nthwd. BA30 35
Oak Glen. Horn. CW31 51
Oak Grange Rd. Guil. AW68 110
Oak Gro. NW2 BQ35 46
Oak Gro. Ruis. BC33 44
Oak Gro. Sun. BC50 73
Oak Gro. W. Wick. CF55 87
Oakgrove Rd. SE20 CC51 87
Oakhall Ct. E11 CH32 49
Cambridge Pk.
Oakhall Rd. E11 CH32 49
Oakham Dr. Brom. CG52 88
Oakhampton Clo. N12 BT28 38
Oakhampton Rd. NW7 BQ29 37
Oakhampton Rd. Rom. CV29 42
Oakhampton Sq. Rom. CV29 42
Oak Hill Epsom BN61 103
Oakhill Esher BJ57 93
Oak Hill, Guil. AU68 109
Oak Hill Surb. BL54 85
Oak Hill Wdf. Grn. CF29 39
Oakhill Av. Pnr. BE30 36
Oakhill Clo. Ash. BK62 102
Oak Hill Clo. Wdf. Grn. CF29 39
Oak Hill Ct. SE23 CC46 77
Oak Hill Ct. Wdf. Grn. CF29 39
Oakhill Cres. Surb. BL54 85
Oak Hill Cres. Wdf. Grn. CF29 39
Oakhill Dr. Sun. BB49 73
Oak Hill Dr. Surb. BL54 85
Oakhill Gdns. Wdf. Grn. CG30 40
Oakhill Gro. Surb. BL53 85
Oak Hill Ms. NW3 BT35 47
Oak Hill Pk. NW3 BS35 47
Oakhill Path Surb. BL53 85
Oakhill Pl. SW15 BS46 76
Oakhill Rd.
Oakhill Rd. SW15 BR46 75
Oakhill Rd. SW16 BX51 86
Oakhill Rd. Ash. BK62 102
Oak Hill Rd. Beck. CF51 87
Oak Hill Rd. Orp. CN54 88
Oakhill Rd. Reig. BS71 121
Oakhill Rd. Rick. AU28 34
Oak Hill Rd. Rom. CS26 41
Oakhill Rd. Surb. BL53 85
Oakhill Rd. Sutt. BS55 86
Oakhill Rd. Wey. AV57 91
Oak Hill Way NW3 BS35 47
Oakhouse Rd. Bexh. CR46 79
Oakhurst Wok. AP58 91
Oakhurst Av. Barn. BU26 38
Oakhurst Av. Bexh. CQ44 69
Oakhurst Clo. E17 CG31 49
Oakhurst Gdns. E4 CG26 40
Oakhurst Gdns. E17 CG31 49
Oakhurst Gdns. Bexh. CQ43 69
Oakhurst Gro. SE22 CB45 67
Oakhurst Rise Cars. BU58 95
Oakhurst Rd. E7 CH35 49
Oakhurst Rd. Enf. CC21 30
Oakhurst Rd. Epsom. BN57 94
Oakhurst Rd. Kings. On T. BL50 75
Oakington Ave. Amer. AS23 25
Oakington Ave. Hayes. BA42 63
Oakington Av. Har. BF33 45
Oakington Av. Wem. BL34 46
Oakington Dr. Sun. BD51 84
Oakington Manor Dr. Wem. BM35 46
Oakington Rd. W9 BS38 56
Oakington Way N8 BX32 47
Oakland Dr. S. Ock. DB39 60
Oakland Gdns. Brwd. DE25 122
Oaklands N21 BX27 38
Oaklands Chess. BK56 93
Oaklands Ken. BZ61 105
Oaklands Twick. BG47 74
Oaklands Av. N9 CB25 30
Oaklands Av. Esher BG54 84
Oaklands Av. Hat. BR17 19
Oaklands Av. Islw. BH43 64
Oaklands Av. Rom. CT31 50
Oaklands Av. Sid. CN47 78
Oaklands Av. Th. Hth. BY52 86
Oaklands Av. Wat. BC26 35
Oaklands Av. W. Wick. CE55 87
Oaklands Clo. Bexh. CQ46 79
Oaklands Clo. Grav. DF49 81
Oaklands Clo. Orp. CN53 88
Oaklands Clo. Sev. CZ57 99
Oaklands Ct. SE26 CB49 77
Oaklands Ct. Wat. BC23 26
Oaklands Dr. Enf. BY21 29
Oaklands Est. SW4 BW46 76
Oaklands Gdns. Ken. BZ60 96
Oaklands Gro. W12 BP40 55
Oaklands La. Barn. BP24 28
Oaklands La. St. Alb. BM13 10
Oaklands La. West. CH60 97
Oaklands Pk. Av. Ilf. CM34 49
Oaklands Rd. N20 BR26 37
Oaklands Rd. NW2 BQ35 46
Oaklands Rd. SW14 BN45 65
Oaklands Rd. W7 BH41 64
Oaklands Rd. Bexh. CQ45 69
Oaklands Rd. Brom. CG50 78
Oaklands Rd. Dart. CX47 80
Oaklands Rd. Wal. Cr. CA16 21
Oakland Way Epsom BN57 94
Oak La. E14 CD40 57
Oak La. N2 BT30 38
Oak La. N11 BW29 38
Oak La. Egh. AR48 72
Oak La. Islw. BH45 64
Oak La. Pot. B. BX17 20
Oak La. Sev. CT68 116
Oak La. Twick. BJ47 74
Oak La. Wind. AN44 61
Oak La. Wok. AT61 100
Oaklawn Rd. Lthd. BH62 102
Oakleafe Gdns. Ilf. CL31 49
Oaklea Pass. Kings-on-t. BK52 84
Oakleigh Av. N20 BT27 38
Oakleigh Av. Edg. BM30 37
Oakleigh Av. Surb. BM54 85
Oakleigh Clo. N20 BU27 38
Oakleigh Ct. Edg. BN30 37
Oakleigh Cres. N20 BU27 38
Oakleigh Dr. Rick. BA25 26
Oakleigh Gdns. N20 BT26 38
Oakleigh Gdns. Edg. BL28 37
Oakleigh Gdns. Orp. CN56 97
Oakleigh Pk. Av. Chis. CL51 88
Oakleigh Pk. N. N20 BT27 38
Oakleigh Pk. S. N20 BU26 38
Oakleigh Rd. Pnr. BE29 36
Oakleigh Rd. Uxb. BA36 53
Oakleigh Rd. N. N20 BT27 38
Oakleigh Rd. S. N11 BV27 38
Oakleigh Way, Mitch. BV51 86
Oakleigh Way Surb. BM54 85
Oakley Av. W5 BM40 55
Oakley Av. Bark. CN36 58
Oakley Av. Croy. BX56 95
Oakley Clo. W7 BH40 54
Oakley Clo. Wey. AX56 92
Oakley Cres. N1 BY37 56
City Rd.
Oakley Cres. Slou. AP40 52
Oakley Dr. Brom. CK55 88
Oakley Dr. Rom. CX28 42
Oakley Dr. Sid. CM47 78
Oakley Gdns. N8 BX32 47
Oakley Gdns. SW3 BU43 66
Oakley Gdns. Bans. BS61 104
Oakley Green Rd. Wind. AK44 61
Oakley Ho. W5 BM40 55
Oakley Park, Sid. CP47 79
Oakley Pl. SE1 CA42 67
Oakley Rd. N1 BZ36 57
Oakley Rd. SE25 CB53 87
Oakley Rd. Brom. CK55 88
Oakley Rd. Har. BH32 45
Oakley Rd. Warl. CB62 105
Oakley Sq. NW1 BW37 56
Oakley St. SW3 BU42 66
Oak Lodge Av. Chig. CM28 40
Oak Lodge Clo. Stan. BJ28 36
Oak Lodge Clo. Walt. BD56 93
Oak Lodge Dr. W. Wick. CE54 87
Oakmead Av. Brom. CH53 88
Oakmeade Pnr. BF29 36
Oakmead Gdns. Edg. BN28 37
Oakmead Rd. SW12 BV47 76
Oakmead Rd. Croy. BW53 86
Oakmere Av. Pot. B. BT20 20
Oakmere Clo. Pot. B. BT19 20
Oakmere La. Pot. B. BT19 20
Oakmere Rd. SE2 CO43 69
Oakmoor Way Chig. CN28 40
Parkes Rd.
Oakmount Pl. Orp. CM54 88
Oak Piece Epp. CS16 23
Oak Ridge, Dor. BJ73 119
Oakridge Av. Rad. BH20 18
Oakridge La. Rad. BH20 18
Oakridge La. Wat. BG21 27
Oakridge La. Wat. BH20 18
Oakridge Rd. Brom. CF49 77
Oak Rise Buck. H. CJ27 40
Oak Rd. Cat. CA64 105
Oak Rd. Cob. BE61 102
Oak Rd. Epp. CN18 22
Oak Rd. Erith CS43 69
Oak Rd. Erith. CU44 69
Oak Rd. Grav. DH48 81
Oak Rd. Grays. DE43 71
Oak Rd. Green. CZ46 80
Oak Rd. Lthd. BJ63 102
Oak Rd. N. Mal. BN51 85
Oak Rd. Orp. CO57 98
Oak Rd. Reig. BS70 121
Oak Rd. Rom. CW30 42
Oak Rd. West. CM66 115
Oakroyd Av. Pot. B. BR20 19
Oakroyd Clo. Pot. B. BR20 19
Oak St. Bakers La. W5 BK40 54
Grove, The,
Oaks Av. SE19 BZ49 77
Oaks Av. Felt. BE48 74
Oaks Av. Rom. CS30 41
Oaks Av. Wor. Pk. BP55 85
Oaks Clo. Lthd. BJ64 102
Oaksford Av. SE26 CB49 77
Oakshade Rd. Brom. CF49 77
Oakshade Rd. Lthd. BG60 93
Oakshaw Rd. SW18 BS47 76
Oakside, Uxb. AW35 44
Oak Side, Uxb. AW36 53
Oaks La. Croy. CB56 96
Oaks La. Ilf. CN31 49
Oaks Rd. Croy. CB56 96
Oaks Rd. Ken. BY60 95
Oaks Rd. Reig. BT70 121

Oaks Rd. Stai. AX46 73
Oak's Rd. Wok. AS62 100
Oaks, The, SE18 CM42 68
Oaks, The, Epsom BO60 94
Oaks, The Hayes BA37 53
Oaks, The, Ruis. BB33 44
Oaks, The, Wey. AW60 92
Oak St. Hem. H. AY15 8
Oak St. Rom. CS31 50
Oak Stubbs La. Maid. AJ41 61
Oaks Way Cars. BU57 95
Oaks Way. Epsom. BP63 103
Oaks Way Ken. BZ60 96
Oaks Way Surb. BK55 84
Oakthorpe Rd. N13 BY28 38
Oak Tree Clo. BP12 10
Lemsford Rd.
Oaktree Av. N13 BY27 38
Oak Tree Clo. W13 BK39 54
Pinewood Gro.
Oak Tree Clo. Guil. AR67 109
Oak Tree Clo. Guil. AU68 109
Oak Tree Clo. Stan. BK29 36
Oak Tree Clo. Vir. W. AR53 82
Oak Tree Ct. Borwd. BK25 27
Oak Tree Dell, NW9 BN32 46
Oak Tree Dri. Guil. AR68 109
Oak Tree Dr. N20 BS26 38
Oak Tree Gdns. Brom. CH49 78
Oaktree Garth. Welw. G. C. BR8 5
Oak Tree Pl. NW8 BT38 56
Oakview Gro. Croy. CD54 87
Oakview Rd. SE6 CE49 77
Oak Village, NW5 BV35 47
Oak Walk, Saw. CP7 6
Oak Way N14 BV26 38
Oakway SW20 BQ52 85
Oak Way, W3 BO40 55
Oak Way. Ash. BM61 103
Oakway Brom. CF51 87
Oak Way Croy. CC53 87
Oak Way, Felt. BB47 73
Oakway. Grays. DD40 71
Oak Way, Reig. BT71 121
Oakway, Wok. AP63 100
Oakway Clo. Bex. CQ46 79
Oakway La. Brom. CF51 87
Oakways, SE9 CL46 78
Oakwood Wal. Abb. CG21 31
Roundhills
Oakwood Wall. BV58 95
Oakwood Av. N14 BW26 38
Oakwood Av. Beck. CF51 87
Oakwood Av. Borwd. BM24 28
Oakwood Av. Brom. CH52 88
Oakwood Av. Brwd. DF25 122
Oakwood Av. Mitch. BT51 86
Oakwood Av. Pur. BY59 95
Oakwood Av. Sthl. BF40 54
Oak Wood Chase Horn. CW32 51
Oakwood Clo. N14 BW25 29
Oakwood Clo. Chis. CK50 78
Oakwood Clo. Dart. CX47 80
Oakwood Clo. Red. BV70 121
Oakwood Clo. Red. BX71 121
Oakwood Clo. Wdf. Grn. CK29 40
Oakwood Ct. W14 BR41 65
Oakwood Cres. N21 BX25 29
Oakwood Cres. Grnf. BJ36 54
Oakwood Dri. Bexh. CS45 69
Oak Wood Dri. Leath. BB67 110
Oakwood Dr. Edg. BN29 37
Oakwood Dr. St. Alb. BK13 9
Oakwood Gdns. Ilf. CN34 49
Oakwood Gdns. Orp. CM55 88
Oakwood Gdns. Sutt. BS55 86
Oakwood Hill Loug. CK25 31
Oakwood Pde. Enf. CA25 30
Queen Anne's Pl.
Oakwood Park Rd. N14 BW26 38
Oakwood Pl. Croy. BY53 86
Oakwood Rise Long. DC52 90
Oakwood Rd. NW11 BS31 47
Oakwood Rd. SW20 BP51 85
Oakwood Rd. Croy. BY53 86
Oakwood Rd. Orp. CM55 88
Oakwood Rd. Pnr. BC30 35
Oakwood Rd. Red. BY68 113
Oakwood Rd. St. Alb. BE18 18
Oakwood Rd. Vir. W. AR53 82
Oakwood Rd. Wok. AP63 100
Oakwood Vw. N14 BW25 29
Oakworth Rd. W10 BQ39 55
Oasthouse Way Orp. CO52 89
Oast Rd. Oxt. CG69 115
Oast Way Hart. DC53 90
Oates Rd. Rom. CR28 41
Oatfield Rd. Orp. CN54 88
Oatfield Rd. Tad. BP64 103
Oatland Rise E17 CD30 39
Oatlands Av. Wey. BA56 92
Oatlands Chase, Wey. BB55 83
Oatlands Clo. Wey. BA56 92
Oatlands Ct. Wem. BK35 45
Oatlands Dr. Slou. AO39 52
Oatlands Dr. Wey. AZ56 92
Oatlands Grn. Wey. BA55 83
Oatlands Mere, Wey. BA55 83
Oatlands Rd. Enf. CC23 30
Oatlands Rd. Tad. BR63 103
Oat La. EC2 BZ39 57
Oban House, E14 CF39 57
Oban Rd. SE25 BZ52 87
Oban St. E14 CF39 57
Obelisk Ride, Egh. AP50 72
Oberstein Rd. SW11 BT45 66
Oborne Clo. SE24 BY46 76
Observatory Gdns. W8 BS41 66
Observatory Rd. SW14 BO45 65
Occupation La. SE18 CL44 68
Occupation La. W5 BK42 64
Occupation Rd. SE17 BZ42 67
Manor Pl.
Occupation Rd. W7 BJ42 64
Occupation Rd. Bolv. CQ41 69
Occupation Rd. Wat. BC25 26
Ocean Est. E1 CC38 57
Ocean St. E1 CC39 57
Masters St.
Ockenden Clo. Wok. AS62 100
Ockenden Rd.
Ockenden Rd. Wok. AS62 100
Ockendon Rd. N1 BZ36 57
Ockendon Rd. Upmin. CY35 51
Ockendon Rd. Upmin. CZ36 60
Ockham Clo. Orp. CO50 79
Ockham La. Cob. BA63 101
Ockham La. Wok. AY63 101
Ockham Mill La. Wok. AX63 101
Ockham Rd. Wok. AZ64 101
Ockley Ct. Sutt. BT56 95
Ockley La. Red. BX67 113
Ockley Rd. SW16 BX49 76
Ockley Rd. Croy. BX54 86
Ockleys Md. Gdse. CC68 114
Octagon Rd. Watt. BB58 92
Octavia Rd. Islw. BH45 64
Octavia St. SW11 BU44 66
Octavius St. SE8 CE43 67
Odard Rd. E. Mol. BF52 84
Oddesey Rd. Borwd. BM23 28
Odell St. SE5 CA42 67
Odessa Rd. E7 CG35 49
Odessa Rd. NW10 BP37 55
Odessa St. SE16 CD41 67
Odger St. SW11 BU44 66
Offa St. St. Alb. BG13 9
Offenham Rd. SE9 CK49 78
Offerton Rd. SW4 BW45 66
Offham Slope N12 BR28 37
Offley Rd. SW9 BY43 66
Offord Clo. N17 CB29 39
Offord Rd. N1 BX36 56
Offord St. N1 BX36 56
Ogard Rd. Hodd. CF11 12
Ogilby St. SE18 CK42 68
Oglander Rd. SE15 CA45 67
Ogle St. W1 BW39 56
Oglethorpe Rd. Dag. CQ34 50
Ohio Rd. E13 CG38 58
Oil Mill La. W6 BP42 65
Okeburn Rd. SW17 BV49 76
Okehampton Cres. Well. CO43 69
Okehampton Rd. NW10 BQ37 55
Okemore Gdns. Orp. CP52 89
Olaf St. W11 BQ40 55
Old Ave. Wey. AV60 91
Old Av. Wey. BA57 92
Old Bailey, EC4 BY39 56
Old Barn Clo. Sutt. BR57 94
Old Barn La. Rick. AY25 26
Old Barn La. Whyt. CA61 105
Old Barn Rd. Epsom BN62 103
Old Barn Way Bexh. CS45 69
Old Barrowfield, E15 CG37 58
Oldberry Rd. Edg. BN29 37
Old Bethnal Green Rd. E2 CB38 57
Old Bexley La. Bex. CS48 79
Old Bexley La. Dart. CT47 79
Old Bond St. W1 BW40 56
Oldborough Rd. Wem. BK34 45
Old Brewery Mews NW3 BT35 47
Hampstead High St.
Old Bridge St. Kings. On T. BK51 84
Thames St.
Old Broad St. EC2 BZ39 57
Old Bromley Rd. Brom. CF49 77
Old Burlington St. W1 BW40 56
Oldbury Pl. W1 BV38 56
Oldbury Rd. Cher. AV54 82
Oldbury Rd. Enf. CB23 30
Old Cavendish St. W1 BV39 56
Old Change Ct. EC4 BZ39 57
Peters Hill.
Old Chapel Rd. Swan. CS54 89
Old Chertsey La. Stai. AV49 72
Old Chertsey Rd. Wok. AQ58 91
Oldchurch Gdns. Rom. CS33 50
Old Church La. NW9 BN34 46
Old Church La. Stan. BJ28 36
Oldchurch Rise Rom. CT33 50
Old Church Rd. E1 CC39 57
Old Church Rd. E4 CE28 39
Oldchurch Rd. Rom. CS33 50
Old Church St. SW3 BT42 66
Old Claygate La. Esher BJ57 93
Old Common Rd. Cob. BC60 92
Old Compton St. W1 BW40 56
Old Cote Dr. Houns. BF43 64
Old Ct. W5 BL39 55
Hillcrest Rd.
Old Ct. Ash. BL63 103
Old Court Pl. W8 BS41 66
Old Court Rd. Guil. AQ71 118
Old Crabtree La. Hem. H. AY14 8
Old Crown Rd. Brwd. CY23 33
Old Dean. Hem. H. AT17 16
Old Deer Park Gdns. Rich. BL45 65
Old Devonshire Rd. SW12 BV47 76
Old Dock Clo. Rich. BM43 65
Old Dover Rd. SE3 CH43 68
Old Downs Hart. DC53 90
Old Drive, The, Welw. G. C. BP8 5
Olden La. Pur. BY59 95
Old Esher Clo. Walt. BD56 93
Old Esher Rd. Walt. BD56 93
Old Farleigh Rd. Sth. Croy. CC58 96
Old Farm Av. N14 BW26 38
Old Farm Av. Sid. CM47 78
Old Farm Clo. Houns. BE45 64
Old Farm Gdns. Swan. CT52 89
Old Farm Pass. Hamptn. BG51 84
Old Farm Rd. Guil. AR69 118
Old Farm Rd. Hamptn. BE50 74
Old Farm Rd. West Dr. AX41 63
Old Farm Rd. E. Sid. CO48 79
Old Farm Rd. W. Sid. CN48 78
Old Ferry Dr. Stai. AR46 72
Oldfield Cir. Nthlt. BG36 54
Oldfield Clo. Amer. AS23 25
Oldfield Clo. Brom. CK52 88
Oldfield Clo. Grnf. BH35 45
Oldfield Clo. Stan. BJ28 36
Oldfield Dr. Wal. Cr. CD17 21
Oldfield Farm Gdns. Grnf. BG37 54
Oldfield Gro. SE16 CC42 67
Oldfield La. Grnf. BG38 54
Oldfield Rd. N16 CA34 48
Oldfield Rd. NW10 BO36 55
Oldfield Rd. SW19 BR50 75
Oldfield Rd. Bexh. CQ44 69
Oldfield Rd. Brom. CK52 88
Oldfield Rd. Hamptn. BE51 84
Oldfield Rd. Hem. H. AV14 7
Oldfield Rd. St. Alb. BK16 18
Oldfields Rd. Sutt. BR55 85
Old Fishery La. Hem. H. AV15 7
Old Fold La. Barn. BR23 28
Old Fold Vw. Barn. BQ24 28
Old Force Clo. Stan. BJ28 36
Old Ford La. Barn. BR23 28
Old Forge Clo. Wat. BC20 17
Old Forge Rd. Enf. CA22 30
Old Forge Rd. Shep. AZ53 83
Old Forge Way, Sid. CO49 79
Old Fox Clo. Cat. BY64 104
Old Fox Footpath. Sth. Croy. CA58 96
Old Garden. The. Sev. CS65 107
Old Gloucester St. WC1 BX39 56
Old Hall Clo. Pnr. BE30 36
Old Hall Dr. Pnr. BE30 36
Oldhams Ter. W3 BN40 55
Old Harpenden Rd. St. Alb. BH12 9
Old Hatch Manor, Ruis. BB33 44
Old Herns La. Welw. G. C. BT7 5
Old Hertford Rd. Hat. BQ11 10
Old Highway, Hodd. CE10 12
Old Hill Orp. CM57 97
Old Hill, Wok. AR63 100
Oldhill St. N16 CB33 48
Old Homesdale Rd. Brom. CJ52 88
Old Ho. Clo. SW19 BR49 75
Old Ho. Clo. Epsom BO58 94
Old House Ct. Hem. H. AY13 8
Old House Croft, Harl. CN10 6
Oldhouse La. Harl. CJ12 13
Oldhouse La. Kings L. AY21 26
Old House La. Wal. Abb. CG15 13
Old House Rd. Hem. H. AY13 8
Old Jamaica Rd. SE16 CB41 67
Old James St. SE15 CB45 67
Old Jewry, EC2 BZ39 57
Old Kenton La. NW9 BM32 46
Old Kingston Rd. Wor. Pk. BN55 85
Old Lane. Cob. AZ62 101
Old Lodge La. Pur. BX60 95
Old Lodge Way Stan. BJ28 36
Old London Rd. Dor. BK67 111
Old London Rd. Epsom BP62 103
Old London Rd. Epsom. BP63 103
Old London Rd. Harl. CP10 6
Old London Rd. Harl. CP11 14
Old London Rd. Leath. BC66 110
Old London Rd. St. Alb. BG14 9
Old London Rd. Sev. CQ61 107
Old Maidstone Rd. Sid. CQ50 79
Old Malden La. Wor. Pk. BN55 85
Old Malt Way, Wok. AR62 100
Old Manor Dr. Islw. BG46 74
Old Manor Gdns. Guil. AU73 118
Old Manor Rd. Til. DG45 71
Old Manor Way Bexh. CS44 69
Old Manor Yd. SW5 BS42 66
Earl's Ct. Rd.
Old Maple, Hem. H. AY10 8
Old Marsh La. Maid. AJ41 61
Old Marylebone Rd. NW1 BU39 56
Old Mill Ct. E18 CJ31 49
Old Mill La. Maid. AH41 61
Old Mill La. Red. BY67 113
Old Mill La. Uxb. AW39 53
Old Mill Rd. SE18 CM43 68
Old Mill Rd. Kings L. BA20 17
Old Mill Rd. Uxb. AW34 44
Old Montague St. E1 CA39 57
Old Nazeing Rd. Brox. CE14 12
Old Nichol St. E2 CA38 57
Old North St. WC1 BX39 56
Theobalds Rd.
Old Oak Ave. Couls. BU63 104
Old Oak Av. Couls. BU62 104
Old Oak Common Way, W3 BO40 55
Old Oak Est. W12 BO40 55
Old Oak La. NW10 BO38 55
Old Oak Rd. W3 BO40 55
Old Orchard. Harl. CM12 13
Old Orchard Sun. BD51 84
Old Orchard, Wey. AY59 92
Old Palace La. Rich. BK46 74
Old Palace Rd. Croy. BY55 86
Old Palace Rd. Guil. AQ71 118
Old Palace Rd. Wey. AZ55 83
Old Palace Yd. Rich. BK46 74
Old Paradise St. SE11 BX42 66
Old Pk. Wey. AV60 91
Old Park Av. SW12 BV46 76
Old Pk. Av. Enf. BZ24 30
Old Parkbury La. St. Alb. BH18 18
Old Pk. Gro. Enf. BZ24 30
Old Park La. W1 BV40 56
Oldpark Ride, Wal. Cr. CA20 21
Old Pk. Ridings N21 BY25 29
Old Pk. Rd. N13 BX28 38
Old Park Rd. SE2 CO42 69
Old Pk. Rd. Enf. BY24 29
Old Pk. Rd. S. Enf. BY24 29
Old Pk. Vw. Enf. BY24 29
Old Perry St. Chis. CN50 78
Old Perry St. Grav. DF47 81
Old Pol Hill, Sev. CS60 98
Old Portsmouth Rd. AR74 118
Old Pottery Clo. Reig. BS71 121
Old Pye St. SW1 BW41 66
Old Quebec St. W1 BU40 56
Old Queen St. SW1 BW41 66
Old Rectory Clo. Tad. BP65 103
Old Rectory Dr. Hat. BP12 10
Old Rectory Gdns. Edg. BM29 37
Old Rectory Ho. SW19 BR49 75
Old Rectory La. Leath. BB66 110
Old Rectory La. Uxb. AV33 43
Old Rectory Rd. Ong. CU20 23
Old Rectory Rd. Ong. CV20 24
Old Redding Har. BF28 36
Old Redstone Dr. Red. BV71 121
Old Reigate Rd. Bet. BM70 120
Old Reigate Rd. Dor. BL70 120
Oldridge Rd. SW12 BV47 76
Old Rd. SE13 CG45 68
Old Rd. Dart. CS46 79
Old Rd. Enf. CC23 30
Old Rd. Harl. CP8 6
Old Rd. Rom. CV23 33
Old Rd. Rom. CV24 33
Old Rd. Wey. AV57 91
Old Rd. E. Grav. DG47 81
Old Rd. W. Grav. DF47 81
Old Ruislip Rd. Nthlt. BD37 54
Olds Approach. Wat. BA26 35
Old School La. Bet. BM72 120
Old Schools La. Epsom BO58 94
Old Slade La. Iver. AV41 62
Old South Lambeth Rd. SW8 BX43 66
Old Station Hill, Chis. CL51 88
Old Station La. Stai. AS46 72
Old Station Rd. Hayes. BB41 63
Old Station Rd. Knockholt CQ58 98
Old Station Rd. Loug. CK25 31
Oldstead Rd. Brom. CF49 77
Old St. E13 CH37 58
Old St. EC1 BZ38 57
Old Terry's Lodge Rd. Sev. CZ61 108
Old Terrys Lodge Rd. Sev. DA60 99
Old Town SW4 BW45 66
Old Town Croy. BY55 86
Old Tye Ave. West. CK61 106
Old Uxbridge Rd. Rick. AV29 34
Old Walk. The. Sev. CV62 108
Old Watford Rd. St. Alb. BE18 18
Old Watling St. Grav. DG49 81
Oldway La. Slou. AL40 61
Old Westhall Clo. Warl. CC63 105
Old Woking Rd. Wok. AT63 100
Old Woolwich Rd. SE10 CF43 67
Olernder Clo. Orp. CM56 97
Oley Pl. E1 CC39 57
Olga St. E3 CD37 57
Olinda Rd. N16 CA32 48
Oliphant St. W10 BQ38 55
Oliver Av. SE25 CA52 87
Oliver Clo. E10 CE34 48
Oliver Clo. Hem. H. AY15 8
Oliver Clo. St. Alb. BG17 18
Oliver Cres. Farn. CW54 90
Oliver Gro. SE25 CA52 87
Olive Rd. E13 CJ38 58
Olive Rd. NW2 BQ35 46
Olive Rd. SW19 BT50 76
Olive Rd. W5 BK41 64
Olive Rd. Dart. CV47 80
Oliver Rd. E10 CE34 48
Oliver Rd. E17 CF32 48
Oliver Rd. Brwd. DD25 122
Oliver Rd. Hem. H. AY15 8
Oliver Rd. N. Mal. BN51 85
Oliver Rd. Rain. CT37 59
Oliver Rd. Sutt. BT56 95
Oliver Rd. Swan. CS52 89
Oliver's Av. Berk. AU11 7
Olive St. Rom. CS31 50
Ollard's Gro. Loug. CJ24 31
Olleberrie La. Rick. AU19 16
Ollerton Grn. E3 CD37 57
Ollerton Rd. N11 BW28 38
Olliffe St. E14 CF41 67
Olmar St. SE1 CB43 67
Olney Rd. SE17 BY43 66
Olron Cres. Bexh. CP46 79
Olven Rd. SE18 CM43 68
Olveston Wk. Cars. BT53 86
Olyffe Av. Well. CO44 69
Olympic Way, Wem. BM34 46
Oman Av. NW2 BP35 46
O'meara St. SE1 BZ40 57
Omega Pl. N1 BX37 56
Caledonian Rd.
Omega Rd. Wok. AT61 100
Omega St. SE14 CD44 67
Ommaney Rd. SE14 CC44 67
Ondine Rd. SE15 CA45 67
One Pin La. Slou. AO35 43
One Tree Clo. SE23 CC46 77
One Tree Hill Rd. Guil. AT71 118
Ongar Clo. Rom. CP32 50
Ongar Clo. Wey. AV56 91
Ongar Clo. Wey. AW56 92
Ongar Hill, Wey. AW57 92
Ongar Pl. Brwd. DB27 42
Ongar Place, Wey. AW57 92
Ongar Rd. SW6 BS43 66
Ongar Rd. Brwd. CX19 24
Ongar Rd. Brwd. CY24 33
Ongar Rd. Brwd. CZ19 24
Ongar Rd. Brwd. DA26 42
Ongar Rd. Epp. CO18 23
Ongar Road. Ong. CY14 15
Ongar Rd. Rom. CO24 32
Ongar Rd. Wey. AW56 92
Ongar Way Rain. CT37 59
Onra Rd. E17 CE33 48
Onslow Av. Rich. BL46 75
Onslow Av. Sutt. BR58 94
Onslow Clo. E4 CF27 39
Onslow Clo. Wok. AT62 100
Onslow Ct. Surb. BH54 84
Onslow Way
Onslow Cr. Chis. CL51 88
Onslow Cres. SW7 BT42 66
Old Brompton Rd.
Onslow Cres. Wok. AT62 100
Onslow Dr. Sid. CP48 79
Onslow Gdns. E18 CH31 49
Onslow Gdns. N10 BV32 47
Onslow Gdns. N21 BY25 29
Onslow Gdns. SW7 BT42 66
Onslow Gdns. Ong. CX17 24
Onslow Gdns. Sth. Croy. CB59 96
Onslow Gdns. Surb. BH54 84
Onslow Gdns. Wall. BW57 95
Onslow Ms. W. SW7 BT42 66
Cranley Pl.
Onslow Rd. Croy. BX54 86
Onslow Rd. Guil. AR70 118
Onslow Rd. N. Mal. BP52 85
Onslow Rd. Rich. BL46 75
Onslow Rd. Watt. BB56 92
Onslow Sq. SW7 BT42 66
Onslow St. EC1 BY38 56
Clerkenwell Rd.
Onslow St. Guil. AR71 118
Onslow Way Surb. BH54 84
Onslow Way, Wok. AV61 100
Ontario St. SE1 BY41 66
On The Hill Wat. BE27 36
Opal Mews, Ilf. CL34 49
Ley St.
Opal St. SE11 BY42 66
Openshaw Rd. SE2 CO42 69
Openview, SW18 BT47 76
Ophir Ter. SE15 CB44 67
Opossum Way Houns. BD45 64
Oppidans Ms. NW3 BU36 56
Oppidans Rd. NW3 BU36 56
Orange Ct. E1 CB40 57
Hermitage Wall
Orange Hill Rd. Edg. BN29 37
Orange Pl. SE16 CC41 67
Orangery La. SE9 CK46 78
Orange St. WC2 BW40 56
Orange Tree Hill Hav. CS28 41
Orantham Clo. Edg. BL27 37
Orbain Rd. SW6 BR43 65
Orbel St. SW11 BU44 66
Orbital Cres. Wat. BB21 26
Orb St. SE17 BZ42 67
Orchad Av. Berk. AQ13 7
Orchard Ave. Wey. AV59 91
Orchard Ave. Wind. AN44 61
Orchard Av. N3 BS31 47
Orchard Av. N14 BW26 38
Orchard Av. N20 BT27 38
Orchard Av. Ashf. BA50 73
Orchard Av. Belv. CQ43 69
Orchard Av. Berk. AQ13 7
Orchard Av. Brwd. DC27 122
Orchard Av. Croy. CD54 87
Orchard Av. Dart. CU47 79
Orchard Av. Felt. BA46 73
Orchard Av. Grav. DG49 81
Orchard Av. Houns. BE43 64
Orchard Av. Mitch. BV54 86
Orchard Av. N. Mal. BO51 85
Orchard Av. Rain. CV38 60
Orchard Av. Sthl. BE40 54
Orchard Av. Surb. BJ54 84
Orchard Av. Wat. BC19 17
Orchard Clo. SW20 BQ52 85
Orchard Clo. Ashf. BA50 73
Orchard Clo. Bans. BS60 95
Orchard Clo. Bexh. CQ44 69
Orchard Clo. Bish. CS7 6
Orchard Clo. Borwd. BL24 28
Orchard Clo. Bush. BG26 36
Orchard Clo. Edg. BL29 37
Orchard Clo. Egh. AT49 72
Orchard Clo. Hem. H. AZ12 8
Orchard Clo. Hert. BW13 11
Orchard Clo. Lthd. BB65 101
Orchard Clo. Lthd. BG64 102
Orchard Clo. Pot. B. BX17 20
Orchard Clo. Rad. BH22 27
Orchard Clo. Rick. AU24 25
Orchard Clo. Ruis. BA33 44
Orchard Clo. St. Alb. BH14 9
Orchard Clo. Sev. CV63 108
Orchard Clo. S. Ock. DB38 60
Orchard Clo. Surb. BJ54 84
Orchard Clo. Uxb. AW36 53
Orchard Clo. Wat. BB23 26
Orchard Clo. Wem. BL36 55
Orchard Clo. Wok. AT61 100
Orchard Cotts. Brwd. DC32 123
Orchard Ct. Edg. BL28 37
Orchard Ct. Islw. BG44 64
Thornbury Av.
Orchard Ct. Wor. Pk. BP54 85
Orchard Cres. Edg. BN28 37
Orchard Cres. Enf. CA23 30
Orchard Croft, Harl. CO10 6

Orchard Dri. Rick. AU24 25
Orchard Dr. SE3 CF44 67
Orchard Dr. Ash. BK63 102
Orchard Dr. Edg. BL28 37
Orchard Dr. Epp. CN21 31
Orchard Dr. Grays. DD41 71
Orchard Dr. St. Alb. BF17 18
Orchard Dr. Uxb. AX38 53
Orchard Dr. Wat. BB23 26
Orchard Dr. Wok. AS61 100
Orchard End, Wey. BB55 83
Orchard End Ave. Amer. AP23 25
Orchard Est. SE13 CE44 67
Orchard Gdns. Chess. BL56 94
Orchard Gdns. Epsom BN60 94
Orchard Gdns. Lthd. BE67 111
Orchard Gdns. Sutt. BS56 95
Orchard Gdns. Wal. Abb. CF20 21
Orchard Gate, NW9 BO31 46
Orchard Gate Esher BG54 84
Orchard Gate, Grnf. BJ36 54
Orchard Grn. Orp. CN55 88
Orchard Gro. Croy. CD54 87
Orchard Gro. Edg. BM30 37
Orchard Gro. Ger. Cr. AR30 34
Orchard Gro. Har. BL32 46
Orchard Gro. Orp. CN55 88
Orchard Hill SE13 CE44 67
Coldbath St.
Orchard Hill Cars. BU56 95
Orchard Hill Dart. CT46 79
Orchard La. SW20 BP51 85
Orchard La. Amer. AO22 25
Orchard La. Brwd. CZ25 33
Orchard La. E. Mol. BG53 84
Orchard La. Wdf. Grn. CJ28 40
Orchard Leas, Wok. AV61 100
Orchardleigh Lthd. BJ64 102
St. Nicholas Hill.
Orchardleigh Av. Enf. CC23 30
Orchard Mains, Wok. AR63 100
Orchardmede N21 BZ25 30
Orchard North. The. Epp. CO19 23
Orchard Piece Ing. DC18 24
Orchard Pl. E14 CG40 58
Orchard Pl. N17 CA29 39
Orchard Pl. Brom. CH51 88
Orchard Rise Croy. CD54 87
Orchard Rise Kings. On T. BN51 85
Orchard Rise, Rich. BM46 75
Orchard Rise, E. Sid. CN46 78
Orchard Rise, W. Sid. CN45 68
Orchard Rd. N6 BV33 47
Orchard Rd. SE3 CG44 68
Orchard Rd. Barn. BR24 28
Orchard Rd. Beac. AO28 34
Orchard Rd. Belv. CR42 69
Orchard Rd. Brom. CJ51 88
Orchard Rd. Chess. BL56 94
Orchard Rd. Ch. St. G. AR27 34
Orchard Rd. Dag. CR37 59
Orchard Rd. Dor. BJ72 119
Orchard Rd. Enf. CC25 30
Orchard Rd. Grav. DE48 81
Orchard Rd. Guil. AP71 118
Orchard Rd. Guil. AS73 118
Orchard Rd. Guil. AT68 109
Orchard Rd. Hamptn. BE50 74
Orchard Rd. Hayes BC40 53
Orchard Rd. Houns. BE46 74
Orchard Rd. Kings. On T. BL52 85
Orchard Rd. Mitch. BV54 86
Orchard Rd. Orp. CL56 97
Orchard Rd. Orp. CP58 98
Orchard Rd. Reig. BS70 121
Orchard Rd. Rich. BM45 65
Orchard Rd. Rom. CR30 41
Orchard Rd. Sev. CT61 107
Orchard Rd. Sev. CT64 107
Orchard Rd. Sid. CN49 78
Orchard Rd. S. Ock. DB38 60
Orchard Rd. Sth. Croy. CB60 96
Orchard Rd. Sun. BC50 73
Orchard Rd. Sutt. BS56 95
Orchard Rd. Swans. DC46 81
Orchard Rd. Twick. BJ46 74
Orchard Rd. Well. CO45 69
Orchard Rd. Wind. AQ46 72
Orchardson St. NW8 BT38 56
Orchard Sq. Brox. CD15 12
Orchards South. The. Epp. CO19 23
Orchards, The, Saw. CQ6 6
Orchard St. E17 CD31 48
Orchard St. W1 BV39 56
Orchard St. Dart. CW46 80
Orchard St. Hem. H. AX15 8
Orchard St. St. Alb. BG14 9
Orchard, The, N21 BZ25 30
Orchard, The, NW11 BS32 47
Orchard, The, SE3 CF44 67
Orchard, The, W4 BN42 65
Orchard, The, W5 BK39 54
Orchard, The Dor. BK73 119
Orchard, The, Houns. BG44 64
Orchard, The, Kings L. AZ18 17
Orchard, The, Welw. G. C. BQ7 5
Orchard Vw. Uxb. AX38 53
Orchard Way, Ashf. AY48 73
Orchard Way Chig. CO27 41
Orchard Way Croy. CD54 87
Orchard Way. Dart. CV48 80
Orchard Way. Enf. CA24 30
Orchard Way Esher BG57 93
Orchard Way. Hem. H. AT17 16
Orchard Way. Oxt. CH70 115
Orchard Way, Pot. B. BS18 20
Orchard Way, Reig. BS72 121
Orchard Way. Rick. AW26 35
Orchard Way. Sev. CX62 108
Orchard Way Sutt. BT56 95
Orchard Way. Tad. BR66 112
Orchard Way, Wal. Cr. BY17 20
Orchard Way, Wey. AW56 92
Orchard Way, Wok. AU66 109
Orchard Waye, Uxb. AX37 53
Orchd. Mead. Hat. BO12 10
Orchehill Ave. Ger. Cr. AR31 43
Orchehill Rise. Ger. Cr. AS32 43
Orchid Rd. N14 BW26 38
Orchid St. W12 BP40 55
Orchid Way. Rom. CW29 42
Orde Hall St. WC1 BX39 56
Ordell Rd. E3 CD37 57
Ordnance Clo. Felt. BC48 73
Ordnance Cres. SE10 CG41 68
Ordnance Hill, NW8 BT37 56
Ordnance Rd. E16 CG39 58
Ordnance Rd. SE18 CL43 68
Ordnance Rd. Enf. CC22 30
Ordnance Rd. Grav. DH46 81
Oregon Av. E12 CK35 49
Oregon Sq. Orp. CM54 88
Oreston Lane. Leath. BC67 110
Oreston Rd. Rain. CV38 60
Orford Ct. SE27 BY48 76
Orford Gdns. Twick. BH48 74
Orford Rd. E17 CE32 48
Orford Rd. E18 CH31 49
Organ La. E4 CF27 39
Oriel Clo. Mitch. BW52 86
Holly Way
Oriel Ct. Mitch. BW52 86
Oriel Gdns. Ilf. CK31 49
Oriel Pl. NW3 BT35 47
Oriel Rd. E9 CC36 57
Oriel Way Nthlt. BF36 54
Oriental Clo. Wok. AS62 100
Oriental Rd. Wok. AS62 100
Oriental St. E14 CE40 57
Orient Rd. Til. DG45 71
Orient St. SE11 BY42 66
West Sq.
Orion Way. Nthwd. BB28 35
Orissa Rd. SE18 CN42 68
Orkney St. SW11 BV44 66
Dagnall St.
Orlando Gdns. Epsom BN58 94
Orlando Rd. SW4 BW45 66
Orleans Rd. SE19 BZ50 77
Orleans Rd. Twick. BJ47 74
Orleston Gdns. Orp. CQ56 98
Orleston Ms. N7 BY36 56
Orleston Rd. N7 BY36 56
Orley Farm Rd. Har. BH34 45
Orlick Rd. Grav. DK48 81
Orlop St. SE10 CG42 68
Ormanton Rd. SE26 CB49 77
Orme Ct. W2 BS40 56
Orme Ct. Ms. W2 BS40 56
Orme La.
Orme La. W2 BS40 56
Ormeley Rd. SW12 BV47 76
Orme Ms. W2 BS40 56
Orme Ct.
Orme Rd. Kings. On T. BM51 85
Ormerod Gdns. Mitch. BV51 86
Ormesby Dr. Pot. B. BQ19 19
Ormesby Gdns. Grnf. BG37 54
Ormesby Way, Har. BL32 46
Orme Sq. W2 BS40 56
Ormiston Gro. W12 BP40 55
Ormiston Rd. SE10 CH42 68
Ormond Av. Hamptn. BF51 84
Ormond Av. Rich. BK46 74
Ormond Rd.
Ormond Clo. WC1 BX39 56
Boswell St.
Ormond Cres. Hamptn. BF51 84
Ormond Dr. Hamptn. BF50 74
Ormonde Av. Epsom BN58 94
Ormonde Av. Orp. CM55 88
Ormonde Ct. SW15 BQ45 65
Upr. Richmond Rd.
Ormonde Gte. SW3 BU42 66
Ormonde Rise Buck. H. CJ26 40
Ormonde Rd. SW14 BM45 65
Ormonde Rd. Nthwd. BA28 35
Ormonde Rd. Wok. AR61 100
Ormonde Ter. NW8 BU37 56
Ormond Ms. WC1 BX38 56
Guilford St.
Ormond Rd. N19 BX33 47
Ormond Rd. Rich. BK46 74
Ormond Yd. SW1 BW40 56
Duke Of York St.
Ormsby Pl. N16 CD34 48
Victorian Gro.
Ormsby St. E2 CA37 57
Ormskirk Rd. Wat. BD28 36
Ornan Rd. NW3 BU35 47
Oronsay, Hem. H. AZ14 8
Oronsay Wk. N1 BZ36 57
Marquess Est.
Orphanage Rd. Wat. BD23 27
Orpheus St. SE5 BZ44 67
Orpingley Rd. N7 BX34 47
Orpington By-pass Orp. CP56 98
Orpington Gdns. N18 CA27 39
Orpington Rd. N21 BY26 38
Orpington Rd. Chis. CN51 88
Orpin Rd. Red. BY67 113
Orris Ms. W6 BQ42 65
Beadon Rd.
Orsett Heath Cres. Grays. DG41 71
Orsett Ms. W2 BS39 56
Orsett Rd. Grays. DD42 71
Orsett St. SE11 BX42 66
Orsett Ter. W2 BT39 56
Orsett Ter. Wdf. Grn. CJ29 40
Orsman Rd. N1 CA37 57
Orton St. E1 CB40 57
Hermitage Wall.
Orville Rd. SW11 BT44 66
Orwell Clo. Wind. AO45 61
Orwell Ct. N5 BZ35 48
Orwell Gdns. Reig. BS71 121
Orwell Rd. E13 CJ37 58
Osbaldeston Rd. N16 CA34 48
Osberton Rd. SE12 CH46 78
Osbert St. SW1 BW42 66
Vincent Sq.
Osborn Clo. E14 CE40 57
Osborne Av. Stai. AY47 73
Osborne Clo. Beck. CD52 87
Osborne Clo. Horn. CU32 50
Osborne Gdns. Th. Hth. BZ51 87
Osborne Gro. E17 CD32 48
Osborne Mews. Wind. AO44 61
Osborne Rd. E7 CH35 49
Osborne Rd. E9 CD36 57
Osborne Rd. E10 CE34 48
Osborne Rd. N4 BX33 47
Osborne Rd. N13 BY27 38
Osborne Rd. NW2 BP36 55
Osborne Rd. W3 BM41 65
Osborne Rd. Belv. CQ42 69
Osborne Rd. Brox. CE13 12
Osborne Rd. Brwd. DA25 33
Osborne Rd. Buck. H. CH26 40
Osborne Rd. Dag. CQ35 50
Osborne Rd. Egh. AS50 72
Osborne Rd. Enf. CC23 30
Osborne Rd. Horn. CU32 50
Osborne Rd. Houns. BE45 64
Osborne Rd. Kings. On T. BL50 75
Osborne Rd. Pot. B. BS18 20
Osborne Rd. Red. BV69 121
Osborne Rd. Sthl. BF39 54
Osborne Rd. Th. Hth. BZ51 87
Osborne Rd. Wal. Cr. CD17 21
Osborne Rd. Walt. BC54 83
Osborne Rd. Wat. BD22 27
Osborne Rd. Wind. AO44 61
Osborne Sq. Dag. CQ35 50
Osborne St. SE17 BZ42 67
Osborne St. Slou. AP41 62
Osborn Gdns. NW7 BQ29 37
Osborn St. E1 CA39 57
Osborn Ter. SE3 CG45 68
Osbourne Av. Kings L. AY17 17
Osbourne Clo. Felt. BD49 74
Oscar St. SE8 CE44 67
Oseney Cres. NW5 BW35 47
Osgood Av. Orp. CN56 97
Osgood Gdns. Orp. CN56 97
O'shea Gro. E3 CD37 57
Osidge La. N14 BV26 38
Osiers Rd. SW18 BS45 66
Osier St. E1 CC38 57
Cephas Av.
Osier Way, Mitch. BU53 86
Oslac Rd. SE6 CE49 77
Oslo Ct. NW8 BU37 56
Osman Clo. N15 BZ32 48
Tewkesbury Rd.
Osman Rd. N9 CB27 39
Osmond Clo. Har. BG34 45
Osmond Gdns. Wall. BW56 95
Osmund St. W12 BO39 55
Braybrook St.
Osnaburgh St. NW1 BV38 56
Osnaburgh Ter. NW1 BV38 56
Osnaburgh St.
Osney Wk. Cars. BT53 86
Osney Way, Grav. DJ48 81
Ospringe Ct. SE9 CM46 78
Ospringe Rd. NW5 BW35 47
Osric Pth. N1 CA37 57
Ossian Rd. N4 BX33 47
Ossie Dr. Iver AU40 52
Ossington Bldgs. W1 BV39 56
Moxon St.
Ossington Clo. W2 BS40 56
Ossington St.
Ossington St. W2 BS40 56
Ossory Rd. SE1 CB42 67
Ossulston Est. NW1 BW38 56
Ossulston St. NW1 BW37 56
Ossulton Pla. N2 BT31 47
Ossulton Way
Ossulton Way. N2 BT31 47
Ostade Rd. SW2 BX47 76
Osten Ms. SW7 BS41 66
Osterberg Rd. Dart. CW45 70
Osterley Av. Islw. BG43 64
Osterley Ct. Islw. BG44 64
Osterley Cres. Islw. BH44 64
Osterley Gdns. Th. Hth. BZ51 87
Osterley La. Sthl. BF42 64
Osterley Pk. Rd. Sthl. BE41 64
Osterley Pk. Vw. Rd. W7 BH41 64
Osterley Rd. N16 CA35 48
Osterley Rd. Islw. BH43 64
Oster St. St. Alb. BG13 9
Oswald Clo. Lthd. BG64 102
Oswald Rd. Lthd. BG64 102
Oswald Rd. St. Alb. BH14 9
Oswald Rd. Sthl. BE40 54
Osward Croy. CD58 96
Osward Rd. SW17 BU48 76
Oswin St. SE11 BY42 66
Oswyth Rd. SE5 CA44 67
Otford Clo. Bex. CR46 79
Otford Clo. Brom. CL52 88
Otford Cres. SE4 CD46 77
Otford La. Sev. CQ59 98
Otford Rd. Sev. CU63 107
Otis St. E3 CF38 57
Otley App. Ilf. CL32 49
Otley Dr. Ilf. CL32 49
Otley Rd. E16 CJ39 58
Otley Rd. Chesh. AP18 16
Otley Ter. E5 CC34 48
Otley Way Wat. BD27 36
Otlinge Clo. Orp. CP52 89
Ottawa Gdns. Dag. CS36 59
Ottawa Rd. Til. DG44 71
Ottaway St. E5 CB34 48
Otterbourne Rd. E4 CF27 39
Otterburn Gdns. Islw. BJ43 64
Otterburn St. SW17 BU50 76
Otterden Clo. Orp. CN56 97
Otterden St. SE6 CE49 77
Otterfield Rd. West Dr. AY40 53
Otter Gds. Hat. BP13 10
Ottermead La. Cher. AU57 91
Otter Rd. Grnf. BG38 54
Otterspool La. Wat. BE22 27
Otterspool Way Wat. BE23 27
Ottesbrook St. SE14 CD43 67
Otto Clo. SE26 CB48 77
Sydenham Hill
Otto St. SE17 BY43 66
Ottway's Av. Ash. BK63 102
Ottway's La. Ash. BK63 102
Otways Clo. Pot. B. BS19 20
Oulton Clo. E5 CB34 48
Southwold Rd.
Oulton Cres. Bark. CN35 49
Oulton Cres. Pot. B. BQ19 19
Oulton Rd. N15 BZ32 48
Oulton Rd. Pot. B. BQ19 19
Oulton Way Wat. BE28 36
Oundle Av. Bush. BG25 27
Ousden Clo. Wal. Cr. CD18 21
Ousden Dr. Wal. Cr. CD18 21
Ouseley Rd. SW12 BU47 76
Ouseley Rd. Wind. AR47 72
Outer Circle, NW1 BV38 56
Outfield Rd. Ger. Cr. AR29 34
Outgate Rd. NW10 BO36 55
Outing's La. Brwd. DA21 33
Outram Rd. E6 CK37 58
Outram Rd. N22 BW30 38
Outram Rd. Croy. CA55 87
Outram St. N1 BX37 56
Outward La. Red. BZ71 114
Outwich St. EC3 CA39 57
Houndsditch.
Outwood La. Couls. BU62 104
Outwood La. Couls. BU63 104
Outwood La. Tad. BS64 104
Oval Gdns. Grays. DE41 71
Oval Pl. SW8 BX43 66
Oval Rd. NW1 BV36 56
Oval Rd. Croy. BZ55 87
Oval Rd. N. Dag. CR37 59
Oval Rd. S. Dag. CR37 59
Oval, The, E2 CB37 57
Oval, The, Bans. BS60 95
Oval, The Guil. AQ71 118
Oval, The, Sid. CO47 79
Oval Way, SE11 BX42 66
Oval Way. Ger. Cr. AS31 43
Ovenden Rd. Sev. CP63 107
Over Brae, Beck. CE50 77
Overbrook. Leath. AZ68 110
Overbrook Wk. Edg. BL29 37
Buckingham Rd.
Overbury Av. Beck. CE52 87
Overbury Cres. Croy. CF58 96
Overbury Rd. N15 BZ32 48
Overbury St. E5 CC35 48
Overcliffe, Grav. DF46 81
Overcliffe Rd. Grays. DE42 71
Overcliff Rd. SE13 CE45 67
Overcourt Clo. Sid. CO46 79
Blackfen Rd.
Overdale . Ash. BL61 103
Overdale, Dor. BK71 119
Overdale. Red. BZ70 114
Overdale Av. N. Mal. BN51 85
Overdale Rd. W5 BK41 64
Overdown Rd. SE6 CE49 77
Overhill Gdns. SE22 CB47 77
Overhill Rd. SE22 CB47 77
Overhill Rd. Pur. BY58 95
Overhill Way Beck. CF53 87
Overlea Rd. E5 CB33 48
Overmead, Sid. CM47 78
Overmead Swan. CT53 89
Overstand Clo. Beck. CE53 87
Overstone Rd. W6 BQ41 65
Overstream, Rick. AW24 26
Over, The, Misbourne. Ger. Cr. AT32 43
Overton Clo. NW10 BN36 55
Overton Clo. Islw. BH44 64
Overton Dr. E11 CH33 49
Overton Dr. Rom. CP33 50
Overton Gdns. Croy. CD54 87
Overton Rd. E10 CD33 48
Overton Rd. N14 BX25 29
Overton Rd. SE2 CP41 69
Overton Rd. SW9 BY44 66
Overton Rd. Sutt. BS57 95
Overton's Yd. Croy. BZ55 87
Overy Liberty Dart. CW47 80
Overy St. Dart. CW46 80
Ovesdon Av. Har. BE33 45
Oveton Way. Lthd. BF66 111
Ovington Gdns. SW3 BU41 66
Ovington Ms. SW3 BU41 66
Ovington Sq. SW3 BU41 66
Ovington St. SW3 BU42 66
Owen Clo. Hayes BC38 53
Owen Rd. N13 BZ28 39
Owen Rd. Hayes BC38 53
Owens Way, Rick. AZ24 26
Owen Way NW10 BN35 46
Owgan Close SE5 BZ43 67
Elmington Estate
Owlets Hall Clo. Rom. CW31 51
Ownstead Gdns. Sth. Croy. CA59 96
Ownstead Hill Croy. CF58 96
Oxberry Av. SW6 BR44 65
Oxdowne Clo. Cob. BF60 93
Oxenden Wd. Rd. Orp. CO57 98
Oxendon Dr. Hodd. CE12 12
Oxendon St. SW1 BW40 56
Oxenford St. SE15 CA45 67
Oxenhill Rd. Sev. CW62 108
Oxenpark Av. Wem. BL33 46
Oxestalls Rd. SE8 CD42 67
Oxfield Clo. Berk. AQ13 7
Oxford Ave. Grays. DG42 71
Oxford Ave. Hayes. BB43 63
Oxford Av. SW20 BR51 85
Oxford Av. Horn. CX31 51
Oxford Av. Houns. BF43 64
Oxford Av. St. Alb. BK14 9
Oxford Clo. N9 CB27 39
Oxford Clo. Ashf. BA50 73
Oxford Clo. Grav. DJ48 81
Oxford Clo. Mitch. BW52 86
Oxford Ct. Felt. BD49 74
Oxford Cres. N. Mal. BN53 85
Oxford Dr. Ruis. BD34 45
Oxford Gdns. N20 BT26 38
Oxford Gdns. N21 BZ26 39
Oxford Gdns. W4 BM42 65
Oxford Gdns. W10 BQ39 55
Oxford La. Guil. AR71 118
Oxford Rd. E15 CF36 57
Oxford Rd. N4 BY33 47
Oxford Rd. N9 CB27 39
Oxford Rd. NW6 BS37 56
Oxford Rd. SE19 BZ50 77
Oxford Rd. SW15 BR45 65
Oxford Rd. W5 BK40 54
Oxford Rd. Cars. BU57 95
Oxford Rd. Cat. CA66 114
Oxford Rd. Enf. CB25 30
Oxford Rd. Ger. Cr. AO31 43
Oxford Rd. Guil. AR71 118
Oxford Rd. Har. BG32 45
Oxford Rd. Ilf. CM35 49
Oxford Rd. Red. BU70 121
Oxford Rd. Rom. CW29 42
Oxford Rd. Sid. CO49 79
Oxford Rd. Tedd. BG49 74
Oxford Rd. Uxb. AW34 44
Oxford Rd. Uxb. AX36 53
Oxford Rd. Wall. BW56 95
Oxford Rd. Wdf. Grn. CJ28 40
Oxford Rd. N. W4 BM42 65
Oxford Rd. S. W4 BM42 65
Oxford Sq. W2 BU39 56
Oxford St. W1 BV39 56
Oxford St. Bark. CL36 58
Oxford St. Wat. BC25 26
Oxford Way. Cat. CA66 114
Oxford Way Felt. BD49 74
Oxfort Ct. Brwd. DB28 42
Oxgate Gdns. NW2 BP34 46
Oxgate La. NW2 BP34 46
Oxhawth Cres. Brom. CL53 88
Oxhey Av. Wat. BD26 36
Oxhey Dr. Nthwd. BC28 35
Oxhey La. Wat. BE26 36
Oxhey Rd. Wat. BD25 27
Ox La. Epsom BP58 94
Oxleas Clo. Well. CM44 68
Oxlease Dr. Hat. BP13 10
Oxleay Av. Har. BF33 45
Oxleay Ct. Har. BF33 45
Oxleigh Clo. N. Mal. BO53 85
Oxley Clo. Rom. CV30 42
Oxleys Rd. NW2 BP34 46
Oxleys Rd. Wal. Abb. CH20 22
Oxleys, The, Harl. CQ9 6
Oxlow La. Dag. CQ35 50
Oxonian St. SE22 CA45 67
Oxshott Av. Cob. BF61 102
Oxshott Ri. Cob. BE60 93
Oxshott Rise. Cob. BE60 93
Oxted Clo. Mitch. BT52 86
Oxted Rd. Gdse. CC68 114
Oxtoby Way, SW16 BW51 86
Oyster Hill. Epsom. BN65 103
Oyster La. Wey. AY59 92
Pachesham Dr. Lthd. BH61 102
Pachesham Park, Lthd. BJ61 102
Pacific Rd. E16 CH39 58
Packet Boat La. Uxb. AX39 53
Packham Rd. Grav. DF48 81
Packhorse Clo. St. Alb. BK11 9
Packhorse La. Borwd. BN20 19
Packhorse La. Borwd. BO22 28
Packhorse La. Pot. B. BN18 19
Packhorse Path Stai. AV49 72
South St.
Packhorse Rd. Ger. Cr. AS31 43
Packhorse Rd. Sev. CS65 107
Packington Sq. N1 BZ37 57
Packington St. N1 BY37 56
Packmores Rd. SE9 CM46 78
Padbury Ct. E2 CA38 57
Padcroft Rd. West Dr. AX40 53
Paddenswick Ct. W6 BP41 65
Paddenswick Rd.
Paddenswick Rd. W6 BP41 65
Paddington St. W1 BV39 56
Paddock Clo. SE26 CC49 77
Paddock Clo. Har. BF35 45
Paddock Clo. Oxt. CG69 115
Paddock Ct. S. Dnth. CY51 90
Paddock Gdns. SE19 CA50 77
Paddock Rd. NW2 BP34 46
Paddock Rd. Bexh. CQ45 69
Paddock Rd. Ruis. BD34 45
Paddocks Clo. Ash. BL62 103
Paddocks Clo. Orp. CP55 89
Paddocks Rd. Guil. AT68 109
Paddocks, The, Barn. BU24 29
Chalk La.
Paddocks, The Guil. AU70 118
Paddocks, The, Lthd. BF66 111
Leatherhead Rd.
Paddocks, The, Wem. BM34 46
Paddocks, The, Wey. BB55 83
Paddocks, The Barn. BU24 29

Paddocks Way. Ash. BL62 103
Paddocks Way. Ash. BL63 103
Paddocks Way. Cher. AW54 83
Paddock, The, Brox. CE13 12
Paddock, The Dor. BG72 119
Paddock, The. Ger. Cr. AR28 34
Paddock, The, Hat. BP11 10
Lemsford Rd.
Paddock, The. Slou. AQ44 62
Paddock, The, Uxb. AZ35 44
Paddock, The. West. CM66 115
Paddock Way, Hem. H. AV13 7
Paddock Way. Oxt. CG69 115
Paddock Way. Wok. AT60 91
Padfield Rd. SE5 BZ45 67
Padgets, The, Wal. Abb. CG20 22
Honey La.
Padnall Rd. Rom. CP31 50
Padstow Rd. Enf. BY23 29
Padua Rd. SE20 CC51 87
Pagden St. SW8 BV44 66
Pageant Rd. St. Alb. BG14 9
Pageant Wk. Croy. CA55 87
Page Clo. Harrow BL32 46
Page Cres. Croy. BY57 95
Page Cres. Erith CT43 69
Page Gdns. Chis. CL51 88
Page Green Rd. N15 CB32 48
Page Green Ter. N15 CA32 48
Page Hth. La. Brom. CJ52 88
Page Hth. Villas Brom. CJ52 88
Pagehurst Rd. Croy. CB54 87
Page Rd. Felt. BA46 73
Page's Hill N10 BV30 38
Page's La. N10 BV30 38
Page St. NW7 BP29 37
Page St. SW1 BW42 66
Page's Wk. SE1 CA42 67
Paget Av. Sutt. BT55 86
Paget Clo. Hamptn. BG49 74
Paget Gdns. E6 CK39 58
Paget Rise SE18 CL43 68
Paget Rd. N16 BZ33 48
Paget Rd. Ilf. CL35 49
Paget Rd. Slou. AS42 62
Paget Rd. Uxb. BA38 53
Paget St. EC1 BY38 56
Paget Ter. SE18 CL43 68
Paglesfield Brwd. DE25 122
Rayleigh Rd.
Pagnell St. SE14 CD43 67
Pagoda Av. Rich. BL45 65
Pagoda Gdns. SE3 CF44 67
Paignton Rd. N15 CA32 48
Paignton Rd. Ruis. BC34 44
Paine's Brook Rd. Rom. CW29 42
Paine's Brook Way. Rom. CW29 42
Paines Clo. Pnr. BE31 45
Paines Hill. Oxt. CJ69 115
Paines La. Pnr. BE30 36
Pains Clo. Mitch. BV51 86
Painters Ash La. Grav. DE48 81
Painters La. Enf. CD21 30
Painters Rd. Ilf. CN31 49
Paisley Rd. N22 BY30 38
Paisley Rd. Cars. BT54 86
Pakeman St. N7 BX34 47
Pakenham Cl. SW12 BV47 76
Balham Pk. Rd.
Pakenham St. WC1 BX38 56
Pakes Way, Epp. CN22 31
Palace Av. W8 BS40 56
Palace Clo. Kings L. AY18 17
Palace Ct. NW6 BS35 47
Palace Ct. W2 BS40 56
Palace Ct. Brom. CH51 88
Palace Ct. Har. BL32 46
Palace Court Gdns. N10 BW30 38
Palace Gdns. Buck. H. CJ26 40
Palace Gdns. Enf. BZ24 30
Palace Gdns. Surb. BH54 84
Palace Gdns. Ms. W8 BS40 56
Palace Gdns. Ter. W8 BS40 56
Palace Gdns. Ter. W8 BS41 66
Palace Gte. W8 BT41 66
Palace Gates Rd. N22 BW30 38
Palace Grn. Croy. CD57 96
Palace Gro. SE19 CA50 77
Palace Gro. Brom. CH51 88
Palace Mews Enf. BZ24 30
Palace Gdns.
Palace Rd. N8 BW32 47
Palace Rd. N11 BW29 38
Palace Rd. SE19 CA50 77
Palace Rd. SW2 BX47 76
Palace Rd. Brom. CH51 88
Palace Rd. E. Mol. BG52 84
Palace Rd. Kings-on-t. BK52 84
Palace Rd. Ruis. BE35 45
Palace Rd. West. CL64 106
Palace Sq. SE19 CA50 77
Palace St. SW1 BW41 66
Palace Vw. SE12 CH48 78
Palace Vw. Brom. CH52 88
Palace Vw. Croy. CD55 87
Palace Vw. Rd. E4 CE28 39
Palamos Rd. E10 CE33 48
Palatine Rd. N16 CA35 48
Palermo Rd. NW10 BP37 55
Palestine Gro. SW19 BT51 86
Palewell Clo. Orp. CO51 89
Palewell Common Dr. SW14 BN46 75
Palewell Pk. SW14 BN46 75
Paley Gdns. Loug. CL24 31
Palfrey Clo. St. Alb. BG12 9
Palfrey Pl. SW8 BX43 66
Palgrave Av. Sthl. BF40 54
Palgrave Rd. W12 BO41 65
Palins Way. Grays. DD40 71
Palissy St. E2 CA38 57
Pallas Rd. Hem. H. AY12 8
Pallet Way SE18 CJ44 68
Tellson Av.
Palliser Rd. W14 BR42 65
Palliser Rd. Ch. St. G. AQ27 34
Pall Mall SW1 BW40 56
Pall Mall E. SW1 BW40 56
Pall Mall Pl. SW1 BW40 56
Palmar Cres. Bexh. CR45 69
Palmar Rd. Bexh. CR44 69
Palmarsh Clo. Orp. CP52 89
Palm Av. Sid. CP50 79
Palmeira Rd. Bexh. CP45 69
Palmer Av. Bush. BF25 27
Palmer Av. Grav. DH49 81
Palmer Av. Sutt. BQ56 94
Palmer Clo. Houns. BF44 64
Palmer Cres. Kings-on-t. BL52 85
Palmer Pl. N7 BY35 47
Palmer Rd. E13 CH38 58
Palmer Rd. NW10 BO36 55
Palmer's Ave. Grays. DE42 71
Palmers Clo. Red. BV71 121
Palmersfield Rd. Bans. BS60 95
Palmers Gro. Wal. Abb. CG14 13
Palmers La. Enf. CB23 30
Palmers Moor La. Iver AW38 53
Palmers Pass. SW14 BN45 65
Palmers Rd.
Palmer's Rd. E2 CC37 57
Palmers Rd. N11 BW28 38
Palmers Rd. SW14 BN45 65
Palmers Rd. SW16 BX51 86
Palmers Rd. Borwd. BM23 28
Palmerston Clo. Welw. G. C. BQ8 5
Palmerston Clo. Wok. AS60 91
Palmerston Ct. E17 CD31 48
Palmerston Rd.
Palmerston Cres. N13 BX28 38
Palmerston Cres. SE18 CM43 68
Palmerston Gdns. Grays DB42 70
Palmerston Gro. SW19 BS50 76
Palmerston Rd. E7 CH35 49
Palmerston Rd. E17 CD31 48
Palmerston Rd. N22 BX29 38
Palmerston Rd. SE18 CM43 68
Palmerston Rd. SW14 BN45 65
Palmerston Rd. SW19 BS50 76
Palmerston Rd. W3 BN41 65
Palmerston Rd. Buck. H. CH27 40
Palmerston Rd. Cars. BU56 95
Palmerston Rd. Grays DB43 70
Palmerston Rd. Har. BH31 45
Palmerston Rd. Orp. CM56 97
Palmerston Rd. Rain. CV37 60
Palmerston Rd. Sutt. BT56 95
Palmerston Rd. Th. Hth. BZ53 87
Palmerston Rd. Twick. BH46 74
Palmer St. SW1 BW41 66
Palmer St. W10 BQ40 55
Palmers Way, Wall. Cr. CD18 21
Palm Gro. W5 BL41 65
Palm Gro. Guil. AR68 109
Palm Rd. Rom. CS32 50
Palm St. E3 CD38 57
Pamber St. W10 BQ39 55
Pamela Av. Hem. H. AY15 8
Pamela Gdns. Pnr. BC32 44
Pampisford Rd. Pur. BY59 95
Pams Way Epsom BN56 94
Pancake La. Hem. H. BA14 8
Pancras La. EC4 BZ39 57
Qn. Victoria St.
Pancras Rd. NW1 BW37 56
Pancroft Rom. CO24 32
Pandora Rd. NW6 BS36 56
Panfield Mews Ilf. CL32 49
Panfield Rd. SE2 CO41 69
Pangbourne Av. W10 BQ39 55
Pangbourne Dr. Stan. BK28 36
Panmuir Rd. SW20 BP51 85
Panmure Rd. SE26 CB48 77
Pannard Pl. Sthl. BF40 54
Pansy Gdns. W12 BP40 55
Pantile Rd. Wey. BA56 92
Pantile Row. Slou. AT42 62
Pantiles Clo. Wok. AQ62 100
Pantiles, The, NW11 BR31 46
Pantiles, The, Bexh. CQ43 69
Pantiles, The, Brom. CJ52 88
Pantiles, The, Bush. BG26 36
Butts, The,
Panton St. SW1 BW40 56
Haymarket
Panyer Alley EC4 BY39 56
Newgate St.
Papercourt La. Wok. AU64 100
Papworth Gdns. N7 BX35 47
Parade Mans. NW4 BP32 46
Parade Ms. SW2 BY48 76
Norwood Rd.
Parade, The, Brwd. DB27 42
Kg. Edward Rd.
Parade, The, Dart. CT46 79
Crayford Way
Parade, The, Epsom BN60 94
Parade, The, Esher BH57 93
Parade, The, S. Ock. CY41 70
Parade, The Sun. BB50 73
Parade, The, Sun. BC50 73
Parade, The. Wind. AL44 61
Paradise Clo. Wal. Cr. CB17 21
Paradise Cotts. Rich. BL46 75
Paradise Rd.
Paradise Hill, Brox. CB16 21
Paradise Pass. N7 BY35 47
Ingham Rd.
Paradise Rd. SW4 BX44 66
Paradise Rd. Rich. BK46 74
Paradise Row E2 CB38 57
Bethnal Green Rd.
Paradise Row, Wal. Abb. CF20 21
Paradise St. SE16 CB41 67
Paradise Wk. SW3 BU43 66
Paradise Wood La. Hem. H. AX14 8
Paragon Gro. Surb. BL53 85
Paragon Mews SE1 BZ42 67
Searles Rd.
Paragon Pl. SE3 CG44 68
Paragon Pl. Surb. BL53 85
Paragon Rd. E9 CB36 57
Paragon Row SE17 BZ42 67
Paragon, The, SE3 CG44 68
Parbury Rise Ches. BL57 94
Parbury Rd. SE23 CD46 77
Parchmore Rd. Th. Hth. BY51 86
Parchmore Way Th. Hth. BY51 86
Pardoner St. SE1 BZ41 67
Pardon St. EC1 BY38 56
Dallington St.
Pares Clo. Wok. AR61 100
Parfett St. E1 CB39 57
Parfrey St. W6 BQ43 65
Parham Dr. Ilf. CL32 49
Parham Way N10 BW30 38
Paringdon Rd. Harl. CL13 13
Paris Gdn. SE1 BY40 56
Parish La. SE20 CC50 77
Parish La. Slou. AO34 43
Park App. Well. CO45 69
Park Ave. Harl. CP12 14
Park Av. E6 CL37 58
Park Av. E15 CG36 58
Park Av. N3 BS30 38
Park Av. N13 BY27 38
Park Av. N18 CB28 39
Park Av. N22 BX30 38
Park Av. NW2 BP36 55
Park Av. NW10 BL37 55
Park Av. NW11 BS33 47
Park Av. SW14 BO45 65
Park Av. Bark. CM36 58
Park Av. Barn. BT25 29
Park Av. Brom. CG50 78
Park Av. Brwd. DE26 122
Park Av. Bush. BD24 27
Park Av. Bush. BE23 27
Park Av. Cars. BV57 95
Park Av. Cat. CA65 105
Park Av. Egh. AU50 72
Park Av. Enf. BZ25 30
Park Av. Grav. DF47 81
Park Av. Grav. DH47 81
Park Av. Grays DA43 70
Park Av. Houns. BF46 74
Park Av. Ilf. CL33 49
Park Av. Mitch. BV50 76
Park Av. Orp. CK55 88
Park Av. Orp. CO55 89
Park Av. Pot. B. BT20 20
Park Av. Rad. BJ20 18
Park Av. Ruis. BA32 44
Park Av. St. Alb. BJ13 9
Park Av. Stai. AR46 72
Park Av. Stai. AV50 72
Park Av. Sthl. BE41 64
Park Av. Upmin. CZ33 51
Park Av. Wat. BC24 26
Park Av. Wdf. Grn. CH28 40
Park Av. W. Wick. CF55 87
Park Av. E. Epsom. BP57 94
Park Avenue Mews, Mitch. BV50 76
Park Av.
Park Av. N. N8 BW31 47
Park Av. N. NW10 BP35 46
Park Av. Rd. N17 CB29 39
Park Av. S. N8 BW31 47
Park Av. W. Epsom BP57 94
Park Barn Dr. Guil. AP69 118
Park Barn Est. Guil. AP70 118
Park Boul. Rom. CT30 41
Park Chase, Guil. AS70 118
Park Chase Wem. BL35 46
Park Cl. Hat. BQ12 10
Park Clo. NW2 BP34 46
Park Clo. NW10 BL38 55
Park Clo. SW1 BU41 66
Park Clo. W8 BR42 65
Park Clo. W14 BR41 65
Park Clo. Bet. BM73 120
Park Clo. Bush. BD24 27
Park Clo. Cars. BU57 95
Park Clo. Esher BF57 93
Park Clo. Har. BH30 36
Park Clo. Hmptn. BG51 84
Park Clo. Houns. BG46 74
Park Clo. Kings. On T. BM51 85
Park Clo. Lthd. BG65 102
Park Clo. Rick. AZ28 35
Park Clo. Walt. BB55 83
Park Clo. Wey. AW58 92
Park Clo. Wind. AO44 61
Park Copner Dr. Leath. BB67 110
Park Copse, Dor. BK71 119
Park Corner. Wind. AM45 61
Park Cor. Ms. W. W1 BV38 56
Park Corner Rd. Grav. DC49 81
Park Ct. N12 BT28 38
Park Ct. Harl. CN10 6
Park Ct. Kings. On T. BK51 84
Park Ct. Lthd. BF66 111
Church Rd.
Park Ct. N. Mal. BN52 85
Park Ct. Wall. BX56 95
Park Ct. Wem. BL35 46
Park Ct. Wok. AS62 100
Park Cres. N3 BS29 38
Park Cres. W1 BV38 56
Park Cres. Borwd. BL24 28
Park Cres. Enf. BZ24 30
Park Cres. Erith CS43 69
Park Cres. Har. BH30 36
Park Cres. Hem. H. AZ11 8
Park Cres. Horn. CU33 50
Park Cres. Ms. E. W1 BV38 56
Gt. Portland St.
Park Cres. Ms. W. W1 BV39 56
Park Cres. Rd. Erith CS43 69
Park Croft Edg. BN30 37
Parkcroft Rd. SE12 CG47 78
Parkdale N11 BW29 38
Bounds Green Rd.
Parkdale Cres. Wor. Pk. BN55 85
Parkdale Rd. SE18 CN42 68
Park Dr. N21 BZ25 30
Park Dr. NW11 BS33 47
Park Dr. SW14 BN45 65
Park Dr. W3 BM41 65
Park Dr. Dag. CS34 50
Park Dr. Har. BF33 45
Park Dr. Har. BG29 36
Park Dr. Pot. B. BS19 20
Park Dr. Rom. CS31 50
Park Dr. Upmin. CX35 51
Park Dr. Wok. AS62 100
Park Drive Clo. SE7 CK42 68
Park End Brom. CG51 88
Park End Rd. Rom. CT31 50
Parker Ave. Til. DH44 71
Parker Clo. E16 CK40 58
Parker St.
Parke Rd. SW13 BP44 65
Parke Rd. Sun. BC52 83
Parker Rd. Croy. BZ56 96
Parker Rd. Grays. DC42 71
Parkers La. Ash. BL63 103
Parker's Row SE1 CA41 67
Parker St. E16 CK40 58
Parker St. WC2 BX39 56
Parker St. Wat. BC23 26
Parkes Rd. Chig. CN28 40
Park Farm Dr. Guil. AP70 118
Park Farm, E. Guil. AP70 118
Park Farm Rd. Brom. CJ51 88
Park Farm Rd. Kings. On T. BL50 75
Parkfield. Sev. CW65 108
Parkfield Ave. Amer. AO22 25
Parkfield Av. SW14 BO45 65
Parkfield Av. Felt. BC48 73
Parkfield Av. Har. BG30 36
Parkfield Av. Nthlt. BD37 54
Parkfield Av. Uxb. AZ38 53
Parkfield Clo. Edg. BM29 37
Parkfield Clo. Nthlt. BE37 54
Parkfield Cres. Felt. BC48 73
Parkfield Cres. Har. BG30 36
Parkfield Cres. Ruis. BE34 45
Parkfield Dr. Nthlt. BD37 54
Parkfield Gdns. Har. BF31 45
Parkfield Rd. NW10 BP36 55
Parkfield Rd. SE14 CD44 67
Parkfield Rd. Felt. BC48 73
Parkfield Rd. Har. BG34 45
Parkfield Rd. Nthlt. BE37 54
Parkfield Rd. Uxb. AZ34 44
Parkfields SW15 BQ45 65
Park Fields. Harl. CH11 13
Parkfields. Welw. G. C. BQ8 5
Parkfields Av. NW9 BN33 46
Parkfields Av. SW20 BP51 85
Parkfields Rd. Kings. On T. BL49 75
Parkfield St. N1 BY37 56
Parkfield Way Brom. CK53 88
Park Flds. Croy. CD54 87
Park Fm. Clo. N2 BT31 47
Park Fm. Clo. Pnr. BC32 44
Park Fm. Rd. Upmin. CW35 51
Park Gdns. E10 CE33 48
Park Gdns. NW9 BM31 46
Park Gdns. Erith CS42 69
Park Gdns. Kings. On T. BL50 75
Park Gate N21 BX26 38
Park Gate SE3 CG45 68
Park Gate W5 BK39 54
Mount Av.
Park Gate Clo. Kings. On T. BM50 75
Warboys App.
Parkgate Cres. Barn. BS23 29
Park Gte. Gdns. SW14 BN46 75
Parkgate Rd. SW11 BU43 66
Parkgate Rd. Reig. BS71 121
Parkgate Rd. Wall. BV56 95
Parkgate Rd. Wat. BD22 27
Park Gro. E15 CH37 58
Park Gro. N11 BW29 38
Park Gro. Bexh. CS45 69
Park Gro. Brom. CH51 88
Park Gro. Ch. St. G. AR24 25
Park Gro. Edg. BL28 37
Park Grove Rd. E11 CG34 49
Park Hall Rd. N2 BU31 47
Park Hall Rd. SE21 BZ48 77
Parkham St. SW11 BT44 66
Parkhead Gdns. NW7 BO28 37
Park Hill SE23 CB48 77
Park Hill SW4 BW46 76
Park Hill W5 BK39 54
Park Hill Brom. CK52 88
Park Hill Cars. BU57 95
Park Hill, Harl. CP9 6
Park Hill, Loug. CJ25 31
Park Hill Rich. BL46 75
Park Hill Clo. Cars. BU56 95
Parkhill Clo. Horn. CV34 51
Park Hill Ct. SW17 BU48 76
Beeches Rd.
Park Hill Gdns. Croy. CA55 87
Park Hill Rd.
Park Hill Rise Croy. CA55 87
Parkhill Rd. E4 CF26 39
Parkhill Rd. NW3 BU35 47
Parkhill Rd. Bex. CQ47 79
Park Hill Rd. Brom. CF51 87
Park Hill Rd. Croy. CA55 87
Parkhill Rd. Epsom BO59 94
Park Hill Rd. Hem. H. AW13 8
Park Hill Rd. Sev. CW62 108
Park Hill Rd. Sid. CM48 78
Park Hill Rd. Wall. BV57 95
Parkholme Rd. E8 CA36 57
Park Horsley. Leath. BC68 110
Park Ho. N21 BX26 38
Park Ho. Dr. Reig. BR71 120
Park House Gdns. Twick. BK46 74
Park Ho. Pass. N6 BV33 47
Parkhouse St. SE5 BZ43 67
Parkhur Rd. Sutt. BT56 95
Parkhurst, Epsom BN58 94
Parkhurst Gdns. Bex. CQ47 79
Parkhurst Rd. E12 CL35 49
Parkhurst Rd. E17 CD31 48
Parkhurst Rd. N7 BX35 47
Parkhurst Rd. N11 BV28 38
Parkhurst Rd. N17 CB30 39
Parkhurst Rd. N22 BX29 38
Parkhurst Rd. Bex. CR47 79
Parkhurst Rd. Guil. AQ70 118
Parkland Ave. Slou. AR42 62
Parkland Av. Rom. CT30 41
Parkland Av. Upmin. CX35 51
Parkland Clo. Hodd. CE10 12
Parkland Clo. Sev. CV68 117
Parkland Ct. W11 BR41 65
Parkland Cres. Ashf. AZ48 73
Parkland Gro. Ashf. AZ49 73
Parkland Rd. Ashf. AZ49 73
Parklands Chig. CM27 40
Parklands, Guil. AT70 118
Parklands, Oxt. CG69 115
Parklands Surb. BL53 85
Parklands, Wal. Abb. CF19 21
Parklands Clo. Chig. CM27 40
Parklands Ct. Houns. BD44 64
Parklands Dr. N3 BR31 46
Parklands Epp. CP18 23
Parklands Rd. SW16 BV49 76
Parklands Rd. Wdf. Grn. CH29 40
Parkland Way Ong. CW18 24
Park La. E15 CF37 57
High St.
Park La. N9 CA27 39
Park La. N17 CB29 39
Park La. W1 BU40 56
Park La. Ash. BL62 103
Park La. Brox. CB15 12
Park La. Brox. CD13 12
Park La. Cars. BV56 95
Park La. Couls. BW64 104
Park La. Croy. BZ55 87
Park La. Har. BF34 45
Park La. Harl. CM10 6
Park La. Hat. BR16 19
Park La. Hat. BS16 20
Park La. Hayes BB39 53
Park La. Hayes BC43 63
Park La. Hem. H. AX14 8
Park La. Horn. CT32 50
Park La. Horn. CU36 59
Park La. Reig. BR71 120
Park La. Rich. BK45 64
Park La. Rom. CP32 50
Park La. St. Alb. BM15 10
Park La. Sev. CV65 108
Park La. Sev. CX62 108
Park La. Sev. CX64 108
Park La. Slou. AQ41 62
Park La. Slou. AT45 62
Park La. S. Ock. CW40 60
Park La. Sutt. BR57 94
Park La. Swan. CV51 90
Park La. Tedd. BH50 74
Park La. Uxb. AW29 35
Park La. Wal. Cr. CB17 21
Park La. Wal. Cr. CC20 21
Park La. Wem. BL35 46
Park La. W. Wick. CE54 87
Park La. Clo. N17 CB29 39
Park La.
Park Lawn Ave. Epsom. BM60 94
Park Lawn Rd. Wey. AZ56 92
Park Lawns Wem. BL35 46
Parklea Clo. NW9 BO30 37
Parkleigh Rd. SW19 BS51 86
Parkleys Rich. BK49 74
Park Mans. NW4 BP32 46
Parkmead SW15 BP46 75
Park Mead Har. BF34 45
Park Mead, Harl. CL10 6
Parkmead Loug. CL25 31
Park Mead Sid. CO46 79
Pk. Meadow. Hat. BQ12 10
Park Ms. Hmptn. BG49 74
Park Nook Gdns. Enf. BZ22 30
Parkpale La. Bet. BM73 120
Park Pde NW10 BO37 55
Park Pde. W3 BM41 65
Park Pde. Pnr. BE29 36
Park Pl. SW1 BW40 56
Park Pl. W3 BM42 65
Park Pl. W5 BK40 54
Park Pl. Hmptn. BG50 74
Park Pl. Mitch. BU52 86
Park Pl. Wem. BL35 46
Park Pl. Wind. AO44 61
Kings Rd.
Park Pl. Gdns. W2 BT39 56
Park Pl. Vill.
Park Pl. Vill. W2 BT39 56
Park Ri. Lthd. BJ64 102
Park Ri. Clo. Lthd. BJ64 102
Park Ridings. N8 BY31 47
Park Rise, Berk. AP12 7
Park Rise. Har. BH30 36
Park Rise Rd. SE23 CD47 77
Park Rd. E6 CJ37 58
Park Rd. E10 CE33 48
Park Rd. E12 CH33 49
Park Rd. E15 CH37 58

Park Rd. E17	CD32	48
Park Rd. N2	BT31	47
Park Rd. N8	BW31	47
Park Rd. N11	BW29	38
Park Rd. N14	BW26	38
Park Rd. N15	BY31	47
Park Rd. N18	CA28	39
Park Rd. NW1	BU38	56
Park Rd. NW4	BP33	46
Park Rd. NW8	BU38	56
Park Rd. NW9	BN33	46
Park Rd. NW10	BN37	55
Park Rd. SE7	CK43	68
Park Rd. SE25	CA52	87
Park Rd. SW19	BT50	76
Park Rd. SW20	BP50	75
Park Rd. W4	BN43	65
Park Rd. W7	BH40	54
Park Rd. Amer.	AP22	25
Park Rd. Ash.	BL62	103
Park Rd. Ashf.	AZ49	73
Park Rd. Bans.	BS61	104
Park Rd. Barn.	BR24	28
Park Rd. Barn.	BT24	29
Park Rd. Beck.	CD50	77
Park Rd. Brom.	CH51	88
Park Rd. Brwd.	DA27	42
Park Rd. Bush.	BF25	27
Park Rd. Cat.	CA65	105
Park Rd. Dart.	CW48	80
Park Rd. Dart	CX47	80
Park Rd. E. Mol.	BG52	84
Park Rd. Egh.	AT49	72
Park Rd. Enf.	CD21	30
Park Rd. Esher	BF56	93
Park Rd. Felt.	BD49	74
Park Rd. Grav.	DG48	81
Park Rd. Grays.	DD42	71
Park Rd. Guil.	AR70	118
Park Rd. Hayes	BB39	53
Park Rd. Hem. H.	AX14	8
Park Rd. Hmptn.	BF49	74
Park Rd. Hodd.	CE12	12
Park Rd. Houns.	BF46	74
Park Rd. Ilf.	CM34	49
Park Rd. Islw.	BJ44	64
Park Rd. Ken.	BY61	104
Park Rd. Kings. On T.	BK51	84
Hampton Wick.		
Park Rd. Kings. On T.	BL49	75
Park Rd. N. Mal.	BN52	85
Park Rd. Orp.	CP53	89
Park Rd. Oxt.	CG67	115
Park Rd. Pot. B.	BV18	20
Park Rd. Rad.	BJ21	27
Park Rd. Red.	BU69	121
Park Rd. Rich.	BL46	75
Park Rd. Rick.	AY26	35
Park Rd. Shep.	AZ54	83
Park Rd. Slou.	AO37	52
Park Rd. Stai.	AW46	73
Park Rd. Sun.	BC50	73
Park Rd. Surb.	BL53	85
Park Rd. Sutt.	BR57	94
Park Rd. Swan.	CT52	89
Park Rd. Swans.	DC46	81
Park Rd. Tedd.	BH50	74
Park Rd. Twick.	BK46	74
Park Rd. Uxb.	AX37	53
Park Rd. Wal. Cr.	CC20	21
Park Rd. Wall.	BV55	86
Park Rd. Wall.	BV56	95
Park Rd. Wat.	BC23	26
Park Rd. Wem.	BL36	55
Park Rd. Wok.	AS62	100
Park Rd. Wok.	AT62	100
Park Rd. E. W3	BM41	65
Park Rd. N.		
Park Rd. E. Kings. On T.	BL49	75
Park Rd. N. W3	BM41	65
Park Rd. N. W4	BN42	65
Park Rd. W. Kings. On T.	BL49	75
Park Row SE10	CF42	67
Park Royal Rd. NW10	BN38	55
Park Royal Rd. W3	BN38	55
Parks Hill, Ash.	BL63	103
Parkshot Rd. Rich.	BK45	64
Parkside N3	BS30	38
Parkside NW2	BP34	46
Parkside NW7	BO29	37
Parkside SE3	CG43	68
Parkside SW19	BQ47	75
Parkside Buck. H.	CH27	40
Parkside. Grays.	DE41	71
Parkside, Hamptn.	BG49	74
Parkside Hmptn.	BG49	74
Parkside Sid.	CO48	79
Park Side Sutt.	BR57	94
Park Side, Wey.	AW58	92
Parkside Ave. Til.	DG44	71
Parkside Av. SW19	BQ49	75
Parkside Av. Bexh.	CS44	69
Parkside Av. Brom.	CK52	88
Parkside Av. Rom.	CS31	50
Parkside Clo. Leath.	BB66	110
Parkside Cres. Surb.	BN53	85
Parkside Cross Bexh.	CT44	69
Parkside Dr. Edg.	BM27	37
Parkside Dr. Wat.	BB23	26
Parkside Gdns. SW19	BQ49	75
Parkside Gdns. Barn.	BU26	38
Parkside Gdns. Couls.	BV62	104
Parkside Rd. Belv.	CS42	69
Parkside Rd. Houns.	BF46	74
Parkside Rd. Nthwd.	BB28	35
Parkside St. SW11	BV44	66
Battersea Pk. Rd.		
Parkside Ter. N18	BZ28	39
Parkside Way Har.	BF31	45
Park Spring Gro. Iver	AT36	52
Park Sq. Esher	BF56	93
Park Sq. E. NW1	BV38	56
Park Sq. Ms. NW1	BV38	56
Park Sq. W. NW1	BV38	56
Parkstead Rd. SW15	BP46	75
Parkstone Av. N18	CA29	39
Parkstone Av. Horn.	CW32	51
Parkstone Rd. SE15	CB44	67
Rye La.		
Park St. N1	BZ37	57
Park St. SE1	BZ40	57
Park St. W1	BV40	56
Park St. Berk.	AQ12	7
Park St. Croy.	BZ55	87
Park St. Guil.	AR71	118
Park St. Hat.	BQ12	10
Park St. Slou.	AP41	62
Park St. Slou.	AU43	62
Park St. Tedd.	BH50	74
Park St. Wind.	AO44	61
Park Street La. St. Alb.	BF18	18
Park Ter. Green.	DB46	80
Park Ter. Wor. Pk.	BP54	85
Park, The, N6	BV32	47
Park, The, NW11	BS33	47
Park. The SE19	CA50	77
Park, The, W5	BK40	54
Park, The, Cars.	BU56	95
Park, The Lthd.	BF65	102
Park. The. Lthd.	BF66	111
Park, The, St. Alb.	BJ12	9
Park, The, Sid.	CO49	79
Parkthorne Clo. Har.	BF32	45
Parkthorne Dr. Har.	BF32	45
Parkthorne Rd. SW12	BW47	76
Parkvale Rd. SW6	BR44	65
Park Vw. N5	BZ35	48
Park Vw. N21	BX26	38
Park Vw. W3	BN39	55
Park View. Berk.	AQ13	7
Park View. Hat.	BQ11	10
Park Vw. Hodd.	CE12	12
Park Vw. N. Mal.	BO52	85
Park Vw. Pnr.	BE30	36
Park View, Pot. B.	BT20	20
Park Vw. Sev.	CP65	107
Park Vw. S. Ock.	CW40	60
Park Vw. Wem.	BM35	46
Park Vw. Cres. N11	BW28	38
Park Vw. Est. E2	CC37	57
Park Vw. Gdns. NW4	BQ32	46
Park View Gdns. Bark.	CN37	58
Park View Gdns. Ilf.	CK31	49
Woodford Av.		
Park Vw. Rd. N3	BS30	38
Park Vw. Rd. N17	CB31	48
Park Vw. Rd. NW10	BO35	46
Parkview Rd. SE9	CL47	78
Park Vw. Rd. W5	BL39	55
Park View Rd. Cat.	CD64	105
Parkview Rd. Croy.	CB54	87
Park View Rd. Pnr.	BC29	35
Park Vw. Rd. Sthl.	BF40	54
Park Vw. Rd. Well.	CO45	69
Park Village East NW1	BV37	56
Park Village West NW1	BV37	56
Park Vill. SE3	CH43	68
Park Vill. Rom.	CP32	50
Parkville Rd. SW6	BR43	65
Park Vista SE10	CF43	67
Park Wk. SW10	BT43	66
Park Wk. Ash.	BL62	103
Rectory La.		
Park Wk. Barn.	BT24	29
Parkway N14	BX27	38
Park Way N20	BU28	38
Parkway NW1	BV37	56
Park Way NW11	BR32	46
Parkway SW20	BQ52	85
Park Way Bex.	CT48	79
Park Way, Brwd.	DC26	122
Parkway Croy.	CE58	96
Parkway, Dor.	BJ71	119
Park Way E. Mol.	BF52	84
Park Way Edg.	BM30	37
Park Way Enf.	BY23	29
Park Way Felt.	BC47	73
Park Way Ilf.	CN34	49
Park Way, Lthd.	BF65	102
Park Way. Rain.	CU38	59
Park Way. Rick.	AX26	35
Parkway Rom.	CT30	41
Park Way Ruis.	BC33	44
Parkway, Saw.	CQ6	6
Parkway, Uxb.	AZ36	53
Parkway Wdf. Grn.	CJ28	40
Park Way. Welw. G. C.	BQ8	5
Parkway, Wey.	BA56	92
Parkway Clo. Welw. G. C.	BQ8	5
Parkway Ct. St. Alb.	BJ15	9
Drakes Dr.		
Parkway, The Iver	AU37	52
Parkway, The, Cranford Sthl.	BC42	63
Park West W2	BU39	56
Park West Pl. W2	BU39	56
Parkwood N20	BU27	38
Parkwood Beck.	CE50	77
Parkwood Brwd.	DB22	33
Parkwood Av. Esher	BG54	84
Park Wood Clo. Bans.	BQ61	103
Parkwood Dri. Hem. H.	AV13	7
Parkwood Gro. Sun.	BC52	83
Parkwood Rd. SW19	BR49	75
Park Wood Rd. Bans.	BQ61	103
Park Wood Rd. Bex.	CQ47	79
Parkwood Rd. Islw.	BH44	64
Parkwood Rd. Red.	BX70	121
Parkwood Rd. West.	CK64	106
Park Wood Vw. Bans.	BQ61	103
Park Works Rd. Red.	BX70	121
Parlaunt Rd. Slou.	AT42	62
Parliament Ct. NW3	BU35	47
Parliament Hl. NW3	BU35	47
Parliament Sq. SW1	BX41	66
Parliament St. SW1	BX41	66
Parma Cres. SW11	BU45	66
Parmiter Pl. E2	CC37	57
Parmiter St.		
Parmiter St. E2	CB37	57
Parnall Rd. Harl.	CM12	13
Parndon Wood Rd. Harl.	CM13	13
Parnell Clo. Edg.	BM27	37
Parnell Clo. Wat.	BB18	17
Parnell Rd. E3	CD37	57
Parnham St. E14	CD39	57
Parolles Rd. N19	BW33	47
Paroma Rd. Belv.	CR41	69
Paronage Leys. Harl.	CN11	13
Parr Av. Epsom	BP58	94
Parris Croft, Dor.	BK73	119
Parrock Av. Grav.	DH47	81
Parrock Rd. Grav.	DH47	81
Parrock St. Grav.	DG46	81
Parrots Clo. Rick.	AZ25	26
Parr Rd. E6	CJ37	58
Parr Rd. Stan.	BK30	36
Parrs Pla. Hamptn.	BF50	74
Parry Av. E6	CK39	58
Parry Clo. Epsom	BP57	94
Parry Grn. Slou.	AS42	62
Parry Pl. SE18	CL42	68
Parry Rd. SE25	CA52	87
Parry St. SW8	BX43	66
Parsifal Rd. NW6	BS35	47
Parsloe Rd. Epp.	CL14	13
Parsloo Rd. Harl	CL13	13
Parsloes Av. Dag.	CP36	60
Parsonage Cl, Warl.	CD61	105
Parsonage Clo. Dor.	BG72	119
Parsonage La.		
Parsonage Clo. Hayes	BB39	53
Parsonage Field Brwd.	DB22	33
Parsonage Gdns. Enf.	BZ23	30
Parsonage La. Dor.	BG72	119
Parsonage La. Enf.	BZ23	30
Parsonage La. Hat.	BP15	10
Parsonage La. Sid.	CQ49	79
Parsonage La. Slou.	AO36	52
Parsonage La. S. Dnth.	CX50	80
Parsonage La. Wind.	AN44	61
Parsonage Manorway. Belv.	CR43	69
Parsonage Rd. Ch. St. G.	AQ27	34
Parsonage Rd. Egh.	AR49	72
Parsonage Rd. Hat.	BP15	10
Parsonage Rd. Rain.	CV37	60
Parsonage Rd. Rick.	AX26	35
Parsonage St. E14	CF42	67
Parsons Cres. Edg.	BM27	37
Parsons Field Bans.	BQ61	103
Parsonsfield Clo. Bans.	BQ61	103
Parsonsfield Rd. Bans.	BQ61	103
Parsons Grn. SW6	BR44	65
Parsons Grn. La. SW6	BS44	66
Parsons Gro. Edg.	BM27	37
Parson's Hill SE18	CL41	68
Powis St.		
Parsons La. Dart.	CU48	79
Parson's Mead Croy.	BY54	86
Parsons Mead E. Mol.	BG52	84
Parsons Pightle. Couls.	BY63	104
Parson's Rd. E13	CJ37	58
Parson St. NW4	BQ31	46
Parthenia Rd. SW6	BS44	66
Partingdale La. NW7	BQ28	37
Partridge Clo. Bush.	BF26	36
Partridge Clo. Chesh.	AP17	16
Partridge Dr. Orp.	CM55	88
Partridge Gn. SE9	CL48	78
Partridge Mead Bans.	BQ61	103
Partridge Rd. N22	BX30	38
Partridge Rd. Harl.	CM12	13
Partridge Rd. St. Alb.	BG11	9
Partridge Rd. Sid.	CN48	78
Partridge Way N22	BX30	38
Parvis Rd. Wey.	AW60	92
Pasadena Clo. Hayes	BC41	63
Pascal St. SW8	BW43	66
Pascoe Rd. SE13	CF46	77
Pasley Rd. SE17	BY42	66
Pasonage Clo. Wat.	BB18	17
Pasquier Rd. E17	CD31	48
Passage, The, Rich.	BL45	65
Quadrant, The.		
Passey Pl. SE9	CK46	78
Passfields W14	BR42	65
Passfields Dr. E14	CE39	57
St. Leonard's Rd.		
Passmore Gdns. N11	BW29	38
Passmore St. SW1	BV42	66
Pastens Rd. Oxt.	CJ69	115
Pasteur Gdns. N18	BY28	38
Paston Cres. SE12	CH47	78
Paston Rd. Hem. H.	AX12	8
Pastor St. SE11	BY42	66
Pasture Clo. Bush.	BG26	36
Pasture Clo. Wem.	BJ34	45
Pasture Rd. SE6	CG47	78
Pasture Rd. Dag.	CQ35	50
Pasture Rd. Wem.	BJ34	45
Pastures Clo. Wor. Pk.	BQ55	85
Pastures, The, N20	BR26	37
Pastures, The Hat.	BP13	10
Pastures, The, Welw. G. C.	BS9	5
Pasture, The, St. Alb.	BF15	9
Patcham Ct. Sutt.	BT57	95
Patcham Ter. SW8	BV44	66
Patch. The. Sev.	CT64	107
Paternoster Clo. Wal. Abb.	CG19	22
Paternoster Hill, Wal. Abb.	CG19	22
Paternoster Row EC4	BY39	56
St. Pauls Churchyard		
Paternoster Sq. EC4	BY39	56
Warwick La.		
Paterson Rd. Ashf.	AX49	73
Pater St. W8	BS41	66
Pates Manor Dr. Felt.	BA47	73
Pathfield Rd. SW16	BW50	76
Path, The, SW19	BS51	86
Pathway, The, Rad.	BH21	27
Pathway, The, Wat.	BD26	36
Pathway, The, Wok.	AV66	109
Patience Rd. SW11	BU44	66
Patio Clo. SW4	BW46	76
Patmore Est. SW8	BW44	66
Pat More La. Watt.	BB57	92
Patmore Link, Hem. H.	BA13	8
Patmore St. SW8	BW44	66
Patmore Way Rom.	CR28	41
Patmos Rd. SW9	BY43	66
Paton Clo. E3	CE38	57
Paton St. EC1	BZ38	57
Patricia Ct. Well.	CO43	69
Wickham La.		
Patricia Dr. Horn.	CW33	51
Patrick Connolly Gdns. E3	CF38	57
Talwin St.		
Patrick Rd. E13	CJ38	58
Patrington Clo. Uxb.	AX38	53
Patriot Sq. E2	CB37	57
Patrol Pl. SE6	CE46	77
Patshull Rd. NW5	BW36	56
Patten All. Rich.	BK46	74
Ormond Rd.		
Patten Av. Rich.	BK46	74
Ormond Rd.		
Pattenden Rd. SE6	CD47	77
Patten Rd. SW18	BU47	76
Patterdale Clo. Brom.	CG50	78
Patterdale Rd. SE15	CC43	67
Patterdale Rd. Dart.	CY47	80
Patterson Ct. SE19	CA50	77
Patterson Rd. SE19	CA50	77
Pattison Rd. NW3	BS34	47
Pattison Wk. SE18	CM42	68
Sandbach Pl.		
Paul Clo. E15	CG37	58
Paul St.		
Paulet Rd. SE5	BY44	66
Paul Gdns. Croy.	CA55	87
Paulham Rd. Har.	BK31	45
Paulin Dr. N21	BY26	38
Pauline Cres. Twick.	BG47	74
Paulinus Clo. Orp.	CP51	89
Pauls La. Hodd.	CE12	12
Pauls Pl. Ash.	BM62	103
Paul St. E15	CF37	57
Paul St. EC2	BZ38	57
Paultons Sq. SW3	BT43	66
Paulton's St. SW3	BT43	66
Old Church St.		
Pauntley St. N19	BW33	47
Paved Ct. Rich.	BK46	74
King St.		
Paveley St. W1	BU38	56
Pavement Mews Rom.	CP33	50
Pavement, The, SW4	BW45	66
Pavet Clo. Dag.	CR36	59
Pavilion Gdns. Stai.	AW50	73
Pavilion Rd. E15	CG38	58
Springfield Rd.		
Pavilion Rd. SW1	BU41	66
Pavilion Rd. SW19	BR49	75
Pavilion Rd. Ilf.	CK33	49
Pavilion Way Ruis.	BD34	45
Pawleyne Rd. SE20	CC50	77
Pawson's Rd. Croy.	BZ53	87
Paxford Rd. Wem.	BJ34	45
Paxton Ave. Slou.	AO41	61
Paxton Ct. Rich.	BL44	65
Paxton Gdns. Wok.	AU59	91
Paxton Pl. SE27	CA49	77
Paxton Rd. N17	CA29	39
Paxton Rd. W4	BO43	65
Paxton Rd. Berk.	AR13	7
Paxton Rd. Brom.	CH50	78
College Rd.		
Paxton Rd. St. Alb.	BH14	9
Paxton Ter. SW1	BV42	66
Churchill Gdns. Rd.		
Paycock Rd. Harl.	CL12	13
Payne Rd. E3	CE37	57
Old Ford Rd.		
Paynesfield Av. SW14	BN45	65
Paynesfield Rd. Bush.	BH26	36
Paynesfield Rd. West.	CJ63	106
Paynes La. Wal. Abb.	CF15	12
Payne St. SE8	CD43	67
Peabody Av. SW1	BV42	66
Peabody Bldgs. WC1	BX38	56
Peabody Clo. SE10	CE44	67
Devonshire Dr.		
Peabody Est. EC1	BZ38	57
Peabody Est. N17	CA30	39
Peabody Est. SE1	BY40	56
Peabody Est. SE24	BY47	76
Peabody Est. SW11	BU45	66
Peabody Est. W6	BQ42	65
Peabody Trust SW3	BU43	66
Chealsea Manor St.		
Peaceful Row Grays	DB43	70
Peace St. E1	CB38	57
Peaches Clo. Sutt.	BR57	94
Peachey La. Uxb.	AX39	53
Peach Tree Av. West Dr.	AY39	53
Peachum Rd. SE3	CG43	68
Peacock St. SE17	BY42	66
Peacock St. Grav.	DH47	81
Peacock Wk. N6	BV33	47
Chomeley Cres.		
Peacock Wk. Dor.	BJ72	119
Rose Hill		
Peacock Yd. SE17	BY42	66
Iliffe St.		
Peahen Ct. EC2	CA39	57
Bishopsgate		
Peakes La. Wal. Cr.	CA17	21
Peakes Way, Wal. Cr.	CA17	21
Peaketon Av. Ilf.	CJ31	49
Peak Hill, SE26	CC49	77
Peak Hl. Av. SE26	CC49	77
Peak Hl. Gdns. SE26	CC49	77
Peaks Hill Pur.	BW58	95
Peaks Hill Rise. Pur.	BX58	95
Peak, The, SE26	CC49	77
Pea La. Upmin.	DA36	60
Peal Gdns. W13	BJ38	54
Pearcefield Av. SE23	CC47	77
Pear Clo. NW9	BN31	46
Pearcroft Rd. E11	CF34	48
Peardon St. SW8	BV44	66
Peareswood Gdns. Stan.	BK30	36
Pearfield Rd. SE23	CD48	77
Pearle Rd. E. Mol.	BF51	84
Pearl Rd. E17	CE31	48
Pearl St. E1	CB40	57
Penang St.		
Pearman St. SE1	BY41	66
Pearscroft Ct. SW6	BS44	66
Pearscroft Rd. SW6	BS44	66
Pearson's Av. SE14	CD44	67
Tanner's Hill		
Pearson St. E2	CA37	57
Pears Rd. Houns.	BG45	64
Pearswood Rd. Erith	CT43	69
Peartree Av. Ashf.	BA49	73
Pear Tree Av. West Dr.	AY39	53
Peartree Chase. S. Ock.	CA37	60
Pear Tree Clo. Brwd.	DB22	33
Peartree Clo. Erith	CS44	69
Peartree Clo. Mitch.	BU51	86
Peartree Clo. Welw. G. C.	BR8	5
Peartree Ct. EC1	BY38	56
Peartree Ct. Welw. G. C.	BR8	5
Peartree Gdns. Dag.	CO35	50
Peartree Gdns. Rom.	CR30	41
Peartree La. Brwd.	DB22	33
Peartree La. Welw. G. C.	BR8	5
Peartree Mead. Harl.	CO12	14
Peartree Rd. Enf.	CA24	30
Peartree Rd. Hem. H.	AW13	8
Pear Tree Rd. Wey.	AW56	92
Pear Trees, Brwd.	DE29	122
Pear Tree St. EC1	BY38	56
Pear Tree Wk. Wal. Cr.	BZ16	21
Peary Pl. E2	CC38	57
Kirkwall Pl.		
Peascod Pl. Wind.	AO44	61
Peascod St.		
Peascod St. Wind.	AO44	61
Peasecroft Rd. Hem. H.	AZ15	8
Pease Hill. Sev.	DC57	99
Peatmore Ave. Wok.	AW61	101
Pebble Clo. Tad.	BO67	112
Pebble Hill. Leath.	BA70	110
Pebblehill Rd. Bet.	BO69	120
Pebblehill Rd. Tad.	BO68	112
Pebble La. Epsom.	BL64	103
Pebble La. Lthd.	BL65	103
Pebworth Rd. Har.	BJ34	45
Peckarmans Wood, SE26	CB48	77
Peckford Yd. SW9	BY44	66
Peckford Pl.		
Peckham Gro. SE15	CA43	67
Peckham High St. SE15	CA44	67
Peckham Hill St. SE15	CB43	67
Peckham Pk. Rd. SE15	CB43	67
Peckham Rd. SE5	CA44	67
Peckham Rd. SE15	CA44	67
Peckham Rye, SE15	CB45	67
Peckham Rye, SE22	CB45	67
Pecks Hill. Wal. Abb.	CG14	13
Peckwater St. Est. NW5	BW35	47
Peckwater St. NW5	BW35	47
Islip St.		
Pedlars End. Ong.	CU14	14
Pedlars Way N7	BX36	56
Pedley St. E1	CA38	57
Pedro St. E5	CC34	48
Pedworth Rd. SE16	CC42	67
Peek Cres. SW19	BQ49	75
Peel Clo. Wind.	AN45	61
Peel Dr. Ilf.	CK31	49
Peel Gro. E2	CC37	57
Peel Prec. NW6	BS37	56
Peel Rd. E18	CG30	40
Peel Rd. NW6	BR37	55
Peel Rd. NW9	BP31	46
Peel Rd. Har.	BH31	45
Peel Rd. Orp.	CM56	97
Peel Rd. Wem.	BK34	45
Peel St. W8	BS40	56
Peel Way. Rom.	CW30	42
Peel Way, Uxb.	AY39	53
Peerless St. EC1	BZ38	57
Peer Way Horn.	CW33	51
Pegamoid Rd. N9	CC27	39
Pegasus Pl. SE11	BY43	66
Clayton St.		
Pegasus Rd. Croy.	BY57	95
Pegelm Gdns. Horn.	CW33	51
Peggotty Waye, Uxb.	AZ39	53
Pegg Rd. Houns.	BC43	63
Pegley Gdns. SE12	CH48	78
Pegmire La. Wat.	BF23	27
Pegrams Rd. Harl.	CM12	13
Pegwell St. SE18	CN43	68
Pekin Clo. E14	CE39	57
Pekin St. E14	CE39	57
Peldon Ct. Rich.	BL45	65
Peldon Pass. Rich.	BL45	65
Sheen Rd.		
Peldon Road North. Harl.	CL11	13

Pelham Av. Bark. CN37 58
Pelham Clo. SE5 CA44 67
Pelham Ct. SW3 BU42 66
Fulham Rd.
Pelham Ct. Hem. H. BA13 8
Pelham Ct. Stai. AW49 73
Pelham Pl. SW7 BU42 66
Pelham Rd. E18 CH31 49
Pelham Rd. N15 CA31 48
Pelham Rd. N22 BY30 38
Pelham Rd. SW19 BS50 76
Pelham Rd. Beck. CC51 87
Pelham Rd. Bexh. CR45 69
Pelham Rd. Grav. DF47 81
Pelham Rd. Ilf. CM34 49
Pelham Sq. SW7 BU42 66
Pelham St. SW7 BT42 66
Pelham's Wk. Esher BF55 84
Pelhams Wat. BD21 27
Pelier St. SE17 BZ43 67
Pelinore Rd. SE6 CG48 78
Pellant Rd. SW6 BR43 65
Pellatt Gro. N22 BY30 38
Pellatt Rd. SE22 CA46 77
Pellerin Rd. N16 CA35 48
Pelling Hill, Wind. AQ47 72
Pelling St. E14 CE39 57
Pellipar Cl. SE18 CK42 68
Hillreach
Pellipar Clo. N13 BY27 38
Pellipar Gdns. SE18 CK42 68
Ogilby St.
Pellipar Rd. SE18 CK42 68
Pell St. E1 CB40 57
Pelly Rd. E13 CH37 58
Pelter St. E2 CA38 57
Diss St.
Pelton Av. Sutt. BS58 95
Pelton Rd. SE10 CG42 68
Pembar Av. E17 CD31 48
Pember Rd. NW10 BQ38 55
Pemberton Av. Rom. CV31 51
Pemberton Clo. St. Alb. BG15 9
Pemberton Gdns. N19 BW34 47
Pemberton Gdns. Rom. CQ32 50
Pemberton Rd. N4 BY32 47
Pemberton Rd. E. Mol. BG52 84
Pemberton Row, EC4 BY39 56
E. Harding St.
Pemberton Ter. N19 BW34 47
Pembridge Av. Twick. BE47 74
Pembridge Cres. W11 BS40 56
Pembridge Gdns. W2 BS40 56
Pembridge La. Brox. BZ14 12
Pembridge La. Hert. BZ13 12
Pembridge Ms. W8 BS43 66
Earls Ct. Rd.
Pembridge Ms. W11 BS40 56
Pembridge Pl. W2 BS40 56
Pembridge Pl. W8 BS42 66
Pembridge Rd. W11 BS40 56
Pembridge Sq. W2 BS40 56
Pembridge Studios W8 BS42 66
Pembridge Vill. W11 BS40 56
Pembroke Av. Enf. CB23 30
Pembroke Av. Har. BJ31 45
Pembroke Av. Surb. BM53 85
Pembroke Av. Walt. BD56 93
Pembroke Cl. SW1 BV41 66
Pembroke Clo. Bans. BS62 104
Pembroke Clo. Brox. CD15 12
Church La.
Pembroke Clo. Horn. CW31 51
Pembroke Dr. Wal. Cr. BY18 20
Pembroke Gdns. W8 BR42 65
Pembroke Gdns. Dag. CR34 50
Pembroke Gdns. Wok. AT62 100
Pembroke Rd.
Pembroke Gdns. Clo. W8 BS41 66
Pembroke Ms. W8 BS41 66
Earl's Ct. Rd.
Pembroke Pl. W8 BS41 66
Pembroke Pl. Edg. BM29 37
Pembroke Pl. Islw. BH44 64
Pembroke Rd. E17 CE32 48
Pembroke Rd. N8 BX31 47
Pembroke Rd. N10 BV29 38
Pembroke Rd. N13 BZ27 39
Pembroke Rd. N15 CA32 48
Pembroke Rd. SE25 CA52 87
Pembroke Rd. W8 BR42 65
Pembroke Rd. Brom. CJ51 88
Pembroke Rd. Erith CS42 69
Pembroke Rd. Grnf. BF38 54
Pembroke Rd. Ilf. CN33 49
Pembroke Rd. Mitch. BV51 86
Pembroke Rd. Nthwd. BA27 35
Pembroke Rd. Ruis. BB33 44
Pembroke Rd. Sev. CU66 116
Pembroke Rd. Wem. BK34 45
Pembroke Rd. Wok. AT62 100
Pembroke Sq. W8 BS41 66
Pembroke St. N1 BX36 56
Gifford St.
Pembroke Studios W8 BR41 65
Pembroke Vill. W8 BS41 66
Pembroke Vill. Rich. BK45 64
Pembroke Way. Hayes. BA41 63
Pembury Av. Wor. Pk. BP54 85
Pembury Clo. E5 CB35 48
Pembury Clo. Brom. CG54 88
Pembury Clo. Couls. BV60 95
Pembury Ct. Hayes. BA43 63
Pembury Cres. Sid. CQ48 79
Pembury Est. E5 CB35 48
Pembury Gro. E5 CB35 48
Pembury Pl. E5 CB35 48
Pembury Rd.
Pembury Rd. E5 CB35 48
Pembury Rd. N17 CA30 39
Pembury Rd. SE25 CB52 87
Pembury Rd. Bexh. CQ43 69
Pemdevon Rd. Croy. BY54 86
Pemell Clo. E1 CC38 57
Colebert Av.
Pemerich Clo. Hayes. BB42 63
Penang St. E1 CB40 57
Farthing Flds.
Penarth St. SE15 CC43 67
Penberth Rd. SE6 CF47 77
Penbury Rd. Sthl. BE42 64
Pencraig Way SE15 CB43 67
Pendall Rd. Red. BY69 121
Penda Rd. Erith CR43 69
Hengist Rd.
Penda Rd. Erith. CS43 69
Pendarves Rd. SW20 BQ51 85
Pendell Ave. Hayes. BB43 63
Pendennis Clo. Wey. AW60 92
Pendennis Rd. N17 BZ31 48
Pendennis Rd. SW16 BX49 76
Pendennis Rd. Orp. CP55 89
Pendennis Rd. Sev. CV65 108
Penderel Rd. Houns. BF46 74
Penderry Ri. SE6 CF48 77
Penderyn Way N7 BW35 47
Carlton Rd.
Pendle Rd. SW16 BV50 76
Pendlestone Rd. E17 CE32 48
Pendleton Rd. Red. BU71 121
Sandpit Rd.
Pendleton Rd. Reig. & Red. BT72 121
Pendragon Rd. Brom. CG48 78
Pendrell Rd. SE4 CD44 67
Pendrell St. SE18 CM43 68
Pendridge Clo. Enf. CB22 30
Pen Dr. Uxb. AV32 43
Penerley Rd. SE6 CE47 77
Penerley Rd. Rain. CU39 59
Penfold La. Bex. CP48 79
Penfold Pl. NW1 BU39 56
Penfold Rd. N9 CC26 39
Penfold St. NW1 BT38 56
Penfold St. NW8 BT38 56
Penford Gdns. SE9 CJ45 68
Penford St. SE5 BY44 66
Pengarth Rd. Bex. CP46 79
Penge La. SE20 CC50 77
Pengelly Clo. Wal. Cr. CB18 21
Burygreen Rd.
Penge Rd. E13 CJ37 58
Penhall Rd. SE7 CJ42 68
Penhill Rd. Bex. CP47 79
Penhurst Rd. Ilf. CL29 40
Penhurst Rd. Pot. B. BT19 20
Penhurst Rd. Th. Hth. BY53 86
Penine Way. Hayes. BA43 63
Peninsular Clo. Felt. BA46 73
Peninsular Rd. Til. DG45 71
Penistone Rd. SW16 BX50 76
Penistone Wk. Rom. CV29 42
Penkeith Dr. Har. BG34 45
Penlow Rd. Harl. CM12 13
Penman Clo. St. Alb. BF17 18
Pen Meadow, Slou. AQ37 52
Penmon Rd. SE2 CO41 69
Pennack Rd. SE15 CA43 67
Sumner Rd.
Pennack Street SE15 CA43 67
Willowbrook Estate
Pennant Ms. W8 BS42 66
Pennant Terr. E17 CD30 39
Pennard Rd. W12 BQ41 65
Pennards, The. Sun. BD52 84
Penn Clo. Grnfd. BF37 54
Penn Clo. Har. BK31 45
Penn Clo. Rick. AU25 25
Penn Ct. Chis. CL51 88
Penner Cl. SW19 BR48 75
Queensmere Rd.
Pennethorne Clo. E9 CC37 57
Victoria Pk. Rd.
Pennethorne Rd. SE15 CB43 67
Penney Clo. Dart. CV47 80
Penn Gdns. Rom. CR29 41
Penn Gaskell La. Ger. Cr. AS28 34
Pennine Dr. NW2 BQ34 46
Pennine La. NW2 BQ34 46
Pennine Dr.
Pennine Way Bexh. CT44 69
Pennine Way, Grav. DF48 81
Pennine Way, Hem. H. AY12 8
Pennington Clo. Rom. CR28 41
Pennington Gro. Wey. BB55 83
Pennington Rd. AR29 34
Penningtons, The Amer. AP22 25
Pennington St. E1 CB40 57
Pennins Av. Guil. AP69 118
Penn La. Bex. CP46 79
Penn Rd. N7 BX35 47
Penn Rd. Rick. AV26 34
Penn Rd. St. Alb. BG17 18
Penn Rd. Slou. AO38 52
Penn Rd. Slou. AR44 62
Penn Rd. Wat. BC23 26
Penn St. N1 BZ37 57
Penn Way. Rick. AU25 25
Pennyfields, E14 CE40 57
Penny Flds. Brwd. DB28 42
Junction Rd.
Penny La. Shep. BB54 83
Pennylets Grn. Slou. AP36 52
Pennymead Dri. Leath. BB67 110
Pennymead. Harl. CO11 14
Pennypot La. Wok. AO59 91
Penpoll Rd. E8 CB36 57
Penpool La. Well. CO45 69
Penrhyn Av. E17 CD30 39
Penrhyn Cres. E17 CE30 39
Penrhyn Cres. SW14 BO45 65
Penrhyn Gdns. Kings-on-t. BK52 84
Penrhyn Gro. E17 CE30 39
Penrhyn Rd. Kings-on-t. BL52 85
Penrith Clo. Red. BU70 121
Penrith Cres. Horn. CU35 50
Penrith Rd. N15 BZ32 48
Penrith Rd. Ilf. CN29 40
Penrith Rd. N. Mal. BN52 85
Penrith Rd. Rom. CX29 42
Penrith Rd. Th. Hth. BZ51 87
Penrith St. SW16 BW50 76
Pen Rd. Ger. Cr. AR30 34
Penrose Av. Wat. BE27 36
Penrose Gro. SE17 BZ42 67
Penrose House, SE17 BZ42 67
Penrose Rd. Lthd. BG64 102
Penrose St. SE17 BZ42 67
Penryn St. NW1 BW37 56
Penry St. SE1 CA42 67
Marcia Rd.
Pensbury Pl. SW8 BW44 66
Pensbury St. SW8 BW44 66
Penscroft Gdns. Borwd. BN24 28
Pensford Av. Rich. BM44 65
Penshurst Av. Sid. CO46 79
Penshurst Clo. Ger. Cr. AR30 34
Penshurst Gdns. Edg. BM28 37
Penshurst Grn. Brom. CG53 88
Penshurst Rd. E9 CC36 57
Penshurst Rd. N17 CA29 39
Penshurst Rd. Bexh. CQ44 69
Penshurst Way Sutt. BS57 95
Pensmead Ter. E4 CF28 39
Mead Cres.
Pentelowe Gdns. Felt. BC46 73
Pentire Clo. Upmin. CZ32 51
Pentire Rd. E17 CF30 39
Pentland Hem. H. AY12 8
Mendip Way
Pentland Av. Shep. AZ53 83
Pentland Rd. Bush. BG25 27
Pentlands Clo. Mitch. BV52 86
Pentland St. SW18 BT46 76
Pentley Clo. Welw. G. C. BQ6 5
Pentley Pk. Welw. G. C. BQ6 5
Pentlow St. SW15 BQ45 65
Pentlow Way Buck. H. CK26 40
Pentney Rd. E4 CF26 39
Pretoria Rd.
Pentney Rd. SW12 BW47 76
Pentney Rd. SW19 BR51 85
Midmoor Rd.
Penton Av. Stai. AV50 72
Penton Dr. Stai. AW51
Penton Dr. Wal. Cr. CC18 21
Penton Gro. N1 BY37 56
Penton Hook Rd. Stai. AW51
Penton Pl. SE17 BY42 66
Penton Pl. WC1 BX38 56
Penton Rd. Stai. AV50 72
Penton St. N1 BY37 56
Pentonville Rd. N1 BX37 56
Pentreath Av. Guil. AP71 118
Pentrich Av. Enf. CB22 30
Pentridge St. SE15 CA43 67
Pentyre Av. N18 BZ28 39
Penwerris Av. Islw. BG43 64
Penwith Rd. SW18 BS48 76
Penwortham Rd. SW16 BV50 76
Penwortham Rd. Sth. Croy. BZ58 96
Penylan Pl. Edg. BM29 37
Penywern Rd. SW5 BS42 66
Penzance Clo. Uxb. AX30 35
Penzance Gdns. Rom. CX29 42
Penzance Pl. W11 BR40 55
Penzance Rd. Rom. CX29 42
Penzance St. W11 BR40 55
Peony Clo. Brwd. DA25 33
Lavender Av.
Peony Gdns. W12 BP40 55
Curve, The.
Pepler Rd. SE15 CA43 67
Peplins Clo. Hat. BR16 19
Peplins Way, Hat. BR16 19
Peploe Rd. NW6 BQ37 55
Pepper Alley Loug. CG23 31
Peppercroft St. Grav. DG47 81
Pepper Hill, Grav. DE48 81
Pepper St. SE1 BZ41 67
Pepys Clo. Ash. BL62 103
Pepys Clo. Dart. CX45 70
Pepys Clo. Grav. DE48 81
Pepys Clo. Slou. AT43 62
Pepys Clo. Til. DH44 71
Pepys Clo. Uxb. AZ35 44
Pepys Cres. Barn. BQ25 28
Pepys Rd. SE14 CC44 67
Pepys Rd. SW20 BQ50 75
Pepys St. EC3 CA40 57
Perceval Av. NW3 BU35 47
Perch St. E8 CA35 48
Percival Ct. N17 CA29 39
High Rd.
Percival Gdns. Rom. CP32 50
Percival Rd. SW14 BN46 75
Percival Rd. Enf. CA24 30
Percival Rd. Felt. BB48 73
Percival Rd. Horn. CV32 51
Percival Rd. Orp. CL55 88
Percival St. EC1 BY38 56
Percival St. SE2 CP41 69
Harrow Manorway
Percival Way Epsom BN56 94
Percy Av. Ashf. AZ49 73
Percy Bryant Rd. Sun. BB50 73
Percy Circus, WC1 BX38 56
Percy Gdns. Enf. CC25 30
Percy Gdns. Hayes BB38 53
Percy Gdns. Islw. BJ45 64
Percy Gdns. Wor. Pk. BN54 85
Percy Ms. W1 BW39 56
Rathbone Pl.
Percy Pl. Slou. AQ44 62
Percy Rd. E11 CG33 49
Percy Rd. E16 CG38 58
Percy Rd. N12 BT28 38
Percy Rd. N21 BZ26 39
Percy Rd. NW6 BS38 56
Percy Rd. SE20 CC51 87
Percy Rd. SE25 CA53 87
Percy Rd. W12 BP41 65
Percy Rd. Bexh. CQ44 69
Percy Rd. Guil. AQ69 118
Percy Rd. Hamptn. BF50 74
Percy Rd. Ilf. CO33 50
Percy Rd. Islw. BJ45 64
Percy Rd. Mitch. BV54 86
Percy Rd. Rom. CR30 41
Percy Rd. Rom. CR31 50
Percy Rd. Twick. BF47 74
Percy Rd. Wat. BC24 26
Percy St. W1 BW39 56
Percy St. Grays. DE43 71
Percy St. Wok. AS62 100
Percy Way Twick. BG47 74
Peregrine Rd. Ilf. CO28 41
Peregrine Rd. Sun. BB51 83
Peregrine Wk. Rain. CU36 59
Perham Rd. W14 BR42 65
Perifield, SE21 BZ47 77
Perimeade Rd. Grnf. BK37 54
Perimeter Rd. Red. BW73 121
Periton Rd. SE9 CJ45 68
Perivale Gdns. W13 BJ38 54
Bellevue Rd.
Perivale Gdns. Wat. BC20 17
Perivale La. Grnf. BJ38 54
Perkins Clo. Wem. BJ35 45
Perkins Ct. Ashf. AY49 73
Fairholme Rd.
Perkins Rents, SW1 BW41 66
Old Pye St.
Perkins Rd. Ilf. CM32 49
Perpins Rd. SE9 CM46 78
Perran Rd. SW2 BY47 76
Perrers Rd. W6 BP42 65
Perrin Clo. Ashf. AY49 73
Perring Est. E3 CE39 57
Perrin Rd. Wem. BJ35 45
Perrins Ct. NW3 BT35 47
Hampstead High St.
Perrins La. NW3 BT35 47
Perrins Wk. NW3 BT35 47
Perrott St. SE18 CM42 68
Perry Av. W3 BN39 55
Perry Clo. Rain. CS37 59
Perry Clo. Uxb. AZ39 53
Perry Croft. Wind. AM45 61
Perryfield Way NW9 BN32 46
Broadway, The.
Perryfield Way NW9 BO32 46
Perryfield Way Rich. BJ48 74
Perry Gdns. N9 BZ27 39
Perry Gro. Dart. CX45 70
Perry Gth. Nthlt. BD37 54
Perry Hall Clo. Orp. CO54 89
Perry Hall Rd. Orp. CN54 88
Perry Hill. Wal. Abb. CG15 13
Perry Hl. SE6 CD48 77
Perry Hl. Est. SE23 CD48 77
Perry How Wor. Pk. BO54 85
Perrymans Farm Rd. Ilf. CM32 49
Perry Mead Bush. BF26 36
Perry Mead Enf. BY23 29
Perrymead St. SW6 BS44 66
Perryn Rd. SE16 CB41 67
Perryn Rd. W3 BN40 55
Perry Rise SE23 CD48 77
Perry Rd. Harl. CM12 13
Perry Rd. S. Ock. CW40 60
Perry St. Gdns. Chis. CN50 78
Perrysfield Rd. Wal. Cr. CD16 21
Perrys La. Orp. CO60 98
Perry Spring. Harl. CP12 14
Perry St. Chis. CM50 78
Perry St. Dart. CT45 69
Perry St. Grav. DF47 81
Perry St. Shaw, Chis. CN50 78
Perry Val. SE23 CC48 77
Persant Rd. SE6 CG48 78
Persfield Clo. Epsom BO58 94
Pershore Gro. Cars. BT53 86
Perth Av. NW9 BN33 46
Perth Av. Hayes BD38 54
Perth Clo. N22 BY29 38
Perth Clo. SW20 BP51 85
Perth Rd. E10 CD33 48
Perth Rd. E13 CH37 58
Perth Rd. N4 BY33 47
Perth Rd. N22 BY30 38
Perth Rd. Bark. CM37 58
Perth Rd. Beck. CF51 87
Perth Rd. Ilf. CL32 49
Perth Ter. Ilf. CM33 49
Perwell Av. Har. BE33 45
Perwell Ct. Har. BE33 45
Pescot Hill, Hem. H. AW12 8
Peter Av. NW10 BP36 55
Peterborough Av. Upmin. CZ33 51
Peterborough Gdns. Ilf. CK33 49
Peterborough Ms. SW6 BS45 66
Peterborough Rd. E10 CF32 48
Peterborough Rd. SW6 BS44 66
Peterborough Rd. Cars. BT53 86
Peterborough Rd. Guil. AP69 118
Peterborough Rd. Har. BH33 45
Peterborough Vill. SW6 BS44 66
Peter Clo. Berk. AP12 7
Petergate, SW11 BT45 66
Peterhill Clo. Ger. Cr. AS28 34
Peterlee Ct. Hem. H. AY11 8
Peters Ave. Oxt. CF68 114
Peters Av. St. Alb. BK16 18
Peters Clo. Stan. BK29 36
Petersfield Av. Rom. CW29 42
Petersfield Av. Slou. AQ40 52
Petersfield Av. Stai. AX49 73
Petersfield Clo. N18 BZ28 39
Petersfield Clo. Rom. CX29 42
Petersfield Cres. Couls. BX61 104
Petersfield Ri. SW15 BP47 75
Petersfield Rd. W3 BN41 65
Petersham Av. Wey. AY59 92
Petersham Clo. Rich. BK48 74
Petersham Clo. Sutt. BS56 95
Petersham Clo. Wey. AY59 92
Petersham Dr. Orp. CN51 88
Petersham Gdns. Orp. CN51 88
Petersham Dr.
Petersham La. SW7 BT42 66
Petersham Ms. SW7 BT41 66
Petersham Pl. SW7 BT41 66
Petersham Rd. Rich. BK46 74
Petersham Way Orp. CO52 89
Peters Hill EC4 BZ39 57
Carter La.
Peter's La. EC1 BY39 56
Cowcross St.
Peters Path SE26 CB49 77
Wells Park Rd.
Peterstone Rd. SE2 CO41 69
Peterstow Clo. SW15 BR48 75
Princes Way
Peter St. W1 BW40 56
Peterswood Harl. CM13 13
Petherton Rd. N5 BZ35 48
Petley Rd. W6 BQ43 65
Peto Pl. NW1 BV38 56
Peto St. S. E16 CG40 58
Petre Clo. Brwd. DE32 123
Petridge Rd. Red. BU73 121
Petten Clo. Orp. CP54 89
Petten Gro. Orp. CP54 89
Petters Rd. Ash. BL61 103
Pettits Boul. Rom. CT30 41
Pettits Clo. Rom. CT30 41
Pettits La. Brwd. DC22 33
Pettits La. Rom. CT30 41
Pettits La. N. Rom. CS30 41
Pettits Pl. Dag. CR35 50
Pettits Rd. Dag. CR35 50
Pettley Gdns. Rom. CS32 50
Petts Gro. Av. Wem. BK35 45
Petts Hill Nthlt. BF35 45
Petts La. Shep. AZ52 83
Pett St. SE18 CK42 68
Pett's Wd. Rd. Orp. CM53 88
Petty France, SW1 BW41 66
Petworth Clo. Nthlt. BE36 54
Petworth Clo. Sutt. BS55 86
Petworth Gdns. SW20 BP52 85
Petworth Gdns. Uxb. BA37 53
Petworth Rd. N12 BU28 38
Petworth Rd. Bexh. CR46 79
Petworth St. SW11 BU44 66
Petworth Way Horn. CT35 50
Petyt Pl. SW3 BU43 66
Petyward SW3 BU42 66
Pevensey Av. N11 BW28 38
Pevensey Av. Enf. BZ23 30
Pevensey Clo. Houns. BG43 64
Pevensey Rd. E7 CG35 49
Pevensey Rd. SW17 BT49 76
Pevensey Rd. Felt. BD47 74
Peveril Dr. Tedd. BG49 74
Pewley Bank, Guil. AS71 118
Pewley Hill, Guil. AR71 118
Pewley Way, Guil. AS71 118
Pewsey Clo. E4 CE28 39
Peyton Pl. SE10 CF43 67
Pheasant Clo. Berk. AR13 7
Pheasant Hill. Ch. St. G. AR27 34
Pheasant Rise. Chesh. AO20 16
Pheasants Way. Rick. AW26 35
Pheasant Wk. Ger. Cr. AR28 34
Phelps Clo. Sev. CZ57 99
Phelp St. SE17 BZ42 67
Phelps Way. Hayes. BB42 63
Phene St. SW3 BU43 66
Philanthropic Rd. Red. BV71 121
Philan Way Rom. CS29 41
Philbeach Gdns. SW5 BS42 66
Philchurch St. E1 CB39 57
Ellen St.
Philipa Way. Grays. DG42 71
Philip Clo. Brwd. DA25 33
Philip Gdns. Croy. CD55 87
Philip La. N15 BZ31 48
Philipot Path, SE9 CK46 78
Philippa Gdns. SE9 CJ46 78
Philip Rd. SE15 CB45 67
Philip Rd. Rain. CT38 59
Philip Rd. Stai. AX50 73
Philip St. E13 CH38 58
Phillida Rd. Rom. CX30 42
Phillimor Clo. Rad. BH21 27
Phillimore Clo. W8 BS41 66
Phillimore Gdns. NW10 BQ37 55
Phillimore Gdns. W8 BS41 66
Phillimore Pl. W8 BS41 66
Phillimore Pl. Rad. BH21 27
Phillimore Wk. W8 BS41 66
Phillip Av. Rom. CS33 50
Phillip Av. Swan. CS52 89
Phillip Clo. Rom. CS33 50
Phillipers Wat. BD21 27
Phillipp St. N1 CA37 57
Phillips Clo. Dart. CU46 79
Phillips Way Brom. CH51 88
Lowland Av.
Philpot La. EC3 CA40 57
Philpot La. Wok. AR59 91
Philpot St. E1 CB39 57
Phineas Pett Rd. SE9 CK45 68
Phipp's Bri. Rd. SW19 BT51 86
Phipps Hatch La. Enf. BZ22 30
Phipp's Ter. SW19 BT51 86
Phipp St. EC2 CA38 57
Phobe Rd. Hem. H. AY12 8
Phoebeth Rd. SE4 CE46 77
Phoenix Clo. Nthwd. BB28 35

Phoenix Dr. Kes. CJ55 88
Phoenix Lo. Mans. W6 BQ42 65
Brook Green
Phoenix Rd. NW1 BW38 56
Phoenix Rd. SE20 CC50 77
Phoenix St. WC2 BW39 56
Stacey St.
Phoenix Way Houns. BD43 64
Phygtle. Th. Ger. Cr. AS29 34
Phyllis Av. N. Mal. BP53 85
Phyllis Ct. NW3 BS34 47
Picardy Manorway Belv. CR41 69
Picardy Rd. Belv. CR42 69
Picardy St. Bel. CR41 69
Piccadilly, W1 BV40 56
Piccadilly Pl. W1 BW40 56
Swallow St.
Piccotts End La. Hem. H. AX12 8
Piccotts End Rd. Hem. H. AX11 8
Pickard St. EC1 BY38 56
Moreland St.
Pickering Av. E6 CL37 58
Pickering Ms. W2 BS39 56
Bishop's Br. Rd.
Picket Croft, Stan. BK30 36
Pickets Clo. Bush. BH26 36
Pickets St. SW12 BV47 76
Pickett's, Welw. G. C. BQ6 5
Picketts Lock La. N9 CC27 30
Pickford Clo. Bexh. CQ44 69
Pickford La. Bexh. CQ45 69
Pickford Rd. Bexh. CQ45 69
Pickford Rd. St. Alb. BJ14 9
Sutton Rd.
Pick Hill, Wal. Abb. CH19 22
Pickhurst Grn. Brom. CG54 88
Pickhurst La. W. Wick. CG53 88
Pickhurst Mead Brom. CG54 88
Pickhurst Pk. Brom. CG53 88
Pickhurst Rise W. Wick. CF54 87
Pickins Piece. Slou. AT44 62
Pickle Herring St. SE1 CA40 57
Pickmoss La. Sev. CU61 107
Pickwick Gdns. Grav. DE48 81
Pickwick Pl. Har. BH33 45
Pickwick Rd. SE21 BZ47 77
Pickwick St. SE1 BZ41 67
Pickwick Way Chis. CM50 78
Picquets Way Bans. BR61 103
Picton Pl. W1 BV39 56
Picton St. SE5 BZ43 67
Piedmont Rd. SE18 CM42 68
Pield Heath Av. Uxb. AZ38 53
Pield Heath Rd. Uxb. AY38 53
Piercing Hill, Epp. CM21 31
Pier Head Cotts. E14 CE41 67
Piermont Green SE22 CB46 77
Peckham Rye
Piermont Rd. SE22 CB46 77
Upland Rd.
Pierrepoint Rd. W3 BM40 55
Pier Rd. E16 CL40 58
Pier Rd. Erith CT43 69
Pier Rd. Felt. BC46 73
Pier Rd. Grav. DF46 81
Pier Rd. Est. E16 CL41 68
Pierson Rd. Wind. AL44 61
Pier St. E14 CF42 67
Pier Ter. SW18 BS45 66
Pigeonhouse La. Couls. BT66 113
Pigeon La. Hamptn. BF49 74
Piggot St. E14 CD39 57
Pike Gdns. SE1 BY40 56
Pike La. Upmin. CZ35 51
Pikes End. Pnr. BC31 44
Pikes Hill Epsom BO60 94
Pilgrimage St. SE1 BZ41 67
Pilgrim Clo. St. Alb. BG17 18
Pilgrim Hill Orp. CQ51 89
Pilgrim Hl. SE27 BZ49 77
Pilgrims Clo. Brwd. CZ25 33
Pilgrim's Clo. Dor. BJ69 119
Pilgrims Ct. SE3 CH44 68
Pilgrim's La. NW3 BT35 47
Pilgrims La. Brwd. CY24 33
Pilgrims La. Cat. BY66 113
Pilgrims La. Oxt. CH66 115
Pilgrims La. Oxt. CJ65 106
Pilgrims Rise Barn. BU25 29
Pilgrims Rd. Swans. DC45 71
Pilgrim St. EC4 BY39 56
Pilgrims Way. Dart. CX47 80
Pilgrims Way. Dor. BG70 119
Pilgrim's Way. Dor. BJ69 119
Pilgrims Way. Dor. & Bet. BL70 120
Pilgrims' Way. Guil. AO73 118
Pilgrims Way. Guil. AR72 118
Pilgrims Way. Reig. BR69 120
Pilgrims Way. Reig. BS69 121
Pilgrims Way. Sev. CY61 108
Pilgrims Way Sth. Croy. CA57 96
Pilgrims Way. West. CL65 106
Pilgrims Way. West CO64 107
Pilgrims' Way. E. Sev. CV61 108
Pilgrims Way. W. Sev. CS61 107
Pilkington Rd. SE15 CB44 67
Pilkington Rd. Orp. CL55 88
Pillions, The Hayes BA38 53
Pillmans Clo. Sid. CO50 79
Piltdown Rd. Wat. BD28 35
Pilton Rd. SW6 BS44 66
Pimlico Rd. SW1 BV42 66
Pimlico Wk. N1 CA38 57
Pimpernel Way. Rom. CV29 42
Pinceybrook Rd. Harl. CM13 13
Pinchbeck Rd. Orp. CN57 97
Pinchfield. Rick. AU28 34
Pinchin St. E1 CB40 57
Pincott Lane. Leath. AZ68 110
Pincott Rd. SW19 BT50 76
Pincott Rd. Bexh. CR46 79
Pindar Rd. Hodd. CF11 12
Pindar St. EC2 CA39 57
Pindock Ms. W9 BS38 56
Pineapple Rd. Amer. AP23 25
Pine Av. Grav. DH47 81
Pine Av. W. Wick. CE54 87
Pine Cl. Swan. CT52 89
High St.
Pine Clo. N14 BW26 38
Pine Clo. Hayes BB38 53
Pine Clo. Ken. BZ62 105
Pine Clo. S. Ock. DB38 60
Pine Clo. Stan. BJ28 36
Pine Clo. Swan. CT52 89
Pine Clo. Wal. Cr. CC17 21
Pine Clo. Wey. AW59 92
Pine Clo. Wok. AR61 100
Pine Coombe Croy. CC56 96
Pine Ct. Upmin. CX35 51
Pine Cres. Brwd. DE25 122
Pine Cres. Cars. BT59 95
Pine Cft. Hem. H. AY16 17
Pinecroft Pnr. BF29 36
Pine Dene. Lthd. BF66 111
Pinefield Clo. E14 CE40 57
Pine Gdns. Ruis. BC33 44
Pine Gdns. Surb. BM53 85
Pineglade Orp. CK56 97
Pine Gro. N4 BX34 47
Pine Gro. N20 BR26 37
Pine Gro. SW19 BR49 75
Pine Gro. Bush. BE23 27
Pine Gro. Hat. BS16 20
Pine Gro. St. Alb. BE18 18
Pine Gro. Wey. AZ56 92
Pine Grove Mt. Wey. BA56 92
Pine Hill Epsom BN61 103
Pinehurst Wk. Orp. CN54 88
Pinelands Clo. SE3 CG43 68
St. John's Pk.
Pine Needles La. Sev. CU65 107
Pine Ridge Cars. BV57 95
Pine Rd. N11 BV27 38
Pine Rd. NW2 BQ35 46
Pine Rd. Wok. AR63 100
Pines Av. Enf. CC21 30
Pines Rd. Brom. CK51 88
Pines, The, N14 BW25 29
Pines. The. Grays. DD40 71
Pines, The Pup. BY60 95
Pines. The Pur. BY56 95
Pines, The, Wdf. Grn. CH27 40
Pine St. EC1 BY38 56
Pinetree Hill Rd. Wok. AU61 100
Pine Wk. Bans. BU62 104
Pine Wk. Cat. CA64 105
Pine Wk. Cob. BD60 93
Pine Wk. Leath. BB67 110
Pine Wk. Surb. BM53 85
Pine Wk. E. Cars. BT59 95
Pine Wk. W. Cars. BT58 95
Pine Way, Egh. AQ50 72
Pine Wd. Sun. BC51 83
Pinewood Ave. Sev. CV64 108
Pinewood Av. Pnr. BF29 36
Pinewood Av. Rain. CU38 59
Pinewood Av. Sid. CN47 78
Pinewood Av. Wey. AX58 92
Pinewood Clo. Croy. CD55 87
Pinewood Clo. Ger. Cr. AS33 43
Pinewood Clo. Iver. AU36 52
Pinewood Clo. Orp. CM54 88
Pinewood Clo. St. Alb. BK13 9
Pinewood Clo. S. Le H. DK42 71
Pinewood Clo. Wok. AT61 100
Pinewood Dr. Orp. CM56 97
Pinewood Dr. Stai. AW49 73
Pinewood Gdns. Hem. H. AW13 8
Pinewood Grn. Iver AU36 52
Pinewood Gro. W13 BK39 54
Pinewood Gro. Wey. AW58 92
Pinewood Pk. Wey. AW59 92
Pinewood Rd. SE2 CP43 69
Pinewood Rd. Brom. CH52 88
Pinewood Rd. Felt. BC48 73
Pinewood Rd. Hav. CS28 41
Pinewood Rd. Iver AT36 52
Pinewood Rd. Vir. W. AQ52 82
Pinewood Way, Brwd. DE25 122
Pinewood. Welw. G. C. BR9 5
Pinfold Rd. SW16 BX49 76
Pinfold Rd. Bush. BE23 27
Pinkham Way, N10 BV29 38
Pinks Hill Swan. CT53 89
Pinkwell Ave. Hayes. BA42 63
Pinkwell La. Hayes. BA42 63
Pinley Gdns. Dag. CO37 59
Pinnacle Hill Bexh. CR45 69
Pinnacles Wal. Abb. CG20 22
Roundhills
Pinnate Pl. Welw. G. C. BR10 5
Pinn Clo. Uxb. AX39 53
Pinnell Pl. SE9 CJ45 68
Pinnell Rd. SE9 CJ45 68
Pinner Ct. Pnr. BF31 45
Pinner Cres. Pnr. BE32 45
Pinner Grn. Pnr. BD30 36
Pinner Hill Pnr. BD30 36
Pinner Hill Rd. Pnr. BD30 36
Pinner Pk. Av. Har. BF30 36
Pinner Pk. Gdns. Har. BG30 36
Pinner Rd. Nthwd. BB30 35
Pinner Rd. Pnr. BE31 45
Pinner Rd. Wat. BD25 27
Pinner Vw. Har. BG32 45
Pinnicks Av. Grav. DG47 81
Pinn Way, Ruis. BA33 44
Pinto Way, SE3 CH45 68
Piper Clo. N7 BX35 47
Piper Rd. Kings-on-t. BM52 85
Pipers Clo. Cob. BD61 102
Pipers End, Vir. W. AR52 82
Pipers Grn. NW9 BN32 46
Pipers Grn. La. Edg. BL27 37
Pipewell Rd. Mitch. BU53 86
Pippbrook Gdns. Dor. BJ71 119
London Rd.
Pippens. Welw. G. C. BR6 5
Piquet Rd. SE20 CC51 87
Pirbright Cres. Croy. CF57 96
Pirbright Rd. SW18 BR47 75
Pirie Rd. E16 CH40 58
Pirrip Clo. Grav. DK48 81
Pishiobury Dr. Saw. CP7 6
Pishiobury Rd. CP6 6
Pitcairn Clo. Rom. CR31 50
Pitcairn Rd. Mitch. BU50 76
Pitcairn St. SW8 BV45 66
Pitchfont La. Oxt. CH66 115
Pitchford St. E15 CF36 57
Pit Farm Rd. Guil. AT70 118
Pitfield Est. N1 CA38 57
Pitfield St. N1 CA38 57
Pitfield Way, NW10 BN36 55
Pitfield Way, Enf. CC23 30
Pitfold Clo. SE12 CH46 78
Pitfold Rd. SE12 CH46 78
Pitlake Croy. BY55 86
Pitmans Field, Harl. CN10 6
Pitman St. SE5 BZ43 67
Pit Path, Lthd. BK63 102
Pitsea Pl. E1 CC39 57
Pitsea St.
Pitsea St. E1 CC39 57
Pitshanger La. W5 BJ38 54
Pitsmead Av. Brom. CH54 88
Pitt Cres. SW19 BS49 76
Pittman Clo. Brwd. DE28 122
Brentwood Rd.
Pitt Rd. Epsom. BO60 94
Pitt Rd. Orp. CM56 97
Pitt Rd. Th. Hth. BZ53 87
Pittsfield, Welw. G. C. BQ6 5
Pitts Head Ms. W1 BV40 56
Pitts Rd. Slou. AO40 61
Pitt Street SE15 CA44 67
Sumner Estate
Pitt St. W8 BS41 66
Pittville Gdns. SE25 CB52 87
Pit Wood Grn. Tad. BQ63 103
Pix Farm La. Berk. AT14 7
Pixfield Ct. Brom. CG51 88
Pixham La. Dor. BK70 119
Pixholme Gro. Dor. BK70 119
Pixie Cres. Hem. H. AV1L 7
Pixley St. E14 CD39 57
Pixton Way Croy. CD58 96
Place Farm Rd. Brwd. DA21 33
Place Farm Rd. Red. BZ68 114
Place House La. Couls. BX63 104
Placket Way. Slou. AL40 61
Plain, The, Epp. CO18 23
Plaistow Grn. Brom. CH50 78
Plaistow Gro. E15 CG37 58
Plaistow Gro. Brom. CH50 78
Plaistow La. Brom. CH50 78
Plaistow Park Rd. E13 CH37 58
Plaistow Rd. E15 CG37 58
Plaitford Clo. Rick. AY27 35
Plane Av. Grav. DE47 81
Plane St. SE26 CB48 77
Plantagenet Clo. Wor. Pk. BN56 94
Plantagenet Gdns. Rom. CP33 50
Plantagenet Pl. Rom. CP33 50
Broomfield Rd.
Plantagenet Rd. Barn. BT24 29
Plantation Dr. Orp. CP54 89
Plantation La. Warl. CD63 105
Plantation Rd. Amer. AP22 25
Plantation Rd. Erith. CU43 69
Plantation Rd. Swan. CU50 79
Plantation, The, SE3 CH44 68
Plantation Walk, Hem. H. AW12 8
Plantation Way. Amer. AP22 25
Plashet Gdns. Brwd. DD28 122
Plashet Gro. E6 CJ36 58
Plashet Rd. E13 CH37 58
Plashetts Bish. CS7 6
Plassy Rd. SE6 CE47 77
Plato Rd. SW2 BX45 66
Platts Av. Wat. BC24 26
Platt's La. NW3 BS35 47
Platts Rd. Enf. CC23 30
Platt St. NW1 BW37 56
Platt, The, SW15 BQ45 65
Plawsfield Rd. SE20 CC51 87
Plaxtol Clo. Brom. CJ51 88
Plaxtol Pl. SE10 CH42 68
Westcombe Hill
Plaxtol Rd. Erith. CR43 69
Playfield Av. Rom. CS30 41
Playfield Cres. SE22 CA46 77
Playfield Rd. Edg. BN30 37
Playford Rd. N4 BX34 47
Playgreen Way, SE6 CE48 77
Playhouse Yd. EC4 BY39 56
Pleany Cl. N15 BY31 47
Pleasance Rd. SW15 BP45 65
Pleasance Rd. Orp. CO51 89
Pleasance, The, SW15 BP45 65
Pleasance Rd.
Pleasant Gro. Croy. CD55 87
Pleasant Pl. N1 BY36 56
Pleasant Pl. Har. BG33 45
Pleasant Pl. Walt. BD57 93
Pleasant Rise. Hat. BQ11 10
Pleasant Row NW1 BV37 56
Camden High St.
Pleasant Vw. Erith CT42 69
Pleasant Vw. Orp. CL56 97
Pleasant Way, Wem. BK37 54
Pleasure Pit Rd. Ash. BM62 103
Plender Pl. NW1 BW37 56
Plender St.
Plender St. Est. NW1 BW37 56
Plender St. NW1 BW37 56
Pleshey Rd. N7 BW35 47
Plevna Cres. N15 CA32 48
Plevna Rd. N9 CB27 39
Plevna Rd. Hamptn. BF51 84
Plevna St. E14 CF41 67
Shepstone St.
Plevna St. E14 CF41 67
Pleydell Av. SE19 CA50 77
Pleydell Av. W6 BO42 65
Pleydell Ct. EC4 BZ39 57
Fleet St.
Plimsoll Rd. N4 BY34 47
Plimsoll St. E14 CE39 57
Plough All. E1 CB40 57
Hermitage Wall
Plough Est. SE8 CC42 67
Plough Hill, Pot. B. BX18 20
Plough La. SE22 CA46 77
Plough La. SW17 BS49 76
Plough La. SW19 BS49 76
Plough La. Berk. AT11 7
Plough La. Cob. BC62 101
Plough La. Pur. BX58 95
Plough La. Rick. AV20 16
Plough La. Slou. AQ37 52
Plough La. Wall. BX56 95
Plough La. Clo. Wall. BX56 95
Plough Lees La. Slou. AP40 52
Plough Pl. EC4 BY39 56
New Fetter La.
Plough Rise, Upmin CZ33 51
Plough Rd. SW11 BT45 66
Plough Rd. Brent. BK43 64
Brent Way
Plough Rd. Epsom BN58 94
Plough St. SW11 BT45 66
Plough Way, SE16 CC42 67
Plough Yd. EC2 CA38 57
Hearn St.
Plover Clo. Stai. AV48 72
Plover Gdns. Upmin. CZ33 51
Plovers Baron. Brwd. DB21 33
Plovers Mead Brwd. DB21 33
Ployters Rd. Harl. CM13 13
Plucking Pl. Sthl. BE41 64
Plumbers Row, E1 CB39 57
Plumbridge St. SE10 CE44 67
Plum Garth, Brent. BK42 64
Plum La. SE18 CL43 68
Plummer La. Mitch. BU51 86
Plummer Rd. SW4 BW46 76
Plumpton Av. Horn. CW35 51
Plumpton Clo. Nthlt. BF36 54
Plumpton Rd. Hodd. CF11 12
Plumstead Common Rd. SE18 CL43 68
Plumstead High St. SE18 CN42 68
Plumstead Rd. SE18 CL42 68
Plumtree Ct. EC4 BY39 56
Shoe La.
Plumtree Mead Loug. CL24 31
Pluto Rise, Hem. H. AY12 8
Plymouth Dr. Sev. CV65 108
Plymouth Pk. Sev. CV65 108
Plymouth Rd. E16 CH39 58
Plymouth Rd. Brom. CH51 88
Plympton Rd. NW6 BR36 55
Plympton St. NW8 BU38 56
Plymstock Rd. Well. CP43 69
Pocketsdell La. Hem. H. AR17 16
Pocklington Clo. NW9 BO30 37
Pocock St. SE1 BY41 66
Podmore Rd. SW18 BT45 66
Poet's Rd. N5 BZ35 48
Pointers Rd. Cob. BA61 101
Point Hl. SE10 CF43 67
Point Pleasant, SW18 BS45 66
Point, The, Ruis. BB35 44
Poland St. W1 BW39 56
Polaym Garth. Welw. G. C. BQ7 5
Polbrook Rd. SE3 CJ44 68
Polebrook Rd. SE3 CJ45 68
Pole Cat Alley Brom. CG55 88
Polecroft La. SE6 CD48 77
Pole Hanger La. Hem. H. AV12 7
Pole Hill Rd. E4 CF26 39
Pole Hill Rd. Uxb. AZ38 53
Pole La. Ong. CT12 14
Polesden Gdns. SW20 BP51 85
Polesden La. Wok. AV65 100
Polesden Rd. Dor. BF68 111
Poles Hill, Rick. AV20 16
Polesteeple Hill, West. CJ62 106
Polesworth Rd. Dag. CP36 59
Police Sta. Rd. Walt. BD57 93
Police Stn. La. Bush. BF26 36
School La.
Pollard Ave. Ger. Cr. AV32 43
Pollard Clo. E16 CH40 58
Munday Rd.
Pollard Clo. N7 BX35 47
Pollard Clo. Chig. CO28 41
Pollard Hatch. Harl. CL12 13
Pollard Rd. N20 BU27 38
Pollard Rd. NW9 BO33 46
Broadway, The,
Pollard Rd. Mord. BT53 86
Pollard Rd. Wok. AT61 100
Pollard Row, E2 CB38 57
Pollards. Rick. AU28 34
Pollards Clo. Loug. CJ25 31
Pollards Clo. Wal. Cr. BZ18 21
Pollards Cres. SW16 BX52 86
Pollards Hill E. SW16 BX52 86
Pollards Hill N. SW16 BX52 86
Pollards Hill S. SW16 BX52 86
Pollards Hill W. SW16 BX52 86
Pollards Oak Cres. Oxt. CH69 115
Pollards Oak Rd. Oxt. CH69 115
Pollard St. E2 CB38 57
Pollards Wd. Rd. SW16 BX52 86
Pollards Wood Rd. Oxt. CH69 115
Pollard Wood Hill. Oxt. CH68 115
Pollen St. W1 BW39 56
Hanover St.
Polsted La. Guil. AO73 118
Polsted Rd. SE6 CD47 77
Polthorne Gro. SE18 CM42 68
Poltimore Ms. W3 BN41 65
Mill Hill Gro.
Poltimore Rd. Guil. AQ71 118
Polworth Rd. SW16 BX49 76
Polygon Ms. W2 BU39 56
Polygon Rd. NW1 BW37 56
Polytechnic St. SE18 CL42 68
Pomeroy Clo. Amer. AO23 25
Pomeroy Cres. Wat. BC21 26
Pomeroy Sq. SE14 CC43 67
Pomeroy St.
Pomeroy St. SE14 CC44 67
Pomfret Rd. SE5 BZ45 67
Flaxman Rd.
Pompadour Clo. Brwd. DB28 42
Queen St.
Pond Clo. SE3 CG44 68
Pond Clo. Uxb. AX30 35
Pond Cotts. SE21 CA47 77
Pond Ct. Ash. BL62 103
Marlo, The,
Pond Croft. Hat. BO12 10
Pondcroft. Welw. G. C. BR8 5
Ponder St. N7 BX36 56
Pondfield Cres. St. Alb. BJ11 9
Pondfield La. Brwd. DD27 122
Pondfield Rd. Brom. CG54 88
Pondfield Rd. Dag. CR35 50
Pondfield Rd. Ken. BY61 104
Pondfield Rd. Orp. CL55 88
Pond Grn. Ruis. BB34 44
Pond Hill Sutt. BR57 94
Pond Hill Gdns. Sutt. BR57 94
Pond Ho. SW3 BU42 66
Pond La. Ger. Cr. AQ30 34
Pond La. Sev. CZ66 117
Pond Meadow, Guil. AP70 118
Pond Piece. Lthd. BF60 93
Pond Pl. SW3 BU42 66
Pond Pl. Ash. BL62 103
Pond Rd. E15 CG37 58
Pond Rd. Egh. AU50 72
Pond Rd. Hem. H. AZ16 17
Pond Rd. Wok. AQ63 100
Pondside Clo. Hayes. BA43 63
Pond Sq. N6 BV33 47
Pond St. NW3 BU35 47
Pond Walk, Upmin. CZ34 51
Pond Way, Tedd. BK50 74
Pondwicks Clo. St. Alb. BG14 9
Pondwood Rise Orp. CN54 88
Ponler St. E1 CB39 57
Ponsard Rd. NW10 BP38 55
Ponsford St. E9 CC36 57
Ponsonby Pl. SW1 BW42 66
Ponsonby Rd. SW15 BP47 75
Ponsonby Ter. SW1 BW42 66
Pontefract Rd. Brom. CG49 78
Ponton Rd. SW8 BW43 66
Pontosie Clo. Sev. CT64 107
Pont St. Ms. SW1 BU41 66
Pont St. SW1 BU41 66
Pontypool Wk. Rom. CV29 42
Pony Chase Cob. BE60 93
Pool Cl. E. Mol. BF53 84
Poole Clo. Ruis. BB34 44
Poole Ct. Rd. Houns. BE44 64
Poole Rd. E9 CC36 57
Poole Rd. Epsom BN57 94
Poole Rd. Horn. CX33 51
Poole Rd. Wok. AS62 100
Pooles Cotts. Rich. BK48 74
Clifford Rd.
Pooles La. Dag. CQ37 59
Pooles Pk. N4 BY34 47
Poole St. N1 BZ37 57
Poole Way, Hayes BB38 53
Pooley Av. Egh. AT49 72
Pooley Green Clo. Egh. AV49 72
Pooley Green Rd. Egh. AT49 72
Pooley's Lane. Hat. BP15 10
Poolmans Rd. Wind. AL45 61
Pool Rd. E. Mol. BE53 84
Poolsford Rd. NW9 BO31 46
Pootings Rd. Eden. CM70 115
Pope Rd. Brom. CJ53 88
Pope's Av. Twick. BH48 74
Popes Clo. Amer. AP22 25
Popes Clo. Slou. AT43 62
Popes Gro. Croy. CD55 87
Pope's Gro. Twick. BH48 74
Popes La. W5 BK41 64
Popes La. Oxt. CG70 115
Popes La. Wat. BC22 26
Popes Rd. SW9 BY45 66
Popes Rd. Wat. BB19 17
Pope St. SE1 CA41 67
Popham Clo. Felt. BE48 74
Popham Gdns. Rich. BM45 65
Marksbury Av.
Popham Rd. N1 BZ37 57
Popham St. N1 BY37 56
Poplar Ave. Amer. AP23 25
Poplar Av. Grav. DH49 81
Poplar Av. Lthd. BJ64 102
Poplar Av. Mitch. BU51 86
Poplar Av. Orp. CL55 88
Poplar Av. Sthl. BF41 64
Poplar Av. West Dr. AY40 53
Poplar Bath St. E14 CE40 57
Lawless St.
Poplar Clo. Ing. DC19 24
Poplar Clo. Pnr. BD30 36
Poplar Clo. Slou. AV44 62
Poplar Clo. Wat. BC19 17
Poplar Ct. SW19 BS49 76

Poplar Cres. Epsom. BN57 94
Poplar Fm. Clo. Epsom BN57 94
Poplar Gdns. N. Mal. BN51 85
Poplar Gro. W6 BQ41 65
Poplar Gro. N. Mal. BN52 85
Poplar Gro. Wem. BN34 46
Poplar Gro. Wok. AS63 100
Poplar High St. E14 CE40 57
Poplar Mt. Belv. CR42 69
Poplar Pl. W2 BS40 56
Poplar Rd. SE24 BZ45 67
Poplar Rd. SW19 BS51 86
Poplar Rd. Ashf. BA49 73
Poplar Rd. Guil. AS74 118
Poplar Rd. Lthd. BJ64 102
Poplar Rd. Sutt. BR54 85
Poplar Rd. Uxb. AX35 44
Poplar Rd. Uxb. AX36 53
Poplar Rd. S. SW19 BS52 86
Poplar Row, Epp. CN22 31
Poplars Av. NW2 BQ36 55
High Rd.
Poplars Av. Hat. BN12 10
Poplars Clo. Hat. BN12 10
Poplars Clo. Ruis. BB33 44
Poplar Shaw, Wal. Abb. CG20 22
Poplars Rd. E17 CE32 48
Poplars, The, N14 BV25 29
Poplars, The, Hem. H. AW14 8
Poplars, The, Rom. CO24 32
Poplars, The, St. Alb. BJ15 9
Poplar St. Rom. CS31 50
Poplar Walk, SE24 BZ45 67
Poplar Wk. Croy. BZ54 87
Poplar Way Ilf. CM31 49
Ashurst Drive
Poppin's Ct. EC4 BY39 56
St. Bride St.
Poppleton Rd. E11 CG32 49
Poppy Clo. Brwd. DA25 33
Porchester Clo. Horn. CW32 51
Woodlands Av.
Porchester Gdns. W2 BS40 56
Porchester Ms. W2 BS39 56
Porchester Pl. NW1 BW36 56
Agar Gro.
Porchester Pl. W2 BU39 56
Porchester Rd. W2 BS40 56
Porchester Rd. Kings-on-t. BM51 85
Porchester Sq. W2 BS40 56
Porchester Ter. W2 BT39 56
Porchester Ter. N. W2 BS40 56
Porchfield Clo. Grav. DH48 81
Porchfield Clo. Sutt. BS58 95
Hulverston Clo.
Porch Way N20 BU27 38
Porcupine Clo. SE9 CK48 78
Porden Rd. SW2 BX45 66
Porlock Av. Har. BG33 45
Porlock Rd. Enf. CA26 39
Porlock St. SE1 BZ41 67
Portal Clo. SE27 BY48 76
Portal Clo. Ruis. BC35 44
Portal Clo. Uxb. AY36 53
Port Ave. Green. DA46 80
Port Cres. E13 CH38 58
Portcullis Lo. Rd. Enf. BZ24 30
Baker St.
Portelet Rd. E1 CC38 57
Porten Rd. W14 BR41 65
Porter's Av. Dag. CO36 59
Porters Clo. Brwd. DA26 42
Greenshaw
Porter, S Wood, St. Alb. BH11 9
Porter's Rd. W2 BT39 56
Porter St. W1 BU39 56
Baker St.
Porters Way. West Dr. AY41 63
Porteus Rd. W2 BT39 56
Porthcawe Rd. SE26 CD49 77
Porthester Mead. Beck. CE50 77
Port Hill. Orp. CO59 98
Porthkerry Av. Well. CO45 69
Portinscale Rd. SW15 BR46 75
Portland Av. N16 CA33 48
Portland Av. Grav. DG48 81
Portland Av. N. Mal. BO54 85
Portland Av. Sid. CO46 79
Portland Cres. SE9 CK48 78
Portland Cres. Felt. BA49 73
Portland Cres. Grnf. BF38 54
Portland Cres. E. Stan. BK30 36
Portland Cres. W. Stan. BK30 36
Portland Dr. Red. BW68 113
Portland Gdns. N4 BY32 47
Portland Gdns. Rom. CP32 50
Portland Gro. SW8 BX44 66
Lansdowne Way
Portland Pl. W1 BV38 56
Portland Pl. Epsom BO59 94
Portland Rise N4 BY33 47
Portland Rise Est. N4 BY33 47
Portland Rd. N15 CA31 48
Portland Rd. SE9 CK48 78
Portland Rd. SE25 CB52 87
Portland Rd. W11 BR40 55
Portland Rd. Ashf. AY49 73
Portland Rd. Brom. CJ49 78
Portland Rd. Dor. BJ71 119
Portland Rd. Grav. DE46 81
Portland Rd. Grav. DG47 81
Portland Rd. Hayes BB38 53
Portland Rd. Kings. On T. BL52 85
Portland Rd. Mitch. BU51 86
Portland Rd. Sthl. BE41 64
Portland St. SE17 BZ42 67
Portland St. St. Alb. BG13 9
Portland Ter. Rich. BK45 64
Portley La. Cat. CA64 105
Portman Av. SW14 BN45 65
Portman Bldgs. NW1 BU38 56
Portman Clo. W1 BV39 56
Portman Clo. Bex. CS47 79
Portman Dr. Wdf. Grn. CJ30 40
Portman Gdns. NW9 BN30 37
Portman Ms. S. W1 BV39 56
Portman Pl. E2 CC38 57
Portman Rd. Kings. On T. BL51 85
Portman Sq. W1 BV39 56
Portman St. W1 BV40 56
Portmeadow Wk. SE2 CP41 69
Portmore Gdns. Rom. CR28 41
Portmore Park Rd. Wey. AY56 92
Portnall Dr. Vir. W. AP53 82
Portnall Rise, Vir. W. AP53 82
Portnall Rd. W9 BR38 55
Portnall Rd. Vir. W. AP53 82
Portnall's Clo. Couls. BV61 104
Portnall's Rise Couls. BV61 104
Portnalls Rd. Couls. BV62 104
Portobello Ct. W11 BR40 55
Portobello Ms. W11 BS40 56
Portobello Rd.
Portpool La. EC1 BY39 56
Portree St. E14 CF39 57
Portsdown Av. NW11 BR32 46
Portsdown La. Edg. BM28 37
Portsea Ms. W2 BU39 56
Kendal St.
Portsea Pl. W2 BU39 56
Kendal St.
Portsea Rd. Til. DH44 71
Portslade Rd. SW8 BW44 66
Portsmouth Av. Surb. BJ54 84
Portsmouth Bldgs. NW1 BU39 56
Portsmouth Rd. Cob. BB60 92
Portsmouth Rd. Cob. BD59 93
Portsmouth Rd. Esher BE58 93
Portsmouth Rd. Esher BG56 93
Portsmouth Rd. Wok. AW65 101
Portsmouth Rd. Wok. AZ62 101
Portsmouth St. WC2 BX39 56
Portugal St.
Portsoken St. E1 CA40 57
Portswood Pl. SW15 BO46 75
Danebury Av.
Portugal Gdns. Twick. BG48 74
Portugal Rd. Wok. AS61 100
Portugal St. WC2 BX39 56
Portway, E15 CG37 58
Portway Epsom. BP58 94
Portway Cres. Epsom BP58 94
Portway Gdns. SE18 CJ43 68
Post House La. Lthd. BF66 111
Post Meadow, Iver AU38 52
Post Office Alley Hamptn. BF51 84
Thames St.
Post Office App. E7 CH35 49
Post Office La. Slou. AR39 52
Postway Ms. Ilf. CL34 49
Clements Rd.
Potier St. SE1 BZ41 67
Potkiln La. Beac. AO30 34
Potten End. Berk. AT12 7
Potter Clo. Mitch. BV51 86
Potterne Clo. SW19 BQ47 75
Castlecombe Dr.
Potter St. Hill. Pnr. BC29 35
Potters Clo. Loug. CK23 31
Potter's Fields, SE1 CA40 57
Potters Gro. N. Mal. BN52 85
Potter's La. SW16 BW50 76
Potter's La. Bans. BR61 103
Potter's La. Barn. BS24 29
Potters La. Borwd. BN23 28
Potters La. Guil. AT66 109
Potters La. Wok. AT65 100
Potters Lane, Wok. AU67 109
Potter's Rd. Barn. BS24 29
Potter St. Pnr. BC30 35
Potters Way, Reig. BT72 121
Pottery La. W11 BR40 55
Portland Rd.
Pottery Rd. Bex. CS48 79
Whenman Av.
Pottery Rd. Brent. BL43 65
Pottery St. SE16 CB41 67
Wilson Gro.
Pott St. Est. E2 CB38 57
Pott St. E2 CB38 57
Bethnal Green Rd.
Pouchen End La. Hem. H. AU14 7
Pouchen Hill La. Hem. H. AU13 7
Poulcott, Stai. AS46 72
Poulett Gdns. Twick. BJ47 74
Poulett Rd. E6 CK37 58
Poulner Way, SE15 CA43 67
Poulton Av. Sutt. BT55 86
Poultry, EC2 BZ39 57
Cheapside
Pound Clo. Surb. BK54 84
Pound Clo. Wal. Abb. CG15 13
Pound Ct. Dr. Orp. CM55 88
Pound Crescent, Lthd. BG64 102
Poundfield Gdns. Wok. AU63 100
Poundfield Rd. Loug. CL25 31
Pound La. NW10 BP36 55
Pound La. Epsom BN59 94
Pound La. Sev. CP61 107
Pound La. Sev. CV65 108
Pound Park Rd. SE7 CJ42 68
Pound Pl. SE9 CL46 78
Pound Rd. Bans. BR62 103
Pound Rd. Cher. AW54 83
Pound St. Cars. BU56 95
Poundwell. Welw. G. C. BS8 5
Pounsley Rd. Sev. CT64 107
Pountney Rd. SW11 BV45 66
Poverest Rd. Orp. CN53 88
Powder Mill La. Dart. CW48 80
Powder Mill La. Twick. BE47 74
Powell Clo. Edg. BL29 37
Powell Clo. Guil. AP71 118
Powell Gdns. Dag. CR35 50
Powell Rd. E5 CB34 48
Powell Rd. Buck. H. CJ26 40
Powells Clo. Dor. BJ73 119
Powell's Wk. W4 BO43 65
Power Rd. W4 BM42 65
Powers Ct. Twick. BK47 74
Cambridge Pk.
Powerscroft Rd. E5 CC35 48
Powerscroft Rd. Sid. CP50 79
Powis Gdns. NW11 BR33 46
Powis Gdns. W11 BR39 55
Powis Ms. W11 BR39 55
Powis Pl. WC1 BX38 56
Powis Rd. E3 CE38 57
Powis Sq. W11 BR39 55
Powis St. SE18 CL41 68
Powis Ter. W11 BR39 55
Powlett Pla. NW1 BV36 56
Harmood St.
Pownall Gdns. Houns. BF45 64
Pownall Rd. E8 CA37 57
Pownall Rd. Houns. BF45 64
Powster Rd. Brom. CH49 78
Powy's Clo. Bexh. CP43 69
Powys La. N13 BX28 38
Powys La. N14 BX28 38
Poyle Rd. Guil. AS71 118
Poyle Rd. Slou. AV45 62
Poynder Rd. Til. DG44 71
Poynders Ct. SW4 BW46 76
Poynders Gdns. SW4 BW47 76
Poynders Hill, Hem. H. BA14 8
Poynder's Rd. SW4 BW46 76
Poynings Clo. Orp. CO55 89
Poynings Rd. N19 BW34 47
Poynings. The. Iver. AV42 62
Poynings Way N12 BS28 38
Poynings Way. Rom. CW30 42
Poyntell Cres. Chis. CM50 78
Poynter Rd. Enf. CA25 30
Poynton Rd. N17 CB30 39
Poyntz Rd. SW11 BU44 66
Poyser St. E2 CB37 57
Old Bethnal Grn. Rd.
Prae Clo. St. Alb. BF13 9
Praed Ms. W2 BT39 56
Norfolk Pl.
Praed St. W2 BT39 56
Pragel St. E13 CJ37 58
Pragnell Rd. SE12 CH48 78
Prague Pl. SW2 BX46 76
Prah Rd. N4 BY34 47
Prairie Clo. Wey. AW55 83
Prairie Rd. Wey. AW55 83
Prairie St. SW8 BV44 66
Pratt Ms. NW1 BW37 56
Pratt St.
Pratts La. Walt. BD56 93
Pratt St. NW1 BW37 56
Pratt Wk. SE11 BX42 66
Prayle Gro. NW2 BQ33 46
Prebend St. N1 BZ37 57
Precinct Rd. Hayes BC40 53
Premier Ave. Grays. DE41 71
Premier Pl. SW15 BQ45 65
Putney High St.
Prendergast Rd. SE3 CG45 68
Prentice Pl. Harl. CP12 14
Prentis Rd. SW16 BW49 76
Prentiss Ct. SE7 CJ42 68
Prescelly Pl. Edg. BL30 37
Prescot Rd. Slou. AV44 62
Prescot St. E1 CA40 57
Prescott Av. Orp. CL53 88
Prescott Grn. Loug. CM24 31
Prescott Rd. Wal. Cr. CD17 21
Pressland St. W10 BR39 55
Kensal Rd.
Press Rd. NW10 BN34 46
Press Rd. Uxb. AX36 53
Prestage St. E14 CF40 57
Quixley St.
Prestburg Rd. N. Mal. BO53 85
Prestbury Cres. Bans. BU61 104
Prestbury Rd. E7 CJ36 58
Prestbury Sq. SE9 CK49 78
Prestead Rd. SW11 BU45 66
St. John's Hill.
Preston Clo. SE1 CA42 67
Preston Clo. Twick. BH48 74
Preston Ct. Shep. AZ53 83
Preston Rd.
Preston Dr. E11 CJ32 49
Preston Dr. Bexh. CP44 69
Preston Dr. Epsom BO57 94
Preston Gdns. NW10 BO36 55
Preston Gdns. Enf. CD22 30
Preston Gdns. Ilf. CK32 49
Preston Gro. Ash. BK62 102
Preston Hill. Chesh. AO18 16
Preston Hill. Har. BL32 46
Preston La. Tad. BQ63 103
Preston Pk. N3 BR30 37
Preston Pl. NW2 BP36 55
Belton Rd.
Preston Pl. NW6 BP36 55
Preston Pl. Rich. BL46 75
Preston Rd. E4 CF29 39
Preston Rd. E11 CG32 49
Preston Rd. E15 CF37 57
Preston Rd. SE19 BY50 76
Preston Rd. SW20 BO50 75
Preston Rd. W10 BQ40 55
Preston Rd. Grav. DF47 81
Preston Rd. Har. BL33 46
Preston Rd. Rom. CV28 42
Preston Rd. Shep. AZ53 83
Preston Rd. Slou. AR40 52
Preston's Rd. E14 CF40 57
Preston Waye, Har. BL33 46
Prestwick Clo. Sthl. BE42 64
Prestwick Rd. Wat. BC28 35
Prestwood, Slou. AQ39 52
Prestwood Av. Har. BJ31 45
Prestwood Clo. Har. BJ31 45
Prestwood Dr. Rom. CS28 41
Prestwood St. N1 BZ37 57
Wenlock Rd.
Pretoria Av. E17 CD31 48
Pretoria Clo. N17 CA29 39
Pretoria Cres. E4 CF26 39
Pretoria Rd. E4 CF26 39
Pretoria Rd. E11 CF33 48
Pretoria Rd. E16 CG38 58
Pretoria Rd. SW16 BV50 76
Pretoria Rd. Cher. AV54 82
Pretoria Rd. Ilf. CL35 49
Pretoria Rd. Rom. CS31 50
Pretoria Rd. Wat. BC24 26
Pretoria Rd. N. N18 CA29 39
Prey Heath Clo. Wok. AR65 100
Prey Heath Rd. Wok. AQ65 100
Preyost Rd. N11 BV27 38
Price Clo. NW7 BR29 37
Price Clo. SW17 BU48 76
Price Rd. Croy. BY56 95
Price's La. Reig. BS72 121
Prices St. SE1 BY40 56
Pricklers Hill Barn. BS25 29
Prickley Wd. Brom. CG54 88
Prideaux Pl. WC1 BX38 56
Prideaux Rd. SW9 BX45 66
Pridham Rd. E. Th. Hth. BZ52 87
Pridham Rd. W. Th. Hth. BZ52 87
Priestfield Rd. SE23 CD48 77
Priest Hill, Egh. & Wind. AR48 72
Priestlands Pk. Rd. Sid. CN48 78
Priestley Gdns. Rom. CO32 50
Priestley Rd. Mitch. BV51 86
Priestley Way, E17 CC31 48
Priestley Way NW2 BP33 46
Priests Av. Rom. CS30 41
Priests Ct. EC2 BZ39 57
Foster La.
Priest, S Fld. Brwd. DE28 122
Priest, S La. Brwd. DC26 122
Priest Wk. Grav. DK48 81
Prima Rd. SW9 BY43 66
Primley Lane, Bish. CS6 6
Primrose Av. Enf. BZ23 30
Primrose Av. Rom. CO33 50
Primrose Cl. Hat. BP13 10
Primrose Clo. E18 CH30 40
Primrose Clo. Har. BE34 45
Primrose Ct. E15 CF36 57
Angel La.
Primrose Field. Harl. CN12 13
Primrose Gdns. NW3 BU36 56
Primrose Gdns. Bush. BF26 36
Primrose Gdns. Ruis. BD35 45
Primrose Glen. Horn. CW31 51
Primrose Hill, EC4 BY39 56
Primrose Hill, Brwd. DB27 42
Primrose Hill, Kings L. AZ17 17
Primrose Hill Orp. CN58 97
Primrose Hl. Ct. NW3 BU36 56
Primrose Hl. Rd. NW3 BU36 56
Primrose La. Maid. AG43 61
Primrose Path, Wal. Cr. CB19 21
Primrose Rd. E10 CE33 48
Primrose Rd. E18 CH30 40
Primrose Rd. Walt. BD56 93
Primrose St. EC2 CA39 57
Primrose Way, Wem. BK37 54
Primula St. W12 BP39 55
Prince Albert Sq. Red. BU73 121
Prince Alberts Rd. Wind. AP43 62
Prince Alberts Wk. Wind. AP43 62
Prince Arthur Ms. NW3 BT35 47
Perrins La.
Prince Arthur Rd. NW3 BT35 47
Prince Charles Rd. SE3 CG44 68
Prince Consort Dr. Chis. CM51 88
Prince Consort Rd. SW7 BT41 66
Princedale Rd. W11 BR40 55
Prince Edward Rd. E9 CD36 57
Prince Edward St. Berk. AR13 7
Prince George Av. N14 BW24 29
Prince George Rd. N16 CA35 48
Prince George Rd. SW19 BT51 86
Prince Georges Av. SW20 BQ51 85
Prince Henry Rd. SE7 CJ43 68
Prince Imperial Rd. Chis. CL50 78
Prince Imperial Way SE18 CL43 68
Prince John Rd. SE9 CK46 78
Princelet St. E1 CA39 57
Prince Of Wales Cres. NW1 BV36 56
Prince Of Wales Dr. SW11 BU44 66
Prince Of Wales Rd. E16 CJ39 58
Prince Of Wales Rd. NW4 BP31 46
Prince Of Wales Rd. NW5 BV36 56
Prince Of Wales Rd. SE3 CG44 68
Prince Of Wales Rd. Red. BY74 121
Prince Of Wales Rd. Sutt. BT55 86
Prince Of Wales Ter. W4 BO42 65
Devonshire Rd.
Prince Of Wales Ter. W8 BS41 66
Prince Pk. Hem. H. AW14 8
Prince Philip Ave. Grays. DD40 71
Prince Regent Rd. Houns. BG45 64
Prince Rd. SE25 CA53 87
Prince Rupert Rd. SE9 CK45 68
Princes Ave. Dart. CX47 80
Prince's Av. N10 BV31 47
Princes Av. N13 BY28 38
Prince's Av. N22 BW30 38
Princes Av. NW9 BM31 46
Princes Av. W3 BM41 65
Princes Av. Cars. BU57 95
Princes Av. Enf. CD21 30
Princes Av. Grnf. BF39 54
Princes Av. Orp. CN53 88
Princes Av. Sth. Croy. CB61 105
Princes Av. Surb. BM54 85
Prince's Av. Wat. BB25 26
Princes Av. Wdf. Grn. CH28 40
Princes Clo. NW9 BM31 46
Princes Clo. Berk. AQ12 7
Princes Clo. Edg. BM28 37
Princes Clo. Epp. CS16 23
Princes Clo. Sid. CP48 79
Princes Clo. Tedd. BG49 74
Princes Ct. Wem. BL35 46
Prince's Dr. Har. BH31 45
Princes Dr. Lthd. BH59 93
Princesfield Rd. Wal. Abb. CH20 22
Princes Gdns. SW7 BT41 66
Princes Gdns. W3 BM39 55
Princes Gdns. W5 BK38 54
Princes Gte. SW7 BU41 66
Princes Gte. Ct. SW7 BT41 66
Exhibition Rd.
Princes Gte. Ms. SW7 BT41 66
Princes La. N10 BV31 47
Prince's Ms. SW7 BT42 66
Princes Ms. W2 BS40 56
Prince, S Rd. Rom. CW23 33
Princes Pk. Rain. CU36 59
Princes Pk. Av. NW11 BR32 46
Princes Park Av. Hayes BA40 53
Princes Park Cir. Hayes BA40 53
Princes Park Clo. Hayes BA40 53
Princes Pk. La. Hayes BA40 53
Princes Park Par. Hayes BA40 53
Princes Pl. W11 BR40 55
Prince's Plain Brom. CK54 88
Princes Rise, SE13 CF44 67
Princes Rd. N18 CC28 39
Princes Rd. SE20 CC50 77
Princes Rd. SW14 BN45 65
Prince's Rd. SW19 BS50 76
Princes Rd. W13 BJ40 54
Mattock La.
Princes Rd. Ashf. AY49 73
Princes Rd. Buck. H. CJ27 40
Princes Rd. Dart. CU46 79
Princes Rd. Dart. CY47 80
Princes Rd. Felt. BB48 73
Princes Rd. Grav. DG49 81
Prince's Rd. Ilf. CM31 49
Princes Rd. Kew. BL44 65
Prince's Rd. Kings. On T. BM51 85
Prince's Rd. Red. BU71 121
Princes Rd. Rich. BL46 75
Princes Rd. Rom. CU32 50
Princes Rd. Tedd. BG49 74
Prince's Rd. Wey. AZ56 92
Princess Ave. Wind. AN45 61
Princess Av. N3 BS30 38
Princess Av. Wem. BL34 46
Carlton Av.E.
Princess Cres. N4 BY34 47
Princess Gdns. Wok. AT61 100
Princess Margaret Rd. S. Le H. DK41 71
Princess May Rd. N16 CA35 48
Princess Mews NW3 BT35 47
Princess Pde. Dag. CR37 59
Whitebarn La.
Princess Pde. Orp. CL55 88
Princes Sq. W2 BS40 56
Princess Rd. NW1 BV37 56
Princess Rd. NW6 BS37 56
Princess Rd. Croy. BZ53 87
Princess Rd. Swan. CU50 79
Princess Rd. Wok. AT61 100
Princess St. SE1 BY41 66
Princes St. EC2 BZ39 57
Princes St. N17 CA29 39
Queen St.
Prince's St. W1 BV39 56
Princes St. Bexh. CQ45 69
Princes St. Grav. DG46 81
Princes St. Rich. BL46 75
Princes St. Sutt. BT56 95
Princes Ter. E13 CH37 58
Princes Ter. W3 BN41 65
Church Rd.
Prince St. SE8 CD43 67
Prince St. Wat. BD24 27
Princes Vw. Dart. CX47 80
Princes Way, SW19 BQ47 75
Princes Way. Brwd. DD27 122
Prince's Way Buck. H. CJ27 40
Princes Way Croy. BX57 95
Princes Way Ruis. BE35 45
Princes Way W. Wick. CG56 97
Princethorpe Rd. SE26 CC49 77
Princeton St. WC1 BX39 56
Pringle Gdns. SW16 BW49 76
Printer St. EC4 BY39 56
Gough Sq.
Printing House La. Hayes. BB41 63
Printing House Yd. E2 CA38 57
Hackney Rd.
Priolo Rd. SE7 CJ42 68
Prior Av. Sutt. BT57 95
Prior Boulton St. N1 BY36 56
Compton Rd.
Prioress St. SE1 BZ41 67
Prior Gro. Chesh. AO18 16

Priors Croft E17 CD30 39
Priors Cft. Wok. AT64 100
Priors Field Nthlt. BD36 54
Priorsford Av. Orp. CO52 89
Priors Gdns. Ruis. BD35 45
Priors Mead, Enf. CA23 30
Priors Mead. Lthd. BF66 111
Priors Pk. Horn. CV34 51
Priors, The Ash. BK63 102
Prior St. SE10 CF43 67
Priory Av. E4 CD27 39
Priory Av. E17 CE32 48
Priory Av. N8 BW31 47
Priory Av. W4 BO42 65
Priory Av. Harl. CP8 6
Priory Av. Orp. CM53 88
Priory Av. Sutt. BQ56 94
Priory Av. Uxb. AX31 44
Priory Av. Wem. BH35 45
Priory Br. SW14 BO45 65
Priory Clo. E4 CD27 39
Priory Clo. E18 CH30 40
Priory Clo. N14 BW25 29
Priory Clo. N20 BR26 37
Priory Clo. Beck. CD52 87
Priory Clo. Brox. CD15 12
Priory Clo. Brwd. DA25 33
Priory Clo. Chis. CK51 88
Priory Clo. Dart. CV46 80
Priory Clo. Hamptn. BE51 84
Priory Clo. Hodd. CE12 12
Priory Clo. Ruis. BB33 44
Priory Clo. Stan. BH27 36
Priory Clo. Sun. BC50 73
Priory Clo. Uxb. AW34 44
Priory Clo. Uxb. AX31 44
Priory Clo. Wem. BH35 45
Priory Clo. Wok. AU60 91
Priory Cotts. Uxb. AX31 44
Priory Ct. E17 CD30 39
Priory Ct. SW8 BW44 66
Priory Ct. St. Alb. BH14 9
Old London Rd.
Priory Ct. Est. E17 CD30 39
Priory Cres. SE19 BZ50 77
Priory Cres. Sutt. BQ56 94
Priory Cres. Wem. BJ34 45
Priory Dr. SE2 CP42 69
Priory Dr. Reig. BS71 121
Priory Dr. Stan. BH27 36
Priory Gdns. N6 BV32 47
Priory Gdns. N8 BW31 47
Priory Gdns. SW13 BO45 65
Priory Gdns. W5 BL38 55
Priory Gdns. Berk. AR13 7
Priory Gdns. Dart. CV46 80
Priory Gdns. Hamptn. BE50 74
Priory Gdns. Uxb. AX31 44
Priory Gdns. Walt. BC55 83
Priory Gdns. Wem. BJ35 45
Priory Grn. Stai. AW49 73
Priory Green Est. N1 BX37 56
Priory Gro. SW8 BX44 66
Priory Gro. Rom. CW27 42
Priory Hill. Dart. CV46 80
Priory Hill Wem. BJ35 45
Priory La. SW15 BO46 75
Priory La. E. Mol. BF52 84
Priory La. Farn. CW54 90
Priory Mead Brwd. DB21 33
Priory Ms. SW8 BW44 66
Priory Pde. Wem. BH35 45
Priory Pk. SE3 CG45 68
Priory Pk. Rd. NW6 BR37 55
Priory Pk. Rd. Wem. BJ35 45
Priory Path. Rom. CW27 42
Priory Pl. SW15 BO45 65
Upr. Richmond Rd.
Priory Pl. Dart. CV46 80
Priory Rd. E6 CJ37 58
Priory Rd. N8 BW31 47
Priory Rd. NW6 BS37 56
Priory Rd. SW19 BT50 76
Priory Rd. W4 BN41 65
Priory Rd. Bark. CM36 58
Priory Rd. Chess. BL55 85
Priory Rd. Croy. BY54 86
Priory Rd. Dart. CV45 70
Priory Rd. Dart. CV46 80
Priory Rd. Ger. Cr. AR31 43
Priory Rd. Hamptn. BE50 74
Priory Rd. Houns. BG46 74
Priory Rd. Loug. CK24 31
Priory Rd. Reig. BS71 121
Priory Rd. Rich. BM43 65
Priory Rd. Rom. CW27 42
Priory Rd. Sutt. BQ56 94
Priory St. E3 CE38 57
Bromley High St.
Priory Ter. NW6 BS37 56
Priory Ter. Sun. BC50 73
Priory, The, SE3 CG45 68
Priory, The. Gdse. CB69 114
Priory Vw. Bush. BH26 36
Priory Wk. SW10 BT42 66
Priory Wk. St. Alb. BH15 9
Priory Way Har. BF31 45
Priory Way. Slou. AQ43 62
Priory Way Sthl. BD41 64
Priscilla Rd. E3 CE38 57
Pritchards Rd. E2 CB37 57
Priter Rd. SE16 CB41 67
St. James's Rd.
Priter Way. SE16 CB41 67
Private Rd. Enf. BZ25 30
Private Rd. Grav. DD47 81
Private Rd. S. Ock. CX41 70
Private Rd. Wal. Cr. BZ19 21
Priyor Clo. Wat. BB19 17
Probert Rd. SW2 BY45 66
Probyn Rd. SW2 BY48 76
Procter Gdns. Lthd. BF66 111
Procter St. WC1 BX39 56
High Holborn
Profumo Rd. Walt. BD56 93
Progress Way N22 BY30 38
Progress Way Croy. BX55 86
Progress Way Enf. CB25 30
Promenade Approach Rd. W4 BO43 65
Promenade De Verdun Pur. BW59 95
Promenade, The, W4 BO44 65
Prospect Clo. SE10 CF44 67
Point Hill
Prospect Clo. SE26 CB49 77
Wells Park Rd.
Prospect Clo. Belv. CR42 69
Prospect Clo. Houns. BE43 64
Prospect Clo. Ruis. BD33 45
Prospect Cotts. SW18 BS45 66
Point Pleasant
Prospect Cres Twick. BG46 74
Prospect Gro. Grav. DH47 81
Prospect Hill, E17 CE31 48
Prospect La. Egh. AQ49 72
Prospect Pla. Brom. CH52 88
Prospect Pl. N2 BT31 47
Prospect Pl. N17 CA29 39
Prospect Pl. NW2 BR34 46
Prospect Rd.
Prospect Pl. Epsom BO60 94
Prospect Pl. Grav. DH47 81
Prospect Pl. Grays. DD43 71
Prospect Pl. Rom. CS30 41
Prospect Pl. Stai. AV49 72
Prospect Ring N2 BT31 47
Prospect Rd. E17 CD32 48
Prospect Rd. NW2 BR34 46
Prospect Rd. SE26 CB49 77
Prospect Rd. Barn. BS24 29
Prospect Rd. Horn. CW31 51
Prospect Rd. St. Alb. BG14 9
Prospect Rd. Sev. CV65 108
Prospect Rd. Surb. BK53 84
Prospect Rd. Wdf. Grn. CJ29 40
Prospect Val. SE18 CK42 68
Prospect Wk. E2 CC38 57
Prospero Rd. N19 BW33 47
Protheroe Rd. SW6 BR43 65
Prothero Gdns. NW4 BP32 46
Prout Gro. NW10 BO35 46
Prout Rd. E5 CB34 48
Providence Ct. W1 BV40 56
Providence La. Hayes. BA43 63
Providence Pl. Epsom BO59 94
Providence Rd. West Dr. AY40 53
Providence Ter. Reig. BS70 121
Provost Dwellings N1 BZ37 57
Provost Rd. NW3 BU36 56
Provost St. N1 BZ37 57
Prowse Av. Bush. BG27 36
Prowse Pl. NW1 BW36 56
Bonny St.
Pruden Clo. N14 BW27 38
Prune Hill, Egh. AR50 72
Prusom St. E1 CB40 57
Pryors, The, NW3 BT34 47
Puck La. Wal. Abb. CF18 21
Pudding La. EC3 BZ40 57
Pudding La. Chig. CN26 40
Pudding La. Hem. H. AW12 8
Pudding La. Sev. CX64 108
Church Rd.
Pudding Mill La. E15 CE37 57
Puddledock EC4 BY40 56
Upper Thames St.
Puddledock La. Dart. CT49 79
Puers La. Beac. AP29 34
Pulborough Rd. SW18 BR47 75
Pulborough Way Houns. BD45 64
Pulford Rd. N15 BZ32 48
Pulham Av. N2 BT31 47
Puller Rd. Barn. BR23 28
Puller Rd. Hem. H. AW14 8
Pulleyns Av. E6 CK38 58
Pulleys Clo. Hem. H. AV13 7
Pulleys La. Hem. H. AV12 7
Pullman Ct. SW2 BX47 76
Pullman Gdns. SW15 BQ46 75
Pulross Rd. SW9 BX45 66
Pulteney Clo. E3 CD37 57
Pulteney Rd. E18 CH31 49
Pulteney Ter. N1 BX37 56
Pulton Rd. SW6 BS43 66
Puma Ct. E1 CA39 57
Commercial St.
Pump All. Brent. BK43 64
High St.
Pump Hill Loug. CK23 31
Pumping Station Rd. W4 BO43 65
Pump La. Chesh. AP20 16
Pump La. Epp. CL15 13
Pump La. Hayes. BB41 63
Pump La. Orp. CR56 98
Pump Pail N. Croy. BZ55 87
Pump Pail S. Croy. BZ55 87
Punchbowl La. Dor. BK71 119
Punch Bowl La. Hem. H. & St. Alb. BA12 8
Pundersons Gdns. E2 CB38 57
Purbeck Av. N. Mal. BO53 85
Purbeck Dri. Wok. AS60 91
Purbeck Dr. NW2 BQ34 46
Purbeck Rd. Horn. CU33 50
Purberry Gro. Epsom BO58 94
Purbrock Av. Wat. BD21 27
Purbrook Clo. Red. BW67 113
Purbrook Est. SE1 CA41 67
Purbrook St. SE1 CA41 67
Purcell Cres. SW6 BR43 65
Purcell Rd. Grnf. BF39 54
Purcells Av. Edg. BM28 37
Purcells Clo. Ash. BL62 103
Purcell St. N1 CA37 57
Purcer's Cross Rd. SW6 BR44 65
Purcers Rd. SW6 BR45 65
Purchese St. NW1 BW37 56
Purdy St. E3 CE38 57
Purex Rd. Grnf. BG37 54
Purfleet Art Rd. S. Ock. CX41 70
Purfleet By-pass CX42 70
Purfleet Rd. S. Ock. CX41 70
Purford Grn. Harl. CO11 14
Purland Clo. Dag. CQ33 50
Purland Rd. SE28 CN41 68
Purleigh Av. Wdf. Grn. CK29 40
Purley Av. NW2 BR34 46
Purley Bury Av. Pur. BZ59 96
Purley Bury Clo. Pur. BZ59 96
Purley Clo. Ilf. CL30 40
Purley Ct. Pur. BY58 95
Purley Downs Rd. Pur. BZ58 96
Purley Hill Pur. BY59 95
Purley Knoll Pur. BX59 95
Purley Oaks Rd. Sth. Croy. BZ58 96
Purley Pk. Rd. Pur. BY58 95
Purley Pl. N1 BY36 56
Islington Pk. St.
Purley Rise Pur. BX59 95
Purley Rd. N9 BZ27 39
Purley Rd. Pur. BY59 95
Purley Rd. Sth. Croy. BZ57 96
Purley Vale Pur. BY60 95
Purley Way Croy. BX54 86
Purlieu Way, Epp. CN21 31
Purlings Rd. Bush. BF25 27
Purney's Rd. SE9 CJ45 68
Purrett Rd. SE18 CN42 68
Pursley Rd. NW7 BP29 37
Purves Rd. NW10 BQ37 55
Putney Br. App. SW6 BR45 65
Putney Hth. SW15 BP47 75
Putney Hth. La. SW15 BQ46 75
Putney High St. SW15 BQ45 65
Putney Hl. SW15 BQ46 75
Putney Pk. Av. SW15 BP45 65
Putney Pk. La. SW15 BP45 65
Putney Rd. Enf. CC21 30
Puttenham Clo. Wat. BD27 36
Putters Cft. Hem. H. AY11 8
Puttocks Cl. Hat. BQ15 10
Puttocks Dr. Hat. BQ15 10
Pyecombe Cor. N12 BR28 37
Pyenest Rd. Harl. CL12 13
Pyghtle, The, Uxb. AW33 44
Pykhill. Grays. DG41 71
Pylbrook Rd. Sutt. BS55 86
Pyle Hill, Guil. AS66 109
Pyle Hill, Wok. AR65 100
Pym Clo. Barn. BT25 29
Pymers Mead, SE21 BZ47 77
Pymme's Clo. N13 BX28 38
Pymmes Gdns. N. N9 CA27 39
Pymmes Gdns. S. N9 CA27 39
Pymmes Grn. Rd. N11 BV27 38
Pymmes Rd. N13 BX29 38
Pymms Gdns. Barn. BU24 29
Pym Pl. Grays. DD42 71
Pynchester Clo. Uxb. AZ34 44
Pyne Rd. Surb. BM54 85
Pynestgreen Grn. Wal. Abb. CH22 31
Pynham Clo. SE2 CO41 69
Pynnacles Clo. Stan. BJ28 36
Pypers Hatch. Harl. CN11 13
Pyrcroft Rd. Cher. AV54 82
Pyrford Common Rd. Wok. AU61 100
Pyrford Heath, Wok. AV61 100
Pyrford Rd. Wey. AW60 92
Pyrford Rd. Wok. AW61 101
Pyrford Woods Clo. Wok. AV61 100
Pyrford Woods Rd. Wok. AV61 100
Pyrland Rd. N5 BZ35 48
Pyrland Rd. Rich. BL46 75
Pyrles Grn. Loug. CL23 31
Pyrles La. Loug. CL23 31
Pyrmont Gro. SE27 BY48 76
Pyrmont Rd. W4 BM43 65
Pyrmont Rd. Ilf. CM34 49
Pytchley Cres. SE19 BZ50 77
Pytchley Rd. SE22 CA46 67
Quadrangle, The Guil. AQ71 118
Quadrangle, The, Welw. G. C. BQ7 5
Quadrant Arc. Rom. CT32 50
Quadrant Clo. NW4 BP32 46
Quadrant Gro. NW5 BU35 47
Quadrant Rd. N1 BZ36 57
Essex Rd.
Quadrant Rd. Rich. BK45 64
Quadrant Rd. Th. Hth. BY52 86
Quadrant, The, SE24 BZ46 77
Quadrant, The, SW20 BR51 85
Quadrant, The, Bexh. CP43 69
Quadrant, The, Grays CY42 70
Quadrant, The, Rich. BK46 74
Quadrant, The, St. Alb. BJ12 9
Quadrant, The, Wey. AZ56 92
Quaggy Wk. SE3 CH45 68
Quainton St. NW10 BN34 46
Quaker Clo. Sev. CV65 108
Quaker La. Islw. BJ44 64
Quaker La. Wal. Abb. CF20 21
Quakers Clo. Hart. DC52 90
Quakers Course NW9 BO30 37
Quaker's Hall La. Sev. CV64 108
Quakers La. Pot. B. BS18 20
Quaker St. E1 CA38 57
Quaker's Wk. N21 BZ25 30
Quality Ct. WC2 BY39 56
Chancery La.
Quality St. Red. BV67 113
Quantock Clo. Hayes. BA43 63
Quantock Clo. Slou. AT42 62
Quantock Gdns. NW2 BQ34 46
Quantock Rd. Bexh. CT44 69
Quantocks Hem. H. AY12 8
Malvern Way
Quarles Clo. Rom. CR29 41
Quarley Way SE15 CA43 67
Quarrendon Rd. Amer. AO23 25
Quarrendon St. SW6 BS44 66
Quarr Rd. Cars. BT53 86
Quarry, Guil. AR71 118
Quarry Clo. Couls. BX57 95
Quarry Clo. Couls. BX61 104
Quarry Clo. Oxt. CG68 115
Quarry Hill. Grays. DD42 71
Quarry Hill. Sev. CV65 108
Quarry Pk. Rd. Sutt. BR57 94
Quarry Rise Sutt. BR57 94
Quarry Rd. SW18 BT46 76
Quarry Rd. Oxt. CG68 115
Quarry Spring. Harl. CO11 14
Quartermaine Av. Wok. AS64 100
Quartermass Clo. Hem. H. AW13 8
Quartermass Rd. Hem. H. AW13 8
Quarter Mile La. E10 CE35 48
Quaves Rd. Slou. AQ41 62
Quebec Ave. West. CM66 115
Quebec Ms. W1 BU39 56
Quebec Rd. Hayes. BD39 54
Quebec Rd. Ilf. CL33 49
Quebec Rd. Til. DG44 71
Quebec Sq. West. CM66 115
Queen Adelaide Rd. SE20 CC50 77
Queen Alexandra's Ct. SW10 BR49 75
Queen Ann Clo. Esher BH58 93
Queen Anne Av. Brom. CG52 88
Queen Anne Gdns. Mitch. BU52 86
Qn. Anne Rd. E9 CD36 57
Queen Anne's Clo. Twick. BG48 74
Queen Annes Gdns. W5 BL41 65
Queen Anne's Gdns. Enf. CA25 30
Queen Anne's Gate, SW1 BW41 66
Queen Annes Gro. W4 BO41 65
Bedford Rd.
Queen Annes Gro. W5 BL41 65
Queen Anne's Gro. Enf. BZ26 39
Queen Anne's Pl. Enf. CA25 30
Queen Anne's Rd. Wind. AO45 61
Queen Anne St. W1 BV39 56
Queen Ann Gate Bexh. CP45 69
Regency Way
Queen Ann Ms. W1 BV39 56
Chandos St.
Queen Anns Gdns. Lthd. BJ64 102
Up. Fairfield Rd.
Queen Anns Ter. Lthd. BJ64 102
Up. Fairfield Rd.
Queenborough Gdns. Ilf. CL31 49
Queenbury Clo. Rick. AU24 25
Queen Caroline Est. W6 BQ42 65
Queen Caroline St. W6 BQ42 65
Queen Clo. Wey. BB57 92
Queen Eleanor Clo. Ash. BL63 103
Queen Eleanor's Rd. Guil. AP71 118
Queen Elizabeth Clo. N16 BZ34 48
Queen Elizabeth Rd. E17 CD31 48
Qn. Elizabeth Rd. Kings. On T. BL51 85
Queen Elizabeth's Dr. N14 BW26 38
Queen Elizabeth's Dr. Croy. CF58 96
Qn. Elizabeths Gdns Croy. CF58 96
Qn. Elizabeths Dr.
Queen Elizabeth St. SE1 CA41 67
Queen Elizabeth Wk. N16 BZ33 48
Queen Elizabeth Wk. Wall. BW56 95
Queen Elizabeth Way, Wok. AS63 100
Queenhill Rd. Sth. Croy. CB58 96
Queenhithe, EC4 BZ40 57
Queen Margaret's Gro. N1 CA35 48
Queen Mary Av. Mord. BQ53 85
Queen Mary Av. Wat. BB24 26
Queen Mary Clo. Wok. AU61 100
Queen Mary Rd. SE19 BY50 76
Queen Mary Rd. Shep. BA51 83
Queen Mary's Av. Cars. BU57 95
Queen Marys Dri. Wey. AV58 91
Queens Acre Sutt. BQ57 94
Queen St. Pl. EC4 BZ40 57
Queens Alley Epp. CN19 22
Hemnall St.
Queen's Av. N3 BT29 38
Queen's Av. N10 BV31 47
Queen's Av. N20 BT27 38
Queen's Av. N21 BY26 38
Queen's Av. Felt. BD49 74
Queens Av. Grnf. BF39 54
Queens Av. Stan. BK31 45
Queen's Av. Wat. BB24 26
Queen's Av. Wdf. Grn. CH28 40
Queens Av. Wey. AX59 92
Queensberry Ms. W. SW7 BT42 66
Queen's Gte.
Queensberry Pl. SW7 BT42 66
Queensberry Way SW7 BT42 66
Harrington Rd.
Queensborough Ct. N3 BR31 46
N. Circular Rd.
Queensborough Pass. W2 BT40 56
Queensborough Ter.
Queensborough Ter. W2 BT40 56
Queensbridge Ms. Islw. BH46 74
Queensbridge Pk. Islw. BH46 74
Queensbridge Rd. E2 CA36 57
Queensbridge Rd. E8 CA36 57
Queensbury Pl. Rich. BK46 74
Retreat Rd.
Queensbury Rd. NW9 BN33 46
Queensbury Rd. Wem. BL37 55
Queensbury Sta. Par. Edg. BL31 46
Queensbury St. N1 BZ36 57
Morton Rd.
Queen's Cir. SW11 BV43 66
Queens Clo. Dg. BM28 37
Queens Clo. Tad. BP66 112
Queens Clo. Wind. AQ46 72
Queen's Club Gdns. W14 BR43 65
Queens Ct. NW11 BR32 46
Queens Ct. SE23 CC48 77
Queens Ct. W5 BK39 54
Queen's Wk.
Queen's Ct. Rich. BL46 75
Queens Ct. St. Alb. BJ13 9
Queens Ct. Wem. BL35 46
Queen's Cres. NW5 BV36 56
Queen's Cres. Rich. BL46 75
Queens Cres. St. Alb. BJ12 9
Queenscroft Rd. SE9 CJ46 78
Queensdale Cres. W11 BQ40 55
Queensdale Pl. W11 BR40 55
Queensdale Rd. W11 BQ40 55
Queensdale Wk. W11 BR40 55
Queensdown Rd. E5 CB35 48
Queens Dri. Rick. AV25 25
Queens Dr. E10 CE33 48
Queen's Dr. N4 BY34 47
Queens Dr. W3 BL39 55
Queens Dr. Guil. AQ69 118
Queens Dr. Lthd. BG59 93
Queen's Dr. Slou. AS37 52
Queen's Dr. Surb. BJ54 84
Queen's Dr. Surb. BM54 85
Queens Dr. Wal. Cr. CE20 21
Queens Dr. Wat. BB19 17
Queen's Elm Sq. SW3 BT42 66
Queen's Gdns. NW4 BQ32 46
Queen's Gdns. W2 BT40 56
Queens Gdns. W5 BK38 54
Queens Gdns. Dart. CX47 80
Queens Gdns. Houns. BE43 64
Queens Gdns. Rain. CS37 59
Queens Gdns. Upmin. CZ32 51
Queen's Gte. SW7 BT41 66
Queen's Gte. Gdns. SW7 BT41 66
Queens Gate Gdns. SW15 BR46 75
Queensgate Gdns. Chis. CM51 88
Prince Consort Dr.
Queen's Gte. Ms. SW7 BT41 66
Queen's Gte Pl. SW7 BT41 66
Queen's Gte. Pl. Ms. SW7 BT41 66
Queen's Gte. Ter. SW7 BT41 66
Queen's Gro. NW8 BT37 56
Queens Gro. Rd. E4 CF26 39
Queens Hd. Wk. Brox. CD15 12
High Rd.
Queens Head St. N1 BY37 56
Raleigh St.
Queen's Ho. Tedd. BH50 74
Queensland Av. N18 BZ29 39
Queensland Av. SW19 BS51 86
Queensland Pl. N7 BY35 47
Queensland Rd.
Queensland Rd. N7 BY35 47
Queens La. Ashf. AY49 73
Clarendon Rd.
Queens Mans. NW4 BP32 46
Queen's Mkt. E13 CJ37 58
Queensmead, NW8 BT37 56
Queensmead Av. Epsom BP58 94
Queens Mead Rd. Brom. CG51 88
Queensmere Clo. SW19 BQ48 75
Queensmere Rd. SW19 BQ48 75
Queen's Ms. W2 BS40 56
Salem Rd.
Queensmill Rd. SW6 BQ43 65
Queen, S Rd. Brwd. DB27 42
Queens Pde. Clo. N12 BU28 38
Hollyfield Av.
Queens Pk. Ct. W10 BQ38 55
Queen's Pk. Gdns. Felt. BC48 73
Queens Park Rd. Cat. CA65 105
Queens Pk. Rd. Rom. CW30 42
Queen's Pl. Mord. BS52 86
Queen's Pl. Wat. BD24 27
Queen's Place, Watt. BB56 92
Queens Prom. Kings-on-t. BK52 84
Queen Sq. WC1 BX38 56
Queen's Ride SW13 BP45 65
Queen's Rise, Rich. BL46 75
Queen's Rd. E11 CF33 48
Queen's Rd. E13 CH37 58
Queen's Rd. E17 CD32 48
Queen's Rd. N3 BT30 38
Queens Rd. N9 CB27 39
Queen's Rd. N11 BX29 38
Queen's Rd. NW4 BQ32 46
Queen's Rd. SW14 BN45 65
Queen's Rd. SW19 BR50 75
Queens Rd. W5 BL39 55
Queen's Rd. Bark. CM36 58
Queens Rd. Barn. BQ24 28
Queen's Rd. Beck. CD51 87
Queens Rd. Berk. AQ12 7
Queen's Rd. Brom. CH51 88
Queen's Rd. Buck. H. CH27 40
Queens Rd. Chis. CL50 78
Queen's Rd. Croy. BY53 86
Queens Rd. Egh. AS49 72

Queen's Rd. Enf. CA24 30
Queens Rd Epp. CR16 23
Queen's Rd. Erith CT43 69
Queens Rd. Felt. BC47 73
Queens Rd. Grav. DH48 81
Queens Rd. Guil. AR70 118
Queens Rd. Hayes BB39 53
Queen's Rd. Hmptn. BF49 74
Queen's Rd. Houns. BF45 64
Queens Rd. Ilf. CM34 49
Queen's Rd. Kings. On T. BM50 75
Queen's Rd. Loug. CK24 31
Queen's Rd. Mord. BS52 86
Queens Rd. N. Mal. BO52 85
Queens Rd. Rich. BL47 75
Queens Rd. Slou. AP40 52
Queens Rd. Slou. AQ44 62
Queen's Rd. Sthl. BE41 64
Queens Rd. Surb. BH53 84
Queens Rd. Sutt. BS59 95
Queen's Rd. Tedd. BH50 74
Queen's Rd. Twick. BJ47 74
Queens Rd. Uxb. AX38 53
Queens Rd. Wal. Cr. CD20 21
Queen's Rd. Wall. BV56 95
Queen's Rd. Wat. BD23 27
Queens Rd. Watt. BB56 92
Queen's Rd. Well. CO44 69
Queens Rd. West Dr. AY41 63
Queens Rd. Wey. AZ56 92
Queens Rd. Wind. AM42 61
Queens Rd. Wind. AO44 61
Queens Rd. Wok. AO62 100
Queen's Rd. W. E13 CH37 58
Queen's Row SE17 BZ43 67
Queen's Sq., The, Hem. H. AY13 8
Queen's Ter. E13 CH37 58
Queen's Ter. NW8 BT37 56
Queen's Ter. Islw. BJ45 64
Queen's Ter. Wind. AO45 61
Queens. The. Dr. Rick. AV26 34
Queensthorpe Rd. SE26 CC49 77
Queenstown Gdns. Rain. CT38 59
Queenstown Rd. SW8 BV45 66
Queen St. EC4 BZ40 57
Queen St. N17 CA29 39
Queen St. Bexh. CQ45 69
Queen St. Brwd. DB28 42
Queen St. Cher. AW54 83
Queen St. Croy. BZ55 87
Queen St. Erith CT43 69
Queen St. Grav. DG46 81
Queen St. Kings L. AW19 17
Queen St. Mayfair. W1 BV40 56
Queen Street. Ong. LZ14 15
Queen St. Rom. CS32 50
Queen St. St. Alb. BG13 9
Queensville Rd. SW12 BW47 76
Queens Wk. E4 CF26 39
Green Wk.
Queen's Wk. NW9 BN34 46
Queen's Wk. SW1 BW40 56
Queens Wk. W5 BK38 54
Queens Wk. Ashf. AX49 73
Queen's Wk. Har. BH31 45
Queen's Wk. Ruis. BD34 45
Queensway NW4 BQ32 46
Queensway, W2 BS40 56
Queensway Croy. BX57 95
Queensway Enf. CB24 30
Queen's Way Felt. BD49 74
Queensway, Hat. BP12 10
Queensway, Hem. H. AX13 8
Queensway Orp. CM53 88
Queensway, Red. BU70 121
Queensway Sun. BC51 83
Queensway Wal. Cr. CD20 21
Longcroft Dr.
Queensway Walt. BD56 93
Queensway W. Wick. CG55 88
Queensway Ong. CW16 24
Queensway, The, Ger. Cr. AR31 43
Queenswell Av. N20 BU28 38
Queenswood Av. E17 CF30 39
Queenswood Av. Brwd. DE25 122
Queenswood Av. Hmptn. BF50 74
Queenswood Av. Houns. BE44 64
Queenswood Av. Th. Hth. BY53 86
Queenswood Av. Wall. BW56 95
Queenswood Ct. SW4 BX46 76
Queenswood Cres. Wat. BC20 17
Queenswood Gdns. E11 CH33 49
Queen's Wood Rd. N10 BV32 47
Queenswood Rd. SE23 CC48 77
Queenswood Rd. Sid. CN46 78
Queenswood Rd. Wok. AO63 100
Queen Victoria Av. Wem. BK36 54
Queen Victoria St. EC4 BY40 56
Quemerford Rd. N7 BX35 47
Quendon Dr. Wal. Abb. CF20 21
Quentin Pl. SE13 CG45 68
Quentin Rd. SE13 CG45 68
Quentin Way, Vir. W. AQ52 82
Quenton Pl. SE13 CG45 68
Quen Way, Brwd DE26 122
Quernmore Clo. Brom. CH50 78
Quernmore Rd. N4 BY32 47
Quernmore Rd. Brom. CH50 78
Querrin St. SW6 BT44 66
Quex Ms. NW6 BS37 56
Quex Rd. NW6 BS37 56
Quickberry Pl. Amer. AO23 25
Quickett St. E3 CE38 57
Quickley La. Rick. AU25 25
Quickley Rise. Rick. AU25 25
Quickmoor La. Kings L. AW20 17
Quick Rd. W4 BO42 65
Quicks Rd. SW19 BS50 76
Quick St. N1 BY37 56
Quickswood NW3 BU36 56
Quickwood Clo. Rick. AV25 25
Quiet Clo. Wey. AW56 92
Quiet Nook Kes. CJ55 88
Quill Hall La. Amer. AP22 25
Quill La. SW15 BQ45 65
Quilot, The, Watt. BB56 92
Quilp St. SE1 BZ41 67
Redcross Way
Quilter Gdns. Orp. CP54 89
Quilter Rd. Orp. CP54 89
Quilter St. E2 CA38 57
Quinbrookes, Slou. AR39 52
Quinces Cft. Hem. H. AW12 8
Quinta Dr. Barn. BP25 28
Quinton Av. SW20 BR51 85
Quinton Clo. Beck. CF52 87
Quinton Clo. Wall. BV56 95
Quinton Rd. Surb. BJ54 84
Quinton St. SW18 BT48 76
Quixley St. E14 CF40 57
Quorn Rd. SE22 CA45 67
Raan Rd. Amer. AP22 25
Rabbit Row W8 BS40 56
Kensington Mall
Rabbits Rd. E12 CK35 49
Rabbits Rd. S. Dnth. CZ51 90
Rabbs Mill, Uxb. AX37 53
Rabies Heath Rd. Red. CA70 114
Raby Rd. N. Mal. BN52 85
Raby St. E14 CD39 57
Raccoon Way Houns. BD44 64
Rachels Way Chesh. AO20 16
Cresswell Rd.
Rack Rd. W3 BM41 65
Racquet Ct. EC4 BY39 56
Fleet St.
Racton Rd. SW6 BS43 66
Radbourne Av. W5 BK42 64
Radbourne Clo. E5 CC35 48
Glyn Rd.
Radbourne Cres. E17 CF31 48
Radbourne Rd. SW12 BW47 76
Radburn Clo. Harl. CO13 14
Radcliffe Av. NW10 BP37 55
Radcliffe Av. Enf. BZ23 30
Radcliffe Gdns. Cars. BU57 95
Radcliffe Path SW8 BW44 66
St. Rule St.
Radcliffe Rd. N21 BY26 38
Radcliffe Rd. Croy. CA55 87
Radcliffe Rd. Har. BJ30 36
Radcliffe Sq. SW15 BQ46 75
Radcliffe Way Nthlt. BD38 54
Radcot Ave. Slou. AU41 62
Radcot St. SE11 BY42 66
Raddington Rd. W10 BR39 55
Radfield Way Sid. CM47 78
Radford Rd. SE13 CF46 77
Radipole Rd. SW6 BR44 65
Radland Rd. E16 CG39 58
Radlett Av. SE26 CB48 77
Radlett Park Rd. Rad. BJ20 18
Radlett Pl. NW8 BU37 56
Radlett Rd. Rad. BK20 18
Radlett Rd. Rad. BK21 27
Radlett Rd. Rad. BL20 19
Radlett Rd. St. Alb. BH18 18
Radlett Rd. Wat. BD24 27
Radley Av. Ilf. CO35 50
Radley Gdns. Har. BL31 46
Radley La. E18 CH30 40
Radley Ms. W8 BS41 66
Radley Rd. N17 CA30 39
Radleys Mead Dag. CR36 59
Radlix Rd. E10 CE33 48
Radnor Av. Har. BH32 45
Radnor Av. Well. CO46 79
Radnor Clo. Mitch. BX52 86
Radnor Ct. Red. BU70 121
Linkfield St.
Radnor Cres. Ilf. CK32 49
Radnor Gdns. Enf. CA23 30
Radnor Gdns. Twick. BH48 74
Radnor Ho. Twick. BJ48 74
Radnor Ms. W2 BT39 56
Radnor Pl. W2 BU39 56
Radnor Rd. NW6 BR37 55
Radnor Rd. SE15 CB43 67
Radnor Rd. Har. BG32 45
Radnor Rd. Twick. BH47 74
Radnor Rd. Wey. AZ55 83
Radnor St. EC1 BZ38 57
Radnor Ter. SW8 BX43 66
South Lambeth Rd.
Radnor Ter. W14 BR42 65
Radnor Wk. SW3 BU42 66
Radnor Wk. Croy. CD53 87
Radnor Way NW10 BM38 55
Radnor Way. Slou. AS42 62
Radstock Av. Har. BJ31 45
Radstock St. SW11 BU43 66
Parkgate Rd.
Radstock Way. Red. BW67 113
Radstock Way. Red. BX68 113
Radstone Ct. Wok. AS62 100
Hill Vw. Rd.
Raeburn Gdns. Barn. BP25 28
Raeburn Av. Dart. CU46 79
Raeburn Av. Surb. BM54 85
Raeburn Clo. NW11 BS32 47
Raeburn Clo. Kings. On T. BK50 74
Lower Teddington Rd.
Raeburn Ho. Kings. On T. BK50 74
Raeburn Rd. Edg. BM30 37
Raeburn Rd. Hayes BA37 53
Raeburn Rd. Sid. CN46 78
Raeburn St. SW2 BX45 66
Rafford Way Brom. CH51 88
Raft Rd. SW18 BS46 76
Ragged Hall La. St. Alb. BE15 9
Ragge Way Sev. CW63 108
Landway, The,
Raggleswood Chis. CL51 88
Rag Hill Rd. Wst. J64 106
Raglan Av. Wal. Cr. CC20 21
Raglan Clo. Reig. BT69 121
Raglan Ct. Sth. Croy. BY56 95
Raglan Ct. Wem. BL35 46
Raglan Gdns. Wat. BC26 35
Raglan Rd. E17 CF32 48
Raglan Rd. SE18 CL42 68
Raglan Rd. Belv. CQ42 69
Raglan Rd. Brom. CJ52 88
Raglan Rd. Enf. CA26 39
Raglan Rd. Reig. BS69 121
Raglan Rd. Wok. AP62 100
Raglan St. NW5 BV36 56
Raglan Way Nthlt. BG36 54
Ragley Clo. W3 BM41 65
Rags La. Wal. Cr. CA17 21
Ragstone Rd. Slou. AO41 61
Rahn Rd. Epp. CN19 22
Rahn Rd. Epp. CO19 23
Raider Clo. Rom. CR30 41
Raikes La. Dor. BC74 119
Railey Ms. NW5 BW35 47
Leverton St.
Railpit. Warl. CG61 106
Railshed Rd. Twick. BJ45 64
St. Margaret's Rd.
Railston Way Wat. BD27 36
Railton Rd. SE24 BY45 66
Railway App. SE1 BZ40 57
Railway App. Cheam BR57 94
Railway Approach, Cher. AV54 82
Railway App. Har. BH31 45
Railway App. Twick. BJ47 74
Railway App. Wall. BV56 95
Railway Arches SE8 CE43 67
Deptford High St.
Railway Av. SE16 CC41 67
Railway Cotts. Ilf. CN29 40
Railway Cotts. St. Alb. BH10 9
Railway Gro. SE14 CD43 67
Railway Ms. W10 BR39 55
Ladbroke Gro.
Railway Pass. Tedd. BJ50 74
Clarence Rd.
Railway Pl. EC3 CA40 57
Fenchurch St.
Railway Pl. SW19 BR50 75
Hartfield Rd.
Railway Pl. Belv. CR41 69
Railway Rd. Tedd. BH49 74
Railway Side SW13 BO45 65
White Hart La.
Railway Sq. Brwd. DB27 42
Railway St. N1 BX37 56
Railway St. Grav. DD46 81
Railway St. Rom. CP33 50
Railway Ter. E17 CF30 39
Railway Ter. SE13 CE46 77
Railway Ter. Felt. BC47 73
Railway Ter. Slou. AP40 52
Railway Ter. Stai. AV49 72
Rainborough Clo. NW10 BN36 55
Rainbow St. SE5 CA43 67
Raine St. E1 CB40 57
Rainham Clo. SE9 CN46 78
Rainham Clo. SW11 BU46 76
Rainham Rd. NW10 BQ38 55
Rainham Rd. Rain. CT36 59
Rainham Rd. N. Dag. CR34 50
Rainham Rd. S. Dag. CR35 50
Rainhill Way, E3 CE38 57
Rainsborough Av. SE8 CD42 67
Rainsford Rd. NW10 BM38 55
Rainsford St. W2 BU39 56
Sale Pl.
Rainsford Way. Horn. CU33 50
Rainton Rd. SE7 CH42 68
Rainville Rd. W6 BQ43 65
Raisins Hill Pnr. BC31 44
Raith Av. N14 BW27 38
Raleana Rd. E14 CF40 57
Raleigh Av. Hayes BC39 53
Raleigh Av. Wall. BW56 95
Raleigh Clo. N13 BZ27 39
Raleigh Clo. NW4 BQ32 46
Raleigh Clo. Pnr. BD33 45
Raleigh Clo. Ruis. BB34 44
Raleigh Ct. Beck. CE51 87
Raleigh Ct. Stai. AW49 73
Leacroft
Raleigh Ct. Wall. BV57 95
Raleigh Dr. N20 BU27 38
Raleigh Dr. Esher BG56 93
Raleigh Dr. Surb. BN54 85
Raleigh Gdns. Mitch. BU51 86
Raleigh Rd. N8 BY31 47
Raleigh Rd. SE20 CC50 77
Raleigh Rd. Enf. BZ24 30
Raleigh Rd. Felt. BB48 73
Raleigh Rd. Rich. BL45 65
Raleigh Rd. Sthl. BE42 64
Raleigh St. N1 BY37 56
Raleigh Way N14 BW26 38
Raleigh Way Felt. BD49 74
Ralliwood Rd. Ash. BM63 103
Ralph St. SE1 BZ41 67
Ralston St. SW3 BU42 66
Tedworth Sq.
Rama Ct. Har. BH34 45
Ramaney Dr. Enf. CD22 30
Rambler Clo. SW16 BW49 76
Rambler La. Slou. AR41 62
Ramblings, The, E4 CF28 39
Ram Gorse, Harl. CL10 6
Ramilles Clo. SW2 BX46 76
Ramilles St. W1 BW39 56
Gt. Marlborough St.
Ramillies Pl. W1 BW39 56
Ramillies Rd. NW7 BO27 37
Ramillies Rd. W4 BN42 65
Ramillies Rd. Sid. CO46 79
Rampart St. E1 CB39 57
Commercial Rd.
Rampayne St. SW1 BW42 66
Ram Pl. E9 CC36 57
Chatham Pl.
Rampton Clo. E4 CE27 39
Ramsay Gdns. Rom. CV30 42
Ramsay Rd. E7 CG35 49
Ramsay Rd. W3 BN41 65
Ramsbury Rd. St. Alb. BH14 9
Ramscroft Clo. N9 CA26 39
Ramsdale Rd. SW17 BV49 76
Ramsden Clo. Orp. CP54 89
Ramsden Rd.
Ramsden Dr. Rom. CR29 41
Ramsden Rd. N11 BU28 38
Ramsden Rd. SW12 BV46 76
Ramsden Rd. Erith CS43 69
Ramsden Rd. Orp. CO54 89
Ramsey Clo. Brox. CD14 12
Ramsey Clo. Hat. BT17 20
Ramsey Clo. St. Alb. BJ14 9
Ramsey Ct. N8 BW32 47
Ramsey Rd. NW9 BO32 46
Broadway, The,
Ramsey Rd. Th. Hth. BX53 86
Ramsey St. E2 CB38 57
Ramsey Wk. N1 BZ36 57
Marquess Est.
Ramsey Way N14 BW26 38
Windsor Ct.
Ramsgate St. E8 CA36 57
Ramsgill App. Ilf. CN31 49
Ramsgill Dr. Ilf. CN32 49
Rams Gro. Rom. CQ31 50
Ramus Wd. Av. Orp. CN56 97
Rancliffe Gdns. SE9 CK45 68
Rancliffe Rd. E6 CK38 58
Randal Cres. Reig. BS71 121
Randall Av. NW2 BO34 46
Randall Clo. Slou. AS42 62
Randall Dr. Horn. CV35 51
Randall Pl. SE10 CF43 67
Randall Rd. SE11 BX42 66
Randall Rd. Rom. CT32 50
Randall Row SE11 BX42 66
Randalls Cres. Lthd. BJ63 102
Randalls Dr. Brwd. DF25 122
Randalls Farm La. Lthd. BJ63 102
Randall's Mkt. E14 CE39 57
Ricardo St.
Randalls Pk. Av. Lthd. BJ63 102
Randalls Ride. Hem. H AX12 8
Randalls Rd. Lthd. BH63 102
Randalls Rode, Hem. H. AX12 8
Randell's Rd. N1 BX37 56
Randle Rd. Rich. BK49 74
Randlesdown Gdns. SE6 CE48 77
Randlesdown Rd. SE6 CE49 77
Randles La Sev. CP60 98
Randolph App. E16 CJ39 58
Baxter Rd.
Randolph Av. W9 BT38 56
Randolph Clo. Bexh. CS45 69
Randolph Clo. Kings. On T. BN49 75
Randolph Clo. Slou. AS42 62
Randolph Clo. Wok. AP62 100
Randolph Cres. W9 BT38 56
Randolph Gdns. NW6 BS37 56
Randolph Ms. W9 BT38 56
Randolph Rd. E16 CJ39 58
Randolph Rd. E17 CE32 48
Randolph Rd. W9 BT38 56
Randolph Rd. Epsom. BO60 94
Randolph Rd. Sthl. BE41 64
Randolph St. NW1 BW36 56
Randon Clo. Har. BF30 36
Ranelagh Av. SW6 BR45 65
Ranelagh Av. SW13 BP44 65
Ranelagh Br. W2 BS40 56
Ranelagh Clo. Edg. BM28 37
Ranelagh Dr. Edg. BM28 37
Ranelagh Dr. Twick. BJ45 64
Ranelagh Est. SW15 BQ44 65
Ranelagh Gdns. E11 CJ32 49
Ranelagh Gdns. SW6 BR45 65
Ranelagh Gdns. W4 BN43 65
Grove Pk. Gdns.
Ranelagh Gdns. Grav. DF47 81
Ranelagh Gdns. Ilf. CK33 49
Ranelagh Gro. SW1 BV42 66
Ranelagh Pl. N. Mal. BO53 85
Ranelagh Rd. E6 CL37 58
Ranelagh Rd. E11 CG35 49
Ranelagh Rd. E15 CG37 58
Ranelagh Rd. N17 CA31 48
Ranelagh Rd. N22 BX30 38
Ranelagh Rd. NW10 BO37 55
Ranelagh Rd. SW1 BW42 66
Lupus St.
Ranelagh Rd. W5 BK41 64
Ranelagh Rd. Hem. H. AZ13 8
Ranelagh Rd. Red. BU70 121
Ranelagh Rd. Sthl. BD40 54
Ranelagh Rd. Wem. BK35 45
Ranfurly Rd. Sutt. BS55 86
Rangefield Rd. Brom. CG49 78
Rangemoor Rd. N15 CA32 48
Range Rd. Grav. DJ47 81
Rangers Rd. E4 CG26 40
Rangers Sq. SE10 CF44 67
Range Way, Shep. AZ54 83
Rangoon St. EC3 CA39 57
Northumberland Alley
Ranleigh Gdns. Bexh. CQ43 69
Ranmere Clo. Red. BV69 121
Ranmere St. SW12 BV47 76
Ranmoor Clo. Har. BG31 45
Ranmoor Gdns. Har. BG31 45
Ranmore Av. Croy. CA55 87
Ranmore Comm. Rd. Dor. BD70 119
Ranmore Path Orp. CO52 89
Ranmore Rd. Couls. BX62 104
Ranmore Rd. Dor. BG70 119
Ranmore Rd. Dor. BJ71 119
Ranmore Rd. Sutt. BQ58 94
Rannoch Rd. W6 BQ43 65
Rannock Dr. NW9 BN33 46
Ranskill Rd. Borwd. BM23 28
Ransom Rd. SE7 CJ42 68
Ranston St. NW1 BU39 56
Rant Meadow, Hem. H. AZ14 8
Ranulf Rd. NW2 BR35 46
Ranwell Clo. E3 CD37 57
Ranworth Clo. Erith CT44 69
Ranworth Clo. Hem. H. AX14 8
Ranworth Rd. N9 CC27 39
Ranworth Rd. Hem. H. AX14 8
Raphael Ave. Til. DG44 71
Raphael Av. Rom. CT30 41
Raphael Rd. Grav. DH47 81
Raphael St. SW7 BU41 66
Rasher Mead, Dor. BK73 119
Rashleigh St. SW8 BV44 66
Rashleigh Way. Hort. K. CY52 90
Rasper Rd. N20 BT27 38
Rastell Av. SW2 BW48 76
Ratcliffe Cross St. E1 CC39 57
Ratcliffe La. E14 CD39 57
Ratcliffe Rd. Uxb. AX38 53
Ratcliff Orchard E1 CC40 57
Ratcliff Rd. E7 CJ35 49
Rathbone Mkt. E16 CG39 58
Rathbone Pl. W1 BW39 56
Rathbone St. E16 CG39 58
Rathbone St. W1 BW39 56
Rathcoole Av. N8 BX31 47
Rathcoole Gdns. N8 BX32 47
Rathfern Rd. SE6 CD47 77
Rathgar Av. W13 BJ40 54
Rathgar Clo. N3 BR30 37
Rathgar Clo. Red. BV73 121
Rathlin, Hem. H. AZ14 8
Rathlin Wk. N1 BZ36 57
Marquess Est.
Rathmell Dr. SW4 BW46 76
Rathmore Rd. SE7 CH42 68
Ratmore Rd. Wal. Abb. CG20 22
Rat's La. Loug. CH22 31
Rattray Rd. SW2 BY45 66
Ratty's La. Hodd. CF12 12
Raul Rd. SE15 CB44 67
Raveley St. NW5 BW35 47
Ravel Gdns. S. Ock. CW39 60
Ravel Rd. S. Ock. CW39 60
Raven Clo. Rick. AX26 35
Raven Ct. Hat. BP13 10
Ravendale Rd. Sun. BB51 83
Ravenet St. SW11 BV44 66
Ravenfield Rd. SW17 BU48 76
Ravenfield Rd. Welw. G. C. BR8 5
Ravenhill Rd. E13 CJ37 58
Ravenna Rd. SW15 BQ45 65
Ravenor Pk. Rd. Grnf. BF38 54
Raven Rd. E18 CJ30 40
Raven Row E1 CB39 57
Ravensbourne Av. Brom. CF50 77
Ravensbourne Av. Ilf. CL30 40
Ravensbourne Av. Stai. AY47 73
Ravensbourne Cres. SE6 CD47 77
Ravensbourne Est. Brom. CF49 77
Ravensbourne Gdns. W13 BJ39 54
Ravensbourne Gdns. Ilf. CL30 40
Ravensbourne Pk. SE6 CD47 77
Ravensbourne Pk. Cres. SE6 CD47 77
Ravensbourne Rd. SE6 CD47 77
Ravensbourne Rd. Brom. CH52 88
Ravensbourne Rd. Dart. CU45 69
Ravensbourne Rd. Twick. BK46 74
Ravensbury Av. Mord. BT53 86
Ravensbury Gro. Mitch. BT52 86
Ravensbury La. Mitch. BT52 86
Ravensbury Path Mitch. BT52 86
Ravensbury Rd. SW18 BS48 76
Ravensbury Rd. Orp. CN52 88
Ravenscar Rd. Brom. CG49 78
Ravenscar Rd. Surb. BL55 85
Ravens Clo. Brom. CG51 88
Ravens Clo. Enf. CA23 30
Ravens Clo. Wok. AO61 100
Ravens Ct. Sun. BB51 83
Ravenscourt Av. W6 BP42 65
Ravenscourt Clo. Horn. CW34 51
Ravens Ct. Clo. Ruis. BA33 44
Ravenscourt Dr. Horn. CW34 51
Ravenscourt Gdns. W6 BP42 65
Ravenscourt Gro. Horn. CW34 51
Ravenscourt Pk. W6 BP42 65
Ravenscourt Pl. W6 BP42 65
King St.
Ravenscourt Rd. W6 BP41 65
Ravenscourt Rd. Orp. CO51 89
Ravenscourt Sq. W6 BP41 65
Ravenscraig Rd. N11 BW28 38
Ravenscroft Av. NW11 BR33 46
Ravenscroft Av. Wem. BL33 46
Ravenscroft Clo. E16 CH39 58
Ravenscroft Pk. Barn. BQ24 28
Ravenscroft Pk. Rd. Barn. BQ24 28
Ravenscroft Rd. E16 CG39 58
Ravenscroft Rd. W4 BN42 65
Ravenscroft Rd. Beck. CC51 87
Ravenscroft Rd. Wey. BA59 92
Ravenscroft St. E2 CA37 57
Ravensdale Av. N12 BT28 38
Ravensdale Rd. N16 CA33 48
Ravensdale Rd. Houns. BE45 64
Ravens Dell. Hem. H. AV13 7
Ravensdon St. SE11 BY42 66
Ravensfield. Slou. AR41 62
Ravensfield Clo. Dag. CP35 50
Ravensfield Gdns. Epsom BO56 94

Ravenshaw St. NW6	BR35	46
Ravenshill Chis.	CL51	88
Ravenshurst Av. NW4	BQ31	46
Ravens La. Berk.	AR13	7
Ravenslea Rd. SW12	BU47	76
Ravens Mead. Ger. Cr.	AS28	34
Ravensmead Rd. Brom.	CF50	77
Ravensmere Epp.	CO19	23
Ravenstone Rd. N8	BY31	47
Ravenstone Rd. NW9	BO32	46
Broadway, The.		
Ravenstone St. SW12	BV47	76
Ravens Way SE12	CH46	78
Ravenswold. Ken.	BZ61	105
Ravenswood Bex.	CQ47	79
Ravenswood Ken.	BZ57	96
Ravenswood Av. Surb.	BL55	85
Ravenswood Av. W. Wick.	CF54	87
Ravenswood Clo. Croy.	BY55	86
Ravenswood Rd.		
Ravenswood Clo. Rom.	CR28	41
Ravenswood Ct. Kings. On T.	BN50	75
Ravenswood Ct. Wok.	AS62	100
Hill Vw. Rd.		
Ravenswood Cres. Har.	BE34	45
Ravenswood Cres. W. Wick.	CF54	87
Ravenswood Gdns. Islw.	BH44	64
Ravenswood Pk. Nthwd.	BC29	35
Ravenswood Rd. E17	CE31	48
Ravenswood Rd. SW12	BV47	76
Ravenswood Rd. Croy.	BY55	86
Ravensworth Rd. NW10	BP38	55
Ravensworth Rd. SE9	CK48	78
Ravent Rd. SE11	BX42	66
Ravey St. EC2	CA38	57
Ravine Gro. SE18	CN43	68
Rawcester Clo. SW18	BR47	75
Rawdon Dr. Hodd.	CE12	12
Rawlings Clo. Orp.	CN56	97
Rawlings La. Beac.	AO27	34
Rawlings St. SW3	BU42	66
Rawlins Clo. Sth. Croy.	CD57	96
Rawson St. SW11	BV44	66
Despard Av.		
Rawstone Wk. E13	CH37	58
Rawstorne Pl. EC1	BY38	56
Rawstorne St.		
Rawstorne St. EC1	BY38	56
Raybarn Rd. Hem. H.	AW12	8
Rayburn Rd. Horn.	CX33	51
Raydean Rd. Barn.	BS25	29
Raydon Rd. Wal. Cr.	CC19	21
Theobalds La.		
Raydons Gdns. Dag.	CQ35	50
Raydons Rd. Dag.	CQ35	50
Raydon St. N19	BV34	47
Rayfield, Epp.	CN18	22
Ray Field. Welw. G. C.	BQ6	5
Rayfield Clo. Brom.	CK53	88
Rayford Av. SE12	CG47	78
Rayford Clo. Dart.	CV46	80
Ray Gdns. Bark.	CO37	59
Ray Gdns. Stan.	BJ28	36
Rayleas Clo. SE18	CL44	68
Rayleigh Av. Tedd.	BH50	74
Rayleigh Clo. Brwd.	DE25	122
Rayleigh Ct. N22	BZ30	39
Rayleigh Ct. Kings. On T.	BM51	85
Cambridge Rd.		
Rayleigh Rise Sth. Croy.	CA57	96
Rayleigh Rd. N13	BZ27	39
Rayleigh Rd. SW19	BR51	85
Rayleigh Rd. Brwd.	DD25	122
Rayleigh Rd. Wdf. Grn.	CJ29	40
Rayley La. Epp.	CQ14	14
Ray Lodge Rd. Wdf. Grn.	CJ29	40
Raymead NW4	BQ31	46
Raymead Av. Th. Hth.	BY53	86
Raymead Clo. Loug.	CM25	31
Raymead Clo. Lthd.	BH64	102
Raymead Way, Lthd.	BH64	102
Raymer Ct. St. Alb.	BH13	9
Raymer Clo.		
Raymere Gdns. SE18	CM43	68
Raymond Av. E18	CG31	49
Raymond Av. W13	BJ41	64
Raymond Bldgs. WC1	BX39	56
Raymond Clo. SE26	CC49	77
Raymond Clo. Slou.	AV44	62
Raymond Cres. Guil.	AP71	118
Raymond Gdns. Chig.	CO27	41
Raymond Rd. E13	CJ36	58
Raymond Rd. SW19	BR50	75
Raymond Rd. Beck.	CD52	87
Raymond Rd. Ilf.	CM33	49
Raymond Rd. Slou.	AT42	62
Raymonds Clo. Welw. G. C.	BR9	5
Raymonds Plain. Welw. G. C.	BR9	5
Raymond Way Esher	BJ57	93
Raymouth Rd. SE16	CB42	67
Rayne Ct. E18	CG31	49
Rayner's Ct. Har.	BF33	45
Rayners Cres. Nthlt.	BC38	53
Rayners Gdns. Nthlt.	BC38	53
Rayner's La. Har.	BF33	45
Rayners Rd. SW15	BQ46	75
Rayner St. E9	CC36	57
Raynes Av. E11	CJ33	49
Raynham Av. N18	CB29	39
Raynham Rd. N18	CB28	39
Raynham Rd. W6	BP42	65
Raynham Ter. N18	CB28	39
Raynor Clo. Sthl.	BE40	54
Raynors Clo. Wem.	BK35	45
Raynton Clo. Har.	BE33	45
Raynton Clo. Hayes	BB38	53
Raynton Dr. Hayes	BB38	53
Raynton Dr. Hayes	BC38	53
Raynton Rd. Enf.	CC22	30
Ray Rd. E. Mol.	BF53	84
Rays Ave. Wind.	AM43	61
Rays Av. N18	CC28	39
Rays Rd. N18	CB28	39
Ray St. EC1	BY38	56
Ray Walk N7	BX34	47
Andover Est.		
Raywood St. SW8	BV44	66
Readens, The, Bans.	BU61	104
Readgold St. W11	BQ40	55
Reading Arch Rd. Red.	BU70	121
Reading La. E8	CB36	57
Reading Rd. Nthlt.	BF35	45
Reading Rd. Sutt.	BT56	95
Readings, The Harl.	CN12	13
Readings, The Rick.	AV24	25
Reading Way NW7	BR28	37
Read Rd. Ash.	BK62	102
Reads Rest La. Tad.	BS63	104
Read Way, Grav.	DH49	81
Reardon Path E1	CB40	57
Reardon St. E1	CB40	57
Reaston St. SE14	CC43	67
Rebble Rd. Swans.	DC46	81
Reckinham Rd. Guil.	AQ69	118
Reckitt Rd. W4	BO42	65
Record St. SE15	CC43	67
Recovery St. SW17	BU49	76
Recreation Av. Rom.	CS32	50
Recreation Av. Rom.	CW30	42
Recreation Rd. SE26	CC49	77
Recreation Rd. Brom.	CG51	88
Recreation Rd. Guil.	AR70	118
Recreation Rd. Sthl.	BE42	64
Recreation Way Mitch.	BW52	86
Rector St. N1	BZ37	57
Rectory Chase Brwd.	DB22	33
Rectory Chase, Brwd.	DB31	51
Rectory Chase, Brwd.	DC31	123
Rectory Clo. E4	CE27	39
Brindwood Rd.		
Rectory Clo. N3	BR30	37
Rectory Clo. Ash.	BL63	103
Rectory Clo. Dart.	CT45	69
Rectory Clo. Guil.	AU69	118
Rectory Clo. Hat.	BU12	11
Rectory Clo. Shep.	AZ52	83
Rectory Clo. Sid.	CO49	79
Rectory Clo. Stan.	BJ28	36
Rectory Clo. Surb.	BK54	84
Rectory Clo. Wey.	AY60	92
Rectory Clo. Wind.	AN44	61
Rectory Cres. E11	CJ32	49
Rectory Field. Harl.	CL12	13
Rectory Field Cres. SE7	CJ43	68
Rectory Gdns. N8	BX31	47
Rectory Gdns. SW4	BW45	66
Rectory Gro.		
Rectory Gdns. Hayes.	BA42	63
Rectory Gdns. Nthlt.	BE37	54
Rectory Gdns. Upmin.	CZ34	51
Rectory Grn. Beck.	CD51	87
Rectory Grn. La. Bet.	BO69	120
Rectory Gro. SW4	BW45	66
Rectory Gro. Croy.	BY55	86
Rectory Gro. Hamptn.	BE49	74
Rectory La. SW17	BV50	76
Rectory La. Ash.	BL62	103
Rectory La. Bans.	BU60	95
Rectory La. Berk.	AR13	7
Rectory La. Edg.	BM29	37
Rectory La. Kings L.	AZ17	17
Rectory La. Loug.	CL23	31
Rectory La. Lthd.	BE66	111
Rectory La. Pot. B.	BN19	19
Rectory La. Rad.	BM19	19
Rectory La. Rick.	AX26	35
Rectory La. Sev.	CV66	117
Rectory La. Sev.	DB64	108
Rectory La. Sid.	CO49	79
Rectory La. Stan.	BJ28	36
Rectory La. Surb.	BJ54	84
Rectory La. Wall.	BW55	86
Rectory La. West.	CP65	107
Rectory La. Wey.	AY60	92
Rectory Pk. Sth. Croy.	CA60	96
Rectory Pk. Av. Nthlt.	BE38	54
Rectory Pl. SE18	CL42	68
Rectory Rd. E12	CK35	49
Rectory Rd. E17	CE31	48
Rectory Rd. N16	CA34	48
Rectory Rd. SW13	BP44	65
Rectory Rd. W3	BM40	55
Rectory Rd. Beck.	CE51	87
Rectory Rd. Couls.	BS66	113
Rectory Rd. Dag.	CR36	59
Rectory Rd. Hayes	BC39	53
Rectory Rd. Houns.	BC44	63
Rectory Rd. Kes.	CJ57	97
Rectory Rd. Sthl.	BE41	64
Rectory Rd. Sutt.	BS55	86
Rectory Rd. Swans.	DC47	81
Rectory Rd. Til.	DH43	71
Rectory Rd. Welw. G. C.	BP6	5
Rectory Rd. West.	CK65	106
Rectory Sq. E1	CC39	57
Rectory Way, Uxb.	AZ34	44
Rectory Wood, Harl.	CM10	6
Reculver Ms. N18	CB28	39
Lyndhurst Rd.		
Reculver Rd. SE16	CC42	67
Red Anchor Clo. SW3	BU43	66
Redan Pl. W2	BS40	56
Redan St. W14	BQ41	65
Redan Ter. SE5	BZ44	67
Flaxman Rd.		
Redberry Gro. SE26	CC48	77
Redbourne Av. N3	BS30	38
Redbourn Rd. Hem. H.	AZ11	8
Redbourn Rd. St. Alb.	BE12	9
Redbridge Gdns. SE5	CA44	67
Dalwood St.		
Redbridge La. E. Ilf.	CJ32	49
Redbridge La. W. E11	CH32	49
Red Bull Yard EC4	BZ40	57
Upr. Thames St.		
Redburn St. SW3	BU43	66
Redburn Ter. Enf.	CC25	30
South St.		
Redbury Clo. Rain.	CV39	60
Redcar Clo. Nthlt.	BF36	54
Redcar Rd. Rom.	CW28	42
Redcar St. SE5	BZ43	67
Redcastle Clo. E1	CC40	57
Juniper St.		
Red Cedars Rd. Orp.	CN54	88
Redchurch St. E2	CA38	57
Redcliffe Clo. SW5	BS42	66
Redcliffe Gdns. SW10	BS42	66
Redcliffe Gdns. Ilf.	CL33	49
Redcliffe Ms. SW10	BS42	66
Redcliffe Pl. SW10	BT43	66
Redcliffe Rd. SW10	BT42	66
Redcliffe Sq. SW10	BS42	66
Redcliffe St. SW10	BS43	66
Redclose Av. Mord.	BS53	86
Redclyffe Rd. E6	CJ37	58
Red Ct. Slou.	AP40	52
Redcroft Rd. Sthl.	BG40	54
Red Cross, Reig.	BS70	121
Redcross Pl. SE1	BZ41	67
Redcross Way		
Redcross Way SE1	BZ41	67
Reddons Ct. Rd. Rom.	CW31	51
Redden Ct. Rd. Horn.	CW31	51
Reddings, Hem. H.	AY14	8
Reddings. Welw. G. C.	BQ7	5
Reddings Av. Bush.	BF25	27
Reddings Clo. NW7	BO28	37
Reddings, The, NW7	BO27	37
Reddington Clo. Sth. Croy.	CA58	96
Reddington Dr. Slou.	AS42	62
Reddins Rd. SE15	CB43	67
Redditch Ct. Hem. H.	AY11	8
Reddons Rd. Beck.	CD50	77
Reddown Rd. Couls.	BW62	104
Reddy Rd. Erith	CT43	69
Rede Pl. W2	BS39	56
Redesdale Gdns. Islw.	BJ43	64
Redesdale St. SW3	BU42	66
Redfern Av. Twick.	BF47	74
Redfern Gdns. Rom.	CV30	42
Redfern Rd. NW10	BO36	55
Redfern Rd. SE6	CF47	77
Brownhill Rd.		
Redfield La. SW5	BS42	66
Redford Av. Couls.	BV60	95
Redford Av. Th. Hth.	BX52	86
Redford Av. Wall.	BX57	95
Redford Rd. Wind.	AL44	61
Redford Way, Uxb.	AX36	53
Redgate Dr. Brom.	CH55	88
Redgate Ter. SW15	BQ46	75
Lytton Gro.		
Redgrave Rd. SW15	BQ45	65
Redhall Dr. Hat.	BO14	10
Redhall La. Hat.	BO14	10
Red Hall La. Rick.	AY23	26
Redheath Clo. Wat.	BC20	17
Red Hill Chis.	CL49	78
Red Hill. Cob.	BA61	101
Redhill Uxb.	AU33	43
Redhill Dr. Edg.	BN30	37
Redhill Rd. Cob.	AZ59	92
Redhill St. NW1	BV37	56
Redholm Vill. N16	BZ35	48
Winston Rd.		
Red House La. Bexh.	CP45	69
Red Ho. La. Walt.	BC55	83
Red Ho. Rd. Croy.	BW53	86
Redhouse Rd. West.	CJ64	106
Redington Gdns. NW3	BS35	47
Redington Rd. NW3	BS35	47
Redlands Couls.	BX57	95
Redlands Couls.	BX61	104
Redlands Gdns. E. Mol.	BE52	84
Redlands Rd. Enf.	CD23	30
Redlands Rd. Sev.	CT65	107
Redlands Way SW2	BX47	76
Red La. Dor.	BL74	120
Red La. Esher	BJ57	93
Red La. Oxt.	CH69	115
Redlaw Way Se16	CB42	67
Bonamy Estate West The		
Redleaf Clo. Belv.	CR43	69
Redleaves Av. Ashf.	AZ50	73
Redlees Clo. Islw.	BJ45	64
Red Lion Clo. Orp.	CP53	89
Red Lion Ct. EC4	BY39	56
Fleet St.		
Red Lion Cres. Harl.	CP12	14
Red Lion Hl. N2	BT30	38
Red Lion La. SE18	CL44	68
Red Lion Lane. Harl.	CP12	14
Red Lion La. Hem. H.	AZ16	17
Red Lion La. Rick.	AW21	26
Red Lion La. Wok.	AP58	91
Red Lion Rd. Surb.	BL55	85
Red Lion Rd. Wok.	AP58	91
Red Lion Row SE17	BZ43	67
Boundary La.		
Red Lion Sq. WC1	BX39	56
Red Lion Sq. Hmptn.	BF51	84
Red Lion St. WC1	BX39	56
Theobalds Rd.		
Red Lion St. Rich.	BK46	74
Red Lion Yd. Wat.	BD24	27
Red Lo. Cres. Bex.	CS48	79
Red Lo. Rd. Bex.	CS48	79
Red Lodge Rd. W. Wick.	CF54	87
Redman's Pl. Sev.	CV66	117
Redman's Rd. E1	CC39	57
Redmead La. E1	CB40	57
Redmead Rd. Hayes.	BB42	63
Redmore Rd. W6	BP42	65
Red Oak Clo. Orp.	CL55	88
Red Oaks Mead, Epp.	CM22	31
Red Pl. W1	BV40	56
Park St.		
Redpoll Way SE2	CP41	69
Maran Way		
Redpoll Way Belv.	CP41	69
Maran Way		
Red Post Hl. SE21	BZ45	67
Red Post Hl. SE24	BZ45	67
Redrick La. Harl.	CN8	6
Redriffe Rd. E13	CG37	58
Redriff Est. SE16	CD41	67
Redriff Rd. SE16	CC41	67
Redriff Rd. Rom.	CR30	41
Red Rd. Bet.	BN69	120
Red Rd. Borwd.	BL24	28
Red Rd. Brwd.	DA28	42
Red Rose La. Ing.	DC18	24
Redruth Clo. Rom.	CW28	42
Redruth Rd. Rom.	CW28	42
Redruth Wk. Rom.	CW28	42
Redstart Clo. Croy.	CF58	96
Redstone Hill, Red.	BV70	121
Redstone Hollow, Red.	BV71	121
Redstone Mans. Red.	BV70	121
Redstone Pk. Red.	BV70	121
Redstone Rd. Red.	BV71	121
Redston Rd. N8	BW31	47
Red St. Grav.	DD50	81
Redvers Rd. N22	BY30	38
Redvers Rd. Warl.	CC62	105
Redwald Rd. E5	CC35	48
Redway Dr. Twick.	BG46	74
Redwing Clo. Croy.	CC59	96
Redwing Clo. Sth. Croy.	CC58	96
Redwood Clo. Ken.	BZ60	96
Redwood Clo. Uxb.	AZ37	53
Redwood Dr. Hem. H.	AY14	8
Redwood Gdns. Chig.	CO28	41
Red Wood Mt. Reig.	BS69	121
Reece Ms. SW7	BT42	66
Reechfield Rd. Welw. G. C.	BR9	5
Reedan Clo, St. Alb.	BF18	18
Reed Av. Orp.	CM55	88
Reed Clo. E16	CH39	58
Plymouth Rd.		
Reed Clo. SE12	CH46	78
Reede Gdns. Dag.	CR35	50
Reede Rd. Dag.	CR36	59
Reede Way. Dag.	CR36	59
Reedham Pk. Av. Pur.	BY61	104
Reedham St. SE15	CB44	67
Reed Pl. NW1	BW36	56
Rochester Pl.		
Reed Pond Wk. Rom.	CT30	41
Reed Rd. N17	CA30	39
Reedsfield Rd. Ashf.	AZ49	73
Reeds La. Ton.	DC68	117
Reedworth St. SE11	BY42	66
Reenglass Rd. Stan.	BK28	36
Rees Gdns. Croy.	CA53	87
Reesland Clo. E12	CL35	49
Rees Rd. Red.	BU70	121
High St.		
Rees St. N1	BZ37	57
Reets Farm Clo. NW9	BO32	46
Reeve Rd. Maid.	AG43	61
Reeve Rd. Reig.	BT72	121
Reeves Av. NW9	BN33	46
Reeves Clo. Brwd.	DA20	24
Reeves Corner, Croy.	BY55	86
Church St.		
Reeves Cres. Swan.	CS52	89
Reeves La. Harl.	CJ13	13
Reeves Ms. W1	BV40	56
Reeves Rd. E3	CE38	57
Reform Row N17	CA30	39
Reform St. SW11	BU44	66
Regal Clo. W5	BK39	54
Regal Ct. N18	CA28	39
Regal Field Clo. Guil.	AP68	109
Regal La. NW1	BV37	56
Regents Park Rd.		
Regal Way Har.	BK32	45
Regan Clo. Guil.	AQ68	109
Regan Way N1	CA37	57
Regarder Rd. Chig.	CO28	41
Regarth Av. Rom.	CT32	50
Regency Clo. W5	BL39	55
Regency Clo. Chig.	CM28	40
Regency Clo. Hamptn.	BE49	74
Regency Dri. Wey.	AV60	91
Regency Ms. NW10	BO36	55
High Rd.		
Regency Mews Islw.	BH46	74
Regency St. SW1	BW42	66
Regency Wk. Croy.	CD53	87
Regency Way Bexh.	CP45	69
Regent Av. N13	BY28	38
Regent Av. Uxb.	AZ36	53
Regent Clo. Har.	BL32	46
Regent Clo. Houns.	BC44	63
Regent Clo. Wey.	AX58	92
Regent Cres. Red.	BU69	121
Linkfield La.		
Regent Ho. Surb.	BL53	85
Regent Pl. W1	BW40	56
Warwick St.		
Regent Pl. Croy.	CA54	87
Regent Rd. SE24	BY46	76
Regent Rd. Epp.	CN18	22
Regent Rd. Surb.	BL53	85
Regents Av. N13	BY28	38
Regents Clo. Grays.	DE41	71
Regents Clo. Rad.	BJ20	18
Regents Clo. Sth. Croy.	CA57	96
Regents Clo. Whyt.	CA62	105
Regents Dri. Kes.	CJ56	97
Regents Pk. Est. NW1	BV38	56
Regents Pk. Rd. N3	BR31	46
Regents Pk. Ter. NW1	BV37	56
Oval Rd.		
Regent Sq. E3	CE38	57
Regent Sq. WC1	BX38	56
Regent Sq. Belv.	CR42	69
Regents Row E8	CB37	57
Regent St. NW10	BQ38	55
Kilburn La.		
Regent St. SW1	BW40	56
Regent St. W1	BV39	56
Regent St. W4	BM42	65
Regent St. Wat.	BC22	26
Regina Cl. Barn.	BQ24	28
Reginald Rd. E7	CG36	58
Reginald Rd. SE8	CE43	67
Reginald Rd. Nthwd.	BB30	35
Reginald Rd. Rom.	CX30	42
Reginald Sq. SE8	CE43	67
Regina Rd. N4	BX33	47
Regina Rd. SE25	CB52	87
Regina Rd. W13	BJ40	54
Regina Rd. Sthl.	BE42	64
Regis Way SE17	BY43	66
Regnart Bldgs. NW1	BW38	56
Euston St.		
Reid Ave. Cat.	BZ64	105
Reid Clo. Pnr.	BC31	44
Reidhaven Rd. SE18	CN42	68
Reid St. N1	BY37	56
Reigate Av. Sutt.	BS55	86
Reigate Hill. Reig.	BS68	113
Reigate Hill Clo. Reig.	BS69	121
Reigate Hill Rd. Reig.	BS70	121
Reigate Rd. Bet.	BN70	120
Reigate Rd. Brom.	CG48	78
Reigate Rd. Dor.	BK71	119
Reigate Rd. Epsom	BP58	94
Reigate Rd. Ilf.	CN34	49
Reigate Rd. Lthd.	BK65	102
Reigate Rd. Reig.	BS70	121
Reigate Rd. Reig.	BS74	121
Reigate Way Wall.	BX56	95
Reighton Rd. E5	CB34	48
Reinters Cotts. Rich.	BK48	74
Relf Rd. SE15	CB45	67
Relinque Rd. SE26	CD49	77
Relko Ct. Epsom	BN59	94
Rembrandt Dr. Grav.	DE48	81
Rembrandt Rd. SE13	CG45	68
Rembrandt Rd. Edg.	BM30	37
Rembrant Way Walt.	BC55	83
Remington Rd. N15	BZ32	48
Remington St. N1	BY37	56
Remnant St. WC2	BX39	56
Kingsway		
Remus Rd. E3	CD36	57
Remus Rd. E3	CE36	57
Monter Rd.		
Rendlesham Av. Rad.	BH22	27
Rendlesham Rd. E5	CB35	48
Rendlesham Rd. Enf.	BY22	29
Rendlesham Way. Rick.	AU25	25
Renforth St. SE16	CC41	67
Renfrew Rd. SE11	BY42	66
Renfrew Rd. Houns.	BD44	64
Renfrew Rd. Kings. On T.	BN50	75
Renmans, The, Ash.	BL61	103
Renmuir St. SW17	BU50	76
Rennell St. SE13	CF45	67
Renness Rd. E17	BX31	47
Rennets Clo. SE9	CM46	78
Rennets Wood Rd. SE9	CM46	78
Rennie Clo. Ashf.	AX48	73
Rennie St. SE1	BY40	56
Rennie Ter. Red.	BV71	121
Renown Clo. Croy.	BY54	86
Renown Clo. Rom.	CR30	41
Rensburg Rd. E17	CC32	48
Renters Av. NW4	BQ32	46
Renton Dr. Orp.	CP54	89
Renwick Rd. Bark.	CO38	59
Rephidim St. SE1	BZ41	67
Replingham Rd. SW18	BR47	75
Reporton Rd. SW6	BR43	65
Repository Rd. SE18	CK43	68
Repton Ave. Hayes.	BA42	63
Repton Av. Rom.	CU31	50
Repton Av. Wem.	BK35	45
Repton Clo. Cars.	BU56	95
Repton Ct. Beck.	CE51	87
Repton Dr. Rom.	CU31	50
Repton Gdns. Rom.	CU31	50
Repton Gro. Ilf.	CK30	40
Repton Rd. Har.	BL31	46
Repton Rd. Orp.	CN55	88
Repton St. E14	CD39	57
Repton Way, Rick.	AZ25	26
Repulse Clo. Rom.	CR30	41
Reservoir Rd. N14	BW25	29
Reservoir Rd. SE4	CD44	67
Reservoir Rd. Loug.	CH23	31
Reservoir Rd. Ruis.	BA32	44
Reson Way, Hem. H.	AW14	8
Restell Clo. SE3	CG43	68
Reston Clo. Borwd.	BM22	28
Reston Path Borwd.	BM22	28
Reston Path. Borwd.	BM23	28
Reston Pl. SW7	BT41	66
Palace Gte.		
Restons Cres. SE9	CM46	78
Retcar St. N6	BV34	47
Retford Clo. Rom.	CW29	42
Retford Path. Rom.	CX29	42
Retford Rd. Rom.	CW29	42
Retingham Way E4	CE27	39
Retreat Clo. Har.	BK32	45
Retreat Pl. E9	CC36	57
Retreat Rd. Rich.	BK46	74
Retreat Ter. Brent.	BK43	64
Brickfield Clo.		
Retreat, The, NW4	BQ31	46
Heading St.		

GREATER LONDON STREET ATLAS

Retreat, The, NW9 BN32 46
Highfield Av.
Retreat, The, SE15 CC44 67
Retreat, The, SW14 BO45 65
South Worple Way
Retreat, The Amer. AS23 25
Retreat, The, Brwd. DA26 42
Costead Manor Rd.
Retreat, The, Brwd. DD25 122
Retreat, The Egh. AR49 72
Retreat, The, Grays. DD43 71
Retreat, The, Har. BF33 45
Retreat, The, Nw9 BN32 46
Retreat, The, Orp. CO57 98
Retreat, The, Surb. BL53 85
Retreat, The, Th. Hth. BZ52 87
Retreat, The, Wor. Pk. BP55 85
Retreat Way Chig. CO27 41
Revell Clo. Lthd. BF64 102
Revell Dr. Lthd. BF64 102
Revell Rise SE18 CN43 68
Revell Rd. Kings. On T. BM51 85
Revell Rd. Sutt. BR57 94
Revelon Rd. SE4 CD45 67
Revelstoke Rd. SW18 BR48 75
Reventlow Rd. SE9 CM47 78
Reverdy Rd. SE1 CB42 67
Revesby Rd. Cars. BT53 86
Review Rd. NW2 BO34 46
Review Rd. Dag. CR37 59
Rewell St. SW6 BT43 66
Rewley Rd. Cars. BT53 86
Rex Av. Ashf. AZ50 73
Rex Clo. Rom. CR29 41
Rex Pl. W1 BV40 56
Reydon Av. E11 CJ32 49
Reynard Clo. Brom. CL52 88
Blackbrook La.
Reynard Dr. SE19 CA50 77
Reynardson Rd. N17 BZ29 39
Reynards Way, St. Alb. BE18 18
Reynolds Av. E12 CL35 49
Reynolds Av. Ches. BL57 94
Reynolds Av. Rom. CP33 50
Reynolds Clo. NW11 BS33 47
Reynolds Clo. Cars. BU54 86
Reynolds Clo. Hem. H. AW13 8
Reynolds Cres. St. Alb. BJ11 9
Reynolds Dr. Edg. BL31 46
Reynolds Pl. SE3 CH43 68
Reynolds Rd. SE15 CC45 67
Reynolds Rd. W4 BN41 65
Reynolds Rd. Hayes. BD38 54
Reynolds Rd. N. Mal. BN54 85
Reynolds Way Croy. CA56 96
Rhea St. E16 CK40 58
Rheidol Ter. N1 BY37 56
Rheola Clo. N17 CA30 39
Rhoda St. E2 CA38 57
Rhodes Av. N22 BW30 38
Rhodesia Rd. E11 CF34 48
Rhodesia Rd. SW9 BX44 66
Rhodes Moorhouse Ct. Mord. BS53 86
Rhodes St. N7 BX35 47
Rhodes Way Wat. BD23 27
Rhodeswell Rd. E14 CD39 57
Rhododendron Ride, Egh. AP49 72
Rhodrons Av. Chess. BL56 94
Rhondda Gro. E3 CD38 57
Rhyl Rd. Grnf. BH37 54
Rhyl St. NW5 BV36 56
Rhyme Rd. SE13 CF45 67
Rhys Av. N11 BW29 38
Rialto Rd. Mitch. BV51 86
Ribblesdale Hem. H. AY12 8
Wharfedale
Ribblesdale Av. Nthlt. BF36 54
Ribblesdale Av. N8 BX31 47
Ribblesdale Rd. SW16 BV50 76
Ribbleside Rd. Dart. CY47 80
Ribchester Av. Grnf. BH38 54
Ribston Clo. Brom. CK54 88
Ricardo Rd. Wind. AO46 72
Ricardo St. E14 CE39 57
Ricards Clo. Surb. BL54 85
Ricards Rd. SW19 BR49 75
Ricebridge La. Reig. BP72 120
Richards Av. Rom. CS32 50
Richards Clo. Har. BJ32 45
Richards Clo. Uxb. AZ37 53
Richard's Cotts. W3 BN40 55
Churchfield Rd.
Richardson Clo. Hayes. BA43 63
Richardson Clo. St. Alb. BL17 19
Richardson Ms. NW1 BW38 56
Warren St.
Richardson Place. St. Alb. BM14 10
Richardson Rd. E15 CG37 58
Richards Pl. E17 CE31 48
Richards Pl. SW3 BU42 66
Richards Rd. Cob. BF60 93
Richard St. E1 CB39 57
Richard St. E16 CH39 58
Richbell Clo. Ash. BK62 102
Richbell Pl. WC1 BX39 56
Emerald St.
Richborne Ter. SW8 BX43 66
Richborough Rd. NW2 BQ35 46
Rich Clo. West. CH62 106
Richfield Rd. Bush. BG26 36
Richford Rd. E15 CG37 58
Richford St. W6 BQ41 65
Richings Way, Iver. AV41 62
Richland Av. Couls. BV60 95
Richlands Av. Epsom. BP56 94
Richmer Rd. Erith CT43 69
Richmond Av. E4 CF28 39
Richmond Av. N1 BX37 56
Richmond Av. NW10 BQ36 55
Richmond Av. SW20 BR51 85
Richmond Av. Felt. BB46 73
Richmond Av. Uxb. AZ36 53
Richmond Br. Rich. & Twick. BK46 74
Richmond Bldgs. W1 BW39 56
Dean St.
Richmond Clo. Epsom. BO60 94
Richmond Clo. Lthd. BF65 102
Richmond Clo. Wal. Cr. CC18 21
Dewhurst Rd.
Richmond Ct. SW20 BP51 85
Richmond Rd.
Richmond Cres. E4 CF28 39
Richmond Cres. N1 BY37 56
Richmond Cres. N9 CB26 39
Richmond Cres. Slou. AQ40 52
Richmond Cres. Stai. AV49 72
Richmond Dr. Shep. BA53 83
Richmond Dr. Wat. BB23 26
Richmond Gdns. NW4 BP31 46
Richmond Gdns. Har. BH29 36
Richmond Grn. Croy. BX55 86
Richmond Gro. N1 BY36 56
Halton Rd.
Richmond Gro. Surb. BL53 85
Richmond Hl. Rich. BL46 75
Richmond Hl. Ct. Rich. BL46 75
Richmond Ms. W1 BW39 56
Dean St.
Richmond Pk. Rd. SW14 BN46 75
Richmond Pk. Rd. Kings. On T. BL51 85
Richmond Rd. E4 CF26 39
Richmond Rd. E7 CH35 49
Richmond Rd. E8 CA36 57
Richmond Rd. E11 CF34 48
Richmond Rd. E17 CD32 48
Richmond Rd. N2 BT30 38
Brighton Rd.
Richmond Rd. N3 BT30 38
Chamberlain Rd.
Richmond Rd. N11 BX29 38
Richmond Rd. N15 CA32 48
Richmond Rd. SW20 BP51 85
Richmond Rd. W5 BL41 65
Richmond Rd. Barn. BS25 29
Richmond Rd. Couls. BV61 104
Richmond Rd. Croy. BX55 86
Richmond Rd. Grays. DE43 71
Richmond Rd. Ilf. CM34 49
Richmond Rd. Islw. BJ45 64
Richmond Rd. Kings. On T. BK49 74
Richmond Rd. Pot. B. BT19 20
Richmond Rd. Rom. CT32 50
Richmond Rd. Stai. AV49 72
Richmond Rd. Th. Hth. BY52 86
Richmond Rd. Twick. BJ47 74
Richmond St. E13 CH37 58
Richmond Ter. SW1 BX41 66
Richmond Ter. Ms. SW1 BX41 66
Parliament St.
Richmond Way, E11 CH34 49
Richmond Way W12 BQ41 65
Richmond Way W14 BQ41 65
Richmond Way, Lthd. BF65 102
Richmond Way, Rick. BA24 26
Richmount Gdns. SE3 CH45 68
Rich St. E14 CD40 57
Rickard Clo. SW2 BX47 76
Ricketts Hill Rd. West. CJ62 106
Rickett St. SW6 BS43 66
Rickman Cres. Wey. AW55 83
Rickman Hill Couls. BV62 104
Rickman Hill Rd. Couls. BV62 104
Rickmans La. Slou. AP35 43
Rickmans La. Slou. AP36 52
Rickman St. E1 CC38 57
Mantos Rd.
Rickmansworth By-pass. Rick. AX26 35
Rickmansworth La. Ger. Cr. AS29 34
Rickmansworth Rd. Amer. AO22 25
Rickmansworth Rd. Nthwd. AZ28 35
Rickmansworth Rd. Pnr. BC30 35
Rickmansworth Rd. Rick. AV24 25
Rickmansworth Rd. Rick. AX26 35
Rickmansworth Rd. Uxb. AX30 35
Rickmansworth Rd. Wat. BB24 26
Ricksons Lane. Leath. AZ67 110
Rickyard, Guil. AO70 118
Ridding La. Grnf. BH35 45
Riddings La. Harl. CO13 14
Riddlesdown Av. Pur. BZ59 96
Riddlesdown Rd. Pur. BZ59 96
Riddons Rd. SE12 CJ48 78
Riders Way. Gdse. CC69 114
Ride, The, Brent. BJ42 64
Ride, The, Enf. CC24 30
Ride, The, Leath. BB66 110
Ridgdale Rd. E3 CE37 57
Ridge Av. N21 BZ26 39
Ridge Av. Dart. CT46 79
Ridgebrook Rd. SE3 CJ45 68
Ridgebrook Ter. SE3 CJ45 68
Ridge Clo. NW4 BQ30 37
Ridge Clo. NW9 BN31 46
Ridge Clo. Bet. BM72 120
Ridge Clo. Houns. BF45 64
Ridge Crest. Enf. BX23 29
Ridgecroft Clo. Bex. CS47 79
St. Mary's Rd.
Ridgegate Clo. Reig. BT69 121
Ridge Grn. Red. BX72 121
Ridge Grn. Clo. Red. BX72 121
Ridge Hill, Pot. B. BN18 19
Ridge Hl. NW11 BR33 46
Ridgehurst Av. Wat. BB20 17
Ridge La. Pot. B. BO20 19
Ridge La. Wat. BB21 26
Ridge Langley Sth. Croy. CB58 96
Ridgemead Rd. Egh. AQ48 72
Ridgemount, Guil. AQ71 118
Ridgemount Av. Couls. BV62 104
Ridgemount Av. Croy. CC55 87
Ridgemount Clo. SE20 CB50 77
Ridgemount Gdns. Enf. BY23 29
Ridge Pk. Pur. BW58 95
Ridge Rd. N8 BX32 47
Ridge Rd. N21 BZ26 39
Ridge Rd. NW2 BR34 46
Ridge Rd. Mitch. BV50 76
Ridge Rd. Sutt. BR54 85
Ridge Rd. W. Red. BW66 113
Ridge St. Wat. BC22 26
Ridge, The, Bex. CQ47 79
Ridge, The, Cat. CE66 114
Ridge, The, Couls. BX60 95
Ridge, The, Epsom BN62 103
Ridge, The Guil. AR73 118
Ridge, The, Orp. CM55 88
Ridge, The, Pur. BW58 95
Ridge, The, Surb. BM53 85
Ridge, The, Twick. BG47 74
Ridge, The Wok. AT62 100
Ridge, The, Way Sth. Croy. CA58 96
Ridge Vw. Clo. Barn. BQ25 28
Ridgeview Rd. N20 BS27 38
Ridgeway N14 BX27 38
Ridgeway, Berk. AP13 7
Ridgeway Brom. CH55 88
Ridgeway, Brwd. DD26 122
Ridge Way Dart. CT46 79
Ridgeway, Dart. CZ49 80
Ridgeway Epsom BN59 94
Ridge Way Felt. BE48 74
Ridgeway, Grays. DF42 71
Ridge Way, Iver AV40 52
Ridgeway, Rick. AW26 35
Ridgeway Rom. CW30 42
Ridgeway, Walt. BB54 83
Ridgeway, Wdf. Grn. CJ28 40
Ridgeway, Welw. G. C. BS8 5
Ridgeway, Wok. AR61 100
Ridgeway Av. Barn. BU25 29
Ridgeway Av. Grav. DG48 81
Ridgeway Clo. Dor. BJ72 119
Ridgeway Rd.
Ridgeway Clo. Lthd. BG60 93
Ridgeway Clo. Red. BU71 121
Ridgeway Cres. Orp. CN55 88
Ridgeway Cres. Gdns. Orp. CN55 88
Ridgeway Dr. Brom. CH49 78
Ridgeway Gdns. Ilf. CK32 49
Ridgeway Rd. E4 CF26 39
Ridgeway Rd. Dor. BJ72 119
Ridgeway Rd. Islw. BH43 64
Ridgeway Rd. Red. BU70 121
Ridgeway Rd. Wok. AV61 100
Ridgeway Rd. The. Pot. B. BU21 29
Ridgeway, The, E4 CE27 39
Ridgeway, The, N3 BS29 38
Ridgeway, The, N11 BU28 38
Ridgeway, The, NW7 BP27 37
Ridgeway, The, NW9 BN31 46
Ridgeway, The, NW11 BR33 46
Ridgeway, The, W3 BM41 65
Ridgeway, The Amer. AO23 25
Ridgeway, The, Croy. BX55 86
Ridgeway, The, Enf. BV21 29
Ridgeway, The, Enf. BY23 29
Ridgeway, The, Ger. Cr. AR31 43
Ridgeway, The Guil. AT71 118
Ridgeway, The, Har. BE32 45
Ridgeway, The, Har. BF32 45
Ridgeway, The, Har. BK32 45
Ridgeway, The. Lthd. BG60 93
Ridgeway, The Lthd. BG65 102
Ridgeway, The, Pot. B. BV17 20
Ridgeway, The, Rad. BJ21 27
Ridgeway, The, Rom. CU31 50
Ridgeway, The, Ruis. BC33 44
Ridgeway, The, St. Alb. BJ11 9
Ridgeway, The, Stan. BK29 36
Ridgeway, The Wat. BB22 26
Ridgeway Wk. Nthlt. BE36 54
Ridgeway West, Sid. CN46 78
Ridgewell Clo. Dag. CR37 59
Ridgewell Rd. E16 CJ39 58
Ridgmont Gdns. Edg. BN28 37
Ridgmont Rd. St. Alb. BH14 9
Ridgmount Gdns. WC1 BW38 56
Ridgmount Rd. SW18 BS46 76
Ridgmount St. WC1 BW39 56
Store St.
Ridgway, SW19 BQ50 75
Ridgway Clo. Wok. AR61 100
Ridgway Gdns. SW19 BQ50 75
Ridgway Ms. SW19 BR50 75
Ridgway Pl. SW19 BR50 75
Ridgway Rd. SW9 BY45 66
Ridgway, The, Sutt. BT57 95
Riding Court Rd. Slou. AR43 62
Ridinge, The Amer. AO21 25
Riding Hill Sth. Croy. CB60 96
Riding Horse St. W1 BV39 56
Riding La. Ton. & Sev. CY71 117
Ridings Av. Enf. BY24 29
Ridings La. Wok. AZ65 101
Ridings Rd. Kings. On T. BN49 75
Ridings, The, W5 BL39 55
Ridings, The Ash. BK62 102
Ridings, The Ches. AR21 25
Ridings, The. Cob. BF59 93
Ridings, The, Epsom BO61 103
Ridings, The. Iver. AV42 62
Ridings, The, Loug. CJ24 31
Ridings, The Reig. BT69 121
Ridings, The, Sun. BC51 83
Ridings, The, Surb. BM53 85
Ridings, The, Tad. BR63 103
Ridings, The, West. CK62 106
Ridings, The Wey. AV57 91
Riding, The, NW11 BR33 46
Golders Green Rd.
Riding, The Wok. AT60 91
Ridlands La. Oxt. CJ68 115
Ridlands Ri. Oxt. CK68 115
Ridler Rd. Enf. CA22 30
Ridley Av. W13 BJ41 64
Ridley Clo. Brom. CG52 88
Ridley Clo. Rom. CU30 41
Ridley Rd. E7 CJ35 49
Ridley Rd. E8 CA35 48
Ridley Rd. NW10 BP37 55
Ridley Rd. SW19 BS50 76
Ridley Rd. Brom. CG52 88
Ridley Rd. Warl. CC62 105
Ridley Rd. Well. CO44 69
Ridley Several SE3 CH44 68
Blackheath Pk.
Ridout St. SE18 CK42 68
Ridsale Rd. SE20 CB51 87
Riefield Rd. SE9 CM46 78
Riesco Dr. Croy. CC57 96
Riffel Rd. NW2 BQ35 46
Rifle Butts Alley Epsom. BO60 94
Rifle Ct. SE11 BY43 66
Kennington Pk. Rd.
Rifle Pl. W11 BQ40 55
Rifle St. E14 CE39 57
Rigault Rd. SW6 BR44 65
Rigby Clo. Croy. BY55 86
Rigby Gdns. Grays. DG42 71
Rigby La. Hayes. BA40 53
Rigby La. Hayes. BA41 63
Rigby Mews Ilf. CL34 49
Rigden St. E14 CE39 57
Rigeley Rd. NW10 BP38 55
Rigg App. E10 CC33 48
Rigge Clo. Wok. AQ64 100
Riggindale Rd. SW16 BW49 76
Riley Rd. SE1 CA41 67
Riley Rd. Enf. CC22 30
Riley St. SW10 BT43 66
Ringcroft Rd. N7 BY35 47
Madras Pl.
Ringers Rd. Brom. CH52 88
Ringford Rd. SW18 BR46 75
Ringlestone Clo. West Dr. AY43 63
Ringley Pk. Av. Reig. BT71 121
Ringley Pk. Rd. Reig. BT70 121
Ringmer Av. SW6 BR44 65
Ringmer Pl. N21 BZ25 30
Ringmore Ri. SE23 CB47 77
Ringmore Rd. Walt. BD55 84
Ring Rd. D. Hayes BC40 53
Ringshall Rd. Orp. CO52 89
Ringslade Rd. N22 BX30 38
Ringstead Rd. SE6 CE47 77
Ringstead Rd. Sutt. BT56 95
Ring, The, W2 BT40 56
Ringway N11 BW29 38
Ringway Sthl. BE42 64
Ring Way Rd. St. Alb. BG17 18
Ringwold Clo. Beck. CD50 77
Aldersmead Rd.
Ringwood Av. N2 BU30 38
Ringwood Av. Croy. BX54 86
Ringwood Av. Horn. CV34 51
Ringwood Av. Orp. CP58 98
Ringwood Av. Red. BU69 121
Ringwood Clo. Pnr. BD31 45
Ringwood Rd. E17 CD32 48
Ringwood Way N21 BY26 38
Ringwood Way Hamptn. BF49 74
Ripley Av. Egh. AS50 72
Ripley-by-Pass, Wok. AX65 101
Ripley By Pass. Wok. AV66 109
Ripley Clo. Croy. CF57 96
Ripley Clo. Slou. AS42 62
Ripley Gdns. SW14 BN45 65
Ripley Gdns. Sutt. BT56 95
Ripley Lane. Leath. HZ66 110
Ripley La. Wok. AY65 101
Ripley Rd. E16 CJ39 58
Ripley Rd. Belv. CR42 69
Ripley Road. Guil. AW67 110
Ripley Rd. Hmptn. BF50 74
Ripley Rd. Ilf. CN34 49
Ripley Vw. Loug. CL22 31
Ripley Way, Hem. H. AV13 7
Ripley Way, Wal. Cr. CB18 21
Riplington Ct. SW15 BP47 75
Ripon Clo. Guil. AP69 118
Ripon Clo. Nthlt. BF36 54
Ripon Gdns. Chess. BK56 93
Ripon Gdns. Ilf. CK32 49
Ripon Rd. N9 CB26 39
Ripon Rd. N17 BZ31 48
Ripon Rd. SE18 CL43 68
Ripon Way Borwd. BN24 28
Rippersley Rd. Well. CO44 69
Ripple Rd. Bark. CM36 58
Ripplevale Gro. N1 BX36 56
Rippolson Rd. SE18 CN42 68
Ripston Rd. Ashf. BA49 73
Risborough Dr. Wor. Pk. BP54 85
Risborough St. SE1 BY41 66
Risdon St. SE16 CC41 67
Risebridge Chase Rom. CT29 41
Risebridge Rd. Rom. CT30 41
Risedale Clo. Hem. H. AY15 8
Risedale Hill, Hem. H. AY15 8
Risedale Rd. Bexh. CR45 69
Risedale Rd. Hem. H. AY15 8
Riseldine Rd. SE23 CD46 77
Rise Pk. Boul. Rom. CT30 41
Rise Pk. Pde. Rom. CT30 41
Rise, The, E11 CH32 49
Rise, The, N13 BY28 38
Rise, The, NW7 BO29 37
Rise, The, NW10 BN34 46
Rise, The Amer. AO22 25
Rise, The, Borwd. BL25 28
Rise, The, Buck. H. CJ26 40
Rise, The, Couls. BW60 95
Rise, The, Dart. CT45 69
Rise, The, Edg. BM28 37
Rise, The, Epsom BO58 94
Rise, The, Grav. DJ49 81
Rise, The, Grnf. BJ35 45
Rise, The, St. Alb. BG16 18
Rise, The Sev. CV67 117
Rise, The, Sid. CP47 79
Rise, The, Sth. Croy. CC58 96
Rise, The Uxb. AY37 53
Riseway, Brwd. DC27 122
Rising Hill Clo. Nthwd. BA29 35
Risinghill St. N1 BX37 56
Risingholme Clo. Bush. BF26 36
Risingholme Clo. Har. BH30 36
Risingholme Rd. Har. BH30 36
Risings, The, E17 CF31 48
Risley Av. N17 BZ30 39
Rita Rd. SW8 BX43 66
Ritches Rd. N15 BZ32 48
Ritchie Rd. Croy. CB53 87
Ritchie St. N1 BY37 56
Ritchings Av. E17 CD31 48
Ritcroft Clo. Hem. H. AZ14 8
Ritcroft St. Hem. H. AZ14 8
Ritherdon Rd. SW17 BV48 76
Ritson Rd. E8 CB36 57
Ritter St. SE18 CL43 68
Ritz Ct. Pot. B. BS19 20
Rivaz Pl. E9 CC36 57
Rivenhall Gdns. E18 CG31 49
River Av. N13 BY27 38
River Av. Hodd. CE11 12
River Av. Surb. BJ54 84
River Bank N21 BZ26 39
River Bank, SE10 CF41 67
Riverbank E. Mol. BH52 84
River Bnk. Surb. BH53 84
River Clo. E11 CJ32 49
River Clo. Rain. CU39 59
River Clo. Ruis. BB32 44
River Clo. Surb BK53 84
Rivercourt Rd. W6 BP42 65
Riverdale Dr. Wok. AS64 100
Riverdale Gdns. Twick. BK46 74
Riverdale Rd. SE18 CN42 68
Riverdale Rd. Bex. CQ47 79
Riverdale Rd. Erith. CR42 69
Riverdale Rd. Felt. BE49 74
Riverdale Rd. Twick. BK46 74
Riverdene Edg. BN27 37
Riverdene Rd. Ilf. CL34 49
River Dr. Upmin. CY32 51
Riverfield Rd. Stai. AV50 72
River Front Enf. BZ24 30
River Gdns. Cars. BV55 86
River Gdns. Felt. BD46 74
River Grove Pk. Beck. CD51 87
River Hill, Sev. CW68 117
Riverholme Dr. Epsom BN58 94
River La. Lthd. BG64 102
River La. Rich. BK47 74
Rivermead Clo. Wey. AX57 92
River Mead Ct. SW6 BR45 65
Ranelagh Gdns.
River Meads Av. Twick. BF48 74
River Meads Est. Twick. BF48 74
Rivermill, Harl. CM10 6
Rivermount, Walt. BB54 83
River Nook Clo. Walt. BD53 84
River Pk. Gdns. Brom. CF50 77
River Park Rd. N22 BX30 38
River Pl. N1 BZ36 57
River Reach, Tedd. BK49 74
Broom Water
River Reach, Tedd. BK50 74
River Rd. Bark. CN37 58
River Rd. Brwd. CZ28 42
River Rd. Buck. H. CK26 40
River Rd. Stai. AV51 82
Riversdale Rd. N5 BY34 47
Riversdale Rd. Rom. CR29 41
Riversdale Rd. Surb. BJ53 84
Rivers End Rd. Hem. H. AX15 8
Riversfield Rd. Enf. CA24 30
Riverside NW4 BP33 46
Riverside, SE7 CH41 68
Riverside, Dor. BK70 119
Riverside, Guil. AR69 118
Riverside, Stai. AR47 72
Riverside, Stai. AT48 72
Riverside, Twick. BJ47 74
Riverside Av. Brox. CE14 12
Riverside Av. E. Mol. BG53 84
Riverside Clo. W7 BH38 54
Riverside Clo. Kings-on-t. BK52 84
Riverside Clo. St. Alb. BH14 9
Riverside Clo. Stai. AV50 72
Riverside Clo. Stai. AV51 82
Riverside Clo. Wall. BV55 86
Riverside Dr. W4 BN43 65
Riverside Dr. Esher BF56 93
Riverside Dr. Mitch. BU53 86
Riverside Dr. Rich. BJ48 74
Riverside Dr. Rick. AX26 35
Riverside Dr. Stai. AV49 72
Riverside Dr. Stai. AV51 82
Riverside Gdns. W6 BP42 65
Riverside Gdns. Berk. AQ12 7
Riverside Gdns. Enf. BZ23 30
Riverside Gdns. Wem. BL37 55
Riverside Pl. Stai. AX46 73
Riverside Rd. E15 CF37 57
Riverside Rd. N15 CB32 48
Riverside Rd. SW17 BS49 76

Riverside Rd. St. Alb. BH14 9
Riverside Rd. Sid. CQ48 79
Riverside Rd. Stai. AV50 72
Riverside Rd. Stai. AX46 73
Riverside Rd. Walt. BE56 93
Riverside Rd. Wat. BC25 26
Riverside, Shep. BB54 83
Riverside Wk. SE1 BX41 66
Riverside Wk. Bex. CP47 79
Riverside Wk. Islw. BH45 64
Riverside Way Dart. CW46 80
Riversmead, Hodd. CE12 12
Riversmead, Wey. AY60 92
Rivers Rd. Slou. AS41 62
River St. EC1 BY38 56
River St. Wind. AO43 61
River Ter. W6 BQ42 65
Crisp Rd.
River Ter. Berk. AQ12 7
River Vw. Enf. BZ24 30
River Vw. Grays. DF42 71
River View Gdns. SW13 BP43 65
River Vw. Gdns. Twick. BH48 74
Riverview Gro. W4 BM43 65
Riverview Pk. SE6 CE48 77
Riverview Rd. W4 BM43 65
Riverview Rd. Epsom. BN55 85
Riverview Rd. Epsom BN56 94
River View Rd. Green. DA46 80
River Wk. Uxb. AX35 44
River Wk. Walt. BC53 83
Riverway N13 BY28 38
River Way SE10 CG41 68
River Way Epsom BN56 94
Riverway, Harl. CO9 6
River Way Loug. CK25 31
Riverway, Stai. AW51 83
River Way Twick. BF48 74
Riverwood La. Chis. CM51 88
Rivey Clo. Wey. AV60 91
Rivfield La. Saw. CQ5 6
Rivington Av. Wdf. Grn. CJ30 40
Rivington Ct. NW10 BO36 55
Rivington Ct. NW10 BP37 55
Longstone Av.
Rivington St. EC2 CA38 57
Rivulet Rd. N17 BZ29 39
Rixon Ho. SE18 CL43 68
Rixsen Rd. E12 CK35 49
Roach Rd. E3 CE36 57
Roads Pl. N4 BW34 47
Hornsey Rd.
Roads Pl. N4 BX34 47
Roakes Av. Wey. AW55 83
Roan St. SE10 CE43 67
Roasthill La. Wind. AL43 61
Robart House, E11 CG33 49
Robb Rd. Stan. BJ29 36
Robbs Clo. Hem. H. AW12 8
Robe End. Hem. H. AV12 7
Robert Adam St. W1 BV39 56
Roberta St. E2 CB38 57
Robert Av. St. Alb. BF15 9
Robert Clo. W9 BT38 56
Robert Clo. Chig. CN28 40
Robert Clo. Pot. B. BR20 19
Robert Clo. Walt. BC56 92
Robert Gentry Ho. W14 BR42 65
Robert Ms. NW1 BW38 56
Hampstead Rd.
Roberton Dr. Brom. CJ51 88
Robert Owen Ho. SW6 BQ44 65
Robert Rd. Slou. AO34 43
Roberts Alley W5 BK41 64
Church Gdns.
Robertsbridge Rd. Cars. BT54 86
Roberts Clo. Rom. CU30 41
Roberts Clo. Stai. AX46 73
Park Rd.
Roberts La. Ger. Cr. AT28 34
Robertson Rd. E15 CF37 57
Robertson St. SW8 BV45 66
Roberts Rd. E17 CE30 39
Roberts Rd NW7 BR29 37
Roberts Rd. Belv. CR42 69
Roberts St. Wat. BD25 27
Robert St. E2 CB37 57
Old Bethnal Green Rd.
Robert St. E16 CL40 58
Robert St. NW1 BV38 56
Robert St. SE18 CM42 68
Robert St. WC2 BX40 56
Savoy Pl.
Robert St. Croy. BZ55 87
High St.
Roberts Way, Egh. AR50 72
Robina Clo. Bexh. CP45 69
Brunswick Rd.
Robin Clo. Rom. CS29 41
Robin Gro. N6 BV34 47
Robin Gro. Brent. BK43 64
Robin Gro. Harrow BL32 46
Robin Hill. Berk. AR13 7
Robin Hill Dr. Chis. CK50 78
Wood Dr.
Robin Hood Clo. Mitch. BW52 86
Robinhood Clo. Slou. AM40 61
Robin Hood Clo. Wok. AP62 100
Robin Hood Cres, Wok. AP62 100
Robin Hood Dr. Bush. BE23 27
Robin Hood Dr. Har. BH29 36
Robin Hood Grn. Orp. CO53 89
Robin Hood La. E14 CF39 57
Robin Hood La. SW15 BO48 75
Robin Hood La. Bexh. CQ46 79
Robin Hood La. Guil. AS65 100
Robin Hood La. Guil. AS66 109
Robin Hood La. Hat. BP12 10
Common, The.
Robin Hood La. Mitch. BW52 86
Robin Hood La. Sutt. BS56 95
Robin Hood Meadow. Hem. H. AY11 8
Robin Hood Rd. SW19 BO49 75
Robin Hood Rd. Brwd. DB26 42
Robin Hood Rd. Wok. AP62 100
Robin Hood Way SW15 BO49 75
Robin Hood Way SW20 BO49 75
Robin Hood Way Grnf. BH36 54
Robin Hood Yd. EC1 BY39 56
Leather Lane
Robinia Av. Grav. DE47 81
Robinia Clo. Chig. CN29 40
Robin Md. Welw. G. C. BS6 5
Robin Rd. Hem. H. AZ14 8
Robins Clo. Uxb. AX39 53
Robin's Ct. SE12 CJ48 78
Robins Ct. Beck. CF51 87
Robins Dale, Wok. AO62 100
Robinsfield, Hem. H. AW13 8
Robins Gro. Kes. CH55 88
Robins Nest Hill. Hert. BW11 11
Robinson Av. Wal. Cr. BY17 20
Robinson Cres. Bush. BG27 36
Robinson Rd. E2 CC37 57
Robinson Rd. SW17 BU50 76
Robinson Rd. Dag. CR35 50
Robinsons Clo. W13 BJ39 54
Robins Orchard. Ger. Cr. AS29 34
Robins, The, Brwd. DB21 33
Robin St. SW3 BU42 66
Flood St.
Robinsway Wal. Abb. CG20 22
Roundhills
Robinsway Walt. BD56 93
Robins Wy. Hat. BO14 10
Robin Way, Guil. AQ68 109
Robin Way Orp. CO52 89
Robin Way, Pot. B. BX17 20
Robin Way, Stai. AV48 72
Robsart St. SW9 BX44 66
Robson Clo. Enf. BY23 29
Robson Clo. Ger. Cr. AR28 34
Robson Rd. SE27 BY48 76
Robyn's Way. Sev. CT64 107
Roch Av. Edg. BL30 37
Rochdale Rd. E17 CE33 48
Rochdale Rd. SE2 CO42 69
Rochelle St. E2 CA38 57
Swanfield St.
Roche Rd. SW16 BX51 86
Rochester Av. E13 CJ37 58
Rochester Av. Brom. CH51 88
Rochester Av. Felt. BB48 73
Rochester Clo. SE3 CJ45 68
Rochester Clo. Enf. CA23 30
Rochester Clo. Sid. CO46 79
Rochester Dri. Bexh. CR46 79
Rochester Dr. Pnr. BD32 45
Rochester Gdns. Croy. CA55 87
Rochester Gdns. Ilf. CK33 49
Rochester Mews NW1 BW36 56
Rochester Rd.
Rochester Pl. NW1 BW36 56
Rochester Rd. NW1 BW36 56
Rochester Rd. Dart. CX47 80
Rochester Rd. Grav. DJ47 81
Rochester Rd. Nthwd. BB31 44
Rochester Row, SW1 BW42 66
Rochester Sq. NW1 BW36 56
Rochester St. SW1 BW42 66
Rochester Row
Rochester Ter. NW1 BW36 56
Rochester Wk. Reig. BS73 121
Castle Dr.
Rochester Way SE3 CH44 68
Rochester Way SE9 CH44 68
Rochester Way Dart. CT47 79
Rochester Way, Rick. AZ24 26
Roche Wk. Cars. BT53 86
Rochford Av. Brwd. DD25 122
Rochford Av. Loug. CM24 31
Rochford Av. Rom. CP32 50
Rochford Av. Wal. Abb. CF20 21
Rochford Clo. E13 CJ37 58
Boleyn Rd.
Rochford Clo. Brox. CD16 21
Rochford Clo. Horn. CU36 59
Rochford Grn. Loug. CM24 31
Rochford St. NW5 BU35 47
Rochford Wk. E8 CB36 57
Wilman Gro.
Rochford Way Croy. BX53 86
Rock Av. SW14 BN45 65
South Worple Way
Rockbourne Rd. SE23 CC47 77
Rockchase Gdns. Horn. CW32 51
Rockcliffe Av. Kings L. AZ18 17
Rockdale Rd. Sev. CU66 116
Rockells Pl. SE22 CB46 77
Rockfield Rd. Oxt. CG68 115
Rockford Av. Grnf. BJ37 54
Rock Gro. SE16 CB42 67
Blue Anchor La.
Rockhall Rd. NW2 BQ35 46
Rockhampton Rd. SE27 BY49 76
Rockhampton Rd. Sth. Croy. BZ57 96
Rock Hill, SE26 CA49 77
Rock Hill Orp. CR57 98
Rockingham Av. Horn. CU32 50
Rockingham Clo. Uxb. AX37 53
Rockingham Est. SE1 BZ41 67
Rockingham Par. Uxb. AX37 53
Rockingham Rd. Uxb. AW 53
Rockingham St. SE1 BZ41 67
Rocklands Dr. Stan. BJ30 36
Rocklands Rd. SW15 BR45 65
Rock La. Dag. CR35 50
Rockley Rd. W14 BQ41 65
Rockmead Rd. E9 CC37 57
Rockmount Rd. SE18 CN42 68
Rockmount Rd. SE19 BZ50 77
Rockshaw Rd. Red. BW67 113
Rocks La. SW13 BP44 65
Rock St. N4 BY34 47
Rockware Av. Grnf. BH37 54
Rockways Barn. BO25 28
Rockwell Gdns. Dag. CR35 50
Rockwell Rd. Dag. CR35 50
Rockwells Ct. SE19 CA49 77
Rockwells Gdns. SE19 CA49 77
Rockwood Gdns. Wdf. Grn. CH27 40
Whitehall La.
Rockwood Pl. W12 BQ41 65
Shepherds Bush Grn.
Rocky La. Reig. BU67 113
Rocliffe St. N1 BY37 56
Rocque La. SE3 CG45 68
Rodborough Rd. NW11 BS33 47
Rodd La. EC3 CA40 57
Roden Clo. Harl. CQ9 6
Roden Gdns. Croy. CA53 87
Rodenhurst Rd. SW4 BW46 76
Roden St. N7 BX34 47
Roden St. Ilf. CL34 49
Roden Way, Ilf. CL34 49
Roden St.
Roderick Rd. NW3 BU35 47
Roding Av. Wdf. Grn. CK29 40
Roding Ho. Wdf. Grn. CK29 40
Roding La. Buck. H. CJ27 40
Roding La. N. Wdf. Grn. CJ30 40
Roding La. S. Ilf. CJ31 49
Roding Rd. E5 CC35 48
Roding Rd. Loug. CK25 31
Rodings, The, Upmin. CY32 51
Rodings, The, Wdf. Grn. CJ29 40
Snakes La.
Roding St. E7 CH35 49
Oakhurst Rd.
Roding Trading Est. Bark. CL36 58
Roding Vw. Buck. H. CJ26 40
Roding Vw. Ong. CX17 24
Roding Way. Rain. CV37 60
Briscoe Rd.
Rodmarton St. W1 BU39 56
Rodmell Slope N12 BR28 37
Rodmere St. SE10 CG42 68
Rodmill La. SW2 BX47 76
Rodney Av. St. Alb. BJ14 9
Rodney Clo. Croy. BY54 86
Rodney Clo. N. Mal. BO52 85
Rodney Clo. Pnr. BE33 45
Rodney Ct. W9 BT38 56
Rodney Cres. Hodd. CE11 12
Rodney Gdns. Guil. AT70 118
Rodney Gdns. Kes. CH56 97
Rodney Gdns. Pnr. BC32 44
Rodney Pl. E17 CD30 39
Rodney Pl. SE17 BZ42 67
Rodney Pl. SW19 BT51 86
Rodney Rd. E11 CH31 49
Rodney Rd. SE17 BZ42 67
Rodney Rd. Mitch. BU51 86
Rodney Rd. N. Mal. BO53 85
Rodney Rd. Ong. CW18 24
Rodney Rd. Walt. BC55 83
Rodney St. N1 BX37 56
Rodney St. SE18 CL41 68
Rodney Way. Rom. CR30 41
Rodney Way. Slou. AV44 62
Rodona La. Wey. BA59 92
Rodsley Pl. SE15 CB44 67
Commercial Way
Rodsley St. SE1 CB43 67
Old Kent Rd.
Rodway Rd. SW15 BP47 75
Rodwell Clo. Ruis. BD33 45
Rodwell Ct. Wey. AV57 91
Rodwell Pl. Edg. BL29 37
Rodwell Rd. SE22 CA46 77
Roebourne Way, E16 CL40 58
Pier Rd.
Roebuck Clo. N17 CA29 39
High Rd.
Roebuck Gdns. Slou. AM40 61
Roebuck La. Buck. H. CJ26 40
Roebuck Rd. Chess. BM56 94
Roebuck Rd. Ilf. CO28 41
Roedean Av. Enf. CC23 30
Roedean Clo. Enf. CC23 30
Roedean Cres. SW15 BO46 75
Roe End, NW9 BN31 46
Roe Fields Clo. Hem. H. AW15 8
Roe Grn. NW9 BN32 46
Roe Green Cl. Hat. BO13 10
Roe Green La. Hat. BO12 10
Roehampton Clo. SW15 BP45 65
Roehampton Clo. Grav. DJ47 81
Roehampton Dr. Chis. CM50 78
Roehampton Gate, SW15 BO46 75
Roehampton High St. SW15 BP47 75
Roehampton La. SW15 BP45 65
Roehampton Vale SW15 BO48 75
Roe Hill Cl. Hat. BO13 10
Roe La. NW9 BM31 46
Roestock Gdns. St. Alb. BO14 10
Roestock La. St. Alb. BN15 10
Roe Way Wall. BX57 95
Rofant Rd. Nthwd. BB29 35
Roffes La. Cat. BZ66 114
Roffey Clo. Pur. BY61 104
Roffey St. E14 CF41 67
Roger's Cl. Cat. CB64 105
Rogers Clo. Couls. BY62 104
Rogers Gdns. Dag. CR35 50
Rogers La. Slou. AP36 52
Rogers Mead. Gdse. CB69 114
Rogers Rd. E16 CG39 58
Rogers Rd. SW17 BT49 76
Rogers Rd. Dag. CR35 50
Rogers Rd. Grays. DE42 71
Rogers Ruff. Nthwd. BA30 35
Roger St. WC1 BX38 56
Rojack Rd. SE23 CC47 77
Rokeby Gdns. Wdf. Grn. CH30 40
Rokeby Rd. SE4 CD44 67
Rokeby St. E15 CF37 57
Roke Clo. Ken. BZ60 96
Roke Lodge Rd. Ken. BY60 95
Roke Rd. Ken. BY61 104
Roker Park Av. Uxb. AY35 44
Rokesby Clo. Well. CM44 68
Rokesly Av. N8 BX32 47
Roland Gdns. SW7 BT42 66
Roland Gdns. SW10 BT42 66
Roland Gdns. Felt. BE48 74
Roland Rd. E17 CF32 48
Roland St. St. Alb. BJ13 9
Roland Way SW7 BT42 66
Roland Way Wor. Pk. BO55 85
Roles Gro. Rom. CP31 50
Rolfe Clo. Barn. BU24 29
Rolfe Rd. SE7 CK42 68
Rollesby Rd. Chess. BM57 94
Rolleston Av. Orp. CL53 88
Rolleston Clo. Orp. CL54 88
Rolleston Rd. Sth. Croy. BZ57 96
Roll Gdns. Ilf. CL32 49
Rollings Clo. Rick. AW26 35
Rollins St. SE15 CC43 67
Rollit Cres. Houns. BF46 74
Rollit St. N7 BY35 47
Hornsey Rd.
Rollo Rd. Swan. CT50 79
Rolls Bldgs. EC4 BY39 56
Fetter La.
Rollscourt Av. SE24 BZ46 77
Rolls Park Av. E4 CE28 39
Rolls Park Rd. E4 CE28 39
Rolls Pass. EC4 BY39 56
Chancery La.
Rolls Rd. SE1 CA42 67
Rollswood. Welw. G. C. BR9 5
Rolt St. SE8 CD43 67
Roman Clo. Felt. BC46 73
Roman Clo. Rain. CS37 59
Romanhurst Av. Brom. CG52 88
Romanhurst Gdns. Brom. CG52 88
Roman Rise SE19 BZ50 77
Roman Rd. E2 CC38 57
Roman Rd. E3 CC38 57
Roman Rd. E6 CK38 58
Roman Rd. N10 BV29 38
Roman Rd. W4 BO42 65
Roman Rd. Epsom. BL65 103
Roman Rd. Grav. DE48 81
Roman Rd. Ilf. CL36 58
Roman St. Hodd. CE11 12
Romans Way. Wok. AW61 101
Roman Villa Hill. S. Dnth. CY50 80
Roman Way N7 BX36 56
Roman Way, Croy. BY55 86
Roman Way, Enf. CA25 30
Romany Gdns. E17 CD30 39
Mcentee Ave.
Romany Gdns. Sutt. BS54 86
Romany Rise Orp. CM54 88
Romany Rd. Grav. DF48 81
Romany Rd. Wok. AO60 91
Roma Rd. E17 CD31 48
Romberg Rd. SW17 BV48 76
Romborough Gdns. SE13 CF46 77
Romborough Way, SE13 CE46 77
Romeland, St. Alb. BG13 9
Romeland, Wal. Abb. CF20 21
Romeland Hill, St. Alb. BG13 9
Romero Sq. SE9 CJ45 68
Romeyn Rd. SW16 BX48 76
Romford Cres. Rom. CT33 50
Romford Rd. E7 CG36 58
Romford Rd. E12 CG36 58
Romford Rd. E15 CG36 58
Romford Rd. Chig. CO27 41
Romford Rd. Ong. CW19 24
Romford Rd. S. Ock CW39 60
Romford St. E1 CB39 57
Romilly Dr. Wat. BE28 36
Romilly Rd. N4 BY34 47
Romilly St. W1 BW40 56
Rommany Rd. SE27 BZ48 77
Romney Chase Horn. CW32 51
Romney Chase, Horn. CX32 51
Romney Clo. N17 CB30 39
Romney Clo. NW11 BT33 47
Romney Clo. Ashf. BA49 73
Romney Clo. Chess. BL56 94
Romney Clo. Har. BF33 45
Romney Dr. Brom. CJ50 78
Romney Dr. Har. BF33 45
Romney Gdns. Bexh. CQ44 69
Romney Rd. SE10 CF43 67
Romney Rd. Hayes BA37 53
Romney Rd. N. Mal. BN53 85
Romney St. SW1 BW41 66
Romola Rd. SE24 BY47 76
Romsey Clo. Slou. AS41 62
Romsey Dr. Slou. AO34 43
Romsey Gdns. Dag. CP37 59
Romsey Rd. Dag. CP37 59
Ronald Av. E15 CG38 58
Ronald Clo. Beck. CD52 87
Ronald Rd. Rom. CX30 42
Ronalds Rd. N5 BY35 47
Ronald's Rd. Brom. CH51 88
Ronaldstone Rd. Sid. CN46 78
Rona Rd. NW3 BV35 47
Rona Wk. N1 BZ36 57
Marquess Est.
Rondu Rd. NW2 BR35 46
Ronelean Rd. Surb. BL55 85
Ronfearn Av. Orp. CP53 89
Ronneby Clo, Wey. BB55 83
Ronson Way, Lthd. BJ64 102
Ronver Rd. SE12 CG47 78
Rook Clo. Rain. CU37 59
Rook Dean. Sev. CS64 107
Rookeries Clo. Felt. BC48 73
Rookery Clo. NW9 BO32 46
Rookery Clo. Lthd. BG65 102
Rookery Cres. Dag. CR36 59
Rookery Dri. Dor. BF72 119
Rookery Dr. Chis. CL51 88
Rookery Gdns. Orp. CP53 89
Rookery Grays DA43 70
Rookery La. Brom. CJ53 88
Rookery La. Wal. Abb. CF18 21
Rookery Rd. SW4 BW45 66
Rookery Rd. Ing. DB17 24
Rookery Rd. Orp. CK58 97
Rookery Rd. Stai. AW49 73
Rookery, The Dor. BF72 119
Rookery, The, Wat. BC26 35
Rookery Vw. Grays. DE42 71
Rookery Way, NW9 BO32 46
Rookery Way. Tad. BR67 112
Rookesley Rd. Orp. CP54 89
Rooke Way SE10 CG42 68
Glenister Rd.
Rookfield Av. N10 BW31 47
Rookfield Clo. N10 BW31 47
Cranmore Way
Rook Hill Cat. BY65 104
Rook La. Cat. BX65 104
Rookley Clo. Sutt. BS58 95
Hulverston Clo.
Rooks Hill, Rick. AX24 26
Rooks Hill. Welw. G. C. BQ8 5
Rooksmead Rd. Sun. BB51 83
Rookstone Rd. SW17 BU49 76
Rookwood Av. Loug. CM24 31
Rookwood Av. N. Mal. BP52 85
Rookwood Av. Wall. BW56 95
Rookwood Clo. Grays. DD42 71
Rookwood Clo. Red. BY67 113
Rookwood Gdns. E4 CG27 40
Whitehall Rd.
Rookwood Gdns. Ilf. CO29 41
Rookwood Gdns. Loug. CM24 31
Rookwood Rd. N16 CA32 48
Roomcroft Clo. Wok. AU61 100
Roomcroft Dr. Wok. AU61 100
Roosevelt Way Dag. CS36 59
Roothill La. Bet. BM73 120
Ropemakers Flds. E14 CD40 57
Ropemaker St. EC2 BZ39 57
Ropers Av. E4 CE28 39
Roper St. SE9 CK46 78
Roper Way, Mitch. BV51 86
Ropery St. E3 CD38 57
Rope Wk. Sun. BD52 84
Rope Wk. Gdns. E1 CB39 57
Commercial Rd.
Rope Yard Rails. SE18 CL41 68
Ropley St. E2 CB37 57
Shipton St.
Rosa Alba Ms. N5 BZ35 48
Kelross Rd.
Rosa Av. Ashf. AZ49 73
Rosaline Rd. SW6 BR43 65
Rosamond St. SE26 CB48 77
Rosary Clo. Houns. BE44 64
Rosary Clo. Pot. B. BS18 20
Rosary Gdns. SW7 BT42 66
Rosary Gdns. Ashf. AZ49 73
Rosary, The, Egh. AV51 82
Rosavale Rd. SW6 BR43 65
Roscoe St. EC1 BZ38 57
Roseacre. Oxt. CH70 115
Rose Acre, Saw. CP5 6
Roseacre Clo. W13 BJ39 54
Roseacre Clo. Horn. CW33 51
Curtis Rd.
Roseacre Gdns. Guil. AV73 118
Roseacre Rd. Well. CO45 69
Rose Alley. SE1 BZ40 57
Roseary Clo. West Dr. AX42 63
Rose Av. E18 CH30 40
Rose Av. Grav. DJ47 81
Rose Av. Mitch. BU51 86
Rose Av. Mord. BT53 86
Rose Bank, SE20 CB50 77
Rose Bank, Brwd. DB27 42
Rosebank Epsom BN60 94
Rosebank, Wal. Abb. CG20 22
Rosebank Av. Horn. CV35 51
Rosebank Av. Wem. BH35 45
Rosebank Cotts. Wok. AS64 100
Rosebank Gdns. E3 CD37 57
St. Stephens Rd.
Rosebank Gdns. W3 BN39 55
York Rd.
Rosebank Gro. E17 CD31 48
Rosebank Rd. E3 CD37 57
Norman Gro.
Rosebank Rd. E17 CE32 48
Rosebank Rd. W7 BH41 64
Rosebank Vill. E17 CE31 48
High St.
Rosebank Way W3 BN39 55
Roseberry Av. EC1 BY38 56
Roseberry Clo. Mord. BQ53 85
Roseberry Clo. Upmin. CZ32 51
Roseberry Gdns. Dart. CV47 80
Roseberry Gdns. Orp. CN55 88
Roseberry Gdns. Upmin. CZ32 51
Roseberry Gdns. Upmin. CZ33 51
Roseberry Pl. E8 CA36 57
Roseberry Rd. Epsom. BN63 103
Roseberry St. SE16 CB42 67
Rosebery Av. E12 CK36 58
Rosebery Av. EC1 BY38 56
Rosebery Av. N17 CB30 39
Rosebery Av. Epsom. BO60 94
Rosebery Av. Har. BE35 45
Rosebery Av. N. Mal. BO51 85
Rosebery Av. Sid. CN47 78
Rosebery Av. Th. Hth. BZ51 87
Rosebery Cres. Wok. AS64 100
Rosebery Gdns. N4 BY32 47

Rosebery Gdns. N8 BX32 47
Rosebery Gdns. W13 BJ39 54
Rosebery Gdns. Sutt. BS56 95
Rosebery Rd. N9 CB27 39
Rosebery Rd. N10 BW30 38
Rosebery Rd. SW2 BX46 76
Rosebery Rd. Bush. BF26 36
Rosebery Rd. Grays. DC43 71
Rosebery Rd. Houns. BG46 74
Rosebery Rd. Kings-on-t. BM51 85
Rosebery Rd. Sutt. BR57 94
Rosebery Sq. Kings-on-t. BM51 85
Rosebine Av. Twick. BG47 74
Rosebriar Wk. Wat. BB21 26
Rosebrook Villas E17 CD31 48
High St.
Rosebury Rd. SW6 BS44 66
Rosebury Vale, Ruis. BB33 44
Rosebushes Epsom BP61 103
Rose Cott. W5 BK40 54
Western Rd.
Rose Ct. SE26 CB48 77
Rose Ct. Pnr. BD31 45
Nursery Rd.
Rosecourt Rd. Croy. BX53 86
Rosecroft Av. NW3 BS34 47
Rosecroft Clo. Orp. CP53 89
Rosecroft Dr. Wat. BB22 26
Rosecroft Gdns. NW2 BP34 46
Rosecroft Gdns. Twick. BG47 74
Rosecroft Rd. Sthl. BF38 54
Rosecroft Wk. Pnr. BD32 45
Rosecroft Wk. Wem. BK35 45
Rose & Crown Ct. EC2 BZ39 57
Foster La.
Rose & Crown La. W6 BQ42 65
Talgarth Rd.
Rose & Crown Yd. SW1 BW40 56
King St.
Rosedale, Ash. BK62 102
Rosedale Orp. CL55 88
Rosedale, Wal. Cr. CA17 21
Rosedale, Welw. G. C. BR6 5
Rosedale Av. Hayes BA39 53
Rosedale Av. Wal. Cr. CB18 21
Rosedale Clo. SE2 CO41 69
Finchale Rd.
Rosedale Clo. Dart. CX47 80
Rosedale Clo. St. Alb. BE18 18
Rosedale Clo. Stan. BJ29 36
Rosedale Cotts. W7 BH41 64
Rosedale Gdns. Dag. CO36 59
Rosedale Rd. E7 CJ35 49
Rosedale Rd. Dag. CO36 59
Rosedale Rd. Epsom. BP56 94
Rosedale Rd. Grays. DE42 71
Rosedale Rd. Rich. BL45 65
Rosedale Rd. Rom. CS30 41
Rosedale Way, Wal. Cr. CB17 21
Rosedene NW6 BQ37 55
Rosedene Av. SW16 BX48 76
Rosedene Av. Croy. BX54 86
Rosedene Av. Grnf. BF38 54
Rosedene Av. Mord. BS53 86
Rosedene Ct. Ruis. BB33 44
Rosedene Gdns. Ilf. CL31 49
Rosedene Ter. E10 CE34 48
Rosedew Rd. W6 BQ43 65
Rose Dri. Chesh. AO19 16
Rosefield. Sev. CU65 107
Rosefield Gdns. E14 CE40 57
Morant St.
Rosefield Gdns. Cher. AU57 91
Rosefield Rd. Stai. AW49 73
Rose Garden Clo. Edg. BL29 37
Rose Gdns. W5 BK41 64
Rose Gdns. Felt. BC48 73
Rose Gdns. Sthl. BF38 54
Rose Gdns. Wat. BC25 26
Rose Glen, NW9 BN31 46
Rose Glen Rom. CT33 50
Rosehatch Av. Rom. CP31 50
Rose Heath. Hem. AV13 7
Roseheath Rd. Houns. BE46 74
Rose Hill, Dor. BJ71 119
Rosehill Esher BJ57 93
Rose Hill Hamptn. BF51 84
Rose Hill Sutt. BS55 86
Rosehill Av. Sutt. BT54 86
Rose Hill Av. Wok. AR61 100
Rosehill Clo. Hodd. CD12 12
Rosehill Gdns. Grnf. BH35 45
Rosehill Gdns. Sutt. BS55 86
Rosehill Gdns. Wat. BA19 17
Rosehill Pk. W. Sutt. BS54 86
Rosehill Rd. SW18 BT46 76
Rosehill Rd. West. CJ62 106
Roseland Cl. N17 BZ29 39
Roselands Av. Hodd. CD11 12
Rose La. Rom. CP31 50
Rose La. Wok. AX64 101
Rose Lawn Bush. BG26 36
Roseleigh Clo. Twick. BK46 74
Rosemary Av. N3 BS30 38
Rosemary Av. N9 CB26 39
Rosemary Av. E. Mol. BF52 84
Rosemary Av. Enf. BZ23 30
Rosemary Av. Houns. BD44 64
Rosemary Av. Rom. CT31 50
Rosemary Clo. S. Ock. DB38 60
Rosemary Clo. Uxb. AZ39 53
Rose Mary Cres. Guil. AP68 109
Rosemary Dr. Ilf. CJ32 49
Rosemary Gdns. SW14 BN45 65
Rosemary La.
Rosemary Gdns. Chess. BL56 94
Rosemary Gdns. Dag. CQ33 50
Rosemary La. SW14 BN45 65
Rosemary La. Egh. AT52 82
Rosemary Rd. Well. CN44 68
Rosemary St. N1 BZ37 57
Rose Mead BO33 46
Rose Mead, Pot. B. BT18 20
Rosemead Av. Felt. BB48 73
Rosemead Av. Mitch. BW52 86
Rosemead Av. Wem. BL35 46
Rosemead Clo. Red. BT71 121
Rosemead Gdns. Brwd. DF24 122
Rosemont Av. N12 BT29 38
Rosemont Cotts. Wem. BL37 55
Rosemont Ct. W3 BM40 55
Rosemont Rd.
Rosemont Rd. NW3 BT36 56
Rosemont Rd. W3 BM40 55
Rosemont Rd. N. Mal. BN52 85
Rosemont Rd. Rich. BL46 75
Rosemoor St. SW3 BU42 66
Rosemount Harl. CL12 13
Rosemount Av. Wey. AW60 92
Rosemount Dr. Brom. CK52 88
Rosemount Rd. W13 BJ39 54
Rosenau Cres. SW11 BU44 66
Rosenau Rd. SW11 BU44 66
Rosendale Rd. SE21 BZ47 77
Rosendale Rd. SE24 BZ47 77
Rosendale St. E5 CB34 48
Roseneath Av. N21 BY26 38
Roseneath Clo. Orp. CP57 98
Roseneath Rd. SW11 BV46 76
Roseneath Wk. Enf. BZ24 30
Rosens Wk. Edg. BM27 37
Rosenthal Rd. SE6 CE46 77
Rosenthorpe Rd. SE15 CC46 77
Roserton St. E14 CF41 67
Rosert St. E14 CF41 67
Manchester Rd.
Rosery, The, Croy. CC53 87
Roses La. Wind. AL44 61
Roses, The, Wdf. Grn. CG29 40
Bunces La.
Rose St. WC2 BX40 56
Floral St.
Rose St. Grav. DD46 81
Rose Trees, Guil. AT71 118
Rosetta St. SW8 BX43 66
Rose Vale, Hodd. CE12 12
Rosevale Rd. SW6 BR44 65
Rose Vall. Brwd. DB27 42
Roseveare Rd. SE12 CJ49 78
Roseville Av. Houns. BF46 74
Roseville Rd. Hayes BC42 63
Rosevine Rd. SW20 BQ51 85
Rose Wk. Pur. BW59 95
Rose Wk. St. Alb. BK12 9
Rose Wk. Surb. BM53 85
Rose Wk. W. Wick. CF55 87
Roseway SE21 BZ46 77
Rosewood Bex. CT49 79
Rosewood Av. Grnf. BJ35 45
Rosewood Av. Horn. CU35 50
Rosewood Dr. Shep. AY53 83
Rose Wood Gdns. Wall. BV57 95
Rosewood Gro. Sutt. BT55 86
Rosher Clo. E15 CF36 57
Rosher Rd. E15 CF36 57
Rosina St. E9 CC35 48
Roskell Rd. SW15 BQ45 65
Roslin Rd. W3 BM41 65
Roslin Way, Brom. CH49 78
Roslyn Clo. Brox. CD14 12
Roslyn Clo. Mitch. BT51 86
Roslyn Gdns. Rom. CT30 41
Roslyn Rd. N15 BZ32 48
Rosmead Rd. W11 BR40 55
Rosoman St. EC1 BY38 56
Rossall Clo. Horn. CU32 50
Rossall Cres. NW10 BL38 55
Ross Av. NW7 BR28 37
Ross Av. Dag. CQ34 50
Ross Cl. Hat. BP11 10
Ross Clo. E4 CF27 39
Ross Clo. Hayes. BA42 63
Ross Cres. Wat. BC21 26
Rossdale Sutt. BU56 95
Rossdale Dr. N9 CC25 30
Rossdale Dr. NW9 BN33 46
Rossdale Rd. SW15 BQ45 65
Rosse Ms. SE3 CH44 68
Rossendale St. E5 CB34 48
Rossindale Rd. Houns. BF46 74
Rossington Av. Borwd. BL22 28
Rossington St. E5 CB34 48
Rossiter Clo. Slou. AS42 62
Rossiter Rd. SW12 BV47 76
Rossland Clo. Bexh. CR46 79
Rosslyn Av. E4 CG27 40
Rosslyn Av. SW13 BO45 65
Rosslyn Av. Barn. BU25 29
Rosslyn Av. Dag. CQ33 50
Rosslyn Av. Felt. BC46 73
Rosslyn Av. Rom. CW30 42
Rosslyn Clo. Hayes BA39 53
Rosslyn Clo. W. Wick. CG55 88
Rosslyn Ct. Wok. AQ62 100
St. John's Rd.
Rosslyn Cres. Har. BH31 45
Rosslyn Cres. Wem. BL35 46
Rosslyn Cres. N. Har. BH31 45
Rosslyn Cres. S. Har. BH32 45
Rosslyn Hl. NW3 BT35 47
Rosslyn Pk. Ms. NW3 BT35 47
Rosslyn Rd. E17 CF31 48
Rosslyn Rd. Bark. CM36 58
Rosslyn Rd. Twick. BK46 74
Rosslyn Rd. Wat. BC24 26
Rossmore Ct. NW1 BU38 56
Rossmore Rd. NW1 BU38 56
Ross Oak Rd. Berk. AQ13 7
Ross Pde. Wall. BV57 95
Ross Rd. SE25 BZ52 87
Ross Rd. Cob. BD60 93
Ross Rd. Dart. CU46 79
Ross Rd. Twick. BG47 74
Ross Rd. Wall. BW56 95
Ross Way, SE9 CK45 68
Rossway La. Berk. AO13 7
Rostella Rd. SW17 BT49 76
Rostrevor Av. N15 CA32 48
Rostrevor Gdns. Hayes BB40 53
Rostrevor Gdns. Iver AU37 52
Rostrevor Gdns. Sthl. BE42 64
Rostrevor Mews SW6 BR45 65
Rostrevor Rd. SW6 BR44 65
Rostrevor Rd. SW19 BS49 76
Rotary St. SE1 BY41 66
Rothbury Av. Rain. CU39 59
Rothbury Gdns. Islw. BJ43 64
Rothbury Rd. E9 CD36 57
Rothbury Wk. N17 CB29 39
Park La.
Rother Clo. Wat. BD20 18
Rotherfield Rd. Enf. CC22 30
Rotherfield St. N1 BZ36 57
Rotherhill Av. SW16 BW50 76
Rotherhithe New Rd. SE16 CB42 67
Rotherhithe Old Rd. SE16 CC42 67
Rotherhithe St. SE16 CB41 67
Rotherhithe Tunnel App. E14 CD40 57
Rothermere Rd. Croy. BX56 95
Rotherwick Hill W5 BL38 55
Rotherwick Rd. NW11 BS33 47
Rotherwood Rd. SW15 BQ45 65
Rothery St. N1 BY37 56
Gaskin St.
Rothesay Av. SW20 BR51 85
Rothesay Av. Grnf. BG36 54
Rothesay Av. Rich. BM45 65
Rothesay Rd. SE25 BZ52 87
Rothes Rd. Dor. BJ71 119
Rothfield Rd. Cars. BV56 95
Rothsay Rd. E7 CJ36 58
Rothsay St. SE1 CA41 67
Rothschild Rd. W4 BN41 65
Rothschild St. SE27 BY49 76
Roth Wk. N7 BX34 47
Andover Est.
Rothwell Gdns. Dag. CP37 59
Rothwell Rd. Dag. CP37 59
Rothwell St. NW1 BU36 56
Rotten Row, SE3 CG44 68
Rotten Row, SW7 BU41 66
Rotten Row, SW11 BU43 66
Rouel Rd. SE16 CB41 67
Rougemont Av. Mord. BS53 86
Rough Down Rd. Hem. H. AW15 8
Roughetts La. Red. CA68 114
Rough Rew, Dor. BJ73 119
Rough Rd. Wok. AO64 100
Roughs. The. Nthwd. BB27 35
Rough, The, Leath. BA66 110
Rough Villas Rd. Hem. H. AW15 8
Rough Wood Clo. Wat. BB22 26
Roughwood La. Ch. St. G. AS25 25
Roughwood La. Ch. St. G. AS26 34
Roundabout's, The Dor. BE71 119
Roundacre Est. SW19 BQ48 75
Round Ash Way. Hart. DC53 90
Roundaway Rd. Ilf. CK30 40
Round Gro. Croy. CC54 87
Roundhay Clo. SE23 CC48 77
Round Hedge Mews. Enf. BX22 29
Roundhill Clo. Wok. AT63 100
Roundhill Dr. Enf. BX24 29
Roundhill Dr. Wok. AT62 100
Roundhills, Wal. Abb. CF20 21
Roundhills, Wal. Abb. CG20 22
Roundhill Way. Cob. BF59 93
Roundhill Way, Guil. AP70 118
Round Hl. SE26 CB48 77
Roundmead Av. Loug. CL24 31
Roundmead Clo. Loug. CL24 31
Roundmoor Dr. Wal. Cr. CD18 21
Round Oak Rd. Wey. AY55 83
Roundtable Rd. Brom. CG48 78
Roundtree Rd. Wem. BJ36 54
Round Way, Egh. AV49 72
Roundways, The, Ruis. BB34 44
Roundway, The, N17 BZ29 39
Roundway, The, Esher BH57 93
Roundway, The Wat. BB25 26
Roundwood Clo. Ruis. CL51 88
Roundwood, Kings L. AY17 17
Roundwood Av. Brwd. DD26 122
Roundwood Clo. Ruis. BA33 44
Roundwood Dri. Welw. G. C. BQ7 5
Roundwood Gro. Brwd. DD26 122
Roundwood Pk. Av. NW10 BP37 55
Roundwood Rd. NW10 BO36 55
Round Wood Rd. Amer. AP22 25
Round Wood Vw. Bans. BQ61 103
Roundwood Way Bans. BQ61 103
Rounton Rd. E3 CE38 57
Rounton Rd. Wal. Abb. CG20 22
Roupell Rd. SW2 BX47 76
Roupell St. SE1 BY40 56
Rousebarn La. Rick. AY22 26
Rousebarn La. Wat. BB24 26
Rouse Gdns. SE21 CA49 77
Rous Rd. Buck. H. CK26 40
Routh Rd. SW18 BU47 76
Rover Av. Ilf. CN29 40
Rowallan Rd. SW6 BR43 65
Rowan Av. E4 CD29 39
Rowan Av. Egh. AV49 72
Rowan Clo. SW16 BW51 86
Rowan Clo. Guil. AR69 118
Rowan Clo. Reig. BT71 121
Rowan Clo. St. Alb. BF19 18
Rowan Clo. Uxb. AW30 35
Rowan Ct. SE12 CG47 78
Rowan Cres. SW16 BW51 86
Rowan Cres. Dart. CV47 80
Rowan Gdns. W6 BQ42 65
Bute Gdns.
Rowan Gdns. Croy. CA55 87
Rowan Grn. Couls. BV64 104
Rowanhurst Dr. Slou. AO35 43
Rowan Pl. Hayes BB40 53
Rowan Rd. SW16 BW51 86
Rowan Rd. W6 BQ42 65
Rowan Rd. Bexh. CQ45 69
Rowan Rd. Brent. BJ43 64
Rowan Rd. Swan. CS52 89
Rowan Rd. West Dr. AX42 63
Rowans. Welw. G. C. BS6 5
Rowans, The, N13 BY27 38
Rowans, The, Ger. Cr. AR31 43
Rowans, The Hem. H. AW13 8
Rowans, The Sun. BB49 73
Rowantree Clo. N21 BZ26 39
Rowantree Rd. N21 BZ26 39
Rowantree Rd. Enf. BY23 29
Rowan Wk. N2 BT32 47
Rowan Wk. Brom. CK55 88
Rowan Wk. Hat. BP14 10
Rowan Wk. Horn. CV31 51
Rowan Way, Rom. CP31 50
Rowbarns Way. Leath. BB68 110
Rowben Clo. N20 BS26 38
Row Croft, Hem. H. AV14 7
Rowcross St. SE1 CA42 67
Rowdell Rd. Nthlt. BF37 54
Rowden Pk. Gdns. E4 CE29 39
Rowden Rd.
Rowden Rd. E4 CE29 39
Rowden Rd. Beck. CD51 87
Rowden Rd. Epsom. BM56 94
Rowditch La. SW11 BV44 66
Rowdon Av. NW10 BP36 55
Rowdon La. Sev. CV60 99
Rowdon. La. Sev. CV61 108
Rowdown Cres. Croy. CF58 96
Rowdowns Rd. Dag. CQ37 59
Rowe Gdns. Bark. CN37 58
Rowe La. E9 CC35 48
Urswick Rd.
Rowena Cres. SW11 BU44 66
Rowen Grn. Brwd. DC27 122
Rowe Wk. Har. BF34 45
Rowfant Rd. SW17 BV47 76
Row Hill. Wey. AV57 91
Rowhill Rd. E5 CB35 48
Rowhill Rd. Dart. CT50 79
Row Hill St. NW3 BU35 47
Rowhurst Av. Lthd. BH62 102
Rowington Clo. W2 BS39 56
Rowland Av. Har. BK31 45
Rowland Clo. Wind. AL45 61
Rowland Ct. E13 CG38 58
Rowland Ct. E16 CG38 58
Beaconsfield Rd.
Rowland Cres. Chig. CN28 40
Fairview Dr.
Rowland Gro. SE26 CB49 77
Rowland Hill Av. N17 BZ29 39
Rowland Hill St. NW3 BU35 47
Rowland Rd. SW4 BW45 66
Rowlands Av. Pnr. BF28 36
Rowlands Rd. Dag. CQ34 50
Rowland Wk. Hav. CT27 41
Rowland Way, Ashf. BA50 73
Rowlatt Clo. Dart. CV49 80
Rowlatt Rd. Dart. CV49 80
Rowlett Dr. St. Alb. BF14 9
Rowley Av. Sid. CO47 79
Rowley Clo. Wat. BE25 27
Rowley Clo. Wem. BL36 55
Rowley Gdns. N4 BZ33 48
Rowley Grn. Rd. Barn. BO25 28
Rowley La. Borwd. BN23 28
Rowley La. Borwd. BN23 28
Rowley La. Slou. AR37 52
Rowley Mead Epp. CP16 23
Rowley Rd. N15 BZ32 48
Rowley Ter. NW5 BV36 56
Rowlls Rd. Kings-on-t. BL52 85
Rowney Gdns. Dag. CO36 59
Rowney Gdns, Saw. CP7 6
Rowney Rd. Dag. CO36 59
Rowney Wood, Saw. CP6 6
Rowns Way Loug. CK24 31
Rowntree Rd. Twick. BH47 74
Rowse Clo. E15 CF37 57
Rowsley Av. NW4 BQ31 46
Rowstock Gdns. N7 BW35 47
Rowton Rd. SE18 CM43 68
Roxborough Av. Har. BG33 45
Roxborough Av. Islw. BH43 64
Roxborough Pk. Har. BH33 45
Roxborough Rd. Har. BG32 45
Roxbourne Clo. Nthlt. BD36 54
Roxburgh Av. Upmin. CY35 51
Roxburgh Rd. SE27 BY49 76
Roxburn Way, Ruis. BB34 44
Roxby Pl. SW6 BS43 66
Roxeth Ct. Ashf. AZ49 73
Roxeth Grn. Av. Har. BF34 45
Roxeth Gro. Har. BF35 45
Roxeth Hill Har. BG34 45
Roxford Clo. Shep. BB53 83
Roxley Rd. SE13 CE46 77
Roxton Gdns. Croy. CE56 96
Roxwell Rd. W12 BP41 65
Roxwell Rd. Bark. CO37 59
Roxwell Way, Wdf. Grn. CJ29 40
Roxy Av. Rom. CP33 50
Royal Arc. SW1 BW40 56
Pall Mall
Royal Av. SW3 BU42 66
Royal Av. Wal. Cr. CD20 21
Royal Av. Wor. Pk. BO55 85
Royal Cir. SE27 BY48 76
Royal Clo. Uxb. AY39 53
Royal Clo. Wor. Pk. BO55 85
Royal College St. NW1 BW36 56
Royal Cres. W11 BQ40 55
Royal Cres. Ruis. BE35 45
Royal Cres. Ms. W11 BQ40 55
Royal Exchange Bldgs. EC3 BZ39 57
Cornhill
Royal Hl. SE10 CF43 67
Royal Hospital Rd. SW3 BU43 66
Royal La. Uxb. & West Dr. AY38 53
Royal Mint St. E1 CA40 57
Royal Naval Pl. SE14 CD43 67
Hereford Pl.
Royal Oak Ct. N1 CA38 57
Royal Oak Rd. E8 CB36 57
Wilton Way.
Royal Oak Rd. Bexh. CQ46 79
Royal Oak Rd. Wok. AR62 100
Royal Oak Shopping Cen. Pur. BY54 86
Royal Pde. SE3 CG44 68
Royal Pde. W5 BL38 55
Western Av.
Royal Pde. Chis. CM50 78
Royal Pier Rd. Grav. DG46 81
Royal Pl. SE10 CF43 67
Royal Rd. E16 CJ39 58
Royal Rd. SE17 BY43 66
Royal Rd. Dart. CX49 80
Royal Rd. St. Alb. BJ13 9
Royal Rd. Sid. CP48 79
Royal Rd. Tedd. BG49 74
Royal St. SE1 BX41 66
Royal Victor Pl. E3 CC37 57
Old Ford Rd.
Royce Clo. Brox. CD14 12
Roycraft Av. Bark. CN37 58
Roycraft Clo. Bark. CN37 58
Roycroft Clo. E18 CH30 40
Roydene Rd. SE18 CN43 68
Roydon Cl. SW11 BU44 66
Reform St.
Roydon Clo. Loug. CK26 40
Roydon Rd. Harl. CK10 13
Roydon St. SW11 BV44 66
Royd Way. Cob. BF60 93
Roy Gdns. Ilf. CN31 49
Roy Gro. Hamptn. BF50 74
Royle Clo. Ger. Cr. AS29 34
Royle Clo. Rom. CU32 50
Royle Cres. W13 BJ38 54
Roymount Ct. Twick. BH48 74
Roy Rd. Nthwd. BB29 35
Roysdon Rd. Rom. CW29 42
Royston Av. E4 CE28 39
Royston Av. Sutt. BT55 86
Royston Av. Wall. BW56 95
Royston Chase, Wey. AY59 92
Royston Clo. Houns. BC44 63
Royston Clo. Walt. BC54 83
Royston Ct. Rich. BL44 65
Royston Ct. Surb. BM55 85
Royston Gdns. Ilf. CJ32 49
Royston Gro. Pnr. BE29 36
Royston Pk. Rd. Pnr. BE29 36
Royston Rd. SE20 CC51 87
Royston Rd. Dart. CT46 79
Royston Rd. Rich. BL46 75
Royston Rd. St. Alb. BJ14 9
Royston Rd. Wey. AY59 92
Roystons, The, Surb. BM53 85
Royston St. E2 CC38 57
Rozel Rd. SW4 BW44 66
Rubastic Rd. Sthl. BC41 63
Rubens Rd. Nthlt. BD37 54
Rubens St. SE6 CD48 77
Ruberoid Rd. Enf. CD24 30
Ruby Rd. E17 CE31 48
Ruby St. SE15 CB43 67
Ruccles Brice Rd. Ashf. AX49 73
Ruckholt Clo. E10 CE34 48
Ruckholt Rd. E10 CE35 48
Rucklers La. Kings L. AW17 17
Rucklidge Av. NW10 BO37 55
Rudall Cres. NW3 BT35 47
Willoughby Rd.
Ruddigore Rd. SE14 CD43 67
Ruddles Way. Wind. AL44 61
Rudd St. SE18 CL42 68
Ruden Way Epsom BP61 103
Rudford Rd. SE16 CC42 67
Rudge Rd. Wey. AV56 91
Rudland Rd. Bexh. CR45 69
Rudloe Rd. SW12 BW47 76
Rudolph Rd. E13 CG37 58
Rudolph Rd. NW6 BS37 56
Rudolph Rd. Bush. BF25 27
Rudwick Clo. Wal. Cr. CD17 21
Ashdown Cres.
Rudyard Gro. NW7 BN29 37
Ruffetts Clo. Sth. Croy. CB57 96
Ruffetts, The, Sth. Croy. CB57 96
Ruffetts Way Tad. BR62 103
Rufford St. N1 BX37 56
Rufus Clo. Ruis. BE34 45
Rufus St. EC1 CA38 57
Old St.
Rugby Av. N9 CA26 39
Rugby Av. Grnf. BG36 54
Rugby Av. Wem. BJ35 45
Rugby Clo. Har. BH31 45
Rugby Gdns. Dag. CP36 59
Rugby La. Sutt. BQ58 94
Rugby Rd. NW9 BM31 46
Rugby Rd. W4 BO41 65
Rugby Rd. Dag. CO36 59
Rugby Rd. Twick. BH46 74
Rugby St. WC1 BX38 56
Rugby Way, Rick. AZ25 26
Rugged La. Wal. Abb. CJ20 22
Rugg St. E14 CE40 57
Ruislip Clo. Grnf. BF38 54

Ruislip Rd. Nthlt. BD37 54
Ruislip Rd. E. Grnf. BG38 54
Ruislip St. SW17 BU49 76
Rumballs Clo. Hem. H. AZ15 8
Rumballs Rd. Hem. H. AZ15 8
Rumbold Rd. SW6 BS43 66
Rumbold Rd. Hodd. CF11 12
Rumford Pl. Erith CT43 69
Rumsey Rd. SW9 BX45 66
Runciman Clo. Orp. CP58 98
Runcorn Cres. Hem. H. AY11 8
Runcorn Pl. W11 BR40 55
Rundell Cres. NW4 BP32 46
Rundells. Harl. CO13 14
Runham Rd. Hem. H. AY14 8
Runham St. SE17 BZ42 67
Runnelfied Har. BH34 45
Runnemede Ct. Egh. AT49 72
Runnemede Rd. Egh. AS49 72
Running Horse Yd. Brent. BL43 65
Pottery Rd.
Running Waters, Brwd. DD28 122
Runn Way, E7 CH35 49
Runnymede SW19 BT51 86
Runnymede Clo. Twick. BF46 74
Runnymede Cres. SW16 BW51 86
Runnymede Gdns. Grnf. BG37 54
Runnymede Gdns. Twick. BF46 74
Runnymede Rd. Twick. BF46 74
Runrig Hill. Amer. AP21 25
Runsley. Welw. G. C. BR6 5
Runtley Wood La. Guil. AS66 109
Runton St. N19 BW33 47
Runway, The, Ruis. BD35 45
Rupack St. SE16 CC41 67
St.Mary Church St.
Rupert Av. Wem. BL35 46
London Rd.
Rupert Gdns. SW9 BY44 66
Rupert Rd. N19 BW34 47
Rupert Rd. NW6 BR37 55
Rupert Rd. W4 BO41 65
Rupert Rd. Guil. AQ71 118
Rupert St. W1 BW40 56
Rural Pl. SE14 CC44 67
Rural Vale, Grav. DF47 81
Rural Way, SW16 BV50 76
Rural Way, Red. BV70 121
Ruscoe Rd. E16 CG39 58
Ruscombe Dr. St. Alb. BG16 18
Rusham Park Av. Egh. AS50 72
Rusham Rd. SW12 BU46 76
Rusham Rd. Egh. AS50 72
Rushbrook Cres. E17 CD30 39
Rushbrook Rd. SE9 CM48 78
Rushcroft Rd. E4 CE29 39
Rushcroft Rd. SW2 BY45 66
Rushdene SE2 CP41 69
Rushdene Av. Barn. BU26 38
Rushdene Clo. Nthlt. BD37 54
Rushdene Cres. Nthlt. BD37 54
Rushdene Rd. Brwd. DB26 42
Rushdene Rd. Pnr. BD32 45
Rushden Gdns. NW7 BQ29 37
Rushden Gdns. Ilf. CL30 40
Rushdon Clo. Grays. DD41 71
Rushen Wk. Cars. BT54 86
Rushes Mead. Harl. CN12 13
Rushet Rd. Orp. CO51 89
Rushett Clo. Surb. BJ54 84
Rushett Dr. Dor. BJ73 119
Rushett Gdns. Surb. BJ54 84
Rushett La. Chess. BK59 93
Rushett Rd. Surb. BJ54 84
Rushetts Rd. Reig. BT72 121
Rushett's Rd. Sev. CZ57 99
Rushey Clo. N. Mal. BN52 85
Rushey Grn. SE6 CE47 77
Rushfield, Pot. B. BQ20 19
Rushfield, Saw. CQ6 6
Rushford Rd. SE4 CD46 77
Rush Grn. Gdns. Rom. CS33 50
Rush Grn. Rd. Rom. CR33 50
Rushgrove Av. NW9 BO32 46
Rushgrove St. SE18 CK42 68
Rush Hill Rd. SW11 BV45 66
Rushleigh Av. Wal. Cr. CC18 21
Rushley Clo. Grays. DE40 71
Rushmead Rich. BJ48 74
Rushmead. Sev. CX62 108
Rushmead Clo. Croy. CA56 96
Rushmead Clo. Edg. BM27 37
Rushmere Av. Upmin. CY35 51
Rushmere La. Ches. AQ17 16
Rushmoor Clo. Guil. AP69 118
Rushmoor Clo. Pnr. BC31 44
Rushmoor Clo. Rick. AX27 35
Rushmore Clo. Brom. CK52 88
Rushmore Ct. Wor. Pk. BP55 85
Rushmore Cres. E5 CC35 48
Rushmore Hill Orp. CP58 98
Rushmore Rd. E5 CC35 48
Rusholme Rd. SW15 BQ46 75
Rusholme Rd. Dag. CR34 50
Rushout Av. Har. BJ32 45
Rushton Av. Wat. BC21 26
Rushton St. N1 BZ37 57
Rushworth Gdns. NW4 BP31 46
Rushworth Rd. Reig. BS70 121
Rushworth St. SE1 BY41 66
Ruskin Av. E12 CK36 58
Ruskin Av. Felt. BB46 73
Ruskin Av. Rich. BM43 65
Ruskin Av. Upmin. CY33 51
Ruskin Av. Wal. Abb. CG20 22
Ruskin Av. Well. CO45 69
Ruskin Clo. NW11 BS32 47
Ruskin Clo. Wal. Cr. CA16 21
Hammond St. Rd.
Ruskin Ct. N21 BX26 38
Ruskin Dr. Orp. CN55 88
Ruskin Dr. Well. CO45 69
Ruskin Dr. Wor. Pk. BP55 85
Ruskin Dr. Wor. Pk. BQ54 85
Ruskin Gdns. W5 BK38 54
Ruskin Gdns. Har. BL32 46
Ruskin Gdns. Rom. CU30 41
Ruskin Gro. Dart. CX46 80
Ruskin Gro. Well. CO44 69
Ruskin Pk. Ho. SE5 BZ45 67
Ruskin Rd. N17 CA30 39
Ruskin Rd. Belv. CR42 69
Ruskin Rd. Cars. BU56 95
Ruskin Rd. Grays. DG42 71
Ruskin Rd. Islw. BH45 64
Ruskin Rd. Stai. AV50 72
Ruskin Rd. Sthl. BE40 54
Ruskin Wk. N9 CB27 39
Ruskin Wk. SE24 BZ46 77
Ruskin Wk. Brom. CK53 88
Rusland Av. Orp. CM55 88
Rusland Rd. Har. BH31 45
Rusper Ct. SW9 BX44 66
Clapham Rd.
Rusper Rd. N22 BY30 38
Rusper Rd. Dag. CP36 59
Russel Av. St. Alb. BG13 9
Russelcroft Rd. Welw. G. C. BQ7 5
Russell Av. N22 BY30 38
Russell Clo. NW10 BN36 55
Russell Clo. Amer. AR23 25
Russell Clo. Beck. CE52 87
Russell Clo. Bexh. CH45 69
Russell Clo. Brwd. DA26 42
Russell Clo. Dart. CU45 69
Russell Clo. Ruis. BD34 45
Russell Clo. Tad. BP66 112
Russell Clo. Wok. AR61 100
Russell Ct. SW1 BW40 56
Cleveland Row.
Russell Ct. Chesh. AO18 16
Russell Ct. Lthd. BJ64 102
Russell Ct. St. Alb. BF18 18
Black Boy Wd.
Russell Cres. Wat. BB21 26
Russell Dr. Stai. AX46 73
Russell Gdns. N20 BU27 38
Russell Gdns. NW11 BR32 46
Russell Gdns. W14 BR41 65
Russell Gdns. Rich. BK48 74
Russell Gdns. Ms. W14 BR41 65
Russell Grn. Clo. Pur. BY58 95
Russell Gro. NW7 BO28 37
Russell Gro. SW9 BY43 66
Russell Hill Pur. BX58 95
Russell Hill Pl. Pur. BY55 86
Russell Hill Pl. Pur. BY59 95
Russell Hill Rd. Pur. BY58 95
Russell La. N20 BU27 38
Russell La. Wat. BA21 26
Russell Pl. SW1 BW42 66
Vauxhall Bridge Rd.
Russell Pl. Hem. H. AW15 8
Russell Pl. S. At. H. CX51 90
Russell Rd. E4 CD28 39
Russell Rd. E10 CE32 48
Russell Rd. E16 CH39 58
Russell Rd. E17 CD31 48
Russell Rd. N8 BW32 47
Russell Rd. N13 BX29 38
Russell Rd. N15 CA32 48
Russell Rd. N20 BU27 38
Russell Rd. NW9 BO32 46
Russell Rd. SW19 BS50 76
Russell Rd. W14 BR41 65
Russell Rd. Buck. H. CH26 40
Russell Rd. Enf. CA22 30
Russell Rd. Grav. DH46 81
Russell Rd. Grays. DD42 71
Russell Rd. Nthlt. BG35 45
Russell Rd. Nthwd. BA27 35
Russell Rd. Shep. AZ54 83
Russell Rd. Til. DF44 71
Russell Rd. Twick. BH46 74
Russell Rd. Walt. BC53 83
Russell Rd. Wok. AR61 100
Russell's Footpath SW16 BX49 76
Russell Sq. WC1 BW38 56
Russells Ride, Wal. Cr. CD19 21
Russell St. E13 CH37 58
Russell St. WC2 BX40 56
Russell Rd. Mitch. BU52 86
Russel St. Wind. AO44 61
Russet Cl. Stai. AV46 72
Russet Clo. Uxb. BA38 53
Russet Cres. N7 BX35 47
Stockorchard Cres.
Russett Clo. Orp. CO56 98
Russett Way Swan. CS51 89
Russet Way SE13 CE44 67
Conington Rd.
Russia La. E2 CC37 57
Russia Row, EC2 BZ39 57
Milk St.
Russington Rd. Shep. BA53 83
Rusthall Av. W4 BN42 65
Rustic Av. SW16 BV50 76
Rustic Clo. Upmin. CZ33 51
Rustic Pl. Wem. BK35 45
Rustington Wk. Mord. BR54 85
Ruston Av. Surb. BM54 85
Ruston Clo. W11 BR39 55
St.Marks Rd.
Ruston Ms. W11 BR39 55
Ruston St. E3 CD37 57
Rust Sq. SE5 BZ43 67
Rutford Rd. SW16 BX49 76
Ruth Cl. Epsom. BM60 94
Ruthen Clo. Epsom BN60 94
Rutherford Clo. Sutt. BT57 95
Rutherford Way Bush. BG26 36
Rutherglen Rd. SE2 CO43 69
Rutherland St. SW1 BW42 66
Rutherwick Rise BX62 104
Rutherwick Rise Couls. BX57 95
Rutherwyke Clo. Epsom BP57 94
Rutherwyk Rd. Cher. AV54 82
Ruthin Rd. SE3 CH43 68
Ruthven Av. Wal. Cr. CC20 21
Ruthven St. E9 CC37 57
Lauriston Rd.
Rutland App. Horn. CW32 51
Rutland Approach, Horn. CX32 51
Rutland Av. Sid. CO47 79
Rutland Av. Slou. AO39 52
Rutland Clo. SW14 BN45 65
Rutland Clo. SW19 BU50 76
Rutland Rd.
Rutland Clo. Bex. CP47 79
Rutland Clo. Chess. BL57 94
Rutland Clo. Dart. CV46 80
Rutland Clo. Red. BU70 121
Rutland Ct. SE5 BZ45 67
Rutland Dr. Horn. CW32 51
Rutland Dr. Horn. CX32 51
Rutland Dr. Mord. BR53 85
Rutland Gdns. N4 BY32 47
Rutland Gdns. SW7 BU41 66
Rutland Gdns. W13 BJ39 54
Rutland Gdns. Croy. CA56 96
Rutland Gdns. Dag. CP35 50
Rutland Gdns. Rich. BK47 74
Rutland Gte. SW7 BU41 66
Rutland Gate Belv. CR41 69
Rutland Gate Brom. CG52 88
Rutland Gte. Ms. SW7 BU41 66
Rutland Gro. W6 BP42 65
Rutland Ms. S. SW7 BU42 66
Rutland St.
Rutland Ms. St. SW7 BU42 66
Ennismore Ms. Gdns.
Rutland Pk. NW2 BQ36 55
Rutland Pk. SE6 CD48 77
Rutland Rd. E7 CJ36 58
Rutland Rd. E9 CC37 57
Rutland Rd. E11 CH32 49
Rutland Rd. E17 CE32 48
Rutland Rd. SW19 BU50 76
Rutland Rd. Har. BG32 45
Rutland Rd. Hayes. BA42 63
Rutland Rd. Ilf. CL35 49
Rutland Rd. Sthl. BF38 54
Rutland Rd. Twick. BG48 74
Rutland St. SW7 BU41 66
Rutland Wk. SE6 CD48 77
Rutland Way Orp. CP53 89
Rutlish Rd. SW19 BS51 86
Rutson Rd. Wey. AY60 92
Rutter Gdns. Mitch. BT52 86
Rutters Clo. West Dr. AZ41 63
Ruttesland St. N1 CA37 57
Hoxton St.
Rutts Ter. SE14 CC44 67
Ruvigny Gdns. SW15 BQ45 65
Ruxbury Rd. Cher. AU53 82
Ruxley Clo. Epsom. BM56 94
Ruxley Clo. Sid. CP50 79
Ruxley Cres. Esher BJ57 93
Ruxley La. Epsom BM57 94
Ruxley Ridge Esher BJ57 93
Ryan Clo. SE3 CJ45 68
Ryarsh Cres. Orp. CN56 97
Rycott Path. SE22 CB47 77
Lordship La.
Rycroft Cres. Barn. BP25 28
Rycroft La. Sev. CT68 116
Ryculff Sq. SE3 CG44 68
Rydal Clo. SW16 BW49 76
Rydal Clo. Pur. BZ60 96
Rydal Ct. NW4 BR30 37
Rydal Cres. Grnf. BJ37 54
Rydal Dr. Bexh. CQ44 69
Rydal Gdns. NW9 BO32 46
Rydal Gdns. SW15 BO49 75
Rydal Gdns. Houns. BF46 74
Rydal Gdns. Wem. BK33 45
Rydal Rd. SW16 BW49 76
Rydal Way Enf. CC25 30
Rydal Way Ruis. BD35 45
Ryde Heron, Wok. AP62 100
Rydens Av. Walt. BC55 83
Rydens Av. Walt. BD55 84
Rydens Clo. Walt. BD55 84
Rydens Gro. Walt. BD56 93
Rydens Rd. Walt. BC55 83
Rydens Rd. Walt. BD54 84
Rydens Way, Wok. AT63 100
Ryder Clo. Brom. CH49 78
Ryder Clo. Bush. BF25 27
Ryder Clo. Hem. H. AT17 16
Ryder Gdns. E6 CL39 58
Ryder Gdns. Rain. CT36 59
Ryders Av. Hat. BO13 10
Ryder's Ter. NW8 BT37 56
Ryder St. SW1 BW40 56
Ryde's Av. Guil. AP69 118
Rydes Clo. Wok. AT63 100
Ryde's Hill Cres. Guil AP68 109
Rydes Hill Est. Guil. AP69 118
Ryde's Hill Rd. Guil. AP69 118
Ryde, The, Hat. BQ11 10
Ryde, The, Stai. AW51 83
Ryde Vale Rd. SW12 BV48 76
Rydings. Wind. AM45 61
Rydons Clo. SE9 CK45 68
Rydons La. Couls. BZ63 105
Rydons Pk. Walt. BD55 84
Rydon St. N1 BZ37 57
St.Paul St.
Rydons Wood Clo. Couls. BZ63 105
Rydston Clo. N7 BX36 56
Sutterton St.
Ryebrook Clo. Lthd. BJ62 102
Ryebrook Rd. Lthd. BJ62 102
Rye. Clo. Bex. CR46 79
Rye Clo. Guil. AP69 118
Ryecoates Mead, SE21 CA47 77
Rye Cres. Orp. CP54 89
Ryecroft Harl. CL11 13
Ryecroft. Hat. BO13 10
Ryecroft. Wind. AM45 61
Ryecroft Av. Ilf. CL30 40
Ryecroft Av. Twick. BF47 74
Ryecroft Clo. Hem. H. BA14 8
Ryecroft Ct. St. Alb. BL13 10
Fourways
Ryecroft N17 CA31 48
Ryecroft Rd. SE13 CF46 77
Ryecroft Rd. SW16 BY50 76
Ryecroft Rd. Orp. CM53 88
Ryecroft Rd. Sev. CU61 107
Ryecroft St. SW6 BS44 66
Ryedale SE22 CB46 77
Ryefield Orp. CP55 89
Ryefield Av. Uxb. AZ36 53
Ryefield Cres. Pnr. BC30 35
Ryefield Path, SW15 BP47 75
Ryefield Rd. SE19 BZ50 77
Ryefield Rd. Croy. CC60 96
Ryehill Ct. N. Mal. BO54 85
Rye Hill Est. SE15 CC45 67
Rye Hill Pk. SE15 CC45 67
Rye Hill Rd. Epp. CO15 14
Rye Hill Rd. Harl. CM13 13
Ryeland Clo. West Dr. AY39 53
Ryelands. Welw. G. C. BR9 5
Ryelands Clo. Cat. CA64 105
Macaulay Rd.
Ryelands Cres. SE12 CJ46 78
Rye La. SE15 CB44 67
Rye La. Sev. CT63 107
Rye La. Sev. CU61 107
Rye Rd. SE15 CC45 67
Rye Rd. Harl. CG10 13
Rye Rd. Hodd. CE11 12
Rye, The, N14 BW26 38
Rye Wk. SW15 BQ46 75
Chartfield Av.
Rye Way, Edg. BL29 37
Ryfold Rd. SW19 BS48 76
Ryhope Rd. N11 BV28 38
Rylandes Rd. NW2 BP34 46
Ryland Rd. NW5 BV36 56
Rylands Rd. Sth. Croy. CB58 96
Rylett Cres. W12 BO41 65
Rylett Rd. W12 BO41 65
Rylston Rd. N13 BZ27 39
Rylston Rd. SW6 BR43 65
Rymer Rd. SW18 BT45 66
Alma Rd.
Rymer Rd. Croy. CA54 87
Rymer St. SE24 BY46 76
Rymill Clo. Hem. H. AT17 16
Rymill St. E16 CL40 58
Rysbrack St. SW3 BU41 66
Rysted La. West. CM66 115
Rythe Ct. Surb. BJ54 84
Rythe Rd. Esher BH56 93
Sabbarton St. E16 CG39 58
Victoria Dock Rd.
Sabella Ct. E3 CE37 57
Mostyn Gro.
Sabella St. SE1 BY40 56
Sabina Rd. Grays. DH42 71
Sabine Rd. SW11 BU45 66
Sabines Rd. Rom. CV23 33
Sable Clo. Houns. BD45 64
Sable St. N1 BY36 56
Sach Rd. E5 CB34 48
Sackville Av. Brom. CH54 88
Sackville Clo. Har. BG34 45
Sackville Clo. Sev. CU64 107
Sackville Cres. Rom. CW30 42
Sackville Est. SW16 BX48 76
Sackville Gdns. Ilf. CK33 49
Sackville Rd. Dart. CV48 80
Sackville Rd. Sutt. BS57 95
Sackville St. W1 BW40 56
Sacombe Rd. Hem. H. AV12 7
Saddington St. Grav. DH47 81
Saddlers Mead. Harl. CO11 14
Saddlescombe Way N12 BS28 38
Saddleworth Rd. Rom. CV29 42
Saddleworth Sq. Rom. CV29 42
Sadie St. SE5 BZ44 67
Orpheus St.
Sadler Clo. Mitch. BU51 86
Sadlers Clo. Guil. AU70 118
Sadlers Ride E. Mol. BG51 84
Sadlers Way, Epsom. BN63 103
Sadlier Rd. St. Alb. BH14 9
Saffron Clo. NW11 BR32 46
Saffron Clo. Hodd. CD11 12
Saffron Hill EC1 BY38 56
Saffron La. Hem. H. AW13 8
Saffron Platt, Guil. AQ68 109
Saffron Rd. Rom. CS30 41
Saffron St. EC1 BY39 56
Saffron Hill
Safron Clo. Brwd. DE32 123
Saftesbury Rd. Cars. BT54 86
Sail St. SE11 BX42 66
Sainsbury Rd. SE19 BZ49 77
St. Agatha's Dr. Kings. On T. BL50 75
Latchmere Rd.
St. Agathas Gro. Cars. BU54 86
St. Agatha's Wk. Kings. On T. BM50 75
Alexandra Rd.
St. Agnell's La. Hem. H. AY11 8
St. Agnes Clo. E9 CC37 57
Gore Rd.
St. Agnes Pl. SE11 BY43 66
St. Aidan's Rd. SE22 CB46 77
St. Aidan's Rd. W13 BJ41 64
St. Aidan's Way, Grav. DJ48 81
St. Albans Av. E6 CK38 58
St. Albans Av. W4 BN42 65
St. Albans Av. Felt. BD49 74
St. Albans Av. Upmin. CZ34 51
St. Albans Av. Wey. AZ55 83
St. Albans Clo. NW11 BS33 47
North End Rd.
St. Alban's Clo. Grav. DH48 81
St. Alban's Cres. N22 BY30 38
St. Alban's Cres. Wdf. Grn. CH29 40
St. Alban's Gdns. Grav. DH48 81
St. Albans Gdns. Tedd. BJ49 74
St. Alban's Gro. W8 BS41 66
St. Albans Gro. Cars. BU54 86
St. Albans Hill, Hem. H. AY15 8
St. Albans La. NW11 BS33 47
West Heath Br.
St. Alban's Ms. W2 BT39 56
Edgware Rd.
St. Albans Pl. W1 BY37 56
St. Alban's Rd. NW5 BV34 47
St. Alban's Rd. NW10 BO37 55
St. Albans Rd. Barn. BQ22 28
St. Albans Rd. Dart. CW47 80
St. Albans Rd. Epp. CP18 23
St. Albans Rd. Hat. BO12 10
St. Albans Rd. Hat. BP12 10
St. Albans Rd. Hem. H. AX14 8
St. Albans Rd. Ilf. CN33 49
St. Alban's Rd. Kings. On T. BL50 75
St. Albans Rd. Pot. B. BO19 19
St. Albans Rd. Reig. BS70 121
St. Albans Rd. St. Alb. BJ11 9
St. Alban's Rd. Sutt. BR56 94
St. Albans Rd. Wat. BC23 26
St. Albans Rd, Wat. BD20 18
St. Albans Rd. Wat. BD21 27
St. Alban's Rd. Wdf. Grn. CH29 40
St. Albans Rd. East, Hat. BP12 10
St. Albans Rd. West. Hat. BN12 10
St. Alban's St. SW1 BW40 56
Jermyn St.
St. Albans St. Wind. AO44 61
St. Alban's Ter. W6 BR43 65
St. Alfege Pass. SE10 CF43 67
Roan St.
St. Alfege Rd. SE7 CJ43 68
St. Alphage Ct. NW9 BN31 46
St. Alphages Gdns. EC2 BZ39 57
St. Alphege Rd. N9 CC26 39
St. Alphonsus Rd. SW4 BW45 66
St Andrew's Ave. Wind. AM44 61
St. Andrews Av. Horn. CU35 50
St. Andrews Av. Wem. BJ35 45
St. Andrew's Clo. N12 BT28 38
St. Andrews Clo. NW2 BP34 46
St. Andrews Clo. Brwd. DC27 122
St Andrews Clo. Epp. CS15 14
St. Andrew's Clo. Islw. BH44 64
St. Andrews Clo. Reig. BS71 121
St. Mary's Rd.
St. Andrew's Clo. Ruis. BD34 45
St. Andrews Clo. Shep. BA52 83
St. Andrews Clo. Stan. BK30 36
St. Andrews Clo. Wind. AQ46 72
St. Andrews Ct. SW18 BT48 76
Waynflete St.
St Andrew's Cres. Wind. AM44 61
St. Andrew's Dr. Orp. CO53 89
St. Andrews Dr. Stan. BK30 36
St. Andrews Grn. Welw. G. C. BR8 5
St. Andrew's Gro. N16 BZ33 48
St. Andrew's Hill EC4 BY39 56
St. Andrew's Ms. N16 CA33 48
Dunsmure Rd.
St. Andrews Pl. NW1 BV38 56
St. Andrew's Rd. E11 CG32 49
St. Andrew's Rd. E13 CH38 58
St. Andrew's Rd. N9 CC26 39
St. Andrew's Rd. NW9 BN33 46
St. Andrews Rd. NW10 BP36 55
St. Andrews Rd. NW11 BR32 46
St. Andrew's Rd. W3 BO40 55
St. Andrew's Rd. W7 BH41 64
St. Andrew's Rd. W14 BR43 65
St. Andrews Rd. Cars. BU55 86
St. Andrew's Rd. Couls. BV61 104
St. Andrew's Rd. Croy. BZ56 96
St. Andrews Rd. Enf. BZ24 30
St. Andrews Rd. Hem. H. AX15 8
St. Andrew's Rd. Ilf. CK33 49
St. Andrews Rd. Rom. CS32 50
St. Andrews Rd. Sid. CP48 79
St. Andrews Rd. Surb. BK53 84
St Andrews Rd. Til. DF44 71
St. Andrews Rd. Uxb. AY37 53
St. Andrews Sq. Surb. BK53 84
St. Andrew St. EC4 BY39 56
St. Andrew St. W14 BR43 65
St. Andrews Wk. Cob. BC61 101
St. Andrews Way. Oxt. CK69 115
St. Anne's Av. Stai. AX47 73
St. Anne's Clo. N6 BV34 47
St. Anne's Ct. W1 BW39 56
Wardour St.
St. Anne's Gdns. NW10 BL38 55
St. Anne's Rd. E11 CF34 48
St. Annes Rd. Brwd. DE23 122
St. Anne's Rd. Cher. AV53 82
St. Anne's Rd. Har. BH32 45
St. Anne's Rd. St. Alb. BK17 18
St. Annes Rd. Uxb. AX31 44
St. Anne's Rd. Wem. BK35 45
St. Ann's Bark. CM37 58
St. Ann's Clo. Cher. AV53 82
St. Ann's Cres. SW18 BT46 76
St. Ann's Gdns. NW5 BV36 56
Queen's Cres.
St. Anns Hill Rd. Cher. AU53 82
St. Ann's Hl. SW18 BS46 76
St. Anns La. SW1 BW41 66
Old Pye St.

St. Ann's Pk. Rd. SW18 BT46 76
St. Ann's Pass. SW13 BO45 65
Cross St.
St. Ann's Rd. N9 CA27 39
St. Ann's Rd. N15 BY32 47
St. Anns Rd. SW13 BO44 65
St. Anns Rd. W11 BQ40 55
St. Ann's St. SW1 BW41 66
St. Anns St. Bark. CM37 58
Morley Rd.
St. Ann's Ter. NW8 BT37 56
St. Ann's Vill. W11 BQ40 55
St. Ann's Way Sth. Croy. BY57 95
St. Anselms Ct. SW16 BX49 76
St. Anselms Pl. W1 BV40 56
Davies St.
St. Anselms Rd. Hayes. BB41 63
St. Anthony's Av. Wdf. Grn. CJ29 40
St. Anthonys Clo. Hem. H. AZ14 8
St. Anthony's La. Swan. CU51 89
St. Anthony's Rd. E7 CH36 58
St. Anthony's Way. Felt. BB45 63
St. Arvans Clo. Croy. CA55 87
St. Asaph Rd. SE4 CC45 67
St. Aubyns Av. SW19 BR49 75
St. Aubyn's Av. Houns. BF46 74
St. Aubyn's Clo. Orp. CN55 88
St. Aubyn's Gdns. Orp. CN55 88
St. Aubyn's Rd. SE19 CA50 77
St. Audrey Av. Bexh. CR44 69
St. Audreys Cl. Hat. BP13 10
St. Augustine Rd. Grays. DG42 71
St. Augustine's Av. W5 BL37 55
St. Augustines Av. Brom. CK53 88
St. Augustine's Av. Sth. Croy. BZ57 96
St. Augustine's Av. Wem. BL34 46
St. Augustine, S Clo. Brox. CD13 12
St. Augustine, S Dr. Brox. CD13 12
St. Augustine's Rd. NW1 BW36 56
St. Augustines Rd. Belv. CQ42 69
St. Austell Clo. Edg. BL30 37
St. Austell Rd. SE13 CF44 67
St. Awdry's Rd. Bark. CM36 58
St. Awdry's Wk. Bark. CM36 58
St. Barnabas Clo. Beck. CF51 87
St. Barnabas Rd. E17 CE32 48
St. Barnabas Rd. Mitch. BV50 76
St. Barnabas Rd. Sutt. BT56 95
St. Barnabas Rd. Wood. Grn. CH30 40
St. Barnabas St. SW1 BV42 66
St. Barnabas Ter. E9 CC35 48
St. Barnabas Vil. SW8 BX44 66
Guildford Rd.
St. Bartholomew's Rd. E6 CK37 58
St. Benedict's Av. Grav. DJ48 81
St. Benet Pl. EC3 BZ40 57
Gracechurch St.
St. Benets Gro. Cars. BT54 86
St. Bernard's Croy. CA55 87
St. Bernard's Rd. E6 CJ37 58
St. Bernards Rd. St. Alb. BH13 9
St. Bernards Rd. Slou. AR41 62
St. Blaise Av. Brom. CH51 88
St. Botolph Rd. Grav. DE48 81
Pepper Hill
St. Botolph Row EC3 CA39 57
Houndsditch
St. Botolph's Ave. Sev. CU65 107
St. Botolph's Rd. Sev. CU65 107
St. Botolph St. EC3 CA39 57
St. Bride's Av. Edg. BL30 37
St. Brides Clo. SE2 CP41 69
St. Katherines Rd.
St. Bride's Pass. EC4 BY39 56
Dorset Rise
St. Bride St. EC4 BY39 56
St. Catharine, S Rd. Brox. CE13 12
St. Catherines Clo. Wok. AR63 100
St. Catherines Ct. W4 BO42 65
Newton Gro.
St. Catherine's Dr. SE14 CC44 67
Kitto Road.
St. Catherines Dr. Guil. AQ72 118
St. Catherine's Rd. E4 CE27 39
St. Catherines Rd. Ruis. BA32 44
St. Cecilia Rd. Grays. DG42 71
St. Chads. Gdns. Rom. CQ33 50
St. Chads Pl. WC1 BX38 56
St. Chads Rd. Rom. CQ32 50
St. Chads St. WC1 BX38 56
St. Chad4s Dr. Grav. DJ48 81
St. Charles' Pl. W10 BR39 55
Chesterton Rd.
St. Charles Rd. Brwd. DA26 42
St. Charles Sq. W10 BQ39 55
St. Christopher Rd. Uxb. AX39 53
St. Christophers Clo. Islw. BG44 64
Thornbury Rd.
St. Christopher's Pl. W1 BV39 56
Barrett St.
St. Clair Cl. Oxt. CF68 114
St. Clair Clo. Ilf. CK30 40
St. Clair Clo. Reig. BT70 121
St. Clair Dr. Wor. Pk. BP55 85
St. Clair Rd. E13 CH37 58
St. Clair's Rd. Croy. CA55 87
St. Clare St. EC3 CA39 57
Minories
St. Clements Av. Grays. DA43 70
St. Clement's La. WC2 BX39 56
Portugal St.
St. Clement's Rd. Grays. DB43 70
St. Clement St. N7 BY36 56
Offord Rd.
St. Clement Way, Uxb. AX39 53
St. Cloud Rd. SE27 BZ49 77
St. Columba's Clo. Grav. DJ48 81
St. Crispin's Clo. Sthl. BE39 54
St. Crispins Way. Cher. AU58 91
St. Cross St. EC1 BY39 56
St. Cuthbert's NW3 BS34 47
St. Cuthberts Gdns. Pnr. BE29 36
Westfield Pk.
St. Cuthbert's Rd. NW2 BR36 55
St. Cuthberts Rd. Hodd. CF10 12
St. Cyprian's St. SW17 BU49 76
St. David Clo. Uxb. AX39 53
St. David's Clo. Hem. H. BA14 8
St. Davids Clo. Iver AU37 52
St. Davids Clo. Reig. BT70 121
St. David's Clo. Wem. BN34 46
St. Davids Clo. W. Wick. CE54 87
St. David's Cres. Grav. DH49 81
St. David's Dr. Edg. BL30 37
St. David, S Dr. Brox. CD13 12
St. Davids Pl. NW4 BP33 46
St. David's Rd. Swan. CT50 79
St. Denis Rd. SE27 BZ49 77
St. Dionis Rd. SW6 BR44 65
St. Donatt's Rd. SE14 CD44 67
St. Dunstan's Alley EC3 CA40 57
Idol La.
St. Dunstan's Av. W3 BN40 55
St. Dunstans Clo. Hayes BB42 63
St. Dunstan's Clo. Hayes BC42 63
St. Dunstan's Dr. Grav. DJ49 81
St. Dunstan's Gdns. W3 BN40 55
St. Dunstan's Av.
St. Dunstan's Hill EC3 CA40 57
St. Dunstan's Hill Sutt. BR57 94
St. Dunstan's La. EC3 CA40 57
Idol La.
St. Dunstans La. Beck. CF53 87
St. Dunstans Rd. E7 CJ36 58
St. Dunstan's Rd. SE25 CA52 87
St. Dunstan's Rd. W6 BQ42 65
St. Dunstans Rd. W7 BH41 64
St. Dunstans Rd. Felt. BB48 73
St. Dunstan's Rd. Houns. BC44 63
St. Edmunds Av. Ruis. BA32 44
St. Edmunds Clo. NW8 BU37 56
St. Edmunds Ter.
St. Edmunds Clo. SE2 CP41 69
St. Katherines Rd.
St. Edmunds Dr. Stan. BJ30 36
St. Edmunds La. Twick. BF47 74
St. Edmund's Rd. N9 CB26 39
St. Edmunds Rd. Dart. CX45 70
St. Edmunds Rd. Dart. CX46 80
St. Edmunds Rd. Ilf. CK32 49
St. Edmunds Ter. NW8 BU37 56
St. Edmunds Way, Harl. CP9 6
St. Edwards Clo. NW11 BS32 47
Finchley Rd.
St. Edwards Clo. Croy CF58 96
St. Edwards Clo. Croy. CF59 96
St. Edwards Way Rom. CS31 50
St. Egberts Way E4 CF26 39
St. Elmo Rd. W12 BO40 55
St. Erkenwald Rd. Bark. CM37 58
St. Ermins Hill SW1 BW41 66
Broadway
St. Ervan's Rd. W10 BR39 55
St. Faith's Rd. SE21 BY47 76
St. Fidelis Rd. Erith CS42 69
St. Fillans Rd. SE6 CF47 77
St. Francis Clo. Orp. CN53 88
St. Francis Clo. Wat. BC26 35
St. Francis Rd. SE22 CA45 67
St. Francis Rd. Erith CS42 69
West St.
St. Francis Rd. Uxb. AV32 43
St. Francis Way, Brwd. DA27 42
St. Francis Way. Grays. DH42 71
St. Gabriel's Rd. NW2 BQ35 46
St. Gabriel St. SE11 BY42 66
St. George's Ave. Grays. DE42 71
St. George's Av. E7 CH36 58
St. George's Av. N7 BW35 47
St. George's Av. NW9 BN31 46
St. George's Av. W5 BK41 64
St. George's Av. Horn. CW33 51
St. Georges Av. Sthl. BE40 54
St. Georges Av, Wey. AZ57 92
St. George's Circus SE1 BY41 66
St. Georges Clo. NW11 BR32 46
St. George's Clo. Wem. BJ34 45
St. Georges Clo. Wey. BA56 92
St. Georges Clo. Wind. AM44 61
St. George's Ct. E6 CK38 58
St. Georges Ct. W8 BT41 66
St. George's Cres. Grav. DH49 81
St. George's Dr. SW1 BV42 66
St. George's Dr. Wat. BE27 36
St. Georges Est. Amer. AQ23 25
St. Georges Fields W2 BU39 56
Albion St.
St. George's Gdns. Epsom. BO60 94
St. George's La. EC3 BZ40 57
Pudding La.
St. Georges Ms. NW1 BU36 56
Regents Pk. Rd.
St. George, S Dr. Uxb. AY34 44
St. George's Pl. Twick. BJ47 74
Church St.
St. George's Rd. E7 CH36 58
St. George's Rd. E10 CF34 48
St. Georges Rd. N9 CB27 39
St. George's Rd. N15 CA32 48
St. George's Rd. N21 BX27 38
St. Georges Rd. NW11 BR32 46
St. George's Rd. SE1 BY41 66
St. George's Rd. SW19 BR50 75
St. George's Rd. W4 BN41 65
St. George's Rd. W7 BH40 54
St. George's Rd. Beck. CE51 87
St. George's Rd. Brom. CK51 88
St. George's Rd. Dag. CQ35 50
St. George's Rd. Enf. CA22 30
St. George's Rd. Felt. BD49 74
St. Georges Rd. Hem. H. AX15 8
St. George's Rd. Ilf. CK33 49
St. George's Rd. Kings. On T. BM50 75
St. Georges Rd. Mitch. BV52 86
St. Georges Rd. Orp. CM53 88
St. George's Rd. Rich. BL45 65
St. George's Rd. Sev. CU64 107
St. George's Rd. Sid. CP50 79
St. Georges Rd. Swan. CT52 89
St. George's Rd. Twick. BJ46 74
St. George's Rd. Wall. BV56 95
St. George's Rd. Wat. BC22 26
St. George's Rd. Wey. AX56 92
St. Georges Rd. Wey. BA57 92
St. George's Rd. W. Brom. CK51 88
St. Georges Sq. E7 CH36 58
St. George's Sq. SW1 BW42 66
St. George's St. Cat. BZ64 105
St. Georges Ter. NW1 BU36 56
Regents Pk. Rd.
St. George St. W1 BV39 56
St. George's Way SE15 CA43 67
St. Georges Way Croy. BZ55 87
St. German's Bungs. SE3 CG44 68
St. German's Pl. SE3 CH44 68
St. German's Rd. SE23 CD47 77
St. Giles Av. Dag. CR36 59
St. Giles Av. Pot. B. BP20 19
St. Giles Circus W1 BW39 56
St Giles Clo. Dag. CR36 59
St. Giles Clo. Orp. CM56 97
St. Giles High St. WC2 BW39 56
St. Giles Rd. SE5 CA43 67
St. Giles, S Av. Uxb. BA35 44
St. Gothard Rd. SE27 BZ49 77
St. Gregory's Cres. Grav. DJ48 81
St. Helena Rd. SE16 CC42 67
St. Helena Ter. Rich. BK46 74
Friars La.
St. Helens Clo. Uxb. AX39 53
St. Helens Ct. Epp. CO18 23
St. Helens Ct. Rain. CU38 59
St. Helen's Cres. SW16 BX51 86
St. Helen's Gdns. W10 BQ39 55
St. Helen's Pl. EC3 CA39 57
Bishopsgate
St. Helens Rd. SE2 CP41 69
St. Helen's Rd. SW16 BX51 86
St. Helens Rd. W13 BJ40 54
Dane Rd.
St. Helen's Rd. Ilf. CK32 49
St. Helier Av. Mord. BT54 86
St. Helier's Av. Houns. BF46 74
St. Helier's Rd. E10 CF32 48
St. Heliers Rd. St. Alb. BJ11 9
St. Hilda's Av. Ashf. AY49 73
St. Hilda's Clo. NW6 BQ36 55
St. Hildas Clo. Wok. AO62 100
St. Hilda's Rd. SW13 BP43 65
St. Hilda's Way, Grav. DJ49 81
St. Hilds's Clo. Ashf. AY49 73
St. Huberts Clo. AS34 43
St. Huberts La. Ger. Cr. AS34 43
St. Hugh's Rd. SE20 CB50 77
St. Hugh's Rd. SE20 CB51 87
Ridsdale Rd.
St. Ives Clo. Welw. G. C. BR5 5
St. Ivians Dr. Rom. CU31 50
St. Jame's Av. Beck. CD52 87
St. James Av. Epsom BO59 94
St. James Av. Ong. CW18 24
St. James' Av. Sutt. BS56 95
St. James Clo. Epsom. BO60 94
St. James Clo. Ruis. BD34 45
St. James Clo. Wok. AQ62 100
St. James' Ct. N22 BX29 38
St. James' La. Green. CZ47 80
St. James Pl. Dart. CV46 80
St James Pl. Enf. CC25 30
South St.
St. James' Rd. E15 CG35 49
St. James Rd. N9 CB27 39
Queens Rd.
St. James Rd. Mitch. BV50 76
St James Rd. Pur. BY60 95
St. James Rd. Surb. BK53 84
St. James' Rd. Sutt. BS56 95
St. James's SE14 CD44 67
St. James's Av. E2 CC37 57
St. James's Av. N20 BU27 38
St. James's Av. W13 BJ40 54
St. James's Av. Grav. DG47 81
St. James's Av. Hmptn. BG49 74
St. James's Clo. N20 BU27 38
St. James's Clo. SW12 BU48 76
St. James's Dr.
St. James's Clo. N. Mal. BO53 85
St. James's Cott. Rich. BL46 75
Paradise Rd.
St. James's Cres. SW9 BY45 66
St. James's Dr. SW17 BU47 76
St. James's Gdns. W11 BR41 65
St. James's Gro. SW11 BU44 66
Battersea Pk. Rd.
St. James's La. N10 BV31 47
St. James, S Rd. Brwd. DB27 42
St. James's Pk. Croy. BZ54 87
St. James's Pass. EC3 CA39 57
Duke's Pl.
St. James's Path E17 CD32 48
St. James's Pl. SW1 BW40 56
St. James's Rd. Cars. BU55 86
St. James's Rd. Croy. BY54 86
St. James's Rd. Grav. DG47 81
St. James's Rd. Hmptn. BF49 74
St. James's Rd. Kings-on-t. BK51 84
St. James's Rd. Sev. CU64 107
St. James's Rd. Wal. Cr. BZ17 21
St. James's Rd. Wat. BC25 26
St. James's Row EC1 BY38 56
Clerkenwell Clo.
St. James's Sq. SW1 BW40 56
St. James's St. E17 CD32 48
St. James's St. SW1 BW40 56
St. James's St. W6 BQ42 65
St. James's St. Grav. DG46 81
St. James's Ter. Ms. NW8 BU37 56
St. James's Vill. SE18 CM42 68
St. James's Wk. EC1 BY38 56
Sekforde St.
St. James Walk SE15 CA44 67
Sumner Estate
St. James Wk. Iver. AV41 62
St. James Way Sid. CQ49 79
St. Jeromes Gro. Hayes BA39 53
St. Joan's Rd. N9 CA27 39
St. Johns, Dor. BK73 119
St. Johns Av. N11 BU28 38
St. John's Av. NW10 BO37 55
St. John's Av. SW15 BQ46 75
St. John's Av. Epsom BO59 94
St. Johns Av. Harl. CP9 6
St. John's Av. Lthd. BJ64 102
St. John's Church Rd. E9 CC35 48
Urswick Rd.
St. Johns Church Rd. Dor. BE73 119
St. John's Clo. Guil. AQ71 118
St. Johns Clo. Pot. B. BT20 20
St. John's Clo. Rain. CU36 59
St. John's Clo. Wem. BL35 46
St. John's Cotts. SE20 CC50 77
Maple Rd.
St. John's Cotts. Rich. BL45 65
Kew Foot Rd.
St. John's Ct. N4 BY34 47
St. Johns Ct. Buck. H. CJ26 40
St. Johns Ct. Islw. BH44 64
St. Johns Ct. St. Alb. BJ12 9
Beaumont Av.
St. John's Cres. SW9 BY45 66
St. Johns Dr. Wind. AM44 61
St. Johns Est. N1 BZ37 57
St. Johns Est. SE1 CA41 67
St. Johns Est. SW11 BT44 66
St. John's Gdns. W11 BR40 55
St. John's Gro. N19 BW34 47
St. John's Gro. SW13 BO44 65
Terrace Gdns.
St. John's Gro. Rich. BL45 65
Kew Foot Rd.
St. John's Hill Couls. BY62 104
St. Johns Hill Pur. BY57 95
St. John's Hill Pur. BY61 104
St. John's Hill. Sev. CV64 108
St. John's Hill Rd. Wok. AQ63 100
St. John's Hl. SW11 BT46 76
St. John's Hl. Gro. SW11 BT45 66
St. John's La. EC1 BY38 56
St. John, S Av. Brwd. DB28 42
St. John's Pde. Sid. CO49 79
St. John's Pk. SE3 CG43 68
St. John's Pass. SW19 BR50 75
St. Johns Rise, Wok. AQ62 100
St. John's Rd. E4 CE28 39
St. John's Rd. E6 CK37 58
St. John's Rd. E16 CH39 58
St. John's Rd. E17 CE30 39
St. John's Rd. N15 CA32 48
St. Johns Rd. NW11 BR32 46
St. John's Rd. SE20 CC50 77
St. John's Rd. SW11 BU45 66
St. John's Rd. SW19 BR50 75
St. John's Rd. Bark. CG37 58
St. Johns Rd. Cars. BU55 86
St. John's Rd. Croy. BY55 86
St. Johns Rd. Croy. BY55 86
Silverdale Rd.
St. John's Rd. Dor. BG72 119
St. Johns Rd. E. Mol. BG52 84
St. John's Rd. Epp. CN18 22
St. John's Rd. Erith CS42 69
St. John's Rd. Felt. BE49 74
St. Johns Rd. Grav. DH47 81
St. Johns. Rd. Grays. DG42 71
St. John's Rd. Guil. AQ71 118
St. John's Rd. Har. BH32 45
St. John's Rd. Hem. H. AW14 8
St. John's Rd. Ilf. CM33 49
St. John's Rd. Islw. BH44 64
St. John's Rd. Islw. BJ45 64
St. John's Rd. Kings. On T. BK51 84
St. John's Rd. Loug. CK23 31
St. John's Rd. Lthd. BK64 102
St. Johns Rd. N. Mal. BN52 85
St. John's Rd. Orp. CM53 88
St. Johns Rd. Red. BU71 121
St. John's Rd. Rich. BL45 65
St. John's Rd. Rom. CS28 41
St. John's Rd. Sev. CU64 107
St. Johns Rd. Sid. CO49 79
St. John's Rd. Slou. AQ40 52
St. Johns Rd. Sthl. BE41 64
St. John's Rd. Sutt. BS55 86
St. Johns Rd. Uxb. AW37 53
St. John's Rd. Wat. BC23 26
St. John's Rd. Well. CO45 69
St. John's Rd. Wem. BK35 45
St John's Rd. Wind. AN44 61
St. John's Rd. Wok. AQ62 100
St. John's Sq. EC1 BY38 56
Clerkenwell Rd.
St. John's St. W10 BQ39 55
Harrow Rd.
St. John's Ter. E7 CH36 58
St. John's Ter. SE18 CM43 68
St. John's Ter. W10 BQ38 55
Harrow Rd.
St. Johns Ter. Enf. BZ22 30
St. Johns Ter. Rd. Red. BU71 121
St. John St. EC1 BY37 56
St. John's Vale SE8 CE44 67
St. John's Vill. N19 BW34 47
St. John's Way N19 BW34 47
St. Johns Well La. Berk. AQ12 7
St. John's Wood Ct. NW8 BT38 56
St. John's Wood Rd.
St. John's Wood High St. NW8 BT37 56
St. John's Wood Pk. NW8 BT37 56
St. John's Wood Rd. NW8 BT38 56
St. John's Wood Ter. NW8 BT37 56
St. Joseph's Dr. Sthl. BE40 54
St. Joseph's Rd. N9 CB26 39
St. Jude's Rd. E2 CB37 57
St. Jude's Rd. Egh. AR49 72
St. Jude St. N16 CA35 48
St. Julian's Clo. SW16 BY49 76
St. Julian's Farm Rd. SE27 BY49 76
St. Julians Hill, St. Alb. BG15 9
St. Julians Rd. NW6 BR37 55
St. Julians Rd. St. Alb. BG14 9
St. Julians Rd. Sev. CW68 117
St. Justin Clo. Orp. CP52 89
St. Katharine's Precinct NW1 BV37 56
Outer Circle
St. Katharine's Way, E1 CA40 57
St. Katherine's Cross. Red. CA70 114
St. Katherine's Rd. SE2 CP41 69
St. Katherine's Rd. Cat. CB66 114
St. Keverne Rd. SE9 CK49 78
St. Kilda Rd. W13 BJ40 54
St. Kilda Rd. Orp. CN54 88
St. Kilda's Rd. N16 BZ33 48
St. Kildas Rd. Brwd. DA26 42
St. Kilda's Rd. Har. BH32 45
St. Laurence Dr. Brox. CD15 12
High Rd.
St. Lawrence Clo. Edg. BL29 37
Whitchurch La.
St. Lawrence Clo. Orp. CP52 89
St. Lawrence Clo. St. Alb. BE19 18
St. Lawrence Clo. Wat. BB18 17
St. Lawrence Dr. Pnr. BC32 44
St. Lawrence Gdns. Ing. DC19 24
St. Lawrence Rd. SW9 BY44 66
St. Lawrence Rd. Upmin. CY34 51
St. Lawrence, Rue De Wal. Abb. CF20 21
John Foxe Pl.
St. Lawrence St. E14 CF40 57
St. Lawrence Ter. W10 BR39 55
St. Lawrence Way, St. Alb. BE19 18
St. Leonards Av. E4 CF29 39
St. Leonard's Av. E14 CE39 57
St. Leonards Av. Har. BK32 45
St. Leonard's Clo. Well. CO45 69
Hook La.
St. Leonard's Ct. SW14 BN45 65
St. Leonard's Rd.
St. Leonards Cres. St. Alb. BK10 9
St. Leonards Gdns. Houns. BE43 64
St. Leonards Gdns. Ilf. CM35 49
St Leonard's Hill. Wind. AM45 61
St. Leonard, S Rd. Wal. Abb. CF15 12
St. Leonard, S Rd. Wal. Abb. CG15 13
St. Leonard's Rise Orp. CM56 97
St. Leonard's Rd. E14 CE39 57
St. Leonards Rd. NW10 BN38 55
St. Leonard's Rd. SW14 BM45 65
St. Leonard's Rd. W13 BK40 54
St. Leonards Rd. Amer. AP21 25
St. Leonards Rd. Croy. BY55 86
St. Leonards Rd. Epsom. BQ63 103
St. Leonard's Rd. Esher BH57 93

St. Leonards Rd. Surb. BJ53 84
St. Leonards Rd. Surb. BK53 84
St. Leonard's Rd. Wal. Abb. CF16 21
St. Leonard's Rd. Wal. Abb. CG16 22
St. Leonards Rd. Wind. AN45 61
St. Leonard's Sq. NW5 BV36 56
St. Leonards Sq. Surb. BK53 84
St. Leonard's St. E3 CE38 57
St. Leonards Ter. SW3 BU42 66
St. Leonards Wk. Iver. AV41 62
St Leon Ave. Wind. AO44 61
St. Loo Av. SW3 BU43 66
St. Louis Rd. SE27 BZ49 77
St. Loy's Rd. N17 CA30 39
St. Luke Clo. Uxb. AX39 53
St. Luke's Clo. SE25 CB53 87
St. Luke's Av. SW4 BW45 66
St. Luke's Av. Enf. BZ22 30
St. Lukes Av. Ilf. CL35 49
St. Lukes Ms. W11 BR39 55
St. Lukes Pass. Kings. On T. BL51 85
St. Lukes Pl. St. Alb. BJ14 9
St. Luke's Rd. W11 BR39 55
St. Luke's Rd. Whyt. CA62 105
St. Luke's Rd. Wind. AQ46 72
St. Lukes Sq. E16 CG39 58
St. Luke's St. SW3 BU42 66
St. Luke's Yd. W9 BR30 55
St. Malo Av. N9 CC27 39
St. Margaret's NW3 BS34 47
St. Margarets Bark. CM37 58
St. Margarets, Guil. AS70 118
St. Margaret's Av. N15 BY31 47
St. Margaret's Av. N20 BT27 38
St. Margarets Av. Ashf. AZ49 73
St. Margaret's Av. Har. BG34 45
St. Margarets Av. Sid. CM48 78
St. Margaret's Av. Sutt. BR55 85
St. Margarets Av. Uxb. AZ38 53
St. Margarets Clo. Berk. AR13 7
St. Margarets Clo. Iver AU37 52
St. Margaret's Clo. Orp. CO55 89
St. Margaret's Cres. SW15 BP46 75
St. Margaret's Cres. Grav. DJ48 81
St. Margaret's Dr. Twick. BJ46 74
St. Margarets Gate, Iver AU37 52
St. Margaret's Gro. SE18 CM43 68
St. Margaret's Gro. Twick. BJ46 74
St. Margaret's Pass. SE13 CG45 68
St. Margaret's Path SE18 CM42 68
St. Margaret's Pl. SW1 BW41 66
Spencer Pl.
St. Margaret's Rd. E12 CJ34 49
St. Margaret's Rd. N17 CA31 48
St. Margarets Rd. NW10 BQ38 55
St. Margaret's Rd. SE4 CD45 67
St. Margaret's Rd. W7 BH41 64
St. Margaret's Rd. Beck. CC52 87
St. Margaret's Rd. Edg. BM28 37
St. Margarets Rd. Grav. DF47 81
Perry St.
St. Margarets Rd. Ruis. BA32 44
St. Margarets Rd. S. Dnth. CZ50 80
St. Margaret's Rd. Twick. BJ45 64
St. Margaret's St. SE18 CM42 68
St. Margarets St. SW1 BX41 66
St. Margaret's Ter. SE18 CM42 68
St. Margaret's Way, Hem. H. BA13 8
St. Marg. Rd. Couls. BV64 104
St. Mark's Clo. Barn. BS24 29
St. Mark's Cres. NW1 BV37 56
St. Marks Gro. SW10 BS43 66
St. Mark's Hill Surb. BL53 85
St. Marks Pl. SW19 BR50 75
Wimbledon Hill Rd.
St. Marks Pl. W11 BR39 55
St Mark's Pl. Wind. AO44 61
St. Mark's Rise E8 CA35 48
St. Mark's Rd. SE25 CB52 87
St. Marks Rd. W5 BL40 55
Common, The.
St. Marks Rd. W7 BH41 64
St. Marks Rd. W10 BQ39 55
St. Marks Rd. Brom. CH52 88
St. Mark's Rd. Enf. CA25 30
St. Mark's Rd. Epsom BQ62 103
St. Marks Rd. Mitch. BU51 86
St. Mark's Rd. Tedd. BJ50 74
St Mark's Rd. Wind. AO44 61
St. Marks Sq. Grav. DF49 81
St. Martha's Av. Wok. AS64 100
St. Martin Clo. Uxb. AX39 53
St. Martins App. Ruis. BB33 44
St. Martin's Av. E6 CJ37 58
St. Martins Av. Epsom. BO60 94
St. Martins Clo. SE2 CP41 69
St. Helens Rd.
St. Martins Clo. Brwd. DE26 122
St. Martin's Clo. Enf. CB23 30
St. Martins Clo. Epsom. BO60 94
St Martins Clo. Leath. BB68 110
St. Martins Clo. West Dr. AX41 63
St. Martin's Ct. WC2 BX40 56
St. Martin's La.
St. Martins Ct. Ashf. AX49 73
St. Martins Dr. Eyns. CV56 99
St. Martins Drive Walt. BD55 84
St. Martin's La. WC2 BX40 56
St. Martin's Le Grand EC1 BZ39 57
St. Martins Meadows. West. CP65 107
St. Martin's Ms. WC2 BX40 56
Adelaide St.
St. Martin's Rd. N9 CB27 39
St. Martin's Rd. SW9 BX44 66
St. Martin's Rd. Dart. CW46 80
St. Martins Rd. West Dr. AX41 63
St. Martins St. WC2 BX40 56
Whitcomb St.
St. Mary Abbot's Pl. W8 BR41 65
St. Mary Abbots Ter. W14 BR41 65
St. Mary At Hill EC3 CA40 57
Lwr. Thames St.
St. Marys Av. Wall. BV55 86
St. Mary Axe EC3 CA39 57
St. Mary Church St. SE16 CC41 67
St. Mary Clo. N17 CB30 39
Kemble Rd.
St. Mary Rd. E17 CE32 48
St. Marys Bark. CM37 58
St. Mary's App. E12 CK35 49
Church Rd.
St. Mary's Ave. Nthwd. BB28 35
St. Mary's Av. E11 CH32 49
St. Mary's Av. N3 BR30 37
St. Mary's Av. Brom. CG52 88
St. Mary's Av. Stai. AX47 73
St. Mary's Av. Sthl. BF42 64
St. Mary's Av. Tedd. BH50 74
St. Marys Av. Wal. Cr. CC18 21
St. Marys Clo. E12 CK35 49
Church Rd.
St. Mary's Clo. Chess. BL57 94
St. Mary's Clo. Epsom BO57 94
St. Mary's Clo. Grav. DH48 81
St. Mary's Clo. Lthd. BG65 102
St. Mary's Clo. Orp. CO51 89
St. Marys Clo. Stai. AX47 73
St. Marys Cres.
St. Mary's Clo. Sun. BC52 83
St. Marys Clo. Uxb. AW31 44
St. Mary's Clo. Wat. BC24 26
St. Mary's Cotts. SW19 BS51 86
St. Mary's Rd.
St. Mary's Ct. E6 CK38 58
St. Mary's Ct. W5 BK41 64
St. Mary's Rd.
St. Mary's Cres. NW4 BP31 46
St. Mary's Cres. Hayes BB40 53
St. Mary's Cres. Hayes BC40 53
St. Mary's Rd.
St. Mary's Cres. Islw. BG43 64
St. Mary's Cres. Stai. AX47 73
St. Marys Dr. Felt. BA47 73
St. Marys Dr. Sev. CT65 107
St. Mary's Gdns. SE11 BY42 66
St. Marys Gr. West. CJ62 106
St. Mary's Gro. N1 BY36 56
St. Mary's Gro. SW13 BP45 65
St. Marys Gro. W4 BM43 65
St. Mary's Gro. Rich. BL45 65
St. Marys La. Upmin. CX34 51
St. Mary's La. Upmin. DB33 51
St. Mary's Ms. W2 BT39 56
St. Mary, S Av. Brwd. DD25 122
St. Mary, S La. Upmin. DC33 123
St. Mary, S'rd. Wok. AR62 100
St. Mary's Rd. E10 CF34 48
St. Mary's Rd. E13 CH37 58
St. Mary's Rd. N8 BX31 47
High St.
St. Mary's Rd. N9 CB26 39
St. Mary's Rd. NW10 BO37 55
St. Mary's Rd. NW11 BR33 46
St. Mary's Rd. SE15 CC44 67
St. Mary's Rd. SE25 CA52 87
St. Mary's Rd. W5 BK40 54
St. Mary's Rd. Barn. BU26 38
St. Mary's Rd. Bex. CS47 79
St. Marys Rd. E. Mol. BG53 84
St. Mary's Rd. Grays. DG42 71
St. Marys Rd. Green. CZ45 70
St. Mary's Rd. Hayes BB40 53
St. Mary's Rd. Hem. H. AX13 8
St. Mary's Rd. Ilf. CM34 49
St. Mary's Rd. Lthd. BJ64 102
St. Mary's Rd. Merton SW19 BS51 86
St. Mary's Rd. Reig. BS71 121
St. Marys Rd. Slou. AS40 52
St. Mary's Rd. Sth. Croy. BZ58 96
St. Marys Rd. Surb. BK53 84
St. Marys Rd. Surb. BK54 84
St. Mary's Rd. Swan. CS52 89
St. Marys Rd. Uxb. AV32 43
St. Marys Rd. Uxb. AW31 44
St. Marys Rd. Wal. Cr. CC18 21
St. Mary's Rd. Wat. BC24 26
St. Mary's Rd. Wey. BA56 92
St. Mary's Rd. Wimb. SW19 BR49 75
St. Mary's Rd. Wok. AR62 100
St. Marys Rd. Wor. Pk. BO55 85
St. Mary's Sq. W2 BT39 56
St. Mary's Ter. W2 BT39 56
St. Mary St. SE18 CK42 68
St. Mary's Wk. SE11 BY42 66
St. Mary's Wk. Hayes BB40 53
St. Marys Wk. St. Alb. BJ11 9
St. Mary's. Way. Ger. Cr. AR30 34
St. Marys Way Long. DC52 90
St. Mathew's Rd. SW2 BX45 66
St. Matthew Clo. Uxb. AX39 53
St. Matthew Rd. Red. BU70 121
St. Matthew's Av. Surb. BL54 85
St. Matthew's Clo. Rain. CU36 59
St. Matthew's Dr. Brom. CK52 88
St. Matthews Rd. W5 BL40 55
Common, The.
St. Matthews Row E2 CB38 57
St. Matthew St. SW1 BW41 66
Old Pye St.
St. Matthias Clo. BO32 46
St. Maur Rd. SW6 BR44 65
St. Merryn Clo. SE18 CM43 68
St. Meryl Est. Wat. BE27 36
St. Michael's Alley EC3 BZ39 57
Cornhill
St. Michael's Av. N9 CC26 39
St. Michael's Av. NW2 BQ35 46
St. Michaels Av. Hem. H. AZ14 8
St. Michael's Av. Wem. BM36 55
St. Michaels Clo. N3 BR30 37
Hendon La.
St. Michaels Clo. N12 BU28 38
St. Michaels Clo. SE2 CP41 69
St. Helens Rd.
St. Michael's Clo. Brom. CK52 88
St. Michael's Clo. Walt. BD55 84
St. Michael's Cres. Pnr. BE32 45
St. Michael's Gdns. W10 BR39 55
Ladbroke Gro.
St. Michael, S Rd. Brox. CD13 12
St. Michael's Rise Well. CO44 69
St. Michael's Rd. SW9 BX44 66
St. Michael's Rd. Ashf. AZ49 73
St. Michael's Rd. Cat. BZ64 105
St. Michael's Rd. Croy. BZ54 87
St. Michaels Rd. Grays. DG42 71
St. Michael's Rd. Wall. BW56 95
St. Michaels Rd. Well. CO45 69
St. Michaels Rd. Wok. AU60 91
St. Michael's St. SE8 CD44 67
Tanner's Hill
St. Michael's St. W2 BT39 56
St. Michaels St. St. Alb. BF13 9
St. Michael's Ter. N22 BX30 38
St. Michaels Vw. Hat. BP11 10
Cornerfield
St. Mildred's Ct. EC2 BZ39 57
Poultry
St. Mildred's Rd. SE12 CG47 78
St. Monica's Rd. Tad. BR64 103
St. Neots Rd. Rom. CW29 42
St. Nicholas Ave. Lthd. BF66 111
St. Nicholas Av. Horn. CU34 50
St. Nicholas Clo. Amer. AQ23 25
St. Nicholas Clo. Uxb. AX39 53
St. Nicholas Dr. Shep. AZ54 83
St. Nicholas Glebe SW17 BV49 76
St. Nicholas Gro. Brwd. DE28 122
St. Nicholas Hill, Lthd. BJ64 102
St. Nicholas La. Chis. CK51 88
St. Nicholas Mnt. Hem. H. AV13 7
St. Nicholas Rd. SE18 CN42 68
St. Nicholas Rd. Surb. BH53 84
St. Nichola's Rd. Sutt. BS56 95
St. Nicholas St. SE8 CE44 67
Lucas St.
St. Nichola's Way Sutt. BS56 95
St. Norbert Gn. SE4 CD45 67
St. Norbert Rd. SE4 CC46 77
St Norman's Way Epsom BP58 94
St. Olaf's Rd. SW6 BR43 65
St. Olaves Clo. AV50 72
St. Olave's Est. SE1 CA41 67
St. Olave's Rd. E6 CL37 58
St. Olaves Wk. SW16 BW51 86
St. Omer Rd. Guil. AT71 118
St. Omer's Ridge, Guil. AT71 118
St. Oswalds Pl. SE11 BX42 66
St. Oswald's Rd. SW16 BY51 86
St. Oswulf St. SW1 BW42 66
Erasmus St.
St. Pancras Ct. N2 BT30 38
St. Pancras Way NW1 BW36 56
St. Pancras Way Est. NW1 BW36 56
St. Pancras Way
St. Patrick's Gdns. Grav. DH48 81
St. Patricks Pl. Grays. DG42 71
St. Paul Clo. Uxb. AX39 53
St. Paul's Alley EC4 BY39 56
St. Paul's Churchyard
St. Paul's Av. NW2 BP36 55
St. Paul's Av. SE16 CC40 57
St. Pauls Av. Har. BL32 46
St. Pauls Av. Slou. AP40 52
St. Pauls Churchyard EC4 BY39 56
St. Paul's Clo. Ashf. BA49 73
St. Paul's Clo. Chess. BK56 93
St. Pauls Clo. Hayes. BA42 63
St. Pauls Clo. Houns. BE44 64
St. Pauls Clo. S. Ock. CW40 60
St. Paul's Cray Est. Chis. CN52 88
St. Paul's Cray Rd. Chis. CM50 78
St. Paul's Cres. NW1 BW36 56
St. Paul's Dr. E15 CF35 48
St. Paul's Pl. N1 BZ36 57
St. Pauls Pl. St. Alb. BJ13 9
St. Paul's Rd. N1 BY36 56
St. Pauls Rd. N17 CB29 39
St. Paul's Rd. Bark. CM37 58
St. Paul's Rd. Brent. BK43 64
St. Paul's Rd. Dor. BJ72 119
St. Paul's Rd. Erith CS43 69
St. Pauls Rd. Hem. H. AX13 8
St. Pauls Rd. Rich. BL45 65
St. Paul's Rd. Stai. AU50 72
St. Paul's Rd. Th. Hth. BZ52 87
St. Pauls Rd. Wok. AT62 100
St. Paul's Rd. E. Dor. BJ71 119
St. Paul's Rd. W. Dor. BJ72 119
St. Paul's Shrubbery N1 BZ36 57
St. Paul's Rd.
St. Pauls Sq. Brom. CG51 88
Church Rd.
St. Paul's St. E3 CD39 57
St. Pauls Ter. SE17 BY43 66
St. Paul St. N1 BZ37 57
St. Paul's Way E3 CD39 57
St. Paul's Way N3 BS29 38
St. Pauls Way Wal. Abb. CF20 21
Rochford Av.
St. Paul's Way Est. E14 CD39 57
St. Pauls Wood Hill Orp. CN51 88
St. Peter's Av. E17 CG31 49
St. Peter's Av. N18 CB28 39
St. Peters Av. Ong. CW16 24
St. Petersburgh Ms. W2 BS40 56
St. Petersburgh Pl. W2 BS40 56
St. Peters Clo. E2 CB38 57
St. Peters Clo. Barn. BP25 28
St. Peters Clo. Bush. BG26 36
St. Peters Clo. Chis. CM50 78
St. Peters Clo. Ger. Cr. AS30 34
St. Peters Clo. Ilf. CN31 49
St. Peters Clo. Rick. AW26 35
Church La.
St. Peter's Clo. Ruis. BD34 45
St. Peters Clo. Wind. AQ46 72
St. Peters Clo. Wok. AU63 100
St. Peters Ct. SE3 CG45 68
St. Peters Ct. Ger. Cr. AS30 34
St. Peter's Gro. W6 BP42 65
St. Peter, S Clo. St. Alb. BG13 9
St. Peter, S Rd. Brwd. DA28 42
St. Peter, S St. St. Alb. BG13 9
St. Peter's Rd. N9 CB26 39
St. Peter's Rd. SW6 BR44 65
Filmer Rd.
St. Peter's Rd. W6 BP42 65
St. Peter's Rd. Croy. BZ56 96
St. Peters Rd. E. Mol. BF52 84
St. Peters Rd. Grays. DG42 71
St. Peters Rd. Kings-on-t. BM51 85
Cambridge Rd.
St. Peters Rd. St. Alb. BH13 9
St. Peter's Rd. Stai. AV50 72
St. Peter's Rd. Sthl. BF39 54
St. Peter's Rd. Twick. BJ46 74
St. Peters Rd. Uxb. AX39 53
St. Peters Rd. Wok. AT63 100
St. Peter's Sq. W6 BP42 65
St. Peters St. N1 BY37 56
St. Peter's St. Sth. Croy. BZ56 96
St. Peters Ter. SW6 BR43 65
Reporton Rd.
St. Peter's Vill. W6 BP42 65
St. Peter's Way N1 CA36 57
De Beauvoir Sq.
St. Peters Way W5 BK39 54
St. Peters Way. Hayes. BA42 63
St. Peters Way. Rick. AT24 25
St. Philip's Av. Wor. Pk. BP55 85
St. Philip Sq. SW8 BV44 66
St. Philip's Rd. E8 CB36 57
St. Philips Rd. Surb. BK53 84
St. Philips St. SW8 BV44 66
St. Philips Way N1 BZ37 57
Linton St.
St. Pinnocks Av. Stai. AW51
St. Quentin Rd. Well. CN45 68
St. Quintin Av. W10 BQ39 55
St. Quintin Gdns. W10 BQ39 55
St. Quintin Rd. E13 CH37 58
St. Raphael's Way NW10 BN36 55
St. Regis Clo. N10 BV30 38
St. Romans Clo. Barn. BT22 29
St. Ronans Cres. Wdf. Grn. CH29 40
St. Rule St. SW8 BW44 66
St. Saviours Av. Dart. CW46 80
St. Saviours Est. SE1 CA41 67
St. Saviour's Rd. SW2 BX46 76
St. Saviour's Rd. Croy. BY53 86
St. Silas Pl. NW5 BV36 56
St. Silas St. NW5 BV36 56
St. Simons Av. SW15 BQ46 75
St. Stephen's Ave. Ash. BL61 103
St. Stephens Av. E17 CF32 48
St. Stephens Av. W12 BP40 55
St. Stephens Av. W13 BJ39 54
St. Stephens Av. St. Alb. BF14 9
St. Stephens Clo. E17 CE32 48
St. Stephen's Clo. NW8 BU37 56
St. Stephens Clo. St. Alb. BF15 9
St. Stephen's Clo. Sthl. BF39 54
St. Stephens Cres. W2 BS39 56
St. Stephen's Cres. Th. Hth. BY52 86
St. Stephens Gdns. W2 BS39 56
St. Stephens Gdns. Twick. BK46 74
St. Stephens Hill, St. Alb. BG14 9
St. Stephens Ms. W2 BS39 56
Chepstow Rd.
St. Stephen, S Cres. Brwd. DD28 122
St. Stephens Pl. Twick. BK46 74
St. Stephen's Rd. E3 CD37 57
St. Stephen's Rd. E6 CJ36 58
St. Stephens Rd. E17 CE32 48
St. Stephens Rd. W13 BJ39 54
St. Stephen's Rd. Barn. BQ25 28
St. Stephen's Rd. Enf. CC22 30
St. Stephen's Rd. Houns. BF46 74
St. Stephens Rd. West Dr. AX40 53
St. Stephen's Row EC4 BZ39 57
Walbrook
St. Stephen's Ter. SW8 BX43 66
Saints, The, Wat. BD20 18
Saints Wk. Grays. DH42 71
St. Swithin's La. EC4 BZ40 57
St. Swithun's Rd. SE13 CF46 77
St. Teresa Wk. Grays. DG42 71
St. Theresa's Rd. Felt. BB45 63
St. Thomas Ct. Bex. CR47 79
St. Thomas Dr. Orp. CM54 88
St. Thomas Dr. Pnr. BE30 36
St. Thomas Rd. E16 CH39 58
St. Thomas Rd. N14 BW26 38
St. Thomas Rd. Belv. CS41 69
St. Thomas Rd. Brwd. DB27 42
St. Thomas's Av. Grav. DG48 81
St. Thomas's Clo. Wal. Abb. CH20 22
St Thomas's Drive. Guil. AY69 110
St. Thomas's Gdns. NW5 BV36 56
Queen's Cres.
St. Thomas's Gdns. Ilf. CM36 58
St. Thomas's Pl. E9 CC36 57
St. Thomas's Rd. N4 BY34 47
St. Thomas's Rd. NW10 BO37 55
St. Thomas's Rd. W4 BN43 65
St. Thomas's Sq. E9 CB36 57
St. Thomas St. SE1 BZ40 57
St. Thomas's Way SW6 BR43 65
St. Ursula Rd. Sthl. BF39 54
St. Ursulas Gro. Pnr. BD32 45
St. Vincent Dr. St. Alb. BJ15 9
St. Vincent Est. E14 CD40 57
St. Vincent Rd. Twick. BG46 74
St Vincent Rd. Walt. BC55 83
St. Vincent's Ave. Dart. CX46 80
St. Vincent's Rd. Dart. CW46 80
St. Vincents Rd. Dart. CX46 80
St. Vincent St. W1 BV39 56
Aybrook St.
St. Vincents Way, Pot. B. BT20 20
Saintway, The, Stan. BH28 36
St. Wilfreds Clo. Barn. BT25 29
St. Wilfreds Rd.
St. Wilfred's Rd. Barn. BT25 29
St. Winifred's Av. E12 CK35 49
St. Winifreds Clo. Chig. CM28 40
St. Winifred's Rd. Tedd. BJ50 74
St. Winifred's Rd. West. CK62 106
St. Winifrid's Wk. SE17 BY43 66
Lorrimore Rd.
Sakins Croft. Harl. CN12 13
Salamanca Pl. SE1 BX42 66
Salamanca St.
Salamanca St. SE1 BX42 66
Salamanca St. SE11 BX42 66
Salamons Way Rain. CT39 59
Salcombe Dr. Mord. BQ54 85
Salcombe Dr. Rom. CQ32 50
Salcombe Gdns. NW7 BQ29 37
Salcombe Rd. E17 CD33 48
Salcombe Rd. Ashf. AY49 73
Salcombe Way Ruis. BC34 44
Salcomb Way, Hayes BB38 53
Salcot Cres. Croy. CF58 96
Salcote Rd. Grav. DJ49 81
Salcott Rd. SW11 BU46 76
Salcott Rd. Croy. BX55 86
Salehurst Clo. Har. BL32 46
Salehurst Rd. SE4 CD46 77
Salem Pl. Croy. BZ55 87
Salem Rd. W2 BS41 66
Porchester Gdns.
Sale Pl. W2 BU39 56
Sale, The, E4 CG28 40
Salford Rd. SW2 BW47 76
Salisbury Av. N3 BR31 46
Salisbury Av. Bark. CM36 58
Salisbury Av. St. Alb. BJ13 9
Salisbury Av. Sutt. BR57 94
Salisbury Av. Swan. CU52 89
Salisbury Clo. Amer. AP23 25
Salisbury Clo. Pot. B. BT19 20
Salisbury Clo. Upmin. CZ34 51
Salisbury Ct. EC4 BY39 56
Salisbury Cres. Wal. Cr. CC19 21
Theobalds La.
Salisbury Gdns. SW19 BR50 75
Salisbury Gdns. Welw. G. C. BR8 5
Salisbury Pl. W1 BU39 56
Salisbury Plain NW4 BQ32 46
Brent St.
Salisbury Rd. E4 CE27 39
Salisbury Rd. E7 CH36 58
Salisbury Rd. E10 CF34 48
Salisbury Rd. E12 CJ35 49
Salisbury Rd. E17 CF32 48
Salisbury Rd. N4 BY32 47
Salisbury Rd. N9 CB27 39

Salisbury Rd. N22 BY30 38
Salisbury Rd. SE25 CB53 87
Salisbury Rd. SW19 BR50 75
Salisbury Rd. W13 BJ41 64
Salisbury Rd. Bans. BS60 95
Salisbury Rd. Barn. BR24 28
Salisbury Rd. Bex. CR47 79
Salisbury Rd. Brom. CK53 88
Salisbury Rd. Cars. BU57 95
Salisbury Rd. Dag. CR36 59
Salisbury Rd. Dart. CY47 80
Salisbury Rd. Enf. CD22 30
Salisbury Rd. Felt. BD47 74
Salisbury Rd. Gdse. CC69 114
Salisbury Rd. Grav. DF47 81
Salisbury Rd. Grays. DE43 71
Salisbury Rd. Har. BG32 45
Salisbury Rd. Hodd. CF11 12
Salisbury Rd. Houns. BD45 64
Salisbury Rd. Ilf. CN34 49
Salisbury Rd. N. Mal. BN52 85
Salisbury Rd. Pnr. BC31 44
Salisbury Rd. Rich. BL45 65
Salisbury Rd. Rom. CU32 50
Salisbury Rd. Sthl. BE42 64
Salisbury Rd. Uxb. AW37 53
Salisbury Rd. Wat. BC23 26
Salisbury Rd. Welw. G. C. BR8 5
Salisbury Rd. Wok. AS63 100
Salisbury Rd. Wor. Pk. BN56 94
Salisbury Row SE17 BZ42 67
Salisbury Sq. EC4 BY39 56
Salisbury St. NW8 BU38 56
Salisbury St. W3 BN41 65
Salisbury Walk N19 BW34 47
Girdlestone Est.
Salix Clo. Sun. BC50 73
Salmen Rd. E13 CG37 58
Salmon Bldgs. E14 CD39 57
Salmond Clo. Stan. BJ29 36
Salmonds Gro. Brwd. DE28 122
St. Nicholas Gro.
Salmon La. E14 CD39 57
Salmon Rd. Belv. CR42 69
Salmon Rd. Lthd. BD68 111
Salmons La. Cat. CA63 105
Salmons La. W. Cat. CA63 105
Salmons Rd. N9 CB26 39
Salmons Rd. Chess. BL57 94
Salmon St. NW9 BM33 46
Salomons Rd. E13 CJ39 58
Salop Rd. E17 CC32 48
Saltash Clo. Sutt. BR56 94
Saltash Rd. Ilf. CM29 40
Saltash Rd. Well. CP44 69
Salt Box Hill. West. CH60 97
Saltcoats Rd. W4 BO41 65
Greenend Rd.
Salterford Rd. SW17 BV50 76
Salters Clo. Berk. AP12 7
Salter's Hill SE19 BZ49 77
Salters Rd. E17 CF31 48
Salter St. E14 CE40 57
Salterton Rd. N7 BX34 47
Saltford Clo. Erith CT42 69
Salt Hill Ave. Slou. AO40 61
Salt Hill Clo. Uxb. AY35 44
Salt Hill Dr. Slou. AO40 61
Salt Hill Way. Slou. AO40 61
Saltoun Rd. SW2 BY45 66
Saltram Cl. N15 CA31 48
Saltram Cres. W9 BR38 55
Saltwell St. E14 CE40 57
Saltwood Clo. Orp. CP56 98
Salusbury Rd. NW6 BR37 55
Salvador SW17 BU49 76
Salvia Gdns. Grnf. BJ37 54
Salvin Rd. SW15 BQ45 65
Salway Clo. Wdf. Grn. CG29 40
Salway Pl. E15 CF36 57
Broadway
Salway Rd. E15 CF36 57
Salwey Cres. Brox. CD13 12
Samantha Rd. E10 CD33 48
Markhouse Rd.
Samels Ct. W6 BP42 65
Sth. Black Lion La.
Samian Gt. St. Alb. BE15 9
Samos Clo. SE3 CG43 68
Samos Rd. SE20 CB51 87
Sampleoak La. Guil. AV73 118
Sampson St. E1 CB40 57
Samson St. E13 CJ37 58
Samuel Lewis Bldgs. SE5 BZ44 67
Samuel Lewis Dws. SW6 BS43 66
Vanston Pl.
Samuel Lewis Trust Bldgs. E8 CB35 48
Samuel Lewis Trust Dws. N1 BY36 56
Samuel St. SE18 CK42 68
Sancroft Clo. NW2 BP34 46
Sancroft Rd. Stan. BJ30 36
Sancroft St. SE11 BX42 66
Sanctuary Clo. Dart. CV46 80
Sanctuary Clo. Uxb. AX29 35
Sanctuary St. SE1 BZ41 67
Sanctuary, The, Bex. CP46 79
Sanctuary, The, Mord. BS53 86
Sandall Clo. W5 BL38 55
Sandall Rd. NW5 BW36 56
Sandall Rd. W5 BL38 55
Sandal Rd. N18 CB28 39
Sandal Rd. N. Mal. BN53 85
Sandal St. E15 CF37 57
Sanday Clo. Hem. H. AZ14 8
Sandbach Pl. SE18 CM42 68
Sandbanks Hill. Dart. DA50 80
Sandbourne Av. SW19 BS51 86
Sandbourne Rd. SE4 CD44 67
Sandbrook Rd. N16 CA34 48
Sandby Grn. SE9 CK45 68
Sandcliff Rd. Erith CS42 69
Sandcross La. Reig. BR72 120
Sandcross La. Reig. BS72 121
Sandells Av. Ashf. BA49 73
Sandell St. SE1 BY41 66
Sanders Clo. Hamptn. BG49 74
Sanders Clo. Hem. H. AY15 8
Sanders Clo. St. Alb. BK17 18
Sandersfield Gdns. Bans. BS61 104
Sandersfield Rd. Bans. BS61 104
Sanders La. NW7 BQ29 37
Sanders La. Wok. AQ64 100
Sanderson Clo. SW4 BW47 76
Sanders Pl. NW7 BQ29 37
Sanders Rd. Hem. H. AY15 8
Sanderstead Av. NW2 BR34 46
Sanderstead Clo. SW4 BW47 76
Atkins Rd.
Sanderstead Ct. Av. Sth. Croy. CB60 96
Sanderstead Hill Sth. Croy. CA59 96
Sanderstead Rd. E10 CD33 48
Sanderstead Rd. Orp. CO53 89
Sanderstead Rd. Sth. Croy. BZ57 96
Sanders Way N19 BX33 47
Hornsey Rise
Sandes Pl. Lthd. BJ62 102
Sandfield Gdns. Th. Hth. BY52 86
Sandfield Pass. Th. Hth. BZ52 87
Sandfield Rd. St. Alb. BJ13 9
Sandfield Rd. Th. Hth. BY52 86
Sandfield Ter. Guil. AR71 118
Sandford Av. N22 BZ29 38
Sandford Av. Loug. CL24 31
Sandford Clo. E6 CK38 58
Sandford Rd.
Sandford Rd. E6 CK38 58
Sandford Rd. Bexh. CQ45 69
Sandford Rd. Brom. CH52 88
Sandford Row SE17 BZ42 67
Sandford St. SW6 BS43 66
Sandgate Rd. N18 CB28 39
Sandgate Rd. Well. CP43 69
Sandgate St. SE15 CB43 67
Sandhills Wall. BW56 95
Sandhills La. Vir. W. AS53 82
Sandhills Rd. Reig. BS71 121
Sandhurst Av. Har. BF32 45
Sandhurst Av. Surb. BM54 85
Sandhurst Clo. NW9 BM31 46
Sandhurst Clo. Sth. Croy. CA58 96
Sandhurst Ct. SW2 BX45 66
Sandhurst Dr. Ilf. CN35 49
Sandhurst Rd. N9 CC25 30
Sandhurst Rd. NW9 BM31 46
Sandhurst Rd. SE6 CF47 77
Sandhurst Rd. Bex. CP46 79
Sandhurst Rd. Orp. CO55 89
Sandhurst Rd. Sid. CN48 78
Sandhurst Rd. Til. DH44 71
Sandhurst Way Sth. Croy. CA57 96
Sandifield Hat. BP14 10
Far-end
Sandiford Rd. Sutt. BR55 85
Sandiland Cres. Brom. CG55 88
Sandilands Croy. CB55 87
Sandilands. Sev. CS64 107
Sandilands La. SW6 BS44 66
Sandilands Rd. SW6 BS44 66
Sandison St. SE15 CA45 67
Sandlands Gro. Tad. BP65 103
Sandlands Rd. Tad. BP65 103
Sandland St. WC1 BX39 56
Sandlewood Av. Cher. AV55
Sandlewood Rd. Felt. BC48 73
Sandling Rise SE9 CL48 78
Sandmere Clo. Hem. H. AZ14 8
St. Albans Rd.
Sandmere Rd. SW4 BX45 66
Sandon Cl. Esher BG54 84
Sandon Pl. Ong. CX18 24
Sandon Rd. Wal. Cr. CC18 21
Sandover Rd. SE5 CA43 67
Sandow Av. Horn. CV34 51
Sandown Av. Dag. CS36 59
Sandown Av. Esher BG56 93
Sandown Clo. Houns. BC44 63
Sandown Ct. Esher BF56 93
Sandown Cres. Hayes. BB41 63
Sandown Rd. SE25 CB53 87
Sandown Rd. Couls. BV61 104
Sandown Rd. Esher BG56 93
Sandown Rd. Grav. DH49 81
Sandown Rd. Wat. BD22 27
Sandown Way Nthlt. BE36 54
Sandpiper Rd. Croy. CC59 96
Sandpiper Rd. Sth. Croy. CC58 96
Sandpit Cres. St. Alb. BJ12 9
Sandpit Gro. Hert. BV12 11
Sandpit Hall Rd. Wok. AQ59 91
Sandpit La. Brwd. CZ25 33
Sandpit La. Brwd. CZ26 42
Sandpit La. St. Alb. BH13 9
Sandpit La. St. Alb. BJ12 9
Sandpit Rd. Brom. CG49 78
Sandpit Rd. Dart. CV45 70
Sandpit Rd. Welw. G. C. BR9 5
Sandpits Head, Guil. AO68 109
Sandpits Rd. Croy. CC56 96
Sandpits Rd. Rich. BK48 74
Sandpitt Rd. Red. BU71 121
Sandra Clo. N22 BZ30 39
New Rd.
Sandra Clo. Houns. BF46 74
Sandridgebury La. St. Alb. BH11 9
Sandridge Clo. Har. BH31 45
Sandridge La. St. Alb. BK11 9
Sandridge Rd. St. Acb. BH12 9
Sandringham Av. SW20 BR51 85
Sandringham Clo. Enf. CA23 30
Sandringham Clo. Ilf. CM31 49
Sandringham Gdns.
Sandringham Ct. W9 BT38 56
Sandringham Ct. Har. BF34 45
Sandringham Cres. Har. BF34 45
Sandringham Dr. Ashf. AX49 73
Sandringham Dr. Well. CN44 68
Sandringham Gdns. N8 BX32 47
Sandringham Gdns. N12 BT29 38
Sandringham Gdns. Houns. BC43 63
Sandringham Gdns. Ilf. CM31 49
Sandringham Ms. W5 BK40 54
High St.
Sandringham Rd. E7 CJ35 49
Sandringham Rd. E8 CA35 48
Sandringham Rd. E10 CF32 48
Sandringham Rd. N22 BZ31 48
Sandringham Rd. NW2 BP36 55
Sandringham Rd. NW11 BR33 46
Sandringham Rd. Bark. CN35 49
Sandringham Rd. Brom. CH49 78
Sandringham Rd. Brwd. DA25 33
Sandringham Rd. Houns. AX46 73
Sandringham Rd. Nthlt. BF36 54
Sandringham Rd. Pot. B. BS18 20
Sandringham Rd. Th. Hth. BZ53 87
Sandringham Rd. Wat. BD22 27
Sandringham Rd. Wor. Pk. BP55 85
Sandrock Pl. Croy. CC56 96
Sandrock Rd. SE13 CE45 67
Sandrock Rd. Dor. BF72 119
Sandsend La. SW6 BS44 66
Sandstone Rd. SE12 CH48 78
Sandtoft Rd. SE7 CH43 68
Sandwell Cres. NW6 BS35 47
Sumatra Rd.
Sandwich St. WC1 BX38 56
Sandy Bank Rd. Grav. DG47 81
Sandy Bury Orp. CM55 88
Sandy Clo. Twick. BJ47 74
Sandy Clo. Wok. AU62 100
Sandycombe Rd. Felt. BC47 73
Sandycombe Rd. Rich. BL45 65
Sandycombe Rd. Twick. BK46 74
Sandycroft, SE2 CO43 69
Sandycroft Rd. Amer. AR22 25
Sandy Dr. Cob. BF59 93
Sandy Hill Av. SE18 CL42 68
Sandyhill Rd. Ilf. CL35 49
Sandy Hill Rd. Wall. BW58 95
Sandy La. Bet. BO71 120
Sandy La. Bush. BG24 27
Sandy La. Cob. BE59 93
Sandy La. Cob. BE60 93
Sandy La. Dart. DB48 80
Sandy La. Grays DA42 70
Sandy La. Grays. DG43 71
Sandy La. Guil. AO73 118
Sandy La. Mitch. BV51 86
Sandy La. Nthwd. BB27 35
Sandy La. Nthwd. BC27 35
Sandy La. Orp. CO54 89
Sandy La. Orp. CP51 89
Sandy La. Oxt. CF68 114
Sandy La. Oxt. CH67 115
Sandy La. Rain. CW40 60
Sandy La. Red. BW71 121
Sandy La. Red. BY69 121
Sandy La. Reig. BP71 120
Sandy La. Rich. BK48 74
Sandy La. Sev. CV65 108
Sandy La. Sev. DA66 117
Sandy La. Sutt. BR58 94
Sandy La. Tad. BR65 103
Sandy La. Tedd. BJ50 74
Sandy La. Vir. W. AS52 82
Sandy La. Walt. BC53 83
Sandy La. Wok. AU61 100
Sandy La. Wok. AU65 100
Sandy La. Est. Rich. BK48 74
Sandy La. N. Wall. BW56 95
Sandy La. S. Wall. BW58 95
Sandy Lodge La. Nthwd. BB27 35
Sandy Lodge Rd. Rick. AZ27 35
Sandy Lodge Way. Nthwd. BB29 35
Sandymount Av. Stan. BK28 36
Sandy Ri. Ger. Cr. AS30 34
Sandy Ridge Chis. CK50 78
Sandy Rd. NW3 BS34 47
Sandy Rd. Wey. AW57 92
Sandy's Row E1 CA39 57
Sandy Way. Cob. BF59 93
Sandy Way Croy. CD55 87
Sandy Way, Walt. BB54 83
Sandy Way, Wok. AU62 100
Sanfoin End, Hem. H. AZ12 8
Sanford St. SE14 CD43 67
Sanford Ter. N16 CA34 48
Sanford Wk. N16 CA34 48
Smalley Rd.
Sanford Wk. SE14 CD43 67
Sanger Av. Chess. BL56 94
Sangley Rd. SE6 CE47 77
Sangley Rd. SE25 CA52 87
Sangora Rd. SW11 BT45 66
Strathblaine Rd.
Sansom Rd. E11 CG34 49
Sansom St. SE5 BZ43 67
Sans Wk. EC1 BY38 56
Woodbridge St.
Santers La. Pot. B. BR20 19
Santley St. SW4 BX45 66
Santos Rd. SW18 BS46 76
Sanway Clo. Wey. AY60 92
Sanway Rd. Cob. AY61 101
Sanway Rd. Wey. AY60 92
Sanwood, Guil. AQ71 118
Sapho Pk. Grav. DJ49 81
Sappers Clo. Saw. CQ6 6
Sapphire Rd. SE14 CD42 67
Saracens Rd. Hem. H. AZ13 8
Saracen St. E14 CE39 57
Sarah St. N1 CA38 57
Sara Pk. Grav. DJ49 81
Saratoga Rd. E5 CC35 48
Sardinia St. WC2 BX39 56
Kingsway
Sarjant Path SW19 BR48 75
Queensmere Rd.
Sark Clo. Houns. BF43 64
Sark Clo. Houns. BF44 64
Sutton Rd.
Sark Wk. E16 CH39 58
Sarnesfield Rd. Enf. BZ24 30
Sarratt La. Rick. AW23 26
Sarratt Rd. Rick. AW22 26
Sarre Rd. NW2 BR35 46
Sarre Rd. Orp. CP53 89
Sarsen Av. Houns. BE44 64
Sarsfield Rd. SW12 BU47 76
Sarsfield Rd. Grnf. BJ37 54
Sartor Rd. SE15 CC45 67
Sarum Dr. Wey. BB55 83
Sarum Grn. Wey. BB56 92
Sarum Pl. Hem. H. AY11 8
Satchwell Rd. E2 CA38 57
Bethnal Green Rd.
Saturn Way, Hem. H. AY12 8
Saunders Copse, Wok. AQ64 100
Saunders La. Wok. AP64 100
Saunders Ness Rd. E14 CF42 67
Saunders Rd. SE18 CN42 68
Saunders Rd. Uxb. AY36 53
Saunders St. SE11 BY42 66
Saunderton Rd. Wem. BJ35 45
Saunton Ave. Hayes. BB43 63
Saunton Rd. Horn. CU34 50
Savage Gdns. E6 CK39 58
Savage Gdns. EC3 CA40 57
Savernake Rd. N9 CB25 30
Savernake Rd. NW3 BU35 47
Savile Gdns. Croy. CA55 87
Savile Row W1 BW40 56
Saville Clo. N. Mal. BO53 85
Saville Cres. Ashf. BA50 73
Saville Gdns. Croy. CA55 87
Saville Rd. E16 CK40 58
Saville Rd. W4 BN41 65
Saville Rd. Rom. CQ32 50
Saville Rd. Twick. BH47 74
Saville Row Wdf. Grn. CH29 40
Savill Gdns. SW20 BP52 85
Savona Clo. SW19 BQ50 75
Savona Est. SW8 BW43 66
Savona St. SW8 BW43 66
Savoy Ave. Hayes. BB42 63
Savoy Clo. Edg. BM28 37
Savoy Clo. Uxb. AW33 44
Savoy Clo. Uxb. AX30 35
Savoy Ct. WC2 BX40 56
Strand
Savoy Hill WC2 BX40 56
Savoy La. Uxb. AW32 44
Savoy Pl. WC2 BX40 56
Savoy Rd. Dart. CV46 80
Savoy St. WC2 BX40 56
Savoy Way WC2 BX40 56
Carting La.
Sawells, Brox. CD14 12
Sawkins Cl. SW19 BR48 75
Queensmere Rd.
Sawley Rd. W12 BP40 55
Sawpit Lane. Guil. AY69 110
Sawtry Clo. Cars. BT54 86
Sawyers Clo. Dag. CS36 59
Sawyers Clo. Wind. AM43 61
Sawyers La. Borwd. BJ23 27
Sawyers La. Pot. B. BQ20 19
Sawyer, S Hall La. Brwd. DB26 42
Sawyer St. SE1 BZ41 67
Sawyers Way, Hem. H. AY13 8
Saxby St. SW2 BX47 76
Saxham Rd. Bark. CN37 58
Saxlingham Rd. E4 CF27 39
Saxon Av. Felt. BE48 74
Saxonbury Av. Sun. BC51 83
Saxonbury Gdns. Surb. BK54 84
Saxon Clo. Brwd. DD27 122
Saxon Clo. Grav. DE48 81
Saxon Clo. Rom. CW30 42
Saxon Clo. Slou. AS41 62
Saxon Clo. Uxb. AY39 53
Saxon Dr. W3 BM39 55
Saxon Gdns. Sthl. BE40 54
Saxon Ho. Felt. BE48 74
Saxon Pl. Hort. K. CY53 90
Saxon Rd. E6 CK38 58
Saxon Rd. N22 BY30 38
Saxon Rd. SE25 BZ53 87
Saxon Rd. Ashf. BA50 73
Saxon Rd. Brom. CG50 78
Saxon Rd. Dart. CW49 80
Saxon Rd. Ilf. CL36 58
Saxon Rd. Sthl. BE40 54
Saxon Rd. Walt. BD55 84
Saxon Rd. Welw. BP5 5
Saxon Rd. Wem. BM34 46
Saxon Wk. Sid. CP50 79
Cray Rd.
Saxon Way N14 BW25 29
Saxon Way, Reig. BR70 120
Saxon Way, Wal. Abb. CF20 21
Saxony Par. Hayes BA39 53
Saxton Clo. SE13 CF45 67
Saxville Rd. Orp. CO52 89
Sayesbury Av. Saw. CP5 6
Sayesbury Rd. Saw. CQ6 6
Sayes Ct. Est. SE8 CD42 67
Sayes Ct. Gdns. SE8 CD42 67
Sayes Ct. Rd. Orp. CO52 89
Sayes Ct. St. SE8 CD43 67
Sayward Clo. Chesh. AO18 16
Scabharbour Rd. Sev. CV70 117
Scad's Hill Clo. Orp. CN53 88
Scales Rd. N17 CA31 48
Scampston Ms. W10 BQ39 55
Scampton Rd. Houns. AY46 73
Southampton Rd.
Scandrett St. E1 CB40 57
Wapping High St.
Scarba Wk. N1 BZ36 57
Marquess Est.
Scarborough Clo. Sutt. BR59 94
Scarborough Clo. West. CJ62 106
Scarborough Rd. E11 CF33 48
Scarborough Rd. N4 BY33 47
Scarborough Rd. N9 CC26 39
Scarbrook Rd. Croy. BZ55 87
Scarle Rd. Wem. BK36 54
Scarlet Rd. SE6 CG48 78
Scarsbrook Rd. SE3 CJ45 68
Scarsdale Gro. SE5 CA43 67
Neate St.
Scarsdale Rd. SE5 CA43 67
Scarsdale Rd. Har. BG34 45
Scarsdale Vill. W8 BS41 66
Scarth Rd. SW13 BO45 65
Scatterdells La. Kings L. AV18 16
Scatterdells La. Kings L. AW18 17
Scawen Rd. SE8 CD42 67
Scawfell St. E2 CA37 57
Scaynes Link N12 BS28 38
Sceaux Est. SE5 CA44 67
Sceptre Rd. E2 CC38 57
Sceyness Link N12 BS28 38
Chanctonbury Way
Schofield Rd. SE3 CH43 68
Scholars Rd. E4 CF26 39
Scholars Rd. SW12 BW47 76
Scholars Wk. Hat. BP14 10
Scholefield Rd. N19 BW33 47
School Alley Twick. BJ47 74
Schoo La. Welw. BU6 5
School Clo. Guil. AR69 118
Schoolfield Rd. Grays DA43 70
School Gdns. Berk. AT12 7
School Green La. Epp. CS16 23
School Hill. Red. BW67 113
Schoolhouse La. E1 CC40 57
School Ho. La. Tedd. BJ50 74
School La. Beac. AO29 34
School La. Brwd. DE29 122
School La. Bush. BF26 36
School La. Ch. St. G. AQ27 34
School La. Dor. BG72 119
School La. Egh. AT49 72
School La. Ger. Cr. AR30 34
School Lane. Guil. AY69 110
School La. Harl. CN10 6
School La. Hat. BQ12 10
School La. Hat. BU12 11
School La. Hort. K. CY52 90
School La. Kings. On T. BK51 84
Park Rd.
School Lane. Leath. AZ68 110
School La. Lthd. BF66 111
School La. Lthd. BG65 102
School La. Ong. CS12 14
School Lane. Ong. CZ10 15
School Lane. Ong. DA11 15
School La. Pnr. BE31 45
School La. Sev. CW64 108
School La. Sev. CZ59 99
School La. Sev. & Ton. DC67 117
School La. Shep. AZ53 83
School La. Slou. AQ36 52
School La. Surb. BM54 85
School La. Swan. CU51 89
School La. Tad. BP66 112
School La. Well. CO45 69
School La. Welw. BO5 5
School La, Wey. AW56 92
School La. Wok. AZ64 101
School Mead, Wat. BA19 17
School Pass. Kings. On T. BL51 85
School Pass. Sthl. BE40 54
School Pl. E1 CB38 57
Buckhurst St.
School Rd. E12 CK35 49
School Rd. NW10 BN38 55
School Rd. W4 BN42 65
Belmont Rd.
School Rd. Ashf. AZ49 73
School Rd. Brwd. CZ22 33
School Rd. Chis. CM51 88
School Rd. Dag. CR37 59
School Rd. E. Mol. BG52 84
School Rd. Grav. DH48 81
School Rd. Hmptn. BG50 74
School Rd. Houns. BG45 64
School Rd. Kings. On T. BK51 84
Park Rd.
School Rd. Ong. CT18 23
School Rd. Pot. B. BT18 20
School Rd. Sev. DA64 108
School Rd. West Dr. AX43 63
School Rd. Av. Hamptn. BG50 74
School Row. Hem. H. AV14 7
School Wk. Slou. AQ40 52
School Wk. Sun. BC52 83
School Way N12 BT28 38
School Way N12 BT29 38
School Way Dag. CP34 50
Schubert Clo. Borwd. BK25 27
Schubert Rd. SW15 BR46 75
Scillonian Rd. Guil. AQ71 118
Sclater St. E1 CA38 57
Scobie Pl. N16 CA35 48
Amhurst Rd.
Scoresby St. SE1 BY40 56

Scorton Av. Grnf. BJ37 54
Scotch Common W13 BJ39 54
Scot Gro. Pnr. BE29 36
Scotland Bridge Rd. Wey. AW59 92
Scotland Gn. N17 CA30 39
Scotland Grn. Rd. Enf. CC25 30
Scotland Grn. Rd. N. Enf. CC24 30
Scotland Rd. Buck. H. CJ26 40
Scots Clo. Stai. AX47
Scotsdale Clo. Orp. CN52 88
Scotsdale Clo. Sutt. BR57 94
Scotsdale Rd. SE12 CH46 78
Scotshall La. Warl. CF61 105
Scots Hill, Rick. AY25 26
Scots Hill Clo. Rick. AY25 26
Scotswold Wk. N17 CB29 39
Waverley Rd.
Scotswood Wk. N17 CB29 39
Northumberland Pk.
Scott Clo. Epsom. BN56 94
Scott Clo. West Dr. AY42 63
Scott Cres. Erith CT44 69
Scott Cres. Har. BF33 45
Scott Ellis Gdns. NW8 BT38 56
Scottes La. Dag. CP33 50
Valence Av.
Scott Lidgett Cres. SE16 CB41 67
Scott Rd. Grav. DH49 81
Scott Rd. Grays. DQ42 71
Scotts Av. Brom. CF51 87
Scotts Av. Sun. BB50 73
Scotts Dr. Hamptn. BF50 74
Scotts Fm. Rd. Epsom BN57 94
Scotts Grove Clo. Wok. AO60 91
Scotts Grove Rd. Wok. AO60 91
Scott's La. Brom. CF52 87
Scotts La. Walt. BD56 93
Scotts Mill Rd. Rick. AY25 26
Scott's Rd. E10 CF33 48
Scotts Rd. W12 BP41 65
Scott's Rd. Brom. CH50 78
Scott's Rd. Sthl. BD41 64
Scott St. E1 CB38 57
Scotts Way. Sev. CT64 107
Scotts Way. Sun. BB50 73
Scotts Wol. Clo. Bush. BE23 27
Scotts Wol. Rd. Bush. BE23 27
Scoulding Rd. E16 CG39 58
Roger's Rd.
Scouler St. E14 CF40 57
Harrap St.
Scout App. NW10 BN35 46
Scout La. SW4 BW45 66
Scout Way NW7 BN28 37
Scovell Rd. SE1 BZ41 67
Scrafton Rd. Ilf. CL34 49
Scrattons Ter. Bark. CP37 59
Scriven St. E8 CA37 57
Scrooby St. SE6 CE46 77
Scrubbits Rd. Rad. BJ21 27
Scrubs La. NW10 BP38 55
Scrubs La. W10 BP38 55
Scrutton Clo. SW12 BW47 76
Scrutton St. EC2 CA38 57
Scudamore La. NW9 BN31 46
Scudders Hill Fawk. DA53 90
Scutari Rd. SE22 CB46 77
Scylla Rd. SE15 CB45 67
Seaborough Rd. Grays. DH41 71
Seabrook Dr. W. Wick. CF55 87
Seabrooke Ri. Grays. DD43 71
Seabrook Gdns. Rom. CR33 50
Seabrook Rd. Dag. CP34 50
Seabrook Rd. Kings L. BA17 17
Seaburn Clo. Rain. CT38 59
Seacoal La. EC4 BY39 56
Seacourt Rd. SE2 CP41 69
Seacourt Rd. Slou. AT42 62
Seacroft Gdns. Wat. BD27 36
Seafield Rd. N11 BW28 38
Seaford Rd. E17 CE31 48
Seaford Rd. N15 BZ31 48
Seaford Rd. W13 BJ40 54
Seaford Rd. Enf. CA24 30
Seaford Rd. Houns. AX46 73
Sandringham Rd.
Seaford St. WC1 BX38 56
Seaforth Av. N. Mal. BP53 85
Seaforth Clo. Rom. CT29 41
Seaforth Dr. Wal. Cr. CC20 21
Seaforth Gdns. N21 BX26 38
Seaforth Gdns. Epsom BO56 94
Seaforth Gdns. Wdf. Grn. CJ28 40
Seaforth Pl. SW1 BW41 66
Buckingham Gate
Seager Pl. E3 CD39 57
Burdett Rd.
Seagrave Clo. E1 CC39 57
Seagrave Clo. Wey. AZ57 92
Seagrave Rd. SW6 BS43 66
Seagry Rd. E11 CH32 49
Sealand Rd. Houns. AZ46 73
Sealand Wk. Nthlt. BD38 54
Wayfarer Rd.
Seal Chart. Sev. CY64 108
Seal Dr. Sev. CW64 108
Seale Hill, Reig. BS71 121
Seal Hill. Sev. CX64 108
Seal Hollow Rd. Sev. CV65 108
Sealord Clo. Ruis. BA34 44
Seal Rd. Sev. CV64 108
Seal St. E8 CA35 48
Seamans Clo. St. Alb. BG16 18
Searches La. Wat. BC17 17
Searches La. Wat. BD17 18
Searchwood Rd. Warl. CB62 105
Searle Clo. SW11 BU43 66
Searles Rd. SE1 BZ42 67
Sears St. SE5 BZ43 67
Seasprite Clo. Nthlt. BD38 54
Seaton Av. Ilf. CN35 49
Seaton Clo. E13 CH38 58
New Barn St.
Seaton Clo. Twick. BG46 74
Seaton Dr. Ashf. AY48 73
Seaton Gdns. Ruis. BC34 44
Seaton Pl. NW1 BW38 56
Seaton Rd. Dart. CU47 79
Seaton Rd. Hayes. BA42 63
Seaton Rd. Hem. H. AX15 8
Seaton Rd. Mitch. BU51 86
Seaton Rd. St. Alb. BK17 18
Seaton Rd. Twick. BG46 74
Seaton Rd. Well. CP43 69
Seaton Rd. Wem. BL37 55
Seaton St. N18 CB28 39
Sebastian Av. Brwd. DD25 122
Sebastian St. EC1 BY38 56
Sebastopol Rd. N9 CB28 39
Sebbon St. N1 BY36 56
Sebert Rd. E7 CH35 49
Sebright Pass. E2 CB37 57
Sebright Rd. Barn. BQ23 28
Sebright Rd. Hem. H. AW14 8
Secker Cres. Har. BG30 36
Secker St. SE1 BY40 56
Second Ave. Harl. CN11 13
Second Av. E12 CK35 49
Second Av. E13 CH38 58
Second Av. E17 CE32 48
Second Av. N18 CC28 39
Second Av. NW4 BQ31 46
Second Av. SW14 BO45 65
Second Av. W3 BO40 55
Second Av. W10 BR38 55
Second Av. Brwd. DB20 24
Second Av. Dag. CR37 59
Second Av. Enf. CA25 30
Second Av. Grays DA43 70
Second Av. Hayes BB40 53
Second Av. Hayes BC40 53
Glebe Rd.
Second Av. Rom. CP32 50
Second Av. Walt. BC53 83
Second Av. Wat. BD21 27
Second Av. Wem. BK34 45
Second Clo. E. Mol. BG52 84
Second Cross Rd. Twick. BG48 74
Second Way Wem. BM35 46
Secretan Rd. SE5 CA42 67
Sedcote Rd. Enf. CC25 30
Sedding St. SW1 BV42 66
Sloane Sq.
Seddon Rd. Mord. BT53 86
Sedgebrook Rd. SE3 CJ44 68
Sedgecombe Av. Har. BK32 45
Sedgefield Clo. Rom. CV28 42
Sedgefield Cres. Rom. CW28 42
Sedgeford Rd. W12 BP40 55
Sedgehill Rd. SE6 CE49 77
Sedgemere Av. N2 BT31 47
Sedgemere Rd. SE2 CP41 69
Sedgemoor Dr. Dag. CR35 50
Sedge Way SE6 CG47 78
Sedgewick Av. Uxb. AZ36 53
Sedgmoor Pl. SE5 CA43 67
Sedgwick Rd. E10 CF34 48
Sedgwick St. E9 CC35 48
Sedleigh Rd. SW18 BR46 75
Sedlescombe Rd. SW6 BS43 66
Sedley Pl. W1 BV39 56
Oxford St.
Sedley Rise Loug. CK23 31
Seeley Dr. SE21 CA49 77
Seelig Av. NW9 BP33 46
Seely Rd. SW17 BV50 76
Seer Green La. Beac. AP29 34
Seer Mead. Beac. AO29 34
Seething La. EC3 CA40 57
Seething Wells La. Surb. BK53 84
Sefton Av. NW7 BN28 37
Sefton Av. Har. BG30 36
Sefton Clo. Orp. CN52 88
Sefton Clo. Slou. AP37 52
Sefton Pad. Slou. AQ36 52
Sefton Rd. Croy. CB54 87
Sefton Rd. Epsom BN58 94
Sefton Rd. Orp. CN52 88
Sefton St. SW15 BQ45 65
Sefton Way, Uxb. AX39 53
Sekforde St. EC1 BY38 56
Selan Gdns. Hayes BC39 53
Selbie Av. NW10 BO35 46
Selborne Av. E12 CL35 49
Selborne Av. Bex. CQ47 79
Selborne Gdns. NW4 BP31 46
Selborne Gdns. Grnf. BJ37 54
Selborne Rd. E17 CD32 48
Selborne Rd. N14 BX27 38
Selborne Rd. N22 BX30 38
Selborne Rd. SE5 BZ44 67
Selborne Rd. Croy. CA55 87
Selborne Rd. Ilf. CL34 49
Selborne Rd. N. Mal. BO51 85
Selborne Rd. Sid. CO49 79
Selbourne Av. Surb. BL55 85
Selbourne Av. Wey. AW58 92
Selbourne Clo. Wey. AW58 92
Selbourne Rd. E17 CD32 48
Selbourne Sq. Gdse. CC68 114
Selby Av. St. Alb. BG13 9
Selby Chase Ruis. BC34 44
Selby Clo. Chess. BL57 94
Selby Gdns. Sthl. BF38 54
Selby Grn. Cars. BU54 86
Selby Rd. E11 CG34 49
Selby Rd. E13 CH39 58
Selby Rd. N17 CA29 39
Selby Rd. SE20 CB51 87
Selby Rd. W5 BJ38 54
Selby Rd. Ashf. BA50 73
Selby Rd. Cars. BU54 86
Selby St. E1 CB38 57
Selcroft Rd. SE10 CG42 68
Selcroft Rd. Pur. BY59 95
Selden Rd. SE15 CC44 67
Selden Wk. N7 BX34 47
Andover Est.
Seldon Hill, Hem. H. AX14 8
Selhurst New Rd. SE25 CA53 87
Selhurst Pl. SE25 CA53 87
Selhurst Rd. N9 BZ27 39
Selhurst Rd. SE25 CA53 87
Selinas La. Dag. CQ33 50
Selkirk Rd. SW17 BU49 76
Selkirk Rd. Twick. BG48 74
Sellers Hall Clo. N3 BS29 38
Sellincourt Rd. SW17 BU49 76
Sellindge Clo. Beck. CD50 77
Sellon Ms. SE11 BX42 66
Sellons Av. NW10 BO37 55
Selma Ho. W12 BP39 55
Du Cane Rd.
Selous St. NW1 BW37 56
Selsdon Av. Sth. Croy. BZ57 96
Selsdon Clo. Rom. CS30 41
Selsdon Clo. Surb. BL53 85
Selsdon Cres. Sth. Croy. CC58 96
Selsdon Pk. Rd. Sth. Croy. CC58 96
Selsdon Rd. E11 CH33 49
Selsdon Rd. E13 CJ37 58
Selsdon Rd. NW2 BO34 46
Selsdon Rd. SE27 BY48 76
Selsdon Rd. Sth. Croy. BZ56 96
Selsdon Rd. Wey. AW59 92
Selsey Cres. Well. CP44 69
Selsey Pl. N6 CA35 48
Crossway
Selsey St. E14 CE39 57
Selvage La. NW7 BN28 37
Selway Clo. Pnr. BC31 44
Selwins Clo. Horn. CV32 51
Selwood Clo. Stai. AX46 73
Selwood Gdns. Stai. AX46 73
Selwood Pl. SW7 BT42 66
Selwood Rd. Brwd. CZ27 42
Selwood Rd. Chess. BK56 93
Selwood Rd. Croy. CB55 87
Selwood Rd. Sutt. BR54 85
Selwood Rd. Wok. AT63 100
Selwood Ter. SW7 BT42 66
Selworthy Clo. E11 CH32 49
New Wanstead
Selworthy Rd. SE6 CD48 77
Selwyn Av. E4 CF29 39
Selwyn Av. NW10 BN36 55
Selwyn Av. Hat. BN13 10
Selwyn Av. Ilf. CN32 49
Selwyn Av. Rich. BL45 65
Selwyn Ct. SE3 CG45 68
Selwyn Ct. Edg. BM29 37
Selwyn Cres. Hat. BO12 10
Selwyn Cres. Walt. BD54 84
Selwyn Cres. Well. CO45 69
Selwyn Dr. Hat. BN13 10
Selwyn Grn. Walt. BD54 84
Selwyn Rd. E3 CD37 57
Selwyn Rd. E13 CH37 58
Selwyn Rd. N17 CA31 48
Selwyn Rd. N17 CB31 48
High Cross Rd.
Selwyn Rd. N. Mal. BN53 85
Selwyn Rd. Orp. CO52 89
Selwyn Rd. Til. DF44 71
Selwyn Rd. Walt. BC55 83
Semaphore Rd. Guil. AS71 118
Semley Pl. SW1 BV42 66
Semley Rd. SW16 BX51 86
Semper Clo. Wok. AP62 100
Semper Rd. Grays. DH41 71
Semphill Rd. Hem. H. AY15 8
Send Hill Rd. Wok. AU65 100
Send Hill Rd. Wok. AU66 109
Sendmarsh Rd. Wok. AU65 100
Send Rd. Wok. AT65 100
Seneca Rd. SW4 BX45 66
Seneca Rd. Th. Hth. BZ52 87
Senga Rd. Wall. BV54 86
Senhouse Rd. Sutt. BQ55 85
Senior St. W2 BS39 56
Senlac Rd. SE12 CH47 78
Sennon Rd. Enf. CA26 39
Senrab St. E1 CC39 57
Sentinal Sq. NW4 BQ31 46
September Way, Stan. BJ29 36
Septimus Pl. Enf. CB25 30
Ermine Side.
Sequoia Clo. Bush. BG26 36
Sequoia Gdns. Orp. CN54 88
Sequoia Pk. Pnr. BF29 36
Serbin Clo. E10 CG33 49
Sergeants Green La. Wal. Abb. CJ20 22
Sergehill La. Wat. BC16 17
Serle St. WC2 BX39 56
Sermon Dr. Swan. CS52 89
Sermon La. EC4 BZ39 57
Carter La.
Serpentine Grn. Red. BW68 113
Serpentine Rd. W2 BU40 56
Serpentine Rd. Sev. CV65 108
Service La. Ing. DB19 24
Service Rd. SE13 CF45 67
Service Rd. Wind. AL44 61
Setchell Rd. SE1 CA42 67
Seton Gdns. Dag. CP36 59
Settle Rd. E13 CH37 58
Settle Rd. Rom. CX28 42
Settles St. E1 CB39 57
Settrington Rd. SW6 BS44 66
Seven Arches Rd. Brwd. DB27 42
Seven Arches Rd. Brwd. DC27 122
Seven Hills Rd. Cob. BB60 92
Seven Hills Rd. Iver. AT35 43
Sevenhills Rd. Iver AU36 52
Seven Hills Rd. Watt. BB57 92
Seven Kings Rd. Ilf. CN33 49
Sevenoaks By-pass, Sev. & Ton. CV69 117
Sevenoaks Clo. Bexh. CR45 69
Martens Av.
Sevenoaks Clo. Rom. CV28 42
Sevenoaks Rd. SE4 CD46 77
Sevenoaks Rd. Orp. CN56 97
Sevenoaks Rd. Orp. CN57 97
Sevenoaks Rd. Sev. CU62 107
Sevenoaks Rd. Sev. DA65 108
Sevenoaks Way Sid. CO50 79
Seven Sisters Rd. N4 BX34 47
Seven Sisters Rd. N7 BX34 47
Seven Sisters Rd. N15 BX34 47
Seventh Av. E12 CK35 49
Seventh Av. Enf. CB25 30
Severalls Ave. Chesh. AO18 16
Severn Av. Rom. CU31 50
Severn Dr. Enf. CB22 30
Severn Dr. Esher BJ55 84
Severn Dr. Upmin. CY32 51
Severn Dr. Upmin. CZ32 51
Severn Mead, Hem. H. AY12 8
Severn Rd. S. Ock. CW39 60
Severns Field Epp. CO18 23
Severn Way NW10 BO35 46
Severn Way, Wat. BD20 18
Severn Way Wat. BD21 27
Severus Rd. SW11 BU45 66
Seville St. SW1 BU41 66
Sevington Rd. NW4 BP32 46
Sevington St. W9 BS38 56
Seward Rd. W7 BJ41 64
Seward Rd. Beck. CC51 87
Sewardstone Gdns. E4 CE25 30
Sewardstone Rd. E2 CC37 57
Sewardstone Rd. E4 CE26 39
Sewardstone St. Wal. Abb. CF20 21
Sewardstone Way, Wal. Abb. CF21 30
Seward St. EC1 BY38 56
Sewdley St. E5 CC34 48
Sewell Clo. St. Alb. BL13 10
Sewell Rd. SE2 CO41 69
Sewell St. E13 CH38 58
Sexton Clo. Rain. CT37 59
Seyhours Harl. CK12 13
Seymer Rd. Rom. CS31 50
Seymour Av. N17 CB30 39
Seymour Av. Epsom BP58 94
Seymour Av. Mord. BQ53 85
Seymour Clo. E. Mol. BG53 84
Seymour Clo. Pnr. BE30 36
Seymour Ct. E4 CG27 40
Seymour Ct. N10 BV30 38
Seymour Ct. NW2 BP34 46
Seymour Cres. Hem. H. AY13 8
Seymour Gdns. Felt. BD49 74
Seymour Gdns. Ilf. CK33 49
Seymour Gdns. Ruis. BD33 45
Seymour Gdns. Surb. BL53 85
Seymour Gdns. Twick. BJ47 74
Seymour Ms. W1 BV39 56
Seymour Pl. SE25 CB52 87
Seymour Pl. W1 BU39 56
Seymour Rd. E4 CE26 39
Seymour Rd. E6 CJ37 58
Seymour Rd. E10 CD33 48
Seymour Rd. N3 BS29 38
Seymour Rd. N8 BY32 47
Seymour Rd. N9 CB27 39
Seymour Rd. SW18 BR46 75
Seymour Rd. SW19 BQ48 75
Seymour Rd. W4 BN42 65
Seymour Rd. Berk. AP12 7
Seymour Rd. Cars. BV56 95
Seymour Rd. Ch. St. G. AR28 34
Seymour Rd. E. Mol. BG53 84
Seymour Rd. Grav. DF48 81
Seymour Rd. Hmptn. BG49 74
Seymour Rd. Kings. On T. BK51 84
Seymour Rd. Mitch. BV54 86
Seymour Rd. St. Alb. BH12 9
Seymour Rd. Slou. AO41 61
Seymour Rd. Til. DF44 71
Seymours Loug. CL23 31
Seymour St. W1 BU39 56
Seymour St. W2 BU39 56
Seymour Ter. SE20 CB51 87
Selby Rd.
Seymour Vill. SE20 CB51 87
Seymour Wk. SW10 BT42 66
Seymour Way, Sun. BB50 73
Seyssel St. E14 CF42 67
Shaa Rd. W3 BN40 55
Shackelton Av. Sthl. BE40 54
Shacklands Rd. Sev. CR59 98
Shackleford Rd. Wok. AT64 100
Shacklegate La. Tedd. BH49 74
Shackleton Rd. Slou. AP40 52
Shacklewell Grn. E8 CA35 48
Shacklewell La.
Shacklewell La. E8 CA35 48
Shacklewell Rd. N16 CA35 48
Shacklewell St. E2 CA38 57
Shadbolt Clo. Wor. Pk. BO55 85
Shad Thames SE1 CA40 57
Shadwell Dr. Nthlt. BE38 54
Shadwell Pl. E1 CC40 57
Shadybush Clo. Bush. BG26 36
Shady La. Wat. BC23 26
Shaef Way. Tedd. BJ50 74
Shafter Rd. Dag. CS36 59
Shaftesbury Loug. CJ24 31
Shaftesbury Av. W1 BW40 56
Shaftesbury Av. WC2 BW40 56
Shaftesbury Av. Barn. BT24 29
Shaftesbury Av. Enf. CC23 30
Shaftesbury Av. Felt. BC46 73
Shaftesbury Av. Har. BF33 45
Shaftesbury Av. Har. BK32 45
Shaftesbury Av. Sthl. BF42 64
Shaftesbury Ct. N1 BZ37 57
Shaftesbury Cres. Stai. AX50 73
Shaftesbury La. Dart. CX45 70
Shaftesbury Rd. E4 CF26 39
Shaftesbury Rd. E7 CJ36 58
Shaftesbury Rd. E10 CE33 48
Shaftesbury Rd. E17 CE32 48
Shaftesbury Rd. N18 CA29 39
Shaftesbury Rd. N19 BX33 47
Shaftesbury Rd. Beck. CD51 87
Shaftesbury Rd. Epp. CN18 22
Shaftesbury Rd. Rich. BL45 65
Shaftesbury Rd. Rom. CT32 50
Shaftesbury Rd. Wat. BD24 27
Shaftesbury Rd. Wok. AT62 100
Shaftesburys, The, Bark. CM37 58
Shaftesbury St. N1 BZ37 57
Shaftesbury Way Twick. BH48 74
Wellesley Rd.
Shaftesbury Way, Twick. BJ48 74
Shaftesbury Waye Hayes BC39 53
Shafto Ms. SW1 BU41 66
Cadogan Sq.
Shafton Rd. E9 CC37 57
Shaftsbury Rd. Beck. CD51 87
Croydon Rd.
Shaftsbury Way, Kings L. BA17 17
Shafts Ct. EC3 CA39 57
Shaggy Calf La. Slou. AQ40 52
Shakespeare Av. N11 BW28 38
Shakespeare Av. NW10 BO37 55
Shakespeare Av. Felt. BC46 73
Shakespeare Av. Hayes BC39 53
Shakespeare Cres. E12 CK36 58
Shakespeare Cres. NW10 BN37 55
Shakespeare Dr. Har. BL32 46
Shakespeare Gdns. N2 BU31 47
Shakespeare Ho. N14 BW27 38
Shakespeare Rd. E17 CC30 39
Shakespeare Rd. N3 BS30 38
Shakespeare Rd. NW7 BO28 37
Shakespeare Rd. SE24 BY46 76
Shakespeare Rd. W3 BN40 55
Shakespeare Rd. W7 BH40 54
Shakespeare Rd. Bexh. CQ44 69
Shakespeare Rd. Dart. CX45 70
Shakespeare Rd. Rom. CT32 50
Shakespeare Rd. Til. DG44 71
Shakespeare Rd. Wey. AX56 92
Shakespeare Sq. Ilf. CM29 40
Shakespeare St. Wat. BC22 26
Shakespeare Wk. N16 CA35 48
Shakespeare Way Felt. BD49 74
Shakespear St. Wat. BC23 26
Shakletons Ong. CX17 24
Shalcomb St. SW10 BT43 66
Shal Cross Dr. Wal. Cr. CD18 21
Shaldon Dr. Mord. BR53 85
Shaldon Dr. Ruis. BD34 45
Shaldon Rd. Edg. BL30 37
Shaldon Way Walt. BD55 84
Shale Grn. Red. BW68 113
Shalfleet Dr. W10 BQ40 55
Shalford Rd. Guil. AR72 118
Shalimar Gdns. W3 BN40 55
Shalimar Rd. W3 BM40 55
Hereford Rd.
Shallcross Cr. Hat. BO14 10
Shallons Rd. SE9 CL49 78
Shalston Rd. SW14 BM45 65
Shalston Vill. Surb. BL53 85
Sham Rd. SW16 BX51 86
Shamrock Clo. Lthd. BG64 102
Shamrock Rd. Croy. BX53 86
Shamrock Rd. Grav. DJ47 81
Shamrock St. SW4 BW45 66
Clapham Manor St.
Shamrock Way N14 BV26 38
Shandon Rd. SW4 BW46 76
Shand St. SE1 CA41 67
Shandy St. E1 CC39 57
Shanklin Gdns. Wat. BD28 36
Shanklin Rd. N8 BW32 47
Shanklin Rd. W15 CB31 48
Shanklin Rd. Sutt. BS58 95
Shanklin Way SE15 CA43 67
Hordle Prom. S.
Shannon Clo. Sthl. BE42 64
Ringway
Shannon Gro. SW9 BX45 66
Shannon Way. S. Ock. CW40 60
Shantock Hall La. Hem. H. AS18 16
Shantock La. Hem. H. AS18 16
Shap Cres. Cars. BU54 86
Shap St. E2 CA37 57
Shardcroft Av. SE24 BY46 76
Shardeloes Rd. SE14 CD45 67
Shards Sq. SE15 CB43 67
Sharland Rd. Grav. DH48 81
Sharman Ct. Sid. CO49 79
Carlton Rd.
Sharman St. E14 CE39 57
Broomfield St.
Sharnbrooke Clo. Well. CP45 69
Sharney Ave. Slou. AT42 62
Sharon Clo. Epsom BN60 94
Sharon Clo. Surb. BK54 84
Sharon Gdns. E9 CC37 57
Sharon Rd. W4 BN42 65
Sharon Rd. Enf. CD23 30
Sharpe Croft. Harl. CM11 13
Sharpes Lane, Berk. AT14 7
Sharples Hall St. NW1 BU36 56
Regents Pk. Rd.
Sharps La. Ruis. BA33 44
Sharp Way. Dart. CW45 70
Sharratt St. SE15 CC43 67
Sharsted St. SE17 BY42 66
Sharvel La. Nthlt. BC37 53
Shaw Av. Bark. CQ37 59

Shawbridge Harl. CM12 13
Shawbrooke Rd. SE9 CJ46 78
Shawbury Rd. SE22 CA46 77
Shawbury Rd. Grnf. BF38 54
Shaw Clo. Bush. BH27 36
Shaw Clo. Cher. AU57 91
Shaw Clo. Epsom BO59 94
Shaw Clo. Sth. Croy. CA59 96
Shaw Clo. Wal. Cr. CC17 21
Shaw Cres. Brwd. DE24 122
Shaw Cres. Sth. Croy. CA59 96
Shaw Cres. Til. DG44 71
Shawfield Pk. Brom. CJ51 88
Shawfield St. SW3 BU42 66
Shawford Ct. SW15 BP47 75
Shawford Rd. Epsom BN57 94
Shaw Gdns. Bark. CQ37 59
Shawley Cres. Epsom BQ62 103
Shawley Way Epsom BP62 103
Shawline Cres. E17 CD30 39
Shaw Rd. Brom. CG48 78
Shaw Rd. Enf. CC23 30
Shaw's Cotts. SE23 CD48 77
Shaw Way Wall. BX57 95
Shaxton Cres. Croy. CF58 96
Shearing Dr. Cars. BT54 86
Shearling Way N7 BX36 56
Shearman Rd. SE3 CG45 68
Sheath's La. Lthd. BF60 93
Sheaveshill Av. NW9 BO31 46
Sheeby Way, Slou. AQ40 52
Sheen Common Dr. Rich. BM45 65
Sheen Ct. Rich. BM45 65
Sheen Court Rd. Rich. BM45 65
Sheendale Rd. Rich. BL45 65
Sheenewood, SE26 CB49 77
Sheen Gate Gdns. SW14 BN45 65
Sheen La. SW14 BN46 75
Sheen Pk. Rich. BL45 65
Sheen Rd. Orp. CN52 88
Sheen Rd. Rich. BL46 75
Sheen Way. Wall. BX56 95
Sheen Wood SW14 BN46 75
Sheepbarn La. War. CG59 97
Sheepcot Dr. Wat. BD20 18
Sheepcote. Welw. G. C. BS9 5
Sheepcote Clo. Houns. BC43 63
Sheepcote La. SW11 BU44 66
Sheepcote La. Orp. CQ53 89
Sheepcote Rd. Har. BH32 45
Sheepcote Rd. Hem. H. AY13 8
Sheepcote Rd. Wind. AN42 61
Sheepcotes Rd. Rom. CP31 50
Sheepcot La. Wat. BC20 17
Sheepcot La. Wat. BD21 27
Sheepfold La. Amer. AO23 25
Sheepfold Rd. Guil. AP69 118
Sheep Hill, Sev. DB66 117
Sheephouse Grn. Dor. BE73 119
Sheephouse La. Dor. BE73 119
Sheephouse Rd. Hem. H. AY14 8
Sheephouse Way N. Mal. BN54 85
Sheeplands Av. Guil. AU69 118
Sheep La. E8 CB37 57
Sheep Wk. Epsom. BN64 103
Sheep Wk. Reig. BR69 120
Sheep Walk, Shep. AY54 83
Sheepwalk Lane. Leath. BB70 110
Sheepwalk Lane. Leath. BC70 110
Sheering Lower Rd. Saw. CR6 6
Sheering Mill La. Saw. CQ6 6
Sheering Rd. Harl. CP9 6
Sheering Rd. Harl. CQ8 6
Sheering Rd. Harl. CQ9 6
Sheerwater Ave. Wey. AV59 91
Sheerwater Rd. Wey. AV60 91
Sheethanger La. Hem. H. AW15 8
Sheet St. Wind. AO44 61
Sheet Street Rd. Wind. AO46 61
Sheffield Dr. Rom. CX28 42
Sheffield Gdns. Rom. CX28 42
Sheffield St. WC2 BX39 56
Portugal St.
Sheffield Ter. W8 BS41 66
Shefton Rise Nthwd. BC29 35
Sheila Clo. Rom. CR29 41
Sheila Rd. Rom. CR29 41
Sheilings, The, Horn. CW32 51
Shelbourne Clo. Pnr. BE31 45
Shelbourne Rd. N17 CB30 39
Shelburne Rd. N7 BX35 47
Shelbury Clo. Sid. CO48 79
Shelbury Rd. SE22 CB46 77
Sheldon Av. N6 BU33 47
Sheldon Av. Ilf. CL30 40
Sheldon Clo. Reig. BS71 121
Lymden Gdns.
Sheldon Ct. Guil. AS71 118
Lwr. Edgeborough Rd.
Sheldon Rd. N18 CA28 39
Sheldon Rd. NW2 BQ35 46
Sheldon Rd. Bexh. CQ44 69
Sheldon Rd. Dag. CQ36 59
Sheldon St. Croy. BZ55 87
Sheldrake Pl. W8 BS41 66
Sheldwick Ter. Brom. CK53 88
Shelford Pl. N16 BZ34 48
Stoke Newington Ch. St.
Shelford Rise SE19 CA50 77
Shelford Rd. Barn. BQ25 28
Shelgate Rd. SW11 BU46 76
Shellbank La. Dart. DA49 80
Shelley Av. E12 CK36 58
Shelley Av. Grnf. BG38 54
Shelley Av. Horn. CT34 50
Shelley Clo. Bans. BQ61 103
Shelley Clo. Edg. BM28 37
Shelley Clc. Grnf. BG38 54
Shelley Clo. Hayes BC39 53
Shelley Clo. Orp. CN55 88
Shelley Clo. Slou. AT42 62
Shelley Cres. Houns. BD44 64
Shelley Cres. Sthl. BE39 54
Shelley Dri. Well. CN44 68
Shelley Gdns. Wem. BK34 45
Shelley Gro. Loug. CK24 31
Shelley Rd. NW10 BN37 55
Shelley Rd. Brwd. DE26 122
Shelley Rd. Har. BH31 45
Shelleys La. Sev. CO61 107
Shellgrove Ms. N16 CA35 48
Shellgrove Rd.
Shellow Road Ong. DB13 15
Shell Rd. SE13 CE45 67
Shellwood Rd. SW11 BU44 66
Shellwood Rd. Reig. BN74 120
Shelly Clo. Ong. CW16 24
Shelson Av. Felt. BB48 73
Shelton Av. Warl. CC62 105
Shelton Clo. Warl. CC62 105
Shelton Rd. SW19 BS51 86
Shelton St. WC2 BX39 56
Shelvers Grn. Tad. BQ64 103
Shelvers Spur, Tad. BQ64 103
Shelvers Way. Tad. BQ64 103
Shemerdine Clo. E3 CD39 57
Shen Clo. Sev. CV67 117
Shenden Way, Sev. CV67 117
Shenfield Cres. Brwd. DC27 122
Shenfield Gdns. Brwd. DD25 122
Shenfield Grn. Brwd. DD26 122
Shenfield Pl. Brwd. DC26 122
Shenfield Rd. Brwd. DB27 42
Shenfield Rd. Brwd. DC26 122
Shenfield Rd. Wdf. Grn. CH29 40
Shenfield St. N1 CA37 57
Shenley Av. Ruis. BB34 44
Shenley Hill Rad. BJ21 27
Shenley La. St. Alb. BJ16 18
Shenley Rd. SE5 CA44 67
Shenley Rd. Borwd. BM24 28
Shenley Rd. Dart. CX47 80
Shenley Rd. Hem. H. AZ11 8
Shenley Rd. Houns. BE44 64
Shenstone Clo. Dart. CS45 69
Shenstone Gdns. Rom. CV30 42
Shephard Clo. Enf. CB22 30
Shepherdess Pl. N1 BZ38 57
Shepherdess Wk.
Shepherdess Wk. N1 BZ37 57
Shepherd Mkt. W1 BV40 56
Shepherd's Bush Grn. W12 BQ41 65
Shepherd's Bush Market W12 BQ41 65
Shepherds Bush Pl. W12 BQ41 65
Shepherd's Bush Rd. W6 BQ42 65
Shepherd's Clo. N6 BV32 47
Shepherds Clo. Rom. CP32 50
Shepherds Grn. Chis. CM50 78
Shepherds Grn. Hem. H. AV14 7
Shepherd's Hill N6 BV32 47
Shepherds Hill, Guil. AQ69 118
Shepherd's La. E9 CC35 48
Shepherds La. Dart. CU47 79
Shepherd's La. Guil. AP69 118
Shepherd, S Hill, Rom. CX30 42
Shepherds Path NW3 BT35 47
Lyndhurst Ter.
Shepherds Path Nthlt. BD36 54
Shepherds Pl. W1 BV40 56
Lees Pl.
Shepherd's Rd. Wat. BB24 26
Shepherd St. E3 CE38 57
Shepherd St. W1 BV40 56
Shepherd St. Grav. DE47 81
Shepherd's Wk. NW3 BT35 47
Hampstead High St.
Shepherds Wk. Epsom BM64 103
Shepherds Way. Chesh. AO20 16
Shepherd's Way, Guil. AS72 118
Shepherds Way, Hat. BT17 20
Shepherds Way. Rick. AW26 35
Shepherds Way Sth. Croy. CC57 96
Shepiston La. Hayes. AZ42 63
Shepley Clo. Cars. BV55 86
Shepley Clo. Horn. CV35 51
Shepley Dr. Ascot. AO53 82
Shepley End, Ascot. AO53 82
Sheppards Clo. St. Alb. BH12 9
Sheppard St. E16 CG38 58
Shepperton Court Dr. Shep. AZ53 83
Shepperton Rd. N1 BZ37 57
Shepperton Rd. Orp. CM53 88
Shepperton Rd. Shep. AY52 83
Shepperton Rd. Stai. AX52 83
Sheppey Clo. Erith. CU43 69
Sheppey Gdns. Dag. CP36 59
Sheppey Rd.
Sheppey Rd. Dag. CO36 59
Sheppey, S La. Kings L. BA18 17
Sheppey Wk. N1 BZ36 57
Marquess Est.
Sheppy Pl. Grav. DG47 81
Shepstone St. E6 CL40 58
Sherard Rd. SE9 CK46 78
Sheraton Dr. Epsom BN59 94
Sheraton St. W1 BW39 56
Wardour St.
Sherborne Av. Enf. CC23 30
Sherborne Av. Sthl. BF42 64
Sherborne Cres. Cars. BU54 86
Sherborne Gdns. W13 BJ39 54
Sherborne Gdns. Rom. CR28 41
Sherborne La. EC4 BZ40 57
King William St.
Sherborne Rd. Felt. BA47 73
Sherborne Rd. Orp. CN53 88
Sherborne Rd. Sutt. BS55 86
Sherborne St. N1 BZ37 57
Sherborne Wk. Lthd. BK64 102
Windfield
Sherborough Rd. N15 CA32 48
Sherbourne Clo. Epsom BP62 103
Sherbourne Clo. Slou. AV44 62
Sherbourne Dr. Vir. W. AO53 82
Sherbourne Dr. Wind. AM45 61
Sherbourne Gdns. NW9 BM31 46
Sherbourne Rd. Chess. BL56 94
Sherbourne Way, Rick. AZ24 26
Sherbrooke Clo. Bexh. CQ45 69
Sherbrooke Clo. Bexh. CR45 69
Sherbrooke Gdns. E6 CK39 58
Sherbrooke Rd. SW6 BR43 65
Sherbrook Gdns. N21 BY26 38
Shere Av. Sutt. BQ58 94
Shere Clo. Chess. BK56 93
Sheredan Rd. E4 CF28 39
Sheredes Dr. Hodd. CD13 12
Shere Road. Guil. AW70 110
Shere Rd. Ilf. CL32 49
Shere Road. Leath. AZ68 110
Shere Rd. Leath. BA71 110
Sherfield Ave. Rick. AX27 35
Sherfield Gdns. SW15 BO46 75
Sherfield Rd. Grays. DD43 71
Sheridan Clo. Rom. CV29 42
Sheridan Cres. Chis. CL51 88
Penn Gdns.
Sheridan Gdns. Har. BK32 45
Sheridan Rd. E7 CG34 49
Sheridan Rd. E12 CK35 49
Sheridan Rd. Bel. CR42 69
Sheridan Rd. Bexh. CQ45 69
Sheridan Rd. Rich. BK48 74
Sheridans Rd. Lthd. BG66 111
Sheridan Ter. Nthlt. BF35 45
Sheridan Walk Cars. BU56 95
Park Hill.
Sheriden Rd. SW19 BR51 85
Sheringham Av. E12 CK35 49
Sheringham Av. N14 BW25 29
Sheringham Av. Felt. BC48 73
Sheringham Av. Rom. CS32 50
Sheringham Av. Twick. BE47 74
Sheringham Dr. Bark. CN35 49
Sheringham Rd. N7 BX36 56
Sheringham Rd. SE10 CC51 87
Sherington Av. Pnr. BF29 36
Sherington Rd. SE7 CH43 68
Sherland Rd. Twick. BH47 74
Sherlies Av. Orp. CN55 88
Shermanbdry Pl. Erith CT43 69
Shermanbury Pl. Erith CT43 69
Sherman Rd. Brom. CH51 88
Shernbroke Rd. Wal. Abb. CG20 22
Shernells Way SE2 CO42 69
Shernhall St. E17 CF31 48
Sherrard Rd. E7 CJ36 58
Sherrard Rd. E12 CJ36 58
Sherrards Pk Rd. Welw. G. C. BQ7 5
Sherrards Way Barn. BS25 29
Sherrick Gn. Rd. NW10 BP35 46
Sherriff Rd. NW6 BS36 56
Sherringham Av. N17 CB30 39
Sherrock Gdns. NW4 BP31 46
Sherwin Rd. SE14 CC44 67
Sherwood. Grays. DC40 71
Sherwood Av. E18 CH31 49
Sherwood Av. SW16 BW50 76
Sherwood Av. Grnf. BH36 54
Sherwood Av. Hayes BC38 53
Sherwood Av. Pot. B. BR19 19
Sherwood Av. Ruis. BB32 44
Sherwood Av. St. Alb. BJ12 9
Sherwood Clo. SW15 BP45 65
Sherwood Clo. Slou. AS42 62
Sherwood Clo. Wok. AP62 100
Sherwood Cres. Reig. BS72 121
Sherwood Gdns. Bark. CM36 58
Sherwood Park Av. Sid. CO47 79
Sherwood Pk. Rd. Mitch. BW52 86
Sherwood Pk. Rd. Sutt. BS56 95
Sherwood Rd. NW4 BQ31 46
Sherwood Rd. SW19 BR50 75
Sherwood Rd. Couls. BW61 104
Sherwood Rd. Croy. CB54 87
Sherwood Rd. Har. BG34 45
Sherwood Rd. Hmptn. BG49 74
Sherwood Rd. Ilf. CM31 49
Sherwood Rd. Well. CO44 69
Sherwoods Rd. Wat. BE26 36
Sherwood St. N20 BT27 38
Sherwood St. W1 BW40 56
Brewer St.
Sherwood Ter. N20 BT27 38
Sherwood Way W. Wick. CE55 87
Shetland Rd. E3 CD37 57
Shevon Way, Brwd. CZ28 42
Shey Copse, Wok. AU62 100
Shieldhall St. SE2 CP42 69
Shield Rd. Ashf. BA49 73
Shiliber Wk. Chig. CN27 40
Shilitoe Av. Pot. B. BQ19 19
Shilling St. N1 BY36 56
Cross St.
Shillington St. SW11 BU44 66
Shillitoe Rd. N13 BY28 38
Shimmings, The Guil. AT70 118
Shinfield St. W12 BQ39 55
Shinglewell Rd. Erith. CR43 69
Ship All. E1 CB40 57
Wellclose Sq.
Shipbourne Rd. Sev. & Ton. CY69 117
Shipfield Clo. West. CJ64 106
Shipford Path SE23 CC48 77
Ship & Half Moon Pass. SE18 CL41 68
Ship Hill, West. CJ64 106
Shipka Rd. SW12 BV47 76
Ship La. SW14 BN45 65
Ship La. S. At H. CV51 90
Ship La. Ock. CW40 60
Shipman Rd. E16 CH39 58
Shipman Rd. SE23 CC48 77
Ship & Mermaid Row SE1 BZ41 67
Weston St.
Ship St. SE8 CE44 67
Ship Tavern Pass. EC3 CA39 57
Lime St.
Shipton Clo. Dag. CP34 50
Shipton Rd. Uxb. AY35 44
Shipton St. E2 CA38 57
Shipway Ter. N16 CA34 48
Victorian Rd.
Shirburn Clo. SE23 CC47 77
Shirbutt St. E14 CE40 57
Shirebrook Rd. SE3 CJ45 68
Shirehall Clo. NW4 BQ32 46
Shirehall Gdns. NW4 BQ32 46
Shirehall La. NW4 BQ32 46
Shirehall Pk. NW4 BQ32 46
Shirehall Rd. Dart. CV49 80
Shire La. Ger. Cr. AT27 34
Shire La. Orp. CK57 97
Shire La. Orp. CN56 97
Shire La. Rick. AT25 25
Shire Mead Borwd. BL25 28
Shires, The, Rich. BL49 75
Shirland Ms. W9 BR38 55
Shirland Rd. W9 BR38 55
Shirley Ave. Couls. BY63 104
Shirley Ave. Wind. AM44 61
Shirley Av. Bex. CP47 79
Shirley Av. Croy. CC54 87
Shirley Av. Red. BU73 121
Shirley Av. Sutt. BR58 94
Shirley Av. Sutt. BT56 95
Shirley Ch. Rd. Croy. CC55 87
Shirley Clo. Brox. CD15 12
Westlea Rd.
Shirley Clo. Dart. CV45 70
Shirley Clo. Houns. BG46 74
Shirley Clo. Wal. Cr. CB18 21
Shirley Cres. Beck. CC52 87
Shirley Dri. Houns. BG46 74
Shirley Gdns. W7 BH40 54
Shirley Gdns. Bark. CN36 58
Shirley Gdns. Horn. CV34 51
Shirley Gro. N9 CC26 39
Shirley Gro. SW11 BV45 66
Shirley Hills Rd. Croy. CC56 96
Shirley Ho. Dr. SE7 CJ43 68
Shirley Oak Rd. Croy. CC54 87
Shirley Pk. Rd. Croy. CB54 87
Shirley Pl. Wok. AO62 100
Shirley Rd. E15 CG36 58
Shirley Rd. W4 BN41 65
Shirley Rd. Croy. CB54 87
Shirley Rd. Enf. BZ24 30
Shirley Rd. St. Alb. BH14 9
Shirley Rd. Sid. CN48 78
Shirley Rd. Wall. BW58 95
Shirley Rd. Wat. BB19 17
Shirley St. E16 CG39 58
Shirley St. N1 BX37 56
Shirley Way Croy. CD55 87
Shirlock Rd. NW3 BU35 47
Mansfield Rd.
Shobden Rd. N17 BZ30 39
Shoebury Rd. E6 CK36 58
Shoe La. EC4 BY39 56
Shoe La. Harl. CQ11 14
Sholdon Gdns. Orp. CP53 89
Shonk's Mill Rom. CU22 32
Shooters Av. Har. BK31 45
Shooters Dri. Wal. Abb. CG14 13
Shooters Hill, SE18 CK44 68
Shooters Hill, Well. CK44 68
Shooter's Hill Rd. SE3 CF44 67
Shooter's Hill Rd. SE18 CF44 67
Shooters Rd. Enf. BY22 29
Shootersway, Berk. AO12 7
Shootersway La. Berk. AP13 7
Shoot Up Hl. NW2 BR35 46
Shoplands, Welw. G. C. BQ6 5
Shord Hill Ken. BZ57 96
Shord Hill Ken. BZ61 105
Shoredliche Clo. Uxb. AY34 44
Shoreditch High St. E1 CA38 57
Shore Est. E9 CC36 57
Shore Gro. Felt. BF48 74
Shoreham Clo. SW18 BS46 76
York Rd.
Shoreham Clo. Bex. CP47 79
Stansted Cres.
Shoreham La. Orp. CR57 98
Shoreham La. Sev. CQ59 98
Shoreham La. Sev. CT64 107
Shoreham Rd. Orp. CO51 89
Shoreham Rd. Sev. CU59 98
Shoreham Rd. E. Houns. AY46 73
Shoreham Rd. W. Houns. AY46 73
Shoreham St. SW18 BS46 76
Barchard St.
Shoreham Way Brom. CH53 88
Shore Pl. E9 CC36 57
Shore Rd. E9 CC36 57
Shores Rd. Wok. AS60 91
Shore St. SW19 BT51 86
Shore, The Grav. DE46 81
Shorncliffe Rd. SE1 CA42 67
Shorndean St. SE6 CF47 77
Shorne Clo. Sid. CO46 79
Park Mead.
Shornefield Clo. Brom. CL52 88
Shorrolds Rd. SW6 BR43 65
Shortcroft Rd. Epsom BO57 94
Shortcrofts Rd. Dag. CQ36 59
Shorter Av. Brwd. DC26 122
Short Gate N12 BR28 37
Shortland Rd. E10 CE33 48
Shortlands W6 BQ42 65
Shortlands. Hayes. BA43 63
Shortlands Av. Ong. CW16 24
Shortlands Clo. N18 BZ27 39
Shortlands Gdns. Brom. CG51 88
Shortlands Grn. Welw. G. C. BR8 5
Shortlands Gro. Brom. CF51 87
Shortlands Ms. W6 BQ42 65
Shortlands Rd. Brom. CF52 87
Shortlands Rd. Kings. On T. BL50 75
Short La. Oxt. CH69 115
Short La. St. Alb. BE18 18
Short La. Stai. AY47 73
Shortmead Dr. Wal. Cr. CD19 21
Short Rd. E11 CG34 49
Short Rd. E15 CF37 57
Short Rd. W4 BO43 65
Shorts Croft NW9 BM31 46
Shorts Gdns. WC2 BX39 56
Shorts Rd. Cars. BU56 95
Short St. NW4 BQ31 46
Short St. SE1 BY41 66
Short Way N12 BU29 38
Short Way SE9 CK45 68
Short Way. Amer. AO22 25
Short Way Twick. BG47 74
Shortwood Av. Stai. AW48 73
Shotfield Wall. BV57 95
Shothamger Way, Hem. H. AU16 16
Shottendane Rd. SW6 BS44 66
Shottfield Av. SW14 BO45 65
Shoulder Of Mutton All. E14 CD40 57
Narrow St.
Shouldham St. W1 BU39 56
Showers Way Hayes BC40 53
Shrapnel Rd. SE9 CK45 68
Shrewsbury Av. SW14 BN45 65
Shrewsbury Av. Har. BL31 46
Shrewsbury Clo. Surb. BK55 84
Shrewsbury Cres. NW10 BN37 55
Shrewsbury Ho. SW3 BU43 66
Shrewsbury Ho. Surb. BL55 85
Shrewsbury La. SE18 CL44 68
Shrewsbury Ms. W2 BS39 56
Chepstow Rd.
Shrewsbury Rd. E7 CJ35 49
Shrewsbury Rd. N11 BW29 38
Shrewsbury Rd. NW10 BO37 55
Shrewsbury Rd. W2 BS39 56
Shrewsbury Rd. Beck. CD52 87
Shrewsbury Rd. Cars. BU53 86
Shrewsbury Rd. Red. BU70 121
Shrewsbury Wk. Islw. BJ45 64
South St.
Shrewton Rd. SW17 BU50 76
Shroffold Rd. Brom. CG49 78
Shropshire Clo. Mitch. BX52 86
Shropshire Rd. N22 BX29 38
Shroton St. NW1 BU39 56
Shrubberies, The, Chig. CM28 40
Shrubberies, The, E18 CH30 40
Shrubbery Gdns. N21 BY26 38
Shrubbery Rd. N9 CB27 39
Shrubbery Rd. SW16 BX49 76
Shrubbery Rd. Grav. DH47 81
Shrubbery Rd. S. Dnth. CY51 90
Shrubbery Rd. Sthl. BF40 54
Shrubbery, The, Upmin. CY34 51
Shrubbs Hill. Wok. AO58 91
Shrubhill Rd. Hem. H. AV14 7
Shrubland Est. E8 CA36 57
Shrubland Gro. Wor. Pk. BQ55 85
Shrubland Rd. E8 CA37 57
Shrubland Rd. E10 CE33 48
Shrubland Rd. E17 CE32 48
Shrubland Rd. Bans. BR61 103
Shrublands Av. Berk. AQ13 7
Shrublands Av. Croy. CE55 87
Shrublands Clo. N20 BT26 38
Shrublands Clo. Chig. CM29 40
Shrublands Rd. Berk. AQ12 7
Shrublands, The, Pot. B. BR20 19
Shrubs Rd. Rick. AY28 35
Shuna Wk. N1 BZ36 57
Marquess Est.
Shurland Gdns. SE15 CA43 67
Rosemary Rd.
Shurlock Av. Swan. CS51 89
Shuttle Clo. Sid. CN47 78
Shuttle Mead Bex. CQ47 79
Shuttle Rd. Dart. CU45 69
Shuttle St. E1 CA38 57
Buxton St.
Shuttleworth Rd. SW11 BT44 66
Sibella Rd. SW4 BW44 66
Sibley Gro. E12 CK36 58
Sibthorpe Rd. SE12 CH47 78
Sibthorp Rd. Hat. BQ15 10
Sibthorp Rd. Mitch. BU51 86
Sibton Rd. Cars. BU54 86
Sicilian Av. WC1 BX39 56
Bloomsbury Way
Sickert Ct. N1 BZ36 57
Sickle Cnr. Dag. CR38 59
Sicklefield Clo. Wal. Cr. CA16 21
Sidbury Av. SW6 BR45 65
Sidbury St. SW6 BR44 65
Sidcup By-pass Sid. CM48 78
Sidcup High St. Sid. CO49 79
Sidcup Hill Sid. CO49 79
Sidcup Hill Gdns. Sid. CP49 79
Sidcup Rd. SE9 CJ47 78
Sidcup Rd. SE12 CJ47 78
Siddons La. NW1 BU38 56
Siddons Rd. N17 CB30 39
Siddons Rd. SE23 CC48 77
Siddons Rd. Croy. BY55 86
Side Rd. E17 CD32 48
South Gro.
Side Rd. Uxb. AU33 43
Sidewood Rd. SE9 CM47 78
Sidford Pl. SE1 BX41 66
Sidmouth Av. Islw. BH44 64

Sidmouth Clo. Wat. BC27 35
Sidmouth Dr. Ruis. BC34 44
Sidmouth Rd. E10 CF34 48
Sidmouth Rd. NW2 BQ36 55
Sidmouth Road SE15 CA44 67
Sumner Estate
Sidmouth Rd. Orp. CO53 89
Sidmouth Rd. Well. CP43 69
Sidmouth St. WC1 BX38 56
Sidney Av. N13 BX28 38
Sidney Boyd Ct. NW6 BS36 56
Sidney Gdns. Brent. BK43 64
Boston Manor Rd.
Sidney Gdns. Sev. CV62 108
Sidney Gro. N1 BY38 56
Wakley St.
Sidney Rd. E7 CH34 49
Sidney Rd. N22 BX29 38
Sidney Rd. SE25 CB53 87
Sidney Rd. SW9 BX44 66
Sidney Rd. Beck. CD51 87
Sidney Rd. Epp. CM21 31
Sidney Rd. Har. BG31 45
Sidney Rd. Sutt. BS56 95
Sidney Rd. Twick. BJ46 74
Sidney Rd. Wal. Cr. CE20 21
Sidney Rd. Walt. BC54 83
Sidney St. Est. E1 CC39 57
Sidney Sq. E1 CC39 57
Sidney St. E1 CB39 57
Sidney St. Stai. AW49 73
Sidworth St. E8 CB36 57
Siemens Rd. SE18 CJ41 68
Sigdon Rd. E8 CB35 48
Sigers, The, Pnr. BC32 44
Sigismund St. SE10 CG41 68
Silas St. Est. NW5 BV36 56
Silbury St. N1 BZ38 57
East Rd.
Silcester Ct. Th. Hth. BY52 86
Silchester Ms. W10 BQ40 55
Walmer Rd.
Silchester Rd. W10 BQ39 55
Silcote Rd. SE5 CA42 67
Albany Rd.
Silecroft Rd. Bexh. CR44 69
Silesia Bldgs. E8 CB36 57
London La.
Silex St. SE1 BY41 66
Silkfield Rd. NW9 BO32 46
Silkham Rd. Oxt. CF67 114
Silkins, The, Rom. CT30 41
Silk Mill Rd. Wat. BC26 35
Silk Mills Path SE13 CF44 67
Silkmore Lane. Leath. HZ66 110
Silkstream Rd. Edg. BN30 37
Silk St. EC2 BZ39 57
Silsden Cres. Ch. St. G. AR27 34
Silsoe Rd. N22 BX30 38
Silver Birch Av. E4 CD29 39
Silver Birch Av. Epp. CQ17 23
Silver Birch Clo. Dart. CT49 79
Silver Birch Clo. Uxb. AY35 44
Silver Birch Clo. Wey. AV59 91
Silverbirch Wk. NW3 BU36 56
Maitland Park Vw.
Silvercliffe Gdns. Barn. BU24 29
Silver Clo. Har. BG29 36
Silver Clo. Sutt. BR56 94
Silver Cres. W4 BM42 65
Silverdale SE26 CC49 77
Silverdale Enf. BX24 29
Silverdale Stai. AW49 73
Leacroft
Silverdale Ave. Lthd. BG60 93
Silverdale Av. Ilf. CN32 49
Silverdale Av. Walt. BB55 83
Silverdale Av. Watt. BB56 92
Silverdale Clo. W7 BH40 54
Cherington Rd.
Silverdale Clo. W13 BH40 54
Silverdale Clo. Har. BE35 45
Silverdale Dr. Horn. CU35 50
Silverdale Dr. Sun. BC51 83
Silverdale Gdns. Hayes BC41 63
Silverdale Rd. E4 CF29 39
Silverdale Rd. Bexh. CR44 69
Silverdale Rd. Bush. BE25 27
Silverdale Rd. Hayes. BB41 63
Silverdale Rd. Orp. CM52 88
Silverdale Rd. Orp. CO52 89
Silver Dell, Wat. BB21 26
Silverhall St. Islw. BJ45 64
Silver Hill. Ch. St. G. AQ27 34
Silverholme. Har. BK33 45
Silverland St. E16 CK40 58
Silver La. Pur. BW59 95
Silver La. W. Wick. CF55 87
Silverleigh Rd. Th. Hth. BX52 86
Silverlocke Rd. Grays. DE43 71
Silvermere Av. Rom. CR28 41
Silvermere Rd. SE6 CE47 77
Silver Pl. W1 BW40 56
Lexington St.
Silver Rd. Grav. DJ48 81
Silversmiths Way, Wok. AR62 100
Silver Spring Clo. Erith CR43 69
Silversted La. West. CM64 106
Silverston Way Stan. BK29 36
Silver St. EC2 BZ39 57
Wood St.
Silver St. N18 BZ28 39
Silver St. Enf. BZ24 30
Silver St. Rom. CO24 32
Silver St. Wal. Abb. CF20 21
Silver St. Wal. Cr. BZ18 21
Silverthorn Dr. Hem. H. AZ15 8
Silverthorne Gdns. E4 CE27 39
Silverthorne Rd. SW8 BV44 66
Silverton Rd. W6 BQ43 65
Silvertown By-pass E16 CJ40 58
Silvertown Way E16 CG39 58
Silvertree Clo. Walt. BC55 83
Silver Wk. SE16 CD40 57
Silver Way Rom. CR31 50
Silverwood Clo. Beck. CE50 77
Brackley Rd.
Silvester Rd. SE22 CA46 77
Silvester St. SE1 BZ41 67
Silwood Est. SE16 CC42 67
Silwood St. SE16 CC42 67
Simla Clo. SE14 CD43 67
Chubworthy St.
Simmil Rd. Esher BH56 93
Simmons Clo. N20 BU27 38
Simmons Clo. Slou. AT42 62
Common Rd.
Simmons La. E4 CF27 39
Simmons Pl. Grays. DD40 71
Simmons Rd. SE18 CL42 68
Brookhill Rd.
Simmons Wk. E15 CF35 48
Waddington Rd.
Simmons Way N20 BU27 38
Simm's Clo. Cars. BU55 86
Simms Rd. SE1 CB42 67
Simnel Rd. SE12 CH47 78
Simon Cl. W11 BS40 56
Portobello Rd.
Simon Dean. Hem. H. AT17 16
Simonds Rd. E10 CE34 48
Simone Dr. Ken. BZ02 106
Simons Clo. Cher. AU57 91
Simons Wk. E15 CF35 48
Simons Wk. E15 CF36 57
Simons Wk. Egh. AR50 72
Simplemarsh Rd. Wey. AW56 92
Simpson Rd. Houns. BE46 74
Simpson Rd. Rain. CT36 59
Simpson Rd. Rich. BK49 74
Simpsons Rd. E14 CE40 57
Simpsons Rd. Brom. CH52 88
Simpson St. SW11 BU44 66
Simrose Ct. SW18 BS46 76
Sims Clo. Rom. CT31 50
Junction Rd.
Sims Wk. SE3 CG45 68
Lee Rd.
Sims Wk. SE12 CG45 68
Sinclaire Clo. Enf. CA23 30
Sinclair Gdns. W14 BQ41 65
Sinclair Gro. NW4 BQ32 46
Sinclair Rd. E4 CD28 39
Sinclair Rd. W14 BQ41 65
Sinclare Clo. Enf. CA23 30
Carterhatch La.
Sincots Rd. Red. BU70 121
Lwr. Bridge Rd.
Sinderby Clo. Borwd. BL23 28
Sinderby Clo. Borwd. BL23 28
Singapore Rd. W13 BJ40 54
Singer St. EC2 BZ38 57
Cowper St.
Singles Cross La. Sev. CP60 98
Single St. Orp. CL60
Singleton Clo. Horn. CT35 50
Cowdray Way
Singleton Clo. Horn. CU35 50
Cowdray Way
Singleton Rd. Dag. CQ35 50
Singleton Scarp N12 BS28 38
Singlewell Rd. Grav. DG48 81
Singret Pl. Uxb. AX38 53
Sinnott Rd. E17 CC30 39
Sion Rd. Twick. BJ47 74
Sipsom La. West Dr. AZ43 63
Sipson Clo. West Dr. AZ43 63
Sipson Rd. West Dr. AY41 63
Sipson Rd. West Dr. AZ43 63
Sipson Way. West Dr. AZ44 63
Sir Alexander Clo. W3 BO40 55
Sir Alexander Rd.
Sir Alexander Rd. W3 BO40 55
Sirdar Rd. N22 BY31 47
Sirdar Rd. SW17 BV50 76
Grenfell Rd.
Sirdar Rd. W11 BQ40 55
Sirdar Strand, Grav. DJ49 81
Sir Thom. More Est. SW3 BT43 66
Sirus Rd. Nthwd. BC28 35
Sisley Rd. Bark. CN37 58
Sispara Gdns. SW18 BR46 75
Sissinghurst Rd. Croy. CB54 87
Sisters Av. SW11 BU45 66
Sistova Rd. SW12 BV47 76
Sittingbourne Av. Enf. BZ25 30
Sitwell Gro. Stan. BH28 36
Siverst Clo. Nthlt. BF36 54
Siviter Way Dag. CR36 59
Siward Rd. N17 BZ30 39
Siward Rd. SW17 BT48 76
Siward Rd. Brom. CH52 88
Six Acres, Hem. H. AZ15 8
Six Bells La. Sev. CV66 117
Sixth Ave. W10 BR38 55
Sixth Av. E12 CK35 49
Sixth Av. Enf. CA25 30
Sixth Av. Hayes BB40 53
Sixth Av. Wat. BD21 27
Sixth Cross Rd. Twick. BG48 74
Skardu Rd. NW2 BR35 46
Skeena Hl. SW18 BR47 75
Skeet Hill La. Orp. CQ54 89
Skeffington Rd. E6 CK37 58
Skelbrook St. SW18 BS48 76
Skelgill Rd. SW15 BR45 65
Skelton Rd. E7 CH36 58
Skeltons La. E10 CE33 48
Skelwith Rd. W6 BQ43 65
Sketty Rd. Enf. CA24 30
Skibbs La. Orp. CQ56 98
Skid Hill La. War. CG60 97
Skiers St. E15 CF37 57
Skillet Hill, Wal. Abb. CH21 31
Skimpans Cl. Hat. BQ15 10
Skin Market Pl. SE1 BZ40 57
Skinner Ct. E2 CB37 57
Parmiter St.
Skinner Pl. SW1 BV42 66
Bourne St.
Skinners La. Ash. BK62 102
Skinners La. Garlick Hill EC4 BZ40 57
Queen Victoria St.
Skinner St. EC1 BY38 56
Skipsey Av. E6 CK38 58
Skipton Dr. Hayes. BA42 63
Skipton St. SE1 BY41 66
Keyworth St.
Skipworth Rd. E9 CC37 57
Skomer Wk. N1 BZ36 57
Marquess Est.
Skylark Rd. Uxb. AU33 43
Sky Peals Rd. Wdf. Grn. CF30 39
Skywood Rd. St. Alb. BJ11 9
Slackesbury Hatch. Harl. CL11 13
Sladebrook Rd. SE3 CJ45 68
Slade Ct. Cher. AU57 91
Sladedale Rd. SE18 CN42 68
Slade Gdns. SW9 BX44 66
Slade Gdns. Erith CT44 69
Slade Grn. Rd. Erith CT44 69
Slade Grn. Rd. Erith. CU43 69
Slade Oak La. Ger. Cr. AT31 43
Slade Rd. Cher AU57 91
Slades Clo. Enf. BY24 29
Slade's Cotts. Chis. CL49 78
Slades Dr. Chis. CM48 78
Slades Gdns. Enf. BY23 29
Slades Hill Enf. BY24 29
Slades Rise Enf. BY24 29
Slade, The, SE18 CN43 68
Slade, The, Enf. BY24 29
Slagrove Pl. SE13 CE46 77
Slaidburn St. SW10 BT43 66
Slaithwaite Rd. SE13 CF45 67
Slapleys, Wok. AS63 100
Sleaford Grn. Wat. BD27 36
Sleaford St. SW8 BW43 66
Sleap Cross Gdns, St. Alb. BM14 10
Sleapshyde La. St. Alb. BM14 10
Sleath Walk, SW19 BT51 86
Brangwyn Cres.
Sleddale Hem. H. AY12 8
Wharfedale
Sleep Farm Rd. Grays. DG41 71
Sleets End, Hem. H. AW12 8
Slewins La. Horn. CV32 51
Slimmons Dr. St. Alb. BJ11 9
Slines Oaks Rd. Cat. CE64 105
Slingsby Pl. WC2 BX40 56
Long Acre
Slippers Pl. SE16 CB41 67
Slipshatch Rd. Reig. BQ72 120
Slipshoe St. Reig. BR70 120
Sloane Av. SW3 BU42 66
Sloane Av. Orp. CM55 88
Sloane Ct. E. SW3 BV42 66
Sloane Ct. W. SW3 BV42 66
Sloane Gdns. SW1 BV42 66
Sloane Sq. SW1 BU42 66
Sloane St. SW1 BU41 66
Sloane Ter. SW1 BV42 66
Sloane Wk. Croy. CD53 87
Sloans Way. Welw. G. C. BR6 5
Slough La. NW9 BN32 46
Slough La. Bet. BP69 120
Slough La. Epp. CS15 14
Slough La. Epsom BN66 112
Slough Rd. Iver AU38 52
Slough Rd. Slou. AP42 62
Slough Rd. Wind. AO42 61
Sloughs, The Bet. BP69 120
Sly St. E1 CB39 57
Cannon St. Rd.
Small Acre, Hem. H. AV13 7
Smallbrook Ms. W2 BT39 56
Craven Rd.
Smallbury Av. Islw. BH44 64
Small Croft. Welw. G. C. BS7 5
Smalley Clo. N16 CA34 48
Smalley Rd.
Smalley Rd. N16 CA34 48
Smallford La. St. Alb. BM14 10
Small's Hill Rd. Reig. BP74 120
Smallwood Rd. SW17 BT49 76
Smardale Rd. SW18 BT46 76
Alma Rd.
Smarden Clo. Belv. CR42 69
Essenden Rd.
Smarden Gro. SE9 CK49 78
Prestbury Sq.
Smart Clo. Rom. CU30 41
Smarts Heath La. Wok. AQ65 100
Smarts Heath Rd. Wok. AQ65 100
Smart's La. Loug. CJ24 31
Smart's Pl. N18 CB28 39
Fore St.
Smarts Pl. WC2 BX39 56
Stukeley St.
Smarts Rd. Grav. DG48 81
Smart St. E2 CC38 57
Smeaton Rd. SW18 BS47 76
Smeaton Rd. Wdf. Grn. CK28 40
Smedley St. SW4 BW44 66
Smedley St. SW8 BW44 66
Smeed Rd. E3 CE36 57
Smithambottom La. Pur. BW59 95
Smithamdowns Rd. Pur. BW60 95
Smithers, The Bet. BM71 120
Smithfield St. EC1 BY39 56
Smithies Rd. SE2 CO42 69
Smith Rd. Reig. BR72 120
Smiths Cres. St. Alb. BM14 10
Smiths La. Eden. CM70 115
Smith's La. Wal. Cr. BZ16 21
Smith's La. Wind. AM44 61
Smithson Rd. N17 BZ30 39
Smith Sq. SW1 BX41 66
Smith St. E16 CG39 58
Smith St. SW3 BU42 66
Smith St. Surb. BL53 85
Smith St. Wat. BD24 27
Smith Ter. SW3 BU42 66
Smithwood Clo. SW19 BR47 75
Smithy Clo. Tad. BR66 112
Smithy La. Tad. BR67 112
Smithy St. E1 CC39 57
Smoke La. Reig. BS71 121
Smooth Field Est. Houns. BF45 64
Smug Oak La. St. Alb. BF18 18
Smyrks Rd. SE17 CA42 67
Smyrna Rd. NW6 BS36 56
Smythe Rd. S. At. H. CX51 90
Smythe St. E14 CE40 57
Smythwood, Wok. AQ61 100
Snag La. Sev. CM59 97
Snag La. Sev. CN58 97
Snakes Hill. Brwd. CY23 33
Snakes La. Wdf. Grn. CH28 40
Snape Spur, Slou. AP39 52
Snaresbrook Dr. Stan. BK28 36
Snaresbrook Rd. E11 CG31 49
Snarsgate St. W10 BQ39 55
Snatts Hill. Oxt. CG68 115
Snead St. SE14 CD43 67
Sneath Av. NW11 BR33 46
Sneldon Clo. Wal. Cr. CA16 21
Snelgar Rd. Wok. AS62 100
Snelling Av. Grav. DF48 81
Snellings Rd. Walt. BD56 93
Snells La. Amer. AQ23 25
Snell's Pk. N18 CA29 39
Sneyd Av. NW2 BQ35 46
Snodland Clo. Orp. CL58 97
Snowbury Rd. SW6 BS44 66
Snowden Av. Uxb. AZ37 53
Snowdon Clo. Wind. AL45 61
Snowdon Cres. Hayes. BA41 63
Snowdon St. EC2 CA38 57
Snowdrop Path. Rom. CV29 42
Snowerhill Rd. Bet. BO71 120
Snow Hill, EC1 BY39 56
Snow Hill Cotts. Chesh. AP15 7
Snows Fields, SE1 BZ41 67
Snowshill Rd. E12 CK35 49
Soames Md. Brwd. DA20 24
Soames St. SE15 CA45 67
Soames Wk. N. Mal. BO51 85
Socket La. Brom. CH53 88
Soham Rd. Enf. CD22 30
Soho Sq. W1 BW39 56
Soho St. W1 BW39 56
Soho Sq.
Solander Gdns. Est. E1 CC40 57
Solebay St. E1 CD38 57
Solebay St. E3 CD38 57
Solecote. Lthd. BF66 111
Sole Farm Ave. Lthd. BE66 111
Sole Farm Rd. Lthd. BE66 111
Solefelds Rd. Sev. CU67 116
Solent Rd. NW6 BS35 47
Solent Rd. Houns. AY46 73
Solesbridge Clo. Rick. AV24 25
Solesbridge La. Rick. AV24 25
Solesbridge La. Rick. AW23 26
Soley Ms. N1 BY38 56
Percy St.
Solid La. Brwd. CZ23 33
Solna Av. SW15 BQ46 75
Solna Rd. N21 BZ26 39
Solomon's Pass. SE15 CB45 67
Solomons Terr. N20 BT26 38
Solom's Ct. Rd. Bans. BT62 104
Solon New Rd. SW4 BX45 66
Solon Rd. SW2 BX45 66
Solway, Hem. H. AY12 8
Solway Clo. Houns. BE45 64
Solway Rd. N22 BY30 38
Solway Rd. SE22 CB45 67
Somaford Gro. Barn. BT25 29
Somali Rd. NW2 BR35 46
Somerby Rd. Bark. CM36 58
Somerden Rd. Orp. CP54 89
Somerfield Clo. Tad. BR63 103
Somerfield Rd. N4 BY34 47
Somerford Clo. Pnr. BC31 44
Somerford Est. N16 CA35 48
Somerford Gro. N16 CA35 48
Somerford Rd. N17 CB29 39
Somerford St. E1 CB38 57
Brady St.
Somerhill Av. Sid. CO47 79
Somerhill Rd. Well. CO44 69
Someries Rd. Hem. H. AV12 7
Somerleyton Pass. SW9 BY45 66
Mayall Rd.
Somerleyton Rd. SW9 BY45 66
Somersby Gdns. Ilf. CK32 49
Somers Cres. W2 BU39 56
Somerset Av. SW20 BP51 85
Somerset Av. Chess. BK56 93
Somerset Av. Well. CN46 78
Somerset Clo. N. Mal. BO53 85
Somerset Clo. Wdf. Grn. CH30 40
Harold Rd.
Somerset Est. SW11 BT44 66
Somerset Gdns. N6 BV33 47
Somerset Gdns. SE13 CE44 67
Somerset Gdns. SW16 BX52 86
Somerset Gdns. Horn. CX33 51
Somerset Gdns. Tedd. BH49 74
Somerset Rd. E17 CE32 48
Somerset Rd. N18 CA28 39
Somerset Rd. NW4 BQ31 46
Somerset Rd. SW19 BQ48 75
Somerset Rd. W4 BN41 65
Somerset Rd. W13 BJ40 54
Somerset Rd. Barn. BS25 29
Somerset Rd. Brent. BK43 64
Somerset Rd. Dart. CU46 79
Somerset Rd. Enf. CE22 30
Somerset Rd. Har. BG32 45
Somerset Rd. Kings. On T. BL51 85
Somerset Rd. Orp. CO54 89
Somerset Rd. Red. BT71 121
Somerset Rd. S. Le H. DK41 71
Somerset Rd. Sthl. BE39 54
Somerset Rd. Tedd. BH49 74
Somerset Sq. W14 BR41 65
Somerset Way. Iver. AV41 62
Somerset Waye Houns. BE43 64
Somersham Rd. Bexh. CQ44 69
Somers Ms. W2 BU39 56
Radnor Pl.
Somers Pl. SW2 BX47 76
Somers Rd. E17 CD31 48
Somers Rd. Hat. BQ15 10
Somers Rd. Reig. BS70 121
Somers Sq. Hat. BQ15 10
Somers Way Bush. BG26 36
Somerton Av. Rich. BM45 65
Somerton Clo. Pur. BY61 104
Somerton Rd. NW2 BQ34 46
Somerton Rd. SE15 CB45 67
Somertons Clo. Guil. AQ69 118
Somertrees Av. SE12 CH48 78
Somertrees Rd.
Somertrees Rd. SE12 CH48 78
Somervell Ct. Har. BF35 45
Somervell Rd. Har. BH35 45
Somerville Rd. SE14 CC44 67
Somerville Rd. SE20 CC50 77
Somerville Rd. Rom. CP32 50
Somerville Rd. Wind. AO42 61
Sonderburg Rd. N7 BX34 47
Sondes Pl. Dri. Dor. BH71 119
Sondes St. SE17 BZ43 67
Sonia Ct. Har. BH32 45
Sonia Gdns. N12 BT28 38
Sonia Gdns. NW10 BO35 46
Sonia Gdns. Houns. BF43 64
Sonning Rd. SE25 CB53 87
Sopers Rd. Pot. B. BX18 20
Sophia Rd. E10 CE33 48
Sophia Rd. E16 CH39 58
Sophia St. E14 CE40 57
Sopwell La. St. Alb. BG14 9
Sopwith Rd. Houns. BD43 64
Sorrel Wk. Rom. CT31 50
Sorrento Rd. Sutt. BS55 86
Sotheby Rd. N4 BY34 47
Sotheron Rd. SW6 BS43 66
Sotheron Rd. Wat. BD24 27
Soudan Rd. SW11 BU44 66
Souldern Rd. W14 BQ41 65
Souldern St. Wat. BC25 26
South Access Rd. E17 CD33 48
South Acre NW9 BO30 37
South Africa Rd. W12 BP40 55
Southall La. Houns. BC43 63
Southall Way, Brwd. CZ28 42
Southampton Bldgs. WC2 BY39 56
Southampton Gdns. Mitch. BX53 86
Southampton Pl. WC1 BX39 56
Southampton Rd. NW5 BU35 47
Southampton Rd. Houns. AY46 73
Southampton Row, WC1 BX39 56
Southampton St. WC2 BX40 56
Southampton Way, SE5 BZ43 67
South App. Nthwd. BA27 35
South Ash Rd. Sev. DB58 99
South Audley St. W1 BV40 56
South Av. E4 CE26 39
South Av. Cars. BU57 95
South Av. Egh. AU50 72
South Av. Rich. BM44 65
Sandycombe Rd.
South Av. Sthl. BE40 54
South Av. Gdns. Sthl. BE40 54
South Bank, Chis. CM49 78
Southbank Surb. BJ54 84
South Bank Surb. BL53 85
South Bnk. West. CM66 115
South Bank Lo. Surb. BL53 85
South Bank Rd. Berk. AP12 7
South Bank Ter. Surb. BL53 85
South Boltons Gdns. SW10 BS42 66
South Border Pur. BW59 95
Southborough Clo. Surb. BK54 84
Southborough La. Brom. CK53 88
Southborough Rd. Brom. CK53 88
Southborough Rd. Surb. BL54 85
Southbourne Brom. CH54 88
Southbourne Av. NW9 BO30 37
Southbourne Clo. Pnr. BE33 45
Southbourne Cres. NW4 BR31 46
Southbourne Gdns. SE12 CH46 78
Southbourne Gdns. Ilf. CM35 49
Southbourne Gdns. Ruis. BC33 44
Southbridge Pl. Croy. BZ56 96
Southbridge Rd. Croy. BZ55 87
Southbridge Way Sthl. BE41 64
Southbrook, Saw. CQ6 6
Southbrook Rd. SE12 CG46 78
Southbrook Rd. SW16 BX51 86
Southbury Av. Enf. CB25 30
Southbury Rd. Enf. CA24 30
S. C. G. Smallholdings Rd. Epsom BQ60 94
South Church Ct. N13 BX28 38
Palmerston Cres.
Southchurch Rd. E6 CK37 58
South Circular Rd. SE23 CC47 77
South Circular Rd. Rich. BM43 65
South Clo. N6 BV32 47

South Clo. Barn. BR24 28
South Clo. Bexh. CP45 69
South Clo. Dag. CR37 59
South Clo. Mord. BS53 86
South Clo. Pnr. BD30 36
South Clo. Pnr. BE33 45
South Clo. St. Alb. BF16 18
South Clo. Twick. BF48 74
South Clo. West Dr. AY41 63
South Clo. Wok. AR61 100
Southcombe St. W14 BR42 65
Southcote Av. Felt. BB48 73
Southcote Av. Surb. BM54 85
Southcote Beech, Wok. AR61 100
Southcote Rise, Ruis. BA33 44
Southcote Rd. E17 CC32 48
Southcote Rd. N19 BW35 47
Southcote Rd. SE25 CB53 87
Southcote Rd. Red. BW68 113
Southcote Rd. Sth. Croy. CA58 96
S. Cottage Dri. Rick. AV25 25
S. Cottage Gdns. Rick. AV25 25
South Cres. WC1 BW39 56
Southcroft Av. Well. CN45 68
Southcroft Av. W. Wick. CF55 87
Southcroft Rd. SW16 BV50 76
Southcroft Rd. SW17 BV50 76
Southcroft Rd. Orp. CN55 88
South Cross Rd. Ilf. CL32 49
Southdale Chig. CM29 40
Southdean Gdns. SW19 BR48 75
South Dene NW7 BN27 37
South Dolphin Rd. Sun. BB51 83
Southdown Av. W7 BJ41 64
Southdown Clo. SW20 BQ50 75
Crescent Rd.
Southdown Cres. Har. BF33 45
South Down Cres. Ilf. CN32 49
Southdown Rd. SW20 BQ51 85
Southdown Rd. Cars. BV58 95
Southdown Rd. Cat. CD64 105
Southdown Rd. Hat. BP14 10
Southdown Rd. Horn. CU33 50
Southdown Rd. Walt. BE56 93
South Dri. Dor. BK71 119
South Dr. SW11 BU44 66
South Dr. Bans. BU60 95
South Dr. Brwd. DB28 42
South Dr. Couls. BW61 104
South Dr. Orp. CN56 97
South Dr. Pot. B. BX18 20
South Dr. Rom. CV31 51
South Dr. Ruis. BB33 44
South Dr. Sutt. BR58 94
South Dr. Vir. W. AQ54 82
South Ealing Rd. W5 BK41 64
South Eastern Av. N9 CA27 39
South Eaton Pl. SW1 BV42 66
South Eden Pk. Rd. Beck. CE53 87
South Edwardes Sq. W8 BR41 65
South Emmwood Clo. Hem. H. AZ13 8
South End. W8 BS41 66
St. Alban's Gro.
South End Croy. BZ56 96
South End. Lthd. BF66 111
Southend Arterial Rd. Brwd. DB32 51
Southend Arterial Rd. Brwd. DC32 123
Southend Arterial Rd. Rom. CV30 42
Southend Arterial Rd. Upmin. CZ32 51
South End Clo. NW3 BU35 47
South End Rd.
Southend Clo. SE9 CL46 78
Southend Cres. SE9 CL46 78
South End Gn. NW3 BU35 47
Southend La. SE6 CD49 77
Southend La. SE26 CD49 77
Southend Rd. E6 CK36 58
Southend Rd. E18 CH30 40
South End Rd. NW3 BU35 47
Southend Rd. Beck. CE50 77
Southend Rd. Grays. DE42 71
South End Rd. Rain. CU37 59
Southend Rd. Wdf. Grn. CH30 40
South End Row W8 BS41 66
Southerby Mews N5 BY34 47
Southerby Rd.
Southerland Rd. N9 CB26 39
Southern Av. SE25 CA52 87
Southern Av. Felt. BC47 73
Southern Dr. Loug. CK25 31
Southern Gro. E3 CD38 57
Southernhay Loug. CJ24 31
Southern Link Rd. Hat. BO14 10
Southern Perimeter Rd. Houns. AY46 73
Southern Pl. Swan. CS52 89
Southern Rd. E13 CH37 58
Southern Rd. N2 BU31 47
Southern Rd. S. Ock. DB39 60
Southern Row W10 BR38 55
Southerns La. Couls. BT65 104
Southerns La. Couls. BT66 113
Southern St. N1 BX37 56
Southern Way. Harl. CL12 13
Southern Way. Harl. CP12 14
Southern Way Rom. CR32 50
Southerton Rd. W6 BQ41 65
Southey Rd. N15 CA32 48
Southey Rd. SW9 BY44 66
Southey Rd. SW19 BS50 76
Southey St. SE20 CC50 77
Southey Wk. Til. DG44 71
Southfield Barn. BQ25 28
Southfield. Welw. G. C. BQ9 5
Southfield Av. Wat. BD22 27
Southfield Clo. Uxb. AZ38 53
Southfield Clo. Wind. AL42 61
Southfield Pk. Har. BF31 45
Southfield Pl. Wey. AZ58 92
Southfield Rd. N17 CA30 39
Avenue, The,
Southfield Rd. W4 BO41 65
Southfield Rd. Chis. CN52 88
Southfield Rd. Enf. CB25 30
Southfield Rd. Hodd. CE11 12
Southfield Rd. Sev. CZ57 99
Southfield Rd. Wal. Cr. CD19 21
Southfields NW4 BP30 37
Southfields E. Mol. BH53 84
Southfields Av. Ashf. AZ50 73
Southfields Cotts. W7 BH41 64
Southfields Gdns. Twick. BH49 74
Southfields Rd. SW18 BS46 76
Southfields Rd. Cat. CE64 105
Southfleet Rd. Grav. DF47 81
Milroy Av.
Southfleet Rd. Orp. CN55 88
Southfleet Rd. Swans. DC47 81
South Gdns. SW19 BT50 76
South Gate. Harl. CM11 13
South Gate Av. Felt. BA49 73
Southgate Circle N14 BW26 38
Southgate Gro. N1 BZ36 57
Southgate Rd. N1 BZ37 57
Southgate Rd. Pot. B. BT20 20
Southgate St. Grays CY42 70
South Green Clo. Red. BY67 113
South Gro. E17 CD32 48
South Gro. N6 BV33 47
South Gro. N15 BZ32 48
South Gro. Cher. AV53 82
South Grove Ho. N6 BV33 47
South Hall Dr. Rain. CU39 59
South Hill, Chis. CK50 78
South Hill, Guil. AR71 118
South Hill Av. Har. BG34 45
South Hill Gro. Har. BH35 45
South Hill Rd. Brom. CG52 88
South Hill Rd. Hem. H. AX13 8
South Hl Pk. NW3 BU35 47
South Hl. Pk. Gdns. NW3 BU35 47
Southill La. Pnr. BC31 44
Southill Rd. Chis. CK50 78
Southill St. E14 CE39 57
South Island Pl. SW9 BX43 66
South Lambeth Pl. SW8 BX43 66
South Lambeth Road
South Lambeth Rd. SW8 BX43 66
Southland Rd. SE18 CN43 68
Southlands Av. Orp. CM56 97
Southlands Gro. Brom. CK52 88
Southlands La. Oxt. CE70 114
Southlands Rd. Brom. CJ53 88
Southlands Rd. Uxb. AV35 43
Southland Way Houns. BG46 74
South La. Kings-on-t. BK52 84
South La. N. Mal. BN52 85
South La. N. Mal. BO54 85
South La. W. N. Mal. BN52 85
Southlea Rd. Slou. AQ44 62
South Ley. Welw. G. C. BR9 5
South Lo. NW8 BT38 56
South Lodge Av. Mitch. BX52 86
South Lodge Cres. Enf. BW24 29
South Lodge Dr. N14 BW24 29
Southly Clo. Sutt. BS55 86
South Mall, N9 CB27 39
South Mall, The, N9 CB27 39
Knights La.
Southmead Epsom BO57 94
South Mead, Red. BU69 121
Southmead Cres. Wal. Cr. CD18 21
South Meadow La. Wind. AO43 61
South Meadows, Wem. BL35 46
Park Lawns
Southmead Rd. SW19 BR47 75
South Mimms By-Pass, Pot. B. BO19 19
South Molton La. W1 BV39 56
South Molton St. W1 BV39 56
Southmont Rd. Esher BH55 84
Southmoor Wk. E9 CD36 57
Trowbridge Est.
Southold Rise, SE9 CK48 78
Southolm St. SW11 BV44 66
Southover N12 BS27 38
Southover, Brom. CH49 78
South Pde. SW3 BT42 66
South Parade W4 BN42 65
South Park. Ger. Cr. AS32 43
South Park. Sev. CU66 116
South Pk. Clo. N. Mal. BN52 85
South Pk. Ct. Beck. CE50 77
South Pk. Cres. SE6 CG47 78
South Park Cres. Ger. Cr. AS31 43
South Pk. Cres. Ilf. CM34 49
South Park Dr. Ger. Cr. AS31 43
South Pk. Dr. Ilf. CN34 49
South Pk. Est. SE16 CB41 67
South Park Gdns. Berk. AQ12 7
South Pk. Hill Rd. Sth. Croy. BZ56 96
South Park La. Red. CB71 114
South Park Ley Rd. Cat. CC63 105
South Pk. Rd. SW19 BR50 75
South Pk. Rd. Ilf. CM34 49
South Pk. Ter. Ilf. CM34 49
South Park Vw. Ger. Cr. AS31 43
South Pk. Way Ruis. BD36 54
South Path. Wind. AO44 61
South Pl. SW19 BQ50 75
Thornton Rd.
South Pl. Enf. CC25 30
South St.
South Pl. Harl. CO9 6
South Pl. Surb. BL54 85
South Pl. Ms. EC2 BZ39 57
South Pl.
Southport Rd. SE18 CM42 68
South Ridge, Wey. AZ58 92
South Riding, St. Alb. BF18 18
South Rise Cars. BU58 95
South Rd. N9 CB26 39
South Rd. SE23 CC48 77
South Rd. SW19 BT50 76
South Rd. W5 BK42 64
South Rd. Amer. AO21 25
South Rd. Edg. BM30 37
South Rd. Egh. AR50 72
South Rd. Erith CT43 69
South Rd. Felt. BD49 74
South Rd. Guil. AQ69 118
South Rd. Hamptn. BE50 74
South Rd. Harl. CO9 6
South Rd. Rick. AU25 25
South Rd. Rom. CQ32 50
South Rd. S. Ock. DB40 60
South Rd. Sthl. BE40 54
South Rd. Twick. BG48 74
South Rd. West Dr. AY41 63
South Rd. Wey. AZ58 92
South Rd. Wey. BA56 92
South Rd. Wok. AR60 91
South Rd. Wok. AR61 100
South Row, SE3 CG44 68
South Row Enf. CC25 30
Southsea Av. Wat. BC24 26
Southsea Rd. Croy. BY54 86
Southsea Rd. Kings-on-t. BL52 85
South Side W6 BO41 65
Southside. Ger. Cr. AR31 43
South Side Common SW19 BQ50 75
Southspring, Sid. CM47 78
South Sq. NW11 BS32 47
South St. W1 BV40 56
South St. Brom. CH51 88
South St. Brwd. DB27 42
South St. Dor. BJ72 119
South St. Enf. CC25 30
South St. Epsom BN60 94
South St. Guil. AR71 118
South St. Islw. BJ45 64
South St. Rain. CS37 59
South St. Rom. CT32 50
South St. Stai. AV49 72
South Ter. SW7 BU42 66
South Ter. Dor. BJ72 119
South Ter. Surb. BL53 85
South, The, Glade, Bex. CQ47 79
South Vale, SE19 CA50 77
South Vale Har. BH35 45
Southvale Rd. SE3 CG44 68
South View Brom. CJ51 88
South Vw. Dart. CT46 79
South View Ave. Til. DG44 71
South View Av. NW10 BO35 46
Southview Cl. Swan. CT52 89
Willow Av.
South View Clo. Bex. CQ46 79
Southview Clo. Wal. Cr. CA16 21
Southview Cres. Ilf. CL32 49
South View Dr. E18 CH31 49
Southview Dr. Upmin. CX34 51
Southview Gdns. Wall. BW57 95
South View Rd. N8 BW31 47
Southview Rd. Brom. CF49 77
Southview Rd. Cat. CE65 105
South Vw. Rd. Dart. CV48 80
South View Rd. Ger. Cr. AR31 43
South View Rd. Grays. DB43 70
South Vw. Rd. Loug. CK25 31
South View Rd. Pnr. BC29 35
South View Rd. Warl. CB63 105
Southviews Sth. Croy. CC58 96
South Vill. NW1 BW36 56
Southville Clo. Epsom BN57 94
Southville Clo. Felt. BB47 73
Southville Cres. Felt. BB47 73
Southville Rd. Felt. BB47 73
Southville Rd. Surb. BJ54 84
South Wk. Hayes BA39 53
South Wk. Reig. BS70 121
South Wk. W. Wick. CG55 88
Southwark Br. EC4 BZ40 57
Southwark Br. SE1 BZ40 57
Southwark Bridge Rd. SE1 BY41 66
Southwark Gro. SE1 BZ40 57
Southwark Park Rd. SE16 CA42 67
Southwark St. SE1 BY40 56
Southwater Clo. E14 CD39 57
South Way N9 CC27 39
South Way N11 BW29 38
Ringway
Southway N20 BS27 38
Southway NW11 BS32 47
Southway SW20 BQ52 85
South Way Brom. CH54 88
South Way Cars. BT58 95
South Way Croy. CD55 87
Southway, Guil. AP70 118
South Way Har. BF31 45
Southway Wall. BW56 95
South Way, Wat. BA20 17
South Way, Wem. BL35 46
South Way, Wal. Abb. CE21 30
South Weald Rd. Brwd. DA27 42
Southwell Av. Nthlt. BF36 54
Southwell Gdns. SW7 BT41 66
Southwell Grove Rd. E11 CG34 49
Southwell Rd. SE5 BZ45 67
Southwell Rd. Croy. BY53 86
Southwell Rd. Harrow BK32 45
Southwest Rd. E11 CF33 48
South Wharf Rd. W2 BT39 56
Southwick Ms. W2 BT39 56
Southwick St.
Southwick St. W2 BU39 56
Southwirk Pl. W2 BU39 56
Southwold Dr. Bark. CO35 50
Southwold Rd. E5 CB34 48
Southwold Rd. Wat. BD22 27
Southwood Ave. Cher. AU57 91
Southwood Av. N6 BV33 47
Southwood Av. Couls. BW61 104
Southwood Av. Kings. On T. BN51 85
Southwood Av. Wok. AO62 100
Southwood Clo. Brom. CK52 88
Southwood Clo. Wor. Pk. BQ54 85
Southwood Ct. NW11 BS32 47
Southwood Dr. Surb. BN54 85
Southwood Gdns. Esher BJ55 84
Southwood Gdns. Ilf. CL31 49
Southwood La. N6 BV33 47
Southwood Lawn Rd. N6 BV33 47
Southwood Rd. SE9 CL48 78
South Worple Av. SW14 BO45 65
South Worple Way
South Worple Way, SW14 BN45 65
Sovereign Clo. W5 BK39 54
Sowerby Clo. SE9 CK46 78
Sowrey Av. Rain. CT36 59
Spacewaye Felt. BC46 73
Spackmans Way. Slou. AO41 61
Spa Clo. SE25 CA51 87
Spa Dr. Epsom. BM60 94
Spa Green Est. EC1 BY38 56
Spa Hill, SE19 BZ51 87
Spain Hall Rd, Ong. DB13 15
Spalding Rd. SW17 BV49 76
Spanby Rd. E3 CE38 57
Spangate, SE3 CG45 68
Spaniards Clo. NW11 BT33 47
Spaniards End NW3 BT33 47
Spaniards Rd. NW3 BT34 47
Spanish Pl. W1 BV39 56
Spanish Rd. SW18 BT46 76
Spareleaze Hill Loug. CK25 31
Sparepenny La. Eyns. CV54 90
Sparkbridge Rd. Har. BH31 45
Spa Rd. SE16 CA41 67
Sparrow Dr. Orp. CM54 88
Sparrow Farm Rd. Epsom. BP56 94
Sparrow Fm. Dr. Felt. BD47 74
Sparrow Grn. Dag. CR34 50
Sparrows Herne Bush. BF26 36
Sparrows La. SE9 CM47 78
Sparrows Way Bush. BG26 36
Sparrows Herne
Sparrowswick Ride, St. Alb. BG11 9
Sparsholt Rd. N19 BX33 47
Sparsholt Rd. Bark. CN37 58
Sparta St. SE10 CE44 67
Spearman St. SE18 CL43 68
Spear Ms. SW5 BS42 66
Spearpoint Gdns. Ilf. CN31 49
Spears Rd. N19 BX33 47
Speart La. Houns. BE43 64
Spedan Tower, NW3 BS34 47
Speedgate Hill Fawk. DA55 90
Speedwell St. SE8 CE43 67
Speer Rd. Surb. BH54 84
Speke Hill, SE9 CK48 78
Speke Rd. Th. Hth. BZ51 87
Speldhurst Clo. Brom. CG53 88
Speldhurst Rd. E9 CC36 57
Speldhurst Rd. W4 BN41 65
Spelman St. E1 CA39 57
Spelthorne Gro. Sun. BB50 73
Spelthorne La. Ashf. BA51 83
Spence Av. Wey. AY60 92
Spencer Av. N13 BX29 38
Spencer Av. Hayes BC39 53
Spencer Av. Wal. Cr. CA16 21
Spencer Clo. NW10 BL38 55
Spencer Clo. Orp. CN55 88
Spencer Clo. Uxb. AX38 53
Spencer Clo. Wdf. Grn. CJ28 40
Spencer Clo. Wok. AU60 91
Spencer Ct. NW8 BT37 56
Spencer Ct. SW20 BP51 85
Spencer Rd.
Spencer Ct. Rich. BK49 74
Spencer Dr. N2 BT32 47
Spencer Gdns. SE9 CK46 78
Spencer Gdns. SW14 BN46 75
Spencer Hill SW19 BR50 75
Spencer Hl. Rd. SW19 BR50 75
Spencer Pk. SW18 BT46 76
Spencer Pass. E3 CB37 57
Dinmont St.
Spencer Pl. SW1 BW41 66
Greycoat Pl.
Spencer Pl. Croy. BZ54 87
Spencer Rise, NW5 BV34 47
Spencer Rd. E6 CJ37 58
Spencer Rd. E17 CF30 39
Spencer Rd. N11 BW28 38
Spencer Rd. N17 CB30 39
Spencer Rd. SW18 BT45 66
Spencer Rd. SW20 BP51 85
Spencer Rd. W3 BN40 55
Spencer Rd. W4 BN43 65
Spencer Rd. Brom. CG50 78
Spencer Rd. Cat. BZ64 105
Spencer Rd. Cob. BC61 101
Spencer Rd. E. Mol. BG53 84
Spencer Rd. Har. BH30 36
Spencer Rd. Ilf. CN33 49
Spencer Rd. Islw. BG44 64
Spencer Rd. Mitch. BU54 86
Spencer Rd. Mitch. BV52 86
Spencer Rd. Rain. CS38 59
Spencer Rd. Slou. AS42 62
Spencer Rd. Sth. Croy. CA56 96
Spencer Rd. Twick. BH48 74
Spencer Rd. Wem. BK34 45
Spencers Croft. Harl. CO12 14
Spencers Gte. St. Alb. BH12 9
Spencer St. EC1 BY38 56
Spencer St. St. Alb. BG13 9
Spencer St. Sthl. BD41 64
Spencer Wk. SW15 BQ45 65
Spencer Wk. Rick. AW25 26
Spencer Wk. Til. DG44 71
Spencer Way, Hem. H. AW12 8
Spencer Way, Red. BV73 121
Spenser Av. Wey. AZ58 92
Spenser Cres. Upmin. CY33 51
Spenser Gro. N16 CA35 48
Spenser Rd. SE24 BY46 76
Spenser St. SW1 BW41 66
Spensley Wk. N16 BZ34 48
Spen St. Grav. DG47 81
Speranza St. SE18 CN42 68
Sperling Rd. N17 CA30 39
Spert St. E14 CD40 57
Spey Side N14 BW25 29
Spey Way Rom. CT29 41
Spezia Rd. NW10 BP37 55
Spicers Field. Lthd. BG60 93
Spicer St. St. Alb. BG13 9
Spices Yd. Croy. BZ56 96
South End.
Spielman Rd. Dart. CW44 70
Spiers Clo. N. Mal. BO53 85
Spigurnell Rd. N17 BZ30 39
Spikes Br. Rd. Sthl. BE39 54
Spillbutters Brwd. DA21 33
Spilsby Rd. Rom. CV29 42
Spilsey Clo. NW9 BO30 37
Spindles. Til. DG43 71
Spinel Clo. SE18 CN42 68
Spinnells Rd. Har. BE33 45
Spinners Wk. Wind. AO44 61
Spinner, The, SW16 BW48 76
Spinney Clo. N. Mal. BO53 85
Spinney Cress Rd. Slou. AN40 61
Spinney Dr. Felt. B47 73
Spinney Gdns. Dag. CQ35 50
Spinney Hill. Wey. AV56 91
Spinney Oak, Brom. CK51 88
Spinneys, The, Brom. CK51 88
Spinney, The, N21 BY26 38
Spinney, The, SW16 BW48 76
Spinney, The, Barn. BS23 29
Spinney, The, Epsom. BP63 103
Spinney, The Lthd. BF65 102
Spinney, The, Ong. CX18 24
Green Wk.
Spinney, The Pur. BY55 86
Spinney, The Pur. BY59 95
Spinney, The, Sid. CQ49 79
Spinney, The, Stan. BL28 37
Spinney, The, Sun. BC51 83
Spinney, The, Sutt. BQ56 94
Spinney The Wat. BC23 26
Spinney, The, Wem. BJ34 45
Spinney Way. Sev. CM59 97
Spinning Wheel Mead. Harl. CO12 14
Spire Clo. Grav. DG47 81
Spring Gro.
Spires, The, Dart. CV48 80
Spital Hth. Dor. BK71 119
Spital La. Brwd. CZ27 42
Spital Sq. E1 CA39 57
Spital St. E1 CA39 57
Spital St. Dart. CV46 80
Spondon Rd. N15 CB31 48
Tynemouth Rd.
Spook Hill, Dor. BJ74 119
Spooners Dr. St. Alb. BG17 18
Sportsbank St. SE6 CF47 77
Spottons Gro. N17 BZ30 39
Spout Hill Croy. CE56 96
Spout La. Stai. AW46 73
Spratt Hall Rd. E11 CH32 49
Spratts Alley. Cher. AV57 91
Spratts La. Cher. AV57 91
Spray St. SE18 CL42 68
Spreighton Rd. E. Mol. BF53 84
Sprimont Pl. SW3 BU42 66
Sprinfield Rd. Guil. AS71 118
Springall St. SE15 CB43 67
Springate Fld. Slou. AS41 62
Spring Av. Egh. AS50 72
Springbank N21 BX25 29
Springbank Av. Horn. CV35 51
Springbank Rd. SE13 CF46 77
Spring Bottom. Red. BY67 113
Springbourne Ct. Beck. CF51 87
Spring Bridge Ms. W5 BK40 54
Spring Bridge Rd.
Spring Bridge Rd. W5 BK40 54
Spring Clo. Borwd. BM23 28
Spring Clo. Sutt. BR57 94
Spring Clo. Uxb. AX30 35
Springcopse Rd. Reig. BT71 121
Spring Cott. Surb. BK53 84
St. Leonards Rd.
Spring Ct. Guil. AQ68 109
Spring Ct. Sid. CO48 79
Spring Court Rd. Enf. BY22 29
Springcroft Av. N2 BU31 47
Spring Crofts Bush. BF25 27
Springdale Rd. N16 BZ35 48
Spring Dr. Pnr. BC32 44
Springett Pl. Amer. AP22 25
Springfield E5 CB33 48
Springfield Bush. BG26 36
Springfield, Epp. CN19 22
Springfield. Oxt. CF68 114
Springfield, Wal. Abb. CG20 22
Springfield Av. N10 BW31 47
Springfield Av. SW20 BR52 85
Springfield Av. Brwd. DF26 122
Springfield Av. Hamptn. BF50 74

Springfield Av. Swan. CT52 89
Springfield Clo. Chesh. AO20 16
Springfield Clo. Pot. B. BT19 20
Springfield Clo. Rick. AZ25 26
Springfield Clo. Stan. BJ27 36
Springfield Clo. Wok. AP62 100
Springfield Dr. Ilf. CM32 49
Springfield Est. SW8 BW44 66
Springfield Gdns. E5 CB33 48
Springfield Gdns. NW9 BN32 46
Springfield Gdns. Brom. CK52 88
Springfield Gdns. Ruis. BC33 44
Springfield Gdns. Upmin. CY34 51
Springfield Gdns. Wdf. Grn. CJ29 40
Springfield Gdns. W. Wick. CE55 87
Springfield Gro. SE7 CJ43 68
Springfield Gro. Sun. BC51 83
Springfield La. NW6 BS37 56
Springfield La. Wey. AZ56 92
Springfield Meadows, Wey. AZ56 92
Springfield Mt. NW9 BN32 46
Springfield Rd. E4 CG26 40
Springfield Rd. E6 CK36 58
Springfield Rd. E15 CG38 58
Springfield Rd. E17 CD32 48
Springfield Rd. N11 BV28 38
Springfield Rd. N15 CB31 48
Springfield Rd. NW8 BT37 56
Springfield Rd. SE26 CB49 77
Springfield Rd. SW19 BR49 75
Springfield Rd. W7 BH40 54
Springfield Rd. Ashf. AY49 73
Springfield Rd. Bexh. CR45 69
Springfield Rd. Brom. CK52 88
Springfield Rd. Brox. CD13 12
Springfield Rd. Chesh. AO19 16
Springfield Rd. Dor. BF72 119
Springfield Rd. Epsom BQ58 94
Springfield Rd. Grays. DF40 71
Springfield Rd. Har. BH32 45
Springfield Rd. Hayes BD40 54
Springfield Rd. Hem. H. AY13 8
Springfield Rd. Kings. On T. BL52 85
Springfield Rd. St. Alb. BJ14 9
Springfield Rd. St. Alb. BM13 10
Springfield Rd. Slou. AT43 62
Springfield Rd. Tedd. BJ49 74
Springfield Rd. Th. Hth. BZ51 87
Springfield Rd. Twick. BF47 74
Springfield Rd. Wal. Cr. CD19 21
Springfield Rd. Wall. BV56 95
Springfield Rd. Well. CO45 69
Springfield Rd. Wind. AN44 61
Spring Fields, Welw. G. C. BP9 5
Springfield Wk. NW6 BS37 56
Springfield Wk. Orp. CM54 88
Farm Av.
Spring Gdns. SW1 BW40 56
Spring Gdns. Dor. BJ71 119
Spring Gdns. E. Mol. BG53 84
Spring Gdns. Horn. CU35 50
Spring Gdns. Orp. CO57 98
Spring Gdns. Rom. CS32 50
Spring Gdns. Wall. BW56 95
Spring Gdns. Wat. BD21 27
Spring Gdns. Wdf. Grn. CJ29 40
Spring Gdns. Wk. Sell. BX42 66
Goding St.
Spring Glen. Hat. BO13 10
Spring Gro. E3 CE37 57
Old Ford Rd.
Spring Gro. W4 BM42 65
Spring Gro. Grav. DG47 81
Spring Gro. Loug. CJ25 31
Spring Gro. Lthd. BF65 102
Spring Gro. Cres. Houns. BG44 64
Spring Gro. Rd. Houns. BF44 64
Spring Gro. Rd. Rich. BL46 75
Springhall La. CQ6 6
Springhall Rd. Saw. CQ6 6
Springhaven, Guil. AT70 118
Springhead Rd. Erith CT43 69
Springhead Rd. Grav. DE48 81
Springhead Rd. Sev CW62 108
Spring Hill E5 CB33 48
Spring Hills, Harl. CL10 6
Spring Lake Stan. BJ28 36
Spring La. E5 CB33 48
Spring La. SE25 CB53 87
Spring La. Hem. H. AW12 8
Spring La. Oxt. CF69 114
Spring La. Sev. DA64 108
Spring La. Slou. AM40 61
Spring Pk. Av. Croy. CC55 87
Spring Pk. Dr. N4 BZ33 48
Spring Pk. Dr. Beck. CF51 87
Spring Pk. Rd. Croy. CC55 87
Spring Pass. SW15 BQ45 65
Embankment, The,
Spring Pl. NW5 BV35 47
Spring Pond Meadow. Brwd. DB21 33
Springpond Rd. Dag. CQ35 50
Springrice Rd. SE13 CF46 77
Spring Rise, Egh. AS49 72
Spring Rd. Felt. BB48 73
Spring Shaw Clo. Sev. CS65 107
Springs, The Brox. CD16 21
Spring St. W2 BT39 56
Spring St. Epsom BO58 94
Spring St. Harl. CM9 6
Springvale Bexh. CR45 69
Spring Vale Dart. CV47 80
Spring Vale. Green. DB46 80
Spring Vale Clo. Swan. CT50 79
Springvale Est. W14 BR41 65
Springvale Rd. Brent. BL42 65
Springvale Ter. W14 BQ41 65
Spring Villa Rd. Edg. BM29 37
Spring Wk. Brox. CC14 12
Springwater Clo. SE18 CL44 68
Springwell Ave. Rick. AW27 35
Springwell Av. NW10 BO37 55
Springwell Clo. SW16 BX49 76
Springwell La. Rick. AW27 35
Springwell Rd. SW16 BX49 76
Springwell Rd. Houns. BD44 64
Springwood Clo. Uxb. AX30 35
Springwood Cres. Edg. BM27 37
Spring Woods, Vir. W. AQ52 82
Springwood Wk. St. Alb. BK12 9
Sprowston Ms. E7 CH35 49
Sprowston Rd. E7 CH35 49
Sprucedale Gdns. Croy. CC56 96
Spruce Hill. Harl. CN13 13
Spruce Hills Rd. E17 CE30 39
Sprules Rd. SE4 CD44 67
Spurfield E. Mol. BF52 84
Spurgate, Brwd. DD26 122
Spurgate Bowray. Brwd. DD27 122
Spurgeon Av. SE19 BZ51 87
Spurgeon Rd. SE19 BZ51 87
Spurgeon St. SE1 BZ41 67
Spurling Rd. SE22 CA45 67
Spurling Rd. Dag. CQ36 59
Spurrell Av. Bex. CS49 79
Spur Rd. N15 BZ31 48
Philip La.
Spur Rd. SW1 BW41 66
Spur Rd. Bark. CM38 58
Spur Rd. Edg. BL28 37
Spur Rd. Felt. BC46 73
Spur Rd. Islw. BJ43 64
Spur Rd. Orp. CO55 89
Spur Rd. Est. Edg. BL28 37
Spurstowe Ter. E8 CB35 48
Square, The, Berk. AT11 7
Square, The, Cars. BV56 95
Square, The, Ilf. CL33 49
Square, The, Rich. BL45 65
Quadrant, The,
Square, The, Saw. CQ6 6
Square, The Wat. BC22 26
Square, The, Wdf. Grn. CH28 40
Square. The. West Dr. AW44 63
Square. The. Wok. AY61 101
Squarey St. SW17 BT48 76
Squires Bridge Rd. Shep. AY52 83
Squires La. N3 BS30 38
Squires Mt. NW3 BT34 47
East Heath Rd.
Squires Rd. Hem. H. AY10 8
Squires Rd. Shep. AZ52 83
Squires Way Dart. CS49 79
Squires Wood Dr. Chis. CK50 78
Bullerswood Dr.
Squirrel Clo. Houns. BD45 64
Squirrels Clo. Lthd. BF65 102
Squirrels Grn. Wor. Pk. BO55 85
Squirrels Heath Av. Rom. CU31 50
Squirrels Hth. La. Rom. CV31 51
Squirrel's Hth. Rd. Rom. CW31 51
Squirrel's La. Buck. H. CJ27 40
Squirrels, The, SE13 CF45 67
Squirrels, The, Pnr. BE31 45
Squirrels Way Epsom BN61 103
Squirries St. E2 CB38 57
Stable End Orp. CM55 88
Stable Inn Bldgs. WC2 BY39 56
Southampton Bldgs.
Stable La. Beac. AO29 34
Stables Way, SE11 BY42 66
Stable Yd. Rd. SW1 BW40 56
Stacey Av. N18 CC28 39
Stacey Clo. E10 CF32 48
Stacey Clo. Grav. DJ49 81
Stacey St. WC2 BW39 56
Stackhouse St. SW3 BU41 66
Pavilion Rd.
Stacklands Clo. Sev. CZ57 99
Stacklands Rd. Welw. G. C. BP9 5
Stack La. Hart. DC53 90
Stacy Path SE5 BZ43 67
Elmington Estate
Stadium Rd. SE18 CK43 68
Stadium Rd. Dart. CT46 79
Crayford Rd.
Stadium St. SW10 BT43 66
Staffa Rd. E10 CC33 48
Stafford, Harl. CQ9 6
Stafford Av. Horn. CV31 51
Stafford Av. Wall. BX56 95
Stafford Clo. N14 BW25 29
Stafford Clo. NW6 BS38 56
Stafford Clo. Sutt. BR57 94
Stafford Clo. Wal. Cr. CB18 21
Stafford Ct. W8 BS41 66
Stafford Cripps Est. EC1 BZ38 57
Stafford Ms. NW6 BS38 56
Stafford Pl. SW1 BW41 66
Stafford Pl. Rich. BL47 75
Stafford Rd. E3 CD37 57
Stafford Rd. E7 CJ36 58
Stafford Rd. NW6 BS38 56
Stafford Rd. W3 BN41 65
Stafford Rd. Brox. CE13 12
Stafford Rd. Cat. CA65 105
Stafford Rd. Har. BG30 36
Stafford Rd. N. Mal. BN52 85
Stafford Rd. Ruis. BB35 44
Stafford Rd. Sid. CN49 78
Stafford Rd. Wall. BW57 95
Staffordshire St. SE15 CB43 67
Stafford St. W1 BW40 56
Stafford Ter. W8 BS41 66
Stafford Way, Sev. CV67 117
Staff St. EC1 BZ38 57
Cranwood St.
Stagbury Av. Couls. BU62 104
Stagbury Clo. Couls. BU63 104
Stag Clo. Edg. BM30 37
Staggart Grn. Chig. CO29 41
Stag Green Av. Hat. BQ11 10
Stag Hill Rd. Guil. AQ71 118
Stag La. NW9 BN30 37
Stag La. SW15 BO48 75
Stag La. Berk. AQ12 7
Stag La. Buck. H. CH27 40
Stag La. Edg. BN30 37
Stag La. Rick. AU25 25
Stag Pl. SW1 BW41 66
Stahlton La. Brwd. DC30 123
Stainash Cres. Stai. AW49 73
Stainbank Rd. Mitch. BV52 86
Stainby Rd. N15 CA31 48
Colsterworth Rd.
Stainer St. SE1 BZ40 57
Staines Av. Sutt. BQ55 85
Staines By-pass, Egh & Stai. AT49 72
Staines By-pass, Stai. & Ashf. AW49 73
Staines Clo. Cher. AV53 82
Staines Clo. Wal. Cr. CD17 21
Staines La. Cher. AV53 82
Staines Rd. Felt. AZ47 73
Staines Rd. Felt. BC46 73
Staines Rd. Ilf. CM35 49
Staines Rd. Stai. AS47 72
Staines Rd. Stai. AW50 73
Staines Rd. Stai. AW51 83
Staines Rd. Twick. BF48 74
Staines Rd. E. Sun. BC50 73
Staines Rd. W. Ashf. & Sun. AZ50 73
Stainford Clo. Ashf. BA49 73
Stainforth Rd. E17 CE31 48
Stainforth Rd. SW11 BU44 66
Stainforth Rd. Ilf. CM33 49
Staining La. EC2 BZ39 57
Gresham St.
Stainmore Clo. Chis. CM50 78
Stainsbury St. E2 CC37 57
Royston St.
Stainsby Pl. E14 CE39 57
Stainsby Rd. E14 CE39 57
Stainton Rd. SE6 CF46 77
Stainton Rd. Enf. CC23 30
Staleys Rd. Sev. DC63 108
Stalham St. SE16 CB41 67
Stalisfield Pla. Orp. CL58 97
Stambourne Way, SE19 CA50 77
Stambourne Way W. Wick. CF55 87
Stamford Brook Av. W6 BO41 65
Stamford Brook Rd. W6 BO41 65
Stamford Clo. N15 CB31 48
Stamford Rd.
Stamford Clo. Har. BH29 36
Stamford Clo. Pot. B. BT19 20
Stamford Clo. Sthl. BF40 54
Stamford Ct. W6 BO42 65
Stamford Dr. Brom. CG52 88
Stamford Gdns. Dag. CP36 59
Stamford Green Rd. Epsom. BM60 94
Stamford Gro. E. N16 CB33 48
Oldhill St.
Stamford Gro. W. N16 CB33 48
Oldhill St.
Stamford Hill N16 CA34 48
Stamford Hill Est. N16 CA33 48
Stamford Ho. W12 BP41 65
Stamford Rd. E6 CK37 58
Stamford Rd. N1 CA36 57
Stamford Rd. N15 CB32 48
Stamford Rd. Dag. CO37 59
Stamford Rd. Wat. BC23 26
Stamford St. NW8 BT38 56
Stamford St. SE1 BY40 56
Stamp Pl. E2 CA38 57
Stanborough Av. Borwd. BM22 28
Stanborough Grn. Welw. G. C. BQ9 5
Stanborough La. Welw. G. C. BQ9 5
Stanborough Pass. E8 BT36 56
Ngsland High St.
Stanborough Rd. Welw. G. C. BP9 5
Stanbridge Rd. SW15 BQ45 65
Stanbrook Rd. SE2 CO41 69
Stanbrook Rd. Grav. DF47 81
Stanbury Av. Wat. BB22 26
Stanbury Rd. SE15 CB44 67
Stancroft, NW9 BO32 46
Standard Rd. NW10 BN38 55
Standard Rd. Belv. CR42 69
Standard Rd. Bexh. CQ45 69
Standard Rd. Enf. CD22 30
Standard Rd. Houns. BE45 64
Standard Rd. Orp. CL58 97
Standen Av. Horn. CV34 51
Standen Rd. SW18 BR47 75
Standfield, Wat. BB19 17
Standfield Gdns. Dag. CR36 59
Standfield Rd. Dag. CR35 50
Standish Rd. W6 BP42 65
Standring Rise, Hem. H. AW15 8
Stand Rd. Wat. BD27 36
Stane St. Dor. BJ74 119
Stane St. Lthd. BL66 112
Stane Way, SE18 CJ43 68
Staneway Epsom BP58 94
Stanfield Rd. E3 CD37 57
Stanford Clo. Rom. CR32 50
Stanford Clo. Ruis. BA32 44
Stanford Clo. Wdf. Grn. CK28 40
Stanford Gdns. S. Ock. CZ40 60
Stanford Pl. SE17 CA42 67
Old Kent Rd.
Stanford Rivers Rd. Ong. CW19 24
Stanford Rd. N11 BU28 38
Stanford Rd. SW16 BW51 86
Stanford Rd. W8 BS41 66
Stanford Rd. Grays. DE41 71
Stanford St. SW1 BW42 66
Vincent Sq.
Stanford Way SW16 BW51 86
Stangate Cres. Borwd. BN24 28
Stangate Gdns. Stan. BJ28 36
Stanger Rd. SE25 CB52 87
Stanham Pl. Dart. CU45 69
Stanham Rd. Dart. CU46 79
Stanhope Av. N3 BR31 46
Stanhope Av. Brom. CG54 88
Stanhope Av. Har. BG30 36
Stanhope Bldgs. SE1 BZ41 67
Redcross Way
Stanhope Gdns. N4 BY32 47
Stanhope Gdns. N6 BV32 47
Stanhope Gdns. NW7 BO28 37
Stanhope Gdns. SW7 BT42 66
Stanhope Gdns. Dag. CQ34 50
Stanhope Gdns. Ilf. CK33 49
Stanhope Gte. W1 BV40 56
Stanhope Gro. Beck. CD53 87
Stanhope Heath, Stai. AX46 73
Stanhope Ms. E. SW7 BT42 66
Stanhope Gdns.
Stanhope Ms. S. SW7 BT42 66
Gloucester Rd.
Stanhope Pk. Rd. Grnf. BG38 54
Stanhope Pl. W2 BU39 56
Stanhope Rd. E17 CE32 48
Stanhope Rd. N6 BW32 47
Stanhope Rd. N11 BV28 38
Stanhope Rd. N12 BT28 38
Stanhope Rd. Barn. BQ25 28
Stanhope Rd. Bexh. CQ44 69
Stanhope Rd. Cars. BV57 95
Stanhope Rd. Croy. CA55 87
Stanhope Rd. Dag. CQ34 50
Stanhope Rd. Grnf. BG39 54
Stanhope Rd. Rain. CU37 59
Stanhope Rd. St. Alb. BH13 9
Stanhope Rd. Sid. CO49 79
Stanhope Rd. Swans. DC46 81
Stanhope St. NW1 BW37 56
Stanhope Ter. W2 BT40 56
Stanhope Way, Stai. AX46 73
Stanier Clo. SW5 BR42 65
Aisgill Av.
Stanlake Rd. W12 BP40 55
Stanlake Vill. W12 BQ40 55
Stanley Av. Bark. CN37 58
Stanley Av. Beck. CF51 87
Stanley Av. Dag. CQ33 50
Stanley Av. Grnf. BG37 54
Stanley Av. N. Mal. BP53 85
Stanley Av. Rom. CU31 50
Stanley Av. St. Alb. BF16 18
Stanley Av. Wem. BL36 55
Stanley Clo. Couls. BX62 104
Stanley Clo. Horn. CV34 51
Stanley Clo. Rom. CU31 50
Stanley Clo. Uxb. AX37 53
Stanley Clo. Wem. BL36 55
Stanley Cotts. Slou. AP40 52
Stanley Ct. Rd. Islw. BG44 64
Stanley Cres. W11 BR40 55
Stanley Cres. Grav. DH49 81
Stanley Gdns. NW2 BQ35 46
Stanley Gdns. SW17 BV50 76
Ashbourne Rd.
Stanley Gdns. W3 BO40 55
Stanley Gdns. W11 BR40 55
Stanley Gdns. Sth. Croy. CB59 96
Stanley Gdns. Wall. BW57 95
Stanley Gdns. Ms. W11 BR40 55
Kensington Pk. Rd.
Stanley Gdns. Rd. Tedd. BH49 74
Stanley Grn. Slou. AS42 62
Stanley Gro. SW8 BV44 66
Stanley Gro. Croy. BY53 86
Stanley Hill Amer. AO23 25
Stanley Hill Ave. Amer. AO23 25
Stanley Park Dr. Wem. BL36 55
Stanley Pk. Rd. Cars. BU57 95
Stanley Pass. NW1 BX37 56
Stanley Rd. E4 CF26 39
Stanley Rd. E10 CE32 48
Stanley Rd. E12 CK35 49
Stanley Rd. E15 CF37 57
Stanley Rd. E18 CG30 40
Stanley Rd. N2 BT31 47
Stanley Rd. N9 CA26 39
Stanley Rd. N10 BV29 38
Stanley Rd. N11 BW29 38
Stanley Rd. NW9 BP33 46
Broadway, The,
Stanley Rd. SW14 BM45 65
Stanley Rd. SW19 BS50 76
Stanley Rd. W3 BN41 65
Stanley Rd. Brom. CH52 88
Stanley Rd. Cars. BV57 95
Stanley Rd. Croy. BY54 86
Stanley Rd. Enf. CA24 30
Stanley Rd. Enf. CC25 30
Stanley Rd. Grav. DF47 81
Cooper's Rd.
Stanley Rd. Grays. DD42 71
Stanley Rd. Har. BG34 45
Stanley Rd. Horn. CV34 51
Stanley Rd. Houns. BG45 64
Stanley Rd. Ilf. CM34 49
Stanley Rd. Mitch. BV50 76
Stanley Rd. Mord. BS52 86
Stanley Rd. Nthwd. BC30 35
Stanley Rd. Orp. CN54 88
Stanley Rd. Sev. DA58 99
Stanley Rd. Sid. CO48 79
Stanley Rd. Sthl. BE40 54
Stanley Rd. Sutt. BS57 95
Stanley Rd. Swans. DC46 81
Stanley Rd. Twick. BG48 74
Stanley Rd. Wat. BD24 27
Stanley Rd. Wem. BL36 55
Stanley Rd. Wok. AS61 100
Stanley Rd. N. Rain. CT37 59
Stanley Rd. S. Rain. CT37 59
Stanley Sq. Cars. BU58 95
Stanley St. E6 CL40 58
Stanley St. SE8 CD43 67
Stanley St. Ashf. AY49 73
Stanley Way Orp. CO53 89
Stanley Wood. Amer. AP23 25
Stanmer St. SW11 BU44 66
Stanmore Gdns. Rich. BL45 65
Stanmore Gdns. Sutt. BT55 86
Stanmore Hill Stan. BJ27 36
Stanmore Pl. NW1 BV37 56
Arlington Rd.
Stanmore Rd. E11 CG33 49
Stanmore Rd. N15 BY31 47
Stanmore Rd. Belv. CS42 69
Stanmore Rd. Rich. BL45 65
Stanmore Rd. Wat. BC23 26
Stanmore St. N1 BX37 56
Stanmore Ter. Beck. CE51 87
Stanmore Way Loug. CL23 31
Stanmount Rd. St. Alb. BF16 18
Stannard Cres. E6 CL39 58
Stannard Rd. E8 CB36 57
Stannary St. SE11 BY43 66
Stansfield Rd. SW9 BX45 66
Stansfield Rd. Houns. BC44 63
Stansgate Rd. Dag. CR34 50
Stanstead Clo. Brom. CG53 88
Stanstead Dr. Hodd. CE11 12
Stanstead Rd. E11 CH32 49
Stanstead Rd. SE6 CC47 77
Stanstead Rd. SE23 CC47 77
Stanstead Rd. Cat. BZ67 114
Stanstead Rd. Hodd. CE11 12
Stanstead Rd. Houns. AY46 73
Stansted Clo. Horn. CV36 60
Stansted Cres. Bex. CP47 79
Stanswood Gdns. SE5 CA43 67
Sedgmoor Pl.
Stanthorpe Rd. SW16 BX49 76
Stanton Av. Tedd. BH50 74
Stanton Clo. Epsom. BM56 94
Stanton Clo. Wor. Pk. BQ55 85
Stanton Rd. SW13 BO44 65
Stanton Rd. SW20 BQ51 85
Stanton Rd. Croy. BZ54 87
Stantons, Harl. CL10 6
Stantons Harl. CL11 13
Stanton Sq. SE26 CD49 77
Stanton St. SE15 CB44 67
Stanton Way. Slou. AS42 62
Stanway Clo. Chig. CN28 40
Tine Rd.
Stanway Gdns. W3 BM40 55
Stanway Gdns. Edg. BN29 37
Stanway St. N1 CA37 57
Stanwell Clo. Stai. AX46 73
High St.
Stanwell Gdns. Stai. AX46 73
Stanwell Moor Rd. Stai. AW48 73
Stanwell Moor Rd. West Dr. AW43 63
Stanwell New Rd. Stai. AW48 73
Stanwell Rd. Ashf. AY48 73
Stanwell Rd. Felt. AZ47 73
Stanwell Rd. Slou. AT45 62
Stanwell Rd. Slou. AU45 62
Stanwick Rd. W14 BR42 65
Stanworth St. SE1 CA41 67
Millstream Rd.
Stanwyck Dr. Chig. CM28 40
Stanwyck Gdns. Rom. CU28 41
Stapenhill Rd. Wem. BJ34 45
Staplefield Clo. SW2 BX47 76
Staplefield Clo. Pnr. BE29 36
Stapleford Av. Ilf. CN32 49
Stapleford Clo. SW19 BR47 75
Beaumont Rd.
Stapleford Clo. Kings-on-t. BM52 85
Vincent Rd.
Stapleford Gdns. Rom. CR29 41
Stapleford Rd. Rom. CR25 32
Stapleford Rd. Wem. BK36 54
Stapleford Way, Bark. CO38 59
Bastable Av.
Staplehurst Clo. Reig. BT72 121
Staplehurst Rd. SE13 CF46 77
Staplehurst Rd. Cars. BU57 95
Staplehurst Rd. Reig. BT72 121
Staple Inn Bldgs. WC1 BY39 56
Holborn
Staple Lane. Guil. AX69 110
Staple's Rd. Loug. CJ24 31
Staple St. SE1 BZ41 67
Stapleton Cres. Rain. CU36 59
Stapleton Gdns. Croy. BY56 95
Stapleton Hall Rd. N4 BX33 47
Stapleton Rd. SW17 BV48 76
Stapleton Rd. Bexh. CQ43 69
Stapleton Rd. Borwd. BM22 28
Stapley Rd. Belv. CR42 69
Stapley Rd. St. Alb. BG13 9
Stapylton Rd. Barn. BR24 28
Starboard Ave. Green. DA46 80
Starboard Way, E14 CE41 67
Tiller St.
Starch House La. Ilf. CM30 40
Starcross St. NW1 BW38 56
Starfield Rd. W12 BP41 65
Star & Garter Hl. Rich. BL47 75

Star Hill Dart. CT46 79
Star Hill, Wok. AR63 100
Star Hill Rd. Sev. CQ61 107
Starkleigh Way, SE16 CB42 67
Egan Way
Star La. E16 CG38 58
Star La. Couls. BV64 104
Star La. Epp. CO18 23
Star La. Orp. CP52 89
Starling Clo. Buck. H. CH26 40
Starling Clo. Pnr. BD31 45
Starling La. Pot. B. BX17 20
Star Path Nthlt. BF37 54
Star Rd. W14 BR43 65
Star Rd. Islw. BG44 64
Star Rd. Uxb. BA38 53
Starrock La. Couls. BU63 104
Starrock Rd. Couls. BV63 104
Star St. E16 CG39 58
Star St. W2 BT39 56
Starts Clo. Orp. CL55 88
Starts Hill Av. Orp. CL56 97
Starts Hill Rd. Orp. CL56 97
Starts Rd. Orp. CL55 88
Starvecrow Clo. Ton. DB71 117
Starwood Clo. Wey. AX59 92
Star Yd. WC2 BY39 56
Staten Gdns. Twick. BH47 74
Statham Gro. N16 BZ34 48
Statham Gro. N18 CA28 39
Station App. E7 CH35 49
Woodford Rd.
Station App. E11 CG34 49
Station App. N11 BV28 38
Station App. SE3 CH45 68
Station App. SE26 CC49 77
Station App. SW6 BR45 65
Station App. SW11 BU45 66
St. Johns Hill
Station App. W3 BN41 65
Kingswood Rd.
Station Approach W13 BH40 54
Station App. Bex. CR47 79
High St.
Station App. Bexh. CQ44 69
Pickford La.
Station App. Bexh. CS44 69
Barnehurst Rd.
Station Approach Buck. H. CJ28 40
Station App. Chelsfield CO56 98
Station App. Chis. CK50 78
Elmstead Woods.
Station App. Chis. CL51 88
Station App. Couls. BW61 104
Station App. Dart. CW46 80
Station App. Debden CM24 31
Station App. Dor. BK70 119
Station App. E. Croy. BZ55 87
Station App. Elt. SE9 CK46 78
Station App. Epsom BN60 94
Station App. Ewell East. BP58 94
Station App. Ewell W. BO58 94
Station App. Ger. Cr. AS32 43
Station App. Grays CX42 70
Station App. Grays. DD43 71
Station App. Grnf. BJ36 54
Station App. Har. BH33 45
Station App. Hatch End BE29 36
Station App. Hayes CG54 88
Station App. Hem. H. AW15 8
Station App. Hinchley Wd. BH55 84
Station App. Loug. CK25 31
Station App. Mott. SE9 CK47 78
Station App. Nthwd. BB29 35
Station App. Orp. CN55 88
Station App. Pnr. BE31 45
Station Approach, Pot. B. BR19 19
Station App. Pur. BY59 95
Whytecliffe Rd.
Station App. Rich. BM44 65
Station App. Rick. AU24 25
Station App. Ruis. BC35 44
Station App. St. Mary Cray CO52 89
Station Approach, Shep. BA53 83
Station App. Slou. AP40 52
Station App. Stai. AW49 73
Station App. Sthl. BE41 64
Station App. Stoneleigh BO56 94
Station App. Sun. BC51 83
Station App. Swan. CT52 89
Station App. Upr. Warl. CA62 105
Station App. Uxb. AU33 43
Station App. Uxb. AW33 44
Station App. Uxb. AZ36 53
Station Approach, Vir. W. AR52 82
Station App. Wal. Cr. CD18 21
Station App. Wal. Cr. CD20 21
Station App. Wat. BB24 26
Station App. Well. CO44 69
Station App. West Dr. AY40 53
Station App. Wey. AW59 92
Station App. (Cray.) Dart. CT46 79
Station Rd.
Station App. E. Red. BU71 121
Station App. Elm Pk. Horn. CU35 50
Station App. N. Sid. CO48 79
Station Rd.
Station Approach Nth. Sid. CO48 79
Station Rd.
Station Approach Rd. Tad. BQ64 103
Station Approach Rd. Til. DG45 71
Station App. Southgate N14 BW26 38
Station Approach Sth. Sid. CO48 79
Station Rd.
Station App. W. Red. BU71 121
Station Ave. Cat. CB65 105
Station Av. Ewell W. BO58 94
Station Av. N. Mal. BO52 85
Station Av. Rich. BM44 65
Station Pde.
Station Av. Watt. BB56 92
Station Bldgs. Hayes CG54 88
Station Clo. N3 BS30 38
Station Clo. Hat. BR16 19
Station Clo. Hmptn. BF51 84
Station Clo. Pot. B. BR19 19
Station Clo. Pot. B. BS19 20
Station Cres. N15 BZ31 48
Station Cres. SE3 CH42 68
Station Cres. Ashf. AX49 73
Station Cres. Wem. BJ36 54
Station Dri. NW1 BW38 56
Station Est. Elmers End CC52 87
Station Est. Rd. Felt. BC47 73
Station Garage Mews SW16 BW50 76
Estreham Rd.
Station Gdns. W4 BN43 65
Station Gate, SE16 CC41 67
Station Gro. Wem. BL36 55
Station Hill, Hayes CH55 88
Station La. Brwd. DE32 123
Station La. Edg. BM29 37
Station La. Horn. CV34 51
Station Parade E11 CH32 49
High St.
Station Pde. NW2 BQ36 55
Station Pde. W3 BM39 55
Station Pde. Chipstead BU62 104
Station Parade, Vir. W. AR52 82
Station Pk. Sev. CU65 107
Station Pass. E18 CH30 40
Maybank Rd.
Station Path, Stai. AV49 72
Station Pl. N4 BY34 47
Station Rise, SE27 BY48 76
Norwood Rd.
Station Rd. E7 CH35 49
Station Rd. E10 CF34 48
Station Rd. E12 CJ35 49
Station Rd. E15 CF36 57
Station Rd. E17 CD32 48
Station Rd. N3 BS30 38
Station Rd. N11 BV28 38
Station Rd. N17 CB31 48
Station Rd. N18 CA28 39
Silver St.
Station Rd. N19 BW34 47
Junction Rd.
Station Rd. N22 BX30 38
Station Rd. NW4 BP32 46
Station Rd. NW7 BO28 37
Station Rd. NW10 BO37 55
Station Rd. SE20 CC50 77
Station Rd. SW13 BO44 65
Station Rd. W5 BL39 55
Station Rd. BJ71 119
Station Rd. Amer. AO23 25
Station Rd. Ash. BL61 103
Station Rd. Ashf. AY49 73
Station Rd. Barkingside CM31 49
Station Rd. Barn. BS25 29
Station Rd. Belmont BS58 95
Station Rd. Belv. CR41 69
Station Rd. Berk. AR12 7
Station Rd. Bet. BO69 120
Station Rd. Bexh. CQ45 69
Station Rd. Borwd. BM24 28
Station Rd. Brom. CH51 88
Station Rd. Brox. CD13 12
Station Rd. Cars. BU56 95
Station Rd. Cat. CD64 105
Station Rd. Cher. AV54 82
Station Rd. Chess. BL56 94
Station Rd. Chig. CL27 40
Station Rd. Chingford E4 CF26 39
Station Rd. Claygate BH56 93
Station Rd. Cob. BE62 102
Station Rd. Crayford. CT47 79
Station Rd. Dag. CP33 50
Station Rd. Egh. AS49 72
Station Rd. Epp. CO19 23
Station Rd. Epp. CR17 23
Station Rd. Esher BG55 84
Station Rd. Ger. Cr. AS32 43
Station Rd. Grav. DD46 81
Station Rd. Grav. DD49 81
Station Rd. Green. DA46 80
Station Rd. Guil. AS73 118
Station Rd. Hampton BK51 84
Station Rd. Hanwell W7 BH40 54
Station Rd. Har. BH31 45
Station Rd. Har. CM9 6
Station Rd. Harl. CP8 6
Station Rd. Harold Wd. CW30 42
Station Rd. Hat. BQ15 10
Station Rd. Hayes. BB41 63
Station Rd. Hayes. BB42 63
Station Rd. Hem. H. AW14 8
Station Rd. Hmptn. BF51 84
Station Rd. Houns. BF45 64
Station Rd. Ilf. CL34 49
Station Rd. Ken. BZ60 96
Station Rd. Kings L. AZ18 17
Station Rd. Kings. On T. BM51 85
Station Rd. Knockholt CQ58 98
Station Rd. Long. DC52 90
Station Rd. Loug. CK24 31
Station Rd. Lthd. BJ64 102
Station Rd. Motspur Pk. BP53 85
Station Rd. Norwood Junc. SE25 CA52 87
Station Rd. Orp. CN55 88
Station Rd. Pnr. BE31 45
Station Rd. Pot. B. BX18 20
Station Rd. Rad. BJ21 27
Station Rd. Red. BU70 121
Station Rd. Red. BW67 113
Station Rd. Rick. AX26 35
Station Rd. St. Alb. BM13 10
Station Rd. St. Mary Cray CP52 89
Station Rd. Saw. CQ5 6
Station Rd. Sev. CQ59 98
Station Rd. Sev. CT63 107
Station Rd. Sev. CU59 98
Station Rd. Sev. CU61 107
Station Rd. Shep. BA53 83
Station Rd. Shortlands CG51 88
Station Rd. Sid. CO49 79
Station Rd. Slou. AT41 62
Station Rd. S. Dnth. CX51 90
Station Rd. S. Ock. DB38 60
Station Rd. Stai. AS46 72
Station Rd. Sun. BC50 73
Station Rd. Swan. CT52 89
Station Rd. Tedd. BH49 74
Station Rd. Thames Ditton BH54 84
Station Rd. Til. DJ43 71
Station Rd. Twick. BH47 74
Station Rd. Upmin. CY34 51
Station Rd. Upr. Warl. CA62 105
Station Rd. Uxb. AX38 53
Station Rd. Wal. Cr. CE20 21
Station Rd. Wat. BC23 26
Station Rd. Welw. G. C. BR5 5
Station Rd. W. Croy. BZ54 87
Station Rd. W. Wick. CF54 87
Station Rd. Wey. AW59 92
Station Rd. Wey. AX56 92
Station Rd. Winchmore Hill N21 BY26 38
Station Rd. Wok. AP59 91
Station Rd. Wok. AS62 100
Station Rd. E. Oxt. CG67 115
Station Rd. Gidea Pk. Rom. CU31 50
Station Rd. N. Belv. CR41 69
Station Rd. N. Har. BF32 45
Station Rd. N. Red. BW67 113
Station Rd. S. Red. BW67 113
Station Rd. W. Oxt. CG68 115
Station Row, Guil. AS73 118
Station Sq. Pett's Wd. CM53 88
Station Sq. St. Mary Cray CO52 89
Station St. E15 CF36 57
Station St. E16 CL40 58
Station St. Grav. DD46 81
Station Ter. NW10 BQ37 55
Station Ter. SE5 BZ44 67
Station Rd.
Station Vw. Grnf. BG37 54
Station Vill. NW7 BQ29 37
Bittacy Hill
Station Way Cheam BR57 94
Station Way Claygate BH57 93
Station Way Roding Vall. CJ28 40
Station Way. Welw. G. C. BQ7 5
Station Yd. Twick. BJ47 74
Staunton Rd. Kings. On T. BL50 75
Staunton Rd. Slou. AO39 52
Staunton St. SE8 CD43 67
Staveley Cl. N7 BX35 47
Penn Rd.
Staveley Clo. E9 CC35 48
Churchill Wk.
Staveley Gdns. W4 BN44 65
Staveley Rd. W4 BN43 65
Staveley Rd. Ashf. BA50 73
Staveley Way, Wok. AP62 100
Staverton Rd. NW2 BQ36 55
Staverton Rd. Horn. CV32 51
Stavordale Rd. N5 BY35 47
Stavordale Rd. Cars. BT54 86
Stayne End, Vir. W. AQ52 82
Stayners Rd. E1 CC38 57
Stayton Rd. Sutt. BS55 86
Steadman Clo. Bex. CT48 79
Stead St. SE17 BZ42 67
Steam Farm La. Felt. BB45 63
Stean St. E8 CA37 57
Stebbing Way, Bark. CO37 59
Stebondale St. E14 CF42 67
Stedman Clo. Uxb. AZ34 44
Steedman St. SE17 BY42 66
Steeds Rd. N10 BU30 38
Steeds Way Loug. CK24 31
Steele Rd. E11 CG35 49
Steele Rd. E15 CG37 58
Steele Rd. N17 CA31 48
Steele Rd. NW10 BN37 55
Steele Rd. W4 BN41 65
Steele Rd. Islw. BJ45 64
Steele's Ms. NW3 BU36 56
Steele's Rd. NW3 BU36 56
Steel's La. E1 CC39 57
Devonport St.
Steel's La. Lthd. BF60 93
Steen Way, SE22 CA46 77
Dulwich Gro.
Steep Clo. Orp. CN57 97
Steep Hill, SW16 BW48 76
Steep Hill. Wok. AO57 91
Steeple Clo. SW6 BR45 65
Steeple Clo. SW19 BR49 75
Steeplestone Clo. N18 BZ28 39
Steerforth St. SW18 BS48 76
Steerlands Bush. BF26 36
Steer's Mead, Mitch. BU51 86
Stella Rd. SW17 BU50 76
Stelling Rd. Erith CS43 69
Stembridge Rd. SEI0 CB51 87
Stents La. Cob. BE63 102
Stepgates Mead La. Cher. AW54 83
Stephen Av. Rain. CU36 59
Stephen Clo. Egh. AU50 72
Stephendale Rd. SW6 BS45 66
Stephen House, E1 CB40 57
Stephen Rd. Bexh. CS45 69
Stephens Clo. Pnr. BD32 45
Stephens Gro. SE13 CF45 67
Stephen's Ms. W1 BW39 56
Gresse St.
Stephenson Ave. Til. DG44 71
Stephenson Rd. W7 BH39 54
Stephenson St. E16 CG38 58
Stephenson St. NW10 BO38 55
Stephenson Way NW1 BW38 56
Stephens Rd. E15 CG37 58
Stephen St. W1 BW39 56
Stepney Causeway, E1 CC39 57
Stepney Green E1 CC39 57
Stepney Grn. Dws. E1 CC39 57
Hayfield Pass
Stepney High St. E1 CC39 57
Stepney Way, E1 CB39 57
Sterling Av. Edg. BL28 37
Sterling Av. Wal. Cr. CC20 21
Sterling Rd. Enf. BZ22 30
Sterling Rd. Enf. BZ23 30
Sterling St. SW7 BU41 66
Montpelier Pl.
Sterndale Rd. W14 BQ41 65
Sterndale Rd. Dart. CW47 80
Sterne St. W12 BQ41 65
Sternhall La. SE15 CB44 67
Sternhold Av. SW2 BW48 76
Sterry Cres. Dag. CR35 50
Sterry Dr. E. Mol. BH53 84
Sterry Dr. Epsom BO56 94
Sterry Gdns. Dag. CR36 59
Sterry Rd. Bark. CN37 58
Sterry Rd. Dag. CR35 50
Sterry St. SE1 BZ41 67
Stevedale Rd. Well. CP44 69
Stevenage Cres. Borwd. BL23 28
Stevenage Rise, Hem. H. AY11 8
Stevenage Rd. E12 CL36 58
Stevenage Rd. SW6 BQ43 65
Stevens Av. E9 CC36 57
Stevens Clo. Beck. CE50 77
Stumps Hill La.
Stevens Clo. Bex. CS49 79
Stevens Cott. NW2 BP36 55
High Rd.
Stevens Grn. Bush. BG26 36
Stevenson Clo. Erith. CU43 69
Stevenson Rd. Slou. AO34 43
Stevens Rd. Dag. CO34 50
Stevens's La. Esher BJ57 93
Stevens Way, Chig. CN28 40
Steventon Rd. W12 BO40 55
Steward Clo. Wal. Cr. CD18 21
Stewards Clo. Epp. CO20 23
Steward's Green Rd. Epp. CO19 23
Steward's Green Rd. Epp. CO20 23
Steward St. E1 CA39 57
Steward Wk. Rom. CT32 50
Stewart Av. Shep. AZ52 83
Stewart Av. Slou. AP39 52
Stewart Clo. NW9 BN32 46
Stewart Clo. Maid. AH44 61
Stewart Clo. Wat. BB19 17
Stewart Rd. E15 CF35 48
Stewarts Av. Upmin. CX34 51
Stewartsby Clo. N18 BZ28 39
Stewart's La. SW8 BV43 66
Stewarts Rd. SW8 BW44 66
Stewart's Rd. Hamptn. BE50 74
Stewart St. E14 CF41 67
Stewart's Wk. SW3 BU42 66
Stewart Way, Stai. AW50 73
Stew La. EC4 BZ40 57
Broken Wharf
Steyne Rd. W3 BM40 55
Steyning Clo. Ken. BY61 104
Steyning Gro. SE9 CK49 78
Steynings Way N12 BS28 38
Steyning Way Houns. BD45 64
Steynton Av. Bex. CP48 79
Sth Birkbeck Rd. E11 CF34 48
Sth Black Lion La. W6 BP42 65
Sth. Common Rd. Uxb. AY36 53
Sth. Countess Rd. E17 CD31 48
Sth. Croxted Rd. SE21 BZ48 77
Sth. Eldon Pl. EC2 BZ39 57
Sth. Esk Rd. E7 CJ36 58
Sth. Hill Rd. Grav. DH47 81
Sth. Kent Av. Grav. DE46 81
Sth. Lodge W5 BK40 54
Webster Gdns.
Sth. Molton Rd. E16 CH39 58
Sth. Norwood Hl. SE25 CA51 87
Sth. Tenter St. E1 CA40 57
Sth. Vw. Ct. Wok. AS62 100
Constitution Hill
Sth. View Rd. Ash. BK63 102
Sth. Western Rd. Twick. BJ46 74
Stickland Rd. Belv. CR42 69
Stickleton Clo. Grnf. BF38 54
Stifford Clays Rd. Grays. DC40 71
Stifford Est. E1 CC39 57
Stifford Hill. S. Ock. DB40 60
Stifford Ho. E1 CC39 57
Stifford Rd. S. Ock. CZ40 60
Stilecroft. Harl. CO12 14
Stilecroft Gdns. Wem. BJ34 45
Stile Hall Gdns. W4 BM42 65
Stile Path Sun. BC52 83
Stiles Clo. Brom. CK53 88
Stillingfleet Rd. SW13 BP43 65
Stillington St. SW1 BW42 66
Stillness Rd. SE23 CD46 77
Stilton Cres. NW10 BN36 55
Stirling Clo. Bans. BR62 103
Stirling Clo. Rain. CU38 59
Stirling Clo. Uxb. AX38 53
Stirling Clo. Wind. AL44 61
Stirling Dr. Orp. CO56 98
Stirling Rd. E13 CH37 58
Stirling Rd. E17 CD31 48
Stirling Rd. N17 CB30 39
Stirling Rd. N22 BY30 38
Stirling Rd. SW9 BX44 66
Stirling Rd. W3 BM41 65
Stirling Rd. Har. BH31 45
Stirling Rd. Hayes BC40 53
Stirling Rd. Houns. AY46 73
Southampton Rd.
Stirling Rd. Twick. BF47 74
Stirling Rd. Pth. E17 CD31 48
Stirling St. SW7 BU41 66
Stirling Wk. Surb. BM53 85
Stirling Way, N18 BZ28 39
Stites Hill Rd Cat. BY64 104
Stiven Cres. Har. BE34 45
Stk. Station App. Red. BX71 121
Stoats Nest Rd. Couls. BX60 95
Stoats Nest Village Couls. BX61 104
Stockbreach Cl. Hat. BP12 10
Stockbreach Rd. Hat. BP12 10
Stockdale Rd. Dag. CQ34 50
Stockdales Rd. Wind. AM42 61
Stockdove Way Grnf. BH38 54
Stockers Farm Rd. Rick. AX27 35
Stockers La. Wok. AT63 100
Stockfield Brwd. CZ22 33
Stockfield Av. Hodd. CE11 12
Stockfield Rd. SW16 BX48 76
Stockfield Rd. Esher BH56 93
Stock Hill, West. CJ61 106
Stocking La. Hert. BW11 11
Stocking La. Hert. BY12 11
Stockingswater La. Enf. CD23 30
Stockland Rd. Rom. CS32 50
Stock La. Dart. CV49 80
Stockley Clo. West Dr. AZ41 63
Stockley Rd. West Dr. AZ40 53
Stockley Rd. West Dr. AZ42 63
Stock Orchard Cres. N7 BX35 47
Stock Orchard St. N7 BX35 47
Stockport Rd. SW16 BW51 86
Stocksfield Rd. E17 CF31 48
Stocks La. Brwd. CZ22 33
Stock St. E13 CH37 58
Stockton Gdns. N17 BZ29 39
Stockton Gdns. NW7 BN27 37
Stockton Rd. N17 BZ29 39
Stockton Rd. N18 CB29 39
Stockton Rd. Reig. BS72 121
Stockwell Av. SW9 BX45 66
Stockwell Clo. Wal. Cr. CB17 21
Stockwell Gdns. SW9 BX44 66
Stockwell Grn. SW9 BX44 66
Stockwell La. SW9 BX44 66
Stockwell La. Wal. Cr. CB17 21
Stockwell Pk. SW9 BX45 66
Stockwell Park Cres. SW9 BX44 66
Stockwell Park Rd. SW9 BX44 66
Stockwell Rd. SW9 BX44 66
Stockwell St. SE10 CF43 67
Stockwood St. SW11 BT45 66
Plough Rd.
Stocton Rd. Guil. AR70 118
Stodart Rd. SE20 CC51 87
Sto Elmo Cres. Slou. AO38 52
Stofield Gdns. SE9 CJ48 78
Stoford Clo. SW19 BR47 75
Southmead Rd.
Sto Johns Rd. Dart. CY47 80
Stoke Av. Ilf. CO29 41
Stoke Clo. Cob. BE61 102
Stoke Common Rd. Slou. AQ35 43
Stoke Ct. Dr. Slou. AP37 52
Stokefields, Guil. AR71 118
Stoke Gdns. Slou. AP40 52
Stoke Grn. Slou. AQ38 52
Stokenchurch St. SW6 BS44 66
Stoke Newington Church St. N16 BZ34 48
Stoke Newington Common N16 CA34 48
Stoke Newington High St. N16 CA34 48
Stoke Newington Rd. N16 CA35 48
Stoke Pl. NW10 BO38 55
Stoke Poges La. Slou. AP40 52
Stoke Rd. Cob. BD61 102
Stoke Rd. Guil. AR70 118
Stoke Rd. Kings. On T. BN50 75
Stoke Rd. Rain. CV37 60
Stoke Rd. Slou. AP40 52
Stoke Rd. Walt. BD55 84
Stokesby Rd. Chess. BL57 94
Stokesheath Rd. Lthd. BG59 93
Stokesley St. W12 BO39 55
Stokes Rd. E6 CK38 58
Stokes Rd. Croy. CC53 87
Stoke St. Cob. BD61 102
Stoke Wood La. Slou. AP35 43
Stompits Rd. Maid. AG43 61
Stompond La. Walt. BC55 83
Stonard Rd. N13 BY27 38
Stonard Rd. Dag. CO35 50
Stonards Hill Epp. CO18 23
Stonards Hill Loug. CK25 31
Stondon Pk. SE23 CD47 77
Stondon Rd. Ong. CX18 24
Stondon Wk. E6 CJ37 58
Stonebridge Est. E8 CA37 57
Stonebridge Pk. NW10 BN36 55
Stonebridge Rd. N15 CA32 48
Stonebridge Rd. Grav. DD46 81

Stonebridge Way Wem. BM36 55
Stone Bldgs. WC2 BX39 56
Stone Clo. West Dr. AY40 53
Stonecot Clo. Sutt. BR54 85
Stonecot Hill Sutt. BR54 85
Stonecroft Av. Iver. AV39 52
Stonecroft Rd. Erith CS43 69
Stonecroft Way Croy. BX54 86
Stone Cross, Harl. CM10 6
Stonecross, St. Alb. BH13 9
Stonecross Rd. Hat. BP11 10
Stone Cross Rd. Swan. CS53 89
Stonecutter St. EC4 BY39 56
Shoe La.
Stonefield Clo. Bexh. CR45 69
Stonefield Clo. Ruis. BE35 45
Stonefield Way, SE7 CJ43 68
Green Bay Rd.
Stonefield Way Ruis. BE35 45
Stonegrove Edg. BL28 37
Stone Gro. Ct. Edg. BL28 37
Stone Gro. Gdns. Edg. BL28 37
Stonehall Av. Ilf. CK32 49
Stone Hall Rd. N21 BX26 38
Stoneham Rd. E5 CB34 48
Stoneham's Hill. Dart. CT45 69
Stonehill Clo. SW14 BN46 75
Stonehill Cres. Wok. AS57 91
Stonehill Grn. Rd. Dart. CS50 79
Stonehill Rd. SW14 BN46 75
Stonehill Rd. W4 BM42 65
Wellesley Rd.
Stonehill Rd. Wok. AR58 91
Stonehills. Welw. G. C. BQ7 5
Stonehills Ct. SE21 CA48 77
Stone Ho. Ct. EC3 CA39 57
Houndsditch
Stonehouse Gdns. Cat. CA66 114
Stonehouse La. Grays CZ43 70
Stonehouse La. Sev. CP58 98
Stonehouse Rd. N11 BW28 38
Stonehouse Rd. Sev. CP58 98
Stoneings La. Sev. CN62 106
Stonelea Rd. Hem. H. AY14 8
Stoneleigh Av. Enf. CB22 30
Stoneleigh Av. Wor. Pk. BP55 85
Stoneleigh Clo. Wal. Cr. CC20 21
Stoneleigh Ct. Ilf. CK31 49
Stoneleigh Cres. Epsom BO56 94
Stoneleigh Dr. Hodd. CE10 12
Stoneleigh Pk. Av. Croy. CC53 87
Stoneleigh Pk. Rd. Epsom BO57 94
Stoneleigh Pl. W11 BQ40 55
Stoneleigh Rd. N17 CA30 39
Chestnut Rd.
Stoneleigh Rd. N17 CA31 48
Stoneleigh Rd. Cars. BU54 86
Stoneleigh Rd. Ilf. CK31 49
Stoneleigh Rd. Oxt. CK68 115
Stoneleigh, Saw. CQ5 6
Stoneleigh St. W11 BQ40 55
Stonell's Rd. SW11 BU46 76
Chatham Rd.
Stonemead. Welw. G. C. BQ5 5
Stone Ness Rd. Grays. DA43 70
Stonenest St. N4 BX33 47
Evershot Rd.
Stone Pk. Av. Beck. CE52 87
Stone Pl. Wor. Pk. BP55 85
Stone Place Rd. Green. CZ46 80
Stone Rd. Brom. CG53 88
Stones Alley Wat. BC24 26
Stones End St. SE1 BZ41 67
Stones La. Dor. BG72 119
Stone's Rd. Epsom BO59 94
Stone St. Croy. BY56 95
Stone St. Grav. DG47 81
Stone St. Sev. CY65 108
Stone St. Sev. CZ66 117
Stoneswood Rd. Oxt. CH68 115
Stonewood Dart. DB48 80
Stonewood Rd. Erith CT42 69
Stone Yard La. E14 CF40 57
Stoney Brook, Guil. AP70 118
Stoney Ct. Welw. G. C. BS7 5
Stoneycroft Clo. SE12 CG47 78
Stoneycroft Rd. Wdf. Grn. CK29 40
Stoneydown Av. E17 CD31 48
Stoneyfield Rd. Couls. BX62 104
Stoneyfields Gdns. Edg. BN28 37
Stoneyfields La. Edg. BN28 37
Stoneylands Ct. Egh. AS49 72
Stoneylands Rd. Egh. AS49 72
Stoney La. E1 CA39 57
Stoney La. SE19 CA50 77
Stoney La. Hem. H. AT17 16
Stoney La. Kings L. AV19 16
Stoney Meade. Slou. AN40 61
Stoney Pl. Wind. AO44 61
Stoney St. SE1 BZ40 57
Stonhouse St. SW4 BW45 66
Stonny Croft, Ash. BL62 103
Stonor Rd. W14 BR42 65
Stony Hill Esher BE57 93
Stony La. Amer. AS22 25
Stony La. Ong. CU15 14
Stony La. Ong. CV16 24
Stony Path Loug. CK23 31
Stonyshotts, Wal. Abb. CG20 22
Stopford Rd. E13 CH37 58
Stopford Rd. SE17 BY42 66
Store Gdns. Brwd. DE25 122
Store Rd. E16 CL41 68
Store St. E15 CF35 48
Store St. WC1 BW39 56
Storey Rd. E17 CD32 48
Storey Rd. N6 BU32 47
Storey's Gate. SW1 BW41 66
Storey St. E16 CL40 58
Storey St. Hem. H. AX15 8
Stories Ms. SE5 CA44 67
Stories Rd. SE5 CA45 67
Stork Rd. E7 CG36 58
Storksmead Rd. Edg. BO29 37
Storks Rd. SE16 CB41 67
Stormont Av. N6 BU33 47
Stormont Rd. SW11 BV45 66
Stormont Way Chess. BK56 93
Stormount Dr. Hayes. BA41 63
Stornaway Strand, Grav. DJ49 81
Stornoway Hem. H. AZ14 8
Northend
Storrington Rd. Croy. CA54 87
Stortford Rd. Hodd. CE11 12
Stothard St. E1 CC38 57
Colebert Av.
Stoughton Av. Sutt. BQ56 94
Stoughton Rd. Guil. AQ69 118
Stour Av. Sthl. BF41 64
Stourcliffe St. W1 BU39 56
Stour Clo. Kes. CJ56 97
Stour Clo. Slou. AN41 61
Stourhead Clo. SW19 BQ47 75
Castlecombe Dr.
Stourhead Gdns. SW20 BP51 85
Stour Rd. E3 CE36 57
Stour Rd. Dag. CR34 50
Stour Rd. Dart. CU45 69
Stour Rd. Grays. DG42 71
Stourton Av. Felt. BF49 74
Stour Way, Upmin. CZ32 51
Stovell Rd. Wind. AN43 61
Stowage, The, SE8 CE43 67
Stowe Cres. Ruis. BA32 44
Stowe Gdns. N9 CA26 39
Stowell Av. Croy. CF58 96
Stowe Pl. N15 CA31 48
Stowe Rd. W12 BP41 65
Stowe Rd. Orp. CO56 98
Stow, The, Harl. CN10 6
Stowting Rd. Orp. CN56 97
Stox Mead Har. BG30 36
Stracey Rd. E7 CH35 49
Stracey Rd. NW10 BN37 55
Strachen Pl. SW19 BQ50 75
Stradbroke Dr. Chig. CL29 40
Stradbroke Gro. Ilf. CK31 49
Stradbroke Rd. N5 BZ35 48
Balfour Rd.
Stradbrooke Gro. Buck. H. CJ26 40
Stradella Rd. SE24 BZ46 77
Strafford Av. Ilf. CL30 40
Strafford Clo. Pot. B. BS19 20
Strafford Gate, Pot. B. BS19 20
Strafford Rd. W3 BN41 65
Bollo Bridge Rd.
Strafford Rd. Barn. BR24 28
Strafford Rd. Houns. BE45 64
Strafford Rd. Twick. BJ47 74
Strahan Rd. E3 CD38 57
Straight Rd. Rom. CU28 41
Straight Rd. Wind. AQ46 72
Straight, The, Sthl. BE41 64
Straitsmouth SE10 CF43 67
Straits, The Wal. Abb. CE19 21
Strakers Rd. SE22 CB45 67
Strand WC2 BX40 56
Strand Clo. Epsom. BN63 103
Strand La. WC2 BX40 56
Temple Pl.
Strand On The Green W4 BM43 65
Strangeways, Wat. BB21 26
Stranraer Rd. Houns. AY46 73
Southampton Rd.
Stranraer Way, N1 BX36 56
Gifford St.
Stratfield Dr. Brox. CD13 12
Stratfield Rd. Borwd. BL24 28
Stratford Av. W8 BS41 66
Stratford Av. Uxb. AY37 53
Stratford Clo. Bark. CO36 59
Stratford Clo. Dag. CS36 59
Stratford Gro. SW15 BQ45 65
Stratford Pl. W1 BV39 56
Stratford Rd. E13 CG37 58
Stratford Rd. NW4 BQ31 46
Stratford Rd. W8 BS41 66
Stratford Rd. Hayes BC38 53
Stratford Rd. Sthl. BE42 64
Stratford Rd. Th. Hth. BY52 86
Stratford Rd. Wat. BC23 26
Stratford St. E14 CE41 67
Stratford Vill. NW1 BW36 56
Stratford Way, Hem. H. AW15 8
Stratford Way, Wat. BB23 26
Strathan Clo. SW18 BR46 75
Strathaven Rd. SE12 CH46 78
Strathblaine Rd. SW11 BT45 66
Strathbrook Rd. SW16 BX50 76
Strathcona Ave. Lthd. BE67 111
Strathcona Rd. Wem. BK34 45
Strathdale SW16 BX49 76
Strathdon Dr. SW17 BT48 76
Strathearn Ave. Hayes. BB43 63
Strathearn Av. Twick. BF47 74
Strathearn Pl. W2 BU40 56
Strathearn Rd. SW19 BS49 76
Strathearn Rd. Sutt. BS56 95
Stratheden Rd. SE3 CH44 68
Strathfield Gdns. Bark. CM36 58
Strathleven Rd. SW2 BX45 66
Strathmore Clo. Cat. CA64 105
Strathmore Gdns. N3 BS30 38
Hervey Clo.
Strathmore Gdns. W8 BS40 56
Strathmore Gdns. Edg. BM30 37
Strathmore Gdns. Horn. CT33 50
Strathmore Rd. SW19 BS48 76
Strathmore Rd. Croy. BZ54 87
Strathnairn St. SE1 CB42 67
Strathray Gdns. NW3 BU36 56
Strath Ter. SW11 BU45 66
Strathville Rd. SW18 BS48 76
Strathyre Av. SW16 BX52 86
Stratmore Rd. Tedd. BH49 74
Stratton Av. Enf. BZ22 30
Stratton Av. Wall. BW58 95
Stratton Chase Dr. Ch. St. G. AQ26 34
Stratton Clo. SW19 BS51 86
Stratton Clo. Bexh. CQ45 69
Stratton Clo. Edg. BL29 37
Stratton Clo. Houns. BF44 64
Strattondale St. E14 CF41 67
Stratton Dr. Bark. CN35 49
Stratton Gdns. Sthl. BE39 54
Stratton Rd. SW19 BS51 86
Stratton Rd. Bexh. CQ45 69
Stratton Rd. Rom. CX28 42
Stratton Rd. Sun. BB51 83
Stratton St. W1 BV40 56
Stratton Wk. Rom. CX28 42
Strauss Rd. W4 BN41 65
Strawberry Hill Clo. Twick. BH48 74
Strawberry Hill Rd. Twick. BH48 74
Strawberry La. Cars. BU55 86
Strawberry Vale N2 BT30 38
Strawberry Vale Twick. BJ48 74
Strawfields. Welw. G. C. BS7 5
Strayfield Rd. Enf. BY21 29
Stream Ct. SW16 BX48 76
Streamdale SE2 CO43 69
Stream La. Edg. BM28 37
Streamway Belv. CQ43 69
Streatfield Av. E6 CK37 58
Streatfield Rd. Har. BK31 45
Streatfield St. E14 CD39 57
Streatham Clo. SW16 BX48 76
Leigham Ct. Rd.
Streatham Common N. SW16 BX49 76
Streatham Common S. SW16 BX50 76
Streatham High Rd. SW16 BX49 76
Streatham Hill, SW2 BX48 76
Streatham Hl. Est. SW16 BX48 76
Streatham Pl. SW2 BX47 76
Streatham Rd. SW16 BU51 86
Streatham Rd. Mitch. BU51 86
Streatham St. WC1 BX39 56
Streatham Vale SW16 BW51 86
Streathbourne Rd. SW17 BV48 76
Streatley Pl. NW3 BT35 47
Streatley Rd. NW6 BR36 55
Street Cobham, Cob. BC60 83
Street, The, Ash. BL62 103
Street, The Bet. BO70 120
Street, The Guil. AR73 118
Street, The, Guil. AW69 110
Street, The, Kings L. AW19 17
Street, The, Leath. AZ67 110
Street. The, Lthd. BD67 111
Street, The Lthd. BG64 102
Street, The, Ong. CY17 24
Street. The. Sev. DB56 99
Street. The. Sev. DB64 108
Streimer Rd. E15 CF37 57
Strelley Way, W3 BO40 55
Stretton Rd. Croy. CA54 87
Stretton Rd. Rich. BK48 74
Stretton Way Borwd. BL22 28
Strickland Av. Dart. CW45 70
Strickland Row. SW18 BT47 76
Strickland St. SE8 CE44 67
Stride Rd. E13 CG37 58
Stringer Ave. Guil. AR67 109
Strode Rd. E7 CH35 49
Strode Rd. N17 CA30 39
Strode Rd. NW10 BP36 55
Strode Rd. SW6 BR43 65
Strode's Cres. Stai. AX49 73
Strode St. Egh. AT49 72
Stroma Clo. Hem. H. BA14 8
Strone Rd. E7 CJ36 58
Strone Rd. E12 CJ36 58
Strongbow Cres. SE9 CK46 78
Strongbow Rd. SE9 CK46 78
Strongbridge Clo. Har. BF33 45
Stronsa Rd. W12 BO41 65
Stronsay Clo. Hem. H. AZ14 8
Strood Av. Rom. CS33 50
Stroud Clo. Wind. AL45 61
Stroud Cres. SW15 BP48 75
Stroude Rd. Egh. AT50 72
Stroude Rd. Egh. AT51 82
Stroude Rd. Vir. W. AS53 82
Stroudes Clo. Wor. Pk. BO54 85
Stroud Farm Rd. Maid. AG43 61
Stroud Field Nthlt. BD36 54
Stroud Gate Har. BF35 45
Stroud Grn. Gdns. Croy. CC53 87
Stroud Green Rd. N4 BX33 47
Stroud Grn. Way Croy. CB54 87
Stroud Rd. SE25 CB53 87
Stroud Rd. SW19 BS48 76
Stroud Way, Ashf. AZ50 73
Strutton Av. Grav. DF48 81
Strutton Ground, SW1 BW41 66
Strype St. E1 CA39 57
Leyden St.
Stuart Av. NW4 BP33 46
Stuart Av. W5 BL40 55
Stuart Av. Brom. CH54 88
Stuart Av. Har. BE34 45
Stuart Av. Walt. BC54 83
Stuart Clo. Brwd. DA25 33
Stuart Clo. Uxb. AZ36 53
Stuart Clo. Wal. Cr. CB19 21
Stuart Clo. Wind. AM44 61
Stuart Cres. N22 BX30 38
Stuart Cres. Croy. CD55 87
Stuart Cres. Hayes BA39 53
Stuart Cres. Reig. BS72 121
Stuart Evans Clo. Well. CP45 69
Stuart Gdns. Tedd. BH49 74
Stuart Mantle Way Erith CS43 69
Stuart Pl. Mitch. BU51 86
Stuart Rd. NW6 BS38 56
Stuart Rd. SE15 CC45 67
Stuart Rd. SW19 BS48 76
Stuart Rd. W3 BN40 55
Stuart Rd. Bark. CN36 58
Dawson Av.
Stuart Rd. Barn. BU26 38
Stuart Rd. Grav. DG46 81
Stuart Rd. Grays. DD42 71
Stuart Rd. Har. BH31 45
Stuart Rd. Reig. BS72 121
Stuart Rd. Rich. BJ48 74
Stuart Rd. Th. Hth. BZ52 87
Stuart Rd. Warl. CB63 105
Stuart Rd. Well. CO44 69
Stuart Rd. Welw. BP5 5
Stuart Way, Vir. W. AQ52 82
Stuart Way. Wind. AM44 61
Stubbers La. Upmin. CZ36 60
Stubbings Hall La. Wal. Abb. CF17 21
Stubbs Clo. Dor. BK72 119
Stubbs End Clo. Amer. AP21 25
Stubbs Hill, Dor. BK72 119
Stubbs Hill. Orp. CP60 98
Stubbs La. Tad. BR67 112
Stubbs Wood. Amer. AP21 25
Stucley Pl. NW1 BV37 56
Camden High St.
Stucley Rd. Houns. BG43 64
Studdridge St. SW6 BS44 66
Stud Grn. Wat. BC19 17
Studholme Ct. NW6 BS35 47
Studholme St. SE15 CB43 67
Studio Dr. Wem. BM34 46
Empire Way
Studland Clo. Sid. CN48 78
Studland Rd. SE26 CC49 77
Studland Rd. W7 BG39 54
Studland Rd. Kings. On T. BL50 75
Studland Rd. Wey. AY60 92
Studland St. W6 BP42 65
Studley Av. E4 CF29 39
Studley Ct. Sid. CO49 79
Studley Dr. Ilf. CJ32 49
Studley Gra. Rd. W7 BH41 64
Studley Rd. E7 CH36 58
Studley Rd. SW4 BX44 66
Studley Rd. Dag. CP36 59
Stukeley Rd. E7 CH36 58
Stukeley St. WC2 BX39 56
Stumble Hill, Ton. DB68 117
Stumps Hl. La. Beck. CE50 77
Stumps La. Whyt. CA62 105
Sturdy Rd. SE15 CB44 67
Sturge Av. E17 CE30 39
Sturgeon Rd. SE17 BY42 66
Sturges Field, Chis. CM50 78
Sturgess Av. NW4 BP33 46
Sturge St. SE1 BZ41 67
Sturmer Way N7 BX35 47
Stockorchard Cres.
Sturrock Clo. N15 BZ31 48
Ida Rd.
Sturry St. E14 CE39 57
Sturt St. N1 BZ37 57
Stutfield St. E1 CB39 57
Stychens Clo. Red. BZ70 114
Stychens La. Red. BZ69 114
Stylecroft Rd. Ch. St. G. AR27 34
Style Rd. Slou. AR41 62
Styles End. Lthd. BF67 111
Styles Gdns. SW9 BY45 66
Styles Way Beck. CF52 87
Succombe Hill. Warl. CB63 105
Sudbourne Rd. SW2 BX46 76
Sudbrooke Rd. SW12 BU46 76
Sudbrook Gdns. Rich. BK48 74
Sudbrook La. Rich. BL47 75
Sudbury Av. Wem. BK34 45
Sudbury Ct. Dr. Har. BH34 45
Sudbury Ct. Rd. Har. BH34 45
Sudbury Cres. Brom. CH50 78
Sudbury Cres. Wem. BJ35 45
Sudbury Cft. Wem. BH35 45
Sudbury Gdns. Croy. CA55 87
Sudbury Heights Av. Grnf. BH35 45
Sudbury Hill Har. BH34 45
Sudbury Hill Clo. Wem. BH35 45
Sudbury Par. Wem. BJ35 45
Sudbury Rd. Bark. CN35 49
Sudeley St. N1 BY37 56
Sudlow Rd. SW18 BS46 76
Sudrey St. SE1 BZ41 67
Sudridge Hill. Sev. CP62 107
Suez Av. Grnf. BH37 54
Suez Rd. Enf. CD24 30
Suffield Rd. E4 CE28 39
Suffield Rd. N15 CA32 48
Suffield Rd. SE20 CC51 87
Suffolk Ct. Ilf. CN32 49
Suffolk Gro. SE16 CC42 67
Hawkstone Rd.
Suffolk La. EC4 BZ40 57
Suffolk Pl. E17 CD31 48
Suffolk Pl. SW1 BW40 56
Suffolk St.
Suffolk Rd. E13 CG38 58
Suffolk Rd. N15 BZ32 48
Suffolk Rd. NW10 BO36 55
Suffolk Rd. SE25 CA52 87
Suffolk Rd. SW13 BO43 65
Suffolk Rd. Bark. CM36 58
Suffolk Rd. Dag. CS35 50
Suffolk Rd. Dart. CW46 80
Suffolk Rd. Enf. CB25 30
Suffolk Rd. Grav. DH46 81
Suffolk Rd. Har. BE32 45
Suffolk Rd. Ilf. CN32 49
Suffolk Rd. Pot. B. BR19 19
Suffolk Rd. Sid. CP50 79
Suffolk Rd. Wor. Pk. BO55 85
Suffolk St. E7 CH35 49
Suffolk St. SW1 BW40 56
Suffolk Way, Horn. CX31 51
Sugar House La. E15 CF37 57
Sugar Lane, Berk. AT14 7
Sugar Loaf Wk. E2 CC38 57
Sugden Rd. SW11 BV45 66
Sugden Rd. Surb. BJ54 84
Sugden St. SE5 BZ43 67
Sugden Way, Bark. CN37 58
Sulgrave Rd. W6 BQ41 65
Sulina Rd. SW2 BX47 76
Sulivan Ct. SW6 BS44 66
Sulivan Rd. SW6 BS45 66
Sullivan Av. E16 CJ39 58
Sullivan Clo. SW11 BU45 66
Ingrave St.
Sullivan Ct. SW6 BS45 66
Sullivan Cres. Uxb. AX30 35
Sullivan Rd. E. Mol. BF52 84
Sullivan Rd. Til. DG44 71
Sullivan Way Borwd. BK25 27
Sultan Rd. E11 CH31 49
Sultan St. SE5 BZ43 67
Sultan St. Beck. CC51 87
Sumatra Rd. NW6 BS35 47
Sumburgh Rd. SW12 BV46 76
Summer Av. E. Mol. BH53 84
Summer Ct. Rd. E1 CC39 57
W. Arbour St.
Summer Dale, Welw. G. C. BQ6 5
Summerfield Hat. BP14 10
Hollyfield
Summerfield Av. NW6 BR37 55
Summerfield Clo. St. Alb. BK16 18
Summerfield Clo. Wey. AW56 92
Summerfield La. Surb. BK55 84
Summerfield Rd. W5 BJ38 54
Summerfield Rd. Loug. CJ25 31
Summerfield Rd. Wat. BC21 26
Summerfield St. SE12 CG47 78
Summer Gdns. E. Mol. BH53 84
Summer Hayes Clo. Wok. AS60 91
Summer Hayes Clo. Wok. AS61 100
Summer Hill, Chis. CL51 88
Summerhill Clo. Orp. CN56 97
Summerhill Ct. St. Alb. BH13 9
Avenue Rd.
Summerhill Gro. Enf. CA25 30
Summerhill Rd. N15 BZ31 48
Summerhill Rd. Dart. CV47 80
Summer Hill Vill. Chis. CL51 88
Summerhouse Av. Houns. BE44 64
Summerhouse Dr. Bex. CS49 79
Summerhouse La. Uxb. AW29 35
Summerhouse La. Wat. BG23 27
Summerhouse La. West Dr. AX43 63
Summer House Rd. N16 CA34 48
Summerhouse Way, Wat. BB18 17
Summerland Gdns. N10 BV31 47
Muswell Hill Broadway
Summerlands Av. W3 BN40 55
Summerlands Rd. St. Alb. BK11 9
Ridgeway, The,
Summerlea. Slough. AN41 61
Summerlee Av. N2 BU31 47
Summerlee Gdns. N2 BU31 47
Summerley St. SW18 BS48 76
Summer Rd. E. Mol. BG53 84
Summersby Rd. N6 BV32 47
Summers Clo. Wey. AZ59 92
Summers La. N12 BT29 38
Summers Row. N12 BU29 38
Summers St. EC1 BY38 56
Back Hill
Summerstown SW17 BT48 76
Summertrees Sun. BC51 83
Summerville Gdns. Sutt. BR57 94
Summerville Rd. Dart. CW46 80
Summerwood Rd. Islw. BH46 74
Summit Av. NW9 BN32 46
Summit Clo. N14 BW27 38
Summit Clo. NW2 BR35 46
Summit Clo. NW9 BN31 46
Summit Clo. Edg. BM29 37
Summit Clo. Wey. AV56 91
Summit Dr. Wdf. Grn. CJ30 40
Summit Est. N16 CB33 48
Summit Rd. E17 CE31 48
Summit Rd. Nthlt. BF36 54
Summit. The Loug. CK23 31
Summit Way N14 BV27 38
Summit Way, SE19 CA50 77
Sumner Av. SE15 CA44 67
Sumner Rd.
Sumner Bldgs. SE1 BZ40 57
Sumner St.
Sumner Gdns. Croy. BY54 86
Sumner Pl. SW7 BT42 66
Sumner Pl. Ms. SW7 BT42 66
Sumner Pl.
Sumner Rd. SE15 CA43 67
Sumner Rd. Croy. BY54 86
Sumner Rd. Har. BG33 45
Sumner Rd. S. Croy. BY54 86
Sumner St. SE1 BY40 56
Sumpter Yd. St. Alb. BG13 9
Sun All. Rich. BL45 65
Sunbeam Rd. NW10 BN38 55
Sunbridge Rd. Croy. CA54 87
Sunbury Av. NW7 BN28 37

Sunbury Av. SW14 BN45 65
Sunbury Ct. Rd. Sun. BD51 84
Sunbury Cres. Felt. BB48 73
Sunbury Gdns. NW7 BN28 37
Sunbury La. SW11 BT44 66
Sunbury La. Walt. BC53 83
Sunbury Rd. Felt. BB48 73
Sunbury Rd. Sutt. BQ55 85
Sunbury Rd. Wind. AO43 61
Sunbury St. SE18 CK41 68
Suncourt Erith CT44 69
Suncroft Pl. SE26 CC48 77
Sundale Av. Sth. Croy. CC58 96
Sunderland Av. St. Alb. BJ13 9
Sunderland Ct. SE22 CB47 77
Sunderland Mt. SE23 CC48 77
Sunderland Rd. SE23 CC48 77
Sunderland Rd. W5 BK41 64
Sunderland Rd. Houns. AY46 73
Southampton Rd.
Sunderland Ter. W2 BS39 56
Sunderland Way E12 CJ34 49
Sundew Av. W12 BP40 55
Sundial Av. SE25 CA52 87
Sundon Cres. Vir. W. AQ53 82
Sundorne Rd. SE7 CH42 68
Sundown Av. Sth. Croy. CA59 96
Sundown Pl. Ilf. CL34 49
Ilford Hill
Sundown Rd. Ashf. BA49 73
Sundridge Av. Brom. CJ51 88
Sundridge Av. Well. CM44 68
Sundridge Clo. Dart. CX46 80
Sundridge Ho. Brom. CH49 78
Sundridge La. Sev. CO62 107
Sundridge Rd. Wok. AT63 100
Sunfields Pl. SE3 CH43 68
Sun Hill Fawk. CX55 90
Sunland Av. Bexh. CQ45 69
Sun La. SE3 CH43 68
Sun La. Grav. DH48 81
Sunleigh Rd. Wem. BL37 55
Sunley Gdns. Grnf. BJ37 54
Sunmead Clo. Lthd. BH64 102
Sunmead Rd. Hem. H. AX13 8
Sunmead Rd. Sun. BC52 83
Sunna Gdns. Sun. BC51 83
Sunningdale Av. W3 BO39 55
Sunningdale Av. Bark. CM37 58
Sunningdale Av. Felt. BE48 74
Sunningdale Av. Rain. CU38 59
Sunningdale Av. Ruis. BD33 45
Sunningdale Clo. Stan. BJ29 36
Sunningdale Gdns. NW9 BN32 46
Sunningdale Rd. Brom. CK52 88
Sunningdale Rd. Rain. CU36 59
Sunningdale Rd. Sutt. BR55 85
Sunningfields Cres. NW4 BP30 37
Sunningfields Rd. NW4 BP30 37
Sunning Hill, Grav. DF48 81
Sunninghill Rd. SE13 CE44 67
Sunnings La. Upmin. CW36 60
Sunningvale Ave. West. CJ61 106
Sunningvale Ave. West. CJ62 106
Sunningvale Clo. West. CJ61 106
Sunny Bank SE25 CB52 87
Sunny Bank. Epsom BN61 103
Sunny Bank. Warl. CD62 105
Sunny Bank Rd. Pot. B. BS20 20
Sunny Cres. NW10 BN36 55
Sunnycroft Clo. Islw. BG44 64
Sunnycroft Gdns. Upmin. CZ33 51
Sunnycroft Rd SE25 CB52 87
Sunnycroft Rd. Houns. BF44 64
Sunnycroft Rd. Sthl. BF39 54
Sunnydale, SE12 CH46 78
Sunnydale Orp. CL55 88
Sunnydale Gro. NW7 BN29 37
Sunnydell, St. Alb. BF16 18
Sunnydene Av. E4 CF28 39
Sunnydene Av. Ruis. BC33 44
Sunnydene Clo. Rom. CW29 42
Sunnydene Rd. Pur. BY60 95
Sunnydene St. SE26 CD49 77
Sunnyfield NW7 BO27 37
Sunnyfield, Hat. BQ11 10
Sunnyfield Rd. Chis. CO52 89
Sunny Gdns. Rd. NW4 BP30 37
Sunnyhill Rd. SW16 BX49 76
Sunny Hill Rd. Ger. Cr. AU29 34
Sunnyhill Rd. Hem. H. AW13 8
Sunny Hl. NW4 BP31 46
Sunnyhurst Clo. Sutt. BS55 86
Sunnymead Ave. Chesh. AP17 16
Sunnymead Av. Mitch. BW52 86
Sunnymead Rd. NW9 BN33 46
Sunnymead Rd. SW15 BP46 75
Sunnymede Chig. CO27 41
Sunnymede Av. Cars. BT59 95
Sunnymede Av. Epsom BO58 94
Sunnymede Dr. Ilf. CL32 49
Sunnymede Gdns. Wem. BK36 54
Sunny Nook Gdns. Sth Croy BZ57 96
Selsdon Rd.
Sunny Ri. Cat. BZ65 105
Sunnyside SW19 BR50 75
Sunny Side Walt. BD53 84
Sunnyside Dr. E4 CF26 39
Sunnyside Gdns. Upmin. CY34 51
Sunnyside Pass. SW19 BR50 75
Sunnyside Rd. E10 CE33 48
Sunnyside Rd. N19 BW33 47
Sunnyside Rd. NW2 BR34 46
Sunnyside Rd. W5 BK40 54
Sunnyside Rd. Epp. CN19 22
Sunnyside Rd. Ilf. CM34 49
Sunnyside Rd. Tedd. BG49 74
Sunnyside Rd. E. N9 CB27 39
Sunnyside Rd. N. N9 CB27 39
Sunnyside Rd. S. N9 CA27 39
Sunny, The, Rd. Enf. CC23 30
Sunny Vw. NW9 BN32 46
Sunny Way N12 BU29 38
Sun Pass. Wind. AO44 61
Peascod St.
Sunray Ave. West Dr. AX41 63
Sunray Av. SE24 BZ45 67
Sunray Av. Brom. CK53 88
Sun Ray Av. Brwd. DF25 122
Sunray Av. Surb. BM55 85
Sunrise Av. Horn. CV34 51
Sunrise Clo. Felt. BE48 74
Sunrise Cres. Hem. H. AY15 8
Sun Rd. Swans. DC46 81
Sun St. Pass. EC2 CA39 57
Sunset Av. E4 CE26 39
Sunset Av. Wdf. Grn. CG28 40
Sunset Dri. Hav. CU28 41
Sunset Dr. Hav. CU28 41
Sunset Gdns. SE25 CA51 87
Sunset Rd. SE5 BZ45 67
Sunset Vw. Barn. BR23 28
Sunshine Way, Mitch. BU51 86
Sun Sq. Hem. H. AX13 8
High St.
Sunstone Grn. Red. BX68 113
Sun St. EC2 BZ39 57
Sun St. Wal. Abb. CF20 21
Sunwell St. SE15 CB44 67
Surbiton Ct. Surb. BK53 84
Surbiton Cres. Surb. BL53 85
Surbiton Hall Clo. Kings-on-t. BL52 85
Surbiton Hill Pk. Surb. BL53 85
Surbiton Hill Rd. Surb. BL52 85
Surbiton Pk. Ter. Kings-on-t. BL52 85
Surbiton Rd. Kings-on-t. BK52 84
Surgeon St. SE18 CL41 68
Surly Hall Wk. Wind. AM44
Surman Cres. Brwd. DE26 122
Surrendale Pl. W9 BS38 56
Surrey Cres. W4 BM42 65
Chiswick High Rd.
Surrey Dr. Horn. CW31 51
Surrey Gdns. W4 BM42 65
Chiswick High Rd.
Surrey Gdns. Lthd. BB64 101
Surrey Gro. SE17 CA42 67
Surrey La. SW11 BU44 66
Surrey Ms. SE27 CA49 77
Hamilton Rd.
Surrey Mt. SE23 CB47 77
Surrey Rd. SE15 CC46 77
Surrey Rd. Bark. CN36 58
Surrey Rd. Dag. CR35 50
Surrey Rd. Har. BG32 45
Surrey Rd. W. Wick. CE54 87
Surrey Row. SE1 BY41 66
Surrey Sq. SE17 CA42 67
Surrey St. E13 CH38 58
Surrey St. WC2 BX40 56
Temple Pl.
Surrey St. Croy. BZ55 87
Surrey Ter. SE17 CA42 67
Surrey Sq.
Surridge Clo. Rain. CV38 60
Surridge Gdns. SE19 BZ50 77
Surr St. N7 BX35 47
Surry Gro. Sutt. BT55 86
Susan Clo. Rom. CR31 50
Susannah St. E14 CE39 57
Susan Rd. SE3 CH44 68
Susan Wood Chis. CL51 88
Sussex Av. Islw. BH45 64
Sussex Av. Rom. CW29 42
Sussex Clo. N19 BX34 47
Sussex Clo. Ch. St. G. AQ27 34
Sussex Clo. Ilf. CK32 49
Radnor Cres.
Sussex Clo. N. Mal. BO52 85
Sussex Clo. Reig. BT71 121
Sussex Clo. Slou. AQ41 62
Sussex Clo. Twick. BJ46 74
Westmorland Clo.
Sussex Cres. Nthlt. BF36 54
Sussex Gdns. N4 BZ32 48
Rosebery Gdns.
Sussex Gdns. SW9 BY45 66
Sussex Gdns. W2 BT39 56
Sussex Gdns. Chess. BK57 93
Sussex Ms. NW1 BU38 56
Sussex Place
Sussex Ms. E. W2 BT40 56
Clifton Pl.
Sussex Pla. Erith. CR43 69
Sussex Pl. W2 BT39 56
Sussex Pl. W6 BQ42 65
Sussex Pl. Slou. AQ41 62
Sussex Rd. E6 CL37 58
Sussex Rd. SW9 BY45 66
Sussex Rd. Brwd. DA28 42
Sussex Rd. Cars. BU57 95
Sussex Rd. Dart. CX47 80
Sussex Rd. Erith CR43 69
Sussex Rd. Har. BF32 45
Sussex Rd. N. Mal. BO52 85
Sussex Rd. Orp. CP53 89
Sussex Rd. Sid. CO49 79
Sussex Rd. Sth. Croy. BZ57 96
Sussex Rd. Sthl. BD41 64
Sussex Rd. Uxb. BA35 44
Sussex Rd. Wat. BC22 26
Sussex Rd. W. Wick. CE54 87
Sussex Sq. W2 BT40 56
Sussex St. E13 CH38 58
Sussex St. SW1 BV42 66
Sussex Way, N7 BW33 47
Sussex Way, N19 BW33 47
Sussex Way Barn. BV25 29
Sutcliffe Clo. NW11 BS32 47
Sutcliffe Clo. Bush. BG24 27
Sutcliffe Rd. SE18 CN43 68
Sutcliffe Rd. Well. CP44 69
Sutherland Ave. West. CJ62 106
Sutherland Av. W9 BS38 56
Sutherland Av. W13 BJ39 54
Sutherland Av. Hayes BC42 63
Sutherland Av. Orp. CN53 88
Sutherland Av. Pot. B. BW17 20
Sutherland Av. Sun. BB51 83
Sutherland Av. Well. CN45 68
Sutherland Clo. Barn. BR24 28
Sutherland Ct. NW9 BM32 46
Sutherland Gdns. SW14 BO45 65
Sutherland Gdns. Sun. BB51 83
Sutherland Gdns. Wor. Pk. BP54 85
Sutherland Gro. SW18 BR46 75
Sutherland Gro. Tedd. BH49 74
Sutherland Pl. W2 BS39 56
Sutherland Rd. E3 CD37 57
Sutherland Rd. E17 CC30 39
Sutherland Rd. N17 CB29 39
Sutherland Rd. W4 BO43 65
Sutherland Rd. W13 BJ39 54
Sutherland Rd. Belv. CR41 69
Sutherland Rd. Croy. BY54 86
Sutherland Rd. Enf. CC25 30
Sutherland Rd. Sthl. BE39 54
Sutherland Rd. Path. E17 CC31 48
Sutherland Row, SW1 BV42 66
Sutherland St.
Sutherlands Av. Sun. BC51 83
Sutherland Sq. SE17 BZ42 67
Sutherland St. E3 CD37 57
Sutherland St. SW1 BV42 66
Sutherland Wk. SE17 BZ42 67
Sutherland Way, Pot. B. BW17 20
Sutlej Rd. SE7 CJ43 68
Sutterton St. N7 BV36 56
Blundell St.
Sutton Ave. Slou. AR41 62
Sutton Av. Wok. AP63 100
Sutton Clo. Brox. CD13 12
Sutton Clo. Loug. CK26 40
Sutton Clo. Pnr. BC32 44
Sutton Common Rd. Sutt. BR54 85
Sutton Ct. W4 BN43 65
Sutton Ct. Rd. E13 CJ38 58
Sutton Ct. Rd. W4 BN43 65
Sutton Ct. Rd. Sutt. BT57 95
Sutton Ct. Rd. Uxb. AZ37 53
Sutton Cres. Barn. BQ25 28
Sutton Dene Houns. BF44 64
Sutton Dws. N1 BY36 56
Sutton Dws. SE8 CC42 67
Sutton Dws. SW3 BU42 66
Sutton Dws. W10 BQ39 55
Sutton Gdns. Croy. CA53 87
Sutton Gdns. Red. BW68 113
Sutton Grn. Bark. CN37 58
Saxham Rd.
Sutton Green Rd. Guil. AS66 109
Sutton Gro. Sutt. BT56 95
Sutton Hall Rd. Houns. BF43 64
Sutton La. W4 BN42 65
Sutton La. Houns. BE45 64
Sutton La. Slou. AT43 62
Sutton La. Sutt. BS59 95
Sutton La. S. W4 BN43 65
Sutton Pk. Rd. Sutt. BS57 95
Sutton Path Borwd. BM23 28
Sutton Pl. E9 CC35 48
Sutton Pl. Slou. AT43 62
Sutton Rd. E13 CG38 58
Sutton Rd. E17 CC30 39
Sutton Rd. N10 BV30 38
Sutton Rd. Bark. CN37 58
Sutton Rd. Houns. BF44 64
Sutton Rd. St. Alb. BJ14 9
Sutton Rd. Wat. BD24 27
Sutton Row, W1 BW39 56
Suttons Av. Horn. CV34 51
Suttons Gdns. Horn. CV34 51
Suttons La. Horn. CV35 51
Suttons Parkway Upmin. CW35 51
Sutton Sq. Houns. BE44 64
Sutton St. E1 CC40 57
Sutton Way W10 BQ38 55
Sutton Way Houns. BE44 64
Swabey Rd. Slou. AT42 62
Swaby Rd. SW18 BT47 76
Swaffham Way N22 BY29 38
Swaffield Rd. SW18 BS47 76
Swaffield Rd. Sev. CV64 108
Swain Rd. Th. Hth. BZ53 87
Swains Clo. West Dr. AY41 63
Swain's La. N6 BV34 47
Swainson Rd. W3 BO41 65
Swain's Rd. SW17 BU50 76
Swaisland Rd. Dart. CU46 79
Swaislands Dri. Dart. CT46 79
Crayford Way
Swaislands Dr. Dart. CT46 79
Crayford Way
Swakeleys Dr. Uxb. AZ35 44
Swakeleys Rd. Uxb. AY35 44
Swalecliffe Rd. Belv. CR42 69
Swale Clo. S. Ock. CW39 60
Swaledale Rd. Dart. CY47 80
Swale Rd. Dart. CU45 69
Swallands Rd. SE6 CE48 77
Swallow Clo. Bush. BF26 36
Swallow Clo. Stai. AV49 72
Swallowdale, Iver AU38 52
Swallowdale Sth. Croy. CC58 96
Swallowdale St. Iver AU38 52
Swallowdale La. Hem. H. AZ12 8
Swallow End. Welw. G. C. BR8 5
Swallowfield Rd. SE7 CH42 68
Swallow Fields, Grav. DF48 81
Swallow Fields. Welw. G. C. BR8 5
Swallowfield Way. Hayes. BA41 63
Swallow Gds. Hat. BP13 10
Swallow St. W1 BW40 56
Piccadilly
Swallow St. Iver AU38 52
Swallow Wk. Rain. CU36 59
Swanage Rd. E4 CF29 39
Swanage Rd. SW18 BT46 76
Swanage Waye Hayes BD39 54
Swan Av. Upmin. CZ33 51
Swanbourne Dri. Horn. CV35 51
Swanbourne Dr. Horn. CV35 51
Swanbridge Rd. Bexh. CR44 69
Swan Clo. Felt. BE49 74
Swan Clo. Orp. CO52 89
Swan Ct. N20 BT27 38
Swan Ct. SW3 BU42 66
Swanfield Rd. Wal. Cr. CD20 21
Swanfield St. E2 CA38 57
Swanhill. Welw. G. C. BS6 5
Swan La. EC4 BZ40 57
Wharfside
Swan La. N20 BT27 38
Swan La. Brwd. CZ22 33
Swan La. Dart. CT47 79
Swan La. Guil. AR71 118
Swanley Bar La. Pot. B. BS17 20
Swanley By-pass Swan. CS52 89
Swanley Cres. Pot. B. BS18 20
Swanley La. Swan. CT52 89
Swanley Rd. Well. CN44 68
Swanley Village Rd. Swan. CU51 89
Swan Mead, SE1 CA41 67
Swan Ms. SW9 BX44 66
Stockwell Rd.
Swan Mill Gdns. Dor. BK70 119
Swann's Meadow. Lthd. BF66 111
Swan & Pike Rd. Enf. CE22 30
Swan Rd. SE7 CJ41 68
Swan Rd. SE16 CC41 67
Swan Rd. Felt. BE49 74
Swan Rd. Iver AV39 52
Swan Rd. Sthl. BF39 54
Swan Rd. West Dr. AX41 63
Swans Clo. St. Alb. BL14 10
Swanscombe Rd. W4 BO42 65
Swanscombe Rd. W11 BQ40 55
Swanscombe Rd. Swans. DC46 81
Swansea Rd. Enf. CC24 30
Swansfield La. Green. DA47 80
Swansland Gdns. E17 CD30 39
Mcentee Ave.
Swanston Path. Wat. BD27 36
Swan St. SE1 BZ41 67
Swan St. Islw. BJ45 64
Swan Ter. Wind. AN43 61
Swanton Gdns. SW19 BQ47 75
Swanton Rd. Erith. CR43 69
Swan Wk. SW3 BU43 66
Swan Wk. Rom. CT32 50
Swan Way Enf. CC23 30
Swan Wf. EC4 BZ40 57
Wharfside
Swanwick Clo. SW15 BO47 75
Swanworth La. Dor. BJ67 111
Swan Yd. N1 BY36 56
Highbury Stn. Rd.
Swanzy Rd. Sev. CV63 108
Sward Rd. Orp. CO53 89
Swaton Rd. E3 CE38 57
Swaylands Rd. Belv. CR43 69
Swaynesland Rd. Eden. CK70 115
Swayne's La. Guil. AV70 118
Swedenborg St. E1 CB40 57
Swedewborg Gdns. E1 CB40 57
Sweeney Cres. SE1 CA41 67
Sweeps La. Egh. AS49 72
Sweeps La. Orp. CP53 89
Sweet Briar. Welw. G. C. BS8 5
Sweetbriar Clo. Hem. H. AW12 8
Sweet Briar Grn. N9 CA27 39
Briary La.
Sweet Briar Gro. N9 CA27 39
Sweetbriar La. Epsom BN60 94
Sweet Briar Wk. N18 CA28 39
Sweetcroft La. Uxb. AY36 53
Sweetenham Wk. SE18 CM42 68
Sandbach Pl.
Sweetmans Av. Pnr. BD31 45
Sweets Way N20 BT27 38
Swete St. E13 CH37 58
Sweyne Rd. Swans. DC46 81
Sweyn Pl. SE3 CH44 68
Sweyn Rd. Green. DB46 80
Swievelands Hill Rd. West. CH63 106
Swift Clo. Har. BF34 45
Swift Clo. Hayes BB39 53
Swift Clo. Upmin. CZ33 51
Swift Rd. Felt. BD49 74
Swiftsden Way, Brom. CG50 78
Swift St. SW6 BR44 65
Swinborn Ct. SE5 BZ45 67
Basingdon Way.
Swinbourne Gdns. Til. DG44 71
Swinbrook Rd. W10 BR39 55
Swinburne Av. E12 CK35 49
Swinburne Cres. Croy. CC53 87
Swinburne Rd. SW15 BP45 65
Swinderby Rd. Wem. BL36 55
Swindon Clo. Ilf. CN34 49
Salisbury Rd.
Swindon Clo. Rom. CW28 42
Swindon Gdns. Rom. CW28 42
Swindon La. Rom. CW28 42
Swindon St. W12 BP40 55
Swinford Gdns. SW9 BY45 66
Swingate La. SE18 CN43 68
Swing Gate La. Berk. AR14 7
Swinnerton St. E9 CD35 48
Swinton Clo. Wem. BM33 46
Swinton Pl. WC1 BX38 56
Swinton St.
Swinton St. WC1 BX38 56
Swiss Av. Wat. BB24 26
Swiss Clo. Wat. BB24 26
Swithland Gdns. SE9 CK49 78
Swyncombe Av. W5 BJ42 64
Sybourn St. E17 CD33 48
Sycamore App. Rick. BA25 26
Sycamore Av. W5 BK41 64
Sycamore Av. Hat. BP13 10
Sycamore Av. Hayes BB40 53
Sycamore Av. Sid. CN46 78
Sycamore Av. Upmin. CX35 51
Sycamore Clo. Bush. BE23 27
Sycamore Clo. Ch. St. G. AQ27 34
Sycamore Clo. Nthlt. BE37 54
Sycamore Clo. Wat. BC21 26
Sycamore Clo. West Dr. AY40 53
Sycamore Dean. Chesh. AO17 16
Sycamore Dr. St. Alb. BG17 18
Radlett Rd.
Sycamore Dr. Swan. CT52 89
Sycamore Gdns. W6 BP41 65
Sycamore Gro. NW9 BN33 46
Sycamore Gro. N. Mal. BN52 85
Sycamore Ri. Ch. St. G. AQ27 34
Sycamore Rd. SW19 BQ50 75
Sycamore Rd. Amer. AO22 25
Sycamore Rd. Ch. St. G. AQ27 34
Sycamore Rd. Dart. CV47 80
Sycamore Rd. Guil. AR70 118
Sycamore Rd. Rick. BA25 26
Sycamore Wk. Ilf. CM31 49
Civic Way
Sycamore Wk. Slou. AS39 52
Sycamore Way Th. Hth. BY53 86
Sydenham Av. SE26 CB49 77
Sydenham Hill, SE23 CB47 77
Sydenham Hill, SE26 CB47 77
Sydenham Pk. SE26 CC49 77
Sydenham Pk. Rd. SE26 CC48 77
Sydenham Rise SE23 CB48 77
Sydenham Rd. SE26 CC49 77
Sydenham Rd. Croy. BZ54 87
Sydenham Rd. Guil. AR71 118
Sydmons St. SE23 CC47 77
Sydner Rd. N16 CA35 48
Sydney Av. Pur. BX59 95
Sydney Cl. SW3 BT42 66
Sydney Cres. Ashf. AZ50 73
Sydney Gro. NW4 BQ32 46
Sydney Gro. Slou. AO39 52
Sydney Ms. SW3 BT42 66
Sydney Ms. Clo. SW7 BT42 66
Sydney Pl. SW7 BU42 66
Sydney Rd. E11 CH32 49
Sydney Rd. N8 BY31 47
Sydney Rd. N10 BV30 38
Sydney Rd. SE2 CP41 69
Sydney Rd. SW20 BQ51 85
Sydney Rd. W13 BJ40 54
Sydney Rd. Bexh. CP45 69
Sydney Rd. Enf. BZ24 30
Sydney Rd. Felt. BC47 73
Sydney Rd. Guil. AS71 118
Sydney Rd. Ilf. CM30 40
Sydney Rd. Rich. BL45 65
Sydney Rd. Sid. CN49 78
Sydney Rd. Tedd. BH49 74
Sydney Rd. Til. DG44 71
Sydney Rd. Wat. BB25 26
Sydney Rd. Wdf. Grn. CH28 40
Sydney Sq. SE15 CB43 67
Latona Rd.
Sydney St. SW3 BU42 66
Sykecluan. Iver. AV41 62
Sykeings. Iver. AV41 62
Sylvana Clo. Uxb. AY37 53
Sylvan Av. N3 BS30 38
Sylvan Av. N22 BX29 38
Sylvan Av. NW7 BO29 37
Sylvan Av. Horn. CW32 51
Sylvan Av. Rom. CQ32 50
Sylvan Clo. Grays. DC42 71
Sylvan Clo. Hem. H. AZ14 8
Sylvan Clo. Sth. Croy. CB58 96
Sylvan Clo. Wok. AT62 100
Sylvan Gdns Surb. BK54 84
Sylvan Gro. SE15 CB43 67
Sylvan Hl. SE19 CA51 87
Sylvan Rd. E7 CH36 58
Sylvan Rd. E11 CH32 49
Sylvan Rd. E17 CE32 48
Sylvan Rd. SE19 CA51 87
Sylvan Rd. Ilf. CM34 49
Sylvan Rd. Est. SE19 CA51 87
Sylvan Way, Dag. CO34 50
Sylvan Way, Red. BV71 121
Sylvan Way W. Wick. CG56 97
Sylverdale Rd. Croy. BY55 86
Sylverdale Rd. Ken. BY60 95
Sylvester Av. Chis. CK50 78
Sylvester Gdns. Ilf. CO28 41
Sylvester Rd. E8 CB36 57
Sylvester Rd. E17 CD33 48
Sylvester Rd. N2 BT30 38
Sylvester Rd. Wem. BK35 45
Sylvia Av. Brwd. DE27 122
Sylvia Av. Pnr. BE29 36
Sylvia Ct. Wem. BM36 55
Sylvia Gdns. Wem. BM36 55
Symes Ms. NW1 BW37 56
Symonds Clo. Sev. CZ56 99
Symondshyde La. Hat. BM9 5
Symons St. SW3 BU42 66
Syon La. Islw. BH43 64
Syon Pk. Gdns. Islw. BH43 64
Syracuse Av. Rain. CV38 60
Tabard Garden Est. SE1 BZ41 67
Tabard St. SE1 BZ41 67
Tabarin Way Epsom BQ61 103
Tabernacle Av. E13 CH38 58
Tabernacle St. EC2 BZ38 57
Tableer Av. SW4 BW46 76
Tabor Gdns. Sutt. BR57 94
Tabor Gro. SW19 BR50 75
Tabor Rd. W6 BP41 65

Tabrums Way. Upmin. CZ33 51
Tachbrook Est. SW1 BW42 66
Tachbrook Rd. Felt. BB47 73
Tachbrook Rd. Sthl. BD41 64
Tachbrook Rd. Uxb. AX37 53
Tachbrook St. SW1 BW42 66
Tackbrook Ms. SW1 BW42 66
Longmore St.
Tadema Rd. SW10 BT43 66
Tadlows Clo. Upmin. CX35 51
Tadmor Clo. Sun. BB52 83
Tadmor St. W12 BQ40 55
Tadorne Rd. Tad. BQ64 103
Tadworth Av. N. Mal. BO53 85
Tadworth Ct. Tad. BQ64 103
Tadworth Pde. Horn. CU35 50
Tadworth Rd. NW2 BP34 46
Tadworth St. Tad. BQ65 103
Taffy's How Mitch. BU51 86
Tait Rd. Croy. CA54 87
Takeley Clo. Rom. CS30 41
Talacre Rd. NW5 BV36 56
Talbey Rd. N7 BX35 47
Talbot Ave. Slou. AS41 62
Talbot Av. N2 BT31 47
Talbot Av. Wat. BE26 36
Talbot Clo. N15 CA31 48
Talbot Rd.
Talbot Clo. Reig. BS74 121
Lymden Gdns.
Talbot Ct. EC3 BZ40 57
Gracechurch St.
Talbot Cres. NW4 BP32 46
Talbot Gdns. Ilf. CO34 50
Talbot Houses. SW3 CG44 68
Talbot Pl. SE3 CG44 68
Talbot Pl. Slou. AR44 62
Talbot Rd. E6 CK37 58
Talbot Rd. E7 CH35 49
Talbot Rd. N6 BV32 47
Talbot Rd. N15 CA31 48
Talbot Rd. N22 BW30 38
Talbot Rd. NW10 BO36 55
Talbot Rd. W11 BR39 55
Talbot Rd. W13 BJ40 54
Talbot Rd. Ashf. AX49 73
Talbot Rd. Brom. CH52 88
Talbot Rd. Cars. BV56 95
Talbot Rd. Dag. CQ36 59
Talbot Rd. Har. BH30 36
Talbot Rd. Hat. BP11 10
Talbot Rd. Islw. BJ45 64
Talbot Rd. Rick. AY26 35
Talbot Rd. Sthl. BE42 64
Talbot Rd. Th. Hth. BZ52 87
Talbot Rd. Twick. BH47 74
Talbot Rd. Wem. BK36 54
Talbot Sq. W2 BT39 56
Talbot Yd. SE1 BZ40 57
Borough High St.
Taleworth Clo. Ash. BK63 102
Taleworth Rd. Ash. BK63 102
Talfourd Pl. SE15 CA44 67
Talfourd Rd. SE15 CA44 67
Talgarth Rd. W6 BQ42 65
Talgarth Rd. W14 BQ42 65
Talisman Clo. SE26 CB49 77
Talisman Way Epsom BQ61 103
Talisman Way, Wem. BL34 46
Tallack Clo. Har. BH29 36
Tallack Rd. E10 CD33 48
Tall Elms Clo. Brom. CG53 88
Tallis Gro. SE7 CH43 68
Tallis St. EC4 BY40 56
Tallon Rd. Brwd. DF25 122
Tally Ho. Cor. N12 BT28 38
Tally Rd. Oxt. CK69 115
Talma Gdns. Twick. BH46 74
Talmage Clo. SE23 CC47 77
Talma Rd. SW2 BY45 66
Talwin St. E3 CE38 57
Tamar Clo. Upmin. CZ32 51
Tamar Dr. S. Ock. CW39 60
Tamar Grn. Hem. H. AY11 8
Tamarisk Clo. S. Ock. DB38 60
Tamarisk Rd. S. Ock. DB38 60
Tamarisk Sq. W12 BO40 55
Tamar Sq. Wdf. Grn. CH29 40
Tamar St. SE7 CJ42 68
Tamar Way. Slou. AT42 62
Tamesis Strand, Grav. DJ49 81
Tamian Way Houns. BD45 64
Tamplin Ms. W9 BS38 56
Warlock Rd.
Tamworth Av. Wdf. Grn. CG29 40
Tamworth Gdns. Pnr. BD30 36
Tamworth La. Mitch. BV51 86
Tamworth Pk. Mitch. BV52 86
Tamworth Pl. Croy. BZ55 87
Tamworth Rd. Croy. BY55 86
Tamworth St. SW6 BS43 66
Tancier La. Wind. AO43 61
Tancred Rd. N4 BY32 47
Tandridge Dr. Orp. CM54 88
Tandridge Gdns. Sth. Croy. CA60 96
Tandridge Hill La. Gdse. CD68 114
Tandridge La. Oxt. CE69 114
Tandridge Rd. Warl. CC63 105
Tanfield Av. NW2 BO35 46
Tanfield Rd. Croy. BZ56 96
Tangent Rd. Rom. CV30 42
Tangier Rd. Guil. AT71 118
Tangier Rd. Rich. BM45 65
Tangier Way Tad. BR62 103
Tangier Wd. Tad. BR62 103
Tanglewood, Cher. AQ55 82
Tanglewood Clo. Croy. CC55 87
Tanglewood Clo. Stan. BH27 36
Tanglewood Clo. Wok. AU61 100
Tangley Gro. SW15 BO46 75
Tangley La. Guil. AP68 109
Tanglyn Av. Shep. AZ53 83
Tangmere Cres. Horn. CU36 59
Tangmere Gdns. Nthlt. BD37 54
Tangmere Way NW9 BO30 37
Tan House La. Brwd. CX24 33
Tanhouse Rd. Oxt. CF69 114
Tanhurst Wk. SE2 CP41 69
Alsike Rd.
Tanhurst Walk Belv. CP41 69
Lanridge Rd.
Tankerton Rd. Surb. BL55 85
Tankerton St. WC1 BX38 56
Argyle Wk.
Tankerville Rd. SW16 BW50 76
Tankhill Rd. Grays CX42 70
Tank La. Grays CX42 70
Tankridge Rd. NW2 BP34 46
Tanners Dean, Lthd. BK64 102
Tanners End La. N18 CA28 39
Tanners Hill, Bet. BM71 120
Tanner's Hl. SE8 CD44 67
Tanners La. Ilf. CM31 49
Tanner St. SE1 CA41 67
Tanner St. Bark. CM36 58
Tannery Clo. Dag. CR34 50
Tannery La. Wok. AU65 100
Tannsfield Clo. Hem. H. AY12 8
Tannsfield Rd. SE26 CC49 77
Tannsmore Clo. Hem. H. AY12 8
Tanrides Rd. Orp. CM54 88
Tanswell Est. SE1 BY41 66
Tanswell St. SE1 BY41 66
Tansy Clo. Rom. CV29 42
Tansy Croft. Welw. G. C. BS7 5
Tantallon Rd. SW12 BV47 76
Tant Av. E16 CG39 58
Tantony Gro. Rom. CP31 50
Tany's Dell, Harl. CO9 6
Tanza Rd. NW3 BU35 47
Tapestry Clo. Sutt. BS57 95
Tapiar Way N17 CA31 48
Tapley St. E14 CF39 57
Taplow St. N1 BZ37 57
Tapner's Rd. Reig. BO73 120
Tappesfield Rd. SE15 CC45 67
Tapster St. Barn. BR24 28
Taransay, Hem. H. AZ14 8
Tarbay La. Wind. AK45 61
Tarbert Rd. SE22 CA46 77
Tarbert Wk. E1 CC39 57
Juniper St.
Target Clo. Felt. BB46 73
Tariff Rd. N17 CB29 39
Tarleton Gdns. SE23 CB48 77
Tarling Rd. E16 CG39 58
Tarling Rd. N2 BT30 38
Oak La.
Tarling St. Est. E1 CC39 57
Tarling St. E1 CB39 57
Tarn Bank Enf. BX25 29
Tarnwood Pk. SE9 CK47 78
Tarnwood Pk. Est. SE9 CK47 78
Tarnworth Rd. Rom. CX28 42
Tarrington Rd. SW16 BW49 76
Tarry La. SE8 CD42 67
Yeoman St.
Tartar Rd. Cob. BD60 93
Tarver Rd. SE17 BZ42 67
Tarves Way. SE10 CE43 67
Norman Rd.
Tasker Rd. NW3 BU35 47
Tasker Rd. Grays. DG41 71
Tasman Ct. Ashf. BB50 73
Warren Rd.
Tasman Ho. Til. DG44 71
Leicester Rd.
Tasmania Ter. N18 BZ29 39
Tasman Rd. SW9 BX45 66
Tasso Rd. W6 BR43 65
Tatam Rd. NW10 BN36 55
Tate Clo. Lthd. BK65 102
Tate Rd. E16 CK40 58
Tate Rd. Sutt. BS56 95
Tatnell Rd. SE23 CD46 77
Tatsfield Approach Rd. West. CH65 106
Tatsfield Av. Wal. Abb. CF15 12
Tatsfield La. West. CK64 106
Tattenham Cnr. Rd. Epsom BO62 103
Tattenham Cres. Epsom BP62 103
Tattenham Gro. Epsom BP62 103
Tattenham Way Tad. BQ62 103
Tattersall Clo. SE9 CK46 78
Tatum St. SE17 BZ42 67
Taunton Ave. Cat. CA65 105
Taunton Av. SW20 BP51 85
Taunton Av. Houns. BG44 64
Taunton Clo. Bexh. CS44 69
Taunton Clo. Sutt. BS54 86
Taunton Dr. Enf. BY24 29
Slades Rise.
Taunton La. Couls. BY63 104
Taunton Pl. NW1 BU38 56
Taunton Rd. SE12 CG46 78
Taunton Rd. Grav. DD46 81
Taunton Rd. Grnfd. BF37 54
Taunton Rd. Rom. CV28 42
Taunton Vale, Grav. DH48 81
Taunton Way, Stan. BL31 46
Tauton Ave. Couls. BY63 104
Tauton Dr. Enf. BY24 29
Tauton Dr. Red. BW68 113
Taverners, Hem. H. AY12 8
Taverners Clo. W11 BR40 55
Addison Av.
Tavistock Av. Grnf. BJ37 54
Tavistock Av. St. Alb. BG15 9
Tavistock Clo. Pot. B. BT19 20
Tavistock Clo. Rom. CV30 42
Tavistock Clo. Stai. AX50 73
Shaftesbury Cres.
Tavistock Cres. W11 BR39 55
Tavistock Cres. Mitch. BX52 86
Tavistock Gdns. Ilf. CN35 49
Tavistock Gro. Croy. BZ54 87
Tavistock Pl. N14 BV25 29
Tavistock Pl. WC1 BW38 56
Tavistock Rd. E7 CG35 49
Tavistock Rd. E15 CG36 58
Tavistock Rd. E18 CH31 49
Tavistock Rd. N4 BZ32 48
Tavistock Rd. NW10 BO37 55
Tavistock Rd. W11 BR39 55
Tavistock Rd. Brom. CG52 88
Tavistock Rd. Cars. BT54 86
Tavistock Rd. Croy. BZ54 87
Tavistock Rd. Edg. BL30 37
Tavistock Rd. Uxb. BA35 44
Tavistock Rd. Wat. BD23 27
Tavistock Rd. Well. CP44 69
Tavistock Rd. West Dr. AX40 53
Tavistock Sq. WC1 BW38 56
Tavistock St. WC2 BX40 56
Tavistock Ter. N19 BW34 47
Tavistock Wk. Cars. BT54 86
Taviton St. WC1 BW38 56
Tavy Br. SE2 CP41 69
Tawney Common Epp. CR18 23
Tawneys Rd. Harl. CN12 13
Tawny Av. Upmin. CX35 51
Tawny Way, SE16 CC42 67
Tayben Av. Twick. BH46 74
Taybridge Rd. SW11 BV45 66
Taylor Clo. N17 CB29 39
Northumberland Pk.
Taylor Clo. Hamptn. BG40 74
Taylor Clo. Rom. CR29 41
Taylor Rd. Ash. BK62 102
Taylor Rd. Mitch. BU50 76
Taylor Rd. Rich. BM44 65
Taylor Rd. Wall. BV56 95
Taylors Av. Hodd. CE12 12
Taylors Bldgs. SE18 CL42 68
Spray St.
Taylors Grn. W3 BO39 55
Long Dr.
Taylors La. NW10 BO36 55
Taylors La. SE26 CB49 77
Taylors La. Barn. BR23 28
Taylors Rd. Chesh. AO18 16
Taylor St. SE18 CL42 68
Taymount Grange, SE26 CC48 77
Taymount Ri. SE23 CC48 77
Tayport Cl. N1 BX36 56
Tayport Clo. N1 BX36 56
Gifford St.
Tay Way Rom. CT30 41
Taywood Rd. Nthlt. BE38 54
Teale St. E2 CB37 57
Tealing Dr. Epsom BN56 94
Teather St. SE5 CA43 67
Southampton Way.
Tebworth Rd. N17 CA29 39
Church Rd.
Tedder Clo. Chess. BK56 93
Tedder Clo. Ruis. BC35 44
Tedder Clo. Uxb. AY36 53
Tedder Gdns. E6 CK39 58
Tedder Rd. Hem. H. AZ13 8
Tedder Rd. Sth. Croy. CC57 96
Teddington Clo. Epsom BN58 94
Teddington Pk. Tedd. BH49 74
Teddington Pk. Rd. Tedd. BH49 74
Tedworth Gdns. SW3 BU42 66
Tedworth Sq. SW3 BU42 66
Tees Av. Grnf. BH37 54
Tees Clo. Upmin. CY32 51
Teesdale, Hem. H. AY12 8
Teesdale Av. Islw. BJ44 64
Teesdale Est. E2 CB38 57
Teesdale Gdns. Islw. BJ44 64
Teesdale Rd. E11 CG32 49
Teesdale Rd. Dart. CY47 80
Teesdale St. E2 CB37 57
Tees Rd. Rom. CV27 42
Tee, The, W3 BO39 55
Teevan Clo. Croy. CB54 87
Teevan Rd. Croy. CB54 87
Teggs La. Wok. AV61 100
Teignmouth Clo. SW4 BW45 66
Teignmouth Clo. Edg. BL30 37
Teignmouth Gdns. Grnf. BJ37 54
Teignmouth Rd. NW2 BQ35 46
Teignmouth Rd. Well. CP44 69
Telcote Way Ruis. BD33 45
Telegraph Hill NW3 BS34 47
Telegraph La. Esher BJ57 93
Telegraph Ms. Ilf. CO33 50
Eastwood Rd.
Telegraph Rd. SW15 BP46 75
Telegraph St. EC2 BZ39 57
Telemann Sq. SE3 CH45 68
Telephone Pl. SW6 BR43 65
Telferscot Rd. SW12 BW47 76
Telford Av. SW2 BW47 76
Telford Clo. Wat. BD21 27
Telford Ct. St. Alb. BH14 9
Alma Rd.
Telford Rd. N11 BW29 38
Telford Rd. NW9 BO33 46
Broadway, The.
Telford Rd. SE9 CM48 78
Telford Rd. W10 BR39 55
Telford Rd. St. Alb. BK17 18
Telford Rd. Sthl. BF40 54
Telford Ter. SW1 BW43 66
Churchill Gdns. Rd.
Telford Way, W3 BO39 55
Telham Rd. E6 CL37 58
Tell Gro. SE22 CA45 67
Tellisford Esher BF56 93
Tellson Av. SE18 CJ44 68
Telscombe Clo. Orp. CN55 88
Telston La. Sev. CT62 107
Temme Av. E15 CG36 58
Temperance St. St. Alb. BG13 9
Temperley Rd. SW12 BV47 76
Tempest Av. Pot. B. BT19 20
Tempest Rd. Egh. AU50 72
Tempest Way. Rain. CU36 59
Templar Ho. NW2 BR36 55
Templar Pl. Hamptn. BF50 74
Templars Av. NW11 BR32 46
Templars Cres. N3 BS30 38
Templar St. SE5 BY44 66
Temple Av. EC4 BY40 56
Temple Av. N20 BT26 38
Temple Av. Croy. CD55 87
Temple Av. Dag. CR33 50
Temple Bar Rd. Wok. AP63 100
Temple Clo. N3 BR30 37
Temple Clo. Wal. Cr. CB19 21
Temple Clo. Wat. BB23 26
Templecombe Rd. E9 CC37 57
Templecombe Way Mord. BR53 85
Temple Croft, Ashf. BA50 73
Templedene Av. Stai. AW50 73
Temple Field Clo. Wey. AW57 92
Temple Fortune Hl. NW11 BS32 47
Temple Fortune La. NW11 BR32 46
Temple Gdns. NW11 BR32 46
Temple Gdns. Rick. AZ28 35
Temple Gdns. Stai. AV51 82
Temple Gro. NW11 BS32 47
Temple Gro. Enf. BY24 29
Temple Hill, Dart. CW46 80
Temple Hill Sq. Dart. CW46 80
Temple La. EC4 BY39 56
Templeman Clo. Pur. BY57 95
Templeman Clo. Pur. BY61 104
Templeman Rd. W7 BH39 54
Temple Mead. Harl. CH10 13
Temple Mead, Hem. H. AX12 8
Templemead Clo. W3 BO39 55
Carlisle Av.
Temple Mead Clo. Stan. BJ29 36
Templemere, Wey. BA55 83
Temple Mill Rd. E15 CE35 48
Temple Mills La. E15 CE35 48
Templepan, Rick. AY22 26
Temple Pk. Uxb. AZ38 53
Temple Pl. WC2 BX40 56
Templer Ave. Grays. DG42 71
Temple Rd. E6 CK37 58
Temple Rd. N8 BX31 47
Temple Rd. NW2 BQ35 46
Temple Rd. W4 BN41 65
Temple Rd. W5 BK41 64
Temple Rd. Croy. BZ56 96
Temple Rd. Epsom BN59 94
Temple Rd. Houns. BF45 64
Temple Rd. Rich. BL45 65
Temple Rd. Wind. AO44 61
Temple Sheen, SW14 BN45 65
Temple Sheen Rd. SW14 BM45 65
Temple St. E2 CB37 57
Temple, The, SW1 BW40 56
Templeton Av. E4 CE27 39
Templeton Clo. SE19 BZ51 87
Templeton Pl. SW5 BS42 66
Templeton Rd. N15 BZ32 48
Temple Way Sutt. BT55 86
Templewood W13 BJ39 54
Templewood Av. NW3 BS34 47
Templewood Dell. Welw. G. C. BQ6 5
Templewood Gdns. NW3 BS34 47
Tempsford Av. Borwd. BN24 28
Temsford Clo. Har. BG30 36
Ten Acre La. Egh. AU51 82
Tenbury Clo. E7 CJ35 49
Romford Rd.
Tenby Av. Har. BJ30 36
Tenby Clo. Rom. CQ32 50
Tenby Gdns. Nthlt. BF36 54
Tenby Rd. E17 CD32 48
Tenby Rd. Edg. BL30 37
Tenby Rd. Enf. CC24 30
Tenby Rd. Rom. CQ32 50
Tenby Rd. Well. CP44 69
Tenchley's La. Oxt. CJ69 115
Tench St. E1 CB40 57
Tenda Rd. SE16 CB42 67
Tendring Rd. Harl. CM12 13
Tendring Way, Rom. CP32 50
Tenham Av. SW2 BW48 76
Tenham Ter. SW3 BU42 66
Tenison Ct. W1 BW40 56
Kingly St.
Tenison Way, SE1 BX40 56
Tenniel Ct. W2 CJ40 58
Porchester Gdns.
Tennison Av. Borwd. BM25 28
Tennison Clo. Couls. BY63 104
Tennison Rd. SE25 CA52 87
Tennis St. SE1 BZ41 67
Tenniswood Rd. Enf. CA23 30
Tennyson Ave. Grays. DD41 71
Tennyson Av. E11 CH33 49
Tennyson Av. E12 CK36 58
Tennyson Av. NW9 BN31 46
Tennyson Av. N. Mal. BP53 85
Tennyson Av. Twick. BH47 74
Tennyson Av. Wal. Abb. CG20 22
Tennyson Clo. Felt. BC46 73
Tennyson Ct. Rich. BK49 74
Tennyson Rd. E10 CE34 48
Tennyson Rd. E15 CG36 58
Tennyson Rd. E17 CD32 48
Tennyson Rd. NW6 BR37 55
Tennyson Rd. NW7 BP28 37
Tennyson Rd. SE20 CC50 77
Tennyson Rd. SW19 BT50 76
Tennyson Rd. W7 BH40 54
Tennyson Rd. Ashf. AY49 73
Tennyson Rd. Brwd. DE26 122
Tennyson Rd. Dart. CX46 80
Tennyson Rd. Houns. BG44 64
Tennyson Rd. Rom. CU29 41
Tennyson Rd. St. Alb. BF16 18
Tennyson Rd. Well. CN44 68
Shelley Dri.
Tennyson Rd. Wey. AY56 92
Tennyson St. SW8 BV44 66
Tennyson Wk. Grav. DE48 81
Tennyson Wk. Til. DG44 71
Tennyson Way. Horn. CU34 50
Tenplars Dr. Har. BG29 36
Tensing Av. Grav. DF48 81
Tensing Rd. Sthl. BF41 64
Ten St. EC2 BZ39 57
Tentelow La. Sthl. BF42 64
Tenterden Clo. NW4 BQ31 46
Tenterden Dr. NW4 BQ31 46
Tenterden Gdns. NW4 BQ31 46
Tenterden Gdns. Croy. CB54 87
Tenterden Gro. NW4 BQ31 46
Tenterden Rd. N17 CA29 39
Tenterden Rd. Croy. CB54 87
Tenterden Rd. Dag. CQ34 50
Tenterden St. W1 BV39 56
Tenter Gro. E1 CA39 57
Brune St.
Tenter St. EC2 BZ39 57
Moor La.
Tent St. E1 CB38 57
Tenzing Rd. Hem. H. AZ13 8
Terborch Way, SE22 CA46 77
Dulwich Gro.
Tercel Path Chig CQ28 41
Terence Clo. Grav. DJ48 81
Terling Clo. E11 CG34 49
Terling Rd. Dag. CR34 50
Terlings, The, Brwd. DA27 42
Kavanagh Rd.
Terminus Pl. SW1 BV41 66
Terminus St. Harl. CM10 6
Terminus St. Harl. CM11 13
Tern Gdns. Upmin. CZ33 51
Tern Way Brwd. CZ28 42
River Rd.
Terrace Gdns. SW13 BO44 65
Terrace Gdns. Wat. BC23 26
Terrace Hill Croy. BY55 86
Terrace La. Rich. BL46 75
Friars Stile Rd.
Terrace Rd. E9 CC36 57
Terrace Rd. E13 CH37 58
Terrace Rd. Walt. BC54 83
Terrace St. Grav. DG46 81
Terrace, The, N3 BR30 37
Hendon La.
Terrace, The, NW6 BS37 56
Terrace, The, SW13 BO44 65
Terrace, The, W14 BR42 65
Terrace, The Dor. BK72 119
Ter. The Grav. DG46 81
Terrace, The, Kings. On T. BK51 84
Church Gro.
Terrace. The. Maid. AH41
Terrace, The, Rich. BL46 75
Terrace, The, Sev. CS64 107
Terrace, The, Wey. AY56 92
Terrace Wk. Dag. CQ35 50
Terrapin Rd. SW17 BV48 76
Terrick Rd. N22 BX30 38
Terrick St. W12 BP39 55
Terrilands, Pnr. BE31 45
Terront Rd. N15 BZ32 48
Testard Rd. Guil. AR71 118
Testers Clo. Oxt. CH69 115
Testerton St. W11 BQ40 55
Testwood Rd. Wind. AL44 61
Tetcott Rd. SW10 BT43 66
Tetherdown, N10 BV30 38
Tethys Rd. Hem. H. AY12 8
Tetterby Way SE16 CB42 67
Bonamy Estate West The
Teversham La. SW8 BX44 66
Tevin Clo. St. Alb. BK11 9
Teviot Ave. S. Ock. CW39 60
Teviot Clo. Well. CO44 69
Stuart Rd.
Teviot St. E14 CF38 57
Tewin Hill. Welw. BU5 5
Tewin Rd. Hem. H. BA13 8
Tewin Rd. Welw. G. C. BR7 5
Tewkesbury Av. SE23 CB47 77
Tewkesbury Av. Pnr. BE32 45
Tewkesbury Clo. N15 BZ32 48
Tewesbury Rd.
Tewkesbury Clo. Wey. AX59 92
Tewkesbury Gdns. NW9 BM31 46
Tewkesbury Rd. N15 BZ32 48
Tewkesbury Rd. Cars. BT54 86
Tewkesbury Ter. N11 BW29 38
Tewson Rd. SE18 CN42 68
Teynham Av. Enf. BZ25 30
Teynham Grn. Brom. CH53 88
Teynton Ter. N17 BZ30 39
Thackeray Ave. Til. DG44 71
Thackeray Av. N17 CB30 39
Thackeray Clo. SW19 BQ50 75
Thackeray Clo. Uxb. AZ39 53
Thackeray Dr. Rom. CO33 50
Thackeray Rd. E6 CJ37 58
Thackeray Rd. SW8 BV44 66
Thackeray St. W8 BS41 66
Thackery Clo. Har. BF33 45
Thakeham Clo. SE26 CB49 77
Thames Av. Dag. CS38 59
Thames Av. Grnf. BH37 54
Thames Av. Hem. H. AY11 8
Thames Bank. SW14 BN44 65
Thames Clo. Cher. AX54 83
Thames Clo. Hamptn. BF51 84
Thames Clo. Rain. CU39 59
Thames. Dr. Grays. DG42 71

Thamesfield Ct. Shep. BA54 83
Russell Rd.
Thameshill Av. Rom. CS30 41
Thameside, Tedd. BK50 74
Thames Mead Walt. BC53 83
Thames Meadow E. Mol. BF51 84
Thames Pl. E14 CD40 57
Thames Prom. Twick. BJ45 64
Thames Rd. E16 CJ40 58
Thames Rd. W4 BM43 65
Thames Rd. Bark. CN38 58
Thames Rd. Dart. CT44 69
Thames Rd. Grays. DD43 71
Thames Rd. Slou. AT42 62
Thames Side, Stai. AW51 83
Thames Side, Tedd. BK50 74
Thames Side, Wind. AO43 61
Thames St. SE10 CE43 67
Thames St. Hmptn. BF51 84
Thames St. Kings. On T. BK51 84
Thames St. Stai. AV49 72
Thames St. Sun. BC52 83
Thames St. Walt. BB54 83
Thames St. Wey. AZ55 83
Thames St. Wind. AO44 61
Thames Vw. Grays. DG42 71
Thames View Est. Bark. CN37 58
Thames Village W4 BN44 65
Thanescroft Gdns. Croy. CA55 87
Thanet Pl. Croy. BZ56 96
Thanet Rd. Bex. CR47 79
Thanet Rd. Erith CT43 69
Thanet St. WC1 BX38 56
Thane Vill. N7 BX34 47
Thanington Ct. SE9 CN46 78
Tharp Rd. Wall. BW56 95
Thatcham Gdns. N20 BT26 38
Thatchers Cft. Hem. H. AY11 8
Thatchers La. Guil. AO67 109
Thatches Gro. Rom. CQ31 50
Thavies Inn, EC1 BY39 56
St. Andrew St.
Thaxted Rd. SE9 CM48 78
Thaxted Rd. Buck. H. CJ26 40
Thaxted Wk. Rain. CT37 59
Thaxted Way, Wal. Abb. CF20 21
Thaxton Rd. W14 BR43 65
Thayers Farm Rd. Beck. CD51 87
Thayer St. W1 BV39 56
Thaynesfield, Pot. B. BT19 20
Theatre St. SW11 BU45 66
Theberton St. N1 BY37 56
The Courtyard N1 BY36 56
Barnsbury Terr.
The Downs. Hat. BP13 10
Theed St. SE1 BY40 56
Thelma Gdns. SE3 CK44 68
Thelma Gdns. Felt. BE48 74
Thelma Gro. Tedd. BJ50 74
Blackmores Gro.
The Mount Dr. Reig. BT69 121
Theobald Cres. Har. BF30 36
Theobald Rd. E17 CD33 48
Theobald Rd. Croy. BY55 86
Theobalds Ave. Grays. DE42 71
Theobalds Av. N12 BT28 38
Theobalds Clo. Pot. B. BX18 20
Theobalds La. Wal. Cr. CB19 21
Theobalds Park Rd. Enf BY21 29
Theobalds Rd. WC1 BX39 56
Theobalds Rd. Pot. B. BX18 20
Theobald St. SE1 BZ41 67
Theobald St. Rad. BJ21 27
Theobald St. Rad. BL23 28
Theodore Rd. SE13 CF46 77
Thepps Clo. Red. BX72 121
Therapia La. Croy. BW54 86
Therapia La. Croy. BX53 86
Therapia Rd. SE22 CB46 77
Theresa Rd. W6 BP42 65
Theresa St. W6 BP42 65
Therfield Rd. St. Alb. BG12 9
Thermopylae Gte. E14 CE42 67
The Sandlings N22 BY30 38
Theseus Walk N1 BY37 56
Nelson Pl.
Thesiger Rd. SE20 CC50 77
Thessaly Rd. SW8 BW43 66
The Street, Bish. CS7 6
Thetford Cl. N22 BY29 38
Thetford Clo. N15 CA32 48
Norfolk Av.
Thetford Gdns. Dag. CQ37 59
Thetford Rd. Ashf. AY49 73
Thetford Rd. Dag. CP37 59
Thetford Rd. N. Mal. BN53 85
Thetford Rd. N. Mal. BO53 85
Theydon Gdns. Rain. CT36 59
Theydon Gro. Epp. CO18 23
Theydon Gro. Wdf. Grn. CJ29 40
Theydon Pk. Rd. Epp. CN22 31
Theydon Pl. Epp. CN19 22
Theydon Rd. E5 CC34 48
Theydon Rd. Epp. CM20 22
Theydon St. E17 CD33 48
Thicket Cres. Sutt. BT56 95
Thicket Gro. SE20 CB50 77
Thicket Gro. Dag. CP36 59
Thicket Rd. SE20 CB50 77
Thicket Rd. Sutt. BT56 95
Thick, The West Dr. AY39 53
Thickthorne La. Stai. AX50 73
Third Ave. Harl. CK11 13
Third Av. E12 CK35 49
Third Av. E13 CH38 58
Third Av. E17 CE32 48
Third Av. W3 BO40 55
Third Av. W10 BR38 55
Third Av. Dag. CR37 59
Third Av. Enf. CA25 30
Third Av. Hayes BB40 53
Third Av. Rom. CP32 50
Third Av. Wat. BD21 27
Third Av. Wem. BK34 45
Third Clo. E. Mol. BG52 84
Third Cross Rd. Twick. BG48 74
Third Way, Wem. BM35 46
Thirkleby Clo. Slou. AO40 61
Thirlby Rd. Edg. BN30 37
Thirleby Rd. SW1 BW41 66
Thirlmere Av. Grnf. BJ38 54
Thirlmere Dr. St. Alb. BJ14 9
Thirlmere Gdns. Nthwd. BA29 35
Thirlmere Gdns. Wem. BK33 45
Thirlmere Rd. N10 BV30 38
Thirlmere Rd. SW16 BW49 76
Thirlmere Rd. Bexh. CS44 69
Thirlstane St. Alb. BH13 9
Lemsford Rd.
Thirsk Clo. Nthlt. BF36 54
Thirsk Rd. SE25 BZ52 87
Thirsk Rd. SW11 BV45 66
Thirsk Rd. Borwd. BM22 28
Thirsk Rd. Mitch. BV50 76
Thirza Rd. Dart. CW46 80
Thistlecroft, Hem. H. AW14 8
Thistlecroft Gdns. BK30 36
Stan.
Thistlecroft Rd. Walt. BD56 93
Thistledene E. Mol. BH53 84
Thistledene Wey. AV60 91
Thistledene Av. Har. BE34 45
Thistledene Av. Rom. CR28 41
Thistle Gro. SW10 BT42 66
Thistle Gro. Welw. G. BT9 5
C.
Thistlemead Chis. CL51 88
Thistle Mead Loug. CL24 31
Thistle Rd. Grav. DJ47 81
Thistles, The Hem. H. AW13 8
Thistlewaite Rd. E5 CB34 48
Thistle Wd Cres. Croy. CF59 96
Thistleworth Clo. Islw. BG43 64
Thomas A'becket Clo. BH35 45
Wem.
Thomas Baines Rd. SW11 BT45 66
Thomas Clo. Brwd. DC27 122
Thomas Doyle St. SE1 BY41 66
Thomas Dr. Grav. DH48 81
Thomas La. SE6 CE47 77
Thomas More St. E1 CB40 57
Thomas Rd. E14 CD39 57
Thomas St. SE18 CL42 68
Thompson Avenue SE5 BZ43 67
Thompson Av. Rich. BM45 65
Thompson Clo. Slou. AS42 62
Thompson Rd. SE22 CA46 77
Thompson Rd. Dag. CQ34 50
Thompson Rd. Uxb. AY37 53
Thomson Cres. Croy. BY54 86
Thomson Rd. Har. BH31 45
Thong La. Grav. DJ49 81
Thong La. Sev. DC64 108
Thoresby St. N1 BZ38 57
Thorkhill Gdns. Surb. BJ54 84
Thorkhill Rd. Surb. BJ54 84
Thorley Clo. Wey. AW60 92
Thorley Gdns. Wok. AW60 92
Thorley Rd. Grays. DD40 71
Thornaby Gdns. N18 CB29 39
Thornash Clo. Wok. AR61 100
Thornash Rd. Wok. AR61 100
Thornash Way, Wok. AR61 100
Thorn Av. Bush. BG26 36
Thorn Bank, Edg. BM29 37
Thorn Bank, Guil. AQ71 118
Thornbank Clo. Stai. AW46 73
Thornbridge Rd. Iver AU37 52
Thornbury Av. Islw. BG43 64
Thornbury Gdns. Borwd. BN24 28
Thornbury Rd. SW2 BX46 76
Thornbury Rd. Islw. BG43 64
Thornby Rd. E5 CC34 48
Thorncliffe Rd. SW2 BX46 76
Thorncliffe Rd. Sthl. BE42 64
Thorn Clo. Brom. CL53 88
Thorn Clo. Nthlt. BE38 54
Thorncombe Rd. SE22 CA46 77
Thorncroft, Hem. H. AZ14 8
Thorncroft Horn. CU32 50
Thorncroft Dr. Lthd. BJ65 102
Dorking Rd.
Thorncroft Rd. Sutt. BS56 95
Thorncroft St. SW8 BX43 66
Thorndales, Brwd. DB28 42
Thorndean St. SW18 BT48 76
Thorndene Av. N11 BV26 38
Thorndon Av. Brwd. DE31 123
Thorndon Clo. Orp. CN51 88
Thorndon Gdns. Epsom BO56 94
Thorndon Gte. Brwd. DE28 122
Thorndon Rd. Orp. CN51 88
Thorndyke Av. Nthlt. BD37 54
Thorne Clo. E11 CG35 49
Thorne Clo. E16 CG39 58
Thorne Clo. Ashf. BA50 73
Thorne Clo. Erith CS43 69
Thorne Clo. N. Mal. BN52 85
Thorneloe Gdns. Croy. BY56 95
Thorne Pass. SW13 BO44 65
White Hart La.
Thorne Rd. SW8 BX43 66
Thorne Rd. N. Mal. BN52 85
Thornes Clo. Beck. CF52 87
Thorne St. E16 CG39 58
Thorne St. SW13 BO45 65
Thornet Wd. Rd. Brom. CL52 88
Thorney Hedge Rd. W4 BM42 65
Thorney La. Iver AV40 52
Thorney La. S. Iver. AV41 62
Thorney Mill Rd. Iver. AW41 63
Thorney St. SW1 BW42 66
Thornfield Av. NW7 BR30 37
Thornfield Rd. W12 BP41 65
Thornfield Rd. Bans. BS62 104
Thornford Rd. SE13 CF46 77
Thorngate Rd. W9 BS38 56
Thorngrove Rd. E13 CH37 58
Thornham Gro. E15 CF35 48
Thornham St. SE10 CE43 67
Thornhaugh St. WC1 BW38 56
Russell Sq.
Thornhill Av. SE18 CN43 68
Thornhill Av. Surb. BL55 85
Thornhill Cres. N1 BX36 56
Thornhill Epp. CS16 23
Thornhill Gdns. E10 CE34 48
Thornhill Gdns. Bark. CN36 58
Thornhill Rd. E10 CE34 48
Thornhill Rd. N1 BY36 56
Thornhill Rd. Croy. BZ54 87
Thornhill Rd. Nthwd. BA28 35
Thornhill Rd. Surb. BL55 85
Thornhill Rd. Uxb. AZ35 44
Thornhill Sq. N1 BX36 56
Thorn La. Rain. CV37 60
Thornlaw Rd. SE27 BY49 76
Thornley Ct. N17 CB29 39
Thornley Dr. Har. BF34 45
Thornley Pl. SE10 CG42 68
Caradoc St.
Thornridge Brwd. DA26 42
Greenshaw
Thornsbeach Rd. SE6 CF47 77
Thornsett Pl. SE20 CB51 87
Thornsett Rd. SE20 CB51 87
Thornsett Rd. SW18 BS47 76
Thornton Ave. West Dr. AY41 63
Thornton Av. SW2 BW47 76
Thornton Av. W4 BO42 65
Thornton Av. Croy. BX53 86
Thornton Clo. Guil. AQ69 118
Thornton Clo. West Dr. AY41 63
Thornton Ct. SW20 BQ53 85
Thornton Dene Beck. CE51 87
Thornton Gdns. SW12 BW47 76
Thornton Gro. Pnr. BF29 36
Thornton Hl. SW19 BR50 75
Thornton Pl. W1 BU39 56
Thornton Rd. E11 CF34 48
Thornton Rd. SW12 BW47 76
Thornton Rd. SW14 BN45 65
Thornton Rd. SW19 BQ50 75
Thornton Rd. Barn. BR24 28
Thornton Rd. Belv. CR42 69
Thornton Rd. Brom. CH49 78
Thornton Rd. Cars. BT54 86
Thornton Rd. Cars. BU54 86
Thornton Rd. Croy. BX54 86
Thornton Rd. Ilf. CL35 49
Thornton Rd. Pot. B. BT18 20
Thornton Rd. E. SW19 BQ50 75
Thornton Rd.
Thornton Row Th. Hth. BY53 86
Thornton's Fm. Av. Rom. CS33 50
Thornton St. St. Alb. BG13 9
Thornton Way. NW11 BS32 47
Thorntree Rd. SE7 CJ42 68
Thornville St. SE8 CE44 67
Thornwood Rd. SE13 CG46 78
Thornwood Rd. Epp. CO18 23
Thorogood Gdns. E15 CG35 49
Thorogood Way Rain. CT37 59
Thorold Clo. Sth. Croy. CC58 96
Thorold Rd. N22 BX29 38
Thorold Rd. Ilf. CL34 49
Thoroughfare, The, Tad. BP65 103
Thorparch Rd. SW8 BW44 66
Thorpebank Rd. W12 BP40 55
Thorpe By-Pass, Egh. AT52 82
Thorpe Clo. Croy. CF59 96
Thorpe Clo. Horn. CV32 51
Parkstone Av.
Thorpe Clo. Nthlt. BE36 54
Thorpe Clo. Orp. CN55 88
Thorpe Cres. E17 CD30 39
Thorpe Cres. Wat. BC26 35
Thorpedale Gdns. Ilf. CL31 49
Thorpedale Rd. N4 BX34 47
Thorpefield Clo. St. BK12 9
Alb.
Thorpe Hall Ms. W5 BK39 54
Eaton Rise.
Thorpehall Rd. E17 CF30 39
Thorpe Lea Rd. Egh. AT50 72
Thorpe Rd. E6 CK37 58
Thorpe Rd. E7 CG35 49
Thorpe Rd. E17 CF30 39
Thorpe Rd. N15 CA32 48
Thorpe Rd. Bark. CM36 58
Thorpe Rd. Cher. AU52 82
Thorpe Rd. Kings. On T. BL50 75
Thorpe Rd. St. Alb. BG14 9
Thorpe Rd. Stai. AU50 72
Thorpes Clo. Guil. AQ69 118
Thorpe St. E1 CA39 57
Wentworth St.
Thorpewood Av. SE26 CB48 77
Thorsden Clo. Wok. AS63 100
Thorsden Ct. Wok. AS62 100
Guildford Rd.
Thorsden Way, SE19 CA49 77
Oaks Av.
Thorton Cres. Couls. BX63 104
Thorverton Rd. NW2 BR34 46
Thoydon Rd. E3 CD37 57
Thrale Rd. SW16 BW49 76
Thrale St. SE1 BZ40 57
Thrawl St. E1 CA39 57
Threadneedle St. EC2 BZ39 57
Three Arch Rd. Red. BU72 121
Three Cherrytrees La. AZ11 8
Hem. H.
Three Close La. Berk. AR13 7
Three Colts La. E2 CB38 57
Three Colt St. E14 CD39 57
Three Corners Bexh. CR44 69
Three Corners, Hem. H. AZ14 8
Three Gates, Guil. AU69 118
Three Gates Rd. Fawk. DA54 90
Three Horseshoes Rd. CL12 13
Harl.
Three Households. Ch. AP28 34
St. G.
Three Kings Ct. EC4 BY39 56
Gough Sq.
Three Kings Rd. Mitch. BU52 86
Three Kings Yd. W1 BV40 56
Three Mill La. E3 CF38 57
Three Nun Ct. EC2 BZ39 57
Aldermanbury.
Three Oak La. SE1 CA41 67
Three Oaks Clo. Uxb. AY34 44
Three Pears Rd. Guil. AU70 118
Threshers Pl. W11 BR40 55
Thriffwood, SE23 CC48 77
Thrift Fm. Rd. Borwd. BN23 28
Thrift Grn. Brwd. DD27 122
Thrifts Mead, Epp. CN22 31
Thrift, The. Dart. DB48 80
Thrigby Rd. Chess. BL57 94
Throckmorten Rd. E16 CH39 58
Throgmorton Av. EC2 BZ39 57
Throgmorton St. EC2 BZ39 57
Throwley Clo. SE2 CP41 69
Throwley Rd. Sutt. BS56 95
Thrums, The Wat. BC22 26
Thrupp Clo. Mitch. BV51 86
Thrupp's Av. Walt. BD56 93
Thrupp's La. Walt. BD56 93
Thrush Av. Hat. BP13 10
Thrush La. Pot. B. BX17 20
Thrush St. SE17 BZ42 67
Thruxton Way, SE15 CA43 67
Thumbswood. Welw. G. BS9 5
C.
Thumpers, Hem. H. AY12 8
Thurbarn Rd. SE6 CE49 77
Thurgood Row, Hodd. CE11 12
Thurland Rd. SE16 CB41 67
Thurlastone Pde. Shep. BA53 83
High St.
Thurlby Clo. Harrow. BJ32 45
Gayton Rd.
Thurlby Clo. Wdf. Grn. CK28 40
Thurlby Rd. SE27 BY49 76
Thurlby Rd. Wem. BK36 54
Thurleigh Av. SW12 BV46 76
Thurleigh Rd. SW12 BU46 76
Thurleston Av. Mord. BR53 85
Thurlestone Av. N12 BU29 38
Thurloe Clo. SW7 BU42 66
Thurloe Ct. SW3 BU42 66
Fulham Rd.
Thurloe Gdns. Rom. CT32 50
Thurloe Pl. SW7 BT42 66
Thurloe Pl. Ms. SW7 BT42 66
Thurloe Pl.
Thurloe Sq. SW7 BU42 66
Thurloe St. SW7 BT42 66
Thurloe Wk. Grays. DD41 71
Thurlow Gdns. Ilf. CM29 40
Thurlow Gdns. Wem. BK35 45
Thurlow Hl. SE21 BZ47 77
Thurlow Pk. Rd. SE21 BY47 76
Thurlow Rd. NW3 BT35 47
Thurlow Rd. W7 BJ41 64
Elthorne Pk. Rd.
Thurlow Rd. W13 BJ41 64
Park Rd.
Thurlow St. SE17 BZ42 67
Thurlow Ter. NW5 BU35 47
Thurlstone Av. Ilf. CN35 49
Thurlstone Clo. Shep. BA53 83
Thurlstone Rd. SE27 BY48 76
Thurlston Rd. Ruis. BC34 44
Thurlton Clo. Wok. AS61 100
Thurnby Ct. Twick. BH48 74
Thurrock Lodge La. DC41 71
Grays.
Thursland Rd. Sid. CQ49 79
Thursley Cres. Croy. CF57 96
Thursley Gdns. SW19 BQ48 75
Thursley Rd. SE9 CK48 78
Thurso Clo. Rom. CX29 42
Thurso St. SW17 BT49 76
Thurstans Harl. CM13 13
Thurston Rd. SE13 CE44 67
Thurston Rd. SW20 BP50 75
Thurston Rd. Slou. AP39 52
Thurston Rd. Sthl. BE39 54
Thurtle Rd. E2 CA37 57
Thwaite Clo. Erith CS43 69
Thyra Gro. N12 BS29 38
Tibbatts Rd. E3 CE38 57
Tibbenham Wk. E13 CG37 58
Tibberton Sq. N1 BZ37 57
Popham Rd.
Tibbet's Ride, SW15 BQ47 75
Tibbetts Clo. SW19 BQ47 75
Tibbs Hill Rd. Wat. BB18 17
Ticehurst Rd. SE23 CD48 77
Tichborne Wd. Rick. AU28 34
Tichmarsh Epsom BN58 94
Tickford Clo. SE2 CP41 69
Tidal Basin Rd. E16 CG40 58
Tidenham Gdns. Croy. CA55 87
Tideswell Rd. SW15 BQ45 65
Tideswell Rd. Croy. CE55 87
Tidey St. E3 CE39 57
Tidford Rd. Well. CN44 68
Tidsworth Rd. E3 CE38 57
Tidworth Rd. E3 CE38 57
Tidy's La. Epp. CO18 23
Tiepigs La. W. Wick. CG55 88
Tierney Rd. SW2 BX47 76
Tiger Way. E5 CB35 48
Tilbrook Rd. SE3 CJ45 68
Tilburstow Hill Rd. CC69 114
Gdse.
Tilbury Clo. SE15 CA43 67
Willowbrook Rd.
Tilbury Clo. Orp. CO51 89
Tilbury Gdns. Til. DG45 71
Tilbury Hotel Rd. Til. DG45 71
Tilbury Mead. Harl. CO12 14
Tilbury Rd. E6 CK37 58
Tilbury Rd. E10 CF33 48
Tilbury Rd. Brwd. DF31 123
Tilbury Sq. Hayes BD39 54
Tildesley Rd. SW15 BQ46 75
Tile Croft, Welw. G. C. BQ6 5
Tile Fm. Rd. Orp. CM55 88
Tile Gate Rd. Harl. CN12 13
Tile Gate Rd. Ong. CS13 14
Tilehouse La. Ger. Cr. AV30 34
Tilehouse La. Uxb. AV31 43
Tilehouse Rd. Guil. AS72 118
Tilehouse Way Uxb. AV32 43
Tilehurst La. Dor. & BL72 120
Bet.
Tilehurst Rd. SW18 BT47 76
Tilehurst Rd. Sutt. BR56 94
Tile Kiln Clo. Hem. H. AZ14 8
Tile Kiln Cres. Hem. H. AZ14 8
Tile Kiln La. N6 BW33 47
Tile Kiln La. N13 BZ28 39
Tile Kiln La. Bex. CS48 79
Tile Kiln La. Hem. H. AZ14 8
Tile Kiln La. Uxb. AZ33 44
Tilers, Way, Reig. BT72 121
Tileyard Rd. N7 BX36 56
Tilford Av. Croy. CF58 96
Tilford Gdns. SW19 BQ47 75
Tilia Rd. E5 CB35 48
Till Av. Farn. CW54 90
Tiller St. E14 CE41 67
Tillett Clo. NW10 BN36 55
Tilley La. Epsom. BM65 103
Tilleys La. Stai. AV49 72
Tillingbourne Gdns. N3 BR31 46
Tillingbourne Grn. Orp. CN52 88
Tillingbourne Rd. Guil. AS73 118
Tillingbourne Way. N3 BR31 46
Tillingbourne Gdns.
Tillingdown Hill. Cat. CB64 105
Tillingdown La. Cat. CB65 105
Tilling Down La. Cat. CB66 114
Tillingham Way N12 BS28 38
Tillotson Rd. N9 CA27 39
Tillotson Rd. Har. BF29 36
Tillotson Rd. Ilf. CL33 49
Tillotson St. E1 CC39 57
Tillwicks Rd. Harl. CO11 14
Tilman St. E1 CB39 57
Tilney Ct. EC1 BZ38 57
Old St.
Tilney Dr. Buck. H. CH27 40
Tilney Rd. Dag. CQ36 59
Tilney Rd. Sthl. BD42 64
Tilney St. W1 BV40 56
Tilson Gdns. SW2 BW47 76
Tilson Ho. SW2 BX47 76
Tilson Rd. N17 CB30 39
Tilstone Ave. Wind. AM42 61
Tilstone Clo. Wind. AM42 61
Tilt Clo. Cob. BE61 102
Tilton Rd. Sev. DC63 108
Tilt Rd. Cob. BD61 102
Tiltwood, The, W3 BN40 55
Acacia Rd.
Tiltyard App. SE9 CK46 78
Timber Clo. Chis. CL51 88
Timber Clo. Lthd. BG67 111
Timbercroft Epsom BN56 94
Timbercroft. Welw. G. BR6 5
C.
Timbercroft La. SE18 CN43 68
Timber Dene. NW4 BQ30 37
Timberhill Rd. Cat. CB65 105
Timber Slip Dr. Wall. BW58 95
Timber St. EC1 BZ38 57
Baltic St.
Timbertop Rd. West. CJ62 106
Timberwharf Rd. N16 CB32 48
Timothy Rd. E3 CD39 57
Timperley Gdns. Red. BU69 121
Timplings Row, Hem. H. AW12 8
Timsbury Wk. SW15 BP47 75
Foxcombe Rd.
Tim's Way, Stai. AV49 72
Tindal St. SW9 BY44 66
Tinderbox Alley. SW14 BN45 65
North Worple Way.
Tine Rd. Chig. CN28 40
Tinglefield, Pot. B. BS18 20
Tinkers La. Wind. AL44 61
Tinsley Rd. E1 CC39 57
Tintagel Clo. Epsom BO60 94
Tintagel Cres. SE22 CA45 67
Tintagel Dr. Stan. BK28 36
Tintagel Gdns. SE22 CA45 67
Oxonian St.
Tintagel Rd. Orp. CP55 89
Tintells Lane. Leath. AZ67 110
Tintern Av. NW9 BM31 46
Tintern Clo. SW15 BR46 75
Tintern Clo. Slou. AO41 61
Tintern Gdns. N14 BX26 38
Tintern Rd. N22 BZ30 39
Tintern Rd. Cars. BT54 86
Tintern St. SW4 BX45 66
Tintern Way Har. BF33 45
Tinto Rd. E16 CH38 58
Tinworth St. SE11 BX42 66
Tippendell La. St. Alb. BF16 18
Tippetts Clo. Enf. BZ23 30
Tipps Cross La. Brwd. DA20 24
Tips Cross Mead DA21 33
Tipthorpe Rd. SW11 BV45 66
Tipton Dr. Croy. CA56 96
Tiptree Clo. Horn. CX33 51
Tiptree Cres. Ilf. CL31 49
Tiptree Rd. Ruis. BC35 44
Tiree Clo. Hem. H. AZ14 8
Tirlemont Rd. Sth. BZ57 96
Croy.
Tirrell Rd. Croy. BZ53 87

Tisbury Rd. SW16 BX51 86
Tisdall Pl. SE17 BZ42 67
Titan Rd. Hem. H. AY12 8
Titchborne Row. W2 BU39 56
Hyde Park Cres.
Titchfield Rd. Cars. BT54 86
Titchfield Rd. Enf. CD22 30
Titchfield Wk. Cars. BT54 86
Titchwell Rd. SW18 BT47 76
Tite Hill, Egh. AR49 72
Tite St. SW3 BU42 66
Tithe Barn Clo. St. Alb. BG15 9
Tithe Barn Dr. Maid. AJ42 61
Tithebarns Lane. Wok. AW66 110
Tithe Barn Way Nthlt. BC37 53
Tithe Clo. NW7 BP30 37
Tithe Ct. NW4 BP30 37
Tithe Farm Av. Har. BF34 45
Tithe Farm Clo. Har. BF34 45
Tithe La. Stai. AT46 72
Tithepit Shaw La. Warl. CB62 105
Tithe Wk. NW7 BP30 37
Titian Av. Bush. BH26 36
Titley Clo. E4 CE28 39
Titmus Clo. Uxb. BA39 53
Titsey Hill, Oxt. CH65 106
Titsey Rd. Oxt. CH67 115
Tiverton Av. Ilf. CL31 49
Tiverton Dr. SE9 CM47 78
Tiverton Gro. Rom. CX28 42
Tiverton Rd. N15 BZ32 48
Tiverton Rd. N18 CA28 39
Tiverton Rd. NW10 BQ37 55
Tiverton Rd. Edg. BL30 37
Tiverton Rd. Houns. BF44 64
Tiverton Rd. Pot. B. BT19 20
Tiverton Rd. Ruis. BC34 44
Tiverton Rd. Wem. BL37 55
Tiverton St. SE1 BZ41 67
Tiverton Way, Chess. BK56 93
Tivoli Rd. N8 BW32 47
Tivoli Rd. SE27 BZ49 77
Tivoli Rd. Houns. BE45 64
Tivoli Way. SE27 BZ49 77
Holderness Way.
Tobin Clo. NW3 BU36 56
Todds Walk N7 BX34 47
Andover Est.
Toft Ave. Grays. DE42 71
Tokenhouse Yd. EC2 BZ39 57
Tokyngton Av. Wem. BL36 55
Toland Sq. SW15 BP46 75
Tolcarne Dr. Pnr. BC30 35
Tolcarne Dr. Pnr. BC31 44
Toley Av. Wem. BL33 46
Tolhurst St. SE4 CD45 67
Foxwell St.
Tollers La. Coul. BX63 104
Tollesbury Gdns. Ilf. CM31 49
Tollet St. E1 CC38 57
Tollgate Av. Red. BU73 121
Tollgate Clo. Rick. AV24 25
Tollgate Dr. SE21 CA48 77
Tollgate Gdns. NW6 BS37 56
Tollgate Rd. E16 CJ39 58
Tollgate Rd. Dart. CY47 80
Tollgate Rd. Dor. BJ73 119
Tollgate Rd. St. Alb. BN15 10
Tollgate Rd. Wal. Cr. CC21 30
Tollington Pk. N4 BX34 47
Tollington Pl. N4 BX34 47
Tollington Rd. N7 BX35 47
Tollington Way. N7 BX34 47
Tollpit End, Hem. H. AW12 8
Tolmers Av. Pot. B. BX17 20
Tolmers Gdns. Pot. B. BX18 20
Tolmers Rd. Pot. B. BX17 20
Tolmers Sq. NW1 BW38 56
Tolpits Clo. Wat. BB25 26
Tolpits La. Wat. BA26 35
Tolpits La. Wat. BB25 26
Tolsford Rd. E5 CB35 48
Clarence Rd.
Tolson Rd. Islw. BJ45 64
Toludene Clo. Wok. AP62 100
Tolver Ct. Brwd. DB27 42
Tower Hill.
Tolverne Rd. SW20 BQ51 85
Tolworth Clo. Surb. BM54 85
Tolworth Gdns. Rom. CP32 50
Tolworth Pk. Rd. Surb. BL55 85
Tolworth Rise N. Surb. BM54 85
Tolworth Rise S. Surb. BM54 85
Tolworth Rd. Surb. BL55 85
Tomahawk Gdns. Nthlt. BD38 54
Javelin Way
Tomlins Gro. E3 CE38 57
Tomlinson Clo. E2 CA38 57
Tomlins Orchard, Bark. CM37 58
Tomlins Wk. N7 BX34 47
Andover Est.
Tomlyns Clo. Brwd. DF25 122
Tom Mann Clo. Bark. CN37 58
Tom's Cft. Hem. H. AY14 8
Toms Hill, Rick. AY21 26
Tom, S La. Kings L. AZ18 17
Tomswood Hill, Ilf. CL29 40
Tomswood Rd. Chig. CL29 40
Tonbridge Clo. Bans. BU60 95
Tonbridge Cres. Har. BL31 46
Tonbridge Rd. E. Mol. BE53 84
Tonbridge Rd. Rom. CV29 42
Tonbridge Rd. Sev. CV67 117
Tonbridge Rd. Ton. & Sev. DB67 117
Tonbridge St. WC1 BX38 56
Tonfield Rd. Sutt. BR54 85
Tonge Clo. Beck. CE53 87
Tonsley Hill. SW18 BS46 76
Tonsley Pl. SW18 BS46 76
Tonsley Rd. SW18 BS46 76
Tonsley St. SW18 BS46 76
Tonstall Rd. Epsom BN59 94
Tonstall Rd. Mitch. BV51 86
Tonwick Rd. Wind. AN42 61
Tooke Clo. Pnr. BE30 36
Took's Ct. EC4 BY39 56
Cursitor St.
Toolands Rd. Islw. BJ44 64
Tooley St. SE1 BZ40 57
Tooley St. Grav. DE47 81
Toorack Rd. Har. BG30 36
Toot Hill Rd. Ong. CT18 23
Tooting Bec. Gdns. SW16 BW49 76
Tooting Bec. Rd. SW17 BV48 76
Tooting Gro. SW17 BU49 76
Tooting High St. SW17 BU49 76
Toots Wd. Rd. Brom. CG53 88
Topaz St. SE11 BX42 66
Topcliffe Dr. Orp. CM56 97
Top Dartford Rd. Swan. CT50 79
Topham Sq. N17 BZ30 39
Topham St. EC1 BY38 56
Top Ho. Rise E4 CF26 39
Topiary Sq. Rich. BL45 65
Topland Rd. Ger. Cr. AR29 34
Toplands Ave. S. Ock. CX40 60
Topley St. SE9 CJ45 68
Top Pk. Beck. CF53 87
Top Park. Ger. Cr. AR32 43
Topsfield Rd. N8 BX32 47
Topsham Rd. SW17 BU48 76
Top Wk. Cat. CD64 105
Torbay Rd. NW6 BR36 55
Torbay Rd. Har. BE34 45
Torbridge Clo. Edg. BL29 37
Torbrook Clo. Bex. CQ46 79
Torcross Dr. SE23 CC48 77
Torcross Rd. Ruis. BC34 44
Tor Gdns. W8 BS41 66
Tor La. Wey. BA59 92
Tormead Clo. Brom. CG50 78
Tormead Clo. Sutt. BS57 95
Tormead Rd. Guil. AS70 118
Tormount Rd. SE18 CN43 68
Toronto Av. E12 CK35 49
Toronto Rd. E11 CF35 48
Toronto Rd. Ilf. CL33 49
Toronto Rd. Til. DG44 71
Torquay Gdns. Ilf. CJ31 49
Torquay St. W2 BS39 56
Harrow Rd.
Torrance Clo. Horn. CU33 50
Torrance Rd. SE3 CJ44 68
Torrans Wk. Grav. DJ49 81
Torrens Rd. E15 CG36 58
Torrens Rd. SW2 BX46 76
Torrens Sq. E15 CG36 58
Torrens St. N1 BY37 56
Torre Wk. Cars. BU54 86
Torriano Av. NW5 BW35 47
Torriano Cotts. NW5 BW35 47
Torriano Av.
Torriano Est. NW1 BW35 47
Torridge Gdns. SE15 CC45 67
Torridge Rd. Th. Hth. BY53 86
Torridge Walk, Hem. H. AY11 8
Torridon Rd. SE6 CF47 77
Torridon Rd. SE13 CF47 77
Torrington Av. N12 BT28 38
Torrington Clo. N12 BT28 38
Torrington Pk.
Torrington Clo. Esher BH57 93
Torrington Dr. Har. BF35 45
Torrington Dr. Loug. CM24 31
Torrington Dr. Pot. B. BT19 20
Torrington Gdns. N11 BW29 38
Torrington Gdns. Grnf. BK37 54
Torrington Gdns. Loug. CM24 31
Torrington Gro. N12 BU28 38
Torrington Pk. N12 BT28 38
Torrington Pl. WC1 BW39 56
Torrington Rd. E18 CH31 49
Torrington Rd. Berk. AQ13 7
Torrington Rd. Dag. CQ33 50
Torrington Rd. Esher BH57 93
Torrington Rd. Grnf. BK37 54
Torrington Rd. Ruis. BB34 44
Torrington Way Mord. BS54 86
Tor Rd. Well. CP44 69
Torr Rd. SE20 CC50 77
Torver Rd. Har. BH31 45
Torver Way Orp. CM55 88
Torwood Clo. Berk. AP13 7
Torwood La. Whyt. CA63 105
Torwood Rd. SW15 BP46 75
Totham Lo. SW20 BP51 85
Richmond Rd.
Tothill St. SW1 BW41 66
Totnes Rd. E16 CH39 58
Totnes Rd. Well. CO43 69
Totnes Wk. N2 BT31 47
Tottenhall Rd. N13 BY29 38
Tottenham Court Rd. W1 BW38 56
Tottenham Green E. N15 CA31 48
Tottenham Grn. W. N15 CA31 48
Town Hall App.
Tottenham La. N8 BX32 47
Tottenham Ms. W1 BW39 56
Tottenham St.
Tottenham Rd. N1 BZ36 57
Tottenham Sq. N1 CA36 57
Tottenham St. W1 BW39 56
Totterdown St. SW17 BU49 76
Totteridge Clo. N20 BS27 38
Totteridge La. N20 BP27 37
Totteridge Rd. Enf. CC22 30
Totternhoe Clo. Har. BK32 45
Totton Rd. Th. Hth. BY52 86
Totty St. E3 CD37 57
Toulmin Dr. St. Alb. BG11 9
Toulmin St. SE1 BZ41 67
Tournay Rd. SW6 BR43 65
Tovey Av. Hodd. CE11 12
Towcester Rd. E3 CE38 57
Tower Bridge. CA40 57
Tower Bridge App. E1 CA40 57
Tower Bridge Rd. SE1 CA41 67
Tower Cl. Epp. CS15 14
Tower Clo. SE20 CB50 77
Tower Clo. Berk. AQ13 7
Tower Clo. Grav. DJ49 81
Tower Clo. Ilf. CM29 40
Tower Clo. Orp. CN55 88
Tower Clo. Wok. AR62 100
Tower Ct. N16 CA33 48
Tower Gdns. Rd. N17 BZ30 39
Tower Gro. Wey. BB54 83
Tower Hamlets Rd. E7 CG35 49
Tower Hamlets Rd. E17 CE31 48
Tower Hill, EC3 CA40 57
Tower Hill, Brwd. DB27 42
Tower Hill, Dor. BJ72 119
Tower Hill, Kings L. AV18 16
Tower Hill Rd. Dor. BJ72 119
Tower La. Reig. BT68 113
Tower Ms. E17 CE31 48
High St.
Tower Pl. EC3 CA40 57
Tower Ri. Rich. BL45 65
Tower Rd. NW10 BP36 55
Tower Rd. Belv. CS42 69
Tower Rd. Bexh. CR45 69
Tower Rd. Dart. CV47 80
Tower Rd. Epp. CN18 22
Tower Rd. Orp. CN55 88
Tower Rd. Tad. BQ65 103
Tower Rd. Twick. BH48 74
Tower Royal EC4 BZ39 57
Cannon St.
Towers Av. Uxb. BA38 53
Towers Pl. Rich. BL46 75
Eton St.
Towers Rd. Hem. H. AY13 8
Towers Rd. Pnr. BE30 36
Towers Rd. Sthl. BF38 54
Towers. The Ken. BZ57 96
Towers, The Ken. BZ61 105
Tower St. WC2 BW39 56
Towers Walk, Wey. AZ57 92
Tower Ter. N22 BX30 38
Mayes Rd.
Tower Vw. Croy. CD54 87
Towfield Rd. Felt. BE48 74
Town Centre, Hodd. CE12 12
Towncourt Cres. Orp. CM53 88
Town Ct. La. Orp. CM54 88
Town Court Path. N4 BZ33 48
Town End High St. Cat. CA64 105
Towneymead Nthlt. BE37 54
Townfield. Rick. AX26 35
Town Field La. Ch. St. G. AR27 34
Townfield Rd. Hayes BB40 53
Town Fields. Hat. BP12 10
Townfield Sq. Hayes BB40 53
Townford Rd. Dor. BJ72 119
Town Hall App. N15 CA31 48
Town Hall App. N16 CA35 48
Milton Bro.
Town Hall Av. W4 BN42 65
Town Hall Rd. SW11 BU45 66
Townholm Cres. W7 BH41 64
Town La. Stai. AX46 73
Townley Ct. E15 CG36 58
Faraday Rd.
Townley Rd. SE22 CA46 77
Townley Rd. Bexh. CQ46 79
Townley St. SE17 BZ42 67
Townmeade Rd. Rich. BM44 65
Townmead Est. SW6 BS45 66
Town Meadow Rd. Brent. BK43 64
High St.
Townmead Rd. SW6 BS45 66
Townmead Rd. Wal. Abb. CF20 21
Town Quay, Bark. CL37 58
Town Quay Stai. AW52 83
Blacksmythe La.
Town Rd. N9 CB27 39
Townsend Av. N14 BW28 38
Townsend Av. St. Alb. BH13 9
Townsend Dr. St. Alb. BG12 9
Townsend La. NW9 BN33 46
Townsend Rd. N15 CA32 48
Townsend Rd. Ashf. AY49 73
Townsend Rd. Sthl. BE40 54
Townsend St. SE17 BZ42 67
Townsends Yd. N6 BV33 47
Townsend Way. Nthwd. BB29 35
Townshend Est. NW8 BU37 56
Townshend Rd. NW8 BU37 56
Townshend Rd. Chis. CL49 78
Townshend Rd. Rich. BL45 65
Townshend Ter. Rich. BL45 65
Townside. Harl. CP11 14
Townslow La. Wok. AX61 101
Townson Av. Nthlt. BC37 53
Townson Way Nthlt. BC37 53
Town, The, Enf. BZ24 30
Town Tree Rd. Ashf. AZ49 73
Town Wf. Islw. BJ45 64
Towton Rd. SE27 BZ48 77
Toxsowa Ho. SE21 CA47 77
Toynbee Rd. SW20 BQ51 85
Toynbee St. E1 CA39 57
Toys Hill. Eden. CP70 116
Toys Hill West. CO69 116
Tracery, The, Bans. BS61 104
Tracey St. SE11 BY42 66
Tracious Clo. Wok. AQ61 100
Tracious La. Wok. AQ61 100
Tracy Av. NW2 BP35 46
Tracy Ct. Stan. BK29 36
Tracyes Rd. Harl. CO12 14
Tradescant Rd. SW8 BX43 66
Trading Est. W3 BM38 55
Trafalgar Av. N17 CA29 39
Trafalgar Av. SE15 CA42 67
Trafalgar Av. Brox. CD14 12
Trafalgar Av. Wor. Pk. BQ54 85
Trafalgar Dr. Walt. BC55 83
Trafalgar Gdns. E1 CC39 57
Trafalgar Gro. SE10 CF43 67
Trafalgar Pl. N18 CB28 39
Trafalgar Rd. SE10 CF43 67
Trafalgar Rd. SW19 BS50 76
Trafalgar Rd. Dart. CW48 80
Trafalgar Rd. Grav. DG47 81
Trafalgar Rd. Rain. CT37 59
Trafalgar Rd. Twick. BG48 74
Trafalgar Sq. WC2 BW40 56
Trafalgar St. SE17 BZ42 67
Trafalgar Ter. Har. BG33 45
Nelson Rd.
Trafford Rd. Th. Hth. BX53 86
Tramway Av. E15 CF36 57
Broadway
Tramway Av. N9 CB26 39
Tramway Path Mitch. BU53 86
Tranby Pl. E9 CC35 48
Tranmere Rd. N9 CA26 39
Tranmere Rd. SW18 BT47 76
Tranmere Rd. Twick. BF47 74
Tranquil Dale, Bet. BO69 120
Tranquil Rise Erith CT42 69
Tranquil Vale, SE3 CG44 68
Transept St. NW1 BU39 56
Transmere Clo. Orp. CM53 88
Transport Av. Brent. BJ43 64
Tranton Rd. SE16 CB41 67
Trapps La. Chesh. AQ20 16
Trapp, S La. Chesh. AO19 16
Trap's Hill Loug. CK24 31
Traps La. N. Mal. BO51 85
Travanion Rd. W14 BR43 65
Travellers La. Hat. BP13 10
Travellers Way Houns. BD44 64
Travers Rd. N7 BY34 47
Trawley Rd. SW6 BS45 66
Traysiea, Uxb. AX37 53
Treacy Clo. Bush. BG27 36
Treadgold St. W11 BQ40 55
Treadway St. E2 CB37 57
Treadwell Rd. Epsom BO61 103
Treaty Rd. Houns. BF45 64
Treaty St. N1 BX37 56
Trebeck St. W1 BV40 56
Curzon St.
Trebellan Dr. Hem. H. AY13 8
Treble Rd. Swans. DB46 80
Trebovir Rd. SW5 BS42 66
Treby St. E3 CD38 57
Trecastle Way N7 BW35 47
Carleton Rd.
Tredegar Rd. E3 CD37 57
Tredegar Rd. N11 BW29 38
Tredegar Rd. Dart. CU48 79
Tredegar Sq. E3 CD38 57
Tredegar Ter. E3 CD38 57
Trederwen Rd. E8 CB37 57
Tredown Rd. SE26 CC49 77
Tree Bourne Rd. West. CJ62 106
Treebys Ave. Guil. AR67 109
Tree Clo. Rich. BK47 74
Tree Mt. Ct. Epsom BO60 94
Treen Av. SW13 BO45 65
Tree Rd. E16 CJ39 58
Treeside Clo. West Dr. AX42 63
Tree Tops, Brwd. DB26 42
Tree Tops, Grav. DG49 81
Tree Tops Clo. Belv. CQ42 69
Tree Tops Clo. Nthwd. BA28 35
Treewall Gdns. Brom. CH49 78
Tree Way, Reig. BS69 121
Trefgarne Rd. Dag. CR34 50
Trefil Walk N7 BX35 47
Warlters Rd.
Trefoil Rd. SW18 BT46 76
Trefusis Wk. Wat. BB23 26
Tregaron Av. N8 BX32 47
Tregarvon Rd. SW11 BV45 66
Tregelles Rd. Hodd. CE11 12
Tregenna Av. Har. BE35 45
Tregenna Clo. N14 BW25 29
Trego Rd. E3 CD36 57
Tregothnan Rd. SW9 BX45 66
Tregunter Rd. SW10 BS43 66
Trehaven Pde. Reig. BS72 121
Hornbeam Rd.
Trehearn Rd. Ilf. CM29 40
Treherne Ct. SW17 BV49 76
Treherne Rd. SW9 BY44 66
Trehern Rd. SW14 BN45 65
Trehurst St. E5 CD35 48
Trelawney Est. E9 CC36 57
Trelawney Rd. Ilf. CM29 40
Trelawn Rd. E10 CF34 48
Trelawn Rd. SW2 BY46 76
Trelawny Ave. Slou. AR41 62
Treloar Gdns. SE19 BZ50 77
Tremadoc Rd. SW4 BW45 66
Tremaine Clo. SE4 CE44 67
Tremaine Rd. SE20 CB51 87
Trematon, Tedd. BK50 74
Tremlett Gro. N19 BW34 47
Tremlett Mews. N19 BW34 47
Junction Rd.
Trenance Gdns. Ilf. CO34 50
Trenchard Av. Ruis. BC35 44
Trenchard Clo. Stan. BJ29 36
Trenchard Clo. Walt. BD56 93
Trenchard Ct. Mord. BS53 86
Trenchard Rd. Maid. AG43 61
Trenchard St. SE10 CF42 67
Trenches La. Slou. AT40 52
Trenham Dr. Warl. CC61 105
Trenholme Clo. SE20 CB50 77
Trenholme Rd. SE20 CB50 77
Trenholme Ter. SE20 CB50 77
Trenmar Gdns. NW10 BP38 55
Trent Av. W5 BK41 64
Trent Av. Upmin. CY32 51
Trent Gdns. N14 BV25 29
Trentham Cres. Wok. AT64 100
Trentham Dr. Orp. CO53 89
Trentham Rd. Red. BV71 121
Trentham St. SW18 BS47 76
Trentham Way, Red. BU71 121
Trent Rd. SW2 BX46 76
Trent Rd. Buck. H. CH26 40
Trent Way, Hayes BB37 53
Trentwood Side Enf. BX24 29
Treport St. SW18 BS47 76
Tresco Clo. Brom. CG50 78
Hillbrow Rd.
Trescoe Gdns. Har. BE33 45
Trescoe Gdns. Rom. CS28 41
Tresco Gdns. Ilf. CO34 50
Tresco Rd. SE15 CB45 67
Tresco Rd. Berk. AP12 7
Tresham Cres. W1 BU38 56
Tresham Rd. Bark. CN36 58
Tresham Wk. E9 CC35 48
Churchill Wk.
Tresilian Sq. Hem. H. AY11 8
Tressillian Cres. SE4 CE45 67
Tressillian Rd. SE4 CD45 67
Treswell Rd. Dag. CQ37 59
Tretawn Gdns. NW7 BO28 37
Tretawn Pk. NW7 BO28 37
Trevanion Rd. W14 BR42 65
Treve Av. Har. BG33 45
Trevelance Way, Wat. BD20 18
Trevelyan Av. E12 CK35 49
Trevelyan Clo. Dart. CW45 70
Trevelyan Cres. Har. BL30 46
Trevelyan Gdns. NW10 BQ37 55
Trevelyan Rd. E15 CG35 49
Trevelyan Rd. SW17 BU49 76
Trevelyan Way, Berk. AQ12 7
Trevelyn Ct. N. Mal. BO54 85
Trevereux Hill. Oxt. CK69 115
Treveris St. SE1 BY40 56
Bear Lane.
Treverton Est. W10 BQ39 55
Treverton St. W10 BQ38 55
Treville St. SW15 BP47 75
Treviso Rd. SE23 CC47 77
Farren Rd.
Trevithick Dr. Dart. CW45 70
Trevithick Rd. Dart. CW46 80
Trevithick St. SE8 CE42 67
Watergate St.
Trevone Gdns. Pnr. BE32 45
Trevor Clo. Barn. BT25 29
Trevor Clo. Brom. CG54 88
Trevor Clo. Islw. BH46 74
Trevor Clo. Nthlt. BD37 54
Trevor Clo. Stan. BH29 36
Trevor Ct. Stai. AW46 73
Horton Rd.
Trevor Cres. Ruis. BB35 44
Trevor Gdns. Edg. BN30 37
Trevor Gdns. Nthlt. BD37 54
Trevor Pl. SW7 BU41 66
Trevor Rd. SW19 BR50 75
Trevor Rd. Edg. BN30 37
Trevor Rd. Hayes. BB41 63
Trevor Rd. Wdf. Grn. CH29 40
Trevor Sq. SW7 BU41 66
Trevor St. SW7 BU41 66
Trevose Rd. E17 CF30 39
Trevose Way Wat. BD27 36
Trewenna Dr. Pot. B. BT19 20
Trewince Rd. SW20 BQ51 85
Trewint St. SW18 BT48 76
Trewsbury Rd. SE26 CC49 77
Triangle, Wok. AR62 100
Triangle Pl. SW4 BW45 66
Triangle Rd. E8 CB37 57
Triangle, The, Bark. CM36 58
Park Av.
Triangle, The, Hamptn. BG51 84
Triangle, The, Kings-on-t. BN51 85
Trident Gdns. Nthlt. BD38 54
Jetstar Way
Trident Rd. Wat. BB20 17
Trident Way, Sthl. BC41 63
Triggs Clo. Wok. AR63 100
Triggs La. Wok. AR63 100
Trigon Rd. SW8 BX43 66
Trilby Rd. SE23 CC48 77
Trimmer Wk. Brent. BL43 65
Netley Rd.
Trim St. SE14 CD43 67
Trinder Gdns. N19 BX33 47
Trinder Rd. N19 BX33 47
Trinder Rd. Barn. BQ25 28
Trindles Rd. Red. BX71 121
Tring Av. W5 BL40 55
Tring Av. Sthl. BE39 54
Tring Av. Wem. BM36 55
Tring Clo. Ilf. CM32 49
Tring Clo. Rom. CW28 42
Tring Gdns. Rom. CW28 42
Tring Grn. Rom. CW28 42
Tringham Clo. Cher. AU56 91
Tring Rd. Berk. AO11 7
Tring Wk. Rom. CW28 42
Trinidad Gdns. Dag. CS36 59
Trinidad St. E14 CD40 57
Trinity Av. N2 BT31 47
Trinity Av. Enf. CA25 30
Trinity Ch. Rd. SW13 BP43 65
Trinity Church Sq. SE1 BZ41 67
Trinity Clo. NW3 BT35 47
Hampstead High St.
Trinity Clo. Brom. CK54 88
Trinity Clo. Houns. BE45 64
Trinity Clo. Nthwd. BB29 35
Trinity Clo. Stai. AX46 73
Trinity Clo. Sth. Croy. CA58 96
Trinity Cotts. Rich. BL45 65
Trinity Rd.
Trinity Ct. N1 CA37 57
Trinity Cres. SW17 BU48 76

Trinity Est. SE8 CD42 67
Trinity Gdns. E16 CG39 58
Trinity Gdns. SW9 BX45 66
Trinity Grn. E1 CC38 57
Trinity Gro. SE10 CF44 67
Trinity La. Wal. Cr. CD19 21
Trinity Pl. Bexh. CQ45 69
Trinity Pl. Wind. AO44 61
Trinity Ri. SW2 BY47 76
Trinity Rd. N2 BT31 47
Trinity Rd. N22 BX29 38
Trinity Rd. SW17 BT46 76
Trinity Rd. SW18 BT46 76
Trinity Rd. SW19 BS50 76
Trinity Rd. Ilf. CM31 49
Trinity Rd. Rich. BL45 65
Trinity Rd. Sthl. BE40 54
Trinity Sq. EC3 CA40 57
Trinity St. E16 CG39 58
Trinity St. SE1 BZ41 67
Trinity St. Enf. BZ23 30
Trinity Way. W3 BO40 55
Trio Pl. SE1 BZ41 67
Tripps Hill Clo. Ch. St. G. AQ27 34
Tripton Rd. Harl. CN11 13
Trisian Sq. SE3 CG45 68
Tristram Clo. E17 CF31 48
Tristram Rd. Brom. CG49 78
Triton Sq. NW1 BW38 56
Triton Way, Hem. H. AY12 8
Tritton Av. Croy. BX56 95
Tritton Rd. SE21 BZ48 77
Triumph Clo. Hayes. BA43 63
Trodd's La. Guil. AU70 118
Trojan Way Croy. BX55 86
Trolling Down Hill. Dart. CY48 80
Tronsay Wk. N1 BZ36 57
Marquess Est.
Troon St. E1 CD39 57
Trosley Av. Grav. DG48 81
Trosley Rd. Belv. CR43 69
Trossachs Rd. SE22 CA46 77
Trothy Rd. SE1 CB42 67
Trots La. West. CM67 115
Trotsworth Av. Vir. W. AS52 82
Trotters Bottom Barn. BP22 28
Trotters La. Wok. AQ59 91
Trotters Rd. Harl. CO12 14
Trott St. SW11 BT44 66
Troughton Rd. SE7 CH42 68
Troutbeck Rd. E14 CD44 67
Trout La. West Dr. AX40 53
Trout Rise, Rick. AW24 26
Trout Rd. West Dr. AX40 53
Troutstream Way, Rick. AW24 26
Trouville Rd. SW4 BW46 76
Trowbridge Rd. E9 CD36 57
Trowbridge Rd. Rom. CV29 42
Trowers Way, Red. BV69 121
Trowley Rise, Wat. BB19 17
Trowlock Av. Tedd. BK50 74
Trowlock Way. Tedd. BK50 74
Broom Rd.
Troy Ct. W8 BS41 66
Troy Rd. SE19 BZ50 77
Troy Town. SE15 CB45 67
Nutbrook St.
Trucks Alley Swan. CR51 89
Truesdale Dr. Uxb. AX31 44
Trulock Ct. N17 CB29 39
Trulock Rd. N17 CB29 39
Truman's Rd. N16 CA35 48
Truman St. SE16 CB41 67
Trumper's Way W7 BH41 64
Trumper Way, Uxb. AX37 53
Trumpetshill Rd. Reig. BP71 120
Trumpington Dr. St. Alb. BG15 9
Trumpington Rd. E7 CG35 49
Trumpsgreen Av. Vir. W. AR53 82
Trumpsgreen Rd. Vir. W. AR53 82
Trumpsgreen Rd. Vir. W. AR54 82
Trumps Mill La. Vir. W. AS53 82
Trump St. EC2 BZ39 57
King St.
Trundlers Way Bush. BH26 36
Trundle St. SE1 BZ41 67
Weller St.
Trundley's Rd. SE8 CC42 67
Trundley's Ter. SE8 CC42 67
Truro Gdns. Ilf. CK33 49
Truro Rd. E17 CD32 48
Truro Rd. N22 BX29 38
Truro Rd. Grav. DH48 81
Truro St. NW3 BV36 56
Truro Wk. Rom. CV29 42
Truro Way, Hayes BB38 53
Truslove Rd. SE27 BY49 76
Trussley Rd. W6 BQ41 65
Trustings Clo. Esher. BJ57 93
Trustons Gdns. Horn. CU33 50
Trycewell La. Sev. DB64 108
Tryfan Clo. Ilf. CJ32 49
Tryon St. SW3 BU42 66
Trys Hill, Cher. AT55 82
Tuam Rd. SE18 CM43 68
Tubbenden Clo. Orp. CN55 88
Tubbenden Dr. Orp. CM56 97
Tubbenden La. Orp. CM56 97
Tubbs Rd. NW10 BO37 55
Tubs Hill. Sev. CU65 107
Tubwell Rd. Slou. AQ37 52
Tucker St. Wat. BD25 27
Tuckley Gro. Wok. AV65 100
Tuck Rd. Rain. CU36 59
Tudor Av. Hmptn. BF50 74
Tudor Av. Rom. CU31 50
Tudor Av. Wal. Cr. CB19 21
Tudor Av. Wat. BD22 27
Tudor Av. Wor. Pk. BP55 85
Tudor Clo. NW3 BU35 47
Tudor Clo. NW7 BP29 37
Tudor Clo. NW9 BN34 46
Tudor Clo. SW2 BX46 76
Tudor Clo. Ashf. AY49 73
Tudor Clo. Bans. BR61 103
Tudor Clo. Brwd. DD25 122
Tudor Clo. Chess. BL56 94
Tudor Clo. Chig. CL27 40
Tudor Clo. Chis. CK51 88
Tudor Clo. Cob. BE60 93
Tudor Clo. Couls. BY62 104
Tudor Clo. Dart. CU46 79
Tudor Clo. Lthd. BE65 102
Tudor Clo. Pnr. BC32 44
Tudor Clo. Sth. Croy. CB61 105
Tudor Clo. Sutt. BQ57 94
Tudor Clo. Wal. Cr. CB19 21
Tudor Clo. Wall. BW57 95
Tudor Clo. Wdf. Grn. CH28 40
Tudor Clo. Welw. BP5 5
Tudor Ct. E17 CD32 48
Tudor Ct. SE9 CK45 68
Tudor Ct. N. Wem. BM35 46
Tudor Ct. S. Wem. BM35 46
Tudor Cres. Ilf. CL29 40
Tudor Cres. Sev. CV61 108
Tudor Dr. Kings. On T. BK49 74
Tudor Dr. Mord. BQ53 85
Tudor Dr. Rom. CU31 50
Tudor Dr. Sev. CV61 108
Tudor Dr. Walt. BD54 84
Tudor Dr. Wat. BD22 27
Tudor Est. NW10 BM38 55
Tudor Gdns. NW9 BN34 46
Tudor Gdns. SW13 BO45 65
Treen Av.
Tudor Gdns. W3 BM39 55
Tudor Gdns. Rom. CU31 50
Tudor Gdns. Upmin. CY34 51
Tudor Gdns. W. Wick. CF55 87
Tudor Gro. E9 CC36 57
Tudor Hill, Hem. H. AX14 8
Tudor Pl. W1 BW39 56
Gresse St.
Tudor Pl. Mitch. BU50 76
Tudor Rd. E4 CE29 39
Tudor Rd. E6 CJ37 58
Tudor Rd. E9 CB37 57
Tudor Rd. N9 CB26 39
Tudor Rd. SE19 CA50 77
Tudor Rd. SE25 CB53 87
Tudor Rd. Ashf. BA50 73
Tudor Rd. Bark. CN37 58
Tudor Rd. Barn. BS24 29
Tudor Rd. Beck. CE52 87
Tudor Rd. Brox. CD14 12
Tudor Rd. Hamptn. BF50 74
Tudor Rd. Har. BG30 36
Tudor Rd. Hayes BA39 53
Tudor Rd. Houns. BG45 64
Tudor Rd. Kings. On T. BM50 75
Tudor Rd. Pnr. BD30 36
Tudor Rd. St. Alb. BH11 9
Tudor Rd. Sthl. BE40 54
Tudor Sq. Hayes BA39 53
Tudor St. EC4 BY39 56
Tudor Wk. Bex. CQ46 79
Tudor Wk. Wat. BD22 27
Tudor Way N14 BW26 38
Tudor Way. W3 BL41 65
Tudor Way Orp. CM53 88
Tudor Way. Rick. AW26 35
Tudor Way, Uxb. AZ36 53
Tudor Way, Wal. Abb. CF20 21
Tudor Way. West Dr. AY42 63
Tudor Way. Wind. AM44 61
Tudor Well Clo. Stan. BJ28 36
Old Church La.
Tudway Rd. SE3 CJ45 68
Tudway Rd. SE9 CJ45 68
Tufnail Rd. Dart. CW46 80
Tufnell Park Rd. N7 BW35 47
Tufter Rd. Chig. CN28 40
Tufton Gdns. E. Mol. BF51 84
Tufton Rd. E4 CE28 39
Tufton St. SW1 BW41 66
Tugela Rd. Croy. BZ53 87
Tugela St. SE6 CD48 77
Tulip Clo. Brwd. DA25 33
Poppy Clo.
Tulip Clo. Rom. CV29 42
Tulip Ct. Pnr. BD31 45
Nursery Rd.
Tullerie St. E2 CB37 57
Tulse Clo. Beck. CF52 87
Tulse Hill, SW2 BY46 76
Tulse Hl. Est. SW2 BY46 76
Tulsemere Rd. SE27 BZ48 77
Tumber St. Epsom BN66 112
Tumblefield Rd. Sev. DC60 99
Tumbler Rd. Harl. CO11 14
Tumblewood Rd. Bans. BR61 103
Tuncombe Rd. N18 CA28 39
Tunfield Rd. Hodd. CE10 12
Tunis Rd. W12 BP40 55
Tunley Rd. NW10 BO37 55
Tunley Rd. SW17 BV47 76
Tunmarsh La. E13 CH38 58
Tunmers End. Ger. Cr. AR30 34
Tunnel Av. SE10 CF40 57
Tunnel Gdns. N11 BW29 38
Tunnel Wood Clo. Wat. BB22 26
Tunnel Wood Rd. Wat. BB22 26
Tunnmead, Harl. CO10 6
Tunsgate, Guil. AR71 118
Tuns La. Slou. AO40 61
Tunstall Av. Ilf. CO29 41
Tunstall Clo. Orp. CN56 97
Tunstall Rd. SW9 BX45 66
Tunstall Rd. Croy. CA54 87
Tunstall Wk. Brent. BK42 64
Ealing Rd.
Tunworth Clo. NW9 BN32 46
Tunworth Cres. SW15 BO46 75
Tures Clo. Uxb. AZ38 53
Turfhouse La. Wok. AP58 91
Turin Ct. Egh. AR49 72
Turin Rd. N9 CC26 39
Turin St. E2 CB38 57
Turkey St. Enf. CB21 30
Turk's Row. SW3 BU42 66
Turle Rd. N4 BX33 47
Turle Rd. SW16 BW51 86
Turley Clo. E15 CG37 58
Turmore Dale. Welw. G. C. BQ8 5
Turnagain La. EC4 CM39 58
Farringdon St.
Turnagain La. Dart. CU48 79
Turnage Rd. Dag. CQ33 50
Turnant Rd. N17 BZ30 39
Lordship La.
Turnberry Way Orp. CM54 88
Turnbull Clo. Green. CZ47 80
Turner Av. N15 CA31 48
Turner Av. Mitch. BU51 86
Turner Av. Twick. BG48 74
Turner Clo. NW11 BS32 47
Turner Clo. Hayes BA37 53
Turner Dr. NW11 BS32 47
Turner Rd. E17 CF31 48
Turner Rd. Bush. BG24 27
Turner Rd. Dart. DA48 80
Turner Rd. Edg. BL30 37
Turner Rd. N. Mal. BN54 85
Turner Rd. West. CJ59 97
Turners Clo. Ong. CW18 24
Turner's Hill, Hem. H. AY14 8
Turners Hill, Wal. Cr. CC18 21
Turners La. Walt. BC57 92
Turners Rd. E3 CD39 57
Turner St. E1 CB39 57
Turner St. E16 CG39 58
Turners Way. NW11 BT33 47
Wildwood Rd.
Turner's Wood NW11 BT33 47
Wildwood Rd.
Turners Wood Dr. Ch. St. G. AR27 34
Turneville Rd. W14 BR43 65
Turney Rd. SE21 BZ47 77
Turney Rd. W14 BR43 65
Turnham Grn. Ter. W4 BO42 65
Turnham Rd. SE4 CD46 77
Turnmill St. EC1 BY38 56
Turnoak Av. Wok. AS63 100
Turnoak La. Wok. AS63 100
Turnpike Ct. Bexh. CP45 69
Crook Log.
Turnpike Dr. Orp. CP58 98
Turnpike La. N8 BX31 47
Turn Pike La. Uxb. AY37 53
Turnpike Link Croy. CA55 87
Turnpin La. SE10 CF43 67
King William Wk.
Turnstones. The. Wat. BE21 27
Turnville Rd. W14 BR44 65
Turp Ave. Grays. DE41 71
Turpentine La. SW1 BV42 66
Sutherland St.
Turpin Av. Rom. CR29 41
Turpington Clo. Brom. CK54 88
Turpington La. Brom. CK54 88
Turpin's La. Wdf. Grn. CK28 40
Turpin Way Wall. BV57 95
Turquand St. SE17 BZ42 67
Turret Gro. SW4 BW45 66
Turtle Rd. SW17 BT48 76
Turton Mkt. Wem. BL35 46
Turton Rd.
Turton Rd. Wem. BL35 46
Turton Way. Slou. AO41 61
Turville St. E2 CA38 57
Old Nichol St.
Tuscan Rd. SE18 CM42 68
Tuskar St. SE10 CG42 68
Tuttlebee La. Buck. H. CH27 40
Tuxford Clo. Borwd. BL22 28
Twedwell Clo. Brom. CK52 88
Tweedale Rd. Cars. BT54 86
Tweed Glen Rom. CS29 41
Tweed Grn. Rom. CS29 41
Tweed La. Bet. BM72 120
Tweedmouth Rd. E13 CH37 58
Tweed Way Rom. CS29 41
Tweedy Rd. Brom. CH51 88
Twelve Acre Clo. Lthd. BE65 102
Twelve Acres. Welw. G. C. BR9 5
Twickenham Br. Rich. BK46 74
Twickenham Br. Twick. BK46 74
Twickenham Clo. Croy. BX55 86
Twickenham Gdns. Grnf. BJ35 45
Twickenham Gdns. Har. BH29 36
Twickenham Rd. E11 CF34 48
Twickenham Rd. Felt. BE49 74
Twickenham Rd. Islw. BJ46 74
Twickenham Rd. Rich. BK45 64
Twickenham Rd. Tedd. BJ49 74
Twigs Clo. Erith CT43 69
Twilley St. SW18 BS47 76
Twinches La. Slou. AN40 61
Twineham Grn. N12 BS28 38
Twining Av. Twick. BG48 74
Twinn Rd. NW7 BR29 37
Twinoaks. Cob. BF60 93
Twisden Rd. NW5 BV35 47
Twitchells La. Beac. AP29 34
Twitton La. Sev. CS61 107
Two Arces. Welw. G. C. BR9 5
Two Dells Lane. Chesh. AP16 16
Two Waters Rd. Hem. H. AX15 8
Twybridge Way. NW10 BN36 55
Twyford Abbey Rd. NW10 BL38 55
Twyford Av. N2 BU31 47
Twyford Av. W3 BM40 55
Twyford Cres. W3 BM40 55
Twyford Pl. WC2 BX39 56
Kingsway
Twyford Rd. Cars. BT54 86
Twyford Rd. Har. BF33 45
Twyford Rd. Ilf. CM35 49
Twyford St. N1 BX37 56
Tyas Rd. E16 CG38 58
Tybenham Rd. SW19 BR52 85
Tyberry Rd. Enf. CB24 30
Tyburn La. Har. BH33 45
Tyburns, The, Brwd. DE27 122
Tycehurst Gdns. Ilf. CM35 49
Tycehurst Hill Loug. CK24 31
Tydcombe Rd. Warl. CC63 105
Tye Green Village. Harl. CN12 13
Tye La. Epsom BN67 112
Tye La. Orp. CM56 97
Tyers St. SE11 BX42 66
Tyers Ter. SE11 BX42 66
Tyeshurst Clo. SE2 CQ42 69
Tykeswater La. Borwd. BK23 27
Tylecroft Rd. SW16 BX51 86
Tylehost, Guil. AQ68 109
Tyler Gro. Dart. CW45 70
Tyler Rd. Beck. CE51 87
Tylers Causeway. Hert. BW14 11
Tylers Clo. Gdse. CB68 114
Tylers Clo. Loug. CK26 40
Tylers Est. SE1 CA41 67
Tylers Gate, SE1 CA41 67
Tylers Gate, Har. BL32 46
Tylers Grn. Rd. Swan. CS53 89
Tylers Hill Rd. Chesh. AP18 16
Tylers La. Harl. CJ13 13
Tylers Rd. Harl. CJ13 13
Tyler St. SE10 CG42 68
Tylers Way Wat. BG24 27
Tylney Av. SE19 CA49 77
Tylney Croft. Harl. CM12 13
Tylney Rd. E7 CJ35 49
Tylney Rd. Brom. CJ51 88
Tyndall Rd. E10 CF34 48
Tyndall Rd. Well. CN45 68
Tyne Cdns. S. Ock. CW40 60
Tyne Clo. Upmin. CY32 51
Tynedale Rd. Bet. BM72 120
Tyneham Rd. SW11 BV44 66
Tynemouth Dr. Enf. CB22 30
Tynemouth Rd. N15 CA31 48
Tynemouth Rd. Mitch. BV50 76
Tynemouth St. SW6 BT44 66
Tyne Rd. Ilf. CM34 49
Tynley Gro. Guil. AR67 109
Type St. E2 CC37 57
Tyrawley Rd. SW6 BS44 66
Tyrell Gdns. Wind. AM45 61
Tyrell Rise Brwd. DB28 42
Chindits La.
Tyrells Clo. Upmin. CX34 51
Tyrone Rd. E6 CK37 58
Tyron Way, Sid. CN49 78
Tyrrell Av. Well. CO46 79
Tyrrell Rd. SE22 CB45 67
Tyrrells Hall Clo. Grays. DE42 71
Tyrrells Wood Dr. Lthd. BL65 103
Tyrrel Way NW9 BO33 46
Tyrwhitt Ave. Guil. AQ68 109
Tyrwhitt Rd. SE4 CE45 67
Tysea Clo. Harl. CN12 13
Tysea Hill. Rom. CT26 41
Tysea Rd. Harl. CN12 13
Tysoe Av. Enf. CD22 30
Tysoe St. EC1 BY38 56
Tyson Rd. SE23 CC47 77
Tyssen Pl. E8 BT36 56
Ramsgate St.
Tyssen Rd. N16 CA34 48
Stoke Newington High St.
Tyssen St. E8 CA36 57
Tytherton Rd. N19 BW34 47
Tyttenhanger La. St. Alb. BK14 9
Tyttenhanger La. St. Alb. BL15 10
Uamvar St. E14 CE39 57
Uckfield Gro. Mitch. BV51 86
Uckfield Rd. Enf. CC22 30
Udall Gdns. Rom. CR29 41
Udall St. SW1 BW42 66
Vincent Sq.
Udney Pk. Rd. Tedd. BJ50 74
Uffington Rd. NW10 BP37 55
Uffington Rd. SE27 BY49 76
Ufford Clo. Har. BF29 36
Ufford Rd. Har. BF29 36
Ufford St. SE1 BY41 66
Ufton Gro. N1 BZ36 57
Ufton Rd. N1 BZ36 57
Ullathorne Rd. SW16 BW49 76
Ulleswater Rd. N14 BX28 38
Ullswater Clo. SW15 BN49 75
Ullswater Clo. Brom. CG50 78
Ullswater Clo. Hayes BB37 53
Ullswater Cres. SW15 BN49 75
Ullswater Cres. Couls. BW61 104
Ullswater Cres. Couls. BX57 95
Ullswater Rd. SE27 BY48 76
Ullswater Rd. SW13 BP43 65
Ullswater Rd. Hem. H. AZ14 8
Ullswater Way. Horn. CU35 50
Ulstan Clo. Cat. CE65 105
Ulster Gdns. N13 BZ28 39
Ulster Pl. NW1 BV38 56
Ulundi Rd. SE3 CG43 68
Ulva Rd. SW15 BQ45 65
Ravenna Rd.
Ulverscroft Rd. SE22 CA46 77
Ulverstone Rd. SE27 BY48 76
Ulverston Rd. E17 CF30 39
Ulwyn Av. Wey. AY60 92
Ulysses Rd. NW6 BR35 46
Umberston St. E1 CB39 57
Umbria St. SW15 BP46 75
Umfreville Rd. N4 BY32 47
Ummer Gro. Borwd. BK25 27
Underacres Clo. Hem. H. AZ13 8
Underbridge Way Enf. CD24 30
Undercliff Rd. SE13 CE45 67
Underhill Barn. BS25 29
Underhill Pk. Rd. Reig. BS69 121
Underhill Rd. SE22 CB46 77
Underne Av. N14 BV27 38
Underriver House Rd. Sev. CX68 117
Undershaft EC3 CA39 57
St. Mary Axe
Undershaw Rd. Brom. CG48 78
Underwood Croy. CF57 96
Underwood Rd. E1 CB38 57
Underwood Rd. E4 CE28 39
Underwood Rd. Cat. CA66 114
Underwood Row N1 BZ38 57
Underwood St. N1 BZ38 57
Underwood, The, SE9 CK48 78
Undine St. SW17 BU49 76
Uneeda Dr. Grnf. BG37 54
Union Cotts. E15 CG36 58
Union Ct. E15 CF37 57
Union Ct. EC2 CA39 57
Wormwood St.
Union Ct. Ilf. CL34 49
Ilford Hill
Union Gro. SW8 BW44 66
Union La. Islw. BJ44 64
Park Rd.
Union Rd. E17 CD32 48
Union Rd. N11 BW29 38
Union Rd. SW4 BW44 66
Union Rd. SW8 BW44 66
Union Rd. Brom. CJ53 88
Union Rd. Croy. BZ54 87
Union Rd. Wem. BL36 55
Union Row N18 CB29 39
Union Sq. N1 BZ37 57
Union St. E15 CF37 57
Union St. SE1 BY41 66
Union St. Barn. BR24 28
Union St. Kings-on-t. BK51 84
Union Wk. E2 CA38 57
Unity Rd. Enf. CC22 30
University Pl. Erith. CR43 69
Belmont Rd.
University Pl. Erith CR44 69
Becton Pl.
University Rd. SW19 BT50 76
University St. WC1 BW38 56
Unwin Av. Felt. BA46 73
Unwin Clo. SE15 CB43 67
Unwin Rd. Islw. BH45 64
Upbrook Ms. W2 BT39 56
Upcerne Rd. SW10 BT43 66
Upchurch Clo. SE20 CB50 77
Woodbin Gro.
Upcroft, Wind. AN45 61
Upcroft Av. Edg. BN28 37
Updale Clo. Pot. B. BQ20 19
Updale Rd. Sid. CN49 78
Upfield Croy. CB55 87
Upfield Rd. W7 BH38 54
Uphall Av. Ilf. CL35 49
Uphall Rd. Ilf. CL34 49
Upham Pk. Rd. W4 BO42 65
Uphill Dr. NW7 BO28 37
Uphill Dr. NW9 BN32 46
Uphill Gro. NW7 BO28 37
Uphill Rd. NW7 BO28 37
Upland Ct. Rd. Rom. CW30 42
Upland Rd. E13 CG38 58
Upland Rd. SE22 CB46 77
Upland Rd. Bexh. CQ45 69
Upland Rd. Cat. CE63 105
Upland Rd. Epp. CM16 22
Upland Rd. Sth. Croy. BZ56 96
Upland Rd. Sutt. BT57 95
Uplands, SW16 BY49 76
Uplands, Ash. BK63 102
Uplands Beck. CE51 87
Uplands, Welw. G. C. BQ6 5
Uplands Av. E17 CC30 39
Uplands Clo. SW14 BM46 75
Uplands Clo. Ger. Cr. AS33 43
Uplands Clo. Sev. CT65 107
Uplands Ct. N21 BY26 38
Uplands Dr. Hat. BS16 20
Uplands End Wdf. Grn. CK29 40
Uplands Pk. Rd. Enf. BY24 29
Uplands Rd. N8 BX32 47
Uplands Rd. Barn. BV26 38
Uplands Rd. Brwd. DC28 122
Uplands Rd. Ken. BZ61 105
Uplands Rd. Orp. CO54 89
Uplands Rd. Rom. CP31 50
Uplands Rd. Wdf. Grn. CK29 40
Uplands, The, Ger. Cr. AS33 43
Uplands, The, Loug. CK24 31
Uplands, The, Ruis. BC33 44
Uplands, The, St. Alb. BE18 18
Uplands Way N21 BY25 29
Uplands Way. Sev. CT65 107
Upland Way Epsom BQ62 103
Upminster Rd. Horn. CW34 51
Upminster Rd. N. Rain. CV38 60
Upminster Rd. S. Rain. CU38 59
Upney La. Bark. CN35 49
Upnor Way SE17 CA42 67
Uppark Dr. Ilf. CM32 49
Upr. Abbey Rd. Belv. CQ42 69
Upper Addison Gdns. W14 BR41 65
Upper Ashlyns Rd. Berk. AQ13 7
Upper Austin Lodge Rd. Eyns. CV56 99
Upper Av. Grav. DF51 81
Upr. Bardsey Wk. N1 BZ36 57
Marquess Est.

Upper Barn, Hem. H. AY15 8
Upr. Belgrave St. SW1 BV41 66
Upr. Berkeley St. W1 BU39 56
Upr. Beulah Hl. SE19 CA51 87
Upr. Bray Rd. Maid. AH42 61
Upr. Brentwood Rd. Rom. CV31 51
Upr. Bridge Rd. Red. BU70 121
Upr. Brighton Rd. Surb. BK53 84
Upper Brockley Rd. SE4 CD45 67
Upper Brook St. W1 BV40 56
Upper Butts Brent. BK43 64
Upr. Caldy Wk. N1 BZ36 57
Marquess Est.
Upr. Cavendish Av. N3 BS31 47
Upr. Cheyne Row SW3 BU43 66
Upper Church Hill. Green. CZ46 80
Upr. Clapton Rd. E5 CB33 48
Upper Corner Pl. Ch. St. G. AQ27 34
Upr. Cornsland, Brwd. DB27 42
Upper Court Rd. Cat. CE65 105
Upr. Court Rd. Epsom BN59 94
Upr Culver Rd. St. Alb. BH12 9
Upr Dagnal St. St. Alb. BG13 9
Upr. Drayton Pl. Croy. BY55 86
Upper Dr. West. CJ62 106
Upr. Edgeborough Rd. Guil. AS71 118
Upper Elmers End Rd. Beck. CD52 87
Upr. Fairfield Rd. Lthd. BJ64 102
Upr. Farm Rd. BE52 84
Upper Feild Rd. Welw. G. C. BR9 5
Upr. Fosters NW4 BQ32 46
Upr. Green E. Mitch. BU51 86
Upr. Green Rd. Ton. DB68 117
Upr. Green W. Mitch. BU51 86
Upper Grosvenor St. W1 BV40 56
Upr. Grotto Rd. Twick. BH48 74
Upper Ground SE1 BY40 56
Upper Gro. SE25 CA52 87
Upr. Grove Rd. Belv. CQ43 69
Upr. Guildown Rd. Guil. AQ72 118
Upr. Gulland Wk. N1 BZ36 57
Marquess Est.
Upper Haliford Rd. Shep. BB52 83
Upper Hall Pk. Berk. AR13 7
Upr. Ham Rd. Rich. BK49 74
Upper Handa Wk. N1 BZ36 57
Marquess Est.
Upper Harley St. NW1 BV38 56
Upr Heath Rd. St. Alb. BH12 9
Upr High St. Epsom. BO60 94
Upper Highway, Kings L. BA19 17
Upper Highway, Wat. BA20 17
Upr. Hill Rise, Rick. AW25 26
Upper Hill Vw. Rd. Pnr. BE29 36
Upper Hitch, Wat. BE27 36
Upr. Holly Hill Rd. Belv. CR42 69
Upper James St. W1 BW40 56
Beak St.
Upper John St. W1 BW40 56
Beak St.
Upr Lattimore Rd. St. Alb. BH13 9
Upr. Lismore Wk. N1 BZ36 57
Marquess Est.
Upper Mall W6 BP42 65
Upr. March La. Hodd. CE12 12
Upr Marlborough Rd. St. Alb. BH13 9
Upper Marsh SE1 BX41 66
Upper Mealines. Harl. CO12 14
Upr. Montagu St. W1 BU39 56
Upr. Mulgrave Rd. Sutt. BR57 94
Upr. North St. E14 CE39 57
Upr. Paddock Rd. Wat. BE25 27
Upr. Palace Rd. E. Mol. BG52 84
Upper Park, Harl. CL10 6
Upr. Pk. Loug. CJ24 31
Upr. Pk. Rd. N11 BV28 38
Upper Pk. Rd. NW3 BU35 47
Upr. Park. Rd. Belv. CR42 69
Upr. Park Rd. Brom. CH51 88
Upr. Park Rd. Kings. On T. BM50 75
Upper Phillimore Gdns. W8 BS41 66
Upr. Pillory Downs. Cars. BV60 95
Upper Pines Bans. BU62 104
Upr. Rainham Rd. Horn. CT33 50
Upr. Ramsey Wk. N1 BZ36 57
Marquess Est.
Upr. Richmond Rd. SW14 BM45 65
Upr. Richmond Rd. SW15 BM45 65
Upr. Richmond Rd. Rich. BM45 65
Upper Rd. E13 CH38 58
Upper Rd. Uxb. AU33 43
Upper Rd. Wall. BW56 95
Upr. Rose Hill, Dor. BJ72 119
Upper Ryle, Brwd. DA28 42
Upr. St. Martin's La. WC2 BX40 56
Long Acre
Upper Sales, Hem. H. AV14 7
Upr. Selsdon Rd. Sth. Croy. CA57 96
Upr. Sheppey Wk. N1 BZ36 57
Marquess Est.
Upr. Sheridan Rd. Belv. CR42 69
Coleman Rd.
Upr. Shirley Rd. Croy. CC55 87
Upper Shot. Welw. G. C. BS7 5
Upper Spring La. Sev. DA64 108
Upper Sq. Islw. BJ45 64
Upper Staithe W4 BN44 65
Upper Station Rd. Rad. BJ21 27
Upper Stoneyfield. Harl. CL11 13
Upper St. N1 BY37 56
Upr. Sunbury Rd. Hamptn. BE51 84
Upr. Sutton La. Houns. BF44 64
Upper Swaines, Epp. CN18 22
Upper Tail. Wat. BE27 36
Upr. Teddington Rd. Kings. On. T. BK50 74
Upr. Teddington Rd. Tedd. BK50 74
Upper Ter. NW3 BT34 47
Windmill Hill
Upper Thames St. EC4 BY40 56
Upr. Tollington Pk. N4 BY33 47
Upperton Rd. E13 CJ38 58
Upperton Rd. Guil. AR71 118
Upperton Rd. Sid. CN49 78
Upr. Tooting Pk. SW17 BU48 76
Upr. Tooting Rd. SW17 BU49 76
Upr. Town Rd. Grnf. BF38 54
Upr. Tulse Hill SW2 BX47 76
Upr. Walthamstow Rd. E17 CF31 48
Upr. West St. Reig. BR70 120
Upr. Wickham La. Well. CO45 69
Upr. Wimpole St. W1 BV39 56
Upper Woburn Pl. WC1 BW38 56
Upper Wood. Harl. CK12 13
Uppingham Av. Stan. DJ30 36
Upsdell Av. N13 BY29 38
Upshire Rd. Wal. Abb. CG19 22
Upshire Rd. Wal. Abb. CH20 22
Upshot La. Wok. AV62 100
Upstall St. SE5 BY44 66
Upton Av. E7 CH36 58
Upton Av. St. Alb. BG13 9
Upton Clo. Bex. CQ46 79
Upton Clo. St. Alb. AP41 62
Upton Pk.
Upton Clo. St. Alb. BG16 18
Upton Court Rd. Slou. AQ41 62
Upton Dene Sutt. BS57 95
Upton Gdns. Har. BJ32 45
Upton Gro. Slou. AP41 62
Upton La. E7 CH37 58
Upton Lo. Clo. Bush. BG26 36
Upton Pk. Slou. AP41 62
Upton Park Rd. E7 CH36 58
Upton Rd. N18 CB28 39
Upton Rd. SE18 CM43 68
Upton Rd. Bexh. CQ45 69
Upton Rd. Houns. BF45 64
Upton Rd. Slou. AQ41 62
Upton Rd. Th. Hth. BZ51 87
Upton Rd. Wat. BC24 26
Upway N12 BU29 38
Upway. Ger. Cr. AS30 34
Upwood Rd. SE12 CG46 78
Upwood Rd. SW16 BX51 86
Uranus Rd. Hem. H. AY12 8
Urban Av. Horn. CV34 51
Urlwin St. SE5 BZ43 67
Urmston Dr. SW19 BR47 75
Ursula St. SW11 BU44 66
Urswick Gdns. Dag. CQ36 59
Urswick Rd. E9 CC35 48
Urswick Rd. Dag. CQ36 59
Usher Rd. E3 CD37 57
Usk Rd. SW11 BT45 66
Usk Rd. S. Ock. CW39 60
Usk St. E2 CC38 57
Usk St. E16 CG40 58
Utterton Way, Red. BT72 121
Uvedale Clo. Croy. CF59 96
Uvedale Rd. Dag. CR34 50
Uvedale Rd. Enf. BZ25 30
Uvedale Rd. Oxt. CG68 115
Uverdale Rd. SW10 BT43 66
Uxbridge Cir. Uxb. AY35 44
Uxbridge Gdns. Felt. BD48 74
Uxbridge Rd. W3 BJ40 54
Uxbridge Rd. W5 BJ40 54
Uxbridge Rd. W12 BP40 55
Uxbridge Rd. W13 BJ40 54
Uxbridge Rd. Felt. BD48 74
Uxbridge Rd. Hmptn. BF49 74
Uxbridge Rd. Kings-on-t. BK52 84
Uxbridge Rd. Pnr. BC30 35
Uxbridge Rd. Rick. AV27 34
Uxbridge Rd. Rick. AW27 35
Uxbridge Rd. Slou. AQ41 62
Uxbridge Rd. Slou. & Iver AS39 52
Uxbridge Rd. Sthl. BF40 54
Uxbridge Rd. Uxb. & Hayes AZ38 53
Uxbridge St. W8 BS40 56
Uxendon Cres. Wem. BL33 46
Uxendon Hill Wem. BL33 46
Vache La. Ch. St. G. AR27 34
Valance Av. E4 CG26 40
Vale Av. Borwd. BM25 28
Vale Clo. W9 BT38 56
Vale Clo. Brwd. CZ25 33
Vale Clo. Couls. BX60 95
Vale Clo. Twick. BJ48 74
Vale Cotts. Brom. CH52 88
Vale Ct. W9 BT38 56
Vale Ct. Wey. BA55 83
Vale Cres. SW15 BO49 75
Valecroft Pnr. BE32 45
Vale Dr. Barn. BR24 28
Vale End SE22 CA45 67
Grove Vale
Vale Farm Rd. Wok. AS62 100
Vale Gro. N4 BZ33 48
Vale Gro. W3 BN40 55
Vale Gro. Slou. AP41 62
Vale La. W3 BM39 55
Valence Av. Dag. CP33 50
Valence Cir. Dag. CP34 50
Valence Ho. Dag. CQ34 50
Valence Rd. Erith CS43 69
Valence Wood Rd. Dag. CP34 50
Valencia Rd. Stan. BK28 36
Valency Clo. Nthwd. BB28 35
Valentine Av. Bex. CQ48 79
Valentine Ct. SE23 CC48 77
Valentine Pl. SE1 BY41 66
Valentine Rd. E9 CD36 57
Valentine Rd. Har. BG34 45
Valentine Row SE1 BY41 66
Valentines Rd. Ilf. CL33 49
Valentines Way Rom. CS34 50
Vale Of Heath NW3 BT34 47
East Heath Rd.
Vale Pl. W14 BQ41 65
Spring Vale Ter.
Valerie Clo. St. Alb. BJ13 9
Valerie Ct. Bush. BG26 36
Vale Rise NW11 BR33 46
Vale Rd. E7 CH36 58
Vale Rd. N4 BZ33 48
Vale Rd. Brom. CL51 88
Vale Rd. Bush. BE25 27
Vale Rd. Chesh. AO16 16
Vale Rd. Dart. CU47 79
Vale Rd. Esher BH58 93
Vale Rd. Grav. DE47 81
Vale Rd. Mitch. BW52 86
Vale Rd. Sutt. BS56 95
Vale Rd. Wey. BA55 83
Vale Rd. Wind. AM44 61
Vale Rd. Wor. Pk. BO55 85
Vale Rd. N. Surb. BL55 85
Vale Rd. S. Surb. BL55 85
Vale Row N5 BY34 47
Gillespie Rd.
Vale Royal N7 BX36 56
Valeswood Rd. Brom. CG49 78
Vale Ter. N4 BZ32 48
Vale, The, N10 BV30 38
Vale, The, N14 BW26 38
Vale, The, NW11 BQ34 46
Vale, The, SW3 BT43 66
Vale, The, W3 BO40 55
Vale, The, Brwd. DB26 42
Vale, The, Couls. BW60 95
Vale, The, Croy. CC55 87
Vale, The, Felt. BC46 73
Vale, The, Houns. BE43 64
Vale, The, Ruis. BD34 45
Vale, The, Sun. BC50 73
Vale, The, Wdf. Grn. CH29 40
Vale. The. Ger. Cr. AR30 34
Valetta Gro. E13 CG37 58
Valetta Rd. W3 BO41 65
Valette St. E9 CB36 57
Vale Way. Horn. CU35 50
Valiant Clo. Nthlt. BD38 54
Ruislip Rd.
Valiant Clo. Rom. CR30 41
Vallance Rd. E1 CB38 57
Vallance Rd. E2 CB38 57
Vallance Rd. N22 BW30 38
Vallentin Ct. E17 CF31 48
Vallentin Rd.
Vallentin Rd. E17 CF31 48
Valley Av. N12 BT28 38
Valley Clo. Dart. CT46 79
Valley Clo. Loug. CK25 31
Valley Clo. Pnr. BC30 35
Valley Clo. Wal. Abb. CF19 21
Valley Clo. Wdf. Grn. CH29 40
Valley Dr. NW9 BM32 46
Valley Dr. Grav. DH49 81
Valley Dr. Sev. CU66 116
Valleyfield Rd. SW16 BX49 76
Valley Flds. Cres. Enf. BY23 29
Valley Gdns. SW19 BT50 76
Valley Gdns. Wem. BL36 55
Valley Grn. The, Welw. G. C. BQ7 5
Valley Gro. SE7 CJ42 68
Valley Hill Loug. CK26 40
Valley Ms. Twick. BJ48 74
Cross Deep
Valley Rise, Wat. BC20 17
Valley Rd. N12 BT28 38
Valley Rd. SW16 BX49 76
Valley Rd. Belv. CR42 69
Valley Rd. Berk AP12 7
Valley Rd. Brom. CG51 88
Valley Rd. Dart. CT46 79
Valley Rd. Fawk. DB53 90
Valley Rd. Ken. BZ60 96
Valley Rd. Orp. CO51 89
Valley Rd. Rick. AV25 25
Valley Rd. Rick. AW25 26
Valley Rd. St. Alb. BH11 9
Valley Rd. Uxb. AY37 53
Valley Rd. Welw. G. C. BP8 5
Valley Side E4 CE27 39
Valley Side, Hem. H. AV13 7
Valley, The Guil. AR72 118
Valley Vw. Barn. BR25 28
Valley Vw. Green. DA46 80
Valley Vw. West. CJ62 106
Valley Vw. Gdns. Ken. CA57 96
Valley Vw. Gdns. Ken. CA61 105
Valley Wk. Croy. CC55 87
Valley Wk. Rick. BA25 26
Valley Way. Ger. Cr. AR32 43
Valliant Clo. Nthlt. BD38 54
Valliere Rd. NW10 BP38 55
Valliers Wood Rd. Sid. CM47 78
Vallis Way W13 BJ39 54
Vallis Way Chess. BK56 93
Valmar Rd. SE5 BZ44 67
Valnay St. SW17 BU49 76
Valognes Av. E17 BX30 38
Valonia Gdns. SW18 BR46 75
Vambery Rd. SE18 CM43 68
Vanbrough Cres. Nthlt. BD37 54
Vanbrugh Clo. Orp. CN54 88
Vanbrugh Fields SE3 CG43 68
Vanbrugh Hill SE3 CG42 68
Vanbrugh Hill SE10 CG42 68
Vanbrugh Pk. SE3 CG43 68
Vanbrugh Pk. Rd. SE3 CG43 68
Vanbrugh Pk. Rd. W. SE3 CG43 68
Vanbrugh Rd. W4 BN41 65
Vanbrugh Ter. SE3 CG44 68
Vance St. SE14 CD43 67
Vancouver Cotts. Epsom BN59 94
Vancouver Rd. SE23 CD48 77
Vancouver Rd. Edg. BM29 37
Vancouver Rd. Hayes BC38 53
Vancouver Rd. Rich. BK49 74
Vanda Cres. St. Alb. BH14 9
Vanderbilt Rd. SW18 BS47 76
Vandome Clo. E16 CH39 58
Vandon Pass. SW1 BW41 66
Petty France
Vandon St. SW1 BW41 66
Van Dyck Av. N. Mal. BN54 85
Vandyke Clo. SW15 BQ46 75
Vandyke Clo. Red. BU69 121
Vandyke Cross SE9 CK46 78
Vandy St. EC2 CA38 57
Vane Clo. Harrow BL32 46
Vanessa Clo. Belv. CR42 69
Vanessa Wk. Grav. DJ49 81
Vanessa Way Bex. CS48 79
Vane St. SW1 BW42 66
Vincent Sq.
Vanguard Clo. Croy BY54 86
Vanguard Clo. Rom. CR30 41
Vanguard St. SE8 CE44 67
Vanguard Way Wall. BX57 95
Vanoc Gdns. Brom. CG48 78
Vansittart Dr. Wind. AN44 61
Vansittart Rd. E7 CG35 49
Vansittart Rd. Wind. AN44 61
Vansittart St. SE14 CD43 67
Vanston Pl. SW6 BS43 66
Vantage Rd. Slou. AN41 61
Vantorts Clo. Saw. CQ6 6
Vantorts Rd. Saw. CQ6 6
Vant Rd. SW17 BU49 76
Varcoe Rd. SE16 CB42 67
Vardens Rd. SW11 BT45 66
Varden St. E1 CB39 57
Varley Rd. E16 CH39 58
Varna Rd. SW6 BR43 65
Varna Rd. Hamptn. BF51 84
Varndell St. NW1 BW38 56
Varney Clo. Hem. H. AV13 7
Varney Clo. Wal. Cr. CB17 21
Varney Rd. Hem. H. AV13 7
Vartry Rd. N15 BZ32 48
Vassall Rd. SW9 BY43 66
Vauban Est. SE16 CA41 67
Vauban St. SE16 CA41 67
Vaudrey Clo. E1 CC38 57
Vaughan Av. NW4 BP32 46
Vaughan Av. W6 BO42 65
Vaughan Av. Horn. CV35 51
Vaughan Gdns. Ilf. CK33 49
Vaughan Pl. SE15 CB43 67
Vaughan Rd. E15 CG36 58
Vaughan Rd. SE5 BZ44 67
Vaughan Rd. Har. BG32 45
Vaughan Rd. Surb. BJ54 84
Vaughan Rd. Well. CN44 68
Vaughan Way Dor. BJ71 119
Westcott Rd.
Vaux Cres. Walt. BC57 92
Vauxhall Bridge BX42 66
Vauxhall Bridge Rd. SW1 BW41 66
Vauxhall Clo. Grav. DF47 81
Vauxhall Cross SW8 BX43 66
Vauxhall Gdns. Sth. Croy. BZ57 96
Vauxhall Gdns. Est. SE11 BX42 66
Vauxhall Gro. SW8 BX43 66
Vauxhall Pl. Dart. CW47 80
Vauxhall Rd. Hem. H. AZ13 8
Vauxhall St. SE11 BX42 66
Vauxhall Wk. SE11 BX42 66
Vectis Gdns. SW17 BV50 76
Vectis Rd.
Vectis Rd. SW17 BV50 76
Veda Rd. SE13 CE45 67
Veevers Rd. Reig. BT72 121
Vega Cres. Nthwd. BB28 35
Vegal Cres. Egh. AQ49 72
Vega Rd. Bush. BG26 36
Velde Way SE22 CA46 77
Dulwich Gro.
Venables St. NW8 BT38 56
Vencourt Pl. W6 BP42 65
King St.
Venetian Rd. SE5 BZ44 67
Venetia Rd. N4 BY32 47
Venetia Rd. W5 BK41 64
Venette Clo. Rain. CU39 59
Venner Rd. SE26 CC49 77
Venners Clo. Bexh. CT44 69
Venn St. SW4 BW45 66
Venour Rd. E3 CD38 57
Maidman St.
Ventnor Av. Stan. BJ30 36
Ventnor Gdns. Bark. CN36 58
Ventnor Rd. SE14 CC43 67
Ventnor Rd. Sutt. BS57 95
Ventor Dr. N20 BS27 38
Venture Clo. Bex. CQ47 79
Elmwood Dr.
Venue St. E14 CF39 57
Venus Hill. Her. H. AT19 16
Veny Cres. Horn. CV36 60
Vera Av. N21 BY25 29
Vera Rd. SW6 BR44 65
Verbena Clo. S. Ock. DB39 60
Verbena Gdns. W6 BP42 65
Verdan Rd. Bexh. CQ44 69
Verdant Ct. SE6 CG47 78
Verdant La. SE6 CG47 78
Verdayne Av. Croy. CC55 87
Verdayne Gdns. Warl. CC61 105
Verderers Rd. Chig. CO28 41
Verdun Rd. SE18 CO43 69
Verdun Rd. SW13 BP43 65
Vereker Dr. Sun. BC52 83
Vereker Rd. W14 BR42 65
Vere Rd. Loug. CM24 31
Vere St. W1 BV39 56
Vermont Rd. SE19 BZ50 77
Vermont Rd. SW18 BS46 76
Vermont Rd. Sutt. BS55 86
Verney Clo. Berk. AP12 7
Verney Gdns. Dag. CQ35 50
Verney Rd. SE16 CB42 67
Verney Rd. Dag. CQ35 50
Verney Rd. Slou. AT42 62
Verney St. NW10 BN34 46
Verney Way SE16 CB42 67
Vernham Rd. SE18 CM43 68
Vernon Av. E12 CK35 49
Vernon Av. SW20 BQ51 85
Vernon Av. Enf. CD21 30
Vernon Av. Wdf. Grn. CH29 40
Vernon Clo. Cher. AU57 91
Vernon Clo. Epsom BN57 94
Vernon Clo. Orp. CO52 89
Vernon Clo. St. Alb. BG14 9
Vernon Clo. Sev. CZ58 99
Vernon Ct. NW2 BR34 46
Vernon Cres. Barn. BV25 29
Vernon Cres. Brwd. DD27 122
Vernon Dr. Stan. BJ30 36
Vernon Dr. Uxb. AX30 35
Vernon Pl. WC1 BX39 56
Bloomsbury Way
Vernon Rise WC1 BX38 56
Percy Circus
Vernon Rise Grnf. BG35 45
Vernon Rd. E3 CD37 57
Vernon Rd. E11 CG33 49
Vernon Rd. E15 CG36 58
Vernon Rd. E17 BX32 47
Vernon Rd. N8 BY31 47
Vernon Rd. SW14 BO45 65
Vernon Rd. Bush. BE25 27
Vernon Rd. Felt. BB48 73
Vernon Rd. Ilf. CN33 49
Vernon Rd. Rom. CS28 41
Vernon Rd. Sutt. BT56 95
Vernon Rd. Swans. DC46 81
Vernon Sq. WC1 BX38 56
Penton Rise
Vernon St. W14 BR42 65
Vernon Wk. Tad. BQ63 103
Vernon Way, Guil. AP70 118
Vernon Yd. W11 BR40 55
Portobello Rd.
Verona Dr. Surb. BL55 85
Verona Gdns. Grav. DJ49 81
Verona Rd. E7 CH36 58
Upton La.
Veronica Clo. Rom. CV29 42
Veronica Rd. SW17 BV48 76
Veronique Gdns. Ilf. CM32 49
Verran Rd. SW12 BV47 76
Balham Gro.
Ver Rd. St. Alb. BG13 9
Versailles Rd. SE20 CB50 77
Verulam Av. E17 CD32 48
Verulam Av. Pur. BW59 95
Verulam Clo. Welw. G. C. BR8 5
Verulam Rd. Grnf. BF38 54
Verulam Rd. St. Alb. BG13 9
Verulam St. EC1 BY39 56
Verwood Rd. Har. BG30 36
Vespan Rd. W12 BP41 65
Vesta Av. St. Alb. BG15 9
Vesta Rd. SE4 CD44 67
Vesta Rd. Hem. H. AY12 8
Vestris Rd. SE23 CC48 77
Vestry Ms. SE5 CA44 67
Vestry Rd. E17 CE32 48
Vestry Rd. SE5 CA44 67
Vestry Rd. Sev. CV63 108
Vestry St. N1 BZ38 57
Vevey St. SE6 CD48 77
Veysey Gdns. Dag. CR34 50
Viaduct Bldgs. EC1 BY39 56
Saffron Hill
Viaduct Pl. E2 CB38 57
Viaduct St. E2 CB38 57
Viaduct, The, E18 CH30 40
Vian Av. Enf. CD21 30
Vian St. SE13 CE45 67
Vibart Gdns. SW2 BX47 76
Vicarage Av. SE3 CH44 68
Vicarage Av. Egh. AT49 72
Vicarage Clo. Brwd. CZ28 42
Vicarage Clo. Egh. AT49 72
Vicarage Clo. Erith CS43 69
Vicarage Clo. Lthd. BF66 111
Vicarage Clo. Pot. B. BU18 20
Vicarage Clo. Ruis. BA33 44
Vicarage Clo. St. Alb. BG15 9
Vicarage Clo. Tad. BR65 103
Vicarage Ct. W8 BS41 66
Vicarage Gate
Vicarage Ct. Felt. BA47 73
Vicarage Cres. SW11 BT44 66
Vicarage Dr. SW14 BN46 75
Vicarage Dr. Bark. CM36 58
Vicarage Dr. Grav. DE46 81
Vicarage Dr. Maid. AH41 61
Vicarage Farm Rd. Houns. BE44 64
Vicarage Flds. Walt. BD53 84
Vicarage Gdns. SW14 BN46 75
Vicarage Gdns. W8 BS41 66
Vicarage Gdns. Mitch. BU52 86
Vicarage Gte. W8 BS41 66

Vicarage Gate. Guil.	AQ71	118
Vicarage Gro. SE5	BZ44	67
Vicarage La. E6	CK38	58
Vicarage La. E15	CG36	58
Vicarage La. Chig.	CM27	40
Vicarage La. Epp.	CR15	14
Vicarage La. Epsom	BP58	94
Vicarage La. Grav.	DK48	81
Vicarage La. Hem. H.	AT17	16
Vicarage La. Ilf.	CM33	49
Vicarage La. Kings L.	AY18	17
Vicarage La. Lthd.	BJ64	102
Vicarage La. Stai.	AS47	72
Vicarage La. Stai.	AX52	83
Vicarage La. Wok.	AU66	109
Vicarage Pk. SE18	CM42	68
Vicarage Path N8	BW33	47
Vicarage Pl. Slou.	AQ41	62
Vicarage Rd. E10	CE33	48
Vicarage Rd. E15	CG36	58
Vicarage Rd. N17	CB30	39
Vicarage Rd. SE18	CM42	68
Vicarage Rd. SW14	BN46	75
Vicarage Rd. Berk.	AT11	7
Vicarage Rd. Bex.	CR47	79
Vicarage Rd. Croy.	BY55	86
Vicarage Rd. Dag.	CR36	59
Vicarage Rd. Egh.	AT49	72
Vicarage Rd. Egh.	AT50	72
Vicarage Rd Epp.	CP18	23
Vicarage Rd. Horn.	CU33	50
Vicarage Rd. Kings. On T.	BK51	84
Vicarage Rd. Sun.	BB49	73
Vicarage Rd. Sutt.	BS56	95
Vicarage Rd. Tedd.	BJ49	74
Vicarage Rd. Twick.	BG46	74
Vicarage Rd. Twick.	BH48	74
Vicarage Rd. Wat.	BC26	35
Vicarage Rd. Wdf. Grn.	CK29	40
Vicarage Rd. Wok.	AO59	91
Vicarage Rd. Wok.	AS64	100
Vicarage Wk. Walt.	BC54	83
Vicarage Way NW10	BN34	46
Vicarage Way. Ger. Cr.	AS32	43
Vicarage Way Har.	BF33	45
Vicarage Way. Slou.	AU43	62
Vicarage Wood, Harl.	CO10	6
Vicars Clo. E15	CH37	58
Vicars Clo. Enf.	CA23	30
Vicars Hl. SE13	CE45	67
Vicar's Moor La. N21	BY26	38
Vicars Rd. NW5	BV35	47
Vicars Wk. Dag.	CO34	50
Vicerage Way. Hem. H.	AT16	16
Viceroy Ct. NW8	BU37	56
Viceroy Rd. SW8	BX44	66
Hartington Rd.		
Vickers Rd. Erith	CS42	69
Victor App. Horn.	CV33	51
Victor Gdns. Horn.	CV33	51
Victor Gro. Wem.	BL36	55
Victoria Arc. Sthl.	BE40	54
Victoria Ave. Grays.	DE41	71
Victoria Av. E6	CJ37	58
Victoria Av. EC2	CA39	57
New St.		
Victoria Av. N3	BR30	37
Victoria Av. Barn.	BT24	29
Victoria Av. E. Mol.	BF52	84
Victoria Av. Grav.	DG47	81
Victoria Av. Houns.	BE46	74
Victoria Av. Rom.	CR29	41
Victoria Av. Sth. Croy.	BZ58	96
Victoria Av. Surb.	BK54	84
Victoria Av. Uxb.	AZ36	53
Victoria Av. Wall.	BV55	86
Victoria Av. Wem.	BM36	55
Victoria Clo. Barn.	BT24	29
Victoria Clo. Grays	DE41	71
Victoria Av.		
Victoria Clo. Hayes	BA39	53
Victoria Clo. Rick.	AX26	35
Nightingale Rd.		
Victoria Clo. Wey.	BB55	83
Victoria Cotts. N10	BV30	38
Victoria Ct. W3	BM41	65
Victoria Ct. Wem.	BM36	55
Victoria Cres. N15	CA32	48
Victoria Cres. SE19	CA50	77
Victoria Cres. SW19	BR50	75
Victoria Cres. Hayes	AW40	53
Victoria Cres. Iver	AV40	52
Victoria Dr. SW19	BQ47	75
Victoria Embankment SW1	BX41	66
Victoria Gdns. W11	BS41	66
Church St.		
Victoria Gdns. Houns.	BE44	64
Victoria Gdns. West.	CJ61	106
Victoria Gro. N12	BT28	38
Victoria Gro. W2	BS40	56
Victoria Gro. W8	BT41	66
Victoria Hill Rd. Swan.	CT51	89
Victoria La. Barn.	BR24	28
Victoria La. Hayes.	BA42	63
Victoria Ms. NW6	BS37	56
Victoria Ms. SW4	BV45	66
Victoria Rise		
Victorian Rd. N16	CA34	48
Victoria Pk. Rd. E9	CB37	57
Victoria Pk. Sq. E2	CC38	57
Victoria Pl. Epsom	BO59	94
Victoria Pl. Rich.	BK46	74
Victoria Rise SW4	BV45	66
Victoria Rd. E4	CG26	40
Victoria Rd. E13	CH37	58
Victoria Rd. E17	CF30	39
Victoria Rd. E18	CH30	40
Victoria Rd. N4	BX33	47
Victoria Rd. N18	CA28	39
Victoria Rd. N22	BW30	38
Victoria Rd. NW4	BQ31	46
Victoria Rd. NW6	BR37	55
Victoria Rd. NW7	BO28	37
Victoria Rd. NW10	BN39	55
Victoria Rd. SW14	BN45	65
Victoria Rd. W3	BN39	55
Victoria Rd. W5	BJ39	54
Victoria Rd. W8	BT41	66
Victoria Rd. Bark.	CL36	58
Victoria Rd. Barn.	BT24	29
Victoria Rd. Berk.	AR13	7
Victoria Rd. Bexh.	CR46	79
Victoria Rd. Brom.	CJ53	88
Victoria Rd. Brwd.	DB28	42
Victoria Rd. Buck. H.	CJ27	40
Victoria Rd. Bush.	BF26	36
Victoria Rd. Chis.	CL49	78
Victoria Rd. Couls.	BW61	104
Victoria Rd. Dag.	CR35	50
Victoria Rd. Dart.	CV46	80
Victoria Rd. Erith	CT43	69
Victoria Rd. Felt.	BC47	73
Victoria Rd. Grav.	DF47	81
Victoria Rd. Guil.	AS71	118
Victoria Rd. Ilf.	CL32	49
Victoria Rd. Kings. On T.	BL51	85
Victoria Rd. Mitch.	BU50	76
Victoria Rd. Red.	BV71	121
Victoria Rd. Rich.	BL44	65
Victoria Rd. Rom.	CT32	50
Victoria Rd. Ruis.	BC33	44
Victoria Rd. Sev.	CU66	116
Victoria Rd. Sid.	CN48	78
Victoria Rd. Slou.	AQ40	52
Victoria Rd. Stai.	AV48	72
Victoria Rd. Sthl.	BE41	64
Victoria Rd. Surb.	BK53	84
Victoria Rd. Sutt.	BT56	95
Victoria Rd. Twick.	BJ47	74
Victoria Rd. Uxb.	AX36	53
Victoria Rd. Wal. Abb.	CF20	21
Victoria Rd. Wat.	BC22	26
Victoria Rd. Wey.	AX56	92
Victoria Rd. Wey.	BA55	83
Victoria Rd. Wind.	AM42	61
Victoria Rd. Wok.	AO62	100
Victoria Rd. Wok.	AS62	100
Victoria Sq. SW1	BV41	66
Beeston Pl.		
Victoria St. E15	CG36	58
Victoria St. SW1	BV41	66
Victoria St. Belv.	CQ42	69
Victoria St. Egh.	AR50	72
Victoria St. St. Alb.	BG13	9
Victoria St. Slou.	AP41	62
Victoria St. Wind.	AO44	61
Victoria Ter. N4	BY33	47
Victoria Ter. Dor.	BJ71	119
Victoria Ter. Har.	BG33	45
Victoria Vills. Rich.	BL45	65
Victoria Way SE7	CH42	68
Victoria Way. Wey.	BA55	83
Victoria Way. Wok.	AS62	100
Victor Rd. N7	BX34	47
Victor Rd. NW10	BP38	55
Victor Rd. SE20	CC50	77
Victor Rd. Har.	BG31	45
Victor Rd. Tedd.	BH49	74
Victor Rd. Wind.	AO45	61
Victor, S Cres. Brwd.	DD27	122
Victor Vill. N9	BZ27	39
Victor Wk. Horn.	CV33	51
Victory Av. Mord.	BT53	86
Victory Park Rd. Wey.	AX56	92
Victory Pl. SE17	BZ42	67
Victory Pl. SE19	CA50	77
Victory Rd. SW19	BT50	76
Victory Rd. Berk.	AQ12	7
Victory Rd. Cher.	AW54	83
Victory Rd. Rain.	CU37	59
Victory Sq. SE5	BZ43	67
Victory Way Rom.	CR30	41
View Clo. N6	BU33	47
View Clo. Chig.	CM28	40
View Clo. Har.	BG31	45
View Clo. West.	CJ61	106
Viewfield Rd. SW18	BR46	75
Viewfield Rd. Sid.	CP47	79
Viewland Rd. SE18	CN42	68
Viewlands Ave. Sev.	CN63	106
View Rd. N6	BU33	47
View Rd. Grays.	DD43	71
View Rd. Pot. B.	BT19	20
View, The, SE2	CQ42	69
View, The Grav.	DH47	81
Viga Rd. N21	BY25	29
Viggory La. Wok.	AR61	100
Vigilant Clo. SE26	CB49	77
Vigilant, The, SE26	CB49	77
Vigilant Way, Grav.	DJ49	81
Vigors Cft. Hat.	BO13	10
Vigo St. W1	BW40	56
Viking Rd. Grav.	DE48	81
Viking Rd. Sthl.	BE40	54
Viking Way Brwd.	DA25	33
Viking Way. Sev.	CZ57	99
Villa Clo. Grav.	DK48	81
Villacourt Rd. SE18	CO43	69
Village Clo. E4	CF28	39
Village Green Ave. West.	CK62	106
Village Grn. Rd. Dart.	CU45	69
Village Green Way, West.	CK62	106
Village La. Slou.	AO33	43
Village Rd. N3	BR29	37
Village Rd. Egh.	AU52	82
Village Rd. Enf.	BZ26	39
Village Rd. Enf.	CA25	30
Village Rd Uxb.	AV34	43
Village Rd. Uxb.	AW33	44
Village Rd. Wind.	AK41	61
Village, The, SE7	CJ43	68
Village, The, Ong.	DB13	15
Village Way NW10	BN35	46
Village Way SE21	BZ46	77
Village Way. Amer.	AR23	25
Village Way, Ashf.	AY49	73
Village Way Beck.	CE52	87
Village Way Pnr.	BE33	45
Village Way Sth. Croy.	CB60	96
Village Way E. Har.	BE33	45
Villa Rd. SW9	BY45	66
Villas Rd. SE18	CM42	68
Villa St. SE17	BZ42	67
Villiers Av. Surb.	BL53	85
Villiers Av. Twick.	BE47	74
Villiers Clo. E10	CE34	48
Villiers Clo. Kings-on-t.	BL52	85
Villiers Ct. N20	BT26	38
Villiers Path Surb.	BL53	85
Villiers Rd. NW2	BP36	55
Villiers Rd. Beck.	CC51	87
Villiers Rd. Islw.	BH44	64
Villiers Rd. Kings-on-t.	BL52	85
Villiers Rd. Slou.	AO39	52
Villiers Rd. Sthl.	BE40	54
Villiers Rd. Wat.	BE25	27
Villiers St. WC2	BX40	56
Villier St. Uxb.	AX37	52
Vincam Clo. Twick.	BF47	74
Vincent Av. Cars.	BT59	95
Vincent Av. Surb.	BM54	85
Vincent Clo. Barn.	BS24	29
Vincent Clo. Brom.	CH52	88
Vincent Clo. Cher.	AV54	82
Vincent Clo. Couls.	BU63	104
Vincent Clo. Esher	BF55	84
Vincent Clo. Ilf.	CM29	40
Vincent Clo. Lthd.	BF65	102
Vincent Clo. West Dr.	AZ43	63
Vincent Ct. NW4	BQ31	46
Vincent Dr. Shep.	BB52	83
Vincent Gdns. NW2	BO34	46
Vincent Rd. E4	CF29	39
Vincent Rd. N15	BZ31	48
Vincent Rd. N22	BY30	38
Vincent Rd. SE18	CL42	68
Vincent Rd. W3	BN41	65
Palmerston Rd.		
Vincent Rd. Cher.	AV54	82
Vincent Rd. Couls.	BW61	104
Vincent Rd. Croy.	CA54	87
Vincent Rd. Dag.	CQ36	59
Vincent Rd. Houns.	BD44	64
Vincent Rd. Islw.	BG44	64
Vincent Rd. Kings-on-t.	BM52	85
Vincent Rd. Rain.	CV38	60
Vincent Rd. Wal. Cr.	CD17	21
Vincent Rd. Wem.	BL36	55
Vincent Row. Hamptn.	BG50	74
Vincent's Dr. Dor.	BJ72	119
Vincents La. Dor.	BJ71	119
Vincents Path Nthlt.	BD36	54
Vincent Sq. SW1	BW42	66
Vincent Sq. West.	CJ60	97
Vincent's Rd. Dor.	BJ71	119
Vincent St. E16	CG39	58
Vincent St. SW1	BW42	66
Vincent Ter. N1	BY37	56
Vincent Wk. Dor.	BJ71	119
Arundel Rd.		
Vince St. EC1	BZ38	57
Vine Av. Sev.	CU65	107
Vine Clo. Stai.	AW46	73
Vine Clo. Surb.	BL53	85
Vine Clo. Sutt.	BT55	86
Vine Clo. Welw. G. C.	BR7	5
Vine Clo. West Dr.	AZ42	63
Vine Ct. E1	CB39	57
Vine Ct. Har.	BL32	46
Vine Court Rd. Sev.	CV65	108
Vinegar All. E17	CE31	48
Vine Gdns. Ilf.	CM35	49
Vinegar Yd. SE1	CA41	67
St. Thomas St.		
Vine Gro. Uxb.	AZ36	53
Vine Hill EC1	BY38	56
Vine La. SE1	CA40	57
Vine La. Uxb.	AY37	53
Vine Pl. Houns.	BF45	64
Vineries Clo. West Dr.	AZ43	63
Vineries End NW7	BP28	37
Vineries, The, N14	BW25	29
Vineries, The, Enf.	CA24	30
Vine Rd. E15	CG36	58
Vine Rd. N17	CD29	39
Love La.		
Vine Rd. SW13	BO45	65
Vine Rd. E. Mol.	BG52	84
Vine Rd. Orp.	CN57	97
Vine Rd. Slou.	AP36	52
Vinery Vill. NW8	BU38	56
Park Rd.		
Vine St. Br. EC1	BY38	56
Farringdon Rd.		
Vines Av. N3	BS30	38
Vines La. Ton.	CY70	117
Vine St. EC3	CA39	57
Vine St. W1	BW40	56
Vine St. Rom.	CS31	50
Vine St. Uxb.	AX37	53
Vine Way, Brwd.	DB26	42
Vine Yd. SE1	BZ41	67
Sanctuary St.		
Vineyard Av. NW7	BR29	37
Vine Yard Clo. SE6	CE47	77
Vineyard Hill, Pot. B.	BV18	20
Vineyard Hill Rd. SW19	BR49	75
Vineyard Pass. Rich.	BL46	75
Vine Yard Path SW14	BN45	65
North Worple Way		
Vineyard Rd. Felt.	BC48	73
Vineyard Rd. Pot. B.	BV18	20
Vineyard Row, Kings. On T.	BK51	84
Vineyard, The, Rich.	BK46	74
Vineyard, The, Welw. G. C.	BR7	5
Vineyard Wk. EC1	BY38	56
Pine St.		
Viney Bank. Croy.	CD58	96
Viney Rd. SE13	CE45	67
Vining St. SW9	BY45	66
Vinlake Av. Uxb.	AZ34	44
Vinson Clo. Orp.	CO54	89
Vintners Pl. EC4	BZ40	57
Viola Av. SE2	CO42	69
Viola Av. Felt.	BD46	74
Viola Av. Stai.	AY47	73
Viola Clo. S. Ock.	DB38	60
Viola Sq. W12	BO40	55
Violet Av. Enf.	BZ22	30
Violet Av. Uxb.	AY39	53
Violet Gdns. Croy.	BY56	95
Violet Hill NW8	BT37	56
Violet La. Croy.	BY56	95
Violet Rd. E3	CE38	57
Violet Rd. E17	CE32	48
Violet Rd. E18	CH30	40
Violet St. E2	CB38	57
Three Colts La.		
Violet Way, Rick.	AX24	26
Virgil Dr. Brox.	CD15	12
Virgil St. SE1	BX41	66
Virginia Av. Vir. W.	AR53	82
Virginia Clo. Ash.	BK62	102
Skinners La.		
Virginia Clo. Stai.	AX52	83
Blacksmythe La.		
Virginia Dr. Vir. W.	AR53	82
Virginia Gdns. Ilf.	CM30	40
Virginia Rd. E2	CA38	57
Virginia Rd. Th. Hth.	BY51	86
Virginia St. E1	CB40	57
Virginia Wk. Grav.	DH50	81
Viscount Gro. Nthlt.	BD38	54
Wayfarer Rd.		
Viscount Rd. Stai.	AX47	73
Viscount St. EC1	BZ38	57
Viscount Way. Houns.	BB44	63
Vista Av. Enf.	CC23	30
Vista Dr. Ilf.	CJ32	49
Vista, The, SE9	CJ46	78
Vista Way Har.	BL32	46
Vivash Clo. Hayes	BB41	63
Vivian Av. NW4	BP32	46
Vivian Av. Wem.	BM35	46
Vivian Clo. Wat.	BC27	35
Vivian Gdns. Wat.	BC26	35
Vivian Gdns. Wem.	BM35	46
Vivian Gro. SE15	CB45	67
Vivian Rd. E3	CD37	57
Vivian Way N2	BT32	47
Vivienne Clo. Twick.	BK46	74
Voce Rd. SE18	CM43	68
Voewood Clo. N. Mal.	BO53	85
Vogan Clo. Reig.	BS72	121
Voltaire Rd. SW4	BW45	66
Voltaire Way, Hayes	BB40	53
Voluntary Pl. E11	CH32	49
Vorley Rd. N19	BW34	47
Voss Ct. SW16	BX50	76
Voss St. E2	CB38	57
Vulcan Clo. Wall.	BX57	95
Vulcan Rd. SE4	CD44	67
Vulcan Ter. SE4	CD44	67
Vulcan Way Croy.	CG58	97
Vyner Rd. W3	BN40	55
Vyner, S Way, Uxb.	AZ35	44
Vyner St. E2	CB37	57
Vyne, The Bexh.	CR45	69
Vyse Clo. Barn.	BQ24	28
Wadding St. SE17	BZ42	67
Waddington Ave. Couls.	BY63	104
Waddington Clo. Couls.	BY63	104
Waddington Rd. E15	CF35	48
Waddington Rd. St. Alb.	BG13	9
Waddington St. E15	CF36	57
Waddington Ter. Bexh.	CR46	79
Waddington Way, SE19	BZ50	77
Waddon Clo. Croy.	BY55	86
Waddon Ct. Rd. Croy.	BY56	95
Waddon Ind. Est. Croy.	BX56	95
Waddon Marsh Way Croy.	BX54	86
Waddon New Rd. Croy.	BY55	86
Waddon Pk. Av. Croy.	BY56	95
Waddon Rd. Croy.	BY55	86
Waddon Way Croy.	BY57	95
Wade Av. Orp.	CP54	89
Wade Rd. E16	CJ39	58
Leyes Rd.		
Wade's Gro. N21	BY26	38
Wade's Hill N21	BY26	38
Wades La. Tedd.	BJ49	74
Wadeson St. E2	CB37	57
Wades Pl. E14	CE40	57
Wades, The Hat.	BP14	10
Wade, The, Welw. G. C.	BR9	5
Wadeville Av. Rom.	CQ32	50
Wadham Av. E17	CE29	39
Wadham Clo. Shep.	BA54	83
Wadham Gdns. Grnf.	BG36	54
Wadham Rd. E17	CE30	39
Wadham Rd. SW15	BR45	65
Wadham Rd. Wat.	BB19	17
Wadhurst Rd. W4	BN41	65
Wadley Clo. Hem. H.	AY14	8
Wadley Rd. E11	CG33	49
Wadsworth Clo. Grnf.	BK37	54
Wadsworth Rd. Grnf.	BJ37	54
Wager St. E3	CD38	57
Waggon Clo. Guil.	AP70	118
Waggon La. N17	CB29	39
Waghorn Rd. E13	CJ37	58
Waghorn Rd. Har.	BK31	45
Waghorn St. SE15	CB45	67
Wagner St. SE15	CC43	67
Ilderton Rd.		
Wagon La. N17	CB29	39
Wagon Rd. Barn.	BS21	29
Wagon Way, Rick.	AX24	26
Waid Clo. Dart.	CW46	80
Wain Clo. Pot. B.	BS18	20
Wainfleet Av. Rom.	CS30	41
Wainford Clo. SW19	BQ47	75
Windlesham Rd.		
Wainwright Av. Brwd.	DE25	122
Waite Davies Rd. SE12	CG47	78
Waite St. SE15	CA43	67
Waithman St. EC4	BY39	56
Pilgrim St.		
Wakefield Cres. Slou.	AP36	52
Wakefield Gdns. SE19	CA50	77
Wakefield Gdns. Ilf.	CK32	49
Wakefield Rd. N11	BW28	38
Wakefield Rd. N15	CA32	48
Wakefield Rd. Rich.	BK46	74
Wakefield St. E6	CJ37	58
Wakefield St. N18	CB28	39
Wakefield St. WC1	BX38	56
Wakehams Hill Pnr.	BE31	45
Wakehams Hl. Pnr.	BE31	45
Wakeham St. N1	BZ36	57
Wakehurst Path. Wok.	AU60	91
Wakehurst Rd. SW11	BU46	76
Wakeling Rd. W7	BH39	54
Wakeling St. E14	CD39	57
Wakelin Rd. E15	CG37	58
Wakeman Rd. NW10	BQ38	55
Wakemans Hill Av. NW9	BN32	46
Wakering Rd. Bark.	CM36	58
Wake Rd. Loug.	CJ22	31
Wakley St. EC1	BY38	56
Walberswick St. SW8	BX43	66
Walbrook, EC4	BZ40	57
Walburgh St. E1	CB39	57
Walburton Rd. Pur.	BW60	95
Walcorde Av. SE17	BZ42	67
Browning St.		
Walcot Sq. SE11	BY42	66
Waldeck Gro. SE27	BY48	76
Waldeck Rd. N15	BY31	47
Waldeck Rd. SW14	BN45	65
Lower Richmond Rd.		
Waldeck Rd. W4	BM43	65
Waldeck Rd. W13	BJ39	54
Waldeck Rd. Dart.	CW47	80
Waldeck Ter. SW14	BN45	65
Lower Richmond Rd.		
Waldegrave Av. Tedd.	BH49	74
Waldegrave Gdns. Twick.	BH48	74
Waldegrave Gdns. Upmin.	CX34	51
Waldegrave Pk. Twick.	BH49	74
Waldegrave Rd. N8	BY31	47
Waldegrave Rd. SE19	CA50	77
Waldegrave Rd. W5	BL39	55
Waldegrave Rd. Brom.	CK52	88
Waldegrave Rd. Dag.	CP34	50
Waldegrave Rd. Twick.	BH49	74
Waldegrove Croy.	CA55	87
Waldemar Av. SW6	BR44	65
Waldemar Av. W5	BK40	54
Waldemar Rd. SW19	BS49	76
Walden Av. N13	BZ28	39
Walden Av. Chis.	CK49	78
Walden Av. Rain.	CS38	59
Walden Clo. Belv.	CQ42	69
Walden Gdns. Th. Hth.	BX52	86
Waldenhurst Rd. Orp.	CP54	89
Walden Park Rd. Wok.	AR61	100
Walden Pl. Welw. G. C.	BQ7	5
Walden Rd. N17	BZ30	39
Lordship La.		
Walden Rd. Chis.	CK50	78
Walden Rd. Horn.	CV32	51
Walden Rd. Welw. G. C.	BQ7	5
Waldens Clo. Orp.	CP54	89
Waldenshaw Rd. SE23	CC47	77
Waldens Rd. Orp.	CQ54	89
Waldens Rd. Wok.	AR62	100
Walden St. E1	CB39	57
Walden Way, NW7	BQ29	37
Walden Way. Horn.	CV32	51
Walden Way, Ilf.	CN29	40
Waldo Pl. Mitch.	BU50	76
Waldo Rd. NW10	BP38	55
Waldo Rd. Brom.	CJ52	88
Waldram Cres. SE23	CC47	77
Waldram Pk. Rd. SE23	CC47	77
Waldram Pl. SE23	CC47	77
Waldram Cres.		
Waldron Gdns. Brom.	CF52	87
Waldronhyrst Croy.	BY56	95
Waldron Ms. SW3	BU43	66
Waldron Rd. SW18	BT48	76
Waldron Rd. Har.	BH33	45
Waldrons, The, Croy.	BY56	95
Waldrons, The. Oxt.	CG69	115
Waldron Yd. Har.	BG34	45
Waleran Bldgs. SE1	CA42	67
Old Kent Rd.		
Walerand Rd. SE13	CF44	67
Wales Av. Cars.	BU56	95
Wales Farm Rd. W3	BN39	55
Walfield Av. N20	BS26	38
Walford Rd. N16	CA35	48
Walford Rd. Dor.	BK73	119
Walford Rd. Uxb.	AX37	53
Walfrey Clo. Harl.	CP9	6
Walfrey Gdns. Dag.	CQ36	59
Walham Gro. SW6	BS43	66
Walham Rise, SW19	BR49	75
Walham Yd. SW6	BS43	66
Walham Gro.		
Walkden Rd. Chis.	CL49	78
Walker Av. Ong.	CY14	15
Walkers Ct. W1	BW40	56
Peter St.		
Walkerscroft Mead SE21	BZ47	77
Walker St. E14	CE39	57
Walkfield Dr. Epsom.	BP62	103

Walkford Way SE15 CA43 67
Walkley Rd. Dart. CU46 79
Walks, The, N2 BT31 47
Walk, The, Horn. CW34 51
Walk, The, Pot. B. BS19 20
Walk, The Sun. BB50 73
Walk, The, Wind. AN42 61
Wallace Cres. Cars. BU56 95
Wallace Flds. Epsom BO59 94
Wallace Rd. E15 CG38 58
Wallace Rd. N1 BZ36 57
Wallace Rd. Grays. DD41 71
Wallasey Cres. Uxb. AZ34 44
Wallbutton Rd. SE4 CD44 67
Wallcote Av. NW2 BQ33 46
Wall End Rd. E6 CK36 58
Wallenger Av. Rom. CU31 50
Waller La. Cat. CA65 105
Waller Rd. SE14 CC44 67
Wallers Clo. Wdf. Grn. CK29 40
Wallers Way, Hodd. CE10 12
Wallflower St. W12 BO40 55
Wallgrave Rd. SW5 BS42 66
Wallgrave Rd. W8 BS43 66
Wallhouse Rd. Erith. CU43 69
Wallingford Av. W10 BQ39 55
Wallingford Rd. Uxb. AW38 53
Wallingford Wk. St. Alb. BG15 9
Wallington Ct. Wall. BV57 95
Wallington Rd. Ilf. CN33 49
Wallington Sq. Wall. BV57 95
Wallis Clo. SW11 BT45 66
Wayland Rd.
Wallis Clo. Dart. CT48 79
Wallis Pk. Grav. DD46 81
Wallis Rd. E9 CD36 57
Wallis Rd. Sthl. BF39 54
Wallis's Cotts. SW2 BX47 76
Wallorton Gdns. SW14 BN45 65
Wall St. N1 BZ36 57
Wallwood Rd. E11 CF33 48
Wallwood St. E14 CD39 57
Wally St. E1 CC39 57
Walmer Clo. Rom. CR30 41
Walmer Gdns. W13 BJ41 64
Walmer Rd. W11 BR40 55
Walmer Ter. SE18 CM42 68
Walmgate Rd. Grnf. BJ37 54
Walmington Fold N12 BS29 38
Walm La. NW2 BQ36 55
Walney Wk. N1 BZ36 57
Marquess Est.
Walnut Ave. West Dr. AZ41 63
Walnut Clo. Cars. BU56 95
Park Hill,
Walnut Clo. Epsom BO61 103
Walnut Clo. Hayes BB40 53
Walnut Clo. Ilf. CM31 49
Civic Way
Walnut Ct. Welw. G. C. BR9 5
Walnut Grn. Bush. BE23 27
Walnut Gro. Enf. BZ25 30
Walnut Gro. Welw. G. C. BR9 5
Walnuts Rd. Orp. CO54 89
Walnut Tree Av. Dart. CW48 80
Walnut Tree Clo. Chis. CM51 88
Walnut Tree Clo. Guil. AR70 118
Walnut Tree Clo. Hodd. CE12 12
Walnut Tree Cotts. SW19 BR49 75
Church Rd.
Walnut Tree Cres. Saw. CQ5 6
Walnut Tree La. Wey. AX59 92
Walnut Tree Rd. SE10 CG42 68
Walnut Tree Rd. Brent. BL43 65
Walnut Tree Rd. Dag. CQ34 50
Walnut Tree Rd. Erith CT42 69
Walnut Tree Rd. Houns. BE43 64
Walnut Tree Rd. Shep. BA52 83
Walnut Tree Wk. SE11 BY42 66
Walnut Way Buck. H. CJ27 40
Walnut Way Ruis. BD36 54
Walnut Way Swan. CS51 89
Walpole Av. Couls. BU62 104
Walpole Av. Rich. BL44 65
Walpole Clo. W13 BK41 64
Walpole Clo. Pnr. BF29 36
Walpole Ct. Twick. BH48 74
Walpole Cres. Tedd. BH49 74
Walpole Gdns. W4 BN42 65
Walpole Gdns. Twick. BH48 74
Walpole Pl. Tedd. BH49 74
Walpole Rd. E6 CJ36 58
Walpole Rd. E17 CD31 48
Walpole Rd. E18 CG30 40
Walpole Rd. N17 BZ30 39
Walpole Rd. SE14 CD43 67
Walpole Rd. SW19 BT50 76
Walpole Rd. Brom. CJ53 88
Walpole Rd. Croy. BZ55 87
Walpole Rd. Surb. BL54 85
Walpole Rd. Tedd. BH49 74
Walpole Rd. Twick. BH48 74
Walpole Rd. Wind. AQ47 72
Walpole St. SW3 BU42 66
Walpole Way Barn. BQ25 28
Walrond Av. Wem. BL35 46
Walsham Rd. SE14 CC44 67
Walsham Rd. Felt. BC47 73
Walsh Cres. Croy. CG59 97
Walshford Way Borwd. BM22 28
Walsh Pl. Pnr. BC30 35
Walsingham Gdns. Epsom BO56 94
Walsingham Pk. Chis. CM51 88
Walsingham Rd. E5 CB34 48
Walsingham Rd. Croy. CF58 96
Walsingham Rd. Enf. BZ24 30
Walsingham Rd. Orp. CO51 89
Walsing Rd. Mitch. BU53 86
Walters Mead Ash. BL62 103
Woodfield La.
Walters Rd. SE25 CA52 87
Walters Rd. Enf. CC25 30
Walter's St. E2 CC38 57
Walter St. Kings. On T. BL51 85
Canbury Pass.
Walters Yd. Brom. CH51 88
Walter Ter. E1 CC39 57
Walterton Rd. W9 BR38 55
Walter Wk. Edg. BN29 37
Waltham Ave. Guil. AQ68 109
Waltham Ave. Hayes. BA41 63
Waltham Av. NW9 BM32 46
Waltham Clo. Dart. CU46 79
Waltham Clo. Orp. CP54 89
Waltham Ct. Har. BF30 36
Waltham Dr. Edg. BM30 37
Waltham Gdns. Enf. CC22 30
Waltham Rd. Cars. BT54 86
Waltham Rd. Cat. CB64 105
Waltham Rd. Sthl. BE41 64
Waltham Rd. Wal. Abb. CG16 22
Waltham Rd. Wdf. Grn. CK29 40
Walthamstow Av. E4 CD29 39
Waltham Way E4 CD28 39
Waltheof Av. N17 BZ30 39
Waltheof Gdns. N17 BZ30 39
Walthorne Gdns. Dag. CR36 59
Walton Av. Har. BE35 45
Walton Av. N. Mal. BO52 85
Walton Av. Sutt. BR55 85
Walton Bridge Rd. Shep. BA53 83
Walton Clo. NW2 BP34 46
Walton Clo. Har. BG31 45
Walton Cres. Har. BE35 45
Walton Dr. Har. BG31 45
Walton Gdns. W3 BM39 55
Walton Gdns. Brwd. DE25 122
Walton Gdns. Felt. BB49 73
Walton Gdns. Grnf. BH35 45
Walton Gdns. Wal. Abb. CE20 21
Walton Gdns. Wem. BL34 46
Walton Grn. Croy. CE58 96
Walton La. Shep. BA54 83
Walton La. Wey. AZ55 83
Walton Pk. Walt. BD55 84
Walton Pk. La. Walt. BD55 84
Walton Pl. SW3 BU41 66
Walton Rd. E12 CL34 49
Walton Rd. E13 CJ37 58
Walton Rd. Bush. BD24 27
Walton Rd. Epsom. BN64 103
Walton Rd. Epsom BO62 103
Walton Rd. Grays. DG41 71
Walton Rd. Har. BG31 45
Walton Rd. Hodd. CE11 12
Walton Rd. Rom. CQ29 41
Walton Rd. Sid. CO48 79
Walton Rd. Walt. BD53 84
Walton's Hall Rd. S. Le H. DK41 71
Walton St. SW3 BU42 66
Walton St. Enf. BZ23 30
Walton St. St. Alb. BH12 9
Walton St. Tad. BP65 103
Walton Ter. SW8 BX43 66
South Lambeth Rd.
Walton Ter. Wok. AT61 100
Walton Way W3 BM39 55
Walton Way Mitch. BW52 86
Walverns Clo. Wat. BD25 27
Walworth Rd. SE17 BZ42 67
Walworth St. SE17 BZ42 67
Walwyn Av. Brom. CJ52 88
Wambrook Clo. Brwd. DE26 122
Wanborough Dr. SW15 BP47 75
Wandle Bank, SW19 BT50 76
Wandle Bank Croy. BX55 86
Wandle Ct. Epsom BN56 94
Wandle Ct. Gdns. Croy. BX55 86
Wandle Rd. SW17 BU48 76
Wandle Rd. Croy. BX55 86
Wandle Rd. Croy. BZ55 87
Wandle Rd. Mord. BT52 86
Wandle Rd. Wall. BV55 86
Wandle Side Croy. BX55 86
Wandle Side Wall. BV55 86
Wandle Way Mitch. BU53 86
Wandon Rd. SW6 BS43 66
Wandsworth Br. Rd. SW6 BS44 66
Wandsworth High St. SW18 BS46 76
Wandsworth Plain, SW18 BS46 76
Wandsworth Rd. SW8 BV45 66
Wangey Rd. Rom. CP33 50
Wanless Rd. SE24 BZ45 67
Wanley Rd. SE5 BZ45 67
Wanlip Rd. E13 CH38 58
Wannions Clo. Chesh. AQ18 16
Wannock Gdns. Ilf. CL29 40
Wan Rd. S. Ock. DB38 60
Wansbeck Rd. E9 CD36 57
Wansbury Way. Swan. CU53 89
Wansey St. SE17 BZ42 67
Wansford Clo. Brwd. CZ27 42
Wansford Pk. Borwd. BN24 28
Wansford Rd. Wdf. Grn. CH30 40
Wanstead Clo. Brom. CJ51 88
Wanstead La. Ilf. CJ32 49
Wanstead Park Av. E12 CJ33 49
Wanstead Park Rd. Ilf. CJ32 49
Wanstead Pl. E11 CH32 49
Wanstead Rd. Brom. CJ51 88
Wansunt Rd. Bex. CS47 79
Wantage Rd. SE12 CG46 78
Wantz La. Rain. CU38 59
Wantz Rd. Dag. CR35 50
Wapping Dock St. E1 CB40 57
Cinnamon St.
Wapping High St. E1 CB40 57
Wapping La. E1 CB40 57
Wapping Wall, E1 CC40 57
Wapseys La. Slou. AP32 43
Wapshott Rd. Stai. AV50 72
Warbank Clo. Croy. CG58 97
Warbank Cres. Croy. CG58 97
Warbeck Rd. W12 BP40 55
Warberry Rd. N22 BX30 38
Warboys App. Kings. On T. BM50 75
Warboys Cres. E4 CF28 39
Warboys Rd. Kings. On T. BM50 75
Warburton Clo. Har. BG30 36
Warburton Rd. Twick. BF47 74
Warburton Ter. E17 CE30 39
War Coppice Rd. Cat. BZ67 114
Wardale Clo. SE16 CB41 67
Southwark Pk. Rd.
Ward Ave. Grays. DD42 71
Ward Clo. Erith CS43 69
Wardell Field NW9 BO30 37
Warden Av. Har. BE33 45
Warden Av. Rom. CS28 41
Warden Ct. Har. BE33 45
Warden Rd. NW5 BV36 56
Wardens Gro. SE1 BZ40 57
Ward Gdns. Slou. AM40 61
Ward Hatch, Harl. CO9 6
Ward La. Warl. CC61 105
Wardle St. E9 CC35 48
Wardley St. SW18 BS47 76
Wardo Av. SW6 BR44 65
Wardour St. W1 BW39 56
Ward Rd. E15 CF37 57
Ward Rd. N19 BW34 47
Ward Rd. SW19 BT51 86
Wardrobe, The, Rich. BK46 74
Old Palace Yard
Wards La. Borwd. BH23 27
Wards Rd. Ilf. CM33 49
Ward St. SE11 BX42 66
Ward St. Guil. AR71 118
Wareham Clo. Houns. BF45 64
Wareham St. N1 BZ37 57
Rushton St.
Waremead Rd. Ilf. CL32 49
Warenford Way Borwd. BM23 28
Warenne Rd. Lthd. BG64 102
Ware Rd. Hodd. CE10 12
Warescot Clo. Brwd. DA26 42
Warescot Rd. Brwd. DA26 42
Warfield Rd. NW10 BQ39 55
Warfield Rd. Felt. BB47 73
Warfield Rd. Hamptn. BF51 84
Wargrave Av. N15 CA32 48
Wargrave Rd. Har. BG34 45
Warham Rd. N4 BY32 47
Warham Rd. Har. BH30 36
Warham Rd. Sth. Croy. BY56 95
Warham St. SE5 BY43 66
Waring Clo. Orp. CN57 97
Waring Dr. Orp. CN57 97
Waring Rd. Sid. CP50 79
Waring St. SE27 BZ49 77
Warkworth Gdns. Islw. BJ43 64
Warkworth Rd. N17 BZ29 39
Warland Rd. SE18 CM43 68
Warland Rd. Sev. CZ58 99
Warley Av. Dag. CQ33 50
Warley Av. Hayes BC39 53
Warley Gap, Brwd. DA29 42
Warley Hall La. Upmin. DC33 123
Warley Hill, Brwd. DA29 42
Warley Par. NW9 BO31 46
Warley Rd. N9 CC27 39
Warley Rd. Brwd. DA29 42
Warley Rd. Hayes BC39 53
Warley Rd. Ilf. CL30 40
Warley Rd. Upmin. CY30 42
Warley Rd. Wdf. Grn. CH29 40
Warley St. E2 CC38 57
Warley St. Brwd. DB32 51
Warley St. Upmin. DB33 51
Warlingham Rd. Th. Hth. BY52 86
Warlock Rd. W9 BR38 55
Warlters Clo. N7 BX35 47
Warlters Mews N7 BX35 47
Warlters Rd. N7 BX35 47
Warltersville Rd. N19 BX33 47
Warmark Rd. Hem. H. AV12 7
Warmington Rd. SE24 BZ46 77
Warmington St. E13 CH38 58
Warminster Gdns. SE25 CB51 87
Warminster Rd. SE25 CA51 87
Warminster Sq. SE25 CB51 87
Warminster Way, Mitch. BV51 86
Warndon St. SE16 CC42 67
Warneford Pl. Wat. BE25 27
Warneford Rd. Har. BK31 45
Warneford St. E9 CB37 57
Warner Av. Sutt. BR55 85
Warner Clo. E15 CG35 49
Warner Clo. NW9 BO33 46
Warner Clo. Hayes. BA43 63
Warner Clo. Slou. AM40 61
Warner Par. Hayes. BA43 63
Warner Pl. E2 CB37 57
Warner Rd. E17 CD31 48
Warner Rd. N8 BW31 47
Warner Rd. SE5 BZ44 67
Warner Rd. Brom. CG50 78
Warners Av. Hodd. CD13 12
Warners Clo. Wdf. Grn. CH28 40
Warners End Rd. Hem. H. AW13 8
Warner's La. Kings. On T. BK49 74
Warner St. EC1 BY38 56
Warnford Rd. Orp. CN56 97
Warnham Court Rd. Cars. BU57 95
Warnham Rd. N12 BU28 38
Warple Way, W3 BO40 55
Warren Av. E10 CF34 48
Warren Av. Brom. CG50 78
Warren Av. Orp. CN56 97
Warren Av. Rich. BM45 65
Warren Av. Sth. Croy. CC57 96
Warren Av. Sutt. BR58 94
Warren Cl. Hat. BP11 10
Warren Clo. N9 CC26 39
Warren Clo. Bexh. CR46 79
Warren Clo. Esher BF56 93
Warren Clo. Slou. AS41 62
Warren Clo. Tad. BR65 103
Warren Ct. Beck. CD50 77
Warren Ct. Chig. CM28 40
Warren Ct. Sev. CV66 117
Warren Cres. N9 CA26 39
Warren Cutting, Kings. On T. BN50 75
Warren Dale, Welw. G. C. BQ6 5
Warrender Rd. N19 BW34 47
Warrender Rd. Chesh. AP18 16
Warrender Way Ruis. BC33 44
Warren Dr. Grnf. BF38 54
Warren Dr. Horn. CU35 50
Warren Dr. Orp. CO56 98
Warren Dr. Ruis. BD33 45
Warren Dr. S. Surb. BN54 85
Warren Dr. Tad. BR64 103
Warren Dr. Tad. BS65 104
Warren Dr. N. Surb. BM54 85
Warreners La. Wey. BA57 92
Warren Fld. Epp. CO19 23
Charles St.
Warren Field, Iver AU37 52
Warren Flds. Stan. BK28 36
Warren Gdns. E15 CF35 48
Warren Gdns. Orp. CO56 98
Warrengate La. Pot. B. BQ19 19
Warrengate Rd. Hat. BQ17 19
Warren Green. Hat. BP11 10
Warren Gro. Borwd. BN24 28
Warren Hill Epsom BN61 103
Warren Hill Lough. CJ25 31
Warren Hill Ho. Loug. CH25 31
Warren Ho. Kings. On T. BN50 75
Warren La. SE18 CL41 68
Warren La. Brwd. CZ23 33
Warren La. Grays DB42 70
Warren La. Lthd. BG59 93
Warren La. Oxt. CG70 115
Warren La. Stan. BH27 36
Warren La. Wok. AW62 101
Warren Mead Bans. BQ61 103
Warrenne Rd. Bet. BN71 120
Warren Pk. Kings. On T. BN50 75
Warren Pk. Warl. CC62 105
Warren Pk. Rd. Sutt. BT57 95
Warren Pond Rd. E4 CG26 40
Warren Ri. N. Mal. BN51 85
Warren Rd. E4 CF27 39
Warren Rd. E10 CF34 48
Warren Rd. E11 CJ32 49
Warren Rd. NW2 BO34 46
Warren Rd. SW19 BU50 76
Warren Rd. Ashf. BB50 73
Warren Rd. Bans. BQ60 94
Warren Rd. Bexh. CR46 79
Warren Rd. Brom. CH55 88
Warren Rd. Bush. BG26 36
Warren Rd. Croy. CA54 87
Warren Rd. Dart. CW48 80
Warren Rd. Grav. DD49 81
Warren Rd. Guil. AS71 118
Warren Rd. Ilf. CM32 49
Warren Rd. Kings. On T. BN50 75
Warren Rd. Orp. CN56 97
Warren Rd. Pur. BY59 95
Warren Rd. Reig. BS70 121
Warren Rd. St. Alb. BG15 9
Warren Rd. Sid. CP48 79
Warren Rd. Twick. BG46 74
Warren Rd. Uxb. AY35 44
Warren Rd. Wey. AW58 92
Warren St. Ms. W1 BW38 56
Warren St.
Warren, S The, Hart. DC53 90
Warren St. W1 BW38 56
Warren Ter. Rom. CP31 50
Warren, The, E12 CK35 49
Warren, The, Ash. BL63 103
Warren, The, Cars. BT58 95
Warren, The Grav. DH49 81
Warren, The, Hayes BC39 53
Warren, The, Houns. BE43 64
Warren, The, Leath. BB68 110
Warren, The, Rad. BJ20 18
Warren, The, Tad. BR65 103
Warren, The, Wor. Pk. BN56 94
Warren, The, Dr. E11 CJ33 49
Warren Wk. SE7 CJ43 68
Warren Way NW7 BR29 37
Warren Way. Welw. G. C. BR5 5
Warren Way, Wey. BA56 92
Warren Wd. Rd. Brom. CG55 88
Warren Wood Clo. Brom. CG55 88
Warrick Gro. Croy. CA55 87
Warriner Av. Horn. CV34 51
Warriner Gdns. SW11 BU44 66
Bushwood Rd.
Warrington Cres. W9 BT38 56
Warrington Gdns. W9 BS38 56
Warwick Av.
Warrington Gdns. Horn. CV32 51
Warrington Rd. Croy. BY55 86
Warrington Rd. Dag. CP34 50
Warrington Rd. Har. BH32 45
Warrington Rd. Rich. BL46 75
Hermitage, The,
Warrington Spur, Wind. AQ47 72
Warrington Sq. Dag. CP34 50
Warrington St. E13 CH38 58
Warrior Av. Grav. DH49 81
Warrior Rd. SE5 BY43 66
Warrior Sq. E12 CL35 49
Warsaw Clo. Ruis. BC36 53
Warspite Rd. SE18 CK41 68
Warton Rd. E15 CF37 57
Warwick Av. W2 BS38 56
Warwick Av. W9 BS38 56
Warwick Av. Edg. BM27 37
Warwick Av. Egh. AU51 82
Warwick Av. Har. BE35 45
Warwick Av. Pot. B. BW17 20
Warwick Av. Stai. AX50 73
Warwick Clo. Bush. BH26 36
Warwick Clo. Hamptn. BG50 74
Warwick Clo. Orp. CO55 89
Warwick Cotts. Barn. BT25 29
Warwick Ct. WC1 BX39 56
Warwick Ct. Surb. BL55 85
Warwick Cres. W2 BT39 56
Warwick Cres. Hayes BB38 53
Warwick Dene W5 BL40 55
Warwick Dr. SW15 BP45 65
Warwick Dr. Wal. Cr. CC17 21
Warwick Est. W2 BS39 56
Warwick Gdns. N4 BZ32 48
Warwick Gdns. W14 BR41 65
Warwick Gdns. Ash. BK62 102
Warwick Gdns. Ilf. CL33 49
Warwick Gdns. Rom. CV31 51
Warwick Gdns. Surb. BH53 84
Warwick Gdns. Th. Hth. BY52 86
Warwick Gro. E5 CB33 48
Warwick Gro. Surb. BL54 85
Warwick Ho. St. SW1 BW40 56
Warwick La. EC4 BY39 56
Warwick La. Upmin. CW38 60
Warwick La. Wok. AQ63 100
Warwick Pl. W5 BK41 64
Warwick Rd.
Warwick Pl. W9 BT39 56
Warwick Pl. Grav. DD46 81
Warwick Pl. Uxb. AX36 53
Warwick Pl. West Dr. AX40 53
Warwick Pl. Ms. W9 BT39 56
Warwick Pl. N. SW1 BW42 66
Warwick Rd. E4 CE28 39
Warwick Rd. E11 CH32 49
Warwick Rd. E12 CK35 49
Warwick Rd. E15 CG36 58
Warwick Rd. E17 CD30 39
Warwick Rd. N11 BW29 38
Warwick Rd. N18 CA28 39
Warwick Rd. SE20 CB52 87
Warwick Rd. SW5 BR42 65
Warwick Rd. W5 BK41 64
Warwick Rd. W14 BR42 65
Warwick Rd. Ashf. AY49 73
Warwick Rd. Barn. BS24 29
Warwick Rd. Borwd. BN24 28
Warwick Rd. Couls. BW60 95
Warwick Rd. Enf. CD22 30
Warwick Rd. Houns. BC45 63
Warwick Rd. Kings. On T. BK51 84
Warwick Rd. N. Mal. BN52 85
Warwick Rd. Rain. CV38 60
Warwick Rd. Red. BU70 121
Warwick Rd. St. Alb. BH12 9
Warwick Rd. Sid. CO49 79
Warwick Rd. Sthl. BE41 64
Warwick Rd. Surb. BH53 84
Warwick Rd. Sutt. BT56 95
Warwick Rd. Th. Hth. BY52 86
Warwick Rd. Twick. BH47 74
Warwick Rd. Well. CP45 69
Warwick Rd. West Dr. AY40 53
Warwick Row, SW1 BV41 66
Warwick's Bench, Guil. AS72 118
Warwick's Bench Rd. Guil. AS72 118
Warwick Sq. EC4 BY39 56
Warwick Sq. SW1 BW42 66
Warwick St. W1 BW40 56
Warwick Ter. SE18 CM43 68
Warwick Way, SW1 BV42 66
Warwick Way, Rick. BA24 26
Warwick Wold Rd. Red. BY68 113
Washington Ave. Hem. H. AY11 8
Washington Av. E12 CK35 49
Washington Clo. Reig. BS69 121
Washington Rd. E6 CJ36 58
St. Stephen's Rd.
Washington Rd. E18 CG30 40
Washington Rd. SW13 BP43 65
Washington Rd. Kings-on-t. BM51 85
Washington Rd. Wor. Pk. BP55 85
Wash La. Barn. BQ21 28
Washneys La. Orp. CO60 98
Washpond La. Warl. CF62 105
Wash Rd. Brwd. DE25 122
Wash Rd. Pot. B. BP20 19
Wastdale Rd. SE23 CC47 77
Watchfield Ct. W4 BN42 65
Watchgate. Dart. CY49 80
Watchlytes. Welw. G. C. BT7 5
Watch Mead. Welw. G. C. BS7 5
Watcombe Cotts. Rich. BM43 65
Bushwood Rd.
Watcombe Pl. SE25 CB52 87
Watcombe Rd. SE25 CB53 87
Waterbank Rd. SE6 CE48 77
Waterbeach Rd. Dag. CP35 50
Watercroft Rd. Sev. CQ58 98
Waterdale Rd. SE2 CO43 69
Waterdale St. Grav. DE48 81
Waterden Clo. Guil. AS71 118
Waterden Rd. E15 CE35 48
Waterden Rd. Guil. AS71 118
Water End Rd. Berk. AT12 7
Waterer Gdns. Tad. BR62 103
Waterer Rise Wall. BW57 95
Waterer Rd. N20 BT27 38
Waterers Rise, Wok. AO62 100
Waterfall Clo. N14 BW27 38
Waterfall Rd.
Waterfall Clo. Vir. W. AQ52 82
Waterfall Cotts. SW19 BT50 76

Waterfall Rd. N11 BV28 38
Waterfall Rd. N14 BV28 38
Waterfall Rd. SW19 BT50 76
Waterfield, Tad. BP63 103
Water Field. Welw. G. C. BS7 5
Waterfield Dr. Warl. CB62 105
Waterfield Dr. Warl. CC63 105
Waterfield Grn. Tad. BP63 103
Waterfields, Lthd. BJ63 102
Waterford Rd. SW6 BS43 66
Watergate, EC4 BY40 56
Tudor St.
Watergate Wat. BD27 36
Watergate St. SE8 CE43 67
Watergate Wk. WC2 BX40 56
Waterhall Av. E4 CG27 40
Waterhead Clo. Erith CT43 69
Waterhouse La. Ken. BZ63 105
Waterhouse La. Red. CA69 114
Waterhouse La. Tad. BR64 103
Waterhouse Moor. Harl. CN11 13
Waterhouse St. Hem. H. AX13 8
Water La. E15 CG36 58
Water La. Berk. AR13 7
Water La. Brwd. CY23 33
Water La. Cob. BE61 102
Water La. Harl. CK12 13
Water La. Hem. H. AT18 16
Water La. Ilf. CN34 49
Water La. Kings L. AZ18 17
Water La. Kings. On T. BK51 84
Water La. Lthd. BD66 111
Water La. Oxt. CH66 115
Water La. Rich. BK46 74
Water La. Sid. CQ48 79
Water La. Twick. BJ47 74
Water La. Wat. BD24 27
Waterloo Br. SE1 BX40 56
Waterloo Br. WC2 BX40 56
Waterloo Cres. Felt. BC47 73
Waterloo Est. E2 CB37 57
Waterloo Gdns. E2 CC37 57
Waterloo Gdns. Rom. CT32 50
Waterloo Ms. SE5 BZ43 67
Elmington Rd.
Waterloo Pl. NW6 BR36 55
Willesdon La.
Waterloo Pl. SW1 BW40 56
Waterloo Pl. Rich. BL45 65
Quadrant, The
Waterloo Pl. Rich. BM43 65
Waterloo Rd. E6 CJ36 58
Waterloo Rd. E7 CG35 49
Wellington Rd.
Waterloo Rd. E10 CE33 48
Waterloo Rd. NW2 BP33 46
Waterloo Rd. SE1 BX40 56
Waterloo Rd. Brwd. DB26 42
Waterloo Rd. Epsom BN59 94
Waterloo Rd. Ilf. CM30 40
Waterloo Rd. Rom. CT32 50
Waterloo Rd. Sutt. BT56 95
Waterloo Rd. Uxb. AX37 53
Waterloo St. EC1 BZ38 57
Lever St.
Waterloo Ter. N1 BY36 56
Waterloo Wk. E9 CC35 48
Churchill Wk.
Waterlow Ct. NW11 BS33 47
Waterlow Rd. N19 BW33 47
Waterlow Rd. Reig. BT71 121
Waterman Clo. Wat. BC25 26
Waterman St. SW15 BQ45 65
Watermead La. Cars. BU53 86
Watermead Rd. SE6 CE49 77
Water Mill Clo. Rich. BK48 74
Water Mill La. N18 CA28 39
Water Mill Way Felt. BE48 74
Water Mill Way. S. Dnth. CX51 90
Waterperry La. Wok. AP58 91
Water Rd. Wem. BL37 55
Waters Dr. Stai. AV48 72
Watersedge, Epsom BN56 94
Watersfield Way, Edg. BK29 36
Waters Gdns. Dag. CR35 50
Waterside, Beck. CD51 87
Waterside Chesh. AO20 16
Waterside Dart. CT46 79
Waterside, Kings L. AZ18 17
Waterside, Uxb. AX39 53
Waterside. Welw. G. C. BS7 5
Waterside Clo. SE16 CB41 67
Bevington St.
Waterside Pla. NW1 BV37 56
Princess Rd.
Waterside Rd. Guil. AR69 118
Waters Mead. Harl. CL13 13
Waterson Rd. Grays. DG42 71
Waterson St. E2 CA38 57
Watersplash La. Hayes BC42 63
Watersplash Rd. Shep. AZ52 83
Waters Rd. SE6 CG48 78
Waters Rd. Kings-on-t. BM51 85
Waters Side Way Wok. AQ62 100
Winnington Way
Waters Sq. Kings-on-t. BM52 85
Water St. WC2 BY40 56
Maltravers St.
Water St. Kings. On T. BL51 85
Canbury Pass.
Waterton Av. Grav. DJ47 81
Water Tower Hill Croy. BZ56 96
Waterville Rd. N17 BZ30 39
Waterway Rd. Lthd. BJ64 102
Waterworks La. E5 CC34 48
Lea Bridge Rd.
Waterworks Rd. SW2 BX46 76
Watery La. SW20 BR51 85
Watery La. Brox. CD16 21
Watery La. Cher. AV54 82
Watery La. Hat. BO13 10
Watery La. Hayes. BB42 63
Watery La. Nthlt. BD37 54
Watery Lane. Ong. CV11 15
Watery Lane. Ong. DA13 15
Watery. La. Sev. CY64 108
Watery La. Sid. CO50 79
Watery La. Wok. AO58 91
Wates Way Mitch. BU53 86
Watford By-pass Borwd. BJ26 36
Watford Clo. SW11 BU44 66
Petworth St.
Watford Clo. Guil. AS70 118
Watford Flds. Rd. Wat. BD25 27
Watford Rd. E16 CH39 58
Watford Rd. Borwd. BK25 27
Watford Rd. Har. BJ33 45
Watford Rd. Kings L. AZ18 17
Watford Rd. Nthwd. BB29 35
Watford Rd. Rick. AZ25 26
Watford Rd. St. Alb. BF17 18
Watford Rd, Wat. BF22 27
Watford Rd. Wat. BF23 27
Watford Way. NW4 BN28 37
Watford Way. NW7 BN28 37
Wathen Rd. Dor. BJ71 119
Watkin Rd. Wem. BM34 46
Watkinson Rd. N7 BX36 56
Watling Av. Edg. BN30 37
Watling Clo. Hem. H. AY11 8
Watling Ct. EC4 BZ39 57
Watling St.
Watling Gdns. NW2 BR36 55
Watling Knoll, Rad. BH20 18
Watling St. EC4 BZ39 57
Watling St. Bexh. CR45 69
Watling St. Borwd. BK23 27
Watling St. Grav. DE48 81
Watling St. Rad. BH19 18
Watling St. St. Alb. BD10 9
Watlington Gro. SE26 CD49 77
Watlington Rd. Harl. CP9 6
Watling Vw. St. Alb. BG15 9
Watney Rd. SW14 BN45 65
Watney's Rd. Mitch. BW53 86
Watson Av. E6 CL36 58
Watson Av. Sutt. BR55 85
Watson Clo. N16 BZ35 48
Matthias Rd.
Watson Clo. SW19 BU50 76
Watson Rd. Dor. BG72 119
Watson Rd. Wok. AS61 100
Watsons Av. St. Alb. BH12 9
Watsons Ms. W1 BU39 56
Crawford Pl.
Watson, S Wk. St. Alb. BH14 9
Watson's Rd. N22 BX30 38
Watson's St. SE8 CD43 67
Watson St. E13 CH37 58
Watsons Yd. NW2 BO34 46
Wattendon Rd. Ken. BY61 104
Wattisfield Rd. E5 CC34 48
Watt's Bri. Rd. Erith. CT43 69
Watts Cres. Grays CY42 70
Watts Farm Par. Wok. AP58 91
Watts Gro. E3 CE39 57
Watt's La. Chis. CL51 88
Watts La. Tad. BQ64 103
Watts La. Tedd. BJ49 74
Watts Mead. Tad. BQ64 103
Watts Rd. Surb. BJ54 84
Watts St. E1 CB40 57
Wat Tyler Rd. SE10 CF44 67
Wauthier Clo. N13 BY28 38
Wavell Clo. Wal. Cr. CD17 21
Wavell Dr. Sid. CN46 78
Wavel Ms. NW6 BS36 56
Wavendene Av. Egh. AT50 72
Wavendon Av. W4 BN42 65
Waveney Av. SE15 CB45 67
Waveney, Hem. H. AY11 8
Waverley Av. E4 CD28 39
Waverley Av. Ken. CA61 105
Waverley Av. Surb. BM53 85
Waverley Av. Sutt. BS55 86
Waverley Av. Twick. BE47 74
Waverley Av. Wem. BL36 55
Waverley Clo. E18 CJ30 40
Waverley Clo. Brom. CJ53 88
Waverley Clo. Hayes. BA42 63
Waverley Cres. SE18 CM42 68
Waverley Cres. Rom. CV29 42
Waverley Dri. Cher. AU56 91
Waverley Dr. Cher. AU55
Waverley Dr. Vir. W. AQ52 82
Waverley Gdns. NW10 BL37 55
Waverley Gdns. Bark. CN37 58
Waverley Gdns. Grays. DD41 71
Waverley Gdns. Ilf. CM30 40
Waverley Gdns. Nthwd. BC30 35
Waverley Gro. N3 BQ31 46
Waverley Pl. NW8 BT37 56
Waverley Pl. Lthd. BJ64 102
Church Rd.
Waverley Rd. E17 CF31 48
Waverley Rd. E18 CJ30 40
Waverley Rd. N8 BW32 47
Waverley Rd. N17 CA30 39
Waverley Rd. N17 CB29 39
Waverley Rd. SE18 CM42 68
Waverley Rd. SE25 CB52 87
Waverley Rd. Cob. BF60 93
Waverley Rd. Enf. BY24 29
Waverley Rd. Epsom BP57 94
Waverley Rd. Har. BE33 45
Waverley Rd. Rain. CU38 59
Waverley Rd. St. Alb. BG12 9
Waverley Rd. Sthl. BF40 54
Waverley Rd. Wey. AZ56 92
Waverley Wk. W2 BS39 56
Waverley Way Cars. BU57 95
Waverton Rd. SW18 BT47 76
Waverton St. W1 BV41 66
Wavertree Ct. SW2 BX47 76
Wavertree Rd. E18 CH30 40
Wavertree Rd. SW2 BX47 76
Wave Tock Side. Brwd. CY23 33
Waxlow Cres. Sthl. BF39 54
Waxlow Rd. NW10 BN37 55
Waxwell Clo. Pnr. BD30 36
Waxwell La. Pnr. BD30 36
Waxwell Ter. SE1 BX41 66
Waycross Rd. Upmin. CZ33 51
Waye Av. Houns. BC44 63
Wayfarer Rd. Nthlt. BD38 54
Wayland Av. E8 CB35 48
Wayland Rd. SW11 BT45 66
Waylands Swan. CT52 89
Waylett Pl. Wem. BK34 45
Waynefleet Tower Av. Esher BF55 84
Wayneflete Sq. W10 BQ40 55
Waynflete Av. Croy. BY55 86
Waynflete St. SW18 BT48 76
Wayre Rd. Harl. CP9 6
Wayside NW11 BR33 46
Wayside, SW14 BN46 75
Way Side, Kings L. AW18 17
Wayside, Pot. B. BT20 20
Wayside Av. Bush. BG25 27
Wayside Av. Horn. CV34 51
Wayside Clo. N14 BW25 29
Wayside Clo. Rom. CT31 50
Wayside Ct. Twick. BK46 74
Arlington Rd.
Wayside Gdns. SE9 CK49 78
Wayside Gro.
Wayside Gdns. Dag. CR35 50
Wayside Gro. SE9 CK49 78
Wayside Mews, Ilf. CL32 49
Gaysham Av.
Wayside, The Hem. H. AZ14 8
Way, The Reig. BT70 121
Wayville Rd. Dart. CX47 80
Way Volante, Grav. DJ49 81
Weald Bridge Rd. Epp. CS15 14
Weald Clo. Brom. CK55 88
Weald Clo. Brwd. DA27 42
Weald Clo. Sev. CU70 116
Weald Clo. Sev. CV70 117
Weald Hall La. Epp. CP16 23
Weald La. Har. BG30 36
Weald Park Way, Brwd. CZ27 42
Weald Rise Har. BH29 36
Weald Rd. Brwd. CX26 42
Weald Rd. Sev. CU67 116
Weald Rd. Uxb. AZ37 53
Weald Sq. E5 CB34 48
Rossington St.
Wealdstone Rd. Sutt. BR55 85
Weald, The, Chis. CK50 78
Weald, The Grav. DF50 81
Weald Way. Cat. CA67 114
Weald Way, Hayes BB38 53
Weald Way, Reig. BT72 121
Weald Way Rom. CR32 50
Wealdwood Gdns. Pnr. BF29 36
High Banks Rd.
Weale Rd. E4 CF27 39
Weall Grn. Wat. BC19 17
Weardale Ave. Dart. CY47 80
Weardale Gdns. Enf. BZ23 30
Weardale Rd. SE13 CF45 67
Wear Pl. E2 CB38 57
Bethnal Green Rd.
Wearside Rd. SE13 CE45 67
Wear St. E2 CB38 57
Teesdale St.
Weatherhall Clo. Wey. AW57 92
Weavers Clo. Grav. DG47 81
Weavers La. SE1 CA40 57
Weavers La. Sev. CV64 108
Weaver St. E1 CB38 57
Weaver Wk. SE27 BY49 76
Webb Clo. Slou. AR42 62
Webber Clo. Erith. CU43 69
Webber Row. SE1 BY41 66
Webber St. SE1 BY41 66
Webb Est. E5 CB33 48
Webb Gdns. E13 CH38 58
Kelland Rd.
Webb's Alley, Sev. CV66 117
Webbs Rd. SW11 BU45 66
Webbs Rd. Hayes BC38 53
Webb St. SE1 CA41 67
Webster Clo. Cob. BF60 93
Webster Clo. Uxb. AX38 53
Webster Clo. Wal. Abb. CG20 22
Webster Gdns. W5 BK40 54
Webster Rd. E11 CF34 48
Webster Rd. SE16 CB41 67
Webster Vill. W5 BK40 54
Webster Gdns.
Wedderburn Rd. NW3 BT35 47
Wedderburn Rd. Bark. CM37 58
Wedgewood Clo. Epp. CO18 23
Theydon Clo.
Wedgewood Clo. Nthwd. BA29 35
Wedgewood Way. SE19 BZ50 77
Beulah Hill.
Wedhey Harl. CM11 13
Wedlake Clo. Horn. CW33 51
Wedlake St. W10 BR38 55
Kensal Rd.
Wedmore Av. Ilf. CL30 40
Wedmore Gdns. N19 BW34 47
Holloway Rd.
Wedmore Ms. N19 BW34 47
Wedmore St.
Wedmore Rd. Grnf. BG38 54
Wedmore St. N19 BW34 47
Wednesbury Gdns. Rom. CW29 42
Wednesbury Grn. Rom. CW29 42
Wednesbury Rd. Rom. CW29 42
Weech Rd. NW6 BS35 47
Weekes Dr. Slou. AN40 61
Weekley Sq. SW11 BT45 66
Th. Baines Rd.
Weetfield Av. Sth. Croy. BZ60 96
Weetman St. SE10 CG41 68
Weigall Rd. SE12 CH46 78
Weighhouse St. W1 BV40 56
Weighton Ms. SE20 CB51 87
Weighton Rd.
Weighton Rd. SE20 CB51 87
Weighton Rd. Har. BG30 36
Weind, The Epp. CN21 31
Weint. The. Slou. AU43 62
Weinurst Gdns. Sutt. BT56 95
Weir Clo. Bex. CR47 79
Weirdale Av. N20 BU27 38
Weir Hall Av. N18 BZ29 39
Weir Hall Clo. N17 BZ29 39
Weir Hall Gdns. N18 BZ28 39
Weir Hall Rd. N17 BZ29 39
Weir Hall Rd. N18 BZ29 39
Weir Pl. Stai. AV51 82
Weir Rd. SW12 BW47 76
Weir Rd. SW19 BS49 76
Weir Rd. Cher. AW54 83
Weir Rd. Walt. BC53 83
Weirs Pass. NW1 BW38 56
Chalton St.
Weiss Rd. SW15 BQ45 65
Welbeck Av. Brom. CH49 78
Welbeck Av. Hayes BC38 53
Welbeck Av. Sid. CO47 79
Welbeck Clo. N12 BT28 38
Welbeck Clo. Borwd. BM24 28
Welbeck Clo. Epsom BP57 94
Welbeck Clo. N. Mal. BO53 85
Welbeck Rd. E6 CJ38 58
Welbeck Rd. Barn. BT25 29
Welbeck Rd. Cars. BU54 86
Welbeck Rd. Har. BF33 45
Welbeck Rd. Sutt. BT55 86
Welbeck St. W1 BV39 56
Welbeck Wk. Cars. BT54 86
Welbeck Rd.
Welbeck Way. W1 BV39 56
Welbourne Rd. N17 CA31 48
Welby St. SE5 BY44 66
Welcomes Rd. Ken. BZ61 105
Welders La. Beac. AP29 34
Weldon Clo. Ruis. BC36 53
Weldon Way. Red. BW68 113
Welfare Rd. E15 CG36 58
Welford Pl. SW19 BR49 75
Welham Cl. Hat. BQ15 10
Welham Rd. SW17 BV49 76
Welhouse Rd. Cars. BU54 86
Wellacre Rd. Har. BJ32 45
Welland Gdns. Grnf. BH37 54
Wellands Clo. Brom. CK51 88
Welland St. SE10 CF43 67
Creek Rd.
Well App. Barn. BQ25 28
Wellbrook Rd. Orp. CL56 97
Wellbury Ter. Hem. H. BA13 8
Well Cl. E1 CB40 57
Well Clo. Ruis. BE34 45
Well Clo. Wok. AR62 100
Wellclose Sq. E1 CB40 57
Wellclose St. E1 CB40 57
Wellclose Sq.
Wellclose St. St. Alb. BG13 9
Wellcome Av. Dart. CW45 70
Wellcott Clo. E11 CJ32 49
Warren Rd.
Well Ct. EC4 BZ39 57
Queen St.
Well Ct. NW8 BT37 56
Well Ct. NW8 BT38 56
Well Croft, Hem. H. AW13 8
Wellcroft Clo. Welw. G. C. BS9 5
Wellcroft Rd. Slou. AN40 61
Welldale Rd. SE16 CC42 67
Welldon Cres. Har. BH32 45
Well End La. Borwd. BN22 28
Wellen Rise, Hem. H. AY15 8
Weller Clo. Amer. AP22 25
Weller Rd. Amer. AP22 25
Wellers Ct. NW1 BX37 56
Weller St. SE1 BZ41 67
Wellesford Clo. Bans. BR62 103
Wellesley Ave. Iver. AV41 62
Wellesley Ave. Nthwd. BB28 35
Wellesley Av. W6 BP41 65
Wellesley Av. Nthwd. BC28 35
Wellesley Ct. W9 BT38 56
Wellesley Ct Rd. Croy. BZ55 87
Wellesley Gro.
Wellesley Cres. Pot. B. BR20 19
Wellesley Cres. Twick. BH48 74
Wellesley Gro. Croy. BZ55 87
Wellesley Pl. NW5 BV35 47
Wellesley Rd. E11 CH32 49
Wellesley Rd. E17 CE32 48
Wellesley Rd. N22 BY30 38
Redvers Rd.
Wellesley Rd. W4 BM42 65
Wellesley Rd. Brwd. DB26 42
Wellesley Rd. Croy. BZ55 87
Wellesley Rd. Har. BH32 45
Wellesley Rd. Ilf. CL34 49
Wellesley Rd. Slou. AQ41 62
Wellesley Rd. Sutt. BT57 95
Wellesley Rd. Twick. BG48 74
Wellesley St. E1 CC39 57
Welley Dr. Slou. AS45 62
Welley Dr. Stai. AS45 62
Welley Rd. Stai. AS45 62
Welley Rd. Stai. AS46 72
Wellfarm Rd. Whyt. CB63 105
Well Field Hart. DC52 90
Wellfield Av. N10 BV31 47
Wellfield Clo. Hat. BP12 10
Wellfield Rd.
Wellfield Rd. SW16 BX49 76
Wellfield Rd. Hat. BP11 10
Wellfields Rd. Loug. CL24 31
Wellfield Wk. SW16 BX49 76
Wellgarth Gdns. Grnf. BJ36 54
Wellgarth Rd. NW11 BS33 47
Well Hall Rd. SE9 CK45 68
Wellham Rd. Uxb. AX37 53
Well Hill Orp. CR57 98
Well Hill La. Orp. CR57 98
Well Hill Rd. Sev. CS57 98
Wellhouse La. Barn. BQ24 28
Wellhouse La. Bet. BN72 120
Wellhouse Rd. Beck. CD52 87
Wellington Arch. SW1 BV42 66
Wellington Av. E4 CE27 39
Wellington Av. N9 CB27 39
Wellington Av. N15 CA32 48
Wellington Av. Houns. BF46 74
Wellington Av. Pnr. BE30 36
Wellington Av. Sid. CO46 79
Wellington Av. Vir. W. AQ52 82
Wellington Av. Wor. Pk. BQ56 94
Wellington Clo. E4 CE27 39
Wellington Av.
Wellington Clo. W11 BS39 56
Ledbury Rd.
Wellington Clo. Dag. CS36 59
Wellington Cotts. Leath. BB68 110
Wellington Cres. N. Mal. BN52 85
Wellington Dr. Dag. CS36 59
Wellington Gdns. SE7 CJ42 68
Wellington Gdns. Hmptn. BG49 74
Wellington Hill, Loug. CH22 31
Wellingtonia Av. Hav. CS27 41
Wellington Pass. E11 CH32 49
Wellington Rd.
Wellington Pl. N2 BU32 47
Wellington Pl. NW8 BT38 56
Wellington Rd. E6 CK37 58
Wellington Rd. E7 CG35 49
Wellington Rd. E10 CD33 48
Wellington Rd. E11 CH32 49
Wellington Rd. E17 CD31 48
Wellington Rd. NW8 BT37 56
Wellington Rd. NW10 BQ39 55
Wellington Rd. SW19 BS48 76
Wellington Rd. W5 BK41 64
Wellington Rd. Ashf. AY49 73
Wellington Rd. Belv. CQ42 69
Wellington Rd. Bex. CP46 79
Wellington Rd. Brom. CJ52 88
Wellington Rd. Cat. BZ64 105
Wellington Rd. Croy. BY54 86
Wellington Rd. Dart. CV46 80
Wellington Rd. Enf. CA26 39
Wellington Rd. Felt. BB46 73
Wellington Rd. Har. BH31 45
Wellington Rd. Hmptn. BG49 74
Wellington Rd. Orp. CO53 89
Wellington Rd. Pnr. BE29 36
Wellington Rd. St. Alb. BJ14 9
Wellington Rd. St. Alb. BK16 18
Wellington Rd. Til. DG45 71
Wellington Rd. Wat. BC23 26
Wellington Rd. N. Houns. BE45 64
Wellington Rd. S. Houns. BE45 64
Wellington Row, E2 CA38 57
Wellington Sq. SW3 BU42 66
Wellington St. E5 CB34 48
Wellington St. SE18 CL42 68
Wellington St. WC2 BX40 56
Wellington St. Grav. DH47 81
Wellington Ter. Har. BG33 45
Wellington Way. E3 CE38 57
Wellington Yd. Rich. BK46 74
George St.
Welling Way SE9 CM45 68
Welling Way Well. CM45 68
Well La. SW14 BN46 75
Well La. Brwd. CZ24 33
Well La. Harl. CL10 6
Well La. Wok. AR62 100
Wellmeade Dr. Sev. CU67 116
Wellmeadow Rd. SE6 CG46 78
Wellmeadow Rd. W7 BJ42 64
Wellow Wk. Cars. BT54 86
Well Pass. NW3 BT34 47
Well Path, Wok. AR62 100
Well Rd. NW3 BT34 47
Well Rd. NW10 BQ38 55
Well Rd. Barn. BQ25 28
Well Rd. Pot. B. BU17 20
Well Rd. Sev. CV62 108
Well Row. Hert. BX12 11
Wells Clo. Nthlt. BD38 54
Wells Cres. SE5 CA43 67
Wells Dr. NW9 BN33 46
Wells Gdns. Dag. CR35 50
Wells Gdns. Ilf. CK33 49
Wells Gdns. Rain. CT36 59
Wellshouse Rd. NW10 BO39 55
Wellside Clo. Barn. BQ24 28
Wellside Gdns. SW14 BN46 75
Wells Ms. W1 BW39 56
Wellsmoor Gdns. Brom. CL52 88
Wells Pk. Rd. SE26 CB48 77
Wells Pl. W5 BK40 54
Wellsprings Cres. Wem. BM34 46
Wells Rise, NW8 BU37 56
Wells Rd. W12 BQ41 65
Wells Rd. Brom. CK51 88
Wells Rd. Epsom. BM60 94
Wells St. W1 BW39 56
Wellstead Av. N9 CC26 39
Wellstead Rd. E6 CL37 58
Wells Ter. N4 BY34 47
Wells, The, N14 BW26 38
Wellstones Wat. BC24 26
Well St. E9 CB36 57
Well St. E15 CG36 58
Wells Way, SE5 BZ43 67

Wellswood Clo. Hem. H. AZ13 8
Well Way, Epsom. BM61 103
Wellwood Clo. Couls. BX56 95
Wellwood Clo. Couls. BX60 95
Wellwood Rd. Ilf. CO33 50
Welsford St. SE1 CB42 67
Welsh Clo. E13 CH38 58
Welshpool St. E8 CB37 57
Weltje Rd. W6 BP42 65
Welton Rd. SE18 CN43 68
Welwyn Av. Felt. BB46 73
Welwyn Ct. Hem. H. AY11 8
Welwyn St. E2 CC38 57
Globe Rd.
Welwyn Way, Hayes BB38 53
Wembley Hill Rd. Wem. BL34 46
Wembley Park Dr. Wem. BL35 46
Wembley Rd. Hamptn. BF51 84
Wembley Way, Wem. BM36 55
Wemborough Rd. Stan. BK30 36
Wembury Rd. N6 BV33 47
Wemyss Rd. SE3 CG44 68
Wendela Clo. Wok. AS62 100
Wendela Ct. Har. BH34 45
Wendell Rd. W12 BO41 65
Wend End Ct. Slou. AP37 52
Wendley Dri. Wey. AV58 91
Wendling Rd. Sutt. BT55 86
Wendon St. E3 CD37 57
Wendover Dr. N. Mal. BO53 85
Wendover Pl. Stai. AV40 72
Wendover Rd. NW10 BO37 55
Wendover Rd. SE9 CJ45 68
Wendover Rd. Brom. CH52 88
Wendover Rd. Stai. AV49 72
Wendover Way Bush. BG25 27
Wendover Way Orp. CO53 89
Wendover Way, Well. CO46 79
Wend, The, Couls. BW60 95
Wendy Clo. Enf. CA25 30
First Av.
Wendy Cres. Guil. AQ69 118
Wendy Way, Wem. BL37 55
Weneth Hall Rd. Ilf. CK31 49
Wenloch Edge, Dor. BK72 119
Wenlock Rd. N1 BZ37 57
Wenlock Rd. Edg. BM29 37
Wenlocks La. Ing. DB20 24
Wenlock St. N1 BZ37 57
Wennington Rd. E3 CC37 57
Grove Rd.
Wennington Rd. Rain. CU38 59
Wensley Av. Wdf. Grn. CG29 40
Wensley Clo. Rom. CR28 41
Wensleydale, Hem. H. AY12 8
Wensleydale Av. Ilf. CK30 40
Wensleydale Gdns. Hamptn. BF50 74
Wensleydale Pass. Hamptn. BF51 84
Wensleydale Rd. Hamptn. BF50 74
Wensley Rd. N18 CB29 39
Wensum Way. Rick. AX26 35
Wentbridge Path Borwd. BL22 28
Wentland Rd. SE6 CF48 77
Wentworth Av. N3 BS29 38
Wentworth Av. Sth. Croy. CB61 105
Wentworth Clo. N3 BS29 38
Wentworth Clo. Ashf. AZ49 73
Reedsfield Rd.
Wentworth Clo. Mord. BS54 86
Wentworth Clo. Orp. CN56 97
Wentworth Clo. Surb. BK55 84
Wentworth Clo. Wat. BB22 26
Wentworth Clo. Wok. AW64 101
Wentworth Cres. Hayes. BA41 63
Wentworth Dr. Dart. CU46 79
Wentworth Dr. Pnr. BC32 44
Wentworth Dr. Vir. W. AP52 82
Wentworth Gdns. N13 BY28 38
Wentworth Hill, Wem. BL33 46
Wentworth Ms. E3 CD38 57
Eric St.
Wentworth Pk. N3 BS29 38
Wentworth Rd. E12 CJ35 49
Wentworth Rd. NW11 BR32 46
Wentworth Rd. Barn. BQ24 28
Wentworth Rd. Croy. BY54 86
Wentworth Rd. Sthl. BD42 64
Wentworth St. E1 CA39 57
Wentworth Way Pnr. BD31 45
Wentworth Way. Rain. CU38 59
Wentworth Way Sth. Croy. CB60 96
Wenvoe Av. Bexh. CR44 69
Wernbrook St. SE18 CM43 68
Werndee Rd. SE25 CB52 87
Werrington St. NW1 BW37 56
Werter Rd. SW15 BR45 65
Wesley Av. NW10 BN38 55
Wesley Av. Houns. BE44 64
Wesley Clo. Har. BG34 45
Wesley Clo. Orp. CP52 89
Wesley Clo. Wal. Cr. BZ17 21
Wesley Rd. E10 CF33 48
Wesley Rd. NW10 BN37 55
Wesley Rd. Hayes BC39 53
Wesley St. W1 BV39 56
Weymouth St.
Wessex Av. SW19 BS52 86
Wessex Bldgs. N19 BW34 47
Wedmore St.
Wessex Clo. Ilf. CN32 49
Suffolk Rd.
Wessex Clo. Kings. On T. BM51 85
Gloucester Rd.
Wessex Dr. Erith CT44 69
Wessex Dr. Pnr. BE29 36
Wessex Gdns. NW11 BR33 46
Wessex Rd. Houns. AW45 63
Wessex St. E2 CC38 57
Wessex Way. NW11 BR33 46
Westacott, Hayes BB39 53
Westacres Esher BE57 93
Westall Rd. Loug. CL24 31
Westanley Ave. Amer. AO23 25
West App. Orp. CM53 88
West Arbour St. E1 CC39 57
West Av. E17 CE31 48
West Av. N3 BS29 38
West Av. NW4 BQ32 46
West Av. Hayes BB40 53
West Av. Hayes BC40 53
West Av. Pnr. BE32 45
West Av. Red. BV73 121
West Av. St. Alb. BF16 18
West Av. Sthl. BE40 54
West Av. Wall. BX56 95
West Av. Watt. BB58 92
West Av. Rd. E17 CE31 48
West Bank. N16 CA33 48
West Bank, Bark. CL37 58
West Bank, Dor. BH72 119
West Bank, Enf. BZ23 30
Westbank Rd. Hamptn. BG50 74
W. Barnes La. N. Mal. BP52 85
West Barnes La. N. Mal. BP53 85
West Beech Rd. N22 BY31 47
Westbere Dr. Stan. BK28 36
Westbere Rd. NW2 BR35 46
Westbourne Av. N9 CB27 39
Fastbournia Av.
Westbourne Av. W3 BN30 55
Westbourne Av. Sutt. BR55 85
Westbourne Br. W2 BT39 56
Westbourne Clo. Hayes BD38 54
Westbourne Cres. W2 BT40 56
Westbourne Dr. SE23 CC48 77
Westbourne Dr. Brwd. CZ28 42
Westbourne Gdns. W2 BS39 56
Westbourne Gte. W2 BS39 56
Westbourne Gr. W11 BR40 55
Westbourne Gro. Ms. W11 BS39 56
Westbourne Gro.
Westbourne Gro. Ter. W2 BS39 56
Westbourne Pk. Ms. W2 BS39 56
Westbourne Gdns.
Westbourne Pk. Pass. W2 BS39 56
Westbourne Pk. Rd. W2 BR39 55
Westbourne Pk. Rd. W11 BR39 55
Westbourne Pk. Vill. W2 BS39 56
Westbourne Pl. N9 CB27 39
Eastbournia Av.
Westbourne Rd. N7 BY36 56
Arundel Sq.
Westbourne Rd. SE26 CC50 77
Westbourne Rd. Bexh. CP43 69
Westbourne Rd. Croy. CA53 87
Westbourne Rd. Felt. BB48 73
Westbourne Rd. Stai. AW50 73
Westbourne Rd. Uxb. AZ38 53
Westbourne St. W2 BT40 56
Westbourne Ter. W2 BT39 56
Westbourne Ter. Ms. W2 BT39 56
Westbourne Ter. Rd. W2 BT39 56
Westbridge Rd. SW11 BT44 66
Westbrook, Maid. AJ42 61
Westbrook Av. Hamptn. BE50 74
Westbrook Clo. Barn. BT24 29
Westbrook Cres. Barn. BT24 29
Westbrook Dr. Orp. CP54 89
Westbrooke Cres. Well. CP45 69
Westbrooke Rd. Sid. CM48 78
Westbrooke Rd. Well. CP45 69
Westbrook Rd. SE3 CH44 68
Westbrook Rd. Houns. BE43 64
Westbrook Rd. Th. Hth. BZ51 87
Westbrook Sq. Barn. BT24 29
Westbury Av. N22 BY31 47
Westbury Av. Esher BH57 93
Westbury Av. Sthl. BF38 54
Westbury Av. Wem. BL36 55
Westbury Clo. Ruis. BC33 44
Westbury Clo. Shep. AZ53 83
Burchetts Way
Westbury Dr. Brwd. DA27 42
Westbury Gro. N3 BS29 38
Westbury La. Buck. H. CH27 40
Westbury Pl. Brent. BK43 64
Hamilton Rd.
Westbury Rd. E7 CH35 49
Westbury Rd. E17 CD31 48
Westbury Rd. N11 BX29 38
Westbury Rd. N12 BS29 38
Westbury Rd. SE20 CC51 87
Westbury Rd. W5 BL39 55
Westbury Rd. Bark. CM37 58
Westbury Rd. Beck. CD52 87
Westbury Rd. Brom. CJ51 88
Westbury Rd. Brwd. DB27 42
Westbury Rd. Buck. H. CH27 40
Westbury Rd. Buck. H. CJ27 40
Westbury Rd. Croy. BZ53 87
Westbury Rd. Felt. BD47 74
Westbury Rd. Ilf. CK34 49
Westbury Rd. N. Mal. BN52 85
Westbury Rd. Nthwd. BA28 35
Westbury Rd. Wat. BC25 26
Westbury Rd. Wem. BL36 55
Westbury St. SW8 BW44 66
Westbury Ter. E7 CH36 58
Westbury Ter. Upmin. CZ34 51
Westbury Ter. West. CM66 115
Westbush Clo. Hodd. CD10 12
Westcar La. Walt. BC57 92
West Central St. WC1 BX39 56
New Oxford St.
Westchester Dr. NW4 BQ31 46
West Clo. N9 CA27 39
West Clo. Ashf. AY49 73
West Clo. Barn. BP25 28
West Clo. Barn. BV24 29
West Clo. Grnf. BG37 54
West Clo. Hodd. CE11 12
West Clo. Rain. CU38 59
West Clo. Wem. BL33 46
Westcombe Av. Croy. BX53 86
Westcombe Ct. SE3 CG43 68
Westcombe Dr. Barn. BS25 29
Westcombe Hill, SE3 CH42 68
Westcombe Pk. Rd. SE3 CG43 68
West Common, Ger. Cr. AR32 43
West Common Clo. Ger. Cr. AS32 43
West Common Rd. Brom. CH55 88
West Common Rd. Uxb. AX35 44
W. Common Rd. Uxb. AX36 53
Westcoombe Av. SW20 BO51 85
Westcote Rise, Ruis. BA33 44
Westcote Rd. SW16 BW49 76
West Cotts. NW6 BS35 47
Westcott Clo. Croy. CE58 96
Westcott Cres. W7 BH39 54
Westcott Rd. SE17 BY43 66
Westcott Rd. Dor. BH72 119
Westcott St. Dor. BF72 119
Westcott Way Sutt. BQ58 94
Westcott Waye, Uxb. AX37 52
West Ct. SE18 CL43 68
Prince Imperial Way
West Ct. Wem. BK34 45
Westcourt Av. Grav. DG48 81
West Cres. Wind. AM44 61
West Cres. Rd. Grav. DG40 01
Westcroft Clo. NW2 BR35 46
Westcroft Est. NW2 BR35 46
Westcroft Gdns. Mord. BR52 85
Westcroft Rd. Cars. BV56 95
Westcroft Sq. W6 BO42 65
Westcroft Wy. NW2 BR35 46
West Cromwell Rd. SW5 BR42 65
West Cromwell Rd. W14 BR42 65
Westdale Rd. SE18 CL43 68
W. Ddrayton Rd. Uxb. AY39 53
Westdean Av. SE12 CH47 78
Westdean Cl. SW18 BS46 76
Denton St.
West Dene Sutt. BR57 94
Park La.
Westdene Dr. Rom. CV28 42
West Dene Way, Wey. BB55 83
West Dolphin Rd. Sun. BB51 83
Westdown, Lthd. BF67 111
Westdown Rd. E15 CF35 48
Westdown Rd. SE6 CE47 77
West Drayton Park Ave. West Dr. AY41 63
West Dr. N8 BW31 47
Redston Rd.
West Dr. SW11 BU43 66
West Dr. SW16 BW49 76
West Dr. Ascot. AO53 82
West Dr. Cars. BT58 95
West Dr. Har. BG29 36
West Dr. Sutt. BQ58 94
West Dr. Tad. BQ62 103
West Dr. Vir. W. AO53 82
West Dr. Wat. BC21 26
West Dr. Gdns. Har. BG29 36
West Eaton Pl. SW1 BV42 66
Wested La. Swan. CU54 89
West Ella Rd. NW10 BO36 55
West End, Sev. CW62 108
West End Av. E10 CF32 48
West End Av. Pnr. BD31 45
West End Gdns. Esher. BE56 93
West End Gdns. Nthlt. BD37 54
West End La. NW6 BS35 47
West End La. Barn. BQ24 28
West End La. Esher BE57 93
West End La. Esher BF56 93
West End La. Hat. BT12 11
West End La. Hayes. BA43 63
West End La. Pnr. BD31 45
West End La. Slou. AP37 52
West End Rd. Ruis. BB33 44
West End Rd. Sthl. BE40 54
Westerdale, Hem. H. AY12 8
Westerdale Rd. SE10 CH42 68
Westerfield Rd. N15 CA32 48
Wester Folds Clo. Wok. AU62 100
Westergate Rd. SE2 CQ43 69
Westerham Av. N9 BZ27 39
Westerham Clo. Wey. AX57 92
Westerham Dr. Sid. CO46 79
Westerham Rd. E10 CE32 48
Westerham Rd. Kes. CJ58 97
Westerham Rd. Oxt. CG68 115
Westerham Rd. Sev. CR65 107
Westerham Rd. West. CJ60 97
Westerley Cres. SE26 CD49 77
Western Av. NW9 BQ32 46
Western Av. W3 BJ38 54
Western Av. W5 BJ38 54
Western Av. Brwd. DB26 42
Western Av. Dag. CS36 59
Western Av. Egh. AT52 82
Western Av. Epp. CN19 22
Western Av. Grnf. BJ38 54
Western Av. Rom. CV30 42
Western Av. Ruis. BC36 53
Western Av. Uxb. AX35 44
Western Av. Uxb. BA36 53
Western Circus, W3 BO40 55
Western Ct. N3 BS29 38
Western Ct. W3 BN39 55
York Rd.
Western Dr. Shep. BA53 83
Western Gdns. W5 BM40 55
Western Gdns. Brwd. DB27 42
Western La. SW12 BV47 76
Western Pde. Barn. BS25 29
Western Perimeter Rd. Houns. AW45 63
Western Perimeter Rd. Houns. AX46 73
Western Rd. E13 CJ37 58
Western Rd. E17 CF32 48
Western Rd. N2 BU31 47
Western Rd. N22 BX30 38
Western Rd. SW9 BY45 66
Western Rd. SW19 BT51 86
Western Rd. W5 BK40 54
Western Rd. Brwd. DB27 42
Western Rd. Epp. CN19 22
Western Rd. Mitch. BT51 86
Western Rd. Rom. CT32 50
Western Rd. Sthl. BD42 64
Western Rd. Sutt. BS56 95
Western Rd. Wal. Abb. CG14 13
Western St. E15 CF36 57
Western Trading Est. NW10 BN38 55
Westernville Gdns. Ilf. CM33 49
Western Vn. Hayes. BB41 63
Western Way Barn. BS25 29
West Farm Av. Ash. BK62 102
West Farm Clo. Ash. BK63 102
West Farm Dr. Ash. BK63 102
West Ferry Est. E14 CE42 67
West Ferry Rd. E14 CE40 57
Westfied Rd. Guil. AS68 109
Westfield, N6 BV34 47
West Field, SW13 BO45 65
Cross St.
Westfield Harl. CN11 13
Westfield, Sev. CV64 108
Westfield, Welw. G. C. BS7 5
Westfield, Ash. BL62 103
Westfield Av. SW13 BO45 65
Westfield Av. Wat. BD22 27
Westfield Av. Wok. AS64 100
Westfield Clo. Enf. CD24 30
Westfield Clo. Grav. DH49 81
Westfield Clo. Sutt. BR56 94
Westfield Clo. Wal. Cr. CD19 21
Westfield Dr. Har. BK32 45
Westfield Dr. Lthd. BF64 102
Westfield Gdns. Har. BK31 45
Westfield Gro. Wok. AS63 100
Westfield La. Harrow. BK31 45
Westfield La. Slou. AR40 52
Westfield Pde. Wey. AX58 92
Westfield Pk. Pnr. BE29 36
Westfield Rd. N8 BX31 47
Westfield Rd. NW7 BN27 37
Westfield Rd. SE18 CJ41 68
Westfield Rd. W13 BJ40 54
Westfield Rd. Beck. CD51 87
Westfield Rd. Berk. AP12 7
Westfield Rd. Bexh. CS44 69
Westfield Rd. Croy. BY55 86
Westfield Rd. Dag. CQ35 50
Westfield Rd. Hodd. CD11 12
Westfield Rd. Houns. BC44 63
Westfield Rd. Mitch. BU51 86
Westfield Rd. Surb. BK53 84
Westfield Rd. Sutt. BR56 94
Westfield Rd. Walt. BE54 84
Westfield Rd. Wok. AR64 100
Westfields SW13 BO45 65
Railway Side.
Westfields, St. Alb. BF14 9
Westfields, St. Alb. BF15 9
Westfields Rd. W3 BM39 55
Westfield Wk. Wal. Cr. CD19 21
Westfield Way, Ruis. BB34 44
Westfield Way, Wok. AS64 100
West Gdns. E1 CB40 57
West Gdns. SW17 BU50 76
West Gdns. Epsom BO58 94
West Gate. SE16 CC41 67
West Gate. Harl. CM11 13
West Gate. Ms. W10 BQ38 55
West Row.
Westgate Rd. SE25 CB52 87
Westgate Rd. Beck. CE51 87
Westgate Rd. Dart. CV46 80
Westgate St. E8 CB37 57
Westgate Ter. SW10 BS42 66
Westglade Ct. Har. BK32 45
West Green Rd. N15 BY31 47
West Gro. SE10 CF44 67
West Gro. Walt. BC56 92
West Gro. Wdf. Grn. CJ29 40
Westgrove La. SE10 CF44 67
West Halkin St. SW1 BV41 66
West Hall Ct. N6 BV34 47
West Hallows, SE9 CJ47 78
Westhall Park Rd. Warl. CC63 105
Westhall Rd. SE5 BY43 66
West Hall Rd. Rich. BM44 65
Westhall Rd. Warl. CB62 105
Westhall Rd. Warl. CB63 105
West Ham La. E15 CG36 58
West Hampstead Ms. NW6 BS36 56
West Harding St. EC4 BY39 56
Fetter La.
Westharold Swan. CS52 89
West Hatch Manor, Ruis. BB33 44
Westhay Gdns. SW14 BM46 75
West Heath. Av. NW11 BS33 47
West Hth. Clo. NW3 BS34 47
West Heath Clo. Dart. CT46 79
West Heath Ct. NW11 BS33 47
West Heath Dr. NW11 BS33 47
West Hth. Gdns. NW3 BS34 47
West Heath La. Sev. CU67 116
West Hth. Rd. NW3 BS34 47
West Heath Rd. SE2 CP43 69
West Heath Rd. Dart. CT46 79
West Hill SW15 BQ47 75
West Hill SW18 BQ47 75
West Hill, Ash. BL63 103
West Hill Dart. CV46 80
West Hill Epsom BN60 94
West Hill Har. BH34 45
West Hill, Orp. CK59 97
West Hill Sth. Croy. CA58 96
West Hill, Wem. BL33 46
West Hill Ave. Epsom. BM60 94
West Hill Bk. Oxt. CF68 114
Westhill Clo. Grav. DG47 81
Leith Pk. Rd.
West Hill Ct. SW18 BR46 75
West Hill Rd.
West Hill Dr. Dart. CV46 80
West Hill Rise. Dart. CV46 80
West Hill Rd. SW18 BR46 75
Westhill Rd. Hodd. CD11 12
West Hill Rd. Wok. AR63 100
West Hill Way N20 BS26 38
Westholm NW11 BS31 47
West Holme Erith CS44 69
Westholme Orp. CN54 88
Westholme Gdns. Ruis. BC33 44
Westhorne Av. SE9 CH47 78
Westhorne Av. SE12 CH47 78
Westhorpe Gdns. NW4 BQ31 46
Westhorpe Rd. SW15 BQ45 65
Westhouse Clo. SW19 BR47 75
Westhumble St. Dor. BJ69 119
Westhurst Dr. Chis. CL49 78
West Hyde La. Ger. Cr. AS29 34
West India Dock Rd. E14 CD39 57
W. Kent Av. Grav. DE46 81
West Kentish Town Est. NW5 BV35 47
Westlake Clo. N13 BY27 38
Westlake Rd. Bex. CP46 79
Blondon Rd
Westland Av. Horn. CW33 51
Westland Ct. Epsom BN60 94
Westland Dr. Brom. CG55 88
Westland Dr. Hat. BR17 19
Westland Rd. Wat. BC23 26
Westlands Ct. Epsom BN61 103
Westlands Ter. SW12 BW46 76
Gaskarth Rd.
Westlands Way. Oxt. CF67 114
Westland Vw. Grays. DD40 71
West La. SE16 CB41 67
West La. Dor. BD73 119
Westlea Av. Wat. BE21 27
Westlea Cres. St. Alb. BM14 10
Westlea Rd. W7 BJ41 64
Westlea Rd. Brox. CD15 12
Westleigh Av. SW15 BP46 75
Westleigh Av. Couls. BV61 104
Westleigh Dr. Brom. CK51 88
Westleigh Gdns. Edg. BM30 37
Westley Wood. Welw. G. C. BS7 5
West Lodge Av. W3 BM40 55
Westlyn Clo. Rain. CV38 60
West Mall W8 BS40 56
West Malling Way. Horn. CV35 51
Westmead, SW15 BP46 75
Westmead Epsom BO57 94
Westmead Ruis. BD35 45
W. Mead. Welw. G. C. BS9 5
Westmead, Wind. AN45 61
Westmead Rd. Sutt. BT56 95
West Meads, Guil. AP71 118
West Mede Chig. CM29 40
Westmere Dr. NW7 BN27 37
Westminster Av. Th. Hth. BY51 86
Westminster Br. SE1 BX41 66
Westminster Br. SW1 BX41 66
Westminster Bridge Rd. SE1 BX41 66
Westminster Clo. Ilf. CM30 40
Westminster Clo. Tedd. BJ49 74
Cambridge Rd.
Westminster Ct. St. Alb. BG14 9
Westminster Dr. N13 BX28 38
Westminster Gdns. Bark. CN37 58
Westminster Gdns. Ilf. CM30 40
Westminster Ms. W2 BS40 56
Shrewsbury Rd.
Westminster Rd. N9 CB26 39
Westminster Rd. W7 BH40 54
Westminster Rd. Sutt. BT55 86
Westmoat Clo. Beck. CF50 77
Westmont Rd. Esher BH55 84
Westmoor Gdns. Enf. CC23 30
Westmoor Rd. Enf. CC23 30
Westmoor St. SE7 CJ41 68
Westmoreland Bldgs. EC1 BZ39 57
Aldersgate St.
Westmoreland Dr. Sutt. BS57 95
Westmoreland Pl. SW1 BV42 66
Westmoreland Pl. W5 BK39 54
Mount Av.
Westmoreland Rd. SE17 BZ43 67
Westmoreland Rd. Brom. CG53 88
Westmoreland Rd. Har. BF32 45
Westmoreland St. W1 BV39 56
Westmoreland Ter. SW1 BV42 66
Westmoreland Way Mitch. BW52 86
Westmore Rd. West. CJ63 106
Westmore Rd. West. CJ64 106
Westmorland Av. Horn. CV32 51
Westmorland Av. Well. CN45 68
Westmorland Clo. E12 CJ33 49
Westmorland Clo. Twick. BJ46 74
St.Margaret's Rd.
Westmorland Rd. E17 CE32 48
Westmorland Rd. NW9 BL31 46
Westmorland Rd. SW13 BO44 65
West Mount Ave. Amer. AO23 25
Westmount Rd. SE9 CK44 68
West Oak, Beck. CF51 87
Westoe Rd. N9 CB27 39
Weston Av. E. Mol. BE52 84
Weston Av. Surb. BH54 84
Weston Av. Wey. AW56 92

Weston Clo. Brwd. DE26 122
Weston Clo. Couls. BX63 104
Weston Dr. Stan. BJ30 36
Weston Gdns. Islw. BG44 64
Weston Grn. Dag. CQ35 50
Weston Grn. Surb. BH54 84
Weston Grn. Rd. Esher BG54 84
Weston Grn. Rd. Surb. BH54 84
Weston Gro. Brom. CG50 78
Weston Gro. Wok. AV61 100
Weston Park. N8 BX32 47
Weston Pk. Kings. On T. BL51 85
Fairfield West.
Weston Pk. Surb. BH54 84
Weston Pk. Clo. Surb. BH54 84
Weston Rise, WC1 BX38 56
Weston Rd. W4 BN41 65
Weston Rd. Brom. CG50 78
Weston Rd. Dag. CQ35 50
Weston Rd. Enf. BZ23 30
Weston Rd. Guil. AQ70 118
Weston Rd. Surb. BH54 84
Weston St. SE1 BZ41 67
Weston Way. Wok. AV61 100
Weston Yd. SE1 BZ41 67
Weston St.
Westover, NW3 BS34 47
Westover Clo. Sutt. BS58 95
Hulverston Clo.
Westover Rd. SW18 BT47 76
Westow Hill, SE19 CA50 77
Westow St. SE19 CA50 77
West Palace Gdns. Wey. AZ55 83
West Park, SE9 CK48 78
West Pk. Av. Rich. BM44 65
West Park Clo. Rom. CQ32 50
West Park Hill, Brwd. DA27 42
West Park Rd. Epsom. BL59 94
West Pk. Rd. Rich. BM44 65
West Pl. SW19 BQ49 75
West Point. Slou. AL40 61
Westpole Av. Barn. BV24 29
Westport Rd. E13 CH38 58
Westport St. E1 CC39 57
West Poultry Av. EC1 BY39 56
Charterhouse St.
West Quarters. W12 BP39 55
Du Cane Rd.
Westray, Hem. H. AZ14 8
West Ridge Clo. Hem. H. AV13 7
West Ridge Gdns. Grnf. BG37 54
West Riding, St. Alb. BE18 18
West Riding, St. Alb. BF18 18
West Rd. E15 CG37 58
West Rd. N17 CB29 39
West Rd. SW3 BU42 66
West Rd. SW4 BW46 76
West Rd. SW14 BN45 65
West Rd. W5 BL39 55
West Rd. Barn. BV26 38
West Rd. Berk. AQ12 7
West Rd. Chess. BK59 93
West Rd. Felt. BA46 73
West Rd. Guil. AS71 118
West Rd. Harl. CO9 6
West Rd. Kings. On T. BN51 85
West Rd. Reig. BS71 121
West Rd. Rom. CQ32 50
West Rd. Rom. CS33 50
West Rd. Saw. CO5 6
West Rd. S. Ock. DA38 60
West Rd. West Dr. AY41 63
West Rd. Wey. AZ58 92
West Row. W10 BQ38 55
Westrow Dr. Bark. CO35 50
Westrow Gdns. Ilf. CN34 49
West St. La. Cars. BU56 95
West Sheen Vale, Rich. BL45 65
Westside NW4 BP30 37
West Side, SW18 BT46 76
West Side, Common, SW19
BQ49 75
West Smithfield. EC1 BY39 56
West Sq. SE1 BY41 66
West Sq. SE18 CK42 68
West Sq. Iver AV39 52
West St. E11 CG34 49
West St. E17 CE32 48
West St. EC2 BZ39 57
Moorgate
West St. WC2 BW39 56
Litchfield St.
West St. Bexh. CQ45 69
West St. Brom. CH51 88
West St. Cars. BU55 86
West St. Croy. BZ56 96
West St. Dor. BJ71 119
West St. Epsom BN60 94
West St. Epsom BO58 94
West St. Erith CS42 69
West St. Grav. DG46 81
West St. Grays DB43 70
West St. Grays. DD43 71
West St. Har. BG33 45
West St. Reig. BR70 120
West St. Sutt. BS56 95
West St. Wat. BC23 26
West Temple Sheen, SW14
BM45 65
West Tenter St. E1 CA39 57
West Thurrock Art Rd. CZ41 70
Grays.
West Towers Pnr. BD32 45
West Valley Rd. Hem. H. AX16 17
West View NW4 BQ31 46
West View. Chesh. AO18 16
West View, Felt. BA47 73
Westview. Hat. BP11 10
West Vw. Lough. CK24 31
West View Av. Whyt. CA62 105
West View Clo. NW10 BO35 46
West Vw. Cres. N9 CA26 39
West View Dr. Wdf. Grn. CJ30 40
West View Rise, Hem. H. AX13 8
West Vw. Rd. Dart. CW46 80
West View Rd. St. Alb. BG13 9
West Vw. Rd. Swan. CS53 89
West Vw. Rd. Swan. CU52 89
West View Rd. Warl. CB63 105
Westville Rd. W12 BP41 65
Westville Rd. Surb. BJ54 84
West Wk. W5 BL39 55
West Wk. Barn. BV26 38
West Walk. Harl. CM11 13
West Wk. Hayes BC40 53
Westward Dri. Amer. AR23 25
Westward Ho, Guil. AS69 118
Westward Rd. E4 CD28 39
Westward Way, Har. BL32 46
West Warwick Pl. SW1 BW42 66
West Way, NW10 BN35 46
Westway SW20 BP52 85
Westway, W12 BO40 55
West Way, Brwd. DA27 42
West Way Cars. BT58 95
Westway. Cat. BZ64 105
West Way Croy. CD55 87
West Way, Edg. BM29 37
Westway, Guil. AP69 118
West Way Houns. BE44 64
Westway Orp. CM53 88
West Way Pnr. BD31 45
West Way. Rick. AW26 35
West Way, Ruis. BB33 44
West Way. Sev. CT64 107
West Way, Shep. BA53 83
West Way, Wal. Abb. CE21 30
West Way. West. CM66 115
West Way W. Wick. CG53 88
West Way Clo. SW20 BP52 85
West Way Gdns. Croy. CC55 87
Westway Gdns. Red. BV69 121
Westways Epsom BO56 94
Westwell App. SW16 BX50 76
Westwell Rd.
Westwell Clo. Orp. CP54 89
Westwell Rd. SW16 BX50 76
Westwick Gdns. W14 BQ41 65
Westwick Gdns. Houns. BC44 63
Westwick Row, Hem. H. BA13 8
Westwood Ave. Wey. AV59 91
Westwood Av. SE19 BZ51 87
Westwood Av. Brwd. DA28 42
Westwood Av. Har. BF35 45
Westwood Clo. Amer. AR23 25
Westwood Clo. Esher BG55 84
Westwood Clo. Pot. B. BS18 20
Westwood Clo. Ruis. AZ32 44
Westwood Gdns. SW13 BO45 65
Westwood Hill. SE26 CB49 77
Westwood La. Well. CN45 68
Westwood Pk. SE23 CB47 77
Westwood Rd. E16 CH40 58
Westwood Rd. SE26 CB49 77
Westwood Rd. SW13 BO45 65
Westwood Rd. Couls. BW62 104
Westwood Rd. Grav. DC50 81
Westwood Rd. Ilf. CN33 49
West Wood Side, Bex. CQ47 79
West Yoke Rd. Fawk. DA55 90
Wetheral Dr. Stan. BJ30 36
Wetherby Clo. Nthlt. BF36 54
Wetherby Gdns. SW5 BS42 66
Wetherby Ms. SW5 BS42 66
Bolton Gdns.
Wetherby Pk. Wey. BB56 92
Wetherby Pl. SW7 BT42 66
Gloucester Rd.
Wetherby Rd. Borwd. BL23 28
Wetherby Rd. Enf. BZ22 30
Wetherby Way Chess. BL57 94
Wetherden St. E17 CD33 48
Wetherell Rd. E9 CC37 57
Wetherill Rd. N10 BV30 38
Wexford Rd. SW12 BU47 76
Wexham Pk. La. Slou. AQ38 52
Wexham Rd. Slou. AQ40 52
Wexham St. Slou. AQ38 52
Weybanks. Wok. AY61 101
Wey Barton, Wey. AY60 92
Weybourne St. SW18 BT48 76
Weybridge Park, Wey. AZ56 92
Weybridge Rd. Th. Hth. BY52 86
Weybridge Rd. Wey. AX55 83
Weybridge St. SW11 BV44 66
Culvert Rd.
Wey Clo. Wey. AW60 92
Wey Ct. Epsom BN56 94
Wey Ct. Wey. AX58 92
Weydown Clo. SW19 BR47 75
Princes Way.
Weyhill Rd. E1 CB39 57
Holly St.
Weylond Rd. Dag. CQ34 50
Wey Manor Rd. Wey. AX58 92
Weyman Rd. SE3 CJ44 68
Weymarks, The, N17 BZ29 39
Weymead Clo. Cher. AX54 83
Weymouth Av. NW7 BO28 37
Weymouth Av. W5 BK41 64
Weymouth Ct. Sutt. BS57 95
Weymouth Dr. Hayes BB38 53
Weymouth Ms. W1 BV39 56
Weymouth Pl. E2 CA37 57
Weymouth Ter.
Weymouth St. W1 BV39 56
Weymouth St. Hem. H. AX15 8
Weymouth Ter. E2 CA37 57
Weymouth Wk. Stan. BJ29 36
Wey Rd. Wey. AY55 83
Wey Side Clo. Wey. AY59 92
Weyside Gdns. Guil. AR69 118
Weyside Rd. Guil. AQ70 118
Weystone Rd. Wey. AY56 92
Whadcoat St. N4 BY34 47
Whalebone Av. Rom. CQ32 50
Whalebone Gro. Rom. CQ32 50
Whalebone La. E15 CG36 58
Whalebone Lane North. CQ29 41
Rom.
Whalebone La. S. Rom. CQ32 50
Whaley Rd. Pot. B. BT20 20
Whally St. E1 CC39 57
Wharfdale Rd. N1 BX37 56
Wharfedale, Hem. H. AY12 8
Wharfedale Gdns. Th. BX52 86
Hth.
Wharfedale St. SW10 BS42 66
Wharf La. Berk. AO11 7
Wharf La. Rick. AY26 35
Wharf La. Twick. BJ47 74
Wharf La. Wok. AX62 101
Wharf Pl. E2 CB37 57
Wharf Rd. E15 CF37 57
Wharf Rd. N1 BZ37 57
Wharf Rd. Brox. CD15 12
Wharf Rd. Brwd. DB27 42
Wharf Rd. Enf. CD25 30
Wharf Rd. Grays. DC43 71
Wharf Rd. Hem. H. AW14 8
Wharf Rd. Stai. AR47 72
Wharfside, EC4 BZ40 57
Wharf St. E16 CG39 58
Wharley Hook. Harl. CN12 13
Wharncliffe Dr. Sthl. BG40 54
Wharncliffe Gdns. NW8 BT38 56
St. John's Wood Rd.
Wharncliffe Gdns. SE25 CA51 87
Wharncliffe Rd. SE25 BZ51 87
Wharncliffe St. E2 CC37 57
Royston St.
Wharton Rd. Brom. CH51 88
Wharton St. WC1 BX38 56
Whateley Rd. SE20 CC50 77
Whateley Rd. SE22 CA46 77
Whateley Rd. Guil. AQ68 109
Whatley Av. SW20 BQ52 85
Whatman Rd. SE23 CC47 77
Whatmore Clo. Stai. AW46 73
Wheatash Rd. Wey. AW55 83
Wheat Barn. Welw. G. C. BT7 5
Wheatfields, Enf. CC23 30
Wheathill Rd. SE20 CB51 87
Wheat Knoll Ken. BZ61 105
Wheatland Rd. Slou. AQ41 62
Wheatlands Rd. SW17 BV48 76
Wheatlands, The, Houns. BF43 64
Wheatley Clo. Saw. CP6 6
Wheatley Clo. Welw. G. BS9 5
C.
Wheatley Cres. Hayes BC40 53
Wheatley Gdns. N9 CA27 39
Wheatley Rd. Islw. BH45 64
Wheatley Rd. Welw. G. BR8 5
C.
Wheat Leys, St. Alb. BK12 9
Wheatley St. W1 BV39 56
Marylebone St.
Wheatley Ter. Rd. Erith CT43 69
Wheatley Way. Ger. Cr. AS29 34
Wheatsheaf Clo. Cher. AU57 91
Wheatsheaf Clo. Wok. AS61 100
Wheatsheaf Hill Orp. CQ58 98
Wheatsheaf La. SW8 BX43 66
Wheatsheaf La. Borwd. BN22 28
Wheatsheaf La. Stai. AV50 72
Wheatsheaf Rd. Rom. CT32 50
Wheatstone Rd. W10 BR39 55
Wheat St. W1 BV39 56
Marylebone St.
Wheeler Ave. Oxt. CF68 114
Wheelers, Epp. CN18 22
Wheelers Cross, Bark. CM37 58
Wheelers La. Bet. BM71 120
Wheelers La. Brwd. CX24 33
Wheelers La. Epsom. BM60 94
Wheelers La. Hem. H. AY14 8
Wheelers Orchard. Ger. AS29 34
Cr.
Wheel Fm. Dr. Dag. CS34 50
Wheelwright St. N7 BX36 56
Wheler St. E1 CA38 57
Whellock Rd. W4 BO41 65
Whenman Av. Bex. CS48 79
Wherwell Rd. Guil. AR71 118
Whetstone Clo. N20 BT27 38
Whetstone Pk. WC2 BX39 56
Gate St.
Whetstone Rd. SE3 CJ44 68
Whewell Rd. N19 BX34 47
Whichcote Gdns. Chesh. AO20 16
Whickcliffe Gdns. Wem. BM34 46
Whidborne St. WC1 BX38 56
Whinfell Clo. SW16 BW49 76
Whinfell Way, Grav. DJ49 81
Whinyates Rd. SE9 CK45 68
Whippendale Way, Orp. CO51 89
Whippend Clo. Orp. CO51 89
Whippendell Rd. Wat. BB25 26
Whippendell Rd. Wat. BC25 26
Whipps Cross Rd. E11 CF32 48
Whiskin St. EC1 BY38 56
Gloucester Way
Whisper Wood, Rick. AW24 26
Whistler Gdns. Edg. BL30 37
Whistler St. N5 BY35 47
Whiston Rd. E2 CA37 57
Whitakers Way Loug. CK23 31
Whitbread Rd. SE4 CD45 67
Whitburn Rd. SE13 CE45 67
Whitby Av. NW10 BM38 55
Whitby Av. Brwd. DE29 122
Whitby Clo. West. CH62 106
Whitby Gdns. NW9 BM31 46
Whitby Gdns. Sutt. BT55 86
Whitby Rd. Har. BG34 45
Whitby Rd. Ruis. BC34 44
Whitby Rd. Sutt. BT55 86
Whitby St. E1 CA38 57
Whitcher Clo. SE14 CD43 67
Chubworthy St.
Whitcher Pl. NW1 BW36 56
Rochester Rd.
Whitchurch Av. Edg. BL29 37
Whitchurch Clo. Edg. BL29 37
Whitchurch Gdns. Edg. BL29 37
Whitchurch La. Edg. BK29 36
Whitchurch Rd. Rom. CV28 42
Whitcomb St. WC2 BW40 56
White Acre NW9 BO30 37
Whitear Wk. E15 CF36 57
White Av. Grav. DF48 81
Whitebarn La. Dag. CR37 59
Whitebeam Av. Brom. CL54 88
Whitebeam Clo. SW9 BX43 66
Whitebeams Hat. BP14 10
White Beam Way. Tad. BP64 103
White Beans, St. Alb. BG17 18
Whitebream Tower E17 CD31 48
Oatland Rise.
Whitebridge Clo. Felt. BB46 73
White Broom Rd. Hem. H.
AV12 7
Whitebutts Rd. Ruis. BD34 45
Whitechapel High St. E1 CA39 57
Whitechapel Rd.
Whitechapel Rd. E1 CB39 57
White Church La. E1 CB39 57
White City Est. W12 BP40 55
White City Rd. W12 BP40 55
Whitecliffe Rd. Pur. BY59 95
White Clo. Slou. AO40 61
White Conduit St. N1 BY37 56
Whitecote Rd. Sthl. BF39 54
White Craig Clo. Pnr. BF28 36
White Craig Clo. Stan. BL31 46
Everton Dr.
Whitecroft, St. Alb. BJ15 9
Whitecroft Clo. Beck. CF52 87
Whitecroft Way Beck. CF53 87
Whitecross Pl. EC2 BZ39 57
White Cross Row. Rich. BK46 74
Water La.
Whitecross St. EC1 BZ38 57
White Downs, Dor. BC73 119
Whitefield Av. NW2 BQ33 46
Whitefield Av. Pur. BY61 104
Whitefield Clo. Orp. CP52 89
Whitefields Rd. Wal. CC17 21
Cr.
Whitefoot La. Brom. CF49 77
Whitefoot Ter. Brom. CG48 78
Whiteford Rd. Slou. AP39 52
Whitefriars Av. Har. BG30 36
Whitefriars St. EC4 BY39 56
Whitefrost Hill, Red. BU70 121
White Gdns. Dag. CR36 59
White Gate Gdns. Har. BH29 36
White Gates Clo. Rick. AZ24 26
Whitehall E7 CH35 49
Forest St.
Whitehall, SW1 BX40 56
Whitehall Clo. Chig. CO27 41
Whitehall Clo. Uxb. AX37 53
Whitehall Clo. Wal. CG14 13
Abb.
Whitehall Ct. SW1 BX40 56
Whitehall Cres. Chess. BK56 93
Whitehall Farm La. Vir. AS52 82
W.
Whitehall Gdns. E4 CG26 40
Whitehall Gdns. W3 BM40 55
Whitehall Gdns. W4 BM43 65
Whitehall La. Buck. H. CH27 40
Whitehall La. Egh. AS50 72
Whitehall La. Erith CT44 69
Whitehall La. Grays. DE43 71
Whitehall La. Reig. BR72 120
Whitehall Park N19 BW33 47
Whitehall Pk. Rd. W4 BM43 65
Whitehall Pl. SW1 BX40 56
Whitehall Rd. E4 CG27 40
Whitehall Rd. W7 BJ41 64
Whitehall Rd. Brom. CJ53 88
Whitehall Rd. Grays. DE42 71
Whitehall Rd. Har. BH33 45
Whitehall Rd. Th. Hth. BY53 86
Whitehall Rd. Uxb. AX37 53
Whitehall St. N17 CA29 39
White Hands Clo. Hodd. CD12 12
Whitehart Av. Uxb. BA39 53
White Hart Clo. Hayes. BA43 63
White Hart Clo. Sev. CV68 117
White Hart Dr. Hem. H. AY14 8
White Hart La. N17 BX30 38
White Hart La. N22 BX30 38
White Hart La. SW13 BO44 65
White Hart La. Brwd. DB27 42
White Hart La. Hem. H. AS17 16
White Hart La. Rom. CR30 41
White Hart Rd. SE18 CN42 68
White Hart Rd. Hem. H. AZ14 8
Whitehart Rd. Orp. CO54 89
White Hart Rd. Slou. AO41 61
Whitehart Slip Brom. CH51 88
White Hart St. SE11 BY42 66
White Hart Wood, Sev. CV68 117
White Hart Yd. SE1 BZ40 57
Borough High St.
Whitehart Yard, Cher. AW54 83
Whitehaven St. NW8 BU38 56
Whitehead Clo. SW18 BT47 76
Whitehead Clo. Dart. CV48 80
Whiteheads Gro. SW3 BU42 66
Whiteheath Av. Ruis. BA33 44
White Hedge Dr. St. BG12 9
Alb.
White Hill. Berk. AR12 7
White Hill. Chesh. AO18 16
White Hill. Couls. BU65 104
White Hill, Hem. H. AV14 7
White Hill. Rick. AZ29 35
White Hill, Welw. BP5 5
White Hill. Welw. G. C. BS7 5
White Hill Clo. Chesh. AO18 16
Whitehill La. Grav. DH48 81
White Hill La. Red. BZ67 114
Whitehill La. Wok. BA65 101
Whitehill Rd. Dart. CU46 79
Whitehill Rd. Grav. DH48 81
Whitehill Rd. Long. DB51 90
Whitehills Rd. Loug. CL24 31
Whitehorn Av. West Dr. AY40 53
White Horse Alley EC1 BY39 56
Cowcross St.
White Horse Dr. Epsom BN60 94
White Horse Hill. Chis. CK49 78
White Horse La. E1 CC38 57
Whitehorse La. SE25 BZ52 87
Whitehorse La. St. Alb. BK16 18
Whitehorse La. St. Alb. BL16 19
White Horse Rd. E1 CD39 57
White Horse Rd. E6 CK38 58
Whitehorse Rd. Croy. BZ54 87
White Horse Rd. Wind. AL45 61
White Horse St. W1 BV40 56
White Horse Yd. EC2 BZ39 57
Coleman St.
White Ho. SW11 BT44 66
Whitehouse Av. Borwd. BM24 28
Whitehouse Clo. Ger. AS29 34
Cr.
Whitehouse Ct. N14 BW27 38
Whitehouse Dr. Stan. BJ28 36
Whitehouse Dr. Stan. BK28 36
London Rd.
Whitehouse Est. E10 CF32 48
White House La. Guil. AR68 109
Whitehouse La. Wat. BC16 17
Whitehouse Rd. Enf. BZ23 30
White House Rd. Sev. CT68 116
Whitehouse Way N14 BV27 38
Whitehouse Way, Iver AU38 52
White Kennett St. E1 CA39 57
White Knobs Way. Cat. CB66 114
Whiteland Ave. Rick. AT24 25
White La. Guil. AU71 118
White La. Oxt. CH65 106
Whiteleaf Rd. Hem. H. AX15 8
Whiteledges W13 BK39 54
Whitelegg Rd. E13 CG37 58
Whiteley Clo. Wind. AM43 61
Whiteley Rd. SE19 BZ49 77
Whiteley's Cotts. W14 BR42 65
Whiteley Way Felt. BF48 74
White Lion Hl. EC4 BY40 56
White Lion Rd. Amer. AP23 25
White Lion St. N1 BY37 56
White Lion St. Hem. H. AX15 8
White Lodge Clo. NW3 BT33 47
White Lodge Est. SE19 BZ50 77
White Lyons Rd. Brwd. DB27 42
Kings Rd.
Whitemore Rd. Guil. AR68 109
Whiteoak Dr. Beck. CF51 87
White Orchard N20 BR26 37
White Orchards, Stan. BJ28 36
White Post Farn. CX54 90
White Post La. E9 CD36 57
White Post St. SE15 CC43 67
White Rd. E15 CG36 58
White Rd. Bet. & Tad. BM70 120
White Rose La. Wok. AS62 100
Whites Av. Ilf. CN32 49
Whites Grounds SE1 CA41 67
Whites Grounds Est. SE1 CA41 67
White Shack La. Wat. AY22 26
Whites La. Slou. AQ43 62
White's Row. E1 CA39 57
Whites Sq. SW4 BW45 66
Nelson's Row
Whitestile Rd. Brent. BK42 64
Whitestone La. NW3 BT34 47
Heath St.
Whitestone Wk. NW3 BT34 47
North End Way
Whitestone Walk, Hem. AW12 8
H.
White St. Sthl. BD41 64
White Stubb La. Hert. BX13 11
White Stubbs La. Brox. BZ14 12
Whitethorn. Welw. G. BS8 5
C.
Whitethorn Av. Couls. BV61 104
Whitethorn Gdns. Croy. CB55 87
Whitethorn Gdns. Enf. BZ25 30
Whitethorn Gdns. Horn. CV32 51
Whitethorn St. E3 CE38 57
Whitewaits, Harl. CN10 6
White Way. Lthd. BF66 111
Whitewebbs Enf. BY21 29
Whitewebbs La. Enf. CA21 30
Whitewebbs Way, Orp. CN51 88
White Wood Rd. Berk. AQ13 7
Whitfield Pl. W1 BW38 56
Whitfield St.
Whitfield Rd. E6 CJ36 58
Whitfield Rd. SE3 CF44 67
Whitfield Rd. Bexh. CQ43 69
Whitfield St. W1 BW38 56
Whitfield Way. Rick. AV26 34
Whitford Gdns. Mitch. BU52 86
Whitgift Av. Sth. Croy. BY56 95
Whitgift St. SE11 BX42 66
Whitgift St. Croy. BZ55 87
Whiting Hill Est. Barn. BP25 28
Whitings Rd. Barn. BQ25 28
Whitland Rd. Cars. BT54 86
Whitley Clo. Stai. AY46 73
Whitley Rd. N17 CA30 39
Whitley Rd. Hodd. CE11 12
Whitlock Dr. SW18 BR47 75
Whitman Rd. E3 CD38 57
Whitmoor La. Guil. AR66 109
Whitmore Ave. Grays. DD40 71
Whitmore Gdns. NW10 BQ37 55
Whitmore Rd. N1 CA37 57
Whitmore Rd. Beck. CD52 87
Whitmore Rd. Har. BF33 45

Whitmores Clo. Epsom BN61 103
Whitnell Way SW15 BQ46 75
Chartfield Av.
Whitnell Wy. SW15 BQ46 75
Whitney Av. Ilf. CJ31 49
Whitney Rd. E10 CE33 48
Whitney Wk. Sid. CQ50 79
Maidstone Rd.
Whitstable Clo. Beck. CD51 87
Whittaker Av. Rich. BK46 74
Whittaker Rd. E6 CJ36 58
Whittaker Rd. Sutt. BR55 85
Whittaker St. SW1 BV42 66
Bourne St.
Whitta Rd. E12 CJ35 49
Whittel Gdns. SE26 CC48 77
Whitting Av. Bark. CL36 58
Whittingstall Rd. SW6 BR44 65
Whittingstall Rd. Hodd. CE11 12
Whittington Av. EC3 CA39 57
Leadenhall St.
Whittington Av. Hayes BB39 53
Whittington Ct. N2 BU32 47
Whittington Rd. N22 BX29 38
Whittington Rd. Brwd. DE25 122
Whittington Way Pnr. BE32 45
Whittlebury Clo. Cars. BU57 95
Whittle Clo. Sthl. BF39 54
Whittle Rd. Houns. BC43 63
Whittlesea Path Har. BG30 36
Whittlesea Rd. Har. BG29 36
Whittlesey St. SE1 BY40 56
Whitton Av. E. Grnf. BH35 45
Whitton Av. W. Nthlt. BF35 45
Whitton Clo. Grnf. BJ36 54
Whitton Dene Houns. BF46 74
Whitton Dr. Grnf. BJ36 54
Whitton Manor Rd. Islw. BG46 74
Whitton Rd. Houns. BF45 64
Whitton Rd. Twick. BH46 74
Whitton Waye Houns. BF46 74
Whitwell Rd. E13 CH38 58
Whitwell Rd. Wat. BD21 27
Whitworth Rd. SE18 CL43 68
Whitworth Rd. SE25 CA52 87
Whitworth St. SE10 CG42 68
Whopshot Av. Wok. AR61 100
Whopshot Clo. Wok. AR61 100
Whopshot Dr. Wok. AR61 100
Whorlton Rd. SE15 CB45 67
Whybridge Clo. Rain. CT37 59
Whymark Av. N22 BY31 47
Whytecroft Houns. BD43 64
Whyteleafe Rd. Cat. CA63 105
Whyteleaf Hill. Whyt. CA63 105
Whyteville Rd. E7 CH36 58
Wickenden Rd. Sev. CV64 108
Wickersley Rd. SW11 BV44 66
St.John's Hill
Wicker St. E1 CB39 57
Wicket, The, Croy. CE56 96
Wickford Clo. Rom. CW28 42
Wickford Dr. Rom. CW28 42
Wickford St. E1 CC38 57
Wickham Av. Croy. CD55 87
Wickham Av. Sutt. BO56 94
Wickham Chase W. Wick. CF54 87
Wickham Clo. Enf. CB24 30
Wickham Clo. N. Mal. BO53 85
Wickham Clo. Uxb. AX30 35
Wickham Ct. Rd. W. Wick. CF55 87
Wickham Cres. W. Wick. CF55 87
Wickham Fld. Sev. CT61 107
Wickham Gdns. SE4 CD45 67
Wickham La. SE2 CO42 69
Wickham La. Egh. AT50 72
Wickham Rd. E4 CF29 39
Wickham Rd. SE4 CD45 67
Wickham Rd. Beck. CE51 87
Wickham Rd. Croy. CC55 87
Wickham Rd. Grays. DH41 71
Wickham Rd. Har. BG30 36
Wickham St. SE11 BX42 66
Wickham St. Well. CN44 68
Wickham Way Beck. CF52 87
Wickhurst Rd. Sev. CT69 116
Wick La. E3 CD36 57
Wick La. Egh. AP50 72
Wickliffe Av. N3 BR30 37
Wicklow St. WC1 BX38 56
Wick Rd. E9 CC36 57
Wick Rd. Egh. AQ51 82
Wick Rd. Tedd. BJ50 74
Wicks Rd. Rick. AU28 34
Wick Way, St. Alb. BJ12 9
Wickwood St. SE5 BY44 66
Wid Clo. Brwd. DE25 122
Widdecombe Av. Har. BE34 45
Widdenham Rd. N7 BX35 47
Widdin St. E15 CF36 57
Widecombe Clo. Rom. CV30 42
Widecombe Ct. N2 BT32 47
Widecombe Gdns. Ilf. CK31 49
Widecombe Rd. SE9 CK48 78
Widecombe Way N2 BT32 47
Widecroft Rd. Iver AV39 52
Widegate St. E1 CA39 57
Sandy's Row.
Wide Way Mitch. BW52 86
Widgeon Way Wall. BX57 95
Widley Rd. W9 BS38 56
Widmore Dr. Hem. H. AZ12 8
Widmore Lo. Rd. Brom. CJ51 88
Widmore Rd. Brom. CH51 88
Widmore Rd. Uxb. AZ38 53
Widworthy Hayes, Brwd. DD26 122
Wieland Rd. Nthwd. BC29 35
Wigan Ho. E5 CB33 48
Wiggenhall Rd. Wat. BC24 26
Wiggie La. Red. BV69 121
Wiggington Av. Wem. BM36 55
Wiggins La. Rich. BK48 74
Wiggins Mead NW9 BO30 37
Wiggins & Pointers Cotts. Rich. BK48 74
Ham St.
Wightman Rd. N4 BY31 47
Wightman Rd. N8 BY31 47
Wigley Bush La. Brwd. CZ27 42
Wigley Rd. Felt. BD48 74
Wigmore Pl. W1 BV39 56
Wigmore Rd. Cars. BT55 86
Wigmores North. Welw. G. C. BQ7 5
Wigmores Sth. Welw. G. C. BQ8 5
Wigmore St. W1 BV39 56
Wigmore Wk. Cars. BT55 86
Wigram Rd. E11 CJ32 49
Wigram Sq. E17 CF31 48
Wigston Rd. E13 CH38 58
Wigton Gdns. Stan. BL30 37
Wigton Rd. E17 CD30 39
Wigton Rd. Rom. CW28 42
Wigton Way. Rom. CW28 42
Wilberforce Rd. N4 BY34 47
Wilberforce Rd. NW9 BP32 46
Wilberforce Way. SW19 BQ50 75
Wilberforce Way, Grav. DH49 81
Wilbraham Pl. SW1 BV42 66
Wilbury Av. Sutt. BR58 94
Wilbury Rd. Wok. AR62 100
Wilbury Way N18 BZ28 39
Wilby Ms. W11 BR40 55
Wilby Rd. SE5 BZ44 67
Grove La.
Wilcot Av. Wat. BE26 36
Wilcox Rd. SW8 BX43 66
Wilcox Rd. Sutt. BS56 95
Wilcox Rd. Tedd. BG49 74
Wild Acres, Wey. AX59 92
Wild Ct. WC2 BX39 56
Wildcroft Gdns. Edg. BK29 36
Wildcroft Manor SW15 BQ47 75
Bristol Gdns.
Wildcroft Rd. SW15 BQ47 75
Wilde Clo. Til. DH44 71
Coleridge Rd.
Wildernesse Ave. Sev. CW64 108
Wildernesse Mt. Sev. CV64 108
Wilderness Rd. Chis. CL50 78
Wilderness Rd. Guil. AP71 118
Wilderness Rd. Oxt. CF68 114
Wilderness Rd. Oxt. CG68 115
Wilderness, The, Hamptn. BF49 74
Park Rd.
Wilders Clo. Wok. AR62 100
Wilderton Rd. N16 CA33 48
Wildfell Rd. SE6 CE47 77
Wild Grn. Slou. AT42 62
Wild Hatch NW11 BS32 47
Wild Hill Rd. Hat. BS14 11
Wild Oaks Clo. Nthwd. BB29 35
Wild's Rents. SE1 CA41 67
Wild St. WC2 BX39 56
Wildwood. Nthwd. BA29 35
Wildwood Av. St. Alb. BE18 18
Wildwood Clo. CG47 78
Wildwood Clo. Leath. BB66 110
Wildwood Clo. Wok. AV60 91
Wildwood Clo. Wok. AV61 100
Wildwood Ct. Ken. BZ61 105
Wildwood Rise. NW11 BT33 47
Wildwood Rd. NW11 BT33 47
Wilford Rd. Croy. BZ53 87
Wilford Rd. Slou. AS42 62
Wilfred Av. Rain. CU39 59
Wilfred St. SW1 BW41 66
Wilfred St. Wok. AR62 100
Wilfred Turney Est. W6 BQ41 65
Wilfrid Gdns. W3 BN39 55
Wilhelmena Ave. Couls. BW63 104
Wilkes Rd. Brwd. DE25 122
Wilkins Clo. Hayes. BB42 63
Wilkin's Green La. Hat. BN13 10
Wilkinson Clo. Dart. CW45 70
Wilkinson Rd. E16 CJ39 58
Wilkinson St. SW8 BX43 66
Willan Rd. N17 BZ30 39
Willard Est. SW8 BV45 66
Willcocks Clo. Chess. BL55 85
Willcott Rd. W3 BM40 55
Will Crook's Gdns. SE9 CJ45 68
Willenhall Av. Barn. BS25 29
Willenhall Rd. SE18 CL42 68
Willersley Av. Orp. CM55 88
Willersley Av. Sid. CN47 78
Willersley Clo. Sid. CN47 78
Willesden Grn. NW2 BQ36 55
Willesden La. NW2 BQ36 55
Willesden La. NW6 BQ36 55
Willes Rd. NW5 BV36 56
Willets La. Uxb. AV35 43
Willets La. Uxb. AV36 52
Willett Clo. Nthlt. BD38 54
Willett Clo. Orp. CN53 88
Willett Clo. Th. Hth. BY53 86
Willett Rd. Th. Hth. BY53 86
Willett Way Orp. CM53 88
Willet Way. SE16 CB42 67
Egan Way
Willey Broom La. Cat. BY66 113
Willey Farm La. Cat. BZ66 114
Willey La. Cat. BZ66 114
William Barefoot Dr. SE9 CK49 78
William Bonney Est. SW4 BW45 66
William Clo. Rom. CS30 41
William Ellis Clo. Wind. AQ46 72
William Fourth St. WC2 BX40 56
William Guy Gdns. E3 CF38 57
Talwin St.
William Hayne Gdns. Wor. Pk. BQ55 85
William Ms. SW1 BU41 66
William Morris Clo. E17 CD31 48
William Morris Ho. W6 BQ43 65
William Parnell Ho. SW6 BS44 66
William Rd. NW1 BV38 56
William Rd. SW19 BR50 75
William Rd. Cat. BZ64 105
William Rd. Guil. AR70 118
William Rd. Sutt. BT56 95
Williams Av. E17 CD30 39
Williams Gro. N22 BY30 38
William's La. SW14 BN45 65
Williams La. Mord. BT53 86
Williamson Clo. SE10 CG42 68
Lenthorpe Rd.
Williamson St. N7 BX35 47
Williamson Way NW7 BR29 37
Williams Rd. W13 BJ40 54
Williams Rd. Sthl. BE42 64
Williams St. Slou. AP40 52
Williams Ter. Well. CN44 68
William St. E10 CE32 48
William St. E15 CF36 57
William St. N12 BT28 38
Lodge La.
William St. N17 CA29 39
William St. SW1 BU41 66
William St. Bark. CM36 58
William St. Berk. AR13 7
William St. Bush. BD24 27
William St. Cars. BU55 86
William St. Grav. DG47 81
William St. Grays DD43 70
William St. Grays. DD43 71
William St. Wind. AO44 61
Williams Way Rad. BJ21 27
William Ter. Croy. BY57 95
William Willisom Est. SW19 BR47 75
Willifield Way NW11 BS31 47
Willingale Clo. Brwd. DF25 122
Fairview Av.
Willingale Clo. Loug. CM23 31
Willingale Clo. Wdf. Grn. CJ29 40
Willingale Rd. Ing. DC16 24
Willingale Rd. Loug. CM24 31
Willingale Road. Ong. CZ14 15
Willingale Road. Ong. DB15 15
Willingdon Rd. N22 BY30 38
Willingham Clo. NW5 BW35 47
Leighton Rd.
Willingham Ter. NW5 BW35 47
Willingham Way Kings-on-t. BM52 85
Willington Rd. SW9 BX45 66
Willis Av. Sutt. BU57 95
Willis Rd. E15 CG37 58
Willis Rd. Croy. BZ54 87
Willis Rd. Erith CS42 69
Willis St. E14 CE39 57
Willmore End. SW19 BS51 86
Willmot Clo. N2 BT31 47
Willoughby Av. Croy. BX56 95
Willoughby Clo. Brox. CD14 12
Willoughby Dr. Rain. CT36 59
Willoughby Gro. N17 CB29 39
Willoughby La. N17 CB29 39
Willoughby Pk. Rd. N17 CB29 39
Willoughby Rd. N8 BY31 47
Willoughby Rd. NW3 BT35 47
Willoughby Rd. Kings. On T. BL51 85
Willoughby Rd. Slou. AT41 62
Willoughby Rd. Twick. BK46 74
Willow Av. SW13 BO44 65
Willow Av. Sid. CO46 79
Willow Av. Swan. CT52 89
Willow Av. Uxb. AX35 44
Willow Av. Uxb. AX36 53
Willow Av. West Dr. AY40 53
Willow Bnk. SW6 BR45 65
Willowbank Rich. BJ48 74
Willow Bridge Rd. N1 BZ36 57
Willowbrook Gro. SE15 CA43 67
Willowbrook Rd. SE15 CA43 67
Willow Brook Rd. Stai. AY48 73
Willow Clo. W5 BK39 54
Willow Clo. Bex. CQ46 79
Willow Clo. Brent. BK43 64
Willow Clo. Brom. CK53 88
Willow Clo. Brwd. DB22 33
Willow Clo. Brwd. DD25 122
Willow Clo. Buck. H. CJ27 40
Willow Clo. Erith. CU44 69
Willow Clo. Horn. CU34 50
Willow Clo. Orp. CO54 89
Willow Clo. Slou. AU43 62
Willow Clo. Th. Hth. BY53 86
Willow Clo. Wal. Cr. CA16 21
Willow Clo. Wey. AV59 91
Willow Cotts. Rich. BM43 65
Waterloo Pl.
Willow Cott. Rd. Cars. BU53 86
Willow Ct. Edg. BL28 37
Willowcourt Av. Har. BJ32 45
Willow Cres. St. Alb. BK13 9
Willow Cres. E. Uxb. AX35 44
Willow Cres. W. Uxb. AX35 44
Willowdene N6 BU33 47
Denewood Rd.
Willowdene Brwd. CZ25 33
Ongar Rd.
Willowdene Bush. BH26 36
Willow Dene, Pnr. BD30 36
Willowdene Clo. Twick. BG47 74
Willowdene Ct. Brwd. DB28 42
Warley Mt.
Willow Dr. Barn. BR24 28
Willow End N20 BS27 38
Willow End, Surb. BL54 85
Willowfield Harl. CM12 13
Willow Gdns. N16 CA34 48
Cazenove Rd.
Willow Gdns. Houns. BF44 64
Willow Gdns. Ruis. BB34 44
Willow Grn. Dor. BJ73 119
Willow Gro. E13 CH37 58
Willow Gro. SE1 CA42 67
Curtis St.
Willow Gro. Chis. CL50 78
Willow Gro. Ruis. BB34 44
Willow Gro. Welw. G. C. BQ5 5
Willowherb Wk. Rom. CV29 42
Willow La. Amer. AP24 25
Willow La. Mitch. BU53 86
Willow La. Wat. BC25 26
Willow Mead Chig. CO27 41
Willowmead Clo. W5 BK38 54
Brenthan Way
Willowmere Esher BG56 93
Willow Path Wal. Abb. CG20 22
Mason Way
Willow Pl. SW1 BW42 66
Francis St.
Willow Pth. Epsom. BM60 94
Willow Rd. NW3 BT35 47
Willow Rd. W5 BL41 65
Willow Rd. Dart. CV47 80
Willow Rd. Enf. CA24 30
Willow Rd. Erith. CU44 69
Willow Rd. N. Mal. BN52 85
Willow Rd. Red. BT71 121
Willow Rd. Rom. CQ32 50
Willow Rd. Slou. AV44 62
Willow Rd. Wall. BV57 95
Willows Av. Mord. BS53 86
Willows Clo. Pnr. BD30 36
Willows. The. Grays. DE43 71
Willows, The, St. Alb. BJ15 9
Willows, The, Wey. AY60 92
Willow St. E4 CF26 39
Willow St. EC2 CA38 57
Willow St. Rom. CS31 50
Willow Tree Clo. Hayes BD38 54
Willowtree Clo. Uxb. BA34 44
Willow Tree La. Hayes BD38 54
Willow Val. Chis. CL50 78
Willow Vale W12 BP40 55
Willow Vale, Lthd. BF65 102
Willow View SW19 BT51 86
Willow Wk. E17 CD32 48
Willow Wk. N2 BT30 38
Willow Wk. N15 BY31 47
Willow Wk. N21 BX25 29
Willow Wk. SE1 CA42 67
Willow Walk, Cher. AW54 83
Willow Wk. Croy. CE55 87
Willow Wk. Dart. CV45 70
Willow Wk. Egh. AR49 72
Willow Wk. Ilf. CL34 49
Station Rd.
Willow Wk. Orp. CL55 88
Willow Wk. Sutt. BR55 85
Willow Walk, Upmin. CZ33 51
Willow Way N3 BS29 38
Willow Way, SE26 CB48 77
Willow Way Epsom BN57 94
Willow Way. Gdse. CB69 114
Willow Way, Guil. AR68 109
Willow Way. Hat. BO14 10
Willow Way, Hem. H. AW12 8
Willow Way, Pot. B. BS20 20
Willow Way Rad. BH21 27
Willow Way, Rom. CX29 42
Willow Way, St. Alb. BF17 18
Willow Way Sun. BC52 83
Willow Way Twick. BF48 74
Willow Way Wem. BJ34 45
Willow Way, Wey. AX59 92
Willow Way, Wok. AR64 100
Willow Wd. Cres. SE25 CA53 87
Wills Cres. Houns. BF46 74
Wills Gro. NW7 BP28 37
Willshaw St. SE14 CE44 67
Willson Rd. Egh. AQ49 72
Willwood Way NW3 BT33 47
North End Rd.
Willy St. WC1 BX39 56
Gt.Russell St.
Wilman Gro. E8 CB36 57
Wilmar Clo. Hayes BA38 53
Wilmar Clo. Uxb. AX36 53
Wilmar Gdns. W. Wick. CE54 87
Wilmar Way Sev. CW63 108
Landway, The.
Wilmer Clo. Kings. On T. BL49 75
Wilmer Cres. Kings. On T. BL49 75
Wilmer Gdns. N1 CA37 57
Wilmerhatch La. Epsom. BM62 103
Wilmer Ho. Kings. On T. BL49 75
Wilmerlee Clo. E15 CF36 57
Wilmer Way N14 BW28 38
Wilmington Av. W4 BN43 65
Wilmington Av. Orp. CP55 89
Wilmington Ct. Rd. Dart. CU48 79
Wilmington Gdns. Bark. CM36 58
Wilmington Sq. WC1 BY38 56
Wilmot Clo. N3 BT30 38
Sylvester Rd.
Wilmot Pl. NW1 BW36 56
Wilmot Pl. W7 BH40 54
Wilmot Rd. E10 CE34 48
Wilmot Rd. N17 BZ31 48
Wilmot Rd. Dart. CU46 79
Wilmot Rd. Pur. BY59 95
Wilmots Clo. Reig. BT70 121
Wilmot St. E2 CB38 57
Wilmot Way Bans. BS60 95
Wilmount St. SE18 CL42 68
Wilna Rd. SW18 BS47 76
Wilna Yd. SW18 BS47 76
Wilna Rd.
Wilrose Cres. SE2 CO42 69
Wilsham St. W11 BQ40 55
Wilshere Av. St. Alb. BG15 9
Wilsman Rd. S. Ock. CA37 60
Wilsmere Dr. Har. BH29 36
Wilsmere Dr. Nthlt. BE35 45
Wilsmere Dr. Nthlt. BE36 54
Wilson Av. Mitch. BU50 76
Wilson Clo. Dag. CS36 59
Wilson Gdns. Har. BG33 45
Wilson Gro. SE16 CB41 67
Wilson Rd. E6 CJ38 58
Wilson Rd. SE5 BZ44 67
Wilson Rd. Chess. BL57 94
Wilson Rd. Har. BG33 45
Wilson Rd. Ilf. CK33 49
Wilson's Pl. E14 CD39 57
Salmon La.
Wilsons Rd. W6 BQ42 65
Wilson St. E13 CH37 58
Wilson St. E17 CF32 48
Wilson St. EC2 BZ39 57
Wilson St. N21 BY26 38
Wilson Way, Wok. AR61 100
Wilton Av. W4 BO42 65
Wilton Ct. N10 BV30 38
Wilton Cres. SW1 BV41 66
Wilton Cres. SW19 BR51 85
Wilton Cres. Wind. AL45 61
Wilton Dr. Rom. CS29 41
Wilton Gdns. Walt. BD54 84
Wilton Gro. SW19 BR50 75
Wilton Gro. N. Mal. BO53 85
Wilton La. Beac. AO29 34
Wilton Ms. SW1 BV41 66
Wilton Pde. Felt. BC48 73
Wilton Pk. Ct. SE18 CL43 00
Prince Imperial Rd.
Wilton Pl. SW1 BV41 66
Wilton Pl. Wey. AX58 92
Wilton Rd. N10 BV30 38
Wilton Rd. SW1 BV41 66
Wilton Rd. SW19 BU50 76
Wilton Rd. Barn. BU24 29
Wilton Rd. Houns. BD45 64
Wilton Rd. Ilf. CL35 49
Wilton Rd. Red. BU71 121
Wilton Row SW1 BV41 66
Wilton Sq. N1 BZ37 57
Wilton St. SW1 BV41 66
Wilton Ter. SW1 BV41 66
Wilton Way E8 CB36 57
Wilton Yd. W10 BQ40 55
Bard Rd.
Wiltshire Av. Horn. CW31 51
Wiltshire Clo. SW3 BU42 66
Wiltshire Gdns. Twick. BG47 74
Wiltshire La. Pnr. BB31 44
Wiltshire Rd. N1 BZ37 57
Wiltshire Rd. SW9 BY45 66
Wiltshire Rd. Orp. CO54 89
Wiltshire Rd. Th. Hth. BY52 86
Wilverley Cres. N. Mal. BO53 85
Wimbart Rd. SW2 BX47 76
Wimbledon Clo. SW20 BQ50 75
Wimbledon Hl. Rd. SW19 BR50 75
Wimbledon Pk. Est. SW19 BR47 75
Wimbledon Pk. Rd. SW18 BR48 75
Wimbledon Pk. Rd. SW19 BR48 75
Wimbledon Rd. SW17 BT49 76
Wimbolt St. E2 CB38 57
Wimborne Av. Hayes BC39 53
Wimborne Av. Orp. CN52 88
Wimborne Av. Red. BU73 121
Wimborne Av. Sthl. BF42 64
Wimborne Clo. SE12 CG46 78
Wimborne Clo. Epsom. BO60 94
Wimborne Clo. Saw. CP6 6
Wimborne Dr. NW9 BM31 46
Wimborne Dr. Pnr. BD33 45
Wimborne Gdns. W13 BJ39 54
Wimborne Gro. Wat. BB22 26
Wimborne Rd. N9 CB27 39
Wimborne Way Beck. CC52 87
Wimbourne Clo. Buck. H. CH27 40
Wimbourne Ct. N1 BZ37 57
Wimbourne Rd. N17 CA30 39
Wimbourne St. N1 BZ37 57
Wimpole Clo. Kings-on-t. BL51 85
Wimpole Ms. W1 BV39 56
Wimpole Rd. West Dr. AX40 53
Wimpole St. W1 BV39 56
Winans Wk. SW9 BY44 66
Wincanton Cres. Nthlt. BF35 45
Wincanton Gdns. Ilf. CL30 40
Wincanton Rd. SW18 BR47 75
Wincanton Rd. Rom. CV27 42
Winchcombe Rd. Cars. BT54 86
Winchcomb Gdns. SE9 CJ45 68
Winch Dells, Hem. H. AZ15 8
Winchelsea Av. Bexh. CQ43 69
Winchelsea Clo. SW15 BQ46 75
Chartfield Av.
Winchelsea Cres. E. Mol. BG51 84
Winchelsea Rd. E7 CH34 49
Winchelsea Rd. N17 CA31 48
Winchelsea Rd. NW10 BN37 55
Winchelsey Rd. Sth. Croy. CA57 96
Winchendon Rd. SW6 BR44 65
Winchendon Rd. Tedd.. BG49 74
Winchester Av. NW9 BM31 46
Winchester Av. Houns. BE43 64
Winchester Av. Upmin. CZ33 51
Winchester Clo. Brom. CG52 88
Winchester Clo. Enf. CA25 30
Winchester Clo. Esher BF56 93
Winchester Clo. Kings. On T. BM50 75

Winchester Clo. Slou. AV44 62
Rodney Way
Winchester Cres. Grav. DH48 81
Winchester Dr. Pnr. BD32 45
Winchester Ms. NW3 BT36 56
Winchester Rd.
Winchester Pk. Brom. CG52 88
Winchester Pl. E8 CA35 48
Kingsland High St.
Winchester Pl. N6 BV33 47
Winchester Pl. W3 BN41 65
Park Rd. E.
Winchester Rd. E4 CF29 39
Winchester Rd. N6 BV33 47
Winchester Rd. N9 CA26 39
Winchester Rd. NW3 BT36 56
Winchester Rd. Bexh. CP44 69
Winchester Rd. Brom. CG52 88
Winchester Rd. Felt. BE48 74
Winchester Rd. Har. BL31 46
Winchester Rd. Hayes. BB43 63
Winchester Rd. Ilf. CM34 49
Winchester Rd. Nthwd. BB31 44
Winchester Rd. Nthwd. BC30 35
Winchester Rd. Orp. CO56 98
Winchester Rd. Twick. BJ46 74
Winchester Rd. Walt. BC54 83
Winchester Sq. SE1 BZ40 57
Winchester Wk.
Winchester St. SW1 BV42 66
Winchester St. W3 BN41 65
Winchester Wk. SE1 BZ40 57
Winchester Way, Rick. AZ25 26
Winchfield Clo. Har. BK32 45
Winchfield Rd. SE26 CD49 77
Winchfield Way. Rick. AX26 35
Winchmore Hill Rd. N14 BW26 38
Winchmore Hill Rd. N21 BW26 38
Winchstone Clo. Shep. AY52 83
Winckley Clo. Har. BL32 46
Wincott St. SE11 BY42 66
Wincrofts Dr. SE9 CM45 68
Windborough Rd. Cars. BV57 95
Windermere Av. N3 BS31 47
Windermere Av. NW6 BR37 55
Windermere Av. SW19 BS52 86
Windermere Av. Horn. CU35 50
Windermere Av. Ruis. BD33 45
Windermere Av. St. Alb. BJ14 9
Windermere Av. Wem. BK33 45
Windermere Clo. Dart. CU47 79
Windermere Clo. Hem. H. BA14 8
Windermere Clo. Orp. CL55 88
Windermere Ct. SW13 BO43 65
Windermere Gdns. Ilf. CK32 49
Windermere Gro. Wem. BK33 45
Windermere Av.
Windermere Rd. N10 BV30 38
Windermere Rd. N19 BW34 47
Holloway Rd.
Windermere Rd. SW15 BO49 75
Windermere Rd. SW16 BW51 86
Windermere Rd. W5 BK41 64
Windermere Rd. Bexh. CR44 69
Windermere Rd. Bexh. CS44 69
Windermere Rd. Couls. BX61 104
Windermere Rd. Croy. CA54 87
Windermere Rd. Sthl. BE39 54
Windermere Rd. W. Wick. CG55 88
Windermere Way, Red. BU70 121
Winders Rd. SW11 BU44 66
Windfield, Lthd. BJ64 102
Windfield Clo. SE26 CC49 77
Windham Av. Croy. CF58 96
Windham Rd. Rich. BL45 65
Wind Hill. Ong. CU13 14
Windhover Way, Grav. DJ49 81
Winding Shot, Hem. H. AW13 8
Windings, The, Sth. Croy. CA59 96
Winding Way, Dag. CP34 50
Winding Way Har. BH35 45
Windlass Pl. SE8 CD42 67
Windlesham Gro. SW19 BQ47 75
Windlesham Rd. SW19 BQ47 75
Windlesham Rd. Wok. AO58 91
Windley Clo. SE23 CC48 77
Windmill Av. Epsom BO59 94
Windmill Av. St. Alb. BK11 9
Windmill Clo. Cat. BZ64 105
Coulsdon Rd.
Windmill Clo. Sun. BB50 73
Windmill Clo. Surb. BK54 84
Windmill Clo. Upmin. CX34 51
Windmill Clo. Wal. Abb. CG20 22
Windmill Dr. SW4 BV46 76
Windmill Dr. Lthd. BK65 102
Windmill Dr. Reig. BU69 121
Windmill Dr. Rick. AY25 26
Windmill End Epsom BO59 94
Windmill Gdns. Enf. BY23 29
Windmill Gro. Croy. BZ53 87
Windmill Hill Enf. BY24 29
Windmill Hill, Kings L. AV19 16
Windmill Hill, Ruis. BB33 44
Windmill La. E15 CF36 57
Windmill La. Barn. BO25 28
Windmill La. Bush. BG26 36
Windmill La. Epsom BO59 94
Windmill La. Grnf. BG38 54
Windmill La. Sthl. BG40 54
Windmill La. Surb. BJ53 84
Windmill La. Wal. Cr. CD18 21
Windmill Rd. N18 BZ28 39
Windmill Rd. SW18 BT46 76
Windmill Rd. SW19 BP47 75
Windmill Rd. W4 BO42 65
Windmill Rd. W5 BK42 64
Windmill Rd. Brent. BK42 64
Windmill Rd. Croy. BZ54 87
Windmill Rd. Dag. CQ34 50
Windmill Rd. Ger. Cr. AR29 34
Windmill Rd. Hem. H. AY13 8
Windmill Rd. Hmptn. BF49 74
Windmill Rd. Mitch. BW53 86
Windmill Rd. Sev. CU68 116
Windmill Rd. Sev. CU70 116
Windmill Rd. Slou. AO40 61
Windmill Rd. Slou. AR35 43
Windmill Rd. Sun. BB51 83
Windmill Rd. Wind. AN44 61
Windmill Row, SE11 BY42 66
Windmill St. W1 BW39 56
Windmill St. Bush. BH26 36
Windmill St. Grav. DG47 81
Windmill Wk. SE1 BY40 56
Windmill Way, Reig. BT69 121
Windmill Way, Ruis. BB33 44
Windmore Av. Pot. B. BQ19 19
Windover Av. NW9 BN31 46
Windridge Clo. St. Alb. BF15 9
Windridge Rd. St. Alb. BD15 9
Windrush Ave. Slou. AT42 62
Windrush Clo. W4 BN43 65
Bolton Rd.
Windrush Clo. Uxb. AY35 44
Windrush La. SE23 CC48 77
Winds End Clo. Hem. H. AZ12 8
Windsland Ms. W2 BT39 56
London St.
Windsor Ave. Grays DD41 71
Windsor Ave. Rick. AW26 35
Windsor Av. E17 CD30 39
Windsor Av. SW19 BT51 86
Windsor Av. E. Mol. BF52 84
Windsor Av. Edg. BM28 37
Windsor Av. N. Mal. BN53 85
Windsor Av. Sutt. BR55 85
Windsor Av. Uxb. AZ37 53
Windsor Clo. N3 BR30 37
Windsor Rd.
Windsor Clo. Borwd. BM23 28
Windsor Clo. Guil. AP71 118
Powell Clo.
Windsor Clo. Har. BF34 45
Windsor Clo. Nthwd. BC30 35
Windsor Clo. Wal. Cr. CB18 21
Windsor Clo. Welw. BP5 5
Windsor Ct. N14 BW26 38
Windsor Court Rd. Wok. AP58 91
Windsor Cres. Har. BF35 45
Windsor Cres. Wem. BM34 46
Windsor Dr. Ashf. AX49 73
Windsor Dr. Barn. BU25 29
Windsor Dr. Dart. CU46 79
Windsor Dr. Orp. CO57 98
Windsor Gdns. Hayes. BA41 63
Windsor Gro. SE27 BZ49 77
Windsor Park Rd. Hayes. BB43 63
Windsor Pl. SW1 BW42 66
Francis St.
Windsor Rd. E4 CE28 39
Chivers Rd.
Windsor Rd. E7 CH35 49
Windsor Rd. E10 CE34 48
Windsor Rd. E11 CH33 49
Windsor Rd. N3 BR30 37
Windsor Rd. N7 BX34 47
Windsor Rd. N13 BY27 38
Windsor Rd. N17 CB30 39
Windsor Rd. NW2 BP36 55
Windsor Rd. W5 BK40 54
Windsor Rd. Barn. BQ25 28
Windsor Rd. Bexh. CQ45 69
Windsor Rd. Brwd. DA25 33
Windsor Rd. Dag. CQ34 50
Windsor Rd. Egh. AR47 72
Windsor Rd. Enf. CC21 30
Windsor Rd. Grav. DG48 81
Windsor Rd. Har. BG30 36
Windsor Rd. Horn. CV33 51
Windsor Rd. Houns. BC44 63
Windsor Rd. Ilf. CL35 49
Windsor Rd. Kings. On T. BL50 75
Windsor Rd. Maid. AG41 61
Windsor Rd. Rich. BL44 65
Windsor Rd. Sid. CO50 79
Windsor Rd. Slou. AQ35 43
Windsor Rd. Slou. AQ43 62
Windsor Rd. Stai. AS46 72
Windsor Rd. Sthl. BE41 64
Windsor Rd. Sun. BC50 73
Windsor Rd. Tedd. BG49 74
Windsor Rd. Th. Hth. BY51 86
Windsor Rd. Wat. BD22 27
Windsor Rd. Welw. BP5 5
Windsor Rd. Wind. AO42 61
Windsor Rd. Wok. AO56 91
Windsor Rd. Wor. Pk. BP55 85
Windsor St. N1 BY37 56
Windsor St. Cher. AW53 83
Windsor St. Uxb. AX36 53
Windsor Ter. N1 BZ38 57
Windsor Wk. SE5 BZ44 67
Windsor Walk, Wey. AZ56 92
Windsor Way, Wok. AU61 100
Winds Ridge, Wok. AU66 109
Windus Rd. N16 CA33 48
Windus Wk. N16 CA33 48
Alkham Rd.
Windward Clo. Enf. CC21 30
Windy Hill, Brwd. DE26 122
Windyridge Clo. SW19 BQ49 75
Wine Office Ct. EC4 BY39 56
Winern Glebe, Wey. AY60 92
Winford Dr. Brox. CD14 12
Winforton St. SE10 CF44 67
Winfrith Rd. SW18 BT47 76
Wingate Cres. Croy. BW53 86
Wingate Rd. W6 BP41 65
Wingate Rd. Ilf. CL35 49
Wingate Rd. Sid. CP49 79
Sidcup-hill
Wingate Rd. Sid. CP50 79
Sidcup Hill
Wingfield Clo. Brwd. DD27 122
Wingfield Clo. Wey. AW58 92
Wingfield Gdns. Upmin. CZ32 51
Wingfield Ms. SE15 CB45 67
Wingfield St.
Wingfield Pl. Sid. CN48 78
Wingfield Rd. E15 CF35 48
Wingfield Rd. E17 CE32 48
Wingfield Rd. Grav. DG47 81
Wingfield Rd. Kings. On T. BL50 75
Wingfield St. SE15 CB45 67
Wingfield Way Ruis. BC35 44
Wingford Rd. SW2 BX46 76
Wingletye La. Horn. CW31 51
Wingletye La. Horn. CX32 51
Wingley La. SW16 BW48 76
Wingmore Rd. SE24 BZ45 67
Wingrave Cres. Brwd. CZ28 42
Wingrave Rd. W6 BQ43 65
Wingrove Rd. SE6 CG48 78
Wing Way, Brwd. DB26 42
Winifred Av. Horn. CV35 51
Winifred Gro. SW11 BU45 66
Marjorie Gro.
Winifred Rd. SW19 BS51 86
Winifred Rd. Couls. BV61 104
Winifred Rd. Dag. CQ34 50
Winifred Rd. Dart. CU46 79
Winifred Rd. Erith CT42 69
Winifred Rd. Hamptn. BF49 74
Winifred Rd. Hem. H. AX15 8
Winifred St. E16 CK40 58
Winifred Ter. Enf. CA26 39
Winkers Clo. Ger. Cr. AS30 34
Winkers La. Ger. Cr. AS30 34
Winkfield Rd. E13 CH37 58
Winkfield Rd. N22 BY30 38
Winkfield Rd. Wind. AM46 61
Winkley St. E2 CB38 57
Canrobert St.
Winkworth Pl. Bans. BR60 94
Winkworth Pl. Bans. BS60 95
Winkworth Rd. Bans. BS60 95
Winlaton Rd. Brom. CF49 77
Winn Common Rd. SE18 CN43 68
Winnings Wk. Nthlt. BD36 54
Winnington Clo. N2 BT32 47
Winnington Rd. N2 BT32 47
Winnington Rd. Enf. CC22 30
Winnington Way, Wok. AQ62 100
Winnock Rd. West Dr. AX40 53
Winn Rd. SE12 CH47 78
Winns Av. E17 CD31 48
Winns Ms. N15 CD31 48
Grove Park Rd.
Winns Ter. E17 CE30 39
Winsbeach E17 CF31 48
Winscombe Cres. W5 BK38 54
Winscombe St. N19 BV34 47
Winscombe Way Stan. BJ28 36
Winsford Rd. SE6 CD48 77
Winsford Ter. N18 BZ28 39
Winsham Gro. SW11 BV46 76
Winslade Rd. SW2 BX46 76
Winslade Way SE6 CE47 77
Winsland Ms. W2 BT39 56
Winsland St.
Winsland St. W2 BT39 56
Winsley St. W1 BW39 56
Winslow Clo. Pnr. BC32 44
Winslow Gro. E4 CG27 40
Hoppett Rd.
Winslow Rd. W6 BQ43 65
Winslow Way Felt. BE48 74
Winslow Way Walt. BD55 84
Winsor Ter. E6 CL39 58
Winstanley Rd. SW11 BT45 66
Winstead Gdns. Dag. CS35 50
Winston Av. NW9 BO33 46
Winston Clo. Har. BH29 36
Winston Clo. Rom. CR31 50
Winston Ct. Har. BF29 36
Winston Dr. Cob. BE62 102
Winstone Clo. Rom. CR31 50
Marlborough Rd.
Winston Rd. N16 BZ35 48
Winston Way, Pot. B. BS20 20
Winston Way, Wok. AT63 100
Winstre Rd. Borwd. BM23 28
Winter Av. E6 CK37 58
Winterborne Av. Orp. CM55 88
Winterbourne Rd. SE6 CD47 77
Winterbourne Rd. Dag. CP34 50
Winterbourne Rd. Th. Hth. BY52 86
Winter Box Wk. Rich. BL46 75
Kings Rd.
Winterbrook Rd. SE24 BZ46 77
Winterdown Gdns. Esher BE57 93
Winterdown Rd. Esher BE57 93
Winterfold Clo. SW19 BR48 75
Winterhill Way, Guil AT68 109
Winterscroft Rd. Hodd. CD11 12
Winters Rd. Surb. BJ54 84
Winterstoke Gdns. NW7 BP28 37
Winterstoke Rd. SE6 CD47 77
Winters Way, Wal. Abb. CH20 22
Winterton Pl. SW10 BT43 66
Winterwell Rd. SW2 BX46 76
Winthorpe Rd. SW15 BR45 65
Winthrop Pl. E1 CB39 57
Winthrop St.
Winthrop St. E1 CB39 57
Winton App. Rick. BA25 26
Winton Av. N11 BW29 38
Winton Clo. N9 CC26 39
Winton Cres. Rick. AZ25 26
Winton Dr. Rick. AZ25 26
Winton Dr. Wal. Cr. CD18 21
Winton Gdns. Edg. BL29 37
Whitchurch La.
Winton Rd. Orp. CL56 97
Winton Way, SW16 BY49 76
Winvale. Slou. AP41 62
Winwood, Slou. AR39 52
Wippendell Hill, Kings L. AX18 17
Wisbech Rd. Croy. BZ53 87
Wisborough Rd. Sth. Croy. CA58 96
Wise La. NW7 BP28 37
Wise La. West Dr. AX41 63
Wiseman Rd. E10 CE34 48
Wisemans Gdns. Saw. CP6 6
Wiseman St. E16 CL40 58
Wise Rd. E15 CF37 57
Wise's La. Hat. BQ17 19
Wise's La. Sev. DC57 99
Wiseton Rd. SW17 BU47 76
Wishart Rd. SE3 CJ44 68
Wisley La. Wok. AX61 101
Wisley Rd. SW11 BU46 76
Wisley Rd. Orp. CO50 79
Wisteria Clo. Brwd. DB25 33
Lavender Av.
Wisteria Clo. Orp. CL55 88
Wisteria Gdns. Swan. CS51 89
Wisteria Rd. SE13 CF45 67
Witan St. E2 CB38 57
Coventry Rd.
Witches La. Sev. CT65 107
Witham Clo. Loug. CK25 31
Witham Rd. SE20 CC52 87
Witham Rd. Dag. CR35 50
Witham Rd. Horn. CU32 50
Witham Rd. Islw. BG44 64
Withens Clo. Orp. CP52 89
Witherby Clo. Croy. CA56 96
Witherfield Way, SE16 CB42 67
Egan Way
Witherings, The, Horn. CW32 51
Witherington Rd. N5 BY35 47
Withers Mead NW9 BO30 37
Withers Pl. EC1 BZ38 57
Old St.
Witherston Way, SE9 CL48 78
Withey Clo. Wind. AM44 61
Witheygate Av. Stai. AW50 73
Withies, The Lthd. BJ63 102
Withycombe Rd. SW19 BQ47 75
Victoria Dr.
Withycroft, Slou. AS39 52
Withy Mead E4 CF27 39
Witley Ct. Sthl. BE32 45
Witley Cres. Croy. CF57 96
Witley Gdns. Sthl. BE42 64
Witley Rd. N19 BW34 47
Holloway Rd.
Witney Clo. Uxb. AY35 44
Witney Path, SE23 CC48 77
Wittenham Clo. Slou. AQ40 52
Wittenham Way E4 CF27 39
Wittersham Rd. Brom. CG49 78
Witton Gdns. E. Mol. BF52 84
Wivenhoe Rd. SE15 CB45 67
Wivenhoe Rd. Bark. CO37 59
Wiverton Rd. SE26 CC50 77
Wix Hill. Leath. AZ68 110
Wix Rd. Dag. CP37 59
Wix's La. SW4 BV45 66
Woburn Av. Epp. CN22 31
Woburn Av. Horn. CU35 50
Woburn Av. Pur. BY59 95
Woburn Clo. Bush. BG25 27
Woburn Hill, Wey. AX55 83
Woburn Pl. WC1 BW38 56
Woburn Rd. Cars. BU54 86
Woburn Rd. Croy. BZ54 87
Woburn Sq. WC1 BW38 56
Woburn Wk. WC1 BW38 56
Wodeham St. E1 CB39 57
Woffingham Clo. Kings. On T. BK51 84
Woffington Clo. Tedd. BK50 74
Upr. Teddington Rd.
Woking Clo. SW15 BO45 65
Wokingdon Rd. Grays. DG41 71
Woking Rd. Guil. AR67 109
Woking Rd. Wey. AV60 91
Woldham Rd. Brom. CJ52 88
Woldingham Rd. Cat. CF66 114
Woldingham Slines New Rd. Cat. CB63 105
Wolds Dri. Orp. CL56 97
Wolfe Clo. Brom. CH53 88
Wolfe Clo. Hayes BC38 53
Ayles Rd.
Wolfe Cres. SE7 CJ42 68
Wolferton Rd. E12 CK35 49
Wolffe Gdns. E15 CG36 58
Wolfington Rd. SE27 BY49 76
Wolf La. Wind. AL45 61
Wolf La. Wind. AM45 61
Wolfram Clo. SE13 CG46 78
Wolfs Hill. Oxt. CH69 115
Wolfs Rd. Oxt. CH68 115
Wolfs Row. Oxt. CH68 115
Wolfstan St. W12 BO40 55
Wolfs Wood. Oxt. CH69 115
Wolmer Clo. Edg. BM28 37
Wolmer Gdns. Edg. BM27 37
Wolseley Av. SW19 BS48 76
Wolseley Gdns. W4 BM43 65
Wolseley Rd. E7 CH36 58
Wolseley Rd. N8 BW32 47
Wolseley Rd. N22 BX30 38
Wolseley Rd. W4 BN42 65
Wolseley Rd. Har. BH31 45
Wolseley Rd. Mitch. BV54 86
Wolseley Rd. Rom. CS33 50
Wolseley St. SE1 CA41 67
Wolsen St. E1 CC39 57
Sidney St.
Wolsey Av. E6 CL38 58
Wolsey Av. E17 CD31 48
Wolsey Av. Surb. BH53 84
Wolsey Clo. Houns. BG46 74
Wolsey Clo. Kings. On T. BM51 85
Wolsey Clo. Sthl. BG41 64
Wolsey Clo. Wor. Pk. BO56 94
Wolsey Cres. Croy. CF58 96
Wolsey Cres. Mord. BR54 85
Wolsey Dr. Kings. On T. BL49 75
Wolsey Dr. Walt. BD54 84
Wolsey Gdns. Ilf. CL29 40
Wolsey Gro. Edg. BN29 37
Wolsey Gro. Esher BF56 93
Wolsey Ms. NW5 BW36 56
Caversham Rd.
Wolsey Rd. N1 BZ35 48
Wolsey Rd. Ashf. AY49 73
Wolsey Rd. E. Mol. BG52 84
Wolsey Rd. Enf. CB23 30
Wolsey Rd. Esher BF56 93
Wolsey Rd. Hmptn. BF50 74
Wolsey Rd. Nthwd. BA27 35
Wolsey Rd. Sun. BB50 73
Wolsey Rd. Sun. BC50 73
Wolsey St. E1 CC39 57
Sidney St.
Wolsey Wk. Wok. AS62 100
Ch. St. W.
Wolstonbury N12 BR28 37
Wolvens La. Dor. BF73 119
Wolvercote Rd. SE2 CP41 69
Wolverley St. E2 CB38 57
Bethnal Green Rd.
Wolverton Av. Kings. On T. BM51 85
Wolverton Gdns. W5 BL40 55
Wolverton Gdns. W6 BQ42 65
Wolverton Rd. Stan. BK29 36
Wolverton Way N14 BW25 29
Wolves La. N13 BY29 38
Wolves La. N22 BY29 38
Womersley Rd. N8 BX32 47
Wonersh Way Sutt. BQ58 94
Wonford Clo. Tad. BP66 112
Wonham La. Bet. BO71 120
Wontford Rd. Pur. BY61 104
Wontner Rd. SW17 BU48 76
Woodall Cres. Horn. CW33 51
Wood Av. Grays CY42 70
Woodbank N12 BS28 38
Woodbank Rd. Brom. CG48 78
Woodbarn Way, Wal. Cr. CD19 21
Woodbastwick Rd. SE26 CC50 77
Woodberry Av. N12 BT29 38
Woodberry Av. N21 BY27 38
Woodberry Av. Har. BF31 45
Woodberry Clo. Sun. BC50 73
Woodberry Cres. N10 BV31 47
Woodberry Down N4 BZ33 48
Woodberry Down Est. N4 BZ33 48
Woodberry Gdns. N12 BT29 38
Woodberry Gro. N4 BZ33 48
Woodberry Way E4 CF26 39
Woodberry Way N12 BT29 38
Woodbery Down Epp. CO17 23
Woodbine Clo. Twick. BG48 74
Woodbine Clo. Wal. Abb. CJ21 31
Woodbine Gro. SE20 CB50 77
Woodbine Gro. Enf. BZ22 30
Woodbine La. Wor. Pk. BP55 85
Woodbine Pl. E11 CH32 49
Woodbine Rd. Sid. CN47 78
Woodbines Av. Kings-on-t. BK52 84
Woodbine Ter. E9 CC36 57
Homerton Ter.
Woodborough Rd. SW15 BP45 65
Woodbourne Av. SW16 BW48 76
Woodbourne Clo. SW16 BW48 76
Woodbourne Dr. Esher BH57 93
Woodbridge Av. Lthd. BJ62 102
Woodbridge Clo. Rom. CV28 42
Woodbridge Ct. Wdf. Grn. CK29 40
Vicarage Rd.
Woodbridge Gdns. Lthd. BJ62 102
Woodbridge Hill, Guil. AQ70 118
Woodbridge Hill Gdns. Guil. AQ70 118
Woodbridge La. Rom. CV27 42
Woodbridge Meadows, Guil. AQ70 118
Woodbridge Rd. Bark. CN35 49
Woodbridge Rd. Guil. AR70 118
Woodbridge Rd. Guil. AR71 118
North St.
Woodbridge St. EC1 BY38 56
Woodbrook Clo. Wal. Abb. CG20 22
Woodbrook Rd. SE2 CO43 69
Woodbury Clo. E11 CH31 49
Woodbury Clo. Croy. CA55 87
Woodbury Dr. Sutt. BT58 95
Woodbury Hill Loug. CK23 31
Woodbury Pk. Rd. W13 BJ38 54
Woodbury Rd. E17 CE31 48
Woodbury Rd. West. CK62 106
Woodbury St. SW17 BU49 76
Woodchester Sq. W2 BS39 56
Woodchurch Clo. Sid. CM48 78
Woodchurch Rd. NW6 BS36 56
Wood Cl. Hat. BP12 10
Wood Clo. E2 CB38 57
Wood Clo. NW9 BN33 46
Wood Clo. Amer. AQ23 25
Wood Clo. Bex. CT48 79
Wood Clo. Har. BG33 45
Wood Clo. Wind. AO45 61
Woodclyffe Dr. Chis. CL51 88
Woodcock Dell Av. Har. BK33 45
Woodcock Hill Borwd. BM25 28
Woodcock Hill Har. BK32 45
Woodcock Hill, St. Alb. BK10 9
Woodcombe Cres. SE23 CC47 77

Wood Common. Hat. BP11 10
Woodcote Av. NW7 BQ29 37
Woodcote Av. Horn. CU35 50
Woodcote Av. Th. Hth. BY52 86
Woodcote Av. Wall. BV58 95
Woodcote Clo. Enf. CC25 30
Woodcote Clo. Epsom BN60 94
Woodcote Clo. Kings. On T. BL50 75
Woodcote Dr. Pur. BW58 95
Woodcote End Epsom BN61 103
Woodcote Grn. Rd. Epsom BN61 103
Woodcote Grn. Rd. Wall. BW58 95
Woodcote Gro. Cars. BV59 95
Woodcote Gro. Rd. Couls. BW61 104
Woodcote Hurst Epsom BN61 103
Woodcote La. Pur. BW59 95
Woodcote Pk. Av. Pur. BW59 95
Woodcote Pk. Rd. Epsom BN61 103
Woodcote Pl. SE27 BY49 76
Woodcote Rd. E11 CH33 49
Woodcote Rd. Epsom BN60 94
Woodcote Rd. Orp. CM54 88
Woodcote Rd. Wall. BV57 95
Woodcote Side, Epsom. BM61 103
Woodcote Valley Rd. Pur. BW60 95
Woodcote Village Pur. BW59 95
Woodcourt Clo. Wal. Cr. CC18 21
Wood Cres. Hem. H. AX14 8
Woodcrest Rd. Pur. BX60 95
Woodcrest Wk. Reig. BU69 121
Woodcroft N21 BX26 38
Woodcroft, SE9 CK48 78
Woodcroft Grnf. BJ36 54
Woodcroft Av. NW7 BO29 37
Woodcroft Av. Stan. BJ30 36
Woodcroft Cres. Uxb. AZ37 53
Woodcroft Rd. Chesh. AO17 16
Woodcroft Rd. Th. Hth. BY53 86
Woodcutters Ave. Grays. DE41 71
Wood Dene Leath. BG58 93
Wood Dene. Lthd. BG59 93
Wood Dr. Chis. CK50 78
Wood Dr. Sev. CT66 116
Woodedge Clo. E4 CG26 40
Forest Side
Woodend SE19 BZ50 77
Wood End Esher BG55 84
Wood End, Hayes BB39 53
Wood End. Lthd. BK66 111
Wood End, St. Alb. BG17 18
Woodend Sutt. BT55 86
Wood End Av. Har. BF35 45
Wood End Clo. Nthlt. BG35 45
Wood End Clo. Slou. AO34 43
Woodend Clo. Wok. AQ63 100
Woodend Gdns. Enf. BX24 29
Wood End Gdns. Nthlt. BG35 45
Wood End Grn. Rd. Hayes BA39 53
Wood End La. Nthlt. BF36 54
Woodend Rd. E17 CF30 39
Wood End Rd. Har. BG35 45
Woodend, The, Wall. BV58 95
Wood End Way Nthlt. BG35 45
Wooder Gdns. E7 CG35 49
Woodfall Av. Barn. BR25 28
Woodfall Rd. N4 BY33 47
Woodfall St. SW3 BU42 66
Wood Farm Rd. Hem. H. AY14 8
Woodfarrs, SE5 BZ45 67
Woodfield Ave. Nthwd. BB28 35
Woodfield Av. NW9 BO31 46
Woodfield Av. SW16 BW48 76
Woodfield Av. W5 BK38 54
Woodfield Av. Cars. BV57 95
Woodfield Av. Grav. DG48 81
Woodfield Av. Wem. BK34 45
Woodfield Clo. SE19 BZ50 77
Woodfield Clo. Ash. BK62 102
Woodfield Clo. Couls. BW63 104
Woodfield Clo. N. Mal. BO53 85
Woodfield Clo. Red. BU70 121
Woodfield Cres. W5 BK38 54
Woodfield Dr. Barn. BV26 38
Woodfield Dr. Rom. CU31 50
Woodfield Gdns. W9 BR39 55
Woodfield Rd.
Woodfield Gdns. N. Mal. BO53 85
Woodfield Gro. SW16 BW48 76
Woodfield Hill. Couls. BV63 104
Woodfield La. SW16 BW48 76
Woodfield La. Ash. BL62 103
Woodfield La. Hat. BT15 11
Woodfield Pl. W9 BR39 55
Woodfield Rise Bush. BG26 36
Woodfield Rd. W5 BK38 54
Woodfield Rd. W9 BR39 55
Woodfield Rd. Ash. BK62 102
Woodfield Rd. Surb. BH55 84
Woodfield Rd. Welw. G. C. BR8 5
Woodfields. Sev. CS65 107
Woodfields, The, Sth. Croy. CA59 96
Woodfield Way N11 BW29 38
Woodfield Way. Horn. CV33 51
Woodfield Way, Red. BU70 121
Woodfield Way, St. Alb. BK12 9
Woodford Av. Ilf. CJ31 49
Woodford Bridge Rd. Ilf. CJ31 49
Woodford Cres. Pnr. BC30 35
Woodford New Rd. E17 CG31 49
Woodford New Rd. E18 CG31 49
Woodford New Rd. Wdf. Grn. CG31 49
Woodford Pl. Wem. BL33 46
Woodford Rd. E7 CH35 49
Woodford Rd. E11 CG33 49
Woodford Rd. E18 CG33 49
Woodford Rd. Wat. BC23 26
Wood Gate, Wat. BC20 17
Woodgate Av. Chess. BK56 93
Woodgate Cres. Nthwd. BC29 35
Woodgavil Bans. BR61 103
Woodger Rd. W12 BQ41 65
Goldhawk Rd.
Woodgrange Av. N12 BT29 38
Woodgrange Av. W5 BL40 55
Woodgrange Av. Enf. CB25 30
Woodgrange Av. Har. BK32 45
Woodgrange Clo. Har. BK32 45
Woodgrange Gdns. Enf. CB25 30
Woodgrange Rd. E7 CH35 49
Woodgreen La. Wal. Abb. CH20 22
Woodgreen Rd. Wal. Abb. CJ20 22
Woodhall Av. SE21 CA48 77
Woodhall Av. Pnr. BE30 36
Woodhall Clo. Uxb. AX35 44
Woodhall Ct. Welw. G. C. BR8 5
Woodhall Dr. SE21 CA48 77
Woodhall Dr. Pnr. BD30 36
Woodhall Gate Pnr. BD29 36
Woodhall La. Rad. BL21 28
Woodhall La. Wat. BD27 36
Woodhall La. Welw. G. C. BR8 5
Woodhall Rd. Pnr. BD29 36
Woodham Ct. E18 CG31 49
Woodham La. Wey. AV59 91
Woodham La. Wey. AX58 92
Woodham La. Wok. AT60 91
Woodham Park Rd. Wey. AV58 91
Woodham Park Way. Wey. AV59 91
Woodham Rise, Wok. AT61 100
Woodham Rd. SE6 CF48 77
Woodham Rd. Wok. AS61 100
Woodham Rd. Wok. AT60 91
Woodham Waye. Wok. AT60 91
Woodhatch Rd. Reig. & Red. BT72 121
Woodhatch Spinney Couls. BX57 95
Woodhatch Spinney Couls. BX61 104
Woodhaven Gdns. Ilf. CL31 49
Brandville Gdns.
Woodhaven Gdns. Ilf. CM31 49
Brandville Gdns.
Woodhaw, Egh. AT49 72
Woodhayes, SW19 BQ50 75
Woodhayes Rd. SW19 BQ50 75
Woodhead Dr. Orp. CN55 88
Woodheyes Rd. NW10 BN35 46
Woodhill, SE18 CK41 68
Woodhill Harl. CN13 13
Woodhill Ave. Ger. Cr. AS32 43
Woodhill Cres. Har. BK32 45
Woodhill, Wok. AU66 109
Woodhouse Av. Grnf. BH37 54
Woodhouse Clo. Grnf. BH37 54
Woodhouse Clo. Hayes. BB41 63
Woodhouse Gro. E12 CK36 58
Woodhouse Rd. E11 CG34 49
Woodhouse Rd. N12 BT29 38
Woodhurst Av. Orp. CL53 88
Woodhurst Av. Wat. BD21 27
Woodhurst Dr. Uxb. AV32 43
Woodhurst Pk. Oxt. CG68 115
Woodhurst Rd. SE2 CO42 69
Woodhurst Rd. W3 BN40 55
Woodhurst Rd. Oxt. CG68 115
Woodhyrst Gdns. Ken. BY57 95
Woodhyrst Gdns. Ken. BY61 104
Wooding Grove. Harl. CL11 13
Woodington Clo. SE9 CL46 78
Woodison St. E3 CD38 57
Woodknoll Dr. Brom. CK51 88
Woodland App. Grnf. BJ36 54
Whitton Dr.
Woodland Ave. Wind. AM45 61
Woodland Av. Brwd. DD25 122
Woodland Av. Guil. AQ71 118
Woodland Av. Hem. H. AW14 8
Woodland Av. Slou. AO40 52
Woodland Clo. NW9 BN32 46
Woodland. Clo. Brwd. DE25 122
Woodland Clo. Epsom BO57 94
Woodland Clo. Uxb. AZ34 44
Woodland Clo. Wdf. Grn. CH27 40
Woodland Ct. Oxt. CF67 114
Woodland Ct. Oxt. CG67 115
Woodland Cres. SE10 CG43 68
Woodland Dri. Leath. BB67 110
Woodland Dr. St. Alb. BK12 9
Woodland Dr. Wat. BB23 26
Woodland Gdns. N10 BV32 47
Woodland Gdns. Croy. CC59 96
Woodland Gdns. Islw. BH45 64
Woodland Gdns. Sth. Croy. CC58 96
Woodland Gro. SE10 CG42 68
Woodland Gro. Wey. BA56 92
Woodland Hl. SE19 CA50 77
Woodland La. Rick. AU24 25
Woodland Ri. Oxt. CG68 115
Woodland Ri. Sev. CW65 108
Woodland Rise, N10 BV31 47
Woodland Rise Grnf. BJ36 54
Woodland Rise. Welw. G. C. BQ7 7
Woodland Rd. E4 CF26 39
Woodland Rd. N11 BV28 38
Woodland Rd. SE19 CA49 77
Woodland Rd. Loug. CK24 31
Woodland Rd. Rick. AU28 34
Woodland Rd. Th. Hth. BY52 86
Woodlands NW11 BR32 46
Woodlands SW20 BQ52 85
Woodlands Har. BF31 45
Woodlands Ave. Wey. AV60 91
Woodlands Av. E11 CH33 49
Woodlands Av. N12 BT29 38
Woodlands Av. W3 BM40 55
High St.
Woodlands Av. Berk. AR13 7
Woodlands Av. Berk. AU11 7
Woodlands Av. Horn. CV32 51
Woodlands Av. N. Mal. BN51 85
Woodlands Av. Red. BU71 121
Woodlands Av. Rom. CQ32 50
Woodlands Av. Ruis. BD33 45
Woodlands Av. Sid. CN47 78
Woodlands Av. Wor. Pk. BO55 85
Woodlands Clo. NW11 BR32 46
Woodlands Clo. Borwd. BM24 28
Woodlands Clo. Brom. CK51 88
Woodlands Clo. Cher. AT58 91
Woodlands Clo. Esher BH57 93
Woodlands Clo. Ger. Cr. AT32 43
Woodlands Clo. Grays. DF41 71
Woodlands Clo. Hem. H. AW14 8
Woodlands Clo. Swan. CT52 89
Woodlands Clo. Wey. BA56 92
Woodlands Dr. Har. BH29 36
Woodlands Dr. Hodd. CE13 12
Woodlands Dr. Kings L. BA17 17
Woodlands Dr. Sun. BD51 84
Woodlands Dr. Wat. BC23 26
Woodlands Gdns. E17 CG31 49
Woodford New Rd.
Woodlands Gro. Couls. BV62 104
Woodlands Gro. Islw. BH44 64
Woodlands La. Cob. BF62 102
Woodlands Pde. Ashf. BA50 73
Hogarth Av.
Woodlands Pk. Bex. CS49 79
Woodlands Pk. Guil. AT70 118
Woodlands Pk. Tad. BM69 120
Woodlands Pk. Wey. AV56 91
Woodlands Pk. Rd. N15 BY32 47
Woodlands Pk. Rd. SE10 CG43 68
Woodlands Rise Swan. CT51 89
Woodlands Rd. E11 CG34 49
Woodlands Rd. E17 CF31 48
Woodlands Rd. N9 CC26 39
Woodlands Rd. SW13 BO45 65
Woodlands Rd. Bexh. CQ45 69
Woodlands Rd. Brom. CK51 88
Woodlands Rd. Bush. BE24 27
Woodlands Rd. Enf. BZ23 30
Woodlands Rd. Epsom. BM61 103
Woodlands Rd. Guil. AR68 109
Woodlands Rd. Har. BH32 45
Woodlands Rd. Hem. H. AZ17 17
Woodlands Rd. Ilf. CM34 49
Woodlands Rd. Islw. BG45 64
Woodlands Rd. Islw. BH44 64
Woodlands Rd. Lthd. BE67 111
Woodlands Rd. Lthd. BG62 102
Woodlands Rd. Orp. CO57 98
Woodlands Rd. Red. BU71 121
Woodlands Rd. Rom. CT31 50
Woodlands Rd. Rom. CX30 42
Woodlands Rd. Sev. CX60 99
Woodlands Rd. Sthl. BD40 54
Woodlands Rd. Surb. BK54 84
Woodlands Rd. Vir. W. AR52 82
Woodlands Rd. Wey. AV60 91
Woodlands Rd. East, Vir. W. AR52 82
Woodlands Rd. West, Vir. W. AR52 82
Woodlands St. SE13 CF47 77
Woodlands, The, N14 BV26 38
Woodlands, The, SE13 CF47 77
Woodlands, The, SE19 BZ50 77
Woodlands, The Amer. AO21 25
Woodlands, The, Esher BG55 84
Woodlands, The, Ger. Cr. AS32 43
Woodlands, The, Islw. BH44 64
Woodlands, The, Orp. CO57 98
Woodlands, The, Wall. BV58 95
Woodlands Way, SW15 BR46 75
Woodlands Way Ash. BL62 103
Woodfield La.
Woodlands Way, Ash. BM61 103
Woodland Ter. SE7 CK42 68
Woodland Ter. SE18 CK42 68
Woodland View. Chesh. AO20 16
Woodland Wk. SE10 CG42 68
Woodland Way N21 BY27 38
Woodland Way, NW7 BO29 37
Woodland Way NW11 BS32 47
Woodland Way, SE2 CP42 69
Woodland Way. Cat. CA67 114
Woodland Way Croy. CD54 87
Woodland Way, Epp. CM21 31
Woodland Way, Mitch. BV50 76
Woodland Way Mord. BR52 85
Woodland Way Ong. CW18 24
Woodland Way Orp. CM52 88
Woodland Way Pur. BY60 95
Woodland Way Surb. BM55 85
Woodland Way, Tad. BR64 103
Woodland Way, Wal. Cr. BY17 20
Woodland Way Wdf. Grn. CH27 40
Woodland Way W. Wick. CE56 96
Woodland Way, Wey. BA56 92
Wood La. N6 BV32 47
Wood La. NW9 BN33 46
Wood La. W12 BQ39 55
Wood La. Cat. BZ65 105
Wood La. Dag. CP35 50
Wood La. Dart. CY49 80
Wood La. Horn. CU35 50
Wood La. Islw. BH43 64
Wood La. Iver AU38 52
Wood Lane. Ong. DC13 15
Wood La. Ruis. BA33 44
Wood La. Slou. AN41 61
Wood La. Slou. AO35 43
Wood La. Stan. BJ27 36
Wood La. Tad. BR62 103
Wood La. Wdf. Grn. CG28 40
Wood La. Wey. BA58 92
Wood La. Wok. AO62 100
Wood La. Clo. Iver AU38 52
Wood Lane End, Hem. H. AZ13 8
Woodlawn Cres. Twick. BF48 74
Woodlawn Dr. Felt. BD48 74
Woodlawn Rd. SW6 BQ43 65
Woodlea Dr. Brom. CG53 88
Woodlea Est. Brom. CG53 88
Woodlea Gro. Nthwd. BA29 35
Woodlea Rd. N16 CA34 48
Woodleigh Av. N12 BU29 38
Woodleigh Gdns. SW16 BX48 76
Woodley Clo. SW17 BU50 76
Woodley Hill. Chesh. AO20 16
Woodley Rd. Orp. CP55 89
Wood Lodge La. W. Wick. CF55 87
Woodman La. E4 CG25 31
Woodman Path Chig. CN29 40
Woodman Rd. Brwd. DB28 42
Woodman Rd. Couls. BW61 104
Woodman Rd. Hem. H. AY14 8
Woodmans Ct. Stan. BL30 37
Woodmansterne La. Bans. BS61 104
Woodmansterne La. Cars. BU59 95
Woodmansterne Rd. SW16 BW50 70
Woodmansterne Rd. Cars. BU58 95
Woodmansterne Rd. Couls. BW61 104
Woodmansterne St. Bans. BU61 104
Wood Meads Epp. CO18 23
Woodmere, SE9 CK47 78
Woodmere Av. Croy. CC54 87
Woodmere Av. Wat. BD22 27
Woodmere Clo. Croy. CC54 87
Woodmere Gdns. Croy. CC54 87
Woodmere Way Beck. CF53 87
Wood Mt. Hat. BP12 10
Woodmount Swan. CS54 89
Woodnook Rd. SW16 BV49 76
Woodpecker Clo. N9 CB25 30
Woodpecker Clo. Bush. BG26 36
Woodpecker Mt. Croy. CD58 96
Woodpecker Rd. SE14 CD43 67
Woodpecker Way, Wok. AR65 100
Woodplace Clo. Couls. BW63 104
Woodplace La. Couls. BW62 104
Woodplace La. Couls. BW64 104
Woodquest Av. SE24 BZ46 77
Woodridden Hill, Wal. Abb. CJ21 31
Woodride Barn. BT23 29
Wood Ride Orp. CM52 88
Woodridge Way. Nthwd. BB29 35
Woodridings Av. Pnr. BE30 36
Woodridings Clo. Pnr. BE29 36
Woodriffe Rd. E11 CF33 48
Wood Rise, Guil. AP69 118
Wood Rise Pnr. BC32 44
Wood Rd. E16 CH39 58
Wood Rd. Shep. AZ52 83
Wood Rd. West. CJ62 106
Woodrow, SE18 CK42 68
Woodrow Av. Hayes BB39 53
Woodrow Clo. Grnf. BJ36 54
Woodruff Av. Guil. AT69 118
Woods Av. Hat. BP12 10
Woods Av. Hat. BP13 10
Woods Bldgs. E1 CB39 57
Durward St.
Woodseer St. E1 CA39 57
Woodsford Sq. W14 BR41 65
Woodshire Rd. Dag. CR34 50
Woodside NW11 BS32 47
Woodside, SW19 BR50 75
Woodside Buck. H. CJ27 40
Woodside, Lthd. BF64 102
Woodside Orp. CO56 98
Woodside. Tad. BR67 112
Woodside, Wat. BC22 26
Woodside Ave. Amer. AO21 25
Woodside Av. N6 BU32 47
Woodside Av. N12 BS28 38
Woodside Av. SE25 CB53 87
Woodside Av. Chis. CL49 78
Woodside Av. Esher BH54 84
Woodside Av. Walt. BC56 92
Woodside Av. Wem. BL37 55
Woodside Clo. Amer. AO22 25
Woodside Clo. Bexh. CS45 69
Woodside Clo. Brwd. DE25 122
Woodside Clo. Ger. Cr. AS30 34
Woodside Clo. Rain. CV38 60
Woodside Clo. Stan. BJ28 36
Woodside Clo. Surb. BN54 85
Woodside Clo. Vir. W. AQ53 82
Woodside Clo. Wem. BL37 55
Woodside Clo. Wok. AO62 100
Woodside Ct. Croy. CB54 87
Woodside Ct. Rd. Croy. CB54 87
Woodside Cres. Sid. CN48 78
Woodside Dr. Dart. CT49 79
Woodside End. Wem. BL37 55
Woodside Epp. CP16 23
Woodside Gdns. E4 CE28 39
Woodside Gdns. N17 CA30 39
Woodside Grange Rd. N12 BS28 38
Woodside Grn. SE25 CB53 87
Woodside Gro. N12 BT27 38
Woodside Hill. Ger. Cr. AS30 34
Woodside La. N12 BS27 38
Woodside La. Bex. CP46 79
Woodside La. Hat. BR15 10
Woodside La. Hat. BS15 11
Woodside, Leath. BA66 110
Woodside Pk. SE25 CB53 87
Woodside Pk. Av. E17 CF32 48
Woodside Pk. Rd. N12 BS28 38
Woodside Pl. Wem. BL37 55
Woodside Rd. E13 CJ38 58
Woodside Rd. N22 BX29 38
Woodside Rd. SE25 CB53 87
Woodside Rd. Amer. AO22 25
Woodside Rd. Bexh. CS45 69
Woodside Rd. Brom. CK53 88
Woodside Rd. Cob. BF60 93
Woodside Rd. Guil. AP70 118
Woodside Rd. Kings. On T. BL50 75
Woodside Rd. N. Mal. BN51 85
Woodside Rd. Nthwd. BB29 35
Woodside Rd. Nthwd. BC29 35
Woodside Rd. Pur. BW60 95
Woodside Rd. St. Alb. BE18 18
Woodside Rd. Sev. CP65 107
Woodside Rd. Sev. CU65 107
Woodside Rd. Sid. CN48 78
Woodside Rd. Sutt. BT55 86
Woodside Rd. Wat. BC19 17
Woodside Rd. Wdf. Grn. CH28 40
Woodside Rd. Welw. G. C. BR5 5
Woodside Vw. SE25 CB53 87
Woodside Vw. Sev. CR58 98
Woodside Way Croy. CC53 87
Woodside Way, Mitch. BV51 86
Woodside Way, Red. BV71 121
Woodside Way, Red. BV73 121
Woods Ms. W1 BV40 56
Woodsome Clo. Wey. BA57 92
Woodsome Rd. NW5 BV34 47
Woods Pl. SE1 CA41 67
Woodspring Rd. SW19 BR48 75
Woods Rd. SE15 CB44 67
Woodstead Gro. Edg. BL29 37
Woods, The, Nthwd. BC28 35
Woods, The, Uxb. AZ35 44
Woodstock Surb. BK55 84
Woodstock Ave. Slou. AR42 62
Woodstock Av. NW11 BR33 46
Woodstock Av. W13 BJ41 64
Woodstock Av. Islw. BJ46 74
Woodstock Av. Rom. CX28 42
Woodstock Av. Sthl. BE38 54
Woodstock Av. Sutt. BR54 85
Woodstock Clo. Bex. CQ47 79
Woodstock Clo. Stan. BL30 37
Woodstock Ct. SE12 CH46 78
Woodstock Cres. N9 CA25 30
Woodstock Dr. Uxb. AY35 44
Woodstock Gdns. Beck. CE50 77
Woodstock Gdns. Hayes BB39 53
Woodstock Gdns. Ilf. CO34 50
Woodstock Gro. W12 BQ41 65
Woodstock, Guil. AW67 110
Woodstock La. Esher BJ57 93
Woodstock Rise Sutt. BR54 85
Woodstock Rd. E7 CJ36 58
Woodstock Rd. E17 CF30 39
Woodstock Rd. N4 BY33 47
Woodstock Rd. NW11 BR33 46
Woodstock Rd. W4 BO42 65
Woodstock Rd. Brox. CD13 12
Woodstock Rd. Bush. BH26 36
Woodstock Rd. Cars. BV56 95
Woodstock Rd. Couls. BV61 104
Woodstock Rd. Croy. BZ55 87
Woodstock Rd. Wem. BL37 55
Woodstock Rd. N. St. Alb. BJ12 9
Woodstock Road S. St. Alb. BJ13 9
Woodstock St. E16 CG39 58
Woodstock St. W1 BV39 56
Oxford St.
Woodstock Ter. E14 CE40 57
Woodstock Way, Mitch. BV51 86
Woodstone Av. Epsom. BP56 94
Wood St. E17 CF31 48
Wood St. EC2 BZ39 57
Wood St. W4 BO42 65
Wood St. Barn. BQ24 28
Wood St. Grav. DD46 81
Wood St. Grays. DE43 71
Wood St. Kings. On T. BK51 84
Wood St. Mitch. BU54 86
Wood St. Red. BW68 113
Wood St. Swan. CV51 90
Woods Wy. Lthd. BH60 93
Woodsyre Est. SE26 CA49 77
Wood, The, Surb. BL53 85
Woodthorpe Rd. SW15 BP45 65
Woodthorpe Rd. Ashf. AX50 73
Wood Vale N10 BW32 47
Wood Vale SE23 CB47 77
Woodvale Av. SE25 CA52 87
Wood Vale Est. SE23 CB47 77
Wood View. Chess. BK59 93
Wood Vw. Grays. DE41 71
Wood View, Hem. H. AW12 8
Wood View, Pot. B. BW17 20
Woodview Av. E4 CF28 39
Woodview Clo. Sev. CZ57 99
Woodview Clo. Sth. Croy. CB60 96
Woodview Rd. Swan. CS51 89
Woodville SE3 CH44 68
Woodville Clo. Tedd. BJ49 74
Woodville Ct. Wat. BC23 26
Woodville Gdns. NW11 BQ33 46
Hendon Way
Woodville Gdns. W5 BL39 55
Woodville Gdns. Ilf. CL31 49
Woodville Gdns. Ruis. BA33 44
Woodville Gro. N16 CA35 48
Woodville Rd.

Woodville Pl. Cat. BZ64 105
Woodville Rd. E11 CG33 49
Woodville Rd. E17 CD32 48
Woodville Rd. E18 CH30 40
Woodville Rd. N16 CA35 48
Woodville Rd. NW6 BR37 55
Woodville Rd. NW11 BQ33 46
Woodville Rd. W5 BK39 54
Woodville Rd. Barn. BS24 29
Woodville Rd. Mord. BS52 86
Woodville Rd. Rich. BJ48 74
Woodville Rd. Th. Hth. BZ52 87
Woodville St. SE18 CK42 68
Woodvill Rd. Lthd. BJ63 102
Woodward Av. NW4 BP32 46
Woodward Clo. Grays. DD42 71
Woodwarde Rd. SE22 CA46 77
Woodward Gdns. Dag. CO36 59
Woodward Rd. Dag. CO36 59
Woodward Ter. Green. CZ46 80
Woodway, Brwd. DD26 122
Woodway, Guil. AT70 118
Wood Way Orp. CL55 88
Wood Way, Sev. CT64 107
Woodway Cres. Har. BJ32 45
Woodwaye Wat. BD26 36
Woodwell St. SW18 BT46 76
North Side
Wood Wharf, SE10 CF43 67
Woodyard La. SE21 CA47 77
Woodyates Rd. SE12 CG46 78
Woolacombe Rd. SE3 CH44 68
Woolacombe Way. Hayes. BB42 63
Woolaston Rd. N4 BY32 47
Umfreville Rd.
Wooler St. SE17 BZ42 67
Woolf Wk. Til. DH44 71
Coleridge Rd.
Woolhampton Way Chig. CO27 41
Woollam Cres. St. Alb. BG11 9
Woollard St. Wal. Abb. CF20 21
Woollard Way Ing. DC19 24
Woolmans Clo. Brox. CD14 12
Woolmead Av. NW4 BP33 46
Woolmer Dr. Hem. H. BA13 8
Woolmer Gdns. N18 CB29 39
Woolmer Rd. N18 CB28 39
Woolmongers La. Ing. DA19 24
Woolmore St. E14 CF40 57
Woolneigh St. SW6 BS45 66
Wool Rd. SW20 BP50 75
Woolsey Rd. Hem. H. AX14 8
Woolstone Rd. SE23 CC48 77
Woolwich Church St. SE18 CK41 68
Woolwich Common SE18 CL43 68
Woolwich High St. SE18 CK41 68
Woolwich Industrial Est. SE28 CN41 68
Woolwich Manor Way, E16 CL40 58
Woolwich New Rd. SE18 CL42 68
Woolwich Rd. SE2 CP43 69
Woolwich Rd. SE7 CG42 68
Woolwich Rd. SE10 CG42 68
Woolwich Rd. Belv. CP43 69
Woolwich Rd. Bexh. CR45 69
Wooster Gdns. E14 CF39 57
Wooton Dr. Hem. H. AY11 8
Wootton Clo. Horn. CV32 51
Wootton Gro. N3 BS30 38
Station Rd.
Wootton St. SE1 BY41 66
Worbeck Rd. SE20 CB51 87
Worcester Av. N17 CB29 39
Worcester Av. Enf. CB22 30
Worcester Av. Upmin. CZ34 51
Worcester Clo. Croy. CD55 87
Worcester Clo. Mitch. BV51 86
Worcester Cres. NW7 BO27 37
Worcester Cres. Wdf. Grn. CH28 40
Worcester Gdns. Grnf. BG36 54
Worcester Gdns. Ilf. CK33 49
Worcester Gdns. Sutt. BS57 95
Worcester Gdns. Wor. Pk. BO55 85
Worcester Pk. Rd. Wor. Pk. BN55 85
Worcester Rd. E12 CK35 49
Worcester Rd. E17 CC30 39
Worcester Rd. SW19 BR49 75
Worcester Rd. Guil. AP69 118
Worcester Rd. Hat. BO12 10
Worcester Rd. Reig. BS70 121
Worcester Rd. Sutt. BS57 95
Worcester Rd. Uxb. AX39 53
Wordsworth Av. E12 CK36 58
Wordsworth Av. E18 CG31 49
Wordsworth Av. Grnf. BG38 54
Wordsworth Clo. Rom. CV30 42
Wordsworth Clo. Til. DH44 71
Coleridge Rd.
Wordsworth Dr. Sutt. BQ56 94
Wordsworth Pde. N8 BY31 47
Alfoxton Av.
Wordsworth Rd. N16 CA35 48
Wordsworth Rd. SE20 CC50 77
Wordsworth Rd. Hamptn. BE49 74
Wordsworth Rd. Har. BH31 45
Wordsworth Rd. Wall. BW57 95
Wordsworth Rd. Well. CN44 68
Wordsworth Rd. Wey. AX56 92
Wordsworth Wk. NW11 BS31 47
Wordsworth Way Dart. CX45 70
Wordsworth Way. West Dr. AY42 63
Worfield St. SW11 BU43 66
Worgan St. SE11 BX42 66
Worgate St. N1 BZ37 57
Rushton St.
Worland Rd. E15 CG36 58
World' End La. N21 BX25 29
Worlds End, Cob. BC60 92
Worlds End Epsom BN61 103
Worlds End La. Orp. CN57 97
Worlds End Pass. SW10 BT43 66
Worley Rd. St. Alb. BG13 9
Worlidge St. W6 BQ42 65
Worlingham Rd. SE22 CA45 67
Wormholt Est. W12 BO40 55
Wormholt Rd. W12 BP40 55
Wormley Lo. Clo. Brox. CD15 12
High Rd.
Wormley West End, Brox. CA15 12
Wormwood St. EC2 CA39 57
Wornington Rd. W10 BR38 55
Wornington Yd. W10 BR38 55
Wornington Rd.
Woronzow Rd. NW8 BT37 56
Worple Av. SW19 BQ50 75
Worple Av. Islw. BJ46 74
Worple Av. Stai. AW50 73
Worple Clo. Har. BE33 45
Worple Rd. SW19 BQ51 85
Worple Rd. SW20 BQ51 85
Worple Rd. Epsom BN61 103
Worple Rd. Islw. BJ45 64
Worple Rd. Lthd. BJ64 102
Worple Rd. Lthd. BK65 102
Worple Rd. Stai. AW50 73
Worple Rd. Stai. AW51 83
Worple Rd. Ms. SW19 BR50 75
Worplesdon Rd. Guil. AP67 109
Worple St. SW14 BN45 65
Worple Way Har. BE33 45
Worple Way, Rich. BL46 75
Worrin Clo. Brwd. DC26 122
Worrin Rd. Brwd. DC26 122
Worship's Hill. Sev. CT65 107
Worship St. EC2 BZ38 57
Worslade Rd. SW17 BT49 76
Worsley Bri. Rd. SE26 CD49 77
Worsley Bri. Rd. Beck. CD49 77
Worsley Rd. E11 CG35 49
Worsopp Dr. SW4 BW45 66
Worsted Grn. Red. BW68 113
Worth Clo. Orp. CN56 97
Worthfield Clo. Epsom BN57 94
Worthing Clo. E15 CG37 58
Worthing Rd. Houns. BE43 64
Worthington Rd. Surb. BL54 85
Worthydown Ct. SE18 CL43 68
Prince Imperial Rd.
Wortley Rd. E6 CJ36 58
Wortley Rd. Croy. BY54 86
Worton Gdns. Islw. BG44 64
Worton Rd. Islw. BG45 64
Worton Way Islw. BG44 64
Wotton Dri. Dor. BD73 119
Wotton Grn. Orp. CP52 89
Wotton Rd. NW2 BQ35 46
Wotton Way Sutt. BQ58 94
Wouldham Rd. E16 CG39 58
Wrabness Way, Stai. AW51 83
Wragby Rd. E11 CG34 49
Wray Av. Ilf. CL31 49
Wray Comm. Rd. Reig. BT70 121
Wray Cres. N4 BX34 47
Wrayfield Av. Reig. BT70 121
Wrayfield Rd. Sutt. BQ55 85
Wraylands Dr. Reig. BT69 121
Wray La. Reig. BT68 113
Wray Park Rd. Reig. BS70 121
Wray Rd. Sutt. BR58 94
Wraysbury Rd. Stai. AT48 72
Wrays Way, Hayes BB38 53
Wrekin Rd. SE18 CM43 68
Wren Av. NW2 BQ35 46
Wren Av. Sthl. BE42 64
Wren Clo. Sth. Croy. CC58 96
Wren Cres. Bush. BG26 36
Wren Cres. Wey. AX56 92
Wren Gdns. Dag. CP35 50
Wren Gdns. Horn. CT33 50
Wren Pl. Brwd. DB27 42
Wren Rd. SE5 BZ44 67
Wren Rd. Dag. CP35 50
Wren Rd. Sid. CP49 79
Wrens Av. Ashf. BA49 73
Wrensfield, Hem. H. AW13 8
Wrens Hill, Lthd. BG61 102
Wren St. WC1 BX38 56
Gray's Inn Rd.
Wrentham Av. NW10 BQ37 55
Wrenthorpe Rd. Brom. CG49 78
Wren Wood. Welw. G. C. BS7 5
Wrenwood Way Pnr. BC31 44
Wrestlers Clo. Hat. BQ11 10
Hillfield
Wrexham Rd. E3 CE37 57
Wrexham Rd. Rom. CV27 42
Wrexham Rd. Slou. AQ41 62
Wricklemarsh Rd. SE3 CH44 68
Wrigglesworth St. SE14 CC43 67
Wright Rd. Houns. BC43 63
Wright's Alley, SW19 BQ50 75
Wrightsbridge Rd. Rom. CW27 42
Wrights Bldgs. SE1 CA41 67
Grange Rd.
Wright's La. W8 BS41 66
Wrights La. Brwd. DB21 33
Wright's Rd. E3 CD37 57
Wright's Rd. SE25 CA52 87
Wrights Row Wall. BV56 95
Wrights Wk. SW14 BN45 65
North Worple Way
Wrigley Clo. E4 CF28 39
Avenue, The,
Writtle Wk. Rain. CT37 59
Wrotham Rd. NW1 BW36 56
St. Pancras Way.
Wrotham Rd. W13 BJ40 54
Mattock La.
Wrotham Rd. Barn. BR23 28
Wrotham Rd. Grav. DF51 81
Wrotham Rd. Well. CP44 69
Wroths Path Loug. CK23 31
Wrottesley Rd. NW10 BP37 55
Wrottesley Rd. SE18 CL43 68
Wroughton Rd. SW11 BU46 76
Wroughton Ter. NW4 BP31 46
Babington Rd.
Wroxall Rd. Dag. CP36 59
Wroxham Av. Hem. H. AX14 8
Wroxham Gdns. N11 BW29 38
Wroxham Gdns. Enf. BY21 29
Wroxham Gdns. Pot. B. BQ19 19
Wroxton Rd. SE15 CB44 67
Wrythe Grn. Rd. Cars. BU55 86
Wrythe La. Cars. BT54 86
Wulfstan St. W12 BO39 55
Wyatt Clo. Hayes BC39 53
Wyatt Clo. Nthlt. BE36 54
Wyatt Clo. Sev. DC63 108
Wyatt La. Wind. AL45 61
Wyatt Pk. Rd. SW2 BX48 76
Wyatt Rd. E7 CH36 58
Wyatt Rd. N5 BZ34 48
Wyatt Rd. Stai. AW49 73
Wyatts Clo. Rick. AW24 26
Wyatt's Green La. Brwd. DB21 33
Wyatt's Green Rd. Brwd. DB21 33
Wyatts La. E17 CF31 48
Wyatts Rd. Rick. AV24 25
Wybert St. NW1 BV38 56
Munster Sq.
Wyborne Way, NW10 BN36 55
Wyburn Av. Barn. BR24 28
Wyche Gro. Sth. Croy. BZ57 96
Wych Elm, Harl. CM10 6
Wych Elm Clo. Horn. CX32 51
Wych Elm Pass. Kings. On T. BL50 75
Wych Elm Rise, Guil. AS72 118
Wych Elm Rd. Horn. CX32 51
Wychelms, St. Alb. BF17 18
Wycherley Cres. Barn. BS25 29
Wychford Dr. Saw. CP6 6
Wych Hill, Wok. AR63 100
Wych Hill La. Wok. AS63 100
Wych Hill Waye, Wok. AR63 100
Wychill Rise, Wok. AR63 100
Wychling Clo. Orp. CP54 89
Wychwood Av. Edg. BK29 36
Wychwood Av. Th. Hth. BZ52 87
Wychwood Clo. Edg. BK29 36
Wychwood Gdns. Ilf. CK31 49
Wychwood Wk. Edg. BK29 36
Wychwood Way. Nthwd. BB29 35
Wycliffe Clo. Well. CN44 68
Wycliffe Rd. SW19 BS50 76
Wycliffe Rd. Grav. DF47 81
Wyclif St. EC1 BY38 56
Wycombe Gdns. NW11 BS34 47
Wycombe Rd. N17 CB30 39
Wycombe Rd. Ilf. CK32 49
Wycombe Rd. Wem. BM37 55
Wydehurst Rd. Croy. CB54 87
Wydell Clo. Mord. BQ53 85
Wydeville Manor Rd. SE12 CH49 78
Wyecliffe Gdns. Red. BW68 113
Wye Clo. Ashf. AZ49 73
Wye Clo. Orp. CN54 88
Wye Rd. Grav. DH48 81
Wye St. SW11 BT44 66
Wye, The Hem. H. AZ11 8
Wyeth's Rd. Epsom BO60 94
Wyevale Clo. Pnr. BC31 44
Wyfields Ilf. CL30 40
Wyfold Rd. SW6 BR44 65
Wyhill Wk. Dag. CS36 59
Wyke Gdns. W7 BJ41 64
Wykeham Av. Dag. CP36 59
Wykeham Av. Horn. CV32 51
Wykeham Grn. Dag. CP36 59
Wykeham Hill, Wem. BL33 46
Wykeham Rd. NW4 BQ31 46
Wykeham Rd. Guil. AU70 118
Wykeham Rd. Har. BJ31 45
Wyke Rd. E3 CE36 57
Wyke Rd. SW20 BQ51 85
Wylands Rd. Slou. AT42 62
Wyldfield Gdns. N9 CA27 39
Latymer Rd.
Wyld Way, Wem. BM36 55
Wyleu St. SE23 CD47 77
Wylie Rd. Sthl. BF41 64
Wyllen Clo. E1 CC38 57
Wyllyotts Clo. Pot. B. BR19 19
Wylo Dr. Barn. BO25 28
Wymering Rd. W9 BQ38 55
Wymond St. SW15 BQ45 65
Wynaud Ct. N22 BX29 38
Palmerston Rd.
Wyncham Av. Sid. CN47 78
Wynchgate N14 BW26 38
Wynchgate Har. BH29 36
Wynchlands Cres. St. Alb. BK13 9
Wyncote Way Sth. Croy. CC58 96
Wyncroft Clo. Brom. CK52 88
Wyndale Av. NW9 BM32 46
Wyndcliff Rd. SE7 CH42 68
Wyndcroft Clo. Enf. BY24 29
Wyndham Av. Barn. BU26 38
Wyndham Av. Cob. BC60 92
Wyndham Clo. Orp. CM54 88
Wyndham Cres. N19 BW34 47
Wyndham Cres. Houns. BF46 74
Wyndham Est. SE5 BZ43 67
Wyndham Ms. W1 BU39 56
Upr. Montagu St.
Wyndham Pl. W1 BU39 56
Wyndham Rd. E6 CJ36 58
Wyndham Rd. SE5 BY43 66
Wyndham Rd. W13 BJ41 64
Wyndham Rd. Kings. On T. BL50 75
Wyndham St. W1 BU39 56
Wyneham Rd. SE24 BZ46 77
Wynell Rd. SE23 CC48 77
Wynford Gro. Orp. CO52 89
Wynford Rd. N1 BX37 56
Wynford Way, SE9 CK48 78
Wynlie Gdns. Pnr. BC30 35
Wynndale Rd. E18 CH30 40
Wynne Rd. SW9 BY44 66
Wynn's Av. Sid. CN46 78
Lyndon Av.
Wynn's Av. Sid. CO46 79
Lyndon Av.
Wynnstay Gdns. W8 BS41 66
Wynnstow Pk. Oxt. CG69 115
Wynter St. SW11 BT45 66
Wynton Gdns. SE25 CA52 87
Wynton Gro. Walt. BC55 83
Wynton Pl. W3 BM39 55
Wynyard Clo. Rick. AW21 26
Wynyard Ter. SE11 BX42 66
Aveline St.
Wyre Gro. Edg. BM27 37
Wyre Gro. Hayes BC42 63
Wyresdale Cres. Grnf. BH38 54
Wyte Leaf Clo. Ruis. BA32 44
Wythburn Pl. W1 BU39 56
Seymour Pl.
Wythenshawe Rd. Dag. CR34 50
Wythens Wk. SE9 CL46 78
Southend Cres.
Wythes Clo. Brom. CK51 88
Wythes Rd. E16 CK40 58
Wythfield Rd. SE9 CK46 78
Wyvenhoe Rd. Har. BG34 45
Wyver Ct. St. Alb. BH13 9
Avenue Rd.
Wyvern Clo. Dart. CV47 80
Wyvern Clo. Orp. CO55 89
Wyvern Rd. Pur. BY58 95
Wyvil Est. SW8 BX43 66
Wyvil Rd. SW8 BX43 66
Wyvis St. E14 CE39 57
Yabsley St. E14 CF40 57
Yalding Clo. Orp. CP52 89
Yalding Rd. SE16 CB41 67
Yale Ct. NW6 BS35 47
Yarborough Rd. SW19 BT51 86
Runnymede
Yardbridge, Sutt. BS58 95
Hulverston Clo.
Yardley Clo. E4 CE25 30
Yardley Clo. Reig. BS69 121
Yardley La. E4 CE25 30
Yardley St. WC1 BY38 56
Yard Mead, Stai. AT48 72
Yarm Ct. Rd. Lthd. BK65 102
Yarmouth Cres. N15 CB32 48
Yarmouth Pl. W1 BV40 56
Brick St.
Yarmouth Rd. Wat. BD22 27
Yarm Way, Lthd. BK65 102
Yarnton Way SE2 CP41 69
Yarnton Way. SE2 CR41 69
Yarrow Side. Amer. AQ23 25
Yateley St. SE7 CJ41 68
Yates Ct. NW2 BQ36 55
Yeading Av. Har. BE34 45
Yeading Gdns. Hayes BC39 53
Yeading La. Hayes BC39 53
Yeading La. Fork Hayes. BD38 54
Yeading Wk. Har. BE32 45
Yeate St. N1 BZ36 57
Yeatman Rd. N6 BU32 47
Yeats Clo. SE13 CF44 67
Eliot Pk.
Yeats Clo. Red. BT72 121
Yeldham Rd. W6 BQ42 65
Yellowpine Way Ilf. CO28 41
Yelverton Rd. SW11 BT44 66
Yenston Clo. Mord. BS53 86
Yeomans Acre Ruis. BC32 44
Yeomans Meadow, Sev. CU66 116
Yeomans Ms. Islw. BG46 74
Yeomans Mews Islw. BH46 74
Yeomans Rd. Hem. H. AZ10 8
Yeomans Row SW3 BU41 66
Yeoman St. SE8 CD42 67
Yeomans Way, Enf. CB23 30
Yeomen Way, Ilf. CM29 40
Yeo St. E3 CE39 57
Yeoveney Clo. Stai. AU48 72
Yeovil Clo. Orp. CN55 88
Yerbury Rd. N19 BW34 47
Yester Dr. Chis. CK50 78
Yester Pk. Chis. CK50 78
Yester Rd. Chis. CL50 78
Yetty Way Brom. CH51 88
Church Rd.
Yevele Way. Horn. CW33 51
Yew Av. West Dr. AY40 53
Yewdale Clo. Brom. CG50 78
Yewfield Rd. NW10 BO36 55
Yew Gro. NW2 BQ35 46
Yewlands, Hodd. CE12 12
Yewlands, Saw. CQ6 6
Yewlands Clo. Bans. BT61 104
Yews Av. Enf. CB21 30
Yew Tree Bottom Rd. Epsom BP61 103
Yew Tree Clo. N21 BY26 38
Yew Tree Clo. Brwd. DD25 122
Yew Tree Clo. Chesh. AQ18 16
Yew Tree Clo. Couls. BU63 104
Yew Tree Clo. Hem. H. AW14 8
Yew Tree Clo. Well. CO44 69
Yew Tree Clo. Wor. Pk. BO54 85
Yew Tree Dri. Guil. AR68 109
Yew Tree Dr. Cat. CA66 114
Yewtree Gdns. Epsom. BM61 103
Yew Tree Gdns. Rom. CQ32 50
Yew Tree Gdns. Rom. CS32 50
Yewtree La. Dor. BF69 119
Yew Tree La. Reig. BS69 121
Yew Tree Rd. W12 BO40 55
Yewtree Rd. Beck. CD52 87
Yew Tree Rd. Dor. BJ70 119
Yew Tree Rd. Slou. AQ41 62
Yew Tree Rd. Uxb. AY37 53
Yew Trees, Egh. AU52 82
Yew Trees Shep. AY52 83
Laleham Rd.
Yew Tree Wk. Houns. BE46 74
Yew Tree Way Croy. CD58 96
Yewtree Wlk. Pur. BZ58 96
Yew Wk. Har. BH33 45
Yiewsley By-pass, Uxb. & West Dr. AZ39 53
Yiewsley Sta. Rd. West. Dr. AY40 53
Yoakley Rd. N16 CA34 48
Yolande Gdns. SE9 CK46 78
Yonge Pk. N4 BY34 47
York Ave. Wind. AN44 61
York Av. SW14 BN46 75
York Av. W7 BH40 54
York Av. Hayes BA39 53
York Av. Sid. CN48 78
York Av. Slou. AO39 52
York Av. Stan. BJ30 36
York Bldgs. WC2 BX40 56
Watergate Wk.
York Clo. SE5 BZ44 67
York Clo. W7 BH40 54
York Clo. Brwd. DC26 122
York Clo. Kings L. AZ18 17
York Ct. Borwd. BN23 28
York Ct. Mord. BS52 86
York Cres. Loug. CK24 31
Yorke Gdns. Reig. BS70 121
Yorke Rd. Reig. BS70 121
Yorke Rd. Rick. AZ25 26
York Gdns. N18 CB29 39
York Gdns. Walt. BD55 84
York Gate N14 BX26 38
York Gte. NW1 BV38 56
York Gro. SE15 CC44 67
York Hill, SE27 BY48 76
York Hill Loug. CK23 31
York Hill Loug. CK24 31
York Ho. Pl. W8 BS41 66
Yorkland Av. Well. CN45 68
York Ms. NW5 BV35 47
York Mews Ilf. CL34 49
York Rd.
York Pl. W7 BH40 54
York Pl. WC2 BX40 56
Villiers St.
York Pl. Grays. DD43 71
York Pl. Ilf. CL34 49
York Rd.
York Pl. Wind. AO44 61
York Rise, NW5 BV34 47
York Rd. E4 CD28 39
York Rd. E7 CH36 58
York Rd. E10 CF34 48
York Rd. E17 CC32 48
York Rd. N11 BW29 38
York Rd. N18 CB29 39
York Rd. N21 BZ26 39
York Rd. NW9 BO32 46
Broadway, The,
York Rd. SE1 BX41 66
York Rd. SW11 BS46 76
York Rd. SW18 BS46 76
York Rd. SW19 BS50 76
York Rd. W3 BN39 55
York Rd. W5 BK41 64
York Rd. Barn. BT24 29
York Rd. Brent. BK42 64
York Rd. Brwd. DC26 122
York Rd. Croy. BY54 86
York Rd. Dart. CW47 80
York Rd. Grav. DE47 81
York Rd. Grav. DH48 81
York Rd. Guil. AR71 118
York Rd. Houns. BF45 64
York Rd. Ilf. CL34 49
York Rd. Kings. On T. BL50 75
York Rd. Nthwd. BC30 35
York Rd. Rain. CT36 59
York Rd. Rich. BL46 75
Albert Rd.
York Rd. St. Alb. BH13 9
York Rd. Sth. Croy. CC58 96
York Rd. Sutt. BS57 95
York Rd. Tedd. BH49 74
York Rd. Uxb. AX36 53
York Rd. Wal. Cr. CD20 21
York Rd. Wat. BD25 27
York Rd. West. CH63 106
York Rd. Wey. AX59 92
York Rd. Wey. BA56 92
York Rd. Wind. AN44 61
York Rd. Wok. AR63 100
Yorkshire Gdns. N18 CB28 39
Yorkshire Grey Pla. NW3 BT35 47
Heath St.
Yorkshire Rd. E14 CD39 57
Yorkshire Rd. Mitch. BX53 86
York Sq. E14 CD39 57
York St. W1 BU39 56
York St. Bark. CL37 58
Abbey Rd.
York St. Mitch. BV54 86
York St. Twick. BJ47 74
York Ter. NW1 BV38 56
York Ter. Enf. BZ22 30
York Ter. Erith. CR44 69
Yorkton St. E2 CB37 57
York Way N1 BW36 56
York Way N7 BW36 56
York Way N20 BU27 38
York Way Chess. BL57 94
York Way Felt. BE48 74
York Way Wat. BD21 27

York Way, Welw.	BP5	5
York Way Ct. N1	BX37	56
Young Field, Hem. H.	AV13	7
Youngmans Clo. Enf.	BZ23	30
Young Rd. E16	CJ39	58
Youngs Rise, Welw. G. C.	BP8	5
Youngs Rd. Ilf.	CM32	49
Young St. W8	BS41	66
Young St. Lthd.	BH65	102
Youngstroat La. Wok.	AS59	91
Yoxley App. Ilf.	CM32	49
Yoxley Dr. Ilf.	CM32	49
Yukon Rd. SW12	BV47	76
Zambra Way. Sev.	CW63	108
Zampa Rd. SE16	CC42	67
Zander Ct. E2	CB38	57
St. Peters Clo.		
Zangwill Rd. SE3	CJ44	68
Zealand Ave. West Dr.	AX43	63
Zealand Rd. E3	CD37	57
Zelah Rd. Orp.	CO54	89
Zennor Rd. SW12	BV47	76
Zenoria St. SE22	CA45	67
Zermatt Rd. Th. Hth.	BZ52	87
Zetland St. E14	CE39	57
Zig Zag Rd. Ken.	BZ61	105
Zig-zag Rd. Tad.	BL69	120
Zion Pl. Th. Hth.	BZ52	87
Zion Rd. Th. Hth.	BZ52	87
Zion St. Grav.	DG47	81
Zoar St. SE1	BY40	56
Zoffany St. N19	BW34	47
Ashbrook Rd.		